The
LONDON
Encyclopædia

The
LONDON
Encyclopædia

Edited by Ben Weinreb
and Christopher Hibbert

MACMILLAN LONDON

Design by Robert Updegraff
Picture research by Juliet Brightmore

ISBN 0 333 32556 7

First published 1983 by
Macmillan London Limited
London and Basingstoke

Associated companies in Auckland, Dallas,
Delhi, Dublin, Hong Kong, Johannesburg,
Lagos, Manzini, Melbourne, Nairobi,
New York, Singapore, Tokyo, Washington
and Zaria

The publishers would like to express their gratitude to
The Observer for their generous support in the preparation of
this book.

Filmsetting and computerized indexing by
Filmtype Services Limited, Scarborough
Printed in Hong Kong

Endpapers: Detail from *A Balloon View
of London as seen from Hampstead*, 1851

Contents

Acknowledgements

In an encyclopædia such as this the debt to previous writers is of course prodigious; but it has been considered impracticable to enumerate the many hundreds of books which have been consulted, although some of these, such as the Greater London Council's *Survey of London* and Sir Nikolaus Pevsner's *Buildings of England*, have proved indispensable. We are deeply grateful to the authors and editors of them all. We are also grateful to the archivists and librarians throughout the Greater London area for their unstinting help, as well as to the members of London's numerous historical societies who have taken so much trouble to answer our questions and, in several cases, to compile the relevant entries. A list of contributors to the *Encyclopædia* is given opposite: but we would also like to express our thanks to all those whose help and encouragement have contributed so much to its completion. We are in particular grateful to Michael Alcock, the director at Macmillan who has been responsible for the *Encyclopædia* since his firm first undertook to publish it; to Esther Jagger, who has helped us edit every entry; to Robert Updegraff, who has designed the book; to Juliet Brightmore, who has collected and chosen the illustrations; to Geoff Barlow, who has been responsible for the production; to our respective wives, Joan Weinreb and Susan Hibbert, for their invaluable help in a variety of ways; and to Ralph Hyde of the Guildhall Library, who has made his unrivalled knowledge available to us all.

CHRISTOPHER HIBBERT
Spring 1983

Contributors

R.D. Abbott
Ann Arnold
Phyllis Auty
Keith Bailey
Victor Belcher
Josephine Birchenough
Mervyn Blatch
Mary Boast
Richard Bowden
Jane Bowen
Nicholas Boyarsky
Bromley Local
  History Society
James Bull
Hilary Burr
R.M. Burton
W.F. Bynum
Andrea Cameron
Mary Clark
Nancy Clark
Peter Clark
Patricia Clarke
Paul Clayden
Peter Clayton
Peter A. Clayton
J.A.R. Clench
Paul Clifford
Douglas Cluett
Cecil Clutton
J.T. Cooper
John W. Collier
C.A. Cornish
Mary Cosh
Ann Cottingham
Jeremy Cotton
A.H. Cox
Margaret Cox
A.D. Croft
B.R. Curle
Lucy Dargue
Marie P.G. Draper
Ann Ducker
Edmonton Hundred
  Historical Society
Esther Eisenthal
Julia Elton
Brian D. Evans
R.F. Farmer
Keith Fletcher
Jacqueline Fortey

Caroline Francis
Kenneth Gay
W.H. Gelder
Laurence Gillam
Colin Glover
J.S. Golland
Sarah Good
Edwin Green
J.W. Green
Erica Griffiths
Michael Hallett
Gabrielle Harris
C.W. Harrison
A.N. Harrisson
Jennifer Hartley
T.O. Haunch
Frances Hawes
Winifred M. Heard
E.G. Heath
Gerald Heath
Geoffrey Hewlett
Jennifer Hewlett
Christopher Hibbert
Edward Hibbert
Kate Hibbert
Susan Hibbert
Paul Hodges
Geoffrey Hollingworth
Valerie Hope
Peter Hounsell
James Howgego
Penny Howman
James Howson
Cecilia Hull
Richard Jeffree
Patricia M. Jenkyns
Colm Kerrigan
Jane Kimber
Sonia Kinahan
Henry Law
James Leasor
Vivienne McAuliffe
Phyllis McDougall
Margaret Mair
Eric de Maré
Dawn Marriott
Hester Marston-
  Smedley
A.L.J. Matthews
D.J. Montier

James Mosley
Margaret Mundy
Paddy Musgrove
Norman H. Nail
Stanley Newens
B.N. Nunns
Bernard Nurse
Robert Oakley
C.B. O'Beirne
Mary O'Connor
Archie Onslow
David Owen
M.A. Pakenham-Walsh
D.O. Pam
K.R. Pearce
Angela Perkins
Alan Piper
Francis Pollen
Thérèse Pollen
C.W. Plant
Patricia Pratt
John A. Prichard
Ruislip, Northwood
  and Eastcote Local
  History Society
Jan Reid
R.N.G. Rowland
Donald Rumbelow
Fiona Rutherford
Frank Sainsbury
A.J. Salmon
Jane Salmon
Alicia Salter
Ann Saunders
R.A.M. Scott
Clare Segal
John Selmon
Anthony Shaw
J.C.M. Shaw
Philip Shelbourne
Francis Sheppard
Joanna Sheppard
Margery M. Smith
Bob Smyth
Stanmore and Harrow
  Historical Society
Ann Strawson
Veronica Steel
Edmund Street
Tessa Street

Allyce Tessier
John Turner
E.E. Vella
Vestry House Museum,
  Walthamstow
Heather Waddell
Hugh Walker
Priscilla Waller
Julian Watson
Ben Weinreb
Joan Weinreb
B.T. White
Gordon White
Godfrey Whitelock
F.J. Whyler
Gwen Wilcox
Michael Wilcox
Audrey Wild
E.J. Willson
Emma Woodcraft
Ron Woollacott
Priscilla Wrightson
Humphrey Wynn
George Wynne Willson

Introduction

The London Encyclopædia contains within a single volume the record of its streets and buildings, people and events. The first book to do this was John Stow's *Survay of London*, published in 1598. His was both a history and a guide-book. 'What London hath been of ancient time men may here see, as what it is now every man doth behold,' he wrote.

Stow's book is printed on 252 small leaves, less than half the size of this one. The largest and most detailed history is today the responsibility of a permanent department of the Greater London Council. It too is called *The Survey of London*. Publication, which began eighty-five years ago, has now reached volume 42 (though as some are in several parts there are actually fifty-eight volumes). By the time it is finished there will be more than double that number.

Stow draws a parallel with Rome, 'the chief city of the world who drew her originall from Gods, Goddesses and demy Gods . . . so London deriveth itself from the very same originall'. Then he describes its walls, rivers, gates, towers, castles, sports and pastimes and finally each City ward, street by street, giving us the history of churches and charities, the halls of City companies, the fine houses and much else. The Greater London *Survey* does the same, except that neither pagan gods nor sports and pastimes come within its scholarly and exacting terms of reference, but every street and every building of interest is recorded, listing the former occupants and detailing its architectural history.

This encyclopædia aims to lie somewhere between the two.

Since Stow there have been many other surveys and histories, but we have taken as our model Wheatley and Cunningham's *London Past and Present* of 1891, which in its turn is based upon Cunningham's *Handbook for London* of 1849, the earliest historical survey to be arranged in alphabetical form. Peter Cunningham, Clerk to the Audit Office, both wrote and edited many books. Work on the *Handbook* took him seven years, during which, he says, he 'left no known source likely to afford new information neglected', concluding: 'I am still so much in love with my subject that I shall continue to collect for a new and improved edition of my work whether called for by the public or not.' It was called for, and a second edition appeared the next year.

His story is a sad one. When he was twenty-six he discovered in the Audit Office a document containing various references to Shakespeare which was published by the Shakespeare Society. A number of years later it was suspected of having been forged, and by Cunningham himself. Although he was not directly accused, investigations revealed irregularities in the Audit Office which resulted in his retirement from government service and his disappearance from the literary scene. This did not diminish the debt of subsequent London historians, which they have always acknowledged. (The document itself continued to be treated with suspicion by Shakespearean scholars, but in 1930 it was subjected to chemical and microscopic examination and proved to be completely authentic.)

After Peter Cunningham's death, his brother Francis spent his last years on the *Handbook*'s revision but, says Wheatley, 'though energetic in the search for information he put little of it on paper'. Then James Thorne, the author of the *Handbook to the Environs of London*, took over the work, but he too died before he had finished. Finally it was given to H.B. Wheatley, who then completely rewrote it, adding a wealth of literary allusion. This became the *London Past and Present* referred to above, and it was the necessary revision and extension of Wheatley and Cunningham out of which the present encyclopædia has grown. By now, however, there were not only ninety more eventful years to be included, but London had become Greater London, extending her boundaries by hundreds of miles. So if a new book was to take shape, comparable with its predecessors and yet contained in a single volume, once again it had to be entirely rewritten.

Wheatley was a man of learning and industry. In another work he edited the diary of Samuel Pepys but, in conformity with the proprieties of his time, omitted all that was indelicate. This same reticence is observed in his writings on London. We are less inhibited, and when an incident or anecdote illustrates or enhances an entry it is told, we hope, with the smell and gusto of the period in which it occurred. The intervening years have also uncovered lost records which shed new light on old tales, enabling us to correct attributions, clarify identities and amend errors which repetition had hardened into history. It is, of course, possible that in spite of infinite care, we ourselves have lent credibility to further errors for future editors to discover. We have been chroniclers engaged in the recording of facts rather than historians concerned with their cause and consequence. It has been our task to compress within a paragraph that which has sometimes been the subject of a book and, like Stow, to set down concisely and in plain words what is generally known and held to be true.

Of course the account of streets and buildings is the story of the people who have lived in them, so that interspersed between the lists of names and dates there sometimes springs to life a man or woman, long since dead, whose wit or wisdom, triumph or tragedy, transcends the sequence of events and imprints upon our mind the vivid picture of their person or the haunting echo of their voice. The recital of these same unvarnished lists of names reminds us 'that in this court did Goldsmith walk' or 'on that spot a maypole stood' or here, beneath the traffic's unrelenting surge, could once be heard on cobbled stones the trundle of a hangman's cart.

Fourteen years ago I began work on this book as an intermittent and spare-time occupation, without realising the enormity of the labour involved. Penny Howman worked on it with me for a time, as did Peter Clayton, but it was my wife Joan who brought order and system to the mounting records and it was her unflagging determination that kept it going when there was no end in sight. In 1977 my friend James Price advised me that a seasoned and experienced partner might more speedily bring the book to fruition, hence in 1979 I was joined, at his suggestion, by Christopher Hibbert and later that year the book was accepted by Macmillan.

My name is first on the title page because I was the initiator, but it is also testimony to Christopher Hibbert's generosity of spirit, for if typography were accurately to reflect the content, his name would be printed much the larger. It is due to his breadth of scholarship, to his skill and clarity as a writer, and to his firm, fair editorial hand that *The London Encyclopædia* has reached completion.

BEN WEINREB
Spring 1983

Abbey Lodge Built probably in 1824 or 1825 by Decimus Burton, it adjoined the northern end of HANOVER TERRACE. In 1845 Elizabeth Gurney, daughter of the head of the Quaker banking family and niece of Elizabeth Fry, the reformer, married Baron Ernest Christian Ludvig de Bunsen; her father, who lived at 20 HANOVER TERRACE, gave them the villa as a wedding present; the Gothic arches and castellations were probably added at this time. The de Bunsens lived there till their deaths in 1903. The remainder of the lease was purchased by their friend, the Austrian painter and sculptor Emil Fuchs, who was patronised by Edward VII. In 1911 he sold the last 13 years of the lease to Baroness Deichmann, the de Bunsens' elder daughter. In 1928 the house was demolished and a block of flats, which bears its name, built in its place.

Abbey Mills Pumping Station *Abbey Lane, E15.* Victorian sewage pumping plant disguised under Moorish towers and a Slavic dome with an interior like a Byzantine church. It was designed by Bazalgette and Cooper and built in 1865–8 as part of Bazalgette's main drainage scheme for London (*see* DRAINS AND SEWERS).

Abbey Orchard Street *SW1.* Between OLD PYE STREET and GREAT SMITH STREET. It was built after the GREAT FIRE on the site of the medieval orchard of WESTMINSTER ABBEY. The Roman Catholic Chapel of St Ann was built in the 1860s.

Abbey Road *NW6, NW8.* Began as a lane leading to KILBURN PRIORY from which it takes its name. The stuccoed individual villas, each set in its own garden, which began to appear from 1830 onwards, are now subdivided or have given way to blocks of flats. John MacWhirter the painter had his residence at No. 1 from 1888 to 1911; the main living-room was a galleried hall. No. 3 is EMI's recording studio, used by the pop group, the Beatles, who named the album issued from it *Abbey Road*. Nos 5 and 7, a pair of villas, are in a remarkable Gothic Tudor style. Opposite them stands the Baptist Church designed by W.G. Habershon and Pite and consecrated in 1863.

Abbey Street *SE1.* Takes its name from BERMONDSEY ABBEY which covered Bermondsey Square and the ground between Grange Walk and Long Walk. The street is on the line of the nave of the Abbey

Abbey Mills Pumping Station. The galleried engine house inside is as extravagant as the Byzantine exterior.

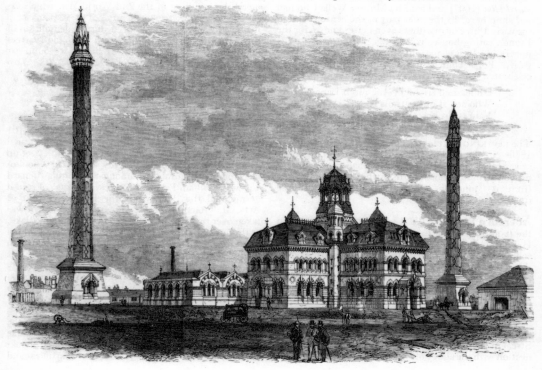

church. 'The Bermondsans,' wrote a correspondent in the *Gentleman's Magazine* in 1808, 'for a love of alteration have this year contrived a new road of no perceptible use or convenience through the very heart of the existing walls of the Abbey.' The principal gateway of the Abbey was removed for this purpose. The eastern gateway in Grange Walk had already been demolished in 1760.

Abbey Wood *SE2.* Lies east of WOOLWICH on the eastern boundary of the London Borough of GREENWICH. Modern Abbey Wood was originally part of the extensive marshes of PLUMSTEAD and Lesnes (later ERITH) manors which were enclosed in the early 13th century by the monks of the 12th-century Lesnes Abbey. The Abbey was closed before the DISSOLUTION, and from the 18th century the marshes were used by the WOOLWICH ARSENAL. During the 19th century weapons, missiles and tanks were tested and some of the Arsenal's moated enclosures still survive north of THAMESMEAD. By the end of the century Abbey Wood Station had been built on the North Kent line, taking its name from the surviving woods south of the Lesnes Abbey remains, and giving it to the area that subsequently developed. During 1900–14 over 1,500 homes were built on the Bostall Estate, and in the 1950s the LONDON COUNTY COUNCIL developed the Abbey Wood Estate. The parish church of St Michael dates from 1908 (Sir Arthur Blomfield and Sons).

Abchurch Lane *EC4.* First mentioned as Abbechurche Lane in 1291. ST MARY ABCHURCH is near the south end. The name is, perhaps, a corruption of Upchurch, as the church is on slightly rising ground. In the early 17th century the lane was renowned for the cakes referred to in John Webster's *Northward Hoe* (1607) and sold by Mother Wells who had her shop here. In the later part of the century and in the early 18th century it was even better known for the French eating-house, PONTACK'S, whose exact site is uncertain. It was patronised by Evelyn, Wren and Swift. Pope chided John Moore, 'author of the celebrated worm powder', who lived here in 1737:

> Oh learned friend of Abchurch Lane
> Who sett'st our entrails free
> Vain is thy art, thy powder vain
> Since worms will eat 'een thee.

The new KING WILLIAM STREET which was built in the 1830s cut the lane in two. In 1855 excavations for a sewer revealed a 36 ft length of Roman ragstone wall, probably running northwards up the middle of the lane from its junction with Nicholas Passage. The GRESHAM CLUB is at No. 15.

Abercorn Place *NW8.* Lies in ST JOHN'S WOOD on the HARROW SCHOOL Estate and is named after James Hamilton, 1st Duke of Abercorn, a governor of the school. Building had begun there by the 1830s. Today, the houses present a fascinating mixture from that date to the present day. Nos 13 and 15 have pretty, early 19th-century façades, overlaid with pebble dash. Charles Robert Leslie RA lived at No. 2, and T.H. Huxley was at No. 26 from 1861 to 1872.

Abingdon Road *W8.* First begun as Newland Street in 1817; the present name recalls the parish connection with the abbey of Abingdon. In 1894 the Coun-

tess von Arnim, author of *Elizabeth and her German Garden*, is said to have stayed at Abingdon Mansions.

Abingdon Street *SW1.* The early Abingdon Street can be seen on Norden's map of about 1593 linking OLD PALACE (YARD) with MILLBANK. At the northern end stood the south gate of the PALACE OF WESTMINSTER, and at the south end the ditch boundary of THORNEY ISLAND which is now represented by GREAT COLLEGE STREET. From about 1690 a mansion stood at the south-west end; initially known as Lindsay House, it was later the residence of the Earl of Abingdon, and by 1708 occupied by the Earl of Carnarvon. When the King came to PARLIAMENT the state coach drawn by eight horses used to turn round in the yard of the house. The lane was briefly known as Lindsay Lane, but by 1750 was known as Dirty Lane, 'narrow, pestered with coaches and inconvenient', and for this reason after an Act of Parliament in that year it was widened and renamed Abingdon Street as part of the general approach improvements to the new WESTMINSTER BRIDGE. The houses that survived until the 2nd World War dated from this time. From about 1820 Thomas Telford lived at No. 24, where he died in 1834. In 1932 Harold Clunn described 'one long terrace of shabby Georgian houses . . . largely inhabited by Members of Parliament'. Concerning their proximity to the Houses of Parliament, he added, 'Its appearance suggests the dustman sitting on the doorsteps of the nobleman's mansion.' Clunn probably echoed the prevailing sentiments; but in 1938 the new Georgian Group of the Society for the Protection of Ancient Buildings moved into No. 27 and successfully petitioned against its demolition by the George V Memorial Committee. This was one of the early preservationist triumphs. But only four houses survived the bombing of the 2nd World War which exposed the JEWEL TOWER behind. The remains of a medieval quay were discovered during demolition of the remaining houses. In 1963–6 Abingdon Street Garden was created. Beneath is an underground car park. In the garden is the bronze, *Knife Edge Two Piece*, by Henry Moore (1962).

Abney Park Cemetery *see* CEMETERIES.

Ackermann's *101 Strand.* Rudolph Ackermann, printer and bookseller, bought the lease of No. 101 Strand in 1794. The site had formerly been occupied by WORCESTER HOUSE. In 1750 William Shipley set up Shipley's Academy here, a highly successful school of drawing which numbered amongst its pupils Richard Cosway, William Pars and Francis Wheatley. From it germinated the Society for the Encouragement of Arts, Manufactures and Commerce. The school was taken over by Henry Pars in 1763; and William Blake, at the age of ten, 'was put to Mr Par's drawing-school in the Strand'. For a period, it became the British Forum and was used by John Thelwall for his *Elocutionary Lectures* and political speeches closely linked with the LONDON CORRESPONDING SOCIETY. When these were suppressed by the Government in 1794 Ackermann, having bought the lease, reopened the premises as a school for drawing. In 1796 he transferred here his print shop (started at 96 STRAND the previous year). In 1806 he closed his school to make room for his expanding business as a print-seller, bookseller, publisher and dealer in fancy articles and

An aquatint of Ackermann's Library for Works of Art in 1813. It was the first shop in London to be lit solely by gas.

materials for artists. Ackermann had been the first to employ refugees from the French Revolution, and contemporary accounts say that seldom in his shop were there less than 50 nobles, priests and ladies of distinction working on screens, flower stands and the colouring of prints. From this address, he began publishing in 1808 his great series of books with coloured aquatints, the *Microcosm of London*, *The History of the University of Oxford* and *Cambridge*, and many others (all of which appeared first in monthly parts), also his famous *Repository of Arts, Literature, Commerce and Manufacturing* which ran from 1809 to 1828. He opened here the first art library in England (it is described in the 1813 volume of his *Repository of Arts*). From 1813, he held every Wednesday a literary reception to which flocked authors, artists, patrons and visiting foreigners. It was said for many years to be 'the meeting place of the best social life in London'. It was the first shop in London 'to be lit solely by Gas which burns with a purity and brilliance unattainable by any other mode of illumination hitherto attempted'. In 1827 Ackermann returned to 96 STRAND, rebuilt for him by J.B. Papworth.

Acton *W3*. There has been sporadic human habitation for 300,000 years in this area which was once watered by the now piped STAMFORD BROOK and its tributary the BOLLO ('bull hollow') on their course to the THAMES at HAMMERSMITH. Anglo-Saxons established the name (Old English *actun*, the settlement among the oaks), but documentation of this comes only in the 12th century. In *Domesday Book*, Acton was merely an anonymous part of the Bishop's manor of FULHAM. Rural but conveniently close to London, it was a favoured retreat for the wealthy and influential until a century ago. Among notable

residents were Francis Rous, the Puritan divine and Provost of Eton, who lived at Bank House, at the west end of the High Street (demolished in 1870); Richard Baxter, the nonconformist divine, who recorded in his memoirs that, during the GREAT FIRE, charred leaves of books from the burning warehouses round ST PAUL'S were picked up near his house; Sir Matthew Hale, the Lord Chief Justice, who took over Baxter's house and is commemorated in Hale Gardens; Sir John Fielding, the blind BOW STREET magistrate, who lived at Broomcroft, Acton Green which was demolished in about 1870; Edward Bulwer Lytton, who wrote *Rienzi* at Berrymead in 1835–6; and Dr John Lindley, the botanist, who lived at Bedford House in what became BEDFORD PARK and later at Fairlawn, Acton Green which was demolished in about 1879.

The town earned more than local fame during the Civil War, when in November 1642 the Royalists attempted an advance on London and the local Parliamentarian garrison helped to repulse them in an engagement that began at BRENTFORD and spread into Acton. Then, throughout the 18th century, the minor spa of Acton Wells attracted health- and pleasure-seekers from many parts.

The nucleus of the town, on the Uxbridge Road 5 miles from MARBLE ARCH, lies round the mother-church of St Mary, whose first rector known by name is recorded in 1228. It was entirely rebuilt in 1865–77. Daughter-parishes were formed following an Enclosure Commissioners' award of 1859 which consolidated the strip-holdings on the former common fields, and entailed new roads across the re-apportioned areas. The result was a remarkable rise in population, from 3,000 in 1861 to 38,000 in 1901. Some 65,000 now live here.

Down to the mid-19th century the economy was

3

agricultural, but there was a rug-mill in the Steyne (Old English *stæne*, a stony place) from the early 1800s. Later came brickfields, and by 1900 there were 180 laundries in South Acton, which was colloquially known as 'Soapsuds Island'. The subsequent growth of engineering and miscellaneous manufacturing encouraged the claim made in the 1930s that Acton was the biggest industrial centre south of Coventry. Improved transport assisted in development. The PADDINGTON CANAL of 1801 and a great mainline and suburban railway complex, begun in 1839, facilitated communication with all parts; buses provided good services from the 1850s; and a horse-tramway of 1878 was electrified in 1901.

The earliest recorded residence is Berrymead, held by ST PAUL's from 1232 until Henry VIII exchanged it for other property and gave it to the Russells of Bedford. Occupants include Marquesses of Halifax and Dukes of Kingston. A daughter of one of the latter, Lady Mary Pierrepoint, eloped from here with Edward Wortley Montagu and became a famous traveller and letter-writer. The house was rebuilt in 1802 in the Gothic taste and fancifully renamed The Priory; it was saved when the grounds were built on in the 1880s but in May 1982 was derelict. West of Berrymead was Mill Hill Park, built over in the 1870s by William Willett, the builder mainly remembered for his campaign for 'Daylight Saving'. Derwentwater House, demolished in 1909, was leased in 1720 by the widow of the Jacobite Earl of Derwentwater, beheaded in 1716.

Most of East Acton was in 1657 inherited by the GOLDSMITHS' COMPANY under the will of John Perryn, a goldsmith from Bromyard in Worcestershire. Perryn's house, once known as Foster's and later as the Manor House, was rebuilt in about 1715–20 but gradually decayed and was pulled down in 1911. Goldsmiths are commemorated in the street names hereabout, including Sir Thomas Vyner, LORD MAYOR in 1653, who married John Perryn's widow. The Company's pleasing almshouses of 1811 face Acton Park, opened to the public in 1888. The massive Government Building in Bromyard Avenue (built to the designs of J.G. West in 1922), St Saviour's church for the deaf (designed by Sir Edward Maufe, 1927); and ST AIDAN's CHURCH (Roman Catholic, 1961) are noteworthy. The golf links in East Acton became a municipal housing estate in 1920. All the roads here have names associated with golf, such as Long Drive, the Fairway and Brassie Avenue.

North-westwards was the Acton Aerodrome, where pioneer flights were made, and adjoining this is the Great Western Railway's garden village of 1923. Friar's Place, on land owned in the 14th century by ST BARTHOLOMEW THE GREAT, SMITHFIELD, fell down in the 1880s; an ice-cream plant, The Friary, is now here. Southward, the archetypal garden suburb of BEDFORD PARK, founded in 1875, lies partly in CHISWICK. Nearby South Acton has been completely redeveloped by the local authority over recent years.

Actuaries' Company see CITY LIVERY COMPANIES.

Adam and Eve Tea Gardens *Tottenham Court.* Tottenham Court was a popular place of amusement in the 17th century. George Wither, in *Britain's Remembrances* (1628), said:

And Hogsdone, Islington and Tottenham Court
For cakes and cream had then no small resort.

In 1645 a maidservant and two others were fined 1s apiece for 'drinking at Tottenhall Court on the Sabbath daie'. Wycherley in the *Gentleman Dancing Master* (1673) couples 'a ramble to Totnam Court' with the other fashionable diversions of visiting the MULBERRY GARDEN and VAUXHALL. The Adam and Eve existed at least as early as 1718 on the site of the manor house at the northern end of TOTTENHAM COURT ROAD. In the 18th century it had a long room with an organ, bowling alleys and extensive gardens with arbours for tea drinking. On 13 May 1785 Vincenzo Lunardi, the balloonist, took off from the HONOURABLE ARTILLERY COMPANY ground on his maiden flight and descended here within 20 minutes. 'He was immediately surrounded by great numbers of the populace and though he proposed re-ascending they were not to be dissuaded from bearing him in triumph on their shoulders.' Towards the end of the 18th century the gardens became hemmed in with houses and were frequented by criminals and prostitutes. In the early 19th century they were shut by the magistrates. They were reopened as a tavern in 1813. In 1838 a description of them reads: 'A house standing alone, with spacious trees in the rear and at the sides, and a forecourt with large timber trees, and tables and benches for out of door customers. In the gardens were fruit trees, and bowers, and arbours for tea drinking parties. In the rear there were not any houses; now there is a town.'

Adam Street *WC2.* Takes its name from the Adam brothers who designed the ADELPHI. Few of their buildings remain. No. 7, the offices of the *Lancet*, with honeysuckle pilasters and lacy ironwork, is one attractive survival.

Adams Row *W1.* On the GROSVENOR ESTATE, it extends from SOUTH AUDLEY STREET to CARLOS PLACE. It was laid out in the 1720s to provide stables and coach-houses for the mansions in nearby GROSVENOR SQUARE, and probably takes its name from one of the builders.

Addington *Surrey.* Referred to as Eddington in *Domesday Book*, the name probably means 'estate in Eadda's territory'. In its 12th-century St Mary's church five Archbishops of Canterbury were buried. From 1807 the nearby ADDINGTON PALACE was their country residence. To the west of the palace in 1929 a 5 ft high brick-lined subterranean passage was discovered. According to local legend this passage, once linked to the remains of a monastery, was used by Henry VIII to reach Wickham Court when he was in love with Anne Boleyn. Addington Cricket Club dates from 1743. The Cricketers' Inn was built in 1847 on the site of a Tudor tavern. The village lies in a Conservation Area but 403 acres of farmland nearby were laid out by the Corporation in 1935 as New Addington, one of the earliest 'overspill' housing developments.

Addington Palace *Croydon, Surrey.* The site is mentioned in *Domesday Book* and was owned by the Leigh family from 1447. In about 1770 Barlow Trecothick, LORD MAYOR of London, MP and City merchant, bought the estate. He employed Robert Mylne to design the house, the central portion of the present palace. In 1807 the ECCLESIASTICAL COMMISSIONERS purchased the estate, then 3,500 acres, for the Archbishops of Canterbury. Archbishops Manners-Sutton, Howley, Sumner, Longley, Tait and Benson all lived here. But Frederick Temple, Benson's successor, decided that the Archbishops could no longer afford to do so. In the face of strong opposition, including the intervention of Queen Victoria, he sold the property and moved to Canterbury. The estate was bought by Frederick English, a South African diamond merchant. He commissioned Norman Shaw to extend the house and alter its interior. Shaw's work cost English £70,000. The greatest alteration was the removal of the first floor in the Great Hall. The estate also has a chapel with pews by Christopher Wren from the CHURCH OF THE HOLY SEPULCHRE, HOLBORN. The gardens were redesigned by 'Capability' Brown, whose landscaping is now obscured by two golf courses (*see* GOLF CLUBS). On English's death in 1909 the palace was sold. In the 1st World War it served as a hospital and between the wars as a country club. In 1951 CROYDON Corporation purchased the estate. Since 1953 the palace has been leased to the ROYAL SCHOOL OF CHURCH MUSIC.

Addiscombe *Surrey*. Situated north-west of ADDINGTON. Within CROYDON manor, by the 13th century it was known as enclosed land belonging to Eadda who was probably also associated with ADDINGTON. Farm buildings, the 17th-century Parsons Farm and Herons Croft, are relics of the rural environment. In 1702 John Evelyn's son-in-law built Addiscombe Place on the site of a Tudor house, reputedly to Vanbrugh's design and with decoration by Thornhill. In 1809 the estate was sold to the East India Company as a military academy, and sold again, in 1863, for development. The house was demolished and roads within the estate named after East India men such as Warren Hastings.

Of the academy, India House survives. In the early 19th century, when Addiscombe was still a hamlet, the young Thackeray was a resident. The railway arrived and the population gradually grew. In 1870 the church of St Paul's (E. Buckton Lamb) was opened and rededicated to St Mary Magdalene in 1874. The parish of Addiscombe was formed in 1879. Literary figures such as Tennyson, Carlyle and Longfellow were entertained by Lady Ashburton at Ashburton House (demolished 1912–13). A BLUE PLAQUE at 20 Outram Road commemorates the residence here of Frederick George Creed, electrical engineer and inventor of the teleprinter.

Addison Avenue *W11*. Takes its name from Joseph Addison who once lived at HOLLAND HOUSE. Tree-lined and with a vista closed by the church of ST JAMES, Norlands, the road dates from the early 1840s. The attractive two-storey paired houses were built to various designs, those in the northern part of the road probably being designed by F.W. Stent.

Addison Bridge Road *W14*. Where the underground railway goes beneath the east end of HAMMERSMITH ROAD and the west end of KENSINGTON HIGH STREET. Samuel Taylor Coleridge lived for a short time at No. 7. Harold Laski, the teacher and political philosopher, lived at No. 5 in 1926–50.

Addison Road *W14*. Like ADDISON AVENUE, it takes its name from Joseph Addison. Among the notable inhabitants of this road, begun in the 1820s, have been two distinguished statesmen, David Lloyd George, who lived at No. 2, 1928–36, and Chaim Weizmann, a founding father and first President of the State of Israel, who resided at No. 67, 1916–19. No. 8 was designed by Halsey Ricardo for Sir Ernest Debenham in 1905–6. The church of St Barnabas was built in 1829 in the Tudor Gothic style to the designs of Lewis Vulliamy. John Galsworthy lived at No. 14 in 1905–13.

Addiscombe House, Croydon, in 1834, by then a military seminary of the East India Company which bought it in 1809.

Addle Hill *EC4*. Addle may derive from the Saxon word *adel*, meaning noble. Formerly Addle Street, it ran down to UPPER THAMES STREET from CARTER LANE. In 1244 it was mentioned as Adhelingestrate; in 1279–80 as Athelingestrate. The nearby WATLING STREET had the same name at this time. In 1596 it was first mentioned as Adling Hill, but in 1598 Stow wrote, 'In Addle Street or Lane, I find no monuments.' The descriptive Addle Hill probably co-existed with the formal Addle Street. In 1600 Dekker's *Shoemakers' Holiday* was printed by Valentine Sons who described themselves as 'dwelling at the foote of Adling Hill, neere Bainards Castle, at the signe of the White Swanne'. After 1863 the southern end was demolished for the creation of QUEEN VICTORIA STREET. In 1939 an extension to Faraday House further truncated the street, leaving the present short cul-de-sac off CARTER LANE.

Adelaide Gallery Properly known as the 'National Gallery of Practical Science, Blending Instruction with Amusement', it stood on the north side of the LOWTHER ARCADE. In the early 1830s it contained some 250 machines, devices and scientific models such as a pocket thermometer, a gas mask, an oxyhydrogen microscope, a steam gun and, later, demonstrations of daguerreotypes, electricity and magnetism. In the 1840s the gallery became an amusement hall and in 1852 the Royal Marionette Theatre. The LOWTHER ARCADE was demolished in 1904.

The long room of the Adelaide Gallery in about 1830. It contained some 250 machines and scientific models.

Adelaide Hotel *and* **Victoria Hotel** *Euston Station*. These two four-storey hotels built at the London and North Western Railway terminus in Euston Square were designed by Philip Hardwick in 1839 and were erected on either side of the Screen (*see* EUSTON STATION). At the Victoria, on the left, the only meal available was breakfast, other meals being served at the 141-bedroom Adelaide (later Euston Hotel) opposite. The two hotels were connected by an ugly block built over the road in 1881. Damaged in the 2nd World War, they were both demolished in 1963 to make way for the new station.

Adelaide Street *WC2*. Named as a compliment to Queen Adelaide in the reign of whose husband,

William IV, the west STRAND improvements were carried out.

Adelphi *WC2*. An imposing riverside development of 24 terraced houses designed and built by John, Robert, James and William Adam. (*Adelphoi* is Greek for brothers.) The 3-acre site had formerly been the grounds of DURHAM HOUSE which was demolished after the Restoration when a network of courts was built there. By the mid-18th century the area had become a slum and most of the buildings were in ruins. In 1768 the Duke of St Albans granted the brothers a 99-year lease on the site for £1,200 per annum and work began. Large numbers of Scottish labourers were brought to work on the site at a cheap rate and bagpipes were played daily. A series of arches and subterranean streets were built to counteract the slope from the STRAND to the river. In 1771 Parliament passed an Act giving permission for the river to be embanked, thus crushing the opposition of the CORPORATION OF LONDON who claimed the river bed. Walpole asserts the decision was due to the King's influence:

> Four Scotchmen, by the name of Adams
> Who keep their coaches and their madams,
> Quoth John in sulky mood to Thomas
> Have stole the very river from us.
> O Scotland, long has it been said
> Thy teeth are sharp for English bread
> What seize our bread and water too
> And use us worse than jailors do;
> 'Tis true, 'tis hard; 'tis true.
> Ye friends of George, and friends of James,
> Envy us not our river Thames;
> The Princess, fond of raw-boned faces,
> May give you all our posts and places;
> Take all to gratify your pride,
> But dip your oatmeal in the Clyde.

In 1772 the building of houses began. No expense was spared. Some of the best painters and craftsmen of the time worked on the interiors including Angelica Kauffmann, Cipriani and Zucchi. The brothers ran into financial difficulties. The Government refused to lease the cellars for storing gunpowder because they flooded at high tide; and the development was remote from the fashionable West End. In 1773 an Act was passed allowing a lottery to be held to raise money to complete the scheme. The lottery was held the next year at JONATHAN'S COFFEE HOUSE, CHANGE ALLEY. There were 4,370 tickets costing £50 each, for 108 prizes. Thus the Adams remained precariously solvent. Soon afterwards the development was complete. As its centrepiece was the Royal Terrace of 11 houses which was presented as a 41-bay architectural unit with unifying central and flanking pilasters. On each side were ADAM STREET and Robert Street and, behind, John Street, James Street and William Street. In 1864–70 the VICTORIA EMBANKMENT was built in front of the Terrace, depriving it of its riverside position. In 1867 the Adelphi Vaults were 'in part occupied as wine cellars and coal wharfs, their grim vastness, a reminder of the Etruscan Cloaca of Old Rome'. Here, according to Tombs, 'the most abandoned characters have often passed the night, nestling upon foul straw; and many a street thief escaped from his pursuers in these dismal haunts before the introduction of gaslight and a vigilant police.' These vaults can still be seen in Lower Robert Street off York

The south front of the Adams' development, the Adelphi. The vaults were 'a reminder of the Etruscan Cloaca of Old Rome'.

Buildings. In 1872 the Royal Terrace lost much of its charm when its façade was cemented over and its wrought iron balconies were removed. The arches were also underpinned. In 1936–8 the Royal Terrace block was demolished and replaced by a building by Colcutt and Hemp, shamelessly called Adelphi and sporting bold zodiacal symbols. The streets have been renamed and renumbered several times. John Street and Duke Street now form JOHN ADAM STREET and James Street and William Street are now named DUR-HAM HOUSE STREET. Only a few of the original houses remain, one of the most attractive being No. 7 ADAM STREET, the offices of the *Lancet*. The Adelphi concept was shortly afterwards imitated by the Adams' staid rival, Sir William Chambers, at SOMERSET HOUSE with its raised riverside terrace.

Adelphi Terrace *WC2*. Robert and James Adam lived here in 1773–8; so did Dr Johnson's friend, Topham Beauclerk, in 1772–6; and David Garrick in 1772–5. His widow continued to live here for a further 43 years after his death, dying in 1822. A room from the demolished house was reconstructed at the VIC-TORIA AND ALBERT MUSEUM. The quack doctor, James Graham, had his Temple of Health here in 1778–81 before moving to SCHOMBERG HOUSE, PALL MALL. His Temple was hung with 'walking sticks, ear trumpets, visual glasses, crutches, etc. left and here placed as most honourable trophies by deaf, weak, paralytic and emaciated persons, cripples etc. who being cured had no longer need of such assistance'. Graham's 'celestial bed' for conceiving perfect children was hired out at £100 per night. In 1781 Emma Lyon, later Lady Hamilton, is said to have posed for him as the Goddess of Health. A resident in 1881–1901

was Richard D'Oyly Carte, producer of the Savoy Operas. Sir Arthur Blomfield had his office here in 1864–8. Thomas Hardy studied architecture under him during 1864–7. Hardy then returned to Dorches-ter, claiming that his health had suffered from the stench of the mud at low tide. He recollected, 'I sat there, drawing inside the easternmost window of the front room on the first floor, occasionally varying the experience by idling on the balcony. I saw from there the Embankment and Charing Cross Bridge built and, of course, used to think of Garrick and Johnson. The rooms contained fine Adam mantelpieces in white marble on which we used to sketch caricatures in pen-cil.' Charles Booth, the shipowner, social reformer and author of *Life and Labour of the People in London*, lived here from 1894 to 1901. The LONDON SCHOOL OF ECONOMICS moved here in its third year of life. Miss Charlotte Payne Townshend, benefactor and friend of the Webbs, took the two upper storeys so that she could help with the social side of the school. In 1898 she married George Bernard Shaw and the couple lived here until 1929 when demolition threatened. The LONDON SCHOOL OF ECONOMICS moved to its own building in CLARE MARKET in 1902.

Adelphi Theatre *Strand, WC2*. (Formerly Sans Pareil, 1806–19; Adelphi, 1819–29; Theatre Royal, New Adelphi, 1829–67; Royal Adelphi, 1867–1901; Century, 1901–2; Royal Adelphi, 1902–40.) Opened in 1806 by John Scott, a local tradesman, to launch his daughter as an actress. It was sold in 1819 to Jones and Rodwell who put on burlettas and dramatised versions of Walter Scott's novels. In 1821 Moncrieff's dramatisation of Pierce Egan's *Tom and Jerry, or Life in London* had over 100 performances, a long run in

7

those days. In 1834 the first sinking stage in England was installed. From 1837 to 1845 popular dramatisations of Dickens's novels were performed here. In 1844 Madame Celeste and Ben Webster took over the management. They produced 'Adelphi dramas', mostly written by J.B. Buckstone, of which the best were *The Green Bushes* (1845) and *The Flowers of the Forest* (1847). The theatre was rebuilt in 1858 by T.H. Wyatt to look like the Opéra Comique in Paris. In the 1880s and 1890s it was famous for melodramas produced by G.R. Sims, Henry Pettit and Sydney Grundy. Among them were *In the Ranks* (1883), *The Harbour Lights* (1885) and *The Bells of Hazlemere* (1887). In 1897 a real drama took place outside the theatre when William Terris, the leading actor, was shot by a lunatic. In 1900 the theatre was rebuilt by Ernest Runtz. In 1904–8 Otho Stuart's management was noted for its productions of modern drama and Shakespearean revivals. From 1908 to 1922 musical comedies were staged. The most successful of these were *The Quaker Girl* (1908), *Tina* (1915), *High Jinks* (1916), *The Boy* (1917), *The Naughty Princess* (1920) and *The Golden Moth* (1921). These were followed by dramas, musical comedies and revues. Outstanding productions were the revue *Clowns in Clover* (1927) and the musical comedy *Mr Cinders* (1929). The theatre was again rebuilt by Ernest Schaufelberg in 1930. It reopened with *Evergreen* produced by C.B. Cochran. The seating capacity is 1,500.

Admiral's Walk *NW3*. Extends from HAMPSTEAD GROVE to Lower Terrace. Takes its name, as does Admiral's House, from the 18th-century admiral, Matthew Barton, who, although a HAMPSTEAD resident, never in fact lived here. The house was built in about 1700, and Fountain North, a naval officer who bought it in 1791, constructed the quarterdeck on the roof where Admiral Barton has long and wrongly been supposed to have fired salutes on special occasions. Other residents of the house have included Sir George Gilbert Scott and Sir John Fortescue.

Admiralty *Whitehall, SW1*. In the early 17th century naval business was done at Wallingford House during the ownership of the 1st Duke of Buckingham, the Lord High Admiral. This was burned down in 1694 and replaced by Wren's Admiralty, a building mainly taken up with residential accommodation for the First Sea Lord and his officers. This in turn was replaced in 1722–6 by Thomas Ripley's existing building which incorporated interior features from the previous building, notably the carved wood garlands and nautical instruments above the Board Room fireplace which are possibly by Grinling Gibbons. The date 1695 is carved on a quadrant to the right of the fireplace. Its heavy portico was 'deservedly veiled', in Horace Walpole's phrase, by Robert Adam's graceful screen in 1759–61. In 1786–8 ADMIRALTY HOUSE was built to the south for the First Lord of the Admiralty. Nelson lay in state here in 1806. William, Duke of Clarence, while First Lord in 1827–8, enlarged the entrance in the screen for his carriage. In 1894–5 Leeming and Leeming's extension was built on the garden of ADMIRALTY HOUSE. The building was badly damaged in the 2nd World War and there was a fire in 1955. Restoration was completed in 1958.

Admiralty Arch *The Mall, SW1*. Built in 1910 to the design of Sir Aston Webb as part of the Queen

The board room of the Admiralty in the early 19th century. The carved wood garlands are possibly by Grinling Gibbons.

Victoria memorial scheme, it is the terminal point of THE MALL, leading into TRAFALGAR SQUARE. It comprises three identical deep arches, each with wrought-iron gates. The gate in the central arch is opened only on ceremonial occasions.

Admiralty House *Whitehall, SW1*. Built in 1786–8 by Samuel Pepys Cockerell as a residence for the First Lord of the Admiralty. In 1894–5 an extension to the ADMIRALTY was built in the garden. The summer house by William Kent was moved to BUCKINGHAM PALACE. Among the First Lords of the Admiralty who have used the house are Earl Grey (1806), Thomas Grenville (1806–7), the Duke of Clarence, afterwards William IV (1827–8), Lord Tweedmouth (1905–8), Winston Churchill (1911–15 and 1939–40), A.J. Balfour (1915–16), Austen Chamberlain (1931), and Duff Cooper (1937–8).

Aeolian Hall *135–137 New Bond Street, W1*. Opened in January 1904 with a recital by the Orchestrelle Company who had taken over the Grosvenor Art Gallery in 1903 and converted it into a concert hall with seating for some 500 people. An organ was built for it and a small gallery added at the back. In 1941 it was taken over by the BBC as a broadcasting studio. It was closed in 1975. (*See also* SOTHEBY'S.)

Aerated Bread Co. *17 Camden Road, NW1*. Opened their first tea shop in the STRAND in 1861, several years before the first Lyons' tea shop (*see* LYONS' CORNER HOUSES). Over the next century hundreds of branches and many tea shops were opened all over the Greater London area. The tea shops have now all closed.

Agar Town The 72-acre area is now covered by the approaches to ST PANCRAS STATION. When William Agar leased the land in 1810 it was open fields and the intended route of the REGENT'S CANAL. Agar protested about the canal and the route was changed. In 1831 part of the estate was sublet, and overnight a shanty town developed with no proper drainage. In 1851 Dickens called it an 'English suburban Connemara .... A complete bog of mud and filth with deep cart-ruts, wretched hovels, the doors blocked up with mud, heaps of ashes, oyster shells and decayed vegetables. The stench of a rainy morning is enough to knock down a bullock.' In 1866 it was taken over by the Midland Railway Company after the ECCLESIASTICAL COMMISSIONERS had refused to renew the Agar family lease. The town was demolished to make way for the new terminal. Tom Sayers, the pugilist, lived in Agar Town for many years; and Dan Leno was born here in 1861.

Air Pilots' and Air Navigators' Guild *see* CITY LIVERY COMPANIES.

Airports HOUNSLOW was London's original civil aerodrome, appointed as such when civilian flying was resumed after the 1st World War. But on 29 March 1920 CROYDON was made the London Customs Air Port and HOUNSLOW was closed. In 1923 a Civil Aviation Advisory Board report on London's aerodrome facilities recommended the retention and enlargement of CROYDON. Consequently this aerodrome was improved and extended and, on 30 January 1928, came into operation as the new Airport of London, being officially opened on 2 May. After the 2nd World War the Government decided that CROYDON and NORTH-OLT would be used as London airports in the immediate post-war period, and on 1 January 1946 the site of a new London Airport at Heathrow was handed over by the Air Ministry to the Ministry of Civil Aviation. In March NORTHOLT came into temporary use as a civil airport (on loan from the RAF to the MCA) and later that month Heathrow was named London Airport, being opened as London (Heathrow) Airport on 31 May 1946 when direct services between the United States and the United Kingdom were started.

In 1952 the Government approved the development of Gatwick (which had had a brief but not very successful pre-war existence) and in 1954 a White Paper proposed that it should be developed as a second main airport to serve London. Elizabeth II opened the new Gatwick Airport on 9 June 1958 and in the following year the former London Airport at Croydon was closed. Development had continued at Heathrow where, on 16 December 1955, the Queen had opened the first three permanent buildings in the Central Area set in the middle of the pattern of the airport's parallel runways. Gatwick was also developed, and on 1 April 1966 the newly formed British Airports Authority took over responsibility for both airports.

During the 1970s further improvements were made at Gatwick, including runway extension and new and enlarged terminal facilities, opened by Prince Charles on 9 June 1978. Shortly after that date Heathrow, for the first time, handled a record total of 106,841 passengers in one day. In nine days in August 1980 the number of passengers handled exceeded 100,000; on 31 August that year the number was 112,880. The total area of London (Heathrow) Airport is 2,810 acres. The Piccadilly Line underground was extended to Heathrow in 1977, Heathrow Central Station being opened on 16 December that year.

Albany *Piccadilly, W1.* The house was originally built in 1770–4 for the 1st Viscount Melbourne to the design of Sir William Chambers. Melbourne House, as it was then known, was soon afterwards exchanged by Lord Melbourne for the WHITEHALL mansion of Frederick, Duke of York and Albany. In 1802 it was sold to Alexander Copland, a young builder, who commissioned Henry Holland to convert the house into

chambers for bachelors. This was done and two large blocks were built on each side of the garden. These blocks were separated – and still are separated – by a paved and covered walk, the rope walk, leading from the PICCADILLY entrance into BURLINGTON GARDENS. The BURLINGTON GARDENS lodges remain, though the entrance gate on the PICCADILLY front and the shops which Holland built on either side of it have disappeared. Residents – women in recent years as well as men – have included Henry Holland himself, Lord Brougham, Charles Wyndham, Palmerston, Sir Robert Smirke, Canning, 'Monk' Lewis, Byron, George Basevi, Gladstone, Bulwer-Lytton, T.B. Macaulay, Sir Thomas Beecham, Aldous Huxley, Sir Arthur Bryant, Prince Littler, Terence Rattigan, Viscount Lee of Fareham, Antony Armstrong-Jones, Malcolm Muggeridge, Dame Edith Evans, J.B. Priestley, Graham Greene, Sir Harold Nicolson, Lord Clark, Margaret Leighton, Terence Stamp and Edward Heath. There are 69 sets of chambers.

Albany Empire *Douglas Way, Deptford, SE8.* The very first purpose-built Community Theatre in Britain, it forms part of the Albany Community Centre and the performances staged are often based on local issues. It was designed by Howell, Killick, Patrick and Amiss.

Albany Street *NW1.* Extends from south to north across the circle of REGENT'S PARK. It was laid out progressively during the 1820s, and takes its name from the title of Prince Frederick, Duke of Albany, George IV's younger brother. It is an interesting street with the back premises of the ROYAL COLLEGE OF PHYSICIANS at its southern end, CHRIST CHURCH in the centre, and the REGENT'S PARK BARRACKS to the north. The Queen's Head and Artichoke public house at Nos 30–32, rebuilt about the turn of this century, still occupies the site on the corner with Longford Street which a courageous earlier proprietor leased when REGENT'S PARK was first planned – as far as is known, he was the first person to take up a lease on the new estate. Sir Edward Jenner occupied both Nos 8 and 12 at different times; Francis Trevelyan Buckland, the naturalist, lived at No. 37 in 1865–80; the Rossetti family at No. 45; Henry Mayhew at No. 55; and Edward Lear stayed at No. 61. Nos 140–148 have fine stucco for they were built by William Nosworthy, Nash's own plasterer. Nos 119–217 are of the original building and unspoiled. Just south of CHRIST CHURCH stood a curious building, demolished in 1968. It was constructed as an Ophthalmic Hospital to extend the work undertaken gratuitously by Sir William Adams at York Hospital in CHELSEA, of treating soldiers suffering from eye disease contracted during the Egyptian campaigns against Napoleon. Later, Sir Goldsworthy Gurney, the inventor, took over the lease and built himself a steam-carriage in the yard which he tried out around the Park before driving it to Bath in July 1829. Later, the hospital was used as a factory for Perkins and Bacon's 'steam guns', a prototype of the modern machine gun. Thereafter, the building was used for a variety of warehouse purposes. The White House Hotel, which has 600 rooms, is on the east side.

Albemarle Street *W1.* After the death in exile of Edward Hyde, Earl of Clarendon, in 1674 his great palace and grounds in PICCADILLY, known as

CLARENDON HOUSE, were sold to the 2nd Duke of Albemarle. In 1683 Albemarle sold the whole property to a group of 'rich bankers and mechanics' (to quote John Evelyn), headed by John Hinde, a CITY goldsmith, who immediately afterwards began to organise the development of the area (then called Albemarle Ground) for building, the embryo streets soon being known by their present names of Albemarle Street, BOND STREET, DOVER STREET and STAFFORD STREET. The principal speculator was Sir Thomas Bond, a financier in high favour at Court, who in 1684 agreed with John Hinde's syndicate to take building leases of considerable parts of Albemarle Ground. Bond's two partners were Henry Jermyn, created Baron Dover in 1685, and Margaret Stafford, an unmarried lady of ancient Northamptonshire lineage, from whom DOVER STREET and STAFFORD STREET take their names. Unfortunately, however, Sir Thomas Bond died in 1685, and Hinde was declared bankrupt two years later, thereby occasioning numerous lawsuits. Consequently the progress of building was extremely slow, and although on the southern part of Albemarle Ground there were already many fine houses, it could still be said in 1720 of the northern part 'that it is not to this Day finished, and God knows when it will. So that it lyeth like the Ruins of Troy, some [houses] having only the Foundations begun, others carry'd up to the Roofs, and others covered, but none of the Inside Work done.' And 25 years later the northern extremities of Albemarle and Dover Streets were still unbuilt. In 1708 the southern part of Albemarle Street was said to contain 'excellent new Building, inhabited by Persons of Quality', and several early 18th-century houses still survive – notably Nos 7, 37 (a small run-of-the-mill house little outwardly altered, excepting the insertion of a shop window), 47, 49 and 50. No. 5, a large house with a pedimented centre window on the first floor, dates from about 1765. No. 7 was for many years occupied by Grillon's Hotel, where Louis XVIII stayed for two days in great pomp in 1814 on his way back to France. No. 50 (its front now wholly covered with stucco) has since 1812 been the home of John Murray, the publishers, *inter alia*, of Byron, Jane Austen and George Crabbe. This was the great literary *salon* of Regency London. Here Byron first met Sir Walter Scott, and it was here that after his death Byron's memoirs were burnt, being judged too salacious for publication.

In the 18th century distinguished residents of Albemarle Street included the Prince of Wales (later George II); George Berkeley, the philosopher and Bishop of Cloyne; Robert Harley, 1st Earl of Oxford, the statesman; Johann Zoffany, the painter; and the architect, Robert Adam. But after about 1800 Albemarle Street ceased to be largely residential. In 1799 the ROYAL INSTITUTION of Great Britain had settled near the north end, and in 1838 its extensive premises were given a handsome stone façade, containing 14 giant Corinthian columns (by Lewis Vulliamy). On the west side BROWN'S HOTEL (where Theodore Roosevelt and his wife spent their honeymoon) took over and still occupies half-a-dozen tall stucco-fronted houses; and the building of the ROYAL ARCADE (which extends from Albemarle Street to BOND STREET) marked another stage in the advancing tide of commerce. No. 24, at the north-west corner, formerly occupied by GARRARD'S, the jewellers, and now by a bank, is a fine stone building of 1911 by Sir Ernest George and Yates.

Today offices, shops and art galleries, all of a very superior kind, predominate. The Parker Gallery, London's oldest firm of print dealers, founded in 1750, is at No. 2; Thomas Agnew and Sons (founded 1817), dealers in works of art, at No. 3.

Albert Bridge *Chelsea–Battersea*. A curious three-span bridge was constructed by R.M. Ordish on his 'straight–link suspension' system in 1871–3. It was built as a cantilever structure, each half supported by 16 straight wrought-iron bars radiating from the top of the highly ornamental cast-iron towers. The side girders of the parapets were hung from vertical steel suspenders. Thus it was a hybrid type of bridge containing elements of both cantilever and suspension. The 1884 suspension members were overhauled by Sir Joseph Bazalgette in 1884. In 1971–3 the deck was strengthened to take increased traffic loads.

Albert Bridge Road *SW11*. Extends from ALBERT BRIDGE along the west side of BATTERSEA PARK to Battersea Park Road. Norman Douglas occupied a flat in Albany Mansions, 1913–17; *Old Calabria* was published while he was living here, and *South Wind* soon after his return to Capri.

Albert Dock *see* ROYAL GROUP OF DOCKS.

Albert Embankment *SE1*. Broad riverside road, just under a mile long, built on the east bank of the Thames opposite MILLBANK by Sir Joseph Bazalgette in 1866–70. Small timber and boat building yards were swept away and land reclaimed from the river at a cost of £1,014,525. Fragments of Delft pottery were found during the digging of the foundations, relics of the Lambeth potteries which had existed here since Elizabethan times (*see* LAMBETH POTTERY). ST THOMAS'S HOSPITAL and LAMBETH PALACE are at the northern end; the southern end covers the site of the VAUXHALL pleasure gardens. Between them the Embankment is now lined with tall office blocks, a rare exception being a Victorian public house, the Crown Tavern, on the corner of Tinworth Street. Lambeth Bridge House was built in 1939–40 for the Ministry of Public Buildings and Works and is now occupied by the Department of the Environment. The LONDON FIRE BRIGADE Headquarters, designed by E.P. Wheeler, was opened by George V in 1937.

Albert Gate *SW1*. The site of a bridge over the WESTBOURNE (*see* KNIGHTSBRIDGE). In 1730 the Serpentine was formed by damming the WESTBOURNE (*see* HYDE PARK) but the old watercourse was used to channel off surplus water. In 1809 the entire neighbourhood was flooded and for several days people were rowed over here from CHELSEA by THAMES boatmen. The WESTBOURNE was diverted into a sewer in 1826. The two old inns which used to stand here, the FOX AND BULL and the White Hart, were both demolished in 1841 and replaced by two large stuccoed buildings built by Thomas Cubitt. They were nicknamed 'The Two Gibraltars' because it was said that they would never be taken. One is now the French Embassy. The gate into HYDE PARK was erected in 1846. The stags on the piers came from the Ranger's Lodge, GREEN PARK and were modelled from prints by Bartolozzi.

Albert Hall *Kensington Gore, SW7.* In 1851 Prince Albert suggested that, with the profits of the GREAT EXHIBITION, a site in South Kensington should be bought for museums, schools, colleges and a central hall containing libraries, a lecture theatre and exhibition rooms. GORE HOUSE was accordingly purchased for that purpose by the commissioners in 1852. The next year Prince Albert asked Gottfried Semper, architect of the Dresden Opera House, to draw up plans for a hall but these were not used. In 1858 Henry Cole, Chairman of the Society of Arts, had plans made by Captain Francis Fowke of the Royal Engineers for a massive concert hall to hold 15,000 but these, also, were not used and the project was temporarily shelved. After Prince Albert's death in 1861 a public fund was opened to finance the ALBERT MEMORIAL and a hall. Seven architects drew up plans for the hall, among them Sir George Gilbert Scott, whose designs were chosen. But barely enough money was raised to cover the cost of the memorial and the hall scheme was again dropped. In 1863 Cole revived the idea, proposing to finance the building by selling the 999-year leasehold of seats. Over 1,300 seats were sold at £100 each, entitling the owner to free attendance at every performance in the hall, an arrangement only partly modified today by the agreement of the seat owners on about 80 occasions each year. In 1865 new designs by Captain Fowke, influenced by Semper's opera house, were approved by the Prince of Wales. The Great Exhibition commissioners gave £50,000 and promised the site at a peppercorn rent of 1s a year which is still paid annually on 25 March. Fowke died in December 1865 and Colonel H.Y. Darracott Scott took over. In 1868 Queen Victoria laid the foundation stone (now behind two seats in block K at the rear of the stalls) and then unexpectedly announced that 'Royal Albert' was to be added to the existing title 'Hall of Arts and Sciences'. Two years later the hall was declared open by the Prince of Wales in place of his mother who was overcome by emotion. The notorious echo was first discovered when the Bishop of London prayed during the ceremony and the 'Amen' reverberated round the building. It has been said that the only place where a British composer can be sure of hearing his work twice is at the Albert Hall. Sir Thomas Beecham said it could be used for a hundred things but music wasn't one of them. The hall is oval – with exterior measurements of 272 ft by 238 ft – and has a capacity of over 8,000 but safety regulations reduce this figure to about 7,000. Its glass and iron dome is 135 ft high internally. The high frieze around the outside wall is by Armitage, Pickersgill, Marks and Poynter and illustrates 'The Triumph of Arts and Letters'. The 150 ton organ by Willis (reconstructed by Harrison and Harrison) had nearly 9,000 pipes and was the largest ever when built. A steam engine worked the bellows. Bruckner played it at the inaugural concert (*see* ORGANS).

In 1877 the Wagner Festival was held, with six concerts conducted by Wagner himself. In the 1880s a dance floor was installed and exhibitions and assaults-at-arms were occasionally held. In 1886 the first of a series of concerts given by Dame Adelina Patti took place. In the 1890s charity balls, bazaars and festivals were held. On one occasion the owners of seats J894 and J895, the Misses Mirchouse, insisted on having a trapdoor cut in the dance floor so they could reach their seats and enjoy the dancing around them. In 1900 Madame Albani gave her farewell concert. In 1906 a record audience of 9,000 heard the first gramophone concert. In 1911 the Shakespeare Ball, which was held just before the coronation of George V, was attended by 80 visiting royals. Another grand ball was held three years later to celebrate 100 years of peace between England and the USA. In 1919 the first boxing contest was held in the hall. The prize was a gold trophy presented by George V. In 1923 the first performance was given of Longfellow's *Hiawatha*, set to music by Coleridge-Taylor; and from 1930 to 1940 *Hiawatha* was performed annually. In 1941 the 47th Season of Sir Henry Wood's Promenade Concerts moved here after the bombing of the QUEEN'S HALL and the 'Proms' have since been held here annually. In 1953 the Coronation Ball was held here as it had been in 1937. In 1968, with a government interest-free loan of £40,000, the acoustics were improved by hanging saucer-like shapes from the roof. In 1970–1 the hall was cleaned and restored for its centenary. The Corps of Honorary Stewards comprises about 70 volunteer ushers who receive a pair of tickets in return for each attendance. All tickets are printed on the site.

H.Y. Darracott Scott's proposed design in 1867 for the 'Hall of Arts and Sciences' to be erected at Kensington. When she laid the foundation stone Queen Victoria prefaced the original name with 'Royal Albert'.

Albert Hall Mansions *Kensington Gore, SW7.* Three six-storey blocks designed by Norman Shaw and erected in 1880–7. They were the first flats to be built in the Dutch style and were widely imitated. All had bathrooms, lifts and wine cellars.

Albert Memorial *Kensington Gardens, SW7.* In 1862 a public meeting was convened at the MANSION HOUSE by the LORD MAYOR, William Cubitt, to discuss the raising of funds for a national memorial to Prince Albert. Queen Victoria was asked to choose the design of the memorial. She formed a committee to advise her, on which sat the Earl of Derby, the Earl of Clarendon, Sir Charles Eastlake and Lord Mayor Cubitt. They rejected the first idea of a memorial obelisk and asked several architects to submit plans. George Gilbert Scott, James Pennethorne, T.L. Donaldson, P.C. Hardwick, M. Digby Wyatt, Charles Barry and E.M. Barry competed. The Queen chose Scott's design. The ROYAL SOCIETY OF ARTS (the Prince had been their president) collected small subscriptions from all over the country. In 1863 Parliament voted £50,000 towards the memorial. Gladstone delayed its construction by haggling over the cost which did not

11

go unnoticed by the Queen. The Irish refused to subscribe and did not carry out their contract for granite.

The Queen took a close interest in the enterprise. On 1 July 1872 she inspected the memorial which was now completed except for the central statue of the Prince. She did not express an opinion, but Scott was knighted. On 3 July the hoardings were removed and the public admitted. There was no official unveiling ceremony.

In 1876 the 14 ft high statue of the Prince by John Foley was erected. The delay had been caused by the death of the first sculptor, Baron Marochetti, whose 1867 model had proved unsatisfactory. The memorial is 175 ft high and cost £120,000. The Gothic canopy is inlaid with mosaics, enamels and polished stone and is topped by an inlaid cross. There are no less than seven tiers of statuary ascending from the base. The outer corners are marked by massive marble groups of 'Asia', sculpted by J.H. Foley, 'Europe', by Patrick Macdowell (Gibson had refused the commission), 'Africa' by William Theed and 'America' by John Bell. On the corners of the podium are 'Agriculture' by Calder Marshall, 'Manufactures' by Weekes, 'Commerce' by Thornycroft and 'Engineering' by Lawlor, all in marble. Around the base of the memorial is a white marble frieze, with 169 life-size figures, by H.H. Armstead and J.B. Philip: on the east side, painters; on the north, architects; musicians and poets on the south; and sculptors on the west. Philip was responsible for 87 of them. Enshrined above is the mighty bronze statue of Prince Albert, seated and holding the catalogue of the GREAT EXHIBITION. On the pillars of the memorial are bronze statues by Philip of 'Astronomy', 'Chemistry', 'Geology' and 'Geometry'; and above, in niches, 'Rhetoric', 'Medicine', 'Philosophy' and 'Physiology' by Armstead. Mosaics in the arches are by Salviati's and show 'Poetry', 'Painting', 'Architecture' and 'Sculpture'. In niches on the spires are gilt bronze figures designed by J. Redfern of 'Faith', 'Hope', 'Charity' and 'Humility', with 'Fortitude', 'Prudence', 'Justice' and 'Temperance' at the corners. Above them are eight gilt bronze angels designed by Philip.

The memorial was initially acclaimed but towards the end of the century a reaction set in. Modern opinion tends to equivocation. For Osbert Sitwell in 1928 it was 'that wistful, unique monument of widowhood . . . that gilded and pensive giant on his dais under the Gothic canopy, strewn with white mosaic daisies of a blameless life'.

Albert Saloon *Shepherdess Walk, Hoxton.* First licensed in 1843 and later known as the Albert Theatre, it was unique in that it had two stages, built at right-angles, one with an open-air auditorium and the other with the proscenium opening into the saloon for wet weather performances. It was never successful and a licence was refused in 1852 for lack of maintenance. It closed in 1853.

Albery Theatre *St Martin's Lane, WC2.* A large Edwardian theatre built in 1903 by W.G.R. Sprague for Charles Wyndham and first known as the New Theatre after the street opposite, New Row. From 1905 to 1913 it was used for six months each year by Fred Terry and Julia Neilson. Many of their most successful plays were first seen here, including *The Scarlet Pimpernel* (1905). Dion Boucicault the Younger became manager in 1915. *Peter Pan* was produced at Christmas between 1915 and 1919. In 1916 Somerset Maugham's *Caroline* was performed, and in 1920 Noël Coward's first play, *I'll Leave It To You*, which ran for five weeks. The first London production of Shaw's *St Joan* was given in 1924 with Sybil Thorndike in the title role. In 1926 *The Constant Nymph* began its run of 587 performances. In it John Gielgud made his first appearance at the theatre. In 1932 there was a black and white production of *Twelfth Night* starring Arthur Wontner and Jean Forbes Robertson. In 1933 Gordon Daviot's play *Richard of Bordeaux* established Gielgud's reputation. In 1944, after the bombing of the OLD VIC and SADLER'S WELLS, the New Theatre became the base for both companies. SADLER'S WELLS returned home in 1944 and the OLD VIC in 1950. Gielgud, Olivier, Edith Evans, Michael Redgrave and Ralph Richardson all performed here in Shakespeare. *The First Gentleman* (1945), a play by Norman Ginsbury, and *The Gioconda Smile* (1948) by Aldous Huxley had long runs. In the 1950s there were many outstanding productions including *The Cocktail Party* (1950) by T.S. Eliot, *Dear Charles* (1952), *The Young Elizabeth* (1952), *I Am a Camera* (1954), *The Remarkable Mr Pennypacker* (1955), *Under Milk Wood* (1956) by Dylan Thomas, *Gigi* (1956), and *The Long, the Short and the Tall* (1959). Between 1960 and 1966 Lionel Bart's musical *Oliver* had a record run of 2,618 performances. *Oliver* was revived in 1977, and, later, *Pal Joey* with Sian Phillips. The name of the theatre was changed in 1973 from New to Albery in honour of Sir Bronson Albery, the theatre director. The seating capacity is 879.

Albion Tavern *153 Aldersgate Street.* One of the biggest of London's Victorian taverns. Dinners were given here by several of the CITY LIVERY COMPANIES and by the East India Company for newly appointed Governors of India.

Aldermanbury *EC2.* The name means alderman's manor and dates from the 14th century. The alderman was possibly Aethelred, son-in-law of Alfred the Great, Alderman of Mercia and Governor of London. Aldermanbury was perhaps the site of the first GUILDHALL or a castle used by English kings before Edward the Confessor established his palace at WESTMINSTER. In 1678–80 Judge Jeffreys, while Recorder of London, had a house opposite ST MARY ALDERMANBURY. The street was bombed in the 2nd World War. In 1965–9 the remains of ST MARY'S CHURCH were shipped to Fulton, Missouri to be rebuilt as a memorial to Winston Churchill. At No. 20 is the Chartered Insurance Institute. The GUILDHALL LIBRARY is on the east side. A board in Aldermanbury Square lists the name of ALDERMEN and Common Councilmen (*see* COURT OF COMMON COUNCIL).

Alderman's Walk *EC2.* In the 17th century it led to a large house and garden belonging to Francis Dashwood, alderman of Walbrook Ward. On 18th-century maps it is marked Dashwood's Walk.

Aldermen The aldermen of the CITY OF LONDON never had anything in common – except their title – with the aldermen of other cities and boroughs in England; and, since the latter have now been abolished, they are in a sense unique. They have a Court of their own dating from 1200, when 'five and twenty of the more discreet men of the City were sworn to take counsel on behalf of the City, together with the Mayor'. In 1319 Edward II decreed that aldermen should be retired annually and not re-elected; but from 1377 each ward elected its own alderman for life, unless he resigned for personal reasons or by the wishes of the Court. This practice has continued to the present day, with one slight adjustment, made in 1975, to the effect that aldermen should retire at the age of 70. A candidate for the office must be a Freeman (*see* FREEDOM OF THE CITY) and on election by his ward must be approved by the Court of Aldermen. Should the Court not approve him after three successive appearances before them they may themselves choose a suitable person. The City Election Act of 1727 confirmed the right of the Court of Aldermen to approve or veto the decisions of the Common Council, but this right was annulled by the repeal of the Act in 1746.

All the aldermen are Justices of the Peace, who not only sit in judgment in the MANSION HOUSE and Guildhall Justice Rooms (*see* GUILDHALL), but also appoint the Magistrates' Clerks for those courts. The Court of Aldermen have responsibilities in association with the CITY OF LONDON POLICE; and the CITY LIVERY COMPANIES come under their authority. They have the right to present petitions direct to the Crown, and with the LORD MAYOR they attend the Privy Council and sign the documents proclaiming the succession of the Sovereign.

Aldermen wear a scarlet gown trimmed on the front edges and sleeves with sable, or a 'violet' (really indigo) gown similarly trimmed with bear fur on occasions as directed by the City Ceremonial Book. Those who have been LORD MAYORS or 'passed the Chair' wear the chains they wore as SHERIFF with the addition of the Sword and Mace to their shrieval badges, and a symbolic Cap of Dignity attached to the back of their gowns. Their ceremonial headgear is a black silk cocked hat with steel chain ornament.

Aldersgate City gate, first built by the Romans. The road through it probably linked up with WATLING STREET, and seems to have been constructed after the city wall, possibly to replace the north gate of the fort. But its name is Saxon and means Gate of Ealdred. In 1335 it was resolved that the gate should be covered with lead and a small house made under it for the gatekeeper. In the room above was the workshop of John Day, printer of *The Folio Bible* (1549), Foxe's *Book of Martyrs* (1563), Roger Ascham's *Scholemaster* (1570) and Tyndale's *Works* (1572). In 1603 James I entered London through it for the first time as king. It was rebuilt in 1617. In 1660 Pepys saw the limbs of traitors on it. Damaged in the GREAT FIRE, it was repaired and beautified in 1670, and demolished in 1761. The gate stood opposite No. 62 ALDERSGATE STREET.

Aldersgate Street *EC1*. Named after the ALDERSGATE, one of the gates in the CITY wall which stood opposite No. 62. The church of ST BOTOLPH ALDERSGATE, mentioned in 1135, is the first recorded building here. In 1289 a house named Redehall was let to Henry le Waleys, the Lord Mayor. In 1352 Henry, Lord Percy, built a house in the street which Henry IV's Queen later used as a clothes store; it was thereafter known as Queen Jane's Wardrobe. The Brotherhood

of the Holy Trinity, which was to be suppressed by Edward VI, was founded here in 1446. Trinity Court marks the site of their house. Several Elizabethan noblemen had their mansions here: among these was Petre House, home of the Petre family from 1552 to 1639. Stow said that the COOKS' COMPANY had a hall opposite the church at the beginning of the 17th century. By then Lord Percy's house had become a printing office. In 1618 John Taylor, the water poet, set out in his 'Pennyles Pilgrimage' from London to Edinburgh from the Bell Inn. In about 1639 John Milton kept a boarding school in Maidenhead Court, 'a spacious house', according to his own account, 'for myself and my books where I again with rapture renewed my literary pursuits'. In 1644 Thanet House, later known as Shaftesbury House, was built for the Earl of Thanet by Inigo Jones. In the Civil War Petre House was used as a prison. Richard Lovelace, the Royalist poet, was kept there in 1648. 'Aldersgate resembleth an Italian street more than any other in London', wrote Howell in 1657, 'by reason of the spaciousness and uniformity of buildings, and the straightness thereof, with the convenient distance of the houses; on both sides whereof there are divers fair ones.' The Duke of Lauderdale is said to have had a mansion here at this time. The BISHOP OF LONDON, burnt out of his house in ST PAUL'S CHURCHYARD during the GREAT FIRE, took over Petre House – the fire not having reached this far north – and renamed it London House. Princess Anne was brought here by Bishop Compton when she deserted her father in 1688. The Duke of Monmouth hid in Thanet House after his rebellion in 1685. In 1728 John Wesley attended a Moravian meeting house in the street and wrote in his journal, 'Went very unwillingly to a Society in Aldersgate Street where one was reading Luther's *Preface to the Epistle to the Romans*. About a quarter before nine while he was describing the changes which God makes in the heart through faith in Christ, I felt my heart strangely warmed.' Eight years later the street was described as 'being very spacious and long and although the buildings are old and not uniform yet many of them are very good and well-inhabited'. In 1750 Shaftesbury House became the City Lying-In Hospital and, after the hospital's removal to CITY ROAD, the first general dispensary in London. London House was burned down in 1768, having been an upholsterer's workshop for some years; and in 1882 Shaftesbury House was demolished. At No. 150 between 1750 and 1836 George Seddon and his descendants carried on business as cabinet-makers. Among the most skilful craftsmen in the trade, they made furniture for SOMERSET HOUSE as well as for Windsor Castle. In 1925 IRONMONGERS' HALL was built at No. 35. The area was heavily bombed in the 2nd World War. The east side of the street forms part of the BARBICAN redevelopment. The LONDON SALVAGE CORPS is at No. 140.

Aldford House *Park Lane*. Designed by Eustace Balfour and Turner for Alfred Beit, the German-born financier who made a fortune in South Africa. A grandiose, stone-faced house with mullion windows, it was built in 1897 and filled with artistic treasures including a fine collection of Italian Renaissance bronzes and Murillo's *Prodigal Son* series. It was demolished in 1931, scarcely more than 30 years after it was built, when purchasers of such houses could very rarely be found. It was replaced in 1932 by the present structure designed by Val Myers.

Aldford Street *W1*. Built in the 1730s on the GROSVENOR ESTATE. It was first known as Chapel Street because the GROSVENOR CHAPEL stood opposite in SOUTH AUDLEY STREET. In 1886 it was renamed after a village on the Grosvenor family's Cheshire estate. Beau Brummel lived at No. 13 in 1816. The house from which Harriet Westbrook eloped with Shelley in 1811 was at No. 23. John Gilbert Winant, the American Ambassador, lived at No. 7 in 1941–6.

Aldgate One of the six original gates to the City built by the Romans. The road through it led out to the east and Colchester, once the capital city of England. The Saxons called it Ealdgate, old gate. It was rebuilt at some time between 1108 and 1147. In 1215, the year of Magna Carta, the Barons came through it on their way to lay siege to the TOWER. Between 1374 and 1385 the room above was leased to Geoffrey Chaucer. In 1471, during the Wars of the Roses, the Bastard of Fauconberg, at the head of 5,000 men, demanded entrance. The citizens let him in but then lowered the portcullis and routed his force. Mary Tudor entered London through this gate in 1553 for the first time as Queen. Princess Elizabeth waited with a guard of honour of 2,000 men to meet her. The gate was rebuilt in 1606–9 when Roman coins were found in the original foundations. It was demolished in 1761 and briefly re-erected at BETHNAL GREEN. Its site is now covered by the corner of the street known as ALDGATE and Duke's Place.

Aldgate *EC3*. Extends from Aldgate High Street to the junction of FENCHURCH STREET and LEADENHALL STREET. It takes its name from the Roman gate. The bronze, *Ridirich*, at Wingate House is by Keith McCarter (1980).

Aldgate Pump Now at the junction of LEADENHALL STREET and FENCHURCH STREET. The present stone fountain is several yards to the west of the original pump. A well called Alegate Well is mentioned adjoining the City wall in the time of King John. A free-standing structure is shown at this point on Braun and Hogenberg's map of 1574. This may be the same as St Michael's Well shown on the 'Agas' map of about 1633. Stow mentions 'a fair well where now a pump is placed' and recounts the execution of the Bailiff of Romford, Essex, on a gibbet 'near the well within Aldgate': 'I heard the words of the prisoner for he was executed upon the pavement of my door where I then kept house.' In the 1860s the pump was moved several feet to the west for street widening. Proposals for its removal were resisted by the inhabitants. The present stone pump with a brass dog's head spout dates from 1870–1. Following an adverse report on the quality of the water by the Medical Officer of Health for the CITY the well was closed and the pump connected to the New River Company's supply in 1876 (*see* WATER SUPPLY). The pump no longer dispenses water.

Aldwych *WC2*. The crescent link between the STRAND and KINGSWAY. The new route between HOLBORN and STRAND was officially opened in 1905. George Laurence Gomme, a London historian and clerk to the LONDON COUNTY COUNCIL, was largely responsible for promoting the name Aldwych for the new street. It first appears in 1398 and the early DRURY LANE was known as the 'Via de Aldwych'. Traditionally this was the area called Aldwic, meaning old settlement, which King Alfred magnanimously allotted to the defeated Danes.

Work on clearing the area started in 1900. Streets demolished included Wych Street and Newcastle Street. The GAIETY THEATRE was also demolished. The STRAND was widened at the same time. Despite the 1905 opening and the laying out of the route, buildings followed slowly. The twin STRAND and ALDWYCH THEATRES and the WALDORF HOTEL appeared in 1905–8; and Inveresk House, which was designed by Mewès and Davis for the *Morning Post*, in 1907. But on the eastern side Aldwych House, for example, dates from 1922–3. The southern segment, too, emerged tardily, with AUSTRALIA HOUSE in 1912–18, BUSH HOUSE in three stages, 1923, 1930 and 1935, and INDIA HOUSE in 1928–30. Ivor Novello died in a flat on the top floor of No. 11. At the east end is the Gladstone statue (*see* STATUES).

Aldwych Theatre *Aldwych, WC2*. Designed in 1905 by W.G.R. Sprague for Charles Frohman and Seymour Hicks. It opened with Hicks and Ellaline Terris, his wife, in a revival of *Bluebell in Fairyland*. This was followed mostly by musical comedies but *The Bad Girl of the Family* (1909), a drama by Frederick Melville, had a long run. Hicks left the theatre in 1910; and from 1919 to 1920 it was managed by C.B. Cochran. In 1924 *It Pays to Advertise*, a farce presented by Tom Walls and Leslie Henson, had 598 performances. From 1925 to 1933 the Aldwych farces written by Ben Travers were staged, beginning with *A Cuckoo in the Nest* (1925) followed by *Rookery Nook* (1926), *Thark* (1928) (this had 401 performances), *Plunder* (1928), *A Cup of Kindness* (1929), *A Night Like This* (1931), *Dirty Work* (1932) and *A Bit of a Test* (1933). In 1960, the theatre became the London home of the Royal Shakespeare Company. Since then it has housed many new Shakespearean productions and plays by modern playwrights including *Becket* (1961) by Anouilh and *The Homecoming* (1965) by Pinter. In 1964 a series of World Theatre Seasons began. The RSC's 8½ hour production of *Nicholas Nickleby* in the 1980s was a triumph. The seating capacity of the theatre is 1,004.

Alexander Place *SW7*. Formerly Alfred Place, this was built in 1840 by James Bonnin to designs by George Basevi acting on behalf of John Alexander, the owner of the THURLOE ESTATE.

Alexander Square *SW3*. Built in the late 1820s by George Basevi and named after the owner of the THURLOE ESTATE, John Alexander. George Godwin, the architect, lived at No. 24; and George Augustus Sala, the journalist, at No. 1.

Alexandra Hotel *Knightsbridge*. A small smart hotel much patronisd by country peers. Remarkably little seems to be known about it. It was opened in 1863, the year in which Princess Alexandra of Denmark married the Prince of Wales. It was almost in the middle of St George's Place which was the name of the south side of KNIGHTSBRIDGE between ST GEORGE'S HOSPITAL and WILTON PLACE and immediately to the east of OLD BARRACK YARD on which

Agricultural House (1956) stands today. In the latter part of the 19th century it was on a par with CLARIDGE'S. It survived as a ruin after heavy bomb damage in the 2nd World War. As the plan to rebuild it as offices in the early 1950s never materialised it was totally demolished.

Penny-farthing bicycle race in the grounds of Alexandra Palace in 1886.

Alexandra Palace *Muswell Hill, N22.* In May 1873 the reconstructed international exhibition building of 1862 (*see* EXHIBITIONS) was formally opened as North London's rival to the CRYSTAL PALACE. It was named in honour of Princess Alexandra, Princess of Wales. Sixteen days later it burnt to the ground after a red-hot coal had fallen from a workman's brazier. Encouraged by the attendance figures, the private company who owned it decided to rebuild immediately. The architects were Meeson and Johnson. It was reopened in 1875 with a large hall, concert room, reading room, theatre and offices covering 7 acres in all. However the venture was not successful. The *Golden Guide to London* of 1884 devoted twice as much space to the CRYSTAL PALACE. It listed the attractions of Alexandra Palace as music festivals and flower, fruit, dog and horse shows. In the grounds were a racecourse, archery and cricket grounds, a circus which could seat 3,000 spectators, a Japanese village, a lake and examples of domestic architecture from foreign countries. Attempts to make it a rival firework centre to the CRYSTAL PALACE were a failure.

In the 1st World War it was used first as a barracks, then for Belgian refugees and later for German prisoners of war, who landscaped the grounds. In 1936 part was acquired by the BBC for television studios and the world's first television transmitter was erected. On 26 August 1936 the first transmission took place – *Here's Looking at You*, a variety show introduced by Leslie Mitchell. On 2 November regular transmissions began. On 10 October 1955 the first experimental television colour tests were made. In 1956 the Television Centre was moved to SHEPHERD'S BUSH, though Alexandra Palace was still used for recording the television programmes for the

Open University. Around it are the 480 acres of ALEXANDRA PARK.

In July 1980 much of the building was destroyed by a fire.

Alexandra Park *N22.* The Park, in which ALEXANDRA PALACE is sited, covers 220 acres of the former Tottenham Wood Farm acquired in 1863 by the Alexandra Park Co. There are now public gardens and various sporting facilities including a ski slope and playing fields, allotments and Cadets' Training Centres.

From 1900, when the Park and Palace were purchased by Private Act of Parliament, administration was in the hands of Trustees. In 1965 this was handed over to the GREATER LONDON COUNCIL who on 1 January 1980 passed it to the HARINGEY Borough Council.

Alexandra Road *NW8.* Built about 1863, one of the first of 67 roads and streets in the Greater London area which bear the name of Edward VII's popular Queen. Lillie Langtry, the King's mistress, lived here behind a high brick wall at Leighton House, now demolished. The eastern end of Alexandra Road became Langtry Road in 1967.

Alhambra *Leicester Square (east side).* Opened in 1854 as the Royal Panopticon of Science and Art: the idea was conceived by Edward Clarke, the founder of the London Electrical Society. It was grandly Moorish in style with two minarets. The building was designed by T. Hayter Lewis. Under a huge dome, a 97 ft high fountain constantly played. The organ, made by Hill and Co., was considered one of the country's best. But Londoners did not want to come and look at scientific apparatus and models of machinery, whatever the surroundings, and Clarke went bankrupt. The exhibits were sold in 1856. The building reopened as the Alhambra Palace, a circus, in 1858. When Queen Victoria and her family came to see 'Black Eagle, the Horse of Beauty', success was assured. A licence for music and dancing was granted. The Alhambra became a music-hall in 1860. The following year there was an appearance by Blondin, just back from crossing the Niagara Falls on a tightrope, and Leotard, 'the daring young man on the flying trapeze [who flew] through the air with the greatest of ease'. In 1864 Frederick Strange took over as manager and began the spectacular ballets for which the Alhambra was famous until the 1st World War. In 1870 Strange's licence was not renewed after 'Wiry Sal' had raised her foot 'higher than her head several times towards the audience and had been much applauded'. Strange continued to hold Promenade Concerts; but he was taken to court and fined and the theatre was closed. Three months later he was granted a licence for stage plays. The theatre was burned down in 1882. Rebuilt behind the original façade by Perry and Reed, it reopened in 1883. The next year the music and dancing licence was restored and the Alhambra became a music-hall again. Revues replaced variety in 1912. 1916 saw the production of *The Bing Boys Are Here* with George Robey, and Violet Lorraine singing 'If You Were the Only Girl in the World'. A Diaghilev ballet season was staged in 1919. *Waltzes from Vienna* began its run of 607 performances in 1931. In 1933 de Basil's Ballets Russes de Monte Carlo came for three weeks and stayed four

Acrobats at the Alhambra, Leicester Square. It was known as the Royal Panopticon of Science and Art in 1854–8.

months. In 1935 *Tulip Time* had 427 performances. The theatre was demolished in 1936. The ODEON cinema covers the site.

All Hallows Barking (by the Tower) *Byward Street, EC3.* In 675 Eorconweald, Bishop of London, founded an abbey at BARKING, Essex for his sister Ethelburga and endowed it with the land upon which this church was built. It is variously mentioned as All Hallows and St Mary's. Excavations revealed the foundations of an aisleless Saxon church and two other churches built *c.* 1000–1060. A stone doorway of reused Roman tiles and Kentish ragstone remains. In 1189–99 Richard I built a Lady Chapel north of the church. There is a tradition that his heart was buried in it. A shrine to the Blessed Virgin is said to have been erected by Edward I. Edward IV endowed a chantry for saying masses. Richard III founded a college of priests. In 1547 the Lady Chapel was demolished, and in 1548 the college was dissolved but was restored in 1613. In 1634–5 the church was partially rebuilt. On 4 January 1649 27 barrels of gunpowder exploded beside the churchyard, blowing up over 50 houses including the Rose Tavern where the parish dinner was being held, and causing many deaths. In 1658–9 the tower was rebuilt. It was the only London church to have building work carried out under the Commonwealth. After the GREAT FIRE Pepys climbed up to the top of this tower and there saw 'the saddest sight of desolation'. In 1813 the church was repaired.

In 1922 it became the headquarters of TOC H, the organisation for Christian fellowship founded by the vicar, the Revd F.T.B. Clayton, at Poperinghe, Belgium in the 1st World War. In 1925 the Memorial Chapel in the crypt was created.

In 1940 the church was bombed. There remained only the tower, the walls, a few monuments, some 17th-century sword-rests, 17 brasses dating from 1389 to 1651 and a font cover ascribed to Grinling Gibbons. In 1949–58 the church was rebuilt by Seely and Paget with donations from benefactors all over the world. The pulpit came from the bombed church of ST SWITHIN LONDON STONE, the font was carved from

Gibraltar rock and the altarpiece of the *Last Supper* was painted by Brian Thomas. In the crypt is a small museum of local Saxon and Roman remains.

Bishop Launcelot Andrews was christened here in 1555 and William Penn in 1644. Judge Jeffreys was married here in 1667 and John Quincy Adams, later sixth President of the United States of America, in 1797. Bishop Fisher was buried here after his execution in 1535 but moved later to ST PETER AD VINCULA. Also buried here were Henry Howard, Earl of Surrey, after his execution in 1547, and Archbishop Laud after his execution in 1645. Surrey's body was moved to Framlingham, Suffolk, in 1614 and Laud's to St John's College, Oxford, in 1663.

All Hallows *Bread Street.* Sometimes known as All Hallows Watling Street. It is first mentioned in 1221. It was enlarged in 1349 and the chapel was added in 1350. In 1531 services were suspended for a month after a fight between two priests. Both had to do penance by walking in procession from ST PAUL'S to CHEAPSIDE. In 1559 the steeple was struck by lightning and demolished. After being extensively repaired in 1625 the church was destroyed by the GREAT FIRE. In 1680–4 it was rebuilt by Wren at a cost of £3,348 7s 2d. In 1876 the site and materials were sold for £32,254 and All Hallows Poplar was built with the proceeds. Most of the fittings went to this church which was destroyed in the 2nd World War but the font cover went to ST ANDREW BY THE WARDROBE, the organ case to ST MARY ABCHURCH, the pulpit to ST VEDAST and the carvings and plate to ST MARY-LE-BOW to which the small parish of 2½ acres was united. The remains of the dead were moved to the CITY OF LONDON CEMETERY. In 1954 the churchyard was removed. Watling House now stands on the church site at the south-east corner of BREAD STREET and WATLING STREET. Several medieval LORD MAYORS were buried here and John Milton was christened here in 1608.

All Hallows *Bromley by Bow (Devons Road), E3.* Built in 1873–4, to the designs of Ewan Christian, with part of the proceeds from the sale of the site of ALL HALLOWS STAINING. Bombed in 1940, it was rebuilt in 1954 by A.P. Robinson of Caröe and Partners.

All Hallows *Hampstead (Savernake Road), NW3.* The foundation stone of this, the finest of James Brooks's works, was laid by the Duchess of Teck in 1892, and the church was consecrated in 1901, the year of the architect's death. The chancel was built by Sir Giles Gilbert Scott in 1913. Long and low, without a tower, the structure of the building is immediately expressed in the particularly massive buttresses which stretch right up at a steep diagonal to the projected vault. The effect is particularly impressive on the north side.

Internally, tall and slender piers separate the nave from the aisles which are of equal height, forming a hall church. In the upper parts of the nave the brickwork is exposed but otherwise the stone used is Ancaster limestone. There are large windows in the aisles and a wheel window at the west end. The pulpit came from ST PETER, VERE STREET.

All Hallows *Honey Lane.* A small parish of just over one acre, first mentioned in 1235. In 1540 Thomas Garrard, a former rector, was burnt at

SMITHFIELD for heresy. After being repaired in 1625 the church was destroyed in the GREAT FIRE and not rebuilt. In 1670 the parish was united with ST MARY-LE-BOW. The site was covered first by HONEY LANE MARKET, then by the CITY OF LONDON SCHOOL, and since 1963 by the offices of the Sun Life Assurance Co.

All Hallows *Lombard Street*. Also known as All Hallows Grass Church, it was first mentioned in 1053. It was rebuilt 1494–1516. The stone porch from the PRIORY OF ST JOHN OF JERUSALEM was incorporated. Soon after being repaired in 1622 it was burned down in the GREAT FIRE. In 1686–94 it was rebuilt by Wren as a simple rectangle with an apse at the east end. It cost £8,058 15s 6d and was the last of Wren's City churches to be completed. In 1735 Wesley mounted the pulpit to discover that he had forgotten his notes. A woman in the congregation, aware of his predicament, called out, 'Cannot you trust God for a sermon?' He never used notes again. In 1864 the parish acquired those of ST BENET GRACECHURCH and ST LEONARD EASTCHEAP and, in 1876, the parish of ST DIONIS BACKCHURCH. The church was closed in 1937 and the site was sold to BARCLAY'S BANK for their head office. It was demolished in 1938–9. The tower was reconstructed as part of ALL HALLOWS, NORTH TWICKENHAM which, with All Saints Queensbury, was built on the proceeds of the sale. The parishes were united with ST EDMUND THE KING.

All Hallows London Wall *83 London Wall, EC2*. Built on a bastion of the Roman city wall. It is first mentioned at the beginning of the 12th century. In 1474 a cell for anchorites was built next to the chancel wall. This was later occupied by Simon the Anker, a famous recluse who lived in it for 20 years, writing here *The Fruyte of Redemcyon* which was printed by Wynkyn de Worde in 1514. A new aisle was built in 1528–9. The church was extensively repaired in 1613–27. It escaped destruction in the GREAT FIRE and was rebuilt in 1765–7 by George Dance, the Younger, having returned from Italy. In later life he referred to it as 'my first child'. It cost £2,941. The altar painting of *St Paul Receiving his Sight from Ananias* was copied by his brother, Nathaniel Dance-Holland, from Pietro da Cortona's painting which hangs in the Church of the Conception, Rome. The building was repaired in 1891 and in 1954 made a guild church. The parish was united with ST BOTOLPH WITHOUT BISHOPSGATE. In 1960–2 it was restored by David Nye. It is now the headquarters of the Council for Care of Churches and a Christian Art Centre.

All Hallows *North Twickenham (Chertsey Road), Middlesex*. The white stone church tower is all that remains of ALL HALLOWS, LOMBARD STREET. In 1938–9, when the original church was pronounced unsafe, a decision was taken to remove the 104 ft tower to North Twickenham where Robert Atkinson erected a simple brick structure beside it to accommodate the fine 17th-century reredos and 18th-century furnishings which had been the gift of bankers to the original church. The porch came from the dissolved PRIORY OF ST JOHN, CLERKENWELL, and a gate which has bars and spikes adorned with emblems of death used to stand in the alley leading to the church. In the vestibule is a tablet to Thomas Vardon and his six children, five of whom died before they were one year old.

All Hallows *Shirlock Road, NW3*. A fine church by James Brooks built in 1889 of Kentish ragstone. The chancel is by Sir Giles Gilbert Scott (1913).

All Hallows Staining *Mark Lane*. First mentioned in 1177. The origin of the name Staining is uncertain. Possibly it is from the church having been built of stone when others were made of wood, or from the land belonging to the manor of Staines. It was rebuilt in about 1450. In 1554 Queen Elizabeth I, while still a princess, gave thanks here for her release from the TOWER and presented the church with new bell ropes as the bells had 'been music to her ears'. Repaired in 1630, the church survived the GREAT FIRE, but in 1671 it collapsed because of excessive burials. Rebuilt in 1674–5, it was demolished in 1870 except for the 15th-century tower. The site was sold to the CLOTHWORKERS' COMPANY for £12,418 on condition that they did not build on the land and kept the tower in good order. ALL HALLOWS BROMLEY BY BOW was built on the proceeds. The parish was united to ST OLAVE HART STREET. A late 16th-century bell from the church is now in GROCERS' HALL.

All Hallows *Tottenham (Tottenham Church Lane), N17*. The brick south porch dates from the 15th century. William Butterfield built the east end of the church in 1875.

All Hallows the Great *Upper Thames Street*. Also known as All Hallows at the Hay, All Hallows in La Corderie, All Hallows in the Ropery, and All Hallows the More, it is first mentioned in 1235. In 1447 Henry VI founded a grammar school. In 1598 Stow described it as 'a fair church with a large cloister on the south side ... but foully defaced and ruinated'. Rebuilt in 1627–9, it was burned down in the GREAT FIRE, and was again rebuilt by Wren at a cost of £5,541 9s 2d in 1677–83, having acquired the parish of ALL HALLOWS THE LESS in 1670. The tower and north aisle were demolished in 1876 to enable QUEEN VICTORIA STREET to be widened. In 1876–7 the tower and vestry were rebuilt on the south side. In 1893–4 it was demolished, except for the tower and vestry, under the Union of City Benefices Act, and the parish was united with ST MICHAEL PATERNOSTER ROYAL. The site was sold to a brewery company for £13,129 16s, which financed the building of All Hallows, GOSPEL OAK. The altarpiece and bells were moved to the new church, the organ case, figures of Moses and Aaron, woodwork, plate and a window to ST MICHAEL PATERNOSTER ROYAL, the pulpit to ST PAUL HAMMERSMITH, and the sounding board, altar rails and a chancel screen to ST MARGARET LOTHBURY. In 1939 the tower and vestry were bombed. In 1954 the parish was united with ST JAMES GARLICKHYTHE. In 1969 the churchyard was removed and Mondial House was built on the site.

All Hallows the Less *Upper Thames Street*. Stood over the gateway to a big house. It is first mentioned in 1216. Burned down in the GREAT FIRE, it was not rebuilt. The parish was united with ALL HALLOWS THE GREAT.

All Saints *Camden Town, NW1*. One of three chapels-of-ease which were erected by the surveyor William Inwood, and his son Henry William Inwood, in 1824, after they had finished ST PANCRAS NEW CHURCH. It was first known as the Camden Chapel and became All Saints only in 1920. It has been used by the Greek Cypriot community since 1948. The bold semicircular porch in the Ionic style and much of the decoration shows the influence of the younger Inwood's travels in Greece.

All Saints *Chingford.* In the 12th century the church belonged to the Dean and Chapter of ST PAUL'S. The north wall probably dates from this era; the south aisle and arcade were built in the late 13th century; and the tower soon afterwards. Reconstruction took place in the 15th century and a porch was added in the 16th. During the following centuries the building became unstable: the aisle walls were heightened and thus overloaded, and ivy almost completely covered the church. In 1844 the dedication to St Peter and St Paul was transferred to the new church at Chingford Green. Residential development around the church in the early 20th century led to its rebuilding in 1930 by C.C. Winmill (financed by Louisa Heathcote), and its subsequent functioning as a chapel-of-ease to St Peter and St Paul.

All Saints *Church Street, N9.* Consists of a west tower of three stages with angle buttresses, a nave, aisles and a projecting chancel. It is chiefly constructed of Kentish ragstone and dates mainly from the 15th century. The north side was refaced in stock brick in 1774. The south aisle is an addition of 1889. Re-set in the south wall is the remains of a Norman doorway. The churchyard contains many interesting memorials, including the grave of Charles Lamb who died in Edmonton in 1834.

All Saints *East India Dock Road, E14.* Built in 1821-3 to the designs of Charles Hollis. In 1821 the parish of POPLAR was created and the parishioners raised over £30,000 for the construction of this expensive church. Although Hollis won the competition for the design, it has been suggested that he plagiarised the plans of Joseph Scoles. The church is built in Portland stone, with an Ionic porch, a Corinthian interior and a steeple after Wren and Gibbs. In the 1950s the vicar, Arthur Chandler, undertook the rebuilding of the interior and removed the more ornate features, including the galleries on cast-iron columns. The Chapel of St Frideswide recalls the church of that name which was bombed and demolished in the 2nd World War.

All Saints *Ennismore Gardens, SW7.* This church now belongs to the Russian Orthodox Church. It was built in the 1840s to the designs of Vulliamy. The Italianate west front is by C. Harrison Townsend, architect of the HORNIMAN MUSEUM. The campanile was added in the 1870s. In the interior there are tall iron Corinthian columns, a small clerestory and a gallery on three sides. The decoration is in the Arts and Crafts style, for much of which Heywood Sumner was responsible.

All Saints *Foots Cray, Sidcup, Kent.* Originated as a wooden building in 900. It was rebuilt in stone about 1330, the chantry chapel added 20 years later, and the nave extended in 1862-3. The parish formerly included LONGLANDS.

All Saints *Fulham (Church Gate), SW6.* Most of what one sees from PUTNEY BRIDGE of the felicitously sited parish church of FULHAM is a rebuilding of 1880-1. Only the tower of Kentish ragstone is medieval, but even this was refaced in 1845 when the thin wooden spire was removed. What lifts All Saints out of the ordinary is its long association with the BISHOPS OF LONDON and its wealth of monuments: the finest in any outer London church after CHELSEA OLD CHURCH; they are mainly of the 17th century.

Bishop Waldhere of London obtained the Fulham lands from the Bishop of Hereford early in the 8th century, thus establishing the long connection between FULHAM and the BISHOPS OF LONDON.

A painting, dated 1690, in the tower shows John Hudnett, beadle and sexton, in a red coat with a quart pot and churchwarden's pipe.

The episcopal connection is underlined by the fact that in the churchyard at the east end of the church are no fewer than eight tombs of former BISHOPS OF LONDON, and another two in the north-east corner.

All Saints *Kingston-upon-Thames, Surrey.* Much of this attractive church dates from the 15th century. The brick tower, however, is 18th-century. Restoration work was carried out in 1886 by John Brandon and John Pearson.

All Saints *Margaret Street, W1.* On the site of the Margaret Chapel which was built in about 1760 for Deists. It later became a proprietary chapel. In 1839-45 Frederick Oakley made it the centre of the High Church Tractarian Movement. His successor, William Upton Richards, and the Ecclesiological Society joined together to rebuild the chapel as a model church in the Gothic style. William Butterfield was appointed architect. The foundation stone was laid in 1850 but the building took many years to complete due to disagreements between the sponsors and the architect. It was consecrated in 1859 by Dr Tait, Bishop of London. Ruskin said it was 'the first piece of architecture I have seen built in modern days which is free from all signs of timidity and incapacity'; and G.E. Street thought it 'not only the most beautiful but the most vigorous, thoughtful and original' of the Gothic Revival churches. It was the first important building where brick was used decoratively. Its spire is 227 ft high. The interior is richly decorated with granite, marble, alabaster and tiles. Above the altar were frescoes by William Dyce but they deteriorated and were covered by panels painted by Ninian Comper in 1909. The tile panel of the Nativity which decorates the windowless north aisle is by Alexander Gibbs. Additions to the church include the Lady Chapel's reredos and canopy by Comper (1911), the pyx by Comper (1930), and the south aisle screen by Laurence King (1962). Included on the small site as an integral part of the scheme were a vicarage and choir school. The latter is now used by the Institute of Christian Studies.

All Saints *Notting Hill, W11.* Built in 1852-5 to the designs of William White, nephew of Gilbert White, the naturalist. There is an unusually tall west tower in four stages. The Lady Chapel is by Sir Ninian Comper. The interior was restored after bombing in the 2nd World War.

All Saints *Orpington, Kent.* Originally Saxon, it contains examples of late Norman work and several succeeding styles. Nicholas de Ystele, rector until 1370, is

18

buried in the west porch, which he had built. The 13th-century tower was partly destroyed by lightning in 1771; it was capped with a shingled spire and this, too, was struck by lightning in 1809. In 1957–8 the church was enlarged by an unusual method: the south wall of the nave was replaced by arches leading into a new church facing south. The new building is on the site of Bark Hart House, which was demolished in the 1950s (*see* ORPINGTON).

All Saints *Sydenham, SE26*. Built in 1901 by G.H. Fellowes Prynne. The interior is incomplete; only three bays of the nave and aisle were built. The church was consecrated in 1903.

All Saints *Tooting Graveney, SW17*. In the *Domesday* survey of 1086 TOOTING and STREATHAM MANOR are shown as held by the Abbey of Bec Helluoin in Normandy – hence TOOTING BEC – from which the great Archbishops Lanfranc and Anselm came to England in Norman times. All Saints was built in 1904–6 out of funds bequeathed by Lady Augusta Georgiana Sophia Brudenell-Bruce in memory of her husband. The architect was L. Temple Moore. It is one of the finest and largest parishes in South London. Many of the furnishings were collected by the first vicar from Italy and France, and date back to the Renaissance. In addition to being a place of worship, the church is frequently used for musical recordings.

All Saints *Upper Norwood, SE19*. Built in 1827–9 by James Savage as a chapel-of-ease to CROYDON parish church. It was originally a rectangular building with galleries and box pews. It seated 800 and cost £6,632. The tower and spire were added in 1841 and the chancel in 1861. The church was painted by Pissarro when he was living in Palace Road during the Franco-Prussian War; and mentioned by Dickens in *David Copperfield*. Vice-Admiral Robert Fitzroy, who captained HMS *Beagle* on the voyage which took Darwin to the Galapagos Islands, was buried in the churchyard.

All Saints *Wandsworth (High Street), SW18*. The first mention of the church was in 1234, when John de Panormo was granted a dispensation 'to hold the Church of Wandsworth', as well as one in Italy. The oldest part of the present structure is the tower, built in 1630, replacing a steeple. The tower was repaired and raised one storey in 1841, to accommodate a peal of eight bells. The north aisle was built in 1724, while most of the rest dates from the rebuilding of 1780. Further alterations and additions were made in the 19th century, including a new chancel by E.W. Mountford. The interior has Adam-like Doric columns of wood, painted as marble, with a frieze and enriched cornice. Old memorials include a brass of 1420 to a soldier of Henry V and monuments to Susannah Powell (1630) and Alderman Henry Smith (1627).

All Saints *West Dulwich (Rosendale Road), SE21*. This towering brick structure in the Gothic style is one of the most ambitious of late 19th-century churches. Sited on a steep slope, it dominates Rosendale Road from a considerable height. It was built in 1888 by G.H. Fellowes Prynne, at a cost of £16,000, on land donated by DULWICH COLLEGE. Money was not available, however, to complete the design and the proposed lofty tower was never built. J.B.S. Comper

restored the church in 1952 and erected a small bell tower at the point where Fellowes Prynne intended his tower to have been.

All Saints *West Ham, E15*. Has a history going back to the beginning of the Middle Ages. At one time it belonged to STRATFORD LANGTHORNE ABBEY. Rebuilt about 1180 by the Norman lord of the manor, it was greatly enlarged in the 13th century. The 74 ft high tower was erected early in the 15th century and the church reached its present form in the 16th century when the chapels on either side of the chancel were completed, the North Chapel in Tudor brick being the finest part architecturally. The whole lies in a spacious churchyard.

The prosperity that came to WEST HAM after the Reformation is reflected in the monuments to Sir Thomas Foot, the first LORD MAYOR in Cromwell's Commonwealth, and that to James Cooper (d.1743) and his wife, with excellent carved standing figures. Another LORD MAYOR, Sir Robert Smyth, is also commemorated, as are other persons of substance who lived in WEST HAM.

Two curiosities are worth noting: one is the font dated 1707, bearing the names of three churchwardens instead of the usual two (the ancient parish was once divided into three Wards and the custom continues); the other is the clock in the tower, made in 1857 to Lord Grimthorpe's design, and the prototype of BIG BEN.

All Souls *Langham Place, W1*. Designed by John Nash, as part of his great scheme for REGENT STREET and REGENT'S PARK, and built in 1822–4. Because of the

John Nash, architect of All Souls, Langham Place, remarked of this 1824 Cruikshank cartoon that criticism had exalted him.

19

intractability of property owners in the area, Nash was unable to continue the northward sweep of REGENT STREET as he wished and was forced to push it westwards. His solution was to build this church as a terminal feature where REGENT STREET turns left into PORTLAND PLACE. Its combination of a Greek peristyle and a spire was ridiculed at the time and the portly Nash was caricatured as impaled upon it. The church is faced with Bath stone, and the interior is galleried and bright in blue and gold. The altarpiece by Richard Westall was a gift from George IV, Nash's patron. Bombed in the 2nd World War, All Souls was restored and rededicated in 1957. It seats 1890. The restoration was carried out by H.S. Goodhart-Rendel.

All Souls *Loudoun Road, NW8*. By Wadmore and Baker, 1865, and altered by Nicholson and Corlette in 1904.

Alleyn's School *Townley Road, SE22*. Came into existence as a result of a reorganisation by Act of Parliament in 1882 of Alleyn's College of God's Gift at Dulwich (*see* DULWICH COLLEGE). Alleyn's School replaced the Lower School of Alleyn's College. New buildings were opened in 1887. Other buildings followed and in 10 years numbers rose from 250 to 680. Alleyn's was a pioneer among day schools in introducing a house system in 1907. New building, held up by the 1st World War, was partially carried out before 1939 but premises for the Junior School were not built till 1964. The school was evacuated during the 2nd World War, returning to DULWICH in 1945. Financial difficulties in post-war years led to it becoming a direct grant school (*see* EDUCATION) from 1958, an arrangement which ended in 1976 when it became an independent school. Girls were admitted from this time and in 1980 there were 890 pupils of whom 204 (at all levels) were girls.

Allsop Place *NW1*. Runs unobtrusively behind BAKER STREET Station. It takes its name from William Allsop, a local farmer, whose buildings occupied the site now filled by the underground station.

Almack's Assembly Rooms *King Street, St James's*. A suite of fashionable assembly rooms designed by Robert Mylne in 1765 and named after the first proprietor, William Almack. A voucher of admission to a weekly ball was 'the seventh heaven of the fashionable world'. The guest lists were strictly controlled by seven ladies of high rank. Henry Luttrell wrote:

> All on that magic list depends;
> Fame, fortune, fashion, lovers, friends:
> 'Tis that which gratifies or vexes
> All ranks, all ages, and both sexes.
> If once to Almack's you belong,
> Like monarchs, you can do no wrong;
> But banished thence on Wednesday night,
> By Jove you can do nothing right.

All the gentlemen had to wear knee breeches and white cravats. Even the Duke of Wellington was denied entrance one night because he had trousers on. The success of the rooms declined from 1835 as less noble guests were admitted, and in 1863 the fashionable balls came to an end, though dinners, concerts and other balls continued under different managements. In 1893

part of the building was taken over by Messrs Robinson and Fisher, auctioneers, the rest being let as shops. It was bombed in the 2nd World War. In 1949–50 a block of offices known as Almack House was built on the site.

Almack's Club *Pall Mall*. Founded at No. 50 PALL MALL in 1762 by William Almack, who had opened a tavern at No. 49 in 1759. Almack undertook to provide the members of his club with dinner, newspapers and gambling. A condition of membership was that no gentleman who joined should belong to ARTHUR'S. In 1764 the club split into two others which became known as BOODLE'S and BROOKS'S. A further two, shorter-lived, clubs also met on Almack's premises. These were the Macaroni, a club for 'travelled young men with long curls and spyingglasses', which was begun in 1764 and lasted until 1772; and the Ladies' Coterie, a fashionable club for both sexes (1769–71). Almack's success with his clubs induced him to open ALMACK'S ASSEMBLY ROOMS as a rival to Mrs Cornelys's Assembly Rooms at CARLISLE HOUSE, SOHO SQUARE.

Alperton *Middlesex*. First recorded as Ealhbert's farm in 1199, it emerged in the 19th century as a local centre for brick and tile manufacture. Hitherto it had been agricultural. Passenger traffic on pleasure trips plied the GRAND UNION CANAL which was opened through Alperton in 1801. Industrial activity was established alongside the canal in the second half of the 19th century. Residential development in Alperton was spurred on by the opening of the railway (now PICCADILLY LINE) in 1903. The granite, *Teamwork*, outside the offices of Taylor Woodrow in Hanger Lane is by David Wynne (1958).

Plate 9 of Hogarth's Industry and Idleness. The Idle Apprentice, *betrayed by a prostitute, is arrested in Alsatia.*

Alsatia The precincts of the former WHITEFRIARS MONASTERY which extended from the TEMPLE to WHITEFRIARS STREET and from FLEET STREET to the THAMES. After the monastery was dissolved by Henry VIII the buildings and land were granted to the royal physician, William Butte. They fell into disrepair and speculative builders plundered them. In 1580 the inhabitants of the area claimed to be exempt from the jurisdiction of the CITY and the Queen allowed their claim. Their privileges were confirmed by charter by James I in 1608. The area became a hotbed of crime and was known as Alsatia after Alsace, the long disputed territory between France and Germany. In 1688

Thomas Shadwell described it in his *Squire of Alsatia*. Macaulay said that 'at any attempt to extradite a criminal, bullies with swords and cudgels, termagant hags with spits and broomsticks poured forth by the hundred and the intruder was fortunate if he escaped back to Fleet Street, hustled, stripped and jumped upon.' Even the warrant of the Chief Justice of England could not be executed without the help of a company of musketeers. In 1697 the privileges were abolished but it was many years before the area became law abiding. In 1747, when Hogarth published his *Industry and Idleness*, he showed in Plate 9 the Idle Apprentice being arrested in a cellar in Blood Bowl House near FLEET STREET, having been betrayed by his whore.

Ambassadors Theatre *West Street, WC2*. Designed in 1913 as a pair with the ST MARTIN'S THEATRE by W.G.R. Sprague. In 1914 Charles B. Cochran staged *Odds and Ends*, the first of the intimate revues, followed by *More Odds and Ends* (1915) and *Pell Mell* (1916). Alice Delysia starred in them all. From 1919 to 1930 the theatre was managed by H.M. Harwood. Among his outstanding productions were *A Grain of Mustard Seed* (1920), *The White Headed Boy* (1920) by Lennox Robinson, and *Deburau* (1921) in which Ivor Novello made his debut. Vivien Leigh made her first West End appearance here in 1935 in *The Mask of Virtue*. *The Gate Revue*, first produced at the Gate Theatre, had 449 performances here in 1939. During the BLITZ the theatre was kept open with 'lunch, tea and sherry performances' by the Ballet Rambert. Since then the main successes have been the revues *Sweet and Low* (1943), *Sweeter and Lower* (1944) and *Sweetest and Lowest* (1946), *Little Lambs Eat Ivy* (1948) and *The Mousetrap*, the thriller by Agatha Christie, which started its run on 25 November 1952. This was transferred to the ST MARTIN'S THEATRE in 1975. The seating capacity of the Ambassadors is 460.

Amen Court *EC4*. Probably so called after the words recited by the medieval clergy of ST PAUL'S during their processions round the precincts, as with AVE MARIA LANE and, possibly, PATERNOSTER ROW. Sydney Smith, a canon of ST PAUL'S, lived at No. 1 in 1831–4 and R.H. Barham, a minor canon and author of the *Ingoldsby Legends*, in 1839–45.

America Square *EC3*. Built between 1768 and 1774 at the same time as the CIRCUS and the CRESCENT. It was designed by George Dance the Younger for middle-class merchants and sea captains and was based on GROSVENOR and CAVENDISH SQUARES. The origin of the name is unknown but probably merchants dealing with America lived here. In 1836 the London and Blackwall Railway encroached on the square. It was bombed in 1941 and none of the original houses now remains. Baron Meyer de Rothschild lived at No. 14, which has since been demolished.

American Church *see* WHITEFIELD'S TABERNACLE.

Ampton Street *WC1*. Named after the Calthorpe family's Suffolk manor (*see* CALTHORPE ESTATE). It was built in 1821–7 and incorporated into Ampton Place 20 years after its completion. A few of the original houses remain. Thomas and Jane Carlyle lodged here in

1831–2. Ampton Street Baptist Chapel (Field Lane Centre) is in Cubitt Street.

Amsterdam Coffee House *Behind the Royal Exchange*. A celebrated early coffee house established about 1675. It moved twice, first from BARTHOLOMEW LANE to Sweeting's Rents, then to BIRCHIN LANE. Titus Oates was arrested here on 10 May 1684. Seamen were engaged at the Amsterdam for the Hudson's Bay Company. The house did not survive the 18th century.

Ancaster House *Richmond Hill, Surrey*. Adjoining RICHMOND PARK and built in 1772 probably as a shooting box for the Duke of Ancaster. It stands in a beautiful spot at the top of RICHMOND HILL opposite the STAR AND GARTER HOME. Near the end of the 18th century the house was acquired by Sir Lionel Darrell, who was a friend of George III. There is a story that Sir Lionel needed extra land to build greenhouses and applied for permission to build on Park land. After interminable bureaucratic delays, he mentioned the problem to George III who was riding in the Park. The king dismounted, marked out a plot of land with a stick and within a short time the land was Sir Lionel's. The Darrells gave brilliant parties and their daughters were called 'the dancing Darrells' by Horace Walpole. Sir Lionel died in 1803 and the house passed to his daughter, Amelia. She virtually closed it down, kept her father's room locked for over 60 years, and when it was opened after her death in 1864, it was exactly as it had been the day he died. There was even a dust-covered copy of *The Times*. At the turn of the century the house narrowly escaped demolition; it is now staff-quarters for the STAR AND GARTER HOME.

Anchor Inn *1 Bankside, SE1*. An 18th-century riverside inn complete with minstrels' gallery, old oak beams and cubby holes to hide fugitives from the CLINK PRISON. Its predecessor dated back to the 15th century and was probably known to Shakespeare. It could have been the little ale house on BANKSIDE where Pepys 'staid till it was dark and saw the fire grow' on 2 September 1666. Henry Thrale, the brewer and friend of Dr Johnson, once owned it. A viewing platform gives an excellent view of ST PAUL'S. The inn contains a collection of Elizabethan objects found during renovations and a model of the GLOBE THEATRE which stood nearby.

Andrew's Crosse *WC2*. A short street named after a house called Crown Court or Andrew's Cross which stood in CHANCERY LANE in the 16th century. It belonged to the PRIORY OF ST JOHN OF JERUSALEM.

Anerley *SE20*. Lies between PENGE and SOUTH NORWOOD. A hilly part of Penge Common, the district known as Anerley did not develop until the 19th century. The Common was enclosed following the 1827 Act, and the wide Anerley Road planned. The rebuilt Robin Hood public house at the junction of Anerley and Croydon Roads had been a hostelry notorious for highwaymen who frequented the Common. The name Anerley (from a northern dialect and meaning alone or lonely) was that of a house belonging to a William Sanderson who offered land to the South Eastern Railway. Anerley Station was opened in 1839 and the railway engineer, Joseph Gibbs, managed to use much of the Croydon Canal track (cut in 1801) for the railway. Anerley Gardens were opened west of the station in 1841 and provided entertainment and diversion for London visitors. They were closed in 1868, probably as a result of competition from the newly-opened CRYSTAL PALACE. A residential area developed and the parish of St Paul's was formed in 1861. Victorian houses, such as the present Oaklands Nursing Home, appeared along the tree-lined Anerley Road, and the residents were involved in such cultural organisations as the Anerley Philharmonic Society. The young H.G. Wells played in the fields round about, and Walter de la Mare lived in Thornsett Road. Limericks about Anerley were written by Edward Lear and Rupert Brooke. In 1965 Anerley became part of the London Borough of BROMLEY.

Angel *24 Rotherhithe Street, SE16.* Dates back to the 15th century when the monks of BERMONDSEY ABBEY used to keep a tavern here. It was originally known as the Salutation but after the Reformation this name was changed to the Angel. Part of the inn is built on piles over the river and there are trapdoors in the floor which must have been useful to local smugglers. Samuel Pepys was a regular visitor here and mentions it in his diary. In one of the bars there is a contract dated 1682 by which the house was sold for £500. A balcony over the river gives splendid THAMES views. Judge Jeffreys is said to have sat here to watch pirates being hanged at EXECUTION DOCK opposite.

The Angel Hotel, now a bank, in 1890. A coaching inn had stood on this site since Jacobean times.

Angel, Islington *Islington High Street, N1.* The Angel, the nearest staging post to London on the GREAT NORTH ROAD, was from Jacobean times a coaching inn opposite some large elms. Until the new PENTONVILLE ROAD was completed in 1757 and the CITY ROAD in 1761, traffic from the north entered the CITY by Goswell Road, and SMITHFIELD by St John Street. Near the inn were lairs for cattle bound for SMITHFIELD. The Angel was especially useful to travellers by night, when the fields towards the CITY were dangerous. Those journeying outwards were escorted by armed patrol from Wood's Close (Northampton Street) to ISLINGTON.

The inn was entirely rebuilt in 1819, subsequently much altered, and rebuilt again in 1899 as a LYONS' CORNER HOUSE, with its great dome a noted landmark. Visitors to the ROYAL AGRICULTURAL HALL made a night of it both here and at COLLINS' MUSIC HALL. But about 1960 the Angel closed, to remain derelict until restored as a bank in 1981–2.

The name 'Angel, Islington' is not strictly accurate, for the parish boundary runs down the middle of the

road. The *Gentleman's Magazine* of October 1823 related that, at some unspecified date, ISLINGTON refused burial to a pauper found 'at the corner of the Back-road' (Liverpool Road), so that CLERKENWELL, having buried him, claimed the Angel corner as theirs. Since the beginning of this century the Angel junction has been a major traffic bottleneck, ambitious attempts to solve it ending in stalemate and planning blight. Wholesale rebuilding on the south-west corner, and road widening in 1981–2, have caused great changes.

Until 1764 ISLINGTON turnpike was in the High Street, at first near White Lion Street. It was removed about 1790 to Liverpool Road corner, and in 1808 shifted again, because of accidents, to a point halfway between the two. Near the turnpike were the old resort, the Three Hats, and another famous coaching inn, the Peacock.

Although the west side beyond Liverpool Road is named Upper Street, Islington High Street continues on the east. This site is mostly demolished – including the former Grand Theatre, or Philharmonic Hall, of 1860 – or scheduled for redevelopment. It passes behind free-standing blocks, of which the southernmost (destroyed in the 1970s) was built in 1850 as a fashionable shopping 'bazaar'. The next adjoining, formerly a transformer station in the style of Newgate Gaol for the tramways, now echoes the bazaar theme as a two-storey antiques 'Mall'.

Beyond High Street, Camden Passage was once a quiet alley where Alexander Cruden, author of the *Biblical Concordance*, died in 1770. It was promoted in the 1960s to become a lively centre for antique and bric-à-brac shops and stalls.

Angell Town *see* BRIXTON.

Annesley Lodge *Platt's Lane, NW3.* Art Nouveau, L-shaped house designed by C.F.A. Voysey (1895) for his father. The best example of his work in London.

Apollo Theatre *Shaftesbury Avenue, W1.* Designed for musicals in 1901 by Lewen Sharp. Early successes were *The Three Little Maids* (1902), *The Girl from Kays* (1902), *Veronique* (1904) and *Tom Jones* (1907) in which Cicely Courtneidge made her London debut. From 1908 to 1912 the theatre was the home of the Follies. Since then it has consistently staged successful plays but has never been the home of a great management. In 1917 *Inside the Lines* by Earl Derr Biggers had 421 performances. In 1919 Ian Hay's comedy, *Tilly of Bloomsbury*, was a big success. In 1930 the farce, *Almost a Honeymoon*, had 394 performances. From 1934 to 1937 Marion Lorne starred in plays written by her husband, Walter Hackett, including *Hyde Park Corner* (1934), *Espionage* (1935), *The Fugitives* (1936) and *London after Dark* (1937). In 1936 Ian Hay's comedy *Housemaster*, which had 662 performances, began its run. The best productions of the 1940s and 1950s were Terence Rattigan's *Flare Path* (1942), a revival of Coward's comedy, *Private Lives* (1944), *Off the Record* (1947), *The Happiest Days of Your Life* (1948), *Seagulls over Sorrento* (1950).

Apollo Victoria *Wilton Road, SW1.* Formerly the New Victoria Cinema, it was taken over in 1979 by Apollo Victoria UK Ltd and completely redecorated and converted to a theatre for the presentation of full-scale musicals. It opened on 2 February 1980 with 'pop' concerts engaging the best known stars in this field, among them Shirley Bassey, Cliff Richard and Sammy Davis Jnr. On 17 August 1981 it presented a revival of *The Sound of Music*, directed by John Fearnley, with Petula Clark, Michael Jayston, Honor Blackman and June Bronhill, the most expensive musical presented in Britain. The seating capacity is 2,750.

Apothecaries' Garden *see* CHELSEA PHYSIC GARDEN.

Apothecaries' Hall *Blackfriars Lane, EC4*. The site of the Hall, which formerly belonged to Lady Howard of Effingham, was purchased in 1632. The building was destroyed by the GREAT FIRE and reconstructed in 1688 by Thomas Locke. The premises exist almost unchanged today, apart from some modifications in 1779 and 1927. Inside there is a fine panelled court room. There are portraits of James I and Charles I, a sketch of John Hunter by Reynolds and a bust of Gideon de Laune, apothecary to James I, who died in 1659, father of 37 children. Other fine features are the 1671 banisters and an ormolu candelabrum of 1736. The dining capacity is about 150. For the Society *see* CITY LIVERY COMPANIES.

Apothecaries' Society *see* CITY LIVERY COMPANIES.

Arbitrators' Company *see* CITY LIVERY COMPANIES.

Archbishop's Park *Lambeth, SE1*. Formed out of the grounds of LAMBETH PALACE. In the late 19th century the Archbishops gradually allowed the local children access to play, and in 1880 24,000 children assembled to celebrate the centenary of the Sunday Schools' foundation by Robert Raikes and offered the Prince and Princess of Wales a lusty rendering of 'Onward Christian Soldiers'.

The 20-acre Park was formally opened to the public in 1901 and although still owned by the Archbishopric is now administered by the GLC. There is a children's playground at the northern end, the remainder being grass and pathways bordered by trees and shrubs.

Archer Street *W1*. Originally known as Arch Street and first mentioned in 1675; the reason for its present name is unknown. The reclining, draped nude over the first-floor window of the London Orchestral Association at Nos 13–14 is *Euterpe*, the muse of lyric poetry, by Charles Petworth (1921).

Archery Considered to be an important stratagem of war from an early period of English history. Successive monarchs encouraged military training with bow and arrow in villages and towns throughout the land. 'Cause public proclamation to be made,' declared one Act of 1369, 'that everyone of the said city London strong in body, at leisure times and on holydays, use in their recreation bows and arrows.' Popular amusements such as handball and football were forbidden under pain of imprisonment. Throughout the 14th and 15th centuries practice at the butts was commonplace, providing ready-trained bowmen for the frequent wars of that period. The fields just outside the limits of medieval London provided the necessary space and earthen butts were set up by youths and men who, with

A Finsbury Archer shown on a ticket issued in 1676. The ticket gives notice of an 'Elevenscore Target' in the 'New Artillery Ground'.

their longbows of yew, aimed at a 'mark' or 'clout' using the same skills so familiar to their forefathers.

Henry VIII strongly supported the use of archery and 'for the better defence of the realm by the science and feat of shooting' in 1537 founded the Guild of St George, a body of élite soldiery which became the HONOURABLE ARTILLERY COMPANY of London. The decline of archery practice began and some of the causes for this were said to be 'new and crafty games such as slidethrift shove ha'penny, unchaste interludes, bargains of incontinence and bear-baiting'. In addition urban growth began to make shooting with bows and arrows both difficult and dangerous.

Elizabeth I set up a commission in order to restore old London archery grounds to their original state, but in 1595 the longbow was declared to be obsolete and its popularity faded. In 1627 an even greater drive was made to revive archery in the CITY OF LONDON. Archery regiments were formed in each ward and once a year they were led into the fields to practise and shoot for prizes. The change from military training with the bow to a more competitive and peaceful use had begun. One of the most popular forms of shooting was 'rovers' in which distance was striven for. Special marks were set up in FINSBURY and ST GEORGE'S FIELDS and MOORFIELDS and these were popular areas until urban encroachment at the end of the 18th century again forced changes. Some of the citizens 'using the exercise of archery' now began shooting on the Artillery Ground at FINSBURY. The FINSBURY Archers flourished for about 100 years and died out in 1770, but surviving members formed the Toxophilite Society

23

(later to become Royal) in 1781. Their first headquarters was at Leicester House in LEICESTER SQUARE and they were patronised by the Prince Regent. Other societies were founded at about this time and a regular form of target shooting was established. This has remained standard practice.

Many of the shooting grounds in and about London have been swallowed up by the spread of development but reminders of the great Regency revival are still to be found. The Archery Tavern in BAYSWATER stands on one site and the Butts at the ELEPHANT AND CASTLE on another, and the pleasure grounds of VAUXHALL, RANELAGH and the BAYSWATER TEA GARDENS, among others, all provided an archery range as part of their attractions.

Changes in political attitudes drove the Royal 'Tox' from REGENT'S PARK, and modern development forced this society to move to Buckinghamshire, abandoning their old shooting ground which was just a bow-shot from MARBLE ARCH. Today the sport of archery, based on the general rules and conduct laid down centuries ago, continues in the activities of numerous clubs in and about London pursuing their ancient art in the same way that generations of Londoners have done before them.

Architectural Association *34–36 Bedford Square, WC1.* Founded on 8 October 1847 at Lyon Inn Hall in the STRAND at a meeting attended by over 100 architectural students. The first President, Robert Kerr, took the initiative in freeing students from the bondage of the articled pupil system of education and in developing a school offering education 'for architects by architects', with an increasing membership throughout the world. In 1859 the AA moved to No. 9 CONDUIT STREET where it shared accommodation with the ROYAL INSTITUTE OF BRITISH ARCHITECTS. In 1892 the school moved to 56 GREAT MARLBOROUGH STREET, and in 1901 when a day school was introduced, the AA moved once again to No. 18 TUFTON STREET (built in 1869 but since demolished), previously the Royal Architectural Museum. In 1917 it moved to BEDFORD SQUARE. Here there has been a succession of distinguished Principals: Robert Atkinson, Howard Robertson, E.A. Rowse, G.A. Jellicoe, Frederick Gibberd, R. Gordon-Brown, K. Furneaux Jordan, Michael Pattrick, W.A. Allen, Dr Otto Koenigsburger and Michael Lloyd. In 1970, after negotiations to amalgamate the AA school with the IMPERIAL COLLEGE OF SCIENCE AND TECHNOLOGY had been broken off, a new life began under the chairmanship of Alvin Boyarsky who was elected by students and staff. The AA is a combination of learned society, club, and school of architecture.

Architectural Museum *Tufton Street.* Designed by George Somers Clarke and Ewan Christian in 1869, it was the first headquarters of the ARCHITECTURAL ASSOCIATION. It contained a fine collection of architectural models, plaster casts and damaged medieval work which was handed over to the VICTORIA AND ALBERT MUSEUM when the ARCHITECTURAL ASSOCIATION moved to BLOOMSBURY. The building was rebuilt in 1935 and afterwards became the NATIONAL LIBRARY FOR THE BLIND.

Archway Road *N6, N19.* Extends from Great North Road, N6, to Upper Holloway, N19. In 1809 an Act of Parliament empowered Robert Vazie to raise £60,000 to construct a 750 ft tunnel through HIGHGATE HILL and thus underpass the notoriously steep gradient. The subsequent works aroused considerable interest: one Sunday, in April 1812, 800 people came to watch. But in the early morning of 13 April the tunnel, which had by then progressed 130 ft, collapsed because too few bricks had been used in its lining and the quality of the cement was poor. The failure occasioned a burlesque 'Operatic Tragedy' at the LYCEUM THEATRE, *Highgate Tunnel – The Secret Arch*. Instead of the tunnel a cutting through the hill was then proposed and, indeed, because of the collapsed tunnel, partially existed. But across the top of the hill had run the ancient Hornsey Lane linking HIGHGATE and HORNSEY and the construction company dared not close it. The Highgate Archway was thus conceived as a viaduct to carry Hornsey Lane over the new cutting which became Archway Road. John Nash was commissioned to design the viaduct which he did in the style of a Roman aqueduct with a lofty arch and three low arches above to carry the lane. It was 36 ft high and 18 ft wide. It was replaced in 1897 by a cast-iron arch designed by Sir Alexander Binnie.

Archway Road was opened on 21 August 1813. Tolls were 'not exceeding' 6d per horse and carriage, 3d for horse or mule not drawing a carriage and 1d for a pedestrian. The tollgate was at the corner of Lidyard Road. It was removed and tolls ceased in 1871.

Argyll House *Argyll Street.* Built between 1735 and 1750 by Archibald Campbell, who succeeded his brother as 3rd Duke of Argyll in 1743. The house was occupied in 1750–62 by the Duke's mistress, Mrs Shireburn, to whom he left his entire property in England. From 1808 to 1860 it was owned by the 4th Earl of Aberdeen, Queen Victoria's Prime Minister during the Crimean War until succeeded by Palmerston. The house was demolished in 1864. Its site is covered by the LONDON PALLADIUM.

Argyll Lodge *Campden Hill.* Also known at various times as Bedford Lodge and Cam House, it was built in about 1815 by John Tasker who probably also designed it. The 6th Duke of Bedford, and later his widow, lived here in 1823–53. The Duchess's social gatherings were splendid occasions. The house was occupied from 1853 to 1900 by the 8th Duke of Argyll who presided over a meeting at which the ROYAL AERONAUTICAL SOCIETY was founded. The house was demolished in 1955 to make way for HOLLAND PARK COMPREHENSIVE SCHOOL.

Argyll Rooms *Little Argyll Street.* Fashionable rooms during the Regency. They were opened on the north-east corner of the street in 1806 by Henry Francis Greville, the dilettante son of Fulke Greville and cousin of the 1st Earl of Warwick. Byron had Greville and his customers in mind when he wrote:

Behold the new Petronius of the day,
Our arbiter of pleasure and of play!
There the hired eunuch, the Hesperian choir
The melting lute, the soft lascivious lyre,
The song from Italy, the step from France,
The midnight orgy, and the mazy dance,
The smile of beauty, and the flush of wine
For fops, fools, gamesters, knaves and lords combine,

Each to his humour – Comus all allows
Champaign, dice, music or your neighbour's spouse.

In 1812 Greville, by then 'an elegant ruin', handed over the management to Stephen Slade, his Conductor of the Household. In 1813 a ball was held here by four leading dandies of the day, Brummel, Alvanley, Pierrepoint and Mildmay, to celebrate their gambling successes. The Prince Regent was invited although he was not on speaking terms with either Mildmay or Brummel. He ignored them both, but spoke to Alvanley, provoking the comment from Brummel, 'Alvanley, who's your fat friend?' In 1813 further popularity was brought to the rooms by the Philharmonic Society concerts which were held here until 1830. In 1819 Slade was forced to sell out by the REGENT STREET Commissioners who found a temporary tenant in the Royal Harmonic Institution. Alterations to the buildings began in the autumn of 1819 but it was found to be in such bad repair that John Nash completely rebuilt it. The rooms were reopened in 1820. Balls, masquerades and plays continued to be well attended. Liszt aged 12 played here in 1823, Weber in 1826 and Mendelssohn in 1829. The building was burned down in 1830. Shops were put up instead, and in 1919 these were replaced by DICKINS AND JONES.

Argyll Street *W1*. Built in the 1730s on land belonging to John Campbell, 2nd Duke of Argyll, one of the Duke of Marlborough's leading generals. His brother, the 3rd Duke, built ARGYLL HOUSE on the east side. Major General William Roy, founder of the Ordnance Survey, lived at No. 10 from 1779 until his death in 1790. Madame de Staël was living at No. 30 in 1814, having been banished from France by Napoleon. Anthony Salvin Senior, the architect, lived here 1850–61, as did another architect, Richard Norman Shaw, from 1864 to 1877. Dr Francis Milman, George III's physician, lived at No. 33 from 1782 to 1798. The Argyll Arms at No. 18, a fine Victorian public house, stands on a site occupied by a tavern of the name since 1740. The LONDON PALLADIUM is at Nos 7–8.

Arkley *Hertfordshire*. Lies west of HIGH BARNET on the ROMAN ROAD from London to St Albans. It occupies part of Barnet Common which was woodland from the time of the Saxon settlement of BARNET, and, in the 18th century, as a haunt of highwaymen, proved hazardous to travellers and coaches journeying to and from London and the north. Arkley was named during the 19th century when the opening of East Barnet and High Barnet stations on the Great Northern Railway led to the residential building up of the whole area. Around Barnet Common 'a little settlement of neat residences and "villas" grew up'. Arkley windmill (restored in 1930) dates from this mid-Victorian era. St Peter's church was built in 1840 as a private chapel by Enosh Durant. In 1899 the church was given a new chancel, and in 1920 a chapel built for what was, by then, the parish church.

After the 2nd World War there was further expansion of residential areas but the village is still surrounded by open spaces such as Rowley Green and Dyrham Park, and the Barnet Road running into Wood Street, HIGH BARNET, overlooks fields and pastures from its high ridge. As part of BARNET Urban District since 1905, Arkley was included in the London Borough of BARNET in 1965.

Arkwright Road *NW3*. Built in 1871; the derivation of its name is unknown. Tobias Matthay, the pianist and teacher, lived at No. 21 in 1902–9. Myra Hess was one of his pupils.

Arlington Street *SW1*. The land here was granted by Charles II in 1681 to Henry Bennet, Earl of Arlington, who immediately sold it to a Mr Pym. It was built up in the late 1680s. Barbara Castlemaine, Duchess of Cleveland, Charles II's mistress, lived here in 1691–6. In the 18th century Horace Walpole called it 'the Ministerial Street' as so many members of the government lived here. Walpole himself was born here in 1717 at No. 17, the home from 1716 of his father Sir Robert who in 1742 moved to No. 5 where he died in 1745. Charles James Fox lived at No. 9 in 1804–6. No. 16 was occupied by Lord North and later by the Duchess of Rutland whose friend, the Duke of York, George IV's brother, died here in 1827 deeply in debt. Other residents of the street included Lady Mary Wortley Montagu and William Pulteney, Earl of Bath. In 1800 at their lodgings in the street Lord and Lady Nelson had their final quarrel about Emma Hamilton and parted. No. 21 (now occupied by the National Association of British and Irish Millers) was possibly designed by William Kent. No. 22 (the Eagle Star Insurance Co.) was certainly designed by Kent (and completed by Stephen Wright). It was built between about 1740 and 1755 for Henry Pelham. Although much redecorated in the 1880s there are still some fine interiors by Kent. Two other fine 18th century houses in the street were demolished in the 20th century: one, designed by Sanderson Miller and built about 1760, was the only Gothic house in central London dating from the middle of the 18th century; the other, an early 18th-century house, was remodelled by Robert Adam for the Dundas family and contained the Dundases' Boucher-Neilson tapestries brought here from Moor Park in the 1780s. The Arlington Restaurant is on the west side; the RITZ HOTEL on the corner of Piccadilly; Hampton and Sons, the estate agents, at No. 6. Arlington House, a block of flats at Nos 17–20, was built to the designs of Michael Rosenauer in 1936.

Armourers' and Brasiers' Company *see* CITY LIVERY COMPANIES.

Armourers' and Brasiers' Hall *81 Coleman Street, EC2*. Stands on a site leased in 1346 and purchased in 1428. The hall survived the GREAT FIRE, but was rebuilt by William Creswell in 1795. It was later demolished and the present building, by J.H. Good, was erected in 1840. It contains an important collection of early plate. The dining capacity is about 80. For the Company, *see* CITY LIVERY COMPANIES.

Army and Navy Club *36–39 Pall Mall, SW1*. Founded in 1837 by various officers returned from service in India who were dismayed by the long waiting lists at both the UNITED SERVICE CLUB and the Junior United Service Club. They had enlisted the help of Sir Edward Barnes, a former commander-in-chief in India, and had originally proposed to call it the Army Club, but when the Duke of Wellington was asked to become Patron he agreed on condition that membership should also be open to officers of the

Royal Navy and the Marines. The membership was at first limited to 1,000 but by 1844 had risen to 1,358, most of them junior officers, by 1851 to 1,600, by 1878 to 2,350 and by 1922 to 2,400. The entrance fee was fixed at 15 guineas (raised to 20 guineas in 1839 and to 25 guineas in 1845). The annual subscription (5 guineas at first) was raised to 6 in 1845, to 10 in 1878 and to 14 in 1920. The club's first premises were on the corner of King Street and St James's Square in a house vacated by the OXFORD AND CAMBRIDGE UNIVERSITY CLUB which had moved to new premises in Pall Mall. The Army and Navy soon outgrew this club-house and moved first to LICHFIELD HOUSE, No. 12 St James's Square, then in 1848 to a large building designed for them in Pall Mall by C.O. Parnell and Alfred Smith. It was modelled on Sansovino's Palazzo Cornaro on the Grand Canal in Venice and had a most imposing but space-wasting entrance hall. In 1916 rooms on the top floor were converted into sleeping accommodation for members. The club-house was renovated and extended in the 1920s; but in 1963 it was demolished and a new club-house was built on part of the site by T.P. Bennett and Son.

The club is often known as 'the Rag', a nickname bestowed upon it by one of its members, Captain Billy Duff, who, entering it late one night in its early days and calling for supper, complained that the bill of fare was so meagre it was a mere 'rag and famish affair', alluding to the Rag and Famish, a cheap gaming-house and brothel in a turning off CRANBOURN STREET. The Club has good collections of pictures of naval and military subjects and portraits of distinguished soldiers and sailors. There are also two portraits, attributed to Sir Peter Lely, of Nell Gwynne who was supposed to have lived in a house occupying part of the site (*see* PALL MALL). There is, however, no portrait of Mary Davis, another of Charles II's mistresses, who did in fact own a house at this address from 1675 to 1687.

Parnell and Smith's Army and Navy Club of 1848, modelled on Sansovino's Palazzo Cornaro on the Grand Canal in Venice.

Army and Navy Stores Ltd *Victoria Street, SW1*. In 1871 a group of army and navy officers formed a co-operative where officers and men and their families could buy provisions at a discount, with prices lower than in the WEST END. Coffee, for instance, was 1s 7d a pound instead of 2s 4d. They took over premises built as a distillery to the designs of Mayhew and Calder, in 1864. By 1874, to ensure adequate supplies at low prices, they began to develop their own factories. A dispute in 1879 resulted in a split and the formation

of the Junior Army and Navy Stores in York House, WATERLOO PLACE. Decline in membership resulted in a change of policy and in 1918 the store opened to the public. Sir Aston Webb was commissioned to redesign the frontage in 1920. The first public television performance took place here in 1926. In 1977 the store was completely rebuilt by Elsom, Pack and Roberts and is now called Army and Navy Victoria.

The house and grounds of Arnos Grove, now Southgate House, in 1784, some 60 years after it was built.

Arnos Grove *Southgate, N14*. Now called Southgate House, it was built for James Colebrook in 1723. It was purchased by John Walker in 1777 and passed from him to his son, Isaac Walker, the father of the seven famous cricketing brothers, one of whom, V.E. Walker (who was born in the house), was surpassed in fame only by W.G. Grace. Indeed, their portraits hang side by side at Lord's. There are very fine murals on the stairs by Lanscroon. The house is now the headquarters of the Legal and General Assurance Society.

Arras Medallion. A great hoard of gold coins, medallions and treasure, probably the war chest of Constantius Chlorus, was found at Beaurains, near Arras, northern France, in 1922. One of the several medallions, a large ten-aureus piece, has a direct bearing on the history of Roman London. The obverse shows a bust of Constantius Chlorus as Caesar, facing right, cuirassed and draped, wearing a laurel wreath. The inscription gives his name and titles: FL(avius) VAL(erius) CONSTANTIVS NOBIL(issimus) CAES(ar). On the reverse is a scene with the victorious Constantius on horseback approaching a suppliant who kneels before a fortified gateway to greet him. Beneath the figure the letters LON identify the place as Londinium, or the figure as a personification of the place. In the lower part of the medallion a fully manned Roman war galley is shown proceeding to the right, and beneath it are the letters PTR. They indicate that the piece was struck at the mint of Trier in Germany. The legend reads: REDDITOR LVCIS AETERNAE – the Restorer of Eternal Light. The scene is a reference to the arrival of Constantius in London after having defeated the troops of the usurper Emperor Allectus in a battle somewhere in Hampshire. Constantius hurried on to London while part of his naval forces made their way up the Thames. His swift action almost certainly saved the city from being sacked by the rebel troops.

This is the earliest known representation of Londinium but, since the medallion was struck in Trier, the die engraver had probably never seen the city. The fortified gateway depicted on the reverse is very probably an example of artistic licence and bears a strong resemblance to the great Porta Nigra, still standing at Trier, with which the engraver would have been familiar.

The Arras Medallion is kept in the Bibliothèque Nationale, Paris, but electrotype copies may be seen in the BRITISH MUSEUM and the MUSEUM OF LONDON. The former also possesses some of the other medallions and gold coins from the hoard.

Arsenal Football Club *see* FOOTBALL CLUBS.

Arthur Street *EC4.* Built in 1829 as part of the approaches to the new LONDON BRIDGE over Miles Lane and Martin's Lane. Until 1911 it was known as Arthur Street West to distinguish it from the eastern section of the street now known as Monument Street. The street may have been named after Sir George Arthur, a hero of the Napoleonic Wars, who received the FREEDOM OF THE CITY OF LONDON and a sword in recognition of his services.

Arthur's Club *St James's Street.* Derived its name from Robert Arthur, son of John Arthur, assistant to Francis White, and himself once proprietor of White's Chocolate House (*see* WHITE'S CLUB). Robert Arthur occupied 69 ST JAMES'S STREET (designed in 1826–7 by Thomas Hopper) in the middle years of the 18th century; and, after his death in 1761, his daughter married Robert Mackreth, her father's former billiard marker and head waiter, who purchased estates in Surrey and was knighted. In his time 69 ST JAMES'S STREET was known as Arthur's Chocolate House, and as such was very popular. 'Everything goes on as it did,' wrote Lady Hervey in 1756. 'Luxury increases – all public places are full, and Arthur's is the resort of old and young; courtiers and anti-courtiers; nay, even of ministers.' Arthur's Club, a descendant of the chocolate house, seems to have been founded in 1811. The members were for 'the most part country gentlemen of a type which has done much for our land in the past. They took their duties seriously, and upheld the traditions of country life.' It was always an expensive club: the original subscription was 20 guineas. There hung in the hall a portrait of Kitty Fischer, the daughter of a German staymaker, who was one of the most celebrated courtesans of her time. It was a tradition of the club that she had been kept for a time by a fund to which all its members subscribed. But, since she died over 40 years before the Club was founded, it was more likely that, if she was kept by subscription at all, it would have been by the Miles Club which was established in the house some time between the departure of WHITE'S and the foundation of Arthur's. The portrait was moved to PRATT'S after Arthur's closed down. Upon its closure several of its members were admitted into the CARLTON CLUB.

Artillery Lane *E1.* Built in about 1682 on the Old Artillery Ground which was known in Stow's day as Tasel Close because of the prickly-headed plants used in treating cloth. The land once belonged to the Prior of ST MARY SPITAL. It was leased to an artillery company in

1537–80. In 1540 the hospital was dissolved but the land continued to be used for military training. In the 17th century there were constant disputes between the Tower Ordnance and the HONOURABLE ARTILLERY COMPANY who both claimed the land had been granted to them. In 1641 the HAC moved to their present ground in FINSBURY. The Tower Ordnance continued to practise here but it became increasingly dangerous as the surrounding areas were built on. In 1682 the artillery ground itself was sold for building. There is a fine Georgian shop front of about 1757 at No. 56.

Artillery Row *SW1.* Takes its name from the artillery practice which used to take place here. Butts had been erected in the area in obedience to an ordnance of Elizabeth I. Artillery House was built in about 1930 to the designs of Maurice Webb. The redbrick block, Westminster Palace Gardens, is by C.J.C. Pawley (1897).

Arts Club *40 Dover Street, W1.* Inaugurated in 1863 by the amateur artist Arthur Lewis, Ellen Terry's brother-in-law, who lived at Moray Lodge, KENSINGTON where his fellow-members of the Artists' Rifle Corps used to meet. The club's first house was at 17 HANOVER SQUARE, but in 1896 it moved to its present address. After severe bomb damage in the 2nd World War the house was reconstructed; it was again remodelled in the 1970s, the club requiring smaller premises. Dickens, George Du Maurier, Whistler, Rossetti and Swinburne were all members. Thomas Hughes, author of *Tom Brown's Schooldays*, was the first chairman. Dame Laura Knight became its first female member at the age of 90. There are now some 150 women among its 1,100-odd members. In recent years the Authors' Club has also moved to 40 Dover Street from WHITEHALL COURT.

Arts Theatre *Great Newport Street, WC2.* A club theatre founded in 1927 by Walter Payne, Bronson Albery, W.E. Gillespie and others for staging unlicensed and avant garde plays. Among its early successes were *Young Woodley* (1928), *The Lady with a Lamp* (1929), *Musical Chairs* (1931), *Richard of Bordeaux* (1932) and *Viceroy Sarah* (1934). From 1942 to 1953 a miniature National Theatre was run here by Alec Clunes. The first production of *The Lady's Not for Burning* by Christopher Fry was staged here in 1948. From 1953 to 1963 the theatre was managed by Campbell Williams. His most successful productions were *Waiting for Godot* (1955) and *Waltz of the Toreadors* (1956). In 1967 the UNICORN THEATRE FOR CHILDREN took over the theatre to give children's plays for eight months of the year. Since then Tom Stoppard's *Dirty Linen* has been successfully produced here. The seating capacity is 337.

Arundel House *Highgate.* The house of Sir William Cornwallis, one of Elizabeth I's courtiers. The Queen visited him in 1589, 1593 and 1594. James I was entertained here in 1604 with Ben Jonson's masque *Penates*. In 1626 Sir Francis Bacon died in the house which then belonged to the Earl of Arundel. He had caught a chill while trying to preserve a dead chicken in snow and was too ill to travel home. In 1694 the western half was demolished and Old Hall (17 South Grove) was built in its place. The eastern half was demolished in 1828.

The view from the roof of Arundel House, from where Wenceslaus Hollar drew his celebrated view of London in 1647.

Arundel House *Strand*. Site of the medieval town house of the Bishops of Bath and Wells. In 1539 the house was given to William Fitzwilliam, Earl of Southampton, reverting to the Crown on his death in 1542. It was granted to Thomas Seymour, brother of the Protector, Somerset, in 1545. Somerset's amorous approaches to Princess Elizabeth are said to have been made here. In 1549 Seymour was executed for treason and the house was sold to Henry Fitz Alan, 12th Earl of Arundel, for just over £40. Fitz Alan died in 1580 and was succeeded by his grandson, Philip Howard, who was brought to trial for high treason and died in the TOWER in 1595. The house was granted in 1603 to Charles, Earl of Nottingham; but in 1607 was transferred to Thomas Howard who was restored to the Earldom of Arundel. From 1615 he began collecting the Arundel Marbles, the first great art collection in England. When he died there were 37 statues, 128 busts and 250 inscribed marbles besides many other fragments. They were described by Selden in *Marmora Arundeliana*, published in 1628. In 1626–8 he was confined in his house, having offended the Duke of Buckingham and Charles I. Wenceslaus Hollar had an apartment at Arundel House and from the roof drew his view of London which was published in 1647. In 1646 Thomas Howard died abroad; and after his death Arundel House was used as a garrison. During the Commonwealth distinguished visitors were received here. At the Restoration it was returned to Thomas's grandson, Henry, 6th Duke of Norfolk, another great collector. The ROYAL SOCIETY met here, 1666–74, having lost their previous meeting place in the GREAT FIRE. In 1667 they were presented with the Earl's library. He gave his marbles to Oxford University. The house was demolished in 1678. HOWARD, NORFOLK, SURREY and ARUNDEL STREETS were built on the site.

Arundel Street *WC2*. Built in about 1678 by the Earl of Arundel as a means of raising money for financing a new town house designed by Wren which he hoped to build on a riverside site to the south of the old ARUNDEL HOUSE in the STRAND. The street was first developed on the east side only so that the ugly backs of the houses would not spoil the view from the Earl's new garden. However, he abandoned his plan and

went to live in ST JAMES'S SQUARE. In the next ten years the street was completed and at first was very fashionable. John Evelyn lived at his son's house here for a time in 1686 and Thomas Rymer, the critic and historian, died here in 1713. In 1716 John Gay wrote in his *Trivia*:

Behold that narrow street which steep descends,
Whose building to the slimy shore extends;
Here Arundel's fam'd structure rear'd its frame,
The street alone retains the empty name:
Where Titian's glowing paint the canvas warm'd
And Raphael's fair design, with judgment, charm'd,
Now hangs the bellman's song and pasted here
The coloured prints of Overton appear.
Where statues breath'd the work of Phidias' hands,
A wooden pump, or lonely watch-house stands.

At the upper end of the street was the Crown and Anchor Tavern, meeting place of political agitators during the 18th and 19th centuries.

Ashbridge Street *NW1*. A small street near to LISSON GROVE north of the MARYLEBONE ROAD, it began its existence about 1834 as Great Exeter Street. Its name was changed in 1939 in honour of Arthur Ashbridge, the Marylebone District Surveyor, whose fine collection of local history material is now the pride of the public library. On the west side is an early block of galleried workers' dwellings, kept spruce and up-to-date and so likely to be preserved.

Ashburnham House *Little Dean's Yard, SW1*. Built in the 1660s and, in Sir Nikolaus Pevsner's opinion, 'the best example in London of a progressive and stately mid-c17 house'. The architect may have been John Webb. It was built for the Ashburnham family and sold by John, Earl Ashburnham to the Crown in 1730. The Cotton Library of Manuscripts (*see* BRITISH MUSEUM) was deposited here in 1731 when the house was occupied by the King's librarian and several of the volumes were lost in a fire that same year. The building is now part of WESTMINSTER SCHOOL.

Ashcroft Theatre *Fairfield Hall, Park Lane, Croydon, Surrey*. Part of the Fairfield Halls designed by Robert Atkinson and Partners and opened by the Queen Mother on the 2 November 1962. It consists of Fairfield Hall, primarily a concert hall but also adapted for stage performances, film shows, boxing and other entertainments; the Arnhem Gallery, which commemorates the link between the towns of Croydon and Arnhem, as well as the theatre. The project was conceived by the CROYDON Council in 1955 and the theatre was built on part of a site which was known as the Fair Field (where an annual fair had been held from 1314 to the middle of the 19th century) and which was bought by the Council in 1934. The theatre is named after CROYDON-born Dame Peggy Ashcroft. The seating capacity is 748.

Asprey and Co. Ltd *165–166 New Bond Street, W1.* William Asprey, a member of a family of skilled craftsmen of Huguenot descent, was working in MITCHAM in 1781, specialising in calico and silk printing. He then began to make fitted dressing cases. In the 1830s his son Charles Asprey moved to 49 NEW BOND STREET, and in 1848 to the present premises at 165–166 NEW BOND STREET, where the firm still designs and makes many articles in its own workshops. Since the time of Queen Victoria it has supplied the Royal Family with fine jewellery, silverware and ornate objets d'art. It remains a family business.

Assembly House *292 Kentish Town Road, NW5.* Originally a meeting point for people who would gather here to make up a party before leaving for HAMPSTEAD HEATH and the north in the sometimes vain hope that numbers would frighten off highwaymen. Built towards the end of the 19th century, this public house has magnificent glasswork and mirrors, and a painting depicting an earlier Assembly House Tavern which stood on the site.

Astley's Amphitheatre *Westminster Bridge Road.* Philip Astley was a man 'with the proportions of a Hercules and the voice of a Senator' who was honourably discharged from the cavalry in 1768 and given his horse as a leaving present. He bought another horse at SMITHFIELD and began giving unlicensed open-air equestrian displays in the fields of SOUTHWARK. Receiving a licence as a reward after a chance incident in which he helped George III subdue a spirited horse near WESTMINSTER BRIDGE, he erected a canvas-covered ring near the bridge in 1769 and called it the 'Royal Grove'. After a fire in 1794, the Royal Grove was rebuilt as Astley's Amphitheatre.

Pony racing at Astley's Amphitheatre before its destruction by fire in 1803.

Clowns, including Grimaldi, acrobats and conjurors appeared, as well as equestrians. Sword fights and exotic melodramas were also presented. In *Sketches by Boz* Dickens, who loved Astley's, described how everything there was 'delightful, splendid and surprising'. The Amphitheatre was rebuilt after another fire in 1803, and again after a third fire in 1841. It was rebuilt for the last time in 1862 when, for a short time, it became the New Westminster Theatre Royal. It was demolished in 1893.

Astoria Theatre *157 Charing Cross Road, WC2.* Built in 1927, to the designs of Frank Verity, as a luxury cinema on the site of a building used for the manufacture of preserves. It was colloquially known as 'The Jam Factory'. It was taken over by the Cooney-Marsh Group and adapted as a theatre, opening in 1977 with a musical, *Elvis*.

Astwood Mews *SW3.* Built on the Thurloe estate and named in 1873, it takes its name from the village in Buckinghamshire where John Thurloe spent much of his life.

The entrance hall of the Athenaeum, the club house in Pall Mall designed by Decimus Burton.

Athenaeum *107 Pall Mall, SW1.* The most intellectually élite of all London's clubs, founded in 1824 in the apartments of the ROYAL SOCIETY at SOMERSET HOUSE for artists, writers and scientists by John Wilson Croker, the politician and writer who first coined the term 'Conservative' and whom Macaulay detested 'more than cold boiled veal!' It was first known as 'The Society', taking its present name when it moved to Pall Mall in 1830. (The Athenaeum in Rome was a university for the study of science and literature founded by the Emperor Hadrian.) The club-house was designed by Decimus Burton. John Henning's frieze above the main windows is a reconstruction of that on the Parthenon. Club members wanted an ice house instead, but Croker insisted on the frieze:

> I'm John Wilson Croker
> I do as I please
> They ask for an ice house
> I'll give them a frieze.

Above the entrance porch is E.M. Baily's large gilt

statue of Athene, Goddess of Wisdom, Industry and War (1829). In 1899 the attic storey was added by Collcutt. Past and present members include the majority of Prime Ministers, Cabinet Ministers, Archbishops, Bishops and major literary figures.

Athlone House *Hampstead Lane, N6.* Edward Brook, a key figure in the development of synthetic chemicals, built this mansion, whose large square tower looks out over HAMPSTEAD HEATH. It was designed by Solomon and Jones (1871). He called it Caen Wood Towers, and lived there from 1871 to 1881. During the 1st World War it was used as a military hospital. After the war Sir Robert Waley Cohen bought the house and lived in it from 1919 to 1942 when it became an Air Ministry building. Later it was used as a nurses' training school; and since 1955, renamed Athlone House, it has been a recovery unit of the MIDDLESEX HOSPITAL.

Atmospheric Railway In 1845 the London and Croydon Railway Company experimented with this revolutionary form of rail transport. It dispensed with the locomotive and was operated by means of pneumatic power picked up from a conductor pipe between the tracks and provided by pumping stations built at 3 mile intervals. These were designed by W.H. Breakespear to resemble Early Gothic churches, with tall chimneys. In 1846 an entirely atmospheric line was operating from FOREST HILL to WEST CROYDON, with the first rail flyover in the world at NORWOOD, to cross the Brighton line. It reached high speeds, but its silent approach caused near-accidents and passengers found themselves occasionally having to push. The engineer was William Cubitt. The railway was abandoned in 1846, due to technical difficulties.

Aubrey House *Aubrey Road, W8.* Named after Aubrey de Vere, the first Lord of KENSINGTON Manor. It is the last surviving country house in KENSINGTON, dating back to the 1690s when it was built as a well house over a newly discovered medicinal spring. This scheme failed but the house continued as a private dwelling, save for a period, 1830–54, when it was used as a private boarding school for young ladies. Probably its most notable inhabitant was Lady Mary Coke who resided here 1767–88 and employed James Wyatt to redecorate the drawing room, but the house is best known for its association with the Alexander family who purchased it in 1873 and whose descendants still reside here. The family was much concerned with local philanthropic work, particularly in the fields of social welfare and housing. W.C. Alexander was a patron of the arts who early recognised Whistler's talents and gave him commissions. His fine art collection was bequeathed to the nation in 1965. Cicely Alexander was painted by Whistler in *An Arrangement in Grey and Green*, now in the NATIONAL GALLERY. Aubrey Road was built in 1859.

Audley Square *W1.* Near the south end of the east side of SOUTH AUDLEY STREET, it is not really a square at all. The frontage of the short range of houses built here in the second half of the 18th century was set back a few feet from the line of frontage of the rest of the east side of SOUTH AUDLEY STREET, and the whole terrace was rather confusingly called Audley Square. All except the southernmost of the original houses have been

demolished, and most of the rest of Audley Square is now occupied by a multi-storey garage.

Austin Friars *EC2.* Named after the leading Augustinian monastery in England founded in 1253 by Humphrey de Bohun, Constable of England, on returning from a crusade. Its boundaries were marked by LONDON WALL, COPTHALL AVENUE and THROGMORTON STREET. In 1354 Humphrey de Bohun (a descendant of the founder) built a larger church for the monks. During the PEASANTS' REVOLT Wat Tyler attacked the monastery, and dragged out 13 Flemings from its sanctuary and beheaded them. In 1513 Erasmus lodged here and complained of the difficulty of getting good wine; and in 1529 Miles Coverdale, one of the monks, worked on his translation of the Bible here. Many illustrious people were buried within the hallowed precincts including the founder, Humphrey de Bohun; Hubert de Burgh, builder of WHITEHALL PALACE; Edward, son of the Black Prince; Richard Fitz Alan, Earl of Arundel and Surrey; Edmund, son of Joan Plantaganet; John de Vere, 12th Earl of Oxford, and his son, Aubrey; many of the Barons killed at the Battle of Barnet during the Wars of the Roses; and Edward Stafford, 3rd Duke of Buckingham.

After the DISSOLUTION OF THE MONASTERIES Sir William Paulet, 1st Marquess of Winchester, took over the monastic buildings and built himself a town house on their site. In 1550 the nave of the church was given to Dutch refugees by Edward VI but the rest was used for storing corn, coal and wine. The ancient monuments were sold for £100 and lead from the roof stripped off. In 1600 the choir, tower and transepts were demolished; and two years later the Marquess of Winchester sold his house to John Swinnerton, a merchant. Fulke Greville wrote to his neighbour, the Countess of Shrewsbury, to tell her that her house and Lady Warwick's had been included in the sale. 'He could not conceive your ladyship would willingly become a tenant to such a fellow.' In 1844 the remaining part of the house was divided into warehouses. In 1862 the church was burnt down. Rebuilt the next year by Edward I'Anson and William Lightly, it was bombed in 1940 and rebuilt again in 1950–6.

Australia House *Strand, WC2.* The Australian High Commission. It is a very grand piece of Beaux Arts designed by A. Marshall Mackenzie and A.G.R. Mackenzie and built in 1912–18. It incorporates the earlier Victoria State Building of 1907. Flanking the entrance are *Exploration and Agriculture* by H. Palmer and on the cornice *The Horses of the Sun* by Bertram Mackennal.

Australian Avenue *Barbican.* Built in about 1894 between BARBICAN and JEWIN CRESCENT on the site of Fig Tree Court and Trafalgar Place. Several of the warehouses in the street were used by Australian merchants. It was completely destroyed in the 2nd World War.

Ave Maria Lane *EC4.* An 'Ave Maria Aly' is recorded in 1506, but the present name is first mentioned in 1603 by Stow who said it was 'so called of text writers and bead makers dwelling therein'. A later suggestion is that the name marks a stage in the processions of the Cathedral clergy as in AMEN COURT. It appears to have been an important link between Newgate Hill and

LUDGATE HILL because it was widened to 18 ft in the improvements which were carried out after the GREAT FIRE. Its proximity to the book trade in PATERNOSTER ROW determined its later character. In 1687 a large part of the library of William Cecil, Queen Elizabeth's Lord Chancellor, was sold at the sign of the Bear. In Queen Anne's time the Black Boy Coffee House was the main place for book auctions. In 1698 Christopher Bateman, the bookseller, moved from HOLBORN to the corner of Ave Maria Lane and PATERNOSTER ROW at this time; and every Saturday in winter the Earls of Oxford, Pembroke and Winchilsea and the Duke of Devonshire would meet at his shop. Thomas Britton, the small-coal merchant who had established his celebrated musical club in Jerusalem Passage in 1678 and collected books on the occult sciences, joined these noble collectors in his blue smock with a coal sack over his shoulders.

Avenue House   *East End Road, Finchley N3.* With its landscaped grounds and rare trees, this house was left to the people of FINCHLEY by Henry C. ('Inky') Stephens, who died in 1918. His father had invented the famous blue-black ink in 1832. The son bought Avenue House in 1874, making considerable additions to the original building, which dates from 1859. These included, in 1884, a large drawing room – used as its council chamber by the Finchley council when bombed out of its premises in 1940 – and, on the first floor, Stephens's private laboratory which still exists, complete with work benches and bunsen burners. The nearby stable yard (1880) has charming decorative features.

The house was a hospital for airmen until 1925; it was a public library in the 1930s. Today it houses the BARNET Borough Arts Council and is a meeting place for the Finchley Society and other local organisations. The pleasant grounds are a public park.

Avery Hill   *SE9.* The park was opened to the public in 1903, having been purchased by the LONDON COUNTY COUNCIL the previous year. It now comprises 86 acres with facilities for cricket, football, rugby, hockey, putting and tennis and a children's playground. The domed Winter Garden, damaged by a flying bomb in the 2nd World War, was reopened in 1962. The adjoining mansion is now a teachers' training college. The GREATER LONDON COUNCIL maintains 17 acres as its central plant nursery which supplies shrubs and bedding plants for its parks and other sites.

Avery Hill College   *Bexley Road, SE9.* Opened in 1906 as the first local authority residential college for training women students. It admitted men in 1959 and opened its MILE END annexe in 1968. As a result of the recent college closures and amalgamations it is now the only free-standing College of Education surviving to be supported by the INNER LONDON EDUCATION AUTHORITY. The main college is located on the north side of AVERY HILL PARK, just to the east of ELTHAM.

Avery Row   *W1.* Extending from BROOK STREET to GROSVENOR STREET, it marks the course of the TYBURN, which here formed the boundary between the GROSVENOR ESTATE and the CORPORATION OF THE CITY OF LONDON's Conduit Mead estate (*see* CONDUIT STREET). It probably takes its name from Henry Avery, a bricklayer active hereabouts in the 1720s and 1730s.

B

Babmaes Street *SW1*. A cul-de-sac built in about 1665 and named after Baptist May, Charles II's friend and Keeper of the Privy Purse, who was granted the land.

Baden-Powell House Museum *Queen's Gate, SW7*. Housed in the Scout Association's international hostel, the museum illustrates the life of Lord Baden-Powell from his days as an officer in the Boer War to his time as chief of the organisation of Boy Scouts which he had founded 'to promote good citizenship in the rising generation'. His celebrated hat is here, his sketches and watercolours, the manuscript of his *Scouting for Boys* and, amongst other memorabilia, a loaf of bread baked during the siege of Mafeking in 1899 and one of the tins which, containing chocolate, was sent by Queen Victoria to Baden-Powell's soldiers in South Africa. Designed by Ralph Tubbs, the building opened in 1961.

Arbours, fountains and tea gardens at Bagnigge Wells, one of the most popular of 18th-century spas.

Bagnigge Wells *King's Cross Road*. One of the most popular 18th-century spas, it was probably named after an ancient local family, the Bagnigges. It was reputed to have been the summer retreat of Nell Gwynne who entertained Charles II here with little concerts and breakfasts. In 1757 it belonged to Thomas Hughes, a tobacconist, who asked Dr John Bevis to discover why he could not grow flowers in his garden. Water from the well was found to be full of iron. Another well was sunk and the water from that proved to be a good purgative. In 1758 Hughes opened the gardens daily and charged 3d for tasting the waters. A season ticket cost half a guinea. The banqueting hall of Bagnigge House had been converted into a long room with a distorting mirror one end and an organ the other. The water was brought to a double pump in a small building called the temple. In the grounds were honeysuckle-covered tea arbours, a bun house, skittle alley, bowling green, grotto, flower garden, fish pond, fountain and formal walks edged with holly and box. On the banks of the FLEET RIVER which flowed through the garden were seats, 'for such as chuse to smoke or drink cyder, ale etc which are not permitted in other parts of the garden'. Concerts and other entertainments were frequently held in the pump-room. From 1760 until the end of the 18th century the wells were not only popular but fashionable. In the mornings the pump-room was thronged with water tasters and in the afternoons with tea drinkers. A song published in the *London Magazine* of June 1759 ran:

Ye gouty old souls and rheumaticks crawl on,
Here taste these blest springs, and your tortures are
  gone;
Ye wretches asthmatick, who pant for your breath,
Come drink your relief, and think not of death.
Obey the glad summons, to Bagnigge repair,
Drink deep of its streams, and forget all your care.

The distemper'd shall drink and forget all his pain,
When his blood flows more briskly through every vein;
The headache shall vanish, the heartache shall cease,
And your lives be enjoyed in more pleasure and peace.
Obey then the summons, to Bagnigge repair,
And drink an oblivion to pain and to care.

The prologue to Garrick's *Bon Ton* (1775) mentioned 'Drinking tea on summer afternoons at Bagnigge Wells with china and gilt spoons', as a fashionable pastime. However, mixing with the *bon ton* were pickpockets, prostitutes and highwaymen. Sixteen-string Jack, who was hanged at TYBURN in 1774, was a frequent visitor. By the beginning of the 19th century the wells were no longer fashionable. According to Daniel Lysons they were, in 1810, 'much resorted to by the lower class of tradesman'. And in 1827 Maria Edgeworth wrote, 'The cits to Bagnigge Wells repair, to swallow dust and call it air.' In 1813 the manager went bankrupt and the place was sold. It was reopened in 1814 on a smaller scale; but, although a concert room was built in 1831, it soon afterwards degenerated into a rather disreputable establishment. A London street ballad related the adventures of a costermonger and his girl:

Every evening he was seen
In a jacket and shorts of velveteen
And to Bagnigge Wells then in a bran
New gown she went with the dogs' meat man . . .

The place was closed in 1841 and the site soon afterwards was built on. Set in the later wall of 61–63 King's Cross Road is an inscribed stone: 'This is Bagnigge House Neare the Pinder a Wakefeilde 1680.' It probably marks the north-western limit of the gardens.

Baker Street *W1, NW1*. Laid out from 1755 onwards by William Baker, a speculative builder, on land leased from the PORTMAN ESTATE. A broad thoroughfare, it is today filled with shops and offices; MARKS AND SPENCER have their administrative head-quarters here as does the Abbey National Building Society which occupies a white skyscraper block, designed in the 1920s by J.J. Joass, at the northern end of the street. No. 120 remains comparatively intact except for the insertion of a plate-glass window. It was the home, during the years 1802–6, of the statesman William Pitt the Younger, whose niece, Lady Hester Stanhope, who later became an explorer in Turkey and the Lebanon, kept house and entertained for him. No. 31 was an early home of Bulwer Lytton; Sir Richard Burton, the explorer and Oriental scholar, lived in the street for a while; and Mrs Sarah Siddons, the actress, lived from 1817 till her death in 1831 at No. 27 Upper Baker Street. Her house was demolished to make way for the Underground Station and its place is now taken by the Lost Property Office at No. 226. Baker Street's most famous resident, the detective Sherlock Holmes, created by Sir Arthur Conan Doyle, lived at No. 221B, today the offices of the Abbey National, where an exhibition re-creating his crowded first-floor apartment was held in 1951 as part of the FESTIVAL OF BRITAIN celebrations; it was later reconstructed at a public house bearing the detective's name in NORTHUMBERLAND AVENUE off the STRAND. The Abbey National frequently receives letters asking Holmes for help with insoluble mysteries. The Volunteer, the public house at Nos 245–247, takes its name from the Royal Marylebone Volunteers formed as a defence against Napoleon's army. Druce and Co. at Nos 58–59 were established as cabinet makers at the Baker Street Bazaar in 1822.

Bakerloo Line The Bakerloo Line, opened in 1906 from BAKER STREET to KENNINGTON Road, was the first tube of C.T. Yerkes's comprehensive scheme of electric railways for London. It was also the first underground railway to cross London from north to south. To begin with the line was considered a failure with only 20–30,000 passengers per day, and for a time the six-car trains were reduced to three during peak hours and two during slack hours. At the same time, objections were raised by conservative railway journals, already hostile to Yerkes's American in-fluence, to the name Bakerloo, a word first coined by the *Evening News* for the Baker Street and Waterloo Railway. The *Railway Magazine* wrote, 'For a rail-way itself to adopt its gutter title, is not what we expect from a railway company. English railway officers have more dignity than to act in this manner.' The magazine added that the name was 'unlikely to increase the business of this struggling concern'. However, business did increase, partly helped by the introduction of a graded fare structure of 1d–3d with ½d stages instead of a standard fare of 2d. With the centralisation of the ownership of the underground system the Bakerloo Line was extended so that by 1910 it reached Watford. By 1939, having taken over the STANMORE branch of the METROPOLITAN LINE, the Bakerloo, which had originally covered 3 miles, extended from Watford and STANMORE in the north to ELEPHANT AND CASTLE in the south thus covering 32 miles in all. The section running between STAN-MORE and BAKER STREET became part of the JUBILEE LINE in 1979 (*see also* JUBILEE LINE *and* UNDER-GROUND RAILWAYS).

Bakers' Company *see* CITY LIVERY COMPANIES.

Bakers' Hall *Harp Lane, EC3*. The original Hall was the converted mansion of John Chichele, a 15th-century Chamberlain of London. It was inherited by his daughter, Elizabeth Chichele, and, after her death in 1498, bought by the Company in 1506. This build-ing was burnt in the GREAT FIRE. The Hall was rebuilt soon after, only to be destroyed by fire again in 1715. The third Hall, built in 1719, was destroyed by enemy action in 1940. The present Hall, completed in 1963, by Trehearne and Norman, Preston and Partners, forms the lower portion of a large office block. For the Company *see* CITY LIVERY COMPANIES .

Bakewell Hall 'A spacious building', in the words of Hatton's *New View of London* (1708), on the east side of GUILDHALL, or on the west side of BASINGHALL STREET. A weekly market for woollen cloths had been established here in the 13th century in a house which belonged to John de Banquelle, Alderman of Dowgate ward, which later became the property of Thomas Bakewell. It was rebuilt in 1588 and again in the 1670s, after its destruction in the GREAT FIRE. It was demolished in 1820 to make way for the Bankruptcy Court. It was also known as Blackwell Hall. GRESHAM COLLEGE now covers the site.

Balcombe Street *NW1*. This was begun in 1826 as Milton Street and changed its name in 1886 for reasons unknown. In 1975, a man and his wife were held hos-tage for six days by IRA gunmen at 22B Balcombe Street. Police surrounded the building, and the IRA eventually surrendered without harming their hos-tages.

Baldwin's Gardens *EC1*. Built in 1589 on the site of Brook House and its gardens, the mansion of Fulke Greville, Lord Brooke, by Richard Baldwin, Queen Elizabeth's gardener. It enjoyed the privilege of sanc-tuary for many years; and petty criminals fled here to live unmolested by law until 1697 when the privilege was abolished. Henry Purcell, the composer, took ad-vantage of the protection the place afforded to escape his creditors. After his day the area became a notorious slum much frequented by criminals, and part of the locality known as the Thieves' Kitchen, a training ground for young criminals.

Bales Court *EC4*. Named after Peter Bales, an Elizabethan calligrapher, who lived in the OLD BAILEY near the sign of the Old Dolphin. He advertised him-self as a writing schoolmaster 'that teacheth to write all manner of handes, after a more speedie way than hath heretofore been taught'. He promised his students, 'You may also learne to write as fast as a man speaketh, by the arte of Brachigraphie by him devised, writing but one letter for a word.' He was used to transcribe public documents into book form and employed by Walsingham and Hatton for deciphering codes, forg-ing letters and copying secret documents.

Balham *SW12*. Probably started as a Saxon home-stead on the ROMAN ROAD of Stane Street, which ran from Chichester to London. The estate is recorded in *Domesday Book* as being occupied by a 'squatter'. Its history during the Middle Ages is complicated as it seems to have been split into three separate holdings, one held by the Abbey of Bec, one by BERMONDSEY ABBEY, and the smallest being in private hands. At the time of the Reformation, Balaams Farm of 200 acres was acquired by the Crown and in the 17th century was leased to a Bernard Hide. His solidly built farmhouse lasted until about 1890 when it was demolished to make way for the houses in Emanuel Road. In 1701 the estate was acquired by Peter Du Cane, MP for Colchester, and it remained in his family until 1840. A map of the mid-18th century shows the area still as open country with Balham as a group of half a dozen buildings straddling the main road. Two lanes lead off into the fields, one starting near the George Inn and skirting a tile kiln. By the end of the century there were a number of large houses lining Balham Hill and the High Road. One of these belonged to George Wolf, Consul-General to the Court of Denmark. He was a great friend of John Wesley, who visited him on a number of occasions between 1785 and 1791. More houses were built after the Duke of Bedford had sold Charrington's Farm in 1802. A Mr Borrodaile had a row of desirable villas built along the High Road and, for himself, a large mansion called Bedford Hill House, on the highest point of the estate. A private road, now Bedford Hill, was made from the main road to TOOTING BEC COMMON to provide access to the house. This road with gates and lodges either end, was shared by two other houses, THE PRIORY and Boundaries House.

Many of the residents were leading figures in the CITY OF LONDON, being bankers, merchants and lawyers. At the beginning of the 19th century, the nearest places of worship were at STREATHAM or CLAPHAM, so these wealthy inhabitants held a meeting to propose the founding of a chapel at Balham. Money was raised and the red-brick building with its façade of four Doric columns was opened on 24 April 1808. Amongst the shareholders were William Wilberforce, Henry Thornton and Lord Macaulay. In 1855 it was assigned its own district and became a parish church.

The following year saw the opening of the railway station, giving easier access to the CITY. By the turn of the century there had been a complete transition of Balham from a country village to part of the urban sprawl of London. Houses for the middle and working classes gradually covered the open land. Large villas were built on either side of Bedford Hill and the old estate was developed by Alfred Heaver. New shops appeared in the High Road and by the 1930s most of the old houses had disappeared. One day a year during this period of change, the main road became congested with traffic. This was Derby Day when all sorts of horse-drawn vehicles, ranging from dog-carts to victorias, landaus and gipsy caravans, made their way to Epsom Downs.

During the 2nd World War, Balham was badly damaged by bombing. One particular incident caused great loss of life. A high-explosive bomb blasted a large crater in the High Road, fracturing the water main. This flooded the UNDERGROUND RAILWAY below, where a number of people taking shelter were drowned. A bus later drove into the crater in the dark. Since the end of the war most of the large houses have been turned into flats or bed-sitters. Open space is in short supply, although TOOTING BEC COMMON is ¾ mile to the south-east and WANDSWORTH COMMON the same distance to the north-west. Both were saved in the 1870s from the ravages of further enclosure or use by the railway companies. Although various plans have been made to improve the town centre with better shopping facilities, open spaces and traffic control, the old Roman road will always be a major route in and out of London. A plaque at 99 Nightingale Road indicates the residence here of the preacher, Charles Haddon Spurgeon, in 1857–80. He rebuilt the house in 1869.

Ballooning 'Balloons occupy senators, philosophers, ladies, everybody,' wrote Horace Walpole at the end of 1785 when all London was agog with this latest craze. Ballooning reached London only a few months after the first sensational achievements with hot air and hydrogen balloons in France in 1783. It was an Italian, Count Zambeccari, who made the first small hydrogen balloons seen over London. The first attempt to ascend in one was made in August 1784 by a Frenchman, Dr Moret, from fields now covered by BELGRAVIA. It ended in disaster when the balloon caught fire on the ground and Dr Moret disappeared with the takings; the disappointed spectators wrecked a nearby teahouse. About a month later Vincenzo Lunardi successfully ascended from the Artillery Ground at MOORFIELDS in his own gorgeous red and white silk hydrogen balloon, and flew to Ware. His second balloon carried a Mrs Sage – the first Englishwoman to fly – from ST GEORGE'S FIELDS, Newington Butts as far as HARROW, though her great weight, it is said, almost prevented the balloon from taking off. Londoners saw the first parachute descent from a balloon in England by a Frenchman, M. Garnerin, who ascended from NORTH AUDLEY STREET and landed near ST PANCRAS in 1802; and watched as the great aeronautical showman, Charles Green, who introduced coal gas as a method of inflation, filled his balloon from the PICCADILLY gas-main and flew from GREEN PARK to BARNET, to celebrate the coronation of George IV. There were ballooning displays at many

The ascent of Charles Green's 'monster Nassau Balloon' from Cremorne Gardens in the summer of 1845.

London pleasure gardens including RANELAGH, CREMORNE and VAUXHALL GARDENS. In *Sketches by Boz*, Dickens devoted a chapter to VAUXHALL in which he wrote, 'the balloons went up, and the aerial travellers stood up, and the crowd outside roared with delight, and the two gentlemen who had never ascended before tried to wave their flags as if they were not nervous, but held on very fast all the while; and the balloons were wafted gently away . . .' In 1869 a monster balloon, nearly 100 ft in diameter, made daily ascents from the Lots, waste ground between ASHBURNHAM HOUSE and the THAMES, west of CREMORNE GARDENS, until the balloon, named *The Captive*, one day escaped its moorings and the exhibition was discontinued (*see* LOTS ROAD). The Bedford Arms in Grove Street, CAMDEN TOWN, was noted for balloon ascents from its tea-gardens. So also were the grounds of another public house, the Eyre Arms, in FINCHLEY ROAD.

The development of dirigibles and powered flight led to the end of free ballooning as popular entertainment, but as a minority sport it was well established at BATTERSEA and HURLINGHAM by the 1890s. In 1906 the first official balloon race in Great Britain was organised by the Aero Club from Ranelagh Club Polo Ground, BARNES, and the first international race took place in 1908 from the HURLINGHAM CLUB, FULHAM.

During the 1st World War 'kite balloons' – a form of barrage balloon – with baskets beneath operated them from ROEHAMPTON as spy balloons, and balloon aerodromes were constructed in and around London at ILFORD, HOUNSLOW and NORTHOLT. Emergency landing grounds were built in HYDE PARK, REGENT'S PARK, WIMBLEDON COMMON, BLACKHEATH and in the grounds of BUCKINGHAM PALACE. In the 2nd World War a vast balloon barrage was deployed over London (*see* BLITZ). In more recent times there have been flights of hot air balloons at dawn from WORMWOOD SCRUBS, and in 1977, Silver Jubilee year, 60 or 70 balloons gathered in HYDE PARK but were not able to fly because of unsuitable weather conditions; nevertheless, many of them flew tethered.

Baltic Exchange *St Mary Axe, EC3.* Has, as its primary function, the provision of facilities for the fixing of cargoes for merchant vessels. Most of the world's freight chartering is arranged here and the sale of over half the world's ships. It originated some years before the middle of the 18th century. On 24 May 1744 it was announced in the *Daily Post* that a coffee house in THREADNEEDLE STREET, whose customers were mainly merchants and ships' masters trading in goods from the plantations of the American colonies and the countries of the Baltic seaboard, had changed its name: 'This is to give notice that the house, late the Maryland Coffee House in Threadneedle Street near the Royal Exchange, is now opened by the name of the Virginia and Baltick Coffee House where all foreign and domestic news are taken in and all letters or parcels directed to merchants or captains in the Virginia or Baltick trade will be carefully delivered according as directed.'

By 1810 the increase in business conducted in this coffee house made it necessary for larger premises to be found. So the Antwerp Tavern in THREADNEEDLE STREET was acquired and renamed the Baltic Coffee House. And in 1823 a Baltic Club was formed with a membership of 300 and recognised rules for trading.

After the repeal of the Corn Laws in 1846 foreign trade greatly increased. In 1857 the Baltic bought SOUTH SEA HOUSE from the liquidators of the Royal British Bank. In 1891 the London Shipping Exchange was founded to meet the needs of liner shipping and, since its activities overlapped those of the Baltic and since both organisations were short of space, an amalgamation was proposed and a site, Jeffrey Square, in ST MARY AXE, purchased for a new building. This was constructed in 1900–3 to the designs of T.H. Smith and W. Wimble. A new wing was opened by the Queen in 1956, the foundation stone having been laid by Sir Winston Churchill the year before.

Baltimore House *Bloomsbury.* Built in 1763 for Frederick Calvert, Baron Baltimore, who in 1768 was tried for decoying here a young milliner, Sarah Woodcock. The Duke of Bolton afterwards lived here and it was then known as Bolton House. Bolton was the model for Captain Whiffle in Smollett's *Roderick Random*. Later occupants of the house were Lord Loughborough, the Earl of Rosslyn (in whose time it was known as Rosslyn House); Sir Vicary Gibbs, Chief Justice of Common Pleas; and (in 1839–54) Sir Thomas Noon Talfourd, also Chief Justice of Common Pleas, a playwright and friend of Dickens. During Talfourd's time the house was a meeting place of numerous men of letters and dramatists. When RUSSELL SQUARE was laid out in 1804, this was the only house there. It was later divided into two. No. 67 was built on the site.

Bancroft's School *Woodford Green, Essex.* In 1737 Francis Bancroft, 'late citizen and draper of London', left his money to the DRAPERS' COMPANY to provide almshouses for 24 old men and a chapel and schoolroom for 100 poor boys, with two houses for masters. The early school was in the Mile End Road, but in 1886 the school moved to a 5-acre site in Woodford Green. There new buildings, still financed by the DRAPERS' COMPANY, were designed for the school by Sir Arthur Blomfield. Today the school educates girls as well as boys; all are now day pupils, and there are over 700 of them between the ages of 11 and 19. Many of them are supported by bursaries or scholarships granted by the DRAPERS' COMPANY.

Bank of England *Threadneedle Street, EC2.* After the Stuart kings' borrowing from the ROYAL MINT and the goldsmith bankers had severely damaged government credit, the idea of a National Bank was put forward by William Paterson, a Scottish merchant. It was based on the revolutionary concept of a National Debt whereby the Government could raise money 'upon a Fund of Perpetual Interest'. In 1694 the Government, in need of funds for the French–Dutch war, passed the Bank of England Act granting them the 'Rates and Duties upon the Tunnage of Ships and Vessels, and upon Beer, Ale and other liquors' to be paid as interest to those voluntarily advancing £1,500,000. The money was immediately raised from 633 subscribers and was lent to the Government at a rate of 8 per cent. Sir John Houblon, son of a Huguenot refugee, was elected first Governor with a Deputy and 24 Directors under him. With 19 staff the Bank began business in MERCERS' HALL, then moved to GROCERS' HALL in POULTRY where it stayed until 1734.

The Bank of England from Threadneedle Street, 1797. The gateway is by George Sampson, the screen walls are by Robert Taylor.

The Bank struggled successfully with open competition from other banks until 1708, when the Government prohibited the issue of notes by an association of more than six persons, giving it a virtual monopoly. In 1715 a Jacobite plot to burn the Bank was uncovered; and five years later it weathered the South Sea Bubble crisis. By this time the National Debt had risen to £36,000,000. In 1724 Daniel Defoe remarked, 'No place in the world has so much business done with so much ease.' In 1725 the first fixed notes were issued – for £20, £30, £40, £50 and £100. In 1731 the death of a Director, Humphrey Morice, revealed his embezzlement of £29,000. The full amount was never recovered. In 1734 the Bank moved to premises in THREADNEEDLE STREET in a building designed by George Sampson. It included an impressive pay hall complete with a vast, ornate charcoal-burning stove. It is said that more than one confused customer thrust his notes through the bars of the stove by mistake. By 1766, under Pitt the Elder, the Bank had already become Banker to the Government and to most State Departments. Between 1767 and 1770 Sir Robert Taylor added major extensions to the building, including the Rotunda which was used as an unofficial stock exchange. (The brokers, described in 1806 as 'by no means of reputable description', were finally expelled in 1838). In 1780 the GORDON RIOTERS attempted to capture the bank. The mob was forced back by militia and volunteers, among them John Wilkes. Records say that they used bullets made from melted-down inkwells. The response to the riot was the institution of a permanent military guard (which remained until 1973). In 1781 ST CHRISTOPHER LE STOCKS was demolished and Robert Taylor's offices were built on the site. A major reconstruction of the Bank began in 1788 under the direction of Sir John Soane who designed a magnificent neo-classical building surrounded by a windowless wall. In 1793 the first £5 note was

issued and in the same year the Napoleonic wars began, leading to a severe banking crisis. During these wars the bank earned a nickname when Sheridan, speaking in 1797 in the House of Commons, made reference to 'an elderly lady in the city of great credit and long standing', as a result of which the bank became popularly known as 'The Old Lady of Threadneedle Street'. The French invasion of Wales had precipitated further panic and the Bank could not meet the rush for gold. Payment was suspended until 1821. The need for banking reform was evident. Acts of 1826 and 1833 allowed the formation of joint stock banks and the Bank of England lost its monopoly. In 1830 the Bank's first provincial office was opened in Gloucester. In 1836 a sewer man found a way into the Bullion Room in London. He sent an anonymous note to the Directors offering to meet them there at any hour they named. They did so at a 'dark and midnight hour'. The man was given a large reward for his honesty. During the second half of the 19th century the expansion of the money market, and the influx of foreign capital, consolidated the Bank's position as a central bank. In 1844 the Bank Charter Act limited the issue of notes by other banks, and by the end of the 19th century the Bank was acting as the government's and bankers' bank only, and was no longer accessible to the public. In 1931 the suspension of the Gold Standard meant that the Bank no longer had to sell gold at a fixed price. In the 1920s and 1930s rebuilding by Sir Herbert Baker left only a few interiors and the outside walls intact. In 1946 the Bank of England Act brought the Bank into public ownership and capital stock was transferred to a nominee of the Treasury. A further Banking Act of 1979 gave the Bank legal powers to supervise banks after the collapse of a number of small banking companies. Today the main functions of the Bank are to act as note-issuing authority, as the government and bankers' bank, as manager of the National Debt and as

36

custodian of the nation's gold reserves. The mosaic pavement in the entrance hall is by Boris Anrep. The bronze doors are by Charles Wheeler, who was also responsible for the figures on the façade, which include the Old Lady of Threadneedle Street holding a model of the building on her knee, and the gilt figure of *Ariel* on the dome (1932) as well as the statues of Charles Montagu and Montagu Norman (1932) on the first floor of the central court. The bronze of the Bank's patron saint, St Christopher, in the central court is by R.R. Goulden (1921).

Hollar's view of Bankside in 1647, showing the Bear Garden (upper left), and the Globe on the river front.

Bankside *SE1*. Narrow street along the river bank at SOUTHWARK, formerly lined with wharves and warehouses with splendid views over the river to ST PAUL'S and the CITY. With its numerous brothels and bear baiting the area of Bankside was for long one of medieval London's main centres of dissipation. Also known for much of its length as Stew's Bank, it contained an unconsecrated graveyard for the corpses of women who had worked in the brothels. It was within the estate of the Bishops of Winchester, the LIBERTY OF THE CLINK. Far from condemning the brothels, the bishops drew up a set of rules for them and regulated their opening hours. In 1546 Henry VIII had them closed, but by the 17th century they had reopened and had been joined by theatres: the ROSE in Rose Lane, the SWAN in Paris Garden, the HOPE in BEAR GARDENS and the GLOBE in what is now PARK STREET. Many actors, stage managers and writers lived in the area, among them William Kemp, Edward Alleyn, Philip Massinger, Beaumont and Fletcher, and Philip Henslowe, lessee of the ROSE THEATRE, who owned much property in the area. After their day the area was better known for its gardens, public houses, breweries, foundries and dyers' and glassmakers' works. The Anchor, built in 1770–5, occupies the site of an earlier inn, the Castell on the Hoop. In the 1750s Oliver Goldsmith practised as a physician in 'a humble way' on Bankside. Barclay and Perkins's brewery was near here in PARK STREET (*see* BREWERIES). On a visit to it in 1850 the Austrian General Haynau, whose evil reputation had been spread by Hungarian refugees, was attacked and beaten by draymen and hauled along the street by his long moustache.

Bankside Power Station Like its counterpart at BATTERSEA, Bankside Power Station was designed by Sir Giles Scott. It was opened in 1963 and has a

distinctive large single chimney. It stands on the south side of the THAMES, opposite QUEENHITHE, and occupies the site of the Great Pike Gardens in SOUTHWARK, which in the 14th century supplied fish to religious houses in the area.

Banner Street *EC1*. Built in 1774, mostly by Henry, John and Peter Banner. Henry Banner was City Carpenter at the time. None of their houses remained after damage in the 2nd World War and subsequent housing development.

Banqueting House *Whitehall, SW1*. The only remaining part of the old WHITEHALL PALACE above ground. Designed by Inigo Jones and completed in 1622, it was the first purely Renaissance building in London. The first known Banqueting House at Whitehall was a temporary structure of wood and canvas, built in 1572 for the visit of a French delegation. In 1581 Elizabeth I erected a more permanent building on the same site, for the entertainment of the envoys who had come to negotiate a marriage between the Queen and the Duke of Alençon. It also was made from wood and canvas, but with 292 glass windows and richly painted. James I considered this to be an 'old, rotten, slight-builded shed' and in 1606 it was pulled down. Its replacement was 'very strong and statlie, being every way larger than the first'. It was 120 ft by 53 ft and set out as a theatre. On its opening, in January 1608, Ben Jonson's *The Masque of Beauty* was performed. It was burnt down in 1619.

The new Banqueting House by Inigo Jones was faced with Portland stone and cost £15,653 3s 3d in all. Horace Walpole wrote of it, 'It is so complete in itself that it stands as the model of the most pure and beautiful taste.' It has a gallery, with a stone balustrade, from which the King's subjects could watch him dine. The ceiling, commissioned by Charles I, is painted by Rubens, and celebrates the benefits of wise rule. It is on a vast scale, each cherub being more than 9 ft high. The building was much admired. In 1655, for example, a foreign visitor described it as looking 'very stately, because the rest of the Palace is ill-built, and nothing but a heap of Houses, erected at divers times, and of different Models.'

It was opened in 1622 with a performance of Jonson's *Masque of Angers*, but after the installation of the Rubens ceiling in 1635, masques were performed in a new wooden building nearby, lest the lamp smoke should damage the paintings.

The Banqueting House was used for a variety of state and court ceremonies, including the reception of foreign embassies, the traditional Maundy Thursday observances, the St George's Day dinner for Knights of the Garter, and the 'touching' for King's Evil (scrofula).

On 30 January 1649 King Charles I walked for the last time across the Banqueting House, and out through a window (there is a controversy as to which) on to the scaffold. Here he made a brief speech, declaring himself 'the Martyr of the People', before he was beheaded. Charles II celebrated his restoration in the hall in 1660. The building also formed the background to the Glorious Revolution: James II added a weather vane to the north end to warn him of a 'Protestant wind' which might carry his son-in-law over the sea from Holland, and it was in this hall too that William and Mary were offered the joint sovereignty by the

Charles I was executed in 1649 on a scaffold outside Inigo Jones's Banqueting Hall, Whitehall.

assembled nobility and commons on 13 February 1689.

The fire of 1698 marked the end of the ceremonial significance of the Banqueting House. It was converted by Wren into the CHAPEL ROYAL, as the old chapel had been burnt. In 1809 it became the Chapel of the HORSE GUARDS. It remained their chapel until 1829 when it was restored and again used as the Chapel Royal until 1890. In 1890 it was granted as a museum to the ROYAL UNITED SERVICES INSTITUTE. In 1963 it was redecorated in its original colours and opened to the public.

Barbers' Company *see* CITY LIVERY COMPANIES.

Barbican *EC2*. Named after an outer fortification of the City, possibly a watch-tower. Stow said it was pulled down by Henry III in 1267 after the war with the Barons. During the 16th and 17th centuries several wealthy and important people lived here. Garter House near the eastern end of the street was built at the beginning of the 16th century for Thomas Wriothesley, Garter King-of-Arms. From the end of the 16th century until it was destroyed by fire in 1687 it was the town house of the Earls of Bridgewater. Next door was Willoughby House, used by the Conde de Gondomar, Spanish Ambassador during Elizabeth I's reign. John Milton lived in the Barbican between 1645 and 1649. *L'Allegro* and *Comus* were probably written at this time. Maitland, writing in 1756, said that the street was inhabited by tradesmen, 'especially salesmen for apparel both new and old'. In the 2nd World War 35 acres to the south were completely laid waste. In 1956 Duncan Sandys, the Minister of Housing and Local Government, proposed that 'a genuine residential neighbourhood, incorporating schools, shops, open spaces and amenities' should be created in this devasta-ted area, even if it meant 'foregoing a more remunerative return on the land.' The proposal was accepted and in 1958 the site was compulsorily pur-chased by the CITY OF LONDON and the LONDON COUNTY COUNCIL. The architects, Chamberlin, Powell and Bon, were commissioned to prepare a plan. It was eventually decided to build flats to accom-modate 6,500 people, some of them in tower blocks over 400 ft high, the highest in Europe at that time. Shops and offices were also built as well as a new GUILDHALL SCHOOL OF MUSIC AND DRAMA, a new MUSEUM OF LONDON, the Halls of the IRONMONGERS' COMPANY and of the BARBERS' COMPANY, and the CITY OF LONDON SCHOOL FOR GIRLS. The parish church is ST GILES CRIPPLEGATE. (*See also* BARBICAN CENTRE FOR ARTS AND CONFERENCES.)

Barbican Centre for Arts and Conferences *Barbican, EC2*. London's equivalent of the Pompidou Centre in Paris and the Lincoln Center in New York, it lies in the middle of the BARBICAN development between two 43-storey blocks of flats, with a view towards ST PAUL'S CATHEDRAL. The area was heavily bombed during the BLITZ and the architects Chamber-lin, Powell and Bon drew up the first plans for its redevelopment in 1955.

The Centre held its first commercial event, the an-nual general meeting of a large City company, on 30 April 1981 and was officially opened by the Queen on 3 March 1982, having cost approximately £153 million. It is the largest complex to have been built by one firm of architects and has the most extensive flat roof in Europe. The buildings, which cover 20 acres, are on ten levels, the lowest being 17 ft below sea level.

The art gallery, on two storeys with 15,000 sq ft of exhibition space, is one of the largest in London. There are three cinemas, with seating capacities of

280, 255 and 153 respectively. The concert hall consists of three curved tiers with a seating capacity of 2,026. The stage can be extended over the front two rows of seats to make room for a choir. Acoustics are improved by balls attached to the ceiling and by hardboard covering on the undersides of the seats. The hall is the home of the LONDON SYMPHONY ORCHESTRA which plays up to five concerts a week over three four-week seasons a year. The Royal Shakespeare Company, founded in 1875, moved from the ALDWYCH and WAREHOUSE THEATRES on 3 March 1982 to become the resident company of the 1,166-seat theatre.

Barclay's Bank *160 Piccadilly, W1.* Designed by William Curtis Green in 1922 as a showroom for Wolseley Motors Ltd, whose cars were displayed to advantage on the marble floors of the exotic Renaissance interior. The company was bankrupt, however, by 1926 and the showroom was sold to Barclay's who commissioned Curtis Green to convert it into a bank. As the original design for the exterior had been influenced by a bank in Boston admired by Curtis Green, he had merely to apply a few touches of detail to the outside such as the extra ironwork and bronze doors. The interior was enriched with lacquered decoration in the Japanese style which adorned tables, chairs, desks, cabinets and standard lamps. The Venetian red paint on the banking hall columns is said to be 26 coats thick.

Barclay's Bank Ltd *Lombard Street, EC3.* Created by the merger of 20 private banks in 1896, this leading clearing bank has direct links with London banking in the 17th and 18th centuries. Barclay and Co. was originally a goldsmiths' business established in about 1694 by John Freame of the Black Spread Eagle in LOMBARD STREET (on the site of the present Bank's headquarters). The Barclay family entered the partnership in 1736, and were subsequently joined by the Bevan and Tritton families. Their acquisitions included Spooner, Attwood and Co. (established at FISH STREET HILL in 1801) and Ransom, Bouverie and Co. of PALL MALL, founded in 1786. The amalgamation of 1896 also embraced Goslings and Sharpe of the Three Squirrels in FLEET STREET. This bank had originally been a goldsmith's concern, established by Henry Pinckney in about 1650. Barclay's Bank's later amalgamations included the London Provincial and South Western Bank, which brought its large network of London branches into Barclay's in 1918, and Martin's Bank in 1968. Martin's had evolved from a goldsmith's business established by Sir Thomas Gresham, founder of the ROYAL EXCHANGE in the late 16th century. Based at the Grasshopper in LOMBARD STREET, the firm was operating as a bank by the beginning of the 18th century. It subsequently became a leading clearing bank, with strong branch representation in London and the north-west. Today Barclay's Bank (excluding its extensive international business) is represented by 350 branches in the London area, while the upper echelons of the Bank continue to include representatives of the founding families of the original private banks.

Barham House *and* **Park House** *33 and 35 High Street, Hampton, Middlesex.* The house now forming these two houses was in being by about 1650. With 16 hearths it rivalled the house that became GARRICK'S

VILLA as the largest house in HAMPTON. In the 1670s it was owned by Henry Cooke, Master of the Children of the CHAPEL ROYAL, and composer of the music written for Charles II's coronation. Henry Cooke left the house to his pupil and son-in-law, Pelham Humfrey, who succeeded to the office of Master of the Children. Henry Cooke taught most of the composers of the English School of the Restoration, among them John Blow and Henry Purcell. A later owner (1714–61) was Anne Bynns, who married Sir John Shadwell as his second wife. Sir John was the son of Thomas Shadwell, Dryden's successor as Poet Laureate. He became Physician-in-Ordinary to Queen Anne and was present at her death. From 1812 to 1844 the house was used as a 'Young Gentlemen's Boarding Academy' and shortly after was divided into two. The right-hand part, Park House, was the first headquarters of the Hampton Local Board in 1890–4, and one of the rooms was used as Hampton's first public library. Both houses are in private ownership.

Baring Brothers and Co. Ltd *Bishopsgate, EC2.* The oldest merchant bank in London, this business was established by John and Francis Baring in QUEEN STREET in 1763. It was originally a merchant house, chiefly concerned with the wool trade, but banking for overseas customers emerged as a major part of the business before 1800. Clients of the firm, which was known as Baring Brothers and Co. after 1807, included the governments of the United States (from 1803), the Argentine (1824) and Russia (1846). The Barings, owing to their early success, could afford to employ Lawrence to paint their family portraits. Although many merchant banks retain family portraits, only Barings have custody of real works of art in this field. The *conversazione* between the partners, commissioned by Sir Francis Baring in 1806–7, is one of Lawrence's masterpieces. The firm was reconstructed as a limited company in 1891 and its activities now include advice on mergers, acquisitions and new issues. The firm's headquarters, at 8 BISHOPSGATE since 1805, were rebuilt by Norman Shaw in 1881; the site was redeveloped in 1975.

Barking *Essex.* Derives its name from Berecingum – 'Berica's people'. It lies east of the RODING RIVER and between the THAMES to the south and ILFORD to the north. It was one of the earliest Saxon settlements in Essex, with the town developing beside BARKING ABBEY at the head of Barking Creek. The parish was included in the Manor of Barking. ILFORD and Chadwell wards in the north were also part of the ecclesiastical parish of Barking until 1830 and of the civil parish until 1888.

After the DISSOLUTION many landowners in Barking were London merchants, several becoming LORD MAYORS OF LONDON, including Sir Crisp Gascoyne, first occupant of the present MANSION HOUSE, whose great granddaughter, Frances, married James Cecil, 2nd Marquess of Salisbury.

For 500 years the most important industry in Barking was fishing; in the middle of the 19th century some 220 Barking smacks were crewed by 1,370 men and boys. But by the end of the century the fleet had moved to Yarmouth and Gorleston, whence rapid railway transport sped the fish to London. The coming of the railway to Barking in 1854 hastened expansion of the town over surrounding farms and market gardens. The population of 21,547 in 1901 reached 78,170 in 1951 but has since declined by some 1,200 a year.

Industries are now concentrated towards the south-west, near the RODING and between Ripple Road (A13) and the THAMES. Barking Power Station, one of the largest in Europe, closed in 1981 after 56 years' production. A freightliner terminal opened in 1972 on some 30 acres of railway sidings south of Ripple Road. That part of Barking west of the RODING and containing Beckton gas works was amalgamated with EAST HAM into the London Borough of NEWHAM. In 1965 Barking was amalgamated with DAGENHAM into the London Borough of Barking and DAGENHAM.

The South-East Essex Technical College designed by J. Stuart was opened in 1936. This is now the Barking Precinct of the NORTH-EAST LONDON POLYTECHNIC. The Town Hall and Assembly Hall, designed in 1936 by Herbert Jackson and Reginald Edmonds respectively, were delayed by the war and not built until 1954–8. Barking railway station was rebuilt in 1956–61. BARKING HOSPITAL was partly rebuilt and enlarged in 1963–6. A new Central Library opened in 1974 and there are several modern office blocks. Post-war housing developments include the Thames View, Lintons, and Gascoigne estates. Part of the main shopping area, East Street, has been made into a pedestrian precinct; and the area surrounding ST MARGARET'S CHURCH and BARKING ABBEY declared a conservation area. Elizabeth Fry, the prison reformer, was buried in the Quaker burial ground, which is now a public garden.

Barking Abbey The greatest Benedictine nunnery in the country at the time of the DISSOLUTION. It was founded in about AD 666 by St Erkenwald, with his sister, St Ethelburga, as first Abbess. Later Abbesses included two more saints (Hildelitha and Wlfhildis), three queens (Alftrudis, widow of King Edgar; Maud, wife of Henry I; and Matilda, wife of King Stephen) and two princesses (Maud, daughter of Henry II; and Maud, daughter of King John). Early endowments of land and property constituted the Manor of BARKING and comprised ILFORD and DAGENHAM as well as BARKING. Other property included ALL HALLOWS BARKING-BY-THE-TOWER. William the Conqueror stayed at Barking after his coronation and confirmed the Abbey charters. The Abbey was dissolved in 1539; its buildings were demolished and their materials used for royal properties at Dartford and GREENWICH. Only the 15th-century Curfew Tower remains intact, with its 12th- or early 13th-century carved stone rood in the chapel over the gateway leading into ST MARGARET'S churchyard. Preserved in the church are a fragment of the shaft of a Saxon carved cross and a black marble slab inscribed with the name of an 11th-century Abbess.

Barking Creek The mouth of the RODING RIVER, which runs down from Essex and through BARKING, once an old market and fishing village lying some 7 miles east of the CITY. The creek runs through the mud between industrial buildings for a mile south of the EAST HAM and BARKING by-pass down to the THAMES. Just west of its mouth is the northern outfall of London's main drainage (*see* DRAINS AND SEWERS) with the works and filter beds of the Main Drainage Metropolis and a jetty projecting into the river for the sludge ships. West of that are gas works. About half a

mile to the east of the mouth by the river rises BARKING Power Station from which extend the cable towers in a bleak – but in certain conditions of light, dramatic – landscape, although one which today hardly conforms to the poet Drayton's description of the creek's 'limpid waters and gay banks'. Opposite the creek on the south bank lie the PLUMSTEAD MARSHES and the ROYAL ARSENAL estate where the new town of THAMESMEAD is still growing and to the east of which lie the southern outfall sewage works.

Barkston Gardens *SW5.* Built in 1886 and named after Barkston Ash, the Yorkshire parliamentary seat of Colonel Robert Gunter, the ground landlord. Ellen Terry lived at No. 22 in 1889–1902.

Barlow Place *W1.* An irregularly shaped yard leading off the south side of BRUTON STREET. It takes its name from the master carpenter Thomas Barlow, surveyor to the nearby GROSVENOR ESTATE, who was active hereabouts in the 1720s.

Barn Elms *Rocks Lane, SW13.* Formerly the manor house of BARNES, held by the Dean and Chapter of ST PAUL'S until 1504 when they leased it to Sir Henry Wyatt. It was forfeited to the Crown on the attainder and execution of his grandson, Sir Thomas Wyatt, for rebellion against Mary I. Sir Francis Walsingham leased the estate in 1579 and entertained Elizabeth I here on three occasions; his son-in-law, the Earl of Essex, also lived here occasionally. In the 17th century it was the subject of lawsuits between the Ferrers and Cartwright families and frequently let to tenants, including the poet, Abraham Cowley, in 1662–5. The gardens were a fashionable resort mentioned by Pepys and Congreve.

Thomas Cartwright rebuilt the manor house in 1694 and a second house on the estate was leased to Jacob Tonson, the publisher and secretary of the KITCAT CLUB, whose members presented him with their portraits by Kneller. His nephew, Jacob II, built a separate gallery for them and acquired land to the west of Barn Elms. In the 1730s the main house became the residence of Sir Richard Hoare (later Lord Mayor of London), whose son, also Sir Richard, extended it and landscaped the grounds. The Hoare family sold the estate to the Hammersmith Bridge Company in the early 1820s. William Cobbett briefly rented the home farm in 1828–30. The house and grounds became the Ranelagh Club from 1884 until 1939, but the house became derelict and was demolished following a fire in 1954. Today, parts of the grounds are used as school playing fields and only a truncated part of the ornamental lake system and the ice-house provide the slightest reminder of the former layout.

Barnes *SW13.* According to *Domesday Book*, the manor (*berne*=barn) was in the possession of the canons of ST PAUL'S but certain dues were payable to the Archbishop of Canterbury as Lord of the Manor of MORTLAKE. Barnes should, however, properly be considered as a separate manor. The Dean and Chapter of ST PAUL'S held it throughout the Middle Ages and still retain the right to nominate the rector. Until the early 19th century the village was considered remote as the normal approaches were either from the river or by foot across the common. The only road led from MORTLAKE along the Terrace by way of the High

Street and the present Church Road to the entrance of BARN ELMS. The construction of CASTELNAU in 1827 and Lonsdale Road in 1846 to provide access from HAMMERSMITH BRIDGE, and the arrival of the railway, also in 1846, heralded a century of large-scale development. On the other hand, the shape of the village centre with its large green and pond has remained intact and retains a leafy, rural character which is bolstered further by the spacious common to the south.

In an island of houses on the common at Mill Hill is the site of the former windmill and the original miller's house (now part of Mill Hill Lodge). In the mid-18th century there was an uninterrupted view of the Rectory (now STRAWBERRY HOUSE), the church, the Homestead and Byfield House (now demolished). Further large houses stood around the green and pond, including MILBOURNE HOUSE. Humbler dwellings and shops lined the High Street but, apart from the uneven stretch of houses in BARNES TERRACE, the village was orientated away from the river.

Brewing was a local industry and there were a number of inns, most of which have disappeared or have been rebuilt. The Sun, still a popular resort near the pond, retains its 18th-century building and the former Rose, of Jacobean timber-framed construction, is now 70 High Street (Barnes Community Association). St Michael's and All Angels, Westfields, is by Charles Innes (1891–3). A BLUE PLAQUE at MILBOURNE HOUSE, Station Road, commemorates the residence here of the novelist Henry Fielding.

Barnardo's Homes see DR BARNARDO'S HOMES.

Barnes Common *and* **Barn Elms Common** *SW13*. Barnes Common covers about 120 acres and was used jointly by the townships of BARNES and PUTNEY until 1589 when a dispute arose, the outcome of which was that the men of BARNES refused to allow the men of PUTNEY to use the Common. Before being drained in the second half of the 19th century, the Common was virtually marshland and natural history societies, then as now, found it an interesting area for research. The adjoining area of Barn Elms Common (54½ acres) is administered by the INNER LONDON EDUCATION AUTHORITY and provides playing fields for various schools.

Barnes Railway Bridge *Chiswick–Barnes*. The oldest bridge remaining below RICHMOND. It was built in 1846–9 by Joseph Locke and J.E. Errington for the London and South Western Railway. It is a cast-iron arch bridge with open spandrels vertically ribbed and now disused. Another wrought-iron bowstring bridge was built alongside it on the downstream side in 1891–5.

Barnes Terrace *SW13*. A piecemeal ribbon development facing the river and containing a number of 18th- and early 19th-century houses retaining original features including much attractive early ironwork. Past residents have included the actor John Moody (No. 11); the playwrights John O'Keefe (No. 30) and Richard Brinsley Sheridan; the Art Nouveau designer Christopher Dresser; the writer W.E. Henley (No. 9) and the composer Gustav Holst (No. 10). Outside their house, No. 28, the master spy the Comte d'Antraigues and his wife, the singer Mme St-Huberty,

were murdered by their Italian valet. All the houses mentioned still exist.

Barnet *see* EAST BARNET, HIGH BARNET *and* FRIERN BARNET.

Barnet General Hospital *Wellhouse Lane, Barnet, Hertfordshire*. Built in 1834 as a workhouse and then called the Barnet Institution. In 1895 an infirmary for 60 beds was added. In 1913 the main hospital block was built and it was named the Wellhouse Hospital. In 1939 additional wards were built and in 1948 the National Health Service took over the administration. In 1951 it was given its present name. There are 413 beds.

Barnsbury *Islington, N1*. Standing on the high ridge of Islington hill, until the 1820s Barnsbury commanded views to HIGHGATE and the CITY. Reed Moat Fields, a moated mound on the site of Mountford House, Barnsbury Square, is popularly identified as the camp of Suetonius Paulinus during his campaign against Boudicca. In fact it belonged to a moated grange of Barnsbury or Bernersbury manor, part of the larger Yseldon manor, held of the canons of ST PAUL'S from the late 13th century until 1532 by Ralph de Berners and his descendants, from whom the name derives. Barnsbury's land extended far beyond today's suburb, from below HIGHGATE almost to the ANGEL. After passing, chiefly by marriage, through the wealthy local families of Fowler, Fisher and Halton, it was devised by Sir William Halton in 1754 to his godson William Tufnell Jolliffe. In 1822 the trustees of Jolliffe's descendant, William Tufnell, a minor, secured a private Act enfranchising the land, which was then disposed of on leases. Thus rural Barnsbury joined the building boom.

In the hilltop fields, near the present corner of Barnsbury and Dewey Roads, was the WHITE CONDUIT, once the CHARTERHOUSE water supply. Open-air religious and political gatherings were held here; and City holiday-makers flocked to the White Conduit House and its gardens. In the 1780s aristocratic cricket was played on the grounds of a tea house and dairy owned by Thomas Albion Oldfield (*see* WHITE CONDUIT CLUB). Cricket subsequently moved to LORD'S; the Albion tea house became a public house; and the field was built over.

On the site of College Cross, farther north, the Loyal Islington Volunteers exercised in the 1790s. Richard Laycock's, one of Islington's two longest-surviving dairy farms (*see* LIVERPOOL ROAD), remained with its cattle lairs until after SMITHFIELD closed in 1855. Market and botanic gardens also flourished here, notably Harvey's (*see* LIVERPOOL ROAD) and that of Dr William Pitcairn, President of the ROYAL COLLEGE OF PHYSICIANS (1775–85), who created a 5-acre garden now covered by Almeida Street and Waterloo Terrace.

Between 1812 and 1820 the REGENT'S CANAL's famous Islington tunnel, 970 yds long, was excavated under the hill, from Muriel Street, west of the White Conduit, to Colebrooke Row, with a handsome arch at either end. A granite and York stone retaining wall at the Barnsbury end was demolished in 1981 during massive council housing development.

At first by degrees, then wholesale from the 1820s, Barnsbury's pond-strewn pastures and gardens were broken up for brick-maker's clay and built over to form a middle-class residential suburb. Chief among new estates were the CLOUDESLEY, or STONEFIELD (1824 onwards), MILNER-GIBSON (1829–41), Cubitt's Manchester Terrace (now 222–266 LIVERPOOL ROAD) and College Cross (1827 onwards), the DRAPERS' COMPANY'S Lonsdale Square (1838–43), and the Thornhill family's 86 acres on the western hillside above CALEDONIAN ROAD (1840s–50s). Barnsbury's idiosyncratic squares, villas and terraces, many of them still a feature of the district, date from this period. Its few public buildings were naturally sited along its perimeter, in LIVERPOOL ROAD: the 18th-century workhouse, replaced in 1872 by an odd turreted building used as the Relieving Office and until 1969 as the Registrar's Office; the London Fever Hospital (1848); and the ROYAL AGRICULTURAL HALL (1862).

With the extension of railways, Barnsbury's new population of prosperous tradesmen, minor professional men and private school proprietors moved to still newer suburbs, and its status declined. From the end of the century it became, like much of ISLINGTON, a shabby district of absentee landlords and small tenancies. Since the 2nd World War whole streets have been demolished, many replaced by council estates, some planted as a park. Streets in the White Conduit area left waste since the 1960s are, in the 1980s, to become part of a housing association development.

Barons Court *Fulham, W14.* A late 19th-century development to the west of NORTH END ROAD, given the name by its owner, Sir William Palliser, in allusion to the Court Baron held by the Lord of the Manor. The roads of the estate form a series of parallelograms from Perham Road to the railway, many of them being named after members of the Palliser family and their estates. On the west side is QUEEN'S CLUB.

Bartholomew Close *EC1.* Named after the nearby church of ST BARTHOLOMEW THE GREAT. In 1633 Hubert le Sueur lived here while making the equestrian statue of Charles I now in TRAFALGAR SQUARE (*see* STATUES). John Milton hid in the Close for some time in the spring of 1660 until the Act of Oblivion pardoned him for seditious works. In 1697, 'next door to Mr Downinge's the Printers', William Hogarth was born, the son of a scholar turned bookseller's hack. In 1725 Benjamin Franklin worked in Palmer's Printing Office in the former Lady Chapel of ST BARTHOLOMEW THE GREAT. Washington Irving took lodgings here when he visited England as a young man. At No.87–88 is BUTCHERS' HALL.

Bartholomew Fair Founded at SMITHFIELD by Rahere, court jester to Henry I, who, taken ill during a pilgrimage to Rome and determined to reform his life, had founded a Priory and Hospice dedicated to St Bartholomew in 1102 (*see* ST BARTHOLOMEW'S HOSPITAL). The Priory received a very considerable income from the tolls of the fair which were granted to it by royal charter in 1133. Bartholomew became the greatest cloth fair in the country, being held annually for three days from the eve of St Bartholomew's Day. Even after he was made Prior, Rahere, as Lord of the Fair, was not above performing juggling tricks at the fair.

The CORPORATION OF LONDON held a cattle fair at the same time and Priory and CITY constantly disputed the rights to tolls. In 1445 they became joint Lords of the Fair. In 1538, after the Priory's dissolution, its rights were granted to Sir Richard Rich. Even then disagreements continued as the rival authorities wrangled over the fair's finances until an uneasy peace was patched up between them in 1596 and in 1604 the CORPORATION took over control. In the 17th century St Bartholomew's became more important as a centre of general entertainment than as a cloth fair and there were numerous booths where strolling players, wrestlers, dwarfs, fire-eaters and tight-rope walkers performed. Ben Jonson's play *Bartholomew Fair* gives a good idea of what the fair was like in the early part of the century. Surprisingly, the fair was not suppressed by the Puritans and Richard Harper, visiting it in 1641, wrote a long description of it, including an account of 'Hocus Pocus with three yards of tape or ribbon in his hand, showing the art of legerdemain to the admiration and astonishment of a company of cockoloaches'. Sir John Shorter, LORD MAYOR of London, came to open the fair with the usual ceremonies in 1688 and in drinking the traditional tankard of wine with the Keeper of NEWGATE flapped the lid of his tankard down so loudly that his horse shied and threw him. He died the next day.

For the next 150 years the entertainments flourished. The Prince of Wales made a visit in great state in 1740. The fair became renowned for the fine quality of the presentations in its many theatrical booths. After a visit in 1825 William Hone reported in his *Every Day Book* seeing 'four lively little crocodiles hatched from eggs at Peckham by steam, Womball and his menagerie, a glass blower in a glass wig blowing tea cups for 3d each'. The City authorities saw the fair as encouraging public disorder and, having bought the rights in 1830 from Lord Kensington, were finally in a position to suppress it in 1855. It was replaced in 1866 by SMITHFIELD MARKET.

Bartholomew Lane *EC2.* Named after the vanished church of ST BARTHOLOMEW-BY-THE-EXCHANGE.

Barton Street *SW1.* Takes its name from Barton Booth, the actor and husband of the 1st Duke of Marlborough's mistress, who owned land in the area. Built in the 1720s and still largely 18th-century, the houses are much sought after by members of Parliament. T.E. Lawrence was living at No. 14 in 1922 where, in the attic above the office of the architect Sir Herbert Baker, he 'found a haven of peace'.

Basil Street *SW3.* First known as North Street at its east end and as Upper North Street at its west end. It was cut in 1773 as a service road to Henry Holland's development of HANS TOWN. Mr Harrod considered the area evil and dangerous in the 1880s; but the prosperity and expansion of his store gradually eliminated the slums. Most of the modern blocks of flats date from the 1890s when much of the redevelopment of the area was carried out. The Basil Street Fire Station was built in 1904. The Basil Street Hotel (113 bedrooms) was built in 1910 upon the original KNIGHTSBRIDGE underground station which had been completed in 1905 – the lounge was made out of the old booking-hall and a ventilating shaft still runs right through the building.

The Capital Hotel (60 bedrooms) is at Nos 22–24. The name of the street was changed in 1906 for reasons unknown.

Basilica *see* FORUM.

Basinghall Street *EC2*. The Basings, a wealthy and influential City family of the 13th century, had a house here which gave its name to the street and the CITY Ward. Stow wrongly said the house became BAKEWELL HALL. The WEAVERS' COMPANY had their hall here from the 15th century until 1856, the COOPERS' from 1547 until 1867, the GIRDLERS' from 1431 to 1940, and the MASONS' from 1483 to 1864. Until 1899 the Church of ST MICHAEL BASSISHAW stood on the east side. Hugh Myddelton, goldsmith, banker and creator of the NEW RIVER, had his office in this street. He was one of the first British tobacco smokers and used to sit in the doorway chatting and sharing a pipe with Sir Walter Ralegh, much to the amazement of passers-by. GRESHAM COLLEGE is at No. 73. The stainless-steel abstract in front of Wool-gate House is *Ritual* by Antanas Brazdys (1969).

Basketmakers' Company *see* CITY LIVERY COMPANIES.

Bateman Street *W1*. Formerly known as Queen Street, it was described by Strype in 1720 as 'a Place not very considerable, having on the North side dead Walls, which generally are dirty and ill-kept'. This north side was built up in the 1770s, much of the south side – which was originally developed in the 1680s – having been rebuilt in the 1730s. Its present name – in use since 1884 – is derived from the Viscounts Bateman of MONMOUTH HOUSE. The Carlisle Arms at No. 2 and the Dog and Duck at No. 18 occupy sites where taverns of the same name have existed since 1752 and 1734 respectively.

Bath Club *43 Brook Street*. Founded in 1894 by two members of the CARLTON CLUB and some of their friends who lamented the fact that there was no club in London where they could swim. They consequently took the Marquess of Abergavenny's house in DOVER STREET and converted the ballroom into a swimming bath. After this house had been burned down in 1941, the club moved for a short time to the LANSDOWNE CLUB, and then to the CONSERVATIVE CLUB in ST JAMES'S STREET (which had no swimming bath). Having merged with the CONSERVATIVE CLUB – to form what was dubbed 'the Lava-Tory' – the Bath moved to the Brook Street address in 1959. The Flyfishers' Club, formerly at WHITEHALL COURT, found a home here. The club closed in June 1981.

Bath House *82 Piccadilly, at the west corner of Bolton Street*. Originally built by the statesman William Pulteney, Earl of Bath, the bitterest opponent of George I's first minister, Robert Walpole. After his death in 1764 it was occupied for a time by the Duke of Portland before being rebuilt in 1821 by Alexander Baring, later Lord Ashburton. He was for many years head of the great banking house of BARING BROTHERS, who featured in a famous quotation of 1818: 'There are six great powers in Europe – England, France, Russia, Austria, Prussia and Baring Brothers.' In about 1900 the interior was remodelled for Sir Julius Wernher, the

financier and philanthropist. The house was demolished in 1960.

Baths *see* PUBLIC LAVATORIES AND PUBLIC BATHS.

Bathurst Mews *W2*. Perhaps the only mews in London where horses are still kept – the Bathurst Riding Stables. The Royal Toxophilite Society used land on this site for archery during the 1830s. The ARCHERY TAVERN in Bathurst Street records this connection with a fine collection of engravings. For the derivation of the name *see* STANHOPE TERRACE.

Batson's Coffee House *17 Cornhill*. Established in the 1690s it was, according to the *London Gazette*, 'much frequented by men of intelligence for conversation'. It was also used as a business address by a variety of traders including Turkey merchants, silk brokers, exchange brokers and Russia merchants. It was, in addition, a house of call for physicians who, in the words of the *Connoisseur*, 'flock together like birds of prey watching for carcases at Batson's'. Sir William Blizzard, the distinguished surgeon, regularly attended here for consultation and was said to have been the last medical man in London to do so. It also attracted quacks; and at one time the 'Right New Cold Drawn Linseed-Oyl which is so famous for the distempers, Pthisick, colds and the only remedy for the plurisie' was available here. Sir William Brown, the physician, continued to be a customer in his eighties. One day in 1771 he presented himself in his fine lace coat and fringed white gloves to show himself to the Lord Mayor. Another customer commented that he looked very well. 'I have', he explained, 'neither wife nor debts.' The house is believed to have closed in the 1830s.

Battersea *SW11, SW8*. First recorded in a charter of AD 693, granting Batrices Ege to the Abbess of BARKING. The name means Badric's Island, the original site being surrounded by water or marshland. The existence of a Saxon settlement has been confirmed by excavations. Earlier occupation is indicated by objects of stone, bronze and iron, found mainly in the THAMES, the best-known example being the Battersea Shield, now in the BRITISH MUSEUM. The old village was centred on Battersea Square. To the north-east was ST MARY'S church, which is mentioned in *Domesday Book*. The old church was replaced by the present building in 1777, although some of the earlier memorials and stained glass have been retained. Next to the church was the manor house, a large, rambling building. The greater part was demolished in 1778 and the rest early this century. The panelling and plaster ceiling from the Cedar Room were sold and re-erected in Philadelphia. A short distance away is OLD BATTERSEA HOUSE, built about 1699 in the style of Wren. In danger of being demolished in 1930, it became a private home; it has recently been renovated and is probably the finest domestic building in the area. Nearby are the Vicarage and Devonshire House, two 18th-century survivals. In the Square is another building from the reign of Charles II, the Raven public house. This Dutch-gabled inn has remained relatively unaltered for the last 300 years.

Until the late 19th century the chief local occupation was market gardening, the soil in the area being particularly fertile. The main crops were carrots, melons, lavender and the famous local asparagus sold in 'Battersea bundles'. Although the area was mainly agricultural, several industrial concerns developed from the late 17th century. These included a pottery, copperworks, a lime kiln, chemical works, docks, wharves and several windmills. One of the latter was the strange 'horizontal mill', which was worked by a set of internal vertical paddles. In 1806, Marc Brunel set up his veneer works, adding machinery for making boots and shoes a few years later. For a short time Theodore Janssen manufactured his BATTERSEA ENAMELS at York House, the first example of the use of transfer printing on porcelain. The beginning of change came with the opening of the London and Southampton Railway in 1838 with its terminus at NINE ELMS. Next to the station a large depot and repair works grew up, creating many new jobs. Housing for the workers was required, and thus started the flood of new buildings. Within 30 years a great tangle of railway lines criss-crossed Battersea, today all part of British Rail. The Nine Elms yard has now gone, replaced by the NEW COVENT GARDEN MARKET. During the late 19th century new factories were established, such as Price's Candle Factory, Morgan Crucible Company, Garton Hill's Glucose Works and the Nine Elms Gas Works. Smaller concerns included laundries, a glove factory, starch and chemical works.

With the influx of new industry the population increased at a great rate. In 1801 it was just over 3,000, climbing to over 107,000 in 1881 and reaching a peak in 1901 of nearly 169,000. This meant that more houses were needed – many of the large estates, mainly in the southern half of Battersea, were sold to speculators and they were soon covered by rows of new homes. Gone are the original five houses of Bolingbroke Grove as well as the homes of William Wilberforce and Henry Thornton which faced CLAPHAM COMMON. A few survive, such as The Shrubbery, Gilmore House and Hollywood.

Down by the THAMES was an area known as Battersea Fields. Over the years the area had been drained and had become one of the most fertile areas near London. A rather lonely place, it was ideal for the duel that took place between the Duke of Wellington and the Earl of Winchilsea. Along the riverside were places of refreshment and entertainment, including the notorious Red House. The area acquired an unsavoury reputation and through public agitation a part of it was developed as BATTERSEA PARK. In 1885 some of the remaining land was used to erect the Albert Palace, a huge structure of iron and glass which, sadly, was demolished within ten years. The rest of the open land was used for housing, such as the model development of the Shaftesbury Park Estate, built in 1872–7 by the Artisans', Labourers' and General Dwellings Company on the site of a market garden. From its first meeting in November 1900, the new Metropolitan Borough of Battersea was fully aware of its responsibilities. In 1901, the Lombard Road generating station was built by the Works Department and part of the street lighting converted to electricity. The same year the Nine Elms Baths were opened. Housing too was not neglected, the old Latchmere allotments being used to build council houses, officially opened by John Burns. This programme of civic improvements was continued for the next 20 years.

The fibreglass sculpture of a male nude, *Archimedes*, in Lombard Road is by Edwin Russell (1962). A plaque at No. 61 Shelgate Road commemorates the residence here of Edward Thomas, the essayist and poet. Another plaque at Battersea Vicarage, No. 42 Vicarage Crescent, commemorates the residence of Edward Adrian Wilson, the Antarctic explorer and naturalist, who lived here – it was then a mission house – when he was studying medicine in 1896.

Battersea Bridge *Chelsea–Battersea*. The first bridge was built of wood to the designs of Henry Holland in 1771–2. It replaced the regular ferry between CHELSEA and BATTERSEA. Then the only bridge between WESTMINSTER and PUTNEY, it transformed CHELSEA from a village to a small town. It was dangerous to shoot the arches and boats were often wrecked when they collided with the piers. It was demolished in 1881 but is remembered by the misty Nocturnes and etchings of Whistler. It was replaced in 1886–90 by the present bridge with five cast-iron arches, designed by Sir Joseph Bazalgette.

Battersea Enamel Small objects, such as snuff-boxes and plaques, made in a workshop at York House, BATTERSEA, in the years 1753–6 under the management of John Brooks who perhaps invented the process of transfer printing by which many of the objects were decorated.

Battersea Park *SW11*. Situated on the former common fields of the Manor of BATTERSEA, the history of which can be traced back to the time of *Domesday Book*. It may have been the point where Julius Caesar crossed the THAMES to subdue the Catuvellauni tribe. In about 1560 the river was roughly embanked and it was here in 1671 that Colonel Blood hid in the reeds intending to shoot Charles II who was bathing. The Colonel confessed at his subsequent trial for his audacious attempt to steal the Crown Jewels that 'his arm was checked by an awe of majesty'. (*See* TOWER OF LONDON.)

In 1829 the Duke of Wellington fought a duel here with Lord Winchilsea who had accused the Duke of treachery to the Protestant cause and treason against the Constitution. Winchilsea kept his hand at his side when the Duke's second gave the order to fire. The Duke consequently fired wide. Winchilsea then fired into the air and tendered an apology.

The Red House Tavern, an Elizabethan building of red brick adjoining the fields, attracted the riff-raff of London and nearby were grounds for pigeon and sparrow shooting. In summer gipsies camped on the fields. On Sundays fairs were held with horse and donkey racing, roundabouts, theatres, comic actors, dancers, conjurors and fortune tellers, gambling, drinking booths and hawkers and vendors of all kinds of articles. Thousands of people were landed by boat and eventually the Government was forced to intervene.

At that time the fields comprised low marshes intersected by black streams and ditches and separated from the river only by a narrow raised causeway. Following suggestions by Thomas Cubitt in 1843 to Queen Victoria's Commission for Improving the Metropolis, an Act was passed in 1846 to enable the Commissioners to form a Royal Park in Battersea Fields at a cost not exceeding £200,000; 320 acres were purchased, 198 of which were to form the park, the remainder being leased for building. The surface was raised and the park laid out under the direction of

Henry Holland's wooden Battersea Bridge, depicted by Greaves in a watercolour of 1858.

Sir James Pennethorne. The park was opened in 1853. In 1860 a lake was excavated and in 1864 the sub-tropical garden was laid out. In 1885 the Albert Palace from the Dublin Exhibition of 1872 was erected at the south end of the park for concerts and art exhibitions, but these were rarely successful and the building was demolished in 1894.

In 1896 the park was crowded with those who had fallen for the new craze of bicycling. Hundreds came to practise or to watch the participants who were forbidden initially to ride in HYDE PARK. Battersea Park became and remained fashionable for this pastime.

In 1951 the FESTIVAL OF BRITAIN Gardens were laid out by Osbert Lancaster and John Piper. In the park now there are a children's zoo, a deer park, playing fields, a running track and tennis courts. There is also a fairground which opens on Easter Sunday with a parade of floats and closes in September each year. Annual events held there include the start of the VETERAN CAR RUN to Brighton and outdoor sculpture exhibitions in summer; and on the Sunday before the opening of the ROYAL TOURNAMENT the performers march past. The stone sculpture, *Three Standing Figures*, is by Henry Moore (1948) and the bronze, *Single Form*, by Barbara Hepworth (1961–2).

Battersea *or* West London Extension Railway Bridge *Chelsea–Battersea.* The five-span wrought-iron bridge, highly reminiscent in form of the cast-iron SOUTHWARK BRIDGE, was built in 1861 by William Baker of the London and North-Western Railway which was part owner, with the Great Western, of the

West London Extension Railway. The line connected the West London Railway with CLAPHAM JUNCTION. The WLR had been so frequently lampooned in *Punch* for going from nowhere to nowhere that it was known as 'Mr Punch's Railway'.

Battersea Power Station The great power station at Kirtling Street, BATTERSEA was designed by Sir Giles Scott, architect of Liverpool Anglican Cathedral, and opened in 1937. It originally had a 300 ft high fluted chimney at each end, but has since been doubled in size and has two chimneys at the ends. The vapour issuing from the four chimneys is white, having been separated from sulphur and other impurities by smoke-washing apparatus. There is a plaque in the wall commemorating Michael Faraday.

Battle of Britain Museum *see* ROYAL AIR FORCE MUSEUM.

Bayham Street *NW1.* Built early in the 19th century for artisans and named after Bayham Abbey, seat of the ground landlord, the Marquess of Camden. In 1822–5 Charles Dickens and his parents lived at No. 16, a small house of four rooms, basement and garret which was rented for £22 a year. It stood in a row of 40. Dickens described its surroundings in *Dombey and Son*: 'There were frowzy fields, and cow-houses, and dung hills, and dust-heaps, and ditches, and gardens, and summer-houses, and carpet-beating grounds ... little tumuli of oyster shells in the oyster season, and of lobster shells in the lobster season, and of broken crockery and faded cabbage leaves in all seasons . . . posts, and rails, and old cautions to trespassers, and backs of mean houses, and patches of wretched vegetation.' The house was demolished in 1910. The window of Dickens's room in the garret is preserved at DICKENS HOUSE, DOUGHTY STREET.

Baynard's Castle *see* CASTLE BAYNARD.

Bayswater *W2.* The southern part of PADDINGTON, covering the area south of the railway, Bayswater probably takes it name not, as is sometimes stated, from Ralph Baynard, friend of William the Conqueror, but from Bayard's Watering, the chief of the district's springs, situated near QUEENSWAY, which served originally as a natural drinking place for horses. In 1439 WESTMINSTER ABBEY granted a water supply from this source, the Bayswater Conduit, to the CITY OF LONDON. This flowed until 1812, when the water pipes interfered with plans for the development of the BISHOP OF LONDON's estate. For all its air of permanence and solidity, most of Bayswater is less than 150 years old. Development began with Tyburnia, at the eastern end of the BAYSWATER ROAD, bounded to the north by Sussex Gardens, or Grand Junction Road as it was first known. This road was planned as a bypass to link up with MARYLEBONE ROAD. After CONNAUGHT PLACE had been built between 1807 and 1815, Samuel Pepys Cockerell began to plan a lavish estate for the BISHOP OF LONDON's trustees, including a huge crescent overlooking HYDE PARK. CONNAUGHT SQUARE, with the streets immediately surrounding it and St George's Burial Ground, was started during the 1820s. Cockerell died in 1827. His successor was George Gutch who had previously worked as surveyor to the GRAND JUNCTION CANAL Company. George Ledwell Taylor and George Wyatt, with his brother Matthew, are thought to have acted as consultant architects to the estate, assisting Gutch. His approach to TYBURNIA was more practical and modern than Cockerell's, as shown in his final plan for the area, published in 1838. He abandoned the main crescent and introduced a series of connected squares, which though confusing to motorist, traffic engineer and even pedestrian today, have a pleasing variety.

Tyburnia, known more prosaically today as the Hyde Park Estate, though attempts to revive the name persist, was at once popular. Thackeray, for example, made 18 Albion Street his first home after his marriage, living here in 1836–7 with his mother and stepfather. Here his daughter, Anne, was born. As it was within quite easy reach of the CITY, wealthy merchants

George Train's 'improved street railway carriage' passing Marble Arch on its way from Bayswater, then the height of fashion, to Paddington in 1861.

and fashionable Victorian society moved readily into the large houses of Bayswater. It may never have quite managed to rival BELGRAVIA, as had been the original intention, but it had instant appeal for the middle and upper middle classes. Architecturally, it reflects every shade of change in Victorian style. The transition from the chaste three-storey brick houses of the early Connaught Street area to the four- and five-storey stucco-faced mansions of the 1830s and later, with their attractive plasterwork ornamentation above and colonnaded entrances below, can be seen in close proximity. The influence of Nash and the REGENT'S PARK terraces may be observed. Hyde Park Gardens, designed by John Crake in the 1830s, is one of the best examples, with an extravagantly laid-out mews behind the entrances, while the main rooms look south over the park. The beautiful curved brick façade at the corner of Kendal and Connaught Streets was copied later in grander style as at the Victoria public house in SUSSEX PLACE.

However, these gigantic mansions inevitably deteriorated, and since the 1930s, when leases began to expire, the CHURCH COMMISSIONERS have completely rebuilt large sections of the area. Practical town houses now surround St John's, Hyde Park Crescent, one of the focal points of Tyburnia, whilst behind, Anthony Minoprio's Water Gardens and surrounding tower blocks of the early 1960s impressively set off the surviving 19th-century houses. Only the south side of GLOUCESTER SQUARE remains and No. 34, where Robert Stephenson, the railway engineer, lived in 1847–59, has been rebuilt. Stephenson was godfather to Lord Baden-Powell, who was born at 11 STANHOPE TERRACE in 1857. SUSSEX SQUARE has been almost totally rebuilt, as has much of Hyde Park Street where W.H. Smith, founder of W.H. SMITH AND SON, lived at No. 12 in 1858–74. As the success of Tyburnia became apparent, the impetus of building spread rapidly to the west, and Bayswater's magnificent terraces and squares were completed by around 1860. One of the grandest conceptions was LANCASTER GATE, while one of the oddest is the pair of perfectly matching dummy house fronts at 23–24 Leinster Gardens, built to conceal the surfacing of the DISTRICT and CIRCLE LINE. At 37–38 Queen's Gardens, Herbert Spencer, the philosopher, lived in 1866–90, rowing on the Serpentine for relaxation. Colonel Crompton's home in Porchester Gardens was the first private house in London to be lit effectively by electricity in 1879. Later he installed the lighting at Windsor Castle and the LAW COURTS. Several well-known literary figures lived in Bayswater, CRAVEN HILL being a particular centre. At 26 Bishop's Bridge Road (now demolished) George Smith of Smith and Elder, the publishers of *Jane Eyre*, entertained Charlotte and Anne Brontë when they first visited London in 1848.

Towards the boundary with KENSINGTON is an area where many developers had a hand in the 1850s, when WESTBOURNE GROVE was becoming a shopping centre. Beyond PALACE COURT and facing KENSINGTON PALACE GARDENS is the tiny Boundary House, built right over the ditch marking the ancient division between KENSINGTON and PADDINGTON. ORME SQUARE and surroundings date from Regency times, while in Bishop's Bridge Road the development of the Colonnades, designed by Farrell Grimshaw Partnership as a shopping centre with flats above, was completed in 1975. The Hallfield Estate, opposite, built by Messrs

Drake and Lasdun for the Borough Council after the last war, breaks the uniformity of the terraces more successfully. The break is helped by trees, which are a feature everywhere in Bayswater. Much of the area is still residential, though in recent years hotels have mushroomed. The Inverness Court Hotel, built in 1912, is among the earliest, but boarding-houses of every description have always flourished here.

Bayswater Road *W2*. Part of the Roman Via Trinobantia, this is one of London's most pleasing tree-lined main roads. Its houses and terraces face HYDE PARK and span over 200 years of different styles. The Swan and Black Lion public houses date from the 18th century, when this was a turnpike road, while Hyde Park Towers, a block of flats completed in 1980 beside Leinster Terrace, has a discretion contrasting sharply with the ROYAL LANCASTER HOTEL. HYDE PARK PLACE is dominated by Albion Gate, built in 1936 by S. Warwick. Hyde Park Gardens (*see* BAYSWATER) and LANCASTER GATE are 19th-century building at its most assured. Sir James Barrie, the playwright, lived from 1902 to 1909 at No. 100, on the corner of Leinster Terrace, where amongst other works he wrote *Peter Pan*; the smaller houses nearby were built as St Agnes Villas in the 1820s. Elms Mews follows the line of the much older Elms Lane. The extravagant late Victorian Orme Court and Palace Court flank tiny ORME SQUARE. In 1861 George Train, an American, experimented with a horse-drawn tram along the Bayswater Road. The Edwardian Coburg Hotel has 125 bedrooms; the modern London Embassy Hotel (194 bedrooms) at No. 150 is by R. Seifert and Partners (1972).

Beadles In the CITY OF LONDON there are four types of official known as beadles. (1) The office of Ward Beadle existed in the early 15th century; its holder was responsible for supervision of the Watch, the lighting, cleaning and maintenance of the streets, the expulsion from the ward of thieves, rogues and other undesirables and a careful watch on taverns. Today he is the personal attendant of the ALDERMAN of his WARD and is attired in a splendid gown and tricorne hat. He assists the ALDERMAN to robe on ceremonial occasions. (2) Each CITY LIVERY COMPANY has its beadle, a general factotum to the Master, Wardens and Court of Assistants and the liaison officer between them and the rest of the Company. He is the Clerk's right-hand man and a useful intermediary between him and the public. On state occasions he carries a mace and leads the Master Wardens in procession. He is sometimes regarded as a sort of sergeant-major, but Blackham records that one Company Beadle returned to his post after service in the 1st World War with the rank of Brigadier-General. (3) The Parish Beadles, gowned and bearing silver-headed staves, attend with the parish clerks and the clergy of the CITY parishes on ceremonial occasions and assist them in other ways. (4) Finally there are the Beadles who are guardians of security and provide information to visitors. These are exemplified by the Beadle of GUILDHALL, resplendent in frock-coat and gold-laced top hat; the Beadle at the BANK OF ENGLAND, in braided gown and cocked hat and bearing a wand; and the ROYAL EXCHANGE Beadles, who support the COMMON CRYER when he reads a Royal Proclamation from the Exchange steps.

Beak Street *W1*. Built in three parts. The western end to Warwick Lane was part of the ancient highway between OXFORD CIRCUS AND PICCADILLY. In about 1689 the section to Bridle Lane was developed by Thomas Beak, a Queen's Messenger. The eastern end was built in about 1718. This part was known as Silver Street until 1883. At No. 23 there is a fine Regency shop front. No. 40 is the site of the Crown Inn frequented by Newman Noggs in *Nicholas Nickleby*. It was demolished in 1921. Canaletto lodged at No. 41 with Richard Wiggan, a cabinet maker, between 1749 and 1751. It was from this address that Canaletto advertised his picture, *A View of St James's Park*, which would be shown to 'any gentleman that will be pleased to come to his house'. John Wilkes at No. 79 is the only survivor of the several firms of gunmakers that used to be found in SOHO.

Bear Gardens Bear and bull baiting seem to have been introduced into England by Italians in the reign of King John for whom a display was put on at Ashby-de-la-Zouch in Leicestershire. But the first reference to the so-called sport in London is at BANKSIDE in 1546. Henry VIII came here; and Elizabeth I brought the French and Spanish ambassadors. In 1604 Edward Alleyn, founder of DULWICH COLLEGE, was appointed Master Overseer and Ruler of the Bears, Bulls and Mastiff Dogs. As well as on Bankside, there were bear gardens at TOTHILL FIELDS, HOCKLEY IN THE HOLE, SAFFRON HILL and ISLINGTON. They were less well attended in the 17th century than they had been in the 16th, but the sport remained popular. Cromwell tried to suppress it but failed. Pepys took his wife to a display in August 1666 and 'saw some good sport of the bulls tossing the dogs, one into the very boxes'. But he thought it a 'very rude and nasty pleasure'. So did Evelyn, who in June 1670 went with some friends 'to the Beare Gardens, where was cock-fighting, dog-fighting, bear and bull baiting .... One of the bulls tossed a dog full into a lady's lap, as she sate in one of the boxes at a considerable height from the arena. Two poor dogs were killed, and so all ended with the ape on horseback, and I most heartily weary of the rude and dirty pastime.' Soon after this the BANKSIDE bear garden was closed; but others continued until as late as 1835 when the sport was at last forbidden by law.

Bear Gardens Museum and Arts Centre *1 Bear Gardens, Bankside, Southwark, SE1*. Founded in 1972 in an area which was crucial to the development of the English theatre. The museum exhibits illustrate the history of this theatre to the mid-17th century. There is a replica of a small early 17th-century theatre with seating for 120 which presents workshop performances of Elizabethan drama as well as Renaissance music, puppeteers and dancers.

Bear Street *WC2*. Probably named after Augustine Beare, a glazier who worked on the houses here, or after a public house which stood here (the Bear and Staff is now at No. 7). The street was first laid out in the early 1670s. It has since been much reduced in size by the construction of CHARING CROSS ROAD and the widening of CRANBOURN STREET. None of the original houses remains.

Beating the Bounds This ancient ceremony takes place in the CITY and its Liberties from time to time.

Formerly carried out on one of the three Rogation Days before Ascension Day, it has since the Reformation taken place on Ascension Day itself. The custom was for the priest and people of a parish, led by the BEADLE and churchwardens, to perambulate the boundaries to confirm the extent of it, and to press the charity school boys into service and bump them into the boundary walls to help them remember the exact spot. It was also the practice to beat the boys with willow wands where no wall existed, for the same purpose. Today the boys carry the wands and thrash the buildings at certain points along the parish boundary. Their perambulation is simplified by the CITY's leaden boundary marks which are set in the walls of buildings crossing the boundary line. It was until recently possible to see between the GUILDHALL LIBRARY corridor and the GUILDHALL ART GALLERY the marks of four parishes whose boundaries intersected at that point.

Beauchamp Place *SW3*. Extends from BROMPTON ROAD to PONT STREET, and until 1885 known as Grove Place. It was built on land forming part of the site of Hermitage House, a country retreat of the singer Angelica Catalani. Noted for its restaurants and small shops, it has held an annual shopping festival to advertise its attractions in recent years.

Beaufort Gardens *SW3*. The most recent of the streets south of BROMPTON ROAD. The origin of its name is uncertain. Architecturally it represents the nadir of the stucco terraced house and was developed in the 1870s. In earlier days there had been a row of cottages along the road with a pasture behind them, ending, as the street does now, at the old parish boundary. By 1885 it had become a good address with a preponderance of military occupants and, later, their widows.

Beaufort House *Chelsea*. Sir Thomas More's house built in about 1521. Erasmus said it was 'not mean, nor invidiously grand, but comfortable'. At a distance was More's building for devotion, study and retirement. To the south were two riverside courtyards; to the north acres of gardens and orchards where More is said to have tied heretics to trees and flogged them. The household was strictly ruled. Everybody had to attend prayers, the servants were not allowed to play games and the sexes were segregated at either end of the house. In 1535 More was taken to the TOWER for refusing to swear the Oath of Supremacy and was beheaded later that year on TOWER HILL. Later owners of the house included Sir Robert Cecil in 1597–9, Lionel Cranfield, Charles I's Lord Treasurer, in 1619–25 (he added the Inigo Jones archway now at CHISWICK HOUSE), the 1st Duke of Buckingham in 1627–8, Bulstrode Whitelocke, Keeper of the Great Seal, in 1628–49, and the Duke of Beaufort in 1682–1738. In 1738 it was bought by Sir Hans Sloane, the naturalist. Two years later it was demolished and in 1766 BEAUFORT STREET built on its site.

Beaufort Street *SW3*. Built on the site of BEAUFORT HOUSE in 1766. Mrs Gaskell lived at No. 7 in 1811 and from 1827 to 1829.

Engraving by Kyp of Beaufort House, Chelsea, c.1695, when the house belonged to the Duke of Beaufort.

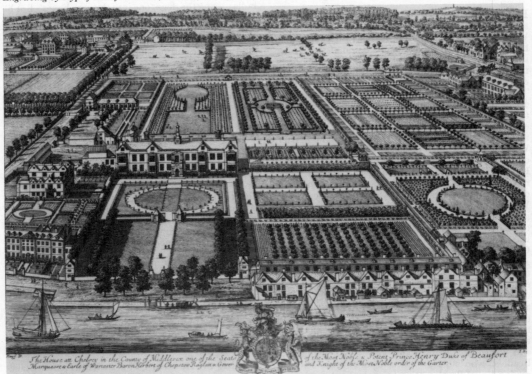

Beaumont Street *W1*. Laid out after 1778 across the site of MARYLEBONE GARDENS which had been leased out for building to Sir Beaumont Hotham. The historian John Richard Green lived at No. 4. Today the KING EDWARD VII HOSPITAL FOR OFFICERS occupies the eastern side.

Beckenham *Kent*. Beckenham Manor, held by the Rokele family at the time of *Domesday Book*, covered much of what is now Shortlands, as well as modern Beckenham. The name is derived from 'Beohha's village'. The Duke of Suffolk entertained Henry VIII here when the King was journeying to Hever. Part of the manor house, which is thought to date back to the 13th century, remains as the Old Council Hall. The manor lands were split up and enclosed in the Middle Ages, and several large estates were formed, including Langley and Kelsey. Langley Park mansion was burned down in 1913, but Langley Court, built in the 1880s, remains and has become a medical laboratory. Kelsey mansion has gone, but the lodge survives. Kelsey Park, with the river Beck flowing through it, is one of several attractive local parks. Beckenham Place, built by John Cator in 1773, had been a family mansion, a school, a sanatorium and a golf clubhouse. In 1982 adaptation for use as a theatre museum was planned. Cator, a local benefactor whose name is remembered in Cator Park, also owned the 18th-century Clock House, and when this was demolished in 1896 the clock from the stable block from which it took its name was removed to Beckenham Place.

Beckenham was a small village until the 19th century. There was a cage for drunkards (demolished in 1856) in the High Street. Few of the old buildings are left in the residential, business and shopping developments of modern Beckenham, but two old inns in the High Street remain: the Three Tuns and the George, a coaching inn dating back to at least 1662. The almshouses in Bromley Road were built in 1694 and renovated in 1881. There has been a church on the site of St George's since the early 12th century, though nothing of this building survives. The 14th-century church was, in turn, replaced by a Victorian Gothic building which was restored after bomb damage in the 2nd World War. It is claimed that the 13th-century lychgate is the oldest in the country.

West Wickham is an attractive residential district to the south of Beckenham. Wickham Court, the manor house, was rebuilt in 1480 for Sir Henry Haydon. It has a variety of architectural styles, with Tudor chimneys and castellated walls. It is now an Arts College. Among the local open and wooded spaces is Coney Wood, containing oak trees which Millais depicted in his painting *The Proscribed Royalist*.

Becontree Estate *Essex*. Built by the LONDON COUNTY COUNCIL between the wars on 4 square miles of flat land, over half in DAGENHAM, a third in BARKING and under a sixth in ILFORD, it provides nearly 27,000 homes. The intention of forming a new local government area with its own town centre was never carried out, and the recent policy of selling houses has given purchasing tenants the chance to break out of their neo-Georgian uniformity into a heterogeneous rash of neo-Palladianism, bankers' Georgian, mock Tudor, pebble-dash, and vertical crazy paving.

Beddington in 1792. Drawing by William Ellis showing the seat of the Carews, owners of the manor of Beddington since the 14th century.

Beddington *Surrey*. One of the spring-line villages on the belt of Thanet Sand from which the River WANDLE rises, it has yielded evidence of occupation from at least the Middle Stone Age. The name probably means 'Beada's settlement'; but who or what Beada was is unknown. Roman occupation is shown by coffined burials from Beddington Park, cremation urns from the site of a modern cemetery, and a bath-house, thought to belong to a villa, discovered in 1871 and re-excavated in 1981. At the time of *Domesday*, in 1186, there were two Beddington Manors, one with two WANDLE watermills. These manors were united by 1381 under Nicholas Carew, who established here a new branch of an important family of Norman origin (*see* CAREW MANOR). The name of Carew was to be borne locally for 500 years; and it was the break-up of the Carew estates in 1859 that turned the village into a London suburb. In 1915, on former Carew farm land, a Royal Flying Corps base for the air defence of London was established. This was the genesis of what became, in 1920, CROYDON Aerodrome: London's major AIRPORT until 1939. In 1915, also, Beddington combined with WALLINGTON to form an urban district, gaining borough status in 1937. Beddington Church (St Mary's) dates in part from a 14th-century rebuilding, and contains a Norman font, many Carew memorials, and a William Morris organ screen.

Beddington Corner *Surrey*. The name (perhaps originally 'estate of Beada') can be seen on a name plate on the Goat public house at Mill Green, Mitcham Junction, although the area never had any official administrative existence. It is where the parish boundaries of MITCHAM and CARSHALTON met at right angles, with the old Beddington parish ending in the corner so formed. Place naming at this point is indeed very confused, since this part of Beddington became part of WALLINGTON when that parish was formed in 1887; HACKBRIDGE, also with no official existence, merges with Beddington Corner on the south; and the nearby Mitcham Junction Station (over the borough boundary) gives a postal district name to this part of the London Borough of SUTTON. The small community of Beddington Corner was based mainly on the cluster of WANDLE Mills – where the 'Goat' bridge now crosses the river – merged today in the Wandle Trading Estate. Market gardens, watercress beds and a lavender and peppermint distillery also were here earlier this century. Three public houses served the community and still exist. One, the Skinners Arms, commemorates the leather industry hereabouts. A small combined chapel and National School was built on Mill Green in the 19th century and demolished early in the 20th. Here, a stream crossing the Green (on the edge of Mitcham Common) carries into the River WANDLE the cleansed effluent from Beddington Sewage Works which forms so large a part of its flow from here to the THAMES. Here, too, a branch of the SURREY IRON RAILWAY entered Beddington on its way to the Hackbridge Mills.

Bedford Coffee House *Covent Garden*. First mentioned in 1730, it stood on the north-east corner 'under the piazza' near the COVENT GARDEN THEATRE. According to the *Connoisseur* of 13 January 1754, it was 'crowded with men of parts. Almost everyone you meet is a polite scholar and a wit. Jokes and *bon-mots* are echoed from box to box; every branch of literature is critically examined, and the merit of every production of the press, or performance of the theatres, weighed and determined.' It was a favourite haunt of the actors David Garrick, Samuel Foote and James Queen, and of Fielding, Pope, Sheridan, Smollett, William Hickey and Horace Walpole. It was here that the Revd James Hackman sat on the evening of 7 April 1779 waiting for the performance of *Love in a Village* to end at the COVENT GARDEN THEATRE. On the appearance in the street of Martha Ray, the singer and mistress of Lord Sandwich, Hackman, whose love for her was not requited, shot her dead. In his diary entry for 10 December 1793 Joseph Farington, the landscape painter, recorded, 'The meeting of the Academy did not break up till past twelve o'clock, when Hamilton, Smirke and myself went to the Bedford Coffee House where we found Tyler, Rooker, Dance, Lawrence, Westall. We staid till four in the morning.' The first meeting of the Sublime Society of Beef-Steaks was held here in 1808 (*see* BEEF-STEAK SOCIETY).

Bedford College *Regent's Park, NW1*. Founded in 1849 by Mrs Elizabeth Jesser Reid to give women a liberal education. It takes its name from its first home in BEDFORD SQUARE. In 1880, two years after the UNIVERSITY OF LONDON had opened its examinations to women, the college became a School of the University. In 1909, as Bedford College for Women, it received a Royal Charter and shortly afterwards in 1913 moved to its present site in REGENT'S PARK as tenant of the Crown. In 1965 a Supplementary Charter allowed the college to admit men undergraduates and it now has a student body of about 1600 – undergraduate and postgraduate – in 20 different departments in the Faculties of Arts and Science. The college stands on the site of SOUTH VILLA which was demolished in 1926 to make way for a new teaching block. Of the original teaching and residential blocks (Basil Champneys, 1913) only some remain. The rest was destroyed by enemy action in 1941 (the staff and students had been evacuated to Cambridge) and have been replaced and extended by a succession of architects. The latest development (1981) includes designs by Sir Hugh Casson. The college is tenant of three other of the Regency villas in the park, THE HOLME (1819 by Decimus Burton), ST JOHN'S LODGE (1817 by John Raffield, extended in 1846 by Barry) in the INNER CIRCLE, and HANOVER LODGE (1827 to designs by Nash – incorporated into a hall of residence in 1964)

in the OUTER CIRCLE. The college has had a line of distinguished women principals, including Dame Emily Penrose (1893–8), Dame Margaret Tuke (1907–29) and Miss Geraldine Jebb (1930–52). In 1972 the college completed its conversion to a college of mixed sexes by appointing its first male principal, Dr John N. Black. Former students include George Eliot and Elizabeth Blackwell. It was announced in 1982 that the college was to merge with ROYAL HOLLOWAY COLLEGE.

Bedford Estates The chief metropolitan estates of the Earls and Dukes of Bedford were COVENT GARDEN and BLOOMSBURY where many of the streets bear Russell family names and titles or names from their country estates. COVENT GARDEN was granted in 1552 to John Russell, the 1st Earl, for services to the Crown. Its development in the 1630s was of great importance to London's history, it being the first suburb built outside the CITY OF LONDON to be regulated by building covenants and financed by the leasehold system. These factors and its architectural pattern, attributed to Inigo Jones, made COVENT GARDEN a prototype which landlords and developers followed for the next 250 years. The two 'patent' theatre companies, founded by Charles II, settled in the area and, together with the taverns and coffee houses for which it became famous, attracted the literary and artistic world of the 18th and early 19th centuries. Charles II also issued the charter which in 1670 recognised and regulated the market for fruit and vegetables and, later, flowers. This provided the Russell family with much of its wealth but, eventually, owing to hostility towards the ducal ownership of a public food market and contemporary tax legislation, the whole estate was sold in 1914. After much heated debate, the market moved to NINE ELMS in 1974 and the buildings, erected in 1828–30 to designs to Charles Fowler, were purchased and restored by the GREATER LONDON COUNCIL in 1974–80. BLOOMSBURY was granted to the 1st Earl of Southampton in 1550, also for services to the Crown. It began to be developed by the 4th Earl of Southampton in the 1660s with the building of what are now known as BLOOMSBURY SQUARE and GREAT RUSSELL STREET. His daughter and heiress, Rachel, married Lord William Russell, whose father became 1st Duke of Bedford in 1669 and after his death in 1723 BLOOMSBURY became part of the Bedford Estates. Its development over the next century continued in a series of squares and terraced streets, up to and over the EUSTON ROAD, attracting the professional and academic tenant. The growth of the BRITISH MUSEUM in the 19th century and the foundation of the UNIVERSITY OF LONDON in the 20th decreased the extent of the estate and encouraged the growth on the remainder of the hotel and lodging-house industry.

Bedford House *Bloomsbury Square, see* SOUTHAMPTON HOUSE, BLOOMSBURY SQUARE.

Bedford House *Covent Garden*. Built in about 1586 for the 3rd Earl of Bedford to replace an earlier family mansion on the south side of the STRAND. The house was two storeys high and had a gabled front with a turret behind the west end. There was a courtyard in front and stables to the east. Behind the house was a large garden. In 1700 the 5th Earl (and 1st Duke of Bedford) died and left the property to his grandson,

Wriothesley Russell. The young Duke saw that fashionable society was moving westwards and decided to continue to live with his mother at SOUTHAMPTON HOUSE, BLOOMSBURY, and to demolish Bedford House. In 1705 the furniture was accordingly moved to BLOOMSBURY and in 1705–6 the house demolished. Its site was laid out for the building of SOUTHAMPTON STREET, TAVISTOCK STREET and TAVISTOCK ROW.

Bedford Lodge *Kensington.* Also known as Argyll Lodge and Cam House, it was built by John Tasker and first occupied in 1815. Distinguished residents included the 6th Duke of Bedford (1823–39), the 8th Duke of Argyll (1853–1900) and Sir Walter G.F. Phillimore (later Lord Phillimore). The house was demolished in 1955.

Bedford Park, London's first garden suburb, built in 1875–81 to designs by Norman Shaw.

Bedford Park *Turnham Green, W4.* London's first garden suburb, built in 1875–81 on the grounds of an old Georgian house known as Bedford House. Dr John Lindley, curator of the gardens of the ROYAL HORTICULTURAL SOCIETY, was its owner in the 1860s and the preservation of his trees played a major part in planning the suburb. After Lindley's bankruptcy the house was let to a civil engineer whose daughter, Agnes Fulton, married Jonathan Carr in 1873. The idea of creating a middle-class commuting 'village' was Jonathan Carr's and was made possible by the opening of the railway station at Turnham Green in 1869, with trains running from RICHMOND to CLAPHAM JUNCTION and then by the extension of the Metropolitan District Line from HAMMERSMITH to EALING Broadway in 1879. E.W. Godwin was appointed architect, but having designed a few houses he was dismissed for incompetence and replaced by Norman Shaw. The layout of the suburb and the design of most of the houses are Shaw's. Also his are the church of ST MICHAEL AND ALL ANGELS and the Tabard Inn, both built in 1880. Shaw soon fell out with Carr, and his pupil Maurice B. Adams took over and added the parish hall and chapel and the Chiswick School of Art and Craft. Other architects designed individual houses in the suburb. No. 14 South Parade, built in 1889, was an early house by Voysey. The first inhabitants of Bedford Park had a reputation for being 'arty' and were satirised in a verse ballad published in the December 1881 edition of *The St James's Review*:

Now he who loves aesthetic cheer
and does not mind the damp,
May come and read Rossetti here
by a Japanese-y lamp.

Thus was a village builded
for all who are aesthete,
Whose precious souls it fill did,
with utter joy complete.

For floors were stained and polished,
and every hearth was tiled,
And Philistines abolished,
by culture's gracious child.

G.K. Chesterton called it Saffron Park in *The Man Who Was Thursday*.

Bedford Place *WC1.* Connects BLOOMSBURY SQUARE with RUSSELL SQUARE. It was constructed in 1801–5 on the site of BEDFORD HOUSE by James Burton. Here lived (1806–7) Edward Jenner, pioneer of small-pox vaccination; also Richard Cumberland, the dramatist, remembered as the model for Sir Fretful Plagiary in Sheridan's *The Critic*. Now the well-preserved houses are occupied by hotels and hostels. No. 38 is the office of the CLOCKMAKERS' COMPANY.

Bedford Row *WC1.* Extends south from THEOBALDS ROAD. It is a wide Georgian street well restored after bomb damage. It was originally developed by Nicholas Barbon in 1684; but only two of his houses survive. Nos 42–43 have heavy sash windows flush with the wall which were forbidden by early 18th-century fire codes. These can be seen also in No. 36, whereas No. 35 has recessed windows so is clearly later. The street was formerly called Bedford Walk after William Harpur's charity at Bedford. He was LORD MAYOR of London in 1561. After the Reformation he refounded Bedford School and endowed it with 13 acres of hunting land in HOLBORN. In 1761 Sir John Holt, Lord Chief Justice, described it as a 'very handsome, straight and well built street, inhabited by persons of distinction.' In about 1724–44 the Crown Coffee House, where the rules of whist were drawn up, was here. Henry Addington was born in a house here in 1757. James Mingay, QC, nicknamed 'Iron Hand Mingay', lived at No. 25 in 1792–6. John Abernethy, the founder of ST BARTHOLOMEW'S HOSPITAL Medical School, lived at No. 14. No. 10 is the Institute of Printing, founded in 1961. Round the corner at the south end of the street is an old hand pump.

Bedford Square *WC1.* The only complete Georgian Square left in BLOOMSBURY. It was built in 1775–80 on the BEDFORD ESTATE and probably designed by Thomas Leverton, William Scott and Robert Grews. The central house on each side is stuccoed and pilastered; the rest are of plain brick with wrought-iron balconies to the first-floor windows and doors decorated with COADE STONE. Several interiors have fine chimney-pieces and ceilings painted by Angelica Kauffmann and Antonio Zucchi. Until 1893 the square was sealed off by gates and tradesmen were required to deliver goods in person. Henry Cavendish, the scientist and grandson of the 2nd Duke of Devonshire, lived at No. 11 from 1796 until his death in 1810. Lord Loughborough, the Lord Chancellor, lived at

No. 6 in 1787–96, and Thomas Leverton at No. 13 in 1796–1824. Lord Eldon, the Lord Chancellor, moved into No. 6 in 1804 and remained here until about 1819. The Prince Regent came to see him in 1802 and, told that he was ill and could see no one, walked upstairs and tried every door until he found the right one. He sat down and asked Eldon to appoint his friend Jekyll a Master in Chancery. Eldon refused, whereupon the Prince settled back in his chair, exclaiming, 'How do I pity Lady Eldon!' 'Good God!' cried the Chancellor, 'what is the matter?' 'Oh, nothing,' came the reply 'except that she will never see you again, for here I remain until you promise to make Jekyll a Master in Chancery.' The appointment was made.

During the Corn Law riots of 1815 the house was broken into by the mob and all the windows smashed, which led a wit to remark that Eldon, who was not remarkable for his hospitality, had at last begun to keep open house. Eldon seized one of the mob by the collar and said to him, 'If you don't mind what you are about you will be hanged.' 'Perhaps so, old chap,' the man replied. 'But I think it looks now as if you will be hanged first.' A noose was put up ready on the lamp post outside. For three weeks Eldon was besieged in the house and the only way he could get to WESTMINSTER HALL was through the gardens of the BRITISH MUSEUM which communicated with his own property at the back. He was always accompanied by Townsend, the Bow Street Runner (see BOW STREET). Eldon prided himself upon the care with which he looked after the wards of his court, so the public were much amused when his own daughter eloped from the house to marry the architect George S. Repton. Later residents of the square have included William Butterfield, the architect, at No. 42 in 1886–1900; Sir Johnston Forbes-Robertson, the actor, at No. 22 in 1888–1937; Sir Seymour Hicks, the actor-manager and author, at No. 53 in 1901–8; and H.H. Asquith at No. 44 in 1921–4. Other residents have included Thomas Wakley, founder of *The Lancet*, at No. 35 and Anthony Hope, the novelist, at No. 41. The square is no longer residential, most of the houses now being used as offices particularly by architects and publishers. The ARCHITECTURAL ASSOCIATION is at No. 19; the building was refurbished by Rick Mather (1980). Leading publishers in the square include Jonathan Cape (No. 30), Frederick Warne (No. 40), Hodder and Stoughton (No. 47), Michael Joseph (No. 44), Heinemann Educational (No. 22); British Museum Publications (No. 6). The Publishers' Association is at No. 19. The garden is private.

Bedford Street *WC2*. Built between 1633 and 1640 to the west of BEDFORD HOUSE. From about 1635 to 1637 Sir Francis Kynaston had his academy, the Museum Minerva, on the west side of the street opposite the churchyard gates. Here young aristocrats 'were taught armes, artes and all generous qualities'. In 1720 Strype said that it was 'a handsome broad street with very good houses which since the Fire of London [had been] generally taken up by eminent tradesmen'. In 1748–51 James Quin, the actor, lived here. Benjamin West, the American painter, took lodgings in the street in about 1763. From the middle of the 19th century it became a centre of publishing. William Heinemann had premises here in 1889–1911, Macmillan in 1864–97, Edward Arnold in 1891–1905 and G.P. Putnam and Sons in 1891–1936. Nos 10–13,

Aldine House, designed by E. Keynes Purchase in 1911, were for many years occupied by J.M. Dent which had had offices in the street since 1898.

Bedlam *see* BETHLEHEM ROYAL HOSPITAL.

Beech Street *EC2*. The name is thought to be derived from a piece of land known as the Beche which used to border the street. The Abbot Ramsey's Inn was here from the 12th century until the Reformation when it passed into the hands of Sir Drewe Drewery and became known as Drewery House. Prince Rupert is said to have lived in it but it was more probably Drury House, STRAND, that he occupied. The date of demolition is unknown.

Beechwood House *Hampstead Lane, N6*. Built in 1834 in the former Fitzroy Park (*see* FITZROY HOUSE) for a barrister, Nathaniel Basevi, to the designs of his brother George Basevi. The exterior is little changed but the interior has been completely remodelled in the early Georgian style by W.B. Simpson of Wimperis, Simpson and Guthrie.

Beefeaters The Yeoman Warders of the TOWER OF LONDON. Their Tudor uniform is similar to that of the QUEEN'S BODYGUARD OF THE YEOMEN OF THE GUARD. They were originally appointed by Edward VI. Their popular name may well have been derived from their fondness for roast beef, but it has also been suggested that it comes from the French *buffetier*. 'Eater' was once a synonym for servant, and is used in this sense in Jonson's *Epicoene, or The Silent Woman* (1609). The Old English *hlaf-oeta* (loaf-eater) meant a menial servant.

Beefsteak Club *9 Irving Street, WC2*. After the dissolution of the BEEF-STEAK SOCIETY, a new club was founded which perpetuated the name since the members hoped to rent a room at the LYCEUM THEATRE where the BEEF-STEAK SOCIETY had met. As it happened, that room was not available; and the first meeting of the club was held on 11 March 1876 in the rooms in KING WILLIAM STREET. The move to the present address took place in 1896. The club premises are a single room over a shop. The membership is extremely varied. Politicians, actors, writers and scholars sit together at the long table, taking places in the order in which they arrive. The steward and waiters are all called 'Charles'.

Beef-Steak Society A club of 24 men of noble or gentle birth founded by John Rich, manager of COVENT GARDEN THEATRE and George Lambert, the scene painter, in 1735. It met for a beef-steak dinner every Saturday evening from November to June. The society's badge was a gridiron. Its members wore a uniform of blue coats and buff waistcoats and buttons bearing the motto, 'Beef and Liberty'. The society used a room in COVENT GARDEN THEATRE until it burnt down in 1808 and it was then transferred to the BEDFORD COFFEE HOUSE. From 1809 to 1830 it met at the LYCEUM THEATRE until that, too, was destroyed by fire. In 1830–8 it again used the BEDFORD COFFEE HOUSE but later went back to the LYCEUM. Lord Brougham and George IV and his brothers, the Dukes of York and Sussex, were members of the Sublime Society of Beef-Steaks, as it had come to be called. It closed in 1867.

Beeston Gift Almshouses *Consort Road, SE15.* In 1582 Cuthbert Beeston, a girdler, gave some land in SOUTHWARK for charitable use. The estate was sold in 1824 to enable the approach road to LONDON BRIDGE to be widened. A year later the Charity Commissioners obtained a site in Nunhead Road, now Consort Road, and Beeston's Gift Almshouses were built to house retired members of the GIRDLERS' COMPANY. The terrace of six stuccoed Tudor-style houses was completed in 1834. The single-storey wings were added in the 1960s and reflect the design and scale of the main terrace. The original building was restored and, together with the new additions, won a Civic Trust Heritage Year Award in 1975.

Belair *Gallery Road, Dulwich, SE21.* Built in 1785 by John Willes, to designs attributed to Robert Adam, on land leased from the College of God's Gift at DUL-WICH (*see* DULWICH COLLEGE). Originally known as College Place, it stood in about 25 acres of ground with a lake. Despite tradition, it seems unlikely that the lake is one of the arms of the River EFFRA, along which Elizabeth I once made a triumphal progress. The house changed hands several times and 10 acres were sold to the London, Chatham and Dover Railway Company to build the railway in the 1860s. The last occupant was Sir Evan Spicer, the paper magnate and chairman of the LONDON COUNTY COUNCIL, who lived there until 1938 and kept a farm in the grounds. In 1945 the estate was leased by SOUTHWARK Borough Council for sports and recreation. The house, which had been altered in the 19th century, was left derelict until 1963, when it was rebuilt. The interior, though modernised, retains its original spiral staircase. It is now used for meetings and other functions, and the land is an attractive park and sports area. The stable block dates from the 18th century and the lodge from the 19th century.

HMS Belfast *Symon's Wharf, Vine Lane, SE1.* Built in 1939, she was, at 11,000 tons, the largest cruiser ever built for the Royal Navy. She was opened to the public in 1971.

Belgrave Square *SW1.* Takes its name from a Leicestershire village (*see* BELGRAVIA). In 1826 the owner of the land, Earl Grosvenor, later 1st Marquess of Westminster (*see* GROSVENOR ESTATE), obtained an Act of Parliament enabling him to build on it and came to an agreement with Thomas Cubitt, the builder, who, in turn, came to an agreement with three bankers of Swiss extraction, George and William Haldimand and Alexander Prevost. The young architect employed was Sir John Soane's clever pupil, George Basevi, Benjamin Disraeli's cousin. The damp clay was dug from the ground and made into bricks on the site, and the excavations filled with soil from ST KATHARINE'S DOCK. The north and east sides were built first, and the more exuberant west and south side after it had become clear that the development was going to be financially rewarding. The houses are large and stuccoed; there are 12 in the south terrace and 11 in the terraces on the other three sides. Large detached houses are sited at the four corners of the Square which extends to 10 acres. There are Seaford House, No. 37, at the south-east corner, on the corner of Chapel Street, which was designed for Lord Sefton by Philip Hardwick and built in 1842–6; No. 24 at the south-west corner, designed by H.E. Kendall for Thomas Read Kemp (who built Kemp Town at Brighton) and completed in 1834; No. 12 at the north-west corner, designed by Sir Robert Smirke for Lord Brownlow and built in about 1830; and No. 49 at the north-east corner, designed for Sidney Herbert, probably by Cubitt himself, and built in 1847. Other distinguished residents included the Duke of Bedford at No. 15 and the Earl of Essex who lived at No. 9. Essex was married, for the second time, in 1838, the year before his death, to Catherine Stephens, the singer, who remained in Belgrave Square until her own death in 1882. No. 36 was rented for £2,000 a year by Queen Victoria for her mother, the Duchess of Kent, while apartments were being prepared for her at KEN-SINGTON PALACE. In 1854 Henry Labouchere was living at No. 27, Earl Grey at No. 30, the Earl of Eglintoun at No. 10 and the Earl of Ellesmere at No. 18. Later in the 19th century rich and aristocratic occupants included the Earl of Pembroke (No. 6), Earl Beauchamp (No. 13), and the Earls of Faversham (No. 19), Albemarle (No. 39) and Clanwilliam (No. 32). The Duke of Connaught lived at No. 41 and the Dowager Marchioness Conyngham at No. 36.

The east side of Belgrave Square in 1827, while still under construction to the designs of George Basevi.

The Square is no longer residential and the houses are now mostly embassies or offices. Embassies here are the Syrian Arab (No. 8), the Portuguese (No. 11), the Austrian (No. 18), the German Federal Republic (No. 23), the Spanish (No. 24), the Norwegian (No. 25), the German Democratic Republic (No. 34), and the Turkish (No. 43). The Ghana High Commission is at No. 13; the Trinidad and Tobago High Commission at No. 42; the Malaysian High Commission at No. 45; and the Saudi Arabian Consulate at No. 30. The Country Landowners' Association is at No.16, the ROYAL COLLEGE OF PSYCHIATRISTS at No. 17, the ROYAL COLLEGE OF VETERINARY SURGEONS at No. 32, the ROYAL COLLEGE OF DEFENCE STUDIES at No. 37, the Institute of Physics at No. 47, the Spiritualist Association of Great Britain at No. 33, the Institute of Practitioners in Advertising at No. 44, the Nature Conservancy Council at Nos 19–20 and the Royal Agricultural Society of England at No. 35. On the wall of the Norwegian Embassy at No. 25 are two reliefs in COADE STONE depicting cherubs in artistic and country pursuits. A plaque reads, 'In 1776 these two Coade stone reliefs were affixed to the Danish–Norwegian consulate in Wellclose Square, Stepney. In 1968 the reliefs were erected on this Embassy by courtesy of the Greater London Council.' The statue on the east side of the gardens (which are private) is of Simon Bolivar (*see* STATUES).

Belgravia Takes its name from Belgrave on the northern outskirts of Leicester, once a small village where the owners of the land, the Grosvenor family, had an estate (*see* GROSVENOR ESTATE). In medieval times, when it was known as the Five Fields because it was intersected by footpaths cutting it into five, it was a flat, treeless area where sheep and donkeys were put out to graze. Watercress grew by the banks of the WESTBOURNE which meandered through it and which was crossed by a wooden bridge known as Bloody Bridge, perhaps because of the number of violent robberies committed there. It remained a haunt of footpads and highwaymen until well on into the 18th century; and it was never safe to cross the fields at night. In 1728 a gentleman was found murdered with one side of his face and five fingers cut off. And in 1749 a muffin man was blinded and robbed. Since it was fairly remote from London, duels also often took place here. In the daytime, however, it was a pleasant enough locality. Swift, walking through the fields to London in 1711, saw haymakers at work and wrote of the sweet smell of the 'flowery meads'. Later there were market gardens where asparagus and other succulent vegetables were grown. On holidays Londoners came out to shoot duck and to watch bull baiting and cock fighting. In 1726, after George III moved to BUCKINGHAM HOUSE, a row of 'fair houses' was built in what is now GROSVENOR PLACE on the east side of the fields. Twenty years later the Lock Hospital for Women was built nearby. On the northern edge of the fields there were barracks and Richard Tattersall's salerooms (*see* TATTERSALL'S). But otherwise there was no building worth speaking of until the 1820s when Lord Grosvenor came to an agreement for developing the estate with Thomas Cubitt, the Norfolk-born son of a carpenter, a highly successful entrepreneur, described by *The Builder* in an obituary as 'a great builder and a good man'. Over the next thirty-odd years Belgravia was built as a stuccoed rival to MAYFAIR for the well-to-do, with BELGRAVE SQUARE as its centrepiece. It was fashionable from the beginning, though Disraeli did not like it. He considered it 'as monotonous as Marylebone, and so contrived as to be at the same time insipid and tawdry'. It is still largely residential, still fashionable and still expensive.

Bell Street *NW8*. Laid out across Bell Field off LISSON GROVE in 1759. In recent years, a second-hand furniture market has grown up here, Saturday being the most active day.

Bell Yard *EC4*. Named after the Bell Inn which stood in CARTER LANE. The first record of its existence is in 1424 and the last in 1708. In 1598 Richard Quyney wrote a letter at the Bell Inn to 'my loveing good ffrend and countryman Mr Wm Shackespere'. This is the only extant letter to Shakespeare. Charles Dickens often went to a later Bell Inn, on the corner of CARTER LANE, when he was writing *David Copperfield*.

Bellamy's Coffee House *Westminster*. Established at the end of the 18th century, it was attached to the old House of Commons and frequented by Members who spoke highly of its chops and steaks and port. It was also known as Bellamy's Kitchen. The last words of William Pitt the Younger were alleged to have been: 'I think I could eat one of Bellamy's pork pies.' It seems to have escaped destruction in the fire of 1834 which destroyed the PALACE OF WESTMINSTER but had closed before the end of the century.

Belle Sauvage *Ludgate Hill*. First documented in 1452 as Savage's Inn, otherwise known as the Bell on the Hoop. Before there were any theatres in London, plays were performed in the courtyard. According to the puritanical William Prynne, the Devil once made a personal appearance during a performance of Marlowe's *Dr Faustus*. Pocahontas, the Indian princess, was a guest here in 1616–17. In 1676 an advertisement claimed that the inn had 40 rooms and stabling for 100 horses. In 1683 a very strange beast called 'a Rynoceros lately brought from the West Indies' was exhibited here. In the 18th century it was one of the City's great coaching inns. It was demolished in 1873 when a printing works was built on the site. When this building was bombed in 1940 almost a million books were destroyed. The site was cleared and made into a garden in 1967.

Bellingham *see* SOUTHEND.

Bellmoor *Hampstead, NW3*. This name is now borne by a monstrous block of flats. It stands at the high point of HAMPSTEAD, across the road from the Whitestone Pond, at the site of a group of four houses which were converted into one by Thomas J. Barratt, the historian of HAMPSTEAD. On the roof of the principal house, Bellmoor, was a bell, one of the alarm bells of old HAMPSTEAD. Barratt lived here from 1877 to 1914, and declared in his famous history that when he first occupied the house he could, through a telescope on a clear day, 'see sailing vessels tacking on the Thames at or beyond Gravesend'. The old house was demolished to make way for the present-day flats which bear a plaque acknowledging Barratt's occupation and stating that the building stands 435 feet 7 inches above sea level, and 16 feet 7 inches above the top of the cross on the dome of ST PAUL'S.

A coach leaving for Cambridge from the Belle Sauvage, Ludgate Hill, a great coaching inn of the 18th and early 19th centuries.

Belmont *Surrey.* Owes much of its growth to the station built in 1865 when the SUTTON to Epsom Downs Railway was built. It has a solid Edwardian core with a small shopping street near the station and a considerable modern spread between the core and the edge of the Banstead Downs. In recent years the building of a large council estate on former hospital grounds has increased the population considerably. The name ('beautiful hill') is probably an early 18th-century invention, a more romantic version of the older names of 'Little Hill', or, as it was known to the rakes who frequented a gambling club on the Downs' edge, just off the London–Brighton turnpike road, 'Little Hell'. The club site is now covered by Belmont Railway Station. The California public house, founded in 1860 on the Brighton Road, is so called because its original landlord had made his fortune in America.

Belsize In the 14th century Belsize was a sub-manor of HAMPSTEAD owned by Roger de Brabazon, Lord Chief Justice to Edward III. He left it to the monks of WESTMINSTER ABBEY on the condition that they said Mass daily for his soul and for those of Edmund of Lancaster and his wife Blanche. In 1542 the monastery which had been established at Belsize was dissolved and WESTMINSTER ABBEY was given the land. During Elizabeth I's reign Armagil Waad, the explorer and friend of William Cecil, leased the estate. He was succeeded by his son, William, Clerk of Elizabeth's and James I's Councils. In 1663, the Royalist soldier Daniel O'Neill took over the lease and rebuilt the manor house 'at vast expense' for his beautiful wife, Catherine (formerly governess of Charles I's daughter, Mary), who had been created Countess of Chesterfield in 1660. (It remained in the Chesterfield family until 1807.) In 1668 Samuel Pepys paid a visit and thought the gardens the most noble he had ever seen. In 1700 it was sublet to one Povey, a retired coal merchant, who built a chapel where couples could marry for 5s provided they held their wedding breakfast in the grounds. After Povey's day it was sublet to an entertainer named Howell who opened 'pleasure gardens for ladies and gentlemen during the summer season'. In 1721 the Prince and Princess of Wales visited these gardens where 'three to four hundred coaches sometimes packed the drive'. For amusement there was hunting of both deer and foxes, racing, music and dancing. The gardens were closed in 1740 and the house thereafter let to wealthy families. Spencer

Perceval, the future Prime Minister, lived in it from 1798 until 1807 when the lease was sold to four Hampstead businessmen. The house was demolished in 1854 and its ground built over. The name is commemorated in BELSIZE PARK and several roads and streets in that area between HAMPSTEAD and PRIMROSE HILL.

Belvedere *Kent.* Known until 1858 as Lessness Heath, this part of ERITH took the name Belvedere from the house which was its principal residence. Built in the reign of George II, Belvedere House was bought in 1751 by Sampson Gideon, a Jewish merchant who supported the government financially during the Jacobite Rebellion. As a reward his Christian son, also called Sampson, was made a baronet in 1759, and became Baron Eardley in 1789. In 1764 he largely rebuilt the house to the designs of James 'Athenian' Stuart. The Eardley family greatly influenced local affairs, especially Sir Culling Eardley, who, following the opening of the North Kent Railway in 1849, developed the Victorian village. He gave it All Saints church, which, designed by W.G. and E. Habershon in 1853–61 which became the parish church of Belvedere in 1861. In 1865 Belvedere House was purchased as a home by the Royal Alfred Merchant Seamen's Institution. Damaged during the 2nd World War, it was replaced by a modern building in 1959, demolished in turn after the Royal Alfred left in 1979. The village remained largely rural until the 1930s, when the surrounding farms and orchards were taken for suburban housing estates.

Meanwhile Lower Belvedere, also known by its ancient manorial name of Picardy, was developed from the 1860s onwards, and became a separate parish in 1916. Its parish church of St Augustine, begun in 1914, was not completed until 1956. Apart from Crossness Sewerage Works, dating from 1865, Belvedere marshes remained, until recently, open land liable to occasional inundations from the THAMES, as, notably, in 1953. They are now dominated by Belvedere Power Station, opened in 1962, and are being steadily built over by the major housing development of THAMESMEAD.

Belvedere Road *SE1.* Commemorates the Belvedere pleasure gardens which opened on the site of the present ROYAL FESTIVAL HALL in 1718. It was formerly known as Narrow Wall and, at the southern end, Pedlar's Acre – a pedlar is said to have bought the land

55

after his dog had discovered treasure there while scratching around in the earth. Once he had dug up the treasure he had given the land to the parish on condition that his portrait and that of his dog were perpetually preserved in painted glass on one of the windows of the church of ST-MARY-AT-LAMBETH. Here are the QUEEN ELIZABETH HALL, the PURCELL ROOM, the HAYWARD GALLERY, the NATIONAL FILM THEATRE and the BRITISH FILM INSTITUTE. The Shell Centre, designed by Sir Howard Robertson in 1962, is one of the largest office blocks in the world. It covers 7½ acres. The stone bell carved with shells, the trademark of the Shell Co., which stands by a garage entrance is by Eric Aumonier (1959).

Bennet Street *SW1*. Built in the 1680s on land granted by Charles II to Henry Bennet, Earl of Arlington. None of the original houses survives. Lord Byron lived at No. 4 while writing *The Corsair* and *The Bride of Abydos* in 1813–14.

Bentinck Street *W1*. Takes its name from William Bentinck, 2nd Duke of Portland, on whose estate it lies. Building began in 1765 and the houses have changed surprisingly little since the historian Edward Gibbon occupied No. 7 from 1774 till 1790 and began to write his *Decline and Fall of the Roman Empire* there. Sir James Mackenzie, author of *Diseases of the Heart*, lived at No. 17.

Bentley Priory *Common Road, Stanmore, Middlesex*. Founded in 1170 by Ranulf de Glanville, Chief Justiciary of England, its name derives from *beonet* (coarse grass) and *leah* (clearing). The present building, designed by Sir John Soane, dates from 1777. From 1788 it was the property of the Marquess of Abercorn and home of the Prime Minister, Lord Aberdeen. The dowager Queen Adelaide, widow of William IV, rented the Priory in 1848 and lived there until her death the following year. Sir Hugh Kelk, the railway engineer, was the next owner, followed by Sir Frederick Gordon, who converted it into a hotel. From 1902 to 1924 the Priory was used as a girls' school, and finally it became the property of the RAF. From here Sir Hugh Dowding directed the Battle of Britain in 1940.

Bentley Priory Park *Stanmore, Middlesex*. Forms part of the Green Belt (*see* PLANNING) and covers an area of 163 acres of which nearly 10, including the man-made Summerhouse Lake and its surrounding woodland, comprise a nature reserve with restricted access. The open land is used primarily for grazing animals, under the supervision of the Nature Conservancy Council.

Berkeley Hotel *Wilton Place, SW1*. A luxury hotel, smaller than most, it was designed by Brian O'Rourke and opened in 1972. It originally stood at the east corner of PICCADILLY and BERKELEY STREET, and occupied the site of the old Gloucester Coffee House and Hotel, which in 1805 supplied 'good soups, dinners, wines and beds'. Later it was rebuilt as the St James's Hotel before becoming the Berkeley Hotel in 1897. Named after Lord Berkeley of Stratton whose house stood nearby in the 17th century, it became highly fashionable in the 1930s and 1940s. The BRISTOL HOTEL, built in 1971, stands on the original site.

The present hotel (152 rooms) stands at the northern end of the 'Five Fields', part of the GROSVENOR ESTATE.

Berkeley House *Piccadilly*. One of half a dozen great mansions put up on the north side of PICCADILLY soon after the Restoration. It was built in 1665 by Hugh May for the 1st Lord Berkeley of Stratton, the Royalist commander in the Civil War. In 1672 John Evelyn, who had a hand in the design of the large garden, dined with Berkeley, 'in his new house, or rather Palace, for I am assured it stood him in neare 30,000 pounds, and truely is very well built, and has many noble roomes in it . . .!' After Lord Berkeley's death in 1678 his widow sold strips of land on either side of the garden for building BERKELEY STREET and STRATTON STREET. Evelyn 'could not but deplore that sweet place should be so much straight'nd and turned into tenements'. In 1692–5 Princess Anne lived here after a quarrel with her sister, Queen Mary. In 1696 the house was bought by the 1st Duke of Devonshire and renamed DEVONSHIRE HOUSE. In 1733 a fire, caused by a pot of glue boiling over while workmen breakfasted, completely gutted the house. It was rebuilt in 1734–7 by William Kent for the 3rd Duke of Devonshire (*see* DEVONSHIRE HOUSE).

Berkeley Square *W1*. Takes its name from the 1st Lord Berkeley of Stratton, the Royalist commander in the Civil War, who soon after the Restoration acquired extensive lands to the north of PICCADILLY (now the Berkeley Square and HILL STREET area) and built himself a great house fronting PICCADILLY. In 1696 BERKELEY HOUSE was sold by his descendants to the 1st Duke of Devonshire, but with a proviso that the view directly to the north of the house, so far as Lord Berkeley's other lands extended, should never be spoiled by building upon them. This condition was in fact respected for over 200 years, for to the north of the gardens of BERKELEY (later DEVONSHIRE) HOUSE lay those of LANSDOWNE HOUSE, and beyond them the garden in the centre of Berkeley Square. And, until after its demolition in 1924, the first houses to be seen, some 500 yards away from the windows of DEVONSHIRE HOUSE, were the houses on the north side of Berkeley Square, which stood on the GROSVENOR ESTATE.

As originally laid out in the 1730s, Berkeley Square therefore consisted only of long ranges of large houses on the east and west sides, the principal developers of which were Edward Cock and Francis Hillyard, carpenters. None of these houses survives on the east side, which is now dominated by the ungainly mass of the showrooms and offices known as Berkeley Square House (1937–8). But on the west side Nos 42–46 and 49–52 form a very fine group of mid-18th-century houses, and even the rebuilt No. 47 has the virtue of being by Ernest George and Peto (1891). Nos 45 and 46 are a splendid stone-faced pair, No. 45 probably by John Devall, mason, 1744. Clive of India lived here from 1761 until his death in the house from an overdose of laudanum in 1774. No. 44, described by Sir Nikolaus Pevsner as 'the finest terrace house of London', was built by William Kent in 1742–4 for Lady Isabella Finch, a Maid of Honour to Princess Amelia. Its reticent façade belies its magnificent interior, and Horace Walpole, who was a frequent visitor to the house, thought that the staircase was 'as beautiful a piece of scenery and, considering the space, of art as can be imagined'. In later years the Prince Regent often dined here with Lord and Lady Clermont, and today it is beautifully maintained by its present occupants, the Clermont Club.

The northern part of the west side is now mostly occupied by large modern 'prestige' office blocks, but on the north side, on the GROSVENOR ESTATE, Nos 27 and 28 date from the early 1820s, and were perhaps designed by Thomas Cundy the Elder. The builder of No. 28 was Thomas Cubitt. No. 25 is a handsome block of flats (now used as offices) of 1905–6 by Frank T. Verity, its site formerly occupied by the fashionable Thomas's Hotel.

Max Beerbohm said that Berkeley Square 'has no squareness', and (apart from the Georgian houses on the west side) it certainly has little beauty now. On the south side, formerly occupied by the garden of LANS-DOWNE HOUSE, now stands a large brick block of 1936. Despite the enduring popularity of the song, no nightingale has sung in Berkeley Square for many years (if ever). The general aspect of the Square is, however, redeemed by over 30 enormous plane trees which are said to have been planted in 1789 and are among the finest specimens of this tree in the whole of London. In the centre of the garden is a little pump house with a Chinese roof of about 1800. Formerly there was an equestrian statue of George III, but the garden's only other adornment now is a marble statue (1858) of a nymph pouring water from a vase into a basin, by Alexander Munro, one of the Pre-Raphaelites.

Notable former inhabitants of the Square included William Pitt the Elder; Charles James Fox (1802–3); Field-Marshal Lord Clyde, better known as Sir Colin Campbell, hero of the Indian Mutiny; Sydney Smirke, architect; John Cam Hobhouse, Byron's friend; and George Canning at No. 50. The florists, Moyses Stevens Ltd, were established in about 1872 at No. 146 Victoria Street by a Miss Moyses who had married a Mr Stevens. The firm moved to Berkeley Square in 1934.

Berkeley Street *W1.* Extends northward from PIC-CADILLY to BERKELEY SQUARE. Its site formed part of the lands acquired soon after the Restoration by the 1st Lord Berkeley of Stratton (*see* BERKELEY SQUARE). In the 1680s his widow began to dispose of outlying portions of the large garden behind the house, and by 1698 houses were being built along the east side of Berkeley Street. Alexander Pope later lived in one of them, and it was to the same house that in 1765 Mr Chaworth was brought after being mortally wounded at the STAR AND GARTER inn in PALL MALL in the famous duel with Lord Byron, great-uncle of the poet. Mrs Howard, mistress of Louis Napoleon (later Napoleon III), was a later resident here.

None of these houses survives, and almost all of the present buildings in Berkeley Street were put up in the 20th century. On the west side there was in fact no building at all until after the demolition of DEVON-SHIRE (previously BERKELEY) HOUSE in 1924. This side of Berkeley Street is now dominated by the side elevation of the vast new Devonshire House (1924–6), and further north by the equally large offices of THOMAS COOK, the travel agents. Both of these, and nearly all the buildings on the east side, have shops at street level, and today Berkeley Street is chiefly famous for its expensive car showrooms and for the BRISTOL and MAYFAIR HOTELS. The Empress Restaurant at No. 16 (Wimperis and Arber 1901) was originally the dining room of the Empress Club established in 1897 by some of Queen Victoria's Ladies-in-Waiting. Thomas Cook, the travel agents at No. 45, were established in the 1840s by a lay preacher and temperance campaigner from the Midlands.

Bermondsey *SE1, SE16.* The district on the THAMES at the north of the modern London Borough of SOUTHWARK. It lies west of ROTHERHITHE, east of LONDON BRIDGE, is bounded on the south by the OLD KENT ROAD, and is served by TOWER BRIDGE. The name may derive from 'Beormund's eye (island)', and may at one time have belonged to a Saxon lord of that name when the area can have been little more than a morass. In 1082 Aylwin Child founded the Cluniac BERMONDSEY ABBEY (hence Abbey Street) and its monks embanked the river here and cultivated the surrounding land, using St Saviour's Dock as its port. Shad Thames runs east from the present Tower Bridge Road and then south into the junction of TOOLEY STREET and Jamaica Road. The land here was once owned by the KNIGHTS TEMPLAR and Shad Thames is a corruption of St John at Thames. In TOOLEY STREET stood the London houses of the Abbots of St Augustine's, Canterbury, and of Battle, and the house of the Prior of Lewes. Tooley, the name of the street running behind the warehouses between London Bridge and Tower Bridge, is a corruption of St Olaf, Norway's king and ally of Ethelred against the Danes, who was murdered in 1030. A medieval church dedicated to him stood in TOOLEY STREET for centuries but its 1740 version was demolished in 1928 for the benefit of HAY'S WHARF Co.

Cherry Garden Pier projects into the river at Bermondsey Wall East and is a reminder of the Restoration pleasure gardens beside the river here which Pepys visited. Another resort was founded in 1766 in what is now Spa Road by one Thomas Keyse, a painter. When a chalybeate spring was found here in 1770 the place became a spa. JACOB'S ISLAND in Bermondsey was a notorious slum in the mid-19th century, described by both Mayhew and Dickens. In 1869 a tunnel was constructed under the river between TOWER HILL and TOOLEY STREET, the engineer being P.W. Barlow, designer of the erstwhile Lambeth suspension bridge (*see* LAMBETH BRIDGE) and of ST PANCRAS STATION train shed. This was the second tunnel under the river, the first being Brunel's between WAPPING and ROTHERHITHE. Barlow's tunnel of cast-iron rings was only 7 ft in diameter but it was important as the prototype of London's later tube railways. At first it contained a passenger railway, then became a footway, and in 1894, when TOWER BRIDGE was built, it was used to take water mains. In 1836 the first London passenger terminus was opened in Bermondsey near LONDON BRIDGE for the London to Greenwich Railway, the outcome of which was LONDON BRIDGE STATION, owned by the Southern Railway before railways were nationalised after the 2nd World War. The first line ran for 4 miles on 878 brick arches. The Croydon Railway, to which it became linked, was opened in 1839, starting at the BRICKLAYERS ARMS STATION in OLD KENT ROAD (now a goods depot). In industry Bermondsey has been associated in the past not only with brewing but also with leather, represented by BERMONDSEY LEATHER MARKET in Weston Street, though the industry there has died. The 3½ miles of riverside were once an important wharfage

Hoefnagel's painting of a wedding festivity in Bermondsey in the late 16th century.

area with rows of warehouses, the most famous being those of the HAY'S WHARF Co. lying between LONDON BRIDGE and TOWER BRIDGE on the Upper Pool, a business founded in 1651 by Alexander Hay. The company built a new office block here in 1931, designed in the modern style of the period by Goodhart-Rendel. All the premises are now to be demolished and a new development for the riverside here is being planned. The parish church is ST MARY MAGDALEN, Bermondsey Street, rebuilt in 1680 on the site of a medieval church probably constructed by BERMONDSEY ABBEY for tenants and labourers on the Abbey lands. Other notable churches are ST JAMES, Thurland Road (1829), and the Roman Catholic church of the Most Holy Trinity, Dockhead (rebuilt 1960).

Bermondsey Abbey In 1082 Aylwin Child, a wealthy and prominent citizen, founded a priory dedicated to St Saviour. The buildings took seven years to complete and covered the ground which now lies between Grange Walk and Long Walk. In 1089 the first four monks arrived from the monastery of La Charité on the Loire. They belonged to the Cluniac order, a strict branch of the Benedictines. One of them named Petreius became the first prior. In 1094 William Rufus gave them the surrounding manor. Henry I later gave them land in ROTHERHITHE, DULWICH, SOUTHWARK and Whaddon, besides advowsons of churches in Kent. In 1115 Princess Mary, daughter of Malcolm III of Scotland and wife of the Count de Boulogne, died at the priory while visiting England and was buried here. In 1117 the Rood of Grace, a Saxon cross, was found nearby in the THAMES. It was thought to have dropped from heaven and to have miraculous powers. It consequently attracted hundreds of pilgrims every year.

In 1140 King Stephen freed the priory from paying tolls and taxes and gave it the right to hold a court of law. He also endowed it with land in SOUTHWARK, the Manor of Grave and the church of Writtle. In 1154 an early parliament met at the priory, a group of clergy and nobles selected by Henry II for the first time on merit alone. In 1213 Prior Richard founded an almonry for indigent children and necessitous converts and dedicated it to St Thomas. It was later amalgamated with another in SOUTHWARK founded by St Mary's Priory and became ST THOMAS'S HOSPITAL. A monastic school existed at this time which was highly thought of. Henry III gave permission to the monks to hold a weekly market and an annual fair at CHARLTON. In 1290 Edward I gave them the manors of Hallingbury, Wideford, Cowyk, Upton and RICHMOND. In 1324 John de Causancia, the prior, and some of his monks were arrested for harbouring rebels, probably supporters of Thomas, Earl of Lancaster, after his defeat at Boroughbridge two years earlier. In 1373 Edward III appointed Richard Dunton as the first English prior, his predecessors having all been French.

In 1380 Richard II drew up a charter freeing the monastery from its parent house of La Charité. Money which had previously been sent abroad was spent on rebuilding the cloister and refectory. In 1387 the nave was re-roofed and new windows were put in the presbytery. In 1397 Thomas, Duke of Gloucester, murdered at Calais – probably on the orders of his nephew Richard II – was temporarily buried here before being moved to WESTMINSTER ABBEY. In 1399 the priory became an abbey on instructions from Pope Boniface IX. In 1436 Catherine de Valois, widow of Henry V, was banished to the abbey after her long-standing secret marriage to Owen Tudor was discovered. She died six months later. In 1437 the body of Joanna of Navarre, Henry IV's queen, lay here before being buried at Canterbury. In 1486 Elizabeth Woodville, widow of Edward IV, was sent here by order of the Council, after a rebellion in Ireland. She died here six years later.

The abbey was surrendered to Henry VIII in 1537–8. Abbot Robert Wharton was granted a large pension of £333 6s 8d a year and later became Bishop of Hereford. In 1541 the abbey buildings were granted to Sir Robert Southwell, Master of the Rolls. Within months he sold them to Sir Thomas Pope, Treasurer of the Court of Augmentations, who pulled down most of the buildings and used the stone to build himself a large residence known as BERMONDSEY HOUSE. The Rood of Grace was set up on Horsleydown Common where it stood until attacked by a Protestant mob in 1559. With the wealth he accumulated from the DISSOLUTION OF THE MONASTERIES, Sir Thomas Pope founded Trinity College, Oxford and many of the books from the monastic libraries and probably some from Bermondsey were transferred there. The gate hooks of the abbey remain in Grange Walk and there is a 14th-century salver from the abbey in the parish church of ST MARY MAGDALENE.

Bermondsey House *Bermondsey.* Stood on the present site of Bermondsey Square. It was built in 1541 with the stones of BERMONDSEY ABBEY by Sir Thomas Pope, Treasurer of the Court of Augmentations. Orchards, gardens, barns, pastures and ponds covered the 20-acre site. From about 1567 it was used by the Earl of Sussex as a town house. Queen Elizabeth visited him here in 1570 for the first time and, in 1583, attended his death-bed in the house. The family apparently ceased to live here after 1595.

Bermondsey Leather Market *Leather Market, SE1.* Built in Weston Street in 1879 to serve the local tanning industry. There had been tanners in Bermondsey since the early Middle Ages. In 1392 the butchers of London were ordered to deposit skins and offal there. The industry made use of the tidal streams and the nearby oak bark. Citizens are said to have fled to the area during the GREAT PLAGUE, believing the smell from the works would protect them. In 1703 the leather industry was granted a charter by Queen Anne and BERMONDSEY became the major leather-working centre. The market was a roofed square, piled high with skins, in the centre of a large block of buildings. Dickens describes the market as reeking with evil smells and the workers in rawhide aprons and gaiters. Parts of the leather industry survive but the market is no longer in use.

Bermondsey Street *E1.* Now a conservation area, this street led in the Middle Ages from the THAMES to BERMONDSEY ABBEY on the site of Abbey Street and Bermondsey Square (noted today for its Friday antiques market). ST MARY MAGDALEN, Bermondsey parish church, rebuilt 1680, with later alterations, has a beautifully restored interior. Buildings of interest in the street include No. 78, probably 17th-century, and the old watchhouse at the corner of Abbey Street. Old warehouses and street names, such as Tanner Street, Leathermarket Street and Morocco Street, provide evidence of Bermondsey's former leather industry.

Bernard Street *WC1.* Built in 1799–1802 by James Burton on the FOUNDLING HOSPITAL estate and named after Sir Thomas Bernard, the Hospital Treasurer in 1795–1806. Roget, compiler of the famous *Thesaurus,* lived here in 1808–43, as did Roger Fry, artist and art critic, in 1927–34. (*See* BLOOMSBURY GROUP.)

Berners Street *W1.* Laid out on land acquired in 1654 by Josias Berners of Woolverstone Hall in Suffolk and developed by his descendant, William Berners. Building began on it in 1746 and with NEWMAN STREET, CHARLOTTE STREET and RATHBONE PLACE it became a part of MARYLEBONE's artistic colony, London's earliest *Quartier Latin*, in the second half of the 18th century. John Opie RA, the portrait painter known as the 'Cornish Wonder', lived from 1791 till his death in 1807 at No. 8, with Henry Fuseli for neighbour at No. 13; Benjamin Robert Haydon recalls a visit to the latter in 1804: '. . . I saw a little, bony hand slide round the edge of the door, followed by a little, white-headed lion-faced man in an old flannel dressing-gown, tied round his waist with a piece of rope, and upon his head the bottom of Mrs Fuseli's work-basket.'

Several of the houses were built by Sir William Chambers who resided at No. 53, designed by himself, from 1769 to 1807; before its demolition, it was a finely appointed dwelling with beautiful door-cases. Sir Robert Smirke lived in the street in 1807 and a third architect, Thomas Hardwick, died at No. 55 in 1829. Samuel Taylor Coleridge lodged with his friends, the Morgans, at No. 71 from 1812 to 1816, and it was to No. 54 that Theodore Hook sent all manner of unwanted goods in what became known as the Berners Street Hoax. The Berners Hotel occupies the site of Messrs Marsh, Stacey, Fauntleroy and Graham's bank which failed when Henry Fauntleroy was convicted of forgery; he was hanged on 30 November 1824. Arthur Sanderson and Sons Ltd, the wallpaper and fabric manufacturers at Nos 52–53, were established at 17 SOHO SQUARE in 1860 and moved here five years later.

Berwick Street *W1.* Built between 1687 and 1703, it was probably named after the Duke of Berwick, an illegitimate son of James II, who may have been a protector of James Pollett, the Roman Catholic ground landlord. In 1720 Strype described it as 'a pretty handsome strait street, with new well built houses much inhabited by the French where they have a church'. In fact they had two: L'Ancienne Patente, and L'Église du Quarré. There are several houses dating from the 1730s, Nos 26, 31–32, 46–48, 50–52, 69–71, 77, and 79–81. The Green Man public house at No. 57 occupies a site where there has been a tavern since at least 1738. The lively Berwick Street Market seems to have begun some time in the 18th century when shopkeepers began displaying their goods on the pavement, but it did not receive official recognition until 1892. In the 19th century, the street was in the middle of a densely crowded slummy area: there were many cases of CHOLERA here in 1854. Now it is a typical SOHO street. The Blue Posts public house at No. 22

occupies a site where there has been a tavern of either this name, or called the Three Blue Posts, since at least 1739. Kemp House (1959–61) is by L.C. Holbrook.

Bessborough Gardens *SW1*. Built in about 1841 and named after John Ponsonby, Baron Duncannon of Bessborough, First Commissioner of Woods and Forests (hence also DUNCANNON STREET and Ponsonby Place and Terrace). The CROWN ESTATE COMMISSIONERS are at No. 1. The Queen Mother's Commemorative Fountain, in aluminium, is by Sir Peter Shepheard (1980). In 1982 much of the square had been demolished for road improvements.

Bethlehem Royal Hospital (*Bedlam*). Founded in 1247 by Sheriff Simon Fitz Mary as the Priory of St Mary Bethlehem outside BISHOPSGATE. The priory is known to have had a hospital attached in 1329 but this was probably for general complaints, and it was not until 1377 that 'distracted' patients were looked after, that is to say were kept chained to the wall by leg or ankle and, when violent, ducked in water or whipped. In 1346 the MAYOR and CORPORATION took the priory and hospital under their protection; and in 1547, when the priory was dissolved, they bought the site from the King and re-established the hospital as a lunatic asylum. In 1557 the asylum was placed under the government of BRIDEWELL. In 1675–6 it was moved to a building in MOORFIELDS which was designed by Robert Hooke and which Evelyn said was very beautiful and similar in design to the Tuileries. It cost £17,000.

At the entrance stood Cibber's statues of *Madness* and *Melancholy*, 'great Cibber's brazen brainless brothers', as Pope called them. They were, in fact, of painted Portland stone. They were modelled on inmates, one of whom was said to have been Oliver Cromwell's porter. Visitors had been allowed in to look at the inmates since the beginning of the 17th century and Bedlam had become one of the sights of London. The chained patients were placed in cells in galleries like caged animals in a menagerie. The asylum received large sums of money from the visitors until 1770 when it was decided that they 'tended to disturb the tranquility of the patients' by 'making sport and diversion of the miserable inhabitants', and that admission should be by ticket only. The lot of the patients had by then been improved by the work of John Howard and public sympathy engendered by the mental illness of George III. Whips were no longer used.

In 1800 James Lewis, the hospital surveyor, reported the building unsafe and drew up designs for a new building at LAMBETH, which were accepted. This new building was finished in 1815 and 122 patients were brought to it in hackney coaches from MOORFIELDS. The next year blocks for criminal lunatics were added at the request of the government. Further blocks at the rear and a dome and portico to the central block were added in 1835 by Sydney Smirke. The first resident medical officer, Dr W. Charles Hood, was appointed in 1851. Among those under his care was Augustus Pugin. In 1864 the criminal patients were moved to Broadmoor.

After the 1st World War a new hospital was begun at ADDINGTON, Surrey, to which the patients were moved in 1930. The present Bethlem Royal Hospital is at BECKENHAM, Kent (*see* MAUDSLEY HOSPITAL). Lord Rothermere bought the grounds of the old hospital and gave them to the LONDON COUNTY COUNCIL as a park in memory of his mother, Geraldine Mary Harmsworth (*see* GERALDINE MARY HARMSWORTH PARK). In 1936 the central block of the old hospital, whose wings had been demolished, became the home of the IMPERIAL WAR MUSEUM.

Bethlem Royal Hospital *see* BETHLEHEM ROYAL HOSPITAL.

Bethnal Green *E1, E2, E3*. The poorest district of London in Victorian times, though two centuries

Robert Hooke's Bethlehem Royal Hospital, built in the 1670s and compared by John Evelyn to the Tuileries in Paris.

For a few pence and a meal men break stones in the Labour Yard of the Bethnal Green Employment Association in 1868.

earlier it was a pleasant country area attracting wealthy residents. The name, thought to mean 'Blida's corner', is of Saxon origin and the BISHOP OF LONDON, who was Lord of the Manor of STEPNEY which then included Bethnal Green, had a residence where the LONDON CHEST HOSPITAL now stands. In the Bishop's Wood nearby, the ALDERMEN and SHERIFFS of London once spent May Day in the reign of Henry VI. The legend of the Blind Beggar of Bethnal Green may have originated about this time.

The centre of the village was the Green (the present Bethnal Green Gardens). A large mansion called Kirby's Castle was built there in 1570. It belonged to Sir William Ryder, Deputy Master of TRINITY HOUSE, when Pepys kept his diary there during the GREAT FIRE. It later became the Bethnal House Lunatic Asylum. Sir Balthazar Gerbier, painter and courtier, and Robert Ainsworth, the lexicographer, kept schools in Bethnal Green; and William Caslon, the printer, retired here in about 1758.

The urban invasion from the south-western corner began towards the end of the 17th century with the spread of the silk-weaving industry from SPITALFIELDS. When Bethnal Green was made a separate parish from STEPNEY in 1743 it was claimed that the 'hamlet contains above eighteen hundred houses, and is computed to have more than fifteen thousand inhabitants ... consisting chiefly of weavers, dyers and other dependents ... crowded into narrow streets and courts ... three or four families in a house'. In 1777 John Wesley recorded in his *Journal*, 'I began visiting those of our Society who lived in Bethnal Green. Many of these I found in such poverty as few can conceive without seeing it.' By 1840 it was estimated that six times as many looms were employed in Bethnal Green as in the former weaving centres at SPITALFIELDS and Mile End New Town. The decline of the industry at this time aggravated distress in the area, although other industries soon developed in its place. These were also based on the home and the small workshop, and included furniture, clothes and boot and shoe manufacture. In 1889 Charles Booth found that almost 45 per cent of the population lived below subsistence level – the highest proportion in London. The 'Jago' district around Old Nichol Street was particularly notorious for crime and poverty. The Victorians introduced several improvements intended to help the area. The Bishop's Wood, later known as Bonner's Fields, was purchased by the Crown and laid out as VICTORIA

PARK in the 1840s. Angela Burdett-Coutts erected a drinking fountain in the park, a block of flats – Columbia Square – and COLUMBIA MARKET. The East London branch of the VICTORIA AND ALBERT MUSEUM, now called the BETHNAL GREEN MUSEUM, was opened in 1872. Oxford House, a university settlement, was established in 1884, the same year as TOYNBEE HALL. The pet market in CLUB ROW and the flower market in COLUMBIA ROAD reflect the traditional interests of the inhabitants in animals and flowers.

Bethnal Green has been completely transformed during the present century by slum clearance, the building of large council estates, the loss of most of its industries and the decline of its population from the peak of about 130,000 in 1901 to about one-third of this number by the 1960s. In 1965 the Metropolitan Borough of Bethnal Green created in 1900 became a part of the present London Borough of TOWER HAMLETS. The Bethnal Green Gardens conservation area incorporates most of the older buildings left and is the only part to retain something of the former village atmosphere.

Bethnal Green Museum *Cambridge Heath Road, E2.* The doll and toy department of the VICTORIA AND ALBERT MUSEUM. The main iron structure, designed by Charles Young, formed part of the temporary buildings erected in 1856 at SOUTH KENSINGTON. It was removed in 1872 to its present site where it was encased in a brickwork exterior designed by James Wild and erected under the supervision of Major-General Henry Scott. The sgraffito panels which form a frieze are the work of students of the National Art Training School, now the ROYAL COLLEGE OF ART, who were provided with designs by F.W. Moody.

The museum contains a fine collection of dolls' houses, dolls, model furniture, toys and indoor games, model theatres, puppets, optical toys and children's books. As well as children's costumes, it has an important series of wedding dresses and a display of SPITALFIELDS SILKS, once the main industry of the locality. In addition it houses a collection of Japanese arms and armour, a unique display of Continental sculpture and decorative art, furniture, ceramics, glass and metalwork from the 1830s to the present day, and an important collection of sculpture by Auguste Rodin. The bronze nude, *The Eagle Slayer*, in the grounds is by John Bell (1847, erected here 1927).

Bethnal Green Road *E2.* While an outline of part of the road appears on Gascoyne's 1703 map, its present form dates from improvements by the METROPOLITAN BOARD OF WORKS in 1879, including the construction of a completely new section from BRICK LANE to Shoreditch High Street. On 3 March 1943, 173 people were killed during a panic at the entrance to Bethnal Green Underground Station which was then being used as an air-raid shelter.

Beulah Hill *SE19.* Once a gravel lane across Norwood Common (*see* UPPER NORWOOD) called Beggar's Hill, because of the gipsies that frequented the area. Like BEULAH SPA, it appears to take its name from Bewlys Coppice and in the enclosure plans for the area was to form part of the 'new town of Beulah'. From the 1830s to the 1880s a fine residential road developed, with villas, large family homes and mansions. Mendelssohn stayed with Thomas Attwood (organist at

ST PAUL'S CATHEDRAL) at Roselawn in 1829 and 1832, and composed there; Dickens visited Springfield, which is reputed to be the setting for the meeting between David Copperfield and Dora Spenlow. Little Menlo was the home of Colonel Gourard, Thomas Edison's representative in England; and Charles Haddon Spurgeon, the Baptist preacher, purchased a mansion called Westwood in 1880. In 1953, the 'Beulah Hill Treasure Trove', consisting of gold nobles and silver groats from the reign of Edward III, was found in a garden. Many of the original houses have been demolished to make way for modern flats, Tivoli Lodge (see BEULAH SPA), Innisfail, and part of St Joseph's College, once known as Grecian Villa, being among those that remain.

Beulah Spa Situated in UPPER NORWOOD in an area now bounded by BEULAH HILL, Spa Hill and Grange Road. The discovery of the mineral spring has been attributed to the miraculous recovery of a sick horse grazing nearby. Its curative properties were certainly known in the 18th century. John Davidson Smith, owner of this section of the Manor of Whitehorse, employed the architect Decimus Burton in 1828 to convert Bewlys Coppice into a health resort and place of entertainment. It opened as the Royal Beulah Spa and Gardens in 1831 and its attractions included an octagonal reading room, a terrace, a maze, an orchestra, a camera obscura and an archery ground, set in beautiful rural surroundings. Military bands played, there was dancing and fortunes were told by local gipsies (see GIPSY HILL). The well was protected by a thatched wigwam-shaped hut and was declared to be 'one of the purest and strongest of the saline spas in the country'. Coaches ran several times daily to the Spa from CHARING CROSS. Mrs Fitzherbert, the Earl and Countess of Munster and the Duke of Gloucester were among the visitors. But by the mid-1840s it was in decline and in 1854 it was eclipsed by the arrival of the CRYSTAL PALACE in NORWOOD. Tivoli Lodge, the rustic entrance lodge, is relatively unchanged, but all that remains of the Spa itself is an area of open ground called the Lawns.

Beverley Brook Rose in SUTTON, flowing northwards between RICHMOND PARK and WIMBLEDON COMMON to Earlsfield and thence to the THAMES near PUTNEY BRIDGE. In 1880 an application was made by the District Railway to run a line from PUTNEY along the Beverley Brook valley to KINGSTON and SURBITON, but this was refused and the line was constructed to Wimbledon to connect with South-Western Railway services to those places.

Bevis Marks EC3. Corruption of Burics Marks, the town house of the Abbot of Bury St Edmunds which once stood here. The Spanish and Portuguese synagogue covers its site. Dickens spent a whole morning wandering through the street to find a house suitable to describe as the 'little habitation' where Sampson Brass, the lawyer in The Old Curiosity Shop, had his office – a small dark house, 'so close upon the footway that the passenger who rakes the wall brushes the dim glass with his coat sleeve – much to its improvement, for it is very dirty'.

Bexley Kent. This London Borough was formed in 1965 by uniting BEXLEY, ERITH, CRAYFORD and SIDCUP.

Bexley village, at the intersection of two ancient roads and a ford on the River CRAY, was a manor of the Archbishop of Canterbury from AD 814 until the time of Henry VIII. In Domesday Book it was said to have three mills, and it remained a thriving agricultural centre until the 20th century. Its attractive situation and nearness to London drew wealthy people to it, and the houses and parklands of some of them remain today like oases in the monotony of modern suburbia. HALL PLACE is the most outstanding of them. DANSON PARK has a Palladian villa by Robert Taylor (1765) in grounds landscaped by 'Capability' Brown for Sir John Boyd; an earlier owner of this estate, John Styleman, of the East India Company, founded the almshouses (1755) still in use in Bexley High Street. The Chapel House, a cottage with a spire stuck on it to add charm to the vista from Danson House, stands incongruously by a busy roundabout in nearby Blendon. The antiquary John Thorpe lived at Bexley for much of his life; his High Street House (1761) still graces the town. St Mary's church contains some 12th-century elements. It has a striking octagonal shingled tower.

Bexleyheath Kent. For centuries an open heath, crossed by the Roman road from London to Dover, suddenly blossomed into a new township early in the 19th century. Many of its early inhabitants worked at textile-printing factories at CRAYFORD but later in the century market gardening was developed on a large scale. Bexleyheath rapidly outgrew BEXLEY village in population, and became the centre of local government after 1880.

THE RED HOUSE was built in 1859 by Philip Webb for William Morris. Dante Gabriel Rossetti considered it 'more a poem than a house'.

Bickley Kent. Apart from a small hamlet, Cross-in-Hand, which had one residence, later known as Farrants from the name of its owner, this whole area was formerly scrubland, suitable only for hunting. Before the mid-18th century there was a hunting lodge known as Highway Bush, owned by Thomas Jukes. In 1759 the area came under the ownership of John Wells, whose family had for many years carried on business at DEPTFORD as shipbuilders. Under the Wells's ownership the modern Bickley appeared. The mansion Bickley Hall was built in 1780 by John Wells on the site of the old hunting lodge. Much of the surrounding waste of furze and briar was cleared to become pleasure grounds attached to the Hall. The winding lanes through the area were replaced by thoroughfares.

John Wells died a bachelor in 1794. It is believed that the name he chose for his house came from Bickleigh in Devon, where a branch of the family lived. The estate remained in the possession of the Wells family for some years and it is reported that one of them, also a John Wells, when he was 70 years of age was involved with a banking firm that failed. He walked out of Bickley Hall with his Bible in one hand, his gun in the other, these being his only remaining possessions. After the estate had passed through a number of hands, it was bought in 1861 by George Wythes, a wealthy contractor, who sold it in 2- and 5-acre plots for the building of large houses with extensive grounds. A church dedicated to St George was built in 1863 and part of the parklands were converted into cricket pitches. They are now the grounds of the Bickley Park Cricket Club. The house became a preparatory school for boys. Bickley is in the London Borough of BROMLEY.

In May 1858, 16 horses drew the new 13 ton bell 'Victoria' to the Clock Tower, Westminster Palace.

Big Ben *Palace of Westminster, SW1.* The soubriquet was originally given to the Great Bell of Westminster and has since been extended to include the bell, clock and St Stephen's Tower of the Houses of Parliament. The architect of the Houses of Parliament, Sir Charles Barry, was not ultimately responsible for the provision of bell and clock, and that part of the rebuilding of the PALACE OF WESTMINSTER is therefore dealt with here.

In 1840 the foundation stone of the new Houses of Parliament was laid, a feature of the design being a clock tower about 320 ft high. In 1844 Barry applied to Parliament for authority to provide a clock for the clock tower. He had an understanding with Benjamin Vulliamy, the Queen's clockmaker and Master of the CLOCKMAKERS' COMPANY, who was to design it. Barry promised Parliament that it would be an eight-day clock, show the time on four 30 ft diameter dials, chime the quarter-hours on eight bells and strike the hours on a 14 ton bell. The First Lord of Her Majesty's Woods, Forests, Land Revenues and Buildings added that it would be 'a noble clock', indeed a king of clocks, the biggest and best in the world, within sight and sound of the throbbing heart of London.

In 1845 Vulliamy submitted his design and working drawings, but when the Commissioners for rebuilding received an appeal from E.J. Dent to let him compete for the construction of the clock, a heated controversy arose over Barry's amicable arrangement with Vulliamy. Under pressure, the Commissioners announced an open competition in 1846, the terms to be formulated by the Astronomer Royal, Professor George Biddell Airy, who himself had designed the important clock of the ROYAL EXCHANGE. Airy demanded an accuracy that astonished the horological trade: the first stroke of each hour should be correct to within one second, and the performance should be checked twice a day at the ROYAL OBSERVATORY, Greenwich, by telegraph. Though his conditions were widely regarded as impractical in a large mechanism partially exposed to the elements, Airy was adamant and five years of bitter controversy followed. Vulliamy's design was dismissed by Airy as merely 'a village clock of a very superior character'. At the GREAT EXHIBITION in 1851 Airy was impressed by the large clock which now surmounts KING'S CROSS STATION, the minute hands of which moved every half-second instead of the then usual thirty seconds. Made by Dent, its designer was Edmund Beckett Denison, an abrasive lawyer whom Airy invited to be co-adjudicator of the competition, no doubt as a formidable ally in the political battles surrounding the clock. In 1852 the contract was at last given to Dent and production started, but following Dent's death in 1853 the work was continued by his stepson, Frederick Dent. At about this time Airy resigned as co-referee, having been eclipsed by Denison. In 1854 the clock was finished, but as the Tower was not complete the clock remained on test in Dent's workshop for the next five years. Denison devised the double three-legged gravity escapement in which a 6 cwt pendulum is regulated by a scape wheel of about ¼ oz, the pendulum remaining unaffected by wind pressures and other external influences. Visually the clock has been compared to a big flat-bed printing press. It is about 15½ ft long by 4 ft 7 ins wide, and weighs about 5 tons. The 2½ ton drive weights suspended in the tower are steadied by revolving vanes when the strike mechanism is in operation. The total cost was £4,080.

In 1856 a great bell was cast by Messrs Warner of CRIPPLEGATE in their Stockton-on-Tees works, and was brought to London by sea and up the THAMES. Denison had insisted on his own mixture of metals – 22 parts of copper to 7 of tin – which the bellfounders refused to endorse, declaring themselves responsible only for the casting. Despite Warner's miscalculation of the quantity of metal required, which in consequence ran short during the casting, the bell weighed 16 tons instead of the 14 intended. When quarter-chime bells had been cast at CRIPPLEGATE to match its tone, all were suspended on trial cat-gallows in PALACE YARD. The great bell was fitted with a 7 cwt clapper, but as the tone was unsatisfactory during the following months, Denison gradually increased the weight of the clapper. In 1857 when a 13 cwt clapper was used, it caused a 4 ft crack and the bell was pronounced 'porous, unhomogeneous, unsound and a defective casting'.

Public interest in these proceedings was intense, and it was about this time that the great bell of Westminster became known as Big Ben. There are two theories as to the origin of the name, though neither can be proved. During the debate in the House on the naming of the new bell, it is said that the large Chief Commissioner of Works, Sir Benjamin Hall, was speaking when a Member called out, 'Why not Big Ben?' There is, however, no record of this in *Hansard*. The second theory is that the bell is named after the popular boxer, Benjamin Caunt, who was the publican of the Coach and Horses in St Martin's Lane, and who weighed 18 stone. On 23 September 1857 Caunt fought an epic 60 rounds with Nathaniel Langham, the only man who had ever beaten the famous Tom Sayers. No decision was reached but his retirement thereafter virtually coincided with the destruction of the great bell in Palace Yard in October. In 1858 the metal from the cracked bell was broken up and used in recasting by George Mears of the WHITECHAPEL BELL FOUNDRY. Mears obtained Denison's approval of the bell before it left the foundry and stipulated that it should not be struck by a hammer of more than 4 cwt. Sixteen horses pulled the bell on an open flat cart through crowd-lined streets. It weighed 13 tons, 10¾ cwt and 15 lbs and rendered the note E. It is decorated with the Royal Arms and Portcullis of Westminster, with low-relief Gothic tracery round the crown, and an inscription round the outer lip: 'This bell was cast by George Mears of Whitechapel for the clock of the Houses of Parliament under the Direction of Edmund Beckett Denison QC in the 21st year of the reign of Queen Victoria in the year of our Lord MDCCCLVIII.' The four quarter bells are the original Warner ones and weigh 3 tons 18 cwt, 1 ton 13 cwt, 1 ton 6 cwt and 1 ton 1 cwt respectively. After the clock and bells had been placed in position the 2½ ton cast-iron hands were found to be too heavy for the mechanism to move, so they were replaced by much lighter gunmetal hands. When Dent found that the minute hands fell several feet each time they passed the vertical he designed hollow 14 ft long copper minute hands weighing only about 2 cwt, which at last proved satisfactory. The 9 ft long gunmetal hour hands, weighing about 6 cwt, remain. The 40 ton clock faces had been reduced by Augustus Welby Pugin from the proposed 30 ft diameter to 22½ ft for aesthetic reasons. Each minute space is 1 ft square. The faces were illuminated at night by 60 gas jets which were replaced in 1912 by electric lighting.

On 31 May 1859 the clock and bell became operational. Until 1913, when automatic winding gear was installed, it used to take two men 32 hours to wind the clock which, from the outset, was very accurate. The 13 ft long pendulum, weighing 685 lb, could easily be regulated by the addition or subtraction of very small weights, usually (old) pennies, the addition of one causing the clock to gain two-fifths of a second in 24 hours. The chimes imitated those of St Mary's church in Cambridge, where Denison had been an undergraduate. These had been arranged from the aria in Handel's *Messiah*, 'I know that my redeemer liveth'. Traditionally the lines

> All through this hour Lord be my Guide
> And by Thy Power no foot shall slide

accompany the chimes.

When the bell cracked within a few months it was discovered that Denison had fitted a 7 cwt hammer despite Mears's stipulation of a 4 cwt maximum. This hammer can now be seen at the foot of the Terrace Stairs within the Houses of Parliament. When the depth of the crack was probed it was decided that it was not necessary to recast the bell. It was tuned slightly to prevent the smaller 4 cwt hammer from aggravating the crack, which was restrained by a slot cut in the lip, and it no longer sounds an E note. During the intervening three years the hour was struck on a quarter bell and at last in 1862 the cracked Big Ben resumed service. In 1910 he tolled for the first time for the funeral of a monarch, King Edward VII, and again in 1936 and 1952 for the funerals of King George V and King George VI. On 31 December 1923 the midnight chimes were broadcast for the first time to herald the New Year.

In 1940 the land line that telegraphed the clock's performance to the ROYAL OBSERVATORY was destroyed and was never repaired, for so accurate was the clock that on only 18 days in the previous year had it been more than one second out of time. On 10 May 1941 when the HOUSE OF COMMONS was destroyed in an air raid and the belfry stage of the tower was damaged and the clock-face shattered, the clock became one and a half seconds inaccurate. It stopped three times during the war, once when a workman left a hammer in the mechanism and jammed it, again in 1944 when the pendulum suspension spring broke, and a third time on 25 January 1945 when snow and ice froze the hammer mechanism in the exposed belfry. In 1956 the clock mechanism was overhauled and three of the faces were reglazed. In 1968 the tower was found to be leaning 9½ ins to the north-west, but checks made since have revealed no appreciable change.

There was at one time a cell in St Stephen's Tower in which were incarcerated any agitators causing trouble in the PALACE OF WESTMINSTER. The last of the rioters to be confined there, in 1902, was Emmeline Pankhurst, the leader of the Suffragette movement.

Biggin Hill *Kent*. Means 'hill by a building'. In the 19th century there were a few small houses here, most of them on the main road to Westerham. There were two or three large houses including Aperfield Court. Lord Stanhope was the landowner. John Westacott, of Cudham Lodge Farm, allowed one of his fields, which was flatter than the others, to be used for occasional landings by the clumsy aeroplanes of that time. Early in the 1st World War the airfield was used for night emergency landings and a wireless testing station was established. Courses on wireless telegraphy were held. These soon became very popular since a course at 'Biggin on the Bump', as the aerodrome was called, meant comfortable accommodation at the Bell Hotel, BROMLEY. In 1917 Aperfield Court with its spacious grounds, about 2 miles from the aerodrome, was requisitioned and a powerful wireless transmitter installed for ground control of fighter aeroplanes. The aerodrome brought about development of the area. Houses were built, roads improved and public transport services provided. Aperfield Court was demolished in 1920 and a few years later, when the aerodrome was being further developed and extended, Lord Stanhope agreed to sell the whole property, including Cudham Lodge Farm. The aerodrome played a great part in the Battle of Britain (*see* BLITZ). In 1951 Major the Revd Vivian Symons moved to the living of St Mark's, Biggin Hill. It was a 50-year-old iron building which had never been consecrated. To rebuild it he obtained permission to use material from a war-damaged church, All Saints' PECKHAM, 17 miles away. Standing on a lorry facing this church, he is reported to have commanded in a loud voice, 'In the name of Jesus Christ be thou removed to Biggin Hill.' Working with volunteer labour, but quite often alone, he built St Mark's, 'The Moving Church'. It took him three years.

Billingsgate Market *Isle of Dogs, E14.* Opened on 19 January 1982, three days after the old BILLINGSGATE MARKET was closed. Built on a 13½ acre site around a renovated warehouse in the WEST INDIA DOCKS, the new market cost £11 million. One of the few remnants of the old market to be preserved here is the Billingsgate Bell. The clock in the middle of the main market area is a fibre-glass copy of the original. The porters no longer wear the leather helmets which were used by the porters on the former site, fork-lift trucks now being used for heavy weights.

Billingsgate Market *Lower Thames Street, EC3.* Famous for fish and bad language. For many centuries Billingsgate and QUEENHITHE were the main wharfs in the CITY for the mooring of fishing vessels and landing their cargoes. QUEENHITHE was at first the more important but Billingsgate gradually superseded it, masters of ships preferring to use the wharf below LONDON BRIDGE rather than attempt its awkward passage. The first toll regulations for the Market in existence date from 1016. Corn, malt and salt, as well as fish, were landed at least as early as the 13th century; and, by the reign of Elizabeth I, 'victuals and fruit' as well. Billingsgate became 'a free and open market for all sorts of fish' in 1698, when an Act of Parliament was passed to break the monopoly of a group of fishmongers. The foul and abusive language used there became notorious. Stow thought its name was derived from 'some owner of the place, happily named Beling or Biling'. In 1749 HUNGERFORD MARKET opened in competition but did not take much business away from Billingsgate.

Until 1850 the market consisted only of shed buildings, the open space by the dock being 'dotted with low booths and sheds, with a range of wooden houses with a piazza in front on the west, which served the salesmen and fishmongers as shelters, and for the purpose of carrying on their trade.' The porters' bobbing hats, so named after the charge they made to carry the fish

Market trading in 1937, outside the new Billingsgate Market, built to the designs of Sir Horace Jones, the City Architect, in the 1870s.

from the wholesaler to the retailer, are said to have been modelled on the leather helmets worn by Henry V's bowmen at Agincourt. In 1850 the market was rebuilt to the designs of J.B. Bunning. This proved inadequate for the ever-increasing trade and the existing market building, designed by Sir Horace Jones, City Architect to the CORPORATION OF LONDON, was begun in 1874 and opened by the LORD MAYOR in July 1877. It has a practical iron interior, conceived with the needs of the wholesale fish trade in mind, but the exterior is somewhat in the French Renaissance style with mansard roofs and pavilions at either end surmounted by golden dolphins on the weather vanes. Yet the site was never practical and in 1883 it was reported that 'the deficiencies of Billingsgate and its surrounds are a great scandal to London'. It was not until the 1970s, however, that the CITY CORPORATION, owners of the site, decided to close the market here and build a new one on the ISLE OF DOGS. The move to the new 13½ acre site, which was developed at a cost of £11 million, took place at the beginning of 1982. Sir Horace Jones's former market was listed as a Grade II building.

The old Thames-side market closed on 16 January 1982 and the site was sold for £22 million to the London and Edinburgh Investment Trust. One of the few relics taken to the new site was the old bell, which rang to announce the beginning of trading there on 19 January 1982.

Billiter Square *EC3.* Takes its name from the belleyesterers or bellfounders who lived in the area. Voltaire took lodgings here during his exile in England. Disraeli's maternal grandfather, Nathan Basevi, and Cardinal Manning's father, William Manning, Director of the BANK OF ENGLAND, both lived here.

Billiter Street *EC3.* Strype, writing in 1720, said the street used to be 'full of poor and ordinary houses inhabited by beggarly people', the origin of the saying 'a bawdy beggar of Billiter Lane'.

Bills of Mortality Weekly returns of deaths compiled from the 16th century by the Company of Parish Clerks, representing 109 parishes in and near London. Notoriously inaccurate, after 1836 they were superseded by the Registrar General's returns.

Birchin Lane *EC3.* Thought to be derived from an old English word meaning lane of the barbers. In the 16th and 17th centuries it was known for men's ready-made clothes shops. Thomas Babington Macaulay, the historian, lived here as a boy. David Garrick, who had been a wine merchant before becoming an actor, used to visit Tom's Coffee House here to keep in touch with his old friends.

Birdcage Walk *SW1.* Site of James I's aviary which was enlarged by his grandson, Charles II. The walk was created as part of the post-Restoration remodelling of ST JAMES'S PARK. Up to 1828 only the Hereditary Grand Falconer (the Duke of St Albans) and the Royal Family could drive down it. Mrs George Norton, who was accused of adultery with Melbourne, lived here. To the east are the graceful backs of the 18th-century houses of QUEEN ANNE'S GATE. To the west are the WELLINGTON BARRACKS. The bronze, *Reclining Mother and Child*, is by Henry Moore.

Birkbeck Bank *High Holborn.* Built in 1895–6 to the designs of Thomas E. Knightley. A fantastic building decorated with DOULTON's majolica. The lower part had medallions with portraits of artists, engineers and inventors from Raphael, Michelangelo and Leonardo da Vinci to Bessemer, Brunel and James Watt. The building was demolished to make way for National Westminster House by Gordon Charraton of the J. Seymour Harris Partnership (1965–8).

Birkbeck College *Malet Street, WC1.* Founded in 1823 at the Crown and Anchor Tavern in the STRAND by, among others, Dr George Birkbeck, a physician of OLD BROAD STREET. It opened the next year as the London Mechanics' Institution in Dr Lindsay's Chapel in Monkwell Street (*see* MONKWELL SQUARE) and was the first college of education in England to provide for people earning their living during the day; 1,300 students were enrolled in the first year. In 1825 the college moved to Southampton Buildings. At the opening of the lecture theatre Dr Birkbeck and Henry Brougham made speeches on how the education of the working classes would not subvert society. In a wave of enthusiasm other mechanics' institutions opened at SPITALFIELDS, HACKNEY, DEPTFORD, ROTHERHITHE, BERMONDSEY, HAMMERSMITH and CHISWICK. In 1830 women were admitted; and in 1833 the committee considered the propriety of allowing females to use the front entrance. In 1858 the University of London was given a new charter which allowed anybody to sit for a degree. This caused a dramatic rise in the number of students at the college, from 300 in 1858 to 3,000 in 1868. In 1866 it was renamed the Birkbeck Literary and Scientific Institution. In 1883–5 a new college was built in FETTER LANE, and in 1891 it was made part of the City Polytechnic. This was disbanded in 1907 and

An evening lecture in 1877 at the Birkbeck Literary and Scientific Institution, later renamed Birkbeck College.

the institution was renamed Birkbeck College. It was made a school of the UNIVERSITY OF LONDON in 1920 and granted a Royal Charter in 1926. In 1951 it moved to BLOOMSBURY, to new buildings designed by Charles Holden. Past students include Annie Besant, Ramsay MacDonald and Arthur Wing Pinero. C.E.M. Joad was head of the Department of Philosophy in 1930–53. In 1981 there were 2,420 students.

Bishop's Court *WC2.* Takes its name from the Bishops of Chichester whose mansion off CHANCERY LANE (*see* LINCOLN'S INN) came into the possession of Ralph Neville, the then Bishop and Chancellor, in the early 13th century.

Bishop's Gate City gate first built by the Romans. Ermine Street, leading to the north, began here. In the 7th century it was rebuilt by Eorconweald, Bishop of London, and again rebuilt by the Hansa merchants in 1471 and by the CITY authorities in 1731. It was demolished with the other CITY gates in 1760. It stood in the present BISHOPSGATE opposite CAMOMILE STREET.

Bishops of London Melitus, who became the third Archbishop of Canterbury in 619, was consecrated Bishop of London in about 604. He was leader of the second band of missionaries sent by Pope Gregory to reinforce Augustine at Canterbury in 601. After his death in about 624 the see was vacant until the consecration of St Cedda in 664. There have been 112 Bishops since Cedda. (*See also* FULHAM PALACE.)

Bishop's Park *SW6.* Extends along the river front between PUTNEY BRIDGE and FULHAM FOOTBALL CLUB ground with some adjacent areas amounting in all to almost 27 acres. Formerly part of the Manor of FULHAM, the land was controlled by the Lord of the Manor, the BISHOP OF LONDON. It includes Bishop's Meadow, Bishop's Walk, Prior's Bank, Fielder's Meadow and the ornamental gardens in the former moat (dating from an early Danish invasion) around FULHAM PALACE, all of which were successively opened to the public with appropriate local fanfares between 1900 and 1924. Facilities now include a cricket pitch, an ornamental pool, an artificial beach for children, an open-air theatre and a refreshment pavilion.

Bishopsgate *EC2.* Named after BISHOP'S GATE which stood opposite CAMOMILE STREET. In Tudor and Elizabethan times rich merchants had their houses here. Among them were the mansions of Sir Thomas Gresham (demolished 1768), Sir John Crosby (*see* CROSBY HALL) and Sir Paul Pindar (*see* PAUL PINDAR'S HOUSE). Before Shakespeare's time plays were performed at the Bull Inn. One of the actors was Burbage who obtained a licence from Queen Elizabeth to erect a building specially designed for theatrical performances. Bishopsgate is now mostly filled with Victorian office blocks. There are three churches, ST ETHELBURGA, ST HELEN and ST BOTOLPH. At the northern end are DIRTY DICK'S, the BISHOPSGATE INSTITUTE and LIVERPOOL STREET STATION. The 600 ft NATIONAL WESTMINSTER TOWER, designed by R. Seifert and Partners, is the tallest building in London and was officially opened by the Queen in June 1981. No. 5 was built in 1877 to the designs of Thomas Chatfield Clarke. Susanna Annesley, mother of John Wesley, was born at No. 7 Spital Yard, Bishopsgate, in 1669.

Bishopsgate Institute *230 Bishopsgate, EC2.* The Charity Commissioners' scheme for the Bishopsgate Foundation received royal approval in 1891. It consolidated the parochial charities of ST BOTOLPH WITHOUT BISHOPSGATE, the income being devoted to amenities for the public in general and the parishioners of ST BOTOLPH in particular. The Bishopsgate Institute was opened in 1894 in a fine Romanesque building by Harrison Townsend. It contains a reference library mainly devoted to London history, a public lending library and an important collection of London prints and drawings. It also has a lecture hall seating 450 persons and is the headquarters of the London and Middlesex Archaeological Society.

Black Death The name given to a particularly severe epidemic of bubonic plague (*Pasteurella pestis*) which spread disastrously in Europe in the 14th century and raged in England between 1347 and 1350. It reached London by 29 September 1348 and was widespread in the city by 1 November. Though this plague had been endemic in the East for centuries, had often been recorded in London and other parts of England in the early Middle Ages, and was to recur in a number of later occasions, notably in London in 1665 (*see* GREAT PLAGUE), the 14th-century epidemic made its ineradicable mark on history because of its virulence and the resulting heavy loss of life. It was said to have killed half the population of England and an even higher proportion of the population of London where the disease spread rapidly because of the narrow, busy and filthy streets, crowded houses and appalling sanitary conditions.

The onset of the disease was sudden. Its symptoms were inflammatory swellings, haemorrhages, high fever, agonising thirst and delirium. The primitive remedies of the time were unavailing. Death followed rapidly. At the time, the cause of the disease was unknown and often attributed to supernatural causes or seen as the coming of the end of the world, though it was later established (1905) that it was carried by

infected rats and their fleas. It has been suggested that the plague was brought to England from France when the wool trade was re-established after Edward III's return to London in 1347 following his success at the Battle of Crécy and the capture of Calais. The disease raged in all parts of London during the winter of 1348, its impact accentuated by the extremely cold and wet weather. PARLIAMENT, due to meet at WESTMINSTER in January 1349, was prorogued by the King who announced that 'a plague of deadly pestilence had broken out in the said place, and had daily increased in severity so that great fears were entertained for the safety of those coming there at that time'.

The plague reached its height between February and Easter. London BURIAL GROUNDS were soon filled and new ones had to be consecrated, the most important being at SOUTHWARK where, it was said, 200 bodies were buried daily, additional to burials in churchyards elsewhere. Contemporary estimates of plague deaths in London vary from 50,000 to 100,000, but these are mere guesses (*see* POPULATION). However, there is incontestable evidence that the number of deaths was very great. Wills proved before the Court of Hustings increased tenfold in the plague years and show that whole families were wiped out. Guild records indicate that eight wardens of the CUTLERS' COMPANY died in 1349 and all six men appointed wardens of the HATTERS' COMPANY in 1347 were dead by the summer of 1350. In May 1349, in the monastery of WESTMINSTER, the Abbot and 27 monks died and were buried in a mass grave in the cloister. With one exception, all the brothers and sisters of the Hospital of St James died in that same month. The one survivor was appointed Warden of the Hospital in May 1349 but was dead by 1353. There seems to have been no great exodus from the city to avoid the disease as happened in the plague epidemic of 1665, since areas outside London were equally affected.

The Black Death burnt itself out in the early 1350s, but the population losses and chaos it had caused resulted in great social changes in London, not least of which were the attempts to improve hygiene and sanitation as seen in the King's proclamation in 1361 to the MAYOR and SHERIFFS, ordering greater control of the slaughter of cattle within the city to prevent 'the putrid blood running down the streets and the bowels cast into the Thames whence abominable and most filthy stench proceeds causing sickness and many other evils'. It ordered that 'all bulls, oxen, hogs and other gross creatures' be killed at either STRATFORD or KNIGHTSBRIDGE.

Black Friar *174 Queen Street, EC4.* Stands on the site of the BLACKFRIARS MONASTERY. It is the only Art Nouveau public house in London. It is a wedge-shaped building, erected in 1875, the ground floor being remodelled in 1905 by H. Fuller Clark. The outside is covered with mosaics and carved figures by Henry Poole (1903). Inside the bars are decorated with multi-coloured marble, with bronze figures of monks shown about their daily activities. The snack bar under the adjoining railway arch was added by Clark in 1919 and is furnished with sculptures by Poole and A.T. Bradford.

Black Friday Both Friday 6 December 1745, when news reached London of the Young Pretender's arrival in Derby, and Friday 11 May 1866, when the bankers, Overend, Gurney and Co., suspended payment and provoked financial panic in the City, have been thus described.

Black Lion Lane *Hammersmith, W6.* Runs from the riverside, east of HAMMERSMITH TERRACE to King Street, bisected by the GREAT WEST ROAD. It gets its name from the Black Lion Public House, which dates from the 18th century and has a skittle alley. Facing it, the old Black Lion stairs lead down to the river. The road includes a number of attractive small early 19th-century houses and ST PETER'S church.

Blackfriars Barge *see* ROMAN BOATS AND BARGES.

Robert Mylne's Blackfriars Bridge under construction in July 1766. From an engraving by Paul Sandby.

Blackfriars Bridge *Blackfriars–Southwark.* The first bridge was designed by Robert Mylne and built in 1760–9. Constructed with nine semi-elliptical Portland stone arches, it strongly reflected the influence of Piranesi, with whom Mylne had spent much time when in Rome. This bridge, the third to span the THAMES in London, cost £230,000 and was mainly paid for by fines that had accumulated from men refusing the post of SHERIFF. It was officially known as William Pitt Bridge but the public insisted on calling it Blackfriars. In 1780 GORDON RIOTERS broke down the toll gates and stole the money. It was freed from tolls in 1785. It was replaced in 1860–9 by the present structure (designed by Joseph Cubitt and H. Carr) of five wrought-iron arches faced with cast iron on granite piers. Queen Victoria opened it on the same day as HOLBORN VIADUCT. So unpopular was she at the time that she and John Brown, her Scottish servant, who rode behind her in the state carriage, were hissed in the STRAND. The bridge was widened on the west side from 70 ft to 105 ft in 1907–10.

Blackfriars Monastery In 1221 a community of Dominicans was founded in CHANCERY LANE by Hubert de Burgh. In 1250 and 1263 the annual General Chapter, attended by more than 400 friars, met there. In 1278 Robert Fitzwalter gave them BAYNARD'S CASTLE and MONTFICHET TOWER on the river as a site for a larger monastery. Edward I gave them permission to demolish part of the City wall. Under the patronage of the King the monks became rich and influential. Several distinguished men and women are buried here, some of them in monk's habit. Among them were Hubert de Burgh and Katherine Parr's father and mother. In 1294 a quay was built for the

monks and their lands were extended to BRIDEWELL and PUDDLE DOCK. In 1311 PARLIAMENT met here. From 1322 to 1323 the monastery was used as a depository for state records; and in 1343, 1370, 1376 and 1378 as a meeting place of the Court of Chancery. In 1382 the 'Earthquake Council', summoned by the Archbishop of Canterbury to examine Wycliffe's doctrines, met here. During the meeting an earthquake shook the CITY. Wycliff said that although the council had denounced his teachings, God had denounced its judgement with this omen. Henry VI's Privy Council often met here. In 1450 the Black Parliament was summoned here, hence its name. In 1522 the Emperor Charles V stayed at the monastery as a guest, and in 1529 a court sat here to hear the divorce case against Catherine of Aragon. In July the Papal Legate adjourned the court for the summer, precipitating Wolsey's fall. In November the Blackfriars Parliament met to bring a Bill of Attainder against him. The monastery was dissolved in 1538. It was valued at £104 15s 5d. The church plate was taken to the King's Jewel House and the buildings granted to Sir Thomas Cawarden, Keeper of the Royal Tents and Master of the Revels. Most of the monastery was demolished, including the church, but privilege of sanctuary continued. In Mary's reign Cawarden had to provide a new church for the parishioners to worship in. This was ST ANN BLACKFRIARS. In 1556–84 the monks' frater or refectory was used as the BLACKFRIARS PLAYHOUSE and again in 1597–1655 by the second BLACKFRIARS PLAYHOUSE. In the 17th century Blackfriars was a fashionable residential area. Ben Jonson had a house here in about 1607. Shakespeare bought one in IRELAND YARD in 1613. Van Dyck lived here in 1632–41. In 1666 the remaining parts of the monastery and ST ANN's church were destroyed in the GREAT FIRE. In 1735 privileges of sanctuary were ended by an Act of Parliament. In 1890 an arcade from the monastery was discovered and re-erected at SELSDON PARK, Surrey. In 1900 pointed arches, capitals and bases were found and in 1915 a length of wall was uncovered. In 1925 part of the choir, 7 ft long, 3 ft high, and 3 ft 3 ins thick, was discovered and re-erected at St Dominic's Priory, HAVERSTOCK HILL. The only surviving part of the monastery *in situ* is a fragment of wall in IRELAND YARD. The monastery is commemorated by name in Blackfriars Court, Lane and Passage, Friar Street, Church Entry and Blackfriars Road (*see also* PRINTING HOUSE SQUARE).

Blackfriars Playhouse The first Blackfriars theatre was opened in 1578 by Richard Farrant, Master of the Children of the Chapel at Windsor, in the frater of the former monastery. It had previously been used as a house by Lord Cobham and others. Farrant's family lived on the ground floor with the theatre above. As the Court of Common Council still claimed jurisdiction over the area, public playhouses were not allowed, but Farrant evaded this rule by calling it a private theatre where the choir boys could practise 'for the better trayning them to do her Majestie service'. Farrant died in 1580 and, under different management, the theatre lasted only four more years. In 1596 James Burbage bought the building, intending to convert it to a public theatre, but he died before the work was completed. Local residents objected to the opening of a public playhouse and alterations had to be made to convert it to a private theatre. It had three

galleries and could hold 600 to 700 people. On its completion in 1597 Richard Burbage, James's son, leased the theatre to Henry Evans, one of Farrant's successors, and Nathaniel Gyles, Master of the Children of the Chapel Royal. The boy actors were very popular and rivalled the adult companies. Shakespeare (*Hamlet*, Act 2, Scene 2) bitterly refers to 'an eyrie of children, little eyases, that cry out on the top of question, and are most tyrannically clapped for't: these are now the fashion, and so berattle the common stages – so they call them – that many wearing rapiers are afraid of goose-quills, and dare scarce come thither'. In 1608 a performance of *The Conspiracy and Tragedy of Charles, Duke of Byron* gave such offence to the French Ambassador that the company was suppressed. Shortly afterwards, Burbage took six of his fellow actors (including Shakespeare) into partnership to run the theatre. The King's Men acted here and doubtless many of Shakespeare's plays were performed. The theatre was closed by the Puritans in 1642 and demolished in 1655. PLAYHOUSE YARD, EC4 marks the site.

The western Blackfriars Railway Bridge in 1864. It was built over the Thames to take the London, Chatham and Dover Railway.

Blackfriars Railway Bridges *Blackfriars–Southwark*. The western bridge was built in 1862–4 by Joseph Cubitt and F.T. Turner to take the London, Chatham and Dover Railway over the river to a junction with the Metropolitan Railway. A wrought-iron lattice girder bridge, carried on splendid Romanesque cast-iron columns with massive pylons at the abutments bearing the railway's insignia, it was designed in conjunction with Cubitt's new BLACKFRIARS (road) BRIDGE, keeping the piers in the same line. It is now disused.

The eastern bridge was built in 1884–6 by John Wolfe-Barry and H.M. Brunel. Of five wrought-iron arches faced with cast iron, it was originally known as St Paul's Bridge as it carried the Holborn Viaduct Station Co. railway (nominally independent but actually a branch of the bankrupt LCDR) over the river from a station on the north side called St Paul's, subsequently (1937) renamed Blackfriars.

Blackfriars Road *SE1*. A wide main road almost a mile long laid out in 1770–1800 between BLACKFRIARS BRIDGE and St George's Circus. Until 1829 it was known as Great Surrey Street. It ran across ST GEORGE'S FIELDS. In 1671 CHRIST CHURCH was built on part of Paris Garden Manor. In 1731 a chalybeate

spring was discovered near the present IMPERIAL WAR MUSEUM and by 1754 around this had grown the fashionable St George's Spa which was visited by hundreds of people each day. Water was sold in flasks for 4d a gallon. After 1770 its popularity declined and in 1787 the pump room shut. In 1772 the Magdalen Hospital for penitent prostitutes moved here from WHITECHAPEL. It moved on to STREATHAM in 1868, and PEABODY BUILDINGS were built on its site. In 1782 the SURREY THEATRE was opened for dramatic and equestrian entertainments by Charles Dibdin, the song writer, and Charles Hughes, the trick horse rider. In 1783 the Surrey Chapel was built for Rowland Hill, the nonconformist preacher. After his death in 1833 he was buried beneath his pulpit. The chapel was closed in 1881 and in 1910 converted into a boxing arena known as the Ring. This was destroyed by enemy action in the 2nd World War. The rest of the road also suffered badly. Since then many new offices and council flats have been built. The INDIA OFFICE LIBRARY is at No. 197. UAC House by the bridge covers the site of the Rotunda (later the Surrey Institution), a celebrated meeting place for political and other organisations in the 19th century.

Blackfriars Station *Queen Victoria Street, EC1*. Known as St Paul's Station until 1937, it was one of the London, Chatham and Dover Railway's group of CITY stations. It opened in 1886, and was at the northern end of the bridge built in 1864 to carry seven tracks across the THAMES and into the CITY. A red, Italianate building, it was small in size but large in ambition. Cut into its columns were the names of European cities that once were the destination of the LCDR's trains, among them Brindisi, Marseilles and St Petersburg. The District Railway's Blackfriars Station had opened across the road in 1870 and St Paul's progressively lost passengers to the extending UNDERGROUND system. Rebuilt in 1977, it is now largely a through station, with the exception of a few trains in the peak hours.

Blackheath *SE3*. The windswept table land south of GREENWICH PARK. It probably derives its name from Bleak Heath. Lying on the direct road from London to Canterbury and Dover, it has a very long history. Watling Street crossed it (*see* ROMAN ROADS). Both Roman and Saxon remains have been found. The Danes camped there in 1011–13, having captured Alfege, the Archbishop of Canterbury whom they murdered, probably on the site of ST ALFEGE's church, down the escarpment in GREENWICH. Wat Tyler in 1381 assembled his peasants here (*see* PEASANTS' REVOLT). It was here that John Ball preached his revolutionary sermon including the famous lines 'When Adam delved and Eve span, who was then the gentleman?' and was executed for his pains. Jack Cade in 1450 also camped here (*see* CADE'S REBELLION). But the only actual battle that took place was in 1497 when Henry VIII defeated Michael Joseph and his Cornish rebels.

The Heath was also associated with happy events, however. Henry V was welcomed here after the Battle of Agincourt in 1415, though, as Holinshed recorded, 'he seemed little to regard such vaine pompe and shewes as were in triumphant sort devised for his welcoming home . . . . He would not suffer his helmet to be carried before him . . . neither would he suffer any ditties to be made and sung by minstrels of his glorious

The country road from Blackheath to Lewisham in about 1825.

victorie.' In 1540 a gorgeous scene of pageantry was staged when Henry VIII went to meet Anne of Cleves. A more enduring source of joy was the welcome for Charles II when he returned in 1660. As a fine place of assembly, the Heath was used for revivalist meetings in the 18th century by both Wesley and Whitefield after whom 'Wat Tyler's Mound' was renamed 'Whitefield's Mound'. It was also used for military reviews and for recreational purposes. The first golf club in England, the Royal Blackheath, was founded here in the reign of James I in 1608. It amalgamated with Eltham Golf Club in 1923 (*see* GOLF CLUBS). In 1689 the first fair was held, a cattle fair. Evelyn thought it was to 'enrich the new tavern'. Fairs are still held every summer. The BLACKHEATH RUGBY CLUB is the oldest in Britain and its members still play on the nearby Rectory Fields.

The Heath had a sinister reputation for highwaymen, crossed as it is by Shooters Hill Road. Pepys, going to visit his friend Evelyn, passed a gibbet where a bloated body was hanging. Jerry Cruncher, taking the 'recalled to life' message to Mr Lorry in the opening scenes of *A Tale of Two Cities*, caused great alarm to the guard and passengers of the Dover coach. It was not until the development of the area in the late 18th century as a residential suburb that it was considered safe. Around the Heath are some fine old houses including the sweeping crescent of the PARAGON, MORDEN COLLEGE and CHESTERFIELD HOUSE. All Saints' church was built in 1857–67 to the designs of Benjamin Ferrey. The CHURCH OF THE ASCENSION is in Dartmouth Row.

In contrast to the long history of Blackheath, the Village is comparatively modern. When the speculative building began in the late 18th century there were only two cottages, no parish and no parish church until All Saints' was built. The complex of shops, now known as the 'Village', grew up according to the law of supply and demand. They catered, as they mostly do now, for a well-to-do upper middle-class clientele. During the 1840s and 1850s very rapid development took place. In 1849 the opening of the railway brought Blackheath within very easy reach of London. The handsome Victorian houses on Shooters Hill Road and other roads not far from the Village, now inevitably turned into flats, convey an excellent picture of the prosperity and popularity of the growing community.

It was also an intellectual community with a close corporate life of its own. One of its chief interests was in schools. There were a great many, good, bad and indifferent. Salem House, where David Copperfield suffered under Mr Creakle, is supposed to be modelled on one of the worst of them. Few of them lasted for very long. Disraeli went to a school kept by the Revd John Potticary which was in existence from 1805 to 1831. Miss Louisa Browning, an aunt of Robert Browning, kept a school from the 1830s to 1861, and Elizabeth Garrett Anderson, the first woman doctor in England, was one of her pupils. A much longer-lived institution was the Blackheath Proprietary School, which was initiated at a meeting in January 1830. It was owned by the shareholding proprietors who were entitled to send or nominate a boy to the school. From its inception it was a success. It was opened in October 1831. A succession of excellent headmasters, and an intelligent home background for the pupils, contributed to its distinguished record. Opening with an enrolment of 25, by 1864 it had a school list of 275 boys and 15 masters. It remained open until 1907. In 1857 the School for the Sons and Orphans of Missionaries was opened in a new neo-Gothic building in Independence Road. This was a boarding school with some 50 pupils. By 1912 it had outgrown its accommodation, moved to Eltham and changed its name to ELTHAM COLLEGE, still a flourishing day and boarding school for boys and no longer confined to the sons of missionaries. Blackheath High School for Girls, founded in 1880, was and is a notable institution as one of the first schools in the country to offer girls a proper education.

The growing community also needed some place for assembly and entertainment. The Green Man, at the top of Blackheath Hill, now commemorated only in the name of a bus stop, had a large hall which had served as a meeting place for years, but in 1869 Alexandra Hall (now Lloyd's Bank) was opened and proved a good investment to the proprietor. Even that was not enough and in 1870, when the rollerskating mania started, the Rink and the Rink Hall were built, on the site of the present post office. Half the rink was enclosed, thus forming an excellent hall suitable for entertainment, dramatic performances and concerts. Paderewski played there; Mme Adelina Patti sang there; Stanley lectured on his experiences in Africa. It could seat up to 1,000 people. It was not, however, entirely satisfactory for concerts because of the noise from the railway. In 1881 the Conservatoire of Music was founded with 60 pupils. By 1895 it had nearly 1,000 and was able to build its own premises and a concert hall. It still flourishes. The Art School, founded at the same time, had in 1896 300 pupils and its own studios, but was forced to close in 1916. Both these institutions were run on a non-profit-making basis. People were willing to give time and money for the enrichment of the life of the community. The Blackheath Preservation Society, founded in 1938, continues to try to maintain the character of the Village. Distinguished residents of Blackheath have included Sir Arthur Eddington, the mathematician and astrophysicist, at No. 4 Bennett Park in 1906–14; James Glaisher, the astronomer, meteorologist and pioneer of weather forecasting, at No. 20, from about 1863 to the 1890s; Donald McGill, the cartoonist famous for his saucy seaside postcards, at No. 5 Bennett Park, in 1931–9; and Sir James Clark Ross, the polar explorer, at No. 2 Eliot Place. Nathaniel Hawthorne, the American author, stayed at No. 4 Pond Road in 1856; and Charles Gounod, the French composer, stayed at No. 15 Morden Road in 1870.

Blacksmiths' Company *see* CITY LIVERY COMPANIES.

Blackwall *E14*. A district of POPLAR on the north bank of the THAMES between the ISLE OF DOGS and near the mouth of the River LEA. Blackwall Reach was a convenient place for larger vessels to moor and Blackwall was an important point of access to the THAMES, with a direct route by land through POPLAR and RATCLIFF to London which avoided the long detour by river around the ISLE OF DOGS. The Blackwall shipyard, begun in the late 16th century, continued, under various owners, to repair and build ships, particularly for the East India Company in the 17th and 18th centuries, until the remnant was closed by 1980. Part of the yard, the BRUNSWICK DOCK, was incorporated into the EAST INDIA DOCKS, opened in 1806. However, Blackwall was best known as a place of arrival and departure. The Virginia Settlers under Captain John Smith set sail from here in 1606 to found the first permanent colony in America. The East India

Dock Company reconstructed the wharf known as Brunswick Pier to accommodate passenger steamers and shortly afterwards passengers were brought to this point by the London and Blackwall Railway (1840–1926). Brunswick Pier was a popular place from which to view the traffic on the river but was closed after the 2nd World War to make way for the Brunswick Wharf Power Station which now occupies most of Blackwall and the site of the EAST INDIA DOCKS.

Blackwall Tunnel *Blackwall–Greenwich*. The northbound tunnel, 4,410 ft long, was built in 1891–7 by Sir Alexander Binnie. It was the second tunnel under the THAMES. Much of it was driven with a 'Greathead' tunnelling shield and compressed air. The combination of these techniques, used for the first time here, was a major development in underwater tunnelling. The tunnel is lined with cast-iron segments filled with concrete and faced in white-glazed bricks. The internal diameter is 24 ft. The southern tunnel house in red sandstone was designed by Thomas Blashill. The southbound tunnel was built to the designs of Mott, Hay and Anderson in 1960–7. It is 2,870 ft long and has an internal diameter of 27½ ft. The modernistic streamlined ventilation shafts are by the Architects' Department of the GREATER LONDON COUNCIL.

Blackwell Hall *see* BAKEWELL HALL.

Blandford Square *NW1*. Built on the northern point of the PORTMAN ESTATE and named after family property near Blandford Forum in Dorset, it is now nothing but a sawn-off stump of a turning, three of its sides having been amputated to build MARYLEBONE STATION. But from 1860 to 1865 Mary Anne Evans, better known as the novelist George Eliot, lived at No. 16. She later moved northwards to The Priory, 21 North Bank, which also was subsequently demolished to make way for the Great Central Railway.

Blandford Street *W1*. Lies on the PORTMAN ESTATE off BAKER STREET and is named after the Portmans' seat at Bryanston near Blandford Forum in Dorset. No. 48, formerly No. 2, was the premises of George Piebau, the bookbinder, who employed the scientist Michael Faraday in his penniless boyhood.

Blenheim Road *NW8*. A unit in the original 1830s development of the HARROW SCHOOL Estate – more than a century after his death, the victories of the Duke of Marlborough were still worth commemorating. It is one of 44 streets or roads in London so named. Sir Charles Santley, the singer, once lived at No. 13. On the northern side stands a row of small, neat, pretty detached early 19th-century cottages. The western half of the street becomes Blenheim Terrace, with a good parade of shops.

Blenheim Street *W1*. On the Conduit Mead Estate (*see* CONDUIT STREET) is a short side street connecting NEW BOND STREET with WOODSTOCK STREET. Its name commemorates the Duke of Marlborough's great victory of 1704.

Blitz The word is from the German *Blitzkrieg*, meaning 'lightning war'. The heavy bombing of London began on 7 September 1940. Although air attacks

A suburban street after a 2nd World War air raid. This particular bomb demolished two houses and seriously damaged many others.

had been expected by the Government, the civil defence organisations were not sufficiently prepared. Gas attacks and massive daylight raids had been anticipated. It was presumed that mass burials in quicklime would be necessary; but the need for vast shelters for use night after night, and for many months, was not envisaged. Before September 1940 the German air force's targets had been mostly the Royal Air Force bases in England; but the bombing of London had been specifically ordered by Hitler as a revenge and reprisal for the bombing of German cities by the Royal Air Force.

Immediately before the war, British scientists had hurriedly prepared for service a chain of rudimentary radar stations. By the summer of 1939 there were 18 stations able to detect aircraft approaching at a medium or high level for a distance of about 100 miles. They were then known as Radio Direction Finding Stations. The air-raid warning signal, the 'alert', was a two-minute siren wail, rising and falling in pitch. In London the alarm was taken up by one BOROUGH after another as the German bombers approached. The 'all clear' was a steady blast on the siren. The course of the THAMES was a great help to the German navigators. Londoners came to expect particularly heavy raids during full-moon periods, and these were known as 'bombers' moons'. Once over the target area, the raiders dropped heavy high-explosive bombs and small but effective incendiary bombs. In later weeks land-mines also caused great devastation. People could do little to protect themselves against 550 lb high-explosive bombs except run for cover, but incendiaries could be extinguished, if discovered soon enough, by completely covering them with sand or a shovelful of earth. Putting them in water, however, caused an immediate explosion. Later in the offensive the incendiaries were dropped in clusters known as 'baskets'.

In the beginning the British night-fighters were not very effective. They also made aiming more difficult for the anti-aircraft gunners. The searchlights assisted the defence by illuminating the bombers and by dazzling the enemy bomb aimers. But once the bomber was caught in the searchlight, if the fighters were at a higher altitude, the raider was invisible to them. Barrage balloons were controlled by RAF Balloon Command operating on sites in parks and open spaces. The

balloons were 62 ft long and 25 ft in diameter at their widest part, with a hydrogen capacity of 19,000 cu ft. They successfully discouraged dive-bombing and low-level attacks. The anti-aircraft fire was inaccurate but the sound it made gave some comfort and encouragement to the citizens of London, although one BOROUGH asked for the removal of the batteries as the thunderous noise was cracking the lavatory pans of the council houses.

For 57 nights London was bombed every night and sometimes during the day. A total of 18,800 tons of high explosive was dropped in night attacks between 7 September 1940 and 11 May 1941. Some of the boroughs most seriously affected were HOLBORN, the CITY, WESTMINSTER, SHOREDITCH, SOUTHWARK and STEPNEY. On 12 September an unexploded bomb buried itself under ST PAUL'S CATHEDRAL close to the south-west tower, threatening the foundations. After three days it was finally extricated and driven away on a lorry to be exploded in HACKNEY MARSHES where it made a crater 100 ft in diameter. Throughout every attack on London the cathedral survived as a result of vigilant fire watching, although all the buildings in its neighbouring areas were flattened one after another.

BUCKINGHAM PALACE was deliberately attacked by a lone German raider on the morning of 13 September. On the night of 15–16 October 410 bombers dropped 538 tons of high explosive killing over 400 civilians with more than 900 seriously injured. At least 900 fires were reported and practically all rail transport was brought to a standstill. Up to 13 November an average of 160 bombers dropped approximately 200 tons of high explosive and 182 canisters of incendiaries nightly.

Throughout the Blitz the PORT OF LONDON was never completely out of action nor was the general chaos totally uncontrollable. During one night the fires in Quebec Yard and SURREY COMMERCIAL DOCKS were considered by the LONDON FIRE BRIGADE to be 40 times bigger than the inferno which had destroyed the BARBICAN in 1938. In peace time 1,850 fire pumps were sufficient to fight outbreaks of fire in the whole of Great Britain. By the end of December 1940 there were 2,000 pumps in the CITY alone, and the LONDON FIRE BRIGADE had 20,000 auxiliary firemen as well as 2,000 regulars. Fire-watching – reporting fires and extinguishing incendiaries – became better organised and was worked on a rota system in private premises and public buildings.

The Government had an evacuation scheme for school children from London into the country, but parents were not compelled to send their children away. Very few private firms or organisations removed their headquarters from London unless their premises were bombed out. The raids caused very little absenteeism. Shortly after returning from work many men and women then reported for duty as air-raid wardens, fire-watchers or ambulance drivers. Several train services were out of action for months at a time. Boats were operated on the THAMES because central London and the Boroughs south of the river had practically no bus services due to unexploded bombs and other damage causing roads to be sealed off.

Although rationed, food was relatively plentiful, but when GAS and ELECTRICITY supplies were disrupted cooking it became a problem. Householders shared their facilities or improvised field-kitchens in the streets and gardens, burning bomb-damaged furniture

People being entertained by a concert party while sheltering from a 2nd World War air raid in Aldwych underground station.

and woodwork. One day water spurted from the gas stoves of PIMLICO!

For some people every night for months was spent in their Anderson shelters – two walls of corrugated steel sunk into the ground with a mound of earth on top. These shelters (named after the then Home Secretary, Sir John Anderson) were cheap and could protect six people against practically anything except a direct hit. However, only a quarter of the population had a garden to put an Anderson shelter in and an acute shortage of steel stopped their production. The Government erected brick and concrete communal shelters designed to protect about 50 people. They were used by the residents of one street or block of flats. They were badly built, badly ventilated, cold, dark and damp with chemical lavatories which stank. They were also unpopular as they were known to collapse if a bomb fell nearby. The hospitals with underground vaults turned them into casualty wards and sleeping quarters for nurses. By November 1941 most Londoners were not using specially erected shelters. Some slept under the stairs, in cupboards or in the basement of their own homes. Those who could left the city every night for the country. A large area of caves in the hills of Chislehurst, Kent, became a temporary home for hundreds of people.

Official policy rejected the use of the UNDERGROUND stations as shelters, but as it was necessary only to buy a platform ticket to gain entry, hundreds of people camped on the stations every night for weeks. The deepest tube stations were more or less invulnerable but a high explosive bomb could penetrate at least 50 ft through solid ground. The tubes were dry and well lit and the raids inaudible: 79 stations in Greater London became shelters with 177,000 people using

them. Three disused stations were reopened. The then incomplete LIVERPOOL STREET extension, which ran under part of the EAST END, accommodated 10,000 shelterers. As the line was not being used for transport and many of the people were homeless, some stayed down for many weeks for most of the time. On 17 September 1940 a bomb scored a direct hit on the MARBLE ARCH station which was filled with shelterers. The explosion ripped the tiles from the walls and these became deadly projectiles adding greatly to the number of casualties. At BALHAM on 14 October 600 people were involved when a bomb smashed through the water mains, electric cables, gas conduits and sewers. Water and rubble cascaded on to the platform, causing a river 3 ft deep. There was a similar tragedy at BANK station in January 1941 when over 100 people were killed. Shelterers felt a certain safety in the tubes, but the lack of adequate sanitation and washing facilities, overcrowding and insufficient ventilation made the air appalling. Rats, fleas and lice flourished. The Government was concerned that typhoid would become a hazard.

The steel-framed buildings in the WEST END provided protection and in some cases comfort. In the basement of the DORCHESTER HOTEL, the Turkish baths were converted to accommodate guests, with rows of beds, some with reservation signs on them in the names of the more fortunate and VIPs. The underground banqueting hall at the SAVOY HOTEL was divided into one part for diners and the other for a dormitory – with a special section for notorious snorers. For several days at the RITZ HOTEL the cooking was done on two up-turned electric radiators. The first week of the Blitz closed the theatres, the WINDMILL being the first to reopen after only ten days. In

PARLIAMENT on 8 October, Churchill turned his wit on the German air force. Announcing that casualities were less than one-tenth of those expected, he said, 'Statisticians may amuse themselves by calculating that after making allowances for the law of diminishing returns, through the same house being struck twice or three times over, it would take ten years at the present rate for half the houses of London to be demolished. And after that, of course, progress would be much slower.'

In March 1941 a nightclub which had been advertised as the safest in town received a direct hit. It was the CAFÉ DE PARIS whose mirror-covered walls, copied from the ballroom of the *Titanic*, were shattered by bomb blast and caused terrible casualties. The club had been crowded with officers on leave; one woman had an injured leg washed with champagne, while looters stole jewellery from the dead and wounded.

Bomb blasts sometimes had extremely odd effects: a girl in POPLAR was taking a bath when her house was hit. The bath was blown upside down with the girl still in it, thus providing her with shelter from the tons of brick rubble under which she was buried. The rescuers found a beautiful, naked, uninjured but acutely embarrassed young lady. Perhaps more unfortunate was the woman in MAYFAIR who was hurled into the street, still in her bath. A man blown out of his bedroom risked his life going back into the house for a clothes brush.

In all over 15,000 people were killed and more than 3,500,000 houses damaged or destroyed. Although the raids caused enormous suffering and hardship, they helped to cement national unity.

Blomfield Street *EC2*. Renamed after Charles James Blomfield, Bishop of London in 1828–57, who had been rector of ST BOTOLPH WITHOUT BISHOPSGATE earlier in his career. Finsbury House at No. 23, formerly the London Mission House, was designed by E.C. Robins and built in 1877.

Bloody Sunday The dispersal by police and soldiers of a Socialist demonstration in TRAFALGAR SQUARE, which led to two deaths in the crowd, took place on Sunday 13 November 1887.

Bloomfield Terrace *SW1*. Built in the early 19th century, it takes its name from Charles James Blomfield (*sic*) who became Bishop of London in 1828, hence BLOMFIELD STREET which is near ST BOTOLPH WITHOUT BISHOPSGATE where he was once rector and Blomfield Crescent, Road and Villas on what was formerly the see of London's estate in PADDINGTON. Blomfield consecrated the nearby church of ST BARNABAS in 1850.

Bloomsbury Has no definite boundaries, but is generally considered to be the area bounded by TOTTENHAM COURT ROAD, EUSTON ROAD, GRAY'S INN ROAD, and on the south, NEW OXFORD STREET, BLOOMSBURY WAY and THEOBALDS ROAD. TOTTENHAM COURT ROAD and GRAY'S INN ROAD follow the lines of ancient routes into London. EUSTON ROAD was originally the New Road built to drive cattle from the west to SMITHFIELD avoiding OXFORD STREET and HOLBORN. THEOBALDS ROAD was part of the route along which James I rode to his favourite hunting ground in Hertfordshire. NEW OXFORD STREET was a continuation of OXFORD STREET opened in 1847 to clean up a notorious slum rookery and to enable traffic to pass west from HIGH HOLBORN without winding round ST GILES HIGH STREET.

Part of Bloomsbury is recorded in *Domesday Book* as having vineyards and 'wood for 100 pigs'. The name derives from Blemondisberi, meaning the 'bury' or manor of Blemond, after William Blemond, who acquired it in the early 13th century. His son dug Blemond's Dyke on the southern border which was still traceable in the 19th century as a common sewer.

The manor came into the hands of Edward III at the end of the 14th century and he gave it to the Carthusian monks of the London CHARTERHOUSE. At the DISSOLUTION OF THE MONASTERIES in the 16th century the land was seized again by the Crown and granted to Thomas Wriothesley. The latter, much in the royal favour, was made Lord Chancellor in 1545 and Earl of Southampton in 1547. His descendant, the 4th Earl of Southampton, moved to a manor house in Bloomsbury early in the 17th century. It must have been called SOUTHAMPTON HOUSE before the Civil War, since in 1643 there is a record of the COURT OF COMMON COUNCIL ordering 'two batteries and a breastwork at Southampton House'. In 1657 the Earl pulled down the old manor house and began rebuilding 'at the bottom of the Long Field'. His new house was completed in 1660 and the Earl then laid out a square south of the house and called it Southampton Square (now BLOOMSBURY SQUARE). In 1665 John Evelyn came to dinner and described it as 'a noble square or Piazza – a little towne'. Though not the first London square, it was the first to be so named, and was the beginning of the development of an area characterised by squares to this day. Other great houses were soon built nearby, notably Montague House in 1678 (now the BRITISH MUSEUM) and Thanet House, now Nos 99–106 GREAT RUSSELL STREET.

In the late 17th century the powerful Russell family, already established in COVENT GARDEN, acquired an interest when Rachel, Lady Vaughan, the widowed daughter of the Earl of Southampton and heiress to Bloomsbury, married William Lord Russell, second son of the 5th Earl of Bedford, who became heir to the Russell fortune when his elder brother died in 1678. However, in 1683 William was involved in the Rye House Plot, a conspiracy to kill Charles II and secure a Protestant succession. Despite a spirited defence by Rachel, he was executed in LINCOLN'S INN FIELDS. The family was reinstated in 1694 when William's father, the 5th Earl of Bedford, was created Duke of Bedford and Marquess of Tavistock in recognition of his son's sacrifice to the Protestant cause. Rachel and William's son inherited the Southampton Estates and the Russell fortune and became the 2nd Duke of Bedford.

Both the 3rd and 4th Dukes married granddaughters of Sarah Churchill, 1st Duchess of Marlborough, who thought Southampton House 'the handsomest, the most agreeable and the best turned out' she had ever seen, and who was influential in getting the name changed to Bedford House. Bloomsbury was growing and becoming fashionable, though still close to the countryside. 'Healthful Great Russell Street' was built to link Bedford House and the square with TOTTENHAM COURT ROAD. The poet Gray, living in a terrace of houses in SOUTHAMPTON ROW in 1759, wrote that it was 'so rus-in-urbish I believe I shall stay here'.

Fanny Burney, living in QUEEN SQUARE in 1771, wrote that they had a beautiful view of the verdant hills of HAMPSTEAD and HIGHGATE.

The 4th Duke of Bedford, who was fond of Bath, would have liked to build a circus, but he died in 1771 and his second wife, Gertrude Leveson Gower, controlled the estate while her son was a minor. She continued development, building BEDFORD SQUARE and GOWER STREET. When he came of age, the 5th Duke was not interested in living in Bloomsbury and in 1800 BEDFORD HOUSE was demolished and a terrace of houses built on the site by James Burton. Under the 6th Duke the estate was developed north and east, principally by James Burton and Thomas Cubitt through building leases. The result was an irregular, but controlled and planned series of handsome squares and roads, which became a favourite area for writers, painters and musicians, as well as the lawyers who found it very convenient for the INNS OF COURT. The squares had a life of their own, with a surrounding system of minor streets, mews and smaller houses which were used for service quarters. They were closed by gates until these were abolished by Act of Parliament in 1893.

During this century Bloomsbury became less fashionable as institutions began to take over. The trend had already begun in 1755 when the BRITISH MUSEUM was started on the site of MONTAGU HOUSE. In 1866 a resident described it as 'a very unfashionable area, though very respectable'. But it was still a home for lawyers, scholars, artists and writers – notable the BLOOMSBURY GROUP. Now it is dominated by the UNIVERSITY OF LONDON and numerous hospitals and learned institutions as well as by the BRITISH MUSEUM. Modern development has obliterated a large number of the Georgian buildings, but many still remain.

Bloomsbury Central Baptist Church *Shaftesbury Avenue, WC2.* Leading church of the English Baptist movement designed by John Gibson and built in 1845–8. The interior was rebuilt by J.B. Shearer Associates in 1964.

Bloomsbury Group An association of friends, mostly writers and artists, active in the earlier years of the 20th century, who subscribed to the philosopher G.E. Moore's belief that 'by far the most valuable things . . . are . . . the pleasures of human intercourse and the enjoyment of beautiful objects . . . It is they . . . that form the rational ultimate end of social progress.' Among the best known of the group, several of whom lived in BLOOMSBURY, were Vanessa and Clive Bell, David Garnett, E.M. Forster, Roger Fry, Duncan Grant, Lytton Strachey, John Maynard Keynes and Virginia and Leonard Woolf.

Bloomsbury Place *WC1.* Built soon after the completion of BLOOMSBURY SQUARE to give its residents access to SOUTHAMPTON ROW. Sir Hans Sloane lived at No. 4 in 1695–1742.

Bloomsbury Square *WC1.* Laid out south of his house in the early 1660s for Thomas Wriothesley, 4th Earl of Southampton (*see* BLOOMSBURY). Around it were smaller houses for servants, stables and a market, now Barter Street, south-west of the square with bookshops and cabinet makers. The land round the square was let off in plots of varying size under building leases

which stipulated that the lessee built houses of appropriate size and character. The 'little Towne' became one of the most sought-after suburbs of London and in its early days was so fashionable that foreign princes were carried to see it as one of the wonders of England.

The house formerly known as SOUTHAMPTON HOUSE was renamed BEDFORD HOUSE in 1734. In 1765 the SPITALFIELDS weavers attacked the house because the Duke of Bedford had criticised a bill putting additional duties on imported silks. The house was demolished in 1800 when the 5th Duke of Bedford obtained two Acts of Parliament for developing his estate. It was replaced with terraced houses by James Burton. These still survive. The gardens were laid out in 1800 by Humphry Repton and in 1816 the statue of Charles James Fox, by Westmacott, was erected facing north up BEDFORD PLACE (*see* STATUES). Apart from James Burton's terrace on the north, none of the original houses remains. In 1928 the east side was filled by the Liverpool and Victoria Friendly Society's offices designed by W. Long. CAMDEN Council built a car park under the gardens in 1971–3. On the south side No. 45 was the Earls of Chesterfield's family home and has a plaque, decorated with cherubs, to the 2nd and 4th Earls. No. 2, in what Pevsner dismissed as 'debased vaguely Northern Renaissance style', was the COLLEGE OF PRECEPTORS. They moved out in 1971 and it is now a training centre run by the chartered accountants Coopers and Lybrand. On the west at No. 5 Dr Radcliffe, physician to William III, Queen Mary and Queen Anne, lived in 1704–14. Isaac D'Israeli, author and father of Benjamin, lived at No. 6 from 1817 to 1829. Robert Willan, the dermatologist, lived at No. 10. No. 16–17 is an early 18th-century building, later remodelled by Nash. It was the home of the PHARMACEUTICAL SOCIETY, whose name is writ in large letters under the cornice, but was compulsorily purchased in 1976 when the area fell under the shadow of the proposed development of the BRITISH LIBRARY. Lord Chief Justice Mansfield's house on the east side was sacked and burnt by GORDON RIOTERS in 1780. Two of the ringleaders, Charles King and John Gray, were hanged outside. Also on the east side lived Herbert Spencer, the philosopher, in 1862–4; Sir Edwin Lutyens, the architect, in 1898–1914; and Lord Chief Justice Ellenborough in 1803. In Bloomsbury Place in the north-east corner of the square there is a BLUE PLAQUE to Sir Hans Sloane, physician and benefactor of the BRITISH MUSEUM. Charles Sedley, the dramatist, had a house in the square in 1691–1701; as did Richard Steele, the author, in 1712–15; and Mark Akenside, the poet, in 1750–9.

Bloomsbury Street *WC1.* Extends from NEW OXFORD STREET to BEDFORD SQUARE. The large Edwardian Ivanhoe Hotel (250 bedrooms) is at No. 9. Thames and Hudson, the publishers, are at Nos 30–34. Previously known as Charlotte Street, the street was given its present name in 1894.

Bloomsbury Way *WC1.* Extends from 28 NEW OXFORD STREET to 4A BLOOMSBURY SQUARE. ST GEORGE'S church is on the north-west side. The late Victorian Kingsley Hotel (169 bedrooms) is beside it. Sidgwick and Jackson, the publishers, are at No. 1 Tavistock Chambers. R. Seifert and Partners, the architects, are at Chesterfield House.

Blue Ball Yard *SW1*. Approached through a narrow archway on the west side of ST JAMES'S STREET, the coach houses here, now used as garages, were built in 1741–2.

Blue Coat School *see* CHRIST'S HOSPITAL.

Blue Plaques Placed by the GREATER LONDON COUNCIL to indicate houses, or the sites of houses, where distinguished people lived. The idea was proposed by William Ewart, the reformer; and the ROYAL SOCIETY OF ARTS originally administered the scheme. The first plaque was placed in 1867 on the house where Lord Byron was born, in Holles Street, WESTMINSTER. Shortly after the formation of the LONDON COUNTY COUNCIL in 1888, the Earl of Rosebery, its first chairman, suggested that responsibility for the placing of the plaques should pass to the Council. The scheme is now administered by the Historic Buildings Division of the GREATER LONDON COUNCIL. The first plaques were not of uniform design. The most common type, however, was circular and made of chocolate-brown terracotta.

There are now over 350 authorised Blue Plaques in London. Inevitably, there is also a fair number of unofficial plaques. For instance, in SOUTH STREET, MAYFAIR, a circular blue plaque, lacking only the GLC imprint, commemorates the residence of Skittles, 'the last Victorian courtesan'. To qualify for a genuine plaque, a candidate must have been dead for at least 20 years and have been born more than 100 years ago. The person should be known to the 'well-informed passer-by' and his or her work 'deserve recognition'. He or she should have made some important positive contribution to human welfare or happiness.

Bluecoat School *Caxton Street, SW1*. Founded in about 1688 as a charity for 50 poor boys of the parish of ST MARGARET, WESTMINSTER. They were taught to 'read, write, cast accounts and the catechism'. The school's first buildings were in Duck Lane. In 1709 William Greene, owner of the Stag BREWERY, financed the building of the existing school house on land rented from the Dean and Chapter of WESTMINSTER ABBEY, and 20 girls were admitted in 1713. In 1869 the Dean and Chapter gave the governors the freehold of the school on condition that they could nominate two poor girls and two poor boys from time to time. The girls' section was closed in about 1876; and in 1898 the school was taken over by the Vestry of ST MARGARET, WESTMINSTER, and made part of Christchurch National Schools. The building was used as a school until 1939. During the 2nd World War it was an army store and afterwards a meeting place for guides and youth clubs. In 1954 it was bought by the NATIONAL TRUST. There is a statue of a charity boy in his blue coat over the doorway.

Board of Green Cloth An ancient institution of the Royal Household, presided over in the past by the Lord Steward, now by the Master of the Household. It is said to take its name from the green cloth which covered the table at which its business is conducted. Its jurisdiction is now limited to the licensing of certain premises within what was known as the VERGE OF THE COURT. Upon his appointment the Master of the Household is made a Justice of the Peace for this purpose. There are five other members of the Board, one the Chief Metropolitan Magistrate. The Board meets in February each year.

Boar's Head Tavern *Great Eastcheap*. One of the largest and most famous of the 16th-century taverns in EASTCHEAP. Shakespeare mentions it; plays were performed in it. It was destroyed in the GREAT FIRE together with its neighbours, the Chicken, the Plough and the Three Kings. It was rebuilt after the Fire in brick. A stone carved with the head of a boar and the date, 1668, was inset above the door. Vine branches elaborately carved in wood, surmounted with small figures of Falstaff, were set each side of the door. Boswell mentioned the inn to Johnson as the 'very tavern where Falstaff and his joyous companions met' and added that the members of a club met here and assumed Shakespeare's characters. Goldsmith wrote his *Reverie* in the tavern. William Pitt and William Wilberforce once spent a convivial evening here in a party in memory of Shakespeare. It was demolished, no longer a tavern but a gunsmith's shop, to make way for the approaches to LONDON BRIDGE in 1831.

Bollo *Boller Brook*, as it was called in 1826, rose in WEST ACTON, crossed under Bull Hollow Bridge – from which it probably takes its name – and followed the line of Bollo Lane, then running eastwards to TURNHAM GREEN to join the other two source streams of STAMFORD BROOK.

Bolsover Street *W1*. Originally called Norton Street, it lies on the north-eastern quarter of the PORTLAND ESTATE. Named after a Derbyshire estate of the Cavendish family, it was laid out in the 1720s–50s. The original houses have been replaced by flats and offices. The artist Richard Wilson lived at No. 24, and David Wilkie had lodgings at No. 8 when he was struggling to establish himself as a painter. B.R. Haydon tells in his diary of how he broke the good news of the favourable reception of Wilkie's *Village Politicians* in the ROYAL ACADEMY exhibition of 1806: 'We huzzaed and, taking hands, danced round the table till we were tired.' The ROYAL NATIONAL ORTHOPAEDIC HOSPITAL, founded in 1838, occupies Nos 54–57.

Bolt Court *EC4*. Small court off Fleet Street probably named after a vanished inn, the Bolt-in-Tun. Dr Johnson lived at No. 8 between 1776 and 1784 when he died here. 'Behind the house was a garden, which he took delight in watering,' Sir John Hawkins wrote, '. . . and the whole of the two-pair-stairs floor was made a repository for his books, one of the rooms thereon being his study.' It was not a large house but he took in those 'whole nests of people', as Mrs Thrale described them, who depended upon his charity. Here he wrote his masterpiece, *The Lives of the Poets*. The house was burned down in 1819. William Cobbett occupied No. 11 in 1802 when publishing the first numbers of his *Political Register* and *The Parliamentary Debates* which were later taken over by his printer, Luke Hansard.

Bolton Gardens *SW5*. Take their name from William Bolton whose descendants owned land here for generations. The poet, journalist and humanist Sir Edwin Arnold lived at No. 31 where he died in 1904. Sir William Orpen, the painter, lived at No. 8 South Bolton Gardens.

Bolton Street *W1.* Extending from PICCADILLY to CURZON STREET, it takes its name from the Duke of Bolton, for whom in 1696 sewer pipes were being laid to serve his property nearby. In 1708 this was the westernmost street in London. Most of the buildings are now modern blocks of offices or flats, but Nos 15–20 on the east side form a good basically 18th-century range. Madame D'Arblay (formerly Fanny Burney) lived at No. 11 and Henry James at No. 3.

The Boltons *SW10.* Probably takes its name from the Bolton family who owned adjacent land in the early 19th century. Built in the decade 1850–60 to plans by George Godwin, the two facing crescents have always been select. Some of its palatial mansions are now occupied by organisations, but private residents remain and have included Jenny Lind and, more recently, Douglas Fairbanks Jnr. St Mary's, West Brompton, finely set in the central garden and also designed by Godwin, was consecrated on 22 October 1850. BOUSFIELD PRIMARY SCHOOL won an architectural award for its London County Council architects, Chamberlin, Powell and Bon, in 1956. Its site includes the former home of the author Beatrix Potter, creator of Peter Rabbit.

Bon Marché *442–444 Brixton Road.* The first shop in England to be purpose-built as a department store. It was established in 1877 by a printer from TOOTING, James Smith, who had won a great deal of money the year before at Newmarket races. He named his emporium after the famous Bon Marché in Paris. His sales staff lived in a large block he built especially for them. Rosebery Smith, as he now called himself, was not successful as a shopkeeper and went bankrupt. The store, however, enjoyed success under subsequent owners, but declined after the 2nd World War and, after a short time as a market known as Brixton Fair, it was closed.

Bond Court *Walbrook, EC4.* Named after William Bond, Alderman of Walbrook Ward in 1649.

Bond Street *W1.* The only street to extend across the full depth of MAYFAIR from PICCADILLY to OXFORD STREET. It was built in two stages. Old Bond Street, as the southern end between PICCADILLY and BURLINGTON GARDENS is now known, formed part of Albemarle Ground, where the principal speculator in 1684 was Sir Thomas Bond (*see* ALBEMARLE STREET). Almost all the rest of the street, extending northward to OXFORD STREET and now known as New Bond Street, was situated on the CORPORATION OF THE CITY OF LONDON's Conduit Mead Estate (*see* CONDUIT STREET). There was some building here between BURLINGTON GARDENS and CLIFFORD STREET soon after 1700, but the main northward thrust had to wait until the great building boom of the early 1720s.

As early as 1736 it was already being said that 'there is nothing in the whole prodigious length of the two Bond Streets . . . that has anything worth our attention', and Bond Street has never been noted for its architectural distinction. A few unremarkable 18th-century houses do survive, notably at ASPREY's, Nos 165–169 New Bond Street, where the ground floor now has splendid Victorian shop-fronts; and it was as a luxury shopping street that the whole of Bond

Bond Street fashionables caricatured by Gillray in his 'High Change in Bond Street–ou–La Politesse du Grande Monde', 1796.

Street very quickly became famous. Shop-gazing being as popular in Georgian times as now, Bond Street also became a fashionable promenade for the *beau monde*, and many shopkeepers let off part of their upper rooms as lodgings. Distinguished lodgers here, often for only very short stays, have included James Thomson, author of the words of 'Rule Britannia' (who put up at a milliner's); Dean Swift (1727); George Selwyn (1751); Edward Gibbon (1758); William Pitt the Elder, 1st Earl of Chatham (1766); Laurence Sterne, who died here in 1768; James Boswell (1769), who first met his hero, General Paoli, here; Sir Thomas Lawrence (1791–4); and Admiral Nelson at Nos 147 and 103 New Bond Street in 1797–8, followed in about 1811–13 (in a different house) by Lady Hamilton, shortly before her imprisonment for debt.

During a promenade here in Bond Street in its late 18th-century heyday, Charles James Fox wagered with the Prince of Wales as to how many cats would be seen on either side of the street; and choosing the sunny side, won his bet with a tally of thirteen to none. Despite a considerable amount of piecemeal rebuilding during the last 100 years, Bond Street has never lost its fashionable pre-eminence as a shopping centre; but visually it is totally different from its counterparts in the broad boulevards of Paris. Throughout most of its length it is still narrow, and many of the shops are still little more than 20ft wide. But they include such world-famous names in the field of art as Ackermann's, established in PALL MALL in 1783, and Agnew's, established in 1817 (at Nos 4 and 43 Old Bond Street respectively); as well as Wildenstein's, founded in Paris in 1875 and opened in London in 1933; the Fine Art Society, established in 1876 by Longman, the publisher, with an Art Nouveau shop front designed by E. Godwin, and SOTHEBY's (at Nos 147, 148 and 34–35 New Bond Street respectively). Harmers of London, the stamp auctioneers founded by H.R. Harmer in 1918, are at No. 41 New Bond Street. Saint Laurent (Rive Gauche), the 'gentlemen's fashion house', are at Nos 72 and 113. Also in New Bond Street are Cartier Ltd, established in Burlington Street in 1902 (Nos 175–176); Chappell and Co., established as music publishers in 1811 (No. 50); FENWICK's department store (No. 63), founded in Newcastle in 1882 and opened in Bond Street in 1891; MAPPIN AND WEBB, the goldsmiths (No. 6); RUSSELL AND BROMLEY, the boot and shoe retailers (Nos 24–25); Tessier Ltd, the jewellers and silversmiths founded by Lewis de Tessier in 1811 and established here in 1856 (No. 26); Rowe's of Bond Street, the children's outfitters, founded in 1913, at No. 170; S.J. Phillips Ltd, the jewellers and dealers in antique plate founded in 1869 (No. 139); the White House Ltd, the linen suppliers established in 1906 (No. 51); Cameo Corner Ltd, the antique jewellers, founded in 1908 at No. 1 OXFORD STREET and later at No. 26 MUSEUM STREET where Queen Mary had a special seat reserved for her (No. 22); Bentley and Co. Ltd, the jewellers, at No. 65 in a shop where there has been a jewellers' business for more than 100 years; and Wallace Heaton, the photographic equipment retailers at No. 119 from 1919 to 1936 (No. 127). In Old Bond Street are H.M. Rayne Ltd, the shoemakers founded in 1889, at No. 16; Benson and Hedges Ltd, the tobacconists founded in the 1860s and at their present address since 1873, at No. 13; Yardley of London Ltd, founded in 1801, at No. 33; Sac Frères, the amber specialists, a family business since 1910, at No. 45; Truefitt and Hill, the gentlemen's hairdressers established in 1805, at No. 23; Carrington and Co. Ltd, the jewellers patronised by Queen Victoria and Queen Alexandra (whose crown for Edward VII's coronation was made by the firm), at No. 25; and at No. 28 Charbonnel et Walker, the chocolate manufacturers whose business was established in 1874 by Mlle Charbonnel – she was befriended by the Prince of Wales, later Edward VII, and her chocolates were the delight of Ellen Terry. The Time-Life Building by Michael Rosenauer (1952–3) is at Nos 153–157 – the bronze on the terrace, *Draped Reclining Figure* (1953), is by Henry Moore. Opposite on the east side is the WESTBURY HOTEL. The ancient Egyptian sculpture in igneous rock (*c*.1600 BC) over the entrance to SOTHEBY's, the oldest outdoor sculpture in London, was erected here in 1917.

Bonham's *Montpelier Galleries, Montpelier Street, SW1 and New Chelsea Galleries, 65–69 Lots Road, SW10.* Fine art auctioneers founded in 1793 by William Charles Bonham and George Jones who opened a small gallery in LEICESTER SQUARE, moving later to OXFORD STREET, then 1930 to NEW BURLINGTON STREET and in 1956 to their present address.

Boodle's Club *28 St James's Street, SW1.* A smart social and non-political club founded in 1762 by William Almack and named after its first manager. The club originally met at ALMACK's in PALL MALL. In 1783 it moved to its present elegant club house which was designed by John Crunden in 1775 for the Savoir Vivre Club. Its members were mostly country gentlemen but also included Edward Gibbon and William Wilberforce. Beau Brummell and the Duke of Wellington were members too. It acquired an early reputation for high gambling and good food. The two principal rooms were redecorated in 1821–4 by John B. Papworth who also designed the front bay-window. In the piazza are Henry Moore's bronzes *Goslar Warrior* (1979) and *Reclining Mother and Child* (1978), and Anthony Caro's metal abstract, *Fathom* (1976).

Borough High Street *SE1.* Once the main road to the south and the terminus for coaches when LONDON BRIDGE was too narrow to carry them into the city. In the 17th century, according to Thomas Dekker, it was full of inns, 'a continued ale house with not a shop to be seen between'. The most famous were the GEORGE, the BEAR, the QUEEN's HEAD, and the WHITE HART. Near the WHITE HART were the MARSHALSEA and KING's BENCH PRISONS. A pillory stood in the middle of the street until 1620. SOUTHWARK FAIR was held here. In 1676 fire swept the northern end, destroying many of the old buildings; and in 1830 most of the remaining old buildings on the west side were demolished for a street-widening scheme and the realignment of LONDON BRIDGE. The yard at No. 50 has the only remaining half-timbered house with an overhanging upper floor. Brandon House, No. 180, the large office building completed in 1981, stands on the site of Suffolk Place, residence in the 16th century of Charles Brandon, Duke of Suffolk. The bronze figure of a soldier on a stone plinth (the memorial to the dead of both World Wars) and the bronze reliefs of battleships and biplanes are by P. Lindsey Clark (1924).

Borough Market *Southwark, SE1.* Claims have been made that this is the oldest fruit and vegetable market in London, a successor to the one that caused a nuisance by spreading on to the southern end of LONDON BRIDGE in 1276. A map of 1542 shows the market place south of St Margaret's church in the High Street. Edward VI granted the market a Charter vesting the market rights in the LORD MAYOR and

Street widening in Borough High Street, 1830. St Saviour's, later Southwark Cathedral, is on the right.

citizens of the CITY. In 1671 Charles II confirmed the Charter and fixed the market boundaries, along the High Street from LONDON BRIDGE to St Margaret's Hill. By 1754 it caused such chaos and traffic congestion that the CITY petitioned Parliament to relieve them of their rights. An Act was accordingly passed which abolished the old market but gave leave for the parishioners of St Saviour's church to set up a new market on another site. The market began again in Rochester Yard. The buildings were designed by H. Rose in 1851 with additions by E. Habershon in 1863–4. Market profits go to the parish of St Saviour for rate rebates.

Bostal Heath *and* **Woods** *SE2*. Comprise nearly 80 acres acquired for the public in the 1890s. The district provided a large number of the 20,000 who marched with Jack Cade's ill-fated insurrection in 1450 (*see* CADE'S REBELLION).

Boston House *Chiswick, W4*. The largest house in the group of 18th-century houses known as Chiswick Square, situated in Burlington Lane, just west of Church Street. It is said to have been built by Henry D'Auverquerque, Viscount Boston, Earl of Grantham, and contains some panelled rooms. Legends about the ghost of a Lady Boston, murdered there by her husband, have no foundation. For the greater part of the 19th century it was a boarding school for girls. It has been suggested as the basis for Miss Pinkerton's Academy in *Vanity Fair* but it is more likely that Thackeray had in mind Walpole House in CHISWICK MALL. In 1981 there were proposals to make Boston House into four residential units and build additional houses in the garden.

Boston Manor House *Boston Manor Road, Brentford, Middlesex*. First heard of in the 14th century when it belonged to the nuns of ST HELEN BISHOPSGATE. At the Reformation it was taken over by the crown. In 1547 Edward VI gave it to Protector Somerset; but in 1552 it was taken back again when the Protector was attained. In 1572 Queen Elizabeth gave it to Robert, Earl of Leicester, who within the year sold it to Sir Thomas Gresham, founder of the ROYAL EXCHANGE and owner of the neighbouring OSTERLEY PARK. After the death of Gresham's wife it was occupied by his stepson, Sir William Reade. In 1662 Lady Reade built the present manor house – a fine three-storey Jacobean building with remarkable plaster ceilings and chimneypieces. A few years later the house was sold to James Clitherow from whose descendants it was bought by the Brentford Urban District Council with 40 acres of land in 1921. Damaged in the 2nd World War, it was reopened after repairs in 1963 and occupied by the National Institute of Houseworkers. It is now leased by the Over Forty Association for Women Workers who have turned the house, apart from state rooms, into flats for their members.

Botany Bay *Enfield, Middlesex*. This hamlet, which grew up after the enclosure of ENFIELD CHASE in 1777, lies at the junction of East Lodge with the Ridgeway in the centre of the Chase. Nearby is East Lodge on the site of one of the three original keepers' lodges, and to the north St Nicholas House, formerly called North Lodge, built in the 1730s. The place was so remote from civilisation that some Victorian humorist called it Botany Bay. It had its public house, the Robin Hood, its blacksmith's shop where the Lawrence family were smith and wheelwright from early in the 19th century, and a chapel, originally of the Huntingdon Connection. Henry Mayhew, the author of *London Labour and the London Poor* and founder of *Punch*, lived at Holly Cottage here. The hamlet now lies secure from developers in the heart of the GREEN BELT.

Botolph Lane *EC3*. Named after a vanished church, ST BOTOLPH BILLINGSGATE. ST GEORGE BILLINGSGATE also once stood in the lane. Wren is thought to have lived here while ST PAUL'S was being built; the house was demolished in about 1906.

Boundary Road *NW8*. Laid out from 1842 onwards, it marks the northern boundary of the parish of ST MARYLEBONE and divides it from its northern neighbour, HAMPSTEAD. The Day Centre at No. 48 is by Evans and Shalev (1979).

Bourchier Street *W1*. Formerly known as Hedge Lane, then as Milk Alley and after 1838 as Little Dean Street. In 1937 it was given its present name in commemoration of the Revd Basil Bourchier, a rector of ST ANNE SOHO, who died in 1934. The congregation of the Huguenot chapel known as L'Eglise du Quarré moved to a church here (since demolished) in about 1769.

Bourdon House *Davies Street, W1*. Takes its name from its first occupant, William Bourdon. It was built in 1723–5, perhaps by Thomas Barlow, the estate surveyor, and was originally a free-standing two-storey house placed end-on to DAVIES STREET, its pedimented five-bay principal front facing south into a walled garden now bounded on the south side by Bourdon Street. In the middle of the 18th century two bays were added on the north side on the DAVIES STREET front, which probably occasioned important internal rearrangements. Later (probably in 1864–5) an extra storey was added. In 1909 the ground landlord, the 2nd Duke of Westminster, ordered extensive repairs and the addition of a substantial new three-storey wing to the south-east of the original house. This was done by Eustace Balfour, the estate surveyor, with his usual discrimination in such matters. After he had vacated GROSVENOR HOUSE in 1916, the enlarged Bourdon House became the Duke's town house until his death in 1953. It is now used as a show-room for antiques. Though much altered, the old part of the house still contains a good 18th-century staircase, panelling and chimneypieces.

Bourdon Place *W1*. On the GROSVENOR ESTATE, it is a short side street connecting GROSVENOR HILL and BOURDON STREET, and takes its name from BOURDON HOUSE.

Bourdon Street *W1*. On the GROSVENOR ESTATE, it is a narrow street extending eastward from DAVIES STREET near BOURDON HOUSE into what was originally a network of mews providing stabling for the great houses in GROSVENOR STREET. In Victorian times several blocks of artisans' dwellings were built here, and most of the stables and coach houses have now been converted to garages, 'bijou' residences or offices.

Bourne and Hollingsworth Ltd *116–128 Oxford Street.* Mr Bourne and Mr Hollingsworth set up a fancy drapers' shop in 1894 in WESTBOURNE GROVE. In 1902 they moved to 116–118 OXFORD STREET, and slowly acquired the rest of the block, including a brothel, a 'nest of Polish tailors', and Savory's cigarette factory. Between 1922 and 1928 they built one of the largest modern drapery stores, designed by Slater and Moberly. In 1982 the stores were due to close.

Bouverie Street *EC4.* Built in about 1799 on the site of WHITEFRIARS Priory and named after the ground landlords, the Pleydell-Bouveries, Earls of Radnor. A crypt from the monastery is preserved beneath No. 30. Hazlitt lived with his son on the site of No. 6 in 1829, having separated from his second wife. The *Daily News* began at Nos 19–22 in 1845 with Charles Dickens as editor, Douglas Jerrold as assistant editor, Dickens's father as manager and his father-in-law as music critic. John Forster was also on the staff. The street is mostly taken up with newspaper offices, including the *Sun* and the *News of the World* in a building at No. 30 designed by A.A.H. Scott in 1930. The offices of *Punch* were at No. 10 for many years until their removal to Tudor Street in 1969. The Newspaper Publishers' Association is at No. 64.

Match-makers in the East End, 1871. At Bryant and May's factory in Bow there was a successful match-girls' strike in 1888.

Bow *E3.* An important bridgehead on the main road from London to Essex over the River LEA. The crossing used by the the Romans at OLD FORD had become inadequate and too dangerous by the early 12th century, so the highway was diverted further to the south (now the Whitechapel, Mile End and Bow Roads). Maud, the wife of Henry I, is said to have had the original stone bridge built here. Shaped like a bow, it gave the area its name, and has been rebuilt many times, most recently in 1973. Bow became a centre for the unloading of goods, especially grain, brought down the River LEA from Hertfordshire for the London market. A milling industry grew up along this part of the river, and by 1311 Bow was sufficiently populated to have its own chapel. ST MARY'S was enlarged in the 15th century but Bow did not become a parish separated from ST DUNSTAN STEPNEY until 1719. The church in Bow Road is the only relic left of the former medieval village that once surrounded it. By the 18th century calico printing and scarlet dyeing

were flourishing along the banks of the LEA. The open land around the village was used for arable farming, pasture and nursery gardens and an annual fair was held near the present Fairfield Road. The famous blue and white porcelain ware known as Bow china was manufactured on the Essex side of the river at STRATFORD, although early experiments were perhaps carried out at Bow.

In 1801 the population was still small – about 2,000 inhabitants – and it was not until the second half of the 19th century that rapid industrial development and growth in population brought Bow into the suburban fringes of London. But it was only to be engulfed soon afterwards by London's relentless expansion eastwards. Many factories started up in the 1850s and 1860s producing, amongst other commodities, soap, hemp-cloth, rubber and matches. The largest of the LEA-side factories, Bryant and May's match factory, combined the use of timber brought up the Lea Navigation Canal with that of chemicals and employed over 5,600 workers in 1875. It was the scene of the successful match-girls' strike in 1888, and the first attempt to organise unskilled women workers into a trade union. The population of Bow had more than doubled between 1861 and 1871 and reached its peak of 42,000 by 1901. Because communication with Central London was direct and easy and further improved by the extension of the DISTRICT Underground Railway to Bow in 1902, Bow retained a considerable residential population of CITY workers with the more affluent living in the roads immediately to the north of Bow Road. At 39 Bow Road a small garden has been laid out as a memorial to George Lansbury who lived here most of his life, represented the area in Parliament for about 20 years and was leader of the Labour Party in 1931–5. His decision to resign and fight a by-election in 1912 for the suffragette cause brought Sylvia Pankhurst to Bow where she founded the East London Federation of Suffragettes. Bow became a part of the Metropolitan Borough of POPLAR in 1900.

Bow Bells The peal of bells of ST MARY-LE-BOW, CHEAPSIDE which were destroyed by bombing in 1941. In 1472 a City mercer provided for the Bow bells to be rung every night at 9 o'clock, and in 1520 a larger bell was given to sound 'a retreat from work'. It is said of an authentic COCKNEY that he is born within the sound of Bow Bells. Before the 2nd World War the BBC used Bow Bells as a time signal and during the war broadcast their peal to enemy-occupied countries.

Bow Lane *EC4.* It was previously known as Cordwainer Street after the shoemakers who lived here, then as Hosier Lane after the hosiers who succeeded them. The present name is after the church of ST MARY-LE-BOW and dates from the 16th century. The 17th-century traveller Thomas Coryat, author of *Coryat's Crudities*, lived here.

Bow Porcelain The workshop where this soft-paste porcelain was made was founded at Stratford Langthorne by a glass merchant named Edward Heylyn and an Irish painter, Thomas Frye. In 1744 they took out a patent for their material, one of whose ingredients was an imported china clay. Among the objects which they produced were cups, bowls, mugs and many figures, in the manner of those produced at CHELSEA. Their quality declined after Frye's retirement in 1759. In 1775 the workshop equipment was moved to Derby.

Bow Road *E3*. Part of the main road from London to Essex and East Anglia, it begins at St Clement's Hospital, built in 1849 as the City of London Union Workhouse. Opposite the hospital there is a terrace of houses built in 1822. George Lansbury lived in No. 39, bombed during the 2nd World War. Further east, ST MARY STRATFORD-LE-BOW was built in the early 14th century but has been much added to. The large town hall is by E. Culpin (1937). The stone panels depicting craftsmen who worked on it are by David Evans (1938). The Gothic fountain in front of the old LNER station is by R. Plumbe (1872).

Bow Street *WC2*. Built in the shape of a bow between 1633 and 1677. It originally ran from FLORAL STREET to TAVISTOCK STREET and was later extended northwards to LONG ACRE and southwards to the STRAND via WELLINGTON STREET. In the 17th and early 18th centuries it was, according to Strype, 'well inhabited and resorted unto by gentry for lodgings'. Robert Harley, the manuscript collector, was born here in 1661. Grinling Gibbons, the woodcarver, lived here in 1678–1721, Jacob Tonson, the publisher, in 1707, William Wycherley in 1715, Charles Macklin, the actor, in 1743–8, Henry Fielding in 1749–53, John Fielding, the magistrate, in 1754–80 and John Rich, manager of Covent Garden Theatre (*see* COVENT GARDEN (ROYAL OPERA HOUSE)), in 1754–61. Samuel Johnson told Boswell that he, too, had lodged here for a while. In 1732 the first Covent Garden Theatre was built. By 1743 there were eight licensed premises in the street. In the early 19th century it was notorious for brothels. In 1856–60 the Floral Hall (*see* COVENT GARDEN) was added by Edward Barry as an extension to the opera house. No. 1, from about 1671 to 1749, was the site of WILL'S COFFEE HOUSE which was founded by William Urwin and patronised by Pepys, Dryden, Gay, Pope, Addison, Steele, Swift, Johnson and Wycherley. In 1740 the BOW STREET MAGISTRATES' COURT was opened by Thomas de Veil, JP for MIDDLESEX, and from here the famous Bow Street Runners later operated. In 1749 Henry Fielding was appointed magistrate and on his death in 1754 he was succeeded by his half-brother, John (*see* BOW STREET MAGISTRATES' COURT). At No. 6 David Garrick and Peg Woffington were living in 1742–4. They did much entertaining and Fanny Burney wrote, 'In graceful deportment and in natural magnetism and in tact she was a hostess so attractive that her receptions were crowded with people of distinction, and the table was never presided over so charmingly as when she was at the head of it.' But Johnson, who often spoke ill of Garrick, with whom he had travelled to London from Lichfield (although allowing no one else to denigrate him), recalled with distaste how cross Garrick was when Peg put an extravagant amount of tea in the pot. The Telephone Exchange on the east side is by G.R. Yeats (1964–7).

Bow Street Magistrates' Court *Bow Street, WC2*. The first Bow Street magistrate was Col. Thomas De Veil, a former army officer who established his office and court at his house at No. 4 on the western side of the street in 1740, a house which had been built in 1703–4 by James Browne, a surgeon.

The second Bow Street magistrate was Henry Fielding, a barrister as well as a novelist. To supplement the inadequacies of the parish constables and watchmen, Henry Fielding established a mobile group of six volunteer 'thief-takers' who proved to be the originals of the body which later came to be known as the Bow Street Runners. They were at first part-time employees and allowed to retain reward money paid for convictions and to undertake private commissions. They wore no uniform. It was not until the turn of the century that the name 'Bow Street Runner' came into general use. In 1751 Fielding's half-brother, John, became his assistant and followed him as the third Bow Street magistrate in 1754. He was knighted in 1761. Although blind, his court work was adequate for the time and he also pursued crime with vigour and success. He was given the improbable credit of being able to recognise 3,000 thieves by their voices. In 1763 Boswell described his court-room as 'a back hall'. The house was attacked in the GORDON RIOTS but little damage was done.

When the Metropolitan Police Act of 1829 created a single uniformed force of 1,011 men for the London area, the Bow Street Runners were excluded from the new body and remained under the control of their own magistrates' office until 1839 when they were disbanded. The Metropolitan Police Courts Act 1839 converted the magistrates' offices into magistrates' courts and the magistrates became normal members of the judiciary without any police responsibilities. The old offices at Nos 3 and 4 were pulled down in 1887 as part of an improvement scheme in connection with COVENT GARDEN MARKET. In 1879–80 the present Magistrates' Court on the eastern side of the street was built at a cost of £38,400 to the designs of Sir John Taylor. It houses three courts, including that of the Metropolitan Chief Magistrate before whom all extradition applications are heard. There is also a METROPOLITAN POLICE historical museum, not open to the public.

Bowes Park *N11, N13, N14, N22*. A late Victorian suburb on the borders of WOOD GREEN and SOUTHGATE. Housing development started in the mid-1870s and continued spasmodically until the 1st World War. In its early days Bowes Park was highly respectable and was one of the most desirable suburbs in NORTH LONDON. Bowes Park Station (opened 1880) was once one of the busiest on the Great Northern Railway's London network. The area today has a distinctly shabby-genteel flavour.

Bowman's Coffee House *St Michael's Alley, Cornhill*. According to Aubrey, this was the first coffee house in London. It was established in about 1652 by Christopher Bowman, coachman to a Turkey merchant who set him up in business. It was four years, Aubrey said, before another coffee house was set up in London. This was the RAINBOW in FLEET STREET. Another authority, Oldys, maintains that 'the use of Coffee in England was first known in 1657, when Mr Daniel Edwards, a Turkey merchant, brought from Smyrna to London one Pasqua Rosee, a Ragusean youth, who prepared this drink for him every morning. But the novelty thereof drawing too much company to him, he allowed his said servant, with another of his son-in-laws, to sell it publicly and they set up in the first coffee house in London in St Michael's Alley in

Watermen present an address to Queen Caroline at Brandenburgh House during the proceedings against her in the House of Lords.

Cornhill. But they separating Pasqua kept on the house, and he who had been his partner obtained leave to pitch a tent and sell the liquor in St Michael's Churchyard.'

Bowyers' Company *see* CITY LIVERY COMPANIES.

Brackley Street *EC1*. Viscount Brackley was the title given to the eldest son of the Earls of Bridgewater whose town house stood close by in BRIDGEWATER SQUARE. The street was first built in the 17th century and was completely rebuilt in 1892–6.

Bradford Avenue *EC1*. A street of warehouses built in the 1890s opposite the Midland Railway Goods Depot in REDCROSS STREET. It was bombed in the 2nd World War and its site now forms part of the BARBICAN redevelopment.

Bradmore House *Broadway, Hammersmith.* Built in 1739 as an addition to Butterwick House (demolished in 1836). At one time the property of the Impey family (Sir Elijah, friend of Warren Hastings, was born there), it became a school but was demolished in 1913 by the London Omnibus Company. The garden front was re-erected to form the front of the bus garage, where it remains in a sadly botched state. Panelling from the house is in the GEFFRYE MUSEUM.

Brandenburgh House *Fulham.* Built in Charles I's reign for Sir Nicholas Crisp. It became the headquarters of General Fairfax in 1647, but in 1660 it was returned to Sir Nicholas who had helped General

Monck plan the Restoration. In 1683 it was bought by Prince Rupert of the Rhine who settled it on his mistress, Margaret Hughes, for ten years. In 1792 it was bought by the Margrave of Brandenburg-Anspach who decorated it in lavish style and made it a centre of fashionable society. He died here in 1806. The Margravine, who was not received at Court because she had lived with him while her husband, the 6th Earl of Craven, was still alive, was deeply interested in amateur theatricals for which she had a theatre built in the grounds. In 1820 Queen Caroline, the eccentric wife of George IV, stayed here before the proceedings against her for adultery in the House of Lords. (She gave thanks in ST PAUL'S CHURCH, HAMMERSMITH when the Bill was abandoned.) She died here in 1821 a few weeks after being shut out of WESTMINSTER ABBEY at her husband's coronation. The next year the house was sold and demolished. The DISTILLERS' COMPANY's distillery to the south of Crisp Road marks the site.

Bread Street *EC4*. Once an important route from CHEAPSIDE market to QUEENHITHE dock. It was the site of the bread market of medieval London; also of the MERMAID TAVERN from about 1411 to 1666, and SADDLERS' HALL in 1454–1641. The SHERIFFS had a compter on the west side of the street before the WOOD STREET COMPTER was built in 1555. One Randall Tytley complained to Thomas Cromwell about 'the heavy charges for beds there and, any charity bread drink or cheare, the keeper will suffer none to come to them lest it hinder his own custom . . . if any one be in arrear for one night's lodgings . . . he is thrust into the hole and kept till he has sold all his clothes and then there is no remedy but to Newgate with him which has been the murder of many a tall man and true.' In 1608 John Milton was born at the sign of the Spread Eagle (the family crest). The street was burnt in the GREAT FIRE; and devastated by bombs in the 2nd World War. The BANK OF ENGLAND administrative offices are at No. 4.

Bread Street Compter An ancient prison for debtors under the control of the City SHERIFF. Its prisoners were transferred to the new WOOD STREET COMPTER in 1555.

Bread Street Hill *EC4.* Before QUEEN VICTORIA STREET was cut in 1867–71 it continued BREAD STREET south to the river. John Donne was born here in 1573.

Brent The London Borough of Brent was created in 1965 by the union of the former Boroughs of WEMBLEY and WILLESDEN. Its component parts, with only a few exceptions like QUEENSBURY, are derived from hamlets of probably Saxon origin.

Brent Town Hall, Forty Lane, was built in 1937–9 for WEMBLEY Urban District Council to designs by Clifford Strange, who earlier had worked for T.S. Tait, the English innovator of a style of brick architecture practised by the Dutchman, Dudok. The site for the Town Hall was acquired in 1934 and a public architectural competition was established with Stanley H. Hamp as the assessor. Although Strange was awarded first prize, the working details when it came to actual construction were debated in committee and provoked substantial opposition from local residents and councillors alike. Building operations began in 1937 when the Council was granted borough status. The plan form is asymmetrical with an off-centre main entrance which enables the offices, library and great hall to be separated from each other. Its 350 ft frontage is set back 160 ft from Forty Lane, but this horizontal emphasis is countered by the vertical plane of the taller entrance piece and two-storey windows of the office block. A similar concern for detail is expressed within the building. The result was a new concept in town hall design.

Brent Cross Shopping Centre *NW4.* At the centre of three major trunk roads and an easy car ride for over 1,250,000 people, Brent Cross was built by Bernard Engle and Partners on a virgin site covering 52 acres. It opened on 2 March 1976. On two floors, the length of the main mall is 610 ft. There are marble floors. An elaborate fountain under the main dome dominates the central well. The centre contains two department stores, four large stores, a supermarket and 82 individual shops.

Brentford *Middlesex.* Often referred to as the county town of the former County of MIDDLESEX, but this is questionable as it was never a corporate town, although the Parliamentary elections took place here for a number of years. It formerly consisted of Old Brentford, which formed part of the parish of EALING until well into the first part of the 19th century, and New, or as it sometimes appears, West Brentford which was in the parish of HANWELL until 1744. The two areas were joined together under the Brentford Local Board in 1875. The name Brentford refers to the ford over the River Brent and first appears as Breguntford in 705. Brentford Bridge at the western end of the High Street existed at least as early as the 13th century.

A number of local historical events, including the battle at Brentford between Edmund Ironside, King of the English, and Canute in 1016, are commemorated on a granite column in Ferry Lane erected in 1909.

Brentford has always had considerable importance from its position on the main road from London to the west, where ferries crossing the THAMES to Surrey were replaced by the first KEW BRIDGE in 1759. During the Civil War, in 1642, a battle was fought at Brentford, after which the Royalists went on towards London only to be turned back at TURNHAM GREEN. Brentford originally consisted of buildings along and near to the High Street, but expanding industry led to the development of streets of small houses north of it in the 19th and early 20th centuries. A great deal of Brentford has been rebuilt since the 2nd World War, including most of the High Street. Apart from the church of ST LAWRENCE, houses in the BUTTS, and BOSTON MANOR HOUSE, there are now few buildings of earlier date than the 19th century. The gas works, which in 1821 belonged to the Brentford Gaslight Company and had spread to both sides of the High Street, have almost disappeared since gas ceased to be made there in 1963. The water works at KEW BRIDGE, started in 1835, have closed. Tower blocks of flats are on part of the site but some of the original steam pumping engines remain to form a section of the museum organised by the Kew Bridge Engine Trust. The former Great Western Railway Dock by the THAMES has been replaced by houses, flats and a marina. The GRAND UNION CANAL still enters the THAMES here but is no longer busy with commercial traffic. Brentford Fruit and Vegetable Market, built near KEW BRIDGE in 1893, was transferred to North Hyde, near HESTON, in 1974. The elevated section of the M4 motorway from Chiswick Flyover starts above the GREAT WEST ROAD and then bears slightly north, allowing the motorist a brief view of Brentford and BOSTON MANOR HOUSE.

Brent Lodge Park *W7.* A major new park being created by the Borough of EALING along the valley of the BRENT RIVER. The area of 850 acres is the nearest natural open space to central London west of KENSINGTON GARDENS. The existing parkland and recreational facilities are to be unified into a continuous whole approximately 4½ miles long and, on average, ½ mile wide. Footpaths and riverside walks will allow the natural beauty of the area to be enjoyed without interfering with existing golf courses and other facilities.

Buildings included within the area are the 12th-century church of St Mary the Virgin and Wharncliffe Viaduct designed by Brunel in 1837 to carry the Great Western Railway over the valley on a series of eight elliptical arches. Above a series of locks known as the Hanwell Flight the GRAND UNION CANAL meets the road and railway. The point of intersection comprises three bridges, one above the other, and is one of Brunel's engineering masterpieces. The locks have been scheduled as an Ancient Monument.

Brent Reservoir *see* WELSH HARP RESERVOIR.

Brent River Rises in south Hertfordshire as the Dollis Brook and is joined in NEASDEN by the Silk Stream. Below the junction it has been dammed up to form the WELSH HARP or BRENT RESERVOIR to provide water for the GRAND JUNCTION CANAL. Between 1793 and 1798 3 miles of it were converted to form the beginning of the canal, which leaves it at GREENFORD. The WELSH HARP is used today for rowing, sailing and swimming and is also the home of numerous interesting water birds. In 1890 it was said that above the Welsh Harp sewage flowed down the Brent and that between HANWELL and EALING even the water rats had fallen victims to the foulness of the stream. Today the pollution comes from industrial waste and foaming detergents, but efforts continue to be made by local authorities to clean up the river. The Brent runs into the THAMES at Brentford Lock, now a fashionable residential area looking across the river to KEW GARDENS.

Brentford Football Club   *see* FOOTBALL CLUBS.

Brentham Garden Estate   *Ealing, W5.* Comprises 60½ acres in the north of EALING, formerly part of Pitshanger Farm (*see* PITSHANGER MANOR), and bounded on the North by Western Avenue. Ealing Tenants Ltd, registered in 1901, was the first co-operative tenants' society, and grew out of Henry Vivian's co-operative building firm, General Builders Ltd. Vivian, a carpenter, trade unionist and MP, was a founder member and first chairman of Ealing Tenants Ltd. The estate was built up between 1901 and 1915 and included 650 houses, a club and institute, recreation grounds and allotments. Raymond Unwin and Barry Parker, designers of Letchworth Garden City, were consulted on the layout of roads. The houses were designed by F. Cavendish Pearson and G. Lister Sutcliffe in a mixture of vernacular styles that avoid uniformity. Since 1969 the area has been designated a Conservation Area.

Brewer Street   *W1.* Built in the 1670s on land which for the most part had belonged to Sir William Pulteney. It was in its early days sometimes known as Wells Street after the builder who developed much of it. Its present name commemorates the breweries of Thomas Ayres and Henry Davis, both now demolished, which existed on the north side in the 18th century. Nos 12, 40, 42, 44 and 80–82 date from the early to mid-18th century. David Hume, the Scottish philosopher and historian, lived at No. 7 between 1767 and 1769. Nos 63–65 cover the site of the HICKFORD ROOMS. The present character of the street may be gauged from the names over some of its premises: Quartet Films Ltd; Fuji restaurant; Commercial and General Travel Service; United Kingdom Bartenders' Guild; David Schayek, solicitors; Blum, manufacturing furriers; Toasty Bars Snack Bar; Target Records; William Hill, turf accountants; Mister George Boutique; Andy, alteration tailor; Barrett's Liquormart; Grodzinski and Co., bakers; Soho Cinema; Doc Johnson's sex-shop. In fact, it is a characteristic SOHO street.

BREWERIES   London has long enjoyed a reputation for good beer, and allusions to London ale occur in the writings of Chaucer and his contemporaries. The BREWERS' COMPANY, one of the oldest of the CITY of London craft guilds, received its Royal Charter in the 15th century, but had been organised in the time of Henry IV. Among its liverymen and Masters have been most of the great names in brewing from then to

the present day. In the course of time some breweries have closed and others amalgamated, but the following deserve to be mentioned:

Albion Brewery   *333–335 Whitechapel Road, E1.* Built in 1808. The first tenant was John Hoffman. The brewery was acquired by Philip Blake and James Mann in 1819. Blake died in 1834 and Robert Crossman and Thomas Paulin joined the business in 1846. Much ambitious rebuilding took place in 1855, and in 1899 Albion introduced the first bottled brown ale in England. The company was still in the hands of the Mann, Crossman and Paulin families in 1904. In 1911 the SIDNEY STREET riots took place next door to the brewery. The firm was amalgamated with Watney, Combe and Reid in 1959. It later became Watney, Mann and Truman.

Anchor Brewery   *Mile End Road, E1.* In 1757 the brewery firm of Westfield and Moss moved from BETHNAL GREEN to the MILE END ROAD. In 1766 John Charrington purchased a third of the shares, buying another third in 1769 and the rest in 1783. He was Master of the BREWERS' COMPANY in 1785. His son Nicholas, who succeeded him in the business, died in 1827. In 1833 the firm absorbed the company of Steward and Head. Nicholas was succeeded by his grandsons Charles, who died in 1873, and Frederick, who died in 1877. During this time the brewery was considerably enlarged. Its first steam engine was installed in 1828; its last was scrapped in 1927 when electric power was adopted. Forty other London breweries were absorbed between 1833 and 1930 and three others between 1950 and 1954. Horses were used for haulage up to 1946.

Draymen carting casks of ale from the brewery of Truman, Hanbury and Co., Brick Lane, in 1842.

Black Eagle Brewery   *91 Brick Lane, E1.* The site of the Brick Lane brewery was leased in 1660 to John Stott, who laid the ground out in streets, one of which was Black Eagle Street, from which the Brewery took its name. Part of the land was sublet to Thomas Bucknall, on whose death Joseph Truman acquired the lease. He was succeeded by his sons Joseph and Benjamin. Joseph retired in 1730, leaving Benjamin to carry on the business, which he did to such good purpose that Black Eagle became famous for its 'porter' or black stout and by 1760 was third in size of all London porter firms. Benjamin was knighted on the accession of George III and carried on until his death in 1780. Sampson Hanbury took over, and when he died in 1835 Black Eagle was producing annually 200,000 barrels of porter and steam power had been introduced. Thomas Buxton joined the firm in 1808, subsequently becoming a partner and being created a baronet by Queen Victoria. In 1873 Truman's was the largest brewery company in the world. It became a public company in 1888, but continued to be led by descendants of the Hanbury, Buxton and Pryor families. The building has been enlarged from time to time and important additions were made in 1977, but the original owner's and head brewer's houses remained in 1982 when the firm had become Watney, Mann and Truman.

City of London Brewery According to John Stow, a brewery stood in his time on the south side of CANNON STREET. It was owned first by a Mr Pott and then by Henry Campion, who died in 1588. He was succeeded by his son Abraham who was followed by *his* son Richard, who was head of the brewery when it was destroyed in the GREAT FIRE. In 1744 the Hour Glass Brewery was established on the site by Sir William Calvert (Lord Mayor in 1748–9) at 89 UPPER THAMES STREET. After a bad fire it was taken over and rebuilt in 1805 by Robert Calvert and in 1862 the City of London Brewery Company was established. The entire site of medieval Coldharbour was acquired in 1894 and imposing new buildings erected. The buildings were destroyed by enemy action in 1941 and the company removed to 6 Albert Court, Kensington Gore. It afterwards moved back to the CITY and became the City of London Brewery and Investment Trust Ltd at 77 LONDON WALL.

Courage (Eastern Ltd) *Horselydown Lane, SE1.* The Horselydown Brewery was founded in 1787 by John Courage, who paid £615 for the buildings. The firm was merged in 1955 with Barclay, Perkins and Co.

Courage Ltd *7 Anchor Terrace, Southwark Bridge Road, SE1.* In 1710 the Anchor Brewery was owned by a Mr Halsey, who amassed a large fortune supplying beer to the Army and then sold his business to Ralph Thrale of STREATHAM. Thrale died in 1758 and was succeeded by his son, Henry (whose wife was the friend and benefactor of Dr Samuel Johnson). Under Henry Thrale's management the brewery became the fourth largest in London. On his death in 1781 Dr Johnson became one of his executors and the business was sold to Barclay and Perkins. Lord Lucan told the story that 'Johnson appeared bustling about with an ink-horn and pen in his buttonhole, like an exciseman; and on being asked what he really considered to be the value of the property, answered, "We are not here to sell a parcel of boilers and vats, but the potentiality of growing rich beyond the dreams of avarice."' A disastrous fire destroyed the buildings in 1832, but they were rebuilt and extended and in 1889 were said to be one of the sights of London. They were reconstructed and modernised in 1960. They are believed to cover the site of Shakespeare's GLOBE THEATRE.

Fuller, Smith and Turner Ltd *Griffin Brewery, Chiswick, W4.* There was a brewery on this site in Elizabethan times. In 1685 it passed to the Mawson family, who leased it to William Harvest in 1740. John Thompson and David Roberts acquired the freehold in 1782. On Roberts's death Thompson was joined by his son Douglas Thompson who ran the brewery after he died and in 1816 named it the Griffin when Reid's brewery in Liquorpond Street ceased to use the name. In 1821 Philip Wood, brother of Matthew Wood, Lord Mayor of London in 1815, was called in to reorganise

the business and in 1829 was joined by John Fuller. When Fuller died in 1839 he was succeeded by his son John Bird Fuller, who was joined in 1845 by Henry Smith of Romford and his head brewer John Turner. The Beehive in BRENTFORD was acquired in 1910 and Siches' Brewery in 1923, and the present limited company was formed in 1929.

Griffin Brewery Richard Meux and Mungo Murray had already bought an ancient brewhouse in 1757 when they built their new Griffin Brewery in 1763 in Liquorpond Street (now part of Clerkenwell Road). By 1795 Andrew Reid, a rich City merchant of Scottish extraction, had joined Meux and invested £10,000 – which met the cost of installing a mammoth vat – and the Griffin had become one of the largest breweries in London. It was sold in 1809 after disagreements between the partners, and the business was reorganised with Andrew Reid as the senior partner. Reid died in 1841 but the firm prospered and the brewery did not close until 1899 after amalgamation with Watney and Combe.

Horseshoe Brewery *Tottenham Court Road.* Took its name from a nearby tavern, the successor to which adjoins the DOMINION CINEMA today. It was built about 1810 for Henry Meux, who installed in it a giant vat, then a prestige feature of leading London breweries. In 1814 the vat burst its hoops, and the ensuing flood of beer swept through the walls, demolishing three adjoining houses and causing the death of eight people. The damage was repaired, the building extended and the business carried on. The brewery was not demolished until 1922.

Lion Brewery Goding's Lion Brewery stood on the south bank of the THAMES in LAMBETH and was built as a storehouse to the designs of Francis Edwards in 1836. With its rusticated ground floor and giant pilasters it was a prominent riverside landmark, and it was widely believed that the lion of COADE STONE which surmounted it contained the formula for that much esteemed material. The building ceased to be used in 1924 and was badly damaged by fire in 1931. It was demolished for the FESTIVAL OF BRITAIN and the SOUTH BANK development in 1951. The lion was preserved, but no formula for Coade stone was found inside it (*see* COADE LION).

Plough Brewery Standing on the boundary between CLAPHAM and BATTERSEA, it began as 'Mr Combs's Brewery' opposite the Nag's Head in 1801. By 1822 it had expanded and become the Clapham Brewery. From 1825 to 1885 the land on which it stands belonged to the Revd Augustus Hewitt, and a legal declaration by Mr Hewitt's nephew in 1886 describes it as the Plough Brewery, its name having been changed by Thomas Woodward when he took it over in 1868. Woodward bought it in 1886 and with his wife and son ran it until his death in 1900. It was sold in 1913 to William Biddell with the right to use Woodward's name for the beer. Young and Co.'s Brewery took it over in 1924, using it as a store. H. and G. Simonds purchased the site in 1925 and Courage and Barclay occupied it in 1943. The building fell into disrepair and was purchased by J.W. Marston and Son in 1968, being now leased for business purposes. Its equipment has been preserved in the interests of industrial archaeology.

Stag Brewery In 1420 Thomas Greene was Master of the BREWERS' COMPANY and members of his family were associated with the Brewhouse at

WESTMINSTER ABBEY. They continued to brew in WESTMINSTER after the suppression of the monasteries, and in 1641 a William Greene became the first brewer at the Stag brewhouse in WESTMINSTER. He was joined by his cousin, John, in 1657. At the Restoration William was knighted and later created a baronet. John's son William rebuilt and enlarged the brewery in 1715. On his death in 1732 it passed to his brother, Thomas, and thence to the latter's grandson, Edward, whose incompetence almost ruined it. On Edward's death it was leased to Moore, Elliot and Co., later Elliot, Watney and Co. John Elliot died in 1829 and his son, John Lettsom Elliot, took over, being joined by James Watney of WANDSWORTH in 1837. The brewery lost much of its adjoining land with the coming of VICTORIA STREET, VICTORIA STATION and the District Railway. Watney took over the management and held it to his death in 1884, following which his son James founded Watney and Co. In 1898 the firm joined its two great rivals to become Watney, Combe and Reid. It survived two wars, but the Stag Brewery was closed in the redevelopments in the area in 1959, the site now being occupied by the 27-storey headquarters of Associated Portland Cement.

Wandsworth (Young and Co.) *Wandsworth High Street, SW18.* A brewery had existed on this site in WANDSWORTH since the 17th century when Charles Allen Young bought an interest in it in 1831. He installed two beam engines in 1835 and 1867, both still working perfectly, as are the two great coppers (one of which was set up in 1869) with a capacity of 14,652 gallons for brewing the malt and hops. The brewery specialises in making the real ale which is increasingly popular today. Its five teams of horses deliver beer three times daily to the 47 Young's inns in the London area.

Whitbread and Co. *Chiswell Street, EC1.* Samuel Whitbread, the son of a Bedfordshire yeoman, was apprenticed to a London brewer in 1736. By 1742 he was able to set up in business in a small way in partnership with the brothers, Godfrey and Thomas Shewell. His first brewery was in WHITECROSS STREET in the City. In 1750 he moved to the King's Head brewery in CHISWELL STREET which was improved for him by some of the leading engineers of the day, including John Rennie. His brewery was visited in 1787 by George III and Queen Charlotte. When Whitbread died in 1798 his brewery brewed 200,000 gallons in one year – a record for London. Although beer was last brewed here in April 1976, the buildings are preserved close by the BARBICAN development. The OVERLORD EMBROIDERY is housed here and Samuel's famous Porter Tun Room has now been converted into a banqueting suite.

Woodyard Brewery Some time during the 17th century a timber yard in Castle Street, ST MARTIN-IN-THE-FIELDS, was taken over by John Shackly as a cooperage, and on his death in 1722 his son carried on the business as a cooper and small brewer. In 1739 William Gyfford took over, taking his brother, Joseph, into partnership and developing a large brewery which they named 'Woodyard' after a passage nearby. Their trade improved rapidly and in 1759 the Gyffords acquired new premises off TOTTENHAM COURT ROAD. Harvey Christian Combe (LORD MAYOR of London 1799–1800) took over the Woodyard in 1787 with Joseph Delafield and other partners and the business became known as Combe's Brewery. Combe

amalgamated with Watney and Reid in 1898 and the Woodyard Brewery closed in 1905.

Brewers' Company *see* CITY LIVERY COMPANIES.

Brick Lane *E1, E2.* Bricks and tiles were manufactured nearby in the 16th century, and by the middle of the following century the southern end of the lane was being built up. The Black Eagle BREWERY, newly rebuilt by Arup Associates (1976) has been here since the late 17th century, and some of the houses to the south of the brewery (Nos 65–79) were built by Joseph Truman in 1705–6. The London Jamme Majid was built as a chapel for French Protestants in 1742 and before becoming a place of worship for local Muslims had been used as such by Methodists and Jews.

Brick Street *W1.* So called because of the adjacent brick kiln which formerly stood here. It leads northward off PICCADILLY and soon bends westward to end up in OLD PARK LANE. Most of its course follows an old field boundary, and today it is still little more than a narrow lane flanked by the backs of big buildings in PICCADILLY and HERTFORD STREET.

Bricklayers Arms Station *Pages Walk, SE1.* Built by the South Eastern and London and Croydon Railway Companies as their London terminus to force the Greenwich Company to lower the tolls for the use of their station at LONDON BRIDGE. Designed by Lewis Cubitt and named after a nearby coaching inn, it opened in 1844. The next year agreement was reached with the Greenwich Company and thereafter the station became mainly a goods depot, being used in particular for the traffic in sheep and cattle. But it had brief revivals of use for passenger traffic, notably during the years 1849–52 and 1932–9. Princess Alexandra of Denmark arrived at Bricklayers Arms when she came to London in 1863 for her marriage to the future King Edward VII. In 1982 the station was a parcels depot.

Bridewell A royal palace built in 1515–20 for Henry VIII on the banks of the FLEET RIVER. It was named after a holy well nearby dedicated to St Bride. The building was a large rambling brick structure round three courtyards. In 1522 Charles V, the Holy Roman Emperor, was entertained here with pageants, music, tennis and feasts. A wooden footbridge was built across the FLEET so that the Emperor could reach his lodgings in BLACKFRIARS MONASTERY. In 1525 Henry VIII installed Henry Blount, his illegitimate son, here as Earl of Nottingham and Duke of Richmond and Somerset. It was here that preliminary conferences took place with the papal legate on the King's divorce in 1528. And on 30 November 1529 Catherine of Aragon probably last saw her husband when they dined together here.

Between 1531 and 1539 the palace was leased to the French Ambassador. In 1553 it was the scene of Holbein's painting *The Ambassadors*. In that same year Edward VI gave the palace to the CITY for the reception of vagrants and homeless children and for the punishment of petty offenders and disorderly women. Queen Mary Tudor confirmed Edward VI's charter in 1556 and the CITY took possession, turning the palace into a prison, hospital and workrooms. There were other Bridewells in London: one at WESTMINSTER and

An early 19th-century imaginary reconstruction of Bridewell Palace c.1660, showing the entrance to the Fleet River.

another at CLERKENWELL, besides several hundred others throughout the country. Prisoners were sent here for a short term only. Invariably flogging was a part of the punishment. Public flogging sessions took place twice a week in front of the prison court. The Junior Beadle beat the prisoners' bare backs until the president of the court knocked on a table with a hammer. Orphans of FREEMEN OF THE CITY and later destitute children were also accommodated here and apprenticed to tradesmen for seven years. They wore a blue uniform which was renewed annually at Easter when they attended the Spital Sermon. In 1628 a ducking stool was set up on the river bank. And in 1638 stocks were built. In the Civil War Cromwell's troops billeted themselves at Bridewell until they received their pay.

Most of the old buildings were destroyed in the GREAT FIRE and rebuilt in 1666–7. In 1675 a schoolmaster was appointed to teach the apprentices to read and write. A doctor was appointed in 1700. (No other prison had medical staff until 1775.) In 1788 prisoners were given straw for their beds. (Other London prisons provided neither straw nor beds.) In 1791 the flogging of females was abolished. And the next year the weekly inspection of prisons was established. A new prison section was built in 1797. The entire prison was brought under state control in 1833 before being closed in 1855 when prisoners of both sexes were transferred to HOLLOWAY. The buildings were demolished in 1863–4 except for the Gateway built in 1802 (*see* NEW BRIDGE STREET). The rest of the site was first covered by DE KEYSER'S ROYAL HOTEL and since 1931 has been occupied by the Unilever Building.

Bridge House Estates   The revenue of the Bridge House Estates Committee comes from properties which were given or bequeathed for the upkeep of the old LONDON BRIDGE which was completed in 1209. The income from these properties has since financed the cost and maintenance of the Corporation's four bridges – BLACKFRIARS BRIDGE, LONDON BRIDGE,

SOUTHWARK BRIDGE and TOWER BRIDGE – across the THAMES, thus avoiding a heavy burden on the rates.

Bridge House Hotel   *London Bridge Station.* Probably the first railway hotel in the world, it was erected close to LONDON BRIDGE STATION by the Hay's Wharf Company. By the end of the century it had come into the possession of the proprietors of the St James's Restaurant, PICCADILLY. Its use as a hotel ceased in the mid-1960s; it subsequently became business premises.

Bridge Street   *SW1.* Built in 1739–50 to connect WESTMINSTER BRIDGE with PARLIAMENT STREET. It covers the site of the Woolstaple founded in the reign of Edward I as one of ten official markets for wool in England. Coleridge lodged in the street in 1801. The south side was removed in 1866–7 to open up NEW PALACE YARD and WESTMINSTER HALL to public view. Sir Charles Barry, the architect of the new PALACE OF WESTMINSTER, was born in one of the houses demolished.

Bridgewater House   *Barbican.* Originally known as Garter House, it was built at the eastern end of the BARBICAN, for Thomas Wriothesley, who succeeded as Garter King of Arms in 1504. At the end of the 16th century it became the town house of the Earls of Bridgewater. It was burned down in 1687 in a fire in which two of the Earl's children died. BRIDGEWATER SQUARE was built on the site.

Bridgewater House   *Cleveland Row, SW1.* Built by Lord Francis Leveson Gower, second son of the 1st Duke of Sutherland and heir to the Bridgewater estates. He was created Earl of Ellesmere in 1846. Having inherited CLEVELAND HOUSE, he discovered it to be in a dangerous condition and had it demolished. Bridgewater House was built on the site to the grand Italianate designs of Charles Barry and completed in 1854. The picture gallery had already been opened to the public in 1851. Damaged in an air raid in the 2nd World War, it was restored in 1948–9 by Robert Atkinson and Partners and sold by the 5th Earl of Ellesmere to the Legal and General Assurance Society. It was then let to the British Oxygen Company, and later occupied by Tube Investments until 1980 when it was offered for sale at about £10 million.

Bridgewater Square *EC1.* In 1688 Sir Christopher Wren and George Jackson of Chipping Warden bought for £4,400 the site of Bridgewater House which had been destroyed by fire with the loss of two of Lord Bridgewater's sons. Among those who took building plots were Nicholas Hawksmoor and Edward Strong. The square was residential until the middle of the 19th century. All the original houses have now been demolished or rebuilt.

Bristol Hotel *3 Berkeley Street, W1.* Built on the site of the old BERKELEY HOTEL by Chapman and Taylor in 1971. There are 197 bedrooms.

Britannia Hotel *40 Grosvenor Street, W1.* Built in 1966–9 to the designs of R. Seifert and Partners on the site of an ale house where members of the Cabinet were first informed of Wellington's victory at Waterloo. There are 436 bedrooms.

Britannia Theatre *High Street, Hoxton.* Built in 1841 as the Britannia Saloon by Sam Lane on the site of an Elizabethan tavern known as the Pimlico which Shakespeare is said to have frequented. The entertainments provided were free, only refreshments being paid for. In 1850 the Brit, as it was generally known, was converted into a theatre. It was enlarged to accommodate 3,000 people in 1858. When Lane died in 1871 his widow, Sara Lane the actress, took over the management, appearing here in pantomime as principal boy until she was over 70. After her death the theatre became a cinema and was destroyed in the BLITZ.

British Academy *20–21 Cornwall Terrace, NW1.* The national learned society for the humanities and social sciences corresponding to the ROYAL SOCIETY in the field of the natural sciences. By the end of the 19th century the work of the ROYAL SOCIETY, and its Fellowship, had come to be entirely concentrated on the natural sciences, and the British Academy was therefore founded by a group of scholars in the humanities and granted a Royal Charter in 1902. Among its founding fathers were Morley, Bryce, Balfour, Murray, Jebb, Bury, Dicey, Maitland, Skeat and Leslie Stephen. Lord Reay was the first President and Israel Gollancz its first Secretary. Later Fellows have included Beatrice Webb, Mortimer Wheeler, Bertrand Russell, Beveridge, L.B. Namier, Curzon, Keynes, M.R. James, Mallowan, Gilbert Murray, Kathleen Kenyon, Stenton and Flinders Petrie. Since its foundation the Academy has occupied various sites. At first it had no rooms of its own and met at the BRITISH MUSEUM. In 1926, with the authority of the Chancellor of the Exchequer (then Winston Churchill), it was given rooms in BURLINGTON GARDENS (now housing the MUSEUM OF MANKIND); in 1968 it moved to BURLINGTON HOUSE; and in 1982 it moved to a house in CORNWALL TERRACE, REGENT'S PARK. Each of these moves has been a sign of the growth of the

Academy's work and responsibilities. It now has about 320 Ordinary Fellows (about 20 are elected each year and the maximum is 350) and about 250 Corresponding (or Overseas) Fellows. Election is on the basis of high distinction in the humanities or social sciences. The Academy grant-aids the 11 British Schools and Institutes abroad, and supports the humanities in a number of other ways. It receives a Government grant for these purposes. It also administers certain private funds, mainly devoted to archaeology, awards, medals and prizes, and offers an annual programme of lectures. Its *Proceedings*, which include the lectures delivered and biographical memoirs of deceased Fellows, are published annually. The memoirs now constitute the major biographical record for British scholarship in the 20th century. It also publishes a wide range of fundamental texts and aids to scholarship.

British Architectural Library *66 Portland Place and 21 Portman Square, W1.* Founded in 1835 at the first public meeting of the (ROYAL) INSTITUTE OF BRITISH ARCHITECTS when Sir Charles Barry, a year or two before winning the competition for the HOUSES OF PARLIAMENT, presented a handsome cheque to the infant Institute 'to assist in the object of collecting standard works which I consider to be of paramount importance'. About the same time Sir John Drummond Stewart, connoisseur and amateur architect, gave a sumptuous collection of 17th and 18th century architectural drawings. These two gifts encouraged members to present their own drawings as exemplars, including measured drawings of Gothic and Classical buildings prepared for the benefit of articled pupils unable to afford the cost of travelling to the original buildings. The gradual accumulation of material, both from members and generous donors, has resulted nearly 150 years later in a priceless collection of books, manuscripts and drawings, which is one of the world's leading architectural libraries. The library contains some 120,000 books, 700 current periodicals, 50,000 photographs and 100,000 manuscripts covering architecture of all periods and countries. The range of subjects includes theory, design, building types, interiors, environment, planning, landscape design, construction, building methods, the allied arts, sociology and management. The manuscript collection includes work by Wren, Kent, Chambers, Nash and famous 19th-century architectural families such as the Smirkes, the Wyatts, the Scotts, and important 20th-century collections, notably the massive correspondence files of Sir Edwin Lutyens. By 1971 space at PORTLAND PLACE had become limited and the Drawings Collection was moved to No. 21 Portman Square. This collection of 250,000 drawings is the most comprehensive in the world. Although it is predominantly British in character, there are important groups of continental drawings, including Rubens's original designs for his *Palazzi di Genova*, and, of unique importance, the Burlington–Devonshire collection representing (along with Inigo Jones, John Webb and Lord Burlington himself), practically all of the surviving designs of the most influential architect in history, Andrea Palladio. The books and drawings which make up the library are essentially a working collection as well as an archive, and provide an active current information service not only for architects but also for the construction industry, and the general public.

Since it is owned by the RIBA and receives no outside financial support, a British Architectural Library Trust has been established.

British Broadcasting Corporation *see* BROAD-CASTING HOUSE.

British Council *10 Spring Gardens, SW1.* Established in 1934, and granted a Royal Charter in 1940, the British Council has as its aims the promotion of a wider knowledge of Britain and the English language and the development of closer cultural relations between Britain and other countries. It has offices world-wide, working independently of British embassies or high commissions, teaching English, running libraries, mounting exhibitions and in every way providing information about Britain to anyone overseas who asks for it. In Britain, many overseas visitors and students study aspects of British life under the auspices of the British Council. SPRING GARDENS, where the Council's headquarters now stands, was once a pleasure garden where it was reported there was 'continual bibbing and drinking wine all day under the trees'. The offices also extend along the north side of CARLTON HOUSE TERRACE, where controversy was caused when a 'delightful 19th-century mews' was demolished to make way for them. These headquarters offices, designed by Howard V. Lobb and Partners, were opened in 1975.

British Film Institute *127–133 Charing Cross Road, WC2.* Founded in 1933, the Institute is primarily responsible for the development of film as an art. Its Production Board offers financial and technical assistance to both new and experienced film makers. The Institute runs the National Film Archive and the NATIONAL FILM THEATRE and publishes the magazines *Sight and Sound* and the *Monthly Film Bulletin*.

British Library Formed in 1973 by bringing together three major national institutions – the British Museum Library, the National Central Library, and the National Lending Library for Science and Technology. It is entitled to receive a copy of each new publication in Britain and has its main Reading Room in the BRITISH MUSEUM, although it is not part of the Museum. It occupies a number of buildings in Greater London, and one, for the headquarters of the Lending Division, in West Yorkshire. The Reference Division, of which the NEWSPAPER LIBRARY is part, is the most comprehensive research library in Britain and is used by scholars from all over the world. It contains nearly 10 million printed books and large collections of Western and Oriental manuscripts, charts and rolls, seals, maps, music, Greek, Latin and Egyptian papyri, Government papers of all countries and periods, and postage stamps. The Science Reference Library, the principal British public reference library for contemporary scientific literature, includes an important collection of literature on world patents. The Lending Division, which has no service for direct borrowing by individuals, is the largest library in the world engaged in lending between libraries and other corporate organisations both domestic and foreign, having access to many millions of books in other libraries to augment its own 2½ million volumes and current periodicals. It is a centre for translation and for the disposal by

libraries of unwanted publications. The Bibliographical Division, responsible for the Copyright Receipt Office, publishes *The British National Bibliography* weekly from works deposited there, and a number of specialist catalogues and indexes of publications in Britain. The Division also houses the National Serials Data Centre with its international links, its computerised service giving access to a variety of data bases. The Library is concerned with the improvement and extension of its services and has an active Research and Development Department entitled to award grants and contracts to outside bodies engaged in this field.

The growing need for more storage space (2 miles of new shelves annually), reading rooms, offices, conservation and staff facilities has long been recognised, and plans for a new building to bring the Library under one roof were finally approved in 1980. The architect is Colin St John Wilson, the site close to ST PANCRAS STATION, and the first part of Stage 1, which will house many of the London operations of the Library, is scheduled for completion in 1991.

British Medical Association *Tavistock Square, WC1.* Founded in Worcester in 1832 as the Provincial Medical and Surgical Association by Sir Charles Hastings and about 50 of his medical colleagues. The present building is on the site of the house occupied by Charles Dickens. It was built in 1913, designed by Sir Edwin Lutyens for the Theosophical Society. The BMA bought the building in 1923 and commissioned Lutyens to extend it. There are approximately 66,000 members of the association, which publishes the *British Medical Journal* and 13 specialist journals.

British Museum *Great Russell Street, WC1.* Originated in an offer by the physician and collector, Sir Hans Sloane, who died in 1753 and suggested in his will that Parliament might like to buy for £20,000 his works of art, antiquities and natural history collections which had cost him about £50,000 to assemble. The offer was accepted and a Foundation Act was passed the same year authorising the purchase not only of the Sloane Collection but also of the Harleian Collection of Manuscripts. These manuscripts formed part of the library which had been founded by Robert Harley, 1st Earl of Oxford and his son Edward, the 2nd Earl, and were bought for £10,000 from the 2nd Earl's heiress, the Duchess of Portland. The Act also provided for 'one general repository for the better reception of the said collections, and of the Cottonian Library, and of the additions thereto'. The Cottonian Library and antiquities had been assembled by the Cotton family from the late 17th century onwards. They had been displayed originally at Cotton House, WESTMINSTER, whose site is now covered by the House of Lords; then at ESSEX HOUSE, STRAND; and from 1731 at ASHBURNHAM HOUSE, LITTLE DEAN'S YARD, which had been purchased by the Government in order to house them for the nation to whom they had been presented in 1700.

To raise money for the purchase, housing and maintenance of these collections a sum of £300,000 was raised by public lottery. Of this £10,250 was paid in 1755 for MONTAGU HOUSE, BLOOMSBURY. A further £12,873 was spent upon repairs and on 15 January 1759 the museum was opened to the public, but only for three hours a day and only to a very limited number

The British Museum in 1852, after Montagu House had been replaced by Robert Smirke's classical façade and portico.

of people who were obliged to make application in writing, 'which writing shall contain the applicants' names, condition, and places of abode, also the day and hour at which they desire to be admitted . . . If the applicants are approved by the principal librarian, the applicants, on applying at the porter's lodge at the time named, will receive printed tickets enabling them to see the collection [but] no more than ten tickets are to be delivered out for each hour of admittance, which tickets when brought by the respective persons therein named are to be shown to the porter; who is thereupon to direct them to a proper room appointed for their reception till their hour of seeing the Museum be come, at which time they are to deliver their tickets to the proper officer of the first department: and that five of the persons producing such tickets be attended by the under librarian, and the other five by the assistant in each department . . . . Each company [is to] keep together in that room to which the officer who attends them shall then be [and at the end of the hour they must] remove out of the apartment, to make room for fresh companies.' These stringent regulations continued in force until 1808 when they were partially relaxed; but it was not until 1879 that unrestricted access to the galleries was permitted.

The foundation collections were augmented year after year by purchases and gifts of all kinds. In 1757 George II presented the Royal Library of 10,500 volumes collected by British monarchs from Henry VIII to Charles II, a gift which brought with it the privilege of receiving a copy of every book registered at STATIONERS' HALL. In 1772 Sir William Hamilton's collection of antique vases was acquired; in 1801 French plunder captured after Bonaparte's defeat at Alexandria, including the Rosetta Stone; in 1805 Charles Towneley's collection of classical sculptures, previously displayed in Towneley's house in what is

now QUEEN ANNE'S GATE; in 1807 the Lansdowne manuscripts containing state papers and correspondence of prominent figures from the reign of Henry VI to that of George III and law reports from Henry VIII's to Charles II's; in 1813 Francis Hargreaves's collection of 500 law manuscripts; in 1816 marbles from the Parthenon and Erechtheum which had been brought back from Greece by Lord Elgin; and in 1823 George III's library of 120,800 volumes came into the Museum's possession. Gifts and bequests came from David Garrick of old plays; from Captain James Cook of items from the South Sea Islands; from Sir Joseph Banks of ethnographical collections, botanical specimens and 16,000 volumes on natural history; from Thomas Grenville of a library of over 20,000 books; from the 13th Earl of Derby of a large zoological collection; from John Doubleday of 2,433 casts of medieval seals; from William Yule of Persian, Arabic and Hindustani manuscripts; from the trustees of Henry Christy of a great ethnographical collection; from Lady Raffles of the Javanese collections formed by Sir Stamford Raffles; from A.W. Franks of a large collection of Chinese and Japanese pottery as well as Greek and Roman antiquities. The BANK OF ENGLAND presented coins and medals; the East India Company zoological specimens; the ROYAL SOCIETY their Museum of Curiosities.

This rapidly accumulating material soon outgrew the limited space available in MONTAGU HOUSE and the temporary structures which were erected around it. In 1823, therefore, work began on an extensive building programme which was to continue for several years. The architect chosen was Robert Smirke who planned a large quadrangle with an open courtyard behind MONTAGU HOUSE. The King's Library was the first to be built in 1823–6. A west wing followed in 1831–4, a north wing in 1833–8; and work began on an entirely new front in 1842. This involved the demolition of MONTAGU HOUSE and its substitution by the fine classical Greek façade with its portico, decorated on its pediment with an ornamental group representing the progress of civilisation, which can be seen with pleasure today. On 19 April 1847 the new Central Hall was opened.

In 1852–7 the courtyard was converted into the Reading Room in accordance with a plan suggested by Sir Anthony Panizzi, Principal Librarian of the Museum, 1856–66. This beautiful Reading Room beneath its huge copper dome, one of the largest in the world, was designed by Sydney Smirke and has been used by scores of great scholars and writers from Thomas Carlyle and George Bernard Shaw to Lenin and Marx. In 1882–4 a further gallery was added for the Halicarnassus sculptures, which had been obtained through the offices of Sir Stratford Canning, British Ambassador in Constantinople, and a wing was constructed for the Newspaper Library and the Department of Prints, Drawings and Manuscripts.

The Museum's congestion was much relieved in 1881 when the natural history collections began to be moved to SOUTH KENSINGTON (*see* NATURAL HISTORY MUSEUM). In 1904–5 a NEWSPAPER LIBRARY was built at COLINDALE. The need for this addition became even more apparent in 1911 with the passing of the Copyright Act which laid down that a copy of every book, periodical or newspaper published in Great Britain must be deposited at the museum. In 1914 the Edward VII Galleries, designed by Sir John Burnet, were completed. In 1937 the North Library was constructed, and a West Gallery for the Parthenon sculptures was completed in 1938 at the expense of Lord Duveen.

Recent acquisitions have included the Sutton Hoo treasure hoard which had been found buried in a ship as a memorial to a 7th-century Anglo-Saxon king (1939); the Mildenhall hoard of 4th-century Roman silver (1942); and a 4th-century Roman pavement found in almost perfect condition in Devon (1963).

This great national collection of antiquities and prints and drawings contains an extraordinarily rich variety of treasures. Among them may be found, in addition to those already mentioned, 67 ivory chessmen made in Scandinavia in the 12th century; the royal gold cup of the Kings of France and England made in Paris in 1380; an Iron Age shield discovered at BATTERSEA; Egyptian mummies; a 4th-century Greek Bible; the 7th-century Lindisfarne gospels; two of the four extant copies of Magna Carta; the Diamond Sutra of 868, the world's oldest printed document, found in a cave in northern China; the log-book of the *Victory*; Shakespeare's first folio of 1623; and Captain Scott's diary. A purpose-built gallery for clocks and watches was opened in 1975. The extension of the Museum in MUSEUM STREET is by Colin St John Wilson and Partners (1980).

British Museum (Natural History) *see* NATURAL HISTORY MUSEUM.

Britton Street *EC1*. Built in 1719 and until 1936 known as Red Lion Street after the tavern of that name (now demolished). The antiquarian John Britton served as apprentice here to the landlord, his uncle, and complained of being confined in 'damp, murky

cellars'. The architects Yorke, Rosenberg and Mardall designed their own offices at No. 24.

Britton's Court *Whitefriars Street, EC4*. Formerly a neat yard with 18th-century houses, now a service bay to offices in BOUVERIE STREET. A crypt beneath it is the only surviving part of the Priory of the Carmelites, the WHITEFRIARS.

Brixton *SW2, SW9*. First recorded in 1067 as Brixistane, meaning 'at the stone of Brihtsige', it gave its name to the north-eastern district or hundred in the County of Surrey, extending a little beyond the present Boroughs of SOUTHWARK, LAMBETH and WANDSWORTH. Hundreds were often called not after their chief town, but after the spot where the men of the hundred assembled for deliberation, most likely in the middle of an uninhabited moor. The present centre of Brixton remained largely waste land until the beginning of the 19th century, the main centre of settlement being around STOCKWELL with isolated settlements at Brixton Hill and Coldharbour Lane. Rush Common, a swathe of common land extending from the centre of Brixton up Brixton Hill, was enclosed in 1810; and with the opening of VAUXHALL BRIDGE in 1816, improved access to central London led to a process of suburban development, chiefly for CITY businessmen. At first this took the form of ribbon development along the frontage of the original country lanes which form the present main roads; but as London grew and land values increased, side roads began to be formed to open up the back lands of market gardens, paddocks and exhausted brickfields for new housing. The consecration of ST MATTHEW's church (designed by Charles Porden) in 1824 provided a focal point for the new community. Other surviving buildings from this period include No. 46 Acre Lane (1808), Trinity Homes (1822) and 1–5 St Matthew's Road (1825–7).

This early 19th-century development was suburban in character, with houses set well back from the road in generous gardens – partly due to building lines laid down by the Rush Common Inclosure Act. In most cases the actual development was piecemeal, with small groups of houses being erected by different builders. The largest single development, and one of the last in suburban character, was Angell Town, laid out in the 1850s on the east side of Brixton Road, and so named after a family which owned land in LAMBETH from the late 17th century until well into the 20th. It consisted of a careful arrangement of wide curving streets opening off Wiltshire Road as the main axis, with the new St John's church (built in 1853 to the designs of Benjamin Ferrey) as the focal point. Small parts of the estate survived postwar redevelopment, notably Angell Terrace at 341–361 Brixton Road (1855–60, recently restored), though the large Italianate houses in St John's Crescent are more typical.

With the coming of the railways in the 1860s, the character of development changed to denser, humbler housing for clerks and skilled workmen taking advantage of quick and cheap access to central London. The neighbourhoods around LOUGH-BOROUGH JUNCTION, Railton, Ferndale and Milkwood Roads date mainly from the 1860s and 1870s, while Brixton Hill was developed in the 1880s and 1890s as tram and horse-bus services extended southward from WESTMINSTER.

As a major route centre with a growing local population, Brixton rapidly became an important shopping centre. The old building lines were increasingly flouted, and Electric Avenue was opened in 1888 with shops behind covered arcades as one of the first shopping streets lit by electricity. Between the two World Wars, fully covered shopping arcades were built, and the LONDON COUNTY COUNCIL allowed shops on the east side of Brixton Road to move their frontages forward in exchange for widening the road, so that the old forecourts disappeared.

Towards the end of the 19th century, the social character of the area was changing, with many of the large old houses being used as lodging houses, particularly for people working in the theatre who took advantage of the easy access to the WEST END. Music-hall stars living in the area included Dan Leno (in Akerman Road) and Fred Karno (in Southwell Road). None of Brixton's own theatres survives, but the Ritzy Cinema (1910) is one of the oldest purpose-built cinemas still in use anywhere. Between the wars, many of the large early 19th-century houses fell into decline and were demolished to make way for flats both private (Brixton Hill) and local authority (Tulse Hill), though small pockets of semi-detached houses of the 1930s can be found.

From 1948, the availability of lodging houses in easy reach of central London led to the settlement of West Indian immigrants in the Brixton area, initially in the Somerleyton Road and Akerman Road areas and later around Railton Road. At the same time several old neighbourhoods were replaced by Council estates, chiefly on the north-east side of Brixton and in the TULSE HILL area. In site of the weakening of community ties by the turnover of population, the neighbourhoods to the south-west of Brixton were able to resist LAMBETH Council proposals for large-scale redevelopment, the economic case for which was faltering by the mid-1970s anyway, and a number of housing improvement schemes were started instead.

Although Brixton is sometimes supposed to be a black ghetto, a supposition strengthened by the riots here in 1981, blacks and Asians in that year represented only 29 per cent of the population: 62 per cent were whites, the rest mostly Cypriots, Maltese, Chileans and Vietnamese.

Brixton Market *Atlantic Road, SW9*. A general market with a strong West Indian flavour, it grew up in the 19th century with the main market under the railway arches and stalls lining Electric Avenue (which had been lit by ELECTRICITY in the 1880s). It became known for its fairground atmosphere and eccentric characters. In 1952 a petition against the closure of the market showed that regular customers came from as far afield as ORPINGTON and ENFIELD.

Brixton Prison *Jebb Avenue, SW2*. Opened in 1820 as a Surrey House of Correction. 'Situate in one of the most open and salubrious spots', it was designed by Chawner, the County Surveyor, the main cell blocks being arranged in the form of a rough crescent with the Governor's house in the centre. When the high wall and gatehouse were finished, 25 prisoners were sent, as an experiment, to help construct the main buildings: unfortunately three escaped and the Governor was dismissed. Built for 175, the usual number confined was about 400, hence, despite its excellent

The treadmill was set up at Brixton Prison in 1821 and connected to the millhouse which contained corn-grinding machinery.

situation, it was one of the unhealthiest of all London prisons. It was a hard-labour prison: the treadmill, invented by Sir William Cubitt, was set up in 1821 and connected to the millhouse which contained corn-grinding machinery. In 1851 the prison moved to WANDSWORTH and Brixton Gaol was sold. Then the Government decided to substitute penal servitude at home for transportation so it bought Brixton for female convicts in 1853. With additions and alterations, accommodation for 700 was made. The prisoners here washed all the clothes for PENTONVILLE, MILLBANK PENITENTIARY and Brixton. Some went to great lengths to improve their appearance. One, it was said, managed to stiffen her stays with wires withdrawn from her windows. It was not until she 'fainted away in chapel one day, a victim to extra-tight lacing, that the misappropriation of the wires was discovered'. Converted into a military prison in 1882, in 1897 Brixton was returned to the Prison Commissioners. After reconstruction it was reopened as a male prison in 1902. In 1973 20 prisoners escaped together; and in 1980 an IRA man awaiting trial escaped with two others. Brixton now houses unconvicted adults from London and the Home Counties and persons serving sentences of up to 18 months. In 1982 it had 771 prisoners (with a certified normal accommodation of 504).

Brixton Windmill *Windmill Gardens, SW2*. The nearest surviving windmill to the centre of London, it was built in 1816 for Ashby and Sons, local millers, in an area which remained open fields until 1850. The mill continued in use on wind power until 1862, by which time the neighbourhood had become too built-up for it to function efficiently, the business being transferred to watermills at MITCHAM. In 1902, however, the mill was put back into use, driven at first by steam and later by a gas engine, instead of sails. In 1957 the mill was bought by the LONDON COUNTY COUNCIL and later restored to its original condition. It is now in the care of LAMBETH COUNCIL. Repeated attacks by vandals, however, have obliged the Council to abandon attempts to maintain it. In 1982 a local group, the Windmill Gardens Community Association, was trying to keep vandals away.

Broad Sanctuary *SW1*. The open area between WESTMINSTER ABBEY and the MIDDLESEX GUILDHALL.

It is so called after the Sanctuary Tower which once stood to the north and in which, despite its name, fugitives from justice were not always safe. In Richard II's reign Judge Tresilian was dragged from it and hanged at TYBURN; in 1440 the Duchess of Gloucester, accused of witchcraft after melting a wax image of the King, was denied entrance; and in 1472, Henry Holland, Duke of Exeter, who claimed sanctuary after the Battle of BARNET, was found drowned in the THAMES after his wife Anne (Edward IV's sister) had divorced him. In 1483 Elizabeth Woodville, widow of Edward IV, fled here with her six children after Richard of Gloucester had taken her eldest son, Edward V, to the TOWER. He later persuaded her to give him her other son, Richard, Duke of York, to be a companion to his brother. Both were murdered within two months (*see* TOWER OF LONDON). Elizabeth I restricted the right of sanctuary to debtors. James I totally abolished it in 1623. On the south side, with a gatehouse leading into DEAN'S YARD, are Gothic stone-faced offices of 1854 by Sir Gilbert Scott who also designed the memorial column to Old Westminsters (*see* MEMORIALS) which marks the approximate site of the GATEHOUSE PRISON. The MIDDLESEX GUILDHALL is by J.S. Gibson. Edmund Burke lived in a house which was demolished when Scott's Gothic block was built. Isaac Newton lodged in Broad Sanctuary in 1689 and Sir John Hawkins, the musicologist and 'un-clubbable' biographer of Samuel Johnson, whose literary executor he was, died in a house here in 1789.

Broad Street Station, the terminus of the North London Railway, was designed by William Baker and opened in 1865. Only two of its platforms are in use today.

Broad Street Station *EC2*. Built as the terminus of the North London Railway and opened in 1865. The design in the best Town Hall style was by William Baker, first chief engineer of the London and North Western Railway, which controlled the NLR and paid the major part of the cost of the station. Broad Street was planned as the terminus for a network of railways linking the London and Birmingham Railway, and other depots in North London, with the London docks, originally for freight purposes. But by the time this network was developed, a huge passenger traffic was ready to use it. Before the turn of the century Broad Street was London's third-busiest station (after LIVERPOOL STREET and VICTORIA), but it lost most of its passengers to buses, trams and the tube. The main station block was closed in 1950. Only two platforms are now in use by the present North London Line for services to RICHMOND and Watford.

Broad Walk *Regent's Park, NW1*. A spacious avenue of trees running north to south like a chord across the eastern side of the Outer Circle. Its southern half is bordered by herbaceous flower beds, well tended and of an extraordinary variety in colour. Enormous stone urns are planted with flowers. The Parsee Fountain (1869) in granite and marble by an unknown Parsee sculptor was the gift of Sir Cowasjeen Jehangir.

Broadbent Street *W1*. On the GROSVENOR ESTATE, it is a short side street extending from GROSVENOR STREET to BOURDON STREET and was until 1936 known as Little Grosvenor Street.

Broadcasting House *Portland Place, W1*. Five years after the British Broadcasting Company's daily programmes started from Savoy Hill on 14 November 1922 (*see* BROADCASTING) there had been such expansion in radio that new premises were needed in central London. In 1928 a site was chosen at the corner of PORTLAND PLACE and LANGHAM STREET. This site had formerly been occupied by a house built in 1780–3 on part of the gardens of Foley House (*see* LANGHAM) to the designs of James Wyatt who built it for his own use. It was originally known as 'Mr Wyatt's House' and later as the second Foley House. It was demolished in 1928 and many of the mantelpieces and fittings went to the VICTORIA AND ALBERT MUSEUM. The site was due to be developed for flats when bought by the BBC. The architects had to produce a building that was not only in keeping with the Adam and Regency style of the surroundings but one which would provide 22 studios entirely sound-insulated. Their answer was to plan an inner core of studios with an outer shell and the building, first occupied on 2 May 1932, remains unaltered externally to the present day. The architect was G. Val Myers who worked initially with the BBC's engineer, Marmaduke Tudsbery. Like a great ship, its prow is aimed at the heart of London.

Broadcasting House cost £350,000 and within months it was found to be far too small. St George's Hall, on the south side of ALL SOULS, was taken over in 1933 for variety shows (it was destroyed by bombs early in the 2nd World War) and a disused roller-skating rink was turned into four studios at MAIDA VALE. In the 1960s the huge office and studio block was added to the north to the designs of H.R. Robinson. The coat of arms and the carving on the balcony of Broadcasting House were designed by the architect, G. Val Myers, and the external sculpture by Eric Gill who took Shakespeare's Ariel as the symbol of broadcasting. Over the main entrance he portrayed Prospero sending Ariel out into the world. On the first floor directly over the entrance hall is the Council Chamber and, on the third floor, the Board Room where the Director-General and the Governors meet to make the policy decisions which affect the whole of the country's public service broadcasting.

Despite the great Television Centre at SHEPHERD'S BUSH and the scores of regional and local offices and studios all over the United Kingdom, Broadcasting House is still today synonymous with the BBC. It came near to destruction in the 2nd World War. Its gleaming white Portland stone was painted battleship grey but the German bombers found it. On 15 October 1940 a bomb exploded in the heart of the building, killing seven people. The Nine O'Clock News, read by Bruce Belfrage, continued through the blast. Less than two months later a landmine exploded in the middle of PORTLAND PLACE and it took seven hours to put out the fire that spread through Broadcasting House. Still the programmes went out. Staff lived and slept on the premises and the Concert Hall became a dormitory with a curtain of blankets hung across the room.

Broadway *SW1*. The site of a hay market which was opened in the reign of James I and continued here until the beginning of the 18th century. Dick Turpin is said to have lived for a time in a nearby court. The Broadway Chapel, built in 1642 by the bequest of a prebendary of WESTMINSTER ABBEY, once stood here. It was used as stables in the Civil War, and prisoners captured at the Battle of Worcester were kept here. They were treated so badly that 1,200 died and were buried in TOTHILL FIELDS. In 1847 it was replaced by Christ Church, designed by Ambrose Poynter. This was bombed in the 2nd World War. The Telephone Exchange, designed by W.S. Frost and built in 1959–62, stands on the site. At No. 55 is the head office of the London Transport Executive, built in 1927–9 to the designs of Charles Holden. It is decorated with Epstein's stone figures *Night and Day* (1929) and reliefs of the winds by Henry Moore, Eric Gill, Allan Wyon, Eric Aumonier, A.M. Gerard and F. Rabinovitch. NEW SCOTLAND YARD is on the north-east side. The Feathers public house is at No. 20.

Broadwick Street *W1*. Building began in 1686, and the street was finished in 1736. The wider western end was originally known as Broad Street, and the narrow eastern part as Edward Street after Edward Wardour who lived nearby. Both parts of the street were renamed Broadwick Street in 1936. It was in its early days a fashionable place, but by the middle of the 18th century, the houses were mostly occupied by tradesmen and shopkeepers. Nos 60–74 (even) and 51–67 (odd), although very much altered, date from this period. William Blake was born at No. 74 (then No. 28) in 1758. His father, a hosier in circumstances comfortable enough to encourage his interest in art, sent him, at the age of ten, to Par's drawing-school in the STRAND. Four years later, he was apprenticed to James Basire, engraver to the SOCIETY OF ANTIQUARIES; and in 1778 he became a student at the recently formed ROYAL ACADEMY. In 1782 he married Catherine Boucher, a BATTERSEA market-gardener's daughter, with whom he set up in lodgings at 23 Green Street, Leicester Fields. In 1784 he opened a print-seller's shop in the house next door to the one in which he had been born, No. 27 (now No. 72), the next year moving to POLAND STREET.

The John Snow public house on the corner of LEXINGTON STREET at No. 39 used to be known as the Newcastle-upon-Tyne, but was given its new name in 1956 in honour of Dr John Snow who was largely responsible for having the handle of the nearby pump chained up during the CHOLERA epidemic of 1854, being convinced that the disease was water-borne. The epidemic was particularly severe in the street, the inhabitants of only 12 of the 49 houses escaping death. The Crown public house, which used to stand at No. 60, on the corner of DUFOUR'S PLACE on a site occupied by a tavern since at least 1740, has now been replaced by the Charles Norton old people's centre. The Lion Brewery, which flourished in the street

from 1801, was demolished in 1937 to make way for Trenchard House.

Brockley *SE4*. North of FOREST HILL and south of NEW CROSS, Brockley (perhaps from 'Broca's wood') straddles the old boundary between the parishes of DEPTFORD and LEWISHAM. In the reign of Henry II it was given to the Premonstratensian canons who may have settled here briefly before moving to Bayham (Sussex) in 1200. In the 1520s Cardinal Wolsey used the estate to endow his abortive Cardinal College, Oxford. The DEPTFORD portion came ultimately to the Wickhams, Drakes and Tyrwhitt-Drakes of Shardeloes, Amersham (Bucks), thus accounting for several local street names.

Brockley remained agricultural until the last century, the only building of note being the Brockley Jack, rebuilt in 1898 but formerly a curious, rambling hostelry, reputedly a haunt of highwaymen. After 1850 substantial development spread south and west from Lewisham High Road (now Lewisham Way). Here in a house at the junction of Wickham Road and Lewisham High Road, Marie Lloyd spent the unhappy years of her first marriage; Charles Stewart Parnell and Kitty O'Shea are said to have used No. 112 Tresillian Road for clandestine meetings; while Edgar Wallace skulked from his creditors at 6 Tresillian Crescent, where he is commemorated by a BLUE PLAQUE. Development of the southern part of Brockley, around Crofton Park Station, was generally later and more workaday, a mixture of terrace houses for 'clerkly classes' and local authority flats and houses. Here lies Hilly Fields whose 'windswept views' were saved from development by public agitation in 1896. The park is dominated by Brockley County School, a building which began life in the 1890s as the Church Schools Company's West Kent Grammar School. The large double cemetery, half for DEPTFORD and half for LEWISHAM, opened in 1856–8 to replace the overcrowded parish churchyards.

Brockley Cemetery *see* CEMETERIES.

Brockwell Park *and* **Hall** *SE24*. Like BRIXTON WINDMILL, a reminder of the area's rural past. The original Brockwell Hall stood near the present Norwood Road, but was demolished before the erection of the present Brockwell Hall in 1811–13, for John Blades, a wealthy glass manufacturer who had bought the house and 60 acres of grounds in 1809. The house was designed by D.R. Roper and later work to the enlarged grounds was directed by J.B. Papworth. Residential development of the grounds was first considered by Blades in the 1820s, but had not proceeded far when he died in 1829.

By the 1880s much of the BRIXTON and HERNE HILL area had been densely covered with houses, and the local authorities set aside funds to provide a park, purchasing the hall and 78 acres of grounds in 1891 after it was offered at a lower price than a smaller estate in Brixton Hill. The park was opened to the public by Lord Rosebery, chairman of the LONDON COUNTY COUNCIL, in 1892. T.L. Bristow, MP for Norwood in 1885–92, who was largely responsible for the project, died of a heart attack at the ceremony. Access from the Brixton direction and extension of the Park to its present size of 84 acres were only achieved by the piecemeal acquisition of the remainder of the estate which was completed in 1922.

The layout of the Park, including the ponds, was carried out by the LONDON COUNTY COUNCIL; but the walled garden dates from the mid-18th century while the former chapel (with classical portico) and coach house are contemporary with Brockwell Hall itself. An open-air swimming pool was added in 1937.

Broderers' Company *see* CITY LIVERY COMPANIES.

Broken Wharf *EC4.* An inquiry in 1249 was told that the joint owners of the wharf, the Abbots of Chertsey and the Abbots of Hamme, had quarrelled for 40 years about mending it. It was so called, according to Stow, because of its 'being broken and fallen into the Thames'. In 1594 a horse-powered engine was installed in a brick water-house erected by Bevis Bulmer for supplying water to CHEAPSIDE and FLEET STREET in lead pipes (*see* WATER SUPPLY).

Bromley *Kent.* The manor of Bromley ('wood with broom shrubs'), formed in 862, was owned from Saxon times by the Bishops of Rochester, who built BROMLEY PALACE as a manor house and continued as lords of the manor until 1845. A market town of long standing, Bromley's first charter for a market was granted in 1205. A second, in 1447, changed market day from Tuesday to Thursday, and granted two annual fairs. The fairs are no longer held, but the market continues. The parish church of SS Peter and Paul dates back to the 13th century. Dr Johnson's wife, Tetty, was buried here in 1752 – owing to his friendship with Dr John Hawkesworth, a distinguished local resident. Tetty's grave-slab survived when the church, rebuilt in the 1790s, was destroyed by a bomb in 1941. A new church building, combined with the restored tower and designed by J. Harold Gibbon, was consecrated in 1957. In 1866 H.G. Wells was born at 47 High Street, son of a local shopkeeper and cricketer, and he spent his early years in Bromley. The building was demolished with others in 1930s, and a plaque on a more modern shop marks the site. The new CHURCHILL THEATRE and Central Library were opened in 1977. To the north-east, Sundridge Park mansion is an outstanding example of 18th-century architecture, built under the direction of Repton, Nash and James Wyatt. Much of its land now belongs to the GOLF CLUB, and the house itself is a management centre.

Further to the north-east is the residential area of Mottingham, where Dr W.G. Grace spent his last years and died (at Fairmount, Mottingham Lane) in 1915. HAYES and KESTON, with their extensive commons, lie to the south of Bromley. Hayes Place, which was demolished in 1934, was built for William Pitt who died there in 1778. William Pitt the Younger also lived there. At the neighbouring Holwood, which he had bought (and which has now been turned into offices), he and William Wilberforce discussed the abolition of the slave trade under a tree known as the Wilberforce Oak. Only the stump of this tree remains, but there is an inscription on a nearby seat. Keston Common, more wooded than Hayes Common, contains ponds fed by 'Caesar's Well', and in nearby Holwood Park is Caesar's Camp, once an ancient British encampment. Keston church, a blend of Norman and Early English, is thought to have been built on the site of a Romano-

British cemetery. In the churchyard is the grave of Mrs Craik, author of *John Halifax, Gentleman*. A plaque on 20 Church Road, Shortlands, records that Alexander Muirhead, the electrical engineer, lived here. He established his factory at Elmers End in the 1890s.

Bromley-by-Bow Palace South of the Old Priory in St Leonard's Street, Bromley-by-Bow, stood a house which was known as the Old Palace. Dating from the 17th century, it was sometimes called Queen Anne's Palace and was built of brick with a plain front and flanking pyramidal towers. The rooms inside it were noteworthy for handsome stucco ceilings, Jacobean panelling, William and Mary carving and marble floors. One of these rooms is preserved at the VICTORIA AND ALBERT MUSEUM. Traditionally associated with James I, its design has been attributed to John Thorpe. It was divided into two merchants' houses about 1750, when the wing towers were reduced in height and the mullioned windows replaced by sash ones. Despite great public indignation it was demolished in 1893 to make way for a LONDON COUNTY COUNCIL Board School. Its demolition was the inspiration for the *Survey of London* (*see* HISTORIANS).

Bromley College *London Road, Bromley, Kent.* The College, founded by Bishop Warner, was built in the late 17th century as a hospital or almshouse for 'twentie poore widows of orthodox and loyall clergiemen'. The original building – a quadrangle with cloisters – remains little changed externally. A second quadrangle was added in a similar style in the early 1800s, and further homes added in 1840 for the widows' daughters who could only live in the College while their mothers were alive. The College continues in its original function today, and is the oldest building of its kind in England.

Bromley Common *Kent.* For centuries an area of about 300 acres of wasteland, overgrown with gorse, heather, fern and broom, through which various tracks passed. Part of the Common was Lammas or half-yearly land, which could be used by local people for six months of the year. The owner, the Bishop of Rochester, had the full use of the land between 5 April and 10 October each year. As late as the mid-18th century, the main coach road from London to Tunbridge Wells was, when it crossed the Common, little more than a track. Evelyn records in his diary that in June 1652 he was robbed on Bromley Common. When James Norman took up residence here in 1755, he had posts put up and painted white in order to mark the roadway. In 1798 a highwayman was hanged on the Common for stealing His Majesty's mail. The first part of the Common was enclosed by an Act of Parliament of 1764. About 60 years later, by an Act of 1821, the rest of the Common was enclosed. New roads, ditches, fences and drains were laid; and, in addition to the few farms and houses which previously existed, a considerable development took place providing residential accommodation. Bromley Town spread out over what had been common land. Horse races had been held here in the 18th century and were said to have been patronised by Frederick, Prince of Wales. In 1864, these were established on a more regular basis. Races and steeplechases were held four times a year until the race course was closed in 1874. It then became a golf course.

Holy Trinity church was built in 1839; St Luke's in 1886; and St Augustine's in 1913. The most prominent residence on Bromley Common was James Norman's house, The Rookery. Later, another residence in the area, Elmfield, was bought by a member of the same family of bankers who enlarged and developed their holdings. Charles Darwin (*see* DOWNE) referred to one of them as 'my clever neighbour, Mr Norman'. They are remembered today by Norman Park.

Bromley Palace *Rochester Avenue, Bromley, Kent.* Built in Norman times as a manor house by the Bishops of Rochester, who owned it until 1845. Bishop John Warner left money for repairing the Palace and for the founding of BROMLEY COLLEGE. In 1669 John Evelyn found the Palace 'now repairing after the dilapidations of the late rebellion'. Bishop Thomas Sprat was arrested here (while composing a sermon in the orchard) for his alleged part in a plot to restore James II; and Francis Atterbury, who entertained Pope and Matthew Prior here, was also imprisoned for Jacobite sympathies.

The waters of St Blaise's Well in the grounds were widely used for medicinal purposes. The old palace was demolished, and a new building replaced it in 1775. With modern wings added, it was until recently used as a college. It now belongs to Bromley Council and is used for council offices.

Bromley St Leonard *E3, E14.* A Benedictine convent dedicated to St Leonard was founded south of the later village of BOW, probably about AD 1100; and Chaucer may have had this nunnery in mind when he described the Prioress, Madame Eglantine, in his Prologue to the *Canterbury Tales*, as speaking French 'after the scole of Stratford atte Bowe'. After the DISSOLUTION, the convent's lady chapel became the parish church; but 19th-century rebuilding, 20th-century bomb damage and the construction of the northern approach road to the BLACKWALL TUNNEL have destroyed all that was left of the church, although some of the churchyard remains off Bromley High Street.

Until the 19th century, land in the area was largely used for farming and market gardening, with industry along the River LEA devoted to calico bleaching, milling grain or distilling. The population numbered about 3,500 by 1811 although almost half the houses were small cottages occupied chiefly by Irish labourers. The parish was divided by the LIMEHOUSE Cut and the North London Railway running south to the docks. This improvement in communications, however, enabled the extensive area of Bow Common in the south-west to be developed for industry. The abundance of water supplied by the LIMEHOUSE CUT, good transport facilities and the remote position made the area attractive for gasworks, brickfields and chemical works. Much of the south-eastern part was acquired for the EAST INDIA DOCKS. The TOWER HAMLETS CEMETERY took land in the north-western district and numerous streets for housing were laid out in the second half of the 19th century. Thus the population rose to 24,000 by 1861 and reached its peak of about 70,000 in 1891. The poorest and roughest area, lying between the Limehouse Cut and Devons Road, was nicknamed the 'Fenian Barracks' because the Irish who lived there were said to send more police to hospital than any other block of streets in London. In 1900

Bromley became a part of the Metropolitan Borough of POPLAR. Much of the 19th-century housing has been demolished to make way for modern council estates or the approach road to the BLACKWALL TUNNEL. A BLUE PLAQUE on the wall of Kingsley Hall, Powis Road, commemorates Mahatma Gandhi's stay at this social settlement in 1931.

Brompton *SW1, SW3.* As 'Broom Farm' it is recorded as early as 1294 and was an outlying hamlet of KENSINGTON on its southern boundary. The area, which straddles the parish boundary between KNIGHTS-BRIDGE and EARLS COURT, was known for its market gardens and nursery grounds from the 17th century. The most famous, BROMPTON PARK NURSERY, was founded in 1681 by George London and his most famous partner was Henry Wise, one-time Superintendent of the Royal Gardens. The nursery, part of whose site is today occupied by the VICTORIA AND ALBERT MUSEUM, achieved a European reputation but there were many others in the locality and Faulkner as late as 1820 could tabulate some 520 acres devoted to these purposes and to farming generally.

Brompton remained sparsely built up until late into the 19th century and in 1886 the population totalled 45,700 as against 127,800 in the remainder of the parish. As late as 1871 the local Medical Officer of Health could make the point that Brompton had a lower mortality rate than Cheltenham, then considered the healthiest town in England. Such a reputation encouraged not only well-to-do residents but also hospitals, of which the best-known is BROMPTON HOSPITAL founded in 1842 as the Hospital for Consumption and Diseases of the Chest. By contrast BROMPTON CEMETERY (architect Benjamin Baud, 1840) is amongst the largest of the metropolitan cemeteries and contains the graves of many famous persons. It is now administered by the Department of the Environment.

Brompton Cemetery *see* CEMETERIES.

Brompton Hall *Brompton.* Traditionally supposed to have been the country house of Lord Burleigh in the reign of Queen Elizabeth who 'occasionally honoured' him with a visit. It stood a short way south of GROVE HOUSE. It was modernised in the 18th century by a Mrs Griffiths, the widow of a clergyman, who discovered 'the arms of Queen Elizabeth, carved in oak, and curiously inlaid with gold' above the chimneypiece in the dining-room. It was bought by the Metropolitan and District Railways in the 1860s and demolished in 1874 when the Railways sold their surplus lands to speculative builders.

Brompton Hospital *Fulham Road, SW3.* Opened in 1842 at a time when hospitals denied admission to consumptive patients. (One of the Standing Orders of ST GEORGE'S HOSPITAL formally stated: 'No person shall be admitted as an in-patient who shall be labouring under any contagious disease or *whose case shall be consumptive*.') In 1841 a poor clerk in the employ of a firm of London solicitors, Baxter, Rose and Norton, was taken ill with consumption. One of the partners, Philip Rose, tried unsuccessfully to get him into hospital. So angry was Rose, and so concerned that consumption was a national scourge, that he collected his personal friends together at his house, 41 HANS PLACE. At this meeting, with Rose's partner, Baxter, in the chair, it was resolved that a hospital called the Hospital for Consumption and Diseases of the Chest be built. As a result of enormous efforts by Rose (who later received a baronetcy), in June 1842 the Committee of Management advertised for a house in the neighbourhood of BROMPTON, KNIGHTSBRIDGE, upper CHELSEA or PADDINGTON, which 'should be suitable for in-patients'. They settled on Manor House, Chelsea, near the ROYAL HOSPITAL. A ten-year lease was taken and 20 in-patients were admitted. In 1843, at the second Anniversary Dinner, Charles Dickens said, 'If this charity had not existed, the doors of no sick house within London's wide bounds would have been open to these poor persons. Before this hospital was founded they would have suffered, lingered, pined and died in their poor homes without a hand stretched out to help them in their slow decay.' Manor House very soon proved to be too small. A site was chosen at BROMPTON, a 'village in Kensington remarkable for the salubrity of its air'. In 1844 the foundation stone was laid by the Prince Consort. The architect was Frederick John Francis. A west wing was opened in 1846; an east wing in 1854; and a south block on the other side of FULHAM ROAD in 1879. The architect for these extensions was Thomas H. Wyatt. Early in the 20th century a medical school for postgraduate students was set up. In 1948 the hospital was taken over by the National Health Service. And the next year it was opened as the Institute of Diseases of the Chest. It is responsible for postgraduate teaching jointly with the LONDON CHEST HOSPITAL and NATIONAL HEART HOSPITAL. It has 352 beds.

Herbert Gribble's drawing of Brompton Oratory, which was built to his design in 1878–84.

Brompton Oratory *Brompton Road, SW1*. The London Oratory of St Philip Neri, a Roman Catholic church served by priests of the Institute of the Oratory, founded by St Philip Neri at Rome in the 16th century. They settled at Brompton in 1847. In 1878–84 the ornate Baroque church, based on the mother church of Chiesa Nuova, Rome was built to the designs of Herbert Gribble, incorporating a magnificent Italian altarpiece and the high altar from St Servatius Maestricht. Marble statues of the apostles by Mazzuoli came from Siena Cathedral. St Peter in the nave is a copy of the statue in St Peter's Rome. Until WESTMINSTER CATHEDRAL opened in 1903 the Oratory was the centre of Roman Catholic activity in London. In 1892 Cardinal Manning's funeral took place here. In 1896 Chevalliaud's marble statue of Cardinal Newman was erected outside.

Brompton Park House *Brompton*. The house, which once stood on the site of the VICTORIA AND ALBERT MUSEUM, was for over 40 years, until his death in 1738, occupied by Henry Wise, the gardener, who was a partner in the BROMPTON PARK NURSERY. In 1784 the mansion was converted into three smaller houses in one of which the 3rd Lord Holland was living when his future wife, Lady Elizabeth Vassal (*see* HOLLAND HOUSE), bore him his illegitimate son. When the Royal Commissioners for the GREAT EXHIBITION of 1851 acquired the freehold of all the houses, they were for a time used by the South Kensington Museum (*see* VICTORIA AND ALBERT MUSEUM) before being demolished in 1899.

Brompton Park Nursery *Brompton*. Founded in 1681 by George London and three other gardeners, it was described by Stephen Switzer, 34 years later, as 'the noblest Nursery of the World'. The great gardener Henry Wise (*see* BROMPTON PARK HOUSE) was associated with it for several years until his partner, London, died in 1714, when he sold it to two of their assistants. In its heyday the Nursery covered over 100 acres south of KENSINGTON ROAD and supplied trees, shrubs and plants for most of the large gardens of London, several of which were landscaped by its proprietors.

Brompton Road *SW1, SW3, SW7*. The ancient track to the village of BROMPTON, it now extends from KNIGHTSBRIDGE to FULHAM ROAD. There have been a number of modern encroachments but much of the 19th- and early 20th-century building remains. HARROD'S by Stevens and Munt (1901–5) is at Nos 87–135. BROMPTON ORATORY is at the junction with CROMWELL ROAD and behind it is the Gothic HOLY TRINITY church built in 1829 to the designs of Thomas Leverton Donaldson. There are two pleasant Victorian public houses, the Crown and Sceptre at No. 132, and the Bunch of Grapes at No. 207. In the modern block at No. 70 are the Independent Broadcasting Authority and a number of sporting organisations, including the Amateur Athletics Association, the Amateur Boxing Association and the Sports Council. At Nos 2–10 is the Scotch House department store which was founded by the Gardiner brothers who travelled from Glasgow to London to sell tweeds and tartans in the 1830s. The Tartan Room has a collection of over 300 tartans. The sculpture *Triga*, three stone horses, by Franta Belsky, stands on the building at No. 44 (1958). The National Fur Company at No. 241 was established in 1878 in SLOANE STREET, moving to Brompton Road shortly afterwards. WARING AND GILLOW are at No. 191.

Brompton Square *SW3*. Small attractive square built in about 1824. Stéphane Mallarmé, the French poet, stayed at No. 6 in 1863. Francis Place, the political reformer, lived at No. 21 in 1833–51.

Brondesbury *NW6*. Situated north-west of KILBURN along the EDGWARE ROAD. The district contains the highest land in WILLESDEN and may possibly have been a hill-fort close to Roman WATLING STREET. In the 11th and 12th centuries ST PAUL'S carved out prebendal estates from the parish of WILLESDEN and the prebend of Bronnesburie was named after a 12th-century canon named Brand. By the Middle Ages thick forest had gradually been reduced to meadow and pasture, although in the 17th century 69 acres of

97

woodland still survived. At that date cattle were kept and a milkhouse and cheese-room existed. In 1788 Lady Sarah Salusbury purchased the leasehold of the Brondesbury estate, combining it with that of the prebend of Bounds. Repton landscaped the grounds of the house for which William Wilkins supplied Gothic designs. From the mid-19th century the outward expansion of London had its effect and by the end of the century the house had become a school. The Hampstead Junction line arrived and from the late 1860s the development of housing for merchants and City professionals was under way. R.B. King's Christ Church was opened in 1866 and in 1867 the new district, incorporating the old prebends of Brondesbury, Bounds and Mapesbury (after the 12th-century prebendary Map), was named Brondesbury. By the beginning of the 20th century the population had increased over eightfold. Brondesbury Park was developed, extending to Willesden Green. Brondesbury Park Station was opened (1908) and in 1909 the district became an additional ward of WILLESDEN Urban District. Brondesbury had a large Jewish population and Baron Meyer de Rothschild and Sir Anthony de Rothschild were buried in the CEMETERY on Willesden Lane (opened 1873). Although many of the large houses were converted into flats following the 2nd World War, Brondesbury still retained its character as a high-class residential area within the municipal borough of WILLESDEN. In 1965 when Willesden amalgamated with WEMBLEY Urban District it became part of the London Borough of BRENT.

Brook Street *W1.* Extends from HANOVER SQUARE to GROSVENOR SQUARE. It takes its name from the TYBURN, which flows beneath it at the intersection with AVERY ROW. Building began at the east end on the CITY OF LONDON's Conduit Mead estate in the early 18th century, and the portion west of South Molton Lane, which is on the GROSVENOR ESTATE, was all developed between 1720 and 1729. Although described in 1736 as 'For the most part nobly built and inhabited by People of Quality', Brook Street was never as fashionable as GROSVENOR STREET, and in the early 19th century several private hotels had established themselves here, of which the most famous was CLARIDGE'S.

A few fine houses still survive. The most famous of these is No. 25, occupied by George Frederick Handel in 1723–59. Nos 66 and 68, both built by the architect Edward Shepherd in 1725 (the former containing two splendidly decorated rooms), are now occupied by the Grosvenor Office. No. 76, now used as offices, was built by Colen Campbell, who lived here from 1726 until his death in 1729. No. 39 was largely rebuilt by Jeffry Wyatt (latterly Sir Jeffry Wyatville), who lived here in 1804–40. No. 69, occupied since 1927 by the SAVILE CLUB, contains a splendid interior, done in the Louis XV style in about 1890 for J. Pierpont Morgan's son-in-law, by W.O.W. Bouwens van der Boijen, a Parisian architect of Dutch extraction. Most of the other houses have been rebuilt, generally since about 1850, and are now chiefly used as offices. Notable residents included (at No. 68) William Pitt, later 1st Earl of Chatham, in 1757, and the 1st Earl of Woolton in 1947–57. At No. 72 Edward Shepherd, the architect, lived in 1726–9; and at No. 47 (now demolished) Henry Addington, later Prime Minister, in 1787–90.

Brooke House *Park Lane.* Built in 1870 for Sir Dudley Coutts Marjoribanks by T.H. Wyatt. An enormous and opulent house on six floors, it was subsequently purchased by King Edward VII's friend, the multi-millionaire Sir Ernest Cassel, who filled it with old masters, with all kinds of objets d'art from Renaissance bronzes to English silver and Chinese jade, and with equally decorative women. Cassel died here in 1921 and the house was demolished 12 years later.

Brooke Street *EC1.* Site of the house of Sir Fulke Greville, Lord Brooke, adviser to Queen Elizabeth and James I and patron of Ben Jonson and Shakespeare. It disappeared in about 1680. Philip Yorke, Lord Chancellor in 1736–56, was a clerk in chambers here. Chatterton, the poet, committed suicide at a house on the site of No. 39 by swallowing arsenic in 1770. The church of ST ALBAN THE MARTYR HOLBORN occupies part of the site of Thieves' Kitchen, a training ground for young criminals which had established itself in the area.

Brook's Mews *W1.* On the GROSVENOR ESTATE, it extends from BROOK STREET to AVERY ROW. It was laid out in the 1720s to provide stables and coach houses for the mansions in BROOK STREET and GROSVENOR HOUSE, on to which it backs.

Brooks's Club *60 St James's Street, SW1.* A smart, social and non-political club founded in 1764 by William Almack. It met at ALMACK'S in PALL MALL until 1778 when it moved to Henry Holland's new club house in St James's Street under the management of William Brooks, a wine merchant and moneylender. It soon established a reputation for heavy gambling. Horace Walpole said 'a thousand meadows and cornfields were staked at every throw'. Charles James Fox did so badly that he had to borrow from the waiters. It later became the Whigs' Club. Fox, Pitt, Reynolds, Garrick, Horace Walpole, Wilberforce, Palmerston and Hume were members. Sheridan was black-balled three times by George Selwyn on the grounds that his father had been on the stage, and was elected at last through a ruse of George IV, then Prince of Wales, who detained Selwyn in conversation in the hall when the ballot was in progress. Daniel O'Connell was also a member. When elected in 1822 John Campbell, later Lord Campbell, the Lord Chancellor, wrote, 'To belong to it is a feather in my cap. Indeed since we lost our estates . . I am inclined to think that my election at Brooks's is the greatest distinction our house has met with. The Club consists of the first men for rank and talent in England.'

Broomfield House *Southgate, N14.* Shown on the earliest map of the parish, drawn in the second half of the 16th century. The owner was Geoffrey Walkaden. By the end of Elizabeth's reign Alderman Sir John Spencer lived here; he sold it to Joseph Jackson and it remained in the Jackson family for nearly 200 years until Mary Jackson married William Tash. After his death it passed to the Powys family, who usually let the house; their most distinguished tenant was Sir Ralph Littler, the barrister. The park and house were purchased by SOUTHGATE Council in 1903. Inside there is a fine staircase hall of about 1725 with murals by Lantscroon. The house is now a museum run by the

London Borough of ENFIELD. There are changing exhibitions of local history and a permanent display of bones, stuffed birds and animals, and pictures. There is also a Victorian nursery. The park contain a model boat pond, three lakes with waterfowl, gardens of remembrance and facilities for bowls and tennis.

Broomwood Road *SW11*. Takes its name from Broomwood House, formerly Broomfield, where William Wilberforce lived when he was conducting his campaign against slavery. There is a plaque commemorating the house, which was demolished in 1904, on No. 111.

Brothers' Steps *see* FIELD OF THE FORTY FOOT-STEPS.

Brown's Hotel *Dover Street, W1*. In 1837 James Brown, a former manservant, opened a hotel at 23 DOVER STREET. He was probably supported financially by his ambitious and efficient wife, Sarah, a former lady's maid to Lady Byron. The hotel prospered and in the next eight years Brown acquired Nos 21, 22 and 24, the present frontage of the hotel. In 1859 he sold out to J.J. Ford, already owner of Ford's Hotel in MANCHESTER SQUARE, and in 1882 Ford's son Henry took over the management. In 1876 Alexander Graham Bell stayed here and from the hotel made the first successful telephone call in the country to Henry Ford at RAVENSCOURT PARK about 5 miles away. Theodore Roosevelt was a guest in 1886 and walked from here to his wedding at ST GEORGE'S, HANOVER SQUARE. In 1889 Henry Ford acquired St George's Hotel (named after the church) in ALBEMARLE STREET, which backed on to the DOVER STREET hotel. In 1905 Franklin and Eleanor Roosevelt spent their honeymoon here. King George II of the Hellenes spent his nine years of exile here. In Room 36 the Dutch Government declared war on Japan in the 2nd World War. Cecil Rhodes and Rudyard Kipling were two of many distinguished patrons. There are 135 bedrooms, 17 family apartments and five suites.

Bruce Castle *Lordship Lane, Tottenham, N17*. An Elizabethan manor house in the then familiar shape of an E, said by local tradition to stand on the site of a castle built by Robert the Bruce's father. Certainly the manor belonged to the Scottish royal family until the 14th century. The house has been much altered. It was rebuilt in about 1670 by Henry Hare, 2nd Baron Coleraine; and the east wing was added by the Townsend family in the 18th century. To the west of the house is a 16th-century round tower of unknown purpose. Lord Coleraine is believed to have locked up in it his second wife who escaped only by throwing herself off the parapet holding a baby. Her ghost is said to repeat the action each year on a November night. In 1827 Rowland Hill bought the house and began a private school here. He left it after a breakdown in his health in 1833, but the school continued until 1891 when the house was acquired by the local authority. It now holds a local history museum, a library, a postal museum illustrating the development of the postal service and the regimental museum of the Middlesex Regiment, with pictures, uniforms, medals and trophies captured in the Maori War, Zulu War, Boer War, at the Battle of Hong Kong and in Korea.

Brunel University *Uxbridge, Middlesex*. In 1962 over 150 acres of former horticultural land to the south of UXBRIDGE were acquired by the rapidly expanding Brunel College of Advanced Technology, established at ACTON in 1957. Richard Sheppard (Richard Sheppard, Robson and Partners) was appointed architect of the new site. The College obtained its Charter in 1966, and the move to UXBRIDGE began the following year. The University, which is noted for its engineering studies and links with industry, has about 4,350 students. It takes its name from Isambard Kingdom Brunel, the engineer, whose Great Western Railway passed through ACTON.

Brunswick Dock A large and important dock in the 18th century, named after the ducal house in honour of George III. It formed the basis for the

William Daniel's aquatint of Brunswick Docks, 1803. The Mast House (centre) held a crane for fitting masts to tall ships.

EAST INDIA DOCKS. Built as a private speculation in 1789 by a Mr Perry (and so often called Perry's Dock), it covered some 8 acres into which had been absorbed the small Blackwall Dock of 1½ acres built during the reign of Charles II for the East India Company. The Blackwall was, in fact, the first wet dock with gates on to the THAMES. Pepys mentions his visit to it in 1661 as Secretary to the Navy and inspected 'a brave new merchantman', the *Royal Oak*, which had been built there. Neither the Blackwall nor the Brunswick was used for handling cargoes but only for ship-building and fitting out, although the Brunswick did come to possess some warehouses for storing whalebones and blubber. A painting by William Daniell of 1803 shows the Brunswick Dock tightly packed with ships, protected from the wind by a row of trees, and having as its main feature a large tower containing a crane for raising or fitting masts to the tall ships. This Mast House was 120 ft high and remained a conspicuous landmark at the EAST INDIA DOCKS until 1862.

Brunswick Square *WC1*. Named after Caroline of Brunswick, wife of the Prince Regent. Planned by Samuel Pepys Cockerell to balance with MECKLEN-BURGH SQUARE on the other side of the FOUNDLING HOSPITAL grounds, and built in 1795–1802. In his report to the Governors of the Hospital, Cockerell wrote that the object of the squares was to retain for the hospital 'the advantages of its present open situation' and to provide an architectural setting so 'as rather to raise than depress the Character of this Hospital itself as an Object of National Munificence'. All the original buildings have been replaced. On the north is the School of Pharmacy of LONDON UNIVERSITY (founded 1842), built in 1939–70 to designs by Herbert J. Rowse. Also the offices of the THOMAS CORAM FOUNDATION with a statue of Captain Coram (*see* STATUES) outside. On the west are terraced and cantilevered apartments by Patrick Hodgkinson (1969–72), forming the Brunswick Centre of shops, restaurants and a cinema. To the south is International Hall, a students' hostel of LONDON UNIVERSITY. Virginia and Adrian Stephen shared a four-storey house in the square with John Maynard Keynes, Duncan Grant and Leonard Woolf. Virginia and Leonard left when they married in 1912. Their friend E.M. Forster lived in the square in 1929–39. John Hunter, physician and Vice-President of the FOUNDLING HOSPITAL, whose name is remembered in Hunter Street, lived here in 1803–9. Isabella in Jane Austen's *Emma* praised BRUNSWICK SQUARE: 'Our part of London is so very superior to most others . . . We are so very airy.'

Bruton Lane *W1*. Extends from BRUTON STREET to the junction of HAY HILL and BERKELEY STREET. Its irregular course follows the boundary between the fields known as Brick Close which were acquired by the 1st Lord Berkeley of Stratton after the Restoration, and Conduit Mead, sometime the property of the CORPORATION OF LONDON (*see* CONDUIT STREET).

Bruton Place *W1*. L-shaped in plan, it extends from the north-east corner of BERKELEY SQUARE to BRUTON STREET. Its site forms part of the lands acquired by the 1st Lord Berkeley of Stratton soon after the Restoration, and it provided stables and coachhouses for the great houses in BERKELEY SQUARE and BRUTON STREET. Nos 36 and 38, of about 1890, still

retain the hoists by which sacks of grain were raised to the lofts. The Guinea public house at No. 30 occupies a site where a tavern is believed to have existed since the 15th century.

Bruton Street *W1*. Extends from BERKELEY SQUARE to NEW BOND STREET. Most of its site forms part of the lands acquired soon after the Restoration by the 1st Lord Berkeley of Stratton, the Civil War commander, from whose country estate near Bruton in Somerset it takes its name. Building began in about 1738, and some of the original houses survive, though in much altered form – notably, on the south side, Nos 12–13, and, on the north side, Nos 23–25 (probably by Isaac Ware, 1739), 27–29 and 31–33 (consecutive), almost all of which now have shop-fronts at street level. No. 17, now demolished, was latterly the town house of the Earl of Strathmore, and here, on 21 April 1926, his daughter, then the Duchess of York, gave birth to Princess Elizabeth, now Queen Elizabeth II.

Notable inhabitants include Richard Brinsley Sheridan, dramatist, in about 1786, and George Canning, later Prime Minister, in about 1809. Norman Hartnell, the first London couturier to take a fashion show and dress collection to Paris, started his business at No. 26 in 1924. Holland and Holland, at No. 13, have been making guns since 1830. The Lefevre Gallery at No. 30 was founded in 1926.

Bryanston Place *W1*. On the PORTMAN ESTATE, it takes its name from Bryanston, the Portman family seat in Dorset. Sir Roderick Impey Murchison, the geologist, was a resident from 1826 to 1838 at No. 3 where he was visited not only by scientists but by men concerned with literature and the arts, such as Hallam, Lockhart, Chantrey, Bulwer Lytton and Sydney Smith.

Bryanston Square *W1*. Takes its name from the Portman family seat in Dorset and lies on the PORTMAN ESTATE to the west of BAKER STREET. Begun in 1812 by David Porter, a builder who had started life as a chimney-sweep, the houses, each with a shallow bow-window, face on to an elongated, apsidal-ended rectangle of garden, set around with railings, and, nowadays, an outer ring of parking-meters. Wyndham Place, running north from the Square, leads to ST MARY's church, designed by Sir Robert Smirke and dedicated in 1824. Bryanston Square is celebrated in literature, for Mr March, in C.P. Snow's *The Conscience of the Rich* (1958), lived at No. 17, and it provides the title and the setting for Algernon Cecil's *A House in Bryanston Square* (1945). Mustapha Pasha Reschid, Turkish statesman and reformer, lived as ambassador at No. 1 in 1839.

Bryanston Street *W1*. First appears in the ST MARYLEBONE Rate Books in 1766; it is named after the Dorset seat of the ground landlords, the Portman family. On the corner with Old Quebec Street is the CHURCH OF THE ANNUNCIATION, a lofty Gothic building by Walter Tapper (1912–14).

Buckingham Gate *SW1*. Extends from VICTORIA STREET to BUCKINGHAM PALACE. There are a few 18th-century houses still remaining in the street, including No. 16 which was built in about 1706, perhaps to the designs of Captain Winde. Wilfrid Scawen Blunt, the diplomat, poet and traveller, lived in the house next door. The nearby house at No. 20 is by Sir Reginald Blomfield (1895). The corner house, No. 10, was built in 1854 by Sir James Pennethorne for the DUCHY OF CORNWALL offices which are still here: the columns between the railings are decorated with the Prince of Wales's feathers. St James's Court (1899) is by C.J. Chirney Pawley. The Westminster Chapel (Evangelical Independent) was originally built in 1840–1 'for divine worship according to the Congregational faith'. Schools and vestries were added in 1843; almshouses in 1859; and the congregation having outgrown it, the chapel was demolished and the present chapel erected in its place to the designs of W.F. Poulton in 1863–5. Wellington House replaces the former Wellington House by Palgrave and Company (1908). Spenser House is by Chapman Taylor and Partners (1980–1). William Gladstone was living at No. 20 in 1889 and H.G. Wells at No. 52 in 1924.

Buckingham House *Pall Mall*.
One of the great Pall Mall mansions, named after George Nugent-Temple-Grenville, 1st Marquess of Buckingham, who inherited it from his uncle. It had previously belonged to Thomas Pitt, grandfather of William Pitt, 1st Earl of Chatham. The house was rebuilt in the 1790s to the designs of Sir John Soane. It was sold in 1847 by the 2nd Duke of Buckingham. The CARLTON CLUB occupied the house in 1854–5 while its club-house was being rebuilt. Thereafter it was occupied by the War Office until 1906. It was demolished in 1908 and the ROYAL AUTOMOBILE CLUB was built on the site.

Buckingham House (The Queen's House) *St James's Park*.
Built in 1702–5 for John Sheffield, 1st Duke of Buckingham and Normanby, by William Winde. The Duke had previously lived at Arlington House but, dissatisfied with both building and site, he had that house demolished and his new red-brick house built partly on land of which he owned the freehold and partly on land which he held on lease

from the Crown. The leasehold land was known as the Mulberry Garden, formerly a walled garden planted with thousands of mulberry trees which James I had created in the hope of promoting the culture of silk. A few weeks after its completion, Macky described Buckingham House as 'one of the great beauties of London, both by reason of its situation and its building. It is situated at the west end of St James's Park, fronting the Mall and the great walk; and behind it is a fine garden, a noble terrace (from whence, as well as from the apartments, you have a most delicious prospect) and a little park with a pretty canal.' The Duke himself told a friend: 'The avenues to this House are along St James's Park, through rows of goodly elms on one hand, and gay flourishing limes on the other; that for coaches, this for walking; with the Mall lying between them. This reaches to my iron pallisade that encompasses a square court, which has in the midst a great bason with statues and waterworks; and from its entrance rises all the way imperceptibly, 'till we mount to a Terrace in front of a large Hall, paved with square white Stones mixed with a dark coloured marble; the walls of it covered with a set of pictures done in the school of Raphael.' The Duke died in 1721 and his widow, who claimed to be an illegitimate daughter of James II by Catharine Sedley, entered into negotiations for the disposal of the property to the Prince of Wales (afterwards George II). Nothing came of these negotiations, however, and it was to be George III who bought the property for £28,000 in 1762 from the Duke's illegitimate son, Sir Charles Sheffield. Furniture and pictures were taken here from HAMPTON COURT and KENSINGTON, and the King and Queen slept here for the first time in September. In 1775 the house was transferred to the Queen for life in exchange for SOMERSET HOUSE which had been made over to the newly founded ROYAL ACADEMY OF ARTS. It was here that Dr Johnson had his celebrated meeting with George III in the library. From time to time extra rooms were added to house the King's growing collections; and the Queen's House became more of a palace than the family home that the King had originally

Buckingham House, built in 1702–5 for the 1st Duke of Buckingham and Normanby, was bought by George III in 1762.

William Heath's 1829 caricature of John Bull questioning John Nash about the excessive cost of building Buckingham Palace.

intended to possess. In 1800 James Wyatt built a new grand staircase with a main and two branching flights which swept majestically up to the first floor beneath ceilings painted by Laguerre. After the Queen's death in 1818, her eldest son, by then Prince Regent, determined to build a larger and even grander house on the site; this eventually became BUCKINGHAM PALACE.

Buckingham Palace *SW1*. Soon after he came to the throne, King George IV announced that CARLTON HOUSE was no longer a sufficiently grand and imposing residence for a King of England. He decided that it would have to be demolished and a new palace built to replace BUCKINGHAM HOUSE, his parents' London house where all his brothers and sisters had been born. He had had this idea in mind for some time, and had estimated in 1819 that a new palace could be built for £500,000. This being £350,000 more than 'the utmost sum' which – so the Prime Minister informed him – the government would be prepared to spend 'in the present circumstances of the country', the project had for the moment to be dropped. It was soon revived, however, and Sir John Soane, hoping that he would be asked to prepare the designs as an attached architect to the Board of Works, produced plans for a new palace in GREEN PARK. But the King preferred the site of BUCKINGHAM HOUSE which, since his mother's death had become known as the King's House, PIMLICO; and, maintaining that 'early associations [endeared him] to the spot', and pointing out the advantages of the large gardens, he insisted that the new palace must be built there. He also insisted that the architect must be John Nash. He had his way; and the House of Commons authorised a sum that 'might not be less

than £200,000' for the 'repair and improvement' of the King's House, PIMLICO. The Government's intention that the old house merely be repaired and improved was no deterrent to the King who was determined to have something entirely new built of Bath stone. So Nash retained the shell of the earlier house and a good deal of the plan, but what gradually emerged was much larger and much more expensive than the Government had envisaged. By the time the original estimate of £252,690 had been increased to £331,973, the work was far from completed; and all manner of costly building materials had arrived on the site, including 500 massive blocks of veined Carrara marble.

The basic design was a three-sided court open at the east, in front of which was to stand the MARBLE ARCH as the main entrance into the forecourt. But the ornamentations seemed to most observers, as they seemed to Thomas Creevey, who sallied forth to see the alterations in February 1827, the 'devil's own'. Other critics complained of the 'square towers at the sides and wretched inverted egg-cup at the top'. Nash was questioned about this 'egg-cup' at a select committee appointed to enquire into the expense of public buildings. His answers were confusing:

'Is any light conveyed from the top of the dome?'
'None at all.'

'Then it is purely an ornamental part of the building?'
'It forms the ceiling of the room underneath.'

'That is one of the state rooms?'
'No, it is over one of the state rooms.'

'Will you inform the committee whether any useful part of the building is lighted by means of the dome.'

'There is no light from the dome, but the cavity of the dome is necessary to make the room underneath the dome of a proper height.'

'Is it a room of great utility?'
'No, nothing but a common bedroom.'

In 1828 Wellington became Prime Minister. Nash went to see him with a proposal that the wings, which did not meet with the King's approval, should be pulled down and rebuilt, to which the Duke replied crossly, 'If you expect me to put my hand to any additional expense, I'll be damned if I will.' But the work, once begun, could not very well be abandoned; and month after month it went on, mounting towards an ultimate total of £700,000, excluding the cost of the MARBLE ARCH.

The King did not live to see the palace finished. His brother, William IV, never lived there either; and when Queen Victoria came to the throne in 1837 it was scarcely habitable. The drains were faulty; there were no sinks for the chambermaids on the bedroom floors; few of the lavatories were ventilated; the bells would not ring; some of the doors would not close; and many of the thousand windows would not open. After Nash's dismissal in 1830, Edward Blore was appointed architect and it was he who finished the building, replaced Nash's dome by an attic and, in 1847, enclosed the courtyard by adding the east front – the front facing THE MALL, which is the one familiar to the public today – an operation which involved the removal of the MARBLE ARCH to its present position at the top of PARK LANE. In 1853–5 the ballroom block was added by Sir James Pennethorne.

By then the Queen had grown fond of the palace. 'I have been so happy there,' she wrote in her diary in 1843 when leaving the palace for one of the other royal residences. Her son, Edward VII, who was born and died here, grew fond of the palace too, once he had cleared out the jumble of unwanted objects with which the Queen had filled it during her long life, had had it redecorated and had rearranged the furniture and pictures. In the time of George V, though the official receptions were as grand as ever, the atmosphere of the palace became much more domesticated. To their eldest son, indeed, it became positively stuffy. 'The vast building', he wrote in his memoirs after he had become Duke of Windsor, 'with its stately rooms and endless corridors and passages, seemed pervaded by a curious, musty smell that still assails me whenever I enter its portals. I was never happy there.' As King he was once seen jumping out of a window and running away across the garden to avoid an unwelcome confrontation with his private secretary. His brother George VI, who shared most of their father's tastes and was innately and unalterably conservative, liked the palace much better and was deeply distressed when it was bombed in the war and the chapel, in his own words, was 'wrecked'.

Since the war the palace has once again been renovated and redecorated. And whatever adverse criticisms may be made of the work of both Nash and Blore concerning the interior of the building – whose east front was replaced in 1913 by the present Portland stone façade designed by Sir Aston Webb – there are several rooms of surpassing grandeur.

There are some 600 rooms in all in the Palace, including those used by the staff as offices for the various members of the Royal Household and the domestic

The Long (picture) Gallery in Buckingham Palace. Begun by George IV, the palace was not finished until Victoria was on the throne.

quarters. The rooms occupied privately by the Royal Family are few in number. The Queen and the Duke of Edinburgh have a suite of about 12 rooms on the first floor of the north wing overlooking GREEN PARK. On the second floor, overlooking the Mall, are two suites for Prince Charles and Princess Anne. There is also a sitting-room for the Ladies-in-Waiting. On the north side is the covered swimming-pool.

The gardens of the palace, landscaped by W.T. Aiton, extend to HYDE PARK CORNER and cover some 45 acres. They are graced by expansive lawns, a lake, and a wide variety of flowers and trees including one of the mulberry trees planted by James I in what was then the Mulberry Garden. Here in the summer garden parties are held, usually three each year for about 8,000 guests. The south wing of the palace contains the QUEEN'S GALLERY.

The forecourt of the palace is patrolled by sentries of the Brigade of Guards in full dress uniform. On most mornings the CEREMONY of Changing the Guard takes place here. When the Queen is in residence the Royal Standard, her personal flag, flies at the palace's masthead.

Buckingham Palace Hotel *2 Buckingham Gate, SW1.* One of the largest hotels in Victorian London. It was built as the Palace Hotel in 1860–1 to the designs of James Murray. Fifteen bays wide, with a projecting cornice and Italianate in style, it faced the south side of BUCKINGHAM PALACE. It was much favoured by families from the counties who came to London for the season. It now serves as offices for the British Transport Authority.

Buckingham Palace Road *SW1.* Known as Chelsea Road in the 18th century, it led from the village of CHELSEA to BUCKINGHAM HOUSE and was much frequented by highwaymen. In 1752 the residents of CHELSEA offered £10 for the capture of a particularly troublesome highwayman. VICTORIA STATION dominates much of the eastern side. On the west side, towards the southern end, is the reference department of the Westminster City Library. The Coach Station at the southern end was built in 1931–2 to the designs of Wallis Gilbert and Partners and the Air Terminal in 1939 to the designs of A. Lakeman. The Portland stone sculpture over the entrance is by E.R. Broadbent (1935). The GROSVENOR HOTEL is also at the south end. At the north end are the QUEEN'S GALLERY and the ROYAL MEWS.

Edward Stephens, the sculptor, died in Buckingham Palace Road in 1882. Until its closure in the 1960s Frederick Gorringe, the drapery store, stood at No. 75. Established in 1858, it was much patronised by Ladies of Queen Victoria's Household. Overton's, the restaurateurs in Terminus Place, were established here in 1872. They also have a restaurant and oyster bar in ST JAMES'S STREET. John Broadwood and Sons, the pianoforte makers, were established in SOHO in the 1740s by Broadwood, a Scottish cabinet maker, and Jacob Tschudi, a Swiss harpsichord maker. The Central Music Library at No. 160 is the biggest public music library in the south of England.

Buckingham Street *WC2.* Built in about 1675 on the site of YORK HOUSE, the former mansion of the Dukes of Buckingham. Samuel Pepys came to live at No. 12 in 1679 and remained there until 1688 when he moved to No. 14. This house, occupied by Pepys until 1701, was afterwards taken by Robert Harley, later Earl of Oxford, who began here his celebrated collection of manuscripts. After Harley's departure in 1714, the house was occupied by Lord Torrington in 1714–16 and then by the Earl of Lichfield. It was the Salt Office from 1735 to 1788. It was rebuilt in 1791–2. Chambers on the first floor were occupied by William Etty from 1824 until 1827 when he moved to the top floor where he painted some of his best-known pictures and where he remained until 1848. The first-floor chambers which he had vacated were taken by his fellow-painter, Clarkson Stanfield, whose son, George Clarkson Stanfield, was born here in 1828. In the basement in 1824–6 Sir Humphrey Davy carried out experiments on the prevention of corrosion on ships' hulls. The actress Peg Woffington lived at No. 9 in 1755–7; David Hume and Jean-Jacques Rousseau at No. 10 in 1766; and Samuel Taylor Coleridge at No. 21 in 1799. At No. 15 Peter the Great stayed in 1698 and Henry Fielding lived in 1735. In 1833 Charles Dickens took chambers on the top floor. Several 17th- and 18th-century houses remain. In 1878 the Society for the Protection of Ancient Buildings, founded the previous year by William Morris, moved into offices at No. 9.

Bucklersbury *EC4.* An ancient CITY street first mentioned in the 14th century. It was named after the Buckerel family who were powerful in the CITY in the 12th century. Their fortified house (*bury*) stood back from the street in POULTRY. In 1183 this was sold to Hasculf de Tania. From 1505 to 1511 Sir Thomas More lived here in a large house where his four children were born. Erasmus stayed with him in 1506 and 1508 when he wrote *Moriae Enconium*. The title is a pun on More's name. In Shakespeare's time the street was known for its apothecaries, and in *The Merry Wives of Windsor* he mentions the peculiar smell of Bucklersbury. In 1863 the street was cut in two by QUEEN VICTORIA STREET.

Buck's Club *18 Clifford Street, W1.* Takes its name from Captain Herbert Buckmaster who, with other young officers of the Household Cavalry, conceived the idea of forming it while on the Western Front in the 1st World War. It opened in June 1919. Buck's Fizz, a mixture of champagne and orange juice, though well known in Paris long before the club's foundation, is said to have been invented by its first barman.

Budge Row *EC4.* A narrow alley, which once formed part of the Roman WATLING STREET, named after the budge or lamb-skin dealers who used to live in it.

Builders' Company *see* CITY LIVERY COMPANIES.

Builders' Merchants' Company *see* CITY LIVERY COMPANIES.

Building Centre *Store Street, WC1.* Opened in 1931 as a permanent exhibition and information service for all interested in building. There are temporary exhibitions of architecture and allied subjects.

Building Crafts Training School *153 Great Titchfield Street, W1.* The School is administered by the CARPENTERS' COMPANY and was founded in 1893. It provides short specialist training courses, notably in woodworking and stonemasonry, for those involved in the construction and maintenance of buildings. The School has links with the JOINERS' AND CEILERS' COMPANY, as well as the TYLERS AND BRICKLAYERS' and the MASONS' and the courses are designed to give firms in these and other related industries the opportunity to provide specialist craft training for their employees.

Building Regulations *see* PLANNING.

Bull and Mouth *St Martin's-Le-Grand.* A large inn and coaching office for travellers from all parts of England and Scotland. It was demolished at the end of the 19th century when the GENERAL POST OFFICE covered the site. The inn sign is in the MUSEUM OF LONDON.

Bull Inn *Bishopsgate Street Within.* A coaching inn and carrier's office for travellers from the eastern counties. Thomas Hobson, the celebrated carrier and livery-stable keeper, on whom Milton wrote two humorous epitaphs, continued to drive here from Cambridge until, far advanced into his seventies, he had to suspend his journeys in 1630 on account of the plague. It was his refusal to allow any horse to leave his stables except in its proper turn that is supposed to have given rise to the saying 'Hobson's Choice'. Plays were performed in the courtyard before Richard Burbage built the GLOBE. The inn was demolished in 1866.

Bull's Head *Clare Market.* The favourite resort of Dr John Radcliffe, the witty physician to King William III and Queen Mary, whose patients often pretended to be ill for the pleasure of his company. He was in the Bull's Head when news came that he had lost £5,000 by the capture of a ship in which he had invested money. 'With a smiling countenance' he commented

Bunhill Fields in 1866. Burials first took place here in 1665, during the Great Plague. The last burial was in 1854.

that he had 'no more to do but go up 250 pairs of stairs to make [himself] whole again'. The Artists' Club, of which Hogarth was a member, used to meet here.

Bunhill Fields *City Road, EC1.* Originally one of the three great fields in the Manor of FINSBURY, the name, probably derived from Bone Hill, is unexplained, as it was in use before the removal to the area in 1549 of cartloads of bones from the Charnel House in ST PAUL'S CHURCHYARD. In the mid-17th century, the CORPORATION OF LONDON, which had leased the fields since 1315, decided to make a new burial ground at Bunhill for use in the GREAT PLAGUE. It was enclosed by a brick wall and gates in 1665–6. It does not appear, however, to have been used for the burial of plague victims, but as an ordinary cemetery. It was known for a time as 'Tyndall's burial ground'. No evidence of the consecration of the ground has been found, and it was much used by nonconformists who were here able to bury their dead without the use of the Common Prayer Book. It has been called 'The Cemetery of Puritan England'. After the Burials Act of 1852, Bunhill Fields was closed. The final burial, of a 15-year-old girl, took place in January 1854.

By Act of Parliament in 1867 the CORPORATION OF LONDON undertook to preserve this ground and maintain it for the use of the public. There remain, now shaded by great plane trees, the monuments to John Bunyan (1688); Susannah Wesley, mother of John and Charles and 17 others (1742); General Fleetwood, son-in-law of Cromwell (1692); Daniel Defoe (1731), a monument erected in 1870 as a result of an appeal to boys and girls by the weekly newspaper, the *Christian World*; Dr Isaac Watts, the 'father of the English Hymn' (1748); and William Blake (1827). In the adjoining Quaker graveyard lies George Fox (1691), founder of the Society of Friends. The spiked gate at the north-east corner was put up to deter body-snatchers.

Bunhill Row *EC1.* Named after BUNHILL FIELDS. It was already built up when Stow compiled his *Survey of London* in 1598. John Milton had a house here from the time of his third marriage to Elizabeth Minshull in 1662 until his death in 1674. During that time he wrote *Paradise Lost, Paradise Regained* and *Samson Agonistes*.

Burberry Ltd *18 Haymarket, SW1.* Thomas Burberry started in business in Basingstoke in 1856. He developed a fabric inspired by the smock frocks worn by shepherds and farmers – which were warm in winter, cool in summer and adequately weatherproof – for which he revived the name 'gabardine'. He and his two sons moved to London in 1899 and in 1901 took premises at 30–35 HAYMARKET. Early open-air motoring made it essential to have coats for wind, dust, cold and rain, as well as motor caps and tie-on hoods. These the firm supplied as well as Burberry-proofed silk dust coats for hot weather. They also supplied clothing for the armed forces, polar expeditions and mountaineering. In 1912 the firm moved to 18 HAYMARKET which was designed by Walter Cave, with Tuscan columns below and giant Ionic columns above.

Burdett Road *E3, E14.* Constructed by the METROPOLITAN BOARD OF WORKS to link the riverside hamlets with VICTORIA PARK, it was opened in 1862. It was named after Miss (later Baroness) Angela Burdett-Coutts. Another philanthropist, William Cotton, provided part of the land and contributed towards the cost of the road. St Paul's church is by Robert Maguire (1960).

Burgh House *New End Square, NW3.* A fine Queen Anne house built in 1703. Seventeen years later it was occupied by Dr William Gibbons, physician to the HAMPSTEAD WELLS. In 1822, the Rev. Allatson Burgh, vicar of ST LAWRENCE JEWRY, bought the house for £2,645, and gave it his name. The Royal East Middlesex Militia had their headquarters and officers' mess in Burgh House for 30 years, from 1858; they were followed by a succession of private owners, the last of whom, in the 1930s, was Captain George Bainbridge, son-in-law of Rudyard Kipling who often visited his daughter here. Acquired by HAMPSTEAD Borough Council in 1946, it housed a Citizens' Advice Bureau in the basement and was used as a community centre; but the structure deteriorated so badly that CAMDEN Council, which had become responsible for its maintenance, closed it in 1963. Local opposition to proposals to convert it into offices or to demolish it led to the formation of the Burgh House Trust. The house is let at a peppercorn rent to the Trust which runs it as a local museum and exhibition centre. Concerts and lectures are also given here.

Burgon Street *EC4.* Named after John Burgon, Dean of Chichester, a prominent Victorian clergyman, who in 1872 led the opposition to the appointment of Arthur Stanley, Dean of Westminster, as select preacher to the University of Oxford.

BURIAL GROUNDS During the 17th century, the central districts of London became so densely populated that it was no longer possible to find room to bury the dead in the small churchyards of the parish churches. The deceased were disposed of with little ceremony; bodies were buried in groups in pits; graves were dug so close together and so shallow that often only an inch or two separated one coffin from another and each from the surface of the ground. Substantial numbers of bodies were disposed of in pits beneath the floor-boards of chapels and schools, where congregations and children gathered and breathed the foul air. In an effort to remedy these horrors, the inner London parishes began to establish burial grounds away from the churches, on the edge of the then built-up area. These burial grounds remained in use until the Burial Acts of the 1850s caused them to be closed. Many of them have since been built over; but some, following the foundation of the Metropolitan Gardens Association in 1882, became, and remain now, public gardens. A number are listed here. The most famous of them all, BUNHILL FIELDS, has a separate entry (*see also* CEMETERIES).

Burial Ground of St John, Clerkenwell *Benjamin Street, EC1.* Consecrated by the Bishop of Lincoln in 1755. Now an attractive garden with trees and flowering shrubs. The only remaining tombstone, dated 1815, is in the east wall.

East Greenwich Pleasaunce *Chevening Road, SE3.* This pleasant garden has been, since 1857, the last resting place of thousands of sailors. It was the burial ground for Royal Naval pensioners from the old GREENWICH Hospital. In 1875, when a railway tunnel was cut through the old Infirmary Burial Ground, further to the west, 3,000 bodies were moved to this place, and a plaque commemorates them. Many other original tombstones remain in place.

Garden of St Mary *Aldermanbury Square, EC2,* see ST MARY ALDERMANBURY.

Huguenot Burial Ground *East Hill, Wandsworth, SW18.* This small cemetery was opened in 1687 as the burial ground for the French Church which stood opposite All Saints' church and was the place of worship of the Huguenot refugees who settled in WANDSWORTH during the 16th and 17th centuries. Later known as 'Mount Nod', the ground was enlarged in 1700 and again in 1735. It was closed in 1854, and later reopened as a garden for the public. In 1911 a memorial was erected to the memory of the Wandsworth Huguenots.

Jewish Burial Ground *Queen's Elm, Fulham Road, SW3.* This small site was purchased for £400 by a society of Jews in 1815, and opened as a burial ground the same year. Some 300 persons were buried here, their gravestones marked with inscriptions in Hebrew and English. Special manuscript copies of prayers inscribed on vellum, for use at the burial services, were presented by Mr Victor Abraham and remained in use until the cemetery was closed in 1885. The ground remains closed and inaccessible behind high brick walls.

Lambeth High Street Recreation Ground *SE11.* Archbishop Tenison gave this area to the parish of ST MARY LAMBETH in 1703 because of the urgent need for more burial space. It was enlarged in 1814, but closed by Order in Council in 1853. By 1880 it had become 'very unsightly', but the Vestry tidied it up and it became a public open space in 1884.

Long Lane Recreation Ground *SE1.* The wording of a granite tablet set in a wall of this recreation ground tells its history: 'The Property of the Six Weeks Meeting of the Society of Friends. This tablet has been placed here by Order of the Said Meeting. The burial ground, purchased in 1697, was extensively used for Friends' burials until closed by Order of the Privy Council in 1885. 8th Month (August) 1895.'

Moravian Burial Ground *King's Road, SW3.* Count Nicholas Ludwig von Zinzendorf, the leader of the Moravian movement in England, gave this piece of land, which had once been part of the SLOANE ESTATE, for the establishment of a church and burial ground. About 400 people have been buried here since the first interment in 1751. The ground, which covers about an acre, is laid out in the form of a cross, with each of the four quarters being reserved for a special group: married men; married women; single men; and single women. Each grave is marked by a simple headstone, laid flat in the grass, and all of them the same size, so that whatever the disparities of the departed's fortunes in life, they are equal in death. Because of the Brethren's custom of burying only one person in a grave, and that one very deep, the burial ground was excepted from the Burial Acts of the 1850s and permitted to remain open.

Paddington Gardens *Paddington Street, W1.* This was the extension burial ground for the old parish church of ST MARYLEBONE which stood in MARYLEBONE HIGH STREET until it was demolished in 1949. The ground was consecrated in 1733 and nearly 100,000 burials took place, including those of the architect Robert Adam; and Francis Wheatley, artist of the 'Cries of London'. Maintained as a public garden since 1886, the gravestones are arranged round the walls 'like chairs before a dance'. George Stubbs was buried in the old parish church in 1806.

Postman's Park *King Edward Street, EC1.* Overlooked by tall office blocks and the back of a GPO building, this gloomy little park was converted from the churchyards of ST LEONARD FOSTER LANE and ST BOTOLPH ALDERSGATE in 1880. Tombstones are stacked around the edge of the garden (*see separate entry*).

Royal Hospital Burial Ground, *Chelsea, SW3.* A cemetery for Chelsea Pensioners and others who worked in the ROYAL HOSPITAL. The first interment, of a Simon Box, took place in 1692. The Hospital seems to have preserved its inmates to a great age: William Hiseland was born in 1620 and died in 1732, 'a veteran, if ever soldier was'; he served in the Army for 80 years, and 'When an 100 years old he took unto him a wife'. Deaths are recorded of: Robert Cumming, in 1767, aged 116, and Joshua Cueman in 1794, aged 123, though their graves can no longer be traced. Also buried here were Sir William Fawcett, KB, Governor of the Hospital (1804); and Dr Charles Burney (1814), the musician and organist at the Hospital and father of Fanny; and two women, Christiana Davis and Hannah Bell, who joined the Army and were only discovered to be women when wounded in the Crimean War. By the time the ground was closed in 1854 more than 10,000 burials had taken place.

St Andrew's Gardens   *Gray's Inn Road, WC1.* The burial ground of ST ANDREW, HOLBORN, consecrated in 1754. Sixty-nine victims of a CHOLERA epidemic were buried here in one pit in 1832; the pit was still open and uncovered the following day. Opened as a public space and garden in 1885.

St George's Fields   *Albion Street, W2.* These 'fields', which at one time the burial ground for ST GEORGE, HANOVER SQUARE, and later used for an archery ground and games fields, and for allotments, have now been covered by a well-laid-out council-flat development. Only one small strip of open ground remains, with tombstones standing three deep along the north wall. This area is now used for a nursery school.

St George's Gardens   *Brunswick Square, WC1.* Joint burial ground of ST GEORGE THE MARTYR, QUEEN SQUARE, and ST GEORGE, BLOOMSBURY. Opened in 1715, and known as Nelson's Burial Ground after Robert Nelson, a 'pious and learned writer' who died that year and was the first to be buried here. It was laid out as a public open space in 1885.

St James's Gardens   *Hampstead Road, NW1.* Originally covering 4 acres, now much reduced, this was the burial ground for ST JAMES, PICCADILLY. A chapel-of-ease (demolished) was built and consecrated in 1793. Many thousands were buried here, including George Morland (1804); Lord George Gordon, of the GORDON RIOTS (1793); and John Hoppner (1810). The area was turned into public gardens in 1887.

St Martin's Gardens   *Pratt Street, NW1.* Formerly known as Camden Town Cemetery, which was consecrated by the BISHOP OF LONDON in 1805 as the burial ground for the dead of the parish of ST MARTIN-IN-THE-FIELDS. Charles Dibdin (1814) is buried here under a memorial erected by the KENTISH TOWN Musical Society. In the middle of the 19th century the churchwardens tried to dispose of the ground for building. Much local indignation was aroused; there were near-riots, and the builder's workmen were stoned. The plan was abandoned, and the ground was finally laid out by ST PANCRAS Vestry as a public garden and open space in 1889.

St Olave's Burial Ground   *Tooley Street, SE1.* In 1586 a piece of land was leased to the parish of St Olave's for a burial ground by the Governors of St Olave's Grammar School. The lease was to be for 500 years at a yearly rent of 1s 4d. After the formation of the new parish of St John, Horselydown, in 1733, the burial ground served the two parishes. In 1839, when the dangers of these overcrowded grounds were being investigated, it was reported that 'a gravedigger, named Stewart, died of typhus in May last. His wife was buried with him, who also died of typhus.' The ground was closed for burials in 1853 and converted

into a public recreation ground in 1888. The school Governors conveyed the freehold to the Board of Works.

Whitefields Ground   *Tottenham Court Road, W1.* In 1756 George Whitefield built a chapel here and from that date until 1853 the adjoining site was used as a burial ground. Over 20,000 burials took place in that time. There is a story that in 1780 Whitefield wished to have the ground consecrated, but this was refused by the BISHOP OF LONDON; so Whitefield had several cartloads of soil brought from the churchyard of ST CHRISTOPHER-LE-STOCKS (at that time being converted into a garden) and had them spread over his burial ground. After 1853 a Mr Jacobson, who then owned the land, started to dig foundations for a building. Coffins were seen to be cut through and graves desecrated. After a violent local outcry, the land was acquired by the ST PANCRAS Vestry, which opened it as a public space in 1895. Elizabeth Whitefield, wife of George, was buried here in 1768.

Burleigh Street   *WC2.* Built in the 1670s, the southern part on the site of EXETER HOUSE which had once belonged to William Cecil, Lord Burleigh and his eldest son, Thomas, afterwards Earl of Exeter. In 1831–3 St Michael's church was built by James Savage on the south-west corner with EXETER STREET. It was demolished in 1906 and the STRAND PALACE HOTEL was built on the site. In 1856–9 the street was extended northwards to give easier access to COVENT GARDEN MARKET. At No. 14 is the rectory of ST PAUL COVENT GARDEN, designed by William Butterfield (1859–60). None of the original houses remains.

Burlington Arcade in 1819, the year it was built by Samuel Ware for Lord George Cavendish of Burlington House.

Burlington Arcade   *Piccadilly, W1.* A Regency arcade famous for its small shops and tall Beadles. It was designed in 1819 by Samuel Ware for Lord George Cavendish of BURLINGTON HOUSE to prevent passers-by throwing oyster shells and other rubbish into his garden. The arcade was raised by a storey in 1911 to the designs of Professor Beresford Pite who placed over the PICCADILLY entrance the arms of Lord Chesham, its then owner. The Chesham family sold the arcade to the Prudential Assurance Company in 1926 for £333,000. In 1931 the lower of the two triple arches was removed and the entrance redesigned by Beresford Pite and Partners, much to the dismay of *The Architectural Review*: 'How much this later "improvement" is to be regretted. It is in a Michelangelesque provincial manner that gives full scope to the mahogany shopfitting "expert". The whole appearance of the arcade is spoiled. Can Professor Pite have ruined his own masterpiece to satisfy the needs of a committee of shopkeepers?' The arcade was damaged in the 2nd World War and has since been restored. The Beadles ensure obedience to the rules against singing, carrying open umbrellas or large parcels, and running. They used all once to be ex-soldiers of the 10th Hussars, Lord Chesham's regiment, but now any reliable ex-serviceman is considered for the appointment. Among the long-established shops in the Arcade are H. Simmons, the tobacconists, founded in PICCADILLY in 1838.

Burlington Estate *W1*. The principal streets on this famous estate were BURLINGTON GARDENS, CLIFFORD STREET, CORK STREET, NEW and OLD BURLINGTON STREETS and SAVILE ROW. In 1670 the freeholder of these 10 acres was Sir Benjamin Maddox, a Hertfordshire baronet, but a leasehold title to them was acquired in 1670 and 1683 by the 1st Earl of Burlington, the owner of the adjoining BURLINGTON HOUSE, PICCADILLY, and some undistinguished building ensued. But the main development of the estate in its modern layout was carried out by the 3rd Earl between 1718 and 1739, when Colen Campbell, Nicholas Dubois, Henry Flitcroft, William Kent and Giacomo Leoni all worked here. The Burlingtons' leasehold interest (which had passed by inheritance to the Dukes of Devonshire) expired in 1809, by which time about a third of the freeholds of the houses had been sold by Sir Benjamin Maddox's heirs, the Pollen family. Little of the splendid Georgian work by many of the foremost architects of the day now survives.

Burlington Gardens *W1*. On the BURLINGTON ESTATE, it extends from SAVILE ROW to NEW BOND STREET, and contains two fine but very different buildings. No. 7, on the north side and now occupied by the Royal Bank of Scotland, was built in 1721–3 to designs by Giacomo Leoni. The first occupant, from 1724–78, was the 3rd Duke of Queensberry, whose protégé, the poet John Gay, also lived and died here. Its original name of Queensberry House was changed when the Earl of Uxbridge bought it in about 1785. He at once altered and enlarged it (now known as Uxbridge House) to designs by John Vardy the Younger, perhaps assisted by Joseph Bonomi, and the handsome stone-faced front with nine giant pilasters dates from this time, though the porch was added by Phillip Hardwick in 1855. Lord Uxbridge and his son, the Marquess of Anglesey (a hero of Waterloo where he lost a leg), lived here successively until 1854. Soon afterwards it was sold to the BANK OF ENGLAND, and in 1933 it was taken by its present occupants. Almost opposite stands the even larger 13-bay Italianate façade of what was originally the headquarters of LONDON UNIVERSITY. This was built on part of the garden of BURLINGTON HOUSE in 1866–7 to designs by Sir James Pennethorne. After the departure of the University in 1900 the building was occupied for many years by the Civil Service Commission. As the MUSEUM OF MANKIND it is now the home of the Department of Ethnography of the BRITISH MUSEUM. The premises beside the rear entrance to ALBANY were formerly occupied by John Lane, founder of the

publishing house, The Bodley Head, who converted the dining-room of his ALBANY chambers into offices. These premises were later occupied by Bertram Rota, the antiquarian booksellers now in LONG ACRE. Hawes and Curtis, the shirtmakers and tailors at No. 2, were founded in 1913 on the corner of Jermyn Street and Piccadilly Arcade. They moved here in 1947. De la Rue and Co., the engravers and printers at No. 5, were established in about 1816 at 40 Crown Court, FINSBURY SQUARE by Thomas de la Rue who began as a straw hat manufacturer before becoming a stationer.

Burlington House, Piccadilly *W1*. The only survivor of half a dozen great noblemen's mansions built on the north side of PICCADILLY in the 1660s. Although repeatedly altered and enlarged, it still retains one on the finest 18th-century Palladian rooms in the whole country. The original house was designed and partly built in 1664–5 by the architect Sir John Denham for his own occupation. But in 1667 he sold it, still unfinished, to the 1st Earl of Burlington, who employed Hugh May to complete it. In 1714–15 the young 3rd Earl, who was to be the champion of Palladian architecture in England, spent a year in Italy, and on his return employed James Gibbs, an exponent of the Baroque manner, to build a beautiful curved colonnade along the sides of the forecourt. But then he abandoned the Baroque for the Palladian, and in c. 1717–20 it was Colen Campbell, the high priest of

Burlington House in Piccadilly, rebuilt in 1717–20 to designs derived by Colen Campbell from the Palazzo Porto at Vicenza.

Palladianism, who remodelled and repaired the house to designs derived from the Palazzo Porto at Vicenza, and provided a great stone gateway for the Piccadilly entrance to the forecourt. Inside, Campbell's magnificent saloon still survives, with a splendid painted ceiling probably by William Kent, who also did another in the secretary's room. The house became the archetypal resort of Burlington's Palladian disciples, and the poet John Gay wrote of it, 'Beauty within, without Proportion reigns.'

In 1815 the house was bought for £70,000 by Lord George Cavendish, who employed Samuel Ware to insert the present grand staircase and make other internal alterations, several painted ceilings done by Ricci in Lord Burlington's time being retained. In 1854 the Government bought the house for £140,000, and after much debate it finally became the home of the ROYAL ACADEMY and of six great learned societies – the ROYAL SOCIETY (recently removed to CARLTON HOUSE TERRACE), the SOCIETY OF ANTIQUARIES, the LINNEAN SOCIETY, the CHEMICAL SOCIETY, the GEOLOGICAL SOCIETY, and the ROYAL ASTRONOMICAL SOCIETY. To house this galaxy of scholars, Gibbs's colonnade and the gateway were replaced in 1868–73 by heavy Italianate blocks ranged along the PICCADILLY front and two sides of the forecourt, R.R. Banks and E.M. Barry being the architects. (The BRITISH ACADEMY was also housed here until 1982.) Burlington House itself was in 1872 brutally assaulted by Sydney Smirke, whose addition of a second storey destroyed the Palladian proportion so justly admired by Gay and many others. The statues above the windows, by H. Weekes, W. Calder Marshall and J. Durham, represent, from left to right, Phidias, Leonardo da Vinci, Flaxman, Raphael, Michelangelo, Titian, Reynolds, Wren and William of Wykeham. Smirke also provided the spacious exhibition galleries behind the old house, and further alterations and additions were made in 1883–5 by Norman Shaw, mainly between the new galleries and the original house. Major exhibitions are regularly held here. These include the celebrated summer exhibitions of work by living British artists.

Burnt Oak *Edgware, Middlesex.* The name probably derives from the Roman custom of burning a tree to mark a boundary. Until 1920 the area was mainly farmland, well-wooded and with the Silk Stream running through to the BRENT. Plans for the extension of the railway from GOLDERS GREEN led to some development but it was when the LONDON COUNTY COUNCIL planned its satellite community and the Burnt Oak station was completed in 1924 that a more extensive expansion was achieved. The experimental houses were of wood, metal and brick construction. Most of the residents came from overcrowded ST PANCRAS and ISLINGTON and they brought with them their COCKNEY manners and institutions, including an open-air market. Middle-class EDGWARE and MILL HILL looked askance but were soon glad of the artisan skills which the newcomers brought with them. One of the area's principal public houses, the Bald Faced Stag, was a famous coaching inn patronised by generations of travellers from the north.

Burton Court *or* **Burton's Court** *SW3.* About 14 acres of open land with some fine trees, it was named after Sir Edmund Burton who lived in CHELSEA during the reign of Edward VI. It is administered by the ROYAL HOSPITAL. It contains the cricket ground of the Brigade of Guards. Part is used as a playground for children of local residents on payment of a fee.

Burton Street *WC1.* Commemorates James Burton, the Scottish developer, who built this street in 1809–20. Burton himself lived at No. 2 in 1816; and Sydney Smith at No. 54 in 1839–44.

Bury Street *EC3.* At the DISSOLUTION OF THE MONASTERIES this was the site of the Abbot of Bury's town house. It was given to Sir Thomas Heneage who had it demolished and the street built over the site. Dr Isaac Watts, the hymn-writer, was reader at a nonconformist chapel in the street in 1708–28. Josef Haydn lived at No. 1 in 1794 while writing the last five of the Salomon Symphonies. No. 32 was built in 1914 by Hendrik Petrus Berlage, the great Amsterdam-born architect, for a Dutch shipping company.

Bury Street *SW1.* Built in the 1670s and early 1680s on land granted to Henry Jermyn, Earl of St Albans (*see* JERMYN STREET), and probably named after Bury St Edmunds which was near the country house of the Jermyn family. The freehold of the whole street still belongs to the Crown. In 1720 Strype described it as 'a handsome open Street'. The Marlborough Hotel, designed by G.D. Martin and opened in 1899, was at No. 13–14 until the bankruptcy of the lessee in 1902 when the Charity Commission took the building over. Quaglino's Hotel, a favourite resort of the rich in the 1920s, was at No. 16 in a building reconstructed in 1955–8 by T.P. Bennett and Sons. Wilton's restaurant is at No. 27 and Grant's of St James's, the wine merchants, at No. 31. Among the many distinguished occupants of the street have been Dean Swift in 1710 and 1726; Richard Steele in 1707–11; George Brummell's grandfather, William, who kept a lodging-house where Charles Jenkinson, later 1st Earl of Liverpool, once stayed; Tom Moore intermittently in 1805–11 and again in 1826; George Crabbe in 1827; Daniel O'Connell in 1829; and Thomas Creevey in 1832–4.

The Belvedere Tavern in Pentonville Road during the 1870s when there was a very popular racket-court in the gardens.

Busby's Folly *Islington.* The Society of Bull Feathers Hall, a curious drinking fraternity which claimed tolls on gravel carried up HIGHGATE HILL, is recorded in a 1664 tract as meeting at Busby's Folly. It appears on Ogilby's 1675 map and in Camden's *Britannia* (1695), on the brow of Islington Hill in the fields below the ANGEL, and was probably owned by

Christopher Busby, proprietor of the White Lion at ISLINGTON. Like DOBNEY's, it had a bowling-green with a fine southern prospect to the CITY.

Before 1756 when the New Road, now PENTONVILLE ROAD, was extended to the ANGEL, Busby's was known as Penny's or the Penny Folly, its view enhanced by an 'elegant and airy' upper room with 14 windows. In 1769 Zucker, a popular German showman, nightly exhibited for 1s his 'Learned Little Horse' as displayed to the Royal Family, with Mr Jonas's 'curious deceptions' and Mme Zucker on the musical glasses. 'The Little Horse will be looking out of the windows up two pair of stairs every evening before the performances begin.'

The 1770s, when PENTONVILLE PRISON was built in this rural spot, brought increased prosperity – a different fate was to befall DOBNEY's – and in about 1780 the tavern was rebuilt at the corner of the smart Penton Street and renamed Belvedere on account of the view. The Belvedere Gardens, notable for a large, well-frequented racket-court, remained until the 1870s, and the present tavern replaced the old in 1876.

Bush House *Aldwych, WC2.* In 1919 an American, Irving T. Bush, planned a vast trade centre opposite ST MARY LE STRAND, facing up KINGSWAY. Designed by the American architects Harvey W. Corbett and finished in 1935, it was intended as a luxurious showplace in which manufacturers could display and sell their goods. It had, and has, galleried shop-fronts, marble corridors and concourses. But Bush's hopes were never fully realised. The freehold was later bought by the Church in Wales and is now owned by the Post Office Superannuation Fund. In 1940 the British Broadcasting Corporation, hard pressed to accommodate its expanding overseas services, took over much of the office space. The building proved suitable for studios too, and today Bush House to many people is virtually synonymous with the BBC External Radio Services (*see* BROADCASTING).

Bush Lane *EC4.* Probably commemorates the 15th-century tavern called Le Bussh which took its name from the custom of hanging a green branch over tavern doors. Excavations between Bush Lane and SUFFOLK LANE in the 1960s uncovered a warren of walls, some 22 ft thick, which are thought to be the remains of an important civic building of ROMAN LONDON. Earlier excavations had uncovered a tessellated floor which was exhibited in 1714 at the ROYAL SOCIETY as the floor of 'Caesar's tent'. In the later excavations drains, an ornamental pond and a hypocaust system were found.

Bushey *or* **Bushy Park** *and* **Hampton Court Park** Both belonged once to the KNIGHTS HOSPITALLERS OF ST JOHN. They were acquired by Cardinal Wolsey in 1514. In 1526 he gave them, with HAMPTON COURT PALACE, to Henry VIII who in 1538 enclosed them for a royal hunting reserve. After his death in 1547 the enclosing fences were removed and the public permitted access. Although both in Crown ownership, the two parks are physically separated by Hampton Court Road. They extend to 1,099 acres.

The main feature of Bushey Park is the magnificent avenue of horse chestnut trees, laid out on the orders of William III by Sir Christopher Wren. On 'Chestnut

Bushey Park House as it appeared in 1827 when occupied by George IV's brother the Duke of Clarence, later William IV.

Sunday' (the Sunday nearest 11 May) Londoners used to visit the park to picnic and see the chestnut blossom. A fine bronze fountain, surmounted by a statue of Diana the huntress, stands at the southern end of the avenue. It was placed there by Wren in 1714. Near the northern end stands Bushey Park House, built during the reign of George III. Lord North lived here while premier and it was later occupied by William IV when Duke of Clarence. It is now part of the National Physical Laboratory. Both deer and sheep graze in the park and it is extensively used for informal recreation.

Hampton Court Park is more formal than Bushey, as befits the adjunct of a great palace. The immediate environs of the palace comprise formal gardens laid out in the Dutch style in the reign of William and Mary. They are notable for the Great Vine planted in 1769, the Privy Garden with its screen of 12 wrought iron panels by the 17th-century ironworker, Jean Tijou, and the celebrated maze. Beyond the gardens extends the park, noted for its canal flanked by limes specially imported from Holland by William III. There are two other avenues of trees extending into the park. The southern part is now a golf course and at the north-eastern end is an ice house (*see also* HAMPTON COURT PALACE).

Butchers' Company *see* CITY LIVERY COMPANIES.

Bute House *Brompton.* Built in the 1760s by Robert Adam's brother, James, and apparently occupied by him until he sold it and moved to the ADELPHI. It was later occupied for about ten years by the 1st Marquess of Bute; and in 1833 passed into the hands of Thomas Dowbiggin, the upholsterer, who, with various associates, laid out BUTE STREET in the grounds of the house which was demolished in 1845 or 1846.

Bute House *Kensington.* Also known as Blundell House, it was built by John Tasker and completed in 1812. The 2nd Marquess of Bute lived here from 1830 until 1842 and other aristocratic residents included the Hon William Sebright Lascelles and the 6th Duke of Rutland. The house was demolished about 1913.

Bute Street *SW7*. Laid out in 1846–8 by Thomas Dowbiggin (*see* BUTE HOUSE, BROMPTON). From this time two buildings still remain, the Zetland Arms public house at No. 2 (east side) and the building opposite it which is now numbered 44–46 OLD BROMPTON ROAD. The north end of Bute Street was demolished between 1865 and 1881 when the Metropolitan and District Railways were built between GLOUCESTER ROAD and SOUTH KENSINGTON stations; the rest of it was rebuilt in the 1950s and 1960s.

Button's Coffee House *Russell Street, Covent Garden*. Established in the second decade of the 18th century by Daniel Button, a former servant of the Countess of Warwick, who was set up in business by Joseph Addison who had married the Countess in 1716. Addison made it a great resort for the wits of the day who had, before Dryden's death, met at WILL'S. James Maclean, the highwayman executed at TYBURN in 1750, was observed 'paying particular attention to the barmaid, the daughter of the landlord'. The house was celebrated for its lion's head letterbox which 'opened its mouth at all hours for the reception of such intelligence as shall be thrown into it' and which was 'planted on the western side of the coffee house holding its paws under its chin upon a box which contains everything he swallows.' When Button's closed in about 1751, the lion's head was removed to the Shakespeare Tavern. It was afterwards taken to the BEDFORD COFFEE HOUSE, then to Richardson's Hotel, then to the house of the Duke of Bedford who had it removed to Woburn.

Butts *Brentford, Middlesex*. A square behind the Magistrates' Court at the back of the Market Place, surrounded by a number of good late 17th- or early 18th-century houses, some of which retain original panelling. The name is thought to be derived from it having been a place used for archery practice in the Middle Ages. It was the polling place for MIDDLESEX at parliamentary elections in the 18th and early 19th centuries, including the rowdy occasion when John Wilkes was a candidate in 1768 and 1769.

Byward Street *EC3*. Built by the Metropolitan and District Railway Companies in 1889–1906. For the first few years it was known as Great Tower Street. The present name is derived from the Byward Tower of the TOWER OF LONDON where the password or byword has to be given at night. ALL HALLOWS BARKING is here.

C

Cabinet War Rooms *Treasury Chambers, Parliament Street, SW1.* In 1936, at the instigation of Winston Churchill and others, the basement of the Civil Service buildings between King Charles Street and PARLIAMENT SQUARE was converted and reinforced for use as Cabinet Offices in the event of war. By the end of the war, the Underground War Rooms covered more than 3 acres and were able to accommodate up to 528 persons. In the sub-basement were a canteen, a hospital, a shooting range and other services, with a warren of rooms used as sleeping quarters, devoid of outside light and with ceilings so low that the occupants could not stand upright. There was more head room but little more space or comfort on the basement level, where the senior officers slept and where the offices vital to the war effort were to be found. Here was the sound-proof Cabinet room, where the War Cabinet could, and did, meet if raids or other dangers threatened. The cloth-covered table where they sat is still there, each place with its blotter bearing the name of a Minister. Close by was the Map Room, where the map information of all the war fronts was co-ordinated for the Cabinet and Chiefs of Staff, and from where hourly reports and news were sent out. This Map Room was in operation from the time of the Munich crisis until 1945; and Churchill, when Prime Minister, visited it every day that he was in London. It remains much as it was when in operation, its maps and graphs still on the walls, some of them with the coloured marker pins still in place, and with its central core of one long desk with a battery of old-fashioned telephones, black, red, white and green. Nearby is the bedroom which Churchill could sometimes be persuaded to use if the raids were bad; it is austerely furnished, and has a desk from which he made occasional broadcasts. Another desk was also reserved for his use – a lectern desk where he could work undisturbed, standing up, in a tiny room scarcely larger than a cupboard. In its equally tiny anteroom was a direct telephone line to Washington so that Prime Minister could speak direct to President. Clocks above the telephone gave the time in both capitals.

Cable Street *E1.* Built in the late 18th century, in an area where ropes and cables were manufactured. The original street was only the length of a cable (600 ft) but the name was later extended to other streets. It now stretches from ROYAL MINT STREET to COMMERCIAL ROAD. Nos 194–214 are the only Georgian houses left. The rest of the street is in various stages of redevelopment. Cable Street is known for the 'battle' which took place here on Sunday 5 October 1936. The Fascists, led by Sir Oswald Mosley, planned to march through the East End taking in Cable Street en route. Left-wing parties and the local inhabitants decided to stop them. Barricades were built in Cable Street and fighting broke out between residents and the police who were trying to clear a way

through. Fenner Brockway, then Secretary of the Independent Labour Party, was injured by a police horse and, realising the clash that would occur if the Fascists succeeded in passing, telephoned the Home Office. Mosley was told to cancel the march. The following week windows of every Jewish shop in the MILE END ROAD were smashed.

Riots took place in Cable Street in 1936 when Oswald Mosley's Fascists marched through the East End.

Cadogan Estate In 1717 Charles Cadogan, later 2nd Baron Cadogan of Oakley, married Elizabeth, younger daughter of Sir Hans Sloane (*see* SLOANE ESTATE). On Sloane's death the larger part of his estate passed to Lady Cadogan, a smaller part going to her sister, Sarah, wife of George Stanley of Paultons in Hampshire. Lord Cadogan became Lord of the Manor of Chelsea. Charles Sloane Cadogan, 3rd Baron Cadogan, was created 1st Earl Cadogan (of the second creation) and Viscount Chelsea in 1800. Several streets and squares in Chelsea derive their names from this family's connections. In addition to those separately mentioned, Caversham Street is named after William Cadogan, 1st Baron and 1st Earl (of the first creation) who was created Viscount Caversham in 1718; Elystan Street after Elystan Glodrydd, founder of the 4th Royal Tribe of Wales, supposedly an early ancestor of the Cadogans; Margaretta Terrace after Margaretta Cecilia Munter, wife of William Cadogan; Rosemoor Street after Rosemoor, Torrington, Devon, a Cadogan family house; Paultons Square and Paultons Street after Sarah Sloane's husband's estate in Hampshire; Oakley Street, since William Cadogan was created Baron Cadogan of Oakley in 1718.

Cadogan Gardens *SW3.* A development of the 1890s between KING'S ROAD and SLOANE STREET. At the KING'S ROAD end is No. 25, now a part of PETER JONES department store, but once described as 'the most wonderful house in the world'. It was built by

A.H. Mackmurdo in 1899 for Mortimer Menpes, an artist friend of Whistler. The interior was in an elaborate version of the Japanese style favoured by Whistler and his friends, and the carved panelling, of which there was a large quantity, was made in Japan under the supervision of Menpes himself.

Cadogan Place *SW1*. Terraces of Georgian and Victorian houses overlooking private gardens on the east side of SLOANE STREET. According to Dickens in *Nicholas Nickleby*, Cadogan Place was the connecting link 'between the aristocratic pavements of Belgrave Square and the barbarism of Chelsea'. Mrs Jordan, mistress of the Duke of Clarence and mother of ten of his children, lived at No. 30 in 1811. No. 44 is the 'small borrowed house' where William Wilberforce died in 1833. Other distinguished residents have included Charles Pelham Villiers, the statesman and Corn Laws reformer, and Zachary Macaulay, the philanthropist, whose son, Thomas Babington Macaulay, lived with him 1812–23. The CARLTON TOWER HOTEL is on the north side. The bronzes in the gardens are *Girl with Doves* (south garden, 1970) and *The Dancers* (north garden, 1971), both by David Wynne.

Cadogan Square *SW1*. With PONT STREET, off which it leads, this was one of the first major 19th-century developments in London which favoured red brick rather than stucco. The development was carried out, on land belonging to the CADOGAN ESTATE and SMITH'S CHARITY ESTATE, by the Cadogan and Hans Place Estate Ltd which was registered in 1875 and whose chairman was Colonel W.T. Makins MP, also chairman of the Gas-Light and Coke Co. Ltd. This company sublet most of the land to other companies and building contractors. The north and east sides of the square were built by Trollope and Sons whose architect for some, if not all, of the houses was G.T. Robinson. In the south-west corner are three houses by Norman Shaw, Nos 62 (1882), 68 (1877) and 72 (1877). Nos 64, 66, 70 and 74 are by A.J. Adams. The house in the north-east corner, whose Gothic style contrasts with the so-called 'Queen Anne' style of its neighbours, was designed by G.E. Street for the daughters of James Henry Monk, Bishop of Gloucester, for whom Street had built ST JAMES THE LESS, Thorndike Street. In 1924 Arnold Bennett lived at No. 75 where he wrote *Riceyman Steps* and *Imperial Palace*. The bronze in the gardens, *Dancer with a Bird*, is by David Wynne (1975).

Café Royal *68 Regent Street, W1*. Daniel Nicolas Thévenon, a former Parisian wine merchant, opened a café-restaurant in 1865 at Nos 15–17 GLASSHOUSE STREET. In 1870 he had expanded his premises to include No. 8 AIR STREET and No. 68 REGENT STREET. In the basement were a wine cellar and billiard room. On the ground floor were a café, luncheon bar and a Grill Room designed by Archer and Green. Until they were closed in 1909 the floors above had private rooms. The Domino Room, with its marble-topped tables and red velvet seats, was from the 1890s until the early 1920s a famous and fashionable meeting place for artists and writers. Sickert, Augustus John, Beardsley, Oscar Wilde, Max Beerbohm and Whistler, who signed his bills with a butterfly mark, were all regular customers. In 1894 the Café was the scene of a famous murder

mystery when the night porter, Marius Martin, was found dying with two bullets in his head. In the early part of the 20th century two future kings, Edward VIII and George VI, patronised the Café. An entry in the waiters' instruction book ran, 'Prince of Wales, Duke of York – lunch frequently. Always plain food. No fuss. Call head waiter at once and notify manager.' In 1923–4 the premises were rebuilt by Sir Henry Tanner to conform with other buildings in REGENT STREET's Quadrant. 'They might as well have told us', wrote T.W.H. Crosland, 'that the British Empire is to be pulled down and redecorated.' The present Grill Room, which still preserves the atmosphere of the old Café, stands where part of the Domino Room was; and the Brasserie, which replaced the artists' rendezvous and was removed in 1951, was built in the space now occupied by the restaurant, Le Relais. In the 1930s regular patrons included James Agate, Sir Alan Herbert, Sir Compton Mackenzie, J.B. Priestley and T.S. Eliot.

Cale Street *SW3*. Takes its name from Judith Cale who died in 1717 leaving £6 18s in bequest to six poor widows of CHELSEA, to be distributed on Christmas Day.

Caledonian Club *9 Halkin Street, SW1*. Founded in 1891 by Neville Campbell, it occupied a series of houses, including Derby House, ST JAMES'S SQUARE, before moving to its present address in 1946. Intended as a meeting place for Scottish gentlemen in London, its rules of membership now admit those who have a Scottish grandparent and even Englishmen who have 'the closest association with Scotland' or have 'served in an important capacity in the public service in Scotland'.

Caledonian Market *see* METROPOLITAN CATTLE MARKET AND CALEDONIAN MARKET.

Caledonian Road *N1*. Privately built in 1826 by the Battle Bridge and Holloway Road Co. to link those places, it was first named Chalk Road after its soil. It cut straight across the fields north of Gray's Inn Lane, skirted the then open Thornhill estate and crossed the REGENT'S CANAL by Thornhill Bridge. Below Copenhagen Fields its sole building was for years the large brick orphanage with Doric portico, designed by George Tappen (1828), for sons of indigent London Scots and of Scots killed or disabled on active service. Founded in 1815 and opened in 1819 at HATTON GARDEN, it came to be called the Caledonian Asylum, and Chalk Road was renamed after it. The orphanage, which first received girls in 1846, removed in 1903 to Bushey, Hertfordshire, and the old building was demolished.

The road's earliest houses were Thornhill Terrace (now Nos 106–146) built in 1832; other terraces followed in the 1840s. For some dozen years from 1837 a group of cottages in gardens occupied the west side between the present railway and Brewery Road – the abortive Experimental Gardens or French Colony, founded by the philanthropist Peter Henry Joseph Baume, as a community on Robert Owen's principles – but the roads were unlighted and unpaved, and the cottages deteriorated into slums tenanted by (says Coull) 'the poorest class of people . . . more like a colony in the wilds of Canada than a suburb of London'.

When in the 1860s the few surviving leases ran out, Blundell, Nailour and Frederica Streets were built, but the topography again radically changed with the layout of the 1970s' council estates. In 1840–1 PENTONVILLE Gaol – its name a slight mystery, being far from PENTONVILLE – or 'Model Prison' was built immediately south of the Asylum. In 1852 Caledonian Road Station opened to serve the western extension of the East and West India Docks and Birmingham Railway (now North London Railway), which bridged the street at that point.

Calthorpe Estate This land, lying east of GRAY'S INN ROAD, belonged to the Priory of St Bartholomew (*see* ST BARTHOLOMEW-THE-GREAT) at the DISSOLUTION OF THE MONASTERIES. It came into the hands of the Calthorpe family in the 18th century. In 1823 the 3rd Lord Calthorpe leased part of it to Thomas Cubitt who had already established his building works in GRAY'S INN ROAD.

Calthorpe Street *WC1*. Built in 1821–49. A few of the original houses remain. At No. 20 there is a BLUE PLAQUE to William Richard Lethaby, the architect, who lived here in 1880–91.

Camberwell *SE5*. Lies south of WALWORTH, east of BRIXTON, west of PECKHAM and north of HERNE HILL within the London Borough of SOUTHWARK. Through the district runs Camberwell Road which continues south as DENMARK HILL. It was a village surrounded by fields in the 18th century, famous for its flowers and fruit trees, among which the CAMBERWELL BEAUTY fluttered freely. Priscilla Wakefield in her *Perambulations* of 1809 describes the area as 'a pleasant retreat of those citizens who have a taste for the country whilst their avocations daily call them to town'. Before 1830 the building began that was soon to make all SOUTH LONDON a huge conglomerate urban area. Houses appeared at first along the main roads but, even as late as the mid-19th century, the Camberwell district contained much pasture land, while as 1871 DULWICH to the south had only 700 houses. The most remarkable feature of Camberwell today is the road called CAMBERWELL GROVE which contains many pleasant late Georgian houses and also the modest but charming Grove Chapel of 1819 by Roper. Here, attached to Grove House, the Camberwell Tea Gardens flourished, and the house itself contained a fashionable public ballroom which Dickens describes in *Sketches by Boz*. Camberwell contains a few other Georgian survivals.

In *Domesday Book*, Camberwell is called Ca'brewelle and it is described as a manor of some value. Later documents call it Camwell or Camerwell. The name 'Cam' may have come from an Old Celtic word meaning crooked: the well is said to have been a medicinal spring used by invalids; hence 'the well of the crippled or crooked'. The parish church in Camberwell Church Street was, in fact, dedicated to ST GILES, patron saint of cripples and mendicants. This church was destroyed by fire in 1841 and a new church was opened on the site in 1844 to a design in Gothic style by George Gilbert Scott and W.B. Moffatt. Within are preserved a late 14th-century *sedilia* and *piscina* from the old church. In the churchyard, now cleared as a public open space, are buried John Wesley's shrewish wife Mary, who died in 1781; Miss Lucy

Warner, who was 32 ins high and ran a local school; and James Blake, who sailed the world with Captain Cook.

Where Church Street meets Camberwell Road, DENMARK HILL and Camberwell New Road lies an acre of land which is surrounded by dull buildings and in which nature struggles to assert herself. This is CAMBERWELL GREEN, on which was held at one time an annual fair of ancient origin which rivalled that of GREENWICH and continued down to 1855. On the south side once stood a fine country mansion of classical manner that contained frescoes by Sir James Thornhill. Tradition has it that Sir Christopher Wren once inhabited the house; hence Wren Road which runs across the site. The poet Thomas Hood lived with his family in Camberwell around 1840 and Joseph Chamberlain was born at No. 188 CAMBERWELL GROVE (then No. 3 Grove Hill Terrace).

Camberwell Beauty A butterfly first observed at CAMBERWELL in 1748. The British species, with white border colouring, is now extinct, but migrant Camberwell Beauties from Europe or North America, with yellow border colourings, are occasionally seen. The species is alternatively known as Mourning Cloak.

Camberwell Green *SE5*. In 1842 the former village green of CAMBERWELL was visited by Mendelssohn who there composed his *Spring Song*, originally called *Camberwell Green*. The poet, Robert Browning, was born in Southampton Street nearby. The Green is now the centre of a busy traffic junction and much of its former peace is lost.

Camberwell Grove *SE5*. A tree-lined road of mainly Georgian houses, part of a conservation area covering also Grove Lane, it was built when CAMBERWELL, like other villages in the same radius, was developing as a London suburb. Among well-to-do professional and business residents were the

Camberwell Grove, birthplace of the politician Joseph Chamberlain, as it appeared in the 1870s, its Georgian houses pleasantly shaded by trees.

Chamberlains. Joseph Chamberlain was born in 1836 at No. 188. Grove Chapel was erected in 1819. Earlier the celebrated physician, John Coakley Lettsom, had a country estate stretching from the hill top to the present Lettsom Street. Among his distinguished visitors was James Boswell.

Camberwell Old Cemetery *see* CEMETERIES.

Camberwell School of Arts and Crafts *Peckham Road, SE5*. Opened in 1896 as a technical school to provide instruction in design which would supplement the skills learnt by young craftsmen during their apprenticeship, with the emphasis on the teaching of trade subjects. After 1908 there was a shift in emphasis to the teaching of fine arts and design, which has continued ever since. Special premises were built next to the SOUTH LONDON ART GALLERY by Maurice Bingham Adams in memory of Lord Leighton. The cost was underwritten by John Passmore Edwards, editor and philanthropist, who contributed to countless charitable organisations in and around London.

Cambridge Circus *WC2*. Formed at the junction of CHARING CROSS ROAD and SHAFTESBURY AVENUE and named after the Duke of Cambridge who opened CHARING CROSS ROAD in 1887. The PALACE THEATRE was built in 1891. Opposite it were the tropical outfitters, Alkit Ltd, a family firm since the early 1930s, whose closing-down sale was held in February 1982.

Cambridge Gate *NW1*. Built in 1876–80 by Archer and Green as an addition to CAMBRIDGE TERRACE. It takes its name from Adolphus, Duke of Cambridge, one of George IV's younger brothers. It covers the site of Decimus Burton's COLOSSEUM which was demolished in 1875.

Cambridge Heath Road *E1, E2*. The name comes from a heath, now built over, at the northern end of the road. The original name for the southern end of the road was Dog Row, tradition having it that kings living in the TOWER OF LONDON kept their dogs here for hunting in EPPING FOREST. Buildings of interest include the Library, opened in 1922; the BETHNAL GREEN MUSEUM, opened in 1872; and Bethnal Green Hospital, opened in 1900. The library was adapted for use as such from a block of the Bethnal House Asylum which had been opened in 1896. The adaptation was supervised by the borough surveyor, A.E. Darby. The Bethnal Green Hospital (originally Infirmary) was designed by Giles, Gough and Trollope. The church of St John on Bethnal Green is on the east side. The sculpture of a woman holding a fish, which was once a fountain on the corner of Malcolm Place, is by Frank Dobson (1963).

Cambridge Square *W2*. Rebuilt after the 2nd World War. Its earlier residents included Robert Stephenson, the railway engineer, at No. 15, in 1844–7, before he moved to Gloucester Square; William Ewart, pioneer of public libraries, at No. 6 in 1843–69; and Thomas Rhodes Armitage, founder of the National Institute for the Blind, at No. 33 in 1866–86.

Cambridge Street *SW1*. Extends from Hugh Street to Lupus Street in PIMLICO. It was built in about 1850 and named after the Duke of Cambridge since the owners of the land, the Grosvenors, had run out of family names. Aubrey Beardsley lived at No. 114 in 1893–5. The flats at Nos 76–78 are by Foggo and Thomas (1969).

Cambridge Terrace *NW1*. A short line of houses on the south-east side of REGENT'S PARK. It was built in 1825 by Richard Mott to designs by John Nash. Like CAMBRIDGE GATE it takes its name from the title of Adolphus, Duke of Cambridge.

Cambridge Theatre *Seven Dials, WC2*. Built for Bertie A. Meyer by Wimperis, Simpson and Guthrie in 1930. The interior was designed by Serge Chermayeff. In its early years seasons of ballet and films alternated with plays. In 1944 Johann Strauss's operetta, *A Night in Venice*, ran for 433 performances. From 1946 to 1948 the theatre was the home of the New London Opera Company, founded by Jay Pomeroy. The seating capacity is 1,280.

Camden Church *Peckham Road*. This was once the only 18th-century church in CAMBERWELL, built as a chapel for the followers of Selina, Countess of Huntingdon, the vigorous promoter of Evangelical Revivalism among the wealthier and more powerful classes. It was enlarged in 1814 and in 1854 Sir George Gilbert Scott built the chancel in the Byzantine style.

Camden Place *Chislehurst, Kent*. Named by a later owner after the historian William Camden, who lived here in the early 17th century. In 1813 the then owner, Thomas Bonar, and his wife were murdered here by a manservant. After this the house passed through various hands until it came into the possession of Nathaniel Strode, who had connections with the court of Napoleon III. Strode added wings to the house, and installed 18th-century French panelling which survives. The house was furnished in the French style, and Empress Eugénie and her son, and later Napoleon III, came here in exile, living quietly. Napoleon III died at Camden Place in 1873, and Empress Eugénie left in 1881. Strode then returned to the house and lived there until his death in 1890. After this, the house and park were sold. Much of the property is now a golf course and Camden Place itself a club-house (*see* GOLF CLUBS, Chislehurst Golf Club).

Camden Square *NW1*. V.K. Krishna Menon, the Indian politician and High Commissioner, lived at No. 57 in 1924–47. George James Symons, the meteorologist, lived at No. 62 in 1868–1900, where for those 32 years he kept a daily record of the weather. He was a fellow of the ROYAL SOCIETY and twice President of the Royal Meteorological Society, whose highest award is the Symons Memorial Gold Medal.

Camden Town *NW1*. The Manor of Cantelowes, which probably stood east of the northern end of present-day Royal College Street, was held at the time of *Domesday Book* by the Canons of ST PAUL's and was stated to contain 'plenty of timber in the hedgerows, good pastures for cattle, a running brook, and two 20d rents'. The Manor passed through various hands, and though the house seems to have disappeared by the early 18th century, the land had by then been acquired by a John Jeffreys of Brecknock Priory. His granddaughter and heiress married in 1749 Sir Charles Pratt, later 1st Earl Camden. At that time it was a quiet country area, supporting 'fields of cows'; but in 1791 Lord Camden granted leases for the erection of 1,400 houses, and in the same year a Frenchman, Vital de St Bel, founded the Veterinary College of London (now ROYAL VETERINARY COLLEGE) and became its first principal. The College, built by a footpath which later became Royal College Street, was established with a view to reforming farriery.

Building was not at first rapid or widespread and even in the early part of the 19th century 'the rural lanes, hedgeside roads and lovely fields made Camden Town the constant resort of those who . . . sought its quietude and fresh air to reinvigorate their spirits'. But the spreading tentacles of London, bringing with them urban poverty, penetrated the area, and after 1820, when a stretch of the REGENT'S CANAL was constructed eastwards through Camden Town, bringing coal wharves and merchants and some small industry, the area could no longer be called rural. Charles Dickens, who lived as a boy in No. 16 Bayham Street (now demolished), described in *Dombey and Son* the 'frowzy fields, and cow-houses, and dunghills, and dust-heaps'. During the 30 or 40 years after 1830, while house building continued, the real upheaval was caused by the coming of the railway. Huge areas were necessary for the loading and shunting operations of first the London and Birmingham, and later the Midland, Railways. But though Nash, too, described most of the houses being built as 'mean', it was still a respectable enough district for Frances Mary Buss to write, in 1850, when planning her NORTH LONDON COLLEGIATE SCHOOL: 'Of all the various suburbs of our vast metropolis, this district . . . is perhaps more thickly inhabited by professional men than any other.' The Buss family – Frances's father was one of the illustrators of *Pickwick Papers* – lived at 46 Camden Street (now No. 12) where the NORTH LONDON COLLEGIATE SCHOOL opened with 35 pupils in April 1850. At that time much of the area was undeveloped: it is said that the last fatal duel was fought here in an open field near the secluded Brecknock Arms in 1843 when Lieutenant Munro killed his brother-in-law, Lieutenant-Colonel Fawcett. However, most of the open spaces were soon covered; and small industries developed, notably the manufacture of musical instruments, telescopes and scientific instruments, and clothing, and by the end of the century 'Camden Town, which as recently as 1870 had been a residential quarter of wealth and even fashion . . . had become largely a place of business; among the residents servants were rare and in nearly every house there was a lodger.' The Working Men's College transferred here in 1905 (*see* CROWNDALE ROAD).

The local population has been greatly increased over the past 100 years by Irish immigrants. These were joined in the 20th century by Greek Cypriots who found occupation as dressmakers, tailors, bakers and shoemakers, and opened Greek cafés and confectioners. There has been large-scale post-war redevelopment of the earliest built-up areas east of Camden High Street, and since the middle of this century, in a new swing of the pendulum, there has been a steady return of residents from the professional classes.

Camden Town Group Both a style of painting and a society of artists, the moving spirit in both cases being Walter Sickert. Theories as to the derivation of the name vary from the purely geographical – Sickert had for several years rented studios and lodgings around MORNINGTON CRESCENT – to the more sensational view that the recently perpetrated CAMDEN TOWN murders would help publicise their name. Since 1905 Sickert (at 47 the eldest of the group) had held open house at his studio in FITZROY STREET. Here paintings were displayed for anyone who cared to come, and they attracted a small but faithful clientele. Though never intended to represent either a movement or a school, the Fitzroy Group, as Sickert and his friends were then known, did come to be associated with certain characteristics which are now given the blanket term of Camden Town Painting. Favourite themes were nudes in shabby lodgings, informal portraits and unpretentious landscapes of NORTH LONDON. A nucleus of the group, which was united in its dissatisfaction with the New English Art Club, decided, in 1911, to set up a rival exhibiting body which they called the Camden Town Group. Initially it consisted of 16 members (women were not accepted) including Augustus John, Henry Lamb, Wyndham Lewis, Lucien Pissarro and Sickert. They exhibited at the Carfax Gallery in BURY STREET, St James's, but after two financially disastrous shows they sought larger premises at the Goupil Gallery. Ironically, by the time the Camden Town Group was formed the Camden Town style of painting was fast disappearing as each of its members began to explore new stylistic avenues. It was finally dissolved in 1913 and its members rejoined their colleagues of the Fitzroy Group to form the larger and more important LONDON GROUP which still survives today.

Camelford House *Oxford Street.* Designed for his own occupation, by Thomas Pitt, 1st Baron Camelford, younger brother of William Pitt, 1st Earl of Chatham. Camelford, 'very amiable and very sensible', in Horace Walpole's opinion, gave advice on the decoration of STRAWBERRY HILL. Camelford House, though plain outside, had a splendid interior with particularly fine plasterwork. Occupied for a time by the Prince Regent's daughter, Princess Charlotte, it was demolished shortly before the 1st World War.

Camomile Street *EC2.* Named after the medicinal camomile plant which probably grew here. The street runs along the line of the Roman city wall, a bastion of which was uncovered in 1876. Part of its statuary is now in the MUSEUM OF LONDON. BISHOP'S GATE stood at the northern end of the street.

Campden Hill *W8.* The name both of a road and an area, the latter is derived from the Campden House Estate although ratebooks do not use the designation before 1827. During the 17th century the area, still mostly open ground, saw the erection of a number of country mansions, notably HOLLAND HOUSE, CAMPDEN HOUSE and AUBREY HOUSE. The road Campden Hill, on part of the PHILLIMORE ESTATE, was laid out by 1817 and gave access to seven houses standing in extensive grounds, the builder and probable designer being John Tasker. Only one of these, Thorpe Lodge, still survives within the grounds of HOLLAND PARK COMPREHENSIVE SCHOOL. This and the modern

Campden House School for Girls, Kensington, in the 19th century. Earlier pupils at the establishment included the daughters of Samuel Johnson's friend Topham Beauclerk.

extensions to QUEEN ELIZABETH COLLEGE now cover the sites of the original houses, all of which had distinguished residents at various times. These included the historian, Thomas Babington Macaulay, who lived at Holly Lodge from 1856 until his death in 1859. The original, and first, LONDON COUNTY COUNCIL BLUE PLAQUE is incorporated into the front of the new hall of residence which was built on the site in 1968. The watertower on the hill's summit, which appears in both G.K. Chesterton's *The Napoleon of Notting Hill* and Barrie's *Peter Pan*, was demolished in 1970.

Campden Hill Road *W8*. Built up in the 1860s with large houses for wealthy men who came here for their health. It is named after CAMPDEN HOUSE. At No. 80, South Lodge, formerly the home of Sir James South (*see* OBSERVATORY GARDENS), Violet Hunt and Ford Madox Ford held their salon at the beginning of this century. It was a meeting-place of H.G. Wells, Arnold Bennett, Joseph Conrad, Henry James, Ezra Pound and Wyndham Lewis. John Galsworthy lived at No. 82 in 1897–1903. At the south end of the road is Kensington Central Library, built to the design of E.Vincent Harris in 1960. QUEEN ELIZABETH COLLEGE and HOLLAND PARK COMPREHENSIVE SCHOOL are on the west side.

Campden Hill Square *W8*. Built in 1827–38 on CAMPDEN HILL by J.F. Hanson. It was known as Notting Hill Square until 1893, when residents petitioned for a change of name. The Christian philosopher and teacher, Evelyn Underhill, lived at No.50. John McDouall Stuart, the Australian explorer, lived at No. 9 in 1866. On a tree on the north side of the garden a plaque reads: 'J.M.W. Turner R.A. landscape painter Born 1775 Died 1851 often painted sunsets near this tree.'

Campden House *Kensington*. Built in about 1612 for Sir Baptist Hicks who was created Viscount Campden of Campden, Gloucestershire in 1628. There was probably an earlier house on the site which was enlarged and refronted. In 1660 Charles II was entertained here for two weeks after his Restoration. Princess Anne (later Queen) lived here in 1691–6 with her son William, Duke of Gloucester. In 1707–21, the house was occupied by the Dowager Countess of Burlington whose son Richard Boyle, 3rd Earl of Burlington, the architect, spent part of his childhood here. Having passed through several hands after Campden's death, the house and the surrounding land were sold in 1751 to Stephen Pitt whose descendants still own part of the estate. Towards the end of the 18th century the house was converted into a girls' boarding school, to which were sent the daughters of Samuel Johnson's friend, Topham Beauclerk, and George Selwyn's adopted daughter. In 1847 William Frederick Woolley rented the house and spent considerable sums on restoration, including the addition of a private theatre. Here it was that Charles Dickens acted in a charity performance of *The Lighthouse* by Wilkie Collins in July 1855. Early in the morning of 23 March 1862 the house was gutted by fire and this led to a celebrated law case over the insurance money which Woolley won. The house was rebuilt in the original style but finally demolished in about 1900, and its site is today a communal garden for the surrounding blocks of flats and houses.

Canning Place *W8*. Semi-detached villas built about 1846 and named after George Canning who lived at Orford Lodge, GLOUCESTER ROAD in 1809–27. Alfred Stevens, the sculptor and architect, lived at No. 7 in 1856.

Canning Town *E16.* Industrial and residential district to the south-west of NEWHAM with a station (original building, 1846) on the North Woolwich railway line. It and the constituent and adjacent districts, variously named as Hallsville, Victoria Docks and Tidal Basin, developed from about 1850 to house the labourers in the Victoria Docks, the coal wharves on Bow Creek and the works which developed on Thames-side. The name was possibly given in honour of Lord Canning, the Governor-General of India. Hallsville took its name from Mr Hall, the landlord, and Tidal Basin from the tidal basin at the entrance to the Victoria Dock from the river. The names Tidal Basin, which had a station on the North Woolwich line from 1858 to 1943, and Hallsville have gone out of use. Victoria Docks is no longer a placename but continues in the Victoria Docks and North Woolwich postal district, E16. Much of the original 19th-century property was of poor quality in a poor environment and received very adverse comment in the Board of Health report of 1855. There was considerable poverty in the neighbourhood up to the 2nd World War and Canning Town and CUSTOM HOUSE were the main centres for the work of several settlements which were established in WEST HAM. The Mayflower Family Centre, founded by the Revd David Sheppard (now Bishop of Liverpool) in 1958, in the premises of the former Dockland Settlement, and the Mansfield House University Settlement, founded by Mansfield College, Oxford in 1880, continue to work in the area. Apart from the Victoria Dock, Canning Town's principal industry was the Thames Ironworks and Shipbuilding Co., founded on Bow Creek in 1846. By the time of its closure in 1912 it had built about 900 vessels from gunboats to dreadnoughts, including a large number for British and foreign navies. The district suffered very badly in the air raids of the 2nd World War and the Keir Hardie Estate now covers the most badly devastated areas. The estate, which was one of the largest areas of comprehensive development in the country, was named after the first Labour MP whom West Ham, South sent to WESTMINSTER in 1892. The remainder of the district has been progressively redeveloped by the WEST HAM and NEWHAM Councils including the provision of the new RATHBONE MARKET (1963) in the Barking Road to replace a well-known East London street market.

Cannon Place *Hampstead, NW3.* Stretches from CHRIST CHURCH, where the Victoria Tea Gardens once were, to Squires Mount. Sir Flinders Petrie, the egyptologist, lived in No. 5 from the 1890s until 1932, and is commemorated by a BLUE PLAQUE. Another BLUE PLAQUE is on the wall of Cannon Hall, the early 18th-century house which gives the road its name. Here Sir Gerald Du Maurier, actor-manager, lived in 1916–34. The house, and Cannon Lodge, also dating from the early 18th century, are presumably so named because of the old cannon outside, some of which were used as hitching-posts. Earlier occupants of Cannon Hall included a succession of magistrates who used to hold courts in the house; and in the walls of the property, though round the corner in Cannon Lane, are the grim door and two tiny barred windows of the old HAMPSTEAD parish lockup. It was in use from 1730 for nearly 100 years, as a plaque records. The doorway is now used as one of the entrances to Cannon Hall.

Cannon Row *SW1.* A narrow alley running north from BRIDGE STREET named after the canons of St Stephen's Chapel (*see* PALACE OF WESTMINSTER) who had their lodgings here. Later noblemen built houses here. The Montagues, Earls of Manchester, had a house here which was later made into tenements, known as Manchester Buildings, in one of which lived James Macpherson, author of the poems of Ossian. Later these tenements were occupied by supporters of Daniel O'Connell, the Irish politician in the 1830s. Lincoln House, the 16th-century mansion of Henry, 2nd Earl of Lincoln, was also here. So was Derby House, the residence of the Earls of Derby in the 16th century. John Pym died here in 1643 and his body lay in state to disprove rumours it had been eaten by lice. Pepys's haunt, the RHENISH WINE HOUSE, was here. At another tavern, the Rummer and Grapes, was one of London's earliest lodges of Freemasons which was in existence in 1716.

By the middle of the 19th century it had become, as Dickens described it in *Nicholas Nickleby*, a 'street of gloomy lodging houses . . . a sanctuary of Smaller Members of Parliament . . . . There are legislators in the parlours, in the first floor, in the second, in the third, in the garrets; the small apartments reek with the breath of deputations and delegates.' It is now best known for its police station.

Cannon Street *EC4.* The old Cannon Street extended from DOWGATE HILL to GRACECHURCH STREET. In the middle of the 12th century it was known as Candelwrithe Street, later as Candlewick Street, in allusion to the candle makers who lived there, and the modern name is a corruption of these. In the 1850s it was extended to ST PAUL'S CHURCHYARD. It was badly damaged in the 2nd World War, especially at the west end. ST AUGUSTINE'S CHURCH was left with only its tower which now forms the entrance to ST PAUL'S Choir School. The CORDWAINERS lost their 18th-century hall, the fourth on the site since 1483. It is now St Paul's Garden. St Swithin's Church opposite CANNON STREET STATION was also destroyed. LONDON STONE, which was embedded in the church's wall, is now in the wall of the Oversea-Chinese Banking Corporation which was built on the site at No. 111. Bracken House at No. 10 was designed for the *Financial Times* by Sir Albert Richardson. The LONDON CHAMBER OF COMMERCE was founded in 1881 at No. 69. The Chamber's present building was designed by Gunton and Gunton and built in 1938–58. The bronze *Icarus* in Old Change Court is by Michael Ayrton (1973).

Cannon Street Railway Bridge Built in 1863–6 by John Hawkshaw and John Wolfe-Barry to carry the South Eastern Railway across the river. It has five spans of shallow plate girders on cast-iron fluted Doric piers. It was widened in 1886–93. The capitals and ornamental brackets were removed in 1979. (*See also* BLACKFRIARS RAILWAY BRIDGE.)

Cannon Street Station *EC4.* Stands where the Hanseatic merchants had their steelyard from the 10th century until 1598 (*see* STEELYARD). The station, which was opened in 1866, was designed by John Hawkshaw for the South Eastern Railway as its CITY terminus. The original building was a massive

Cannon Street Station, designed by John Hawkshaw, was opened in 1866. The railway bridge was built in 1863–6.

structure of high walls carrying an almost semi-circular single-span arch over the tracks. This roof was 680 ft long and at its apex 106 ft high. The walls ended in twin stone towers standing on either side of the northern end of the bridge across the river. The Cannon Street Hotel (by E.M. Barry) was built between the station and the street, in 1867, but was converted to offices in 1931. The station was severely damaged by bombs in the 2nd World War. In 1958, Hawkshaw's arched roof was removed and during the 1960s the station was almost entirely remodelled, to include office blocks, shops and a pedestrian walkway. However, the original walls and the two riverside towers remain. Cannon Street is largely a commuter station, bringing office workers into the CITY. By 1970, over 37,000 passengers were arriving each weekday morning during the peak hours.

Canonbury *Islington, N1.* Covers part of the lands of the former Canonbury manor, which extended between present-day UPPER STREET, ESSEX ROAD and St Paul's Road (once named Hopping Lane, where presumably hops were grown). Apart from the manor-house enclosures, the land was open fields and rich dairy pastures, beyond the straggling high-road village of ISLINGTON. From the mid-17th century (after the Marquesses of Northampton ceased to live there as lords of the manor) to the late 18th, its population must have consisted largely of summer visitors at CANONBURY TOWER.

Opposite the Tower was Canonbury Tavern, converted into an ale-house from manorial farm buildings, and partly enclosed within the old park walls. Beside it was a picturesque pond, much painted by artists, and finally filled in about 1850. The tavern was greatly enlarged in the 18th century, improved with tea-gardens, and became popular for club dinners. The present tavern of about 1850, which unfortunately lost its top storey through dry rot in the 1950s, is a favourite – indeed famous – local public house.

In 1770 John Dawes, a stockbroker, leased Canonbury manor grounds and buildings, demolishing some

of the buildings and altering others. On the south range he built (says Nelson) 'a villa' – Canonbury House – 'and three other good dwelling houses', in one of which he lived before acquiring Highbury manor lands. In about 1800 Jacob Leroux secured a building lease of over 19 acres and built the north-west range of what is now Canonbury Square, and the handsome 37-house Compton Terrace facing UPPER STREET.

The 1820s saw Canonbury developing as a pretty suburb along the lines of BARNSBURY, though with rather more fine villas and grandly proportioned houses, and enhanced by bosky surroundings and the NEW RIVER, whose last loop in the fields near Astey's Row was straightened to facilitate building. Expansion in the 1840s–50s included Canonbury Park North and South, laid out across 'Canonbury Field' by the Marquess of Northampton, and the group of roads called 'Alwyne' after one of the Northampton family names. Some of the old manor garden survives, with the two Elizabethan garden houses incorporated in Alwyne Villas and Alwyne Place.

In 1907, during the restoration of CANONBURY TOWER, King Edward Hall was built alongside it as a recreational club for the Marquess's estate residents here and in CLERKENWELL; and in 1952, when the Tavistock Repertory Company leased the Tower, this hall became the Tower Theatre. Much of the area is now freehold, but the remaining estate was, in 1931, settled by the 6th Marquess on trustees, by whom it has since been managed, still retaining the family connection.

While it declined in the earlier part of this century to 'shabby-genteel', the district never lost its style. Writers, artists and publishers lived here, including George and Weedon Grossmith at 5 Canonbury Place, Evelyn Waugh in 1928 at 17a Canonbury Square, and George Orwell at 27 Canonbury Square in 1945. The 2nd World War left bomb-sites in Canonbury Park, and as these gaps were filled the area was rediscovered, restored and in places rebuilt. Creation in the 1970s of the Marquess Estate, an imaginative complex of flats, involved demolition of several 1860s' streets between

ESSEX ROAD and the NEW RIVER. Although, since the war, the river has ended at Green Lanes, simulated stretches are maintained in park areas near Astey's Row and south of St Paul's Road – the latter containing a pretty brick circular hut often supposed to be Jacobean, but probably an early 19th-century linesman's hut.

Canonbury Road *see* NEW NORTH ROAD.

Canonbury Tower *Canonbury Place, N1*. The base of ISLINGTON's most famous historic building appears to be extremely ancient, incorporating pre-Roman work; and, according to some sources, 24 ley-lines passed through the site of its unusually large square newel. Canonbury manor belonged in Saxon times to the BISHOPS OF LONDON, passing under the Normans to the de Berners family with BARNSBURY manor. In 1253 it was granted by Ralph de Berners to the Canons of ST BARTHOLOMEW'S PRIORY, SMITH-FIELD, and was thence known as the Canons' Burgh or Canonbury. The Tower and probably much of the extant mansion were built by its last Prior, William Bolton, whose rebus, a bolt piercing a tun, survives at 6 Canonbury Place and on two garden buildings now in Alwyne Villas. On dissolving the Priory in 1539 Henry VIII gave the manor to Thomas Cromwell, but on Cromwell's attainder a year later it reverted to the Crown. Edward VI exchanged it for other land with John Dudley, Duke of Northumberland, who himself then forfeited it for treason. Lord Wentworth, who obtained Canonbury House from Queen Mary, sold it to a rich cloth merchant, John Spencer, later knighted and Lord Mayor in 1594.

Canonbury Tower, Islington, built by the last Prior of St Bartholomew's, Smithfield. An engraving of 1819 after A.C. Pugin.

Spencer embellished the buildings, especially the Tower, from which in 1599 his daughter Elizabeth reputedly was lowered in a basket to elope with the penniless Lord Compton, who was disguised as a baker's boy. Sir John disinherited his daughter, but was tricked into reconciliation by Queen Elizabeth's summoning him to sponsor the child of an impoverished young couple, whom he discovered to be his own grandson.

Lord Compton, created Earl of Northampton in 1618, leased Canonbury House (1616–25) to Sir Francis Bacon, and apart from a period in the 1650s–60s the Spencers ceased to live there. Later it was let as lodgings, and tenants of its apartments included the encyclopaedist, Ephraim Chambers, who died there in 1740, Oliver Goldsmith (1762–4), and for a time Washington Irving. Two of the Tower rooms contain Elizabethan panelling and elaborate chimneypieces, and the buildings also have contemporary plaster ceilings, one dated 1599. Since 1952 the restored Tower has been leased by the Tavistock Repertory Company.

The Canons *Madeira Road, Mitcham, Surrey*. The site of a grange farm of the Augustinian Canons of ST MARY OVERIE, SOUTHWARK who served the Parish Church of St Peter and St Paul from 1259. They dug the carp pond and built the stone dovecote (dated 1511). After the DISSOLUTION, the farm had many owners until bought by Robert Cranmer, a City merchant, in 1656 as part of the manor of MITCHAM. His son, John, had the present house built in 1680 and the Cranmer family resided in it from 1741 until 1843. The obelisk in the grounds was erected by the Revd Richard Cranmer to commemorate the appearance of a spring during the extremely dry summer of 1822. The Cranmer family, and later the Simpsons who married into it, maintained ownership of The Canons until 1939 when it was sold to MITCHAM Council.

Canons Park *Middlesex*. Situated between STAN-MORE and EDGWARE, about 10 miles north of London along the EDGWARE ROAD. It was part of the land held at the time of *Domesday Book* by Roger de Rames, in STANMORE manor. In the 14th century the Augustinian Canons of ST BARTHOLOMEW, SMITHFIELD, were granted land in LITTLE STANMORE together with its church of ST LAWRENCE which had existed since the early 12th century. The estate was subsequently referred to as Canons in the manor of Whitchurch – Whyt Churche being a description of ST LAWRENCE. In 1604 the estate was bought by Sir Thomas Lake, Secretary of State to James I, and the manor house rebuilt, traditionally by John Thorpe. At the beginning of the 18th century when Mary Lake married James Brydges, created Duke of Chandos in 1729, the church, Lake Almshouses to the north (augmented 1693), and the manor house were still the only buildings of any importance away from WATLING STREET in the wooded parish. Chandos had made his fortune as Paymaster General to the Duke of Marlborough and his estates included 1,492 acres of LITTLE STANMORE of which Canons comprised 481 acres. The grounds of the estate were laid out as a park by Dr Alexander Blackwell. Life at Canons was considered the height of fashion in its time although Pope saw fit to satirise it as Timon's villa in his *Epistle on False Taste* (1731). In 1747 the 2nd Duke was obliged to break up the house to pay off debts and only the gateway on to

EDGWARE ROAD remains. The subsequent owner built a modest Georgian house on the site and Repton later carried out some landscaping. The existence of the Park meant that by the 19th century there were still relatively few buildings in LITTLE STANMORE, and development on the west side of the road north of EDGWARE was only possible following the gradual sale of the Canons estate from the 1880s. By 1919, after the opening of the Canons Park terminus of the METROPOLITAN LINE, houses appeared along EDGWARE ROAD and Whitchurch Lane, and during the next decade when the UNDERGROUND was extended from GOLDERS GREEN, the developer, George Cross, began building along the new Canons Drive. The detached and semi-detached houses appearing in the Park helped satisfy the need of the growing population of its immediate neighbour EDGWARE. The parkland character was preserved to the design of A.J. Butcher, and the main tree-lined Drive and the lake are legacies of Chandos's park. In 1929 the NORTH LONDON COLLEGIATE SCHOOL bought the extended Georgian house and some of its grounds, and in 1934 LITTLE STANMORE became part of HARROW Urban District which acquired most of the remaining land on the Canons estate.

Capel Bedyddwyr Cymreig (Welsh Baptist Church) *30 Eastcastle Street, W1*. Arose out of the need for a place of worship where the Welsh language was used, and a centre for cultural and social activities for Welsh people living in London. The original hall was soon found to be too small and the present building was erected in 1889 to the designs of Owen Lewis. The Chapel offers an imposing frontage to the street, with tall columns and a pair of staircases leading to the interior. This is essentially a preaching and discussion hall with seating concentrated upon the pulpit, centrally placed at the east end, above which the organ rises in an impressive manner. The massively coved ceiling had to be cut away so that the pipes could be heightened. Above this is a small clerestory with a flat roof. A gallery, supported on fluted columns and enclosed with an attractive wrought-iron screen, encircles the interior. Below the platform on which the pulpit rests is a tiled area for baptismal immersion. A frequent visitor to the chapel, when he was in London, was David Lloyd George.

Capel Court *EC2*. Named after the Capel family who had a house on this site in the 16th century. Sir William Capel was Lord Mayor in 1503. Until 1973 the court led to the STOCK EXCHANGE.

Capital Radio *Euston Centre, Euston Road, NW1*. Occupies the first floor of a building designed by the Sidney K. Firman Partnership and completed in the late 1960s. It started on 16 October 1973 as the second independent radio station. Its offices, originally in PICCADILLY, were moved with the seven studios and four editing rooms in late 1973. It holds a franchise for general and entertainment broadcasting. It is on the air 24 hours a day over an official 30-mile area, and has between four and five million listeners.

Carburton Street *W1*. Takes its name from Carburton, Nottinghamshire, which was part of the dowry of Henrietta Cavendish when she married Edward Harley (*see* HARLEY STREET). The Regent

Centre Hotel (350 bedrooms) is by Raymond Spratley, 1973.

Cardinal House *see* FARADAY HOUSE.

Cardinal's Wharf *Bankside, SE1*. Probably takes its name from Cardinal Wolsey, who was Bishop of Winchester (*see* BANKSIDE) in 1529–30. A plaque here reads: 'Here lived Sir Christopher Wren during the building of St Paul's Cathedral. Here also in 1502 Catherine Infanta of Castile and Aragon afterwards first Queen of Henry VIII took shelter on first landing in London.'

Carew Manor *Beddington, Surrey*. The Great Hall of the house, now a school, has an impressive and probably unique 15th-century roof, resembling the arch-braced hammer-beam roof of ELTHAM PALACE. Its true construction was for years disguised by applied moulded decoration. Formerly known as Beddington Park, Place or House, this was once a medieval moated manor house. It was rebuilt at least three times; most recently before 1866 when it became an orphanage. A dovecote and an orangery wall (probably early 18th-century) survive. BEDDINGTON is believed to be the first place in this country where oranges were planted in the open ground (by Sir Francis Carew who died in 1611).

Carey Lane *EC2*. Although Stow says that the name was derived from a man named Kery, it more probably came from an old English girl's name, Kiron. It was once known as Kyron Lane.

Carey Street *WC2*. Takes its name from Nicholas Carey, who owned land hereabouts in the reign of Charles I. Several distinguished lawyers have lived in the street, including Blackstone, who wrote his *Commentaries* here, and John Scott, later Lord Eldon. Henry Mayhew, author of *London Labour and the London Poor*, began his working life here as a clerk in his father's law office, 'very little to the satisfaction of any of the parties concerned'. The chambers known as New Court are by Alfred Waterhouse. On the south side is an entrance to the LAW COURTS.

Carlisle House *Lambeth*. Built for the Bishop of Rochester in about 1197 and rebuilt some 20 years later when it was known as La Place. In 1531 Richard Rose, a cook, tried to poison Bishop Fisher but the Bishop 'eats no pottage that daie' and 14 guests died instead. Rose was boiled to death at SMITHFIELD. In 1539 the house was taken over by the Bishop of Carlisle. During the Commonwealth it was sold. At the Restoration it was returned to the then Bishop but he never used it. In 1690–1730 a part was leased as a pottery, in 1730–63 as a tavern, and in 1763–86 to a dancing master. From about 1786 to 1826 it was an academy for young gentlemen. It was demolished in 1827 when smaller houses were built on the site between Hercules Road and Carlisle Lane.

Carlisle House *Soho Square*. Occupied at the end of the 17th century by the 2nd Earl of Carlisle; in the middle of the 18th by the Neapolitan Ambassador; and from 1760 by Theresa Cornelys, a Viennese opera singer and courtesan. Casanova claimed paternity of one of her children. Mrs Cornelys (whose real name was

Imer) rented the house and its furniture for her celebrated assembly rooms which those who could afford her tickets attended for dancing, cards, operatic concerts and masquerades. The venture proved most successful: Smollett referred to the rooms in *Humphrey Clinker* as surpassing 'all description'; and Fanny Burney, writing in 1770 at the age of 18, thought 'the magnificence of the rooms, splendour of the illuminations and embellishments, and the brilliant appearance of the company exceeded anything I ever before saw. The apartments were so crowded we had scarce room to move, which was quite disagreeable, nevertheless, the flight of apartments both upstairs, and on the ground floor seemed endless.' Popular and fashionable though they were, however, the rooms were unable to withstand the challenge, first of ALMACK'S, which Horace Walpole suggested in 1764 might 'swallow Mrs Cornelys up', then of the PANTHEON, which was opened in January 1772. Mrs Cornelys responded by making her rooms and entertainments finer than ever; but the debts she had accumulated, and the fines she had to pay for allowing unlicensed dramatic performances on her premises, ruined her. She was arrested at the suit of her creditors in October 1772 and imprisoned in the KING'S BENCH. She was declared bankrupt and Carlisle House was assigned to her creditors, one of whom was Thomas Chippendale, the cabinet-maker.

For a time the rooms remained open for public receptions on Sundays when, in the words of an American visitor who was taken to them in November 1780, 'The employment of the company is simply walking through the rooms; being allowed tea, coffee, chocolate, lemonade, orgeat, negus, milk, etc; admission by ticket, cost, three shillings . . . The ladies were rigged out in gaudy attire, attended by bucks, bloods, and macaronies, though it is also resorted to by persons of irreproachable character.' On weekdays concerts and masquerades were also still held; but the rooms had seen their best days and by 1783 had closed. The premises passed into the hands of a music publisher a few years later and were demolished in 1791. ST PATRICK's Roman Catholic church covers part of the site.

Carlisle Place

SW1. Extends south from VICTORIA STREET west of WESTMINSTER CATHEDRAL. It takes its name from George Howard, Viscount Morpeth and Earl of Carlisle, who was in charge of the government department responsible for its development in the 1850s (hence also Morpeth Terrace). Cardinal Manning lived at No. 22, 'a cavernous house', in 1873–92. The large building on the west side houses the Convent of the Daughters of Charity of St Vincent de Paul who have been here since 1859. They run a hostel here for girls in distress and a day centre for vagrants. There is also a school and a day nursery.

Carlos Place

W1. A short curved street connecting GROSVENOR SQUARE with MOUNT STREET. It was laid out in 1891–3 to improve communications between GROSVENOR SQUARE and BERKELEY SQUARE. The large private houses on the curved eastern side are by J.E. Trollope of Giles, Gough and Trollope, 1891–3. On the west side the CONNAUGHT HOTEL (until 1917 the Coburg) has occupied premises on this site since 1815. The present building of 1894–6 is by Lewis H. Isaacs and Henry L. Florence.

Carlton Club

69 St James's Street, SW1. Founded in 1832 after a general election in which only 179 Tories were returned out of a total membership of the House of Commons of 658, the intention being to form a social club which could serve as a meeting-place for Conservatives anxious to restore the fortunes of their party and to oppose the Reform Bill. A short lease was taken of 2 CARLTON HOUSE TERRACE to the end of 1835 when the club took apartments at the CARLTON HOTEL, Regent Street until premises, designed by Sir Robert Smirke, had been built in Pall Mall. These premises were extended by Sir Robert's brother, Sydney, in the 1840s and demolished in 1854 to make way for a new club house designed by Sydney Smirke and George Basevi and modelled on Sansovino's Library of St Mark's at Venice. Among its early members were the Dukes of Cumberland and Gloucester, and W.E. Gladstone. Disraeli was elected in 1836 when membership had become prized by all ambitious Conservatives, and the Club had begun to exercise the kind of functions now performed by the Conservative Central Office. The number of members was at first fixed at 700, raised to 800 in 1833 and to 900 in 1857 when it was resolved that the political views of those who wished to join must be 'in accordance with those entertained by the great body of the Carlton Club'. And, although it was not until 1912 that members were specifically required by the club rules to 'profess the principles and objects' of the Conservative Party, it was indicated to those whose political allegiances were in doubt that they were no longer welcome. 'A scene took place at the Carlton Club on Monday evening which has excited much attention,' the Marquess of Downshire wrote in 1852 when the Peelites, of whom Gladstone was one, were at loggerheads with the rest of the party. 'While Mr Gladstone was reading a newspaper, certain Tory members of the House of Commons came into the room, and employed extremely insulting language to the Right Hon. gentleman, telling him among other things that he had no right to belong to a Conservative Club, but ought to be pitched out of the window in the direction of the Reform Club.' Gladstone resigned in 1860. Disraeli, of course, continued as a member; and although, as he once confessed, he hated clubs, he often thought it advisable to look in. He did so, for instance, on 13 April 1867 after a splendid speech in the House. A member proposed a toast to him and he was loudly cheered; he was asked to stay to supper but he declined, preferring to go home to his wife who was waiting up for him with his favourite pie and a bottle of champagne. A few years later it was 'resolved unanimously' that the great man should be 'invited to a Banquet by the Members of the Club'.

In the 20th century the club continued to play an important part in Conservative politics: it was at a meeting here in 1911 that Bonar Law was elected Leader of the Conservative Party and here also in 1922 that it was decided that the Conservatives would withdraw their support from Lloyd George's coalition government. 'The Carlton is a beastly club infected by the worst of the species viz: – the bore political,' Balfour told Lord Curzon. 'But you are quite right to belong to it. It must be suffered like long hours and constituents as a necessary though disagreeable accompaniment of a political career.'

In 1925, soon after its façade of Caen stone had been renewed by Sir Reginald Blomfield, No. 7

CARLTON GARDENS was bought from the Earl of Dudley and became the Carlton Club Annexe to which ladies could be invited and in which at dinner evening dress was compulsory. In the main part of the club some members still continued to wear silk hats in the daytime; and although the 26th Earl of Crawford, who died in 1913, was said to have been the last member to wear a top hat while eating in the coffee-room, Lord Clanwilliam continued to wear his elsewhere in the club until his death in 1953.

The requirement that members should adhere to the principles of the Conservative Party and be British subjects still obtains. Nearly all Conservative Prime Ministers, including, in recent years, Churchill, Eden, Macmillan and Heath, have been members of the club.

Carlton Gardens *SW1*. John Nash's extension of CARLTON HOUSE TERRACE built in 1830–3. Prince Louis Napoleon (later Napoleon III) lived in exile at No. 1 in 1839–40. It afterwards became the official residence of the Foreign Secretary. It is now occupied by the Metals Society. Field Marshal Earl Kitchener lived at No. 2 in 1914–15. Palmerston occupied No. 4 as Foreign Secretary in 1847–55, A.J. Balfour in 1874–97 and 1908–29, Lord Curzon in 1898, and the Free French forces in the 2nd World War. On the wall beneath the Cross of Lorraine is inscribed General de Gaulle's message to the French people, broadcast after the fall of France in 1940. The house was rebuilt by Sir Reginald Blomfield in 1923–4. Sidney Herbert, the Secretary for War, was at No. 5 in 1846–51; Gladstone at No. 6 in 1838–41. The Royal Fine Art Commission is at No. 2. The statue of Lord Curzon is by Mackennal (*see* STATUES).

Carlton Hotel *Haymarket*. Designed by C.J. Phipps to form part of the same block as HER MAJESTY'S THEATRE, the hotel was completed by Lewis H. Isaacs and Henry L. Florence. After leaving the SAVOY HOTEL, César Ritz took over the Carlton, engaged Escoffier as chef, and employed the architect, Mewès, to do the interiors in the style of the Paris Ritz, with a magnificent Palm Court. The hotel opened in 1899. Three years later Ritz received the news of the postponement of Edward VII's coronation. After weeks of preparation for the grand season that was to follow, the news brought about a nervous breakdown from which Ritz never recovered. The hotel closed in 1939, was bombed in the 2nd World War and remained empty until demolished in 1957–8. NEW ZEALAND HOUSE now stands on the site.

Carlton House *Pall Mall*. Built at the beginning of the 18th century for Henry, Lord Carlton, it was purchased in 1732 by Frederick, Prince of Wales, whose widow, Augusta, George III's mother, continued to live there until her death in 1772, considerably enlarging it and adding to it the house next door which was bought from George Bubb Doddington. George III granted the use of the house to his eldest son, provided he undertook 'all repairs, taxes and the keeping of the garden'. The gardens, which stretched as far down as MARLBOROUGH HOUSE and had been laid out by William Kent, were particularly attractive; but the house was unremarkable and in poor repair. The Prince of Wales instructed Henry Holland, whose work at BROOKS'S CLUB he had much admired, to reconstruct it. Work began in the early autumn of 1783 and was to continue intermittently for nearly 30 years at a cost which the inordinately extravagant Prince was

The Prince of Wales, later George IV, at a garden party in 1784 in the grounds of Carlton House, laid out by William Kent. The previous year Henry Holland had begun the lavish and costly reconstruction of the house itself.

123

himself to admit was 'enormous'. Adjoining houses were bought and demolished to make way for new wings; a fine Corinthian portico was added; inside a splendid hall, decorated with Ionic columns of brown Siena marble, led to an octagon and a graceful double staircase. Above were the state apartments, the Prince's exotic bow-windowed bedroom, his dressing-room and bathroom. Beyond the music room there was a drawing-room decorated in the Chinese taste for which agents were sent to China to buy furniture; the mercer's bill alone came to £6,817 and £441 was spent on lanterns. All the rooms in the house were as expensively decorated and furnished, many of them with exquisite pieces from France, several of which are now at BUCKINGHAM PALACE. The result in the opinion of the novelist, Robert Plumer Ward, was worthy to stand comparison with Versailles, although Robert Smirke, the rather staid architect of the BRITISH MUSEUM and many other public buildings in London, considered it 'overdone with finery'.

It was the scene of several extraordinarily grand receptions and balls, notably a splendid fête on 19 June 1811 to celebrate the inauguration of the Prince's Regency, an entertainment which Thomas Moore thought more magnificent than any ever given, and an equally wonderful fête given for 2,000 guests in 1814 as a tribute to Wellington, for which special buildings, designed by John Nash – who was responsible also for new Corinthian rooms in the house – were erected in the beautiful gardens. The Regent's only child, Princess Charlotte, was born here in 1796 and married here in 1816. Splendid as the house was, however, when the Regent came to the throne as George IV he decided that it was not fine enough for his new dignity. Another large palace would, therefore, have to take its place. It was demolished and a terrace of houses was built upon its site and in the garden (see CARLTON HOUSE TERRACE). Its columns were used in the portico of the NATIONAL GALLERY; several of its fireplaces and doors were removed to BUCKINGHAM PALACE and Windsor Castle; and some of the armorial stained glass from the conservatory was incorporated in the windows at Windsor. But little else remains of a residence which Horace Walpole, during its reconstruction, described as likely to be 'the most perfect palace' in Europe.

Carlton House Terrace *SW1*. Two magnificent terraces by John Nash built in 1827–32 on the site of CARLTON HOUSE. Gladstone lived at No. 4 in 1856 and at No. 11 in 1857–75; Palmerston at No. 5 in 1840–6; and Lord Curzon at No. 1 in 1905–25. William Crockford, founder of CROCKFORD's Gaming Club, occupied No. 11 in 1842–4, and Earl Grey No. 13 in 1851–7 and in 1859–80. After severe damage in the 2nd World War the façade was restored and the interior much altered. The ROYAL COLLEGE OF PATHOLOGISTS is at No. 2; the TURF CLUB at No. 5; the ROYAL SOCIETY at No. 6; the INSTITUTE OF CONTEMPORARY ARTS at No. 12; the annexe of the NATIONAL PORTRAIT GALLERY at No. 15; and at No. 17 the FEDERATION OF BRITISH ARTISTS.

Carlton Mews *Warwick House Street*. Designed by Nash for those who lived in CARLTON HOUSE TERRACE. Originally, carriages were kept on the ground floor, horses on the first floor which was reached by a ramp, and grooms and other servants on the floor above. Later the mews were converted into attractive houses approached by a narrow entry off COCKSPUR STREET. They were demolished in the 1960s.

Carlton Theatre *Haymarket*. Built in 1926 by a syndicate called the Carlton Theatre Co., to the designs of Frank T. Verity and S. Beverley. It opened in April 1927 under the direction of Gilbert Miller with *Lady Luck*, a musical by Firth Shephard, with Leslie Henson, Laddie Cliff, Phyllis Monkman and Madge Eliot. This ran for 324 performances and was followed by *The Yellow Mask*, a musical drama by Edgar Wallace. An American import, *Good News*; a revue, *In Other Words*, with George Robey; and a revival of *The Merry Widow* were a prelude to its conversion in April 1929 to a cinema. It was sold in 1930 to the Paramount Film Co. Its seating capacity as a theatre was 1,500. The Carlton Cinema has recently been converted into two cinemas.

Carlton Tower Hotel *Cadogan Place, SW1*. A luxury hotel for a time known as the Sonesta Tower Hotel. It was built in 1961 to the designs of Michael Rosenauer. The beaten copper panels on the south face are the *Four Seasons* by Elizabeth Frink (1961), and the murals in the lobby are by Feliks Topolski. There are 244 bedrooms.

Carlyle Square *SW3*. A pleasant leafy square built in about 1830 on some market gardens and named Oakley Square after a title of the Cadogan family (*see* CADOGAN ESTATE). Its name was changed in 1872 in honour of Thomas Carlyle who was living in CHEYNE ROW (*see* CARLYLE'S HOUSE).

Carlyle's House *24 Cheyne Row, SW3*. One of a terrace of redbrick houses built in 1708. In 1834 Thomas Carlyle came to London from Craigenputtock in search of a house and finally settled on No. 5 Cheyne Row (now No. 24). 'It is notable how at every new visit your opinion gets a little hitch the *contrary* way from its former tendency,' he wrote to his wife. 'I nevertheless still feel a great liking for this excellent old house .... Chelsea is unfashionable; it was once the resort of the Court and the great, however; hence numerous old houses in it, at once cheap and excellent .... The House itself is eminent antique; wainscotted to the very ceiling, and has been all new-painted and repaired .... And then as to room, Goody! .... Three storeys beside the sunk storey, in every one of the three apartments ....' His wife approving of the house, it was taken on a yearly tenancy at £35 a year. They moved in in June and subsequently entertained many of the leading intellectuals and writers of the day including Ruskin, Dickens, Mazzini, Leigh Hunt and Kingsley. In the basement kitchen Tennyson and Carlyle used to smoke into the chimney so that Mrs Carlyle would not take offence at the fumes. *The French Revolution*, *Latter Day Pamphlets* and *Frederick the Great* were written in the attic which Carlyle unsuccessfully tried to soundproof in 1853. In 1881 he died in the drawing-room on the first floor. The house is much as the Carlyles left it. Most of the furniture, pictures and books are theirs. Carlyle's hat still hangs on the peg and there is no electricity to brighten the wainscoted corridors.

Carmen's Company *see* CITY LIVERY COMPANIES.

Carnaby Street *W1*. Laid out in the 1680s and named after Karnaby House which was built in 1683 on the east side of the street by Richard Tyler, a bricklayer. Many of its first inhabitants were Huguenots. By the middle of the 19th century most houses were in the hands of tradesmen and shopkeepers. In 1957 John Stephen, John Vince and Andreas Spyropoulus opened a men's boutique which was soon surrounded by other small shops selling colourful clothes and accessories for both sexes. By the 1960s the street was world-famous and had entered the *Oxford English Dictionary*: 'Carnaby Street *n* (usu.*attrib.*) Fashionable clothing for young people.' Many of the boutiques remain, but the *éclat* is no more. Inderwick and Co., the tobacconists at No. 45, were founded in WARDOUR STREET (then known as Prince's Street) in 1797 by John Inderwick. He started the fashion for Meerschaum pipes and purchased a mine in the Crimea to ensure supplies for his shop.

Carnegie Libraries Founded by Andrew Carnegie, the Scottish-born steel industrialist who emigrated to America in 1848 and made a huge fortune there. On his retirement he devoted himself to philanthropy and, in various English-speaking countries, provided the money for a large number of libraries on condition that the local authorities found sites and maintained the buildings. Money was provided for 380 library buildings in the United Kingdom. Many of these were in London and several still remain.

Caroline Gardens *Asylum Road, SE15*. Formerly the Licensed Victuallers' Benevolent Asylum. There are nearly 200 houses and a chapel set in 6 acres of grounds. The houses were erected between 1828 and 1866 to provide homes for retired members of the licensed victualling trade. The central feature is the shell of the chapel which was severely damaged in the 2nd World War. There remains the portico of six Ionic columns surmounted by a pediment and tower designed by H. and E. Rose. The Licensed Victuallers' Benevolent Institution moved to Denham, Bucks, in 1959 and the entire property was taken over and rehabilitated by the London Borough of SOUTHWARK to house local old people. The buildings were renamed Caroline Gardens after a former resident, Caroline

Secker, the widow of James Secker, a Royal Marine who served with Nelson at the Battle of Trafalgar.

Carpenters' Company *see* CITY LIVERY COMPANIES.

Carrington Street *W1*. A short cul-de-sac leading off the south side of SHEPHERD STREET. It evidently takes its name from Nathan Carrington, who owned land hereabouts at the time of its first development in the mid-18th century.

Carshalton *Surrey*. A spring-line village, always famous for its waters. One of the two main courses of the River WANDLE is formed by the town ponds. These ponds have always tended to impede through-traffic, and helped to preserve Carshalton's historic centre, now designated a conservation area of outstanding interest. The name at the time of *Domesday*, in 1186, was Aultone, formerly Aewiell-tun; probably 'settlement by the spring'. The 'Cars' prefix first appears as Kers or Cres – possibly either a cross or [water] cress. The manorial history is complex: five manors in the time of Edward the Confessor were united by *Domesday* and subsequently split in two. One sub-manor was associated with a house latterly known as Carshalton Place, demolished earlier this century. Part of its park remains as a public park – as does that of a more famous house which met a similar fate: The Oaks, which was once owned by the Earls of Derby and saw the origins of the Derby and Oaks horse-races. The Grove Park, through which the WANDLE flows, includes the last reconstruction of another sub-manor house: Stonecourt. A fine 18th-century house which survives is CARSHALTON HOUSE. Carshalton church (All Saints) dates in part from the 12th and 13th centuries and contains many fine monuments. As well as trout and walnuts, and the many industries associated with the WANDLE Mills (snuff, paper, leather, oil, copper and calico bleaching), Carshalton, and its sister villages of BEDDINGTON and WALLINGTON, were for many years associated with the extensive lavender and mint growing and processing based on MITCHAM. A plaque at No. 19 Park Hill commemorates the residence here of William Hall White (Mark Rutherford), the novelist.

Carshalton House *Pound Street, Carshalton, Surrey*. This house, now a convent school (St Philomena's), was built by Edward Carleton before

Carshalton House, 'from its healthy and pleasant situation, styled ... the Montpelier of England'.

1710. Subsequent owners were Dr John Radcliffe, royal physician and Oxford University benefactor, and Sir John Fellowes, Sub-Governor of the South Sea Company, who was almost certainly the builder of the unique Waterhouse and the 'Hermitage' in the garden, and who made other additions and alterations to house and garden in 1716–21. The beautiful Blue, or Adam, Room was probably the creation of the Hon. Thomas Walpole (nephew of the Prime Minister, Robert). Other owners included Admiral Lord Anson and Lord Chancellor Hardwicke. The house has been a school of various kinds since 1847.

Carter Lane *EC4*. Named after two 14th-century local tax payers, Stephen and Thomas Le Charatter. Before a right of way was established through ST PAUL'S CHURCHYARD the lane was one of the CITY'S main thoroughfares. Guy Fawkes and his fellow conspirators used to meet here at the Hart's Horn Tavern.

Carthusian Street *EC1*. Built in about 1699 and named after the Carthusian Priory of CHARTERHOUSE.

Cartwright Gardens *WC1*. A crescent, formerly Burton Crescent. It was built in 1807 by James Burton and renamed after Major John Cartwright, the political reformer, who campaigned for universal suffrage, vote by ballot, annual parliaments and the abolition of slavery. He lived at No. 37 from 1820 until his death in 1824. In 1831 a bronze seated statue of him by George Clarke was set up in the gardens (*see* STATUES). Edwin Chadwick, the sanitary reformer, lived at No. 1 in 1838–9; Sir Rowland Hill at No. 2 in 1837–9; and Sydney Smith at No. 20 in 1835–6 and at No. 34 in 1836–9. Now the east side is occupied by Hughes Parry Hall, Commonwealth Hall and Canterbury Hall, residential halls of LONDON UNIVERSITY. On the west side are hotels.

Castelnau *SW13*. Known as Bridge Road until 1896, it is the main approach to BARNES from HAMMERSMITH BRIDGE. It was constructed by the Hammersmith Bridge Co. in 1827 and initially developed by the Boileau family of MORTLAKE (their house there being named after their ancestral home, Castelnau de la Garde, near Nîmes). The original Castelnau Villas (Nos 91–125 and 84–122) were designed by Henry Laxton and advertised in 1842. They were built as semi-detached pairs with uniform façades, although some latitude was permitted in the design of the coachhouses. In spite of later alterations and accretions, this remains one of the most satisfying of early Victorian developments. The Boileau Arms also opened in 1842 near the bridge where rows of shops came later. Holy Trinity Church, designed by the local Thomas Allom, was consecrated in 1868 to serve the new community. Other houses, no longer standardised and often detached, were built to the north and south, completing the thoroughfare and reflecting changes in style.

Castle Baynard Built on the banks of the THAMES at BLACKFRIARS by Bairnardus or Baynard, a Norman who came over with William the Conqueror. It was given by Henry I to Robert Fitzwalter. Tradition has it that in King John's reign another Robert Fitzwalter's daughter, Matilda, caught the King's eye. Neither father nor daughter would agree to her becoming the King's mistress. Robert fled to France but

Matilda was caught, carried off to the TOWER and poisoned with powder on a poached egg. Later Robert acquitted himself well in a tournament, and was allowed to return home and to rebuild his castle, which had been destroyed in his absence. In 1275 yet another Robert Fitzwalter gave the site to the Archbishop of Canterbury for the foundation of a house and church for the Dominicans, from which BLACKFRIARS takes its name.

Fitzwalter built a new castle on the riverside east of BLACKFRIARS. This castle, by then royal property, was rebuilt after a fire in 1428, by Humphrey, Duke of Gloucester, younger brother of Henry V. In 1461 Edward IV was proclaimed King at Baynard's. It was here also that, in 1483, the Duke of Buckingham offered the crown to Richard of Gloucester, according to tradition. Henry VII rebuilt the castle in 1487, and it was used by Henry VIII for lavish banquets. Catherine of Aragon, Anne Boleyn and Anne of Cleves all lived here for some time, Anne of Cleves being the last royal person to make it a permanent home. In 1553 both Lady Jane Grey and Mary Tudor were proclaimed Queen here. Queen Elizabeth was entertained here by the Keeper, the Earl of Pembroke, to a dinner and fireworks display; and in 1660, according to Pepys, Charles II came to the castle for supper. In 1666 the GREAT FIRE destroyed the castle except for one turret which survived until 1720. Excavations were undertaken in 1972–4 by the GUILDHALL MUSEUM, Department of Urban Archaeology. They revealed the remains of a tower, probably of the 15th century, and possibly that which survived until 1720; a stone-lined dock; and parallel limestone walls running east to west, presumably the remains of the pre-1428 curtain walls, one of which had been repaired and extended in brick in the 15th century. The limits of a 16th-century addition to the castle were defined; and the north gateway was located. This last discovery revealed that the gateway's foundations were part of the Roman riverside city wall, whose existence had been the subject of argument for many years.

Castle Court *EC3*. The GEORGE AND VULTURE at No. 3 occupies a site where taverns have stood since at least the 15th century. Dickens was a frequent customer and used it for several scenes in the *Pickwick Papers*.

Catford *SE6*. In early times the Catford area, being low-lying, was liable to flood, and there are several bequests in late medieval wills towards the building of a causeway. Fordmill, a river mill near Catford Hill, is mentioned in *Domesday Book*; it survived as a corn mill until the end of the 19th century. Until the 18th century Catford was a small scattered hamlet, agriculture being the main occupation of its inhabitants where the ground was not too wooded or waterlogged. There were one or two grand houses, such as Place House, Catford Hill, where Queen Elizabeth I stayed, according to local legend. It is said that on 23 July 1518 the Papal Legate, Cardinal Campeggio, was entertained at Rushey Green Place, another mansion, by its owner William Hatcliffe.

The coming of the railway to Catford Bridge in 1857 accelerated development in the area; and in the late 19th century, streets were built radiating from Rushey Green on land which had been fields, or the grounds of properties such as Rosenthal House, the home of

Cruikshank's reconstruction of the police raid on the house in Cato Street where conspirators planned to murder the cabinet in 1820.

Alexander Rowland, inventor of macassar hair oil. The pound for straying animals at Rushey Green was removed; old weather-boarded cottages pulled down; and the stream which formerly flowed beside the road disappeared in 1855 when the clay bed was pierced during the laying of a sewer. In the last 100 years Catford has become a busy, populous suburb. Some well-known landmarks have fallen victim to new development: the old Town Hall (1875), formerly the offices of the LEWISHAM Board of Works, was demolished in 1968 and replaced by a modern building; a large Victorian church, St Laurence's (by H.R. Gough, 1886), was pulled down in 1967; and the Gaumont and Eros Cinemas (the Eros, formerly the Lewisham Hippodrome, was designed by Frank Matcham) were both demolished in 1960 to make way for an office block.

Catherine Street *WC2*. In the 1630s the northern part between RUSSELL STREET and EXETER STREET was built and named Brydges Street after the family into which the 4th Earl of Bedford, the ground landlord, had married. It appears by that name in Fielding's *Tom Jones*. From about 1632 to 1688 the Fleece Tavern stood on the corner of TAVISTOCK STREET. In 1660 Pepys mentioned that 'a Scottish Knight was killed basely the other day at the Fleece in Covent Garden where there had been a great many formerly killed'. In 1663 the THEATRE ROYAL DRURY LANE was opened. In 1673 the street was extended south to the STRAND. The new part was named Catherine Street after the Queen, Catherine of Braganza. Throughout the 18th century the street was as disreputable as DRURY LANE. Gay wrote:

O may thy virtue guard thee through the roads
Of Drury's mazy courts and dark abodes!
The harlots' guileful paths, who nightly stand
Where Catherine Street descends into the Strand.

In 1794 three taverns were prosecuted here as 'common nuisances'; and as late as 1847 tradesmen complained that prostitutes were driving away customers. In one of the several taverns in the street, the White Hart, the SAVAGE CLUB was organised. In 1872 the whole street was renamed Catherine Street. In 1900 the southern portion was swept away when ALDWYCH was built. In 1929 the DUCHESS THEATRE opened. The Opera Tavern at No. 23 was built in 1879 to the designs of John Treacher.

Catherine Wheel Alley *E1*. Named after the Catherine Wheel, a galleried coaching inn which stood at the end of the alley in BISHOPSGATE. The inn is first recorded in 1708. In 1895 it was partly destroyed by fire and the rest was demolished in 1911. The inn sign is said to have been derived from the arms of the TURNERS' COMPANY.

Cato Street *W1*. On the PORTMAN ESTATE, it is one of a group of streets with classical names, Homer and Virgil being its companions. It was laid out with mean houses and mews in 1803. In the stable loft of No. 6 (now No. 1A) the Cato Street Conspirators made their plans to murder the entire cabinet as they dined with Lord Harrowby at No. 44 GROSVENOR SQUARE on 23 February 1820. The Ministers were to be slaughtered in the dining-room and the heads of Lord Sidmouth, the Home Secretary, and that of one of his strongest supporters, Lord Castlereagh, were to be carried off in a bag. After the assassinations the conspirators intended assaulting COUTTS' BANK, capturing the cannon in the Artillery Ground, and GRAY'S INN, taking the MANSION HOUSE, BANK and TOWER, burning the barracks and proclaiming a provisional government. But one of the conspirators, probably George Edwards, betrayed them. On 23 February a detachment of Coldstream Guards and a few BOW STREET officers entered the loft. Arthur Thistlewood, a former estate agent and army officer, the leader of the conspirators, ran through one of the police officers, Richard Smithers, with his sword. Several conspirators were taken prisoner and hustled into the hackney carriages bound for BOW STREET but 11 escaped. Thistlewood was caught the next day in a house at Little Moorfields. On 1 May 1820 five ringleaders – James Ings, William Davidson, John Brunt, Richard Tidd and Arthur Thistlewood – were hanged at NEWGATE. They were spared being drawn and quartered because of public sympathy for them. (The man suspected of hanging them was later attacked in the street and almost castrated.) Five others were transported. Nothing was heard of the rest. 'The Ministers have had a narrow escape,' Lord Althorp observed, 'for nothing would have been more easy than to have murdered them in the way it was intended.' In 1827 the name of the alleyway was changed to Horace Street but a century later, when time had overlaid violence with romance, it became Cato Street again. Today, the little houses have been rebuilt as smart town apartments, but the loft remains, slightly battered, with a BLUE PLAQUE to remind us of what happened there on the night of 23 February 1820.

Cavalry and Guards Club *127 Piccadilly, W1.* Founded in 1890 as a proprietary club by an officer of the 20th Hussars. It became a members' club in 1895. It has always occupied its present premises which have been enlarged since its foundation. Unlike some other gentlemen's clubs, the Cavalry has always been tolerant of women guests. Edward VIII, as Prince of Wales, was often to be found here. The library is believed to be the best cavalry library in the world. Members are still limited to those who have been commissioned in cavalry and yeomanry regiments or in the HONOURABLE ARTILLERY COMPANY. The club was merged with the GUARDS CLUB in 1976.

Cavendish Hotel *Jermyn Street, SW1.* A modern luxury hotel built by Maurice Hanna. It opened in 1966 on the site of the old Cavendish Hotel. There has been a hotel on this site since the end of the 18th century. It was known as Miller's at the beginning of the 19th century, the Orléans in the early 1830s, and the Cavendish since 1836. The old Cavendish became famous under the eccentric management of Edward VII's friend, Mrs Rosa Lewis, 'the Duchess of Jermyn Street', who had been a kitchen maid in the house of the Comte de Paris and then cooked for the Prince of Wales (later Edward VII), Lady Randolph Churchill, and others. She ran a catering service for Edwardian house parties, and became a very close friend of Sir William Eden and Lord Ribblesdale (a room in the new hotel is named after him; the Sub Rosa Bar after her). She also acted as concierge of apartments at 55 Eaton Terrace where the Prince could take his mistresses, but after he was crowned he did not see her again. She expanded the catering service and bought the Cavendish Hotel in 1904, remaining there until her death in 1952. At the outbreak of the 1st World War, she hung the portrait of the Kaiser upside down in the servants' lavatory – 'the only throne fit for old Willie'. During the 2nd World War when the Cavendish was damaged in an air raid she stayed at the HYDE PARK HOTEL where she was an appallingly difficult guest. Evelyn Waugh portrayed her manner of speaking, and

the way she ran her hotel, in the character of Lottie Crump of Shepheard's Hotel, DOVER STREET, in *Vile Bodies*. She was extremely cross with 'the little swine' and refused to admit him into the hotel. By 1945, however, he was forgiven. He had lunch there in September and, as he recorded in his diary, she kissed him. There are 255 bedrooms.

Cavendish Place *W1.* Built soon after CAVENDISH SQUARE was completed. G.E. Street, the architect, lived at No. 14.

Cavendish Square *W1.* Laid out by John Prince for Edward Harley, 2nd Earl of Oxford, as the first development on his estate. It was named after the earl's wife, Lady Henrietta Cavendish Holles. Building began in 1717 but was held up by the bursting of the South Sea Bubble in 1720. In 1721–4 ST PETER VERE STREET and the OXFORD MARKET were built to stimulate further development. On the north side the Duke of Chandos planned to build his town house. Two wings were built by Edward Shepherd in 1724–8 but the centre block was never completed. In 1743 the site was acquired by the SOCIETY OF DILETTANTI for an academy which was never built. Eventually in about 1771 Nos 11–14 were built on the site by a Mr Tuffnell. The statue of George Bentinck was erected in 1851 (*see* STATUES). During the past 50 years most of the houses have been replaced by offices and flats. Tootal's is by Adams, Holden and Pearson (1937) and John Lewis by Slater, Moberly and Uren (1939). In 1971 an underground car park opened in the centre. Lady Mary Wortley Montagu lived at No. 5 in 1723–38. Captain and Mrs Horatio Nelson lived in the square in 1791; and Quintin Hogg, founder of the Regent Street Polytechnic (*see* POLYTECHNIC OF CENTRAL LONDON) in 1885–98. At Nos 11–14 is the Convent of the Holy Child linked by an arch which bears Epstein's *Madonna and Child* (1953), his 'passport to eternity'. Princess Amelia, daughter of George II, lived at No. 16 in 1761–80; H.H. Asquith at No. 20 in 1895–1908; George Romney, the painter, at No. 32 in 1775–97, and Sir Martin Archer Shee, 1797–1827. The surgeon, pathologist and neurologist, Sir Jonathan Hutchinson, lived at No. 15 from 1874 for most of the rest of his life.

Caxton Hall *Caxton Street, SW1.* Designed by Lee and Smith in 1878 as the WESTMINSTER City Hall. It is now used for concerts and public meetings, but was better known for its registry office. Between Caxton Hall and VICTORIA STREET is a bronze scroll on a plinth inscribed: 'This tribute is erected by the Suffragette fellowship to commemorate the courage and perseverance of those men and women who, in the long struggle for votes for women, selflessly braved derision, opposition and ostracism, many enduring physical violence and suffering. Nearby Caxton Hall was historically associated with women's suffrage meetings and deputations to Parliament.'

Caxton Street *SW1.* Takes its name from William Caxton who set up his printing press in WESTMINSTER in the 1470s. CAXTON HALL is on the north side; the BLUECOAT SCHOOL is on the south. The St Ermin's Hotel (242 bedrooms) was built in 1887 to the designs of E.T. Hall. The Social Democrats met here on 26 March 1981 to form their party.

Thomas Malton's aquatint of the north side of Cavendish Square in 1800.

Cecil Court *WC2.* Narrow pedestrian precinct between 24 CHARING CROSS ROAD and 93 ST MARTIN'S LANE, lined with antiquarian and secondhand bookshops. Abraham Raimbach, the engraver, was born here in 1776.

CEMETERIES By the 19th century the small BURIAL GROUNDS established by the parishes of inner London to relieve the overcrowding in the churchyards had themselves become so packed with bodies as to constitute a danger to the health of the neighbourhoods surrounding them. The condition of graveyards everywhere was becoming a public scandal. Bodies were often scarcely buried; old coffins were dug up and cast aside to make room for the newly dead; and none was safe from the attentions of body snatchers and grave robbers. In 1824 George Frederick Carden began a campaign in *The Penny Magazine* for the formation of public cemeteries, and he caused a petition to be presented to the HOUSE OF COMMONS in 1830, praying for the removal of graveyards 'to places where they would be less prejudicial to the health of the inhabitants'. Between 1837 and 1841 Parliament authorised the establishment of seven commercial cemeteries more or less in a ring outside the residential suburbs. These were the cemeteries of KENSAL GREEN, WEST NORWOOD, HIGHGATE, NUNHEAD, ABNEY PARK, BROMPTON and TOWER HAMLETS. But by 1850 it had become clear that these cemeteries would not take very long to fill; and the public, in any case, was demanding the right to burial in non-profit-making establishments. In that year there was an 'Act to make better provision for the Interment of the Dead in or near the Metropolis', and the plans were entrusted to a General Board of Health. As the *Illustrated London News* reported

soon afterwards, however, the Board, 'after devising several gigantic schemes for providing cemeteries at remote distances from London . . . found the difficulties they had to contend with insurmountable.' So the Act was repealed and replaced by another which enabled local burial boards, elected by the vestries, to take the necessary steps to establish places of burial. Thereafter most new cemeteries were run by public bodies. The total area of London's cemeteries is about 3,000 acres. Most of them are described below (*see also* BUNHILL FIELDS, BURIAL GROUNDS *and* HIGHGATE CEMETERY).

Abney Park Cemetery *Stamford Hill, N16.* The town house of Sir Thomas Abney, a leading nonconformist of his day and Lord Mayor of London 1700–1, stood here. For 30 years Dr Isaac Watts, the hymnwriter, lived here with him, and a monument to Watts by E.H. Baily stands on the site of the house. Watts is buried in BUNHILL FIELDS. The 30-acre cemetery, owned by the Abney Park Cemetery Company, was opened by the LORD MAYOR in 1840. The Company refused consecration of the ground, and 30 per cent of all burials were of Dissenters, making it 'the heir of Bunhill Fields'. William Hosking designed the Egyptian lodges, the entrance gates and the Gothic chapel, and the cemetery was extensively planted with trees and shrubs. By 1843 Loudon wrote of 'one of the most complete arboretums in the neighbourhood of London, all the trees and shrubs being named'. Buried here are William Hone, bookseller and writer (1842), James Braidwood, Superintendent of the LONDON FIRE BRIGADE (1861) and William Booth, founder of the SALVATION ARMY (1912). In 1978 the cemetery, untended, overgrown and damaged by vandals, was bought for £1 by the London Borough of HACKNEY which is carrying out restoration.

Brockley Cemetery *Brockley Road, SE4.* Opened as a cemetery within the parish of ST PAUL'S DEPTFORD in 1858. Some 131,000 people have been buried here, including Maria Clousen, a domestic servant aged 17, who was murdered by an unknown assailant in 1871 and for whom a memorial was erected by public subscription.

Brompton Cemetery *Old Brompton Road, SW10.* The West of London and Westminster Cemetery Company bought 40 acres of land from Lord Kensington in 1837, though their cemetery was not consecrated until 1840. Benjamin Baud won the competition for the best design for the walls, chapels, catacombs and buildings. He envisaged a formal design of a wide main avenue leading from the entrance to a large, domed, octagonal chapel. From this Anglican chapel, long arms of catacombs were to reach out to form a 'Great Circle' on each side of which it was planned to build a further chapel, one for Roman Catholics and one for Dissenters. But the company soon ran into financial difficulties, and though the central octagonal chapel was built, and remains, the two smaller ones were never constructed. Nor were the catacombs fully completed, though they do form the 'Circle', and extend a short way beyond it. More catacombs were built along the western wall. Baud had difficulty in getting paid for the work that was done, and it was soon evident that the company could not continue. After long haggling over the price, the cemetery was bought in 1852 by the General Board of Health, and thus became the first London cemetery under state control. It was soon filled – the 'Great Circle' overflowing with tilting graves and memorials. It is now maintained by the Department of the Environment who in 1980 applied for permission to lay out the cemetery as a public space and 'for this purpose to remove certain tombstones'. Buried here are Dr Benjamin Golding, founder of CHARING CROSS HOSPITAL (1863); Francis Fowke, architect of the ALBERT HALL (1865); George Borrow (1881); Sir Henry Cole, organising genius of the GREAT EXHIBITION and the VICTORIA AND ALBERT MUSEUM (1882) and Emmeline Pankhurst, Suffragette (1928).

Camberwell Old Cemetery *Forest Hill Road, SE22.* Established by the Burial Board of ST GILES' CHURCH, SOUTHWARK in 1856. The Anglican chapel and a small Roman Catholic chapel were both demolished during the 2nd World War. The Victorian lodge remains. F.J. Horniman, of the HORNIMAN MUSEUM, is buried here (1906). In 1927 Camberwell New Cemetery was opened nearby in Brenchley Gardens, SE23, and imaginatively planted with shrubs. Both CAMBERWELL cemeteries are now full, and burials are once more taking place in NUNHEAD CEMETERY. All three cemeteries are administered by the Borough of SOUTHWARK.

City of London Cemetery *Aldersbrook Road, Manor Park, E12.* More than half a million interments have taken place in this, the largest municipal cemetery in Europe, since it was opened in 1856. The Commissioners of Sewers of the CITY OF LONDON, under the pressures caused by the closing of many CITY churchyards, started in 1853 to look for a site for a cemetery to the north east. 200 acres of land at LITTLE ILFORD, in Essex, the site of the old Manor of Aldersbrook, were bought for £30,721. By this purchase, the Commissioners acquired certain commoners' rights over WANSTEAD FLATS and EPPING FOREST. This enabled the CITY CORPORATION to sue private landowners who had been enclosing forest land into their estates, and thus preserve EPPING FOREST for free public use. The cemetery was designed by William Haywood, the chief engineer to the Commissioners of Sewers. Under his direction curving roads were built leading to the three Gothic chapels; the Aldersbrook Lake, once famous for its carp, tench and perch, was drained and its site used to form Catacomb Valley; and the whole area was carefully landscaped with gardens, trees and shrubberies. Several enclosures were formed to contain the remains of those buried in the old CITY churchyards, which were closed and cleared during the extensive Victorian rebuilding of the CITY. There are imposing monuments to, among others, the reburied dead of ST MARY, ALDERMANBURY and ST MARY SOMERSET. In 1902 a crematorium was built, one of the first in the country. A second was added in 1973. The cemetery is now administered by the CORPORATION OF THE CITY OF LONDON, who maintain the 9 miles of roads and acres of cultivation to a high standard.

Dogs' Cemetery *Kensington Gardens, W2.* Packed tightly together in a neglected garden behind Victoria Lodge, on the north-east corner of KENSINGTON GARDENS, are the graves and memorials of more than 200 cherished pets. It is thought that the first burial to take place here was in 1880 when a dog belonging to the Duke of Cambridge, at that time Ranger of HYDE PARK and ST JAMES'S PARK, was run over outside Victoria Gate, and died in the Lodge. It soon became fashionable for pets to be buried in this little cemetery, and the graves of birds, cats and monkeys as well as dogs are to be found here.

Golders Green Crematorium *Hoop Lane, NW11.* By the end of the 19th century, the number of cremations had increased to such an extent that the London Cremation Society was formed to plan and build a crematorium within easy reach of central London. Golders Green Crematorium was opened by Sir Henry Thompson, President of the Cremation Society of England, in 1902. Since then over a quarter of a million cremations have taken place here. The group of Romanesque buildings, which include three chapels used for cremation services, and a cloister and memorial chapel, was designed by Sir Ernest George, and 12 acres of well-landscaped memorial gardens were laid out behind them. Those who have been cremated here include Sir Henry Irving (1905), W.S. Gilbert (1911), Anna Pavlova (1931), Rudyard Kipling (1936), Sigmund Freud (1939), Neville Chamberlain (1940), Stanley Baldwin (1947), Tommy Handley (1949), George Bernard Shaw (1950), Kathleen Ferrier (1953), Sir Alexander Fleming (1955), Ralph Vaughan Williams (1958), and T.S. Eliot (1965).

Hampstead Cemetery *Fortune Green Road, NW6.* Opened in 1878, this cemetery successfully combines pre-1914 extravagance with more modern restraint, Victorian disorder with present-day lawn-graves. Its twin chapels and lodge were designed by Charles Bell. In its 26 acres, of an attractive uneven shape, there are over 16,000 graves, among them those of Kate Greenaway (1901); Lord Lister, originator of antiseptic surgery (1912); Bernard Quaritch (1899); the Grand Duke Michael of Russia, who lived for a time at KENWOOD HOUSE (1929); Marie Lloyd (1922); Denis Brain, the horn-player (1957); and Gladys Cooper, the actress (1971).

Jewish Cemetery *Brady Street, Whitechapel, E1.*
In 1761 a group of Jewish traders acquired a lease of 'a certain brickfield situate on the north side of Whitechapel Road, between the Ducking Pond there and Bethnal Green Church ... to be used as a burial ground.' A further piece of land was added in 1795. When the ground was filled, it was decided to raise one portion by several feet of earth, so as to form a cemetery above a cemetery. The result is a large flat-topped mound; because of the double layer of graves, the headstones are in places erected back to back. Baron Nathan Meyer de Rothschild was buried here (1836). The cemetery was closed in 1858.

Jews' Cemetery *Pound Lane, Willesden, NW10.*
The Home Office issued a licence in 1871 authorising the use of this site 'consisting of 9 acres, as a Cemetery for the Jews of London'. It was consecrated on 5 October 1873, and the first interment took place the same day. According to Jewish custom, the Chief Rabbi, the Revd Dr Nathan M. Adler, assisted in digging the first grave. Buried here are members of the de Rothschild family; Charles Clore, financier, (1979); and Sir John Cohen, founder of Tesco stores (1979).

Kensal Green Cemetery *Harrow Road, W10.* All Souls Cemetery, KENSAL GREEN, was the first of the great commercial cemeteries to be opened in London. According to the *Penny Magazine* it was the 'first practical attempt to remedy a great public inconvenience'. The General Cemetery Company was founded in 1830, and the following year 54 acres of land south of the HARROW ROAD were bought for £9,400; 800 trees were soon planted, and a prize of 100 guineas was announced for the best designs for a chapel and entrance gates. The competition was won, in 1832, by H.E. Kendall with a Gothic design; but the Chairman, Sir John Dean Paul, urged a Greek Revival plan, and his will prevailed. The cemetery is entered by a large Doric arch incorporating offices and a residence. Three 'gravelled roads of sufficient width for carriages' diverge, two following the northern and southern perimeters, and the third, central avenue leading to the Anglican Chapel with Doric porch and flanking colonnades. Beneath the chapel are extensive catacombs, once served by hydraulic lift. At the east end of the cemetery is an Ionic nonconformist chapel, now much decayed. Along the north wall is a colonnade covering further public catacombs. Minutes of the General Cemetery Company indicate that the designs were the work of the company's surveyor, John W. Griffith, though the detailed drawings are signed by William Chadwick. In January 1833, 39 acres were consecrated by the BISHOP OF LONDON, the remaining 15 acres being reserved for Dissenters. By 1839 the cemetery was described as 'a flourishing concern', the original £25 shares being already worth £52. The burial of the Duke of Sussex, sixth son of King George III, in 1843, and that of his sister, Princess Sophia, six years later, marked the social acceptance of the 'gardens for the deceased'. The Duke was a radical royal personage who is said to have been appalled at the confusion and bickering over protocol at William IV's funeral at Windsor. 'I would not be buried there after this fashion for all the world,' he declared, and stipulated burial at Kensal Green in his will. Also buried here are J.C. Loudon, the landscape architect (1843); Thomas Hood, the poet (1845); the Revd Sydney Smith, the writer and wit (1845); Sir Mark Isambard Brunel

(1849) and his wife Sophia, joined in 1859 by their son Isambard Kingdom Brunel; Charles Kemble, the actor (1854); Joseph Hume, the Radical (1855); W.M. Thackeray (1863); James Miranda Barry, Inspector General of the Army Medical Department, who at death was found to be a woman (1865); Leigh Hunt (1859); Anthony Trollope (1882); Wilkie Collins (1889); and Charles Blondin, tight-rope walker (1897). The cemetery is still owned and managed by the General Cemetery Company, the only one of the original seven big cemeteries to have remained under the management of its founding company. It is celebrated in G.K. Chesterton's 'The Rolling English Road':

For there is good news yet to hear and fine things to be seen
Before we go to Paradise by way of Kensal Green.

Kensington Cemetery *Uxbridge Road, Hanwell, W7.* The *West London Observer* reported in October 1855 the consecration by the BISHOP OF LONDON of the 'new Burial Ground for the populous and wealthy parish of Kensington'. In 1929 the Council for the Royal Borough opened a second cemetery at Gunnersbury Avenue, W3. A black marble obelisk inscribed 'Katyn, 1940' commemorates the 14,500 Polish prisoners-of-war who disappeared in 1940, of whom 4,500 were later found in mass graves at Katyn, near Smolensk. Erected in 1976, it was designed by Louis Fitzgibbon and Count Stefan Zamoyski. General Bor-Komorowski (1966), the Polish general who led the ill-fated Warsaw uprising in 1944, is buried here.

New Southgate Cemetery *Brunswick Park Road, N11.* Originally called the Great Northern Cemetery, this was one of the few private cemeteries to be founded after the Burial Acts of the 1850s and it remains in the control of the founding company, the Great Northern Cemetery Co. Ltd. It was opened in 1861, the site well planted with trees, its tall-spired Gothic chapel standing at the centre of a series of concentric avenues. The architect was Alexander Spurr. On the western side, shaded by yew trees, huge vault slabs cover the remains of the dead removed from the SAVOY CHAPEL in the STRAND. Many of the names incised into the slabs are those of Hanoverian courtiers.

Nunhead Cemetery *Linden Grove, SE15.* This, the 'Cemetery of all Saints', was the second (after HIGHGATE) to be planned by the London Cemetery Company. The 30-acre site was opened for burials in 1840. It was laid out by J.B. Bunning who also designed the gates and lodges; while the pinnacled Gothic chapels were built to designs by Thomas Little. The cemetery contains, on its wooded hillside, many large old family vaults and a memorial to the five 'Scottish martyres' who campaigned for Parliamentary Reform and were transported in 1793. The memorial was erected in 1851 from funds collected by Joseph Hume, MP. The inscription, which is an extract from the speech, in his own defence, of Joseph Gerrald, one of the five, reads, 'The experience of all ages should have taught our rulers that persecution can never efface principles.' By the middle of the 20th century the cemetery had been allowed to fall into total disrepair and suffered badly from vandalism. The delicate Anglican chapel was ruined and is now a roofless shell, the Dissenters' chapel had been demolished and many graves destroyed. Nunhead was closed in 1969. A special Act of Parliament in 1975 enabled the Borough of SOUTHWARK to take it over, and clearing and restoration are being undertaken. One of Bunning's lodges will be restored. Since April 1980 the cemetery has again been open for burials.

Putney Vale Cemetery *SW15*. The first interment in this 38-acre cemetery, which lies between the peace of WIMBLEDON COMMON and the noisy A3 road, took place in June 1891. Since then there have been over 45,000 burials, including those of Lillie Langtry (1929), Jacob Epstein (1959) and Lord Ismay (1965). A crematorium was opened in 1938. Clement Attlee was cremated here in 1967, and Clementine Churchill in 1977.

St Mary's Roman Catholic Cemetery *Harrow Road, NW10*. This is an entirely separate cemetery from All Souls KENSAL GREEN, though the two are adjacent and not now visibly separated. The Catholic Cemetery was opened in 1858, though the chapel and lodge, designed by S.J. Nichols, were not built until 1860. In the first eight years some 12,500 burials took place, 'many of the Irish migrants of the Great Famine finding their last resting place here'. Cardinal Wiseman (1865) and Cardinal Manning (1892) were both initially buried here, though both were later removed to WESTMINSTER CATHEDRAL. Buried here also were the poets Francis Thompson (1907) and Alice Meynell (1922); and Sir John Barbirolli (1970).

St Marylebone Cemetery *East End Road, Finchley, N2*. In 1855 the Burial Board of the parish of ST MARYLEBONE opened a 25-acre cemetery in a 'retired and rural spot' in FINCHLEY. The architects, Barnett and Birch, designed a Gothic Episcopal chapel with a 'crocketed' spire, and a plain Dissenters' chapel set on one side with its area of unconsecrated ground divided from the rest by ornamental posts and chain fencing. The cemetery is now administered by the City of WESTMINSTER. Sir J. Austen Chamberlain (1937) and the conductor, Leopold Stokowski (1977) are buried here.

St Pancras and Islington Cemeteries *High Road, N2*. The first of the new cemeteries established after the 1850 Burials Act. The ST PANCRAS Vestry purchased the land, part of the old FINCHLEY COMMON, in 1853 and sold 30 acres of it to the parish of ST MARY, ISLINGTON, the following year. The two cemeteries were enlarged by the joint purchase of a further 107 acres of farmland in 1877. Although within the same perimeter, they are separately administered. In St Pancras Cemetery is buried the first of the PEARLY KINGS, Henry Croft (1930), and an effigy of him in top hat and pearly suit stands above his grave.

Tower Hamlets Cemetery *Southern Grove, E3*. The City of London and Tower Hamlets Cemetery Company opened this, the farthest east of the early commercial cemeteries, in 1841. The ground was consecrated by the BISHOP OF LONDON in September and the first interment took place on the same day. The cemetery seems very soon to have become overgrown, making a dense green enclave in the EAST END, and a great many graves were crowded in, so close to each other that they show, says J.S. Curl, 'a curious air of Cockney togetherness even in death'. Most of the stones commemorate inhabitants of the immediately surrounding boroughs, among them foreigners whose first London homes were in the East End. In 1887 Tower Hamlets saw the burial of Alfred Linnell, a young man ridden down and fatally injured by a mounted policeman in NORTHUMBERLAND AVENUE. His funeral became a demonstration against the miserable conditions of the working classes. The procession passed through the West End, down FLEET STREET and CHEAPSIDE, and by the time it reached ALDGATE was big enough to take almost an hour to pass by. William Morris walked beside the coffin and spoke at the graveside. The Cemetery's chapel and lodges were damaged in the 2nd World War, and later demolished. Since 1966 Tower Hamlets has been maintained by the GREATER LONDON COUNCIL.

West Norwood Cemetery *Norwood High Street, SE27*. In 1837 the South Metropolitan Cemetery Company bought 40 acres of land in the hamlet of Norwood. Sir William Tite became architect to the company, and designed a cemetery with two Perpendicular Gothic chapels set at the top of sloping lawns, among groups of fine trees. The cemetery was consecrated by the Bishop of Winchester, and the first burial took place in December 1837. Five years later, land in the north-east corner was acquired for a Greek cemetery and many handsome mausolea were erected, notably that of Augustus Ralli (1872), as well as a Greek Doric mortuary chapel. Tite's Anglican and Dissenters' chapels were damaged in the 2nd World War and later demolished. By 1966 the cemetery was over-full and over-grown. It was bought by the Borough of LAMBETH with the intention of turning some parts into a nature park, with headstones and monuments preserved. A 'Tombstone Trail' has been devised which leads past the graves of NORWOOD notables. These include Sir William Cubitt, the civil engineer (1861); Mrs Isobel Beeton, the cookery writer (1865); Dr William Marsden, founder of the ROYAL FREE and ROYAL MARSDEN HOSPITALS (1867); Sir Henry Doulton, inventor of DOULTON WARE (1897); Sir Henry Bessemer, inventor of the process for converting cast iron into steel (1898); and Sir Henry Tate (1899), who gave the TATE GALLERY to the nation.

Willesden Lane Cemetery *NW6*. Originally called Paddington Cemetery, these 25 acres were consecrated by the BISHOP OF LONDON in July 1855. At the centre of a symmetrical layout of intersecting roads and paths the designer Thomas Little placed two chapels linked by porches, robing-rooms and gateways. In recent years the City of WESTMINSTER has removed many of the headstones and grassed over a large part of the cemetery, but a number of Victorian tombs and mausolea remain. Arthur Orton, the Titchborne claimant (1898), is buried here but his grave is unmarked.

Woolwich Cemetery *King's Highway, SE18*. Opened in 1856 by the Burial Board of the Borough of WOOLWICH. The original Gothic Anglican chapel remains in use, though the nondenominational one has been demolished, and the lodge rebuilt in 1969. Many of the gravestones have been removed and the sloping 32 acres are now grassed over to enhance the remaining memorials and some magnificent beech trees. A huge cross commemorates the 550 people who died in the disaster of the paddle steamer *Princess Alice*, which sank after a collision in the THAMES in 1878 while returning to WOOLWICH after a pleasure trip to Sheerness.

Cenotaph *Whitehall, SW1*. National memorial to the 'Glorious Dead' of both world wars, designed in Portland stone by Sir Edwin Lutyens (1919–20) to replace a temporary plaster one put up for the Allied Victory Parade in 1919. The lines of the cenotaph (from the Greek words *kenos*, empty, and *taphos*, tomb) are slightly convex and concave, representing infinity. It is devoid of any religious symbols, the flags of the three services and the Merchant Navy being the only adornment. A service attended by the monarch and leading politicans is held annually on the Sunday nearest the eleventh day of the eleventh month at 11 a.m.

The Old Bailey's Justice Hall, whose court room was left open to reduce the risk of prisoners infecting others with gaol fever (typhus).

Central Criminal Court   *Old Bailey, EC4.* The first Old Bailey Sessions House in regular use was erected in 1539 beside NEWGATE PRISON at a cost of £6,000 and replaced by a new building in 1774. The name Old Bailey is that of a street which passes nearby. These Sessions which from time immemorial had exercised criminal jurisdiction over the London area and adjoining counties were superseded by the Central Criminal Court in 1834. The normal area of jurisdiction of the present Court is that of Greater London. The present Session House, designed by E.W. Mountford on the site of NEWGATE PRISON, was opened by King Edward VII in 1907. It contained four court rooms and offices and, with the 1972 extension by McMorran and Whitby, now houses 19 court rooms. Four others nearby are available. Daytime accommodation is provided by 70 cells for prisoners in custody. The height from the ground to the head of the bronze *Justice* statue (*see* STATUES) on the dome above the entrance hall is 212 ft. Damage by enemy action in 1941 was severe. It was also attacked by IRA bombers in 1973.

The Judges of the Court include the Lord Chancellor, the Lord Chief Justice, all High Court judges, the ALDERMEN of the CITY OF LONDON, the RECORDER and the COMMON SERJEANT (the resident judges), and circuit judges assigned to the Court. By tradition at certain times the judges carry posies of sweet smelling flowers, a reminder of the malodours and gaol fever associated with the old NEWGATE PRISON. The notorious Judge Jeffreys was COMMON SERJEANT in 1671 and RECORDER in 1678. Among many famous trials held in the old Sessions House were those of Penn and Mead (1670) which established the independence of jurors; Franz Muller (1864); Adelaide Bartlett (1886); and Oscar Wilde (1895). In the 1907 building, Dr H.H. Crippen (1910); Frederick Seddon (1912); George Joseph Smith, the 'Brides-in-the-

Bath' murderer (1915); Edith Thompson and Frederick Bywaters (1923); William Joyce ('Lord Haw-Haw') (1945); George Neville Heath (1946); J.R. Christie (1953) and Peter Sutcliffe, the 'Yorkshire Ripper' (1981).

Central Hall   *Storey's Gate, SW1.* Chief Methodist church designed by Lanchester and Richards and built in 1905–11 in an ornate French style on the site of the ROYAL AQUARIUM. Early use was made of steel framing. The hall (capacity 2,700) is used for organ recitals, concerts, public meetings and examinations as well as church services and in 1948 held the first assembly of the United Nations.

Central Line   The Prince of Wales (later King Edward VII) inaugurated the original section of the Central London Railway, between BANK and SHEPHERD'S BUSH, on 27 June 1900. It was a fully electrified tube railway, with white painted tunnels 60–110 ft below the surface, crimson locomotives hauling smart passenger cars, and electric lifts. These features, together with the flat fare of 2d along an extremely busy route, made the 'Twopenny Tube' an instant success – it was the first really modern tube and Londoners welcomed it warmly. The only problem was the vibration caused by the locomotives, which were therefore replaced by multiple-unit trains. Although the Central was originally intended as 'a line for Londoners, supplying a rapid shuttlecock service between main centres' and not as a trunk line, it was extended westward to EALING BROADWAY in 1920; and later, after its takeover by LONDON TRANSPORT, extensions eastward to LEYTON and westward to RUISLIP were planned. Work was stopped by the outbreak of war in 1939, and the new tunnels were adapted as air-raid shelters, bomb-proof stores and war material factories, the largest of which was the Plessey factory stretching over nearly 5 miles. After the war, extensions to east and west were opened, the last one under private ownership being to WOODFORD and Newbury Park in 1947. Some of the new stations were very striking, notably Newbury Park (designed by Oliver Hill) which won the FESTIVAL OF BRITAIN award for architectural merit. After nationalisation in 1948 surface lines were extended to WEST RUISLIP and to Ongar, bringing the total length of the Central up to 51¼ miles (*see also* UNDERGROUND RAILWAYS).

An early photograph of the Bank Station of the 'Twopenny Tube', as this section of the Central Line was first known. The station was opened in 1900.

Central Markets *EC1 see* SMITHFIELD.

Central Office of Information *Hercules Road, SE1.* This non-ministerial, non-policy-making 'common service' department, set up in 1946, provides information and publicity material as required by other government departments.

Central School of Art and Design *Southampton Row, WC1.* The Central School of Arts and Crafts was founded in 1896 by the Technical Education Board of the LONDON COUNTY COUNCIL, its first Principal being William Lethaby, art adviser to the Board. It was originally situated at Morley Hall, REGENT STREET, and accommodated 80 students. In 1908 it moved to a new building in Southampton Row, built to the designs of the architect W.E. Riley, and it is today maintained by the INNER LONDON EDUCATION AUTHORITY. It has places for 450 full-time students in fine art, graphic design, industrial design, ceramics, jewellery design, theatre design, textile design, history of art and liberal studies. The building was extended in 1963 and the substitution of 'Design' for 'Crafts' in the name probably dates from its transfer to the ILEA. Many famous artists have taught in the School, including Ruskin Spear, and several have studied here, including James Fitton.

Central School of Speech and Drama *Embassy Theatre, Eton Avenue, NW3.* Founded in 1906 by Elsie Fogerty who joined Sir Frank Benson in premises at the ROYAL ALBERT HALL. The choice of name was intended to indicate an avoidance of extremism in the training of the students. This training gradually evolved into courses for actors and stage managers, for speech therapists and for teachers. The school moved to the Embassy Theatre in 1956 and is designated by the INNER LONDON EDUCATION AUTHORITY, from which it receives a grant, as an independent specialised institution.

Ceremonies One of London's oldest ceremonies, apart from the CORONATION of the sovereign, is the distribution of the Royal Maundy on Maundy Thursday. Although it is now held in a different place each year, and in the Middle Ages took place wherever the monarch was in residence, it was, and still is, often held in London – at GREENWICH PALACE, the BANQUETING HOUSE, ST PAUL'S CATHEDRAL or WESTMINSTER ABBEY. The custom originated in the 12th century when Henry I's 'good Queen Maud' washed and kissed the feet of the poor at WESTMINSTER in memory of Jesus at the Last Supper. Elizabeth I had the feet washed before she performed the token ceremony and changed the custom of presenting the royal gown into a gift of money. William III was the last monarch to kiss the feet, and during the 18th and 19th centuries the monarch ceased to attend. The custom was revived by George V and the Queen has taken a keen interest and nearly always distributes the Royal Maundy herself.

Ceremony for the Accession is well established. On the death of the sovereign the Heralds assemble on the Friary Court Balcony of ST JAMES'S PALACE and after a fanfare by the State Trumpeters, the Garter King of Arms proclaims the successor. This is repeated at CHARING CROSS and then at TEMPLE BAR, which is ceremonially closed. Behind the Bar stand the LORD MAYOR, ALDERMEN and high officers of the CITY, and the CITY MARSHAL challenges Her Majesty's Officers of Arms. After the Proclamation has been made, the LORD MAYOR declares, 'Admit the cavalcade' and they proceed into the CITY and read the Proclamation at the corner of CHANCERY LANE and on the steps of the ROYAL EXCHANGE.

The distribution of the Royal Maundy in the Banqueting House, engraved in 1777 after a drawing by Grimm.

TEMPLE BAR is also ceremonially closed when the monarch enters the CITY in state. She is met by the LORD MAYOR who presents the City's Pearl Sword. It used to be the custom to surrender the sword, but when Charles I entered the CITY in 1641 the sword was returned immediately, and now the Queen merely touches the hilt. The LORD MAYOR then carries the sword before her.

Some of our rulers are commemorated by annual ceremonies. Every 30 January, the anniversary of his execution, there is a service by Charles I's statue in TRAFALGAR SQUARE and a wreath laying ceremony at the BANQUETING HOUSE. Tribute is paid to Cromwell's memory every 3 September beside his statue outside the HOUSES OF PARLIAMENT. Charles II is remembered on Oak Apple Day at the CHELSEA HOSPITAL early in June. His statue is decked with oak branches and the Pensioners parade, in their uniforms, wearing oak leaves. They give three cheers for 'Our Pious Founder' and three cheers for the sovereign.

The CITY has many ceremonies of its own, one of the most impressive being the handover from the old to the new LORD MAYOR on the day before the LORD MAYOR'S SHOW, known as the Silent Change. The ALDERMEN and High Officers assemble in GUILDHALL, with members of the public. After the Lord Mayor Elect has made his solemn Declaration the LORD MAYOR surrenders his seat to him in silence, and in silence the symbols of office – the Sword and Mace, the Crystal Sceptre, the Seal and City Purse – are handed over, the City Plate is signed for and the ALDERMEN come forward to shake the hand of their new LORD MAYOR.

The ceremony of the Loving Cup, a feature of City banquets, is also wordless. In AD 978 King Edward the Martyr was assassinated while drinking the stirrup cup presented to him by the treacherous Elfrida. It is believed this is the origin of the ritual in which three people rise simultaneously and, while one drinks, another lifts the cover and the third protects the drinker's back – and so the cup is passed round the company.

The LORD MAYOR receives certain ceremonial presentations at the MANSION HOUSE. Near the beginning of his year the BUTCHERS' COMPANY present a boar's head, which used to be payment for land which they used 'for cleansing the entrails of beasts'. In the autumn the FRUITERERS' COMPANY present fruits, as they have done for over 200 years since the 'Fruit Meters', collectors of tolls on all fruits entering the CITY, were abolished and an annual presentation to the LORD MAYOR substituted for the payment. One of the most charming ceremonies is the presentation of a perfect red rose on 24 June as a rent for a bridge built across SEETHING LANE by Lady Knollys in the 14th century.

Every October the Quit Rents Ceremony is held at the LAW COURTS in the STRAND, when the CITY pays a quit rent to the QUEEN'S REMEMBRANCER for holdings at the Moors, Shropshire and the Forge at ST CLEMENT DANES. For the Moors the COMPTROLLER AND CITY SOLICITOR pays a billhook and a hatchet, and for the Forge six horseshoes and 61 nails. The QUEEN'S REMEMBRANCER also presides at the Trial of the Pyx in the GOLDSMITHS' HALL when the coins of the realm are tested in an ancient ceremony.

Some ceremonies commemorate famous men. At ST OLAVE, HART STREET, where Samuel Pepys and his wife used to worship, an annual service is held in his memory and the LORD MAYOR lays a wreath in front of his memorial. At ST BOTOLPH, ALDGATE, the staff and pupils of the SIR JOHN CASS SCHOOL remember their benefactor. He was said to have died from a haemorrhage while signing his will and the blood stained his quill pen, so they each wear a red plume.

Just outside the CITY, the TOWER is locked every night in the 700-year-old Ceremony of the Keys. The Yeoman Warder with his escort locks the West Gate, the Middle Tower and the Byward Tower. At the Bloody Tower archway he is challenged by the sentry and replies that he brings 'Queen Elizabeth's Keys'. At the close of the ceremony the Chief Warder raises his Tudor bonnet and cries 'God preserve Queen Elizabeth' and the guard respond 'Amen' just as the clock tolls 10 p.m. A bugler sounds the Last Post and the Chief Warder goes to the Queen's House and hands the Keys to the Resident Governor for safe keeping till the morning.

The Druids celebrate the Spring Equinox in a ceremony on Tower Hill Terrace and the Autumn Equinox on PRIMROSE HILL.

On 6 January, in a 700-year-old ceremony during the Royal Epiphany Gifts service at the CHAPEL ROYAL, ST JAMES'S PALACE, officials of the Royal Household offer up gifts of gold, frankincense and myrrh in the name of the sovereign whose personal participation lapsed in the time of George II. The frankincense is afterwards given to an Anglican church where incense is used, the myrrh to Nashdom Abbey; and the gold is returned to the BANK OF ENGLAND and its cash equivalent spent on charitable purposes.

Early in January the opening session of the CENTRAL CRIMINAL COURT is attended by the LORD MAYOR who, accompanied by the SHERIFFS, the SWORD-BEARER, the COMMON CRYER and the CITY MARSHAL, leads a procession from the MANSION HOUSE to the OLD BAILEY.

On the Saturday nearest to 22 February Boy Scouts and Girl Guides gather in WESTMINSTER ABBEY on the shared birthday of Lord and Lady Baden-Powell and lay wreaths on the Baden-Powell Memorial.

On Ash Wednesday the Cakes and Ale Sermon is delivered in ST PAUL'S CATHEDRAL by the chaplain of the STATIONERS' COMPANY whose members have walked in procession from STATIONERS' HALL. This ceremony is maintained in accordance with the wishes of a Stationer who died in the reign of James I. Cakes and ale are given out before or after the service.

On Easter Sunday afternoon there is a carnival parade in BATTERSEA PARK of floats, bands, early flowers from the Scilly Islands and fanciful hats, which has evolved from the custom of Victorian ladies promenading in the Park to display their new spring bonnets. On Easter Monday in the Inner Circle, REGENT'S PARK, there is a display of horse-drawn vehicles, both commercial and private, known as the Harness Horse Parade.

On 21 May representatives of Henry VI's foundations, Eton College and King's College, Cambridge, meet at Wakefield Tower in the TOWER OF LONDON, where he was murdered on that day in 1471. Lilies from Eton and roses from King's are placed on the spot where he was slain.

On 28 September the Sheriffs elected by the CITY LIVERY COMPANIES on Midsummer Day proceed in procession with the LORD MAYOR, other Liverymen and CITY officers, from the MANSION HOUSE to

GUILDHALL where they are presented with their chains of office.

On 21 October there is a naval parade, in memory of Nelson's victory at Trafalgar, down the MALL to TRAFALGAR SQUARE where a service is held and wreaths are laid at the foot of NELSON'S COLUMN.

Special annual church services with ceremonies include the Court of Common Council Service in January at the church of ST LAWRENCE JEWRY in GRESHAM STREET to which the LORD MAYOR and his officers walk in procession from the GUILDHALL before the first sitting of the newly elected COURT OF COMMON COUNCIL; the Clowns' Service at Holy Trinity church, Dalston, in early February when a wreath is laid on the memorial to Grimaldi; the Blessing of the Throats at the Roman Catholic church of ST ETHELDREDA, ELY PLACE, on 3 February to commemorate St Blaise, patron saint of those suffering from throat infections; the Bridewell Service at ST BRIDE'S, FLEET STREET on the second Tuesday in March to commemorate Edward VI's foundation of the BRIDEWELL ROYAL HOSPITAL in 1553; and, also in March, the Oranges and Lemons Service at ST CLEMENT DANES, when the children of St Clement Danes Primary School attend a short service and are each given an orange and lemon. Shortly before Easter the united guilds of the CITY OF LONDON hold their annual service at ST PAUL'S CATHEDRAL. On Good Friday the Butterworth Charity is celebrated at ST BARTHOLOMEW-THE-GREAT, SMITHFIELD, when hot cross buns and coins are left on tombstones after the 11 o'clock service. (They used to be for 'poor widows of the parish' but are now given to children.) On or near 5 April John Stow's Quill Pen ceremony is held at the church of ST ANDREW UNDERSHAFT, LEADENHALL STREET. On the second Wednesday after Easter the Spital Sermon is preached to the Governors of CHRIST'S HOSPITAL and the BRIDEWELL, in ST LAWRENCE JEWRY, and in the same church on a Sunday in May the Dunkirk Veterans hold their annual service. On the first Sunday in October the PEARLY KINGS AND QUEENS attend the Pearly Harvest Festival Service in ST MARTIN-IN-THE-FIELDS. On the second Tuesday in October the year's wine harvest is celebrated at ST OLAVE'S CHURCH, HART STREET, attended by the Masters and Wardens of the Worshipful Companies of Vintners and Distillers. On or near 22 November a service is held at the CHURCH OF THE HOLY SEPULCHRE WITHOUT NEWGATE, in honour of St Cecilia, patron saint of music. During this service, which was inaugurated in the 16th century and revived in 1946, having lapsed in the 19th century, distinguished organists and choirs from ST PAUL'S CATHEDRAL and WESTMINSTER ABBEY perform church music.

Special customs include the leaving of buns on Good Friday at the WIDOW'S SON inn, BOW; swearing on the Horns in May and September at HIGHGATE, where visitors can swear an oath in front of a mock judge and become 'Freemen of Highgate'; and Pancake Day Races on Shrove Tuesday in LINCOLN'S INN FIELDS (see also BEATING THE BOUNDS, SWANS and TROOPING THE COLOUR).

Chagford Street *NW1*. On the PORTMAN ESTATE. It takes its name from Chagford in Devon, one of the main stannary towns of Dartmoor. Viscount Portman was Lord Warden of the Stannaries. In an alleyway near DORSET SQUARE, a privately erected plaque

proclaims that Bentley Motor Cars were first made here.

Chalcot Gardens *NW3*. Takes its name from Chalcot Farm (see CHALK FARM) on whose land it was built. Arthur Rackham, the illustrator, lived at No. 16, a house built in 1881 and enlarged in 1889 to the designs of C.F.A. Voysey.

Chalk Farm *NW3*. Situated east of PRIMROSE HILL, at the lower end of HAVERSTOCK HILL. The Anglo-Saxon Chaldecote (cold cottages) suggests that habitations existed there in early centuries, possibly as shelters for travellers up the bleak hill to HAMPSTEAD. The area constituted part of the prebendal manor of Rugmere and was given to Eton College by Henry VI in the 15th century. It was still farmland and pasture in the 17th century when Upper Chalcot Farm was located at the end of the present England's Lane, and Lower Chalcot was an inn known as the White House. This inn was probably on the site of the ancient manor house and later became known as Chalk House Farm – an 18th-century corruption of Chalcot's Farm. In 1854 it was rebuilt as the present Chalk Farm Tavern and formed a centre for popular entertainment, with a tea garden, dancing and wrestling nearby. The area was developed into middle-class respectability in the 19th century: from 1820 Eton College built roads with names such as Eton Villas, Provost Road and Fellows Road, and from 1840 Lord Southampton sold the property around Chalk Farm itself. In 1851 the construction of the London to Birmingham Railway ended at Chalk Farm (now PRIMROSE HILL Station) and the ROUND HOUSE was built near the GRAND UNION CANAL to house the turntable of the terminus. The 20th century saw the arrival of the NORTHERN LINE at Adelaide Road Station, now Chalk Farm, and the increase of smaller dwellings and blocks of flats. In 1965 CAMDEN Council replanned the central 35 acres of the Eton Estate as Chalcots Estate, and, with CAMDEN, Chalk Farm became part of the London Borough of CAMDEN.

Chancery Lane *WC2*. Once known as New Street but the name was changed to Chancellors Lane in 1377 when Edward III took over the House for Converted Jews for the use of the Keeper of the Rolls of Chancery. This was demolished in 1896 and the PUBLIC RECORD OFFICE was extended over the site. Ralph Neville, Bishop of Chichester and Chancellor of England, had his house nearby (see CHICHESTER RENTS). Cardinal Wolsey is believed to have lived at the HOLBORN end of the lane for some time, emerging every morning at eight o'clock and riding his crimson-caparisoned mule to WESTMINSTER, escorted by two pillow bearers, two cross bearers and four footmen, and carrying an orange filled with vinegar to ward off the smell of the streets and crowds. Thomas Wentworth, Earl of Strafford, was born in Chancery Lane in his grandfather's house in 1593. Izaak Walton, author of *The Compleat Angler*, lived here in 1627–44. He was churchwarden of ST DUNSTAN IN THE WEST in which there is a memorial window to him. Jacob Tonson, the celebrated bookseller and one of the founders of the KIT-KAT CLUB, started his shop at the FLEET STREET end in 1678. He published here the works of Dryden, Congreve, Vanbrugh, Addison and Steele and purchased the copyright of *Paradise Lost* of which he published a fine illustrated edition in 1688. His business was continued by his nephew and great-nephew who both bore the same name. SERJEANTS' INN was in the lane from the 15th century until it was dissolved in 1876. No. 57 was occupied in 1824 by William Pickering who had started three years before publishing the Diamond Classics on which cloth was used for the first time to bind books. He published the best designed and most consistently elegant books in the 19th century. The LAW SOCIETY is at No. 113 in a building designed by Lewis Vulliamy (1831) with additions by Charles Holden (1902). The LONDON SILVER VAULTS, established in 1885, are in the basement of Nos 53–64. Lincoln's Inn Gateway (see INNS OF COURT) is on the west side. Heralds announce the accession of a new sovereign from the end of the lane. The Hodgson's Rooms of SOTHEBY PARKE BERNET are at No. 115.

Chandos House *Chandos Street, W1*. Built in 1769–70 by Robert and James Adam for the 3rd Duke of Chandos, and one of the finest Adam houses extant. It was the Austro-Hungarian embassy, 1815–71. Lavish parties were given here by Prince Esterhazy when he was ambassador in 1815–42. In 1871 the house was acquired by the Duke of Buckingham and Chandos in whose family it remained until 1905. In 1905–24 it was the home of the Countess of Stafford; and in 1924–7 it was owned by the Earl of Shaftesbury. Viscount Kemsley lived here in 1927–63. From 1964 it was occupied by the ROYAL SOCIETY OF MEDICINE.

Chandos House *St James's Square, SW1*. This mansion once stood on the site now occupied by Nos 9, 10 and 11. The Earl of St Albans moved here from his house in the south-east corner of the Square (see NORFOLK HOUSE *and* ST JAMES'S SQUARE) in 1676; and it was then known as St Albans House. It became known as Ormonde House after 1682 when St Albans sold it for £9,000 to James Butler, Earl of Ormonde. In 1720 it passed into the hands of the Duke of Chandos (see CANONS PARK), having been occupied for a time successively by the French and Spanish ambassadors. Chandos's mounting debts obliged him to sell it in 1735 to Benjamin Timbrell, the builder, who demolished the mansion and, with the help of Henry Flitcroft, erected three smaller houses on the site. No. 9 was bought by the Hoare banking family who lived here until 1888. No. 10, as a plaque on the wall indicates, was the home of William Pitt the Elder from 1759 until 1762. The Victorian Prime Minister, the Earl of Derby, lived here between 1837 and 1854, and Derby's political opponent, Gladstone, rented the house in 1890. No. 11 was occupied from 1798 to 1817 by Alexander Davison, Nelson's prize agent, after work had been carried out on it by the Adam brothers for a previous owner, Sir Rowland Winn. The ground floor was altered by Messrs Trollope and Sons in 1877 who erected the portico and balcony. The three houses, now known as Chatham House, are occupied by the ROYAL INSTITUTE OF INTERNATIONAL AFFAIRS.

Chandos Place *WC2*. Built in 1631–8 and named after the 3rd Lord Chandos, father-in-law of the 4th Earl of Bedford, the ground landlord. The Charing Cross Medical School was built 1881–9 (see CHARING CROSS HOSPITAL). Claude Duval, the highwayman, was arrested at the Hole-in-the-Wall, a tavern which

stood on the site of the Victorian public house, the Marquis of Granby, at No. 51.

Chandos Street *W1*. Built in 1725 and named after James Brydges, Duke of Chandos, who owned all the land between the site of his proposed town house in CAVENDISH SQUARE and his country house, CANONS at EDGWARE. The Medical Society of London was founded at No. 11 by John Coakley Lettsom, the Quaker physician, in 1773. At the corner of Queen Anne Street is CHANDOS HOUSE.

Change Alley *Cornhill, EC3*. Named after the ROYAL EXCHANGE nearby. Now lined with banking buildings but once famous for its coffee houses, especially JONATHAN'S and GARRAWAY'S.

Chapel Royal *St James's Palace, SW1*. The Chapel Royal and the imposing gatehouse are the main surviving parts of the Tudor Palace built by Henry VIII. The Chapel is famous chiefly for being the nursery of church music. It employed the finest English church musicians and numbered amongst those who served in it such talented organists as Thomas Tallis, William Byrd and Henry Purcell. It was Queen Anne who moved the choral foundation from the BANQUETING HOUSE in WHITEHALL to ST JAMES'S PALACE. Although much of the building itself dates from the time of redecoration in about 1836, the ceiling, decorated with names and cyphers of William IV and Queen Adelaide, matches the original ceiling of 1540 which commemorated the short-lived marriage of Henry VIII and Anne of Cleves. Charles I received here the Sacrament of Holy Communion on 30 January 1649 before crossing the park to his execution in WHITEHALL. Happier occasions were the marriage of Queen Victoria and the Prince Consort in the chapel in 1840 and the wedding of George V (then Duke of York) to Princess May of Teck in 1893.

Chapels Royal Developed from the priests and choirs, their vestments and chalices, which used to accompany the peripatetic households of the early medieval kings. When the King's court became more settled they were established as oratories in his palaces. Although commonly referred to as such, not all royal chapels are Chapels Royal. The Chapels Royal in London are those at HAMPTON COURT PALACE, ST JAMES'S PALACE and the TOWER (the Chapels of St John and St Peter ad Vincula). There are also royal chapels at BUCKINGHAM PALACE and in the STRAND (see SAVOY CHAPEL). The Dean of the Chapels Royal has offices in ST JAMES'S PALACE.

Chapel Street *SW1*. Built in 1775–1811 and named after the Lock Hospital Chapel, situated here. The hospital was built in 1746 'for females suffering from disorders contracted by a vicious course of life'. The buildings were demolished in 1846 (see GROSVENOR PLACE).

Chapter Coffee House *Paternoster Row*. From its earliest days, in about 1715, this was the haunt of booksellers, writers and men of letters. It was famous for its punch. Meetings of the Congers, an association of booksellers 'for the purpose of diminishing their individual risk in publications of an expensive character . . . by dividing the venture into shares', were held here. It was noted for its plentiful supply of books, pamphlets and newspapers. In 1773 James Boswell was directed to the Chapter in his search for files of the *Public Advertiser*. Charlotte and Anne Brontë stayed here on their first visit to London. The house was turned into a tavern in the 1880s.

Charing Cross *WC2.* The busy area at the junction of the STRAND, WHITEHALL and COCKSPUR STREET. In the reign of Edward I it was a small hamlet whose name, Charing, was probably derived from the Old English *cierran*, to turn: the road from Bath turned north-west at the river bank here where the river bends. When Edward I's wife, Eleanor of Castile, died at Harby in Nottinghamshire in 1290 he had crosses erected at the 12 places where the funeral cortege had rested on its way to WESTMINSTER ABBEY. This was the last cross. It was the work of the King's mason, Richard of Crundale, and perhaps of Richard's son, Roger. Made of Caen stone, it was surrounded by Corfe marble statues of Queen Eleanor by Alexander of Abingdon. It stood where the statue of Charles I now is (*see* STATUES). It was pulled down, much decayed, on the orders of Parliament in 1647. Some of the stone was used for paving in WHITEHALL, some for making knife handles. On its site a fish shop was established. This in turn was pulled down at the Restoration when eight regicides were executed here. Among them was Colonel Thomas Harrison who was required to meet his end at 'the railed place where Charing Cross stood' with 'his face towards the Banqueting House at Whitehall'. Evelyn did not witness the executions of the regicides, but 'met their quarters, mangled and cut and reeking as they were brought from the gallows in baskets'. Six years later a more cheerful sight was a Punch and Judy show given by an Italian puppeteer; it was said to be the first such show to be seen in England. At Charing Cross proclamations were read and offenders were pilloried. The RUMMER TAVERN and its successor the SALOPIAN TAVERN were both situated here, as, for more than 200 years, was DRUMMOND'S BANK. At the beginning of the 17th century it was said that anyone who wanted to know what was going on in London had merely to go to Charing Cross to be told; and in reply to Boswell's observation that he liked the cheerfulness of FLEET STREET, 'owing to the quick succession of people' to be perceived passing through it, Johnson said, 'Why, sir, Fleet Street has a very animated appearance; but I think the full tide of human existence is at Charing Cross.'

In 1863 a replica of the cross, which still can be seen there, was created in the forecourt of CHARING CROSS STATION at a cost of £1,800 to the London, Chatham and Dover Railway Company. Founded on drawings of the original cross, it was designed by A.S. Barry. The eight statues of Queen Eleanor are by Thomas Earp.

Charing Cross Hospital *Fulham Palace Road, W6.* Founded in 1818 by Benjamin Golding. Three years previously, as a medical student at ST THOMAS'S HOSPITAL, he had written, 'I opened my house in the year 1815 to such poor persons as desired gratuitous advice and presented myself daily for all such applicants from eight o'clock in the morning until one in the afternoon.' He was a young man of means living in LEICESTER PLACE, off LEICESTER SQUARE. He was much influenced by Thomas Guy, a great benefactor

of ST THOMAS'S HOSPITAL in the previous century, who subsequently built his own hospital (*see* GUY'S HOSPITAL). In 1818 Golding set up his hospital at 16 SUFFOLK STREET by the back door of the HAYMARKET THEATRE, calling it 'The West London Infirmary and Dispensary'. No new hospital had been founded in London since the MIDDLESEX nearly 80 years previously. In an official report to the Prince Regent at that time the area north, east, and south of Golding's new Infirmary was described as follows: 'The distress and misery have become insupportable. The inhabitants are mostly Irish labourers, costermongers and characters of doubtful calling. It is impossible to convey an accurate description of the filth and wretchedness of this locality or the scenes enacted there.' In 1823 the infirmary moved to 28 VILLIERS STREET with accommodation for 12 beds. In 1827 the name was changed to Charing Cross Hospital and plans began for erecting a much larger hospital. Assisted by many members of the Royal Family, including the Duchess of Kent, Queen Victoria's mother, funds were raised. Decimus Burton was chosen as architect. In 1831 the foundation stone was laid by the Duke of Sussex, brother of the new King, William IV. The Duke was very interested in medicine and announced in the HOUSE OF LORDS that he was arranging in his will for his body to be opened and examined by surgeons. The hospital was opened in 1834 with 60 beds. Golding was keen from the outset to incorporate a medical school (other hospitals had no schools as such) which he achieved in 1822. In 1826 the UNIVERSITY OF LONDON was founded and this body gave great support to the medical school which got a much better lecture theatre in Decimus Burton's building. Distinguished early students were David Livingstone, the African missionary and explorer, and Thomas Henry Huxley. In 1863 Golding died having given his whole life to the hospital. As the century advanced further buildings were added and by 1904 there were 278 beds. In 1911 the medical school became a college of the UNIVERSITY OF LONDON. In 1921 Philip Inman was appointed Secretary and Superintendent. He soon became an extremely successful fund raiser, much assisted by the theatrical profession, the hospital being the nearest to theatreland. He even crossed the Atlantic and begged very successfully in New York. In 1936 he became chairman. After the 2nd World War plans were made for rebuilding. In 1948 the hospital was taken over by the National Health Service and in 1957 designated to move to FULHAM PALACE ROAD to occupy the site of FULHAM HOSPITAL which was to be demolished. The new hospital (which contains 805 beds) and its medical school were designed by Ralph Tubbs and opened on 22 May 1973.

Charing Cross Hotel *Strand, WC2.* Built in 1863–4 by E.M. Barry above CHARING CROSS STATION. It was one of the first buildings in London to be faced with artificial stone. The rooms were richly ornamented and the dining-room one of the most opulent in London. Barry's original roof line has been replaced by a straight horizontal double storey. The Eleanor Cross stands in the forecourt (*see* MEMORIALS). There are 210 bedrooms.

Charing Cross *or* **Hungerford Railway Bridge** *Charing Cross–Waterloo.* The nine-span wrought-iron lattice girder bridge was designed by Sir John Hawkshaw to carry the South Eastern Railway over the river

Charing Cross Hotel, one of the first buildings in London to be faced with artificial stone, was designed by E.M. Barry.

to its new West End terminus at CHARING CROSS. Completed in 1864, it incorporated a footbridge. It replaced Brunel's Hungerford Suspension Bridge of 1841–5, built to serve Hungerford Market, though utilising two of its piers (the chains were used to complete Brunel's Clifton suspension bridge). An argument used by the railway company in support of the demolition of the suspension bridge was that the smell from the river, particularly in the summer, was so bad that no one used it. The cross girders were replaced in a major overhaul in 1979.

Charing Cross Road *WC2*. After the completion of REGENT STREET, the need for additional improvements in communications between PICCADILLY CIRCUS and CHARING CROSS northwards to TOTTENHAM COURT ROAD and BLOOMSBURY became imperative. In 1877, therefore, Parliament granted the METROPOLITAN BOARD OF WORKS powers to construct the thoroughfares to be known as SHAFTESBURY AVENUE and Charing Cross Road. The route of the two streets was planned by the Board's architect, George Vulliamy, and their engineer, Sir Joseph Bazalgette. Charing Cross Road was essentially to be a widening of Crown Street and Castle Street, so the street pattern of this part of London was changed far less than that of the districts to the west by the construction of REGENT STREET. As with SHAFTESBURY AVENUE, the building of Charing Cross Road resulted in the demolition of some of the most squalid slums in London; but the need to provide new housing for the families displaced impeded the rate of work and the road was not finished until the late 1880s. Architecturally it was a disaster. Sandringham Buildings which glowered down upon the southern half of the road were a characteristic example. Consisting mostly of three-room tenements and designed to house 900 people, they were opened by the Prince and Princess of Wales in 1884. Further north, on the west side of the street before the intersection with Shaftesbury Avenue known as CAMBRIDGE CIRCUS, the Welsh Presbyterian Church is not so depressing. It was built in 1887 to the designs of John Cubitt for the Trustees of the Welsh Calvinist Methodist Connection whose previous chapel in Gerrard Place (then known as Nassau Street) had been acquired by the METROPOLITAN BOARD OF WORKS for the construction of SHAFTESBURY AVENUE. Built three years later was Westminster City Hall which, designed by Robert Walker, was enlarged in 1902. Also dating from the 1880s is the Cambridge Public House at No. 93 which was built in 1887 and

known until 1891 as the King's Arms, the name of a tavern which had stood on or near the site since at least 1744. The other Victorian public house in the road, the Excelsior at No. 167, which was built in 1889 on a site occupied by a tavern since at least 1759, has now been turned into a snack bar. The ASTORIA CINEMA was originally built in 1892 as a warehouse for Messrs Crosse and Blackwell. The well designed building at Nos 127–131 was built in 1897 by Sir Banister Fletcher for Messrs Alfred Goslett and Co. Ltd, the builders' merchants, who occupied it until a few years ago, and gave their name to Goslett Yard. It is now occupied by the BRITISH FILM INSTITUTE and Collet's International Bookshop. There are three theatres in the road, the GARRICK, WYNDHAM'S and the PHOENIX. ST MARTIN'S SCHOOL OF ART was opened in 1939 on the site of St Martin's Almshouses. At the north end of the road, where ST GILES'S CIRCUS links it to OXFORD STREET, TOTTENHAM COURT ROAD and NEW OXFORD STREET, towers R. Seifert and Partners' massive block, Centre Point. The road is famous for its shops selling musical instruments and for its bookshops. The best known of these are Zwemmer's at Nos 76–80, and FOYLE'S who have occupied Nos 121 and 123, on the corner of MANETTE STREET, since 1913. Anello and Davide Ltd, the theatrical shoemakers who have made footwear for numerous stage and ballet stars, including Alicia Markova and Anna Pavlova, are at Nos 92–94. G. Smith and Sons, the tobacconists at No. 74, were founded in 1869. At No. 84 once stood Marks and Co.'s bookshop. Helene Hanff began writing letters to this shop in 1945; and on the correspondence was based her book *84 Charing Cross Road*.

Charing Cross Station *Strand, WC2*. Designed by John Hawkshaw, consulting engineer to the South Eastern Railway, and opened in 1864. It was built on the site of the old HUNGERFORD MARKET. As at CANNON STREET, the tracks were roofed by a single great arch, here of 164 ft span, rising to nearly 100 ft above the six platforms. The CHARING CROSS HOTEL was built at the same time as the station. In the station forecourt stands a replica by Barry of the Eleanor Cross which had marked the last resting place of Edward I's Queen before her burial in WESTMINSTER ABBEY (*see* CHARING CROSS). In 1905, during roof maintenance, the arch above the tracks collapsed, killing six people and destroying the Avenue Theatre next door (*see* PLAYHOUSE THEATRE). Charing Cross was the West End terminus of the SER and remains the main line station nearest to the heart of London. Over 111,000 passengers use the station each weekday, of whom nearly 39,000 arrive during the morning rush hour.

Charles Street *W1*. On Lord Berkeley's estate (*see* BERKELEY SQUARE), it extends from BERKELEY SQUARE to Waverton Street, its western end, narrower than the rest, bending slightly northward where it approaches the boundary of the estate. Charles was a name in common use in the Berkeley family – hence, probably, the street's name. Building began in about 1745–50, the master carpenter John Phillips (whose workshop is said to have been at No. 27A) being the principal undertaker of the substantial houses erected. Some of these still survive, notably Nos 39–41 and 48 on the south side, and Nos 10 and 16–18 on the north, a few with their original iron lampholders and stone obelisks in front of the doorways. No. 37, now the home of the ENGLISH SPEAKING UNION, is an expensive amalgamation of 1890 of three houses by W. Alwright for Lord Revelstoke. Here also is the 82-bedroomed Chesterfield Hotel. Flats, apartments and offices now predominate in Charles Street.

Former inhabitants include Edward Gibbon, 1758; Edmund Burke, 1780–5; John Hoppner 1785–1810; Beau Brummell, 1792; the Duke of Clarence, later William IV, at No. 22, 1826; Sydney Smith, 1835–9; Admiral Sir Edward Codrington, victor of Navarino; and Lord Rosebery, Prime Minister and 1st Chairman of the LONDON COUNTY COUNCIL, at No. 20 where he was born in 1847.

Charles II Street *SW1.* Known as Charles Street until 1939, it was completed in 1689 on land granted to the Earl of St Albans (*see* JERMYN STREET). Strype described it in 1720 as 'large and handsome'. At the beginning of the 19th century John Stewart, 7th Earl of Galloway, had a large house on the site of No. 29 in which the Earl of Liverpool, later Prime Minister, lived in 1809–10. The premises of the JUNIOR UNITED SERVICES CLUB stood on the north side until their demolition in 1955, when construction began of the present building at No. 11 designed for the United Kingdom Atomic Energy Authority by Trehearne and Norman, Preston and Partners in association with Leslie C. Norton.

Charlotte Street *W1.* Begun in 1787 and named after Queen Charlotte, wife of George III. An artists' quarter from the late 18th century onwards until, in the 1950s, the pleasant, shabby house-fronts gave way to curtain walling. George Morland had lodgings here in 1796. Richard Wilson, the landscape painter, lived at No. 8 in 1773–9 (also at No. 69 in 1773 and at No. 78 in 1771–2). At Nos 15–17 stood the Percy Chapel, built in 1764–6 by William Franks and demolished 1867. William Wilberforce worshipped here. Charles Dibdin, the song writer and dramatist, lived at No. 30 in 1808; John Nash at No. 36 in 1824. St John the Evangelist, designed by Hugh Smith in 1846 and bombed in 1945, stood on the site of No. 74. John Constable lived at No. 76 in 1822–37. Here he finished *The Lock*, *Salisbury Cathedral* and *Hampstead Heath* among many other works. Sir Robert Smirke, the architect, lived at No. 81 in 1786–1804; and Daniel Maclise at No. 85 in 1835–7. On the corner with Tottenham Street stood the SCALA THEATRE. The street is celebrated for its numerous restaurants. These include Bertorelli's at No. 19 and L'Etoile (founded 1906) at No. 30. Bertorelli's was founded by four Italian brothers in 1912 and in 1982 was still managed by the son of one of them.

Charlton *SE7.* One of the few communities in inner London to have retained its distinctive village features. Parish church, manor house, the short but attractive village street and the last remnant of the village green stand in close proximity. Cerletone is reported in *Domesday Book* but its earlier origins can be clearly demonstrated. In 1915 an excavation took place of a large hill fort in what is now Maryon Park revealing evidence that a native British settlement had been there right through the four centuries of Roman occupation. Unfortunately, this splendid monument was destroyed by quarrying soon after the excavation.

Charlton is dominated by CHARLTON HOUSE, a magnificent Jacobean mansion built by Adam Newton in 1612. Newton's great wealth also benefited the nearby parish church of ST LUKE, which was rebuilt in 1630 with money given by Newton's executors. In the village is an old public house, the Bugle Horn, built from two cottages and still retaining some 18th-century timbers. In Fairfield Grove are the parish almshouses, rebuilt by Sir Richard Baynes in about 1710.

Until 1872 Charlton was the scene every October of the notorious CHARLTON HORN FAIR, held until 1820 on the village green. When the green was largely taken into the grounds of CHARLTON HOUSE in the 1820s it was moved to Fairfield where its indecencies and frequent riots continued until it was suppressed by Order in Council in 1872.

In the last century the marshes of Lower Charlton were developed for industrial use and the slopes of the hill on which Charlton stands were extensively quarried. Between the communities of Old and New Charlton are two pleasant parks, Maryon and Maryon Wilson Parks, named after the family that owned the manor until 1925. These are the last remnants of the village's ancient forest formerly known as Hanging Wood.

Charlton Athletic Football Club *see* FOOTBALL CLUBS.

Charlton Horn Fair The origins of the fair are uncertain. Tradition has it that the right to hold the fair was granted by King John to a miller in recompense for the King having seduced his wife after a hunting expedition in the vicinity. The miller was granted all the land visible from CHARLTON to the bend of the river beyond ROTHERHITHE. The miller's amused neighbours christened the river boundary of his property 'Cuckold's Point' and the fair Horn Fair, horns being the sign of the cuckolded husband. The parish church of CHARLTON is ST LUKE'S and the fair took place on 18 October, St Luke's Day. St Luke is often depicted writing beside an ox and cow, whose horns are very prominent: this too could be the origin of the Fair's name. The only known Charter relating to CHARLTON is of 1268 when permission was given to the Prior of BERMONDSEY for a fair on the Feast of the Trinity. This, however, existed separately from the Horn Fair and ended in the mid-17th century. The fair reached its heyday in Charles II's reign when thousands of people visited CHARLTON by boat dressed as kings, queens and millers with horns on their heads. Later, people came to CHARLTON by river steamer. The fair ended in 1872.

Charlton House *SE7.* One of the finest specimens of Jacobean architecture in the country, it was built for Adam Newton, tutor to Prince Henry, son of James I. The house was completed in the year in which Prince Henry died (1612). The architect is not known but architectural historians usually attribute it to John Thorpe. The traditional attribution to Inigo Jones is discredited but it is felt that the orangery (now a public lavatory) displays many signs of Jones's handiwork. When Adam Newton died in 1630 his son succeeded to the estate. Eventually the manor came to the Maryon Wilson family who held it until 1925 when it was bought by GREENWICH Borough Council and,

A Carthusian monastery founded in 1370 became the Charterhouse, shown here in Sutton Nicholl's engraving of c.1750.

subsequently, became a community centre and library. It is of red brick relieved with white stone quoins and dressings and is in the shape of a shallow H. House, orangery, stables and park have survived intact except that the north wing of the house was destroyed in the 2nd World War and later rebuilt.

Chartered Accountants' Company *see* CITY LIVERY COMPANIES.

Chartered Accountants' Hall *Moorgate Place, EC2.* The original hall, designed by John Belcher, was built in 1890–3. Belcher's partner, J.J. Joass, built an extension in 1930–1 as a continuation of the earlier design. In 1959 William Whitfield was commissioned to design a further extension, including a Great Hall. The new headquarters of the INSTITUTE OF CHARTERED ACCOUNTANTS were opened by the Queen in May 1970. In addition to the Council Chamber, Guests' Room, Members' Room, reception rooms and committee rooms, there are a library with over 26,000 books on accounting, law, finance and taxation and a restaurant. The collection of modern silver, designed by Gerald Benney, comprises some 600 pieces.

Chartered Insurance Institute Museum *20 Aldermanbury, EC2.* Founded in 1897, it contains various fire insurance relics, old policies and advertisements as well as what is probably the best collection of British insurance offices' fire marks in the world.

Chartered Secretaries' and Administrators' Company *see* CITY LIVERY COMPANIES.

Chartered Surveyors' Company *see* CITY LIVERY COMPANIES.

Charterhouse *Charterhouse Square, EC1.* In 1350–1 Sir Walter de Manny, one of Edward III's bravest knights, bought 13 acres of ground adjoining Pardon Churchyard and gave it to the CITY as a burial ground for victims of the BLACK DEATH. A small chapel stood on the site of CHARTERHOUSE SQUARE. In 1370 Manny founded a Carthusian monastery on the site. John Luscote, a Carthusian from Hinton, Somerset, and seven other monks moved into temporary buildings. And in 1371 the House of the Salutation of the Mother of God, otherwise known as Charterhouse, received its foundation charter. Henry Yevele, Edward III's master mason, took charge of building operations. By the end of 1371 the first cells were ready. A 'cell' consisted of a two-storey house which stood in its own garden. Each had a workroom, oratory, bedroom, living-room and wood-store. The monks lived alone and usually ate alone except on Sundays and feast days when they went to the refectory. They could talk to each other on Sundays after refectory when they went for a three-hour walk outside the monastery. They had no personal possessions and were not allowed meat. In 1372 Manny died and was buried in the chapel before the high altar. His funeral was attended by Edward III and the royal children. John of Gaunt endowed 500 masses to be said for his soul. By 1398 19 cells had been built but another five were still incomplete. In 1405 the weekly walk was stopped because of the distractions of BARTHOLOMEW FAIR. Between 1499 and 1503 Sir Thomas More prayed at the monastery and wore a hair shirt in penance. In 1535 Prior John Houghton and two other Carthusian priors invited Thomas Cromwell to a discussion on the King's supremacy. He sent them to the TOWER as rebels and tried them at WESTMINSTER for 'treacherously machinating and desiring' to deprive the King of his title as Supreme Head of the Church. All were sentenced to death. And on 4 May 1535 they, and another monk from SYON, were drawn on hurdles to TYBURN where they were hanged and, while still alive, cut down and quartered. One of Prior Houghton's arms was put up over the priory gate but it fell down three days later and was buried in a secret place. Cromwell then installed agents in the monastery to report on the monks. Their books were confiscated and sermons were preached to convert them. On 19 June three more monks were hanged at TYBURN. In 1536 Cromwell appointed William Trafford as prior. The next year 20 monks signed the Oath of Supremacy. Ten who refused to sign were sent to NEWGATE where they were chained upright. Nine died of starvation and the survivor, William Horn, was transferred to the TOWER until his execution at TYBURN three years later. In 1537 Prior Trafford surrendered the monastery to the King who used it for storing hunting tents. It was acquired in 1545 by Sir Edward North, Chancellor of the Court of Augmentations, and two years later sold to John Dudley, Duke of Northumberland, possibly as a residence for his son, Guildford Dudley, and his daughter-in-law, Lady Jane Grey. He himself had adequate accommodation at DURHAM HOUSE in the STRAND. In August that year, on the death of Edward VI, Lady Jane Grey was proclaimed Queen. Northumberland was subsequently executed on TOWER HILL and Charterhouse was given back to North in spite of the fact that he had signed the declaration at GREENWICH in favour of Queen Jane. In November 1558 Queen Elizabeth stayed for five days with North and received homage from her nobles and assembled ambassadors. She left to spend a vigil in the TOWER before her coronation. The procession was 'headed by gentlemen and knights and lords and after came all the trumpets blowing and then came all the heralds in array and my Lord of Pembroke bore the Queen's sword. Then came her Grace on horseback in purple velvet with a sash around her neck and sergeants-at-arms about her Grace. And next after rode Robert Dudley, her master of horse and so the guard with halberds. There was such shooting of guns as never was heard before.' In July 1561 Elizabeth stayed again with North for three days and made another royal progress through the CITY even more splendid than the first. After this North, ruined financially by the visit, retired to live in the country, and in 1565 Charterhouse was sold to Thomas Howard, 4th Duke of Norfolk, who renamed it Howard House. His plans to marry Mary Queen of Scots led first to his imprisonment at the TOWER, then to his house arrest at Howard House, and finally, in 1572, to his execution. In 1573 the house was let to the Portuguese Ambassador for some years; and from 1593–5 it was the home of George Clifford, Earl of Cumberland, and his family. In 1601 it was given by Elizabeth to Thomas Howard, second son of the 4th Duke of Norfolk and Admiral of the Fleet, for services to his country. He rarely used it, preferring to go to Audley End, though in 1603 Elizabeth stayed one day with him here. And in May that year, her successor, James I, stayed for four days on his arrival in London. He created 133 new knights in the Great Chamber and made Howard his Lord Chamberlain. In May 1611 Thomas Sutton, 'esteemed the richest commoner in England', bought the house for £13,000 as a school for 44 poor boys and a hospital for 80 poor gentlemen. Though he died in December that year it was not until exactly three years later that his embalmed body was brought from CHRIST CHURCH GREYFRIARS to be reburied in the Charterhouse Chapel beneath a fine

tomb carved by Nicholas Stone and Nicholas Janssen. The first boys were admitted in 1614 and a schoolmaster with a salary of £20 per annum and an usher with £10 were appointed. They were allowed to supplement their meagre incomes by taking additional fee-paying boys. But in the early years numbers never rose above 100. When John Russell was appointed headmaster in 1811 at the age of 24, he introduced the Madras system of pupils teaching pupils. Numbers rose dramatically. In 1818 there were 238 boys and by 1825 there were 480. Parents began to remove their children, however, and by 1835 there were only 99 boys left. Having gradually recovered its reputation, the school moved to Godalming in 1872. Among those who were pupils at the London Charterhouse were Richard Lovelace, Richard Steele, John Wesley, Joseph Addison, Sir William Blackstone, Lord Ellenborough, Robert Baden-Powell, Sir Henry Havelock, Sir Charles Eastlake, George Grote, Sir Johnstone Forbes-Robertson, Lord Liverpool and William Thackeray who describes the school in *The Newcomes*, thinly disguised as Greyfriars. In 1875 part of the building was sold to MERCHANT TAYLORS' SCHOOL which also moved to the country in 1933. In 1941 most of the old buildings were destroyed in an air raid. They were restored by Mottistone and Paget. In 1949 ST BARTHOLOMEW'S HOSPITAL Medical School, designed by Easton and Robertson, was built on part of the Great Cloister. The Charterhouse pensioners still live in the surviving old buildings. Above the 17th-century library is the Great Chamber which is said to have been the finest Elizabethan room in England before it was bombed. The chapel, once the monks' Chapter House, incorporates 14th-century walls. Buried in it, besides Thomas Sutton, are Lord Ellenborough, whose monument is by Chantrey, and Dr Matthew Raine, a headmaster who died in 1811, and whose memorial is by Flaxman.

Charterhouse Square *EC1*. Georgian houses built between 1700 and 1775. Some have fine ironwork and doorways. Thackeray lodged here with a Mrs Boyes while a pupil at CHARTERHOUSE School.

Chase Farm Hospital *Enfield, Middlesex*. Founded as a farm school for orphans in 1894. In 1930 it was converted for use as a home for the elderly. In 1939 it was used as an emergency hospital. The National Health Service took over in 1948 since when it has been used as an acute general hospital. It has 600 beds.

Chatelain's *Covent Garden*. A famous French ordinary, where meals could be obtained at fixed prices and regular hours. It was established in the reign of Charles II, and was celebrated as a meeting place for wits in the late 17th century. Pepys records two visits in 1668. On the first occasion he complains, 'A dinner cost us 8s 6d apiece, a base dinner which did not please us at all.' But later he fared better 'with musick and good company . . . and mighty merry till ten at night'. References to this ordinary in fiction suggest it attracted those with false pretensions.

Chatham House *St James's Square see* CHANDOS HOUSE, ST JAMES'S SQUARE.

Cheam *Surrey*. Derives its name from the Saxon Kaggaham, the village by the stumps, the stumps possibly being those of large trees on the clay knoll where St Dunstan's, the original church, now stands. They were felled to build the original farmhouses. The earliest settlement was probably of the 6th century. Unlike SUTTON, Cheam, although on the railway from 1847, did not become a Victorian suburb and while a slow expansion occurred in Victorian and Edwardian times, Cheam remained essentially a Surrey farming village until the 1920s. Because a relatively iron-free clay could be dug locally, Cheam became in the 13th to 15th centuries a centre of pottery manufacture. Suburban expansion came in the late 1920s and the 1930s, both on the northern clay lands which had been Cheam common and on the southern chalk lands. Cheam, south of the railway, is a fine example of the larger, more expensive and better-quality suburban development of the later 1930s with detached houses in spacious grounds. The late development of suburban building in Cheam resulted in the old village centre being encapsulated in the new development but, because the 2nd World War cut short further growth, the centre was not entirely rebuilt. Part of central Cheam is a late 1930s' Tudor revival-style shopping area, but several 17th- to early 19th-century houses of the old village remain. WHITEHALL, a large timber-framed house of about 1530 with 17th- and early 19th-century additions, is open to the public. The area is almost wholly residential although there are some businesses in North Cheam. St Dunstan's church is a 6th-century foundation but was rebuilt in the Victorian Gothic style in 1864 to the designs of F.E. Pownall. The chancel of the medieval church survives in the churchyard to the south of the Victorian church. On the chalkland of south Cheam was a large hare warren built in the 1690s. It consisted of a warrener's cottage and 50 or so acres enclosed in a substantial brick wall, the south side of which was pierced at intervals with shuttered openings. The hares lived and bred in the warren and, when coursing was practised on the Downs, were driven by beaters through the openings. The cottage has gone and the area of the warren is now built over, but the brick wall survives along Onslow Avenue and Warren Avenue and, along the former, the outlet openings can still be seen.

Cheapside *EC2*. The chief market place of medieval London. (*Ceap* or *chepe* was the Old English word for market.) It was sometimes known as West Cheap to distinguish it from EASTCHEAP. Each craft guild lived and worked in a special area nearby: the bakers in BREAD STREET, goldsmiths in GOLDSMITHS ROW between BREAD and FRIDAY STREETS, fishmongers in FRIDAY STREET, shoemakers and curriers in Cordwainer Street, pepperers (grocers) in Sopers Lane, mercers between POULTRY and Sopers Lane, poulterers in POULTRY, dairymen in MILK STREET, cutlers on the north side of Cheapside at the east end and saddlers at the west end. Cheapside was infamous for its brawling apprentices. Chaucer relates in *The Cook's Tale*:

There was a prentice living in our town,
Worked in the victualling trade and he was brown . . .
At every wedding would he sing and hop
And he preferred the tavern to the shop.
Whenever any pageant or procession
Came down Cheapside, goodbye to his profession.
He'd leap out of the shop to see the sight
And join the dance and not come back that night!

The market declined after Henry III ordered fish, corn and salt to be unloaded at DOWGATE and QUEENHITHE Wharves and the STOCKS MARKET to be established. Water conduits stood at either end of the street. The Great Conduit was at the east end and the Little Conduit at the west. On special occasions, such as when Edward I brought his wife Eleanor to London and at the birth of the Black Prince, the conduits ran with wine. By ST MARY-LE-BOW was a fountain known as the Standard. Punishments were often carried out by it. In 1293 three men had their right hands cut off here for rescuing a prisoner; and in 1326 Walter Stapleton, Treasurer to Edward II, was beheaded. Two fishmongers were also beheaded in 1351. During the PEASANTS' REVOLT Wat Tyler beheaded Richard Lions here; and in 1450 Jack Cade decapitated Lord Say. There was also a pillory in Cheapside. In 1372 Nicholas Mollere was pilloried for an hour with a whetstone round his neck for spreading false rumours; in 1382 a BREAD STREET cook was put there for selling stale conger and the fish was burnt under his nose; and in 1611 a man named Floyd was whipped from WESTMINSTER to Cheapside pillory and there branded on the face. At the corner of WOOD STREET was the Cheapside Cross built in 1290 by order of Edward I at one of the resting places of Queen Eleanor's coffin (*see* CHARING CROSS). It was three storeys high and was decorated with statues of the Pope, the Virgin and Child and the Apostles. In the 16th century it was constantly attacked by Puritans; and in 1643 it was demolished by workmen protected by soldiers 'to

Cheapside as it appeared in 1638, when Marie de' Medici came to visit her daughter Henrietta Maria, Queen of Charles I.

143

cleanse that great street of superstition'. Tournaments were held in the 14th century on open ground to the north, 'the stone pavement being covered with sand, that the horses might not slide when they strongly set their feet to the ground'. One tournament was held in 1330 to celebrate the birth of the Black Prince. Once the stand used by Queen Philippa and her ladies collapsed. The carpenters were sent for and would have been punished but the Queen pleaded for them. A stone stand was then built. In memory of it Wren built a balcony on ST MARY-LE-BOW when he rebuilt the church after the Great Fire.

In 1118 Thomas Becket was born in a house at the corner of IRONMONGER LANE. The site was later occupied by the HOSPITAL OF ST THOMAS OF ACON which was founded by Becket's sister, and later still by MERCERS' HALL. Stow wrote in 1598, 'On the south side of Cheapside there were houses that were of old time but sheds where a woman sold seeds, roots and herbs now by encroachments on the high street ... largely builded on both sides outward and also upward some three, four or five stories high.' In the GREAT FIRE, ST MARY-LE-BOW, ST PETER WEST CHEAP, ST MICHAEL AT CORN, and the MERCERS' and SADDLERS' HALLS were all destroyed. ST MARY-LE-BOW was rebuilt by Wren, MERCERS' HALL by Edward Jarman and SADDLERS' HALL by an unknown architect, but the other two churches were left as ruins. In 1720 Strype said Cheapside was, 'a very spacious street adorned with lofty buildings, well inhabited by goldsmiths, linen drapers, haberdashers and other great dealers'. In the middle of the 19th century it rivalled the WEST END as a shopping centre. In 1861 John Keats lived in a house opposite IRONMONGER LANE while composing his first volume of poetry. At the turn of the century, large and costly blocks of chambers, offices, warehouses and shops were built. In 1912 a hoard of early 17th-century jewellery was dug up, presumably left by a goldsmith fleeing from the plague or fire. ST MARY-LE-BOW, SADDLERS' and MERCERS' HALLS were destroyed in the 2nd World War. All have been rebuilt between tall blocks of offices. At the corner of WOOD STREET are three shops two storeys high; they were built by the parishioners of St Peter, West Cheap in 1687. No. 73 contains a 17th-century staircase which was in the previous house on the site. Sir Christopher Wren is said to have built it for the Lord Mayor, William Turner.

Chelsea *SW3, SW10*. The origin of the name is disputed. Spellings such as Chelcheya and Chelchythe are among many which appear on old documents. It is likely that it means 'Chalk Wharf' and traces of chalk can be seen at low tide in the River THAMES. Offa, King of the Mercians, held a Synod in Chelsea about AD 787 and a church was probably built in AD 799. Chelsea is mentioned in *Domesday Book* as a village in MIDDLESEX. During the Middle Ages there are occasional mentions of Chelsea and its famous inhabitants such as Sir Reginald Bray, Lord of the Manor in 1485, and the Lawrence family in the 16th century. The arrival in 1520 of Sir Thomas More, who built himself a country house and who is commemorated in CHELSEA OLD CHURCH, set Chelsea firmly in its place in history. In the 16th century it became known as a 'Village of Palaces'. The Duke of Norfolk, the Earl of Shrewsbury and Henry VIII himself all had splendid houses here. Queen Elizabeth I lived as a

child under the care of her father's surviving wife, Katherine Parr, and her husband, Lord High Admiral Seymour. The most famous monument in Chelsea is the ROYAL HOSPITAL, begun in 1682 by Christopher Wren as a home for old soldiers, which it still is. The story of Nell Gwynne inspiring the idea has little foundation in fact, though she was among its early benefactors. Chelsea was a home of writers such as Swift and Addison and later Carlyle and Leigh Hunt, and was renowned for gatherings of intellectuals. The great reputation that it has for art really began with the CHELSEA PORCELAIN WORKS and the illustrations done for publications by the CHELSEA PHYSIC GARDEN. Later Whistler, Rossetti, and other famous artists living in Chelsea gave the place a distinctive character. In 1900 the Chelsea Borough Council was formed; its first Mayor was Earl Cadogan. When the London Government Act of 1963 ended Chelsea's life as a separate entity, the last Mayor was that Earl Cadogan's grandson. On 1 April 1965, the amalgamation of KENSINGTON and Chelsea took place and the Royal Borough of KENSINGTON and Chelsea was formed. Although Chelsea has changed considerably in the last century, and although there is hardly a day when some building is not destroyed to be replaced by a modern structure, it still has a character all its own.

Chelsea Arts Club *143 Old Church Street, SW3*. Towards the end of the last century a great many artists had settled in CHELSEA. Many of them met at the Six Bells Public House (now the Bird's Nest) in the KING'S ROAD. By 1891 it was felt that more permanent premises were necessary; so a group of artists rented the upper part of 181 KING'S ROAD as a club from James Christie, a founder member, along with James Abbott McNeill Whistler, Philip Wilson Steer, Frank Brangwyn, George Clausen and the sculptor, Thomas Stirling Lee, who became the first chairman. In 1902 they moved to their present premises at No. 143 OLD CHURCH STREET, a low rambling house with a beautiful garden. Other founder members were Walter Sickert, Fred Pegram and W.H. Townsend, art editor of *Punch*. Many distinguished artists have been members of the Club – Augustus John, Stephen Spurrier, Sir Alfred Munnings, Henry Tonks and Sir Charles Wheeler. The Chelsea Arts Ball was held originally at the club and then at the ALBERT HALL. It finally became so riotous that it was stopped in 1959.

Chelsea Barracks *Chelsea Bridge Road, SW1*. The first barracks, designed for 1,000 foot guards by George Moore, were built in 1861–2 on the east side of the newly constructed Chelsea Bridge Road. In 1960–6 they were completely rebuilt by Tripe and Wakeham.

Chelsea Bridge *Chelsea–Battersea*. The first bridge, designed by Thomas Page, was built in 1851–8. It was a suspension bridge with cast-iron towers. Many human bones and Roman and British weapons were found during the digging of the foundations, showing that a battle must have been fought here. It was freed from tolls in 1879, and in 1934 replaced with a suspension bridge by Rendel, Palmer and Tritton.

Chelsea Bun House *Jew's Row (Pimlico Road)*. 'Rrrrrrrare Chelsea Buns' are mentioned by Swift who was there in 1711 and got a stale one for a penny. The Bun House was a single-storey building projecting over the pavement and in its heyday was kept by Richard Hand. The interior was decorated with foreign clocks and a strange collection of natural and artificial rarities. George II and Queen Caroline and, later, George III, Queen Charlotte and all the Princesses were among Hand's customers. According to a local poet the buns were:

Fragrant as honey and sweeter in taste!
As flaky and white as if baked by the light,
As the flesh of an infant soft, doughy and slight.

On Good Fridays crowds of 50,000 were said to wait outside. In 1793 Mrs Hand 'respectfully informed her friends and the public that in consequence of the great concourse of people which assembled before her house at a very early hour on the morning of Good Friday last by which her neighbours (with whom she has always lived in friendship and repute) have been much alarmed and annoyed ... she is determined, though much to her loss, not to sell Cross Buns on that day to any person whatever but Chelsea Buns as usual.' In 1804, with the closure of RANELAGH GARDENS, trade fell off. However, on Good Friday 1839, 240,000 buns were sold. The house was demolished in 1839.

Chelsea College *Manresa Road, SW3.* Originally the South Western Polytechnic, the foundation stone was laid on 29 June 1891 by the Prince of Wales. The second of the great polytechnics, it originally contained what is now the CHELSEA SCHOOL OF ART. The architect was J.M. Brydon who also designed the Chelsea Public Library and CHELSEA OLD TOWN HALL. There were strict rules of government, forbidding alcoholic drinks, political movements and religious denominations. Men and women had separate entrances. In 1922 it was renamed Chelsea Polytechnic and in 1963 designated a College of Advanced Technology. In 1962, after the Robbins Report, it became a college of the UNIVERSITY OF LONDON. The Royal Charter of Incorporation into the UNIVERSITY OF LONDON was granted on 22 December 1971. In 1980 it acquired the site and buildings of the COLLEGE OF ST MARK AND ST JOHN.

Chelsea Common *SW3.* (Sometimes called Heath and incorrectly Chelsea Green.) This open space once had gravel pits and a large pond. Certain houses, including CHELSEA MANOR HOUSE, now destroyed, once the home of Hans Sloane, had right of pasture on this land. The owners of old SHREWSBURY HOUSE raised two cows and one heifer, EVANS FARM six cows and three heifers. Troop reviews were held on the Common at the time of the Civil War. Later volunteers, mostly from the CITY, drilled and exercised here. The Common is now surrounded by shops with a small ornamental green and garden in the centre.

Chelsea Embankment *also* **Embankment Gardens** *SW3.* Broad riverside road, just over three-quarters of a mile long, built at a cost of £269,591 in 1871–4 and flanked by gardens on land recovered by the embankment from the muddy foreshore of the river. It extends from CHELSEA BRIDGE to ALBERT BRIDGE. Constructed by the METROPOLITAN BOARD OF WORKS it was designed by Sir Joseph Bazalgette and opened by the Duke and Duchess of Edinburgh in

May 1874. It has a dual purpose: a fine riverside thoroughfare, it also covers the main sewer of this part of London. Embankment Gardens form a crescent, on the western corner of which stands Shelley House, now a nurses' residence, built to the designs of Edmund Warren and lived in by Charles St John Hornby, the printer and connoisseur, who died in 1946. The Ashendene Press which he had founded in Hertfordshire was moved to a cottage in the garden of Shelley House and functioned there until 1936. George Frederick Robinson, 1st Marquess of Ripon, Liberal statesman and Viceroy of India in 1880–4, lived at Turner's Reach House (No. 9). OLD SWAN HOUSE (No. 17) was built in 1875 by Norman Shaw. George Eunorphopolos lived at No. 7 with his famous collection of oriental frescoes, ceramics and sculptures now mainly in the BRITISH MUSEUM. Most of the houses on the Embankment are divided into flats. The fibreglass figure of *The Boy David* is by E. Brainbridge Copnall (1975). An inscription on the plinth reads, 'The original Boy David statue ... the model for the Carabiniers' memorial at Hyde Park Corner ... was presented to the Borough of Chelsea in 1963 but was later stolen.' (For the Carabiniers' Memorial *see* MEMORIALS.)

Chelsea Flower Show   The May Flower Show of the ROYAL HORTICULTURAL SOCIETY has been held (with the exception of some war years) in the grounds of the ROYAL HOSPITAL since May 1913.

Chelsea Football Club   *see* FOOTBALL CLUBS.

Chelsea Hospital *Royal Hospital Road, SW3.* Founded by Charles II for veteran soldiers, an idea inspired by the Hôtel des Invalides in Paris and by a similar hospital for the Irish Army. It stands on the site of an unsuccessful College of Theology established in 1618 by Dr Sutcliffe, Dean of Exeter. Archbishop Laud called it 'Controversy College'. After 40 years it closed and the government took over the building for Dutch and Scottish prisoners of war who were supervised here by John Evelyn. In 1666 it was granted to the ROYAL SOCIETY but it was too dilapidated for them to use. In 1681, Sir Stephen Fox, the first Paymaster General, outlined the idea of the hospital to Charles II. The next year Christopher Wren was appointed architect and the King laid the foundation stone. 476 old pensioners were admitted in 1689. The building was finished in 1692. It was constructed around three courtyards, the centre one opening to the south, the side ones to the east and west respectively. In the centre one a statue of Charles II was erected (*see* STATUES). The building remains more or less unchanged except for minor alterations made by Robert Adam in 1765–82 and the stables which were added to the west by Sir John Soane in 1814. Carlyle called the hospital, 'quiet and dignified and the work of a gentleman'. The main north block contains the Central Saloon flanked by the Hall and Chapel. The hall is panelled and in it hangs a large painting of Charles II on horseback by Antonio Verrio. In 1807 General Whitelock was cashiered here after his court martial for surrendering the fortress of Monte Video. In 1852, from 10 to 17 November, the Duke of Wellington lay in state. So many people filed past his coffin that two of them were killed in the crush. The Chapel is also panelled and decorated with flags captured in battle. Over the altar is a painting of the

Chelsea Hospital, built by Wren and finished in 1692. This 1744 view also shows the Rotunda in Ranelagh Gardens (right).

Resurrection by Sebastiano Ricci. The east and west wings are dormitories. At the southern end of the west wing is the Governor's House. The State Room is panelled and has a fine limewood carving over the fireplace by William Emmett. Royal portraits line the walls, among them those of Charles I and his family by Van Dyck, Charles II by Lely and William III by Kneller. To the west of the hospital is the infirmary. The original one was the home of Sir Robert Walpole in 1723–43. It was destroyed by a landmine in 1941 and rebuilt with 80 beds in 1961. East of the Hospital is a small museum illustrating the hospital's history. Every May the CHELSEA FLOWER SHOW is held in the grounds. The granite obelisk was erected in the grounds in 1853 in memory of the men who died at Chilianwalla in 1849 (*see* MEMORIALS). To the south-west of the hospital is the NATIONAL ARMY MUSEUM (*see also* CHELSEA PENSIONERS).

Chelsea Manor House Built in about 1536 by Henry VIII on the river to the east of the former manor house. He gave the house to Katherine Parr as a wedding present in 1543 and after his death in 1547 she retired to it. Thomas Seymour came here to woo the Queen, giving rise to the suspicious relationship with Princess Elizabeth which was held against him at his trial. In 1548 Katherine died here and the house was given to John Dudley, 1st Duke of Northumberland. After Northumberland's execution his widow continued to live here until her own death in 1555. She is buried in CHELSEA OLD CHURCH. Anne of Cleves, Henry VIII's fourth wife, died here in 1556. From 1559 to 1587 the house was the home of Anne, Duchess of Somerset, widow of the Protector. In 1591 Queen Elizabeth gave it to Charles Howard, Earl of Nottingham, Lord High Admiral and she often visited him here. From 1639 to 1649 the house belonged to James, Duke of Hamilton. He built a large extension to the west. The whole was seized by Parliament in 1653. In 1660

it was sold to Charles Cheyne and in 1712 bought by Hans Sloane who leased it before coming to live here with his great natural history collection in 1742. He wished the government to buy the house as a museum but the collection was, however, moved to BLOOMSBURY where it formed the nucleus of the BRITISH MUSEUM. Not long after Sloane's death the manor house was demolished. Nos 19–26 CHEYNE WALK cover the site.

Chelsea Manor Street *SW3*. Previously known as Manor Street, it became known by its present name in 1937. Close to the site of the former CHELSEA MANOR HOUSE, it runs from ST LUKE's churchyard, crosses the KING'S ROAD and leads towards CHELSEA EMBANKMENT. It contains the main Chelsea Post and Sorting Office, and several blocks of flats, including a PEABODY ESTATE.

Chelsea Old Church (All Saints) *Cheyne Walk, SW3*. Documentary evidence suggests that there was a Norman church on this site in 1157, but not until 1290 was it named All Saints' church.

The nave, built in the classical style, leads into the medieval chancel, the altar and barley sugar altar rails of which are 17th-century. The chapels off the chancel were originally private. The north chapel, about 1325, belonged to the Lord of the Manor of CHELSEA, who could see the altar through the squint still to be found in the east arch. In this chapel is a free-standing triumphal arch commemorating Richard Jervoise, son of the wealthy occupant of CHELSEA MANOR HOUSE. Sir Thomas More rebuilt the south chapel in 1528 for his own private worship. The capitals of the pillars leading to the chancel are traditionally attributed to Hans Holbein the Younger. In the sanctuary is a monument to More. His first wife's Gothic altar tomb is here, and he intended it to be the tomb of himself and his second wife, but after his execution in 1535 his head was buried in Canterbury. His tribute on the monument to Alice, his second wife, says, about his son and three daughters:

> To them such love was by Alicia shown,
> In stepmothers, a virtue rarely known,
> The world believed the children were her own.

In the More chapel is the tomb, badly damaged, of the Duchess of Northumberland, mother-in-law of Lady Jane Grey, mother of Robert Dudley, Earl of Leicester, and grandmother of Sir Philip Sidney. Among other memorials is a plaque to Henry James and a sculpture to Lady Jane Cheyne, a great benefactress to the village of Chelsea. Sir John Fielding and Thomas Shadwell, the dramatist, are both believed to have been buried here, but no certain evidence has been found.

The marble font dates from 1673 but the cover is a reproduction. There are six chained books, the only chained books in any London church, the gift of Sir Hans Sloane, whose monument by Joseph Wilton stands in the churchyard. The bell which hangs in the porch was a gift, in 1679, in thanksgiving for safety from drowning in the river, and is inscribed 'The GVIFT of the Honourable William Ashburnham esqvier cofferer to his Majesties household.'

Ashburnham is one of the many parishioners to be commemorated in the kneelers embroidered for the church since the 2nd World War. Among others thus remembered are Bartholomew Nutt, the ferryman of Chelsea Reach, and Thomas Doggett, founder of DOGGETT'S COAT AND BADGE RACE. The distinguished are many and include Henry VIII who married Jane Seymour privately here before their state wedding in 1536.

Chelsea Old Church was very badly damaged by bombing in 1941, when five firewatchers were killed. It was restored (architect Walter Godfrey) after the war on its old foundations. A ring of eight bells was installed in the Silver Jubilee year of Queen Elizabeth II and was cast around the third bell which has a long Chelsea history reaching back in all probability to the reign of Elizabeth I.

Chelsea Old Town Hall *King's Road, SW3.* CHELSEA's Town Hall until the amalgamation with KENSINGTON in 1965, it is now used by several municipal services. Chelsea Public Library occupies some of the ground floor. Among many important events held here was the reception and presentation of an address by the Vestry of the Parish of CHELSEA to Sir George White, Governor of the ROYAL HOSPITAL, who had led the defence of Ladysmith in the Boer War. The hall was built to the design of J.M. Brydon in 1886 but extended in 1906–8 by L.R. Stokes who lived in MULBERRY WALK. Still used for functions, it is decorated by murals portraying CHELSEA's association with the arts, literature and science. These were painted by several artists, their work being chosen from an open competition held in 1912 and judged by John Singer Sargent, Philip Wilson Steer and A.E. Ricketts. In 1914, after heated discussion, the Borough Council decided to remove the mural on literature because it contained a portrait of Oscar Wilde (it also contained portraits of George Eliot and Thomas Carlyle). But, mainly because of the outbreak of war, this resolution was not carried out. A Roll of Chelsea Freemen is displayed. The names include that of Sir Alexander Fleming who lived in DANVERS STREET and of whom there is also a bust, unveiled in 1956.

Chelsea Park Gardens *SW3.* This group of houses built soon after the 1st World War on the east side of BEAUFORT STREET has no particular history, but its name commemorates the park which once covered the area now bounded by KING'S ROAD, FULHAM ROAD, Park Walk and OLD CHURCH STREET. Once a part of Sir Thomas More's estate, it was used for a few years in the 18th century as a silk farm. A house belonging to the Henniker-Wilson family stood here until its demolition in 1876. Sir Alfred Munnings, President of the ROYAL ACADEMY, lived at No. 96 in 1920–59.

Chelsea Pensioners The Royal Hospital, CHELSEA, more familiarly known as CHELSEA HOSPITAL, was founded by Charles II as a home for veteran soldiers. The in-pensioners, about 420 in number, are divided into six companies. Men over 65 (55 if unable to earn a living) are boarded, lodged, clothed, nursed when ill, and receive a small weekly allowance. Their uniform, navy blue in winter and light scarlet in summer, dates from the 18th century. A three-cornered hat is worn on special occasions such as Oak Apple Day (29 May) when pensioners parade in the central quadrangle, in honour of their royal founder's birthday (*see* CEREMONIES). On this occasion oak foliage decorates the large statue of Charles II (*see* STATUES) and sprigs are carried by pensioners. In autumn a Harvest Festival parade takes place.

Chelsea Physic Garden. This mid-19th-century lithograph shows the famous cedars of Lebanon, planted in 1683.

Chelsea Physic Garden *Swan Walk, SW3.* The second oldest physic garden in the country (the first being founded at Oxford in 1621), it was established by the APOTHECARIES' COMPANY in 1676 on ground they had leased three years earlier intending to build a boat house for their state barge. In 1683 the first cedar trees to grow in England were planted here (the last one died in 1903). In 1684 John Evelyn visited Mr Walls, the keeper, and was much impressed with 'the subterraneous heat conveyed by a stove under the conservatory all vaulted with brick so as he has the doors and windows open in the hardest of frosts'. In 1732 cotton seed sent from here to America to James Oglethorpe, the colonist of Georgia, helped to establish the industry there. In 1736 Linnaeus visited the garden to collect plants and dried specimens. Between about 1700 and 1737 Mrs Elizabeth Blackwell drew 500 plants to illustrate her *Curious Herbal* to help her husband out of financial difficulties. In 1772 Sir Hans Sloane, the Lord of the Manor, presented the garden to the APOTHECARIES' COMPANY on condition they gave 2,000 dried plants to the ROYAL SOCIETY at the rate of 50 per annum and maintained the garden for 'the manifestation of the glory, power and wisdom of God, in the works of creation'. A statue of Sloane by Rysbrack stands in the centre of the garden (*see* STATUES). Botanical research is still carried on here. Since 1683 there has been a mutual exchange of plants and seeds with botanic gardens throughout the world. There is the earliest rock garden in the country, constructed of old building stone from the TOWER OF LONDON and some basaltic lava brought from Iceland by Sir Joseph Banks. In 1681 the first greenhouse and stove in England were built. In addition to the Herb Garden with modern and historical medicinal and culinary plants, there are many exotic shrubs and trees collected from all parts of the world, including a 30 ft high olive tree (*Olea europaea*), the biggest in Britain, which produced seven pounds of edible olives in 1976; and a Chinese willow pattern tree (*Koelreuteria paniculata*).

Chelsea Porcelain Works *Lawrence Street.* Founded in about 1745 and run during its most prosperous periods by Nicholas Sprimont, who appears to have been manager and whole or part owner until 1769. The production is usually divided by collectors into the following periods, defined by the marks. Triangle period (about 1745–9): a small production of wares and figures, many of them in the white. Raised Anchor period (about 1749–52): increasing sophistication is shown in the figures and in the painting of wares. Red Anchor period (about 1752–8): the most prosperous and artistically successful period (many of the best figures date from this time; these are probably modelled by Joseph Willems). Gold Anchor period (about 1758–79): a smaller production, mainly of luxury items including many vases and scent-bottles, with increased use of coloured grounds and elaborate gilding in the Sèvres manner. Chelsea-Derby period (about 1770–84). After a short interval, when the factory was owned by James Cox, it was resold to William Duesbury, who ran it in tandem with his Derby porcelain factory. Neo-classical forms were introduced during this period. In 1784 the Chelsea factory closed and all moveable stock and models removed to Derby. A legend that Dr Johnson attempted to make porcelain at the Chelsea factory is probably based on a misunderstanding.

Chelsea Rectory *Old Church Street, SW3.* Stands on the east side of OLD CHURCH STREET, within a brick wall. It has been rebuilt on several occasions but parts date back to about 1566. There is a magnificent garden (*see* GARDENS). Among many famous rectors of CHELSEA were the Hon. Valerian Wellesley, Charles Kingsley and Gerald Blunt.

Chelsea School of Art *Manresa Road, SW3.* Opened by Sir Isaac Hayward on 25 March 1965. Before that it formed part of Chelsea Polytechnic, now Chelsea College. It is one of London's best known, and possibly at times most fashionable, art schools. It offers graduate and postgraduate courses in fine art, printmaking, sculpture, ceramics and design. The school has several annexes where students have studio space to work in. Most lecturers are well known British artists. The Liberal Studies department offers art history and other art related subjects and the college has

an excellent library. The sculpture in the forecourt, *Two-piece Reclining Figure*, is by Henry Moore (1959, placed here 1969).

Chelsea Square *SW3.* Originally called Trafalgar Square. When the LONDON COUNTY COUNCIL renamed many streets in the 1920s the oldest established thoroughfares kept their original names. Chelsea's Trafalgar Square existed long before the one in WESTMINSTER, but the name of the latter far more famous square could hardly be altered, so that of CHELSEA was changed. Two beautiful white houses, Nos 41 and 42, designed by Oliver Hill (1935), sharing a magnificent garden with very old trees, stand on the west side.

Chelsea Waterworks Company Incorporated in 1723 'for the better supplying the City and Liberties of Westminster and parts adjacent with water'. There were 2,000 shares of £20 each and the tide-mill works were established near the THAMES on a site now covered by the CHURCHILL GARDENS Estate. The low-lying canals were filled at high tide and the water retained until low tide by sluice gates. Later these were opened to run a water-mill that in turn ran the pumps. By 1726 the waterworks supplied reservoirs in HYDE PARK and ST JAMES'S PARK and preparations were being made to lay pipes 'through all Westminster including Grosvenor Square, Hanover Square and all places adjacent'. A horse mill pumped the water to the higher ground near GROSVENOR SQUARE. In 1729 the ST JAMES'S PARK reservoir was enlarged, indicating continued expansion. The following year the Company received £2,500 compensation from the Crown for relinquishing the right to have water pipes in KENSINGTON GARDENS which were being improved by Queen Caroline. In 1733 the capital of the Company was increased from £40,000 to £70,000 by a new share issue. At this time the Company was charging £150 p.a. to supply water to KENSINGTON PALACE and the Round Pond. It was also permitted to take the overflow from the Serpentine in HYDE PARK. And, in 1736, the HYDE PARK reservoir (on the east side of the park opposite STANHOPE GATE) was enlarged. It supplied KENSINGTON PALACE and 'the new buildings about Oliver's Mount', and the 'Northern parts of Westminster'. The Company introduced the first iron main in London in 1746. Two atmospheric engines were installed in 1741–2, but the tide-mill continued to assist them until at least 1775. In 1755 a new cut was made from the THAMES to near BUCKINGHAM HOUSE garden wall. The cuts and canals were eventually to extend over 89 acres of today's PIMLICO. By 1767, 1,750 tons of water were pumped daily. From 1803 water began to be taken directly from the river. In 1823 the GROSVENOR CANAL was built; and in 1826 the GREEN PARK reservoir cleaned and deepened. In 1827 a petition to the HOUSE OF COMMONS by Sir Francis Burdett alleged that 'the water taken from the River Thames at Chelsea, for the use of the inhabitants of the western part of the metropolis, being charged with the contents of the great common sewers, the drainings from dunghills, and laystalls, the refuse of hospitals, slaughter houses, colour, lead and soap works, drug mills and manufactories, and with all sorts of decomposed animal and vegetable substances, rendering the said water offensive and destructive to health, ought no longer to be taken up by any of the water companies

Chelsea Waterworks in 1725, the source of supply for reservoirs in Hyde Park and St James's Park.

from so foul a source.' In 1829 the Company became the first to introduce slow sand filtration in order to purify their river water. The filter was designed by the Company's engineer, James Simpson, and comprised successive beds of loose brick, gravel and sand. The scheme cost £12,000. In 1835 the Company was supplying two million gallons daily to 13,000 houses. In 1856 new works were established at SURBITON, adjoining those of the LAMBETH WATERWORKS COMPANY. Three new reservoirs at PUTNEY HEATH supplied the old Chelsea works. After 1876 the intake came from near Walton, 5 miles upstream. In 1902 the Metropolitan Water Board took over the functions of the Company (*see* WATER SUPPLY).

Chelsfield *Kent*. In *Domesday Book* it is referred to as Cillesfelle. The *Textus Roffensis* of 1122 refers to Cilesfeld. There are various conjectures about the derivation of the name. *Feld* means field or plain. The Old English *ceol* was a personal name; *ceorl* means a Saxon freeman; *ceald* is Saxon for cold; whilst *cisil* is Anglo-Saxon for gravel. All have been suggested. The church, which stands some distance from the village, is dedicated to St Martin of Tours. It was rebuilt in the 13th century but has been little altered since. Sir Otho de Grandison was Lord of the Manor in 1300, and in his will dated 1369, he asked that if he died at Chelsfield, he should be buried in the church there. Later the property came into the possession of the DUCHY OF LANCASTER. It then passed through various hands until in the 18th century it was acquired by Brass Crosby, Lord Mayor of London in 1770–1. It is still essentially a village, though in the London Borough of BROMLEY.

Cheltenham Terrace *SW3*. This attractive short street faces the grounds of the DUKE OF YORK'S HEAD-QUARTERS, its name probably chosen by the builder of ST LEONARD'S TERRACE who was born in Gloucestershire. A large block of flats, Whitelands House, now stands at the corner with the KING'S ROAD, on the site of an 18th-century building of interesting history. This was a girls' school in 1772. It was purchased in

1842 by the National Society for Training School-mistresses and named Whitelands Training College – it later moved to PUTNEY. In 1881 John Ruskin instituted a May Day Festival which he regularly attended and at which he presented a copy of *Sesame and Lilies* to each May Queen. The headquarters of the British Union of Fascists was here until the beginning of the 2nd World War.

Chenies Street *WC1*. Built in about 1776 on the BEDFORD ESTATE and named after a manor in Buckinghamshire belonging to Anne Sapcote, wife of John Russell, 1st Earl of Bedford. Madame d'Arblay, the novelist and diarist, better known by her maiden name, Fanny Burney, lived at No. 23 in 1812–13.

Cherry Garden Pier *Rotherhithe, SE16*. A landing stage for Cherry Garden, a popular 17th-century retreat. Pepys left 'singing finely' after his visit in 1664. J.M.W. Turner painted the *Téméraire* from here. At this point ships sound their hooters if they want TOWER BRIDGE raised.

Chesham Place *SW1*. Built in 1831 and named after Chesham in Buckinghamshire where the Lowndes family, who owned the land, had a country estate. Lord John Russell lived at No. 37 in 1841–57 and 1859–70. George Harvey, the American Ambassador, lived at No. 29 in 1922. The Embassy of the Republic of Zaire is at No. 26; the Finnish Embassy at No. 38; the Embassy of the State of Qatar at No. 27. The Ladbroke Belgravia Hotel is at No. 20. The bronze, *Flora*, is by Fritz Koenig (1978). The handsome new West German Embassy completed in 1979 is by the Munich architects, Walther and Bea Betz.

Cheshire Cheese, Ye Olde *Wine Office Court, Fleet Street, EC4*. Familiarly known as 'The House', this old oak-beamed public house retains much of the atmosphere of the London chophouse of the late 18th and 19th centuries. It was frequented by Charles Dickens who allegedly chose to sit at the table to the right of the fireplace in the ground-floor room opposite the bar. A portrait over the fireplace in the bar depicts a waiter, William Simpson, resting a hand on this table in 1829. Its once celebrated puddings made of beef steaks, kidneys, oysters, larks, mushrooms and spices, each weighing 50–80 lb, are mentioned in Galsworthy's *Forsyte Saga*. A notice outside lists the 15 reigns in which the place has been in existence and another proclaims its celebrated visitors: 'Here came Johnson's friends, Reynolds, Gibbon, Garrick, Dr Burney, Boswell and others of his circle. In the 19th century came Carlyle, Macaulay, Tennyson, Dickens (who mentions the Court in *A Tale of Two Cities*), Forster, Hood, Thackeray, Cruikshank, Leech and Wilkie Collins. More recently came Mark Twain, Theodore Roosevelt, Conan Doyle, Beerbohm, Chesterton, Dowson, Le Gallienne, Symons, Yeats and a host of others in search of Dr Johnson's "The Cheese".' There is no direct evidence of Johnson ever having been to the Cheshire Cheese, but as WINE OFFICE COURT is one of the approaches to GOUGH SQUARE it seems most unlikely that he did not. The Victorian journalist, Cyrus Redding, recalled having met people who had seen Johnson and his friends here. In particular Redding mentioned a very old gentleman who remembered Johnson nightly at the Cheshire Cheese. After moving from INNER TEMPLE LANE Johnson preferred it to the MITRE and the ESSEX HEAD because 'nothing but a hurricane would have induced him to cross Fleet Street'.

An eccentric parrot named Polly was once a much admired inhabitant. On Armistice Night 1918 this bird imitated the popping of a champagne cork 400 times and then fainted. On its death, aged 40, in 1926 obituaries appeared in 200 newspapers.

Chessington *Surrey*. A small village in 1900, Chessington grew rapidly after the 1st World War and was amalgamated with the Urban District of SURBITON in 1933. The southern fringe towards Leatherhead is still rural today and marks the limit of the GREATER LONDON COUNCIL County Boundary. TELEGRAPH HILL at 248 ft is the highest point in KINGSTON Borough. On nearby Castle Hill are earthworks, the site of a medieval moated homestead or farmhouse, listed as an Ancient Monument. Below Winey Hill stands Burnt Stub, a castellated, pseudo-Gothic 19th-century mansion now incorporated into Chessington Zoological Gardens, the largest privately owned zoo in the country, founded in 1931.

The parish church of St Mary the Virgin in Garrison Lane has much medieval work in its structure, mainly 13th-century. The building is of flints with a timbered porch. A short, shingled spire rises from the western tower. The nave and chancel display Early English lancet windows. The east window of two lights was inserted in the 17th century. There is much interesting woodwork, including the timbered nave pillars, the chancel roof and the arcading of a *sedilia* on the chancel south wall. The vestry door is 14th-century. Restorations were carried out in 1853 and 1870. Of its valuable furniture, the most prized is a silver chalice, one of the smallest in the country, being only 3⅜ inches high. It bears the date 1568 and the mark of its London maker. Chessington Hall, sold in 1913 and subsequently demolished, was a favourite resort of the 18th-century novelist and diarist Fanny Burney. It was the home of Samuel Crisp whom Miss Burney referred to as 'Daddy Crisp'.

Chester Square *SW1*. A smaller version of EATON SQUARE laid out in 1840 by Thomas Cubitt. ST MICHAEL'S CHURCH on the west side is by Thomas Cundy, 1844. Mary Wollstonecraft Shelley, widow of the poet and author of *Frankenstein*, died at No. 24 in 1851. Matthew Arnold lived at No. 2 from 1839 until 1867 when he was 'fairly driven out of Chester Square, partly by the number of our children, partly by the necessity of a better school for the boys'. He moved to HARROW. John St Loe Strachey, editor of the *Spectator*, was living at No. 76 in 1926. Queen Wilhelmina of the Netherlands had her secretariat at No. 77 in 1940–5.

Chester Terrace *NW1*. Takes its name from one of George IV's youthful titles, Earl of Chester. Designed by John Nash, it was built by James Burton in 1825. One of the most handsome and successful of the terraces, its characteristic features are the archways which link the individual parts. The original intention was to place a statue on top of each of the 52 Corinthian capitals which adorn the façade but, after the work had been put in hand, John Nash decided the statues looked absurd and they were withdrawn. The terrace was carefully restored after the 2nd World War, the units remaining as houses.

Chesterfield Gardens *W1*. A short cul-de-sac leading off the north side of CURZON STREET. It was laid out in mid-Victorian times on part of the gardens of CHESTERFIELD HOUSE. On the west side are vast blocks of modern flats, but on the east side is a fine range of five opulent stone-faced houses put up when the street was formed.

Chesterfield Hill *W1*. Known as John Street until 1940, it was originally part of Lord Berkeley's lands (*see* BERKELEY SQUARE), and takes its old name from one of the three Lords Berkeley called John. It extends from CHARLES STREET to FARM STREET, and building began here in the 1740s. At the west corner of John Street and CHARLES STREET formerly stood the Berkeley Chapel, built about 1750, where the Revd Sydney Smith later made his reputation as a preacher. Near the south end there are still some good 18th-century houses.

Chesterfield House *Great Stanhope Street*. Palladian-style mansion built in 1748-9 by Isaac Ware for Philip, 4th Earl of Chesterfield, brilliant and witty author of the *Letters to his Son* and recipient of the famous letter of rebuke from Samuel Johnson. Among other features, the house contained marble columns and the grand staircase from the demolished CANONS PARK, Edgware. 'The staircase particularly will form such a scene, as is not in England,' wrote Lord Chesterfield, 'The expense will ruin me, but the enjoyment will please me.' At the house-warming party the Duke of Hamilton fell in love with the beautiful Miss Gunning and married her two days later with a curtain ring at the Mayfair Chapel, CURZON STREET. In 1870 part of the garden, which Lord Chesterfield had thought 'a scene of verdure', was leased for the development of CHESTERFIELD GARDENS. The 6th Earl of Harewood lived here after his marriage to the Princess Royal. The house was demolished in 1937.

Chesterfield House *Greenwich see* RANGER'S HOUSE, Greenwich.

Chesterfield Street *W1*. Extends from CURZON STREET to CHARLES STREET. The houses on the west side originally backed on to the garden of CHESTER-FIELD HOUSE. Today all but one of the houses on both sides are still basically 18th-century, and this is probably the least altered street in the whole of MAYFAIR. Somerset Maugham, the playwright and novelist, lived here, at No. 6, in 1911–19.

Cheval Place *SW7*. Originally a small cul-de-sac running north to stables at the west end of Brompton Row. ST JOHN'S CHAPEL (now BONHAM'S auction rooms) was built in 1769 and Cheval Lane ran down beside the chapel to give access to the fields north of Brompton Row. It became gradually built up with stables, cow sheds, a smithy and small poor-class houses some of which remain behind the prettified exteriors. Its name is derived from *cheval*, horse. The stables here were much frequented by French residents of BROMPTON.

Cheyne Gardens *SW3*. These houses at the southern end of CHELSEA MANOR STREET were built in about 1890. They replaced the first houses which had been built not long after 1712 when the new owner of the Manor of CHELSEA, Sir Hans Sloane, began the development of his property by building on the garden of CHELSEA MANOR HOUSE.

Cheyne Place *SW3*. Twentieth-century houses and flats of varying styles on the north side of ROYAL HOSPITAL ROAD overlooking CHELSEA PHYSIC GARDEN.

Cheyne Row *SW3*. A charming row of Queen Anne Houses on the west side built in 1703 on property leased from Lord Cheyne. Thomas Carlyle lived at No. 24 from 1834 and died there in 1881. He was visited by almost every literary celebrity of the day. The house was acquired for the nation in 1895 and passed to the NATIONAL TRUST in 1936 (*see* CARLYLE'S HOUSE). At the northern end is the CHURCH OF THE HOLY REDEEMER built in 1895 on the site of Orange House where William De Morgan had a warehouse and showroom for his pottery in 1876–82. He lived at No. 30. A plaque at No. 10 commemorates Margaret Damer Dawson, a pioneer of women in the police force.

Cheyne Walk *SW3*. Like CHEYNE Court, GARDENS, MEWS, PLACE and ROW, it takes its name from the Cheyne family who were lords of the manor of Chelsea from 1660 to 1712. Cheyne Walk extends from ALBERT BRIDGE to CREMORNE ROAD and contains many beautiful Queen Anne houses and others of interesting later design. Among them is No. 3, lived in by Sir John Goss, organist of ST PAUL'S CATHEDRAL, and Admiral Henry Smyth, one of the founders of the ROYAL GEOGRAPHICAL SOCIETY. In 1942 the NATIONAL TRUST acquired the house for the Benton Fletcher collection of musical instruments (now at FENTON HOUSE, HAMPSTEAD). No. 4, built in 1718, has a beautiful doorway and wrought iron work, as have Nos 5 and 15. Those of No. 5 are believed to have come from LINDSEY HOUSE. George Eliot lived at No. 4 at the end of her life. The artists, William Dyce and Daniel Maclise, also lived here for a time. No. 5 was occupied for many years by a miser named John Camden Neild who left his fortune to Queen Victoria. No. 6 was built by Sir John Danvers in about 1718. Dr Domincetti, an Italian, moved into the house in 1765 and spent over £37,000 in building brick and wood structures in the garden. He introduced medicated baths and treated thousands of patients. Heavily in debt, he left this house in 1782. Nos 7–12 were built in the 1880s. No. 10 was lived in by Earl Lloyd George in 1924–5 and later by Archbishop Lord Davidson. Nos 15–17 were built in 1717–19. No. 16, designed by John Witt, is known as Queen's House. In 1862 Dante Gabriel Rossetti, Algernon Swinburne and

Parrott's 1841 lithograph shows Cheyne Walk's Queen Anne houses with (left) the Old Church, and (right) Sir Hans Sloane's tomb.

George Meredith took the house jointly. Rossetti kept a small zoo, including many peacocks who were so distressingly noisy that subsequent Cadogan leases include a clause prohibiting the keeping of these birds. The house became a meeting place for poets and artists during the years 1871–81. No. 17 was for a time the home of Thomas Attwood, a pupil of Mozart and organist of ST PAUL's in 1796. No. 18, known as DON SALTERO's, was a coffee house originally established in 1695 further along Cheyne Walk. It was moved to No. 18 in 1718 by James Salter, a barber and former servant of Sir Hans Sloane. He built up a bizarre collection of curios given him by Sir Hans Sloane and others. After his death his daughter ran a comic museum here until 1799 when the contents were sold for £50. The house then became a tavern and was rebuilt in 1867. Nos 19–20 date from about 1760 and replaced the New Manor House built in Tudor times. Nos 38 and 39 were designed by C.R. Ashbee in the 1890s. Nos 46–48 are of about 1711. After the King's Head and Eight Bells (on the site of a much older public house) are Carlyle Mansions where Henry James lived and died, and the Cheyne Hospital for Children, now the Spastic Children's Day Centre. Both are of red brick and were built in about 1880. Beyond CHELSEA OLD CHURCH are Roper Gardens, created on the site of Lombard Terrace which was bombed in the 2nd World War. CROSBY HALL stands on the corner of DANVERS STREET. On the west side of BEAUFORT STREET are No. 91, formerly Belle Vue Lodge and No. 92, Belle Vue House, both built in 1771 with attractive Venetian style windows. Mrs Gaskell was born at No. 93 in 1810. Nos 96–100 form LINDSEY HOUSE. No. 96 was occupied by the painter, Whistler, in 1866–78. No. 97 had a succession of owners but was unoccupied for 108 years. It is said to contain the original staircase of the old house. No. 98 was the home of John Martyn in 1840–54. Sir Marc Brunel, engineer, designer and builder of the THAMES TUNNEL and his son Isambard, designer of the *Great Eastern*, lived here. No. 101 was where Whistler lived when he first came to CHELSEA and where he met the Greaves brothers, Walter and Henry, who lived at No. 103. Hilaire Belloc lived at No. 104 in 1901–5. No. 109 was the home of the painter Philip Wilson Steer from 1898 until his death in 1942. No. 119 was the home of J.M.W. Turner who lived there under the name of Booth (*see* TURNER'S HOUSE). Beyond BATTERSEA BRIDGE and opposite LINDSEY HOUSE lies the Chelsea Basin where many houseboats are moored. Cheyne Walk is rich in sculpture: P. Lindsay Clark's *Boy with Cat* bronze (1925); David Wynne's bronze *Boy with a Dolphin* (1975) opposite Albert Bridge; west of the bridge, *Atlanta*, nude bronze by Francis Derwent Wood (1929); in Roper Gardens, Epstein's unfinished relief of a nude girl (1972) and Gilbert Ledward's bronze, *Awakening* (1965); and at the west end of the gardens in which Carlyle's statue stands (*see* STATUES) is Charles Pibworth's stone birdbath (1933).

Chichester Rents *WC2*. Takes its name from the Bishops of Chichester whose mansion off CHANCERY LANE (*see* LINCOLN'S INN) came into the possession of Ralph Neville, the then Bishop and Chancellor, in the early 13th century.

Chief Commoner The spokesman and acknowledged leader of the COURT OF COMMON COUNCIL is always the Chairman of the City Lands and BRIDGE HOUSE ESTATES Committee of the CORPORATION OF LONDON. This is their senior committee, having been founded in 1592. It administers those funds of the CITY OF LONDON which derive from its rights and privileges as an ancient corporation. The Chairman has thus acquired a special status; the expression 'Chief Commoner' was used to describe him by 1880 and has gradually become his official title. A new Chairman is elected every year.

Child and Co. *1 Fleet Street, EC4*. Francis Child, who inherited the Blanchard family's old-established goldsmith's business, began banking at the Marygold by Temple Bar in 1673. Rebuilt in 1879, the bank has remained at the same site to the present day. Child and Co. developed a small but influential clientele in London society with strong connections with the legal profession and the Oxford colleges. In 1924, after the death of the 8th Earl of Jersey (the senior partner), the business was sold to Glyn, Mills and Co. The bank is now the Child's Branch of WILLIAMS AND GLYN'S BANK.

Child's Coffee House *Warwick Lane*. Established at the end of the 17th century and much frequented by clergymen, lawyers and by doctors from the nearby College of Physicians. In September 1716 the proprietress of Child's was defrauded of a large sum of money by one Dr Mead when 'she received a note by the penny post, which appeared to come from Dr Mead ... saying that a parcel would be sent there for him from Bristol, containing ... drugs ... and begging her to pay the bearer ... The bundle was brought, the money paid; the Doctor declared his ignorance of the transaction, the parcel was opened, and the contents found to be rags.' Many references to visits by James Boswell are to be found in his *London Journal*. It closed soon after Boswell's death.

Chingford *E4*. Situated north of WALTHAMSTOW, between the River LEA and EPPING FOREST. Chingford was the Saxon 'ford of the dwellers by the stumps' where pile dwellings were built in the marshland by the LEA. The Bourne River, renamed the Ching, flows down the eastern boundary, through HIGHAMS PARK and WALTHAMSTOW towards the LEA. The original settlement was probably in this region but by the 12th and 13th centuries settlement had occurred in forest clearings on higher ground. Fisheries existed by the 11th century and a church by the 12th, probably on the site of ALL SAINTS which was named by 1397. The clay soil of the eastern ridge encouraged potteries and brick-making. There was royal deer hunting in the area until the 17th century and Henry VIII, after acquiring the manor of Chingford St Paul's from the Dean and Chapter of ST PAUL's, was responsible for much forest clearance. His project for Fairmead Park in the north of the parish was abandoned, but a standing from which to view the hunt, the so-called Queen Elizabeth's Hunting Lodge, survives. Larkshall farmhouse dates from the 16th century and Pimps Hall, bought by Sir George Monoux of WALTHAMSTOW in 1538, has a surviving 17th century barn and dovecote. By the 17th century there was a route near the LEA leading from Waltham Abbey to WALTHAMSTOW and London, and a bridge crossed the river at Cook's Ferry, between the present Banbury and Girling reservoirs. Dairy farming predominated and the rural landscape with small villages such as those at Chingford Hatch and Chingford Green changed little until the late 19th century. The weatherboarded Carbis Cottage is a contemporary example of many of its kind. R.B. Heathcote, rector of ALL SAINTS (1829–65), whose family had come into possession, in the previous century, of the manor of Chingford Earls (owned by the Earl of Essex in the 15th century) was responsible for a new rectory (1829), Friday Hill House (Lewis Vulliamy, 1839; now a community centre) and a new parish church of St Peter and St Paul (Lewis Vulliamy, 1844; addition by Sir Arthur Blomfield, 1903) at Chingford Green. In the 19th century, the Pole Hill obelisk was also erected (1824). This marked the direction of true north from GREENWICH until the meridian was moved 19° eastwards in 1850. Urban development followed the Great Eastern Railway's extension from WALTHAMSTOW to Chingford in 1873, while the 1878 Epping Forest Act ensured that 300 acres were reclaimed as parkland and recreation grounds now within easy reach of London. At the beginning of the 20th century the EAST LONDON WATERWORKS CO. acquired marshland on the LEA and created the present-day landscape of reservoirs (King George V, 1913; William Girling, 1951). In 1965 Chingford became part of the London Borough of WALTHAM FOREST.

Chippendale's Workshop *60–61 St Martin's Lane*. Let as a workshop to Thomas Chippendale and his partner, James Rannie, in 1754. That same year Chippendale published his *Gentleman and Cabinet-maker's Director*, the first comprehensive trade catalogue of its kind, which contained illustrations of his designs. David Garrick ordered furniture for his house in the ADELPHI, Teresa Cornelys for CARLISLE HOUSE, SOHO SQUARE, Lord Mansfield for KENWOOD and Lord Shelburne for LANSDOWNE HOUSE, BERKELEY SQUARE. Chippendale died in 1779 leaving the business to his eldest son, who had been trained in his father's workshop and who was declared bankrupt in 1804. 'The beautiful Mahogany Cabinet Work of the first class, including many articles of great taste and of the finest workmanship,' was auctioned in two days.

Chislehurst *Kent*. The name is derived from the Saxon for a wood on gravel. It is centred on its wooded common, and has many old buildings. The manor was bought in 1611 by Sir Thomas Walsingham of neighbouring SCADBURY, and the two manors were held jointly thereafter. The Walsinghams were eminent in public life: Sir Edward was Lieutenant of the TOWER OF LONDON, and Sir Francis, born at SCADBURY, was Queen Elizabeth I's Secretary of State. Although the moated manor house was pulled down in the 18th century, the Walsinghams are remembered locally. The village sign depicts Queen Elizabeth knighting Thomas Walsingham when she visited him here in 1597. Sir Thomas was patron of Christopher Marlowe, the poet and playwright, who spent some time here. The old Tiger's Head Inn derives its name from the Walsingham family crest.

On the Common, which has been well protected, is the village cockpit – a rare survival, as cockfighting was prohibited from 1834. The old Poor House, where at one time the daily ration was one herring and three potatoes, was built on the Common in 1759. Later used as a school and as tenements, it has been part of St Michael's Orphanage since 1855. Nearby buildings, including schools and the Crown public house, were erected on land taken from the Common at a yearly rent of 'two fat pulletts'. There was a windmill until 1876, also partly on Common ground, and it is said that when Napoleon III was at CAMDEN PLACE the French Republic had spies at the top of the mill, and the Emperor had counter-spies at the bottom.

To the west are Chislehurst Caves, remains of chalk mines said to date from Roman times. These underground passages, now open to the public, have had many uses, and formed an extensive air-raid shelter, including a church, in the 2nd World War. The coming of the railway in 1865 meant an increased demand for housing from people needing to travel to London, but development was not so rapid here as in neighbouring districts. A number of the older, large houses were, however, eventually demolished and their grounds became housing estates, fields were built over, and the High Street has been greatly changed in recent years; but the protected Common and other public woodlands and recreation grounds, and the number of preserved old buildings, help to give a feeling of space and reserve Chislehurst's individuality.

Chiswell Street *EC1*. The origin of the name is unknown. In 1741 George Dance, the architect, was born in the street and lived here until 1775, the year in which James Lackington, the celebrated bookseller, began business here. At the west end is Whitbread's BREWERY which has been here since Samuel Whitbread, founder of the firm, moved from OLD STREET in 1750. George III and Queen Charlotte came to inspect it. H.W. Caslon and Co., the type founders and designers of the famous Caslon typeface, had their foundry here in the 18th century. Over the door of Diana House (No. 34) is Fleischmann's gilded concrete *Diana* (1953).

Chiswick *W4*. About 6 miles west of HYDE PARK CORNER, Chiswick is situated in a loop of the River THAMES south of ACTON, with HAMMERSMITH to the east and BRENTFORD to the west. There is uncertainty as to the origin of its name which some say means Cheese Farm, and others the village by the Stony Beach. It does not appear in *Domesday Book* as at that time it was part of the BISHOP OF LONDON's Manor of FULHAM. The original village grew up by the THAMES round the old parish church of ST NICOLAS, the houses being mostly by the river and along what is now Church Street and the southern end of Chiswick Lane. From early times there were hamlets beside the river at STRAND-ON-THE-GREEN and at TURNHAM GREEN along the main road to the west. During later medieval times the parish comprised two manors, the Manor of Sutton and the Prebendal Manor, both of which belonged to the Dean and Chapter of ST PAUL'S. Until the mid-19th century Chiswick was still a comparatively rural place of large estates, such as CHISWICK HOUSE, GROVE HOUSE AND SUTTON COURT, interspersed with farms, market gardens and numerous smaller houses in their own grounds. In 1801 the population was only 3,235, growing to 15,663 in 1881 and 28,513 in 1901. Like many other places Chiswick did not begin to develop until the coming of the railways. The first station was opened in 1849 on what is now the Southern Region and in 1869 TURNHAM GREEN Station and Gunnersbury, then known as Brentford

153

Road, were opened. Horse-trams between HAMMER-SMITH and KEW BRIDGE were started in 1882 to be succeeded in 1901 by the electric trams of the London United Tramway Company whose original headquarters and power station in Chiswick High Road, just west of Young's Corner, are now the Stamford Brook Garage of London Transport buses. Gradually the big houses were demolished and their grounds built upon. SUTTON COURT was pulled down in 1896 and a block of flats built on the site. Although much of the GROVE HOUSE estate had been developed the house and its immediate surroundings survived until 1928. Near and along Chiswick High Road houses which had stood in their own grounds gradually disappeared in the 19th century to be replaced by shops, flats or smaller houses. Many, such as Belmont House, Arlington House, Heathfield House and Linden House, are commemorated in street names. The final infilling between the High Road and the river did not take place until between the two wars. One reason for the rather slow development of Chiswick was probably that much of the land was owned by the Dukes of Devonshire, the owners of CHISWICK HOUSE. In 1822 the ROYAL HORTICULTURAL SOCIETY leased land from the Duke of Devonshire to establish gardens at Chiswick. Wavendon Avenue, Hadley Gardens and part of Barrowgate Road are now on the site. The Society gave up most of its land in 1870 but retained 10 or 11 acres until 1904 when they transferred the gardens to Wisley. As the population grew the old parish was divided and in the 19th century the churches of Christchurch, Turnham Green, St Paul, Grove Park and St James, Gunnersbury, were built while St Michael's, Sutton Court was not built until 1909.

Chiswick has never been industrial but what is now Fuller, Smith and Turner's BREWERY began as a small local brewery some 300 years ago. In 1866 John Thornycroft, elder son of the eminent sculptor, Thomas Thornycroft, started the shipbuilding yard near the old parish church which grew into a world famous firm, building ships for the British and foreign navies, and which was finally transferred to Woolston, Southampton in 1904. The opening of the

CHISWICK BRIDGE across the THAMES in 1933 and the building of the road to serve it began to break up the old rural aspect of Chiswick. This change in the appearance of the area was continued after the 2nd World War by the completion of the GREAT WEST ROAD. Many changes since 1945 include the replacement of the Chiswick Empire Theatre by a tall office block, and the building of a tower block at Gunnersbury Station as well as development of war damaged areas and other parts with new council and private flats, houses and offices.

Chiswick Bridge *Chiswick–Mortlake.* Built in 1933 with three concrete arches with Portland stone facing by A. Dryland with Sir Herbert Baker. It takes the Great Chertsey Road (A316) over the river. It is the finishing point of the UNIVERSITY BOAT RACE.

Chiswick House *Burlington Lane, W4.* A magnificent country villa modelled on Palladio's Villa Rotonda at Vicenza by the 3rd Earl of Burlington in 1725–9. The interior's spectacular plaster ceilings and Inigo Jones-inspired fireplace are by William Kent. The Earl lived in an adjacent Jacobean mansion (which was demolished in 1758) and used the new villa for displaying his works of art and entertaining groups of his friends who included Pope, Swift, Handel, Gay, Rysbrack and Bishop Berkeley. The villa was inherited in 1753 by the 4th Duke of Devonshire. In 1788 James Wyatt added wings to the north and south for the 5th Duke (these were demolished in 1952). In 1806 Charles James Fox died here; and in the same room George Canning died in 1827. In 1892 the 8th Duke moved to Chatsworth and the house became a private mental home. It was purchased by the MIDDLESEX County Council in 1928 and was subsequently well restored by the Ministry of Works. The gardens, laid out by Kent and Bridgman, were the first in England to break with the formal Dutch tradition. They were long neglected and many of the follies fell down or were demolished. There remain an Ionic temple, a Doric column, statues of Caesar, Pompey and Cicero brought from Hadrian's Villa at Tivoli, two obelisks (one incorporating a Roman tombstone),

Chiswick House as it appeared in 1745. The old Jacobean mansion which can be seen to the right was demolished in 1758.

a cascade, an avenue of urns and sphinxes, a rustic house, a deer house, Inigo Jones's gateway from BEAUFORT HOUSE, CHELSEA, James Wyatt's bridge of 1788 and a large conservatory attributed to Joseph Paxton.

Chiswick Mall *Chiswick, W4.* Runs beside the THAMES from the bottom of Church Street to the HAMMERSMITH border. Although the houses appear to date from the 17th to the 20th centuries it is likely that some are older and have been refaced. Bedford and Eynham Houses, not far from the junction with Church Street, were originally one, built, or rebuilt, about the middle of the 17th century by Edward Russell, son of the 4th Earl of Bedford. Red Lion House, opposite the Draw Dock, was the Red Lion Inn until the 1st World War. Said House was the home of Sir Nigel Playfair, the actor-manager, who in the 1920s was well-known for his productions at the old LYRIC THEATRE, HAMMERSMITH. Walpole House is named after the Walpole family, some of whom, including the Hon. Thomas Walpole, nephew of Sir Robert Walpole, are buried in Chiswick church. The house is said to have been the home of Barbara, Duchess of Cleveland, favourite of Charles II. Later it was a school, at which Thackeray was a boarder, and which is thought to have suggested Miss Pinkerton's Academy in *Vanity Fair*. The houses at the eastern corner of Chiswick Lane are built on the site of College House, originally the Manor House of the Prebendal Manor and demolished in 1875. It came to be called College House when leased by WESTMINSTER SCHOOL in 1570 as a retreat from London in time of plague. In the 19th century it was the home of the Chiswick Press, from which many books were issued between 1810 and 1852 by the Charles Whittinghams, uncle and nephew. Daniel O'Connell had lodgings in Chiswick Mall when a law student in 1796. Herbert Beerbohm Tree lived here in 1904–5.

Cholera As trade routes opened in the early 19th century between Europe and the East, cholera spread from India, where it was endemic. The disease reached Britain in October 1831, and within the next few months there were over 6,000 deaths. In 1848–9 some 14,000 people died out of 30,000 cases. There were 10,675 deaths in 1854; and in 1866 more than 5,000 died within three weeks.

Cholera was universally dreaded because no cure existed. As a bacterial disease of the gut, first symptoms were painless diarrhoea, followed by vomiting and dehydration of the body. The disease had a 50 per cent mortality, either within hours, or at the most within two days of its onset.

Some medical authorities believed that cholera was caused by an aerial poison produced by the putrefaction of bodies or rotting vegetables. Dr John Snow, the 40 year-old vice-president of the Westminster Medical Society, and Queen Victoria's obstetrician, disagreed with this theory. He believed that cholera was water-borne, for the highest casualty rates were from those who drew water from a pump in Broad Street. Dr Snow persuaded the authorities to remove the handle from this pump, and the incidence of cholera in the area quickly dropped.

During the third epidemic, Snow found that the worst areas of cholera were SOUTHWARK and VAUXHALL. Both districts obtained water from a part of the THAMES contaminated by sewage from ships and the CITY itself. Cholera had apparently been re-introduced to London aboard ships arriving from the Baltic, and discharging untreated sewage into the THAMES. Snow's theory met with initial opposition, but was later vindicated and resulted in great improvements to London's sanitation and WATER SUPPLY arrangements. (*See also* DRAINS AND SEWERS.)

Christ Church *Albany Street, W1.* Built to the designs of James Pennethorne in 1837 in yellow brick with a slender tower and spire. The interior was remodelled in 1867 by William Butterfield, who had earlier designed the font and choir stalls. The stained glass window of the *Sermon on the Mount* was designed by D.G. Rossetti and executed by William Morris.

Christ Church *Blackfriars Road, SE1.* Built in 1671 on part of PARIS GARDEN Manor, it was rebuilt in 1738 and again, after being bombed in the 2nd World War, in 1959. The old chancel was incorporated. The modern stained glass depicts SOUTHWARK'S industries.

Christ Church *Down Street, W1.* Built in the Decorated style in 1865 to the designs of F. and H. Francis. It was enlarged in 1868.

Christ Church Greyfriars *Newgate Street.* The first church built on the site was for Franciscan Friars in 1225 (*see* GREYFRIARS MONASTERY). The heart of Queen Eleanor of Provence, the wife of Henry III, was buried here in 1291 and from then on royal patronage was marked. In 1306 Margaret, the second Queen of Edward I, began rebuilding the church. She died before it was completed and was buried before the high altar. The church was finished in 1348. In size it was second only in the CITY to ST PAUL'S, being 300 ft long, 89 ft wide and 64 ft high. In 1526 a friar recorded 765 burials to date. Many people were buried in a monk's habit to ease their passage to heaven. The monastery was dissolved in 1538. Thereafter the church was at first used to store wine plundered from French ships. In 1547 the chancel was renamed Christ Church and given a parish comprising the former parishes of ST NICHOLAS SHAMBLES, ST EWIN, and part of ST SEPULCHRE. The King's Printer set up his presses in the nave. The gravestones were broken up and the costly materials sold to the Lord Mayor, Sir Martin Bowes, for £50. Destroyed in the GREAT FIRE, the church was rebuilt by Wren in 1687–1704 on the foundations of the old chancel. It was one of his most expensive churches costing £11,778 9s 6d. Inside he put steep side galleries possibly so that the masters from CHRIST'S HOSPITAL could keep an eye on their charges.

Among those buried here were Queen Margaret (1318), Queen Isabella, wife of Edward II (1358), her daughter Joan de la Tour, Queen of Scotland (1362) and Elizabeth Barton, the Holy Maid of Kent, who was hanged at TYBURN in 1534 for preaching against Henry VIII's second marriage. Apart from the steeple, which was erected in 1701–4, the church was destroyed in the BLITZ. The steeple was destroyed by Lord Mottistone in 1960.

Christ Church *Lancaster Gate.* Built on the site of a market garden in 1854–5 to the design of F. and

H. Francis. There were immense congregations in 1879–84 during the incumbency of William Boyd Carpenter, later Bishop of Ripon. Many of the parishioners were wealthy and for many years on Hospital Sunday over £1,000 was collected at Matins: Christ Church consequently became known as 'the Thousand Pound church'. It was demolished, because of structural damage, in 1978.

Christ Church *Spitalfields, E1*. Designed in 1720, it is a grand example of Nicholas Hawksmoor's work. It was one of those churches commissioned to be built under the Fifty New Churches Act of 1711 by which the newly-elected High Church Tory Government celebrated its victory. The money for this venture was raised by a tax on coal. It originally served the Huguenot refugees who had joined the small group of silkweavers living and working in the green fields of Spital. They built up a prosperous community and today more than half of the 18th-century gravestones bear French names. The church has suffered some disastrous 19th-century alterations, largely the work of Ewan Christian, carried out after the church had been struck by lightning in 1841. It is still, however, distinctly one of Hawksmoor's masterpieces. The massive portico of four Tuscan columns and barrel-vaulted arch in the middle is tied to the separate composition of the body of the church by the unusual tower with its octagonal spire – simplified in the 19th century – topped by a delicate finial. The interior conforms to the basilican plan with a rich simplicity of columns and aisles. There are two splendid 18th-century monuments in curved niches on either side of the chancel. The one on the south side was erected in 1737 by John

One of the finest of all Hawksmoor's churches, Christ Church Spitalfields, as it appeared in 1815.

Peck to his father, Edward Peck. It is the work of Thomas Dunn, the mason-contractor who built Christ Church. Edward Peck, who owned a number of houses in the neighbourhood, was one of the original Commissioners of the 'Fifty Churches' and it was he who laid the foundation stone of the church. The second monument on the north side is by the sculptor, John Flaxman. It is to the memory of the banker, Sir Robert Ladbroke, who was Lord Mayor in 1747. In 1965, the sale of ST JOHN'S, SMITH SQUARE, helped towards making it financially possible to embark on a plan to repair the neglected fabric of this fine example of what has come to be known as 'English Baroque'. But, although the flat coffered ceiling has been restored, the church has been out of regular use for some time, and, despite the fact that it is slowly coming back to life with concerts and occasional religious services, the interior still has a forlorn look. The crypt is used as a rehabilitation centre for alcoholics.

Christ Church *Streatham, SW2*. Built in the Italian basilican style in 1840–1 to the designs of John Wild. The campanile rises sheer to a height of 113 ft.

Christ Church *Wanstead (Wanstead Place), E11*. Built of ragstone by Sir George Gilbert Scott in 1861. The north tower is over the porch. The spire and south aisle were added later. The furnishings are unremarkable but there is good Kempe glass in the east window and an attractive Gothic organ case at the east end of the north aisle, serving as a reredos to the aisle altar.

Christchurch *Cosway Street, NW1*. Built in 1822–4 by Philip Hardwick, this church is notable for its east front with Ionic portico before the domed tower which has a large rectangular colonnaded upper stage.

Christchurch *Christchurch Street, SW7*. Brick church built to the designs of Edward Blore in the 1830s. Minor alterations were made in 1900–1 to the designs of W.D. Caröe; new porches were built, the front was extended and a church-room added. The pulpit was brought from ST JAMES GARLICK HILL in 1876 and the organ is from ST MICHAEL QUEENHITHE.

Christchurch *Newgate Street see* GREYFRIARS MONASTERY.

Christ the King *Gordon Square, WC1*. One of the best Gothic Revival churches in the country, designed by Raphael Brandon in 1853 for the Catholic Apostolic Church, a sect begun by Edward Irving at the Church of Scotland REGENT SQUARE. There he encouraged the congregation to stand up and 'utter'. It was frowned upon by his fellow ministers; and Irving was expelled. With some faithful followers he built his own church in Duncan Street ISLINGTON but died in 1834, the year it was finished. Since then the movement has lost its impetus and his followers have dwindled. This church is now used by LONDON UNIVERSITY.

Christ the Saviour *Ealing Broadway, W5*. Originally known as Christchurch, it was built in 1850–2 to the design of Sir George Gilbert Scott. It was paid for by the private benefaction of Miss Rose Frances Lewis in memory of her father. It was designed in the Early English style and built of Kentish rag and Bath stone,

An auction sale of pictures at Christie's. Aquatint after Rowlandson and Pugin in 1808.

with west tower and spire. Interior decoration was added in 1906 by G.F. Bodley but most of the glass was replaced after war damage. St George's Chapel was completed in 1919. It replaces St Mary's (the original parish church) as rebuilt by Teulon in 1866–73.

Christie, Manson and Woods *8 King Street, SW1.* Fine art auctioneers established in 1766 by James Christie, a former midshipman in the Navy who had resigned his commission to become an assistant to Mr Annersley, a COVENT GARDEN auctioneer. He first established himself in business at Great Castle Street, moving in 1767 to an unidentified house in PALL MALL. The following year he moved to Nos 83–84 and in 1770 to No. 125 next door to where Gainsborough was then living. He himself lived at No. 84 until his death in 1803. When he began in PALL MALL he auctioned everything from chamber pots to sedan chairs, but by the turn of the century his sale rooms had become the fashionable place for art sales, doubtless owing much to his friendship with Reynolds, Garrick, Sheridan and Gainsborough. The French Revolution provided a steady flow of paintings. In 1823 his son, another James, moved the business to its present address in KING STREET, where it has remained ever since. In 1831 James Christie took into partnership William Manson. Thomas Woods became a partner in 1859. The last member of the Christie family to take part in the business was James J.B. Christie who retired in 1889. The premises were bombed in the 2nd World War and, after an exile at Derby House and SPENCER HOUSE, the firm returned in 1953 to offices reconstructed behind J. MacVicar Anderson's façade of 1893–4 which had survived. The firm also has premises in OLD BROMPTON ROAD. From £1,760,000 in 1957, annual turnover had increased by 1979 to £125,000,000.

Christ's Hospital *Newgate Street.* Founded in 1553 by Edward VI ten days before his death, as a hospital for orphans. The distinctive long blue coats

and yellow stockings, which the boys still wear, date almost from this time. The colour of the stockings is said to have been chosen to keep away the rats from the boys' ankles. The hospital was given the old GREYFRIARS MONASTERY buildings. 380 children were collected but 'many of them, taken from the dunghill, when they came to swete and cleane keping and to pure dyett, dyed downe righte.' Before long there was a school attached, with a grammar master, writing master, music master, two other teachers and a matron for the girls who became fewer and fewer as time went on. The school was, and is, also known as the Blue Coat School, because of the uniform. In the 17th century the children were often hired out as mutes for funerals. In 1666 many of the buildings were burnt in the GREAT FIRE. Most were rebuilt under the superintendence of Wren. The actual work appears to have been carried out by Hooke and Oliver. Wren began work on designs for the writing school, which were completed by Hawksmoor. New buildings for the girls were opened at Hertford in 1704. Coleridge and Charles Lamb came to the school in 1782 and Leigh Hunt in 1791.

Christ's Hospital and Christchurch, Newgate Street. The old buildings were destroyed in the Great Fire, and rebuilt by Wren.

157

Other, earlier, pupils were William Camden, the antiquary, and Edward Stillingfleet, the eloquent Bishop of Worcester. Edmund Campion, the Roman Catholic martyr, also seems to have attended the school. Thomas Barnes, one of the great editors of *The Times*, was at the school with Leigh Hunt. In 1902, a new school by Aston Webb and Edward Ingress Bell was built at Horsham, Sussex and the GENERAL POST OFFICE was extended over the site of the demolished buildings in London. On St Matthew's Day (21 September) some of the boys return to the CITY to attend a special service with the LORD MAYOR and ALDERMEN at ST SEPULCHRE'S HOLBORN and to have tea at the MANSION HOUSE.

HMS Chrysanthemum Moored in KING'S REACH opposite the TEMPLE, a sloop of the 1st World War which, with HMS WELLINGTON, now serves as the headquarters of the London Division of the Royal Naval Reserve.

Church Commissioners for England *Millbank, SW1.* Established in 1948 by the amalgamation of the Ecclesiastical Commissioners (established in 1836) and Queen Anne's Bounty (established in 1704). Their work includes the management of the capital assets of the Church of England, the proper distribution of the income therefrom and various administrative duties, among which are the payment of clergy stipends and pensions, the building up of capital and the funding of special schemes. Residential property in London belonging to the Commissioners consists mainly of (a) the HYDE PARK Estate ('up-market') between BAYSWATER ROAD, EDGWARE ROAD and SUSSEX GARDENS; (b) the MAIDA VALE Estate ('middle market') mainly to the north of the GRAND UNION CANAL and west of the EDGWARE ROAD; and (c) the 'Octavia Hill' Estates (for residents of modest means) in LAMBETH, WATERLOO, BRIXTON, WALWORTH, VAUXHALL, WESTMINSTER, STOKE NEWINGTON and MAIDA VALE. Their commercial property in London includes offices and shops in various parts of the area, but notably the Paternoster Development in the CITY and the narrow but valuable plot bounded by VICTORIA STATION, VICTORIA STREET, the ARMY AND NAVY STORES and WESTMINSTER CATHEDRAL.

Church End *N3 see* FINCHLEY.

Church Entry *EC4.* Led to the church of ST ANN BLACKFRIARS which was destroyed in the GREAT FIRE. The small churchyard remains.

Church Gate *Fulham, SW6.* A lane leading from Fulham High Street which existed from at least the 14th century and which once had the vicarage of ALL SAINTS on its south-east side. The vicarage was demolished in 1934 and replaced by a public garden. Two of the old houses in the lane survive: Nos 5 and 6, both built in the late 17th century. The Sir William Powell Almshouses by ALL SAINTS' CHURCH were founded in the reign of Charles II and removed from their original site in the High Street in 1869 to their present Gothic style block of 12 dwellings, designed by J.P. Seddon. Steeple Close (the name commemorates the church tower which was known as the steeple), a development of the 1960s by J.J. de Segrais, was built on the site and grounds of Temple House at No. 7.

Church House *Great Smith Street and Dean's Yard, SW1.* Designed by Sir Herbert Baker as a replacement for an earlier building which had been erected as the administrative headquarters of the Church of England. The foundation stone was laid by Queen Mary on 26 June 1937 and the building completed in 1939. On 10 June 1940, King George VI opened the new Church House and attended the first session of the Church Assembly in the Great Circular Hall. Later that year the Assembly Hall was damaged by a bomb and six people were killed. The rest of the building was requisitioned by the Government, and throughout the war thereafter it became the alternative meeting place of both HOUSES OF PARLIAMENT: the Lords sat in the Convocation Hall and the Commons in the Hoare Memorial Hall. Oak panels in both Halls commemorate this use.

By October 1946 some administrative offices of the Church Assembly had returned to Church House, and the Church Assembly was able to return for its autumn session in 1950. The remainder of the administrative offices returned in 1968. Church House has become an important national centre for conferences and meetings. The statue of Christ above the DEAN'S YARD entrance is by Charles Wheeler.

Church of the Annunciation *Bryanston Street, W1.* Designed in the Edwardian Gothic style by Sir Walter Tapper and completed in 1914, it stands on the site of Quebec Chapel, built in 1787 by the Portmans to commemorate Wolfe's victory at Quebec in 1759. The scholarly Henry Alford, editor of the *Contemporary Review*, who became Dean of Canterbury in 1857, was appointed minister of this chapel in 1853 and while serving here published seven volumes of sermons. The chapel was purchased from the Portman family by a public subscription organised by the chaplain, Edward Bickersteth Ottley, in 1894. In 1911 the chapel was demolished, and a petition was presented to Parliament by the Vestry to build the present church.

Church of the Ascension *Blackheath (Dartmouth Row), SE3.* Originally known as Dartmouth Chapel, it was built between 1690 and 1695 with money provided by Susannah Graham, widow of Raynold Graham, who had purchased the Manor of LEWISHAM in 1640. Graham sold the Manor to his nephew by marriage, George Legge, who was later to become the first Lord Dartmouth. Susannah, who was the great-aunt of George Washington, 1st President of the United States, endowed the Chapel in perpetuity in 1697. From the original building a charming coffered apsidal chancel framed in coupled columns and piers with gilded capitals survives. Most of the rest was rebuilt in 1824 although part of the nave is believed to be from a design by Sir Christopher Wren.

Despite its being the private chapel of the Earls of Dartmouth, it became a chapel-of-ease for LEWISHAM and was used as the parish church in time of need, that is to say, 1774–7 when Lewisham church was undergoing repairs and rebuilding, and again in 1831 when it was badly damaged by fire. In 1883 the Chapel became the parish church of a separate ecclesiastical district under the dedication of Church of the Ascension.

After damage in the 2nd World War only the western gallery was retained and this was cut back.

Church of the Ascension *Lavender Hill, SW11.* This brick church designed by James Brooks was built in the late 1870s, completed by Micklethwaite and consecrated in 1883.

Church of the Holy Redeemer *Exmouth Market, EC1.* Built on the site of the SPA FIELDS CHAPEL in 1887–1906 to the Italian Renaissance designs of John Dando Sedding, a master of the Art Workers' Guild, whose work was completed by his assistant, Henry Wilson.

Church of the Holy Redeemer and St Thomas More *Cheyne Row, SW3.* One of the few Victorian Roman Catholic churches in the classical tradition. Edward Goldie, the architect of ST JAMES'S, SPANISH PLACE, reluctantly abandoned the fashionable Gothic Revival and made his designs in the Renaissance style in order to please his client, Canon Cornelius Keen. When the church was opened in 1895, people were critical of the bleak 'concert-hall' appearance of the interior. Goldie argued that shortage of money and the limitations of the site had made a domed church in the 'Oratorian manner' impossible. The Marquess of Ripon, Viceroy of India and a convert to Roman Catholicism, was one of the subscribers to the building. A memorial tablet was put up on his death in 1909. The dedication to St Thomas More was added in 1935 after his canonisation; and an altar, containing a bone from his vertebrae, was erected in his honour.

Church of the Holy Sepulchre without Newgate *Holborn Viaduct, EC1.* Has curious associations. It was founded by Rahere in 1137 and dedicated to the martyred King Edmund. Like the Church of the Holy Sepulchre in Jerusalem, it was built just outside the north-west gate of the City. It was for this reason that the knights of the Crusades found it an appropriate place from which to set out for the Holy Lands; and thus it acquired its present name. It was rebuilt in 1450 by Sir John Popham, Treasurer to Henry VI, and became the largest parish church in the City. It was in the early 17th century that a parishioner called Robert Dowe instituted a grisly practice. The night before an execution a bellman walked along a tunnel which connected the church with NEWGATE prison, tolling a handbell and reciting:

All you that in the condemned hold do lie,
Prepare you for tomorrow you shall die.
Watch all and pray the hour is drawing near
That you before the Almighty must appear.
Examine well yourselves. In time repent
That you may not to eternal flames be sent.
And when St Sepulchre's bell tomorrow tolls
The Lord have mercy on your souls.

The last awesome lines were shouted through the keyhole of the condemned cell. In the morning, the Great Bell of Bailey would solemnly intone from the tower of St Sepulchre as the prisoners were led out. When they reached the church gate they would receive a nosegay. The custom was dropped in 1744. Robert Dowe's handbell, however, is displayed in a case inside the church, near the entrance to the blocked-up tunnel. The GREAT FIRE did not completely destroy St Sepulchre and it was possible to rebuild on the same foundations. The fan vault of the porch and the arches under the tower are original 15th-century. Because the Vestry were impatient to start the work of restoration, they refused to wait for Wren and employed his master mason, Joshua Marshall, to do the work. The church was reopened in 1670. Since then the outside has been altered twice to suit the whim of fashion, once in 1790, and again in 1879 when the tower was restored and given its over-large pinnacles. The spacious interior is a pot-pourri of differing architectural styles. The north chapel contains some 15th-century material. It was dedicted to St Stephen; but in 1955 it became the Musicians' Chapel and the memorial windows were erected in 1963. At the end of the south aisle is the Regimental Chapel of the ROYAL FUSILIERS. Traces of the GREAT FIRE can be seen on a *piscina* set in the south wall. Several interesting people are buried in the church: John Rogers, the Vicar, the first Protestant to be burnt in the reign of Mary Tudor, Roger Ascham, the tutor of Elizabeth I, and Captain John Smith, the intrepid Governor of Virginia whose body was brought back here for burial. A brass plate on the wall of the south chapel recounts his adventures. Sir Henry Wood was christened in the church in 1870. He learnt to play the organ here and when he died in 1944 his entombed ashes formed the centre piece for the Musicians' Chapel. St Sepulchre still retains its large parish, and is involved in many CITY functions. It is also the Headquarters of the ROYAL SCHOOL OF CHURCH MUSIC and so provides the setting for many concerts.

Church of the Immaculate Conception *Farm Street, W1.* Popularly known as 'Farm Street', this church is the headquarters of the English Jesuits, the successors of that small band of Englishmen, mostly Oxford graduates who, in the reign of Elizabeth I, could not accept the separation from Rome and the abolition of the Mass. They left for the Continent in order to join the newly-formed Society of Jesus, and then returned secretly to England. At the risk of their lives they toured the country in disguise, celebrating the Mass, administering the sacraments and preaching to those who still adhered to the old Church of Rome, but who had been cut off from its teaching and practices. In 1829 the Act of Catholic Emancipation was passed, and Catholics, who had had to resort to embassy chapels in order to hear Mass, could once again build churches. In 1844 Joseph Scoles was commissioned by the Jesuits to design a church on a site they had acquired in a back street of a district that had once been part of HAY HILL Farm. The building, designed in the Decorated Gothic style, with its south façade inspired by the west front of Beauvais Cathedral, was completed in five years. The entrance from MOUNT STREET and that on the north side are of a later date. Originally the only way in was from FARM STREET. This main entrance leads into a nave flanked by piers of red granite, through a wide chancel arch to the sanctuary at the north end of the church. There is a clear view of the splendid Pugin high altar and reredos – a gift of the Duke of Norfolk. Above is a nine-light window, derived from the east window of Carlisle Cathedral. The mosaics below it are 19th-century Venetian. The marble communion rails have panels of lapis lazuli. The outer aisles and sumptuous chapels are late Victorian, the work of Henry Clutton, Romaine-Walker and A.E. Purdie. The glass in the rose window was replaced after the 2nd World War by Evie Hone; the window in the Lourdes chapel is also

159

by her; the one next to the Calvary chapel is by her friend and pupil, Patrick Pollen, and was executed in 1953. Soon after the opening of the church in 1849, the powerful preaching tradition of the Jesuit Fathers attracted large congregations. Among the many distinguished people who sought instruction was Henry Manning, the future Cardinal. His reception took place in 1851. Disraeli, when dying on 18 April 1881, sent for Father James Clare SJ. He arrived at the bedside too late. The Prince of Wales attended a Requiem in 1889 for the Archduke Rudolf of Austria. In 1921 there was a Requiem for Sir Ernest Cassel. To the surprise of many, he had been a Catholic for 30 years. Lloyd George, representing the Liberal Party on the occasion of another Requiem, was approached by the sacristan as he and his fellow dignitaries prepared to seat themselves prominently alongside the coffin. 'Gentlemen', the sacristan exclaimed, 'you cannot go in the sanctuary dressed as you are; you must put on these cassocks.' And he dressed them up like choir boys. For a time after the 2nd World War the Pulpit Dialogues, made famous by Father Bernard Vaughan in 1901, were reintroduced. Since 1963, when 'Farm Street' became a parish church, it has been the scene of many fashionable weddings and christenings.

Church of Our Lady of the Assumption and St Gregory *Warwick Street, W1*. Formerly the Chapel of the Portuguese Embassy, then that of the Bavarian Embassy. Destroyed in the GORDON RIOTS, it was rebuilt in 1788 with a red brick front to the street. The ground-floor windows were inserted when there was little cause to fear they would be smashed by a Protestant mob. The interior was remodelled by J.F. Bentley in the 1870s when the statue known as Our Lady of Warwick Street was erected. The large relief of the *Assumption* is by J.E. Carew (1853).

Church Row *NW3*. This, the most attractive street in HAMPSTEAD, extends from FROGNAL to FITZJOHN'S AVENUE. Many of the early 18th-century houses remain unspoiled. Those on the south side are all of about 1720. W.M. Thackeray's daughter, Anne Thackeray Ritchie, described it as 'an avenue of Dutch red-faced houses, leading demurely to the old church tower that stands guarding its graves in the flowery churchyard'. The tower is that of the parish church of ST JOHN. H.G. Wells was living at No. 17 when *Ann Veronica* and *The History of Mr Polly* were published. Among other famous inhabitants have been Wilkie Collins, George Gilbert Scott, William Rothenstein, George du Maurier, Cecil Sharp and Compton Mackenzie. Thomas Park, the 'Poetical Antiquary', and his son, John James Park, authors of the first history of HAMPSTEAD, lived at No. 18.

Church Street *NW8*. First entered in the Rate Books for 1808, it leads to ST JAMES'S CHURCH in PADDINGTON. A market, established before 1914, still flourishes today with furniture and antiques at the eastern (LISSON GROVE) end, and food-stuffs – meat, fish and vegetables with a West Indian flavour – in the western half.

Churchill Gardens *Grosvenor Road, SW1*. Award-winning scheme of flats and maisonettes for 6,500 people designed by A.J.P. Powell and J.H. Moya (1950–62) for WESTMINSTER City Council. The rooms are heated from waste hot water pumped under the river from BATTERSEA POWER STATION. A covered shopping centre, a restaurant, four public houses and an underground car park are included in the 30 acre site.

Churchill Hotel *30 Portman Square, W1*. A luxury hotel with 489 bedrooms on nine storeys built in 1970 to the designs of Stone, Toms and Partners. It is much favoured by well-to-do Americans.

Churchill Theatre *High Street, Bromley, Kent*. Opened by the Prince of Wales in 1977 on the site of the New Theatre, Bromley which had offered a variety of entertainment, including plays, lectures, music-hall and minstrel shows since 1889. In 1930 after a period of some 30 years as a cinema the New Theatre reverted to a repertory theatre with the backing of the Rank organisation, presenting, amongst others, the Hulberts, Frankie Howerd, and Michael Bentine. After its destruction by fire in 1971, the theatre was rebuilt by the London Borough of BROMLEY and named the Churchill Theatre.

Circle Line The Circle was built by the Metropolitan Railway and the District Railway. Soon after the completion of the first section of the METROPOLITAN LINE plans were made for an 'Inner Circle', linking the two ends of the METROPOLITAN. The Metropolitan Railway built the section from PADDINGTON to SOUTH KENSINGTON, opened in 1868, and the Metropolitan District Railway (later called the DISTRICT) built the section from SOUTH KENSINGTON to MANSION HOUSE, completed in 1871. The two companies had originally been expected to amalgamate but relations between them deteriorated, partly over the division of receipts from the Circle, and partly because of personal animosity between the chairmen of the two companies. It was CITY interests that finally forced them to complete the Circle and the last link, between MANSION HOUSE and ALDGATE, was opened in 1884. The METROPOLITAN and the DISTRICT both worked their trains all round the Circle. The two companies came together later to experiment with electrification for the Circle, though after the DISTRICT was taken over by an American, C.T. Yerkes, it was his preferred method of electrification that was used for the Circle. Electrification was completed in September 1905, and the running time of Circle trains was reduced from 70 to 50 minutes for the round trip. Since then there have been no major alterations to the line, though obviously equipment, rolling stock and stations have changed with the times (*see also* DISTRICT LINE, METROPOLITAN LINE *and* UNDERGROUND RAILWAYS).

Circus *EC3*. Built in 1768–74 at the same time as the CRESCENT and AMERICA SQUARE to the designs of George Dance the Younger who was probably influenced by John Wood's development at Bath. With the CRESCENT this was a novel introduction to a London of straight streets and squares. None of the original houses remains.

Circus Road *NW8*. Laid out on the EYRE ESTATE in St John's Wood from 1824 onwards. Its name probably commemorates the Grand Circus planned but never realised; its layout appears on a plan issued by Spurrier and Phipps in 1794. The most remarkable feature was

the pairs of semi-detached villas that surrounded the Circus; as far as is known, this was the first appearance of an arrangement that later became a domestic commonplace. No. 58 Circus Road (formerly No. 26) was the home of Douglas Jerrold, the author, dramatist and wit, in 1854–6.

Citadel *The Mall, SW1.* A fortress and bunker, with foundations 30 ft deep, built beside the ADMIRALTY by W.A. Forsyth in 1940–1 to provide bombproof protection for the Admiralty communication rooms. The exterior is constructed of compressed pebble and flint blocks.

City and Guilds of London Institute *76 Portland Place, W1.* Following a meeting of representatives of the CITY CORPORATION and the CITY LIVERY COMPANIES, presided over by the LORD MAYOR and held at the MANSION HOUSE, the City and Guilds of London Institute was incorporated by Royal Charter in 1878 for the advancement of technical and scientific education. In its first year it held examinations in 28 centres in 7 subjects for 202 candidates; in its 70th year its examinations were held in over 1,000 centres in 151 subjects for 58,500 candidates, including 4,500 from overseas. The Institute's operations today include the City and Guilds College – the engineering section of the IMPERIAL COLLEGE OF SCIENCE AND TECHNOLOGY – in EXHIBITION ROAD, and the City and Guilds of London Art School, 124 Kennington Park Road, SOUTHWARK which, established in 1897, became independent in 1971.

City Barge *Strand-on-the-Green, W4.* Known as the Navigator's Arms when it was first built in 1484. Much of the original building was demolished in the 2nd World War. Queen Elizabeth I granted a Royal Charter to the inn which was renamed after the LORD MAYOR of London's State Barge, the *Marie Celeste*, which was moored nearby. The bar contains a 'Parliamentary clock', open-faced to avoid the tax which would have been imposed had it been covered by a glass door.

City Chamberlain A High Officer of the CORPORATION OF LONDON. He used to be elected in COMMON HALL but in 1979 this was changed to election by the COURT OF COMMON COUNCIL. The first known Chamberlain was one John Wacher who took office in 1237. The responsibilities of the office have grown over the centuries with the increase of the CITY's wealth and financial importance. The Chamberlain is the CORPORATION's financial adviser, accountant, treasurer and banker. As well as running the budget of a modern local authority, he administers the CITY's ancient funds. These are City's Cash, which comes from property and is used to maintain the CITY's four schools and to defray the costs of the Mayoralty (*see* LORD MAYOR), and the income from BRIDGE HOUSE ESTATES which maintains the CITY's four road bridges. The Chamberlain takes part in CITY ceremonial and admits Freemen to the FREEDOM OF THE CITY in his court in GUILDHALL.

City Corporation *see* CORPORATION OF LONDON.

City Livery Club *Sion College, Victoria Embankment, EC4.* Founded in 1914 to 'bind together in one organisation liverymen of the various guilds . . . in service to the Ancient Corporation and in maintenance of the priceless City churches'. Initially meeting at DE KEYSER'S ROYAL HOTEL, the club moved first to ST BRIDE'S INSTITUTE, then to Williamson's Hotel, BOW LANE, then to the Chapter House, ST PAUL'S CHURCHYARD, and from there to BUTCHERS' HALL before settling at SION COLLEGE.

CITY LIVERY COMPANIES It has long been the practice in many countries for men in a particular trade to band together to promote their interests. In London various craft guilds were established as early as the 12th century and many more were formed during the 13th and particularly the 14th and 15th centuries. Often these were associated with religious fraternities, designed to guarantee decent burial and masses for the souls of the dead. The established guilds or mysteries (less confusingly spelt misteries, from the Italian *mestiere* – a trade) fulfilled a wide variety of functions. Medieval thought was not dominated by costs and competition. Policy was based on giving fair value. The typical guild decided who could work or trade in its craft; it controlled prices and wages, working conditions and welfare. It exercised vigorous quality control with wide powers of inspection and confiscation, coupled with severe punishment for poor workmanship. In return it received monopoly powers. Guild members were eventually known as liverymen because they wore a distinctive livery or uniform. They were governed by a Master and usually two Wardens, supported in due course by a Court of Assistants. Often there were also freemen and a yeomanry. These tended to be the craft workers while the liverymen were the employers. Promotion from one class to another could occur and no doubt depended on status. In spite of struggles to introduce democracy, the organisation has remained oligarchical up till today. Entry can be by three methods, patrimony (the right of a son born when his father was a liveryman), apprenticeship (after serving for a definite period to learn a trade) and redemption (straight payment for the privilege of entry). The third is naturally the most expensive. The proportions elected by the three methods vary from Company to Company. All liverymen receive the FREEDOM OF THE CITY for which they take a separate oath and pay a separate fee. Liverymen still play a part in the organisation of the CITY in that they form the sole electorate for choosing each year the LORD MAYOR and the SHERIFFS. The first mention of Companies was in 1180 when several were fined as 'adulterine', i.e. existing without official authorisation. The typical Company officially started when its draft ordinances were approved by the LORD MAYOR and ALDERMEN. Later it would probably receive a Royal Charter and at a disconnected date the right to bear arms. The CITY authorities also granted a livery and assigned an order of precedence. This order is an approximate but not exact indication of the date of establishment. It has not changed much with time and the table of precedence enacted by the Court of Aldermen in 1514 differs little from that of today. The Middle Ages were a period of manoeuvring for power, with disputes between Companies and the CITY, between one Company and another – often over precedence or in fields of overlapping interests – and inside individual Companies between the classes of member or even between Master and Livery.

Struggles between Companies could be riotous and violent. In 1267 there was a pitched battle between the GOLDSMITHS and the TAYLORS with CLOTHWORKERS and CORDWAINERS joining in, and in 1340 a similar affray between the FISHMONGERS and SKINNERS. In both cases lives were lost and the ringleaders subsequently hanged. All combined to keep out the feared foreigners, though eventually some, such as the Huguenots, had to be admitted. Yet out of these stresses developed the practice of municipal administration which influenced national government. Characteristically it was the commercial merchant companies that became most wealthy and powerful. The craft-based Companies made less money. Twelve Companies gradually became outstandingly important and were named as the 'Great' Companies, all others being referred to as 'Minor'. Status was shown by mounting elaborate pageants, which were the forerunners of the current LORD MAYOR'S SHOW.

The Reformation passed with less effect than might have been predicted. Although all property and endowments devoted to religious observances for the repose of the souls of the dead and similar 'superstitious practices' were confiscated, Companies were often able to repurchase the confiscated property. Late Tudor and Stuart times brought severe financial pressures from the Crown. The practice of granting to favoured courtiers monopolies that conflicted with Company rights introduced great complications. Some Stuart monarchs recalled the earlier charters and regranted them for heavy fees. The Companies were virtually forced to finance plantations of English and Scottish workers in Ulster in 1608 and a similar scheme in Virginia in 1610. Many Companies had to sell their plate to raise the cash. Smoother waters were entered in the 18th century but these concealed great dangers. Partly because of admission by patrimony and partly because many trades left London and moved elsewhere in the country, many of the Companies became less and less representative of their crafts. Furthermore their monopoly powers became an intolerable restriction on the development of trade. Consequently in many cases their controlling powers lapsed and the original reasons for their existence disappeared. Numbers in some Companies dwindled almost to vanishing point by the middle of the 19th century. Then, because of changed social habits and Victorian prosperity, the trend was reversed and for more than 100 years numbers have steadily increased. Paradoxically it was this loss of effective power that enabled the Companies to survive. In Europe various revolutions between 1789 and 1864 swept away the guilds as repositories of inherited power, a violent solution that was not needed in England.

The popular image of Livery Companies may be one of gargantuan meals eaten in palatial surroundings. Reality is different. Certainly liverymen enjoy their occasional dinners but the Companies do much for public good. Since they are private organisations and have no shareholders, they do not publish accounts; usually only the Court of Assistants is aware of the financial position. But the great majority engage in substantial charitable and educational activities. Many take an interest in the industry from which they sprang, or perhaps in a modern successor industry. This is supported by prizes, awards, research fellowships and scholarships in appropriate educational establishments. The wealthier Companies have founded and financed university departments or built complete colleges. Many combined to set up the CITY AND GUILDS OF LONDON INSTITUTE. A very wide range of charities is afforded powerful help, each Company making its own choice. The present trend is against the formerly popular almshouses, financial help being given instead. The funds for such uses originated partly in wise purchases of land and property long ago and partly in bequests from benevolent members.

Between 1709 and 1930 no Livery Companies were established but the last 50 years have seen the appearance of 17 new Companies, making a present total of 94. Two or three of these recently established companies represent new crafts but the majority cover specialist professional interests, the Liveries being open only to appropriately qualified persons.

Brief notes follow on each Company and a longer account of the great Companies. After each name the figure in brackets shows its position in the table of precedence. As it is often impossible to state the year of foundation, the date of the original Ordinances and of the first Charter are quoted, omitting all later steps. Where they exist or used to exist, information is given on the Halls. If a Company does not have a Hall or office, the address quoted is that of the Clerk. Certain of the finer Halls have separate entries.

Actuaries' Company *(91)* *5 New Bridge Street, EC4.* Granted its Livery in 1979. Admission is limited to professionally qualified actuaries. A Trust has been established for charitable and educational activities but so recently that policy has not yet been formulated. Although the permitted Livery is 300, it will be long before that figure is achieved.

Air Pilots' and Air Navigators' Guild *(81)* *30 Eccleston Street, SW1.* Established in 1929 and granted its Livery in 1956. It is composed of qualified and experienced pilots and navigators and promotes the highest standards of air safety and professional competence. It gives authoritative advice to Government, makes 12 awards for distinguished service and has a benevolent fund. The Livery numbers about 400 plus 1,200 Freemen.

Apothecaries' Society *(58)* *Blackfriars Lane, EC4.* Apothecaries were members of the GROCERS but their specialised training and knowledge caused them to break away. They received their first Charter in 1617. Their powers were steadily extended into the realm of surgeons and physicians. Since 1815 those who pass the LMSSA examination are fully qualified as general practitioners. Specialist diplomas were added later. The retailing of drugs has been given up. The Livery of over 1,000 is almost entirely composed of medical professionals. William and John Hunter, Jenner, pioneer of the smallpox vaccination, Sir Humphrey Davy, inventor of the safety lamp, Oliver Goldsmith, Oliver Cromwell and John Keats were members. For the Hall *see* APOTHECARIES' HALL.

Arbitrators' Company *(93)* *75 Cannon Street, EC4.* Granted its Livery in 1981, the Company already has over 100 Liverymen, who must be Fellows of the Chartered Institute of Arbitrators. A charitable trust is being formed for relief and education within the profession.

Armourers' and Brasiers' Company *(22)* *81 Coleman Street, EC2.* The Armourers were instituted by Ordinance in 1322, receiving their first Charter in 1453. After absorbing the Blacksmiths in 1515, and later the Helmet Makers and Armour Repairers, workers in brass and copper were incorporated in 1708. Progress in metallurgy is encouraged by research fellowships; scholarships at Oxford; and prizes to Sheffield cutlery apprentices and to students of metallurgy and engineering at Sheffield College of Technology and the CITY AND GUILDS OF LONDON INSTITUTE. The Livery numbers about 120. For the Hall *see* ARMOURERS' AND BRASIERS' HALL.

Bakers' Company *(19)* *Harp Lane, Lower Thames Street, EC3.* Mentioned in 1155 and received its first Charter in 1486 for bakers of white bread. Bakers of brown bread were incorporated in 1569. Severe penalties were inflicted on inefficient bakers, the control powers lasting until 1805. Nowadays one-third of the Livery of over 350 is connected with the trade. Training is supported by awards at the CITY AND GUILDS OF LONDON INSTITUTE, the Federation of Bakery Students and the National Bakery School at the POLYTECHNIC OF THE SOUTH BANK. For the Hall *see* BAKERS' HALL.

Barbers' Company *(17)* *Monkwell Square, Wood Street, EC2.* Mentioned in 1308 and received its first Charter in 1462. Barbers early assisted monks in surgery and when monks were forbidden to practise, barbers took over and were senior to surgeons, who joined them in 1540 but who later broke away and established their Royal College in 1800 (*see* MEDICINE *and* ROYAL COLLEGE OF SURGEONS). Many surgeons are in the Livery of nearly 200. General charities assist the needy and support training. Barber-Surgeons' Hall, first built in Monkwell Street in the mid-15th century, was extended in 1605 and in 1635. Much was burnt in 1666 and rebuilt. After reductions in 1784 and 1869, all was destroyed in 1940. The new Hall was opened in 1969, Kenneth Cross followed by Lawrence King and Partners being the architects. Dining capacity is about 120.

Basketmakers' Company *(52)* *87–95 Tooley Street, SE1.* An operative craft Company constituted in 1569. Livery was granted in 1825 and a Royal Charter in 1937. The Company is interested in blind craftsmen and technical training and encourages the craft and apprentices. It is now very strong in the City civic field with a Livery of over 460 and many Freemen.

Blacksmiths' Company *(40)* *41 Tabernacle Street, EC2.* Certainly existed in 1494 and received their first Charter in 1571, when they joined with the Spurriers. Earlier blacksmiths were official toothdrawers. There is a Prime Warden plus three Wardens. They now support the CITY AND GUILDS OF LONDON INSTITUTE, award trophies at several rural shows and contribute to many charities. The Livery numbers nearly 250. The former Hall existed in Lambeth Hill (the site now occupied by the SALVATION ARMY Headquarters) from 1494 to 1666, when it was destroyed. A new Hall was opened in 1671 but fell out of use, and the lease terminated in 1785.

Bowyers' Company *(38)* *7 Chandos Street, W1.* Mentioned in 1371 on separation from the Fletchers; received Arms in 1488 and a Charter in 1621. The trade has disappeared but there is a long history of support for Cambridge University. Medals and prizes are given for archery contests. The Livery numbers about 75. A former Hall at the corner of HART STREET and Monkwell Street was burnt down in 1666.

Brewers' Company *(14)* *Aldermanbury Square, EC2.* The first record is dated 1292 and the first Charter was granted in 1437. The Company is intimately connected with the trade, and the Livery of about 80 is composed of directors of London brewery companies (*see* BREWERIES). The Company is Trustee of schools at Potters Bar and Aldenham and administers two sets of almshouses and other charities. The Hall was in existence in ADDLE STREET in 1418, as recorded in the then Clerk's record book, which still survives. It was burnt down in 1666 and its replacement opened in 1673. This was destroyed in 1940. Its successor, designed by Sir Hubert Worthington and opened in 1960, has a dining capacity of 70.

Broderers' Company *(48)* *11a Bridge Road, East Molesey, Surrey.* Existed in a corporate form by 1376 and received its first Charter in 1561. From early medieval times, English embroidery was famous throughout Europe. Nowadays a new Trust maintains two apprentices at the ROYAL SCHOOL OF NEEDLEWORK, awards a prize at the CITY OF LONDON SCHOOL FOR GIRLS, supports the MacIntyre Homes and helps general charities. The Livery is slightly over 100. The former Hall existed in Gutter Lane from 1515 but was burnt in 1666. Rebuilt but little used, it was let and became a warehouse in the 19th century. It was destroyed in 1940 and the site sold in 1957.

Builders' Company *(94)* *127 Thomas More House, Barbican, EC2.* Founded in 1976 and granted Livery in 1981, the 330 members are all architects, engineers, surveyors or builders. Charitable support is given to education in building and civil engineering and to numerous other causes.

Builders' Merchants' Company *(88)* *128 Queen Victoria Street, EC4.* This new Company was granted its Livery in 1977. The Livery, numbering about 160, are professionals closely connected with the trade. A charitable fund makes grants to certain charities connected with the trade and/or the CITY OF LONDON.

Butchers' Company *(24)* *87 Bartholomew Close, EC1.* An adulterine guild was mentioned in 1179. Ordinances for a limited area were issued in 1331 and general Ordinances in 1423. The first Charter came in 1605. The present Livery of about 500 has many connections with the trade. Charities cover necessitous freemen and dependents. The first Hall in MONKWELL STREET dated from the second half of the 15th century. The next Hall near ST BARTHOLOMEW'S HOSPITAL was destroyed in 1666. Its successor in PUDDING LANE (1667–77) was again burnt, rebuilt in 1829–30 and compulsorily purchased in 1882. The following Hall (1884–5) in Bartholomew Close was bombed in 1915, again in 1944 and rebuilt in 1960, seating 128.

Carmen's Company *(77)* *81–87 Gresham Street, EC2.* Separated from the Woodmongers, the Carmen were established in 1668 but received a Charter only in 1946. The transport industry is strongly represented on the Livery of nearly 400. The Company contributes to the CITY OF LONDON SCHOOLS and to general charities, has a special relationship with the Royal Corps of Transport and presents a shield to transport organisations.

Carpenters' Company *(26)* *Throgmorton Avenue, EC2.* Received Ordinances in 1333 and the first Charter in 1477. They run the BUILDING CRAFTS TRAINING SCHOOL in Great Titchfield Street, award educational bursaries, have almshouses in Godalming, govern Rustington Convalescent Home and have special relations with the Carpenters' Company of Philadelphia. The Livery is about 130. The Hall of 1429 was near the City Wall and surrounded by a garden which saved it

163

in the GREAT FIRE. It was demolished in 1876 and reopened nearby in 1880, then destroyed in 1941. The new Hall, designed by Austen, Hall and Partners, was opened in 1960. It contains excellent examples of modern carpentry, and its dining capacity is about 230.

Chartered Accountants' Company *(86) 81–87 Gresham Street, EC2.* In 1977 the Company was granted its Livery which already numbers over 250 professionally qualified accountants. A charitable trust has been established to support charities in the CITY and the profession. The Company gives a substantial prize to the best student of the year and in 1980 began assisting training in the Commonwealth.

The existing professional headquarters of the INSTITUTE OF CHARTERED ACCOUNTANTS are used as their Hall.

Chartered Secretaries' and Administrators' Company *(87) 16 Park Crescent, W1.* This new Company was granted its Livery in 1977. The Livery of over 180 is confined to members of the INSTITUTE OF CHARTERED SECRETARIES AND ADMINISTRATORS. Formal links have been established with the Royal Army Pay Corps. A bursary is offered through the CITY UNIVERSITY and prizes through polytechnics and colleges.

Chartered Surveyors' Company *(85) 12 Great George Street, SW1.* The Company was granted its Livery in 1977 and its Arms in 1979. The Livery, approaching 260, is composed of professional members of the ROYAL INSTITUTION OF CHARTERED SURVEYORS. It assists the education of students and presents prizes to students of land economy at Reading, Cambridge, Aberdeen and Cirencester.

Clockmakers' Company *(61) 2 Greycoat Place, Westminster, SW1.* Heavy church clocks were made by BLACKSMITHS but skilled clockmakers received their first Charter in 1631. Today 70 per cent of the Livery of nearly 300 are connected with the trade. A prize is given annually for the best horological student and a splendid collection of clocks and watches maintained at GUILDHALL (*see* GUILDHALL CLOCK MUSEUM).

Clothworkers' Company *(12) Dunster Court, Mincing Lane, EC3.* Several guilds were connected with textiles and one was fined as adulterine in 1180. In 1528 the Fullers who had been incorporated in 1480 and the Shearmen, incorporated in 1508, combined to form the Clothworkers. The combined Company succeeded to the precedence of the Shearmen and became 12th of the 'Great Twelve'. Samuel Pepys was Master in 1677–8. Modern representation of the clothworking trade is slight, but the early wealth of the Company is now deployed in notable charitable and educational activities. The Departments of Textile Industries and of Colour Chemistry and Dyeing in Leeds University originated in foundations of the Clothworkers, who still support them financially and aid other projects in the University. The Company has also been a leading supporter of the CITY AND GUILDS OF LONDON INSTITUTE. The secondary and higher education of women is a particular interest, with help for girls' schools and places for women at Oxford and Cambridge. Help for the blind has long been a particular priority. The Company is recognised as a leading source of assistance in this field. Often the charities supported are those with little popular appeal or of a new type. The Livery numbers about 205. The Hall of the Shearmen stood on a site in MINCING LANE acquired in 1456. The first Hall was built about 1472 and was taken over by the Clothworkers in preference to that of the FULLERS. The second Hall on the same site was completed in 1549 and a third one in 1633. This was destroyed in the GREAT FIRE but rebuilt by 1668. Because of poor foundations it had to be demolished in 1855, and the fifth Hall, by Samuel Angell, the Company's architect, was opened in 1860. That was destroyed in 1941 and the present Hall, designed by H. Austen Hall, was opened in 1958. The accommodation includes a Livery Hall, Reception Room, Library, Drawing Room, Court Room and Court Luncheon Room.

Coachmakers' and Coach Harness Makers' Company *(72) 9 Lincoln's Inn Fields, WC2.* Received a Charter in 1677. Nowadays there are close connections with transport industries. Prizes are given in motor vehicle competitions, the CITY AND GUILDS OF LONDON INSTITUTE is supported, and occasional awards are presented for outstanding advances in transport. There are a Master, three Wardens and a Livery of about 370. The former Hall was purchased from the Scriveners' Company in 1703, rebuilt in 1842–3 and 1870, but totally destroyed by fire in 1940. It was noteworthy as the meeting place of the Protestant Association which provoked the GORDON RIOTS.

Cooks' Company *(35) 49 Queen Victoria Street, EC4.* A fraternity was formed in 1311 and received its first Charter in 1482. Technical colleges in London are supported and prizes given to the CITY AND GUILDS OF LONDON INSTITUTE and the Army Catering Corps. There are also charities. The Livery, limited to 75, is headed by a Master, Second Master and two Wardens. The former Hall, on a site in ALDERSGATE STREET purchased in 1500, survived the GREAT FIRE. A new Great Hall was added in 1674 which was destroyed and rebuilt in 1764, but both were burnt down in 1771 and not rebuilt. The Company still owns the site.

Coopers' Company *(36) 13 Devonshire Square, EC2.* A fraternity existed by 1422 and received its first Charter in 1501. Members made standard barrels for beer, wines and spirits. The Coopers' Company and Coborn School at UPMINSTER is supported, also needy persons in TOWER HAMLETS, Egham and BATTERSEA, and Benevolent Trusts. Unusually, the whole Livery of over 250 elect Master and Wardens. In 1522 a Hall was constructed in BASINGHALL STREET. A timber Hall was built alongside in 1547 and lasted until 1666. The next Hall was completed in 1670 and demolished in 1865. The third Hall lasted from 1868 to 1940. The present mid-18th-century house acquired in 1957 contains offices and a Court Room renovated in 1976, with E.W. Palmer as architect.

Cordwainers' Company *(27) 30 Fleet Street, EC4.* Received ordinances in 1272 and their first Charter in 1439. They worked in Cordoba goatskin leather and later made shoes, leather bottles and harness. They now support Cordwainers' Technical College, the CITY AND GUILDS OF LONDON INSTITUTE and the CITY UNIVERSITY. A very wide range of charities helps nurses, the blind, the deaf and dumb, clergymen's widows, ex-servicemen and almshouses. The Livery numbers 135. The former Hall was in the gardens around ST PAUL'S CATHEDRAL on a site acquired at the end of the 14th century. The first Hall was rebuilt in 1577, again after the GREAT FIRE, and once more in 1788, but was destroyed in 1941 after which the site was compulsorily purchased.

Curriers' Company *(29) 43 Church Road, Hove, East Sussex.* The first ordinances of 1300 dealt with price and quality; those of 1415 were general. A Charter was granted in 1605. Curriers dressed, levelled and greased the tanned leather. Always rather small, the present Livery numbers about 75. Technical colleges are supported and there are charities for the needy, particularly old curriers. A former Hall existed from 1484, then in 1516 a site on CRIPPLEGATE was acquired, on which a Hall was erected before 1587. This was burnt down in 1666, rebuilt by 1670 and demolished in 1820. It was followed by others; the last, by John Belcher, was built in 1874–6, sold to the CHARTERED INSTITUTE OF SECRETARIES in 1920, and eventually destroyed in 1940.

Cutlers' Company *(18)* *Warwick Lane, EC4*. An organised craft early in the 13th century, they received their first Charter in 1416. In the early 17th century the trade concentrated in Sheffield but surgical instrument making remained in London, where apprentices are fostered. Scholarships are awarded to Oxford and Cambridge and at the CITY OF LONDON SCHOOL. The Livery numbers 100. For the Hall *see* CUTLERS' HALL.

Distillers' Company *(69)* *1 Vintners Place, EC4*. The Charter and Arms granted in 1638 were resisted by the CITY which eventually accepted enrolment in 1658, with powers to produce spirits, vinegar, etc., supervised by Sir Theodore de Mayerne, a French Huguenot who had been physician to Charles I. The Livery of about 200 are mainly distillers and wine merchants, and grant distilling scholarships.

Drapers' Company *(3)* *Throgmorton Street, EC2*. An association of drapers was in existence in the 12th century and is first mentioned when Henry Fitzailwin, first Mayor of London, left them his property in the parish of St Mary, Bothaw. It received its first Charter in 1364. The Grant of Arms was made in 1439, the document being the oldest surviving English grant of arms. The wool trade was of the highest importance in medieval times and the Company grew to great wealth and influence, its members dealing at different periods with both export and import of wool cloth. As with similar Companies, connections with the trade greatly diminished but the Drapers retained their influence, coupled with political power, supplying LORD MAYORS about 100 times to the CITY. Through the centuries they have been made trustees for a wide range of educational and welfare charities. They are deeply involved with the management of BANCROFT'S at WOODFORD and Howell's at Denbigh, as well as QUEEN MARY COLLEGE of the UNIVERSITY OF LONDON which was established through their generosity. They also support four almshouses and a block of flats for the elderly, award pensions to the needy and make educational and welfare grants. The Drapers' Charitable Fund was established in 1959 to make grants for a variety of good causes, including research fellowships, medical, social and educational projects generally. The Livery numbers approximately 230. For the Hall *see* DRAPERS' HALL.

Dyers' Company *(13)* *Dowgate Hill, EC4*. The Dyers' Guild was mentioned in 1188 and received its first Charter in 1471. About one third of the present Livery of over 100 are engaged in the dyeing or chemical industries. They support a school in Norwich, Leeds University, a gold medal for outstanding research and prizes to the CITY AND GUILDS OF LONDON INSTITUTE. Thirty almshouses are owned at Crawley. The Dyers share with the VINTNERS the privilege of keeping SWANS on the THAMES. For the Hall *see* DYERS' HALL.

Fan Makers' Company *(76)* *107–111 Fleet Street, EC4*. Following immigration of French fanmakers, the Company received its first Charter in 1709. The craft was at its peak in the 18th century. Now it gives prizes to the National College of Heating, Ventilating, Refrigeration and Fan Engineering, also for fan design in London schools, and supports aeronautical research at Cranfield Institute of Technology. The Livery numbers about 195. As a Hall the parish hall of ST BOTOLPH WITHOUT BISHOPSGATE has been shared with the church since 1952. The building was a former schoolroom dating from 1861. It has been extensively restored and redecorated and includes oak panelling of 1726. The dining capacity is 80.

Farmers' Company *(80)* *7–8 King's Bench Walk, Temple, EC4*. Grew out of the cooperative work of the Agriculture Fund of 1939–45. It was granted a Livery in 1952 and a Charter in 1955. Most of the Livery, numbering about 275, are farmers. It makes grants for travelling expenses to study farming overseas and operates an advanced farm management course at Wye College.

Farriers' Company *(55)* *3 Hamilton Road, Cockfosters, N14*. A Fellowship was formed in 1356 which gained a Charter in 1674. An increasing proportion of the Livery of about 375 is connected with horses. Since 1891 examinations and registration of smiths have been organised, now supported by apprenticeships, to ensure the supply of competent farriers. Medals are awarded in shoeing competitions.

Feltmakers' Company *(63)* *53 Davies Street, W1*. The first Charter was not received until 1667, the Company having been incorporated by Letters Patent in 1604. Many of their members were previously HABERDASHERS. Later competition (for felt hats) came from silk and machines. When Elizabeth I was greeted by a company of hatters on a visit to the City she commented on their 'superior bearing and lusty loyalty', and announced that 'such journeymen must be gentlemen'. The Livery numbers about 230.

Fishmongers' Company *(4)* *Fishmongers' Hall, EC4*. This important Company is one of the very few old Companies that still perform their original function. All fish sold in the CITY and its environs must first be inspected by the Company's officials, known as fish-meters, to ensure its fitness for human consumption. There is still an appreciable representation of working fishmongers in the Livery which numbers nearly 300. A predecessor guild was fined as adulterine in 1154 and the Company received its first Charter in 1272. It is governed by a Prime Warden, five other Wardens and a Court of 28. The religious importance of fish in the medieval diet brought great wealth and influence. Originally there were saltfishmongers and stockfishmongers, who after previous amalgamations and separations were finally united in 1536. The most famous fishmonger is Sir William Walworth who as Lord Mayor in 1381 broke the Peasants' Revolt by stabbing Wat Tyler in the presence of the young Richard II (*see* PEASANTS' REVOLT). In 1714 an actor named Doggett presented a coat and silver badge to be rowed for annually by six young Thames WATERMEN. Since Doggett's death, the Company has organised this event (*see* DOGGETT'S COAT AND BADGE RACE). Educationally, the Fishmongers have for long supported and administered Gresham's School, Holt, being still the Trustees. They are deeply involved in the City and Guilds of London Art School and support the

CITY AND GUILDS OF LONDON INSTITUTE. They are intimately concerned with salmon and fresh water fishing as well as shell fish throughout the country and support research. For the Hall *see* FISHMONGERS' HALL.

Fletchers' Company *(39)* *College Hill Chambers, EC4.* In 1371 a petition by the Arrow Makers to be separated from the BOWYERS was accepted and ordinances granted in 1403. ARCHERY is still supported by prizes for Royal Toxophilite Society competitions and help provided to disabled archers to acquire special equipment. Charities are directed towards the CITY and archery. The Livery numbers about 110. The former Hall existed in ST MARY AXE at the beginning of the 16th century but was burnt down in 1666 and not rebuilt. The site was not sold until 1933.

Founders' Company *(33)* *13 St Swithin's Lane, EC4.* The original founders cast brass and bronze objects such as candlesticks and water pots. Ordinances were conferred in 1365 and a Charter in 1614. Nearly half of the present Livery of 150 is engaged in the foundry industry. For long the Company was responsible for marking all brass weights in the CITY. It now supports research, organises seminars and annually tours the industry in Great Britain and overseas. For the Hall *see* FOUNDERS' HALL.

Framework Knitters' Company *(64)* *51 Dulwich Wood Avenue, SE19.* Originated in the first successful knitting machine, supposedly invented by a Cambridge graduate to gain the love of a lady. The Charter was awarded in 1657, when the Company became very prosperous. Later the industry tended to move to Leicester and Nottingham, where many of the Livery of 225 live. The former Hall stood in prosperous times in REDCROSS STREET but later bad times led to its sale to the CORPORATION in 1821.

Fruiterers' Company *(45)* *1 Serjeants Inn, EC4.* After a mention in 1292, the Company received Ordinances in 1463 and its first Charter in 1605. It inspected all fruit entering the CITY and assessed the duty. Over half the present Livery of about 260 is associated with the trade. Support is given to East Malling Research Station, Wye College and similar bodies.

Furniture Makers' Company *(83)* *Grove Mills, Cranbrook Road, Hawkhurst, Kent.* The early craft was in the hands of such Companies as the TURNERS and the UPHOLDERS. In 1952 a Guild was formed which was granted a Livery in 1963. The Livery, numbering about 250, is limited to makers, retailers and designers of furniture. Many scholarships are given to promote the craft and good design.

Gardeners' Company *(66)* *College Hill Chambers, EC4.* In 1345 gardeners successfully petitioned to sell produce publicly. The first Charter was granted in 1605. The Company was the sanitary cleansing authority. It presents bouquets to CORONATIONS and royal marriages and an annual offering to the LORD MAYOR. The Company encourages CITY floral displays and church gardens in Greater London. The Livery numbers 250.

Girdlers' Company *(23)* *Basinghall Avenue, EC2.* After earlier mentions, Letters Patent were granted in 1327 and the first Charter in 1449. Medieval girdles had symbolic importance and one is still presented to the Sovereign at the CORONATION. Scholarships are awarded at Corpus Christi and Girton Colleges, Cambridge. Two adjoining sets of almshouses are maintained and general charities supported. The Livery numbers 80. The Hall is on a site owned since 1431 and extended in 1505. It was destroyed in 1666 and rebuilt in 1681. Again destroyed in 1940, it was charmingly rebuilt by C. Ripley and reopened in 1961 with a garden containing a mulberry tree descended from a tree of 1750. A precious possession is a notable Indian carpet of 1634.

Glass Sellers' Company *(71)* *6 Eldon Street, EC2.* Medieval table glass was imported but in 1664 the Company gained its Charter and soon promoted lead crystal glass. Most of the major glass companies are represented in the Livery of 150. Although not a wealthy Company it gives an annual award for excellence in the industry and supports many City charities.

Glaziers' Company *(53)* *9 Montague Close, SE1.* The earliest record of the Glaziers is in 1328 but they did not receive their first Charter until 1638. The present Livery of about 255 includes some with trade connections. Prizes are given for practical glazing and stained glass design. There is also a travelling scholarship and grants are made to churches for stained glass preservation. The Hall was first mentioned in 1601 in Five (Fye) Foot Lane off QUEEN VICTORIA STREET, which was leased from the FISHMONGERS. This was lost in the GREAT FIRE and not rebuilt. In 1978, a great new Hall, designed by William Holford, was opened. It is shared with the SCIENTIFIC INSTRUMENT MAKERS and includes many commercial offices. The dining capacity is 340.

Glovers' Company *(62)* *Bakers' Hall, Harp Lane, EC3.* Ordinances of the Guild were made in 1349 and the first Charter was granted in 1639. Now the Company presents gloves to the Sovereign when crowned and annually to the LORD MAYOR and Lady Mayoress. The best leathercraft student at Nene College receives an award. One-third of the Livery of 265 is connected with the industry. The former Hall in Beech Lane, CRIPPLEGATE existed during the 18th and 19th centuries but had to be given up in 1882 for financial reasons.

Gold and Silver Wyre Drawers' Company *(74)* *40A Ludgate Hill, EC4.* The drawing of fine gold-coated silver thread for use in brocade and later in uniforms is now reduced to a single maker. The Charter was granted in 1693 and the Livery in 1780. The trade is still represented in the Livery of about 350. The principal charity is the London Homes for the Elderly.

Goldsmiths' Company *(5)* *Foster Lane, EC2.* The Goldsmiths' Fraternity was fined as adulterine in 1180 and received its first Charter in 1327. In 1300 gold and silver were first hallmarked with a leopard's head by the wardens of the craft. This craft body became one of the most wealthy and powerful of the 'Great Companies'. It had absolute responsibility for the quality of gold and silver objects (recently adding platinum) which had to be marked in GOLDSMITHS' HALL (hence hallmarking) before they could be sold. A particular responsibility is that of determining that the precious metal content of the coin of the realm does not fall below the legally prescribed minima, an operation carried out in the Trial of the Pyx each year since 1248 (*see* CEREMONIES). The practice of using promissory notes that grew up among the Goldsmiths of the 17th century was the forerunner of modern banking, of which the goldsmith, Sir Francis Child, is regarded as the father. Many of the Livery are associated with the craft. The officers consist of a Prime Warden and three other Wardens. The Company each year makes grants to well over a hundred charities, mostly for the benefit of Londoners. They have been munificent supporters of education and took a leading part in establishing the CITY AND GUILDS OF LONDON INSTITUTE. They founded GOLDSMITHS' COLLEGE and established a Chair of English at Oxford, of Metallurgy at Cambridge and of Microbiology at the UNIVERSITY OF LONDON. Particular interest is shown in extending the breadth of experience of schoolteachers. They have an outstanding silver plate collection, organise exhibitions and design competitions, give grants and travelling awards. The Livery numbers nearly 250. For the Hall see GOLDSMITHS' HALL.

Grocers' Company (2) *Princes Street, EC2*. The forerunners of the Grocers were the Pepperers, fined in 1180 as adulterine. They dealt in spices, drugs and tobacco, often coming from Italy and being connected with Italian merchants who had settled in London. They became responsible for inspecting and cleansing or garbling spices and also for regulating the weighing of all heavy imported goods by using the King's Beam, nominating the officers in charge for 350 years. Ordinances were drawn up for the Pepperers in 1345 but by 1373 the company became known as Grocers or properly Grossers because they dealt in bulk, i.e. were wholesale merchants. They became powerful with their first Charter in 1428 but suffered a loss in 1617 when the APOTHECARIES broke away, taking the drug business, and were nearly ruined in 1666 when the GREAT FIRE destroyed the Hall and practically all the rentable property. A century of struggle ensued, followed by a return to prosperity. Now the Company supports three schools at Oundle, the public school and two day schools. It has endowed other schools in London and Oxfordshire which have now passed under local authority control. It regularly supports the CITY AND GUILDS OF LONDON INSTITUTE and provides scholarships at a number of schools. The Grocers support a wide range of charitable activities, with particular emphasis on medical work, as well as the Church and the arts. The Livery numbers about 280. Members of the Company have included Sir John Crosby of CROSBY HALL, William Laxton, founder of Oundle School, General Monck, Heneage Finch, Sir Philip Sidney, Pitt the Elder and Pitt the Younger, and George Canning. For the Hall see GROCERS' HALL.

Gunmakers' Company (73) *48–50 Commercial Road, E1*. Received its first Charter in 1637. This working Company still tests and marks small arms gun barrels for public safety, having shared the task from the end of the 18th century with the Birmingham Proof House. Gunmakers are well represented on the Livery of nearly 150. A Hall was built in 1872 alongside the Proof House in WHITECHAPEL, which itself dates from 1757. This was the only Livery Hall outside the CITY but was sold in 1927. During the repair of war damage, a Court Room was incorporated in the Proof House in 1952.

Haberdashers' Company (8) *Staining Lane, EC2*. The Haberdashers were originally an offshoot of the MERCERS and had two distinct branches. The Hurrers or Cappers made and sold hats, while the Milliners imported fashionable goods from Milan. The first Ordinances were promulgated in 1371 and the first Charter granted in 1448, following a grant of arms in 1446. The various sections were united in 1502 and

became wholesale merchants. In Elizabethan times the Company was associated first with the import of pins and later with their production. These replaced the earlier natural thorns and because of their convenience became very popular. They were also very expensive so that all gentlemen had to allow their ladies 'pin money'. An Association of Pinners with its own Hall was formed but eventually died out. The wealth is represented today by an extraordinary number of educational charities. The Company is responsible for the HABERDASHERS' ASKE SCHOOLS and two schools for boys and for girls in Monmouth, as well as schools at Newport, Shropshire and Bunbury, Cheshire. Almshouses are maintained at Monmouth, Newport and Newland, Gloucestershire. Other charities provide scholarships, augment the stipends of clergymen and support the needy in various localities. The Livery numbers 320. For the Hall see HABERDASHERS' HALL.

Horners' Company (54) *365 Fulham Road, SW10*. A Mistery was recognised by 1375 but the Charter was delayed until 1638. Horners made horn articles such as windows, lanthorns and hornbooks. Now they have connections with plastics and sponsor the Horners' award. A boy at the CITY OF LONDON SCHOOL and another at EMANUEL SCHOOL is helped, also general charities. The Livery number 450.

Innholders' Company (32) *Dowgate Hill, EC4*. After mentions as Hostellers in the 14th and 15th centuries, the first Charter was granted in 1514, the name Innholders distinguishing them from the servant hostlers. The present Livery of a little over 100 has some connections with the trade. Homes for aged persons have been opened at WIMBLEDON, with three at Tunbridge Wells. The Hall, first mentioned in 1522 on the present site, was burnt in 1666 and rebuilt for opening in 1671. It was partly rebuilt in 1885–6, suffered slight damage in the 1st World War and severe damage in the 2nd. In 1950–2, it was partly rebuilt with Col E.D.J. Mathews as architect. Offices and basement were added in 1958–9.

Insurers' Company (92) *Hall of the Chartered Insurance Institute, 20 Aldermanbury, EC2*. The Company was incorporated and granted its Livery in 1979. Membership of the Company, which is limited to 300, is open only to persons wholly or mainly engaged in insurance. A Charitable Trust has been established.

Ironmongers' Company (10) *Barbican, EC2*. A fellowship existed in the 13th century. This was mentioned as a guild in the 14th century, was granted Arms in 1455 and its first Charter in 1463. The early ironmongers were known as ferroners, supplying and sometimes making such articles as bars, rods, horseshoes, and cart wheel tyres (which had to be of closely specified dimensions). The iron used came from the Weald of Sussex and Kent. The Company became important and wealthy and was able to make large contributions to the financial demands of the Crown. It took a prominent part in CITY pageants and in 1409 an Ironmonger LORD MAYOR produced a great play covering the history of the world which took eight days to present. Although a Great Company, it is one of the smallest in numbers and until 1977 the entire Livery formed the Court. The Livery now numbers 100. In 1723 an unusual charity was endowed by Thomas Betton with half his estate 'for the redemption of British slaves in Turkey or Barbary', and did good work. The original almshouses, endowed by Sir Robert Geffrye and built in 1715, now house the GEFFRYE MUSEUM and self-contained flats for 38 elderly people have been built at Hook near Basingstoke. Schools are helped, as are the needy. Exhibitions are granted at Oxford and Cambridge, research on iron and steel is supported at Sheffield University, and an annual award made to the ferrous foundry industry. The preservation of iron objects owned by the NATIONAL TRUST is aided. The Hall originated in 1457 with the purchase of some buildings in FENCHURCH STREET. These were rebuilt in 1587 and unlike many others survived the GREAT FIRE. The Hall was rebuilt in 1745 and suffered some bomb damage in 1917. However, the site was sold and the building demolished. The present site off ALDERS-GATE STREET was purchased in 1922 and the Hall opened in 1925. It was a coincidence that the site had been cleared and drained in 1606 by a Master of the Ironmongers. The Hall narrowly escaped destruction by fire in 1940. It is built in the Tudor style, recalling the Golden Age of craftmanship, using hand-made bricks and iron fittings. The panelled banqueting hall contains a minstrels' gallery and a fine Waterford glass chandelier. The architect was Sydney Tatchall. The dining capacity is 170.

Joiners' and Ceilers' Company *(41)* *8 West Heath Road, SE2*. Joiners make wooden glued joints such as mortice and tenon and use wood pins, whereas carpenters use only nails. Ceilers are wood carvers. A Guild was formed in 1375 and received a Charter in 1571. The Livery of over 100 supports the CITY AND GUILDS OF LONDON INSTITUTE and the BUILDING CRAFTS TRAINING SCHOOL. The former hall in UPPER THAMES STREET was built between 1518 and 1551 and burnt in 1666. It was rebuilt and again burnt in 1694. The next Hall of 1696 was let in 1799 but once more burnt in 1811. It was rebuilt as a warehouse but destroyed in 1940. The site was sold.

Launderers' Company *(89)* *34 Broadhurst, Ashtead, Surrey*. Formed as a guild in 1960, they were granted their Livery in 1977. This numbers about 150 and is composed of professionals engaged in laundering and dry cleaning. A benevolent Trust supports laundry students by scholarships, medals and books, particularly at the Derby College of Nottingham University, the Sail Training Association and Outward Bound scheme.

Leathersellers' Company *(15)* *St Helen's Place, EC3*. Received Ordinances on dyeing of leather in 1372 and the first Charter in 1444. The Pouchmakers joined in 1573. Exhibitions, scholarships or fellowships are awarded at English universities. The CITY AND GUILDS OF LONDON INSTITUTE and particularly the National Leathersellers' Centre at Northampton are supported. Almshouses at BARNET are administered, also COLFE'S SCHOOL and almshouses at LEWISHAM. The Livery numbers 150. For the Hall *see* LEATHERSELLERS' HALL.

Loriners' Company *(57)* *2–5 Benjamin Street, EC1*. Ordinances were issued in 1261, and a Charter in 1711. Loriners are makers and vendors of bridles, spurs, stirrups, bits and other metal parts for harness, mainly for horses. Always prominent in CITY affairs, the Company maintains a close trade connection, awarding training bursaries and conducting an annual examination in Lorinery. There are over 300 Liverymen. The former Hall existed until 1860 and its site is marked by a plaque on LONDON WALL.

Makers of Playing Cards' Company *(75)* *1 Serjeants Inn, Fleet Street, EC4*. The Charter is dated 1628 and the Livery granted in 1792. A Crown duty was payable to discourage importation of foreign cards. Special presentation packs are issued annually. An extensive collection of cards is maintained. The Livery of nearly 150 includes senior makers. A Trust controls charitable donations.

Marketors' Company *(90)* *25 Pebworth Road, Harrow*. A guild was formed in 1975 which became constituted as a Livery Company in 1977. The Livery, numbering about 140, is limited to persons engaged in marketing at a high level. An education and charitable Trust has been established.

Masons' Company *(30)* *9 New Square, Lincoln's Inn, WC2*. The first regulations were promulgated in 1356, Arms granted in 1472, the Livery in 1481 and a Charter in 1677. The Livery of about 100 includes architects and construction-industry representatives. Awards are made to stonemason apprentices and the Building Crafts Training School and the Vauxhall College of Further Education supported, as are charities. The Hall was on a site leased in 1463 from the Convent of Holy Trinity, off BASINGHALL STREET. The buildings were purchased in 1562 but were burned down in 1666. The rebuilt Hall was sold in 1865 but the site is still known as Masons' Avenue.

Master Mariners' Company *(78)* *Victoria Embankment, WC2*. The Company first met in 1926, received its Charter in 1930 and its Livery in 1932, the first new Livery for 223 years. It is limited to Master Mariners of at least five years' competency and has a Livery of 300. It publishes nautical information and aids nautical schools, needy navigating officers or dependents. The Hall is unique, being HQS WELLINGTON, a former sloop. It was acquired in 1947. The accommodation includes a spacious Hall with dining capacity of 108, offices, library and a model room.

Mercers' Company *(1)* *Ironmonger Lane, EC2*. The Mercers were originally leading London merchants who dealt in many articles, but particularly in textiles. They exported wool and woollen cloth and imported linen, silk and velvets. The term 'mercer' is derived from the French word *mercier*, meaning 'small ware dealer'. The Company's earliest ordinances are dated 1347 and it received its first royal charter in 1394. By the reign of Elizabeth I many Mercers were no longer connected with their original trade. The present Livery numbers about 250. Among famous Mercers were William Caxton, Dean Colet, Sir Thomas More, Sir Thomas Seymour, Richard Whittington (who founded almshouses for 13 poor citizens of London, now transformed into a housing complex for 45 elderly persons at East Grinstead), Sir Thomas Gresham (founder of the ROYAL EXCHANGE and of the Gresham Lectures, transferred to the CITY UNIVERSITY in 1966), Sir Rowland Hill and Lord Baden Powell. In education the Company has administered Dean Colet's ST PAUL'S SCHOOL since 1509 and in 1903 opened ST PAUL'S GIRLS' SCHOOL on the same foundation. Its own London school (*see* MERCERS' SCHOOL) has had to be closed after 400 years, but it still retains close links with Collyer's VI Form College at Horsham, Dauntsey's School at West Lavington and Abingdon School, all founded by Mercers. Annual grants are made to the CITY AND GUILDS OF LONDON INSTITUTE and to other educational bodies. The Company administers WHITTINGTON COLLEGE and TRINITY HOSPITAL at GREENWICH. It also maintains close associations with units of the Royal Navy, the Army and the Royal Air Force. In 1698 the Mercers made the first attempt to run a life assurance scheme, but in 1745 they had to hold a lottery to meet their commitments and the scheme was abandoned. For the Hall see MERCERS' HALL.

Merchant Taylors' Company *(7 or 6)*   *30 Threadneedle Street, EC2.* The Company's most lucrative activities in medieval times were the making of tents and the padded linen tunics worn under armour. In due course it became the inspecting authority for the measures used in selling cloth in the CITY and at Fairs. Its first Charter was granted in 1327. Its curious order of precedence resulted from a dispute with the SKINNERS, solved in 1484 by the LORD MAYOR who ruled that one Company should be sixth in one year and seventh in the next. The two Companies now dine together regularly. A quarrel with the GOLDSMITHS in 1267 ended less happily. After a pitched battle in which many were killed, the leaders were executed. The City historian John Stow, the cartographer John Speed and Sir Christopher Wren were all members of the Company and Titus Oates a pupil at the School. The Company still governs MERCHANT TAYLORS' SCHOOL at NORTHWOOD, and is interested in Merchant Taylors' Schools for boys and for girls at Crosby, Liverpool, as well as Wolverhampton Grammar School. Exhibitions and scholarships are awarded at Oxford and Cambridge and other educational establishments supported. In the LEWISHAM area are maintained 32 small almshouses, 28 on another neighbouring site and two blocks of housing in the form of self-contained flats. Many grants are made to the needy and financial help given to two London churches. The Livery numbers about 300 but has had no connection with the trade since the 17th century. The Hall has stood on its present site, acquired in 1331, from some date between 1347 and 1392. It lost the roof and interior in the GREAT FIRE but was restored by Jarman and reopened in 1671. In it James I was splendidly entertained on his arrival in London and it is reputed to be the scene of the first singing of the National Anthem in 1607 under the direction of John Bull. It was again severely damaged in 1940 but the Library, the Court Room and the Great Kitchen (used continuously since 1425) survived. The reconstructed Hall was opened in 1959. In the Hall itself small sections of the clay 14th-century floor, of the tile floor of 1646 and of the stone floor of 1675 have been left visible. Other fine rooms are the Drawing Room and the Great Parlour. Precious possessions include two fine funeral palls of 1490 and 1520 and the Account Book goes back to 1397. The architect of the restored Hall was Sir Albert Richardson and its dining capacity is 250.

Musicians' Company *(50)*   *4 St Paul's Churchyard, EC4.* The Musicians received Ordinances in 1350 and were incorporated in 1500. Awards are made to singers, composers, advanced organ students and students at schools of music throughout the country including the military schools such as the Royal Naval College of Music and KNELLER HALL. There are also other charitable funds for musical objects. The Livery numbers about 150.

Needlemakers' Company *(65)*   *4 Staple Inn, Holborn, WC1.* After unsuccessful applications, a Charter signed by Oliver Cromwell was granted in 1656. Needlemakers moved from demolished houses on LONDON BRIDGE to Redditch, where the industry is supported by prizes and awards of the honorary freedom. The Company almost disappeared in 1870 but revived with London support. The Livery numbers 225.

Painter-Stainers' Company *(28)*   *9 Little Trinity Lane, EC4.* Painters (Ordinances 1283 and 1466) worked on cloth and Stainers (mentioned 1268) on wood and metal. They united in 1502, receiving their first Charter in 1581. Many prizes are given to the CITY AND GUILDS OF LONDON INSTITUTE and other colleges. Charities are widely spread, especially for the blind. The Livery numbers some 375. Members have included Sir Godfrey Kneller, Antonio Verrio, Richard Lovelace, Sir Peter Lely and Sir James Thornhill. For the Hall *see* PAINTER-STAINERS' HALL.

Pattenmakers' Company *(70)*   *6 Raymond Buildings, Gray's Inn, WC1.* The mistery was mentioned in 1379 and received its Charter in 1670. A patten was an undershoe to raise the ordinary shoe above the mud. The shoe trade is well represented in the Livery of over 200. Prizes are given in competitions and scholarships to CITY schools. Charities are concentrated towards 'young enterprise'.

Paviors' Company *(56)*   *Cutlers' Hall, Warwick Lane, EC4.* Received Ordinances in 1479 but the 1672 Charter was opposed by the CORPORATION. In addition to constructing streets and pavements, the Company was responsible for removing scavenging pigs. The Livery of 250 is representative of the industry. A Chair of Highway Engineering is operated through the CITY UNIVERSITY. LONDON UNIVERSITY is also supported.

Pewterers' Company *(16)*   *Oat Lane, EC2.* Articles were applied for in 1348, the first Charter granted in 1473 and accounts date from 1451. The Livery numbers 105. Research is financed at the Institute of Neurology and the CITY UNIVERSITY. School scholarships are awarded and the CITY AND GUILDS OF LONDON INSTITUTE and Art School supported. The first Hall in LIME STREET was built in 1496 on a site bought in 1484 and still owned. It was burned in 1666. The next Hall of 1670 had good interior decorations but these were burned in 1840 and the Hall demolished in 1932. The Oat Lane Hall was opened in 1961 with panelling and three chandeliers from LIME STREET.

Plaisterers' Company *(46)*   *1 London Wall, EC2.* The Company was incorporated by its first Charter in 1501. The Livery numbers about 195. Pensioners are nominated for two Trusts administered by the MERCHANT TAYLORS. The Company was a Founder of the CITY AND GUILDS OF LONDON INSTITUTE and still supports it, and a register of skilled plasterers is maintained. The first Hall in Addle Street dated from 1556 and was destroyed in 1666. Wren designed the 1669 Hall, which was burned in 1882. The present Hall and office block were opened in 1972 with a Great Hall of 300 dining capacity, a Livery Hall, Court Room and Mott Room (so called after the Mott family who supplied three clerks to the Company), all with Adam-style plasterwork and decoration.

Plumbers' Company *(31)*   *218 Strand, WC2.* Granted Ordinances in 1365 and the first Charter in 1611. Medieval plumbers made glazing, cisterns and large roofs and certified lead weights. A register of plumbers was maintained until 1960. The Company is active in the building industry, sponsoring various awards and prizes. A gold medal is awarded annually.

The Livery numbers about 275. The Former Hall stood in Chequer Yard, BUSH LANE from 1532. After destruction in 1666 it was rebuilt, but was demolished in 1863 to make way for CANNON STREET STATION.

Poulters' Company *(34)* *7–8 King's Bench Walk, Temple, EC4*. Received Ordinances from 1368 and a Charter in 1665. It controlled the sale of rabbits, pigeons, game, poultry and swans. About 60 per cent of the Livery of 150 are connected with poultry and frozen food. An annual grant is made to the Game Conservancy, Fordingbridge. Nepton's Charity helps elderly people in ILFORD and BARKING. Former Halls existed between 1610 and 1666.

Saddlers' Company *(25)* *Gutter Lane, EC2*. Perhaps following an Anglo-Saxon predecessor, the first Charter may have been granted in 1272, succeeded by incorporation in 1395. The Livery of nearly 100 retains close connections with saddlery. Prizes are given at the CITY AND GUILDS OF LONDON INSTITUTE, CORDWAINERS' COLLEGE, horse trials and show jumping. The CITY UNIVERSITY and ALLEYN'S SCHOOL are helped and pensions granted. The first Hall in FOSTER LANE dated from the end of the 14th century. It was destroyed in 1666 and rebuilt by 1670. That Hall was damaged by fire in 1815 and burnt out in 1821. Its successor was destroyed in 1940. The present Hall, designed by L. Sylvester Sullivan, was opened in 1958 with a dining capacity of 150. It possesses a 1508 funeral pall and a 1619 ballot box.

Salters' Company *(9)* *Fore Street, EC2*. In 1394 a Fraternity and Guild of Corpus Christi, which was composed of salters, was founded. This was further licensed in 1467 and a Charter granted in 1559. Salt was essential in the medieval preservation of meat and fish. It was imported from the west coast of France and landed at QUEENHITHE, later at BILLINGSGATE, whence it was measured out and distributed by the Company's saltmeters. They also dealt in flax, hemp and many chemicals such as potash. This gave them a continuing interest in the chemical industry and today the Livery of about 150 includes an appreciable representation of scientists. Inevitably there were disputes with other Companies, such as the TALLOW CHANDLERS, who were concerned with salt sauces. There is a long history of educational support in schools, colleges and universities; and in 1918 an important step was taken in the foundation of the Salters' Institute of Industrial Chemistry, designed particularly to help young chemists complete their training. This awarded fellowships and still provides scholarships and prizes. The Salters also organise refresher courses for school teachers of chemistry and give grants for books and equipment. Research in industrial chemistry has been assisted at some universities and technical colleges. General charities include administration of almshouses at Watford and Maidenhead and help for other charities.

The first Hall was built in BREAD STREET in 1454 and was rebuilt after destruction by fire in 1539. In 1641 Oxford House in ST SWITHIN'S LANE was purchased but both this and the hall in BREAD STREET were lost in the GREAT FIRE in 1666. By 1668 a new Hall was built on the Oxford House site. In 1695 this was extended to include a piazza. A completely new Hall, with an impressive Ionic portico by E. Carr, replaced it between 1824 and 1827. This in turn was destroyed by fire in 1941 and the site sold. A modern new Hall, designed by Sir Basil Spence, was opened in FORE

STREET in 1976. This possesses a splendid ash panelled Banqueting Hall with a dining capacity of 120, committee rooms, court room and office accommodation.

Scientific Instrument Makers' Company *(84)* *9 Montague Close, SE1*. The Livery of about 200 is limited to scientific instrument makers and distinguished users. It was formed in 1955 and granted its Livery in 1964. Fellowships are awarded at Massachusetts Institute of Technology, a Teaching Fellowship at Girton College, and prizes at the CITY UNIVERSITY and the CITY AND GUILDS OF LONDON INSTITUTE. The Hall at the south west corner of LONDON BRIDGE is shared with the GLAZIERS' COMPANY.

Scriveners' Company *(44)* *4 Wilton Mews, SW1*. Ordinances were formulated in 1373 and the Charter granted in 1617. Formerly, legal documents had to written by Scriveners in Latin. The Company still has jurisdiction over London public notaries. Many of the present Livery of about 170 are connected with the legal profession. A charitable fund exists for members and their relatives. The former Hall in NOBLE STREET was occupied from 1631. It was destroyed in the GREAT FIRE, rebuilt but sold in 1703 to the COACH AND HARNESS MAKERS.

Shipwrights' Company *(59)* *Ironmongers' Hall, Barbican, EC2*. The Free Shipwrights received Ordinances in 1428 and the Foreign (Rotherhithe) Shipwrights a Charter in 1612, but a legal decision caused the latter's demise. In 1782 the present Company received its Livery, which, numbering 500, is restricted to persons with British maritime interests. Charitable and educational support is given to maritime objectives, including apprentices. The former Hall stood in RATCLIFF from the beginning of the 17th century to the end of the 18th century when it was destroyed.

Skinners' Company *(6 or 7)* *8 Dowgate Hill, EC4*. Deriving from two religious brotherhoods, founded in the 12th and 13th centuries, the Skinners received their first Charter in 1327. They controlled the fur trade and became wealthy because the wearing of furs was restricted to the upper classes as an obvious indication of dignity. This sense of importance led to disputes on precedence with other Companies, notably the FISHMONGERS' and the MERCHANT TAYLORS'. In the latter case in 1484 the Mayor ruled that the two Companies should occupy the 6th and 7th positions in alternate years and entertain each other regularly, arrangements which still apply. The Company is governed by a Master and four Wardens. The Master is chosen by trying a hat on various Liverymen but miraculously it is usually found to fit only the First Warden. The present Livery of about 300 has only slight connections with the fur trade. There are notable educational activities. In 1553 a Skinner, Sir Andrew Judd, built a school, Tonbridge, of which the Company became governors at his death. In the same town, the Judd School was established in 1888. In Tunbridge Wells the Skinners' School for boys was founded in 1886 and a similar school for girls set up in 1889 at STAMFORD HILL. Scholarships are awarded at Oxford and Cambridge and support given to the CITY UNIVERSITY. Among general charities is one for assisting young men with vocational training.

The Hall has probably existed on its present site since 1380. It was burned down in 1666. The rebuilt Hall was refronted in 1778 by a handsome façade facing DOWGATE HILL. This was designed by R. Jupp and incorporates Ionic pilasters supporting an entablature and pediment. Alterations were made to the Hall in 1847 by G. Moore. Serious war damage was sustained in 1941 and 1944. The dining-hall of the restored building is distinguished by a fine series of 15 panels by Frank Brangwyn. Its dining capacity is 160. The adjacent elegant Old Court room is now used for luncheons and small receptions. On the first floor the Court Room is fitted with 17th-century cedar panelling. A fine 18th-century Russian glass chandelier hangs in the Outer Hall.

Solicitors' Company (City of London) *(79) Cutlers' Hall, Warwick Lane, EC4.* The Company was founded in 1908, granted its Livery in 1944 and its Charter in 1957. Membership is limited to CITY solicitors and it acts as the local law society. Prizes are given in the LAW SOCIETY examinations and CITY and professional charities supported. The Livery numbers 420.

Spectacle Makers' Company *(60) Apothecaries' Hall, Blackfriars Lane, EC4.* The Company was granted its Charter in 1629 but its Livery not until 1809. The majority of the Livery of about 300 are concerned with the trade but the greatest public service has been the examinations since 1898 to qualify opticians to practise; there are over 4,000 qualified Freemen. Optical research is supported.

Stationers' and Newspaper Makers' Company *(47) Stationers' Hall, EC4.* A Brotherhood was established in 1403 and chartered in 1557. It controlled publication of books which until 1911 were registered at Stationers' Hall. The Livery of 450 is totally connected with the trade. The Company's School (1858) moved to HORNSEY in 1895. Trade and general charities are supported, also travelling scholarships. The present site off LUDGATE HILL was bought in 1611. This was burned in 1666, rebuilt by 1673, and refronted in 1800 by Robert Mylne. A wing was rebuilt in 1888. Having suffered severely in the 2nd World War the Hall was restored in 1950–6 with Geoffrey Gurney as architect. The dining capacity is 183.

Tallow Chandlers' Company *(21) 4 Dowgate Hill, EC4.* Tallow candles were used for ordinary illumination, wax for churches. The Company also dealt in vinegar, salt, sauces and oils. It was granted its first Charter in 1462. The present Livery of 160 includes representatives of the oil trades. Awards are made to oil craft apprentices and to Selwyn College, Cambridge and Bembridge School. The present Hall site was purchased in 1476, the Hall being destroyed in 1666. Rebuilt in 1672 by John Caines and Edward Jarman, the building still survives though considerably damaged in the 2nd World War. The panelling in the Parlour and Court Room survives from the 1670s. The restoration of 1947–55 was planned by Edmund Mathews and Professor Richardson, providing a Banqueting Hall seating 90.

Tin Plate Workers' Company Alias Wireworkers *(67) 71 Lincoln's Inn Fields, WC2.* Evolved from the IRONMONGERS, they joined with the Wireworkers in 1425 and received a Charter in 1670. The modern Livery of about 195 has connections with the electrical wire industry. Awards are made of scholarships, bursaries and for craftsmanship.

Tobacco Pipe Makers' and Tobacco Blenders' Company *(82) 154 Fleet Street, EC4.* Earlier Companies existed from 1619 to 1642, from 1663 to 1864, with a re-establishment in 1954 and a Livery granted

in 1960. Many Liverymen, totalling over 170, are connected with the trade. Considerable financial support is given to Sevenoaks School; others helped include boys' clubs and the GUILDHALL SCHOOL OF MUSIC.

Turners' Company *(51) 1 Serjeants' Inn, EC4.* A Society received Ordinances in 1478 and the Company its first Charter in 1604. Turners made wooden cups, platters and ale measures, as well as furniture and machine tools. The modern Livery of about 170 includes many engineers. Numerous engineering, woodworking and design awards are made and financial help is given to a number of charities. A former Hall stood in PHILPOT LANE from 1591. This was destroyed in 1666 but rebuilt in 1670. It was given up in 1737 and a new Hall acquired in COLLEGE HILL. This was sold in 1766 and not replaced.

Tylers' and Bricklayers' Company *(37) 6 Bedford Row, WC1.* Tilers laid roof, floor and wall tiles, the latter becoming known as bricks in the 16th century. A Charter was granted in 1568. Nearly one half of the present Livery of about 100 is associated with building. A Trust supports charities, the BUILDING CRAFTS TRAINING SCHOOL and makes awards for outstanding buildings. A former Hall existed in LEADENHALL STREET from the 16th century and was one of the few to escape the GREAT FIRE. Not used by the Company after 1767, when it became the synagogue of Dutch Jews, it was rebuilt in the early 19th century and the site sold in 1915.

Upholders' Company *(49) 56 Kingsway, WC2.* Was associated with upholstery and bedding with a wide range of second-hand goods. Mentioned in 1360, a petition was granted in 1474 and a Charter in 1626. The present Livery of 200 includes Master Upholsterers. A gold medal is awarded to the trade and dependants of craftsmen are assisted. A former Hall existed in LAMBETH HILL. It was burnt down in 1666 and not replaced.

Vintners' Company *(11) Upper Thames Street, EC4.* Originally divided into *Vinterarii* (wine importers) and *Tabernarii* (innkeepers), the former being the more important. The Company received a Charter in 1364 which granted it a monopoly of trade with Gascony, followed in 1437 by a grant of incorporation. The Company's extensive powers over the trade are still reflected in the privilege of some free Vintners of selling wine at approved sites free of excise licence. There is a legend that in 1363 the Vintners feasted at one time the five kings of England, France, Scotland, Denmark and Cyprus, in memory of which distinction the number five is mentioned in the Company's toasts and five cheers are given instead of the usual three. Another historic relic is the sweeping clean of the street before the installation day procession to church, recalling its medieval muddy condition. The Vintners share with the DYERS and the Crown the ownership of all SWANS on the THAMES, their cygnets being marked with two nicks on the beak on the annual Swan Upping Voyage. About a quarter of the present Livery of some 300 belong to the wine trade. A 1973 Charter authorised the setting up of the Wine Standards Board with certain responsibilities for enforcing the EEC Wine Laws. Education in wine is encouraged by a travel scholarship and a bursary and by participation in founding the Master of Wine examination. Close connections are maintained with all appropriate trade, educational and benevolent associations. The Company's almshouses are now at Nutley, Sussex.

The first Hall stood from 1357 and in 1446 the Company was bequeathed the present UPPER THAMES STREET site. That was destroyed in 1666 but by 1671 the Hall was rebuilt by Roger Jarman as master craftsman. It still survives, having suffered only minor damage in the 2nd World War. The Court Room is splendidly panelled. The main Hall has a dining capacity of 140. A fine staircase of 1673 leads to an impressive late 19th-century drawing-room. Among interesting possessions are a tapestry of 1466, a hearse cloth given to the Company in 1539 and a painting after Van Dyck showing St Martin (the Vintners' patron saint) dividing his cloak with the beggar. Outside the Hall on the corbel of the west wall is the painted COADE STONE *Vintry Schoolboy* by an unknown sculptor, c. 1840.

Watermen and Lightermen's Company *see* WATERMEN AND LIGHTERMEN.

Wax Chandlers' Company *(20) Gresham Street, EC2.* Collective action was recorded in 1330, the first Ordinances were granted in 1358 and the first Charter in 1484. The present Livery numbers about 80. Close connections exist with the British Bee Keepers' Association. The London Parochial and Bexley United Charities are supported, also the CITY UNIVERSITY and the CITY AND GUILDS OF LONDON INSTITUTE and CHRIST'S HOSPITAL. The Hall passed to the Company in 1544 but was destroyed in 1666. Rebuilt by Edward Jarman in 1668–70, it was replaced in 1793 and again in 1853 to the designs of Charles Fowler, a Past-Master. This was destroyed in 1940 and, with Seely and Paget as architects, rebuilt in 1956–8. The dining capacity is 60. Two floors are let as offices.

Weavers' Company *(42) 1 The Sanctuary, SW1.* Existing in 1130, the Weavers are the oldest Livery Company, receiving their first Charter in 1155. A complicated history includes the splitting off of other textile Companies and temporary suppression. About one third of the present Livery of 130 is connected with textiles. Valuable awards are made in textile technology and craft. Almshouses at WANSTEAD shelter 40 persons. The first Hall in BASINGHALL STREET was burnt down in 1666. It was rebuilt in the 1680s by Edward Jarman and demolished in 1856. A block of offices replaced the Hall and the site was sold in 1962.

Wheelwrights' Company *(68) Greenup, Milton Avenue, Gerrards Cross, Bucks.* Received a Charter in 1670 conferring strict powers over wheel making to promote public safety. Court meetings demanded dignified dress. The Livery of 275 still supports road safety by awarding prizes. It operates three charitable Trust funds in aid of needy dependants of Wheelwrights, also general charities.

Woolmen's Company *(43) 192–198 Vauxhall Bridge Road, SW1.* Incorporated by prescription in 1522, the Company engaged in the winding, packing and selling of raw wool. One third of the present Livery of about 130 is concerned with wool. Wool studies are encouraged at Leeds University by scholarships and prizes, also the Clothing and Footwear Institute. Wool and CITY charities are supported.

COMPANIES WITHOUT LIVERY

Parish Clerks' Company *14 Dale Close, Oxford.* The membership of about 100 is limited to London parish clerks who prefer to wear gown and cassock instead of livery. Based on a religious fraternity existing from 1274, the first Charter was received in 1442.

A former Hall existed in CLARK'S PLACE but was confiscated in 1547. Its replacement in 1562 in Brode (Broad) Lane was destroyed in 1666. The third Hall was opened in SILVER STREET in 1671. This was damaged in 1765 and destroyed in 1940, the site being subsequently sold.

Watermen and Lightermen of the River Thames *18 St Mary-at-Hill, EC3.* Founded by Act of Parliament in 1555, the Company until 1908 was the licensing authority for all watermen, who in Stuart times numbered some 20,000. They constantly opposed the building of a second bridge. Even now there are several thousand Freemen. Almshouses and pensions for Freemen are maintained, also a Trust for after-school education. For the Hall *see* WATERMEN AND LIGHTERMEN'S HALL.

City Marshal The third of the Household Officers of the LORD MAYOR. He shares the administration of engagements and daily attendance upon the LORD MAYOR with the SWORDBEARER and the COMMON CRYER and SERJEANT-AT-ARMS. Letters patent of Queen Elizabeth I dated 1595 gave powers to a marshal to maintain order in the CITY. Today he controls the marshalling of most civic processions and calls the names of the members thereof in their proper order. He also challenges troops exercising the privilege of marching through the CITY with drums beating, bayonets fixed and colours flying.

City of London The area ruled by the LORD MAYOR and CORPORATION OF LONDON covers some 677 acres, or slightly over one square mile, including the TEMPLE precinct. On the west it reaches TEMPLE BAR and HOLBORN BARS, on the north SMITHFIELD and MOORFIELDS, on the east ALDGATE and TOWER HILL and on the south the River THAMES. While it can be assumed that there was a settlement in the area before the Romans came – Tacitus, writing about AD 67, refers to it as a flourishing trading city – no reliable evidence has come to light regarding its origins. The name is said to derive from Lyn-dun – the fortified town on the lake – from the wide stretch of water which formerly stood above the navigable part of the THAMES. London history really starts with Aulus Plautius, who was ruler of Britain under the Emperor Claudius, AD 43–50. The Romans settled down to colonising the city which they called LONDINIUM, and transforming it into a highly civilised community. Archaeologists have discovered the sites of the Great Basilica and FORUM in LEADENHALL, a TEMPLE OF MITHRAS in BUCKLERSBURY and a handsome tessellated pavement in the same area; among many other relics now in the MUSEUM OF LONDON in the BARBICAN is a reasonably authentic reconstruction of a Roman house interior in the City. Some refinements of Roman life, like central heating, disappeared after the departure of the Romans and re-appeared only in the late 19th century (*see also* ROMAN LONDON). How the Romans named their streets is not known, but it is certain that they built a bridge over the THAMES near the site of the present LONDON BRIDGE and that they built a stout wall round the city, the area of which was then about 330 acres – one and a half times as big as Verulamium (the modern St Albans). The wall was 3¼ miles in length and contained six main gates to the trunk roads. Much of it stood until the late 18th century, when it was demolished as an obstruction. All that survives

The old City of London gates were all demolished before the end of the 18th century, with the exception of Temple Bar (8). The rest are (1) Aldgate, (2) Bishopsgate, (3) Moorgate, (4) Cripplegate, (5) Aldersgate, (6) Newgate, and (7) Ludgate.

now consists of fragments built into later construction, as at CRIPPLEGATE and Cooper's Row. The riverside portion had been demolished by about 1150.

Little is known about London after the withdrawal of the Roman Legions in AD 410 until it was occupied by the Saxon invaders in the 6th century. In 604 Ethelbert, first Christian King of Kent, founded ST PAUL'S CATHEDRAL and is said to have had a palace in ALDERMANBURY, occupied by succeeding Saxon kings until Edward the Confessor moved to WESTMINSTER about 1060. When William the Conqueror arrived in 1066 he built the TOWER OF LONDON outside the City's east wall in order to keep an eye on its inhabitants, but was statesman enough to grant them a charter confirming the rights which they had enjoyed under Edward the Confessor. Henry I allowed them to appoint their own SHERIFF and in 1215 a charter of King John confirmed their right to elect a MAYOR and CORPORATION provided that each new MAYOR be presented to him or his Justiciar or Chief Minister. During the Middle Ages the craft guilds or CITY LIVERY COMPANIES grew up, and as time went on came to represent the citizens in their choice of a MAYOR.

In due course the efficiency of the City's government became manifest; and in 1585 it was taken as a model for the administration of the city of WESTMINSTER. Perhaps the most famous of the medieval Mayors of London was Richard Whittington, folk hero and wealthy merchant, who served in the office four times and contributed to the building of GUILDHALL and GUILDHALL LIBRARY.

LONDON BRIDGE was completed in 1209, and remained the only stone bridge over the THAMES for five and a half centuries and the only one in the City until Mylne's BLACKFRIARS BRIDGE of 1769. Built on 19 arches it had shops or houses on both sides of its narrow carriage way and a chapel dedicated to St Thomas of Canterbury embodied in its construction. At its southern end was the Bridge Gate, over which the heads of malefactors were displayed on spikes as a warning to would-be criminals.

During the latter part of the Tudor dynasty the country in general and London in particular underwent testing times. The monastic establishments were suppressed (*see* DISSOLUTION OF THE MONASTERIES); the churches turned Protestant under Henry VIII, back to Catholic under Mary I and to Protestant again under Elizabeth I. The currency was debased and there was mass unemployment. Sir Thomas Gresham restored the currency and built the ROYAL EXCHANGE as a meeting-place for the City merchants who launched an export drive of world-wide proportions. Great trading companies sprang up – the Muscovy Company, the Turkey Company, the Levant Company, the Virginia Company, and in 1600 the most famous of all, the Honourable East India Company, which maintained an army and a navy in India and developed a mercantile fleet with standards of service, discipline and maintenance never exceeded since. It was not only in the world of commerce that the City of London was distinguished in Tudor and Stuart times. Chaucer and Spenser were born here and Shakespeare had associations here. The chroniclers, John Stow and Alderman Fabyan, were natives of the City. William Dobson and William Hogarth, leading painters of their age, were both City-born, as was Inigo Jones, architect of the BANQUETING HOUSE and London's first town planner.

Perhaps the greatest influence on the development of the City were its twin disasters of the 17th century, the GREAT PLAGUE of 1665 and the GREAT FIRE of 1666. The plague was introduced by the Norwegian brown rat which came to London in trading ships. It had arrived some years before, and there were large numbers of deaths from it for several decades previously; but it reached its height in 1665, with many of the citizens moving out to Essex and Kent and the mortality among those remaining in London so heavy that mass burials were carried out in large plague pits on the fringes of the City. Buildings in the City were mostly small, cramped and ill-constructed, and sanitation was so primitive that it was said that with a westerly wind London could be smelt from Tilbury, so disease spread rapidly. During the summer of 1666 a long hot spell made matters worse. As is normal in England, the dry weather brought a strong easterly wind, and when a fire was accidentally started in a bakery in PUDDING LANE near LONDON BRIDGE on the night of 3 September it developed into a conflagration which destroyed two thirds of the City before the flames were extinguished four days later. The Fire destroyed the ROYAL EXCHANGE, ST PAUL'S CATHEDRAL and many handsome City halls; but it also destroyed many rotten buildings and exterminated the Norwegian brown rats.

The Commission appointed to plan the rebuilding included Robert Hooke, Edward Jerman, Peter Mills and Sir Christopher Wren. Ambitious designs were produced by Wren, John Evelyn and Valentine Knight, all of them involving alteration of the street plan, which would have taken a lot of time. Time, however, was what the City could not spare, since its very existence depended on commerce and it needed to get back to work. So the rebuilding had to be more realistic, that is to say modelled on the old street plan, but with buildings of brick and stone. Wren rebuilt ST PAUL'S in a Renaissance style and 49 of the City's parish churches in a variety of attractive designs of his own, and put an ugly and incongruous clerestory with a flat roof over the Gothic walls of the burnt-out GUILDHALL. Jerman rebuilt the ROYAL EXCHANGE and designed other buildings. Wren also designed the Fire MONUMENT, a fluted stone column 202 ft high with a viewing platform and a cap of gilded flames at the top.

During the 18th century more handsome buildings sprang up – the BANK OF ENGLAND, the new EAST INDIA HOUSE, IRONMONGERS' HALL, the MANSION HOUSE designed by George Dance the Elder, and the neo-Gothic façade of GUILDHALL by his son and namesake. The following century saw the rebuilding of GOLDSMITHS' HALL and FISHMONGERS' HALL and the replacement of two famous bridges – the 620-year-old LONDON BRIDGE by John Rennie's bridge in 1831 and the century-old BLACKFRIARS BRIDGE by Sir Horace Jones's splendid Victorian structure. Both bridges necessitated the cutting of new streets for their approaches – KING WILLIAM STREET, PRINCE'S STREET and MOORGATE for LONDON BRIDGE and QUEEN VICTORIA STREET for BLACKFRIARS. A further bridge – SOUTHWARK BRIDGE – led directly via QUEEN STREET and KING STREET to GUILDHALL, and the railways built bridges into the City at CANNON STREET and BLACKFRIARS. The picturesque TOWER BRIDGE, the bascules of which can be raised to admit ships to the Upper Pool, was opened in 1894 by the Prince of Wales (afterwards Edward VII).

Jerman's ROYAL EXCHANGE was destroyed by fire and replaced by the present building by William Tite. Smirke's GENERAL POST OFFICE was erected in ST MARTIN'S-LE-GRAND, subsequently being superseded by the present GENERAL POST OFFICE in King Edward Building across the road. Wren's clerestory and roof in GUILDHALL were replaced by a more fitting wooden open roof by Sir Horace Jones. Large commercial buildings were put up, a notable example being the PRUDENTIAL ASSURANCE building in HOLBORN. The CITY CORPORATION augmented the educational facilities already provided within its boundaries by the wards and parishes, the CITY LIVERY COMPANIES and the great religious foundations by building a public school for boys in MILK STREET (subsequently removed to VICTORIA EMBANKMENT) and one for girls in Carmelite Street; and also a school of music and drama in John Carpenter Street (see CITY OF LONDON SCHOOLS and GUILDHALL SCHOOL OF MUSIC AND DRAMA). The HOLBORN valley was bridged and CANNON STREET and BISHOPSGATE STREET widened. A new system of sewers did much to combat the outbreak of CHOLERA in the 1830s and 1840s and occasioned a great deal of useful work in the large-scale mapping of the City. Charles Pearson, City Solicitor in 1839–62, pioneered efforts to connect the City by rail with the termini of the main line railways and eventually the METROPOLITAN, London's first underground line, ran from FARRINGDON via KING'S CROSS to PADDINGTON and was opened in 1863 (see UNDERGROUND RAILWAYS). By the end of the century the City had four main line termini – LIVERPOOL STREET, FENCHURCH STREET, CANNON STREET and HOLBORN VIADUCT – and its first deep 'Tube' UNDERGROUND RAILWAYS to WATERLOO and STOCKWELL. The London General Omnibus Company was formed in 1855, and by 1900 a network of bus routes covered the whole of London, including the City, and trams reached the City boundaries from all directions. Motor buses appeared on the City streets in 1908 and gradually ousted the horse bus. Electricity took over as the motive power for trams and underground railways and even some suburban lines of the main line railways (see also TRANSPORT).

During the 1st World War there were air raids on the City. The GENERAL POST OFFICE in ST MARTIN'S-LE-GRAND was damaged and the beautiful IRONMONGERS' HALL in FENCHURCH STREET demolished. Much fine building took place during the 1920s and 1930s including extensive additions to the BANK OF ENGLAND by Sir Herbert Baker, Royal Mail House in LEADENHALL STREET by Sir Edwin Cooper and the startling *Daily Express* building in FLEET STREET by Ellis and Clarke in collaboration with SIR OWEN WILLIAMS.

The 2nd World War outdid the GREAT FIRE of 1666 in its destruction in the City. GUILDHALL itself was burnt out and everything around it and to the north of it between ALDERSGATE and MOORGATE was completely laid waste. ST PAUL'S CATHEDRAL was damaged and the NEWGATE, BLACKFRIARS and TOWER HILL areas flattened. The total devastated area roughly equalled that after the GREAT FIRE, but the rebuilding took considerably longer. This was partly because underground works such as drains, gas and water pipes and electric supply lines had to be dealt with but mainly because the operation involved massive replanning, much of which was altered as work went on. Some of the City churches were beyond repair, but most were rebuilt, and in their open setting among the new buildings gained much in appearance. One of them, ST MARY ALDERMANBURY, was taken down stone by stone and re-erected at Westminster College in Fulton, Missouri, USA as a memorial to Sir Winston Churchill.

North of GUILDHALL, the extension of LONDON WALL westwards to ALDERSGATE and the erection of the BARBICAN – an extensive residential complex with a museum, an arts centre and the CITY OF LONDON SCHOOL FOR GIRLS (removed from BLACKFRIARS) – form one of the two greatest recent achievements in the City's reconstruction. The other was the replacement of Rennie's LONDON BRIDGE of 1831 by a graceful new bridge designed by the City Engineer, Harold King, and William Holford and Partners. The building was carried on without interrupting traffic in and out of the City, and, being paid for out of the City's Cash, at no cost to the ratepayers.

Today the City of London, with its many centuries of history, its traditions of craft guilds and commerce, state pageantry and national hospitality and its exemplary system of local government, stands as an example of careful husbandry, civic pride and national dignity. Its chief citizen, the LORD MAYOR, who is also Admiral of the PORT OF LONDON, Head of the City Lieutenancy and Chancellor of the CITY UNIVERSITY, is the host of princes and presidents, the organiser of world-wide charity and the champion of the rights of his citizens. He ranks before all except the Sovereign in the City, and his permission must be sought for the entry of troops into the City – even those regiments who by tradition are privileged to march through it with bayonets fixed, drums beating and colours flying. Between 1971 and 1981 the City's work force was reduced from about 500,000 to some 360,000. Three-quarters of these are office workers, nearly all of whom live elsewhere. Only about 8,000 people now live in the City, most of them custodians of office buildings and their families and the occupants of the BARBICAN housing development.

City of London Cemetery *see* CEMETERIES.

City of London Club *19 Old Broad Street, EC2.* Founded in 1832 by a group of prominent bankers, merchants and shipowners under the chairmanship of John Masterman, MP. The first meetings took place at members' offices and at the GEORGE AND VULTURE, ST MICHAEL'S ALLEY. The Duke of Wellington, Sir Robert Peel and Baron Nathan Meyer de Rothschild were among the original members. The Palladian club house was built in 1833–4 to the design of Philip Hardwick. It occupies part of the site of SOUTH SEA HOUSE. The club was originally intended for bankers, merchants and shipowners, and now only 'principals' of firms or the sons of existing members qualify for membership. There is a quota of solicitors and stockbrokers in the club. In the early 1970s the club was threatened by plans for the adjacent NATIONAL WESTMINSTER TOWER. Conservationists fought to obtain listed status for the building, which was granted in 1974. In return for land elsewhere, the bank agreed to finance the restoration of the club. Max Gordon, the architect who restored the building at a cost of £2,000,000, describes the juxtaposition of the Palladian club and the tower as 'architectural schizophrenia'. The combined entrance and annual subscription fees are the most expensive in London.

City of London Coat of Arms Argent, a cross gules, in the first quarter a sword in pale, point upwards, of the last. Crest: on a wreath of the colours. A dragon's sinister wing argent charged on the underside with a cross throughout gules. Supporters: on either side a dragon argent charged on the undersides of the wings with a cross throughout gules. Motto: *Domine dirige nos*. Arms 'anciently recorded'. Crest (on a peer's helmet) and supporters confirmed and granted 30 April 1957.

City of London Corporation *see* CORPORATION OF LONDON.

City of London Freemen's School The City of London Freemen's Orphan School was founded in 1854 and opened in BRIXTON for the education of orphans of Freemen (*see* FREEDOM OF THE CITY). Social improvements as time went on led to a gradual falling off of applications for admission to the school, and in 1926 it was moved to Ashtead Park in Surrey as a fee-paying boarding school, the word 'Orphan' being dropped from its name. Today many Freemen send their children to it as fee-paying pupils, but orphans of Freemen are still eligible to be admitted as Foundationers. The school is co-educational and also accepts day pupils from the Ashtead area.

City of London Police The genesis of the present City of London Police force is the City Day Police which was formed in 1784 in the aftermath of the GORDON RIOTS. By 1824 it was no longer strictly a Day Police but a Night Police, too. In 1838 it was totally reorganised together with the CITY's archaic constables and watchmen. The old systems were abandoned and the Day Police and Nightly Watch of 500 men were brought into being under the command of a Superintendent. Under Home Office pressure further changes were demanded. The City of London Police Act (1839), which is still its constitutional authority, replaced the Superintendent with a Commissioner and changed the name of the force to the City of London Police. The force had no legal jurisdiction to act beyond the boundaries of the one square mile. Originally the CITY was divided into six divisions with a headquarters at 26 OLD JEWRY. This former CITY merchant's warehouse, counting house and dwelling house was bought in 1841 as the Commissioner's official residence. It ceased to be used as such in 1863 but housed the administrative offices instead.

In 1910 the force reached its peak strength of 1,181 men with an additional 150 allowed for private service. The same year saw the murder of three CITY police officers and the crippling of two others in the events which led up to the famous siege of SIDNEY STREET. In 1914 the number of divisions was reduced from six to four; these were A Division, MOOR LANE; B Division, SNOW HILL; C Division, BISHOPSGATE; D Division, CLOAK LANE. In 1937 the City Police bought its first two wireless cars. In 1940 MOOR LANE A Division was totally destroyed in the BLITZ. It was never reformed and the ground was divided between the remaining three divisions.

In 1946 the Metropolitan and City Police Company Fraud Department was formed. In the first year it investigated 290 cases of fraud. Five Fraud Squad officers were sworn in as Metropolitan constables so that they could operate beyond the CITY boundary. The CITY's first policewomen were not recruited until 1949 when a woman police sergeant and six women constables were added to the strength.

In 1946 a national Police Act removed the restrictions

on police operating beyond their force boundary. The following year CLOAK LANE was closed down and replaced by a new divisional station at WOOD STREET. The present force has three main divisions; B Division, SNOW HILL; C Division, BISHOPSGATE; D Division, WOOD STREET. Transport and communications are the responsibility of A Department which is based at D Division. Finance, personnel and administration is dealt with by B Department which is based at the OLD JEWRY headquarters. In addition, there is a Criminal Investigation Department, Cheque Squad, Dog Section and Mounted Branch. The Fraud Squad's work is becoming increasingly more complex with its investigations into international fraud. There is a small museum at the WOOD STREET divisional station. (*See also* POLICE).

City of London Polytechnic *117–119 Houndsditch, EC3.* Formed in 1970 by the amalgamation of the City of London College, the Sir John Cass College and the King Edward VII Nautical College. The Business School (previously the City of London College) provides courses in economics, accountancy, management and banking and has close links with the CITY. The School of Navigation offers courses in maritime operations and civil aviation and incorporates a ship-manoevring tank, planetarium and radar simulator suite. The School also has its own sea-going radar and research vessel. The Sir John Cass School of Science and Technology has a long tradition of collaboration with industry going back to 1907 when it ran courses to prepare mining engineers for work in the Empire. A student from the Sir John Cass School of Art recently achieved distinction by helping to design tableware for the White House in Washington.

The City of London School in Milk Street, off Cheapside, in the 1830s, before moving to its present site on the Victoria Embankment.

City of London School *Victoria Embankment, EC4.* John Carpenter, Town Clerk of London, who died in 1442, left property in his will to provide income to maintain in perpetuity 'four boys born within the City of London who shall be called in the vulgar tongue "Carpenter's Children" to assist at divine service in the choir of the [GUILDHALL] chapel aforesaid

on festival days, and to study at schools most convenient for them on ferial days. . . .' For many years these 'Carpenter's children' boarded in a college adjacent to the chapel until this was dissolved by Henry VIII in 1536. For the next three centuries they continued to be housed, fed and clothed by the Carpenter bequest and educated at various London schools. By the early 19th century the endowment had so increased in value that the CORPORATION OF LONDON, led by Warren Stormes Hale, first Chairman of the Schools Committee, and later LORD MAYOR, decided to build its own school, thereby using the bequest for wider educational purposes. In 1834 an Act of Parliament permitted the establishment of the City of London School which thereafter received substantial financial assistance from the Carpenter bequest and still today provides for Carpenter scholars. The school was opened in 1837 on a site in MILK STREET off CHEAPSIDE, but grew so rapidly that in 1883 it moved to buildings on its present site on VICTORIA EMBANKMENT. New buildings for classrooms, science laboratories, sports, arts and a Junior School were added in 1926, 1937 and during the 1950s. By 1980 plans had been completed for rebuilding the school on a new site east of BLACKFRIARS BRIDGE between QUEEN VICTORIA STREET and the river but building was delayed by economic problems. The school is governed and financed (with the aid of the Carpenter bequest) by the CORPORATION OF THE CITY OF LONDON. It is an independent school administered by a Board of Governors appointed by the COURT OF COMMON COUNCIL. In 1981 there were 780 pupils. Distinguished old boys include H.H. Asquith, the prime minister; Lord Evans, the physician; Sir Sidney Lee, the biographer; Arthur Rackham, the artist; Sir Walter Raleigh, the critic; the writers, Kingsley Amis and James Leasor; and the cricketer, J.M. Brearley.

City of London School for Girls *Barbican, EC2.* An independent school of 640 pupils. It was established by the CORPORATION OF LONDON in 1881 in accordance with the will of one William Ward for 'the religious and virtuous education of girls'. It was opened in 1894 in Carmelite Street adjoining the GUILDHALL SCHOOL OF MUSIC, and moved in 1973 to new buildings in the BARBICAN overlooking ST GILES, CRIPPLEGATE.

City Remembrancer A High Officer of the CORPORATION OF LONDON elected by the COURT OF COMMON COUNCIL. His office dates from the reign of Elizabeth I and he is the traditional channel of communication between the CORPORATION and the Court and Ministers of the Crown. As a law officer he must guard the CITY's age-old rights and privileges against any infringements by outside bodies. He advises the CORPORATION on all parliamentary matters which may affect them and has the right to attend PARLIAMENT and promote CORPORATION bills. He arranges the CITY's participation in public and civic ceremonies and organises the ceremonial and invitations when the CORPORATION is host at the GUILDHALL or the MANSION HOUSE (*see also* CEREMONIES).

City Road *EC1.* Extends in a long westerly curve from FINSBURY SQUARE, across OLD STREET to ISLINGTON High Street. It was built in 1761. In April 1777 John Wesley laid the foundation stone of his chapel (*see* WESLEY'S HOUSE AND CHAPEL). Opposite this on the west side of the road is BUNHILL FIELDS Burial Ground. And immediately south of BUNHILL FIELDS are the headquarters of the HONOURABLE ARTILLERY COMPANY and their training ground, the Artillery Ground, once the exercising fields of the City's TRAINED BANDS. The London Club, one of the earliest cricket clubs, used to play matches here; in one of them their president, Frederick, Prince of Wales, father of George III, received a blow from a ball which led to his death. Here, too, Lunardi made the first balloon ascent in England in 1784. Eagle Dwellings at No. 212 are built on the site of the EAGLE TAVERN, the tea-gardens and music-rooms celebrated in the nursery rhyme. There are two hospitals in the road, ST MARK'S HOSPITAL FOR DISEASES OF THE RECTUM AND COLON and MOORFIELDS EYE HOSPITAL. ST MATTHEW'S HOSPITAL is approached from Shepherdess Walk. The granite obelisk at the junction with Old Street and East Street was erected by the Metropolitan Board of Works (1876).

City Temple *Holborn Viaduct, EC1.* A large non-conformist church built in 1874 to replace a chapel in POULTRY. In the 1920s it was made famous by Dr F. Norwood and Leslie Wethered. Subjects such as birth control were then freely discussed. After severe damage in the 2nd World War it was rebuilt by Seely and Paget in 1958, with the addition of a theatre.

City Terminus Hotel *Cannon Street Station.* Designed by E.M. Barry, this hotel, later renamed the Cannon Street Hotel, was opened in May 1867. Although a huge building, the main rooms occupied most of it and there were being only about 84 bedrooms. In July 1920 representatives of various bodies met here to set up the Communist Party of Great Britain. The hotel closed down in 1931 but rooms were kept open for public meetings, the remainder being converted to offices and let under the name of Southern House. The building was reconstructed after the 2nd World War to the designs of the architect J.G.L. Poulson.

City University *Northampton Square, EC1.* Founded in 1896 as the Northampton Polytechnic, it became a university in 1966. The Chancellor is the LORD MAYOR and graduation ceremonies are held in GUILDHALL. Its early reputation rested upon the faculties of engineering, physical sciences and ophthalmic optics, but its teaching and research now also include social sciences, business studies and the arts. The original building, College Building, was completed in 1896 to the designs of Edward W. Mountford. The site of Connaught Building was purchased in 1908 and the architect then appointed was W. Campbell Jones. The building was opened in 1932. Drysdale Building forms part of the modern development and was handed over in stages in 1969–70. Tait Building was handed over in 1974. The architects of these later developments were Richard Sheppard, Robson and Partners.

In 1979–80 there were about 2,300 undergraduate students half of them enrolled in the various departments of technology. There were 770 postgraduate students. There are three modern halls of residence: Northampton Hall, Bunhill Row, EC1 (opened in 1964); Finsbury Hall, Bastwick Street, EC1 (opened

in 1972), and Heyworth Hall, Bastwick Street (opened in 1976).

City University Club *Cornhill, EC3.* Founded in the late 19th century for graduates of Oxford and Cambridge working in the City. All university graduates are now eligible.

Civil Service Stores *425 Strand, WC2.* Founded in 1864 by a group of clerks in the General Post Office who clubbed together to buy and share half a chest of tea. The result, a saving of 9d a pound, prompted them to extend their operations to coffee, sugar and other groceries. In January 1865 they formed the Post Office Supply Association with 40 members, a venture which proved so popular that in April 1865 membership was opened to all civil servants. Thereafter the name was changed to the Civil Service Supply Association, whose first premises were in VICTORIA STREET. In 1900 the Association moved to 425 STRAND, and in 1927 became a public company. After that date it became a comprehensive department store and severed its links with the Civil Service. It was closed down in 1982 after a severe fire.

Clapham *SW4.* Formerly spelt Clopeham or Clappeham, the name means village or homestead on the hill. The earliest reference is in the register of Chertsey Abbey where it is stated that, in the time of King Alfred, a Saxon noble named Aelfrid gave 30 hides of land in the manor of Clappeham to his wife, Werburgha. During the 11th century the manor became the home of a Danish nobleman, Osgod Clapha, and it is said that at the marriage feast of Osgod Clapha's daughter in 1042, Hardacanute, King of England, fell senseless in a fit of intoxication and died shortly afterwards. Clopeham is mentioned in *Domesday* as belonging to the De Mandeville family, who continued to hold the manor for several generations. Thereafter it changed hands many times, remaining a small village until the 17th century when inhabitants of London, fleeing first from the GREAT PLAGUE and later from the GREAT FIRE, began to settle there. In the reign of James I, the Manor was bought by Dr Henry Atkyns, Physician to the King, allegedly with money given to him by the King in gratitude for his having saved the life of the infant Prince Charles. Memorials of various members of the Atkyns family can be seen in ST PAUL'S CHURCH.

By the end of the 17th century Clapham had become a popular place of suburban residence. In 1690 the first stage coach service was established, the coach running once a day to and from GRACECHURCH STREET, braving the highwaymen of the then wild and rural CLAPHAM COMMON. A number of handsome private houses in the Queen Anne style were built, remaining examples of which can be seen at Nos 39, 41 and 43 Old Town. Among those who moved from London to this newly fashionable area was the diarist Samuel Pepys who, it was recorded by John Evelyn in 1703, 'lived at Clapham in a very noble house and sweate place where he enjoyed the fruit of his labour in great prosperity.' This 'noble house' was that built by Sir Dennis Gauden (remembered today in Gauden Road) on the north side of the Common. The marshland now known as CLAPHAM COMMON was drained in 1760 and thereafter constantly improved, enabling Thackeray to write in *The Newcomers* that 'of all the pretty suburbs that still adorn our metropolis there are few that exceed in charm Clapham Common.'

During the 18th century Clapham became a centre of Evangelism and the home of the so-called CLAPHAM SECT. On the west and south sides of the Common some fine houses formerly inhabited by members of the CLAPHAM SECT remain, but those with the most interesting associations have been destroyed. Broomwood, where Wilberforce lived, was at the corner of what is now Broomwood Road, and at the corner of Cavendish Road is the site of Cavendish House where the chemist and philosopher, Henry Cavendish, lived and died. Between 1713 and 1720 a row of fine Georgian houses was built on the north side of CLAPHAM COMMON, some of which still stand. There is a tradition that Captain Cook lived at No. 22 North Side, and on the third floor is a balcony known locally as Captain Cook's quarterdeck. The church of HOLY TRINITY on CLAPHAM COMMON was completed in 1776.

Among those who lived in or had associations with Clapham in the 19th century were the poets Thomas Hood and Shelley, whose first wife Harriet Westbrook was a pupil at a school on CLAPHAM COMMON from which she eloped with Shelley in September 1811. Macaulay Road perpetuates the name of the historian Lord Macaulay who spent his childhood in Clapham. Sir Charles Barry, designer of the HOUSES OF PARLIAMENT, lived and died at a house called The Elms, still standing on North Side, and Lytton Strachey and Thomas Burke were born and brought up in the area. John Francis Bentley, who designed WESTMINSTER CATHEDRAL, lived at No. 43 Old Town, CLAPHAM COMMON in 1876–94. John Burns, the statesman, lived at No. 110 North Side, CLAPHAM COMMON from 1914 and John Walter, founder of The Times, at Gilmore House, No. 113 North Side, in 1774–84. The arrival of the railways and the boom in industry in neighbouring BATTERSEA in the late 19th century led to large influxes of people into Clapham and to the many rows of terraced houses which so largely contribute to its present-day character. It is now part of the London Boroughs of WANDSWORTH and LAMBETH.

Clapham Common *SW4*. In 1722, Christopher Baldwin arranged the draining and planting of this land. In 1722 a raid was ordered on the vermin infesting the Common and 10s was paid for killing nine hedgehogs and seven polecats. In 1781 a fair previously held here was abolished and in 1816 the parish Vestry directed that swine should not be allowed loose on the Common. The Duke of Cumberland's army camped here in 1745, the year of the Jacobite Rebellion. The Common became surrounded in the 18th and 19th centuries by impressive houses of City merchants, philanthropists and others including Samuel Pepys in 1700–3 and, later, Wilberforce and Lord Macaulay (*see* CLAPHAM SECT). Many trees were planted including Spurgeon's Tree, a poplar so named since a man was killed by lightning whilst sheltering beneath it in 1859 and on the following Sunday the Revd C.H. Spurgeon took as his text: 'Be ye also ready, for in such an hour as ye think not the Son of Man cometh' (Matthew XXIV, 44). There was also (until a gale in 1893) 'Captain Cook's Tree' which was probably planted by the eldest son of the explorer, who lived on the Common and called the balcony behind the house his 'quarterdeck.' By this tree stood those who wished to air their social, religious and political opinions. The Common extends to 220 acres. On the north side is the *Woman of Samaria* fountain with stone figures of a woman offering water to an old woman with a crutch. It is by Sir Charles Barry and was erected here in 1894. (*See also* CLAPHAM.)

Clapham Junction *SW11*. Originally a country cross-roads with the Falcon Inn providing travellers with refreshments. The change came with the arrival of the railway in 1839. At first only a signal box, the station opened in 1863. With the growth of housing and the different railway companies running services through the Junction, it became a major commuter centre. At one time it was the busiest in the world with

Jackson, the runner, displaying his agility in a hopping match on Clapham Common in 1827.

over 2,500 trains passing through every day. Shops soon sprang up to cater for the growing population, including Arding and Hobbs department store. This was first built on the corner of LAVENDER HILL and St John's Road in 1885 but destroyed by fire on 20 December 1909, the heat cooking meat in a butcher's shop across the road. Immediately rebuilt, it still serves the area today. The Junction also became a centre for entertainment with music-halls such as the GRAND THEATRE, the Shakespeare Theatre, LAVENDER HILL, providing more serious entertainment; and by 1920 there were at least eight cinemas in the neighbourhood. The area has now become more important than the old village and today is the major centre of BATTERSEA.

Clapham Sect A group of rich Anglican Evangelicals, including Zachary Macaulay, James Stephen and William Wilberforce, who believed that religion must be manifested in good works. They worked for the abolition of the slave trade, the spread of missionary work and the improvement of moral standards at home. According to an article in *The Times* of 31 January 1879 they also organised benevolence, they revived religion, they reformed manners and were the first to take in hand the education of the people. Their name was given them by Sydney Smith because most of their number lived in the district, Wilberforce in a house called Broomfield on the south-west side of CLAPHAM COMMON, and Macaulay, for a time, in Clapham High Street.

Clapton *E5.* Situated on ground rising west of the River LEA. Roman burial remains have been found in the area, and it seems from its name that a farm on a hillock existed by the Saxon era. A medieval pilgrim route from London to Waltham Abbey ran through Lower Clapton and Upper Clapton between STAMFORD HILL and HACKNEY. In the 16th century Brooke House (demolished 1954), on the site of the present Brooke School, was owned by Henry Algernon Percy, 6th Earl of Northumberland, and visited by Henry VIII. Fulke Greville, 1st Lord Brooke, lived there in the following century when the garden was praised by Evelyn. Agriculture was still predominant and the area supplied London's bread when St Thomas's church was opened (1773, enlarged 1829) to serve the hamlet. During the 18th century John Howard, the penal reformer, and Major John André, hanged by Washington as a spy, were born in Clapton (the former on the Laura Place site); and a nonconformist seminary was opened (and shortly closed). By the end of the 19th century development was such that only a strip of old open common survived as Clapton Common, with factories nearby. Middle-class villas replaced many 18th-century houses – as late as the 1930s Upper Clapton had a reputation as a very respectable residential area. The 20th century saw the opening of the 33½ acre Springfield Park on the banks of the LEA and the erection of council flats. In 1965 Upper and Lower Clapton were incorporated into the London Borough of HACKNEY.

Clare Market *WC2.* Takes its name from a market established in the 17th century on land belonging to John Holles, Earl of Clare. In 1720 Strype described the market as being 'very considerable and well served with provisions, both flesh and fish; for besides the butchers in the shambles, it is much resorted to by the country butchers and higglers'. It was here, after his escape from NEWGATE, that Jack Sheppard obtained the butcher's blue smock and woollen apron which he was wearing when captured at FINCHLEY. At the end of the 19th century the market was described as 'a cluster of narrow dirty streets and passages lined chiefly with butchers' and greengrocers' shops ... supplemented by long lines of greengrocers', fishmongers' and miscellaneous stalls and barrows – a crowded, noisy and unsavoury place'. All the market buildings were swept away in the KINGSWAY and ALDWYCH improvement scheme of 1900–5. Buildings for the LONDON SCHOOL OF ECONOMICS have since been erected here.

Clarence House *Stable Yard Road, St James's Palace, SW1.* Gracious stuccoed house reconstructed for William, Duke of Clarence, by John Nash on the site of his old lodgings. It was finished in 1828. In 1830 William became King and, because BUCKINGHAM PALACE was not finished, he continued to live here. He tried ST JAMES'S PALACE for a time, but found there was so little room that he and his Queen had to move all their books and letters out of the rooms before levées. So a passage to connect the palace with Clarence House was built. On King William's death in 1837 Princess Augusta, George III's daughter, took the house until her own death three years later. In 1840–61, Clarence House was the home of Queen Victoria's mother, the Duchess of Kent; and from 1866 to 1900 it was the official residence of Prince Alfred, Duke of Edinburgh. Another storey was added in 1873. In 1900–42 it was used by Queen Victoria's third son, the Duke of Connaught. During the remainder of the 2nd World War it was the headquarters of the Red Cross and the St John's Ambulance Brigade. In 1947–50 it was the home of Princess Elizabeth before her accession. Princess Anne was born here. In 1953 the Queen Mother moved here with Princess Margaret, who now lives at KENSINGTON PALACE. Although twice remodelled and enlarged, and restored after bomb damage in the 2nd World War, three storeys remain of Nash's building as well as a number of ceilings and mantelpieces of the same period. The house contains many valuable paintings from the Queen Mother's private collection.

Clarence Terrace *NW1.* Takes its name from William IV's earlier title, Duke of Clarence. It was the smallest of the terraces, consisting originally of 12 houses, designed by Decimus Burton. Its 'elegant correctness' led to other official commissions for the young architect. Wilkie Collins was living at No. 2 in 1859, the year in which he launched *All the Year Round*, a periodical edited by himself and Charles Dickens, and in which he published his most successful novel, *The Woman in White*. The same house was, in the present century, the home of Louis Macneice, 1954–63. William Charles Macready, the actor, was living at No. 5 in 1848, when he was playing Wolsey in *Henry VIII* at the THEATRE ROYAL DRURY LANE; and No. 8 was the home of Sir John Blundell Maple, 1876–1903.

Clarendon House *Piccadilly.* One of half a dozen great mansions built on the north side of PICCADILLY in the 1660s. It was the short-lived home of

Clarendon House in Piccadilly, described by Pepys as 'the finest pile I ever did see in my life'.

Edward Hyde, Earl of Clarendon, Charles II's faithful companion in exile and his Lord Chancellor, whose daughter had married James, Duke of York, the future James II. The grandeur of his house, designed by Sir Roger Pratt, matched his powerful position at Court, and Pepys described it as 'the finest pile I ever did see in my life'. But its great cost – over £40,000 – and the unpopularity of his policies proved Clarendon's undoing. He was popularly supposed to have acquired his wealth by all sorts of dishonest means and, in June 1667, a representation of a gibbet was set up before the main gates, inscribed 'Three sights to be seen: Dunkirk, Tangier and a barren Queen', in reference to the sale of Dunkirk to France, the failure of the Tangier expedition, and the inability of the queen to provide an heir. Soon afterwards he was dismissed and fled to France, where he spent the remaining seven years of his life in completing his great *History of the Rebellion*, the profits of which later helped to construct the Clarendon Building at Oxford, to house the university press. His house in PICCADILLY was demolished in 1683, and soon afterwards a group of speculators, headed by Sir Thomas Bond, began to lay out BOND STREET, DOVER STREET and ALBEMARLE STREET on the site.

Clareville Grove *SW7*. Takes its name, as does Clareville Street, from Clareville Cottage which once stood in OLD BROMPTON ROAD. The first houses, small but with quite big gardens, were built in the 1820s on land that had formerly been used mostly as nursery gardens. No. 2, which has since been extended, was leased in 1826, No. 16, which has not been much altered outside, in 1832 and No. 9, whose outward appearance has been changed, in 1828. There has been a good deal of more recent building, but the area retains much of its original intimate atmosphere.

Clarges Street *W1*. Extending from PICCADILLY to CURZON STREET, it probably takes its name from Sir Thomas Clarges, the friend and trustee of Sir William Pulteney who died in 1691. Building began in the early 18th century, and on the west side some Georgian houses still survive, though much altered. Charles James Fox lived at No. 46 in 1803, but the house (now stuccoed) must have looked very different in his day. At Nos 33 and 34 the doorways were handsomely embellished in the later 18th century with COADE STONE in the manner of those in BEDFORD SQUARE, BLOOMSBURY. Other notable inhabitants included Lady

Hamilton, Nelson's mistress; Edmund Kean, the actor; Daniel O'Connell, the Irish statesman; and Thomas Babington Macaulay, the historian. Modern blocks of offices and apartments now encumber almost the whole of the east side.

Claridge's *Brook Street, W1*. William Claridge, while a butler in a noble household, saved enough to buy a small hotel in BROOK STREET. In 1855 he acquired the neighbouring Mivart's Hotel, which had been established in 1808. In 1860 Baedeker described it as the 'first hotel in London'. It was bought by the Savoy Co. in 1895 and rebuilt in red brick 1895–9, to the design of C.W. Stephens, with interiors by Sir Ernest George. It was extended in 1931 by Oswald Milne. It is well established as the London hotel most appropriately equipped to house the rich and the royal. There are 262 bedrooms.

Clark's Place *EC2*. Named after Parish Clerks' Hall (*see* CITY LIVERY COMPANIES) which once stood here. There was also an almshouse here for impoverished parish clerks, their wives and widows. It was described by Stow in 1598 as 'a fair entrie or court to the common hall of the Parish Clerks'. The Marine Society at No. 5 was founded in 1756 by Jonas Hanway to help poor boys go to sea.

Clattern Bridge *Kingston-upon-Thames, Surrey*. Stands in the High Street over the Hogsmill River (which joins the THAMES at this point), a tributary which rises near Ewell and was once famous for its watermills. The structure consists of three circular arches and dates from the late 12th century. It is now a Scheduled Ancient Monument. In early days scolding wives were ducked in the river here as a means of correction.

Clayhill *Middlesex*. Situated north of ENFIELD on gravel slopes west of the LEA valley. By the 16th century a small settlement at the edge of ENFIELD CHASE bore the name, possibly after a family who had resided in the parish for centuries. The oldest surviving buildings are the Fallow Buck and the Rose and Crown which Dick Turpin's grandfather is said to have kept. By the 18th century houses were scattered along Clay Hill; Claysmore was bought in 1847 by the Huguenot Bosanquet family. In 1857 J.P. St Aubyn's church of St John was built as a chapel-of-ease to St Andrew's, ENFIELD, but became the district church ten years later. Although urban development began in the early 20th century it was checked by GREEN BELT legislation and Clayhill remains very rural. In 1911 the 62 acres of Hilly Fields Park was bought by ENFIELD Urban District Council as a public open space.

Cleaves Almshouses *Kingston-upon-Thames, Surrey*. Derive from a bequest made by William Cleave, an ALDERMAN of the CITY OF LONDON, who died in 1667. They stand in London Road and are built of brick with six houses on each side of a central gabled entry. The family arms of the founder are displayed above this in colour. Originally this charity provided a home for six poor men and six poor women.

Clements Lane *EC4*. Named after the church of ST CLEMENT EASTCHEAP which stands at the southern end. Until the early 19th century the lane extended as far south as CANNON STREET, but it was cut short in 1831 by the formation of KING WILLIAM STREET. The many pieces of Roman glass, glass slag and an iron mould found here with them between 1865 and 1878 suggest it was the site of a glass factory. The banking firm of Rogers, Olding and Co. founded by the father of Samuel Rogers, the poet, was situated here during the Regency. Dositej Obradovic, the Serbian man of letters, lived at No. 27 in 1784.

Cleopatra's Needle *Victoria Embankment, WC2.* A granite obelisk nearly 60 ft high and weighing about 186 tons which was cut from the quarries of Aswan and, in about 1475 BC, transported down the Nile to be erected at Heliopolis. It was carved with dedications to various gods and symbols representing the Pharaoh Tethmosis III. The names of Ramses II and of Cleopatra were added later. The obelisk was moved to Alexandria probably upon orders of the Roman Emperor Augustus or, so an unlikely tradition has it, as a memorial to a son whom Julius Caesar had by Cleopatra. For centuries the obelisk stood at Alexandria before it toppled over into the sand. It was lying there when presented to the British in 1819 by the Turkish Viceroy of Egypt, Mohammed Ali. It was considered impossible to move it to England, however, until General Sir James Alexander, who had seen similar obelisks in Paris, suggested to an English engineer in Alexandria, John Dixon, that he should turn his mind to the problem. Erasmus Wilson, a surgeon, offered £10,000 to finance the project upon which Dixon was to spend a further £5,000. Dixon built an iron cylindrical pontoon in which the obelisk was towed out to sea off Alexandria in September 1877. During a gale in the Bay of Biscay, in which six

The 186-ton Cleopatra's Needle arrived from Alexandria in 1878 and was erected on Victoria Embankment.

seamen were drowned, the Needle was almost lost. But it was eventually towed into a Spanish port and reached London in January 1878. It was originally intended to erect it in front of the HOUSES OF PARLIAMENT but as the site there was found to be subsiding it was put up instead in its present position on the EMBANKMENT, between WATERLOO and HUNGERFORD BRIDGES. Buried beneath it were various articles including that morning's newspapers, a set of coins, a razor and a box of pins, four Bibles in different languages, Bradshaw's *Railway Guide* and photographs of 12 of the best-looking Englishwomen of the day.

Clerkenwell *EC1.* North and slightly uphill from the CITY and SMITHFIELD, on fertile meadowland watered by abundant springs and the FLEET RIVER, Clerkenwell grew up as a hamlet serving the 12th-century monastic foundations, St Mary's Nunnery and the PRIORY OF ST JOHN OF JERUSALEM. In the 14th century the CHARTERHOUSE was founded to the south-east. St Mary's drew its water supply from the *Fons Clericorum* or Clerks' Well, which later gave its name to the parish; mystery plays were performed both here and at the Skinners' Well, one of many whose sites were lost during later building. The FLEET, or River of Wells, was hereabouts called Turnmill Brook from its function in the local agricultural community; a neighbouring street named after it, however, became notable for its brothels.

When the monasteries were dissolved by Henry VIII their buildings were dismantled or turned to Protestant and secular use (*see* DISSOLUTION OF THE MONASTERIES). St Mary's Church, rededicated to ST JAMES, survived as a parish church, and in 1788–91 was rebuilt, being ruinous, by James Carr, a local architect who modelled its spire on ST MARTIN-IN-THE-FIELDS. The monastic land was given to the new Tudor nobility. Families who built mansions here included the Cavendishes, Dukes of Newcastle, the grounds of whose gloomy house, north of ST JAMES'S CHURCH, incorporated most of the nunnery cloister: this survived intact until the1790s, and its foundations were rediscovered in the 1970s but were then largely destroyed. Local street names commemorate the Earls of Albemarle, the Berkeleys – Sir Maurice was standard-bearer to two Tudor kings – and the Earls of Ailesbury, whose house was north of the old Priory church and who used its choir as a private chapel and its 12th-century crypt as a wine cellar. The Challoners built a large house, often associated with the Cromwell family, in Clerkenwell Close, opposite Newcastle House. The Earls of Northampton had a mansion halfway up St John Street.

Among important developments in James I's reign was the completion of the NEW RIVER, the CITY's first piped domestic water supply, in 1613, when the 'bason' or New River head was opened by its promoter, Hugh Myddelton, in fields above Clerkenwell (*see* WATER SUPPLY). In 1611 the CHARTERHOUSE was endowed by the rich Thomas Sutton as a school and almshouse for poor gentlemen. Hermitage Fields, former Hospitaller property north of the village, were bequeathed in 1613 by Dame Alice Owen for a school and almshouses, in memory of her 'astonishing deliverance' as a girl from an accidental shot by a bowman. Owen's School and Almshouses, administered by the BREWERS' COMPANY, were rebuilt on their St John Street site in 1840, and a girls' school was added in 1886. In 1971–6 the schools moved to Potter's Bar.

Clerkenwell's position and water supply made it a natural overspill for the CITY. In 1612 the first sessions house, Hicks Hall, was built by Sir Baptist Hicks, mercer and JP, at the foot of St John Street, courts having been formerly held in SMITHFIELD taverns. Its successor was in CLERKENWELL GREEN (see OLD MIDDLESEX SESSIONS HOUSE). In 1615 a prison to relieve BRIDEWELL was erected in fields north of New-castle House, later joined by a second 'New Prison' or House of Detention, to relieve NEWGATE. This Bridewell was demolished in 1804 having been made redundant by a new model House of Correction still farther north in Coldbath Fields (1794) (see COLD-BATH FIELDS PRISON); and the New Prison was rebuilt in 1845–6. A workhouse built beside the prisons in 1662 to serve a union, or 'corporation' of parishes, gave its name to Corporation Row. In 1692 the Society of Friends acquired the workhouse, which in 1786 was taken into the prison precincts when the Friends moved to Rawstorne Street, where they also ran a school: this moved to CROYDON in 1825.

In Charles II's time, as the Court moved westwards, the great houses were abandoned to merchants and craftsmen, particularly during the GREAT PLAGUE and after the GREAT FIRE. Newcomers to skilled crafts, and foreigners such as French Huguenot refugees, who were discouraged by restrictive guild practices, settled outside the CITY, so Clerkenwell became a centre for clock- and watch-makers, jewellers, printers and their ancillary workers. Gin distillers, including Booth's, Gordon's and Nicholson's, and brewers such as Whit-bread's (see BREWERIES), profited from the good water supply. Clerkenwell was thus rapidly urbanised, though London's building line still ended at Corpora-tion Row.

Fine new town houses included those of Red Lion Street (1719; now Britton Street) built by Simon Michell, a rich magistrate, who with his wife also re-stored the remains of St John's Priory church in con-temporary style to serve from 1723 as a second parish church. The British Order of St John acquired this in 1931. No. 2 Albemarle Street still contains a fine George I interior behind an 1870s' façade. St John's Square was also surrounded by good houses, such as Bishop Gilbert Burnet's on the west side, from which he witnessed the looting of the church in the Sacheverell riots (see RIOTS). This house was destroyed for the building of CLERKENWELL ROAD in 1879. On the north side John Wilkes was born in 1727, of a family later linked with Booth's, the distillers, and with the assassin of Abraham Lincoln. Other notable residents were Izaak Walton, who had retired to CAM-BERWELL GREEN by 1650 from his linen-draper's busi-ness; and Thomas Britton, a gifted coal-dealer, in whose house in JERUSALEM PASSAGE famous musicians performed.

Rediscovery of medieval springs, with their sup-posed medicinal qualities, brought fame and fashion to Clerkenwell's airy hillside, starting with the wells found in 1683 in the garden of Thomas Sadler's music house, thenceforward named SADLER'S WELLS, and in about 1685, the ISLINGTON SPA or New Tunbridge Wells. By the 1730s at least a dozen gardens provided entertainment varying in sophistication from milk and cheesecakes (local specialities) to tea, coffee, music and dancing, shaded walks, and raree shows. Among these were the ENGLISH GROTTO, Merlin's Cave, and the LONDON SPA. Though in decline from the 1770s, several lingered until about 1840, frequented by CITY tradesmen and apprentices, when Clerkenwell's fields had surrendered to crowded alleys and industrial grime.

In London's expansion after the Napoleonic wars, as Clerkenwell's population rocketed, its fine streets became slums – especially the new Northampton Es-tate, laid out round Northampton Square with streets named after family titles and estates (Spencer, Ashby, Compton) but without control over subdivision of the plots. The manor house, long abandoned to become a private asylum and then a school, was demolished, and on its site in 1869 rose the vast Martyrs' Memorial Church, itself destroyed in the 2nd World War and now replaced by shops and flats. Houses were turned into workshops and tenements; squalid courts and alleys were notorious; the FLEET RIVER became a rank sewer. SMITHFIELD cattle market, protected by CITY interests, intensified health hazards until its removal in 1855. Branches of the metal industry expanded, while women slaved in clothing and millinery sweatshops. Ragged Schools, and a 'crippleage' for handicapped girls which was founded in Sekforde Street by John Groom, a young philanthropist, could barely touch the problem.

Victorian clearances, which drove broad thorough-fares across acres of slums and added to the numbers of homeless, were here represented by FARRINGDON ROAD and CLERKENWELL ROAD; while in 1862 the new Metropolitan Railway alongside FARRINGDON ROAD brought further demolition.

Poverty and overcrowding combined with political and social dissatisfaction to make Clerkenwell a centre of radicalism. In 1816 a meeting addressed by 'Orator' Henry Hunt at Spa Fields led to a rather inept attempt to storm the TOWER; and in 1832 a clash between the new police and unemployed demonstrators in Cold Bath Fields ended in bloodshed and the 'Clerkenwell Riot'. CLERKENWELL GREEN became a political meeting-place and the start of Chartist and other processions. A disastrous attempt to free Fenian prisoners from the House of Detention, by blowing up the wall, achieved only destruction and death in the densely-populated Corporation Row.

At length the old prisons were replaced by the HUGH MYDDELTON SCHOOL; and COLD BATH FIELDS PRISON in 1889 by MOUNT PLEASANT POST OFFICE Parcels Dept. Even the Sessions House moved in 1921 to Newington Butts.

The Borough of FINSBURY, incorporating both Cler-kenwell and St Luke's, was formed in 1899, the new Vestry Hall in ROSEBERY AVENUE becoming its Town Hall. In 1898 the Northampton Institute, precursor of the Northampton Polytechnic and CITY UNIVERSITY (1966), was founded in St John Street. On the other hand SADLER'S WELLS, Clerkenwell's famous subur-ban theatre, ended as a music-hall and cinema; other entertainment was minimal and recreational space al-most non-existent.

In this century population has steadily declined, whole ancient streets have been demolished as slums, industry has decayed and schools have closed. In 1965 the small borough was unwillingly merged with ISLINGTON (though its identity remains distinct).

Today the rebuilt (1931) SADLER'S WELLS receives visiting companies, while institutions like the Museum of the Order of St John (see ST JOHN'S GATE) provide an historical focus. Though much has been levelled since the war, restoration has taken place on the NEW RIVER and WOODBRIDGE ESTATES. Firms are still closing, and SMITHFIELD is threatened, yet Clerkenwell Craftsmen, now established at Penny Bank Chambers and in Clerkenwell Close and Cornwell House, provide some hope for the future.

Clerkenwell Close *EC1*. Formerly known as St Mary's Close, from the old Benedictine nunnery of St Mary. ST JAMES's church is on the east side.

Clerkenwell Green *EC1*. Now a backwater bypassed by CLERKENWELL ROAD, this was once the centre of a semi-rural village, a short distance south of ST JAMES's church. In the 17th century it was ringed with houses of the nobility and CITY knights, and planted with trees, the last of which blew down in 1796. By the 18th century it had lost its grass, but still had a pound, pillory and watch-house, and a turnstile at the entrance to Clerkenwell Close. On the west side the MIDDLESEX SESSIONS HOUSE was built in 1779–82 on the site of older buildings. During Victorian times the Green was a well-known centre for political, especially radical, meetings, from Chartists to Home Rulers. On 13 November 1887, after a meeting convened by the London Patriotic Club (now the Marx Memorial Library) and addressed by William Morris and others, it was a departure point for the march of protesters to TRAFALGAR SQUARE which ended as BLOODY SUNDAY. With CLERKENWELL's now greatly reduced population the Green today sees little activity.

Convicts exercising in the grim prison yard of Clerkenwell's House of Detention, demolished in 1890.

Clerkenwell House of Detention *Clerkenwell Close*. Built in 1616. Jack Sheppard and his mistress, Edgeworth Bess, were imprisoned here in 1724 but escaped by sawing through the bars. The prison was rebuilt in 1775 and again in 1847. In 1867 an unsuccessful attempt was made to rescue two Fenian prisoners, Burke and Casey. Not only was the prison wall blown down but the row of houses opposite, killing six people and injuring 50. The prison was closed in 1877 and demolished in 1890.

Clerkenwell Road *EC1*. A new thoroughfare of the METROPOLITAN BOARD OF WORKS between GRAY'S INN ROAD and GOSWELL ROAD was opened in April 1878 at a cost of £1,600,000, linking NEW OXFORD STREET – THEOBALDS ROAD with OLD STREET and SHOREDITCH. The street characteristically cut through a maze of slums, including Liquorpond Street, then traversed the Italian district round SAFFRON HILL, bridged the FLEET valley and Metropolitan Railway by FARRINGDON ROAD, narrowly missed CLERKENWELL GREEN, sliced the fine 18th-century Red Lion Street (now Britton Street) and, destroying Bishop Burnet's house, cut a ruthless swathe through the old priory precinct of St John's Square. Between St John Street and GOSWELL ROAD it incorporated old Wilderness Row – where Thackeray lived as a CHARTERHOUSE schoolboy – widening the narrow lane by cutting through the top of the CHARTERHOUSE grounds.

It quickly became a warehouse-lined tram route. At the western end the typically bleak Cavendish Mansions (1882) contrast with the LONDON COUNTY COUNCIL's more imaginative Bourne Estate opposite (W.E. Riley, 1901–2). In the Italian section is the Roman Catholic church of ST PETER, and at the corner of Britton Street the handsome redbrick Holborn Union Offices (1886), now ISLINGTON Borough Council's Engineering Dept. Between the railway and Britton Street were once densely packed alleys, including Lamb and Flag Court with its Ragged School. Booth's Distillery, established in Turnmill Street by 1778, now occupies the whole block. Penny Bank Chambers, another Model Dwellings tenement (1879), were restored in 1980 for the Clerkenwell Craftsmen.

Cleveland House *Cleveland Row*. Built in the 1620s for Thomas Howard, who became Earl of Berkshire in 1625, and then known as Berkshire House. In 1666 the house was occupied by Edward Hyde, Earl of Clarendon, while he was waiting for CLARENDON HOUSE to be completed in PICCADILLY. It was evidently bought in 1668 by Charles II for his mistress, Barbara Villiers, Countess of Castlemaine, who was created Duchess of Cleveland in 1670 when Berkshire House was renamed accordingly. The Duchess improved and extended it. She sold it in the late 1680s to a building speculator who in 1700 disposed of it to John Egerton, 4th Earl of Bridgewater. Francis Egerton, 3rd Duke of Bridgewater, entirely rebuilt the house in the 1790s and assembled there an important collection of pictures. He died without issue and left the house to his nephew, who became Marquess of Stafford in 1803 and Duke of Sutherland in 1833. He continued his uncle's restoration of the house and added to the collection of pictures which he opened to the public. Cleveland House was inherited by his second son who, finding the fabric in a dangerous condition, demolished it in 1840–1 and built BRIDGEWATER HOUSE on the site.

Cleveland Row *SW1*. Named after Barbara Villiers, Duchess of Cleveland, Charles II's most grasping mistress, to whom CLEVELAND HOUSE, which stood here until its demolition in 1840–1, belonged. Captain Marryat, the novelist, lived at No. 5 in 1822–7. STORNOWAY HOUSE is at No. 13.

Cleveland Street *W1*. Built in about 1745–70 on land owned by Charles Fitzroy, Duke of Southampton, a descendant of Charles II's Duchess of Cleveland. It is now mostly occupied by buildings of the

MIDDLESEX HOSPITAL. Samuel Morse, the American inventor of the Morse Code, lived at No. 141 in 1812–15.

Clifford Street   *W1.* On the BURLINGTON ESTATE, it extends from SAVILE ROW to NEW BOND STREET, and takes it name from Elizabeth Clifford, great-grandmother of the 3rd Earl of Burlington, from whom much of his wealth came. Building began here in about 1719, and several very fine original houses still survive – Nos 4, 5, 8 and 9 on the north side, and Nos 16, 17 and 18 on the south side, the last of which has been occupied by BUCK'S CLUB since its foundation here by Captain H.J. Buckmaster in 1919. No. 8 has a splendid staircase, ornamented with *trompe l'oeil* decoration, probably by Sir James Thornhill. Most of the buildings (of whatever age) in Clifford Street are now used as offices, some having high-quality shops at street level. Henry Addington, 1st Viscount Sidmouth, Prime Minister, lived at No. 7 (demolished) in about 1805–8 and 1816–24. Scott Adie, the kilt and tartan specialists at No. 14A, were at 115 REGENT STREET in the 1860s. They moved to 38 CONDUIT STREET in the 1920s and to 29 CORK STREET in the 2nd World War. They still have part of a bale of cloth from which one of Queen Victoria's cloaks was cut.

Clifton Gardens   *W9.* May have been named in honour of Brunel's suspension bridge at Clifton, which was completed in 1864. Sir Ambrose Fleming, the scientist and electrical engineer who taught at UNIVERSITY COLLEGE, lived at No. 9 in the 1890s. It is now part of the Worsley Hotel.

Clifton Hill   *NW8.* Built in the mid-19th century and perhaps named after Brunel's suspension bridge at Clifton which was under construction at this time. William Powell Frith, the painter, lived at No. 114 from 1896 until his death in 1909.

Clink Prison   *Southwark.* Origin of the expression 'in the clink'. It was a small prison in the Bishop of Winchester's park (*see* WINCHESTER HOUSE). Stow said it was for people who broke the peace on BANKSIDE and in the brothels. It is first mentioned in 1509. Bishop Hooper and John Bradford were both imprisoned here before their execution in 1555. When WINCHESTER HOUSE and park were sold after the Civil War the prison probably fell into disuse. In 1761 it was described a 'a very dismal hole where debtors are sometimes confined, but little used'. Burned down in the GORDON RIOTS, it was not rebuilt. It is commemorated by CLINK STREET.

Clink Street   *SE1.* This narrow, cavernous street, overshadowed by Victorian warehouses, was the site of the notorious CLINK PRISON. The Bishops of Winchester had their London estate here, known as the LIBERTY OF THE CLINK. The 14th-century rose window and other vestiges of WINCHESTER HOUSE survive. In the 16th century the 'Clink', the bishop's prison, housed both Protestant and Catholic prisoners of conscience. The Clink bollards were erected in 1812. St Mary Overie Dock is probably 'the tideway where ships are moored' mentioned in *Domesday Book*. Parishioners of St Saviour's (now SOUTHWARK CATHEDRAL) formerly claimed landing rights here.

Clipstone Street   *W1.* Built about 1720–50 and named after the Duke of Portland's estate at Clipstone, Nottinghamshire. G.F. Watts was living at No. 1 in 1838 and at No. 14 in 1840.

Clissold Park   *Stoke Newington, N16.* 53 acres opened by Lord Rosebery in 1889 after acquisition by the METROPOLITAN BOARD OF WORKS. It was named after the Revd Augustus Clissold, the eminent Swedenborgian who had been a curate at the neighbouring church of St Mary's in the early 19th century. The curate wished to marry one of the daughters of the tenant who had a lease from the Ecclesiastical Commissioners at a yearly rental of £109 'and a fat turkey'. Unfortunately the father objected to the match and even threatened to shoot the messengers whom the lovers were forced to employ. They had to wait for him to die before they married and the curate obtained the property. The nearby Queen Elizabeth's Walk commemorates the time when the Queen reputedly visited the local manor, which was owned by a branch of the Dudley family, in the difficult times before she became Queen. Clissold House, a large brick villa of 1790 with a Doric verandah, overlooks the lake. It was originally occupied by Jonathan Hoare, a member of the banking family. Later it was known as Crawshay's Farm after the tenant who opposed the marriage of his daughter to Augustus Clissold.

Cloak Lane   *EC4.* Probably named after the open sewer which ran down the street into the WALBROOK, *cloaca* being Latin for sewer. The church of ST JOHN THE BAPTIST UPON WALBROOK stood in the lane from the 12th century until the GREAT FIRE. Romano-British remains found in the area include a tessellated pavement and some timber structures thought to have been part of a wooden bridge which spanned the brook.

Clockmakers' Company   *see* CITY LIVERY COMPANIES.

Cloth Fair   *EC1.* Named after BARTHOLOMEW FAIR, held annually at SMITHFIELD from the 12th century until 1855. Until Elizabeth I's reign BARTHOLOMEW FAIR was England's main cloth fair to which merchants travelled from all parts of Europe. Cloth Fair itself was generally inhabited by drapers and merchants, Inigo Jones's father among them. Until recently some old leaning houses typical of those built after the GREAT FIRE were still standing, but they have now all gone except No. 41 which is much restored.

Clothworkers' Company   *see* CITY LIVERY COMPANIES.

Cloudesley Estate   *Islington, N1.* A piece of ground called 'the Stoney Field, otherwise the Fourteen Acres' (actually over 16) was bequeathed in trust to ISLINGTON parish in 1517 by Richard Cloudesley among many pious bequests – apparently as expiation for sins, for he also called for numerous masses and 'solemn obits'. Disturbances were in fact reported at his grave in ST MARY's churchyard, until a torchlight exorcism seems to have brought him peace. Cloudesley's bequest, used for the poor and for church repairs (extended in 1811 to other churches) survived the Reformation, perhaps because of its charitable purpose. By 1809, when the CITY CORPORATION considered the ground for a cattle market in place of SMITHFIELD, its value was nearly £23,000. In 1824 the trustees let it on 81-year building leases, and from 1825 the square and terraces now named Cloudesley and Stonefield were built in various pleasing styles, as BARNSBURY's earliest 'estate'. Holy Trinity Church (now disused), a brick echo of King's College Chapel, Cambridge, was designed by the young Charles Barry for the square. From the 1970s ISLINGTON Council restored many houses, then much decayed, and the street barrier represents a small survival of the famous 1970s' experimental BARNSBURY traffic scheme.

The Club Later known as the Literary Club, it was founded by Joshua Reynolds and Samuel Johnson. Its meetings were originally held every Monday evening at seven at the TURK'S HEAD, GERRARD STREET. The membership was at first limited to nine, the same number as had constituted the earlier IVY LANE CLUB, though it afterwards rose to 35. The first members included John Hawkins, Oliver Goldsmith, Edmund Burke and Johnson's young friends, Bennet Langton and Topham Beauclerk. The conversation was chiefly literary, but all manner of subjects were discussed, only politics being excluded. Johnson led the conversation, 'as, indeed,' Hawkins observed, 'he did everywhere'. When Goldsmith proposed a larger membership on the grounds that the present members had travelled thoroughly over each other's minds, Johnson angrily retorted, 'Sir, you have not travelled over *my* mind, I promise you.' Although Garrick was an intimate friend of several members of the Club, he was not admitted until 1773. According to Hawkins the reason for this was that Johnson, who was still envious of his former pupil's success and affected to despise his profession, refused to have him elected, protesting, 'He will disturb us by his buffoonery.' Boswell, on the other hand, contended that it was Garrick's conceit that prevented his becoming a member. When told of its formation, Garrick evidently said to Reynolds, 'I like it much, I think I shall be of you.' '*He'll be of us!*' expostulated Johnson when informed of Garrick's comment. 'How does he know we will *permit* him. The first Duke in England has no right to hold such language.'

It was Hawkins's request to be excused paying his share of the Club supper, on the grounds that he had not eaten anything, that prompted Johnson's famous comment upon him, 'We all scorned him and admitted his plea. For my part I was such a fool as to pay my share for wine, though I never tasted any. But Sir John was a most *unclubable* man.'

Charles James Fox was later admitted a member but did not talk much. Boswell heard Edward Gibbon remark that 'Fox could not be afraid of Dr Johnson; yet he certainly was very shy of saying anything in Dr Johnson's presence'. When Gibbon himself was put forward for membership in 1774 he was rejected.

Club Row *E2*. The origin of the name is unknown. The market, for live animals, reptiles and birds, has been traced back to the 18th century and may have arisen out of the local Huguenots' interest in caged birds. Concern over the welfare of birds and animals has long accompanied transactions there, but their sale continues, mostly in nearby Sclater Street.

Coachmakers' and Coach Harness Makers' Company *see* CITY LIVERY COMPANIES.

Coade Lion *Westminster Bridge (southern side)*. Also known as the South Bank Lion, it was made in Eleanor Coade's (*see* COADE STONE) LAMBETH factory in 1837. Painted red, it was placed over the entrance arch of the Lion Brewery next to HUNGERFORD BRIDGE and was a prominent feature of London's riverside. After a visit to London in 1893 Emile Zola wrote, 'It amused me greatly, this British Lion waiting to wish me good morning.' It disappeared a few years before the brewery was demolished in 1949, but reappeared in 1951 and formed part of the decorations for the FESTIVAL OF BRITAIN. Afterwards, at the request of George VI, it was removed to the entrance of WATERLOO STATION, and in 1966 re-erected on its present site. It is 12 ft high, 13 ft long and weighs 13 tons. A similar lion went to the rugby football ground at TWICKENHAM.

The Coade Artificial Stone Manufactory, Lambeth, in 1820, where this special terracotta was manufactured until 1840.

Coade Stone An artificial stone, the most weatherproof ever made, used as decoration on many 18th-century London buildings and for statues, busts and other ornaments. A special kind of terracotta, developed in a yard at LAMBETH, was patented by Richard Holt in the 1720s. After the lapse of the patent in the 1760s Mrs Eleanor Coade, the head of a south London family business, took over Holt's yard where an improved version of his terracotta was made by the addition of other materials including finely ground quartz or glass. The Coade manufactory offered a large variety of designs and several distinguished sculptors worked in the material, including John Flaxman and both John Bacons. This Coade Artificial Stone Manufactory was closed in 1840 and the secret of the composition was lost, but several examples of Coade stonework can still be seen in London. These include the COADE LION on WESTMINSTER BRIDGE; ornamented keystones in BEDFORD SQUARE, HARLEY STREET and QUEEN ANNE'S GATE; the frieze, *Tragedy and Comedy*, by Flaxman, on the ROYAL OPERA HOUSE, COVENT GARDEN; the playing children at the Royal Norwegian Embassy at No. 25 BELGRAVE SQUARE; the arms and supporters of the Worshipful Company of SKINNERS at their Hall in DOWGATE STREET the statue of Minerva by Flaxman on the east façade of the National Gallery, originally intended to represent Britannia on the top of MARBLE ARCH; the frieze on the west façade of BUCKINGHAM PALACE by William Croggan; the eight large Grecian females at the church of

ST PANCRAS, Upper Woburn Place; the table-tomb of Captain William Bligh at ST MARY LAMBETH; the statues of the boy and girl pupils beside the entrance to FAN MAKERS' Hall, once ST BOTOLPH's parish school; and the coat of arms and medallions of George III and Queen Charlotte on the façade of TRINITY HOUSE.

The Coal Exchange in Lower Thames Street was one of the earliest cast iron buildings in London.

Coal Exchange *Lower Thames Street*. An early cast iron building, it had a fine rotunda with an adjacent 100 ft tower designed by J.B. Bunning and decorated by Sang in 1847–9. The remains of a Roman hypocaust were found 13 ft below the surface while the foundations were being dug. Prince Albert opened the building, the last occasion on which the state barge was used. The floor of the Exchange was made of wood inlaid in the shape of a mariner's compass. A wind dial helped auctioneers calculate the time of arrival of coal shipments. Above the floor were three tiers of balconies and dealers' offices. It was roofed by a glass dome. In defiance of protest, the building was demolished in the 1960s.

Coal Hole *Carting Lane, Strand, WC2*. A public house, partly underground, founded in the early 19th century when it was used by the coal-heavers who worked on the THAMES. It has many theatrical connections. The Wolf Bar is named after a club, founded by the actor Edmund Kean, for repressed husbands who were not permitted to sing in their baths.

Cock Lane *EC1*. In the 14th century the only licensed walk for prostitutes. On the corner of GILTSPUR STREET is a fat gilt cherub marking Pie Corner where the GREAT FIRE of 1666 is reputed to have stopped. In January and February 1762 No. 33 was visited by thousands of people hoping to hear the scratchings of the COCK LANE GHOST.

Cock Lane Ghost Reported to have manifested itself at No. 33 COCK LANE in 1762 to an 11-year-old girl, the daughter of William Parsons, officiating clerk of the church of ST SEPULCHRE. The girl claimed to have heard knockings and scratchings while lying in bed and Parsons alleged that the noises were made by the ghost of his sister-in-law, Fanny, who had recently died of smallpox; but a friend of

the family, who claimed to be able to interpret such signs, said the sounds indicated that the ghost had been a victim of arsenic poisoning. The manifestation attracted great attention and crowds gathered at No. 33 COCK LANE to witness the phenomenon. In a letter to Montagu, Walpole tells how he went to the house in the company of the Duke of York and others. He was disappointed, however, as he was informed that the ghost would not make itself heard until seven o'clock the next morning. He also mentions the readiness of surrounding alehouses to exploit the great interest shown by the public. The girl was removed to the house of the rector of ST JOHN's, CLERKENWELL who invited a group of distinguished men, including Dr Johnson, to come and investigate the phenomenon. They heard nothing and correctly concluded that the girl had been making the noises herself. Johnson wrote an *Account of the Detection of the Imposture in Cock Lane* which was later published in the *Gentleman's Magazine*. The satirical poet, Charles Churchill, used the incident in *The Ghost*, where Johnson is portrayed as 'Pomposo', a credulous visitor.

Cock Pit *St Andrew's Hill, EC4*. A public house dating from the 16th century, it would probably have been familiar to William Shakespeare who lived for a time nearby. As the name suggests, it was originally famous for its cockfights. After cockfighting was banned in 1849, the name was changed to the Three Castles. A few years ago, when the inside was redecorated to recreate the cockpit and the original spectators' gallery, the original name was readopted.

Victorian customers in the Cock Tavern, Fleet Street. Famous for its chops, it replaced the 16th-century Cock Ale House.

Cock Tavern *22 Fleet Street, EC4*. Built in 1887 to replace a 16th-century inn originally known as the Cock Alehouse, which stood opposite. It faced MIDDLE TEMPLE Gate and became famous for its chops, steaks and porter. Pepys was a satisfied customer. On 23 April 1668 he came here with Mrs Knipp, the actress, 'drank, and eat a lobster, and sang, and mightily merry'. Afterwards he 'did tocar her corps all over and besar sans fin her, but did not offer algo mas; and so back led her home' where his wife later playfully waved a pair of red-hot tongs at him. Dickens used to come here. So did Tennyson whose 'Will Waterproof's Lyrical Monologue' was 'made' at the Cock:

O plump head-waiter at the Cock,
To which I most resort,
How goes the time? 'Tis five o'clock.
Go fetch a pint of port:
But let it not be such as that
You set before chance-comers
But such whose father-grape grew fat
On Lusitanian summers.

Cockfosters *Hertfordshire*. The name derives from the Chief Forester of ENFIELD CHASE whose house, now a hotel, WEST LODGE PARK, is nearby. Cockfosters is on the edge of ENFIELD CHASE, part of which survives in TRENT PARK which dates back to pre-Norman times. Its suburban development followed the extension of the PICCADILLY LINE in 1935. The station was designed by Charles Holden.

Cockney Derived from the Middle English, *cokeney*, meaning cock's egg, a misshapen egg such as those sometimes laid by young hens. As applied to human beings it meant an effeminate person or a simpleton, particularly a weak man from a town as opposed to a tougher countryman. In the 17th century it came to mean specifically, pejoratively or banteringly, a Londoner. It is now used, without disrespect, of both Londoners and their accent.

Cockney School A term applied pejoratively by J.G. Lockhart, the critic, biographer and novelist, to certain early 19th-century London writers including William Hazlitt, Leigh Hunt, Shelley and Keats who, in Lockhart's opinion, used rhymes in their verse which lacked classical purity.

Cockpit Theatre *Drury Lane, WC2*. Built in 1609 by John Best for cockfighting. It was converted to a theatre by Christopher Beeston in 1616. The next year a group of drunken apprentices burnt it down. It was soon rebuilt and renamed the Phoenix Theatre, although the old name was sometimes also used. It was closed by the Puritans in 1642 but plays continued to be performed surreptitiously. It was reopened at the Restoration. A joint company of actors under Killigrew and Davenant probably used it. The THEATRE ROYAL opened in DRURY LANE in 1663 and the Cockpit, unable to withstand the competition, is last recorded as being used as a theatre in 1664.

Cockspur Street *SW1*. Perhaps named after spurs for fighting cocks which were sold here, or after the Cock Tavern which stood at the end of SUFFOLK STREET in the 17th century. In 1747 John Broughton, self-styled boxing champion of England, opened an academy between Cockspur Street and the HAYMARKET THEATRE at which boxing gloves were used for the first time. In the late 19th century the street was full of small shops selling luxuries. In 1871 the Rugby Football Union was founded at the Pall Mall Restaurant here by 32 representatives of 21 clubs. Cockspur Street is now mostly occupied by the head offices of the big shipping companies and travel agents. The Sun Life Assurance Co. of Canada and the Royal Bank of Canada are at Nos 2–4. M.C. Wyatt's statue of George III is here (*see* STATUES).

Cocoa Tree Chocolate House *Pall Mall*. First mentioned in 1698, it occupied various sites in PALL MALL and from 1799 to about 1835 was at No. 64 ST JAMES'S STREET. The Cocoa Tree was used as a sign after chocolate was first brought to England in 1652. In 1657 Roger North wrote, 'the use of coffee houses seems newly improved by a new invention called chocolate houses.' The house was frequented by Tories in the early 18th century. In the 1745 rebellion it was thought of as the headquarters of the Jacobites. In 1746 Walpole wrote to Montagu that when the Duke of Cumberland offered Mordaunt the Pretender's coach, if he would drive up to London, Mordaunt replied, 'That I will, Sir, and drive till it stops of its own accord at the Cocoa Tree.' In 1746 it was converted into a private club which became notorious for gambling. In 1780 Walpole wrote to Mann, 'Within this week there has been a cast at hazard at the Cocoa Tree, the difference of which amounted to a hundred and fourscore thousand pounds.' The club was still in existence at the end of the 19th century, but seems to have closed soon afterwards.

Cogers' Hall *Bride Lane, Fleet Street*. The Honourable Society of Cogers, which was established about 1755 in SHOE LANE, met here in the 19th century. The Society's members were mostly young politicians, barristers and law students anxious to obtain practice in public speaking. The name Cogers came from the Latin *cogito*. Members were not obliged to speak, but 'for the good of the house' were required to drink. The building was demolished in the 1890s.

Convicts in an overcrowded dormitory of Cold Bath Fields Prison in the 1860s.

Cold Bath Fields Prison Built in 1794 in a district so called from a well of cold water discovered in 1697, the prison soon became notorious for its severity. Southey and Coleridge wrote in *The Devil's Thoughts*:

As he went through Coldbath Fields he saw
A solitary cell;
And the Devil was pleased, for it gave him a hint
For improving his prisons in Hell.

In 1820 Thistlewood and the other CATO STREET conspirators were kept here for a few days before they were moved to the TOWER. The prison was closed in 1877 and demolished in 1889. The Parcels Post Office in FARRINGDON ROAD was built on the site.

Coldharbour On the north bank of the THAMES, slightly east of where CANNON STREET STATION now

Coldharbour, in Thames Street, as it appeared before its destruction in the Great Fire.

stands, was Coldharbour, once the residence of merchants and noblemen, purchased by Sir John de Pulteney in 1334 and sometimes called Pulteney's Inn. In 1553 it was granted to George Talbot, Earl of Shrewsbury, and it appears in maps of that time as Shrewsbury House. It was burnt in the GREAT FIRE, but was rebuilt and used by the WATERMEN'S COMPANY for a Hall. The Company moved to ST MARY-AT-HILL in 1778 and the site was subsequently occupied by the City of London BREWERY.

Coleman Street *EC2*. Street of great antiquity probably named after the charcoal burners or coalmen who used to live here. In 1598 Francis Bacon was confined in a handsome house here after he had been arrested for debt. In 1642 the five MPs whom Charles I had tried to arrest in the Commons hid in the street, which was a stronghold of Puritanism. On the west side of the street stood the church of ST STEPHEN COLEMAN which was bombed in the 2nd World War. The ARMOURERS' AND BRASIERS' HALL is at No. 81.

Colham *Middlesex*. One of the largest manors in the locality at the time of *Domesday Book*, it was later overshadowed by the development of UXBRIDGE, one of its constituent villages. The name survives today at Colham Green, about half a mile south of HILLINGDON Village.

Colindale *NW9*. The name probably derives from the River Colne. Colindale lies along the western boundary of HENDON, south of BURNT OAK and north-east of KINGSBURY. It shared in the inter-war development of HENDON but is more famous for three notable institutions: the Newspaper Library (*see* BRITISH LIBRARY), the Metropolitan Police Training Centre (*see* POLICE) and the Central Public Health Laboratory. The latter is under the authority of the Department of Health and among its functions has a special role in the detection of disease.

Coliseum Theatre *St Martin's Lane, WC2*. (CalledLondon Coliseum 1904–31.) Designed by Frank Matcham in 1904 for Oswald Stoll as a variety house with a magnificent florid Edwardian interior. The globe on top used to revolve but was stopped after a legal battle with WESTMINSTER City Council. It was the first theatre in England to have a revolving stage and the first in Europe to have lifts. It is now London's largest theatre, with a capacity of 2,558. Ellen Terry, Edith Evans, Lillie Langtry and Sarah Bernhardt

appeared here in variety shows. Diaghilev's Russian Ballet gave seasons here in 1918, 1924 and 1925. From 1932 it staged musical spectaculars interspersed with ballet and variety. Among the best remembered is *White Horse Inn* (1931). It was a cinema from 1961 until 1968 when it opened as the new home of the Sadler's Wells Opera Company.

College Hill *EC4*. Earlier names were Royal Street or Tower Royal, after the resident wine merchants from La Riole near Bordeaux. In the 15th century Richard Whittington had a house on College Hill which was so called because, in order to ensure a safe passage to heaven for his soul, he founded the College of St Spirit and St Mary with five priests in the church of ST MICHAEL PATERNOSTER ROYAL and an almshouse next door. Whittington's College was dissolved by Henry VIII and the almshouse was moved to HIGHGATE in 1808. The MERCERS' SCHOOL occupied the almshouse site between 1808 and 1894. Nos 21–22A have fine 17th-century stone gateways.

College of Arms *Queen Victoria Street, EC4*. The fine 17th-century home of the royal heralds. Part of the royal household from Edward I's reign or earlier, they were granted their first charter by Richard III in 1484 and were also given Coldharbour, a house in UPPER THAMES STREET. When Richard lost his throne in 1485 Henry VII ousted them. Mary I granted them another charter in 1555 and gave them Derby Place which was built on the present site for Thomas Stanley, Earl of Derby, in the late 15th century. This was burned down in the GREAT FIRE but the heralds' charters, rolls and records were saved. In 1671–8 the College was rebuilt to the designs of Maurice Emmett, Master Bricklayer to the Office of Works. The building was preserved from fire in the heavy bombing of May 1941 by a change in wind. The wrought iron gates and railings, which had formerly stood at Goodrich Court, Herefordshire were presented to the College in 1956 by an American benefactor. The College is still very active, examining and recording pedigrees and granting armorial bearings. The Earl Marshal (a title always held by the Duke of Norfolk) arranges State occasions such as CORONATIONS, STATE OPENINGS OF PARLIAMENT and proclamations in England, Wales and Ulster. Under him the chief officers are the Kings of Arms (Garter, Clarenceux and Norray and Ulster King of Arms); the heralds, York, Richmond, Windsor, Somerset, Lancaster and Chester; and the Pursuivants Portcullis, Rouge Dragon, Rouge Croix and Bluemantle. Each has his own room.

College of Preceptors *Originally in* BLOOMSBURY, *now at Theydon Bois with an office in the* LIBRARY ASSOCIATION. Founded in 1846 by 'middle class schoolmasters', i.e. teachers in private schools, for the purpose of promoting sound learning. They received a Royal Charter in 1849. There were at that time qualifications for masters in public and elementary schools, but none for the private schools, so the College introduced qualifications at three levels – Associate, Licentiate and Fellowship. The Licenciate was, and still is, recognised as the equivalent of a university degree, and teachers take the qualifications of the College as evidence for further professional study.

The College started examination of pupils in 1850,

Late 17th-century Stanley Grove, one of Chelsea's loveliest houses, is now part of the College of St Mark and St John.

followed several years later by Oxford and Cambridge and later London, and these examinations were the forerunners of the School Certificate and GCE examinations. In the 1960s the College began examinations for 15-year-olds in the secondary modern schools, which were the forerunners of the CSE examination. The College are no longer involved in the examination of pupils. Their first office was in GREAT RUSSELL STREET, from where they moved to No. 28 BLOOMSBURY SQUARE and then to QUEEN SQUARE. In 1887 they built No. 2 BLOOMSBURY SQUARE. In 1973 the building was taken over because of the proposed development of the BRITISH LIBRARY, so the College moved out to their present address in Theydon Bois, Essex.

College of St Mark and St John *King's Road, SW10.* (Colloquially known as 'Marjohn.') Stanley Grove, one of CHELSEA's most beautiful houses, built by the Stanley family at the end of the 17th century, still stands here. It was once occupied by Sir William Hamilton, Secretary to Lord Elgin, who, while supervising the removal of the Parthenon marbles, made plaster casts of part of the frieze, which he placed on the walls of the house where they still remain in what is known as the Hamilton Room. In 1840 the whole site became the College of St Mark, a training college for Church of England teachers. The first principal was Derwent Coleridge, son of the poet, and the Assembly Hall still bears his name. In 1923 the College of St John was transferred here from BATTERSEA. In the 1950s a fine new campus was added. When it seemed likely that the new West Cross Road would cut right through it – though this did not materialise – the College moved to Plymouth. In 1980 the whole site was acquired by CHELSEA COLLEGE. A very fine garden includes a rare weeping willow tree over 150 years old. Lewis Casson, the actor, a student at the original college and sometime President of Equity, maintained that the idea of the National Union of Teachers was first discussed under the thorn tree in the garden. Certainly, one of the

original officers of the Union was a student of this College.

College Road *Dulwich, SE21.* The longest road in DULWICH. The earliest section runs from the old College to DULWICH COMMON. Part of the original Highway through Dulwich, it includes a number of fine Georgian houses with interesting features. Bell House, built in 1767 by Alderman Thomas Wright, had a bell on its roof to sound the alarm when fire broke out in the village and to summon local people to fill the fire engine from the Butcher's Pond nearby. Pickwick Cottage is supposed to be the home Dickens had in mind for Mr Pickwick (*see* DULWICH VILLAGE). The road petered out at the Common until 1787, when John Morgan replaced what had been a woodland track to the south with a private road (*see* DULWICH TOLL GATE). Morgan's Road became Penge Road and finally College Road, when DULWICH COLLEGE moved to its present site in 1870.

College Street *EC4.* Formerly known as Paternoster Lane, after the church of ST MICHAEL PATERNOSTER ROYAL, and as Great Elbow Lane because of its 'bending', as Stow put it. It was renamed in 1830 to commemorate Whittington's College (*see* COLLEGE HILL). INNHOLDERS' HALL is on the south side.

Colliers Wood *SW19.* Situated between MERTON and TOOTING GRAVENEY. Colliers Wood was originally woodland where charcoal was presumably burnt for fuel. Settlement was early on the fertile banks of the River WANDLE and farms existed by the time of the Conquest, when the manor of neighbouring MERTON belonged to William I. Colliers Wood High Street follows the track of Stane Street (*see* ROMAN ROADS) and would have been the route of King and Court between London and Guildford or Winchester. The foundation of Merton Priory in the 12th century increased traffic, and for centuries, although within Mitcham parish, Colliers Wood depended on MERTON for services and supplies. From the 16th century

Huguenot and Flemish refugees developed calico printing and felt manufacture, and textile mills existed into the 19th century, polluting the once pure WANDLE. The 18th century saw the introduction of toll gates on the Epsom road, including the Merton Singlegate (dismantled about 1870), and the appearance on the High Street of some buildings which still survive. Following the construction of the WIMBLEDON to TOOTING railway branch, the late 18th-century Colliers Wood House (demolished about 1904) – replacing the 16th-century house of Sir Nicholas Carew of BEDDINGTON – was sold for development, together with its Lower TOOTING Estate, towards the end of the 19th century. Roads such as Rutland, Boyd and Miller commemorate residents. Christchurch was opened in 1874 to meet the needs of a growing, mainly working-class population. In the 20th century the UNDERGROUND RAILWAY station (Charles Holden, 1926) took the name Colliers Wood. Conor P. Fahy's Roman Catholic church of St Joseph was opened in 1965. The London Borough of MERTON, created in 1965, includes Colliers Wood.

Collins' Music Hall *Islington Green*. Opened by Sam Collins in 1862 in the Lansdowne Arms public house as the Lansdowne Musical Hall. Difficulties with the licensing authority led to its almost immediate closure. Collins, having enlarged and redecorated it and obtained a licence, reopened it as Collins' Music Hall (colloquially known as 'The Chapel on the Green') on 4 November 1863. He was the star of his own theatre, singing mostly Irish songs composed for him, though he was, in fact, a Londoner. He died at the age of 38 in 1865 and his widow took control. The entertainment provided was not of a very high standard, comprising mostly comic songs but, as ladies were admitted and drink could be consumed during the performance, its popularity continued for years. During the 2nd World War it was taken over by Lew Lake. Its character changed but its appeal was sustained as a relic of an earlier age until it was destroyed by fire in 1956. Its seating capacity was 600.

Colney Hatch A former hamlet on the borders of SOUTHGATE and FRIERN BARNET. A large mental hospital was built here in 1851. Extensive housing development took place after the opening of the Great Northern Railway in 1850. The name Colney Hatch mental hospital became too closely associated with the district and was renamed NEW SOUTHGATE.

Colonnade House *Blackheath, SE3*. There is little to differentiate the history of this house, which adjoins THE PARAGON to the west, from that of THE PARAGON AND PARAGON HOUSE. It too was built by Michael Searles, suffered a decline, was for many years a boarding house, was restored by Bernard Brown and turned into flats with a communal garden. Like THE PARAGON it now belongs to the Trustees of MORDEN COLLEGE.

Colosseum *Cambridge Gate*. A huge rotunda in REGENT'S PARK designed for a panorama by Decimus Burton in 1824–7. Views of London, sketched by a Mr Horner from a precarious crow's nest on top of ST PAUL'S CATHEDRAL, were first shown. After its initial success its popularity declined. A proposal to turn it

into an opera house came to nothing. It was demolished in 1875 (*see also* PANORAMAS).

The Colosseum in Regent's Park was designed for a panorama by Decimus Burton in the 1820s. The building was pulled down in 1875.

Columbia Market *Bethnal Green*. A short-lived market conceived and financed by the philanthropist, Baroness Burdett-Coutts, as an attempt to wean the costermongers from the streets. Designed by H.A. Darbishire, and opened in 1869 in a rough East End area just east of Shoreditch church and Hackney Road, it was said to have cost £200,000. It was an open quadrangle surrounded by elaborate market buildings including a galleried mock Gothic hall with immensely tall granite shafts. Bells in the clock tower sounded a hymn tune every quarter-hour. The costermongers preferred the streets and, despite persistent efforts, the market failed. It was taken over for a short time by the CITY CORPORATION but was returned to the Baroness in 1874, briefly reopened in 1884, then let as workshops, and finally demolished in 1958.

Columbia Road *E2*. The flower market here is a successor of COLUMBIA MARKET, established by Baroness Burdett-Coutts.

Comedy Theatre *Panton Street, SW1*. Designed in 1881 by Thomas Verity and financed by J.H. Addison for Alexander Henderson. For the first four years comic operas were produced. From 1885 to 1888 it was managed by Violet Melnotte who introduced dramas and comedies to the theatre. Among her successful productions were *The Silver Shield*, a comedy by Sydney Grundy, and *Erminie*, a comic opera which starred Marie Tempest. In 1887 Herbert Beerbohm Tree produced *The Red Lamp*, a drama by W. Outram Tristam. In 1888 to 1892 and again in 1896 to 1899 Charles Hawtrey was manager and produced farces and comedies. In 1902 *Monsieur Beaucaire*, a romantic opera by Frederick Lonsdale and André Messager, was produced by Lewis Waller. It had 430 performances, and restored the prestige of the theatre. From 1907 to 1909 Marie Tempest appeared regularly in comedies. The theatre was partially reconstructed in 1911. In 1914 *Peg O' My Heart* with Laurette Taylor ran for 710 performances. Between 1915 and 1918 revues staged here included Cochran's *Half-Past Eight*

190

The Gothic Columbia Market, Bethnal Green, opened in 1869, was conceived as an attempt to wean costermongers from the streets.

(1915) and Charlot's *This and That* and *See-Saw* (both 1916). *Bubbly* (1917) and *Tails Up* (1918), two musicals by J.H. Turner and Philip Braham, had long runs. From 1922 to 1925 the theatre was managed by J.E. Vedrenne. His main success was *The Silent House* (1927), a play by John Brandon and George Pickett which had 420 performances. The theatre was again reconstructed in 1933, and again in the 1950s. The seating capacity is 820.

Commercial Road *E1, E14*. Built by the Commercial Road Co. in the first decade of the 19th century to facilitate the transport of goods from the newly opened EAST and WEST INDIA DOCKS to the edge of the CITY, the road ended at Back Church Lane until 1870, when the METROPOLITAN BOARD OF WORKS extended it to WHITECHAPEL HIGH STREET. Of the many streets and squares that were developed on either side of the thoroughfare in the early 19th century, Albert Gardens remains almost intact.

Commercial Street *E1*. The section from WHITECHAPEL to CHRISTCHURCH, SPITALFIELDS, opened in 1845, and the remainder, north to SHOREDITCH High Street, in 1858. TOYNBEE HALL, at the WHITECHAPEL end, was founded by Canon Barnett in 1884 and was the first of the university settlements in the East End. Near the SHOREDITCH end of the street stands the first block of PEABODY BUILDINGS, opened in 1864.

Commissioner of the City of London Police Appointed by the LORD MAYOR, ALDERMEN and COMMON COUNCIL of the CITY OF LONDON authority under section 3 City of London Police Act (1839), subject to the approval of Her Majesty as signified by one of Her Majesty's principal Secretaries of State. Under section 9 of the same Act the Commissioner makes all appointments to the force (*see also* CITY OF LONDON POLICE).

Common Cryer and Serjeant-at-Arms The second of the three Household Officers of the LORD MAYOR. He shares the administration of engagements and daily attendance upon the LORD MAYOR with the SWORDBEARER and the CITY MARSHAL. His office is probably the oldest of the three and was established well before 1338, when it was held by one of the King's serjeants-at-arms. In 1559 he is referred to as the Common Cryer and Serjeant-at-Arms. He bears the Mace before the LORD MAYOR and at COMMON HALL he proclaims silence and opens the proceedings calling, 'Oyez, Oyez, Oyez. You good members of the Livery . . . draw near and give your attendance.'

Common Hall The electoral assembly in GUILDHALL unique to the CITY OF LONDON. It is summoned by the LORD MAYOR for the election of the LORD MAYOR and the SHERIFFS and some minor traditional officers. Originally all Freemen (*see* FREEDOM OF THE CITY) could attend, but since the 15th century the franchise has been limited to members of the CITY LIVERY COMPANIES and this was confirmed by Statute in 1724. The election of the two SHERIFFS is held on Midsummer's Day, 24 June, by show of hands. On Michaelmas Day, 29 September, the Liverymen choose two ALDERMEN who have served the office of SHERIFF, from whom the Court of ALDERMEN elect the LORD MAYOR by ballot. In either case the date is adjusted so that the election does not fall at the weekend, and if a poll is demanded it is held a fortnight later.

Common Serjeant A Judge at the CENTRAL CRIMINAL COURT and Deputy to the RECORDER OF LONDON. The first known Common Serjeant was

Gregory de Norton in 1319. He was son of the first Recorder, Geoffrey de Norton. The Common Serjeant was originally elected by the MAYOR, ALDERMEN and Commonalty; but since the Local Government Act of 1888 his appointment has been vested in the Crown, though it is approved by the CORPORATION OF LONDON who pay his salary. Outside the CENTRAL CRIMINAL COURT his main duty is at COMMON HALL where he submits names of candidates at the elections of the LORD MAYOR and the SHERIFFS. He also attends and advises, when required, the LORD MAYOR and the Courts of ALDERMEN and COMMON COUNCIL and attends the LORD MAYOR on public and ceremonial occasions.

Commons, Open Spaces and Footpaths Preservation Society *25A Bell Street, Henley-on-Thames, Oxon.* Founded in 1865 as the Commons Preservation Society, it is the oldest of the national environmental societies. Its initial purpose, which was almost wholly successful, was to save the London commons, HAMPSTEAD HEATH, WIMBLEDON COMMON and WANDSWORTH COMMON. As its present name (assumed in the 1920s) implies, the Society is now concerned with wider issues including public rights of way. It was formerly at 11 King's Bench Walk, EC4.

Commonwealth Institute *Kensington High Street, W8.* Founded in 1887 as the Imperial Institute to commemorate Queen Victoria's Golden Jubilee, and then situated in IMPERIAL INSTITUTE ROAD. The present building, designed by Sir Robert Matthew and Johnson-Marshall, was opened by the Queen in 1962. Of striking design, it has a hyperboloid roof of Zambian copper. Many gifts from Commonwealth countries were also used in the building. The Institute is funded by the Foreign and Commonwealth Office; and spacious galleries on three floors display continuous and changing exhibitions on every Commonwealth country, associated state, and dependency. The Art Gallery displays fine art, sculpture, craftwork and tribal art. The 430-seat cinema daily shows varied types of relevant material, and is also used as a theatre for poetry recitals, music and drama. In the Activities Room educational programmes are conducted, with Commonwealth teachers incorporating such subjects as costume, music, art and cookery from their own countries in the instruction. In addition the Institute offers accommodation to business firms for conferences and seminars. The setting, with gardens and lawn, can be used for outdoor exhibitions and functions. The comprehensive library and Resource Centre with its collection of books, gramophone records and audio-visual learning aids is open to the general public for loan and reference.

Comptroller and City Solicitor A High Officer of the CORPORATION OF LONDON elected by the COURT OF COMMON COUNCIL. His is an amalgamation of several ancient posts. That of City Solicitor dates from 1545. He is Vice-Chamberlain and Conveyancing Officer for the CORPORATION. He conducts all the CORPORATION's legal proceedings and is legal adviser to the Commissioner of Police CITY OF LONDON (*see* POLICE). He is also Clerk of Enrolments to the ancient Court of Hustings, and Attorney-in-Waiting to the LORD MAYOR when the latter presides over a WARD-MOTE. He is Custodian of the Keys to the City Seal and

participates in City ceremonial, especially the Quit Rents Ceremony (*see* CEREMONIES) at the LAW COURTS in the STRAND.

Conduit Street *W1.* Extends from NEW BOND STREET to REGENT STREET. It was laid out in the early 18th century on the CITY OF LONDON's Conduit Mead estate, which also included NEW BOND STREET and which had been acquired by the CORPORATION in the 15th century to safeguard the conduits supplying the CITY with water. Only a very few of the original houses now survive – notably Nos 42, 43 and 47. The finest building is No 9, designed by James Wyatt in 1779 for Robert Vyner MP, a Lincolnshire country gentleman. It is a beautiful three-bay stuccoed composition with giant Ionic pilasters and pedimented first-floor windows. In Victorian times it was occupied by the ROYAL INSTITUTE OF BRITISH ARCHITECTS and now provides an appropriately chic home for the London headquarters of Christian Dior. Nearby, Rolls-Royce motors have their elegant showrooms, as do two world-famous pianoforte makers – Blüthner and Steinway. Near the west end are the galleries of the ROYAL SOCIETY OF PAINTERS IN WATER COLOURS, while opposite, on the south side, is the recently erected WESTBURY HOTEL. Much of the rest of the street is occupied by the offices of airlines and travel agents. Charles James Fox was born in Conduit Street in 1749; and James Boswell, William Wilberforce and George Canning all lived here briefly. J. and E. Atkinson, the perfumers at No. 26, were founded at the beginning of the 19th century in GERRARD STREET. Outside the shop was chained a bear whose grease, perfumed with attar of roses, was sold as a pomatum to the Prince Regent. The shop moved to 39 Bond Street in 1826, and in 1832 to 24 OLD BOND STREET. The firm has been at its present address since 1972. Collingwood's, the jewellers, established by a cockfighting impresario and friend of the Prince Regent, moved to Conduit Street in 1837 and are now at No. 46.

Congregational Memorial Hall Trust *2 Fleet Lane, Farringdon Street, EC4.* The original Congregational Memorial Hall of Victorian Gothic design was erected on the site of the FLEET PRISON in 1872 to commemorate the bicentenary of the ejection of 2,000 ministers on the passing of the Act of Uniformity in 1662. The Trades Union Congress of 27 February 1900, at which the Labour Party was founded, was held at the Memorial Hall and the General Strike of 1926 was run from it. It was demolished in 1969 and replaced in 1972 by a new building, named Caroone House, of which the present Memorial Hall is part. The new Memorial Hall has an entrance in Fleet Lane and contains the Congregational Library, offices, also committee rooms and a hall which are let for meetings. The remainder of the building is occupied by the Post Office.

Connaught Hotel *Carlos Place, W1.* In 1803 Alexander Grillon opened a hotel in ALBEMARLE STREET and some years later another in Charles Street, GROSVENOR SQUARE, later renamed CARLOS PLACE. In 1896 Auguste Scorrier, the owner, rebuilt it to the designs of Isaacs and Florence and renamed it the Coburg Hotel. At the outbreak of the 1st World War, in deference to anti-German feeling, it was renamed the Connaught Hotel. The hotel's monogram was thus able to remain unchanged. Between the wars it was best known as the London home for landed families, since it was equidistant from BUCKINGHAM PALACE and HARLEY STREET, and many of them retained permanent suites. In the 2nd World War it was the London headquarters of General de Gaulle. There are 89 bedrooms. The hotel's restaurant is one of the best in London.

Connaught Place *W2.* The building of this terrace, between 1807 and 1815, with final additions a little later, began to make the area north of HYDE PARK fashionable. The earliest house was built by the Duke of Gloucester, Earl of Connaught, from whom the terrace takes its name. The house was apparently built for Lady Augusta de Ameland, the so-called Duchess of Sussex, whose marriage in 1793 to the sixth son of George III had been declared invalid. She lived here from 1808 for 20 years. No. 7 was the home in 1813–14 of Queen Caroline, also of Princess Charlotte after her banishment from court. In 1883–92 Lord Randolph Churchill lived at No. 2; and Elinor Glyn, the novelist, lived at No. 11 in 1934–7.

Connaught Rooms *61–65 Great Queen Street, WC2.* Built on the site of a house occupied by the Marquess of Normanby. On 1 May 1775 the foundation stone was laid for a new masonic hall which was opened on 23 May 1776. This was found to be inadequate and, at Thomas Sandby's suggestion, the Freemasons' Tavern was built in the 1780s. This became one of London's most celebrated taverns. In 1905 the old building was demolished and new, larger premises were constructed to the designs of Brown and Barrow. These, the Connaught Rooms, are now the largest permanent banqueting hall in London. The name commemorates the Duke of Connaught, who was Grand Master of the Freemasons. They comprise 27 sumptuous rooms providing facilities for exhibitions, conferences, banquets and dinners for up to 2,500 people. Many functions of the CITY LIVERY COMPANIES are held here, also dinners given by masonic charitable institutions. (*See also* FREEMASONS' HALL.)

Connaught Square *W2.* Dating from the 1820s, this most elegant square was the earliest to be built in this corner of BAYSWATER. Marie Taglioni, the ballerina, lived at No. 14 in 1875–6 and at No. 6 in 1877–9; and Albert Fonblanque, editor of the *Examiner* and friend of Thackeray and Forster, at No. 44 in 1840–72.

Connaught Theatre *see* ROYAL AMPHITHEATRE.

Conservative Club *74 St James's Street, SW1.* Founded in 1840. The club's premises were designed by George Basevi the Younger and Sydney Smirke and erected in 1843–5 on the site of the THATCHED HOUSE TAVERN. The exterior is in a Palladian design with rusticated ground floor and Corinthian pilasters on the upper floor. The rooms inside are well proportioned and the Dining Room and Library face ST JAMES'S PALACE. The centre of the interior is a square room with a circular upper gallery under a circular dome. The rooms, hall, staircase and upper vestibule were decorated by Sang (who executed the encaustic paintings in the old COAL EXCHANGE) and Naundorff.

Constitution Arch *Hyde Park Corner, SW1.* Designed by Decimus Burton, and erected in 1828 near APSLEY HOUSE, it was known as Wellington Arch

The Conservative Club in St James's was designed by George Basevi and Sydney Smirke in 1843–5.

and then as the Green Park Arch. Matthew Cotes Wyatt's statue of Wellington (*see* STATUES) which once stood on top of it was removed to Aldershot in 1883 when the arch was moved to the top of CONSTITUTION HILL. It is now surmounted by a bronze group, the *Quadriga*, by Adrian Jones, a former officer in the 3rd Hussars. The £17,000 cost of this sculpture was met by Lord Michelham, a Jewish financier, who presented it in 1912 in memory of his friend, Edward VII. Michelham's 11-year-old son served as a model for the boy who pulls at the reins of the four horses harnessed to the *quadriga* as an immense figure of Peace descends upon them from heaven. Jones held a dinner for eight people inside one of the horses shortly before the completion of his four years' labour on the group. Inside the arch is a police station which, after the one in TRAFALGAR SQUARE, is the smallest in London.

Constitution Hill *SW1*. A pleasant avenue dividing GREEN PARK from the walled gardens of BUCKINGHAM PALACE. It is still lined with trees and old lamp posts, despite recent attempts to remove them. Nobody knows how it got its name. One theory is that Charles II took constitutional walks here. He was said to have been walking here one day when his brother, the Duke of York (later James II), returned from hunting on HOUNSLOW HEATH accompanied by a large party of guardsmen. Surprised to see the King walking with so few attendants, the Duke 'thought His Majesty exposed himself to some danger'. 'No kind of danger, James,' the King replied. 'For I am sure no man in England will take away my life to make you King.' Constitution Hill, was, however, the site of three attempts made on Queen Victoria's life – in 1840, 1842 and 1849. In 1850 Sir Robert Peel was fatally injured when thrown from his horse by the wicket gate leading into GREEN PARK after calling at the Palace.

Convent of the Sacred Heart *Hammersmith Road, W6*. Believed to be the only place in London which has always been in Roman Catholic possession. A convent stood here long before the Reformation. It escaped destruction at the time of the DISSOLUTION OF THE MONASTERIES because of its lack of endowment. After the Reformation it became a girls' school run by nuns who were at first obliged to wear disguise. Titus Oates had the place searched and accused the headmistress of harbouring Jesuits; but he was unable to obtain a conviction through lack of proof. In 1795 a community of Benedictines from Dunkirk, fleeing from the Revolution, took the building over and founded a girls' school. The school continued until 1869 when it moved to Devon. A Roman Catholic seminary known as St Thomas's was then built on the site at the instigation of Archbishop Manning. The architect was J.F. Bentley whose plans, drawn up in 1875, were realised in 1876–88. The seminary was replaced by a convent and school in 1893. The Sacred Heart Roman Catholic High School (ILEA) and Sacred Heart RC Primary School (ILEA) are now here.

Conway Hall *25 Red Lion Square, WC1*. Built in 1929, the Hall is the home of the South Place Ethical Society (founded 1839) and was named after its 19th-century minister, Moncure Conway. A favourite meeting place for all kinds of function, the large Hall accommodates 500, the small hall 100, and there are three smaller rooms. All are available for hire.

Although the Society became agnostic in 1869, it retains the tradition of Sunday meetings and organises many other activities. The celebrated chamber music concerts begun in 1887 take place every Sunday from October to April.

Cooks' Company *see* CITY LIVERY COMPANIES.

Cook's Road *SE11*. A short road in KENNINGTON extending south-east from the north of KENNINGTON PARK. The bronze, *Two-Piece Reclining Figure No.3*, in the Brandon Estate is by Henry Moore (1961).

Coombe, Surrey Derives its name from *cwm* – a hilltop. The site of a Roman settlement, it is mentioned in *Domesday Book* as having three manors. During the early 19th century the local landowners were Lord Liverpool, Prime Minister during the Regency and under George IV; and, later, the Duke of Cambridge, cousin to Queen Victoria. They both lived at Coombe House, a 16th-century building demolished in 1933. The estate devolved on the Fitzgeorges, the Duke's children by a morganatic marriage, and was finally sold in 1932. In the 16th century Cardinal Wolsey piped water from Coombe Springs to HAMPTON COURT. Three conduit houses of Tudor brickwork survive. In Coombe Hill Road is a 15th-century timber-framed building, Coombe Wood House, removed from Colchester, Essex, in 1911, by being dismantled in sections and re-erected. It has been empty for some 30 years.

Many celebrated and wealthy people lived in this area some 80–100 years ago, including John Galsworthy, who was born here and used the place as 'Robin Hill' in his novel cycle *The Forsyte Saga*.

CO-OPERATIVE SOCIETIES Owe their origin to 'certain poor inhabitants of Hull' who, in 1795, formed a co-operative to build their own mill so as to protect themselves from the effects of the rising cost of bread. In the following years several co-operative congresses were held throughout the country, including one in London in 1832. In 1863 a London Association for the Promotion of Co-operation was established; and in 1879 the foundation stone of a warehouse was laid in Leman Street, E1. This building was followed by the construction and opening of several others in the Greater London area, which were intended 'to supply all the constant needs of the worker and his wife, their children and their home'. There are now four retail co-operative societies in London, each of which is based on the recognised co-operative principles of open membership, democratic control, limited interest on capital and dividend in proportion to trade. These societies run shops and department stores throughout Greater London which are supplied with goods by the Co-operative Wholesale Society. They have their own dairies, and are the largest funeral directors in the area. They also make substantial grants for various educational purposes, and are closely associated with or affiliated to the Labour Party or the Co-operative Party. These societies are:
London Region Co-operative Retail Services *54 Maryland Street, E15*. This was formed in 1981 and developed from the London Co-operative Society (founded 1921) which itself developed from the Stratford Society (founded 1862).

Copenhagen Fields, Islington, 1834. Trade Unionists meet to carry a petition to the King on behalf of the Tolpuddle Martyrs.

Royal Arsenal Co-operative Society *125–157 and 132–152 Powis Street, Woolwich, SE18.* Founded 1868.

Enfield Highway Co-operative Society *548–590 Hertford Road, N9.* Founded 1872.

South Suburban Co-operative Society *99 London Road, Croydon, Surrey.* This was founded in 1914 but its origins can be traced back to the Brixton Society, founded in 1864, and the Reigate Society, founded in 1863.

Coopers' Company *see* CITY LIVERY COMPANIES.

Copenhagen House *Islington.* A part 17th-century gabled mansion situated on the hill between Maiden Lane and HOLLOWAY, possibly built as a hostelry for visiting Danes when the King of Denmark came to James I's court in 1606. Or it may have been named after its supposed occupation by the Danish ambassador during the GREAT PLAGUE. Its magnificent uninterrupted view over London and up to HIGHGATE made it popular from the 1750s as a tea-garden. It was also licensed for wine and beer, with ninepins and skittles in the grounds. Fives-playing, introduced by a young assistant from Shropshire, proved a great favourite, the Irish champion John Cavanagh playing notable matches here.

In 1780 a public subscription after the landlady, Mrs Harrington, suffered a brutal robbery, enabled the owner to build on a Long Room for tea-drinking, with a smoking-room below. Tooth, a later landlord, encouraged a rougher clientele, with bulldog fights and bull-baiting; but his licence was suspended in 1816.

Paths converged on Copenhagen Fields from all directions, and its popularity for recreation made it also a favourite place for mass meetings, from the LONDON CORRESPONDING SOCIETY during the French Revolution to Dissenters, Chartists and radicals. Louis Kossuth, the Hungarian patriot, addressed a meeting here in 1851. In 1852 the CITY CORPORATION acquired 75 acres here for a new Metropolitan Cattle Market, in order to close SMITHFIELD. The old house was demolished in 1853. The Market tower, built approximately on its site, still survives.

Copthall Avenue *EC2.* Built in 1890 over Leathersellers Buildings and Little Bell Alley and named after Copped Hall, a large house which stood on DOWGATE HILL in the 13th and 14th centuries. The remains of a Roman wharf built beside the WALBROOK have been discovered here.

Coptic Street *WC1.* Originally built after the GREAT FIRE and then known as Duke Street, in honour of the ground landlords, the Dukes of Bedford. To avoid confusion with other Duke Streets in London it was renamed in 1894, the year after a valuable collection of Coptic manuscripts had been brought to the nearby BRITISH MUSEUM. No. 33, now a *pizzeria*, was formerly a dairy, designed in the Art Nouveau style by R.P. Wellcock in 1888 with white tiles and a sunflower motif.

Coram Fields *WC1.* On the former site of the FOUNDLING HOSPITAL which was founded in the 18th century by Thomas Coram whose work is carried on by the THOMAS CORAM FOUNDATION FOR CHILDREN. Coram Fields themselves are now a children's playground, administered by CAMDEN Borough Council, to which unaccompanied adults may be refused admission. However since the 1880s the former burial ground in the adjoining St George's Gardens has been beautifully laid out as a public garden, where even adults may find refuge.

Coram Street *WC1*. Built in 1800–4 on the FOUNDLING HOSPITAL Estate and named after Captain Coram, the founder. Thackeray lived here in 1837–43. His eldest daughter, Anne, was born here in 1838. In the *Ballad of Eliza Davis*, he wrote:

> P'raps you know the foundling Chapel,
> Where the little children sing
> Lord I like to hear on Sunday,
> Them there pretty little things.

After the birth of their third child Mrs Thackeray had a mental breakdown. She never recovered and a few years later Thackeray gave up the house. Mr Todd in *Vanity Fair* lives in Great Coram Street as it was then called. It is now redeveloped with hotels on the south and shops on the north. John Leech lived here in 1837, and Edward Fitzgerald in 1843.

Corbets Tey *see* UPMINSTER.

Cordwainers' Company *see* CITY LIVERY COMPANIES.

Cork Street *W1*. On the BURLINGTON ESTATE, it extends from BURLINGTON GARDENS to CLIFFORD STREET, and takes its name from the Earls of Burlington's ancillary Earldom of Cork. Development began here in 1718 – on the west side only, the east side being occupied for many years by the back gardens of the houses on the west side of OLD BURLINGTON STREET. None of the original houses now survives, but Nos 7 and 19–20 date from 1814–18. All the rest of the buildings here are either Victorian or more modern offices, generally with shops at street level, mostly occupied by art galleries including the three Waddington Galleries (founded between 1957 and 1981) and the Redfern Gallery (founded in 1923), or tailors. Abigail Masham, confidante of Queen Anne, and her husband, 1st Baron Masham, lived at No. 5 in 1725–36; and Alexander Pope stayed at No. 7 in about 1739–40. Alan McAfee, the shoemakers at No. 5, were established in 1910. HENRY POOLE AND CO., the tailors, are at No. 10.

Corn Exchange *Mark Lane and Seething Lane, EC3*. A public granary was established in London in 1438. By 1521 the CITY was regularly supplied with corn by the CORPORATION and the CITY LIVERY COMPANIES. Each of the 12 great Companies purchased its own supply which was stored at Bridge House, at the SOUTHWARK end of LONDON BRIDGE, where baking ovens were built. Other ovens were built at the Companies' Halls. By the middle of the 17th century it had been accepted, however, that private trading would be more efficient than corporate buying and selling; and, at the same time, most of the Companies' Halls and ovens were destroyed in the GREAT FIRE. Thereafter corn was landed at QUEENHITHE and BILLINGSGATE and carried by packhorse to the two main London corn markets, CORNHILL and CHEAPSIDE, BREAD STREET being the market for baked bread. At the beginning of

Samples under inspection in the Corn Exchange, Mark Lane, 1842.

the 18th century the Metropolitan Corn Market was established at Bear Quay, THAMES STREET. At about this time also an agency system was applied to the corn trade. This had arisen from the practice of various Essex farmers, who frequented a tavern in WHITECHAPEL, of leaving samples of corn with the innkeeper to be sold on commission, and from the later employment of agents to act for the farmers. The agents set up stands in many places until the first Corn Exchange, open to the sky, was built in MARK LANE in 1749. It was extended and partly rebuilt in 1827, and a New Exchange adjoining it was constructed in 1828. The old Exchange was again extended and roofed over in 1850, and rebuilt in the 1880s with an Italianate façade by E. I'Anson. In 1929 the two Exchanges were amalgamated. The building was badly damaged by bombs in 1941, but rebuilt and reopened in 1954 on a site covering two-thirds of the space occupied by the two former Exchanges. The remainder of the site was used for the construction of an eight-storey office block to the design of T.E. Heysham. The new Corn Exchange was reconstructed in 1973. Goods traded on the exchange include all types of imported and home-grown cereals, pulses, flour, agricultural seeds, all types of animal feedstuffs, oil seeds and fertilisers.

Cornhill *EC3*. The highest hill in the CITY, site of the Roman BASILICA and of a medieval grain market which gave it its present name. It was long celebrated for its pillory for false dealers, its stocks and its prison known as the Tun, which was used particularly for night-walkers. Daniel Defoe, who had had a hosier's shop in the nearby Freeman's Court, spent a day in the pillory in 1703 for issuing his *The Shortest Way with the Dissenters*. At the corner of LOMBARD STREET and Cornhill, Thomas Guy, founder of GUY'S HOSPITAL, had his bookshop. No. 39 is the site of the house in which the poet Thomas Gray was born in 1716. From the 16th to the 19th centuries Cornhill and its surrounding alleys abounded in well-known coffee-houses, such as GARRAWAY'S. The offices of the

196

Traffic in Cornhill in 1788 passes the Royal Exchange on the right. St Paul's is at the bottom of the hill.

publishers, Smith and Elder, were at No. 65 from 1816 until about 1868. Among their authors were Thackeray, Leigh Hunt, Mrs Gaskell and the Brontës. Anne and Charlotte Brontë came here to prove they were Acton and Currer Bell. The *Cornhill* magazine was first published here in 1859; Thackeray was its editor. His last two novels, *The Adventures of Philip* and *Denis Duval*, were serialised in it. ST MICHAEL'S church is on the corner of St Michael's Alley, and ST PETER-UPON-CORNHILL between Nos 54 and 55. A third church, ST BENET FINK, was burned down in the GREAT FIRE; it was rebuilt by Wren in 1679 and Cardinal Newman was baptised here in 1801. But the rebuilding of the ROYAL EXCHANGE entailed its demolition in 1844. Most of Cornhill is now occupied by commerical blocks of the late 19th and early 20th centuries. No. 65 is by Edward I'Anson (1871). The drinking fountain at the corner of the ROYAL EXCHANGE, *Motherhood*, is by Jules Dalou.

Cornwall Terrace *NW1*. Takes its name from an earlier title of George IV, Duke of Cornwall. Designed

by Decimus Burton, it was the first terrace to be completed in REGENT'S PARK. It consists of 19 houses, the westernmost, No. 10, terminating in an elegant bow window, running through two storeys and adorned with caryatids. Since the 2nd World War it has been well restored and now houses the offices of the British Land Company, a property-owning enterprise. In 1982 the BRITISH ACADEMY moved to Nos 20–21.

Coronation Stone *Kingston-upon-Thames, Surrey*. A weathered slab of grey sandstone mounted on a stone plinth outside the Guildhall in the High Street and surrounded by a railing of Saxon design. According to tradition at least seven Saxon kings were crowned on this stone, from Edward the Elder in 900 to Ethelred the Unready in 979. Set into the plinth is a coin of the reign of each of these kings.

Coronations The coronation ceremony is over 1,000 years old. It was first planned by St Dunstan, Archbishop of Canterbury, for the crowning of King Edgar at Bath in 973. Since 1066 every coronation has taken place in WESTMINSTER ABBEY. In that year two kings were crowned – Harold in January, and on Christmas Day the victorious William I, whose coronation was marred because the Norman soldiers on guard outside the Abbey thought the shouts of acclaim were a sign of rebellion and began killing the Saxons. Throughout the centuries some sovereigns have had ill omens at their coronations. A bat swooped round the head of Richard I as he assumed the crown. Richard II lost a shoe as he left the Abbey. Charles I wore white, which many said was unlucky. James II's crown wobbled and nearly fell during the procession to WHITEHALL. (This Catholic King heard mass at St James's Palace but submitted to Anglican rites at his coronation.) George IV was determined to have a magnificent ceremony and Parliament voted £243,000 for it. It was indeed magnificent, even though it was held on an exceptionally hot July day and the king appeared 'distressed almost to fainting' in his full robes and

Engraving after T. H. Shepherd's drawing of Cornwall Terrace, Regent's Park, in 1827.

The coronation of James II in Westminster Abbey on St George's Day, 1685.

heavy wig during the five-hour service. Lady Cowper said he looked 'more like the victim than the hero of the fête'. Once revived with sal volatile he recovered sufficiently to wink at Lady Conyngham until the sternly admonitory sermon of the Archbishop of Canterbury induced a more serious mood. Meanwhile his rejected Queen Caroline was trying to force her way in to the Abbey, but all doors were barred against her.

William IV thought the ceremony 'a pointless piece of flummery' in the words of his biographer, Philip Ziegler; and looked comical rather than regal and 'very infirm in his walk'. There was great splendour for Victoria's coronation procession in June 1838. The bewildered Turkish Ambassador kept muttering: 'All this for a woman!' Victoria arrived at the Abbey 30 minutes late, but despite her youth (she was 18) 'performed her part with great grace and completeness'. Other participants did not do so well. Peers, generals and maids-of-honour scrabbled inelegantly for coronation medals tossed about by the Treasurer, and the Queen's ladies proved utterly incompetent to cope with their own trains and manage hers. Lord Rolle tripped and fell down the stairs to the throne, and the congregation cheered as he shakily picked himself up and climbed again towards the Queen's outstretched hand. There was confusion over the presentation of the Orb; and the ruby Ring, designed for her little finger, was painfully forced on to the fourth. Once the Bishop of Bath accidentally turned over two pages at once and nearly ended the service prematurely.

Edward VII was to have been crowned in June 1902 but the coronation was postponed until August because of his serious illness. When the ceremony took place the ancient Archbishop of Canterbury caused great confusion. He almost fell over with the Crown, was only just prevented from putting it on the wrong way round, and had to be helped up after paying homage to the King on behalf of the church. In consequence of past mishaps, there were careful preparations for George VI's coronation in May 1937, but even so rehearsals in the Abbey were chaotic, with the Archbishop of Canterbury wandering about crying 'Where is the Lord of the Manor of Worksop?' (who had the right to present an embroidered glove). There was dismay when the Orb was lost, until the six-year-old Princess Margaret was found playing with it on the floor. The King recorded his own worries, particularly over the reading, and whether his Crown would be the right way round; but despite some anxious moments all went well.

Queen Elizabeth II's coronation in June 1953 was well rehearsed, dignified and well ordered, thanks to the calm organisation of the Archbishop of Canterbury and the Earl Marshal. The only adverse factor was the weather, but the pouring rain could not diminish the enthusiasm of the huge crowds. It was the first coronation to be televised. The coronation of her father, George VI, had been the first 'to be recorded by cinematography' and the first coronation photographs were taken at that of her grandfather, George V, in 1911.

The order of service closely followed the *Liber Regalis* written and illustrated in the 14th century and kept in WESTMINSTER ABBEY. In it the parts to be played by the various dignitaries and officials in the rite are carefully laid down. The Queen walked into the Abbey at the end of a procession of 250, pausing first at the area, between the Choir and the Sanctuary, known as the Theatre. There were the three chairs used during the ceremony by the Sovereign – the Chair of State; the Throne; and King Edward's Chair, holding the Stone of Scone which was first used for the coronation of Edward II in 1308. In the rite, known as the Recognition, the Archbishop presented the Queen to the congregation and asked if they were willing to do homage and service. All cried 'God Save Queen Elizabeth' and the trumpets sounded. The Oath followed and the Presentation of the Bible, and then the Communion Service began. After the Creed the Queen took her place in King Edward's Chair, clad in a simple white gown, for the Anointing. She was invested with the royal robes and ornaments: the Jewelled Sword, the Armills (gold bracelets of sovereignty and wisdom), the Orb and Sceptre and the Coronation Ring. Then everyone in the Abbey rose as the Archbishop of Canterbury, having dedicated St Edward's Crown, raised it on high and solemnly lowered it on to the Queen's head. All shouted 'God Save the Queen', the trumpets sounded and the guns of the TOWER OF LONDON fired a Royal Salute. The enthronement followed and then the Queen received the homage of the Princes and Peers. After the Homage the drums beat and the trumpets sounded and all cried 'God Save Queen Elizabeth, Long live Queen Elizabeth, May the Queen live for ever.' The Queen and Prince Philip then retired to St Edward's Chapel where the Queen was arrayed in her Royal Purple Robe and the weighty St Edward's Crown was replaced by the lighter Imperial State Crown. Finally the newly crowned Queen moved with her great procession through the Abbey to the West Door to the sounds of the National Anthem and the pealing of bells.

A Coronation Banquet used to be held in WESTMINSTER HALL, where the Barons of the Cinque Ports carried the canopy over the King's head and the King's Champion rode in full armour into the Hall and challenged to mortal combat any who might dispute his right to the title. The Hereditary Champions were for centuries the Dymokes of Scrivelsby and, although the custom was discontinued after George IV's coronation, they have other coronation duties nowadays. At James II's Coronation Banquet the Champion fell in full armour as he dismounted to kiss the King's hand, while at George III's banquet, although the Champion did well, one of his companions, Lord Talbot, could not prevent his horse from entering the Hall backwards. All went well at the last Challenge in 1821, when, after no one had taken up the Gauntlet, George IV drank to the Champion from a gold cup which, having drunk from it himself, the Champion took away with him as his rightful trophy. The peers enjoyed an excellent meal, while their wives and children, who were allowed to watch from the rows of seats above, looked on hungrily, though one thoughtful peer tied a cold capon in his handkerchief and tossed it up to his family.

Corporation of London The CITY OF LONDON has no Charter of Incorporation although it has served as a pattern for many other municipalities which do have Charters. The composition of its governing body in order of precedence is: LORD MAYOR, SHERIFFS,

ALDERMEN and COURT OF COMMON COUNCIL. Until the 18th century the Court of ALDERMEN was mainly responsible for the government of the CITY, but the day-to-day administrative work was gradually taken over by the COURT OF COMMON COUNCIL and the aldermanic body developed into what has been loosely described as an Upper House. The work of the modern ALDERMEN is dealt with separately under that heading. The Court of ALDERMEN sits under the LORD MAYOR and meets some 15 times a year in its own Court Room, a quorum consisting of 12 ALDERMEN apart from the LORD MAYOR, that is to say half the total number of ALDERMEN.

The COURT OF COMMON COUNCIL arose out of the ancient folkmoot or husting of elected members of the commonalty meeting with the ALDERMEN to govern the CITY, and has worked so well that in 1837 the Municipal Corporations Commission reported that the City of London Corporation was the only one in the kingdom which did not need reform. The Court is presided over by the LORD MAYOR and must be attended by him, or in his unavoidable absence his *locum tenens* (who must be a former LORD MAYOR), two other ALDERMEN and at least 38 Common Councilmen.

The meetings take place twice monthly in GUILDHALL except during the summer recess. The LORD MAYOR sits in the centre of the dais, with those ALDERMEN who have 'passed the Chair' on his right and the junior ALDERMEN on his left. The two SHERIFFS sit at the ends of the rows of ALDERMEN. In front of the LORD MAYOR and ALDERMEN on the dais is a long table at which the principal officers of the Corporation sit facing the Hall. Chief of these is the CITY CHAMBERLAIN, the CITY's banker and treasurer, custodian of the City's Cash and head of the Court which admits candidates for the FREEDOM OF THE CITY and personally greets those distinguished people who have been awarded the Honorary Freedom by order of the Corporation. On his right sit the Town Clerk, Deputy Town Clerk and two other officials from the Town Clerk's Office, and at the end of the table the Principal Clerk to the Chamberlain. On his left are the COMPTROLLER, who is also the City Solicitor and acts as the Vice-Chamberlain, conveyancing officer and legal adviser; the Remembrancer, whose duties are parliamentary, legal and ceremonial; the Medical Officer of Health for the City and Port of London; the City Surveyor; the City Engineer and the City Planning Officer. In front of the long table is a small table on which rest the Sword and Mace, the responsible Household Officers – the SWORDBEARER and the COMMON CRYER – sitting on either side. The CITY MARSHAL stands by the steps which lead up to the dais. The Common Councilmen are seated in the body of the Hall on chairs arranged in rows at right angles to the dais and facing inwards, the front row on each side being occupied by the Chairmen of Committees. The Town Clerk conducts the business.

The Committees of the Corporation are at present as follows: City Lands (the Chairman of which is known as the Chief Commoner), BRIDGE HOUSE ESTATES and GRESHAM COMMITTEE – all of these are concerned with the City's estates; Coal and Corn and Finance and Rates Finance, dealing with the administration of the City's income; Education, responsible for the City's three public schools; Music, mainly concerned with the GUILDHALL SCHOOL OF MUSIC AND DRAMA;

Epping Forest and Open Spaces, and the Committee of Managers of West Ham Park – both concerned with the various open spaces belonging to the City; a group of Committees devoted to the Corporation's domestic affairs; General Purposes, responsible *inter alia* for the MANSION HOUSE; Establishment; Freedom Applications; Privileges; GUILDHALL Reconstruction; Corporation Benevolent; and finally, those Committees relating to the City's various public services – Housing, Library, Litter Act, Licensing Planning, Joint Markets Advisory, POLICE, Port and City of London Health, Planning and Communications, Barbican and Social Services. There are also a Policy and Parliamentary Committee and a MUSEUM OF LONDON Committee (with a membership one-third Corporation, one-third GREATER LONDON COUNCIL and one-third HM Treasury).

Cosway Street *NW8*. Lies on the PORTMAN ESTATE just north of the MARYLEBONE ROAD. First rated in 1795 and originally called Stafford Street, it changed its name in 1905 in honour of the miniaturist, Richard Cosway, who was baptised in ST MARYLEBONE PARISH CHURCH in 1740. In this street stands CHRISTCHURCH, designed by Philip Hardwick and consecrated in 1825.

Cottage Place *SW3*. An ancient track leading north from Brompton Lane to a cowshed near the parish boundary. It formed the western boundary of the BROMPTON SQUARE estate developed by William Farler in 1826. On the west was built the Church of Holy Trinity in 1826–9. The little cottages and garages on the east side date from the 1920s and 1930s. The tall houses Nos 7 and 9 were a rather seedy hotel in the early 1930s. The building at the south end was the Old Brompton Road Station of the PICCADILLY LINE, built in 1905, closed in 1934 and later incorporated into the Territorial Army drill hall.

Cotton Street *Barbican*. In 1892–4 the CITY CORPORATION built a street of drapers' warehouses over the site of several alleys. It ran from AUSTRALIAN AVENUE to HARE COURT but was completely destroyed in the 2nd World War.

Coulsdon *Surrey*. Colesdone, the present Old Coulsdon, was held by the Abbey of Chertsey for 800 years. St John's church, with its rare *sedilia* and *piscina*, was rebuilt in 1260. Sir Nicholas Carew of BEDDINGTON acquired the manor in 1537 from Henry VIII but was executed for high treason in 1539. A cricket team from Coulsdon and Caterham in 1731 challenged 'any 11 men in England'. In 1766 the club played the first recorded match with three stumps and two bails. 'Gentleman' Jackson won his first prize fight in 1788 at Smitham Bottom (modern Coulsdon) against Mr Fewterel in the presence of the Prince Regent, who rewarded the winner with a bank note. The first public railway in the world, the SURREY IRON RAILWAY, was extended in 1805 south to Merstham, passing through Smitham. At Smitham over 40 coaches a day called at the Red Lion on the Brighton run. In 1820 a bystander asked George IV, 'Where's your wife, George?' during the proceedings against Queen Caroline, so he afterwards avoided the Red Lion. This public house was also the site of the first fatality of the London to Brighton VETERAN CAR RUN

when, in 1901, 'Edgar Crundy of South Norwood was summonsed for furiously driving a motor car. . . . The police evidence as to speed was conflicting, various estimates ranging from 16 to 153 m.p.h.' Cane Hill Mental Hospital was sited in 1883 on the Portnalls Estate where 30 years later a pre-glacial hippopotamus, now in the HORNIMAN MUSEUM, was discovered.

Coulsdon Commons *Surrey*. The Commons of Farthingdown, Riddlesdown, COULSDON and KENLEY, about 18 miles due south of the CITY, were acquired by the CORPORATION in 1883. The four commons cover approximately 430 acres and are maintained in their natural state.

County Hall *SE1*. This monumental building, occupying one of the most splendid sites in London, stands on the south side of the THAMES beside WESTMINSTER BRIDGE. It is now the headquarters of the GREATER LONDON COUNCIL, but was built by that Council's predecessor, the LONDON COUNTY COUNCIL. When the LONDON COUNTY COUNCIL came into being in 1889 it inherited inadequate offices in SPRING GARDENS, near TRAFALGAR SQUARE, and in 1905 it decided to provide itself with more suitable premises by acquiring this riverside site, then occupied by a clutter of wharves, timber yards and factories which formed an ugly eyesore when viewed from the EMBANKMENT on the other side of the THAMES. A public competition for the design of the new building was held (one of the unsuccessful competitors being Edwin Lutyens) and the winner was Ralph Knott, whose only large building this was to be.

Soon after excavation of the site had begun in 1909 the battered remains of a Roman boat were discovered (*see* ROMAN BOATS AND BARGES). Work ceased in 1916 owing to the war, but was resumed in 1919, and the building was opened by King George V on 17 July 1922, though the northern riverside section was not completed until 1933. Subsequently two more blocks of offices were built at the back fronting York Road, the external designs of which (provided by the Council's own Architect's Department) are similar to the main block, though simpler in general appearance. The whole complex was finished in 1963. Knott's block is in a free 'Edwardian Renaissance' style and is faced with Portland stone except at the base where, like the river wall in front, it is finished in granite. In addition to two basements it has six storeys, the top two being set in the roof above a heavy overhanging cornice and lit by dormer windows projecting from the long roof slopes, which are laid with red Italian tiles. The building is planned round a number of internal courtyards, with the Council Chamber placed at its heart. The two principal entrances are from Westminster Bridge Road (for the use of members of the Council only) through a vaulted approach, reminiscent of Piranesi, to the fine principal courtyard; and from the centre of the long, somewhat monotonous, east front, which lacks the focal point provided on the river front by the colonnaded crescent, central *flèche* and end pavilions. The sculptures above the first-floor windows are by Ernest Cole and Alfred Hardiman.

County Hall Boat *see* ROMAN BOATS AND BARGES.

Court of Arches The chief court of the Archbishops of Canterbury, so called because it was originally held in the parish church of ST MARY-LE-BOW in CHEAPSIDE, otherwise known as Sancta Maria de Arcubus, which was destroyed in the GREAT FIRE. The court was then moved to the rebuilt Hall of the Advocates at DOCTORS' COMMONS in KNIGHTRIDER STREET. When the Society of Advocates was incorporated by Royal Charter in 1768 the Dean of the Arches (i.e. the judge) became *ex officio* the President of the College. The right to practise in the Court was confined to advocates and proctors. The Court's jurisdiction in matrimonial and testamentary matters was superseded by the legislation of 1857 which set up the new Divorce and Probate Courts. Today the Court of Arches is the Court of Appeal of the Archbishop of Canterbury, with a further appeal lying to the Judicial Committee of the Privy Council.

Court of Common Council Arose from the ancient folkmoot or husting – a Saxon word meaning 'house thing' or indoor meeting – of members of the 'commonalty' of the CITY OF LONDON. These men, elected by their WARDS, had by the 14th century come to share the government of the CITY with the ALDERMEN. In due course the Court of Common Council assumed most of the duties of the Court of ALDERMEN, and since the 18th century has been the effective governing body of the CITY. Today it is summoned and presided over by the LORD MAYOR, who also has the power to dissolve it. Each of the 26 WARDS of the CITY elects a number of its FREEMEN – varying from four to twelve according to the size of the WARD – to the office of Common Councilman (not, as in other municipalities, 'Councillor'). Elections take place annually, but an efficient member of the Court is

The Court of Common Council meeting in their chamber in the Guildhall in 1808. Since the 18th century the Court has been the City's governing body.

usually re-elected unless he is unwilling to stand again. Those who stand for election are mainly liverymen of Guilds or CITY LIVERY COMPANIES, but some appear in the Corporation lists simply as 'A Freeman'. There are no political parties, but this in no way diminishes the fury of debate when occasion demands. An attempt was made on one occasion to introduce politics into Common Council elections, but the candidate concerned was not elected. The annual election of Common Councilmen takes place at a Wardmote (*see* WARDS AND WARDMOTES) on 20 December.

The robe of a Common Councilman, worn at the first Court of a mayoralty and on other occasions as set out in the Corporation Ceremonial Book, is known as a mazarine gown, from its soft blue colour, said to have been favoured by Cardinal Mazarin. Its short sleeves are trimmed with fitch fur. At GUILDHALL receptions and other functions those Common Councilmen who are members of the Special Reception Committee concerned exercise general supervision over the proceedings, wearing their mazarine gowns with white gloves and bearing their wands of office.

Courtauld Institute Galleries *Woburn Square, WC1.* Fine collection of Impressionist and other paintings housed in a redbrick building constructed in 1958 to the designs of Charles Holden. Part of Samuel Courtauld's personal art collection was given to LONDON UNIVERSITY at the time of the Institute's foundation, and the rest bequeathed on his death in 1947. The collection has been added to by bequest of Roger Fry (1934), Lord Lee of Fareham (1947), Robert Witt (1952), Mark Gambier-Parry (1966), and William Spooner (1967). In 1978 Count Antoine Seilern bequeathed his superb collection of Old Master paintings and drawings to the Institute.

Courtauld Institute of Art *20 Portman Square, W1.* An institute of the UNIVERSITY OF LONDON. A generous endowment given by Samuel Courtauld and the support of Viscount Lee of Fareham and Sir Robert Witt led to its foundation in 1931. In 1932 the lease of 20 PORTMAN SQUARE was given to the Institute by Samuel Courtauld and in that year the first students were accepted. The house is one of the first designed by Robert Adam who built it in 1773–5 for the Dowager Countess of Home (*see* HOME HOUSE). The Institute was the first establishment in Britain to offer the study of art history as an academic discipline in its own right and the first to award an honours degree in the history of European art and architecture.

Courtfield Gardens *SW5.* Built in about 1873 on the Courtefield, a big field at EARL'S COURT. Sir George Gilbert Scott lived at No. 39 in 1877–8.

Cousin Lane *EC4.* Named, according to Stow, after 'William Cosin that dwelled there in the [reign] of Richard II, as divers his predecessors had done before him'.

Coutts and Co. *440 Strand, WC2.* One of the oldest surviving banks in London. It was founded by John Campbell, who set up as a goldsmith banker in 1692 at 'the sign of The Three Crowns in the Strand'. This symbol, incorporating Campbell's initials, is used by the bank today. After his death in 1712 the business passed to his partner, George Middleton, an extremely able banker, who married one of Campbell's daughters. In 1716, shortly before he ceased to trade as a goldsmith, he had one very important customer, the Prince of Wales, later George II, who purchased some gold plate; this transaction proved to be the first link between the bank and the Royal Family. In 1727 Middleton took his brother-in-law, George, into partnership, and twelve years later they moved to 59 STRAND.

In 1755, eight years after Middleton's death, James Coutts, son of an Edinburgh banker, married George Campbell's niece and was made a partner. Five years later his youngest brother, Thomas, joined him and, through his industry and acumen, established the bank in a high position, numbering among his friends and customers many famous political and aristocratic figures. Under Thomas's control the bank held the Royal Accounts of George III, since when every succeeding sovereign has maintained an account at Coutts.

Thomas died in 1822, leaving an enormous fortune, which passed in 1837 to one of his granddaughters, Angela Burdett, a passionate philanthropist. Associated with many of her social reforms and private charities was Charles Dickens, a close friend and a customer of the bank, which had numbered among its clients many household names since the late 18th century. These included such diverse figures as the 1st Duke of Wellington, Sheridan, Sir Walter Scott, Sir Joshua Reynolds, Sir Henry Irving and Lord Tennyson.

In 1904, after 165 years at No. 59, the bank (which had been known as Coutts and Co. since 1822) moved to 440 STRAND, premises designed by MacVicar Anderson on a site running through a triangular block which had been built by John Nash for commerical purposes in 1831. Between 1973 and 1978 this site was redeveloped to the designs of Frederick Gibberd and Partners, affording a new bank and offices for Coutts, while retaining the Nash façades, including four famous 'pepper-pot' corner cupolas.

Coutts, now a self-contained unit in the NATIONAL WESTMINSTER BANK Group, operates 16 branches in the Greater London area, four of them under one roof at 440 STRAND. But despite its progressive outlook and modern banking methods, certain traditions survive; every member of the male staff must be clean-shaven and wear a frock-coat. The present Chairman is Mr David Money-Coutts, a descendant of Thomas Coutts.

Covent Garden *WC2*. The area in which Covent Garden stands – circumscribed by the present LONG ACRE, ST MARTIN'S LANE, DRURY LANE and an irregular line parallel with the STRAND – once belonged to the Abbey (or Convent) of St Peter at Westminster (*see* WESTMINSTER ABBEY). Mostly pastureland, the central part was enclosed by a fence, later replaced by a wall. After the DISSOLUTION OF THE MONASTERIES the land was granted by the Crown to John Russell, 1st Earl of Bedford. The 3rd Earl built BEDFORD HOUSE on the land north of the STRAND where SOUTHAMPTON STREET now is. Francis Russell, who succeeded his cousin as 4th Earl in 1627, was anxious to make money as a building speculator and secured for £2,000 a licence for the building to the north of his garden wall of a number of houses 'fitt for the habitacions of *Gentlemen* and men of ability'; and he paid a further £2,000 later as a fine for works done before the licence was

issued. He called in as architect Inigo Jones, the King's Surveyor of Works. Jones, the son of a SMITHFIELD cloth worker, had been apprenticed as a joiner in ST PAUL'S CHURCHYARD, but after showing exceptional talents as an artist and designer he had gone to Italy to study the works of the great masters of design, and had come home with a deep admiration for the style associated with the name of the brilliant Paduan architect, Palladio. The buildings he had since designed in London such as the BANQUETING HOUSE and the NEW EXCHANGE in the STRAND reveal how strongly the classical manner he had admired in Italy influenced his own genius. They came in for much criticism from those who preferred the old familiar styles. The new square which he built for the Earl of Bedford, consisting of ST PAUL'S church and three sides of a square of tall terraced houses looking inwards on to a large open courtyard, seemed particularly strange to the Londoner who had not been on the Continent. Even Evelyn, who had been to Livorno and liked the Piazza d'Arme there, was not impressed by Jones's version. The houses which were completed by 1639 had front doors opening on to vaulted arcades in the manner of the Italian architect, Sebastiano Serlio, and pleasant gardens with coach houses and stabling at the back. They soon found rich and fashionable tenants who were prepared to pay up to £150 a year. For some time the piazza – a name later applied not to the entire square but to the arcades only – was one of the most sought after residential addresses in London. Soon, however, the rich and aristocratic families, who had been the early occupants of the houses, were less easily induced to take them, since they preferred the developments further west, such as ST JAMES'S SQUARE; while the spread of a market in the square accelerated the decline of its fashionable status. None of the original houses remains, although Bedford Chambers, on the north side, built to the designs of Henry Clutton in 1877–9, provides a tolerable imitation of their former appearance. Among the 17th-century occupants of the square were Thomas Killigrew, the dramatist, in 1636–40 and 1661–2, Sir Peter Lely in 1662–80 and Sir Godfrey Kneller from 1682 to about 1702.

The market came into existence towards the middle of the 17th century, and in 1670 the 5th Earl of Bedford and his heirs were granted by royal charter the right to hold a market for flowers, fruit, roots and herbs in Covent Garden and to collect tolls from the dealers. The market gradually expanded: 22 shops with cellars were built in 1677–8 against the garden wall of BEDFORD HOUSE, and when the house was demolished a row of 48 shops was built nearer the middle of the piazza within the railings. Larger and more solidly constructed shops appeared in 1748. Coffee houses began to spring up around them. The best known was the Bedford, patronised by Fielding, Goldsmith, Boswell, Garrick, Pope, Sheridan and Walpole. Here Hogarth quarrelled with Charles Churchill, a quarrel which resulted in Hogarth's print *The Bruiser* and Churchill's *Epistle to Hogarth*. Hogarth shows Covent Garden in his engraving *Morning*, part of *The Four Times of Day*. In the early 18th century Covent Garden was popular with artists and actors. James Thornhill had his academy here in 1722–34. John Rich, the theatre manager, had a house here in 1743–60 and Charles Macklin in 1753–5. Samuel Scott lived in nearby Tavistock Row from about 1736–47; so did Richard Wilson in 1748–50. By the middle of the 18th century nearly all the well-to-do had moved west. Their houses had been converted into seedy lodging houses and an astonishing number of Turkish baths, many of which were brothels. Sir John Fielding, the magistrate, called it the great square of Venus and said, 'One would imagine that all the prostitutes in the kingdom had picked upon the rendezvous.' John Cleland's delightfully saucy heroine, Fanny Hill, had lodgings in Covent Garden which 'by having been, for several successions, tenanted by ladies of pleasure, the landlord of them was familiarized to their ways; and provided the rent was duly paid, everything else was as easy and commodious as one could desire.' In 1722 22 gambling dens were counted. Duels were fought in the taverns. Press gangs and mohocks roamed the streets at night. Local elections held outside the church were rowdy affairs, with bricks and dead cats thrown at candidates.

By the early 19th century the character of the market as well as of the neighbourhood had been transformed. Traders in crockery, poultry, bird-cages, locks and old iron had moved in, giving the growers and dealers in fruit and vegetables excuses to flout the rules of the market and to complain about the payment of tolls. In an attempt to bring order out of chaos, the 6th Duke of Bedford obtained an Act of Parliament to redefine his authority in 1813; but in 1826 the family solicitor still complained that the market displayed a 'total want of that systematic arrangement, neatness and accommodation which tends obviously to facilitate and increase public convenience.' What was required was a new Act of Parliament to replace the faulty one of 1813 and, in particular, to authorise a schedule of tolls, and a large new building where the tradesmen could carry on their business in regularly assigned areas. This building, designed by Charles Fowler, was completed in the early 1830s at a cost of some £70,000 and, in the words of the *Gardener's Magazine*, was 'a structure at once perfectly fitted for its various uses; of great architectural beauty and elegance; and so expressive of the purposes for which it is erected, that it cannot by any possibility be mistaken for anything else than what it is.' Scarcely more than 25 years later, however, *Building News* maintained that it no longer deserved its old reputation, not on account of its own faults but because the trade had grown so fast that the accommodation was no longer sufficient, and because better accommodation could be given. But the building was renovated rather than reconstructed, the only important improvements being the provision of iron roofs in the 1870s and 1880s. The east terrace conservatories were replaced by an office building in 1901–2. Meanwhile other market buildings had been constructed. The Floral Hall to the south of the ROYAL OPERA HOUSE was opened in 1860; the Flower Market, designed by William Rogers, in 1870–1; and the Jubilee Market, designed by Lander, Bedells and Crompton, in 1904. The Floral Hall, designed by E.M. Barry, originally had an arched glass roof carried on cast iron columns and a glass dome, but these had to be replaced after a fire in 1956.

The activities of the market – in which nearly 1,000 porters were employed at weekly wages of between 30s and 45s – were supervised by twelve officials of the BEDFORD ESTATES and seven policemen hired from the METROPOLITAN POLICE. But the market remained an unruly and ill-organised place and the Bedford family were anxious to divest themselves of it. The 9th Duke offered it to the METROPOLITAN BOARD OF WORKS and the CITY CORPORATION but neither was willing to take it over. It was eventually sold by the 11th Duke in 1918 to a private company which had been formed for the purpose, the Covent Garden Estate Co. Ltd. This Company endeavoured unsuccessfully to sell it to the LONDON COUNTY COUNCIL in 1920. Although condemned the following year by the Ministry of Food as being 'altogether inadequate to the necessities of the trade', the market remained at Covent Garden for another half century. It was at last sold in 1962 to the Covent Garden Market Authority who acquired it and some nearby properties for £3,925,000; and in 1974 it moved away to NINE ELMS (*see* NEW COVENT GARDEN MARKET).

The restoration of Covent Garden market was taken over by the GREATER LONDON COUNCIL. Fowler's market building has been converted into many smaller units, mostly specialist shops and eating places, with offices on the first floor. The Flower Market is now the LONDON TRANSPORT MUSEUM. (*See also* BEDFORD ESTATES *and* COVENT GARDEN MARKET.)

Covent Garden Market London's best-known fruit and vegetable market, it began in 1656 as a few temporary stalls erected in the garden of Bedford House, home of the Earl, later Duke, of Bedford. Ten years later it was attracting attention because of the amount of rubbish left at the end of the day. In 1670 the Earl was granted a licence by Charles II to hold a market every day of the year except Sunday and Christmas. In 1678 the lease was sold to Adam Piggot and others for £80, giving them the right to erect permanent shops against the garden wall and to buy and sell fruit, flowers, roots and herbs. By the end of the 17th century it was a thrice-weekly market grouped under a few trees at the south side of the square. It was popular, but no match for STOCKS MARKET, and by 1710 it was still no more than a few sheds amidst a fashionable residential area. In 1748 the sheds begin to get upper storeys and potters moved into the area. The same year the Vestry of ST PAUL's presented a petition to the Duke complaining of the nuisance of the market, and £4,000 was spent on rebuilding. The closure of the STOCKS MARKET in 1737 brought a sudden increase in trade to Covent Garden. In 1771 Edmund Burke recorded that he sold £14 worth of carrots in the market and could have sold them for twice as much. There is also a record of a seedsman selling lavender, herbs and live hedgehogs here; the latter were kept by Londoners as pets to eat beetles. At the beginning of the 19th century the market began to get out of control. The closure of the FLEET MARKET in the 1820s brought more business and it became increasingly congested. In 1828 an Act was passed for the improvement and regulation of the market place. And in the ensuing three years a new market place, designed by Charles Fowler, was built. The market thereafter became a lively, colourful place where fashionable Londoners liked to mingle with farmers, costermongers and flower-girls. Dickens took a room nearby and wrote that he would go and gaze at the pineapples in the market when he had no money. By the end of the 19th century the market had five sections: the Row area, the Flower Market, the Russell Street area, the Floral Hall and the Charter Market. *Punch* responded to this expansion by launching a campaign against the tyranny

Covent Garden in the early 18th century still had temporary market buildings. St Paul's church is on the left.

of vegetables at 'Mud Salad Market'. In 1904 the Jubilee Market was built by Cubitt and Howard to cater for foreign flowers. In 1918 the whole site was sold by the 9th Duke of Bedford to the Covent Garden Estate Co. – a private company owned by the Beecham family. In 1961 the company was taken over by the Covent Garden Market Authority by Act of Parliament. Suggestions for an alternative site for the market had been made since the 18th century. They included St Pancras, Waterloo, the Foundling Hospital Estate, Seven Dials, Wood Lane and Beckton. But in 1973 the market moved to a 64 acre site at NINE ELMS, BATTERSEA. (*See also* COVENT GARDEN *and* NEW COVENT GARDEN.)

Covent Garden (Royal Opera House) *Bow Street, WC2.*

The first theatre was designed by Edward Shepherd for John Rich, the pantomimist and harlequin. It was the most luxurious ever built in London and when it opened in 1732 Hogarth engraved Rich's triumphal entry. James Quin was the leading

A half-price riot at Covent Garden Theatre in 1763.

actor until Garrick and Macklin replaced him. In 1734 Mr Matter and Mlle Sallé performed a new dance called *Pygmalion*, said to have been the first *ballet d'action* ever presented on the stage. Between 1734 and 1737 Handel wrote for Covent Garden *Samson*, *Judas Maccabaeus*, *Belshazzar*, *Solomon*, *Theodora*, *Jeptha* and many other oratorios. In 1738 Peg Woffington made her debut and continued to be a great attraction until she collapsed playing Rosalind in *As You Like It* in 1747. John Rich died in 1761 and was succeeded as manager in 1763 by his son-in-law, John Beard. Riots broke out in 1763 when entry at half-price after the third act was refused. All the benches of the boxes and pit were entirely torn up, the glass and chandeliers broken and the lining of the boxes cut to pieces. The wooden pillars were cut away between the boxes: if the insides of them had not been iron they would have brought the galleries down. The piano was played for the first time in public at the theatre in 1767 when Thomas Harris took over the management from John Beard. In 1773 *She Stoops to Conquer* had its première. Goldsmith was so worried that he brought his friends from the Literary Club to clap and did not watch until the last act. In 1775 Sheridan's *The Rivals* was first performed here. In 1789 Charles Macklin, then 89 years old, forgot his lines in his most famous role of Shylock and had to be led off the stage. In 1792 major alterations costing £30,000 were made by Henry Holland. The price of a gallery seat was raised from 1s to 2s. Such a commotion ensued that it had to be reduced again. In 1803 John Kemble bought a share in the management from Thomas Harris. Five years later the theatre was destroyed by fire. The BEEF-STEAK CLUB lost their stock of wine and Handel's organ was burned with many of his manuscripts.

Financial aid came from the Prince Regent and others, and within months a new theatre was being built.

The second theatre, opened in 1809, was designed by Robert Smirke and modelled on the Temple of Minerva at Athens. Under the portico was Flaxman's frieze of literary figures (*see* COADE STONE). To help offset the cost of rebuilding, prices were raised, sparking off the Old Price Riots which continued for 61 nights until the management gave way. During 1810–24 Henry Bishop was musical director. He adapted Scott's novels for opera and was responsible for the first performances in English of Mozart's *Don Giovanni* (1817), *Marriage of Figaro* (1819) and Rossini's *Barber of Seville* (1818). Mrs Siddons's farewell performance was given in 1812. In 1820 Thomas Harris died, leaving his share of the management to his son, Henry. Soon after John Kemble retired and left his share to his younger brother, Charles. Harris continually quarrelled with his partner and the theatre deteriorated. In 1823 Kemble discarded the traditional costumes for his revival of *King John* and had a completely new set designed by Planché. In 1824–6 Carl Maria von Weber was musical director. *Oberon* was first performed under his direction in 1826. After Weber's death in 1826 Kemble found himself in financial difficulties. The bailiffs took over in 1829. A public appeal saved the theatre temporarily and Charles Kemble's daughter, Fanny, revived its popularity. In 1833 Edmund Kean had a stroke during a performance of *Othello* and had to be carried off. A series of short managements followed Kemble's retirement in 1833. In 1837–9 William Charles Macready was in charge. Limelight was first used by him. In 1847 Giuseppe Persiani, the Italian composer, bought the lease after HER MAJESTY'S THEATRE had refused to produce one of his operas. He brought with him most of the theatre's leading singers, including Giulia Grisi; and after alterations Covent Garden reopened as the Royal Italian Opera House. Frederick Gye became manager in 1849 and in his day Verdi's *Rigoletto* (1853) and *Il Trovatore* (1855) had their English premières. In 1855 it was subleased to John Anderson who had already lost two theatres by fire. On the last day of his lease he lost a third. Only Flaxman's frieze survived.

The third theatre was designed by E.M. Barry in 1858. Flaxman's reliefs were incorporated under the portico. The theatre remained virtually unchanged until a huge extension programme was put in hand in the early 1980s. The first phase was officially opened in July 1982. At a cost of £9.75 million, it extends the building the full length of FLORAL STREET, as far as St James Street, while retaining the style of Barry's building. New rehearsal studios and dressing-rooms have been provided, while scene-making shops, a fly-tower, a cafeteria and an enlarged stage are planned. Gollins, Melvin, Ward and Partners are the architects.

In 1861 Adelina Patti made her debut as Amina in *La Sonnambula*. She then appeared every year until 1885. In the 1860s there were unsuccessful attempts to introduce opera in English. In 1867 HER MAJESTY'S THEATRE was burned down and, without competition, Covent Garden flourished. *Don Carlos* (1867), *Lohengrin* (1875) and *Aïda* (1876) had their first performances in England here. Gye died in 1878 and ten years later Augustus Harris became manager. He remained at Covent Garden for eight years, and this was one of its most successful periods. He engaged the leading singers of the day, installed electric light and

took great interest in scenery and costumes. In 1892 *The Ring*, conducted by Mahler, was performed for the first time in England. 1900 saw the English première of Puccini's *Tosca* and 1905 *Madame Butterfly's* première in England. The first performance of *The Ring* in English was given in 1907. There were seasons by Thomas Beecham in 1910 and 1913. Richard Strauss's operas *Elektra* and *Salome* had their English premières in 1910 and *Der Rosenkavalier* in 1913. During the 1st World War the theatre was used as a government store. Beecham was musical director in 1919–20. In these years over 100 operas were performed in English, but although the season was an artistic success it was a financial disaster and Beecham left. Managements constantly changed but none made a profit. In 1929 the lease expired and the theatre was threatened with demolition. In 1932 the Royal Opera Company took a new lease and asked Beecham to become principal conductor, elevating him to artistic director the next year, a post he held until 1939. During the 2nd World War the theatre was used as a dance hall. It reopened in 1946 as the National Opera House, financed by the Council for the Encouragement of Music and the Arts, the forerunner of the ARTS COUNCIL. Erich Kleiber was musical director. The Royal Ballet was formed from the SADLER'S WELLS Ballet and the Royal Opera from the Carl Rosa, the Sadler's Wells Opera and other pre-war opera companies. Since then Covent Garden has concentrated on lavish productions. Most of the world's great opera and ballet stars have performed here. It has also held the London premières of *The Olympians* (1949) by Sir Arthur Bliss, *Pilgrim's Progress* (1951) by Vaughan Williams, *Billy Budd* (1951), *Gloriana* (1953), *A Midsummer Night's Dream* (1961) and *Curlew River* (1964) by Sir Benjamin Britten, *Troilus and Cressida* (1954) by Sir William Walton, and *The Midsummer Marriage* (1955) by Sir Michael Tippett. Between 1961 and 1967 Sir George Solti was musical director. The seating capacity of the theatre is 2,141.

Covent Garden Theatre *see* COVENT GARDEN (ROYAL OPERA HOUSE).

Coventry Street *W1*. Built in 1681 and named after Henry Coventry, Charles II's Secretary of State, who had a house nearby. From its earliest times it was known rather as a place of entertainment than as a residential street. Writing in 1846 J.T. Smith commented, 'There is a considerable number of gaming-houses in the neighbourhood at the present time, so that the bad character of the place is at least two centuries old, or ever since it was built upon.' Once well known for its LYONS' CORNER HOUSE and SCOTT'S RESTAURANT, it now contains many smaller and less recommendable eating-places. Part of SCOTT's once elegant premises is now a Wimpy Bar, other parts, reflecting the changed nature of the area, were in 1980 occupied by Harmony Time, a 'sex aid shop', and Cherry's night-club. The PRINCE OF WALES THEATRE is on the south side of the street, on the corner of Oxendon Street. Opposite it is the Rialto Cinema which was built with a large basement restaurant in 1912–13. This basement was later converted into the Café de Paris, a well-known nightclub of the 1930s, which, as a dance hall, still exists. It was bombed in 1941 when a large number of customers and the bandleader were killed. In the 19th century it was a street of shops as well as of places of entertainment. Lambert's, the goldsmiths, silversmiths and jewellers, stood at Nos 10, 11 and 12 until the demolition of their premises soon after the 1st World War. Established in 1803, their Georgian shopfront was the largest to survive into the 20th century.

Cowley *Middlesex*. The manor belonged to WEST-MINSTER ABBEY both before and after the Conquest, and the parish church of St Laurence was presumably built by the monks or their tenants in the 12th century. The district remained an agricultural village until considerable residential development took place before and after the 2nd World War.

Cowley Street *SW1*. The street name commemorates Barton Booth, the actor, a former pupil of WESTMINSTER SCHOOL who had a house at COWLEY near UXBRIDGE where he was buried. The street was built in 1722 and is still largely 18th-century. The houses are much sought after by Members of Parliament.

Cowper's Court *EC3*. The name of this alley dates from about 1765 and commemorates Sir William Cowper who had a large house nearby in the early 17th century. It was earlier known as Fleece Passage after a tavern in CORNHILL which was destroyed by fire in 1748. The JERUSALEM COFFEE HOUSE began in this alley in the 1730s, if not before.

Cox and Co. *Pall Mall, SW1*. Now the Cox and King's Branch of LLOYD'S BANK, the business was established when Richard Cox became Regimental Agent to the 1st Foot Guards in 1758. By 1815 the firm was acting as agent and banker to most other Army regiments. Cox and Co., originally based in ALBEMARLE STREET, moved to the present address in 1923. The banking business of Henry S. King, Army agents (established in 1816), was purchased in 1922 and in the following year Cox and King's was amalgamated with LLOYD'S BANK.

Cox's Museum *Spring Gardens*. An 18th-century museum of mechanical works of art in precious and semi-precious stones, including a peacock which screeched and spread its tail when the hour struck (now in the Hermitage, Leningrad) and a silver swan that dipped its beak and appeared to glide over water (now in the Bowes Museum, Barnard Castle). The valuable objects were said to be worth £197,000. They were assembled by James Cox, a jeweller, who employed Nollekens and Zoffany as designers. Boswell, who visited the Museum in 1772 on Samuel Johnson's recommendation, was much impressed by them: 'The mechanism and rich appearance of the jewels were both very wonderful and very pleasing.' They were on display, however, for only three years, the collection being sold in 1775. The exhibition hall, formerly a Huguenot chapel and a concert hall where Mozart had made his London début, was then used for a variety of purposes, including Wigley's Auction Rooms, and between 1809 and 1820, for three months of the year, by the Society of Artists in Water-Colours, until its demolition in about 1825.

Craig's Court *SW1*. Built in 1702. Harrington House, now part of the telephone exchange, was also

built in that year. The Sun Fire Office was established here in 1726. George Romney had his first London home here in 1763–7.

Cranbourn Street *WC2*. Built in the 1670s on the SALISBURY ESTATE, and like Cranbourn Passage and Cranbourn Alley, which were also developed at this time, named after Cranborne, Dorset, the family's country estate. William Hogarth was apprenticed here in 1713 to Ellis Gamble, a silver-plate engraver, who kept a shop under the sign of the Golden Angel. In 1720 Hogarth designed his own trade card: 'W. Hogarth Engraver at ye Golden Ball ye Corner of Cranborne Alley Little Newport Street Aprill ye 29, 1720.' According to his biographer, Hogarth's two sisters kept a linen draper's shop nearby. J.T. Smith, Joseph Nollekens's biographer, said that his father once asked James Barry, the Irish painter, if he had ever seen Hogarth. 'Yes, once,' Barry replied. 'I was walking with Joe Nollekens through Cranbourne Alley when he exclaimed: "There, there's Hogarth!" "What!" said I, "that little man in the sky-blue coat?" Off I ran, and though I lost sight of him only for a moment or two, when I turned the corner into Castle Street, he was patting one of two quarrelling boys on the back . . . .'

In 1843 the street was widened and made to form a continuation of COVENTRY STREET eastwards to LONG ACRE. The Warner Cinema stands on the site of DALY'S THEATRE. The LONDON HIPPODROME – a theatre designed by Frank Matcham for H.E. Moss to provide 'a circus show second to none in the world, combined with elaborate stage spectacles impossible in any other theatre' – was converted in 1957 into the theatre–restaurant, the Talk of the Town.

Crane Court *EC4*. First mentioned in 1662, it was burned down in the GREAT FIRE and rebuilt. Dr Edward Browne, President of the (ROYAL) COLLEGE OF PHYSICIANS, lived here at the beginning of the 18th century. His house was purchased in 1710 by the ROYAL SOCIETY who held their meetings here until their removal to SOMERSET HOUSE in 1780. Newton regularly attended them. The house was later rented by the Philosophical Society. Coleridge delivered his course of 12 lectures on Shakespeare in the main room, beginning on 18 November 1819. The building was burned down in 1877. The first numbers of *Punch* were printed in the court in 1841 and those of the *Illustrated London News* in 1842.

Cranford *Middlesex*. Once described as 'the prettiest village in Middlesex', it is now a typical London suburb and many of the old houses have been demolished. In *Domesday Book*, the manor of Cranforde had a priest, implying there was a church. In the 13th century the manor was divided into two. Cranford St John was given to the KNIGHTS TEMPLAR, and in the 14th century passed to the KNIGHTS OF ST JOHN OF JERUSALEM. Cranford Le Mote went to the Abbey of Thame. The two manors came together in 1603 when they were conveyed to Sir Roger Aston, an official at James I's court. Elizabeth, Lady Berkeley bought the manor in 1618 and the family retained it for 300 years (*see* CRANFORD HOUSE). In 1931 only 200 people lived in Cranford. During the 1930s urban development took place along the Bath Road, causing many of the 18th-century houses to be demolished. In

1964 the M4 motorway was built across the northern part of Cranford Park. Once situated within the park, Cranford Rectory in Church Road now stands isolated beside the motorway. The east wing is a 17th-century timber-framed building, refaced with 18th-century brick and extended. It was the Rectory from 1774 to 1938. It is now a private house. Stansfield House is the only remaining 18th-century house in the High Street. It was the Rectory from 1938 to 1980. The Cage in the High Street was built in about 1838. One of only two surviving cages in the METROPOLITAN POLICE area, it housed offenders overnight before their appearance in front of the magistrates.

Cranford House *Cranford, Middlesex.* The manors of Cranford Mote and Cranford St John were brought together in 1603. They were purchased by Elizabeth Lady Berkeley in 1618. The 17th-century manor house appeared to be the nucleus to which extensive additions were made by James Berkeley, 3rd Earl of Berkeley, about 1720, virtually creating a new house. A southward extension of the main block, in the same style, was made about 70 years later by Frederick Augustus Berkeley, the 5th Earl. The garden front was made symmetrical and an oval entrance hall was created on the east side. At this time also, apparently, a secret shaft was built descending from the Countess's room to the cellars, from where an underground passage led to the grounds. The 5th Earl's alleged first marriage to the Countess (Mary Cole) led to the celebrated affair of the Berkeley succession. Cranford House became ruinous after the Berkeleys left in 1918 and was demolished in 1945. The underground cellars, with stone piers and brick vaults, still exist, however, together with the early 18th-century stables. The ha-ha that surrounded the house also remains, and in the park is a formalised stretch of the River Crane with a late 18th-century bridge carrying the driveway to the house and parish church. The park was opened to the public in 1935. The adjoining Avenue Park was once attached to Avenue House, a fine 18th-century house demolished in 1949.

Cranham *Essex.* The old hamlet of Cranham is found where the streets of UPMINSTER stretch out to the fields of Essex. The nearby railway bridge over St Mary's Lane carries the Grays branch line as it swings southwards. But the church of All Saints is almost hidden along a lane (the Chase), leading off the main road, in a rural situation protected from the main thrust of development northwards. Re-erected in 1874 in a 14th-century style, it is famous for being the last resting place of the founder of the state of Georgia, USA – General James Oglethorpe. After a life of many vicissitudes, he retired to Cranham, dying in 1785. Nearby is Cranham Hall, rebuilt after Oglethorpe's mansion was pulled down in 1789. Some of the original structure may have been incorporated in the new three-storey stucco-fronted building; 16th-century garden walls survive from old Cranham Hall.

Thomas Crapper and Co. Ltd *King's Road.* Thomas Crapper came to London from Yorkshire at the age of 11 in 1848. Employed at first by a plumber in CHELSEA, he set up in Marlborough Road in 1861 as a sanitary engineer on his own account and expanded his business into the large Marlborough Works at Nos 50, 52 and 54 Marlborough Road, the site being covered by a block of flats built in the 1930s in what is now DRAYCOTT AVENUE. His firm became celebrated for their water closets, though his name is not, as is commonly supposed, a derivation of the vulgar verb with which their use is associated (*crap* is Middle English from the Dutch *krappe*). The firm's premises at No. 120 KING'S ROAD are now occupied by Dorothy Perkins, the ladies' outfitters.

Craven Hill *W2.* The descendants of the 1st Earl of Craven acquired a small estate here in the 1730s in order to transfer a pest house from the country into SOHO, where he had first built it after the GREAT PLAGUE of 1665. There was no plague-pit on this site as is sometimes supposed. Before the existing houses were built, Craven Hill Cottages stood on the north side of Craven Hill. Here during the 1830s William Fox, Unitarian Minister, lived at No. 5 with his housekeeper, Eliza Flower, the friend of Robert Browning; her circle included William Macready, Thomas Carlyle, Harriet Martineau and others. At No. 4, during the same period, lived Vincent Novello, the musician, whose daughter, Mary, lived at No. 9, after marrying Charles Cowden Clarke, friend of John Keats. Craven Hill Gardens, designed by Douglas Stephen and Partners, were completed in 1973.

Craven Road *W2.* Tommy Handley, the radio comedian, lived in a flat at No. 34 until his death in 1949.

Craven Street *WC2.* An ancient street known as Spur Alley until it was redeveloped in about 1730, when the Craven family owned the land. Grinling Gibbons lived in the street at one time. Heinrich Heine, the German poet, lived at No. 32 from April to August 1827; Henry Flitcroft, the architect, at No. 33 in 1731; Benjamin Franklin at No. 36 in 1757–62, when he was acting for the Colony of Pennsylvania, and again from 1764–72 when he moved to another house, since demolished, in the street with his landlady of whom he had grown fond. He returned to America in 1775. Dr Charles West, the founder of GREAT ORMOND STREET Hospital, lived at No. 40 in 1840–2. James Smith, the author and humorist, who died at his house in Craven Street in 1839, wrote:

In Craven Street, Strand, ten attorneys find place,
And ten dark coal barges m6or'd at its base;
Fly, Honesty, fly! seek some safer retreat,
For there's *craft* in the river, and *craft* in the street.

To this Sir George Rose responded:

Why should Honesty fly to some safer retreat,
From attorneys and barges, 'od rot 'em? –
For the lawyers are *just* at the top of the street,
And the barges are *just* at the bottom.

Several of the 18th-century terraced houses survive.

Crawford Street *W1.* Laid out from 1795 onwards, it takes its name from Tarrant Crawford, a Dorset property of the Portman family, on whose estate it lies. A considerable number of the 18th-century houses remain intact, with delicate window-bars and pretty ironwork balconies; their ground floors are now, for the most part, shops. Messrs Meacher, Higgins and Thomas, chemists on the corner with Montagu Street, established as a pharmacy in 1814, have a magnificent iron lantern projecting from the first floor.

Cray A river which rises in ORPINGTON and flows northwards through St Mary Cray, St Paul's Cray, FOOTS CRAY and North Cray, eventually joining the Darenth to flow into the THAMES near Dartford. At the end of the 18th century there were still mills along its upper length.

Crayford *Kent.* Here the invading Jutes are said to have won their decisive victory over the Britons in AD 457. It stands at the point where the ROMAN ROAD from London to Dover crosses the River CRAY. It has a remarkable history as an industrial centre. There was an iron mill here by 1570, and in the following century Cresheld Draper, who was lord of the manor, established a linen-bleaching industry from which textile printing later grew and has continued to the present day. In the 19th century the manufacture of chemicals, carpets and optical instruments was introduced; brick-making was for many years an important local activity; and celluloid knife handles, called in the trade Crayford Ivory, were first made here.

The greatest developments followed Hiram Maxim's decision in 1888 to make his machine-gun here, for Crayford became an armaments centre, flourishing in war-time and depressed in peace. In 1903 Vickers (who had taken over Maxim's) made the first Wolseley motor cars here during a slump in the armaments business. The 1st World War saw a vast expansion of Vickers's activities; and the production of aircraft was introduced. Their work-force grew from 300 to 14,000 in the war years; many well-designed houses and other buildings were erected, including a canteen, which later became Crayford's town hall. Again in the 2nd World War Vickers's factories in Crayford were fully extended on military products. In more recent times they have diversified into general engineering.

Many of Crayford's older buildings were pulled down and replaced in the 1930s, and some were destroyed in air raids. St Paulinus's church, which dates from Norman times, has unusual features. It was enlarged about 600 years ago by doubling its width, and so has a single arcade down the centre of the nave. Interesting memorials include one to Sir Cloudsley Shovel, who rose from cabin boy to admiral in the Royal Navy, but lost his life in a shipwreck off the Scilly Isles in 1707.

Slade Green, one mile north of Crayford and in former times part of the manor of Howbury, was largely developed about 1900 to house workers on the railway.

Crayford became an urban district in 1920, and was incorporated in the new London Borough of BEXLEY in 1965.

Creed Lane *EC4.* In the 14th and 15th centuries it was known as Spurriers' Row because spur makers lived here. By Elizabeth I's reign they had been replaced by writers of religious texts and so the lane was renamed appropriately. The first edition of Spenser's *Shepheard's Calender* was printed by Hugh Singleton at the sign of the Gylden Tunne here in 1579. James 'Athenian' Stuart, the architect, was born here in 1713.

Cremorne Gardens *Chelsea.* Opened as the Cremorne Stadium in 1832 by Charles Random de Berenger, who called himself Baron de Beaufain and

The dancing platform at Cremorne Gardens in 1847.

the Baron de Berenger, an inventor of guns and a brilliant shot, not long since emerged from the KING'S BENCH where he had been imprisoned for stock exchange frauds. His house, Cremorne House or Cremorne Farm, had previously belonged to the Earl of Cremorne whose wife was a descendant of William Penn. Formerly, when known as Chelsea Farm, it had belonged to the Earl of Huntingdon whose wife was founder of that famous religious body known as the Countess of Huntingdon's Connection. De Berenger's Stadium, so its prospectus said, was 'established for the tuition and practice of skilful and manly exercises generally'. These included swimming, rowing, shooting, fencing and boxing. There was also 'a Ladies' Links' with a clubroom which gentlemen were not permitted to enter unless 'by consent of the ladies occupying such'. The sporting club did not, however, prove as profitable as the Baron had hoped and, under the management of Renton Nicholson, a former pawnbroker's assistant who had become proprietor of the Garrick's Head in BOW STREET, the place was soon offering all kinds of other diversions from mock tournaments and pony races, to performances by Tom Matthews, the clown, evening dances and balloon ascents. It was from here that Charles Green, 'the intrepid aeronaut', made one of his famous ascents in a balloon accompanied by a lady and a leopard. In the 1840s the grounds, extending to about 12 acres, were reopened as pleasure gardens with a banqueting hall, a theatre, an American bowling-saloon, an orchestra, grottoes and 'delightful lavender bowers' which could accommodate 1,500 people. The grand entrance was in the KING'S ROAD where a huge star illuminated the pay-box. Entertainments included firework displays, more and more spectacular balloon ascents, a circus and side shows. In the season they were open for 15 hours a day for an entrance fee of 1s. In 1855, during a pageant re-enacting the storming of a fort at Sebastopol, the stage collapsed beneath 500 bayonet-carrying soldiers. In 1861 Madame Genevieve crossed the THAMES from here on a tightrope. In 1864 Goddard went up successfully in his Montgolfier Fire Balloon. But 'The Flying Man', intending to descend in his balloon, *The Czar*, from 5,000 ft, drifted on to the spire of ST LUKE's church, Sydney Street, with fatal results. By the 1880s the gardens had acquired a bad reputation under the direction of John Baum who 'had not the character of his predecessors, nor a hand strong enough to restrain the vagaries of his more troublesome clients'. The minister of the Chelsea

Baptist Chapel issued a pamphlet in which Cremorne was condemned as the 'nursery of every kind of vice'. Baum sued for libel but, although he won the case, was awarded only a farthing damages. He was now ill and in debt, and when his licence became due for renewal in 1877 his application was withdrawn. The gardens were then closed and their contents put up for auction. LOTS ROAD POWER STATION covers most of the site. Cremorne Road commemorates it.

Cremorne Road *SW10*. In the late 1770s Thomas Dawson, Baron Dartrey, bought a house in west CHEL-SEA near the THAMES known as Chelsea Farm. He was created Viscount Cremorne in 1785 and the house was subsequently known as Cremorne House. During the 1830s it was used as a sporting club, and then from 1845 to 1877 the grounds were developed as CREMORNE GARDENS. Several streets of small houses were built after the Gardens closed, but these have now gone and WORLD'S END estate occupies the site.

Crescent *EC3*. Built in 1768–74 at the same time as the CIRCUS and AMERICA SQUARE. It was designed by George Dance the Younger, who seems to have been influenced by John Wood's development at Bath. It was the earliest crescent in London. Several of the original houses remain.

Cricket Memorial Gallery *Lord's Cricket Ground, St John's Wood, NW8*. Originated in 1865, when the Honorary Secretary of the MARYLEBONE CRICKET CLUB advertised for gifts to establish a cricket museum at LORD'S. Until 1953 both the exhibits in the museum and the books in the library were housed in the Members' Pavilion, but in that year they were moved to a gallery opened as a memorial to cricketers who gave their lives in the two world wars. Portraits of great cricketers, old photographs of teams, bats, memorabilia of W.G. Grace and the urn containing the Ashes – those of a bail burned by Australian supporters mourning their defeat by the MARYLEBONE CRICKET CLUB in 1883 – are among the many exhibits of interest to the game's enthusiasts.

Cricklewood *NW2*. Lies north-east of WILLES-DEN, half in BRENT and half in BARNET, bisected by the EDGWARE ROAD. It is a mainly residential district with some light industry, notably Smith's Industries at Staples Corner. The area was completely rural until the late 19th century when the district transformed by several phases of development carried out by land-owners such as All Souls College Oxford and George Furness of Roundwood House, Willesden. Only Ox-gate Farmhouse survived, bought by an employee of Costain's, the contractors, who were obliterating everything else. The name of the area is probably derived from a dialect word meaning 'bend' and describes the shape of the wood that once grew here.

Crime As defined by L. Owen Pike, crime 'is that which the law declares to be crime, or for which the state recognises a punishment . . . . The meaning of the term necessarily varies with the laws at various times, but can at any time be determined by reference to the laws which are in force.' Recent theories suggest that increased crime coincides with troughs of economic depression. It is possible that such conclusions might be drawn from the statistics of the past 150 years with

The notorious highwayman James Maclean robbing Horace Walpole and Lord Eglington on Hounslow Heath.

a fair degree of certainty. Beyond that such statistics as exist must be regarded with some suspicion. In many cases they have been drawn from ballads, chap-books, broadsides and 'gallows literature' generally. London crime before the 16th century is scarcely more than anecdotal. In the Court Rolls there are references to fights 'without a light and with edged weapons'; single-line entries in the inquest records hinting at suspicious deaths; monastic forgeries to justify long-standing privileges; whippings and pilloryings for vagrancy or trading malpractices; and a rise in the number and savagery of punishments after outbreaks of murder and lawlessness such as those that accompanied CADE'S REBELLION, the PEASANTS' REVOLT and RIOTS of Lon-don apprentices. These scattered references neverthe-less indicate that crime was endemic in London life. William Bullein's *A Dialogue against the Pestilence* (1564) rails against 'the wild rogue and his fellows, having two or three other harlots for their turn, with picklocks, handsaws, long hooks, ladders, etc., to break into houses, rob, murder, steal, and do all mischief in the houses of true men, utterly undoing honest people to maintain their harlots . . . . No man shall be able to keep a penny, no, scant his own life in a while. For they that dare attempt such matters in the city of London, what will they do in houses smally guarded, or by the highway?'

A contributory cause of crime in Tudor London was the growing army of beggars attracted to the capital by its size, the criminal opportunities it offered and the unlikelihood of arrest. In 1517 the estimated number of London beggars was about 1,000. As the result of enclosures, a growing population and the DISSOLU-TION OF THE MONASTERIES, it had risen by 1594 to over 12,000. These beggars constituted an army that had its own organisation and private language. 'Priggers of prancers' were horse-stealers, there were 'abram-men' who counterfeited insanity, 'hookers' or 'anglers', 'rufflers,' 'upright-men' and 'palliards'. Lon-don was 'Rome-ville'. In addition to the beggars there were rapidly growing numbers of discharged soldiers and sailors; in 1569 500 of them threatened to loot BARTHOLOMEW FAIR. Church sanctuaries had always guaranteed freedom from arrest but, although such places had theoretically been swept away, the rights of sanctuary still persisted, because the law was too weak to suppress them. London's three principal sanctuaries which became rookeries were at WESTMINSTER, ST MARTIN'S-LE-GRAND and WHITEFRIARS. Other rookeries existed in places such as the MINT, HOUNDS-DITCH, BARBICAN and SMITHFIELD. South of the river were the BANKSIDE brothels. In an ale-house near BILLINGSGATE there was a school 'set upp to learne younge boyes to cutt purses. There were hung up two devises, the one was a pockett, the other was a purse. The pocket had in yt certen cownters and was hunge aboute with hawkes bells and over the topp did hannge, a little sacring bell; and he that could take owt a cownter without any noyse, was allowed to be a publique Foyster; and he that could take a peece of sylver owt of the purse without the noyse of any of the bells, he was adjudged a judiciall Nypper. Nota that a Foister is a pick-pockett, and a Nypper is termed a Pickepurse, or a Cutpurse.' According to *The Devil's Cabinet Broke Open* (1658), gangs were commanded by Captains or Superiors; novices had to be tested and trained; each man carried 'his private badge whereby the Society may know what he is when they meet him; the Robbers bear always a glove hanging and made fast by one finger; the Cheats button their doublets by intercession one buttoned and the next unbuttoned; the *Stafadours* always stroke moustaches every three or four steps; the cutpurses have a little white mark in their hatbands etc.' In the WHITEFRIARS sanctuary in 1691, in a pitched battle with the authorities, 70 sanctuary men were arrested and the ringleader hanged in FLEET STREET.

The professional thief-takers were as corrupt as the system they served. From 1712 until he was hanged in 1725 the London underworld was ruled by a criminal genius; this was the self-styled 'Thieftaker-General of Great Britain and Ireland', Jonathan Wild. As thief-taker he sent more than 100 persons to the gallows; in doing so, he brought the London underworld under his control. He had armies of thieves, prostitutes, highwaymen, pickpockets and burglars working for him; he had a detachment of 'Spruce Prigs' – former valets and footmen, trained by a dancing master – always ready to go to Court 'on Birth-nights, to Balls, Operas, Plays, and Assemblies, for which Purpose they were furnished with lac'd Coats, brocade Waistcoats, fine Perriwigs, and sometimes equipp'd with handsome Equipages, such as Chariots, with Footmen in Liveries, and also *Valets-de-Chambres*, the Servants all being Thieves like the Master'. Wild had 'a List of *seven thousand* Newgate-birds, now in Services in this City, and parts adjacent, all with Intent to rob the Houses they are in'. He had warehouses to conceal the vast amounts of stolen goods, teams of artists to break up and make unidentifiable the watches, snuff-boxes and jewellery that were shipped across to Holland for disposal. To maintain control of this criminal empire he often put his life at risk; when he died he had the scars of 17 sword and pistol wounds on his body, while his skull was morticed together with silver plates where it had been fractured. After Wild's death his empire was broken up among smaller gangs. Crime continued unabated and thieves robbed with impunity. Within a few years the streets had grown so dangerous that, in Horace Walpole's words, one was 'forced to travel even at noon as if one was going into battle'. The old sanctuaries had largely disappeared but other rookeries of crime had taken their place. As London continued its haphazard growth it seemed to many observers that it might have been designed specifically to facilitate crime. Henry Fielding, writing in 1751, commented, 'Whoever indeed considers the Cities of London and Westminster, with the late vast Addition of their Suburbs; the great irregularity of their Buildings, the immense Number of Lanes, Alleys, Courts and Bye-places; must think,

that, had they been intended for the very purpose of Concealment, they could scarce have been better contrived. Upon such a view, the whole appears as a vast Wood or Forest, in which a Thief may harbour with as great Security, as wild Beasts do in the Desarts of Africa or Arabia.'

Working in gangs 20–30 strong the underworld enjoyed near-immunity from arrest. One gang, numbering nearly 100 men, was not only proficient in 'every Art of Cheating, Thieving, and Robbing', but had 'Officers and a Treasury' and if caught 'rotten Members of the Law to forge a Defence for them, and a great Number of False Witnesses ready to support it'. Gangs of highwaymen were active all around the capital and made frequent forays into London; among them was the Gregory gang which included in its band Dick Turpin. The CITY boundary remained a hiding-place for the underworld. SMITHFIELD and SAFFRON HILL were known as 'Jack Ketch's Warren'. The old Red Lion Inn had a sliding plank over which wanted men escaped across the FLEET ditch by rolling from an upstairs window to a room on the other side. MOOR-FIELDS was known as 'Sodomites' Walk' because of the blackmailing activities of the young men who would pounce on innocent passers-by and threaten to charge them before a magistrate. BLACKFRIARS was 'the haunt of strolling prostitutes, thieves and beggars'. Rag Fair, on and about TOWER HILL, was 'a Sort of Fair with Raggs and Old Cloths which . . . for the most part are the ill got Effects of Thieves and Robbers. . . .' By 1787 it stretched from the TOWER through the MINORIES and HOUNDSDITCH. In FLEET STREET and LUDGATE HILL traders complained of the prostitutes and bullies between ST PAUL'S and TEMPLE BAR. 'They create a bustle and try over the pockets of unsuspecting persons; till at length, having marked out one, the accomplice shoves him hard up against other persons (usually some of the gang) who naturally repress the intrusion. Thus wedged in they hit him over the head with a stick, when he, to save his hat, or to resent the insult, lifts up his arms. A third or fourth still further behind gives one more shove, rams his flat hand hard against the belly of the person marked out to be done and pulls out his watch.'

In the early part of the 18th century London was gripped by an unprecedented wave of lawlessness. This was partly due to the lack of police. Henry Fielding blamed the heavy gin-drinking, particularly in such notorious rookeries as ST GILES-IN-THE-FIELD and BLOOMSBURY, and on gambling, 'a school in which most highwaymen of great eminence have been bred'. His half-brother, John, while agreeing with him, blamed immigration and thought that 'if some restraint could be laid on the imported Irish it would be another means of preventing a great many robberies in this country. There are certainly a much greater number of Jews and Irish than can possibly gain subsistence by honest means.' Immigration, as a cause of crime, was to be a recurrent theme.

One rich source of plunder was the shipping and the warehouses to the east of LONDON BRIDGE. In 1800 Colquhoun estimated that more than 3,000 ships and vessels discharged or received, in one year, over 3,000,000 packages. River pirates plundered the West Indian merchants of an estimated £250,000 annually. Such pirates were considered the most dangerous of river thieves as they were strong enough to loot ships by day as well as by night in spite of the guards set over them. Almost as great a threat to the merchants were the watermen working in collusion with the watchmen; they would steal hogsheads of sugar, coffee and tallow. Meanwhile mudlarks scoured the shoreline for coal and snatched any object of value that could be sold to London's network of receivers.

The Industrial Revolution brought about new techniques in forging coins and banknotes. There were about 40–50 private mints in London. Two or three people could stamp and finish £200 worth of halfpennies in six days. So great was the profit that trading in counterfeit become an industry in itself; immense quantities were 'regularly sent from London to the Camps during the summer season; and to persons at the sea-ports and manufacturing towns, who again sell in retail to the different tradesmen and others who pass them at the full *import* value.' There was a concurrent growth in pornography concentrated on HOLYWELL STREET, which disappeared with the construction of the ALDWYCH. One raided dealer was found to possess 'no less than 12,346 obscene prints, 393 books, 351 copper plates, 188 lithographic stones and 33½ cwts of letterpress....'

The growth in industrialisation led to social unrest and the desperation of a few who saw in violence the only way of changing society. In 1812 the Prime Minister, Spencer Perceval, was shot down in the lobby of the HOUSE OF COMMONS. Eight years later the CATO STREET conspirators planned to assassinate the Cabinet as it sat at dinner. Assassination attempts were made on the lives of successive sovereigns.

Colquhoun in his *Treatise on the Police of the Metropolis* was at pains to point out the connecting 'chain by which these criminal people extend and facilitate their trade; *nourishing*, *accommodating*, and supporting one another'. Half the hackney coachmen in London were said to be 'flashmen' in league with thieves. In CHEAPSIDE 'a multitude of thieves and pickpockets, exhibiting often in their dress and exterior the appearance of gentlemen and men of business, assemble every evening in gangs, watching at the corners of every street, ready to *hustle* and *rob*, or to *trip up the heels* of the *warehouse-porters and the servants of shopkeepers carrying goods*; or at the doors of warehouses, at dusk and at the time they are locked, to be ready to seize loose parcels when unperceived; by all which means, aided by a number of other tricks and fraudulent pretences, they are but too successful in obtaining considerable booty.'

Prostitution was one of the more obvious features of the 19th-century underworld. HAYMARKET, where the greatest number of prostitutes operated, was known as 'Hell Corner'. Mayhew gives the trades of some who were taken into custody: there were hatters and trimmers, laundresses, milliners, servants, shop girls and fishwives. Demand always exceeded supply. Foreign prostitutes were imported. Brothels abounded in the HAYMARKET, LEICESTER SQUARE and SOHO areas. A police magistrate observed, 'About this town, within our present district of Westminster, or halfway down the Strand towards Temple-bar, there would every night be found above five hundred or one thousand of that description of wretches: how they can gain any profit by their prostitution one can hardly conceive.' Near the BANK OF ENGLAND they were said to stand in rows like hackney-coaches. In still more striking contrast was the appalling area down by the Ratcliff Highway, Bluegate Fields, and Shadwell High

Street where they strolled about 'bare-headed, in dirty-white muslin and greasy, cheap blue silks with originally ugly faces horribly seamed with small-pox, and disfigured by vice ....' In one room Mayhew found a Lascar half-stupefied with opium and a woman with hands so filthy that mustard and cress might have been grown on them. In 1857 it was estimated that one house in 60 was a brothel and one woman in every 16 a whore. *The Lancet* estimated that London had 6,000 brothels and about 80,000 prostitutes. Child prostitution was commonplace, partly because it was generally supposed that the act of deflowering could cure venereal disease.

A large proportion of London's criminals were children. Thousands of them were neglected and prowled daily about the streets, begging and stealing to survive. Mayhew wrote, 'They are to be found in Westminster, Whitechapel, Shoreditch, St Giles's, New Cut, Lambeth, the Borough, and other localities. Hundreds of them may be seen leaving their parents' homes and low lodging-houses every morning, sallying forth in search of food and plunder.' As they grew up so they extended their stealing over the whole of the metropolis. Some stole from shops, others crept into lobbies and house entrances on various pretexts, stealing as the opportunity arose. As they became more skilful some turned to picking pockets, house-breaking and burglary. The more hardened they became the more willing they were to use violence. Garrotting, like mugging, reached almost epidemic proportions. 'More brutal and inexpert thieves press the fingers of both hands into the victim's throat; others use a short stick, which is passed across the throat from behind, and hauled back at both ends.'

Statistics began to be regularly compiled in the 19th century but the picture they give is apt to be an incomplete one. Confusion often resulted because of the want of any proper means of identifying offenders by such means as fingerprints and photographs. The problem is highlighted by the following comment by the Chaplain of CLERKENWELL Gaol in 1887. 'We take very little notice of names and ages in prison, as from various reasons they are apt to alter with each entrance. Thus Frederick Lane, age 15, has just been sentenced to eighteen months' imprisonment. He has previously been in custody as Alfred Miller, aged 15, John Smith, aged 16, John Collins, aged 16, John Kate, aged 17, John Klythe, aged 17, and John Keytes, aged 17. In 1883 he is 15; in 1881 he was 17.'

In 1867 a new dimension was added to London crime with the bombing of the CLERKENWELL prison and the attempted rescue of Fenian prisoners. It was a precedent that the Dynamiters followed in 1883–4. Bombs were successfully exploded at *The Times* offices, Government offices in WHITEHALL and at SCOTLAND YARD itself. Immigrants, many of them political refugees fleeing Tsarist pogroms, found refuge in the EAST END. Some began to form fighting funds for their particular causes by carrying out 'expropriations' or robberies. One particular group of Latvian anarchists murdered three policemen while carrying out just such an expropriation.

For the first 20 years or so of the present century criminal statistics vary little. But now they are being recorded with far greater accuracy and it is beginning to be possible to foresee trends in crime. In the decade from 1930 to 1940 the figures begin to rise and, apart from temporary recessions, have continued to rise ever since. In 1938 the number of known indictable crimes was 95,280; by 1977 this had risen to 568,972. Between 1955 and 1965 thefts and fraud accounted for about 80% of London's crime.

In the 1940s and 1950s there was a marked increase in prostitution, gambling, fraud and protection rackets in London. Certain gangs came to the fore. In the 1950s those of Jack 'Spot' Comer and Billy Hill were notorious. Other gangs, such as the Messina brothers, controlled prostitution. The Richardson gang controlled much criminal activity in SOUTH LONDON, the Kray brothers in the EAST END. Both these gangs have now been destroyed but others have since emerged.

The greatest change in the past two decades has been the growth of violence generally and the rise of the so-called urban guerrillas. (*See also* POLICE.)

Cripplegate One of the CITY gates built by the Romans, it stood at the northern end of WOOD STREET. The derivation of the name is obscure: perhaps it came from cripples begging there, perhaps from the Anglo-Saxon word *crepel* meaning an underground passage, or perhaps from the legend that some cripples were miraculously cured when Edmund the Martyr's body was brought through the gate in 1010. In 1244 it was rebuilt by the BREWERS' COMPANY. In the 14th century the room over the gate was used as a prison. During the Wars of the Roses Henry VI and Margaret of Anjou arrived at Cripplegate after their victory over Warwick the Kingmaker at St Albans in 1461. Pro-Yorkist citizens promised them food as long as they kept out of the CITY, but just as the waggons were rolling through, the news came that Warwick and Edward, later Edward VI, were about to re-enter London. The waggons were called back and the Lancastrians had to retire hungry to the north. The gate was again rebuilt in 1491. In 1554 one of Wyatt's rebels was hanged here. In 1558 Elizabeth I passed into the CITY in state for the first time as Queen, 'the mayor riding with Garter King-at-Arms and carrying a sceptre before her'. The gate was demolished in 1760 so the street could be widened, and the materials sold to a Mr Blagden, a carpenter of COLEMAN STREET, for £91.

Cripplegate Bastion *see* LONDON WALL.

Cripplegate Foundation *2–8 Wilson Street, EC2.* The Cripplegate Institute was built under the provisions of a scheme of the Charity Commissioners dated 23 February 1891, using the parochial charities of ST GILES, CRIPPLEGATE. It is an educational and cultural centre for residents and workers in the western half of the CITY OF LONDON, especially ST GILES's parish. It formerly stood at the corner of Golden Lane, and contained a theatre, public lending library, swimming bath and secretarial college. With the development of the BARBICAN area the Cripplegate Foundation moved to Wilson Street, MOORFIELDS, and the secretarial college was discontinued. The Schools Foundation is now administered by 24 trustees appointed by the main Foundation, the LORD MAYOR and CORPORATION, the UNIVERSITY OF LONDON and the CITY UNIVERSITY, the Rector of ST GILES being a trustee *ex officio*. It manages and supports the LADY ELEANOR HOLLES SCHOOL for girls at HAMPTON, providing sixth-form scholarships and bursaries for third-form scholars.

Crisp Street *E14.* The original street was laid out around 1840 and named after a member of the local landowner's family. There was a street market here from the 1860s until a new market was built on the nearby Lansbury Estate. This opened as part of the FESTIVAL OF BRITAIN in 1951.

Criterion Restaurant *Piccadilly.* Built at a cost of about £80,000 on the south side of PICCADILLY CIRCUS in 1870–4 by Thomas Verity for Spiers and Pond, the railway caterers, on the site of the noted White Bear Inn. Extended in 1878 and 1885, the restaurant was one of the earliest buildings to use ornamental tile work for decoration. The Long Bar had a grand gilded ceiling. There were big rooms for functions, with a concert hall in the basement. This became the CRITERION THEATRE. The banqueting rooms were standing empty in 1982.

Criterion Theatre *Piccadilly Circus, W1.* Designed in 1874 by Thomas Verity as an annexe of Spiers and Pond's restaurant and one of the first theatres to be built entirely underground. It opened with *An American Lady*, a comedy written by the manager, H.J. Byron, who also acted in it. From 1875 to 1899 Charles Wyndham managed the theatre, and from 1879 until his death in 1919 he was the lessee. In 1877 *Pink Dominoes*, a farce by James Albery, had 555 performances. In 1879 *Betsy*, another comedy, was a big success. In 1883–4 the interior was reconstructed, electricity installed and the ventilation improved. In 1886 Mary Moore acted in the farce, *The Man with Three Wives*. She became Wyndham's leading lady and eventually married him in 1916. Between 1893 and 1897 several of Henry Arthur Jones's plays were first performed, including *The Bauble Shop* (1893), *The Case of Rebellious Susan* (1894), *The Physician* (1897) and *The Liars* (1897). The theatre was remodelled in 1902. In 1915 Walter Ellis's farce *A Little Bit of Fluff* had 1,241 performances. Wyndham died in 1919 and left the theatre to Mary Moore, who owned it until her death in 1931 when it passed to her son, Sir Bronson Albery. In 1919 *Lord Richard in the Pantry*, a comedy, had 576 performances and ran for two years. In 1921 *Ambrose Applejohn's Adventure*, starring Charles Hawtrey, had 455 performances. Marie Tempest made several successful appearances between 1926 and 1929. In 1933 *Fresh Fields*, a comedy by Ivor Novello, had a long run. So did Terence Rattigan's comedy *French Without Tears* (1936) which had 1,039 performances. During the 2nd World War the theatre was used as a BBC studio. Since reopening it has housed many famous plays including Beckett's *Waiting for Godot*. The seating capacity is 592.

Crockford's A private club and gambling house established in 1828 at No. 50 ST JAMES'S STREET, 'composed of the chief aristocracy of England'. Its chef, Eustace Ude, was paid £1,200 a year, and among its members were several men who did not gamble, including the Duke of Wellington. 'No one', wrote Captain Gronow, 'can describe the splendour and excitement of the early days of Crockey.' It took its name from William Crockford, who had once kept a fish stall near TEMPLE BAR and who died a millionaire in 1844. The club house was designed by Benjamin and Philip Wyatt in 1827 and altered in 1870–5 by C.J. Phipps. Its decorations are said to have cost £94,000. After

Crockford's death the premises were sold by his widow and were occupied in turn by the Naval, Military and Civil Service Club, the Wellington (a restaurant), auction rooms, the offices of the London and Paris Hotel Company, and, in 1874, by the DEVONSHIRE CLUB.

Crofton *Kent*. Originally one of ORPINGTON's four manors, it later belonged to ST THOMAS'S HOSPITAL. Development started in a modest way soon after the coming of the railway in 1868, and was intensified after the opening of PETTS WOOD Station in 1928.

Cromwell Gardens *later* **Florida Gardens** *Brompton*. Stood on a 6 acre site south of CROMWELL ROAD, approximately where Courtfield Road now runs. The name was taken from the adjacent CROMWELL HOUSE. The gardens, with arbours and musical entertainments, were in existence by 1762. Illustrations in the *Sunday Ramble* for 1776 show that they had quickly acquired a dubious reputation. Charles Hughes, builder of the original SURREY THEATRE, gave equestrian performances here. From about 1781 the gardens were taken over by a botanist who planted cherries, strawberries and unusual flowers which patrons could gather. The name was then changed to Florida Gardens. A dining-room and bowling-green were constructed and, in 1784, the attractions of FIREWORKS and air balloon displays added (*see* BALLOONING). By 1797 the proprietor was bankrupt; and Maria, Duchess of Gloucester, obtained the site to build a villa, Maria Lodge, later Orford Lodge, which was demolished in about 1850 (*see* GLOUCESTER ROAD).

Cromwell House *104 Highgate Hill, N6*. A two-storey house, in deep red brick, with a basement and attic, built in about 1637–8 for the Sprignell family. There was no connection with Cromwell, and the house did not carry his name until 1833. In the 1860s, the roof was rebuilt with a row of dormer windows and a cupola. By this time Cromwell House had been a boys' school for some years; early this century it was used by the HOSPITAL FOR SICK CHILDREN, GREAT ORMOND STREET as a convalescent home. For some years between the wars it was the home of Sir Truby King's Mothercraft Training Society; and it is now occupied by the Montfort Missionary Society. Inside are two plaster ceilings, copies of the originals which were damaged by fire in 1865, and a fine elaborate early 17th-century oak staircase. The staircase was at one time decorated with carved military figures; but these were stolen early in the 1980s.

Cromwell Place *SW7*. Like CROMWELL ROAD it takes its name from CROMWELL HOUSE and was largely developed by Charles James Freake (*see* CROMWELL ROAD *and* EXHIBITION ROAD). Sir John Lavery, the painter, lived at No. 5 from 1899 to 1940.

Cromwell Road *SW7 and SW5*. Work on this road, which now extends for a mile westwards from the VICTORIA AND ALBERT MUSEUM to Earl's Court Road, began in 1855 under the terms of an agreement made between the Royal Commissioners for the GREAT EXHIBITION of 1851 (*see* EXHIBITION ROAD) and Henry Browne Alexander, whose family owned the land (mostly market gardens) through which part of the road was to pass, and William Jackson, a building speculator. The name, chosen by Prince Albert, who

did 'the lion's share' of the work of framing the Commission's policy, commemorates a house known as Hale House or Cromwell House which stood on the junction between Cromwell Road and QUEEN'S GATE and in which the Protector is traditionally supposed to have lived for a time. Some of the first houses to appear were built by Charles James Freake (*see* EXHIBITION ROAD). Amongst those that remain are Nos 15–29 (odd). No. 21, a large mansion which Freake himself occupied from 1860 until his death, is now the ROYAL COLLEGE OF ART School of Fashion Design. No. 33, now demolished, was sold by Freake to the Duke of Rutland. Nearby houses were occupied by the Earl of Durham, Lord Cairn and Lord Blantyre. At the east end of the road on the north side the NATURAL HISTORY MUSEUM was built opposite CROMWELL PLACE. Next door to it is BADEN-POWELL HOUSE and further down the West London Air Terminal by Sir John Burnett, Tait and Partners (1963) surrounded by Victorian houses which have mostly been converted into hotels and flats. The huge redbrick block of flats at the EARL'S COURT end, Moscow Mansions (No. 224), is as forbidding in its way as the more recently constructed LYCÉE CHARLES DE GAULLE (No. 35). The Venezuelan Embassy is at No. 1; the Embassy of the People's Democratic Republic of Yemen at No. 57. Amongst the numerous hotels are the LONDON INTERNATIONAL at No. 147, designed by George Beech, 1970, with 418 bedrooms; and the LONDON PENTA at No. 97, designed by R. Seifert and Partners, 1977, with 914 bedrooms on 27 storeys. Opposite the VICTORIA AND ALBERT MUSEUM stands Angela Connor's Hopton stone-mix fountain-abstract, the *Yalta Memorial* (1981), commemorating Russian nationals who had served in the 2nd World War and were forcibly repatriated. A plaque on Nos 58–66 says: 'Professor Slobodan Yovanovitch (1869–1958), Serbian historian, literary critic, legal scholar, Prime Minister of Yugoslavia, lived here 1945–1958.'

Crooms Hill *Greenwich, SE10*. The steep and winding ancient road (*crom* means crooked) to the west of GREENWICH PARK. The Spread Eagle at the bottom stands on the site of an old coaching tavern. GREENWICH THEATRE is nearby. Greenwich Park Station, which used to stand opposite, has now been demolished. The oldest house in the road is the Grange, some of whose timbers date from the beginning of the 12th century. The gazebo overlooking the wall of GREENWICH PARK was built in 1672 to the designs of Robert Hooke for Sir William Hooker, Lord Mayor of London and, in Pepys's opinion, 'a plain, ordinary silly man . . . but rich'. It was restored in 1972.

Crosby Hall *Danvers Street, SW3*. The great hall of Crosby Place, the only surviving part of the BISHOPSGATE mansion built for Sir John Crosby, a wealthy grocer, in 1466–75. In 1483 Richard of Gloucester was living here when he first heard of the murder of the princes in the TOWER. In 1532–4 it was owned by Sir Thomas More, but he probably never lived in it. From about 1576 to 1610 it belonged to Sir John Spencer, a wealthy merchant, who added to it, and kept his mayoralty here in 1594–5. Sir Walter Ralegh had lodgings here in 1601. It was often used for the reception of distinguished visitors. In 1621–38, it was the head office of the East India Company; in

213

Crosby Hall, the great hall of Crosby Place, when used as a warehouse in 1819 before its removal to Chelsea.

1672–1769 a Presbyterian Meeting House; in 1770–1853 commercial premises; and in 1842–68 the Crosby Hall Literary and Scientific Institution. In 1868 it became a restaurant. In 1908 it was bought by the University and City Association of London and moved to its CHELSEA site which had once been part of Sir Thomas More's garden (*see* BEAUFORT HOUSE). In 1926–7 it was incorporated into the International Hostel of the British Federation of University Women, a Tudor-style building designed by W. Godfrey. The hall's hammerbeam roof and oriel windows have been preserved. Behind the high table hangs one of the three copies of Holbein's portrait of More with his family (he painted one for each of More's daughters).

Crosby Square *EC3*. Built in about 1671 on part of the site of CROSBY HALL.

Cross Lane *EC3*. In Stow's time it was known as Fowle Lane because of its evil smell. It may have been given its present name because it crossed the churchyard of ST DUNSTAN IN THE EAST, or from a cross on the church.

Crouch End *N8*. Eclipsed Hornsey High Street as the centre of HORNSEY. It is situated in a valley at the eastern end of the Northern Heights and derives its name from the Latin *crux*, meaning cross or cross-roads. It was the meeting place for ancient routes around which a medieval settlement developed. The routes still exist as roads meeting in Crouch End Broadway. Of typical late Victorian appearance, this shopping centre was built at the end of the 19th century, replacing cottages and estates. TOPSFIELD HALL, for example, at the junction of Tottenham and Middle Lanes, was demolished in 1895 and replaced by the four-storey Topsfield Parade of shops, overlooking the 1895 clocktower designed by F.C. Knight and erected to H.R. Williams, chairman of the Local Board, as a testimonial in his own lifetime. The oldest surviving building in the Broadway is the yellow-brick No. 6, Dunn's the bakers, and close to it is the notable Hornsey Town Hall. Built in 1933 and designed by R.H. Uren in brick with a tall, square tower, it won a gold medal from the ROYAL INSTITUTION OF BRITISH ARCHITECTS. It has a grass forecourt with offices and shops around it. At the rear is a modern library (1965) by F. Ley and C. Jarvis containing a large engraved glass window by F.J. Mitchell, depicting a historical map of Hornsey. North of the Broadway in Tottenham Lane is the magnificent turn-of-the-century public house, the Queen's Hotel, designed by J.C. Hill. The extensive Crouch End Playing Fields are in Park Road, an ancient pilgrimage route to the well at MUSWELL HILL.

South of the Broadway on Crouch End is the stone-built Christ Church, designed in 1862 by Arthur Blomfield in the Gothic style. Haslemere Road opposite leads to the upper slopes of Crouch Hill, long known as Mount Pleasant. Down Crouch Hill a pair of Regency houses remain at Nos 118 and 120, and opposite them is the former Congregational Park Chapel, part of it dating from 1854.

Crown *24 Aberdeen Place, St John's Wood, NW8*. Otherwise known as 'Crocker's Folly', this late Victorian public house remains almost intact. It was built in 1898 by Mr Crocker, a local building speculator, who calculated that his hotel would stand at the entrance to MARYLEBONE STATION when this was constructed. Unfortunately, he was half a mile out in his estimate, and the many bedrooms have remained virtually empty ever since. The bars are a delight, with fine marble work, a hooded fireplace and a moulded ceiling. There is also a completely unspoiled Victorian billiard room.

Crown and Treaty *Uxbridge, Middlesex*. Lies at the north-west end of the town. Formerly known as Place House, it probably dates from the early part of the 16th century. It later became known as the Treaty House because of the negotiations held here in 1645 between Parliamentary and Royalist representatives (*see* UXBRIDGE). In the 18th century about two-thirds of the mansion was demolished, and in about 1800 the remaining wing became an inn named the Crown and Treaty House. It is still an inn.

Crown Estate This estate, which includes much valuable property in the West End, used to belong personally to the Sovereign. Much of it was taken from the Church at the time of the Reformation. It is still theoretically in royal hands but, since the reign of George III, it has been surrendered to the Government at the beginning of each new reign in return for the allowances made to the Sovereign. The income derived from the Crown Lands was £6,500,000 in 1977–8. The Estate is managed on the Government's behalf by the Crown Estate Commissioners who have offices in Redhill Street, NW1, Gore Road, E9, Bessborough Gardens, SW1, and at 13–15 CARLTON HOUSE TERRACE, SW1.

Crown Jewels *see* TOWER OF LONDON.

Crown Office Row *Temple, EC4*. Clerks of the Crown drew up their indictments at an office here from the 16th century until 1882. Charles Lamb, the son of a clerk and servant to a bencher of the INNER TEMPLE, was born here in 1775. 'Cheerful Crown Office Row,' Lamb wrote. 'A man would give something to be born in such places.'

Crowndale Road *NW1*. Originally a medieval track leading to ST PANCRAS OLD CHURCH, it was for years known as Fig Lane, and at least one fig tree survived until the end of the 19th century. It is said that a hunting lodge once stood in the lane. The Working Men's College, on the corner of Camden Street, moved here in 1905 from HOLBORN, where it was founded in 1854 as the first adult educational institute in the country.

Croydon

Croydon *Surrey*. Lies 12 miles south of London near the junction of several dry valleys where the ROMAN ROAD from London to Portslade bisected a gap in the North Downs. At the time of *Domesday*, and subsequently, the Archbishops of Canterbury were Lords of the Manor. The name was Crogedene in 962 and Croendene in 1086. It may be derived from *Crocus sativus*: saffron was grown in those days for both dyeing and pharmaceutical purposes. The ancient parish of Croydon comprised over 9,000 acres including NORBURY, UPPER NORWOOD, SHIRLEY, PURLEY and WADDON (with a detached area of SELSDON removed in 1883). ADDINGTON was added in 1928. The Archbishops greatly influenced Croydon. Their manor house, ADDINGTON PALACE, adjoining the parish church of ST JOHN THE BAPTIST was visited by Henry III, Edward I, Henry IV, Henry VII, Henry VIII, Queen Mary and Queen Elizabeth I. James I of Scotland was imprisoned there before becoming king. Six archbishops were buried in the church including in the 16th century John Whitgift, who founded WHITGIFT SCHOOL. The almshouses he endowed still stand in the centre of the town. Croydon became the largest town in East Surrey partly due to good communications. Its railway (horse-drawn) and canal links with London were both in existence by 1809, although used only for freight. The population of 5,743 in 1801 rose to 134,037 by 1901. 'Handsome villas spring up on every side tenanted by City men whose portly persons crowd the trains.' (*London Society*, 1882.) Its plentiful water supply and proximity to the Surrey hills were contributory factors. In 1915 Croydon Airport (*see* AIRPORTS) was opened to defend London, and in 1920 became London's airport. Amy Johnson's record-breaking flight to Australia began there in 1930.

Surrey Street Market, formerly the 'Fleshe-markett', dates back 700 years to the original archbishop's charter. Although still thriving, it is now overshadowed by the department stores and the nearby shopping precincts of the Whitgift Centre and St George's Walk. In 1900, in an early example of municipal redevelopment, the central Middle Row area of narrow streets was rebuilt, it being, in the words of the *Croydon Chronicle* in 1888, 'a human moral piggery that for low depravity either Newcastle or Manchester might match but certainly could not surpass.' The town was severely damaged by bombs in the 2nd World War, and between 1960 and 1970 far-reaching redevelopment took place. Boom conditions and the excellent rail service to London stimulated a modern complex of skyscrapers, municipal buildings and the Fairfield Halls, containing theatre, concert hall and art gallery (*see* ASHCROFT THEATRE).

The small market town, which had its own cricket team as early as 1707, thus became, in 1963, a thriving London Borough with a population of over 330,000. A BLUE PLAQUE at 44 St Peter's Road commemorates the residence of Alfred Russell Wallace, the naturalist, whose *Geographical Distribution of Animals* (1880) was published while he was living here.

Cruft's Dog Show

Cruft's Dog Show Charles Cruft, born in BLOOMSBURY in 1846, became in 1860 James Spratt's assistant, selling 'dog cakes' in HOLBORN. His 'First Great Terrier Show' at the ROYAL AQUARIUM, WESTMINSTER in 1886 attracted 500 entries. His annual shows became Cruft's Dog Shows in 1891 and were soon internationally famous. The Jubilee Show in 1936 had 9,000 entries. He died in 1938. The show was taken over by the Kennel Club some years later, but his name is still given to the annual shows at OLYMPIA.

The old Navy Office in Crutched Friars, from an engraving after Thomas Taylor in 1714.

Crutched Friars

Crutched Friars *EC3*. More commonly known in the 16th century as Hart Street. Stow refers to it thus and uses 'Crowched Friars' to denote the House of the Friars of the Holy Cross which stood here (*crux* is Latin for cross). By 1720 the street was more commonly known by its present name. FENCHURCH STREET STATION lies just north of it.

Crystal Palace

Crystal Palace *Sydenham*. The huge glass conservatory which was designed to house the GREAT EXHIBITION OF 1851. At first a brick building had been proposed, but the estimated cost of £120,000 was considered excessive; and when a drawing of a glass and iron structure by Joseph Paxton appeared in the *Illustrated London News* the Exhibition Committee's interest was aroused. Paxton was superintendent of the Duke of Devonshire's gardens at Chatsworth where he had designed a conservatory which served as a model for his proposed structure. A tender of £80,000 was obtained for its construction, and 2,000 workmen were engaged upon it. The monumental building of 4,000 tons of iron and 400 tons of glass contained 30 miles of guttering and 200 miles of wooden sash bars. When it was finished, squads of soldiers were marched in and ordered to stamp and jump on the floor and roll round shot about, to test its capacity to remain in one piece when crowded with visitors. After the Exhibition it was removed from HYDE PARK and re-erected across the river at SYDENHAM where it was enlarged and divided into courts. For 80 years it was the central

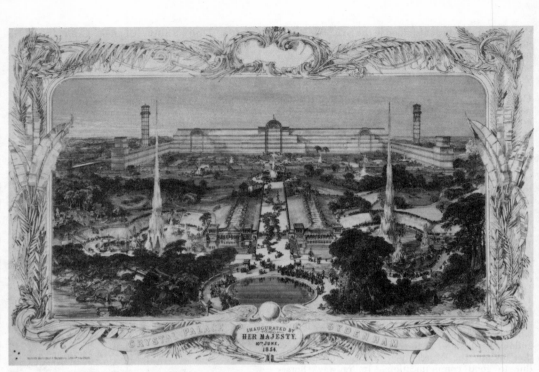

Joseph Paxton's Crystal Palace, after its removal from the Great Exhibition site to Sydenham in 1864.

feature of an amusement park and was used as a concert hall, theatre, menagerie and exhibition rooms. Outside there were fountains supplied by two 300 ft high water towers and a collection of statuary. Firework displays were held regularly (*see* FIRE-WORKS), and, until the opening of WEMBLEY STADIUM in 1924, the Football Association Cup Final was played here. The building caught fire during the night of 30 November 1936 and was destroyed. Only its strange plaster prehistoric animals now survive in CRYSTAL PALACE PARK.

Crystal Palace Football Club *see* FOOTBALL CLUBS.

Crystal Palace Park *SE19.* Situated on SYDEN-HAM HILL, the park comprises 200 acres containing gardens, boating lakes, a zoo, large models of prehistoric animals and extensive sporting facilities which are now some of the best in the country. The National and Youth Sports Centre was opened in 1964. There is a stadium for 12,000 spectators where regular speedway and athletic events are held. The multi-purpose sports hall with seating for 2,000 has an Olympic-size swimming pool and a dry ski slope. The 29 prehistoric monsters are of brick and iron covered with stucco. They are by Waterhouse Hawkins, advised by Professor Richard Owen (1854). The black marble, *Guy the Gorilla*, by the lake is by David Wynne (1962).

Cubitt Town *E14.* A district on the south-east corner of the ISLE OF DOGS which William Cubitt, Lord Mayor of London in 1860–1 and brother of Thomas Cubitt, developed in the 1840s and 1850s to house the growing numbers of workers in the nearby shipyards, docks and factories. Cubitt established timber wharves, saw-mills, a cement factory, pottery and brickfields and built houses in streets which followed the lines of the former marsh drainage ditches. He gave Cubitt Town a church (Christ Church) and leased land along the riverside for industrial use, except for the southern tip which was sold to the Commissioners of the GREENWICH HOSPITAL opposite. As early as the 17th century Wren thought that this was the best place from which to view the GREENWICH HOSPITAL and the land was made into public gardens with an entrance to the Greenwich foot tunnel which opened in 1902. An earlier attempt to make this open space the nucleus of a villa colony had failed because middle-class residents were not attracted to the area. A similar attempt was made in the 1970s with the building of expensive private dwellings overlooking the river; but most of the area has been redeveloped for modern council estates and the new GEORGE GREEN'S SCHOOL.

Cullum Street *EC3.* Built after the GREAT FIRE and named after Sir Thomas Cullum, owner of the land.

Cumberland Hotel *Marble Arch, W1.* A massive eight-storey block with inset pairs of Corinthian pillars, built in 1933 to the designs of F.J. Wills. It faces MARBLE ARCH and PARK LANE. (The original interior was designed by O.P. Bernard who also designed the associated Lyons' Corner House.) There are 894 bedrooms.

Cumberland House *Pall Mall, see* YORK HOUSE, PALL MALL.

Cumberland Market A 19th-century hay and straw market held just north of REGENT'S PARK in a building designed by Nash. Established in the reign of George IV to replace the old market in HAYMARKET.

Cumberland Terrace, the most splendid of all Nash's terraces in Regent's Park, built in 1826–8.

Cumberland Terrace *NW1.* Designed by Nash in 1826–8 and built by William Mountford Nurse with James Thomson as the architect on site. The most splendid of all the terraces in REGENT'S PARK, it was intended to stand opposite the small palace which Nash had originally planned for his princely patron; though the palace was never built, Cumberland Terrace retained its magnificent pediment. It consists of three main blocks linked by decorative arches; the pediment of the central block is adorned with statues, designed by George Bubb, representing Britannia with the 'various arts, sciences, trades, etc., that mark her empire'. After the 2nd World War, it was reconstructed behind the original façade into houses and flats; the architect was K. Peacock. Its name comes from the title of Ernest, Duke of Cumberland, one of George IV's younger brothers.

Cuming Museum *155–157 Walworth Road, SE17.* Developed from the private research collection of general topics which Richard Cuming began in 1782. The Museum now specialises in the archaeological evidence of local history in the SOUTHWARK area from its prehistoric desolate riverside past through the small market town and outlying villages at the foot of LONDON BRIDGE to its present industrial sprawl. Another speciality is the archaeological evidence for London superstitions. The permanent display relates local history and includes Roman funerary sculptures from under SOUTHWARK CATHEDRAL; the badge of one of King Richard III's soldiers; items with Dickensian associations; personal effects of Michael Faraday, who revolutionised electrical generation in the 19th century; sculptures in pottery by George Tinworth, a DOULTON designer; an early 20th-century shop, and the delivery equipment of local family dairies. Exhibits of superstitions from the early 20th century include an acorn ornament for an umbrella handle to ward off lightning; blue beads as a charm against rheumatism; an acorn necklace against diarrhoea; and tusks against the evil eye. Small temporary exhibitions on special aspects of the history of the local community and its environment are held from time to time.

Cunningham Place *NW8.* Takes its name from the Revd William Cunningham, Vicar of HARROW.

Emily Davies, founder of Girton College, Cambridge, lived at No. 17 in 1862–86.

Cuper's Gardens *(Waterloo Road), Southwark.* 17th- and 18th-century pleasure gardens, popularly known as Cupid's Gardens. In 1643 Thomas Howard, Earl of Arundel, bought 3 acres of land and subsequently leased them to his gardener, Abraham Boydell Cuper. It was either Abraham or his son who opened the garden to the public. In 1686 7 acres of adjoining land were leased from the Archbishop of Canterbury and added to the garden. Rocque's map shows a landing-stage on the river called Cuper's Bridge which was the favourite approach to the gardens. They were long and narrow, extending almost as far south as St John's church, with serpentine paths among trees, bushes, and statues and busts brought across the river from ARUNDEL HOUSE in the STRAND. On the west side was a lake. A tavern called the Feathers was connected with the grounds. Entrance cost 1s. In 1708 Hatton described them as 'pleasant gardens and walks with bowling greens ... whither many of the westerly part of the town resort for diversion in the summer season.' In 1738 Ephraim Evans took charge, improved the gardens and built an orchestra where a band played from six until ten o' clock. He announced that care would be taken to keep bad company out and that no servant in livery would be admitted. Watchmen were appointed to protect customers from footpads who approached the gardens by ST GEORGE'S FIELDS. In 1740 Evans died but his widow, known universally as 'The Widow', carried on providing good music and elaborate fireworks and attracting a fashionable clientele numbering the Prince and Princess of Wales and 'many noblemen and their ladies'. In 1753, under a new 'Act for Better Preventing Thefts and Robberies and for Regulating Places of Public Entertainment', a renewal of the licence was refused. But the place remained open as a tea garden; and in 1755 concerts and fireworks were provided once again, though only for subscribers. The gardens were closed in 1760. In 1762 a wine and vinegar distillery was built on the site. This was demolished to make way for the approaches to WATERLOO BRIDGE.

Curriers' Company *see* CITY LIVERY COMPANIES.

Cursitor Street *EC4.* Named after the Cursitors, 24 men first appointed by Nicholas Bacon to issue writs for the COURT OF CHANCERY. Their office was in CHANCERY LANE. Sloman's sponging-house was here; among its many famous temporary inmates were Sheridan and Mme Vestris who was escorted each night to and from the theatre where she was then performing. It is mentioned in Thackeray's *Vanity Fair*, *The Newcomes* and *The Virginians*, and in Disraeli's *Henrietta Temple*, and seems to have been the original of Coavinses' Castle in *Bleak House*. John Scott, the son of a Newcastle coalfactor and afterwards Lord Chancellor and 1st Earl Eldon, lived here after his elopement with Elizabeth Surtees, the daughter of a rich banker.

Curtain *Holywell Lane.* One of the earliest London playhouses, built in about 1576. Between 1597 and 1599 the Chamberlain's Men, a company which included William Shakespeare, probably acted here. Having fallen into disuse about 1625, it was destroyed in the GREAT FIRE.

Curzon Cinema *Curzon Street, W1.* Originally a single-storey building designed by Sir John Burnet, Tait and Partners in 1935. In 1963 the building was reconstructed to incorporate an underground car park, a cinema, a shop, offices and flats. It presents mainly foreign films.

Curzon Place *W1.* A short side-street leading off the south side of CURZON STREET. For vehicular traffic it is a cul-de-sac, but at the south end a narrow covered flight of stairs provides a short-cut to PITT'S HEAD MEWS.

Curzon Street *W1.* Leads grandly out of PARK LANE and peters out between the cliffs of the modern blocks at its east end where an almost unending stream of taxis and cars pass round from Fitzmaurice Place into BOLTON STREET – a favourite short cut from BERKELEY SQUARE to PICCADILLY. Curzon Street extends down the length of what was once Great Brookfield, which in about 1715 came into the possession of Nathaniel Curzon, a Derbyshire baronet of ancient lineage and ancestor of the Marquess Curzon who nearly became Prime Minister in 1923. Building seems to have begun in the great boom of the early 1720s, and to have been largely completed towards the end of the 18th century; but much of the north side remained open for many years thereafter, being flanked by the gardens of CHESTERFIELD HOUSE and Crewe House. The latter occupies the site of the house of Edward Shepherd, the architect and builder active in many parts of MAYFAIR, who died in 1747. His house was later much altered, and is now a late Georgian stucco-fronted mansion with columns, pediment and bow-fronted wings, standing detached and well back from the street. In 1818 it was bought by the 1st Baron Wharncliffe and known for many years as Wharncliffe House, but in 1899 it acquired its present name when the Earl (later Marquess) of Crewe, the statesman, purchased it. It is now the headquarters of the Thomas Tilling Group of companies.

Directly opposite stood the Mayfair Chapel (demolished in 1899), where, before the Marriage Act of 1754, the Revd Alexander Keith performed his illicit marriage ceremonies without banns or licence; over 700 couples were thus wedded in 1742 alone. It was here that the Duke of Hamilton married the beautiful Miss Elizabeth Gunning in 1752, a bed-curtain ring being used in the absence of anything more suitable. Much of Curzon Street is now lined with modern office blocks and hotels. Near the east end there is the Third Church of Christ, Scientist (Lanchester and Rickards, 1910–12). The CURZON CINEMA is at Nos 37–38. There are also still some very fine mid-18th-century terrace houses, mostly on the south side, notably Nos 28, 29, 30 (the last still containing fine work done by Robert Adam in 1771–2) and Nos 47 and 48, the latter very prettily stuccoed around 1840. Between Curzon Place and Derby Street there is a still complete range of very large Georgian houses (Nos 18–23 consecutive). Benjamin Disraeli, Earl of Beaconsfield, died at No. 19 in 1881. George Trumper, the hairdresser, is at No. 9; the Bagatelle Restaurant has been at No. 56 since 1936.

Custom House *Lower Thames Street, EC3.* In 979 King Ethelred levied the first known customs duty. In 1275 the first custom house was built on the Old Wool

Quay east of the present site. It was rebuilt in about 1378 by John Churchman, Sheriff of London, and again in 1559, after its destruction by fire, by William Paulet, Marquess of Winchester. Burned down again in the GREAT FIRE it was rebuilt by Wren in 1669–71. His building was two storeys high and had wings running back to THAMES STREET. In 1714 it was severely damaged when a store of gunpowder blew up nearby; and once more rebuilt in 1717–25 by Thomas Ripley on Wren's foundations. Ripley introduced the first Long Room where customs men received official documents. In 1722 Macky wrote, 'It's a pretty pleasure to see the multitude of payments that are made in a morning. I heard Count Tallard say that nothing gave him so true and great idea of the richness and grandeur of this nation as this, when he saw it after the Peace of Ryswick.' In 1813 David Laing, surveyor of buildings to the Board of Customs, began building a larger custom house to the west of the old one. The old one was burnt down in 1814 and three years later Laing's custom house was completed. In 1825 part of the Long Room crashed into the warehouse below, an accident which was caused by beech piling rotting and which resulted in Laing's dismissal. A new river façade (1,190 ft long) and a new Long Room were built by Robert Smirke at a cost of £200,000. The east wing was bombed in the 2nd World War and was rebuilt to the original plans. Since 1956 the Board of Customs and Excise have also occupied King's Beam House, MARK LANE.

Thomas Ripley's Custom House, rebuilt on the site of an earlier house by Wren and destroyed by fire in 1814.

Custom House *E16.* District of south NEWHAM with station (1855) on the North Woolwich railway line. It took its name from the custom house on the north side of the Victoria Dock and developed as a working-class residential area, mainly from 1880. It was badly damaged by bombing in the 2nd World War. Part of the post-war Keir Hardie Estate, designed by the Borough architect, Thomas E. North, covers its western end. The remainder has been progressively redeveloped by the WEST HAM and NEWHAM Councils. The Albert Dock Hospital originated as the Seamen's Hospital near the western entrance to the Royal Albert Dock in 1890. Sir Patrick Manson, the world authority on tropical medicine, founded a research unit at the hospital in 1893. This became the London School of Tropical Medicine in 1899 and remained at Custom House until it moved to buildings near LONDON UNIVERSITY 25 years later. The present hospital building in Alnwick Road opened in 1937 on a site given by the PORT OF LONDON AUTHORITY which also made a substantial contribution to its cost. West Ham Stadium opened at

Custom House in 1928 and became nationally known as a motor-cycle speedway with a celebrated team. It closed in about 1972 and is now covered by a housing estate, the roads of which are named after speedway stars.

Cutler Street *E1.* Built in about 1734 and earlier known as Scummer Alley, Woolpack Alley and Woolsack Alley. From the mid-18th century the western end of the street has been called Cutler Street, probably because the CUTLERS' COMPANY owned the land. An old clothes market was held here. In 1870 Daniel Kirwan, an American visitor, wrote that there hung in Clothier Street and Cutler Street, 'hundreds and hundreds of pairs of trousers, thousands of spencers, highlows, fustian jackets, some greasy, some unsoiled, shooting-coats, short coats, and cutaways: drawers and stockings, the latter washed and hung up in all their appealing innocence. Milling round were two hundred men, women and children mostly of the Jewish race with here and there a burly Irishman sitting placidly smoking a pipe amid the infernal din.' In 1906 White Street was incorporated at the eastern end. (*See also* CUTLER STREET WAREHOUSES.)

Cutler Street Warehouses *E1.* Built by the East India Company in the late 18th century, they were used for warehousing the Company's goods, mainly tea, until it ceased to operate as a trading company. The warehouses were bought by the St Katharine's Dock Co. in 1835 and in the present century the PORT OF LONDON AUTHORITY continued to use them for storage and trading purposes. What remains of them is at present in the process of being adapted for a variety of uses. The architect of the original warehouses was Richard Jupp. After his death in 1799 he was succeeded by Henry Holland. The main group was completed in 1801. A final small group, designed by Samuel Pepys Cockerell, were finished in 1820.

Cutlers' Hall *Warwick Lane, EC4.* The first Hall, completed in 1285, was in POULTRY. The Cutlers moved to CLOAK LANE early in the 15th century and became owners of a Hall there in 1451. This Hall was rebuilt in 1660–1, but destroyed in the GREAT FIRE. The fourth Hall was opened in 1671. The Cutlers lost their Hall again when it was compulsorily purchased by the District Railway in 1882. The Company moved to WARWICK LANE where a new Hall, designed by T. Tayler Smith and with a terracotta frieze by Benjamin Creswick, was opened in 1887. The building suffered damage in 1941. The dining capacity is 120. For the Company *see* CITY LIVERY COMPANIES.

Cutty Sark *King William Walk, Greenwich, SE10.* The last and most famous of the tea clippers built at Dumbarton in 1869 for the London shipowner, Captain John Willis. Her name comes from Robert Burns's *Tam O'Shanter*. She was still carrying cargoes when she was bought and restored in 1922. Since 1954 she has rested in a specially made dry dock at GREENWICH. Inside is a museum of maritime prints, paintings, relics and the best extant collection of carved and painted figureheads, presented to the Cutty Sark Preservation Society in 1953 by Sidney Cumbers who wore a patch over one eye and went by the nickname of Long John Silver. Alongside is GIPSY MOTH IV.

Cutty Sark Tavern *Ballast Quay, Greenwich, SE10.* There has been an inn on this site for nearly 500 years. The present building was erected in 1804 when it was known as the Union. In 1954 it was renamed the Cutty Sark after the famous tea clipper which is in permanent dry dock nearby. The WHITEBAIT DINNERS were held here from time to time.

D

Dagenham *Essex*. Derives its name from Deccanhaam – 'Daecca's home'. Lying to the east of BARKING and ILFORD, it was an ancient parish extending northwards from the THAMES for some 8 miles to Lambourne End, and was part of the Manor of BARKING, retaining its rural aspect until the 1920s. Dagenham village, towards the south, was probably one of the earliest Saxon settlements in Essex. Beacontree Heath, in the centre, is thought to have been the Saxon meeting place of Becontree Hundred. Chadwell Heath, once the southern fringe of HAINAULT FOREST, and a haunt of highwaymen and footpads, became a separate ecclesiastical parish in 1895. The urbanisation of Dagenham began at Chadwell Heath in about 1900, and developed rapidly after 1918 with both private and council housing, especially the BECONTREE ESTATE and a Civic Centre by E. Berry Webber (1937). Population grew from some 9,000 in 1921 to 114,568 in 1951, but is now declining.

All that remains of the old village, apart from the church of ST PETER AND ST PAUL and the 17th-century vicarage, is the Cross Keys Inn, a timber-framed hall house of about 1500 or earlier, with gabled and formerly jettied cross wings, the oldest secular building in the borough. There are three industrial zones in Dagenham: the marshland between New Road (A13) and the THAMES; Freshwater Road, south of the railway at Chadwell Heath; and part of Rainham Road South in East Dagenham. In 1931 the Ford Motor Company began production at their Thames-side works; May and Baker Ltd moved to East Dagenham in 1934; and in 1958–9 Berger Paints concentrated their processes at Freshwater Road. Telephone Cables, Europe's largest cable manufacturers, began soon after 1900 near Dagenham Dock, a tidal basin constructed by Samuel Williams in 1887 after attempts at turning the 18th-century DAGENHAM BREACH into a dock had failed. Other industries range from Sterling submachine guns to 'the largest pop-corn plant in the world'. Further development since the 2nd World War includes the Heath Park estate, south of Beacontree Heath (designed by Norman and Dawbarn) the Marks Gate estate north of Eastern Avenue (A12) (designed by S.J. Harris, architect to the Borough of DAGENHAM), and Beacontree Heath itself. In 1965, when the municipal boroughs of Dagenham and BARKING were amalgamated into a London Borough, the northern part of Dagenham, including the HAINAULT FOREST area, was amalgamated with ILFORD into the London Borough of REDBRIDGE.

Dagenham Breach Originally a 400 ft gap in the THAMES wall in the early 18th century which resulted in a large mud bank in the THAMES, a danger to shipping requiring an Act of Parliament in 1714 to ensure its repair. When repaired it left behind a 1,000-acre lake which took the name Dagenham Breach and which became an anglers' retreat, though much of it

has now been filled in. The maritime engineer's house, Breach House, was taken over by the Commissioners of Sewers for their meetings and as a meeting place for diners and anglers. It saw the beginning of the 'Ministerial' or WHITEBAIT DINNERS, later held upriver at GREENWICH.

Daly's Theatre *Cranbourn Street*. Designed in 1893 by Spencer Chadwick and C.J. Phipps. It opened under the management of an American, Augustine Daly. The first London performance of Humperdinck's *Hansel and Gretel* was given here in 1895. Also in that year George Edwardes produced *An Artist's Model*, the first of a series of musicals which lasted until the theatre was demolished in 1937. Most successful of these were *The Geisha*, *San Toy* with Marie Tempest, *A Country Girl*, *The Merry Widow* and *The Maid of the Mountains*. The Warner Cinema covers the site.

Danebury Avenue *SW15*. Extends west from Roehampton Lane to Priory Lane. The bronze, *The Bull*, is by R.E. Clatworthy (1961).

Danson Park *Bexleyheath, Kent*. Situated between BEXLEYHEATH and WELLING, Danson Park derives its name from the medieval Dansington first recorded in the Archbishop of Canterbury's survey of his BEXLEY manor in 1284. From the wealthy merchant John Styleman the estate passed in 1751 to the ambitious London alderman, John Boyd. He built the Palladian villa designed by Sir Robert Taylor, with interior decorations by well-known artists including Sir William Chambers. The grounds were landscaped from 1761 by 'Capability' Brown, who planned the large artificial lake now used for sailing. The estate was purchased by BEXLEY Council in 1924 to become a public park. There are about 200 acres. The house and its adjacent stables are now being sympathetically restored for use as offices.

Danvers Street *SW3*. Built in 1696 on the site of Danvers House, home of Sir John Danvers, the regicide. Pepys thought it the 'prettiest contrived' house he had ever seen. The gardens were the first in England to be laid out in the formal Italian style. Dean Swift lived on the west side of the street in 1711 and from there wrote his *Letters to Stella*. Sir Alexander Fleming, the discoverer of penicillin, lived in a flat at No. 20 from 1929 until his death in 1955.

D'Arblay Street *W1*. Laid out in 1735–44 and originally known as Portland Street after the Duke and Duchess of Portland, the ground landlords. It was given its present name in 1909 in commemoration of Fanny Burney who married the French émigré General d'Arblay in 1793 and who lived in nearby POLAND STREET. Nos 2–4, 10, 11, 13, 24 and 25 all date from the time when the street was first built. The George public house at No. 1 (built in 1889) occupies a site where a tavern has existed since 1739.

Dark House Lane *EC4*. In the 14th century it was known as Dark Lane. The present name probably commemorates a tavern called the Darkhouse which stood in THAMES STREET next to BILLINGSGATE MARKET in 1671. Dark House Lane first appears on maps at the end of the 18th century.

Dartmouth Park *NW5*. Situated south of HIGHGATE, in the north-eastern corner of the London Borough of CAMDEN. In 1755 the 2nd Earl of Dartmouth acquired by marriage land on the HIGHGATE estate. It was developed between 1870 and 1885 by the 5th Earl. Dartmouth Park Avenue, Hill and Road were named after his family and Woodsome Road derives from the name of their seat near Huddersfield in Yorkshire.

Dartmouth Street *SW1*. Built in 1705 and named after William Legge, Lord Dartmouth, who was then living in Queen Square, now QUEEN ANNE'S GATE. The Royal Cockpit, featured in Hogarth's picture of 1759, was here. It was built in the late 17th century on land leased by CHRIST'S HOSPITAL to Sir Edward de Carteret. On the expiry of the lease in 1810 it was demolished but matches continued at the new cockpit in TUFTON STREET until 1820. The Fabian Society, founded in 1884, is at No. 11. The Two Chairmen public house was established in about 1756.

Davies Street *W1*. Takes its name from Mary Davies, by whose marriage to Sir Thomas Grosvenor in 1677 the GROSVENOR ESTATE in London, of which it forms part, was established. It extends from BERKELEY SQUARE to OXFORD STREET, and was laid out in the 1720s. The sole survivor of this original work is BOURDON HOUSE, but most of the other houses were

Hogarth's engraving of 1759 of the Royal Cockpit in Dartmouth Street. The blind gambler in the centre is Lord Albemarle Bertie.

small and narrow and occupied by tradesmen. An unsuccessful food market known as the Grosvenor Market was established in 1785–6 south of the junction with South Molton Lane, but it petered out in the mid-19th century. By that time some rebuilding had taken place elsewhere, notably on the site of the garden and offices of No. 66 BROOK STREET, where the handsome stucco-fronted No. 53 Davies Street, now the Grosvenor Office, was erected in about 1836, probably to designs by the estate surveyor, Thomas Cundy the Younger. Opposite is an agreeable public house, the Running Horse, rebuilt in 1839–40. Most of the other buildings in the street now date from after 1900, with shops, offices and banks predominating; but at Nos 4–26 (even) there are some pleasing neo-Georgian flats of 1910–12 by Edward Wimperis and J.R. Best.

De Keyser's, a 400-room hotel built in 1874 on the site of Bridewell Palace.

Dawley House *Dawley Road, Harlington, Middlesex.* The manor of Dawley (and that of HAR-LINGTON) was acquired by Sir John Bennet in 1607, but the house, with extensive formal gardens and a splendid orangery, was a typical late 17th-century mansion. A new house, south-east of this building, with a courtyard and service wings, was built by Charles Bennet, 1st Earl of Tankerville, and completed by 1721. The 2nd Earl sold Dawley, however, and it was eventually purchased by Henry St John, Viscount Bolingbroke, in 1725, after he was permitted to return from exile. James Gibbs was engaged to enlarge the recently completed house and the work was finished by 1728, probably to a plan something like that of Gibbs's Ditchley. Bolingbroke, who consistently called Dawley his 'Farm', entertained there such literary celebrities as Pope, Voltaire, Swift, Gay, Goldsmith and Dryden. He left Dawley in 1735 and eventually sold it to Edward Stephenson, an East India Company merchant who, in turn, sold it in 1755 to Henry Paget, 2nd Earl of Uxbridge. Paget spent a considerable sum on Dawley and was responsible for the estate wall that still largely exists (together with a garden wall), but his heir sold the property and the house was demolished about 1776. A residence was created from the dairy-cum-laundry building and this Dawley House and adjoining land was leased by the Tattersall family for a stud farm in the early 19th century. The final fate of this house was to be used as a radio laboratory by EMI Ltd who demolished it in the 1950s.

De Keyser's Royal Hotel *Embankment, Blackfriars.* Sir Polydore de Keyser came from Belgium and first worked as a waiter. He built a 400-room hotel on the site of BRIDEWELL Palace. It opened in 1874. The hotel, which also catered for GUILDHALL banquets, was a great success, and much patronised by travellers arriving at and departing from BLACKFRIARS STATION. By 1887 de Keyser, having acquired British nationality, became Lord Mayor of London, the first Roman Catholic to be elected to that office since the Reformation. After the 1st World War the hotel was closed down and Unilever House (1930–1) was built on the site.

De Vere Gardens *W8.* Built in about 1875 and named after the De Vere family who had once owned the manor. Many of the houses are now converted to hotels. The Kensington Palace Hotel (320 bedrooms, rebuilt 1952, refurbished 1981) is on the west side; the De Vere Hotel (76 rooms) on the east. Robert Browning lived at No. 29 in 1887–9. After his death in Venice in 1890 his body was brought back to this house to await burial in WESTMINSTER ABBEY. Between 1886 and 1910 Henry James lived at No. 34 where he wrote *The Tragic Muse*, *The Spoils of Poynton*, *What Maisie Knew* and *The Awkward Age*.

Dean Street *W1.* The origin of the name is not known for certain. It may possibly have been bestowed, like that of OLD COMPTON STREET, as a compliment to Henry Compton, Bishop of London, who was Dean of the CHAPELS ROYAL, or less conceivably, in honour of the Vicar of ST MARTIN-IN-THE-FIELDS who was Dean of Bangor, or to commemorate some now forgotten builder or speculator. It was built in the 1680s, and amongst its earliest occupants were several

titled families. By the time of Queen Anne's death, a number of French immigrants had settled here; and, later on in the 18th century, several artists had come to live in the street, including John Francis Rigaud (1774–7), Francis Hayman (1765–76), William Beechey (1791), and the architect, Thomas Hardwick (1783). Before her marriage to Henry Thrale, Samuel Johnson's friend, Hester Lynch Salusbury, also lived here in the early 1760s. So did another of Johnson's friends, Anthony Chamier, the charming and highly intelligent stockbroker, Deputy Secretary of War, and one of the nine founder-members of THE CLUB, who occupied No. 67 in 1764–7. In the middle of the 19th century, several of the houses were still privately occupied, but craftsmen had taken over others; and, as the century progressed, some were turned into restaurants. Rocque's map of 1746 shows No. 21 as the site of the Venetian Ambassador's Chapel. In 1748–63 it was Caldwell's Assembly Rooms in which Mozart, aged seven, played the harpsichord accompanied by his four-year-old sister in 1763. It was later a Dancing Academy, auction room and warehouse and, from 1872 to 1939, St Anne's National School. In 1944 it became the West End Street Synagogue which was rebuilt, 1961–3, by Joseph Fiszpan and now contains the Gallery of the Ben Uri Art Society. No. 23 was taken in 1798 by Henry Morland, the painter's brother, who converted it into Morland's Hotel. George Morland was often to be found here 'upstairs, in the back drawing-room, at work, or rather drinking and talking over his old disasters'. At No. 28, now part of Leoni's Quo Vadis restaurant (which was established by P.G. Leoni in 1926), Karl Marx lived in two small rooms with his family, in 1851–6. Three of his young children died here. A Prussian agent reported the house as being 'in one of the worst, therefore also the cheapest, quarters of London. . . . There is not one clean and good piece of furniture to be found; all is broken, tattered and torn, everywhere clings thick dust, everywhere is the greatest disorder; his manuscripts, books and newspapers lie beside the children's toys, bits and pieces from the wife's work basket, teacups with broken rims, dirty spoons, knives, forks, lamps, an inkwell, tumblers, Dutch clay-pipes, tobacco ash . . . all this on the table . . . But all this gave Marx and his wife not the slightest embarrassment; one is received in the friendliest way.' At No. 29 Joseph Nollekens, the sculptor, was born in 1737, and George Cruikshank, the illustrator, probably lived here in 1811. For several years in the second half of the 18th century, No. 33 was Jack's Coffee House, patronised by Goldsmith and Johnson. Joined to 33A, it was Walker's Hotel in 1813–49. Nelson spent the night here before leaving for Trafalgar. No. 42 was built in 1903–4 by Roger Field and A.D. Collard, for the Royal Ear Hospital. No. 57 was the site of the parish watchhouse, lock-up, fire-engine-house, and vestry. At No. 64, Karl Marx was living between May and December 1850, when he and Engels produced the last numbers of the *Neue Rheinische Zeitung*. No. 75 marks the site of a fine house built in the early 1730s, and often falsely stated to have been the residence of Sir James Thornhill to whom – and to whose son-in-law, Hogarth – the painted staircase hall was equally falsely attributed. Before the house was demolished in 1923 the paintings were taken out and sold in America where the ground-floor rooms were also sold and put on display in the Art

Institute of Chicago. No. 76 was also built in the early 1730s. It was first occupied by the 7th Earl of Abercorn, afterwards by the Hon. Henry Bathurst, the future Lord Chancellor. In 1810 the lease was sold to Philip Rundell whose firm of jewellers did much business with the Royal Family. In 1847 the freehold was bought by a firm of leather curriers and cutters whose successor, Messrs Joseph Clark and Sons, were still in occupation over a hundred years later, as the smell of the premises made clear to the clients of the literary agents, Messrs David Higham Associates, who occupied the three upper floors. No. 78 was occupied in the 1740s by the Irish actress, Peg Woffington, who for a time was David Garrick's mistress. No. 88 has a bow-windowed shop front dating from 1791. No. 91 was the house of William Behnes, the sculptor, between 1823 and 1833. In 1862 it was acquired as a branch of the London Lock Hospital, PADDINGTON. Rebuilt in 1912–13 it became, in 1953–4, the West End Hospital for Nervous Diseases. It is now the West End Reception Centre, a hostel run by the Department of Health and Social Security. Dean Street is now a characteristic SOHO street of restaurants, sex establishments, shops and offices. Gamba Ltd, the theatrical bootmakers at No. 46, were established in 1903 by Luigi Gamba, a former waiter at the SAVOY HOTEL whose fellow-workers there complained of the difficulty of finding comfortable shoes. The firm made ballet shoes for Pavlova and Nijinsky and later for numerous other performers including Fred Astaire, Noël Coward and Ivor Novello.

Deanery Street *W1*. Until comparatively recently known as Dean Street, it was built in the mid-18th century upon an outlying piece of the Manor of KNIGHTSBRIDGE which belonged to the Dean and Chapter of WESTMINSTER – hence its name. It extends in a short gentle curve from PARK LANE to SOUTH AUDLEY STREET, much of the west side being occupied by the back of the DORCHESTER HOTEL. On the opposite side, Nos 2 and 3 are probably 18th-century, and No. 7 has a real and rather rare mid-Georgian projecting porch supported on columns.

Dean's Yard *SW1*. Entered through a gateway from BROAD SANCTUARY, the north side being occupied by the backs of Sir Gilbert Scott's Gothic offices of 1854. Nos 1 and 3 on the west side are also by Scott. CHURCH HOUSE is on the south side, WESTMINSTER ABBEY Choir School on the west and the Abbey itself lies to the east. An archway at this side leads to LITTLE DEAN'S YARD. The Westminster Chapter office is at No. 1. Residents here have included Mrs Purcell, the composer's widow; Charlotte Lennox, the writer and friend of Samuel Johnson; and Edward Gibbon's aunt, Mrs Porten, who kept a boarding-house for the scholars of WESTMINSTER SCHOOL. It was here that Edmund Curll, the bookseller, whose biographies 'added a new terror to death', was decoyed by the boys of the school and tossed in a blanket, an incident referred to in Pope's *Dunciad*.

Debenham and Freebody *44 Wigmore Street*. In the village of Mary-le-Bone in the 18th century, Mr Franks owned a small drapery store. His successor, Thomas Clark, went into partnership with William Debenham in 1813 and their little shop looked over Harley Fields near CAVENDISH SQUARE. In 1818

Clement Freebody married William Debenham's daughter. William Debenham's two sons, William and Frank, joined their father in 1851 and the firm was renamed Debenham, Son and Freebody. The premises were expanded and called Cavendish House. In 1896 other firms were acquired, including the Nicholay Feather and Fur Manufactory which supplied furs to royalty all over Europe; Fosters of WIGMORE STREET who manufactured artificial flowers and feathers; Capper's famous linen house; and Maison Helbronner (established in 1834 in OXFORD STREET, later at 106 NEW BOND STREET), makers of heraldic embroidery. In 1953 S. Bradley and Co., silk mercers and furriers established in 1871, were also acquired.

In 1903 the firm became one of the first of the Post Office business telephone subscribers with a historic telephone number, Mayfair One. Reconstruction began in 1906 to the designs of James Gibson. The new store opened in 1909. By 1926 a Drapery Trust had been formed, and by the 1980s this group controlled over 70 department stores which used the Debenham name, including the former MARSHALL AND SNELGROVE. HARVEY NICHOLS and HAMLEYS who retain their original names, as did SWAN AND EDGAR until their closure. The store at 44 Wigmore Street closed in 1981.

Defoe Chapel *Tooting High Street, SW17*. Erected in 1766, it was commissioned by Mrs Emma Miles, whose husband, Henry, had been the pastor in 1731–63. The congregation was originally formed in 1688 by nonconformists who then met in a private house. In 1889 an attempt to hand the chapel to the Presbyterians was successfully opposed by the London Congregational Union. The building with its simple classical façade was renovated and continued as a place of worship until 1911. Since then it has seen use as a corn shop, auction rooms, waxworks, billiards saloon and now a betting shop. According to local legend, Daniel Defoe was one of the founding group but there is no supporting documentary proof. However, it is known he was a close friend of Joshua Gearing, a leading nonconformist and resident of TOOTING.

Delamere Terrace *W2*. Now almost completely redeveloped as part of the Warwick Estate, among the former inhabitants of this once fashionable terrace were Edmund Wilson, the Antarctic explorer, in 1896; Arabella Barrett, Robert Browning's sister-in-law; and Sir Edmund Gosse, the Victorian man of letters. The derivation of the name is unknown.

Denman Street *W1*. Built in the 1670s by Colonel Thomas Panton. It was first known as Queen Street and described by Strype in 1720 as 'a pretty neat, clean and quiet Street, with good Houses, well inhabited'. In 1862 it was given its present name in honour of Dr Thomas Denman (father-in-law of Matthew Baillie) whose son, Thomas Denman, a future Lord Chief Justice and Queen Caroline's Solicitor-General during the proceedings against her in the House of Lords in 1820, was born here in 1779. The two public houses in the street, the Queen's Head and the Devonshire Arms, stand on sites occupied by taverns since 1738 and 1793 respectively. The PICCADILLY THEATRE on the corner of Sherwood Street opened in 1928.

Denmark Hill *SE5*. The name is derived from Prince George of Denmark, husband of Queen Anne, who is said to have had a house on the east side of Denmark Hill. RUSKIN PARK commemorates John Ruskin, who lived in 1819–43 at 28 HERNE HILL, a continuation of Denmark Hill, and in 1843–72 at 163 Denmark Hill. His writings describe what was then a beautiful semi-rural neighbourhead. Both his houses have gone, but others of the period survive. Sir Henry Bessemer, inventor of the Bessemer steel process, had a mansion and grounds on the site of Bessemer housing estate. KING'S COLLEGE HOSPITAL moved to Denmark Hill in 1913. MAUDSLEY HOSPITAL was built in 1915 with money donated by Dr Henry Maudsley. William Booth Memorial Training College was designed by Sir Giles Gilbert Scott in 1932. Outside are statues of the Salvation Army founders, General and Mrs Booth (*see* STATUES).

Denmark Street *WC2*. Built in the 1680s. The painter Johann Zoffany lived for a time at No. 9. Popularly known as 'Tin Pan Alley', it is a street largely occupied by music publishers, recording studios and musical instrument dealers.

Deptford *SE8, SE14*. Lies on the THAMES south of ROTHERHITHE, north of NEW CROSS, and west of GREENWICH, within the London Borough of LEWISHAM. It was for a time known as West Greenwich and long ago was called Depeford. A deep ford existed across the little River RAVENSBOURNE near its influx into the THAMES just before it widened into Deptford Creek. Later a bridge was built here; and at this bridge Lord Audley and his Cornish rebels were defeated in 1497. Deptford became the last stopping place before London for coaches on the Dover Road. Its main interest is historical, for here, in what was then a fishing village, Henry VIII cradled his navy at the ROYAL DOCK or, as it was called locally, the King's Yard. Queen Elizabeth came to inspect Francis Drake's ship the *Golden Hind* when she conferred a knighthood on the captain. Here a pleasure yacht was built for Charles II; and here Captain Cook's two ships, *Resolution* and *Discovery*, were equipped before his last voyage to the Pacific. The ROYAL VICTORIA VICTUALLING YARD adjoined the west side of the dockyard. The latter closed in 1869, its site becoming the Foreign Cattle Market and, today, Convoy's Wharf. John Evelyn's house, Sayes Court, stood near the ROYAL DOCK and there Peter the Great stayed in 1698 while studying ship building in Deptford. Near his home Evelyn discovered young Grinling Gibbons at work in a cottage and then helped him to grow famous as a wood-carver and sculptor. Sayes Court was demolished in 1729 and a workhouse was built on the site. In 1878 part of its grounds became a recreation area. Sayes Court Street, Czar Street and Evelyn Street commemorate the place.

At Deptford Green stood the mansion of Lord Howard of Effingham, the admiral who fought the Spanish Armada, but that too has vanished. TRINITY HOUSE, which Henry VIII founded in 1514, had its first headquarters at Deptford. The district developed in the 18th century to become a small town with two parishes, ST NICHOLAS and ST PAUL, and by 1801, a census year, the population already numbered 18,000. ST NICHOLAS, the parish church of Lower Deptford, retains most of its medieval tower, though the body of the church, of the late 17th century, was ruined by bombing in the 2nd World War. In Deptford High Street stands the large, fine parish church of Upper Deptford, that of ST PAUL by Thomas Archer. The late 17th-century brick Baptist Meeting House in Deptford Church Street has recently been demolished. In the High Street is the Roman Catholic Church of the Assumption of 1844, no doubt needed here to serve the many Irish employed in Deptford. Some 18th-century houses survive here and there, the best being in Albury Street.

Deptford Park *SE8*. Formerly part of the estate of the Evelyn family, the park now comprises 17 acres with various sporting facilities.

Derby Street *W1*. A short street connecting CURZON STREET with PITT'S HEAD MEWS. In the early 18th century the ground landlord hereabouts was Sir Nathaniel Curzon, a Derbyshire baronet, from whose association with that county the street probably takes its name. All the houses on the east side are basically Georgian, though much altered.

Dering Street *W1*. A short T-shaped street extending from TENTERDEN STREET to NEW BOND STREET and OXFORD STREET. The two arms were originally known as Union Street and Shepherd Street, but in 1886 were renamed Dering Street for reasons unknown. The fine art dealer, Anthony d'Offay, has premises at Nos 9 and 23. His firm, founded in 1965, deals in 20th-century British art at No. 9 (including the works of Epstein, Gill, Wyndham Lewis, Sickert, Stanley Spencer and Gwen John) and in contemporary international art at No. 23.

Derry and Toms *Kensington High Street*. Listed in the London Post Office Directory of 1854 as a 'Toy and Fancy Repository', this little shop was run by Joseph Toms. In 1862 he joined with Charles Derry and by 1870 they had acquired seven shops, using one as a 'Mourning Department'. Over 200 employees lived in. The firm, which prided itself on being the main suppliers to the upper classes of South Kensington, was acquired by JOHN BARKER AND CO. LTD in 1920. A large rebuilding programme was begun in 1930. The new building, designed by Bernard George, opened in 1933, with a restaurant called the Rainbow Room and a roof garden which was embellished with 500 shrubs and trees, a flowing stream on which there were live flamingoes, a Dutch garden and a Spanish garden. On 13 January 1973 Derry and Toms closed down and a few months later it was taken over by Biba, who turned the sedate store into 'a dream emporium for a couple of swinging years'. Later MARKS AND SPENCER LTD and British Home Stores took the premises over. The roof garden has a fine view over London (*see* GARDENS).

Design Centre *28 Haymarket, SW1*. The shop window of the government-sponsored Design Council, originally the Council for Industrial Design founded in 1944. The Centre provides continuing, but changing exhibitions in the consumer, contract and engineering fields, and provides an information service for trade visitors as well as the general public. Exhibitors are listed in the selective Design Index, which numbers approximately 7,000 manufacturers of well-designed British goods.

Devereux Arms *Devereux Court, Strand, WC2.* Originally the GRECIAN COFFEE HOUSE, it was once patronised by Steele. It has a gas-lit oak-panelled bar and a bust of Robert Devereux, Earl of Essex, dated 1676, above the door. It was remodelled in 1843 when it received its present name.

Devereux Court *Strand, WC2.* Takes its name from Robert Devereux, Earl of Essex, whose mansion ESSEX HOUSE once occupied part of the site. The GRECIAN COFFEE HOUSE once stood at No. 20. Remodelled in 1843, it is now the Devereux Hotel. On the façade is a bust of Essex, beneath which is the legend 'This is Devereux Court, 1676'. TOM'S COFFEE HOUSE was also in the court. Devereux Chambers are occupied by barristers. There is an entrance to the TEMPLE.

Devonshire Club A Liberal club founded in 1875 as an alternative to the REFORM CLUB and so called because the Managing Committee first met at Devonshire House. The Duke of Devonshire was elected president; his son, the Marquess of Hartington, became chairman. W.E. Gladstone and other prominent Liberals attended the inaugural dinner. The political qualification for membership survived until 1915. Financial difficulties led, in 1976, to the amalgamation of the club with the East India and Sports Club (*see* EAST INDIA, DEVONSHIRE, SPORTS AND PUBLIC SCHOOLS CLUB). The club's former premises at 50 ST JAMES'S STREET were designed by Benjamin and Philip Wyatt for CROCKFORD'S and are now occupied by the Jamaican High Commission. They were remodelled for the club in the 1870s by C.J. Phipps.

Devonshire House *Piccadilly.* 'A perfectly unpretending building,' in the words of Augustus Hare. It had a 'low-pillared entrance hall' and 'a winding marble staircase with wide shallow steps'. It was built in 1734–7 for William Cavendish, 3rd Duke of Devonshire, on the site of an earlier house, formerly known as BERKELEY HOUSE, which had been burned down. The architect was William Kent who provided the Duke with a splendidly opulent interior in contrast with the simplicity of the outside. In the time of the 5th Duke and his lively, enchanting and extravagant wife, Georgiana, the house became a centre for the Whig opposition to the Tory Government of George III. Charles James Fox, Sheridan and the Prince of Wales were frequent guests. It was here in 1851 that the first performance of Bulwer-Lytton's comedy *Not So Bad As We Seem* was performed before Queen Victoria. The audience sat in the picture gallery; the adjacent library was used for the stage. Dickens, Wilkie Collins, Douglas Jerrold and Mark Lemon were amongst the actors. They were shown upstairs by liveried footmen with epaulettes of silver bullion. The overture was played by the Duke's private band. The house was sold by the 9th Duke in 1918 and in 1924–6 the large block known also as Devonshire House, and designed by Carrère and Hastings, was built on the frontage overlooking PICCADILLY. Offices and the old BERKELEY HOTEL were built in the gardens behind. The 18th-century wrought iron gates were originally made for Lord Heathfield's house at TURNHAM GREEN. In 1837–98 they stood in front of CHISWICK HOUSE and from 1898 to 1921 in front of Devonshire House. They

are now at the PICCADILLY end of the Broad Walk in GREEN PARK.

Devonshire Place *W1.* Built in the early 1790s on the site of MARYLEBONE GARDENS and named after the 5th Duke of Devonshire who was related to the ground landlord, the Duke of Portland. Many of the original houses still stand, and are now used as doctors' and dentists' surgeries. Dr Arthur Conan Doyle had a consulting room at No. 2 in 1891. He wrote, 'Every morning I walked from the lodgings at Montague Place, reached my consulting room at 10 and sat there until three or four with never a ring to disturb my serenity.' To fill in time he wrote the first of the *Adventures of Sherlock Holmes* which was published in *The Strand Magazine*. The novelist, 'Monk' Lewis, lived at No. 9 in 1803–5; and Sir Horace Jones, the architect, at No. 30 in 1887. The LONDON CLINIC is at Nos 18–20.

A bird's eye view of Devonshire Square, built between 1678 and 1708.

Devonshire Square *EC2.* On the site of Fisher's Folly, an Elizabethan mansion built by a goldsmith, Jasper Fisher. From 1620 to 1675 it was the Duke of Devonshire's town house. Part of it was leased in 1666 to Quakers for a meeting-house. Raids were so frequent that George Whitehead, the minister, used to take his nightcap to meetings in anticipation of spending the night in NEWGATE PRISON or BRIDEWELL. In 1675 the house was sold to Nicholas Barbon and others for development. The square and a new Quaker meeting-house were built between about 1678 and 1708. The Quakers moved to FRIENDS HOUSE, EUSTON ROAD in 1926. A few Georgian houses still stand.

Devonshire Street *W1.* Built during the 1780s, partly across the site of MARYLEBONE GARDENS, and named after the Duke of Devonshire (*see* DEVONSHIRE PLACE). Robert and Elizabeth Browning stayed at No. 26 in 1851; and Sir John Herschel the astronomer was at No. 56 in 1824. The INSTITUTE OF CONTEMPORARY HISTORY AND WIENER LIBRARY are at No. 4; the Chilean Embassy at No. 12; and the Royal Society for Asian Affairs at No. 42.

Dickens House *49 Doughty Street, WC1.* The author's only surviving London home. In April 1837 he moved into the house, which he had rented for £80 a year, with his wife, Kate, and their baby, Charles. Kate's sister Mary came to stay with them as well as Dickens's brother Fred. His sisters Fanny and Letitia were frequent visitors. Fanny's husband, Henry Burnett, recalled an evening in the house when Dickens took a little table to the corner of the room to work on *Oliver Twist*, bidding everyone to go on talking and occasionally making a remark himself, 'the feather of his pen still moving rapidly from side to side'. Dickens's daughters, Mary and Kate, were born in the house and, to his infinite distress, his beloved sister-in-law died here. The later chapters of *Pickwick Papers* were written here as well as *Oliver Twist* and *Nicholas Nickleby*. In 1839 Dickens moved to a larger house, 1 DEVONSHIRE TERRACE, REGENT'S PARK, which was demolished in 1960, a block of offices now covering the site. Dickens House was bought by the Dickens Fellowship in 1924. It contains letters, portraits, first editions and some of Dickens's own furniture.

Dickins and Jones Ltd *222–224 Regent Street, W1*. Dickins and Smith opened a shop in 1790 at 54 OXFORD STREET at the sign of the Golden Lion. In 1830 it became Dickins, Sons and Stevens, and in 1835 moved to Nos 232–234, in the recently built REGENT STREET. In 1884 some members of the Dickins family established a silk manufactory in Manchester which supplied the London store. A tradition for fine fabrics is still maintained. In the 1890s the business became known as Dickins and Jones when John Pritchard Jones became a partner. By 1900 the staff totalled 200, most of whom lived in ARGYLL STREET. In 1901 the store was all prepared for a white sale when Queen Victoria died. Most of the stock was dyed black to meet the urgent demand for mourning wear. In 1914 the store became part of the HARRODS group. In 1919 the island site was acquired, and the store rebuilt to the designs of Sir Henry Tanner in 1922. In 1959 the HARRODS group became the House of Fraser.

Dick's Coffee House *Fleet Street*. Also known as Richard's after the first proprietor, Richard Torvor or Turver. It stood near TEMPLE BAR and was opened in 1680. It was particularly popular with country gentlemen. William Cowper, the poet, on reading what he took to be a libel upon himself in a newspaper, rushed out of the premises in a frenzy, intent upon suicide. It became a French restaurant in 1885 and was demolished some years later.

Dilettanti Society (Brooks's) *St James's Street*. A dining-club founded in the 18th century. 'The nominal qualification for the Dilettanti,' wrote Horace Walpole, 'is having been in Italy and the real one being drunk; the two chiefs are Lord Middlesex and Sir Francis Dashwood who were seldom sober the whole time they were in Italy.' Arguably then, and unquestionably later, the Dilettanti Society was more seriously concerned with the arts than Walpole's words imply. In the 18th century they sponsored many of the great books about Greece which inspired the Classical Revival in architecture. Their fine collection of pictures formerly hung on the walls of the ST JAMES'S CLUB, where, since they had no home of their own, their meetings were held after 1922. With the partial merger of the ST JAMES'S CLUB with BROOKS'S the Dilettanti Society also moved to BROOKS'S.

Dilke Street *SW3*. First so called in 1875, it no doubt takes its name from the Dilke family. Sir Charles Dilke was Member of Parliament for CHELSEA in 1868–86.

Dioramas A precursor of the cinema was the Eidophusikon, or 'Various Imitations of Natural phenomena represented by Moving Pictures,' devised

Engraving after T.H. Shepherd's drawing of a dinner of the Dilettanti Society at the Thatched House Club in 1840.

by the painter Philippe de Loutherbourg and set up in LISLE STREET in 1781. It consisted of a 10 ft wide box within which a series of moving and mechanically operated scenes, such as a storm at sea, were displayed. Other precursors were PANORAMAS and the Peepshow of the streets and fairgrounds as depicted by Hogarth in his engraving of SOUTHWARK FAIR. A smart version of the Peepshow was the Cosmorama (from Greek *kosmos*, world, and *orama*, scene or view) opened in ST JAMES'S STREET in 1820 and later moved to REGENT STREET. This became a fashionable meeting-place, its main attraction being a set of 14 peepholes set in the walls and filled with large convex lenses to magnify different scenic effects in perspective dramatised by mirrors and special lighting. Then Jacques Mandé Daguerre, inventor of the first effective form of photography, and skilful painter of *trompe l'oeil*, produced his remarkable Dioramas, the first of which he opened in Paris in 1823. Berlin and London each acquired one. That in London, which Daguerre ran in partnership with Charles-Marie Bouton, pupil of the painter David, was opened in 1823 with two displays: the interior of Canterbury Cathedral and the Valley of Sarnen. Its entrance was on the façade of one of Nash's fashionable new terrace houses facing REGENT'S PARK – Nos 9 and 10 Park Square East. The building, whose façade at least is there today, was designed by the elder Pugin who was working for Nash at the time. Its dark circular auditorium, seating 200, could be rotated through 73 degrees by a boy working a ram engine so that the audience could view two stages alternately; while one proscenium was exposed, the other was closed by the shell of the auditorium wall and could then be rearranged for the next display. A mystified eye-witness thus described one of the most popular tableaux, *A Midnight Mass of St Etienne-du-Mont*: 'At first it is daylight; we see the nave with its chairs; little by little the light wanes and the candles are lighted. At the back of the choir the church is illuminated, and the congregation arriving take their places in front of the chairs, not suddenly, as if the scenes were shifted, but gradually. The midnight mass begins. In this reverent stillness the organ peals out from under the distant vaults. Then the daylight slowly returns, the congregation disperses, the candles are extinguished and the church with its chairs appears as at the beginning. This was magic.'

The magic was achieved by ingenious means. A corridor with black walls behind the proscenium led to the stage, near the back of which was hung the main picture (hence the name: Greek *dia*, through, and *orama*, scene). The paintings, which could be rolled up on huge cylinders, measured 72 ft wide by 40 ft high. They were made of calico and painted with translucent and opaque colours – a forerunner of the wide screen. Behind the painting rose tall windows to light the translucent areas while the opaque areas were lit from directional skylights in the roof of the dark corridor. The lighting effects could be modified, with dramatic effects, by an elaborate system of shutters pulled by cords, some being made of coloured fabric which could overlay one another as required, so that almost limitless mixtures of colours and lighting could be achieved. Solid objects were often placed in front of the painting to heighten the realism. Daylight only was used so that foggy days marred performances. But later Dioramas in London were lit by gas which, though dangerous, could be used to commercial

advantage since the weather could be discounted and displays presented at night. Each spectacle was shown for 15 minutes. In 1851, the year of the GREAT EXHIBITION, Daguerre's Diorama was showing Mount Etna under three effects with organ accompaniment: at sunrise, at sunset, and in glorious eruption. In 1854 the building was converted to a Baptist chapel and in 1981 it was being used by an actors' co-operative. A number of art groups were then trying to restore it.

Dirty Dick's *202–204 Bishopsgate, EC2*. Built in 1745 and rebuilt in 1870, this inn takes its name from Nathaniel Bentley, a well-known dandy whose fiancée died on the eve of their wedding. He locked up the dining room, complete with wedding breakfast, and spent the rest of his life in increasing squalor. 'It is no use,' he is reputed to have said. 'If I wash my hands today, they will be dirty again tomorrow.' When he died in 1809, the house was in ruins, though he was worth a fortune. The cellars are part of the original building, but the present-day cobwebs and dead cats are synthetic.

RRS Discovery *St Katharine's Dock, E1*. Captain R.F. Scott's ship, built in Dundee especially for his first Antarctic expedition in 1901–4. In 1905–12 she carried cargoes for the Hudson Bay Company across the Atlantic; and, in 1915–16, munitions to Russia. In 1925–7 the ship was used for researching into the habits of whales. In 1929–31 she took the British, Australian and New Zealand expedition to the Australian Antarctic. In 1937 she became a training ship for sea scouts; and in 1955 the drill ship of the Royal Naval Reserve. From 1960 she was the recruiting headquarters of the Royal Navy. Formerly moored at VICTORIA EMBANKMENT, the ship was moved after overhaul to ST KATHARINE'S DOCK in March 1980 (*see* HISTORIC SHIP COLLECTION OF THE MARITIME TRUST).

District Line The Metropolitan District Railway Company was set up to raise the extra capital needed to complete an 'Inner Circle' to be created by extending the METROPOLITAN LINE. The company was closely associated with the Metropolitan Railway and the two were expected to amalgamate after completion of the work. The District completed the section from SOUTH KENSINGTON to WESTMINSTER BRIDGE in 1868, from there to BLACKFRIARS in 1870, and thence to MANSION HOUSE in 1871. It also opened a line from SOUTH KENSINGTON to WEST BROMPTON in 1869. However, the two companies fell out over the working of the line and the District began running its own trains in 1871. Hoping to improve its poor financial position, the District extended eastward to HAMMERSMITH in 1874, to RICHMOND in 1877, and from TURNHAM GREEN to EALING BROADWAY in 1879, raising capital under different company names where necessary. Another extension from WEST BROMPTON to PUTNEY BRIDGE was opened in 1880, and the District began running a service to WIMBLEDON in 1889. Meanwhile CITY interests finally forced the District and Metropolitan back into partnership to complete the CIRCLE, which opened in 1884. The District and METROPOLITAN both worked their trains all round, and in addition the District ran trains from HAMMERSMITH to NEW CROSS over the southern part. The District made other enterprising attempts to increase its revenue: it exploited and encouraged exhibition traffic by building a subway from SOUTH KENSINGTON to the exhibition ground and charging 1d toll, and by building a covered way from EARL'S COURT to WARWICK ROAD. Yet another extension, from WHITECHAPEL to BOW, was opened in 1902.

C.T. Yerkes, an American, took over the District in 1901 with the expressed intention of electrifying it. This was completed in 1905, and new multiple-unit open stock was introduced, together with automatic signalling, controlled by track circuits. The geography of the line has not substantially altered since then, though extensive modernisation has of course taken place. The District is now some 30 miles long (*see also* CIRCLE LINE, METROPOLITAN LINE *and* UNDERGROUND RAILWAYS).

Dissolution of the Monasteries

This took place between 1535 and 1540, causing a sudden and wholesale change in the appearance of London and a transformation of its social and religious life. Instigated by Henry VIII and organised by Thomas Cromwell, it began with 'visitations' to religious houses to investigate their administration and the behaviour of their members. The purpose was to find excuses for the suppression of monasteries and the confiscation by the King of their properties and valuables accrued over centuries. Henry VIII had complex and special motives for dissolving monasteries and dispersing members of religious orders. These included his ambition to increase royal power as well as a pressing need for increased revenue. He also had an immediate personal desire to get church approval for divorce from his wife, Catherine, for his marriage to Anne Boleyn and recognition of the legitimacy of her offspring. Failing to get this from the Pope, he turned to the church in England of which the monasteries formed an influential part. Most monastic orders had built their houses in the seclusion of the countryside, but there were about 12 monasteries of different orders in London, some being among the earliest and richest foundations. These included the Benedictine WESTMINSTER ABBEY, the Bridgettine SYON HOUSE and the Carthusian house at SMITHFIELD known as CHARTERHOUSE. London was, however, the main centre for various orders of friars and canons whose lives were dedicated to preaching, teaching and social work among the urban poor. The friars, unlike the monastic orders, did not possess many rich buildings and great tracts of land, but they were extremely successful collectors of money and, through pastoral contacts, were most influential among the London populace. They were, therefore, the first to be investigated and disbanded in London after the initial success of the dissolution of the lesser monasteries in 1536. In London there were 12 main, and many more smaller, houses of friars and canons. These were Augustinians at ALDGATE, Dominicans at LUDGATE, Franciscans at CORNHILL, SMITHFIELD and NEWGATE, and the WHITEFRIARS (Carmelite) in FLEET STREET. There were also some 25 major hospitals (and many minor ones) belonging to religious orders of which eight were large establishments and a number specialised in the care of lepers, the insane and the aged poor. These hospitals included ST THOMAS ACON, ST BARTHOLOMEW'S, St Mary at BISHOPSGATE, the SAVOY hospital, St Mary Bethlehem (BEDLAM) and St John's (later MERCHANT TAYLORS'). Other religious foundations included secular colleges such as the TEMPLE, specialising in

teaching and learning. There were also several nunneries – Benedictines at BISHOPSGATE, Augustinians at CLERKENWELL and SHOREDITCH, Franciscans at the MINORIES. In 1534 all religious orders were required to take oaths supporting the 1534 Acts of Supremacy (recognising the King instead of the Pope as head of the English church) and Succession (accepting the validity of the King's divorce and remarriage). Most members of London's religious houses accepted the oaths, sometimes with the qualification 'in so far as the law of God allow'. But there were several outstanding exceptions, among them the Carthusians of CHARTERHOUSE, priests and nuns of the Bridgettine SYON HOUSE and members of the Franciscan order of Observants at RICHMOND and GREENWICH who had close connections with the court and Queen Catherine. Many Observants refused the oath and continued to preach against the royal divorce, and a number were executed. By the end of the year their London houses, and those elsewhere in England, had been dissolved and their property confiscated. The friars had fled abroad or been cast into prison where many died. With notable exceptions such as CHARTERHOUSE and SYON HOUSE, religious houses in London put up little opposition. A deed of surrender for WESTMINSTER ABBEY was signed by the abbot and 24 monks in 1534 and it was finally suppressed in 1540. Its buildings and school were saved by being secularised and because the abbey became for a brief period (to 1550) the seat of a new bishopric. It was restored as a monastic house under Mary, but again suppressed in 1561. One monk of WESTMINSTER who refused the oath was imprisoned for 20 years, but was alive, aged 86, in the year Elizabeth I died. Most religious houses in London were less fortunate. Their property and possessions were confiscated, and their buildings vandalised. GREYFRIARS was used as a store for herrings and wine. Confiscated property was dealt with by the Court of Augmentations which was specially created in 1536 to conduct the business of suppression. This it did so thoroughly and expeditiously that within five years numerous beautiful buildings which had been landmarks in London were gaunt ruins. Instructions to the Commissioners of the Court were that they were to 'pull down to the ground all the walls of the churches, stepulls, cloysters, fraterys, dorters, chapterhowsys'. Only a few escaped together with some of the hospitals whose work in controlling disease was indispensable; but these too were secularised. Monastic property was occasionally sold by auctioneers handling church and domestic furniture, even candlesticks, pans, cupboards, doors, locks, grates and altars. The trail of destruction left London with insufficient hospitals and places of worship. The Lord Mayor, Sir Richard Gresham, asked that the main CITY hospitals might be taken over by the CORPORATION in order to prevent the spread of disease. He asked also that some monastic churches might be retained for worship 'by reason of the great multitude of people daily resorting to parish churches to the annoyance of parishioners'. The petition was not granted and the routine attendance of London people at daily service fell off. The revenues accruing to the crown were immense, amounting between 1536 and 1540 to about £140,000 per annum when normal crown revenue was £100,000 per annum. In two years, sales of monastic goods brought in £13,787, whilst sales of lands produced £164,495 and £165,459. London's three richest religious houses,

WESTMINSTER, CHARTERHOUSE and SYON, were included among the confiscated properties. The men and women of the suppressed houses, provided they swore the required oaths, received state pensions, varying greatly in size from the £700 per annum for the abbess of SYON, to the average payment of £5 per annum for a man and £3 for women. A number of monks became parish priests, others married (some took nuns as wives, thus enjoying two pensions). The suppression of the monasteries brutally destroyed a way of life that had dominated lay and religious society for over 500 years. The familiar sight of monks, friars and nuns disappeared from London's streets and their influence was speedily eradicated. The Dissolution marked the end of medieval life in London.

Distaff Lane *EC4.* Distaffs for holding unspun wool were made and sold in the lane. In 1850 the original Distaff Lane was swept away when CANNON STREET was extended. The part that remains used to be known as Little Distaff Lane.

Distillers' Company *see* CITY LIVERY COMPANIES.

Dobney's *Islington.* Bowling-greens 'in Islington Fields' are mentioned as early as 1633, and in 1669 Prospect House commanded a fine view from north of them on ISLINGTON Hill across the NEW RIVER COMPANY's fields to the CITY. By 1709 the Company's Upper Pond (the site of Claremont Square) was built immediately south of the greens, which were advertised in 1718 for 'gentlemen bowlers'. They were approached by a carriageway downhill from the gate of the White Lion in Islington High Street.

Dobney or d'Aubigny was a later owner, on whose widow's death in 1760 the place became famed as an equestrian amphitheatre under its next purchaser, Thomas Johnson. In 1767 the main summer attraction 'at the Prospect House, known by the name of Dobney's Bowling-Green' was the show-rider Price from the THREE HATS at Islington. Attractions for 1769 included Philip Jones, a juggler, and the skeleton of a whale. After a spell as a boarding-school, the premises reopened as the Jubilee Tea-Gardens, a fashionable name since Garrick's Shakespeare Jubilee. Nightly at 6.45 p.m. (entrance 1s, boxes and gallery 2s), the improbable horseman, Daniel Wildman, rode standing upright, wearing 'a curious mask of bees'.

The creation of PENTONVILLE suburb from 1773 allowed an easier approach from the new Penton Street, but with the building development the grounds became unkempt. The house, with handsome public rooms on two floors each holding 200, was still popular with CITY apprentices, but by 1780 it had become lecture-rooms and was auctioned the following year. In 1790 Winchester Place (part of Pentonville Road facing the reservoir) was built over the gardens, which finally disappeared in 1810, commemorated only by Dobney's Court off Penton Street. Dobney's fate was in marked contrast with BUSBY'S FOLLY.

Docks The London docks stem from the early quays or hithes of Roman and Saxon times – cuts dug out of the river bank having sides lined with stakes. In the 1970s some original Roman and medieval quays were unearthed at the POOL OF LONDON, preserved by THAMES clay for centuries, including a fine 40 ft quay

by the CUSTOM HOUSE (Lower Thames Street) where Roman galleys tied up. The first wet dock on record was at BLACKWALL. This was enlarged in 1789 as the BRUNSWICK and was mentioned by Pepys in 1661. Apart from that and the HOWLAND GREAT DOCK, built in 1696, London had no large enclosed docks until the early 19th century. Since Roman times ships could be docked at some places along the quays: QUEENHITHE, for example, an indentation of the bank just above LONDON BRIDGE, was used by small craft. Other mooring places have been BILLINGSGATE below LONDON BRIDGE; the mouth of the FLEET where comparatively deep water existed; at PUDDLE DOCK, WAPPING, the TOWER, WHITEFRIARS, and, on the south bank, at St Saviour's and St Mary Overie's. (*See* SOUTHWARK CATHEDRAL). But mostly vessels came to anchor in mid-stream in the POOL below the Bridge, their cargoes being landed by lighters. Smuggling was always rife in the old days but it was curbed when Queen Elizabeth enacted a law to compel all ships to discharge their cargoes under supervision only at certain 'Legal Quays', 17 in number between the Bridge and the TOWER, where duty could be collected. The number proved to be inadequate and before long extra 'Sufferance Wharfs' were added where certain goods bearing low duties could be handled. In 1665 three more 'Legal Quays' were established.

In spite of the GREAT PLAGUE and the GREAT FIRE, trade increased at the port during the 17th century. Early in the 18th century, Defoe made his *Tour* and found on London's river 'about two thousand sail of all sorts, not reckoning barges, lighters or pleasure boats or yatchts', and from the POOL down to BLACKWALL he discovered three wet docks for laying up ships, 22 dry docks for repairing them, and 33 shipyards for building merchantmen. By 1699 BILLINGSGATE had become a free wharf for fish and a fishmarket. Shipping grew during the 18th century and at even greater speed during the 19th, when the Industrial Revolution was in full spate, and the Empire was expanding. By the close of the 18th century docking facilities had become so congested, delays were so serious, warehousing was so inadequate, and pilfering so rife (*see* RIVER POLICE) that drastic action was essential. Only a few warehouses stood on the banks, mainly for storing tobacco in bond; since, after 1714, traders were allowed to store their imports in such warehouses, paying the full duty only when the tobacco was removed. Only one port authority existed, the CITY CORPORATION, which obtained good profits from its monopoly, but as it was inefficient, in 1796 a Parliamentary Committee debated the docking problems and issued a report that condemned the congestion and inadequacy of London's port. As a result a number of large-scale projects were proposed for the building of new docks and shipping facilities but none was carried out. The solution came piecemeal in the building of a number of enclosed docks by private companies in the marshy land east of the TOWER. All of these lie between TOWER BRIDGE and Gallions Reach, a distance of 10 miles, and their sizes range from ST KATHARINE's to the west at 10 acres to the Royal System to the east at 245 acres. The first enclosed dock was opened in 1802, the last in 1921.

The first large, wet, enclosed and protected dock with adequate warehousing was built by the West India Company. Here, cut off from the tides by locks, ships could lie safely at the quays. The dock proved its

Ships under construction and repair in the dockyard at Deptford in the 1730s.

worth immediately and other enclosed docks rapidly followed: the LONDON (1805), the EAST INDIA (1805), the SURREY on the south bank (1807), ST KATHARINE'S (1828), WEST INDIA SOUTH (1829), Royal Victoria (1855), MILLWALL (1868), Royal Albert (1880), King George V (1921) (*see* ROYAL GROUP OF DOCKS). All these docks, except the last, were the products of private enterprise. In their construction and running the CITY CORPORATION took only a nominal part. Many problems, in fact, might have been avoided had an overall authority existed from the beginning. From west to east on the north bank the enclosed docks in turn are ST KATHARINE'S, LONDON, REGENT'S CANAL DOCK (owned by the British Waterways Board), the WEST INDIA and MILLWALL on the ISLE OF DOGS, the EAST INDIA, and finally the vast ROYAL GROUP (Victoria, Albert and George V), while on the south bank, east of ROTHERHITHE, lies the complex of the SURREY COMMERCIAL. Then, far down river on the north side of Greenwich Reach, are TILBURY DOCKS, the only ones still active and now modernised for the new system of containerisation. The various docks have tended to specialise in types of imports: rum and hardwood at the WEST INDIA, for instance, softwood at the SURREY, grain at MILLWALL, wool, sugar and rubber at ST KATHARINE'S, ivory, spices, coffee and cocoa at LONDON. So essential was the defence of the docks that they were built like impregnable castles and protected by special armed police. As the West India Dock Act of 1799 decreed: 'Such of the said Docks, as shall be used for unlading Ships, together with the Quays, Warehouses and other Buildings, shall be inclosed and surrounded by a strong brick or stone Wall, not less than 30 feet high, on all sides, leaving only proper spaces for the Cuts and Entrances into the Dock, and proper Gateways through the Wall; and immediately without the Wall ... there shall be a Ditch, of the width of 12 feet, at least, to be always kept filled with water, 6 feet deep.' In the event, the ditches were taken less seriously than the walls.

For a time, all went well and the shareholders of the

docks 'basked in the sunshine of ten per cent'; but by the end of the century the PORT OF LONDON was again in trouble as a result of free trade, the free run of dock waters by the lightermen, the arrival of the railways (which, like the lightermen, bore away cargoes as soon as they were landed), troubles with labour, fierce competition between the dock companies, and the rivalry of the port of Liverpool. The situation was saved for the next half century by the formation of the PORT OF LONDON AUTHORITY in 1909. But in the 1960s London's docks began to close and the whole of dockland has suffered a sudden, yet almost unnoticed death. The causes are several: the disbanding of the Empire, labour troubles, tardy modernisation, increases in the size of ships, competition from foreign ports, particularly Rotterdam, and the move down river to Tilbury with its new equipment. The chief reason, however, is that large modern ships, now carrying containers, need deep water berths and a quick turnaround, and their owners do not want to waste time travelling up a crowded tidal river or to be delayed by docking. At the time of writing a scheme is afoot to build a huge new dock at Maplin some 50 miles from LONDON BRIDGE, but the future is uncertain since events such as the building of a Channel tunnel would affect docking plans significantly. The dockland area of London awaits huge redevelopments for new purposes and new ways of life.

Dr Barnardo's Homes *Head Office – Tanners Lane, Barkingside, Ilford, Essex.* Thomas John Barnardo was born in Dublin in 1845. In 1866, wanting to become a medical missionary in China, he came to study at the LONDON HOSPITAL. He was appalled by the living conditions of the London poor, especially the children, and started a Ragged School at Hope Place, STEPNEY. One of his pupils, Jim Jarvis, showed him some of the 'lays' where the children slept. Dr Barnardo decided 'to do something about it', and by 1870 he had raised enough money (including contributions from philanthropists like Lord Shaftesbury) to open his first home for destitute lads at Stepney Causeway. In 1874, after the death of a boy he had been forced to turn away for lack of room, he adopted the slogan 'the Ever Open Door' and founded many more homes, schools and clubs for children in need. Today there are 164 homes, schools and other centres throughout the UK. Nowadays Barnardo's aims include keeping children in ordinary family homes, preventing family breakdown through Day Care Services and finding foster homes wherever possible for children in need.

Dr Williams's Trust and Library *14 Gordon Square, WC1*. Daniel Williams, a prominent Presbyterian minister, bequeathed the bulk of his estate in 1716 to trustees for charitable purposes. Included was his library, to which he had added that of Dr William Bates, who had died in 1699, around 10,000 items in all, and intended by him for a public library. For this a building was erected on the east side of REDCROSS STREET, opened in 1729, and long referred to as the Dissenters' Library. Until the withdrawal of the Unitarians from the 'Three Denominations' in 1836 the library was a recognised meeting place for Dissenting associations. A register of births (now in the PUBLIC RECORD OFFICE) was maintained here from 1742 until 1837. Books were added by donation and purchase and on removal to No. 8 QUEEN SQUARE in 1865 there were some 22,000 volumes. In 1873 the library moved to new premises at No. 16 Grafton Street East and in 1890 to University Hall, GORDON SQUARE. Christopher Walton, the theosophist, presented 1,000 volumes in 1876 and in 1882 C.L. Lewes presented over 2,000 items from the library collected by his father, G.H. Lewes, and George Eliot. The collection, now more than 130,000 volumes, is pre-eminent for English nonconformity.

Aquatint after Rowlandson and Pugin of the Common Hall of Doctors' Commons in about 1808.

Doctors' Commons The colloquial name for the College of Advocates and Doctors of Law which was situated near ST PAUL'S CATHEDRAL. In it were housed, from 1572 onwards, the ecclesiastical and Admiralty courts together with the advocates practising therein. These advocates – a wholly separate body from the barristers of the time – enjoyed a monopoly of practice and were required to hold doctorates in the civil (i.e. Roman) law awarded by the Universities of Oxford or Cambridge before being admitted by the

Archbishop of Canterbury to practise in the COURT OF ARCHES which sat originally in the church of ST MARY-LE-BOW in CHEAPSIDE. In 1768 the College was inaugurated by Royal Charter under a President who was the Dean of the Arches for the time being.

A description of the premises and of the court at work is given in Chapter 23 of Charles Dickens's *David Copperfield* and is also mentioned in *The Pickwick Papers* (Chapter 55). With the passing of the Matrimonial Causes Act 1857, the Court of Probate Act of the same year and the High Court of Admiralty Act of 1859, the College ceased to function and the premises were demolished in 1867.

A scene at the Dog and Duck, a popular tavern the waters of whose medicinal spring were recommended by Dr Johnson in 1771.

Dog and Duck *St George's Fields, Lambeth*. So called because of its vicinity to ponds where spaniels hunted duck. The tavern was here by 1642, before the first mention of the medicinal spring which was later to attract so much custom. The waters were first advertised in 1731 and at 4d a gallon were recommended as a cure for gout, stone, the king's evil, sore eyes and inveterate cancers. Many doctors believed in their powers and, in 1771, Dr Johnson wrote to recommend them to Mrs Thrale. In 1769 a bowling-green and swimming bath were added. Shortly after a circus, established nearby in ST GEORGE'S FIELDS, attracted more custom. Gradually thereafter the place's reputation declined and, in 1787, the proprietor had to appeal against the magistrates' decision to refuse a licence. The licence was lost again in 1796; but a freeman of the VINTNERS' COMPANY, who needed no licence, was engaged to solve the problem. In 1799 the Dog and Duck was finally suppressed. In 1811 the buildings were demolished and the BETHLEHEM ROYAL HOSPITAL was built on the site.

Doggett's Coat and Badge Race Thomas Doggett, comedian and joint manager of DRURY LANE THEATRE, who died in 1721, provided in his will 'for procuring yearly on the ffirst day of August for ever the following particulars, that is to say, ffive pounds for a Badge of Silver weighing about twelve ounces and representing Liberty to be given to be rowed by six young Watermen according to my custom eighteen shillings for Cloath for a livery, whereon the said badge is to be put, one pound one shilling for making up the said Livery and Buttons and appurtances to it and Thirty shillings to the clerk of the Watermens Hall All which I would have to be continued for ever yearly in

Rowlandson's watercolour of the finish of Doggett's Coat and Badge Race at the Old Swan, Chelsea.

commemoration of his Majesty King George's happy accession to the British Throne.' The course is 4½ miles from LONDON BRIDGE to Cadogan Pier, CHELSEA and the race is usually held at the end of July. It is the oldest annually contested event in the British sporting calendar. Today light sculling boats have replaced the original heavy standard skiffs; they are rowed against the ebb tide and the average time taken is about 30 minutes. Up to 1950 the race was exclusively professional, but amateurs may now take part provided they do not accept prizes of money if they win.

Dogs' Cemetery *see* CEMETERIES.

Dogs' Home, Battersea *Battersea Park Road, SW8.* Founded at HOLLOWAY in 1860 by Mrs Mary Tealby as 'The Temporary Home for Lost and Starving Dogs'. By 1869 there were about 200 dogs in the home at a time and the neighbours complained about the noise; so in 1871 she moved to BATTERSEA. The Home's peak intake was in 1896, following a LONDON COUNTY COUNCIL muzzling order, when 42,614 dogs were taken in during the year. Now the home has on average 450 at a time, and in 1979 over 17,000 dogs were received and found new homes or restored to their owners. The home has also taken stray cats since 1882. The idea of the Home was ridiculed at first but it soon gained a high reputation and it has helped to control rabies and educate the public to a better consideration of animals. In 1879 the Prince of Wales visited the Home and became its Patron in 1884. Queen Victoria followed his example in 1885 and Queen Elizabeth II became Patron in 1956. The services of the clinic are free to those who cannot afford to pay for them. About three million animals have passed through the home.

Dollis Hill *NW2.* Situated to the west of the EDGWARE ROAD, north of WILLESDEN. One of the highest points in the area, it was probably an early hamlet in a woodland clearing of the extensive MIDDLESEX forest. Willesden manor is mentioned in *Domesday Book*, and was subsequently divided into eight prebends of which OXGATE contained the area to become known as Dollis Hill. By the end of the 16th century, when a group of buildings existed there, it was called Daleson Hill (and, later, Dolly's Hill) presumably referring to a resident's name. Any connection with the Dollis Brook that flows south from BARNET, to enter the WELSH HARP as the River BRENT, just north of Dollis Hill, has not been proved. Arable farming predominated, with dairy-farming increasing in the 19th century when cattle were no longer allowed in the metropolis. In 1823 DOLLIS HILL HOUSE was rebuilt, replacing a small residence. Until the 1890s Dollis Hill remained a 'pretty little hamlet' but by the turn of the century the population had increased eightfold and, in 1901, 96 acres of land around the House were sold to create Gladstone Park in the face of advancing development, for example that of Earl Temple's estate. In 1909 Dollis Hill Station extended the METROPOLITAN LINE and in 1913 St Andrew's Hospital was opened. The 1st World War stimulated the growth of industry and consequently the spread of terraced housing; but in 1933, when the Post Office Research Station was built, much of Dollis Hill was still farmland, unlike the greater part of WILLESDEN. During the 1930s Dollis Hill was built up and by 1939, when the BAKERLOO LINE arrived, it housed a population consisting of many who had moved north and west from BRONDESBURY and KILBURN.

Dollis Hill House *Dollis Hill Lane, NW2.* Built in 1823 by Joseph Finch, the last surviving member of the Company of Moneyers and their Apprentices, Dollis Hill House stands high above WILLESDEN. Despite housing developments, the views towards HARROW and

EALING are still fine. The house, a plain, three-bayed, two-storied Regency building, is said to have inspired Felicia Dorothea Heman's phrase 'the stately homes of England'. It was for many years the home of the Victorian statesman, Lord Aberdeen, and William Gladstone often stayed there when PARLIAMENT was in session. Mark Twain was also a frequent guest. In 1901 the house was purchased by the local authority. In the 1st World War it was used as a hospital. The War Cabinet met here in 1941. It is now used for receptions. About 100 acres of the grounds were laid out as a public recreation area called Gladstone Park.

Dollond and Aitchison Ltd Opticians originally at No. 28 OLD BOND STREET and now with branches all over London. John Dollond was born into a Huguenot family in 1706 and opened a small optical workshop in Vine Street, SPITALFIELDS in 1750, later moving to the Sign of the Golden Spectacles in the STRAND. Lord Nelson bought a telescope from the firm in 1805. The Duke of Wellington was also a customer. James Aitchison who joined the firm towards the end of the 19th century was apprenticed in HIGH HOLBORN in about 1875 and was a pioneer of scientific sight testing.

Dolphin Square *SW1.* A massive block of 1,250 flats, in dull red brick with stone dressings, designed by Cecil Eve and Gordon Jeeves. It covers 7½ acres and, when built in 1937, was the largest such block in Europe. There are shops, a restaurant, a garage and a central garden.

Dominion Cinema *Tottenham Court Road, W1.* Built in 1929 as a theatre by William and T.R. Millburn on the site of Meux's Horseshoe Brewery. It opened with a musical comedy, *Follow Through.* In 1932 it became a cinema, though it is now partly used as a theatre again.

Domus Conversorum *New Street (now Chancery Lane).* Founded in 1233 by Henry III as a hostel for Jewish converts. In 1280 it was decided that converts must practise a trade or cease to receive their allowance. 280 Jews were hanged, and the rest banished, in 1290, for allegedly clipping coins. Their children, however, continued to be admitted to the school which was kept here, and records of 1292 show that allowances of 10½d for a man, and 8d for a woman, were still being made. In 1377 the keeper restored the house at his own expense. Keepers were usually Masters of the Rolls, and it was decided, after the building's restoration, that the house be granted to the Masters. From that time the Chancery rolls were kept in the house. Accounts of allowances to converts cannot be traced after 1608. The chapel, however, was rebuilt by Inigo Jones in 1617; and Donne is said to have preached here. In 1717 the house was demolished and a new residence for the Master of the Rolls built on the site. The PUBLIC RECORD OFFICE has been on the site of the chapel since 1896 and monuments from the chapel, including the 13th-century chancel arch, are preserved in its museum.

Don Saltero's Coffee House *Chelsea.* James Salter, a barber and former servant of Sir Hans Sloane, opened this house on the corner of LAWRENCE STREET in 1675. A few years later he moved to DANVERS STREET where he remained until 1715. He then moved to premises on the site of what is now CHEYNE WALK. Salter was nicknamed Don Saltero by Vice-Admiral Munden who had long been on the coast of Spain where he acquired a fondness for Spanish titles. At first the coffee shop was combined with a barber's. Besides shaving his customers Salter also bled them, pulled out their teeth, played the violin and wrote them verses. Sir Hans Sloane gave him various duplicates from his collection of curiosities and by 1723 Salter, who also received gifts from other benefactors, including Smollett, was advertising 'My Museum Coffee House'. When he died in 1728, his daughter continued to run the business. In 1799 the collection of curiosities was sold. They included 'a starved cat found between the walls of Westminster Abbey when repairing, and a Staffordshire almanac in use when the Danes were in England'. Don Saltero's is mentioned in Fanny Burney's novel, *Evelina.*

Dorchester Hotel *Park Lane, W1.* The early site formed part of the manor of Hyde, given by William the Conqueror to Geoffrey de Mandeville. In the 18th century it was acquired by Joseph Damer. The first large building erected in 1751 was named Dorchester House when Damer became Earl of Dorchester in 1792. Bought by the rich 3rd Marquess of Hertford (who laid the foundations of the Wallace Collection) in the early 19th century, it was renamed Hertford House. After Hertford's death Captain Robert Stayner Holford built a grand mansion (*see* DORCHESTER HOUSE). In 1928 Sir Robert McAlpine and Sons and Gordon Hotels Ltd bought the house to demolish it. Designed by William Curtis Green, the new building opened with a flourish on 18 April 1931. Being of sound reinforced concrete it became the headquarters of General Eisenhower in the 2nd World War. In 1952 extensions were carried out on the DEANERY STREET side with suites designed by Oliver Messel on the floors above. In 1977 it was sold to an Arab consortium. There are 290 bedrooms.

Dorchester House *Park Lane.* Designed by Lewis Vulliamy for the millionaire, R.S. Holford, who asked for, and was provided with, a private palace of monumental grandeur. The outside was closely modelled upon Peruzzi's Villa Farnesina in Rome. Much of the interior, including a fine marble fireplace in the Red Drawing-Room, was designed by Alfred Stevens. Finished in 1857, it was demolished in 1929 to make way for the DORCHESTER HOTEL.

Doric Villas *Regent's Park, NW1.* A pair of substantial houses, numbered as 42 and 43 YORK TERRACE, they were designed by John Nash and built about 1828. The original occupants of No. 43 were the Revd Henry Raikes and Miss Charlotte Finch Raikes, relatives of the diarist, Thomas, at NORTH VILLA. In 1877, Warren William de la Rue moved into No. 43; he was the grandson of the founder of the stamp-printing and playing card firm. Later he acquired No. 42 as well, and arranged internal communication between the two houses. After the 1st World War they were again divided. Ernest Jones, the physician and psychoanalyst, lived at No. 42 from 1923 to 1941. Next door in 1918–29 lived Lady Wyndham, née Mary Moore, the actress wife of the actor-manager Sir Charles Wyndham.

Dorset Garden Theatre *Off Fleet Street*. Also known as Duke's Theatre, it was a magnificent Restoration building costing £9,000, designed by Sir Christopher Wren. The rich auditorium included an ornate proscenium and was surmounted by the Duke of York's arms and a gallery, probably for musicians, flanked by two statues of Melpomene and Thalia. It stood on the river front in the gardens of DORSET HOUSE which had been destroyed by the GREAT FIRE. It was built for Sir William Davenant for the Duke's Men but he died before it was completed. Thomas Betterton and Henry Harris assumed artistic control of the Duke of York's Company but the widowed Lady Davenant held the purse strings. The theatre opened in 1671 with Dryden's *Sir Martin Mar-All*. For two years after the DRURY LANE THEATRE was burned down in 1672, the Dorset Garden was the only first-class theatre in London. In 1672 Wycherley's *Gentleman Dancing Master* was first produced, and 1678 saw the first performance of Dryden's *The Kind Keeper; or Mr Limberham*; this was not well received. In 1682 the Duke's Company amalgamated with the King's Company and moved to the DRURY LANE THEATRE. Although performances by the joint company were still given here, the fashionable audience deserted Dorset Garden which was thereafter used by fencers, wrestlers and for sundry exhibitions. In 1689 it was renamed the Queen's Theatre. It was demolished in about 1720 and five years later the site was a timber yard. The playground of the CITY OF LONDON SCHOOL occupies the site. Near the north-east of JOHN CARPENTER STREET is a plaque bearing the legend: 'In this playground stood the Duke's Theatre. Opened 1671. Demolished 1709.'

Dorset House *Fleet Street, see* SALISBURY HOUSE, FLEET STREET.

Dorset Square *NW1*. From 1787 to 1811, the site of Thomas Lord's first cricket ground. The houses were built soon after Lord removed to ST JOHN'S WOOD and the square was named after the Duke of Dorset, an early patron of the game. Though the south and east sides have been rebuilt, the houses on the north side remain more or less intact. No. 1 served as the Free French Headquarters in the 2nd World War and a plaque, unveiled in 1957, commemorates the men and women who set off from here on missions to Occupied France. A BLUE PLAQUE on No. 28 records the residence of George Grossmith, the actor and co-author, with his brother, of *The Diary of a Nobody*.

Dorset Street *W1*. This little street, first rated in 1793, lies on the PORTMAN ESTATE off BAKER STREET, its name commemorating the Portman home county. Charles Babbage, the mathematician and inventor of the calculating machine, lived at No. 1.

Doughty House *142 Richmond Hill, Surrey*. Replaced the original house occupied by Sir William Richardson in the mid-18th century. The house was called after Elizabeth Doughty who lived there from about 1786. She was a devout Roman Catholic and built the church of St Elizabeth in the Vineyard. She died in 1826. But Doughty House owes its fame to Sir Francis Cook who acquired it in 1849. Sir Francis built up the finest collection of Old Master paintings

in England which became renowned as the Cook Collection. He began this collection around 1860 and it contained some of the best-known works of Filippo Lippi, Dürer, Holbein, Rembrandt, Velasquez, Gainsborough and Turner. Sir Francis added a gallery to the house to hang his collection and at the same time 'Victorianised' the house itself. Over the years the Cook family added to the collection and it included sculptures and bronzes. The collection was finally sold in 1947 and is now scattered around the world in museums and private collections. The gallery has been empty since the collection was dispersed though there have been attempts to open it as a gallery for public exhibitions. An exhibition was held there to celebrate the Queen's Silver JUBILEE in 1977. The house is now turned into flats.

Doughty Street *WC1*. Built in 1792–1810 and named after the ground landlord, Henry Doughty, who inherited the land from his forebears, the Brownlows. William Brownlow, who began Brownlow Street, was the father of Elizabeth Doughty. Her son, George Brownlow Doughty, and his wife continued the development during the 1720s with the help of James Burgess (*see* GREAT JAMES STREET). At No. 14 lived Sydney Smith. A confirmed Londoner, he wrote, 'I have no relish for the country. It is a kind of healthy grave.' No. 48 is DICKENS HOUSE. J.W. Cuddy, the architect, lived at No. 21 in 1828–36; William Butterfield, the architect, at No. 24 in 1848–54; J.M. Levy, founder of the *Daily Telegraph*, at No. 57 in 1850–60. *The Spectator*, first published in 1828, the name having previously been used by the essayists, Addison and Steele, for their periodical which began in 1711, has offices at No. 56.

Douglas House *Lower Petersham Road, Richmond, Surrey*. Built in 1680 for Lord Carleton on the land of the old manor house of the Cole family who had given up their property in Petersham Park to Charles I when he was creating his new RICHMOND PARK. It is an attractive brick building with fine stables (1690) set at right angles on the east side and an unusual semi-circular front wall with wooden rails. The house has a steep sloping roof and a pediment in the centre of the front aspect. In 1725 it was inherited by Kitty Hyde, wife of Charles Douglas, 3rd Duke of Queensberry. The Duchess became famous as a patron of writers and in particular of John Gay whom she virtually adopted. He wrote many of his plays and poems here using her summer house as his study. Later in the century the house was enlarged by her nieces who continued in her tradition by having the Berry sisters and Walter Scott as friends.

In 1969 the house was bought by the Federal Republic of Germany for use as a German school. New buildings for 900 pupils are being erected in the grounds, but the original house and stables are intact and will be preserved.

Doulton and Co. *Pall Mall, SW1*. Founded in 1815 when John Doulton invested his life savings in a partnership in a small LAMBETH pothouse. At first the firm made utilitarian stonewares such as spirit flasks and ink bottles. Its range of products widened in the 1830s to include architectural terracotta and garden wares. John's son, Henry, entered the firm in 1835. It was, however, the manufacture of drainpipes during the sanitary revolution of the 1840s that assured the company's financial success and enabled it to venture into art pottery in the 1860s. Talented students from the local Lambeth School of Art were employed – in particular George Tinworth, who specialised in monumental religious panels, and the Barlow sisters, Hannah and Florence, whose work was usually decorated with animals and birds. Robert Wallace Martin and his brothers, Charles, Walter and Edwin, were also employed by the firm for a short time before setting up their own studio pottery. By 1890, over 300 people, most of them women, were producing art pottery in LAMBETH. In 1877, the company acquired its first factory in Stoke-on-Trent – today it manufactures tableware and figurines – and by the time the LAMBETH factory was closed in 1956, the firm's centre of gravity had shifted to the Midlands. Doulton took over Minton china in 1968 and Webb Corbett glass in 1969. In 1972 the company became part of S. Pearson and Son Ltd. The name Doulton was retained.

Douro Place *W8.* Built in 1846 and named after the Duke of Wellington who had been created Baron Douro after his crossing of the Douro River in 1809. He had been Commander-in-Chief of the Army since 1827. Samuel Palmer, the artist, lived at No. 6 in 1851–61.

Dove *19 Upper Mall, Hammersmith, W6.* One of the most famous of London's riverside inns. The building, which dates back to the 17th century, was opened as the Dove Coffee House in 1796. It has many literary associations: William Morris lived next door; A.P. Herbert used it as a model for the Pigeons in his novel *The Water Gypsies*; James Thomson wrote 'Rule Britannia' here. In 1860 an artist painted two doves on the sign instead of one, which resulted in it being known, erroneously, as the Doves until a new sign was made in1948 and the original name restored. It is said that Charles II and Nell Gwynne drank here. The verandah gives an excellent view of the UNIVERSITY BOAT RACE.

Dover House *Whitehall, SW1.* Designed by James Paine for Sir Matthew Featherstonehaugh and built in 1754–8 on the tilt yard of WHITEHALL PALACE. It was sold in 1787 to Frederick, Duke of York and Albany, younger brother of the Prince Regent. Henry Holland added the circular entrance hall and portico for him. In 1792 the Duke exchanged the house for Lord Melbourne's mansion in PICCADILLY (*see* ALBANY). After Melbourne's death in 1828 it was sold in 1830 to George James Welbore Agar-Ellis, later Baron Dover. It was taken over by the government for offices in 1885. It suffered bomb damage in the 2nd World War, but the restoration was completed in 1955. It is now the Scottish Office.

Dover Street *W1.* Extends from PICCADILLY to HAY HILL and takes its name from Henry Jermyn, Baron Dover, one of Sir Thomas Bond's partners in 1684 in the development of Albemarle Ground (*see* ALBEMARLE STREET). The Duke of Albemarle public house, at the corner of STAFFORD STREET, possesses a date tablet 1696, but the building is very much altered. Inside is a STAFFORD STREET sign of 1686. Nos 25, 26 and 27, on the east side, are a group of large mid-Georgian houses; but by far the best house is No. 37,

built as his town residence by Edmund Keene, Bishop of Ely, in 1772, to designs by Sir Robert Taylor. Its three-bay stone-faced front is a superb example of the purest Palladianism, and despite considerable alteration for the Albemarle Club in 1909, the interior still contains several fine features. Famous residents (sometimes only for very short periods) in Dover Street include John Evelyn, the diarist; Alexander Pope; Samuel Whitbread, the brewer and politician; the architect, John Nash, and Frederic Chopin. Like ALBEMARLE STREET, Dover Street gradually lost its residential character in the 19th century, and BROWN'S HOTEL occupies several houses on the east side. Most of the buildings here are mid- or late 19th-century in date, or of much more recent origin, and at street level high quality shops predominate. Longman and Strongi' th'arm, the jewellers, are at No. 13 and the tailors, Kilgour, French and Stanbury, and Hawes and Curtis, at Nos 33A and 43 respectively. The ARTS CLUB is at No. 40. The sculpture, *Horse and Rider*, at the PICCADILLY end is by Elizabeth Frink (1975).

Dowgate Hill *EC4.* Named after a watergate close to where the WALBROOK entered the THAMES. In the 12th and 13th centuries the usual form of the name was Dunegate or Douuegate. Stow, evidently mistaking the second 'u' for an 'n', said that it was so called because 'of the sodaine descending or going down of that way from St John's Church upon Walbrooke unto the river of Thames'. The name may, in fact, be derived from the Old English name Duua. The TALLOW CHANDLERS' HALL is at No. 4, the SKINNERS' HALL at No.8½, the DYERS' HALL at No. 10.

Down Street *W1.* Extends from PICCADILLY to HERTFORD STREET. It was developed in the 1720s by John Downes, a bricklayer. It is mostly lined with late Victorian red brick houses (now divided into flats). On the west side is CHRIST CHURCH; and, near the corner of PICCADILLY, the red-tiled front of the original HYDE PARK CORNER tube station still survives.

Downe *Kent.* A rural village within 12 miles of CHARING CROSS. The earliest reference to it is in about 1100. A 1287 deed dealing with the transfer of local land was witnessed by John de la Dune, a member of a leading family in the area until the early 15th century. According to a deed of 1547, land at Downe had earlier been owned by Thomas Cromwell, Henry VIII's minister. The first church is believed to have been built in 1291. For the poll tax in the year 1377 the population of Downe was estimated at 167 excluding children under 14 years of age. In 1831 the total population was still only 340. Jacob Verzelini, who was born in Venice in 1522 and came to England in 1571, was granted a royal patent to produce drinking glasses. He amassed a large fortune, bought land at Downe and lived at Downe Court until he died in 1607. In Downe church there is a brass commemorating him, his wife and children. Charles Darwin moved into Down House (so spelled) in 1842 and it was here that he thought and worked for 40 years. He seldom left the village and his most important books were written here. He died at Downe in 1882. Nearby lived his great friends, the Lubbocks. Sir John William Lubbock, a banker, bought High Elms farm in 1808. His son, also Sir John William Lubbock, had the High Elms mansion built in 1842. This house was destroyed by fire in

1967. Other distinguished residents include Sir Arthur Keith, the anthropologist, and Sir Oliver Lodge, the physicist and psychical researcher. Downe is now part of the London Borough of BROMLEY.

Downham *see* SOUTHEND.

Downing Street *SW1.* The earliest building known to have stood on the site was a brewhouse called the Axe which belonged to the Abbey of Abingdon. By the middle of the 16th century it was no longer used. In 1581 Elizabeth I leased the property to Thomas Knyvet, Keeper of WHITEHALL PALACE. After the death of his widow, the property came into the possession of her niece, Elizabeth Hampden, mother of John and aunt of Oliver Cromwell. Soon afterwards the Crown's interest in the property was acquired by Sir George Downing, Member of Parliament for Carlisle and later for Morpeth, who was for many years Resident at The Hague. In about 1680 Downing built a cul-de-sac of plain brick terraced houses. Strype described the street in 1720 as 'a pretty open place especially at the upper end where are four or five very large and well built houses fit for persons of honour and quality; each house having a pleasant prospect into St James' Park with a tarras walk.' James Boswell took lodgings in the street in 1762, and in 1774 Tobias Smollett tried to establish a surgeon's practice here. In 1868 the south side of the street was replaced by Scott's GOVERNMENT OFFICES. Of the original houses only Nos 10, 11 and 12 remain. The eastern part of No. 10 was acquired by the Crown in 1732. George II offered it as a personal gift to Sir Robert Walpole but he would only accept it for his office as First Lord of the Treasury. Since that date it has been the official residence of the Prime Minister although many early Prime Ministers did not live here, preferring to remain in their own grander town houses and letting No. 10 to relatives or junior ministers. It was altered internally by William Kent in 1732–5. The western part of the building was acquired by the Crown in 1763. Interior alterations were carried out by Sir John Soane in 1825. In the late 1950s and early 1960s expensive alterations were made to No. 10 by Raymond Erith. In the foundations remnants of Roman pottery, of a Saxon wooden hut and of WHITEHALL PALACE were found. The western part of No. 11 was bought by the Crown in 1805 for use as the Home Secretary's office but from the beginning it has been used by the Chancellor of the Exchequer. The eastern part was acquired in 1824. No. 12 was bought by the Crown for the Judge Advocate General's official residence in 1803. It is now the Party Whips' office.

Downshire Hill *Hampstead, NW3.* Although the top end of Downshire Hill is now occupied by modern and official buildings, much of the rest consists of charming Regency villas. A large part of the area was developed early in the 19th century by William Woods, who also probably designed the delightful ST JOHN'S church which stands at the junction with Keats Grove. The road is called after the Marquess of Downshire, whose family name happened to be Hill. Before she moved to Wentworth Place (*see* KEATS'S HOUSE), Fanny Brawne lived in Elm House, which then stood on the corner with ROSSLYN HILL, and D.G. Rossetti and his new wife, Elizabeth Siddall, stayed briefly in 1860 in Spring Cottage, which was where the flats, Hampstead Hill Mansions, stand now. Well-known residents of Downshire Hill include Edwin Muir, Gordon Craig, Hilda Carline (first wife of Stanley Spencer) and Sir Roland Penrose. At the Freemasons' Arms, at the bottom of the Hill, is to be found the last remaining Pell Mell court in England (*see* PALL MALL). The house at No. 49A is by Michael Hopkins (1977).

Downshire Hill, Hampstead, in about 1842. To the right is St John's, built as a proprietary chapel.

*Labourers deepening the sewers in Fleet Street, east of
Temple Bar, in 1845.*

Drains and Sewers Until the METROPOLITAN
BOARD OF WORKS (precursor of the LONDON COUNTY
COUNCIL of 1888 and the GREATER LONDON COUNCIL
of 1965) was given the primary duty in 1845 of creating
a properly planned system, London's drainage had
always been rudimentary, chaotic and a chronic danger to health. With the enormous expansion of the
metropolis during the Victorian era, and the recurring
outbreaks of CHOLERA, radical reform became imperative. Before the GREAT FIRE rubbish and excrement lay rotting and stinking in the gullies running
down the middle of the cobbled streets from where it
was occasionally washed away by heavy rainfalls into
ditches, streams and eventually the river. Cesspits
were dug everywhere under the houses and now and
then their contents and those of earth closets would be
carted away to open public laystalls as so-called night-
soil, and this could be carted away again to the market
gardens and fields as manure. Although the water-
closet had been invented by Sir John Harington as far
back as 1596, it could not be generally used until
adequate drains and public water supplies became
available. That the tributaries were open sewers in
medieval times is confirmed in a petition to Parliament
in 1290 by the WHITEFRIARS who declared that the
putrid exhalations from the FLEET overcame the aroma
of their incense and had caused the deaths of several
brethren. Until it was covered over and used as a sewer
the FLEET RIVER was always a 'stinking ditch'. In 1427
came the first of a series of Acts appointing local Commissions of Sewers, but they were mainly concerned
with the drainage of surface water and the prevention
of flooding. In 1531 an Act was passed that remained
statutory until 1848. But the laxity of the Commissioners was notorious, and as late as the mid-19th
century the CITY possessed only some 15 miles of
sewers. Most of London stood above an underground
town of excavated cesspits and many of the parish
sewers were stagnant cesspools. The Metropolitan Improvements of Nash's time laid some useful sewers
below the streets, and Nash himself built a fine one
which still serves below REGENT STREET. Yet these did
little to improve the general situation. Such sewers, in

any case, were still mostly designed to carry away rain
water, and the discharge of excrement or garbage into
them was, indeed, a legal offence – often ignored with
impunity – until well into the 19th century. The
general unconcern about the redolence of old London
is evoked by Pepys in his *Diary* where he records how
his wife stooped in the street 'to do her business', and
another entry reads, 'Going down into my cellar . . . I
put my foot on a great heap of finds . . . by which I find
that Mr Turner's house of office is full and comes into
my cellar, which doth trouble me.' In the reconstruction of the CITY after the GREAT FIRE, the Rebuilding
Act of 1667 gave wide powers of altering, enlarging
and cleaning the CITY sewers, but this lapsed when the
rebuilding was complete. The Metropolis General
Paving Act of 1817 provided for the cleansing of drains
and cesspits, but ten years later the WESTMINSTER
Commission of Sewers stated that the care of road
drainage was the only matter in which the public was
concerned, the rest being a concern of property
owners. Then the Metropolitan Buildings Act of 1844
made mandatory the connecting of all drains to sewers
in new buildings. The census of 1841 had revealed that
over 270,000 houses stood in the metropolis, most of
which had a cesspit below. In poor districts these
would often overflow through the floor boards into the
rooms above. In an attempt to rectify this hideous
situation the Metropolitan Commission of Sewers was
formed in 1847 to amalgamate the eight separate local
bodies nominally responsible for London's drainage.
It decreed that all cesspits must be abolished and so
some 200,000 cesspits suddenly went out of use. The
effect was disastrous, for now all the main sewers and
underground streams discharged their new contents
into the THAMES which was compelled to accept the
ordure of three million human beings. The river
became a huge open sewer. In 1800 salmon had still
been swimming up to London and beyond, but by
mid-century – by which time the population had
doubled – no fish of any kind could survive in the river
and even the SWANS had deserted it.

Most of the 369 sewers emptied either into the river
itself or on to the foreshore only at low tide, and as the
tide rose the outlets became closed and the sewage was
dammed back and became stagnant; while the sludge
carried down stream was regurgitated with the next
incoming tide. At one point, indeed, sewage was
flushed into the river opposite a main intake of London's water supply. In the hot, dry summer of 1858 the
climax arrived in what came to be called the GREAT
STINK when the windows of the HOUSES OF PARLIA-
MENT had to be draped with curtains soaked in
chloride of lime to mitigate the disgusting smell. Tons
of chalk lime, chloride of lime and carbolic acid were
tipped into the river with little effect, and Disraeli
described the noble THAMES as 'a Stygian pool reeking
with ineffable and unbearable horror'.

The worst effect of this improper and *ad hoc*
drainage, however, was not the stink but the appalling
CHOLERA epidemics that smote London for three
decades, most of which occurred in the poorer
districts. It was then thought that Asiatic cholera was
caused by the inhaling of noxious vapours, but then Dr
John Snow proved his theory that cholera was due to
the contamination of drinking water. Not until 1883,
however, was the microbe of cholera isolated by
Robert Koch. But by the year of the GREAT STINK
radical improvements were imminent; for in 1858 a

237

Bill for the purification of the THAMES was passed and the following year Joseph Bazalgette began his gigantic works for providing the whole of London, both north and south of the river, with a properly planned main drainage system. That object had for years been advocated by Sir Edwin Chadwick of the General Board of Health, a body that was closed down in 1854. To his single discredit, Chadwick had supported the scheme for flushing all sewers into the THAMES, but he had pointed out that, whatever was done, a full, large-scale survey of London's levels was the first need. That was begun in 1848 and was the origin of the Ordnance Survey. On its valuable contour maps Bazalgette was able to prepare his huge conception.

One of Chadwick's admirable concerns was to save London's sewage for manure, an old concept of converting filth to tilth that had been practised and preached for centuries. Many large schemes for draining London had been proposed. One was by John ('Mad') Martin, painter and planner, who in 1832 proposed saving manure by draining London's sewers into large reservoirs along the river banks from which it could be distributed by canals, running below arcaded quays, to the countryside. It was an imaginative scheme which, in principle, was not unlike that which Bazalgette was to realise, a principle which the great builder, Thomas Cubitt, who constructed excellent drains for his speculative housing schemes, had already advised in 1843. Like Chadwick, Bazalgette never received the credit he deserves, although he was eventually knighted and has his modest monument (see STATUES) on the EMBANKMENT beside HUNGERFORD RAILWAY BRIDGE. Son of a Royal Naval Commander of French extraction, he joined the staff of the Metropolitan Commission of Sewers on its formation and in 1845 was appointed Chief Engineer to the new Board of Works. He at once began preparing his grand drainage scheme for London. Although the Prince of Wales declared part of it open in 1865, the whole was not completed until 1875. Its effect on the health of Londoners was dramatic: the CHOLERA epidemics were over for good. The scheme consists of a network of sewers at three levels, on both sides of the river, running down to the lowest level of outfall sewers that run eastwards to reservoirs some 26 miles below LONDON BRIDGE – on the north at Beckton just west of BARKING Creek, and on the south at Crossness to the north of the ERITH marshes. Through the outfalls both sewage and surface water are discharged except during excessive rainfalls when the surface water can be run straight into the river. The high- and middle-level sewers discharge by gravitation, while the low-level ones are aided by pumps built at strategic points. At first the outfalls were discharged straight into the river and the sludge was spewed back into London by the tides, but in 1887 the decision was taken to precipitate the sewage chemically, allowing only the effluent to run into the river, the sludge being removed in special ships for discharge into the sea in the Black Deep beyond the Nore. When finished, Bazalgette's scheme consisted of 1,300 miles of sewers, mostly built of stock bricks, 82 miles of which were main intercepting sewers. At DEPTFORD, STRATFORD, PIMLICO and Crossness rose the noble pumping stations of romantic design and masterly engineering which we have come to admire.

Another of Bazalgette's achievements was the building of the great granite ALBERT, VICTORIA and CHELSEA EMBANKMENTS, and he incorporated a length of the northern low-level sewer in the CHELSEA and VICTORIA EMBANKMENTS. London's drainage has been increased and improved greatly, of course, as London has grown, but Bazalgette's works remain at its core. In 1879, after severe flooding, some 12 miles of storm relief sewers were built, and between 1900 and 1914 and again between 1919 and 1935 the LONDON COUNTY COUNCIL made many improvements. In 1936 the old MIDDLESEX County Council began to centralise its 28 small sewage works into one pioneering plant for treating sludge with bacteria, and in 1964 a similar plant was built at Crossness; in 1975 the Beckton plant was extended and improved as the largest of its kind in Europe. In 1974 the Thames Water Authority replaced the GREATER LONDON COUNCIL and local authorities in controlling London's 800 miles of main drainage when it also assumed control of the entire water cycle of the 5,000 square miles of the THAMES basin and catchment area. London's complex sewage system now treats over 2,700 million litres a day at 14 treatment works. The purified effluent flows into the THAMES and its tributaries and the sludge is rendered inoffensive, two-thirds being carried as before by ships 50 miles out to sea and the rest being used as a soil conditioner. A by-product is methane gas which is used to power much of the machinery at the sewage works. The river grows cleaner year by year, and in 1974 the first salmon on the river for 150 years was found trapped in the filters of the West Thurrock Power Station.

Drapers' Company see CITY LIVERY COMPANIES.

Drapers' Gardens *EC2*. Originally the gardens attached to DRAPERS' HALL. In 1541 the DRAPERS' COMPANY took over Thomas Cromwell's house in THROGMORTON STREET. The garden then stretched to LONDON WALL. In 1551 the gardener complained that the herbs were being destroyed by the drying and bleaching of clothes there. An order was consequently made the following year that no one except past and present wardens was to dry linen or woollen clothes in the garden and that strangers were not to play bowls or take the herbs and fruit. After the GREAT FIRE the garden was opened to the general public; it was previously open only to those prepared to pay £3 a year for the privilege. Ned Ward in *The London Spy* says it was a fashionable promenade an hour before dinner time. Between about 1873 and 1886 Drapers' Gardens and THROGMORTON AVENUE were laid out on the site.

Drapers' Hall *Throgmorton Street, EC2*. The first Hall, mentioned in 1425, stood in ST SWITHIN'S LANE and was alleged to have belonged to Henry Fitzailwin, first Mayor of London. The present site, with a spacious mansion, was purchased from Henry VIII to whom it had passed on the attainder of Thomas Cromwell in 1543. From 1660 it was used by General Monk as a headquarters. The mansion was destroyed in the GREAT FIRE and rebuilt by Edward Jarman in 1667. After further damage by fire in 1772, the front was rebuilt by the Adam brothers. Herbert Williams remodelled the Hall in 1868–70, and more alterations were carried out in 1898. The Court Dining Room, with its fine plaster ceiling, and the Clerks' Office, form the only portion which survived the fire of 1772. The garden, with mulberry trees, is a remnant of the original Drapers' Gardens which once stretched to LONDON WALL. For the Company *see* CITY LIVERY COMPANIES.

Draycott Avenue *SW3*. Once the lane which bordered CHELSEA COMMON, it was widened and developed in the mid-19th century. In 1820 an old house on the north side, Blacklands House, was leased by Sir Francis Shuckburgh who, five years later, married Anne-Maria Draycott, whose father owned Henry Holland's PAVILION (now the site of CADOGAN SQUARE). Lady Shuckburgh died in 1846 shortly before the development of the area began.

Draycott Place *SW3*. A street of redbrick houses between DRAYCOTT AVENUE and CADOGAN GARDENS built in about 1891. Admiral of the Fleet Earl Jellicoe lived at No. 25 in 1906–8.

Dreadnought Seamen's Hospital *Greenwich, SE10*. Erected in 1763 to the designs of James Stuart. The Earl of Sandwich was much concerned with the design and structure. It was damaged by fire at the beginning of the 19th century and rebuilt in 1812. It was taken over by the National Health Service in 1948. There are 130 beds for acute cases, mostly merchant seamen, but the hospital occasionally admits local landsmen.

Drummond's Bank *Charing Cross, SW1*. Andrew Drummond, a goldsmith, began banking at the Golden Eagle on the east side of CHARING CROSS in 1717. His customers originally included many of the aristocratic Scottish families living in the neighbourhood. When the bank prospered, Drummond gave up his goldsmith's business in 1737; he moved the bank to its present site on the west side of CHARING CROSS in 1760. After Drummond's death in 1769 his family continued as sole proprietors, and their customers included George III, Josiah Wedgwood, James Smithson and James Whistler. Drummond's Bank, rebuilt in 1877–9, was acquired by the Royal Bank of Scotland in 1924 and is now the Royal Bank's Drummond's Branch.

Drury Lane *WC2*. An ancient highway, formerly known as Via de Aldwych (*see* ALDWYCH), which takes its present name from Sir Thomas Drury who built a house here in the reign of Queen Elizabeth I. John Donne had apartments in this house after his secret marriage to Anne More. In the 16th and 17th centuries, it was a fashionable street. Residents included both the Marquess of Argyll and the Earl of Stirling in 1634–7, Oliver Cromwell in 1646, the Earl of Anglesey in 1669–86, and the Earls of Clare and Craven in 1683. Nell Gwynne had lodgings here. Pepys saw her standing at her door in 1667 in her smock sleeves and bodice. Lavinia Fenton, afterwards Duchess of Bolton and the original Polly Peachum in the *Beggar's Opera*, lived in a coffee house here. In the 18th century, as Gay, Pope and Goldsmith all testified, however, it became a notoriously rowdy locality, notable for its brawls and drunkenness. Plate 3 of Hogarth's *The Harlot's Progress* is set in Drury Lane. Gin shops and prostitutes abounded here. Gay wrote:

O may thy virtue guard thee through the roads
Of Drury's mazy courts and dark abodes!

By the end of the 19th century the area was one of the worst slums in London. Most of these were cleared when KINGSWAY and ALDWYCH were constructed. The PEABODY BUILDINGS constructed to house 1,470 people are at Nos 124–140 on the site of the COCKPIT THEATRE. The New London Theatre Centre is on the east side. The entrance to the THEATRE ROYAL DRURY LANE is in CATHERINE STREET. Brodie and Middleton Ltd, the scenic colourmen, have been a family business since the 1840s. The Drury Lane Hotel at No. 10 (130 bedrooms) was built in 1977. There are 70 original cartoons by Osbert Lancaster in the bar. There has been a public house on the site of the White Hart at No. 191 since the 15th century.

Duchess Street *W1*. Built in the 1770s on the PORTLAND ESTATE and named after Margaret Harley, Duchess of Portland, wife of the ground landlord. One of the houses had been designed by Robert Adam for his friend, Major-General Clerk. It was bought in 1799 by Thomas Hope who redesigned and refurnished it in neo-classical style. On the first floor he arranged his art collections. He and his wife lived above. From 1804 the public were admitted on application 'signed by some persons of known character and taste'. Visitors passed through the Sculpture Gallery designed as a Greek Temple, three Vase Rooms containing over 500 vases, the Indian Room, the Flaxman Room, the Egyptian Room, the Dining Room and the Lararium which contained Egyptian, Hindu and Chinese idols and curiosities. In 1819 an art gallery was added by Hope to house his collection of Dutch and Flemish paintings. On his death in 1831 he left the mansion to his son, Henry. It was sold for demolition in 1851. On the south side of the street are the stable fronts of CHANDOS HOUSE.

Duchess Theatre *Catherine Street, WC2*. A Tudoresque theatre designed in 1929 by Ewen Barr. It opened under the management of Jack de Leon and his sister, Delia. In 1930 *The Intimate Revue* set a record for the London stage by not lasting for even a single performance. In 1933 J.B. Priestley's comedy, *Laburnum Grove*, had 335 performances. In 1934–6 Priestley was associated with the management and his plays *Eden End* (1934) and *Cornelius* (1935) were produced. His wife, Mary Wyndham Lewis, redecorated the theatre. In 1935 Emlyn Williams's thriller *Night Must Fall* ran for a year. Until its closure in 1939 the theatre's main success was Eliot's *Murder in the Cathedral*.

Duchy of Cornwall A private estate vested in the eldest son of the sovereign, or, if there is no son, dormant in the Crown. It covers an area of nearly 130,000 acres, mostly in the West Country, though it also has property in London including a residential estate in KENNINGTON and the OVAL CRICKET GROUND. The Duchy of Cornwall office is at 10 BUCKINGHAM GATE, SW1.

Duchy of Lancaster A collection of estates extending to about 52,000 acres spread all over England which were acquired by the Crown in the Middle Ages and which constitute a private property, not part of the CROWN ESTATE. Part of the Duchy's property is in London, in the STRAND, where the Duke of Lancaster is still a landlord (*see* SAVOY PALACE), and in the CITY.

It is still doubtful, in fact, if the reigning monarch is Duke of Lancaster. King Edward VII, whose mother, Queen Victoria, had been content to travel incognito as the Countess of Lancaster, used the title of Duke when in Paris, though the then Chancellor of the Duchy of Lancaster thought that he had no right to it. In September 1905 a controversy arose in the pages of the *Westminster Gazette* on the subject, and the Chancellor prepared a letter, a copy of which he sent to the King's Private Secretary. This letter put forward the view that the title properly belonged to the descendants of John of Gaunt and did not go with the Duchy whose lands were vested in the sovereign. On this letter the King scrawled the comment: 'I have always imagined that I was Duke of Lancaster, as the Sovereign of England always is. Queen Victoria considered herself so, just as the heir to the throne is Duke of Cornwall, and I have no wish to give up my rights.' The letter was suppressed. The controversy was renewed in the next reign when King George V asked for his health to be drunk in Lancashire as Duke of Lancaster. Charles Hobhouse, the then Chancellor of the Duchy, consulted the Duchy's attorney who expressed the view that it was 'extremely unlikely' that His Majesty was also Duke of Lancaster. Hobhouse reported this opinion to the King who gave him 'a very cold bow indeed' the next time he saw him. The Duchy of Lancaster Office is in WHITEHALL, SW1.

Ducksfoot Lane *EC4*. Corruption of Duke's Foot Lane. It once led to the Duke of Suffolk's house (*see* SUFFOLK LANE).

Dufour's Place *W1*. Built 1719–37 and originally known as Dufour's Court after Paul Dufour, a gentleman of ST JAMES'S, who agreed to spend at least £800 within two years in building good, sound houses on pieces of ground leased to him by William Pulteney. Nos 1–10, though much altered, date from this period.

Duke of York Column *Waterloo Place, SW1*. A memorial to Frederick, second son of George III. It is 124 ft from base to head, of a sufficient height, so it was suggested, to keep the Duke – whose debts amounted to £2,000,000 at his death – out of the way of his creditors. Its cost (about £25,000) was met largely by stopping one day's pay from every soldier in the Army, in which, hitherto, the Duke – an admirable Commander-in-Chief for all his faults – had been a popular figure. The column, designed by Benjamin Wyatt, is of the Tuscan order. Above its capital there are a square balcony, a drum and a dome. The bronze statue of the Duke surmounting all is by Sir Richard Westmacott (1834). After lengthy discussions about which way the statue should face, it was decided that it should look towards the WAR OFFICE in WHITEHALL.

Duke of York Steps *Waterloo Place, SW1*. A fine flight of public steps leading down into THE MALL from WATERLOO PLACE, built soon after Nash's CARLTON HOUSE TERRACE whose front it breaks. The DUKE OF YORK COLUMN towers over it.

Duke of York Street *SW1*. Probably named in honour of James, Duke of York, who succeeded his brother, Charles II, as James II in 1685. It was built

The Duke of York's Column was erected in Waterloo Place in the 1830s as a memorial to King George IV's brother.

in the 1680s on ground granted to the Earl of St Albans (*see* JERMYN STREET). None of the original houses remains. The late Victorian Red Lion public house occupies a site where a tavern of that name has stood since at least 1788. Its interior, embellished with well preserved mahogany and bevelled glass, has been described in *The Architectural Review* as 'a perfect example . . . of the small Victorian Gin Palace at its best'. One of WHEELER's restaurants is on several floors of a building on the corner of Apple Tree Yard. Cecil and Company, the old-established fishmongers, whose shop used appropriately to be opposite at No. 1, are now at No. 23 ROMILLY STREET.

Duke of York's Headquarters *King's Road, SW3*. Consists of a number of buildings of which the main one, and by far the oldest, was designed by John Sanders in 1801 for the Duke of York's school for soldiers' orphans. The girls were moved away to Southampton 12 years later and the boys to Dover in 1909. The council of the Territorial Auxiliary Volunteer Reserve Association, the regimental headquarters of the Royal Corps of Signals, the main office of the Army Benevolent Fund and territorial, infantry and parachute subunits are located here.

Duke of York's Theatre *St Martin's Lane, WC2*. (Trafalgar Square Theatre 1892–4, Trafalgar Theatre 1895). Designed by Walter Emden in 1892 for

Frank Wyatt and his wife, Violet Melnotte. It was the first theatre to be built in ST MARTIN'S LANE. In 1893 the first performance in England of Ibsen's *The Master Builder* was given here. In 1896 *The Gay Parisienne*, a musical comedy with Ada Reeve, ran for 369 performances. From 1897 to 1915 the theatre was managed by the American Charles Frohman who introduced many leading American actors and actresses to London including Maxine Elliott and her husband, Nat Goodwin. Among his successful productions were Barrie's *Admirable Crichton* (1902), *Peter Pan* (1904) which was revived every Christmas until 1914, *What Every Woman Knows* (1908) and Maugham's *Land of Promise* (1914). In 1910 Frohman unsuccessfully tried to introduce the repertory system to the London theatre with Shaw's *Misalliance*, Galsworthy's *Justice*, Granville Barker's *The Madras House* and other plays. In 1916 *Daddy Long-Legs*, a comedy by Jean Webster, ran for 514 performances. During 1923–8 Violet Melnotte managed the theatre. Her first success was the revue *London Calling*, mostly written by Noël Coward. The seating capacity is 641.

Duke Street *SW1*. Laid out on land granted to the Earl of St Albans (*see* JERMYN STREET), building was completed in the 1680s and the street presumably named after Charles II's brother, James, Duke of York, who became James II in 1685. None of the original houses remains. The Chequers at No. 16 occupies a site where a public house has stood since at least 1732. The street is now a centre of fine art dealers and galleries. The building at Nos 1 and 2 by Vincent Harris and T.A. Moodie is an architectural curiosity of 1900–12. Alfred Dunhill, the tobacconists at No. 30, were established in 1907. Their modern headquarters, which incorporates the original premises, contains a pipe and lighter museum.

Duke Street *Mayfair, W1*. Extends from GROSVENOR SQUARE northward across OXFORD STREET to MANCHESTER SQUARE. The part south of OXFORD STREET is on the GROSVENOR ESTATE. Building began here in the 1720s, the houses being inhabited mainly by tradesmen. All this part of Duke Street was rebuilt, chiefly with ranges of shops with flats above, during 1886–96. The two most notable buildings are Alfred Waterhouse's King's Weigh House Church (now the cathedral of the Ukrainian Catholic Church) which was completed in 1891, and C. Stanley Peach's imposing electricity sub-station of 1903–5. A. Nelson and Co., the homeopathic chemists at No. 73, were established in RYDER STREET in 1860 by Ernest Louis Ambrecht whose son, Nelson Ambrecht, changed his name to A. Nelson. The firm moved to Duke Street in 1890.

Duke's Place *EC3*. Once the site of HOLY TRINITY PRIORY, ALDGATE. The priory was dissolved in 1531 and the buildings granted to Sir Thomas Audley. After the stone from the church and steeple had been sold off in cartloads for paving, Audley built himself a mansion which later came into the possession of Thomas Howard, Duke of Norfolk, on his marriage to Audley's daughter, Margaret. Norfolk was beheaded in 1572 and his son, the Earl of Suffolk, sold the house to the CITY OF LONDON. In 1622 the parochial church of St James, Duke's Place was built. Jews were allowed by Cromwell to settle here in 1650 and in 1692 German

and Polish Jews built the Great Synagogue. The SIR JOHN CASS FOUNDATION SCHOOL was built to the design of A.W. Cooksey in 1910.

Belair, one of several fine country houses built at the end of the 18th century in Dulwich.

Dulwich *SE21*. The ancient Manor of Dulwich was a tiny hamlet surrounded by woods and farmland and bordered on its southern edge by the Great North Wood (*see* UPPER NORWOOD). In AD 967, Edgar the Peaceful granted Dilwihs to one of his thanes, but it is not mentioned in *Domesday Book*. Dilewic was among lands given to BERMONDSEY ABBEY by Henry I in 1127 and, although the Manor was subsequently leased, it remained the property of the monks until the DISSOLUTION OF THE MONASTERIES in 1538. Dilwysshe, Dylways and Dullag were other medieval spellings of the name, but Dilewysshe was the most common and is supposed to have been derived from the Old English *dile-wisc*, meaning 'the meadow where the dill grew'. The Manor extended from Champion Hill (then Camberwell Hill) in the north to Vicar's Oak on Sydenham Hill, to the south, and old boundary stones still exist. Lordship Lane defined the eastern boundary between Dulwich and the Manor of Friern, and Croxted Road (then Crokestrete) was to the west. The inhabitants in the Middle Ages, numbering about 100 in 1333, were centred on what is now DULWICH VILLAGE. The Manor lacked a good road through it until well into the 19th century and life there was quiet and insular. Courts which were held regularly by the Abbots at Dulwich Court, and which continued until 1883, documented local disputes; and incidents of cattle straying, tree-felling, illegal brewing and neglect of property are noted frequently in the Court Rolls. Cases of assault were rare, though in 1334 William Hosewode was accused by Richard Rolf of carrying off 'Edith, his wife, together with one cow worth ten shillings, clothes, jewels, and other goods and chattels ...' In 1544, Henry VIII granted to Thomas Calton the Manor of 'Dulwyche' and 'the messuage of Hall Place ...' for £609 and an annual rental of £1 13s 9d. Hall Place, which stood until 1882 on the corner of Park Hall Road and South Croxted Road, may have been the Manor House. In 1605 Calton's grandson, Francis, finding himself in financial difficulties, sold the estate to Edward Alleyn (*see* DULWICH COLLEGE) for £5,000 ('£1,000 more than any other man would have given for it', in Alleyn's opinion.) However, his foundation in 1619 of the College of God's Gift at Dulwich (now DULWICH COLLEGE) and its endowment with his estate was to be the major influence in the future development of the area. In the 17th century, the Manor remained a quiet backwater, although Charles I appears to have made a number of visits to Dulwich Woods for hunting, and instructed that local people should 'forebeare to hunt, chase, molest or hurt the King's stagges'. Roundhead soldiers were less welcome visitors, when, in 1647, they were quartered the Old College and were said to have 'committed great havoc'. In 1665 the GREAT PLAGUE carried off 35 Dulwich victims, including the miller and his family. The grimmest incident in the Manor's history occurred in 1678, when a man who carried the celebrated Dulwich waters to London beat his 12-year-old son to death for falling asleep while at work. Dulwich Wells, located near the corner of Dulwich Common and Lordship Lane, became a fashionable spa in the 18th century. The Green Man Inn (on the site of the present Grove Tavern) provided entertainment for those who came to take the waters. It was later replaced by Dr Glennie's Academy where Byron was a pupil for two years. A number of wealthy and influential individuals began to build houses in Dulwich, although the College restricted leases to 21 years. BELAIR and Casino House, built by Richard Shaw (who defended Warren Hastings) and since demolished, were two mansions built at the end of the 18th century, and large houses were also built in and around the village (see DULWICH VILLAGE). Communications with London were still bad and highwaymen, smugglers and gipsies frequented Dulwich Woods. In 1802, Samuel Matthews, the so-called Dulwich Hermit, was murdered there. Grief-stricken at the death of his wife, he had camped out in a cave in the woods for several years and had been regarded as something of a local curiosity. His murderer was never found. In 1812 Mr Thomas Redman was appointed to provide a horse-patrol to protect travellers from footpads on the road from CAMBERWELL to Dulwich. The social life of the gentry then revolved around the expanding school and the Dulwich Club, a dining club formed in 1772. In the 19th century Dulwich became popular with outside visitors, attracted by the new DULWICH PICTURE GALLERY, its inns and its rural surroundings. In 1832 Arnold's *Magazine of the Fine Arts* claimed that a visit there 'forms one of the most delightful intellectual trips which the neighbourhood of the metropolis affords'; and George Eliot, during a visit in 1859, enjoyed the art gallery, but was more impressed by 'the chestnuts just on the verge of their flowering beauty, the bright leaves of the limes, the rich-yellow brown of the oaks, the meadows full of buttercups.' Acts of Parliament in 1805 and 1808 provided for the enclosure of DULWICH COMMON and extended the length of leases to 63 or 84 years and thus enabled the College to let building land to wealthy business and professional men. The arrival of the CRYSTAL PALACE in NORWOOD in 1854, followed by the railway to CRYSTAL PALACE in 1856, gave added impetus to development. In the 1850s, large estates of substantial villas grew up to the south of the estate and the population had also expanded to the north of the village. John Ruskin, who lived in HERNE HILL, bewailed 'the ghastly squalor of the once lovely fields of Dulwich' caused by the onslaught of visitors to the CRYSTAL PALACE. Sir Henry Bessemer, the inventor of the famous steel process, also lived in a large mansion on HERNE HILL. The College Governors, like many of the local gentry and bourgeoisie, were unenthusiastic about the arrival of the railways. The West End and Crystal Palace Line crossed a corner of College land, but the London, Chatham and Dover Railway met with resistance and the line was not in use until 1863. The Governors insisted that the railway bridges should be built in ornamental iron to the designs of the College architect (of the original eleven, two are left) and many of the existing bridges carry the initials of Alleyn's College. With the railways came the huge growth in housing for the middle and working classes and the population rose from 1,632 in 1851 to 10,247 in 1901. The farms and market gardens of East Dulwich became suburban streets and Victorian roads were built in West Dulwich and HERNE HILL. In 1868 a police station was built and several churches date from the second half of the 19th century, including St John's, Goose Green, St Stephen's, College Road, and St Barnabas, a church for the newly formed parish of Dulwich, built in 1894. The Alleyn Foundation now included three large schools, ALLEYN'S SCHOOL, JAMES ALLEN'S GIRLS' SCHOOL in East Dulwich and DULWICH COLLEGE. New estates have developed in Dulwich in recent years (see KINGSWOOD HOUSE), but due to the Estates Governors' policy of conservation the district has also retained large areas of green space, with woods, a golf course and allotments, DULWICH PARK, many attractive trees and numerous sports and playing fields.

Dulwich College *College Road, SE21*. In the reign of James I, Edward Alleyn, the actor who had made much money controlling licences as 'Master of the Royal Game of Bears, Bulls and Mastiff Dogs' and as part-owner of the baiting house at PARIS GARDEN, bought the manor of DULWICH for £5,000. Being childless, he decided to use it to endow an educational establishment for poor boys on the lines of institutions such as CHARTERHOUSE, WESTMINSTER SCHOOL and MERCHANT TAYLORS. He also made provision for 'Fellows' as at Eton and for 'Alms-people'. In 1613 he employed a bricklayer, John Benson, to build 'a chapell, a schole house and twelve almshouses'. The chapel was consecrated in 1616 and other buildings completed by 1618 were Old College, the lodgings for Master and Warden, a Drawing Room and Parlour. The east wing of these buildings provided accommodation for four fellows, ten scholars and six almsmen. The west wing had six alms-women on the ground floor and a long picture gallery and a library above. The Royal Patent for incorporation of the charity was granted on 21 June 1619. Alleyn spent much time at the school, probably died there in 1626 and was buried in the chapel. During the Civil War the fellows supported the Royalist cause by pawning the College silver; the Roundheads quartered troops on the College, and melted organ pipes and coffins for lead bullets. By the time of the Restoration the College buildings were dilapidated and income was low. Prosperity was restored in the 18th century, but revenue was spent on the wellbeing of the fellows and the reconstruction of buildings rather than on scholars. At the end of the century the College benefited greatly by a bequest of pictures and in 1811–14 Sir John Soane designed the present gallery for them (see DULWICH PICTURE GALLERY). Education resumed its importance in the 19th century and Charles Barry (later architect of the HOUSES OF PARLIAMENT) designed a small grammar school for day boys which was opened near the college in 1842. In 1857 a special Act of Parliament

Dulwich College was founded in the early 17th century. The new buildings by Charles Barry the Younger were opened in 1870.

dissolved the old foundation and was followed by a complete reorganisation giving paramount importance to education by the school which took the title of Alleyn's College of God's Gift at Dulwich. In the 1860s increased land values and railway construction on endowment lands provided funds for extensive building to the designs of Charles Barry the Younger. New buildings were opened by the Prince of Wales on 21 June 1870 and the whole foundation took the title of Dulwich College. But the evident wealth of the foundation had led to criticism in DULWICH and the London parishes associated with Alleyn's bequest. These asserted that it was being lavished on a privileged class instead of being devoted to the poor. After much discussion a new scheme was approved by Parliament in 1882. The governing body instituted by the 1857 act was replaced by two new boards, the Estates Governors and College Governors. The former were required to provide sites for a new ALLEYN'S SCHOOL which became separate from Dulwich College, and a new JAMES ALLEN'S GIRLS' SCHOOL. Thus three schools received sites and income from the bequest which also provided finance for the chapel and gallery at DULWICH. Money was also provided for the Central Foundation Schools in BISHOPGATE and FINSBURY and St Olave's and St Saviour's Grammar School, as well as the almshouses of Alleyn's bequest. The numbers of pupils at Dulwich College rose rapidly from 300 in 1870 to 680 in 1896 and 900 in 1918. There was much rebuilding after the 2nd World War. In 1981 numbers totalled 1,415 boys with a few girls admitted to the Upper Sixth. P. G. Wodehouse often fondly remembered his days at the school. In 1982 the preparatory school was badly damaged by fire.

Dulwich Common *SE21.*

This road passes through what was once the common land of the Manor of DULWICH, following the route of a medieval lane. Rocque's map of 1745 shows Dulwich Common to be about one and a quarter miles long. Edward Alleyn's windmill stood there until 1814, near the existing Mill Pond, and the miller lived in one of the attractive group of weatherboarded and brick cottages, known as Pond Cottages. Crossing the Common could be hazardous, due to its proximity to the Great North Wood (*see* UPPER NORWOOD). In 1800 two highway robberies occurred within an hour. Duels are also supposed to have been fought here. Local people grazed livestock on the Common; but in 1799 John Bowles complained of outsiders taking advantage of these rights. The 1805 'Act for Inclosing Lands in the

Manor of Dulwich' enabled the College to enter into the freehold of about 130 acres of land. Trees were planted on the Common in 1812 and legislation in 1808 to extend leases facilitated the letting of building plots. The Old Blew House and Oakfield are among the few houses built there in the 18th century, but a number of substantial villas, such as Glenlea and Elm Lawn, date from after the enclosure. The new DULWICH COLLEGE, completed in 1870, was built on 40 acres of the land.

Dulwich Hospital *East Dulwich Grove, SE22.*

Opened as an infirmary in 1887 under the local Board of Guardians, it was taken over by the LONDON COUNTY COUNCIL in 1930 and transferred to the National Health Service in 1948. In 1964 it was merged with KING'S COLLEGE HOSPITAL Group. There are 356 beds.

Dulwich Park *SE21.*

In medieval times DULWICH was a small hamlet surrounded by woods and farmland. Charles I hunted in the neighbourhood. One of his yeomen huntsmen-in-ordinary was empowered 'to take from any person or persons offending therein their dogges, hounds, gunnes, crossbowes or other engynes'. Duels were often fought here. In *Captain Blake*, a novel published in 1838, a character observes, 'Now I prefer for the Surrey side and there is not a prettier shooting-ground in Britain than the Dulwich meadows. I think I could mark off as sweet a sod there as ever a gentleman was stretched upon.'

In 1619 Edward Alleyn endowed the College of God's Gift with the manor of Dulwich (*see* DULWICH COLLEGE). In the 1880s the administration of the land was put in the hands of Estates Governors. In 1885 they presented 72 acres to the METROPOLITAN BOARD OF WORKS for public use. The park was opened in 1890 by Lord Rosebery, the first Chairman of the LONDON COUNTY COUNCIL. The GREATER LONDON COUNCIL erected Barbara Hepworth's sculpture *Two Forms (Divided Circle)* in 1970. The park is well known for its azaleas, rhododendrons and rockery.

Dulwich Picture Gallery *College Road, SE21.*

England's oldest public picture gallery, it is owned and administered by Alleyn's College of God's Gift (*see* DULWICH COLLEGE). The nucleus of the collection was bequeathed by Edward Alleyn in 1626. It was greatly enlarged in 1811 when Sir Francis Bourgeois left 371 pictures to the College. Some of them had been collected by the art dealer, Noel Desenfans, for a national gallery in Warsaw which was never formed. Bourgeois also bequeathed £10,000 for the collection's maintenance and £2,000 to repair and beautify the west wing and gallery of the College. But the governors decided to build a new gallery financed partly by themselves and partly by Mrs Desenfans. This gallery was built in 1811–14 to the designs of Sir John Soane. It includes a mausoleum for Mr and Mrs Desenfans and Sir Francis Bourgeois which is probably based on an engraving of an Alexandrian catacomb, published in 1809. Until 1858 the gallery was only open to ticket-bearing members of the public on one day a week. After being bombed in 1944 the gallery and mausoleum were restored in 1947–53 by Arthur Davis and Edward Maufe. The collection includes works by Rembrandt, Cuyp, Van Dyck, Rubens, Poussin, Murillo and Gainsborough.

Dulwich Toll Gate *College Road, SE21.* The sole survivor of the London toll gates, the rest of which were abolished in 1864 (*see* TURNPIKES AND TOLL-BARS). It was set up in 1789 by John Morgan of PENGE who made up the road in 1787 to provide access to grazing leased from the College of God's Gift at Dulwich (*see* DULWICH COLLEGE). The College took over in 1809 and continues to charge tolls to maintain the private road. A board displays rates of 6d 'For every Motor Car, Motor Cycle or Motor Cycle Combination', 2½d 'For Sheep, Lambs or Hogs per score' and so on. Today's rates are 5p for a motor car, 30p for a lorry.

Dulwich Village *SE21.* The name given in 1913 to the main street of DULWICH, once known as the Highway or High Street. It was an ancient way through the medieval Manor and the original hamlet appears to have developed from north to south along it. It remained a tiny place until the 18th century, when Alleyn's College (*see* DULWICH COLLEGE) and the nearby spa at Dulwich Wells (*see* DULWICH) began to attract affluent visitors and residents. Rocque's map of 1762 shows the village extending from the junction of Red Post Hill and Village Way to a point along COLLEGE ROAD some distance beyond the Old College. A number of handsome buildings from this time still exist, including Lyndenhurst (1757) and Pond House (1739), both detached houses in Village Way, and Nos 103 and 105 (1759) and other Georgian houses on the east side of Dulwich Village. The Old Burial Ground, with its Sussex iron gates and railings, was a gift to the people of Dulwich from Edward Alleyn in 1616. Among those buried there were the local victims of the GREAT PLAGUE and Old Bridget, Queen of the Gipsies, in 1768 (*see* GIPSY HILL). When Acts of Parliament in 1805 and 1808 permitted the enclosure of common land and extended leases on the College Estate, the village expanded. The present broad grass verges are the remains of common land, known as the Manor Wastes. The pretty shops and cottages on the west side were built or rebuilt during the 19th century, although some of them have changed little since then. The Crown and the Greyhound (since replaced by the Crown and Greyhound) were popular inns, the latter being the meeting-place of the fashionable Dulwich Club to which Dickens was a frequent visitor. He chose Dulwich as the retirement place for Mr Pickwick, who 'was freqently seen contemplating the pictures in the Dulwich Gallery' and Pickwick Road replaced the Greyhound when it was demolished. As suburban London spread, the green spaces in the village filled out with shops, housing and schools, including the Old Grammar School (*see* ALLEYN'S SCHOOL) in 1842, Dulwich Hamlet in 1884 and Dulwich Infants' School. However, despite the addition of many 20th-century houses, the street retains its rural atmosphere.

Duncan Terrace *N1.* Built in 1768. Charles Lamb was living at No. 64 in 1823–7 when he was writing *Essays of Elia.*

Dunraven Street *W1.* Built in 1757 and first known as New Norfolk Street. Lord William Russell was murdered here by his valet in 1840. In 1940 it was renamed after Lord Dunraven, the politician and yachtsman, who had lived at No. 27 in 1895.

Dunster Court *EC3.* Marked on 17th- and early 18th-century maps as Dunstan's Court. The enormously rich alderman and Lord Mayor, William Beckford, had his counting-house here. The Court was severely damaged in the 2nd World War and the CLOTHWORKERS' HALL was destroyed. Their new neo-Georgian hall was built here to the designs of H. Austen Hall in 1955–8.

Durham House *Strand.* Built as a town house for the Bishop of Durham. Richard le Poor, a 13th-century Bishop, is the first one to have used it. In 1258 Simon de Montfort lived here. One day he offered Henry III temporary shelter from a storm but the King told him 'thunder and lightning I fear much, but by the head of God I fear thee more,' and carried on. In 1502 Catherine of Aragon lodged here before her marriage to Prince Arthur; and in 1516 and 1518 Wolsey lived here. Wolsey owned the house as Bishop of Durham, 1523–9, but only used it while YORK PLACE, WHITEHALL was being rebuilt. In 1529 it was allocated to Anne Boleyn and her father. Cranmer stayed with them so that he could study the question of the King's divorce. In 1536 Bishop Cuthbert Tunstall was forced by the King to exchange the house for COLDHARBOUR and it was given in 1550 to Princess Elizabeth. In 1553 John Dudley, Duke of Northumberland, lived here. The marriage of his son, Guildford, to Lady Jane Grey took place in the chapel. In 1558 Mary I gave Tunstall the house back but before his death the next year, having refused to take the Oath of Supremacy, he had to surrender it again to Elizabeth I, in whose reign Norden described it as 'stately and high, supported with lofty marble pillars. It standeth upon the Thames very pleasantly.' Queen Elizabeth let it to ambassadors and favourites: from 1559 to 1563 to De Quadra, the Spanish Ambassador; in 1566 to Robert Dudley, Earl of Leicester; in 1567–8 to Sir Henry Sidney; in 1572 to the Earl of Essex; and in 1583–1603 to Sir Walter Ralegh. A servant seeing Ralegh exhale tobacco smoke is said to have thrown a tankard of ale over him thinking he was on fire. In 1604 James I, disliking Ralegh, restored the house to the Bishop of Durham. Ralegh protested without effect that he had spent £2,000 on it and that even the poorest artificer was given some notice by his landlord. In 1604 part of the house was given to Robert Cecil, Earl of Salisbury, and incorporated in the gardens of SALISBURY HOUSE. In 1608–9 Cecil built the NEW EXCHANGE on the Strand frontage. Ambassadors continued to be lodged at Durham House. In 1640 the Bishop sold his interest to the Earl of Pembroke who intended to have the house rebuilt by John Webb but the Civil War put an end to such schemes. During the War parliamentary troops were quartered here. In 1660 the house, now much dilapidated, was mostly demolished. The site was redeveloped with poorly built houses which, together with the remaining parts of Durham House, were swept away for the Adam brothers' ADELPHI in 1769–70. DURHAM HOUSE STREET commemorates the mansion.

Durham House Street *WC2.* Takes its name from DURHAM HOUSE which stood on the site. It was formerly known as James Street and William Street after two of the Adam brothers who designed the ADELPHI.

Dutch Church *Old Broad Street, EC2.* Once part of a great Augustinian monastery founded in 1253 by Humphrey Bohun, Earl of Hereford and Constable of England. The church was rebuilt by Bohun's grandson in 1354. Stow had 'not seen the like'. The monastery was dissolved in 1538 and granted to royal favourites who used the church as a stable. Edward VI gave the nave and aisles to Protestant refugees, mostly Dutch and German, in 1550. The rest of the church was used as a granary and coal store; and lead from the roof was sold. Monuments to Humphrey Bohun; Edward, son of the Black Prince; Edmund, half brother of Richard II; John de Vere, 12th Earl of Oxford; his son, Aubrey; and Edward Stafford, Duke of Buckingham, were all removed. The foreign congregation were given 24 days' notice to leave in the reign of Mary I but they returned under Elizabeth I in 1559. In 1600 all but the nave was pulled down by the Marquess of Winchester. In 1862 a fire destroyed most of the building. The church was restored in 1863–5 by Edward l'Anson and William Lightly. Bombed and devastated in the 2nd World War, it was replaced with a sub-classical church by Arthur Bailey in 1950–6. There are windows by Max Nauta, Hugh Easton and William Wilson.

Dyers' Company *see* CITY LIVERY COMPANIES.

Dyers' Hall *10 Dowgate Hill, EC4.* After using a Hall from 1482, the Dyers were given a site and buildings in UPPER THAMES STREET in 1545. This was burnt down in the GREAT FIRE. The replacement was destroyed by fire in 1681. The third Hall, built on DOWGATE HILL in 1731, collapsed in 1768. The next Hall was condemned as unsafe in 1838 before it, too, collapsed. The present Hall, built by Charles Dyer, was opened in 1842. A Roman pavement was found during excavations. For the Company *see* CITY LIVERY COMPANIES.

Dyers' Hall, the fourth hall on this site. Condemned as unsafe in 1838, it later collapsed, as had its predecessor.

Dyott Street *WC1.* Built in about 1672 across Pitance Croft, a field belonging to St Giles Leper Hospital. This was purchased by Henry Bainbridge and the street probably named after one of his married daughters, Jane Dyott. From the mid-18th until the mid-19th century, when NEW OXFORD STREET was built, it was the centre of a most notorious rookery. Its centre-piece was the Rat's Castle, the frequenters of which 'spoke openly of incidents which they had long ceased to blush at but which hardened habits of crime alone could teach them to avow'. At the corner of Streatham Street is one of the earliest buildings erected by the Society for Improving the Condition of the Working Classes. Built in 1848–9 to the design of Henry Roberts, it contained 54 flats, each with a living room, two bedrooms and a scullery off which was a water closet. They were let at 4s a week and those in the basement at 2s. The carved inscription along the string course reads in bold plain letters 'Model Houses for Families'. The offices of *The Bookseller* are at No. 12.

E

Eagle *2 Shepherdess Walk, N1.* Formerly a tea-garden near the SHEPHERD AND SHEPHERDESS it was turned into an early music-hall in 1825, 'the father and mother, the dry and wet nurse of the Music Hall', in the words of John Hollingshead, the journalist and theatrical manager. Jemima Evans and Samual Wilkins go here in Dickens's *Sketches by Boz*. The Eagle later became the Grecian Theatre, a minor theatre for melodrama, music and ballet which achieved some temporary fame because of the acrobatic performances of the manager, George Conquest. Here Marie Lloyd appeared at the age of 14. In 1884 the premises were sold to General Booth for a SALVATION ARMY Centre and were demolished in 1901. Rebuilt that year, the building is now a public house with a good collection of music-hall prints.

The tavern gave rise to the old song:

> Up and down the City Road,
> In and out the Eagle,
> That's the way the money goes,
> Pop goes the weasel!

The weasel was slang for a tailor's iron; pop is slang for pawn. Pop Goes the Weasel was also the name of a country dance in which these words were sung as one of the dancers darted under the arms of the others.

Eagle House *London Road, Mitcham, Surrey.* A Queen Anne building virtually unchanged inside and out and an outstanding example of this period of domestic architecture. The house was built in 1705 for Fernando Mendes, physician to Catharine of Braganza, wife of King Charles II. In 1711 it was leased to a London merchant, James Dolliffe, a founder director of the South Sea Company. His monogram 'JMD' appears above the wrought iron entrance gates. After a succession of domestic owners until 1818, the house was used as a private boarding school until 1855 when the building became an 'Industrial School for paupers and orphans'. It has maintained an educational role ever since, being subsequently a day-nursery, a Special School and now an Adult Education Centre.

Eagle House *High Street, Wimbledon, SW19.* Built in 1613 by Robert Bell, one of the founders of the East India Company. It was originally in red brick although most of this has now been rendered. In the 17th and 18th centuries it was owned by a number of important men, including Marquesses of Bath and William Pitt's foreign minister, Lord Grenville, who used frequently to entertain his cousin, the Prime Minister, here. The building became a private school in the early 19th century and its present name originated in 1860 when Dr Huntingford took over the school and mounted on the central gable the stone eagle brought from his previous school. The building is now used as offices.

Ealing *W5, W13.* Although Ealing is a Saxon settlement ('territory of the people of Gilla'), it does not

The Eagle Tavern, once a tea-garden, became a music hall in 1825.

appear in *Domesday Book*, almost certainly because it was part of the BISHOP OF LONDON's large manor of FULHAM. Ealing is mentioned among his estates in the 12th century and there was a church there from 1130. The village grew up near the church on the road, now St Mary's Road, that led from the UXBRIDGE Road to BRENTFORD which was, until 1863, part of Ealing. The parish of Ealing, therefore, extended from the River BRENT in the north to the River THAMES. Ealing developed slowly until the 19th century in contrast with BRENTFORD. By the 18th century Ealing had established itself as a fashionable spot for country houses, having the advantages of rural seclusion and proximity to London. Elegant houses were built round Ealing Green, including PITSHANGER MANOR at Little Ealing and on the slopes of Castle Bar Hill. Princess Amelia, George III's youngest daughter, lived at GUN-NERSBURY HOUSE from 1761 and at the turn of the century the Duke of Kent, Queen Victoria's father, lived at Castle Hill Lodge whose previous occupant had been Mrs Fitzherbert. The ill-fated Prime Minister, Spencer Perceval, lived at Elm Grove from 1801 until his assassination in 1812. At this time Ealing was also well known for its schools, particularly Great Ealing School, founded in 1698, but enjoying under Dr Nicholas its period of greatest fame when it was said to rival its neighbour HARROW.

By the early decades of the 19th century the area immediately to the south of the Uxbridge Road was being built up. The Great Western Railway laid its main line to the West of England roughly parallel to the Uxbridge Road and opened a station on Haven Green in 1838 but this did not suddenly disrupt Ealing's rural nature. In the middle of the century it was still predominately agricultural with sizeable farms to the north of the railway. In the 1870s and 1880s house building transformed Ealing into what the publicists of the 1890s termed the 'Queen of the Suburbs', famed for its healthy environment, modern accommodation and good amenities. There was no industry and the scant working-class accommodation was largely confined to that area of West Ealing known, after its landlord, as Stevens Town. Standards of building were enforced by the Local Board which had come into existence in 1863 and by their enthusiastic surveyor, Charles Jones; and only houses of high rateable value were built. Development started near the existing centres of population, Uxbridge Road, St Mary's Road and Haven Green. Much of the building was piecemeal and small-scale, reflecting the pattern of land ownership. The only large scale estate that was projected was too ambitious and landed the developer, Henry de Bruno Austin, in the Bankruptcy Court.

Commuting to London on the GWR was possible but not very practicable for Ealing residents. The position was improved by the opening of a station at Castle Hill (West Ealing) and by the construction in 1879 of the Ealing extension of the Metropolitan District Line with stations at Ealing Broadway and Ealing Common. Further District stations were opened at Northfields, South Ealing and later at North Ealing. (The present Northfields Station on the PICCADILLY LINE was built in 1933 to the designs of Charles Holden and S.A. Heaps.) Trams started running along the Uxbridge Road between SHEPHERD'S BUSH and SOUTHALL in 1901. This paved the way for the period of greatest house building, much of it of a cheaper sort, in the first decade of the 20th century when Little Ealing was transformed into Northfields.

Ealing Common *W5.* 47 acres located off Uxbridge Road, EALING. It is almost entirely grassland, bordered with stately chestnut trees. The land was registered under the Commons Registration Act 1965.

Ealing Studios *The Green, Ealing, W5.* Famous for feature films in the 1940s and 1950s, the studios have a long and distinguished film production history. Their origins go back to 1907 when William George Barker, already established as a film producer, bought a house called West Lodge which was set back from Ealing Green, and set up Barker Motion Photography Ltd. He made many spectacular films and by 1912 these studios – in his five-acre garden – were the largest in England. Barker retired from film-making in 1918 and in the 1920s the studios were rented out or used for shorts production. In 1929 the site was bought by Union Studios but they collapsed and it was then acquired by Associated Talking Pictures, a recently formed company, whose head of production was Basil Dean. Sound stages, with the latest equipment, were built to the designs of Robert Atkinson and the first production started in 1931. When Dean resigned in 1938, Michael Balcon took his place and the production company became known as Ealing Studios Ltd. The period from then until the early 1950s saw the making of the famous 'Ealing comedies' and many other significant films, but in 1955 the Ealing complex was sold to the BBC which still uses it.

Earl's Court *SW5.* Originally a small hamlet centred around the site of the present Metropolitan Railway station it derives its name from the courthouse of the Earls of Warwick and Holland, formerly lords of the manor. Notable early residents included John Hunter, the surgeon, at Earl's Court House (since demolished) and James Gunter, confectioner, whose sons were responsible for the development of much of the area in the 19th century. There was a farm here on a site adjacent to the present station until the 1860s when the Metropolitan Railway was built; but by the 1880s much of the area was built up as seen today. After 1914 many of the large houses began to be subdivided or used as hotels and in recent years the area, with a large transient population beside the regular inhabitants, has been called 'Kangaroo Valley' (many Australians stayed here) and the 'Bedsit Jungle'.

Earl's Court Exhibition Hall *SW5.* The present building opened in 1937 and was designed by C. Howard Crane. At that time the largest reinforced concrete building in Europe, its site covers 12 acres. The centre span of the main hall is 250 ft. Entertainment here however goes back to 1887 when J.R. Whitley opened an entertainment ground which made imaginative use of derelict land between railway lines. Permanent features, of which the most famous was the Great Wheel, were supplemented by annual exhibitions and 'spectaculars' such as Buffalo Bill's Wild West Show. The ground closed in 1914. The hall is now mostly used for public exhibitions such as the Boat Show, the ROYAL TOURNAMENT, and the Royal Smithfield Show.

Earlsfield *SW16.* Lies between WANDSWORTH and BALHAM. Earlsfield covers an area originally belonging to Allfarthing manor, itself part of the ancient BATTER-SEA manor. The residential district developed at the end of the 19th century on either side of the London to Southampton railway. Its name was probably derived from that of the wife of the lord of the manor until the 1890s rather than from Earl Spencer who owned land in the vicinity. The 4-acre Garratt Park and 8-acre Garratt Green are remains of WANDS-WORTH's manorial wastelands. Enclosure in the 18th century resulted in protest from the hamlet of Garratt whose residents, until the 19th century, elected a president – the MAYOR OF GARRATT – for their self-protection society in a burlesque of parliamentary elections. St Andrew's, Garratt Lane (E.W. Mountford) was begun in 1889. In 1965 Earlsfield became part of the London Borough of WANDSWORTH.

East Barnet *Hertfordshire*. Situated in a vale east of HIGH BARNET along Pymmes Brook, overlooked by the Church of ST MARY THE VIRGIN on Church Hill. During the Saxon period the area was densely forested: the Saxon word *baernet* means 'a burning' – an area cleared in a forest by fire (*see also* HIGH BARNET, FRIERN BARNET). Until the DISSOLUTION OF THE MONASTERIES the manor belonged to the Abbot of St Albans, and comprised the parishes of both East Barnet and Barnet (i.e. HIGH BARNET). From the 13th century a distinction between land in the two parishes appears to have been made. The village was sparsely inhabited until the Reformation, and soon afterwards mansions began to appear in the estates along the high ridge to the east overlooking Pymmes Brook. The wealthy Thomas Conyers acquired Church Hill House (later Trevor Park) where Lady Arabella Stuart was detained on James I's orders in 1611, from 15 March until her escape on 3 June. Mount Pleasant existed by the beginning of the 17th century, and later, as Belmont, was the residence of the antiquary, Elias Ashmole. Other estates included Buckskin Hall, Monkenfrith, later Oak Hill, Little Grove and Osidge, which dates back to the Saxon era. Many of these names are recorded in park and road names today.

Until the 19th century the parish remained mainly arable and pasture land. Then, in 1849, the Great Northern Railway bought the Lyonsdown estate to build New Barnet Station, and the estate, previously meadow-land, soon developed into a middle-class residential area with a great number of places of worship. The rest of the parish was divided into small lots for building to accommodate a rapidly increasing population. In the village alone, the population grew from about 400 in 1841 to about 4,000 in 1881, and by the end of the century the district had changed from a rural to an urban one. In 1860 the Boys' Farm Home, Church Farm, was founded near ST MARY THE VIRGIN for the training and education of destitute boys.

The 20th century has seen the further residential development of the area. In 1965 the Urban District of East Barnet was incorporated into the London Borough of BARNET.

East Bedfont *Middlesex*. Straddles the Staines road. It was originally built by the Romans for moving their army from London to Silchester. Inhabited since Saxon times, the manor of Bedefunde was owned at the time of *Domesday Book* by Walter Fitz Other, Lord of the Manor of Stanwell. Bedefunde or Bedefunt meant Beda's Spring. For many centuries

the parish of East Bedfont was a tiny rural hamlet containing fewer than 300 inhabitants, entirely surrounded by HOUNSLOW HEATH. The centre of the village surrounds Bedfont Green which is divided by the Staines Road. Until early this century there were two ponds on the Green. On the north side of the Green stands St Mary the Virgin church, the oldest surviving building in the London Borough of HOUNS-LOW. It was built in about 1150 and partially rebuilt in 1865. The Norman chancel arch and two wall paintings of about 1245 survive. Next to the church is Burlington House, built in about 1791 by an unknown architect for the Reed family who lived there until about 1930. It is now an old people's home. Bennetts Farm in Staines Road was built, also by an unknown architect, in about 1700. It was the home of the Hatchett family until about 1900. Still a private house, it is now surrounded by modern buildings. Farming was the main source of work until about 1930. From the mid-19th century some farms became market gardens. For 100 years from about 1750 stage-coaches travelling the Staines Road to the West Country provided employment in the roadside inns, the accompanying stables, and in the many blacksmiths' forges needed for the shoeing of horses and the maintenance of the coaches. Today Heathrow Airport, situated just north of the parish, provides the main source of employment (*see* AIRPORTS). Bedfont had two manors, Pates and Fawns, and both these manor houses survive. Pates Manor in Halton Road is a 16th-century timber-framed building with one wing of about 1495. It was extended and altered over the centuries and reconstructed in 1865. The present owner has restored it to its original condition. Fawns Manor in Bedfont Road is a mid-16th-century timber-framed house, later converted into three cottages, but restored to one house in 1889. The Sherborn family, who have lived in Bedfont from the 14th century, have owned the house for several generations.

East Greenwich Pleasaunce *see* BURIAL GROUNDS.

East Ham *E6, E7, E12*. Ancient parish and former county and parliamentary borough in the county of Essex, incorporated in the London Borough of NEWHAM in 1965. The East Ham postal district is E6, but the borough included the eastern half of FOREST GATE (E7) and the whole of MANOR PARK (E12). During excavations for the Northern Outfall Sewer in the 1860s, a small Roman cemetery was found about 900 yards west of the parish church of ST MARY MAG-DALENE – indicating the possibility of a settlement. There were three hamlets in the parish (in addition to East Ham village) all first mentioned in a document of 1560–14 – Wallend, Plashet and Green Street. Wallend survives as a place name on East Ham's boundary with BARKING. The name probably derives from a wall against the RODING Back River. Plashet, 'an enclosure in a wood', dates back to the time when part of EPPING FOREST came well south of the ROMFORD road into East Ham. Plashet House, first mentioned in the early 17th century, was the home of the Quaker family, the Frys, from 1784–1829. Elizabeth Fry lived here in 1808–29. The house was demolished in about 1883 but the name 'Plashet' is still applied to an area between Katherine Road (named from Elizabeth's eldest daughter) and High Street North, East Ham. Green Street, or

Greenstreet, probably took its name from the old way from the ROMFORD road southward to the marshes. The modern main road, Green Street, follows its course.

The Jesuit missionaries, Campion and Parsons, had a secret printing press in the hamlet for a short time after their arrival in England in 1580. The Tudor mansion, Green Street House (demolished in 1955), was built towards the middle of the 16th century, possibly by its early resident, Richard Breame, a servant of Henry VIII. Breame purchased the manor of East Ham from the king after the dissolution of its previous owner, STRATFORD LANGTHORNE ABBEY. The mansion's popular name 'Boleyn Castle' came from the erroneous tradition that Anne Boleyn lived here during Henry's courtship. Breame also owned a house in GREENWICH which Henry rented ostensibly for Anne's brother, and the tradition regarding Green Street probably arose from a confusion of the two houses. The hamlet's name is now out of use but its immediate area is colloquially known as 'The Boleyn' and modern roads to the east are named after Henry VIII's wives and Anne's brother, Lord Rochford. In 1869, Cardinal Manning bought the house and its 30 acres of grounds for a Roman Catholic reformatory school. This closed in 1906. The site is now occupied by a Roman Catholic church and primary and comprehensive schools and the home ground of WEST HAM UNITED FOOTBALL CLUB. The modern residential district of Upton Park was begun on the Plashet estate after the demolition of the house and spread southward on either side of Green Street to the latter's former hamlet. Upton Park Station (1877) serves the London, Tilbury and Southend line and the DISTRICT LINE. Nearby is Queens Market, built by the NEWHAM Council, to replace an earlier street market. From the 13th century onwards, East Ham did not develop like its larger neighbour, WEST HAM, and remained an agricultural village until the last quarter of the 19th century. In 1851 there were still only 300 houses against WEST HAM's 3,300. Increase began in 1851–81 and the population rose from 1,750 to 10,700. Then, within 20–30 years – growing faster than any comparable town in England – East Ham became one of the dormitory suburbs of London. The population trebled in each of the decades 1881–91 and 1891–1901 and reached 133,500 in 1911. The only major industry was in the south and consisted of the Royal Albert and King George V docks and their ancillary industries, the factories at NORTH WOOLWICH and the BECKTON gasworks. The latter were built in 1868–70 by the Gas-Light and Coke Co. under the governorship of Simon Adams Beck who gave his name to the works and to the district of Beckton built to house the workers. The small area called New Beckton mainly consists of East Ham's first municipal housing project – the erection of 143 dwellings in Savage Gardens in 1901. The name sometimes includes the district of Cyprus to the south. This housing estate was built in 1881 to the north of the newly opened Albert Dock. All its road names derive from persons and places in the news during the previous decade and its place name comes from the Mediterranean island taken over by Britain in 1878. East Ham station (1858) serves the London, Tilbury and Southend line and the DISTRICT LINE. East Ham Memorial Hospital originated in the Passmore Edwards Cottage Hospital (1902). The present main hospital was built alongside in Shrewsbury Road as a memorial to East Ham's war dead and opened in 1929. Both were erected through the efforts of John H. Bethell, MP (later Lord Bethell), who was a major influence in the municipal development of the borough. East Ham's former parish administration was taken over successively by a Local Board in 1879, an Urban District Council in 1895, a Borough Council in 1904, and a County Borough Council in 1915. East Ham was incorporated into the ancient parish of LITTLE ILFORD for local government purposes in 1886. It became a parliamentary borough in 1918, with two seats – North and South. In 1923, East Ham North elected Miss Susan Lawrence. She and Miss Margaret Bondfield became the first women Labour MPs to take their seats in the Commons.

East Harding Street *EC4.* Named after Agas Hardinge who, in 1513, bequeathed lands, tenements and gardens in FETTER LANE and SHOE LANE to the GOLDSMITHS' COMPANY so that two poor goldsmiths' widows could have 1d each a week.

East Heath Road *NW3.* Marked on Rocque's map of 1745, it borders the south-east side of Hampstead Heath. Katherine Mansfield and her husband, John Middleton Murry, lived at No. 17, a house which 'because of its greyness and its size' they christened 'the Elephant'.

The East India Company Museum, Leadenhall Street, in 1858; its exotic contents had all been assembled by Company officials.

East India Company Museum *Leadenhall Street.* Also known as the Oriental Repository, it housed at the Company's headquarters a collection of Indian weapons, agricultural and musical instruments, Buddhist idols, a silver howdah and the 'Man-Tiger-Organ' mentioned by Keats. This was the mechanism which had belonged to Tippoo Sahib, a virulent Anglophobe killed during the capture of Seringapatam in 1799, and which was put on show in the museum in 1808. It represented the sight and sounds of a tiger overwhelming a red-coated Englishman. After the Indian Mutiny of 1857–8, the Company's remaining administrative functions were taken over by the Government, and the museum was moved to Fife House, WHITEHALL YARD. In 1865 its exhibits were moved again to the new India Office where they could not be displayed and were, therefore, stored. Tippoo Sahib's tiger is now at the VICTORIA AND ALBERT MUSEUM. Other items were given to the BRITISH MUSEUM and KEW GARDENS. (*See also* EAST INDIA HOUSE.)

249

East India Company Warehouses *New Street, EC2*. Designed by Richard Jupp and Henry Holland in 1793–1801. Six storeys high and covering about 5 acres, they are now owned by the PORT OF LONDON AUTHORITY.

East India, Devonshire, Sports and Public Schools Club *16 St James's Square, SW1*. The East India United Service Club was founded in 1849 for officers of the East India Company on leave in London and for retired officers of the Company. The inaugural dinner was held at No. 16 St James's Square on 1 January 1850. As well as to East India Company 'servants, clerical, civil, military, naval and medical', membership was open to 'officers of HM's Army and Navy who had served in India, certain law officers in India, and ex-captains of the Company's late maritime service'. The club bought the freehold of No. 16 in 1862 and that of No. 17 the next year and rebuilt both houses in 1865 to the designs of Charles Lee. Two storeys were added in 1939 when the club amalgamated with the Sports Club. It has since amalgamated with the DEVONSHIRE CLUB and with the PUBLIC SCHOOLS CLUB.

East India Dock Road *E14*. Completed in 1810, it joined the new COMMERCIAL ROAD at LIMEHOUSE, giving traffic from the EAST INDIA DOCKS (opened 1806) a straight run to London, by-passing POPLAR High Street. All Saints' church, on the southside of the road, was consecrated in 1823 for the newly created parish of POPLAR. Designed by Charles Hollis, it was remodelled after bomb damage in the 2nd World War. The fibreglass sculpture *The Dockers* in Trinity Gardens is by Sidney Harpley (1962).

East India Docks The trade of the East India Company (founded in 1600) was as important as that of the West at the start of the dock building early in the 19th century, although it was less in volume. It differed from that of the West India Company in being controlled by a single organisation instead of by many individual merchants. It was a rich, powerful, and well-organised body which owned the largest ships that used the PORT OF LONDON. Being so large, these ships never sailed higher up-river than DEPTFORD, well east of the CITY boundaries. The Company's wealth enabled it to employ a competent staff and to protect its valuable cargoes better than most other companies. In 1782 it built itself splendid inland warehouses in the CITY, including some in Cutler Street, which, sold to the St Katharine Dock Company in 1835, were as sound as they had ever been when they awaited the decisions of the developers in the 1970s. The Company therefore had less urgent need to build enclosed docks in London. Nevertheless it followed the trend and in 1803 obtained an Act for new docks. These were opened in 1806 on the site at BLACKWALL which included the old BRUNSWICK DOCK. The joint engineers were John Rennie and Ralph Walker who had been concerned with the WEST INDIA DOCKS. The scheme followed the same pattern of export and import docks lying parallel with one another and having a locked basin giving entrance from the river, the import dock being at 18 acres by far the larger of the two. Tea, silks, indigo and spices from India, and tea and porcelain from China were, of course, major imports. The famous CUTTY SARK, launched in 1869, and now on

view in dry dock at GREENWICH, was one of the tea clippers that once berthed in these docks. Between them, the West and East India Companies saw to the making of a broad new toll road to their docks named Commercial Road.

In 1838 the East India Company's docks were amalgamated with those of the West India Company. In 1943 the Import Dock, like the South Dock of the SURREY COMMERCIAL DOCKS, was pumped dry and spread with bomb rubble as a base for building the concrete caissons for D-Day's Mulberry Harbours. The East India Docks were the first of London's inland docks to be closed down, ending their long life in 1967.

East India House *Leadenhall Street*. The East India Company was incorporated in 1600 when Elizabeth I granted a charter to the 'Company and Merchants of London trading with the East Indies'. The company later became the agent of the British Government in India and remained so until its abolition in 1858, after the Indian Mutiny. The Company's first premises were in the 'great mansion house' of Sir William Craven, father of the Earl of Craven and Lord Mayor in 1610. This house was rebuilt in 1726 and enlarged in 1799. Charles Lamb worked in the new building for 33 years. 'My printed works were my recreations,' he wrote, 'my true works may be found on the shelves in Leadenhall Street filling some hundred folios.' James Mill, the Scottish philosopher and author of the *History of British India* (1817–18), also worked here, eventually as head of his department. His son, J.S. Mill, entered East India House as a clerk in 1823 and also became head of his department. The building was demolished in 1862, and new premises for LLOYD's were built on the site.

East London Waterworks Co. *Old Ford, Bow*. In 1807 30 acres of works were established at OLD FORD, BOW, supplied by the River LEA. The company – whose motto came from Horace: 'Thou, too, shall become one of the honoured founts' – took over the operations of the SHADWELL WATERWORKS COMPANY and the WEST HAM Waterworks which were threatened by dock construction. In 1815 agreement was reached with the NEW RIVER COMPANY to create monopoly service areas. In 1829 the intake was moved higher up the River LEA. The Hackney Waterworks was purchased in 1830, and a canal cut from Lea Bridge across the HACKNEY MARSH to OLD FORD. And in 1861 the construction of new reservoirs at WALTHAMSTOW was started. Five years later a CHOLERA epidemic caused the OLD FORD plant to close. In 1868–71 new supply lines were laid from the THAMES at Sunbury Lock running 19 miles to a new reservoir at FINSBURY PARK. In 1884 the water pipes were invaded by eels, some of them 18 ins long. The Old Ford site was sold in 1892, and in 1902 the Company was taken over by the Metropolitan Water Board (*see* WATER SUPPLY).

East Mount Street *and* **Mount Terrace** *E1*. When Parliament ordered fortifications to be built for the defence of London during the Civil War, an earthen hill was raised on the south side of WHITECHAPEL ROAD. Debris was later added to it, so that it stood higher than the LONDON HOSPITAL when the latter opened alongside it in 1757. The mound was cleared away in the early 19th century.

East Sheen *see* MORTLAKE.

East Smithfield *E1*. Once the whole area east of the TOWER, but now restricted to a small road running south of the ROYAL MINT. During the 13th century a fair was held here annually for 15 days starting on the Feast of Pentecost. In 1348 victims of the BLACK DEATH were buried here and a small chapel built. In 1349 the Cistercian abbey of St Mary Graces was founded by Edward III on his safe return from a stormy sea voyage. He had vowed to build an abbey 'to the honour of God and the Lady of Grace, if she should grant him the grace of coming safe on shore'. He richly endowed it with land and property. It was dissolved by Henry VIII in 1539. Stow wrote in 1598 that it was, 'cleane pulled down by Sir Arthur Darcie, knight and others: In place thereof is built a storehouse for victuals; and convenient ovens for baking of biscuites to serve Her Majesty's ships. The grounds adjoining . . . are employed in building small tenements.' In 1552 Edmund Spenser is said to have been born here:

> Merry London my most kindly nurse
> That to me gave this life's first native source.

The victualling yard remained here into the 18th century. The fibreglass elephants on the gates of Ivory House are by Peter Drew (1973).

Eastbury Manor House *Barking, Essex*. Fine Elizabethan manor house built in the shape of an H. The exact date of the building and the identity of the builder are unknown. In 1605 Lord Monteagle is supposed to have been living here when he received the letter revealing the GUNPOWDER PLOT, but he himself said he received it at HOXTON. In 1796 Daniel Lysons wrote in his *Environs of London* that it had been let for almost 100 years and had become a farmhouse. It was taken over by the NATIONAL TRUST in 1936 and is now owned by the London Borough of BARKING and used as a cultural centre.

Eastcastle Street *W1*. Formerly known as Castle Street East, the name was changed in 1918. It was first rated in 1723 and named after a nearby inn. It is now full of small, wholesale dress show-rooms. Dr Johnson lived in poverty at No. 6 in 1738; during his sojourn there he was introduced to Reynolds 'at the house of some Miss Cotterells'. Sir William Beechey was at No. 12 in 1782 and No. 26 was, from 1773 till his death in 1806, the home of the eccentric painter James Barry who was responsible for the murals which decorate the Lecture Room of the ROYAL SOCIETY OF ARTS. 'His house became almost proverbial for its dirty and ruinous state. He lived quite alone scarcely admitting any visitor and living on bread and apples.'

Eastcheap *EC3*. Site of the medieval meat market. It used to run north past GRACECHURCH STREET; but this section, together with ST MICHAEL CROOKED LANE and the Boar's Head Tavern, was demolished in 1829–31 to make way for KING WILLIAM STREET. A Roman road was discovered three feet below the surface in 1831. The south side of the street was set back in about 1875 when the Metropolitan Railway was built. ST MARGARET PATTENS is at the corner of Rood Lane. Nos 33–35, designed by R.L. Roumieu in 1868, have been described by Sir Nikolaus Pevsner as 'one of the maddest displays in London of gabled Gothic brick'.

Eastcote *Middlesex*. The eastern settlement of the manor of Ruislip, it originally consisted of a small agricultural community dispersed along the River Pinn. The name means 'eastern cottage or shelter'. Ancient ways led northwards to the common waste and these ways still exist as Fore Street, Wiltshire Lane, Joel Street and Catlines Lane. South lay the open fields extending to Down Barnes and Northolt. The High Road is the centre of old Eastcote and retains a line of detached ancient buildings and the more modern Haydon Lodge (in about 1880) built in a striking Elizabethan style to the designs of Sir Ernest George, the architect who also designed the New Cottages further along the High Road. The Old Barn House, now offices, is medieval in origin and Ivy Farm in Wiltshire Lane and Park Farm in Field End Road are 16th century. The enclosure of the open fields following the Ruislip Enclosure Act of 1804 gave Eastcote the rural appearance it maintained until the beginning of the 20th century. Several well-to-do families built houses on ancient sites in the area. Eastcote House was the home of the Hawtreys from about 1532 and was built on the site of a former dwelling. The first Hawtrey, Ralph, was the younger son of the owner of Chequers, now the Buckinghamshire country home of the Prime Ministers, and his family and descendants occupied Eastcote House until the late 19th century. The house was demolished in 1965 but the 17th-century stables and walled garden still exist and there is a dovecote. An occupier of Eastcote House from 1878–88 was Sir Samuel Morton Peto, the railway engineer and contractor. Opposite is the site of Haydon Hall which was built about 1630 by the Countess of Derby. It passed to William, Lord Chandos, and in 1720 was rebuilt by Sir Thomas Franklin. Other owners were the Revd Thomas Clarke of Swakeleys Ickenham (1763) and Dr Adam Clarke, theologian and Methodist divine (1824–32). The house has been demolished and the grounds are a public park. High Grove was built on an ancient site at Hale End and was rebuilt in 1881, after a fire, for Sir Hugh Hume-Campbell to the designs of Edward Prior. It is now used by the Local Authority as a hostel. In 1906 a railway station was opened on the METROPOLITAN LINE. This was followed shortly afterwards by the building of the first of the many estates which sprang up in the district. Eastcote is now a residential suburb within the London Borough of HILLINGDON.

Eaton Place *SW1*. Takes its name from Eaton Hall, Cheshire, the country seat of the ground landlords, the Grosvenors, Earls, Marquesses and later Dukes of Westminster (*see* GROSVENOR ESTATE *and* BELGRAVIA). It was built in 1826–45 by Thomas Cubitt as a secondary development to EATON SQUARE. The earliest houses are at the east end and were completed and first occupied in 1828. Progress westwards was slow, the eastern blocks, designed by Thomas Cubitt's brother, Lewis, being finished by 1835, the centre blocks by 1840 and the western blocks by 1845. The design details are not uniform. In 1828–47 Thomas Cubitt had his office at nine different houses in the street, moving finally round the corner to No. 3 Lyall Street. Lord Kelvin, the scientist, lived at No. 15 for many years and Lord Carson, the strong opponent of Home Rule for Ireland, for a time at No. 5. William Ewart, the social reformer, lived at

No. 16. Lord Avebury, the scientist and author, was born at No. 29 in 1834. Chopin gave his first London recital at No. 99 in 1848. Field-Marshal Sir Henry Wilson was shot by two Irish assassins as he was alighting from a car outside No. 36 in 1922 and died as he was being carried into the house. The Hungarian Embassy is at No. 35.

Eaton Square *SW1*. Takes its name from Eaton Hall, Cheshire (*see* EATON PLACE). It is actually a rectangle divided by KING'S ROAD, the three terraces of unequal size on each of the two longer sides being separated from each other by streets crossing KING'S ROAD at right angles. Construction began in 1826 and was not completed until 1855, the year of the death of its builder, Thomas Cubitt: the irregular detailing of the blocks reflects the long period covered by the development. ST PETER'S CHURCH at the east end antedates the earliest blocks adjoining it. The first house to be finished was occupied by W.H. Whitbread, the brewer. Another early resident was George Fitz-Clarence, the eldest bastard son of William IV, at No. 13. Prince Metternich stayed at No. 44 in 1848. Admiral Sir Edward Codrington died at No. 92 in 1851, Ralph Bernal at No. 75 in 1854, Lord Chancellor Truro at No. 83 in 1855, George Peabody, the American philanthropist, at No. 80 in 1869 and Lord Napier of Magdala at No. 63 in 1890. Lord John Russell lived at No. 48 in 1858 and two other future Prime Ministers, Stanley Baldwin and Neville Chamberlain respectively, at No. 93 in 1920–3 and No. 37 in 1923–35. The Bolivian Embassy is at No. 106 and the Belgian Embassy at No. 103. On the latter is a plaque inscribed, 'Here many Belgians volunteered during World War Two to fight with their allies on land, sea and air to liberate their country. Those who gave their lives will not be forgotten. This plaque was unveiled by Her Majesty Queen Elizabeth, the Queen Mother on 21st June 1964.' The six rectangular gardens are private.

Ebury Square *SW1*. Laid out in 1820 on the site of Ebury Farm, an estate of 430 acres which once belonged to Elizabeth I who often came to eat syllabubs here. In 1676 it became part of the GROSVENOR ESTATE. Some of the early buildings were destroyed in 1860; the rest made way for blocks of modern flats.

Ebury Street *SW1*. Extends from Pimlico Road to GROSVENOR GARDENS on the borders of PIMLICO and BELGRAVIA. It was built on land belonging to Ebury Farm in 1820. It was down this way that George III and his family walked to the CHELSEA BUN HOUSE. At No. 180 the eight-year-old Mozart wrote his first symphony in 1764–5. George Moore, the Irish writer and author of *Conversations in Ebury Street*, lived at No. 121. Tennyson stayed at No. 42 in 1847.

Eccentric Club *9 Ryder Street, SW1*. Founded in 1890 by the theatrical costumier, Jack Harrison, mainly for those connected with the theatre and the music-hall. Dan Leno, George Robey, Sir George Alexander and Sir Charles Wyndham were among the early members; and it was Wyndham who, so it is said, unwittingly gave the club its name when, exasperated by the failure of the committee to choose one, exclaimed that they were a 'bunch of eccentrics'. The club's first premises were at 21 SHAFTESBURY AVENUE. In 1914 it

moved to its present address which had formerly been the Dieudonné Hotel, a well-known *maison de rendezvous*. These premises were badly damaged in the 2nd World War but have since been restored. Few members now have connections with the theatre; most are businessmen. The club does, however, contain a small museum of music-hall mementoes and a private suite of rooms is kept for the Grand Order of Water Rats.

Ecclesiastical Commissioners *see* CHURCH COMMISSIONERS.

Eccleston Square *SW1*. Large stuccoed square built in 1835 by Thomas Cubitt and named after the Duke of Westminster's estate at Eccleston, Cheshire. Matthew Arnold lived at No. 3 in 1877; Winston Churchill in 1908–11 at No. 33 where his son, Randolph, was born. This house was the headquarters of the Labour Party during the General Strike of 1926. The garden is private.

Eccleston Street *SW1*. Built by Thomas Cubitt in about 1835 and named after the Duke of Westminster's estate at Eccleston, Cheshire. Francis Chantrey, the sculptor, lived at No. 13 from 1811 until his death in 1841 and produced much of his best work in a studio at the back of the house.

Eden Lodge *Kensington Gore*. Built in the 1740s, the house was first occupied by John Swinhoe, the proprietor of BROMPTON PARK NURSERY. It was later occupied by James Stephen, great-grandfather of Virginia Woolf. In 1842 it passed into the hands of George Eden, 1st Earl of Auckland, the former Governor-General of India, whose brother, the Bishop of Sodor and Man, and his two sisters inherited his estates. The Royal Commissioners for the Exhibition of 1851, who were able to buy GORE HOUSE on its west side, and the land upon which EXHIBITION ROAD was built on its east, were naturally anxious to acquire Eden Lodge, too. But the Bishop refused to sell since his sister, Emily Eden, was living there, as their brother had requested she should in his will. The house was sold in 1870 to William Lowther, a Member of Parliament and nephew of Lord Lonsdale, who demolished it and built on the site LOWTHER LODGE, now the home of the ROYAL GEOGRAPHICAL SOCIETY.

Edgar Wallace *40 Essex Street, WC2*. Previously known as the Essex Head, this public house stands on the site of an old inn that was named after Robert Devereux, Earl of Essex, favourite of Queen Elizabeth I. Dr Johnson and his friends used to meet here three times a week as a favour to the landlord, Sam Greaves, an old friend of the Thrales. In 1975, the centenary of the birth of Edgar Wallace, the house was renamed. It contains a collection of Wallace mementoes.

Edgware *Middlesex*. The first settlement in Edgware probably developed on Brockley Hill about 2 miles to the north of the modern town centre. With the coming of the Romans this settlement became the posting station and pottery-making centre of Sulloniacae on Watling Street. The earliest known reference to Edgware is in a charter of AD 978 when it was recorded as 'The Old Town Place' within Aegeswer. Aeges was probably a Saxon farmer who built a weir or dam across the Silk Stream for fishing or irrigation purposes. An earlier charter dated 957 also referred to the 'Town Place' but did not mention the village by name. Edgware is not included in *Domesday Book*, but was entered under Little STANMORE as the land of Roger de Rames. The early history of Edgware is, in fact, intimately associated with that of Little STANMORE and the areas they occupied were, and still are, confused.

In 1176 King Henry II confirmed a gift of land in Edgware by the 1st Earl of Salisbury to the PRIORY OF ST BARTHOLOMEW, and in 1216 King John ordered that the Countess of Salisbury should be allowed to retain the manor of Eggeswere on the death of her husband, the second Earl. On the death of the Countess the manor passed to her daughter Ela, who in her turn gave it to her son, Nicholas Longespée, later Bishop of Salisbury, at an annual rent of a sparrowhawk. Ela's husband was William Longespée, an illegitimate half brother of King John. Medieval owners of Edgware included the Knights of St John of Jerusalem, the Priory of St Bartholomew and All Souls College, Oxford.

The parish church of St Margaret at the junction of Watling Street and Station Road has a tower which dates from the 14th century. The rest of the church in redbrick was largely rebuilt in 1764 and again in 1845. Aisles attributed to C.H. Freeman were added in 1928. At Stonegrove on Watling Street almshouses were founded in 1680 by Samuel Atkinson for four aged women and in 1828 by Charles Day for eight aged persons. Both still exist. Timber-framed buildings ranging from the 15th to the 17th century line the west side of the High Street. This area with the war memorial and the mock 16th-century Handel's Smithy (*see* ST LAWRENCE, Little Stanmore) is under consideration as a conservation area. The most interesting buildings in the proposed conservation area are the timber-framed hall house, now shops (Nos. 65 and 67) dating from about 1500, and the 16th-century group of shops and a restaurant (Nos. 97, 99 and 101) near the war memorial. A 17th-century coaching inn with covered wagon way, the White Hart, survives in Edgware High Street, but other early inns including the Chandos Arms have fallen to the onslaught of modern suburbia. The most important of the houses in the neighbourhood was the 18th-century mansion of the Duke of Chandos at CANONS.

The railway first came to Edgware in 1867 but this line was short-lived, and so the area remained largely rural until the coming of the underground from CHARING CROSS in 1924.

Edgware Road

W2. A long straight road lined with office blocks and flats running between OXFORD STREET and ST JOHN'S WOOD along the course of Roman Watling Street which led north, via EDGWARE, to St Albans and Chester. Oliver Goldsmith lodged at a farm off the Edgware Road in 1771–4 when writing *She Stoops to Conquer*. At No. 239 stood the Red Lion Tavern (now demolished) on the site of an earlier tavern where Shakespeare is said to have acted as a strolling player. At No. 258 is a large MARKS AND SPENCER store, built in 1959 on the site of a Penny Bazaar which opened in 1912. At MARBLE ARCH is the Odeon Cinema by T.P. Bennet (1967). The unfortunate painter Benjamin Robert Haydon lived beside the Edgware Road at No. 4 (now 12) Burwood Place where he committed suicide on 22 June

1846. Charles Wesley had lodgings for a while at No. 20.

Edmonton

N9, N18. Before 1881 Edmonton included SOUTHGATE, WINCHMORE HILL, PALMERS GREEN and Bowes. In that year these western districts were formed into the district of SOUTHGATE. Edmonton is situated on the east bank of the River LEA. The ground rises gently to the west. Much of the area is low-lying and until recent times was prone to flooding. There were two main settlements – Lower Edmonton, centred on Edmonton Green, and Upper Edmonton, about a mile to the south. The two became linked by ribbon development along Fore Street in the mid-19th century. The arrival of the Great Eastern Railway's high-level line to LIVERPOOL STREET in 1872 produced dramatic changes. There was a massive influx of working-class people from the East End and a large part of Edmonton was covered with cheap working-class housing, much of it jerry-built. From that time the population rose steeply, finally reaching a peak of 104,000 in 1951. There was also a good deal of industrial development, particularly in the Angel Road area. Since the 2nd World War extensive redevelopment has removed the worst of the slums and has completely altered the appearance of large areas of the district. In 1965 Edmonton joined ENFIELD and SOUTHGATE to form the London Borough of ENFIELD.

Much of Edmonton consists of 19th-century working-class housing interspersed with modern council developments. There is also a fair amount of middle-class housing from between the wars on the borders of ENFIELD and SOUTHGATE. Of the original settlements a fair amount remains. Church Street retains several 18th- and early 19th-century houses and an 18th-century Charity School. Upper Edmonton is represented by scattered survivals from the 18th century along Fore Street. In the 18th and 19th centuries the Bell at Edmonton was a favourite resort of London holiday-makers. It is here that William Cowper's John Gilpin is commended by his wife to take her on their wedding anniversary:

> Tomorrow is our wedding day
> And we will then repair
> Unto the Bell at Edmonton
> All in a chaise and pair.

As is well known, Gilpin's horse bolted with him on it; and in the 19th century the Bell had a sign outside depicting his ride from Ware. The landlord renamed his house the Bell and John Gilpin's Ride. Charles Lamb used to conduct his visitors on their way home as far as 'Gilpin's Bell' where they would have a parting drink with them. He lived at Bay Cottage, now known as Lamb's Cottage, Church Street. He moved there from Chase Side, ENFIELD, in 1833, with his sister, Mary Lamb. He died there in 1834 and was buried in the churchyard of All Saints. John Keats served his apprenticeship to Thomas Hammond, the surgeon, at a cottage on the site of 7 Keats Parade, Church Street.

Edwardes Estate

On the death of the 4th Earl of Holland in 1721, the HOLLAND ESTATE passed to William Edwardes, son of Elizabeth Rich. He had married Francis Edwardes of Haverfordwest, whose family owned large estates in Pembrokeshire. William Edwardes was created Baron Kensington in 1776. The northern part of the estate was sold to Stephen Fox in

1768. Several streets and squares in KENSINGTON and CHELSEA derive their names from the Edwardes family's connections. In addition to those separately mentioned, Longridge Road, Nevern Road, Philbeach Gardens, Marloes Road, Trebovir Road and Templeton Place, as well as Pembroke Road and Pembroke Square, are all named after places in Pembrokeshire.

Edwardes Square *W8*. Built in 1811–19 by a speculative builder, Louis Léon Changeur, on 11 acres leased from the 2nd Lord Kensington. It is named after Lord Kensington's father, William Edwardes. The story that the square was built for officers of Napoleon's army arose from the pro-Napoleonist views of HOLLAND HOUSE across the road, and from a temporary misunderstanding of the Board of Kensington Turnpike Trust that the builder was Colonel Charmilly, who had been denounced as a Napoleonic agent by Earl Grey in 1809. Earls Terrace was built first. Five houses were then added at either end. Leonard Place to the east was demolished in 1926 but Edwardes Place still exists. The east side of the square went up next, followed by the west and finally the south. In 1819 an Act of Parliament was passed regulating the lighting, watching, watering, cleansing and planting of the square. A fine of 5s was to be imposed on anyone who failed to sweep and cleanse the footway in front of his house 'before the hour of 9 o'clock in the forenoon', and a fine of £5 was imposed for 'suffering swine to wander upon said footways and carriageways'. The garden was laid out in 1820 and the gardener's lodge built in Greek Revival style. Mrs Elizabeth Inchbald, the novelist and dramatist, lived at No. 4 Earls Terrace in 1816; George du Maurier, the artist and novelist, at No. 12 Earls Terrace in 1867–70. G. K. Chesterton lived at No. 1 in 1901, and Leigh Hunt in 1840–51 at No. 32, where he wrote *The Old Court Suburb*; *Men, Women and Books*; *Table Talk*; and part of his autobiography. Goldsworthy Lowes Dickinson, the author and humanist, lived at No. 11 with his sisters in 1912–30.

Eel Pie House *and* **Highbury Sluice** *Islington*. A tavern once noted for its pies, presumably made with eels caught from the NEW RIVER. It was a favourite resort for London anglers, and for holidaymakers on their way along the river bank to HORNSEY Wood, especially in the early hours of Palm Sunday. About 60 yards south of it was Highbury Sluice, a small wooden house astride the river where it turned towards NEWINGTON, containing a 'machine' to pipe off water for the HOLLOWAY district. This was the stretch which, in the 17th century, was carried above ground level in the 'Boarded River' aqueduct. In the early 1860s suburban building overtook the once rural area, and No. 57 Wilberforce Road now covers the approximate site of Eel Pie House.

Effra A river which rises in the hills of UPPER NORWOOD, flows through NORWOOD CEMETERY, then alongside Croxted Road to DULWICH, on to HERNE HILL, north-eastwards along BROCKWELL PARK, following the BRIXTON road to KENNINGTON church and turning west to enter the THAMES immediately above VAUXHALL BRIDGE. At BRIXTON it formerly flowed between the BRIXTON road and a farm to the east of it, and is said to have been 12 ft wide and 6 ft deep. It passed under the BRIXTON road at Hazard's Bridge and under Clapham Road at MERTON Bridge, curved round the OVAL and flowed on past VAUXHALL GARDENS and under South Lambeth Road to the THAMES. Below Brixton it was used as a sewer as long ago as the 17th century, but in DULWICH it was still supplying fresh water in 1860 and even today is used as an ornamental lake. Most of its length is, however, now covered in. Its name derives from the Celtic *yfrid* – a torrent.

Egerton Crescent *SW3*. Formerly Brompton New Crescent, this was built in the early 1840s by James Bonnin, probably to the designs of George Basevi, architect to the Trustees of SMITH'S CHARITY ESTATE. Charles James Richardson, the architect and author, lived at No. 22. For the derivation of the name *see* EGERTON TERRACE.

Egerton Gardens *SW3*. Building began in 1886 to the designs of T. H. Smith. The houses replaced earlier 18th-century ones designed by Michael Novosielski. Mortimer House was built in 1887 by William Godwin in the Tudor style by then out of fashion. It replaced an earlier building, Crescent House, erected by Novosielski in the 1780s.

Egerton Terrace *SW3*. Built in 1785 and then known as Michael's Grove, with Michael's Place on either side of it along the main road. Michael Novosielski was the developer and architect of much of the SMITH'S CHARITY ESTATE. At the end of the road, just short of the parish boundary, he built himself a large house, Brompton Grange, in 1790. At the main entrance was a circular drive leading to his house at the east end of a garden which contained a small lake (the stables were entered from YEOMAN'S ROW). Novosielski died young in April 1795 and his widow moved to a smaller house. The Grange was taken by John Braham, the celebrated singer who, however, ruined himself by his disastrous theatrical speculations and had to leave it in 1841. It remained empty until 1843 when it was demolished. Meanwhile in the late 1780s a row of ten houses had been built along the north-east side of the street. With the demolition of the big house, the street was extended to the boundary wall and named Grange Terrace, now Nos 27–41 (odd) on the north-east side and Nos 6–24 (even) on the south-west side. All the original Grove houses except Nos 23 and 25 were demolished when Egerton Place was built in

A caricature by Woodward of anglers in 1796 at the New River Head, Islington, near Eel Pie House.

1886, and much of the north-west end of the estate was redeveloped. The whole was renamed Egerton Terrace after Francis Egerton, 1st Earl of Ellesmere, one of the SMITH'S CHARITY trustees.

Egyptian Hall *Piccadilly*. An exhibition building, officially known as the London Museum, with an Egyptian façade designed by Peter Frederick Robinson in 1811–12, to hold 'upwards of Fifteen Thousand Natural and Foreign Curiosities, Antiques, and Productions of the Fine Arts'. These exhibits belonged to William Bullock, the showman, who had previously displayed most of them at the LIVERPOOL MUSEUM. Soon after the exhibition opened Bullock added to its attractions by opening 'a Roman gallery' and in 1815–16 made £35,000 by a display of Napoleonic relics, including the Emperor's luxurious bullet-proof carriage, an exhibit that drew enormous crowds. Bullock sold the carriage to a coachmaker for £168 and in 1843 it was bought for display by MADAME TUSSAUD'S. The remainder of the Egyptian Hall's contents were sold by auction in 1819. In 1820 the hall was hired by Benjamin Robert Haydon to show his picture, *Christ's Entry into Jerusalem*, from which the artist made a handsome profit. Later exhibitions were of Egyptian art and artefacts, including a tomb found near Thebes, a show of 'Ancient and Modern Mexico', a family of Laplanders 'complete with house and reindeer', 18-year-old Siamese twins, the skeleton of a mammoth, a moving PANORAMA of the Mississippi painted on 3 miles of canvas, and numerous freaks. In 1844 the hall was hired by Phineas T. Barnum for the American dwarf, General Tom Thumb. The hall was demolished in 1905 and the office block at Nos 170–173 PICCADILLY was built on the site.

General Tom Thumb seen arriving at the Egyptian Hall in his miniature coach and four in 1844.

Elder Street *E1*. Forming part of the Tillard Estate in SPITALFIELDS, it was developed in the 1730s. Many of the original houses survive: some have been restored, and a group are being repaired by the Spitalfields Housing Trust. Mark Gertler, the painter, who was born in nearby Gun Street, lived at No. 32.

Eldon Street *EC2*. Built at the end of the 18th century as part of the CITY CORPORATION'S FINSBURY Estate. It is named after Lord Eldon, Lord Chancellor 1807–27. ST MARY MOORFIELDS is on the north side.

Electricity The use of GAS as a source of power for lighting was largely unchallenged until the 1870s when the first public displays of electricity, using arc lamps with carbon electrodes, were conducted. BILLINGSGATE, the GAIETY THEATRE in the STRAND, LONDON BRIDGE STATION and the offices of *The Times* were among the first public buildings to have electric light. In 1878 arc lamps were installed along the 1¼ miles of the EMBANKMENT between CHARING CROSS and WESTMINSTER. But arc lamps were too brilliant, and too expensive to run, for wide application.

The invention of the vacuum filament lamp by Swan and Edison opened up new possibilities. The early supplies were powered by small engines. In 1883 Edison constructed the world's first power station at 57 HOLBORN VIADUCT. It supplied power to the OLD BAILEY and the GENERAL POST OFFICE but had to close in 1886. However, other companies were set up and in 1882 the Electricity Lighting Act gave the right to private companies to obtain provisional orders to dig up the streets or use overhead cables in order to operate in particular areas. The Councils (who granted the orders) were able to buy out the operation after 21 years although another Act six years later lengthened the reversion period to 42 years.

In the early years many small plants, all using different systems, voltages and frequencies, were established. A. and S. Gatti set up a private plant for their restaurant, in the STRAND (*see* GATTI'S). Another early operation was the KENSINGTON COURT Electricity Company which was begun in 1886 when Colonel Crompton persuaded the residents of Kensington Court Estate, just south of KENSINGTON HIGH STREET, to institute a common supply of electricity for lighting. The company grew and amalgamated with others, establishing power stations in KNIGHTSBRIDGE and NOTTING HILL.

In 1883 the Grosvenor Gallery in NEW BOND STREET set up a private lighting supply for the gallery. Like other such installations there were many requests for supply from neighbours. The Gallery expanded and soon supplied, via overhead cables, an area which reached from the THAMES to REGENT'S PARK and from KNIGHTSBRIDGE to the LAW COURTS. Sebastian Ziani de Ferranti became Chief Engineer and, after the London Electricity Supply Company was formed in 1887 to take over the Gallery undertaking, a search was started for a new site for expansion. The site chosen was at DEPTFORD because the land was cheap; it had an unlimited supply of water for cooling; and waterborne coal could easily be unloaded. Rather than negotiate with 24 different authorities to dig up the streets, Ferranti's laid cables alongside railway lines and over railway bridges. The Grosvenor Gallery was used as a distribution centre. Deptford dwarfed the average station of the time but was not the economic success which had been predicted. Delays in construction lost

The Mansion House in 1881 illuminated by electricity, which had been used for street lighting in London since the 1870s.

it some of the market which it was intended to supply. It did, however, set the pattern for future development of large stations supplying a wide area.

By the end of the century there were 30 power stations in London under the control of 16 undertakings. By 1914 the number of power stations had grown to 70. The penalties of an early start in electrical development in London became apparent. Electricity for lighting was sold by a multiplicity of undertakings, public and private, in both alternating and direct current, and on a bewildering number of voltages, frequencies and distribution systems. The supply areas tended to follow local government boundaries. Private companies had gained their foothold in Central London and the West End, where early development had taken place and the Councils were Conservative. Unlike most other large sites, where city corporations had purchased the electricity undertakings operating in their area, municipal ownership in London was to be found mostly in the East End, along the south of the river and in some of the outer suburbs where the progressive parties were in a majority. Ownership of electricity undertakings was a big political issue and the LONDON COUNTY COUNCIL, when under progressive control, made repeated attempts to unify London's supply.

Subsequently there were attempts to rationalise production into larger power stations. This required co-operation between undertakings which was not easy to achieve. A group of east London undertakings took bulk supply from the County of London Company's new station at BARKING (1925) while a group of west London companies established the London Power Co. to build a new power station at BATTERSEA. Battersea is one of the power stations that have become landmarks in London. It is now a listed building.

One area in which electricity had a large impact was in transport. It had a clear advantage over its competitors in the powering of tramways; and the resultant cheap tramway network enabled more workers to travel to and from the suburbs. In 1890 the City and South London tube line opened, operating from KING WILLIAM STREET to STOCKWELL. The Central London tube between BANK and SHEPHERD'S BUSH opened

soon after. Electrification freed commuters from the smoky and unpleasant experience of travelling on the DISTRICT LINE. In 1892 the UNDERGROUND carried 8 million passengers. By 1906 this had risen to 95 million. Between the wars, while electricity made great headway in lighting, gas proved very resilient, especially as gas companies such as the Gas-Light and Coke Co. offered an integrated service. Electricity companies tried to build up a market among lower-income consumers by offering assisted wiring and hire schemes and by greater use of prepayment meters. In Labour's post-war nationalisation most of London became part of the London Electricity Board for distribution purposes, though parts of the suburbs are divided among a number of other boards. Meanwhile large power stations are being built away from centres of population and London's old stations are becoming obsolete and being closed down (*see also* GAS *and* STREET LIGHTING).

Elephant and Castle *SE1*. A traffic junction since at least the 17th century, because the roads to KENNINGTON, WALWORTH and LAMBETH met here. In the mid-18th century the volume of traffic was greatly increased by the building of BLACKFRIARS BRIDGE, the New Kent Road and the London Road. The Elephant and Castle was originally a smithy which was converted to a tavern in about 1760. The origin of its name is uncertain but it may have been named after the sign of the CUTLERS' COMPANY, which dealt in ivory, or after the Infanta of Castille who was once engaged to Charles I; however in the heraldry of the Middle Ages an elephant is nearly always shown with a castle on its back, and in chess sets the castle is sometimes carved on the top of an elephant. The Elephant and Castle became a well-known coaching terminus in the 18th and 19th centuries and later a terminus for trams. The area was devastated in the 2nd World War. It was redeveloped in 1961–6 around two gigantic roundabouts with a covered shopping arcade designed by Boissevian and Osmond, a cinema and buildings for the Ministry of Health by Erno Goldfinger, and the London College of Printing and Graphic Art by LONDON COUNTY COUNCIL architects.

Elizabeth Garrett Anderson Hospital *144 Euston Road, London NW1*. Elizabeth Garrett Anderson, the first woman in England to qualify in medicine, opened the St Mary's Dispensary for Women and Children at 69 Seymour Place in July 1866, having received the LSA diploma in 1865. From the outset it was her ambition to provide a hospital where women could be treated by members of their own sex. At first most of her patients were local women but within a few years they were coming from all over London with gynaecological complaints. As the work increased the need for in-patient treatment became overwhelming and in 1872, when the Dispensary became the New Hospital for Women, a ward of 10 beds was opened by Lord Shaftesbury. The hospital continued to grow and in 1874 it moved to Nos 222 and 224 MARYLEBONE ROAD, where 26 beds were provided.

In 1888 it was moved to its present site. When rebuilding by J.M. Brydon was completed in 1890 the new hospital had 42 beds and was staffed entirely by women. On the death of Elizabeth Garrett Anderson the hospital was given its present name. In 1929 a new wing was opened by Queen Mary who also opened the

The Elephant and Castle has always been notorious as a confused traffic junction. From an aquatint by Pollard, 1826.

Garrett Anderson Maternity Home in 1948. From the earliest days women medical students and many women doctors working all over the world received training here. Since no medical school in England or Scotland would accept her as a pupil, nor any examining body as a candidate, Elizabeth Garrett Anderson had to go for her MD to the Sorbonne where she presented her thesis on migraine. There is now a thriving migraine clinic at the hospital and some of the pioneer work on tyramine and dietary migraine was done here.

In 1948 the 107-bed hospital became part of the ROYAL FREE HOSPITAL Group; in 1972 it was transferred to the North West Metropolitan Regional Hospital Board, and in the 1974 reorganisation the hospital became part of the CAMDEN and ISLINGTON Area Health Authority.

Elizabethan Public Theatres In the Middle Ages plays were performed publicly on church steps by clergy, or in inn yards and elsewhere by lay players. Apart from bull and bear baiting arenas (*see* BEAR GARDENS) there were no theatre buildings until the THEATRE was built at SHOREDITCH in 1576. This was managed by James Burbage and his associates, and plays were performed by a company known as the Chamberlain's Men. This theatre was demolished in 1598. Another theatre in SHOREDITCH, the CURTAIN, was built in 1577–8. It fell into disuse in about 1625 after the severe jurisdiction of the CITY had persuaded theatre managements to move across the river to SOUTHWARK and the LIBERTY OF THE CLINK. On BANKSIDE the ROSE was built in 1586–7, the SWAN in 1594–6, the GLOBE in 1598–19, and the HOPE in 1613–14. All these theatres were round, wooden buildings surrounding an open yard, in which stood the stage overlooked by tiers of galleries (*see also* BEAR GARDENS MUSEUM AND ARTS CENTRE).

Elm Row *NW3*. Built in the 1720s and lined with elm trees. Sir Henry Cole, the art patron and public servant (*see* GREAT EXHIBITION), lived at No. 3 in 1879–80.

Elm Tree Road *NW8*. This little street in ST JOHN'S WOOD, laid out on the EYRE ESTATE in the early 1820s, still retains many of its original small, pretty villas. Thomas Hood, the poet and writer, lived at No. 17 in 1841–4.

Elmers End *Kent*. First mentioned in the 16th-century. Eden Lodge, which was the principal residence, is believed to have been built about 1710, although one source gives the date as 1610. A document dated 1682 relates to an estate known as Eastfield situated at Elmers End. In 1775, when John Cator was Lord of the Manor, a request was made to him to allow 12 small houses to be built there for the use of the 'industrious shepherds and labourers of the parish'. Eden Lodge was at one time known as Gwydyr House, and in 1876 it is shown on the map as Elm Lodge. In 1839 it was extensively damaged by fire and some time after 1856 it was demolished and a new house built. It later became a boys' school, with the grounds at the back being used by the Eden Park Polo Club. Elmers End is now part of the London Borough of BROMLEY.

Elmstead Woods *Kent*. In the 11th century part of the estate of BROMLEY owned by the Bishop of Rochester. For the most part the soil in the area was of inferior quality but the woods at Elmstead were valuable. In 1319 Bishop Hamo de Hethe was elected Bishop of Rochester. The Pope, however, refused to recognise the appointment and granted the see to John de Puteoli, Confessor to Queen Isabella. Long and expensive litigation followed and Bishop Hamo de Hethe was obliged to sell Elmstead Woods. During the reign of Henry VIII the then Bishop of Rochester sold ten loads of timber from Elmstead Woods at 2s a load, to build the *Kathleen Pleasaunce*, one of the ships which took the King's retinue to the Field of the Cloth of Gold. More wood was later taken for shipbuilding; and in 1580 Bishop Young informed Queen Elizabeth that, because of the great reduction of the woodlands, he had not cut down any trees except those required to repair the Bishop's palace at BROMLEY. With the demand for houses for the rapidly increasing population and with the spread of BROMLEY, the woodlands were taken over and houses built. As recently as 1915 Elmstead was referred to as a hamlet; but the railway had arrived by then, making the area easily accessible for commuters to London. Elmstead Woods is now a pleasant suburban area in the London Borough of BROMLEY.

Elsing Spital *(The Priory Hospital of St Mary's within Cripplegate).* In about 1329 William de Elsing, a mercer, founded a small hospital for blind men and women on the site of a former nunnery. It was initially administered by a rector and four secular priests, but in 1342 five Augustinian canons were substituted. Elsing became the first prior. In 1534 the King's supremacy was acknowledged by the prior and canons, but in 1536 the hospital closed. The fate of the patients is unknown but the sisters who had nursed them were given a house nearby, and the prior became the King's chaplain. The chapel was given to the parishioners of ST ALFEGE, London Wall, who moved to it from their ruinous church opposite. Stow said that the other buildings were given to Sir John Williams, Master of the King's Jewels, and that, on the following Christmas Eve, they were burned down. The buildings of the first SION COLLEGE were erected on part of the site. Some 14th-century ruins of the priory can still be seen in LONDON WALL.

Elsworthy Road *NW3.* Probably takes its name from a contractor employed by Eton College, which was endowed with the Manor of Chalcots (*see* CHALK FARM) by Henry VI. Sir Henry Wood, the musician, lived at No. 4 in 1905 – 37.

Eltham *SE9.* This pleasant suburb with its busy High Street was, within living memory, an attractive Kentish village which had grown up on either side of the highway from London to Maidstone. The Saxon community here, confirmed by an entry in *Domesday Book,* was possibly preceded by a small Romano-British community, as traces of a farmstead have been found at the eastern end of Eltham, and the Roman WATLING STREET forms the northern boundary of the parish. Antiquarians have, however, always been drawn to Eltham by the picturesque remains of ELTHAM PALACE, the Tudor building at the moated manor of WELL HALL, and ELTHAM LODGE in the Great Park of the old palace. In addition much of interest can still be found in and around the High Street. At the western end can be seen Queenscroft in Eltham Hill, a restored early 18th-century house with contemporary murals, and the parish church of St John (built in 1875), the latest in a sequence of churches on this site dating back to the Saxon period. Of the four big houses which once stood at this end of the High Street only Cliefden House (built in the early 18th century) with its contemporary stable block, and the delightful Orangery of the now demolished Eltham House, survive, but almost opposite can be seen the early 18th-century and heavily restored Greyhound public house with its two fireplaces taken from ELTHAM PALACE, and the late 17th-century Mellins, formerly a chemist's shop. The Philipot Almshouses, founded in 1694 in the High Street, can now be found in Philipot Path where they were rebuilt in 1931. Further along the High Street, next to the Roman Catholic

church, can be found the 18th-century Eagle House.

Away from the High Street in the Bexley Road stands AVERY HILL, a sumptuous mansion built in 1890 for Col. John North by T.W. Cutler, which is now AVERY HILL COLLEGE, a teachers' training college. This lavish Italianate building incorporates a glass-domed conservatory in which a varied selection of exotic plants are grown.

The transformation of Eltham into a suburb began with the arrival of the two railway lines and the building in the 1930s of the Eltham by-pass (A20). The hamlet of Pope Street became the suburban area of New Eltham and the area to the east of WELL HALL was laid out by Cameron Corbett as a fine Edwardian estate with its own railway station. The need to house munitions workers in the 1st World War provided the impetus for the building of the Progress Estate, still much admired as a small garden city development.

Many famous people have lived in Eltham: Van Dyck; James Sherard, the botanist who produced his *Hortus Elthamensis* in 1732; Kitty O'Shea, whose relationship with Charles Stewart Parnell led to his political downfall; Edith Nesbit, who lived at WELL HALL from 1899 to 1922; Herbert Morrison, the cabinet minister, who lived at No. 55 Archery Road in 1929–60; and Frankie Howerd. Bob Hope was born here.

Eltham College *Mottingham, SE9.* An independent school of 670 pupils, including 10 girls, aged 7 to 18 years. It was established in London in 1842 for the sons of missionaries, and has occupied its present site, a 25-acre estate surrounding an 18th-century mansion, since 1912.

Eltham Lodge *SE9.* A splendid example of Restoration domestic architecture in brick with stone dressings, built in 1664 for Sir John Shaw by Hugh May. Shaw, who had acquired the lease of the Manor of Eltham, found the old palace derelict so built his new house in the Great Park on the site of the Keeper's Lodge. The Shaw family held it until 1820 and, after a succession of tenants, it became in 1889 the club house of the Eltham Golf Club. It is now the headquarters of the Royal Blackheath Golf Club which moved there in 1923 (*see* GOLF CLUBS).

Eltham Palace *SE9.* At the time of the Domesday survey of 1086 the manor of Eltham was in the hands of Odo, Bishop of Bayeux and was held for him by Haimo, sheriff of the county, from whose heirs it passed to the Clare family; then, in 1278, to the de Vesci family; and in 1295 to Antony Bek, Bishop of Durham, who seems to have extensively rebuilt the manor house before presenting both house and manor to Edward, Prince of Wales, son of Edward I and later Edward II. The buildings were again extended by Edward II for Queen Isabella who spent much time here. Edward III was also a frequent visitor and it was here that he received the captive King John II of France. Froissart described Eltham at this time as 'a very magnificent palace which the King possessed seven miles from London'. The improvements to the palace were continued in the reign of Richard II under the supervision of Geoffrey Chaucer, the clerk of works. Among these improvements was a stone bridge, the predecessor of the 15th-century bridge across the moat which still survives. Further additions were made to the palace in the reign of Henry IV, who was married by proxy here to Joan of Navarre in 1402, and in that of Henry VI. The great hall, the most splendid surviving part of the palace, with the third largest hammerbeam roof in England, was constructed in about 1479 and a new chapel (excavated in 1976) was built in the reign of Henry VIII who was often at Eltham in his early years and issued from here the Statutes of Eltham, those regulations of the Royal Household which were drawn up in 1525 by Wolsey who had been installed as Lord Chancellor in the chapel 10 years before. The timbered Chancellor's Lodging was probably built at this time.

Towards the end of his reign Henry rarely came to Eltham, and Elizabeth I even less often. In 1576 Lambard wrote, 'This house by reason of its nearness to GREENWICH hath not been so greatly esteemed.' And when Parliament took possession of it after the execution of Charles I it was reported as being 'much out of repair'. It was sold to Col. Nathaniel Rich who began to pull it down. After a visit in 1656 John Evelyn wrote, 'Both the palace and chapel in miserable ruins, the noble wood and park destroyed by Rich, the Rebel.' When the manor was leased to Sir John Shaw in 1663 he chose to leave the palace in ruins and, appointing Hugh May his architect, rebuilt the manor lodge in the park which survives as Eltham Lodge, the clubhouse of the Royal Blackheath GOLF CLUB. The Great Hall was used as a barn.

When a lease was granted in 1931 to Stephen Courtauld, however, the restoration of the Hall began and was completed by 1937. Courtauld built a new house, designed by Seely and Paget, and redesigned the gardens. The Courtaulds lived at Eltham Palace until shortly before the end of the 2nd World War, when the lease was acquired by the War Department.

Elvaston Place *SW7.* Takes its name from Elvaston Castle in Derbyshire, seat of the Earls of Harrington (*see* HARRINGTON ESTATE). Mostly large mid-Victorian houses converted into flats. The Divan Hotel at No. 31 occupies a house which in the 1950s was one of the best-run brothels in London. The Mauritius High Commission is at Nos 32–33.

Ely Place *EC1.* Site of the Bishops of Ely's London house from the end of the 13th century until 1772. The Bishops used to lodge in the TEMPLE but by 1290, after a quarrel with the KNIGHTS TEMPLAR, the then bishop was living in his own house here. By the end of the century ST ETHELDREDA'S CHURCH had been built beside it. In 1327 the 14-year-old Philippa of Hainault spent Christmas here before her wedding to Edward III. And John of Gaunt lived here from 1381, after his SAVOY PALACE had been wrecked in the PEASANTS' REVOLT, until his death in 1399. It is here that Shakespeare has him reflect on 'This royal throne of kings, this sceptred isle . . . this blessed plot, this earth, this realm, this England.' Henry VIII and Catherine of Aragon came to Ely House in 1531 for a series of banquets lasting five days during which 100 sheep, 51 cows, 91 pigs, 24 oxen, 720 chickens, 444 pigeons, 168 swans and over 4,000 larks were consumed.

In 1576 Elizabeth I obliged the bishop to lease part of the property to her beloved Chancellor, Sir Christopher Hatton, for £10 a year, ten loads of hay and a rose picked at midsummer. While the see was vacant in the 1580s Hatton built himself a house in the garden which he bequeathed to his nephew whose widow married the great lawyer, Sir Edward Coke. It was an unhappy marriage and after Coke's removal from the bench, following his resistance to the encroachments of the royal prerogative, his wife 'divided herself from him and disfurnished his house of whatever was in it, and carried all the moveables and plate she could come by, God knows where, and retiring herself into obscure places.' During the Civil War the house was used first as a prison for royalists, then as a hospital for soldiers and sailors. Lady Coke died in 1648; and at the Restoration in 1660 the Bishops of Ely returned to their part of the property.

On the death of the last Lord Hatton in 1772 his property reverted to the Crown. Ely House had by then become extremely dilapidated, and the Bishop of Ely moved to Ely House, 37 DOVER STREET. The buildings of Ely Place were thereupon demolished, the adjoining church of ST ETHELDREDA's being preserved; and brick terraced houses were built on the site. Sir Charles Barry, the architect, took a house in Ely Place as a young man. Dickens set Mr Waterbrook's house here and in it David Copperfield renews his friendship with Tommy Traddles. As Crown property Ely Place does not form part of the CITY OF LONDON and is exempt from the authority of the LORD MAYOR. It is still a private road, supervised by a top-hatted commissionaire. The police may enter it only if invited.

Emanuel School *Battersea Rise, SW11.* Originated from Emanuel Hospital, which was founded in WESTMINSTER by the will of Anne Sackville, Lady Dacre, in 1594. The school moved to the disused premises of the Royal Victoria Patriotic Fund Orphanage in 1883.

Embankment Gardens *WC2, SW1, SW3.* These comprise the Victoria (BLACKFRIARS BRIDGE to the HOUSES OF PARLIAMENT), the Albert (on the opposite side from WESTMINSTER BRIDGE to VAUXHALL) and the Chelsea (from BATTERSEA BRIDGE to CHELSEA BRIDGE). The idea of riverside gardens on what Gay in his *Trivia* of 1716 described as 'the slimy shore' was first advanced by Sir Christopher Wren in his scheme for rebuilding the CITY in 1666. But it was not until 1870 that, after the expenditure of large sums of money, the Victoria Embankment Gardens were opened to the public. Monuments include a statue of Robert Burns, the poet, and Robert Raikes, the founder of Sunday schools (*see* STATUES). There is also a bandstand for open air concerts.

The Albert Embankment Gardens were more easily constructed at a similar cost and opened in 1869. The site, noted by Samuel Pepys for its boat and shipbuilding in the 17th century, was previously liable to flooding. There is now a fine promenade with a superb view of the HOUSES OF PARLIAMENT.

Embankments Sir Joseph Bazalgette's major work, as Chief Engineer of the METROPOLITAN BOARD OF WORKS, was the main drainage of London (*see* DRAINS AND SEWERS). But he supervised other notable constructions. The most important were the colossal ALBERT, VICTORIA and CHELSEA EMBANKMENTS along the THAMES to the west of the CITY. They have a total length of 3½ miles. Like the main sewage scheme, the embankments were an old concept, often proposed but often delayed. The Romans

The Victoria Embankment under construction in 1864, as seen from King's College, Strand.

first embanked the Thames and, according to Tacitus, they pressed the Britons into the work. The next mention of embanking London's river is in a document of 1367. James I encouraged embanking; and, after the GREAT FIRE, Christopher Wren designed a continuous new embankment for the new CITY to run between BLACKFRIARS and the TOWER, but it was never fully executed. In 1767 the City Corporation embanked a mile of the river side. During the 1830s Sir Frederick Trench produced a grand embanking scheme; and in 1856 John Martin, the painter, proposed another. Bazalgette finally made the old dream a reality in the bold and confident Victorian manner. With their battered walls, thick parapets, occasional landing stages, all faced with granite blocks, with their rhythmical rows of plane trees lining broad avenues, their dolphin-based lamps of cast iron, their lion-headed mooring rings, and general character of solid indestructibility, the Embankments are the most enduring monuments of Victorian enterprise London can offer. When completed they impressed everyone, including Dickens and even Carlyle. Begun in 1868 and completed in 1874, their building required an immense amount of mud shifting and road building as well as an enormous amount of brick, concrete and masonry work. They reclaimed no less than 32 acres of mud and at CHARING CROSS and CHEYNE WALK new public gardens were formed, while the TEMPLE GARDENS were extended. The extent of the reclamation along the VICTORIA EMBANKMENT can be judged by the long distance of the YORK WATERGATE in the EMBANKMENT GARDENS from the river.

Embassy Club *6, 7, 8 Old Bond Street, W1.* Built as a theatre club in the late 19th century and known as the 400 Club until 1920. It presented sophisticated cabaret and was a meeting place for the rich and famous: Edward VIII, then the Prince of Wales, was often to be seen here. It declined with the onset of the 2nd World War but is now moving towards the

recovery of its former position. The seating capacity is 250.

Empire Cinema *and* **Theatre** *Leicester Square, WC2.* The Royal London Panorama was built in 1881 by a French company on the site of SAVILE HOUSE. It opened with scenes from the Charge of the Light Brigade but it was a financial failure and the next year Thomas Verity began converting the building into the Empire Theatre. It reopened in 1884 but its burlesques, operettas and ballets were not well attended. In 1887, after redecoration, it reopened as a music-hall under the management of Augustus Harris and George Edwards. They began the series of spectacular ballets which brought the Empire world-wide fame up to the turn of the century. Katti Lanner was the ballet mistress and among the leading dancers were Adeline Genée, Lydia Kyasht, Phyllis Bedells and Fred Farren. The LONDON COUNTY COUNCIL re-granted the theatre's licence in 1894 on the condition that its notorious promenade was altered. Thin canvas screens were put up to hide it from the auditorium, but on the opening night they were torn down by the audience led by the young Winston Churchill, then a cadet at Sandhurst. In 1905 the first revue, *Rogues and Vagabonds*, was staged and was followed by many others. After the 1st World War variety was interspersed with musical comedies. Among the main successes were *Lilac Domino* (1918), *Irene* (1920), *The Rebel Maid* (1921) and *Lady be Good* (1926). It was closed and demolished in 1927, and in 1928 the Empire Cinema opened on the site.

Endell Street *WC2.* Named after the Revd James Endell Tyler, the rector of ST GILES'S at the time of its construction in the 1840s. In the 17th century there was a bath here, fed by medicinal springs, in which Queen Anne is supposed to have immersed herself from time to time. It was locally known as Queen Anne's Bath. The Swiss Church of London, designed by George Vulliamy (1853), is at No. 79; ST PAUL'S HOSPITAL FOR UROLOGICAL DISEASES is at No. 24.

Endsleigh Street *WC1*. Extends north from GOR-DON SQUARE to Endsleigh Gardens. It was built by Thomas Cubitt and James Sim and named after a place in Devon on the Russell family's estate. The writer, Dorothy Richardson, had a top floor room at No. 7 in 1896–1906 and 1907–11. In her autobiographical novel, *Pilgrimage*, she calls it Tansley Street. On the west is a well-restored terrace housing the LONDON UNIVERSITY institute of education and the John Adams Hall of Residence. Opposite is Hillel House, the headquarters of the Jewish social organisation known as B'Nai B'Rith. No. 6 is the Muslim Institute. The LONDON SCHOOL OF ECONOMICS is at No. 13.

Enfield *Middlesex*. Enfield parish is oblong in shape and bounded to the east by the River LEA. The river marshes provided rich meadow land. Further west lay a broad belt of brick earth which, manured, yielded good arable crops. In the west the boulder clay proved too difficult for animal-drawn ploughs; it remained woodland and was enclosed in 1136 as ENFIELD CHASE. The people had common rights there for fuel, timber and pasture. Enfield existed long before the Domesday survey; indeed by then the area was already fully cultivated. Its centre, formerly the village green, developed into Enfield Town. On the south side lay the manor house, known locally as the 'Palace', on the north Saint Andrew's Church, the Tudor Grammar School and the market square which was created in 1632. The greatest house was Elsyng where Henry VII's rich minister and Speaker of the House of Commons, Sir Thomas Lovell, lived with over a hundred servants. Later it passed to Henry VIII, and the future sovereigns Edward, Mary and Elizabeth spent much of their childhood here. Nearby FORTY HALL was built in 1629 for Sir Nicholas Rainton, the puritan Lord Mayor. The area remained Parliamentarian in the Civil War. The only fighting was a skirmish between local commoners and troops in 1659.

The 18th century saw much poverty, with wood stealing on the chase. Men were hanged for killing the king's deer. It was followed by a period of stagnation, though the Royal Small Arms Factory was opened in 1815. The railway revived the town in 1849 and many new houses were built. Ediswan's, set up in PONDERS END in 1880, was the cradle of the electronics industry. New industrial development followed the opening of the Northmet Power Station in 1903 at Brimsdown. In

The manor house known as the 'Palace' which stood in the centre of Enfield, from a late 18th-century engraving.

the 1920s the Cambridge Road was constructed and further industry followed along its route. During the 1930s a vast number of houses were built over former orchard and nursery land. The population reached a peak of 110,000 in 1951. Enfield was amalgamated with EDMONTON and SOUTHGATE in 1956 to form the London Borough of Enfield. A plaque on Enfield Town station booking hall states that 'John Keats' first school was in a house on this site, demolished 1872.' Another plaque on Westwood Cottage, Chase Side, indicates that Charles Lamb lived here from October 1829 to May 1833. Lamb also lived at No. 85 Chase Side from September 1827 to October 1829.

Enfield Chase *see* TRENT PARK.

English Grotto (*Rosoman Street*), *Clerkenwell*. A small pleasure garden first heard of in 1760. In 1769 Jackson, the proprietor, advertised his 'Grand Grotto Garden and Gold and Silver Fish Repository' as having an enchanted fountain, a wonderful grotto and a water mill which, when set to work, represented fireworks and formed a beautiful rainbow. Admission cost 6d. Nothing is known of the garden after 1780.

Ennismore Gardens *SW7*. Takes its name from William Hare, Viscount Ennismore and Earl of Listowel, who in 1823 bought Kingston House which had been rebuilt by Evelyn Pierrepoint, 2nd Duke of Kingston for his mistress, Elizabeth Chudleigh. The paddocks and gardens were considerable and stretched along the whole length of what is now PRINCE'S GATE and south to the parish boundary. The houses on the east side were built between 1843–6 and named Prince's Terrace. (The Prince of Wales gate to the Park had just been made.) The developer was John Edgar and the architect was H.L. Elmes. Ennismore Mews was created at the same time and the houses must have been very attractive looking westward over the gardens to the village of KENSINGTON. All Saints Church by Lewis Vulliamy was built in 1848. In the 1870s the 3rd Earl of Listowel decided on further development and three huge houses, Alford House, Morcovo House and Bolney House were built down the west side of the terrace, Alford House being designed by Matthew Digby Wyatt for Lady Mary Alford. The north side of the Gardens was then laid out with very large houses with mews behind them, then the west and south sides of the square. Unusually for so late a development, the houses were provided with well-built mews and carriage houses (now Ennismore Garden Mews). Kingston House was demolished in 1929 and the present flats were built on the site. The west side of the Terrace and north side of the Gardens are a later development.

Epping Forest *E11. E17*. A remnant of the primeval forest that stretched from the THAMES to the Wash and from the LEA to the Essex coast. In the forest two Iron Age earthworks remain. Loughton Camp is oval, covers six and a half acres and is surrounded by a rampart and a 45 ft wide ditch. Ambersbury Banks is a rectangular hill fort enclosing 12 acres. Its rampart is still 7 ft high in places and the ditch 22 ft wide and 10 ft deep. Boudicca is said to have used it and fought her last battle with the Romans near here. Having seen that her men were losing, she committed suicide with her daughters by eating poisonous berries near Epping

Pollard's aquatint Turning out the Stag at Buckik Hill *illustrates the Easter Monday hunt in Epping Forest in 1820.*

Upland. In 1030 Waltham Abbey was founded as a collegiate church of secular canons. It was rebuilt in 1060 by King Harold who prayed here on his way back from Stamford Bridge to fight the invading Normans at Hastings. He was buried in the Abbey. In 1177 it was refounded as an Abbey of Augustinian canons.

Early kings, who hunted in the forest, often spent the night at the Abbey. In 1226 Henry III granted the citizens of London the right to hunt in the forest on Easter Monday. The Easter Hunt became a great civic occasion attended by the LORD MAYOR and ALDERMEN. While hunting in the forest in 1536 Henry VIII is said to have heard the gun from the Tower signalling the death of Anne Boleyn. Waltham Abbey was dissolved in 1540. Most of the monastery was demolished but part of the Norman nave was made a parish church. In Edward VI's reign Princess Mary was kept a prisoner at Copt Hall, a house to the north of the forest. Elizabeth I hunted here and often used the hunting lodge at CHINGFORD, which was built in the early 16th century on a hill as a grandstand for the hunt. It is a timbered three-storey building and originally had no outer walls.

After the 17th century monarchs took less interest in hunting and the strict forest laws were not enforced. Highwaymen began to hold up passers-by on the lonely forest roads. In 1698 William III narrowly escaped being kidnapped and had to take refuge for the night in Copt Hall. By 1777 the forest had shrunk through enclosures to 12,000 acres, and by 1851 there were only 6,000 unenclosed acres left. In the 1860s Thomas Willingdale, his son and several others insisted on their right to lop trees in a part of the forest newly enclosed by the Lords of the Manor. They were arrested and sent to prison for malicious trespass. Partly as a result of this the Commons Preservation Society was formed which included among its members Octavia Hill and Sir Thomas Fowell Buxton (*see* COMMONS, OPEN SPACES AND FOOTPATHS PRESERVATION SOCIETY). By 1871 there were only 3,000 acres of forest left. The CORPORATION of the CITY OF LONDON, which owned a small amount of land in the forest, financed a chancery suit against the Lords of the Manor. In 1874 the court ruled that all enclosures made after 1851 were illegal. £250,000 was paid in compensation. An Act of Parliament in 1878 handed over the control of 6,000 acres of forest to the COR-PORATION OF LONDON. In 1882 at High Bench, Queen Victoria and the newly appointed Ranger, the Duke of Connaught, heard the LORD MAYOR declare the forest open and dedicated to the delectation of the public for ever. Small additions made since are Oak Hill (1889), Highams Park, WOODFORD (1891), and Yardley Hill, CHINGFORD (1899). By the late 19th century the Easter Hunt had degenerated into a rowdy affair 'attended by baronets and butchers, dandies and dustmen, tailors and tinkers, nobocracy and snobocracy'. The last was held in about 1882. Epping Forest today is the largest forest of hornbeams in England and is a much used 'lung' of East London. Herds of deer have been here for hundreds of years.

Epping Forest District Museum *39–41 Sun Street, Waltham Abbey, Essex.* A collection of exhibits illustrating daily life in the Epping Forest area from the earliest times to the present day, and housed since 1981 in two timber-framed buildings dating from the 16th and 18th centuries. Two special features of the museum are its Tudor herb garden and a fine oak-panelled room, carved in the reign of Henry VIII, on loan from the VICTORIA AND ALBERT MUSEUM.

Erith *Kent.* Situated where prehistoric trackways met the THAMES, Erith was first recorded in a charter of AD 695. Its name is derived from the Anglo-Saxon 'muddy haven'. Known alternatively throughout the Middle Ages as Erith or Lesnes, the manor was held at the time of *Domesday* by Odo, Bishop of Bayeux. Lord of the manor during the reign of Henry II was Richard de Luci, Justiciar of England, and as an act of penance for his implication in the plot to murder Thomas Becket he founded in 1178 LESNES ABBEY, suppressed by Wolsey in 1525. In 1215 King John issued letters of safe conduct to the barons' party for a meeting with his representatives at Erith church, but no record of the encounter survives. When the PEASANTS' REVOLT broke out in 1381, the first leader of the Kentish rebels was Abel Ker of Erith, who led

The Princess Alice *after colliding with the* Bywell Castle *on the Thames above Erith in 1878, when 700 lives were lost.*

a mob which burst into LESNES ABBEY. Henry VIII founded a naval dockyard at Erith, at which warships built at WOOLWICH, notably the *Great Harry*, were fitted out. The town grew in importance as a river port, but was still sufficiently secluded for the manor house to be rented as a meeting place by the Gunpowder Plotters in 1605. During the 18th and 19th centuries the Wheatley family as lords of the manor influenced the town's development, and their monuments may be seen in the parish church of St John the Baptist, a building of Norman origin heavily restored and enlarged in 1877. With the building of a pier and pleasure gardens in 1842 Erith enjoyed a brief vogue as a watering place. The THAMES above Erith was the scene of two famous 19th-century disasters: the Gunpowder Explosion of 1864, when two powder barges blew up causing widespread havoc, and the sinking of the *Princess Alice* pleasure steamer in 1878 with the loss of 700 lives. After the North Kent Railway opened in 1849 the town developed rapidly as a residential and industrial centre, and the population had reached 15,000 when it was made an Urban District in 1894. Among the multiplying factories whose products made Erith's name known worldwide were the Callender Cable Co. (1880), and the Maxim-Nordenfelt Gun Co. (1887), afterwards Vickers.

With continued housing development at BELVEDERE, Bostall, and Northumberland Heath, Erith became a municipal borough in 1938, with an eventual population of 46,000. The district suffered heavy damage in the air raids of the 2nd World War and the post-war years saw the decline of many of its traditional industries. In 1965 Erith was merged in the London Borough of BEXLEY, and recent redevelopment of the town centre has left little of architectural interest apart from Christ Church, a worthy example of Victorian gothic, built to the designs of J.P. St Aubyn in 1874. The spire was added in 1915.

Ermine Street Named after Arminius (or Hermann), the Saxon hero who routed Varus and the Roman legions at Winfeld on the Weser in Germany AD 9. Coinciding in part with the Romano-British road system, it ran from London north through STOKE NEWINGTON and ENFIELD and on via Lincoln to York. It was one of the four great roads which enjoyed royal protection, and may have entered the CITY from the south near LONDON BRIDGE. The remains of a Roman

Road linking it with WATLING STREET have been found 20 ft below the surface in BUDGE ROW.

Eros (Shaftesbury Memorial Fountain) *Piccadilly Circus, W1.* Symbolic memorial fountain designed by Alfred Gilbert and erected by public donations in memory of the philanthropic 7th Earl of Shaftesbury. It was intended to represent the Angel of Christian Charity, not Eros the God of Love. The first London statue to be cast in aluminium, it was unveiled in 1893 by the Duke of Westminster whilst the Duchess drank from one of the drinking cups supplied – the cup was quickly stolen. The fountain was considerably different from Gilbert's original design. He had planned a large basin into which water cascaded, but the basin that was made was so small that passersby got drenched if the fountain was turned full on. Around the outside was a low wall broken in four places and demolished in 1894. On the western section was a bust of Shaftesbury by Boehm. Gilbert was furious with the memorial committee's interference with his design and did not attend the unveiling. From 1922 to 1931 the memorial stood in the EMBANKMENT GARDENS while the underground station was excavated. Since 1937 it has been boarded up on New Year's Eve and other occasions of public celebrations. In 1939–48 it was kept at Egham. Until the 1940s elderly cockney ladies, euphemistically known as 'flower girls', sat around the memorial and were an integral part of the scene.

Piccadilly Circus during the 1st World War, with Cockney 'flower girls' beneath Eros.

Essex House *Strand.* Once the Outer Temple of the KNIGHTS TEMPLAR. In 1313 it passed to the

Knights of St John who leased it to the Bishops of Exeter. In 1326 Bishop Walter Stapleton was murdered by a mob in CHEAPSIDE and his body dragged back to his house and buried under a dung heap. Henry VIII gave the house to his Secretary of State, William, Lord Paget. In 1563 it passed to Robert Dudley, Earl of Leicester, who rebuilt it. Edmund Spenser often visited him and mentions the house in his *Prothalamion*. In 1588 Leicester died and his stepson, Robert Devereux, Earl of Essex, the Queen's favourite, inherited it. On 8 February 1601, piqued by the Queen's displeasure, Essex gathered some men and unsuccessfully tried to raise the CITY. He was surrounded at Essex House, forced to surrender and taken off to LAMBETH PALACE. Later he was imprisoned in the TOWER and executed for high treason. His son, Robert, came to live here when he came of age. In 1643 the HOUSE OF COMMONS, led by the Speaker, Lord Mayor and Aldermen, came to congratulate him after the Battle of Newbury. In 1646 Robert died and Pepys came to see his body lying in state. In 1674 the estate was sold to Nicholas Barbon, the speculative builder. Charles II had his eye on it as a present for a faithful servant and so most of the house was hastily demolished and the building of ESSEX STREET began soon afterwards. The remaining part was used to house the Cotton Library in 1712–30 (*see* BRITISH MUSEUM). This part was demolished in 1777.

Essex Road *Islington, N1.* One of ISLINGTON's main thoroughfares, its old name, Lower Street, referring to the fall in ground level from UPPER STREET. Beyond New North Road, where it ran into open country, it became Ball's Pond Road. At Astey's Row the NEW RIVER ran diagonally under the street through a 489 yd tunnel to Colebrooke Row, until it was piped in 1861. The street, which still contains many 18th- and early 19th-century houses, was once noted for fine mansions and ancient inns. The latter have all been rebuilt, though the Old Queen's Head, whose famous two-tier-gabled predecessor was pulled down in 1829, contains a 16th-century plaster ceiling and chimneypiece from the original, which had associations with Sir Walter Ralegh and Lord Burleigh. Dr William Hawes, founder in 1774 of the Royal Humane Society, was born in 1736 at the oldest of five successive Thatched House taverns on and near the site of the present public house at Astey's Row.

Of the mansions, opposite Cross Street stood the brick 17th-century Fisher House (later an asylum, demolished 1845), belonging to the related Fisher and Fowler families, both Lords of the Manor of CANONBURY. Ward's Place, fancifully named 'King John's', was a much older timber-framed house south of Greenman's Lane, probably built by Sir Thomas Lovell, Chancellor of the Exchequer to Henry VII and VIII. Renowned for its splendid plasterwork and stained glass, it was destroyed about 1800 after occupation as a smallpox hospital, soap factory and poorhouse. Behind its site are some of the earliest PEABODY BUILDINGS (1865), constructed in the form of an open square.

The Green Man, a Victorian public house, occupies the site of the Lower Street meeting house, ISLINGTON's earliest purpose-built Dissenting chapel, founded in 1744. Two small rows of almshouses in Queen's Head Lane were the CLOTHWORKERS', from 1640 to 1827, and Davis's, endowed by a local carpenter's widow.

These have also been demolished. At Packington Street part of the first Northern District Post Office (1855) survives behind a modern frontage. Other notable buildings are the Public Library of 1916, in Queen Anne style, and the former ABC cinema in Egyptian Art Deco (1930). Narrow lanes of cottages north of Britannia Row traditionally housed watchmakers' craftsmen; their sites were mostly obliterated by the Council's Popham Estate of the 1970s.

Past New North Road and the pretty Annett's Crescent was the grandiose Palladian building of Samuel Ridley's floorcloth manufactory, built in 1812 in open fields; from 1893 it became Probyn's bottling factory, and in the 1970s was restored as Council offices. Ridley lived in a row of bow-fronted Regency villas beyond. These were destroyed in about 1961.

In 1833, in an attempt to divert the slaughter of cattle from SMITHFIELD to the country, John Perkins built 'Islington Market' on 15 acres between the present Northchurch and Baxter Roads. Vested interests ensured his failure; derelict until the CALEDONIAN MARKET was authorised in the 1850s, the ground was then laid out with new streets. A few houses from the market period survive north of Northchurch Road.

Essex Street *WC2.* Built in about 1680 on the site of ESSEX HOUSE by Nicholas Barbon. Tom Cox, the highwayman hanged at TYBURN, who after a hold-up used to scuttle into ST CLEMENT DANES disguised as an old man, committed many of his robberies here. Essex Hall, which was rebuilt after the 2nd World War, is the head church of the Unitarian movement. It stands on the site of the first church, which was established in 1774. The EDGAR WALLACE public house at No. 40 stands on the site of the Essex Head. At the beginning of the 20th century this was a street of publishers. Methuen and Co. and Chapman and Hall were still here in the 1950s. The family firm of Macmillan, founded by Daniel Macmillan in ALDERSGATE STREET in 1843, are now at 4 Little Essex Street. Essex Street still contains some of its original houses. Distinguished residents of the street have included Sir Orlando Bridgeman, Henry Fielding and James Savage, the architect. The small public house, the Cheshire Cheese, at No. 5 Little Essex Street, occupies a site where a tavern has stood since the 16th century.

Eton Villas *NW3.* Takes its name from Eton College, which was endowed with the Manor of Chalcots (*see* CHALK FARM) by Henry VI. Alfred Stevens, the artist who designed the Wellington Memorial in ST PAUL'S CATHEDRAL, lived at No. 9.

Europa Hotel *Grosvenor Square, W1.* A neo-Georgian building occupying a large part of the north side of GROSVENOR SQUARE. Designed by Lewis Solomon, Kaye and Partners, it opened in 1964. There are 275 bedrooms.

Euston Road *NW1.* This was originally the New Road built in 1756 by the 2nd Duke of Grafton to drive cattle from the west to SMITHFIELD MARKET, avoiding OXFORD STREET and HOLBORN. The Capper family, who lived on the south side in the Long Fields, petitioned the House of Commons in vain to forbid the development because they said the clouds of dust raised by the driven cattle would spoil their hay. J.T. Smith, a British Museum official, described the Capper sisters: 'They wore riding habits and men's hats. One used to ride after boys flying kites with a large pair of shears to cut the strings. The other seized the clothes of those who trespassed to bathe.' Capper Street is named after the family.

Euston Square was built in 1827 and named after the ground landlords, the Fitzroys, Dukes of Grafton and Earls of Euston. The New Road was renamed Euston Road in 1857 and the south side of Euston Square was renamed Endsleigh Gardens in 1880. Euston Road is now a main thoroughfare with three of London's main railway termini along its length: EUSTON, where of the original station only the lodges to the Doric portico remain; the pinnacled ST PANCRAS, and the austerely handsome KING'S CROSS. Other notable buildings include the Inwoods' ST PANCRAS NEW CHURCH (1922); the ELIZABETH GARRETT ANDERSON HOSPITAL (1890); FRIENDS' HOUSE with its charming small garden; the Camden Town Hall, formerly the St Pancras Town Hall (opened in 1937), whose flagstaff has more than once flown the Red Flag; and the St Pancras Library and SHAW THEATRE. On the pavement outside the theatre stands the concrete and stainless steel abstract *St Joan* (1971) by Keith Grant. No. 122 (now an outfitters) is the site of the St Pancras Coffee Tavern which was licensed as a theatre in 1881–2. The Euston Theatre of Varieties opened in 1900 at Nos 37–43, became the Regent Theatre 1922–32, then a cinema, and was demolished to make way for an extension to the Town Hall in 1950. At No. 314 (whose site is now part of THAMES TELEVISION) the EUSTON ROAD SCHOOL of Painters was founded. Also in the street are the GLC Fire Station, the WELLCOME FOUNDATION, the Open Space Theatre and the headquarters of the National Union of Railwaymen (Nos 195–203) and the National Union of Mineworkers (No. 222). The offices at No. 250 are by Renton Howard Wood Levin (1981).

Euston Road School William Coldstream, Victor Pasmore and Claude Rogers, who lived and worked in the neighbourhood of FITZROY STREET which was then abounding in studios, founded their School of Drawing and Painting during the late 1930s opposite the north end of the street in EUSTON ROAD. Reacting against the academic pressures of contemporary art schools, and the current preoccupation with abstraction, they sought to foster by example and personal master-pupil contact a return to a more natural impressionistic portrayal of everyday life. Though the school was closed by war, the Pasmore-Rogers style is still recognised as 'Euston Road'.

Euston Station *Euston Road, NW1*. Both the oldest and the newest of London's main line termini. The first station on this site was built for the London and Birmingham Railway. It was planned by Robert Stephenson to replace the earlier terminus at CHALK FARM, and it opened in July 1837. A number of sites had been considered, including one at ISLINGTON and another near MARBLE ARCH, but had been rejected in favour of the area known as Euston Grove, at that time 'a quiet scene of nursery gardens'. The station was built with two platforms, each 420 ft long, one for arrivals, one for departures. Charles Fox designed a 200 ft long double train shed, with 40 ft spans. For the

first year six trains a day ran to HARROW, Watford and Boxmoor, but on 17 September 1838 the 112 miles from Euston to Birmingham were covered for the first time, the journey taking more than 5 hours. Until 1844 steam trains had to be drawn up the steep incline between Euston and CAMDEN TOWN on a fixed winding cable, as they did not have enough power to do it on their own. Trains out of Euston were attached to an endless rope 4,780 yds long and 3 ins thick, worked by two 60 horsepower stationary steam engines. Incoming trains had their engines detached at CAMDEN TOWN and the carriages ran down into the station under the charge of brakemen.

To celebrate the completion of the London and Birmingham Railway, Philip Hardwick designed a screen of two lodges and a 72 ft high portico to stand in front of the station. The portico was a splendid arch with four huge Doric columns, built of Bramley stone, which, in 1838 when they were built, were higher than those of any other building in London. The arch cost £35,000 and the expense was explained in a report to the shareholders: 'The entrance to the London passenger station, opening immediately upon what will necessarily become the Grand Avenue for travelling between the Midland and Northern parts of the Kingdom, the directors thought that it should receive some embellishment.' In 1839 Philip Hardwick added two hotels, one on either side of the portico. The Victoria was a 'Dormitory' serving breakfast only, at 3s 6d to 5s per night; on the other side the Euston provided more comfortable and more conventional service and was managed by a former steward of the ATHENAEUM.

Soon after Euston was opened a passenger commented: 'The booking offices are very fine specimens of architecture, but the waiting rooms are far from corresponding with them in magnificence.' This was not true for long, however, for in 1849 the Great Hall, 'the second splendour of Old Euston', was opened. It was a combined concourse and waiting-room designed by Philip Hardwick the Younger, a magnificent chamber in Roman-Ionic style 125 ft long, 61 ft wide and 62 ft high, with a deeply coffered ceiling. At its northern

Design for Hardwick's Great Hall of Euston Station, 1846–9, with George Stephenson's statue at the foot of the sweeping staircase.

end a curved double flight of steps led to a gallery and vestibule from which doors opened into the general meeting room, the board room, conference room and offices. A morning paper of 28 May 1849 reported, 'The elegant new station ... was yesterday opened for business. ... The decorations of the principal apartments are profuse, chaste and elegant; the general offices are neat, convenient and spacious; the whole, in fact as a railway station is without equal.' In 1852 a marble statue of George Stephenson by E.H. Baily was put up at the foot of the staircase in the Great Hall; and in 1881 the screen and portico were partially hidden by a new block containing a hotel with 141 bedrooms.

This hotel stood until 1963 when it was demolished to make way for a new station. British Rail needed more space for their operations and decided to rebuild Euston. Against strong opposition screen, portico and Great Hall were swept away with the rest. In 1968 Queen Elizabeth II opened the new Euston, a long, low building with a 647 ft long frontage and 18 platforms, designed by R.L. Moorcroft. The main concourse covers an area of some 30,000 sq yds and contains a Travel Centre, shops, a bank and refreshment rooms. A British Rail leaflet declares, 'Simplicity is the keynote in design of the new Euston.' Only the statue of George Stephenson and a stone group of Britannia, and other figures from the Great Hall, survive as reminders of former glories.

D.H. Evans *318 Oxford Street, W1*. In 1879 Dan Harries Evans, the son of a farmer from Llanelly, bought 320 OXFORD STREET, having moved from a small draper's shop in WESTMINSTER BRIDGE ROAD. His wife did the dressmaking, helped by other family members. The store specialised in fashionable lace goods. In 1937 a new store was built to the designs of Louis Blanc.

Evans Farm Listed in 1647 as one of several old properties which had grazing rights on CHELSEA COMMON. Its precise location is not known, but it may have been to the north of KING'S ROAD and east of OLD CHURCH STREET.

Evans Music-and-Supper Rooms *43 King Street, Covent Garden*. Housed in a 17th-century mansion, at one time the residence of Sir Thomas Killigrew, the founder of the THEATRE ROYAL DRURY LANE. The mansion was turned into a hotel in 1774, one of the earliest in London. The ROYAL INSTITUTE OF BRITISH ARCHITECTS rented rooms here in 1853–7. In the 1840s the huge dining-room was converted by W.H. Evans into a song and supper room which was known as Evans Late Joy's, Joy being the name of the previous owner. It became the haunt of wealthy Bohemians. It was the first and most famous of its kind and could perhaps claim to be the origin of the music-hall. Hot meals were served during the performances, which continued well into the morning. Sam Collins, the founder of COLLINS' MUSIC HALL, first sang there. The rooms were taken over in 1844 by 'Paddy' Green, who had been one of Evans's entertainers; he reconstructed the rooms and for some time maintained their reputation. The establishment slowly declined with similar institutions and closed in 1880. It was later taken over by the NATIONAL SPORTING CLUB and during 1930 became the home of the PLAYERS'

THEATRE CLUB, the cast of which, reflecting its origins, were known as the Late Joys. They transferred to the PRINCE CHARLES THEATRE in 1964, where they first appeared before members of the public rather than club members only.

Customers being entertained at Evans Music-and-Supper Rooms in Covent Garden in 1856.

Evelina Children's Hospital *Southwark Bridge Road, SE1*. Opened in 1869 in SOUTHWARK as a model hospital for children, with 30 beds. It was financed by Baron Ferdinand de Rothschild in memory of his wife, Evelina, who had died in childbirth three years earlier.

Everyman Cinema *Holly Bush Vale, NW3*. A small, oddly shaped building, it was constructed in 1883 as a drill hall for the HAMPSTEAD detachment of the 3rd Middlesex Rifle Volunteer Corps. In 1919 the building was redesigned as a theatre under the management of Norman MacDermott, and named the Everyman Theatre after Ben Jonson's comedy *Every Man in his Humour*, which was first performed at the CURTAIN theatre in 1598. Its première was a translation of Benavente's *The Bonds of Interest* in 1920. It presented plays with less commercial appeal than those shown in the West End, including the première of Noël Coward's *The Vortex* in 1924. Coward and the rest of the cast accepted the theatre's ruling that all actors should be paid only £5 a week. Nevertheless, they were sad to leave what one of them called 'that draughty, uncomfortable and loving little theatre'. In 1933 it opened as a cinema with René Clair's comedy *Le Million*. The oldest repertory cinema in the country, it has a policy of showing short seasons of films related to directors, actors, themes and countries. The small art gallery in the foyer mounts exhibitions of mainly lesser known and some famous artists.

Evil May Day Riots erupted in London on 1 May 1517. They were caused by general hostility towards foreign merchants and craftsmen from Flanders, Italy, France and the Baltic who had settled and were working in London. Superior techniques had ensured them a monopoly in a number of lucrative trades. Moreover, the government treated those guilty of dishonest practices with notable leniency. The depressed economic climate intensified the foreigners' unpopularity and May Day rioters expressed the resentment of Londoners in their attacks on foreigners' workshops and houses.

The mob of apprentices, clerics and ruffians was initially incited by a preacher, Dr Beal, at ST PAUL'S Cross, and subsequently led by a disillusioned broker, John Lincoln. The disorder they caused alarmed the authorities. Sir Richard Cholmley, Lieutenant of the TOWER, fired guns, and the Earls of Surrey and Suffolk brought troops in, quelling the violence and taking 400 prisoners. Lincoln and other leaders were hanged, drawn and quartered, and their remains gibbetted.

The surviving prisoners faced the death penalty for the treasonable offence of breaking the peace of Christendom. Henry VIII, on his return from RICHMOND, heard their pleas for mercy at WESTMINSTER HALL. He was accompanied by his Queen, Catherine, his two sisters, Thomas Wolsey, Lord Chancellor, the Council and the LORD MAYOR and CITY ALDERMEN. Queen Catherine, on her knees before Henry, interceded successfully for the female prisoners, but, like Henry's sisters, failed to secure his pardon for the rest. Wolsey, hated for his arrogance and far-reaching political power, was determined to use the incident to gain popularity. Weeping, and offering personal guarantees regarding the prisoners' future conduct, he persuaded the King to be merciful. The prisoners rejoiced, 'took the halters from their necks and danced and sang'.

Execution Dock The dock between WAPPING New Stairs and King Edward's Stairs was the spot where pirates were hanged. Stow wrote, 'The usual place for the hanging of pirates and sea-rovers, at the low-water mark, and there to remain till three tides had overflowed them'. And in *The Gentleman's Magazine* of 1735 it is recorded, 'Williams the pirate was hanged at Execution Dock, and afterwards in chains at Bugsby's Hole, near Blackwall'. People living in the late 19th century could still recall such riverside hangings,

A pirate making his confession to a chaplain before being hanged at Execution Dock, Wapping, c. 1795.

one recorded recollection being of a pirate hanging by the river with a crow on his shoulder pecking his flesh through the iron netting that enclosed the body.

Executions Until the 18th century it was customary for offenders to be taken by cart to some selected place of execution such as TYBURN or SMITHFIELD or sometimes near the scene of their crime. Stow, describing ALDGATE WARD in the the 16th century, vouches for the accuracy of his account of the hanged man's last words by explaining that the gallows were erected on the pavement outside his house. When 13 boys were hanged after EVIL MAY DAY in 1517 portable gallows were set up successively at LEADENHALL, NEWGATE and ALDGATE.

The first permanent London gallows was at TYBURN in 1571. It was innovatory in design, being triangular in shape, possibly for strength and also to face three roads, about 18 ft high with cross beams 8 or 9 ft broad. Eight people could hang from each beam at once. TYBURN was one of several regular places of execution to be found in London which one 18th-century traveller refers to as 'the City of the gallows'. To the east were TOWER HILL and EXECUTION DOCK, where pirates were hanged in chains, and gibbets were on the marshes on both sides of the river. The traveller from the north would see the execution places at SMITHFIELD and NEWGATE prison; and, if riding in from the south, those at KENNINGTON COMMON and, at an earlier date, the heads and quarters on LONDON BRIDGE. Until the end of the 17th century not more than about 50 offences carried the death penalty; in the next century this number rose dramatically, so that by 1819 there were more than 200.

Public executions were intended to act as a deterrent to crime. But young apprentices, who were allowed a holiday on an execution day – also known as 'the Hanging Match' or 'Tyburn Fair' – usually regarded the victims as heroes. The more notorious criminals such as Jack Sheppard and Dr Dodd had previously been put on public view. Crowds flocked to their cells and the turnkeys made hundreds of pounds from the spectators. The Ordinary (the prison chaplain) of NEWGATE often used the time between sentence and execution to compile a 'life' of the prisoner which was usually put on sale on the day of his execution. Collections of such 'lives' eventually made up the *Newgate Calendar*. Occasionally they were dictated by the criminals themselves; at other times they were written by professional hacks who would offer money or, sometimes, 'as handsome a coffin as a man has need of'. The poorer prisoners were glad of the money to settle debts or to provide something for their families. Some prisoners were dressed in their best finery. The highwayman, 'Sixteen-String' John Rann wore a pea-green coat and a huge nosegay as a buttonhole. Others, such as Stephen Gardiner, were clothed in nothing but a shroud; this was sometimes a sign of repentance and sometimes a determination to cheat the hangman from having the victims' clothes, which was one of his perquisites. Few went so far as the Irish woman, Hannah Dagoe, who brawled with the hangman as he tried to stop her from stripping off most of her clothes and throwing them into the crowd. Sometimes a white cockade in the hat or a white dress was worn as a symbol of innocence. The procession from prison to place of execution was escorted by the CITY MARSHAL, javelin-men and constables. Normally three prisoners

267

'Thieftaker-General of Great Britain and Ireland', Jonathan Wild, went to the gallows. By his own admission he had sent more than 70 persons to execution and used to ride in front of the carts announcing that his 'children' were coming. When he made the same journey in 1725 the jeering crowds shouted that this time it was their 'father' who was coming. Some were privileged to ride in their own coaches. Earl Ferrers, who had murdered his steward, wore his wedding suit and rode in his own landau to his execution in 1760. Generally persons who had been convicted of murder were refused this privilege. In 1768 it was denied to an attorney who had been convicted of forgery and wanted to share his coach with a footpad who was to be hanged with him. In cases of treason the ride had to be made backwards, on hurdles, tied to the horses' tails. In Cromwell's case this was done even though he had been dead for two years; the mummified remains of the former Lord Protector were dug up, together with the bodies of Bradshaw (who had sentenced Charles I) and Ireton (Cromwell's son-in-law) and dragged to TYBURN where they were hanged in their shrouds before being decapitated. Their heads were impaled at WESTMINSTER HALL. In 1746 the heads of two unsuccessful Jacobites were placed on TEMPLE BAR where, so Horace Walpole said, 'people make a trade of letting spy-glasses at a halfpenny a look'.

The journey from NEWGATE to TYBURN, along present-day OXFORD STREET to MARBLE ARCH, would last about two hours (see TYBURN). The carts stopped at ST SEPULCHRE'S, and at taverns to allow the prisoners to enjoy last drinks. Inevitably many of them were drunk by the time they reached the gallows. The story of the condemned man promising to pay for his drink 'when he came back' is a recurrent anecdote in many of the 'lives'. Possibly it originated with Jonathan Swift's poem 'Clever Tom Clinch, Going to be Hanged, 1727'. Around the gallows enormous crowds would gather. Pepys, at Colonel Turner's execution in 1664, paid 1s to stand on the wheel of a cart. Around 18th-century TYBURN was erected a stand known, from the cowkeeper who owned it, as 'Mother Proctor's Pews'. In this way, at Earl Ferrer's execution, she made more than £500. Once, when a prisoner was reprieved, some of the seats were destroyed in the riot that followed. 'It was a ribald,

Stephen Gardiner, shrouded as a sign of repentance, about to die on the gallows at Tyburn; engraving from The Newgate Calendar, *1773.*

rode in each cart, either sitting on or beside their coffins, sometimes with a chaplain. Methodist ministers were the first to make this uncomfortable ride regularly. In notorious cases the crowd could be extremely hostile to the prisoners and throw bricks and dead cats. A storm of missiles was showered on Eliza Brownrigg. A more ironic note was struck when the self-styled

At his execution in 1760 Earl Ferrers is watched by a crowd, many of whom occupy Mother Proctor's Pews to the left.

reckless, brutal mob, violently combative, fighting and struggling for foremost places, fiercely aggressive, distinctly abusive.' According to Arthur Griffiths, spectators often had their limbs broken, their teeth knocked out, and sometimes they were crushed to death. At Turner's hanging Pepys estimated the numbers at between 12,000 and 14,000.

Until the end of the 17th century it was usual for prisoners to mount a ladder with the rope about their neck and jump. If their nerve failed them they had to be 'turned off'. Pepys noted that Turner prolonged 'the time by long discourses and prayers, one after another, in hopes of a reprieve; but none came, and at last was flung off the ladder in his cloak.' By the 18th century prisoners were made to stand in a cart which was then drawn away. In their last moments they said prayers, sang a few verses of the Psalms or said goodbye to waiting friends and relatives. As the cart pulled away these rushed forward to speed up the deaths by pulling on their legs or beating at their hearts with fists and stones. Sometimes they tried to support them in the hopes of a late reprieve or of reviving them when cut down. In 1709 John ('half-hanged') Smith was cut down after hanging for quarter of an hour, and successfully revived. Again, in 1740, a hanged man taken to Surgeons' Hall for dissection was resuscitated and was committed again that same evening to NEW-GATE. Several other such cases are recorded. Frequently the struggles that occurred were between the surgeons, who were allowed ten bodies a year for dissection, and the prisoner's friends, who opposed such 'anatomisation'. Having successfully escaped from prison several times the notorious Jack Sheppard had hoped also to escape a premature death; instead his friends, who were waiting to revive him, had to watch helplessly as his body was cut down and tossed about by the crowd who thought that it was wanted for dissection.

Hangmen were hired by the CITY of London SHERIFFS who supervised the executions. Their methods were as crude and frequently as inefficient as those of Jack Ketch who bungled the execution of the Duke of Monmouth in 1685 and whose name was given as a nickname to his successors. Ropes broke; sometimes the hangman was drunk and on one occasion he was arrested for debt as he was on his way to TYBURN. One hangman, Derrick, was sentenced to death for rape but was reprieved by the Earl of Essex whom he subsequently beheaded. The shape of his gallows gives his name to the modern derrick crane, which suggests that he probably winched his victims up to the crossbeam of the gallows. Another hangman, John Price, was hanged for the murder of a woman. A third, Edward Dennis, was sentenced to death for his part in the GORDON RIOTS but was reprieved to hang his fellow-rioters. The longest-serving hangman was the Victorian, William Calcraft, whose bungling inefficiency from 1829 to 1874 prompted the scathing comment of his successor, William Marwood, 'Old Calcraft strangled 'em ... I execute 'em.' Albert Pierpoint, executioner 1931–56, estimated the length of time it took to die under the method of execution in use at that time as, at the maximum, 20 seconds.

In an effort to stamp out the riotous behaviour that accompanied each execution the gallows at TYBURN were demolished in 1783 and executions were carried out at NEWGATE instead. Most of the other notorious places of execution, such as EXECUTION DOCK, had already been abandoned. The last beheading on TOWER HILL, where, over several centuries, more than 300 people had lost their lives, usually by the axe, was of the Jacobite Lord Lovat who, as he laid his head on the block in 1747, smiled with satisfaction as a spectators' stand collapsed, killing 12 of the people who had come to see him die. The last beheadings of all took place outside NEWGATE in 1820, when the five CATO STREET conspirators, who had planned to assassinate the Cabinet, had their heads taken off, not with the axe that had been specially prepared for the occasion, but with a surgeon's knife.

An innovation was the drop that was fitted to the gallows at NEWGATE. A small collapsible platform had been used at Earl Ferrer's execution but as this could be lowered only about 18 ins the dying man could still touch the boards with his toes. Twenty persons could be hanged simultaneously on the new gallows. As late as 1864 five pirates were hanged side by side. NEWGATE was also the place of death of Christian Murphy who had been found guilty of coining offences; she was the last woman to be burned after hanging. When Catherine Hayes was burned in 1726 for murdering her husband, the hangman failed to strangle her, because of the flames burning his hands, and dropped the rope. Burning is more usually associated with near-by SMITHFIELD, particularly the burnings of heretics and martyrs, in the 16th century, when nearly 300 persons were burned at the stake.

Hangings continued to attract crowds well on into the 19th century. About 100,000 people were present when Henry Fauntleroy was hanged for forgery in 1824. When Holloway and Haggerty were hanged in 1807 the crowd was smaller, about 40,000; but when a pieman fell over, he caused a panic in which the

Murderess Catherine Hayes was burned to death in 1726 – the hangman failed to strangle her because the flames burned his hands.

269

crowd fought to get out of the confined space. People were trampled to death or suffocated. By the time the streets had been cleared there were nearly 100 dead and dying. Criticism mounted at the appalling behaviour of the crowds. At Muller's execution in 1864 *The Times* commented that 'robbery and violence, loud laughing, oaths, fighting, obscene conduct and still more filthy language reigned round the gallows far and near.' When the Mannings were hanged on the roof of Horsemonger Lane gaol in 1849 Dickens, who was present, told a friend that he 'felt for some time afterwards almost as if I were living in a city of devils'. His letters to *The Times* urged the abolition of such public spectacles. In 1868 Parliament submitted to public pressure, and thenceforth such executions took place inside the prisons. The last man to be publicly hanged was the Fenian, Michael Barrett, for his part in the CLERKENWELL explosion. From that time on only a black flag fluttering at the prison mast and the deep tolling of the bell gave any outward indication that a hanging was in progress.

NEWGATE was demolished in 1902 but executions continued to be carried out at other London prisons such as PENTONVILLE and HOLLOWAY. When Ruth Ellis was hanged at HOLLOWAY for shooting her lover in 1955, a crowd of about 1,000 surged about the prison gates reading the Execution Notice and protesting at the continuation of such a punishment. No executions have taken place since 1964, and in 1965 an Act was passed abolishing the death penalty for any crime except treason or piracy with violence.

Exeter Change *Strand*. Built in about 1676 on the site of EXETER HOUSE. In it were small shops intended for hosiers, milliners and drapers but most of them remained unlet and had to be leased out as offices. In 1773–1829 Edward Cross had his menagerie here with lions, tigers, monkeys, a hippopotamus that Byron said looked like Lord Liverpool, and a sloth that looked like his valet. One of the most popular exhibits was an elephant named Chunee, an animal weighing 5 tons, who had to be shot in 1826 when he threatened, in a particularly irritable mood, to break down the bars of his cage. A civilian firing squad failed to kill the

Exeter Change, Strand, the site of Edward Cross's menagerie, shortly before its demolition in 1829.

beast, so a party of soldiers had to be called in from SOMERSET HOUSE. They, too, failed in their mission; and a cannon was sent for. Before it arrived, a keeper managed to destroy the badly wounded elephant with a harpoon. Nine butchers took twelve hours to flay the hide. The skinned corpse was then dissected by more than ten surgeons watched by medical students. After the meat had been carted away, Cross displayed the skeleton in the damaged cage. Exeter Change was demolished in 1829, and the menagerie moved to the SURREY ZOOLOGICAL GARDENS. The site is now occupied by BURLEIGH HOUSE and the STRAND PALACE HOTEL.

Exeter Hall *Strand*. A classical building designed by Gandy Deering as a nonsectarian hall for religious and scientific gatherings and for the meetings of various philanthropic organisations. Built in 1829–31 on the gardens of EXETER HOUSE, it was used by the Ragged School Union; the Sacred Harmonic Society; the Bible Society; the Revd Charles Spurgeon, the popular preacher; the anti-slavery movement – Prince Albert attended a meeting of the Anti-Slavery Society here in 1840 – and the Temperance Society, who were concerned to discover that the cellars below were let to a wine merchant. In Barham's *Ingoldsby Legends* of 1840 we read:

Mr David has since had a 'serious call'
He never drinks ale, wine, or spirits at all,
And they say he is going to Exeter Hall
To make a grand speech,
And to preach and to teach
People that 'they can't brew their malt liquor too small'.

The building was acquired by the YOUNG MEN'S CHRISTIAN ASSOCIATION in 1880 and demolished in 1907. The STRAND PALACE HOTEL covers the site.

Exeter House *also at times known as Burghley House and Cecil House, Strand*. Built in Edward VI's reign for Sir Thomas Palmer, who was executed in 1553. Elizabeth I gave it to William Cecil, Lord Burghley, who 'beautifully increased it'. She visited him several times. On one occasion she found him laid up with gout and remarked, 'My lord we make use of you not for the badness of your legs, but for the goodness of your head.' Another time, as she bent to go through a doorway, she told a servant, 'For your master's sake I will stoop but not for the King of Spain.' Burghley died in 1598 and was succeeded by his son, Thomas, who was created Earl of Exeter in 1605. In 1623 Henrietta Maria lodged here before her marriage to Prince Charles. The house was badly damaged by fire in 1627 but was repaired; in 1660 Henrietta Maria returned, as a widow, to worship in the chapel specially set aside for her. After the GREAT FIRE the Admiralty Court, the Prerogative Courts and the Court of Arches sat here until DOCTORS' COMMONS was rebuilt. Anthony Ashley Cooper, 2nd Earl of Shaftesbury, husband of Frances, daughter of the 3rd Earl of Essex, lived here for a time. In 1671 his son, the author of *The Characteristics*, was born here. The son's tutor was John Locke who, as a member of the household, no doubt wrote part of his *Essay Concerning Human Understanding* here. The house was demolished in the 1670s and BURLEIGH STREET, EXETER STREET and EXETER CHANGE were built on its site.

Exeter Street *WC2*. Takes its name from EXETER HOUSE, on part of whose site it was built. Dr Johnson's first lodgings when he came to London from Lichfield were with a staymaker in this street. Part of his tragedy, *Irene*, was written here and his poem, *London*, completed. The inaugural meeting of the LONDON CORRESPONDING SOCIETY was held here at the Bell Tavern in 1792.

Exhibition Road *SW7*. The financial success of the GREAT EXHIBITION of 1851 enabled the Royal Commissioners, with the help of funds voted by Parliament, to purchase a large expanse of land south of Kensington Road at prices in excess of £3,000 an acre. Much of this land had been in the possession of Baron de Graffenried Villars, a Swiss nobleman living in Paris, and of the 5th Earl of Harrington. Almost all of it had been under cultivation, a considerable part as market gardens and nurseries, including the BROMPTON PARK NURSERY. North of these gardens, the GORE HOUSE Estate was also purchased. The Commissioners' intention was to further the aims of the Exhibition and extend 'the influence of Science and Art upon Productive Industry' by building on the land various museums, concert halls, colleges, schools and premises for learned societies. In order to help finance their scheme the Commissioners hoped that private houses would also be built. The names of the three important new roads which were constructed – QUEEN'S GATE, CROMWELL ROAD and Exhibition Road – were all chosen by the Commissioners' President, Prince Albert. Exhibition Road was built under an agreement with a rich and socially ambitious builder, Charles James Freake (for whom his friend, the Prince of Wales, successfully applied for a baronetcy) the son of a publican who had formerly been a coal merchant. Freake's road was subsequently extended southwards by the railway companies responsible for South Kensington Station. On its east side, in the 1860s, Freake built several large houses for well-to-do families in that grandiose, Italianate style which was to characterise the area. Four of these, Nos 69–72, remain. Lord Acton, the historian, owned No. 72 in 1877–90 and let it to Joseph Chamberlain for a year or so in the early 1880s. Close neighbours were Lord Bury, later 7th Earl of Albemarle, Treasurer of Queen Victoria's Household, and the 2nd Baron Methuen, father of the

Field-Marshal. The site of the remainder of Freake's houses in Exhibition Road is now covered by the Hyde Park Chapel of the Church of Jesus Christ of Latter Day Saints, the first Mormon church in London, designed by Sir Thomas Bennett, 1981. Behind the Chapel is another of Freake's developments, PRINCE'S GATE MEWS. Most of Exhibition Road, however, was, and is, occupied by museums, colleges and cultural institutes. At the south-east end is the VICTORIA AND ALBERT MUSEUM whose main entrance is in CROMWELL ROAD. Opposite this is the new extension to the NATURAL HISTORY MUSEUM whose main entrance is also in CROMWELL ROAD. And on this west side of the road may also be found the GEOLOGICAL MUSEUM, the SCIENCE MUSEUM, the City and Guilds College building of the IMPERIAL COLLEGE OF SCIENCE AND TECHNOLOGY, the British Institute of Recorded Sound, and, at the north end opposite the side entrance to the Afghanistan Embassy in PRINCE'S GATE, the ROYAL GEOGRAPHICAL SOCIETY whose main entrance is in KENSINGTON GORE. The ROYAL SCHOOL OF NEEDLEWORK used to occupy a charming building in Exhibition Road next to the IMPERIAL INSTITUTE. It was designed by the Lady Superintendent's brother, Fairfax B. Wade, and completed in 1903. But, like the IMPERIAL INSTITUTE itself, it was demolished for the expansion of IMPERIAL COLLEGE.

Exmouth Street *EC1*. Takes its name from admiral Edward Pellew, who was created 1st Viscount Exmouth for his bombardment of Algiers which compelled the Dey to accept the treaty abolishing Christian slavery. (Hence also Exmouth Market, so called from the Exmouth Arms of about 1816.) The SPA FIELDS CHAPEL stood here until 1879.

Eyre Estate In 1732, Lord Wootton sold land in ST JOHN'S WOOD to Henry Simon Eyre, merchant of London. To this day, the estate remains largely intact and in the possession of the Eyre family (*see also* ST JOHN'S WOOD).

Eyre Street Hill *EC4*. George Morland, the painter, having been arrested for not settling a publican's bill, died in a sponging-house here in 1804 after days of delirium and convulsions. His wife died three days later.

F

Fairfield Road *E3*. Probably laid out in the 1830s, by which time Bow Fair, which gave the road its name, had been abolished for being too rowdy. A dispute at Bryant and May's matchworks on the east side of the road in 1888 led to the famous 'matchgirls' strike', one of the first successful strikes by unskilled workers.

Fairholt Street *SW7*. Part of the early layout of the MONTPELIER development and first called Middle Street. It was built in 1835–40 with small houses, many of which have been refaced. It is named after Fredrick William Fairholt, the engraver and antiquarian, who lived in the area.

Fairs The history of fairs is closely associated with that of markets. The main differences between the two are that markets had a weekly regulation, fairs an annual one, and that markets satisfied the day-to-day needs of small householders while the annual fairs were for larger-scale trading.

Fairs are known to have existed in Anglo-Saxon times, although their charters were not granted until after the Conquest. Many charters date from King John's reign in the early 13th century. Most fairs originated as the result of pilgrims assembling at abbeys and cathedrals on the feast days of their enshrined saints. Religious houses tended to be in the country or small villages which were unable to cope with the numbers of pilgrims. Tented communities sprang up and travelling merchants set up stalls; thus sacred and secular interests coincided. Many charters confirm already existing fairs, change their dates and grant their very considerable incomes to corporations or church interests, these incomes deriving from the right to raise tolls or for 'stallage and pickage', that is to say stalls or poles placed in the ground. Early charters guaranteed the freedom of merchants, as Magna Carta did in 1215. Foreign merchants also required protection very early. Order was enforced at the fairs by officers entrusted with this task and by the Courts of Pie Powder, whose name was derived from the French *pieds poudreux*, signifying that those who were dealt with in them had dirty feet from travelling. Justice in these courts was rough and ready, offenders being tried before a jury of traders. One such court still operated at Hemel Hempstead in 1898.

There are detailed records only of very few of the numerous fairs which once flourished in London. The most important are dealt with individually. The fair at PECKHAM was said to have been founded by King John although no charter survives. Held from 21 July to 3 August next to the Kentish Drovers public house, it was noted for the exhibition of 'curious monsters'. It was abolished in 1827. HAMPSTEAD had a midsummer pleasure fair and nowadays the August Bank Holiday is celebrated with a fair on HAMPSTEAD HEATH. PINNER had a fair on the Wednesday after Whitsun by a Charter of Edward III and still has a fair today.

Edward III also granted a charter to St Katharine's Hospital for a fair on TOWER HILL. CROYDON once had two fairs, the sheep and cattle fair on 2 October and a cherry fair on 5 July, both with 14th-century charters. The EDMONTON fair was remarkable for offering for sale nothing of any utilitarian value. STEPNEY fair, as many other fairs in the suburbs, prospered as London grew in the 17th century and the open spaces once available for fairs in the centre no longer existed. It was founded by Charles II at the instance of the Earl of Cleveland.

The earliest record of a fair at MITCHAM is in 1732. It was held annually thereafter on 12 August. TOTTENHAM COURT fair flourished in the 18th century, being held at the Kings Head Tavern for three days in May. BOW fair took over from MAY FAIR when the latter was suppressed (*see* ST JAMES'S FAIR) and itself met the same fate in 1822. DEPTFORD fair was at its height in the early 19th century, as were the two fairs at BLACKHEATH on 12 May and 11 October, which were both suppressed in 1872. CAMBERWELL fair flourished at the same time and between 10 and 20 August was 'almost as riotous as Greenwich'.

A great many ancient fairs were suppressed in the 19th century, although a survey of 1927 could still list an astonishing total of 1,500 annual fairs in England and Wales, many of these in the London area (*see also* BARTHOLOMEW FAIR, CHARLTON HORN FAIR, FROST FAIRS, GREENWICH FAIR, ST JAMES'S FAIR, SOUTHWARK FAIR *and* WESTMINSTER FAIR).

Falcon Brook Rose in two places – BALHAM and TOOTING – the streams joining near CLAPHAM COMMON, running across WANDSWORTH COMMON to CLAPHAM JUNCTION and thence westwards to the THAMES at BATTERSEA. Originally called Hidaburna, it was renamed Falcon from the crest of the St John family, lords of the manor of BATTERSEA, or possibly from the 18th-century tavern which took its name from the same source. In modern times it forms an outlet into the THAMES for storm water from the sewers.

Falcon Court *EC4*. Named after a house called The Falcon which John Fisher left to the CORDWAINERS' COMPANY in 1547. The court once led to the TEMPLE CHURCH but the way was blocked in 1611. John Murray, the publisher, was born in a house at the corner of the court in 1778. His father had a small publishing business here which Murray took over in 1803. Shortly after the publication of the first cantos of Byron's *Childe Harold* in 1812 Murray moved to ALBEMARLE STREET.

Falcon Square *EC1*. Survives in name only at the south-west corner of LONDON WALL. It was bombed in 1940 together with Falcon Street and Falcon Avenue. All were named after the Castle and Falcon coaching inn which stood opposite the church of ST BOTOLPH ALDERSGATE in the 17th and 18th centuries. John Jasper in *Edwin Drood* stays at the Falcon Hotel when visiting London.

Fan Makers' Company *see* CITY LIVERY COMPANIES.

Fann Street *EC1*. The origin of the name is uncertain but it is thought to be that of a 17th-century landowner or builder.

Faraday House *and* **Cardinal's House** *Hampton Court Green, Middlesex*. Together formed the original Faraday House, named after Professor Michael Faraday who lived there from 1858–67. More than 300 years earlier the house on the site had been the Master Mason's lodging. The house was rebuilt for the Master Mason during Queen Anne's reign. It later became the official house of the Comptroller of Works, and was occupied by Thomas Ripley, Henry Flitcroft, and Sir William Chambers. The latter gave up the house in 1783 and it became the house of the Palace Clerk of Works until the office lapsed in 1835, when it became a 'grace and favour' residence. Hampton Court was greatly enlivened in 1897 with the granting of the house to the Princesses Sophia, Bamba and Catherine Duleep Singh, daughters of the deposed Maharajah Duleep Singh, former ruler of the Punjab, who had been defeated in battle in 1849. Princess Sophia achieved notoriety when she became a militant member of the Women's Suffrage Movement. In 1960 Faraday House was divided, the left-hand part retaining the name and the right-hand part being named Cardinal's House.

Farm Street *W1*. Extends from SOUTH STREET to HILL STREET. It formed part of Lord Berkeley's estate (*see* BERKELEY SQUARE) and takes its name from Hay Hill Farm, as this area was known in the 17th century. (The two parallel streets to the south, it may be noted, are called HAY'S MEWS and HILL STREET, all three constituents of the old name being thus commemmorated.) Building, chiefly of coach-houses and stables, began in the 1740s. Today most of the street is occupied by garages with mews-flats above, and is chiefly famous for the Roman Catholic CHURCH OF THE IMMACULATE CONCEPTION. But Farm House on the south side provides an engaging contrast to all its neighbours.

Farmers' Company *see* CITY LIVERY COMPANIES.

Farnborough *Kent*. Once a Liberty of the DUCHY OF LANCASTER and situated on the chalk of the North Downs. The northern part is mostly suburbia but the southern part more open. In the churchyard of St Giles is a gravestone commemorating Urania Boswell (*see* LOCKS BOTTOM). The church of St Giles was rebuilt in 1639 after the ancient structure had been destroyed in a tempest. The font dates from the 13th or 14th century.

Farriers' Company *see* CITY LIVERY COMPANIES.

Farringdon Market Established for the sale of fruit and vegetables when FLEET MARKET was cleared for the construction of Farringdon Street. At the opening ceremony waggons of vegetables were drawn past by horses decorated with ribbons. The market area was a large paved courtyard surrounded by shops let at 15s a week. The west side of the market was demolished when the approaches to HOLBORN VIADUCT were built. In mid-Victorian times it was celebrated for its cress. Mayhew paints a pathetic picture of the little watercress girls, some no more than seven years old, haggling with the saleswomen before dawn, then shivering in their cotton dresses and threadbare shawls as they tied up the bunches and washed the leaves at the pump before going out into the streets crying, 'Water-creases, four bunches a penny, water-creases!' On an average day they would make 3d or 4d. Today there is a Saturday morning market in Farringdon Road dealing in old and rare books.

Farringdon Road *EC1*. Originally Victoria Street, this thoroughfare, ploughing through some of London's most infamous slums, was projected as early as 1838, enacted in 1840 (though not built until 1845–6) and renamed in 1863. It followed the course of the FLEET RIVER from Middlesex House of Correction or COLDBATH FIELDS PRISON, from BAGNIGGE WELLS (King's Cross Road) over what had been Codpiece or Coppice Row, through the SAFFRON HILL rookeries, destroying among others the notorious West Street or Chick Lane, towards SMITHFIELD and FLEET STREET. Parallel with it, the Metropolitan Railway was opened in 1863, in tunnels at the northern end and from Ray Street to FARRINGDON STATION through a deep brick cutting masked by high walls.

Before this date the surroundings were largely waste ground. Even in 1878 the area was open enough to accommodate the stones of TEMPLE BAR before their removal to Theobalds, though by then many handsome warehouses – some now near-derelict – were being built. They include the 'Venetian palace' at the corner of Greville Street (Nos 25–27), recently restored.

Corporation Buildings, a row of Model Dwellings, were built by the CITY CORPORATION in 1865, largely due to Alderman Sir Sidney Waterlow; and on the other side Farringdon Road Buildings (1876), by the Metropolitan Association for Improving the Dwellings of the Industrious Classes. Both are now demolished. Next to the former was the grim brick Clerkenwell Workhouse, enlarged in 1790, castigated by *The Lancet* in 1865 as among London's worst, and pulled down in 1883. The ornate shop and office block replacing it as Nos 143–155 were themselves long ruinous until restored in 1981.

Farringdon Road now has two newspaper offices, the *Guardian*'s featureless block of 1976 on the site of Corporation Buildings (Nos 119–141) and the concrete *Morning Star* of 1949 at No. 75. The walled stretch opposite above the railway has long been the home of bookstalls, whose half-dozen survivors are now run by a single dealer. At the street's southern end the ruins of the former goods station still stand. At No. 63 Fullerscopes Ltd have been manufacturing telescopes on the premises since 1830.

Farringdon Street *EC4*. Formed in 1737 when the FLEET RIVER was arched over, it was named after William de Farringdone, a 13th-century goldsmith and CITY worthy. In 1737 the STOCKS MARKET, displaced from its MANSION HOUSE site, was moved here.

The Metropolitan Railway cutting parallel to Farringdon Road in 1868, five years after its construction.

It was rebuilt by W. Mountague in 1839 on the west side and renamed the FLEET MARKET. In 1874 it was moved to SMITHFIELD. No. 15 is the site of the FLEET PRISON and the CONGREGATIONAL MEMORIAL HALL.

Fauconberg House *Soho Square*. Occupied from about 1683 to his death in 1700 by Thomas Belasyse, 1st Earl Fauconberg, and from 1753–61 by Arthur Onslow, Speaker of the House of Commons. In Onslow's time a visitor was Samuel Richardson, author of *Pamela*, who, so Samuel Johnson said, 'used to give large vails [tips] to the Speaker Onslow's servants, that they might treat him with respect.' In 1762 Onslow sold the lease to the 4th Duke of Argyll who lived here till his death in 1770. It was then sold to John Grant, a Scottish lawyer and proprietor of West Indian sugar plantations, who commissioned Robert Adam to improve it for him. Some of Adam's drawings are in the SOANE MUSEUM. Grant's executors sold the lease to a victualler who turned it into Wright's Hotel and Coffee House. At the beginning of the 19th century it was in the hands of a firm of musical-instrument makers and in 1858 of Messrs Crosse and Blackwell who had it demolished in 1924 for their new offices (*see* SOHO SQUARE).

Federation of British Artists *17 Carlton House Terrace, SW1*. Established in 1961. The Federation organises annually such exhibitions as the Lord Mayor's Art Award and the City of London Art exhibition and acts as administrators of the MALL GALLERIES. It also provides exhibition facilities for several major London art societies, including the Royal Institute of Oil Painters (founded 1883), the Royal Society of Marine Artists (founded 1939), the Pastel Society (founded 1880), the Royal Society of Miniature Painters, Sculptors and Gravers (founded 1895), the Royal Society of Portrait Painters (founded 1891), the National Society of Painters, Sculptors and Printmakers (founded 1930), the Royal Society of British Artists (founded 1823), the Society of Women Artists (founded about 1855) the New English Art Club (founded 1886), the Society of Graphic Artists (founded 1920), the Society of Portrait Sculptors (founded 1953), the Society of Wildlife Artists (founded 1962) the United Society of Artists (founded 1921) and the ROYAL INSTITUTE OF PAINTERS IN WATER COLOURS.

Feltham *Middlesex*. A Saxon settlement, the name means a home in a field. Although a Domesday manor, it later lost its manorial rights to the neighbouring Kennington Manor. The village was almost totally destroyed by fire in 1634. It was rebuilt soon afterwards, together with the Manor House which was demolished in 1966 and is now the site of the Four Point Garage. Feltham expanded in 1847 with the opening of the London and South Western Railway line to Datchet. The Middlesex County Industrial School opened in 1859 and became a Borstal in 1919. The High Street was re-developed in the mid-1960s with a shopping precinct. Many buildings on the north side were demolished for the dual carriageway. On the south side the Green and pond survived, but other buildings were demolished in the 1970s for the New Chapel Square development designed by Manning Clamp and Partners, and the Philip Morris offices, designed by Trehearne's of Weybridge. St Dunstan's Church in St Dunstan's Road was originally a medieval building of unknown date, completely rebuilt in

1802 with a nave, chancel and battlemented tower with spire. Aisles were added in 1855. In the churchyard is buried William Wynne Ryland, an engraver executed for forgery at TYBURN in 1783. The 17th century vicarage, refronted in the 18th century, is now the Church Centre. Feltham House in Elmwood Avenue is a mid-18th-century house, with interior decoration attributed to James Wyatt. Once the home of the Westmacott family, it now serves as an Officers' Mess for the Royal Army Ordnance Corps.

Feltmakers' Company *see* CITY LIVERY COMPANIES.

Fenchurch Street *EC3*. Ancient street extending from ALDGATE to GRACECHURCH STREET. Its name is derived either from the fenny ground by the banks of the LANGBOURN which ran nearby, or from the hay market in GRACECHURCH STREET, the Latin for hay being *faenum*. Cinerary urns of Celtic origin some 3,000 years old and three Roman pavements have been found here. There were once three churches in the street, ST BENET GRACECHURCH, ST DIONIS BACKCHURCH and ST KATHARINE COLEMAN. On the corner of MARK LANE once stood the King's Head tavern where Princess Elizabeth had a meal of pork and peas after being released from the TOWER in 1554. Another ancient tavern, the Elephant, which still stands at No. 119, was so strongly constructed of stone that it survived the GREAT FIRE and was rebuilt in 1826. The Mitre, a favourite haunt of Pepys, did not, however, survive the Fire. Pepys described the owner, Daniel Rawlinson, who was a great friend of his, 'looking over his ruins' in 1667. Rawlinson was also a tea merchant. His business, founded in 1650, was at the sign of the Crown and Three Sugar Loaves in the street. It was taken over by his son, Thomas Rawlinson, who became Lord Mayor in 1706. On the south side is Plantation House by A.W. Moore, built in 1934–7 and housing the LONDON COMMODITY EXCHANGE and the Rubber Exchange. On the north side near CULLUM STREET is Fountain House, designed by W.H. Rogers and built in 1954–7; it was the first building in London to comprise a low horizontal block and a tall tower: the tower, 14 storeys high, was the first skyscraper erected in the CITY. At No. 71, in a building of 1900 designed by T.E. Collcutt, is LLOYD'S REGISTER OF SHIPPING. FENCHURCH STREET STATION lies farther south. On the wall of the Midland Bank stands W.H. Chattaway's bronze *The Spirit of Enterprise* (1962).

Fenchurch Street Station *Railway Place, EC3*. Opened in 1841 by the London and Blackwall Railway, this was the first railway terminus in the CITY OF LONDON. The line from BLACKWALL had originally ended at MINORIES. Until 1849 no steam locomotives were used. Trains were dragged from BLACKWALL to MINORIES by cables and had to reach FENCHURCH STREET by their own momentum and leave by gravity needing 'only a slight push from the platform staff'. In 1854 a new station, designed by George Berkeley, was opened. This was later also used by the London, Tilbury and Southend Railway. Rebuilt in 1935, Fenchurch Street, now a minor terminus of the Eastern Region, receives over 28,000 passengers in the morning peak hours.

Fenton House *Hampstead Grove, NW3*. Built in 1693. The names of the architect and the first owner are unknown. It takes its name from Philip Fenton, a merchant, who bought it in 1793. It was acquired in 1936 by Lady Binning who bequeathed it to the NATIONAL TRUST in 1952, together with her collections of porcelain, furniture and pictures which included a view of Hampstead Heath supposed at that time to be by Constable, G.F. Watts's *Neptune's Horses* and a landscape by Brueghel the Elder. Since 1952 the house has also held a large collection of early musical instruments assembled by Major George Henry Benton Fletcher, which had been presented to the NATIONAL TRUST in 1937. These are kept in playing order for students and include a 1612 harpsichord probably used by Handel, the property of the Crown.

Festival of Britain *1951* To revive the nation after more than five years of post-war austerity, the Festival Exhibition was held on derelict land on the south side of the THAMES in LAMBETH, a century after the historic GREAT EXHIBITION of 1851. Unlike its predecessor it was actually planned to lose money, but it did set in motion the development of the SOUTH BANK. Among its features were the ROYAL FESTIVAL HALL, the Dome of Discovery, the Skylon obelisk, ornamental fountains and the tower of a former lead shot factory. As part of the Festival BATTERSEA PARK was transformed into a pleasure garden in the manner of VAUXHALL GARDENS, with a tree walk, fountains and a grotto.

Fetter Lane *EC4*. The name, originally Faytor or Faiter Lane and afterwards Fewterers Lane, may be derived from the Old French *faitor*, a lawyer, whose reputation in the Middle Ages was so low that by the 14th century the word had come to mean idler. It was used by Chaucer to describe the impostors and beggars who frequented the lane. It has also been suggested that the name may come from the fetters or lance vests worn on cuirasses, since the armourers who worked for the KNIGHTS TEMPLAR had their workshops here. Stow referred to the lane as Fraitor Street, and it has also been conjectured that the designation may be a false derivation from Frater which might be 'an appropriate title for a street so close to the purlieus of the learned brethren of the Law'. Nathaniel Tomkins, brother-in-law of Edmund Waller and implicated in Waller's Plot, lived at the HOLBORN end of Fetter Lane and was hanged on 5 July 1643 before his front door. Both this end and the FLEET STREET end of the street – where the murderess Sarah Malcome was hanged in 1733 – were often used as places of execution and for other punishments. From the mid-17th century the lane was celebrated for its conventicles. Praise-God Barebone, the rich leather merchant who gave his name to Cromwell's Parliament of 1653 and who was the father of the speculator, Nicholas Barbon, lived in the lane and preached in one of the conventicles here. The Fetter Lane Independent Chapel was founded in 1660. Thomas Bradbury, its pastor in 1714, claimed to have been the first man to have proclaimed George I King, having had private intelligence of the death of Queen Anne. The chapel was rebuilt in 1732. Wesley preached in this new chapel in 1737; and John Spurgeon, father of Charles Haddon Spurgeon, the Calvinistic Victorian preacher, was pastor here. London's first Moravian Chapel was built in the lane before the GREAT FIRE. Richard Baxter gave lectures here for ten years from 1672; Thomas Bradbury in 1720; and later Wesley and George Whitefield both preached here. Famous occupants of the lane have included John Dryden; Thomas Hobbes, author of *Leviathan*; and Tom Paine. It was in a coal-shed in Fetter Lane that Dr Johnson's strange medical friend, Robert Levett, used to meet the prostitute whom he most unwisely married. It was also here, in a house on the east side opposite FLEUR DE LIS COURT, that the notorious Elizabeth Brownrigg, midwife to St Dunstan's Workhouse, maltreated her girl apprentices, one of whom was stripped naked, flogged, imprisoned in a cellar with a chain tightened to the point of suffocation round her neck, and had her tongue cut through with a pair of scissors. The girl eventually died. Mrs Brownrigg was hanged. The PRINTER'S DEVIL public house is at No. 98. From the White Horse at No. 90 coaches used to set out for Oxford and the West Country. Nos 3 and 4 were designed by John Shaw in 1849 as an infants' school. The street was widened in 1841.

Field of the Forty Footsteps Also known as Brothers' Steps, it was the ground behind the present BRITISH MUSEUM upon which two brothers fought a duel in the 1680s over a girl with whom they were both in love. They were both killed. Tradition has it that 40 of their footprints were to be seen here for several years. No grass would grow in the field or upon the bank upon which the girl sat to watch the fight.

A ticket for a display by James Figg, 'Father of the Ring' and owner of Figg's, Marylebone, designed by Hogarth in about 1733.

Figg's *Marylebone*. A 'boarded house' presenting entertainments such as female-fighting, bear- and tiger-baiting and cock- and bull-fights. It was built near the Oxford Road by James Figg, the famous prize-fighter from Thame, Oxfordshire. He died in 1734 and was buried in MARYLEBONE churchyard.

Finch Lane *EC3*. Named after either Ailwin Fink, a money-changer who lived in Finkeslane in 1261–2, or James Finke who lived there in 1231–45. In 1755 James Watt was apprenticed here to the 'philosophical instrument maker', John Morgan. John Henry Newman, later Cardinal Newman, the son of a partner in the banking firm of Ramsbottom, Newman and Co., was born here in 1801.

Finch's Grotto Gardens *Southwark*. Situated on a triangular plot near St George's Road. It was opened by Thomas Finch, a herald painter, in 1760, probably to replace CUPER'S GARDENS which closed in that year. A grotto was built over the medicinal spring. There was one orchestra in the gardens and another in the elaborately decorated octagonal music-room. Musical standards were high, and the gardens attracted artists from COVENT GARDEN and SADLER'S WELLS. In 1771 FIREWORKS and illuminated transparent paintings, 30 ft by 40 ft, were added to the attractions. The grotto was demolished in 1773 and gave way to a skittle ground. The Goldsmith's Tavern succeeded the grotto.

Finchley *N2, N3, N12*. Despite its Saxon name ('wood frequented by finches'), it does not appear in *Domesday*. This is because by 1086 it already formed part of the ecclesiastical manor of FULHAM. By the 13th century, or earlier, Hornsey Park, much of which lay in Finchley, had been emparked by the BISHOP OF LONDON, whose moated castle lay astride the Finchley boundary, where HIGHGATE golf course now is.

On the west, the Dollis Brook separates Finchley from HENDON. Its tributary the Mutton Brook forms part of the southern boundary, and to the south-east Finchley takes in part of HAMPSTEAD GARDEN SUBURB, the ancient SPANIARDS INN and a small part of the grounds of KENWOOD. The eastern part of Finchley once consisted mainly of the notorious Finchley Common, crossed by the GREAT NORTH ROAD and a haunt of highwaymen until its enclosure in 1816.

Much of Finchley lies on boulder clay. Between this and the underlying London clay is a layer of gravel. The best conditions for early settlement were where this lay exposed: thus Nether Street, an ancient local road, links the sites of old farms along the gravel line. Elsewhere, near the gravel, were the three hamlets that formed Finchley's earliest population centres, now fully connected by 20th-century building.

To the south-west, around the parish chuch of ST MARY, was Church End. East End, now East Finchley, sprang up at the northern gate of the Bishop's Park. At the north, WHETSTONE with its many inns was important to travellers on the GREAT NORTH ROAD. North Finchley became a major centre only in the late 19th century, but rapidly became an important shopping district.

In the 14th century the BISHOP OF LONDON allowed travellers to pass through his private park, which had gates at HIGHGATE, the SPANIARDS, and East End. They could then cross the common, instead of using more roundabout routes, to WHETSTONE and beyond. Church End and most agricultural land still lay well west of the busy route and, as late as 1876, was described as 'still rural' and 'not unpicturesque'. This comparative seclusion offered pleasant retreats for the wealthy in the 18th and 19th centuries and some large houses were built, notably along Nether Street, Ballards Lane and East End Road.

More than 90 long-distance coaches passed daily through WHETSTONE by 1835, but early Finchley commuters had their own 8.20 a.m. coach from Church End to the BANK, as well as omnibuses from several other points. It was, however, only with the coming of the Great Northern Railway (now part of the underground NORTHERN LINE) in 1867 that building really intensified. In the next 50 years most large houses, estates and meadow land gave place to mainly middle-class housing. Wentworth, Fallow Lodge, Moss Hall, Woodhouse, and Grass Farm are a few of the old estates which have given their names to modern roads. Remaining old houses include some handsome listed buildings: Park House (1739) in Hendon Lane; FINCHLEY'S MANOR HOUSE (1723) in East End Road; The Limes (1734), now 1339 High Road, and Cornwall House (1795) in Cornwall Avenue.

Three conservation areas have been established. Moss Hall Crescent is a neat Victorian development of substantial houses; Finchley Garden Village is a pre-1st World War development around a central 'green'. The Church End conservation area, based on the original hamlet, includes the parish church, Park House, Christ's College with its distinctive 'pepperpot' tower, AVENUE HOUSE and Grove Lodge, one of the few remaining Victorian houses still bordering the Regent's Park Road, which was cut through fields to Ballards Lane by an Act of Parliament of 1825.

Finchley Road *NW2, NW3, NW8, NW11.* A long road extending north from ST JOHN'S WOOD through SWISS COTTAGE, FROGNAL and GOLDERS GREEN to the NORTH CIRCULAR ROAD. It was built in accordance with an Act of Parliament of 1827. C.B. Fry, the cricketer, lived at 8 Moreland Court. Thomas Hood, the poet, lived at No. 28, Devonshire Lodge, which was built in 1843, and died here in 1845. John Barnes and Co., the department store, formerly at Nos 191–217 in a building by T.P. Bennett and closed in 1981, was established in 1899.

Finchley's Manor House *East End Road, N3.* Built in about 1723 by Thomas Allen, whose family held the manor from 1622 for more than 200 years. An extra floor was added in the 1920s, also a chapel and school premises. Since the early 19th century the house has been used from time to time for educational purposes, and since 1981 as a Jewish seminary and primary school. Although a manor house existed in 1253, no trace of any building earlier than the present one has yet been found.

Finsbury *EC2.* The area was once part of the great fen which lay outside the CITY walls. The manor belonged to a prebend of ST PAUL'S CATHEDRAL. When Fitzstephen wrote his description of London in the 12th century the drier parts were used by the citizens for sport. Apprentices skated on the frozen fen in winter. In 1414 Lord Mayor Thomas Falconer built the Moor

Part of Agas's 16th-century map showing windmills in Finsbury Fields (left) and the kennels of the Lord Mayor's Hunt (centre).

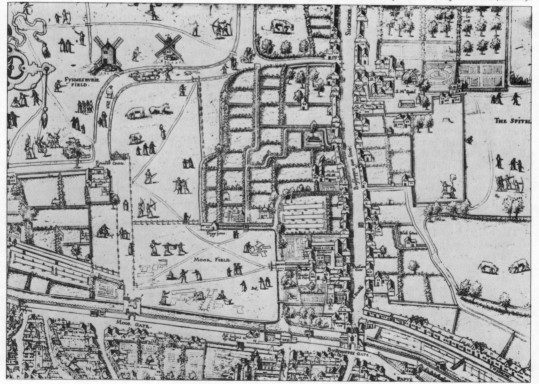

Gate in the City wall 'for ease of citizens that way to pass ... into the fields ... for their recreation'. In about 1511 the Lord Mayor, Roger Acheley, 'caused dikes to be made and the ground to be levelled and made more commodious for passage'. Some years later the citizens, angry about enclosures made on the fields, took the law into their own hands and 'within a short space all the hedges about the towns [ISLINGTON, HOXTON, SHOREDITCH, etc] were cast down and the ditches filled'. In 1548 Protector Somerset, on his return from the Battle of Pinke, was welcomed in Finsbury Fields by the Lord Mayor and Aldermen. Ralph Agas's late 16th-century map shows sheets of cloth lying out to dry, archers, cattle, windmills and the kennels of the Lord Mayor's hunt.

Trees were planted at the beginning of the 17th century and gravel walks made. In 1607 Richard Johnson wrote that the area was 'the garden of this city and a pleasurable place of sweet ayres for citizens to walk in'. In 1641 the HONOURABLE ARTILLERY COMPANY settled in Finsbury. From the time of the Civil War until after the Restoration there was a foundry in the fields where cannon were made. In 1665 BUNHILL FIELDS was made a burial ground for Dissenters. Victims of the GREAT PLAGUE were also buried in the fields in a large pit. After the GREAT FIRE the homeless camped in the fields, 'some under tents, some under miserable huts and hovels; many without a rag or any necessary utensils, bed or board'. In 1667 Pepys walked in Moorfields and found houses two storeys high. He forecast, 'it must become a place of great trade till the City be built'. Building on the fields began at this time but much of Finsbury remained open until the late 18th century. In 1676 BETHLEM HOSPITAL was rebuilt in Moorfields by Robert Hooke. In 1732–3 the Church of ST LUKE OLD STREET was built and given part of the parish of ST GILES CRIPPLEGATE. In 1739 John Wesley took over the old foundry and converted it into a Methodist chapel, preacher's house, school and classrooms. He and Whitefield often preached in the surrounding fields to crowds of 10,000. In 1749 Whitbread's BREWERY moved to CHISWELL STREET. The next year ST LUKE'S HOSPITAL was built by the elder Dance at the west end of WORSHIP STREET. In 1761 the CITY ROAD was built to join the 'new road' from MARYLEBONE. The City of London Lying-in Hospital was built in CITY ROAD in 1770–3. Between about 1775 and 1800 the Finsbury Estate was laid out as a residential suburb by George Dance, with FINSBURY SQUARE as its centrepiece. It became the fashionable area for the medical profession until the late 19th century when the doctors migrated west to HARLEY STREET. In 1778 Wesley's New Chapel was built. In 1790 ST LUKE'S HOSPITAL was rebuilt in OLD STREET.

The borough of Finsbury was created in 1900. It was bounded on the north by ISLINGTON, on the east by SHOREDITCH, on the south by the CITY, and on the west by HOLBORN. Redevelopment of the area started at this time when large office blocks were built, so that it became almost indistinguishable from the main part of the CITY. The Borough of Finsbury was abolished in 1965 and the area was absorbed into an enlarged Borough of ISLINGTON.

Finsbury Circus *EC2*. Laid out in 1815–17 with tall, handsome houses by William Mountague to the designs of George Dance the Younger. The site had been partly occupied by BETHLEM ROYAL HOSPITAL;

the rest of it had been an open field with gravel walks for promenading. On the demolition of the buildings the hospital moved to LAMBETH. None of the original houses remains, all having been rebuilt as offices, the south-west quadrant as Salisbury House by Davis and Emanuel in 1849, the south-east quadrant by Gunton and Gunton in 1901, and in the north-west as Britannic House, now Lutyens House, by Sir Edwin Lutyens in 1924–7.

Finsbury Circus Garden *EC2*. A circular garden, ringed with office buildings, lying between LONDON WALL and MOORGATE, it is a popular rendezvous for City people. In the summer many take their lunch there. There is a fine bowling green and band concerts are sometimes held in the summer.

Finsbury Park *N4*. Comprising 115 acres for sport and recreation, it was purchased at a cost of £472 per acre and opened as one of the earliest municipal parks in 1869. It included the site of the earlier Hornsey Park visited by the boy King Edward V accompanied by his uncle Richard of Gloucester (later Richard III). 'When the Kynge approached nere the cytee,' in the words of Hall's *Chronicle*, 'Edmonde Shawe, goldsmythe, then Mayre of the cytie; with the aldermenne and shreves in skarlet and five hundreth commoners in munraye [violet] receyved his Grace reverently at Hornesay Parke and so conveighed him to the cytie where he entered the fourth day of May, in the fyrst and last yere of his reigne.' (*See also* STROUD GREEN.)

Finsbury Pavement *EC2*. Once a fashionable promenade, a dry footway across the marshy district of MOORFIELDS, it was described by Strype in 1720 as a 'new row of good houses not yet named'. John Keats was born in 1795 at the Swan and Hoop livery stables where his father, who had married the proprietor's daughter, was chief ostler.

Finsbury Square *EC2*. Rectangular square with the CITY ROAD running through the east side – an attempt to recreate a 'West End' atmosphere in the City – designed by George Dance the Younger in 1777–92. All four sides were different. It is said to have been the

The interior c. 1810 of James Lackington's book shop, known as 'The Temple of the Muses', in Finsbury Square.

first public place where gas lighting was permanently installed. From 1778 to 1798 James Lackington, the bookseller, had a shop in the south-east corner of the square called 'The Temple of the Muses'. It had a frontage of 140 ft and was one of the sights of London. On top of the building was a dome with a flagpole which flew a flag when Mr Lackington was in residence. In the middle of the shop was a huge circular counter around which, it was said, a coach and six could have been driven, so large were the premises. A wide staircase led to the 'lounging rooms' and the first of a series of galleries with bookshelves. The books got shabbier and cheaper as one ascended. The shop burned down at the beginning of the 19th century. Only a few of the original houses survived the 2nd World War and the square is now mostly filled with modern buildings. On the summit of Royal London House is a bronze figure of Mercury by James Stephenson which was first exhibited at the ROYAL ACADEMY in 1929. David Livingstone lived here for a short time in 1856. The Austrian composer, Anton Bruckner, stayed at a house on the site of Nos 39–45 in 1871, and began his Second Symphony here.

Fires The narrow, tortuous streets which have characterised London since Saxon times, and the combustible materials from which the houses that lined them were constructed, have meant that the CITY has been ravaged time and again by fire. The first destruction, however, was pre-Saxon; it was inflicted on the newly established Roman trading-centre beside the THAMES and the marks of it can still be seen. When the foundations of today's tower blocks are excavated, a change in the colour of the earth reminds us how completely Boudicca and her tribesmen destroyed the first Roman London of AD 61. The Saxon ST PAUL'S CATHEDRAL was destroyed twice over, first in 961 and then in a more general conflagration in 1087. The medieval building was seriously damaged again in a widespread fire in 1135 when LONDON BRIDGE was partially destroyed also. William Fitzstephen, writing in the last quarter of the 12th century, declared in his description of an otherwise ideal city that 'the only plagues of London are the immoderate drinking of fools and the frequency of fires'. Late in the 12th century it was enacted that the lower parts of all City houses must be made of stone and that all roofs were to be tiled; but the command was largely ineffective. Each ward, however, was required to provide the equipment – poles, hooks, chains and ropes – for the demolition of a burning house, and well-to-do citizens were charged to keep a long ladder available outside the main door in hot weather. Londoners were well aware of the dangers that threatened them. John Stow, searching the City records and recalling the stories told by his parents and grandparents, tells of frequent outbreaks of fire, including serious conflagrations at WESTMINSTER PALACE in 1299, at BAYNARD'S CASTLE in 1428 and at ST PAUL'S CATHEDRAL in 1444. Coming to his own day, he recorded the desolation of the cathedral after the spire, one of the marvels of Europe, was struck by lightning in 1561, the whole fabric being much damaged in the ensuing blaze.

It was not only the CITY that suffered from fires. SOUTHWARK Town Hall and 624 houses besides were consumed on 26 May 1676. With them vanished the WHITE HART INN which Jack Cade had made his headquarters. WHITEHALL PALACE seems to have been particularly unfortunate. James I's first BANQUETING HOUSE there was destroyed in 1619, to be replaced by Inigo Jones's structure which still survives. An eight-hour blaze on 9 April 1691 wiped out the Stone Gallery with Holbein's paintings on the ceilings; a second conflagration, which raged for 17 hours on 4 January 1698, destroyed the rest save for the BANQUETING HOUSE. Other parts of London suffered too: 150 houses were burnt down at WAPPING, for instance, in 1716, and a further 70 in 1725.

A serious fire in the CITY on 28 March 1748 destroyed the houses in and around CHANGE ALLEY and over a million pounds' worth of damage was done in RATCLIFF when a Dutch ketch carrying saltpetre burst into flames. The fire which wiped out the CUSTOM HOUSE on 12 February 1814 destroyed the goods within it as well, including a valuable collection of pictures waiting to have duty paid on them, and Lord Moira's library which was in transit there. In the following year there was a serious fire at the ROYAL MINT.

The first British municipal fire force was set up in Edinburgh in 1824; but although its chief, James Braidwood, moved south in 1833 to take command of the London Fire Engine Establishment it was impossible to save the old PALACE OF WESTMINSTER which was destroyed on 16 October 1834. Two CITY landmarks, LLOYD'S COFFEE HOUSE and the ROYAL EXCHANGE, vanished in flames on 10 January 1838, the carillon bells of the latter chiming out the tune of 'There's Nae Luck aboot the Hoose' before they were melted away. Three years later, on 30 October 1841, a fire at the TOWER OF LONDON destroyed the Grand Armoury and did £250,000 worth of damage to the Bowyer and to Butler's Towers. On 19 August 1843, the first TOOLEY STREET fire broke out. This was a serious enough conflagration, but in the second, on 22 June 1861, the whole south waterfront of the Upper Pool was ablaze. James Braidwood and one of his men died in the flames; and the ruins smouldered on till the end of the year.

ALEXANDRA PALACE in north London has been a particularly susceptible building. Opened in May 1873, it was destroyed a fortnight later on 9 June. It was rebuilt, but a second blaze in July 1980 left it a charred ruin again. Another unlucky building was the storage warehouse, the Pantechnicon (*see* MOTCOMB

Waterside premises ablaze in the second great Tooley Street fire in 1861, when Braidwood, the fire chief, was killed.

THE GREAT FIRE NEAR LONDON BRIDGE.
ON SATURDAY, 22d JUNE, 1861.

STREET), where a blaze on 13 February 1874 destroyed £2,000,000 worth of goods.

The narrow streets and warehouses in the north-west corner of the CITY were peculiarly vulnerable to fire. WOOD STREET and ADDLE STREET were heavily damaged in 1882; and a second fire in the same area on 19 November 1897 wiped out 2½ acres and affected 4 acres. An explosion in SILVERTOWN in 1917 resulted in a fire which caused £2,000,000 worth of damage. MADAME TUSSAUD'S WAXWORKS suffered grievously in 1925; and on 30 November 1936 the CRYSTAL PALACE, which had been reconstructed on SYDENHAM Hill, after having so triumphantly housed the GREAT EXHIBITION of 1851, vanished in flames. The fires of the BLITZ during the winter of 1940–1 did the worst damage to the CITY since the GREAT FIRE. The rest of London suffered with it. (*See also* GREAT FIRE *and* LONDON FIRE BRIGADE.)

Fireworks Displays of fireworks, although given in Rome at least as early as the time of the Emperor Carinus, were rarely seen in London before the reign of Queen Elizabeth I. And while a writer in 1611 claimed that there were then in London 'many men very skilful in the art of pyrotechny and of fireworks', it was not until later in the century that exhibitions of the art were often to be witnessed. There was a display on the THAMES, under the direction of the Master-Gunner, in 1613 to celebrate the marriage of King James's daughter, Elizabeth, to the Prince Palatine but this seems to have been a rather amateurish affair compared to those dramatic entertainments given at that time in Florence at the court of the Medici. The arrival in England of a highly skilled Swedish pyrotechnist, Martin Beckman, led to more exciting displays in London. Beckman, who was honoured with the appointment of Comptroller of the Fireworks in 1697, was responsible for the displays celebrating the coronations of Charles II and James II, as well as for a grand exhibition in St James's Park to mark the return of William III to London in 1695. All these appear to have been memorable performances. But after Beckman's death in 1702 there were few displays of note. The accession of Queen Anne was not celebrated by large-scale fireworks; nor were the coronations of George I and George II. There was a 'grand show' on the THAMES to celebrate the Peace of Utrecht on 7 July 1713 but this was not matched until 1749 when a display was given in GREEN PARK to celebrate the treaty signed at Aix-la-Chapelle the year before. This was directed by a group of Italian pyrotechnists specially brought over for the purpose, including the renowned Signor Ruggieri, and was accompanied by 'a grand overture on warlike instruments' composed for the occasion and conducted by George Frederick Handel. The music was much admired; but, although £8,000 had been expended and over 10,000 rockets were shot into the sky, the fireworks were not as successful as had been hoped, largely because of the disputes between the English and Italian artificers which culminated in one of the Italians drawing his sword against Charles Frederick, the Comptroller of the Royal Laboratory at WOOLWICH, in a fierce quarrel about the use of trains of gunpowder. 'The fireworks by no means answered the expense, the length of preparation, and the expectation that had been raised,' complained Horace Walpole. 'The rockets and whatever was thrown into the air succeeded mighty well, but the wheels and all

The Duke of Richmond's magnificent private firework display on the Thames at Whitehall in 1749.

that was to compose the principal part, were pitiful and ill conducted with no change of coloured fires and shapes ... and lighted so slowly that scarce anybody had patience to wait for the finishing.'

The Duke of Richmond, however, acquired all the fireworks that were left over when the display was concluded at midnight. He then gave a private display, 'a charming entertainment at his town house, the garden of which sloped down to the Thames,' Walpole continued. And this was a very different affair: 'From boats on every side were discharged water-rockets and fires of all kinds; and then the wheels which were ranged along the rails of the terrace were played off; and the whole concluded with the illumination of a pavilion on the top of the slope, of two pyramids on either side and the whole length of the balustrade to the water. ... I really never passed a more agreeable evening.'

By now the ordinary Londoner had become something of a connoisseur of fireworks, for nearly all the city's pleasure gardens gave displays which vied with each other for spectacular and noisy entertainment. At MULBERRY GARDEN, at VAUXHALL, at New Wells, RANELAGH, CUPER'S GARDENS and MARYLEBONE GARDENS, as well as at more disreputable places, these displays attracted enormous crowds. At the rowdier, rougher places, such as the Bear Gardens, Hockley-in-the-Hole, fireworks were tied to the backs of animals. One characteristic handbill announces: 'A green bull to be baited, which was never baited before, and a bull to be turned loose, with fireworks all over him; also a mad ass to be baited. With a variety of bull-baiting and bear-baiting, and a dog to be drawn up with fireworks.' But at places like VAUXHALL and RANELAGH, where the brilliant Morel Torré put on his 'Mount Etna' and 'Forge of Vulcan' spectacles, the displays were works of art.

Throughout the 19th century the Londoners' pleasure in fireworks continued. There was a brilliant display in 1814 when, in that year of peace, the King of Prussia, Tsar Alexander, and the Emperor of Austria's representative, Prince Metternich, visited London. It was under the direction of the Prince Regent's friend, Colonel William Congreve, inventor of the Congreve rocket. And Charles Lamb thought it 'splendent – the Rockets in clusters, in trees and all shapes, spreading about by young stars in the making'. Seven years later the firework display in HYDE PARK given to celebrate George IV's coronation was a surprisingly modest one in view of the fact that all the other celebrations connected with that event had been performed so lavishly and at the enormous cost of £243,000. The display mounted for the coronation of William IV was also a modest event – not so surprisingly. But for the CORONATION of Queen Victoria in 1838 'fireworks were provided on the most liberal scale. They were the same in Hyde Park and in the Green Park.' They presaged a number of splendid displays in the Queen's reign, including brilliant ones in HYDE PARK, GREEN PARK, VICTORIA PARK and on PRIMROSE HILL, to celebrate the end of the Crimean War, and culminating in those given for the Queen's Diamond Jubilee in 1897.

By this time the CRYSTAL PALACE, re-erected at SYDENHAM, had become the place where the people of London flocked for fireworks. Here, on 12 July 1865, was held a 'Grand Competition of Pyrotechnists'. It was the idea of Charles Thomas Brock of the firm of firework manufacturers which was to become a household name. So successful did it prove to be and so successful, too, were the subsequent displays staged at the CRYSTAL PALACE by Brock that in 1869 the board of directors granted him a benefit 'as a mark of their appreciation of his unfailing efforts and outstanding achievements in the field of pyrotechny during the past five seasons.' 'Brock's Benefit' thereafter became a metaphor for spectacular grandeur. As the *Sportsman* observed in 1892, 'Brock's Benefit is almost as familiar among Englishmen, and quite as well known among Londoners, as Bank Holiday itself.' Crowds of over 60,000 people visited the CRYSTAL PALACE to watch the performances. 'One thing we do manage better in England than anywhere else', the *Daily Graphic* commented proudly, 'is our fireworks. Brock is almost a pillar of our constitution, and his annual benefit may, in many senses, be regarded as a benefit to the public.' Two years later the *Daily Telegraph* recorded of the annual show: 'The fireworshippers of London joined in thousands last night in their annual celebration at the temple of pyrotechny for the benefit of the high priest.' And in 1897 the *Daily Graphic* observed, 'The Londoner who has not at one time or another said to himself that he must really go down this year to the Crystal Palace to see the fireworks, is almost as rare as the man who is not moved by the sight of his native land. For the fireworks at the Crystal Palace in general and Brock's benefit in particular are national institutions, and Englishmen are justly proud of them.' These displays came to an end in 1936 when the CRYSTAL PALACE was burned down.

Another fireworks company that has always been based in and around London is Pain's, whose founder Charles Pain manufactured the gunpowder that was used (unknown to him) by Guy Fawkes in his attempt to blow up the HOUSES OF PARLIAMENT and King James I on 5 November 1605. For many years in the last century Pain's Fireworks was situated in the ELEPHANT AND CASTLE district, before moving out to MITCHAM and subsequently to its present location at Dartford – adjacent to the THAMES on the site previously established by the Wells Fireworks Co. Pain's has always specialised in large-scale shows such as that given to celebrate the Queen's Silver Jubilee in 1977 and the wedding of the Prince of Wales and Lady Diana Spencer in 1981.

Fishmongers' Company *see* CITY LIVERY COMPANIES.

Fishmongers' Hall *King William Street, EC4.* The first Hall dated from 1310. The next Hall, on the present site, was bequeathed to the Company in 1434, but was burnt down in the GREAT FIRE. The replacement, designed by Edward Jarman, opened in 1671. This building was demolished to accommodate the new LONDON BRIDGE in 1827. The architect of the next Hall was Henry Roberts. Gilbert Scott was then a junior member of his staff, and made the working drawings for the building which opened in 1834. After severe damage in 1940 it was restored by Austen Hall and reopened in 1951. Besides a fine collection of 17th- and 18th-century plate, the Company owns an embroidered 15th-century funeral pall, two portraits by Romney, Annigoni's first picture of the Queen, river scenes by Samuel Scott and the dagger with which Lord Mayor Walworth (a Fishmonger) killed Wat Tyler at Smithfield in 1381 (*see* PEASANTS' REVOLT). For the Company *see* CITY LIVERY COMPANIES.

Fish Street Hill *EC3.* The main thoroughfare to LONDON BRIDGE before the construction of KING WILLIAM STREET in 1829–35. According to Stow, the Black Prince had a house here. It was one of the authorised places in the CITY for the retail sale of fish. In the 15th century the collapsible stalls under which the earlier fishmongers slept at night began to give way to the permanent houses of the rising merchant class. The street was gorgeously bedecked in 1415 when Henry V and his entourage paraded triumphantly up it after the English victory over the French at Agincourt.

Fish Street Hill, leading past the Monument and St Magnus the Martyr to London Bridge, in 1792, from an engraving after Marlow.

Fitzjohn's Avenue *NW3*. Takes its name from Fitzjohn's in Essex, a property belonging to the Maryon Wilson family (*see* HAMPSTEAD). The portrait painter, Philip de László, lived at No. 3 from 1921 until his death in 1937.

Fitzrovia The name, adopted towards the beginning of the 2nd World War, for that area stretching north from OXFORD STREET to EUSTON ROAD and bounded on the east by GOWER STREET and on the west by GREAT PORTLAND STREET. FITZROY SQUARE is in the north-western corner. The area developed piecemeal and has long been known as a haunt of writers and artists, mostly impecunious. It has also attracted craftsmen, particularly furniture makers.

Fitzroy House *Highgate*. Built in about 1780 for General Charles Fitzroy who was that year created Lord Southampton. It stood on the site of Sherricks Hole Farm whose lands formerly covered the south slope of the ridge between the village of HIGHGATE and KENWOOD. The park, in which there were some magnificent beech trees, was probably laid out by Lancelot 'Capability' Brown. In 1811 the house was acquired by the Duke of Buckingham who entertained here Samuel Rogers, Coleridge and Keats. It was demolished in 1828 and 'several elegant villas' were built in the park, among them BEECHWOOD HOUSE. It is commemorated by Fitzroy Close and Fitzroy Park, N6.

Fitzroy Road *NW1*. For the derivation of the name see FITZROY SQUARE. W.B. Yeats, the poet and dramatist, lived at No. 23.

Fitzroy Square *W1*. Henry Fitzroy was the son of Charles II by Barbara Villiers, Duchess of Cleveland, and was married at the age of nine to the five-year-old Isabella Bennet, only daughter of Lord Arlington. Isabella, 'a swete child if ever there was any', was left a country estate at Euston in Suffolk by her father who also gave her the Manor of Tottenham Court (*see* TOTTENHAM COURT ROAD). Her husband was created Earl of Euston (the title deriving from Arlington's estate) and later Duke of Grafton (hence Grafton Crescent, Place, Road, Way and Yard which were all built in the old Manor of Tottenham Court). Their son Charles Fitzroy, 2nd Duke of Grafton, built the EUSTON ROAD, and their great-grandson, who was created 1st Baron Southampton and married the daughter of Sir Peter Warren (hence Southampton Road, NW5, and WARREN STREET) developed Fitzroy Square, one of London's finest squares. The east and south sides were first to be built to the designs of the brothers Adam in the early 1790s (the south side was destroyed in the 2nd World War but has been replaced). The west and south sides were added in 1825–9. Sir Charles Eastlake, President of the ROYAL ACADEMY, lived at No. 7, 1844–65. Ford Madox Brown lived at No. 37 where, between 1867 and 1882, he regularly entertained Rossetti, Burne-Jones, Holman Hunt, William Morris, Swinburne and Whistler. On No. 21 is a BLUE PLAQUE to Lord Salisbury, Prime Minister. Virginia and Adrian Stephen lived at No. 29 in 1907–11 and gave regular Friday evening readings. They moved to BRUNSWICK SQUARE when their lease expired. George Bernard Shaw lived in the same house in 1887–98 while he was music and drama critic for several papers

and a writer of political and economic tracts for the FABIANS. It then contained, in his own words, 'a mountain of buried books, all wide open'. Roger Fry established the OMEGA WORKSHOPS at No. 33, now part of the London Foot Hospital on the south side. On the north side is St Luke's Hospital for the Clergy. At the south-east corner is the YMCA Indian Students' Union and Hostel by Ralph Tubbs (1953). In the spacious central garden the sculpture, *View II*, is by Naomi Blake (1977). The square is now a pedestrian precinct.

Fitzroy Street *W1*. For the derivation of the name see FITZROY SQUARE. Captain Matthew Flinders, the explorer and navigator, lived at No. 56 in 1813–14.

Flask *77 Highgate West Hill, N6*. Long, low-ceilinged public house built in 1663, rebuilt in 1767, and renovated in 1910. The name commemorates the time when flasks were obtained here to be filled with water from the HAMPSTEAD WELLS. Dick Turpin is said to have hidden here (and, indeed, in every other public house in the area). But it was certainly a resort for Hogarth, Morland, Cruikshank and Karl Marx who is buried just up the road in HIGHGATE CEMETERY. The ancient ceremony of Swearing on the Horns takes place here. This involves kissing a pair of antlers tied to a pole and swearing to drink only strong ale, the reward for which is the Freedom of HIGHGATE and a chance to kiss the prettiest girl in the room.

Fleece Tavern *Covent Garden*. Notorious in the 17th century for the violence of its customers: it was 'very unfortunate for homicides', in the words of John Aubrey. 'There have been several killed there in my time.' Pepys liked the place, however.

Fleet Bridge One of four bridges which once spanned the FLEET. It linked LUDGATE HILL to FLEET STREET. The first bridge, completed in 1431, was stone, 'fair coped on either side with iron pikes'. It bore the emblem of John Welles, Mayor of London, a portrait embraced by angels. He may have been responsible for building the bridge. Tolls were collected here from dealers bringing their produce into the CITY. The GREAT FIRE destroyed the original bridge and a new one was constructed, decorated with pineapples and the CITY OF LONDON COAT OF ARMS. This was demolished in 1765 when the FLEET was directed into what is now FARRINGDON STREET. London's first daily paper, the *Daily Courant*, was printed in 1702, 'against the Ditch at Fleet Bridge'.

Fleet Lane *EC4*. Named after the FLEET RIVER which still flows under FARRINGDON STREET. One of the three bridges across it was at the west end of the lane; it was demolished in 1737 when the river was covered over.

Fleet Market A meat and vegetable market set up when the STOCKS MARKET was demolished. In 1733 an Act of Parliament allowed the Fleet Ditch between FLEET STREET and HOLBORN to be covered over. The new market, designed by George Dean, was built on the bridge. There were two rows of one-storey shops connected by a covered walkway with skylights. A clock and turret stood in the centre. By the early 19th century the market had become dilapidated and it was

A clandestine marriage, known as a Fleet Wedding, between 'A brisk young sailor and his landlady's daughter' in 1747.

cleared in 1826–30 to make way for FARRINGDON STREET.

Fleet Marriages

Clandestine marriages performed without licence, first in the chapel of the FLEET PRISON and from the beginning of the 18th century in nearby taverns and houses, several of which bore signs depicting a male and female hand clasped together above the legend 'MARIAGES Performed Within'. The marriages were mostly conducted by clergymen imprisoned in the Fleet for debt, who were allowed the LIBERTIES OF THE FLEET. According to James Malcolm, author off *Londinium Redivivum*, up to 30 couples were married in a day and almost 3,000 marriages were performed in the four months to 12 February 1705. Fleet Marriages were declared void by Lord Hardwicke's Marriage Act, 1753.

Fleet Prison

Said to have been built soon after the Norman Conquest although it is not recorded until 1170–1. It stood on the east bank of the FLEET RIVER. The post of Keeper was hereditary (the Leveland family held it from 1197–1558). With the appointment went the privilege of receiving the customs duty levied on the Fleet and fees from prisoners for food, lodging and privileges. This was a source of great abuse. Prisoners on payment of fees were allowed to stay away from the prison for days and nights without bail, and many escaped. The prison was divided into several parts and the larger the sum paid to the Keeper the better the accommodation given to the prisoner. There was the prison proper, a prison precinct of about an acre originally surrounded by the moat, and 'the rules', houses which stood outside the moat. Debtors were always kept in the prison proper. During the late Middle Ages the Fleet Prison was particularly used to hold offenders condemned by the King's Council and the Court of Chancery. It was rebuilt in Edward III's reign, and again at the end of the 14th century, having been burned in the PEASANTS' REVOLT.

From Henry VIII's reign until 1641 prisoners convicted by the Court of Star Chamber were sent here.

In 1542–3 the Earl of Surrey, the poet, was imprisoned here, and in the 1550s several martyrs to their faith including Bishop Hooper. In 1601 the poet John Donne was incarcerated for marrying Sir George More's daughter without his consent. The first recorded FLEET MARRIAGE took place in 1613.

The prison was destroyed in the GREAT FIRE, but soon afterwards rebuilt once again. In the new building William Wycherley was imprisoned for debt. In 1691 a debtor called Moses Pitt revealed in his *Cry of the Oppressed* that he had to pay £2 4s 6d to the Keeper on entry for the privilege of being put on 'the gentlemen's side' although the legal fee was 4d. He was also charged 8s every week for his room instead of 2s 4d. He ran out of money after 16 months and was sent to the dungeon where he slept on the floor with 27 companions 'so lowsie that as they either walked or sat down, you might have pick'd lice off from their outward garments'. During 1707–9 William Penn was imprisoned here for debt. In 1729 a parliamentary inquiry on the activities of the Keeper, Thomas Bambridge, found him guilty of the most notorious breaches of his trust, 'of great extortions, and the highest crimes and misdemeanours in the execution of his said office'. He had 'arbitrarily and unlawfully loaded with irons, put into dungeons, and destroyed prisoners for debt, under his charge, treating them in the most barbarous and cruel manner ...' A special Act of Parliament was needed to dismiss him and 20 new rules for future Keepers to observe were drawn up.

In 1774, however, when John Howard inspected the prison, he found it 'crowded with women and children, being riotous and dirty'. Many prisoners were drinking; men and women mixed freely; and there was no medical attention. In 1780 the Gordon Rioters fired the prison and released the inmates. The prison was rebuilt once more in 1781–2. Some years later, on his last visit in 1788, John Howard found conditions no better than on his first. In 1792 a Committee of the House of Commons inspected the prison and suggested new regulations but they were ignored. Suggestions of another Committee set up in 1815 were similarly ignored. Dickens graphically described the early 19th-century prison in *Pickwick Papers*. It was closed in 1842 and demolished four years later. Its site was sold in 1864 to the London, Chatham and Dover Railway Co.

A debtor being dragged in the 'Gaoler's Coach' at Fleet Prison c. 1680, drawn by Moses Pitt, who wrote The Cry of the Oppressed *after his own horrific imprisonment here.*

Fleet River One of London's underground rivers which rises in KENWOOD and HAMPSTEAD ponds and flows down to the THAMES through CAMDEN TOWN, KING'S CROSS and beneath FARRINGDON ROAD, FARRINGDON STREET and NEW BRIDGE STREET. Fleet was the name originally given to the lower part of the river only and is an Anglo-Saxon word meaning tidal inlet. The higher reaches were known as Hole Bourne (HOLBORN), the River of Wells, and Turnmill Brook (there were always many mills along the banks). The Fleet lay to the west of ROMAN LONDON and formed a defensive barrier. The earliest mention of it being used for bringing cargoes into London is in the early 12th century when stones for old ST PAUL'S were brought upstream. In King John's reign the Knights Hospitaller had a wharf at Fleet Lane. They allowed ST BARTHOLOMEW'S HOSPITAL to use it and patients who were too ill to walk to the hospital were landed here. In the 13th and 14th centuries many cutlers lived along the banks and from the 13th to the 16th century tanners worked there. In 1290 the monks of

WHITEFRIARS complained to the King that the smell of the river was so bad that even their incense could not mask it. In 1343 the butchers of NEWGATE STREET were given permission to use a wharf near the FLEET PRISON to cleanse entrails. As the population increased, more refuse and sewage were dumped in the river. It was cleaned out in 1502. Stow in his *Survey of London* of 1598 mentions five bridges over the lower part of the river: Cow Bridge, Holborn Bridge, another by modern Fleet Lane, FLEET BRIDGE and Bridewell Bridge. The river was cleaned again in 1606. But by 1652 it was 'impassable for boats, by reason of the many encroachments thereon made, by the throwing of offal and other garbage by butchers, saucemen and others and by reason of the many houses of office standing over upon it'. The GREAT FIRE of 1666 leaped from bank to bank and burnt down the wharves and houses on either side. Afterwards, under the guidance of Wren and Hooke, the lower 700 yards were deepened and widened and made into a canal with wharves 30 ft wide on either side. To mark the northern end of it Wren redesigned Holborn Bridge. However, boats still did not use the river and the wharves became thoroughfares and rubbish dumps. In 1733 the river was arched over from Holborn Bridge to Fleet Bridge. In 1739 the STOCKS MARKET was moved to make room for the MANSION HOUSE; it was set up over the covered-in river and renamed the FLEET MARKET. In 1766 the river from Fleet Bridge to the THAMES was channelled underground. The FLEET MARKET was moved in 1826–30 and FARRINGDON STREET made. The Fleet is still used as a sewer.

Fleet Street *EC4*. Extends eastwards from TEMPLE BAR as far as LUDGATE CIRCUS. In medieval London it was a main thoroughfare named after the nearby FLEET RIVER which now runs under FARRINGDON STREET and NEW BRIDGE STREET. At this time many prelates lived in the street, among them the Bishops of Salisbury and St Davids and the Abbots of Faversham, Tewkesbury, Winchcombe and Cirencester. The church of ST BRIDE was probably established as early as the 6th century. The church of ST DUNSTAN is first mentioned in 1185. The street that ran between them was the path of contrition for the penitent, the royal route to ST PAUL'S and a regular battleground. In Queen Anne's reign the Mohocks operated here and in the riots of 1763 Wilkites burned a jack boot, symbol of their villain, John Stuart, Earl of Bute. It had long been a showplace for freaks, giants, fire eaters, elephants and other large animals. MRS SALMON'S WAXWORKS at the sign of the Trout was also a big attraction.

Fleet Street's association with printing and publishing is of long standing. Among the early printers and booksellers who established themselves there were the following.

Wynkyn de Worde moved here in about 1500 from Caxton's old house in WESTMINSTER. He rented two houses, a dwelling house and a printing office, for an annual rental of £3 6s 8d. His printing office at the sign of the Sun was on the south side of the street, near the entrance to SHOE LANE where there were a number of bookbinders. The last book he issued was the *Complaint of the too soon maryed* of 1535. He died at the beginning of that year. Altogether, he printed nearly 800 books and made use of at least 17 varieties of devices, in all of which Caxton's initials and device are

Horse-drawn buses and carts in Fleet Street, looking towards Ludgate Hill and St Paul's, in about 1890.

prominent. He also had a shop at ST PAUL'S CHURCHYARD at the sign of Our Lady of Pity.

Richard Pynson, a Norman by birth, appears to have been educated at the University of Paris. He came over in about 1486 and started as a publisher and printer mainly of legal texts, but amongst his books was an edition of Chaucer's *Canterbury Tales*. In 1495 he issued an edition of the *Hecyra* of Terence, probably intended for use at Eton. By 1500 he had printed 84 books. In that year, Pynson and some others brought an action in the Star Chamber against Henry Squire and his companions for assault. It appears to have been one of the usual attacks by natives on foreign workmen then common, but Pynson stated that his servants were so terrorised that they had left him, and his work was consequently at a standstill. The evident outcome of this case was the removal by Pynson in 1500 of his printing office from ST CLEMENT'S parish, which was outside the CITY, to a house within TEMPLE BAR at the corner of CHANCERY LANE and FLEET STREET next to ST DUNSTAN'S CHURCH, which had belonged to the College of St Stephen in WESTMINSTER, and to which he gave the sign of 'the George' or 'St George'. In 1508 he became Printer to the King. He received an annuity of £2 and in 1515 the sum was raised to £4. This position carried with it the title of Esquire and the right to bear arms, which Pynson immediately assumed and which are found the following year in his edition of the *Ship of Fools*. Pynson is known to have printed 371 books. On his death in 1530 he left considerable property in CHANCERY LANE and TOTTENHAM.

On Pynson's death Thomas Berthelet was appointed Printer to the King with an annuity of £4. His shop was 'near to ye cundite at ye signe of Lucrece'. His work was to a great extent official, though he issued many books of general interest and published all the works of Sir Thomas Elyot. Besides being Royal Printer, Berthelet was also bookseller and bookbinder to the King. It is supposed that he brought over to England some Italian workmen, both to work for him and to teach his own men. Berthelet's bindings are almost the first gilt-tooled bindings produced in England and he himself speaks of them as worked in the 'Venetian manner'.

William Rastell printed between 1530 and 1534, at a house in ST BRIDE'S churchyard, more than 30 books including several plays and works by his uncle, Sir Thomas More. He remained a Catholic and, on the accession of Edward VI, retired abroad. In February 1550 his house was seized. When Mary came to the throne he returned; he printed law books and a complete edition of the works of Sir Thomas More in 1557.

John Butler was at one time an assistant to Wynkyn de Worde who, on his death, left him a bequest of £6 worth of printed books. By 1529 he had started in business on his own at the sign of St John Evangelist, issuing in that year an edition of the *Parvulorum institutio ex Stanbrigiana collectione*. Besides this one he produced eight undated books including the *Jeaste of Sir Gawayne*, the *Doctrynale of good servantes*, and the *Convercyon of Swererers*.

John Byddel of Salisbury was also for some time an assistant to Wynkyn de Worde. The first four books which he issued were all printed by de Worde about the beginning of 1534, but after this he printed for himself. In 1535 he was one of de Worde's executors. In the same year he left his former house in FLEET STREET with the sign of 'Our Lady of Pity' and moved to de Worde's house, 'The Sun'. Here he printed steadily until 1544, issuing altogether 50 different books. In 1543 he was imprisoned in the POULTRY COMPTER for printing unlawful books, but was freed after a fortnight's detention.

William Middleton, a printer at the 'sign of the George in Fleet Street', issued numerous law books. In 1543 he was brought before the Privy Council 'for printing off suche bokes as wer thowght to be unlawfull, contrary to the proclamation', and was committed to the FLEET PRISON but let out after a fortnight. He was, however, compelled to pay a fine and send in a list of all books and ballads which he had printed and sold within the past three years. He printed a very large number of books up to 1547, the year of his death.

Richard Tottell started printing in FLEET STREET at 'The Hand and Star' within TEMPLE BAR in 1553. He occupied the same premises for 41 years. In 1553 he was granted a patent to print for seven years all 'duly authorized books on Common Law', and from then on became the leading publisher of legal books. But he was also the publisher of much literature, including Thomas More's *Dialogue of Comfort* (1553) and Lydgate's *Fall of Princes* (1554). His best-known book was the poetry anthology *Tottell's Miscellany*, which first appeared in 1557 and contained 40 poems by Henry Howard, Earl of Surrey, all the 96 poems by Thomas Wyatt which have survived, and more by John Heywood and others.

William Jaggard was in business at 'St Dunstan's Churchyard, Fleet Street' from 1594 to 1608, and at 'The Half Eagle and Key,' BARBICAN from 1608 to 1623. In 1594–5 he published the *Booke of secretes of Albertus Magnus*. In 1599 he collected a number of poems by various authors, and published them under the collective title of *The Passionate Pilgrime, by W. Shakespeare*, but there was little of Shakespeare's work in the volume, which however contained several of Thomas Heywood's poems, abstracted from *Troia Britannica*. About the year 1608 William Jaggard bought the old-established printing business of James Roberts in the BARBICAN, and became printer to the CITY OF LONDON.

John Jaggard, his son, was a bookseller from 1593 to 1623, at 'the Hand and Star in Fleet Street, between the two Temple Gates'. Following a seven-year apprenticeship, from 1584, to Richard Tottell, he published several books of travel, an edition of Bacon's *Essays*, and Richard Carew's *Survey of Cornwall* in 1602.

John Hodgets was at 'The Flower de Luce in Fleet Street, near Feter Lane end' from 1601 to 1625. He was a publisher of plays, among which were John Day's *Ile of Guls* (1606), Dekker's *Honest Whore* (1604), Dekker and Webster's *Westward Hoe* (1607), Thomas Heywood's *A Woman kilde with kindnesse* (1607), and John Marston's *The Dutch Courtezan* (1605).

On 11 March 1702 the first newspaper, The *Daily Courant*, was issued by Edward Mallett but it was soon in the hands of another printer, Samuel Buckley. Later came *The Morning Chronicle*, whose editor, William Woodfall, lived in SALISBURY SQUARE. He left the *Chronicle* to set up *The Diary* in 1789.

Nowadays Fleet Street and the immediate area are dominated by the offices of daily and provincial newspapers and all their related associations. At No. 43 is the National Union of Journalists which was founded in Birmingham in 1907; a Central London branch was formed at a meeting in YE OLDE CHESHIRE CHEESE, WINE OFFICE COURT, in the same year. No. 85, which was designed by Lutyens in 1935, is shared by REUTER'S WORLD NEWS SERVICE, established in 1855 by Baron de Reuter, and the PRESS ASSOCIATION. On the north side of the street is the *Daily Express* at Nos 121–128. It was founded in 1900 by Arthur Pearson and bought by Lord Beaverbrook in 1915. This black glass and chrome building was designed for the newspaper in 1931 by Ellis and Clarke in association with Sir Owen Williams, and was the first curtain wall building constructed in London. The *Daily Telegraph* at No. 135 was founded in 1855 by J.M. Levy and occupies the building designed by Elcock and Sutcliffe in 1928–30. On the south side CHILD'S BANK used to stand at No.1, and next door to it stood the Devil Tavern where Ben Jonson, Pepys and Samuel Johnson were customers. At No. 17 PRINCE HENRY'S ROOM is over the INNER TEMPLE Gateway, a fine example of half-timbered work. At No.22 is the COCK TAVERN. No.32 was occupied by John Murray, the publishers, from 1762 until 1812 when they moved to their present premises in ALBEMARLE STREET. HOARE AND CO., the bankers, occupy No. 37. El Vino, haunt of lawyers and journalists, is at No.47. The company was established in 1879 and acquired their Fleet Street premises in 1923. In November 1982 the Court of Appeal ruled that the wine bar was breaking the law by continuing to refuse to allow women to stand and be served at the bar.

Fletchers' Company see CITY LIVERY COMPANIES.

Fleur de Lis Court *EC4*. Probably named after the house called the Flowerdeluce which existed here in the 16th century. The court originally extended to FLEET STREET but when FETTER LANE was widened in 1841 the southern part was swept away.

Flood Street *SW3*. Named after Luke Thomas

Flood, resident in, and benefactor of, CHELSEA parish in the early 19th century. Dame Sybil Thorndike spent the last years of her life at Swan Court between CHELSEA MANOR STREET and FLOOD STREET, dying there in 1976. Mrs Margaret Thatcher, who became Prime Minister in 1979, lives at 19 Flood Street.

Flood Walk *SW3*. A short road leading off FLOOD STREET, much of it occupied by the Violet Melchett Infant Welfare Centre. The building was a gift from Violet Melchett's husband, the 1st Baron Melchett, and was opened by Queen Mary in 1931. Originally a voluntary service to CHELSEA mothers and children, it has been under the control of the Royal Borough of KENSINGTON and CHELSEA since 1967.

Floods The earliest record of a London flood is dated 1099, and comes in the late *Anglo-Saxon Chronicle*: 'On the festival of St Martin, the sea flood sprung up to such a height and did so much harm as no man remembered that it ever did before.' In 1237 the WOOLWICH MARSHES became a sea, many were drowned and within the Great Hall at Westminster (*see* WESTMINSTER HALL) the lawyers rowed around in wherries. Five years later the river overflowed at LAMBETH for a distance of 6 miles and then in the Great Hall 'men took their horses because the water ran over all' (Stow). The Great Hall was flooded again in 1515 and a contemporary reported in 1579 that fishes were left floundering on the floor of the Hall when the flood subsided. Ben Jonson recalls such a flood:

It was the day, what time the powerful moon
Makes the poor Banksider creature wet its shoon
In its own Hall.

Pepys entered in his *Diary* on 7 December 1663: 'There was last night the greatest tide that ever was remembered in England to have been in this river, all Whitehall having been drowned.' Floods occurred again in 1735, 1791 and 1841. There were three more during the 1870s and in 1881 a surge raised the water 16 ft above the mean water level. Another flood happened the next year. In the bad flood of 1928, 14 people were drowned in the basements of WESTMINSTER, and in 1953 a flood affected the East Coast and the Thames Estuary, when 300 were drowned. If that flood had reached central London the effects would have been appalling.

The traditional defence against flooding is the building of river walls and embankments. After the Thames Flood Act was passed in 1879, this was effected on long stretches of the banks. After the bad flood of 1928 banks were again raised between 1930 and 1935 and they were raised and improved further in 1971 and 1972. This walling and embanking may be effective for a while but cannot go on indefinitely if the whole river is not to be cut off from view. After the floods of 1953 an official inquiry recommended that 'apart from erecting further walls and banks, an investigation should be made into the building of a flood barrier across the Thames'. Debate dragged on for 13 years until the authorities at last realised how urgent the matter had become. A bad flood could affect 45 square miles of London's low-lying land, could overwhelm a million and a quarter people and a quarter of a million buildings, could paralyse the underground railways for months, and seriously curtail gas, water, electricity and telephones. Apart from suffering and death, the cost would run into billions of pounds. The chances of overlapping are now one in 50 every year and of a disastrous flood one in 200. Serious floods occur under certain meteorological conditions, as when a trough of low pressure moves across the Atlantic causing a surge of high water which may turn south above Scotland into the North Sea and down to the shallows of the bottleneck between south-east England and the Low Countries; its height may be increased by northerly gales. The surge may then enter the THAMES estuary on top of a high tide, with devastating results. Such inundations grow yearly more likely for three reasons: the increasing volume of ocean water caused by the melting of the polar ice caps, the tilting of Britain towards the south-east at about one foot each century, and the slow sinking of London on its bed of clay. The tides are thus rising by over two feet every century.

The anti-flood strategy of the GREATER LONDON COUNCIL relies partly on further embanking but mainly on the huge Thames Barrier across Woolwich Reach. As long ago as the 1850s such a barrier was advocated by the philosopher Herbert Spencer and in 1904 a Thames Barrage Association was formed. This proposed a barrier with four locks at Gravesend. Designed by the engineer, T.W. Barber, it would, in effect, have made the whole of the river between Gravesend and LONDON BRIDGE one huge dock accessible at all states of the tide. The practical objections, however, were overwhelming. In 1934 a similar body proposed a barrage at WOOLWICH as a dam with locks and a road across the top, and this received considerable support but also much opposition; then the outbreak of war eliminated any hope of rapid realisation.

The gargantuan Thames Barrier, built under the consultancy of the engineering firm of Rendel, Palmer and Tritton, is not such a dam; it is a vast machine with movable gates. As a result of the Thames Barrier and Flood Prevention Act of 1972, work on it began in 1975 and was completed in 1982. Spanning 520 metres across the river, it has four main shipping gates flanked by six minor ones; the main gates are of steel, as high as a five-storey building, and they rise 20 metres above the water bed; at 61 metres they are as wide as the opening of TOWER BRIDGE. Each, with counterweight, weighs 3,000 tonnes. The gates are pivoted and turn through 90 degrees when opened or closed. When open their curved faces lie face down in concrete cills on the river bed to allow ships to pass over them. Between the gates rise huge concrete piers on which stand structures to house the electro-hydraulic machines that turn the gates, each roofed with sheets of stainless steel in forms that seem to have been inspired by the 'sails' of Sydney's Opera House. Closing the gates will take under 30 minutes, and sealing the upper river from any surge from the sea will prevent the flooding of London in the future. The gates are likely to be closed two or three times a year during the 1980s increasing to a possible ten closures a year during the next century. The final cost of the Barrier and its associated works is likely to be about £500 million, 75 per cent of which is being paid by the Government and the rest by the GREATER LONDON COUNCIL.

Floral Street WC2. Formerly known as Hart Street, its name was changed to one considered more appropriate to its position near COVENT GARDEN. Joe Haines, the comedian, died here in 1701; the actor Barton Booth was living here in 1732. His fellow-actor, Charles Macklin, retired from the stage to open a tavern here, but it was not a success and he was obliged to return to his old profession.

Florence Nightingale Hospital 19 Lisson Grove, NW1. The Institution for Sick Governesses, which was opened in CHANDOS STREET, CAVENDISH SQUARE with 11 beds in 1850, was run by a Lady Superintendent who had under her a cook, kitchenmaid, housemaid and manservant. Nurses were employed when necessary and there was an honorary chaplain. Doctors were unpaid and patients paid only a guinea a week. The hospital moved to No. 1 HARLEY STREET in 1853 and in August of that year Florence Nightingale was appointed Lady Superintendent. She put in a hot water supply to all floors and a windlass for bringing up hot food from the kitchen; she changed the grocer, the coal merchant and the kitchen range; made the hospital nonsectarian; renamed it the Institute for Gentlewomen during Illness, and undertook to receive widows and daughters of clergy, naval, military and professional men. Having achieved these reforms she left for the Crimea in October 1854. In 1909 a new hospital was built in Lisson Grove. It was renamed the Florence Nightingale Hospital for Gentlewomen in 1910. Since 1978 it has been run in conjunction with the Fitzroy Nuffield Hospital. There are 68 beds.

J. Floris Ltd 89 Jermyn Street, SW1. Perfumers established in 1730 by Juan Famenias Floris, a Spaniard from Minorca, who set up his barber's sign at this address. Here he attracted a fashionable clientele for whom he started to create individual perfumes reminiscent of the fragrant flowers of his native land. These scents were soon in such demand that he abandoned the barber's shop and used the premises to display his perfumery in a setting of carved Spanish combs in tortoiseshell and ivory, also for sale.

In 1821 the firm of Floris received a Royal Warrant from George IV. The Spanish mahogany showcases lining the shop were acquired from the GREAT EXHIBITION of 1851. By the end of the 19th century Floris perfumes were world-famous and from 1912 were exported regularly to Europe, the USA and South America. Today, in the same premises, Floris has remained a family firm through seven generations.

Fogs Since Shakespeare refers to 'Drooping fogge as blacke as Acheron', it would seem that London has been troubled by an atmosphere overladen with particles of soot since the 16th century at least. John Evelyn, in his *Fumifugium* (1661), inveighed against 'that Hellish and dismall cloud of sea-coale' which rendered London painful to the lungs of the inhabitants. He recommended the banishing of all noisome trades from the city, and the planting out of flower-beds with 'Pinks, Carnations, Cloves, Stock-gilly-flower, Primroses, Auriculars, Violets ... Cowslips, Lillies, Narcissus, Strawberries ... Spike, Camomile, Balm, Mint, Marjoram, Pempernel, and Serpillum.' The authorities did not, however, take his advice; London continued to burn coal and the pall of soot grew worse. On 27 December 1813 there was a fog so serious that the Prince Regent, having set out for Hatfield House, was forced to turn back at KENTISH TOWN. On the return journey, one of his outriders fell into the ditch. This fog lasted till 3 January 1814; and during this time the Birmingham mail coach took 7 hours to crawl

A caricature illustrating the hazards of fog, 'A thoroughbred November and London Particular', in 1827.

as far westwards as UXBRIDGE. As the century passed, fogs became more frequent, the longest of all probably being that which began in November 1879 and lasted till March of the following year. Charles Dickens described fog as a 'London particular': the opening chapter of *Bleak House* contains his description of the stricken city:

'Fog everywhere. Fog up the river where it flows among green aits and meadows: fog down the river where it rolls defiled among the tiers of shipping, and the waterside pollutions of a great (and dirty) city. Fog on the Essex marshes, fog on the Kentish heights. Fog creeping into the cabooses of collier-brigs; fog lying out on the yards and hovering in the rigging of great ships; fog drooping on the gunwales of barges and small boats. Fog in the eyes and throats of ancient Greenwich pensioners, wheezing by the firesides of their wards; fog in the stem and bowl of the afternoon pipe of the wrathful skipper down in his close cabin; fog cruelly pinching the toes and fingers of his shivering little prentice boy on deck. Chance people on the bridges peeping over the parapets into a nether sky of fog, with fog all round them, as if they were up in a balloon, and hanging in the misty clouds.'

A music-hall song:
> I'm just a little girl, lost in the fog,
> Me and my dog
> Won't some kind gentleman see me 'ome?

celebrated London's winter murkiness. The audience would have referred to the aerial shroud as a 'pea-souper'; and in the twentieth century the poet T.S. Eliot wrote of 'yellow fog that puts its back upon the window-panes'.

Notable London fogs occurred in December 1881; January 1882; November 1901; January–February 1918; November 1921; December 1924; January 1925; February 1927; December 1930; November 1934; December 1935; January and December 1944; November 1947; November–December 1948; and December 1952. This last was reckoned to have caused some 4,000 deaths, excluding those of cattle at SMITHFIELD show. As a result, a Commission of Enquiry was set up and the Clean Air Act was passed in 1956. In January and again in December of that year there were serious fogs – in December, a rabbit was found wandering in KNIGHTSBRIDGE and a duck in LIVERPOOL STREET, both, presumably, having lost their way in the gloom. In December 1957 the fog was the cause of the LEWISHAM rail disaster in which 87 people lost their lives. In addition some 1,000 deaths occurred as a result of atmospheric pollution. Another fog spread in December 1962 but since then, the capital has been free of bad fog.

Foley Street *W1*. Built in about 1745–70 and named after Lord Foley, whose mansion was nearby. He was a cousin of the ground landlord, Edward Harley (*see* PORTLAND ESTATE *and* MARYLEBONE). No. 33 was the home from his birth in 1802 till 1826 of (Sir) Edwin Landseer. From here, at the age of 13, he sent his first picture to the ROYAL ACADEMY. Another artist, Henry Fuseli, lived at No. 37, 1788–1802.

Folly A timber pleasure boat moored at Cuper's Stairs, near the SAVOY, or at BANKSIDE, SOUTHWARK. The open deck had turreted corners, and an enclosed deck below had boxes and curtained compartments for couples to drink in. It is first mentioned by Pepys who visited it in April 1668. Queen Mary II visited the boat in its early days and it was consequently also known as the Royal Diversion. Its reputation declined swiftly and it soon became a place of 'folly, madness and debauchery'. A German visitor, Z.C. Uffenbach, was disgusted in 1710 to find 'innumerable harlots' and prices that were 'prodigious dear'. About 10 years later it had to be suppressed and was chopped up for firewood.

FOOTBALL CLUBS The principal London football clubs are given below with the years in which they were formed and in which they became professional given in brackets.

Arsenal (1886, 1891) *Highbury Stadium, Highbury, N5*. Colours: red and white. Titles: 1st division League Champions, 1930–1, 1932–3, 1933–4, 1934–5, 1937–8, 1947–8, 1952–3, 1970–1. F.A. Cup, 1929–30, 1935–6, 1949–50, 1970–1, 1978–9.

Brentford (1889, 1899) *Griffin Park, Braemar Road, Brentford, Middlesex*. Colours: red, white and black. Titles, 2nd division League Champions, 1934–5. 3rd division League Champions, 1932–3. 4th division League Champions, 1962–3.

Charlton•Athletic (1905, 1920) *The Valley, Floyd Road, Charlton, SE7*. Colours: red and white. Titles: 3rd division League Champions, 1928–9, 1934–5. F.A. Cup, 1947, runners-up, 1946.

Chelsea (1905, 1905) *Stamford Bridge, SW6*. Colours: blue and white. Titles: 1st division League Champions, 1954–5. F.A. Cup, 1970. European Cup Winners' Cup, 1970–1, 1971–2. Football League Cup, 1964–5.

Crystal Palace (1905, 1905) *Selhurst Park, SE25*. Colours: blue and red. Titles: 2nd division League

Champions, 1978–9. 3rd division League Champions, 1920–1. F.A. Cup semi-finals, 1975–6.

Fulham (1879, 1898) *Craven Cottage, Stevenage Road, SW6.* Colours: white and black. Titles: 2nd division League Champions, 1948–9. 3rd division League Champions, 1931–2. F.A. Cup runners-up, 1974–5.

Millwall (1885, 1893) *The Den, Cold Blow Lane, SE14.* Colours: blue and white. Titles: 3rd division League Champions, 1927–8, 1937–8. 4th division League Champions, 1961–2. F.A. Cup semi-finals, 1899–1900, 1902–3, 1936–7.

Orient (1881, 1903) *Leyton Stadium, Brisbane Road, E10.* Colours: red and white. Titles: 3rd division League Champions, 1955–6. F.A. Cup semi-finals, 1977–8.

Queen's Park Rangers (1885, 1898) *Loftus Road, South Africa Road, W12.* Colours: blue and white. Titles: 3rd division League Champions, 1947–8, 1966–7. Football League Cup, 1966–7.

Tottenham Hotspur (1882, 1895) *White Hart Lane, 748 High Road, Tottenham, N17.* Colours: blue and white. Titles: 1st division League Champions, 1951–2, 1960–1. F.A. Cup, 1900–1, 1920–1, 1960–1, 1961–2, 1966–7, 1980–1, 1981–2. Football League Cup, 1970–1, 1972–3. European Cup Winners' Cup, 1962–3.

West Ham United (1900, 1900) *Upton Park, Green Street, E13.* Colours: claret, blue and white. Titles: F.A. Cup, 1963–4, 1974–5, 1979–80. European Cup Winners' Cup, 1964–5.

Wimbledon (1889; semi-professional, 1964) *Plough Lane Ground, Durnsford Road, Wimbledon, SW19.* Colours: blue and yellow. Titles: Southern League Champions, 1974–5, 1975–6, 1976–7.

Foots Cray *Sidcup, Kent.* In earlier times, a Saxon manor with a church, ALL SAINTS. The road to Wrotham was turnpiked in 1751 and bought much activity to the still narrow High Street, while a water-mill of 1767 and its successors laid the foundations for today's surrounding industry. FOOTS CRAY PLACE was burnt down in 1949.

𝕱𝖔𝖔𝖙𝖘 𝕮𝖗𝖆𝖞 𝕻𝖑𝖆𝖈𝖊 *Sidcup, Kent.* A Palladian-style house built in about 1754 for Bourchier Cleeve, probably to the designs of Isaac Ware. It was bought by Kent Education Committee for use as a museum but destroyed by fire in October 1949.

Foots Cray Place, Sidcup, in the 1760s. A view of the Palladian mansion engraved soon after its completion. The architect was probably Isaac Ware.

Fore Street *EC2.* Extended before the CITY wall, hence the name. In 1654 a postern gate was built at the northern end of ALDERMANBURY and Fore Street soon sprang from obscurity to become the chief shopping street in the northern part of the City until the mid-19th century. In 1660 Daniel Defoe, the son of a butcher, was born here; and in 1850 Ebenezer Howard, originator of the garden city movement, the son of a confectioner. SALTERS' HALL is at No. 4. ST GILES CHURCH is the parish church of the BARBICAN. The street used to extend from REDCROSS STREET to FINS-BURY PAVEMENT but a large part was destroyed in the 2nd World War. A stone tablet in the wall at the WOOD STREET corner of Fore Street marks the site where the first bomb fell on the CITY on 25 August 1940.

Forest Gate *E7.* Postal and residential district in the north of NEWHAM extending across both EAST HAM and WEST HAM. Forest Gate station (1841) is on the Eastern Region line and the district also contains Wanstead Park Station on the ST PANCRAS–BARKING line (opened 1894). Woodgrange Park station on the same line is on the Forest Gate–Manor Park boundary. Neither of these station names has become a formal district name. The name Forest Gate, recorded in the WEST HAM parish registers in the second half of the 17th century, derives from the gate placed across the modern WOODFORD road to prevent cattle straying from the Lower Forest (WANSTEAD FLATS) on the main ROMFORD road. The gate was taken down in 1883. The district is roughly coterminous with the manor of Woodgrange and the Hamfrith ('Ham wood-land') estate of the manor of WEST HAM. As with Plashet in EAST HAM, these names date back to the time when EPPING FOREST came well into the north-east of modern NEWHAM. Hamfrith Wood, north of the ROMFORD road, survived until about 1700. Residential development began in about 1850, largely on the extensive land holdings of Samuel Gurney, owner of what is now West Ham Park. Notable among several good-class estates is the Woodgrange Estate of over 1,100 houses built on the approximately 110 acres of Woodgrange Farm by Thomas Corbett and his son A. Cameron Corbett (later 1st Lord Rowallan) between 1877 and 1892. Cameron Corbett also developed large parts of ILFORD, ELTHAM and HITHER GREEN. The Woodgrange Estate is now a conservation area. Forest Gate Hospital, Forest Lane, originated as an industrial school for pauper boys from East London in 1854, served several poor law purposes, and is now largely used as a maternity hospital.

Forest Hill *SE23.* South of BROCKLEY and north of SYDENHAM, Forest Hill was originally simply 'The Forest', part of LEWISHAM parish, bordering the Great North Wood and Westwood Common. HONOR OAK on its northern border is traditionally named from a prominent oak beneath which Elizabeth I is said to have dined. The most interesting pre-Victorian houses are Hill House and Ashberry Cottage, at the corner of Honor Oak Road and Westwood Park. Both claim the distinction of being used by the Duke of Clarence (later William IV) and Mrs Jordan, his mistress from 1791 until 1811, but without firm evidence. Development began with the opening of the Croydon Canal (1809) and its cripplingly uneconomic stair-case of locks up from NEW CROSS. The railway replaced the canal in 1836. During its experiment with 'atmospheric pressure' traction (1845–8), four massive steam pumping engines were installed at Dartmouth Arms (Forest Hill) station. Encouraged by the hill's 'extensive prospects', Victorian suburban development paralleled that of SYDENHAM. Among those attracted to it was Frederick J. Horniman, tea merchant, traveller and inveterate collector, who opened his vast collection of anthropological and musical objects to the public in 1890. The collection eventually outgrew his house, Surrey Mount, and he commissioned the HORNIMAN MUSEUM by C. Harrison Townsend, giving both building and contents to the LONDON COUNTY COUNCIL on completion in 1901.

Forest Hill attracted a sizeable community of German exiles who built their own church in Dacres Road in 1883. Dietrich Bonhoeffer was pastor for two years from 1933, and the new building (1959) is named Dietrich Bonhoeffer Kirche. In this century the district has changed considerably with the widespread replacement of its Victorian houses by flats; but it remains a pleasant suburb. Tom Keating, whose skilful imitations of Constable and Palmer became notorious, is a native of Forest Hill.

Fortess Road *NW5*. Originally a farm track through Fortis Field, land which perhaps belonged to the owners of FORTIS GREEN. In 1856–62 Ford Madox Brown lived at No. 56, where he painted *Work*.

Fortis Green *N10*. Situated north of the ARCHWAY ROAD between EAST FINCHLEY and MUSWELL HILL. The area was part of the ancient forest of MIDDLESEX, and coins found at nearby Cranley Gardens attest to Roman presence on the high ground. In the 13th century the Manor of HORNSEY or HARINGEY was in the possession of the BISHOPS OF LONDON and their wood covered the western part of the parish. Common land was mainly at MUSWELL HILL and Fortis Green, a hamlet named thus at least by the 16th century, probably after the name of a resident. From the end of the century a sudden increase in population led to the building of 'illegal cottages' at Fortis Green, but its major development occurred during the 19th century when Londoners moved north, forcing the contraction of farmland and the appearance of villas and cottages. The opening of the Finchley (1867) and Muswell Hill (1872) stations of the Great Northern Railway transformed it into a residential district: by the turn of the century Onslow and Cranley Gardens were built, shops and flats soon fronted Fortis Green Road, and terraced houses and mansion blocks appeared. Only HIGHGATE WOOD, QUEEN'S WOOD and Coldfall Wood remain relics of the distant past, and much of Coldfall Wood was cleared for council housing in the 1920s. Today Fortis Green still remains linked with the ecclesiastical district of MUSWELL HILL.

Fortnum and Mason Ltd *181 Piccadilly, W1*. In 1705 William Fortnum came to London and was befriended by Hugh Mason, who owned a small shop in ST JAMES'S MARKET. William Fortnum became a footman in the Household of Queen Anne; and, one of his jobs being to refill the royal candelabra, he sold the used candles to the Queen's Ladies. On retiring, with his knowledge of the needs of the Palace household, he opened a grocery shop quite close to the present site, with his friend Mason (who quickly established stables in MASON'S YARD nearby to deal with the deliveries).

Through the East India Company the partners imported many exotic foods such as 'Harts Horn, Gable Worm Seed, Saffron and Dirty White Candy; and by 1788 the shop was also providing many potted foods. During the Peninsular War, and in subsequent wars, officers relied upon Fortnum and Mason to send them the provisions they could not obtain abroad. In 1819 Sir William Edward Parry took 2 cwt of Fortnum and Mason's sweetened cocoa powder on his expedition to find the North West Passage. Visitors to the GREAT EXHIBITION in 1851 came to the store and marvelled at the exotic foods. A tradition of ready-prepared hampers, supplied for this occasion, survives to the present day. There was a special department to attend to the needs of gentlemen's clubs including the ATHENAEUM and BOODLE'S. During the Crimean War Queen Victoria sent a present to Florence Nightingale of a huge consignment of concentrated beef tea. In 1886 a Mr Heinz called and they ordered his whole stock of the newly invented canned food. The shop was completely rebuilt in 1923–5 by Wimperis, Simpson, Guthrie and Fyffe; the firm has now increased its range from food to furniture and clothes. The Fountain Restaurant and Soda Bar is 'a rendezvous for the *beau-monde*'. In 1964 an articulated clock was placed over the main entrance; designed by Berkeley Sutcliffe and sculpted by P.J. Bentham, it has simulated 18th-century figures of Mr Fortnum and Mr Mason, who on the hour turn and bow to each other.

Fortune Theatre *Golden Lane*. A round wooden theatre, modelled on the GLOBE, SOUTHWARK. It was built in 1600 for Edward Alleyn and Philip Henslow and cost £550. A statue of the Goddess of Fortune stood over the entrance. From the profits Alleyn founded the trust which now supports DULWICH ART GALLERY, DULWICH COLLEGE and several other schools. It was burned down in 1621 but was soon rebuilt in brick. The Puritans closed it in 1642 but illegal performances continued. Dismantled by soldiers in 1649, it was completely demolished in 1661. The modern FORTUNE THEATRE is said to look like the old one, but the design was based on an inaccurate early print.

The second Fortune Theatre, in Golden Lane, built to replace the original wooden structure which burnt down in 1621. This one was pulled down in 1661.

Fortune Theatre *Russell Street, WC2.* Designed in 1922–4 by Ernest Schaufelberg, the sculptor of the bronze, *Nude Girl*, on the façade (1924). Laurence Cowen financed the theatre and it opened with his own play, *Sinners*. For many years it housed amateur productions. In 1927 *On Approval*, a farce by Frederick Londsale, was a big success. In 1957 *At the Drop of a Hat* with Michael Flanders and Donald Swann ran for 733 performances. In 1961 *Beyond the Fringe*, a revue by Alan Bennett, Peter Cook, Jonathan Miller and Dudley Moore, ran here for four years. The seating capacity is 432.

Forty Hall *Enfield, Middlesex.* A magnificent house built in 1629–36 for Sir Nicholas Rainton, Lord Mayor of London. It is constructed of red brick with stone quoins and window surrounds. Inside many of the ceilings and much of the panelling is original, as are the fine screen in the dining-room and most of the chimneypieces. From Sir Nicholas ownership passed to his great-nephew, Nicholas Rainton. Throughout the 19th century the house was owned by the Meyer family until 1895, when it was purchased for Sir Henry Ferryman Bowles by his father. The last private owner was Derek Parker Bowles who sold the estate to EN-FIELD Council in 1951. It is now a museum of the London Borough of ENFIELD.

Forum *Cornhill.* The forum was the major open area and market place of ROMAN LONDON, some 600 feet square. On its north side, in the usual position, were the basilica, the legal centre, offices and shops. Colonnades on either side protected the public from the weather, rather more inclement in Britain than in the Mediterranean lands where the plan originated. The larger than life-size bronze head of the Emperor Hadrian found in the THAMES (now in the BRITISH MUSEUM), and fragments of bronze statues, arms and other remains, probably came from honorific statues set up on pedestals in this area.

Foster Lane *EC2.* Foster is a corruption of St Vedast, to whom the church on the east side of the lane is dedicated. Another church dedicated to St Leonard once stood opposite. Before the GREAT FIRE the lane was known for its goldsmiths and jewellers. GOLDSMITHS' HALL still stands at the corner of GRESHAM STREET.

Foubert's Place *W1.* Built at the end of the 17th century, and named after a riding school founded on the south side at that time by Solomon de Foubert, a Huguenot whose family had emigrated to England in 1679 and whose school was carried on by his son, Major Henry Foubert. George II's sons, William Augustus, Duke of Cumberland, and Sir Robert Walpole were both taught here. The school was closed in 1778. A Congregational chapel, known as Craven Chapel, was built here in 1821 by a retired merchant, Thomas Wilson, on land leased from Lord Craven. In the 1830s the chapel had a very large congregation who came from 'over half London' to hear the sermons of the Revd John Leifchild. A lecture hall and school-rooms known as Craven Hall were added in 1873. The lease of the chapel expired in 1898 and the building was sold to the Lion Brewery in BROADWICK STREET which utilised it as stables. It is now used for industrial purposes. Craven Hall was sold to LIBERTY's in 1907 and is now used as a warehouse.

Founders' Company *see* CITY LIVERY COMPANIES.

Founders' Court *EC2.* FOUNDERS' HALL once stood here. The massive bronze doors of the merchant bankers, Brown, Shipley and Co., are by John Poole and were erected in 1975.

Founders' Hall *13 St Swithin's Lane, EC4.* Their first hall was built in FOUNDER'S COURT, LOTHBURY in 1531. Stow said the street got its name from the loathsome noise which came from their forges. The Hall was destroyed by the GREAT FIRE but was rebuilt soon after. In the 1790s sympathisers of the French Revolution used it as a meeting place and it was nicknamed 'the cauldron of sedition'. In the early 19th century Dissenters worshipped here. It was rebuilt in 1845 and soon after let as offices to the Electric Telegraph Co. The founders met in an adjoining house. That, too, was leased to the Telegraph Co. in 1854 and the founders moved to ST SWITHIN'S LANE. Their present Hall was built in 1877–8 to the designs of George Aitchison. For the Company *see* CITY LIVERY COMPANIES.

Foundling Hospital *Guildford Street, WC1.* Founded in 1742 by Captain Thomas Coram, a man of many parts – shipwright, master mariner and philanthropist. After spending some time in Taunton, Massachusetts, he settled in London. When going into the CITY on business he had been frequently shocked by the sight of infants exposed in the streets, abandoned by their parents, 'left to die on dung hills'. After 17 years' philanthropic work among these children he eventually persuaded 21 ladies of 'Nobility and Distinction' and a group of noblemen to petition the King. Some houses were first taken in HATTON GARDEN in 1741. In the first year over a third of the children admitted died. After a long search the ladies purchased 56 acres of Lamb's Conduit Fields (north of LAMB'S CONDUIT STREET) from the Earl of Salisbury for £6,500. Work on the hospital, which was designed by Theodore Jacobsen, began in September 1742 and the boys were removed from HATTON GARDEN in 1745 to the completed west wing. The east wing was then built for the girls who were always segregated from the boys except on Christmas Day. Even in death they were kept apart, there being one mortuary for the boys and another for the girls. Originally entry to the hospital was on a 'first come, first served' basis, but this caused disturbances in the street when the disappointed mothers were asked to take their children elsewhere. So in 1742 the Governors decided on a balloting scheme. Each mother drew a coloured ball from a leather bag. A white ball entitled a child to admission subject to a medical examination. A black ball meant that both mother and child were asked to leave. A red ball entitled a child to be put on a waiting list in case one of the 'white' children was found to be suffering from an infectious disease. Word about the hospital got around all over the country and children appeared in droves. Rules were then made that only a first child of an unmarried mother would be admitted; it had to be under 12 months old and the father must have deserted both mother and child. Lastly, the mother had to have been of good repute before her 'fall'. The accepted babies were sent into the country to foster-parents until they were four or five years old and were then

Mothers seeking admission for their babies at the Foundling Hospital, established by Captain Coram in 1742.

brought back to the hospital to be educated. At 14 the Governors arranged indentures for the boys and watched over them until the end of the apprenticeship. Most joined the Army, while the girls were trained to be ladies' maids.

Hogarth was a great friend and admirer of Coram and a patron and Governor of the hospital to which he presented a fine portrait of Coram, saying that it had given him more satisfaction than any other of his portraits and that he had put more effort into it. At Hogarth's instigation other distinguished artists gave portraits to decorate the Governors' Court Room. This attracted the public to come and see the children and the pictures and to contribute towards the upkeep of the hospital. The plan was so successful that the artists held an annual exhibition of their works. The hospital's other great benefactor was Handel. In 1750 he gave an organ to the chapel and by giving performances of *Messiah* on it with the choir which he himself taught, he raised £7,000. Another method of raising money was to hold ladies' breakfasts and it is recorded that on one occasion they provided 1,028 meals. It was due largely to Handel that the Foundling Hospital became a fashionable place of worship; people rented pews and came from all over London to hear well-known preachers. Dickens was a regular member of the congregation.

In 1926 the hospital moved to Berkhamsted, the HATTON GARDEN site having been bought by Lord Rothermere and others for a children's playground. The buildings were demolished, apart from the entrance arcades. The body of Thomas Coram, the font, pulpit and organ from the chapel were taken to ST ANDREW'S HOLBORN. A new house designed by J.M. Sheppard was erected nearby at 40 BRUNSWICK SQUARE, and the organisation continues to this day as the THOMAS CORAM FOUNDATION FOR CHILDREN.

The Governors had the foresight to remove all their beautiful possessions to the new building, including one of the staircases. The Court Room is an exact representation of the room that Hogarth and his friends, including Reynolds and Gainsborough, decorated with their pictures. The ceiling by Wilton is original. The statue of Coram outside is by William MacMillan (*see* STATUES).

Fournier Street *E1*. Originally Church Street, it was developed while work was in progress on the nearby CHRISTCHURCH, SPITALFIELDS. The attic windows were designed to give maximum light to the weavers who occupied them when the houses ceased to be used solely for domestic purposes.

Fox and Bull *Knightsbridge*. A tavern which once stood on the west corner of ALBERT GATE. Queen Elizabeth I called here occasionally on her visits to Lord Burleigh at BROMPTON. In the 18th century it was frequented by men of fashion. Sir Joshua Reynolds painted a sign for it. George Morland was often to be seen here, usually drunk. The corpse of Harriet Westbrook, Shelley's first wife, was brought here after her drowning (*see* HYDE PARK). When the tavern was demolished in 1835–6 the bodies of several soldiers killed in the Civil War were discovered.

Fox and Hounds *29 Passmore Street, SW1*. One of London's smallest inns, this building has been licensed since the early 19th century, for beer and wine only. Inside it is the nearest equivalent to a small country public house to be found in London. It has cottage-type furniture and old prints.

Foyle's (W. and G. Foyle Ltd) *119–125 Charing Cross Road, WC2*. The biggest bookshop in London.

It was opened here in 1906 by two young brothers, William and Gilbert Foyle, who had failed their Civil Service examinations and, advertising their unwanted textbooks for sale, had realised from the number of replies they received how large a market for such books there was. They first began trading in their own home in Fairbank Street, off the CITY ROAD, then moved to CECIL COURT before settling down in CHARING CROSS ROAD.

The original premises at Nos 121 and 123, which were built in 1903 to the designs of Alfred Burr, were gradually altered and extended, and in 1929 the existing five-floor building was officially opened by the Lord Mayor. In 1916 the firm reconstructed the south side of MANETTE STREET to provide further accommodation for their growing miles of shelving and millions of books.

The firm's numerous distinguished customers have included Eamon de Valera, G.B. Shaw, John Masefield, John Galsworthy, Conan Doyle, and the Sitwells. Aleister Crowley was a regular visitor to the Occult Department. Walt Disney was often seen browsing here among the art books. David Ben-Gurion once spent a whole morning in the Philosophy Department; and Noël Coward claimed that he found inspiration for *Cavalcade* in some old volumes in Foyle's shelves.

Framework Knitters' Company *see* CITY LIVERY COMPANIES.

Frascati's Restaurant *26–32 Oxford Street.* The original building was designed by Collcut in 1893; and redecorated in 1928 by Stanley Hamp. It was a large and handsome establishment with a winter garden, café and grill room. The site is now occupied by the Language Tuition Centre, by Robinson and Partners (1954–8).

Frederick Street *WC1.* Built in 1826–34 on the CALTHORPE ESTATE and named after Frederick, 5th Lord Calthorpe, who was born in 1826. Some of the original houses remain.

Frederick's Place *EC2.* Terraced houses built by the Adam brothers in 1776 on the site of a house which had belonged to Sir John Frederick, Lord Mayor of London in 1661. Benjamin Disraeli was articled to a firm of solicitors at No. 6 in 1821. Setting himself apart from the other clerks, he adopted a style of dress and flamboyant manner which were considered striking even in those early years of the reign of George IV. 'You have too much genius for Frederick's Place,' a woman friend said to him. 'It will never do.'

Freedom of the City Derives from the ancient craft guilds which guarded the interests of individual crafts or trades and made themselves responsible for the quality of training and performance of the practitioners in them. A young man apprenticed to a member of a craft guild served him for several years before appearing before the court of the guild concerned and proving his proficiency. If he did so he was 'made free' of the guild to practise his trade. He had then to be made free of the CITY in order to work there.

Today the Freedom of the City can be acquired by any one of three methods: (1) servitude, which means serving the full term of apprenticeship to a Freeman, applying to the CHAMBERLAIN of London and paying the fee prescribed; (2) patrimony, by which the son or daughter of a Freeman, aged at least 21 and born after the father's enrolment to the Freedom, may be made free on application to the CHAMBERLAIN and payment of a fee; and (3) redemption – admission to the Freedom by payment, on application, sponsored by two liverymen, to the CHAMBERLAIN.

The CHAMBERLAIN of London is the official custodian of the Roll of Freemen, and admissions to the Freedom are made by the Clerk to the Chamberlain's Court. Applications are made and fees paid to him, and approval is given by the Court of ALDERMEN in the case of members of a CITY LIVERY COMPANY and by the COURT OF COMMON COUNCIL in all other cases. All fees paid in respect of applications for admission to the Freedom are devoted to the CITY OF LONDON FREEMEN'S SCHOOL at Ashtead in Surrey. Most of the privileges attaching to the Freedom have long since been rendered unnecessary by the welfare state, but the orphans of Freemen are still eligible for admission to the Freemen's School as foundation scholars.

On admission Freemen receive a certificate of their enrolment and a book of *Rules for the Conduct of Life*, with a warning not to claim to have been awarded the Honorary Freedom of the City. The latter is an honour accorded only to distinguished British citizens for outstanding service to the nation. Honorary Freemen are admitted by the CHAMBERLAIN himself before the LORD MAYOR and CORPORATION in GUILDHALL, and receive their certificate of admission in a gold casket or some other container of special significance. Distinguished service officers may also receive a Sword of Honour. The citations of Honorary Freemen are inscribed in a special record entitled *London's Roll of Fame*.

Freemasons' Hall *Great Queen Street, WC2.* Built in 1927–33 to the designs of H.V. Ashley and F. Winton Newman as a ceremonial and administrative headquarters for the United Grand Lodge of England and known initially as the Masonic Peace Memorial in honour of those English Freemasons who were killed in the 1st World War. The building was opened by the then Grand Master, the Duke of Connaught. The ground floor is occupied by the administrative offices of the Order; the first floor contains the Grand Temple, Library and Museum; the second and third, suites of rooms for masonic meetings. The building is the third to stand in GREAT QUEEN STREET. The first hall, designed by Thomas Sandy, was built in 1775–6 on a small part of the site now occupied by the CONNAUGHT ROOMS which originally had been known as the Freemasons' Tavern. Later developments and rebuildings successively extended the hall and tavern respectively to the west and east along the street. Nothing now remains of Sandby's Hall of 1775 nor of later work by Sir John Soane and Philip Hardwick in the first part of the 19th century. The second Freemasons' Hall, designed by Francis Pepys Cockerell, was constructed in 1864–9. Of this there remains only part of the façade of the Hall together with the former Tavern portion, both today being part of the CONNAUGHT ROOMS in which Cockerell's fine banqueting hall is now the Grand Hall.

Freemen of the City *see* FREEDOM OF THE CITY.

French Protestant Church *Soho Square, W1.* In the 16th century Protestant refugees, fleeing from persecutions on the continent, found asylum in England. Although Edward VI granted them a licence in 1550 to hold their own services, they had, however, no large church of their own until 1893. Until that date they had moved from pillar to post making use of a varied number of available buildings. In 1889 the consistory of their church was in a position to purchase Nos. 8 and 9 SOHO SQUARE and Sir Aston Webb was commissioned to draw up plans. Purchase of the site could not proceed without the permission of the Attorney-General and this delayed the start of work. The congregation, meanwhile, used a Baptist chapel behind No. 7 Soho Square. The church was completed in 1893. It is a four-storeyed block in the Flemish-Gothic style, with living accommodation above the entrance lobby.

Fribourg and Treyer *34 Haymarket, SW1*. Originally established in 1720 by Mr Fribourg at the sign of the Rasp and Crown. By the end of the 18th century Mrs Martha Evans who had married Gottlieb Augustus Treyer from Amsterdam, had come into the business. She and her husband used to live in the shop, with an Adam screen to divide off the living accommodation. Customers would call in for a cigar and a chat. The Evans family continued in a long line to run the shop, and in 1912 No. 33 (originally BURBERRY'S) was added to the premises as well as Arundel Court (renamed Shaver's Place after the 17th-century gaming hall). The earliest mention of cigarettes was in 1852. The shop was well placed, close to the clubs, including BOODLE'S, WHITE'S and BROOKS'S and their patrons numbered, among others, David Garrick, George IV, Beau Brummell, the Marquess of Queensberry, Mrs Fitzherbert, and Dr Jenner. Sidelines included 'Trees and Seeds' and 'Treyer's Portable Soup'. After 261 years the shop was closed in 1981. The HOUSE OF BEWLAY, however, continues to sell Fribourg and Treyer cigarettes. The distinctive façade remains, as No. 34 is a listed building.

Friday Street *EC4*. Used to run between CHEAPSIDE and OLD FISH STREET but since the construction of QUEEN VICTORIA STREET and the bombing of the 2nd World War only a small section between QUEEN VICTORIA STREET and CANNON STREET remains. Stow said it was named after a medieval fish market held here on Fridays. Ekwall suggests it might be a corruption of an Old English name, Frigdaeges. Three churches used to stand in the street: ST MARGARET MOSES, ST JOHN THE EVANGELIST and ST MATTHEW. All were destroyed in the GREAT FIRE. Only ST MATTHEW was rebuilt, but it has been demolished since.

Friends' House *Euston Road, NW1*. Headquarters of the Religious Society of Friends (Quakers) in Great Britain. A neo-Georgian building, built in 1925–7 to the designs of Hubert Lidbetter, it comprises a large meeting house, committee rooms and the central offices of the Society; it also houses its library which was founded in 1673 and contains a fine collection of Quaker literature including George Fox's journal and documents relating to the foundation of Pennsylvania.

Friern Barnet *Middlesex*. Situated north of MUSWELL HILL, with the GREAT NORTH ROAD to the west

and the NORTH CIRCULAR ROAD to the south, it protrudes into Hertfordshire, with EAST BARNET to its north. Originally part of the forest extending throughout MIDDLESEX, the name Barnet derives from the Saxon *baernet*, a burning, that is, a clearing made by fire in a forest (*see also* HIGH BARNET, EAST BARNET). In the 12th century it was referred to as South Barnet or Sarnets (without) Barnet, and in the 13th century as Little Barnet. Friern derives from 'Freren', a name it assumed from the 13th century after the parish, together with its manor of Friern Barnet or WHETSTONE, had been given by the BISHOP OF LONDON to the Knights of St John of Jerusalem. The small Church of St James on Friern Barnet Lane dates back to the late 12th century (the restored south doorway is probably Norman), and the old manor house was known as the first *hospitium* or hostel for travellers north from London.

At that time Friern Barnet Lane was part of the Great North Road, together with Colney Hatch Lane; and it was not until the 14th century when the BISHOP OF LONDON allowed passage through his hunting park that a more direct road was made between HIGHGATE and WHETSTONE. The hamlets of WHETSTONE in the north-west part of the parish, and COLNEY HATCH (hatch possibly meaning 'gate') in the south-east, existed by the end of the 14th century.

At the DISSOLUTION the manor passed to the crown and then to the Dean and Chapter of ST PAUL'S. The manor house no longer existed by 1551 when the Friary House was built and subsequently given by Elizabeth I to Sir Walter Ralegh. From him it passed to the Bacon family, with whom it remained until the 19th century. Elizabeth passed through the village on several occasions on her way from Hatfield to London; in 1553 as Mary's prisoner, and in 1558 in triumph on Mary's death. She is supposed to have stopped to drink at Queen's Well to the east of the church. The extensive woodland of the parish was used by the Queen for hunting. In the 16th century more than 450 acres (about one-third of the parish) were still wooded and the village consisted only of the church, manor house (known also as the Friary), and two farmhouses.

Until the mid-19th century Friern Barnet remained essentially rural, and the Lawrence Campe almshouses built in 1612 are the only buildings to survive that can be said to antedate 1850. They were repaired and restored in the 19th century; St James's was rebuilt and enlarged in 1853. By this date most of the woodland had been cleared and the building of residential areas had begun along new roads such as Friary and Torrington Roads. Ten acres of Hollick Wood were cleared for the Colney Hatch Asylum (*see* FRIERN HOSPITAL).

In 1851 the Great Northern Railway opened COLNEY HATCH station (renamed New Southgate and Friern Barnet in 1923), and during the second half of the century the population of Friern Barnet increased from about 450 to 4,000, mainly in the area around Colney Hatch. The railway allowed people to live outside London and commute into town to work, and the hospital brought people into the area as inmates and staff. In 1892 J. Loughborough Pearson built St John's Church near the hospital on the south side of Friern Barnet Road to serve as a chapel of ease to St James's. It was dedicated in 1911.

From the late 19th century estates and farms were

sold for residential building, much of this carried out during the early decades of this century by Friern Barnet Urban District Council which had been formed in 1895. In 1909 it bought 23 acres around the Friary to make the public Friary Park. During the 1930s the district underwent a series of boundary changes involving FINCHLEY, HORNSEY, SOUTHGATE and WOOD GREEN, and in 1965 it was incorporated into the London Borough of BARNET, sacrificing the atmosphere of village community that had survived to that date.

Apart from Pearson's St John's, Friern Barnet Town Hall, designed by the architects Sir John Brown and Henson, is a notable building as an example of the architecture of the 1940s.

Friern Hospital *New Southgate, N11*. The foundation stone of what was to be England's finest and Europe's largest mental hospital, built to the design of S.W. Dawkes, was laid by the Prince Consort in 1849. It opened in July 1851 as the Middlesex County Pauper Lunatic Asylum on a 140-acre site at COLNEY HATCH in what is now the south-east corner of the London Borough of BARNET with accommodation for 1,250 patients. As plain COLNEY HATCH it came to symbolise madness in the popular mind as BEDLAM had done in previous centuries.

COLNEY HATCH, like most Victorian county asylums, was planned as a largely self-supporting rural community with its own farm, water supply, gas works, brewery, laundry, needle-room, shoemaker, upholsterer and tailor. It even had its own graveyard. Much of the work was done by patients, which reduced their charge on the county rate as well as providing useful occupation.

As the population of London grew, the asylum had to be enlarged, at first by additions to the main building; then, at the turn of the century, by separate villas, and the provision of quarters for nursing staff who had originally slept adjoining their wards. By the time it was taken over by the newly-created LONDON COUNTY COUNCIL in 1889, there were more than 2,000 beds. During the 1st World War the number rose to nearly 3,500. In 1937 it was renamed Friern Hospital to remove old associations.

Frith Street *W1*. Laid out in the late 1670s and early 1680s and evidently named after Richard Frith, a rich builder. It appears on some 18th-century maps, including Rocque's, as Thrift Street. Like other SOHO streets, it had in its early years several aristocratic residents, though fewer foreign occupants than DEAN and GREEK STREETS. As, too, in other parts of SOHO, artists and writers came to live here in the 18th and early 19th centuries. J.A. Gresse, the royal Drawing Master, was living here in 1794, John Constable in 1810–11, John Bell, the sculptor, in 1832–3, Horne Tooke in about 1804, and Arthur Murphy, the actor, in about 1801. Later, tradesmen and craftsmen moved in; then restaurant keepers. No. 5 was built in the 1730s, Nos 6–7 in 1718. But apart from No. 60, which is an original late 17th-century house, scarcely any of the early houses can now be identified from the outside.

At No. 6 William Hazlitt had lodgings in 1830 and wrote his last essays here. Charles Lamb was at his bedside when he died, murmuring, 'Well, I've had a happy life.' The Gothic shop front at No. 15 was installed in 1816 for Charles Clark, bookbinder. Samuel

Romilly, the law reformer, was born in 1757 at No. 18. Mozart lodged with his father and sister in the house of a staymaker, No. 20, when he was nine in 1764–5. His father placed an announcement in *The Public Advertiser* in March 1765; 'Those Ladies and Gentlemen, who will honour him with their Company from twelve to Three in the Afternoon, any Day in the Week ... may, by taking a Ticket, gratify their Curiosity, and not only hear this young Music Master and his Sister perform in private; but likewise try his surprising Musical Capacity, by giving him any thing to play at Sight, or any Music without Bass, which he will write upon the Spot, without recurring to his Harpsichord.' William Macready, the actor, was living at No. 64 in 1816. John Logie Baird lived at No. 22 between 1924 and 1926 and, on 26 January 1926 in his attic room, gave the first public demonstration of television to members of the ROYAL INSTITUTION. The apparatus he used is in the SCIENCE MUSEUM.

Frognal *Hampstead, NW3*. The earliest beginnings of HAMPSTEAD were here. A farm is known to have existed in the area before AD 1000. The Manor of HAMPSTEAD was in the possession of the Monks of WESTMINSTER ABBEY from that date; and in the Domesday survey it was reckoned to have 'land for 3 ploughs'. The first mention of Frognal by that name (although written as Ffrognal) was in the Farm Accounts of 1372. No one knows for certain the derivation of the name; one theory is that in this well-watered area the Manor House was known as 'Frogen-hall' – the Saxon word for frogs being *frogen*. The old Manor Farm House stood in the angle of Frognal and what is now Frognal Lane. The village cattle pond was between the house and the church, and was watered by the Frognal brook, which ran alongside the present road. Manor Courts were almost certainly held in the Great Hall of the Manor Farm House which, by Tudor times, consisted of buildings on three sides of a great yard. The monks held the Manor until the DISSOLUTION in 1539 when it passed into lay hands; the Frognal area was known as the 'Manor Place of Hampstead' in 1543. In 1551 King Edward VI granted the Manor to Sir Thomas Wroth, who thus became the first in a long line of Lords of the Manor, none of whom lived in the Manor House. In fact, the house was never more than a modest farm house. The Tudor building was demolished about 1790 by Thomas Poole, who was at that time farming the land, and who also owned JACK STRAW'S CASTLE. Three houses were built on the site in the next few years, and remain there today. Across the road, at the end of today's Frognal Way, was Priory Lodge (demolished 1924), where in the summer of 1746 Samuel Johnson stayed with his wife. 'Mrs Johnson, for the sake of the country air, had lodgings at Hampstead,' writes Boswell. The country air still survived in 1822, when Maria Edgeworth talked of 'delicious Frognal. Hay-making, profusion of flowers, rhododendrons ... flowering down to the grass.' Frognal Priory was the name given to a 'mock antique structure' built in the first half of the 19th century lower down the hill (Frognal Close is there now). Its owner was a local character known as 'Memory Corner Thompson', so named because he once won a bet that he could name from memory every public house situated at street corners in a certain district of London. His fantastic Gothic house had stained-glass windows, panelled ceilings and an

The house in Frognal designed in 1885 by Norman Shaw for Kate Greenaway, who lived there until 1901.

immense, ornate porch. After Thompson's death it fell into disrepair and was finally pulled down in the last years of the century.

At the top end of Frognal, in the grounds of today's Medical Research Council building, once stood an old Tudor house which in 1725 became the first parish workhouse. These houses have all disappeared, but Frognal still has much of architectural and historic interest. The Old Mansion, among the oldest houses in Hampstead, built in about 1700 though considerably altered, is at No. 94; and of much the same date are Nos 108 and 110. The latter was once a famous tavern, the Three Pigeons, and was later the home of E.V. Knox, once editor of *Punch*. No. 99 dates from 1740; from 1940 to 1942, it was occupied by General de Gaulle. A little further up, built about 1745, is an attractive group of houses by Henry Flitcroft (*see* FROGNAL GROVE). In one of these, No. 103, Ramsay Macdonald lived for a time.

Prominent in the southern part of Frognal is UNIVERSITY COLLEGE SCHOOL, opened in 1907 by King Edward VII. Across the road is the house that Norman Shaw built for Kate Greenaway, who lived there from 1885–1901. Kathleen Ferrier, Anton Walbrook, Ann Ziegler and Webster Booth also lived in Frognal at various times.

Frognal Grove *Hampstead, NW3*. Designed by Henry Flitcroft for his own occupation. The copyhold of Frognal Grove was acquired by Flitcroft in 1741. The house was completed in 1750. It was approached by a celebrated lime walk which had been planted by Edmund Bolesworth, owner of a perfumer's business near TEMPLE BAR, who had previously held the property, then comprising cottages, farms and stabling. The lime entrance avenue is still there, with a right of way for pedestrians along its length. Upon Flitcroft's death in 1769, Frognal Grove devolved upon his son, Henry, who was insane. It was, therefore, let to Edward Montagu, a Master in Chancery and friend of Lord Mansfield, owner of KENWOOD. It was then known as Montagu House. The house subsequently came into the possession of the Street family. George Edmund Street, architect of the LAW COURTS in the STRAND, carried out alterations.

In the 1950s, the house and stables were divided into several residences, though the exterior, facing the lime walk, remains unaltered. An old mounting block, cut from a single slab of stone, can still be seen outside the house. In the 1950s a number of modern houses were also built in the large and beautiful gardens.

Frognal House *Frognal Avenue, Sidcup, Kent.* Once the home of Sir Philip Warwick and later of Earl Sydney, it is sited on the spring line overlooking the Cray valley and was probably an ancient manor. Ownership is recorded from 1253 and parts of the basement are early Tudor. The house was rebuilt in about 1670 and the grounds remodelled under the influence of John Evelyn. In 1917 the Queen's Hospital (later Queen Mary's) was established here and Harold Gillies won recognition for plastic surgery. Frognal was the setting for Conan Doyle's *The Abbey Grange*. After falling into disrepair, the house has since been converted into offices.

Frost Fairs Before 19th-century engineering constructed bridges which minimally impeded the flow of the River THAMES there were many winters when it froze over completely. A sustained period of cold weather was necessary as the icing-over process took time: ice patches formed near the banks and bridges, gradually extending and joining up until a continuous sheet of ice covered the river. So-called 'Fairs' were then held, although they were really just impromptu jollifications as a true fair required a Royal Charter.

In 1564–5 it was recorded that archery and dancing took place on the THAMES. 1683–4 saw 'a mighty frost' with ice between the beginning of December and 4 February. A whole ox was roasted on the ice and there was an entire street of booths from the TEMPLE to SOUTHWARK. A broadsheet entitled *A Winter Wonder of the Thames Frozen Over with Remarks on the Resort thereon* asked: 'And who'd believe to see revived there in January, Bartholomew Fair?'

Charles II, together with members of his family and household, visited the frozen river to view and enjoy the entertainments. Hand printing presses had been set up on the ice to provide people with a permanent memento of the Frost Fair and the King and his party had their names printed on a quarto sheet of Dutch paper, 3½ ins × 4 ins, which can be seen in the MUSEUM OF LONDON.

Further great frosts occurred in 1715–6 and in 1739–40 when it is recorded that some venturers in the STRAND bought a large ox in SMITHFIELD to be roasted whole on the ice; and one, Hodgson, claimed the privilege of felling or knocking down the beast as a right inherent in his family, his father having knocked down the one roasted on the river in the Great Frost of 1684 near Hungerford Stairs.

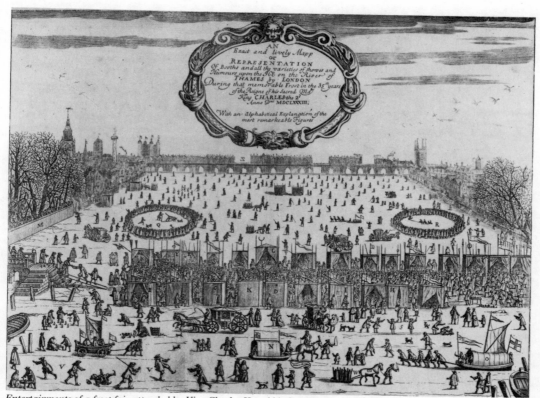

Entertainments of a frost fair attended by King Charles II and his family on the frozen Thames in 1683.

In 1788–9 from PUTNEY BRIDGE down to Redriff was one continual scene of merriment and jollity. The following advertisement appeared in the *Public Advertiser* of 5 January 1789: 'This Booth to let. The present possessor of the premises is Mr Frost. His affairs, however, not being on a permanent footing, a dissolution or bankruptcy may soon be expected and a final settlement of the whole entrusted to Mr Thaw.'

1813–4 saw the greatest frost fair of the century with a grand mall or walk running from BLACKFRIARS BRIDGE and named 'City Road'. Thousands of people paid 2d or 3d entry tolls to the WATERMEN who, done out of their usual means of livelihood by the ice, ensured that no one had access to the Thames without their help by excavating channels in the ice by the banks of the river and then assisting people over them! Once old LONDON BRIDGE was demolished in 1831, the improved flow of the river prevented it from freezing over.

Fruiterers' Company *see* CITY LIVERY COMPANIES.

Fulham *SW6*. The area to the west of CHELSEA was the heart of the Manor of Fulham which was granted to the BISHOPS OF LONDON in the 8th century and which was their country home from about the 11th century. The name is said to be derived from a personal name and to mean Fulla's settlement in a low-lying bend of the river. Fulham seems to have developed not as one village, but as a number of settle-

ments which had to wait until the second half of the 19th century to be linked together. The settlements were: Fulham Town, PARSONS GREEN, WALHAM GREEN, North End and Sands End. Fulham was the 'great fruit and kitchen garden north of the Thames', a place of market and nursery gardens, intermixed with fine houses, built for prosperous Londoners in search of purer air. Fulham Town, with its High Street leading to the ferry, and, after 1729, to the old bridge, was the early centre of the community, having FULHAM PALACE, the home of the BISHOPS OF LONDON until 1973, and the parish church of ALL SAINTS, which stands at the approach to PUTNEY BRIDGE. CHURCH GATE leads to the Church. Opposite, on the site of the Grand Theatre, stands Bridge House, one of the International Computers Limited buildings. Designed by R. Seifert and Partners, it has on its front a sculpture, *Swan Uppers*, by Bainbridge Copnall. The Grand Theatre, opened in 1897, was a commanding building in classical style, with the interior decorated in the manner of Louis XIV. It seated more than 1,000 but, after the advent of the cinema, it closed in 1934.

The NEW KING'S ROAD, the far end of Chelsea's KING'S ROAD, at right-angles to the Bridge, includes FULHAM POTTERY, the south side of PARSONS GREEN and Eelbrook Common. To the north of Eelbrook is WALHAM GREEN, a settlement which can be traced back to the 14th century. North End, most of which is now known as West Kensington, was a later settlement dating from the 16th century. Its centre is NORTH END

All Saints Fulham as seen from the bridge in about 1750 before the removal of the wooden spire.

ROAD which runs to HAMMERSMITH ROAD and on its west side includes BARON'S COURT.

After its junction with Fulham Road, Fulham High Street becomes FULHAM PALACE ROAD. This area was the last part of Fulham to retain its farms and gardens and the rows of streets which lead from it mostly date from the last years of the 19th century and the beginning of the 20th.

The Sands End area, south-west of the NEW KING'S ROAD and extending to the CHELSEA boundary, also retained its open spaces until the 19th century. One remains as South Park. The name Sands End is thought to be derived from the sandy nature of the land exposed by the river in flood. The area was dominated by the gasworks which was responsible for the many rows of small houses built for its workers. In its grounds stands SANDFORD MANOR HOUSE.

Fulham Bridge Yard The yard of the Fulham Bridge public house, a cul-de-sac running northwards from BROMPTON ROAD. The public house was totally demolished, together with No. 62, in 1944 by a flying bomb which came down HANS CRESCENT, just missing the east end of HARROD's. The site is occupied by Silver City House, completed in 1962.

Fulham Carpets and Tapestries Made in a workshop established by a French émigré, Pierre Parisot, from the Savonnerie factory in Paris. The workshop was started in WESTMINSTER and moved to PADDINGTON before being set up in FULHAM in 1753. Although many other workers from the Savonnerie worked for Parisot during the next few years, the high prices charged soon led to the downfall of the workshop, which was closed in 1755.

Fulham Football Club *see* FOOTBALL CLUBS.

Fulham Hospital *Fulham Palace Road.* A conglomeration of buildings constructed in 1849–50 when the Hammersmith and Fulham workhouse was built on this site. A survey of 1854 shows 32 beds reserved for sick men, 50 for women, 6 for lying-in, 16 for idiots, 46 in the infirmary, 12 for infectious cases and 22 for infants. Additional buildings were added in the latter part of the 19th century. In 1884 two doctors were appointed to look after 486 patients. In 1905 a nurses' home and operating theatre were built. The hospital was renamed Fulham Hospital in 1928. In 1930 it was taken over by the LONDON COUNTY COUNCIL. In 1948, with the introduction fo the National Health Service, it was brought under the Fulham and Kensington Hospital Management Committee, and in 1957 it was amalgamated with CHARING CROSS HOSPITAL. A new teaching hospital designed by Ralph Tubbs has been built on the site (*see* CHARING CROSS HOSPITAL).

Fulham Palace *Bishop's Avenue, SW6.* The manor house of the BISHOPS OF LONDON and their official residence until 1973. It is thought that the Bishops had a home in FULHAM from the 11th century. The present brick house dates from the beginning of the 16th century. Its oldest part, built by Bishop Fitzjames, is known as the Fitzjames Quadrangle. This is entered through an archway and on its east side there is a low, battlemented tower, surmounted by a bell turret. The red brickwork has an ever-repeating diaper pattern of dark purple bricks. The east front was rebuilt by Bishop Howley in 1814–5. The chapel was erected by Bishop Tait in 1866–7. The buildings were originally surrounded by a moat which, so Sir Arthur Blomfield suggested in 1856, might have been dug round a Danish camp. Recent excavations suggest, however, that it may have had a Roman origin as a defensive earthwork. The grounds are planted with many rare trees, perhaps by Bishops Grindal and Compton, but more probably by the later Bishops Howley, Blomfield and Jackson. Since 1973 the palace has been leased to the Borough Council.

Fulham Palace Road *Fulham, SW6.* Links FULHAM with HAMMERSMITH and was the old 'Churchway' leading to the parish church of ALL SAINTS before Hammersmith had its own chapel-of-ease to ST PAUL in 1631. It received its present name in 1882. The road ran through fields. The windmill, thought to have been there in the time of the *Domesday* survey, although not mentioned in it, remained until 1794; among the few buildings were the Workhouse and Infirmary built in 1849 (the site of CHARING CROSS HOSPITAL). The last farm, that of William Matyear, was sold after his death in 1910 and developed as the Crabtree housing estate, and as wharves on the riverside.

Fulham Pottery *New King's Road, Fulham, SW6*

Established in 1672 by John Dwight, a former lawyer and skilful artist who succeeded, for the first time in England, in producing continental-type salt-glazed domestic wares of all kinds. He also made portrait busts and statuettes of a high quality, among which is his bust of Prince Rupert in the BRITISH MUSEUM. Continued by his family after his death in 1703, the pottery passed in 1864 to C.I.C. Bailey and in 1889 to the Cheavin family, who concentrated on the production of commercial stoneware, such as drainpipes and water filters. When the demand for these decreased, decorative pottery was designed, including white earthenware vases known as 'Fulham Vases'. A fire in 1918 destroyed most of the old buildings and only those of the late 19th century remained to be demolished in the 1970s, when the site was excavated. A 19th-century bottle kiln has been preserved among the modern office development on the site. Pottery continues to be made and sold, and pottery materials supplied from the adjoining premises.

Fulham Power Station *Townmead Road, SW6*. Designed by G.E. Baker and Preece, Cardew and Rider and opened in 1936. The building contains 20,000 tons of steel, 500,000 rivets and nearly 4,000,000 bricks, and the cranes used in its construction were previously used in the building of Sydney Harbour Bridge in Australia. The coaling jetty on its river front is 120 yards long.

Fulham Road *SW3, SW6, SW10*. Extends from BROMPTON ROAD across FULHAM BROADWAY to FULHAM PALACE ROAD. The road existed from at least the 15th century but its present name dates from the 19th. Earlier names were the King's Highway and the London Road. It was a busy coaching road to Portsmouth and the south-west, though notorious for its bad condition and footpads. At the eastern end at No. 61 stands the Michelin Building erected to the designs of Epinasse in 1910–11 and decorated with Art Nouveau designs. A public house called the Queen's Elm stands at the junction of OLD CHURCH STREET. This succeeded a tavern called the Queen's Tree mentioned in CHELSEA parish books in 1667. Tradition has it that Queen Elizabeth I sheltered in a storm under an elm

tree and said that henceforth it should be called the Queen's tree. Elm Park Gardens are a little further west on the southern side. These were once Victorian houses in single occupation now mainly converted by the local authority into subsidised flats as is Elm Park House, built in 1964. ST STEPHEN'S HOSPITAL occupies a large frontage between Limerston Street and Netherton Grove. Arnold Bennett lived in Netherton Grove when he first came to London. After Stamford Bridge the road passes the grounds of CHELSEA FOOTBALL CLUB and goes through FULHAM BROADWAY. No. 596, the Marist Convent School, includes buildings dating from the 1840s; and No. 624, Vine Cottage, an early 18th-century cottage, is reputed to have been the home of the opera singer, Anastasia Robinson, who became the wife of the 3rd Earl of Peterborough. Until the 1880s there was little development along the road west of FULHAM BROADWAY. It ran by nursery gardens and a few large estates. The ROYAL MARSDEN HOSPITAL is on the south side, the BROMPTON HOSPITAL on the north. Fulham Town Hall opposite FULHAM BROADWAY station was built in 1888–90. Laura Ashley, the dress and fabric designer, moved to No. 157 from PELHAM STREET in 1969. The fabrics for which she has become renowned were originally printed in PIMLICO in 1953 by Bernard Ashley. Henri Gaudier-Brzeska, the sculptor, had a studio at the back of No. 454, now Thomas and Wilson, fibrous plasterers, from 1912 to 1914 when he joined the French Army. He was killed the next year.

Fulwood Place *WC1*. Now redeveloped, this was a Tudor cart track used as the south entrance to GRAY'S INN. Sir George Fulwood acquired it by marriage in about 1580. He blocked the lane and lined it with houses known as Fulwood's Rents. He sold to GRAY'S INN the narrow entrance to South Square used today. In 1589 he was admitted as a member and his son Christopher became a member and later Treasurer. A Royalist, he was killed in the Civil War and his estates confiscated. Until 1697 the street was a place of sanctuary for debtors. From about 1699–1731 Ned Ward, the 'London Spy', had his punch house here. In 1720 Strype wrote of it as 'a place of good resort and taken up with coffee houses, ale houses and houses of entertainment by reason of its vicinity to Gray's Inn.'

Furniture Makers' Company *see* CITY LIVERY COMPANIES.

Furnival Street *EC4*. Formerly known as Castle Street; Tommy Traddles has lodgings here in *David Copperfield*. The name was changed in the 1880s in commemoration of Furnival's Inn (*see* INNS OF CHANCERY).

G

Gaiety Restaurant *335 Strand*. Originally stood on the site of the old EXETER CHANGE on the north side of ALDWYCH (now Inveresk House). It was managed by the railway caterers, Spiers and Pond. It moved to the south side of ALDWYCH in 1904, being part of the buildings by Norman Shaw (with interiors by Ernest Runtz) which had the GAIETY THEATRE in the main corner. Over-large and uneconomic, it closed in 1908. It is now Marconi House.

Gaiety Theatre *Strand*. Opened on 21 December 1868 on a site in the STRAND with entrances in CATHERINE STREET and EXETER STREET, the principal entrance and foyer in the STRAND being the site of the Strand Music Hall which was demolished in 1866. In anticipation of its demolition the properties on each side and at the rear had been acquired discreetly by Lionel Lawson, the proprietor of the *Daily Telegraph*, whose intention was to build an enlarged theatre incorporating a restaurant to be called the Gaiety. A lease of the new theatre was granted by Lawson to John Hollingshead, a journalist. *Thespis*, the first collaboration of Gilbert and Sullivan, was commissioned by Hollingshead for Christmas 1871.

In 1878 electric light was installed in the frontage of the theatre for the first time in England. Although operettas, several by Offenbach, and farces and drama were presented, the main attractions were burlesques, a list of which, produced between 1868 and 1886, filled 18 pages of one of Hollingshead's publications. *Little Jack Sheppard* (1885) was the only joint production of Hollingshead and George Edwards, who had been taken into partnership. Hollingshead retired the following year, leaving Edwards in sole charge. Edwards achieved even greater fame than Hollingshead, initially continuing the same policy before introducing musical comedy. *A Gaiety Girl* (1893) was moderately successful, but he established the vogue for musical comedy with *Shop Girl* (1894), starring Ada Reeve, which ran for 546 performances and which inaugurated the era of the Gaiety Girls, the Stage Door Johnnies and a new element in the aristocratic marriage market. The STRAND improvement scheme necessitated the closure of the theatre on 4 July 1903.

The New Gaiety Theatre, designed by Ernest Runtz and George McLean Ford (with elevations by Norman Shaw) was then in the course of erection on the corner of ALDWYCH and the STRAND. This opened on 26 October 1903 with *The Orchid*, which ran for 559 performances. The cast included Gertie Millar and George Grossmith Jnr. Successful musicals continued to be produced during the war. The two longest running, *Theodore and Co.* (1916), Ivor Novello's first musical score, and *Going Up* (1918), with Evelyn Laye, both had over 500 performances.

Many celebrated performers were associated with the theatre, including Leslie Henson, Stanley Lupino, Laddie Cliff, Jack Hulbert, Cecily Courtneidge and Phillys Dare. Among distinguished managers were Oscar Asche, C.B. Cochran and Firth Shephard. The theatre was demolished in 1957. Citibank House now stands on the site. A plaque on the building gives the date of closure incorrectly as 1938. The seating capacity of the original Gaiety was 2,000 and of the New Gaiety 1,338.

A. W. Gamage Ltd *116–128 Holborn*. In 1878 Arthur Walter Gamage, a Herefordshire farmer's son apprenticed to a draper in the CITY OF LONDON, having saved £40, decided to start on his own. He found a tiny shop with a 5 ft frontage, and hung his motto 'Tall Oaks from Little Acorns Grow' above the door. He and his friend, Frank Spain, who helped cover the cost of the £80 lease and £8 for fittings, slept in the back room and allowed themselves 14s a week for living expenses. At the end of the first year trading had reached £1,632. Through the years Gamage, who bought Spain out, acquired small old properties around the original building. This resulted, in spite of alterations, in his shop becoming a series of rooms, passages, steps and ramps, which made the search for the department required something of an adventure. The variety of goods offered for sale in the 'People's Popular Emporium' covered haberdashery, furniture, gardening, sports and camping equipment and clothing (Gamage was official outfitter to the Boy Scouts' organisation). There was a large zoological department as well as a toy department and a motoring department where cars could be bought in addition to motoring equipment. A 900-page mail order catalogue of 1911 devoted no less than 49 pages to bicycles, motor bicycles and cycling equipment. Gamage is said to have lain in state in this department after his death in 1930. The premises, acquired in 1970 for a £20 million redevelopment scheme, were closed in March 1972. The huge building now on the site was completed in 1980 to the designs of R. Seifert and Partners.

Gardeners' Company see CITY LIVERY COMPANIES.

GARDENS Exceptional gardens in London include those below. (*See also* CHELSEA FLOWER SHOW, GREEN PARK, HYDE PARK, KENWOOD, ROYAL BOTANIC SOCIETY OF LONDON, ROYAL HORTICULTURAL SOCIETY, ROYAL HOSPITAL, ST JAMES'S PARK, VICTORIA EMBANKMENT GARDENS, VICTORIA TOWER GARDENS *and* YORK HOUSE, TWICKENHAM.)

Avery Hill Winter Garden and Nurseries *Bexley, SE9*. The 19 acres of nurseries grow a considerable number of the trees, shrubs and plants for the Greater London Parks; and the Botanical Garden, though small, is laid out like that at KEW GARDENS. The Winter Garden houses plants from all over the world in cool, temperate and tropical sections, the centre dome of the temperate house being 90 ft high.

Barbican Gardens *EC1*. A conservatory in the Arts Centre houses tropical plants. Two gardens in the residential area are laid out like London squares, one mainly of shrubs and trees, including a mimosa.

Buckingham Palace Gardens *SW1*. George III bought the land in 1762, 4 acres of which had once been Mulberry Garden, planted as an unsuccessful silk farm by James I (*see* BUCKINGHAM HOUSE). Later it became a pleasure resort noted by Evelyn in his diary. George IV had the grounds of about 45 acres landscaped from designs by John Nash. After Queen Victoria had made Buckingham Palace her official residence she asked the architect Edward Blore to lay out parterres and shrubberies. The soil removed to construct the lake or fishpond was made into a mound. Here Prince Albert designed walks; and shrubs and trees were planted to screen the stables from the Palace windows. The present garden, enclosed within high walls, consists of great lawns, shrubberies, flowering plants, a lake and numerous fine trees. The privacy enables a great deal of wildlife to flourish. Flamingoes, introduced in 1959, help to keep algae off the lake. (*See also* BUCKINGHAM PALACE.)

Bushy Park *Waterhouse Plantation (Woodland Gardens), Kingston-upon-Thames, Surrey*. This is larger and wilder than the Isabella Plantation in RICHMOND PARK, but Richard Church described them as forming together 'two of the most beautiful man-made scenes that I have found anywhere in Europe'. The woods are chiefly of mature trees underplanted with more recent shrubs; and in the middle a stream has been built.

Cannizaro Park *Wimbledon, SW19*. Sunken terrace and woodland garden.

Chelsea Physic Garden *see separate entry*.

Chelsea Rectory Garden *Old Church Street, SW3*. Two acres of garden with very old trees, including a mulberry believed to have been planted in Elizabeth I's reign.

Chiswick House Garden *Burlington Lane, Chiswick, W4*. The garden is a link between the formal French style of the 17th century and the informal landscape gardening popular in the mid-18th century in Britain. Originally planned by Charles Bridgeman and William Kent, it fell into disrepair until the London Borough of HOUNSLOW began restoration to the original designs, including a more recent addition of a large conservatory and a Victorian parterre. Edward VII lived in the house for a time, and there is an area known as 'The Princes' Gardens' where his sons looked after their own plants. A fine gateway by Inigo Jones came originally from the garden of BEAUFORT HOUSE, CHELSEA. (*See also* CHISWICK HOUSE.)

Dulwich Park *Southwark, SE21*. This was a favourite garden of the late Queen Mary. Rhododendrons, azaleas and silver birch grow in the park, which also contains a rock garden and a display of heather. (*See also* DULWICH PARK.)

Finsbury Circus Garden *EC2*. This garden was threatened with devastation by the Metropolitan Railway Co. in 1862 but saved by the directors, one of whom, Alfred Smee FRS, considered that its 700 shrubs and many fine trees made it the most beautiful of London squares. The trees, Smee wrote, 'carry up large quantities of water into the over-dried atmosphere, and this little forest of trees must play an important and beneficial part in the neighbourhood'. It is the largest open space in the CITY and the CITY

CORPORATION acquired it for public use by Act of Parliament in 1900.

Fulham Palace Gardens *SW6*. Once known for its fine trees, of which several old specimens remain, including cedar and black walnut. The tamarisk was first introduced here by Bishop Grindal, who used to send Queen Elizabeth I presents of fruits from this garden, renowned for its vines. Bishop Compton (1675–1714) did most to make the gardens famous, and admitted students of botany and horticulture.

Greenwich Park *SE10*. Celebrated for its many rare trees: the avenues lined with Spanish chestnut were planted in the 1660s. The park includes a scented garden for the blind; flowerbeds, many filled with old-fashioned plants; the Wilderness, where fallow deer have bred for over 450 years; a bird sanctuary; bronze-age tumuli; and the biggest children's playground in the London Royal Parks. Behind the QUEEN'S HOUSE is one of the longest unbroken herbaceous borders in England – over 900 ft – though not as wide as that at BUCKINGHAM PALACE. (*See also* GREENWICH PARK.)

Hall Place Gardens *Bexley, SE9*. Parkland and grounds of floral bedding displays. There are rock, herb, rose, peat and water gardens, and conservatories. The topiary is designed in the form of the Queen's Beasts.

Ham House Garden *Richmond*. The garden is laid out as in the 17th century. In 1678 John Evelyn recorded in his diary: 'the Parterres, Flower Gardens, Orangeries, Groves, Avenues, Courts, Statues, Perspectives, Fountains, Aviaries, and all this at the banks of the Sweetest River in the World, must needs be admired.' The brick walls and paved courtyards still remain between lawns, gravelled paths, flowers and trees, though the wistaria-covered Orangery is now a tea pavilion. The forecourt was laid out in 1800, with a COADE STONE figure of Father Thames by John Bacon. (*See also* HAM HOUSE.)

Hampton Court Gardens The 50 acres are a blend of Tudor, French, Italian and Dutch gardening styles. Cardinal Wolsey created the original garden with flower-beds, galleries, arbours and a 'mount' on a base of 256,000 bricks, with a three-storeyed summer-house on top. The Maze, constructed for William and Mary, is a version of Wolsey's labyrinth: the shape is triangular and originally consisted of hornbeam, cypress and flowering shrubs, but holly and privet have now been added. In the Tilt Yard, where knights once jousted, is a rose garden, and to the south side of the Palace lie the formal Tudor gardens, with a knot garden planted from old patterns. The long herbaceous border was laid out by William Robinson who disliked formal gardens and developed a style known as 'wild gardening' with flowers appearing throughout the year. The Great Vine, planted in 1769, is now controlled to produce a third of the original 2,200 bunches of grapes each season. The gardens also contain Wren's Chestnut Avenue and Broad Walk; the Wilderness; and the Great Fountain, Pond and Privy Gardens. (*See also* HAMPTON COURT.)

Holland Park *Kensington, W11*. Originally the private park of HOLLAND HOUSE, which stood, according to John Timbs, writing in 1867, among, 'its stately cedars, oaks and planes; its flower-garden, with evergreens clipped into fantastic forms; beds of Italian and old English character, fountains and terraces befitting the architectural garden of this Elizabethan mansion. In the "French Garden", in 1804, was first raised in

England the Dahlia, from seeds sent by Lord Holland from Spain.' Of the 55 acres 28 are now woodland, containing 3,000 species of rare British plants and trees. (*See also* HOLLAND HOUSE AND PARK.)

Inns of Court Gardens *WC2, WC1, EC4.* LINCOLN'S INN, originally the monastery of the Dominicans, was given to the Earl of Lincoln by Edward I when the monks moved to BLACKFRIARS. Following their intensive cultivation the Earl's garden produced abundant fruit, vegetables and flowers. It was separated from LINCOLN'S INN FIELDS by a brick wall and in 1663 a terrace was made against the wall. Pepys brought his wife 'to Lincolne's Inne, and then walked up and down to see the new garden which they are making, and will be very pretty'. The 'Walks' of all the Inns were very fashionable, particularly in Charles II's reign. Now they are open only at lunch-time.

GRAY'S INN gardens, used in early times for ARCHERY and hunting, were laid out under the direction of Francis Bacon when he became a Bencher in 1586. In the north-western corner he built an octagonal summer-house on a mount (demolished in 1755) to view the distant wooded heights of HAMPSTEAD. His elegant flight of steps at the northern end survives, though much of the area was destroyed by bombs in the 2nd World War. One of the oldest trees, still flowering, is a catalpa.

The TEMPLE was separated into Inner and Middle in the reign of Henry VI and the garden of the Inner Temple was divided into several enclosures. Shakespeare here laid the scene of the York and Lancaster red and white roses (*Henry VI*, Pt I, Act II, Scene IV). There were many sundials. One dated 1686 is still on the wall on Pump Court, inscribed 'Shadows we are and like shadows depart'. Charles Lamb, who was born in the TEMPLE, loved Fountain Court which is described by Dickens in *Martin Chuzzlewit*. The ROYAL HORTICULTURAL SOCIETY held here the precursor of the CHELSEA FLOWER SHOW.

Japanese Garden *St Katharine-by-the-Tower, Tower Hamlets, EC3.* Water from fountains drops down on to the garden which is below the level of the road. There is Japanese formal landscaping with rock planting, shrubs and a bridge over a stream. Water falls over a perspex sculpture *Peace and Harmony* by Arthur Fleischmann (exhibited at Osaka 1970, erected here 1980).

Kensington Gardens *Sunken Garden, Orangery, Flower Walk, W8.* A pleached lime tree walk encloses the Sunken Garden, which was laid out again in the reign of Edward VII to reproduce the original. Flowering roses follow the spring bulbs set in beds descending in four tiers from low shrub-covered walls to a central oblong pool surrounded by tubs of miniature cypress. Nearby, across a small green, domed trees of bay and holly line a walk to the Orangery, originally called the Green House. This building was designed by Sir John Vanbrugh in 1704 (with a large stone centrepiece by Nicholas Hawksmoor) for Queen Anne, who used it for entertaining among the exotic scented shrubs. It has recently been restored and refurnished with statues and vases, but is otherwise empty except for slatted seats for visitors. The Flower Walk is surrounded by unusual trees. (*See also* KENSINGTON GARDENS and KENSINGTON PALACE.)

Lambeth Palace Gardens *and* **St Mary at Lambeth Churchyard,** *SE1.* Most of the original palace garden of 16 acres is now a public park; but in Cranmer's time the garden had a unique summer-house of fine workmanship, and his successor, Cardinal Pole, planted white Marseilles fig trees, which have survived for centuries. They still cover part of the old library wall and face on to a group of magnolia trees in the centre of the forecourt. There is a herbaceous border along one wall of the Palace and a small rose garden. The Churchyard of St Mary at Lambeth, beside the Palace, has been made by the Tradescant Trust into a garden, designed by Lady Salisbury, in memory of John Tradescant, father and son, who are buried here with their wives. The tomb is surrounded by newly laid out brick paths with trees and shrubs and a knot garden. (*See also* LAMBETH PALACE *and* ST MARY AT LAMBETH.)

Regent's Park *Queen Mary's Rose Garden and St John's Garden, W1.* The Rose Garden was originally the garden of the Royal Botanic Society of London. In 1839 they leased 18 acres of land, which had formerly been Jenkins' Nursery and were situated within the INNER CIRCLE of REGENT'S PARK. The Society's Summer Flower Shows were held here until 1932, when the garden was renamed after Queen Mary and first planted as a rose garden. This is now five times its original size, with 40,000 bushes, laid out in large beds, each with one variety. The central beds are encircled with roped pillars for climbing roses. The park contains a small lake within the circle, a hillock of winding paths massed with flowering shrubs and trees, and nearby, a rock garden. St John's Garden is entered through a walk of herbaceous borders, into a rose garden of three reducing circles, enclosed in walls of pleached limes.

Richmond Park *Isabella Plantation, Richmond, Surrey.* Originally laid out in 1831, this oval area of woodland, which lies in a shallow saucer of land, has been open to the public since the end of the 2nd World War. Two streams run through it, converging midway and flowing into a lake outside the wood. Two smaller lakes have been constructed within the woodland.

Roof Garden *99 High Street, Kensington, W8.* One and a half acres opened in 1938 and now restored to the original designs. There are a Spanish garden with fountains and palm trees, a Tudor garden and walkway. On the ponds are protected birds, including flamingoes.

Royal Botanic Gardens, Kew *see separate entry.*

St Botolph's Garden *Bishopsgate, EC2.* One of the churchyards, no longer used for interments, which, under the Burial Act of 1855, the churchwardens were responsible for maintaining 'in decent order'. It was laid out as a garden with poplar and plane trees, the flower-beds enriched with terracotta tiles instead of box edging, and fenced with railings from old LONDON BRIDGE. Now maintained by the CITY CORPORATION, it is one of the CITY's largest open spaces, and contains a floodlit hard tennis court. The fountain was built in 1972.

Syon House Gardens *Brentford.* Dr William Turner (the father of English botany) created one of the first botanical gardens in England here and refers in his book *The Names of Herbes* (1548) to the formal walled gardens he laid out on the east and west sides of the house. These were redesigned by Lancelot 'Capability' Brown and the area landscaped with lawns, a lake, and woodland garden. There are many trees, including tulip, cedar and 28 varieties of oak. The dome-shaped mulberry bushes, brought from Persia in 1548, are the oldest in England, and still bear fruit. The Tudor

Garden to the west of the house is now a 6-acre rose garden, with a pergola of stone columns for climbing roses and clematis. The crescent-shaped conservatory, where birds fly freely among the exotic plants, was constructed by Dr Charles Fowler in the 1820s. (*See also* SYON HOUSE.)

Westminster Abbey Gardens *College, Little Cloister and St Katherine's Chapel Gardens, SW1.* The College Garden, one of the oldest gardens in England, was once the infirmary garden of the ancient monastery and was originally planted with healing and culinary herbs. It is now a lawn with paved paths, and trees including planes and pink and white Japanese cherries. On the east and south side are herbaceous borders protected by the high original river boundary walls. To the north are two small gardens; the one known as the Little Cloister is approached through a Norman vaulted passage. In the centre of the garden are a small pool and fountain. A few yards away is St Katherine's Chapel Garden, consisting of a sunken lawn surrounded by flower-beds and overlooked by a clergy house on one side and the remains of the south aisle columns and arch face of the chapel on the other. A row of column bases stands out of the lawn.

Garland's Hotel *Suffolk Street.* Established as a smart and discreet hotel in the 1840s. Henry James and Harriet Beecher Stowe were among its patrons. It was destroyed by bombs in 1943.

Garlick Hill *EC4.* Where garlic was sold. It is now the centre of the fur trade. At the top of the hill is the neo-Georgian Beaver Hall of 1928 where the Hudson's Bay Company hold fur auctions. At the foot of the hill is ST JAMES, GARLICKHYTHE. Sir John Coke, the lawyer, lived here in 1625.

Garnett College *Downshire House, Roehampton Lane, SW15.* The College, which provides training for teachers, first opened in 1946 as the North Western Polytechnic. It became a permanent college in 1950 and was officially named Garnett College in 1953 to commemorate the work of Dr William Garnett, who was the first secretary of the London Technical Education Board set up after the Technical Instruction Act of 1889. In 1963 it moved to its present premises in ROEHAMPTON. Since 1979 the college has had made available to it the use of MANRESA HOUSE, which overlooks RICHMOND PARK and which was designed in the early 1760s by Sir William Chambers, the architect of SOMERSET HOUSE, as a country villa for the 2nd Earl of Bessborough.

Garrard and Co. Ltd *112 Regent Street, W1.* George Wickes, son of James Wickes, an upholsterer of Bury St Edmunds, was apprenticed to a London goldsmith, Samuel Wastell, in 1712. In 1735 he opened a shop on the corner of PANTON STREET and HAYMARKET and took a partner, Edward Wakelin, who ran the business. Wakelin's son, John, became apprenticed to his father in 1766 and registered his mark with William Taylor in 1776. John Wakelin and William Taylor ran the business until 1792 when Robert Garrard joined them. Gaining a controlling interest, he altered the name to Garrard and Co. Queen Victoria appointed them Crown jewellers in 1843 (the lighter crown, seen on her head in the portraits and statues of her in later years, was designed

in 1870). In 1911, for the coronation of George V, they were commissioned to incorporate part of the Cullinan diamond in the Imperial State Crown. The firm moved to ALBEMARLE STREET in 1911. After Robert Garrard Jnr had died in 1881, his descendants carried on the business until 1946. Having taken over the Goldsmiths' and Silversmiths' Co. Ltd, the firm moved to 112 REGENT STREET in 1952.

Garraway's Coffee House *Exchange Alley, Cornhill.* Famed as one of the chief auction houses of the CITY, Garraway's started in 1669, probably with fur sales for the Hudson's Bay Company. Ships were auctioned there; and sales 'by the candle' of sugar, coffee, textiles, spices and salvaged goods including 'damaged rice' were held. Tea was sold here in the 1670s for £10 a pound, Thomas Garraway being the first man in England who sold and retailed tea, recommending it 'for the cure of all disorders'. His house was also famed for its cherry wine, sandwiches, sherry, pale ale and punch. *The Times* of 9 November 1796 contains an advertisement of the sale at Garraway's of 11 properties, including 'a Renter's Share' in the THEATRE ROYAL, DRURY LANE and a family house at 47 CHANCERY LANE. By the 19th century merchants, drug brokers, Turkey merchants and ship brokers were using the house as an address. Garraway's was well known to Charles Dickens and is mentioned in *Pickwick Papers*, *Martin Chuzzlewit*, *Little Dorrit* and *The Uncommercial Traveller* in which the crypt of the building is described: 'There is an old monastery-cript under Garraway's (I have been in it among the port wine), and perhaps Garraway's taking pity on the mouldy men who wait in its public room all their lives, gives them cool house room down there on Sundays.' The house was finally closed down in 1872 and was later demolished to make way for Martin's Bank.

Garrick Club *15 Garrick Street, WC2.* Founded in 1831 by the Duke of Sussex for actors, painters, writers and other artists, although among the early members were a duke (Devonshire), five marquesses, six earls and 12 barons. Later members have included Dickens and Thackeray and Irving (who was black-balled when he first applied). It was named after David Garrick, the actor, whose portrait by Zoffany hangs here. The first club house was a converted family hotel in KING STREET. The present building, designed by Frederick Marrable, was built in 1864. The Garrick owns a very fine collection of theatrical portraits, the nucleus of which was collected by the comedian, Charles Mathews, and sold to the club by his executors in 1835. Its convivial membership now is made up mainly of lawyers, writers and publishers, and those associated with the theatre, television and films.

Garrick Street *WC2.* Built in the 1860s, when the slums of SEVEN DIALS were being cleared, and named after the actor. The GARRICK CLUB is at Nos 13–15.

Garrick Theatre *Charing Cross Road, WC2.* Designed in 1889 by Walter Emden and C.J. Phipps for W.S. Gilbert. A copy of Gainsborough's portrait of David Garrick was hung in the foyer. It opened under the management of John Hare with Pinero's *The Profligate*, starring Forbes-Robertson, Hare, Lewis Waller and Katie Rorke. Hare's management lasted until 1896. His greatest successes were *A Pair of Spectacles* (1890) and *The Notorious Mrs Ebbsmith* (1895), in which he appeared with Mrs Patrick Campbell. From 1900 to 1915 the theatre was managed by Arthur Bourchier. He made his mark when he refused to admit the drama critic of *The Times* in 1903. Among his successful productions were Barrie's *The Wedding Guest* (1900), Pineros' *Iris* (1901), W.S. Gilbert's *The Fairies Dilemma* (1904), Alfred Sutro's *The Walls of Jericho* (1904) and Edward Knoblock's *Kismet* (1911). C.B. Cochran was lessee in 1918–24. In 1935 *Love on the Dole* made Wendy Hiller a star. The seating capacity is 700.

Garrick's House *Hampton Court Road, Hampton, Middlesex*. Formerly called The Cedars. An earlier house on the site was owned by Thomas Simpson, Keeper of BUSHY PARK for 69 years, who continued to work until near to his death at the age of 99 in 1734. The present house was built in about 1769. The first tenant from then until 1776 was the Countess of Pembroke, a noted beauty of her day and Lady-in-Waiting to Queen Charlotte. She lived there while her husband was pre-occupied with his mistress, Miss Hunter, and was a close friend of the Garricks. She was associated with David Garrick in his calamitous Shakespeare Festival at Stratford-on-Avon in 1769. David Garrick bought the house for his nephew, David Garrick, an army officer, who came to the house in 1778 and lived there until his death in 1795. The house is now named after him, and not his famous uncle. It is still in private ownership.

Garrick's Villa *Hampton Court Road, Hampton, Middlesex*. A house belonging to Richard Caswell stood on this site by 1640. The Caswells were wealthy London grocers and the house remained in the hands of the family until 1754, when it was acquired by David Garrick. Robert Adam made a number of alterations, including the addition of the hollow wooden Corinthian pillars. Garrick also built an Orangery in the grounds and a Temple to Shakespeare on the riverside lawn, reached by a tunnel under the road. After Garrick's death in 1779 his widow, Eva, lived there as a recluse until her death in 1822. Her solicitor, Thomas Carr, acquired the house and named it Garrick's Villa. In 1861 it was sold to a London merchant, Silvanus Phillips, who added the west wing in about 1865. The house was converted into eight apartments in 1922. In 1967 these were modernised, houses were built in the grounds (Hogarth Way), and the Orangery was converted into a group of houses by the addition of two wings.

Gas In 1792 William Murdock became the first person to make practical use of gas for lighting his home in Cornwall. The first public display of gas lighting took place in 1805 when Frederick Winsor, a flamboyant Moravian, gave a display of lighting in PALL MALL to celebrate the birthday of the Prince of Wales. The Prince, later to become George IV, gave his patronage to gas. In 1812, after various unsuccessful attempts, the Gas-Light and Coke Co. became the first gas company to receive a charter of incorporation to provide light to the CITY OF LONDON, WESTMINSTER and the borough of SOUTHWARK. It set up its works in GREAT PETER STREET, Westminster. Gas street lamps appeared on WESTMINSTER BRIDGE. Soon several other gas companies, both statutory and non-statutory, were established. Among these were the City of London, the Imperial and the Independent north of the river, and the South London, South Metropolitan and Phoenix south of the river, the latter having bought the rights of supply and mains from the Gas-Light and Coke Co.

Gas supplies then developed separately on each side of the river. Gas street lighting became increasingly widespread because its bright light was considered helpful in the fight against CRIME. However, there was also much apprehension about possible explosions. The advent of Earl Grey's Government in 1830 led to a period of stiff competition between companies. With no defined limits to their supply areas, companies lowered prices and used armies of canvassers to gain clients. During the 1840s OXFORD STREET and TOTTENHAM COURT ROAD were supplied by four different companies from five different gas stations. Payment was by fixed rental rather than by volume, so company workmen sometimes connected clients to other companies' mains while still charging them rental. Quality suffered but there was also a large increase in demand for gas. In the 1840s BUCKINGHAM PALACE and the new HOUSES OF PARLIAMENT went over to gas lighting, as did many theatres. The main market was in lighting, particularly public lighting. Competition had died down by the 1850s and the companies began to negotiate over prices and supply districts. In 1853 the South Metropolitan, Phoenix, London and the Survey Consumers companies agreed by mutual consent on districts in South London. A year later a similar agreement was concluded by the Gas-Light and Coke, Equitable, Western, Imperial and London Companies in North London. There was widespread condemnation of the apparent collusion between companies. The CITY CORPORATION often threatened to take over companies in its area, considering it could offer a better deal through civic ownership. Charles Pearson and others set up the Great Central Gas Consumers' Co. in order to challenge the other companies. This company offered gas at low prices. The other companies lowered their prices and used all available means to thwart Great Central. The fierce competition culminated in the 'Battle of Bow Bridge', when workmen of the Commercial barricaded themselves on Bow Bridge to prevent Great Central workmen from laying their mains in one of the few bridges over the River LEA. Later Great Central raised its prices like the other companies and it became indistinguishable from them.

In 1867, having failed to purchase a site for expansion on HACKNEY MARSHES, the Gas-Light and Coke Co. bought a site at EAST HAM. This marked a new era for gas in London. Although distant from the main area of supply, the site was cheap; its proximity to the THAMES allowed coal to be landed straight from barges; and its large size allowed for the construction of a completely up-to-date plant which was not spatially constructed as the city centre works were. The works were named Beckton after Simon Adams Beck, then Governor of the company. The company began laying its famous 48 in. mains into London. The Imperial Co., which had previously been a far larger organisation, attempted a similar enterprise at BROMLEY-BY-BOW, but the obsolescent design and its inland position put it a disadvantage. Beckton was a resounding success; no other company could match

Rowlandson caricatures Londoners' curiosity at the first public display of London gas lights, in Pall Mall in 1807.

its output or prices. Gradually during the 1870s the Gas-Light and Coke Co. amalgamated with the other companies in north London including the Imperial. Beckton went on to become the world's largest coal gas works. Production stopped in 1976.

A similar process went on about the same time south of the river. The South Metropolitan, its OLD KENT ROAD works having become too restrictive, bought 150 acres at east GREENWICH to build a large new works. In turn the South Metropolitan gradually grew by amalgamation with other companies. In the 1880s the advent of ELECTRICITY began to threaten the gas companies. As electricity made inroads into the lighting market, gas companies began to develop the non-lighting load and started hiring out cookers and water heaters. The invention of the incandescent mantle, and the greater use of the prepayment meter, made gas a more economical and attractive proposition, though it was not until after the 1st World War that gas lighting was put into working-class homes during construction.

During the 2nd World War London's gas companies valiantly attempted to keep production going through the worst of the bombing. By 1945 the Gas-Light and Coke Co. alone accounted for 12 per cent of total national gas sales. In Labour's post-war nationalisation, which set up regional gas boards, London was split between a number of gas boards so that the regions were more or less the same size. The THAMES remained a boundary. The South Metropolitan Co. formed the basis for South Eastern Gas, while the Gas-Light and Coke Co. did likewise for North Thames Gas.

Nationalisation led to rationalisation of productive facilities into fewer and fewer sites. But gas manufacture, which changed over to an oil base from coal, continued in London till the 1970s by which time gas from the North Sea was flowing through the Beckton 48s and all other gas mains (*see also* ELECTRICITY *and* STREET LIGHTING).

Gate Theatre   The first club theatre. It opened in 1925 in a warehouse in FLORAL STREET, COVENT GARDEN for staging experimental and unlicensed plays under the management of Peter Godfrey. In 1927 it moved to VILLIERS STREET. From 1934–40 it was run by Norman Marshall who produced a series of notable productions including *Victoria Regina, Parnell, Oscar Wilde, The Children's House, Of Mice and Men*, and *Distant Point*, as well as an annual Gate Revue. It was closed in 1940 and destroyed by bombs the next year.

Gatehouse Prison   *Westminster*. Built in 1370 by Walter de Warfield, Cellarer of the Abbey, on a site now occupied by the memorial to Old Westminsters in BROAD SANCTUARY. There were two wings at right-angles to each other. On the west side of TOTHILL STREET was a staircases for 'the bringing in and carrying out of robbers, felons and trespassers'. The Abbey Janitor was appointed warder of the prison and in payment received a loaf of bread and flagon of ale daily and a new robe once a year. In October 1618 Sir Walter Ralegh was imprisoned here on the eve of his execution. Richard Lovelace, the Cavalier poet incarcerated here in 1642, wrote 'To Althea' – 'Stone walls do not a prison make, nor iron bars a cage'. In 1672 a female keeper of the prison was tried for the extortion of fees and for treating prisoners 'in a most barbarous manner'. She was fined and removed from office and the custody of the prisoners was given to the Sheriff of MIDDLESEX. In 1689 Samuel Pepys was imprisoned but was quickly released on grounds of ill health. In 1761 Dr Johnson said the building was so offensive that it ought to be pulled down as being a disgrace to the magnificence of the city and a continual nuisance to neighbours and passengers. It was demolished by a chapter order in 1776, though one wall stood until 1836.

Gatti's Music Hall   *Westminster Bridge Road, SE1*. Opened in 1862 as a restaurant by the Gatti family (*see* GATTI'S RESTAURANTS). It became a music-hall in 1865. It was commonly known as Gatti's-in-the-Road or Gatti's-over-the-Water to distinguish it from the brothers' other music-hall at CHARING CROSS, later the PLAYERS' THEATRE. In 1900 Harry Lauder made his first London appearance here. The building was bombed in 1940 and demolished in 1950 to make way for a new road.

Gatti's Restaurants and Cafés A chain of inexpensive restaurants and cafés established by the Italian family of Gatti. They were very successful until the advent of Lyons' teashops in 1894 (*see* LYONS' CORNER HOUSES). The best known was the restaurant as No. 436 Strand, formerly the ADELAIDE GALLERY. The family also ran the Adelphi Theatre Restaurant.

Gayfere Street *SW1.* Built in the 1720s and still largely 18th-century. The houses are much sought after by Members of Parliament.

Geffrye Museum *Kingsland Road, E2.* Originally 14 almshouses, mainly for ironmongers' widows, constructed in 1715 under the bequest of Sir Robert Geffrye, a former Lord Mayor of London and Master of the IRONMONGERS' COMPANY. The museum conversion was completed in 1914, after the building had been purchased by the LONDON COUNTY COUNCIL. It is now administered by the INNER LONDON EDUCATION AUTHORITY. It is situated in the centre of the furniture- and cabinet-making area of London and its permanent displays consist of fully furnished rooms dating from Elizabethan times to the 1930s, with added examples of staircases, panelling and portraits from old London houses.

A 1908 watercolour by Philip Norman of the Ironmongers' Company Almshouses, which in 1914 became the Geffrye Museum.

General Post Office *King Edward Street, EC1.* Originally known as the General Letter Office, it was moved from the Black Swan in BISHOPSGATE to LOMBARD STREET in about 1678. The growth in POSTAL SERVICES during the next century made a much larger building essential. The new building was erected on the site of ST MARTIN-LE-GRAND. Designed by Sir Robert Smirke, it was opened in 1829. The building was used as a combined post office, sorting office and administrative centre, and was lit by a thousand gas burners. It was later increased in size by the addition of two storeys on top and the extension of the base-

Engraving after Pollard of the Royal Mails departing from the General Post Office in St Martin-Le-Grand, 1830. The building was designed by Robert Smirke.

ment. Smirke's old post office building (known as GPO East) was demolished in 1912.

Between KING EDWARD STREET and ST MARTIN-LE-GRAND is a building known as GPO North. It was built of Portland stone in 1890–5 to the plans of Sir Henry Tanner and is now GPO Headquarters. The head carved in stone above the entrance in ST MARTIN-LE-GRAND is of Henry Raikes, who was Postmaster General, 1886–91, and that above the entrance in KING EDWARD STREET is of Arnold Morley, who held the office in 1892–5. On the wall of the building in ST MARTIN-LE-GRAND is a plaque stating that from the roof of the building Guglielmo Marconi made the first public transmission of radio signals on 27 July 1896 under the patronage of William Preece, FRS, Engineer in Chief of the GPO. The development of this site had entailed the demolition of the BULL AND MOUTH coaching inn, whose delightful sign is, however, preserved in the MUSEUM OF LONDON.

King Edward Building, designed by Sir Henry Tanner to house the new General Post Office, was built on the site of CHRIST'S HOSPITAL on the west side of KING EDWARD STREET. The foundation stone was laid by King Edward VII in 1905, and the building was completed in 1911.

Geological Museum *Exhibition Road, SW7.* Originally the Museum of Economic Geology, housed in CRAIG'S COURT, WHITEHALL at the instigation of the first director of the Geological Survey, which had been formed in 1835 to prepare geological maps of Great Britain. This museum, formed to illustrate the useful application of geology and the mineral resources of the country, was moved to the new Museum of Practical Geology. By the 1920s it had outgrown that building and was moved to the present museum designed by J.H. Markham and opened by the Duke of York in 1935. The museum's collection of minerals and fossils now numbers over a million specimens.

Gentlemen-at-Arms *see* HONOURABLE COMPANY OF GENTLEMEN-AT-ARMS.

Geological Society *Burlington House, Piccadilly, W1.* Incorporated by Royal Charter in 1825, the Society's main objective is to promote knowledge concerning the history of the earth through lectures, publications and library services.

George and Vulture *St Michael's Court, Cornhill, EC3*. A restored 18th-century public house used by Charles Dickens as a hostelry for Mr Pickwick during the trial of Bardell versus Pickwick.

George Inn *77 Borough High Street, SE1*. The only galleried coaching inn left in London. It stands on the site of an inn which existed in 1542 and probably in medieval times. The present building dates from 1676. It originally surrounded three sides of the courtyard, but the central and northern wings were demolished for the railway in 1899. Dickens mentions the George in *Little Dorrit*. In summer, performances of Shakespeare's plays are given in the inn yard. The inn now belongs to the NATIONAL TRUST.

George Street *W1*. Running across BAKER STREET and on to the EDGWARE ROAD, George Street was first rated in 1787. Many of the 18th-century houses remain, particularly to the east of BAKER STREET. Thomas Moore, the poet and song writer, lodged at No. 15 (formerly No. 44) in 1799 where 'they have my breakfast laid as snug as possible every morning.' John Buonarotti Papworth, one of the founder members of the RIBA, stayed at No. 11 (now No. 38). Samuel Pepys Cockerell, the architect, lived at No. 43 in 1875–7. Durrant's Hotel (96 bedrooms) was converted to its present use in 1921 from several Georgian lodging houses. The Holiday Inn at No. 134 (243 bedrooms) is by R. Seifert and Partners (1973).

George's Coffee House *Strand*. Stood between DEVEREUX COURT and ESSEX STREET, probably at No. 213. First mentioned in 1723, it seems to have been patronised by wits and men of letters. William Shenstone, the poet, reported it to be 'economical' in 1739, and went there to read pamphlets without having to pay. Lloyd, satirising a scholar in *The Law Student*, writes:

> Supreme at George's he harangues the throng,
> Censor of style, from tragedy to song.

The value offered by the house is often mentioned, as by Tate in his *Epistle to a Young Critic*:

> Tis easy learnt the art to talk by rote:
> At George's 'twill but cost you half a groat

Sir James Lowther, the 'bad earl', a man with a reputation for meanness who had an annual income of £40,000, is said to have returned here once with a bad halfpenny he had been given by the landlady, demanding it be exchanged. In 1804 the house provided an accommodation address for the swindler Henry Perfect who, under aliases such as the Revd Mr Paul and the Revd Mr Bennett, defrauded the Earl of Clarendon. Among more distinguished patrons was Horace Walpole. After 1842, George's is referred to as a hotel or tavern.

Georgian Group *2 Chester Street, SW1*. Founded in 1937 by Lord Derwent 'in order to awaken and direct public opinion to the urgent need to protect the nation's steadily diminishing Georgian heritage and by means of action in Parliament and the Press to rescue from demolition squares, terraces and individual buildings of beauty and importance.' In 1982 there were about 2,000 members.

German Church *Knightrider Street*. Built in 1666–75 by Jacob Jacobsen, Master of the Hanseatic merchants, on the site of HOLY TRINITY THE LESS. The church, rebuilt in 1773, was demolished in about 1867 to make way for QUEEN VICTORIA STREET and the DISTRICT LINE.

German Hospital *Ritson Road, E8*. Opened in 1845 for poor natives of Germany and of German-speaking countries, 'for it must be a comfort to be treated by people speaking their own language'. A German staff was employed. The idea was put forward by the Prussian Ambassador, Christian, Freiherr von Bunsen and his English wife. In 1851 Florence Nightingale met the Bunsens and they persuaded her to visit, for four months, the Kaiserwerth Nursing Home on the Rhine. This she did much against the wishes of her parents. But the visit aroused her interest in nursing. The King of Prussia contributed to the hospital and the committee wished to make him Protector. This annoyed Queen Victoria, who let it be known that she should have been asked first. The matter was resolved by putting the hospital under the joint protection of Queen Victoria, Queen Adelaide (the Queen Dowager), the King of Prussia and Prince Albert, and by decreeing that it would be under the patronage of the British Royal Family. The Duke of Cambridge was elected Chairman. The hospital fulfilled a need and its hundred beds were regularly occupied. The 1st World War did not cause much disturbance. Though the younger doctors were returned to Germany, elderly German physicians were allowed to carry on. In the 2nd World War things were quite different. Together with all the other Germans in England, the staff were interned and British people took their place. The German Hospital thereafter became an English hospital. The National Health Service took it over in 1948 and it is now part of the Hackney Group of hospitals, It has 53 beds for psychiatric and psychogeriatric patients. In the waiting-room are portraits of the 2nd Duke of Cambridge, Crown Princess Victoria of Prussia and her husband Crown Prince Friedrich (later Emperor)

Gerrard Street *W1*. Built in 1677–85 on land belonging to Charles, Lord Gerrard, which was known as the Military Ground, and used as a training area by the MILITARY COMPANY. The developer was Nicholas Barbon, a persuasive, energetic man of insinuating charm and questionable probity who was one of the most active property dealers in Restoration London. The son of Praise-God Barbon (or Barebones), the leather merchant who, nominated by Cromwell and his council of officers, had given his name to one of the Commonwealth's Parliaments, Nicholas Barbon had studied medicine in Holland and had been admitted as an Honorary Fellow to the ROYAL COLLEGE OF PHYSICIANS. Ambitious and enterprising, he protested that it was not worth his while to engage in small ventures: 'that a bricklayer could do. The gain *he* expected was of great undertakings which would rise lustily in the whole.' Gerrard Street was one of these.

The first houses built in the street seem to have been of three substantial storeys with garrets. Two of them were much larger than the rest. These were No. 9, which was originally occupied by Lady Wiseman and is now divided into offices, and the Earl of Devonshire's house which was occupied by the Earl, later

1st Duke of Devonshire, in 1685–90, then by Charles Montagu, 4th Earl of Manchester, and afterwards by the 5th Baron Wharton and the 1st Earl of Scarborough, before being demolished in 1732. By the middle of the 18th century, Gerrard Street had become distinguished less for the number of its aristocratic residents, than for its coffee houses and taverns, and for the number of artists and writers who frequented them and who lived or lodged in the street. John Dryden was one of the first. He came here from LONG ACRE in 1687, and lived at No. 44 where he 'used most commonly to write in the ground-room next to the street'. (A BLUE PLAQUE was erected in error on No. 43.) A few years later James Gibbs, the architect, came to live at No. 18, where he remained until 1726. No. 9, which had once belonged to Lady Wiseman, was a tavern by 1710, and in the 1760s was the famous TURK'S HEAD where Johnson and Reynolds founded THE CLUB. No. 3, at the end of the century, was a coffee house kept by Francis Saulieu. In the early years of the 19th century, when known as the Nassau Coffee House, it was patronised by Benjamin Robert Haydon and David Wilkie. Among other artists and writers who lived in the street were Francis Wheatley and George Morland in 1784, Sir Robert Kerr Porter and John Sell Cotman in 1800–1, and John Crunden, the architect, in 1768. Edmund Burke was living at No. 37 in the 1780s, and in 1775 James Boswell took lodgings at No. 22 with a tailor, 'a very neat first floor at sixteen shillings per week'. In 1820 Charles Kemble, the actor, took lodgings at No. 35. By the end of the 19th century there were several foreign restaurants in the street, the Hôtel des Etrangers at No. 37 (which in 1805–18 had been the offices of the Royal Literary Fund), and the Mont Blanc where G.K. Chesterton and Hilaire Belloc first met in 1900. In 1923 Francis Birrell and David Garnett moved their antiquarian bookshop to No. 30. They let the cellar to Francis and Vera Meynell as the office of the Nonesuch Press, from where they published that year their first book, *The Love Poems of John Donne*. In the 1920s and 1930s it was celebrated for its night-clubs, including that of Mrs Merrick; and in the 1950s for its strip-tease 'clubs' and clip-joints. Now Gerrard Street has largely been taken over by the Chinese.

Gidea Park *Essex*.

To the east of ROMFORD lies the residential suburb of Gidea Park, stretching from Eastern Avenue, a 1930s bypass road, down to the area of Squirrels Heath. It takes its name from Gidea Hall, which lay along the main road towards the former hamlet of Hare Street, once the home of Humphry Repton, the landscape architect. His cottage site is marked by a plaque on a local bank. Gidea Hall mansion was once occupied by Sir Anthony Cooke, a tutor to King Edward VI. One of his daughters married the great Lord Burleigh and another became the mother of Francis Bacon. The grounds of Gidea Hall became a superior garden suburb in 1910. The houses were designed by leading architects after a competition and exhibition. A further exhibition and extension of this estate took place in the 1930s. The Hall served for a while as a focus for the estate but was later demolished. Raphael Park also lies on part of the site. It was given to the town by Sir Herbert Raphael, who was a Liberal Member of Parliament. The name Gidea is possibly derived from the word 'giddy', meaning a foolish building, a folly.

Gieves and Hawkes Ltd *1 Savile Row, W1*.

Originally two firms, they were both founded in the 18th century. Gieves, established in 1785 by Melchizedeck Meredith in Portsmouth, were Nelson's tailors. James Gieve joined the firm in 1852. Hawkes, founded in 1771, were tailors to the Duke of Wellington. The great room at No. 1 SAVILE ROW was the Map Room of the ROYAL GEOGRAPHICAL SOCIETY, 1870–1911. The front part of the building, once the town house of Lord Fairfax, is late 17th-century.

Giltspur Street *EC1*.

Ancient street once known as Knightrider Street because knights used to ride through it on their way to the SMITHFIELD tournaments. Gilt spurs were probably made here later. The Giltspur Street Compter was built by order of the SHERIFFS at the end of the 18th century. It was demolished in 1855. The gilded figure of a little boy on the corner of COCK LANE, by an unknown sculptor, was erected here in 1910 to mark the site where the Great Fire ended. The fountain with a bronze figure of *Peace* in the public gardens at the northern end is by J.B. Philip (1873).

Giltspur Street Compter

A prison for debtors under control of the SHERIFFS, it stood on the east side of the street opposite ST SEPULCHRE'S CHURCH. A heavy rusticated stone building, it was designed by George Dance the Younger, architect to the CORPORATION. It received the prisoners moved from WOOD STREET COMPTER in 1791. It was demolished in 1855 and part of the site was added to the grounds of CHRIST'S HOSPITAL.

Gin Lane

The custom of gin drinking was brought from Holland by William III. Gin was free from tax and could be sold without licence. It was soon obtainable at barbers', grocers', tobacconists', shoemakers' and other tradesmen's shops, from barrows in the street and from dram shops. Between 1727 and 1735 the sale of spirits rose from 3½ to 6½ million gallons. At this time every fourth house in ST GILES was said to sell gin. You could be 'drunk for a penny and dead drunk for twopence'. In 1736 the Middlesex magistrates petitioned Parliament to restrict the sale of spirits. An Act was promptly passed imposing a tax of £1 per gallon and a £50 annual licence on all who sold it. The London mob held a funeral procession for 'Madame Geneva'. Several informers were murdered and gin continued to be drunk under the pseudonyms of 'Ladies' Delight', 'Cuckold's Comfort' and 'King Theodore of Corsica'. In 1743 another ineffective Act was passed. In 1750 Henry Fielding published an *Inquiry* into the increase of London robberies and attributed them to gin drinking. In 1751 Hogarth published *Gin Lane* and *Beer Street*, showing the depths of degradation gin drinking could bring compared with the innocuous effect of beer.

Gipsy Hill *SE19*.

Situated west of CRYSTAL PALACE in the south-eastern corner of the London Borough of LAMBETH. By the 17th century this hill in NORWOOD was already a gipsy haunt and in about 1730 Margaret Finch, the Queen of the Gipsies, settled here. In 1797 under the Vagrancy Act the police raided the encampment but it was not until the passing of the Croydon and Lambeth Enclosure Acts at the beginning of the 19th century that the community of gipsies was dispersed, many of them intermarrying with local people. Until this time the area had been relatively inaccessible. Part of the estate of Lord Thurlow, Lord Chancellor from 1778, was sold at his death in 1806 for development; new roads including Gipsy Hill and Gipsy Road accelerated the process. In the mid-19th century the West End of London and Crystal Palace Railway reached Gipsy Hill. Christchurch (John Giles, 1850–5) was erected and building development followed swiftly.

Gipsy Moth IV *King William Walk, Greenwich, SE10.* Sir Francis Chichester's 54 ft-long sailing ketch in which he made his solo circumnavigation of the world from 27 August 1966 to 28 May 1967. The Queen knighted Chichester on 13 June at the ROYAL NAVAL COLLEGE, using the same sword that Elizabeth I had used when knighting Sir Francis Drake. *Gipsy Moth IV* was placed in permanent dry dock beside the CUTTY SARK for public viewing.

Girdlers' Company *see* CITY LIVERY COMPANIES.

Girls' Public Day School Trust *26 Queen Anne's Gate, SW1.* Originated in 1872 from the National Union for Improving the Education of Women of All Classes, founded by Maria Grey, who was assisted by her sister, Mrs Emily Shirreff, the Dowager Lady Stanley of Alderley and Mary Gurney. The aim was to establish 'good and cheap day schools, for all classes above those attending the public elementary schools', where such schools would find adequate support. Since the withdrawal of the Direct Grant in 1976, formerly applying to all the Trust schools, they have become independent.

The Trust's schools include Blackheath, Bromley, Croydon, Notting Hill and Ealing, Putney, South Hampstead, Sutton, Sydenham and Wimbledon High Schools.

Glass Sellers' Company *see* CITY LIVERY COMPANIES.

Glasshouse Street *W1.* First appeared in the rate-books in 1678 and, in the words of Vol. XXXI of the *Survey of London,* 'perhaps owes its name to the activities of Windsor Sandys in the neighbourhood.... In 1676 Sandys was the partner of John Dwight, the Fulham potter, and in that year they contracted to supply stoneware to the GLASS SELLERS' COMPANY. As early as 1672 Sandys had been general undertaker for cleansing the streets of the parishes of St Martin and St Giles, and it may be conjectured that he used potasium nitrate, or saltpetre, which was produced from night soil as an ingredient for the production of glass.' In 1720 Strype said that the street was 'but meanly built', and that its inhabitants were 'not much to be boasted of'. In 1863 it was incorporated with Tichborne Street, which took its name from Sir Henry Tichborne of Tichborne, Dorset. In Tichborne Street there stood at the end of the 18th century, and the beginning of the 19th, WEEKS'S MECHANICAL MUSEUM, an exhibition of mechanical curiosities. The Museum, which was built over the stabling and coach-houses of the Black Horse Inn at No. 3 Tichborne Street, became a glass and china warehouse in 1837, and in 1859, together with the Black Horse, was sold to Emil Loible and Charles Sonnhammer who turned it into a

beer-hall, skittle-alley and rifle gallery which they called the London Pavilion.

The last performance in this London Pavilion was given on 25 March 1885. The north side of Glasshouse Street is now dominated by the soapy white walls of the REGENT PALACE HOTEL which are built of that sort of *faience* known as Burmantoft Marmo.

Glasshouses In 1549 eight glass blowers from Venice (from where glass had long been imported) came to work in London. They are known to have worked near the TOWER, probably in the Aldgate dining-hall of the dissolved CRUTCHED FRIARS. Soon afterwards they were recalled to Venice, and all but one returned there in 1551. The CRUTCHED FRIARS workshop was taken over by Jean Carre, a glass-maker from Antwerp, in about 1570 and, sometime before 1573, by his manager, Jacopo Verzelini, a Venetian who produced there, among other objects, goblets of soda-lime glass in the Venetian manner. The workshop was destroyed by fire in 1575 and Verzelini moved to BROAD STREET. His works were acquired by Sir Jerome Bowes in 1592 and in 1618 by Sir Robert Mansell who held the sole patent of making 'all sorts of glass with pit-coal'. By the end of the 17th century there seem to have been 24 glasshouses in and around London, making a variety of glass, from mirrors and crown-glass to flint-glass, bottle-glass and window glass, the more important being in SOUTHWARK, RATCLIFF, WAPPING, by the river near the SAVOY, in WHITECHAPEL, GREENWICH, VAUXHALL and on the banks of the FLEET. Their former presence is commemorated by such streets as GLASSHOUSE STREET, W1, Glasshouse Yard, EC1, and Glasshouse Walk, SE11.

It was to a glasshouse in the vicinity of Glass House Alley that Pepys took his cousins on 23 February 1669. 'Had several things made with great content,' he recorded; 'but among others, I had one or two singing-glasses made, which made an echo to the voice, the first that ever I saw; but so thin that the very breath broke one or two of them.'

In 1673 the Duke of Buckingham established a glasshouse at VAUXHALL which made what Evelyn described as 'Large *Vasas* of mettal as cleare & pondrous & thick as Chrystal, also *looking-glasses* far larger & better than any that come from Venice'. This business was carried on until 1780. In the 18th century the great London glass merchants were Thomas Betts and John Akerman, both of whom employed German as well as English glass-cutters. Akerman was Master of the GLASS SELLERS' COMPANY.

Glaves *80–100 New Oxford Street.* Drapers, costumiers and milliners started in 1848 when Henry and Charles Glave opened a small linen drapers' shop at 3½ Scotts Place, Lower Road, ISLINGTON. By 1854 Henry Glave had acquired additional premises at 535–536 OXFORD STREET; and by 1876 he also owned Nos 534 and 537 and Nos 1–5 Royal Arcade. Charles had moved to Nos 204 and 206 ESSEX ROAD, ISLINGTON by 1867. From 1883 until 1924 Henry Glave and then his son, Nolan, had gradually acquired Nos 80–100 NEW OXFORD STREET; and in 1931 a grand new store by Gunton and Gunton was opened. The business survived until 1936. In 1939 the building was taken over for Government offices.

Glaziers' Company *see* CITY LIVERY COMPANIES.

GLC *see* GREATER LONDON COUNCIL.

Glebe Place *SW3*. Runs from the KING'S ROAD to CHEYNE ROW on part of glebe lands belonging to Chelsea Rectory. A small chapel was erected on its east side about 1685 for the many Huguenots who settled in CHELSEA after the revocation of the Edict of Nantes which had given them religious freedom. This was only the second place of worship erected in CHELSEA. It had few windows for safety reasons. A tree grew right under it and is still there. A brickwork cottage (now No. 51) is reputed to have been a hunting lodge of King Henry VIII but this is unlikely. It was used for a long time as the Chelsea Open Air Nursery School. Cooks Ground at the south-west corner of Glebe Place was the site of several educational establishments including Kingsley Sunday Schools (named after Charles Kingsley). This land has now been sold by the INNER LONDON EDUCATION AUTHORITY to the Libyan Government for use as a school.

Glentworth Street *NW1*. Laid out as Park Street in 1809, it changed its name in 1897 in honour of a local resident, Lord Glentworth, who died in 1845. At its northern end is ST CYPRIAN's church, built in 1903 by Sir Ninian Comper, with its lofty white interior and carved rood screen. It developed from a humble mission hall, established some years earlier by the Revd Charles Gutch to serve the poor of the EDGWARE ROAD area. Its founder did not live to see the well-built church for which he had longed.

Globe Theatre *Bankside*. A round wooden theatre built in 1598–9 by Cuthbert and Richard Burbage with materials from THE THEATRE, SHOREDITCH. It was named after its sign, which showed Hercules carrying the world on his shoulders. It was used only during the summer since, except for the stage and galleries, it was not roofed. The company acted at the BLACKFRIARS THEATRE in the winter. It cost 1d for admission to the pit, 2d to the gallery and 3d for a seat. Stools were put on the stage for privileged people. Shakespeare was both a shareholder and a player here. No complete list exists of plays performed, but it is known that Shakespeare's *Richard II*, *Romeo and Juliet*, *King Lear*, *Othello*, *Henry VIII*, *Love's Labour's Lost*, *The Winter's Tale*, *The Taming of the Shrew*, *Macbeth* and *Pericles* were all acted at the Globe. Probably *Henry V*, with its reference to 'this wooden O', was also performed here. In 1613 two cannon, fired during a performance of *Henry VIII*, set the thatch alight and the theatre was destroyed. Everyone escaped unhurt except for one man who had 'his breeches on fire that would perhaps have broyled him if he had not with the benefit of a provident wit put it out with bottle ale'. It was quickly rebuilt with the aid of public subscriptions and a royal grant and reopened in 1614; it is shown on Visscher's map of 1616. It was closed in 1642 by the Puritans and demolished two years later. Its site was on the south side of Park Street.

Globe Theatre *Shaftesbury Avenue, W1*. Designed in 1906 as the Hicks Theatre (the name changed in 1909) by W.G.R. Sprague to match the QUEEN'S THEATRE and financed by Jacobus-Marler Estates for Charles Frohman and Seymour Hicks. It opened with *The Beauty of the Bath*, a musical by Hicks and Cosmo Hamilton. In its early years the theatre's main successes were *Brewster's Millions* (1907), a comedy with Gerald du Maurier, and the farce, *The Glad Eye* (1912). In 1918–27 it was managed by Marie Lohr and her husband, Anthony Prinsep. Other successes included *The Lady's Not for Burning* (1949), by Christopher Fry, which starred John Gielgud and Pamela Brown; in 1950 Anouilh's *Ring Round the Moon* (682 performances); in 1956–8 Coward's comedy, *Nude with Violin*; and *A Man for All Seasons* (1960) by Robert Bolt.

Globe Theatre *Newcastle Street, Strand*. A ramshackle structure backing on to the even more jerry-built Opera Comique, which were together known as 'The Rickety Twins'. It was designed, built and managed by Sefton Parry who hoped to make handsome profits in compensation when the area was demolished, which was even then in contemplation. It was, however, commodious, with a capacity of 1,800. It opened in 1868. The theatre is best remembered for *Charley's Aunt* (1893) which ran for 1,466 performances, and for its association with the famous actor manager, John (later Sir John) Hare, who produced Pinero's *The Gay Lord Quex* (1899), then the most daring play of its time, with himself, Gilbert Howe and Irene Vanbrugh in the cast. In this production, which ran for 300 performances, ladies first smoked cigarettes on stage. The theatre was then known to be drawing to its close as the Strand improvement scheme had been finally approved (*see* STRAND). It closed in March 1902 while under the management of Fred Terry and Julia Neilson, and was soon afterwards demolished. BUSH HOUSE stands on its site.

Gloucester Crescent *NW1*. Takes its name from the Prince Regent's cousin and brother-in-law, William, Duke of Gloucester (*see* REGENT'S PARK). The Italianate terraces were built on the fields of CHALK FARM in the 1840s–50s. The former circular piano factory at No. 43 is now partly occupied by Gerald Duckworth, the publishers. It was built in 1852 by Collard and Collard who assigned different processes to each of the five floors, the pianos being hoisted up and down through a well in the centre, now blocked up.

Gloucester Gate *NW1*. Takes its name from the title of the Duke of Gloucester, husband of Mary, George IV's younger sister. It was designed by Nash and built by Richard Mott with Joseph John Scoles as architect on the site. Scoles did not care for Nash's façade so, hoping to improve it, he doubled the scale of the mouldings on the capitals. Nash, busy in 1827 with building BUCKINGHAM PALACE, never noticed but simply murmured that 'the parts looked larger than he had expected'. The 11 houses, and the detached ones that form part of the group, are still in good condition. The flats at No. 37 are by James Stirling (1967).

Gloucester House *Park Lane, see* GROSVENOR HOUSE.

Gloucester House *137 Piccadilly, at the west corner of Old Park Lane*. Originally built in the early years of the reign of George III. Here Lord Elgin exhibited his famous Greek marbles from the Parthenon, shortly before selling them to the nation in

1816. In that year the house was bought by William Frederick, Duke of Gloucester (grandson of Frederick, Prince of Wales), whose nickname of 'Silly Billy' did not prevent his being elected Chancellor of Cambridge University. He lived here until his death in 1834. After the death of his widow the house was occupied by George, 2nd Duke of Cambridge, a grandson of George III, and for many years Commander-in-Chief of the British Army, whose equestrian statue still adorns WHITEHALL (*see* STATUES). Gloucester House was demolished soon after the Duke's death in 1904.

Gloucester Lodge *Brompton*. Designed by William Tyler for George III's sister-in-law, Maria, Duchess of Gloucester, it was sold by her daughter to George Canning who was living here as Foreign Secretary in the 1820s. It stood opposite the present underground station in GLOUCESTER ROAD (to which it gave its name) and was demolished in the early 1850s when the area was developed after the GREAT EXHIBITION.

Gloucester Place *W1*. Built in 1810 by John Elwes and named after William, Duke of Gloucester, brother of George III. Mary Anne Clarke, daughter of a bricklayer and mistress of the 'Grand Old' Duke of York, the Commander-in-Chief of the Army, occupied No. 62 in 1803–10, living in style with innumerable carriages, ten horses, 20 servants, three cooks and piles of gold plate. In 1809 the Duke deserted her after a parliamentary enquiry found that she had been taking money from Army officers who were hoping for promotion. No. 99 was Elizabeth Barrett's first London home in 1836–8. John Robert Godley, founder of Canterbury, New Zealand, lived at No. 48 in 1860–1; and Wilkie Collins at No. 65 (where he wrote *The Moonstone*) in 1867–88.

Gloucester Road *SW7*. Formerly known as Hogmore Lane, it was given its present name in 1826 in honour of Maria, Duchess of Gloucester, who built a house in this area, Orford Lodge, in 1805. After her death in 1807 her daughter sold the house to George Canning who lived here in 1809–27. Several of his children were born here, including the future Viceroy of India. The house was demolished in 1850. The road extends from CROMWELL ROAD to PALACE GATE. It was started in 1826 but scarcely anything of this period remains other than a few houses at the northern end. The Nicaraguan Embassy is at No. 8, the Bahrain Embassy at No. 98. ST STEPHEN'S CHURCH, by Peacock, (1865), is on the corner of Southwell Gardens. Thorney Court at the northern end is by John R. Harris (1980–81). Sir James Barrie, the dramatist, lived at No. 133 in 1896–1902.

Gloucester Square *W2*. Takes its name from the nearby town house of George IV's cousin and brother-in-law, William, Duke of Gloucester. Robert Stephenson, the engineer, lived at No. 35 from 1847 until his death in 1859.

Glovers' Company *see* CITY LIVERY COMPANIES.

Goat Tavern *3 Stratford Street, W1*. Built originally in 1686 and rebuilt in 1958. There is a life-size figure of a goat as an inn sign. Lord Nelson met Lady Hamilton here. During the 1st World War it was an unofficial club for naval officers until it was declared out of bounds following heavy losses at sea which were attributed to careless talk. In 1736 a trust was set up here for the needy of two local parishes. The inn still contributes to this fund today.

Godliman Street *EC4*. The original of the name is uncertain but it could be derived from *godelmynges*, the skins of young animals which were used by shoemakers. The street originally ran only between CARTER LANE and KNIGHTRIDER STREET but since 1890 has incorporated both Bennet Hill and Paul's Chain.

Godolphin and Latymer School *Hammersmith, W6*. Sir William Godolphin left provison in his will for the relief, maintenance and education of poor scholars. In 1856 the Charity Commission used this income to fund the Godolphin School for boys in Great Church Lane, which flourished until the end of the century when it was decided to convert it to a secondary day school for girls. The Latymer Foundation (*see* LATYMER UPPER SCHOOL) gave financial support, and in 1906 200 girls moved into the converted premises of the old boys' school.

Gog and Magog Two legendary giants, originally known as Gogmagog and Corineus (the former an ancient inhabitant of Britain, the latter a Trojan invader), representing warriors in a supposed conflict which resulted in the founding in 1,000 BC of Albion's capital city, New Troy. Statues of them were paraded in pageants and processions since at least the beginning of the 15th century. They greeted Mary I on her entry into London in 1554 and Elizabeth I in 1558; and have often appeared in the LORD MAYOR'S SHOW. After a time Corineus was forgotten and his antagonist's name was divided into two to serve for them both. There are statues of them in the GUILDHALL and they are, no doubt, the two giants who strike the hour against the bell on the clock of ST DUNSTAN, FLEET STREET.

The Guildhall statues of the legendary giants Gog and Magog, which were destroyed in the Blitz.

Gold and Silver Wyre Drawers' Company *see* CITY LIVERY COMPANIES.

Golden Lane *EC1*. Probably named after a family who owned property here, it used to be known as Golding Lane. One of the early London theatres, the FORTUNE, stood on the east side of the lane between 1600 and 1661. In 1664 Thomas Killigrew began a school for young actors here called The Nursery. Pepys went along to see their productions several times. The last entry in his diary was in 1668 and it is not known how long the school lasted after that. During the 2nd World War the area was devastated. The CRIPPLEGATE INSTITUTE was one of the few buildings to survive. In 1955–62 the west side of the lane to GOSWELL ROAD was redeveloped as a housing estate – a prizewinning design by Chamberlin, Powell and Bon, built around four courts.

Golden Square *W1*. Building began here in 1670 and was completed by the early 1700s. Golden is probably a refined corruption of gelding, the land being formerly used for the grazing of geldings, and consequently known as Gelding's Close. Designed to contain 'such houses as might accommodate Gentry', the square was at first extremely fashionable. Its residents included Barbara Villiers, Duchess of Cleveland (1705–7), James Brydges, later 1st Duke of Chandos (1700–10), and Henry St John, 1st Viscount Bolingbroke (1702–14). In 1720 Strype described it as 'a very handsome place railed round and gravelled with many very good houses inhabited by gentry on all sides'. According to the *Dictionary of National Biography*, William Windham the statesman, whose father came from an old Norfolk family, was born at No. 6 in 1750. By then, however, most of the English aristocratic residents had left for smarter districts to the west; and the square became distinguished for the number of foreign legations that established themselves here – among them those of Bavaria, Brunswick, Genoa, Russia and Portugal. The Portuguese Embassy, at Nos 23–24, was where the Portuguese statesman, Sebastian de Carvalho, Marquis of Pombal, lived as ambassador in 1739–44. The square also became distinguished for the residence of foreign artists, including the Swiss painter, Angelica Kauffmann, who lived at No. 16 from 1767, until she returned to Italy in 1781, having married the Venetian painter, Antonio Zucchi. The Anglo-Irish painter, Martin Archer Shee, later President of the ROYAL ACADEMY, also lived here, at No. 13, during 1796–8. There were several medical men, too, in the square. John Hunter, the Scottish surgeon, lived at No. 31, in 1765–8. Mrs Jordan, the actress and mistress of the Duke of Clarence, later William IV, took No. 30 in 1803 for the three daughters she had had by Richard Ford, whose father Edward Ford was then living at No. 4. None of the original houses remains; but there are four 18th-century domestic buildings. No. 11 was rebuilt in 1778, No. 21 in 1790; Nos 23 and 24 were originally built in the late 17th century and, much altered, were in 1724–88 together occupied by first the Portuguese, then the Bavarian, Legation. In 1788 both houses were bought by Bishop James Talbot, so that the Roman Catholic Church in WARWICK STREET, the CHURCH OF OUR LADY OF THE ASSUMPTION AND ST GREGORY, could be built in the garden behind. No. 23 was then let, and No. 24 used as the Church presbytery. The Revd James Archer, renowned for his sermons, lived here in 1794–1825.

By the time Dickens wrote *Nicholas Nickleby* in 1839, and placed Ralph Nickleby's gloomy house here, Golden Square had deteriorated. 'Two or three violins and a wind instrument from the Opera band reside within its precincts. Its boarding-houses are musical, and the notes of pianos and harps float in the evening time past the head of the mournful statue, the guardian genius of a little wilderness of shrubs, in the centre of the square. On a summer's night, windows are thrown open, and groups of swarthy mustachio'd men are seen by the passer-by lounging at the casements, and smoking fearfully. Sounds of gruff voices practising vocal music invade the evening's silence, and the fumes of choice tobacco scent the air. There, snuff and cigars, and German pipes and flutes, and violins, and violoncello's, divide the supremacy between them. It is the region of song and smoke. Street bands are on their mettle in Golden Square, and itinerant glee-singers quaver involuntarily, as they raise their voices within its boundaries.' Many of the smokers and musicians lived in the boarding-houses and small hotels of which, by the 1860s, there were eight in the square. There were also a number of musical instrument makers, a few architects and engineers and, in 1870, no less than 16 practising solicitors. These were gradually replaced by woollen manufacturers and merchants. In 1900 as many as 70 different firms connected with this trade had premises in the square. When the 1st World War broke out there were only four buildings in the whole square whose occupants were not connected with the woollen trade. Several firms in the trade still have premises here. Other office buildings are now leased by film companies. The ROYAL NATIONAL THROAT, NOSE AND EAR HOSPITAL stands on the corner of UPPER JOHN STREET.

In the 2nd World War the middle of the square was dug up for an air-raid shelter. Afterwards it was paved, and benches and flower pots were put up around the statue that Dickens had described as mournful. This statue is attributed to Nost, and is supposed to represent George II (*see* STATUES).

Golders Green *NW11*. Part of the old parish and manor of HENDON. The name is probably derived from that of an early landholder. Camden (1695) refers to Goulders Green, and other variants are shown on earlier maps. By the middle of the 18th century the forest lands had been cleared and the flat plains of Golders Green were parcelled up into farms. It was to remain agricultural land, with a sparse population of farmers, labourers and the occupants of a few larger country houses, until the beginning of the 20th century. The area was dramatically changed by the development of the NORTHERN LINE in 1905. A tunnel was driven under HAMPSTEAD HEATH (440 ft above sea level at the highest point) to emerge into the totally undeveloped Golders Green fields (220 ft). There was an almost immediate explosion of speculative building and consequently of population. Even so, land was still relatively cheap and the London Crematorium Co. was able to purchase a site for the GOLDERS GREEN CREMATORIUM in 1902 for £6,000.

The largest building in Golders Green is the Hippodrome. This was built to seat 2,300 people and opened as a music hall in 1913 and as a theatre in 1923. It was subsequently acquired by the BBC as a studio. The Manor House Hospital is run by the Trade Union Movement. Its premises include Ivy House, formerly the home of Anna Pavlova (whose last public performance was given at Golders Green Hippodrome). Golders Green is now wholly built up except for the attractive Golders Hill Park. The population of the area was significantly augmented before and after the 2nd World War by the influx of many central European émigrés. St Michael's church is by

A 1908 Underground poster advertising the pleasures of living in the suburban 'sanctuary' of Golders Green.

John T. Lee and Caroe and Passmore (1914–24); St Alban's by Sir Giles Gilbert Scott (1932). Child's Hill to the south was once celebrated for its brick kilns and laundries (*see also* HAMPSTEAD GARDEN SUBURB).

Golders Green Crematorium *see* CEMETERIES.

Goldsmith Street *EC2*. Marked on Rocque's map of 1746 as Gold Street, its name derives from the goldsmiths who used to be found here. John Henderson, the actor known as 'The Bath Roscius', was born here, the son of an Irish factor, in 1747.

Goldsmiths' College (University of London) *New Cross, SE14*. In 1891 the GOLDSMITHS' COMPANY acquired the buildings in New Cross which were originally designed by John Shaw the Younger for the Royal Naval School for the sons of naval and marine officers. The GOLDSMITHS' COMPANY acquired the school as a Technical and Recreative Institute which was to provide classes in art and music and prepare students for external degrees in engineering and science for the UNIVERSITY OF LONDON. A Great Hall and a new south block to the main building, designed by Sir Reginald Blomfield, were added before 1904, when the site and buildings (which today occupy 14 acres) were presented to the UNIVERSITY OF LONDON.

Goldsmiths' Company *see* CITY LIVERY COMPANIES.

Goldsmiths' Hall *Foster Lane, EC2*. The first record of a Hall dates from 1366. It stood on the east side of FOSTER LANE and had formerly been the mansion of Nicholas de Segrave, brother of the Bishop of London. It was rebuilt in 1407 by Sir Drue Barentyn and included a courtyard, an assay office, vaults, an armoury and a granary. The next Hall was built by Nicholas Stone in 1634–6. It was used as the exchequer by Parliamentarians during 1641–60. This building was damaged by the GREAT FIRE, and restored by Edward Jarman in 1669. The present Renaissance-style Hall was built on the same site by Philip Hardwick in 1829–35. After being damaged in the 2nd World War, it was restored by C. James in 1947. The panelling in the Court Room is from the 1669 Hall. For the Company *see* CITY LIVERY COMPANIES.

GOLF CLUBS The principal clubs in the Greater London area include:
Addington Golf Club *Shirley Church Road, Croydon, Surrey*. Founded in 1913. The course was designed by J.F. Abercromby.
Addington Palace Golf Club *Addington Park, Gravel Hill, Croydon, Surrey*. The course was laid over the gardens of ADDINGTON PALACE which were landscaped by 'Capability' Brown in about 1870.
Bush Hill Park Golf Club *Bush Hill, Winchmore Hill, N21*. Founded in 1895 on ground which was formerly the home park of the manorial palace of ENFIELD. Henry VIII settled the property on the young Elizabeth, who resided here for some time before becoming Queen. At the time of the Commonwealth the park supplied 397 oak trees to the Navy. The present club house was originally a Ranger's Lodge.
Chislehurst Golf Club *Camden Place, Chislehurst, Kent*. Founded in 1894 and opened by A.J. Balfour, later Prime Minister. For the club house see CAMDEN PLACE.
Coombe Hill Golf Club *Golf Club Drive, Kingston Hill, Surrey*. The course was laid out by J.F. Abercromby in 1910, and in the words of T. Simpson, the golf course architect, 'ranks as by far the cleverest work done in England up to that time.'
Dulwich and Sydenham Hill Golf Club *Grange Lane, College Road, SE21*. The first six holes were laid out here by Tom Dunn in 1893, to be followed by a few holes designed by Willie Park. H.S. Colt completed the course in 1910. There was a gun site on the course during the 2nd World War. The club house is reputed to be the only one in the world which overlooks a capital city. Peter Oosterhuis played here as a schoolboy.
Fulwell Golf Club *Wellington Road, Hampton Hill, Middlesex*. The club was founded in 1904, and the course architect was J.H. Taylor. Originally farmland, potatoes were grown here in the 1st World War, and wheat in the 2nd.
Home Park Golf Club *Hampton Wick, Kingston-upon-Thames, Surrey*. Founded in 1895, the course was designed by James Braid. According to the golfing writer, Horace Hutchinson, there is evidence of golf being played at nearby Molesey Hurst in the 1760s when Dr Alexander Carlyle of Inveresk went with other Scots to visit Garrick at HAMPTON. 'He had told us to bring golf clubs and balls that we might play at that game on Molesey Hurst. We accordingly set out in good time, six of us in a landau. As we passed through Kensington, the Coldstream Regiment were changing guard, and on seeing our clubs, they gave us three cheers in honour of a diversion peculiar to Scotland.'

313

Langley Park Golf Club *Barnfield Wood Road, Beckenham, Kent*. Founded in 1910, the course was designed by J.H. Taylor. Henry Cotton was the professional here from 1926 to 1932.

London Scottish Golf Club *Windmill Enclosure, Wimbledon Common, Surrey*. In 1865 Lord Elcho, later Earl of Wemyss, and sixteen other members of the London Scottish Rifle Volunteers started the game on the Common by playing round the windmill and Mrs Doggett's cottage, the first club house. By 1871 membership was open to civilians, though control remained with the LSRV and Lord Elcho. There was an annual match against ROYAL BLACKHEATH, followed by dinner at the Dog and Fox. Three rounds of seven holes were played, 14 a side. A separate course was established for ladies in 1872. Here honorary male members were permitted to enter competitions, but were ineligible for prizes. By 1882 the club house was at the Iron Shooting House on the PUTNEY side of the common. There had been a considerable rift in the membership and a Wimbledon club was formed, later known as the ROYAL WIMBLEDON. This club used the same course but found other premises on the Wimbledon side of the common. The annual match with Cambridge University was established in 1879.

Mill Hill Golf Club *100 Barnet Way, NW7*. The course was designed by J.F. Abercromby, and remodelled by H.S. Colt in 1931.

Muswell Hill Golf Club *Rhodes Avenue, Wood Green, N22*. Founded in 1893, it was the pioneer club in north London. Members from the club went to form clubs at HAMPSTEAD and TOTTERIDGE (*see* SOUTH HERTS) to enable them to play the game on Sundays. During the 2nd World War one third of the course was turned over to agriculture.

Northwood Golf Club *Rickmansworth Road, Northwood, Middlesex*. Founded in 1891.

Richmond Golf Club *Sudbrook Park, Richmond, Surrey*. Founded in 1891, the course was designed by Tom Dunn. King George VI was captain of the club when Duke of York. Prince and Princess Arthur of Connaught played here, as also did Sandy Herd, Willie Park, J.H. Taylor and Harry Vardon. For the club house see SUDBROOK PARK.

Romford Golf Club *Heath Drive, Gidea Park, Essex*. Founded in 1894. The course was designed by James Braid. Directors of the Great Eastern Railway made travel concessions to members travelling from central London. The fee for a brake or cab from the station was 6d. Players were advised: 'Accommodation is provided not only for their wants by day, but for their needs at night, large and airy bedrooms being ready for those who wish to taste the sweets of fresh air and invigorating golf at "screech of day", even after a late night.'

Royal Blackheath Golf Club *Court Road, Eltham, SE9*. A Society of Blackheath Golfers was formed in 1608 when the game was played on ground adjacent to GREENWICH PALACE, James I's Scottish courtiers having introduced the game to London. All club records before 1787 were destroyed in a fire, but the earliest trophy survived, a silver club dated 1766. Separate clubs existed for winter and summer golf, the winter club being known as The Knuckle Club. This was founded in 1789 and organised as a masonic lodge, its Gold Medal, now the Spring Medal, being the oldest in the game. Club captains are recorded since 1766, and the office of Field Marshal since 1802. There was

An engraving after Abbott of golfers at Blackheath in 1790, wearing the red coat obligatory on the course.

a new lay-out of seven holes in 1844. The gutta ball arrived in 1848 and the popularity of the game quickly increased. Other clubs were being formed throughout the world with the help of the Blackheath Club. Advancing urbanisation caused the amalgamation with ELTHAM Golf Club in 1923. The course here was designed by James Braid over the grounds of ELTHAM LODGE. Among the many prized possessions from Blackheath housed here is the picture of the *Blackheath Golfer* by Lemuel Abbott. He is depicted in the red coat which had to be worn when playing on the Heath.

Royal Epping Forest Golf Club *Forest Approach, Chingford, E4*. Founded in 1888 when the High Sheriff was elected President, and 60 other members, captained by F.G. Faithfull, paid one guinea a year to belong. The royal prefix was granted in 1889, and the members used the Forest Hotel as their club house. It is now a municipal course.

Royal Mid-Surrey Golf Club *Old Deer Park, Richmond, Surrey*. Founded in 1892. The course was designed by J.H. Taylor who was the professional for 47 years. He was followed by Henry Cotton. The club acquired the 'Royal' prefix in 1926 when the Prince of Wales was captain. S.H. Fry, eight times amateur billiards champion, was a member here and at the age of 80 produced a score of 75. In the words of the 'Happy Golfer', Henry Leach, 'In a special way Mid-Surrey stands for London golf.'

Royal Wimbledon Golf Club *29 Camp Road, Wimbledon Common, SW19*. Founded in 1882. The course was designed by H.S. Colt and modified by C.D. Lawrie. Civilian members of the LONDON SCOTTISH formed the Wimbledon club when further tenancy of the Iron Shooting House was terminated by the commanding officer of the Volunteer Corps. The Royal prefix was granted in 1882. The present club house and course were in use by 1908. The 7th, 10th and 11th holes lie over ground where Caesar's troops are said to have camped. Red coats must still be worn here. Several founder members of the Ladies Golf Union in England came from this club.

Selsdon Park Hotel Golf Club *Addington Road, South Croydon, Surrey*. The course was designed by J.H. Taylor, and opened in 1928. A championship course used by the 1981 Ryder cup teams. Harry Weetman was a professional here.

Shooters' Hill Golf Club *Eaglesfield Road, Shooters' Hill, SE18*. Founded in 1903. The course was designed by Willie Park. It is known as 'the club on the hill', and the views over London were probably appreciated by Roman soldiers marching along the old WATLING STREET. During the 2nd World War, German and Italian prisoners were en-camped on the course, and there was considerable bomb damage.

South Herts Golf Club *Links Drive, Totteridge, N20*. Founded just before the end of the last century, the pioneers were members of the MUSWELL HILL and HAMPSTEAD clubs where there was no Sunday play. Harry Vardon was the professional here for many years, and gave much careful attention to the course. He was followed by Dai Rees. This club is the home of the Hudson Trophy.

Sudbury Golf Club *Bridgewater Road, Wembley, Middlesex*. Formed from the remnants of the Acton Golf Club which was founded in 1896.

Sundridge Park Golf Club *Garden Road, Bromley, Kent*. The course was opened in 1903 by A.J. Balfour, Prime Minister. It was designed by Willie Park Jnr over parkland belonging to SUNDRIDGE PARK, built in 1796.

Upminster Golf Club *114 Hall Lane, Upminster, Essex*. Founded 1928. For the club house *see* UPMINSTER HALL.

Wanstead Golf Club *Overton Drive, Wanstead, E11*. Founded in 1893. The course was designed by Tom Dunn on land formerly belonging to Wanstead House, once the home of the Earl of Mornington and now demolished. The stable block survives and is now the club house.

Wimbledon Park Golf Club *Home Park Road, Wimbledon, SW19*. Founded in 1899. The course was designed round a lake in the grounds of a Tudor man-sion house. Two club houses were lost by fire, and a third by a flying bomb. The course is adjacent to the ALL ENGLAND LAWN TENNIS CLUB.

Other London clubs founded before 1900 are:

Ealing Golf Club, Perivale Lane, Greenford, Middlesex (1898)

Enfield Golf Club, Old Park Road, Windmill Hill, Enfield, Middlesex (1893), designed by James Braid

Hampstead Golf Club, Winnington Road, N2 (1894), nine holes

Hillingdon Golf Club, Dorset Way, Hillingdon, Middlesex (1892), nine holes

Malden Golf Club, Traps Lane, New Malden, Surrey (1894)

Purley Downs Golf Club, Purley Downs Road, Purley, Surrey (1895)

Stanmore Golf Club, Gordon Avenue, Stanmore, Middlesex (1893)

West Middlesex Golf Club, Greenford Road, Southall, Middlesex (1894)

Woodford Golf Club, Sunset Avenue, Woodford Green, Essex (1890).

Goodge Street *W1*. Built on a meadow known as Crab Tree Field which belonged to the wife of John Goodge, a carpenter. Goodge's nephews, Francis and William Goodge, began developing the field in the late 1740s. During 1775–1815 Benjamin West, the President of the ROYAL ACADEMY, had a house here. In 1777 the body of Dr Dodd, the forger hanged at TYBURN, was brought to an undertakers in the street where John Hunter tried unsuccessfully to resuscitate him in a hot bath.

Goodman's Fields Theatre *Ayliffe Street, Whitechapel*. Built in 1733 for the actor, Henry Gif-fard, as 'an entirely new, beautiful convenient theatre' by the same architect as COVENT GARDEN (Edward Shepherd) where 'dramatic pieces were performed with the utmost elegance and propriety'. It was Gif-fard who sent a libellous play, *The Golden Rump*, to Sir Robert Walpole which resulted in the passing of the Licensing Act of 1737. Under it Giffard's own theatre was closed. He later reopened it, charging admission for concerts which preceded and followed the play. In 1741 David Garrick made his debut here as Richard III under the name of Lydall, 'a gentleman who never appeared on any stage'. He was so acclaimed that he drew the audiences away from the patent theatres of COVENT GARDEN and DRURY LANE. In 1742 the theatre was compulsorily closed through the influence of the patent theatres.

Goodman's Fields Theatre *Leman Street, Whitechapel*. In 1729 Thomas Odell, a playwright and deputy Licenser of Plays, converted a shop in Leman Street into a theatre. During the first season Fielding's play, *The Temple Beau*, was first produced. In 1730 the theatre was shut for a while to avoid compulsory closure. In 1731 Odell sold out to his leading actor, Henry Giffard. In 1733 Giffard built another theatre in Ayliffe street, also known as GOODMAN'S FIELDS THEATRE. The old one thereafter seems to have been used for jugglers, rope walkers and other circus acts. In 1751 it was closed and became a warehouse; it was destroyed by fire in 1802.

Goodwin's Court *St Martin's Lane, WC2*. First appears in the rate books in 1690. On the south side is an intact row of 17th-century houses.

Gordon Medical Museum *St Thomas Street, SE1*. Established as a historical medical museum to help medical staff and students in their research. It houses specimens dating back 150 years, including some extraordinarily gruesome examples of contor-tions and additions to the human body. Open to med-ically qualified visitors, staff from GUY'S HOSPITAL and other medical personnel.

Gordon Riots On Friday 2 June 1780 a crowd 50,000 strong assembled in St George's Fields, SOUTHWARK, before marching to Parliament with a petition against the repeal of anti-Roman Catholic

The burning and plundering of Newgate Prison during the Gordon Riots of June 1780.

legislation. The march had been organised by Lord George Gordon, a Member of Parliament and leader of the Protestant Association, but he lost control of the crowd and a squadron of dragoons had to be called in. Some of the demonstrators broke away to plunder the Sardinian and Bavarian Ambassadors' private chapels. On 4 June hostile crowds surrounded and set light to Roman Catholic chapels in MOORFIELDS and SPITAL-FIELDS. By the evening of 5 June the mob had lost interest in Roman Catholics and began a campaign of general destruction, particularly against Irish property and Irishmen. NEWGATE, CLERKENWELL, the FLEET, KING'S BENCH and BOROUGH CLINK were all burned down and their inmates released. LANGDALE'S DIS-TILLERY in HOLBORN was attacked. So was Sir John Fielding's house in BOW STREET. Many of the mob made themselves so drunk that they fell into the flames and became human torches. They attacked on DOWN-ING STREET and tried to storm the BANK OF ENGLAND but were repelled with the help of clerks using bullets made from melted-down ink wells Thereafter it was patrolled at night by a platoon from the Guards in ceremonial bearskins (*see* BANK OF ENGLAND). Next day all was quiet. On 9 June Lord George Gordon was arrested and accused of high treason. He was ac-quitted, but 21 ringleaders were found guilty and hanged. An estimated 850 people lost their lives. Dickens describes the riots in *Barnaby Rudge*.

Gordon Square *WC1*. Begun by Thomas Cubitt in the 1820s and completed some 40 years later by his executors. It was named after the 6th Duke of Bed-ford's second wife, Lady Georgiana Gordon. Few original houses remain, but the terraces have been well restored. Most of the buildings now house depart-ments and institutes of LONDON UNIVERSITY. At the south-west corner is the university church of CHRIST THE KING. Next door is University Hall, opened in 1848 as a hall of residence for Unitarians studying at UNIVERSITY COLLEGE. It now houses the Royal In-stitute of Philosophy and DR WILLIAMS'S LIBRARY. At No. 53 is the PERCIVAL DAVID FOUNDATION OF CHINESE ART. No. 46 was the home of the Stephen family. Virginia lived here in 1905–7; Vanessa and Clive Bell took it over in 1911; and J.M. Keynes lived here in 1916–46. Lytton Strachey lived at No. 51 and wrote *Queen Victoria* here in 1921. This house is now the University Publications Department. Bertrand Russell lived at No. 57 in 1918–19.

Gordon Street *WC1*. Now contains the New University Centre and Students' Union. The east side used to be occupied almost entirely by members of the BLOOMSBURY GROUP. No. 5 was the editorial office in 1930–1 of the magazine *Action*, edited by Sir Oswald Mosley with the help of Sir Harold Nicolson and V. Sackville-West.

Gore House *Kensington Gore*. Built in the middle of the 18th century and subsequently occupied by Ad-miral Lord Rodney, the house belonged in 1808–21 to William Wilberforce. In the 1830s the lease was ac-quired by Byron's friend, the Countess of Blessington, the beautiful Irish writer and witty hostess. Her step-daughter's husband, the gifted dandy, Count D'Orsay, lived nearby until 1839 when he moved in with her, and thereafter the house became one of the most celebrated salons of early Victorian London. An ex-traordinarily wide variety of famous and fashionable people were entertained here, from Wellington and Disraeli, to the morose Prince Louis Napoleon, the ebullient Walter Savage Landor and the lively young Charles Dickens. In 1849 the reckless extravagance of Lady Blessington and Count D'Orsay obliged them to leave London for Paris where she died of apoplexy that same year and where he also died not long afterwards. The sale of their effects, which continued over 12 days and was conducted by Mr Phillips (*see* PHILLIPS), brought enormous crowds to the house. 'I visited Gore House for the last time on the 10th of May,' wrote

T.H. Shepherd's 1850 watercolour of Gore House, once Lady Blessington's mansion; the Albert Hall now occupies the site.

Lady Blessington's friend H.H. Madden, 'the auction was going on. Every room was thronged. The well-known library saloon, in which the conversaziones took place, was crowded – but not with guests. The armchair in which the lady of the mansion was wont to sit, was occupied by a stout, coarse gentleman of the Jewish persuasion, engaged in examining a marble hand, extended on a book. People as they passed through the room, poked the furniture, pulled about the precious objects of art and ornaments which lay on the table. And some made jests. It was the most signal ruin of an establishment I ever witnessed. Here was a total smash, a crash on a grand scale, a sweeping clearance of all the house's treasures.' The next year the house was taken by Alexis Soyer, who for some 12 years had been chef at the REFORM CLUB. He opened a flamboyant restaurant here with a Baronial Banqueting Hall in the grounds. The venture, however, was not a success and the restaurant closed down after five months having lost Soyer £7,000. The house was bought by the Royal Commissioners for the GREAT EXHIBITION. The ALBERT HALL now covers the site.

Goring Hotel *15 Beeston Place, Ebury Street, SW1.* Opened in 1910 and named after its first proprietor, O.R. Goring, and still run by his family. Three extensions had been added by 1926. It claims to have been the first hotel in the world to have central heating and a bathroom to every bedroom. There are now 100 bedrooms.

Gospel Oak *NW3, NW5.* Straddles the border between HAMPSTEAD and KENTISH TOWN. The name derives from the custom of beating the parish bounds during the three days before Ascension Day, a ceremony which included a reading from the Gospel under a large tree, usually an oak. This Gospel Oak probably

stood on the east side of Southampton Road, where it crosses the railway, and it marked the boundary between the parishes of HAMPSTEAD and ST PANCRAS. Many are said to have preached beneath the tree, including St Augustine, Wycliffe and Wesley. Whitefield is more reliably reported to have addressed 'crowded audiences of the working classes'. Until the 19th century, Gospel Oak was a rural area of pastures and watercress beds, watered by a tributary of the FLEET RIVER, although the land around the junction of the present-day Gordon House Road and Highgate Road had, by the late 18th century, some buildings upon it, including the Gordon House Academy, 'an old established Academy kept by Mr Cooper who died suddenly of Apoplexy in the year 1788 whilst sitting at his desk and giving lessons to his pupils'. Gordon House Road itself (Gordon House Lane until 1882) was created in 1806, along a path between KENTISH TOWN and HAMPSTEAD, but Gospel Oak Fields remained and the annual Gospel Oak Fair was held there at Easter until the 1850s. Lords Mansfield, Southampton and Lismore all held land in the area, and all are today remembered in the names of streets.

By the middle of the 19th century, the landowners had seen the possibilities for development: 27 acres around what is now Lismore Circus were sold in 1846 for £10,200. By 1858 plans were being made for the building of a residential development based on a central circus, with six or seven roads radiating from it. These were to be laid out with elegant semi-detached villas in their own gardens. But with the coming of the railways everything changed, here as in so many developing areas on the edge of London. Houses were built, but they were of a 'very humble' kind for humble people. 'The noisiest and most objectionable public house in the district bears the significant sign of the Gospel Oak. It is the favourite resort of navvies and quarrelsome shoemakers.' The North London Railway, the Tottenham and Hampstead Junction Railway and, above all, the Midland Railway, desecrated the fields and open spaces, built stations and shunting-yards; and by 1867 the area designated for the construction of Lismore Circus was still only a 'mud island'. Development finally started there in the 1870s, as it did in the fields north of Mansfield Road, which the railway had cut off from the open spaces of the Heath. There was a carpet beating ground in Fleet Road in 1874, and brickfields were still operating there in 1885. A small church built in Lisburne Road in 1900 (demolished 1971) was the last building to be constructed from bricks from the Gospel Oak brickfields. London Street Tramways depot opened in Cressy Road in the 1880s (the site is now used as the Camden Vehicle Maintenance Depot). Soon all those areas which had escaped the attentions of the railways were covered by houses and small factories to provide homes and employment for the growing population, 'respectable but emphatically working class', which was moving in. The NW3 part of Gospel Oak remains much as planned and built by the late Victorians, though it has become very largely residential. But after the 2nd World War wholesale demolition of the area round Lismore Circus was undertaken by the Council and it was redeveloped in massive estates. Of the earlier streets of small villas, Oak Village and its immediate surroundings are all that have survived.

Goswell Road *EC1*. Named after a garden which Robert de Ufford, Earl of Suffolk, had here and which was called Goswelle. That part of the road from ALDERSGATE STREET to just beyond OLD STREET used to be known as Goswell Street. And it was here that Mr Pickwick lodged with Mrs Bardell. When he opened his window, 'Goswell Street was at his feet; Goswell Street was on his right hand – as far as the eye could reach; Goswell Street extended on his left: and the opposite side of Goswell Street was over the way.' Goswell Road now extends from the ANGEL, ISLINGTON to just north of the BARBICAN.

Gough Square *EC4*. Situated just north of FLEET STREET, to which it has access through BOLT COURT, JOHNSON'S COURT and ST DUNSTAN'S COURT. A family of wool merchants, the Goughs, owned this court in the 18th century. Richard Gough was knighted in consequence of his successful trading with China and India. He died in 1728. Twenty years later Samuel Johnson moved into No. 17, where he lived until 1759 (*see* JOHNSON'S MEMORIAL HOUSE). The Irish dramatist and miscellaneous writer, Hugh Kelly, formerly a staymaker's apprentice, was a well-known figure in the square until his death in 1777. 'He exhibited his fat little figure in a flaming broad silver-laced waistcoat, bag-wig and sword and was so fond of displaying plate on his sideboard that he added to it his silver spurs.'

Government of Greater London Greater London is an area of some 610 sq miles (1,580 sq km). At its broadest points it is 34 miles (55 km) across and 27 miles (43 km) from north to south. Some seven million people live in the area, and many hundreds of thousands more travel into it daily, by train, underground, bus or car, to work or shop or for pleasure. Within the Greater London area there are 31 BOROUGHS, plus the Cities of WESTMINSTER and

London in the centre. Local government is the responsibility of the councils of the BOROUGHS, the ancient CORPORATION OF THE CITY OF LONDON and the GREATER LONDON COUNCIL (GLC). Most local government services are provided by the borough councils and the CITY CORPORATION, but some, which can be better provided on a London-wide basis, are the responsibility of the GLC.

Most of the London boroughs have populations of around 250,000, and their councils consist of about 60 members, elected for four years, generally on a party political basis. They are responsible for local planning, local roads, local housing, welfare, social and amenity services, and in outer London for education, which in inner London is managed by a special committee of the GLC known as the INNER LONDON EDUCATION AUTHORITY. The GLC's duties include traffic management, maintenance of main roads, financial and policy control of London Transport (*see* TRANSPORT *and* UNDERGROUND), refuse disposal and the running of the LONDON FIRE BRIGADE. Inevitably some degree of overlap occurs. To facilitate co-operation the London borough councils have formed the London Boroughs Association, a forum in which they can discuss common problems, co-ordinate their activities, and express their views corporately to the government and to the GLC.

Services for which these elected councils are not responsible include hospitals (provided by four regional health authorities) (*see* MEDICINE), port facilities (the PORT OF LONDON AUTHORITY), water and main drainage (the Thames Water Authority), electricity and gas. The METROPOLITAN POLICE are under the control of the Commissioner of Police of the Metropolis, who is responsible to the government in the person of the Home Secretary. But in the CITY OF LONDON the CITY CORPORATION has its own police force, the CITY OF LONDON POLICE.

Government Offices *SW1*. Sir George Gilbert Scott's Government Offices, built in 1868–73, stretch from WHITEHALL to ST JAMES'S PARK. Scott prepared a Gothic design, but this provided a bitter dispute in Parliament, which became known as the Battle of the Styles. His second effort was in the Byzantine style of the early Venetian palaces, but this was also dismissed, as a 'regular mongrel affair' by Palmerston, who insisted on a Renaissance design. Scott therefore 'bought some costly books on Italian architecture and set vigorously to work'. The Victorian Italianate building which emerged originally housed the Home Office and the India Office, as well as the Foreign Office.

Governor's Palace *Cannon Street, EC4*. Excavations beneath CANNON STREET STATION and the immediately adjacent area in recent years have revealed evidence of a substantial palatial building. A feature of it was the fine plasterwork and an ornamental fountain in a garden. Such an establishment could only be the Roman Governor's residence and it is in an appropriate situation in relation to the other known major public buildings. The soldiers needed for guard duty or ceremonial parades were probably garrisoned in the ROMAN FORT situated in the north-west corner of the city.

Gower Street *WC1*. A long, wide street extending between BEDFORD SQUARE and EUSTON ROAD. Plain

Sir George Gilbert Scott's Foreign Office, built in 1868–73 in the Italianate style, as seen from St James's Park.

brick terraces dating from 1790 remain at the south end. Ruskin thought it the depth of ugliness in street architecture and George Gilbert Scott agreed. It was named after Lady Gertrude Leveson-Gower, daughter of Earl Gower who married the 4th Duke of Bedford and supervised the development. On the west side are the ROYAL ACADEMY OF DRAMATIC ART and UNIVERSITY COLLEGE HOSPITAL; also the Royal National Institute for the Deaf, established in 1911 and opened at No. 105 in 1938 by George VI. On the east side are LONDON UNIVERSITY buildings, including the Biological Sciences building and the SCHOOL OF HYGIENE AND TROPICAL MEDICINE. UNIVERSITY COLLEGE is also on the east side. At No. 136 are H.K. Lewis, the medical publishers founded in 1844 at premises in Gower Place.

On the wall of UNIVERSITY COLLEGE is an elaborate plaque to Richard Trevithick. 'Close to this place' he demonstrated the first locomotive to draw passengers, in 1808. On the wall of the Biological Sciences building is a BLUE PLAQUE to Charles Darwin who lived here in 1838–42 while he wrote his book on coral reefs and part of *The Origin of Species*. On No. 2 at the BEDFORD SQUARE end is a BLUE PLAQUE to Dame Millicent Garrett Fawcett. She and her sisters were interior designers and early exponents of women's suffrage. One of these sisters, Elizabeth Garrett Anderson, was the founder of the maternity hospital bearing her name, now in EUSTON ROAD. On No. 91 is a BLUE PLAQUE to George Dance the Younger who died there in 1825. Other distinguished residents of Gower Street include Lord Chancellor Eldon who lived here in 1791–1804 before he moved to BEDFORD SQUARE; Sir Samuel Romilly, 1798–1802; Giuseppe Mazzini in 1837–40 in his early 20s; and Louis Kossuth, the Hungarian patriot. Sarah Siddons, who lived here in 1784–9, was delighted with her house – 'the back of it is most effec-

tually in the country and delightfully pleasant'. The comedian John Bannister lived in the street in 1815–36, and the artist Peter de Wint in 1827–49. John Millais lived with his parents at No. 7 (then 87) when he was helping to establish the Pre-Raphaelite Movement. On the site of UNIVERSITY COLLEGE HOSPITAL Charles Dickens's mother tried to set up a school when Charles was working in the blacking factory and her husband was in the MARSHALSEA. Twentieth-century writers and intellectuals have also been connected with Gower Street: Anthony Hope, Lady Ottoline Morrell, Katherine Mansfield and J.M. Keynes lived here at various times.

Gracechurch Street *EC3*. Named after the vanished St Benet Grass Church. The corn and hay market of medieval London was held in the street. In the adjacent White Hart Court was the Friends' Meeting-House, the oldest Quaker meeting-house in London; William Penn used to talk here, and in 1670 George Fox was seized here, after the passing of the Conventicles Act, and taken to be questioned by the LORD MAYOR. William Curtis, the botanist and founder of the BOTANICAL MAGAZINE, had an apothecary's shop on the site of No. 51 from about 1770. His fellow-botanist, Peter Collinson, had a wholesale mercer's business at the sign of the Red Lion. William Hone, who was to achieve fame as the author of the *Everyday Book*, opened the Grasshopper Coffee-House in the street in 1830, having failed in various other commercial ventures, including several attempts at book-selling. The Grasshopper, too, was a failure. No. 84 was the site of the Spread Eagle Inn where the young Charles Dickens used to watch the departing coaches; and opposite it was the Swan-with-Two-Necks where he set the scene for Estella's meeting with Pip in *Great Expectations*.

Grafton Street Probably named after Henry Fitzroy, Duke of Grafton, a natural son of Charles II and Barbara Villiers, Duchess of Cleveland. It was, like Litchfield Street (which was presumably named after Barbara Villiers's son-in-law, the Earl of Lichfield, laid out by that energetic speculator, Nicholas Barbon, in the 1680s on the Newport Estate (*see* NEWPORT MARKET). It was totally demolished for the construction of the CHARING CROSS ROAD.

Grafton Street *W1*. An L-shaped street extending from NEW BOND STREET to the north end of DOVER STREET. Its site formed the southern end of Conduit Mead, which in the 17th century belonged to the CORPORATION OF THE CITY OF LONDON (*see* CONDUIT STREET). In 1667 this field was leased by the CORPORATION to the Earl of Clarendon, and after the sale of CLARENDON HOUSE, PICCADILLY, building development was projected on this southern end of Conduit Mead, by then incorporated into Albemarle Ground (*see* ALBEMARLE STREET). But after the bankruptcy of the principal promoter, John Hinde, in 1687, building at the north end of Albemarle Ground ceased, and in 1723 the 2nd Duke of Grafton and three of his neighbours bought the sites of what are now GRAFTON STREET and the north ends of ALBEMARLE and DOVER STREETS in order to preserve the views from their nearby houses.

Rocque's map of 1746 shows this area still open, but in 1771–2 four very large houses, Nos 3–6, were built for the 3rd Duke of Grafton by Sir Robert Taylor on the west side of Grafton Street; and by 1800 the development of the street had been completed. Nos 3–6 still survive, and Nos 4 and 5 have the arms of the CITY CORPORATION unobtrusively emblazoned on their façades. All are now used as offices, and have enormous stone doorcases with Tuscan columns and pediments, as well as fine staircases inside. Lord Brougham lived at No. 4 in 1839–68. Nos 21, 22 and 23, on the east side, are much smaller mid-Georgian houses, each having a Venetian window on the first floor. Notable inhabitants of Grafton Street included Charles James Fox, Admiral Lord Howe, Sir William Harcourt and Henry Irving, the actor, who lived at No. 15a. Today expensive offices and high-quality shops predominate.

Grahame Park *NW9*. Named (following a local competition) after Claude Grahame-White, the aircraft pioneer who started his Grahame-White

Aviation Co. on the site in 1911. It is now a large GREATER LONDON COUNCIL housing estate built in 1965–75. The facilities are of a high standard, though the architecture is often thought brutal and uncompromising. In the plans for Grahame Park, provision was appropriately made for the establishment of the ROYAL AIR FORCE MUSEUM.

Grand Hotel *Northumberland Avenue*. Built in the 1870s after the demolition of Northumberland House. It was a seven-storey, highly ornamented building designed by F. and H. Francis to face TRAFALGAR SQUARE. Its grand Palm Court, excellent restaurants and Winter Garden proved extremely popular. It had 500 bedrooms.

Grand Junction Canal Construction of this canal to the Midlands was begun by a private company towards the end of the 18th century. A section from PADDINGTON to UXBRIDGE was opened in 1801 and joined to the main canal in 1805. It was connected to the REGENT'S CANAL in 1820. During the Napoleonic Wars the workforce declared their loyalty to the Crown and the canal was used for military purposes; but not long afterwards the workers were striking for higher wages, and in 1825 complaints were made of the rowdiness of the 'leggers' who propelled boats through the Grand Junction tunnels by lying on the deck and 'walking' along the tunnel roof with their feet. Passengers were conveyed on the canal five days a week and country excursions were still being advertised well into the mid-19th century. In 1848 the company set up a direct carrying business competing with the railways, but an agreement was reached in 1857. The carrying business was closed in 1876 after heavy claims arising out of the REGENT'S PARK EXPLOSION of 1874. In 1894 the company purchased the GRAND UNION CANAL.

Grand Junction Waterworks Co. Incorporated in 1811. The original intake was at PADDINGTON from the GRAND JUNCTION CANAL. In its prospectus the company promised pure water, a constant supply and cheap rates. None of this was, however, forthcoming. There were early attempts to use stone pipes by the company's engineer, John Rennie; but from 1812 cast-iron pipes were used. In 1820 the intake was changed to the THAMES near CHELSEA HOSPITAL, the canal supply having proved meagre and dirty. In 1855 new works were established above KEW BRIDGE and a six-million-gallon reservoir at

A view of the bridge at Paddington, with passengers being towed down the Grand Junction Canal to Uxbridge in 1801.

CAMPDEN HILL was supplied by a 6–7-mile long main from KEW. In 1896 the construction of two reservoirs at Staines was begun in conjunction with the NEW RIVER and WEST MIDDLESEX WATER COMPANIES. The Metropolitan Water Board took over the functions of the company in 1902 (*see* WATER SUPPLY).

Grand Surrey Canal The chief London canal south of the THAMES. It ran from the SURREY COMMERCIAL DOCKS to CAMBERWELL and was planned originally to reach MITCHAM when it was authorised in 1801. The engineer for the first year was Ralph Dodd and the entrance lock into the THAMES was opened in 1807. The canal never got far beyond PECKHAM. Its use for transport ended in 1836 and it became a line of wharves. The company eventually combined with the Commercial Docks Co. to take over the Surrey Commercial Docks in 1864. In 1908 it was transferred to the PORT OF LONDON AUTHORITY, who closed it in 1971, and it was subsequently drained.

Grand Theatre *21 St John's Hill, Clapham Junction, SW11*. Built to the designs of E.A. Woodrow and opened by Dan Leno in 1900. From then until 1912 it was known as the New Grand Theatre of Varieties, and during 1912–27 as the Grand Theatre of Varieties. It became a cinema in 1950 and a bingo hall in 1973.

Grand Union Canal The original Grand Union Canal was opened in 1814 to link the GRAND JUNCTION and Leicestershire and Northamptonshire Canals, but its narrow locks at Watford and Foxton prevented its use by wide boats. It was purchased in 1894 by the GRAND JUNCTION CANAL CO. which in 1929 joined the REGENT'S CANAL in London, the Warwick and Birmingham, the Warwick and Knapton and the Birmingham and Warwick Junction Canals to form the new Grand Union Canal, with running powers over the Oxford Canal to enable it to link London and Birmingham. This undertaking absorbed the Leicester Navigation, the Loughborough Navigation and the Erewash Canal in 1932. With government aid and at a cost of £1,000,000 vast improvements were carried out in locks and walling between London and Birmingham during the next two years. In 1948 with other waterways it was taken over by the British Transport Commission and in 1963 by the British Waterways Board by whom it is still administered.

The Grange (Museum of Local History) *Neasden, NW10*. In 1810 the century-old stables of a large house called The Grove were converted into a Gothic residence known as The Grange. An L-shaped house was formed, two-storeyed with brick walls 2 ft thick in places. It has windows with Gothic-arched glazing bars and a roof of an unusual double-hipped construction like an inverted W. By the 1860s a two-storeyed gabled porch had been added. The house was a private residence until 1971 when road improvements removed all the outbuildings and the London Borough of BRENT converted The Grange to fulfill a new role as a museum of local history.

Grantham Place *W1*. A short cul-de-sac leading off the east side of OLD PARK LANE. It takes its name from Thomas and John Grantham, building speculators hereabouts in the mid-18th century.

Grapes *76 Narrow Street, E14*. A 16th-century public house surrounded by dockland and holding an early morning licence for dockers. Dickens is said to have used it as the original of the Six Jolly Fellowship Porters in *Our Mutual Friend*. There is a Dickens Room with a balcony giving a very pleasant view of the river.

Graveney A river which rises in UPPER NORWOOD, flows under the London Road at NORBURY, and thence through Lower TOOTING to join the WANDLE in WANDSWORTH on its way to the THAMES.

GRAY'S INN *WC1*. (*See also* INNS OF COURT.) The present site of the Inn was originally occupied by the Manor House of the 'Ancient Manor of Purpoole in Holborn', the London residence of Sir Reginald le Grey, Chief Justice of Chester, who died in 1308. By 1370 the Manor House had become a *hospitium* for lawyers. The area included a windmill and dovecotes with open country to the north. The neighbourhood then contained a number of lakes which have long since vanished. Today a thoroughfare running into GRAY'S INN ROAD opposite Verulam Buildings carries the name Portpool Lane. It is recorded that in 1684 when Nicholas Barbon was building RED LION SQUARE, a little to the west, members of the Inn, resenting the intrusion on the local rural amenities, attacked Barbon's workmen but failed to stop the development. The crest or badge of the Inn is a golden griffin rampant on a black field.

Among the many prominent persons associated with the Inn were Sir William Cecil, 1st Lord Burghley; Nicholas Bacon, keeper of the Great Seal and his more famous son, Francis; Sir James Eyre, Lord Chief Justice; Daniel O'Connell, the Irish statesman who became a student in 1796; Sir Samuel Romilly, the pioneer law reformer and his son, John, Master of the Rolls; T.M. Healey, first Governor-General of the former Irish Free State (1922–8) and Treasurer of the Inn in 1929; Henry Edward Duke, President of the former Probate, Divorce and Admiralty Division of the High Court, who was also Chief Secretary for Ireland (1916–18); Lord Birkenhead, Lord Chancellor; Lords Uthwatt and Devlin, Lords of Appeal in Ordinary; Dame Rose Heilbron, judge of the High Court and Lord Shawcross, Attorney-General in 1945–51 and chief prosecutor at the Nuremberg War Crimes Tribunal. Among literary figures are Sir Philip Sidney, the Elizabethan poet and soldier; William Camden, the historian; Robert Southey, Poet Laureate; Lord Macaulay, who lived at No. 8 South Square; Maurice Baring, the diplomat and novelist, who lived at No. 3 Gray's Inn Place; Hilaire Belloc and Sidney Webb.

Hall. The Hall, which measures 75 ft in length, 35 ft across and 47 ft in height, dates from 1556 and is the centre of the Inn's activities. It contains a notable screen said to be constructed from the wood of a captured Spanish Armada galleon. Although the Hall was destroyed by enemy bombing in May 1941, the screen had been taken to pieces for removal and was rescued largely intact. The oldest of the escutcheons in the windows dates from 1462. The Hall was restored under the supervision of Sir Edward Maufe who was later elected an honorary Bencher. The Hall has been the setting for many celebrated social occasions: Shakespeare's *Comedy of Errors* was first staged here

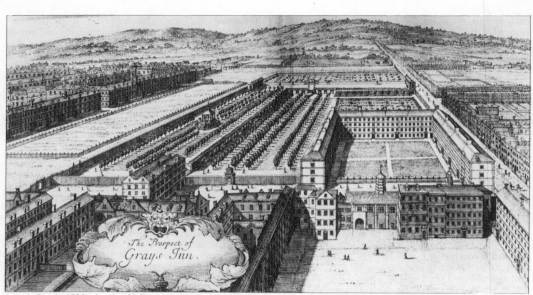

Gray's Inn in 1720, showing Holborn Court, now South Square, and the Hall in the right foreground.

in 1594, the Earl of Southampton, the playwright's patron, then being a member of the Inn. There are portraits of Queen Elizabeth I, Charles I and II, James II, Nicholas and Francis Bacon. The Hall was heated by an open central fire until 1815 when a cast iron stove, removed in 1893, took its place. The Court of Exchequer used to hold out-of-term sittings in the Hall. The Court was absorbed by the High Court in 1881 and hearings removed to the new Royal Courts of Justice in 1883 (*see* LAW COURTS).

Library. The earliest reference to the library, which adjoins the Treasury in South Square, dates from 1555. Rebuilt and enlarged in 1929, with funds supplied by Sir John Holker, a Bencher, it was renamed the Holker Library. In May 1941 it, too, was destroyed by bombs with the loss of 30,000 books. Reconstructed under the supervision of Sir Edward Maufe, it was reopened in 1958 by the Prime Minister, Harold Macmillan, and contains about 36,000 works including many of Commonwealth, American and international law, also a 14th-century copy of Bracton's *De Legibus et Consuetudinibus Angliae* and a number of old chained books. The old records of the inn perished in a fire in the library in 1684.

Chapel. The Chapel has stood on the same site since 1315. When it was rebuilt in 1689, an upper storey containing chambers was omitted. Further restoration took place in 1893. Fortunately, the original stained glass windows had already been removed before the building was destroyed in May 1941. Post-war rebuilding afforded further opportunity to enlarge the Chapel and the original windows were replaced. The east window (1895) commemorates four Archbishops of Canterbury associated with the Inn as members or preachers, John Whitgift, William Juxon, William Laud and William Wake. The pulpit, lectern and pews are of maple wood and were presented to the Inn after the 2nd World War by the Canadian Bar Association. A Roll of Honour listing members who died in both World Wars is on the southern wall.

Squares. The main entrance from HIGH HOLBORN

passes Gray's Inn Chambers (rebuilt 1966) and leads directly into South Square containing the Hall, the Under-Treasurer's Office, Common Room and Library, all four of which were rebuilt after being destroyed by bombing in 1941. The statue on the grass of the square dates from 1912 and commemorates Sir Francis Bacon (*see* STATUES). Charles Dickens as a youth was employed in 1827–8 for a wage of 13s 6d per week as a clerk by an attorney with an office in the former No. 1 Holborn Court, now South Square. Mr Phunky, Mr Pickwick's junior counsel in the case of Bardell v. Pickwick, had chambers close by.

Immediately to the north lies the much larger Gray's Inn Square. Nearly half was destroyed in 1941. The exit to GRAY'S INN ROAD bears the arms of the INNER TEMPLE as a token of the traditional friendship between these Societies (*see* INNER TEMPLE). Mr Perker, solicitor for Mr Pickwick, had his office in Gray's Inn Square. Further north, facing GRAY'S INN ROAD, stand Verulam buildings (1803–11) – Francis Bacon became the 1st Lord Verulam – and to the west of the Walks abutting on THEOBALDS ROAD, Raymond Buildings, named after Lord Chief Justice Sir Thomas Raymond. The Inns of Court School of Law is situated in Gray's Inn Place close to the wrought-iron gates (1723) leading into the Walks from Field Court.

Gardens. Styled 'The Walks', these were laid out by Sir Francis Bacon in 1606 and became very popular in the 17th century with fashionable society and provided a convenient venue for duelling. Samuel Pepys was a frequent visitor. Bacon is believed to have planted the catalpa tree which faces the rear of No. 4 Raymond Buildings.

Most of the accommodation in the Inn is leased to professional tenants – many of them architects and solicitors; barristers occupy less than 20 sets of chambers, although their number is increasing. Many of the top storeys are let as residential flats.

Gray's Inn Road *WC1*. This was the ancient route from the north to the CITY markets. Stow wrote 'this lane is furnished with fair buildings and many tenements on both sides'. General Monck came down the road to restore Charles II. Tom Jones entered into London this way and put up at the Bull and Gate in HOLBORN. Until 1862 it was called Gray's Inn Lane. In 1879–80 it was cleared by the METROPOLITAN BOARD OF WORKS and the roadway was widened. Now it is rather dreary. On the east side used to be the ROYAL FREE HOSPITAL, now moved to HAMPSTEAD. Founded in 1828, it moved into buildings first opened in 1842 as the Light Horse Volunteer Barracks. There were many extensions and the front central block (1895) is still there and now houses the Area Health Authority offices. Opposite is the London Welsh Centre. Nos 192–212, New Printing House Square, were built in 1974 to the designs of R. Seifert and Partners for the offices of *The Times* and *Sunday Times*. The Institute of Laryngology and Otology is at No. 330. At the bottom (HOLBORN) end of the road is the Royal Fusiliers' MEMORIAL. The Eastman Dental Hospital at No. 256 was opened in 1930 and sponsored by George Eastman of Eastman Kodak, Rochester, New York.

Great College Street
SW1. Built in about 1722 and named after WESTMINSTER SCHOOL. It is thought to mark the southern boundary of Thorney Isle, an islet at the mouth of the TYBURN on which the monks built the first church at WESTMINSTER. The precinct wall of the ABBEY dating from about 1374 runs along the north side. At the west end of the street was the King's Slaughter House. Remains of it were found in 1807. Edward Gibbon stayed with his aunt, Mrs Porter, who ran a boarding house in the street, in 1749 and 1758. Nos 16–18 date from 1722. Keats lived at No. 25 in 1819.

Great Cumberland Place
W1. Begun in 1791 on the PORTMAN ESTATE and originally planned as a circus, it was named after George II's son, William Augustus, Duke of Cumberland, the 'butcher' of Culloden. Only a crescent was realised, the central portion of which is today a synagogue.

Great Eastern Hotel
Liverpool Street, EC2. The only hotel in the CITY OF LONDON, the Great Eastern was built close to LIVERPOOL STREET STATION to the designs of Charles E. Barry in 1884. In 1901 a building designed by Colonel Robert Edis was added. It contains an elaborate glass-domed restaurant with dancing sylphs and two Masonic temples. Beneath the hotel was an area called 'the backs' which had tracks and sidings serving the building. A late-night train brought coal for the hotel and took away the hotel refuse and ashes. Sea water was also brought in by train for the sea water baths. There are now 157 bedrooms.

Great Exhibition
1851, Hyde Park. Conceived by Henry Cole when assistant keeper at the PUBLIC RECORD OFFICE and a member of the Council of the Society of Arts of which he was soon to become chairman. In 1850 a Royal Commission was appointed to raise the money. Peel, Gladstone, Russell, the Duke of Devonshire, Cobden, Cubitt, Barry and others sat on it. It was presided over by Prince Albert. Battersea Fields, REGENT'S PARK, PRIMROSE HILL and even the ISLE OF DOGS were suggested as possible sites but eventually HYDE PARK was settled on, much to the horror of *The Times* which forecast that the whole of the park would become 'a bivouac of all vagabonds. Kensington and Belgravia would be uninhabitable and the Season would be ruined.' A competition was held for the design of the building. Over 230 entries were rejected before Joseph Paxton designed his CRYSTAL PALACE, based on the conservatory at Chatsworth where he was superintendent of the gardens. The park's precious trees were incorporated inside the building but so were sparrows, whose droppings spattered the Persian carpets and other exhibits until the Duke of Wellington thought of introducing sparrowhawks. The finished building stood up to the test of gales, hailstorms, 300 workmen jumping in the galleries, and trolleys of cannon balls being trundled up and down.

On 1 May 1851 it was opened by Queen Victoria. A Chinese mandarin suddenly appeared and, after discreet conferences, was put between the Archbishop of Canterbury and the Duke of Wellington. He was later seen showing people round his junk on the THAMES. Queen Victoria came almost every other day in the first three months. The Duke of Wellington took an equal delight in the exhibition and caused a near riot every time he called. Exhibits came from all over the world. There were jewels, including the largest pearl ever found and the Koh-i-Noor diamond, engines of every description, carriages, leather goods, textiles, china, glass and cutlery, including a knife with 300

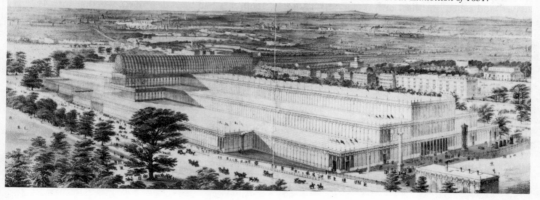

Joseph Paxton's Crystal Palace in its original position in Hyde Park, where it housed the Great Exhibition of 1851.

Cruikshank's image of the world converging upon the Great Exhibition, which was visited by over six million people.

blades. Jones of Dublin sent over a chair of bog yew with arms carved as wolf hounds labelled 'gentle when stroked'. At the intersection of the nave and transepts was a glass fountain 27 ft high which weighed 11 tons. On 15 October the exhibition closed, to the strains of the National Anthem. It had been visited by over six million people, including one woman of 84 who had walked from Cornwall. Three women had been assaulted by a party of Welsh abstainers. £356,000 had been taken at the door and this went towards setting up the South Kensington Arts Centre. The building was taken down in 1852 and re-erected as the CRYSTAL PALACE at SYDENHAM. Prince Albert's model dwelling house was moved to KENNINGTON PARK and the statue of Richard the Lionheart, cast in bronze (*see* STATUES), was re-erected in OLD PALACE YARD. Only the gates stayed in HYDE PARK.

Great Fire *1666*. A little before two o'clock on the night of 2 September 1666 a workman in Farriner's baking house smelt smoke and aroused the household. The baker, his wife and child hurried over the rooftops to safety but their maid, too timid to follow, was burned to death. Helped by a strong wind, the flames spread quickly. The parish constable and watchmen arrived and called out the Lord Mayor, Sir Thomas Bloodworth, who thought it not worth his attention and went back to bed, grumpily observing, 'Pish! A woman might piss it out!'

Later that morning Samuel Pepys found that 300 houses, half LONDON BRIDGE and several churches had disappeared. He watched the riverside warehouses spew wine and spirits into the river, saw people scurrying hither and thither, moving their possessions at the last minute from relative's house to relative's house as each in its turn was threatened. Even the pigeons were reluctant to leave their perches and hovered about until they burned their wings and fell down. Off to WHITEHALL he went, where he was ushered into the presence of the King and his brother James, Duke of York. They had not heard about the fire and seemed much troubled. The King commanded Pepys to tell

the LORD MAYOR to pull down houses in the path of the fire. Pepys found the LORD MAYOR in CANNING STREET 'like a man spent, with a handkerchief about his neck'. On receiving the King's message he cried 'like a fainting woman, "Lord what can I do? I am spent, people will not obey me. I have been pulling down houses but the fire overtakes us faster than we can do it."' That night Pepys went to a little ale house on Bankside and 'there staid till it was dark and saw one entire arch of fire from this to the other side of the bridge and in a bow up the hill above a mile long.'

Next morning at four, Pepys in his nightshirt drove with his valuables to Sir William Rider's house at BETHNAL GREEN. The King and his Council had been up early too and had put the Duke of York in charge of fire-fighting operations. Fire posts manned by civilians, constables and soldiers were set up round the City. Frenchmen, Dutchmen and Papists were locked up for their own protection as rumour grew of a foreign plot. William Taswell, a Westminster schoolboy, saw a Frenchman hit over the head with an iron bar and his brother saw another almost dismembered. Later that morning Pepys found a boat to move the rest of his furniture downstream and buried his wine and Parmesan cheese in the garden. That day the ROYAL EXCHANGE was burned. By 4 September half the CITY had gone. The GUILDHALL and ST PAUL'S were then threatened. Attempts were made to halt the fire at the FLEET RIVER by pulling down houses on either side; but the flames bridged the gap and enveloped BRIDEWELL, the City's corn store, ST BRIDE'S CHURCH and INNER TEMPLE HALL. The Queen arranged to leave for HAMPTON COURT early the next morning. The navy were brought in to blow up houses with gunpowder in TOWER STREET and this succeeded in stopping the flames before the TOWER.

Pepys decided to take his gold and his wife to WOOLWICH. When he returned he expected to see his house gone but it had survived. He climbed the steeple of ALL HALLOWS BARKING and there saw the saddest sight of desolation. 'Everywhere great fires, oil cellars and brimstone and other things burning. The wind had dropped but still there was a blaze at the TEMPLE, HOLBORN and CRIPPLEGATE where the King himself was seen helping the soldiers.'

By the end of the day the worst was over. Another outbreak in the TEMPLE that night was dealt with by the inmates, the Duke of York and his gunpowder being locked out. Nearly 400 acres had been burned within the CITY walls and 63 acres outside them; 87 churches had been destroyed, together with 44 livery halls and 13,200 houses, but miraculously only nine lives had been lost. The refugees camped on the fields outside the City; some under tents, others under miserable huts and hovels with a rag or any necessary utensils, bed or board. The King rode out to speak to them, quelling their fears of a foreign plot, and promised to provide them with bread. Robert Hubert, a Frenchman, confessed to setting fire to the baker's shop and was hanged at TYBURN. Local government was restored as soon as possible. The COURT OF COMMON COUNCIL and the Court of ALDERMEN met at GRESHAM COLLEGE, the CUSTOM HOUSE was set up at Lord Bayning's house in MARK LANE, the Excise Office in SOUTHAMPTON FIELDS, the Hearth Tax Office in LEADENHALL STREET, the Post Office in Brydges Street and the King's Weigh House on the site of

LONDON.

Contemporary engraving of the Great Fire of 1666, which destroyed almost 400 acres within the City walls.

ST ANDREW HUBBARD. A temporary building was put up in the GUILDHALL for the courts. Prisoners and debtors were housed in ALDERSGATE STREET.

Rebuilding was forbidden until owners had cleared debris from the roadway and established their claims to the land, and a Committee had considered redevelopment plans, among which were those of Christopher Wren and John Evelyn. Evelyn wanted an Italianate city of piazzas and wide streets with a quay along the river. Wren had similar ideas, but intended turning the FLEET into a canal and banishing noisy trades from the CITY. Both were rejected as impractical for a commercial city. By November the commissioners had drawn up Bills to give the City authorities power to deal with drainage, water supply and street cleaning. A coal tax was levied to raise revenue for rebuilding public buildings. Private houses were to be rebuilt with 'two storeys for bylanes, three storeys along the river and for streets and lanes of note, four storeys for high streets and mansion houses for citizens of extraordinary quality'. By 1668 the BUTCHERS, CUTLERS and INNHOLDERS had finished their new Halls. By 1669 the GUILDHALL was finished and the PLASTERERS', PEWTERERS', GOLD-SMITHS' and PAINTER-STAINERS' HALLS. In 1670 14 new churches were begun. Soon afterward the CUS-TOM HOUSE, BLACKWELL HALL and the ROYAL EX-CHANGE were finished. By 1672 most of the private houses were completed and life and trade had revived. The MONUMENT, built by Wren in 1671–7, commemorates this Great Fire.

Great George Street *SW1*. Westward extension of BRIDGE STREET, built in 1752–7. One original façade is left, No. 11, part of the ROYAL INSTITUTION OF CHARTERED SURVEYORS, dating from 1756. The Institution's other building was designed by Alfred Waterhouse in 1896–8. Most of the south side was destroyed in 1806 in an improvement scheme. In 1910 the north side was demolished to make way for a large block of government offices designed by J.W. Brydon and Sir Henry Tanner. In 1912 Nos 2–7 were replaced by the INSTITUTION OF CIVIL ENGINEERS, designed by James Miller. William Cubitt, the engineer, lived at No. 6 in 1837–55; Thomas Babington Macaulay at No. 12 in 1839–40; John Wilkes at No. 13 in 1757–63; Robert Peel at No. 36 in 1813; Robert Stephenson at No. 24 in 1857–9; Sir Charles Barry at No. 32 in 1859–70. Lord Byron lay in state for two days at No. 25 in 1824. The NATIONAL PORTRAIT GALLERY was at No. 29 in 1859–70.

Great Globe *Leicester Square*. A large rotunda designed by H.R. Abraham and opened in the Square on 2 June 1851, a month after the opening of the GREAT EXHIBITION. The idea of its construction was conceived by James Wyld, the noted geographer, who

James Wyld's huge model of the earth's surface, which was constructed as the Great Globe in Leicester Square in 1851.

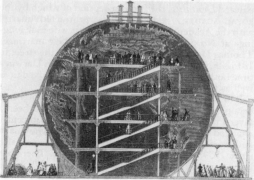

had decided that 'the congregation in London of the different nations and races of our empire and the world' would be 'the proper moment for the completion of a great model of the Earth's surface'. The globe, 40 ft in diameter and 60 ft high, was the largest which had ever been constructed. It was lit by gas and viewed from a four-stage gallery rising from the centre of the floor.

Upon its interior side were 'delineated the physical features of the earth, the horizontal surface being on the scale of an inch to ten miles, and mountains, shown by mechanical devices, on thrice that scale. . . . The walls of the circular passages were hung with the finest maps, and atlases, globes and geographical works were displayed upon tables.' The Globe remained one of the principal attractions of LEICESTER SQUARE for ten years until it was sold, in 1862, to a demolition contractor.

Great James Street *WC1*. The continuation north of THEOBALDS ROAD from BEDFORD ROW. Narrower than the latter, but an elegant and almost complete street of the 1720s. It was named after James Burgess who helped George Brownlow Doughty and his wife, Frances, develop the area. The poet Swinburne lived here in 1872–5 and 1877–8; and Dorothy Sayers occupied a house in the street for a time, as did Leonard and Virginia Woolf and T.S. Eliot. Francis and Vera Meynell ran the Nonesuch Press here in 1924–36.

Great Marlborough Street *W1*. Built at the beginning of the 18th century and named after John Churchill, 1st Duke of Marlborough, whose victory at Blenheim was won in 1704. John Macky, writing in 1714, said, 'It surpasses anything that is called a street in the magnificence of its buildings and gardens and is inhabited by all prime quality.' A less enthusiastic observer 20 years later, however, thought that its character, as 'one of the finest streets' in Europe, must have been due to its length and breadth as the buildings, in his opinion, were 'trifling and inconsiderable'. Many of them were, nevertheless, occupied by the 'prime quality' as Macky had said. Five peers were living here in 1716, including the 1st Earl of Scarborough at No. 12, the least altered of the old houses in the street, which is now a hotchpotch of all kinds of scales and materials.

Other distinguished residents have been Henry Cavendish, the scientist, in 1782–4; Mrs Siddons, the actress, during 1790–1804; Sir Walter Farquhar, the physician, in 1771–97; and Benjamin Robert Haydon, the historical painter, in 1808–17. It was here that he painted *Dentalus*, the frigid reception of which by the ROYAL ACADEMY resulted in his protracted quarrel with the Academicians. Nelson and his wife took lodgings at No. 10 for a time soon after their marriage. Thomas Hardwick, the architect, lived in the street in 1815–25, and Charles Darwin in 1837–8. In Darwin's time both architects and medical men had moved in as well as tailors.

The Marlborough Head public house, which had occupied a site at Nos 37–38, where there had been a tavern of that name since at least 1739, has recently changed its name to the Dog and Trumpet. The Coach and Horses at No. 1, where there has been a tavern also since 1739, still trades under its old name. There has been a police station in the street since 1793; the present Magistrates' Court is at Nos 20–21 in a building erected to the designs of J.D. Butler in 1913. Appropriately, the anatomist, Joshua Brookes, whose brother kept the menagerie in EXETER CHANGE, had his museum here (1786–98) and exhibited in it the bodies of criminals, many of whom had been sentenced in the nearby building. The LONDON COLLEGE OF MUSIC still occupies a building at No. 47 (formerly No. 42) which, although much altered, dates from the early 18th century and has been occupied by the College since 1896. A.W. Blomfield's Church of St John the Baptist which was built in 1885 was, however, demolished in 1937.

The REGENT STREET end of Great Marlborough Street is now marked by two oddly contrasting buildings: the Tudor extravagance of LIBERTY'S, with its leaded windows, hand-made roofing tiles and oak timbers from ancient men-of-war, built to the designs of E.T. and E.S. Hall in 1922–3; and the modernistic Ideal House designed in 1928 by the American architect Raymond Hood (in association with Gordon Jeeves), with its black granite façade decorated with gilt floral mobiles. James Galt and Co, the toy shop at Nos 30–31, is by John Burnet, Tait and Partners (1961).

Great Newport Street *WC2*. One of the first streets to be built in the area, it was named after Mountjoy Blount, Earl of Newport, whose house faced on to what is now LITTLE NEWPORT STREET. The earliest houses were built soon after 1612 when the 2nd Earl of Salisbury granted to John Waller, a yeoman of Sussex, a lease on condition that he would 'sett up severall substantiall and well built dwelling houses'. These cannot have been very satisfactorily constructed for, by 1650, they were occupied by poor tenants who had allowed them to 'go to ruine'. Lord Salisbury, therefore, bought the remainder of the lease from Waller's heirs and granted a new lease to Richard Ryder, later Master Carpenter to Charles II, who contracted to spend a large sum of money on new buildings. This resulted in the north side of the street becoming very fashionable. Oliver St John, 2nd Earl of Bolingbroke, lived here after the Restoration. So did Elizabeth, Countess of Holland, the 1st Earl of Carlisle, the 1st Viscount Townshend, the widow of the 3rd Earl of Anglesey, and the 1st Earl of Halifax. In 1720 Strype wrote that the north side 'hath far the Best Buildings and is inhabited by Gentry; whereas, on the other side dwell ordinary Tradespeople, of which several are of the French Nation.' Later on in the 18th century, several artists came to live in the street. One of these was Sir Joshua Reynolds, who had a house on the site of Nos 10–11 during 1754–60, having moved from apartments in Sir James Thornhill's old house at 104 ST MARTIN'S LANE where he had been joined by his youngest sister, Frances, who kept house for him for many years. Other artists living in the street in the 18th century included Johann Zoffany in 1779, George Romney during 1768–9 and Sir Robert Ker Porter in 1796–9. Josiah Wedgwood, the potter, had a showroom on the corner of Upper St Martin's Lane during 1768–74. It was designed by Joseph Pickford and demolished when UPPER ST MARTIN'S LANE was widened in 1843–6. The one house to survive in the street is No. 5, but this has been defaced by black faience tiling. Next door is the ARTS THEATRE.

Great North Road From Roman times until the 17th century the main road from London to York ran through HIGHGATE, FINCHLEY, Hatfield, Welwyn, Stevenage and Baldock, following the line of the present A10 road and by-passing Ware. In view of the latter's importance as a market town travellers began to deviate from the York Road, and Pepys in 1660 and Defoe in the 1720s were among those who used a road which passed through Ware and which was called the Great North Road. This was badly maintained, narrow and infested by highwaymen until the early 19th century, but by the mid-20th century had become a first-class highway. It enters the CITY from the south at LONDON BRIDGE, proceeding over the Bridge, up KING WILLIAM STREET, via Prince's Street to MOORGATE, thence by way of ISLINGTON, HIGHGATE and FINCHLEY to BARNET and beyond.

Great Northern Hotel *King's Cross, N1.* Set apart from KING'S CROSS STATION, the crescent-shaped building by Lewis Cubitt was opened in 1854. There are 66 bedrooms.

Great Ormond Street *WC1.* Extends from QUEEN SQUARE to MILLMAN STREET. It was probably named after James Butler, the Royalist Commander in Ireland, created Duke of Ormonde at the Restoration. Several early 18th-century houses remain. Nos 41 and 43 have fluted Ionic columns and elaborate segmental pediments. Nos 55 and 57, now the Society for the Protection of Ancient Buildings, are probably by Barbon, who is remembered in Barbon Close opposite the HOSPITAL FOR SICK CHILDREN. The east end of the south side was built in 1720 and carefully restored in 1980. Powis Place marks the site of Powis House, the design for which was published in the first volume of *Vitruvius Britannicus.* It was built at the end of the 17th century for the 2nd Marquess of Powis. It then became the French Embassy, was burned down in 1713, and rebuilt in a grand style at the expense of the French monarchy. On the roof it had a fish pond which could be used as a reservoir in case of fire. Later, from 1764 to 1783, it became the Spanish Embassy. It was demolished towards the end of the 18th century. The Working Men's College was in the street from 1857–1906. (It then moved to Crowndale Road, ST PANCRAS.) John Howard, the prison reformer, lived at No. 23 from 1777 till his death in 1790. No.45, now the Migraine Trust, was where Lord Thurlow, Lord Chancellor, was living in 1784 when the Great Seal was stolen from his house. The north side from LAMB'S CONDUIT STREET to QUEEN SQUARE is taken up by the HOSPITAL FOR SICK CHILDREN and the ROYAL LONDON HOMEOPATHIC HOSPITAL. Thomas Babington Macaulay, the historian, lived for a time in a house on the site which was occupied by his father, Zachary, before taking chambers in GRAY'S INN.

Great Peter Street *SW1.* Extends from the west end of HORSEFERRY ROAD to MILLBANK. WESTMINSTER ABBEY is the Abbey of St Peter's. St Matthew's Church on the north side was built to the designs of Sir George Gilbert Scott in 1849–51; the Lady Chapel is by Sir Ninian Comper, 1892.

Great Plague *1664–5.* 'In the middle of the Christmas Holy-Days', in 1664, Dr Nathaniel Hodges (born in Kensington, educated at Oxford and Cambridge and then practising in WATLING STREET) 'was called to a young man in a Fever, who after two days course of alexiterial medicines, had two Risings about the bigness of a Nytmeg broke out, one on each Thigh'.

These black soft swellings were soon to become familiar as 'plague tokens' and almost certain signs of death, for although Dr Hodges's patient recovered, within the next 18 months 68,576 others were to die of plague in London. In fact, the total was probably nearer 100,000, for public records were inaccurate, and to allay public alarm the weekly 'BILLS OF MORTALITY' sometimes gave causes of death as 'dropsy', 'griping of the guts', 'winde', 'worms', 'French pox', 'frighted', and 'lethargy'. Halfway through the epidemic the parish clerk of ST OLAVE'S, HART STREET, admitted to Samuel Pepys that: 'There died nine this week, though I have returned only six.'

From November 1664 until the following March London lay in the grip of almost continual black frost; even the THAMES was frozen and this cold weather initially held the plague in check. During the second week of April 1665, 398 were officially admitted to have died of plague. By the end of April Lord Clarendon, the Lord Chancellor, noted that 'ancient men', who remembered earlier plague epidemics in 1636 and 1647, were prudently moving their families out of the CITY, and the government realised that London faced a serious epidemic, far worse than these earlier visitations. Powers were given for Justices of the Peace in the CITY and WESTMINSTER to acquire ground to build new pest-houses, as hospitals were called, with special roads to reach them. Three more were built in MARYLEBONE, Soho Fields and STEPNEY. Overcrowding in the wards of all London hospitals was soon so great that visitors had to walk across the beds instead of round them.

King Charles II prorogued Parliament until September – when it was hoped that the epidemic would be over – because many members were anxious to be out of London 'so that they might not hazard themselves'.

May and June were unusually warm months and the plague spread rapidly. Clergymen abandoned their parishes, doctors their patients, and the rich their servants. Everyone who could left London. In June, Samuel Pepys walked up DRURY LANE 'on the hottest day that ever I felt in my life', and saw houses marked with the plague sign: a crude red cross on the front doors.

The few doctors and chemists still remaining in London worked late every night visiting patients and ordering fires to be burned in houses and public places to fumigate the air. Each evening Dr Hodges drank a glass of sack 'to dissipate any Lodgment of the Infection', and although he twice had plague symptoms, he survived. William Boghurst, an apothecary in ST GILES-IN-THE-FIELDS, also refused to leave London and was to dress as many as 40 sores a day.

Servants dismissed by employers who had left London were recruited to drive 'dead-carts' containing the corpses of plague victims. Many London households had contained 50 servants, and since not all could find such work, gangs of unemployed roamed the streets, looting abandoned houses or robbing pedestrians.

Soon graveyards were filled. With layers of bodies only inches beneath the earth, the air stank with the smell of death. The authorities ordered that huge holes should be dug in vacant patches of earth, lined with quicklime, for mass graves or plague-pits.

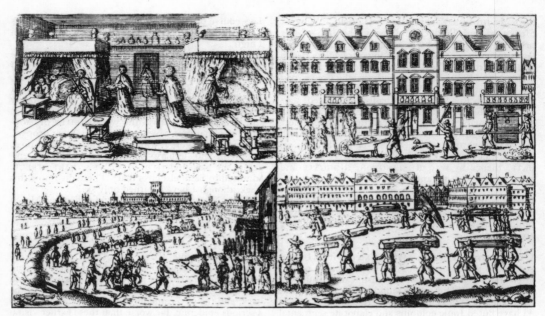

This contemporary broadsheet of the Great Plague shows plague victims in bed, with the dead being carted away.

Grave-diggers, often drunk, worked in shifts, day and night. Even so, it was impossible to bury all the corpses within 24 hours of death, and some lay stacked like wax figures in the streets for two or three days.

The INNS OF COURT were deserted; many shopkeepers went bankrupt for lack of customers. The LORD MAYOR and the Justices of the Peace ordered that all dogs and cats should be killed on the theory that they might spread the plague. Official exterminators were paid 2d for each body – two days' wages for an ordinary labourer. Samuel Pepys calculated that 40,000 dogs and perhaps five times as many cats were destroyed within days. Some were cornered in the streets and clubbed while others were fed poisoned meat, and their rotting corpses added to the general putrefaction. With the removal of so many cats, the real carriers of the plague multiplied. These were the rats, who had fleas on their feet.

Quacks took a calculated risk in remaining, and compounded potions from pepper, urine and salt. Others sold amulets and cordials against the plague or undertook purging, bleeding or crude surgery on plague 'tokens'. Soon these men were among the richest left in London.

Seven hundred and twenty-five Londoners died from plague during the last week of June; on 29 June King Charles and his courtiers left for HAMPTON COURT. By the middle of July more than 1000 were dying each week. In the first week in August the death roll increased to 2020.

In the absence of the King, central government and the administration of London outside the City walls became the responsibility of the Duke of Albemarle. The CITY, which contained 97 parishes, was largely administered by the LORD MAYOR, under whose direction the authorities acted harshly to reduce casualties. All lodgers, visitors, guests and relatives who usually stayed with householders were ordered to leave; they could die where they pleased, so long as they did not die within the CITY boundaries.

When plague was diagnosed in a house everyone was locked inside for 40 days once the infected patients had either recovered or died. Watchmen with sharpened halberds stood guard day and night outside front doors to enforce these orders. Sometimes neighbours ripped down plague notices and overcame these guards to set the inmates free, for conditions inside these locked houses were appalling.

Manufactories closed because coaling coasters from Newcastle would not put into the PORT OF LONDON. Thousands of craftsmen and apprentices were therefore out of work – and also driven from their lodgings by a City ordinance which ruled that anyone found taking in a lodger in the CITY faced the punishment of having their house shut up, as though infected with the plague.

Grass and weeds sprouted in the streets. The carcasses of dogs, cats, pigs and horses swelled up and burst under the summer sun. All day the dead carts trundled to the shouts of their drivers: 'Bring out your dead!'

As the virulence of the plague increased, country towns and villages, which had welcomed earlier refugees because they could fleece them, now posted guards with firearms to turn away all who might have come from London. Guildford magistrates fitted lids and padlocks on their wells to prevent Londoners from drawing water. In Oxford, a constant night watch was set on the four entrances to the city to prevent refugees entering. Letters arriving in the country from London were washed or heated in front of a fire before being read, in an attempt to disinfect them. Thousands of refugees from London wandered wretchedly around the countryside, being pelted with stones and manure. Near Dorchester, a Londoner crawled into a farm hut to die, presumably from plague. So great was the horror of its contagion that locals dug a vast pit into which they tipped the whole building with the corpse inside, rather than move the body.

More than 10,000 Londoners took to the THAMES and lived on boats moored in mid-river. A higher proportion of these survived than any others.

During August and September, panic among sufferers in London became so great that some leaped from their beds and stood 'crying and roaring at their windows', as one doctor reported. Others ran into the streets foaming at the mouth, naked and delirious, and flung themselves into the CRIPPLEGATE plague-pit. Relatives restrained many by lashing them to their beds with ropes or chains.

By the late summer, many grave-diggers and 'dead-cart' drivers were infected; until then, they had appeared curiously immune. Some died at the reins of their carts which, stacked with corpses, moved on aimlessly at the whim of the horses.

During the third week in September, 8297 were officially admitted to have died from plague; Dr Hodges calculated that a truer figure would be 12,000 and the French Ambassador reported to Paris that in his opinion the total was 14,000.

Suddenly the casualties declined. In the last week of September, 4929 died. By the same week in November, the total was down to 900. Although this was partly because of cold weather, evacuees now began to return to a virtually deserted capital. They found forges and manufactories still empty and boarded up, as were the houses in the fashionable areas of COVENT GARDEN and WESTMINSTER. The LORD MAYOR threatened to break into them and seize goods unless the absent owners paid a rate of about 2s towards the cost of burning fires in the streets to fumigate them. On Christmas morning, Samuel Pepys was surprised to see a wedding in progress. He also bought two barrels of oysters from a shop in Great Church Street; life was slowly returning to normal, though a heavy, sweet smell of putrefaction still hung over London like a cloud. It was proposed that the graves should be covered with thousands of tons of lime, but this would have taken weeks to dig out from the chalk pits in Kent and bring to London by barges or carts. Nothing was done, and the smell drifted away as the bodies decayed.

On 1 February 1666 King Charles felt it safe to return to ST JAMES'S to the peal of church bells. As the sovereign's flight had precipitated a mass evacuation of wealthy citizens, so his return encouraged others to do likewise. London soon recovered its usual bustle. But within months the GREAT FIRE was to prove as damaging in terms of property as the plague had been in terms of human life.

A legacy of the plague is the nursery rhyme:

> Ring-a-ring o'roses
> A pocket full of posies
> A-tishoo! A-tishoo!
> We all fall down.

The roses refer to the first rosy-coloured rash, and the ring signifies the round 'tokens' which confirmed the presence of the plague and were usually a sign of approaching death. The posies were herbs and spices that some people carried to sweeten the air. 'A-tishoo! A-tishoo!' refers to sneezing, a common symptom of those close to death.

Great Portland Street *W1*. First rated as John Street in 1726, it runs from north to south across the

PORTLAND ESTATE. It is today lined with wholesale dress show-rooms and offices. James Boswell died in a house on the site of No. 122 in 1795, and Carl Maria von Weber at No. 91 in 1826. Leigh Hunt lived at No. 98 in 1812, and David Wilkie at No. 117 in 1808–9. Pagani's Restaurant at No. 42, with a frontage by Beresford Pite (1903), has been demolished.

Great Pulteney Street *W1*. Built on Sir William Pulteney's estate in the early 18th century, 13 of the original houses survive: Nos 8–13, 23 and 35–40. Few of them were ever occupied by the kind of aristocratic families who came to live elsewhere in the area at this time. Nor has it ever been identified with any particular trade, though Jacob Kirkman, founder of the firm of harpsichord and pianoforte manufacturers, was living at No. 17 between 1739 and 1750, and Burkhardt Tschudi, another harpsichord manufacturer whose son-in-law, John Broadwood, carried on the family business – which continued in the street until 1904 – was living at No. 32 in 1743–74. Josef Haydn was staying at No. 18 in 1791–2. Many of the buildings in the street are now used as offices by firms in the clothing and textile trades.

Great Queen Street *WC2*. Described in the 18th century as the 'first regular street in London', its houses were built in the 1630s and early 1640s. The architect who designed them has been named variously as Peter Mills, Bricklayer to the CITY OF LONDON, John Webb and Inigo Jones. All these houses have now disappeared but some early 18th-century houses remain. Among the people who lived here were Thomas Fairfax, Parliamentary general, in 1647; Lord Chancellor Finch in 1676 when the Mace and Purse were stolen from him; Judge Jeffreys in 1685–7; Thomas Arne, composer of 'Rule Britannia', in 1735–48 and Mary 'Perdita' Robinson, actress, Gainsborough's model and mistress of the Prince of Wales, in 1774. In 1711–20 the first Academy of Drawing and Painting had premises here. Henry Fuseli lived at No. 7 in 1803. William Blake was apprenticed to an engraver at No. 31 in 1771–8. Other distinguished residents were Sir Godfrey Kneller in 1702–23; Sheridan in 1777–82, James Boswell in 1786–8, John Opie, the painter, in 1783–92 and R.H. Barham, author of *The Ingoldsby Legends*, at No. 51 in 1821–4. FREEMASONS' HALL is on the corner of Wild Street.

Great Russell Street *WC1*. In 1101 the land to the south was granted to the Leper Hospital of St Giles (*see* ST GILES IN THE FIELDS), and one of its buildings occupied a site which is now the corner of Great Russell Street and MUSEUM STREET. From the 13th century the Russell family owned all the surrounding land (*see* BLOOMSBURY). In 1662 they leased out building sites along a proposed street line, and the first houses were built in the 1670s. In a map of 1670 it is designated Russell Street, and in another of 1674 Great Russell Street. SOUTHAMPTON HOUSE was completed in about 1657, MONTAGUE HOUSE in 1679 and Thanet House in 1686. From then on much building took place and Strype speaks of it in 1720 as 'a very handsome and well built street . . . an aristocratic area'. In 1777 John Nash, then 25, took a lease on the corner of BLOOMSBURY SQUARE and built two elegant houses with Corinthian pilasters facing the square, and a terrace of six smaller ones along the south side of

Great Russell Street, all with stucco exteriors. Nash himself occupied the one on the corner of Bury Place from 1778 to 1781, but the leases failed to sell and he was declared bankrupt in 1783. They are his first buildings and survive today.

From 1823 onwards the rebuilding and extension of the BRITISH MUSEUM resulted in the progressive replacement of the 17th- and 18th-century houses by blocks of flats like Great Russell Mansions, designed by Hayward in 1893, and respectable family hotels with literary overtones such as the Thackeray (later the YMCA's Helen Graham House), also by Hayward (1888), and two others designed by Sir Thomas Rhind, the Ivanhoe (1910) and the Kenilworth (the last two requisitioned as homes for Maltese families during the 2nd World War). The Central London YOUNG MEN'S CHRISTIAN ASSOCIATION, built in 1911 to the design of R. Plumbe in bulbous, *fin de siècle* baroque with naked stone ladies above the door, was replaced in 1976 by a very angular building designed by the Elsworth Sykes Partnership. In contrast, the YOUNG WOMEN'S CHRISTIAN ASSOCIATION opposite is dignified and Neo-Georgian (1930–2, by Sir Edwin Lutyens). Next door is Congress House (1958) by D. du R. Aberdeen, the headquarters of the TRADES UNION CONGRESS.

At No. 14 lived Charles Kitterbell, 'a small sharp man with an extraordinarily large head and a cast in his eye', as related in Dickens's *Sketches by Boz*; and at No. 46 Randolph Caldecott, the Victorian book illustrator, in 1872–86. It was also the office of A.E. Richardson (later Sir Albert). C. Lovett-Gill lived at No. 47 in 1908–13. Douglas Cockerell, the bookbinder, was at No. 50 from 1898 to 1902, as were George B. Sowerby and his son, conchologists and suppliers of natural history specimens, in 1842–84. Lewis Gruner, adviser to the Prince Consort, was at No. 59 in 1846. No. 72, then No. 43, was occupied by Jones and Willis, church decorators working for Butterfield, Street, Burges and others, from 1862 to about 1910. No. 73 was the early office of the influential Art Union of London; George Godwin, later editor of *The Builder*, was its first secretary in about 1840. At No. 79, or possibly 89, lived John Philip Kemble, the Shakespearean actor, from 1802 to 1816. George du Maurier was at No. 91 in 1863–8. Nos 98–99, Thanet House, was built in 1686. A possible early occupant was the son of Christopher Wren, also Christopher. Topham Beauclerk took it in 1778. He had a library of 30,000 volumes housed in a building which, Horace Walpole remarked, 'reaches halfway to Highgate'. His wife, Lady Diana Beauclerk, was a much admired amateur artist. After his death in 1780 the house was divided into two. In 1821, the area having become intellectual rather than fashionable, Thomas Cubitt divided the house yet again and rebuilt the façade. In the 1920s and 1930s it was the office of Heinemann, the publishers. Auguste Charles Pugin moved to No. 106 in 1823 and started a school for architectural draughtsmen of whom the most famous was his son, Augustus Welby Pugin. The Museum Tavern, refuge over the years of poets and scholars, appears in the first London street directory of 1842 as the British Museum, and continued to be known thus until 1873.

Great St Helen's *EC3*. The original site of CROSBY HALL. Part of it was once known as Crosby Street. It takes its name from ST HELEN'S PRIORY.

Great Scotland Yard *Whitehall, SW1*. Named after a house given to Kenneth III of Scotland by King Edgar when he came to pay homage in 959. Margaret, widow of James IV and sister of Henry VIII, was the last member of the Scottish royal family to stay here. By James I's Act of Union the buildings were converted to offices. Inigo Jones is said to have lived here for a time as Surveyor-General. During the Commonwealth he and Nicholas Stone, the sculptor, buried their money in the garden for safe keeping but later moved it to LAMBETH Marsh. Milton had lodgings in Scotland Yard while he was Cromwell's Latin Secretary. In 1829 a police station was established here which eventually became the headquarters of the Metropolitan Police Force until they moved to NEW SCOTLAND YARD on the VICTORIA EMBANKMENT in 1891. The Civil Service Club is at Nos 13–15.

Great Smith Street *SW1*. Takes its name from Sir James Smith, the ground landlord, who had it laid out in about 1700. There was a TURNPIKE here in the early 19th century. Some of Keats's letters to Fanny Brawne were written from an address in this street. No. 35 was the site of the Architectural Museum (*see* ARCHITECTURAL ASSOCIATION). The public library, opened in 1857 in the former Mechanics' Institute, was the first free public library in London. The present building, designed by F.J. Smith, was opened in 1893, and housed Dean Stanley's bequest (1881) of 3,200 books.

Great Stink The epithet bestowed upon an insupportable stench created in 1858 by a combination of an unusually hot, dry summer and the newly installed sewers which belched into the THAMES. The stench was so bad that river excursions had to be stopped and the windows of the HOUSES OF PARLIAMENT draped with sheets soaked in chloride of lime. Nobody went near the river unless they had to. The same problem occurred occasionally until the late 1860s when Bazalgette's drainage system came into operation. (*See* DRAINS AND SEWERS.)

Great Swan Alley *EC2*. On 6 January 1661 Thomas Venner, a wine cooper, preached to a congregation of Fifth Monarchy Saints in a meetinghouse here urging them to arm themselves and seize the kingdom. For days they ran round the CITY murdering and looting. By 12 January Venner had been caught and tried. He was hanged, drawn and quartered in front of the meeting-house.

Great Titchfield Street *W1*. First rated in 1740 it takes its name from a subsidiary title of the Bentinck family, who were Marquesses of Titchfield in Hampshire as well as Dukes of Portland. Two young musicians were lodging in the street in the 1840s, Frederick Nicholls Crouch, the composer of *Kathleen Mavourneen*, in 1843, and from 1837–41 (in Portland Chambers) William Sterndale Bennett, whose genius as a composer was stifled beneath the load of professional teaching which he undertook. Thomas De Quincey, author of *Confessions of an Opium Eater*, lodged at No. 82; Richard Wilson, the landscape painter, at No. 85 in 1779. Another Academician, Joseph Bonomi, was at No. 76 during 1787–1806. And Ezra Pound evidently passed through at some time between the two World Wars, for in Canto LXXX we read of a character stewing with rage concerning the landlady's *doings* with a lodger unnamed

az waz near Gt Titchfield St next door to the pub 'married wumman, you couldn't fool her'.

Great Tower Street *EC3*. A public house, the Czar's Head, formerly known as the Czar of Muscovy, which used to stand at No. 48 was frequented by Peter the Great when he was learning ship-building at DEPTFORD. William Beckford lived in the street when he was Lord Mayor. ALL HALLOWS, BARKING is on the corner of TOWER HILL. At No. 26 is Christ's Hospital College, the headquarters of CHRIST'S HOSPITAL, and Christ's Hospital Club.

Great Trinity Lane *EC4*. Beaver House here is the London headquarters of the Hudson's Bay Company, originally founded for the purpose of importing the furs and skins obtained from the Indians of British North America. In 1670 Charles II granted a charter to Prince Rupert and 17 noblemen and gentlemen, incorporating them as the 'Foreman and Company of Adventurers of England trading into Hudson's Bay.' In 1821 the Company was amalgamated with the North-West Fur Company of Montreal. In 1870 the possessions of the Company were incorporated with the Dominion of Canada and the headquarters were transferred to Winnipeg, but the London office still auctions 50 different kinds of fur, the smell of the preservative used on the skins pervading the entire area.

Great Turnstile *WC1*. A narrow street leading from HOLBORN into LINCOLN'S INN FIELDS. This and Little Turnstile were mentioned in Tudor times. The old turning stiles prevented grazing cattle from straying on to the highway. Later they probably kept animals being driven to market from wandering into LINCOLN'S INN. From 1750 to 1760 John Smeaton, builder of the Eddystone lighthouse, kept a shop here for making and selling scientific instruments. The offices of the *New Statesman* (founded in 1913) were for many years at No. 10.

Great West Road Built to relieve congestion on the main roads through CHISWICK, BRENTFORD and HOUNSLOW. It had been talked of since early in the 19th century when Brentford High Street was thought inadequate for the then horse-drawn traffic. The first part, opened in 1925, left Chiswick High Road beside Gunnersbury Avenue where the Chiswick Flyover is now. The completion of this section through BRENTFORD and HOUNSLOW was followed by the development of what was often called the 'golden mile' because of the many successful factories which had been built on either side of the Great West Road. These mostly belonged to firms whose products were household names such as Firestone, Pyrene and Gillette. These factories, built in the late 1920s and early 1930s, many with lawns in front, were at that time regarded rather critically as examples of 'modern' architecture and disliked by many people. Now, however, they are of much interest to conservationists as good examples of the architecture of their period, much of which is fast disappearing. The sudden destruction of the Art Deco centre front of the 1928 Firestone building, with its Egyptian look and fine ceramic tiles, in August 1980, led to an outcry and endeavours to ensure that other

factories of the period in the area, such as the Pyrene, Gillette and Coty buildings, should be preserved. During the last few years manufacturing has declined along the Great West Road, and the buildings tend to be used more by importers and distributors than by manufacturers. After the 2nd World War the Great West Road was completed back towards the centre of London, cutting right through CHISWICK and HAMMERSMITH.

Great Western Royal Hotel *formerly* **Great Western Hotel** *Paddington Station, W2*. Built to the designs of Philip Hardwick, it opened on 9 June 1854. It had twin towers each two storeys higher than the five-storey main block and a pediment by John Thomas illustrating *Peace, Plenty, Industry and Science*. It originally had 103 bedrooms and 15 sitting rooms. These were all refurbished in the 1930s. There are now 170 bedrooms.

Great Winchester Street *EC2*. Named after William Paulet, 1st Marquess of Winchester, who was granted part of the priory and precincts of the Augustine friars from Henry VIII in 1539 and pulled down the building for Paulet House, later known as Winchester House. By 1720, according to Strype, the gardens of the house had been built on and 'made into a fair street'. The father of Edmond Halley, the astronomer, was a rich soap-boiler here. MORGAN GRENFELL AND CO., the merchant bankers, are at No. 23 in a building designed by Mewès and Davis (1925).

Great Windmill Street *W1*. Takes its name from a windmill which stood here in the middle of the 17th century. It was described in 1651 as 'well fitted with Staves and other materialls' and had a granary 'strongly built with Bricke and covered with Tile lofted over and commodiously divided for Corne'. It was evidently still there when various builders and speculators, including Col. Panton, began to lay out the street in the 1670s; but it seems not to have survived 50 years later. The street became renowned in the second half of the 18th century for the anatomical theatre which Dr William Hunter opened at No. 16. Hunter, who had come to London from Glasgow in 1740, first lived in COVENT GARDEN, then in JERMYN STREET. He soon became well known as a lecturer and collector of anatomical specimens. In 1766 he bought a large house in Great Windmill Street and asked Robert Mylne, the Scottish architect of BLACKFRIARS BRIDGE, to whom he was related by marriage, to rebuild it for him, providing him with a residence, museum, library, anatomical theatre and dissecting rooms. He lectured there regularly from 1767 until his death in 1783, taking into partnership William Cruikshank and being assisted by his nephew, Matthew Baillie. Cruikshank and Baillie continued the lectures and demonstrations after Hunter's death; and they in turn were followed by other medical men into whose hands the building passed, the specimens being removed in 1807, in accordance with Hunter's will, to Glasgow University. The last lectures were given there in 1831. Thereafter the building became for a time a printing works, then the Hôtel de l'Etoile; and in 1887 was sold to the proprietor of the LYRIC THEATRE of which, greatly altered, it forms a part.

While lectures were being given at No. 16, further

down the street, south of what is now SHAFTESBURY AVENUE, which was to cut across it, a variety of entertainments were given at what became known in 1832 as the Royal Albion Theatre. This was built on land which in the 18th century had been a tennis court and in the earlier part of the 19th century a circus. In the 1840s the building was used by John Dubourg for his mechanical waxworks and 'Grand Centrifugal Railway'. In 1851 Dubourg's partner, Robert Bignell, opened his assembly rooms, calling them the Argyll Rooms which became a haunt of prostitutes and their customers. In 1878 Bignell, who had by this time made a great deal of money, was refused a renewal of his licence for music and dancing, so closed the Argyll Rooms, opening the premises in 1882 as the Trocadero Palace music hall. This no longer survives as a theatre; but the WINDMILL THEATRE still continues its chequered career. The St James's and St Peter's Primary School which was opened here in the 1870s still incongruously remains at No. 23, SOHO's one remaining school. Also, less incongruously, remaining at Nos 45–46 is the St James's Tavern, a public house built in 1896–7 on a site occupied by a tavern, once known as the Catherine Wheel, which had stood here since at least 1733. St Peter's Church which was built in 1860–1 was, however, demolished in 1954. The foundation stone was laid by one prime minister, the 14th Earl of Derby, and the congregation regularly included two others, Lord Salisbury and Gladstone. In 1847 the second Congress of the Communist League was held at No. 20. In 1850–1 Karl Marx gave a course of lectures here in rooms above the present Red Lion public house.

Greater London Council Established in 1965 as part of a major re-organisation of metropolitan local government. By that time the built-up area of London had spread far beyond the confines (117 sq miles) of the jurisdiction of the LONDON COUNTY COUNCIL; the GLC's new area contained 610 sq miles, inhabited by over seven million people. The Council is composed of 92 members, elected for four years. It operates on party political lines, and since 1965 power has alternated in roughly equal successive periods between Labour and Conservatives. The Leader of the Council is elected by the members of the majority party and is the Council's political head. The Chairman of the council is the GLC's ceremonial head and is elected annually by the whole Council. The GLC is responsible for the large-scale strategic administration of the whole Greater London area. Its Greater London Development Plan, approved by the Secretary of State for the Environment in 1976, gives statutory expression to the planning policies for Greater London. Its duties include traffic management, the maintenance of main roads, financial and policy control of London Transport (*see* TRANSPORT *and* UNDERGROUND), provision of land drainage, the disposal of refuse and the running of the LONDON FIRE BRIGADE. Within the inner London area (i.e. the area formerly administered by the LCC) education is controlled by a special committee of the GLC known as the INNER LONDON EDUCATION AUTHORITY.

Grecian Coffee House *Devereux Court*. Stood at No. 19. It is said to have taken its name from one Constantine, variously identified. The first mentions are in the *Tatler* of 1709–10, where it is described as attracting men of learning. It was often referred to as 'the Athenaeum of its day'. An argument over the accent of a Greek word is said to have ended in death by sword for one of the men who went to decide the issue in a duel outside in DEVEREUX COURT. The house also attracted men of medicine and science. Members of the ROYAL SOCIETY, including Sir Isaac Newton and Dr Halley, were patrons. So also was Sir Hans Sloane; it was here that Sarah Mapp, the bonesetter, showed him her skills. By 1803, however, the Grecian advertised itself as frequented by 'gentlemen of the law', rather than literary or medical men. *The Times* of 3 August 1807 reports that one Mr Gordon, a barrister, narrowly escaped when bullets from an air-gun or cross-bow were fired into the coffee house. It appears to have closed in 1843.

Greek Orthodox Cathedral of St Sophia *Moscow Road*, W2. Built in 1877–82 to the Byzantine Revival designs of John Oldrid Scott, Sir Gilbert Scott's second son, to cater for the Greek community in London which had much increased following the war of independence. The richly furnished interior has icon paintings by Ludwig Thiersch, Professor at the German Academy in Athens.

Greek Street W1. Laid out in the late 1670s and early 1680s and named after the Greek Church which stood in Hog Lane. Although from its earliest years there were taverns, coffee-houses and tradesmen's workshops in the street, there were also several aristocratic tenants, including the 5th Earl of Anglesey in 1711–17, and the 4th Earl of Fingall in 1709–17. In 1720, according to Strype, the street was 'well built and inhabited'. There were a number of more or less distinguished artists and musicians amongst the inhabitants. Casanova chose to stay here when he visited London in 1764, and Thomas De Quincey, author of *Confessions of an Opium-Eater*, having run away from Manchester Grammar School in 1802, took lodgings in the street in a house which had 'an unhappy countenance of gloom and unsocial fitfulness due in reality to long neglect of painting and cleansing'. Some of the early 18th-century buildings remain, although most have been refaced. At Nos 12–13, which was once the largest house in the street, Josiah Wedgwood had his London warehouse and showrooms from 1774, after moving from GREAT NEWPORT STREET, until 1797 when the firm again moved, this time to No. 8 ST JAMES'S SQUARE. Some interesting 19th-century shop-fronts also survive: No. 17, where Charles Clagget opened his museum of musical instruments in 1789, is a particularly good example. By the time of its construction many of the houses in the street had been turned into shops and small manufactories, particularly those of leather workers, which until very recently were still to be found here. The public house, the Pillar of Hercules, at No. 7 is on the site of earlier taverns of the same name. It was from its doorway that the starving and opium-addicted Francis Thompson was rescued by Wilfrid Meynell, editor of *Merry England* in whose pages two of Thompson's early poems were published. The Coach and Horses at No. 29 is also on the site of previous taverns which have stood there since at least the 1720s.

Greek Street is now a characteristic SOHO street, though, largely because of the long, dull wall of the

PRINCE EDWARD THEATRE on its south-western side, less lively than its neighbours. At the north-eastern end is the HOUSE OF BARNABAS. There are several well-known restaurants in the street, including the Gay Hussar at No. 2, Au Jardin des Gourmets at No. 5 and L'Escargot at No. 48. The last-named was established by Georges Gaudin at the turn of the century. His motto, 'slow but sure' can be seen outside the restaurant beneath a representation of himself riding a snail.

Green Belt   *see* PLANNING.

Green Park   *SW1*. So called because of its verdure of grass and trees, it comprises about 53 acres between PICCADILLY and CONSTITUTION HILL, bounded in the west by Duke of Wellington Place and in the east by QUEEN'S WALK. It is said to have been the burial ground of the lepers from the hospital of St James's (*see* ST JAMES'S PALACE), which is supposedly why there are no flowers here as there are in the adjoining ST JAMES'S PARK. It was enclosed by Henry VIII and made into a Royal Park by Charles II who laid out walks and built a snow house for cooling drinks in summer. The mound of this snow house can still be seen opposite No. 119 PICCADILLY, surmounted by one of the park's fine plane trees.

In the 18th century the park was a favoured place for duels. It was here that Count Alfieri fought his mistress's husband, Lord Ligonier, bravely returning to the HAYMARKET THEATRE with a sword wound in his arm to sit through the last act and later generously to comment, 'My view is that Ligonier did not kill me because he did not want to, and I did not kill him because I did not know how.' The park was also much frequented by highwaymen: Horace Walpole was but one of numerous gentlemen who were held up here. Many balloon ascents were made here (*see* BALLOON-

ING) and several firework displays given (*see* FIREWORKS). There was a particularly fine display to celebrate the Peace of Aix-la-Chapelle of 1748 for which Handel composed the incidental music. In 1775 a reservoir was built in the north-east corner by the CHELSEA WATERWORKS CO. It was either here or in the Serpentine in HYDE PARK that Shelley's pregnant wife, Harriet Westbrook, whom he had deserted, met her mysterious death by drowning in 1816. It was filled in in 1856. For the celebrations of 1814 a Gothic castle over 100 ft square was erected in the park, and from its battlements there blazed an amazing array of maroons and serpents, Roman candles and Catherine wheels, fire-pots and girandoles. Rocket after rocket shot into the sky, each one containing 'a world of smaller rockets'. And when the dense clouds of smoke, which hid the sombre castle from view for a minute or two, had dispersed there was seen, standing in its place, a brightly illuminated Temple of Concord, its walls displaying allegorical pictures prominent amongst which was *The Triumph of England under the Regency*. On this occasion also there was a spectacular ascent from Green Park when Windham Sadler's balloon 'sprang into the air with its usual velocity and Mr Sadler, who had taken up with him a vast number of programmes of the jubilee ... flung them down again from the sky with much industry and profusion.'

The Broad Walk which cuts across the park from PICCADILLY to the eastern end of CONSTITUTION HILL is part of the design for the QUEEN VICTORIA MEMORIAL. The ornamental iron gates at the southern end were given by the Dominions, while those at the PICCADILLY end were formerly outside DEVONSHIRE HOUSE and were erected here in 1921. The fountain towards the western end surmounted by the bronze figure of *Diana*, sculpted by E.J. Clack, was a gift from the Constance Fund (*see* HYDE PARK) in 1954.

The revolving 'Temple of Concord', erected in Green Park as part of the firework display for the 1814 Peace Celebrations.

Green Street *W1.* Part of the GROSVENOR ESTATE it extends from NORTH AUDLEY STREET to PARK LANE. It probably takes its name from John Green, a builder active here until he came to an untoward end in 1737 by falling down a well in UPPER GROSVENOR STREET. Building had begun in the 1720s, but it was not finished until the 1760s, and Green Street was not fashionable. The only house to survive from this period is Hampden House, (originally two houses, also known as Nos 60 and 61), so called from the long residence (beginning in 1756) of the Hampden family. The architect and first occupant (during 1730–49) of No. 61 was Roger Morris, but in later years both houses have been much altered and enlarged, and are now occupied by the British Standards Institution. Virtually the whole of the rest of Green Street was rebuilt in the 40 years beginning in 1882, large houses with red brick and terracotta or stone dressings predominating. A notable feature of this redevelopment was the provision by the Grosvenor Office of a large communal garden for the houses on the south side between PARK STREET and DUNRAVEN STREET. Most of the houses in Green Street are now divided into flats or used as offices. No. 32, designed in 1897–9 by Sidney R.J. Smith for the 4th Baron Ribblesdale, is now the Brazilian Embassy. William Blake lived at No.23 in 1782–4. The Revd Sydney Smith lived on the north side in 1839–45.

Green Street Green *Kent.* First mentioned as Grenestrete but formerly known as New Chelsfield and in the 19th century as Greenstead Green. Hops were grown in the area and in 1708 there was a small farm brewhouse. The quality of the beer was such that the demand grew. In 1836 John Fox founded the Oak Brewery, with 110 employees. Cottages and houses were built and Green Street Green grew to be a small village. The brewery closed in 1909 and during the 1st World War the buildings were used as barracks. At this time also the nearby ORPINGTON Hospital was built. Green Street Green is now a busy shopping and residential area, forming part of the London Borough of BROMLEY.

Greenford *Middlesex.* Grenan forda is first mentioned in 845, the ford presumably being over the RIVER BRENT which formed part of its southern and eastern boundaries. The manor of Greenford was in the hands of WESTMINSTER ABBEY from before the Norman Conquest until the DISSOLUTION OF THE MONASTERIES in the 16th century. There were three centres to the parish, Greenford Green to the north, the church and manor house in the centre and Stickleton on the hill to the south, all linked by the old north-south road, Oldfield Lane. Greenford remained a secluded and predominantly farming community until the 20th century, although William Henry Perkin's synthetic dyeworks had opened at Greenford Green in 1856. The PADDINGTON arm of the GRAND JUNCTION CANAL cut across the parish in 1801, but the railway did not arrive until 1903 with the opening of the Great Western northern main line and a loop line from Greenford to West EALING.

Industry arrived in advance of housing in the 20th century, with factories near the canal and the railway line which were used for moving raw materials. J. Lyons and Co. Ltd and Rockware Glass were early arrivals, with Glaxo and Aladdin later in the 1930s.

The geography of the area was fundamentally changed by the road development of the 1920s and 1930s when the WESTERN AVENUE was cut east-west and Greenford Road replaced Oldfield Lane as the principal north-south route. Speculative housing followed in the 1930s and the area was largely built up by 1940, although a large open space survives on Horsenden Hill. The main shopping centre developed to the south where Greenford Road and Ruislip Road meet leaving the station isolated on the north side of WESTERN AVENUE. Industry has changed in the last ten years, with factories being replaced by warehousing, and a flyover has been built at the Greenford Road–Western Avenue intersection. Few buildings predate the 1930s development, although Greenford Community Centre (once the private house Greenford Hall), BETHAM SCHOOL and the two churches of HOLY CROSS, in Oldfield Lane, make an interesting group.

Greenhill *Harrow, Middlesex.* The heart of modern HARROW, its shopping centre occupying the area of Station Road, College Road and St Ann's Road, was formerly the tiny hamlet of Greenhill at the foot of Harrow Hill. All that remains to remind us of its former rural atmosphere is a solitary 18th-century weatherboarded barn of Greenhill Farm in High Mead. The origins of the Greenhill family who farmed the area have been traced back to the 14th century. The rapid growth of HARROW from Greenhill dates from the coming of the Metropolitan Railway in 1880. The stone church of St John the Baptist, Greenhill, by J.S. Alder, was built in 1904 on the site of an earlier church built in 1866. Gayton High School (formerly Harrow County School for boys) was built in 1911, and Lowlands Junior College (formerly Harrow County School for girls) in 1913.

Greenwell Street *W1.* A small street running just south of the MARYLEBONE ROAD behind GREAT PORTLAND STREET Underground Station, it was until 1937 known as Buckingham Street. The new name was chosen in honour of the Vestry Clerk, James Hugo Greenwell. John Flaxman, the artist and sculptor, lived at No. 7 from 1796 until his death in 1826.

Greenwich *SE10.* The name is either derived from the Anglo-Saxon, 'green village', or is a Scandinavian name given by the Danes, 'green reach'. In 1011–14 the Danish fleet lay off Greenwich and the men encamped to the east of the present borough. In 1011 they took Alphege, Archbishop of Canterbury, hostage, and brought him to Greenwich where they killed him eight months later when he refused to allow ransom to be paid for his release. Greenwich Manor originally belonged to LEWISHAM Manor. Ethelruda, a niece of King Alfred, gave both to the Abbey of St Peter at Ghent. In 1414 it passed to the Carthusian priory at SHEEN. In 1530 it became Crown property. Edward I seems to have stayed in Greenwich, because in 1300 he made offerings at the chapel of the Virgin Mary. In 1408 Henry IV dated his will from Greenwich. In 1417 the manor passed to Humphrey, Duke of Gloucester, who enclosed the 190 acres of GREENWICH PARK and in 1437 rebuilt GREENWICH PALACE. The Palace was to become a favourite residence of the Tudors, and the birthplace of Henry VIII in 1491, of Mary I in 1515 and of Elizabeth I in 1533. It was frequently used for celebrations, hunting, jousting, balls and banquets. In

1576 the first paupers were admitted to the College of the Poor of Queen Elizabeth, almshouses later controlled by the DRAPERS' COMPANY. In 1605 James I settled the park and palace on his wife, Anne of Denmark. She began the building of the QUEEN'S HOUSE which was completed in 1635 when her daughter-in-law, Queen Henrietta Maria, moved in. In 1613 Henry Howard, Earl of Northampton, founded Norfolk College almshouses for 20 residents, 12 from Greenwich and eight from Shottesham, Norfolk, his birthplace. In 1642 three companies were sent from Parliament to search Greenwich for arms, but found nothing.

Greenwich was not sold after the Civil War, as were most Crown lands, but was retained to become a residence for the Protector. After the Restoration Charles II planned the construction of a new palace. Funds ran out in 1669 when only one wing, now King Charles's building of the ROYAL NAVAL COLLEGE, had been completed. Improvements planned in the park, however, were achieved, to the designs of Le Nôtre in the 1660s. In 1675 the foundation stone of the ROYAL OBSERVATORY was laid and the following year Flamsteed, the first Astronomer Royal, was able to begin his duties. Flamsteed House was built for him to Wren's designs at a cost of only £520. In 1673 Pepys was appointed Secretary for the Affairs of the Navy and his work often brought him to Greenwich. He was able to help friends by obtaining passage for them on the 16 yachts which lay off Greenwich and set sail from here to the continental ports. Nell Gwynne was amongst those who benefited from this favour. When Samuel Atkins, Pepys's pupil, was accused of the murder of Sir Edmund Berry Godfrey in 1678, he produced one Captain Vittles as a witness for his alibi. Atkins, having failed to find Pepys at Derby House to take orders for the day, had decided to spend the afternoon drinking on Vittles's yacht with two ladies. They had been left, inebriated, at BILLINGSGATE at 11.30 at night, two hours after the murder had taken place. Atkins was acquitted.

In 1692 Queen Mary decided that the buildings begun by Charles II should be completed to provide a Royal Naval Hospital for disabled seamen. This is now the ROYAL NAVAL COLLEGE. The buildings were designed by Wren, with Hawksmoor as his assistant. Vanbrugh succeeded Wren and built two houses for himself in the area. VANBRUGH'S CASTLE, to the east of the park, is in the style of a fortress and is said to be England's first folly. In about 1694 the RANGER'S HOUSE was built for the Earl of Chesterfield; it now houses the Suffolk collection of 16th- to 18th-century portraits. In 1710 the roof of the parish church of ST ALPHEGE collapsed and a new church had to be built. This, the present church, consecrated in 1718, was designed by John James of Greenwich, and has a Nicholas Hawksmoor exterior.

In 1737 Samuel Johnson came to Greenwich and took lodgings in Church Street. In 1763 Boswell came to be shown the park and read some of Johnson's lines on it:

On Thames's bank in silent thought we stood:
Where Greenwich smiles upon the silver flood:
Pleased with the seat which gave Eliza birth,
We kneel and kiss the consecrated earth.

Walking in the Park some years later, however, Boswell, asked by Johnson if it were not fine, replied,

'Yes, sir; but not equal to Fleet Street'; and Johnson agreed. Another resident, General Wolfe, set out from here for Quebec and returned in 1759, embalmed, to lie in state, in the family home, Macartney House which was bought by Wolfe's father in 1751 (see STATUES).

The residential area of CROOMS HILL and Gloucester Circus is mostly a Georgian development on the ancient Anglo-Saxon road. One of the houses, The Grange, contains timbers dating from the beginning of the 12th century. In 1809 the people of Greenwich founded the Jubilee Almshouses to commemorate George III's Golden Jubilee. In 1837 the TRAFALGAR TAVERN was built. In 1869 an Act closed the Naval Hospital, and it opened in 1873 as the ROYAL NAVAL COLLEGE, retaining the Infirmary as a Free Hospital for Seamen of All Nations. A year later a tide rose well over 2 ft above the pavement.

In the late 1880s the railway station was built; and towards the end of the century Crowder's Music Hall, now the GREENWICH THEATRE, was opened. The tunnel to the ISLE OF DOGS was constructed at about the same time to enable workers to cross to the WEST INDIA DOCKS. Goddard's Eel and Pie House, a Greenwich institution, was founded in 1890 and still sells cheap pies and jellied eels which meet with the approval of the most fastidious cockney. Londoners also come to Greenwich to shop at Boulton's, the best of Greenwich's celebrated fishmongers, or to visit the open market and the restaurants. They arrive by boat as well as by other forms of transport. In 1954 the CUTTY SARK was brought to dry dock here, and in 1968 GYPSY MOTH IV joined her.

Greenwich Fair There were at one time two fairs at GREENWICH on the Monday, Tuesday and Wednesday of both Easter and Whitsun weeks, the Easter fair being the best known. Heavily loaded steamers brought revellers from London and the roads were crowded with 'cabs, hackney-coaches, "shay carts", coal wagons, stages, omnibuses, sociables, gigs and donkey-chaises'. The fair is mentioned in Thackeray's *Sketches and Travels in London*, where Mr Brown threatens to disinherit his nephew if he is ever found 'as a frequenter of races at Greenwich Fair and such amusements in questionable company'. The best description that exists of the fair at the height of its popularity is by Dickens in *Sketches by Boz*. He calls the fair 'a periodical breaking out, we suppose; a sort of rash; a three days' fever which cools the blood for six months afterwards'. A time-honoured custom at the fair was for young couples to climb the hill to the ROYAL OBSERVATORY and then the young men would drag the girls down again as quickly as possible 'greatly to the derangement of their mobs and bonnet-caps'.

Greenwich Meridian Until the 18th century each country tended to use its own capital as the zero point from which to measure longtitude. In 1767 the *British Nautical Almanack* was first published and became the indispensable handbook for all navigators. At the international conference held at Washington in 1884 it was agreed that the meridian passing through the ROYAL OBSERVATORY at GREENWICH (now marked by a broad brass rail inlaid in concrete) should be the zero or prime meridian from which meridians East and West up to 180° were to be measured.

'Holyday Gambols on Greenwich Hill' during the Easter Fair of 1750.

Greenwich Palace *SE10.* A favourite residence of the Tudor monarchs. It was built by Humphrey, Duke of Gloucester, brother of Henry V, on the banks of the THAMES in 1427. Bella Court, as he called it, was one of the finest houses in England. As was usual at that time, it had a moat and battlements. At the top of Greenwich Hill was a watch-tower. The grounds extended from the THAMES to the top of the hill. In 1433 the Duke was given permission to enclose 200 acres which now form GREENWICH PARK. The Duke's library was the first great library in England owned by a private individual. When he died he left it to Oxford University, where it formed the nucleus of what is now the Bodleian Library. In 1445 he lent the house, for their honeymoon, to Henry VI and Margaret of Anjou who, after Gloucester's arrest in 1447 and sudden death five days later, took it over and renamed it Placentia – the pleasant place. Margaret put in terracotta tiles bearing her monogram, filled the windows with glass and built a landing stage and treasure house. In 1465 Elizabeth Woodville gave birth here to Elizabeth of York, the future wife of Henry VII. In 1466 Edward IV settled the house on his Queen for life. In 1480 Edward IV granted a piece of land for a monastery to Franciscan friars who were given permission by the Pope 'to build a house with church, low bell tower, bell, cloister, frater, dorter, gardens and other necessary offices for the perpetual use and habitation of the friars in Greenwich'. In 1490 Henry VII made Elizabeth Woodville a virtual prisoner in BERMONDSEY ABBEY and took over the palace. The next year his son, the future Henry VIII, was born here. In 1501 his elder brother, Prince Arthur, married Catherine of Aragon in the palace. Arthur died soon afterwards and was succeeded by Henry.

The palace became Henry's favourite residence. He could hawk and hunt in the park and from the windows and leaden roof he could watch the large vessels of London bringing in silk and gold and spices and carrying out wool and metal. Here, too, he could visit his ships-of-war anchored close to the palace. In his day the palace was a complex of buildings round three quadrangles. The main entrance was from the river through a massive gatehouse which led to the central court. Henry added armouries, staffed by German craftsmen, a banqueting hall designed by William Vertue and a large tilt yard. In 1515 Princess Mary, his sister, the widow of Louis XII, married Charles Brandon, Duke of Suffolk, at Greenwich in front of the whole court. In February 1516, Henry's daughter, the future Mary I, was born at Greenwich and baptised in the friars' church. Wolsey was godfather. At Christmas that year the first masquerade was performed in England. From 1529–31 Catherine of Aragon was kept prisoner in the palace for refusing to acknowledge the invalidity of her marriage. In 1533 Anne Boleyn gave birth here to Elizabeth I, who was baptised the next day in the friars' church. After the suppression of the monastery in 1536, 200 monks were thrown into prison where they remained for several years until Sir Thomas Wriotheseley interceded for them and they were allowed to go to Scotland or the Continent. In 1536, at the May Day tournament Anne Boleyn is said to have dropped her handkerchief as a signal to a lover. Henry left early and that night Anne's brother and four of his friends were taken to the TOWER, followed the next day by Anne herself. Henry signed her death warrant at Greenwich, and it was here in 1540 that he was married by proxy to Anne of Cleves. In April 1553 the sickly Edward VI was sent to Greenwich for his health's sake, but he died here in July.

Soon after her accession, his sister, Mary I, invited

the Franciscan friars to return. She rarely came to Greenwich herself. On one of her rare visits a cannon ball, fired in salute, came through the wall of her apartment, 'to the great terror of herself and her ladies', but nobody was hurt. In 1558 Elizabeth I became Queen and soon after banished the Franciscans for ever. She made Greenwich her principal summer residence. It was here that Ralegh put his cloak over a puddle so that she would not get her shoes dirty. In 1573 the Queen revived here the Maundy Ceremony in which she washed the feet of 39 pauper women (having had them washed by three other people first) and gave them food and money. And it was here in 1587 that Elizabeth signed the death warrant of Mary Queen of Scots.

Elizabeth's successor, James I, settled Greenwich on his Queen, Anne of Denmark, for whom the QUEEN'S HOUSE was designed by Inigo Jones. In 1652 the Parliamentarians tried to sell the palace but no buyers could be found; it was stripped of its paintings and furniture and turned into a biscuit factory. Also Dutch prisoners of war were kept here in 1653–4. At the Restoration of 1660 Charles II decided to rebuild the palace rather than restore it. Three new blocks, designed by John Webb, were planned but only the western one had been completed by the time of the King's death. William and Mary preferred the royal palaces at KENSINGTON and HAMPTON COURT, and the remains of the building were demolished to make way for the ROYAL NAVAL HOSPITAL.

Greenwich Park SE10.

Burial mounds suggest that Bronze Age tribes settled here. A Roman built his villa on the east side of the park and many silver and bronze coins dating from 35 BC to AD 425 have been found. A Roman road ran through the park down to GREENWICH, which was then probably a fishing village. In 1427 Humphrey, Duke of Gloucester, brother of Henry V, built himself a house on the river, the forerunner of GREENWICH PALACE. He enclosed a mile-long rectangle of land stretching from the THAMES to Greenwich Hill. In 1433 Henry VI gave him permission to enclose 200 acres of pasture, wood, heath and gorses, the area of the present royal park. On the hill he built a watch-tower. Humphrey died in 1447 and the palace was taken over by Henry VI and made

one of the principal royal residences. From 1515 deer have been kept in the park, originally to provide game for the royal hunts.

Under Henry VIII Greenwich reached the height of royal favour. Henry loved 'to go a-maying' in the park. On the flat ground at the bottom of the hill tilting, shooting at butts, wrestling, fighting with spears and swords, and casting the light and heavy bars took place. In 1526 Henry restored or rebuilt the castle on the hill for younger members of his family and his mistresses. On May Day 1536 at a tournament Anne Boleyn is said to have dropped her handkerchief as a signal to a lover. Henry left early and that night Anne's brother and his friends Norris, Weston, Brereton and Smeaton were arrested and taken to the TOWER, followed by Anne herself the next day.

In 1558, soon after Elizabeth's accession, the CITY OF LONDON provided a spectacular entertainment for her in the park. In 1572 she reviewed companies of 1,400 men raised by the CITY after the Duke of Norfolk's plot. A mock battle then took place 'which had all the appearances of a regular battle except for the spilling of blood'. In 1619 James I enclosed the park with a brick wall costing £2,000. At the Restoration Charles II had the park laid out anew by Le Nôtre, Louis XIV's landscape gardener. The QUEEN'S HOUSE was made the focal point, with tree-lined avenues converging on it. During the 1660s many elms and Spanish chestnuts were planted under the direction of Sir William Boreman, and in 1675 Sir Christopher Wren built the ROYAL OBSERVATORY on the hill on the site of Duke Humphrey's castle. Charles Sackville, Earl of Dorset and Middlesex, was appointed in 1690 as first Ranger of the park with the right to live in the QUEEN'S HOUSE.

Since the 18th century the park has been open to the public. Dr Johnson thought it very fine and composed his poem 'Irene' here. In 1806 Princess Caroline sold her rights as Ranger and moved from the QUEEN'S HOUSE, but continued to live in GREENWICH at MONTAGUE HOUSE until 1811. From 1815–1900 CHESTERFIELD HOUSE was used as the Ranger's residence.

In 1855 a steamboat service between GREENWICH and London began and a year later the first London railway between DEPTFORD and LONDON BRIDGE opened. Two years later the line was extended to

The celebrated view from Greenwich Hill in 1842, showing part of the Royal Observatory on the left, from a lithograph by T.S. Boys.

GREENWICH. As a result GREENWICH became the playground of Londoners at bank holidays and the existing fair was expanded. In 1859 the fair was described as 'little more than a confusion of unwashed and shabbily dressed people, presenting a mobbish appearance'. In 1870 the METROPOLITAN BOARD OF WORKS suppressed the fair as a nuisance to local residents. During 1848–78 a tunnel was made under the park to extend the railway to CHARLTON, WOOLWICH and Gravesend.

In 1930 the statue of General Wolfe was erected and in 1935 the statue of William IV from the CITY was re-erected here (*see* STATUES). During the period 1948–57 the ROYAL OBSERVATORY moved to Herstmonceux in Sussex and the buildings have since been opened as a branch of the NATIONAL MARITIME MUSEUM. The view from Greenwich Hill is famous, giving a panorama of London with the QUEEN'S HOUSE, the ROYAL HOSPITAL and the THAMES in the foreground. The bronze, *Standing Figure and Knife Edge*, is by Henry Moore (1979).

Greenwich Theatre *Crooms Hill, SE10*. Built on the shell of an old music-hall, the Greenwich Hippodrome, which had been acquired with money provided over a long period of fund-raising, by the Greenwich Theatre Trust. Incorporated in the building are a restaurant, picture gallery and jazz club as well as the theatre. This opened in 1969 with *Martin Luther King*, a play with music by Ewan Hooper, the theatre's first director. Many notable artists have since appeared here. The theatre has an intimate auditorium with a seating capacity of 426.

Greenwich Tunnel *Greenwich–Isle of Dogs*. Built in 1897–1902 by Sir Alexander Binnie to replace the ferry in existence since 1676. It was intended as a pedestrian tunnel for the use of dockers working in the WEST INDIA DOCKS. The internal diameter is 11 ft, the length 1,217 ft. There are circular shafts with domed glass roofs for stairs and lifts.

Grenadier *Old Barrack Yard, Wilton Row, SW1*. Originally known as the Guardsman, this was once a mess of the Duke of Wellington's officers. The Duke is reputed to have played cards here, and the house is full of Wellington mementoes, old weapons and military prints. It is reputed to be haunted during September by an officer who was flogged to death after being caught cheating at cards.

Grenville Place *SW7*. On the HOLLAND ESTATE. Sir Walter Cope, who built HOLLAND HOUSE, married Dorothy Grenville. Charles Booth, the pioneer in social research and author of the monumental *Life and Labour of the People of London*, lived at No. 6 in 1875–90.

Gresham Club *Abchurch Lane, EC4*. Founded in 1843 for bankers, merchants and 'professional gentlemen of known respectability'. The premises were originally on the corner of ST SWITHIN'S LANE and LOMBARD STREET. The present building was constructed during the 1st World War. The club has always been celebrated for its port.

Gresham College *Gresham Street, EC2*. Founded in 1579 by Sir Thomas Gresham for the delivery of public lectures on Divinity, Music, Astronomy (Christopher Wren gave these during the Commonwealth), Geometry, Physics, Law and Rhetoric. The lectures began in 1597 at Gresham's house in BROAD STREET which had been left vacant since the death of his widow the year before. In 1645 the Royal Society for the Advancement of Natural Science developed from the weekly meetings of the seven professors. This society was formally instituted by Charles II in 1662. It met at the college until 1710. In 1768 Gresham's house was demolished, but the lectures continued in a room above the ROYAL EXCHANGE. A new college was built in 1843 in GRESHAM STREET to the designs of George Smith. It was replaced in 1911–13 by the present building by Dendy Watney and Sydney Perks. The College has recently been reconstituted as an academic entity by the Joint Trustees, the MERCERS' COMPANY and the CORPORATION OF LONDON, in association with the CITY UNIVERSITY, 'to promote in contemporary circumstances the ideas and ideals of Sir Thomas Gresham in relation to higher education in the City of London'.

Gresham Committee The ROYAL EXCHANGE was built by Sir Thomas Gresham and opened by Queen Elizabeth I in 1570 as a meeting place for CITY merchants. Gresham died in 1579 and entrusted the EXCHANGE to the CITY CORPORATION and to his own livery company, the Mercers. Since then the administration and maintenance of it has been the responsibility of a Committee consisting of members of both bodies. The CORPORATION appoints its own Clerk, but the Clerk to the Grand Committee is the Clerk to the MERCERS' COMPANY.

Gresham Lectures Sir Thomas Gresham, the Elizabethan financier and builder of the first ROYAL EXCHANGE, made provision in his will for 'a college in London for the gratuitous instruction of all who chose to attend the lectures'. He left the ROYAL EXCHANGE half to the CORPORATION OF LONDON and half to the MERCERS' COMPANY, who were to appoint and pay lecturers between them in seven subjects: Divinity, Rhetoric, Geometry, Medical Science, Astronomy, Law and Music. The first lectures were read at Gresham Mansion, which was renamed GRESHAM COLLEGE in 1597. Since 1966 the lectures have been associated with the CITY UNIVERSITY, but the CITY OF LONDON and the MERCERS' COMPANY continue to be Trustees.

Gresham Street *EC2*. Created in 1845 by widening Cateaton Street, MAIDEN LANE, St Anne's Lane and Lad Lane. It is named after Sir Thomas Gresham, founder of the ROYAL EXCHANGE and GRESHAM COLLEGE, which moved to the corner of BASINGHALL STREET in 1842 and was rebuilt in a neo-Palladian style by Dendy Watney and Sydney Perks in 1911–13. Before the road was widened the Swan-with-two-Necks, the terminus for north-bound coaches, stood at the corner of ALDERMANBURY. WAX CHANDLERS' HALL is on the south side. The entrance to HABERDASHERS' HALL is in STAINING LANE. At No. 50 are the shirt makers, Messrs Thresher and Glenny, whose firm made several of the red shirts which were presented to Garibaldi and various other members of the Thousand as a contribution to the fund opened in London for the Sicilian expedition. The GUILDHALL and

ST LAWRENCE JEWRY are in Guildhall Yard adjoining. The Banca Commerciale Italiana occupies No. 42, a building designed by Sancton Wood in 1850–2 and formerly housing the Queen's Assurance Co.

Gresse Street *W1*. Built in about 1767 on the site of his house by Peter Gaspard Gresse, father of John Alexander Gresse, the painter and drawing master to King George III's children, who was known as Grease because he was so fat. The departments of economics, geography, geology, politics and sociology of BIRK-BECK COLLEGE are at Nos 7–15.

Greville Street *EC1*. Named after Sir Fulke Greville, 1st Lord Brooke, the poet and intimate friend of Sir Philip Sidney, whose house, Brooke House, stood here. Greville was murdered in the house by a servant in 1628. Brooke House and its grounds extended over the present Brooke Street as well as Greville Street. Like the nearby HATTON GAR-DEN, it is largely occupied by manufacturing jewellers, and diamond merchants, polishers and setters.

Grey Coat Hospital School *Greycoat Place, SW1*. Founded in 1695 as a school for 40 poor boys and 40 poor girls who wore grey uniforms as shown in the figures of the two pupils on the restored remains of the old school in GREYCOAT PLACE. In 1701 a 17th-century workhouse was bought in TOTHILL FIELDS and converted for the accommodation of the pupils who were found employment when they left. The school was granted a royal charter by Queen Anne in 1706. The school was reorganised in 1874, the boys being sent to other schools and Greycoat Hospital becoming an establishment for the higher education of girls. The school was enlarged in 1955 to take about 600 pupils, new classrooms being built behind the old façade which was restored by Laurence King (*see* GREYCOAT PLACE). It became a Church of England girls' comprehensive school in 1977 with 900 girls. Distinguished old pupils include David Thompson, the explorer of Western Canada, who left in 1784, and Dame Edith Evans, who attended the Lower School which is now in Graham Terrace, SLOANE SQUARE.

Greycoat Place *SW1*. Here stand the remains of GREYCOAT HOSPITAL, founded in 1695. The Queen Anne centre of the building was destroyed in the 2nd World War but was restored with its lantern in 1955 under the supervision of Laurence King. Painted wooden 18th-century figures of a boy and girl pupil in their grey uniforms stand in niches on either side of the doorway. The coat of arms is of COADE STONE.

Greyfriars Monastery *Newgate Street*. In 1224, of nine Franciscan friars who landed in England five stayed at Canterbury and four came to London. For 15 days they stayed as guests of the Dominicans and then took a house on CORNHILL given them by John Travers, Sheriff of London. The following summer they were given land in NEWGATE STREET close to the City abattoir by John Ewin, mercer. It was bounded on the north by the City wall, on the east by KING EDWARD'S STREET and on the south by NEWGATE STREET. The western boundary is unknown. The simple life of the friars, of whom there were 80 by 1243, attracted many admirers and benefactors, notably Margaret, second Queen of Edward I, Queen Isabella

and Queen Philippa (*see* CHRIST CHURCH, GREYFRIARS). In 1349 about 100 friars died in the BLACK DEATH. Queen Isabella was buried here in 1358; and Joan, Queen of Scotland, daughter of Edward II, in 1362. A library was built in 1421–5 at the expense of Richard Whittington who presented it with £400 worth of books.

After the DISSOLUTION OF THE MONASTERIES the church was used for storing war spoils taken from the French, and the other buildings became private dwellings. All the tombs were destroyed in 1547 and the alabaster, marble and brass was sold for £50. The church was renamed CHRISTCHURCH and a parish formed for it from the parishes of ST NICHOLAS SHAMBLES, ST EWIN and ST SEPULCHRE. The parishioners probably used the choir only, as the King's Printer set up his presses in the nave. The decaying buildings were repaired in 1552 and the following year CHRIST'S HOSPITAL, a school for 'poor fatherless children' and others, was established here. After the GREAT FIRE in which some of the buildings were damaged, Wren rebuilt CHRISTCHURCH. The library, which had escaped the fire, was faced with brick in 1778. In 1897 the school moved to Horsham, Sussex, and the remaining monastic buildings were destroyed soon after when the GENERAL POST OFFICE was extended over the site.

Grimsdyke House *Old Redding, Harrow Weald, Middlesex*. A Tudor-style house built to the design of Norman Shaw in 1872 for the artist, Frederick Goodall. It later became the home of W.S. Gilbert. At Grimsdyke he wrote most of his libretti and there he met his death from heart failure while trying to rescue a young lady from drowning in the lake. The house derives its name from the massive linear earthwork, probably of the 5th century, which is visible in the grounds and on the adjacent golf course. Sections of the dyke are also visible in parts of STANMORE and PINNER. A convalescent home and sanatorium between the wars, the house became a hotel in 1970.

Grocers' Company *see* CITY LIVERY COMPANIES.

Grocers' Hall *Princes Street, EC2*. At first the guild had no hall and met in various places including the house of the Abbot of Bury in ST MARY AXE, the house of the Abbot of St Croix, Cornet's Tower, BUCKLERSBURY and the house of Lord Fitzwalter in OLD JEWRY. The first Hall, purchased in 1426, was built on the site of Lord Fitzwalter's town house and opened in 1431. Committees of both HOUSES OF PARLIAMENT met in the Hall in 1642 to discuss Charles I's attempt to arrest the five members. Cromwell and Fairfax were entertained here in 1649: 'The musick was only drums and trumpets, the feast very sumptuous, no healths drunk nor any incivility passed.' Fairfax was presented with a basin and ewer in beaten gold and Cromwell with £300 of gold plate and 200 pieces of gold. At the Restoration in 1660 the company held a feast in celebration and made Charles II the Sovereign Master. They also contributed £540 towards the cost of his coronation. The walls withstood the GREAT FIRE but the roof was destroyed and had to be replaced. The entire Hall was rebuilt in 1668–9 at the expense of Sir John Cutler. It was renovated and enlarged by Sir John Moore in 1682 to make it a fit residence for the LORD MAYOR. He himself kept his mayoralty here and it was later used by some of his successors. From 1690–1734 the premises were used by the BANK OF ENGLAND. The third Hall was badly built in 1802 by Thomas Leverton. Repairs had to be made by Joseph Gwilt in 1827 but, despite these, the building was demolished in 1888. The fourth Hall, designed by Henry C. Boyes, was opened in 1893. Fire damaged the building in 1965. Extensive restoration, undertaken by Beard, Bennett, Wilkins and Partners, was completed in 1970. The dining capacity of the Hall is 150. For the Company see CITY LIVERY COMPANIES.

Grosvenor Canal Constructed in 1725 by the CHELSEA WATERWORKS COMPANY and improved in the 1820s by the GROSVENOR ESTATE. Various commercial concerns, including Cubitt's building yard and Bramah's engineering works, leased land beside it. Much of the canal above Ebury Bridge was later covered by VICTORIA STATION. The lock gates can still be seen beside the Western Pumping Station in GROSVENOR ROAD.

Grosvenor Chapel *South Audley Street, W1.* A modest proprietary chapel of brown brick built by Benjamin Timbrell in 1730 for the newly developed Grosvenor Estate. In 1831 it became a chapel-of-ease to ST GEORGE, HANOVER SQUARE. It was used by American armed forces in the 2nd World War. Buried here are the parents of the Duke of Wellington as well as Lady Mary Wortley Montagu and John Wilkes.

Grosvenor Estate For over 300 years the Grosvenor family or their trustees have owned, and still own, two large estates in what are now some of the most valuable parts of WESTMINSTER. Their lands were acquired in 1677 by the Cheshire Baronet, Sir Thomas Grosvenor, through his marriage to Mary Davies, the 12-year-old daughter and heiress of a London scrivener, Alexander Davies, who had himself inherited them from an old uncle, Hugh Audley, who died at the age of 85 'infinitely rich'. At that time they consisted of 100 acres in MAYFAIR and about 400 acres in what are now BELGRAVIA and PIMLICO, and the annual rental amounted to £2,170.

In MAYFAIR building began in 1720, and was completed in the 1770s; but in BELGRAVIA it did not start on a large scale until the 1820s, and the development of PIMLICO was not finished until mid-Victorian times. Both estates were well laid out, the citadels of GROSVENOR and BELGRAVE SQUARES being surrounded by street after street of substantial terrace houses, those in MAYFAIR being mostly faced with brick, and those in BELGRAVIA and PIMLICO with cream-painted stucco. By 1891 the annual rental of the MAYFAIR estates alone amounted to about £135,000. The Grosvenors were described as 'the wealthiest family in Europe', and their riches were matched by successive advancements in the peerage, culminating in the Dukedom of Westminster in 1874.

Despite the penal taxation of great wealth, the Grosvenors and their trustees have managed to retain the greater part of their tremendous inheritance, the only substantial sale being that of the PIMLICO area. The estate has always been well managed, and has never been allowed to deteriorate; in recent years the trustees have looked overseas, making enormous investments in property in Canada, the USA and elsewhere.

Grosvenor Gardens *SW1.* French Renaissance-style terraces built around two triangular gardens. In the southern garden is a statue of General Foch (*see* STATUES). F.E. Smith, 1st Lord Birkenhead, lived at No. 32 in 1915–30. The London Tourist Board is at No. 26.

Grosvenor Hill *W1.* On the GROSVENOR ESTATE, it is an L-shaped side-street forming a loop with the two ends of BOURDON STREET, and now lined with garages, offices and Victorian artisans' dwellings. Until 1936 and 1947 respectively parts of it were known as Little Grosvenor Mews and Grosvenor Mews.

Grosvenor House Hotel *Park Lane, W1.* Stands on the site once occupied by Gloucester House, the London mansion of George III's brother, the Duke of Gloucester. Robert Grosvenor, 2nd Earl Grosvenor, who was created 1st Marquess of Westminster at the coronation of William IV, occupied the house in the reign of George IV. He built an entrance screen and the celebrated Grosvenor Gallery to the designs of Thomas Cundy the Younger in 1842–3. In 1928 Alfred Octavius Edwards built a nine-wing building with a colonnaded west façade by Sir Edwin Lutyens. The south wing has a block of 150 luxury flats, the north wing 478 bedrooms. The first hotel in London to have a swimming pool, it also had a skating rink during 1929–34. This was in the Great Room which was afterwards used for banqueting and in 1943 for an American Officers' Mess to which Generals Eisenhower and Patton were frequent visitors. It is now used for large social functions of all kinds.

Grosvenor Hotel *101 Buckingham Palace Road, SW1.* Adjacent to VICTORIA STATION, it was built of Bath stone by J.T. Knowles in 1861. It has five storeys and two further storeys of dormers. There are French pavilion roofs on the angles, with much carved foliage. In the spandrels of the arches are medallion portraits (all of Portland stone) of Queen Victoria, Albert the Prince Consort, and Palmerston, among others. The hotel was reconstructed and refurbished in 1892–9. A new annexe set back from the old building line was opened in 1907. There are 356 bedrooms.

Grosvenor *or* **Victoria Railway Bridge** *Victoria–Battersea.* The Eastern side was built in 1858–60 by Sir John Fowler to carry the London, Chatham and Dover Railway into VICTORIA STATION. It was widened in 1902–5. The western side was built in 1865–6 by Sir Charles Fox for the London, Brighton and South Coast Railway. Both bridges are of five wrought-iron arches, and were rebuilt in 1963–7 by Freeman Fox and Partners in steel, the old piers being encased within the new concrete ones.

Grosvenor Place *SW1.* The first building here was the Lock Hospital built in 1746 for 'females suffering from disorders contracted by a vicious course of life'. (The hospital was removed to the HARROW ROAD in 1842 and the building demolished in 1846.) A row of houses overlooking the grounds of BUCKINGHAM HOUSE were erected in 1747. George III tried to buy the land to prevent this, but the Treasury declined to issue the £20,000 required. The rest of the street was constructed in 1805–10, but largely rebuilt when

VICTORIA STREET was made. Henry Campbell-Bannerman lived at No. 6 in 1877–1904; the Duke of Northumberland was living in 1889 at No. 2, a house later occupied by the Duke of Buccleuch. The 5th Earl Stanhope, the historian and President of the SOCIETY OF ANTIQUARIES in 1846, lived at No. 20. Hobart House, Nos 36–42, the headquarters of the National Coal Board since 1947, was designed by Howard and Souster and built in 1937–40. The buildings of ST GEORGE'S HOSPITAL are at the HYDE PARK CORNER end; the Irish Embassy is at No. 17; and THE ROYAL SOCIETY OF HEALTH at No. 13.

Grosvenor Road *SW1*. Extends along the river from CHELSEA BRIDGE to VAUXHALL BRIDGE. Apart from a small Regency terrace at Nos 105–109 next to the William IV public house, most of the buildings are modern blocks of flats overlooking the river. These include the extensive blocks known as DOLPHIN SQUARE and CHURCHILL GARDENS. The WESTERN PUMPING STATION of 1873–5 is on the north side.

Grosvenor Square *W1*. The centre-piece of the 100-acre GROSVENOR ESTATE in MAYFAIR, and, with the exception of LINCOLN'S INN FIELDS, the largest square in London. It was built between about 1725 and 1731, the land being granted in blocks or single plots for long terms; 30 builders or partnerships took leases or sub-leases at the 51 sites, and by 1738 about half of them had become insolvent, though their misfortunes may not have always been due to their undertakings in the square. All the houses were large, and many were handsomely equipped within, prices for them in their early years ranging up to the large sum of £7,500. But despite the stately appearance which both the individual houses and the whole enormous ensemble were evidently intended to provide, attempts to impose architectural uniformity were largely ineffective. The carpenter, John Simmons, did achieve symmetry on the east side, but Edward Shepherd's attempt to provide a Palladian façade on the larger north side was only realised at three houses; and splendid schemes devised by Colen Campbell came to nothing.

From its earliest days Grosvenor Square attracted residents of high social status, over half of whom, until well into the 20th century, were always people of title. The square has never deteriorated socially, due partly to its favourable position close to HYDE PARK, partly to the good fortune of never being infected by any adja-

cent squalid areas, and partly to the watchful management of successive members of the Grosvenor family. The rack rents and fines (or premiums) which they required when the original building leases expired limited potential residents to the very richest people; and once installed, they tended to spend lavishly on the upkeep of their houses, often employing the best architects of the day. Adam, Chambers, Soane, Wyatville, and James and Samuel Wyatt, for instance, all worked in Grosvenor Square. And at Derby House (now demolished) on the west side Adam produced one of his masterpieces. In Victorian times the roll-call of architects here becomes less distinguished; but expenditure on the refurbishment and even the enlargement (usually by additional storeys) of most of the houses continued unabated.

Only two of the original houses now survive, much altered. No. 9, at the north-east corner, is chiefly remarkable for the residence during 1785–8 of John Adams, the first 'minister plenipotentiary' and later President of the USA. No. 38, on the south side, now the Indonesian Embassy, was embellished by John Johnson, probably in 1776 for the 3rd Duke of Dorset. Another notable survivor is No. 4, on the east side, which was rebuilt in 1865–8, by C.J. Freake, to designs by the estate surveyors, Thomas Cundy the Elder and the Younger. Almost all the other houses, of whatever age, perished in the rebuilding schemes inaugurated, rather uncertainly, by the 2nd Duke of Westminster in the 1920s. Detmar Blow, the estate surveyor, called in his former partner, the distinguished French architect Fernand Billerey, to design the *pièce de résistance*, the great north range, but when building had barely begun Blow unexpectedly left the Duke's service. Billerey's fine designs were substantially altered above the cornice level, and although their general manner was followed later on (the south and east sides, where rebuilding was not completed until 1969), the general effect (except on the north side) is weak. On the west side stands the totally different new American Embassy of 1956–60. In the centre of the square stands the British memorial to President Franklin D. Roosevelt (*see* STATUES).

Notable former inhabitants of Grosvenor Square include, on the east side, the Marquess of Rockingham, Prime Minister in 1750–82; Charles Townshend, Chancellor of the Exchequer in 1758–66; Anne Damer, sculptress in 1795–8; Walter Hines Page, American Ambassador, in 1913–18; Lady Cunard in

Thomas Bowles' engraving of Grosvenor Square in 1751. With the exception of Lincoln's Inn Fields it is the largest square in London. It has never lost its status as a prestigious address.

1926–40. On the north side lived Henry Addington, Prime Minister in 1792–5; Lord Lytton, the novelist in 1868–73; John Pierpont Morgan Jnr, the financier, in 1902–43; Lady (Utica) Beecham, wife of Sir Thomas Beecham, the conductor, in 1926–32; the 1st Earl Beatty, Admiral of the Fleet, in 1926–36. On the west side lived Ralph Allen of Bath, intermittently in the 1750s and 1760s, and the 7th Earl of Shaftesbury, the philanthropist, in 1851—85. And on the south side lived the Duchess of Kendal, mistress of George I, in 1728–43; Lord North, the Prime Minister, intermittently between 1753 and 1792; the 3rd Duke of Grafton, the Prime Minister in 1765–8; John Wilkes, the politician, in 1791–7; Viscount Stratford de Redcliffe, the diplomatist, intermittently in 1832–78; and Sir Ernest Cassel, the financier, in 1890–1918. During the 2nd World War, when so many buildings in the square were occupied by American military headquarters, it was nicknamed Eisenhower Platz. A plaque at No. 20 indicates the building where Eisenhower's headquarters were located in 1942. The EUROPA HOTEL is on the north side. The BRITANNIA HOTEL is at No. 40.

Grosvenor Street *W1*. One of the principal streets on the GROSVENOR ESTATE, built in 1720–34. In 1735 it was described as 'a spacious well built street, inhabited chiefly by People of Distinction', and about one third of its residents were titled. About 20 of its 74 houses survive, though much altered by stucco facings or by the addition of porticos and extra storeys. Much of this kind of work was done in Victorian times, but the street retained its predominantly fashionable residential quality until around 1914, and as late as 1910–11 the financier Sir Edgar Speyer built himself a magnificent mansion at No. 46 (now the Japanese Embassy) to designs by Detmar Blow and the French architect Fernand Billerey. But soon after 1918 the GROSVENOR ESTATE abandoned its attempts to maintain the residential quality of the street; several office blocks have since been built, and commerce now predominates. Notable inhabitants include, on the north side, James Stuart, the architect, in 1759–63; Samuel Whitbread, the brewer and politician, in 1792–8; William Huskisson, the statesman, in 1800–3; Sir Humphry Davy, the scientist, in 1816–24; Sir Thomas Stamford Raffles, the colonial governor, in 1825–6; Richard Cobden, the statesman, in 1855–8. On the south side lived Bishop Benjamin Hoadly, in 1726–45; the 3rd Earl of Bute, later Prime Minister, in 1748–52; Robert and James Adam, the architects, in 1758–62; and George Palmer, the biscuit manufacturer, in 1881–7.

Grove *Highgate, N6*. A notable row of houses stretching from the top of West Hill towards Hampstead Lane. Nos 1–6 were built on the site of Dorchester House in the 1680s by William Blake (*see* HIGHGATE). It became HIGHGATE's most elegant street, and was known successively as the Long Walk, Pemberton Walk and later Quality Walk. Coleridge lived in No. 3, the home of his friend, the surgeon James Gillman, for 18 years, and died there in 1834. His long stay is marked by a plaque. J.B. Priestley also lived in No. 3. Roger Fry was born in No. 6. Yehudi Menuhin was living at No. 2 in 1982. Nos 7–12 are built on the site of a house known as The Grove, and were built from 1832 onwards, extending the road as far as Hampstead Lane. John Drinkwater lived at No. 9.

Grove End Road *NW8*. A stretch of road running northwards, linking LISSON GROVE with Abbey Road. The large detached villas which once bordered it were begun about 1818 by a speculative builder, William Hall, who is himself commemorated in Hall Place. W.F. Yeames and P.H. Calderon had their studios at Nos 4 and 16 respectively in the 1880s, but the thoroughfare's greatest ornament was the mansion owned first by J.J. Tissot and then by Sir Lawrence Alma-Tadema from 1886 till his death in 1912. No. 44 (formerly 34) still exists, though now sub-divided into flats. The famous garden colonnade still looks sturdy.

Grove House *Brompton*. This house, which once stood in what is now Cromwell Place and which was demolished in 1857, was the country retreat of the magistrate Sir John Fielding, who believed that all magistrates should 'each have a little country house at some small distance out of town'.

Grove House *Chiswick*. The site is now covered by the houses in Kinnaird Avenue. It is not known when the first Grove House was built but the estate is recorded in the 14th century. From the mid-16th to the mid-18th century it belonged to the Barker family, some of whom represented MIDDLESEX in Parliament. By the early 19th century it was owned by the Duke of Devonshire. The house, much altered in the 18th century, was not demolished until 1928, after the death of the last owner. The grounds were famous for their beautiful trees.

Grove House *100 High Street, Hampton, Middlesex*. Built in 1726–9 by Lady Mary Downing on the site of two earlier houses. Part of one of these remains on the left-hand side. Mary Forrester had been forced to marry, at the age of 13, her cousin George Downing, then aged 15, but they separated very soon afterwards. Downing, who succeeded to a baronetcy in 1711, bequeathed funds for the founding of the Cambridge college named after him. The main feature is a spectacular room with marble floor, domed roof, red and blue stained glass, and dado of Persian tiles, having the appearance of a mosque. This room was added in 1906 by Mr C.J. Stutfield and it gave rise to the supposition that, while serving in the Army, he had been converted to Islam. In fact he was a staunch Anglican and Anglican services were held in the room. There is little doubt that the design was inspired by the Court of the Alhambra, visited by Mr Stutfield while stationed at Gibraltar. The house is now the offices of an engineering firm.

Grove House *Kensington Gore*. Built in the middle of the 18th century on the site of the ALBERT HALL. It was occupied soon afterwards by Anne Pitt, sister of the Earl of Chatham, and described by Horace Walpole as a 'vile *guinguette*, that has nothing but verdure, and prospect, and a parcel of wild trees that have never been cut into any shape'. As though taking these words to heart, Miss Pitt commissioned Robert Adam to carry out certain improvements which, so Mrs Delany said, turned it into 'an uncommonly pretty place'. A later occupant was John Elliott who became physician to the Prince of Wales in the 1770s and told the Queen that he preached to the Prince 'against intemperance as any bishop could have done'. 'And probably,' the Queen commented, 'with like success.' Elliott's divorced wife Grace was one of the Prince's early mistresses and she liked to suppose that her illegitimate daughter was his, though she may equally well have been fathered by one of Grace's numerous other lovers. Samuel Whitbread's widow subsequently lived here for 30 years until her death in 1846. Five years later the house was sold to the Royal Commissioners for the GREAT EXHIBITION of 1851, used for some time as their offices and demolished in 1857.

Grove House *Regent's Park, NW1.* Built in 1823 by Decimus Burton for George Bellas Greenhough, the natural scientist, who lived there till 1856. Particular care was taken with the villa, which occupies one of the most commanding sites on the perimeter of the Park. In 1909–39 it was the home of Sigismund Goetze, artist and benefactor of ST MARYLEBONE, who presented the bronze statue of St George and the Dragon by C. Hartwell RA which stands in front of ST JOHN's church, and the wrought iron gates to Queen Mary's Garden in REGENT'S PARK. He adapted the main drawing-room into a music-room, repainting the walls himself with themes from Ovid's *Metamorphoses*. In 1955 the house was acquired by the Nuffield Foundation and it is now known as Nuffield Lodge.

Grove House formerly **Roehampton Great House** *Roehampton Lane, SW15.* The original house was built in about 1630 by Charles I's Lord Treasurer, Sir Richard Weston, later Earl of Portland. Early owners included Christian, Dowager Countess of Devonshire, who lived here from about 1650 until her death in 1674. A staunch supporter of the Royalist cause, she is perhaps chiefly remembered as the patron of the poet, Edmund Waller, and the political philosopher, Thomas Hobbes, both of whom were visitors to the house. Lord Portland's home was demolished in the late 18th century by Sir Joshua Vanneck, later Lord Huntingfield, who replaced it with a building traditionally attributed to James Wyatt. Wyatt's house (if such it is) forms the core of the present building, which has been the home of the Incorporated Froebel Educational Institute since 1921, and now also contains part of the administration of the ROEHAMPTON INSTITUTE.

Grovelands *Southgate, N14.* Originally called Southgate Grove, Grovelands was built in 1797 to designs by John Nash for Walker Gray. The park was landscaped by Humphry Repton. The Taylor family of Taylor Walker, the brewers, lived there for much of the 19th century until the house was handed over for use as a military hospital during the 1st World War. The best room is undoubtedly the delightful birdcage room. Until recently the house was used as a hospital. In 1981 proposals were made to convert it into offices.

Grub Street Possibly meant a street infested with worms, or more probably it was named after a man called Grubbe. Since the 17th century, when Andrew Marvell coined the phrase 'Grub Street', it has been used in connection with needy authors and literary hacks. Dr Johnson said it was 'much inhabited by writers of small histories, dictionaries and temporary poems'. Foxe, the author of the *Book of Martyres*, had a house here in 1571–87. Since 1830 it has been known AS MILTON STREET.

Guards' Chapel *Wellington Barracks, Birdcage Walk, SW1.* The spiritual home of the HOUSEHOLD DIVISION. It was Dr William Dakins, Chaplain to the Brigade of Guards, who, in 1797, first proposed that troops stationed in London should cease to use conveniently accessible chapels and riding schools for divine worship, and should be given a chapel of their own. The idea was finally realised in 1838. A chapel, known as the Royal Military Chapel, was built at the east end of the barracks. It was described in *The Times* as having a 'neat and imposing exterior, both chaste and elegant'. The architect is not known. The interior, however, was considered plain to the point of ugliness. By 1879 sufficient money had been raised to rectify this and George Edmund Street was commissioned to draw up plans to beautify the chapel with marble, mosaics and stained glass. He also designed an apse in the Byzantine manner. One of the many memorial tablets erected at this time was one to Dr Dakins, whose inspiration the chapel had been.

On 18 June 1944 the chapel was hit by a flying bomb during the Sunday morning service: 121 people were killed and many more injured. As the chapel crashed in ruins, the candles in the six silver candlesticks, a present from King George VI, continued to burn on the undamaged altar. The apse was in fact the only part of the building to survive. A new chapel was designed by Bruce George and dedicated in 1963.

Guards Club *Charles Street.* Established during the Peninsular War for the regiments of Foot Guards. The Prince Regent and the Duke of Wellington had been concerned that the officers returning from Spain in 1810 should have somewhere to meet. It was at first sited opposite WHITE'S in ST JAMES'S STREET. Captain Gronow said that it was at that time 'conducted upon a military system. Billiards and low whist were the only games indulged in. The dinner was, perhaps, better than at most clubs, and considerably cheaper. I had the honour of being a member for several years, during which time I have nothing to remember but agreeable incidents.' Colonel Sebright, 'one of the most eccentric men of the age', was a daily visitor, 'finding fault with everything and everybody connected with the changes taking place in the dress etc. of the army, and of the English gentleman. From the windows of the club he used to gaze at White's and abuse the dandies, especially Brummell and Alvanley, ejaculating, "Damn those fellows; they are upstarts and fit only for the society of tailors!"' The club was afterwards situated successively in PALL MALL, ST JAMES'S STREET, JERMYN STREET and BROOK STREET before moving to Charles Street. Unable to overcome financial difficulties, in 1976 the club merged with the CAVALRY CLUB.

Guild of Freemen of the City of London *40a Dowgate Hill, EC4.* Founded in 1908, primarily for FREEMEN OF THE CITY, who were not necessarily Liverymen. The Guild now has 3,500 members. It administers a number of charities and holds an annual service in ST PAUL'S CATHEDRAL.

Guildhall *EC2.* No records remain of the buildings in which were held meetings of the ancient Court of Husting. But a survey of properties belonging to ST PAUL's dated 1128 mentions a Guildhall; and in it the first MAYOR was installed in 1192. When the rebuilding of Guildhall began in 1411 the arms of the King,

*The south prospect of the medieval Guildhall c. 1700,
having been repaired after severe damage in the Great Fire.*

Henry IV, were accompanied by those of Edward the
Confessor who reigned from 1043 to 1066, so presumably the 15th-century builders believed that the structure which they were replacing had existed in the Confessor's time. To which guild the hall belonged is
uncertain. It has been suggested, however, that it was
the Knighten guild, no longer a military guild at the
time of its dissolution in the 12th century, but a
primarily religious organisation to which the Confessor granted special privileges. This hall seems to
have been just to the west of the present site with an
entrance in ALDERMANBURY. The earlier building, in
the words of an ALDERMAN writing in the year of its
replacement, was merely 'an olde and lytell Cotage',
the new one, however, was 'a fayre and goodly house'.
Work on this house continued for some years, Henry
V helping to reduce its cost by allowing the free
passage of stone by boat and cart, and the executors of
Richard Whittington contributing to the cost of paving
the Hall and glazing some of the windows. The Gothic
porch, which is still the entrance to the Hall from
Guildhall Yard, was finished in 1430 and provided
with statues in niches under canopies. The main structure, 152 ft by 40 ft 6 ins, was completed nine years
later, in 1439; a chapel adjoining it was dedicated in
1444; in 1491 two louvres were built into the roof for
ventilation; and, in 1501, kitchens were added at the
back for the MAYOR's feast. Beneath the Hall was a
large crypt which survives today, the most extensive
medieval crypt in London.

As well as being the centre of civic government
where LORD MAYORS and SHERIFFS were elected and
meetings of the COURT OF COMMON COUNCIL held – as
they still are – Guildhall, as the largest hall in England
after WESTMINSTER HALL, was also used for important
trials, such as that of Anne Askew for heresy in 1546
and the Earl of Surrey for treason in 1547. Lady Jane
Grey was tried here with her husband, Lord Guildford
Dudley, 1553. That year also saw the trial here of
Archbishop Cranmer. And in 1606 the Jesuit, Henry
Garnet, was condemned in the Guildhall for his part
in the GUNPOWDER PLOT.

The medieval building was severely damaged in the
GREAT FIRE during which it stood, so an eye-witness
reported, 'for several hours together after the fire had

taken it, without flames (I suppose because the timber
was such solid oake), in a bright shining coale as if it
had been a palace of gold or a great building of bur-
nished brass.' The exterior walls survived and were
heightened 20 ft and provided with a row of windows
above the 15th-century cornice. The construction of
the flat roof was probably supervised by Wren. In
October 1671 the LORD MAYOR'S BANQUET was held in
the reconstructed hall. The erection of a gallery and
the interior decoration were completed by 1673. In
1789 George Dance removed the statues from the
porch as well as a balcony which had been built over
the gateway for ceremonial occasions, much simplifying the appearance of the Hall on that side.

In 1862 it was decided by the COURT OF COMMON
COUNCIL, on the advice of the City Architect, J.B.
Bunning, to replace the flat roof with an open roof
more in conformity with the medieval style of the rest
of the building. Bunning's designs were amended by
his successor, Sir Horace Jones, who introduced four
turrets at the corners, two pinnacles at the apex of each
end wall and a flèche above the louvre. Jones also
reconstructed the interior of the Hall, repaired the
floor and provided a minstrels' gallery at the west end
and an oak screen at the east. The brass plates, marking official lengths of 100 ft and 66 ft, were set in the
floor in 1878. Official lengths of one foot, two feet and
one yard are on a tablet on the south wall.

In December 1940 Guildhall was set on fire in an air
raid and the roof collapsed on to the floor. Surveying
the ruins, Sir Giles Gilbert Scott reported the 'remarkable fact' that 'the medieval portions of the old Hall
[remained] intact and practically uninjured'. A temporary steel roof was provided to cover them, and
beneath this roof Winston Churchill received the
FREEDOM OF THE CITY in 1943 and a banquet was held
to celebrate the coronation of Elizabeth II in 1953. Sir
Giles Gilbert Scott's proposals for a new roof with
stone arches strengthened with hidden steel trusses
were accepted in 1953. This roof is covered with
Collyweston stone tiles and, on the inside, the oak is
decorated with a series of shields bearing the arms of
the CITY LIVERY COMPANIES. Beneath them the windows, replacing the Victorian stained glass destroyed
in 1940, are patterned with the names and dates of all
the LORD MAYORS OF LONDON interspersed with the
monograms and supporters of the reigning monarchs.
The Lady Mayoress's gallery which was originally
erected in 1910 was rebuilt in 1953. On pedestals in the
West Gallery stand limewood representations of the
fabulous giants, GOG AND MAGOG, by David Evans,
replacing taller effigies carved in 1708 by Captain
Richard Saunders and destroyed, like the windows, in
1940. The banners hanging beneath the clerestory
windows are those of the 12 principal CITY LIVERY
COMPANIES.

The decision by the COMMON COUNCIL to erect
monuments to a few men of national importance was
not taken until the 18th century. The first to be erected, in 1772, was of the Lord Mayor, William Beckford,
by Francis J. Moore. The monument to William Pitt,
Earl of Chatham (by John Bacon, 1782) was followed
by that to William Pitt the Younger (by J.H. Bubb,
1813). Nelson's statue by James Smith was erected in
1810; Wellington's was made by John Bell in 1857.
The bronze of Sir Winston Churchill by Oscar Nemon
was cast in 1958. The memorial by F.W. Pomeroy on
the south wall to the west of the entrance door is to the

officers and men of the ROYAL FUSILIERS (the CITY OF LONDON Regiment) who died in the South African War, 1899–1902. A similar memorial to members, sons of members and officers of the CORPORATION who fell in the 1st World War is in the Porch. Statues of monarchs by Nicholas Stone (*see* GUILDHALL CHAPEL) are on the staircase leading to the old library.

The Livery Hall, intended for the use of LIVERY COMPANIES which do not have halls of their own, was built in 1957 to the design of Sir Giles Gilbert Scott. The Ambulatory on the north side of the Hall was also constructed in 1957 and gives access to the Guildhall offices and kitchens as well as the Livery Hall and the CHAMBERLAIN's Court, a room used for the admission of FREEMEN and the binding of apprentices. In 1971 six new windows for the east crypt, depicting the GREAT FIRE, Chaucer, Caxton, More, Wren and Pepys, were donated by the CLOTHWORKERS' COMPANY and four Common Councilmen. In 1973 the west crypt was restored to its original state. It has one of the finest vaulted ceilings in London. The 19 stained glass windows depict coats-of-arms of the CITY LIVERY COMPANIES. In 1974 the new west wing, designed by Sir Giles Scott Son and Partners, was completed. It contains the GUILDHALL LIBRARY, offices, committee rooms and the ALDERMEN's court room. The Guildhall art collection, at present in store, contains works by Constable, Turner, Millais and Leighton, among others. (*See also* GUILDHALL CHAPEL, GUILDHALL CLOCK MUSEUM, *and* GUILDHALL LIBRARY.)

Guildhall Chapel Completed in the early 14th century and dedicated to St Mary, St Mary Magdalen and All Saints. In 1368 Adam Fraunceys and Henry Frowyk founded a college of priests to serve there. In 1417 the CITY CORPORATION confiscated the college's lands because the priests had neglected their duties. The chapel was rebuilt in the 1430s and early 1440s. In 1542 Bishop Bonner ordered the priests not to enter taverns, wear weapons in the precincts or allow strangers in their rooms. He also imposed fines of 4d for slander and 6s 8d for fighting. The college was suppressed by Edward VI in 1548; and two years later the CORPORATION bought the chapel for £456 13s 4d. It was used by the LORD MAYOR and his retinue for weekly services and at elections and feasts. In about 1620 Nicholas Stone's statues of Elizabeth I, Charles I and Edward VI, which had been carved for the ROYAL EXCHANGE but rejected, were erected on the façade. In 1782 the Corporation adopted ST LAWRENCE JEWRY for their services and converted the chapel to a court room. The building was demolished in 1782 and replaced by a new court designed by William Mountague. The monarchs' statues were moved inside GUILDHALL. In 1886 the court was converted to house the Guildhall Art Gallery (*see* GUILDHALL).

Guildhall Clock Museum *Guildhall Library, Aldermanbury, EC2.* One of the most important horological collections in the country. Much of it was bequeathed to the GUILDHALL by the CLOCKMAKERS' COMPANY which was established by Royal Charter in 1631 'to regulate the craft of clock and watch making within the CITY OF LONDON and ten miles beyond'. The Company's collection and library – originally intended for instructing apprentices – were started in about 1814 and have both been available to the public

since 1872. More recently the Antiquarian Horological Society and the Osborne Index of Watch and Clockmakers' Collections have been added to it.

Guildhall Library *Aldermanbury, EC2.* The original Guildhall Library was formed in about 1423 from money left by Richard Whittington, Lord Mayor of London. The books, mainly theological, were all in manuscript and were chained in their bookcases. Open to all scholars, it can claim to be the first public library financed by a local authority. However, in 1549 the entire collection of books was removed in handcarts by the Duke of Somerset, possibly to furnish his new palace, SOMERSET HOUSE in the STRAND. Nearly 300 years later, in 1828, the CORPORATION OF LONDON opened its second library. It grew rapidly and, in spite of severe losses during the 2nd World War, is the finest source of information on London. The collection includes the most important works of all periods written on London, including an almost complete set of London directories dating from 1677. Equally rich is its collection of prints, maps and drawings which provide a unique topographical and visual record of London over the centuries. It is also an interesting source of genealogical history, with extensive parish registers and heraldic history of prominent London citizens.

A contemporary lithograph after Dalby of Sir Horace Jones's Guildhall Library shortly after its opening in 1872.

Guildhall Museum Founded in 1826 by the Corporation of the CITY OF LONDON, it is now amalgamated with the MUSEUM OF LONDON.

Guildhall School of Music and Drama *Barbican, EC2.* Founded in 1880 by the CORPORATION of the CITY OF LONDON as the GUILDHALL SCHOOL OF MUSIC, the result of a series of successful concerts given by the Guildhall Orchestral and Choral Society. Its conductor, Weist Hill, was made Principal of the new school. It opened with 62 pupils in a disused warehouse in ALDERMANBURY. 'The gentleman who taught the drums gave his lessons in the coal cellar.' By 1887 there were 2,500 pupils and the school moved to a building in John Carpenter Street, BLACKFRIARS, designed by Sir Horace Jones in 1885–7. The names of Tallis, Gibbons, Purcell, Arne and Sterndale Bennett were inscribed on the façade. In 1897 additions to the building were made by Andrew Murray. In 1935 the drama section was added. The school moved to the BARBICAN in 1977. The new buildings were designed by Peter Chamberlin. In 1981 there were 1,550 pupils.

Guilford Street *WC1*. Extends from RUSSELL SQUARE to GRAY'S INN ROAD. It was built mainly by James Burton in about 1793–7. In 1794 the New River Company objected to laying mains there because of the softness of the ground, but were assured that the street had been used 'for nearly 12 months for quite heavy carriages'. The street was named after the Prime Minister Lord North, 2nd Earl of Guilford, who was President of the FOUNDLING HOSPITAL in 1771–92. S.P. Cockerell planned the street with better houses on the west end and less good ones to the east. They range from first to fourth class (*see* PLANNING), but the difference is in the dimensions; there is no obvious change on the outside. Nos 70–73 have Doric façades. The south side has been redeveloped. At the entrance to CORAM'S FIELDS (now the Harmsworth Memorial Playground) are the gates of the FOUNDLING HOSPITAL. On the north side is London House, a residence for overseas students, built in 1935–7 to the designs of Sir Herbert Baker. On the south side Guilford Place leads to LAMB'S CONDUIT STREET. Swinburne, the poet, lived at No. 25 in 1879–90; J.B. Bunning, the architect, at No. 34 in 1830–2; Matthew Digby Wyatt, the architect, at No. 54 in 1852–61; George Augustus Sala, the writer, at No. 64 in 1864–6; and the Revd Sydney Smith at No. 77 in 1803. The stone sculpture of a kneeling girl pouring water from a jug in Guilford Place is by an unknown artist (1870).

Guinness Trust Formed in 1890 by Sir Edward Guinness to provide housing for the urban poor. The first estate was at Brandon Street, WALWORTH. There were also estates at Lever Street, FINSBURY, and Pages Walk, BERMONDSEY – these have been totally reconstructed on site by the Trust. The estates in Vauxhall Square, LAMBETH, and Brandon Street were sold to local authorities for demolition and redevelopment. The four remaining estates, Draycott Avenue, CHELSEA; Columbia Road, BETHNAL GREEN; Snow's Fields, BERMONDSEY; and FULHAM PALACE ROAD are all being partly demolished and partly converted into flats.

Gunmakers' Company *see* CITY LIVERY COMPANIES.

Gunnersbury Park *W3*. Said to be named after Canute's niece, Gunhilda. Few early records of the manor exist but Alice Ferrers, Edward III's mistress, is believed to have held it at one time. In the 15th century it belonged to the Frowick family, then to the Spelmans. In 1658–63 John Webb built a fine Palladian house here for Sir John Maynard, Charles II's law adviser. Princess Amelia, daughter of George II, used the house as her summer residence in 1763–86. Her bath house in the grounds survives. During her ownership William Kent is said to have worked in the gardens. In 1801 the Palladian house was demolished and the estate split into two. At the beginning of the 19th century, the two existing Regency houses were built: Gunnersbury House, probably for Major Morrison, and Gunnersbury Park, for the architect Alexander Copland, by whom it was perhaps designed. In 1835 Nathan Meyer Rothschild bought Gunnersbury Park to which Sydney Smirke carried out alterations in 1836 and added the orangery and the stables. In the 1860s the Gothic folly tower by the fishing pond was built. In 1889 the Rothschilds

bought the smaller house and estate for guests and relatives. The Rothschilds lived here until 1917 when part of the estate was sold for building. In 1926 both houses and 186 acres of land were bought by the Boroughs of ACTON, BRENTFORD and CHISWICK and EALING and opened to the public. In 1965 they were transferred to the new London Boroughs of EALING and HOUNSLOW. The larger house contains a museum whose collections cover archaeology, local history, social history and topography. They include transport, costumes, early views and maps.

Gunpowder Plot *1605*. A conspiracy in which several Roman Catholics planned to blow up King James I, his Queen and his heir, as well as PARLIAMENT, in the hope that their co-religionists would be able to take over the country in the subsequent confusion and thereby obtain the religious toleration which was denied them. The conspirators – Robert Catesby, Thomas Winwith, Thomas Percy, John Wright and Guy Fawkes, among them – rented a cellar under the PALACE OF WESTMINSTER in which Fawkes hid several barrels of gunpowder. But one of those subsequently involved in the plot, Francis Tresham, warned his brother-in-law, Lord Monteagle, not to attend the House on 5 November. Monteagle then apprised the Government of the plot. Fawkes was discovered in the cellar and taken to the TOWER, where, under torture, he gave the names of his fellow-conspirators. Four of these, including Catesby and Percy, were killed while resisting arrest. The others were dragged through the streets, executed and their heads displayed on pikes. Ever since, the cellars of the PALACE OF WESTMINSTER have been ceremonially searched before the STATE OPENING OF PARLIAMENT. And 5 November is annually kept as Guy Fawkes Night with bonfires, FIREWORKS and demands of 'a penny for the guy', an effigy of the most celebrated of the conspirators.

Gunter Estate Robert Gunter, who was created a baronet in 1901, was the son of a famous pastry-cook whose house in EARL'S COURT was known familiarly as Currant Jelly Hall. Gunter developed his father's property and many of the streets he created derive their names from his family's connections, particularly its connections with Yorkshire where Gunter had a country house, Wetherby Grange, hence WETHERBY GARDENS, SW5 and Wharfedale Street, SW10. Barkston Gardens, Bramham Gardens, Collingham Gardens, Gledhow Gardens and Knaresborough Place, SW5, are also named after places in Yorkshire. Gilston Road, SW10 and TREGUNTER ROAD, SW10 take their names from places in Wales where Robert Gunter also had properties including Abergavenny Priory, hence Priory Walk, SW10. Edith Grove, SW10 is named after one of Robert Gunter's daughters.

Gunter's Tea Shop *7–8 Berkeley Square*. The firm was founded in 1757 by an Italian pastry-cook, Domenico Negri, 'making and selling all sorts of English, French and Italian wet and dry sweetmeats', at the sign of the Pineapple – this being the usual emblem of 18th-century confectioners. Twenty years later, Negri took Gunter into partnership, and by 1799 Gunter was running the business on his own and his confectioners, on the east side of BERKELEY SQUARE, had become a famous MAYFAIR rendezvous. The *beau* *monde* flocked there to eat his ices and sorbets, said to be prepared from a secret recipe. A custom grew up that the ices were eaten, not in the shop, but in the Square itself; ladies would remain in their carriages under the trees, their escorts leaning against the railings near them, while the waiters dodged across the road with their orders. For many years, when it was 'not done' for a lady to be seen alone with a gentleman at a place of refreshment in the afternoon, it was perfectly respectable for them to be seen at Gunter's. In August 1843 Jane Carlyle reported to her husband that Darwin had said she 'looked as if I needed to go to Gunter's and have an ice', and that doing so 'revived me considerably'. The other speciality of the house was the renowned, heavily decorated, multi-tiered wedding cakes, which became an essential part of every MAYFAIR wedding. The families who ordered them were likely to have dealt at Gunter's for generations. When the east side of BERKELEY SQUARE was demolished and rebuilt in 1936–7, Gunter's moved to CURZON STREET. The tea shop closed in 1956, though the catering side of the business continued in BRYANSTON SQUARE for a further 20 years.

Gutter Lane *EC2*. A corruption of the 12th-century family name, Goudren, Guthurum or Godrune. The street was originally known as Goudron and later as Gutheran Lane. SADDLERS' HALL is on the west side.

Guy's Hospital *St Thomas's Street, SE1*. In 1721 Thomas Guy bought a plot of land opposite ST THOMAS'S HOSPITAL in St Thomas's Street with the intention of building his own hospital. Guy, a bachelor, was a very successful publisher and printer and had also made an enormous fortune in South Sea Stock. MP for Tamworth and a SHERIFF of the CITY OF LONDON, he had been a great benefactor to ST THOMAS'S. He was much encouraged in his munificence by his friend, the leading physician of the time, Richard Mead. Guy lived to be 80 but died just before the first patients were admitted to his hospital which contained 100 beds. In its early years there were

51 employees whose annual salaries, including those for the butler and his horse, amounted to £1,348 18s 8d. In 1735 a man was paid £20 for killing bed bugs; in 1738–9 an east wing designed by James Steer was added; and in 1744 a lunatic house was built with 20 beds. The west wing was added by Richard Jupp in 1774–80. In 1780 cold, hot and vapour baths were installed. Guy was reburied in 1780 in the chapel under a fine tomb and statue by John Bacon.

John Howard visited the hospital in 1788. He found some wards too low and disapproved of the wooden bedsteads which harboured bugs, but praised the new wards with iron bedsteads, admired the ventilation, sanitary arrangements and baths. In 1793 a new Governor and Treasurer, Benjamin Harrison, was appointed, ruling the hospital for the next 50 years 'despotically without salary'. He tightened up the rules. For example, Rule V stated: 'If any patient curse or swear or use any prophane or lewd Talking, and it was proved on them by two Witnesses, such patient shall, for the first Offence lose their next Day's Diet, for the second Offence lose two Day's Diet, and the third be discharged.' Rule XIII ran: 'If any patient do send to pawn, or sell any of their wearing apparel, the Pawner, the Messenger, the Sellar and the Buyer are to be discharged.'

Richard Bright, appointed to the hospital staff in 1820, was best known for his work on the kidneys (Bright's Disease) – 'the indication of disease to be deduced from an albuminous condition of the urine.' His apparatus for diagnosis was very simple – an iron spoon and a candle. He said, 'If albumen be present you perceive before it reaches the boiling point that it becomes opaque . . .' It was said when he died that no one physician since Harvey had effected so great a revolution in the habits of thought among physicians of his time. His contemporary, Thomas Addison, was almost as famous. Addison's Disease (of the suprarenals) was first described by him. Another contemporary was Thomas Hodgkin who, although he worked at Guy's, was never appointed to the staff. He became world famous for discovering 'a peculiar enlargement of the lymphatic glands and spleen' –

A patient being carried into Guy's Hospital, which was founded by Thomas Guy and opened in 1726.

Hodgkin's Disease. Of the hospital's surgeons at that time the most famous was Astley Cooper. At the age of 21 he was appointed Demonstrator of Anatomy in the medical school at ST THOMAS'S HOSPITAL, the United Hospitals School as it was known, since it served both Guy's and ST THOMAS'S HOSPITAL. With unusual good looks, manners that seldom failed to please, and a unique knowledge of anatomy and dexterity in operating, he had an income of £20,000 a year. He was twice President of the ROYAL COLLEGE OF SURGEONS. The poet John Keats was a student and listened to Astley Cooper's lectures. Keats qualified but never practised. In 1799 Guy's became the first hospital in London to appoint a dental surgeon, and it has been famous for dentistry since.

Towards the end of the 19th century, when W.E. Gladstone was senior governor, much rebuilding of the medical school was undertaken. Guy's suffered very much from bombing in the 2nd World War but its private wing, Nuffield House, built in 1935 and given by Lord Nuffield, survived. In 1940 the Nuffield Nurses' Home extension was built and the York Clinic for psychological illnesses was begun. Recently much building has been accomplished. In 1959–63 an 11-storey surgical tower block was built. There are 894 beds.

Gwydyr House *Whitehall, SW1.* Unpretentious brick house built in 1772 for Peter Burrell, the Surveyor General of Crown Lands probably by John Marquand. In 1795 it was inherited by Baron Gwydyr, his son. In 1838–40 it was leased to the REFORM CLUB while the club house in PALL MALL was being built. Since 1842 it has been used as government offices. It is now the Welsh Office. It has a snuffer on its railings at which link boys once extinguished their torches.

H

Haberdashers' Aske Schools A bequest in the will of Robert Aske, silk merchant and Liveryman of the Worshipful Company of Haberdashers, led to the foundation in 1690 of Haberdashers' Aske School which was first situated in the buildings of the HABER-DASHERS' COMPANY in STAINING LANE. In 1692 the school was moved to premises in HOXTON which were reconstructed in 1825 and again in 1875. In that year also, provision was made for separate education for girls at the school; and in addition, two new schools, for boys and girls respectively, were founded at Hatcham. Between 1898 and 1902 the foundation at HOXTON was moved and two separate schools, designed by the same architect, were built, for boys at HAMPSTEAD and for girls at ACTON. In September 1961 the boys' school at HAMPSTEAD was moved to Elstree, and in 1974, the girls' school was moved from ACTON to a site adjoining the boys' school. Thus in modern times, the Haberdashers' Aske foundation had four schools, two for boys and two for girls, with one of each at Elstree and at Hatcham. The former were classed as Direct Grant Schools until this system was abolished in 1976 when they became independent schools.

Haberdashers' Company *see* CITY LIVERY COMPANIES.

Haberdashers' Hall *Gresham Street, EC2.* The site of the present Hall was bequeathed to the Company in 1478. The original Hall was burnt down in the GREAT FIRE. The next Hall, designed by Sir Christopher Wren, opened in 1668; it suffered serious damage by fire in 1840 and 1864, and was restored. It was finally destroyed by bombs in 1940. The present Hall was incorporated into a block of flats, designed by A.S. Ash, in 1956. The panelling in the Luncheon Room dates from 1730. The Hall also contains a binding parlour for apprentices. Some fine clocks, furniture and interesting portraits have survived the various catastrophes. The dining capacity is 150. For the Company *see* CITY LIVERY COMPANIES.

Hackbridge *Surrey.* An area in the London Borough of SUTTON with no definable boundaries, around the Hackbridge, the bridge which carries the CARSHALTON–London road over the River WANDLE, which at this point formed the boundary between the parishes of CARSHALTON, on the western side, and WALLINGTON on the eastern. The origin of the name is obscure. Early versions include Hakebridge, Hagbridge and Hogbridge. The position of the bridge has shifted somewhat over the centuries, but here the river was a single stream; whilst, upstream, two rivers merged, only to become two streams again almost immediately below. This, therefore, was the obvious place for a bridge. The name came to be applied to the area surrounding the bridge. It merged with CARSHALTON on one side and BEDDINGTON CORNER on the other. In the 18th and 19th centuries the district was one of mills and large riverside estates: the owners or occupiers of the estates often worked the mills as well. Of some eight houses of substance built in this period, standing in grounds ranging from one acre to 77 acres, only one, Strawberry Lodge (now church premises) remains.

Hackford Road *SW9.* In this road in LAMBETH in 1879 Vincent Van Gogh lodged at No. 89 with Mrs Loyer, the French widow of a curate. He was then working at the London branch of the art dealers, Goupil, in SOUTHAMPTON STREET. He fell in love with his landlady's daughter who was engaged to another man.

Hackney *E5, E8, E9, N1, N16.* Situated on the west side of the River LEA with HARINGEY to the north and TOWER HAMLETS to the south. ISLINGTON and the CITY OF LONDON lie to the west. According to William Maitland's *History of London* (1756), 'the village of Hackney being anciently celebrated for the numerous seats of the nobility and gentry, occasioned a mighty resort thither of persons of all conditions from the city of London.' The derivation of the name is doubtful but one suggestion is that it comes from an Anglo-Saxon word *haccan* (to kill with a sword or axe) indicating a place of battle and *ey* meaning a river. Another theory is that it refers to well-watered land or marsh belonging to a Saxon chief named Haca and *eyot*, meaning an island between two branches of a stream. Hackney, as such, is not mentioned in *Domesday Book* because it is believed to have been a hamlet of the manor of Stebeunheath (STEPNEY) with its Lord living at Bishops Hall, BETHNAL GREEN. For many centuries the area was pleasant and open countryside with views stretching for many miles. Hackney was itself a long and scattered village, its main houses being on either side of the road which runs from MILE END via Cambridge Heath to join the main north road at STAMFORD HILL. Midway along this road was the old village centre with its parish church. One of the few buildings now remaining to remind residents of links with the distant past is the tower of this church of St Augustine, said to have been built by the KNIGHTS TEMPLAR about 1300. The old tower owes its survival to an apprehension that the tower of the new church of ST JOHN would not bear the weight of a peal of eight bells. This misgiving proved false and the bells hang in the present church which was completed in 1799.

During the 15th and 16th centuries London was growing and the villages in close proximity were becoming more important as places where the nobility and rich merchants could build homes not too far removed from the CITY. One such house, thought to have been built about 1409, stood at the junction of Upper Clapton Road and Lea Bridge Road. This was known as Brooke House. Until it was extensively

Hackney in the late 19th century, when its largely rural character had been changed by the coming of the railways.

damaged in the 2nd World War it was the home of the Earls of Northumberland and Oxford. Edward de Vere, the 17th Earl of Oxford, who is considered by some to have been the author of Shakespeare's plays, lived here until his death in 1604. Hackney's oldest surviving house was built early in the 16th century. This is Sutton House in Homerton High Street. Thomas Sutton, the founder of CHARTERHOUSE hospital and school, lived here at the beginning of the 17th century. Restored in 1904, it was presented to the NATIONAL TRUST in 1938.

In the 17th and 18th centuries Hackney was regarded as particularly healthy and agreeable and acquired a reputation for gaiety and pleasurable activities. Its gardens were also famous and in Pepys's time pleasure grounds provided a profitable income for Hackney's inhabitants. In his diary, dated 11 June 1664, Pepys records, 'With my wife only to take ayre, it being very warm and pleasant, to Bowe and Old Ford; and thence to Hackney. There light and played at shuffle board, eat cream and good cherries; and so with good refreshment home.' Evelyn also records in his diary on 8 May 1654, 'I went to Hackney to see my Lady Brooke's garden which is one of the neatest and most celebrated in England . . .'

At the opening of the 19th century Hackney was still largely rural in character, but while central and northern Hackney were busy with nursery gardening, industry had been growing to the south and east. Clothing, boot and shoe making and furniture were the main occupations. According to the 1801 census Hackney had by then a population of 12,730. This was to rise to 22,494 in 1821, 53,589 by 1851 and by the beginning of the 20th century the population was over 200,000. With the exception of a few parks Hackney's rural acres disappeared under bricks and mortar.

In this century the period between the Wars and the years following the 2nd World War have seen the demolition of thousands of Georgian and Victorian houses, terraces and squares and the building of many large municipal housing estates. In 1965 Hackney was amalgamated with SHOREDITCH and STOKE NEWINGTON to form a larger local authority unit, the London Borough of Hackney.

Hackney Downs *E5.* In 1837 these were 'lammas lands' with complicated rights affecting seasonal crops grown there. This gave rise to disputes when people tried to help themselves to the freeholder's corn. They are now used for bowls, children's games, fêtes and carnivals. There are about 40 acres.

Hackney Marsh *E5, E9.* A large area (337 acres) of flat meadowland lying to the east of HACKNEY alongside the River LEA. It was purchased by the LONDON COUNTY COUNCIL in 1893 for £75,000. The mills on Mill River, a tributary of the LEA, were owned by the KNIGHTS HOSPITALLERS. They were employed in grinding corn and needle and pin points. In chemical experiments there Prince Rupert invented 'Prince's metal' for the manufacture of guns.

Danish Vikings sailed up the River LEA as far as Ware in the 9th century. King Alfred outwitted them by diverting the river 'soe that where shippes before had sayled, now a small boate could scantily rowe', causing them to run aground. Following draining of the marshes, part of a Roman causeway, coins and a coffin containing a skeleton were discovered in 1757. Dick Turpin and other footpads frequented the nearby White House public house. In the 19th century the area was frequently flooded until the canal system was developed. Bird shooting, hare and rabbit coursing and bull-baiting all took place and fishing was very popular. Football and cricket have now superseded these pastimes.

Hadley Wood *Hertfordshire.* This middle-class housing estate, developed during the last 100 years, lies on the extreme west of the ancient ENFIELD CHASE. The Chase became Crown property in 1399 through the marriage of the Duke of Lancaster (later King Henry IV) to Mary de Bohun. Henry incorporated this inheritance into the DUCHY OF LANCASTER. EN-FIELD CHASE was a royal hunting-ground till 1777, when by special Act of Parliament it was enclosed. Allotments of land were assigned to adjoining parishes; the central 3,000 acres remained the property of the Crown and were sold for agricultural development in 24 lots with 99-year leases. By 1850 the Great Northern Railway main line to London was completed. It passed through the four most westerly lots of Duchy land on which Hadley Wood now stands. The agricultural development required by the 1777 Act not having been very successful, the then leaseholder, Charles Jack, made a new lease with the Duchy and came to an agreement with the Great Northern Railway to develop a housing estate on part of his land if a station was built. By 1884 the station was opened and the first 50 houses were being constructed. By 1941 the lease between the Duchy and the Jack Estate ended prematurely, the Jack Trustees not having fulfilled the conditions. Freeholds of houses and of some land were sold; private housing development increased especially in the 1950s and '60s. Today Hadley Wood consists of some 900 houses. In the 1980s the Duchy still owns a few freeholds and has covenants on most houses. Two buildings of historical interest remain. The Duchy surveyor concerned with the 1777 Act received a gift from the Crown of 152 acres, on which he built himself a mansion. Today, very little altered, it is Hadley Wood Golf Club House. The other building, WEST LODGE PARK, rebuilt in 1832 on the site of the West Bailey Ranger's Lodge in the old CHASE, is now a hotel. Hadley Wood has always been in the Urban District of ENFIELD. It is now part of the London Borough of ENFIELD although the postal address is BARNET. Since 1911 it has had its own church, St Paul's, a chapel-of-ease to Christ Church, COCKFOSTERS.

Haggerston *E2*. That part of the former Metropolitan Borough of SHOREDITCH which lies east of Kingsland Road and to the north of Hackney Road. It is now within the London Borough of HACKNEY. The manor is referred to in *Domesday Book* by the name of Hergotestane: 'Robert Gernon holds of the King two hides in Hergotestane . . . and it is worth forty-five shillings.' The name may have meant 'at the stone of Haergōd' but the spellings from 1220 onwards indicate an original ending in '-turn' and so the meaning may have been 'Haergōd's farm'. In 1255 the Dean and Chapter of ST PAUL's were granted all the manor holdings, but what eventually became of them is uncertain. Part seems to have gone to Hoxton Manor and the major portion to the Priory of St Mary Spital without BISHOPSGATE. After the DISSOLUTION the manor passed through a series of owners until its purchase in 1720 by a Richard Nicholls whose name appears on a map by Peter Chassereau in 1745.

In the 17th century Haggerston was still sufficiently out of London to be the residence of gentlemen of leisure and scholars such as the Astronomer Royal, Edmond Halley, the first observer of the comet which bears his name. In the next century, the area was still predominantly rural, peripheral to the built-up part of London with buildings being concentrated round a green in an angle formed by Nursery Lane (now Laburnum Street) and Haggerston Lane (now Weymouth Terrace). There were few other buildings. Proximity to the CITY encouraged the building of alms-houses by a number of City companies – Drapers', Ironmongers', Framework Knitters' (all on the east side of Kingsland Road) and Goldsmiths' (to the east of the area, north of Hackney Road) (*see* CITY LIVERY COMPANIES). Of these only the Ironmongers' remain. Erected about 1715 from money provided under the will of Sir Robert Geffrye, a former Lord Mayor of London and twice Master of the IRONMONGERS' COMPANY, the building is now owned by the INNER LONDON EDUCATION AUTHORITY, and is a museum of furniture and domestic art (*see* GEFFRYE MUSEUM).

Hainault Forest *Essex*. Like EPPING FOREST, a surviving part of the Royal Forest of Essex. The earliest known form, Henehout (in 1221) indicates 'the community's wood': this corner of the old forest belonged to the abbey of BARKING. The later spelling, suggesting a connection with Edward III's queen, Philippa of Hainault, is misleading. At the ILFORD end of Hainault Forest stood the Fairlop Oak, still recalled by names on the map. Daniel Day, a pump maker of WAPPING, came out each July to collect rent and about 1725 he began the custom, which became annual, of bringing a party of friends and joining with his tenants in a feast below the great tree. After Day's death, Fairlop Fair was kept up until, following a fire in 1805 and the falling of the rest of the tree in 1820, the focal point had gone and the fair petered out. The pulpit of ST PANCRAS church in Upper Woburn Place was made of wood from the tree. Hainault Forest was disafforested in 1851 and became mostly farm land. Much of it later became sports grounds.

Hain's Coffee House *Birchin Lane*. Probably established in 1674, Hain's changed its name to the Marine Coffee House in 1681. Although it was never used as a business address by traders, the Marine was 'a mart of importance'. The first offices of the London Assurance were reached through a passage under the coffee room, and the house has sometimes mistakenly been called the London Assurance Coffee House. It was destroyed in the fire in CORNHILL in March 1748.

Hale House *Kensington*. Also known as Cromwell House, its site is now covered by the crossroads where CROMWELL ROAD passes through QUEEN'S GATE. In the later 17th century it was occupied by the 5th Lord Howard of Effingham and in 1794 it was rented by Edmund Burke in the vain hope that the air of the district might be good for his sickly son. There is an unverifiable tradition that Oliver Cromwell once lived here, hence its alternative name which Prince Albert chose as the name for CROMWELL ROAD when the house was demolished to make way for QUEEN'S GATE in the 1850s.

Half Moon Street *W1*. Extends from PICCADILLY to CURZON STREET and takes its name from a public house which formerly stood at the corner of PICCADILLY. Building evidently began in about 1730, and quite a number of Georgian houses still survive, though, of course, much altered. Nos 7–15 on the east side make a good range, No. 14 (stuccoed now) having had a two-storey projection added in Regency times, supported on thin iron columns. This picturesque effect is repeated on the west side, where No. 26 has a similar projection encompassed with much Regency cast-ironwork. Most of the houses on both sides retain their original frontage-widths even though rebuilt, and some are used as hotels or for apartments. Half Moon Street has, indeed, had apartment houses for a very long time. James Boswell took rooms here in 1768 at 'Mr Russell's, upholsterer', where he was visited by David Hume, David Garrick and of course Dr Johnson. So too, in 1849, did Lola Montez, former protégée of King Ludwig of Bavaria, and it was perhaps from this house that she sallied out to celebrate her bigamous marriage to the rich George Heald, who very opportunely died shortly afterwards, thereby obviating the need for her to go to gaol after the reappearance of her 'first' husband, and enabling her to decamp to foreign parts. But despite this naughty interlude Somerset Maugham in 1930 found Half Moon Street to be 'sedate and respectable. Most of the houses let apartments but this was not advertized [sic] by the vulgarity of a card; some had a brightly polished brass plate, like a doctor's, to announce the fact, and others the word *Apartments* neatly painted on the fanlight.' It was at about this time that Bulldog Drummond, the hero in Sapper's thrillers, lived in Half Moon Street. After the lapse of another 50 years, things have changed relatively little here.

Halfway Street *Sidcup, Kent*. North of the railway, dates from the 15th century and shows occasional traces of once being a busy and pleasant hamlet; but, having suffered the same history as SIDCUP, it is now little more than a road name. Behind lie LAMORBEY PARK and the Oval, a town-planning scheme of 1931. Beyond the Wyncham stream and the River Shuttle, Blackfen and Blendon lie along a crest. Both date from the 13th century and were centred on large houses and grounds which succumbed to developers in the 1930s, aided by new railway stations at Falconwood and Albany Park.

Halkin Street *SW1*. Built in about 1807 and named after Halkin Castle, Flintshire owned by the ground landlord, the Marquess of Westminster. The Belgrave Chapel, designed by Robert Smirke in 1825 and later known as St John's, Belgrave Square, was in this street. It was demolished in 1910. The CALEDONIAN CLUB is at No. 9.

Hall Place *Bexley, Kent*. The name of this house is presumably derived from the 13th-century Bexley family named At-Hall who owned the original property. A former Lord Mayor of London, Sir John Champneys, bought the estate in 1537 and built what is basically a scaled-up version of a late medieval hall house, using stone probably filched from a recently closed monastery. It has a central hall, with parlour and bedroom at one end and domestic offices at the other; a chapel and kitchen projected from the ends of the main block. Robert Austin, also a wealthy Londoner, bought it in 1649 and built a large brick extension, effectively doubling the size of the house but with no attempt to harmonise the new with the old. He also installed a moulded plaster ceiling in the Champneys' principal bedroom which is regarded as one of the finest of the period in Kent. From the Austins it passed to Sir Francis Dashwood, whose descendants let it to tenants. It was a boarding school for most of the 19th century.

Hallam Street *W1*. Built in about 1745–70 and named after Henry Hallam who lived at 67 WIMPOLE STREET. Nos 36–38, the Central Synagogue, designed in a Moorish style by N.S. Joseph in 1870, were destroyed in the 2nd World War and rebuilt in 1958. At No. 44 is the General Medical Council, founded 1858. It is the controlling body of medicine responsible for standards of education and for keeping registers of qualified doctors. Their building is by Eustace Frere (1915). No. 110 was the birthplace of D.G. Rossetti in 1828.

Halsey Street *SW3*. First listed in the Chelsea Road Book in 1846. Probably named after the Revd John Halsey, heir to part of the land on which the street is built.

Ham *Surrey*. Passing through PETERSHAM, one very quickly comes to a large open space of grass and trees. This is Ham Common which reaches as far as Ham Gate to RICHMOND PARK. Variously known as Hamme-juxta-Kyngeston and Ham-with-Hatch, Ham was always a separate manor from PETERSHAM, though from 1637 they shared the same Lord when the two manors were leased to William Murray, 1st Earl of Dysart, of HAM HOUSE. As in PETERSHAM, the Dysarts owned much of the property in Ham. Charles I granted the inhabitants certain rights on Ham Common in return for 483 acres which he took when he was creating his New Park, now RICHMOND PARK. These rights were jealously guarded over the centuries, and when in 1891 the Dysart family tried to restrict them and claim that certain footpaths were private property, they retreated in the face of public outcry.

There are a number of fine 18th-century houses round the Common and in Ham Street which runs from the Common to the river. In Ham Gate Avenue which leads to RICHMOND PARK, stands ORMELEY LODGE. Other houses include the late 17th-century Sudbrook Lodge and Park Gate House built in 1768. In Ham Street are the MANOR HOUSE and Grey Court where John Henry Newman lived until he was seven. He wrote later, 'I dreamed about it when a schoolboy as if it were paradise.' St Andrew's Church on the Common was built in 1831 to the designs of Edward Lapidge. The south aisle was added in 1857. The history of Ham is inextricably bound up with that of HAM HOUSE and its close neighbour PETERSHAM.

Ham House *Surrey*. Has been called the sleeping beauty among country houses. Beautifully situated by the THAMES and surrounded by parkland, it has survived relatively unaltered from the 17th century. In 1678, John Evelyn wrote in his diary, 'After dinner I walked to Ham to see the House and Garden of the Duke of Lauderdale, which is indeed inferior to few of the best Villas in Italy itself; the House furnished like a great Prince's; the Parterres, Flower Gardens, Orangeries, Groves, Avenues, Courts, Statues, Perspectives, Fountains, Aviaries, and all this at the banks of the Sweetest River in the World, must needs be surprising.' It was built in 1610 by Sir Thomas Vavasour, Knight Marshal to James I. The Earls of Dysart lived at Ham for nearly 300 years, the house having been acquired in 1637 by William Murray, 1st Earl of Dysart. As a youth, he held the post of whipping boy to the future Charles I, which entailed being punished for the prince's misdemeanours. But his friendship with the heir to the throne also brought less painful benefits including a peerage and the lease of the manors of HAM and PETERSHAM. His only daughter Elizabeth acquired the title of Countess of Dysart in her own right and the power to hand the title down to her children. Her portrait painted by Sir Peter Lely when she was a young girl hangs in the Round Gallery at Ham and shows a face full of character bearing out Henry Knyvet's description of her as 'a pretty witty lass'. She married first an unambitious man, Sir Lyonel Tollemache, who died in 1669. In 1672, she married John Maitland, Earl of Lauderdale, soon to become Duke, a man more equal to her abilities and ambitions. She had considerable political power, both influencing Cromwell during the Commonwealth, and doing much to further the Royalist cause. The Duke had been held prisoner by the Parliamentarians until the Restoration but quickly regained his former power. He became Secretary for Scotland, a post he held for 20 years. He was a member of the famous ministry called the Cabal. Macaulay wrote of him, '. . . loud and coarse both in mirth and anger, [he] was perhaps, under his outward show of boisterous frankness, the most dishonest man in the whole Cabal.' Ham House then became the home of these two powerful people and was immediately judged too small. Building work began in 1672, the year of their marriage, with the intention of doubling the existing accommodation. But it was on the interior that they spared no expense, creating rooms of such sumptuous splendour as to occasion Evelyn's remark that the rooms were 'furnished like a great Prince's'. The walls were hung with tapestries or other rich fabrics such as damask and velvet, curtains were made to match or contrast, beds were hung with satins, and upholstery was trimmed to match in brilliant colours. Ham House today, meticulously restored, still retains enough of this original splendour to give us some idea of the vivid and glorious effect it once had on admiring visitors. Shortly after the redecorating was finished in 1677, an inventory of the contents was made, and two others were made in 1679 and 1683. The Duke of Lauderdale died in 1682, but the Duchess continued to live at Ham until her death in 1698. The house passed to Lionel Tollemache, 3rd Earl of Dysart, her son by her first marriage. The fortunes of Ham then changed abruptly: the 3rd Earl, feeling it necessary to economise after his mother's extravagances, virtually stripped the house of its splendour and put into storage all its treasures. His grandson Lionel, the 4th Earl, who inherited it in 1727, was described by Horace Walpole, then living across the THAMES at STRAWBERRY HILL, as 'a strange brute'. His son proposed to Walpole's niece, Charlotte, whose portrait by Sir Joshua Reynolds hangs in the Great Hall, and was accepted. During their time the house remained secluded from the world. Soon after Charlotte moved to Ham in 1770, Walpole wrote, 'I went yesterday to see my niece in her new principality of Ham. It delighted me and made me peevish. Close to the Thames, in the centre of all rich and verdant beauty, it is so blocked up and barricaded with walls, vast trees, and gates, that you think yourself an hundred miles off and an hundred years back. The old furniture is so magnificently ancient, dreary and decayed, that at every step one's spirits sink, and all my passion for antiquity could not keep them up.'

Perhaps one of the most remarkable things to survive at Ham is the 17th-century garden, a great rarity as most of the formal gardens of that time were swept away in the 18th and 19th centuries by the fashion for natural landscape gardens.

Hambro's Bank Ltd *Bishopsgate, EC2.* One of the CITY's senior merchant banks, Hambro's was established in 1839 as the London office of C.J. Hambro and Son, merchants and bankers of Copenhagen. Its first office was at 70 OLD BROAD STREET, where the banking business was dominated by Scandinavian connections and, between the 1850s and 1880s, by major loan issues for foreign governments. In 1920 the firm amalgamated with the British Bank of Northern Commerce (founded in 1912) and was renamed Hambro's Bank in 1921; it is now the only merchant bank which calls itself a bank in its title. Five years later Hambro's moved to its present address, 41 BISHOPSGATE, site of the Bank of Northern Commerce's old headquarters.

Hamilton Place *W1.* Originally a short cul-de-sac leading out of PICCADILLY to the southern boundary of HYDE PARK, which then extended further east than now. It takes its name from James Hamilton, who was appointed Ranger of HYDE PARK by his companion, Charles II. In 1869–71 it was connected to PARK LANE in order to relieve the congestion at the southern end of that thoroughfare, and its width was doubled. More recently, in the 1960s, it has itself been relieved of most of its through traffic by the dual carriageway extension of PARK LANE to HYDE PARK CORNER. Most of Hamilton Place is now dominated by the INN ON THE PARK and the INTER-CONTINENTAL HOTEL. No. 5, now Les Ambassadeurs Club, was rebuilt in 1879–81 by W.R. Rogers for Leopold de Rothschild in an appropriately expensive Frenchified classical style, and has dramatic views across the swirling traffic of PARK LANE to the peace of HYDE PARK. No. 4, once the home of the Earl of Lucan (1810), the Duke of Wellington (1814) and Lord Granville (1822), is now the headquarters of the ROYAL AERONAUTICAL SOCIETY.

Hamilton Terrace *NW8.* Laid out in 1829 on the HARROW SCHOOL estate and called after James Hamilton, Duke of Abercorn, a Governor of the School. No. 17 was the home of Sir Joseph William Bazalgette, the civil engineer who created London's drainage system; and at No. 20 lived the musician, Sir George Alexander MacFarren, to be followed in 1900–21 by the artist, William Strang.

Hamley's of Regent Street Ltd *188 Regent Street, W1.* William Hamley founded a toy shop at 231 HIGH HOLBORN called 'Noah's Ark' in 1760. As the business grew, Hamley's descendants opened a branch at 64–66 REGENT STREET and acquired Bland's at 35 NEW OXFORD STREET in 1881. In 1901 the original 'Noah's Ark' was burnt down and reopened at 86–87 HIGH HOLBORN. Inventors of games usually came first to Mr Hamley's stores. A new game called Cossima became very popular, though the name was not, so it was renamed Ping Pong. In 1906 the firm moved to 200–202 REGENT STREET and had a model of Noah's Ark over the door.

Hammersmith *W6.* The most western of the inner London boroughs, it seems to have derived its name from two Anglo-Saxon words meaning 'hammer' and 'smithy'. The first recorded mention of the name was in 1294. Throughout its history Hammersmith has been dominated by the roads along which it developed. It was crossed by two great roads from London; that which ran through KENSINGTON to BRENTFORD and that which ran through BAYSWATER, NOTTING HILL and SHEPHERD'S BUSH to UXBRIDGE.

Hammersmith was part of the Manor of FULHAM which belonged to the BISHOPS OF LONDON from the 8th century. It was a part of the parish of FULHAM until 1834 when its chapel-of-ease, consecrated by Archbishop Laud in 1631, became the parish church of ST PAUL.

Roads still dominate Hammersmith with the GREAT WEST ROAD cutting off the riverside and passing over Hammersmith Flyover which was built in 1961 to relieve the traffic going through HAMMERSMITH BROADWAY, one of the busiest traffic junctions in Greater London. The riverside from HAMMERSMITH BRIDGE to CHISWICK forms an attractive oasis. Most of the buildings date from the 18th century. They include KENT HOUSE and WESTCOTT LODGE in LOWER MALL which is separated from UPPER MALL by Furnivall Gardens. Furnivall Gardens was named after F.J. Furnivall, the English philologist, who founded the Hammersmith Sculling Club for girls and men, now called the Furnivall Sculling Club. They also include an enclosed garden on the site of the old Quaker burial ground which was bombed during the 2nd World War. In UPPER MALL are SUSSEX HOUSE, the SEASONS, the DOVE Inn (an attractive building dating from the early 18th century, originally a coffee-house), River House (next door to KELMSCOTT HOUSE) which retains much of its early 18th-century character and was once the home of T.J. Cobden-Sanderson, the book-binder and printer, RIVERCOURT HOUSE and LINDEN HOUSE.

Apart from traffic congestion, Hammersmith is best known for providing entertainments of all kinds. Those which remain include the WHITE CITY STADIUM, the BBC TELEVISION CENTRE, QUEEN'S PARK RANGERS FOOTBALL CLUB, the PALAIS DE DANSE, OLYMPIA, the new LYRIC THEATRE, the Hammersmith Odeon and the Riverside Studios, no longer making films, but now an arts centre. A plaque at No. 11 Ravenscourt Square indicates that the novelist, Ouida, whom Queen Victoria considered one of the greatest writers of her time, lived here before she moved to the LANGHAM Hotel. Another plaque at No. 27 Stamford Brook Road commemorates the residence here of Lucien Pissarro, the painter, printer and wood engraver. He lived here from 1910 until his death in 1944. Sir Frank Short, the painter and engraver, who was Treasurer of the ROYAL ACADEMY and on the staff of the ROYAL COLLEGE OF ART, lived at No. 56 Brook Green from 1893 to 1944. Leigh Hunt's last home in London was at No. 162 Rowner Road. The huge Cunard International Hotel (640 bedrooms) by Hammersmith Flyover is by T. P. Bennett and Partners (1973).

Hammersmith Bridge *Hammersmith–Barnes*. The first suspension bridge in London, it was built in 1824–7 by William Tierney Clarke with a central span of 422 ft. It was replaced in 1883–7 by the present decorative suspension bridge designed by Sir Joseph Bazalgette who re-used the old piers and abutments. The IRA tried to blow it up in 1939 but the bomb was thrown into the river by a passer-by. The deck girders were replaced in a major overhaul in 1973–6.

Hammersmith Broadway *W6*. Originally the place where roads from SHEPHERD'S BUSH, the riverside and FULHAM crossed the GREAT WEST ROAD to BRENTFORD. It became the focal point of HAMMERSMITH, with coaching inns, among which the George (formerly the White Horse, dating from before 1656), the Clarendon (once the Goat) and the Swan remain, all having been rebuilt. Trains followed the coaches

Hammersmith Bridge, the first suspension bridge in London, in 1827. It was replaced by the present bridge in 1883.

and the DISTRICT, PICCADILLY and METROPOLITAN LINES meet at Hammersmith Broadway Station.

Hammersmith Road

W6, W14. The continuation of KENSINGTON HIGH STREET to HAMMERSMITH BROADWAY. On the north side are OLYMPIA; the CONVENT OF THE SACRED HEART; the WEST LONDON HOSPITAL; and Cadby Hall, the headquarters of J. Lyons and Co. (*see* LYONS' CORNER HOUSES) – a plaque here indicates that Charles Samuel Keene, the artist, lived in a house on the site in 1865–91. Waterhouse's ST PAUL'S SCHOOL which formerly stood here has been demolished and the school has moved to BARNES. The Red Cow at No. 157 occupies a site where a tavern of this name has existed since the beginning of the 18th century. ST MARY'S church is on the south side.

Hammersmith Terrace

Hammersmith, W6. A terrace of 17 houses on the river bank almost running to the borough boundary with CHISWICK. It was probably built about 1755. The houses face the river and have gardens running down to it; the backs, which face the road, mostly have stucco Doric porches. A number of well-known people have lived in them including Philip de Loutherbourg, painter and faith healer, Arthur Murphy, actor and playwright, F.G. Stephens of the Pre-Raphaelite Brotherhood, Sir Emery Walker, engraver, Edward Johnston, calligrapher, and Sir Alan Herbert, author.

Hammett Street

EC3. Built in the late 18th century and named after Benjamin Hammett, Alderman of Portsoken Ward, who speculated in the development of the CRESCENT, the CIRCUS and AMERICA SQUARE nearby. Hammett had been a footman to Alderman 'Vulture' Hopkins. He married a daughter of the banker, Sir James Esdaile of Bunhill Row. Esdaile lent him the money for this development and later took him into partnership.

Hampstead

NW3. When prehistoric tribes lived on the hill at Hampstead they shared it with deer, boars, wild cattle and dense forest. All they left behind were two barrows. The one on PRIMROSE HILL has been flattened but there is still one on PARLIAMENT HILL. Boudicca was said to have been buried there in AD 62, but no remains were found when it was opened in 1894. The Romans built a road to St Albans across the heath. An urn and other utensils were dug up in 1774. It was probably a Saxon farmer who cleared part of the forest for his homestead that gave Hampstead its name. The place is first mentioned in a charter of King Edgar in the 10th century. In 986 King Ethelred confirmed that he had earlier given the manor to the monastery at WESTMINSTER. The Abbot hunted here and put up a gallows on the heath. At the time of *Domesday Book* Ranulph Pevrel held a fifth of the manor. He is thought to be the man who married William the Conqueror's discarded mistress, Ingelrica. By John's reign the Abbot had leased off the rest of the manor. In 1218 Henry III ordered the area to be deforested but few trees were cut down. In 1349 the Abbot and monks came to Hampstead to escape the BLACK DEATH. Nevertheless he and 26 of his monks died. In the 14th century BELSIZE is first mentioned as a sub-manor. When a great flood which would destroy all London was predicted for 1 February 1524, crowds came up the hill to watch. The Prior of St Bar-

tholomew, Smithfield had built a fortress on the hill at HARROW for the event but everyone went home dry at the end of the day. In 1540 WESTMINSTER Monastery was dissolved and the manor was given to Bishop Thirlby of Westminster. Ten years later Thirlby was sent to Norwich in disgrace and the manor was given to Sir Thomas Wroth. In about 1584 a beacon was built on the hill to warn Londoners if the Spanish Armada landed. Hampstead became a separate parish in about 1598, having previously been attached to HENDON. In 1620 the Wroth family sold the manor to Sir Baptist Hicks, later Lord Campden, who sold it to Lord Noel of Riddlington in 1629. In 1653 Hollar engraved a picture of an elm on the heath which measured 28 ft round and had 42 steps inside leading up to a platform which held 20 people. During the GREAT PLAGUE the village was invaded by fleeing Londoners. By the time the judges and lawyers arrived there was no accommodation left and they had, according to local legend, to sleep and hold court under the trees of JUDGE'S WALK. In the 1680s and 1690s parliamentary elections for MIDDLESEX were held on the heath. By the end of the century much of the forest had been cleared for timber to rebuild London after the GREAT FIRE. By 1700 Hampstead spring water, 'of the same nature and equal in virtue with Tunbridge Wells', was being sold in London taverns. In 1701 John Duffield built a pump room in WELL WALK. Fashionable society began to flock to Hampstead (*see* HAMPSTEAD WELLS). A race course was opened near JACK STRAW'S CASTLE; new lodging houses were built; a new tavern was opened; a bowling green was made; bun shops and tea shops thrived. Part of the heath was encroached upon for building. The KIT-KAT CLUB met in summer at the Upper Flask Tavern in HEATH STREET. In 1725 Defoe commented that Hampstead was growing 'from a little village almost to a city'. In 1736 when the end of the world was forecast many people spent an uneventful day on the hill waiting. In 1780 the GORDON RIOTERS came up to Hampstead to attack Lord Mansfield's house at KENWOOD, but were stopped *en route* by the landlord of the SPANIARDS who gave them free drinks until soldiers arrived. By 1801 the population had risen to 4,300. From 1808 and 1814 an Admiralty telegraph stood on Telegraph Hill. It formed a link between CHELSEA HOSPITAL and

Hollar's 1653 engraving of the elm on Hampstead Heath which had 42 steps inside leading to a platform on top.

A view of Hampstead in 1773, from the corner of Pond Street looking up what is now Rosslyn Hill.

Elstree. In 1829 Sir Thomas Maryon Wilson, the Lord of the Manor, petitioned Parliament to let him build on the heath. Local residents protested and when he died 40 years later the matter was still not resolved. Finchley Road was built in 1830 and BELSIZE developed in the 1840s. In 1871 John Maryon Wilson sold his manorial rights to the METROPOLITAN BOARD OF WORKS and the heath was preserved for public use in perpetuity. Many additions have been made since, the largest being PARLIAMENT HILL and East Park Estate (1888), Golders Hill (1898), WYLDES FARM (1907) and KENWOOD grounds in the 1920s. Hampstead was made a borough in 1900. In 1907 the tube station was built 200 ft below ground. HAMPSTEAD GARDEN SUBURB was begun in 1907. In 1964 the Library and swimming bath at SWISS COTTAGE were completed, the first stage of Hampstead Civic Centre, by Spence, Bonnington and Collins. In 1965 Hampstead became part of the new Borough of CAMDEN. The village has always been a popular place. John James Park, writing in 1814, called it 'a select, amicable, respectable and opulent neighbourhood'. Martin Frobisher had a house here. So did Sir Harry Vane; William Pitt, Earl of Chatham; Lord Chancellor Loughborough; Lord Chancellor Mansfield; Leigh Hunt; Byron; Keats (*see* KEATS HOUSE); John Constable; H.G. Wells; Wilkie Collins; Cecil Sharp; Compton Mackenzie; Sir Rowland Hill; Kate Greenaway (at No. 39 FROGNAL in a house designed for her by Norman Shaw); Joanna Baillie (at Bolton House, Windmill Hill in 1806–51); Sigmund Freud (at No. 20 Maresfield Gardens in 1938–9); Romney (at Holly Bush Hill in 1795–1800); Gerald du Maurier (at Cannon Hall, CANNON PLACE in 1916–34); Sir Walter Besant (Frognal End, Frognal Gardens in 1895–1901); Rabindranath Tagore (at No. 3 Villas on the Heath, VALE OF HEATH in 1912); R.L. Stevenson; Anna Pavlova (at Ivy House, North End Road, a house previously occupied by Charles Cockerell, Professor of Architecture at the ROYAL ACADEMY); Ramsay MacDonald (at No. 9 Howitt Road in 1916–23 and No. 103 FROGNAL in 1925–37); Mary Webb, the writer, at No. 12 HAMPSTEAD GROVE; Sir Flinders Petrie, the Egyptologist, at No. 5 CANNON PLACE; Sir Samuel Hoare, the banker, at HEATH HOUSE; John Masefield; Sir Julian Huxley; D. H. Lawrence; J.B. Priestley; George du Maurier (at New Grove House, HAMPSTEAD GROVE in 1874–95); John Galsworthy (at Grove Lodge in 1918–35). Sir George Gilbert Scott lived in 1856–65 at Admiral's House, ADMIRAL'S WALK (*see also* FROGNAL *and* WELL WALK).

Hampstead Cemetery *see* CEMETERIES.

Hampstead Garden Suburb *NW11*. Situated between GOLDERS GREEN and EAST FINCHLEY, the suburb was begun in 1907 to plans prepared by Raymond Unwin and Barry Parker who had designed Letchworth Garden City in 1903. The suburb was the idea of the philanthropist, Mrs (later Dame) Henrietta Barnett, wife of Canon Samuel Barnett, founder of TOYNBEE HALL who, when the extension of the tube to GOLDERS GREEN was planned, conceived the idea of purchasing WYLDES FARM so that 80 acres of it could form an extension to HAMPSTEAD HEATH and the remaining 243 acres form a residential area in which people from all walks of life could live together in pleasant surroundings. In WHITECHAPEL she and her husband had encouraged intellectuals to meet the local people but she felt that this temporary stimulus was not enough and better results could be achieved by the poor and deprived sharing the same environment with more fortunate beings.

In addition to Unwin and Parker, other architects were commissioned to design individual buildings. Among them was Sir Edwin Lutyens who disagreed with many of Mrs Barnett's ideas. She was 'a nice woman', in his opinion, 'but proud of being a Philistine – has no idea beyond a window box full of geraniums, calceolarias and lobelias over which you can see a goose on the green.' Building was in good, vernacular styles, in well-laid-out, tree-lined roads with ingenious closes, varying lines, and respect for contours. The central area is distinguished by terraces of houses and flats designed by Lutyens and by his notable ST JUDE'S CHURCH (named after Canon Barnett's Whitechapel parish), domed Free Church, and Institute. Flats for artisans were built to the north, villas for the middle classes to the west and larger houses for the affluent to the south adjoining the heath. The Orchard for old people and Waterlow Court for working women partly fulfilled Mrs Barnett's ideals, but her ultimate goal of forming an integrated community was never reached as the suburb, which was considerably extended after the 1st World War with good but less impressive domestic architecture, is now predominantly middle class with few shops and no public houses.

Hampstead Grove *NW3*. Until recently this was still a grove, being lined with great trees; but most of them were struck by Dutch Elm disease and had to be felled. FENTON HOUSE occupies a large part of the eastern side of the street. Opposite it is a short row of tiny cottages; Mary Webb, the writer, lived for a while in No. 12. Further north, across the road from FENTON HOUSE garden, stand Old Grove House and New Grove House, both built early in the 18th century. George du Maurier lived in the latter in 1874–95. It is quite probable that one of Hampstead's famous windmills stood just here. Hampstead Grove continues past a small reservoir (1856) to a shrubby area where can be found the old white milestone after which the Whitestone Pond is named. It announces that the spot is 'IV

miles from St Giles Pound' and '4½ miles 29 yards from Holborn Bars'. Sir George Gilbert Scott, the architect, lived at No. 21; John Galsworthy at Grove Lodge.

Hampstead Heath *NW3*. Comprises approximately 800 acres including PARLIAMENT HILL, added in 1888, the formal gardens and animal enclosure of Golders Hill, in 1898, and KENWOOD, in the 1920s. HAMPSTEAD was infested with wolves as late as the 13th century. In the time of Henry VIII it was where the washerwomen performed their services for the nobility and gentry of London. It only became fashionable with the discovery of the springs with their reputed medicinal properties in 1698. Hone described HAMPSTEAD as 'the place of groves'. One of the finest is known as Judge's Walk or Kings Bench Avenue so called since the Courts of Law were transferred there in 1665 at the height of the GREAT PLAGUE. The judges and barristers had to sleep under canvas since accommodation was so scarce. A large Roman sepulchral urn was discovered in 1774 and in 1780 the GORDON RIOTERS attempted to create havoc but were decoyed into drinking by the landlord of the SPANIARDS public house. On the high ground by JACK STRAW'S CASTLE the views are very fine and here was installed a semaphore telegraph as the first stage between CHELSEA and Yarmouth. The Heath was also used for rifle practice during the Napoleonic Wars.

The Heath has always been popular with writers and poets. The KIT-KAT CLUB met at the Upper Flask in East Heath Road. Steele, Pope and Dr Arbuthnot

Farmworkers haymaking on Hampstead Heath in 1780, with distant views of north London.

were members. Later Keats and Shelley were frequent visitors. Charles Dickens who refers to the heath in many of his books often rode to JACK STRAW'S CASTLE. The mantel-tree over the kitchen fireplace there is said to have been made out of the gallows on which the highwayman Jackson was hanged. Nearby the corpse of John Sadleir, the fraudulent MP for Sligo, was found when he poisoned himself there in 1856. Dickens used the story in creating Mr Merdle in *Little Dorrit*.

The local inhabitants have always clung to their rights over the Heath. They fought a long series of legal battles with Sir Thomas Maryon Wilson, Lord of the Manor, between 1831 and 1871 when the Heath was finally saved for the public. The Heath has always been popular and up to 100,000 visitors on one day have been recorded on a Bank Holiday. Fairs are still held at Easter, and on the Spring and Late Summer Bank Holidays. There are also riding and sporting facilities.

Hampstead High Street NW3. Many of HAMP-STEAD's 18th-century buildings are preserved here, though most of the ground floors have been converted into shops. At Stanfield House the painter, Clarkson Stanfield, lived in 1847–65.

Hampstead Water Company An act of 1543–4 had authorised the CITY to convey water from springs at HAMPSTEAD to London. But the supply remained in the hands of the CITY CORPORATION until 1692 when the Hampstead Water Company was formed to lease the 'Springs and reservoirs' from the Corporation whose interest in the water supplies had diminished with the success of the NEW RIVER COMPANY. Despite its name, the Company did not supply water to HAMP-STEAD but to the West End via KENTISH TOWN. In 1777 another reservoir was added to the three in existence. In 1850 Arthur Hassall in *A Microscopic Examination of the Water Supplied to the Inhabitants of London* described the water as coming from 'tolerably clean ponds, but also a large pond in the Vale of Health, full of weeds, swarming with animal life, the receptacle of some dead animals, and into which no inconsiderable amount of sewage passes.' There were also other weedy ponds. 'Regarding them all', Hassall concluded, 'it is impossible to say that the water distributed to the public by this company is in the condition on which a scrupulous regard to health and safety depends.' In 1858 the lowest of the Hampstead ponds was filled in. The east end of Pond Street now occupies the site. The Company was subsequently purchased by the NEW RIVER COMPANY.

Hampstead Way *NW11*. Leads north from HAMPSTEAD HEATH to FINCHLEY ROAD. John Linnell, the painter, lived at Old Wyles, North End Road, Hampstead Way where his friend, William Blake, stayed with him in the 1820s. Sir Raymond Unwin (*see* HAMPSTEAD GARDEN SUBURB) lived in the same house from 1906 to 1940.

Hampstead Wells The earliest mention of a spring in what is now WELL WALK occurs in the time of Charles II when Dorothy Pippin sold water here. The first to draw attention to the medicinal value of the water was Dr Gibbons, a celebrated physician of the early 18th century, who described it as being as good

as any chalybeate water in England. Advertised as being 'of the same nature and virtue as that of Tunbridge Wells', it was sold at the Eagle and Child in FLEET STREET for 3d. a flask, as well as at several other places including the Black Posts, KING STREET and Sam's Coffee House, LUDGATE HILL. In about 1700 a tavern was built at Hampstead, also a coffee room, bowling green and the Great Room (*see* WELL WALK). For the next 20 years all sorts of people, from court ladies to FLEET STREET seamstresses, came to the Wells to dance and listen to the concerts in the Great Room; to promenade in WELL WALK and to gamble and bowl on HAMPSTEAD HEATH. By the end of the first quarter of the 18th century the raffish frequenters of the Wells outnumbered the polite. The Great Room was sold and converted into an episcopal chapel in 1733 and used for church services until 1849. A second spa was launched soon afterwards. This proved fashionable for a time; but towards the end of the century had become as disreputable as its predecessor. The heroine of Fanny Burney's *Evelina* was obliged to refuse the offers of 'inelegant and low bred partners' who 'begged the favour of hopping a dance' with her.

Hampton, Hampton Wick, Hampton Court and Hampton Hill *Middlesex*. The present components of the Anglo-Saxon parish of Hampton, so named from the Saxon words describing the position of the first settlement – the farm in the bend of the river. *Domesday Book* of 1086 gave Earl Algar as the former owner of the manor and Walter de St Valery as the new owner. The manor was acquired by the Knights Hospitaller of St John of Jerusalem in 1236 and occupied by them until leased by Thomas Wolsey in 1514. Wolsey pulled down their manor house and started to build his palace, soon to be transformed into a royal palace for Henry VIII (*see* HAMPTON COURT PALACE). By then Hampton Court resembled a village, most of it within the walls, but with some houses, offices and workshops outside.

Meanwhile Hampton, also known as Hampton-on-Thames, was developing nearly a mile away upstream and Hampton Wick (or Hamlet) a like distance downstream. Hampton was the centre of the parish, where the church was, and the seat of parochial government. The wide separation of Hampton and its hamlet gave rise to a conflict lasting for several generations. The dispute was partly resolved by an agreement of 1698 to divide the parish land and income in the proportion of two to the 'Town' and one to the 'Wick'. With the expansion of Hampton early in the 19th century and the consequent rebuilding of the parish church in 1820–31, Hampton Wick seized the opportunity to build its own church, to form a new parish of St John, and to become independent of Hampton. The name Hampton Court is still used to denote the area adjoining the Palace, although it is not an administrative entity.

Hampton expanded away from the river towards the north along the line of the road to TWICKENHAM and London early in the 19th century, and this gave rise to a new settlement known as New Hampton. By 1863 this part of Hampton had increased to such an extent that a new parish of St James was formed. The church of St James was consecrated in 1863 and the tower with its very tall spire was added in celebration of Queen Victoria's Golden Jubilee in 1887. In response to the wishes of the inhabitants the name was changed from

New Hampton to Hampton Hill, though the hill is not detectable.

In the middle of the 19th century the supply of water became an important industry in Hampton. Although the opportunities for employment were welcomed, Hampton has never ceased to lament the loss of much of its river frontage.

By the end of the 19th century Hampton was also expanding towards the north-west, in the direction of HANWORTH. This part of Hampton was formerly the southern edge of HOUNSLOW HEATH. In the 1860s attempts were made to develop it as a housing estate. This, and subsequent attempts, had only a limited success, but they resulted in the formation of the new parish of All Saints, centred on the church in The Avenue consecrated in 1908.

By 1890 most of the spare land had been taken up for market gardening. During 1884–1914 the number of nurseries grew from one to 49 and until about 1950 the nurserymen prospered. But the time came when the sale of land for housing became more attractive than market gardening. By 1980 the number of nurseries had fallen to one again and some 1,700 houses or apartments were being built in the parish of All Saints. (*See also* BARHAM HOUSE, FARADAY HOUSE, GARRICK'S HOUSE, GARRICK'S VILLA, GROVE HOUSE, HAMPTON COURT HOUSE, MITRE, OLD COURT HOUSE, OLD GRANGE, PRESTBURY HOUSE, ROYAL MEWS *and* WILDERNESS HOUSE.)

Hampton Court Bridge *Hampton Court–East Molesey.* The first bridge on this site was built in 1753 by Samuel Stevens and Benjamin Ludgator. An exotic seven-span timber bridge, it was, despite its flimsy and undulating appearance, a road bridge 20 ft wide and the largest Chinoiserie bridge ever built. Rebuilt in 1778, it was replaced by an iron bridge in 1865. The present structure was built in 1930–3 in reinforced concrete with stone and brickwork facing. W.P. Robinson, the County Engineer of Surrey, in conjunction with Sir Edwin Lutyens, architect, was responsible for the design.

Hampton Court House *Middlesex.* Fronting Hampton Court Green and backing on to BUSHY PARK, was built in about 1757 by George Montagu Dunk, 2nd Earl of Halifax, for his mistress, Mrs Anna Maria Donaldson. Mrs Donaldson was an accomplished singer, appearing at MARYLEBONE GARDENS. After the Earl's death in 1771 the house was let to the Earl of Suffolk; then to the 4th, and memorable, Earl of Sandwich; the Countess of Lincoln (Horace Walpole's cousin); Charles Bingham (later 1st Lord Lucan); Admiral Lord Keith; and the 3rd Earl of Kelly. The owner in 1871, Marmaduke Sampson, added a picture gallery, complete with palm house. In 1883 Thomas Twining, of the family of tea and coffee merchants, bought the house for his daughter and her husband, Auguste de Wette. The de Wettes used the picture gallery as a concert hall and ballroom and entertained on a most lavish scale. In 1945 the house became a home for elderly ladies, and in 1971 the Teddington Theatre Club converted the picture gallery into a modern theatre.

Hampton Court Palace *Middlesex.* On the banks of the THAMES some 15 miles south-west of London, contains some of the finest Tudor architecture in Britain, as well as buildings of great splendour designed by Sir Christopher Wren. Its clean air, pure water, spacious woods and grounds, and the opportunity it offered for the laying out of gardens, arbours and tree-lined walks, made it the favourite country home, hunting lodge and pleasure palace of successive generations of English monarchs. Their personal tastes and the genius of their artists, architects and designers can still be seen in the buildings and gardens and in the art treasures which fill its rooms, galleries and halls.

Thomas Wolsey bought the site in 1514 from the Order of St John of Jerusalem, a year before he became Cardinal and Lord Chancellor of England. The private residence he projected rapidly assumed the proportions and grandeur of a royal palace, with 280 rooms for guests and a staff of nearly 500. The magnificence of his hospitality and entertainments were the wonder of Europe. When Wolsey fell from favour, he presented Hampton Court to Henry VIII in a vain attempt to regain his position; but in 1529 all his goods and lands were declared forfeit to the Crown. Henry moved in at once and began to enlarge the buildings and efface, where possible, traces of its former owner. New courtyards, kitchens, galleries, a new library and guard room were added during his reign. The famous Astronomical Clock, designed by Nicholas Oursian in

Hampton Court Palace in 1751. The 50 acres of gardens are a blend of Tudor, French, Italian and Dutch styles.

1540, was set in Wolsey's great gateway, redecorated and named after Anne Boleyn, Henry's second Queen. Wolsey's arms over the entrance, defaced by Henry, are now restored, and the clock, removed in 1840, was repaired and replaced in 1879, and is still in working order. Henry took great interest in the gardens, planting trees and shrubs, and, a keen huntsman, saw that the estate was well stocked with game. Towers, turrets, a Water Gallery and an elaborate summer house were put up on the south side between the palace and the river and a complex of buildings leading to the water-gate which Henry used when he came to Hampton Court by barge. He brought five of his six wives to live here. Anne Boleyn's badges and initials can still be seen among the carvings and tracery of the Great Hall which Henry built to replace Wolsey's smaller one, though Jane Seymour, who died in the palace having given birth to Henry's only son, Edward VI, had taken her place before the work was finished.

Edward VI spent most of his short life here, and it was here that his successor, Mary Tudor, received Philip II's proposal of marriage, spent her honeymoon, and passed many sad months during the remaining four years of her life, hoping vainly for a child.

Elizabeth first came to live at Hampton Court in 1559, a year after her accession to the throne. She had often stayed there, and, for some weeks in the early part of Mary's reign, had been kept under guard in the Water Gallery, suspected of intriguing to usurp her sister's crown. Her alterations to the palace included a three-storey building to the south-east of Wolsey's lodgings, which still bears her initials and the date 1568; and on the north side of the Great Hall a large room, known as the Horn Room, was converted for the display of a collection of horns and antlers. Elizabeth kept up and improved her father's gardens, working there herself every morning, in the words of a contemporary, 'briskly when alone,' but when others were present, 'she, who was the very image of majesty and magnificence, went slowly and marched with leisure.' Rare plants were brought back from distant lands by Hawkins, Ralegh and Drake for her hot-houses and flower beds, including the tobacco plant and the potato. She kept great pomp and ceremony at Hampton Court, conducting both state and private business here; it was here that her Council debated and decided the fate of Mary, Queen of Scots; and here also that a succession of foreign ambassadors came to suggest husbands for her. She always celebrated Christmas here, lavishly entertaining hundreds of guests in great merriment and pageantry, with banquets, masques, balls, masquerades, plays, music and dancing, tennis in the covered court built by her father (and still in use), and, out-of-doors, shooting, stag-hunting, tilting and coursing. The Great Hall, where plays were presented, is the oldest surviving Elizabethan theatre in England. Armies of carpenters, tailors, silk and buskin weavers, haberdashers and upholsterers were employed to make costumes and scenery; ingenious lighting effects were invented, and even artificial snow fell when required. The Duke of Württemberg, visiting in 1590, recorded in his diary: 'Now this is the most splendid and most magnificent royal palace of any that may be found in England, or indeed in any other Kingdom' and went on to describe one of the Queen's apartments 'in which she is accustomed to sit in State' with its tapestries encrusted with gold and precious stones,

the inlaid tables, fine paintings, musical instruments and ornaments.

James I took his Danish Queen to stay at Hampton Court a few weeks after his accession in 1603, and was determined to maintain the festive atmosphere which had been so marked a feature of Elizabeth's reign. Anne was an enthusiastic actress, and her first Christmas saw the royal party producing and acting in a masque commissioned from Samuel Daniel, with the young Inigo Jones designing and building the scenery. Thirty other plays were acted that Christmas by the visiting King's Companie of Comedians, Shakespeare among them. Soon afterwards, in January 1604, James arranged a Conference of Divines in an attempt to resolve fundamental differences between the Puritans and the Established Church. In this he was not successful, but out of that Conference came the Authorised Version of the Bible. After the Queen's death, in 1619, James visited the palace mainly to indulge his great love of hunting and hawking, and closely supervising, with Inigo Jones, his Surveyor, the management of the estate.

James died in 1625 and his son Charles I, recently married to the sister of Louis XIII, spent his honeymoon there and made it his home for many months during the next few years. The State Rooms were redecorated, the gardens redesigned, Charles being responsible for new ornamental lakes, ponds and fountains. He had a wide channel cut 11 miles long to bring water to feed them, and to supplement the domestic supply installed by Wolsey, making himself in the process very unpopular with his neighbours for despoiling their land. Charles was a great art collector: a catalogue of 1639 shows that nearly 400 pictures, as well as ivories, crystal, porcelain and sculpture, were at Hampton Court. The pictures included the nine canvases by Mantegna, *The Triumph of Caesar*, now cleaned and hung in their own gallery. Charles used the palace as a refuge during the troubled years 1633–42, and five years later, after the Civil War, was held prisoner there for some months by the victorious Parliamentarians. In his absence, Puritan zeal had been at work desecrating the Chapel and destroying 'popish and superstitious pictures and images'. And two years later, a few months after the King's execution, the new Parliament put Hampton Court up for sale: the proceeds were to be used to pay the royal debts and 'for the benefit of the Commonwealth'. But in 1651 the sale was stopped and Cromwell moved in with his family and lived here until his death in 1658. After the Restoration, Charles II applied himself to redecorating and repairing the palace and bringing back many of the tapestries, pictures and articles of furniture sold during the Commonwealth. The gardens in the Home Park were completely redesigned on models he had admired during his exile in France and Holland; the avenues of lime trees radiating from the east front of the State Rooms were replanted or restocked; new fountains and cascades were added. Charles spent his honeymoon at the Palace, visited it constantly to walk and picnic in the parks, entertained a stream of guests from England and abroad, and found the extensive lodgings well suited to housing his many mistresses. Evelyn and Pepys were frequent visitors, Lely came to paint the Court ladies, fashionable Londoners took refuge here from the GREAT PLAGUE in 1665, and a year later Charles stored valuable paintings there while the GREAT FIRE raged. Not a passionate huntsman, unlike so many of his forebears, he put the grounds at the disposal of his guests and was an enthusiastic spectator. Charles's brother, James II, who succeeded him, never lived at Hampton Court, but after the Revolution in 1688 and the accession of William and Mary, the second great rebuilding of the palace began. Taste had moved on, the apartments were 'old-fashioned and uncomfortable' and Sir Christopher Wren, appointed by Charles II as Architect and Surveyor of the Works, was now charged with creating something more in keeping with modern ideas. Originally he intended to demolish the whole palace, except for Henry's Great Hall, and to build 'a new Versailles' in its place, but Mary's early death in 1694, halfway through the first phase, and then a growing shortage of money, forced William to abandon the plan, and only Henry's State Apartments were pulled down. Four splendid new ranges in the classical French Renaissance style were built round the new Fountain Court. Antonio Verrio, Grinling Gibbons, Jean Tijou and Louis Laguerre were among the many notable artists commissioned to decorate the interior and design the intricate wrought-iron and stone work on the outside, on the terraces, and in the gardens. The King and Queen were keenly involved at every stage, virtually living on the site. For the first five years, the Queen, says Wren, pleased herself '. . . in examining and surveying the drawings, contrivances and the whole progress of the present building, and giving thereon her own judgment, which was exquisite.' Work slowed down after her death and the new palace was not ready until 1699, when William moved in. Much had still to be done, and in the next three years William supervised the arrangement of the art treasures he had inherited and augmented, including Mary's collection of fine china, made further changes in the gardens and parks and conducted most of his official business and entertaining here. The Banqueting House near the site of the old Water Gallery dates from this time and incorporates some of the brickwork Wren was instructed to rescue and use 'in lieu of new materials' when the old buildings were demolished.

Work already begun continued during the 12 years of Anne's reign. The Chapel was redecorated by Wren, with carvings, including the great classical reredos, by Grinling Gibbons; and the Queen's Drawing Room and other rooms on the east front were painted with murals by Verrio, Thornhill and others. Many of the rooms were not finished until after her death. Anne increased the size and importance of the Hampton Court Stud, and enjoyed the hunting. In her last years, crippled by gout and dropsy, she devised a method of hunting in a one-horse chaise. She had the parks drained and levelled and special 'chaise-ridings' made, and here she drove in pursuit of the stag, according to Swift 'furiously like Jehu', on one occasion 'no less than forty miles'. But in spite of these prodigious feats, Anne's social life was restricted by her health, and by the heavy debts she had inherited from William for work on the new palace and gardens. The days of costly royal hospitality were already past. The palace lodgings, occupied by Court and other officials, and increasingly by unauthorised persons, had become popular for private entertainments, one of which is said to have been Pope's *Rape of the Lock*.

It was not long before Anne's successor, George I, discovered the charms of Hampton Court. Unpopular and ill-at-ease among an alien people, he retreated there, whenever he could, to enjoy the rigid etiquette of his small German Court and the company of his mistresses, always travelling ceremoniously by the State barges. He took no part in the work of embellishing and finishing the new palace, which continued throughout his reign. His prolonged absences in Hanover gave his son, while Prince of Wales, freedom to invite his friends for river parties and other junketings, but the fun stopped when the King returned and the royal family settled once more into dull domesticity. By 1720 they had left the palace in the hands of caretakers and retired to London. George II brought his own family there in 1728, a year after his accession, and came every summer for the next ten years for stag-hunting and coursing, conducted, according to Mrs Howard, the King's mistress, 'with great noise and violence'. William Kent and Sir John Vanbrugh were engaged to decorate or alter parts of Wren's palace, including the ornate white marble chimneypiece and doorways in the room where the King and Queen dined in public. George II was the last English monarch to reside at Hampton Court. George III's decision not to use it came, according to his son, from having had his ears boxed by his grandfather in the State Apartments while he was still a boy. After his accession in 1760, the palace was managed by a staff of 40, among them 'Capability' Brown, who planted the Great Vine in 1769. George III solved the age-old problem of illegal tenants by his system of 'Grace and Favour' lodgings for needy and deserving people, which is still in existence.

In ensuing years Hampton Court continued to attract the interest and concern of its royal owners. George IV, keenly devoted to the turf, extended and improved the Royal Stud; his successor, William IV, renovated and repaired dilapidated buildings and brought back many of the art treasures for display in the State Rooms. Queen Victoria declared it open to the public 'free and without restriction' on certain days of the week, and in 1851, re-established the Stud which had been entirely sold 15 years earlier. At this time the administration was transferred from the Crown to the Government. The Department of the Environment now superintends the restoration, repairs and decoration, and the care of parks and gardens. (*See also* BUSHEY PARK *and* HAMPTON COURT PARK.)

Hamsell Street *Barbican.* In 1898, the former Redcross Square was renamed after an estate near Tunbridge Wells owned by the GOLDSMITHS' COMPANY, the ground landlords. Soon afterwards warehouses on both sides of the street were destroyed by fire. In the 2nd World War the street was again destroyed and its site now forms part of the BARBICAN redevelopment area.

Hand and Shears *1 Middle Street, Cloth Fair, EC1.* The tavern was erected in the 16th century. Here was established a Court of Piepowder where the stall-holders from the nearby market could settle their disagreements. The name derives from the Lord Mayor of London's opening of Smithfield FAIR by cutting the first piece of cloth. The inn sign depicts this.

Handel Street WC1. Built in 1803–8 on the FOUNDLING HOSPITAL estate and named after George Frederick Handel, a leading patron of the hospital.

Hanging Sword Alley EC4. Presumably takes its name from a street sign mentioned in 1564. The area was once well known for its fencing schools. The alley was once known as Blood Bowl Alley after a notorious night-cellar in which Hogarth laid the scene for plate IX of *Industry and Idleness* and depicted the Idle Apprentice, betrayed by a prostitute, being apprehended by officers of justice (*see* ALSATIA). Jerry Cruncher, the odd-job man and messenger for Tellsun's Bank in Dickens's *A Tale of Two Cities*, has his lodgings in the alley.

Hanover Lodge *Regent's Park, NW1*. Designed in 1827 by Decimus Burton for Colonel Sir Robert Arbuthnot, the house was in 1832–45 the home of Thomas Cochrane, 10th Earl of Dundonald. Accused in 1814 of circulating a report of Napoleon's death in order to manipulate the STOCK EXCHANGE to his own advantage, he was dismissed from the Navy and imprisoned; on his release, he roved the world, serving with the Chilean, Brazilian and Greek navies. In 1831, he was cleared of the charge of fraud and restored to his former rank, eventually serving as an Admiral in the British Navy, 1848–54. From 1848 till 1897 the villa was the property of Matthew Uzielli, the banker, and, after his death in 1860, of his family. In 1911–25 it was the home of Admiral Lord Beatty, and from 1926 the residence of Mrs von Hofmannsthal, née Astor, daughter-in-law of Hugo von Hofmannsthal, poet and librettist of Richard Strauss's *Der Rosenkavalier*. In 1948, the villa was taken over by BEDFORD COLLEGE.

Hanover Square *W1*. Forms the centre-piece of the 13-acre Millfield or Kirkham Close Estate, which was bounded approximately by OXFORD STREET on the north, REGENT STREET on the east, and on the south and west by the backs of the houses in CONDUIT STREET and NEW BOND STREET respectively. The layout of this estate was begun very soon after the accession of the Elector of Hanover as George I in 1714 (hence the name Hanover Square), the principal developer being

the great Whig magnate Lieutenant-General the Earl of Scarbrough, who in 1717–20 was granting building sub-leases here under his own lease from the ground landlord, Sir Benjamin Maddox. Hanover Square was the first of the three great MAYFAIR squares, and the success of the venture was assured by the West End building boom of the early 1720s, and by the erection of the immediately fashionable Church of ST GEORGE on the estate in ST GEORGE STREET. The original houses in the square were large and inhabited by 'persons of distinction' who included several retired generals. Only about half a dozen of these houses now survive, notably No. 24 (of three bays and four storeys, and although now with a shop window, still the least altered); and Nos 16 and 20, the latter by the French Huguenot architect Nicholas Dubois. No. 21 was occupied by Prince Talleyrand in 1830–4. In 1774–5, Sir John Gallini, the Swiss-Italian dancing master, rebuilt No. 4, on the east side, as assembly rooms. For a century the HANOVER SQUARE ROOMS were principally famous for their concerts, at which J.C. Bach, Haydn, Paganini and Liszt all performed at various times. But fashionable receptions were also frequently held. By that time most of the fashionable residents had left Hanover Square long ago, but it was still a favourite home for learned societies and for clubs, of which the most famous was the ORIENTAL CLUB at No. 18 on the west side, built in 1825 to designs by Benjamin Dean Wyatt, and now demolished.

At the south end of the central garden stands a large statue of William Pitt the Younger by Sir Francis Chantrey (*see* STATUES).

Hanover Square Rooms *Hanover Square*. Lord Dillon's house on this site was bought in 1773 by Sir John Gallini who demolished it and built these concert rooms, later known as the Queen's Ancient Concert Rooms, which were opened in 1774. Gallini, Karl Friedrich Angel and Johann Christopher Bach gave a series of subscription concerts here. After a visit in February 1775, the Earl of Malmesbury's brother wrote that it was 'by all accounts by much the most

Daye's view of Hanover Square in 1787, when its original houses were still inhabited by 'persons of distinction'.

362

elegant room in town ... larger than Almack's'. The ceiling was domed and the walls were decorated with paintings by West, Cipriani, Gainsborough and others. Annual performances of *Messiah* were given in these rooms from 1785 until 1848. The Philharmonic Concerts were held here from 1833, and the Amateur Musical Society was established here in 1846. Concerts continued to be held until 1875 when the building was sold to the Hanover Square Club, a general social club which was founded that year, and for which it was adapted by H.E. Tyler. The premises were demolished in 1900.

Hanover Street *W1*. On the Millfield Estate (*see* HANOVER SQUARE), it extends from REGENT STREET to HANOVER SQUARE and was laid out in about the 1720s. None of the original houses survives and almost all the (relatively modern) buildings are in commercial use.

Hanover Terrace *NW1*. Takes its name from George III's other kingdom, Hanover. It was designed in 1822 by John Nash in his most scholarly and restrained manner and was solidly built by John Mackell Aitkens. Its 20 houses are arranged as a single group with one continuous loggia running along the ground floor. Porticoes project at each end and in the centre with Doric pillars linking the first and second floors; the pediments are topped by somewhat precarious statues. The widowed Mrs Collins lived at No. 17 with her sons, Wilkie, the novelist, and Charles and William the artists; in 1852 they gave a dance which 70 artists and writers attended, Charles Dickens presiding over the buffet. Alexander Strahan, Wilkie's publisher, lived at No. 9 in 1874–8. Later residents were Alfred Noyes (at No. 13, 1929–35), H.G. Wells (also at No. 13) in 1937–46 and Edmund Gosse (at No. 17) in 1902–28. Wallis Simpson stayed for a while at No. 7, and Vaughan Williams lived at No. 10 which is today the official residence of the Provost of UNIVERSITY COLLEGE, London.

Hans Crescent *SW1*. Originally cut in 1773 to give access to the new development of HANS TOWN and then called New Street. There were small houses with little gardens back and front. By 1815 the area was deteriorating fast and had by 1850 become a 'rookery'. The prosperity of HARROD'S store saved it, and by 1894 much of the west side of the street had become part of the store. The south-east end of the Crescent, originally Exeter Street, was also cut in 1773. In this street lived the Perrins with whom Miss Hannah Lightfoot is supposed to have stayed. All the buildings in this part were rebuilt or refronted in the 1880s and 1890s when the area was rising rapidly in the social scale and the large building on the south side, now the Knightsbridge Crown Court, was built as the Hans Crescent Hotel in 1903.

Hans Place *SW1*. Built in about 1777 by Henry Holland as a smaller edition of the Place Vendôme, Paris and named after the ground landlord's father-in-law, Sir Hans Sloane (*see* SLOANE ESTATE). On the south side was THE PAVILION, Holland's own house. None of the original houses has survived. Jane Austen stayed at No. 23 with her brother in 1814–15. 'It is a delightful Place,' she told her sister, 'and the garden is quite a Love. I am in the Attic which is the Bedchamber to be preferred.' Whilst she was here the Prince

Regent invited her to Carlton House and permitted her to dedicate *Emma* to him. Shelley lived at No. 1 in 1817. No. 22 was the site of a school kept by M. Saint Quentin, once secretary to the Comte de Moustière, Louis XVI's ambassador in London. Fanny Kemble, Lady Caroline Lamb and Mary Russell Mitford were pupils here. Another pupil, Letitia Landon, the future poet LEL, was born in Hans Place in 1802.

Hans Road *SW3*. The west end of Hans Road was originally known as Birk's Buildings and later as Queen Street after George III's Queen Charlotte. It was cut in 1787 to join up with Elizabeth Street, now also Hans Road (east end), to form an original entrance to the north-west corner of HANS PLACE and as such is part of Holland's original plan for the development of HANS TOWN. In its first state it had respectable small houses with gardens in the rear but it became a slum and in the 1870s Mr Harrod thought them dirty and dangerous. As his store prospered the slum was gradually swept away and the houses on the west side were rebuilt in a far grander style in the 1880s and 1890s. No. 12 was built by Arthur Mackmurdo in 1894 and Nos 14–16 by Charles Voysey in 1891. The houses on the east side were demolished at the time of the extension of Harrods between 1902 and its completion in 1911. The street name was changed to Hans Road in 1886.

Hans Town *Chelsea*. In 1771 Henry Holland, the architect, leased 89 acres from Lord Cadogan. Hans Town (named after Cadogan's father-in-law, Sir Hans Sloane) was built over the next ten years. It comprised HANS PLACE, CADOGAN PLACE, SLOANE STREET, and Holland's private house THE PAVILION. The houses were plain brick terraces for people of moderate means. Fields separated them from WESTMINSTER until the middle of the 19th century when BELGRAVIA was developed. Only a few of the original houses now survive.

Hanway Street *W1*. A narrow crescent running just north of OXFORD STREET and linking it with TOTTENHAM COURT ROAD, it was first mentioned in the Overseers' Survey records in 1723. It takes its name from Major John Hanway, the freeholder who began its development. William Baker, the builder responsible for BAKER STREET, was a resident here.

Hanwell *W7*. Situated on the Uxbridge Road to the west of EALING, Hanwell is bounded on the north and west by the River BRENT. The Anglo-Saxon *han* means stone or rock and possibly refers to an Ice-Age boulder rediscovered in the early 20th century. Saxon graves attest to its ancient settlement, and it is mentioned in *Domesday Book* as an independent manor. Soon afterwards it appears to have become a subsidiary manor of neighbouring GREENFORD under the lordship of the Abbot of WESTMINSTER. The old parish probably included New Brentford (which was dissociated from it in the 18th century) and stretched southwards to the THAMES. The medieval village grew around the church which existed on the site of St Mary's by the 12th century. Hanwell Bridge was important in carrying the road west from London over the BRENT. At the Reformation, Hanwell passed to the BISHOP OF LONDON and by the late 16th century the bridge had already been rebuilt or repaired. In the 18th century there were several inns on the Uxbridge Road and most of the land was enclosed and terraced housing appeared early along the main road. The landscape further changed with the building of the GRAND UNION CANAL in 1794 which straightened the course of the BRENT. But by the beginning of the 19th century there were still only a few houses near the church and along Church Road; and it was not until the opening of Hanwell Asylum (now ST BERNARD'S HOSPITAL) in 1831 that the area was placed firmly on the map. Famous as an 'enlightened' lunatic asylum, it housed about 2,000 inmates by the end of the century. In 1838 the Great Western Railway at Hanwell and Brunel's brick Wharncliffe viaduct had been built bringing, eventually, a growth in population. In 1842 St Mary's, a new and larger parish church by George Gilbert Scott and W.B. Moffatt, was opened. Estates such as Hanwell Park and Hanwell Grove were developed. A real spur to the population increase was the foundation of the Central District School for poorlaw children in 1856 (closed 1933) which at times boasted over 1,000 pupils, including Charlie Chaplin. Smaller working-class housing developed and new inhabitants served light industries in the area. The KENSINGTON and Westminster Cemeteries were opened on either side of the Uxbridge Road. By the 20th century new churches were necessary to serve the increased population, notably Sir Arthur Blomfield's St Mellitus (1910) and Edward Maufe's St Thomas with its east front crucifixion by Eric Gill (1934). In 1926 the Urban District of Hanwell amalgamated with the Borough of EALING. Despite intensive urban development the area around St Mary's still retains its village character.

Hanworth *Middlesex*. Originally the *Domesday* manor of Haneworde, meaning a small village. A Saxon moat, mostly destroyed, protected an unknown building. Early in the 16th century the manor passed to Henry VII who used the house as a hunting lodge. Henry VIII gave it to Anne Boleyn after spending money enlarging and enriching the house. Later owners were Lord Cottington and the 5th Duke of St Albans. The house was destroyed by fire in 1797. Although Hanworth had under 1,000 inhabitants until 1881, the population doubled in 1891–1901 with the building of the Hanworth Farms Estate by William Whiteley, founder of WILLIAM WHITELEY LTD) BAYSWATER. Food sold there was produced at the farms, market gardens, orchards and foodprocessing factories of Hanworth. Hanworth Park House was built in about 1820 on part of the manor grounds. In 1929 Hanworth Airport opened. The *Graf Zeppelin* landed here in 1932. The airport closed in 1946 because of HEATHROW AIRPORT's proximity. Urban developments of semi-detached houses began in the 1930s and continued in the 1950s and 1960s. In Castle Way is Tudor Court, the manor house stables which, gothicised in the 18th-century, survived the 1797 fire and were converted into flats in 1923. The grounds contain the remains of two 16th-century fireplaces from Henry VIII's kitchen. Two alcoves with pediments enclose 16th-century terracotta busts in roundels, part of a set at HAMPTON COURT PALACE. Also in Castle Way is St George's church, built to the designs of James Wyatt in 1812. The west wall incorporates medieval stone from an earlier church. The chancel and spire were added by S.S. Teulon in 1865.

Hanworth Park House *Hanworth, Middlesex*. Built in about 1820 by an unknown architect. The lodges, now demolished, were designed by Thomas Cundy the Elder. The west wing and clock tower were added in about 1857. It was the home of the Perkins family, of Barclay and Perkins, the SOUTHWARK brewers (*see* BREWERIES), and later of the Lafone family. It was purchased in 1916 by J.A. Whitehead of the Whitehead Aircraft Co. The house became a Red Cross Hospital and the park an aerodrome for aircraft built in Whitehead's factory. Later it became a club house and hotel for Hanworth Airport, known in the 1930s as London Air Park. It is now an old people's home.

Harcourt House *Cavendish Square*. Designed in 1722 by Thomas Archer for Robert Benson, Baron Bingley, formerly Ambassador in Madrid. Later acquired by the Harcourt family, a 99-year lease of the house was lost at cards in 1825, by the 3rd Earl Harcourt, to the Duke of Portland for whom Thomas Cundy the Younger carried out certain alterations. The eccentric and reclusive 5th Duke of Portland – who always wore three pairs of socks with his corksoled boots, used a handkerchief three feet square and built an underground tunnel a mile and a half long between Welbeck Abbey and the town of Worksop so that no one would notice his rare excursions to London – had the garden of Harcourt House enclosed by a ground-glass and cast-iron wall 80 ft high. The house, empty for a long period after the Duke's death, was demolished in 1906.

Hare Court *EC4*. South of the point where THE STRAND meets FLEET STREET, between MIDDLE and INNER TEMPLE LANES, this Court was built by Sir Nicholas Hare, the judge who was created Master of the Rolls in 1553 and sat on the commission which tried Sir Nicholas Throckmorton for 'imagining the Queen's death'.

Harefield *Middlesex*. Lies in the north-east corner of MIDDLESEX, adjoining Buckinghamshire on the west and Hertfordshire on the north, in the London Borough of HILLINGDON. The Anglo-Saxon Herefelle means open land used by an army. The moors surrounding Harefield extended south to Moorhall which belonged to the KNIGHTS OF ST JOHN OF JERUSALEM from the 12th century. Part of the west end of the nave of St Mary's, Harefield (restored in the 19th and 20th centuries) probably dates from that century. The north aisle and tower were built in the 16th century when John Newdigate acquired Harefield manor together with Moorhall. The estates remained in the possession of the Newdigate family into the 20th century, and many members are commemorated in the church – two 17th-century tombs by Grinling Gibbons survive. Sir Thomas Egerton lived at Harefield Place (burned 1660 and rebuilt in the 19th century) in the 17th century and was visited by Elizabeth I. Lady Egerton's almshouses date from 1637. Cottages on High Street and Park Lane survive from the 17th century together with the timber-framed King's Arms (extended in the following century). In the 18th century the rural environment began to change: land was enclosed and the GRAND UNION CANAL was built to the west alongside the River Colne. Small factories, limekilns and copper mills soon appeared and, in the 19th century, industry increased. More residences were built – such as the houses on High Street and the cottages at Moorhall – but woods and coverts were planted so that old moorland was reclaimed. By the early 20th century there were still 20 farms in the area, including the 18th-century Highway Farm; but development such as that at Moorhall and Mount Pleasant followed the 1st World War. Surviving mansions were converted for public services: Belhammonds became the Harefield Chest Hospital; Harefield Place (formerly Lodge) became Harefield County Hospital in 1936.

Harefield Place *Uxbridge, Middlesex*. An 18th-century mansion, initially known as Harefield Lodge, designed by Henry Couchman, the property of Sir Roger Newdigate, the antiquary. It became a hospital in 1936. Renovated and extended in 1980–1 under the direction of Fewster and Partners, it is now let as offices.

Harewood House *Hanover Square, W1*. Formerly known as Roxburghe House, it was remodelled in 1776 by Robert Adam for the third Duke of Roxburghe, the book collector, whose library was later housed at his mansion in ST JAMES'S SQUARE. It later passed into the hands of the Lascelles family who lived there until 1895 when the Earl of Harewood sold it to the ROYAL AGRICULTURAL SOCIETY for offices. It was demolished in 1908. The site is now occupied by 13 Hanover Square, by G.D. Martin, 1907–8.

T. Malton's aquatint of Harewood House, Hanover Square, remodelled in the 1770s by Robert Adam. It was demolished in 1908.

Haringey A London Borough formed in 1965 from the former Boroughs of HORNSEY, WOOD GREEN and TOTTENHAM. Largely residential, it contains some light industry, mainly in TOTTENHAM. Harringay is the name of a district in the south of the Borough (*see* HORNSEY).

Harlequin Football Club *see* RUGBY FOOTBALL CLUBS.

Harlesden *NW10*. Mentioned in *Domesday Book* of 1086, but even in the 1830s the settlement remained as a country village with a few grand houses. The London-Birmingham railway was opened in 1837 but was not a focus of local activity until yards and sidings were established there in 1873–94. Harlesden's development took place during the 30 years following 1880 accelerated by a tramway service and the establishment of major industries like Heinz Ltd and United Biscuits. Attractive Victorian properties of this period include the terrace in the High Street from the Royal Oak to the Green Man public houses. In the centre of the High Street is the Jubilee Clock – erected to commemorate Queen Victoria's Jubilee of 1887 – and nearby is All Souls church (1879) by E.J. Tarver with its elaborate octagonal roof.

To the north lies Roundwood Park, now public open space but once the estate of George Furness, a prominent local builder and politician who helped construct the THAMES EMBANKMENT.

Harley Road *NW3*. Probably takes its name from a builder employed by Eton College which was endowed with the Manor of Chalcots (*see* CHALK FARM) by Henry VI – hence also Eton Avenue, Road and Villas, Eton College Road, KING HENRY'S ROAD and various other roads in the area named after Eton and its associations. Dame Clara Butt, the singer, lived at No. 7 in 1901–29.

Harley Street *W1*. World renowned for its medical specialists. First rated in 1753, it was named after Edward Harley, 2nd Earl of Oxford, the ground landlord. Before the doctors moved in, in about 1845, it was a smart residential street. Kitty, Duchess of Wellington, lived at No. 11 in 1809–14 when the Duke was fighting in Portugal, and Sir William Beechey was at No. 13 from 1804–39. Nos 43–49 are occupied by QUEEN'S COLLEGE, an independent girls' public day school founded in 1848 by F.D. Maurice who also founded the Working Men's College. J.M.W. Turner lived at No. 64 in 1804–8; Allan Ramsay, the portrait painter, at No. 67 in 1770–80; Sir Charles Lyell, the geologist, at No. 73 in 1854–75. Gladstone also lived at No. 73 in 1876. No. 38 was the home in 1861 of the writer Barry Cornwall, the pseudonym of Bryan Waller Procter who earned his living as a solicitor. His daughter was Adelaide Ann Procter who wrote *The Lost Chord*. Sir Arthur Wing Pinero lived at 115a in 1909–34. Sir John Herschel, the astronomer, had his residence at No. 56, on whose site now stands a block of flats, Goodwood Court.

Harlington *see* HAYES AND HARLINGTON.

Harmondsworth *Middlesex*. The parish straddles the Bath Road and includes Harmondsworth Village, Sipson, Longford and Heathrow. Its name is derived from Heremod's *worth* (Heremod's enclosure). The Manor was granted by William I to the Abbey of Rouen in 1069 and a priory cell was established in the village. Later the Manor was acquired by William of Wykeham who, in 1391, gave it as part of his endowment of Winchester College. Harmondsworth was important, since traffic from London to the west passed along the Bath Road, bringing prosperity to its many inns, some of which still survive. The stage coach era ended in 1838 when the Great Western Railway opened, but Harmondsworth continued as a farming and market gardening area, selling much of its produce to the London markets. A great change occurred in the 1940s when Heathrow was obliterated to make way for the airport.

Harringay *see* HORNSEY.

Harringay House *Hornsey.* Harringay Park Estate is mentioned as being in the possession of the Cozens family in 1552 and it remained in their ownership until 1750 when the fine old Tudor mansion was pulled down and the estate sold to Edward Gray, a London linen draper. Harringay House (and later the district) probably derived its name from an estate called Farnfields or Fernfields reputed to be a manor in 1549 and called Harringay in the 18th century. In 1789 Edward Gray acquired several fields in the east part of HORNSEY parish where in 1792 he was erecting Harringay House, a stone house with 14 bedrooms on the site of the demolished Tudor mansion in a loop of the NEW RIVER. It was complete in 1796 when Gray was rated for 55 acres. By 1801 Gray also possessed at least 85 acres of the manor of Farnhills or Harringay. In 1809 he acquired 93 acres in the north-west part of the parish and he was assessed at 192 acres in 1829. The estate was split up after his death and the house demolished in 1885–6.

Harringay Stadium Opened by the Greyhound Racing Association in 1927 on a site of 24 acres south of the adjacent railway line. It has stands and terraces for 30,000 spectators and greyhound racing has been carried on continually on the site since it was opened.

Harrington Estate A large estate in South Kensington owned by the Stanhopes, Viscounts Petersham and Earls of Harrington, until sold by the 11th Earl in 1957. Harrington Road, HARRINGTON GARDENS, Stanhope Gardens and Petersham Lane, Mews and Place, SW7, commemorate the family. So do Elvaston Mews and Place, SW7, Elvaston Castle being the family's country house in Derbyshire.

Harrington Gardens *SW7.* Laid out by Ernest George on the HARRINGTON ESTATE in 1882. No. 39 was designed for Sir W.S. Gilbert by George and Peto.

He lived here from 1883 until 1890 when he moved to GRIMSDYKE. No. 39 was exceptional for its time in having a bathroom on every floor, extensive central heating and telephones. The large Gloucester Hotel (559 bedrooms) is by S. Kaye Firmin and Partners (1973).

Harrod's Ltd *(Knightsbridge), 87–135 Brompton Road, SW1.* Henry Charles Harrod, a wholesale tea merchant of EASTCHEAP, took over a small grocer's shop in the village of KNIGHTSBRIDGE in 1849. His son, Charles Digby Harrod, aged 20, bought it in instalments from his father in 1861. By 1867 he had five assistants working for him; and the next year turnover reached £1,000 a week. Harrod moved his family living quarters from the back of the shop to Esher. His cousin, William Kibble, joined him as a partner and they began to sell perfumes, stationery and patent medicines. By 1870 Harrod had sixteen assistants, but his total wages bill was only £15 a week. Staff worked from 7 a.m. to 8 p.m. In 1873 a two-storey extension was built on the back garden, and further premises were acquired the next year. By 1880 nearly 100 assistants were employed. In December 1883 the store was destroyed by fire. Harrod wrote to his customers, 'I greatly regret to inform you that, in consequence of the above premises being burnt down, your order will be delayed in the execution a day or two. I hope, in the course of Tuesday or Wednesday next, to be able to forward it.' In fulfilling this hope Harrod dispatched all his Christmas orders, and his customers were so impressed that by the time the store was rebuilt in 1884 turnover had more than doubled. In 1889 the store was bought for £120,000 and made a limited liability company. Harrod intended to retire but the store did so badly without him that he carried on until 1891 when Richard Burbidge was appointed General Manager. In 1894 Burbidge arranged for the store to close at 7 p.m. each night and at 4 p.m. on Thursdays. In the 1890s a depository was built at BARNES. An advertisement in the *Daily Telegraph* in 1894 could justifiably make the claim, 'Harrods serves the world.' In 1894 the BASIL STREET frontage was acquired and flats and showrooms were built on the site. In 1898 the first escalator in London was installed. An assistant stood

Customers leaving the provisions department at Harrod's by the first escalator to be installed in London, in 1898.

at the top armed with sal-volatile and brandy for nervous customers. In 1901–5 the main part of the present terracotta emporium was built to the designs of Stevens and Munt. The Meat Hall was decorated with tiles depicting hunting scenes designed by W.J. Neatby. Rebuilding was finally completed in 1939. In 1959 Harrod's was bought by the House of Fraser. With a staff of 5,000 it is one of the world's largest stores.

Harrow Road W9. Redevelopment since 1960 and the construction of WESTWAY have transformed the character of the PADDINGTON section of this road, so graphically captured in the film *The Blue Lamp* of 1950. Originally a Celtic track it became, much later, PADDINGTON's high street. The lively northern end (*see also* QUEEN'S PARK) now fulfils this function, but the redevelopment has also left its scars here. The two tall towers of the LONDON COUNTY COUNCIL's Elgin Estate clash with their surroundings. The part of ST MARY'S HOSPITAL until 1968 known as Paddington General Hospital stands on the sites of the Lock Hospital, the first proper Paddington Workhouse, of 1845, and the Paddington Infirmary of 1886, incorporating parts of the earlier buildings. Some 19th-century houses and warehouses remain north of the Paddington Basin. Almshouses were built in 1714 not far from the North Westminster School. Matthew Cotes Wyatt, the sculptor, lived in 1829–62 at the former No. 64 (previously 34 Dudley Grove), near Porteus Road. The Paddington Maintenance Depot, No. 117, is by Bicknell and Hamilton.

Harrow School *Harrow-on-the-Hill, Middlesex.* Founded in 1572 by a local yeoman farmer, John Lyon, who obtained a charter from Queen Elizabeth for this purpose. Though it seems likely that there was an earlier school in the churchyard of St Mary's, the new buildings were completed in 1615, and the original classroom, known as the Fourth Form Room, still exists. Its oak-panelled walls are covered with carved names of former pupils, including Byron, Sir Robert Peel, Sheridan, Anthony Trollope and Sir Winston Churchill. In 1981 there were about 750 boys, living in 11 houses. These include the Head Master's, designed by Decimus Burton in 1845 and Druries, rebuilt by C.F. Hayward in 1868. The Vaughan Library of 1863 and the School Chapel (1855) were both designed by Sir George Gilbert Scott. The original building of the Old Schools was extended in 1820 by Samuel and Charles Cockerell, who added a new wing containing a Speech Room and fitted Tudor-style oriel windows to both wings to match. This speech room became too small with the rapid expansion of the school in the 19th century under two progressive headmasters (C.J. Vaughan and H. Montagu Butler), and a new Speech Room was designed by William Burges for the tercentenary: it was opened in 1877. It is built in semi-circular shape to accommodate the whole school, and is used for school plays and Harrow Songs: these were started in 1869 when John Farmer and Edward Bowen first collaborated; apart from *Forty Years On* a large number of songs is known by every Harrow boy and sung each term with great enthusiasm. Churchill used to come each winter during and after the War to listen to them.

Herbert Baker designed the School's War Memorial, which includes the remarkable Fitch Room, in memory of an Old Boy killed in the 1st World War. Every item in the room is of historical interest.

Her Majesty Queen Elizabeth II opened the new Physics Schools in 1971 and in 1976 Dennis Lennon successfully incorporated a central dining hall into the complex of buildings on the slopes of the Hill. In that year, also, Alan Irvine turned the Old Speech Room into an art gallery and museum.

Surrounding the Hill are 360 acres of sports fields, including a nine-hole golf course and a lake designed by 'Capability' Brown in 1767.

Harrow Weald *Middlesex.* First recorded in 1303 as Waldis, by 1382 it had become Walde and by 1553 Harrow Weald. All Saints church with chancel by J.T. Harrison dates from 1842. The nave and south aisle were added by Butterfield in 1845. Tombs include those of the Crosse and Blackwell families, and of Leefe Robinson VC, who shot down the first Zeppelin in the 1st World War. The northern slopes of Harrow Weald are GREEN BELT land, and Brooks Hill Drive is a designated conservation area. The farm where Anthony Trollope lived as a boy and the cottage home of the actor George Arliss have gone, but at least ten timber-framed buildings survive including Harrow Weald Farm House of about 1500, once the home of the actor Leslie Henson, and the 17th-century inn, the Seven Balls, in Kenton Lane. A brick-making complex survives off Common Road comprising a 17th-century timber-framed house and the one surviving brick-making kiln in the area with contemporary drying sheds. Large houses in Harrow Weald include The Old Barn, moved brick by brick in 1902 from Evesham in Worcestershire, and GRIMSDYKE HOUSE.

Harrow-on-the-Hill *Middlesex.* The word Harrow derives from the Saxon word *hergae*, of which there are many variant spellings and which means a temple or shrine. The earliest known document relating to Harrow is a charter covering a grant of land by Offa, King of Mercia, to Abbot Stidberht of St Albans in AD 767. The grant covered land between Gumeninga Hergae and the Lidding (probably Kenton) Brook. Offa's successor, Cenwulf, confirmed the grant on the

Harrow-on-the-Hill in the late 19th century, with the buildings of Harrow School, founded in 1572, in the background.

reverse side of the document in the year 801, but later seized the land for himself. Cenulf was succeeded as lord of the lands of Harrow by his son, Kenelm, aged seven, but Kenelm was murdered by his half-sister Cwoenthryth. In 825, however, Cwoenthryth was forced by the Council of Clovesho to restore the land at Hergae, amounting to about 16,000 acres, to the church. Gumeninga Hergae referred to in Offa's charter means the temple or shrine of the Gumeningas, the Saxon tribe whose chieftain was Guma or Gumen. *Domesday Book* records that Earl Leofwin held the manor before 1066 but that by 1086 it had passed to Archbishop Lanfranc.

The hill, dominated and graced by the church of ST MARY, has always been the centre of the local community, and the focal point for the outlying hamlets of GREENHILL, ROXETH, Roxbourne, PINNER, HEADSTONE, and SUDBURY. Below the hill, the surrounding countryside was thickly wooded, and afforded good hunting. The King's Head public house, reputed to date from 1535 but rebuilt following a fire in 1750, was used by King Henry VIII as a hunting lodge. From the 13th to the 16th centuries, Crown Street (once called Hog Lane) and Middle Street were the scene of the market and fair. Off West Street is the 17th-century Harrow Pie House, scene of the Piepowder (or *pieds poudreux*) Court, so called from the French because disputes arising at the fair were settled before the participants could clean their dusty feet. The Pie House is now part of a plastics factory and used primarily for storage. The field behind the court for the amusements of the fair is still called High Capers.

The great event in the history of Harrow was the founding of HARROW SCHOOL by John Lyon in 1572. One of the school governors, Sir Gilbert Gerard, lived at a house called Flambards, which took its name from one of the great Harrow families of the 14th century. The present Flambards in High Street dates from the 18th century. During the Civil War, Gerard raised a force of 4,000 men who fought against Charles I; and there is a spot on the hill still called King Charles's Well where the King stopped to water his horses before his surrender to the Scottish army. The old town well, 700 ft deep, is nearby at the top of West Street. Harrow Hill comprises no fewer than eight separate but interlocking conservation areas, each full of buildings of historic interest and high architectural merit, ranging in date from the 17th to the 20th century. Apart from ST MARY'S church and the King's Head, the most important of the buildings on the hill are connected with HARROW SCHOOL. Former noteworthy residents include R.B. Sheridan at The Grove, Charles Kingsley at Kingsley House, London Road; Matthew Arnold at Byron House in Byron Hill Road; Robert Ballantyne at Duneaves which he rebuilt in Mount Park Road when his sons were at the school; and Anthony Trollope at Julians at the foot of the hill on the side towards SUDBURY.

Hart Street *EC3*. The name is probably derived from hearths which are thought to have been made and sold here. It was long supposed that Richard Whittington's house was in this street; but the mansion which was pointed out as his to visitors in the 18th century was built after his death. Samuel Pepys's parish church, ST OLAVE'S, is in this street.

Harvey Nichols and Co. Ltd *109–125 Knightsbridge, SW1*. Benjamin Harvey had a little linen draper's store in 1813 in what was then LOWNDES TERRACE. The proximity to CRYSTAL PALACE in HYDE PARK, and the GREAT EXHIBITION in 1851 helped a thriving business which Harvey left to his daughter, Elizabeth, with the advice to take Colonel Nichols, a silk buyer, into partnership. It is now part of the Debenham Group.

Hatch End *Middlesex*. The suffix 'end' is used in the sense of a part of a larger district, and 'hatch' means a gate, perhaps the gate to Pinner Park. Pinner Park was probably referred to by William the Conqueror when he ordered that the citizens were not to interfere with the deer at HARROW. Records show that the park had an official keeper as long ago as 1314. In 1578 Pinner Park was in the possession of Sir Nicholas Bacon (Lord Keeper of the Great Seal) and later passed to his more celebrated son, Francis Bacon (Lord High Chancellor of England). Pinner Park is now a dairy farm. Interesting buildings in Hatch End include the 17th-century Letchford House in Headstone Lane formerly Hatch End Farm House, now used as office premises; Harrow College of Further Education, formerly Royal Commercial Travellers' School in Uxbridge Road, the foundation stone of which was laid by the Prince Consort; St Anselm's parish church in Westfield Park, by F.E. Jones (1895); and Hatch End Station by G.F. Horsley with its cartouche of the LNWR dated 1911. Old Dove House (demolished) was once the residence of Mr Tilbury, coachbuilder and designer of the two-wheeled tilbury carriage.

Hatchard's *187 Piccadilly, W1*. John Hatchard, bookseller and publisher, opened his shop in 1797 at No. 173 Piccadilly. In 1801 he moved to No. 190 and later to the present address. It quickly became a fashionable rendezvous, obtaining many of its customers from ALBANY opposite, and was as much a club as a bookshop. The daily papers were laid out on the table by the fireplace and there were benches outside for the customers' servants. In 1804 the inaugural meeting of the ROYAL HORTICULTURAL SOCIETY was held in the reading room behind the shop, and William Wilberforce used the same room for anti-slavery meetings. Hatchard was both pious and shrewd and his publishing covered a wide range of interests including *The Christian Observer*, a weekly paper which he began in 1802 and ran until his retirement in 1845, all the publications of the Society for Bettering the Conditions of the Poor, political pamphlets and children's books, including Mrs Sherwood's *History of the Fairchild Family*. He was bookseller to Queen Charlotte, since when the firm has always held the Royal Warrant. Though primarily serving the opulent classes, they have long had a reputation as one of the most literate of bookshops and their regular customers have included Canning, Macaulay, Byron, Palmerston, Peel, Wellington, Gladstone, Thackeray, Oscar Wilde, Bernard Shaw, Lloyd George, G.K. Chesterton, Somerset Maugham, and Cecil Rhodes who ordered all the source books for Gibbon's *Decline and Fall*. John Hatchard died in 1849 and was succeeded by his son Thomas. Since then the business has changed ownership many times, and was bought by the publishers Collins in 1956. It remains one of the most celebrated bookshops in the English-speaking world.

Hatton Garden *EC1.* HATTON HOUSE was built in about 1576 by Sir Christopher Hatton, Elizabeth I's Chancellor, 'who danced with grace and had a very fine form and a very fine face'. In 1659 Evelyn noted in his diary, 'To *Lond* . . . to see the foundations now laying for a longe streete, and buildings in Hatton Garden, designed for a little Towne; lately an ample Garden.' The remains of Hatton House could probably still be seen at that time but had disappeared by 1720. The street was first known as Hatton Street, Hatton Garden being the whole area between LEATHER LANE, SAFFRON HILL, HOLBORN and Hatton Wall. Until the early 19th century it was 'an esteemed situation for gentry, where no shops were permitted but at the lower end', with views over the fields to PENTONVILLE. Cromwell's physician, Dr George Bate, died here in 1688; and William Wycherley, the dramatist, had a house here in the 1670s. In September 1673 Evelyn 'went to see *Paradise*, a roome in *Hatton Garden* furnished with the representations of all sorts of animals, handsomely painted on boards or cloth, & so cut out & made to stand & move, fly, crawll, roare and make their severall cries.' Captain Coram, the founder of the FOUNDLING HOSPITAL, was living here in the 1740s; and Giuseppe Mazzini, the Italian patriot, in exile at No. 5 in 1841–2. Nos 52–53 was the site of the notorious police court, a 'dispensary of summary justice', presided over by Mr Laing, the original of Mr Fang in *Oliver Twist*. At No. 57 Sir Hiram Maxim made his first automatic gun which by 1884 he had perfected so that it could fire 600 rounds a minute.

On the corner of Cross Street a small chapel was built in the 1690s and converted in 1696 into a charity school. It was bombed in the 2nd World War and has been rebuilt as offices behind the façade. The original figures of the charity children are still to be seen. There were some jewellers working in gold and silver in the street by 1836. Since then it has become the centre of the diamond trade. The London Diamond Club is at No. 87, and an elaborate diamond laboratory and computer 'fingerprinting' service in Edney House at No. 15. Nearby in HOLBORN VIADUCT are De Beers, through whom 80 per cent of the world's diamond production is sold.

Hatton House *Ely Place, Holborn.* Built in about 1576 on the orchard of ELY PLACE by Sir Christopher Hatton. After his death in 1591 the house passed to his nephew, William Newport, who took Hatton's name. He married the determined Lady Elizabeth Cecil, daughter of the 1st Earl of Exeter. She retained the house after Hatton's death and her remarriage to the lawyer, Sir Edward Coke. They quarrelled constantly, and there was great dispute over the marriage of their daughter. After the intervention of James I, the girl was married to Sir John Villiers, brother of the court favourite, Buckingham. A banquet was given for the King at the house: 'His Majesty was never merrier nor more satisfied.' The house was demolished at the end of the century to provide a site for 'a little Towne', now HATTON GARDEN.

Havering This London Borough was formed in 1965 from the old Borough of ROMFORD and the Urban District of HORNCHURCH. ROMFORD had become a Borough in 1937. HORNCHURCH had the highest population of any urban district in the country. The name was chosen because a large part of the new London Borough had been within the bounds of the historic Royal Liberty of Havering. (*See also* HAVERING-ATTE-BOWER.)

Havering-atte-Bower *Essex.* This village on its hillside ridge was once dominated by a palace owned by Kings of England from before the Norman Conquest until 1620 when it fell into decay. It was sold during the Commonwealth. It was used by almost every sovereign from Edward the Confessor to the Stuarts. To Havering came Henry I, John and Henry III. Here Edward III invested his child successor Richard II. In 1397 a conspiracy was hatched at Havering to murder the Duke of Gloucester (the uncle of Richard II). Havering also became the official residence of England's Queens, among them Henry VIII's first three wives. At first the Queen's residence was called The Bower, later it was known as Pyrgo. A plan of Havering Palace made under Lord Treasurer Burleigh's direction in 1578 gives us some idea of the rambling nature of the royal palace, which must have covered a large part of the hilltop, close to the present village green. In 1465 Edward IV granted the famous charter of the royal 'Liberty of Havering Atte Bower'. This liberty took in ROMFORD and HORNCHURCH and a large part of the present London borough of HAVERING. Before the charter this area had been part of the Becontree Hundred, but it now became a privileged Manor, having its own law court under a High Steward and many other rights. Beside the Green is the parish church of St John. This was built in 1876–8 on the site of an earlier building which had been one of the chapels of the palace which the inhabitants had reclaimed. The school of Dame Alice Tipping in North Road was founded in 1724. It was rebuilt in 1818 and 1837, Queen Victoria contributing £20. A very unusual building constructed on an oval plan and called the Round House, is thought to have been modelled on a tea-caddy because its owner had prospered as a tea-merchant. It dates from about 1792. This stucco villa was in the early 20th century occupied by the Rev J.H. Pemberton, a famous rose grower who propagated the Alexandra rose. Down Orange Tree Hill lies the Bower House of 1729, a small country house incorporating a coat of arms from the old royal palace. Flitcroft was the architect (his first commission) and many of the stones came from the palace site.

Haverstock Hill *NW3.* Extends from ROSSLYN HILL to Chalk Farm Road. The origins of the name, one of the earliest to be found in the district, are obscure. On the façade of the Convent of the Sisters of Providence, Rowland Hill Street (which takes its name from Rowland Hill who lived at Hampstead Green in 1849–79) the fibreglass statue, *Mater Ecclesiae*, is by Michael Verner (1977).

Hay Hill *W1.* So called from Hay Hill Farm, the name by which the lands around the modern BERKELEY SQUARE were known in the 1690s: this in turn is derived from Ayehille, denoting the ridge or hill of land near the Aye Brook, otherwise known as the TYBURN which flowed along the course of BRUTON LANE to the bottom of Hay Hill. It is said that on this ridge Mary Tudor's troops were drawn up in 1554 to oppose Sir Thomas Wyatt's rebellious forces; and that after his execution on TOWER HILL his head was exhibited here, impaled on a pike. All the buildings on both sides of the street now date from about 1900.

Haydon Square *E1*. Captain John Heydon (or Haydon) was resident in the MINORIES by virtue of being Lieutenant General of the Ordnance under Charles I. Sir Isaac Newton lived here in a house (since demolished) while he was Master of the ROYAL MINT. The area was known as Heydon's Yard when it was first developed in the late 17th century. The GUINNESS TRUST properties that now occupy the square were opened in 1981.

Hayes *Kent*. The name means 'village on the heath'. Roman remains have been found here, including a silver *denarius* of Mark Antony dug up in 1889. A document in the BRITISH MUSEUM dated 1177 refers to John, the rector of Heese, so there was probably a church here at that time. A tax roll of 1301 gives the names of 26 families, which implies a population of about 140. A plague in 1349 swept away about half the village. Elizabeth Montagu took a lease of a house here in 1751. She gathered round her a group of famous literary and cultured men and women, who became known as 'the blue stockings'. William Pitt, Earl of Chatham, conceived a liking for the area and bought Mrs Montagu's house. He rebuilt it as Hayes Place. James Wolfe was summoned to Hayes in 1759. Both Lord Nelson and the Duke of Wellington visited Hayes Place and planted trees. Sir Everard Alexander Hambro, the head of the famous banking firm, later lived at Hayes Place which was demolished in 1933–4. Hambro was a great benefactor of the village. He rebuilt many of the old cottages and made substantial gifts to the church of St Mary the Virgin, a church which contains fragments of a Norman building and which has been repeatedly enlarged. After Hambro's death the area was extensively developed. It is now part of the London Borough of BROMLEY.

Hayes and Harlington *Middlesex*. The parishes of Harlington and Hayes led separate existences until they, together with CRANFORD parish, were brought together in 1930 as the Urban District of Hayes and Harlington. This was changed in 1934 to include only CRANFORD west of the River Crane, with ST DUNSTAN'S and CRANFORD HOUSE. Both Hayes and Harlington are mentioned in the *Domesday* survey. They remained agricultural communities until the GRAND JUNCTION CANAL was cut through the district in 1794, leading to brick-making on a commercial scale. This lasted in a small way until the 1950s. Market gardening is still important in Harlington. The manor of Hayes was in the possession of the Archbishopric of Canterbury at *Domesday* and remained so until the reign of Henry VIII, although the parish stayed a 'peculiar' of Canterbury until the 19th century. Archbishop Anselm occasionally resided in Hayes. In 1530 the grasping behaviour of the farmer of the rectory tithes, Thomas Gold, and his brother Henry, the vicar, caused such resentment among the villagers that there were outbreaks of rioting. Henry Gold later supported Elizabeth Barton, the 'Nun of Kent', and was hanged for treason. In the mid-18th century there were cockfights in the churchyard and the bellringers were a source of trouble, yet the Wesley brothers enjoyed well-behaved congregations at Hayes. Harlington and Dawley manors (*see* DAWLEY HOUSE) had various lay

owners, including Ambrose Coppinger, who entertained Queen Elizabeth in 1602, the Bennets, Bolinbroke, and the Pagets. William Byrd, the composer, lived at Harlington in about 1577–92. TURNPIKE trusts created in the early 18th century for the two main westward routes from London, the Bath Road and the Oxford Road, improved communications with the Metropolis and probably led to the increase in the number of gentlemen's houses in the district. Stephen Storace, composer of many popular light operas, lived at Hayes from about 1788–92; also Alderman Harvey Combe, LORD MAYOR of London in 1799. The Great Western Railway was built through the district in 1838, but had little immediate effect, since Hayes and Harlington Station was not opened until 1864. The London United Electric Tramways line was extended through Hayes to UXBRIDGE in 1904. The attraction of cheap land near London enjoying good rail, canal and road communications with the rest of the country, led to the establishment of manufacturing industry at Hayes, mainly in an area near the railway and the canal. The British Electric Transformer Company (1901) and the Gramophone and Typewriter Co. Ltd (1907 – later EMI) were among the first to open factories. The construction of London Airport at HEATHROW on the site of the Fairey Aviation Company's airfield caused immense changes.

Haymarket *SW1*. Extends southward from COVENTRY STREET to PALL MALL EAST. It was probably due to the presence nearby of the Royal Mews that a market for hay and straw came into being here in the mid-17th century, the name Haymarket first appearing in the parish ratebooks in 1657. In 1661 Charles II appointed an inspector to supervise the market, but in the same year the royal Surveyor of the Works asked that it should be discontinued on the grounds of nuisance. This was not done, but in 1662 an Act provided for a toll to be levied on all hay and straw sold here, and for the money to be used for the repair of the paving. In the following year, however, Charles II granted to his old friend the Earl of St Albans the right to hold a twice-weekly market in the Haymarket for the sale of sheep and cattle. Within a few years the Haymarket evidently became so filthy that James II decided to remove both markets. In 1686 he accordingly granted to St Alban's heir the right to keep his cattle market, and also an annual fair from 1 May for 15 days, in Great Brookfield, Mayfair; and this is the fair (not ST JAMES'S FAIR) from which MAYFAIR takes its name. But his efforts to get rid of the hay and straw market were not so successful, for James Pollett, to whom in 1688 James granted the right to remove it to SOHO, turned out to be a papist, and after the accession of William and Mary his grant was annulled. The whole matter was regulated in 1690 by another Act, and the Haymarket continued to be disrupted by waggons carrying hay and straw (over 26,000 loads being registered in 1827) until 1830, when the market was finally removed to the new Cumberland Market east of REGENT'S PARK.

John Strype described the Haymarket as 'a spacious street of great resort, full of inns and houses of entertainment'. The inns have been replaced by coffee and hamburger bars, but the tradition of 'houses of entertainment' still continues with HER MAJESTY'S THEATRE, the HAYMARKET THEATRE and the ODEON and CLASSIC cinemas. NEW ZEALAND HOUSE, at the south-west corner, joins Canada House, South Africa House and offices of the governments of Hong Kong and Uganda in making TRAFALGAR SQUARE, COCKSPUR STREET and PALL MALL East the citadel of Commonwealth (or former Commonwealth) countries' London headquarters. Only one 18th-century building survives – FRIBOURG AND TREYER's former tobacco shop at No. 34 – but the pleasing stucco-faced buildings at Nos 3 and 4 form part of Nash's rebuilding of SUFFOLK PLACE in the early 1820s. They are occupied by American Express. Most of the rest of the street is now lined with more recent showrooms and commercial buildings, such as BURBERRY's at Nos 18–22, Dewar House at No. 11 (by Frank M. Elgood, 1960–7), London headquarters of the Scotch whisky firm (where hang Landseer's *Monarch of the Glen* and Raeburn's *Macnab*), and at Nos 28–29 the DESIGN CENTRE (by Ward and Austin, interiors by Robert and Roger Nicholson), opened in 1956 for the display of British goods of high quality. In the 18th century, as James Boswell discovered, it was a well-known resort of prostitutes, and by Victorian times had become notorious as 'the great parade ground of abandoned women. Today it is devoted to the more acceptable side of commerce and entertainment.

Haymarket Theatre *(The Theatre Royal), Haymarket, SW1.* The first theatre was built in 1720 by a carpenter named John Potter but as it had no licence he had difficulty in letting it to anyone but amateurs. In 1735–7 it was managed by Henry Fielding. As a result of his satires the theatre closed and censorship was introduced in 1737. The theatre remained derelict until 1744 when it was reopened for a short time by Charles Macklin. It was again reopened in 1747 by Samuel Foote who managed to flout the licensing laws by taking admission money for chocolate and coffee served during the performance. In 1766 the Duke of York and others persuaded Foote to ride a wild horse which threw him and caused him to have his leg amputated. To make amends the Duke obtained a royal patent for the theatre which allowed it to open during the summer months for Foote's lifetime. During 1776 it was managed by George Colman. After Foote's death in 1777 the theatre remained open on an annual licence. During this period all the great actors of the day performed here. In 1794 15 people were crushed to death during the first command performance at the theatre. In 1805 rioting tailors, incensed by Foote's satire, *The Tailors*, had to be dispersed by Life

John Nash's Theatre Royal, Haymarket, was opened in July 1821 on a site next to the derelict old theatre of 1720.

Guards. In 1817 Colman's brother-in-law, David Morris, took over the management. The theatre was rebuilt to the south by John Nash 1820–1. In 1825 Madame Vestris sang *Cherry Ripe* in John Poole's comedy of the same name. In 1837 Samuel Phelps made his London debut as Shylock. In 1853–78 J.B. Buckstone managed the theatre and staged many notable productions. Some say his ghost is still here. During 1880 the Bancrofts were in charge. They began by having the interior remodelled by C.J. Phipps who made the pit into stalls and enclosed the stage to make it the first 'picture frame' stage. In 1887–96 Herbert Beerbohm Tree was manager. During this time Oscar Wilde's *A Woman of No Importance* (1893) and *An Ideal Husband* (1895) were first produced. With the profits he made from *Trilby*, a play by Paul Potter from George du Maurier's novel, Beerbohm Tree was able to build HER MAJESTY'S THEATRE opposite and left to manage it. In 1904 the interior was reconstructed by C. Stanley Peach. In 1911 *Bunty Pulls the Strings*, a comedy by Graham Moffatt, ran for 617 performances. In 1913 *Within the Law* a play by Frederick Fenn and Arthur Wimperis, had 427 performances. Ibsen's *Ghosts* had its first licensed performance in London in 1914. From then until now it has presented and re-presented plays by the best dramatists of their day from Galsworthy and Barrie to Rattigan and Fry.

Hay's Mews *W1.* Originally part of Lord Berkeley's estate *(see* BERKELEY SQUARE), it extends southward from HILL STREET to CHARLES STREET, with another arm extending westward to Waverton Street. It was laid out in the 1740s and 1750s to provide stables and coachhouses for the mansions in BERKELEY SQUARE and the adjacent streets.

Hay's Wharf *SE1.* Begun in 1651 by Alexander Hay, this is the oldest wharf in the PORT OF LONDON. It is also the largest, stretching between LONDON BRIDGE and TOWER BRIDGE. During the 1860s it pioneered cold storage, handling New Zealand butter and cheese as early as 1867. It was rebuilt by H.S. Goodhart-Rendel in 1931.

Hayward Gallery *Queen Elizabeth Hall, Belvedere Road, SE1.* Opened in October 1968 to form part of the SOUTH BANK arts complex. It provides the Arts Council with storage and exhibition space. Designed by Ove Arup and Partners.

Headstone Manor *Headstone Lane, Pinner, Middlesex.* The only surviving moated manor house in the Borough of HARROW. The present house bears the date 1501 but there is one remaining bay of a 14th-century aisled hall. The moat, too, dates from the 14th century. The great barn, expertly restored in 1973, dates from 1533–5. It is 150 ft in length and 30 ft in width. The manor has been a working farm from at least 1344 when it came into the possession of the Archbishops of Canterbury, who used it as a country residence. This seems to confirm the legend that Becket stayed at Headstone on the several occasions when he visited HARROW. Headstone remained a farm until 1923. Headstone Manor house is now unused, but occupied by a caretaker; the great barn is let out for functions; the farm lands are now a recreation ground.

Heal and Son Ltd *196 Tottenham Court Road, W1*. John Harris Heal came to London in 1805 to work with a feather dressing firm; and in 1810 set up on his own at 33 RATHBONE PLACE. After his death, his widow, Fanny, carried on the business, and in 1840 their son, John Harris Heal, took control, and moved to Miller's Stables at 196 TOTTENHAM COURT ROAD. They lived in the old farm house behind the shop. Rebuilding and extensions were completed in 1869. Heal's sons, Ambrose and Harris Heal, and their cousin, Alfred Brewer, joined the firm in 1875. Ambrose Heal Jnr served an apprenticeship as a cabinet maker and joined the firm in 1893. His simple oak Arts and Crafts furniture soon gained a wide following. The bedding factory and part of the premises in TOTTENHAM COURT ROAD were rebuilt to the designs of Smith and Brewer with recessed shop windows behind an arcade in 1916. This front was extended to the south by Sir Edward Maufe in 1938. There was more rebuilding in 1962. The curtain and cabinet factories returned to TOTTENHAM COURT ROAD in 1978–9. The sixth generation of the Heal family still runs the firm.

Heath House *Hampstead, NW3*. A large early 18th-century mansion standing in its own walled grounds at the junction of the roads to GOLDERS GREEN and HIGHGATE, and opposite JACK STRAW'S CASTLE. In 1790 it was bought by Samuel Hoare, banker and 'Quaker of philanthropic spirit and literary sympathies'; and here he entertained many literary lions, including Cowper, Wordsworth and Crabbe. Here, too, came William Wilberforce and other philanthropists who met to discuss the ways and means of having slavery abolished. The house at that time appears not to have had a name; it became known as Heath House in 1880.

Heath Street *Hampstead, NW3*. The lower part of this street (the part below the tube station) came into being as part of the HAMPSTEAD Town Improvements in 1887–9. The street was cut through from the newly constructed Fitzjohn's Avenue, to make a link with the upper part of Heath Street. In the process, the area south of CHURCH ROW, hitherto a maze of little courts and sloping narrow alleys, was levelled and rebuilt. The Drill Hall, built in 1888, became the EVERYMAN THEATRE in 1919 (Noël Coward's *The Vortex* had its first performance here) and the Everyman Cinema in 1933.

The upper part of Heath Street was one of the original tracks through the village of HAMPSTEAD. By the time of Queen Anne it had become a road leading to HAMPSTEAD HEATH and beyond; but leading also to the Upper Flask Tavern, which stood where the former Queen Mary's Maternity Home (closed in 1974) now stands. It was at the Upper Flask that meetings of the famous KIT-KAT CLUB were held. Vanbrugh called it the best club that ever was. The Upper Flask was used by Richardson as the setting for some of the scenes in his novel *Clarissa Harlowe*.

Up the hill from Hampstead Station, past the site of the Village's first cinema on the corner of Back Lane (now a restaurant) is the Baptist Chapel, built in 1860, and further up is the Friends' Meeting House, dated 1907. Higher up still stands NEW END HOSPITAL, first built as a workhouse. Opposite the tube station the building with a prominent clock tower, now occupied by a Building Society, was designed by Lewis

Vulliamy and opened as a fire station in 1873. Heath Street appears always to have been flanked by public houses and restaurants, and this remains true today.

Heathrow *see* AIRPORTS, HARMONDSWORTH, *and* HAYES AND HARLINGTON.

Heathrow Airport *see* AIRPORTS.

Heddon Street *W1*. A short L-shaped street leading off the west side of REGENT STREET. There was building hereabouts in the 1670s, but in the 1720s the area was redeveloped in its present form by the ground landlord, William Pulteney, MP for Heddon, Yorkshire, where he owned considerable property. Today Heddon Street is very much the poor relation of its great neighbours in REGENT STREET and SAVILE ROW, and the buildings are either grey brick Victorian warehouses or of more recent origin.

Heinz Gallery *21 Portman Square, W1*. Part of the ROYAL INSTITUTE OF BRITISH ARCHITECTS it is named after Mr and Mrs Henry J. Heinz II who sponsored the building of this small modern gallery in 1972. Designed by Stefan Buzas and Alan Irvine it gives exhibition space to some of the institute's magnificent collection which, with over 200,000 drawings, is the largest of its kind in the world. The collection dates from 1834. Since 1894 it has been the custodian of the Burlington-Devonshire collection from Chatsworth which not only contains designs by Inigo Jones and John Webb, but almost the whole output of Andrea Palladio's studio. The house was designed by James Adam in 1772 for the collector and connoisseur William Lock of Norbury.

Hemus Place *SW3*. Built by William Hemus Rayner. Formerly known as Bedford Place, it contained the Bedford Hall celebrated for its Pax Robertson Theatre. Many well-known actors, including Esmond Knight, began their careers here.

Hendon *NW4*. In the 14th century the manor of Hendon was in the gift of WESTMINSTER ABBEY. During the BLACK DEATH the area became a haven. Cattle from other places were transported on the hoof, accompanied by one or two grangers, and were retained here until the worst of the plague was over. The oldest buildings in Hendon are the parish church of ST MARY and Church Farm House which dates from the 17th century and is remarkable for its fine chimneys; this is now a local museum. In 1557 William Herbert, Earl of Pembroke, received the manor from the crown. The Herberts held the land for 200 years but did not take up residence. In 1796 David Garrick, the actor, became Lord of the Manor, presented the living to his nephew and bought Hendon Hall (now the HENDON HALL HOTEL) as a residence but did not stay long. The small Garrick Park is the only reminder of his estate and nothing remains of the statuary which he erected in honour of Shakespeare. Between the two World Wars there was considerable industrial development along the western boundary, the EDGWARE ROAD. This consisted largely of light engineering and the aircraft and motor car industries. Hendon became internationally famous for its air displays, based initially on the pioneer work of Grahame-White, De Havilland and Handley Page.

Hendon Air Displays From 1920 to 1937 the Royal Air Force put on 18 annual air displays at Hendon aerodrome in aid of RAF charities.

Although the name of the event changed – the first was referred to as the Royal Air Force Tournament; from 1921 to 1924 it was known as the Royal Air Force Aerial Pageant and from 1925 to 1937 as the Royal Air Force Display – its character did not: its main purposes were to show off the standard of RAF flying skill and to give the public a sight of new military aircraft.

Hendon Hall Hotel *Ashley Lane, NW4.* At the time of *Domesday Book* the original manor belonged to WESTMINSTER ABBEY. In 1550 Bishop Thirlby surrendered it to Edward VI who bestowed it upon Sir Edward Herbert whose descendants held it until the 4th Earl of Powis sold it to David Garrick who owned it in 1756–79. By this time a 17th-century mansion had replaced the Elizabethan manor house. Towards the end of the 18th century this mansion was successively the seat of the Earl of Northampton and Lord Chief Justice Tenterden. Samuel Ware the builder and architect, owned the house in 1840 and largely rebuilt it, adding the portico of four brick columns with rustication and rich Corinthian capitals, entablature and pediment, which are said to have come from CANONS. It is now a Kingsmead Hotel with 52 bedrooms.

Henekey's Long Bar *22–23 High Holborn, WC1.* Originally built in 1430, it was rebuilt, using some of the original materials, in 1923, when the structure became unsafe. The only bar, on the ground floor, is one of the longest in Britain; and on a gallery overhead the enormous vats from which Henekey's bottled their wines and spirits can still be seen. It has an extremely high, arched ceiling which has led to its being nicknamed the Cathedral Pub. Along one wall there are cubicles with swing doors. These were installed at the turn of the century to enable lawyers to speak privately to their clients over lunch or a drink. There is also a unique three-cornered fireplace with no apparent outlet for the smoke, which, in fact, escapes from a chimney running under the floor.

Henrietta Place *W1.* First rated in 1730 and called after Lady Henrietta Cavendish Holles, the wife of Edward Harley, Earl of Oxford; the lands in Marylebone, which became the PORTLAND ESTATE, were her inheritance. The 18th-century houses have all gone but No. 5 was the London residence of James Gibbs who designed ST PETER'S, VERE STREET for the Earl and Countess. The first floor drawing-room of No. 11 was preserved when the house was demolished and has been reconstructed in the VICTORIA AND ALBERT MUSEUM. The Countess of Mornington, the Duke of Wellington's mother, lived at No. 3 for some years till 1831. Charles Bridgeman, gardener to George I, lived at No. 8 in 1726–41; Matthew Cotes Wyatt, the sculptor, at No. 19 in 1808–22.

Henrietta Street *WC2.* Built in 1631–4 and named in honour of Charles I's Queen, Henrietta Maria. Here was the studio of the miniature painter, Samuel Cooper, who was commanded to paint Oliver Cromwell 'warts and all' and later painted Mrs Pepys, 'a most rare piece of work', in the opinion of her husband. It has been completely rebuilt since. It was at the Castle Tavern that Sheridan fought his third duel with

Matthews over Miss Linley. They cut each other up so badly that pistols replaced swords as the fashionable duelling weapon. Samuel Scott, the painter, lived at No. 2 in 1747–58. Jane Austen with her brother, Henry, in 1813–14 at No. 70, the premises of the bankers, Austen, Maunde and Tilson. ST PETER'S HOSPITAL FOR STONE ETC. is at No. 27. Victor Gollancz, the publishers, are at No. 14. Boulestin at No. 2 was first opened as the Restaurant Français on the corner of LEICESTER SQUARE and PANTON STREET in 1925.

Henry VIII's Wine Cellar *Whitehall, SW1.* A portion of this beneath the MINISTRY OF DEFENCE is the only surviving part of Wolsey's palace (*see* YORK PLACE). It is a vaulted undercroft supported by four octagonal pillars. The whole crypt, weighing 800 tons, was lowered 18 ft 9 ins during the rebuilding of Whitehall in the 1950s, without a brick being disturbed, at a cost of £100,000.

Her Majesty's Theatre *Haymarket, SW1.* (Queen's Theatre, 1705–14, King's Theatre, 1714–1837, Her Majesty's, 1837–1902, His Majesty's, 1902–52.) The first theatre was designed in 1704–5 by Sir John Vanbrugh who was just embarking on another successful career as an architect. It was financed by 'persons of quality' for Thomas Betterton's company of actors who were then making do with a converted tennis court in LINCOLN'S INN FIELDS. The theatre opened in 1705 under the management of Vanbrugh and William Congreve with an Italian opera *The Loves of Ergasto*. Congreve dropped out of the management after the first year and Vanbrugh after the second, having lost a lot of money. Colley Cibber blamed the theatre's failure on Vanbrugh's design. 'Every proper quality and convenience of a good theatre had been sacrificed or neglected to shew the spectator a vast piece of architecture. . .' Cibber wrote. 'For what could their vast columns, their gilded cornices, their immoderate high roofs avail when scarce one word in them could be distinctly heard in it? Also the City, the Inns of Court and the middle part of the town which were the most constant support of a theatre . . . were too far out of the reach of an easy walk.' In 1711 Handel's opera *Rinaldo* was performed. It was the beginning of his 40-year association with the theatre during which time many of his oratorios and operas were first performed here. In 1720–28 he

A watercolour of Vanbrugh's Her Majesty's Theatre in 1783, six years before its destruction by fire.

directed the Royal Academy of Music, a company of Italian opera singers formed under royal patronage. Thirteen new operas by Handel were staged at the theatre before the Academy ran out of money and was disbanded. The theatre was destroyed by fire in 1789. An employee named Carrivalli is rumoured to have confessed to arson on his death bed. The theatre was rebuilt by Michael Novosielski as an opera house in 1790–1. It was the largest theatre in England and was used exclusively for operatic productions except for the years 1791–4 when the DRURY LANE company acted here while their theatre was being rebuilt. In 1816–18 John Nash and G.S. Repton remodelled the auditorium and added a colonnade on three sides of the theatre and the ROYAL OPERA ARCADE on the fourth. The years between 1830–50 were the golden age of the opera house. Even the audience in the pit had to wear evening dress. Great operatic stars performed here, including Jenny Lind who made her debut in 1847. *Fidelio* had its English premiere here in 1851. But next year the theatre closed, having lost most of its patrons to COVENT GARDEN. It was reopened in 1856 after COVENT GARDEN had been burned down, but was destroyed in 1867 by a fire thought to have begun by a stove overheating. In 1868–9 it was rebuilt within the shell by Charles Lee. But no tenant could be found for the new building and it remained empty until 1874. In 1878 Bizet's *Carmen* was first performed in England, and in 1882 there was the first complete performance of Wagner's *Ring*. In 1890 the theatre was closed, being heavily in debt, and in 1891 it was demolished except for the ROYAL OPERA ARCADE. The present theatre, designed in French Renaissance style by C.J. Phipps, was built in 1897 on half the site. The southern half was used for the Carlton Hotel which was designed by the same architect and demolished in 1957 to make way for NEW ZEALAND HOUSE. The theatre was financed by Herbert Beerbohm Tree with the profits he had made from *Trilby* at the HAYMARKET THEATRE. In 1904 he founded a dramatic school attached to the theatre which was later to become the ROYAL ACADEMY OF DRAMATIC ART. In 1916 *Chu Chin Chow*, produced by Oscar Asche while Tree was abroad, ran for 2,238 performances. In 1917 Tree died. In 1926 and 1928 there were seasons of Diaghilev's Russian ballet. In 1929 Noël Coward's operetta, *Bitter Sweet* had 697 performances. The main successes of the 1930s and 40s were *The Good Companions* (1931), *The Boy David* (1936) by Barrie, *Lady Behave* (1941), *Follow the Girls* (1945), *Anna Lucasta, Edward My Son* (1947) and many other notable productions.

Heralds' Museum *Tower of London, EC4*. Opened in the old Waterloo Barracks near the White Tower in 1980, its exhibits illustrate the development of heraldry from its origins in the 12th century. (*See also* COLLEGE OF HERALDS).

Hercules Road *SE1*. Extends from No. 79 Westminster Bridge Road to No. 178 LAMBETH ROAD. The CENTRAL OFFICE OF INFORMATION is on the west side. William Blake and his wife lived in a house on the site of No. 23, a 'pretty, clean house of 8 or 10 rooms'. A visitor once came upon them sitting naked in the summer-house where they were reciting passages from *Paradise Lost*. 'Come in,' Blake called out. 'It's only Adam and Eve, you know!'

Hereford House *Bolton Gardens*. An 18th-century mansion that formerly stood to the west of the present Bousfield School. The home of Dion Boucicault, the actor and dramatist, it became for a brief time from 1896 the headquarters of the Wheel Club, a fashionable cycling organisation. The house was demolished in about 1900, its site being covered by the east end of Coleherne Court.

Hereford Road *W2*. This street and others nearby with names from the Welsh borders were developed by William Kinnaird Jenkins of Herefordshire, a lawyer, who bought the estate from the Ladbroke family in 1847. Many different builders were involved and though pleasantly neo-Georgian, the area is architecturally undistinguished. At No. 71 Guglielmo Marconi lived between February 1896 and July 1897 when the world's first patent for wireless telegraphy was granted to him. The Princess Royal public house was built by James Bott, proprietor of the ARCHERY TAVERN.

Hereford Square *SW7*. A small quiet square built in 1847 by Edward Blore and probably named after Hereford Lodge, the large house at the south-west corner. George Borrow lived at No. 22 in 1860–81, and Fanny Kemble at No. 26 in 1884–90.

Herne Hill *SE24*. Situated on ground rising south of LAMBETH with DULWICH to the south-east. Herne Hill was within the ancient manor of Milkwell and is now part of the London Borough of LAMBETH. Canute is said to have rowed up the River EFFRA which once flowed at the foot of Herne Hill; and the herons that doubtless frequented the area were once said to have given it their name. More probably it was named after the Herne family, prominent 17th-century DULWICH residents. By the early 19th century, when John Ruskin spent his boyhood in Herne Hill, it was an affluent rural district of detached houses with large gardens. But it was transformed into a populous lower-class area with the arrival of the railways in the 1860s. St Saviour's (A.D. Gough) was opened in 1867 and

Herne Hill in 1825, then an affluent rural district of large detached houses, in one of which Ruskin spent his childhood.

towards the end of the century 78 acres of the estate of the early 19th-century Brockwell House became BROCKWELL PARK, famous for its Old English Garden. Building continued into the 20th century: notable are the Carnegie Public Library (H. Wakeford and Sons, 1906) and the Sunray Avenue Council Estate of the 1940s. Past residents of the area include Henry Bessemer, Havelock Ellis, Richard Church and Sir Victor Pritchett.

Hertford Street *W1.* Extends eastward from PARK LANE and then turns north to join CURZON STREET. It was laid out during the great building boom of the mid-1760s, and probably took its name from the Hertford Arms, a nearby inn now no longer in existence. There are still some agreeable Georgian houses towards the east end (the west end being dominated by the return fronts of modern hotels in PARK LANE), notably Nos 10–13, 17–19, 36–39 and 45–46. Nearly all the houses here are now used as offices, flats or furnished chambers, but Hertford Street was originally fashionable. At No. 10, designed in 1769–71 by Robert Adam, some of whose interiors still survive, lived General John Burgoyne, commander of the British forces at Saratoga, followed by Richard Brinsley Sheridan, the dramatist and statesman, who was here in 1795–1802. Sir George Cayley, the pioneer of aviation, lived at No. 20, and other famous residents in Hertford Street include Charles Grey, later Earl Grey of the Reform Bill, and in the 1830s Bulwer-Lytton, the novelist.

Hertford Union Canal The Hertford Union is a mere 1¾ miles in length and is known also as Duckett's Cut. It is reached at a junction on the REGENT'S CANAL after passing through Salmon's Lane, Johnson and Mile End Locks. It was acquired from Sir George Duckett in 1855 by the REGENT'S CANAL COMPANY, and provides a connection with the River LEA (or Lee) via three locks. Private boats are required to give a day's notice before passing through.

Hertford Villa *later St Dunstan's, Regent's Park, NW1.* Built in 1825 by Decimus Burton for the Marquess of Hertford, the villa changed its name in 1830 when the Marquess purchased, for £210, the ancient clock with striking figures of GOG AND MAGOG from ST DUNSTAN'S church in FLEET STREET. Francis Charles Seymour Conway, 3rd Marquess of Hertford, was Envoy Extraordinary to Russia and a noted art collector. He was probably the model for the Marquess of Steyne in Thackeray's *Vanity Fair* and for the Marquess of Monmouth in Disraeli's *Coningsby*, and was known as the 'Caliph of Regent's Park'. During 1860–1908 the villa was the home of Henry Hucks Gibbs, Lord Aldenham, merchant banker and bibliophile; his son, the Hon. Vicary Gibbs, MP for St Albans, edited *The Complete Peerage* in collaboration with his uncle, J.E. Cockayne. In 1914 it became the residence of Otto Hahn, an American banker, who allowed it to be used as a training centre for war-blinded soldiers and sailors, thus giving a name to that institution. In 1934 Lord Rothermere acquired the villa and returned the clock to FLEET STREET. In 1937 the house was demolished and another built on the site for Countess Haugwitz-Reventlow, née Barbara Hutton, the daughter of the founder of WOOLWORTH'S. It is today the official London residence of the United States Ambassador.

Heston *Middlesex.* Originally part of the *Domesday* manor of ISLEWORTH, earliest documents record the name as Hegeston, meaning a bushland settlement. For centuries it was a small hamlet, known only for the high quality of its wheat and the fact that Elizabeth I had her bread made from Heston-grown flour. In the 19th century there were several brickfields supplying bricks for developments in London and Birmingham. The railways coming to HOUNSLOW in 1850 and 1883 did not affect Heston. The GREAT WEST ROAD opening in 1925 along the southern boundary led to ribbon development on either side of the road. Heston Airport functioned for private flying in 1929–39. In 1925–39 there were numerous semi-detached housing developments. Such developments have continued since 1950. St Leonard's church, rebuilt in 1866, retains the 14th-century tower and some memorials. The lady chapel has a Robert Adam monument to Robert Child of OSTERLEY PARK who died in 1782. A tablet on the nave's north wall records the burial in the church of Sir Joseph Banks who lived at SPRING GROVE. In the churchyard lies Mrs Ann Brock, nurse to Princess Victoria, later Queen. Another grave is that of Frederick John White, a private in the 7th Queen's Own Hussars, who died from a flogging received as a punishment at HOUNSLOW Barracks in 1846. This resulted in the maximum number of lashes being reduced, and in 1881 to the abolition of flogging in the British Army.

Heythrop College *29–39 Brunswick Square, WC1.* Takes its name from Heythrop House, the baroque mansion in Oxfordshire which once belonged to the Catholic Earls of Shrewsbury and had been a Jesuit College from 1922 to 1969. With other Catholic Theological Colleges, its library and students became incorporated in 1971 by Royal Charter as a School of LONDON UNIVERSITY in the Faculty of Theology and Arts. Its governing body includes representatives of the University, of the English Province of the Society of Jesus, and local authorities. Admission is open to students of all religious affiliations and studies are for degrees in Divinity, Pastoral Theology and of Master and Doctor of Philosophy. Above its entrance is a fine bronze by Epstein of the Virgin and Child.

Hickford Rooms *Brewer Street.* The main London concert hall in the 1740s and 1750s. Mozart, aged nine, gave a recital here in 1765.

High Barnet *Hertfordshire.* Situated on a hill ridge north of the BRENT valley, High or Chipping Barnet (sometimes referred to simply as Barnet) lies on the Great North Road, mid-way between London and St Alban's. Its name derives from the Saxon *baernet*, a burning or conflagration, which suggests its origins in the burnt clearing of an area of ancient forest that stretched through much of MIDDLESEX, Hertfordshire and Essex (*see also* EAST BARNET *and* FRIERN BARNET). Barnet is not mentioned in *Domesday Book*, but was probably founded by the monks of St Albans to whose abbey the manor belonged until the DISSOLUTION. In 1199, King John granted the abbot a charter for the market, hence the name Chipping (=Market) Barnet. The market was held on a site near the church of ST JOHN THE BAPTIST.

High Barnet's position on the main route north out of London accounts for the rapid growth of the town, and High Street and Wood Street are of at least

15th-century origin. Located on such an important thoroughfare, Barnet is linked with several historical events. In the Wars of the Roses the forces of York and Lancaster met at the Battle of Barnet (in fact on Hadley Green to the north) in 1471, and the Earl of Warwick was killed in flight. Elizabeth I frequently passed through on journeys between London and Hatfield; Charles I escaped during the Civil War via Barnet to Oxford; and in 1660 General Monk is supposed to have stopped at the Mitre Inn. The site of the 17th-century militia headquarters lies off the High Street.

Barnet's market and fair made inn-keeping a major livelihood. It became a 'town of inns'; the original Red Lion at the foot of Barnet Hill dates back to the 16th century. Barnet's cattle and horse market was granted a charter by Elizabeth I in 1588, and today's September fair is a rare survivor from medieval times. Livestock would be brought to graze on Barnet Common to the north of the town before sale. Elizabeth was also responsible for the foundation of the Free Grammar School in 1573 (see TUDOR HALL).

From the late 16th century the development of the residential Wood Street, and a series of bequests for the building of almshouses, are evidence of the town's prosperity. James Ravenscroft, a great benefactor whose family chapel is in ST JOHN'S, gave land and funds for Jesus Hospital in Wood Street (1679). Barnet also had a reputation as a spa town both for its air and for the 'Physic Well' on the Common which was frequently visited by Samuel Pepys.

By the end of the 17th century a new road had been made from Hadley Highstone, just north of Barnet, to Hatfield, and the coaching trade became important for Barnet as the first stage out of London, servicing over 150 coaches a day. The heavy use of the GREAT NORTH ROAD resulted in the formation in 1712 of the Whetstone and Highgate Turnpike Trust to pay for road maintenance by the collection of tolls. It was responsible for the levelling of Barnet Hill in 1823 by McAdam, at a cost of £17,000, and for Telford's building of the New Road, now St Albans Road, in 1828. On this road, in 1845, George Gilbert Scott built Christ Church.

The coming of the railways dealt a death blow to the coaching trade and led to a trebling in population since it allowed people to commute to work in London from outside: during the 19th century Barnet's population grew from 1,250 to 5,000. In 1849 the Great Northern Railway bought the Lyonsdown estate, which comprised part of both parishes of Chipping and EAST BARNET, and in 1852 New Barnet Station was opened. In the subsequent years the pastures from EAST BARNET to the foot of Barnet Hill were built up, becoming known as New Barnet. In 1872 a station for a branch service from FINCHLEY was built at the foot of Barnet Hill, on the site of the Barnet Races which were therefore terminated. Residential streets off the main Wood and High Streets were developed. By 1883 much of Barnet Common had been enclosed (a process dating back at least to the Duke of Chandos's enclosure of 135 acres in 1729), and the formal Ravenscroft Gardens were laid out.

High Holborn *WC1*. The continuation of HOLBORN to SHAFTESBURY AVENUE and ENDELL STREET. The KNIGHTS TEMPLAR had their first round church here just beyond HOLBORN BARS. Edwin and Susan Sawle, the confectioners who provided sweet-meats for King James I's children and who were implicated in the Overbury poisoning case, had their shop here. John Milton, at different times before and after the Civil War, occupied two houses here. The George and Blue Boar coaching inn once stood on the site of No. 270. It was here that Cromwell and Ireton intercepted the letter from King Charles I to Henrietta Maria which they found concealed in the saddle of the King's messenger. No. 119 is on the site of the premises of Thomas Earnshaw, the watch and chronometer maker, who carried on business in High Holborn from 1806–29. The neo-Georgian offices at Nos 81–87 known as Templar House were built in 1939 on the site of the Royal Amphitheatre which opened in 1867 with equestrian entertainments. A variety of other performances, including opera and skating, were tried out until the theatre closed in 1886. Before being bombed in the 2nd World War it was used successively as the Holborn Central Hall, the NATIONAL SPORTING CLUB, the YMCA, the Holborn Boxing Stadium and the Stadium Club. The HOLBORN EMPIRE also stood in High Holborn at No. 242. Another theatre, the HOLBORN THEATRE ROYAL, stood on the site of Nos 40–48. After being bombed in the 2nd World War, it was rebuilt as government offices. The Duke's Theatre also stood in High Holborn. This was burned down in 1880. The First Avenue Hotel (300 bedrooms, now demolished) was built on the site. Another large late Victorian hotel, The Inns of Court Hotel (also now demolished) was nearby. Her Majesty's Stationery Office government bookshop is next door at No. 49. Also on the north side at Nos 63–71 is State House, designed by Trehearne and Norman, Preston and Partners (1855–7). The bronze in the forecourt is *Meridian* by Barbara Hepworth (1958–9).

On the south side Pendrell House at No. 284 holds the Meterological Office's London Weather Centre. Also on the south side are the Pearl Assurance Company in a handsome late Edwardian building by Moncton and Newman (1912); and the Princess Louise, a carefully restored Victorian public house, at Nos 208–209. The Westminster Branch of the MOORFIELDS EYE HOSPITAL is at No. 176; the Bow Group at No. 240; and George C. Harrap and Co., the publishers, are at Nos 182–184. The old Town Hall at No. 197 was designed by Warwick and Hall (1906). John Brumfit Ltd, the tobacconists at No. 337, were founded in ST SWITHIN'S LANE in 1864. Their shop in High Holborn, whose façade is well known because of its depiction on 'Old Holborn' tobacco packets, was opened in 1933 and is still run as an 'old-world tobacconist's' and provides special blends for individual customers. Beatties of London Ltd, the model railway dealers, were founded at the beginning of this century. Theirs is one of England's biggest model shops. At the same address, No. 112, is the Railway Club. Kenneth Brown, Baker, Baker, one of London's largest firms of solicitors, are at Nos 296–302. Kodak Ltd, the photographic dealers, formerly of Kodak House, Kingsway, moved from 246, the site of the old HOLBORN EMPIRE, to No. 900 in 1981.

High Timber Street *EC4*. Named after the 13th-century wharf, Timber Hithe, where timber was brought ashore and warehoused.

Highams Park *E4*. Lies between CHINGFORD and WALTHAMSTOW at the eastern boundary of the London Borough of WALTHAM FOREST. In 1768

Anthony Bacon built Higham House, or Highams, on an estate in the north-east corner of WALTHAMSTOW parish, to the design of William Newton. It lay within the ancient manor of Hecham (high home) which was in existence in 1066. In the 1780s the house was altered – the pediment was removed and the porch, cupola and balustraded third storey were added– and in 1793 Repton designed the grounds to include the lake fed from the River Ching. A summerhouse by the lake (demolished in 1831) was constructed with stones from the old LONDON BRIDGE. In 1873 Highams Park Station was opened to the west of the estate and the area around it was immediately developed. The Warner Company (which took its name from the Warner family, owners of Highams) were responsible for terraces of high quality workmanship, such as those between Winchester and Chingford Roads marked with a 'W'. This area subsequently became known as Highams Park. Within years the CORPORATION OF LONDON had bought land near Highams to remain as open space; and in 1891 a further 30 acres of the estate, including the lake, were acquired.

Highbury *N5*. Originated as one of ISLINGTON's six manors. The smaller of its two parts extended south of Islington Green to the CITY ROAD, the larger covered 987 acres, from Newington and Kingsland Greens to Hornsey Lane. This portion, named in a late Anglo-Saxon charter as Tollandune and in *Domesday Book* as Tolentune (Tolla's hill), was in Norman times held of the King by Ranulf. Its moated manor-house, on the east side of Hornsey Road (Kinloch Street), was superseded by another on higher ground – hence 'Highbury' – on the site of Leigh Road. Known also as Newington Barrow, it was later held by Alicia de Barowe, who in 1271 presented the lordship to the PRIORY OF ST JOHN OF JERUSALEM IN CLERKENWELL, which already held an adjoining manor (*see* HOLLOWAY).

The fine Priors' house was burned by Jack Straw's men in the PEASANTS' REVOLT, like Clerkenwell Priory itself; and the Highbury Manor site was afterwards known as Jack Straw's Castle. In 1540 Henry VIII, when he suppressed the Priory, granted Highbury with CANONBURY to Thomas Cromwell, but it reverted to the crown on Cromwell's disgrace. Queen Elizabeth leased it to Sir John Spencer among others (*see* CANONBURY TOWER). In 1611, a survey for Prince Henry, Charles I's elder brother, showed the 'castle' much decayed but the land value greatly increased. Charles finally disposed of the rights after his accession, and it passed through several families, including the Colebrookes from 1723.

The springs of this hilly wooded area supplied CITY and monastic sites from the 15th century, and Strype records a ceremonial inspection of conduits by the LORD MAYOR and ALDERMEN, followed by a hunt and a feast. One conduit head survived in the 1840s in Highbury Fields, opposite 14 Highbury Place. Highbury was also famed till the 1850s for dairy farms, such as the ancient Cream Hall, sited at the angle of modern Legard Road. It was enlarged as a dwelling-house in the 19th century, and destroyed about 1860. The more famous HIGHBURY BARN survived, greatly changed, much longer.

In Highbury Vale (Blackstock Road area), long known as Danebottom from memories of an early battle, the 'Boarded River' carried the NEW RIVER over

Gipsy Lane bridleway (now Mountgrove Road), crossing Hackney Brook behind the present Arsenal Tavern. Later converted to an embankment, this part of the river was diverted eastwards in the 1870s. North of it were EEL PIE HOUSE and Highbury Sluice.

Early building speculation proved unprofitable when the freeholder John Dawes (builder of CANONBURY's first houses) granted leases to John Spiller, who erected 39 fine houses called Highbury Place (1774–9). Highbury Terrace to the north-west, by different entrepreneurs, followed in 1789; but these handsome rows did not launch the expected suburb. Spiller occupied the top house of the exclusive Place; next door at 38 was Abraham Newland, Chief Cashier of the BANK OF ENGLAND, John Nichols, biographer, topographical writer and editor of the *Gentleman's Magazine*, lived at No. 14 from 1803 until his death in 1820; in the 1840s Joseph Chamberlain lived at No. 25. And in 1927–34 Sickert had his painting school and studio at No. 1.

In 1781 Dawes acquired Highbury Manor or 'castle' site with 74 acres from Sir George Colebrooke, and built on it Highbury House, where he died in 1788. A later owner was Alexander Aubert, FRS, an insurance broker and noted amateur astronomer of Swiss extraction, who having built one observatory near DEPTFORD commissioned Smeaton for another at Highbury House. He re-erected ST PETER-LE-POER clock from BROAD STREET in a tower in his grounds. Aubert also organised and commanded the Loyal Islington Volunteers, in 1798–1801. Highbury House was demolished in 1938 for Eton House, flats built by the Old Etonian Housing Association. Opposite the former manor site is Christ Church, built in 1848 for the new parish; and nearby, the Victoria Jubilee clock tower (1897).

In 1826 Highbury College, founded at Mile End in 1783 as an independent theological institution, was opened in extensive grounds above Highbury Vale. Six acres at the vale end were taken in 1913 for the ARSENAL FOOTBALL CLUB. The Greek-style college, later owned by the Church of England, was destroyed by fire in 1946, its site remaining as a garden in Aubert Park; Aubert Court stands on part of its grounds.

Suburban expansion began in the 1820s with Cubitt's villas in Highbury Grove, only two, with some mews, now remaining (Nos 54 and 56 Highbury Park); in 1830 came Park Terrace, opposite. An imaginative project for a huge public park, bounded by Ball's Pond, Stoke Newington reservoirs, SEVEN SISTERS ROAD and the Great Northern Railway was abandoned in the 1850s, though FINSBURY PARK, as small compensation, was formed in 1869, and 27½ acres of

Highbury House in the late 18th century, when the clock from the church of St Peter-le-Poer was re-erected in the tower in the grounds.

Highbury Fields were secured in 1885 and 1891. Highbury, instead of a planned garden village, became developers' prey.

Henry Rydon led off with the affluent Highbury New Park (1853–61) near the NEW RIVER; the Grosvenor Avenue area, slightly less affluent, followed from 1864. Highbury Hill was grand, Aberdeen Park secluded. The latter was an enclave clustered round St Saviour's church where the young John Betjeman worshipped. These estates are now eroded by infilling and demolition and Council flats have replaced many villas. By contrast, later brick and terracotta streets farther north survive almost intact.

Highbury Barn *Islington.* Originally part of the country manor of the Priors of St John, and subsequently within the farm enclosure of Highbury Grange (*see* HIGHBURY). The large 'barn' or dairy-building is mentioned in 1740 as a cakes-and-ale house, whither in the late 1760s Goldsmith and his friends sometimes walked from the TEMPLE. From 1770 to 1818 it was also known as Willoughby's, after a father and son who improved the grounds with a bowling-green and tea-gardens. The younger Willoughby equipped the Barn as a Great Room which became renowned for club dinners. Between about 1835 and 1860, under John Hinton, owner of the Eyre Arms at ST JOHN'S WOOD, and his son, Archibald the place was a 'North London Cremorne'. In the 1840s annual dinners of the Licensed Victuallers catered for 3,000 guests, nearly double the then population of HIGHBURY. In 1854 Archibald Hinton converted the Barn into a concert-hall and, obtaining a dancing licence, in 1858 built the famous *Leviathan*, a 4,000 ft square open-air dancing platform lit by huge gas globes, with an orchestra at one end. Admission was 6d and crowds flocked there on Sunday evenings.

The most notable proprietor was Edward Giovanelli, born Edwards, once a clown at the SURREY THEATRE, who in 1861 further embellished the five-acre grounds with a large supper-room and splendid illuminations, engaging singers and the gymnast Leotard for the season. The Alexandra Theatre was elaborately reconstructed on the old Barn site in 1865 and hailed by *The Times* as a long-wanted theatre for 'the northern portion of the metropolis'. With boxes at a guinea, prices were high. Attractions included Giovanelli and his wife in comedy and pantomime, Blondin and other high-wire performers (one woman fell to her death), music-hall, and the original Siamese twins. But well-to-do inhabitants of the now expanding suburb complained of the crowds' rowdiness and horseplay, and a serious riot in 1869 enabled them next year to prevent renewal of Giovanelli's licence. A successor, E.T. Smith, was also refused; and the Barn finally closed in 1871. Its gardens became overgrown, and by 1883 it was entirely built over. Highbury Tavern (26 Highbury Park) marks a small part of the huge site.

Highbury Fields *N5.* Area of 27½ acres bought in 1885 for £60,000. Wat Tyler's rebels occupied them and destroyed an old priory. Evelyn describes in 1666 how there were gathered after the GREAT FIRE up to '200,000 people of all ranks and degrees dispersed and lying along by their heapes of what they could save

The Leviathan Platform, a 4,000 ft square open-air dancing area lit by huge gas globes, at Highbury Barn.

378

from the fire, deploring their losses and though ready to perish for hunger and destitution, yet not asking one penny for relief.' Tennis and other facilities are now provided and there is a bandstand.

Highbury Quadrant *N5.* The sculpture in cemented iron of two seated men in conversation is by Siegfried Charoux (1959).

Highgate *N6, N19.* Most of Highgate at one time belonged to the BISHOPS OF LONDON, and formed part of their HORNSEY estate. The first community probably grew up round the gate to the Bishop's Park (near today's Gate House public house) and is likely to have included workers connected with the park, as well as a hermit who lived where Highgate School Chapel now stands. The hermit was responsible for maintaining the road from ISLINGTON, and it was the digging of gravel for this purpose which caused the formation of the ponds which used to be in Pond Square but which were filled in in 1864 as they had become stagnant. There was certainly a hamlet in the 13th century, and in the 14th, the BISHOP OF LONDON allowed a road to be built over the hill, as the old one round it was becoming impassable in winter. Along the road the Bishop had toll gates erected, and the one on the top of the hill is said to have given Highgate its name. Legend says that Richard Whittington rested at the bottom of the hill, near today's public house called the Whittington Stone, and here it was that he heard the message peeled by BOW BELLS:

> Turn again Whittington,
> Thrice Lord Mayor of London Town.

A stone on HIGHGATE HILL, WHITTINGTON STONE, commemorates this. In 1593, John Norden wrote of Highgate that it was 'a most pleasant dwelling, yet not so pleasant as healthful' and that many people who came here sick were soon cured by the 'sweet salutarie aire'. Highgate Green, which stretched from present-day Pond Square to THE GROVE, was the centre of the village. Its 'grassy walks and shady avenues were the scenes of exercise and harmless merriment.' Here holidays were celebrated with fairs and games and Morris dancing. In 1565, Sir Roger Cholmley, the village's most notable resident of the time, founded his free school (now HIGHGATE SCHOOL) in a building on the site of the former hermit's chapel. By this time aristocratic members of London's society, escaping the discomforts of the rapidly expanding capital, had taken to building themselves mansions on these pleasant northern heights. These included ARUNDEL, CROMWELL, FITZROY and LAUDERDALE HOUSE. In 1622 an early Congregational chapel was founded in Southwood Lane; such chapels had been banned within five miles of the CITY OF LONDON, and this site was just outside the boundary. Towards the end of the century, William Blake, an eccentric philanthropist, established a hospital for 40 poor or orphaned children who were to receive a basic education. The school, probably the first charity school, got into financial difficulty, even though Blake had built Nos 1–6 THE GROVE as a speculation in an attempt to raise money for its support. After a few years the school had to close and Blake was imprisoned as a debtor. The time for building huge mansions was now temporarily over in Highgate; but some of the existing ones were adapted and lived in by rich CITY merchants and professional men who also built smaller, but very elegant houses here. Highgate had become a place of resort for Londoners. Byron described the taking of the Highgate Oath in *Childe Harold*. There were then about 20 licensed houses in the district, and strangers entering them were required to take a pair of animal horns in their hands and swear a jocular oath:

> ... Both men and maids are sworn,
> And consecrate the oath with dance and draught till morn.

The custom died out towards the end of the 19th

'*Swearing on the Horns' at Highgate, 1906. In earlier times it was regularly performed at some 20 local public houses.*

A coach approaching Holloway Turnpike, beyond which the Archway can be seen crossing Highgate Hill.

century though it has been revived as an occasional ceremony in certain local taverns. During the last century the population of Highgate and the surrounding areas so increased that institutions began to be added to the village. The Whittington Almshouses (*see* WHITTINGTON COLLEGE), at the bottom of HIGHGATE HILL, were built in 1822 by the MERCERS' COMPANY (demolished in the 1970s as a result of road widening). A new church was required, so ST MICHAEL'S was built in 1832. The next year the old chapel in the centre of the village (built in about 1567) was demolished, to be eventually replaced by the Cranley Chapel, built for HIGHGATE SCHOOL in 1866–7. Below St Michael's, HIGHGATE CEMETERY was laid out in 1839. The HIGHGATE LITERARY AND SCIENTIFIC INSTITUTION was also founded in 1839; and in 1850, the Smallpox and Vaccination Hospital (see WHITTINGTON HOSPITAL) was built in Maiden Lane (now Dartmouth Park Hill).

The pressure of traffic up HIGHGATE HILL had been eased early in the 19th century by the construction of the ARCHWAY ROAD and in 1884 Europe's first cable tramway was laid up the hill – though this event was followed by a disaster in 1892 when one of the cars broke loose while ascending the hill. The cable cars were replaced by trams a few years later. Another disaster was narrowly averted on Highgate's other hill – West Hill – in 1837, when the new young Queen Victoria's carriage horses bolted with her and the Duchess of Kent as they were being driven down the hill. The horses were dragged to a halt by the landlord of the Fox and Crown, who promptly received permission to put up the Royal Arms. The Fox and Crown was demolished in 1892, but a plaque commemorates the event; and the Royal Coat of Arms is now in the library at the HIGHGATE LITERARY AND SCIENTIFIC INSTITUTION. The palatial WITANHURST was built at the top of West Hill in 1913. Further down the hill another large house, Holly Lodge, was demolished in 1920 to make way for the HOLLY LODGE ESTATE.

Today Highgate remains an elegant village, still retaining its own identity as a separate community, though bisected by the busy High Street, and divided between three London boroughs. Many old houses still stand, though those unlucky enough to be on main roads are constantly shaken by traffic. Modern

developments include Highpoint 1 and 2, in North Hill, by Lubetkin and Tecton (1938), praised by Le Corbusier as 'the vertical garden city'; housing on West Hill by Ted Levy, Benjamin and Partners, and CAMDEN Council's vast Highgate New Town.

Famous people who have lived in Highgate, in addition to those mentioned in separate items, include Coventry Patmore; A.E. Housman, who wrote *A Shropshire Lad* while living in Byron Cottage, North Hill; Mary Kingsley, who spent her childhood in Southwood Lane; and John Betjeman who spent his at No. 31 West Hill.

Highgate Cemetery *Swain's Lane, N6.* The Cemetery of St James at HIGHGATE lies on the southern slope of Highgate West Hill. It was established by the London Cemetery Company, whose founder, the architect and civil engineer Stephen Geary, designed and planned the cemetery. The original 20-acre site was at one time part of the grounds of a mansion belonging to Sir William Ashurst, who was Lord Mayor of London in 1693. Geary designed an entrance in the form of an archway linking the two chapels with the porter's lodge; a group of buildings of Gothic design, though laid out to a classical plan. The landscape gardener, David Ramsay, designed serpentine roads and footpaths leading upwards through the burial area to the buildings and terrace just beneath ST MICHAEL'S CHURCH. These buildings are approached through an arch flanked by Egyptian columns and obelisks, beyond which is the Egyptian Avenue. The avenue, with tombs on either side, leads under a bridge to the Circle of Lebanon: catacombs built on either side of a circular passageway, each tomb a square compartment with stone shelves for coffins and cast-iron doors. The circle was built around a magnificent cedar tree which grew in Sir William Ashurst's garden and still dominates the cemetery. Steps lead up from the circle to the terrace immediately below the church.

The cemetery was consecrated in May 1839 by the BISHOP OF LONDON and was an immediate success. Not only was it a popular and fashionable place to be buried, it became a tourist attraction to which people thronged to admire the architecture and enjoy the magnificent views over London. 'In such a place the aspect of death is softened,' declared the *Lady's Newspaper* in 1850. Another newspaper reported, 'This undertaking seems eminently successful and to excite some envy among its competitors.' It was so successful that in 1857 an extension was opened on the other side of Swain's Lane, enlarging the total area to 50 acres. The chapels continued in use for both parts, and a bier was used which lowered coffins by hydraulic system into a basement whence they travelled by tunnel under Swain's Lane to the new cemetery. Among those buried in the older Western Cemetery are: George Wombwell, menagerie proprietor (1850), who has a sleeping stone lion on his tomb; Stephen Geary, the architect of the cemetery (1854); Frederick Lillywhite, the 'nonpareil bowler' (1854); J.B. Bunning, the landscape architect (1863); Tom Sayers, the last of the barefisted fighters (1865) – carved on his tomb is the effigy of his huge dog, who was the chief mourner at his funeral, following the coffin alone in a mail-phaeton (10,000 humans also attended); Michael Faraday (1867); Julius Beer, proprietor of the *Observer* from 1870 until his death (1880), in a heavy mausoleum designed by John Oldrid Scott; Mrs Henry Wood, the writer (1887); Carl Rosa (1889) who founded the Opera Company in 1875; Christina Rossetti, poet (1894). And in the Eastern Cemetery lie George Eliot (1880); Karl Marx (1883) (the ugly bust which is his memorial being the constant object of pilgrimage for Communist delegations as well as a target for bombers); Herbert Spencer, radical philosopher (1903); and William Friese-Greene (1921) whose monument was designed by Edwin Lutyens.

By the 1960s, the United Cemetery Company (successors to the London Cemetery Company) had run out of money. The cemetery was totally neglected. Buildings were disintegrating, grounds overgrown, tombs and monuments – all those angels, animals and musical instruments – hidden by undergrowth and broken by vandals. In 1975 a voluntary body, the Friends of Highgate Cemetery, was formed to promote its conservation and secure its preservation and restoration. The following year the London Borough of CAMDEN obtained powers by a special Act of Parliament with a view to acquiring the cemetery. Since then the eastern part has been operated by CAMDEN council, while the Western Cemetery has remained closed except for certain special Visitors' Days. Early in 1981, when it looked as though Highgate Cemetery might finally be closed, the freehold of the land was acquired from the United Cemetery Co., for £50, and is now owned by a company whose directors are members of the Friends of Highgate Cemetery. Conservation and restoration work is to continue.

Highgate Hill *N6, N19*. Runs up the hill from the busy Archway roundabout until it becomes Highgate High Street; it divides HIGHGATE between the boroughs of CAMDEN to the west and HARINGEY and HORNSEY to the east. The road up the steep hill was made in 1386, and was one of the main thoroughfares northward out of London until the construction of the ARCHWAY ROAD in 1813. At the bottom of the hill stands the WHITTINGTON STONE. By the junction with Dartmouth Park Hill, St Joseph's Retreat was opened as a monastery by Cardinal Manning in 1876, and the Romanesque Church of St Joseph was added to the design of A. Vicars, in 1888. The green dome of 'Holy

Joe', surmounted by a plain gold cross, is a local landmark which can be seen for miles. Across the road the Old Crown Tea Gardens flourished until 1900 when they disappeared beneath the present public house. Up the hill on this (east) side is CROMWELL HOUSE, and above it Ireton and Lyndale Houses, Nos 106 and 108, built in the early 18th century, originally as one house. Opposite them is LAUDERDALE HOUSE, which backs on to WATERLOW PARK, and in the wall near this house a plaque marks the site of the cottage in which the poet Andrew Marvell is said to have lived. The cottage was demolished in 1869. Channing School for Girls, founded in 1885, is at the top of the hill.

Highgate Literary and Scientific Institution *South Grove, N6*. Founded at a public meeting in the Gate House Tavern in 1839 'for the promotion of useful and scientific knowledge', the Institution moved in 1840 to the premises it occupies today. The building, formerly a school for Jewish boys, now contains a reading room, lecture hall and a flourishing subscription library, and is the meeting place for many local societies. The impressive Royal Coat of Arms from the wall of the Fox and Crown on West Hill (*see* HIGHGATE) is in the library.

Highgate Road *NW5*. A very old northward route, known until 1870 as Green Street. At its southern end is the Bull and Gate public house, which has been there (though the present building is Victorian) since early in the 18th century. ST JOHN THE BAPTIST, KENTISH TOWN parish church originally a chapel built in 1784 by J. Wyatt, was enlarged and altered in 1845 by J. Hakewill. Just north of the Vine public house is the entrance to College Lane, with the oldest buildings remaining in KENTISH TOWN. Further north is Grove Terrace, an attractive row of houses built in 1780–93.

Highgate School *N6*. Founded in 1565 when Elizabeth I issued Letters Patent authorising Sir Roger Cholmeley to found 'a grammar school . . . for the good education of boys and young men' in HIGHGATE and 'for the relief and support of certain poor in the said town or hamlet'. The endowment property at LUDGATE HILL had the modest annual value of £10 13s 4d. To this was added a grant by Edmund Grindal, Bishop of London, of a ruined chapel and hermitage with two acres. In subsequent years these meagre resources came to be used both for the school and for a chapel-of-ease. By 1571 a small school house had been built at HIGHGATE which provided education for 40 free scholars; and subjects, taught by an appointed master, included Latin and possibly Greek. In 1712 there were also ten boarders. In the 17th and 18th centuries the governors of the school (whose minute book is still extant), continued to spend much of the endowment on the chapel and social services for parishioners, so that by 1816, according to an inspection report on educational charities, Highgate School had fallen into 'complete decay'. When the governors' use of the endowment funds was challenged in a case in the Chancery Court, Lord Eldon ruled in 1827 that the endowment funds should be used for a free grammar school. Revised statutes passed in 1832 separated chapel and school and the bequest money was assigned to the school, which at that time had only 32 pupils. The school was restored to prosperity and success under the long Mastership of the Revd John Dyne

(1839–74). When he retired there were ten assistant masters and 200 boys. New buildings (designed by S.P. Cockerell) and playing-fields had been added and the school had considerable academic success. A Royal Commission on secondary education in the 1860s described the school as 'a very useful institution' doing 'very good work for the upper middle classes', though it considered fees at £18 15s for day boys and £91 for boarders as expensive. Further buildings were added before the end of the 19th century with additional sports facilities and the school changed from rugger to soccer in football. In the 20th century numbers continued to increase and the curriculum was greatly expanded with a new emphasis on science. In 1980 pupils totalled 673 boys (543 day and 130 boarding). Famous pupils have included the etymologist, W.W. Skeat, and the poets Gerard Manley Hopkins and John Betjeman.

Highgate Wood *N6*. Once the property of the BISHOPS OF LONDON, these 70 acres were taken over by the CORPORATION in 1885 and have been kept as far as possible in their natural state. An excellent cricket pitch has been provided and there are also a children's playground and refreshment pavilion.

Highway *E1*. The present road incorporates the notorious Ratcliff Highway. Stow remembered it being built up with small tenements. In the 18th and 19th centuries organised vice relieved generations of sailors of their earnings, despite the warning in the song to 'Mind Ratcliff Highway and the damsels loose'. Mayhew visited dancing rooms there and found 'a certain innate delicacy' among the sailors' women.

Hill Street *W1*. On the Berkeley Estate (*see* BERKELEY SQUARE), it extends from BERKELEY SQUARE to the edge of the estate at Waverton Street, where it bends northwards to enter the GROSVENOR ESTATE and ends at SOUTH AUDLEY STREET. Building began in about 1745, and some of the original houses still survive in altered form; but No. 36 has been little changed outwardly. Apartments and offices now predominate. Residents include the ill-fated Admiral John Byng, Henry Brougham, later Lord Chancellor and Mrs Elizabeth Montagu.

Hillingdon *Middlesex*. At the time of *Domesday Book* it was a small manor centred around the present Hillingdon village, but it later merged with the adjacent manor of Colham. The large medieval parish of Hillingdon then also included the settlements of COLHAM, YIEWSLEY and UXBRIDGE, and totally surrounded the tiny village of COWLEY. The Bishops of Worcester owned property here from 1281, and used the former Hillingdon manor-house as a halt in the pre-Reformation period. The district remained largely rural until last century, when the opening of the GRAND JUNCTION CANAL encouraged the working of gravel and brick-earth deposits to the south. Population growth since 1800 has led to the division of the old parish into six. Today, the village of Hillingdon is dominated by the church of ST JOHN THE BAPTIST which stands on high ground at the junction of Uxbridge Road and Royal Lane. The village character is retained by several attractive properties nearby, notably the Cedar House of about 1580, The Cottage of about 1560 (now the Cottage Hotel), and the Red Lion Inn where King Charles halted briefly in 1646. The parish workhouse, built in 1747 to the south of the village, has now developed into Hillingdon Hospital.

On the reorganisation of local government in Greater London in 1965 the Borough of UXBRIDGE was linked with the urban districts of YIEWSLEY and WEST DRAYTON, HAYES and HARLINGTON, and RUISLIP-NORTHWOOD. The new authority was named the London Borough of HILLINGDON.

Hinde Street *W1*. Built in 1777 onwards by Samuel Adams and named after Jacob Hinde, son-in-law of the ground landlord, Thomas Thayer. Sir Henry Raeburn lived at No. 1, in 1754–65. On the corner with Thayer Street stands Hinde Street Methodist Church built in 1807–10 by the Revd William Jenkins and rebuilt in the 1880s by James Weir.

Historians The first written reference to London occurs in Tacitus's *Annales*, Book XIV, where he describes the destruction of the city by Boudicca's tribesmen; the first view of London is a woodcut illustrating *Chronycle of Englonde* which Wynkyn de Worde printed at WESTMINSTER in 1497; and the first detailed description of the capital is that given by William Fitzstephen as a preface to his life of Thomas Becket. Throughout the Middle Ages, a number of chronicles were kept, the most famous being that ascribed to Robert Fabyan. London's first real historian, however, was John Stow. He was born in 1525, the son of a tallow chandler. He earned his living as a tailor, though from his youth he had a bent for literature. He edited Chaucer's works and Holinshed's *Chronicle*, compiled his own *Summarie of Englyshe Chronicles* which was afterwards called *The Annales of England*, edited Matthew Paris's writings and, then, when well advanced in middle age, he began *A Survey of London*, giving first a brief account of the foundation of the city and then a detailed ward-by-ward perambulation of its streets. It was published in 1598. Stow wrote from his own observation and memory, telling how as a boy he had fetched milk from Farmer Goodman who had the farm which had formerly belonged to the Convent of St Clare beside TOWER HILL, how his father was buried 'as close as may be' to other members of his family in the 'little green churchyard' of ST MICHAEL CORNHILL, and how the fields to the east of the city had 'within a few years [been] made a continual building throughout, of garden-houses and small cottages.' It is from his pages that we can, for the first time, gain a conspectus of London as it once was. But Stow himself gained little from his labours. Of his *Summarie* he declared: 'It hath cost me many a weary mile's travel, many a hard earned penny and pound, and many a cold winter night's study.' In 1603, at the age of 78, he was forced to apply to the newly enthroned James I for a licence to beg. Two years later he was dead, a new edition of his *Annales* being issued within a few days of his demise. In spite of their poverty, his widow set up a handsome memorial to him in the church of ST ANDREW UNDERSHAFT. Carved by Nicholas Johnson, it shows a half-figure of the self-trained scholar seated at his desk, intent upon his work. Every year in April, a service is arranged by the London and Middlesex Archaeological Society at which a fresh quill is put into the hand of the effigy and a short address is given on some aspect of Stow's life and work (*see* CEREMONIES).

Fresh editions of his *Survey*, with continuations, were published at intervals. The sixth and seventh editions were the work of the learned and zealous antiquary, the Revd John Strype who virtually rewrote the book in order to bring it up to date. Strype was the rector of LEYTON for 68 years, being buried at last in his own churchyard at the age of 94. He lies beneath a Latin epitaph which he had himself composed and his collected works fill 19 volumes. In 1908, Charles Lethbridge Kingsford prepared a new edition with notes of Stow's original text and this is still the best.

Stow had many followers. William Maitland produced his *History of London from its foundation by the Romans to the Present Time* in 1739. A profusely illustrated folio volume, it gives not only a history and description of the CITY, but also interesting information on the CITY LIVERY COMPANIES, on London's commercial activities, on the condition of the arts, on places of learning and on charities within the CITY. The Revd John Entick followed with a four-volume *New and Accurate History and Survey* in 1766, illustrated with harsh little engravings; and in 1773 John Noorthouck, 'citizen and stationer', produced his *New History of London* adorned with beautiful plates and an excellent map by Thomas Kitchin of the country 30 miles around London. For amateurs of London were by now becoming aware that the capital, or at least its influence, extended far beyond the boundaries of the CITY and WESTMINSTER: in 1792–96 the Revd Daniel Lysons produced his *Environs of London, being an Historical Account of the Towns, Villages, and Hamlets within twelve Miles of that Capital; Interspersed with Biographical Anecdotes*. This remains one of the most informative and readable studies of its kind. Thomas Pennant, the naturalist, produced his *Some Account of London* in 1790. Of him, Dr Johnson said, 'He observes more things than any one else does.' From his notes, a posthumous *Antiquities of London* was compiled and issued in 1814; his collection of maps, watercolours, drawings and engravings of London were dispersed at auction. Pennant's near contemporary, an American historian and topographer, James Peller Malcolm, produced four volumes of *London Redivivus* (1803–7). His account was 'compiled from parochial records, archives from various foundations, the Harleian MSS and other authentic sources', and is still very useful.

All these writers, save Lysons, kept to the same basic pattern of a history of London followed by a topographical description. But Charles Knight's *London*, issued in 150 weekly parts between 6 March 1841 and 17 February 1844, took a different approach. Each part consisted of a single extended essay on a London topic – the river THAMES and particular buildings were familiar themes, but more general subjects, such as music in the capital, were covered too, while less obvious matters, including old May Day customs and London astrologers, were discussed. Social conditions were given serious consideration, and buildings, such as Horace Walpole's residence at STRAWBERRY HILL, though well outside the boundaries of the CITY and WESTMINSTER, were described. Knight did not write every essay himself; he edited the work of a team which he directed well, illustrating their articles with small, charming engravings.

In 1849, Peter Cunningham produced his *Handbook of London*, a two-volume work which was soon followed by a single-volume second edition. He died before the work could be expanded, but his notes eventually passed to Henry Benjamin Wheatley who added to them his own considerable researches and produced in 1891 his *London Past and Present*, a three-volume topographical dictionary of London which gives details of matters of interest for the whole LONDON COUNTY COUNCIL area. This is still a standard, and a most excellent, reference book. It provided much material for George H. Cunningham's *London: A Comprehensive Survey of its History, Traditions and Historical Associations of Buildings and Monuments Arranged under Streets in Alphabetical Order* (1927). A new edition of Wheatley and Cunningham with much additional material was prepared by John O'Leary. It had reached proof stage by 1976 when the publishers suddenly decided not to issue it. A most valuable set of corrected proofs, with MS. additions, is, however, in the guardianship of the GUILDHALL LIBRARY.

Around the late 19th and early 20th centuries, a number of scholars and enthusiasts were writing on London. John Timbs produced a splendidly encyclopaedic compilation, *Curiosities of London*, with 800 pages full of fascinating details set out in dictionary form. In 1873–8, Walter Thornbury and Edward Walford produced their invaluable six-volume *Old and New London; a Narrative of its History, its People, and its Places*, which contains much information about buildings that have long since vanished. William John Loftie wrote his two-volume *History of London* in 1883; Reginald R. Sharpe produced his *London and the Kingdom*, a discussion of the relationship between the capital and national events, in 1894; and Sir George Laurence Gomme published *The Governance of London* in 1907. Sir Walter Besant wrote numerous volumes on the capital, carefully describing it period by period; Walter Godfrey, for many years the editor of the LONDON TOPOGRAPHICAL SOCIETY's publications, produced his *History of Architecture in and around London* in 1911 (2nd edn. 1962); Walter Bell produced a series of works, including two studies of the GREAT PLAGUE and the GREAT FIRE (1924 and 1920) of particular value; Beresford Chancellor described the cultural and artistic life of the capital in past centuries. Henry Andrade Harben's *Dictionary of London* was published in 1918. It deals only with the CITY but for this it is invaluable. William Kent also produced a *Dictionary of London*, of wider scope, in 1937. A new edition of this was produced in 1970.

Nearer our own day, the tendency has been for London's historians to concentrate on one particular period or aspect of the city's past, and for histories to be written by professional historians rather than enthusiastic amateurs. Of the exceptional books which have appeared in the last 50 years the following comprise but a random selection: *The Growth of Stuart London* by Norman Brett-James (1935); *London Life in the Eighteenth Century* by M. Dorothy George (1925); *A History of London Life* by R.J. Mitchell and M.D.R. Leys (1958); *London, the Unique City* by Steen Eiler Rasmussen (1934); *The Rebuilding of London after the Great Fire* (1940), which started as Professor T.F. Reddaway's postgraduate thesis; *Georgian London* by Sir John Summerson (1945); Barker and Robbins, *History of London Transport*; H.J. Dyos, *Victorian Suburb*; F.M.L. Thompson, *Hampstead*;

Gareth Stedman-Jones, *Outcast London*; Gillian Bebbington, *London Street Names*; and several works by Hermione Hobhouse. To be considered as essential reading are the relevant volumes of the Victoria County History, of Nikolaus Pevsner's *Buildings of England*, and of the Royal Commission on Historical Monuments.

Currently, there are two great London enterprises slowly approaching completion; these are the GREATER LONDON COUNCIL's *Survey of London* and Secker and Warburg's 8-volume *History of London*. The former was instigated in 1894 by C.R. Ashbee who was outraged at the demolition of BROMLEY-BY-BOW PALACE. The first volume appeared in 1900. There are now 40 volumes, each one describing in scholarly detail some particular building, parish or area of London. Until his retirement in 1982 the *Survey*'s editor was Dr Francis Sheppard who was then also editing Secker and Warburg's *History of London*, of which three volumes have so far appeared. These are *London 800–1216: the Shaping of a City* by Christopher Brooke assisted by Gillian Keir (1975); *Hanoverian London, 1714–1808* by George Rudé (1971); and Sheppard's own *London 1808–1870: the Infernal Wen* (1971).

Historic Ship Collection of the Maritime Trust
St Katharine's Dock, E1. The Maritime Trust was founded in 1969 and transferred its most important vessels to St Katharine's Dock, near the TOWER OF LONDON, to form the Historic Ship Collection which opened to the public in 1979. The Collection lies in the East Basin and includes the *Kathleen and May*, a three-masted topsail trading schooner launched in 1900, Captain Scott's famous ship RRS DISCOVERY and five other historic ships. The Nore light vessel, the tug *Challenge*, the steam coaster *Robin* and the sailing barge *Cambria* all have connections with London's river and the THAMES estuary. Several THAMES barges can be seen here as well as various modern cruising vessels.

Hither Green
SE6, SE13. That part of LEWISHAM known as Hither Green extends south from the railway station of that name, on either side of Hither Green Lane which, before the area was built up, was one of the old country roads, running along the crest of the hill between the valleys of the rivers RAVENSBOURNE and QUAGGY. Many of the roads in this area have Scottish street names. They represent the Corbett Estate, built about the turn of the century by A. Cameron Corbett, MP (subsequently 1st Lord Rowallan), whose ambition was to offer well-designed spacious houses – a 'modern Hygeia', a 'Garden of Eden', a desirable area for young families with high ideals – with plenty of places of worship but no public houses. Torridon Road, on this estate, runs due north-south on the GREENWICH MERIDIAN. The educationists and social reformers, Rachel and Margaret McMillan, are commemorated by a plaque on their house, 127 George Lane.

Hoare and Co.
Fleet Street, EC4. The business was founded by Richard Hoare, goldsmith and banker, in about 1672. Originally based at the Golden Bottle in CHEAPSIDE, the firm moved to its present site in FLEET STREET in 1690. Banking displaced the goldsmith business after the 1690s, and early customers included Samuel Pepys, John Evelyn and John

Dryden. The FLEET STREET premises were rebuilt in 1829 and a West End branch was opened at Aldford House, Park Lane, in 1932. The business remains an independent firm, managed and controlled by the Hoare family since 1672.

Hobury Street
SW10. Completed in about 1855 and possibly named after its builder. George Meredith, the poet and novelist, lived at No. 7 in 1857–9.

Hogarth's House
Chiswick, W4. The artist's country retreat from 1749 until the night before his death in 1764 in his town house in Leicester Fields, now LEICESTER SQUARE. He lived here with his wife Jane (who continued to reside at CHISWICK until 1789), his sister Anne, and his widowed mother-in-law who died here in 1757. After Jane Hogarth's death the house passed to her cousin, Mary Lewis, then to the Rev. Henry Francis Cary, translator of Dante into English, and a friend of Charles Lamb. It was first opened as a museum in 1909.

Holbein Gate
Built about 1532, in three storeys, of chequered stone and flint, with two octagonal turrets. There is no evidence that Hans Holbein was employed by Henry VIII until 1536, so it is unlikely that he designed this gate, but he may have occupied lodgings over it. Lady Castlemaine inhabited the lower rooms for several years after 1663 (*see* WHITEHALL PALACE), while the upper storey was in use as the Paper Office by 1672. It was threatened with destruction in the early 18th century: Vanbrugh regretted in 1719 that 'there should be no other expedient found to make way for coaches etc. than destroying one of the greatest curiositys there is in London.' But it was not finally demolished until 1759. The Duke of Cumberland's plan to re-erect the gate in Windsor Great Park was never carried out.

Holborn
EC1. Extends from HIGH HOLBORN to HOLBORN CIRCUS. It takes its name from the Holebourne, a tributary of the FLEET. It was first mentioned as Holeburnstreete in 1249. At that time it was a principal highway for the cartage of wool and hides, corn, cheese and wood to the CITY. It was paved in 1417 and again in 1535. STAPLE INN is at the western end. BARNARD'S INN is also on the south side: Dickens describes Pip as living here with Herbert Pocket in *Great Expectations*. Next to it stood Langdale's distillery which was wrecked in the GORDON RIOTS. FURNIVAL'S INN used to be on the north side. Here Dickens lived in 1834–9 as a bachelor and in the early days of his marriage. He wrote *Pickwick Papers* here. The site is now covered by the offices of the PRUDENTIAL ASSURANCE COMPANY. The once famous store GAMAGE'S is no more. The dramatic *Daily Mirror* building at No. 33 was built in 1957–60 to the designs of Sir Owen Williams and Partners and Anderson, Forster and Walker. Distinguished occupants of Holborn have included Sir Francis Bacon, Sir Thomas More, Fulke Greville, John Milton and John Gerardi, the herbalist, who had his physic garden here and here wrote his *Herball*. Samuel Johnson also lived here for a time.

Holborn
WC2. The area to the north of the STRAND in which are situated LINCOLN'S INN and GRAY'S INN. It is first mentioned in a 10th-century charter in which

King Edgar granted land here to WESTMINSTER ABBEY. The smallest of the former metropolitan boroughs, it is now part of the London Borough of CAMDEN.

Holborn Bars   Stone obelisks surmounted by silver griffins mark the boundary of the CITY OF LONDON, one at the end of GRAY'S INN ROAD, the other at STAPLE INN. These were originally set up in about 1130. Here tolls and commercial dues used to be exacted, and guards prevented the passage of rogues, vagabonds and lepers.

Holborn Circus   *EC1*. Constructed in 1872, the junction of HOLBORN, HOLBORN VIADUCT, HATTON GARDEN, Charterhouse Street, St Andrew's Street and NEW FETTER LANE. The bronze of Prince Albert raising his hat to the CITY OF LONDON is by Charles Bacon (*see* STATUES).

Holborn Empire   *242 High Holborn*. Opened in 1857 by Henry Weston as Weston's Music Hall in a converted building formerly the Holborn Tavern and the Holborn National Schools. It was rebuilt in 1887 by Lander and Bedells to hold 2,500 people. Ernest Runtz rebuilt the façade in 1897. It was bought by Walter Gibbons in 1905 and completely rebuilt by Frank Matcham at a cost of £30,000. Many of the great stars appeared here including Albert Chevalier, Dan Leno, Lottie Collins and Ada Reeve. In 1922–8 the children's play, *Where the Rainbow Ends*, was staged each Christmas. The building was badly damaged by bombs in 1940 and demolished in 1960. Offices for the Pearl Assurance Company were built on the site.

Holborn Restaurant   *218 High Holborn*. A very large establishment, it opened as a restaurant in 1874, having formerly been a casino, swimming-baths and dance hall. Extended and redecorated by T.E. Collcutt in 1896, it had an ornate terracotta Empire Grill, a Grand Restaurant with dancing and cabaret, private dining rooms, three Masonic temples and some 14 other smaller restaurants. Some 960 chairs were listed in the sale of goods before it was demolished in 1955.

Holborn Theatre Royal   *High Holborn*. Designed in 1866 for Sefton Parry, the theatre speculator. It opened with a successful new drama, *Flying Scud: or A Four Legged Fortune* by Dion Boucicault. After that managements came and went in quick succession and the theatre was often closed. In 1878 Clarence Holt and Charles Wilmot made it pay by presenting 'strong' dramas at low prices, but it was destroyed by fire in 1880. A hotel was built on the site. This was damaged in the BLITZ and the site is now covered with First Avenue House, a block of offices at 40–48 High Holborn.

Holborn Viaduct   *EC1*. Designed by William Heywood, the City Surveyor, to bridge the valley of the FLEET and to connect HOLBORN with NEWGATE STREET. The viaduct, which was finished after six years work in 1896, is 1,400 ft long and 80 ft wide and said to have cost £2.5 million. The scheme included the building of HOLBORN CIRCUS, Charterhouse Street and St Andrew's Street. The bridge crossing FARRINGDON STREET is decorated with bronze statues erected in 1868; on the north are *Commerce* and *Agriculture* by Farmer and Brindley and on the south *Science* and *Fine Arts* by H. Bursill. Four Italian Gothic houses stood at the corners of the bridge. Two and a half of them are still there and have in niches statues of Henry Fitzailwyn, the first Mayor; Sir Thomas Gresham, founder of the ROYAL EXCHANGE and GRESHAM COLLEGE, Sir William Walworth, the Lord Mayor who stabbed Wat Tyler; and Sir Hugh Myddelton, pioneer of the NEW RIVER. Queen Victoria opened the viaduct on the same day as BLACKFRIARS BRIDGE. ST ANDREW'S CHURCH is on the south side. The CITY TEMPLE is next door to it.

Holborn Viaduct Station   *EC1*. One of the three linked CITY OF LONDON stations of the London, Chatham and Dover Railway. The line which came over BLACKFRIARS BRIDGE through ST PAUL'S (*see* BLACKFRIARS STATION) and LUDGATE HILL, was finally extended to end at a new street called Holborn Viaduct. The station, a very modest affair, was opened in 1874. The hotel by L.H. Isaacs, built to form the façade, opened in 1877. It was bombed in 1941, and replaced by a 10-storey office block designed by Ronald Ward and Partners. Holborn Viaduct is now a week-days only station, catering mainly for commuter passengers.

T.S. Boys's view of the Holborn Viaduct, completed in 1869 to bridge the valley of the Fleet.

Holford House *Regent's Park*. Designed by Decimus Burton for James Holford, a wealthy merchant and wine importer, the villa was not built till 1832 and was the largest in REGENT'S PARK. Holford lived there till his death in 1853 and the house then became Regent's Park College, a Baptist College for the training of candidates for the ministry. It was heavily bombed during the 2nd World War and was demolished.

Holford Road *NW3*. Takes its name from the Holfords, one of the principal families of HAMPSTEAD from the beginning of the 18th century. The houses on the east side were built on part of the grounds of Holford House, now known as Ladywell Court, which was the family home until about 1860. Baron von Hugel, the theologian, lived at No. 4 in 1882–1903.

Holland Estate All the four manors comprising KENSINGTON were at various times owned by Sir Walter Cope who built Cope's Castle, known as HOLLAND HOUSE after his death when his estates passed to his son-in-law, Sir Henry Rich, later Baron Kensington and 1st Earl of Holland. On the death of the 4th Earl of Holland in 1721 the estate passed to William Edwardes (*see* EDWARDES ESTATE). In 1768 HOLLAND HOUSE and its surrounding land were sold to Henry Fox who had leased it from 1746 and who had been created Baron Holland in 1763. After the death of the 4th Baron Holland in 1859, his widow left the estate to her husband's cousin, Henry Edward Fox-Strangways, Baron Strangways of Woodford Strangways, Dorset and 5th Earl of Ilchester. The names of several streets in this part of Kensington, in addition to Cope Place, W8, Holland Road, W14, Holland Street, W8 (where Walter Crane, the artist, lived in 1892–1915), Ilchester Place, W14, Strangways Terrace, W14, and Woodford Square, W14, reflect these family connections. ADDISON ROAD, W14 takes its name from Joseph Addison, the essayist, who was married to the widow of the 3rd Earl of Holland; Melbury Road, W14 from the Dorset home of the Earls of Ilchester; Russell Gardens, perhaps, from Lord John Russell, an intimate friend of the Holland family.

Holland House *and* **Park** *W8*. The Jacobean mansion originally called Cope Castle was built in about 1606 for Sir Walter Cope, James I's Chancellor of the Exchequer who, at various times, owned all four Manors of KENSINGTON. The architect is unknown, but it might have been John Thorpe who mentions it as 'perfected by me'. The Portland stone gateway in front of the house has been attributed to Inigo Jones and to Nicholas Stone the Elder. King James was an unappreciative guest in 1612; he said that the wind blew through the walls so that he could not lie warm in his bed. Under the terms of Cope's will, his widow inherited the house providing she did not remarry. When she did so it passed to their daughter, Lady Rich, whose husband, Sir Henry, was created Earl of Holland in 1624. Following his execution as a Royalist during the Civil War the house was confiscated by the Parliamentarians. Cromwell is said to have gone into the surrounding fields with General Ireton so that eavesdroppers should not overhear what he had to shout to his deaf son-in-law. After the Civil War the house was restored to Lady Holland who had plays privately performed here in defiance of the laws obtaining during the Commonwealth.

The widow of the 3rd Earl Holland married Joseph Addison who is said to have composed many of his *Spectator* articles pacing the 100 ft Long Gallery with a glass of wine at either end. He died in 1719 at Holland House, saying to his unruly stepson, 'See in what peace a Christian can die.' In 1746 the house was let to Henry Fox, 1st Baron Holland, who bought it in 1763 with money he had made by speculating with public funds when he was Paymaster General. He and his elder son both died in 1774, when the 3rd Baron Holland inherited the estate at one year old. His bride, whom he brought to live at Holland House, had been divorced because of their adultery. Ostracised on this account at Court, she determined to establish a *salon* of her own. Her new husband had been greatly influenced by the liberal views of his uncle, Charles James Fox, who had brought him up and who had grown up here himself; the house became the social centre of Whig politicians and literary men including Earl Grey, George Canning, Richard Brinsley Sheridan, Sydney Smith, Melbourne, Byron, Talleyrand, Wordsworth, Scott, Palmerston, Brougham, Dickens and Macaulay. Although a brilliant and fascinating hostess, Lady Holland was not afraid to speak her mind. Thomas Moore, the Irish poet, said 'Poets inclined to a plethora of vanity would find a dose of Lady Holland now and then very good for their complaint,' but Sydney Smith more flatteringly wrote to her, 'I do not believe all Europe can produce as much knowledge, wit and worth as passes in and out of your door.' In 1802 the Hollands were presented to Napoleon whom ever afterwards they unfailingly supported, even to the extent of sending him jars of plum jam, more than 400 books and a refrigerator when he was in exile on Elba. In 1804, while the family was still abroad, Lord Camelford was shot dead in a duel with Captain Best in the meadows to the west of the house.

After Lord Holland died in 1840 his widow rarely used the house. Their son, the 4th Baron, made considerable renovations and alterations to it. He built the Garden Ballroom in the former 17th-century stables, and arcades and terraces were added to connect the house and the Orangery. He entertained intermittently, but not on the scale of his parents. Queen Victoria and Prince Albert attended two Scottish fêtes held in the grounds in 1849 and 1850. He died in 1859 and, after an interval abroad, his widow returned to Holland House where her lavish entertaining ran her into debt. In 1866 land adjoining BAYSWATER ROAD was sold for building the area now called HOLLAND PARK. In 1873 the land west of Holland Villas Road had also been sold as building land. As she had no children, Lady Holland made the Earl of Ilchester her heir. (He was the head of the elder branch of the Fox family.) When she died here in 1889 Lord Ilchester took possession. His wife was a celebrated hostess of the 1890s and the Edwardian era, and often gave masked balls, garden parties and charity fêtes.

During the 2nd World War the house was bombed and was left derelict until 1952 when the LONDON COUNTY COUNCIL bought the property from the Earl of Ilchester. It proved possible to preserve only the ground storey and the arcades of the central portion, the east wing (which had been badly damaged), and the gateway. The restored east wing has housed, since 1959, part of the King George Memorial Youth Hostel Association. In summer the front terrace of the house forms the setting for open-air plays, ballets, operas and

The Jacobean Holland House, Kensington, in 1769. It became a social centre for the Whigs in the late 18th and early 19th centuries.

concerts, and is known as the Court Theatre. The Garden Ballroom was converted in 1965 for use as a restaurant, and small art exhibitions are held in the Orangery.

There are three formal gardens near the house and Garden Ballroom, the Rose Garden, the Dutch Garden and the Iris Garden. The Dutch Garden, designed in 1812 by Buonaiuti, librarian to the Hollands, consists of flower beds in geometric arrangement, bordered with box. In the mellow brick wall on the north side is an alcove known as Rogers' Seat, over which is an inscription by Lord Holland to his friend Samuel Rogers, the poet and banker. In the smaller Iris Garden Lady Holland is said to have planted the first dahlias ever to have been grown in England. In one corner there is a small 18th-century building believed to have been an ice house. Not far from this is a bronze statue by John Macallan Swan, *The Boy and The Bear Cubs* (1902). The other statues in the park are one by Eric Gill in the Dutch Garden, bronze replicas in the Orangery of the two figures of *The Wrestlers*, and a monument to the 3rd Baron Holland at the end of the Rose Walk by G.F. Watts and Edgar Boehm, 1872 (*see* STATUES).

Holland Park Comprehensive School *W8*. Built in 1956–8 on the sites of MORAY and BEDFORD LODGES and designed by the LONDON COUNTY COUNCIL's Architect's Department. The grounds include Thorpe Lodge which was built by John Tasker in 1808–17 and whose last owner was Montagu Norman (Baron Norman), a Governor of the BANK OF ENGLAND in 1920–44. In 1982 there were about 1,600 pupils.

Hollen Street *W1*. Built in 1715–16 by Allen Hollen, a gentleman of ST JAMES's, and first known as Gresham Street after a wine cooper of COVENT GARDEN, Richard Gresham, from whom Hollen had purchased part of the land. The houses built in these years have all now been demolished.

Holles Street *W1*. First mentioned in the Overseers' Survey for 1723, the street is named after John Holles, Duke of Newcastle who purchased the southern half of the manor of Tyburn (*see* MARYLEBONE) in 1708 for £17,500. His only child and heiress, Lady Henrietta Cavendish, married Edward Harley, Earl of Oxford. The young couple were responsible for the development of the estate. Lord Byron was born at No. 24 on 22 January 1788. Barbara Hepworth's bronze *Winged Figure* was erected on the wall of the John Lewis store in 1963.

Holloway *N7, N17*. The north part of ISLINGTON which was held at the time of *Domesday Book* by the Dean and Chapter of ST PAUL's but which was not part of the manors of BARNSBURY or CANONBURY, was called Tallington or Tolentune. It was made over by them to the two CLERKENWELL foundations, the Priory of St John and the Nunnery of St Mary, which held it until the Reformation. Remains of the moated manor house of Tolentune, the 'Lower Place' which the Hospitallers abandoned for HIGHBURY, survived well past the mid-19th century off Hornsey Road at Kinloch Street. Hercules Road, near SEVEN SISTERS ROAD, was the site of the westerly lands' manor-house. Hornsey Road or Tallington Lane, probably marking the boundary, led in a straight line towards CROUCH END through the hamlet and common land of Stroud or Strood Green, where later (near Hanley Road) stood the oddly-named Japan House as well as Stapleton Hall which was recorded by Jacobean times and eventually became a tavern. Although Hornsey Road and its manor-house were both called 'Duval's' or 'Devil's', any association with the highwayman Claude Duval is fanciful. Hagbush Lane, an ancient thoroughfare wandering west, then north, from the LIVERPOOL ROAD area, never became a highway and was gradually obliterated by about 1830, and its very course was lost.

The name Holloway appears by the 15th century, referring to the sunk or sloughy highway, hence to the 'Upper' and 'Lower' hamlets on its route (*see* HOLLOWAY ROAD). Intersected as it was in the 19th century by busy link roads and by the railway, and covered from the 1860s by gaunt streets and drab houses, the former rural character of the area behind the highroad is now hard to imagine. Pleasant villas for retired CITY men appeared in UPPER HOLLOWAY by the 1820s, when Hanley Road and Tollington Park were laid out, but the latter was built up over only 40 years. In the 1850s land development societies were creating small estates north and south of these roads – the St Pancras

387

Freehold Society favouring names like Liberty, Reform and Franchise Streets, all later renamed and now heavily rebuilt. Drayton Park never developed as intended, remaining today half waste space and railway land.

The largest estate was built on BARNSBURY manor's most northerly lands, then owned by the Tufnell family and hence named TUFNELL PARK. The polygonal Byzantine-style St George's church (1868), semi-derelict for some years, reopened in 1976 as ST GEORGE'S THEATRE.

In 1855, on 32 acres round the hilltop site of COPENHAGEN HOUSE, the Metropolitan Cattle Market replaced SMITHFIELD, with hotels, taverns and a benevolent institution for drovers' widows round its perimeter. A 'rag fair' of bric-à-brac and junk-dealers here became a famous London feature until the 2nd World War; efforts to revive the Caledonian Market on this site afterwards failed; and in 1963 the cattle market and abattoirs also closed. In 1969 the CITY CORPORATION transferred the land to ISLINGTON Borough, which built Council flats over most of the area, retaining only the clock-tower which marks the site of COPENHAGEN HOUSE, and the ornate railings whose distinctive cattle masks were unfortunately stolen.

HOLLOWAY PRISON opened in 1852 on 10 acres beside the then rural Camden Road, which was soon overtaken by building. Expansion of the railways, especially at FINSBURY PARK, and the UNDERGROUND, the spread of industry, and grim housing with no space for parks, made Holloway a synonym for a drab existence – appropriate background in 1910 for the Crippen murder case (he lived in Hilldrop Crescent, now replaced by Margaret Bondfield House). Some streets had a notorious underworld society, like Campbell Road off SEVEN SISTERS ROAD, which has now disappeared under a council estate, and Queensland Road off Hornsey Road, now entirely industrial.

Holloway Prison *Parkhurst Road, N7.* Originally the City House of Correction for both men and women sentenced to short terms of punishment. Designed on the separate system by J.B. Bunning, building was completed in 1852. It was described in 1862 as 'a noble building of the castellated Gothic style ... built on rising ground. [It was] originally purchased by the City Corporation to be used as a cemetery at the time of the cholera in 1832 ... At the back of the prison lie some beautiful green meadows.' It had a central tower copied from Caesar's Tower, Warwick Castle. In 1896 Dr Jameson and his fellow raiders were imprisoned. Used exclusively for women from 1902, Mrs Pankhurst and other suffragettes were imprisoned here, the first in 1906. In 1970 a demolition and rebuilding programme began to the designs of Robert Matthew Johnson-Marshall and Partners. Only two decorative griffins from the old buildings and the famous glass foundation stone inscribed, 'May God preserve the City of London and make this place a terror to evil doers,' have been preserved. The new prison is built of attractive red brick, with trees and planted areas, the lay-out being based on the village-green principle. The rear perimeter wall is designed to a sinuous line to make climbing more difficult. Living accommodation is in units of 16 and 32. Each has common facilities at the centre, including a dining and television room. Rooms are 4-bed or single, with WC. They have large

windows with curtains and broad vertical bands replacing bars, the long pane between two bands opens in casement fashion. There are 42 places for women with children up to 5 years old. There are a hospital, a gymnasium and a swimming pool. It is the major women's prison in the country and takes all types of prisoners. In 1982 its population was 308 (the certified normal accommodation is 247).

Holloway Road *and* **Archway** *N7, N19.* This heavily used section of the GREAT NORTH ROAD, 1¾ miles between Highbury Corner and Archway roundabout, was always an important exit from London. In 1364 Edward III first licensed tolls for gravelling the highway, 'notoriously miry and deep'. The 'hollow way' was turnpiked under the 1717 Act, with a gate near the junction with the Back (Liverpool) Road at Ring Cross, once an execution site whose cross perhaps marked the Knights Hospitallers' territory.

BARNSBURY manor's demesne extended to the area now covered by TUFNELL PARK, and its moated site – between the Odeon Cinema and Mercer's Road – was visible until these lands were first developed, long after the house had vanished. Manor House, mentioned by 1822 as just north of this, was a girls' school.

Hornsey Road, another old highway, turned off south of where the Great Northern Railway bridge was later built. Two ancient bridleways, Mead Lane and Heame Lane, were obliterated by new link roads to CAMDEN TOWN (Camden Road, 1826) and TOTTENHAM (SEVEN SISTERS ROAD). In 1811 Junction Road was made, to connect KENTISH TOWN with the ARCHWAY, itself then building to carry Hornsey Lane across ISLINGTON's northern boundary. Most other roads were Victorian creations.

By the early 19th century Holloway Road was lined with villas and cottages. At Bowman's Lodge, site of an Elizabethan 'archery house' by SEVEN SISTERS ROAD, Edward Lear was born in 1812. A few such houses still survive, especially in UPPER HOLLOWAY (No. 529 might pass for The Laurels, the home of Mr Pooter in the Grossmiths' *Diary of a Nobody*). Holloway Road also drew the carriage trade, but of several famous stores, notably Beale's, (established here 1829), only Jones Bros (established 1867 and now part of the JOHN LEWIS PARTNERSHIP), and Selby's remain. Famous suburban theatres, long demolished, were the Marlborough at No. 383 (1903), now replaced by a Polytechnic department, Parkhurst at No. 401 (1890), and Holloway Empire at No. 564 (1899).

ST MARY MAGDALENE, LOWER HOLLOWAY, was built in 1811 as a chapel-of-ease for ISLINGTON; St John's, UPPER HOLLOWAY (1826–8), was designed by the young Charles Barry, externally a double of his St Paul's, Ball's Pond. Among old taverns rebuilt are the Nag's Head, centre of a busy shopping area; the Half-Moon (No. 471), famed in the 18th century for HOLLOWAY cheesecakes; Mother Red-Cap's (No. 665), half-way house to HIGHGATE; and the Crown (No. 622), traditionally visited by Cromwell.

Public buildings include the POLYTECHNIC OF NORTH LONDON; the handsome Islington Central Library (1906), and the Royal Northern Hospital, moved from Caledonian Road in 1888.

The metamorphosis of Archway junction in the 1970s all but marooned the Archway Tavern (rebuilt 1888) and methodist Central Hall. Beyond, WHITTINGTON HOSPITAL incorporates the former

Smallpox Hospital, removed here to the country from KING'S CROSS in 1841. The present WHITTINGTON STONE was removed during heavy rebuilding to a new spot on HIGHGATE HILL. Whittington Almshouses, built by the MERCERS' COMPANY in 1822, were sacrificed to road-widening in the 1960s. (*See also* UPPER HOLLOWAY.)

Holly Bush *Heath Street, NW3.* An old public house approached by a flight of steps from Heath Street. It was built in 1643. The name derives from the custom of hanging a green branch or bush over the door to advertise the sale of wines or beer. (Hence the saying, 'A good wine needs no bush'.) Until recently the inn had been in the same family for almost 80 years and the interior remained almost unchanged. Dr Johnson drank here, as did Boswell. Romney lived and worked at the neighbouring Romney House.

Holly Bush Hill *NW3.* The residence of George Romney, the painter, is commemorated here by a BLUE PLAQUE. Romney, who had previously occupied a large house and studio at No. 32 CAVENDISH SQUARE, bought the house in 1796, demolished the stables and built instead 'a gallery for pictures and sculpture and enclosed half of the garden under a timber arcade for a riding-house. These costly freaks were a severe strain upon his income, and caused great annoyance to his son.'

Holly Lodge Estate *West Hill, Highgate, N6.* In the villa, Holly Lodge, built in about 1830 by Sir Henry Tempest 'in most beautifully timbered and extensive grounds', lived Thomas Coutts, one of the two founders of COUTTS' BANK; and, later, Baroness Burdett-Coutts. After her death, and that of her husband, the house was demolished and 'London's loveliest garden colony' was created in the 1920s, covering the slope of the hill with rows of detached pseudo-Tudor houses, and tall blocks of flats.

Holly Village *Swain's Lane and Chester Road, Highgate, N6.* Eight picturesque and fanciful Gothic cottages clustered round a green, built in 1865 to the design of Henry Darbishire. Often said to have been erected for the servants of Baroness Burdett-Coutts (*see* HOLLY LODGE ESTATE), Holly Village was in fact constructed as a business venture, and the cottages were let for substantial rents.

Holme This villa, designed in 1818–19 by Decimus Burton for his father, James Burton, the speculative builder who supported John Nash, was the first villa

The Holme, in Regent's Park, was built in 1818–19 by Decimus Burton for his father, James Burton.

to be completed in REGENT'S PARK. The Burton family remained there till 1834. In 1913–35, the house was the property of Sir George Dance, the theatrical producer and song writer. In 1947 The Holme was taken over by BEDFORD COLLEGE for residential and academic purposes.

Holt and Co. *Whitehall, SW1.* This bank (now known as Holt's Branch, WILLIAMS AND GLYN'S BANK) was founded in 1809 by William Kirkland, an Army paymaster. Based in Whitehall Place, Holt and Co became a leading Army agent at the end of the Napoleonic Wars. In 1884 it acquired Lawrie and Son, Army agents of JERMYN STREET (established in 1780), and in 1915 absorbed Woodhead and Co, Navy agents of CHARING CROSS (founded in 1809). Holt and Co was purchased by Glyn, Mills in 1923.

Holy Cross *Greenford (Oldfield Lane), Middlesex.* The two churches of Holy Cross, one medieval, the other built in 1939–41, stand at right-angles to each other in Oldfield Lane, near WESTERN AVENUE. The old church was originally built or rebuilt in the late 15th or early 16th century, but it has been subsequently altered. The exterior is of flint rubble with stone dressings, the tower is weatherboarded. The church contains interesting early 16th-century stained glass which was brought in the 19th century from King's College, Cambridge, and portrays the arms of Catherine of Aragon and Henry VIII as well as those of King's College and Eton College. The font was given in 1638. The church was threatened with demolition in 1951 but after extensive restoration it was reopened in 1956 and continues to be used.

The new church became necessary with the dramatic increase in GREENFORD's population in the 1930s. It was built a few yards west of the old church and orientated north-south. Sir Albert Richardson designed it with a large interior in the form of a hall, constructed mainly of Oregon pine. The low external walls are of Stamford brick and the steeply pitched roof of Stamford tiles is divided by a clerestory, and a type of oriel window at the south end.

Holy Redeemer *Clerkenwell (Exmouth Market), EC1.* Built in 1888–9 in the Italian style and completed later with a projecting south-west campanile and east end, the church is an early example of steel and concrete construction except for the front which is of brick with a round-arched doorway, a rose window and a large pediment. Inside, Corinthian columns support the unbroken entablature. There is a baldacchino over the altar. The organ belonged to the Prince Consort.

Holy Trinity *Clapham Common (North Side), London SW4.* Has one of the greenest settings of any London church. Of little architectural distinction, it is chiefly known as the centre of the CLAPHAM SECT. John Thornton of CLAPHAM, reputed to have been the wealthiest merchant in England at that time, was the founder of the group. He bought the advowson of Holy Trinity, and in 1792 John Venn, a member of the sect, was installed as rector. They had an extempore method of praying aloud which was generally preceded by the words 'Let us engage . . .'

The church was built in 1776. A Bill had been passed in the Commons two years previously to permit the vestry to pull down the dilapidated 12th-century

Holy Trinity, Clapham Common, built in 1776, became the place of worship of the Clapham Sect.

parish church of St Mary's, which stood where ST PAUL'S, RECTORY GROVE stands today, and to commission 'a strong, neat church to contain 800 persons to be built' on this corner of CLAPHAM COMMON. The surveyor, Kenton Couse – a protégé of Lord Burlington's architect friend, Henry Flitcroft (popularly known as 'Burlington's Harry') – designed it. Originally the church was a simple brick box with two tiers of windows, an awkward cupola and a stone turret. There was a small pedimented porch at the west end. This has been replaced by Francis Hurlbatt's Doric colonnade, designed in 1812. Beresford Pite added the chancel in 1902. Inside, the original galleries remain, but the wooden pulpit, which was unusually tall and had occupied a dominant, central position in the church, has been moved and reduced in height. The church was closed after it had been damaged by a rocket in 1945. It was repaired by Thomas T. Ford and reopened in 1952.

The 17th-century parish monuments are at ST PAUL'S, RECTORY GROVE. They include the lovely marble figures from the monument to Sir Richard Atkins – Lord of the Manor of CLAPHAM – and one to Samuel Pepys's clerk and later Commissioner of the Navy, Richard Hewer.

Holy Trinity *Gough Square*. Built in the Norman style in 1837–8 by John Shaw as a chapel-of-ease to ST BRIDE FLEET STREET. THE GOLDSMITHS' COMPANY donated the site. It was altered by A.W. Blomfield in 1873 and demolished in about 1905.

Holy Trinity *Kingsway, WC2*. The first church was known as Holy Trinity, Little Queen Street. It was designed by Francis Bedford and built in 1829–31 on the site of the house where Mary Lamb had stabbed her mother in a fit of madness in 1796. The Commissioners of the Church Building Act of 1818 paid the whole cost of £8,521. It was large enough for a congregation of 2,000. Both the altar and the entrances were at the east end, but in 1880 the altar was removed to the west end. Galleries on either side of the organ were erected for the use of Holborn Charity Children

until they moved to the new Christchurch ENDELL STREET adjoining the workhouse. The church was demolished in 1909, having been undermined by excavations for the PICCADILLY LINE. The present Renaissance-style church was built in 1909–11 by Belcher and Joass. It is modelled on Pietro da Cortona's church of St Maria della Pace, Rome.

Holy Trinity Marylebone *Marylebone Road, NW1*. Built to serve the fashionable residential suburbs which spread north from OXFORD STREET during the late 18th and early 19th centuries. It is one of the 'Waterloo' churches for which a £1 million thanksgiving fund was voted by Parliament in 1821 to mark the nation's deliverance from invasion during the Napoleonic Wars. One of the few churches to have been designed by Sir John Soane – architect of the BANK OF ENGLAND – it is similar to his earlier one of ST PETER WALWORTH. It was completed in 1828 and had a seating capacity of 1,300. The main façade faces south on to GREAT PORTLAND STREET and the altar is at the north end. In his original drawings Soane showed the Ionic columns of the portico as pilasters. The people of MARYLEBONE, suspecting that this was an example of the ST MARYLEBONE vestry's well-known pinch-penny attitude toward church building, raised a subscription to pay for the present free-standing ones. The tower is characteristic of Soane's work. In 1952, the parish was reunited with St Marylebone church, and Holy Trinity became the headquarters of the SOCIETY FOR PROMOTING CHRISTIAN KNOWLEDGE. The church had many distinguished parishioners during the 19th century. Among them were the Duke of Wellington, John Flaxman, the sculptor, J.M.W. Turner, W.E. Gladstone and the astronomer, Sir John Herschel. Florence Nightingale and Lord Roberts of Kandahar were both regular members of the congregation.

Holy Trinity Minories *Haydon Square*. In 1293, Edmund, Earl of Lancaster, brother to Edward I, founded a convent of the Order of St Clare on this site. St Clare, the friend of St Francis of Assisi, was the foundress of the Order, and the nuns were known as Sisters Minoresses. They followed a rule similar to that of the Franciscans. Because of its royal connection, this convent enjoyed the privilege of being a Papal Peculiar, that is to say it was exempt from the jurisdiction of the English bishops. In the plague of 1515 the community and its attendants were all but wiped out. The last abbess surrendered the convent to Henry VIII in 1539. Part of the convent buildings were then used as an armoury for the TOWER OF LONDON and the rest became a workhouse. The chapel was given the name of St Trinities and became the parish church. In 1706 it was rebuilt in a plain, simple style, no bigger than the convent chapel, for 30 to 40 people. When Master of the MINT, (1699–1727), Isaac Newton used to worship here. It has no tower, only a bell turret with a peal of three bells. It continued to be free from the jurisdiction of Canterbury. The head of Lady Jane Grey's father, the Duke of Suffolk – who had been granted the abbey by Edward VI – was discovered in a good state of preservation in a vault in 1852. He had been beheaded on TOWER HILL in 1554. For a time it was displayed in a glass case under the pulpit. It was moved to ST BOTOLPH, ALDGATE in 1893 when the two parishes were joined. Holy Trinity then became a parish room. It was destroyed in the 2nd World War.

The lack of space in the tiny churchyard had been a constant problem to the vestry through the years. In 1689, and again in 1763, they emptied it. No one knows what they did with the corpses. A stone in front of the church with '1745' inscribed on it covered a box filled with bones from the field of Culloden.

Holy Trinity *Prince Consort Road, SW7*. Built in 1902–3 to the designs of G.F. Bodley, it was one of his last works. The church was restored in the 1950s. James Oliver Hannay, who wrote novels under the name of George A. Birmingham, became rector here in 1934.

𝕳𝖔𝖑𝖞 𝕿𝖗𝖎𝖓𝖎𝖙𝖞 𝕻𝖗𝖎𝖔𝖗𝖞 *Aldgate*. Built in the 12th century by the Canons of Augustine, secular priests who lived in small groups according to the rule of St Augustine. Church and State were so intimately connected at that time that the Prior was also an ex-officio Alderman of Portsoken Ward in the CITY. Part of the Priory church originally served the new parish of Christ Church, but this was not a satisfactory arrangement; so the church of ST KATHARINE CREE was built in the precincts of the Priory for the use of the parish. Up until 1414 it was served by a canon appointed by the Prior. After this date, however, the parishioners maintained their own priest. The Priory was the first of the large houses – and the first in London to be dissolved by Henry VIII. In 1532 Parliament confirmed the gift 'to the King, because the Prior had departed from the monastery, leaving it profaned and desolate'. Its closure caused little regret. The Prior as Alderman was not popular and, due to high living, the Priory was seriously in debt. Henry VIII gave it to Lord Audley. He in turn, while happy to keep the rest of the property, offered the church to the parishioners of ST KATHARINE CREE. They, however, refused the gift. It was then pulled down, and the stone sold very cheaply as Londoners still preferred brick and wood for building.

Holy Trinity *Roehampton (Ponsonby Road), SW15*. Built to the designs of G.H. Fellowes Prynne in 1896–8.

Holy Trinity *Sloane Street, SW1*. This church, designed by John Dando Sedding in 1890, is the apotheosis of the Arts and Crafts Movement inspired by William Morris. It replaces a Gothic church by James Savage built in 1830 as a chapel-of-ease to his church of ST LUKE in SYDNEY STREET. This was demolished in 1888 when it could no longer accommodate the increasing number of parishioners in the district. Unfortunately Sedding did not live to see his work completed. His assistant, Henry Wilson, who was appointed his successor, designed the grille behind the altar, at the east end of the north aisle, and the altar rails. The iron railings outside the church in SLOANE STREET are also by him. Many leading artists of the day contributed to the decoration of the interior. The use of several different Italian marbles shows the influence of Ruskin. The large east window is by Sir Edward Burne-Jones and was executed by William Morris.

Holy Trinity *Trinity Church Square, SE1*. Built in 1823–4 to the designs of F.O. Bedford. Although the altar is in its usual position at the east, the portico of six tall Corinthian columns is on the north, opposite a porch on the south.

𝕳𝖔𝖑𝖞 𝕿𝖗𝖎𝖓𝖎𝖙𝖞 𝖙𝖍𝖊 𝕷𝖊𝖘𝖘 *(Knightrider Street)*. So named to distinguish it from HOLY TRINITY PRIORY ALDGATE. It is first mentioned in 1258. John Rogers, the martyr, was rector here in 1532–4. It was rebuilt, largely at the expense of the MERCHANT TAYLORS' and VINTNERS' COMPANIES in 1607–8. After its destruction in the GREAT FIRE Hanseatic merchants from the STEELYARD bought the site for the GERMAN CHURCH and the parish was united with ST MICHAEL QUEENHITHE in 1670. St Michael's was demolished in 1875 and the parish was then united to ST JAMES GARLICKHYTHE. BEAVER HOUSE, GREAT TRINITY LANE now covers the site.

Home House *20 Portman Square, W1*. A superb Robert Adam house built in 1773–7 for Elizabeth, Countess of Home. The interior is one of the finest in London with delicate stucco decoration and inlaid paintings by Antonio Zucchi and Angelica Kauffmann. In 1932 Samuel Courtauld gave the remainder of the lease to the Home House Society for the COURTAULD INSTITUTE OF ART which had been founded the year before.

Homerton *E9*. Situated west of the River LEA between Lower CLAPTON and HACKNEY MARSHES. Known as Hunburh's farm or estate, it was part of the manor of Lordshold which passed in the 14th century from the suppressed KNIGHTS TEMPLAR to the Knights of St John of Jerusalem. The former had already established a mill by the LEA; the badge of the latter was the Lamb and Flag. The hamlet gradually developed, and in the 17th century Sir Thomas Sutton, Paymaster of the Northern Army and Victualler of the Navy, resided at St John's or Sutton House in the High Street. In the 18th century the area was poor and housed the Hackney Union Workhouse (1732) surrounded by fields, nurseries and market gardens. Watercress beds were fed by Hackney Brook. Stephen Ram erected his chapel in 1723 and, later, schools for both girls and boys. In 1823 Homerton College, for Protestant Dissenters, was opened. It moved to

Cambridge in 1843 as a result of the increasing industrialisation of the area. In 1847 Arthur Ashpital's St Barnabas was consecrated and in 1885 the separate parish of St Paul's, Lower Homerton, was formed. By the end of the century factories existed in areas of squalid poverty – Berger paints was already one of the oldest industries in HACKNEY parish – and the Workhouse Infirmary was expanding into the present public hospital. By the early years of the 20th century building development had made Homerton an extension of HACKNEY. In 1965 it became part of the London Borough of HACKNEY.

Honey Lane   *EC2*. Where beekeepers used to live. ALL HALLOWS HONEY LANE was burnt in the GREAT FIRE. On its site HONEY LANE MARKET was set up.

Honey Lane Market   *Cheapside, EC2*. A meat market established after the GREAT FIRE to replace the Cheapside street markets. At the time of Leybourn's survey of city markets it had 105 butchers' stalls though it was known to be the smallest market building in London. In 1691 the building was leased to French refugees for their religious services. In 1773 the market is mentioned as being famous for the quality of its provisions. It was rebuilt by George Dance the Younger in 1787–8. In 1835 the CITY OF LONDON SCHOOL was built upon the site, though provision dealers still lingered in the area till the end of the century.

Honor Oak   *SE23*. Situated to the south of PECKHAM, about 4½ miles distant from CHARING CROSS. For centuries an oak marked the boundary between CAMBERWELL and LEWISHAM. It was situated on One Tree Hill which rises to over 300 ft and stands at the northern end of a series of hills stretching from CROYDON within the ancient Great North Wood. It was reputedly the site of the victory of Suetonius Paulinus over Boudicca in AD 61. Within the manor of CAMBERWELL, it formed part of the estates or honour of the 12th-century Earls of Gloucester. Elizabeth I is said to have rested under the tree and Dick Turpin to have used the hill as a look-out. At the beginning of the 18th century it was, indeed, used by the Admiralty as a beacon hill during the Napoleonic wars and by the East India Company as a semaphore station. The surrounding area remained rural into the 19th century when houses such as that contained within the Sacred Heart Convent School in Honor Oak Rise appeared; in 1873 St Augustine's was built on the south slope of the hill. In the 1880s the oak was struck by lightning and another planted nearby. The hill was a place of public recreation and, when threatened with enclosure by a golf club in 1896, the Enclosure of Honor Oak Protest Committee was formed. This Committee eventually pursuaded the CAMBERWELL Borough Council to acquire the hill for use as an open space (1905). On 11 May 1899 the last perambulation of the parish boundary and psalm-singing at the oak took place. Since the 1950s landslips have occurred, damaging property and moving tons of earth towards Honor Oak Station.

Honourable   Artillery   Company   *Armoury House, City Road, EC1*. Claims to be the oldest military body in the United Kingdom. Founded to supply officers for the City's TRAINED BANDS, it was incorporated in 1537 when Henry VIII granted a charter to an existing body of citizen archers known as 'The Guild of St George'. Their new title in full was 'The Fraternity or Guild of Artillery of Longbows, Crossbows and Handguns'. The Guild became known as the 'Gentlemen of the Artillery Garden'. Until 1642 their training ground was in Artillery Lane, BISHOPSGATE, but since then their headquarters have been in CITY ROAD. Their main object was the defence of London, but its members also fought in foreign wars and served with the fleet against the Spanish Armada. Wren, Pepys, Milton and Cowper, as well as Cowper's John Gilpin, were members. In 1685 the prefix Honourable was first used, though this was not confirmed until the reign of Queen Victoria. On 18 June 1774 the first great cricket match in England (of which the full score exists) was played on the artillery ground between Kent and All England. James Love's 'Cricket, A Heroic Poem' describes the match. In the 1780 GORDON RIOTS the Company performed a peace-keeping role and was later presented with two three-pounder field guns. After the Napoleonic Wars, the company was the only volunteer reserve to survive and in 1860 was made part of the new Volunteer Force which later became the Territorial Army.

Apart from earlier confrontations in RIOTS, the HAC has participated with distinction in two World Wars, providing both combatant and officer-producing units. It has about 400 active and over 2,000 veteran members, the former being trained either in a special reconnaissance role or in gunnery. Both sections have ceremonial duties which include firing salutes and performing as guards of honour. In the LORD MAYOR'S SHOW they participate as pikemen or musketeers. The reigning monarch is normally the company's Captain General.

Honourable   Corps   of   Gentlemen-at-Arms   Founded by Henry VIII. On ceremonial occasions they wear scarlet coats, blue trousers and gilt metal helmets crowned by white swans' feathers. Including the Captain (who is Chief Whip in the House of Lords), the Lieutenant, the Standard Bearer, the Clerk of the Cheque and Adjutant and the Harbinger, there are 32 members. Among their duties is attendance upon the Queen at the STATE OPENING OF PARLIAMENT and at garden parties at BUCKINGHAM PALACE.

Hood Court   *EC4*. A small court leading to HANGING SWORD ALLEY. It was probably named after the poet, Thomas Hood, who was born in POULTRY in 1799.

Hook   *Surrey*. Once known as La Hoke, the name is derived from its shape – a long, thin strip of land – and indicates an 'ancient place'. It was a mere hamlet on the KINGSTON to Leatherhead road until the growth of SURBITON as a large residential area led to a similar growth to the south. It became a separate ecclesiastical parish in 1839, the first St Paul's Church being built at this time. This church was paid for from a legacy left by Mrs Savage, wife of a former vicar of Kingston.

Among the several large estates set back from the main road in the mid-19th century were the Rhodrons, Gosbury Hill and Haycroft. As the value of land for farming decreased and that for urban development increased, these were all, in turn, auctioned off around the turn of this century. The Local Government Act 1894 created urban districts, and Hook was merged with SURBITON as a result. The opening of the Kingston By-Pass in 1927 gave a great impetus to residential and commercial development.

The present St Paul's parish church was built to the designs of Carpenter and Ingelow in 1881–3, the nave and chancel being in one. The details are in the early Decorated style. The stained glass east window, designed by Seddon and executed by S. Belham and Co., is a memorial to the Hare family, the occupants of Gosbury Hill. The south window in the chancel was created by Kempe in 1900. The Victorian architect, John Pollard, designed the font whose cover, consisting of 70 pieces of carved wood, held together by two bolts, shows the Vine of Life leading towards the Crown of Eternity. In the churchyard is the grave of Harry Hawker, the Australian pioneer aviator, who was killed in an air crash in 1921, when flying a Nieuport-Goshawk in preparation for that year's Aerial Derby.

There are also the tombs of John Selfe, his wife and daughter. Selfe created Selfe Park, later Surbiton Park. On his tomb are inscribed the words 'The law of Thy mouth is dearer unto me than thousands of gold and silver'.

Hoop and Grapes *47 Aldgate High Street, EC3.* Claims to be the oldest licensed house in the CITY with foundations dating back to the 13th century. The present timbered and leaning building, with its wooden-framed bow windows, is supposed to date from the 16th century although Pevsner puts it as late 17th-century. There is a listening tube, connecting the bar and cellars, through which the landlord could eavesdrop. The cellars are supposed to contain a tunnel, now sealed off, leading to the TOWER OF LONDON.

Hoover Factory *Western Avenue, Perivale, Middlesex.* Built in 1932 and opened in 1933, it was designed by Wallis Gilbert and Partners, architects famous for their GREAT WEST ROAD factories. Serving as both factory and offices, the original buildings have been extended at the rear by functional blocks but without detracting from the main front elevation. The façade, with white pilasters framing long green-painted windows which give no indication of the first floor level, is flanked by two staircase towers. The white exterior is relieved by bands of dark blue and red faience. The interior was in the Art Deco style. The building was floodlit from the beginning.

Hope House *116 Piccadilly, at the east corner of Down Street.* Built in 1848–9 it housed the famous Hope collection of pictures. This is said to have been one of the first houses in the West End to be built in the French Renaissance style. In 1868 the house was sold to the Junior Athenaeum Club and it was eventually demolished in 1936.

Hope Theatre *Southwark.* After the GLOBE THEATRE was burned down in 1613, the Burbages' rival, Philip Henslowe, took advantage of their misfortune and with Jacob Meade converted a former bear and bull baiting arena into a play house. It was modelled on the SWAN THEATRE and had a movable stage so that bear and bull baiting could still be held. In 1614 Ben Jonson's play *Bartholomew Fair* was first performed here. After 1616 there is no record of plays

being staged and it probably reverted to a baiting arena. It was dismantled in 1656. Its approximate site is marked by the alley named BEAR GARDENS.

Hopton Street *SE1.* In this largely industrial and commercial street leading from BANKSIDE are the charming Hopton's Almshouses, erected in 1752, under the will of Charles Hopton, a fishmonger, and still used as homes for old people. No. 61 is a surviving small house of about 1700.

Horn Tavern *29 Knightrider Street, EC4.* Built in 1665 and mentioned by Dickens in *The Pickwick Papers* as the tavern to which Mr Pickwick sent for two bottles of good wine while he was in the FLEET PRISON.

Hornchurch *Essex.* Before records began, Hornchurch lay at the furthest edge of the ice-sheet which covered England in the great Ice Age. Later, the people of the Bronze Age left evidence of their presence in the neighbourhood and later still the Romans. In 1159 a sub-hospice or priory dedicated to St Nicholas and St Bernard arose on the small hill where St Andrew's church stands today. It was sponsored by Henry II in recognition of the assistance given to royal envoys, travelling through the Alps, by the mother priory of St Bernard in Savoy. It was run by a prior and twelve brothers from Savoy and owned land throughout the present HAVERING Borough. The name Hornchurch originated quite early and appears for instance in 1222 in its latin form – *Monasterium Cornutium* in the Close Rolls. Later in a 1311 deed it is given in English as Hornedecherche. The reason for the name is obscure, but the bull's head was an attractive symbol for official seals, particularly in a town which became so famous for its leather goods. In fact today's High Street was known in the 13th century as Pellestrate or Pelt Street. Even in the 19th century there were three tanyards in the village. In the 1930s and even to a lesser extent in the 1950s Hornchurch High Street and its continuation up Church Hill was lined by ancient, mainly half-timbered buildings, some hidden by later frontages. These have all been swept away, leaving the King's Head on the hill behind the White Hart and the three buildings above, as 17th-century survivors. The King's Head, though considerably altered, retains its charm. Further up the hill is the church of St Andrew, the only church in the country to have a bull's head and horns instead of a cross at the east end. Memorials include the fine 16th-century Ayloffe tomb and a monument by Flaxman to Richard Spencer, as well as the tomb of Thomas Witherings, Postmaster General to Charles I. Beside the church is the Dell, a hollow, once used for pastimes and fair days and the occasional prizefight, now housing an electricity station. Behind Billet Lane stands Langtons, partly 18th-century. It is now a register office, having been presented to the council with its attractive gardens in 1929. The adjacent Fairkytes, fronting Billet Lane, opposite the modern Queen's Theatre, has become an Arts Centre. Fairkytes was originally built in the late 17th century but the façade is Victorian. It was once occupied by Joseph Fry, son of Elizabeth Fry. Drury Falls, at the junction of Upminster Road and Wingletye Lane dates principally from the 16th century, with later additions.

Horners' Company *see* CITY LIVERY COMPANIES.

Horniman Museum *London Road, Forest Hill, SE23.* Founded by Frederick J. Horniman, head of the well-known tea firm, who assembled a large general collection on his travels abroad. In 1890 this collection was opened to the public three times a week at his home, Surrey House, in FOREST HILL. In 1898 the house was demolished and replaced by a new museum, designed in the Art Nouveau style by C. Harrison Townsend. Constructed of stone and red brick, the building consisted of North and South Halls and a clock tower. A decorative mosaic panel stretching the length of the main façade depicts an allegory on the course of human life. When complete in 1901 the museum was presented with its 21 acres of park and gardens to the LONDON COUNTY COUNCIL, as a gift to the people of London.

Hornsey *N8.* Now part of the London Borough of HARINGEY, the former Borough of Hornsey (created in 1903), lies three to six miles north-west of London at the eastern end of the Northern Heights. Much of it is a hilly area with land rising in the west to above 300 ft in MUSWELL HILL, and above 400 ft in HIGHGATE, with two spurs stretching eastwards to the flatter terrain of the LEA Valley. Following the spread of Victorian building the whole area is now a suburb of London, but still retains many open spaces. Hornsey as a name, like HARINGEY and HARRINGAY and other variants, is thought to derive from an Old English word meaning 'the enclosure of Hering or Haer's people' and probably originated as a Saxon settlement in the forest of MIDDLESEX, west of the River LEA. It was to become the parish and manor of Hornsey, nearly 3,000 acres in extent, on ecclesiastical land largely owned by the BISHOPS OF LONDON and used by them for hunting. Settlements were to develop, as well as at Hornsey village, at HIGHGATE, CROUCH END, MUSWELL HILL and later at STROUD GREEN.

Hornsey High Street, site of the parish church and original village, was described in the 19th century as 'long, irregular and scattered'. It once had a pleasant, rural aspect with the NEW RIVER crossing the broad, tree-lined High Street in three places until in 1860 its course was straightened. In 1850 Hornsey railway station was opened at the east end of the village, the first station out of London on the newly-built Great Northern Railway, thus making it possible to work in the city and live in this country area. The large estates were gradually replaced by residential streets and Canon Richard Harvey, appointed rector in 1829 to a village church, retired in 1881 from a town parish.

Hornsey High Street today tends to be infiltrated by small manufacturing works and is visually neglected although its greens remain. Areas north and south have been redeveloped with municipal housing and new schools built. Two 18th-century houses survive, much altered, at No. 69 (Eagle House) and No. 71 (The Manor) adjacent to the fine, flamboyant, Great Northern Railway Tavern of 1897, designed by Henry Rising. Opposite them the tower, built in about 1500, of the former St Mary's parish church still stands but the last of several churches on the site which was built to the designs of James Brooks in 1888, was demolished in 1969. In the churchyard (the burial place of Betsey Trotwood's husband in *David Copperfield*) is the family grave of Samuel Rogers, the banker and poet who declined the poet-laureateship after Wordsworth's death in 1850. At No. 32 High Street, David Greig opened a shop in 1876 which his son was to develop into the well-known chain of provision stores. Priory Park, terminating the High Street, contains a large fountain from ST PAUL'S CHURCHYARD. South of the church in Tottenham Lane, is the tall, brick-built, Holy Innocents church, built in 1877 to the designs of Arthur Blomfield. Next to it is the restored remnant of an early, village school house of 1848. No. 46 Alexandra Road, Hornsey, north-east of the High Street, was the first London address of Arnold Bennett, the novelist, when working as a junior clerk in LINCOLN'S INN in 1890.

Hornton Street *W8.* Built in about 1790, possibly by a Mr Hornton. A Baptist Chapel stood on the east side of the street at the southern end during 1793–1828. In 1960 Kensington Public Library, designed by E. Vincent Harris, was built on the site of The Abbey, a Gothic house which had been constructed in 1880 for a Mr Abbot and bombed in 1944. Herbert Hoover, later President of the USA, lived at the Red House in 1908–18. No. 56 was occupied by Sir Charles Stanford, chairman of the ROYAL COLLEGE OF MUSIC in 1894–1916. The CHELSEA AND KENSINGTON TOWN HALL is on the east side.

Horse Guards *Whitehall, SW1.* In 1649 a small guardhouse was built here in the tilt-yard of

George II, on his way to the House of Lords, passes William Kent's recently completed Horse Guards in 1753.

WHITEHALL PALACE. This was replaced in 1663–5 by a larger building for the horse guards and some of the foot guards. In 1750–8 the present building was constructed to a picturesque Palladian design by William Kent which was executed after his death by John Vardy. Only members of the Royal Family are allowed to drive through the central arch. Hogarth in plate 2 of *The Election* depicted the royal coach emerging with a headless driver as it is impractically low. Until 1872 the building was also the headquarters of the general staff. Subsequently it became the headquarters of LONDON DISTRICT and the HOUSEHOLD DIVISION. Two mounted troopers of the Household Cavalry are posted outside daily from ten o'clock to four and are relieved every hour.

Horse Guards Parade *SW1*. On the site of the tilt-yard of WHITEHALL PALACE. A great tournament was held here in 1540 by Henry VIII and attended by knights from all over Europe. For many years exercises were held here on Elizabeth I's birthday; and from the 17th century reviews, parades and medal presentation ceremonies. The funeral procession of the Duke of Wellington formed up here in 1852. The TROOPING THE COLOUR takes place here. On the parade ground there are bronze statues of the Field Marshals Kitchener, Wolseley and Roberts (*see* STATUES); a Turkish gun 'made by Murad son of Abdullah, chief gunner in 1524, taken in Egypt by the British Army, 1801'; and the Cadiz Memorial (*see* MEMORIALS).

Horseferry Road *SW1*. Extends from Stratton Ground street market on the south side of VICTORIA STREET opposite BROADWAY to LAMBETH BRIDGE. The horse ferry at LAMBETH is believed to be even older than LONDON BRIDGE. It was the only horse ferry allowed on the THAMES near London. The right to collect tolls belonged to the Archbishops of Canterbury who were paid £3,000 in compensation when WESTMINSTER BRIDGE was built. It was still in use in the 19th century. WESTMINSTER HOSPITAL is on the south side; and Westminster Mortuary and Coroner's Court at No. 65.

Horsemonger Lane Gaol *Southwark*. Built as a model prison by George Gwilt in 1791–9. Public executions used to take place outside. It was here in November 1849 that Dickens attended the hangings of Mr and Mrs Manning who killed a friend for his money and buried him under the kitchen floor. He wrote to *The Times*, 'I do not believe that any community can prosper where such a scene of horror as was enacted this morning outside Horsemonger Lane Gaol is permitted. The horrors of the gibbet and of the crime which brought the wretched murderers to it faded in my mind before the atrocious bearing, looks and language of the assembled spectators.' In 1813–15 Leigh Hunt was imprisoned here for a libel on the Prince Regent whom he called 'a fat Adonis of forty'. Byron met Hunt here for the first time. The gaol was closed in 1878 and demolished in 1880. Newington Recreation Ground marks the site.

Hosier Lane *EC1*. Named after the hosiers who lived here in the 14th century. In 1720 Strype wrote that the lane was 'of great resort during the time of ST BARTHOLOMEW'S FAIR all the houses generally being made publick for tippling and lewd sort of people.'

Hospital for Sick Children *Great Ormond Street, WC1*. Founded on the inspiration of Dr Charles West in 1851. Up to that time there was no children's hospital in England, although as early as 1676 L'Hôpital des Enfants Malades had been founded in Paris. In London out of 50,000 persons who died annually, 21,000 were children under ten. An enquiry carried out in 1843 showed that of 2,363 patients in all the hospitals of London, there were only 26 under the age of ten. Children were to all intents and purposes excluded. For example, the LONDON HOSPITAL refused 'all children under seven except such as required amputation or cutting of the stone'. West and his colleagues managed to rent No. 49 GREAT ORMOND STREET on the corner of Powis Place. It had been the home of Dr Richard Mead, a royal physician at the turn of the 17th and 18th centuries. It was originally called the London Hospital for Sick Children but a few months later that name was changed to its present one. No. 48 GREAT ORMOND STREET was incorporated in 1858. Both houses had extensive gardens. Ten beds were originally available and children of both sexes between the ages of two and 12 years suffering from acute or chronic, external or internal, general or local illness were admitted. Smallpox cases were, however, excluded. Children and infants under two years of age were not generally eligible for admission as in-patients, it being 'undesirable on account of their tender age to separate them from their mothers', though they were admitted as out-patients. But infants under two were allowed admission to the new hospital which was designed by E.M. Barry. The foundation stone of this hospital was laid in 1872 in the gardens of the two houses by the Princess of Wales. It was completed in 1877 and had 120 beds. Five years later the two original houses were demolished. In 1893 a new block was opened, bringing the bed numbers up to 240. In 1929 Sir James Barrie made a gift of the copyright of *Peter Pan* covering the stage and film productions of the play, and television and book rights. In 1933 rebuilding began and the foundation stone was laid by the Princess Royal who had been a nurse here. The architect, Stanley Hall, also designed the new Nurses' Home in 1937. The main hospital block was completed in 1938. After the War the Institute of Child Health was evolved here in collaboration with the UNIVERSITY OF LONDON and the Department of Health. Since then there have been considerable extensions. The bronze, *St Christopher with the Infant Christ*, by the door of the Outpatients' Wing, is by Gilbert Ledward (1952). The bronze of *St Nicholas with Three Children* is also by Ledward.

Hospital for Tropical Diseases *4 St Pancras Way, NW1*. Founded in 1899, at the instigation of the distinguished parasitologist, Sir Patrick Manson, and first housed in Albert Dock Hospital (which no longer exists). Manson's School of Tropical Medicine which became known internationally was established here. In 1920 the hospital moved to Endsleigh Gardens where it remained until 1939 when it was closed. After the advent of the National Health Service it was revived as part of UNIVERSITY COLLEGE HOSPITAL in 1951 when it moved to its present site. In 1982 there were 68 beds.

Hospital for Women *29 and 30 Soho Square, W1*. Founded in RED LION SQUARE in 1843 as the Hospital for Diseases of Women, mainly through the efforts of

Dr Protheroe Smith. It was the first hospital in the world to deal exclusively with 'those maladies which neither rank, wealth nor character can avert from the female sex'. There were 11 beds in two wards. In 1845 it was renamed the Hospital for Women, as the earlier title had discouraged many subscribers who thought it only treated venereal diseases. In 1852 it moved to No. 30 SOHO SQUARE where 20 beds could be fitted in. The adjoining house acquired in 1865, was rebuilt by E.L. Bracebridge in 1867–9. In 1882 No. 2 FRITH STREET was acquired and rebuilt 12 years later as an out-patients' department and nurses' home. It was remodelled by H. Percy Adams in 1908. Since the introduction of the National Health Service the hospital has been amalgamated with the MIDDLESEX HOSPITAL. In 1982 there were 78 beds.

Hospital of St Thomas of Acon Cheapside.

In about 1190 a small brotherhood of crusading knights was founded by Thomas Fitz Theobald de Helles and his wife, Agnes, sister of St Thomas Becket. (Acon or Acre in Syria was believed to have been captured through St Thomas's miraculous intervention.) The hospital area which had a frontage of 190 ft to CHEAPSIDE included the site of the house where Becket was born in 1118. His father, Gilbert, was a prominent mercer and, from the beginning, the MERCERS' COMPANY were patrons of the hospital. They held meetings here and prayed in the hospital church which was built in 1248. Sometimes all the CITY LIVERY COMPANIES assembled and on important feast days the LORD MAYOR attended services. The bell for prime signalled the opening of the CITY wicket gates and the bell for vespers the end of trading in CORNHILL and CHEAPSIDE. The hospital was a popular charity and received many bequests. Several early mayors chose to be buried here. In 1296 Edward I granted a charter to the Guild of St Thomas Becket for trading overseas. It developed into the Merchant Adventurers incorporated by Henry VII in 1497. In 1407 the MERCERS bought a chapel within the hospital church and a room for their exclusive use. In 1447 John Neell, Master of the Hospital, and four other London parsons successfully petitioned Henry VI to found five new grammar schools. The school of St Thomas Acons flourished. But in 1510 Richard Adams, the Master, was removed for mismanagement. In 1517–22 the MERCERS' COMPANY built a new hall and a chapel on adjoining land bought from the hospital. In 1518 a visitation by Cardinal Wolsey revealed the hospital had an income of £316 17s 2d. In 1534 the master and six brothers acknowledged the King's supremacy. In September 1538 Cromwell ordered the statue of Becket over the high altar to be taken down and windows bearing his image to be destroyed. The next month the hospital was dissolved, despite Sir Richard Gresham's request that it should continue. The Master was given an annual pension of £66 13s 4d and the brothers a sum of between £5 and £8. The buildings were let. In 1541 the MERCERS' COMPANY bought them for £969 17s 6d and undertook to keep a school for 25 children in the City in perpetuity. This was the origin of the MERCERS' SCHOOL. All the buildings were destroyed in the GREAT FIRE. On 5 September 1666 Pepys 'walking homeward took up a piece of glass of the Mercers' Chapel where much more was so melted and buckled with the heat to be like parchment.' MERCERS' HALL was rebuilt on the same site. Its chapel,

the only one in a City Livery hall, commemorates the occupation of the site by this monastic house. A 16th-century figure of Christ and the 1625 effigy of Richard Fishborne remain.

Hotel Great Central 222 Marylebone Road. Built

across the road from MARYLEBONE STATION, the terracotta seven-storey 700-bedroom hotel with high gable roof and central tower, was designed by Colonel Robert William Edis. Financed and furnished by Sir Blundell Maple (see MAPLE'S), it opened on 1 July 1899, and dwarfed the station. In 1916 the hotel was requisitioned by the government for wounded soldiers. It was again requisitioned in the 2nd World War. In 1982 it was the headquarters of the British Railways Board.

Hôtel Métropole Northumberland Avenue. Built

in the mid-1880s to the designs of F. and H. Francis and J.E. Saunders. The spandrels over the main entrance were carved by H.H. Armsted. It had 550 bedrooms. It is now part of Metropole Buildings.

Houndsditch EC3. Runs along the site of the moat

that bounded the City wall, it is so called, according to Stow, 'from that in old time, when the same lay open, much filth (conveyed forth of the City) especially dead dogges were there laid or cast.' Or its name may be derived from the City Kennels which were in the moat and in which were kept the hounds for the City hunts. Richard of Cirencester said that Edric, believed to be the murderer of Edmund Ironside, was thrown into the ditch on the orders of King Canute, having first been drawn by the heels from CASTLE BAYNARD and then tormented to death by being roasted in the flames of torches. In 1511–71 there was a gun factory here run by three brothers named Owens. Stow said that in his youth there was a field next to Houndsditch owned by HOLY TRINITY PRIORY, ALDGATE where sick people had cottages and that every Friday people came to leave alms for them. However by the time he wrote the Survey in the 1590s Houndsditch had been built up, the ditch had been levelled and carpenters' yards and large houses built on it. Many of the houses were occupied by old clothes sellers, and from these rogues, John Taylor, the Water Poet, considered the street got its name. Its inhabitants suffered severely in the GREAT PLAGUE; and in a large ditch nearby 1,100 bodies were

The synagogue in Duke's Place, Houndsditch, in 1809; it was built to serve a rapidly growing Jewish population.

thrown. Gunfounders cast bronze here in the reign of Henry VIII. It remained an old clothes market throughout the 19th century, and visitors to it were advised 'to leave their watches and valuables at home, and not to take offence at a little "Bishopsgate banter"'. For a 1d fee prospective customers could gain access to a large room with no stalls but large sacks of old clothes placed on the ground. In 1861 Henry Mayhew said it was also 'inhabited by Jewish shopkeepers, warehousemen, manufacturers and inferior jewellers'. In 1927 a group of local businessmen unsuccessfully petitioned the CITY CORPORATION to change the name of the street because its character had so changed.

Hounslow

Middlesex. A corruption of the word Honeslaw or Hundeslawe, the *lawe* meaning rising ground, and *hundes* possibly meaning hounds. The town is divided by the High Street, now the A30 but originally the Roman road from London to Silchester. No archaeological evidence has so far revealed a Roman settlement here. The land between Hounslow and Staines was the Forest of Staines. The first mention of the town of Hounslow appears in 1215 when, after the signing of *Magna Carta*, the Barons organised a tournament in Staines Wood and at the town of Hounslow. In 1214 the Friars of Holy Trinity established a priory on the site of HOLY TRINITY CHURCH providing a hospital for the sick and accommodation for travellers. After the DISSOLUTION OF THE MONASTERIES, only the chapel remained. Hounslow Manor House was built on the site, and demolished in about 1820. Hounslow depended upon travellers for trade and employment. Stage-coaches passed through the town from the 17th century, taking four days to travel from London to Exeter. From 1784 there were regular mail coach services through Hounslow to the West Country. Hounslow Heath stretched for 4,000 acres westwards to Staines, providing cover for the many highwaymen. Gibbets lined the heath between the Staines and Bath Roads reminding highwaymen of their fate, if caught. The heath was also used by the army as a Review Ground from 1686, when James II's standing army was encamped here. In 1793 Hounslow Cavalry Barracks was built, and an infantry barracks added in 1875. The stage-coaches caused Hounslow to prosper, as inns, stables, and blacksmiths' forges were built to cope with the demand. This ceased in about 1840 with the opening of the Great Western Railway. In 1829 Holy Trinity Church was built on the site of the priory, becoming the Parish of Holy Trinity in 1856. (This church was burned down in 1943 and replaced with another in 1963 designed by W.E. Cross.) A school opened in 1831 and a town hall in 1858. The London and South Western Railway station opened in 1850, causing a building development of villas in South Hounslow, and an improvement to the prosperity of the town. The District Railway came in 1883, the station being on the site of the present bus garage. This resulted in building developments in central and north Hounslow. 1919 saw the first civil airport in the country opened on Hounslow Heath, with a daily service between London and Paris. The first flight between England and Australia took off from here in November 1919. Further developments took place in the 1920s and 1930s, particularly after the PICCADILLY LINE reached Hounslow in 1932. Today some of the villas have been replaced by blocks of flats and smaller houses. 1875 saw Hounslow, HESTON and ISLEWORTH

united to form the Urban Sanitary District of HESTON and ISLEWORTH, with Hounslow as the geographical and administrative centre. An Urban District Council was formed in 1894 and borough status was achieved in 1932. In 1965 the London Borough of Hounslow was created, with Hounslow as the official name for the first time.

House of Commons *see* PALACE OF WESTMINSTER.

House of Lords *see* PALACE OF WESTMINSTER.

House of St Barnabas

1 Greek Street, W1. Today provides temporary accommodation for homeless women in an outwardly plain Georgian mansion built in the 1740s. After standing empty for some time it was bought in 1754 for £2,500 by Alderman Richard Beckford, brother of William Beckford, the Lord Mayor, who lived nearby in SOHO SQUARE. The rich plastering and carving of the interior were probably created for Richard Beckford whose executors sold the house with its furnishings nine months later for £6,300. It is one of the finest examples of the English rococo style of the 1750s now surviving in London, though the designer is unknown. There is an impressive cantilevered stone staircase with wrought iron balusters, a later 'crinoline' staircase at the rear and a florid ceiling in the panelled room that is now the Council Chamber. From 1811 the house was used as the administrative offices of the Westminster Commissioners of Sewers and later by the METROPOLITAN BOARD OF WORKS which sold the building to the House of Charity in 1861. The House of Charity had been founded 15 years earlier with the declared intention of affording 'temporary relief to as many destitute cases as possible, and [of having] a Christian effect on the poor population.'

Household Division

Of the seven regiments of Guards, two are Household Cavalry and five are Foot. The reigning sovereign is their Colonel-in-Chief. The regiments concerned are the Life Guards, the Blues and Royals (the latter have been amalgamated since 1969), the Grenadier, Coldstream, Scots, Irish and Welsh Guards. All the regiments, except the Irish and Welsh Guards, which were formed respectively in the reign of Queen Victoria and during the 1st World War, date back to the 17th century. The Major General Commanding LONDON DISTRICT also commands the Division. While the full dress uniforms of the two mounted regiments are quite distinctive, those of the foot guards can only be recognised by the colour or presence of plumes in the bearskins and the arrangement of jacket buttons. The Household Cavalry, with a strength of about 1,600, includes a mounted regiment of some 300 representing both the Life Guards and the Blues and Royals and two armoured regiments, the roles of which are in accordance with other mechanised cavalry units. While the mounted regiment is quartered in KNIGHTSBRIDGE BARRACKS, the other two normally alternate between Windsor and the British Army of the Rhine in Germany. Five of the eight battalions of Foot Guards are likely to be stationed in the London–Windsor area at any one time.

Ceremonial occasions for the Division include TROOPING THE COLOUR on the sovereign's official birthday, CHANGING OF THE GUARD at BUCKINGHAM

PALACE and various guard and escort duties relevant to the mounted or dismounted troops at the HORSE GUARDS, ST JAMES'S PALACE, the TOWER OF LONDON and elsewhere as the occasion demands (*see also* REGIMENTS).

Houses of Parliament *see* PALACE OF WESTMINSTER.

Howard de Walden Estate *see* PORTLAND ESTATE.

Howard Street *WC2*. Named after the Howard family upon part of the site of whose mansion, ARUNDEL HOUSE, the street was built. William Mountfort, the actor, was murdered here in front of his house in 1692 by Lord Mohun and Captain Richard Hill who had both conceived a passion for Mrs Bracegirdle, the actress, and who believed Mountfort responsible for her refusal of their advances. Hill escaped and Mohun, acquitted by his peers, was later killed in a duel by the 4th Duke of Hamilton. William Congreve lived in the house next door to Mrs Bracegirdle's.

Howbury Moated Grange *Slade Green, Erith, Kent*. Lies on the edge of the marshes about a mile north of CRAYFORD. Though now a lonely ruin, it was once the home of an official of the courts of Henry V and Henry VI. It still has a moat around it, dating back to Norman times, when the Manor of Howbury was listed in *Domesday Book*. Several houses occupied the site successively, the last of which, a 17th-century building, suffered damage in the 2nd World War and is now beyond repair. Only the wall of the moat survives as evidence of the turbulent times of its origin. It is of narrow jointed ashlar, probably built in the 12th century. A drawbridge on the west side was removed in 1780 and replaced by a brick one which has now collapsed. Near to the moated grange is Howbury Barn, an excellent example of Jacobean craftsmanship, with a fine timbered queen post roof and English bond brickwork. Its doorposts carry the remains of a mechanism by which shutters could be adjusted during winnowing.

Howland Great Dock A large wet dock built on the banks of the THAMES. In 1695 John Howland, a wealthy landowner of STREATHAM, settled his property at ROTHERHITHE on Wriothesley Russell, Marquess of Tavistock (later the 2nd Duke of Bedford) at his marriage to his daughter and heiress, Elizabeth. The Marquess was only 15 years old at the time, so this seems to have been a marriage of convenience. The Russell family then at once obtained parliamentary permission to build the dock. A contemporary engraving shows a bird's-eye view of the dock with the family mansion on the axis at the far end. The rectangular dock covered 10 acres. It remained London's largest dock for a century and retained its original form until the late 19th century. It could accommodate 120 large merchant ships against the quays, unaffected by the tides from which it was protected by a lock. Rows of trees were planted around it to protect the ships against high winds. The dock was sold in 1763, and then used by whaling ships under the name Greenland Dock. It was eventually absorbed into the complex of the SURREY COMMERCIAL DOCKS. Its engineers seem to have been George Sorocold, who

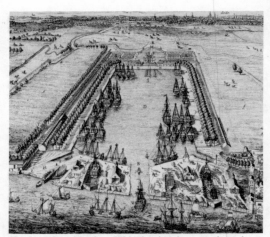

Howland Great Dock c. 1720, showing the trees planted as wind-breaks and the mansion of the Russell family who built the dock.

later improved the waterworks at LONDON BRIDGE, and Thomas Steers who designed the first dock at Liverpool. Their assistant was John Wells, a local shipwright.

Hoxton *N1*. That part of the former Metropolitan Borough of SHOREDITCH which lies to the north of Old Street and the west of Kingsland Road. It is now within the London Borough of HACKNEY. Hoxton is first referred to in *Domesday Book* as a manor of 'three hides' held by the Canons of ST PAUL'S and worth 45s. It was still held by the BISHOP OF LONDON at least until the 14th century. William Fitzstephen's description of the area in the 12th century comments on 'the fields for pasture, and open meadows, very pleasant, into which the river waters do flow, and mills are turned about with a delightful noise. Next lieth a great forest, in which are woody places and for game . . .'

By the 16th century there was a spilling of London's population into this countryside. The wealthy and the fashionable moved into the villages surrounding the city and Hoxton was one of the villages which was developed at this time. Here the rich built homes in pleasant surroundings not too far removed from the court or places of business. Hoxton also became a place of entertainment and recreation. It was in SHOREDITCH that the first theatre was built in London. A poem written at the beginning of the 17th century called 'Tis a mad world at Hogsdon' describes a notorious ale-house in Hoxton Street called the Pimlico. This was later to be the site of the BRITANNIA THEATRE. The 17th and 18th centuries saw the steady growth of the area but it still retained its rural appearance. During the 17th century Hoxton had a reputation for its market and nursery gardens. Later in that century and into the 18th many CITY LIVERY COMPANIES acquired land here for their almshouses. In 1689 Robert Aske left £20,000 to the Haberdashers' Company for the erection of an almshouse for 20 poor single freemen of the Company and schooling for 20 sons of poor freeman. Aske's Hospital in Pitfield Street was therefore erected in 1692 for both these purposes. Rebuilt in 1825 and altered in 1873 it was finally purchased by the LONDON COUNTY COUNCIL for a technical school. It is now the City and East London College, which was formed in 1974 on the amalgamation of the City College for Further Education, Tower Hamlets College for Further Education and the three departments of Walbrook College based north of the Thames. The WEAVERS' COMPANY almshouses erected in 1670 were on the site of the present court and opposite stood the FULLERS' almshouses.

Hoxton Square was laid out towards the end of the 17th century. It was here that one of the first dissenting academies was opened. Here, barred from the universities, Presbyterian and Independent ministers received their theological training, and a liberal education was provided for Dissenters' sons.

By 1801, the population of the whole of SHOREDITCH (of which Hoxton was a part) had grown to 34,766, doubled to 68,564 by 1831 and in 1861 was 129,364. SHOREDITCH rapidly lost its rural aspect. As the population grew the parish of SHOREDITCH was divided and the present parish church of Hoxton, dedicated to St John the Baptist, was erected in 1825–6. In a survey of London life and labour towards the end of the century Hoxton is described as 'one of the worst parts of London, where poverty and overcrowding are characteristic of practically the whole district. Largely owing to conditions in Hoxton, Shoreditch ranks second among eastern area boroughs in the percentage of persons living in poverty.'

Hoxton was renowned at this time for its music halls. In Hoxton Street stood, until 1940, the BRITANNIA Theatre, once noted for its blood-curdling melodrama. Rebuilt in 1858, it became one of the most famous music-halls. MACDONALD'S, also in Hoxton Street, opened in 1864 and the Varieties (in Pitfield Street) in 1870. Near the Britannia stood the Pollock's Toy Theatre shop, immortalised by Robert Louis Stevenson in one of his essays, *Penny Plain and Twopence Coloured* (*see* POLLOCK'S TOY MUSEUM). Overcrowding continued in this part of London right down to the 2nd World War. The area suffered a great deal in the bombing and the former borough of SHOREDITCH energetically reconstructed it. Today there is a considerable amount of new municipal housing and very little can be seen to remind the visitor of Hoxton's past. Famous residents have included Kate Greenaway, the artist, who was born in Cavendish Square in 1896, and James Parkinson, the physician, geologist – and author of *An Essay on the Shaking Palsy* (1817) in which *Paralysis agitans*, known as Parkinson's disease, is described – who lived and practised at No. 1 HOXTON SQUARE.

Hoxton Square *N1*. Built in the 1680s on ground where Ben Jonson fought a duel with an actor named Gabriel Spencer, whom he killed. For punishment he had his left thumb branded, escaping the gallows by benefit of clergy.

Huggin Hill *EC4*. Derived from an Old English word *hoggene* meaning where hogs were kept. In 1964 a Roman bath was discovered here.

Huguenot Burial Ground *see* BURIAL GROUNDS.

Hungerford Market *Charing Cross*. Built in 1682 for Sir Edward Hungerford on the gardens of his

family house which had burnt down in 1669. The market began as a rival to COVENT GARDEN, selling fruit and vegetables, but was soon outclassed. It was rebuilt by Charles Fowler in 1833 with two storeys for selling meat, fish, fruit and vegetables. A bazaar and art gallery were added in 1851. These were burned down in 1854. In 1860 the market was demolished to make way for CHARING CROSS RAILWAY STATION.

Celebrations at the July 1833 opening of the Hungerford Market. Rebuilt by Charles Fowler, it stood until 1860.

Hungerford Railway Bridge *see* CHARING CROSS OR HUNGERFORD RAILWAY BRIDGE.

Hunterian Museum *Royal College of Surgeons of England, 35–43 Lincoln's Inn Fields, WC2.* Based upon the collections of the great 18th-century Scottish surgeon, John Hunter (*see* LEICESTER SQUARE). In his will, Hunter requested that his more than 13,000 specimens, which he had collected over a period of 40 years, should be offered for sale to the British Government. In 1799 £15,000 was granted for their purchase and they were then made over to the Company of Surgeons, soon to become the ROYAL COLLEGE OF SURGEONS. A specially built museum was opened in 1811. This was demolished and rebuilt twice as large in 1837 to accommodate the much expanded collection. Further rooms were added in 1855 and 1891. By the outbreak of war in 1939 the number of specimens had increased to 63,000. In 1941 the College and Museum were badly damaged in an air raid and many of the specimens were destroyed. Most of the anthropological material survived and was transferred to the NATURAL HISTORY MUSEUM. The present museum, containing about 3,500 surviving Hunterian specimens and some 2,500 additional physiological specimens, was opened in 1963.

In Hunter's day most anatomy schools had collections of preserved human specimens for use during demonstrations and lectures, but Hunter himself considered it important that students should study comparative anatomy, so his collections were much more than an assembly of anatomical teaching specimens. The Museum is, therefore, unique and is often referred to as Hunter's 'unwritten book', since it contains evidence of many unpublished investigations. The major sections demonstrate normal structures and the body's ability to adapt, morbid anatomy and reproduction. Among the exhibits are the double-headed skull of a Bengali child, the biceps of a Negro, a vulture's head and the skeleton of an 8 ft tall

A special room was opened in 1811 at the Royal College of Surgeons to house the Scottish surgeon John Hunter's huge collection.

Irishman. Visitors require some knowledge of biology to appreciate the exhibits. Children under 16 are not normally admitted.

H. Huntsman and Sons Ltd *11 Savile Row, W1.* A 'gaiter and breeches maker' had been trading since about 1814 at 125 NEW BOND STREET, when Henry Huntsman joined him in 1849. Huntsman and his two sons were at 41 ALBEMARLE STREET from 1898 and moved in 1919 to 11 SAVILE ROW.

Hurlingham Club *Ranelagh Gardens, SW6.* Hurlingham House was built in 1760 for Dr William Cadogan, an expert on gout. Enlarged by a later owner, it was subsequently acquired by the 3rd Lord Egremont and, in 1867, leased by Frank Heathcote who established a pigeon-shooting club here. This cruel sport was abandoned in 1905. By then polo had become the principal sporting activity of the club. The first polo match was played here in 1874; and in 1875 the rules of the game were formalised by the Hurlingham Club Committee, the forerunner of the Hurlingham Polo Association which still retains the name although the polo grounds were compulsorily purchased for housing by the LONDON COUNTY COUNCIL in 1946. By then other games had been introduced at the club. A skittle alley had been built in 1869. This had been followed by croquet lawns, tennis courts, squash courts, a cricket pitch, a bowling green, a swimming pool and a golf course. All manner of other sporting events are held here, including archery competitions and fencing matches. A reception is traditionally given here by the International Lawn Tennis Club of Great Britain before the

tennis championships at WIMBLEDON. In 1982 the club had about 3,000 members.

Hurlingham Road *Fulham, SW6.* Lies south of the NEW KING'S ROAD. No. 76, The Vineyard, is an early 17th-century house with 18th-century alterations, the home for ten years in the 1920s and early 1930s of Lord Beaverbrook. Hurlingham Park, on the south side, together with a housing estate, occupy the old polo grounds of the HURLINGHAM CLUB.

The Hyde *NW9.* Situated north of the six-mile stone on the EDGWARE ROAD. The Hyde is part of both KINGSBURY and West HENDON. In the 13th century there may have been a group of dwellings at the junction of the Edgware and Kingsbury Roads in what was then a hamlet of HENDON. Its name – meaning the area of 100 Saxon acres (about 120 acres) – occurs by this time. By the end of the 16th century there were about 12 farmhouses and cottages, one of which was known as Hide House. Later, the Bell of Hyde House was a cage for vagabonds opposite the Kingsbury Road. Until the 18th century the area remained grassland, mainly for sheep-farming, endangered by highwaymen on the ancient WATLING STREET. During the 18th century the Duke of Chandos acquired land between his London residence and CANONS PARK which included an area of The Hyde, and new houses and cottages, such as Shell Cottage of 1752, began to appear. Oliver Goldsmith stayed in Hyde Lane in 1771–4. In the 19th century housing became dense and shops were built along the EDGWARE ROAD. The Hyde Brewery was built (1862, demolished in the 1950s). The area became famous for the Kingsbury Reservoir whose northern arm, the WELSH HARP, joined the Silk Stream at the EDGWARE ROAD. Also known as the Brent Reservoir, it was completed in 1835. Although the arrival of the Midland Railway a few years later frightened away much bird-life, it is still designated a 'site of special scientific interest'. By the early 20th century cows were still kept at The Hyde to provide milk for the increasing population of London and its suburbs, but both sides of the EDGWARE ROAD had by then been developed and industry replaced many of the Victorian shops.

Hyde Park *W1, W2, SW7.* The largest of the London parks, extending over 340 acres from BAYSWATER ROAD in the north to KNIGHTSBRIDGE in the south. PARK LANE marks the eastern boundary and in the west, it merges with KENSINGTON GARDENS, this western boundary being a line running from ALEXANDRA GATE across the Serpentine bridge and along Buck Hill Walk to VICTORIA GATE. The park was once one of those properties, Ebury, Neate and Hyde, which comprised the manor of Eia and which were bequeathed to the monks of WESTMINSTER soon after the Conquest by Geoffrey de Mandeville. It was then a haunt of deer, boar and wild bulls. In 1536, at the DISSOLUTION OF THE MONASTERIES, the manor was appropriated by Henry VIII who sold Ebury and Neate and retained Hyde as a hunting ground. Deer were hunted in the park until 1768. Elizabeth also hunted here and inaugurated military reviews which were to be held here for centuries.

The park was opened to the public at the beginning of the 17th century and it soon became fashionable, particularly on May Day, the great day for visiting it.

In about 1642 fortifications were built along the east side to defend the city against Royalist attacks. A large fort stood opposite MOUNT STREET but it was never used. Another fort was built near the present HYDE PARK CORNER and near where MARBLE ARCH now stands there was a strong-point where travellers' credentials were examined. In 1649 Lord Essex's troops camped in the park. Other military camps appeared here in 1665 during the GREAT PLAGUE in 1715, during the Jacobite Rebellion and in 1780 at the time of the GORDON RIOTS.

In 1652 the park was sold by order of Parliament. It was divided into three lots and fetched £17,000. Evelyn indignantly reported the next year that 'the sordid fellow' who had purchased part of it was charging 1s for every coach to enter and 6d for each horse. In 1654 May Day 'was more observed by people going a-maying than for divers years past. Great resort came to Hyde Park, many hundreds of rich coaches and gallants in attire but most shameful powdered hair, men painted and spotted women. But his Highness the Lord Protector went not thither nor any of the Lords of the Council.' Coach races in the park were very popular at this time. On one occasion Cromwell 'provoked the horses [so much] with the whip that they grew unruly and ran so fast that the postilion could not hold them in whereby His Highness was flung out of the coachbox upon the pole, on which he lay with his body and afterwards fell upon the ground. His foot getting hold in the tackling, he was carried away a good while in that posture during which time a pistol went off in his pocket. But at last he got his foot clear and so came to escape.'

At the Restoration in 1660 Charles II took the park back into royal hands and enclosed it for the first time with a brick wall. In his time 'nothing was so much in fashion during the fine weather as a large enclosure called the Tour, and later the Ring, which was the rendezvous of fashion and beauty. Everyone who had either sparkling eyes or a splendid equipage constantly repaired thither and the King seemed pleased with the place.' On May Day 1663 Samuel Pepys decided it might help his career if he took part in the parade and was noticed by the King and Lady Castlemaine. He bought new clothes, including 'painted gloves, very pretty and all the mode' and turned out looking, so his wife recorded, 'mighty noble'. But the horse he hired at the Chequer Inn, CHARING CROSS, proved too high-spirited for him to handle and he was obliged to go home without having come to the King's attention. North of the Ring, in an enclosure known as Buckdean Hill, now Buck Hill, the King had the park restocked with deer.

When William III came to live at KENSINGTON PALACE he had 300 lamps hung from the branches of the trees along the *route du roi* (from which Rotten Row takes its name) between the palace and ST JAMES'S. It was the first road in England to be lit at night. It was hoped that this lighting would deter the highwaymen who were so active in the park of whom one had, in 1687, been hanged for killing a woman who had swallowed her wedding ring to prevent his taking it. The park, however, continued to be plagued by highwaymen: it was here in 1749, when returning from HOLLAND HOUSE, that Horace Walpole was stopped by two highwaymen who threatened him with a blunderbuss and took his watch and eight guineas.

The park was also well known as a duelling ground. Lord Mohun, 'one of the arrantest rakes in town' and the Duke of Hamilton fought their duel here in 1712. 'They fought with so violent an animosity that, neglecting the rules of art they seemed to run on one another, as if they'd tried who should kill first, in which they were both so unhappily successful that the

During the 1814 Peace Celebrations the battle of Trafalgar was re-enacted in Hyde Park. From a contemporary broadsheet.

Lord Mohun was killed outright and the Duke died in a few minutes.' Here also John Wilkes fought Samuel Martin in 1772, Sheridan fought Captain Matthews over Miss Linley in 1772, Lord Thurlow fought Andrew Stuart in 1770 and in 1779 Charles James Fox was slightly wounded in his duel with William Adam, having ignored his second's advice to place his bulky frame sideways to his opponent on the grounds that he was 'as thick one way as another'. Horace Walpole considered this the 'most perfect of all duels. So much good temper, good sense, propriety, easy good humour and natural good nature.'

In 1730 work began for Queen Caroline, a keen landscape gardener, on forming the lake to be known as the Serpentine by damming the WESTBOURNE. Two yachts were put in the water for the Royal Family's use. The powder magazine north of the Serpentine was built in 1805. During the celebrations of 1814 'a Great Fair' was held in the park and ornamental booths and stalls, arcades and kiosks, swings and roundabouts were erected; there were sword swallowers and military bands, fire eaters and the 'fattest ladies of forty in the world', cake-houses and apple stalls; and the battle of Trafalgar was re-enacted on the lake with guns roaring and the French ships sinking in flames to the strains of the National Anthem. 'The whole surface of Hyde Park is dry crumbling sand, not a vestige or hint of grass ever grows there,' Charles Lamb told Wordsworth afterwards, 'booths and drinking places go all round it for a mile and a half I am confident – I might say two miles in circuit – the stench of liquors, bad tobacco, dirty people and provisions conquers the air and we are stifled and suffocated in Hyde Park.' In 1816 Shelley's pregnant wife, Harriet Westbrook, whom he had deserted, met her mysterious death by drowning either in the Serpentine or in the reservoir in GREEN PARK. In 1820 George IV's coronation was celebrated in the park by firework displays and balloon ascents, and in 1822 the statue of Achilles by Westmacott was erected to commemorate Wellington's victories (see STATUES). In 1825 Decimus Burton designed lodges for HYDE PARK CORNER, Grosvenor Gate, Stanhope Gate and Cumberland Gate. In 1826 George Rennie's bridge, which commands such lovely views to WESTMINSTER ABBEY and the PALACE OF WESTMINSTER, was built over the Serpentine dividing it from the Long Water. In that year also 'the most daring feat of all times was carried out on the Serpentine', which in many past hard winters had been crowded with skaters. Mr Henry Hunt, of Hunt's Matchless Blacking, drove one of his company's vans and four horses across the

In January 1826 Henry Hunt of Hunt's Matchless Blacking won a bet by driving a horse-drawn vehicle across the frozen Serpentine.

ice at the broadest part and won 100 guineas from 'a Noble Lord of Sporting Celebrity'. In 1832 the Ranger's Lodge was built.

In 1845 Albert Gate was erected and in 1847 the Prince of Wales's Gate. The GREAT EXHIBITION OF 1851 was held in the CRYSTAL PALACE which was put up near this latter gate between Rotten Row and the Carriage Road. In 1855 150,000 people gathered in the north-east corner of the park to demonstrate against Lord Robert Grosvenor's Sunday Trading Bill. There was no legal right of assembly there then and the police arrived to arrest an inflammatory orator but he had already gone. After more demonstrations the right of assembly was recognised in 1872; and in this part of the park, known as Speakers' Corner, anyone with a mind so to do may now declaim on any subject he chooses, provided he is not obscene or blasphemous, or does not constitute an incitement to a breach of the peace.

In 1860 flowers were first planted in the park by William Nesfield, the architect and landscape gardener, who was often consulted about improvements in the London parks and in 1861 the Italian Water Garden at Victoria Gate was made. These include fountains, an Italianate summer house and Queen Anne's Alcove, which was built to the design of Christopher Wren and moved here from KENSINGTON GARDENS. Beside the fountains is a large bronze statue of Dr Jenner by W. Calder Marshall (see STATUES). The fountain at Grosvenor Gate, designed by Alexander Munro, was put up in 1863; the *Joy of Life* fountain by T.B. Huxley-Jones which stands on the PARK LANE side of the park opposite MOUNT STREET was given by the Constance Fund, an organisation founded in 1944 by Mrs Constance Goetze in memory of her husband. A dogs' cemetery was made at Victoria Gate in 1880 when the Duchess of Cambridge's pet was buried here; the last interment was in 1915. The statue of *Diana* by Feodora Gleichen was erected in 1906; and Sir Henry Tanner's Tea House (later turned into the SERPENTINE GALLERY) was built in 1908. Epstein's bas-relief of *Rima* provoked cries of outrage when it was unveiled by the Prime Minister in 1925. It represents the goddess in *Green Mansions*, the novel by W.H. Hudson, the naturalist and writer, after whom the bird sanctuary in which it stands is named. The Cavalry Memorial was erected in 1924 (see MEMORIALS). The Serpentine Restaurant, designed by Patrick Gwynne, was opened in 1963 and Gwynne's smaller restaurant in the Dell, at the east end of the Serpentine, in 1965. The so-called Standing Stone in the Dell is traditionally said to have been brought here by Charles I from Stonehenge. In fact it is a 7-ton piece of Cornish stone once part of a drinking fountain erected in 1861 and subsequently removed. Near this is a stone recording that 'on this spot stood a conduit house which supplied the precincts of Westminster with water till the spring was cut off by drainage in 1861. The building was removed in 1868 and this memorial erected in 1870 to mark the place where it stood.' In the park are four acres of greenhouses where all the bedding plants for the royal parks are raised. The large bronze group of Pan playing his pipes, a man, a woman their child and a dog running into the park by Edinburgh Gate is by Epstein. More than 9,000 elms in the park have been killed by Dutch elm disease in recent years.

The trunks of three of these, between the bird sanctuary and the Serpentine, were sculpted by first-year students of the CHELSEA SCHOOL OF ART in 1978. Henry Moore's 19 ft high sculpture *The Arch*, carved in 1979 in Roman travertine, a gift of the Henry Moore Foundation, was unveiled on the east bank of Long Water opposite Watts's *Physical Energy* in September 1980. By the east end of the Serpentine is a small artificial stone fountain (originally marble, but this weathered so badly that it was replaced in 1975) by W. R. Colton (1896). Barbara Hepworth's *Family of Man* sculptures were removed in 1982.

Hyde Park Corner *SW1*. When KENSINGTON and KNIGHTSBRIDGE were small communities separate from London, the toll gate here was the entrance to London from the west. In the later 18th century several schemes were put forward for the improvement of the area: Robert Adam in 1778 proposed a triumphal arch with screens as gateways to the royal parks. Jeffry Wyatt put forward other proposals in 1794; and in 1796 John Soane envisaged a new palace in the north-west corner of GREEN PARK. But it was not until BUCKINGHAM PALACE was built in the 1820s that CONSTITUTION ARCH was erected here to the designs of Decimus Burton. On the island upon which the arch stands is a bronze statue of the Duke of Wellington (*see* STATUES) and memorials to the Machine Gun Corps and the Royal Artillery (*see* MEMORIALS). The Hyde Park Screen to the north is also by Decimus Burton and it too was meant to be an imposing feature of the drive from the palace into the park. The carvings on the frieze are by John Herring, the Younger. Opposite the screen on the corner of KNIGHTSBRIDGE and GROSVENOR PLACE stand the buildings of ST GEORGE'S HOSPITAL. The whole area now swarms with traffic beneath which pedestrians walk in the underpasses which were constructed when the LONDON COUNTY COUNCIL improvement scheme for PARK LANE was carried out in the 1960s.

Hyde Park Gate *SW7*. Rows of large, extremely expensive early to mid-Victorian houses, most of them much altered. They have often, in the words of the *Survey of London*, provided houses 'for people of professional and social eminence'. There have been 'several aristocratic residents' and 'many members of Parliament found the street convenient for Westminster. Nearly a score of the 19-century occupants . . . are entered in the *Dictionary of National Biography*, including Sir Leslie Stephen, the *Dictionary's* first editor.' His daughters, Virginia Woolf and Vanessa Bell, were born at No. 22. No. 29 was the home of Sir Roderick Jones, chairman of REUTER's and of his wife, Enid Bagnold, the playwright and novelist who confessed in her memoirs that she was seduced as a young woman by Frank Harris under a table in a private room at the CAFÉ ROYAL. Their house was altered for them by Sir Edwin Lutyens who placed a revolving copper ball on the newel-post of Miss Bagnold's writing-room staircase so that, if she suddenly thought of an idea or a snatch of dialogue in the middle of the night, she could, having leaped out of bed, rush down the staircase and propel herself into the chair by her desk before the inspiration left her. The houses next door, Nos 27 and 28, were the last home of Sir Winston Churchill who bought 28 at the end of the War and 27, mainly for use as office accommodation, later, joining the two houses together. He died here on 24 January 1965. A near neighbour of his at No. 18 was Sir Jacob Epstein who had lived here for about 30 years until his death in 1959. Lord Baden-Powell lived at No. 9 as a boy.

Hyde Park Hotel *66 Knightsbridge, SW1*. Built in 1882 as an expensive apartment block by Archer and Green, with turrets, balconies and pillared porticos.

An engraving after Pollard of the screen at Hyde Park Corner, designed as a park entrance by Decimus Burton in the 1820s.

After a fire in 1904 it was reopened as a hotel in 1908.

As Queen Victoria did not allow signs in HYDE PARK, and the original main entrance was kept for private use by the Royal Family, KNIGHTSBRIDGE became the main entrance. In 1916 Mary Dooley from Dublin came to work here and stayed for 61 years. She married the cellarman and many famous people, including Edward VIII, used to retreat into the still-room for a quiet talk and a coffee or brandy. Queen Mary used to visit the soldiers on leave who occupied the main rooms during the 1st World War. Lord Beaverbrook (then Max Aitken) was staying here in 1916 when he was offered a peerage by Lloyd George and Bonar Law. It was also patronised by Winston Churchill and by Mahatma Gandhi for whom a goat was milked each day. The King of Sweden was a regular guest. Many famous film stars including Valentino stayed in the 1920s. Mme Vacani later gave dancing lessons here to the Princesses Elizabeth and Margaret. During the 2nd World War Rosa Lewis came to stay while her own CAVENDISH HOTEL was being restored after bomb damage. Guests can watch the HOUSEHOLD CAVALRY pass each morning from the restaurant overlooking HYDE PARK. There are 205 rooms and 19 suites restored by David Hicks and others.

Hyde Park Place *W2.* Rebuilt in the early 20th century this terrace suffered bomb damage in the 2nd World War during which the Chapel of the Ascension was destroyed. On the site of No. 5 Dickens worked on *Edwin Drood* in 1870; beside this is the Benedictine Tyburn Convent, founded in 1903, and foreseen by the Jesuit martyr, Gregory Gunne, as he stood on the scaffold at TYBURN in 1585. No. 10, only five ft wide, is claimed to be the smallest house in London. Sir Max Beerbohm lived at No. 12 in 1892–6. St George's Row, built before 1800, originally stood here. It was the home of many artists, including Paul Sandby.

I

Ickenham *Middlesex*. Called Ticheham in *Domesday*, it remained an agricultural community until the third decade of this century. In 1909 it was 'a small quiet village scattered about a tiny patch of green, on which is a picturesque pump'. The turning-point was probably 1922, when the SWAKELEYS estate was sold for residential development. The population, given as 443 in 1921, had risen to 1,741 ten years later. By 1961 it was 10,370. A number of older buildings survive, notably the medieval parish church of ST GILES and the moated 15th-century Manor Farm.

Idol Lane *EC3*. Could be named after a statue outside ST DUNSTAN-IN-THE-EAST, although on 18th-century maps it is spelt Idle Lane. No. 9 is an early 18th-century house.

Ilchester Estate *see* HOLLAND ESTATE.

ILEA *see* INNER LONDON EDUCATION AUTHORITY.

Ilford *Essex*. Today means Great Ilford which, despite being always the larger place, was until the 19th century a hamlet of the huge parish of BARKING, while Little Ilford, a separate parish, has been swept up into Manor Park. Seven miles from London, where the great highway into East Anglia crosses the River RODING, Ilford stands on a slight rise on the east or left bank. The probable meaning of the name is 'ford across the Hyle' (the old name of the RODING). The site has been inhabited from earliest times. Mammoth and other prehistoric bones have been found in several places, mostly near the river; some may be seen in the NATURAL HISTORY MUSEUM. The 'camp' at Uphall is pre-Roman; and Roman remains have been turned up at Valentines and Barkingside.

As part of the lands of the royal abbey of BARKING, Ilford had no significance until about 1140 when, in the reign of Stephen, the Abbess Adeliza founded a leper hospital dedicated to the Blessed Virgin at the crossroads (now the Broadway) at the top of Ilford Hill. The foundation was enlarged about 1180 by Abbess Mary Becket in honour of her martyred brother St Thomas of Canterbury, whose name was added to the dedication. The present chapel, although much restored, is essentially of the 14th century. The 18th-century almshouses, successors to the original lepers' cells, make an attractive group within the high wall of the hospital.

Valentines, built in late Stuart or early Georgian times, is the only large house remaining. It stands in the extensive Valentines Park and is used as offices by REDBRIDGE council. Ilford bridge was the limit of commercial navigation on the RODING. A considerable trade was done in timber, coal, gravel, cement and sand, but this declined sharply in the 1920s and the barge traffic ceased about 1930. St Mary's church in the High Road (James Savage) was built in 1831 but

has had a new chancel. Until its opening the only place of worship was the Hospital Chapel.

Ilford, which has had a railway station since 1839, was an early dormitory suburb: the population increased from 10,913 in 1891 to 179,600 in 1957. Such development has inevitably been in large estates, and there are few notable buildings. The municipal borough, which included Fairlop, Barkingside, Seven Kings, Aldborough Hatch, Goodmayes, much of Hainault and part of Chadwell Heath, is now joined to WANSTEAD and WOODFORD to form the London Borough of REDBRIDGE.

Imperial College of Science and Technology *South Kensington, SW7*. Established in 1907 by Royal Charter 'to give the highest specialised instruction and to provide the fullest equipment for the most advanced training and research in various branches of science, especially in its application to industry.' It became a School of the UNIVERSITY OF LONDON in the following year. It was formed by the federation of three institutions which had settled in SOUTH KENSINGTON at the end of the 19th century: the Royal College of Science, the Royal School of Mines and the City and Guilds College. They had been accommodated on land which the Commissioners for the GREAT EXHIBITION of 1851 had bought with surplus funds, for the purpose of promoting the knowledge of science and art and their application to productive industry. Their amalgamation created one of the world's most prestigious institutions of advanced technological education.

The Royal College of Science traces its origin to the Royal College of Chemistry founded in 1845 by the Prince Consort, its first president. The Royal School of Mines was founded in 1851, while the City and Guilds College was established in 1884 by the CITY AND GUILDS OF LONDON INSTITUTE. Great names of science and technology which are part of the Imperial College heritage include Hofmann, Perkin, T.H. Huxley, Frankland, Roberts-Austen, Percy, Le Neve Foster, Armstrong, Ayrton and Unwin.

Imperial Hotel *Russell Square, WC1*. The original, highly ornate, Victorian hotel by Charles Fitzroy Doll (who also designed the nearby RUSSELL HOTEL) was built in 1905–11 in red brick with terracotta ornaments. It had a grand Winter Garden and Turkish Baths of glazed DOULTON ware. When Gorky stayed here he was visited by Lenin who, always suspicious of hotels, carefully inspected the bedclothes to make sure they were not damp. It was demolished in 1966, and the new Imperial Hotel by C. Lovett, Gill and Partners was opened in June 1969. This retains some of the original statues in the courtyard. In 1982 there were 460 bedrooms.

Imperial Institute *South Kensington*. Designed by T.E. Collcutt and built in 1887–93 for the institute

Queen Victoria arriving in 1893 to open the Imperial Institute.

which had been founded after the Imperial Exhibition of 1886. Apart from its central tower, the building was demolished when the IMPERIAL COLLEGE OF SCIENCE was expanded (*see also* COMMONWEALTH INSTITUTE).

Imperial Theatre *Tothill Street, Westminster*. Part of the grand design of the ROYAL AQUARIUM, a vast building which included an aquarium, concert hall, picture gallery and reading room and was opened on 22 January 1876 by the Duke of Edinburgh. The theatre, known as the Royal Aquarium Theatre, was later incorporated in the west end of the building to the design of A. Bedborough. It opened on 15 April 1876 with *Jo*, an adaptation of Dickens's *Bleak House* which was transferred by Edgar Bruce, with his company, including Jennie Lee, from the GLOBE THEATRE. It failed to live up to the high hopes of its creators and deteriorated into a house of mixed entertainment and low reputation until taken over in 1878–80 by Marie Litton, who revived, among other successes, *Uncle Tom's Cabin* and *She Stoops to Conquer*, and changed the name to the Imperial Theatre. It is remembered mostly for its association with Lillie Langtry who briefly managed it in 1882 and eventually took over the lease in 1900 and completely rebuilt the interior. The work financed by Edgar Cohen was to the design of F.T. Verity. The theatre reopened disastrously on 22 April 1901 with *A Royal Necklace* which was almost immediately withdrawn. The Aquarium building was acquired by the Wesleyan Methodists and demolished in 1903, leaving the theatre standing under a lease which expired in 1907. The interior was then taken

down and incorporated in a cinema, formerly a music hall, in CANNING TOWN. This was burned down in 1931.

Imperial War Museum *Lambeth Road, SE1*. Collects, preserves and displays material and information relating to the two World Wars and other military operations in which Great Britain and the Commonwealth countries have been involved since August 1914. Established by Act of Parliament in 1920 as the Imperial War Museum, it opened at the CRYSTAL PALACE in that year. From 1924 to 1935 it was housed in the former IMPERIAL INSTITUTE at SOUTH KENSINGTON and moved to its present location (a building designed by James Lewis in 1815) which was formerly part of BETHLEM ROYAL HOSPITAL. The Museum sustained some damage from air-raids during the 2nd World War and the galleries were closed to the public from 1940 to 1946. Improvements and extensions were carried out in 1962. In 1968 some losses occurred as the result of a fire.

The surrounding gardens are known as the Geraldine Mary Harmsworth Park in memory of the mother of Viscount Rothermere (*see* BEDLAM).

Incorporated Society of Musicians *10 Stratford Place, WC1*. Established in 1882, incorporated in 1892 and reconstituted in 1928. The Society's main objectives are 'the promotion of the Art of Music and the maintenance of the honour and interests of the Musical profession'. Membership is restricted to full-time professional musicians and the society provides advice on professional matters, opportunities for young artists and a benevolent fund. There are 53 centres throughout the country. Past presidents have included Sir Thomas Beecham, Sir Malcolm Sargent and Yehudi Menuhin.

India House *Aldwych, WC2*. Offices of the High Commissioner designed by Sir Herbert Baker and A.T. Scott in 1928–30. The interiors are by Indian artists.

India Office Library and Records *197 Black-friars Road, SE1*. Once of the finest Oriental library and archive collections in the world, formerly located in the India Office building in WESTMINSTER. Collections in European and Oriental languages have been built up from various sources. Under the 1867 Indian Registration of Books Act, the library was entitled to a copy of every work published in India and Burma. Since 1948 important works from India and Pakistan, in English and Oriental languages, have been added.

Ingestre Place *W1*. Takes its name from Lord Ingestre, later 19th Earl of Shrewsbury, who had proposed the building of a block of artisans' dwellings which were put up here in the 1850s. The street was originally in two parts known as New Street and Husband Street (probably named after Thomas Husbands, a painter who had been granted leases here). Building began at the end of the 17th century. None of the original houses remains.

Inn on the Park *Hamilton Place, W1*. A ten-storey hotel with views over HYDE PARK standing on a wedge-shaped site, between OLD PARK LANE and HAMILTON PLACE. Designed by Michael Rosenauer, it opened in 1970. In 1982 there were 228 bedrooms.

Inner Circle *Regent's Park, NW1*. The inner ring road of REGENT'S PARK was originally planned by Nash to have its sides lined with a double ring of terraces but the scheme was, happily, abandoned. Around its edge stood three villas, THE HOLME, ST JOHN'S LODGE and SOUTH VILLA. The two former remain, unspoiled. During 1838–1932, the centre was occupied by the gardens of the Royal Botanic Society; their place has now been taken by Queen Mary's Rose Garden entered through magnificent gates, the gift of the artist Sigismund Goetze who, under his will, further endowed the Park with the Triton Fountain (1936) designed by William Macmillan and with two bronze sculptures by A.H. Hodge, *The Lost Bow* and *The Mighty Hunter* (1939). Today, the Polygon Restaurant and the OPEN AIR THEATRE stand in the Inner Circle, and around it London's van horses parade on Easter Monday.

Inner London Education Authority (ILEA) Deals with education in the CITY OF LONDON and the twelve inner London Boroughs – CAMDEN, GREENWICH, HACKNEY, HAMMERSMITH, ISLINGTON, KENSINGTON, LAMBETH, LEWISHAM, SOUTHWARK, TOWER HAMLETS, WANDSWORTH and the CITY OF WESTMINSTER. The ILEA is a special committee of the GREATER LONDON COUNCIL.

INNER TEMPLE *EC4*. For the derivation of the name *see* KNIGHTS TEMPLAR. In the second half of the

12th century the KNIGHTS TEMPLAR built a residence in the area of the present Temple and began work on the Round Church which still survives (*see* TEMPLE CHURCH). When the Knights were suppressed in 1312 their property passed to the Knights Hospitallers who leased part of it to lawyers (the predecessors of the barristers of the MIDDLE and Inner Temple) for use as a hostel. On the suppression of the Hospitallers in 1539 all their property, including the Temple area, passed to the Crown. In 1609 James I granted the ownership of the Temple to the Benchers of these two Inns, subject to an obligation to maintain the Church and Master's House. No formal division of property between the Inns took place until 1732. The Outer Temple is that area outside TEMPLE BAR once owned by the KNIGHTS TEMPLAR as part of their residence which was never occupied by the lawyers. All the early Temple records were destroyed in the PEASANTS' REVOLT in 1381. The crest of the Inner Temple depicts the winged horse Pegasus.

Hall The present hall, which faces the southern aspect of the TEMPLE CHURCH, dates from 1955 and was rebuilt by Sir Hubert Worthington in neo-Georgian style. It replaces a Gothic structure erected in 1868–70 by Sydney Smirke in lieu of a medieval hall of the KNIGHTS TEMPLAR which had become inadequate. The new hall incorporates a medieval buttery and crypt. During dining terms a horn is blown at 6.45 to summon members to the hall.

Library Adjoining the hall and Treasury, it was rebuilt by the same architect. When the previous library was destroyed in 1941 some 45,000 books were lost, but today it contains about 95,000 volumes.

Gateway At the northern end of INNER TEMPLE LANE, leading into FLEET STREET, this Gateway has been described by Pevsner as one of the best pieces of half-timber work in London. Above is Prince Henry's Room, named after the elder son of James I. It was possibly once the Council Chamber of the DUCHY OF CORNWALL.

Crown Office Row Rebuilt first by Sydney Smirke in 1863–4 and subsequently by Sir Edward Maufe in 1953–5, the present Crown Office has been situated in the LAW COURTS since 1882. A plaque on the south wall commemorates Charles Lamb who was born in the previous building on this site, where his father was a clerk to a Bencher of the Inn. Thackeray also lived at the former No. 10 in 1848–50.

Dr Johnson's Buildings Erected in 1857, they commemorate Dr Samuel Johnson who lived at No. 1, INNER TEMPLE LANE which once occupied part of the site of the present structure.

Farrar's Building The present building, erected in 1876, stands on the site of the former town house of the Bishops of Ely. James Boswell entered chambers in a previous building on this site so as to be close to his friend, Samuel Johnson.

Francis Taylor Building Named after Sir Francis Taylor, QC, a Bencher for 46 years, it was completed in 1957 by Sir Edward Maufe in late Georgian style.

Harcourt Buildings Rebuilt by Sir Hubert Worthington after the 2nd World War, it is named after Lord Chancellor Harcourt, who was treasurer of the Inner Temple when the original building was erected on this site in 1703.

Hare Court Named after Sir Nicholas Hare, a Bencher, who rebuilt part of the original in 1567, it is better known for its connection with the notorious

Lord Chief Justice Jeffreys who, as a barrister, had chambers on the west side.

King's Bench Walk The greater part was built in red brick in 1677–8 to the designs of Wren; but Nos 9–11, in yellow brick, date from 1814. The original King's Bench Office was burned in 1677. Oliver Goldsmith lived at No. 3 before moving to BRICK COURT. Sir Harold Nicolson and his wife, Vita Sackville-West, used No. 4 as their London residence in 1930–45. George Moore, the novelist and poet, lived at No. 8 from 1888–96. H. Rider Haggard lived at No. 13.

Mitre Court Buildings Dating from 1830, damage by bombing was made good in 1951 under Sir Hubert Worthington. In a previous building on this site lived Sir Edward Coke, legal writer and jurist. Charles and Mary Lamb also lived here in 1800–8 before moving to Inner Temple Lane.

Paper Buildings The original building on this site was erected in 1610 and constructed with lath, timber and plaster. The present building by Sir Robert Smirke dates from 1838. The novelist John Galsworthy had chambers at No. 3 in the 1890s. In Dickens's novel *Barnaby Rudge* Sir John Chester lived in Paper Buildings.

Temple Gardens Building At the south end of MIDDLE TEMPLE LANE and designed by E.M. Barry, it dates from 1878–9, and is markedly out of harmony with the rest of the Temple.

Inner Temple Gardens The entrance gates by Crown Office Row date from 1730 and carry a Griffin as well as a Pegasus in token of the traditional amity between GRAY'S INN and the Inner Temple. Between 1888 and 1913 the ROYAL HORTICULTURAL SOCIETY held their Great Spring Show in the Gardens by courtesy of the Benchers. In the latter year the Show was moved to CHELSEA and has since been known as the CHELSEA FLOWER SHOW.

Among many prominent persons associated with the Inn (in addition to those already referred to) are Lord Howard of Effingham; Thomas Wentworth, 1st Earl of Strafford; Francis Beamont, the dramatist; William Cowper, the poet; George Canning who lived at No. 2, Paper Buildings; Arthur Henry Hallam, the poet; Thomas Hughes, author of *Tom Brown's School Days* and Leslie Stephen, editor of the *Dictionary of National Biography* and father of Virginia Woolf (*see also* INNS OF COURT).

Innholders' Company *see* CITY LIVERY COMPANIES.

INNS OF CHANCERY Why they should have been styled 'Inns of Chancery' is not fully known. Their initial function may have been the training and housing of the medieval Chancery Clerks who were responsible for preparing the writs for all the King's courts. By the middle of the 15th century the Inns had largely been taken over by resident students and solicitors and attorneys and had become preparatory schools for students wishing to be called to the Bar by the INNS OF COURT which had managed to secure a degree of control over the Inns of Chancery. By 1530 Furnival's and Thavies Inns had become affiliated to LINCOLN'S INN, while Staple Inn and Barnard's Inn looked to GRAY'S INN, and Clement's, Clifford's and Lyon's Inns were affiliated to the INNER TEMPLE. After the destruction of the Strand Inn in 1549, the MIDDLE TEMPLE had only one Inn of Chancery, namely New Inn.

Each Inn of Chancery normally comprised a Principal, Ancients (Benchers) and Juniors or Companions (barristers and students). Unlike the INNS OF COURT, the Inns of Chancery – also styled 'Honourable Societies' – had no power to call students to the Bar but in most other respects their constitutions were similar to those of the Inns of Court. By 1600 eight Inns of Chancery were in existence but, with the decline in the educational role of these Inns, students were tending increasingly to enrol directly in the INNS OF COURT. At the same time the attorneys and solicitors, who were being gradually excluded from the INNS OF COURT, took over the Inns of Chancery. By the 18th century the latter had ceased to have any educational function and had become little more than social clubs for attorneys and solicitors. With the establishment of legal education for attorneys and solicitors by the LAW SOCIETY, the anachronistic position of the Inns of Chancery became ever more apparent and only two of them survived the 19th century. The foundation dates here attributed to the Inns are approximate.

Barnard's Inn *1454*. Originally known as Mackworth's Inn and situated on the south side of HOLBORN close to FETTER LANE, the premises came into the ownership of the Dean and Chapter of Lincoln under the will of the Dean of Lincoln, John Mackworth. Subsequently it came into the possession of a society of lawyers headed by a man named Barnard, and became an Inn of Chancery. By the middle of the 19th century the structure had fallen into disrepair. It is described in chapter XXI of Dickens's *Great Expectations*. In 1892 the MERCERS livery company purchased the Inn for £43,000 as premises for the MERCERS SCHOOL. Although the premises survived the 2nd World War intact, the school moved away in 1959 and the buildings are now leased to the PRUDENTIAL ASSURANCE COMPANY.

Clement's Inn *1480*. Derived its name from the nearby church of ST CLEMENT DANES. Together with New Inn and Lyon's Inn, this Inn was situated on the north side of the STRAND close to the western boundary of the LAW COURTS. Part was sold and demolished in 1868 and the rest sold in 1884. The remaining buildings were demolished in 1891. The only subsisting link with the Inn is Clement's Passage which runs eastwards from nearby Houghton Street. Shakespeare's Justice Shallow had lodgings here.

Clifford's Inn *1345*. The Inn occupied part of the southern block between CHANCERY LANE and FETTER LANE on the northern side of FLEET STREET. In 1344 Lady Clifford, the widow of the 6th Baron Clifford, leased the premises to lawyers. In 1618 the freehold was conveyed to them as an Inn of Chancery. Among its students were Sir Edward Coke and James Selden, eminent writers on legal topics. The court which dealt with disputes about boundaries and other associated problems after the GREAT FIRE sat in the Hall of the Inn. The Inn was largely rebuilt in 1767–8. Samuel Butler lived here between 1864 and 1902. In 1903 the Inn was sold for £100,000 of which £77,000 was earmarked for legal education. In 1911 the Society of Knights Bachelor purchased the property for £36,000, retaining it until 1920. In 1934 the Inn was almost entirely demolished and replaced by offices and flats known as Clifford's Inn. The only part of the old Inn extant is Clifford's Inn Passage which leads from FLEET STREET to the former gate house. Leonard and Virginia Woolf lived in the Inn, in 1912–13.

Furnival's Inn *1383*. The Inn derived its name from William de Furnival, 4th Lord Furnival, who leased the property to law students in 1383. LINCOLN'S INN purchased the freehold of the Inn which was situated on the northern side of HOLBORN in 1547. Sir Thomas More was a Reader of the Inn in about 1503. When LINCOLN'S INN declined to renew the lease in 1817 the Society was dissolved. A subsequent lessee demolished the Inn and replaced it by a new building but retained the name of Furnival's Inn. Charles Dickens lived here while working as a reporter on the *Morning Chronicle* in 1834–7, and the *Pickwick Papers* were begun here. In 1879 the PRUDENTIAL ASSURANCE COMPANY moved into a new building designed for them by Alfred Waterhouse adjoining the reconstructed Inn. In 1888 the Company paid LINCOLN'S INN £150,000 for the freehold of this neighbouring property which they demolished in 1897 to allow for the enlargement (under the supervision of Waterhouse) of their existing premises into the present well-known building. The Inn is commemorated by a plaque at the entrance to the building.

Furnival's Inn, an Inn of Chancery, was founded in 1383. This 1818 engraving shows it shortly after the Society was dissolved.

Lyon's Inn *1413*. The INNER TEMPLE in 1583 bought the freehold which was situated where AUSTRALIA HOUSE, BUSH HOUSE and the ALDWYCH now stand. Originally a common tavern, it became an Inn of Chancery in the time of Henry V. The name derives from the sign of the lion which it bore when a hostelry. The Inn had fallen into decay by 1800 and was sold in 1863. The whole area was cleared as part of the former LONDON COUNTY COUNCIL'S KINGSWAY Improvement Scheme of 1899. No trace remains.

New Inn *1485*. Originally a common tavern styled the Inn of Our Lady, the premises were converted into an Inn of Chancery by students who had abandoned another Inn of Chancery (St George's Inn) situated near the OLD BAILEY, which had fallen into disrepair. By the year 1608 the MIDDLE TEMPLE had acquired the freehold. The Inn, part of which was sited on land now occupied by AUSTRALIA HOUSE and the ALDWYCH, was compulsorily acquired in 1899 by the former LONDON COUNTY COUNCIL under its KINGSWAY Improvement Scheme. The only remaining trace of the Inn is New Inn Passage near Houghton Street. Out of the compensation money paid for the acquisition £55,000 was earmarked for legal education.

Staple Inn *1378*. GRAY'S INN purchased the freehold in 1529. The Inn, which has survived physically up to the present, is situated behind a façade of 16th-century

shops on the southern side of HOLBORN facing the southern end of GRAY'S INN ROAD. Originally a wool warehouse – hence the name 'Staple' – it became an Inn of Chancery in 1378. The hall of the Inn dates from 1580. In common with other Inns of Chancery it declined in the 19th century and was sold in 1884. Part was acquired by the PATENT OFFICE and the remainder, in 1886, bought for £68,000 by the PRUDENTIAL ASSURANCE COMPANY who fully restored the Inn. In 1944 it suffered severe damage but was again restored in 1950: most of it is at present occupied by the INSTITUTE OF ACTUARIES, the rest of the building being used as offices. Samuel Johnson had lodgings in the Inn in 1759.

Strand Inn *1294*. Situated on the south side of the STRAND opposite the church of ST MARY-LE-STRAND, this Inn of Chancery was sometimes known as Chester Inn having been previously the property of the Bishop of Chester. It was one of the Inns of Chancery which had been associated with the MIDDLE TEMPLE. It was demolished in 1549 by the Lord Protector Somerset who wanted the site, amongst others, to build a mansion for himself which became known as SOMERSET HOUSE.

Thavies Inn *1348*. The property originally belonged to an armourer called John Thavies who died in 1348. It became attached to LINCOLN'S INN before 1422. LINCOLN'S INN purchased the freehold in 1549. Failure to secure a renewal of their lease in the 1760s resulted in the dissolution of the Society. The sale of the site of the Inn, which was situated in SHOE LANE close by ST ANDREW'S church, HOLBORN, provided part of the money for the construction of STONE BUILDINGS, LINCOLN'S INN.

Inns of Court In relation to the Inns of Court and of CHANCERY the word 'Inn' has always had the special meaning of mansion or town house and, in particular, one used as a hostel for barristers and students. Today there are four Inns of Court, namely LINCOLN'S INN, the MIDDLE TEMPLE, the INNER TEMPLE and GRAY'S INN, while the INNS OF CHANCERY have ceased to exist. Each of the Inns of Court is formally referred to as an 'Honourable Society'. All are wholly independent bodies, not incorporated under any law and fully self-governing save to the extent that in 1974 they delegated certain of their regulatory powers for the sake of uniformity and efficiency to a body known as the Senate of the Inns of Court and the Bar on which individual Inns are represented. Amongst other matters, the Senate is concerned with finance, law reform, legal education and the maintenance of high professional standards through the Bar Council. Each Inn is governed by Benchers (Masters of the Bench) and they alone have the power to call students to the Bar.

The earliest records of the Inns of Court date from 1422 (LINCOLN'S), 1501 (MIDDLE TEMPLE), 1505 (INNER TEMPLE) and 1569 (GRAY'S), but the Inns themselves date from an earlier period, probably from the 14th century, and it is believed that they came into existence for the purpose of teaching, controlling and protecting bodies of 'apprentices' i.e. students and barristers below the rank of SERJEANT-AT-LAW. In 1292 Edward I gave a monopoly of practice in the courts to persons selected by the judges. The need for proper instruction in the English Common Law (not taught in the universities) led to the establishment in the early

13th century of hostels for practitioners and students within easy reach of WESTMINSTER: two of these (New Inn and Thavies Inn) became INNS OF CHANCERY. Legal education at the Inns of Court originally extended over a period of seven or eight years and consisted of lectures given by senior barristers (Readers) followed by discussions. Readers also lectured at the INNS OF CHANCERY. In addition, history, music and dancing were taught with a view to preparing the students to play their part suitably in the higher levels of society.

Legal education, both at the Inns and at the universities, began to decline in the latter half of the 17th century, partly because of the upheavals provoked by the Civil War and partly because of the spread of printing. By the end of the 18th century it had virtually ceased. In 1779 the Bar comprised 15 King's Counsel, 11 Serjeants, 203 Barristers and 12 Advocates (see DOCTORS' COMMONS). With the advance of the 19th century a steady revival took place both at the universities and at the Inns and in 1852 the Council of Legal Education was set up by the Inns of Court. The first compulsory examination for the bar students was held in 1872. By the end of the year 1980 the practising Bar totalled 4,589 of whom 453 were Queen's Counsel. There were 447 women barristers of whom 10 were Queen's Counsel.

Institute of Actuaries *Staple Inn Hall, High Holborn, WC1.* Founded in 1848 and granted its Royal Charter of Incorporation in 1884. Since 1887 the Institute has been housed in Staple Inn (*see* INNS OF CHANCERY).

Institute of Bankers *Lombard Street, EC3.* This Institute was established at 11–12 Clement's Lane in 1879. It moved to Lombard Street in 1951.

Institute of Chartered Accountants of England and Wales *Chartered Accountants' Hall, Moorgate Place, EC2.* Founded as the Institute of Acountants in London at a meeting in the City Terminus Hotel, CANNON STREET, in November 1870. (*See also* CHARTERED ACCOUNTANTS' HALL.)

Institute of Chartered Secretaries and Administrators *16 Park Crescent, W1.* Formed by a group of prominent Company Secretaries in 1891, the Institute was granted a Royal Charter in 1897. The Institute's Headquarters are in Park Crescent, one of the Nash developments of the 1820s.

Institute of Contemporary Arts *Nash House, The Mall, SW1.* Wishing to provide similar facilities for artists in Britain to those enjoyed by American artists at the Museum of Modern Art in New York, Herbert Read and Roland Penrose founded the ICA in 1947. For 21 years its premises in DOVER STREET became a centre for the most advanced thinking in modern art. It moved to the Mall in 1968.

Institute of Contemporary History and Wiener Library *4 Devonshire Street, W1.* The Wiener is a specialised private library (available to accredited researchers who may become members on payment of a moderate fee) with holdings on European history since 1914. There is particular emphasis on German history, National Socialism, extremist movements and modern Jewish history. The library was founded in Amsterdam in 1933 by Dr Wiener, a leading figure in one of Weimar Germany's most influential Jewish organisations. Before the outbreak of the 2nd World War the library was moved to London, and opened at No. 19 MANCHESTER SQUARE on the day the war broke out. It moved in 1956 to 18 ADAM STREET and in 1958 to DEVONSHIRE STREET.

Institute of Directors *116 Pall Mall, SW1.* Founded in 1903 and granted its Royal Charter in 1906. It is the world's largest body representing individual business leaders. In 1978 it moved from BELGRAVE SQUARE to the former UNITED SERVICES CLUB.

Institute of Journalists *Bedford Chambers, Covent Garden, WC2.* Founded in 1884 and incorporated by Royal Charter in 1890. It is the oldest professional organisation of journalists in Britain and is representative of the profession as a whole including radio and television journalists, press photographers and public relations officers.

Institution of Civil Engineers *Great George Street, SW1.* The learned society and qualifying body for the civil engineering profession. Its foundation resulted from a meeting of young engineers at Kendal's Coffee House, FLEET STREET in 1818. Its aims, incorporated in the Royal Charter of 1828, are: 'The General Advancement of Mechanical Science, and more particularly for promoting the acquisition of that species of knowledge which constitutes the profession of a Civil Engineer; being the art of directing the Great Sources of Power in Nature for the use and convenience of man ...' The first President was Thomas Telford, who helped to establish a unique library. Other distinguished Presidents have been Sir John Rennie, Robert Stephenson, Lord Armstrong, Sir Frederick Joseph Bramwell, Sir Benjamin Baker and Sir John Wolfe-Barry. Isambard Kingdom Brunel, Sir William Siemens, Sir Henry Bessemer and Sir Joseph Whitworth have been Members of Council.

Institution of Electrical Engineers *Savoy Place, WC2.* Designed by Stephen Salter. The foundation stone was laid by Queen Victoria in 1886 and the building was completed in 1889. The institution was founded in 1871 as the Society of Telegraph Engineers and in 1880 it became the Society of Telegraph Engineers and Electricians. It adopted its present name in 1888 and received its royal Charter in 1921.

Institution of Mechanical Engineers *1–3 Birdcage Walk, SW1.* Founded in Birmingham in 1847. In 1877 it moved to Victoria Chambers in WESTMINSTER and to its present premises in 1899. These were designed by Basil Slade.

Insurers' Company *see* CITY LIVERY COMPANIES.

Inter-Continental Hotel *1 Hamilton Place, W1.* It was opened in September 1975 at the corner of PARK LANE and PICCADILLY, on the site of an old bomb-damaged mansion house and several other houses. It was designed by F. Gibberd and Partners. There are 500 bedrooms.

International Exhibition *1862*. Henry Cole and Wentworth Dilke suggested to the SOCIETY OF ARTS in 1858 that an international exhibition should be held in 1861, ten years after the GREAT EXHIBITION. But the Franco-Austrian war broke out in 1859 and the exhibition was postponed until 1862. It was officially opened by the Duke of Cambridge in May that year. Tennyson composed an ode for the occasion which was set to music by William Sterndale Bennett. The main exhibition building of glass and iron was designed by Captain Fowke of the Royal Engineers. It was larger than the CRYSTAL PALACE and stood at the southern end of the gardens of the ROYAL HORTICULTURAL SOCIETY in KENSINGTON. The exhibition, which attracted rather more visitors than the GREAT EXHIBITION, was successful enough for Henry Cole to launch another series of international exhibitions in 1871. The exhibition building was mostly demolished in 1864. Some of it was re-erected as the ALEXANDRA PALACE on MUSWELL HILL.

Ireland Yard *EC4*. Named after the family who owned the land in the early 17th century. It covers part of the site of BLACKFRIARS MONASTERY. A few stones from the south wall of the Provincial's Hall, which had the dormitory over it, can be seen here. They are the only remaining relics *in situ*. From 1607 to 1847 it was the churchyard for the parish of ST ANN BLACKFRIARS. In 1613 Shakespeare bought a house nearby for £140. The Deed of Conveyance is in the GUILDHALL LIBRARY. It had a haberdasher's shop on the ground floor and a small yard adjoining it. It was only 600 ft from the BLACKFRIARS THEATRE but Shakespeare leased it at once to a John Robinson. On his death in 1616 he bequeathed it to his daughter, Susanna Hall.

Ironmonger Lane *EC2*. First mentioned as Ysmongeres Lane in 1213, it was inhabited largely by ironmongers until they moved to FENCHURCH STREET in the 15th century. St Thomas Becket is said to have been born in a house at the CHEAPSIDE corner of the lane in 1119. A hospital was founded on the site which was taken over by the MERCERS' COMPANY for their hall in 1540. Their present hall is at the corner of CHEAPSIDE. Two churches once stood in the lane: ST MARTIN POMEROY which was destroyed in the GREAT FIRE and ST OLAVE OLD JEWRY which was demolished except for its tower in 1888. There are parish boundary plaques to both churches outside the entrance to MERCERS' HALL. The basement of No. 11 contains one of the few *in situ* remnants of ROMAN LONDON, a section of a mosaic pavement, with a series of floral motifs set in a geometrical surround carried out in red, yellow, blue and black tesserae, part of a Roman house of the 2nd century. John Boydell, the engraver who became Lord Mayor, lived here and rose every morning at five o'clock, went out to the pump, placed his wig on top of it, and pumped water over his head.

Ironmonger Row *EC1*. Like IRONMONGER LANE, largely inhabited by ironmongers until they moved to FENCHURCH STREET in the 15th century. George Psalmanazar, the eccentric literary impostor who drank 'ten or twelve spoonfuls of laudanum, and very often more' every night, lived here and died in the Row in 1763. Samuel Johnson, much impressed by his piety and the breadth of his knowledge, said that he would 'as soon have thought of contradicting a bishop'.

Ironmongers' Company *see* CITY LIVERY COMPANIES.

Irving Street *WC2*. Formerly known as Green Street, in commemoration of a bowling-green which once stood on the east side of LEICESTER SQUARE, it was first laid out in 1670. When the opening of CHARING CROSS ROAD increased the amount of traffic passing through the street into LEICESTER SQUARE, it became necessary to widen it. Most of the buildings were consequently demolished in the 1890s. It is now a street of small shops and inexpensive restaurants. On the south side at No. 18 are the premises of BERMAN AND NATHAN'S, the theatrical costumiers originally established as military tailors in LEICESTER SQUARE in 1900; and at No. 9 opposite is the BEEFSTEAK CLUB. The street takes its name from Sir Henry Irving, the first actor to receive a knighthood.

Isis *see* TEMPLE OF ISIS.

Islamic Cultural Centre *and* **London Central Mosque** *(Regent's Park), 146 Park Road, NW8*. The first proposals for a London mosque were put forward in the 1920s when the Nizam of Hyderabad instituted a fund for this purpose. No further action was taken until 1940 when Lord Lloyd, Chairman of the BRITISH COUNCIL and former High Commissioner of Egypt, urged by Nashat Pasha, the then Egyptian Ambassador, approached the Prime Minister, Neville Chamberlain. Their proposal received prompt Government support, with the promise of a Treasury grant coupled with funds from Muslim sources to finance the project. A committee under Nashat Pasha was set up, and a site of 2.3 acres at Hanover Gate was purchased out of the funds provided by the British Government. In 1944 the site was formally handed over by the CROWN ESTATE COMMISSIONERS. The building, designed by Frederick Gibberd, was eventually completed in 1978.

Island Gardens *E14*. These 2½ acres of gardens lie by the river on the ISLE OF DOGS with fine views of GREENWICH PARK opposite. A walkway under the THAMES connects with the south shore near the CUTTY SARK clipper. A subterranean forest of elm, oak and fir trees allegedly destroyed by an earthquake, was discovered on the Isle and recorded in Cowper's *History of Millwall*. Both Lysons in 1789 and Pepys in 1665 record finds of fossil nuts and trees here and at BLACKWALL. PEPYS also records the frequent flooding of the area. The gardens were opened in 1895 on the tip of the peninsula. Wren had considered this the best point from which to view Greenwich Hospital.

Isle of Dogs *E14*. The low-lying north bank peninsula created by the great bend in the River THAMES opposite GREENWICH. In the Middle Ages the district was known as Stepney Marsh and came within the hamlet of POPLAR and the parish of STEPNEY. Drainage of the land, probably carried out in the 13th century, enabled a small population to be supported by working the cornfields, meadows and pastureland. A chapel was built for them by 1380. However, Stepney Marsh was submerged once more when the embankment opposite DEPTFORD was breached in 1448. The community was dispersed and the chapel fell into disuse. The origin of the name has never been satisfactorily explained, though it is usually said that it was derived from the royal kennels which were once kept there. The earliest record known is on a map of 1588 and it may simply have been a nickname of contempt. In the 17th century windmills were erected on the western embankment to help drain the land but the Chapel House Farm was still the only dwelling on the Isle of Dogs a century later. Development began in the 19th century when a large portion of the northern part was appropriated for the WEST INDIA DOCKS which were opened in 1802; and in 1805 the Isle of Dogs became an island in fact as well as in name when a canal was cut across the peninsula; this was later incorporated in the WEST INDIA DOCKS. The population grew slowly at first but then rapidly from over 4,000 in 1851 to over 21,000 in 1901 with the development of CUBITT TOWN and MILLWALL. The opening of the MILLWALL DOCKS marked the final disappearance of the old pastureland, although silt dredged from the docks created the mounds in the open space known as 'the mudchute'.

Isle of Dogs Canal Before the great expansion of the docks of the PORT OF LONDON which began in 1802, the inconvenience to ships bound in or out of London of having to round the ISLE OF DOGS caused the CITY OF LONDON to authorise a canal across the neck of the 'Isle' between LIMEHOUSE and BLACKWALL. When this was opened, however, it was found that the passage of the steam paddle tugs required to tow ships through the canal set up a wash which damaged its banks and led to high maintenance costs. When the WEST INDIA DOCKS were opened on the ISLE OF DOGS the canal was closed and transformed into the SOUTH WEST INDIA DOCK.

Isleworth *Middlesex*. There was a neolithic settlement on the banks of the THAMES here, close to the borders with BRENTFORD, but evidence of a sizeable village, known as the Manor of Gristlesworde, with a manor house, two mills and a fishing weir, is not provided until the *Domesday* Survey of 1086. The manor was given to Richard, Earl of Cornwall, in 1227. He built a new manor house, close to the present

Duke of Northumberland public house, and a chapel whose site is unknown. The tower of All Saints church is 14th-century with side walls from the 1705 rebuilding. The present church, completed in 1969 to the designs of Michael Blee, replaced the 18th-century building which was gutted by fire in 1943. Syon Monastery, founded at St Margaret's by a charter of Henry V in 1415, moved in 1431 to the present site of SYON HOUSE. There it remained until Henry VIII dissolved the monasteries, when the site was given to Edward Seymour, Duke of Somerset, who had SYON HOUSE built. A charity school was founded in 1630, which still exists as Isleworth Blue School. In about 1703 Wren reported on the state of the church and drew up plans for rebuilding. These were modified and the resulting church completed in 1706. Several riverside estates were built in the 18th century, making Isleworth a fashionable place in which to live. William Lacy, co-owner of DRURY LANE THEATRE with David Garrick, built Lacy House in about 1750. Later lived in by Richard Brinsley Sheridan, it was demolished in 1830. Isleworth had two ferries; one from the Church closed in 1960, having started in Henry VIII's reign. The second ferry at Railshead started in George III's reign and stopped early this century. Land surrounding the village consisted of either orchards or market gardens. The estates were sold following the opening of the London and South Western Railway to Isleworth in 1849, leading to the first developments of small houses. Pears soap was made in a factory on the London Road in 1862–1962, and many people were employed. The Brentford Union Workhouse was built on the Twickenham Road in 1837, became the Infirmary in 1895, utilising some of the workhouse buildings. The name changed to WEST MIDDLESEX HOSPITAL in 1920. The Thameside wharves provided berths for boats from Scandinavia, bringing wood and coal. There were more housing developments from the early years of this century to the 2nd World War. Since then most developments have been council houses. The Ingrams Almshouses, Mill Platt, were built in 1664 and financed by Sir Thomas Ingram, LORD MAYOR of London. The riverside

Islington High Street c. *1843, showing the Post Office, and a 'Favourite' horse-bus approaching the turnpike gate.*

London Apprentice public house in Church Road was built in about 1741. In Richmond Road are Isleworth House, reconstructed in 1833 for Sir William Cooper, a former chaplain to George III (now an old people's home) and Gordon House, an early 18th-century house with 19th-century additions, containing some of Robert Adam's early work. This is now a further education college. In Twickenham Road are Gumley House which was built in about 1700 for John Gumley, a glassmaker, which has been a Catholic convent school from 1840; and Holme Court, an early 18th-century house, which became a Methodist boys' boarding school and is now used as offices. In 1867 Vincent Van Gogh taught here.

Isleworth Pottery Earthenware made between about 1760 and 1825 in a workshop established by Joseph Shore and Richard and William Goulding. Their mark was S & G.

Islington *N1*. In late Anglo-Saxon times called Gislandune (Gisla's hill), and in *Domesday Book*, Isendone and Iseldone, when its land in the forest of MIDDLESEX was held by the canons of ST PAUL'S. Six manors eventually comprised the parish, the Dean and Chapter disposing of BARNSBURY and CANONBURY to Ralph de Berners, HIGHBURY and Tolentone (*see* HOLLOWAY) to the Knights of St John, to form part of the manor of CLERKENWELL, and retaining the 'Prebend' manor themselves. Much of this residual land, extending from the 'town' of Islington eastwards, passed at different times to the CLOTHWORKERS' COMPANY and others.

Islington, whose earliest church is mentioned in 1317, though the vicars are recorded only from the 15th century, was a natural stopping place for royalty travelling to and from the capital. Henry VI, captured and brought bound to London in 1465, was formally arrested here by the Earl of Warwick; Edward IV and James I on their accession and Henry VII after defeating Lambert Simnel, were ceremonially met here by the LORD MAYOR and ALDERMEN. By the 16th century Islington was noted for handsome, elaborately adorned mansions with gardens and orchards, and Henry VIII, who liked to hunt hereabouts, owned houses both north and south of NEWINGTON GREEN, in the latter of which he supposedly installed his mistresses. This eventually came into the hands of the Parliamentary Mildmay family; it was destroyed in the last century and the site is now Council flats – though Newington Green still has Islington's oldest surviving private houses (1657).

Queen Elizabeth often visited Sir John Spencer at CANONBURY HOUSE; and Sir Thomas Fowler, whose lands adjoined Spencer's and whose house survived until 1850 in Cross Street near Halton Road, had a garden lodge (destroyed 1861) which the Queen especially liked. She also reputedly visited Sir Walter Ralegh at a house in UPPER STREET, and the Earl of Leicester, probably at Ward's Place (*see* ESSEX ROAD).

The hilltop village was soon known as 'merry Islington', renowned for good dairy farms providing London's milk, and pure water from its springs. In the 18th century it rivalled CLERKENWELL as a recreational resort for tea-gardens and amusements, including HIGHBURY BARN, COPENHAGEN HOUSE, the Castle Inn at Colebrooke Row, and the Barley Mow at Frog Lane (now Popham Road). At this last, in 1799, George Morland both painted and drank assiduously.

Less merrily, Islington, being outside the City, was a refuge during plague outbreaks and after the GREAT FIRE. It was also the resort of Dissenters, and in 1557–8 under Queen Mary I, several Protestants, who came to be called the Islington Martyrs, including the Scottish minister, John Rough, were arrested at secret worship, tried and burnt at the stake at SMITHFIELD. From Charles II's reign non-juring clergy settled round NEWINGTON GREEN, setting up meeting-houses and schools, such as Charles Morton's academy where Daniel Defoe and Charles Wesley were educated. Later Mary Wollstonecraft and her sister kept a school here. Samuel Rogers was born here in 1763.

Academies of all kinds for young ladies and gentlemen flourished all over Islington. There was a notable one in Colebrooke Row whose earliest houses were built by the NEW RIVER in 1768. To the north part of the Row, Bird's buildings, the topographical artist Thomas Hosmer Shepherd moved with his family in 1842 from 26 Chapman (now Batchelor) Street, BARNSBURY. At 64 Duncan Terrace, a cottage now no longer detached, Charles Lamb lived in 1823–7, feeling 'like a great lord, never having had a house before'.

Much of the fertile land round Colebrooke Row was used for nursery gardens which were owned with much other property by the Rhodes family; while at Ball's Pond were Barr's and Bassington's nurseries. The landowners profited by the bulding boom in the early 19th century, turning their ground into brickfields which, in turn, in areas like St Peter's and BARNSBURY, became covered with houses. Among the most handsome single streets was Cross Street (about 1780).

The CLOTHWORKERS, who in 1563 had added to their prebendal lands 60 acres bequeathed by Dame Anne Packington, developed in 1846–50 an estate south of ESSEX ROAD, unusual in the regular planning of its broad, straight streets lined with low-rise houses. These included Arlington and Union Squares. The area suffered badly in the 2nd World War, and after repairs the Company sold it in 1945. Since 1937 the Packington Estate proper had been administered by the City Parochial Foundation, which in 1960 sold part to private developers. Islington Council purchased it in 1963, and subsequent demolition and rebuilding (including half of Union Square) of much of the Packington estate were to mark a milestone in conservation legislation.

The CLOTHWORKERS' COMPANY still maintain the Victorian St James's church (1873–5) but have sold the almshouses (1855) – one of Islington's two almshouses now standing. Several had existed off ESSEX ROAD since the 18th century, and in 1829–41 five companies built them in Ball's Pond Road and the neighbouring King Henry's Walk, all in neo-Perpendicular style. Of these only the Metropolitan Benefit Societies' buildings survive.

The REGENT'S CANAL from 1820, and more especially the growth of the railways, increased industry and trade but altered Islington's living patterns. Industries clustered round Belle Isle off York Way, accompanied by hideous slums and later by 'industrial dwellings'. Privileged commuters followed the railways outwards, but throughout the 19th century the population swelled alarmingly. After 1901 Islington declined both in numbers and prosperity. Although rediscovery by the professional classes since the 1960s has revived

The Charms of Dishabille or New Tunbridge Wells. *Taking the waters at Islington Spa in 1733.*

social amenities – like Camden Passage antiques market and small theatres – the borough as a whole (combined with FINSBURY in 1965) has remained depressed, with a serious unemployment and housing problem.

Islington Spa or **New Tunbridge Wells** A chalybeate spring opposite SADLER'S WELLS was analysed by Robert Boyle in 1684 and found to be similar to Tunbridge water, and was patronised in summer for its medicinal properties; gardens and lime-walks adjoined. Ned Ward's verses of 1691 and 1694, when admission was 3d, describe very mixed company in its arbours, coffee-room and dancing and lottery 'sheds'. Long afterwards Lady Mary Wortley Montagu claimed she had introduced it to the fashionable society which flocked here in 1732–3 when George II's daughters, Princesses Amelia and Caroline, attended regularly and were greeted on Princess Amelia's birthday by a 21-gun salute as they crossed Spa Fields. As many as 1,600 took the waters in a day. Lodgings were available; there were weekly public breakfasts, and from 11 to 3, dancing. Poems and pamphlets lauded the gardens' beauties and the waters' cures for 'Hysterics, Vapours, Dropsies, and Swellings of the Legs, Rheumatism, Scurvy, Jaundice ... Want of Digestion, Gravel, Gout, Strangury ...' The reputation of the spa later declined, and Colman's play *The Spleen* (1776) satirises a now bourgeois clientele. In 1803, however, *Londinium Redivivum* describes the gardens' still spacious charm with picturesque trees, pedestals and urns set in open fields. But about 1810 small terraces began to encroach upon them through one of which, Lloyd's Row, a new south entrance was made. The proprietor's house, inscribed 'New Tunbridge Wells, or Islington Spa', survived until this century. A surgeon, Molloy, in 1826 refurbished the pilastered steps displayed glowing testimonials. But demolition of the 40 ft coffee-room began the following year, and in 1840 the gardens were built over, only the spring flowing until the 1860s 'in an obscure nook, amidst a poverty-stricken and squallid [*sic*] rookery of misery and vice'. The humble cottages were damaged during the 2nd World War; and in the 1950s the Spa Green Estate of tall council blocks was built on the site.

Italian Hospital *Queen Square, WC1*. Founded in 1884 by Commendatore Giovanni Battista Ortelli in his private house at No. 41 Queen Square for poor sick Italians. In 1897 an adjoining house in Boswell Street was acquired. In 1898 No. 42 Queen Square was bought. In 1899 the hospital was rebuilt by Thomas Cutler. It now exists as a voluntary hospital outside the National Health Service. The patients are nursed by nuns. In 1982 there were 49 beds.

Iveagh Bequest *see* KENWOOD.

Iverna Gardens *W8*. The Armenian church of St Sarkis was built in 1922 by Calouste Sarkis Gulbenkian, the millionaire, as a memorial to his parents.

Ivy Lane Club *Ivy Lane, Paternoster Row*. Founded by Samuel Johnson in 1749, the club held weekly meetings at the KING'S HEAD. A fellow-member, Sir John Hawkins, said it was 'a great relief' to Johnson to come here after the fatigue of study: 'He generally came to it with both a corporal and mental appetite; for our conversation seldom began till after a supper, so very solid and substantial, as led us to think that with him it was a dinner ... Johnson was, in a short time after our assembling, transformed into a new creature ... His countenance brightened: his mind was made to expand, and his wit to sparkle: he told excellent stories: and in his didactic style of conversation, both instructed and delighted us.' Other members included John Hawkesworth, a writer, Samuel Dyer, a gentleman of no occupation and modest means, a bookseller, a merchant and three doctors. One of these was Johnson's young friend, Richard Bathurst, whom he loved 'above all living creatures'; another was Edmond Barker, whom Johnson so frequently snubbed for being a Unitarian that he did not often attend.

J

Jack Straw's Castle *North End Way, NW3.* A famous old coaching inn on HAMPSTEAD HEATH, rebuilt in 1964 to the designs of Raymond Erith. The original building was named after one of the leaders of the PEASANTS' REVOLT, who burned down the PRIORY OF ST JOHN in CLERKENWELL and who took refuge on the site of the present inn until caught and executed by the King's men. The inn was patronised by Wilkie Collins, Thackeray and Dickens.

Jackson's of Piccadilly *171–172 Piccadilly.* John Jackson was in business as a chandler and oil man as early as 1604. From the 1680s members of his numerous family were pursuing various trades in the PICCADILLY area. Among them, William Jackson was working as a merchant's help in 1685; and his nephew William Jackson, by 1765, as an oil man. By the mid-1820s under Richard Jackson, wax and tallow chandler of 190 PICCADILLY, all the different family businesses were consolidated. The family lived over the shop until about 1840 when the firm moved to Egyptian House, at 171–172 PICCADILLY. It expanded, supplying groceries, wine, tobacco, fruit, poultry and game, soap and perfumery, and, especially, tea. The PICCADILLY shop shut its doors in 1980 though the name is still used for goods supplied to other stores.

Jacob's Island *Bermondsey.* Famous as the site of Bill Sikes's death in *Oliver Twist*. It stands beside the polluted NECKINGER, 'the very capital of cholera'. After being attacked about the fictitious nature of the site, Dickens wrote this defence in the preface to a new edition of the novel: 'In the year 1850 it was publicly declared in London by an amazing alderman that Jacob's Island did not exist and never has existed. Jacob's Island continues to exist like an ill-bred place as it is in the year 1867, though much improved and changed.' A plan from Wilkinson's *Londinia* (1818)

Jacob's Island, Bermondsey, in Victorian times an infamous rookery and the scene of Bill Sikes's death in Oliver Twist.

shows a space between Jacob Street and London Street which probably represents the island. The present-day Jacob Street marks the site.

Jaeger *204 Regent Street, W1.* Clothing store founded in 1884 by Lewis Tomalin, a disciple of Dr Gustav Jaeger, who advocated the exclusive use of animal fibre in clothing. The first shop, which opened in FORE STREET, bore over its door the inscription, 'Dr Jaeger's Sanitary Woollen System'. The cult was taken up by various prominent men: Oscar Wilde was a regular customer and George Bernard Shaw walked about London in a knitted brown Jaeger suit. The fibre was the subject of an enthusiastic leading article in *The Times* on 4 October 1884. Not intended as a commercial venture, the enterprise proved so successful that Tomalin soon expanded it. Jaeger garments were taken by Stanley to Africa when he went in search of Dr Livingstone, by Nansen on his first great Polar voyage and by Scott and Shackleton to the Arctic. By 1900 there were 20 Jaeger shops and a thriving wholesale company.

During the early 1920s Humphrey Tomalin, grandson of the founder, created a new and fashionable image for Jaeger, and in 1935 the company moved to their present address from OXFORD STREET.

Jamaica Coffee House *St Michael's Alley.* Established in the 1670s on part of the glebe land of ST MICHAEL, CORNHILL. Most of its customers were concerned with trade in Jamaica. The house was 'but little damaged' in the CORNHILL fire of 1748 and was not only used as a business address by traders, but also as a place where letters for the island could be left and received. Roach's handbook of 1793 states that the best rum could be obtained at the Jamaica, and that 'one sees nothing but aquatic captains in the trade of that island'. In the middle of the 19th century, the Jamaica was still established as the place for information about the island, for shipping-lists, and was described as 'the best place, above all others, to ascertain any information relative to the mail packets on the West Indies station, or the merchant vessels making these voyages.' The Jamaica Wine House, established in 1869, stands on the site.

Jamaica Road *SE1, SE16.* Takes its name from the former Jamaica Tavern, visited by Pepys, who also visited the Cherry Garden in Cherry Garden Street. The most notable building today is the Roman Catholic church of the Most Holy Trinity, Dockhead, designed by H.S. Goodhart-Rendel and rebuilt in 1960. St James's church nearby in Thurland Road was built in 1829 and rebuilt in 1960, after war damage, by Goodhart-Rendel. Wilson Grove represents a pre-war Borough Council attempt to build a 'garden city' in BERMONDSEY. The bronze, *Draped Seated Woman*, on the Stifford Estate is by Henry Moore (1954–8).

James Allen's Girls' School *East Dulwich Grove, SE22.* In 1741 James Allen, Master of the College of God's Gift of Dulwich (*see* DULWICH COLLEGE), gave to that foundation six houses in KENSINGTON, producing a gross income of £21 6s to provide 'a Schoolmistress or Mistresses for instructing and teaching such and so many poor boys to read, and so many poor girls to read and sew as to the Master shall seem meet.' The new school (the Dulwich Reading Room) was at first housed in an inn, later called the French Horn. Up to 1807 the property's income was £15 per annum, but with renewal of leases it increased to £200 which enabled the school to provide separate rooms for boys and girls. By 1826 numbers were 120. The Dulwich College Act of 1857 made other provision for boys (*see* DULWICH COLLEGE) and led to land being assigned from the College estates for a new girls' school in DULWICH VILLAGE which opened in 1866. A Charity Commissioners' Report of 1878 described the school as an efficient, independent, elementary school for girls with accommodation for 150 and attendance of about 70 girls paying fees of 2d per week if from DULWICH and 4d for others. With the new scheme for the Alleyn's College Foundation in 1881 the Estates Governors assigned three acres and £6,000 to build a new school in East Dulwich Grove. At its opening in 1886 there were 122 pupils. Later the buildings were greatly extended as were the grounds which today cover 20 acres and include the Botany Gardens which have been a special feature of the school since 1896.

Jeannetta Cochrane Theatre *Southampton Row, WC1.* Opened in 1964 as a school for the Theatre Department of the CENTRAL SCHOOL OF ART AND DESIGN. It was named after Jeannetta Cochrane, formerly the head of the Department.

Jenny's Whim *Pimlico.* Tavern and tea gardens which stood at the end of the wooden Ebury Bridge spanning the reservoir of CHELSEA WATERWORKS. It was celebrated for the 'amusing deceptions' in the garden. Devices triggered by hidden springs caused figures of harlequins and monsters to jump up before the unsuspecting. Some of these figures, wrote Henry Angelo, 'were ugly enough to frighten the onlooker'. Floating models on the lake gave the impression of mermaids and fish rising from the water. The price of a pot of beer included entrance to 'Perrot's inimitable Grotto', while a decanter of Dorchester and a turn at duck-hunting cost 6d. Horace Walpole wrote to Montagu in 1750 that Lord Granby had arrived to meet him, 'very drunk from Jenny's Whim'. He had dined there with Lady Fitzroy, whom he was to marry shortly after, and left her playing at brag with friends. The gardens lost popularity towards the end of the 18th century, and by 1804 only the tavern remained. The premises were demolished in 1865 to make room for the extension of VICTORIA STATION.

Jermyn Street *SW1.* Completed in the early 1680s on part of a large area of crown land which had been granted to Henry Jermyn, Earl of St Albans. There is a relief on the façade of No. 73, on the corner of BURY STREET, depicting Charles II handing over the deeds to Jermyn. He was an assiduous courtier who owed his influence to the King's mother, Henrietta Maria, whose secret husband he was reported to be and whose

Vice-Chamberlain he had been appointed in 1628. During the court's exile he enjoyed the complete management of her finances which enabled him to afford a carriage and an excellent table, while other, more scrupulous courtiers were living in penury. At the Restoration he was, in accordance with Henrietta Maria's desire, created an earl and appointed ambassador in Paris where he seems to have found opportunities to increase his already substantial fortune. None of the houses in the street put up in Jermyn's time remains. No. 106 by Treadwell and Martin is a Jacobean pastiche of 1906. The last remaining early 18th-century house has recently been demolished. So have the Savoy Turkish Baths (George Somers Clarke, 1862), for long a feature of the Street at Nos 91–92 until their demolition in 1976.

At first the west end of the street was more fashionable than the east: the 1st Duke of Marlborough had a house at the west end in 1675–84, while at a slightly later time Thomas Gray, the poet, lodged at the other end over 'Robert's the hosiers, or at Frisby's the oilman's'. By the early 19th century the street was noted for its hotels where 'all the articles of consumption' were of the best, and 'the accommodations', much to 'the injury of taverns and lodging-houses', combined 'all the retirement and comforts of home with the freedom of access, egress, and ingress, which one generally expects when abroad'. Among these hotels were Blake's, Reddish's, Miller's, Topham's, the St James's (where Walter Scott stayed) and, later, the Waterloo, afterwards known as Jules. Jules Bar is still on the site at No. 85. The luxury restaurant À L'Ecu de France is at No. 111. The one remaining hotel, however, is the CAVENDISH. The street is now more renowned for its fashionable men's shops. Harvie and Hudson, the shirtmakers (founded in 1929), are at No. 97 which has one of the finest mid-Victorian shop fronts in London. Other shirtmakers are Turnbull and Asser (founded in 1885) at Nos 70–72 in a building of 1902–3 by Reginald Morphen; New and Lingwood (founded in 1865) at No. 53; Hilditch and Key (founded in 1899) at No. 73; and T. Hodgkinson (established since 1849) who have recently moved from No. 112, a building of 1900, also by Reginald Morphen, to No. 23 opposite. Bates, the hatters (founded in 1900), are at No. 21A; RUSSELL AND BROMLEY, the boot and shoe retailers, at No. 95. Old-established shops of a different kind are Floris, the perfumers, at No. 89; Paxton and Whitfield, the provision merchants (founded by a Suffolk cheesemonger at CLARE MARKET in about 1740) at No. 93 where there is as varied a selection of cheeses as any in London; and ALFRED DUNHILL, the tobacconists, at No. 50. Astleys, the tobacconists at No. 109, were established in 1862. The south façade of Simpson's (*see* PICCADILLY) covers the site of the MUSEUM OF PRACTICAL GEOLOGY.

A plaque by the door of No. 87 indicates the site of a house once occupied by Isaac Newton. Other distinguished residents and lodgers in the street include Thomas Lawrence in 1787–90; Sydney Smith in 1811; Tom Moore in 1825; Gladstone in 1832, when he lived over a corn chandler's when first elected to Parliament; and Thackeray in 1842. Thomas Wall, remembered for his ice cream, was born in 1846 at No. 113, now Rowley's Restaurant.

Jerusalem Coffee House *Cowper's Court, Cornhill.* Its early history is undocumented, but by 1776, according to William Hickey, it was 'the general resort of all those who had anything to do with India'; and towards the end of the century, a London directory indicated that many of its customers were 'gentlemen who are, or have been in the service of the Honourable East India Company and the managing owners of the ships employed in their service; also the merchants, policy and insurance brokers concerned with the East India trade. To this coffee house and Lloyd's are transmitted the earliest accounts of the departure, arrival and loss of ships in the company's service and of all important events that happen.' Towards the end of the 19th century the Jerusalem became an exchange for the conduct of shipping business.

Jewel Tower *Westminster Abbey precincts, SW1.* A survival of the PALACE OF WESTMINSTER. Built of Kentish ragstone in 1365–6, it was probably designed by Henry Yevele. On three storeys, and surrounded by a moat, it was used to contain the King's valuables including his jewels, clothes, furs and gold vessels. Its use for this purpose continued until the reign of Henry VII. In 1621–1864 parliamentary records were kept here; thereafter it was used, until 1938, by the Weights and Measures Office. It now houses a collection of pottery and other objects found during excavations in the area.

Jewin Crescent *Barbican.* Built in 1805 to the north of JEWIN STREET on the site of Bull Head Court and Nixons Square. It was originally residential but by the 1880s had been filled with warehouses. Until 1910 there was a brass foundry at the east end. It was completely destroyed in the 2nd World War.

Jewin Street *Barbican.* By the middle of the 12th century Jews had settled in the district in considerable numbers. In 1177 Edward I granted them a patch of ground here for burying their dead. The Barons desecrated the graves in 1215 and took some of the head stones to repair Lud Gate. When the Jews were expelled from England in 1290, their burial ground was granted to William de Monte Forte, Dean of ST PAUL'S. In Stow's time it was being built on. In 1660–4 John Milton lived here whilst writing part of *Paradise Lost.* In 1809–78 a nonconformist chapel, used first by Presbyterians and later by Wesleyan Methodists, stood at the west end of the street. In the 2nd World War the entire street was destroyed.

Jewish Burial Ground *see* BURIAL GROUNDS.

Jewish Cemetery *see* CEMETERIES.

Jewish Museum *Woburn House, Upper Woburn Place, WC1.* The first permanent collection of Jewish items opened to the public in England. In 1931 a proposal was made to Sir Robert Waley Cohen, the vice-president of the United Synagogue, to house a museum in the new Jewish Communal Centre, which was designed by Ernest Joseph. It opened in 1932 and now contains over 1,000 items relating to Anglo-Jewish history, dating from the 13th century.

Jewry Street *EC3.* Formerly known as Poor Jewry because, in Stow's words, 'of old time were certain tenements, called *The Poor Jewry,* of Jews dwelling there.' The Sir John Cass Foundation is at No. 31 (*see*

SIR JOHN CASS SCHOOLS), also the CITY OF LONDON POLYTECHNIC.

Jews' Cemetery *see* CEMETERIES.

Jews' College *11 Montagu Place, Montagu Square, W1.* Founded in 1855 as an Institute of Higher Jewish Studies leading towards both undergraduate (BA Hons) and graduate (M Phil and PhD) degrees as well as Rabbinical Semichah: B Ed degrees for Teachers and also Cantorial Diplomas. The College buildings, which were designed by Yorke, Rosenberg and Mardall (1956–7), include a magnificent library consisting of 60,000 volumes.

Jews' Harp *Marylebone Park.* A well-patronised 18th-century tavern, tea-garden and pleasure ground situated between the present Broad Walk, REGENT'S PARK and the north-east corner of the botanical gardens. It consisted, according to a description given in 1722, of 'a large upper room, ascended by a large outside staircase, for the accommodation of the company on ball-nights; and in this room large parties dined. At the south front of these premises was a large semicircular enclosure with boxes for tea and ale drinkers, guarded by deal-board soldiers between every box, painted in proper colours. In the centre of this opening were tables and seats placed for smokers. On the eastern side of the house there was a trap-ball ground; the western side served for a tennis-hall; there were also public and private skittle grounds.' It is marked on Rocque's map of 1745. Speaker Onslow often came here incognito. It was demolished in 1812.

Jews' Hospital and Orphan Asylum *Knight's Hill, West Norwood, SE27.* The original Jews' Hospital in Mile End, STEPNEY, was founded in 1795. A new building, in the style of a Jacobean mansion in red and black brick, was started in 1861 on 9 acres of land given for charitable purposes by Barnett Meyers. Designed by Tillot and Chamberlain, it cost £23,000. It was enlarged in 1874 and 1897, and in 1876 the MILE END and NORWOOD Asylums amalgamated with it. The original building has since disappeared.

John Adam Street *WC2.* Formerly John Street and Duke Street, it takes its name from one of the brothers Adam, designers of the ADELPHI. Little of the Adams' work remains. Thomas Rowlandson lived in a house on the site, No. 16 in 1803–27; and John Francis Bentley, architect of WESTMINSTER CATHEDRAL, had his offices here in 1868–1902. The LONDON SCHOOL OF ECONOMICS was started here in three small rooms in 1895. The Little Theatre was in this street during 1910–49. The ROYAL SOCIETY OF ARTS is still on the north-west side.

John Carpenter Street *EC4.* Commemorates John Carpenter, town clerk of London in the early 15th century (*see* CITY OF LONDON SCHOOL).

John Islip Street *SW1.* Extends from VAUXHALL BRIDGE ROAD to PAGE STREET. It commemorates John Islip, the last great Abbot of Westminster who died in 1532 (*see* WESTMINSTER ABBEY).

John Lyon School *Middle Road, Harrow, Middlesex.* Originated from the 'English Form' established in 1853 by Dr Vaughan, the headmaster of HARROW SCHOOL, in order to meet one of the original purposes of Harrow's founder, John Lyon, which was to provide an education for the sons of HARROW townsmen. The Lower School of John Lyon, as it was then known, moved to Middle Road in 1876, becoming an independent public school managed by a committee appointed by the governors of HARROW SCHOOL. It became officially known as the John Lyon School in 1956.

John Prince's Street *W1*. First rated in 1723 and formerly known as Princes Street, it was renamed in 1953 after John Prince, the Earl of Oxford's surveyor, who provided the original plan for the development of the Earl's MARYLEBONE ESTATE.

John Roan School *Maze Hill, SE3*. Mixed secondary school founded in the 17th century. John Roan, Yeoman of His Majesty's Harreyers, provided for the foundation in his will: 'To bring up soe many poore town-borne children of East Greenwich aforesaid at schoole that is to reading, writing and cyphering and each of them fortie shillings per annum towards their clothing until each of them shall accomplish the age of fifteen years.' In 1677 a school for boys was opened; and in 1814 successful application was made to the Roan Foundation – on the grounds that Roan stated 'children' in his will – for the establishment of a National School of Industry for girls. In 1872 two new school buildings, one for the boys and one for the girls, were opened. In 1980 the two Roan schools were amalgamated.

John Street *WC1*. Built in 1754 and named after John Blagrave, a carpenter employed by Henry Doughty (*see* DOUGHTY STREET). The Shaftesbury Society and Ragged School Union had their headquarters at No. 32 from 1914.

John's Coffee House *Cornhill*. Established at the end of the 17th century probably by John Painter. It was later taken over by John Shipton. On the plan of the 1748 CORNHILL fire the house was marked as 'greatly scorched'. By the 1750s those listed as frequenting the house included assurance company directors, Turkish merchants, attorneys, brokers and Russian and Italian merchants. In May 1811, John's took subscriptions for 'the relief of the unfortunate sufferers in Portugal who have been plundered and treated by the French armies with the most unexpected and savage barbarity'. It was destroyed in the fire which burnt down the ROYAL EXCHANGE in 1838.

Johnson's Court *EC4*. Referred to as 'Mr Johnson's Court' in 1647, Mr Johnson being a tailor who had owned it in the previous century. Samuel Johnson came to live at what was then No. 7 in 1765. His friends Robert Levett, Anna Williams and his black servant, Frank Barber, all moved in with him. His own apartment was on the first floor. He remained here for ten years. The magazine, *John Bull*, was started here in 1820. And the *Monthly Magazine* also had offices here. Through their letter box Dickens, 'stealthily one evening at twilight', dropped a contribution which was accepted and printed as his first published work. It later appeared in *Sketches by Boz* as 'A Dinner at Poplar Walk'.

Johnson's Memorial House *17 Gough Square, EC4*. This elegant late 17th-century house is the only original house in GOUGH SQUARE, and the only remaining house of those many in which Johnson lived in London. The timber used in its construction is American white and yellow pine which was brought back as ballast in ships trading with the colonies. Johnson lived here in 1746–59 at a rent of £30 a year. In the attic he compiled the famous dictionary with the help of six clerks. Boswell later said that 'it was fitted out like a counting-house'. Reynolds, on a visit to this attic, noticed that 'besides his books, all covered with dust, there was an old crazy deal table and a still worse and older elbow chair having only three legs'. Despite the convulsive movements of his body Johnson managed to sit in this chair without falling over, and when he raised his great bulk out of it he would balance it with his hand or 'place it with great composure against some support'. Johnson's wife Tetty, who in the opinion of his friend, Robert Levett, was 'always drunk and reading romances in her bed where she killed herself by taking opium', died here in 1752. From here in 1755 Johnson despatched a messenger with the last proofs of the dictionary to Andrew Millar, the bookseller, in the STRAND. When he returned Johnson asked what Millar had said. 'Sir,' answered the messenger, 'Thank God I have done with him.' 'I am glad,' said Johnson, 'he thanks God for anything.' Johnson wrote to Samuel Richardson from GOUGH SQUARE when arrested for debt in 1758, and was sent 6 guineas. He moved from the house the next year. By March 1759 he was living in lodgings in STAPLE INN. From there he moved to GRAY'S INN, thence to rooms on the first floor at INNER TEMPLE LANE. He lived for some time at 7 JOHNSON'S COURT before moving to 8 BOLT COURT where he died.

Little is known of 17 GOUGH SQUARE after Johnson's departure until Carlyle visited it in 1832. He was conducted round by the landlord who told him, 'I have spent many a pound and penny on it . . . I let it all in lodgings to respectable gentlemen by the quarter or the month, it's all one to me.' Carlyle described the tiny garden as little larger than a bed quilt. In 1910 the house was purchased by Cecil Harmsworth, reputedly for £3,500, and restored to its original condition. Since 1914 it has been open to the public. In 1929 it became the property of the Dr Johnson's House Trust. The garret suffered damage in the 2nd World War, but was restored with the aid of a £2,250 grant from the Pilgrim Trust. It has been gradually refurnished with 18th-century pieces. The Johnson relics include a first edition of the Dictionary, many portraits of Johnson, his friends and acquaintances, an alleged piece of the Great Wall of China collected by Johnson, a chair from the OLD COCK TAVERN where it was known as Dr Johnson's chair, and Johnson's silver teaspoons and sugar tongs. The adjoining curator's house is the smallest in the City.

Joiners' and Ceilers' Company *see* CITY LIVERY COMPANIES.

Jonathan's Coffee House *Exchange Alley, Cornhill*. Established by Jonathan Miles in about 1680. It became a meeting place for speculators at the time of the South Sea Bubble and is depicted in one of a series of four prints by Bowles on the *Humours of*

Jonathan's Coffee House in Exchange Alley was frequented by speculators at the time of the South Sea Bubble in 1720.

Stock Jobbing. The *Daily Courant* of 21 November 1720 advertised: 'LOST out of a pocket at Jonathan's Coffee House in Exchange Alley on Saturday 19th instant a plain vellum pocket book wherein was a first subscription to the South Sea Company of £1,000 South Sea Bonds. Whoever brings the said book, with the papers therein contained to Mr Johnathan Wilde in the Old Bailey shall have five guineas reward and no questions asked.' The following year Edward Harley wrote to his sister: 'Nothing arises or increases here but uneasiness, discontent and clamour which reigns in every part of the city. The Exchange is the least frequented place of any of it. Jonathan's and Garraway's empty, and no creatures but passengers to be seen in the Alley, nor any trade stirring but what belongs to common necessaries . . .' The house was destroyed and rapidly rebuilt after the CORNHILL fire of 1748, and was much used by stock and insurance brokers. Damaged by fire in 1778, it did not reopen.

Jones Brothers (Holloway) *350 Holloway Road, N7.* In 1867 William Pearce Jones ran away from home in Caernarvon. He acquired an ironmonger's shop in Pear Tree Terrace (now HOLLOWAY ROAD) and sent for his brother to help turn it into a drapery business. Four years later they had four more shops and were selling men's wear, ladies' underwear, bonnets and fancy goods. They also provided entertainers for parties, and later were said to supply evening escorts for lonely ladies. By about 1885 they had more departments selling china, glass, groceries and ironmongery. William P. Jones was one of the retailers who helped to finance the building of John Barnes and Co. Ltd. In 1982 the firm was part of the JOHN LEWIS PARTNERSHIP.

Peter Jones *Sloane Square, SW1.* Peter Rees Jones, son of Thomas Jones, a Monmouthshire hat manufacturer, was born in 1843 and apprenticed to a draper in Carmarthen. He opened his first small shop in HACKNEY in 1868 but quickly moved to SOUTHAMPTON ROW, BLOOMSBURY and from there to Draycott Avenue (then Marlborough Road). In 1877 he acquired 4–6 KING'S ROAD, CHELSEA and by 1884, being the only large draper's (and furnishing) shop in the area, his business was prospering. By the time he died in 1905 his firm occupied most of the block. But by then business had fallen on hard times, and legend has it that in the spring of 1906 John Lewis walked from his OXFORD STREET shop to KING'S ROAD with twenty £1,000 bank notes in his pocket and bought it outright. In 1914 he handed over the chairmanship to his son, Spedan Lewis, who brought it within the John Lewis profit-sharing partnership. Between 1932 and 1936 the new building by Slater, Crabtree and Moberly was erected. Metal framed with glass curtain walling, it was the first of its kind in Britain.

Jubilee Line Originally called the Fleet Line, the Jubilee Line was built to relieve overcrowding on the most heavily-used section of the UNDERGROUND, the BAKERLOO LINE between BAKER STREET and OXFORD CIRCUS (which used to carry 24,000 passengers an hour in peak periods), and to provide a link between the north-east suburbs and central London. Work on the Fleet Line began in 1972; it was rechristened Jubilee in 1977, the Queen's Jubilee year, and was finally completed in April 1979, at a cost of £87 million, which was met by the GREATER LONDON COUNCIL and the government. Minor improvements were carried out at the 13 former BAKERLOO stations north of BAKER STREET, but the main construction work was on the new tunnel between BAKER STREET and CHARING CROSS and new platforms at BOND STREET, GREEN PARK and CHARING CROSS. The rolling stock consists of 33 modern seven-car trains, previously used on the BAKERLOO LINE, but they are to be replaced in the 1980s by trains similar to those used on the VICTORIA LINE. It was at one time planned to extend the line from CHARING CROSS to FENCHURCH STREET and thence to THAMESMEAD in south-east London.

Jubilees *see* ROYAL JUBILEES.

Junior Carlton Club *30 Pall Mall, SW1.* Founded in 1864 to alleviate the waiting list of the CARLTON CLUB. The club house was built to the designs of David Brandon in 1866, enlarged by J. Macvicar Anderson in 1885–6, and rebuilt as part of a new block by Norman Royce in 1967. Inside is Disraeli's round table used for political meetings at his house in Dover Street.

Justerini and Brooks Ltd *61 St James's Street, W1.* Wine merchants established in 1749 by George Johnson and a young Italian, Giacomo Justerini, in premises which in 1820 became known as No. 2 the Colonnade and finally No. 2 PALL MALL. Justerini, the nephew of a Bolognese distiller, had come to London for love of an opera singer, and his special cordials proved so popular that by 1760 he was able to retire, a wealthy man, to Bologna. George Johnson continued in partnership with his son, Augustus, and shortly afterwards the firm received a Royal Warrant from George III, a distinction which has been renewed by every subsequent monarch. In 1831 George's grandson sold the business to Alfred Brooks who renamed it Justerini and Brooks. In 1954, after 205 years in the original premises, the firm moved to 153 NEW BOND STREET, and in 1968 to its present address.

Justice Walk *SW3.* A narrow way connecting LAWRENCE STREET and OLD CHURCH STREET. It is said, rather improbably, to derive its name from John Gregory, a Justice of the Peace who owned property in Gregory Place and KENSINGTON CHURCH STREET and who took walks here.

K

Keats House *Wentworth Place, Keats Grove, Hampstead, NW3.* Built in 1815–16 as a pair of semi-detached houses in a common garden. Charles Wentworth Dilke, the antiquary and critic and grandfather of the Victorian politician, lived in the larger western house and Charles Armitage Brown, the writer on Shakespeare's sonnets, lived in the smaller. John Keats came to Hampstead in 1816 to meet Leigh Hunt who then lived in the VALE OF HEALTH and who introduced him to Dilke and Brown. The next year Keats came to live in Well Walk with his two brothers George and Tom. In 1818 George emigrated to America and Tom died of consumption. Brown, a bachelor, invited John to come to live with him. Keats accepted the invitation. In 1819 Dilke let his house to Mrs Brawne to whose daughter, Fanny, Keats became engaged; but in 1821 Keats died in Rome.

Much of Keats's best work was written in the house, or in the garden where he composed the 'Ode to a Nightingale'.

The two houses were converted into one by Eliza Chester, a retired actress, who bought them in 1838–9 and added the drawing-room on to the east side. Keats House was completely restored in 1974–5.

Kelmscott House *26 Upper Mall, Hammersmith, W6.* Built about 1780 on the site of a warehouse and formerly known as The Retreat. It was the home of Sir Francis Ronalds who in 1816 invented the electric telegraph, having planted 8 miles of cable, insulated in glass tubes, in the garden during his experiments. When Ronalds offered his invention to the Admiralty he received the reply that 'telegraphs are now [at the end of the Napoleonic Wars] totally unnecessary, and no other than the one in use [semaphore] will be adopted.' Part of the telegraph is now in the SCIENCE MUSEUM. George MacDonald, the poet and novelist, lived in the house in 1868–77 when William Morris agreed to rent it from him for £85 a year. Morris renamed it after his Oxfordshire home, Kelmscott Manor, and established here his printing and design works. The riverside house was in very bad repair when he took it over but he thought it 'might be made very beautiful'. In Bernard Shaw's opinion, he succeeded in making it so. 'Nothing in . . . this magical house . . . was there because it was interesting or quaint or rare or hereditary,' Shaw wrote. 'Everything that was necessary was clean and handsome: everything else was beautiful and beautifully presented.' Morris died here on 3 October 1896. The house still contains the fireplace designed by Philip Webb as a wedding gift for Morris and some original Morris wallpaper.

Kenley *Surrey.* Coena's Lea, a woodland glade belonging to Coena, was formerly part of COULSDON.

In a 'dreadful accident' in 1871, the Chancellor of the Exchequer, Robert Lowe, on a penny-farthing bicycle, knocked over a local greengrocer. From a few scattered farms, a forge and the Rose and Crown (where the old Surrey Hunt met) Kenley's population grew around the Caterham branch railway in the late 19th century. There was a 'sea of top hats' at Kenley Station each morning. Kenley Common provided an aerodrome for the defence of London in both World Wars. From here Spencer's dirigible balloon set forth to drop Suffragette leaflets on Parliament but the wind took it south to Caterham. In 1919 a horse trainer named Dyer put his war gratuity on a horse in the Lincoln and with the proceeds bought Welcomes Farm. His subsequent financial failure was followed by the arson of the farm and the murder of his partner, whose mother, through a dream, led the police to the well where her son's body was discovered. Dyer committed suicide.

Kennington *SE11.* A district in the London Borough of LAMBETH, lying west of WALWORTH, north of STOCKWELL and south of LAMBETH parish. In 1774 it was described as 'a village near Lambeth'. The name may derive from the Saxon *kyning-tun*, the town or place of the king, for the area was once a royal manor. In *Domesday Book* it is called Chenintun, at which time it was owned by one Theodoric, a goldsmith, who held it by grant from Edward the Confessor. The Black Prince once had a palace here which is commemorated by the existing BLACK PRINCE ROAD. This remained an occasional residence of royalty down to the reign of Henry VII. James I settled the manor of Kennington on the Prince of Wales, and Charles I, when Prince of Wales, lived for a time in a house built on part of the palace site. As Duke of Cornwall, the Prince of Wales is still ground landlord of a number of Kennington streets and their dwellings (*see* DUCHY OF CORNWALL). Charles I, when Prince of Wales, granted part of the manor to Sir Noel Caron, ambassador to Holland early in the 17th century, who erected here a splendid mansion, the remnants of which vanished early in the 19th century. Part of its site and grounds now form the OVAL CRICKET GROUND.

East of Kennington Park Road lies the flat open space of KENNINGTON PARK, formerly called Kennington Common, at the south end of which lies a public swimming pool. South of it, in the 18th century, where ST MARK'S CHURCH now stands, the gallows of the County of Surrey were erected, and there many of the Scottish rebels were hanged after their trial in 1746. Their bodies were then beheaded and disembowelled, the heads being subsequently displayed on poles on the top of TEMPLE BAR. During the 18th century the Common was a lively fairground in holiday seasons and there preachers could always collect an audience. South-west of the park across

Kennington Common, now Kennington Park, part of the Duchy of Cornwall Estates, in 1830, with (left) St Mark's church.

Camberwell New Road rises Roper's church of St Mark built in 1824 in the Greek Revival style.

Kennington still possesses a number of terraced houses of the late 18th and early 19th centuries, notably in Kennington Park Road, Cleaver Square and Kennington Road. In Black Prince Road and St Michael's Road stand some excellent DUCHY OF CORNWALL flats of 1939 by Louis de Soissons and a pleasant quadrangle of houses for elderly tenants in the Georgian manner of 1914 by Adshead and Ramsey. Charlie Chaplin spent part of his unhappy childhood at No. 287 Kennington Road with his father, his father's mistress and their child. 'The family lived in two rooms,' he recorded, ' and, although the front room had large windows, the light filtered in as if from under water ... The wallpaper looked sad, and the stuffed pike in the glass case that had swallowed another pike as large as itself – the head sticking out of its mouth – looked gruesomely sad.'

Kennington Park *SE1*. Formerly a common of 20 acres and a part of the DUCHY OF CORNWALL estates since it was conferred on Prince Henry by James I. It was the main place of execution for the county of Surrey. The base of the gibbet has been found under St Mark's church. Some of the Jacobites of the 1745 rebellion were hanged, drawn and quartered here. The fiancée of one of them (James Dawson) died on the spot from shock. The last execution was that of a forger in the early 19th century. Both Wesley and Whitefield preached here to large audiences, sometimes 50,000 strong. In August 1639 Whitefield gave his last sermon before leaving for America. The Chartists called a meeting here in 1848 to which hundreds of police were called by the Duke of Wellington but the afternoon ended quietly with rain instead of bullets dispersing the crowd. The park lodge, designed by Henry Roberts, was originally the PRINCE CONSORT'S MODEL LODGE.

In 1818 some of the original common was used for Camberwell New Road and a part thus detached was

the site for the new ST MARK'S CHURCH begun in 1822 despite the fact that the Enabling Act to use the common land was not passed until 1824, six days before consecration. The remaining part was enclosed in 1825. In 1852 Thomas Miller, the poet and novelist, wrote, 'Kennington Common is but a name for a small grassless square, surrounded with houses and poisoned by the stench of vitriol works and by black open sluggish ditches.' The present park, gardens and sports facilities show how much it has changed. The curtailment of the local games of cricket following the laying out of the park caused the establishment of the Oval Cricket Club. This was leased to the SURREY CRICKET CLUB at a low rental in recognition of their former rights. George Tintworth's *Pilgrimage of Life*, in terracotta (1869), which stands in the Park, is the gift of the makers, DOULTON AND CO.

Kensal Green *NW10*. On the boundaries of the Borough of BRENT and the Royal Borough of KENSINGTON and CHELSEA, it formed a natural expansion of KENSAL TOWN and became fashionable after the opening of KENSAL GREEN CEMETERY in 1832. Some housing of this period survives, supplemented by later Victorian terraced properties. Kensal Lodge and Kensal Manor House once stood west of the cemetery and were successively the homes of the novelist W. Harrison Ainsworth in 1835–53 when Dickens, Thackeray, Landseer and many other writers and artists were among his frequent guests.

Kensal Green Cemetery *see* CEMETERIES.

Kensal Town *W10*. Since the 2nd World War this area has been carefully redeveloped, a few cottages, warehouses and derelict wharves still remaining to suggest its original character. It was built in the 1840s following the arrival of the railway and at that time formed part of CHELSEA (*see* QUEEN'S PARK). Before long it developed into an overcrowded slum area, attracting a number of mission halls and workingmen's clubs, some of which can still be seen in Kensal Road; the new warehouses at No. 166 were designed by John Outram (1980). 'Canine Castle' was a notorious 19th-century establishment here for 'lost' dogs, similar to the one vividly described in Virginia Woolf's *Flush*. The Emslie Horniman Pleasaunce, a public garden presented to the LONDON COUNTY COUNCIL by a former MP for Chelsea after whom it is named, dates from 1914. The 30-storey high Trellick Tower has a futuristic fascination, and the Dock, a public house and narrow boat terminus on the corner of Ladbroke Grove, recalls the early days of pleasure trips along the canal. The name Kensal is derived from Kingisholte, or King's wood.

Kensington *W8, W10, W11, W14, SW5, SW7, SW10.* Anglo-Saxon in origin, the name appears in the *Domesday* survey of 1086 as Chenesit, one interpretation of this being Cynesige's farm. The earliest settlement was probably in the vicinity of the present church, ST MARY ABBOTS, on rising ground above the THAMES flood plain. It was along this central east-west ridge rising to the north of the present KENSINGTON HIGH STREET that the earliest development of Kensington subsequently took place. At the Norman Conquest the manor became one of those held by the de Vere family, later Earls of Oxford, and they remained lords of the manor until the early 16th century by which time the original manor had been subdivided. There was probably a church at Kensington from Saxon times, for a priest is mentioned in *Domesday* and the church itself was presented to the Abbey of Abingdon in the early 12th century for medical services rendered to the son of Aubrey de Vere by the abbot, this transfer accounting for its present name.

The parish, the boundaries of which corresponded fairly closely to those of the old metropolitan borough, was largely rural in character and was noted for its market gardens and nurseries in the southern part. This industry was introduced to the area in the late 16th century and flourished until the 19th when the spread of London made the land more profitable for building purposes. The north was mainly arable and, along with the rest of MIDDLESEX, supplied hay to the London market.

From the early 17th century the low ridge of rising ground situated between the present KENSINGTON HIGH STREET and NOTTING HILL Gate became the site of a number of large mansions whose owners found there all the advantages of a country estate within easy reach of London. HOLLAND HOUSE was built in about 1606, CAMPDEN HOUSE in about 1612, and others followed; this aristocratic leavening of the local population was further stimulated in 1689 when William III bought Nottingham House and commissioned Wren and others to turn it into KENSINGTON PALACE. In 1705 John Bowack in his *Antiquities of Middlesex* described Kensington as having '... ever been resorted to by persons of quality ... and is inhabited by gentry and persons of note; there is also abundance of shopkeepers and ... artificers ... which makes it appear rather like part of London, than a country village.'

Although the presence of the Court until 1760 certainly stimulated trade and local employment, the resident population was probably not more than 1,000 by the 1690s, though by the first census of 1801 this had reached 8,556. Its reputation as a healthy locality not only attracted well-to-do residents but brought many visitors for shorter periods. Both Pepys and Evelyn mention excursions of pleasure to Kensington in their diaries and Evelyn described a visit to the BROMPTON PARK NURSERY, one of the most famous nursery gardens of its day. Kensington was also then noted for the proliferation of private schools in the many large houses available. This activity has continued down to the present. Such houses were also suitable as private asylums and there were a number of these in the parish.

The 19th century witnessed a remarkable transformation from a rural parish of less than 10,000 inhabitants, governed in the main by voluntary part-time officials, to a metropolitan borough with a population of 176,628 in 1901. The new borough was administered by a council which employed a large staff of professionals and craftsmen, providing many services unknown a hundred years before. In the interim the physical environment had changed out of all recognition. Gone were the farms and market gardens of the early 1800s, replaced by street after street of new houses. Estate development played an important role in this and early development of the LADBROKE, NORLAND, PHILLIMORE and SMITH'S CHARITY ESTATES was followed in the 1850s by the South Kensington estate of the Commissioners for the GREAT EXHIBITION of 1851. Metropolitan borough status in 1900 was followed, in 1901, by the title of 'Royal' to confer a mark of distinction on the birthplace of Queen Victoria whose youth was spent at KENSINGTON PALACE. The present BOROUGH was formed in 1965 by a merger with CHELSEA.

Kensington and Chelsea Town Hall *Hornton Street, W8.* Completed in 1976 to the designs of Sir Basil Spence. The bronze abstract, *River Form*, is by Barbara Hepworth (1977); the stone relief, *The Sun Worshipper*, by Jacob Epstein (begun in 1910 and placed here in 1980); and the stone, *Lion and Unicorn*, by William Macmillan (1960), who also made the gilded brass figure standing on one foot (1960) which serves as a lightning conductor.

Kensington Canal In 1839, following an agreement made three years before, the Kensington Canal was vested in the West London Railway, and in 1845 it was drained and used for a railway line. It was made in 1827–8 from a rivulet rising in KENSAL GREEN and entering the THAMES at Sandford Creek.

Kensington Cemetery *see* CEMETERIES.

Kensington Church Street *W8.* Once a country lane between NOTTING HILL Gate and KENSINGTON village. A toll gate divided it at Campden Street until 1864. The upper part was known as Silver Street and the lower part as Church Lane. A map of 1734 shows development as far as Kensington Place, then the site of the manor pound. Outside the church of ST MARY ABBOTS was the watch house and parish pump. A few 18th-century houses still stand. The barracks were built in 1905; they now house the Kensington Students Centre. The Carmelite Church of Our Lady of Mount Carmel and

Kensington church c. 1750, with (right) the watch house and what became Kensington Church Street, and (left) the stocks and pump.

St Simon Stow was designed by E.W. Pugin in 1865. It was bombed in 1944 and rebuilt in 1959–60 by Sir Giles Gilbert Scott. Muzio Clementi, the composer, lived at No. 128 in 1820–3.

Kensington Court *W8*. Built on the site of the second Kensington House, this estate of flamboyantly decorated houses dates from 1883, the designs being under the general control of the state architect, J.J. Stevenson, who was responsible for No. 1 (now part of the Milestone Hotel). This was the first private estate to be lit by electricity supplied from a local generating station and the engineer responsible was R.E.B. Crompton who founded the Kensington Court (Electricity) Company in 1886 for this purpose. He lived at No. 40 for some 40 years and carried out many experiments there. This scheme marked the beginning of modern public electricity supply and the generating station (no longer used) can still be seen behind Crompton's house. (*See also* ELECTRICITY.)

Kensington Gardens *W8*. The grounds were originally attached to Nottingham House which in 1689 was bought by William III and converted into KENSINGTON PALACE. In 1690 John Evelyn said that 'a straight new way had been made through the park from the palace to the West End.' Part of this survives as Rotten Row (*see* HYDE PARK). Queen Mary took a great interest in the gardens and had those south of the palace laid out by the royal gardeners, Henry Wise and George London, with box and yew hedges in formal Dutch patterns. *An Account of Gardens near London* described the palace grounds as 'not great nor abounding with fine plants. The orange, lemon, myrtle and other trees they had there in summer were all removed to Mr London's and Mr Wise's greenhouse at Brompton Park a little mile from them. But the walks and grass laid very fine.' In 1702–8 an alcove was built for Queen Anne by Sir Christopher Wren at the end of the walk leading directly south from the palace but was moved to its present position near Marlborough Gate in the late 19th century (*see* HYDE PARK). Queen Anne did not like formal Dutch gardens and had most of

them uprooted. In about 1705 Wise produced a plan for laying out the garden, showing the Round Pond as an oblong, the Serpentine as a chain of ten ponds, and the Broad Walk.

In 1712 Addison mentions in the *Spectator* that a gravel pit to the north had been made into a sunken garden. In about 1726 Wise and Charles Bridgman produced another scheme for the gardens which was adopted. George II opened the gardens on Saturdays to 'respectably dressed people' when the court was at RICHMOND. The Broad Walk became as fashionable as THE MALL had been a century before. In about 1726–7 a small temple was built, probably by William Kent, in the south-east corner of the gardens. It was later incorporated into Temple Lodge but has now been restored and cleared of encumbrances. The Round Pond was filled with water in 1728. George II was 'in the habit of walking every morning alone round the garden,' his great grandson, William IV, told Lord Duncannon, 'and one day a man jumped over the wall, approached the King, but with great respect, and told him he was in distress, and was compelled to ask him for his money, his watch, and the buckles in his shoes. The King gave him what he had about him, and the man knelt down to take off his buckles, all the time with profound respect. When he had got everything, the King told him that there was a seal on the watch-chain of little or no value, but which he wished to have back, and requested he would take it off the chain and restore it.' The man said he would do so provided the King did not mention the robbery to anyone. The bargain was made and the man returned the seal at the same hour on the same spot the next day.

A revolving summer house was built in 1733 in the south-east corner of the gardens on a mount of earth excavated from the Serpentine. Both have now gone. Barracks for the Life Guards were built in 1754 at the south end of the Broad Walk but were demolished in 1841. William IV opened the park to the public all the year round and in 1843 a Flower Walk was made. Kensington Palace Gardens were built on the site of the palace kitchen garden. In 1863 the ALBERT MEMORIAL was begun and completed in 1872. A granite obelisk of

1864 commemorates John Hanning Speke's discovery of the source of the Nile. The statue of Queen Victoria outside her birthplace was erected in 1893 and that of William III in 1907 (see STATUES). The sculpture, *Physical Energy*, is by G.F. Watts (1904). The sunken garden to the east of the palace was created in 1909. The statue of Peter Pan by Sir George Frampton dates from 1912 (see STATUES) and the Elfin Oak, a tree stump carved with small animals by Ivor Innes, was set up in 1928 in the children's playground at the north end of Broad Walk by Black Lion Gate. The original swings here were a gift from J.M. Barrie. Diseased elms along the Broad Walk were cut down and replaced with oak and copper beech in 1953. The park extends to 275 acres. The bronze does and fawns on the top of the Queen's Gate entrance are by P. Rouillard (1919).

Kensington Gate *W8*. Built in the early 1850s partly on the site of a workhouse which had been constructed some 70 years before by the Campden Charities, a trust created in the 17th century for the poor of Kensington by the wills of the 1st Viscount Campden and his wife. The workhouse was demolished when the site became so valuable that it was deemed advisable to build a new and larger one in MARLOES ROAD. The narrow square was originally called Gloucester Square but by 1852 became known as Kensington Gate: a toll gate for travellers between KNIGHTSBRIDGE and KENSINGTON still stood nearby where it was to remain for another 12 or so years. The houses, with Ionic porches and Italianate façades, were designed for the kind of well-to-do families who lived in HYDE PARK GATE and PALACE GATE. The sculptor, Richard Westmacott the Younger, was living with five servants at No. 1 in 1861. It was described by Leigh Hunt as 'having one of those unmeaning rounded towers whose tops look like pepper-boxes, or "Trifles from Margate"'.

Kensington Gore *SW7*. Takes its name from the Old English *gara*, a triangular piece of land left when ploughing irregularly shaped fields. It is a road rich in historical associations. Residents included the composer, William Boyce (1766–79) and John Broadwood, musical instrument maker (1787–1812). At GORE HOUSE resided in turn Admiral Lord Rodney (1784–9), William Wilberforce (1808–21), and the Countess of Blessington with Count Alfred D'Orsay (to 1849), while Alexis Soyer, the famous chef, opened a restaurant there during the GREAT EXHIBITION. The ROYAL GEOGRAPHICAL SOCIETY is at No. 1. The ALBERT MEMORIAL is on the north side; on the south the ROYAL ALBERT HALL and the ROYAL COLLEGE OF ART.

Kensington High Street *W8*. Until the 17th century KENSINGTON was a small country town outside London. In 1689 William III bought Nottingham House and converted it into KENSINGTON PALACE. YOUNG STREET and KENSINGTON SQUARE recently built nearby were used to accommodate courtiers. In 1711–12 Kensington Charity School for boys and girls was built on the north side by John Vanbrugh. To the west of it Lower Phillimore Place was built in 1787 by William Phillimore (see PHILLIMORE ESTATE). By 1800 the high street had been built up as far west as EDWARDES SQUARE and St Mary Abbots Terrace. From 1821 until about 1838 William Cobbett had a house in the high street. Its site is now covered by the

underground railway station which was opened in 1868 by the Metropolitan Railway as part of their extension from EDGWARE ROAD to GLOUCESTER ROAD. In 1869 Our Lady of Victories Roman Catholic Church was built to the designs of G. Goldie. In 1870 John Barker opened two small drapery shops. In 1878 the Town Hall, designed by R. Walker, was built on the site of the charity school; and in 1889 the vestry building which had been built in a Tudor-style by Broadbridge in 1852, was converted into a public library. PONTING'S store was built in about 1893, and the western part of BARKER'S store in 1905, the eastern section being added to the designs of Reginald Blomfield, in 1912–13. In 1926 the Odeon Cinema was built by Julian Leathart. In the 1930s most of the Georgian terraces along the High Street were demolished and replaced by large blocks of flats. In 1933 DERRY AND TOMS store was built to the designs of Bernard George who also designed the rear extension of Barker's (established in Kensington High Street in 1870) which was completed in 1938. In 1958 Our Lady of Victories was rebuilt by Sir Adrian Gilbert Scott after war damage. In 1960 a new public library was opened in HORNTON STREET. Certain Town Hall departments moved into the library's former building. In 1965 the ROYAL GARDEN HOTEL was built to the designs of R. Seifert and Partners replacing Basil Champneys's Royal Palace Hotel of 1890. ST MARY ABBOTS church is on the north side; the Antique Hypermarket at Nos 26–40. The Commonwealth Institute is by Sir Robert Matthew and Johnson-Marshall (1962). The old town hall was partly demolished in June 1982.

Kensington New Town *W8*. A small area to the south of Kensington Road developed in 1837–46 by John Inderwick, a successful businessman, and centred on the inverted L formed by Launceston Place and Victoria Grove. Now the core of a conservation area this little group of streets in late Regency style included shops and a public house in the original design and is an early example of neighbourhood planning. The architectural designs, probably by Joel Bray, are attractive in their variety and their convenience and their position close to the West End soon found them tenants. Today this little area still retains much of its visual attraction and period charm.

Kensington Palace *W8*. Originally a Jacobean house built for Sir George Coppin, it was later purchased by King William III's Secretary of State, the Earl of Nottingham, and hence became known as Nottingham House. Neither William III nor Queen Mary liked WHITEHALL PALACE where the King's chronic asthma was much exacerbated and the Queen felt excessively confined and able to 'see nothing but water or wall'. So, moving out to HAMPTON COURT and keeping WHITEHALL for state and ceremonial purposes, in 1689 they bought Nottingham House, whose grounds strongly appealed to the King, an enthusiastic landscape gardener. Wren was instructed to reconstruct the house and Hawksmoor was appointed Clerk of the Works. The Queen, impatient to move in, went over frequently 'to hasten the workmen', as she put it herself; and, in November, the work having been hurried forward too speedily, 'the additional buildings … being newly covered with lead, fell down in a sudden and hurt several people and killed some, the Queen herself there but little before.' By Christmas, however,

The King's Grand Staircase at Kensington Palace, embellished with a balustrade by Tijou and trompe l'oeil *murals by William Kent.*

work had progressed far enough for the Royal Family to move in. Yet it was far from complete and in February 1690 Evelyn described it as still being 'a patch'd building', though six months later the Queen reported to her husband, 'Kensington is ready.' Even so improvements continued to be made, and a fire in November 1691 led the way to more. During this fire the King and Queen 'stood laughing heartily as the ladies of the court rushed about *en chemise* with needless alarm. Evelyn thought the gardens 'very delicious' and the house itself 'very noble, tho not greate'. It was certainly quite adequate for Queen Anne, who succeeded her brother-in-law, and for her husband, Prince George of Denmark, who, like William III, was asthmatic. Queen Anne decided, however, to have the

gardens altered to conform to the '*English* model'; the Orangery House was built for her in 1704, probably to the designs of Hawksmoor as modified by Vanbrugh. Queen Anne spent much of her time at Kensington in domestic intimacy with her friend, the Duchess of Marlborough, who called her 'Mrs Morley' and whom she called 'Mrs Freeman'. This intimacy was terminated here after a quarrel in which the Duchess crossly complained that she had been 'kept waiting like a Scotch lady with a petition'. The Queen told her to put her feelings in writing and never saw her again. In 1714 Queen Anne died here from an attack of apoplexy brought on by overeating. She left the house 'very much out of repair'; but her successor, George I, liked it because it reminded him of his palace at Herrenhausen in Hanover. He brought over with him a large retinue of German servants and attendants, from mistresses and advisers to trumpeters and plate cleaners; and he appointed William Benson, who had worked for him in Hanover, to replace Wren and to supervise improvements to the house. William Kent also worked here at this time, as did Colen Campbell who was probably responsible for the three state rooms which were constructed in 1718–21. After the death of George I, in his coach on the way to Hanover in 1727, the house became the principal residence of George II and his wife, Caroline. The house was not structurally altered but Queen Caroline spent much of her time rearranging the furniture and pictures and supervising the new layout of the gardens with the help of Charles Bridgman who succeeded Henry Wise as Royal Gardener in 1728. The Broad Walk and the Round Pond were both made at this time (*see* KENSINGTON GARDENS). In 1760 George II died in his water closet and, since his grandson, George III, preferred BUCKINGHAM HOUSE, the house, now more usually known as Kensington Palace, fell into disrepair. After George III's son, the Duke of Kent, was allocated rooms here in 1798, expensive alterations were begun under the direction of James Wyatt. The Duke, however, saw little of them. His debts obliged him to go abroad where he lived with his mistress, Mme St Laurent. In his absence other members of the Royal Family lived here. In 1806 his brother Augustus, Duke of Sussex, moved in and remained for many years, building up a remarkable library of religious books and manuscripts.

Kensington Palace c. 1825. The former Jacobean mansion was reconstructed by Wren and Hawksmoor for William and Mary.

In 1808–13 Caroline, the eccentric Princess of Wales, had apartments here. Her daughter, Charlotte, was a regular visitor until her father discovered she had been left alone in a room with a Captain Hesse and told to enjoy herself. In 1819 the Duke of Kent, having left Mme St Laurent and married Princess Victoria of Saxe-Coburg-Saalfeld the year before, returned to the palace so that his child could be born in England. This child, the future Queen Victoria, was born in a ground-floor room of his apartments on 24 May 1819. In June Princess Victoria was christened here. The Prince Regent, her uncle, created a scene by disagreeing with the choice of names and reducing her mother to tears. After her father's death, the Princess was brought up in the palace by her mother and governess Louise Lehzen, under the strict 'Kensington system' advocated by the Duchess's calculating adviser, Sir John Conroy. On 20 June 1837 she was called from her bed by the Archbishop of Canterbury and the Lord Chamberlain to be told she was Queen. The next day she held her accession council here and managed it so well that both the Duke of Wellington and Charles Greville were deeply impressed. David Wilkie painted the scene, none too accurately. That night she slept away from her mother's room for the first time, and within three weeks had moved to BUCKINGHAM PALACE. The Duke and Duchess of Teck lived here in 1867–80, and their daughter, later Queen Mary, was born here in 1867. From 1880 to 1939 Princess Louise, Queen Victoria's sixth child, lived here. In 1889 the State Apartments were opened to the public on the occasion of Queen Victoria's 70th birthday. In 1912 these Apartments were used for the LONDON MUSEUM which in 1914 was moved to LANCASTER HOUSE. The State Apartments were then closed, being reopened in 1923. In 1950 the LONDON MUSEUM was brought back here and remained until 1975 when its exhibits were removed to be shown later in the MUSEUM OF LONDON. Princess Margaret has apartments in the palace.

Kensington Palace Gardens *W8*. A private road laid out by James Pennethorne in 1843 and lined with opulent mansions built in 1844–70 by distinguished architects. No. 8A is by Owen Jones; No. 12 by Banks and Barry; 12A (the Nepalese Embassy) probably by Decimus Burton, Sydney Smirke and James Murray; No. 13 by Richardson and Tarver; No. 15 by Knowles; Nos 18–19 by T.H. Wyatt and Brandon; No. 20 by Banks and Barry. No. 15A is the Nigerian High Commission; No. 19 the Egyptian Embassy; No. 21 the Lebanese Embassy; No. 25 the Czechoslovakian Embassy (by Sramek, Bacon, Stepanski, with Robert Matthew Johnson-Marshall and Partners, 1969).

Kensington Park Gardens *W11*. This and Kensington Park Road in NOTTING HILL were given their names in the 1840s in the hope that the smart-sounding address would encourage people to come to live here. Sir William Crookes, the scientist, lived at No. 7 Kensington Park Gardens, one of the first houses in England to be lit by ELECTRICITY, from 1880 until his death in 1919.

Kensington Square *W8*. Laid out in about 1681 by Thomas Young. It became highly fashionable when William III bought Nottingham House and converted it into KENSINGTON PALACE. It was originally called Kings Square and until about 1840 was surroun-

ded by fields. Houses on the west, south and north are mostly original, though much altered. Among the inhabitants of the square were the Duchess of Mazarin, 1692–8; Richard Steele, 1708; Talleyrand may have stayed here with Archbishop Herring in the 1790s. J.R. Green, the historian, lived at No. 14 in 1879–83; and Sir Charles Hubert Parry at No. 17 in 1886–1918. Walford Davies and Vaughan Williams both came to him here for music lessons. John Stuart Mill lived at No. 18 in 1837–51. It was here that his maid used Carlyle's manuscript of *The French Revolution* to light the fire. Sir John Simon, the pioneer of public health, lived at No. 40 from 1868–1904. The Church of the Assumption was built to the designs of Goldie in 1875. Mrs Patrick Campbell lived at No. 33 in 1898–1915; Edward Burne-Jones at No. 41 in 1865–7. Burne-Jones wrote, '*Topsy* [William Morris] has given us a Persian carpet which amply furnishes one room. I have a little crib which I call a library, because there I keep my tobacco and my borrowed books.'

Kent House *10 Lower Mall, Hammersmith, W6*. Dates from 1782 and is built of light coloured brick with two great bay-windows, with canted sides, which are carried up both storeys of the house. The doorway is reached by a flight of steps enclosed by a gateway and wrought iron railings. Originally called Mansion House, it was at one time a school and is thought to get its present name from a family who owned much property in the area. It is now the home of the Hammersmith Club Society.

Kent Terrace *NW1*. Takes its name from Edward, Duke of Kent, George IV's younger brother and Queen Victoria's father. It is a plain, severe terrace of houses, facing on to Park Road and backing on to HANOVER TERRACE in REGENT'S PARK. Designed by John Nash, built by William Smith and completed in 1827, its one peculiarity is its 'flat roofs covered in with a recently invented covering called zinc'. E.H. Shepherd, the illustrator of A.A. Milne's Winnie-the-Pooh books, spent his childhood at No. 10.

Kentish Town *NW5*. In medieval times Kentystone and St Pancras seem to have been two names for the same place, a hamlet in a clearing in the great forest of MIDDLESEX. ST PANCRAS was made a prebendal manor by King Ethelbert, and granted to the dean and Chapter of ST PAUL'S in 603. The first mention of ST PANCRAS CHURCH was in Norman times; by 1251 the settlement near the church consisted of no more than 30 houses. However, as the hamlet grew, more houses were built to the north and at least one mansion was in existence in 1415, when William Bruges, first Garter King of Arms, entertained the Emperor Sigismund to an immense feast at his house in Kentish Town. In the 15th century the FLEET RIVER was the cause of a further shift. Because of constant flooding near the church, and to accommodate the growing population in the northern part of the parish, a chapel-of-ease was built in 1449, on what is now the Kentish Town Road, and this became the nucleus of present day Kentish Town. The name is probably a corruption of Ken-ditch; Ken, as in KENWOOD, being the Celtic word for both 'green' and 'river', and the 'ditch' being the FLEET. After the chapel-of-ease was built, the area round the church appears to have been abandoned: 'About this church have bin many buildings now decayed, leaving poor

Pancras without company or comfort.' But Kentish Town flourished, and for the next 300 years was a pleasant village by the FLEET RIVER, encircled by farms and hay-fields and noted for its pure air and clean water. The village was favoured by wealthy outsiders who were glad to build substantial country houses so close to London; but travelling to it could be dangerous. In 1664 the actor, Clun, when returning on horseback to his home in Kentish Town after performing at the King's Theatre, was set upon by footpads and stabbed to death. The antiquarian, Dr Stukely, built a country villa in the early 18th century, which stood roughly on the site of the present-day Bartholomew Place, 'a most agreeable rural retreat . . . absolutely and clearly out of the influence of the London smoak'. Nelson planted trees as a boy in the grounds of his uncle William Suckling's house near the Castle Tavern. The Castle, with its two acres of gardens running down to a stream, was among the most notable of the inns which catered for the many travellers who passed along the road. Others were the Bull and Gate, a main staging post, and the Assembly House which, in 1780, had 'a good trap-ball ground, skittle ground and extensive gardens'. Rebuilt versions of all three remain, without the gardens. Visitors to these inns in the 18th century included Londoners who came on day excursions to enjoy the quiet of the countryside: 'Here are many public houses, it being much resorted to, especially in summer time, by the inhabitants of London.' But the end of the 18th century saw the beginning of a building boom which was to change Kentish Town from a village into a select suburb which was said to be the 'residence of some good families who kept their carriages and suite of servants'. A new parish church, ST JOHN THE BAPTIST, was designed by James Wyatt, and built in 1784. In 1820 Leigh Hunt lived near the Highgate Road (in Mortimer Terrace) where Keats stayed with him, and Mary Shelley, the poet's widow, lived in the Kentish Town Road where she watched Byron's funeral cortège pass by in 1824.

In the 1840s development started in earnest. Speculative builders ensured that farms, pastures and brickfields disappeared beneath rows of villas. Morgan's Farm, which was built in about 1600 for Sir Thomas Hewitt, probably opposite the public house called the Old Farm House, went with the rest. Ford Madox Brown, the artist, lived at 56 Fortess Road in 1856; and Karl Marx was a resident first in Grafton Terrace, in 1856–64, and later in Maitland Park Road where he lived until his death in 1883 (Both these houses have been demolished.) ST MARTIN'S CHURCH by E.B. Lamb, called by Pevsner 'the craziest of London's Victorian churches', was built in Vicar's Road in 1865. After the 1860s the middle-class atmosphere vanished as the Midland Railway developed. Huge tracts of land were acquired for railway undertakings, and soon Kentish Town was transformed into a grimy working-class district, interlaced by railway lines, with many houses in multiple occupation and the FLEET RIVER confined and invisible in an iron pipe. Small industries sprang up; manufacturers of pianos and organs, scientific instruments, suppliers of building materials; and in Angler's Lane (where at the beginning of Queen Victoria's reign local boys had fished in a tributary of the FLEET RIVER), a manufacturer of false teeth. The police station in Holmes Road is by Norman Shaw, 1894–6. At No. 50 Lawford Road lived

George Orwell, who shared a flat here with Rayner Heppenstall in 1935–6.

Kentish Town Road *NW1, NW5.* For centuries the heart of the rural village of KENTISH TOWN. It follows the route of an early road into London from the north and is still heavily used. Between 1440 and 1784 a chapel-of-ease for ST PANCRAS OLD CHURCH stood where Nos 205–213 are today. Near Gaisford Street, on the east side, was the site of Morgan's Farm, a famous 17th-century timbered building demolished during development in the 1840s.

Kenton *Middlesex.* First recorded as the farm of Cena's people in 1251, it initially grew up alongside the Wealdstone Brook. A few old farm buildings can be found scattered around the district but Kenton Grange, which was built in about 1805 and is now an old persons' home, is one of the oldest surviving buildings. The centre of the settlement shifted three-quarters of a mile to the west when a station was opened on the Euston–Watford line in 1912. During 1921–31 Kenton's population rose from 268 to 6,171 and by 1938 its suburban development was virtually complete.

An engraving of Kenwood House, Hampstead, in 1793. It was the home of the Murray family from 1754 to 1922.

Kenwood House *Hampstead Lane, NW3.* Probably originally built by John Bill, the King's Printer, around 1616. In 1694 it came into the possession of William Brydges, Surveyor General of the Ordnance, by whom it was largely demolished and rebuilt. The subsequent brick structure still exists under the 18th-century facade. Sold by Brydges in 1704 at a handsome profit, it changed hands several times before it was purchased in 1754 from Lord Bute by William Murray, later 1st Earl of Mansfield and Chief Justice. Ten years later it was remodelled by Robert Adam who commented that Lord Mansfield 'gave full scope to my ideas'. After Lord Mansfield's death in 1793, his nephew and heir, David Murray, extended the property, engaging the architect, George Saunders. Kenwood remained in the Mansfield family until 1922 when the greater part of the estate was bought from the 6th Earl by the Kenwood Preservation Council to protect it from being sold to a building syndicate. This land, with later acquisitions, was vested in the LONDON COUNTY COUNCIL in 1924 and opened to the public in the following year by King George V. In the same year, Edward Cecil Guinness, 1st Earl of Iveagh, purchased Kenwood House with its remaining 74 acres from Lord Mansfield, and here he installed his collection of pictures which, together with the property, he bequeathed to the nation in 1927. Closed during the 2nd World War, the house became the administrative responsibility of the LONDON COUNTY COUNCIL in 1949 and was reopened in 1950. In 1965 the responsibility passed to the GREATER LONDON COUNCIL.

Before 1793 Kenwood was separated from the HAMPSTEAD–HIGHGATE road by only a forecourt and a high wall, but between 1793 and 1796 the 2nd Earl of Mansfield had the road diverted. This left the house, as it is today, in a secluded setting of garden and park approached by two serpentine drives leading from Hampstead Lane. At the entry to each of these is an octagonal white-brick lodge with gate-piers and gates. The entrance or north front consists of a stucco block by Robert Adam with a central portico rising to the height of the house and surmounted by a pediment. On either side are projecting wings in white Suffolk brick designed by George Saunders which were added in 1793–96. The south front, also by Adam, is composed of a central stucco block, the upper two storeys of which are adorned with slim pilasters. It is flanked on the west by an orangery which was part of the earlier house, and on the east by a library added by Adam. The ornamental details of the façade were restored in 1975 using fibreglass panels which were based on Adam's engravings from his *Works*. These details were originally executed in a patent composition which gave trouble early and caused Lord Mansfield to complain that if Parian marble had been used it could not have cost him as much as Adam's stucco. On a lower level and discreetly sited on the east side of the house is the service wing. Designed by George Saunders, it is in London stock brick of a fine purple-brown variety. Opposite to the service wing and below the terrace is the Brick House, a cold plunge-bath, built about 1755. The park was largely landscaped by the 1st Lord Mansfield who was responsible for the little sham bridge at the east end of the lakes. The siting of the drives, lawns and flower garden adjoining the house may have been inspired by Humphry Repton, who was consulted by the 2nd Earl of Mansfield. The plain brown brick stables near the east entrance, and the farm together with a cottage, dairy and brew-house lying south-west of the west entrance were built by the 2nd Earl of Mansfield and are, presumably, the work of George Saunders.

Robert Adam's library is the principal feature of the interior. Intended as 'a room for receiving company' as well as for housing Lord Mansfield's collection of books, it is rectangular with apsidal ends on the chords of which are pairs of fluted Corinthian columns. The curved ceiling, described by Adam as 'extremely beautiful and much more perfect than that which is commonly called the cove ceiling', is decorated with flat panels of ovals and rectangles. The cornice includes lions and heads of deer, the supporters and crest respectively of Lord Mansfield's armorial bearings.

The south rooms take their shape generally from the pre-Adam house but include some decorative detail by him. The orangery is very plain with an early 18th-century cornice. The music room and the dining-room, by Saunders, are very plain with delicate friezes. The pictures in the house, which form the Iveagh Bequest, include works by Van Dyck, Gainsborough, Guardi, Hoppner, Reynolds, Kauffmann, Landseer, Lawrence, Morland, Rembrandt and Turner. The blue limestone *Monolith* (*Empyrean*) in the grounds is by Barbara Hepworth (1953). The metal *Birdcage* is by Reg Butler (1951).

Keppel Street *WC1*. Built in about 1810 on the BEDFORD ESTATE and named after Lady Elizabeth Keppel, daughter of William Keppel, Earl of Albemarle, and mother of the 5th and 6th Dukes of Bedford. John Constable lived at No. 1 in 1817–21 in a house his friends called 'Ruysdael House'. Anthony Trollope was born in 1815 at No. 6. The LONDON SCHOOL OF HYGIENE AND TROPICAL MEDICINE is here.

Keston *Kent*. The *Domesday* Survey of 1086 calls it Chestan. An Anglo-Saxon charter refers to Cysse Stan, which means the stone of Cyssa. Flint implements and pit dwellings found in the area show that it was occupied as early as 3000 BC. A Roman cemetery has been found together with traces of a villa and a smaller burial site. Keston developed when enclosures of the common land were made in the later Middle Ages. The first large estate in the parish was Holwood, which dates back to 1484 and is known to have been in the possession of Sir Stephen Lennard (who was then Lord of the Manor of WEST WICKHAM) in the 17th century. Among the occupants in the 18th century were Field Marshal Lord Tyrawley, Ambassador to Portugal, who according to one report returned to England with three wives and fourteen children; his daughter, George Anne Bellamy (names given to her by mistake for Georgiana), a celebrated actress and beauty; and, during 1785–1801, William Pitt the Younger. In order to improve the view, Pitt levelled some of the Iron Age earthworks constructed about 200 BC and possibly later used by the Romans. An ancient oak by the public footpath through Holwood was the site where William Wilberforce informed William Pitt that he was resolved to abolish the slave trade. The present Holwood House was built in 1827 by Decimus Burton. Later owners were Lord Chancellor Cranworth and the Earls of Derby. The mansion is now occupied by Seismograph Service Ltd., consultant geophysicists. The remains of the oldest mill in Kent still stand on Keston Common. Inscribed on the mill post is the date 1716. It has not worked since a violent storm in 1878 severely damaged the sails. Keston is now part of the London Borough of BROMLEY.

Kettner's Restaurant *29 Romilly Street, W1*. Established by Auguste Kettner, chef to Napoleon III, in the 1860s, it seems to have been the first foreign restaurant in SOHO – apart from those of the hotels in LEICESTER SQUARE – to have attracted English gourmets. It was celebrated for its comfortable and discreet *cabinets particuliers*. In 1869 a reader of *The Times* wrote a letter recommending Kettner's as a restaurant which had provided him with a dinner which was 'better than he could have obtained at a West-End club'. It was Oscar Wilde's favourite restaurant.

The Royal Mail passing the Star and Garter Hotel and the Kew Bridge Toll Gate in 1835. An engraving after Pollard.

Kew *Surrey*. Situated south of the THAMES between BRENTFORD and CHISWICK. It was called thus (being a neck of land by a landing place) from at least the 14th century when Kew, SHEEN and PETERSHAM were included in KINGSTON parish. Ancient British coins are witness to early settlement encouraged by easy river access and fording of the THAMES at BRENTFORD. From the 16th century courtiers were residing at Kew, close as it was to RICHMOND PALACE: Mary Tudor herself had an establishment there, as did James I's daughter Elizabeth; Sir Peter Lely lived on the site of the Herbarium, which in the 19th century became the home of Ernest, Duke of Cumberland, later King of Hanover. Royal associations continued and Queen Anne gave the site for the church consecrated in 1714. The village with its houses around the Green essentially dates from the end of that century. In 1789 a Purbeck stone KEW BRIDGE (based on designs by James Paine) replaced the wooden arched bridge of 1757. It was replaced yet again by the granite bridge of 1903. In the early 1730s Frederick Prince of Wales leased the property of Sir Henry Capel, renaming the house KEW PALACE, and in 1759 Princess Augusta began the development of Capel's gardens into the present KEW GARDENS. In 1769 Kew was separated from KINGSTON parish, the major part of it soon being taken up by KEW GARDENS. George III bought the Palace freehold, demolishing it in 1803 in order to rebuild (never completed), meanwhile residing at the Old Dutch House, the present KEW PALACE. Throughout the 19th century the church of ST ANNE benefited from royal patronage. In 1892 the Borough of RICHMOND was enlarged to include Kew, which became part of the London Borough of RICHMOND-UPON-THAMES in 1965.

Kew Bridge *Ealing–Kew*. The first bridge was built in 1758–9 by John Barnard with seven timber arches. This was replaced by James Paine's stone bridge in 1784–9. The present bridge by Sir John Wolfe-Barry and Cuthbert Brereton was erected in 1903.

Kew Gardens *see* ROYAL BOTANICAL GARDENS.

Kew Palace *Kew Gardens, Kew*. A small Jacobean mansion, formerly known as the Dutch House, it is the last survivor of a group of royal residences which once stood in, or near, Kew Green. Situated about a mile from Richmond Lodge, the favourite home of George II, the Dutch House was leased by Queen Caroline in 1728 for 99 years for 'the rent of £100 and a fat Doe'. Thereafter it was frequently occupied by members of the Royal Family. In 1731 the house adjacent to it, the former White House, was rented by Frederick, Prince of Wales who, despite his feud with his parents, settled in their immediate vicinity with his family and court. This house, in which George III was born and where he spent much of his boyhood, stood some 50 yards south of the present Palace. A two-storeyed mansion, it had been built of timber and stone in the second half of the 17th century by Sir Henry Capel and featured, according to John Evelyn, a great hall surmounted with a cupola. 18th-century accounts suggest that, apart from the royal apartments, the rooms of the White House were small, dark and draughty, in spite of Prince Frederick's enlargements. The Prince died in 1751 and his widow, Augusta, Dowager Princess of Wales, continued to occupy and improve the property

Frederick, Prince of Wales (father of George III), with his sisters in the gardens of the Dutch House, Kew in 1733.

until her death in 1771, after which George III and Queen Charlotte took possession of it. As the White House, however, was not large enough for the rapidly growing Royal Family, the Dutch House was used as an annexe – at first for the new Prince of Wales and Prince Frederick and later for some of the younger princes.

In 1802 George III caused the White House to be demolished, and most of its furniture and fittings were taken to the Dutch House into which the King moved while awaiting the completion of a new and grandiose palace only 200 yards away. This eccentric edifice, designed by James Wyatt in the Gothic style, was known as the Castellated Palace. Costly and impractical, it was never finished, and the Dutch House remained in royal occupation until Queen Charlotte's death in 1818, after which the Prince Regent ordered its destruction, considering it 'unworthy of Repair, but Execution of the Order was afterwards suspended.' Thereafter the reprieved mansion began to be known as the 'Old Palace' to distinguish it from the Castellated Palace, which was finally demolished in 1827–8. Of the White House, for 72 years a royal residence, only the mid-18th-century kitchen wing survives; a late 17th-century sundial, originally one of a pair at HAMPTON COURT, which was erected by William IV in 1832, marks its site.

The Dutch House was built over the Tudor vaults of an earlier house by Samuel Fortrey, a prosperous London merchant of Dutch parentage, for himself and his wife, Catherine, in 1631. The date, together with their initials, SFC, are commemorated above the main entrance. All that survives of the previous building is a vaulted brick basement containing a well which, as late as 1806, was the only immediately available source of water in the Palace; the reset and much restored linenfold panelling in the library anteroom and, on the 2nd floor, a large Tudor fireplace. The Palace, three-storeyed with attics, is only 70 ft long by 50 ft wide and is built of red brick laid in 'Flemish bond' which gives a rich and varied appearance. The main south front, which faces the site of the former White House, consists of a central block of three bays containing the entrance, and two side wings of shallow projection.

In the garden the older children of George III were instructed in 'practical gardening and agriculture'. A doorway in the garden wall gave access to the river bank. The present garden behind Kew Palace is named the Queen's Garden after Queen Elizabeth II, who opened it to the public in May 1969. It is laid out in the style of a 17th-century garden with herbal plants of the period, much grey stone, and features such as a 'mount' with a rotunda on top.

Kew Railway Bridge *Gunnersbury–Kew*. Built by W.R. Galbraith in 1864–9 for the London and South Western Railway on the short line linking South ACTON Junction with RICHMOND. Wrought-iron lattice girders are carried on ornate cast-iron piers.

Kidbrooke *SE3*. Until the 15th century Kidbrooke was a small but flourishing village, well watered by the three streams from which it derives its name. In the early 12th century Chitebroc possessed a small chapel, subordinate to Charlton church, and by the next century a parish church dedicated to either St Nicholas or St Blaise. However, by 1427–8 the church living was vacant and no new incumbent was appointed. In 1494 there was still no priest and the church was derelict. For reasons as yet unknown the village had died. Until a new church was built in 1867, dedicated to St James, the few inhabitants of Kidbrooke had to attend ST LUKE's church, Charlton or any of the other neighbouring churches. From the demise of the village in the 15th century until suburban development spread over its fields in the 1930s, largely due to the building of the A2 Rochester Way, it was primarily a farming community.

The Red Lion at Kilburn, established in the 15th century, was one of several travellers' inns lying along the Edgware Road.

Kilburn *NW6*. Situated along the EDGWARE ROAD, a major thoroughfare since Roman times. A number of inns catered for travellers. The Red Lion and the Cock, since rebuilt, were established in the 15th century. KILBURN PRIORY was established by the Kele burn in 1130 but by 1600 the Bell Inn had appeared on the site and after 1714 became a fashionable spa.

From the 1840s a regular horse bus service ran along Kilburn High Road and a railway station was established on the main line from EUSTON in 1851–2. The development of the adjoining manor of BELSIZE in the 1840s and the ECCLESIASTICAL COMMISSIONERS' estates in Kilburn Park, as well as the opening of Brondesbury station on the North London Railway in 1860 all brought more people to the area. By 1879, when the Metropolitan Railway arrived, Kilburn was turning into the commercial centre it is today. Buildings of interest include the Kilburn Park housing estate, developed by James Bailey in 1859–67; St Augustine's Church (1880) by J.L. Pearson; Kilburn Polytechnic in Glengall Road designed by A.T. Wakelan; and the Gaumont State Cinema with its dominant tower and richly decorated foyer (1937) by George Coles.

Kilburn Priory *Priory Road, NW6*. A piece of a 15th-century brass 2½ ins long portraying the head of a nun in St Mary's church, Priory Road is all that remains of the little medieval convent that occupied this site. It had been a dependant of WESTMINSTER ABBEY. The present church was built in the Gothic style in 1856 by Horace Francis.

Kilburn Wells In about 1742 the Bell Tavern was fitted up as a pump room where the 'politest companies could come to drink the water from a nearby spring'. The water was a mild purgative, milky in appearance and had a bitterish taste. It was said to be more strongly impregnated with carbon dioxide than any other spring in England. In its day Kilburn rivalled SADLER'S WELLS. In 1773 it was advertised as 'a happy spot equally celebrated for its rural situation and the acknowledged efficacy of its water'. The gardens had been enlarged and improved and 'the houses and offices repainted and beautified in the most elegant manner'. It was open for breakfast. A 'plentiful larder was always provided together with the best of wines and other liquors.' Water tasting continued until the early 19th century when it was superseded by tea drinking. The Bell was demolished in 1863. A stone plaque at first floor level at the corner of Kilburn High Road and Belsize Road marks the site of the spring.

Kiln *Walmer Road, W11*. Situated opposite Avondale Park, this was formerly a pottery kiln standing in a notorious slum area known as the 'Piggeries and Potteries' from its principal 19th-century occupations. The kiln has recently been renovated and forms the dining-room of a house in a new mews development.

King Edward Memorial Park *Shadwell, E1*. Created near the northern end of the ROTHERHITHE TUNNEL in memory of King Edward VII. Formerly a fish market, it was opened in 1922.

King Edward Street *EC1*. Named in 1843 in memory of King Edward VI who founded CHRIST'S HOSPITAL. Earlier names were Stinking Lane, Chick Lane, Blowbladder Street and Butchers' Hall Lane. It was once full of butchers' slaughterhouses but by 1720 Strype said the butchers had left and the street was occupied mainly by milliners and seamstresses. On both sides now are the buildings of the GENERAL POST OFFICE.

King Edward VII's Hospital for Officers *Beaumont House, Beaumont Street, W1*. In 1899 Miss Agnes Keyser and her sister Fanny, at the suggestion of the Prince of Wales, whose friendship they enjoyed, started the hospital in their own house, 17 Grosvenor Crescent, to nurse sick and wounded officers from the South African War. At the end of the Boer War King Edward, as he had then become, insisted that the hospital should be kept open on the ground that there was a great need in times of peace for a place to which sick officers, serving in so many climates all over the world, might gain admission. In 1903 he gave the hospital his name and became its first patron. In 1904 the hospital was moved to 9 GROSVENOR GARDENS, and in 1948, after several more moves, to Beaumont House, where in 1960 they opened a wing for 'patients of the educated middle class of moderate means but not necessarily with service connections'.

King George V Dock *see* ROYAL GROUP.

King Henry's Road *NW3*. Takes its name from Henry VI who gave the land to Eton College which began to develop it in the 1860s. The Holiday Inn of Swiss Cottage (300 bedrooms) is by Dennis Lennon and Partners (1973).

King of Clubs Founded in 1801 by Sydney Smith's brother 'Bobus', later Advocate-General of Bengal, at the CROWN AND ANCHOR TAVERN. Its members included Samuel Rogers, the poet; Richard ('Conversation') Sharp, a rich businessman with literary tastes; J.P. Curran, the Irish orator; Erskine, the Scottish lawyer; Sydney Smith and several others who, like Smith, were regular guests at HOLLAND HOUSE. They met once a month and the conversation according to Francis Horner, one of the founders with Sydney Smith and Francis Jeffrey of the *Edinburgh Review*, 'consisted chiefly of literary reminiscences, anecdotes of authors, criticisms of books, etc.'. The Club was dissolved in 1824.

King of Cockneys A master of the revels chosen by the students of LINCOLN'S INN on 28 December, the Mass of the Holy Innocents, known as Childermass Day.

King Street One of the streets which, once an ancient thoroughfare, disappeared when SHAFTESBURY AVENUE was constructed. Building began in 1677 and was completed in 1692, when it was presumably named in honour of King William III. A few years later, in 1720, Strype described it as 'a pretty good street, but not so broad as most in these parts; yet well inhabited'. In the 18th century it was a centre for goldsmiths and jewellers. It was to her lodgings in this street in 1853, that W.E. Gladstone, then Chancellor of the Exchequer and deeply concerned with the welfare of prostitutes, accompanied a young girl who had accosted him in LONG ACRE as he was walking home from COVENT GARDEN THEATRE. A young man, who had followed them, demanded money or a post in the Inland Revenue. He was subsequently sentenced to a year's hard labour for blackmail, but had served only six months when Gladstone asked the Home Secretary to have him released.

King Street *EC2*. Built after the GREAT FIRE in conjunction with QUEEN STREET and Queen Street Place to form a road from the river to the GUILDHALL.

King Street *SW1*. Laid out on land granted to the Earl of St Albans (*see* JERMYN STREET). Building was completed by 1682 and the street presumably named in honour of Charles II. None of the original houses remains. There were already several fine-art dealers here by the middle of the 18th century. CHRISTIE'S remain at No. 8. Spink and Son are at Nos 5–7 in a building which was redesigned for them in the 1920s and had formerly contained the Feathers, an old public house described in 1899 as 'the latest and highest development in public-house decoration that has so far been reached'. Fischer Fine Art (established in 1972) is at No. 30. The Golden Lion public house occupies a site where a tavern of the same name has stood since at least 1762. ALMACK'S ASSEMBLY ROOMS stood on the south side on the site of the present Almack House at Nos 26–28. At Nerot's Hotel, once one of the most fashionable in London, Nelson met his wife after his return to London from the Battle of the Nile in 1800. The hotel was demolished to make way for the ST JAMES'S THEATRE which was, in turn, demolished for St James's House at Nos 23–24, built to the designs of R. Seifert and Partners in 1959. The balconies are decorated with relief panels on the lowest of which can be seen the heads of Lord Olivier and Vivien Leigh who protested strongly against the theatre's demolition. During his exile in England Napoleon III lived in a house on the north side at the ST JAMES'S SQUARE end.

King Street *WC2.* Built in the 1630s and named after Charles I. Among those who have lived or lodged here are William Lenthall, Speaker of the House of Commons, during the Commonwealth; Thomas Killigrew, the dramatist, in 1637–43; Sir Kenelm Digby, the diplomat and writer, in 1662–85; David Garrick in 1743–5; Coleridge in 1799–1802; and Admiral Edward Russell, Earl of Oxford in 1690–1727. James Quin, the actor, was born here in 1693, Thomas Arne, the composer, in 1710, and Arne's sister, Susannah, who married Theophilus Cibber, one of the best tragic actresses of her day, in 1714. The house in which Admiral Russell and Sir Kenelm Digby lived was converted in 1774 into the first family hotel in London and was known thereafter by the names of its successive owners. Towards the end of the 18th century it belonged to a Mrs Hudson who advertised that it had 'stabling for 100 noblemen and horses'. It eventually came into possession of W.C. Evans who made it famous as EVANS MUSIC-AND-SUPPER ROOMS. It retained the name after its purchase in 1844 by John Green who built on a hall and made it as celebrated for its food as its music. Thackeray was a frequent customer and introduced it often into his books. The building was later occupied by the NATIONAL SPORTING CLUB in 1892–1929. The GARRICK CLUB was founded in King Street in 1831. The headquarters of the Communist Party of Great Britain were at No. 16, MOSS BROS at Nos 20–22. According to Timbs, 'In King Street lived the lady for whom mahogany was first used in England', and a few of the houses in the street still have doors of solid mahogany. None of the original houses, however, survives.

King Street Gate *Whitehall.* Part of WHITEHALL PALACE, it stood south of the HOLBEIN GATE. Completed in 1532, it was a stone, two-storeyed building that had two circular turrets with domed roofs. It had a square central opening, between two circles for pedestrians. Edward Montagu, Earl of Sandwich, lodged here in the mid-17th century, and Samuel Pepys may have had a room in one of the turrets when he acted as secretary to his kinsman and patron in 1655–7. The gate was demolished in 1723.

King William Street *EC4.* Laid out in 1829–35 as an approach to the new LONDON BRIDGE and named after the reigning monarch, William IV. A statue of the King stood opposite the bridge from 1844 until it was moved to GREENWICH in 1935 (*see* STATUES). It marked the site of the Boar's Head Tavern, EASTCHEAP, mentioned by Shakespeare in *Henry IV*, by Washington Irving in his *Sketch Book* and in one of Goldsmith's essays. The Banque Nationale de Paris at No. 123 is by Fitzroy Robinson and Partners (1978).

Kingly Street *W1.* Building began in the 1680s when it was known as King Street. It was described by Strype in 1720 as 'a pretty good Street, having divers very good Houses fit for Gentry'. Many of these were rebuilt in the 1720s and Nos 7–11 and 24 date from this period. There has been a tavern on the site of the King Charles II (formerly the Blue Posts) at No. 18 since at least 1737. The street became known by its present name in 1906.

King's Arms *144 Cheyne Walk, SW10.* A riverside public house dating from the time of Charles II after whom it is named. In 1718 the licensee was Richard Hand, the King's bunmaker.

King's Arms *23 Poland Street, W1.* There has been an inn on this site for over 200 years. The Ancient Order of Druids was revived here in 1781.

King's Bench Prison *Southwark.* Takes its name from the gaols attached to the court of King's

The King's Bench Prison in the early 19th century, after it had become 'the most desirable place of incarceration in London'.

Bench which travelled from town to town. The first prison building stood on the east side of BOROUGH HIGH STREET. In 1554 the martyr, John Bradford was imprisoned here before he was executed. The majority of the prisoners were debtors. In 1653 there were 399 inmates with a collective debt of £900,000. It was at that time and for the duration of the Commonwealth, known as Upper Bench. Prison conditions depended on the prisoner's finances; some had regular allowances from friends, others 'fed like moths upon their clothes'. Richard Baxter, imprisoned by Judge Jeffreys in 1670 for his paraphrase of the New Testament, was joined by his wife and wrote that they 'kept house contentedly as at home, though in a narrower room'. Another notable prisoner in this room was the King of Corsica, imprisoned for debt in 1752. In 1754 an inquiry revealed extortion, cruelty, promiscuity, drunkenness and many other irregularities within the prison. In 1755–8 the prison was moved to a new site in ST GEORGE'S FIELDS. The new building was large and cheerless with 224 rooms and an open courtyard surrounded by a high wall. Wealthy prisoners could buy freedom of the Rules, that was to say 3 square miles surrounding the prison and including taverns and other places of entertainment. In 1759 Tobias Smollett wrote *Sir Lancelot Greaves* while in the prison. In 1768 John Wilkes was imprisoned for libel. In 1770 a mob assembled outside the prison to escort him to the HOUSE OF COMMONS. Soldiers opened fire when they refused to disperse, killing and injuring several people. This became known as the St George's Field Massacre. In 1780 the prison was burned in the GORDON RIOTS and quickly rebuilt. By the early 19th century the prison was notorious for the laxity of its rules. A description of it in 1828 calls it 'the most desirable place of incarceration in London'. The courtyard thronged with life: there were tailors, barbers, hatters, piano-makers, chandlers and oyster-sellers. Drink flowed freely: there were no fewer than 30 gin shops and 120 gallons sold weekly. Affluent inmates dined in style with a regular cook to prepare their meals; poorer prisoners took their turns with a begging box at the gate. In 1815 Lord Cochrane, imprisoned for complicity in certain STOCK EXCHANGE

frauds, staged a dramatic and near disastrous escape attempt to take his seat in Parliament. The rope he was using broke when he was still 20 ft from the ground, but he managed to get away. During the 1840s the prison was amalgamated with the FLEET and the MARSHALSEA PRISONS and was renamed Queen's Bench. In 1850 Dixon, the historian, complained that it had lost the 'buffoonery, scoundrelism, riot and confusion which had formerly made it picturesque'. During the middle years of Queen Victoria's reign arrest for debt was abolished and it was used for a time as a military prison. It was demolished in 1880.

King's College *Strand, WC2.* Founded in 1828 as a rival to UNIVERSITY COLLEGE, the godless institution in GOWER STREET, by the Duke of Wellington, the Archbishops and 30 Bishops of the Church of England. It was granted a royal charter in 1829. The college was built to the designs of Robert Smirke, in 1829–31. At its opening, in October 1831, Bishop Blomfield held a service in the chapel and preached a sermon on the combination of religious instruction with intellectual culture. The college was divided into senior and junior departments. The junior was a school for boys from middle-class families. The senior was a finishing school for young men before they embarked on their careers. Courses were held in religion, natural philosophy, classical studies, history, modern languages, mathematics, medicine, surgery, chemistry and jurisprudence. The governors and the professors (except the linguists) had to be members of the Church of England but the students did not. Dr William Otter was appointed principal. In 1834 associateship of the college was first granted to students who had attended satisfactorily for three years. In 1836 the UNIVERSITY OF LONDON was founded as an examining body but the governors were offended at the exclusion of divinity from the syllabus and advised students to take the Oxford or Cambridge examinations. In 1840 KING'S COLLEGE HOSPITAL was opened in the converted workhouse of the parish of ST CLEMENT DANES, and in 1846 the Theological Department was founded for training Church of England priests. In 1849 the College pioneered evening classes

The Archbishop of Canterbury distributes prizes in the Theatre of King's College in 1841.

in London; Thomas Hardy used them for studying modern languages. In 1908 King's College became a constituent college of the UNIVERSITY OF LONDON.

Among the distinguished men who have taught at the college are Lister, F.D. Maurice, Charles Wheatstone, and James Clerk Maxwell. Major reconstruction and rebuilding of the College began in 1966. The new block facing the STRAND, designed by E.D. Jefferiss Mathews, was completed in 1972. The abstract bronze by the office is *Ultimate Form* by Dame Barbara Hepworth (1972).

King's College Hospital Denmark Hill, SE5. Stems from the foundation of KING'S COLLEGE, STRAND. The Medical Department was established in 1831 and the first King's College Hospital in 1839. A rented building was chosen – ST CLEMENT DANES workhouse in PORTUGAL STREET. It was renovated by Sir Robert Smirke and the first patients were admitted in 1840. In 1852 a wing was added and in 1862 the hospital was completely rebuilt to the designs of Thomas Bellamy at a cost of £45,000. At that time it was considered to be the model hospital in London. In 1877 Professor Joseph Lister, introducer of antiseptic surgery, was invited to join the staff. In 1912 Sir Ronald Ross, the discoverer of the cause of malaria and its means of transmission, also joined the hospital staff with the promise of ten beds in the projected hospital at DENMARK HILL, the foundation stone of which had been laid in 1909. The medical school moved with the hospital, but pre-clinical medical teaching continued (and does to this day) at KING'S COLLEGE. The new hospital, designed by W.A. Pite, was opened in 1913. In 1937 a private patients' block, designed by Collcutt and Hemp, was built. With the advent of the National Health Service four hospitals were added to the King's College Group: the Belgrave Hospital for Children, 1 Clapham Road, SW9 (51 beds), the DULWICH, the ST FRANCIS, and ST GILES HOSPITAL. The new block, designed by W.N.B. George of George Trew, Dunn, Beckles, Willson and Bowes, was opened in 1968. In 1982 King's itself had 663 beds.

King's College School *Southside, Wimbledon Common, SW19.* Originating as the junior department of KING'S COLLEGE it opened in 1831 with 85 pupils. By 1843 there were 500 pupils and the need for larger premises eventually led to the move to WIMBLEDON in 1897.

King's Cross *N1.* When the EUSTON and PENTONVILLE ROADS were cut in 1756 there was a small village here named Battle Bridge. The FLEET RIVER used to flow on the western side of Pancras Road and there was probably a broad ford there, for the name Battle Bridge is a corruption of Broad Ford Bridge. There is no truth in the legend that it was the site of a battle fought between Boudicca and the Romans. In 1731 the highwayman, John Everett, was hanged at TYBURN for holding up a coach here. In the mid-18th century ST CHAD'S WELL became a spa attracting 800–900 people daily. At this time a huge heap of ashes from Harrison's brickworks in GRAY'S INN ROAD accumulated in Battle Bridge Field. It was only removed when the ground was sold in 1826. It was rumoured that the Russians had bought it to help to rebuild Moscow after Napoleon's invasion. From 1746 until about 1846 there was a smallpox hospital here (*see* WHITTINGTON

HOSPITAL). In 1836, at the junction of EUSTON, PENTONVILLE, ST PANCRAS, and GRAY'S INN ROADS there was erected the monument which resulted in the name of the locality being changed to King's Cross. Designed by Stephen Geary, it had an octagonal base decorated with Doric columns and the four patron saints of Britain. At the top of the 60 ft-high monument was a statue of George IV. The base was first used as a police station and later as a public house. The whole structure provoked such unfavourable comment that the statue was taken down in 1842 and the rest three years later. In 1851–2 KING'S CROSS STATION was built on the site of the smallpox hospital.

King's Cross took its name from a monument which, demolished in 1845, had been in turn a police station and a public house.

King's Cross Station *Euston Road, NW1.* Built on the site of the London Smallpox Hospital, in a district formerly known as Battle Bridge. It was called King's Cross to commemorate the monument to George IV which stood at the crossroads near the site from 1830 until 1845. The station, designed by Lewis Cubitt, was built in 1851–2 as the London terminus for the Great Northern Railway, and when it opened it was the biggest station in England. The Midland Railway used it as well until ST PANCRAS STATION opened in 1868. The terminus was the fifth to be built in London and the second to be designed by Cubitt (BRICKLAYERS ARMS was finished in 1844). He set out to make a design that would 'depend for its effect on the largeness of some of its features, its fitness for its purpose, and its characteristic expression of that purpose.' He achieved this with a straightforward functional building: twin train sheds, each 800 ft long and 105 ft wide, closed at the south end by a plain façade of London brick. The central tower, 112 ft high, holds a clock made by Dents for the GREAT EXHIBITION. King's Cross was much admired when it opened and was said to 'wear a magnificent appearance – so much so that Edmund Denison, the Chairman of the Great Northern, had to answer charges of extravagance from some shareholders. 'It is,' Denison riposted, 'the cheapest building for what it contains and will contain, that can be pointed out in London.' Cubitt added the Great Northern Hotel in 1854, placing it to the west of the station on a curved site. Towards the end of the 19th century King's Cross was handling about 250 trains daily.

King's Head Tavern *Fleet Street*. The signboard was a portrait of Henry VIII, in whose reign the tavern probably existed. It was certainly there in the reign of his daughter, Elizabeth I. It was known as a 'Protestant House'. Titus Oates and his fellow conspirators used to meet here. So also did the Green Ribbon Club. The tavern was on the first floor. There were shops below. One of these was the bookshop of Richard Marriott for whom was printed the first edition of Izaak Walton's *The Compleat Angler* (1653). The building was demolished in 1799 for the widening of CHANCERY LANE.

King's Road *SW3, SW6, SW10*. CHELSEA's main artery, it extends from SLOANE SQUARE to FULHAM. The eastern part as far as OLD CHURCH STREET was originally a private road which Charles II used on his way to HAMPTON COURT. Others could use it on production of a copper pass stamped 'The King's Private Roads' on one side and with the King's monogram on the other. It was George III's favourite route to KEW, and ceased to be a private road only in 1830. It is now celebrated for its shops, particularly for its boutiques. On the south side the DUKE OF YORK'S HEADQUARTERS stands between LOWER SLOANE STREET and CHELTENHAM TERRACE, and CHELSEA OLD TOWN HALL beyond CHELSEA MANOR STREET. Between OAKLEY STREET and GLEBE PLACE is an elegant group of houses. Argyll House, No. 211, was designed by the Venetian architect, Giacomo Leoni, in 1723. Next to it, Nos 213 and 215 were built in 1720 and retain their attractive brick fronts. Dr Thomas Arne lived at No. 215 and is thought to have composed *Rule Britannia* here. A plaque on the house commemorates Ellen Terry's residence here in 1904–20. Further on the King's Road bends and behind a large gate lies the MORAVIAN BURIAL GROUND. Moravian Corner is by Chamberlin, Powell and Bon (1970). The next stretch of shops forms the frontage of the Cremorne Estate designed by Edward Armstrong and Frederick MacManus on the site of the CREMORNE GARDENS. Its original gates now stand in Tetcott Road. The COLLEGE OF ST MARK AND ST JOHN stands on the north side of the King's Road on Chelsea Creek. A large part of CHELSEA COLLEGE stands between Carlyle Square and Manresa Road. Beyond it is the Chelsea Fire Station. Further east is the Old Chelsea Burial Ground given to the people of CHELSEA by Sir Hans Sloane and consecrated in 1736. It contains many monuments, including those of Cipriani, the Italian painter and engraver, and John Martyn, the botanist, who introduced peppermint into pharmacy. The Chelsea Society replanned the burial ground, which is now a pleasant open space with seats and flowers, to celebrate Queen Elizabeth II's Jubilee and their own 50th anniversary. The PHEASANTRY stands between Jubilee Place and MARKHAM SQUARE. Givan's Irish Linen Stores at No. 207 were originally opened by George Givan of Belfast at Nos 111–114 NEW BOND STREET in 1899. Dorothy Perkins, the ladies' outfitters at No. 120, occupy a building which was formerly the premises of Thomas Crapper, whose firm, renowned for its water closets, was established in Marlborough Road in 1861. The stone obelisk fountain is dedicated to the memory of Andrew Miller, the bookseller. Its date is 1751, the sculptor unknown.

King's Troop Royal Horse Artillery *see* ST JOHN'S WOOD BARRACKS.

King's Wardrobe *Blackfriars*. Built as a private house in the 14th century by Sir John Beauchamp, Constable of Dover and Warden of the Cinque Ports, who died here in 1359. His executors sold the house soon after his death to Edward III to hold his ceremonial robes which were removed here from the TOWER. Such was the extent of the building that Edward granted the rector of ST ANDREW-BY-THE-WARDROBE 40s for the loss of tithes. The Wardrobe not only held the King's clothes but garments for the entire royal family for weddings, funerals and coronations, 'cloaths of state, beds, hangings and other necessaries for the houses of foreign ambassadors, cloaths of state for Lord Lieutenant of Ireland, Prince of Wales and ambassadors abroad' and robes for the King's ministers and Knights of the Garter. The account books of the Royal Household were also kept here. James I sold many of the old costumes to the Earl of Dunbar 'by whom they were sold,' in the words of Thomas Fuller, 're-sold, and re-re-sold at as many hands almost as Briareus had, some gaining vast estates thereby.' After its destruction in the GREAT FIRE, the Wardrobe was re-established in the SAVOY and later in BUCKINGHAM STREET. The last Master of the Wardrobe, Ralph, Duke of Montagu, died in 1709. The original site was between the church of ST ANDREW and CARTER LANE, and is marked by Wardrobe Place. It is also commemorated by Wardrobe Chambers, Court and Terrace, EC4.

Kingsbury *NW9*. The centre of Kingsbury (the King's burgh or stronghold) had already shifted from its location around St Andrew's church in Old Church Lane to Kingsbury Green after the BLACK DEATH. The old church of St Andrew dates from the 13th century and is surrounded by the remains of a medieval ditch. The church's flint and rubble walls incorporate sarsen corner stones and Roman material which suggests an earlier occupation of the site. Though often referred to as a Saxon church (the modified long and short work of the western quoins being a Saxon feature) other evidence suggests a post-Conquest date. Throughout its history it has suffered from periods of neglect and decay and then in the 19th century from attempts at keen restoration. It was declared redundant in 1977 and has been taken over by the WEMBLEY History Society for museum, workshop and study purposes. The church has three rare bells one of which, by Peter de Weston, dates from about 1340. The fitments include the memorial to William Murray, Earl of Mansfield who lived at KENWOOD, the brass of John Shepard of Kingsbury (1520), and a memorial slab to John Bul of Roe Green, Gentleman and Keeper of the King's Poultry (1621).

The striking form of the 'new' church of St Andrew which adjoins it was designed by Dawkes and Hamilton. The church was originally built in Wells Street, OXFORD CIRCUS in 1845–7. Benjamin Webb, co-founder of the Cambridge Camden Society, was the vicar there in 1862–5, and the composer, Sir Joseph Barnby, was once its organist. Various well-known architects of the period – Street, Pearson, Butterfield and Burges – were called in to 'improve' the interior. The church was declared redundant (the last evensong being in 1931) and was carefully dismantled and re-erected in Kingsbury in 1933–4.

Kingsbury was once the home of Oliver Goldsmith who wrote *She Stoops to Conquer* at Hyde House

Farm. Kingsbury Manor at Roe Green Park, Kingsbury was built in 1899 for the wife of the 3rd Duke of Sutherland. (It was at its converted stables that John Logie Baird received the first combined 'sound and sight transmission' in March 1930.)

Kingsbury's thatched cottages in Slough Lane and Buck Lane were built in the 1920s when the area was still largely rural. They were designed by Ernest George Trobridge, the son of an Irish landscape artist. His ties with the Swedenborgian church provided him with a number of church contracts countrywide during 1908–14. He patented his 'Compressed Greenwood Construction' after the 1st World War. Projects in Kingsbury began in 1921 with the setting up of the local sawmills. They reached their most bizarre in a representation of styles of English architecture through the ages whose castellated forms crown the top of Buck Lane.

Kingston Bridge *Hampton Wick–Kingston*. There has been a bridge at this site since at least medieval times. In 1219 William de Coventry was appointed Master of the Bridge. In 1223 the bridge was endowed with lands for its maintenance. There was a further grant in 1318. In 1376 it is mentioned as being broken down. In 1528 there was yet another grant of land and Henry VIII had his artillery brought over the river here rather than at LONDON BRIDGE lest the latter be damaged by the weight. It was freed from tolls in 1567 and made into a drawbridge in 1661. The present bridge of brick faced with stone was built by Edward Lapidge in 1825–8. This bridge was freed from tolls in 1870. It was widened on the upstream side in 1914.

Kingston Grammar School *70 London Road, Kingston-upon-Thames, Surrey*. Established by Royal Charter in 1561, it probably originated in the Middle Ages in the chapel school of St Mary Magdalen at KINGSTON.

Kingston Polytechnic *Penrhyn Road, Kingston-upon-Thames, Surrey*. Originally created in 1970 by the amalgamation of the KINGSTON College of Technology and the College of Art, the Polytechnic was enlarged in 1975 by its merger with the GIPSY HILL College of Education. Its campuses are only a few minutes from the THAMES and the centre of KINGSTON with its historic market place where Saxon kings were once crowned. While Canbury Park, the main centre for engineering, is a converted aircraft factory, the Gipsy Hill buildings on Kingston Hill are a mixture of large houses and purpose-built accommodation set in woodland. The London Sinfonietta is based at the Gipsy Hill centre and the resident Medici String Quartet gives tuition and coaches string sections of the orchestra.

Kingston Railway Bridge *Hampton Wick–Kingston-upon-Thames*. A cast-iron arch bridge by J.E. Errington, bringing a branch from the London and South Western Railway at TWICKENHAM, was built here in 1860–3. This was replaced by a similar bridge in steel by J.W. Jacomb Hood in 1907.

Kingston-upon-Thames *Surrey*. Has always held a strategic position as the river here was once fordable. Hence its earliest name, Moreford, the Great Ford. In Saxon times it became Cyningestum, that is

to say the King's Estate and finally Kingston. The three fishes embodied in its coat-of-arms refer to the importance of the local fisheries. It is the oldest of the only three Royal Boroughs, a status it has enjoyed since medieval times, its earliest surviving charter that granted by King John in 1200. It holds the ancient right to elect its own High Steward and Recorder.

Until 1750 the bridge was the first above the THAMES after LONDON BRIDGE. A wooden structure, existing from pre-Conquest times, it made the Borough a key point and was often damaged in times of strife. The present stone bridge was opened in 1828 by the Duchess of Clarence (later Queen Adelaide). Newly-designed lamps were installed in 1980. During the Civil War the town was occupied in turn by both armies and one of the first and one of the last skirmishes took place in the area.

For centuries Kingston has been a leading market town in Surrey, a charter of 1628, granted by Charles I, forbidding the holding of any other market within a seven-mile radius. The whole Market Place is a Scheduled Conservation Area, and surrounding it are the famous inns of the Griffin and the Druid's Head. A Jacobean staircase in Chiesman's department store is a relic of the Castle Inn which once stood on the site. The forerunner of Chiesman's was Hide and Co., a firm which had developed from a drapery business begun by Joseph Hide in 1740. Part of Boots, chemists, dates from the 16th century. The town was once a centre for brewing and malting, tanning, milling, boat-building and river barge traffic. Present industries include aviation, chemicals, engineering, plastics, printing, refrigeration and wine products.

Kingston Grammar School was founded by Elizabeth I in 1561. The Market Hall, built in 1838 to the design of C. Helman, replaced an earlier 16th-century structure. It was the town hall until 1935 when it was replaced by a Guildhall designed by Maurice Webb.

Kingston Vale *SW15*. Where the old London to Portsmouth Road dropped from the heights of WIMBLEDON COMMON, before rising again over Kingston Hill, a small village grew up, originally known as Kingston Bottom. Here stood an inn, the Bald-Face Stag, a regular stopping-place for noblemen on their way to HAMPTON COURT, and in the 18th century the haunt of footpads and highwaymen. It closed early this century. Later it was used as a factory for racing cars, the *Bluebird* being built here. In the 19th century the Duchess of Teck lived at WHITE LODGE, RICHMOND PARK which is entered at this point by the Robin Hood Gate. The Duchess's daughter, Princess May, later Queen to George V, often stayed here and attended the parish church of St John the Baptist.

Kingsway *WC2*. The 28-acre Kingsway and ALDWYCH scheme was the last and greatest of the Victorian metropolitan improvements. It cost about £5 million. Although not opened until 1905 by Edward VII and named in his honour, Kingsway was conceived, with NEW OXFORD STREET, SHAFTESBURY AVENUE and CHARING CROSS ROAD as a radical solution to the problem of Victorian traffic congestion. It had a useful by-product of slum clearance and the provision of new homes in adjoining streets. Alternative names suggested for it included King Edward VII Street, Empire Avenue, Imperial Avenue and Connecticut Avenue.

Work in progress on Kingsway, which cost some £5 million. It was opened in 1905 by Edward VII and named in his honour.

The two ancient routes linking the STRAND with HOL-
BORN were DRURY LANE and CHANCERY LANE. Both
were narrow. Plans to replace or widen them had
emerged from the 1830s onwards. The new LONDON
COUNTY COUNCIL referred the problem to their im-
provements committee. In 1892 the 100 ft-wide
Kingsway was conceived to run between the old routes
and to replace both as the main north–south artery.
ALDWYCH is the crescent link between the STRAND and
Kingsway. Demolition, which included the SAR-
DINIAN CHAPEL, began in 1900 and the new route was
laid out. But, despite the 1905 opening ceremony,
buildings rose slowly. The W.H. Smith Building at
No. 7 was one of the earliest, followed by Kodak
House, designed by Sir John Burnet and Thomas Tait
(1910–11). This building (No. 63) was owned in 1982
by Gallaher's, the tobacco manufacturers. After 1912
progress was rapid and by 1916 there were only a few
empty sites. Africa House, built to the designs of
Trehearne and Norman in 1922, was the last major
addition. A feature of the street was the tram subway
to the EMBANKMENT. It was heightened in 1929–31,
closed in 1932 and the southern end reopened as a
traffic underpass in 1964. The ROYALTY THEATRE is at
No. 22. HOLY TRINITY CHURCH is on the west side, St
Angela and St Cecilia on the east.

Kingsway Theatre *Great Queen Street.* Designed
in 1882 by Thomas Verity for comedies. In the early
years its name and management changed frequently.
In 1889 Ibsen's *A Doll's House* had its English
première here. In the drama, *Sins of the Night*, the
actor, Temple E. Crozier, was stabbed to death by
mistake. In 1900 the theatre was acquired by W.S. Pen-
ley with money he had made from *Charley's Aunt*.
It was reconstructed for him by Murray and Foster. In
1902–7 it was leased to Hans Andersen and the German Theatre Company. The interior was reconstructed in 1907 by F.W. Foster. In 1912–13 it was
managed by Granville-Barker and Lillah McCarthy.
Their main successes were *Fanny's First Play* (1912)
by Bernard Shaw and *The Great Adventure* (1913) by
Arnold Bennett. In 1925–6 Barry Jackson with his
Birmingham Repertory Company staged a series of
modern plays and the first modern-dress *Hamlet*. In
1927 *Marigold*, a comedy by Harker and Pryor, began
its run of 642 performances. In 1940 Donald Wolfit
gave a Shakespeare season. Badly damaged in the
BLITZ, it was demolished in 1956. Newton Street was
extended over the site to join GREAT QUEEN STREET.

Kingswood House *Seeley Drive, Dulwich, SE21.*
King's Wood or King's Coppice formed part of the
once extensive woods on the south of Dulwich Manor
(*see* DULWICH). It probably takes its name from the
ownership of Dulwich Manor by King Henry I in the
12th century. The Kings of England were already
hunting here then and continued to do so until the 17th

century. An 18th-century mansion appears to have stood on the site, but the existing mansion was started in 1812 by William Vizard, and enlarged and embellished throughout the 19th century. Outside, it has a Gothic appearance, with castellations and a tower, and inside its panelled rooms have been decorated in a variety of styles. It was surrounded by a self-sufficient 30-acre estate, including a farm, an ornamental lake and a generating plant. Among its owners were James, Baron Hannen, the Divorce Court Judge; Thomas Tapling, philatelist; Lawson Johnson, founder of Bovril (the house was nicknamed 'Bovril Castle') and Samuel, 2nd Baron Vestey. Damaged by air raids in the 2nd World War, the house was acquired by the LONDON COUNTY COUNCIL and Kingswood Estate, with flats, schools, a public house and shops, built in the grounds. The house was threatened with demolition, but was made into a library and Community Centre in 1956 by CAMBERWELL Borough Council. Since 1965 it has been owned by the Borough of SOUTHWARK.

Kinnerton Street *SW1.* Originally built on the GROSVENOR ESTATE as the service road to the west side of WILTON STREET and WILTON CRESCENT and named after a village in Cheshire. It rapidly became a slum and its little courts ended at the west end at the Ranelagh Sewer which was not covered over until 1844. In 1854 it contained a cow-keeper, a saddler, two tailors, a plumber, a wheelwright, a grocer and two purveyors of asses' milk which was much used in hospitals and thought to have therapeutic qualities. The houses have now been converted and prettified.

Kit-Kat Club An influential club of Whig patriots founded in 1700 by Jacob Tonson, the bookseller (*see* STRAND) to ensure a Protestant succession at the end of William III's reign. It is supposed to have been named after the pastry cook Christopher Katt, at whose house the club first met and whose mutton pie its members relished. During the summer members met at Tonson's house at Barn Elms or at the Upper Flask Inn, HAMPSTEAD. Among the members were the Duke of Marlborough, Sir Robert Walpole, Vanbrugh, Addison, Steele, Congreve and Kneller who painted the portraits of all his companions which are now in the NATIONAL PORTRAIT GALLERY. The club came to an end in about 1720.

Kleinwort Benson Ltd *Fenchurch Street, EC2.* With origins as a merchant house in Cuba in 1792, Kleinwort and Sons moved to London in 1830. The growth of its merchant banking was based on strong international links, particularly in eastern Europe. More recently it was active in the unit trust movement. In 1961 the firm merged with Robert Benson, Lonsdale and Co. (founded in 1852) and since 1966 it has owned the bullion dealing firm of Sharps, Pixley and Co. (established in 1803, and now based in LIME STREET, EC3).

Kneller Hall *Whitton, Middlesex.* Built in 1709–11 as a country villa for the court painter, Sir Godfrey Kneller, who may have designed it himself, though it has also been attributed to Wren. It was rebuilt in 1848 by George Mair as a palatial neo-Jacobean mansion. Since 1857 it has been occupied by the Royal Military School of Music founded the same year by the Duke of Cambridge for training army bandsmen and band-masters. The school has been administered by the government from 1865.

Knightrider Street *EC4.* Stow thought it was part of the route knights took from the Tower Royal in WATLING STREET to the tournaments at SMITHFIELD. DOCTORS' COMMONS, ST MARY MAGDALEN and the GERMAN CHURCH all used to be in the street. No. 5 is the site of Thomas Linacre's house where he founded the ROYAL COLLEGE OF PHYSICIANS. The church of ST MARY MAGDALEN stood on the corner of OLD CHANGE until demolished after being badly damaged by fire in 1886. R.H. Barham, author of *The Ingoldsby Legends*, was incumbent for many years and buried there in 1845.

Knights Hospitaller *see* ORDER OF ST JOHN MUSEUM, PRIORY OF ST JOHN OF JERUSALEM, ST JOHN CLERKENWELL *and* ST JOHN GATE.

Knights Templar In 1099 Jerusalem was captured from the Mohammedans, and a desire to see the Holy Places swept over Europe. Pilgrims who set forth were often robbed and sometimes killed while on their way through Palestine. Observing this, nine noble knights formed a brotherhood in arms, and made a solemn vow to devote themselves to the protection of these pilgrims. They were led by a French knight, Hugues de Payens, and were very poor. Impressed by their valour and devotion, King Baldwin of Jerusalem gave them a base on the Temple Platform of Mount Moriah, the space that lies between the famous Dome of the Rock and the Mosque of El Aksa – at that time King Baldwin's own palace, and vulgarly known as the Temple of Solomon. They thus became known as the Knights of the Temple of Solomon of Jerusalem, and later as the Knights Templar. When they built churches in Europe they followed the circular design of the Dome of the Rock. They were also known as the Red Knights because of the big red cross worn on the shoulders of their mantles. The Knights Templar were well established in London by the first half of the 12th century in what is now HIGH HOLBORN, where they built a round church. In 1162 they moved south to the River THAMES by whose banks they built a second round church known as the 'New' Temple to distinguish it from the first (*see* TEMPLE CHURCH). Nearby they built a splendid monastery with two large halls, a 'hall of priests' connected with the temple by a cloister, and a hall of knights. Across the river lay a field where they could exercise their horses. The New Temple was used by the Crown as well as the Templars. King John was living here when summoned by his barons to sign *Magna Carta*. Gifts were showered upon the knights and as owners of property they became wealthy bankers. According to Sir Edward Coke they had 'so great and so large privileges, liberties, and immunities for themselves, their tenants and farmers', that 'no other Order had the like'. Such riches aroused the greed of kings. Philip the Fair of France brought extraordinary and largely unjustified charges for sodomy, blasphemy, and heresy and persuaded Pope Clement to persecute the Order. In London knights were arrested, put into the TOWER, and their property confiscated. Their properties passed in the end to the Knights Hospitaller but not without resistance. Edward II presented the London properties to his cousin, the Earl of Lancaster. Students and professors of the Common Law approached the Earl for lodgings in the Temple and their request was granted.

Knightsbridge *SW1*. The street extending from HYDE PARK CORNER to KENSINGTON ROAD. It takes its name, which dates back to the 11th century, from the village that stood south of HYDE PARK on the road to KENSINGTON. The bridge here crossed the WESTBOURNE near the site of the present ALBERT GATE. There is a legend that two knights fought to the death on it. It was a village celebrated for its taverns, including the Swan, mentioned by Thomas Otway in *The Soldier's Fortune*; the White Hart, which was in existence at least as early as 1631; the World's End, frequented by Pepys; and the FOX AND BULL. It was also a favourite place for duels and was much plagued with highwaymen. There have been many recent encroachments but several of the familiar 19th-century buildings still remain. At the east end are the buildings of the former ST GEORGE'S HOSPITAL. On the other side, facing SLOANE STREET, is the HYDE PARK HOTEL built in 1888 by the architects of WHITEHALL COURT, Archer and Green. And, on the corner of RUTLAND GATE, is Kent House (now the Westminster Synagogue), named after Queen Victoria's father, the Duke of Kent, who lived here for a short time. Sir George Cornewall Lewis, Chancellor of the Exchequer, died here in 1863. T.H. Wyatt's KNIGHTSBRIDGE BARRACKS have, however, been replaced by Sir Basil Spence's building (1970). Other new buildings are, from the east end, the neo-Georgian Agriculture House, Nos 25–31, by Ronald Ward and Partners

Knightsbridge traffic in the late 1920s. The Hyde Park Hotel (centre) was built in 1882.

(1956); the SHERATON PARK TOWER HOTEL, No. 101 by R. Seifert and Partners (1973); Hyde Park House by Guy Morgan and Partners (1963). Bowater House, by Guy Morgan and Partners (1959) replaces two large mansions built by Thomas Cubitt, one of them once occupied by George Hudson, the 'Railway King'. The bronze sculpture outside Mercury House and Knightsbridge House is *The Seer* by Gilbert Ledward. A large block of flats at No. 245 replaces South Lodge, formerly known as Stratheden House, where Lord Chancellor Campbell, who died here in 1861, wrote *Lives of the Lord Chancellors*. Other residents in Knightsbridge, in houses which also no longer exist, were Byron's grandson, the Earl of Lovelace; John Liston the comedian; Elizabeth Inchbald, the novelist and actress, Charles Reade who wrote several of his novels in a house then numbered 70. HARVEY NICHOLS are at Nos 109–25; the French Embassy is at No. 58; the Wellington Club is at No. 116A; and the ROYAL THAMES YACHT CLUB at No. 60. No. 164 was designed by Carl Auböck (1976).

Knightsbridge Barracks *Kensington Road, SW7*. Buildings on the present site were originally erected for the Horse Guards at the end of the 18th century. They held 600 men and 500 horses. In 1857 a riding school and stables designed by Philip Hardwick were added. These buildings gave way to somewhat flamboyant barracks which were completed in 1880 to the designs of T.H. Wyatt, which were demolished in 1966 when their place was taken by barracks surrounding a tower block 270ft high designed by Sir Basil Spence. They provide accommodation for 514 soldiers of the Household Cavalry and 273 horses.

Knightsbridge Green *SW1*. This little passage is the vestigial remains of the village green which originally encompassed the whole area of the Park Mansions (SCOTCH HOUSE) site. It is alleged to have been a plague pit at the time of the BLACK DEATH. It has been steadily encroached upon for the last 400 years. There was a cattle market on the green every Thursday and the hitching posts survived till 1850 though the market ceased in 1805. The maypole went in 1800 and the stocks at the north end in 1805. The animal pound was demolished in 1835. The earliest 19th-century houses were King's Row (now 16–25 BROMPTON ROAD) built in 1785 but since reconstructed. On the south-west side was Grosvenor House, later the home of the Gosling family, bankers. It became a tenement but was bought and demolished by TATTERSALL'S when they built their new headquarters there in 1864.

Kodak Museum *Headstone Drive, Wealdstone, Harrow, Middlesex*. Founded in 1927 and rehoused in 1979 in specially designed premises in the original Kodak Factory Building, erected in 1891. It contains the largest collection of photographic exhibits and apparatus in the country.

L

La Patente Chapel *Berwick Street*. Built in 1688 for Huguenot refugees. In 1694 half the congregation left for a new chapel in SHERATON STREET. By 1707 the rest of the French congregation had dispersed and the chapel was bought by the vestry of ST JAMES'S CHURCH, PICCADILLY as a chapel-of-ease. In 1838–9 the site was sold to the Church Commissioners and a new parish church of St Luke was built, in a Decorated Gothic design by Edward Blore. This was demolished in 1936 and the parish amalgamated with ST ANNE'S, SOHO. Kemp House now marks the site.

The Hippodrome Racecourse on the Ladbroke Estate, Notting Hill, c. 1838, a year after its opening.

Ladbroke Estate Developed in the1840s by James Weller Ladbroke whose family had owned land in North KENSINGTON for about a century. The Hippodrome racecourse was opened in 1837 but proved a failure and closed in 1841. It is commemorated in Hippodrome Place, W11. Thereafter the planning of the estate was entrusted to Thomas Allom, the eastern part being leased in 1844 to W.K. Jenkins of Hereford, hence the street names in the area: Denbigh Road, W11, CHEPSTOW VILLAS, W11, Pembridge Road and Crescent, W11, Pembridge Gardens and Square, W2, and Ledbury Road, W11.

Ladbroke Grove *W10, W11*. This road, the central spine of North KENSINGTON, was begun in the 1830s at its southern end but took a further 40 years to reach the HARROW ROAD. It includes most building styles in the area from the classical villas and stuccoed terraces of the Ladbroke Estate to the peeling, shabby terraces of the north interspersed by council estates of varying age and various public buildings. St John the Evangelist, well situated on its hill, was designed by J.H. Stevens and G. Alexander in the Early English Gothic manner and was consecrated in 1845. Its site occupied the central point of the Hippodrome racecourse which originally circled the hill. The

course, the brainchild of John Whyte, was opened in June 1837 but its success was short-lived as various disputes and the heavy nature of the going led to its closure in 1841. The church of St Michael and All Angels was built in the Romanesque style in 1871 to the designs of James and J.S. Edmeston. Hablot Knight Browne, who illustrated Dickens's novels as 'Phiz', lived at No. 99 in 1872–80.

Lady Eleanor Holles School *Hanworth Road, Hampton, Middlesex*. Founded in 1711 in the ward of CRIPPLEGATE, by the will of Lady Eleanor Holles, the unmarried daughter of the Earl of Clare. Originally a Church of England foundation, it is now non-denominational with 730 girls aged between 7 and 18 years.

Lady Margaret Church *Chatham Street, SE17*. Named after the mother of Henry VII, the Lady Margaret, Countess of Richmond, founder of St John's College, Cambridge, which, in its turn, founded this church. The church was built in 1888–9, and a bust of Lady Margaret was erected in 1920.

Lamb *94 Lamb's Conduit Street, WC1*. Public house named after the engineer who built the conduit underneath the road. It was established in the 18th century. The Victorian interior, restored in 1961, contains much original woodwork and glass with attractively engraved screens. Once a meeting place of various members of the BLOOMSBURY GROUP, it houses a unique collection of music hall photographs.

Lamb and Flag *33 Rose Street, Covent Garden, WC2*. Built in 1623, it is one of the few wooden-framed buildings to survive in central London. The exterior is Georgian. It was once known as the Bucket of Blood because of its association with prizefighters. John Dryden was attacked nearby in 1679 for having written scurrilous verses about Charles II's mistress, the Duchess of Portsmouth.

Lamb's Conduit Street *WC1*. The conduit was an Elizabethan dam made in one of the tributaries of the FLEET RIVER and restored in 1577 by William Lamb, who also provided 120 pails for poor women. He was a chorister of the Chapel Royal and a member of the CLOTHWORKERS' COMPANY. The conduit has been gone for some 200 years but there is a charming statue of a lady with an urn in Guilford Place at the top of the street; and at the entrance to Long Yard there is an ancient stone set in the wall with the inscription 'Lamb's Conduit, the property of the City of London. This pump is erected for the benefit of the Publick.'

Lambeth *SE1, SW8, SW9*. The modern London Borough marches on its east with the Borough of SOUTHWARK and on its west with that of WANDSWORTH.

Lambeth in the 1880s, showing the shot tower and the old Waterloo Bridge, built in 1811–17 and demolished in 1936.

It extends from HUNGERFORD RAILWAY BRIDGE in the north down to STREATHAM in the south, encompassing the parishes and districts of WATERLOO, old Lambeth, KENNINGTON, CLAPHAM, STOCKWELL, BRIXTON, WEST DULWICH, part of HERNE HILL, part of BALHAM, STREATHAM and WEST NORWOOD. It is served by four road bridges across the river: WATERLOO, WESTMINSTER, LAMBETH and VAUXHALL; and by HUNGERFORD RAILWAY BRIDGE, which also takes a footpath. Along its river front rise the NATIONAL THEATRE, the ROYAL FESTIVAL HALL, COUNTY HALL, ST THOMAS'S HOSPITAL and LAMBETH PALACE; and between VAUXHALL and COUNTY HALL runs the ALBERT EMBANKMENT.

Up to the 18th century Lambeth was mostly marshland, fields, and polder dams crossed by a few roads raised against floods – a favoured area for duckshooting. When the Romans arrived it may, indeed, have consisted mainly of a huge, shallow lake (hence possibly Llyn Din, the city on the lake). As in most of south London, the 19th-century urban growth absorbed the small settlements. Nothing before the 18th century survives in Lambeth except the Archbishop's PALACE by the river with its noble brick gatehouse of 1495, and the neighbouring parish church of ST MARY'S. The Manor of Lambeth has been owned by the See of Canterbury since 1197. Before that one of its inhabitants had been King Hardacanute who died here in 1041 while feasting. The PALACE was conveniently placed more or less opposite the PALACE OF WESTMINSTER to which it was linked for centuries by a horse ferry (hence HORSEFERRY ROAD on the north). The Black Prince is believed to have lived in a royal palace at KENNINGTON, and its manor was vested in the Princes of Wales as Dukes of Cornwall in the time of James I. Much of KENNINGTON still belongs to the DUCHY OF CORNWALL, which has built some good housing on its land (*see* KENNINGTON).

On Rocque's map of 1746 a built-up fringe of houses

appears only along the river bank between WESTMINSTER BRIDGE and NINE ELMS, with a few scattered houses along KENNINGTON ROAD, while VAUXHALL, STOCKWELL and BRIXTON are villages and NORWOOD is a forest (the Great North Wood). In the time of William and Mary, Lambeth Wells served medicinal water at LAMBETH WALK. During the first half of the 19th century a good many villas came into being, as at Camberwell Grove, DENMARK HILL and HERNE HILL, and also pleasant terraced houses like the many that survive in KENNINGTON. Some early industries grew up in north Lambeth: the Vauxhall Plate Glass Works (1670–1780), and Coade's artificial stone factory (*see* COADE STONE), established in 1769 on a site now occupied by County Hall. DOULTON's pottery also flourished in Lambeth. North Lambeth grew slummy in Victorian times, but most of the slums have been replaced by municipal flats, some of them high-rise, as around the ELEPHANT AND CASTLE.

The Borough contains many churches, including four late Georgian examples: ST LUKE'S, WEST NORWOOD (1822), ST MARK'S, KENNINGTON (1824), St Mary the Less, Black Prince Road (1824), and the Congregational Church, St Matthew's Road (1828). Some 13 Victorian churches can be found in the Borough. Open spaces include the OVAL CRICKET GROUND, KENNINGTON, CLAPHAM COMMON (on the east corner of which may be found the early 19th-century Crescent Grove), RUSKIN PARK ON DENMARK HILL, KENNINGTON PARK, NUNHEAD CEMETERY, PECKHAM RYE COMMON, STREATHAM COMMON, BROCKWELL PARK (containing Roper's Brockwell Hall, a big house of 1816, Norwood Park, and the SOUTH METROPOLITAN CEMETERY at WEST NORWOOD, established in 1836 and containing many interesting and elaborate Victorian monuments and mausolea. An open space of the past was VAUXHALL GARDENS, lying between Kennington Lane and the EMBANKMENT, which had flourished as a popular resort since the 17th century. Another pleasure resort of the 19th century was the SURREY GARDENS, WALWORTH. Also in Lambeth are KING'S COLLEGE HOSPITAL on DENMARK HILL, WATERLOO STATION, the OLD VIC THEATRE, Brixton Town Hall (1908), and BRIXTON PRISON, Jebb Street. The name probably means a muddy harbour, or possibly a Saxon 'hithe' where lambs were unloaded.

Lambeth Bridge *Westminster–Lambeth.* The first mention of a horse ferry here is in 1513. It was one of the few places on the river where a coach and horses could cross. In 1633 the ferry sank under the weight of Archbishop Laud's belongings when he was moving into LAMBETH PALACE. Oliver Cromwell's coach and horses also sank in 1656. On 9 December 1688 Mary of Modena escaped via the ferry, with the infant Prince James, to France. After the construction of WESTMINSTER BRIDGE in 1750 the ferry closed down. The first bridge on the site (one of four crossings recommended by a Select Committee of 1854) was built in 1861. It was a lattice-stiffened suspension bridge with three spans of 268 ft each, designed by P.W. Barlow. It was freed from tolls in 1877. In 1929–32 it was replaced by the present five-span steel-arch bridge designed by Sir George Humphreys, with Sir Reginald Blomfield as architectural consultant.

Lambeth High Street Recreation Ground *see* BURIAL GROUNDS.

Lambeth Hill *EC4.* Probably named after a 13th-century landowner, Lambertus Wodemongere.

Lambeth Palace *Lambeth Palace Road, SE1.* The Archbishop of Canterbury's official residence. In 1190 Archbishop Baldwin bought part of the Manor of Lambeth from the Convent of St Andrew, Rochester. He intended to form a college of monks here but never did so. Archbishop Hubert Walter acquired the rest of the Manor of Lambeth in 1197 and about three years later he built Lambeth House as a house of Praemonstratensian canons, with his own residence attached. The extent of these early buildings is unknown since all the records have been lost. A chapel is first mentioned in 1228. The vaulted crypt under the existing chapel is 13th-century. In 1378 John Wycliffe was examined in the chapel for 'propositions, clearly heretical and depraved'. In 1381 Wat Tyler's rebels over-ran the palace, burning books, accounts and furniture and smashing open wine casks. Archbishop Simon Sudbury took refuge in the TOWER OF LONDON but was followed there and murdered. In 1432 the Lollards' Tower was built as a water tower by Archbishop Chichele; it is so called because of a legend that Lollards were imprisoned here.

The Tudor gatehouse was built by Archbishop Morton in 1486–1501. Here the Lambeth Dole was handed out three times a week to the poor of LAMBETH, a practice which continued until 1842 when money grants were made instead. In 1534 Thomas More was examined in the Guard Room by Thomas Cromwell and the Lords of the Council for refusing to sign the Oath of Supremacy. In 1553 Queen Mary refitted the palace for Cardinal Pole who died here in 1558 within 12 hours of the death of the Queen. His body lay in state for 40 days. In 1575 Archbishop Matthew Parker (perhaps the original 'nosey parker') died at the palace and was buried in the chapel. In 1601 the Earl of Essex was held here for a night after his unsuccessful rebellion, as it was too dangerous to 'shoot' LONDON BRIDGE after dark. In 1610 Archbishop Bancroft bequeathed his library to his successors; it formed the nucleus of the now extensive ecclesiastical library. Archbishop Laud undertook much restoration work in

Lambeth Palace, the official residence of the Archbishops of Canterbury, c. 1710, showing a coach and horses on the ferry.

the 1630s in the chapel, mending the stained glass windows, renewing the altar and pulpit and putting in pews and a beautiful carved screen (now in the Lollards' Tower). (All this was brought against him at his trial.) Laud was attacked here on 11 May 1640 by 500 London apprentices, but he had moved to the safety of WHITEHALL. He wrote in his diary, 'I had notice and strengthened the house as well as I could, and, God be blessed I had no harm.' In June Evelyn records another attack by 'a rude rabble from Southwark'. After the outbreak of the Civil War, the palace was taken over for public service; and until the Restoration it was used as a prison. Richard Lovelace, the poet, was kept here in 1648–9. During the Commonwealth dances were held in the chapel and the corpse of Archbishop Parker was dug up and reburied under a dung hill. At the Restoration the palace and the manor were returned to the Archbishop; the chapel was repaired and Parker reburied; and the rebuilding of the Great Hall began. In 1780 the GORDON RIOTERS surrounded the palace but failed to get in.

In 1828–34 the structure was rebuilt and extensively restored by Edward Blore, the residential part of the palace being completely reconstructed 'in the best Gothic taste'. The Great Hall was converted into a library and the galleries over the cloisters were rebuilt. The 14th-century Guard Room was also rebuilt, except for the ceiling; and the portraits of Archbishops – among them Warham by Holbein, Laud by Van Dyck, Herring by Hogarth and Secker by Reynolds – which had formerly hung in the Long Gallery, were moved here.

In 1867 the first LAMBETH conference was held by Archbishop Longley. It was attended by 76 Bishops from Britain, the Colonies and America. In 1900 the Archbishop gave 9 acres of the palace grounds to the LONDON COUNTY COUNCIL for a public park (see ARCHBISHOP'S PARK). In 1931 the Memorial fountain to Archbishop Davidson was erected in the courtyard. After damage by bombing in the 2nd World War, the Lollards' Tower was converted into flats by Mottistone and Paget, who also fitted up the galleries above the cloisters as a library and restored the Great Hall.

Lambeth Pottery Tin-glazed earthenware, made here from the 17th century, was much like SOUTHWARK POTTERY for which it is sometimes mistaken. In the 18th century blue and white ware decorated with *chinoiseries* was introduced.

Lambeth Road *SE1*. Extends from St George's Circus to LAMBETH BRIDGE. ST MARY, LAMBETH and St George's Roman Catholic Cathedral (designed by Pugin, 1841) are on the north side, the IMPERIAL WAR MUSEUM on the south. William Bligh, commander of the *Bounty*, lived at No. 100; Sir Philip Barling Ben Greet, the actor-manager, at No. 160 in 1920–36.

Lambeth Walk *SE11*. The market here grew up in the 19th century and by the 1840s was well established. Mayhew notes 164 costermongers' stalls in 1861. Today it is a busy general market seven days a week. The street gave its name to a Cockney dance first made popular in 1937 by Lupino Lane, in the musical *Me and My Gal* at the VICTORIA PALACE.

Lambeth Waterworks Company Started supplying south and west London in 1785 from a

THAMES intake in Belvedere Road near the present FESTIVAL HALL site. A clause in the Act of Incorporation excluded the parishes of ST GEORGE and ST SAVIOURS', SOUTHWARK from the area supplied. In 1802 the main was extended to supply KENNINGTON, 'that respectable and populous neighbourhood'. At that time iron mains began to replace wood. In 1832 a reservoir at STREATHAM HILL was constructed. By 1833 the value of the company's shares had increased tenfold. From 1834 new works and reservoirs were constructed on 16 acres in BRIXTON after an Act of Parliament allowing an extension of the area served. In 1836 part of the site was sold for the construction of BRIXTON PRISON. In 1847 the directors decided to move the intake to a position above the tideway. The new works were at Seething Wells, Thames Ditton, 23 miles above LONDON BRIDGE. By 1868 10 million gallons daily were pumped into the BRIXTON reservoir. But as the supply became polluted, in 1871 the intake was moved to west Molesey. In 1902 the company was taken over by the Metropolitan Water Board (*see* WATER SUPPLY).

Lambeth Wells Situated on what is now LAMBETH WALK. There were two wells, designated 'Nearer' and 'Farther'. The premises, with a 'Great Room' for music and dancing, were opened before 1697. The admission was 3d; but for a special 'Consort of very good musick, with French and Country dancing', which was advertised in 1721, visitors paid 1s. After 1740 a musical society, led by the organist of ST SAVIOUR'S, SOUTHWARK, was formed and met monthly. Lambeth Wells could not compete with the attractions of St George's Spa, and the proprietor was refused a licence in 1755. The premises passed to the Methodists for a meeting hall.

Lamorbey Park *Burnt Oak Lane, Sidcup, Kent*. A 'good house' was built here probably for one James Goldwell in about 1515, being altered in the 1700s and again in the late 1830s and used for education since 1947. The Rose Bruford Training College of Speech and Drama use it by day, and in the evenings Lamorbey Park Adult Education Centre. The London Borough of BEXLEY's Teachers' Training Centre occupy premises in the grounds. The grounds – once about 300 acres – are still partly open space and now cover about 40 acres. Ursula Bloom frequently uses the house as a setting for her novels.

Lancaster Gate *W2*. Possibly named in honour of the Duchy of Lancaster. The BAYSWATER TEA GARDENS flourished here from 1775 until 1850. Earlier still on this site was the physic garden of the botanist and amateur playwright, Sir John Hill. Lancaster Gate itself, designed in 1857 by Sancton Wood, is the most ambitious and successful architectural achievement in BAYSWATER. Beyond the Meath Memorial only the tower now remains of CHRIST CHURCH, which was demolished in 1978 because of structural damage. At No. 108 Prince Eugène Bonaparte, son of the Emperor Napoleon III, stayed in 1872. At No. 69 Lytton Strachey, the critic and biographer, spent his childhood and youth, from 1884, and at No. 74 Bret Harte, the American writer, lived from 1895 until his death in 1902. White's Hotel (61 bedrooms), designed by Hammet and Norton, is one of 16 hotels in the road.

Lancaster House, St James's was rebuilt for Frederick, Duke of York by Benjamin Dean Wyatt in the 1820s.

Lancaster House *Stable Yard, St James's Palace, SW1.* In 1807 Frederick, Duke of York, second son of George III, moved to the 17th-century Godolphin House in Stable Yard and renamed it York House. Ten years later, on the death of Princess Charlotte, he became heir to the throne. Robert Smirke was engaged to rebuild York House to be worthy of his new position but the Duke's brother, George IV, hated Smirke's plans so much that he was replaced as architect by Benjamin Dean Wyatt. Building began in 1825. The house was still unfinished when the Duke died, much in debt, at the Duchess of Rutland's house in ARLINGTON STREET. The government paid off the mortgages on it and sold a lease for £72,000 to one of his many creditors, the Marquess of Stafford. (The money was used to buy VICTORIA PARK.) In 1833 the Marquess was created 1st Duke of Sutherland but died later that year. Stafford House, as it was then known, was roofed but still unfinished. The 2nd Duke asked Wyatt to plan the interior decorations and Smirke to carry them out. Charles Barry was also consulted. In 1841 Smirke added another storey for servants.

The completed mansion was a solid rectangle of Bath stone, three storeys high with a two-storey portico on the front. The interior was decorated in the exuberant French style of Louis XV. The family's rooms and the library were on the ground floor. The staircase was the most spectacular part of the house, decorated with imitation marbles and copies (by Lorenzi) of Veronese's paintings. On the first floor were the state rooms – the State Drawing Room, the Music Room which served also as a State Dining Room, and the Great Gallery which held the Duke's magnificent art collection. Among the paintings were works by Raphael, Tintoretto, Titian, Velasquez, Rubens, Van Dyck, Watteau, Murillo and others.

His wife, Harriet, was a close friend of Queen Victoria and her Mistress of the Robes in 1837–61. The Queen was often a guest at the house and once said, 'I have come from my house to your palace.' It was the rallying point for the Whigs and Liberal politicians. Lord Shaftesbury, Garibaldi and William Garrison, the American abolitionist of slavery, were entertained here and it was the scene of many lavish balls. In 1848 Chopin played for the Queen, Prince Albert and the Duke of Wellington. In 1912 the 4th Duke of Sutherland sold the house to Sir William Lever, later 1st Viscount Leverhulme. He renamed it Lancaster House after his native county. In 1913 he gave the remainder of the lease to the nation so the house could be used for government hospitality and a home for the London Museum (*see* MUSEUM OF LONDON), which remained here until 1946. In 1953 the Coronation Banquet for Elizabeth II was held here. It is now used for government receptions and conferences.

Lancaster Place *WC2.* Built on part of the site of SAVOY Hospital. The offices of the DUCHY OF LANCASTER are on the west side.

Lancaster Terrace *W2.* The 18-storey Royal Lancaster Hotel (436 bedrooms) was designed by T.P. Bennett and Son and opened in 1967.

Lancelot Place *SW7.* Originally a path leading to the fields behind the houses facing KNIGHTSBRIDGE GREEN. In the 1790s small cottages appeared on both sides. In 1817 some of the small houses were demolished and the Trevor Chapel, a large plain building for the Independents, took their place. The Revd John Morrison preached to large congregations for many years here. Before the 2nd World War it became a warehouse. It was demolished after the war and Nos 3–11 were built on the site in 1953. The office development on the east side dates from the early 1960s. The place takes its name from Lancelot Wood, the builder of TREVOR SQUARE. Earlier, across the street stood a public house, the Earl Grey, but this was demolished in 1913 when HARROD's built their garage.

Langbourn One of the Wards of the CITY OF LONDON, in its commercial and banking area, is called Langbourn, and John Stow believed it was so named from a lost stream nearby. There is, however, no evidence of any such stream and the Ward in fact took its name from the word Langebord or Langebrod, a 13th-century version of Lombard. LOMBARD STREET, named after the bankers from Italy who practised in it, runs through it.

The Langham Hotel, built in 1864 for £300,000, was an outstanding example of London's grand Victorian hotels.

Langham *Portland Place, W1.* Built in 1864, to the designs of Giles and Murray, as the Langham Hotel; over 2,000 people were present for the gala opening, including King Edward VII (then Prince of Wales). It was the forerunner of London's grand hotels, costing £300,000 and built in the style of a Florentine palace on seven floors, with 600 rooms including many private suites. It was magnificently furnished in white, scarlet and gold. There were 15,000 yards of carpet and the plaster-relief ceilings and mosaic flooring were by Italian craftsmen. Exiled royalty, statesmen, artists, musicians, writers, all stayed here. Toscanini, Mark Twain, Arnold Bennett, Frank Harris and the notorious swindler, Horatio Bottomley, were among its patrons. The composer Dvorak scandalized the management by asking for a double bedroom for himself and his grown-up daughter, to save money. The exiled Emperor, Napoleon III of France, and many years later another exiled Emperor, Haile Selassie of Ethiopia, stayed at the Langham. Ouida, the bestselling writer of romantic novels, lived at the hotel for several years. She threw lavish receptions, mostly for young guards officers. Many of her novels, including *Under Two Flags*, were written in her boudoir which had black velvet curtains drawn to shut out the daylight. Conan Doyle used the Langham in the plots of some of his novels. It was the essence of Victorian pride and respectability. At the OLD BAILEY in the 1880s, in the case of Carr and Benson, two turf swindlers, a witness gave evidence: 'I knew he must be a perfect gentleman – why, he had rooms at the Langham.'

The land on which the hotel was built was for years the subject of fierce lawsuits. In 1767 Lord Foley built a mansion there, first having secured, after years of legal squabbling, a guarantee from the Duke of Portland that no building could ever be erected in front of the house to obscure the view north to Hampstead and Highgate. That is why today PORTLAND PLACE is 125 ft wide, the width of old Foley House, and among the broadest and most handsome public thoroughfares in London. In 1814 the Foley fortune was squandered and John Nash, the architect, acquired the whole estate in settlement of a debt. He sold part to the Crown and part to Sir James Langham for a new town house with the proviso that he (Nash) should build it. In its brochure the mammoth Langham Hotel, built on the site of Langham House and the nearby Mansfield House, dismissed Nash's most beautiful small church, ALL SOULS in LANGHAM PLACE, as 'that quaint church with its peculiar steeple'. But servants at the Langham had to assemble every morning at seven for prayers led by a clergyman from ALL SOULS. Situated close to BROADCASTING HOUSE and with many BBC associations over the years, ALL SOULS was the scene of fashionable weddings, with receptions across the road at the Langham, until just before the 2nd World War. The nearness of the QUEEN'S HALL made the Langham a popular centre for international musicians and artists. QUEEN'S HALL and the adjoining St George's Hall were destroyed by fire bombs in 1941. Between the wars, as the fashionable centre of London moved west and more luxury hotels were built, the Langham declined in popularity, though aristocratic guests were still faithful patrons. One of the Langham's proudest possessions, the massive water tank holding 38,000 gallons, was to be its final ruin when a German land mine dropped in Portland Place in 1940. Part of the building was shattered but most of the damage was caused by flooding from the giant tank. In 1982 the Langham was owned by the BRITISH BROADCASTING CORPORATION, which used it for offices, studios and the BBC Club.

Langham Place *W1*. First rated in 1815 and named after the landowner, Sir James Langham, whose house occupied part of the site of Foley House which had been demolished in 1814 to make way for the New Street (REGENT STREET) which Nash was planning to link the projected REGENT'S PARK with WESTMINSTER. ALL SOULS CHURCH was constructed on the curve of the road as a pivot. BROADCASTING HOUSE stands at the junction with PORTLAND PLACE. The sculpture, *Prospero and Ariel*, over the main entrance, and the three stone bas-reliefs on the same level, are by Eric Gill. When Langham House was demolished in its turn, it was replaced by the LANGHAM Hotel. St George's Hotel opposite covers the site of the QUEEN'S HALL, bombed in 1941, where Sir Henry Wood's Promenade Concerts were held from 1895 onwards.

Langham Street *W1*. Laid out in the early 19th century, the street takes its name from Sir James Langham, a local magnate. Edmond Malone, the Shakespearean scholar and editor, lived at No. 40 in 1779–1812.

Lansdowne Club *9 Fitzmaurice Place, Berkeley Square, W1*. A club open to both men and women which admits children from the age of six and allows them to become members at 16. The club's premises in LANSDOWNE HOUSE include an indoor swimming pool, four squash courts and a fencing salon. In 1969 600 members of the former International Sportsmen's Club joined; and in 1975 the SAVAGE CLUB rented a suite of rooms on the first floor.

Lansdowne House *Berkeley Square*. Once a marvellous house by Robert Adam, built in 1762–8 and originally completely detached. It was designed for Lord Bute when he was First Lord of the Treasury and sold by him before it was finished to William Petty, 2nd Earl of Shelburne and 1st Marquess of Lansdowne who became Secretary of State for the Southern Department in 1766. The gallery was a later addition, first a library by Joseph Bonomi, then remodelled as a sculpture gallery by George Dance the Younger, and completed by Sir Robert Smirke in 1819. This is still to be seen in the LANSDOWNE CLUB, as is the upper part of the original entrance hall, but much of the rest of the interior disappeared when, in the 1930s, the front was set back about 40 ft to make way for Fitzmaurice Place and the present Lansdowne House was built by Wimperis, Simpson and Guthrie. The main drawing-room and dining-room were preserved, however: the drawing-room is now in the Museum of Arts at Philadelphia, the dining-room at the Metropolitan Museum, New York.

Lansdowne Road *W11*. As with other roads and streets on the LADBROKE ESTATE, this was named after a notable member of the House of Lords, Lord Lansdowne, Lord President of the Council; hence also Clarendon Cross and Road, Stanley Crescent and Gardens and Portland Road. In Lansdowne House, built in 1904 to the designs of William Flockhart, the artists Charles Ricketts, Charles Shannon, Glyn Philpot, Vivian Forbes, James Pryde and F. Cayley Robinson all had studios.

Lant Street *SE1*. Built in 1770–1800 and named after the family who owned the land. Dickens lodged here as a boy while his father was in the MARSHALSEA. Mr and Mrs Garland in *The Old Curiosity Shop* are said to be sketches of the landlord and landlady. In

Pickwick Papers Dickens wrote, 'There is a repose about Lant Street, in the Borough which sheds a gentle melancholy upon the soul. There are always a good many houses to let in the street; it is a by-street too and its dullness is soothing. The majority of the inhabitants either direct their energies to the letting of furnished apartments or devote themselves to the healthful and invigorating pursuit of mangling. The chief features in the still life of the street are green shutters, lodging bills, brass doorplates and bell handles; the principal specimens of animated nature the pot boy, the muffin youth and the baked potato man. The population is migratory, usually disappearing on the verge of quarterday and generally by night. Her Majesty's revenues are seldom collected in this happy valley; the rents are dubious, and the water communication is very frequently cut off.' St Michael's church (now disused) on the north side is by A.S. Newman (1867).

Latymer Upper School *King Street, W6.* The Latymer Foundation dates from 1624, when a Crown Official with a responsible position in the Court of Wards and Liveries, Edward Latymer, made provision in his will for the welfare and education of a small number of men and boys in HAMMERSMITH. The boys first attended a school in FULHAM churchyard. In 1648 they were moved to a school specially built for them in HAMMERSMITH. A new school for 125 boys was built in HAMMERSMITH ROAD in 1863. The buildings were designed by J.M. Kellett. There were 150 boys to begin with; by 1897 the numbers had risen to 300. The trust money was reallocated in 1879. The existing school was renamed Latymer Lower School and continued as such until 1963. The Governors of the Trust opened Latymer Upper School in 1895.

Lauderdale House *Waterlow Park, N6.* The original house was built in the 16th century by Richard Martin, Master of the ROYAL MINT in the reign of Elizabeth I, twice LORD MAYOR and four times Prime Warden of the GOLDSMITHS' COMPANY. Purchased in 1641 by the Countess of Home, the house passed on her death to her daughter, Anne, who married the 2nd Earl of Lauderdale by whom it was completely reconstructed in about 1645. During the Commonwealth General Ireton's brother, John, lived in the house. At the Restoration Lauderdale obtained possession once more. Charles II is said to have borrowed the house as a summer residence for Nell Gwynne; and it was here that she is supposed to have threatened to drop their son out of a window unless his father did something for him immediately. Whereupon the King is said to have called out, 'Save the Earl of Burford!' In 1671, on the death of the Countess of Lauderdale, Ireton bought the house and moved in again. He died in 1677 and thereafter it passed through a succession of hands until, in the 18th century, it became a boarding-house. John Wesley stayed here and thought it must surely be 'the most luxurious boarding-house in England'. In 1812 it became a school. It was bought in 1871 by Sir Sidney Waterlow, who leased it at a low rent to ST BARTHOLOMEW'S HOSPITAL as a convalescent home. In 1889 Waterlow presented it, together with the surrounding park, to the LONDON COUNTY COUNCIL. Lauderdale House was badly damaged by fire in 1963. During the 1970s the Lauderdale House Society was

formed and the house has been restored. It now houses a local museum and a restaurant, and is used for exhibitions and concerts.

Launderers' Company *see* CITY LIVERY COMPANIES.

Laurence Pountney Hill *EC4.* Named after the church of St Laurence Pountney, which was burned down in the GREAT FIRE and not rebuilt. Sir John de Poulteney, who lived nearby, was four times Lord Mayor in the 14th century. The Black Prince lived in his house in 1359. It too was destroyed in the GREAT FIRE. Suffolk House, a tall neo-Gothic building designed by R.B. March in the 1880s, stands on the site of a house which had once belonged to the Duke of Suffolk. It later passed into the hands of the Duke of Buckingham when it became known as the Rose and is referred to as such in Shakespeare's *Henry VIII*. William Harvey, Charles I's physician and discoverer of the circulation of the blood, came to live here with his brother, a rich merchant, after the surrender of Oxford to the Parliamentary forces in 1646. Nos 1 and 2, built in 1703, are the finest early 18th-century houses still to be seen in the CITY.

Lavatories *see* PUBLIC LAVATORIES AND PUBLIC BATHS.

Lavender Hill *Battersea, SW11.* Received its name from the lavender that was grown in the market gardens on the north side of the road. Until the late 18th century it was a coaching route passing through open fields. Then a few large houses were built; by the 1860s urbanisation was taking hold, and many of the houses standing today date from this period.

Law Courts *Strand, WC2.* The Royal Courts of Justice ('the Law Courts') were built in the 19th century to concentrate in one convenient place all the superior courts concerned with civil – i.e. non-criminal – cases. These courts traditionally sat in WESTMINSTER HALL in the legal term time, but out of term used to move to various highly inconvenient locations. In 1865 an amount of £1,453,000 out of public funds was provided for the purchase of the site (then an unsalubrious slum) and £700,000 allocated out of unclaimed funds in Chancery to pay for the new building. G.E. Street was appointed architect. The foundations were laid at a cost of £36,750 in 1871–2 and work on the building, which was to cost £826,000, began in 1874. Six years were allowed for construction, but a combination of labour troubles, bad weather and financial difficulties delayed the completion and formal opening of the new courts by Queen Victoria until 4 December 1882. Street himself had meanwhile died of a stroke in December 1881, his death being widely attributed to the many vexations associated with the project. His statue by H.H. Armstead is in the Main Hall. The building is brick (35 million) faced with Portland stone, and contains more than 1,000 rooms and some three and a half miles of corridors. Over the main entrance are statues of Christ (centre), King Solomon (west) and King Alfred (east), while Moses stands over the back door. The hall, in the centre of the building, is 238 ft long and 80 ft high and contains statues of Sir William Blackstone, author of the *Commentaries on the Laws of England*, and

G.E. Street's early design for the Law Courts. His building, much modified, was opened by Queen Victoria in 1882, a year after his death, which was believed by many to have been caused by the problems and frustrations that attended the project.

Lord Chief Justice Russell, the first Roman Catholic to occupy that post since the Reformation. Gothic arches lead off to the courts and other accommodation. The windows carry the arms of former Lord Chancellors and Lord Keepers of the Great Seal. A museum of legal dress is situated in the hall near the main entrance.

The Supreme Court of Judicature, which since 1875 has replaced the old superior courts of WESTMINSTER, comprises the Court of Appeal, the High Court and the Crown Court. The High Court is made up of the Queen's Bench Division, the Chancery Division and the Family Division. Each Division is concerned with a particular form of civil litigation. However, Queen's Bench Judges also preside over the more important criminal trials in the Crown Court throughout the country, while the Court of Appeal has a Criminal Division to hear appeals in criminal cases.

The original building contained 19 courts but the extension of 1911 (West Green) provided four more and the new Queen's Building (1968) 12 more. To relieve the pressure on the CENTRAL CRIMINAL COURT a number of criminal trials are held in the Queen's Building. A modern 11-storey structure at the rear in CAREY STREET (Thomas More Building) accommodates the Bankruptcy and Companies Courts. In all some 60 courts are in present use. All are equipped for tape recording. On the second Saturday in November the LORD MAYOR elect rides in his coach in procession from the GUILDHALL to the courts to be sworn in by the Lord Chief Justice.

Law Society *Chancery Lane, WC2.* A voluntary organisation of solicitors, originally known as the Law Institute, it dates from 1825. When a royal charter of incorporation was obtained in 1831, it was renamed the Incorporated Law Society. Earlier attempts to raise professional standards resulted in the foundation

in London in 1739 of the Society of Gentlemen Practisers in the Several Courts of Law and Equity, and the creation in 1819 of the Metropolitan Law Society. Both bodies ceased to exist after 1831. Its present title, the Law Society, derives from an amending charter of 1903. The growth of the Society's educational and social activities contributed to the disappearance of the INNS OF CHANCERY in the 19th century.

The Society is governed by a President and Council of 65 members. Membership has grown from 223 at its inception to 7,712 (1901), 10,283 (1931), 20,000 (1967) and 31,625 (1980). This last figure represents about three-quarters of all the solicitors currently on the roll (46,591). The Society has numerous powers and duties imposed upon it in regard to the education and discipline of the profession generally, e.g. it keeps the roll of solicitors, runs a College of Law, administers the Legal Aid Scheme on a nationwide basis, conducts professional examinations and takes action against offending solicitors.

The Law Society's Hall is situated on the west side of CHANCERY LANE at its southern end (No. 113). The building was designed by Lewis Vulliamy in 1831. The stained glass windows depicting the arms of the former Serjeants which were once part of Serjeants' Inn (dissolved in 1877) are now in the Society's Hall. The Society has an extensive library containing some 80,000 books.

Lawrence Lane *EC2.* From the 13th until the 18th century it was known as St Lawrence Lane after the church of ST LAWRENCE JEWRY. Before KING STREET was built it was the main street from CHEAPSIDE to the GUILDHALL. From the 14th century until 1855 a famous tavern called Blossom's Inn stood in the lane.

Lawrence Street *SW2.* One of the oldest streets in the parish, named after a CHELSEA family whose monument is in the CHELSEA OLD CHURCH. The Duchess of Monmouth lived at No. 24. Later Tobias Smollett lived here in 1749–63. CHELSEA PORCELAIN FACTORY was in the north-west corner; shards are still found in some gardens. The houses on the western side were built after the factory buildings were pulled down in 1784. On the east side is a PEABODY BUILDINGS estate, the oldest built by this charity.

Lazard Brothers and Co. Ltd *Moorfields, EC2.* Established in London in 1870, this merchant bank is a close cousin of the Lazard firms established in Paris and New York. The London firm operated primarily as an accepting house, later emerging as a specialist on new issues and takeovers. It was acquired in 1920 by S. Pearson and Sons, the industrial holding company, and in 1960 it purchased Edward de Stein and Co, merchant bankers at AUSTIN FRIARS since 1925.

Le Quarré Church *Berwick Street.* Built in 1694 for French Protestant refugees. Its congregation dwindled in the 1960s and it became an auction room.

Lea *or* **Lee** Rising in Bedfordshire, this river was formerly the boundary between MIDDLESEX and Essex. It joined the THAMES at POPLAR. It may have been used by the Romans as a navigable route to Verulamium; according to the Anglo-Saxon Chronicle, King Alfred's ships pursued the Danes up it in 896. Throughout medieval, Tudor and later times successive authorities have continued to maintain and improve the Lea navigation and it now includes a network of canals. Like most running streams in the Middle Ages it was used for carrying away human sewage and the more disgusting refuse from the butcher's trade. In its upper reaches it was used by Izaak Walton and other devotees of angling, and today, after many years of cleaning up, it furnishes one sixth of London's water supply.

Lea Bridge *E5.* Lies to the west of the River LEA with HACKNEY MARSHES on the opposite bank. The Mill Fields are reputedly the site of the battle in AD 527 between Octa, King of Kent, grandson of Hengest, and the victorious Erchenwein, founder of the kingdom of Essex. There was early settlement on the high ground at CLAPTON to the west of the marshland and probably an early track towards the LEA as part of the route between London and Waltham Abbey. A bridge across the LEA at this point existed by the 18th century and was replaced by an iron bridge in 1820. There was building around the bridge and along Lea Bridge Road, and by the 20th century a mission church dedicated to St James served the hamlet. In 1892 the third and present Lea Bridge was opened, carrying much traffic into LEYTON where Lea Bridge station is situated. The establishment of a marina with recreational facilities at Lea Bridge in the Lea Valley Regional Park in 1967 allowed the traditional pastimes of angling and bathing to continue. In 1965 Lea Bridge became part of the London Borough of HACKNEY.

Leadenhall Market *Gracechurch Street, EC2.* Takes its name from a mansion with a lead roof which belonged to the Neville family in the 14th century. 'Foreigners', that was to say anybody who came from outside London, were allowed to sell their poultry here. In 1377 'foreigners' were given permission also to sell cheese and butter. The house and estate were sold to the CITY CORPORATION in 1411. In 1445 the newly built granary was declared a general market for poultry, victuals, grain, eggs, butter, cheese and such like. Later wool and leather were sold too. Both the market and the mansion were burnt down in the GREAT FIRE. The market was rebuilt round three large courtyards. In the first yard was the beef market. Leather, wool and raw hides were also sold here on certain days. The second yard was for veal, mutton and lamb; but fishmongers, poulterers and cheesemongers had stalls here, too. In the third yard was the herb market, for fruit and vegetables. In 1881 Horace Jones replaced these structures by the present buildings. Meat, poultry, plants, fish, etc. are sold here.

Leadenhall Street *EC3.* Named after the Leadenhall (*see* LEADENHALL MARKET), it extends from CORNHILL to ALDGATE. In it have been found parts of nine tessellated Roman pavements including, in 1803, a particularly fine example at a depth of 9 ft 6 ins. It was first mentioned in the early 17th century and largely rebuilt in the later years of the 19th. ST KATHARINE CREE stands at the corner of Gracechurch Lane. On the corner of LIME STREET once stood EAST INDIA HOUSE, where Charles Lamb worked as a clerk from 1792 to 1825 and John Stuart Mill was employed from 1823 to 1858. Thomas Love Peacock, the novelist, was also employed here. The building was demolished in 1862. Nathaniel Bentley, the notorious 'Dirty Dick', kept at No. 46 a hardware shop, the first glazed hardware shop in London, which he had inherited from his father who had presented a bell to ST KATHARINE CREE in 1754 on condition that it was rung on his birthday as long as he lived (*see* DIRTY DICK'S). At No. 157 was the shop of the nautical instrument dealer, Solomon Gills, in *Dombey and Son*. His sign, the Little Wooden Midshipman, was later moved to the premises of Messrs Norris and Wilson in the MINORIES. LLOYD'S moved here in 1928 to a building designed by Sir Edwin Cooper. The Midland Bank at No. 140, designed by Sir Edwin Lutyens, was completed in 1931; Commercial Union and P & O headquarters at No. 130 by Gollins, Melvin, Ward and Partners in 1969; Nos 36–38 by Yorke, Rosenberg and Mardall in 1973; and the Banque Belge at No. 135, also by Gollins, Melvin, Ward and Partners, in 1978.

Leather Lane *EC1.* The name is probably not derived from the leathersellers who carried on business here but from *leveroun*, the old French word for greyhound, possible the name of an inn: 14th-century spellings of the name are Leveroune and Louverone. In Strype's day there were several inns, 'all indifferent'. In the late 19th century the lane was described as traversing 'a very poor neighbourhood; is much infested with thieves, beggars, and Italian organgrinders; and is in itself narrow and dirty, and lined with stalls and barrows of itinerant dealers in fish, bacon and vegetables, plasterers or image shops, and old clothes; a decidedly unsavoury and unattractive locality.' The market here is still in existence, selling food, clothes and general foods.

Leathersellers' Company *see* CITY LIVERY COMPANIES.

Leathersellers' Hall *St Helen's Place, EC3.* The Company's first Hall, acquired in 1445, was in

LONDON WALL. The nunnery buildings of ST HELEN BISHOPSGATE were purchased in 1543. These were demolished in 1799 and the Company moved to a smaller building nearby. This was burned down in 1819 and rebuilt in 1822 by W.F. Pocock. A new, larger Hall was built opposite by G.A. Wilson and opened in 1878. The old building was let as offices. Having sustained severe damage in 1941 the present Hall was restored by K. Peacock in 1959. The livery hall is almost a perfect 38 ft cube. For the Company *see* CITY LIVERY COMPANIES.

Leaves Green   *Kent*. Takes its name from the Legh family of ADDINGTON. In 1500, when it was mostly common land, it was known as Lese Green. There are still 19½ acres of common. The workhouse for the parish of Cudham was erected here sometime before 1731. The building still stands and is now three cottages. The London Coal and Wine Duties Continuation Act, 1831, provided for a charge to be made on all loads of wine and coal entering the London area. One of the iron posts set up to mark the area still stands at Leaves Green, which is now part of the London Borough of BROMLEY.

Lee   *SE12, SE13*. Until the 1830s a sparsely-populated rural area, running from BLACKHEATH on the north, to the Hundred (later the county) boundary at Grove Park to the south. The ancient parish church of St Margaret's in Lee Terrace is now represented by its ruined tower standing in the old burial ground. Here are buried two Astronomers Royal, Edmond Halley and John Pond; and Robert Cocking, a foolhardy pioneer who fell to his death in the parish while attempting to land from a balloon with an untested parachute. The present church, which stands on the opposite side of the road, built in 1839–41, is a fine example of 'Commissioners' Gothic' probably by John Brown of Norwich. The busy Lee High Road, often jammed with traffic on its way to the Channel ports, virtually bisects the area. Until it was straightened in 1825, the main road took a zig-zag course through the village, the old twists remaining as Old Road. The main settlement was round Lee Green and the Tiger's Head (where the horses were changed, and horse buses stopped) with some half a dozen mansions occupied by wealthy CITY businessmen scattered along the street. Of these, two remain, Pentland House (originally built about 1680) and the Manor House (1771) where Sir Francis Baring, the merchant and banker, lived in 1797–1810. The latter was probably designed by Richard Jupp. An attractive square chapel in Lee High Road is all that survives of the original almshouses (built 1682 and mentioned in John Evelyn's diary). It was built by Christopher Boone, a wealthy CITY merchant who settled in the village in the mid-17th century. (Daniel Boone, the American pioneer, was a collateral descendant of this family.) Behind the chapel are the attractive Merchant Taylors' almshouses (1826).

Speculative building of large houses brought a wave of new well-to-do residents to Lee in the 1830s–50s. With the advent of the railways, many smaller houses were built before the 1st World War. The building of the large LONDON COUNTY COUNCIL estate at Downham between the wars completed the building up of the area. Some of the old farm fields have been preserved in parks and playing fields, retaining the pleasant, spacious, quiet atmosphere of the district. Lee lost its status as a separate community in 1899, when it was amalgamated with LEWISHAM to form the new Metropolitan Borough of LEWISHAM.

Lee Navigation   Runs from Hertford via Ware to Hoddesdon, where it is joined by the River Stort from Bishop's Stortford, and thence south to OLD FORD AND BOW, joining the THAMES at CANNING TOWN. It is 30¾ miles long, has 20 locks and is connected to the REGENT'S CANAL by the Hertford Union Canal and the LIMEHOUSE CUT.

Leicester House   *Leicester Square*. Built in the 1630s by Robert Sidney, 2nd Earl of Leicester, on land which a century earlier had come into the hands of Henry VIII (*see* LEICESTER SQUARE). It was a fairly plain house externally, but extremely large and expensively furnished. For a generation it remained one of the biggest houses in London, celebrated for

A view across farmland from Blackheath towards the village of Lee in about 1825, from a lithograph by T.M. Baynes.

its entertainments: in 1672 John Evelyn dined here with the wife of the 2nd Earl's grandson, the English ambassador in Paris, and was beguiled by Richardson, 'the famous Fire-Eater, who before us devour'd Brimston on glowing coales, chewing and swallowing them downe'. In 1717 the Prince of Wales, who became George II in 1727, moved here from his apartments in ST JAMES'S PALACE from which he had been evicted after a quarrel with his father. He agreed to pay a rent of £500 and, in addition, took over the neighbouring SAVILE HOUSE with which Leicester House was then linked by a covered passage. For ten years Leicester House was frequented by George I's opponents until the old King died and his son was proclaimed his successor outside the gates. Soon afterwards the new King moved out of the house which, in 1742, the 7th Earl agreed to let to Frederick, Prince of Wales, father of the future George III. Prince Frederick died here in 1751, after being hit on the throat by a cricket ball. His widow remained in the house until 1764 when she moved to CARLTON HOUSE; her son, Prince Henry, Duke of Cumberland, continued to live there until 1767.

Seven years later the house was taken over by a naturalist from Lancashire, Ashton Lever, who had assembled an immense collection of fossils, shells and other objects of natural history. The collection remained open to the public at Leicester House until 1788 when it was removed to a rotunda at 3 BLACKFRIARS ROAD. Lever was also interested in archery, an activity to which he had been introduced by his secretary, Thomas Waring, and it was at Leicester House that the Toxopholite Society was formed in 1780 or 1781. After his employer's death, Waring continued to live in part of Leicester House until 1791 when, the 7th and last Earl of Leicester having died and the heiress upon whom Leicester House had devolved having also died, heavily in debt, the estate was auctioned and, in 1791–2, the house demolished. LEICESTER PLACE was laid out across the site of the forecourt and LISLE STREET extended eastwards over the site of the house.

Leicester Place *WC2.* Laid out in the 1790s by Thomas Wright, a banker, on part of the site which had been occupied by LEICESTER HOUSE and its garden. Soon after its construction the SANS SOUCI THEATRE was built here by Charles Dibdin. And in 1793 Robert Barker opened his panorama designed by Robert Mitchell (*see* PANORAMAS). The panorama shows continued until 1864, but in the following year the lease of the property, together with that of the adjoining house, No. 5, was acquired by a French Marist priest, and the two buildings were converted into Notre Dame de France. The crypt of the church is now used by the Centre Charles Péguy, a club for young French people in London, named after the French poet who was killed in 1914. The French general, and former Girondist Foreign Minister, Charles François Dumouriez who, denounced as a traitor by the Jacobins, deserted to the Austrians in 1793, came to live in the street in 1812. The PRINCE CHARLES CINEMA was built as a theatre in 1961–2, as part of the office block known as Charles House, to the design of Carl Fisher and Associates.

Leicester Square *WC2.* In the Middle Ages the land upon which the square was built belonged to the Beaumont family, and to the Abbot and Convent of St

Peter's, WESTMINSTER ABBEY. The Abbot and Convent surrendered their 3 acres to Henry VIII in 1536 and the other 4 acres came into the King's hands the following year upon the death of the last Lord Beaumont's widow. During 1630–48 Robert Sidney, 2nd Earl of Leicester, acquired the land; and in 1631–5 LEICESTER HOUSE was built on the northern part. On the southern part, which had come to be known as Leicester Fields, Leicester Square was laid out in the 1670s for 'the good and benefit of the family, the advancement of their revenue, and the decency of the place before Leicester House'. The houses built in the square were handsome buildings modelled upon those in PALL MALL. At first no shops were allowed, but Lord Leicester's son and heir, the 3rd Earl, permitted the erection of booths in front of the courtyard of Leicester House towards the end of the 17th century. In 1782 a linen draper named Gedge opened a shop on the corner of Cranbourn Street, which had one of the earliest shop fronts in London. Many of the houses in the 17th and 18th century were occupied by aristocratic families, including those of the Earls of Ailesbury, Sunderland, Rockingham, Scarsdale, Westmorland and Deloraine. There were also several artists, writers and professional men among the residents: the poet, Matthew Prior, lived at a house on the site of the present No. 21 between 1699 and 1700; and William Hogarth lived at No. 30 in 1733–64, producing here some of his best-known work, including *Marriage à la Mode*, *Rake's Progress*, *Beer Street*, *Gin Lane*, and *Industry and Idleness*.

While Hogarth was still living in the square, Sir Joshua Reynolds bought a house here, in which he lived from 1760 until his death in 1792. This was No. 47 whose site is now covered by the headquarters of the Automobile Association, Fanum House. During the years of Reynolds's residence in the house, his friend, Samuel Johnson, spoke of his ever-increasing fame and fortune with a kind of wistful envy: 'Reynolds is without a rival and continues to add thousands to thousands'; 'Reynolds gets six thousand a year'; 'Reynolds still continues to increase in reputation and in riches.' Certainly he lived at No. 47 in style. According to one of his assistants he built on a 'splendid gallery for the exhibition of his works, and a commodious and elegant room for his sitters'. Friends as well as sitters were constant callers. Burke and Boswell came, Goldsmith, Garrick, and Fanny Burney. Johnson came to ask Reynolds's advice as to whether or not he ought to accept the state pension which had been offered him in view of his definition of the word in his dictionary as an 'allowance made to any one without an equivalent – in England generally understood to mean pay given to a state hireling for treason to his country.' It was in this house, too, 'at his own fireside', that Reynolds proposed to Johnson the formation of THE CLUB.

Other distinguished residents of the square in the 18th century were Sir Thomas de Veil, the celebrated and lascivious magistrate who lived, in 1729–37, at No. 40 the site of which is now covered by the Leicester Square Theatre; William Cumberland Cruikshank, the surgeon who attended Dr Johnson in his last illness and was resident at No. 49 in 1789–1800; James Stuart, the architect, who lived at No. 35 in 1766–88; and John Singleton Copley, the American painter, who lived in 1776–83 at No. 28, which was then taken over by the Scottish surgeon, John Hunter. Hunter,

An engraving of Leicester Square in 1750. Leicester House was at that time one of the biggest houses in London.

who lived here until his death in 1793, extended the house to provide accommodation for his huge collection of physiological specimens. This collection was purchased for the nation in 1799 and in 1806 was removed to the premises of the ROYAL COLLEGE OF SURGEONS (*see* HUNTERIAN MUSEUM).

Throughout the 18th century the square remained a fashionable area, though by the century's end several foreign craftsmen had moved in and some houses had ceased to be privately occupied. The house on the site of No. 27, for example, which had been occupied until his death in 1724 by the 1st Earl of Rockingham, was soon converted into a *bagnio*; and it was here that the anatomist, Nathanael St André, then a surgeon at WESTMINSTER HOSPITAL, brought Mary Tofts, an illiterate woman from Surrey who claimed that in November 1726, after having been frightened by a rabbit while at work in the fields, she had given birth to a litter of 15 rabbits. St André was convinced of the truth of her account, and claimed to have himself delivered her of two further rabbits or parts of rabbits. The extraordinary story became the talk of London and George I sent a surgeon in his household to investigate the matter. The surgeon, too, claimed that he had delivered the woman of part of another rabbit. From the *bagnio* in Leicester Square, St André sent an invitation to Sir Hans Sloane, then President of the ROYAL SOCIETY, to come to witness her give birth to more rabbits. She was soon afterwards caught trying secretly to buy a rabbit; her imposture was exposed and she confessed it. Some years later there was another notorious affair when Anne Millicent King, who lived at No. 36 in 1757–61, was murdered by her lodger, a Swiss miniature painter, who cut up her body, threw the entrails into the boghouse, and 'carried bits of her about in parcels'.

Towards the middle of the 19th century the character of the square began to change as the construction of NEW COVENTRY STREET led to a great increase in the volume of traffic. Private residents moved out, and

their houses made way for hotels, shops, exhibition centres, museums and cultural institutes. SAVILE HOUSE had already become a museum; in 1835 Dr Hunter's house had been occupied by the National Museum of Mechanical Arts, which closed down the following year; and in 1854 the ROYAL PANOPTICON OF SCIENCE AND ART was opened. Brunet's Hotel, later known as Jaunay's, which had opened in 1800, was but one of several foreign hotels for which the square had become celebrated. Of these the Sablonière and the Cavour were the best known. The Sablonière occupied the south corner of the east side of the square. In later Victorian times the square was also celebrated for its Turkish baths, its oyster rooms, and, above all its theatres: the ALHAMBRA was opened in 1858; the EMPIRE in 1884; and, round the corner in CRANBOURN STREET, DALY'S in 1893 and the HIPPODROME in 1900. So, in the words of the *Survey of London* (vol. XXXIV), 'Leicester Square reached the peak of its fame as a West End centre of diversion during the quarter-century before the outbreak of war in 1914. ... Leicester Square was essentially masculine – its popularity with the *demi-monde* meant that it was no place for unescorted ladies – and when the war engulfed its clientele, nostalgic memories of it were universally evoked by the phrase "Farewell, Leicester Square" in the song "It's a Long Way to Tipperary".'

Today the square, which has been closed to traffic, presents a rather forlorn and decrepit appearance with no identifiable character. Its cinemas, snack bars and restaurants are its principal *raison d'être*. The west side is dominated by Fanum House which, designed for the Automobile Association by Andrew Mather, was begun in 1923 and extended by Leonard Allen and Gordon Jeeves 1956–9. On the south-east corner is the redbrick and biscuit-coloured terracotta Royal Dental Hospital, built in 1899–1901 to the designs of Young and Hall.

The square's garden has not changed in the last century so radically as the square itself. It was originally

Lammas land, that is to say common land available to all the parishioners for drying clothes and for pasturing cattle after Lammas Day, 12 August. The Earl of Leicester was obliged, therefore, to compensate the parishioners for the loss of their rights when he acquired the ground in 1630. The garden of LEICESTER HOUSE was separated from the rest of the ground by a brick wall; and a committee of the Privy Council, appointed by Charles I to arbitrate between Lord Leicester and the parishioners, decided that this ground must be turned by his Lordship 'into Walkes and planted with trees along the walkes and fitt spaces left for the Inhabitantes to drye their clothes there as they were wont, and to have free use of the place.' When building took place around what was now known as Leicester Fields, the contractors were required to rail off the centre and plant it with young elms. By the beginning of the 18th century the wooden rails and posts had been replaced by a brick wall and iron railing; and in 1748 Burchard's statue of George I was placed in the centre of the square (see STATUES).

In 1808 the garden was sold by the Tulk family, into whose hands this part of the Leicester Estate had now passed. The new owner, a dentist living in the square, allowed it to deteriorate; and subsequent owners permitted further degeneration until, towards the middle of the 19th century, it was described as 'very ruinous and dilapidated'. It was in this state when it was acquired by James Wyld, the geographer, who began in 1851 to build in it his GREAT GLOBE. After the demolition of the GREAT GLOBE, the garden continued in a scandalous condition, the playground for the 'unwashed Arabs of Westminster' who 'disported themselves at their own will among the putrifying remains of dogs and cats.' In 1873 it was enclosed by tall wooden hoardings on which were placed advertisements for 'cocoa, cheap trousers, rival circuses, and the largest circulation'. These unsightly spectacles were removed later that same year by order of the Master of the Rolls, who ruled that the garden must be used as a garden and for no other purpose.

It was at this juncture that Albert Grant, the flamboyant MP for Kidderminster, came to the garden's rescue. Grant, who had been born in Dublin and changed his name from Gottheimer, was, in the words of the *Dictionary of National Biography*, 'the pioneer of modern mammoth company promoting'. He had made a fortune by extremely dubious methods and chose to call himself Baron Grant, a title conferred upon him by the King of Italy in return for some services rendered in connection with the Galleria Vittorio Emanuele in Milan. He bought the garden for £11,060 in 1874 and commissioned James Knowles to lay it out. A marble fountain surmounted by a statue of Shakespeare was placed in the centre; and in the corners were placed busts of four great men, three of whom, Hogarth, Reynolds and John Hunter, had lived in the square, and one of whom, Isaac Newton, was supposed to have done but actually lived at 35 ST MARTIN'S STREET. Hogarth's bust is by J. Durham, Reynolds's by H. Weekes, Hunter's by T. Woolner, and Newton's by W. Calder Marshall. When the renovated garden was opened to the public in July 1874, Grant handed over the title deeds to a representative of the Board of Works. The statue of Charlie Chaplin was unveiled in 1981 (see STATUES).

Leicester Street *WC2*. Built on part of the site of LEICESTER HOUSE in the early 1680s. A large house on the site of Nos 10–11 was successively occupied for short periods by the Earls of Manchester and Stamford, then by Lord Newborough, the Duchess of Leeds and the Hon. Arthur Onslow, Speaker of the House of Commons, who remained here from 1727 to 1753 when he moved to the by then more fashionable SOHO SQUARE. In 1805–11, after which he too moved to SOHO SQUARE, the house was occupied by the Scottish surgeon, Sir Charles Bell.

Leighton House, now a museum and art gallery, was designed for himself in 1865 by Lord Leighton and his friend George Aitchison.

Leighton House Museum and Art Gallery *12 Holland Park Road, W14*. A simple redbrick exterior conceals rooms of exotic Eastern splendour. The studio house was built for Lord Leighton of Stretton RA in 1866 to his own designs and those of his friend, George Aitchison. Others of Leighton's friends made contributions to it – Randolph Caldecott, the capitals to the red marble columns; Walter Crane, the mosaic frieze; William De Morgan, tiles and pottery. The fantastic Arab Hall, added in 1877–9 and based on drawings made by Aitchison in Moorish Spain, has a fountain in the mosaic floor, a cupola with stained glass lights, alcoves of Cairene lattice-work and walls covered with floral patterned tiles from Cairo, Damascus and Rhodes which were collected by Leighton and his friends, Sir Caspar Purdon Clarke and Sir Richard Burton.

Lennox Gardens *SW1*. Built on Prince's cricket ground (see PRINCE'S CLUB) after its lease had expired in 1885. The land is part of the SMITH'S CHARITY ESTATE and the gardens were named after a trustee of the charity, the 6th Duke of Richmond and Gordon, whose family name was Lennox. The large redbrick houses were the work of a number of architects but they are all of a style which Osbert Lancaster named 'Pont Street Dutch'. The Uruguayan Embassy is at No. 48.

Lenthall Place *SW7*. Built in about 1872 on the THURLOE ESTATE, it takes its name from William Lenthall, Speaker of the House of Commons in John Thurloe's time.

Lesnes Abbey Woods *Abbey Wood, SE2*. Lesnes Abbey was founded in 1178 by Richard de Luci, Justiciar of England and Lord of the Manor of ERITH, as an act of penance for his support of King Henry II in the dispute with Thomas Becket which culminated in the Archbishop's murder. Belonging to the Augustinian order, the Abbey was never a wealthy foundation, largely due to the expense of repairing the adjacent river walls, and was suppressed by Wolsey in 1525. It then passed through various hands, including those of William Brereton who was involved with Anne Boleyn and executed for treason. From 1633 it spent three centuries in the possession of CHRIST'S HOSPITAL before being taken over by the LONDON COUNTY COUNCIL in 1930. The ruins were excavated under the direction of Sir Alfred Clapham from 1909 onwards, and with the surrounding 200 acres of woodland, famous for their spring daffodils and bluebells, now form one of London's most attractive parks.

John Lewis Partnership *278–306 Oxford Street, W1.* John Lewis was a buyer of silks and dress materials for PETER ROBINSON when a customer encouraged him to set up on his own. In 1864 he took a small shop at 132 OXFORD STREET. By 1892 he had spread along OXFORD STREET to HOLLES STREET, and in 1897 acquired Cavendish Buildings and wished to extend his shop into CAVENDISH SQUARE; he was stopped by a court injunction which he defied, spending three weeks in BRIXTON PRISON in consequence, but later won his point and spoilt the square.

In the early 1900s his son, Spedan Lewis, aware that he, his father and brother were drawing more out of the business than all the rest of the staff together, started to devise a more equitable division of the profits. In 1906 they acquired a controlling interest in PETER JONES, and their profit-sharing schemes continued to develop, culminating in 1929 in the formation of a Trust in which all members of the staff became joint owners of the store and business. They have since developed, absorbed and propagated many other businesses including the Waitrose supermarkets of which there are now eight in the Greater London area. The main store was rebuilt by Slater and Uren in 1958–60. The winged figure on the east wall is by Barbara Hepworth (1963).

Lewisham *SE13.* Now a major shopping centre south of DEPTFORD and north of CATFORD. In 918 Elfrida, daughter (or niece) of Alfred the Great, gave the manor to the Abbey of St Peter at Ghent, Belgium. The ancient parish, centred on the church of ST MARY (rebuilt in restrained classical style by George Gibson in 1774–7), included the modern suburbs of BLACKHEATH, BROCKLEY, FOREST HILL, SYDENHAM, CATFORD and HITHER GREEN. Stone House, built by Gibson for himself in about 1766–74, can be glimpsed at the top of Lewisham Way. Lewisham High Street, whose length so impressed James I that 'he would be king of Lewsham' became fashionable in the 17th and 18th centuries. Its farmhouses were interspersed with mansions, including The Limes where John Wesley retired to rest and write. Limes Grove and the Roman Catholic church of St Saviour and St John (by John Kelly, 1909) mark the site of the house and grounds today. Only one house of any age survives, the former Vicarage on the corner of Ladywell Road, built in 1692–3 by the Revd George Stanhope, Dean of Canterbury. Dean Swift visited him there in 1711. In 1652 an earlier vicar, the Revd Abraham Colfe, founded the Grammar School which still bears his name although

situated now at Lee Green. On the site occupied by the Register Office, his trustees built six almshouses and a chapel in 1664. Another set of almshouses, for six aged females, built in 1840 by John Thackeray of Lewisham, survives where Lewisham High Street becomes Rushey Green. For those less fortunate a new workhouse was built in about 1821, and stands as part of LEWISHAM HOSPITAL, to the south of the main entrance.

The little River RAVENSBOURNE supported a surprising number of water mills (11 in *Domesday Book*), the most notable being the Armoury (later Silk) Mill, which produced steel for GREENWICH armour in the 16th century, musket barrels during the Napoleonic Wars, and gold and silver thread for Victorian uniforms. Only the Riverdale Mill (c.1828) remains as the centrepiece of an office development behind the Riverdale shopping centre. Ladywell Fields adjoining St Mary's church incorporate 30 acres of meadow recorded in *Domesday*. The Lady Well, now buried beneath the access road to Ladywell Station, is recorded in 1592 and was probably a holy well connected with the parish church. Its coping stones can still be seen in front of the old public baths in Ladywell Road.

After 1849 the railways transformed the area. The first superior developments, such as Granville Park, were followed by a network of terraces; and in the High Street the mansions gave way to shops. With little industry until after 1900, Lewisham became a solid, conservative, middle-class suburb. The poet, Ernest Dowson, lived in a house on the site of No. 1 Dowson Court, Belmont Grove; the social reformers Margaret and Rachel McMillan at No. 127 George Lane in 1910–13; Samuel Smiles, author of *Self-Help*, at No. 11 Granville Park. The Clock Tower commemorating Queen Victoria's 1897 Jubilee symbolised the achievement of Metropolitan Borough status in 1900. The years since 1945 have seen fundamental changes, with rebuilding, population changes, and the absorption in 1965 of the more industrial borough of DEPTFORD, creating a varied, almost cosmopolitan society in the Victorian terraces and tower blocks.

Lexington Street *W1.* Building began here in the 1670s, the whole of the street being rebuilt in the 18th century. Few of these houses remain and none is of interest. Most of the street is now occupied by Victorian and Edwardian warehouses, and many of the firms in it are connected with the clothing trade. The northern part of the street was known as Cambridge Street until 1885; the southern part, which leads into BREWER STREET, as Little Windmill Street. Its present name derives no doubt from Robert Sutton, Baron Lexington of Aran, and his successors who inherited the Pulteney Estate. The garage in the street was the second to be built in London on the ramp system (*see* POLAND STREET).

Leyden House *Thames Bank, SW14.* Basically a late 15th-century timber-framed structure behind its plain rendered 18th-century façade. A stone 16th-century fireplace survives inside, but the rear cross-wing was demolished and other early features removed when the house was refurbished in the 1960s. Other early houses, notably Thames Bank House, Tudor Lodge and Thames Cottage, form a most attractive group at the traditional end of the UNIVERSITY BOAT RACE course. It is still a private house.

Leyland House *174–204 Marylebone Road, NW1.*
Designed as Castrol House by Gollins, Melvin, Ward
and Partners (1958–61), based on the Lever Building
in New York, with a 13-storey tower rising from a two-
storey podium. It was one of the earliest post-war curtain wall towers in London.

Leyton *E10.* Situated about 5 miles north-east of
London with the River LEA to the west and WALTHAM-
STOW lying to the north. The ancient parish of Low
Leyton was originally part of the forest of Essex and by
the 14th century included a hamlet called LEYTON-
STONE. Much of the parish was low-lying marshland
by the LEA, rising to more than 100 ft towards EPPING
FOREST. Remains suggest Roman settlement in the
south-west, and a Roman road on the line of Leytonstone High Road ran northwards from London to EP-
PING FOREST and Waltham Abbey. The marshes, liable to flooding and drained by the Dagenham Brook
from WALTHAMSTOW, were fertile farmland from the
Saxon era when Leyton meant a farm on the LEA. A
church existed on the site of ST MARY THE VIRGIN by
1182, and the late 15th-century timber-framed Essex
Hall (remodelled about 1700 and with a 19th-century
porch) survives on the site of the original manor house.
The 16th and 17th centuries saw the arrival of
illustrious and affluent residents, including Thomas
More's grandson, an upholder of Roman Catholicism
in Leyton, and Nathaniel Tench, one of the first
governors of the BANK OF ENGLAND. Mansions appeared, and John Smith's almshouses were built
(1656, rebuilt 1885). Market gardening was a flourishing concern in the 18th century.

In the early 19th century an iron bridge was built
and many acres of Leyton Marshes were soon taken
over by the railway, and by water and gas works. Lea
Bridge station (1840) on the Eastern and Northern
Railway, and Low Leyton (1856, known as Leyton
station from 1868) on the Great Eastern were opened.
In 1897 Temple Mills – associated with a 13th-century
watermill belonging to the KNIGHTS TEMPLAR –
became the Great Eastern's wagon department and
was developed in the 1950s as one of the most modern
of its kind. Rapid population growth continued into
the 20th century with many residents working on the
railways. T.E. Knightley's 52 Bakers' Almshouses
(1857–66) reflect the increased poverty in the area.
Estates such as Grange Park, Barclay Park and Ruckholt Manor were developed; but the 1878 Epping
Forest Act ensured that over 200 acres in Leyton were
preserved as public open land. In 1905 the Leyton
Urban District Council acquired remaining Lammas
land – the relics of common pastureland – for Leyton
Marshes open space and recreation grounds. The or-
ganmakers, R. Spurden Rutt, founded in 1899 when
modern industry appeared around the marshes,
supplied more than 50 churches in Essex and
MIDDLESEX before the firm's closure in the mid-20th
century. Severe bombing during the 1st and 2nd
World Wars resulted in much redevelopment in Leyton. In 1947 the electrified CENTRAL LINE made travel
to London very swift; and in 1965 Leyton became part
of the London Borough of WALTHAM FOREST. Cardinal Wiseman lived in Leyton's Etloe House from 1856.

Leytonstone *E11.* Situated east of LEYTON with
EPPING FOREST to the north. Part of the ancient parish
of LEYTON, Leyton by the stone existed as a hamlet by
the 14th century. It stood on the Roman route from
London to EPPING FOREST, and Leytonstone High
Road became very important for coach traffic in
subsequent centuries. The High Stone is reputedly on
the site of a Roman milestone. In the 16th century
Wallwood in the north was called King's Wood, attest-
ing to its use as a royal hunting ground. Few early
buildings survive: the Pastures youth centre occupies
the site of a 17th-century house (demolished in the
1960s). Amongst notable residents of the 18th century,
David Lewis, poet and friend of Alexander Pope, and
Samuel Bosanquet were responsible for the building of
a chapel-of-ease, opened in 1749, to ST MARY THE VIR-
GIN, LEYTON. Edward Blore's church of St John the
Baptist was built in 1833, and in 1845 Leytonstone
became a parish. Its station on the Great Eastern Railway was opened in 1856 and, with the improved transport, the parish had become a suburban dormitory by
the end of the century. Further separate parishes were
created including Holy Trinity, Harrow Green. Despite extensive 20th-century development and
demolition some earlier buildings have survived:
WHIPP'S CROSS HOSPITAL, then part of the West Ham
Union Infirmary, was from 1903 built around the early
18th-century Forest House (and much extended
thereafter); and an early 19th-century terrace of
houses in Browning Road was designated a conservation area in 1972. John Drinkwater, poet and dramatist, was born in Leytonstone in 1882.

Liberties of the Fleet The area immediately surrounding the FLEET PRISON, in which prisoners were
allowed to live. FLEET MARRIAGES were performed
here.

Liberty and Co. Ltd *210–220 Regent Street, W1.*
Arthur Lasenby Liberty, of a draper's family in
Chesham, Buckinghamshire, worked first for Farmer
and Roger's Great Cloak and Shawl Emporium which
imported shawls from India. Impressed by the
INTERNATIONAL EXHIBITION of 1862, he persuaded
them to start an Oriental warehouse. In 1875 he
opened his own shop at 218a REGENT STREET, calling
it East India House, and selling soft coloured silks
from the East. He was soon also selling Oriental goods
of all kinds, particularly Japanese work and fans. By
1883 he had acquired two shops further south in
Regent Street. A jeweller's shop between them was
circumvented by a humped double staircase over its
entrance, known as the Camel's Back. Later he took
over all the buildings from 140 to 150 REGENT STREET
and named his extended premises Chesham House. By
1925 all had been swept away and replaced by two new
Liberty buildings in an amalgam of styles which
evolved out of the disparate requirements of the conservative controllers of Crown property and the flamboyant imagination of a successful shopkeeper. In
REGENT STREET three massive figures silhouetted
against the skyline look down upon a 115 ft frieze
portraying the wealth of far countries, borne by camel,
elephant and ship sailing towards a statue of Britannia.
This sculptured panorama by Doman and Clapperton
crowns a concave front screened behind classical
columns. Round the corner in GREAT MARLBOROUGH
STREET, but attached by a three-storey bridge over the
intervening Kingly Street, a timber façade fronts a
Tudor-style interior built from the remains of two
men-o'-war, HMS *Hindustan* and HMS *Impregnable*.

This was enhanced by Liberty's own stained glass craftsmen and Italian master carvers. The versatile architects E.T. and E.S. Hall were responsible for both buildings.

Liberty's influence upon late 19th- and 20th-century taste and fashion is immense. Early on they started a handprinting press using their own blocks; and Thomas Wardle, a friend of William Morris, produced for them, at his factory at Leek, block-printed designs on Indian silks. In 1881 Gilbert and Sullivan further enhanced Liberty's fame by using their fabrics for costumes in *Patience*. Some of these costumes were designed by Gilbert himself. In 1884–6 E.W. Godwin, the architect and designer, directed the costume department (at a fee of 1 guinea an hour). It was he who introduced into women's clothes the soft draped lines of the Pre-Raphaelite paintings. Amongst their customers were Ruskin, Alma-Tadema, Burne-Jones, Charles Keene, Rossetti and Whistler. By 1888 Arthur Lasenby Liberty himself was an active participant in the Arts and Crafts Society. Over the years the shop began to sell furniture, silver, pewter, jewellery, wallpapers and much else besides.

Liberty Cinema *South Road, Southall, Middlesex.* Now called the Liberty and showing exclusively Indian films, the Palace Cinema was built in 1929 to the designs of George Cole for United Picture Theatres, later part of Gaumont-British. Somewhat inappropriately, considering its present usage, it is decorated internally and externally in the Chinese manner with coloured faience tiling, pantiled roofs and dragon-head finials; it is unusual in being designed without a circle. Since the Chinese style for cinemas is a rarity, the building has recently been listed.

Liberty of the Clink An area of some 70 acres in SOUTHWARK which was outside the jurisdiction of the City. Most of it was included in the park of WINCHESTER HOUSE. (*See also* BANKSIDE *and* CLINK PRISON.)

Liberty of the Rolls The CITY OF LONDON Liberties are believed to have originated as areas immediately outside the CITY enjoying ecclesiastical privileges or exemptions. Today they come under the jurisdiction of the London Borough in which they lie. The Rolls Liberty was that in which the ROLLS CHAPEL was situated, and consisted of that part of the CHANCERY LANE area which is now in the City of WESTMINSTER.

Library Association *7 Ridgmount Street, WC1.* Founded in 1877 and incorporated by Royal Charter in 1898.

Lichfield House *St James's Square, SW1.* Now numbered 15, it was built in 1678–9 by the speculator Richard Frith and was for a time occupied by the lovely Frances, Duchess of Richmond – the model for Britannia on the old English penny – whose looks so bewitched Charles II and whose favours were denied him. In the 1740s the house belonged to Lord Anson who bequeathed it to his elder brother, Thomas Anson, a rich bachelor, who employed James Stuart, author of *Antiquities of Athens*, to reconstruct it for him and to provide it with its beautiful stone façade. Alterations were carried out in 1791–4 by Samuel Wyatt. It was sold in 1856 to the General Medical Society (now the Clerical, Medical and General Life Assurance Society), which has continued to occupy it ever since.

Lillywhite's Ltd. *Piccadilly Circus, SW1.* The Lillywhites were a well-known cricketing family: Frederick William Lillywhite played for Sussex. He had three sons, one of whom in 1862 took a small stand at an exhibition at 10 Seymour Street, EUSTON SQUARE, selling articles connected with cricket. This led to the opening in 1863 of a retail shop under the name James Lillywhite (the eldest son) at No. 31 HAYMARKET. In 1925 the firm took part of the Criterion Building, constructed to the designs of Thomas Verity in 1870–4. Their catalogue of June 1930 included 'The Lillisport Aviation Suit for Ladies, as designed for Miss Amy Johnson to wear on her historic solo flight to Australia, and approved by all leading women aviators'.

Lime Street *EC3.* Ancient city street named after the lime burners and sellers who once lived here. No. 23 is the site of ST DIONIS BACKCHURCH. The large extension to LLOYD'S was built to the designs of Terence Heysham in 1950–7 and the offices at Nos 12–13 in 1978 to the designs of Richard Sheppard, Robson. Samuel Straker and Sons, the printers, lithographers and stationers at No. 25, were established in about 1820 in LOMBARD STREET.

Limehouse *E14.* The lime oasts or kilns around Limehouse Dock which gave Limehouse its name are known to have been there at least from the 14th century when supplies of chalk were brought from Kent. However, this hamlet of STEPNEY owed its importance to links with the sea and the growth of London as a commercial centre. Many Elizabethan seamen had houses in Limehouse including Sir Humphrey Gilbert, the explorer, and William Borough and Sir Henry Palmer, both Controllers of the Navy. By 1610 there were over 2,000 inhabitants in Limehouse and, as in the neighbouring hamlet of RATCLIFF, about half the working population were mariners. This lively and busy sea-serving community clustered mostly around three streets close to the river. It numbered about 7,000 a hundred years later when Limehouse was considered the easternmost part of London. Hawksmoor's outstanding church of ST ANNE LIMEHOUSE was built to cater for this growing population. Limehouse was one of the main centres in London for shipbuilding in the 18th and early 19th centuries. It was also the first to go into decline although one shipyard, Forrestt's, built many of the country's lifeboats between 1852 and 1890. Alexander II, Tsar of Russia, visited a ropeworks there in 1871, and Dickens often visited his godfather, Christopher Huffam, in Church Row (now Newell Street). The Grapes public house in Narrow Street appears as the Six Jolly Fellowship Porters in *Our Mutual Friend*.

The independent maritime character of Limehouse disappeared with the growth in housing and population and the diminishing importance of the riverside; and Limehouse became a part of the generally industrial East End, a hinterland to the nearby WEST INDIA DOCKS. It became drawn into London (as well as internally divided) by several links, notably the LIMEHOUSE CUT, COMMERCIAL ROAD, the REGENT'S CANAL AND DOCK and the London and Blackwall Railway. The construction of Burdett Road in 1862

Most of Britain's best lifeboats were built at Forrestt's building yard in Limehouse between 1852 and 1890.

connected Limehouse with VICTORIA PARK, and the adjacent Cotton Estate was built over some of the last remaining fields. In 1861 the rector complained that 'the parishioners are for the most part poor, comprising a large number of persons employed at the Docks, and engineering and ship building yards .... There is an increase of low lodging houses for sailors ... and the removal of the more respectable families to other localities.' Special provision was first made for the floating population of Lascars and other foreign ships' crews with the opening of the Strangers' Home for Asiatics in West India Dock Road in 1856, but it was the colony of Chinese who first arrived about 1890 that attracted most attention. Originally mostly sailors employed by the Blue Funnel Line and others operating from the WEST INDIA DOCKS, they rarely numbered more than 300–400 and settled particularly in Pennyfields and Limehouse Causeway. The activities of a few opium smokers and inveterate gamblers were sensationally reported by the press and enlarged by such writers as Thomas Burke and Sax Rohmer. Oscar Wilde's Dorian Gray came here for opium. With the decline in the number of Chinese seamen taking up shore leave, Limehouse gradually gave way to SOHO as the centre of the community. Limehouse suffered considerable bomb damage during the 2nd World War. New council estates have replaced the old slums and few industries remain. There are however some 18th-century survivals including ST ANNE'S CHURCH and houses in Newell and Narrow Streets.

Limehouse Basin *see* REGENT'S CANAL DOCK.

Limehouse Cut Leaves the LEE NAVIGATION just north of Bow Locks and runs south-west to join the REGENT'S CANAL slightly north of its entrance to the THAMES at LIMEHOUSE. It is about 1½ miles in length.

Limes *123 Mortlake High Street, SW14.* Built in the 1720s for the Countess of Strafford. The façade, to which side extensions have been added much later, is

of five bays with a later Tuscan porch; some original interiors survive including the hall and staircase. The house is particularly associated with the long ownership of Naphtali Franks, an Anglo-Jewish merchant, whose riverside garden was particularly admired. Later occupants included Lady Byron (widow of the poet) and Field Marshal Viscount Wolseley. The house became the Council House in 1894 and is at present leased to an international company.

Lincoln's Inn *WC2.* One of the four INNS OF COURT. Founded in the middle of the 14th century, it took its name either from Thomas de Lyncoln, the King's Serjeant of HOLBORN, or from Henry de Lacy, 3rd Earl of Lincoln, one of Edward I's most influential advisers, whose family had acquired land near the church of ST ANDREW, HOLBORN, close to which it may originally have stood. The Earl of Lincoln's crest – a lion rampant purpure – appears in the arms of the Honourable Society of Lincoln's Inn, upon the early 16th-century GATE HOUSE, also upon the archway leading into CAREY STREET. It is believed that before 1348 the Society of Lincoln's Inn occupied the house which later became known as Thavies Inn and then moved to a larger house later known as Furnival's Inn (*see* INNS OF CHANCERY) before finally moving, between 1412 and 1422, to its present site on the western side of CHANCERY LANE where it rented a mansion from the then Bishop of Chichester for an annual payment of £6 13s 4d. The Bishops of Chichester had owned this land for 200 years, the CHANCERY LANE (Chancellor's Lane) derived its name from the fact that it led to the residence of one of them, John de Langton, Chancellor of England for 13 years. The freehold of the property was purchased by the Inn in 1580 for £520. A predecessor of the Bishop was Ralph Neville, Henry III's Chancellor, who is commemorated by the nearby Bishop's Court and CHICHESTER RENTS. The OLD BUILDINGS were completed over the years 1524 to 1613 while the OLD HALL was built between 1489 and 1492. The GATE HOUSE was built in 1518 and work on

457

the CHAPEL began in 1619. At some time during these years, according to John Aubrey, Ben Jonson worked as a bricklayer with his stepfather on this construction. 'He helped with the building of the new structure of Lincoln's Inn,' confirmed Thomas Fuller, 'when, having a trowel in one hand, he had a book in his pocket.' NEW SQUARE dates from 1682–93; STONE BUILDINGS were erected in 1774–80 and 1780; and the NEW HALL and LIBRARY in 1843–5.

One of the earliest of the many distinguished members of Lincoln's Inn was Sir John Fortescue, Chief Justice of the King's Bench (1442) and one of the Inn's four Governors in 1425–30. He is best known as the author of the historical Latin treatise *De Laudibus Legum Angliae*. Another was Sir Thomas More. Other members were Sir Matthew Hale, who was Chief Justice of the King's Bench, as was Lord Mansfield. Later Lord Chancellors who were members included Lords Erskine, Campbell, Brougham and Selborne, while in the present century Lord Haldane and the 1st and 2nd Lords Hailsham have held the office of Lord Chancellor. Lord Denning, Master of the Rolls, is a member of the Inn. The jurist, Jeremy Bentham, was also a member. Among Prime Ministers were Walpole, Pitt the Younger, Canning, Spencer Perceval, Melbourne, Addington and Asquith. Oliver Cromwell and his son, Richard, were students at the Inn, as was William Penn, founder of Pennsylvania. Disraeli and Gladstone were enrolled as students in 1824 and 1833 respectively while Daniel O'Connell, the Irish statesman, was a student in 1794–6 when he moved to GRAY'S INN. Among literary and theatrical figures were John Donne, David Garrick, Sir Henry Newbolt and John Galsworthy.

Lincoln's Inn Archway *Carey Street, WC2*. One of the three principal entrances to the Inn, built in 1697, it leads into NEW SQUARE. As plaques inside the archway indicate, the shields displayed on the walls facing the square bear the arms of Henry Serle and Henry Lacy, 3rd Earl of Lincoln. The premises on either side of the archway are occupied by Wildy and Sons, the law booksellers established here since 1830.

Lincoln's Inn Chapel *WC2*. Built just north of the OLD HALL, probably to the designs of Inigo Jones, in 1619–23. An early example of 17th-century Gothic, it replaced an earlier chapel which was demolished. The foundation stone was laid by John Donne, who had been admitted a member of the Inn on 6 May 1592 and had since been appointed Dean of ST PAUL'S. Donne also preached the consecration sermon on Ascension Day 1623. The chapel has an open undercroft which was intended as a place where the students could 'walk and talk and confer for their learning' and where legal practitioners could meet their clients. Here lie the remains of John Thurloe, Cromwell's Secretary of State, who had chambers in the Inn from 1646 until his death in 1668. The first move towards the Restoration of the Monarchy was made at a secret meeting of 80 Members of Parliament in the undercroft in 1659, and here, on 27 June 1663, Pepys, having walked up and down 'the new garden which they are making and will be very pretty', strolled about 'by agreement'. The building has been much restored. Wren was responsible for work in 1685; James Wyatt designed a new roof and put in a new east window in 1791; and Stephen Salter renovated the entire struc-

ture in 1882. In 1668 Elias Ashmole was married here to the daughter of his fellow-antiquary, Sir William Dugdale. In response to Lord Brougham's urgent request that the rules against the interment of females might be waived, his beloved daughter, 'Tullia', was buried here in 1839 so that when his own time came he might be buried beside her. He died, however, at his château at Cannes and was buried in the cemetery there. Distinguished successors of John Donne as Preachers to the Inn include Bishop Heber. F.D. Maurice, the Christian Socialist, was appointed chaplain in 1846. Several of the chapel windows are attributed to the brothers Bernard and Abraham van Linge. The east windows bear the arms of the Inn's Treasurers from 1608 to 1908, while the arms of members distinguished in fields other than law are contained in another window. The pulpit and communion table are 18th-century.

Lincoln's Inn Fields *WC2*. Evolved from two 'waste common fields', Purse Field and Cup Field, which had been a playground for students from the nearby LINCOLN'S INN since the 14th century. A third field, known as Fickett's Field, which lay to the south and which is now covered by CAREY STREET, PORTUGAL STREET and part of SERLE STREET, became known as Little Lincoln's Inn Fields after development had begun on the other two fields. From 1431 Cup Field was the property of the Hospital of St John, and in the early 16th century Purse Field belonged to the Hospital of St Giles. Both fields were leased by their owners, Purse Field in 1524 to one Katharine Smyth, probably as pasturage for the White Hart, DRURY LANE, and Cup Field in 1529 to John Braythwaite, probably as pasturage for the Ship Inn in the STRAND. Both reverted to the Crown in about 1537 when their owners' estates were seized, but they remained pasturage attached to the two inns. In 1586 Anthony Babington and his 13 accomplices were hanged drawn and quartered 'in the place where they had used to meet and confere of their traitorous practices'. The precise place is unknown but there is a contemporary reference to it as being 'in the fields near Lincolns Inns'. Seven of the conspirators were executed one day and seven the next. Babington was still conscious when eviscerated and because of this cruelty Queen Elizabeth directed that the other conspirators should be hanged until dead. In 1588 the Roman Catholic martyrs, Robert Morton and Hugh More, were executed here because of their faith.

In 1613 Purse Field came into the hands of Sir Charles Cornwallis who applied for a licence to build a house here. The Society of LINCOLN'S INN objected and local justices were ordered to 'restrayne and forbid that building by such effectual means as you shall think meete'. Four years later the Society of LINCOLN'S INN and the four adjoining parishes petitioned that 'for their general Commoditie and health [the fields should be] converted into walkes after the same manner as Morefeildes'. The idea was commended by King Charles I, and the Privy Council urged the various authorities to seek funds for the enterprise 'as a meanes to frustrate the covetous and greedy endeavors of such persons as daylie seeke to fill upp that small remainder of Ayre in those partes with unnecessary and unprofitable Buildinges'. The proposal languished, however, and a Royal Commission was set up in 1618 to hasten 'this greate ornament to the Citie . . . a memorable worke of our tyme to all posteritie'. Inigo Jones, the Surveyor General, was among the Royal Commissioners; and, with his support, a survey was ordered and it was recommended that all 'nuisances, inconveniences and annoyances whatsoever whereby the ayre in those partes' might be 'corrupted or made unwholesome' should be demolished. Nothing came of this recommendation, however; and in the 1630s William Newton of Beddenham, Bedfordshire, who had acquired the leases of both Cup and Purse Field, petitioned Charles I for permission to build 32 houses on them, pointing out the meagre sum of £5 6s 8d which the Crown received annually as freeholder. The Society of LINCOLN'S INN again objected; but this time the licence was granted, though Newton agreed with the Society that the main parts of the fields should 'for ever and hereafter be open and unbuilt'. In this agreement lies the genesis of the square that comprises Lincoln's Inn Fields. By 1641 most of Newton's houses had been built. Although the square thereafter became a fashionable place to live, the grassland overlooked by the brick-built houses was often the scene of fights and robberies and still a place of execution: William, Lord Russell, was beheaded here in 1683, having been found guilty of complicity in the Rye House Plot. A plaque purports to mark the spot in the bandstand in the middle of the gardens. In his *Trivia* (1716) Gay wrote:

Where Lincoln's Inn, wide space, is rail'd around,
Cross not with venturous step; there oft is found
The lurking thief, who, while the daylight shone,
Made the walls echo with his begging tone,
That crutch, which late compassion moved, shall wound
Thy bleeding head, and fell thee to the ground.
Though thou art tempted by the linkman's call,
Yet trust him not along the lonely wall,
In the mid way he'll quench the flaming brand
And share the booty with the pilfering band.

Distinguished residents of the square in the 17th and 18th centuries included Edward Montagu, 1st Earl of Sandwich; the 2nd and 3rd Lords Coventry; Thomas Pelham-Holles, Duke of Newcastle; Robert Sidney, 2nd Earl of Leicester whose daughter, Dorothy, Countess of Sunderland, Edmund Waller commemorated in his love poems as 'Sacharissa'; Robert Bertie, 1st Earl of Lindsey, whose house at Nos 59–60, built in 1640, has been credited to Inigo Jones; and the Duchess of Portsmouth. Another of Charles II's mistresses, Nell Gwynne, had lodgings here in a house in which her son by him, Charles Beauclerk, afterwards 1st Duke of St Albans, was born in 1670. Several great lawyers have lived and worked here, among them Sir William Blackstone, author of *Commentaries on the Laws of England*, on the site of Nos 55–56; and the Lords Chancellor, Lords Somers, Cowper, Macclesfield, Hardwicke, Loughborough, Erskine and Brougham. William Pitt had chambers here in 1778; and Spencer Perceval lived in Lindsey House in 1790–1807. A later Prime Minister, Ramsay MacDonald, also lived here between 1896 and 1911. His six children were born here and his wife died here. A statue of her was erected in the square (*see* STATUES). Nos 12, 13 and 14 were owned by Sir John Soane, the architect, who was a resident of the square between 1792 and 1837 (*see* SOANE MUSEUM).

John Forster, Dickens's friend and biographer,

Newcastle House in 1720, the Lincoln's Inn Fields mansion of the Duke of Newcastle, since rebuilt by Lutyens.

lived at No. 58 where, in 1844, Dickens read *The Chimes* to several of his friends who are depicted in Daniel Maclise's sketch of them that evening. Dickens chose the house as the residence of Sir Leicester Dedlock's lawyer, Mr Tulkinghorn, in *Bleak House*, 'a large house, formerly a house of state . . . let off in sets of chambers now; and in those shrunken fragments of greatness lawyers lie like maggots in nuts'.

There are still some interesting 18th-century houses in the square in addition to the SOANE MUSEUM, although Lindsey House at Nos 59–60, divided into two in the early 1750s and later stuccoed, is the only original house left. Its neighbour at Nos 57–58, whose design it closely follows, is by Henry Joynes (1730). The house on the north-west corner was rebuilt by Lutyens in the style of Powis House which was built in 1685–6 for William Herbert, Marquess of Powis, by Captain William Winde. This was the house which was once owned by Thomas Pelham-Holles, Duke of Newcastle, George II's Prime Minister. The ROYAL COLLEGE OF SURGEONS at Nos 35–43 is by Sir Charles Barry (1835–6) on the site of a house by George Dance the Younger, some of which Barry incorporated in his design. Next door, Nuffield College of Surgical Sciences, a residential college for postgraduates, occupies a neo-Georgian house by A.W. Hall (1956–8). On the other side, at Nos 44–49 is the modern headquarters of the Imperial Cancer Research Fund, designed by Young and Hall (1960). Also on the south side is the neo-Jacobean Land Registry by Sir Henry Tanner (1906). The Queen's solicitors, Messrs Farrer and Co., are on the west side at No. 66. The Association of Certified Accountants have a house on the north side designed in the Palladian style by Greenaway and Newberry (1925), formerly the headquarters of the Chartered Auctioneers' and Estate Agents' Institute before their amalgamation with the ROYAL IN-STITUTION OF CHARTERED SURVEYORS. The gateway to LINCOLN'S INN is on the east side.

Since 1894 the gardens have been open to the public. The Royal Canadian Air Force had their head-quarters in the square in the 2nd World War and this is commemorated by the footpath outside the north side of the gardens, known as Canada Walk. The memorial seat in the gardens has bronze figures by R.R. Goulden. The sculpture by Barry Flanagan was set up in 1980.

Lincoln's Inn Fields Theatre was reconstructed by John Rich in 1714 but, by 1818, had become a china warehouse.

Lincoln's Inn Fields Theatre *Portugal Street.* Opened in 1661 by Sir William D'Avenant for the Duke's Company in a converted tennis court. It was the first London theatre to have a proscenium arch, and D'Avenant was the first to use movable and changeable scenery on the English professional stage. On 28 August 1661 Pepys went to see *Hamlet* which was 'done with scenes very well but above all Betterton did the prince's part beyond imagination'. In 1671 the company moved to DORSET GARDEN THEATRE. In 1672–4 the theatre was used by Thomas Killigrew and his company while the Theatre Royal, Bridges Street was being rebuilt. Thereafter it became a tennis court once more. In 1695 it was refitted as a theatre by Congreve, Betterton, Mrs Bracegirdle and Mrs Barry. It opened with Congreve's *Love for Love*. Mrs Bracegirdle said in the epilogue:

And thus, our audience, which did once resort
To shining theatres to see our sport,
Now find us toss'd into a tennis court.
These walls but t'other day were filled with noise
Of roaring gamesters and yor damme boys;
Then bounding balls and rackets they encompast,
And now they're filled with jests, and flights and bom-bast.

In 1697 Congreve's *The Mourning Bride* was first produced here. It was a great success at the time but is now mainly remembered for its opening line: 'Music has charms to soothe a savage breast.' In 1700 the first production of Congreve's *Way of the World* was presented. In 1704 the company moved to the Queen's Theatre in the HAYMARKET. In December 1714 the theatre was refitted by John Rich. In 1716 the first pantomime was performed, with Rich as Harlequin. There was a riot in the theatre in 1721 after a drunken earl had refused to leave the stage during the play: actors fought with his friends. In 1728 *The Beggar's*

Opera was first produced, making 'Gay rich and Rich gay'. In 1732 Rich moved to COVENT GARDEN. The theatre was afterwards used as a barracks, an auction room and a china warehouse. It was demolished in 1848 to make way for an extension to the museum of the ROYAL COLLEGE OF SURGEONS.

Lincoln's Inn Gatehouse *Chancery Lane, WC2.* One of the three principal entrances to the Inn, it was built in 1517–21 by Sir Thomas Lovell, son of Henry VIII's Chancellor of the Exchequer. Sir Thomas More, one of the Inn's greatest Benchers, contributed to the cost. It bears the Lovells' arms above the doors as well as those of Henry VIII and the Earl of Lincoln (*see* LINCOLN'S INN). The oak doors were made in about 1564. The rooms above are said to have been occupied by the 18-year-old law student, Oliver Crom-well, in 1617.

Linden House *60 Upper Mall, Hammersmith, W6.* Built before 1733, it once had a companion, Grafton House, which had been much altered and was pulled down. Linden House, an attractive brick two-storey house, with an entrance flanked by Ionic columns, has been since 1963 the home of the London Corinthian Sailing Club which was founded in 1894.

Lindsey House *98–100 Cheyne Walk, SW3.* Takes its name from the property in the 1660s from the family of Sir Theodore Mayerne (who had been doctor to James I and Charles I). In the 1670s Lindsey either rebuilt or substantially repaired the house, making it outward-ly much as it appears today. In 1750 it was bought by Count Zinzendorf, who intended it to be part of a large Moravian community. The project did not prosper, but the former stables which were converted to a chapel still stand near the KING'S ROAD facing the MORAVIAN BURIAL GROUND. In the 1770s the house was divided into five separate houses. These have had various dis-tinguished occupiers including James Whistler, who painted the famous portrait of his mother here.

Lindsey Row This was a name used for a while for LINDSEY HOUSE and the adjacent properties – now Nos 91–104 CHEYNE WALK. The two houses nearest to BEAUFORT STREET, Belle Vue House and Belle Vue Lodge, were built in the 1770s at the same time as the original wooden Battersea Bridge.

Linley Sambourne House *18 Stafford Terrace, W8.* The house, from 1874 until his death here in 1910, of Edward Linley Sambourne, the book illustrator and chief political cartoonist of *Punch*. Its interior uniquely reflects the taste of the period in furniture, furnishings, decorations and objets d'art. The collec-tion includes works by artists and cartoonists of the age including Kate Greenaway, Walter Crane, John Leech, George du Maurier and Tenniel, as well as books illustrated by Linley Sambourne. In 1978 the house and its contents were offered to the nation by the Earl and Countess of Rosse (Linley Sambourne's granddaughter) and in 1979 they were bought by the GREATER LONDON COUNCIL. The house is now run by the VICTORIAN SOCIETY.

Linnean Society of London *Burlington House, Piccadilly, W1.* In 1778 the great Swedish naturalist,

Carl Linnaeus, died in Uppsala, and his extensive botanical and zoological collections and library were bought by a young English medical student, himself an industrious botanist, James Edward Smith. The son of a wealthy Norwich merchant, Smith was urged to buy the collections by Sir Joseph Banks. In 1788 (after consultation with Banks) Smith, with the Revd Samuel Goodenough and Thomas Marsham, founded the Linnean Society of London for the promotion of the study of natural history in all its branches, especially in the British Isles. Sir Joseph Banks was one of the first honorary members. This was the first specialist scientific society outside the ROYAL SOCIETY. Its aims were to commemorate Linnaeus, to run a library, to hold meetings and to publish papers and books. The Society was granted a Royal Charter in 1802, the year that Smith was knighted. He had retained Linnaeus's library and collections, which the Society expected to inherit. Instead, after Smith's death they were offered for sale in the open market, and the Society had to raise the money to buy them. They also had to buy Smith's own library and herbarium. These objectives were achieved in 1829. In the 1850s the Linnean Society moved into old BURLINGTON HOUSE, and it was at a meeting of the Society there in July 1858 that Charles Darwin and Alfred Russell Wallace first made known their views on the origin of species by natural selection. Together with the other learned societies which are around the courtyard, the Society was installed in 1873 in its new purpose-built home on the left of the archway at BURLINGTON HOUSE, and remains there today. It has survived as a broadly based inter-disciplinary society, concentrating on the flora and fauna of the Palearctic. Linnaeus's collections and library are preserved, the specimens magnificently housed in a cabinet-lined strongroom, and are available for research to Society members and other specialists, as is the Society's own library with its extensive collection of volumes on natural history and related subjects.

Lisle Street *WC2*. In 1682–3 the western part of the street was laid out in the grounds of LEICESTER HOUSE and in the early 1790s, after LEICESTER HOUSE had been acquired by Thomas Wright, the banker, the street was extended eastwards to join LITTLE NEWPORT STREET. The Earls of Leicester of the 5th creation were also Viscounts Lisle. In the 18th century the street had several aristocratic occupants, including the Earls of Ailesbury and Deloraine. No. 5, which was built in the late 1890s to the design of Frank T. Verity on the site of one of the larger private houses in the street, was at first occupied by the French Club, then by ST JOHN'S HOSPITAL FOR DISEASES OF THE SKIN. A building designed by Thomas Hopper for the Royal Society of Musicians and built in 1808 was demolished in 1931.

Lisson Grove *NW1, NW8*. The name preserves the last echo of the pre-Conquest manor of Lileston, itself a corruption of Lille's *tun* or farm. According to *Domesday Book* there were eight families living here in 1086, and a cluster of houses continued through the Middle Ages, though Lisson Green only enters the Rate Books in 1723 and Lisson Grove does not make its appearance till 1783. Leigh Hunt lived at No. 13 on his release from prison in 1815. B.R. Haydon and the sculptor, Charles Rossi, both had studios at No. 116. The Grove today is a little battered, even squalid, with scarcely a tree in sight. At its southern end is Marylebone Grammar

School (originally the Philological School, founded in 1792), the FLORENCE NIGHTINGALE HOSPITAL and, at Nos 33–35, the Sea Shell, in 1982 possibly the best fish and chip shop in London. Its eastern side, formerly the goods yard of MARYLEBONE STATION, is now an estate developed by Westminster Council. At its northern extremity is the Roman Catholic church of Our Lady, built in 1836 by J.J. Scoles.

Litchfield Street *W1*. Probably named after Edward Lee, 1st Earl of Lichfield, the husband of Charles II's natural daughter, Lady Charlotte Fitzroy, the child of Barbara Villiers, Duchess of Cleveland. It was first laid out in 1684–91 by Nicholas Barbon. In its early years it was a fashionable street with several aristocratic occupants; but most of these had left by the time numerous Huguenot craftsmen came to live here in the middle of the 18th century. The pretty, chubby singer Elizabeth Billington, the mistress, it was rumoured, of both the Duke of Rutland and the future George IV, was said to have been born here in 1768. Dr William Hunter, the Scottish anatomist and obstetrician, had a house here in 1763–7 and Dr Johnson's friend, Saunders Welch, High Constable of HOLBORN, had an office in the street in 1763–7. Both these houses have now been demolished, as were many of those at the western end for the construction of CHARING CROSS ROAD.

Little Ben, outside Victoria Station for over 70 years, was removed for a street widening scheme in 1964 but replaced in December 1981.

Little Ben *Victoria Station, SW1*. Smaller, 30 ft high version of BIG BEN which, until its removal for a street-widening scheme in 1964, was a well-known

461

meeting place for over 70 years. After restoration, including a new mechanism, the clock was replaced in December 1981. The work was paid for by a French oil company in commemoration of the wedding of the Prince of Wales and Lady Diana Spencer, and in acknowledgement of the fact that many French people used to meet here before catching their trains to the channel ports.

Little Britain *EC1.* Narrow, winding street running south of SMITHFIELD, named after the Dukes of Brittany who had a house here before the 16th century. From about 1575 to 1725 it was much inhabited by booksellers. In one of the bookshops here the Earl of Dorset came across *Paradise Lost* for which, the bookseller said, there was no sale: copies were cluttering up his premises and he begged Dorset to help him get rid of them. Milton had lodgings in the street in 1662. In 1711 the *Spectator* was first printed here by Samuel Buckley. The following year, when Samuel Johnson was brought to London at the age of three to be touched by Queen Anne as a cure for his scrofula, he and his mother lodged in the street with Nicholson, the bookseller. Benjamin Franklin also lodged here when he came to London in 1724. Adjoining the site of No. 13 was the house of John Bray, scene of Charles Wesley's evangelical conversion in 1738. Dickens placed the dismal offices of Mr Jaggers, the lawyer in *Great Expectations*, in Little Britain.

Little College Street *SW1.* Built in the 1720s and still largely 18th-century. The houses are much sought after by Members of Parliament.

Little Dean's Yard *SW1.* Approached through an archway from DEAN'S YARD. Here are the buildings of WESTMINSTER SCHOOL and ASHBURNHAM HOUSE. They were built around the yard on the site of the old quarters of the monks of the Abbey.

Little Essex Street *WC2, see* ESSEX STREET.

Little Holland House *40 Beeches Avenue, Carshalton, Surrey.* This house was built in 1902–4 by Frank R. Dickinson, an admirer of the social and artistic ideals of John Ruskin and William Morris, and an amateur practitioner of the Arts and Crafts movement. Building to his own design, and with the help of brothers and friends, Dickinson then filled the house with his own hand-made furniture, metalwork, carvings and paintings. The house was bought in 1972 by the London Borough of SUTTON.

Little Ilford *E12.* Ancient parish in the north-east of NEWHAM, lying on either side of the Romford Road. It appears in the *Domesday* Survey simply as 'Ilford', as the modern (Great) ILFORD was then part of the manor of BARKING. 'Ilford' means the 'ford over the Hile' – an early name of the River RODING which with its Back River formed the parish's eastern boundary. The parish was the smallest (786 acres) in the BECONTREE hundred and had only 85 inhabitants in the first census of 1801. Residential development began in the late 1860s on its north-western border, in the area first known as MANOR PARK. In the late 1890s the land of Little Ilford manor was sold and the whole parish south of the Romford road was covered with housing. The Aldersbrook manor was within the

parish from Tudor times. Situated on the north side of the Romford road, its names derived from the 'old river' – the western arm of the RODING. In 1854, most of its estate was purchased by the CITY OF LONDON for its large CEMETERY. As Aldersbrook was within the ancient bounds of EPPING FOREST, this gave the Corporation a voice in Forest affairs. It became the most powerful influence for the preservation of the Forest from further enclosures, and the Act of 1878, which declared EPPING FOREST open to the people for ever, placed it under the control of the CITY CORPORATION. A small area to the north-west of the cemetery is called Aldersbrook, but the name MANOR PARK is now applied to the majority of the ancient parish and is the postal district. Until recent years Little Ilford survived as an ecclesiastical parish (with the only rector in NEWHAM), although the daughter church of St Michael and All Angels, Romford Road, became the parish church. In 1886 the civil parish of Little Ilford was incorporated with EAST HAM for local government purposes. It retained some independence, with its own School Board from 1887, but it was merged with EAST HAM in 1900.

Little Newport Street *WC2.* Built towards the end of the 17th century and described by Strype in 1720 as 'ordinarily built and inhabited; being much annoyed with Coaches and Carts into the So Ho, and those parts'. Many of its houses are now occupied as offices by film companies. There has been a tavern on the site of the Crown and Grapes at No. 7 since at least 1745, originally known as the Chequers and Feathers but since 1793 by its present name.

Little Pantheon *Spa Fields, Exmouth Street.* Opened in 1770 by William Craven who laid out a garden and built a pantheon at a cost of £60,000. The pantheon was a rotunda with two circular galleries round the interior. It was known as the Little Pantheon to distinguish it from the OXFORD STREET PANTHEON. The 4-acre gardens contained shrubs, fruit trees and a fishpond. A contemporary magazine reported that, whereas the OXFORD STREET PANTHEON attracted the 'nobility', these gardens attracted the 'mobility'. A visitor in 1772 was shocked to find a majority of women patrons, some of whom approached him. In 1774 the business was put up for sale as Craven was bankrupt; and it closed in 1776. Shortly afterwards the SPA FIELDS CHAPEL was built on the site.

Little Theatre *John Adam Street.* A small theatre with 250 seats opened in 1910 by the actress, Gertrude Kingston. It had been converted by Hayward and Maynard from the banking hall of Messrs COUTTS. In 1911 Noël Coward made his stage debut as Prince Mussel in the children's play, *The Goldfish*. Later that year *Fanny's First Play* by Bernard Shaw was performed. It was his first commercial success. After the theatre's destruction in an air raid in 1917, it was rebuilt in 1919–20 by the original architects. In the early 1920s a series of revues were staged in which Jack Hulbert, Cicely Courtneidge and Beatrice Lillie appeared. The best productions of the 1930s were *Lady Precious Stream* (1935) and *Whiteoaks* (1936) by Mazo de la Roche. Bombed in 1941, the theatre was demolished in 1949. A block of offices, the Little Adelphi, at No. 10, now stands on the site.

Little Titchfield Street *W1*. Built in 1760 and named after the ground landlord, William Bentinck, 2nd Duke of Portland, Marquess of Titchfield. The north side is taken up with an extension to the POLYTECHNIC OF CENTRAL LONDON, the south by dress manufacturers' showrooms. Horatia Nelson, Emma Hamilton's and Nelson's week-old child, was brought in her mother's muff to No. 9 to be looked after by Mrs Gibson who was promised that she would be 'handsomely rewarded'.

Little Trinity Lane *EC4*. Covers part of the site of HOLY TRINITY THE LESS. PAINTERS' HALL is at No. 8. It is a centre of the fur trade. The London Auction Mart is at Fur Trade House, No. 25.

Little Venice *W2*. The canal surrounded by trees together with the Rembrandt Gardens make this one of the most unexpected beauty spots in London. Though both Robert Browning (*see* WARWICK CRESCENT) and Lord Byron compared it to Venice, the name seems not to have been generally used until after the 2nd World War. Artists who have worked here in recent years include Lucian Freud and Feliks Topolski. The Rembrandt Gardens were so named in 1975 to mark the 700th anniversary of the founding of Amsterdam and the beginning of a special link between Amsterdam and the City of WESTMINSTER, as recorded on a stone plaque in the gardens.

Liverpool Museum *22 Piccadilly*. An exhibition, originally displayed in Liverpool, of natural and artificial curiosities which had been collected by the showman, William Bullock. It opened in 1809 and a few months later had become 'the most fashionable place of amusement in London'. Jane Austen was among the thousands of visitors. Its success prompted Bullock to open a larger exhibition at the EGYPTIAN HALL.

Liverpool Road *N1*. The 'Back Road' to Upper Street, renamed Liverpool Road in 1822, extended from ISLINGTON turnpike at the High Street – Upper Street junction about 1¼ miles to Ring Cross, near the HOLLOWAY ROAD turnpike. At the High Street end a short terrace named Nowell's Buildings (a plaque dated 1774 is still on No. 28) ended in fields and cattle lairs used by drovers on the way to SMITHFIELD. Beyond, until the 1820s, the road was bordered by market gardens, Jacob Harvey's botanic garden – part of which from 1825 to 1915 formed the grounds of the Church Missionary Institution – and the lairs behind Laycock's, one of ISLINGTON's noted dairy farms which supplied milk to London until the 1860s.

West and east of the road were the CLOUDESLEY or Stonefield and the MILNER-GIBSON ESTATES, both held of Barnsbury Manor, and north of the CLOUDESLEY ESTATE was Gosseyfield, DRAPERS' COMPANY land (the site of Lonsdale Square). Beyond was the well-proportioned Islington Workhouse (1777, enlarged 1802), which succeeded earlier workhouses on other sites. This institution was moved in 1872 to HOLLOWAY and its buildings demolished. Its site was occupied by a small Registrar's office which was in use until 1969.

Among the few early houses were Park Place (1790) (Nos 268–292, demolished 1976 and now Council flats), and at the north-west end Paradise Row of about 1770, raised on a high pavement, much of which survives (Nos 495–507). Between this and Paradise House, an old mansion demolished in the 1830s, ran Hagbush Lane, an ancient packhorse road winding westwards and then north. It here marked the boundary between the manors of BARNSBURY and St John of Jerusalem. Hone, who explored its remnants when it was already engulfed by brickfields and the new Camden Road, records in his *Everyday Book* (1825) that it was 'the *oldest* north road, or ancient bridleway, to and from London and the northern parts of the kingdom'.

South of Paradise House a parochial school was built in 1815, one of several founded by a charity formed in 1710. It was enlarged by Roumieu in 1841 and subsequently rebuilt several times. Opposite is St Mary Magdalene's Churchyard (1812–14, now a public park).

From the 1820s the estates of Barnsbury Manor were developed, until Liverpool Road was lined by individually named terraces. Nos 200–266, between Barnsbury and Islington Park Streets, was Manchester Terrace (1832–7), by Thomas Cubitt.

In 1848 the London Fever Hospital removed from KING'S CROSS to a site adjoining the MILNER-GIBSON ESTATE, predictably arousing fierce opposition from local residents. Later part of the ROYAL FREE HOSPITAL, it closed in 1975. When the (ROYAL) AGRICULTURAL HALL in 1861—2 covered the cattle lairs south of the hospital, the road was almost completely built up. Laycock's farm gave way to Samuel Lewis Buildings in 1910, and while since the 1960s a number of the elegant terraces – whose subsidiary names were abolished in 1855 – have been restored, almost as many have been destroyed. However, Liverpool Road remains one of ISLINGTON's most handsome streets.

During the experimental days of tramways William Curtis, an engineer, applied to demonstrate a 'trambus' here with a flangeless wheel (September 1860), though there is no evidence that he actually did so. In the 1880s the North Metropolitan Co. ran a tram route as a loop to the Archway–Moorgate line, but it proved unprofitable and was closed in 1913 by the London County Council.

Liverpool Street *EC2*. Built in 1829 over a winding street known as Old Bethlem. BETHLEM HOSPITAL once stood to the north. It was renamed after Lord Liverpool, Prime Minister in 1812–27. LIVERPOOL STREET STATION and BROAD STREET STATION are on its northern side. The first edition of the Manifesto of the Communist Party was printed at No. 46.

Liverpool Street Station *EC2*. In 1862 the newly formed Great Eastern Railway started to search for a site for a new CITY station, as an extension of their lines from the then terminus at SHOREDITCH. The site chosen was beside BROAD STREET STATION and near LIVERPOOL STREET, which had just been renamed in honour of Lord Liverpool. Until the end of the 17th century, the BETHLEM HOSPITAL had stood on the site. The original plan was to erect an impressive building, standing as high as BROAD STREET STATION and extending as far as LONDON WALL. But this was not allowed by the CITY authorities, so Edward Wilson's Gothic redbrick station is tucked down, with its platforms well below ground level. Liverpool Street opened in 1874, and after an extension in 1891 it had more platforms than any other station – until VICTORIA STATION was enlarged in 1908. The 18 tracks reduced to six immediately beyond the platforms, a layout that remains to this day. This has not prevented Liverpool Street from being always the busiest London station, handling more daily passengers than any other terminus. There were 157,000 a day in the 1970s, 61,500 of them arriving in the morning rush hour. The GREAT EASTERN HOTEL on the station's east side was designed by Charles Barry but was much added to in 1891–5. A large memorial to the dead of the 1st World War stands in the main booking hall. Field Marshal Sir Henry Wilson unveiled this memorial in 1922 and was assassinated by the IRA on his return home from the ceremony. During the winter of 1944, Tom Driberg described Liverpool Street as 'almost completely squalid' and called it 'this hell hole', but John Betjeman later found it 'the most picturesque and interesting of the London termini'.

Livery Companies see CITY LIVERY COMPANIES.

Livesey Museum 682 Old Kent Road, SE1. Formerly the Livesey Library, the redbrick building was erected in 1890 as 'Camberwell Public Library No. 1' and was the gift of Sir George Livesey, once chairman of the South Metropolitan Gas Co. and a well-known philanthropist. In the 2nd World War the rear part of the building was irreparably damaged by bombing. The former newsroom was thereafter used as a lending library.

Lloyd Baker Estate WC1. Land between present Amwell Street and King's Cross Road, once part of the Knights Hospitallers' 'Commandry Mantells', passed in time to one of James II's 'Seven Bishops', Dr William Lloyd, Bishop of St Asaph's. It formed the dowry of his great-granddaughter Mary, who in 1775 married the Revd William Baker, of Gloucestershire. From 1819 the old clergyman and their son, Thomas Lloyd Baker, developed two of the steep fields for building, with layout and extraordinarily individual houses designed by another father and son, John and William Joseph Booth, of the DRAPERS' COMPANY. The work was attended by fierce disputes with the builders, with neighbouring landowners – the NEW RIVER COMPANY and Lord Northampton – and with Randell, owner of the large tile-kilns in 'Black Mary's', the lower field.

In 1860 William Pinks, aged 31, author of *The History of Clerkenwell*, died at 30 Granville Square. The square, built in 1841, was in its seedier days graphically described in Arnold Bennett's novel (1923) *Riceyman Steps* – steps which, connecting it with King's Cross Road, are now unsympathetically bridged by the London Ryan Hotel. The square's west side, undermined by the railway, had to be rebuilt in the 1870s, and its oversize church, St Philip's (1831–2), by Burton Lamb, was pulled down in 1938.

Unusually for London, the estate remained in the family's hands until the death of Miss Olivia Lloyd Baker in 1975 when it was worth £2 million. Half the property was put up for sale including much of Granville Square, Wharton and Lloyd Baker Streets (but not Lloyd Square), and acquired in 1979 by IS-LINGTON Council.

Lloyd's Leadenhall Street, EC3. A unique insurance market which has no shareholders and accepts

Lloyd's subscription rooms in 1809, from an aquatint after Rowlandson and Pugin.

no corporate liability for risks insured. It is a society of underwriters, all of whom accept insurance risks for their personal profit or loss and are liable to the full extent of their private fortunes to meet their insurance commitments. It originated in a coffee-house kept by Edward Lloyd in Tower Street in the 1680s and from 1692 in Abchurch Lane on the corner of LOMBARD STREET. London had long since been a centre of marine insurance, a practice which seems to have been introduced into England by the Lombards in the 16th century. But before the establishment of Lloyd's and in the days before the creation of marine insurance companies, it was the usual practice for the proprietor of an insurance office to act as broker by taking a policy from one rich and reliable merchant to another until the risk had been fully covered. Once Lloyd's Coffee House was known, however, as a place where ships' captains, shipowners and merchants congregated, and as a centre for obtaining trustworthy shipping news, it soon also became recognised as a place for obtaining marine insurance. But as the 18th century progressed Lloyd's attracted those whom the more respectable customers considered mere and reckless gamblers, as well as such distracting literary figures as Steele; and in 1769 a New Lloyd's Coffee-House was established in Pope's Head Alley for customers seriously and strictly concerned with marine insurance. Here periodical sales of ships 'by candle' were established and the proprietor began publishing his short-lived *Lloyd's News*, the precursor of *Lloyd's List*. Lloyd's Register of Ships was first published in 1760. (In 1797 a dispute over classification methods prompted shipowners to publish their own book which appeared in 1799 and remained a rival register until 1834 when a common problem of finance brought about a reconciliation which resulted in the formation of *Lloyd's Register of Shipping*. This remains an independent classification society (at 71 FENCHURCH STREET), though a close liaison is maintained by members of the Committee of Lloyd's serving on the Register's Committee.

Within a short time the premises in Pope's Head Alley proved to be too small and in 1771, a society with fixed rules having been established, a committee was elected to find new premises. 79 merchants, underwriters and brokers each paid £100 for the purpose. Three years later, having failed to buy suitable premises, 'a very roomy and convenient place' was rented in the ROYAL EXCHANGE. Here the society officially began business on 7 March 1774, and they remained until the fire of 1838. They occupied SOUTH SEA HOUSE for a time, returning to the ROYAL EXCHANGE once it had been rebuilt. In 1925 new buildings for Lloyd's were begun on the site of EAST INDIA HOUSE. Designed by Sir Edwin Cooper they were finished in 1928. A large extension in Lime Street, linked to the main building by a bridge, was built in 1950–7 to the designs of Terence Heysham. The Underwriting Room, where underwriters meet to conduct their business, is in this extension and here, hanging above the rostrum, is the Lutine Bell. This bell originally belonged to the French frigate *La Lutine* which was surrendered to the British at Toulon in 1793 and, as HMS *Lutine*, was used to carry a cargo of gold and silver bullion from England to Germany in 1799. The ship sank in a storm with the loss of all hands. Various attempts were made to recover the cargo; and, in addition to about £100,000 in bullion, the rudder and bell were raised. A chair and table now in Lloyd's library were made from the rudder. The bell, recovered in 1859, is sounded on ceremonial occasions and when important announcements are to be made to the market, two strokes for good news and one stroke for bad. The practice of ringing the bell for every loss at sea has long since been discontinued.

In 1979, following a decision to redevelop Lloyd's LEADENHALL STREET site, Richard Rogers and Partners were commissioned to design a new building to house the Underwriting Room. The scheme involved the demolition of the 1928 building. The main entrance in the LEADENHALL STREET frontage was preserved.

Lloyd's Avenue *EC3*. Built in the late 1890s between FENCHURCH STREET and CRUTCHED FRIARS under the supervision of T.E. Collcutt and B. Emmanuel. Many of the office buildings, most of them undistinguished, are occupied by ship-brokers.

Lloyd's Bank Ltd *Lombard Street, EC3*. Although not all of Lloyd's Bank's head office business was moved to London until 1910, its links with the capital are amongst the oldest and most numerous in the banking community. The Bank had been established as Taylor's and Lloyd's at Birmingham in 1765 and it obtained a London agency (Hanbury, Taylor, Lloyd and Bowman of LOMBARD STREET), as early as 1770. In 1864 the London agency was absorbed by Barnett, Hoare and Co. (probably established at the Black Horse in LOMBARD STREET in the 1660s), which was itself absorbed by Lloyd's in 1884. Renamed Lloyd's Banking Co. in 1865, Lloyd's also acquired Bosanquet, Salt and Co. (established in the 1770s) and joined the LONDON BANKERS' CLEARING HOUSE in 1884. A London office was then built on the site of Bosanquet's bank at 71 LOMBARD STREET (rebuilt as the head office in 1929). Other acquisitions included Praed's and Co., FLEET STREET (founded in 1802 and absorbed in 1891), Twining and Co., the STRAND (1824–92), Herries, Farquhar and Co., ST JAMES'S STREET (1772–1893), COX AND CO. and, in 1918, the Capital and Counties Bank, whose constituent banks included Willis, Percival and Co., LOMBARD STREET (founded in about 1670). By 1910, when 71 LOMBARD STREET became its sole head office, Lloyd's ranked as one of the largest clearing banks. It now has over 150 branches in the London area.

James Lock and Co. Ltd *6 St James's Street, SW1*. James Lock married Mary Davis, and inherited his father-in-law's hatter's business in 1759. The business moved to No. 6 ST JAMES'S STREET in 1764. George James Lock, his son, succeeded in 1799. In 1821 George's son, James Lock, took over. His daughter, Ann, married Charles Whitbourn and their son joined his uncle, James Lock, in 1865. That year James Benning, George Lock's foreman, entered into partnership and when he died his place was taken by his grandson, George James Stephenson, who had started in the firm in 1894. The Whitbourns and Stephensons remain connected with the firm to the present day. Customers included Lord Nelson, who called before leaving London for the last time to settle an account for a hat made specially with a built-in eyeshade, and the Duke of Wellington, who bought here the plumed hat he wore at Waterloo. In 1850 a William Coke had a hard-domed hat designed to fit closely to the head and thus suitable wear for his gamekeepers when chasing poachers. Since Lock's chief suppliers were Thomas and William Bowler in Southwark Bridge Road, this hat became known as a bowler, but in St James's it was called a coke after the man who had ordered it. Scott's the hatters, founded in the early 1870s at No. 1 OLD BOND STREET, became part of the firm in the 1970s.

The Chapel of the Lock Hospital, Southwark, originally built for lepers in the 12th century, was closed in 1760.

Lock Hospital *Southwark*. A leper hospital built probably in the 12th century. Its existence is first recorded on a patent roll of 1315. Its name was derived from the locks or rags which covered the patients' sores. In 1549 ST BARTHOLOMEW'S HOSPITAL took the Lock Hospital over. By the 18th century leprosy was extinct in England and patients with venereal diseases were treated here instead. Other hospitals dealing with the same complaints were called lock hospitals. The Southwark Lock Hospital was closed in 1760. The site is now covered by the junction of Tabard Street and Great Dover Street.

Locket's *Charing Cross*. A celebrated ordinary where meals could be obtained at fixed prices and regular hours. It took its name from the landlord, Adam Locket, who died in 1668. Locket's was much frequented by the gentry, apparently mainly as a meeting place after the theatre, and was renowned for its food.

> At Locket's, Brown's, and at Pontack's enquire,
> What modish kickshaws the nice *beaux* desire,
> What fam'd ragouts, what new invented sallat,
> Has best pretensions to regale the palate.

A royal sign-manual warrant of James II pays 'the sum of £36 to Adam Lockett, for providing Diet for the officers of the Horse Guards that are in waiting'. The house is mentioned in contemporary works of fiction, such as *The Relapse* by Vanbrugh and Congreve's *The Way of the World*. The ordinary's reputation declined after the reign of Queen Anne.

Locks Bottom *Kent*. Probably takes its names from one Lock, who lived in the area in 1776. The White Lion Inn dates from 1626 and was a popular coaching inn. The workhouse at Locks Bottom was opened in 1845 and after 1910 it gradually developed into the present hospital. At Goddendene, now demolished, lived the March family of artists who were responsible for the Canadian National Memorial built here and unveiled by King George VI at Ottawa in 1939. It had taken the family 12 years to design and build. A well-known family of gipsies, reputed to be true-bred Romanies, were the Boswells who lived here with their herd of donkeys. Levi Boswell died in 1924 and over a thousand people attended his funeral. But this funeral was surpassed by that of his widow, Mrs Urania Boswell, who died in 1933. She had forecast her own end and it was estimated that there were 15,000 present.

Lombard Lane *EC4*. Extends southwards from FLEET STREET between Serjeants' Inn and BOUVERIE STREET. The money lenders, the Lombards, used to operate here in the Middle Ages and it is still very much a banking street. COUTTS', LLOYD'S, BARCLAY'S, WILLIAMS AND GLYN'S and the Clydesdale Bank all have premises in this small lane.

Lombard Street *EC3*. Banking centre of London since the Lombard merchants from North Italy settled here in the 12th century. In a house on the site of No. 72 lived Gregory de Rokesley, eight times Mayor of London and one of the richest goldsmiths of his day. BARCLAY'S, LLOYD'S, GLYN MILLS and MARTIN'S all used to have their head offices here. Their medieval banking signs were hung out to celebrate Edward VII's coronation for the first time since Charles II banned them as unsafe. George Beadnell, the banker, with whose daughter, Maria, the young Dickens fell desperately in love, lived next door to Messrs Smith, Payne and Smith's bank at 2 Lombard Street and eventually became the manager. The INSTITUTE OF BANKERS is at No. 10. On the north side is the Church of ST EDMUND THE KING. Another Wren church dedicated to ALL HALLOWS stood here until 1938 when it was demolished. Alexander Pope's father was a linen draper of Lombard Street and the poet was born here in 1688. Frederick John Francis and Horace Francis designed Nos 39–40 in 1868. The Poseidon Fountain

by Sir Charles Wheeler (1969) in George Yard is the gift of BARCLAY'S BANK to the CITY OF LONDON. Also by Wheeler are the bronzes *Hercules and the Lion* and *St George and the Dragon* (both 1962), the one on the corner of Barclay's bank facing George Yard, the other on the first-floor level of the Bank façade.

A Roman pavement being excavated in Bucklersbury in 1869. Roman London was an important trading centre.

Londinium It was the geographical features of the area that brought about the foundation of Roman London. There is no strong evidence of any occupation on the site before the Conquest in AD 43. London stands at the lowest convenient bridging point of the THAMES. There was a way through the marshes from the south and on the north side two gravel hills (now ST PAUL'S and CORNHILL) stood above the flood plain and gave a firm foothold. The combination of these elements of topography and geology gave the site a military importance in the eyes of the Roman army surveyors. Over the 400 years of Roman London's existence the military aspect was obviously to decline after the early years but the civil and governmental elements expanded in an increasing ratio until, eventually, in the 4th century Londinium was granted the title Augusta.

The first Roman settlement must have huddled around the bridgehead; the THAMES was much wider and shallower than it is now. Recent excavation evidence, however, plus alignments of roads coming from the south through SOUTHWARK, suggests that the crossing point was actually the ford at WESTMINSTER (a fact put to a practical test several years ago by the late Lord Noel-Buxton, who was over 6 ft tall). Pottery and coin evidence from the city indicates a possible foundation date late in the reign of Claudius (41–54) or early in the reign of Nero (54–68). Tacitus, when describing the horrors of the attack by Boudicca in 60, wrote that London 'did not rank as a Roman settlement, but was an important centre for business-men and merchandise'. On this basis the general Suetonius decided 'to sacrifice the single city of Londinium to save the province as a whole'. Those who could not move out with the army as it withdrew, the women and old folk 'were slaughtered by the enemy. Verulamium suffered the same fate.' Evidence of the disaster in layers of burnt debris and pottery has been found in many places and can still be seen in the crypt of ALL HALLOWS BY THE TOWER.

The archaeological evidence of recent years shows that there was a basic plan from the beginning for the growth of Londinium, ultimately to extend over the

330 acres it was to occupy when walled in the late 2nd century. Fine wares, glass, jewellery and other objects from the Mediterranean testify to the city's importance as a commercial entrepôt. In the rebuilding after the disaster priority seems to have been given to business premises, no doubt fostered by the benevolent eye of the newly appointed procurator (tax collector), Julius Classicianus. He realised that a harsh reaction after the revolt would not regain lost taxes and is recorded as having set the province on its feet again. The fragments of his grand tomb, erected by his sorrowing wife Julia Pacata, were found on TOWER HILL in 1852 and 1935 and are now restored in the BRITISH MUSEUM. (A copy of the inscription is set into a wall in the Wakefield Gardens, TOWER HILL.)

The nucleus of the new settlement was on CORNHILL, with evidence for a ribbon development particularly along the road west towards NEWGATE (see also LONDON WALL, NEWGATE BASTION). Apart from the actual business premises the most important new buildings to be erected were a basilica and FORUM, a small classical-style temple by CORNHILL, and the GOVERNOR'S PALACE, where the most famous governor of Britain, Julius Agricola, would have resided upon his appointment in the 80s.

Late in the 1st century port facilities were improved with the building of a huge timber revetment, remains of which were found in excavations in Trig Lane. And in about AD 80 a large timber quay was built close to LONDON BRIDGE on the north side of what is now LOWER THAMES STREET. The city had nearly been set on its feet in the early 2nd century; it had seen the visit of the Emperor Hadrian in 122 and the building of a fine new forum that completely dwarfed the previous structure (it was at least four times the size). Disaster struck almost immediately with a fire that destroyed some 100 acres of the central area in the later 120s. It was a blow that, for a while, the city seemed unable to overcome. There is evidence of commercial failing, disregarded public buildings and baths, and even the fort in the north-west corner of the city appears to have been abandoned for a while. A lot of trade was obviously rerouted to the larger of the local tribal capitals that were just beginning to expand. Around 150 Londinium was in a parlous state; indeed, it is even probable that for a while it lost its capital status to one of the other thriving tribal capitals. The tide was turned towards the end of the 2nd century, possibly due to specific interest shown by the Emperor in Rome. It was then that the river-front quay was rebuilt, more massive and longer than before. The encircling city wall (see LONDON WALL) was also built, the evidence for the transportation of its construction materials being found in the Blackfriars barge (see ROMAN BOATS AND BARGES). Trade with Gaul in the bright red luxury samian ware pottery revived (although in the 3rd century it was to be overtaken by large imports of North African imitations). From the Rhineland came *mortaria* and fine glassware. Trade, in fact, began to boom. Probably a lot of the east coast trade with the Rhineland (Germany and Holland) now came back to London. The economic effects of Clodius Albinus's revolt in 192 must have been felt, but were soon overcome when Septimius Severus defeated Albinus and came to Britain himself, to die at York in 211. It was about this time that the province was divided into two, with York as the capital of Britannia Inferior, leaving London less a military and commercial area in the 3rd century and more an administrative city.

Public monuments of some size were erected in the early 3rd century, including a monumental arch (pieces of which have only recently been found and recognised as parts of the 4th-century rebuilding of the river wall). It was also now that the TEMPLE OF ISIS was built and the major building phase of the TEMPLE OF MITHRAS in the WALBROOK is also of this date. A number of large polychrome mosaics from private houses testify to the wealth of certain members of the population, doubtless wealthy merchants or government officials. After this period of magnificence the population seems to have declined (a feature noted in a number of other large Romano-British towns of the period). At the end of the 3rd century came the revolt of Carausius (287–93), followed by that of Allectus (293–6). A mint was opened in London, striking coins for both usurpers (see ROYAL MINT).

That there was still something of commercial value in Londinium is evidenced by the repairs carried out on the wall and the re-use of much 3rd-century and earlier sculpture in it at the end of the 4th century. A huge section of wall still in a remarkable state of preservation was found within the TOWER OF LONDON in 1977. This can almost certainly be ascribed to the known restoration work carried out in 396 at the orders of Stilicho, the great general under the Emperor Honorius. Stilicho had kept the Visigoths at bay in Italy, and when he was executed as the result of a palace intrigue in 408 it left a weak Emperor helpless at Ravenna. The way was open for the barbarians to attack, which itself led to the recall of the legions from Britain by Honorius in 410. Some 50 years later the walls of London were still high and strong enough to afford protection against the Saxons, but it is not known for how long after the mid-5th century the city remained inhabited.

It was probably not for long. There is little archaeological evidence. And the Anglo-Saxons, it is known, especially from several poems, stood in awe and dread and shunned 'the work of giants' as they called the Roman buildings, now standing derelict. (See also ALL HALLOWS BARKING BY THE TOWER, ARRAS MEDALLION, BLACKFRIARS BARGE, COAL EXCHANGE, FORUM, GOVERNOR'S PALACE, IRONMONGER LANE, LONDON STONE, LONDON WALL, LOWER THAMES STREET, ROMAN BATHS, ROMAN BOATS AND BARGES, ROMAN FORT, ROMAN ROADS, ST BRIDE'S, STRAND 'ROMAN' BATH, TEMPLE OF ISIS, TEMPLE OF MITHRAS.)

London Airport see AIRPORTS.

London Apprentice *62 Old Church Street, Isleworth, Middlesex.* Built in the 15th century, this public house now has an 18th-century façade. It stands opposite the spot where the Romans crossed the THAMES in AD 54. There is an Elizabethan ceiling on the first floor, carved by Italian apprentices who stayed here while working on nearby SYON HOUSE. The name, however, derives from the apprentices to the CITY LIVERY COMPANIES who rowed up to ISLEWORTH on their days off, as a painting on one side of the inn shows. Henry VIII, Elizabeth I and Charles II are all alleged to have stayed here. It is scheduled as an ancient monument.

London Bankers' Clearing House *Lombard Street, EC3.* In about 1770 London's private banks established a clearing house at the Five Bells, Dove Court, LOMBARD STREET for the settlement of payments to each other. It proved especially important in dealing with cheque payments. By the 1830s membership of the Clearing House was a jealously guarded privilege and the new joint stock banks (see BANKING) were denied entry until 1854. Facilities for clearing the cheques of country banks were available after 1858. The BANK OF ENGLAND joined in 1864 and by 1900 all the major London-based banks were members. Situated at 10 LOMBARD STREET since 1951, the Clearing House handles nearly 5 million cheques on an average day.

London Bridge The first London Bridge was probably built of wood between AD 100 and 400 during the Roman occupation. In 1014 King Ethelred and King Olaf of Norway burnt down the bridge to divide the Danish forces. Ottar Svarte, a Norse poet, wrote:

> London bridge is broken down
> Gold is won and bright renown.
> Shields resounding
> War horns sounding
> Hildur shouting in the din
> Arrows singing
> Mailcoats ringing
> Odin makes our Olaf win.

(The more familiar version of the nursery rhyme did not appear until the mid-17th century.) In 1091 the bridge was swept away by a gale. Soon afterwards rebuilt, it was burned down in 1136 and then reconstructed in elm. The first stone bridge was begun in 1176 by Peter, Chaplain of ST MARY COLECHURCH. The first mention of houses on the bridge is in 1201. Later pictorial records show it crowded with houses on either side, three to seven storeys high. Near the SOUTHWARK end was Nonsuch House, which was built entirely of wood. Pegs held it together instead of nails. In the centre of the bridge was a chapel dedicated to St Thomas Becket. This, like the bridge itself, was

built by Peter de Colechurch who was buried there. It was important enough to have two priests and four clerks. The bridge had 19 small arches and a drawbridge at the SOUTHWARK end. The river current was so strong that it was impossible to 'shoot the bridge' on a flood tide and dangerous to do so on an ebb tide. Many were drowned attempting to do so: an old proverb said that London Bridge was made for wise men to go over and fools to go under. In 1212–13 fire broke out on the bridge. Sightseers and firefighters found themselves trapped when both ends caught fire. 'Then,' according to Stow, 'came there to aid them many ships and vessels into which the multitude so inadvisedly rushed that, through fire and shipwreck, three thousand people were killed.' When Simon de Montfort attempted to cross the bridge with his prisoner Henry III in 1264, he found that the Lord Mayor had pulled up the drawbridge, locked the gates and thrown the keys into the river. The London citizens then came to his aid, battered down the gates and let him in. During a great frost in 1282 five arches of the bridge were swept away. In 1305 the head of William Wallace, the Scots patriot, was put up above the portico of the gatehouse, and so began a gruesome custom. The heads were parboiled in one of the gatehouse rooms, then dipped in tar to preserve them. In 1357 King John of France rode over the bridge on a white charger, while his captor the Black Prince rode humbly by his side on a small black horse. During the PEASANTS' REVOLT the bridge was closed by order of Lord Mayor Walworth against Wat Tyler, who took it without a fight when he threatened to burn it down. When Isabella of France, aged eight, arrived to marry Richard II in 1395, so great was the crush to see her on the bridge that nine people were killed. In 1384–97 the chapel was rebuilt and enlarged. After his victory at Agincourt Henry V rode over the bedecked bridge accompanied by the Lord Mayor and his retinue; and, seven years later, his body was brought back from Vincennes, accompanied by the Archbishop of Canterbury, 15 bishops, 500 men-at-arms on horses draped in black and 300 torch-bearers. In 1450 the

Visscher's view of London Bridge dated 1616, with traitors' heads above the gate. The houses were removed between 1758 and 1762.

John Rennie's new London Bridge of five stone arches, built up-stream of the old one in 1823–31, was opened by William IV.

drawbridge was lowered to admit Jack Cade and his rebels after they had threatened to burn it down. After his defeat Cade's head was tarred and hoisted above the gatehouse roof. In 1535 Thomas More's head was put up on the bridge. His daughter Margaret Roper later acquired it and is said to have buried it at St Dunstan's, Canterbury. Bishop Fisher's head was also displayed here but it was thrown into the river after a fortnight as it was rumoured to be growing more fair instead of rotting. In 1536 Anne, the baby daughter of a cloth-worker, William Hewett, fell from the bridge into the river but was rescued by an apprentice named Edward Osborn. By the time Anne was of marriageable age her father had become a wealthy man. All her suitors were discarded in favour of Osborn who eventually became Lord Mayor of London. In 1538 the chapel was reduced to two priests only; and two years later to a single priest with an assistant. In 1540 Thomas Cromwell's head was put up on the bridge. In 1554, when Thomas Wyatt and his followers found the bridge shut against them, they delayed in SOUTHWARK until so many cannon faced them that they had to retire to KINGSTON. In 1548 the chapel was turned into a well and its valuables were given to the bridge master. In 1582 Pieter Morice, a German, built mills on two arches of the bridge for pumping drinking water (*see* WATER SUPPLY). In 1598 a German visitor counted over 30 heads on the bridge. In 1633, in a fire begun by a servant leaving a tub of hot ashes under a flight of stairs, half the structure was destroyed. During the Civil War cannon were set up behind the bridge gates but were never used. At the Restoration Charles II rode over the bridge to reclaim his throne, accompanied by 300 gentlemen in cloth-of-silver, 300 soldiers in velvet, troops, trumpeters, City dignitaries and the

Life Guards. The next year the custom of displaying the heads of traitors was discontinued.

In 1758–62 the houses were removed under the supervision of Sir Robert Taylor and George Dance Senior, who also replaced the two central arches with a single navigation span. When this work was completed stones from demolished City gates were used to strengthen the arches. A competition for designs to replace the old bridge as part of the PORT OF LONDON improvements was held in 1799–1801. Thomas Telford submitted his famous scheme for a single-span cast-iron bridge of 600 ft. But not enough was known about the technical factors involved and the whole project was shelved. And in 1823–31 a new bridge of five stone arches upstream of the old bridge was built by Sir John Rennie to his late father's design. This bridge was opened on 1 August 1831 by William IV and Queen Adelaide. KING WILLIAM STREET and MOORGATE were built as approaches. In 1967–72 the present structure of pre-stressed concrete cantilevers forming three spans was built by Mott, Hay and Anderson, with Lord Holford as architectural adviser. It was paid for by the BRIDGE HOUSE ESTATES. Rennie's bridge was sold and re-erected at Lake Havasu City, Arizona.

London Bridge Hotel Built in 1861 on the south side of the London, Brighton and South Coast Railway terminus to the designs of Henry Currey at a cost of over £111,000. It had magnificent reception rooms and 250 bedrooms; but it attracted little custom and in 1893 it was purchased by the London, Brighton and South Coast Railway Board and used for offices. In 1941 it was demolished, having suffered extensive bomb damage during the BLITZ.

London Bridge Station *SE1*. On 8 February 1836, the first passenger train on the first steam railway in London arrived at Spa Road, BERMONDSEY from DEPTFORD. The London and Greenwich Railway Co. set up a temporary terminus at Spa Road and used it for the next ten months until tracks had been laid to London Bridge. The new station had only wooden platforms and no impressive buildings. The London – Croydon Railway, the South Eastern Railway and the London and Brighton Railway began using the station, and more lines had to be laid. A proper station was built in the Italianate style, 1840–4, to a design by Henry Roberts. In 1849 it was rebuilt by Samuel Beazley in two parts – one side for the South Eastern Railway, which had taken over the Greenwich Railway, and the other for the remaining companies which had amalgamated to form the London, Brighton and South Coast Railway. London Bridge Station was very badly damaged in the 2nd World War. The Booking Hall was rebuilt in the late 1970s by the British Rail Architects' Department. It is very much a rush-hour station. About 44,000 people arrive during the morning peak hours. In vaults beneath the station, at 28–34 TOOLEY STREET, is the horror museum known as the London Dungeon.

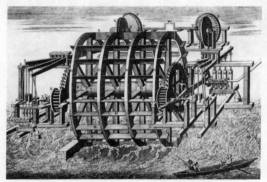

Thames water was first pumped to the City from London Bridge in 1581 by Pieter Morice; the family stayed in business until 1701.

London Bridge Waterworks The first pumped water was supplied to the CITY in 1581 when Pieter Morice was granted a 500-year lease at 10s annually of one of the arches of LONDON BRIDGE. The rapid flow through the bridge turned a wooden waterwheel that enabled water to be pumped to CORNHILL. Similar enterprises had proved successful in Germany and Morice was granted his patent in 1578, following support from Sir Christopher Hatton and a demonstration in which a jet of water was forced over the steeple of ST MAGNUS THE MARTYR. Despite the later reluctance of the CITY to provide a site and help with the cost, the supply started on Christmas Eve 1582. A second arch was leased about this time. The works were completely destroyed in the GREAT FIRE. At the time Morice's descendants were sharing an income of £1,000 a year. By 1668–9 the supply had been resumed. In 1701 Morice's descendants sold the whole undertaking for £38,000 to a goldsmith, Richard Soame. This included a recently granted lease of a third area. Soame also took leases of some of the CITY supply points and thus further hastened the end of free water supplies.

He formed a company with £150,000 capital and shortly afterwards the works were rebuilt. By 1737 there were four waterwheels, capable of pumping an estimated 107,274 gallons per hour. In 1761 a fourth arch was leased, probably to compensate for the reduced water flow caused by improvement to LONDON BRIDGE in the preceding years. At the same time supplies were extended to a limited number of houses in SOUTHWARK; and in 1767 a waterwheel was placed at the SOUTHWARK end of the bridge. An atmospheric engine was installed to supply water when the flow was inadequate to turn the wheels.

In 1817 one of the wooden waterwheels was replaced by an iron one. By 1821 it was estimated that the company supplied four million gallons of water daily to 10,000 customers. Sixty-eight public buildings were supplied. Rates varied from £1 to over £20 according to the quantity used. The water was, as the company admitted, 'foul' when pumped but, after standing for 24 hours, it was 'finer than any other water that could be produced'. The rebuilding of LONDON BRIDGE, sanctioned by Act of Parliament in 1822, meant the end of the waterworks, as water would not rush through its diminished number of piers at the same rate, and the City refused to allow its modern bridge to be disfigured by waterwheels. The leases were transferred to the NEW RIVER COMPANY.

London Central Markets *EC1. see* SMITHFIELD.

London Chamber of Commerce and Industry *69 Cannon Street, EC4*. Launched in the MANSION HOUSE in 1881 following a meeting presided over by the Lord Mayor, William McArthur. It is the largest Chamber of Commerce in the country, with a membership of over 8,500 drawn from all sectors of industry and commerce. Its principal aims are to protect the domestic trade interests of commerce and industry in London and the south-east and to develop the international trade of all British companies. As well as providing a collective voice for its members it helps them individually and provides an extensive range of services. It holds seminars, training courses and meetings, business lunches and receptions, an annual prize-giving in the MANSION HOUSE and an annual banquet in GUILDHALL.

London Chest Hospital *Bonner Road, E2*. In 1848 a group of City men realised the very urgent need of large numbers of people in north and east London for a hospital specialising in diseases of the heart and lungs, particularly tuberculosis which was prevalent then. Most hospitals would not accept tubercular cases (the BROMPTON HOSPITAL was an exception). This new chest hospital was originally opened at No. 6 LIVERPOOL STREET (since demolished) opposite BROAD STREET STATION. In 1849 a site in Bonner's Fields, part of VICTORIA PARK, was acquired for a hospital of 80 beds. In 1851 the Prince Consort laid the foundation stone. Sir Joseph Paxton promised to design a crystal sanatorium in which 'the purity of the atmosphere should be secured by a process of artificial filtration and an equable and pure temperature both in summer and winter, the outer air being admitted by tunnels to the centre of the building'. It was never built as it was considered too expensive. The hospital was then known as the City of London Hospital for Diseases of the Chest and subtitled Victoria Park Hospital.

London Coffee House *Ludgate Hill.* Standing next to ST MARTIN'S CHURCH, the house was established in about 1731 by James Ashley and was also known in the early days as Ashley's London Punch House. In March 1772 James Boswell noticed that its clientele was 'composed principally of Physicians, dissenting clergy and masters of academies'. Joseph Priestley, Benjamin Franklin and other 'honest, ingenious friends' belonged to a club which met here to discuss social and philosophical questions. As it stood within the LIBERTIES OF THE FLEET prison, juries from OLD BAILEY who could not agree upon a verdict were frequently locked up here for the night. A London Directory of 1798 described the house as 'perhaps the most elegant and extensive of any that come under the name of coffee-house in the three kingdoms'. Masonic meetings were frequently held here. It was long a resort for Americans; and in 1851 Mr George Peabody, the philanthropist, gave a dinner for Americans connected with the GREAT EXHIBITION. The house was closed in 1867 and the freehold bought by the CORPORATION.

London College of Music *47 Great Marlborough Street, W1.* Founded in 1887 at a time when there was a considerable increase in demand for musical facilities and education.

London Commodity Exchange *52 Mark Lane, EC3.* Until 1973 this Exchange was in MINCING LANE where, as early as the 10th century, trading in commodities was conducted by galley men, so called because they landed their merchandise, chiefly wines and spices from Mediterranean ports, at Galley Quay in THAMES STREET near the south end of MINCING LANE. After the destruction of the ROYAL EXCHANGE in the GREAT FIRE the various commodity traders conducted their business in coffee-houses, particularly the JAMAICA, the JERUSALEM, and, later, GARRAWAY'S. Many of them continued to do so after the construction of the London Commercial Sale Rooms on the east side of Mincing Lane in 1811. These rooms, as well as most of MINCING LANE, were destroyed by bombs in 1941. Until the formation of the London Commodity Exchange in 1954, its members were housed in Plantation House, EC3 by the London Rubber Exchange. Shareholding member markets are the Coffee Terminal Market Association of London Ltd, the London Cocoa Terminal Market Association Ltd, the London Rubber Terminal Market Association Ltd, the United Terminal Sugar Market Association Ltd, the London Vegetable Oil Terminal Market Association Ltd, the London Wool Terminal Market Association Ltd, the Grain and Feed Trade Association and the Soya Bean Meal Futures Association Ltd. A new market, the Internal Petroleum Exchange, opened in 1981.

London Corresponding Society The most influential of the reform societies which sprang up following the French Revolution and the publication of Tom Paine's *The Rights of Man.* It was founded in 1792 by Thomas Hardy, a shoemaker at the Bell Tavern, EXETER STREET. At the height of its influence (1794–5) it probably had over 5,000 members who were mostly 'tradesmen, mechanics and shopkeepers'. Edmund Burke called it 'the mother of all mischief'. At a meeting at COPENHAGEN HOUSE, ISLINGTON, in 1795, the Society protested against the high taxation and prices due to the French wars. Its aims were peace with France, universal suffrage, annual elected parliaments and the abolition of party politics, with nationwide campaigns to secure these objectives. As well as the Revolutionary Society and other similar bodies, the London Corresponding Society was suppressed within a few years of its foundation by Pitt's government in a programme of legislation prompted by fears of public disorder.

London County Council Established by the Local Government Act of 1888 as successor to the METROPOLITAN BOARD OF WORKS, until superseded by the GREATER LONDON COUNCIL in 1965, it had jurisdiction over some 117 sq miles inhabited (in 1961) by 3,200,000 people. It was composed of 126 councillors elected every three years, plus 21 aldermen elected by the councillors for periods of six years. From 1922 its headquarters were at COUNTY HALL.

It was the first metropolitan authority to be elected directly by the people of London, and party politics were always to the fore in its affairs. From 1889 to 1895 the Progressives (or Liberals) had a majority, but in 1895 they lost to the Moderates (or Conservatives). The Progressives were again in control from 1898 to 1907, but the Moderates held power from 1907–34, when they were ousted by the Labour Party led by Herbert Morrison (later Deputy Prime Minister). The Labour Party retained its majority for the rest of the Council's existence.

Throughout its career successive Acts of Parliament conferred ever wider functions on the LCC, and ultimately its powers were very considerable. It was responsible *inter alia* for main drainage, the control of building methods and materials, the fire service, and (concurrently with the 28 Metropolitan Borough Councils) for housing. By 1938 it had provided over 86,000 new dwellings. It bought out all the London tramway companies and, until the formation of the LONDON PASSENGER TRANSPORT BOARD in 1933, ran all the trams. It built two tunnels under the Thames (BLACKWALL and ROTHERHITHE), rebuilt six bridges (its demolition of old WATERLOO BRIDGE in 1937 drew fierce opposition), laid out KINGSWAY and constructed several by-passes in outer districts. In the 1930s it introduced planning control throughout the whole of its area. In 1938 it initiated the London GREEN BELT, and by 1939 it had more than doubled the acreage of parks and open spaces which it had inherited from the METROPOLITAN BOARD OF WORKS.

After the abolition of the School Board for London in 1904, it became the education authority for the whole of London and managed this, perhaps the most important of all its functions, with such success that in 1965 responsibility for education within the LCC area was not, as originally intended, distributed among the new London Boroughs, but was retained intact by a special committee of the GREATER LONDON COUNCIL known as the INNER LONDON EDUCATION AUTHORITY.

In 1929 its public health functions were vastly enlarged when the duties of the Metropolitan Asylums Board and of the 25 Boards of Guardians of the Poor were transferred to the Council, and the welfare services, hitherto known as indoor or outdoor relief and then renamed public assistance, also became its responsibility.

Close to County Hall, the ROYAL FESTIVAL HALL, now London's principal concert hall, built by the

Council as part of its contribution to the FESTIVAL OF BRITAIN of 1951, provides a fitting monument to the breadth of vision of the LCC and to the quality of much of its work.

London Discount Market   Bills of exchange, by which merchants ordered their agents to make payments at a given date, dominated the finance of London's trade after the 15th century. The discounting of bills, by exchanging them for cash at a discount, brought bills into much wider use in the 18th century, and after the Napoleonic Wars discounting was a key element in London's growth as a financial centre. The business was handled by 'bill brokers', who channelled bills to bankers and others who were prepared to discount for cash, thereby employing surplus funds in areas where working capital was needed. By the mid-1820s some of these brokers were acting as 'discount houses' with their own bill holdings and short-term borrowings. In this role they relied on support from the BANK OF ENGLAND for the discount of their best-quality bills. This support was severely tested by the failure of the largest discount house, Overend, Gurney and Co., in 1866. Recovery was only achieved after the leading discount houses were reconstructed and after the market's emphasis shifted towards international finance. More recently the market has widened to include sterling and eurocurrency loans and certificates of deposit. The relationship with the BANK OF ENGLAND remains of central importance; by borrowing the banks' 'at call' money and relending it to the government and to companies, the market acts as a buffer between the banks and the BANK OF ENGLAND in the control of monetary policy. London's discount business, estimated at between £6 billion and £10 billion each week in the late 1970s, is shared by a group of only eleven discount houses, including Alexander's Discount Co. (established in 1810), Gerrard and National Discount Co. (1870), Gillett Bros Discount Co. (1867) and Union Discount Co. (1866).

London District   *Horse Guards, Whitehall, SW1.* One of the United Kingdom Army Commands. It is responsible for military administration in the CITY OF LONDON, the London metropolitan area and Windsor, together with the barracks at Caterham and the Guards' depot at Pirbright. It is commanded by a Major-General who also commands the HOUSEHOLD DIVISION.

London Docks   Sanctioned by an Act of 1800 and opened at WAPPING in 1805, three years after the WEST INDIA DOCKS. They were then the nearest docks to the CITY. For 21 years the company which ran them enjoyed a valuable monopoly, since all ships arriving in London with tobacco, rice, wine and brandy – except from the East and West Indies – had to unload at London Docks. Their plan consisted of a large Western Dock of 20 acres with a lock into a basin and from there into the river on the south, and an Eastern Dock of seven acres with a basin and locks into the river on the east. The docks were linked by a small Tobacco Dock. The splendid warehouses of brick, with stone plinths and rustications, carved with ammonites and sea patterns, were mostly four storeys high. They stood above remarkable, brick-vaulted wine cellars of

London Docks, amalgamated with St Katharine's Dock in 1864, from an 1890s' photograph.

472

vast extent joined beneath the roads by tunnels and skilfully ventilated. The docks also possessed a great warehouse for wool. Surrounded by the obligatory high walls, the works had a Roman dignity, thanks to the talent of the designer, Daniel Alexander. He was then Surveyor to TRINITY HOUSE for which he built a number of lighthouses. Later he added the colonnades to the QUEEN'S HOUSE, GREENWICH, in honour of Nelson. Much of the work at London Docks, however, was accomplished by John Rennie, who was appointed engineer to the scheme in 1801. The London Docks amalgamated with ST KATHARINE'S DOCK, lying to the west, in 1864. In 1969 they were closed to shipping and the area is being redeveloped.

London Fields *Hackney, E8*. Area of 26½ acres once used for sheep grazing and thus worn bare. By 1866 they had become 'in dry weather a hard, unsightly, dusty plain with a few isolated tufts of turf and in wet weather a dismal impassable swamp'. They were frequented by the riff-raff of London and in the 18th century often by highwaymen. Cricket was played there as early as 1802.

London Fire Brigade After the fall of the Roman Empire there was no organised fire-fighting force in London until William the Conqueror established his *couvre-feu* or curfew law which required people to douse all fires and lights at nightfall. Severe penalties were imposed upon those who broke this law. These penalties were abolished by Henry I despite the fire of 1086 which destroyed a large area of the city. Between the 12th and 16th centuries various attempts were made to introduce BUILDING REGULATIONS, but these were largely ignored and it was not until 1600 that various forms of early fire appliances came into use. These, maintained at the expense of the parishes, were used, for the most part ineffectually, at a large fire in 1633.

After the GREAT FIRE, houses were largely rebuilt in brick and their owners began to insure their premises against fire. Insurance companies were granted charters to provide fire assurances and the fire offices realised that it would be in their own interests to hire men to put out fires in buildings which they insured. Fire engines were introduced and WATERMEN recruited as fire-fighters. Every policy-holder was issued with a metal badge or 'fire mark' to fix to the outside of the building. Frequently when a fire occurred more than one company's brigade arrived on the scene. If the mark was not that of their company they would leave the fire to burn, and in some cases even provoke a fight with a rival brigade. But gradually the brigades began to co-operate with each other and in 1833 their resources were pooled to form the London Fire Engine Establishment, with 19 fire stations.

This force comprised only 80 full-time professionals, known as Jimmy Braiders after James Braidwood, their superintendent. Steam fire engines were invented in Braidwood's time, but he preferred the old manual machines; and the Establishment's failure to preserve the HOUSES OF PARLIAMENT in the fire of 1834, despite valiant efforts, led to widespread criticism of it, which was reinforced by its failure to bring under control for two days a fire in TOOLEY STREET where Braidwood was killed when a wall collapsed on him.

The Government appointed a committee which recommended the formation of a Metropolitan Fire

The London Fire Brigade, then under Eyre Massey Shaw, at practice on the Thames Embankment in 1868.

Brigade under the control of the METROPOLITAN BOARD OF WORKS. The Brigade was established in 1865 and Captain Eyre Massey Shaw, who had succeeded Braidwood as Superintendent of the London Fire Establishment, was appointed its commander. A gifted friend of the Prince of Wales and immortalised in Gilbert and Sullivan's *Iolanthe*, Shaw expanded the use of steam fire engines, introduced telegraph systems and, despite poor finances, increased the strength of the Brigade whose hard-worked men were paid 22s a week.

Twenty-six new fire stations were built in 1867–71, to the designs of Edward Cresy, self-styled 'Architect to the Metropolitan Fire Brigade'. He was succeeded by Alfred Mott who changed the style to 'Secular Gothick'. In 1889 the LONDON COUNTY COUNCIL took over control of the Brigade, and Shaw, who had commanded it in his own way under the METROPOLITAN BOARD OF WORKS, resigned after stormy quarrels.

In 1904 the Metropolitan Fire Brigade became officially known as the London Fire Brigade. The last horse-drawn machines, which had been gradually supplanted by motor appliances, were withdrawn in 1921. After the 1st World War, in which firemen were exempted from war service, the Brigade was vastly improved. New headquarters were constructed on the ALBERT EMBANKMENT by LAMBETH BRIDGE to replace the old headquarters in SOUTHWARK. In the 2nd World War an Auxiliary Fire Service was formed, and in 1941 a National Fire Service came into existence. In Greater London the separate brigades were formed into a single regional force divided into five, and later four, fire forces. Two years after the establishment of the GREATER LONDON COUNCIL in 1963, a new London Fire Brigade came into existence. Between the year of its establishment and 1979 there were 644,640 fires in London; in answering 1,215,444 calls, ten men of the Brigade lost their lives and 1,528 were injured. The Brigade is organised into 11 divisions and has 114 fire stations, a complement of about 6,800 men and over 500 appliances.

London Fire Brigade Museum *Winchester House, Southwark Bridge Road, SE1*. Housed in the former residence of Captain Sir Eyre Massey Shaw, Superintendent of the London Fire Establishment 1861–5 and of the Metropolitan Fire Brigade 1866–91, the museum contains a unique collection of fire brigade historical items.

London Gazette Founded in 1665 as a daily news-letter and first produced in PRINTING HOUSE SQUARE. It is now the official organ of the British Government, in which official announcements are made.

London Group An exhibiting society of English artists, it was formed in 1913 by an amalgamation of the CAMDEN TOWN GROUP, the Futurists and the Vorticists, together with various artists who had shown their work in the Allied Artists' Exhibitions organised by Frank Rutter in the ALBERT HALL in 1908. Among the most distinguished members were Wyndham Lewis and Jacob Epstein. Its first show was held in the Goupil Gallery in May 1914. Sculptors were admitted and a ban on women was lifted. The first president was Harold Gilman. After the 1st World War Roger Fry joined, bringing his BLOOMSBURY friends with him. The group continued after the 2nd World War, exhibiting regularly.

London Hilton Hotel *22 Park Lane, W1*. A 30-storey hotel towering above HYDE PARK. Designed by Lewis Solomon, Kaye and Partners, it opened in 1963. A row of attractive terrace houses formerly occupied the site, one of them a Perpendicular Gothic house of 1847 by W.B. Moffatt (Gilbert Scott's partner). These were bought in 1956 by Charles Clore and demolished. In 1982 there were 509 bedrooms.

London Hippodrome *Hippodrome Corner, Cranbourn Street, WC2*. Built for Edward Moss to the design of Frank Matcham and opened in 1900 as a combined music-hall and circus with a built-in water-tank. Theatrical history was made with several water shows including *Siberia*, *The Redskins* and *The Earthquake*. In December 1912, after a complete reconstruction, the direction was taken over by Albert de Courville who presented successful revues and variety starring such performers as George Robey, Violet Loraine, Morris Harvey, Sophie Tucker and Paul Whiteman with the first of the big dance bands. These were followed by successful musical comedies, among them *Sunny* (1925), *Hit the Deck* (1927), *Mr Cinders* (1929), *Please, Teacher* (1935). Jack Buchanan, Elsie Randolph, Binnie Hale, Bobbie Howes and Cicely Courtneidge all enjoyed long runs here. The seating capacity was 1,340. In 1958 it was reconstructed as the Talk of the Town, a cabaret and restaurant. It closed in 1982.

London Hospital (Mile End) *275 Bancroft Road, E1*. Originally a poor law hospital, it was founded as Mile End Hospital in 1859 and moved to its present site in 1881. It was taken over by the LONDON COUNTY COUNCIL in 1930 and by the National Health Service in 1948. In 1982 there were 376 beds.

London Hospital (St Clement's) *Bow Road, E3*. Built in 1840 as the City of London Infirmary, it now houses the psychiatric part of the LONDON HOSPITAL. In 1982 there were 135 beds.

London Hospital *Whitechapel Road, E1*. Founded in 1740 at a meeting of seven gentlemen at the Feathers Tavern, CHEAPSIDE. The moving spirit was a surgeon named John Harrison, aged only 22, who had just joined the Barber-Surgeons' Company (*see* BARBERS' COMPANY). A house was leased in

Featherstone Street, MOORFIELDS, near where MOORFIELDS EYE HOSPITAL, CITY ROAD now stands. Containing about 30 beds and called the London Infirmary, it was moved in 1741 to Prescott Street near the MINORIES, north-east of the TOWER, just outside the CITY boundary, in an exceedingly bad neighbourhood, full of brothels and drinking houses.

In the early days no deaths were recorded, only occasional discharges for misdemeanours. By 1755 patients were classified as 'cured' or 'relieved'. On discharge they had to give thanks to the Committee and 'their kind benefactors' and then go to their parish churches to give thanks to Almighty God. Any patient refusing to do so was never to be treated again (a black list of these offenders was kept). Nursing not being a recognised profession then, many nurses recruited proved unsuitable and were often discharged for drunkenness. Matters improved when the Gin Laws were passed in 1751, but bed bugs remained a severe problem until well in to the next century. (Professional bug destroyers existed until Victoria's reign.) There were no sinks in the wards and no water flushing system. 'Soil' was carried in buckets by the hospital labourer at night to be dumped in the hospital cesspool or the street. The governors discouraged the teaching of students, maintaining that they financed the hospital for treating 'poor objects', not for the purpose of instruction.

In 1757 new buildings were begun amongst green fields in WHITECHAPEL, to the design of Boulton Mainwaring, the hospital surveyor. This new hospital, finished in 1759, was probably the finest hospital building in London in its time, since the other main hospitals then existing were not rebuilt until well into the next century. Even a primitive water flushing system had been installed. In 1755 the East Wing was added, bringing the number of patients to over 200. In 1778 the West Wing was completed.

Sir William Blizard was the outstanding medical figure at the London towards the end of the century. His ambition was to start a medical school actually at, and associated with, the hospital. Up to this time there were only private schools dissociated from hospitals such as the famous one in GREAT WINDMILL STREET run by the Hunter brothers. After a great struggle and much opposition, he finally succeeded in erecting a one-storey building at the east end of the hospital. Opened in 1785, it contained a chemical laboratory, museum, and dissecting room. Blizard also founded a medical club which was to include 'Gentlemen who are or have been pupils of the hospital'. The members held an annual dinner at the London Tavern. Blizard played an active part in establishing the ROYAL COLLEGE OF SURGEONS, of which he was the first President. As an operating surgeon he was outstanding. His last operation at the age of 84 was an amputation above the knee, the stump healing perfectly, which was very rare in those days. He retired from the active staff of the London at the age of 90.

In 1854 a new medical college was opened, 'the most convenient, salubrious and handsome school in the Metropolis'. In 1866 Thomas John Barnardo, later founder of DR BARNARDO'S HOMES, joined the Medical College as a student. In 1876 Queen Victoria opened a new wing to the hospital which, with 790 beds, was by then the largest hospital in the country. In 1877 a new Medical College and Nurses' Home was opened by the Prince of Wales. In 1890 a new gabled front

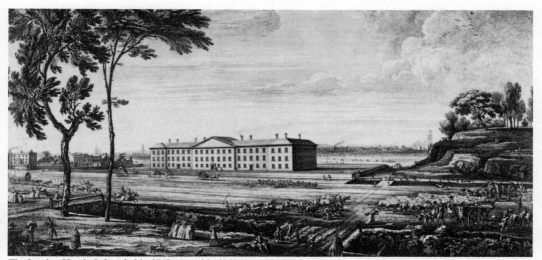

The London Hospital, founded in 1740, moved in 1757 to new buildings among the green fields of Whitechapel.

designed by Roland Plumbe was added to Boulton Mainwaring's original north façade, providing a covered approach from Whitechapel Road.

In 1896 Sydney Holland, later Viscount Knutsford, was elected Chairman of the hospital. From then until his death in 1931 he raised enormous sums for the hospital and practically rebuilt it. He worked in close association with Miss Eva Lückes, who was appointed Matron at the early age of 24. The well-educated daughter of a country gentleman, she was an unusual recruit for the nursing profession in those days. She died, still working at the hospital, in 1919 and Knutsford said, 'To me the loss is the greatest I ever had.' The hospital has been largely rebuilt since the 2nd World War. Mile End and St Clement's Hospitals, now respectively called LONDON HOSPITAL (MILE END) and LONDON HOSPITAL (ST CLEMENT'S), are associated with the main London Hospital, which in 1982 had 718 beds.

London Institution *Finsbury Circus*. Founded in 1806 'for the Advancement of Literature and the Diffusion of Useful Knowledge'. Its meetings were originally held in a house in OLD JEWRY belonging to Sir Robert Clayton. A building designed for the institution by William Brooks was opened on the north side of FINSBURY CIRCUS in 1819. Its large library was celebrated for its topographical books. Hazlitt said that he once saw the first librarian, the Greek scholar Richard Porson, 'with a large patch of coarse brown paper on his nose, the skirts of his rusty black coat hung with cobwebs, and talking in a tone of suavity approaching condescension to one of the managers.' Lectures were given at the Institution by 'eminent scientific and literary men'. The London Institution was demolished in 1936.

London Irish Rugby Football Club *see* RUGBY FOOTBALL CLUBS.

London Library *14 St James's Square, SW1.* Founded at the instigation of Thomas Carlyle who, one day in 1841, spent a frustrating morning in the BRITISH MUSEUM waiting two hours for a book to be delivered to him while Macaulay, much more respectfully attended, was busily working in a private room. Determined to form a library which would make resort to the BRITISH MUSEUM less necessary and which would provide the kind of books not available in the circulating libraries, Carlyle, to use his own word, 'ignited' a group of men prepared to back him in his enterprise. These included the historian Henry Hallam, the philosopher John Stuart Mill and a young barrister, William Douglas Christie, who prepared a pamphlet setting out the object of the library which was stated to be, 'the supply of good books in all department of knowledge. Books in the lighter departments of literature and new books will necessarily be included else the library would not be complete; but new books will not be bought merely because they are new, and much discrimination will necessarily be exercised as to the lighter literature which is the grand stock-in-trade of the ordinary circulating libraries.'

At an inaugural meeting Carlyle propounded his ideas, forcefully condemning both the BRITISH MUSEUM and the circulating libraries, and extolling the advantages of a serious library from which books could be taken home. The response was satisfactory: 500 subscribers prepared to pay an entrance fee of £6 and an annual subscription of £2 were soon found; and the library opened with 3,000 volumes at 49 PALL MALL. Four years later, in 1845, the library moved to its present site in ST JAMES'S SQUARE, where it continued to prosper. By 1893 its stock of books had increased to 167,000. In that year Charles Hagbert Wright arrived as librarian and was to preside over the expansion of the building and the staff which had now become essential. The rebuilding was carried out in 1896–8 to the designs of J. Osborne Smith.

When Wright died in 1940 the stock had risen to 475,000 volumes. Many of these were damaged when in 1944 a bomb fell in nearby MASON'S YARD. But the stock has gradually been replaced and increased and the library now holds almost a million books. It is a general collection on the humanities. It does not contain specialist works on law, medicine, the natural sciences or technology, but in other fields almost every worthwhile book in the major European languages will be found in the catalogue, which is itself a renowned bibliographical reference work. In addition the main reading room contains a wide-ranging selection of current periodicals and learned journals.

The first President of the Library was Lord Clarendon. He was followed by Carlyle who, according to Simon Nowell-Smith, librarian in 1950–6, broke all the rules, refusing to return books when asked, and scribbling scornful comments in their margins. Carlyle was followed by Richard Monckton-Milnes, Tennyson and Sir Leslie Stephen. More recent Presidents have included T.S. Eliot and Lord Clark. In 1980 there were about 6,000 members paying a subscription of £40 a year.

London Metal Exchange *Whittington Avenue, EC3.* Established in LOMBARD STREET in 1877. The need for such an exchange had been apparent since the beginning of the century when Britain, instead of being a net exporter of metals at fairly steady prices, became a large importer at sharply fluctuating prices. Its three main functions are to register daily price quotations; to provide a market where metals can be bought or sold; and to provide facilities for 'hedging', that is to say for all those connected with the metal trade to make offsetting purchases or sales against their own commitments. Dealings take place in minimum quantities of 25 metric tonnes for copper, lead and zinc, 5 metric tonnes for tin and 10,000 troy ounces for silver. The alchemical symbols, used to indicate the metal traded in at any one time, are:

♀ ♃ ♄ ♁ ☽

copper tin lead zinc silver

The origin of these symbols is not known for certain. They were in general use by alchemists in the 13th century.

London Passenger Transport Board *see* LONDON TRANSPORT EXECUTIVE.

London Museum *Kensington Palace.* Founded in 1911 by the 2nd Viscount Esher and the 1st Viscount Harcourt to illustrate the social history of London from the earliest times. Moved from KENSINGTON PALACE to LANCASTER HOUSE in 1914, it was bought for the nation by Lord Leverhulme. It was evacuated during the 2nd World War and returned to KENSINGTON in 1950. It is now amalgamated with the MUSEUM OF LONDON.

London Natural History Society Founded in 1858. Its members are interested in all aspects of natural history, especially in the area within 20 miles of ST PAUL'S CATHEDRAL. It organises lectures, mostly in central London, conducts field meetings which explore the geology, plant and animal life all round the capital, has a large library for the use of members, and publishes two journals annually, the *London Naturalist* and the *London Bird Report*. The Society has recently produced an atlas of the breeding birds of the London area and an atlas of its flowering plants is being prepared. (*See also* LONDON WILDLIFE TRUST.)

London Palladium *Argyll Street, W1.* The site was first used for entertainment by Charles Hengler, who made a permanent home here for his touring circus. The circus premises were later used for ice-skating. In 1910 the luxurious music-hall, built for Walter Gibbons, opened as the Palladium, with a variety bill. Designed by Frank Matcham, it cost £250,000 and had box-to-box telephones and a palm court in Norwegian granite behind the stalls. From the early 1920s spectacular revues were staged here. The most successful were *Rockets* (1922), *Whirl of the World* (1923) and de Courville's *Sky High* (1925). *Peter Pan* was first performed at Christmas in 1930 and was repeated every year until 1938. In the early 1930s the theatre was used as a cinema for three months. The Crazy Gang shows ensured its revival as a theatre; the last of them was *These Foolish Things* (1938). It became officially known as the London Palladium in 1934.

London Pavilion *Piccadilly Circus.* Originally a song-and-supper-room annexe to the Black Horse Inn, it became a music-hall in 1861. The word 'jingoism' originates from a song sung here in 1878 during the Russo-Turkish War:

> We don't want to fight
> But, by Jingo, if we do,
> We've got the ships,
> We've got the men and got the money, too

The original building was demolished in 1885 and a new Pavilion, managed by Edmund Villiers, was built to the designs of Worley and Saunders. The façade still stands. In 1918 it became a theatre and was used for C.B. Cochran's spectacular reviews. It was converted into a cinema in 1934, and closed in 1982.

London Philharmonic Orchestra Formed in 1932 by Sir Thomas Beecham as a result of his failure to agree with the policies of many existing London orchestras. It is now one of the leading orchestras of Europe. It rapidly achieved success and, when Beecham left for the USA at the start of 1939, the players decided to continue as a self-governing orchestra and have remained so. (As a result Beecham founded the ROYAL PHILHARMONIC ORCHESTRA in 1946.) From 1949 the LONDON COUNTY COUNCIL gave the orchestra financial assistance until its building of the ROYAL FESTIVAL HALL in 1957. The orchestra survived this cut in its financing, and by the 1960s was re-established, playing under Sir Adrian Boult, John Pritchard and Sir George Solti. It also made many recordings; in 1964 it became the resident orchestra for the opera at Glyndebourne. Touring extensively, it was the first British orchestra to visit the USSR and China.

London Plane Hybrid between *Platanus orientalis* from south-east Europe and western Asia, introduced early in the 16th century, and *Platanus occidentalis* from North America, introduced from Virginia in 1636. These trees have been planted regularly since the middle of the 18th century in London squares, streets and gardens.

London Pride A pink-flowered saxifrage, *Saxifraga umbrosa*, the flower is also known as none-so-pretty and St Patrick's cabbage.

London Rocket *Sisymbrium irio*, a plant native to the Mediterranean area. It appeared in large numbers in areas destroyed by the GREAT FIRE.

London Rowing Club *Embankment, Putney, SW15.* Founded in 1856, it was the first club to challenge the virtual monopoly of Oxford and Cambridge Universities in rowing at Henley-on-Thames. It was immediately successful in winning the Grand and Steward's Cups and the Diamond Sculls, and has won more races at Henley than any other club. It instituted and organises the Metropolitan Regatta and has been the most successful club in the Tideway Head of the River Race. The club colours are blue and white.

London Salvage Corps *140 Aldersgate Street, EC1.* Set up in 1866 following the Metropolitan Fire Brigade Act of 1865, which laid responsibility for fighting fires in London upon the METROPOLITAN BOARD OF WORKS and gave the fire insurance companies the right to establish a separate salvage force to attend fires and save insured property. Eighteen fire insurance offices became the founder members and since then many other companies and LLOYD'S have been admitted to membership. The original headquarters was at 31 WATLING STREET; it was moved to 63–66 WATLING STREET in 1905 and to their modern purpose-built premises in 1961. Until 1923 the Corps worked with horse-drawn vehicles. Now they have a number of red tenders known as Damage Control Units, of varying sizes.

They worked in conjunction with the LONDON FIRE BRIGADE during the 2nd World War, and have a cordial relationship with them. Whereas the LONDON FIRE BRIGADE aim to extinguish a fire as quickly as possible, the Corps endeavour to prevent damage to property, particularly from smoke and the water used in fire-fighting.

London School of Economics and Political Science *Houghton Street, WC2.* Founded in 1895 to promote 'the study and advancement of Economics or Political Economy, Political Science or Political Philosophy, Statistics, Sociology, History, Geography, and any subject cognate to any of these'. It had been made possible by Henry Hunt Hutchinson, a member of the Fabian Society, who had died the year before, leaving instructions that Sidney Webb and four other trustees were to dispose of the residue of his estate for socially progressive purposes. It was largely based on L'Ecole Libre des Sciences Politiques in Paris, and other schools and universities on the Continent and in America where political and social problems were being studied.

The School's first home was at No. 9 JOHN STREET, ADELPHI. In 1896 it moved to No. 10 Adelphi Terrace, later the house of G.B. Shaw, who was closely connected with Webb in plans for the school. The British Library of Political and Economic Science was started at No. 19 in November 1896. In 1902 the school, which had become a college within the federal UNIVERSITY OF LONDON in 1900, moved to CLARE MARKET. The site had been provided by the LONDON COUNTY COUNCIL and the money for building donated by Passmore Edwards and others. In 1920 Harold Laski, later Professor of Political Science and Chairman of the Labour Party, joined the staff. Among his contemporaries were Friedrich von Hayek, Tooke Professor of Economic Science and Statistics, 1931–50, and Lionel (later Lord) Robbins, Professor of Economics, 1929–61. In 1921 the school was recognised by the University Faculty of Laws; in 1922 by the Faculty of Arts; and in 1963 by the Faculty of Science. New school buildings were opened in 1922; further new buildings came into use in the 1930s and 1960s; and the eight-storey St Clement's extension and the Clare Market Building in 1970. Also in 1970 the school contracted to purchase the five-storey Strand House in PORTUGAL STREET, the head office and warehouse of W.H. SMITH AND CO. After fund-raising conversion work on this building began in 1976 and in July 1978 it was opened as the Lionel Robbins Building. It houses the library, a collection of almost three million items, the most distinguished social science collection in the world.

The first Chairman was Sidney Webb; the Chairman in 1981 was Sir Huw Wheldon. Professor Ralf Dahrendorf was appointed Director in 1974. The school has probably had more influence on the political shape of the present-day world than any other university school.

London School of Hygiene and Tropical Medicine *Gower Street, WC1.* Founded in 1924, and incorporating the London School of Tropical Medicine which was established in 1899, it became part of the UNIVERSITY OF LONDON in 1905. The building was completed in 1929 to the designs of P. Morley Horder and O. Verner Rees.

London Scottish Rugby Football Club *see* RUGBY FOOTBALL CLUBS.

London Silver Vaults *Chancery House, 53–64 Chancery Lane, WC2.* Originating from the Chancery Lane Safe Deposit Co., which was established in 1885, and belonging today to a security company, Sterling Guards Ltd, the London Silver Vaults were reopened on their present underground site in 1953, the former premises having been destroyed during the 2nd World War.

London Spa *Clerkenwell.* In about 1685 a chalybeate spring was discovered in the gardens of the Fountain Inn. John Halhed, the proprietor, claimed his accommodation to be 'suitable to the goodness of the Waters' which Robert Boyle, the chemist, had declared to be 'the strongest and best of those late found out'. The poor were supplied free. In 1714, according to the *Field Spy*, the gardens and spring were very popular.

In 1733, according to *Poor Robin's Almanack*:

Now sweethearts with their sweethearts go
To Islington or London Spaw,
Some go but just to drink the water,
Some for the ale which they like better.

On 17 March 1741 the *Daily Post* recorded, 'On Sunday a custom house officer being intoxicated with spaw ale, in a phrensical fit drew his dagger, and fancying all people that passed to be his enemies, cut and slashed several persons in a most frightful manner, for which being apprehended, he was carried before a justice of the peace and committed to the New Prison.' From about 1754 few people came to drink the waters and the building became a mere tavern. Spa Fields Recreation Ground remains, behind Exmouth Market.

London Stone *Cannon Street, EC4.* Set in a niche in the wall of the Bank of China is a roughly shaped, round-topped stone. Before 1960 it had been in a similar position on the north side of CANNON STREET (opposite the railway station), but set in the wall of ST SWITHIN'S CHURCH. The stone is weathered Clipsham limestone and has no markings except a pair of grooves worn in the top. Its origin is uncertain. It was certainly in place as far back as 1198 when it was referred to as Lonenstane. From at least the late 16th century it has been suggested that it was a Roman milestone, possibly that from which all measurements in the province of Britannia were taken. Its site would be appropriate, since recent excavations have revealed the remains of the GOVERNOR'S PALACE beneath CANNON STREET STATION. More probably it is merely the rounded top of an early wayside Roman funerary monument whose base may still await discovery on the south side of CANNON STREET. When Jack Cade, the Kentish rebel, rode into the City in 1450, calling himself John Mortimer, he struck the stone with his sword and is said to have announced, 'Now is Mortimer Lord of the City' (see CADE'S REBELLION).

London Symphonies Haydn's last 12 symphonies (Nos 93–104) are known as the London Symphonies. They were written in 1791–5, and for years were his only symphonies regularly performed (with such nicknames as 'The Surprise', 'The Clock' 'The London' (No. 104) and 'The Military'). Haydn was invited to London by the impresario Salomon, who commissioned them for his HANOVER SQUARE concerts. Vaughan Williams's *A London Symphony* was written in 1912–13 and incorporates such effects as WESTMINSTER chimes, STREET CRIES and other London sounds.

London Symphony Orchestra The oldest surviving orchestra in London, it has long been recognised as one of the greatest orchestras in the world. It was founded in 1904 after an unresolved dispute between Henry Wood and some 50 members of his celebrated Queen's Hall Orchestra, who as a result left to form their own self-governing body. The inaugural concert at the QUEEN'S HALL was conducted by Hans Richter. Principal conductors since have included Elgar. The orchestra has not only made many tours abroad, but since the 1950s has made numerous award-winning recordings. The orchestra was selected by the CORPORATION OF THE CITY OF LONDON to be resident at the BARBICAN ARTS CENTRE.

London Tavern *Bishopsgate Street Within.* A large tavern rebuilt by William Jupp and William Newton after its destruction by fire in 1765, it was renowned for the excellent meals provided in its dining-room, which could accommodate 355 people. The East India Company used to give its dinners here. John Britton, the antiquary and author with Edward Wedlake Brayley of *The Beauties of England and Wales*, was cellarman for a time, but only a short time as he found 'the confinement and occupation slavish and irksome.' Charles Dickens presided at a meeting here in 1841 for the benefit of the Sanatorium for Sick Authors and Artists, and at the annual dinner in 1851 in aid of the General Theatrical Fund. And it is here in *Nicholas Nickleby* that the public meeting is held 'to take into consideration the propriety of petitioning Parliament in favour of the United Metropolitan Improved Hot Muffin and Crumpet Baking and Punctual

Delivery Company'. On his way to attend this meeting 'Mr Bonney elbowed his way briskly upstairs, receiving in his progress many low bows from the waiters who stood on the landing to show the way, and, followed by Mr Nickleby, dived into a suite of apartments behind the great public room, in the second of which was a business-looking table, and several business-looking people.' The building was demolished in 1876.

London Telecom Tower One of the tallest buildings in London, the London Telecom Tower (formerly known as the Post Office Tower) was built to provide support for aerials which transmit and receive radio, television and telephone calls in and out of London by means of very high-frequency signals, called microwaves. The tower is near the TOTTENHAM COURT ROAD and was completed in 1964. The chief architect was Eric Bedford. The tower is 580 ft high, surmounted by a 39 ft high mast supporting a weather radar aerial, a total height of 620 ft.

London to Brighton Rally *see* VETERAN CAR RUN.

London to Brighton Walk First held officially in September 1919 and, except during the 2nd World War, held annually in September ever since. It is organised by the Surrey Walking Club over a distance of 53 miles, starting at 6 a.m. by the chimes of BIG BEN and finishing on the Esplanade at Brighton. Donald Thompson won the walk eight times between 1955 and 1962, and again in 1967.

London Topographical Society *Bishopsgate Institute, 230 Bishopsgate, EC2.* Founded in 1880 for the reproduction of maps, drawings and plans of London which are issued to members and, whenever sufficient stocks remain, sold to the public. The Society also publishes the *London Topographical Record*, a five-yearly collection of essays and historical and topographical notes.

London Transport Executive In 1929, with a certain amount of competition on the roads from independent bus operators, the London County Council tramways, the UNDERGROUND railways and the London General Omnibus Co. proposed to co-ordinate their services. There was some political opposition to the idea from those who saw it as an attempt by Lord Ashfield, the UNDERGROUND's Chairman, to enlarge his empire. And it was not until 1933, under the National Government, that the London Passenger Transport Board was established by law.

With the outbreak of the 2nd World War the Government assumed control of the London Passenger Transport Board and continued in charge until 1947. In that year the British Transport Commission was set up by the Transport Act, and executive bodies were appointed by it to deal with transport in various parts of the country. One of these took over the whole of the road and rail transport in the London area, and the policies of the London Passenger Transport Board were carried out by the London Transport Executive which superseded it in 1948. The GREATER LONDON COUNCIL has, since its establishment in 1965, been responsible for the overall policy and financial control of London Transport, but the Executive is wholly responsible for its day-to-day management and operation.

London Transport Museum *Floral Market, Covent Garden, WC2.* A small collection of early omnibuses was formed by the London General Omnibus Co. at their CHISWICK works in the 1920s and 1930s. During the 2nd World War this collection, by then enlarged, was moved to Reigate. After the nationalisation of London Transport and the country's railways and the establishment of the British Transport Commission in 1948, a report recommended the preservation of the collection. A new Museum for British Transport in London was accordingly established and its exhibits, which now included paintings and models, were displayed at a redundant London Transport garage at CLAPHAM. They were later moved to a former garden pavilion at SYON HOUSE, where the London Transport Collection was opened in May 1973. In 1978 the Collection was closed at SYON HOUSE and in 1980 the Museum opened in COVENT GARDEN. It represents nearly 200 years of London Transport services. (*See also* RAILWAYS, TRANSPORT *and* UNDERGROUND.)

London University *see* UNIVERSITY OF LONDON.

London Wall The name is still preserved in a road running on or close to its northern boundary from MOORGATE to the BARBICAN (*see next entry*). The wall surrounding LONDINIUM was probably built late in the 2nd century. Since there was no adequate building stone available in the area, Kentish ragstone was brought from quarries near Maidstone down the river Medway, out into the open sea, hugging the coast, and up into the THAMES. One of the barges used in this freighting sank at its moorings and was found and excavated at BLACKFRIARS BRIDGE in 1962 (*see* BLACKFRIARS BARGE).

Nearly 2 miles in length, the wall enclosed an area of some 330 acres, was 6–9 ft wide and about 18 ft high, probably with a catwalk and parapet on top. Its outer face was protected by a 6 ft deep V-cut ditch that varied in width from 9 to 15 ft. When the wall was built it incorporated within its circuit the already existing ROMAN FORT in the north-west corner of the city. This is a partial explanation for the unusual shape of the plan of Londinium. Six gates pierced the wall at ALDGATE, BISHOPSGATE, CRIPPLEGATE, ALDERSGATE, NEWGATE and LUDGATE, with small additional postern gates at ALDERMANBURY and the TOWER.

It was long argued that there had been no river wall, since remains were lacking, but excavations in 1975 in the area of UPPER AND LOWER THAMES STREET produced stratified sections that had collapsed. The late date of the structure was confirmed by the re-use in it of numerous sculptures, altars, and even fragments of a once monumental arch. Some time at the end of the 3rd century bastions were added to the wall for additional defence, generally at a distance of about 210 ft apart. Over 20 bastions are known, some solid-based (again often re-using earlier sculptures), others hollow-based. In 1980 a new bastion was found in Crosswall (between ALDGATE and the TOWER), with a good foundation and the wall standing up to 9 ft high. This is preserved in Bastion House, 8–10 Crosswall. Substantial restorations were carried out in the 390s, part of a massive wall of this date being found in the TOWER OF LONDON in 1977. It may be associated with the work of the general Stilicho in 396, and therefore would be some of the latest Roman work in Britain before the withdrawal in 410.

The wall continued in use long after Roman times. The *Anglo-Saxon Chronicle* records it as being still substantial enough for defence in 457 against the raiding Saxons. Sections can still be seen where medieval work continues above Roman foundations and first courses (for instance in Wakefield Gardens, COOPER'S ROW, and ST ALFEGE's churchyard). It was not until the mid-16th century that the city began to spread substantially beyond the walls; the ditch was noted for its bad odour from being used as a dump for rubbish and dead dogs. Major building and redevelopment in the 18th and especially the 19th centuries led to the destruction of large portions of the wall, that is, when the contractors were able to overcome the substantial Roman work. In a number of instances they gave up the unequal struggle against the Roman masonry and a number of cellars of Victorian warehouses on the north-west sector have apsidal ends, reflecting the shape of the bastion into which they fit.

Sections of the wall can still be seen (travelling east to west) at: the TOWER OF LONDON (Wardrobe Tower); Wakefield Gardens, TOWER HILL; TOC H, THE MINORIES; 8–10 COOPER'S ROW; Roman Wall House, CRUTCHED FRIARS; LONDON WALL, in the underground car park; ST ALFEGE'S CHURCHYARD, just off LONDON WALL; Cripplegate Bastion, beside ST GILES'S CHURCH, CRIPPLEGATE; Noble Street, wall and turret foundations; Newgate Bastion, under the Post Office yard, NEWGATE STREET; and below Amen House, WARWICK SQUARE.

London Wall *EC2.* Extends from ALDERSGATE STREET to BROAD STREET along the line of the City wall. Part of the wall still stands in ST ALFEGE GARDEN and beneath the west end of the street are the remains of the west gate to the Roman fort at CRIPPLEGATE (*see* LONDINIUM). From 1329 to 1536 ELSING SPITAL, an Augustinian priory and hospital for 100 blind men, stood here. When Henry VIII closed it he gave the hospital chapel to the parishioners of ST ALFEGE LONDON WALL, whose own church opposite was in danger of falling down. From about 1623–1886 SION COLLEGE stood on the hospital site. BETHLEM HOSPITAL had its hall opposite BASINGHALL STREET from the middle of the 17th century for over 100 years, and the CURRIERS' COMPANY had theirs on the south side of the street from the 16th century until 1920. In the 2nd World War the area was heavily bombed. The street has now been rebuilt with tall blocks of offices and forms the southern boundary of the BARBICAN redevelopment. PLAISTERERS' HALL is at No. 1. ALL HALLOWS-ON-THE-WALL is on the north side towards the OLD BROAD STREET end. THE MUSEUM OF LONDON, at the junction with ALDERSGATE STREET, was completed in 1976 to the designs of Powell and Moya. In the garden of Brewers' Hall stands *The Gardener*, a bronze by Karin Jonzen, 1971.

London Weekend Television *South Bank TV Centre, Kent House, Upper Ground, SE1.* Occupying the whole of Kent House, opened in 1968 with a franchise for general, entertainment, news and information broadcasting. It operates from 5·15 on Friday evening and all day Saturday and Sunday, thus replacing THAMES TELEVISION at weekends. It broadcasts to the whole of the London area and has a potential 30,000,000 viewers.

London Welsh Rugby Football Club *see* RUGBY FOOTBALL CLUBS.

London Wildlife Trust *1 Thorpe Close, NW10.* Established in 1981 with the aim of actively promoting the conservation and appreciation of plant and animal life within London. It publishes a newsletter, *Wild London*.

Londonderry Hotel *19 Park Lane, W1.* The original LONDONDERRY HOUSE, built in the 1760s and remodelled for the 3rd Marquess of Londonderry by Benjamin and Philip Wyatt, was sold for redevelopment in 1962. The hotel, designed by Lewis Solomon, Kaye and Partners, was built in 1964–7 with extensions in 1966–9. In 1982 there were 150 bedrooms.

Londonderry House *Hertford Street.* Designed in the 1760s by James Stuart for Robert d'Arcy, 4th Earl of Holdernesse, a former Ambassador in Venice, Secretary of State for the Southern Department and Governor of the Prince of Wales, 'a formal piece of dullness' in Horace Walpole's opinion but, in fact, conscientious and sensible. The house was then known as Holdernesse House, its later name being adopted after it was reconstructed between 1825 and 1828 by Benjamin and Philip Wyatt for Lord Castlereagh's brother, the 3rd Marquess of Londonderry. The grand staircase designed by the Wyatts led up to a magnificent ballroom which contained a fine collection of statues by Canova. Two rooms of James Stuart's original house, with beautiful decorated ceilings, survived on the first floor. Dwarfed by the LONDON HILTON built on its north side, the house was sold for redevelopment in 1962 and demolished.

Long Acre *WC2.* Once a narrow strip of market gardens owned by the monks of WESTMINSTER ABBEY. In 1552 it was granted to the 1st Earl of Bedford. In the early 17th century it was owned by the MERCERS' COMPANY. After development began at that time the road itself was always kept in good repair, as it was part of James I's route from WESTMINSTER to Theobalds. At first it was a fashionable address. Nicholas Stone, the sculptor, had a house here in 1615–45, Oliver Cromwell in 1637–43, Lady Mary St John, mother of Viscount Bolinbroke, in 1665–92, and John Dryden, the poet, kept an inn called the Mourning Crown in 1645–53. In the middle of the 17th century Long Acre became a centre of coachbuilding. In 1668 Pepys bought a second-hand coach here for £53 and spent from three in the afternoon until eight at night watching it being painted yellow. In 1772 a Mug House Club, whose members were supporters of George I and 'a mixture of gentlemen, lawyers and tradesmen' met in a great room in this street. The company, according to one of the members, was 'seldom under a hundred. The room was always so diverted with songs and drinking from one table to another, to one another's healths, that there was no room for politicks or anything that can sow'r conversation.'

In the 18th century Long Acre was a centre for cabinet-making and furniture designers. Among those who had workshops here were William Hallett, William Vile, John Cobb, Benjamin Goodison and Thomas Chippendale. In 1850 St Martin's Hall, designed by William Westmacott, was opened for choral singing. It was also used for political and social gatherings. In 1859 Dickens gave his first series of readings here. Burned down and rebuilt in 1860, it was converted to the Queen's Theatre in 1867 and closed in 1878. In 1911 it was taken over by Odhams Press. The building has now been demolished and a block of offices, shops and flats built on the site. Bertram Rota, the booksellers, are at Nos 30–31; Edward Stanford Ltd, the map publishers, are at Nos 12–14. Established at No. 6 CHARING CROSS ROAD in 1852, it is the largest map shop in the world. From the site of Nos 132–135 John Logie Baird broadcast the first television programme in Britain on 30 September 1929.

Long Lane *EC1.* Stow, writing in 1598, said it had recently been built up 'with tenements for brokers and tipplers and such like'. In the 17th and 18th centuries it was known for its second-hand clothes sellers. The father of John Howard, the prison reformer, had an upholstery business here.

Long Lane Recreation Ground *see* BURIAL GROUNDS.

Longlands *Sidcup, Kent.* There are references to a hamlet here in 1635. Longlands House was built in about 1750. The estate was developed from 1870 and the house demolished in about 1886.

Longridge Road *SW5.* On the EDWARDES ESTATE. It takes its name (dating from 1872) from a village in Wales belonging to the family. Marie Corelli lived at No. 47 in 1883–99.

Lord Mayor The head of the CITY CORPORATION, its Chief Magistrate and the Chairman of its two governing bodies, the Court of ALDERMEN and the COURT OF COMMON COUNCIL. The office of mayoralty, though not as old as that of SHERIFF, is of respectable antiquity, being first mentioned in 1189 as the leader of a municipal administrative body modelled on that of a French town. The first holder was Henry Fitzailwyn, described as 'of London Stone', who remained in office from 1192 until his death in 1212; but it was not until 1215, in the mayoralty of Roger Fitz Alan, that King John bestowed a charter on the CITY OF LONDON giving the citizens the right to elect their own Chief Magistrate. The date of that charter is some weeks before John was persuaded to approve the more famous Magna Carta. The Lord Mayor signs himself with his surname only, in the manner of a peer, and adds the title of 'Mayor' – his original title. The first allusion to a Lord Mayor is in a record of proceedings taken *coram domino Majori* in 1283. From then for some 260 years the term 'Lord Mayor' or *Dominus Major* occurs from time to time. From about 1545 the form 'Lord Mayor' was brought into common use, but the title was never specifically granted.

Apart from being the head of the oldest municipal corporation in the world, the Lord Mayor holds a number of offices and has certain privileges. Within the CITY OF LONDON he ranks before everybody except the Sovereign, including princes of the Blood Royal. Outside the CITY on public occasions he ranks immediately after Privy Councillors and is entitled to the style of Right Honourable – a privilege accorded to only one other Lord Mayor in England, one in Ulster and one

The Lord Mayor, William Pickett, presenting the City Sword to George III on the occasion of the King's procession to St Paul's in 1789.

in Wales. He has the constitutional right to seek an audience with the Sovereign through the Lord Chamberlain, and if in office at the time of a Coronation has the privilege of acting at the ceremony as Chief Butler to the Sovereign. For the ceremony – and only on that occasion – he must provide himself with a special robe at a cost of several thousands of pounds at today's prices. As well as Lord Mayor, he is Head of the Lieutenancy, Admiral of the Port of London, Chancellor of the CITY UNIVERSITY and has the password to the TOWER.

Today the Lord Mayor is elected from, and by, the Court of ALDERMEN. Before serving as an ALDERMAN he may or may not have served on the COURT OF COMMON COUNCIL, but he must, before becoming Lord Mayor, have served the office of SHERIFF. He is elected annually, and the normal choice today is the senior of all the ALDERMEN who have not already served as Lord Mayor or, in the official phraseology, 'passed the Chair'. Should the ALDERMAN concerned feel that he will be unable for financial reasons – a Lord Mayor nowadays receives a grant of £80,000 for his year of office from the City CORPORATION, but may be involved in expenditure from his private purse of up to £65,000 – or any other cause to undertake the duties of the mayoralty, he may inform the CORPORATION as soon as possible during the year previous to his anticipated election and ask to be passed over.

The election takes place each year on Michaelmas Day, 29 September, when the liverymen of the craft guilds of CITY LIVERY COMPANIES meet in Common Hall in GUILDHALL to nominate two ALDERMEN who have served as SHERIFF. The ALDERMEN selected then proceed to the Court of ALDERMEN, where their fellow-ALDERMEN normally select the 'first in line' by raising their hands and calling out 'All!'. They encourage the other with cries of 'Next year'. The Lord Mayor elect has now to obtain the Sovereign's approval as laid down by the Charter of 1215, and goes with the RECORDER, the CITY's principal law officer, to the PALACE OF WESTMINSTER to receive this through the Lord Chancellor.

On the Friday preceding the second Saturday in November he is 'admitted' or sworn in by the Town Clerk in GUILDHALL. This ceremony is known as 'the Silent Change', since the symbolic transfer of the various instruments of authority – sword, mace, purse, etc. – to the new Lord Mayor from his predecessor is carried out in complete silence by the officers

concerned. The next day – Lord Mayor's Day – he drives in state – the LORD MAYOR'S SHOW – to the LAW COURTS, where he makes the statutory declaration to the Judges of the Queen's Bench. This declaration was originally made in 1230 before the Barons of the Exchequer. The LORD MAYOR'S SHOW was at first intended to enable the citizens to present addresses to the new Mayor along the route, but today these are presented at GUILDHALL beforehand. On the Monday following the SHOW the Lord Mayor gives a banquet in GUILDHALL in honour of his predecessor and invites the Prime Minister, who normally speaks on behalf of the Government.

The official residence of the Lord Mayor during his year of office is the MANSION HOUSE. His ceremonial robes, apart from the Coronation Robe already referred to, include the Crimson Velvet Reception Robe, worn only in the presence of the Sovereign and dating from the reign of George IV; the Black and Gold Entertaining Gown, worn on civic state occasions; and the aldermanic Scarlet and Violet Gowns, worn at certain meetings of the CORPORATION as directed by the City Ceremonial Book. There is also a plain black robe for mourning and similar occasions. The Lord Mayor's ceremonial headgear, unlike that of his brother ALDERMEN, consists of a black tricorn hat decorated with ostrich feathers; and while other mayors may wear a Chain of Office, he wears the celebrated Collar of SS, consisting of 26 S-shaped links, with alternating knots and roses, all in gold and enamel, joined by a Tudor portcullis from which hangs the Mayoral Jewel. The collar was given by Sir John Allen (d.1544) and enlarged in 1567. The Jewel, surrounded by 24 rose-cut diamonds, was made in 1802 and re-set in 1806. It consists of a cameo of the CITY arms, surrounded by the City motto in blue enamel and wreathed in roses, thistles and shamrock in brilliants and rose diamonds. It replaces a rather ugly jewel made in 1607.

Lord Mayor's Banquet One of the outstanding social events in London, this has been held annually, except during wartime, in GUILDHALL for more than four centuries. The custom of the Lord Mayor's Banquet may be almost as old as the mayoralty itself. At the end of the 15th century kitchens were specially added to GUILDHALL, and in 1501 Sir John Shaa 'was the first that kept his feast there'. Already in 1529 the Lord Chancellor and many peers of the realm were among the guests, and the tradition of annual banquets was well established by 1580 when the Privy Council enquired why the feast had been omitted. By long tradition the LORD MAYOR and the SHERIFFS are the hosts and the Banquet is held on the Monday following the LORD MAYOR'S SHOW. It is given in honour of the 'late Lord Mayor' (as the outgoing LORD MAYOR is always described) and over 700 distinguished guests include the Prime Minister, who makes a major speech reviewing the country's international position. Also present are Cabinet Ministers, representatives of the Commonwealth and other countries, leaders of church, state, commerce and the armed services, and judges in their robes. The LORD MAYOR and Lady Mayoress (with her Maids of Honour) receive the most distinguished guests to the sound of trumpets in the Old Library. Afterwards as they walk round GUILDHALL to take their seats a band in the gallery plays the Mayoral March from Handel's *Scipio*.

481

Lord Mayor's Banqueting House *Oxford Road*. A building erected near the medieval conduit which supplied the CITY with water. The LORD MAYOR and CORPORATION dined here when they made their periodical visits to inspect the conduit heads and to hunt in the locality. The building was demolished in 1757 and the cisterns arched over (*see* STRATFORD PLACE *and* STRATFORD HOUSE).

Lord Mayor's Coach *Museum of London, London Wall, WC2*. Constructed in 1757 by Joseph Berry to the design of Sir Robert Taylor, and used by successive LORD MAYORS ever since. The ALDERMEN were called upon to contribute £60 each and the Lord Mayor £100. The total cost was £1,065. It has no springs but is slung on leather braces, and until 1951 had no brakes. It is elaborately decorated on all panels with paintings attributed to Giovanni Battista Cipriani. The front panel depicts Faith, by a sacrificial altar, supporting Charity, with Hope pointing to the dome of ST PAUL'S. The Genius of the CITY is shown on the back panels; above, she is greeting Riches and Plenty who are pouring fruit and money into her lap, and below, attended by Neptune, she is receiving representatives of Trade and Commerce. On the right-hand side of the coach the picture is of Fame presenting a LORD MAYOR to the Genius with the spire of old ST PAUL'S in the background. On the left-hand door the Genius stands with Mars, the deity of the CITY, who points to a scroll held by Truth which is inscribed 'Henri Fitz Alwin' – the first mayor of the CITY. The coachman's foot-rest is in the form of a scallop shell. The coach weighs 2 tons 17 cwt and it is brought out of the MUSEUM OF LONDON each year for the LORD MAYOR'S SHOW.

Lord Mayor's Show The procession occasioned by the progress of the LORD MAYOR to the LAW COURTS for his oath of office before the Judges of the Queen's Bench. In 1215, five weeks before he was forced to sign *Magna Carta*, King John, hoping for the support of the CITY, granted a new charter which allowed annual elections to be held on condition the LORD MAYOR presented himself to the King or his justices for approval and to 'swear fealty'. During the 13th and early 14th centuries the election and assumption of office took place on 28 October (the feast of St Simon and St Jude) and next day the LORD MAYOR went to WESTMINSTER to seek the King's approval. If the King or his justices were away the LORD MAYOR presented himself to the Constable of the TOWER or his Lieutenant. In 1346 the election day was changed to 13 October, but the visit to WESTMINSTER continued to take place on 29 October until 1752. In 1378 there is the first record of ALDERMEN accompanying the LORD MAYOR, and by 1401 minstrels were in the procession, too. The LORD MAYOR travelled by water for the first time in 1422. In 1452 Sir John Norman provided a magnificent barge with silver oars to take him to WESTMINSTER. In 1501, for the first time, a feast took place, after the procession, at GUILDHALL where new kitchens had been built. This became the annual LORD MAYOR'S BANQUET.

During the 16th and 17th centuries pageants were a popular and important feature of the processions. These were composed by the CITY poets, among whom were Thomas Dekker and John Taylor, the water poet. The 1553 diary of Henry Machyn, an undertaker, provides the first written description of the Show. He saw 'the crafts of London in their best livery with trumpets blowing ... My Lord Mayor landed at Baynards Castle and then came trumpeters blowing,

An engraving after David Roberts's painting of barges in procession on the Thames at Westminster on Lord Mayor's Day, c. 1836.

then came a devil and after came the bachelors all in livery and scarlet hoods, and then came the pageant of St John Baptist gorgeously with goodly speeches and then came all the King's trumpeters . . . and then the Crafts and then my Lord Mayor and good henchmen and then all the Aldermen and Sheriffs and so to dinner.' Some years later William Smith, a haberdasher, wrote in his *Breffe Description of the Royall Citie of London* (1575): 'The day of St Simon and St Jude the Mayor enters into his state and office. The next day he goes by water to Westminster in most triumphant-like manner . . . Next before him goeth the barge of the livery of his own company, decked with their own proper arms; and then the Bachelors barge and so all the companies in order every one having their own proper barge with the arms of their Company. And so passing along the Thames he landeth at Westminster, where he taketh his oath in the Exchequer before the judge there: which done he returneth by water as aforesaid, and landeth at St Paul's Wharf where he and the rest of the Aldermen take their horses and in great pomp pass through Cheapside. And first of all cometh two great standards, one having the arms of the City, and the other the arms of the Lord Mayor's Company; next them two drums and a flute; then an Ensign of the City; and then about seventy or eighty poor men marching two and two, in blue gowns, with red sleeves and caps, every one bearing a pike and a target, whereon is painted the arms of all those that have been Mayors of the same Company that this new Mayor is of. Then two banners one of the King's arms and one of the Mayor's own arms. Then a set of hautboys playing, and after them certain whifflers [armed attendants who cleared the way] in velvet coats and chains of gold with white staves in their hands; then the Pageant of Triumph richly decked, then sixteen trumpeters, eight and eight, having banners of the Mayor's company. Then certain whifflers in velvet coats and chains with white staves as before. Then the Bachelors, two and two, in long gowns with crimson hoods on their shoulders of satin; which Bachelors are chosen every year of the same company that the Mayor is of and serve as gentlemen on that and other festival days to wait on the Mayor . . . After them twelve trumpeters more with banners of the Mayor's company; and then the Drums and Flute of the City and an ensign of the Mayor's Company; and after the Waits of the City in blue gowns, red sleeves and caps, every one having a silver collar about his neck. Then they of the Livery in their long gowns, everyone having his hood on his left shoulder, half black and half red . . . After them follow Sheriffs officers and then the Mayor's officers with other officers of the City as the Common Serjeant and the Chamberlain. Next before the Mayor goeth the Sword Bearer having on his head the cap of honour and the Sword of the City in his right hand, in a rich scabbard set with pearl, and on his left hand goeth the Common Crier of the City with his great mace on his shoulder all gilt. The Mayor hath on a long gown of scarlet and on his left shoulder a hood of black velvet and a rich collar of gold about his neck and with him rideth the old Mayor also in his scarlet gown hood of velvet and a chain of gold about his neck. Then all the Aldermen, two and two, all in scarlet gowns . . . The two Sheriffs come last of all in their black scarlet gowns and chains of gold. In this order they pass along the City to Guildhall where they dine that day to the number of 1000 persons all at the charge of the Mayor and the two Sheriffs. This feast costeth £400 whereof the Mayor payeth £200 and each of the Sheriffs £100. Immediately after dinner they go to St Paul's Church, every one of the aforesaid poor men bearing staffs, torches and targets.'

In 1602, this grand procession also included 'a lyon and a cammell'. In 1605 the pageant was *The Triumph of Reunited Britannia* and featured the giants Gogmagog and Corineus (*see* GOG AND MAGOG). In 1612 Thomas Dekker wrote the pageant *Troia Nova Triumphans*. The next year the 'Pageant of the Triumphs of Truth* was a solemnity unparalleled for cost, art and magnificence at the confirmation and establishment of that worthy and tru nobly minded gentleman Sir Thomas Middleton. On the Thames were five islands artfully garnished with all manner of Indian fruit trees, drugges, spiceries and the like, the middle island having a faire castle especially beautified'. In 1616 the pageant for the Mayor, the fishmonger, John Leman, was a 'lemon tree rich in flowers and fruit with a pelican's nest and the five senses at its foot'. (Such puns are still common.) The *Pageant of the Triumphs of Honour and Industry* in 1617 cost £800. In 1619 the Mayor, William Cockayne, had an artificial cock crowing and flapping his wings in his procession. There was no show in 1625 because of plague and in 1639 the pageants were stopped by the Puritans.

In 1660 a Boscobel oak was carried in the first show after the Restoration. Pepys saw the pageant in 1663 and thought it 'very silly'. There were no pageants in 1665–70 because of the GREAT PLAGUE and the GREAT FIRE. In 1672 the procession for the LORD MAYOR, Robert Hanson, a grocer, was led by a negro riding a camel scattering fruit to the crowd, with Plenty and Concord on either side of him. There was also a throned Indian emperor with Princes of Peru and Mexico at his feet. 'Two extra great giants each of them 15 ft high were drawn by horses in two separate chariots, moving, talking and taking tobacco as they ride along to the great admiration and delight of all the spectators.'

In 1711 Sir Gilbert Heathcote was unsaddled by a drunken flower girl and was thus the last Lord Mayor to ride in the procession on horseback. After this a coach was used. In 1752, at the reformation of the calendar, 11 days were lost, and the date of the show was changed to 9 November. In 1757 the LORD MAYOR'S COACH was built and Sir Charles Asgill was the first to use it. In 1774, for the Lord Mayor John Wilkes, both banks of the river were packed with jubilant mobs cheering wildly and pelting the better-dressed with rubbish. At the ensuing GUILDHALL banquet there were many empty places. 'A mysterious epidemic had swept the West End of the town and their royal highnesses of Gloucester and Cumberland together with the Lord Chancellor, the Chief Justices, the Archbishops and Bishops, the Secretaries of State and most of the leading nobility had found themselves forced to decline my Lord Mayor Wilkes' invitation at which my Lord Mayor grinned all the more pleasantly.'

In 1830 the Reform Bill riots prevented the show taking place. In 1837 Queen Victoria attended the banquet. At TEMPLE BAR she received an address from the senior scholar of CHRIST'S HOSPITAL, an event which is commemorated on the Temple Bar Memorial (*see* TEMPLE BAR). In 1841 an East India ship, drawn by six horses, was in the procession. In 1850 George Godwin wrote to the LORD MAYOR elect suggesting improvements: 'In lieu of the men in mock armour, who have had a long run, you might introduce say, three compositions, typical of Manufacturers, Agriculture and the Arts.' Trade displays are now a regular feature of the Show.

In 1856 the State Barge was used for the last time. In 1882 the procession went to WESTMINSTER HALL for the last time. The new LAW COURTS in the STRAND were henceforth the scene of the presentation. In 1889, when the 700th anniversary of the mayoralty was prematurely celebrated, outstanding MAYORS from each century were impersonated. In 1959 an Act of Parliament was passed to change the date of the procession to the second Saturday in November to avoid traffic congestion. In 1974 Sir Murray Fox's pageant included a model of a giant fox. Nowadays the Show has a theme chosen by the LORD MAYOR. In 1979 the themes were 'Natural Resources and the Environment', in 1980, 'Leadership and Youth and the City Livery Companies', and in 1981 'Transport'.

Lord North Street *SW1*. An almost complete Georgian street dating from 1722. The houses are much sought after by the more well-to-do Members of Parliament. The INSTITUTE OF ECONOMIC AFFAIRS is at No. 2.

Lord Raglan *St Martin-le-Grand, EC1*. One of the oldest tavern sites in the City. The house was originally known as the Bush. After the execution of Charles I, the Royalist landlord changed the name to the Mourning Bush and painted the sign black. It received the present name after the Crimean War, in honour of the commander-in-chief. The cellars date from the original building and incorporate parts of the old Roman Wall.

Lord's Cricket Ground *St John's Wood Road, NW8*. In 1787 a Yorkshireman, Thomas Lord, opened a cricket ground on the site of DORSET SQUARE and formed the MARYLEBONE CRICKET CLUB. He was backed financially by the Earl of Winchilsea and Charles Lennox, members of the WHITE CONDUIT CLUB. The first match was played on the ground in 1787 between MIDDLESEX and Essex. The MCC played their first match in 1788. The first Eton v. HARROW match was played in 1805; Lord Byron was in the losing HARROW side. The first Gentlemen v. Players match was played in 1806. In 1809, forewarned of an increase in rent, Lord moved his turf to North Bank, ST JOHN'S WOOD. Five years later, since the REGENT'S CANAL was planned to cut through the ground, he moved the turf again to the present site.

The first pavilion was a one-room building. In 1822 John Willes, playing for Kent against the MCC, bowled 'straight armed' and was no-balled by the umpire. The pavilion was burnt down in 1825 during the HARROW v. Winchester match; and all the existing records were lost. It was rebuilt soon after by William Ward. Red Indians camped on the pitch in 1844 and gave dancing and archery displays. In 1866 the freehold was acquired by the MCC. In 1867 the grandstand (reconstructed in 1926) and press stand were built. In 1868 the Tavern was rebuilt by Edward Paraire. The MIDDLESEX COUNTY CRICKET CLUB made Lord's their home ground in 1877; and in 1882 the northern terrace for 2,000 spectators was built. The first test played here was in 1884, when the English team beat the

Australians. In 1887 Henderson's Nursery was bought for use as a practice ground. The pavilion was rebuilt by Thomas Verity in 1889–90 at a cost of £21,000. The Mount Stand was built in 1899. The first test match against the West Indies was played in 1928, that against New Zealand in 1931, that against India in 1932, and that against Pakistan in 1954. The Warner Stand (named after Sir Pelham Warner) was opened in 1958. The last Gentlemen v. Players match was played in 1962; after this game professional and amateur status was abolished. In 1966 a block of flats and the new Tavern were built by Davis Hodges. The new Tavern Stand was designed by Kenneth Peacock. In 1970 the Cricket Council, which meets at Lord's, took over from the MCC as the governing body of cricket (*see also* CRICKET MEMORIAL GALLERY). The main entrance gates were designed in 1923 by Sir Herbert Baker 'to the memory of William Gilbert Grace, the great cricketer (1848–1915)'. The stone relief on the ground wall in Wellington Road is by Gilbert Bayes (1934).

Loriners' Company *see* CITY LIVERY COMPANIES.

Lothbury *EC2*. Possibly derives its name from the word *lod*, a drain or cut leading into a larger stream, in this case the WALBROOK; or from the personal name Lod; or from Albertus Loteringus, a canon of ST PAUL's whose burgh (fortified house) was here at the time of the Norman Conquest; or from Lottenbury, a place where founders cast candlesticks and other copper work. Certainly it was largely occupied by coppersmiths in the early Middle Ages. By the early 18th century, however, tradesmen had mostly been replaced by merchants and bankers: Samuel Johnson sometimes used Lothbury as a synonym for the CITY as a whole. The south side is now occupied by the BANK OF ENGLAND. Opposite it is ST MARGARET LOTHBURY. No. 7 was designed by G.S. Clarke the Elder in 1866 and now houses the Overseas Bankers' Club.

Lots Road *SW10*. Commemorates the 'lots' of ground which belonged to Chelsea Manor and over which the parishioners had Lammas rights, that is to say rights to graze their animals at certain times of the year. It was for many years notorious for rough behaviour and fighting. Later it was the scene of more peaceful entertainment, and in 1863 a medieval-style tournament was held here. In 1869 a balloon made several ascents from the 'Lots'; the Balloon Tavern is at No. 114.

Lots Road Power Station *Lots Road, SW10*. Built in 1902–5 to provide power for the DISTRICT LINE, its massive outline and four great chimneys near Chelsea Reach provoked vociferous opposition and *Punch*'s suggestion that an equestrian statue of Thomas Carlyle should be supported by the chimneys. From time to time, notably in 1963, the power station's capacity has been increased.

Loughborough Junction *SW9*. Coldharbour Lane and Loughborough Road are medieval parish lanes, and the name of the Green Man public house at their junction long predates the Victorian public house which stands there now. The name Loughborough, which is to be found several times on the north-east side of BRIXTON, derives from Henry Hastings, created

1st Baron Loughborough and Lord Lieutenant of Leicestershire in 1660. His residence, afterwards known as Loughborough House, stood at the junction of Evendale and Loughborough Roads, in extensive grounds, until its demolition in 1854 when the neighbourhood was becoming more built-up. This building had its origins as the manor house of the Manor of Lambeth Wick, which lay on the north and east sides of BRIXTON. From 1701 this Manor was leased by the Archbishops of Canterbury to Sir Stephen Fox and his descendants, of whom the 3rd Lord Holland was most active in developing the northern part for housing, in 1820–30. Fine examples of this development still survive along Brixton Road, Vassall Road and Camberwell New Road in particular. The Barrington Road and Loughborough Park areas were laid out for housing development in the 1840s by Henry Currey, and much of the latter area has been restored.

During the 1860s the area was dissected by railway lines, and the complex of viaducts at Loughborough Junction itself was completed in 1872 when a branch line to PECKHAM necessitated demolition of houses in Flaxman Road which were scarcely ten years old.

Lovat Lane *EC3*. Used to be known as Love Lane, probably because of the prostitutes who frequented it. The name was changed in 1939 to avoid confusion with Love Lane, EC2, at the behest of a company of fishmongers who suggested its present name because of the number of salmon that arrived daily in BILLINGSGATE from the fishings owned by Lord Lovat. The Abbots of WALTHAM had their inn here from 1218–1540. Sir Thomas Blanke, the Lord Mayor, lived in the house in 1582–3. ST MARY-AT-HILL is on the east side.

Love Lane *EC2*. A haunt of prostitutes in the Middle Ages. ST MARY ALDERMANBURY, which stood at the corner until the 2nd World War, is now re-erected in Fulton, Missouri, USA.

Lovekyn Chapel *Kingston-upon-Thames, Surrey*. Built by the Lovekyn family in the 14th century as a chantry chapel, it stands in London Road opposite the grammar school. It was the only one of its kind to survive the DISSOLUTION. The walls are of varied masonry; the windows are perpendicular. At the east end are two embattled towers. It is now a scheduled ancient monument.

Lower Holloway *N1, N7*. Stretches from HOLLOWAY PRISON in the north down to the back door of KING'S CROSS STATION where once stood COPENHAGEN HOUSE. From the 17th century this house and the surrounding Copenhagen Fields (both still commemorated in the name Copenhagen Street) made a popular excursion for Londoners: 'The resort of Cockney lovers, Cockney sportsmen and Cockney agitators'. During the French Revolution the meeting of the LONDON CORRESPONDING SOCIETY in these fields caused some anxiety, and one meeting was dispersed by the City Light Horse. In the early 19th century the bull-baiting and dog-fights around COPENHAGEN HOUSE became so rowdy that the landlord lost his licence; but after this the tea-gardens were frequented largely by those wishing to enjoy the countryside, particularly during the hay harvest in the nearby fields. In 1834, the metropolitan trade unions met on Copenhagen Fields before forming up to march in protest against the sentences passed on the Tolpuddle Martyrs.

In 1852 COPENHAGEN HOUSE and its grounds, and 75 acres of the fields, were bought by the CORPORATION OF THE CITY OF LONDON and laid out as the CALEDONIAN MARKET, which was opened by the Prince Consort in 1855. It was designed by J.B. Bunning and his high, white central clock-tower remains a historic landmark in an area which, since the closing of the market in the 1960s, has been completely redeveloped as 'a mixture of green open space and red council housing'. For many years, until the outbreak of the 2nd World War, the CALEDONIAN MARKET was also held on Fridays. Here H.V. Morton saw for sale 'the driftwood and wreckage of a thousand lives'.

Bunning also designed another notable institution, HOLLOWAY PRISON. Built in 1851–2 as the City House of Correction, it became a prison for women in 1903. Demolished and rebuilt in 1979, only the entrance gate and towers of Bunning's building remain.

Opposite the prison stood, from 1871, the Camden Road Athenaeum, which housed the Islington Literary and Scientific Institution. This building was also demolished, in 1956. Not far away, in Hilldrop Crescent (where Margaret Bondfield House, a block of council flats, stands) was the semi-detached house into which Dr Crippen moved in 1905 with his second wife, Cora Turner. He poisoned her, fled with Ethel le Neve and passed into history as the first murderer to be caught with the help of radio. The POLYTECHNIC OF NORTH LONDON is in Holloway Road.

Lower James Street *W1. see* LOWER JOHN STREET.

Lower John Street *W1*. This and the other three streets leading into Golden Square, Upper John Street, Lower James Street and Upper James Street are presumably named after John Emlyn and James Axtall, who owned Gelding's Close (*see* GOLDEN SQUARE) when licence to build there was granted in 1673. No. 4 is a house built in about 1685 with an extremely narrow front and originally planned to have but one room on each floor. Nos 5–8 have what Pevsner described as 'an oddly grand mid-Victorian façade of remarkably consistent design, white brick, thirteen bays with gaunt giant pilasters and very long thin windows ... It was apparently from the beginning no more than a warehouse.' Quaritch, the antiquarian booksellers, occupy part of this building. L. Novello and Co. at Nos. 1–3 Upper James Street were founded at No. 67 FRITH STREET in 1829 by J. Alfred Novello, son of Vincent Novello, organist at the Portuguese Embassy Chapel in SOUTH STREET and one of the founders of the London Philharmonic Society in 1813.

Lower Mall *Hammersmith, W6*. Begins a pleasant walk by the river to CHISWICK and runs from below HAMMERSMITH BRIDGE to Furnivall Gardens. The houses, which mostly date from the 18th century but are thought to be built on the sites of earlier ones, include KENT HOUSE, houses with attractive fanlights and balconies, small cottages, boat-houses, the Rutland and Blue Anchor public houses and WESTCOTT LODGE.

Lower Thames Street *EC3*. The eastern part of what used to be Thames Street, UPPER THAMES STREET

485

forming the western part above LONDON BRIDGE. The CUSTOM HOUSE, BILLINGSGATE and ST MAGNUS THE MARTYR are on the south side. In 1981 excavations revealed a large section of a Roman timber wharf built in about AD 80, the massive timbers being perfectly preserved in the water. It was probably constructed by the Roman army under the pacification programme of the governor, Julius Agricola, the wood being floated down river before being extended. The entire wharf may have been a mile long, extending from the present SOUTHWARK BRIDGE to near TOWER BRIDGE.

Lowndes Estate William Lowndes, Secretary to the Treasury and a member of an old Buckinghamshire family, had finalised the purchase of this land by 1723. It consisted of two fields, the northern one on the west side of the WESTBOURNE and the southern one on the east side. They were connected by a narrow neck of land now covered by part of LOWNDES STREET. The stream crossed this neck opposite WHEELER'S restaurant and was not covered over till 1842.

William Lowndes's grandson, also William, decided in the 1820s to develop his estate as the Grosvenors were doing immediately to his east. The northern field, which is now occupied by Lowndes Square and its attendant service streets and mews, had belonged to the Abbots of WESTMINSTER and was mostly occupied by a copse from which the monks had cut their firewood. Later it became a pleasure garden where Pepys roistered in 1660. By 1800 Grove House had been built; this was an anatomical museum and later a builder's yard. In 1827 Thomas Cubitt bought the lease and demolished the house. (The Park Tower Hotel stands on its site.) Cubitt built the east and north sides of Lowndes Square between 1838 and 1849; the west side was started slightly later, in 1844, and the south side was a speculation by Thomas Cubitt's younger brother, Lewis. The square has always been a smart address. Admiral Southey lived at No. 38. Thomas Brassey, the railway contractor, also lived in the Square. The co-trustee of the estate was Charles Lyall, hence Charles Street and Lyall Street, SW1. William Lowndes's wife and sister were both called Harriet, hence Harriet Street and Harriet Walk, SW1.

The Lowther Arcade, designed in 1830, had by the 1860s become celebrated for its splendid toy shops.

Lowther Arcade *Strand*. A shopping arcade about 80 ft long, surmounted with glass domes. Designed by Witherden Young in 1830, it was named after Lord Lowther, who was Chief Commissioner of

Woods and Forests when the improvements in the West STRAND were made. Its small shops mostly sold knicknacks and luxury goods, but by the middle of the century they were nearly all toyshops and the arcade was the delight of Victorian children. It was demolished in 1904 for the construction of COUTTS' BANK.

Ludgate Circus *EC4*. Constructed in 1864–75 at the junction of LUDGATE HILL and FLEET STREET. The FLEET BRIDGE crossed the FLEET here. In a house near the old bridge the first daily newspaper, the *Daily Courant*, was published in 1702. On the corner with Ludgate Hill is the Old King Lud public house, designed by Lewis H. Isaacs in 1870.

Ludgate Hill *EC4*. Named after the Lud Gate which, according to tradition, was built by King Lud in 66 BC. It was probably the Romans who erected it to lead to one of their main burial grounds in the area of what is now FLEET STREET. It was rebuilt in about 1215. From the time of Richard II there was a prison above it for petty criminals. Stephen Forster was imprisoned there as a boy for debt, but a rich widow saw him at the window, paid his debts and eventually married him. He was elected Lord Mayor in 1454. The gate was again rebuilt in 1586 and repaired after being damaged in the GREAT FIRE. Like the other city gates it was demolished in 1760. Statues of Queen Elizabeth I, King Lud and his two sons which decorated it are now outside ST DUNSTAN FLEET STREET. Its site was almost opposite ST MARTIN'S CHURCH. On the north side of the hill from the 15th century until 1873 stood the BELLE SAUVAGE inn.

In the 17th century the hill was a fashionable shopping area. John Evelyn, the diarist, lived at the Hawk and Pheasant in 1658–9. On the north side between 1731 and 1867 was the LONDON COFFEE HOUSE, frequented by Boswell and much favoured by Americans. The father of John Leech, the artist, was proprietor at the beginning of the 19th century. Arthur Clennam in *Little Dorrit* stayed here when he arrived in London from the Continent. Juries from the Old Bailey who could not agree on their verdicts were locked up here for the night. In 1865 the railway viaduct was built by the London, Chatham and Dover Railway to reach LUDGATE HILL STATION, which was on the south side of Pilgrim Street. The station was closed in 1929. A plaque on the bridge records that the *Daily Courant*, England's first daily newspaper was published nearby in 1702.

The hill has been widened twice: first in 1864, when LUDGATE CIRCUS was made, and then in 1897. Halfway up the hill on the north side is ST MARTIN WITHIN LUDGATE. When it was being rebuilt by Wren after the GREAT FIRE the workmen found a tombstone 7 ft by 2 ft 6 ins with a figure of a soldier inscribed 'In memory of Vivius Marcianus of the 2nd Augustan Legion. Januaria Martina, his most devoted wife, set up this monument.' This memorial is now in the Ashmolean Museum, Oxford, but another Roman memorial found in Ludgate Hill in 1806 may be seen at the MUSEUM OF LONDON. It is a hexagonal column inscribed: 'In memory of Claudia Martina, aged 19. Erected by Anencletus, slave of the province, to his most devoted wife. She lies here.' STATIONERS' HALL is in Stationers' Hall Court between Nos 28 and 30.

Ludgate Hill Station *EC4*. Opened in 1865, the second of the three linked CITY stations built by the London, Chatham and Dover Railway. The following year the line was extended to a link with the Metropolitan Railway at Farringdon. Ludgate Hill then became a station at the hub of suburban services which ran to all points of the compass, and as far afield as ENFIELD, RICHMOND, CRYSTAL PALACE and TOTTENHAM. A regular workmen's service ran from LUDGATE HILL to VICTORIA, fares for workmen being 1s a week. The station was remodelled in 1907–12, but was finally closed in 1929.

Lunchtime Comment Club *Connaught Rooms, Great Queen Street, WC2*. Founded in 1919, this is probably the oldest extant luncheon club in London. Eminent speakers address members and their guests.

Lyall Street *SW1*. For the derivation of the name see LOWNDES ESTATE. Thomas Cubitt, the builder, lived at No. 3.

Lyceum Dance Hall *Wellington Street, WC2*. In 1771 the Lyceum, a room for concerts and exhibitions, was built in the grounds of EXETER HOUSE by James Paine for the Incorporated Society of Artists. It was converted to a theatre by Dr Samuel Arnold in 1794 but, being unable to get it licensed as a playhouse, he let it to a circus. By 1799 it was known as the Lyceum Theatre and was presenting mixed entertainment. In 1802 it held MADAME TUSSAUD's first London waxworks exhibition. In 1809–30 and 1838–67 it was the meeting-place of the BEEF-STEAK SOCIETY. In 1809–12 the company from the THEATRE ROYAL, DRURY LANE acted here while their own theatre was being rebuilt after a fire. When they left, the Lyceum retained a licence for the summer season. In 1815 it was renamed the Theatre Royal English Opera House. Rebuilt by Samuel Beazley in 1816, it was destroyed by fire in 1830. WELLINGTON STREET was built over the site.

Rebuilt further west by Beazley in 1834, the theatre reopened as the Royal Lyceum and English Opera House. From 1847 to 1855 it was managed by Mme Vestris and C.J. Mathews. Many brilliant productions were staged in these years. In 1856–9 it was used by the COVENT GARDEN THEATRE Company, whose own theatre had been burned.

In 1871 the management was taken over by Col Hezekiah Bateman to advertise his actress daughters. He engaged a virtually unknown actor, Henry Irving, to take the leading roles. In November 1871 Irving persuaded him to stage *The Bells*, an adaptation by Leopold Lewis of Erckmann-Chatrian's *Le Juif Polonais*. Such was the success of the play that it saved Bateman from ruin and made Irving's reputation. In 1874 Irving's production of *Hamlet* made him supreme among the actors of his day. Bateman died in 1875 and the management was left in the control of his widow and son. That year Irving staged his production of *Macbeth* followed in 1876 by *Othello* and in 1877 by *Richard III*. Irving took control of the management in 1878 and engaged Ellen Terry as his leading lady. During the 1879–80 season he staged his first production of *The Merchant of Venice*, followed in 1882 by *Romeo and Juliet* and *Much Ado about Nothing* and in 1884 by *Twelfth Night*. Irving's production of *Faust* began its 16-months' run in 1885. In 1892 a spectacular production of *King Henry VIII* cost £11,000. In 1893

Tennyson's *Becket* was one of his greatest triumphs. This was followed in 1896 by Irving's production of *Cymbeline*. In 1899, after several failures and a fire that destroyed his store of scenery, Irving parted with control of the management to a company, but he continued to act at the theatre. His production of *Coriolanus* in 1901 was the last of his Shakespearean revivals. In 1902 Ellen Terry left the company; and on 19 July that year Irving made his last appearance at the theatre as Shylock.

In 1902 the LONDON COUNTY COUNCIL required extensive alterations to the theatre which the company could not afford, and it had to close. It was demolished, except for the walls and portico, in 1903, and in 1904 was rebuilt as a music-hall by Bertie Crewe. It opened under the management of Thomas Barrasford and was intended to rival the COLISEUM, but it lasted as a music-hall for only six months. Until 1907 it was often shut. It was then taken by Smith and Carpenter for melodramas. In 1909 it was acquired by the Melville brothers, who continued to produce melodramas. In 1937 one brother died, and the next year the other. Plans were drawn up to redevelop the site with shops and offices. The theatre closed in 1939 but the site was acquired by the LONDON COUNTY COUNCIL for part of an approach road to WATERLOO BRIDGE. When the 2nd World War broke out the scheme was dropped. Since 1945 it has been let as a dance hall.

Lyons' Corner Houses Among the best-known of the larger London restaurants during the first half of the 20th century. They were owned by the firm of J. Lyons and Co. Ltd, which had been established in 1894 by the Salmon and Gluckstein families who were already operating a chain of retail tobacconists in London and the suburbs. The COVENTRY STREET Corner House was built in 1907 to the design of W.J. Ancell, and the westward extension which stood upon the site of PANTON SQUARE was created in 1921–3 to the designs of F.J. Wills. Other Corner Houses were in the STRAND (opened in 1912) and OXFORD STREET (1923). A similar establishment, the Maison Lyons, at the MARBLE ARCH end of OXFORD STREET, was operated by Cumberland Hotels Ltd, an associated company of Lyons. Each of the Corner Houses provided a wide range of food in several restaurants and could maintain reasonable prices by catering on a large scale. The extended COVENTRY STREET premises could seat 4,500 customers; the establishments in the STRAND and OXFORD STREET could each cater for 2,500. Following the closure of its predecessors, a new Lyons' Corner House was opened at 450 STRAND, opposite CHARING CROSS STATION, in June 1981.

The firm of Lyons was also well known for its teashops, immediately recognisable by the exterior decoration of gilt lettering on a white background. The first shop was opened at 213 PICCADILLY; the trading formula of attractive light refreshments was immediately successful, and the teashop chain was eventually extended to 260 premises. Waitresses in these teashops were popularly known as 'Nippies', a name which was registered by Lyons in 1924. Prices were kept low by standardisation of menus, economies of scale, and tight control of costs.

Wherever possible supplies for the teashops were produced at a central depot: for example, production for the London shops was undertaken at the firm's headquarters at Cadby Hall, in Hammersmith Road, HAMMERSMITH, the nucleus of which was the piano factory of Charles Cadby which had been acquired by Lyons in 1895 and gradually extended.

Lyric Theatre *King Street, Hammersmith, W6.*
Opened as the Lyric Opera House in Bradmore Grove on 17 November 1890 with a triple bill including *Puck*, a potted version of *A Midsummer Night's Dream*. Originally the Lyric Hall, it was built in 1888 to the design of Isaac Mason for Charles Cordingley, the proprietor and editor of the *West London Advertiser*; but as it did not conform with the requirements for a dramatic licence it was redesigned by F.H. Francis and Sons in 1890. In 1895 it was almost completely rebuilt to the design of Frank Matcham and opened with *A House of Lies* by Charles Hannan, preceded by a prologue spoken by Mrs Langtry. Its reputation soon declined and by 1907, more often closed than open, it was known as 'The Blood and Flea Pit'.

In 1918 it was rescued by Nigel Playfair, who retained the theatre's original Victorian style and raised it far above local reputation, opening with A.A. Milne's *Make Believe*. Among many notable successes were revivals of *The Beggar's Opera*, which ran for more than three years, *The Cherry Orchard* and *The Way of the World* (1924) with Edith Evans. Ellen Terry made her last stage appearance here in *Crossings* (1925) and A.P. Herbert's *Tantivy Towers* and *Derby Day* were first produced here.

When Playfair left in 1933 the theatre's fortunes ebbed and it had been closed for some time when J. Baxter Somerville revived it in 1944 with many productions destined for success in the West End. *Venice Preserved* with Sir John Gielgud and *Richard II*

with Paul Scofield were both presented here, as well as the first plays of both Harold Pinter (*The Birthday Party*, 1958) and John Mortimer (*Dock Brief*, 1958). But the standard could not be maintained, and the theatre closed in 1966.

In 1974 HAMMERSMITH Council approved plans prepared by their architects' department in consultation with Theatre Projects for a new Lyric in King Street. Frank Matcham's original plasterwork from the 1895 theatre was the centrepiece of the three-tiered auditorium. The new Lyric opened in the presence of the Queen on 18 October 1979 with Shaw's *You Never Can Tell*. The seating capacity is 537.

Lyric Theatre *Shaftesbury Avenue, W1.* Designed by C.J. Phipps in 1888 for Henry J. Leslie, who financed it with the profits he had made at the PRINCE OF WALES THEATRE with the comic opera, *Dorothy*. He transferred the play here and it ran for four months. Marie Tempest appeared in it and in Leslie's subsequent productions, *Doris* and *The Red Hussar*. In the 1890s the theatre specialised in comic operas. The most successful were *La Cigale* (1890), *Little Christopher Columbus* (1893) and *Florodora* (1899). Eleonora Duse made her London debut in 1893 in *La Dame aux Camélias*. In 1896 Wilson Barret's play, *The Sign of the Cross*, had 435 performances. In 1902 the theatre was managed by Forbes-Robertson who presented *Mice and Men*, *Hamlet*, *Othello* and *The Light that Failed*.

In 1906–10 Lewis Waller was manager and staged many revivals. After that for 15 years it staged mostly musicals and in the 1950s and 1960s plays by T. S. Eliot, Robert Morley, Alan Bennett and others.

M

Macclesfield Street *W1*. First mentioned in 1685 and partly rebuilt in 1729–30. The most handsome house in the street, No. 9, was demolished for the construction of SHAFTESBURY AVENUE; but some original features can still be seen at No. 2. Frederick Engels was a lodger here in 1850. It takes its name from Charles Gerrard, 1st Earl of Macclesfield.

Madame Tussaud's Waxworks *Marylebone Road, NW1*. Mme Tussaud arrived in England from France in 1802 with 35 wax figures inherited from her uncle. After travelling around the country with her show she settled in BAKER STREET in 1835. By the time of her death in 1850 the show had become, in Dickens's words, 'something more than an exhibition . . . an institution, with celebrities . . . strictly up to date . . . continuously added to every department of the exhibition'. No expense was spared in clothing the figures in authentic costumes – George IV's coronation and state robes were bought for £18,000 – and in the decoration of the exhibition rooms. The Duke of Wellington was a regular visitor. A painting of him inspecting an effigy of Napoleon and various relics of the Emperor was commissioned from Sir George Hayter in 1852. It hung in the museum until destroyed by fire. The Duke was particularly interested in the Chamber of Horrors and asked to be informed whenever new exhibits were on show there. The entertainment was carried on by Madame Tussaud's sons. In 1884, when it was transferred to its present site, it contained 400 figures. It was damaged by fire in 1925 and by bombs in the BLITZ in 1940, but the casts survived. The exhibits, which include *tableaux* as well as figures, some of them far more successful than others, were visited by 2·5 million in 1978.

Maddox Street *W1*. Extends from REGENT STREET to NEW BOND STREET, thus traversing the Millfield Estate, from the ground landlord of which, Sir Benjamin Maddox, it takes its name (*see* HANOVER SQUARE). Building began soon after 1714. The only survivor is No. 49, on the south side, a very ordinary three-bay early Georgian house with a modern shop at street level. But a number of the original narrow plots do still exist, and many of the buildings (hardly any more than a century old) are used as small shops, restaurants and offices.

Magpie and Punchbowl *86 Bishopsgate, EC2*. On the site of the first hall of the Worshipful Company of Parish Clerks (*see* CITY LIVERY COMPANIES). It was originally known as the Magpie, Punchbowl being added when the tavern was used by Whig politicians who drank punch as opposed to the claret favoured by the Tories.

Magpie and Stump *18 Old Bailey, EC4*. Opposite the OLD BAILEY, the present building was erected during this century, though the foundations are said to date back to the 18th century and the site has an even longer history. Until public hangings were abolished in 1868 the landlord here would let the upper rooms to wealthy people who wished to watch the execution in comfort. Prices charged were up to £50 which included breakfast.

Maida Vale *W9*. At the Battle of Maida in southern Italy a British force under General Sir John Stuart defeated the French in 1806. Very soon after this the first Hero of Maida inn was opened in the EDGWARE ROAD and, as more houses appeared, this section of the road near the canal became known as Maida Hill and later Maida Vale. The name was extended to cover not only the stretch of the EDGWARE ROAD between the canal and KILBURN but also the whole of PADDINGTON north of the canal as far west as QUEEN'S PARK. It is a spaciously laid-out area for the most part, taking its tone from the magnificent mansions and terraces which were built first, in and around WARWICK AVENUE, in the 1840s and 1850s, most of which have survived. The CHURCH COMMISSIONERS have restored much of this area in recent years. St Saviour's church, rebuilt in 1976 by Biscoe and Stanton, blends well with the stucco splendour around it, of which a good example is the Colonnade Hotel on the corner of Castellain Road. The clusters of shops in Clifton Road and Formosa Street add a more human dimension.

Sir John Tenniel, principal cartoonist of *Punch* and illustrator of *Alice in Wonderland*, lived at 10 Randolph Avenue from 1853, when the original house was first built, until 1909. Charles and James Ollier, early publishers of Keats and Shelley, lived in 1816–30 in Maida Hill and Mary Shelley later often stayed with friends nearby. Other famous residents in this area were Sir Ambrose Fleming, the radio engineer, at 9 Clifton Gardens in 1890–6; the poets John Davidson at 19 Warrington Crescent in 1889–1909 and John Masefield at 30 Maida Avenue in 1907–9; Christopher Fry, the dramatist, at No. 37 Blomfield Road between 1950 and 1970; and William Friese-Greene, the pioneer of cinematography, at No. 136 Maida Vale.

During the second phase of building in Maida Vale, around 1860, stucco was abandoned for plain brick. A plan by George Gutch, the early surveyor to the estate, for an enormous circus in Elgin Avenue was changed, and the existing road pattern is seen at its best at the graceful junction of roads by the Warrington Hotel in Sutherland Avenue. The flats along Sutherland and Elgin Avenues were not built until the 1880s but further west the Neeld, Goldney and Rundell families developed Chippenham Road and the streets around it during the 1860s. St Peter's church, Elgin Avenue, was rebuilt in 1976. This area was once called St Peter's Park, as it belonged to WESTMINSTER ABBEY. The remaining streets bordering on QUEEN'S PARK were not completed until the 1890s. They were built mainly by small developers, though it was the United Land Company which introduced the incongruously named Beethoven and Mozart Streets. This grim and characterless part of PADDINGTON, occupied by squatters in the 1970s, is aptly personified by the tragic figure of the poet, Francis Thompson, who lived a life of extreme poverty, flitting from one lodging to another in this area in the 1890s. However, in the last 15 years new Council developments such as the Mozart Estate of 1975 have changed the skyline and set out to meet the housing needs here. At No. 114 Shirland Road stood the Warwick Farm Dairy, built in 1886. It was founded in 1845 behind Warwick Place and is still used as a milk distribution centre. It is a link with the not-so-distant past when this once was farmland. A sense of this remains in the streets north of Sutherland Avenue, the last part of Maida Vale to be built with the bowling-green and tennis courts behind Castellain Road and the Recreation Ground further north. This was rescued as an open space in 1888 after a long struggle led by R. Melville Beachcroft and Lord Randolph Churchill. Here Dr Roger Bannister trained for his four-minute mile. The streets around it are mainly comfortable Edwardian mansion blocks. Vera Brittain and Winifred Holtby lived at Wymering Mansions in 1923–7. The ornate building in Delaware Road where the BBC has had studios since the early 1930s was originally built as a roller-skating rink in 1912. The SPANISH AND PORTUGUESE SYNAGOGUE in Lauderdale Road dates from 1896.

Further north again lies Kilburn Park, between Paddington and the railway, dating from around the time that ST AUGUSTINE'S CHURCH opened, in 1880. By Hall Road, on the site of Vale Court, was the important Pineapple Nursery, opened in 1793 and lasting for nearly a century, run by the Henderson family. The Pineapple Nursery, which specialised in bulbs and decorative plants, gave its name to the Pineapple tollgate which stood just north of the nursery until 1838, gaining notoriety in 1836 from a murder which was committed just outside it.

Maida Vale Hospital for Nervous Diseases 4 *Maida Vale, W9.* Founded in 1866 as the London Infirmary for Epilepsy and Paralysis by Dr Julius Althaus at 19 Charles Street, MARYLEBONE (now Blandford Place). At first only outpatients were treated but in 1868 a small number of inpatients were admitted and a matron was engaged for £10 a year to look after them. In 1873 they were moved to Winterton House, Portland Terrace, REGENT'S PARK, where there were three wards – one female, one male and one private. It was renamed the Hospital for Diseases of the Nervous System, and in 1876 the Hospital for Epilepsy and Paralysis. In 1884 a brain tumour was first diagnosed by Dr A. Hughes Bennett and removed by Sir Rickman John Godlee. The patient survived the operation but died later of meningitis. In 1900–2 a new hospital in MAIDA VALE was built to the designs of Keith Young. By 1913 this hospital had 70 beds. In 1937 it was renamed the Maida Vale Hospital for Nervous Diseases. Since the introduction of the National Health Service, the hospital has been amalgamated with the NATIONAL HOSPITAL, QUEEN SQUARE. In 1982 there were 84 beds.

Maiden Lane *WC2.* Part of an ancient track that ran through the convent garden to ST MARTIN'S LANE.

According to Isaac D'Israeli it is named after a statue of the Virgin Mary which stood at the street corner. From about 1631 to 1728 houses were built along it. In 1727–8 Voltaire, exiled from Paris, lodged at the White Wig Inn. Until 1857 it was a cul-de-sac linked to SOUTHAMPTON STREET by a footpath. Then a way through was made so that Queen Victoria's carriage did not have to turn round after leaving her at the ADELPHI THEATRE. Corpus Christi Roman Catholic Church on the south side was designed by F.H. Pownall in 1873–4. Andrew Marvell lived on the site of No. 9 in 1677. J.M.W. Turner was born on the site of No. 21 over his father's barber shop. RULE'S RESTAURANT is at No. 35.

Maids of Honour Row *The Green, Richmond, Surrey.* George I's son, Frederick George, Prince of Wales (later George II) acquired the Duke of Ormonde's house in the OLD DEER PARK so that he and his wife, Princess Caroline of Anspach, could hold their own court. In 1724 the *British Journal* announced, 'His Royal Highness hath given directions for erecting a new building near his Seat at Richmond to serve as Lodgings for the Maids of Honour attending the Princess of Wales.' The building was, in fact, a terrace of four houses of three storeys and a basement, set off by forecourts with wrought-iron gateways. They correspond to 'Houses of the second sort fronting Streets and Lanes of Note and the River Thames', as laid down by the Committee of Architects in 1667 for the rebuilding of London after the GREAT FIRE. These delightful houses adjoin the gateway to the palace overlooking Richmond Green.

The Maids of Honour cannot have occupied all the houses for long, for in about 1744 John James Heidegger, the Swiss theatre manager, lived at No. 4 and is said to have commissioned the scene painter Antonio Jolli to decorate the entrance hall. The panels show views of Switzerland, Italy and China and emblems of the arts and the seasons.

Makers of Playing Cards' Company *see* CITY LIVERY COMPANIES.

Malden Manor *Old Malden, Surrey.* The name Malden derives from the Saxon *mael* – a cross, and *dun* – a hill. Its two manors are mentioned in *Domesday Book*. In the 13th century the Lord of the Manor, Walter de Merton, gave the Malden lands to found a students' college. A religious house was founded locally, and the money obtained from managing this estate was used to maintain 20 scholars at Oxford University at what became known as Merton College, named after the benefactor.

Today Malden Manor still retains the appearance of a village, and the whole area around Church Road is a scheduled Conservation Area. The Plough Inn has 16th-century features. The Manor House, built of mellowed red brick, dates from the 17th century. The parish church of St John the Baptist stands on a small hill overlooking the Hogsmill River. The original chancel, now a chapel, has walls of flint dating from the 14th century. The old nave, now an aisle, was built in 1610, by the then Lord of the Manor, John Goode, who also donated the cost of the massive western tower. The present nave and chancel were added in 1875. The approach, through trees, is by a timbered and tiled lychgate.

Malet Street *WC1*. Previously known as Keppel Mews North, its present name (authorised in 1907) is taken from Sir Edward Malet who married the daughter of Francis, 9th Duke of Bedford (*see* BEDFORD ESTATE). Dillon's University Bookshop is on the west side. Most buildings are now occupied by departments of the UNIVERSITY OF LONDON, including the SENATE HOUSE. The SCHOOL OF ORIENTAL AND AFRICAN STUDIES is by Denys Lasdun and Partners.

The Mall *SW1*. The Mall was created in about 1660 as part of the post-Restoration improvements to ST JAMES'S PARK. It replaced PALL MALL as the alley for the game thus described in 1621: 'A paille mall is a wooden hammer set to the end of a long staff to strike a boule with, at which game noblemen and gentlemen in France doe play much.' The Mall alley was about ½ mile long, fenced, and with a double row of trees on either side. The design was attributed by Vertue to André Le Nôtre. Pepys saw the game for the first time on 2 April 1661. In the same year Waller lauded the royal play:

> Here a well-polished Mall gives us the joy,
> To our Prince his matchless force employ:
> His manly posture and his graceful mien
> Vigour and youth in all his motions seen;
> No sooner has he touched the flying ball
> But 'tis already more than half the Mall
> And such a fury from his arm has got
> As from a smoking culverin 'twere shot.

Pepys walked in the Park, 'discoursing with the keeper of the Pell Mell, who was sweeping of it, who told me of what the earth is mixed that do floor the Mall, and that over all there is cockle shells powdered and spread to keep it fast, which however in dry weather, turns to dust and deads the ball'. On Ogilby and Morgan's map of 1681 it is still called the Pall Mall and Pall Mall Street. For 150 years the Mall was the fashionable London promenade. 'When I pass the Mall in the evening it is prodigious to see the number of ladies walking there,' said Swift on 5 May 1711. Not all were ladies. As Pope wrote:

> Some feel no flames but at the Court or Ball
> And others hunt white aprons in the Mall.

Its cosmopolitan character was described by the visiting Baron von Pöllnitz in 1733: 'The grand walk they call The Mall is full of people every hour of the day, especially in the morning and evening and their Majesties often walk in it, with the Royal Family, who are attended by only half a dozen Yeomen of the Guard and permit all persons without distinction of rank or character to walk there at the same time with them, for which reason the crowd is sometimes too great, and it forms one of the most diversified scenes imaginable. The ladies always appear in rich dresses, for the English who 20 years ago did not wear gilt lace but in their army, are now embroidered and bedaubed as much as the French. I speak of persons of quality for the citizen still contents himself with a suit of fine cloth, a good hat and wig and fine linen.'

The game itself had passed out of fashion by 1741 and the enclosing fence had been replaced by a low wooden kerb. But the daily social promenades continued. Another visitor, Baron Blelfeld, described it at that time: 'I enter a long and spacious walk they call The Mall. It is now mid-day and I find it thronged with the *beau monde* of both sexes, who pass hastily along. The ladies here wear a kind of "neglige" in which they appear still more charming than in a most laboured dress. Every part of their apparel is extremely neat; instead of a large hoop they have short petticoats and their gowns are elegant not gaudy, they have short cloaks trimmed with lace and little hats of either straw or beaver, or else feathers in their hair, which gives them a very lively, elegant air. It is in this walk that we always meet some of our friends and here we see the ministers, the courtiers, the *petits maîtres* and the *coquettes*; here we learn the news of the day and make our parties until it is time to dress for the Court or dinner.'

The wooden kerb was replaced by one of Portland stone in 1749 and in 1751 The Mall is described as newly gravelled. It remained a fashionable walk as late

The grand walk of the Mall in 1750 when it was full at every hour of the day. From an engraving after Maurer.

as 1774. But in the second decade of the following century Sir Richard Phillip mourned the passing of the fashionable Mall: 'My spirits sank and a tear started into my eyes, as I brought to mind those crowds of beauty, rank and fashion, which, till within these last few years, used to be displayed in the centre Mall of this park on Sunday evenings during the spring and summer. How often in my youth had I been a delighted spectator of the enchanted and enchanting assemblage. Here used to promenade, for one or two hours after dinner, the whole British world of gaiety, beauty and splendour. Here could be seen in one morning the most lovely women in this country of female beauty, all splendidly attired and accompanied by as many well dressed men. What a change, I exclaimed, has a few years wrought in these once happy and cheerful personages. How many of those who on this very spot then delighted my eyes are now mouldering in the silent grave.'

As part of the national memorial to Queen Victoria, The Mall's character was radically altered in 1903–4. The new Mall, as it was called, was conceived as a 115 ft wide processional route linking the ADMIRALTY ARCH and the QUEEN VICTORIA MEMORIAL. It runs just south of the old Mall, which can be seen as the adjoining horse ride, and comprises a 65 ft wide road flanked by 25 ft wide pedestrian avenues of plane trees and galleon-topped lamp posts. From the DUKE OF YORK STEPS to the new arch, the route was entirely new and was not opened until 1911. At the eastern end are the Royal Marines Memorial and a statue of Captain James Cook and, on the south side, a memorial to members of the Royal Artillery killed in the Boer War (see MEMORIALS and STATUES). The CITADEL was built at the beginning of the 2nd World War.

Mall Galleries *The Mall, SW1.* Designed by Kenneth Peacock of the Louis de Soissons partnership and opened on the lower ground floor of Nash's CARLTON HOUSE TERRACE in 1971. The first exhibition held here was of works by members of the Royal Society of British Artists (founded 1823). The galleries are administered by the FEDERATION OF BRITISH ARTISTS.

Mallord Street *SW3.* Between OLD CHURCH STREET and the Vale. Mallord was one of the names of the artist Turner who lived in CHEYNE WALK. No. 28 was built for Augustus John by Robert Van t'Hoff. The house was sold in the 1930s to Gracie Fields. A.A. Milne lived at No. 13 in 1920–39; *Winnie-the-Pooh* was published in 1926.

Manchester Square *W1.* Small square laid out in 1776–88 and named after the Duke of Manchester, the first owner of Hertford House (see WALLACE COLLECTION). A church was planned for the centre but never built. Sir Julius Benedict, the composer, lived at No. 2 in 1845–85; John Hughlings Jackson, the expert on nervous diseases, at No. 3 in 1871–1911; and Lord Milner for a time at No. 14. EMI House is by Gollins, Melvin, Ward and Partners (1909).

Manchester Street *W1.* Built in about 1789 and named after the Duke of Manchester who had a house in MANCHESTER SQUARE. Joanna Southcott, the religious fanatic, lived at No. 38 in 1814. She died there on 27 December 1817, and was buried in ST JOHN'S WOOD churchyard. Admiral Sir Francis Beaufort, inventor of the wind scale, lived at No. 51 in 1822–32.

Mandeville Place *W1.* Built in about 1777 and named after the Duke of Manchester (Viscount Mandeville), who lived in MANCHESTER SQUARE. TRINITY COLLEGE OF MUSIC is at Nos 11–13.

Manette Street *W1.* Built in the early 1690s and first known as Rose Street, probably after a tavern. In 1720 Strype wrote, 'This street hath some indifferent good houses but the greater part is taken up for coach houses and stables'. George III's friend, Mrs Mary Delany, was living here at this time with her first husband. She thought it 'a very unpleasant part of the town'. No. 14 was designed by James Paine in 1770 for the vestry of ST ANNE'S as the parish workhouse. A new storey was added in 1804. The building was used as a workhouse until 1837. The east end of the street is occupied by the return frontages of FOYLE'S bookshop; and at the west end is an archway leading into GREEK STREET by the Pillars of Hercules public house. The street was given its present name in 1895 because of Dr Manette's connections with SOHO mentioned in Dickens's *A Tale of Two Cities*: 'The quiet lodgings of Dr Manette were in a quiet street-corner not far from Soho Square. . . . A quainter corner than the corner where the doctor lived was not to be found in London. There was no way through it, and the front window of the Doctor's lodgings commanded a pleasant little vista of street that had a congenial air of retirement on it.' On the south is Goldbeaters' House. Over the door is a replica of the Goldbeaters' arms mentioned in Chapter 6 of Book 2 of *A Tale of Two Cities*: 'In a building at the back, attainable by a courtyard where a plane-tree rustled its green leaves, church-organs claimed to be made, and silver to be chased, and likewise gold to be beaten by some mysterious giant who had a golden arm starting out of the wall of the front hall.' The original of this golden arm can now be seen at DICKENS HOUSE.

Manor House *The Green, Sidcup, Kent.* Built for Charles Stuart Minshaw to the designs of an unknown architect in the 1780s. It is now Council offices.

Manor House *Ham Street, Ham, Surrey.* Originally built in Queen Anne's reign but greatly enlarged towards the end of the 18th century. It stands in splendid grounds bordering on the avenue that leads to HAM HOUSE, but these gardens like so many in the district are threatened with 'development' for housing. During the 19th century there was a succession of well-known occupants starting with Sir Everard Home, Sergeant Surgeon to George III, George IV and William IV after John Hunter whose pupil and brother-in-law he had been; in 1823 Home destroyed Hunter's papers here after frequently using them in his own work. In 1832 the house was taken over by Lord Dudley Coutts Stuart, a son of the Marquess of Bute and husband of Christine Bonaparte, the daughter of Lucio, Prince of Canino, and niece of Napoleon I. As a Member of Parliament he devoted himself to helping Polish refugees and the cause of Polish independence. During 1868–78 the Manor House was the home of the architect Sir George Gilbert Scott who was responsible for so many Victorian Gothic churches and monuments; he used the gardener's cottage as his drawing-office. It is still a private house.

Manor House *South Road, Southall, Middlesex.* The oldest secular building in SOUTHALL. The house was originally called The Wrenns and there was a house on this site in 1503. Francis Ausiter probably altered this existing house in 1587, a date that appears carved over one of the windows. It remained in the Ausiter family until 1801. The house originally consisted of a central hall with wings. Substantial additions were made in the 18th century and an entirely new wing of cottages with a clock tower was built in the 19th but demolished this century to make way for road widening. The house was bought by SOUTHALL Council in 1913 and since 1970 has been leased to SOUTHALL Chamber of Commerce as offices. The exterior is largely timber-framed with brick infilling but it has been extensively altered and restored and much that is visible is not original. Panelling from the 16th and 17th centuries survives in the interior.

Manor House Hospital *Golders Green, NW11.* In 1914 a precursor to this hospital was established at Yvetôt near Le Havre. It was set up by the Allies' Hospital Benevolent Society and organised as a military hospital for French soldiers – L'Hôpital de l'Alliance. After the 1st World War, when the Society turned to the work of rehabilitating British soldiers by orthopaedic treatment, the War Office was induced to take over the Manor House and 9 acres of ground. When the last rehabilitated soldiers had left, the Society converted the hospital for the treatment of patients suffering from industrial injuries. In 1982 there were 243 beds for acute cases.

Manor Park *E12.* Postal and residential district of north-east Newham with a station (1872) on the Eastern Region line. It covers the ancient parish of LITTLE ILFORD. Its development began in the late 1860s on the land of the Manor House built by James Humphreys, lord of the Manor of WEST HAM, in the 1820s at the eastern extremity of his Hamfrith estate. The manor house survives in Gladding Road, E12 as part of the dairy depot of the London CO-OPERATIVE SOCIETY. It was sold to the Eastern Counties Railway Company when their line cut through the grounds in about 1838 and then leased to William Storrs Fry, son of Elizabeth. After the grounds were sold for development in 1866, Cardinal Manning bought the house for a Roman Catholic school and built the church of St Nicholas adjoining. Fr John Heenan, later Cardinal Archbishop of Westminster, was parish priest in 1937–47. At the turn of the century the lands of LITTLE ILFORD manor were developed for housing and the name of Manor Park came to be applied to the whole area.

Manresa House *Roehampton, SW15.* Formerly known as Bessborough House, then Parkstead, the house was built in about 1750 to the designs of Sir William Chambers for Lord Bessborough. It later became a Roman Catholic Seminary. Gerard Manley Hopkins, the priest and poet, lived and studied here in the 1870s and 1880s.

Man's Coffee House *Charing Cross.* Situated on the waterfront. It was named after Alexander Man, who established the house, and it remained in the family until the death of his son, Edmund Man, in 1728. Man's was one of the earliest coffee houses to be established. It is first mentioned in 1666. Soon afterwards Man was appointed 'Coffee Man' to Charles II, and in 1675 he was granted a patent by the King so that the house could act as 'Intelligence Office for Servants', the first recorded servants' registry. In 1676 Man's became known as the Royal Coffee House and later, after the opening of a Young Man's Coffee House (not a connected establishment), as the Old Man's Coffee House. Man's was frequented by officers whom Bickerstaff described in the *Tatler*, 1709–11, as 'young spruce Beauish non-fighting Officers . . . loaded with more Gold Lace than ever was worn by a thriving Hostess upon her Red Petticoat'. It was also used by Masons for Lodge meetings. There is no mention of Man's after 1741 and in 1749 the Admiralty Coffee House opened on the site.

Mansfield Street *W1.* Built in 1772 by the Adam brothers on the site of a reservoir and named after Viscount Mansfield, Duke of Newcastle. Many Adam houses remain. John Loughborough Pearson, the architect, lived at No. 13 in about 1881–97; Sir Edwin Lutyens in 1919–44. Charles, 3rd Earl Stanhope, the inventor and reformer, lived at No. 20 in 1787–95.

Mansion House *Bank, EC2.* The official residence of the LORD MAYOR OF LONDON for his year of office. Early mayors lived in their own houses and entertained there or in their livery company's hall, using the GUILDHALL for important functions. Evelyn's plan for rebuilding after the GREAT FIRE included a house for the LORD MAYOR and the two SHERIFFS. But although the ALDERMEN reported in 1670 on the possibility of building a permanent residence, nothing was done. And a proposal put forward in 1689 to convert GROCERS' HALL into a mansion house came to nothing. At last in 1728 a committee was appointed by the COURT OF COMMON COUNCIL to find a suitable site. But it was not until 1734, when another committee was appointed to find a site and the SWORDBEARER and COMMON CRYER instructed to draw up a list of accommodation requirements, that the matter was put seriously in hand.

In 1735 the site of the STOCKS MARKET was chosen. Initially James Gibbs, John James, Giacomo Leoni, Batty Langley and Isaac Ware were invited to draw up plans. Less than a month later George Dance, Clerk of the City Works, was ordered to produce designs. These, now in the SOANE MUSEUM, were eventually chosen. Dance probably based his designs on Colen Campbell's WANSTEAD, a Palladian mansion with a heavy portico and inner courtyard. The entrance is to the principal rooms (of which there are now ten) on the first floor. Corinthian pilasters between the bays unite the first and second storeys. There is a further attic storey with balustrade. But originally it did not end there. To achieve height in his two main rooms, the Ball Room and the Banqueting Room (known as the Egyptian Hall), Dance vitiated his Palladianism with two high clerestory extrusions that were dubbed the Mayor's Nest and Noah's Ark. The Egyptian Hall followed the description of Vitruvius, having columns on all sides and the clerestory above. The Ball Room, then called The Dancing Gallery, is on the second floor. The chimneypieces were made by Horsenaile

George Dance's Mansion House c. 1750, showing the 'Mayor's Nest' and 'Noah's Ark', later removed from the roof.

and the woodcarving and stucco work done by John Gilbert, George Fewkes and Humphrey Wilmott. They were built of both marble and stone in order to satisfy the aspirations of the two guilds involved.

In 1739 the foundation stone was laid by the Lord Mayor, Micajah Perry, attended by several aldermen, deputies and the City Musick. Coins minted in 1739 from a guinea to a farthing were placed with the foundation stone whose position is now lost. Dance was given 20 guineas to distribute among the workmen. In 1744 a competition was held for the design of the pediment sculptures between Robert Taylor, L.F. Roubiliac and Henry Cheere. Taylor's design showing *London* trampling on *Envy* and leading in *Plenty* was chosen. A figure of Father Thames watches. In 1752 Dance reported the main structure complete; and the Lord Mayor, Sir Crisp Gascoyne, took up residence though work continued on the interior. The building had cost more than £70,000 and had been paid for out of fines levied by the CITY on ALDERMEN who had refused to act as SHERIFFS. The main Portland stone front is 103 ft wide and has a raised portico of six Corinthian columns.

In 1768 the windows and chandeliers were broken when rioters threw stones because the house was not lit to celebrate John Wilkes's election as Member of Parliament. The windows were broken again by the GORDON RIOTERS in 1780. In 1794–5 the central courtyard was roofed over by Dance the Younger, creating a new saloon. He seized the opportunity to remove the Noah's Ark and thus lowered the ceiling of the Egyptian Hall and altered its 'Egyptian' proportions. In 1795 the Grand Staircase was removed to make way for another two rooms; and in 1835 the entrance steps on either side of the portico were reduced to one flight. In 1842 the Ball Room ceiling was reconstructed as a barrel vault and the attic storey, the Mayor's Nest, was removed. In 1845 the LORD MAYOR's private entrance was created in WALBROOK; and in 1849 the SWORD BEARER's room was converted into the Justice Room, a necessary apartment since the LORD MAYOR is Chief Magistrate of the CITY. This is one of the CITY's two magistrates' courts. Beneath this are ten cells for men and one for women; the female cell resembles a birdcage and is known by this name. Emmeline Pankhurst

was once confined here. During 1854–64 the niches in the Egyptian Hall were filled with marble statuary of figures in national history or characters in the works of English, Scottish and Irish poets, including Alfred the Great, Shakespeare, Alexander the Great and Timon of Athens. This room was further embellished in 1868 when large stained-glass windows by Alexander Gibbs were placed at either end. At the west end the Royal Window depicts the signing of the Magna Carta and the Procession of Elizabeth I in her state barge from the TOWER to WESTMINSTER, while the CITY window at the east end depicts Sir William Walworth killing Wat Tyler and Edward VI entering the CITY after his coronation. There was a general restoration of the whole structure in 1931 when it was refurnished in its original style, few of the original fittings having survived Victorian alterations.

In 1936 the one-millionth telephone to be made – this one in gold – was presented to the Mansion House. In 1937 a doorway was made for lady guests beside the LORD MAYOR's entrance in WALBROOK. The building was damaged in the 2nd World War, and the Egyptian Hall not reopened until 1950. In 1962 a public gallery was added to the Justice Room. The most precious possession of the Mansion House is a set of 18th-century armchairs presented to the LORD MAYOR to commemorate Nelson's victory at the Battle of the Nile. The LORD MAYOR's Chair of State was made in 1780. The Lord Mayor's private secretary and his staff are responsible for the running of the Mansion House and the Household Officers – SWORDBEARER, COMMON CRYER AND SERJEANT-AT-ARMS (or Macebearer) and CITY MARSHAL – have their offices here and attend the LORD MAYOR when he goes out on state occasions.

John Maple and Co. Ltd *141–150 Tottenham Court Road, NW1.* Under the sign of the 'Hen and Chickens', John Maple and James Cook set up a store at 145 TOTTENHAM COURT ROAD in 1841 as wholesale and retail drapers, carpet factors, cabinet makers and furnishing warehousemen. James Cook started a shop called Cook and Maple in Middle Queen's Buildings, KNIGHTSBRIDGE (later HARROD'S), in 1845. By 1851 the partnership was dissolved, and John Maple rebuilt the TOTTENHAM COURT ROAD stores as a single

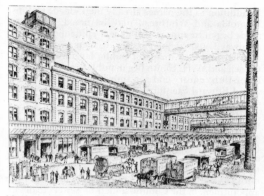

Maple and Co.'s furniture showrooms in Tottenham Place, shortly before the store was rebuilt in 1896.

emporium in his own name. Workshops were in what was then called Tottenham Place where the furniture was hand-made. John Blundell Maple joined his father in 1861, at the age of 16, and by 1884 Maples were offering 'ten thousand Bedsteads in 600 styles for immediate delivery'. John Blundell Maple became an MP in 1887 and in 1892, to commemorate his knighthood, he undertook to rebuild UNIVERSITY COLLEGE HOSPITAL. The store was rebuilt in 1896, by which time the firm supplied furniture for everyone, from the modest middle classes to Queen Victoria, the princes of India, and the Tsar of Russia. In 1905 a Paris branch was opened. In the 1930s a new front was designed by Sir Herbert Baker, reminiscent of his New Delhi style and no doubt as a compliment to the firm's wealthy Indian clientele. At that time it was said to be 'the largest furniture establishment in the world'. It was destroyed by enemy action in 1941. Rebuilding was completed by 1959. During the 1980s the whole block was redeveloped by R. Seifert and Partners with the vast ground floor areas being used as furniture showrooms and the floors above for offices.

Mappin and Webb Ltd *106 Regent Street, W1.* Goldsmiths, silversmiths and jewellers established by Jonathan Mappin, a cutler from Sheffield. The firm was on the south side of POULTRY in 1870 and soon afterwards took over No. 220 REGENT STREET. An OXFORD STREET branch was opened in 1906 at No. 158. This was designed by Belcher and Joass and is still known as Mappin House. New premises were designed for the firm at No. 172 REGENT STREET by J.J. Joass in 1915. There are branches now at No. 170 REGENT STREET and in BOND STREET, FENCHURCH STREET, QUEEN VICTORIA STREET and BROMPTON ROAD.

Maps of London No maps of London of any practical use appeared before the middle of the 16th century. Any modern maps of the CITY at an earlier date are based on historical research and not on old maps. The parent of London maps as we know them no longer exists, but is known from two of the original copper plates from which it was printed. Evidence points to its Continental origin and it appears to be the common source for the small map of London in Braun and Hogenberg's *Civitates Orbis Terrarum*, published in 1572, and the large woodcut map of the CITY attributed

to Ralph Agas and believed, in spite of many ingenious theories to the contrary, to have appeared about 1633. It is of a larger scale than Agas's – about 28 in : 1 mile. Like other London maps of its time, it takes the form of a bird's eye view, and thanks to its large scale shows the principal buildings in quite recognisable detail. It extended from FINSBURY to BANKSIDE and from ST JAMES'S to ALDGATE.

The next large-scale map of London was published in 1658 and was drawn by Richard Newcourt and engraved by William Faithorne. On a scale of 14 in. to 1 mile, it was decorated with views and lists of churches and other features. Various other London maps of small scale and minor importance, mostly of Continental origin, appeared in the years leading up to the GREAT FIRE which disaster had a most significant effect on the map. After the destruction of the CITY, the duty fell on the authorities of settling property claims and boundary disputes. This called for accurate two-dimensional plans and the bird's eye type of map was quite unsuitable. The CITY CORPORATION appointed John Ogilby and his wife's grandson William Morgan to prepare a plan of the devastated area. The result was a large two-dimensional plan of the CITY to a scale of 52 in. to 1 mile, measuring 5×8 ft. This was the first accurate and detailed London map. It was published in 1676 and the only known dated copy is in the GUILDHALL LIBRARY. A 12-sheet map to a smaller scale – 17½ in. to 1 mile – was published in 1681–2 by Morgan, covering the area between FINSBURY, LIMEHOUSE, LAMBETH and ST JAMES'S PARK. The sides of the map were embellished with engravings of London buildings, a picture of Ogilby (who had died soon after the survey was begun) presenting the subscription list to Charles II and his Queen, a prospect of London and a list of peers and officers of state.

The maps so far described, and those which follow, are of course principal examples, and many smaller ones were published over the same period, notably the maps by Wenceslaus Hollar of the destruction inflicted by the GREAT FIRE and the various Dutch maps of the same subject – e.g. Doornick, Venckel and De Wit – as well as the straightforward maps of Morden and Lea, John Oliver and John Overton. There also appeared proposed plans for the rebuilding of the CITY, by Wren, Evelyn and others.

John Ogilby presenting to Charles II the map of London which he was commissioned to prepare after the Great Fire of 1666. It measured 5×8 ft.

Mapmaking and publishing have always tended to run in families; and during the early 18th century the heirs and descendants of 17th-century mapmakers continued in business, examples being Ann Lea and Henry Overton. Thomas Bowles began business in 1712, acquiring part of the stock of Morden and Lea and of John Seller, both 17th-century firms. His brother, John Bowles, set up his business about the same time. The two often worked together, and when Thomas died he was succeeded by John's son, Carington Bowles. Among the many publishers of smaller maps and 'Pocket Plans' of London in the 18th century were Robert Sayer, Emanuel Bowen, Thomas Jefferys, George Foster and George Willdey. Much of their work was derivative. Copying, indeed, was rife until 1734 when the Copyright Act was passed. This was known as 'Hogarth's Act' because of the artist's part in obtaining it after his own works had been pirated. After 1734 the publisher added the words 'Published according to Act of Parliament' to his imprint.

The great event of the mid-18th century in London maps was the coming of John Rocque. One of a family of immigrants from France, he practised land surveying in a modest way at first, but in 1737 began a survey of the whole built-up area of London to a scale of 26 in. to 1 mile. This was completed and published in 1745, engraved by John Pine and published by him and John Tinney. A similar map to half the scale was published in 1755 and another survey by Rocque of 'the country ten miles round' to a scale of 5½ in. to 1 mile appeared in 1746. Both the 1746 maps went into several editions.

The latter half of the 18th century saw the arrival of more publishers of smaller maps of London – John Andrews, John Cary, William Faden, Samuel Fores and Laurie and Whittle, John Fairburn, John Stockdale and John Wallis. The culmination of the 18th-century London map came at the end of the century with Richard Horwood's great survey to a scale of 26 in. to 1 mile of the area between ISLINGTON, LIMEHOUSE, KENNINGTON and BROMPTON, showing the boundaries of local divisions and the number of every house. It was not in fact possible completely to show the house numbers since, although house numbering had begun in 1735, there were still many houses which in 1792 bore no number; but at any rate every house was shown. The production of the map was an expensive undertaking, and it was only with the help of the Phoenix Assurance Company, for whom Horwood had previously done surveying work, that he was able to publish the map in 1799. He was desperately short of money and moved to Liverpool, where he died in poverty after publishing a survey of that city. William Faden acquired the plates of his London map and produced later editions of it in 1807, 1813 and 1819. It is said that a later edition still was planned by James Wyld but was abandoned in anticipation of the large-scale Ordnance Survey of London.

In the 19th century more important names entered the map field. G.F. Cruchley, C. Greenwood, John Wallis and James Wyld (father and son) all published clear and attractive maps during the first half of the century and the map of London to a scale of 8 in. to 1 mile by Christopher and John Greenwood went into nine editions between 1827 and 1854. Cruchley's folding maps of London went into edition after edition well into the second half of the century. In 1851 the GREAT EXHIBITION in HYDE PARK was a great stimulus to the publication of maps and guides for visitors to London.

In addition to the names already mentioned, Collins, Reynolds and Whitbread may be noted. Thematic maps began to appear – drainage, epidemic, railway, tramway, bus, cycling, police districts, water board districts and even maps of public lavatories. Bacon, Cassell and W.H. Smith began publishing maps in the latter 19th century and continued to the present time, as did Edward Stanford, George Philip, John Bartholomew and Geographia Ltd.

Meanwhile in 1791 the first sheets of the 1 in. Ordnance Survey of England had appeared, the London area being covered by 4 sheets as follows: MIDDLESEX (1822), Essex (1805), Surrey (1816) and Kent (1819), and many commercially produced maps of London of the time were based (by permission) on them. The CHOLERA outbreaks of the 1830s and 1840s led to the appointment of the Commissioners of Sewers to devise a unified system of drainage in London, and this in turn called for the accurate large-scale mapping of the metropolitan area with heights above sea level. The Skeleton Survey appeared in 1851 and from it was developed the 5 ft Ordnance Survey of London dated 1875. Subsequent editions of the latter and the smaller 25 in., 6 in. and 1 in. Ordnance Survey maps appeared at intervals up to the 1940s. After the 2nd World War the National Grid mapping of Great Britain was introduced, and the 5 ft survey of London was replaced by the 50 in. or 1:1,250 scale map. Smaller maps were subdivided in scale, so that the present day scales are 1:2,500 (25 in.), 1:10,560 (6 in.), 1:25,000 (2½ in.) and 1:50,000 (1¼ in.). An 'Aerial Mosaic' of actual aerial photographs to the 1:1,250 scale was begun in 1947 but abandoned after the publication of 58 sheets.

The full range of London maps, with a few unimportant exceptions, is held between the Map Room of the BRITISH LIBRARY, GREAT RUSSELL STREET, the GREATER LONDON COUNCIL record room, COUNTY HALL and the GUILDHALL LIBRARY, each of which has examples of most of them. Most London municipal reference libraries have good map sections in their local collections and WESTMINSTER, BUCKINGHAM PALACE ROAD and KENSINGTON AND CHELSEA, PHILLIMORE WALK, are outstanding. The BISHOPSGATE INSTITUTE has a good coverage of London maps, as do such learned societies as the ROYAL GEOGRAPHICAL SOCIETY, KENSINGTON GORE, and the SOCIETY OF ANTIQUARIES OF LONDON, BURLINGTON HOUSE.

Marble Arch *W1*. Designed by John Nash, who based it on the Arch of Constantine in Rome, and constructed at a cost of £10,000, it was erected in 1827 in front of BUCKINGHAM PALACE. The reliefs on the north side were by R. Westmacott, those on the south by Baily. A statue of George IV by Chantrey was intended to be set on the top but stands instead in TRAFALGAR SQUARE. It was moved to its present site at the north-east corner of HYDE PARK in 1851 and islanded in 1908. Only senior members of the Royal Family and the KING'S TROOP ROYAL HORSE ARTILLERY may pass through it.

Marble Hill *Vauxhall*. Stood on the south side of the present VAUXHALL BRIDGE ROAD. It was opened in 1740 by Joseph Crosier who enlarged and illuminated the gardens and provided a 'Long Room' for dancing. In 1752–6 Napthali Hart, teacher of music and dancing, was proprietor. In 1756 it was converted to a coffee house and tavern.

Nash's Marble Arch, originally in front of Buckingham Palace, was removed to the north-east corner of Hyde Park in 1851.

Marble Hill House *Richmond Road, Twickenham, Middlesex.* Situated between Richmond Road and the THAMES is one of the most delightful examples of an 18th-century Palladian villa set in parkland which rolls down to the river. The house was built by Henrietta Howard, the 'exceedingly respectable and respected mistress' of Frederick, Prince of Wales, later George II. She was unhappily married to Charles Howard who later became Earl of Suffolk. They both held posts in the royal household. Caught between an impossible marriage and a precarious position at court, she naturally felt the need to acquire her own house. In 1723 the Prince of Wales gave her £11,500, and with the help of her friends she began to build Marble Hill.

The land was acquired for her by Lord Ilay who also engaged Roger Morris as builder. The plans were drawn up by Lord Herbert, an enthusiastic amateur architect. Roger Morris was more than simply a builder: his function was to interpret Lord Herbert's ideas into a practical design. Work was begun in 1724 and the house was finished in 1729. Another of Henrietta's friends, and also her neighbour, was Alexander Pope who played a large part in planning the park. Pope wrote of Henrietta:

> I know a thing that's most uncommon;
> (Envy, be silent and attend!)
> I know a reasonable woman,
> Handsome and witty, yet a friend.

Together with Charles Bridgman, the landscape gardener, he worked on plans for the park which included a wide lawn on the south side of the house with groves of trees on either side set back to give the best possible view of the THAMES.

It was not until 1731 that Henrietta could begin to enjoy her house. Her court duties changed when she became Countess of Suffolk and she wrote to John Gay, '. . . Every thing as yet promises more happiness for the latter part of my life than I have yet had a prospect of . . . I shall now often visit Marble Hill. . . .' This she did, and spent happy years there entertaining her friends. In 1747 she acquired a new neighbour when Horace Walpole took over STRAWBERRY HILL. He became a firm friend and drew greatly on her memories of court life for his *Memoirs of the Reigns of George I and George II*.

Henrietta died at Marble Hill in 1767. The house then had a succession of tenants and owners. After 1887 it stood empty for many years and fell into a dilapidated state. It was under threat of becoming a building site when in 1901 it was saved and came into the care of the LONDON COUNTY COUNCIL. It has been carefully restored and now belongs to the GREATER LONDON COUNCIL. A glossy mahogany staircase leads to the first-floor rooms whose furniture and decorations resemble as closely as possible those of the original house. Wallpapers have been copied and chairs covered in contemporary canvas-work embroidery.

Marchant's Waterworks Founded in 1694 in Hartshorn Lane to the west of CRAVEN STREET. One of the entrepeneurs was Hugh Marchant. Permission was given by the Western Sewer Commissioners for Marchant to utilise the flow of sewage in the Hartshorn Lane sewer as a power source. Pumps were actuated by the flow of sewage over water wheels placed in the sewer and THAMES water was thus supplied to the expanding WEST END. As the sewer decanted close to the water intake, the scheme was never very successful. In 1761 Lysons described two further pumps, one a windmill in Tottenham Court Road Fields, the other higher up the original sewer beneath TOM'S COFFEE HOUSE in ST MARTIN'S LANE on the site of the LONDON COLISEUM. The former can be seen on Rocque's map of 1746. In 1766 CHARLOTTE STREET was begun on the site. Hartshorn Lane was rebuilt as Northumberland Street in 1760; and in 1775 inhabitants in the vicinity petitioned against the riverside works. It was found that the sewer water 'had not been used for several years past for the original purpose of supplying the inhabitants with water . . . but that the proprietors make use of the said sewer water for no other purpose than to turn a corn mill'. As a result the patent of the waterworks was rescinded in 1779.

Maresfield Gardens *NW3.* Takes its name from Maresfield in Sussex, a property of the Maryon Wilson family (*see* HAMPSTEAD). Sigmund Freud lived at No. 20 in 1938–9.

Margaret Street *W1.* Laid out in 1734 and called after Lady Margaret Cavendish, wife of the 2nd Duke of Portland. In it stands Butterfield's ALL SAINTS CHURCH and Mowbray's long-established bookshop. B.A. Seaby Ltd at No. 11 is the largest coin shop in the world. The firm was founded at OXFORD CIRCUS in 1926 by Bert Seaby who had worked for SPINKS.

Maritime Trust Museum *see* HISTORIC SHIPS COLLECTION.

Mark Lane *EC3.* A corruption of Mart Lane, a name derived from the market held here in the reign of Edward I. The CORN EXCHANGE is on the east side at Nos 52–57. At the corner of FENCHURCH STREET in Star Alley was ALL HALLOWS STAINING which, apart from the tower, was demolished in 1870. Nos 59–61 were built in 1864 as offices for James and John Innes who dealt in property and started the company which is now known as the City of London Real Property Company. The architect was George Aitchison.

Market House *Uxbridge, Middlesex.* A stolid but functional building of 1789 symbolising the past history of the township. Tuscan columns of wood support spacious first-floor rooms and a central turret clock. The ground floor, once open, was originally used for pitching corn, and the first floor served as a corn exchange.

Market Mews *W1*. A long narrow mews extending westward from HERTFORD STREET, it is part of the network of narrow streets and alleys laid out in about 1735 by Edward Shepherd around SHEPHERD MARKET.

Market Place *W1*. This tiny enclave between UPPER REGENT STREET and GREAT TITCHFIELD STREET marks the site of OXFORD MARKET, established in 1724 to serve the Earl of Oxford's newly developed estate (*see* PORTLAND ESTATE). It remained in use till 1882 when the area was redeveloped into offices and showrooms; a few barrows still loiter hopefully in the purlieus.

Marketors' Company *see* CITY LIVERY COMPANIES.

Markham Square *SW3*. Built on a field which was part of Box Farm. The last owner of the farm was Pulham Markham Evans who sold the farmhouse, which stood at the corner of Markham Street and KING'S ROAD, in 1899. The square had been laid out in 1836.

Markham Street *SW3*. Pulham Markham Evans, who gave his name also to MARKHAM SQUARE and Markham Place, was the last owner of Box Farm on this site. The Evans family had Common rights since the '29th year of Elizabeth'. The KING'S ROAD end of Markham Street forms a side of the PHEASANTRY. The old St Luke's Church Schools stood where Markham Street joins CHELSEA COMMON.

Marks and Spencer Ltd *173 and 458 Oxford Street, W1*. In 1884 Michael Marks, a Polish immigrant, opened a market stall in Leeds selling household goods, haberdashery, sheet music and toys. Above the stall the sign read 'Marks's Penny Bazaar – Don't Ask the Price – It's a Penny'. In 1894 he took a partner, Thomas Spencer, and many market stalls were opened around England, together with 'variety chain' stores. In 1907 Michael's son, Simon Marks (later Lord Marks), took over, working closely with his brother-in-law, Israel Sieff (later Lord Sieff). By 1926 they were selling a vast range of merchandise and became a public company. The MARBLE ARCH store, designed by Trehearne and Norman, opened in 1930; and in 1937 the firm bought the building in OXFORD STREET on the site of the PANTHEON of 1772 and of the Bazaar of 1833–4. The façade was dismantled and presented to the GEORGIAN SOCIETY. The building was reconstructed in 1938. It is of black granite and was designed by W.A. Lewis and Partners and Robert Lutyens. The name 'The Pantheon' is commemorated on the frontage. In 1982 there were 42 stores in the Greater London Area.

Marlborough Club *Pall Mall*. Founded in 1869 by the Prince of Wales with the help of a backer whom the Prince's friend, Charles Wynn-Carrington, called 'an old snob named Mackenzie, the son of an Aberdeenshire hatter who had made a fortune in Indigo and got a baronetcy'. There were 400 members, all of them

known personally to the Prince who was the club's President. They included the Dukes of Sutherland, Manchester and St Albans; the Marquess of Ormonde; the Earls of Rosebery and Leicester; William Howard Russell, the Irish war correspondent; Christopher Sykes, who was to bankrupt himself trying to keep up with the Prince's expensive habits; and Colonel Valentine Baker, commanding officer of the Prince's regiment, the 10th Hussars, who was to be cashiered and imprisoned for a year for allegedly assaulting a young lady in a railway carriage. Members were allowed to smoke freely – not the case at WHITE's which the Prince hardly ever entered in consequence. For a time the commodious club premises, designed by David Brandon, included a bowling alley until the residents of PALL MALL complained of the noise and it was roofed over to form a billiard room. In 1917, according to Wynn-Carrington, by then Marquess of Lincolnshire, 'the Marlborough Club was on its last legs. Sir Ernest Cassel [a German Jew] offered to finance it; but the members would not stand that; and King George V saved the club by producing £7,000.' It was described in 1927 as 'probably the most distinguished club in London as to the royalty and nobility among its members'. It closed in 1953 and the building was converted to offices.

Marlborough House *Pall Mall, SW1*. Built for Sarah, Duchess of Marlborough, who obtained a 50-year lease of land adjoining ST JAMES'S PALACE from her friend, Queen Anne. The Duke was unenthusiastic and wrote, 'I have no great opinion of this project, for I am very confident that in time you will be sensible that this building will cost you double the money of the first estimate.' The Duchess invited Wren to design her new house; Vanbrugh had been the Duke's choice for Blenheim Palace. She later recalled that she made Wren promise two things: 'First that he would make the contracts reasonable and not as Crown work ... the other ... that he must make my house strong plain and convenient and that he must give me his word that this building should not have the least resemblance of anything in that called Blenheim which I have never liked ...' The red bricks were brought as ballast from Holland in ships that had carried troops and supplies to the Duke's armies. The Duchess herself laid the foundation stone in 1709 and the house was finished in 1711. The actual design was probably drawn by Christopher Wren the Younger, under the supervision of his father. The Duchess dismissed Wren before completion, feeling that the contractors took advantage of him. She supervised the completion of the unpretentious house herself.

In 1722 the Duke died at Windsor Lodge but his body was brought here to lie in state before burial in WESTMINSTER ABBEY. A series of historical paintings of his battles lines the walls of the central *salon* and the staircases. His widowed Duchess divided her time between her houses at London, Windsor, St Albans and WIMBLEDON. In 1733 she tried to improve access to the house by making a new drive from the front entrance to PALL MALL; she had built the gateway when Sir Robert Walpole bought the leases of the obstructing houses to spite her. The blocked-up arch can still be seen. The Duchess died at Marlborough House in 1744.

In the early 1770s Sir William Chambers added a third storey and put in marble fireplaces. The house remained in the Marlborough family until 1817 when it reverted to the Crown and preparations were made for Princess Charlotte, the heir to the throne, and her husband, Prince Leopold of Saxe-Coburg-Saalfeld, to move in; but she died in childbirth at Claremont Park. Prince Leopold came here alone and lived in it until he accepted the invitation to become the first King of the Belgians in 1831. In 1837–49 the Dowager Queen Adelaide lived here. Between her death and the coming of age of Edward, Prince of Wales, it provided accommodation for the Vernon and Turner collections of pictures, the Government School of Design and the Department of Practical Art (*see* VICTORIA AND ALBERT MUSEUM). For several years the Duke of Wellington's funeral carriage, a product of the School of Design, was exhibited in a shed in the forecourt. It was later moved to ST PAUL'S CATHEDRAL.

In 1861–3 Sir James Pennethorne removed Chambers's attic storey and replaced it with two of his own. The carriage porch was added, a range of rooms to the north, and stables. The work was for the new occupant, Edward, Prince of Wales. The small rooms were enlarged by combining two or even three together. In his time visitors to the house were admitted to the entrance hall by a Scots gillie in Highland dress. In the hall they were met by two scarlet-coated and powdered footmen, their hats and coats being passed to a hall porter in a short red coat with a broad band of leather across his shoulders. A page in a dark blue coat and black trousers would then escort them to a walnut-panelled ante-room on the first floor next door to which the Prince would be waiting to receive them in a cluttered sitting-room. As they passed upstairs they were conscious of the flittings of many maids, all in neat uniform, whose business it was to maintain the character of the Prince's residence as the 'best kept house in London'. It was also, of course, the centre of fashionable society. In 1865 the future George V was born here and in 1903–10 lived here as Prince of Wales. From 1910 to 1925 it was the home of the widowed Queen Alexandra. In the garden are gravestones to her dogs Muff, Tiny and Joss and one to Benny the Bunny. Her own Queen Alexandra Memorial is in MARLBOROUGH ROAD (*see* MEMORIALS). In 1936, on the death of King George V, his widow, Queen Mary, moved here. She died here in 1953. There is a memorial plaque to her, also in Marlborough Road.

In 1959 the house was donated to the Government for use as a Commonwealth Centre, and was opened as such in 1962. It also houses the Commonwealth Foundation. The principal room is the saloon which is two storeys high. On its wall are paintings of the Battle of Blenheim by Louis Laguerre. On the ceiling are Gentileschi's *Arts and Sciences* painted in 1636 for the QUEEN'S HOUSE at GREENWICH but removed by the Duchess of Marlborough by permission of Queen Anne. Beyond is the main conference room with two smaller ones on either side. On the staircases to the first floor are more paintings by Laguerre of the Battles of Ramillies and Malplaquet. There is also Edward VII's smoking-room lined appropriately with bogus books.

Marlborough Place *NW8*. First rated in 1829 and called after John Churchill, Duke of Marlborough, this is one of a group of military names to be found in ST JOHN'S WOOD: Blenheim Place is nearby. Thomas

Huxley lived at No. 38; it is today the Marlborough Hospital. No. 23 has a remarkable Italianate tower.

Marlborough Road *and* **Gate** *St James's Park, SW1*. Originally a private access road from ST JAMES'S PALACE to ST JAMES'S PARK it was closed at the north end by the QUEEN'S CHAPEL. There was a suggestion in 1835 that it should be cut through to PALL MALL, macadamised and opened to the equestrian public, but it was not until 1856 that a similar plan was carried out. This involved relaying the roadway several yards to the west, separating the QUEEN'S CHAPEL from the PALACE. Until THE MALL was built, all the park traffic used Marlborough Road and PALL MALL to approach TRAFALGAR SQUARE. In 1925 a pavement on the west side was added to that on the east, involving further encroachment on ST JAMES'S PALACE land. The Queen Alexandra MEMORIAL is on the garden wall of MARLBOROUGH HOUSE facing Friary Court of ST JAMES'S PALACE. There is also a memorial plaque to Queen Mary with a relief by W. Reid Dick.

Marloes Road *W8*. On the EDWARDES ESTATE. Marloes is a place in Wales. Andrew Lang, the man of letters, lived at No. 1 in 1876–1912.

Marshall and Snelgrove *334–338 Oxford Street*. James Marshall and a Mr Wilson opened a shop at 11 VERE STREET in 1837. John Snelgrove joined them in 1848. A nearby rival was William Debenham. By 1871 James C. Marshall, son of the founder, had taken over and introduced a large mail-order business. Sir Horace Jones designed new premises for the firm in 1870. These were rebuilt in 1968–71 to the designs of Adrian V. Montague and Partners. Marshall and Snelgrove is now part of the Debenham Group.

Marshall Street *W1*. Almost certainly takes its name from Hampstead Marshall, the Berkshire seat of the Earl of Craven, the ground landlord, who allowed the land upon which it was built to be used for pesthouses and burial grounds in 1665 and who bought the freehold from James Baker, great-nephew of Robert Baker, the tailor. It was built in 1733–6. On the east side are seven of the original houses, Nos 7–13, into all of which, other than Nos 7 and 9, shop fronts have been fitted. Most of the west side is now occupied by an electricity station. At Nos 14–18 are the Westminster Public Baths and Wash-houses, which were built in 1928 at a cost of £173,000 on a site where public baths have been since 1851–2. William Blake was born in a house on the site of No. 8.

Marshalsea Prison *Southwark*. The name is derived from an ancient court held by the Steward and Marshal of the king's household. The date of the founding of the prison is unknown but it was attacked by Wat Tyler's rebels in 1381. At that time it stood near the present Mermaid Court. In 1509 Bonner, the usurped Bishop of London, was imprisoned here for the first time – he later died in the Marshalsea. Under Elizabeth I it became one of the most important of London's prisons, second only to the TOWER. It was mainly used for debtors but was also convenient for the incarceration of anybody thought to defy or ridicule authority. In 1609 the poet Christopher Brooke was imprisoned for having witnessed the secret marriage of Anne More to John Donne without her father's consent. In 1613 another poet, George Wither, wrote *Shepherd's Hunting* here. In 1729 the prison was housing more than 300 debtors. Conditions were bad and there was widespread corruption and extortion. An anonymous pamphlet of 1738; *Hell in Epitome*, describes the Marshalsea as

> An old pile most dreadful to the view
> Dismal as wormwood or repenting rue.

General Oglethrope, the friend of Dr Johnson, was so distressed by the state of some prisoners that he raised money to pay off their debts. In the 1770s William Smith described the prison as in bad repair with stairs so dark and ruinous that it was dangerous to go up and down without a candle. In the late 18th century it was moved to just north of St George's church. In 1824 Dickens's father was imprisoned here for debt. In *Little Dorrit* (1856) the heroine is born in the prison and Dickens describes it as 'an oblong pile of barrack building, partitioned into squalid houses standing back to back, so that there were no back rooms; environed by a narrow paved yard, hemmed in by high walls duly spiked at top'. As well as the debtors' prison there was a more confined area for smugglers; those owing customs and excise fines were locked behind an iron-plated door. The prison was closed in 1842.

Marsham Street *SW1*. The continuation of GREAT SMITH STREET. Named after Sir Robert Marsham, forebear of the Earl of Romney. A stone plaque on the west side records: 'This is Marsham Street 1688.' The street is now dominated by the buildings of the Department of the Environment built in 1963–71 to the designs of Eric Bedford in association with Robert Atkinson and Partners. The 9th Church of Christ Scientist on the east side was built in 1928–30 to the designs of Sir Herbert Baker. Locket's Restaurant at Marsham Court is a successor of the ordinary (an eating-house providing meals at a fixed price) at CHARING CROSS.

Martin Lane *EC4*. Named after the church of ST MARTIN ORGAR which was demolished in 1820. Its site is marked by a tall Italianate tower designed as a rectory by John Davies in 1851 but now used as offices.

Martinware Pottery Collection *Public Library, Osterley Park Road, Southall, Middlesex*. Robert Wallace Martin, the eldest of four brothers, founded the firm of R.W. Martin in 1873 in FULHAM. The firm moved to a derelict soap factory between the GRAND UNION CANAL and Havelock Road in SOUTHALL in 1877; and a shop was opened in Brownlow Street, off HOLBORN, the wares having previously been hawked around London in carpet bags. R.W. Martin was the modeller and sculptor, Walter the thrower, Charles, the second brother, kept the shop, and Edwin, the youngest, was the etcher and painter. On the successive death of the brothers, the first English studio potters, output gradually petered out. It finally stopped with the death of R.W. Martin in 1923. The pottery was struck by lightning and gutted in 1943. The collection of Martinware at SOUTHALL Public Library contains birds, toby jugs, grotesques and other pieces.

Marx Memorial Library *37 Clerkenwell Green, EC1*. Built in 1737 as the Welsh Charity School for children for poor Welsh families in London, which in 1772 moved to Gray's Inn Lane. For the next century the small building, subdivided, served as shops and coffee-rooms, and being in a centre of social and political protest, was in 1872–92 the home of the radical London Patriotic Club. In 1892 the Twentieth-Century Press, Social Democratic publishers under Harry Quelch, moved here, backed by William Morris, and were visited by such famous international Socialists as Kropotkin and Eleanor Marx. In 1902–3 Lenin published 17 issues of *Iskra* from here. From 1922 the house was by turns empty and in commercial use, until in 1933 it became the Marx Memorial Library and lecture-rooms.

Mary Ward Centre *Tavistock Place, WC1*. Founded by Mrs Mary Ward in 1890 at University Hall, GORDON SQUARE as a social centre for men and women from all walks of life. In 1891 Marchmont Hall, TAVISTOCK SQUARE was also rented and boys' and men's clubs were started there and concerts and lectures given. In 1894 John Passmore Edwards offered to finance a new building for the settlement and the Duke of Bedford offered a cheap site in TAVISTOCK PLACE. An architectural competition was held for the building which was judged by Norman Shaw. The winners were A. Dunbar Smith and Cecil Brewer, two young residents of University Hall. The building is one of the best examples of Art Nouveau in London. It was opened in 1897 as the Passmore Edwards Settlement. In 1898 Mrs Ward opened here the first play centre in the country and the first school for invalid children. It was renamed the Mary Ward Settlement in 1921, a year after her death.

Marylebone *see* ST MARYLEBONE.

Marylebone Cricket Club (MCC) Formed in 1787 by members of the old WHITE CONDUIT CLUB against whom they played their first match in June 1788 on land leased to Thomas Lord, now the site of DORSET SQUARE (*see* LORD'S CRICKET GROUND). The Earl of Winchilsea and Charles Lennox (later the Duke of Richmond), prominent members of the WHITE CONDUIT CLUB, were largely responsible for the formation of the MCC and the subsequent merger of the two clubs. Thomas Lord obtained ground further west to which the MCC moved in 1811 but yet another move to land at ST JOHN'S WOOD, its present home, was made in 1814. The present ground was purchased in 1866 for £18,000 by the MCC, by which time it had established itself as the supreme authority on the conduct and rules of the game: its decisions were accepted wherever cricket was played. This position was not achieved under the authority of any written document

Early players of the 'Noble Game of Cricket' in 1787 at the White Conduit Club (later the Marylebone Cricket Club).

or legal instrument, but from the integrity and respect in which its leading committee members were held. Moves to expand its activities beyond the boundaries of LORD'S to more northern areas, on the grounds that it was too southern in its outlook, were unsuccessful and not very vigorously pursued; but in 1968 an authority was set up – the MCC Council – which embraced not only the MCC but also the Test and County Cricket Board and the Minor Counties. The president is appointed annually by his predecessor and its secretary by the committee, for indefinite periods. There have been only ten secretaries since its inauguration. The club also has squash courts and a real tennis court (*see* TENNIS COURTS).

Marylebone Gardens Opened in 1650 in the fields at the back of the manor house (*see* MARYLEBONE MANOR HOUSE). There were dog-fights, cock-fights, bear- and bull-baitings, bowling greens and boxing matches. In 1668 Pepys thought the gardens 'a pretty place'. They were much patronised by rich gamblers, ne'er-do-wells and sharpers. John Gay in his *Beggar's Opera* (1728) makes the gardens a haunt of the highwayman Captain Macheath. Dick Turpin did, in fact, come here in the 1730s and it was here, reputedly, that he stole a kiss from Mrs Fountayne, the schoolmaster's wife, telling her she could forever thereafter boast that she had been kissed by the famous Dick Turpin. For a time James Figg, the early 18th-century pugilist, had an amphitheatre here and advertised contests between 'the most eminent professors, both male and female, of the art of defence'. At this time the proprietor of the gardens was John Trusler, father of Dr John Trusler, the eccentric divine and prolific writer who became curate of ST CLEMENT DANES and chaplain to the POULTRY COMPTER.

The gardens were enlarged in 1738 and an entrance fee of 6d was charged to make them more exclusive. A silver season ticket cost half a guinea. No servants in livery were admitted, 'nor persons of ill repute'. The grand walk in the centre was planted with trees which met overhead. Latticed alcoves were spaced at discreet distances on either side. To the south an orchestra played each evening from 6 to 10 o'clock. In 1739 assembly rooms were built for balls, concerts and promenading in wet weather. The refreshments were of a high standard, Mr Trusler's tarts and cakes often being praised in the literature of the time. In 1769 Dr Samuel Arnold, the composer who became conductor of the Academy of Ancient Music in 1789 and organist to WESTMINSTER ABBEY in 1793, leased the gardens which thereafter became well known for the quality of their music. In 1773 Thomas Arne, the prolific composer of *Rule, Britannia* and many other vocal pieces, conducted the orchestra here. In that same year a medicinal spring was discovered and the gardens briefly became a spa. They had also by then become famous for their fireworks. These, in the 1770s, were under the direction of the great pyrotechnist, Morel Torré, whose display Dr Johnson once came to see. In 1778, the gardens were closed. Devonshire Street and Beaumont Street now cover part of the site.

Marylebone Lane *and* **High Street** *W1.* The narrow winding Lane and its broader continuation, Marylebone High Street, represent the nucleus of the old village and indeed, despite rebuilding, retain much of the village character. No. 35, the headquarters of BBC Publications, stands on the site of the Rose of Normandy, once the entrance to MARYLEBONE GARDENS and in the 19th century a music hall in its own right: the music-hall lamps are still set in the pavement outside. At the north end, on the east side, stood the MARYLEBONE MANOR HOUSE, probably built by Thomas Hobson in the early 16th century. It became a school in the 18th and was demolished in 1791. The parish church stood opposite. The first building, dedicated to Our Lady, stood beside the TYBURN and so gave a new name to the area – St Mary-by-the-Bourne, hence MARYLEBONE; it endured from 1400 to 1740 and provided the setting for Tom Rakewell's marriage to the Rich Old Lady, as depicted in Hogarth's

Promenaders in Marylebone Gardens in 1761. The orchestra (right) was conducted at one time by Thomas Arne.

Rake's Progress. Becoming ruinous, it was replaced by a second church which ceded its dignity as parish church to Hardwick's handsome building in 1817 but continued to serve as parish chapel till, damaged by bombs, it was pulled down in 1949. The hymn-writer Charles Wesley, a resident in MARYLEBONE for 17 years, was buried in the churchyard; this has since become a small paved garden with seats but the Wesley monument remains undisturbed. At the northern end of the street, facing on to the MARYLEBONE ROAD, was No. 1 Devonshire Terrace, 'a house of undeniable situation and splendour', which, in 1839–51, was the home of Charles Dickens. During those years, he wrote *The Old Curiosity Shop*, *Barnaby Rudge*, *American Notes*, *Martin Chuzzlewit*, *A Christmas Carol*, *The Chimes*, *The Cricket on the Hearth*, *Dombey and Son*, *The Battle of Life*, *The Haunted Man*, and *David Copperfield*. Grip, his pet raven which he introduced into *Barnaby Rudge*, lived and died here – rather to the relief of the Dickens children whose ankles he would nip unmercifully. The house was later the home of another novelist, George du Maurier. The whole terrace was demolished in the late 1950s and Ferguson House, Nos 15 and 17 Marylebone Road, stands on the site with a large plaque in the entrance, finely carved with a head of Dickens and representations of the characters from the novels written here. The Cordon Bleu Cookery School (London) Ltd is at No. 114 Marylebone Lane; the Constance Spry Flower School at No. 53; and the London College of Dance and Drama at No. 100.

Marylebone Manor House Exchanged in 1544 by Thomas Hobson (then Lord of the Manor of MARYLEBONE) with Henry VIII for church lands taken over by the crown. The King had it converted into a hunting lodge, and his children, Mary, Elizabeth and Edward, all hunted here. James I sold it and it eventually passed into the hands of the Austen family from whom it was purchased at the beginning of the 18th century by John Holles, Duke of Newcastle; soon afterwards the surrounding land was developed. The manor house became a boarding school until it was demolished in 1791. Its gardens were the fashionable MARYLEBONE GARDENS.

The 16th-century Marylebone Manor House, which later became a boarding school, was demolished in 1791.

Marylebone Road *NW1*. Built in 1757 as part of the 'New Road from Paddington to Islington' which had been required by Act of Parliament. Originally known as New Road, its name was changed in 1857.

George Shillibeer started his omnibus service on 4 July 1829 from the YORKSHIRE STINGO tavern to the BANK – the fare was 1s including the use of a newspaper (*see* TRANSPORT). George Morland was living at No. 20 in 1700–1; Leigh Hunt at No. 77 in 1817–19. On the north side are HOLY TRINITY CHURCH, now housing the SOCIETY FOR PROMOTING CHRISTIAN KNOWLEDGE; the ROYAL ACADEMY OF MUSIC; MADAME TUSSAUD'S; the LONDON PLANETARIUM; and the executive offices of F.W. WOOLWORTH AND CO. LTD. And on the south ST MARYLEBONE CHURCH; the WESTERN OPTHALMIC HOSPITAL; and the SAMARITAN HOSPITAL FOR WOMEN. LEYLAND HOUSE is at Nos 172–204.

Marylebone Station *Boston Place, Marylebone Road, NW1*. Designed by H.W. Braddock in 1899 for the Great Central Railway, this was the last main-line terminus to be built in London. Because the residents of ST JOHN'S WOOD and the MARYLEBONE CRICKET CLUB at LORD'S had fought hard against the construction of the last two miles of track, the GCR was short of money by the time their line finally reached London. So Marylebone is a simple and unpretentious station – though the letters 'GCR' are everywhere worked into the wrought-ironwork of its railings. The hotel by Robert William Ellis, quite separate from the station and fronting the Marylebone Road, was also opened in 1899. Since 1962 it has been occupied by the British Railways Board. Despite many threats to turn Marylebone into a parcels depot, in 1982 it was still a small and friendly passenger terminus of the Western Region.

Masonic Peace Memorial *see* FREEMASONS' HALL.

Mason's Arms Yard *W1*. On the Millfield Estate (*see* HANOVER SQUARE), it is a long narrow cul-de-sac leading off the north side of MADDOX STREET. It takes its name from the nearby Mason's Arms public house, which (although now rebuilt in the 'Brewers' Tudor' style) has existed in MADDOX STREET since the 1720s.

Mason's Avenue *EC2*. Extends from 30 COLEMAN STREET to 14 BASINGHALL STREET. Formerly known as Masons' Alley, it was named after the MASONS' COMPANY whose hall, in existence as early as 1410, used to stand here. On the south side is Ye Olde Dr Butler's Head which was established in 1616 by Dr William Butler, physician to James I.

Masons' Company *see* CITY LIVERY COMPANIES.

Master Mariners' Company *see* CITY LIVERY COMPANIES.

Maudsley Hospital *Denmark Hill, SE5*. Founded by Dr Henry Maudsley, a Yorkshireman, the Professor of Medical Jurisprudence at UNIVERSITY COLLEGE HOSPITAL, who offered the LONDON COUNTY COUNCIL £30,000 for the building of a psychiatric hospital on condition that it should deal with early and acute cases, and have an outpatients' department and teaching and research facilities. At a cost of £250,000, it was opened in 1916 and was immediately turned over to mentally damaged army personnel. Maudsley died in January 1918 before the building was vacated by the military. In 1924 the UNIVERSITY OF LONDON recognised the hospital as a medical school and following the 2nd World War the school became the Institute of Psychiatry, part of the British Postgraduate Medical Federation. In 1967 it moved to a new building in De Crespigny Park. It is the main centre in the UK for postgraduate psychiatric education and there are now nine professorial chairs. The hospital is linked with the BETHLEHEM ROYAL HOSPITAL now situated at Beckenham, Kent. For convenience they are known as the Joint Hospital.

Mayfair *W1*. Now denotes the large area bounded on the north by OXFORD STREET, on the east by REGENT STREET, on the south by PICCADILLY and on the west by PARK LANE. It takes its name from the fair which was in 1686–8 transferred from the overcrowded HAYMARKET to Great Brookfield (now the site of CURZON STREET and SHEPHERD MARKET) and which until its suppression in the mid-18th century was held here every year from 1 May for 15 days.

Building began in the 1660s at the south-east corner, near the modern PICCADILLY CIRCUS, and at first advanced westward along the north side of PICCADILLY. But it very soon fanned out northward and by the mid-18th century almost the whole of modern Mayfair had been covered with houses, most of them situated on six great estates – the BURLINGTON, MILLFIELD (*see* HANOVER SQUARE), Conduit Mead (*see* CONDUIT STREET), Albemarle Ground (*see* ALBEMARLE STREET), the Berkeley (*see* BERKELEY SQUARE), the Curzon (*see* CURZON STREET), and by far the largest, the GROS-VENOR, this last being the only one still surviving intact and still in the possession of the descendants of its original developers.

This colossal expansion of the built-up area shifted the centre of gravity of aristocratic London westward from hitherto fashionable COVENT GARDEN and SOHO. But unlike these two already declining areas, Mayfair has always retained its social *cachet*, and even today a good address there is as much sought after as ever. Much of this success was originally due to Mayfair's favourable topographical situation (near the Court of ST JAMES'S (PALACE) and the royal parks) and to the good layout plans provided by the ground landlords. There was a handsome church (ST GEORGE'S), three great SQUARES (HANOVER, BERKELEY and GROSVENOR), and scores of wide straight streets, all interspersed with a dozen or so noblemen's palaces (e.g. BURLINGTON HOUSE, DEVONSHIRE HOUSE and CHESTERFIELD HOUSE). Most of the houses originally had plain brick fronts with three storeys and a basement, and although almost all of them have been very greatly altered by the addition of porticos, stucco facings, window dressings and extra storeys, basically original houses still survive in large numbers. Much of Mayfair, in fact, still has a well-bred Georgian air about it, as can best be seen in little-changed CHESTERFIELD STREET.

There were always other aspects of Mayfair, however, for the residents of the *beau monde* required numerous services close at hand. First, there were the mews which lay between the great streets, and which were originally lined with stables and coach houses and occupied by armies of grooms and coachmen (the other army of domestic servants lived in, either in the

Mayfair, a popular fair of the 18th century, was suppressed in 1764 after complaints from rich local residents.

basements or attics). Many of these mews have in modern times been widened at their entrances, and the stables converted into garages, offices or 'bijou' residences; while in others (e.g. BOURDON STREET and Brown Hart Gardens), blocks of artisans' dwellings contain relatively inexpensive accommodation for the providers of the services still required by the occupants in the great boulevards. Second, there has always been an important commercial presence in Mayfair. Originally this chiefly took the form of small shops for food, fashionable clothing and expensive furnishings and upholstery, the main centres being BOND STREET, MOUNT STREET and SHEPHERD MARKET. But with the passage of time commerce of a much more sophisticated and varied nature has gradually percolated into most parts of Mayfair, particularly the eastern parts, where it is now virtually universal. After the 1st World War domestic servants were less cheap and less plentiful, the great houses became more expensive to service, and although some of them were taken over as foreign embassies, even the richest resident of all, the 2nd Duke of Westminster, found it necessary to abandon GROSVENOR HOUSE to the demolition contractors in favour of something very much smaller (BOURDON HOUSE).

After the 2nd World War this process repeated itself for much the same reasons; but now there was also an acute shortage of office accommodation in London, due to the destruction of large parts of the CITY by bombing. The commercial invasion acquired irresistible momentum. Headquarters for hundreds of famous and not-so-famous firms were established in Mayfair, and banks, advertising and public relations consultants, salesmen of expensive motor cars, travel agencies and airline offices all made their presence conspicuous, either in brand-new blocks or in expensively adapted Georgian houses. Equally conspicuous were the new, smart international hotels which sprang up, chiefly in PARK LANE and GROSVENOR SQUARE.

Mayfair Hotel *Berkeley Street, W1.* When DEVONSHIRE HOUSE was pulled down for redevelopment in

1924–6, this hotel of redbrick with stone facing was built in 1927 in the long gardens which led back to Lansdowne Row. There are a night club, theatre (*see* MAYFAIR THEATRE) and cinema in the building. In 1982 there were 410 bedrooms.

Mayfair Place *W1.* Laid out after the demolition of DEVONSHIRE HOUSE in 1924 upon the site of the garden. It extends from STRATTON STREET to BERKELEY STREET.

Mayfair Theatre *Stratton Street, W1.* Designed by George Beech in 1963 as part of the MAYFAIR HOTEL. It opened with Pirandello's comedy *Six Characters in Search of an Author* which had 295 performances. Since then it has housed the revue *Beyond the Fringe* (1964–6). The seating capacity is 310.

Mayflower *117 Rotherhithe High Street, SE16.* Built about 1550 when it was known as the Shippe. Captain Christopher Jones, master of the *Mayflower*, moored his ship nearby before sailing for America. In 1621 the ship returned. Captain Jones died in ROTHERHITHE, where he was buried in the nearby churchyard of ST MARY'S. The inn was rebuilt in the 18th century and renamed the Spread Eagle and Crown, which it remained until about 20 years ago when it became the Mayflower in honour of the Pilgrims' ship. It is a genuine 17th-century inn, with exposed beams and open fireplaces, and is said to incorporate parts of the *Mayflower* within its structure. It is one of the few inns licensed to sell postage stamps, and in view of the close connection with America, it also has permission to sell American postage stamps. A model of the *Mayflower* hangs outside the entrance. There is a also a milestone to inform the passer-by that it is 2 miles to LONDON BRIDGE.

Mayor of Garratt Garratt (commemorated by Garratt Lane, SW17 and SW18) was a small hamlet between WANDSWORTH and TOOTING. Some of its

The procession of supporters in the mock election of the Mayor of Garratt passing the Leather Bottle Inn in 1782.

inhabitants formed a society to prevent enclosures on the surrounding Common. The society's chairman became known as the Mayor of Garratt. When the common land was released, the custom of electing a Mayor continued and the election became a famous local festival which was attended by as many as 100,000 people. The hustings were erected at Garratt Green near the Leather Bottle which still stands at 538 Garratt Lane, SW17. The candidates were London characters well known for their eccentricity, wit or physical deformities. The Mayor elected at the first recorded election in 1747 was a WANDSWORTH Waterman who stood as Squire Blow-me-down; the last recognised Mayor, elected in 1796, was a muffin-seller who offered himself as Emperor Anti-Napoleon. Samuel Foote, who wrote some of the speeches delivered at these rowdy elections, was the author of *The Mayor of Garratt*, a comedy performed at the HAYMARKET THEATRE in 1763.

Maypole in the Strand Erected in the 16th century on the green outside ST MARY LE STRAND. It was destroyed in 1644 but another, 134 ft high, was put up in its place after the Restoration of 1660 'at which the little children did much rejoice and the ancient people did clap their hands, saying golden days begin to appear.' This, having decayed, was replaced in 1713 and removed five years later when bought by Sir Isaac Newton for a friend in WANSTEAD where it was erected in the park to support what was then the highest telescope in Europe.

MCC *see* MARYLEBONE CRICKET CLUB.

McDonald's Music Hall *High Street, Hoxton*. Opened in 1864 under the management of James Mortimer. Although no larger than the usual long room in those public houses which provided entertainment, it was assembled, rather than built, as a musical hall. As with similar places of entertainment at that time, the basic items of construction, including pillars and roofing, were readily obtained from builders' merchants and put together cheaply. The type of entertainment was in keeping with the building. The management passed in 1866 to James MacDonald Jnr. The hall closed in 1871 and remained empty until 1890 when it was taken over as a Quaker meeting-house, and renamed Hoxton Hall. It is now a Community Centre providing varied entertainment.

Meard Street *W1*. Built in two stages in 1722–32 by John Meard, the carpenter who, in 1718, had put up the spire of ST ANNE'S CHURCH. A row of the later houses, marked by a plaque inscribed 'Meards Street 1732', still survives. In 1824 a congregation of Particular Baptists built Salem Chapel behind No. 8. This was demolished in 1907 and replaced by a garage. In the early 1740s Batty Langley, the architectural writer, occupied No. 9 where with his brother, Thomas, he carried on business as a surveyor and designer of buildings and gardens. He advertised that he made 'Designs for Buildings, Gardens, Parks, etc. in the most grand taste'. He also manufactured an artificial stone which was used for making statues, busts and architectural ornaments. In the same house Elizabeth Flint, whom Samuel Johnson found so entertaining, had lodgings in 1758. She was 'generally slut and drunkard, occasionally whore and thief. She

had, however, genteel lodgings . . . and a boy that walked before her chair. Poor Bet was taken up on a charge of stealing a counterpane, and tried at the Old Bailey. The Chief Justice [John Willes], who loved a wench, summed up favourably and she was acquitted.' After which Bet said, with a 'gay and satisfied air, "Now that the counterpane is *my own*, I shall make a petticoat of it." . . . She got a harpsichord, but Bet could not play; however, she put herself in fine attitudes and drummed. . . . When she found herself obliged to go to jail, she ordered a sedan chair, and bid her foot boy walk before her.'

Mecklenburgh Square *WC1*. Named in honour of Queen Charlotte, formerly Princess of Mecklenburg-Strelitz. It was planned by Samuel Pepys Cockerell to face BRUNSWICK SQUARE on part of the grounds of the FOUNDLING HOSPITAL. Cockerell quarrelled with the Governors of the hospital and was dismissed. Later the differences were overcome and his pupil, Joseph Kay, designed the buildings and the gardens, with Cockerell as honorary consultant. There was extensive damage in the 2nd World War. R.H. Tawney, the historian, lived at No. 21.

Medicine in London London has long had a unique status as a medical centre, particularly since its early position as chief commercial centre, capital and seat of king and court was firmly established. In Anglo-Saxon times, some Graeco-Roman medical elements, folk ideas, herbal lore, superstitions and religious beliefs were mingled in the early vernacular Leech Books of the 9th century. Leeches (from the Anglo-Saxon word for 'medical practitioners') were sometimes clergymen, sometimes laymen. Monastic infirmaries also provided medical care. The more general 'hospitals' from the 12th century had religious origins and broad charitable functions, three of them eventually acquiring more specialised medical and psychiatric relevance: ST BARTHOLOMEW'S HOSPITAL, ST THOMAS'S HOSPITAL and BETHLEHEM ROYAL HOSPITAL. After the DISSOLUTION OF THE MONASTERIES these institutions came under the aegis of the CITY OF LONDON. In addition, these were some leprosaria, for example ST GILES, HOLBORN; small plague hospitals and other medical institutions.

Official medical groups emerged during the Middle Ages. Twelfth-century church prohibitions against clergymen shedding blood encouraged the separation of surgeons and medical practitioners. From the 13th century Oxford and Cambridge produced some physicians with medical degrees, whereas from 1324 an élite Fellowship of Surgeons dominated surgical practices. The Barbers, a guild from 1308, became a CITY LIVERY COMPANY in 1462. In addition to barbery, its members let blood, pulled teeth and performed minor surgery. The Fellowship and Company were amalgamated into the Barber-Surgeons' Company in 1540. Apothecaries sold drugs and other commodities; they were associated with the Spicers, Pepperers and Grocers before receiving a separate charter as the Society of Apothecaries, largely through the efforts of Gideon Delaune. The Society's present building near BLACKFRIARS was built after the GREAT FIRE. Apothecaries treated patients in addition to selling drugs and thus came into conflict with the physicians who, according to an Ecclesiastical Act of 1551, were entitled, under the BISHOP OF LONDON or Dean of

ST PAUL'S, to examine medical practitioners in, and for 7 miles around, London. The Charter of the ROYAL COLLEGE OF PHYSICIANS OF LONDON confirmed and extended these privileges but the efforts of its founder, Thomas Linacre, John Caius and other Tudor physicians failed to turn the College into a liberal, reforming force; and until at least the 17th century it was more concerned with guarding privileges than raising standards. Before the GREAT FIRE, its buildings were located at Amen Corner, near ST PAUL'S. Afterwards, the College stood in WARWICK LANE.

In the period between the BLACK DEATH and the GREAT PLAGUE, plague was the most important and socially disruptive disease of Londoners. More than 150,000 of them perished from plague epidemics between 1624 and 1665 alone. Flight to the comparatively safe countryside was the best preventative but most, especially the poor, had to remain in London where public policy dictated locking up the sick and well together in houses where plague had struck. When plague epidemics threatened, the ROYAL COLLEGE OF PHYSICIANS would publish instructions and prescriptions; many doctors then fled, leaving medical care with officially appointed plague physicians and the remaining surgeons and apothecaries. One of the doctors during the GREAT PLAGUE, Nathaniel Hodges, attributed his preservation during that awful year to his consumption of large quantities of sack, a Spanish wine much beloved by Shakespeare's Sir John Falstaff. Plague victims were buried at night in large plague pits, situated under the present site of LIVERPOOL STREET STATION, in STEPNEY, SOUTHWARK and elsewhere. Plague increased awareness of public health and lay behind the London BILLS OF MORTALITY. Plague and other acute diseases such as fevers and smallpox were described by London doctors such as Thomas Sydenham. Plague disappeared in London after 1665, but fevers, smallpox and phthisis (tuberculosis) were major health hazards throughout the 18th century, which also witnessed much medical activity in London. The voluntary hospital movement (known as such because individuals volunteered annual subscriptions to support the hospitals) began with the foundation of WESTMINSTER HOSPITAL (1719), and by 1750 four other general hospitals had been established in London: GUY'S HOSPITAL, 1725; ST GEORGE'S HOSPITAL, 1733; the LONDON HOSPITAL, 1740; the MIDDLESEX HOSPITAL, 1745. Appointment as physician or surgeon to one of these institutions conferred prestige and the opportunity to increase private practice among the hospital's governors and their families. Surgeons and sometimes physicians used hospital patients in training medical students and apprentices. From the middle of the century smaller specialised hospitals were started, largely for groups (such as pregnant women and those with smallpox or venereal disease) who were denied admission to the general hospitals. St Luke's Hospital (1751) provided additional psychiatric facilities to BEDLAM; private madhouses also catered for both pauper and well-to-do lunatics.

Private initiative also developed medical education, particularly anatomy teaching. William Hunter began his anatomy lectures and dissections in 1745; his school, finally situated in purpose-built accommodation in GREAT WINDMILL STREET, survived till the 1830s and eventually offered instruction in most medical subjects. His younger brother, John Hunter,

taught many surgical students at his house in LEICESTER SQUARE and at ST GEORGE'S HOSPITAL and many other entrepreneurs (mostly former students of the Hunters) started private medical and anatomy schools. These were frequently located near hospitals (and often staffed by hospital doctors), but from the early 19th century, when the hospitals recognised the advantages of having their own medical schools, the private schools could no longer compete. Professional communication among physicians, surgeons and apothecaries was encouraged by organisations like the Medical Society of London.

The 1815 the Apothecaries Act consolidated London's medical educational status, for the Act required all would-be apothecaries throughout England and Wales to register with the SOCIETY OF APOTHECARIES, to take formal courses in medical subjects and pass an examination set by the Society. By the 1830s more than 400 students per year sat the exam. Many found it useful also to become members of the ROYAL COLLEGE OF SURGEONS, this dual qualification – Licentiate of the SOCIETY OF APOTHECARIES and Member of the ROYAL COLLEGE OF SURGEONS: LSA, MRCS – becoming the hallmark of the surgeon-apothecary or 'general practitioner', a phrase increasingly used from the 1830s and championed by Thomas Wakley, founder of the influential weekly, *The Lancet* (1823). From 1840, the forerunner of what became the *British Medical Journal* was also published in London.

A second wave of general hospitals was founded in the early 19th century: (CHARING CROSS HOSPITAL, the ROYAL FREE, UNIVERSITY COLLEGE HOSPITAL, and KING'S COLLEGE HOSPITAL), and the importance of a hospital affiliation for the most successful medical or surgical career encouraged doctors to start additional specialised hospitals, such as those for chest, skin or nervous diseases or the diseases of children. Medical men were also active in the increasingly vocal demands for public health legislation. By the 1830s it was apparent to many that London, like other British cities, had appalling sanitary arrangements. The great CHOLERA epidemics heightened public concern and in 1848 a General Board of Health was established with Edwin Chadwick among its members. In the same year, John Simon, a London surgeon, was appointed Medical Officer of Health to the CITY OF LONDON. Between them, they dominated the public health movement from the 1840s to the 1870s, the 1875 Public Health Act consolidating and extending much previous legislation on housing and sanitation, noxious trades and factory conditions. The importance of clean water had been documented by John Snow during the 1848–54 CHOLERA epidemics, both with a local outbreak in SOHO caused by a contaminated water well in Broad Street, and with systematic surveys of houses supplied by two independent water companies, one drawing water from the THAMES downstream, after the sewage had been dumped in it, the other upstream. Cities like London continued to have higher mortality rates than rural areas until late Victorian times.

The concentration in London of hospitals, specialty medical services, medical corporations such as the ROYAL COLLEGE OF PHYSICIANS, and famous consultant physicians and surgeons, such as those clustered in HARLEY STREET, has insured the continued London dominance of British medical education and medical care. HARLEY STREET has survived the creation of the National Health Service (1948); and London hospital medicine within the NHS has meant that 50 per cent of British doctors still have some of their training in the metropolis.

Melbury Road *W14.* On the ILCHESTER ESTATE, it takes its name (1875) from the Dorset home of the Earls of Ilchester. G.F. Watts lived at Little Holland House with Mr and Mrs Thoby Prinsep for several years. When this house was demolished, Watts built another, also known as Little Holland House, at No. 6 (now the site of Kingfisher House). Here he made his *Physical Energy*, a copy of which is in KENSINGTON GARDENS. The painter Luke Fildes lived at No. 11 (now No. 31) which was designed by Norman Shaw. A fellow-painter, and one who also illustrated Dickens's later work, Marcus Stone, lived at No. 8, another of Norman Shaw's works. Sir William Hamo Thornycroft, the sculptor, lived at No. 2 and Holman Hunt at No. 18. No. 9 (now No. 29) was designed as 'a model residence of the 15th century' by William Burges.

In 1876–81 William Burges built the Tower House in Melbury Road for occupation by himself. From a drawing by Morris Adams.

Melcombe Place *NW1.* On the PORTMAN ESTATE, it takes its name from Melcombe in Dorset where the Portmans owned land. E.M. Forster, the novelist, was born at No. 6 in 1879.

MEMORIALS (See also STATUES.)
Afghan and Zulu War Memorial *Woolwich, SE18.* Granite blocks with bronze trophies of Zulu arms and Afghan weapons by Count Gleichen (1882).
Queen Alexandra *Marlborough Gate, SW1.* One of Sir Alfred Gilbert's last works, this bronze was unveiled in 1932 by the Queen's son, George V. Behind the memorial, which includes a number of bronze allegorical figures on a red granite plinth, is a bronze screen with lamps in the top corners, and below is a fountain.
Army Ordnance Corps *Corner of Francis Street and Artillery Place, SW1.* Memorial to members of the AOC killed in the Boer War, designed by C.M. Jordan (1905). A bronze figure in AOC uniform by F.

Coomans surmounts a granite pedestal from which springs a fountain.
Artemis *Rotten Row, Hyde Park, SW1.* Figure of the Greek goddess, twin sister of Apollo, by Feodora Gleichen (1906).
Belgian War Memorial *Victoria Embankment, WC2 (almost opposite* CLEOPATRA'S NEEDLE). Bronze group by Victor Rousseau of women accompanied by a boy and girl carrying garlands, the setting designed by Sir Reginald Blomfield. Erected in gratitude by those Belgians who spent the 1st World War in Britain.
Braidwood Memorial *33 Tooley Street, SE1.* Marble memorial by S.H. Gardner (1862) at the corner of Hay's Lane to the Superintendent of the LONDON FIRE BRIGADE.
Burghers of Calais *Victoria Tower Gardens, SW1.* Cast of Rodin's group which was set up in the Place Richelieu at Calais in 1895, commemorating the heroism of the six burghers of Calais at the surrender of the town to Edward III in 1347. This cast was placed here in 1915.
Burton Monument *Roman Catholic Cemetery, North Worple Way, SW14.* Although Sir Richard Burton, explorer and translator of the *Arabian Nights*, had no direct connection with MORTLAKE, his body was brought here for burial by his widow, *née* Isabel Arundell, as it was then one of the few Roman Catholic CEMETERIES near London. She took up residence at 65 North Worple Way and supervised the erection of their mausoleum in the bizarre form of a concrete Arab tent with a crucifix above the door. This has recently been restored and the interior may be viewed through a window at the rear. A large collection of Burton memorabilia is on permanent display at the Branch Library in Sheen Lane.
Buxton Memorial Fountain *Victoria Tower Gardens, SW1.* Gothic drinking fountain designed by S.S. Teulon commemorating Sir Thomas Fowell Buxton, leader of the Anti-Slavery Party. It was erected by his son, Charles, in 1865 and stood until 1957 at the northwest corner of PARLIAMENT SQUARE. The eight bronze statuettes of British rulers from Caractacus to Queen Victoria originally around the monument were stolen in 1960 and have been replaced in fibreglass.
Cadiz Memorial *Horse Guards Parade, SW1.* A French mortar mounted on a cast-iron Chinese dragon. The inscription reads, 'To commemorate the raising of the siege of Cadiz in consequence of the glorious victory gained by the Duke of Wellington over the French near Salamanca, 22 July 1812. This mortar cast for the destruction of the great fort, with powers surpassing all others, and abandoned by the besiegers on their retreat, was presented as a token of respect and gratitude by the Spanish nation to HRH Prince Regent.' Known to his contemporaries as the Regent's Bomb (then pronounced bum), it became a favourite subject for caricaturists and is depicted on numerous irreverent prints, often in conjunction with the Regent's then mistress, Lady Hertford.
Carabiniers Memorial *Chelsea Embankment, SW3 (opposite* CHELSEA BRIDGE). Bronze plaque on a redbrick surround by Adrian Jones. The relief depicts a mounted officer with horses and troopers, a memorial to the officers and men of the 6th Dragoon Guards, the Carabiniers, who fell in the Boer War.
Cavalry Memorial *Serpentine Road, Hyde Park, W1.* Originally erected at STANHOPE GATE in 1924, the memorial was moved to its present site when

The Cadiz Memorial, a captured French mortar, satirically known as the 'Regent's Bomb', in Horse Guards Parade in 1816.

PARK LANE was replanned in 1961. The bronze St George, mounted and brandishing his sword over the slain dragon, is by Adrian Jones, himself a cavalryman.

Chilianwalla Memorial *Royal Hospital Grounds, Chelsea, SW3.* Tall granite obelisk by Charles Cockerell, 'To the memory of 255 officers, non-commissioned officers and privates of the 24th regiment who fell at Chilianwalla, 13 January 1849.' Erected 1853.

Civil Service Rifles *Somerset House, Strand, EC2.* Stone column (1919) in memory of the 1,240 officers and men of the Prince of Wales's Own Civil Service Rifles who were killed in the 1st World War.

Crimean Memorial *Royal Artillery Barracks, Woolwich, SE18.* Bronze figure by John Bell (1860) of *Victory* standing on a high granite pedestal inscribed to the officers and men of the Royal Regiment of Artillery who fell during the war with Russia in the years 1854–6.

24th (East Surrey) Division *Battersea Park, SW11.* 1st World War memorial by Eric Kennington (1924). Group of three soldiers.

Eleanor Cross *Charing Cross Station Yard, SW1.* A very high stone and granite memorial designed by E.M. Barry and executed by Thomas Earp in 1863. On the death of Queen Eleanor, the wife of Edward I, her body was brought to London in 1290 to be buried in WESTMINSTER ABBEY. The king ordered 12 crosses to be erected to mark the resting places of the cortège, the last one at CHARING CROSS. The site of the original one, now lost, was in what is now TRAFALGAR SQUARE, then called Charing.

First Aid Nursing Yeomanry *St Paul Knights-*

bridge, SW1. Memorial on north wall to those 'Fannies' who died in the 2nd World War, 13 of them as agents in occupied Europe.

Guards *Horse Guards Road, SW1.* Bronze figures by Gilbert Ledward of soldiers of the five regiments of Foot Guards stand in front of the Portland stone cenotaph designed by H.C. Bradshaw (1926). The inscription reads, 'To the glory of God and in memory of the officers, warrant officers, non-commissioned officers and guardsmen of His Majesty's Regiment of Foot Guards who gave their lives for their King and country during the Great War, 1914–18 and of the officers and men of other units who, while serving with the Guards' Division, ... fell with them. ...' The figures were cast from German guns taken by the Guards.

Guards Crimea Memorial *Waterloo Place, SW1.* By John Bell (date unknown), it commemorates the 2,162 officers, non-commissioned officers and privates of the three (at that time) regiments of foot guards who fell in the Crimean War. On the south side, guarding the memorial, are statues of Florence Nightingale, shown as the 'lady with the lamp' (by Arthur Walker), and her associate and strong supporter Lord Sidney Herbert in peer's robes (by John Foley). On the sides of the bronze pedestals on which they stand are bronze reliefs depicting events in their careers. On the main pedestal, also of granite, are three large bronze figures of guardsmen wearing greatcoats and bearskins. A female figure, stretching out her arms and holding laurel wreaths, is on a stone block behind the soldiers. On either side of the memorial are shields inscribed Alma, Inkerman and Sebastopol, and representations of guns and mortars. There are also two elaborate lamp standards. Russian cannon taken at Sebastopol were melted down and used in components of the memorial.

Imperial Camel Corps *Victoria Embankment Gardens, SW1.* Small bronze by Cecil Brown (1920) of a soldier riding a camel.

Katyn *Gunnersbury Park, W3.* Black granite obelisk 'in remembrance of 14,500 Polish prisoners of war who disappeared in 1940 from camps at Kozielsk, Starobielsk and Ostaszkow of whom 4,500 were later identified in a mass grave at Katyn near Smolensk.' By Louis Fitzgibbon and Count Stefan Zamoysky, and erected after much controversy in 1976.

London Troops *Royal Exchange, EC2.* Memorial to London troops of the 1st and 2nd World Wars, designed by Sir Aston Webb with figures by Alfred Drury.

Machine Gun Corps *Hyde Park Corner, SW1.* Bronze nude figure of David holding a sword in the left hand with wreathed machine guns on either side. 'Erected to commemorate the glorious heroes of the Machine Gun Corps who fell in the Great War, 1914–19. "Saul hath slain his thousands, but David his tens of thousands."' By Francis Derwent Wood (1925).

Medical Officers *British Medical Association, Tavistock Square, WC1.* The iron gates commemorate medical officers who were killed in the 1st World War; those killed in the 2nd World War are commemorated by a fountain with statues by James Woodford (1954).

Mercantile Marine *Trinity Square, EC3.* A pavilion by Lutyens in a memorial garden designed by Maufe, to the memory of the 24,000 men of the Merchant Navy and fishing fleet who 'gave their lives for their country and have no grave but the sea'.

Norwegian Stones *Serpentine, Hyde Park, SW1.* An immense Pre-Cambrian granite rock standing on three smaller ones bearing the inscription: 'This stone was erected by the Royal Norwegian Navy and the Norwegian Merchant Fleet in the year 1978. We thank the British people for friendship and hospitality during the Second World War. You gave us a safe haven in our common struggle for freedom and peace.'

Polish Air Force *Corner of West End Road and Western Avenue, Northolt Aerodrome.* Bronze eagle on a stone base commemorating the Poles who were based at Northolt in the 2nd World War. By M. Lubelski (1948).

Protestant Martyrs *St Bartholomew's Hospital, EC1.* Granite plaque on the wall of the hospital to the martyrs burned near here in 1555–7.

Rangers *Chenies Street, WC1.* Memorial to the 2nd County of London Regiment. It has a bronze of the regiment's badge.

Rifle Brigade *Grosvenor Gardens, SW1.* Figures of three soldiers, one of the 1st World War on the central plinth, with two of the Napoleonic Wars (1800 and 1806), on either side. Inscribed: 'In memory of 11,575 officers, warrant officers and riflemen who fell in the Great War, 1914–18, and in memory of 1329 . . . who fell in the World War, 1939–45.' Bronze by John Tweed (1924).

Rima *Hyde Park.* Memorial, fittingly on the bird sanctuary, to the naturalist W.H. Hudson. The stone monument by Lionel Pearson stands behind a little rectangular pool, and forms the setting for Epstein's relief of *Rima*, a character from Hudson's *Green Mansions*. The sculpture caused a furore in 1925 when it was unveiled, as it was considered obscene.

Royal Air Force *Victoria Embankment, SW1 (opposite former Air Ministry, now Ministry of Defence).* Memorial to the officers and men of the Royal Naval Air Squadron, the Royal Flying Corps and the Royal Air Force who were killed in the two World Wars. A gold eagle surmounts a stone plinth. Designed by Reginald Blomfield and executed by W. Reid Dick 1923, with later inscription.

Royal Artillery *The Mall, SW1 (near Admiralty Arch).* 'Erected by the officers and men of the Royal Artillery in memory of their honoured dead, South Africa, 1899–1902.' Surmounted by a female figure of Peace and a winged horse, with friezes representing horse artillery on the plinth. By W.R. Colton (1910).

Royal Field Artillery *Woolwich Common, SE18.* Obelisk of red granite commemorating the non-commissioned officers and men of the 61st Battery who fell in the Boer War (1903).

Royal Fusiliers *Holborn, WC1 (bottom of Gray's Inn Road).* By Alfred Toft (1924). A soldier, modelled on a sergeant of the regiment, carries a rifle and bayonet.

Royal Marines *The Mall, SW1.* Bronze figures by Adrian Jones of two marines, one wounded, in fighting attitudes. A memorial to those who fell in South Africa and China in 1899–1900. Bronze reliefs by Sir Thomas Graham Jackson depict battles in the two campaigns.

Royal Regiment of Artillery *Hyde Park Corner, W1.* Large Portland stone plinth surmounted by stone field gun and decorated with bas-reliefs of gunners in action. On the south, east and west sides are over-lifesize bronze figures of gunners, and on the north a bronze effigy of a dead soldier beneath which is 'the roll of honour of those whose memory is perpetuated by this memorial'. The inscription reads: 'In proud remembrance of the 49,076 of all ranks in the Royal Regiment of Artillery who gave their lives for King and Country in the Great War 1914–1919'. The sculptor was C. Sargeant Jagger, the base by Lionel Pearson.

Lady Henry Somerset *Victoria Embankment Gardens, SW1.* Bronze statue (1897) of a young girl holding a bowl, which also served as a bird bath, commemorates the social reformer. The bronze was stolen in 1970 and all that remains is the girl's sawn-off feet.

John Hanning Speke *Kensington Gardens, W2.* Polished granite obelisk erected to the explorer in 1866 and inscribed: 'In memory of Speke. Victoria, Nyanza and the Nile, 1864.'

Submariners *Victoria Embankment, SW1.* 'Erected to the memory of the officers and men of the British Navy who lost their lives serving in submarines in 1914–18 and 1939–45.' Bronze relief of submarines, being dragged down by menacing spirits, are flanked by figures of Truth and Justice. By F. Brook Hatch and A.H. Ryan (1922), with alterations to include the dead of the 2nd World War.

Trade Unionists *TUC, 23–28 Great Russell Street, WC1.* Epstein's figure of a man protectively holding a corpse was carved from a 10-ton block of stone. It stands in the courtyard.

Victoria Cross *Old St George's, Woolwich, SE18.* Dedicated to the memory of 'all ranks of the Royal, and late Indian Artillery who won the Victoria Cross' (1920).

Robert Waithman *Salisbury Square, EC4.* The granite obelisk with a gilt top is a memorial to the man who was Lord Mayor in 1823–4.

William Wallace *St Bartholomew's Hospital, EC1.* Tablet on the wall of the hospital to the Scottish patriot who was hanged, drawn and quartered near here in 1305 after his conviction at WESTMINSTER HALL. Erected 1956.

Westminster School *Broad Sanctuary, SW1.* Tall red granite column, designed by Sir George Gilbert Scott (1859–61), and surmounted by a statue of St George killing the dragon. It is inscribed at the base: 'To the memory of those educated at Westminster School who died in the Russian and Indian Wars AD 1854–1859.' These included Field-Marshal Lord Raglan, General Sir Henry William Barnard and Lieutenant General Frederick Markham. The lions at the base are by J.B. Philip. The stone statues higher up are of Edward the Confessor, Henry III (facing the Abbey), Elizabeth I (facing WESTMISTER SCHOOL) and Queen Victoria (facing down VICTORIA STREET). They are by J.R. Clayton (1861).

Yalta *Thurloe Place, SW7.* Memorial to those Russians and their dependants who were forcibly returned to the USSR after the 2nd World War and were for the most part executed there. The symbolic design of a sphere kept in perpetual motion by jets of water is by Angela Connor (1981). The inscription reads: 'This monument was placed here by members of Parliament of all parties and others to commemorate the thousands of innocent men, women and children from the Soviet Union and other Eastern European states who were imprisoned and died at the hands of Communist governments after their repatriation at the conclusion of the Second World War.'

(*See also* ALBERT MEMORIAL, CENOTAPH, CLEOPATRA'S NEEDLE, EROS, DUKE OF YORK COLUMN, MONUMENT, NELSON COLUMN *and* QUEEN VICTORIA MEMORIAL.)

Mercers' Hall *Becket House, Ironmonger Lane, EC2.* In medieval times the Mercers lived and worked in the Mercery, the district in CHEAPSIDE between FRIDAY STREET and ST MARY-LE-BOW. By 1347 they had acquired a meeting place in the HOSPITAL OF ST THOMAS OF ACON in CHEAPSIDE. The hospital had been founded by the sister of St Thomas Becket on the site of his birthplace. By coincidence, Thomas's father, Gilbert Becket, was a Mercer. In 1517 the Company bought the CHEAPSIDE frontage from the hospital and built there a 'Rightly good chapel' with a hall over it, at a cost of £5,000. At the DISSOLUTION the hospital was disbanded, and in 1542 the Company bought the rest of the buildings for £969. These buildings were destroyed in the GREAT FIRE. The Hall was rebuilt in 1672–82 by John Oliver who used plans drawn up by Edward Jarman before his death. The BANK OF ENGLAND rented the Hall in 1694 as their first place of business. The East India Company used the Hall as their Head Office in 1702. A new façade was added on the CHEAPSIDE front in 1879. The old façade is now part of Swanage Town Hall. The Hall was bombed in May 1941. The Hall and Chapel (which is the only one in a Livery Hall) were rebuilt in 1954–8 as part of an office block by E. Noel Clifton of Gunton and Gunton, with Sir Albert Richardson as consultant. The Chapel and Hall incorporated fittings from the old Hall, including some 17th-century woodwork and Victorian stained glass. During excavations a 16th-century figure of Christ was discovered buried in soft earth, 2 feet below ground. The mahogany-panelled Large Court Room and Dining Room contain carvings attributed to Grinling Gibbons. The suite has a series of English crystal 18th- and 19th-century chandeliers. Inside the Hall is a 1546 portrait of Sir Thomas Gresham and the recumbent effigy of Richard Fishborne. The dining capacity of the Hall is 150. For the Company *see* CITY LIVERY COMPANIES.

Mercers' School In 1541 the MERCERS' COMPANY bought property in OLD JEWRY, including two churches and the HOSPITAL OF ST THOMAS OF ACON with which the MERCERS were closely connected, on condition that the Company should maintain a school for 25 poor boys. It is said that a grammar school had existed there since 1447, making it one of London's oldest schools. Fee-paying students were admitted from the late 16th century to supplement the Company's funds, but fees were always relatively low. The school declined in the 18th century due to erratic administration. In 1804 the Company overhauled the syllabus and finances. The school then flourished by providing a commercial education for the professional and middle classes. In 1894, following several moves after the original premises had been destroyed in the GREAT FIRE, the school settled in BARNARD'S INN a building designed by T. Chatfield Clarke for 300 boys. There was little room for expansion, and this, together with the financial problems that arose from the lack of an endowed trust scheme, led to the school's closure in 1959.

Merchant Taylors' Company *see* CITY LIVERY COMPANIES.

Merchant Taylors' School *Sandy Lodge, Northwood, Middlesex.* The Master, Richard Hilles, Wardens and Court of Assistants of the MERCHANT TAYLORS' COMPANY founded the school in 1561. It was situated in Suffolk Lane in the CITY until 1875, when it moved to CHARTERHOUSE SQUARE for 60 years before the need for space led to the move to Sandy Lodge, standing on a site of 256 acres. Since the earliest times there has been a close connection with St John's College, Oxford, as its founder, Sir Thomas White, was a member of the Company and a close friend of Richard Hilles. The library, founded in 1662 by the headmaster, John Goad, boasts a considerable number of fine old books and first editions. It is an independent school with about 60 boarders and about 600 day boys, most of whom enter at 13, although a few

Mercers' Hall, originally built in 1517, became in 1694 the first place of business of the Bank of England.

start at 11 from state schools, including some grant-assisted pupils. Notable old boys include the poet Edmund Spenser; Titus Oates, who was expelled; Gilbert Murray; Sir James Jeans; the artist Samuel Palmer; and Dr F.D. Coggan, the former Archbishop of Canterbury.

Merlin's Mechanical Museum *11 Princes Street, Hanover Square*. A celebrated collection of ingenious mechanical devices or 'scientific toys', as Horace Walpole described them, invented by John Joseph Merlin, assistant to James Cox (*see* COX's MUSEUM), established in PRINCES STREET in the 1770s. Merlin contrived all manner of mechanical novelties from barrel organ-harpsichords to gambling machines. After his death in 1803 the museum closed in 1808.

Mermaid Tavern *29–30 Bread Street*. The earliest-known reference is one of 1411. The inn stood on the west side of the street opposite ST MILDRED's CHURCH. The FISHMONGERS' COMPANY owned it. It was famous as the meeting place of the Friday Street Club (sometimes known as the Mermaid Club) founded by Sir Walter Ralegh. Members included Shakespeare, Donne, Beaumont, Fletcher and Jonson. Beaumont wrote:

What things have we seen
Done at the Mermaid! heard words that have been
So nimble, and so full of subtle flame,
As if that every one from whence they came
Had meant to put his whole wit in a jest,
And had resolv'd to live a fool the rest
Of his dull life . . . .

Keats also wrote *Lines on the Mermaid Tavern*:

Souls of poets dead and gone
What Elysium have ye known,
Happy field or mossy cavern
Choicer than the Mermaid Tavern?

The tavern was destroyed in the GREAT FIRE.

Mermaid Theatre *Puddle Dock, Upper Thames Street, EC4*. Began as a private theatre in 1951 in the house of Bernard Miles and his wife, Josephine Wilson, in ST JOHN's WOOD. The Elizabethan stage was designed by Michael Stringer and C.W. Hodges. In 1953, as part of the coronation festivities, it was erected at the ROYAL EXCHANGE and had such a good reception that on October 1956 the CITY CORPORATION granted 'Bernard Miles and other poor players of London' a lease of a blitzed Victorian warehouse at PUDDLE DOCK for a peppercorn rent. In 1957–9 it was converted by Devereux and Davies into a permanent theatre. The 6 ft-thick Victorian walls and cast-iron pillars at the entrance were retained. On 28 May 1959 the first new theatre in the CITY for 300 years was opened by the LORD MAYOR.

The Mermaid opened with *Lock Up Your Daughters*, adapted by Bernard Miles from Henry Fielding's *Rape upon Rape*. It has since staged many revivals and new plays.

Merton *SW19, SW20*. First mentioned by name in 967 and since it is likely that this area was part of King Harold's holding immediately before the Conquest, it is not surprising that at the *Domesday* survey the Manor was held by King William I. In the Middle Ages Merton was known for its large Augustinian priory, founded in 1114. The Statute of Merton (the earliest on record) was enacted here in 1236. Thomas Beckett was educated at Merton, as also was Walter de Merton, Chief Justice of England and founder of Merton College, Oxford. At the DISSOLUTION the Priory was demolished and the stones were used by Henry VIII to build NONSUCH PALACE, CHEAM. Only the Chapter House foundations remain visible in Station Road, in an area erroneously called Merton Abbey, for the house was never more than a priory. Since the arrival of the Huguenots in the 16th century, calico bleaching and printing has taken place nearby on the banks of the WANDLE and William Morris's workshop (destroyed in the 1940s) and LIBERTY's print works were also located here. The latter firm's 'colour house' of 1742 still survives.

To the south of Merton High Street stood Merton Place, built in 1699 and the only home ever owned by Lord Nelson, who lived here with Sir William and Lady Hamilton in 1801–5. The house was sold soon after Lord Nelson's death and was demolished in about 1823. The names of the local side streets commemorate Nelson's connection with this area. The parish church of ST MARY dates from the 12th century and lies further west in what is now called Merton Park. This was farm land until purchased in 1867 by John Innes, a successful City businessman. He laid out the fields with splendid avenues of trees and holly hedges and, between 1871 and his death in 1904, built the interestingly varied houses which are a distinctive feature of this district. The John Innes Horticultural Institute was established under his will and existed on the site of the present Rutlish School until it was moved in 1953. Merton Park claims to be the forerunner of the Garden Suburbs. At the arrival of the UNDERGROUND in 1926 the estate was extended towards Morden Station.

Metropolitan Board of Works Established in 1855 by the Metropolis Management Act, this was the first metropolitan-wide local authority for London. Its jurisdiction extended over the whole of the metropolitan area as defined by the Registrar General, an area which with minor variations was later to form the County of London. Under the Act the parish vestries were reconstituted as elected bodies, the 23 largest remaining as separate authorities and the smaller parishes uniting to elect 15 district boards. These 38 units of local administration, plus the COURT OF COMMON COUNCIL, in turn chose the members to sit on the Board of Works. There were originally 45 such members, some of the larger parishes having two representatives and the Common Council three. The disadvantages that it was not directly elected and was only given limited powers initially in order to placate the powerful vestries, prevented the Board from becoming a respected or efficient unit of local government. The butt of continual criticism, it was eventually superseded by the LONDON COUNTY COUNCIL in 1889, and the date of its demise was actually brought forward amid accusations of corruption. Nevertheless, despite its shortcomings, the Board's achievements should not be underrated. It undertook the vast main drainage system of London, which was one of the engineering wonders of the 19th century and involved the construction of huge intercepting sewers to carry sewage and surface water to outfall works at Barking Creek and Crossness at ERITH. The VICTORIA, ALBERT and CHELSEA EMBANKMENTS were formed by the Board and several new streets were made including SOUTHWARK STREET, NORTHUMBERLAND AVENUE, CHARING CROSS ROAD and SHAFTESBURY AVENUE. The acquisition of HAMPSTEAD HEATH as a lung for Londoners was another notable triumph even if it was not achieved without much characteristic bickering and delay. Fittingly, perhaps, the person best remembered in connection with the Board was not an administrator, but its chief engineer, Sir Joseph Bazalgette.

Metropolitan Cattle Market *and* **Caledonian Market** After 50 years of struggle the live cattle market was moved from SMITHFIELD to Copenhagen Fields ISLINGTON in 1855. The entrepreneur John Perkin had invested large sums in building a well-equipped marketplace away from the centre of London. After much opposition the 30-acre site was purchased by the CITY OF LONDON CORPORATION and the market opened by Prince Albert. Livestock were sold on Mondays and Thursdays, and on Fridays, among the empty pens, there grew up a general market which became known as the Caledonian because it was adjacent to Caledonian Road, the route used by cattle drovers on their way to Smithfield. It was frequented by Cockney pedlars who dealt in bric-à-brac from emptied attics and lumber rooms and soon became famed for its bargains. By the beginning of this century the cattle market was decreasing and there began a booming interest in antiques. In 1924 the general market was extended to Tuesdays. Stolen goods and general junk flooded in, the 'Caledonian Silver Kings' became notorious and many fortunes were made. A census of 1930 counted 2,100 stalls on one Friday.

Stories of bargains from the 1920s include one woman who bought a long string of black pearls for 7s 6d. The market closed during the 1st World War and, despite numerous petitions, costermongers were not allowed back when it was over. The new Caledonian Market was opened in Bermondsey Street as a dealers' antique market. In 1965 the ISLINGTON site was cleared for a housing development. The original iron railings in Market Road, three of the imposing taverns at the corners and the clock tower marking the site of COPENHAGEN HOUSE, designed by J.B. Bunning, have been preserved.

Metropolitan Drinking Fountain and Cattle Trough Association *426 Lewisham High Street, SE13.* Founded in 1859 by Samuel Gurney, MP (a nephew of Elizabeth Fry), under the title the Metropolitan Free Drinking Association, its purpose was, by ensuring a free supply of pure drinking water, to help to eradicate both CHOLERA and intemperance in the metropolis. The first fountain was put up by Gurney the same year against the wall of ST SEPULCHRE'S, Snow Hill, where it still stands. In 1856 drinking troughs for dogs and for cattle and horses were added to the commitments of the Association, which still maintains drinking fountains all over London.

Metropolitan Line The world's first underground passenger railway. Work began on the line from PADDINGTON to KING'S CROSS and thence to FARRINGDON STREET in February 1860. The railway was constructed by the 'cut and cover' method and, as property was expensive, most of the trenches were dug along roads, the main one being the MARYLEBONE ROAD. W.E. Gladstone and his wife were amongst those who took part in the first trial trip on 24 May 1862. The Fleet

The Metropolitan Cattle Market in 1855, showing Bunning's clock tower which marks the site of Copenhagen House.

ditch sewer burst into the works in FARRINGDON STREET shortly afterwards, but the damage was quickly repaired and the line finally opened on 10 January 1863. Despite the misgivings of the public, who had nicknamed the railway the 'Drain', and the warnings of *The Times* which said it was 'an insult to common sense to suppose that people . . . would ever prefer . . . to be driven amid palpable darkness through the foul subsoil of London', the railway was an instant success. Steam locomotives hauling first-, second- and third-class carriages were used; and in 1864 the Metropolitan Railway was the first to introduce workmen's trains, charging 3d for a return fair. The line was soon extended to HAMMERSMITH (1864) and to MOORGATE (1865), and plans were made for an 'Inner Circle' to link the two ends of the Metropolitan. The section from PADDINGTON to SOUTH KENSINGTON was opened in 1868 and from MOORGATE to ALDGATE in 1876. The section between SOUTH KENSINGTON and MANSION HOUSE was completed in 1871 by the Metropolitan District Railway (later to break away from the Metropolitan and become the DISTRICT LINE). The CIRCLE was finally completed in 1884 and both companies worked their trains all round it; the Metropolitan also ran trains from HAMMERSMITH over the northern part and on to NEW CROSS. The Metropolitan Railway also extended north of BAKER STREET to HARROW. The chairman's aspirations for the Metropolitan to become a main-line railway led to Rickmansworth extension, a through service from BAKER STREET to Verney Junction and the 'Brill branch'. Meanwhile, increased traffic on the underground line was causing problems for steam operation, and on 1 January 1905 the Metropolitan introduced its first electric service, from BAKER STREET to UXBRIDGE. Takeover by the LONDON PASSENGER TRANSPORT BOARD in 1933 and nationalisation in 1948 both led to electrification and modernisation of the underground but closure of the suburban lines: the last through service to stations north of Amersham ran on 9 September 1961, which was also the last day of passenger-train steam working on London Transport lines (*see also* CIRCLE LINE, DISTRICT LINE *and* UNDERGROUND RAILWAYS).

Metropolitan Police *see* POLICE.

Metropolitan Tabernacle *Elephant and Castle, Newington Butts, SE1*. Built for Charles Haddon Spurgeon, the vociferous Baptist preacher, in 1859–61 by W.W. Pocock on the site of the FISHMONGERS' COMPANY Almshouses. Spurgeon was 27 when it opened. He had come to London in 1853 and at the New Park Street Chapel had attracted a large following, eventually hiring the SURREY MUSIC HALL to house his congregation, which subscribed over £31,000 for the new Tabernacle. Spurgeon called it the Tabernacle because he said people were still in the wilderness. It held 6,000. At the rear was a lecture hall holding 900 and a schoolroom for 1,000 children. Here, as at his earlier chapel, 'the crowd was so immense' wrote a contemporary observer, 'that seat holders could not get to their seats. Half an hour before time the aisles were solid blocks and many stood throughout the service, wedged in by their fellows and prevented from escaping by the crowd outside who sealed up the doors and filled up the yard in front and stood in throngs as far as the sound could reach.' From

1855 his sermon was published every week. In 1879 he received a testimonial of £6,263 from his congregation. He died in 1892 and was buried at NORWOOD CEMETERY. Rebuilt after a fire in 1894–9 the chapel was destroyed by enemy action in 1941 and again rebuilt behind its massive portico with 1750 seats in 1959.

The Metropolitan Tabernacle, built in 1849–51 for the Baptist preacher C.H. Spurgeon to house his immense congregations.

Metropolitan Theatre *Edgware Road*. A famous music hall, commonly known as 'The Met'. It stood on the site of the White Lion, a 16th-century inn. In 1836 the inn was rebuilt to include a concert room. In 1862 it was rebuilt again by John Turnham to hold 4,000 people and opened as Turnham's Grand Concert Hall. In 1864 it was renamed the Metropolitan Music Hall after the newly built Metropolitan Railway Line which ran nearby. It was rebuilt by Frank Matcham in 1897. After the 1st World War it was used for variety shows and later as a boxing and wrestling arena and television studios. It was demolished in 1963 to make way for a flyover.

Metropolitan Water Board *see* WATER SUPPLY.

MIDDLE TEMPLE *EC4*. (For the derivation of the name *see* KNIGHTS TEMPLAR; and for a brief account of the early history of the Temple *see* INNER TEMPLE). The crest of the Middle Temple depicts the Pascal Lamb with the flag of innocence.

Hall The original Hall dates from about 1320. The present building was completed in 1573 and contains a striking oak double hammerbeam roof and a notable screen, also of oak. Both survived the onslaught of German bombers in the 2nd World War. The long table on the low dais ('the Bench Table') is 29 ft long, made from a single oak tree and believed to have been given to the Inn by Queen Elizabeth I. Above the Bench Table are paintings of Charles I (1683), the Duke of York (1684), Charles II, Queen Anne (1703) and William III (1725). In front of the Bench Table is a small table traditionally known as 'the Cupboard'. In former days it served as a centre round which the students would gather while debating a topic under the guidance of a senior barrister known as a Reader. On completing his course of lectures, the Reader would become a Bencher. Coats-of-arms of former Readers adorn the walls, dating from 1597 to the present day, the more recent being situated in the Benchers' private

Fountain Court and Middle Temple Hall (right), completed in 1573, from an engraving of 1735 after Nichols.

quarters. The instruction of students is now the responsibility of the Council of Legal Education. It is said that the present Cupboard was made of wood from the hatch of Sir Francis Drake's ship, the *Golden Hind*. The busts of the Caesars on each side of the Hall are believed to date from the mid-1600s. The suits of armour are Elizabethan. A large open fireplace stood in the centre of the Hall until 1830. In early days it was usual for the floor to be covered with rushes as in all of the INNS OF COURT. The Hall was used to stage lavish entertainments including revels, banquets, masques and plays, especially over the period of All Saints (1 November) to Candlemas (2 February). Shakespeare's *Twelfth Night* was produced here on 2 February 1601. To keep their terms, students are today required to dine in the Hall not less than three times in each of 12 terms. During dining terms, by tradition, a horn is blown at 6.30 to summon members to the Hall.

Among many prominent persons associated with the Middle Temple were Edmund Plowden, jurist, Treasurer of the Inn and builder of the Hall, whose bust stands before the screen; the Elizabethan sailors Sir John Hawkins, Sir Francis Drake and Sir Walter Ralegh; Nicholas Wadham, founder of Wadham College, Oxford; Thomas Shadwell, the dramatist; Henry Ireton, the Cromwellian general; William Wycherley and William Congreve, the dramatists; the Duke of Monmouth, illegitimate son of Charles II; the 1st Earl of Clarendon; John Evelyn; Henry Fielding; William Cowper, the poet; Sir William Blackstone, the legal jurist and judge; Edmund Burke; Charles Dickens; Thomas de Quincey; Henry Grattan, the Irish statesman; Theobald Wolfe Tone, the United Irishman; and John Thaddeus Delane, editor of *The Times* from 1841 to 1877. In more recent times members have included Lords Scarman and Wilberforce, Lords of Appeal in Ordinary, and Dame Margaret Booth, a judge of the High Court.

Gate House Provides the main entrance to the Middle Temple from FLEET STREET. In 1520 the existing medieval Gate House was demolished and rebuilt by the Treasurer, Sir Amyas Paulet. This in turn was replaced in 1684 by the present Gate House which was designed by Roger North, a Bencher, and leads into Middle Temple Lane.

Brick Court Oliver Goldsmith had chambers in No. 2 from 1765 till his death in 1774 when he was buried in the north churchyard of the TEMPLE CHURCH. His tombstone survives, but the exact site of the grave is uncertain. *She Stoops to Conquer* was written here. Sir William Blackstone lived immediately below at this time. In 1855 William Makepeace Thackeray occupied these same rooms. Nos 2 and 3 Brick Court suffered major war damage and the site is now part of a car park.

Fountain Court It was by the single jet fountain here that John Westlock met Ruth Pinch in Dickens's *Martin Chuzzlewit*.

Library Rebuilt by Sir Edward Maufe in 1956, its predecessor, which stood in MIDDLE TEMPLE GARDENS, having been destroyed by bombing in 1941. It is known for its very comprehensive collection of American law books and also houses the 16th-century Molyneux Globes which depict the celestial and territorial worlds as then known.

Middle Temple Gardens Lying to the south of FOUNTAIN COURT and extending down to the EMBANKMENT, these contain the new Queen Elizabeth Building (1958) designed by Sir Edward Maufe, which stands on the site of the former Middle Temple Library. Traditionally the Gardens were the scene of the plucking of the red rose of Lancaster and the white rose of York which became associated with the Civil Wars (1455–85) between the Houses of Lancaster and York.

New Court Erected by Nicholas Barbon in 1675 and sold by him to the Middle Temple. Its attribution to

514

Wren has been denied by Sir John Summerson. The entrance to New Court from Devereux Court offers an attractive view of the Inn.

Pump Court One of the oldest parts of the Temple. A pump which formerly existed was destroyed in the 2nd World War and not replaced. A deep well below the pavement served as an emergency water supply during that period. The south side, destroyed in the 2nd World War, was rebuilt to a design by Sir Edward Maufe. Henry Fielding had chambers at No. 4.

Cloisters A brick building was erected over the cloisters in 1612. After a fire in 1688 the INNER TEMPLE wished to have the property re-instated as before, but the Middle Temple, at the suggestion of Nicholas Barbon, pressed for a solid block, thereby gaining extra accommodation. An arbitration award by the Lord Chancellor led to a larger building, designed by Wren and supported by reinforced cloisters below. After the 2nd World War the Cloisters were rebuilt in 1949–50 under the supervision of Sir Edward Maufe. (*See also* INNS OF COURT.)

Middlesex Originally the county of the Middle Saxons, the name Middlesex first appeared in a charter of AD 704. It became a shire early in the 10th century. The first written account of Middlesex as a shire was in the *Domesday* survey, which shows it as divided into six Hundreds – EDMONTON, Elthorne, Gore, HOUNSLOW, Ossulstone and Spelthorne. Middlesex lost much of its area when the County of London was formed on the passing of the Local Government Act of 1888. The new Middlesex County Council met for the first time on 1 April 1889. It ceased to exist on 31 March 1965 when, together with parts of Hertfordshire, Essex, Kent and Surrey, it was taken into the new administrative area of Greater London. The name Middlesex now survives only as a postal address and the name of a County Cricket team.

Middlesex County Cricket Club *Lord's Cricket Ground, St John's Wood, NW8.* Founded officially on 2 February 1864, although teams calling themselves Middlesex had played, from time to time, since the mid-18th century. An organised Middlesex team was formed in 1850, but played only irregularly. Prince's Ground (*see* PRINCE'S CLUB) was the county's home ground in the 1870s, but from that year they have been tenants of LORD'S and have the advantages (and disadvantages) of playing all their home fixtures at the headquarters of cricket. In the early days, Middlesex was primarily an amateur side, producing from public schools and Oxford and Cambridge brilliant batsmen, but few bowlers of quality. They first won the County Championship in 1866 and have produced many of the game's greatest players. Perhaps the most distinguished was Sir Pelham ('Plum') Warner, who captained the county in 1908–20 and led England to victory against Australia in two Test series. He was knighted for services to the game in 1937 and became President of the MCC in 1950–1: a stand at LORD'S has been named after him. E.H. ('Patsy') Hendren, one of the game's best-loved players, made 170 centuries, seven of them in Test matches, and a total of 57,611 runs, the third highest of all times, in a career from 1907 to 1937. The eccentric B.J.T. Bosanquet invented the 'Googly', a right-handed off-break bowled with a leg-break action out of the back of the hand. Also a brilliant batsman, he played a decisive part in

England's winning the Test series against Australia in 1903–4 and 1905. More recently Denis Compton and W.J. ('Bill') Edrich, both famous Test cricketers, each made over 3,000 in the 1947 season (a record), Compton 3,816 (an individual record) and Edrich 3,539. J.M. Brearley captained the County from 1971.

Middlesex Guildhall *Broad Sanctuary, SW1.* Gothic hall designed by J.S. Gibson and built in 1906–13 on the site of Sanctuary Tower (*see* BROAD SANCTUARY). The foundation stone was laid by the Duke of Bedford on 2 May 1912. The stone figures above the doorway facing PARLIAMENT SQUARE were carved by Henry C. Fehr. Since the absorption of the County of MIDDLESEX into Greater London, the quarter sessions for the area have still been held in the Crown Court here.

Middlesex Hospital *Mortimer Street, W1.* Founded in 1745 as the Middlesex Infirmary at Nos 8–10 Windmill Street, about 200 yards east of its present site. The houses were rented from Mr Goodge (*see* GOODGE STREET). The hospital was opened 'for the sick and lame of Soho', with three beds set aside for women in labour. In 1754 an adjacent site of 25 acres was acquired from Mr Berners (*see* BERNERS STREET). The new site was separated from the TOTTENHAM COURT ROAD by ponds and marshland. In May 1755 the Earl of Northumberland laid the foundation stone of the new building, to be called the Middlesex Hospital. Much of the money was raised by Garrick and Handel who gave performances gratis. The new hospital had 64 beds. In 1766 the west wing was added and in 1780 the east wing. In 1791 Samuel Whitbread, the brewer, gave £3,000 to endow a ward for cancer patients who could remain there until 'relieved by art or released by death'. This special interest in cancer has survived in the Middlesex in the two centuries that have followed.

As in other hospitals, the education of medical students was rather haphazard for nearly a century. With the founding of the UNIVERSITY OF LONDON there was a great stimulus to the more efficient teaching of students, and in 1835 the Middlesex built its own medical school next to the west wing. The most enthusiastic supporter of the scheme was Sir Charles Bell, surgeon to the hospital, who discovered in 1811 the distinct functions of the motor and sensory nerves – perhaps the greatest discovery in physiology since Harvey's demonstration of the circulation of the blood 200 years earlier. He is best known among the laity for a type of facial paralysis which he described before the ROYAL SOCIETY in 1821 – ever since known as Bell's palsy. Another great son of the hospital was Bell's contemporary, Sir Henry Halford, one of the most famous London physicians of all time. He had an enormous practice. Physician to four successive monarchs from George III onwards, he became President of the ROYAL COLLEGE OF PHYSICIANS in 1820. As the 19th century progressed many additions and improvements were made. In 1848 additional buildings increased the number of beds to 295 and fireproof staircases were installed. In 1890 the chapel, rich in ornament, was built to the designs of J.L. Pearson. Enormous developments have taken place in the present century, the hospital being rebuilt in 1935, to the designs of A.W. Hall. This was made possible by the energy and skill in fund raising of Lord Webb-Johnson, Surgeon to the hospital and President of the ROYAL COLLEGE OF SURGEONS. In 1929 a private wing was opened, the gift of Lord Woolavington. Another great benefactor, Colonel the Hon. J.J. Astor, Chairman of the hospital for many years, gave the famous Nurses' Home. Other well-known adjuncts are the Cancer Research Laboratories and Cancer Wing in Nassau Street, the Bland-Sutton Institute of Pathology, and the Courtauld Institute of Biochemistry. Since 1959 the Medical School and its many research departments have been largely rebuilt, thanks to generous benefactors including Astor, Sir Edward Lewis, Sir Jules Thorn and the Wolfson Foundation. In 1982 there were 684 beds.

Middlesex Polytechnic *114 Chase Side, N14.*
One of the largest polytechnics in Britain, with over 5,400 full-time students, it was formed in 1973 by the amalgamation of ENFIELD and HENDON colleges of technology and the HORNSEY College of Art. In 1974 TRENT PARK College of Education and New College of Speech and Drama, and in 1977 the College of All Saints, also joined forces with the Middlesex Polytechnic. Located at some ten sites in the boroughs of BARNET, ENFIELD and HARINGEY, the architecture of the polytechnic ranges from a Georgian mansion set in rolling parkland (TRENT PARK) to purpose-built complexes and converted warehouse premises.

Middlesex Street *E1.* Formerly known as Hogge
Lane, it extends from BISHOPSGATE to Aldgate High Street. It was first built up in the late 17th century. Before that several large country houses stood here. One of these was occupied by Gondomar, the Spanish ambassador, another by Hans Jacobson, the King's jeweller, and later by the father of John Strype. His son, the historian of London, was born here in 1643. He is commemorated in STRYPE STREET. As far north as STRYPE STREET, Middlesex Street forms the border between the CITY and TOWER HAMLETS (*see also* PETTICOAT LANE). The Middlesex Street Estate stands on part of the site previously occupied by Artisans Dwellings. In 1884 the City Commissioners of Sewers cleared away several courts to build these five tenement blocks, each five storeys high, three of which had shops on the ground floor.

Midland Bank Ltd *Poultry, EC2.* Established in
Birmingham in 1836, this Bank moved its headquarters to London in 1891 when it acquired the Central Bank of London (founded in 1863) and Lacy, Hartland and Woodbridge of West Smithfield (established 1809). The purchase of the Central gave the Midland membership of the BANKERS' CLEARING HOUSE. Seven years later the Bank purchased the City Bank (established by Royal Charter in 1855), with its network of 21 branches in London; the Midland then moved its headquarters to the City Bank's old office at 5 THREADNEEDLE STREET. In 1918, consolidating its position as one of the largest British clearing banks, the Midland took over the London Joint Stock Bank (founded 1836). This Bank operated 60 branches in London and its constituent businesses included Wright and Co. of PALL MALL (established 1759), T.M. Challis and Son of Smithfield and ISLINGTON (established 1851), and the Imperial Bank (established 1862). The Midland moved to its present head office, designed by Sir Edwin Lutyens and Gotch and Saunders, in POULTRY in 1930. In 1982 the Bank had over 220 branches in the London area and its subsidiary companies included THOMAS COOK LTD and SAMUEL MONTAGU AND CO. LTD.

Midland Grand Hotel *Euston Road.* Built as
part of the Midland Railway terminus by Sir George Gilbert Scott, it opened in 1873 and was considered by Baedeker 'one of the best of the London hotels'. The hotel had lifts and electric bells and, at ground-floor level, refreshment and dining rooms, with wine cellars in the basement. The grand staircase ascended the whole height of the building with cast-iron treads, stone vaulting and painted walls. The main suites were on the first few floors, with comfortable servants' quarters on the top floor. It had 400 bedrooms. It now serves as offices for British Rail.

Milbourne House *Station Road, SW13.* Named
after the Milbourne family who lived there in the 15th century. The rear cross wing, now called Ratcliff House, possibly incorporates a hall and solar of their time, but the main building is constructed of 16th-century brickwork, most noticeable in the characteristic chimneystacks. The façade is mid-18th-century with a handsome doorcase and a slate mansard roof. Inside there is a late 16th-century chimney piece and the remnants of a Jacobean staircase. The house has had many distinguished occupants since its acquisition by Sir Henry Wyatt in 1517–18. In the 1590s it was lived in by Robert Beale, Walsingham's secretary and brother-in-law, who read the death sentence to Mary Queen of Scots. Henry Fielding, the novelist, lived here briefly in 1750–2 and probably wrote *Amelia* during his stay, which is commemorated by a BLUE PLAQUE. It is still a private house.

Mile End *E1, E2.* Mile End was mostly common
land in the Middle Ages, a favourite place of recreation for Londoners and a convenient place close to the CITY for people to gather. During the PEASANTS' REVOLT in 1381 the men of Essex met Richard II here and made their famous demand that no man should be a serf. Two Lord Mayors of London lived here, Henry le Waleis, in whose house in 1299 a parliament was held which confirmed Magna Carta, and Sir Henry Colet, whose son, Dean Colet, was one-time Vicar of ST DUNSTAN'S STEPNEY. However, by the end of the 16th century Stow was complaining that 'this common field, being sometime the beauty of this city on that part is so encroached upon by building of filthy cottages, and with other purpressors, inclosures and lay stalls, that in some places [Mile End Road] scarce remaineth a sufficient highway for the meeting of carriages and droves of cattle'. The western part of Mile End developed so rapidly in the last quarter of the 17th century that it was constituted a separate hamlet of STEPNEY of 1690 known as Mile End New Town. The remainder was then called Mile End Old Town. Despite its name, Mile End New Town was really an extension of SPITALFIELDS. It was claimed in 1690 that the population was mainly composed of 'handicraft tradesman, labourers and artificers', many of whom were presumably weavers. Other industries were established over the next 200 years, including a large dye-house, extensive warehouses for Truman's brewery, metal works, a sugar refinery, saw mill, timber

yard and fish-curing factory. The population of over 5,000 in 1801 reached more than 18,000 a hundred years later.

The more extensive hamlet of Mile End Old Town remained mostly open in the 18th century. Some land on the north side of MILE END ROAD had been acquired for their first burial ground by the Jews who were allowed to resettle in England after 1657. Several almshouses were erected, of which only Trinity Almshouses (built in 1695) are left. BANCROFT'S SCHOOL and Almshouses, on the site of QUEEN MARY COLLEGE, moved to Woodford. The house in Mile End Road where Captain Cook lived in about 1764–76 has been demolished, but many of the 18th-century houses in Stepney Green still remain. During the 19th century most of the hamlet was developed for housing, the population rising to nearly 113,000 people, some employed in local industries but many working in the nearby CITY. Although Mile End was quietly respectable with very little extreme poverty compared to other parts of East London, William Booth began the work of the SALVATION ARMY on Mile End Waste in 1868 and the first DR BARNARDO'S HOME for orphans was founded in 1870 near Ben Jonson Road. A centre for education and recreation, the PEOPLE'S PALACE (now QUEEN MARY COLLEGE) was opened by Queen Victoria in 1887; and C.R. Ashbee established his Guild and School of Handicraft in 1888 in TOYNBEE HALL and then at Essex House, Mile End in 1891. There was a considerable influx of Jewish immigrants spreading from the main area of settlement in WHITECHAPEL from the 1880s, particularly into Mile End New Town, the western part of Mile End Old Town and Stepney Green. The 'Siege of Sidney Street' in 1911 showed that Russian revolutionaries had also sought refuge in Mile End. Mile End became a part of the Borough of STEPNEY in 1900 and Mile End New Town suffered particularly heavily from bomb damage during the 2nd World War. Much of the district has since been rebuilt with council flats, although some 19th-century terraces around Tredegar Square and the roads near Grantley Street, for example, have been recently restored.

Mile End Road *E1, E2.* Already well built up when the TRINITY ALMSHOUSES were opened in 1695. Close by these are a bronze bust and a statue of William Booth (*see* STATUES). The first meetings of the movement that was to become the SALVATION ARMY took place here. Further east, at the back of No. 253, is the first cemetery of the Jews after they were re-admitted to England by Cromwell. A short distance away is the PEOPLE'S PALACE, now part of QUEEN MARY COLLEGE. The new People's Palace (by Campbell-Jones and Smithers, 1936) has five bas-reliefs by Eric Gill (1937). Captain Cook, the explorer, lived in a house on the site of No. 88.

Miles Lane *EC4.* Named after the church of ST MICHAEL CROOKED LANE, demolished in 1831 when KING WILLIAM STREET was built. Miles is an early variant of the name Michael.

Milford Lane *WC2.* Takes its name from the ford which crossed a stream carrying water from the higher land above the STRAND into the THAMES. Once the boundary between the mansions of Lord Essex and the Earl of Arundel, it was a hiding-place for debtors in the

17th century. Sir Richard Baker, author of Sir Roger de Coverley's favourite book, the *Chronicles*, lived here in 1632–9. The resin bronze abstract, *Winged Form*, is by Geoffrey Wickham (1968).

Military Company One of a number of bands of volunteer soldiers which were formed in several parts of the country during the reign of James I and which received direct encouragement from the King through the Privy Council. This company in WESTMINSTER was founded in 1615 and was modelled on the Artillery Company which exercised at SPITALFIELDS. Thomas Holcroft, a professional soldier, was appointed its first captain. The 3½ acres of land acquired for the company's training lay in the north-west part of St Martin's Field and was referred to as the Military Ground, Garden or Yard. On this was later built an armoury house for arms, armour and equipment. Apart from occasional policing, there is no record of the company's military activities. It was known to have been still exercising in 1708; but its association with the Military Ground ceased in 1661 owing to leasing difficulties.

Milk Street *EC2.* The milk market of medieval London was here. St Mary Magdalene's Church, founded in the 12th century in this street, was burned down in the GREAT FIRE and not rebuilt. Sir Thomas More was born here in February 1478. Joseph Chamberlain's father, who was Master of the CORDWAINERS' COMPANY, had a bootmaker's business here between 1830 and 1864.

Mill Hill *NW7.* This area was protected from suburban development by the northern heights of Hampstead until penetration by the NORTHERN LINE, first to GOLDERS GREEN and later to EDGWARE. In the 17th and 18th centuries, however, there were several large houses along the Ridgeway and Totteridge Common. Three LORD MAYORS OF LONDON have lived here: John Wilkes; Sir John Anderson; and Sir Charles Flower. Celia Fiennes, the redoubtable horsewoman, 'the fine lady on a white horse' of the 17th-century rhyme, also lived here. So did Lord William Russell of the Bedford family who was found guilty of implication in the Rye House Plot. Later in the same house at Totteridge Common, Highwood House, lived Sir Stamford Raffles at the end of his short life. His neighbour was William Wilberforce who was responsible in 1833 for the building of the redbrick St Mary's church, described as having 'four pinnacles but no steeple'. Farther along the Ridgeway was the home of Peter Collinson, the eminent botanist, who introduced into this country the hydrangea, the yucca and over 150 other plants from all over the world. On the site of Collinson's house, Ridgeway House, MILL HILL SCHOOL, originally the Dissenters' School, was built in 1807, the main classical frontage being executed by Sir William Tite in 1825. The school is accounted 'an island of nonconformity in a sea of Roman Catholicism' because there are a number of Roman Catholic institutions in the area. The most notable in St Joseph's College, designed by Goldie and Child (1866–71). Students of all nationalities are trained here for mission work. Its graduates are known world-wide as 'the little fathers of Mill Hill'. It was built in 1871 on the initiative of Cardinal Vaughan who lived at Holcombe House on Holcombe Hill, a house distinguished by a Georgian portico and interior decorations by Angelica Kauffmann and Antonio Zucchi who also did work together at KENWOOD, and subsequently married. Holcombe House was built in 1775 by John Johnson for John Anderson, a glove merchant who became LORD MAYOR of London. Next door is St Mary's Abbey, a château-like group of buildings designed by Goldie, Child and Goldie (1889) and now occupied by the Franciscan Sisters of Mill Hill.

In the northern part of Mill Hill there are several groups of 18th-century timber-clad cottages, including the old mill house and the buildings of the local forge. Perhaps the most elegant building in the area is the 18th-century, Adam-style Belmont, opposite Holcombe House, once the home of Wilkes and now serving as the junior school for MILL HILL SCHOOL.

Past the Sheepwash and Angel ponds and the old Methodist church, now the bethel of the Nigerian Brethren of the Star and Cross, past the almshouses built in 1697 by Thomas Nicoll, the local miller, and a group of prize-winning houses built in the 1960s to the designs of Seifert, is St Vincent's Convent and School. Formerly known as Littlebury's it was the home in the 18th century of the brothers Perrean, wine merchants who dabbled in forgery. After a complicated *cause célèbre* which rocked the CITY one of the brothers was executed. Legend associates the place with Nell Gwynne and others of Charles II's mistresses, but none of this is proven. Gladstone, however, certainly stayed here on his visits to MILL HILL SCHOOL.

Nearby is the modern Medical Research Unit whose work ranges from cancer research to investigation of the common cold. The building, designed by Maxwell Ayrton, was ready for occupation in 1939 but was then requisitioned for use as a Women's Royal Naval Service training centre. At Mill Hill East are the Inglis Barracks, once the home of 'The Die-Hards', the Middlesex Regiment, and now of the Royal Engineers and the Army Postal Unit. The main shopping centre, the Broadway, in spite of multiple stores and building societies, still retains something of a village atmosphere. John Keble church in Dean's Lane, between Mill Hill and EDGWARE, is a fine building by D.F. Martin-Smith (1936). John Groom's Crippleage nearby was founded in 1866 in CLERKENWELL, and moved here in 1931.

Mill Hill School   *Mill Hill Village, NW7.* Founded in 1807 by a group of ministers and merchants for the sons of Protestant dissenters. The present school house was designed by (Sir) William Tite in 1827. The chapel was built to the designs of Basil Champneys in 1897. In 1982 there were some 530 pupils aged 12 to 18 years, including about 20 girls. James Murray, who gave a large part of his life to editing the *Oxford English Dictionary*, was a master here from 1870 to 1885. He accounted this time his 'halcyon years'. In the school buildings is the room where he stored the 3 tons of slips on which the quotations for the *Dictionary* were written.

Mill Street   *W1.* On the Millfield estate (*see* HANOVER SQUARE), it is a very short street connecting MADDOX and CONDUIT STREETS. It was originally laid out around 1720 and is now entirely in commercial use.

Millbank   *SW1.* Takes its name from the WESTMINSTER ABBEY mill which once stood at the end of what is now GREAT COLLEGE STREET. In about 1736 Sir Robert Grosvenor demolished the mill and on the site built a house 'with a large court before it and a fine garden behind'. Millbank was then a lonely riverside road leading from WESTMINSTER to CHELSEA through marshy ground and market gardens. In about 1809 Grosvenor's house was demolished to make way for the MILLBANK PENITENTIARY. When Thomas Cubitt began developing PIMLICO in the 1820s, houses were built along MILLBANK for the first time. But, as Dickens observed in *David Copperfield*, MILLBANK remained for the most part 'a melancholy waste': 'A sluggish ditch deposited its mud at the prison walls. Coarse grass and rank weeds straggled over all the marshy land in the vicinity. In one part, carcasses of houses, inauspiciously begun and never finished, rotted away. In another the ground was cumbered with rusty iron monsters of steam-boilers, wheels, cranks,

The gloomy Millbank Penitentiary, completed in 1821, was pulled down in 1903 to make way for the Royal Army Medical College.

pipes, furnaces, paddles, anchors, diving-bells, windmill-sails and I known not what strange objects accumulated by some speculator and grovelling in the dust underneath which, having sunk into the soil of their own weight in wet weather, they had the appearance of vainly trying to hide themselves.' They have mostly been replaced by solid Edwardian office blocks. The CHURCH COMMISSIONERS for England are at No. 1 in a building designed by W.D. Caroë in 1903; and the Crown Agents for Overseas Governments and Administrations in a building designed by J.W. Simpson and erected in 1914–16. At No. 7 is Westminster House, designed by Sir F. Baines in 1928. To the north of the TATE GALLERY, in Bulinga Street, are the buildings of the QUEEN ALEXANDRA MILITARY HOSPITAL, opened by Edward VII and Queen Alexandra in 1905. The ROYAL ARMY MEDICAL COLLEGE is on the corner of Atterbury Street. The huge 387ft high Millbank Tower was built in 1960–3 for the Vickers Group of Companies to the designs of Ronald Ward and Partners. Thames House by Lambeth Bridge is by W.B. Ragan. The bronze abstract by VAUXHALL BRIDGE, *Locking Pieces* is by Henry Moore (1968). It was given by the sculptor to the TATE GALLERY. The widening of Millbank was completed in 1969.

Millbank Penitentiary Built in response to calls for prison reform and based on the ideas of Jeremy Bentham. In 1791 Bentham published *The Panopticon or Inspection House*, setting out novel ideas for prison management. Prisoners were to occupy the circumference of a building like a glazed iron cage, with officers in the centre giving an illusion of perpetual surveillance. They were to be kept silent and separate and encouraged to love labour through sharing what they produced. In 1794 Bentham gained a contract with the government to build a prison based on his ideas. He invested heavily from personal funds but the scheme fell through. In 1813 the government took over and built a modified version of his designs costing £500,000. In 1821 the prison was finally completed. It was in the shape of a six-pointed star and covered 7 acres of low-lying marshy ground near to the river. It was a cold, gloomy building with 3 miles of labyrinthine passages. One warder is recorded as still having to mark his way with a chalk after 7 years' service. It was the largest prison in London and used for men and women awaiting transportation or referral. Prisoners were confined to separate cells; they made shoes and mail bags and were forbidden to communicate with each other for the first half of their sentence. The locality and the diet were extremely unhealthy and in 1822–3 epidemics of scurvy and CHOLERA affected half the population, killing 30. An Act of Parliament cleared the prison, giving a free pardon to the women and dividing the men between the various hulks on the river. The prison was fumigated and conditions improved. Candles were put in the cells; some games were allowed, and education provided.

During the 1830s the young Richard Smith became notorious for his escape attempts. In his first attempt he drilled a hole in a brick arch with a pin and used a ladder made from threads of cotton and rags. But all attempts failed and he died in prison aged 21. In 1843 the penitentiary was converted into an ordinary prison. It was closed in 1890 and demolished in 1903. The ROYAL ARMY MEDICAL COLLEGE stands on the site of the prison.

Millfield Lane *Highgate, N6.* Probably the remains of a track which led from the City via KENTISH TOWN to the Great North Road, it runs from West Hill to KENWOOD. Once Coleridge's favourite country walk, it was here that he first met Keats who, as they parted, said, 'Let me carry away the memory, Coleridge, of having pressed your hand.' Coventry Patmore called it 'the poets' path'. Charles Mathews, the actor, lived in Ivy Cottage from 1819 to 1833, and kept here his famous collection of theatrical portraits (now in the GARRICK CLUB). Charles Lamb paid him a visit which he describes in one of his essays. West Hill Court, designed by W.R. Binney, was built on the site in 1934. The Highgate ponds, on the west side of the Lane, were Elizabethan gravel pits.

Millman Street *WC1.* Planned by S.P. Cockerell and built in 1792–9. Houses were of the 5th class (*see* PLANNING) and all have since been redeveloped. It is named after William Milman (who spelled his name with one 'l'), son of a coffee-house keeper in the STRAND who made his fortune stockjobbing. He built the first Milman Street in the 1680s. John Bellingham was living here in 1812 when he assassinated Spencer Perceval.

Millwall *E14.* The western part of the ISLE OF DOGS gained its name from the mills which stood on the marsh wall in the 17th and 18th centuries and helped to drain the low-lying land. They were removed in the 19th century when industrial premises were erected along the riverside, the most notable of which was John Scott Russell's ship-building yard. It was here that Brunel's *Great Eastern* was built and eventually launched in 1859 after several attempts. It was the largest vessel built in Britain until the 1890s. The MILLWALL DOCK was constructed in 1864–8. MILLWALL FOOTBALL CLUB, dating back to 1885, is thought to have had its origin in the team of Morton's cannedfood factory. After using several grounds on the ISLE OF DOGS, the club crossed the river to its present site in NEW CROSS in 1910. Considerable overcrowding and poverty were still noticeable in Millwall between the wars but bomb damage, closure of the docks and many of the factories, slum clearance and rehousing schemes have since transformed the neighbourhood.

Millwall Dock The Millwall Canal Company was incorporated by an Act of 1864 but immediately changed its name to the Millwall Freehold Land and Dock Company. It bought some 200 acres of marsh land on the ISLE OF DOGS south of the WEST INDIA DOCKS, and here built a dock of 36 acres of water which opened for business in 1868. The dock, designed by John Fowler assisted by William Wilson, was built in the form of a reversed L with an entrance on the west side of the ISLE OF DOGS. An entrance from the east side was projected but never accomplished. The completed scheme included a dry dock 413ft long, the first of its kind to be built by a London dock company. Having ample land, the company later built a railway system to the dock, running through the WEST INDIA DOCK area as a branch line from the BLACKWALL RAILWAY. For a few years, as a fire precaution the trains to the dock were hauled by horses instead of steam engines. The dock became active in grain from the Baltic, but was never very successful financially. When the PORT OF LONDON AUTHORITY took over the dock in 1909, it linked

Brunel's Great Eastern, *which was to be launched in 1859, under construction in the building yard at Millwall.*

the north of the MILLWALL with the WEST INDIA DOCKS system, so making a large complex spreading all over the ISLE OF DOGS and having access to the river to both east and west. All these docks were closed in 1980.

Millwall Football Club *see* FOOTBALL CLUBS.

Milner Street *SW3*. An unusually wide street developed in the late 1850s with several terraces of stuccoed houses and a small country village church, St Simon's, built in 1858–9 by Joseph Peacock. Milner Street once led to Prince's Cricket Ground (*see* PRINCE'S CLUB) where the first Australian touring team played which no doubt accounts for one of its two public houses being called the Australian. The other is the Shuckburgh Arms (*see* DRAYCOTT AVENUE).

Milner-Gibson Estate *Islington, N1*. One of the chief small estates held in copyhold of the manor of BARNSBURY, by the Milner-Gibson family of Theberton, Suffolk. It was enfranchised by a private Act in 1822 by the Lord of the Manor's trustees (*see* BARNSBURY), and the fields between UPPER STREET and the Back Road (LIVERPOOL ROAD) let on 99-year building leases. By 1825 Moon Street and Studd Street were built with artisans' houses, and the old field path became the basis of Theberton Street. At the UPPER STREET corner an ancient house, the Pied Bull, which has associations with the Ralegh family, was rebuilt as a public house.

The estate layout was by Francis Edwards, engineer to the Imperial Gaslight Company and a pupil of Soane. He may himself have designed the first houses with their distinctive giant-pilaster façades. Gibson and Milner Squares, whose names were reversed in Edwards's original plan, are unusually long and rectangular. Building was piecemeal (1828–33), mostly in batches of six, starting with both ends of Theberton Street and Gibson Square south side (1832), now 51–75 Theberton Street. The rest of the square was begun in 1836, and the street's north side completed in a different style (1839). Trinidad Place (82–124 LIVERPOOL ROAD) of 1834 was named after the family's plantations; and the row connecting this with the square's north side, Charles Street, was eventually renumbered 35A–D Gibson Square. Last came the extraordinary 'Venetian' Milner Square (1841), by the ingenious young architects Roumieu and Gough, so dizzyingly vertical that in later, shabbier days it inspired gloom. A classical church intended for the west side was never built. Dr Pitcairn's botanic garden (*see* BARNSBURY) separated the square from UPPER STREET, with only a communicating passage through the east-side houses – isolation which survived the building in the 1840s–50s of Almeida Street on the garden site.

After a long period of multiple tenancies, the area was restored by new owner-occupiers from the 1960s. Milner Square was restored by Islington Council in the 1970s. Construction of the VICTORIA LINE necessitated building a ventilation shaft in Gibson Square gardens. As the result of strong local agitation, this was designed like a temple to harmonise with the surroundings.

Mincing Lane *EC3*. According to Stow, named after the *mynchens* or nuns of ST HELEN'S BISHOPSGATE. The hall of the CLOTHWORKERS' COMPANY is in Dunster Court.

Minet Estate *SE5.* The medieval Manor of Milkwell lay along the boundary between the parishes of CAMBERWELL and LAMBETH, and was split into three portions in 1671. In 1770 the northern portion was purchased by Hughes Minet, grandson of a French Huguenot refugee, and remained in the family's ownership for the next 200 years.

The laying-out of Camberwell New Road in 1818, linking Camberwell Green to the new VAUXHALL BRIDGE, stimulated housebuilding along the relatively short frontages to the new road and on the west side of the Green; some of these houses remain. However, the flat low ground was unattractive to the more prosperous classes who were migrating to the suburbs in the first half of the 19th century, and most of the estate remained market gardens and pasture until 1863, when the London, Chatham and Dover Railway was built along the south-eastern side of the estate. This created a large demand for small suburban houses, so that the remainder of the estate was laid out for residential use by the then freeholder, James Minet, succeeded by his son William in 1885. Restrictive covenants forbade commercial uses, and a number of amenities were provided by the Minet family: St James's church, Longfield Hall and the original Minet Library in Knatchbull Road, and the land for MYATT'S FIELDS donated to the LONDON COUNTY COUNCIL in 1889 and named after a former tenant of market gardening days. William Minet later donated his important collection of Surrey archives to the library, where they remain as the core of LAMBETH's present local history records. In the early 1970s the Minet Estate was purchased by LAMBETH Council.

Ministry of Defence *Whitehall, SW1.* A huge building designed by E. Vincent Harris in 1957. It was erected at a cost of £5 million and provides accommodation for 5,360 civil servants. The main entrance, which is flanked by Sir Charles Wheeler's 30-ton nude sculptures representing *Earth* and *Water*, is on Horse Guards Avenue.

From the latter half of the 19th century the direction of the British Army was in the hands of the WAR OFFICE, based in London and, in particular, WHITEHALL. In 1964 the Ministry of Defence became a government department which absorbed the then existing ministry of the same title (established in the 2nd World War to assist co-ordination), the ADMIRALTY, Air Ministry and WAR OFFICE.

Ministry of Housing *Whitehall, SW1.* Designed in Renaissance style by J.M. Brydon and built between 1898 and 1912. A bridge over KING CHARLES STREET links it to Scott's Home Office (*see* GOVERNMENT OFFICES).

Minories *EC3.* Named, as John Stow related, after 'an abbey of nuns of the order of St Clare, called the Minories, founded by Edmund, Earl of Lancaster, Leicester and Derby, brother to King Edward I in the year 1293. ... This house was surrendered by Dame Elizabeth Salvage, the last abbess there, unto King Henry VIII, in the 30th of his reign, the year of Christ 1539. ... In place of this house is now built divers fair and large storehouses for armour and habiliments of war, with divers workhouses serving to the same purpose.' Although Henry Percy, 9th Earl of Cumberland, lived in great state in a large mansion in the street at the end of the 16th century, the Minories remained 'chiefly of note for the gunsmiths' up till Stow's time (1720). Wheatley wrote in 1891 that it had become 'a place of general trade without a gunsmith from end to end'. Many of its offices are now occupied by shipbrokers, chartering agents and insurance brokers. The church of Holy Trinity of the Minoresses was destroyed in 1940.

Mint Street *SE1.* On the site of a mint established by Henry VIII at Suffolk Place, the house of Charles Brandon, his sister's husband, in about 1543. Brandon was compensated with the Bishop of Norwich's town house in the STRAND. Edward VI continued to use the mint. Mary I gave it to her Archbishop of York, Nicholas Heath. After its demolition in 1557 smaller houses were built on the site. The area around the mint was a recognised sanctuary for debtors and thieves up to the early 18th century. The highwaymen Jack Sheppard and Jonathan Wild both took sanctuary here.

Mitcham *Surrey.* First mentioned by name in 727, it originated from a camp of Anglo-Saxon warriors encouraged to settle by the Romano-British to defend London from attack from the south. An extensive cemetery of this period (AD 450–600) was excavated in the early years of the 20th century in Morden Road. The town has two village greens, and at the *Domesday* survey there were two settlements, Mikleham (big settlement) around what is now the Upper or Fair Green, and Whitford (white ford, or shallow bubbling water) around what is now the Lower or Cricket Green. Only one parish church (ST PETER AND ST PAUL) was built, so presumably by the 13th century the settlements were combined.

In the 16th and 17th centuries, Mitcham was the country home of a number of City and Court notables. Queen Elizabeth stayed in the village five times between 1591 and 1598. The establishment of the Turnpike in 1745 caused the rebuilding of two inns, the White Hart and the King's Head (now the Burn Bullock) which remain substantially unaltered. The Buck's Head inn at the Fair Green, although rebuilt at the turn of the 20th century, is named after the buck's head crest of the Smythe family who owned it in Elizabethan times. The Canons, built in 1680, EAGLE HOUSE, built in 1705, and Park Place, built in 1780, are old mansions owned by the local council. The Parish Rooms at the Cricket Green were built in 1788 as the first Sunday School of the village. This became a day school in 1812.

Cricket has been played on the Green for at least 270 years, since Mitcham Cricket Club was founded in 1707. Many distinguished players learned the game here. An annual August Fair was held on Fair Green until 1924 when it was moved to the Three Kings' Piece. Traditionally this is thought to be a Tudor fair although written records go back only to 1732. Apart from the common, which covers 500 acres, and the two greens, there is another piece of common-land to the north of the parish. This is Figges Marsh, named after William Figge, a local farmer in the mid-14th century.

The cultivation of lavender and medicinal herbs in the Physic Gardens became the main activity in Mitcham between about 1750 and 1880, but declined due to the advent of synthetic chemicals and the rise in the value of land close to London.

Mitcham Common *Mitcham, Surrey.* Area of 460 acres run by a Board of Conservators under an Act of 1891. James I complained that 'lewd people of Mitcham did so much poaching that there was a great scarcity of game which was at one time plentiful'. There was a hunt until the early 19th century. The common now provides a golf course and other sporting facilities. The fair still takes place in summer although the horse sales for which it was famous have been discontinued. A windmill was built in 1806 but was struck by lightning in the 1850s, became disused, and was dismantled in 1905. Anti-aircraft batteries were temporarily installed here to defend London in the 2nd World War.

Mitre *Palace Gate, Hampton Court, Middlesex.* The 'great Inn called the Mytre' was built by Andrew Snape, the King's Sergeant Farrier, in 1666–7. Snape died in 1691 and left it to his son. The second Andrew Snape, who was also the King's Sergeant Farrier, died in 1709, leaving the Mitre to his widow and their son, Andrew. The third Andrew Snape was already set on a distinguished career. He was educated at Eton, gained a scholarship to Cambridge, and in 1711 became headmaster of his former school. In 1719 he became Provost of King's College and in 1723 Vice-Chancellor of Cambridge University. He and his mother failed to redeem the mortgage on the Mitre and it passed out of the hands of the Snape family. About 1782 it was converted to private houses and remained so until 1840, when it was reconverted to an inn. It soon became a social centre for the neighbourhood; many bodies held their dinners here; and it was used as a meeting place by a number of Masonic Lodges. It has provided accommodation for the enormous number of visitors to HAMPTON COURT PALACE ever since the opening of the Palace to the public.

Mitre Court *EC2.* Takes its name from the MITRE tavern which, in existence here as early as 1475, was destroyed in the GREAT FIRE.

Mitre Tavern *Mitre Court, Fleet Street.* Formerly Joe's Coffee House, this was the inn most favoured by Samuel Johnson who declared that a tavern chair was 'the throne of human felicity'. It was here that he arranged to meet Arthur Murphy to discuss with him the pension that Murphy had been deputed by the government to offer him, and here that he had his first long conversation with James Boswell who, having been introduced to him in the parlour behind Thomas Davies's shop on 16 May 1763, came across him by chance a few days later at TEMPLE BAR. Knowing the Mitre to be Johnson's favourite tavern, Boswell asked Johnson to accompany him there, but the latter said it was too late: 'They won't let us in. But I'll go with you another night with all my heart.' The next Saturday they met again by chance at Clifford's Eating House in Butcher Row where Boswell asked Johnson if he would go to the Mitre with him that evening. They did so, had a good supper, two bottles of port and sat talking until after one o'clock in the morning. They met again at the Mitre on 1 July, this time with Goldsmith; and on 6 July Boswell gave a supper party here. In Johnson's time the landlord of the tavern was Henry Cole. Subsequent landlords, naturally anxious to profit by the fame which Boswell's *Life of Samuel Johnson* had bestowed upon the place,

kept a cast of Nollekens's bust in the corner where Johnson had sat and proudly pointed out the great man's favourite chair.

The Fellows of the ROYAL SOCIETY held their anniversary dinner here in 1772 before moving to the CROWN AND ANCHOR. The SOCIETY OF ANTIQUARIES also held dinners here from 1728 to 1753. Hogarth was an occasional customer. Thomas Topham, the strong man of ISLINGTON, who could bend an iron poker to a right angle by striking it on his bare left arm, who could hold back a horse and cart, despite all the driver's efforts to proceed, and who could support five men standing on his body while lying extended between two chairs, demonstrated his extraordinary powers in the tavern in 1733 by rolling up a pewter dish with his fingers. The place ceased to be a tavern in 1788, later became auction rooms and was demolished in 1829 for an extension of HOARE'S BANK.

Mitre Tavern *St James's Market.* Kept by Mrs Voss, aunt of the actress, Anne Oldfield. George Farquhar, the Irish playwright, once found Mrs Oldfield here behind the bar, rehearsing her part in Beaumont and Fletcher's *The Scornful Lady* between intervals of serving drinks. He expressed admiration of her gifts in glowing terms which were passed on by her mother to Vanbrugh, another customer of the house, who, also struck by her abilities, introduced her to John Rich, manager of COVENT GARDEN, by whom she was engaged in 1692 at a weekly salary of 15s.

Mitre Tavern *Wood Street.* Mentioned by Ben Jonson in *Bartholomew Fair* and *Every Man in His Humour* in which two scenes are placed here. It was 'a house of the greatest note in London', according to Pepys who was introduced here to handicap, 'a sport that [he] never knew before, which was very good'. The landlord, William Proctor, died insolvent in the GREAT PLAGUE in 1665 and the tavern was destroyed the following year in the GREAT FIRE.

Monken Hadley *Middlesex.* Situated north of HIGH BARNET and west of HADLEY WOOD and ENFIELD, Monken Hadley is the highest point on the GREAT NORTH ROAD between London and York. The Saxon *head-leah* means a high place cleared in a forest, and, in Saxon times, the area was part of the extensive forest stretching north from ISLINGTON as far as the Wash. In 1136 Geoffrey de Mandeville gave the 'Hermitage of Hadley' to his newly founded Benedictine Monastery of Walden, hence 'Monken' Hadley. At the DISSOLUTION this passed to Thomas, Lord Audley, together with the Church of ST MARY THE VIRGIN.

Hadley's position on the road to London made it the site of the decisive Battle of Barnet fought in 1471 between the Yorkists and the Lancastrians. The memorial obelisk (erected first in 1740 but afterwards moved) stands at Hadley Highstone, north-east of the church. There were famous and infamous visitors: Elizabeth I and Oliver Cromwell are each said to have stayed at the Old Ford Manor House; ENFIELD CHASE to the east remained a favourite royal hunting ground until the 18th century and was notorious for highwaymen such as Dick Turpin.

During the 18th century the village developed from a rural settlement into a residential area. To the few 17th-century buildings, including the surviving Wilbraham almshouses of 1612, were added imposing

Georgian residences such as Mount House and Hadley Manor, the home of William Thackeray's grandfather, and cottages including Livingstone Cottage, home of the explorer in 1857. The Act of 1777 dividing EN-FIELD CHASE allotted about 240 acres to the parishioners in compensation for ancient rights of common, almost doubling the previous parish area.

The present appearance of Monken Hadley was developed in the 19th century. In 1828 Telford's New Road to St Albans was built west from the High Street and, while the green and common remained open, residential streets were built to the south to accommodate some of the growing population of HIGH BARNET and EAST BARNET. In 1889 Monken Hadley was transferred to Hertfordshire for administrative purposes, and then, in 1904, divided between Barnet and East Barnet Urban Districts to be incorporated complete into the London Borough of BARNET in 1965. In 1968 and 1969 the area of Hadley Green and Hadley Common was designated a conservation area.

Monkwell Square *EC2*. The name probably derives from the family of Muchewella, mentioned in the early 12th century, though Stow claimed that it came from a well at the north end which belonged to the Abbot of Garendon and was used by the monks under his charge. The square covers the site of old Monkwell Street and HART STREET. BARBER-SURGEONS' HALL is here.

Monmouth House *Soho Square*. A large mansion built in the early 1680s, around three sides of a courtyard on the south side of the square for James Scott, Duke of Monmouth, the illegitimate son of Charles II. He had lived there for only a few months when he left for the Netherlands. After his unsuccessful rebellion in 1685 he was executed. For a long time the house stood empty while his creditors wrangled. In 1689 a back room was converted into L'Église du Quarré for Huguenot refugees. In 1694 the congregation moved to a larger building in BERWICK STREET, then to Little Dean Street, now BOURCHIER STREET. In 1716 the Duchess of Monmouth sold the house to Sir James Bateman, the Lord Mayor, who remodelled the front, probably to the design of his relation Thomas Archer. No sooner had this been done than, in 1718, Bateman died. His eldest son, William, later 1st Viscount Bateman, lived here until 1739. In 1765–6 it was let to the French Ambassador; in 1768–9 to the Russian Ambassador; and in 1771–2 to John Reney who unsuccessfully tried to set up a boys' school. In 1773 it was demolished. Bateman Buildings now occupy the site.

Monmouth Street *WC2*. Named after the Earls of Monmouth who had property in the area in the 17th century. It ran from what is now CHARING CROSS ROAD to BROAD STREET and was widened to form the eastern part of SHAFTESBURY AVENUE. Throughout the 18th century and for most of the 19th it was famed for its old clothes shops. Gay wrote in his *Trivia*:

Thames Street gives cheeses, Covent Garden fruits, Moorfields old books, and Monmouth Street old suits.

'On Lord Kelly, a remarkable red-faced, drunken lord, coming into a room in a coat much embroidered but somewhat tarnished, Foote said he was an exact representation of Monmouth Street in flames!'

Cruikshank's illustrations, for Dickens's Sketches by Boz, *of the old clothes market in Monmouth Street, 1836.*

Dickens described the street in *Sketches by Boz* in which there is a representation on it by Cruikshank. The name was re-established in the 1930s when Little and Great St Andrew's Streets, which run from Upper St Martin's Lane to the top of Shaftesbury Avenue, were renamed to become the present Monmouth Street.

Monmouth Street Market *Seven Dials*. A well-known Victorian market for old clothes. According to Mayhew, 'Monmouth Street Finery' was a byword for tawdriness and pretence. By the 1860s it was mainly an old boot and shoe market where most of the 'cobbling' was brown paper and blacking. Dickens referred to the market as the 'burial place of fashion'.

Samuel Montagu and Co. Ltd *Old Broad Street, EC2*. This merchant bank was founded in 1853 by Samuel Montagu (later Lord Swaythling) and his brother Edwin Samuel, a Liverpool banker and bullion merchant. The firm was originally based in LEADENHALL STREET and in 1865 it moved to its present address at No. 114 OLD BROAD STREET. Specialising in foreign exchange and bullion dealing, the firm later diversified into foreign loans and other merchant banking services. It is now a member of the London Gold and Silver Markets. In 1960 it absorbed Hart Son and Co. merchant bankers (founded in 1889) and in 1974 amalgamated with Drayton Corporation, a long-established investment group. The enlarged bank became a subsidiary of the MIDLAND BANK in 1973.

Montagu House *Bloomsbury*. The first house on the site was designed by Robert Hooke for Ralph Montagu, later 1st Duke of Montagu, Charles II's Ambassador to Paris, who had married Elizabeth, daughter of the Earl of Southampton and widow of the Earl of Northumberland. It adjoined the gardens of

The entrance hall of Montagu House, Bloomsbury, c. 1800. It was sold in 1755 to accommodate the new British Museum.

SOUTHAMPTON HOUSE, which had been built by his wife's family, and it was, in John Evelyn's opinion, 'a stately and ample palace'. It survived for less than ten years, however, being burned down in a fire in January 1686. The house was immediately rebuilt to the designs, so Horace Walpole thought, of Pierre Puget: certainly several French artists were employed in its decoration. 'What it wants in grace and beauty,' Walpole wrote, 'is compensated by the spaciousness and lofty magnificence of the apartments.' The costs incurred by Montagu were enormous; but, after the death of his first wife, he repaired his fortune by marrying the 2nd Duchess of Albemarle, an extremely rich but insane woman who, having declared she would marry no one but a crowned head, was persuaded to believe that Montagu was the Emperor of China and, in the role of Empress, was served at Montagu House on bended knee. John, the 2nd Duke of Montagu, left his father's grandiose palace for a smaller house on the site of what is now Richmond Terrace; and in 1755 the house was sold for the housing of the newly established BRITISH MUSEUM. It was demolished to make way for Smirke's building in the 1840s.

Montagu House *Portman Square*. Stood diagonally at the north-west corner of the square. It was designed in 1760 by James 'Athenian' Stuart for Mrs Elizabeth Montagu but was not built until 1777–82. Mrs Montagu, one of the leading hostesses of her day, was 'brilliant in diamonds, solid in judgment, critical in talk'. Her literary gatherings were nicknamed the Blue Stocking Society (the origin of the term) by Admiral Boscawen, after the idiosyncrasy of a regular habitué, Mr Benjamin Stillingfleet, who wore blue stockings instead of black silk ones. One of the rooms was decorated with bird feathers. Cowper wrote:

The birds put off their every hue
To dress a room for Montagu.

Another room was painted with jasmine, roses and cupids. Every May Day Mrs Montagu gave a dinner of roast beef and plum pudding to chimney sweeps' climbing-boys. One of them, David Porter, grew up to be a builder and named MONTAGU SQUARE, and MONTAGU PLACE after her. She died here in 1800. The Montagu family owned the house until 1874, leasing it for long periods to noble families. It was then taken over by the ground landlord, Lord Portman, and was recased in red brick. Members of the Portman family lived in the house until it was destroyed in the 2nd World War. The gate-piers survived and are now in the grounds of KENWOOD HOUSE.

The house in Portman Square originally built in 1782 for Mrs Elizabeth Montagu, a leading hostess of her day.

524

Montagu Place *W1.* Built in about 1811 and named after Mrs Elizabeth Montagu of PORTMAN SQUARE who had befriended the builder, David Porter, when he was a poor chimney sweep. Sir Arthur Blomfield, the architect, lived at No. 6 in 1882–98. JEWS' COLLEGE (founded 1855) is at No. 11.

Montagu Square *W1.* A narrow oblong of brick terraced houses designed by Joseph Parkinson as a twin for BRYANSTON SQUARE, it was built in 1811 by David Porter and named after Mrs Elizabeth Montagu of PORTMAN SQUARE. Anthony Trollope lived at No. 39 in 1873–80.

Montague Place *and* **Montague Street** *WC1.* Named after Ralph, Duke of Montagu, who chose to build his lavish mansion near BEDFORD HOUSE, fronting GREAT RUSSELL STREET (*see* MONTAGU HOUSE). Evans Brothers, the publishers, are at Nos 8–11 Montague Street and the BEDFORD ESTATE office at No. 29A.

Montfichet Tower Stood on the river at BLACKFRIARS. It is said to have been built in the reign of William I but is not mentioned in documents until the 1130s. At one time it was occupied by the Barons of Montfichet. In 1275 Robert Fitzwalter, who then owned it, gave it with CASTLE BAYNARD to the Black Friars as a site for their monastery. It was demolished soon afterwards.

Montpelier Place, Square, Street, Terrace *and* **Walk** *SW7.* Built on fields which had belonged to the Moreaus, a rich Huguenot family, in the 18th century. By 1824 the two fields had become the property of John Betts and Thomas Marriott, and in 1826 were laid out for development. The development was slow. Access was obtained in the north-east corner by the purchase of a small piece of land from the Trevor Estate, but elsewhere it was blocked by the Rutland Estate and the BROMPTON SQUARE development. The houses on the east and west sides were built mainly in 1840–5. Some of those in Montpelier Terrace were not built until 1850. It was not a very high-class area, as was shown by the presence of a number of public houses and a butcher's shop. Galsworthy, writing in 1922, was undoubtedly wrong to put Soames Forsyte into it, at No. 62 Montpelier Square, in 1876. But despite its fairly lowly beginnings, the square rose rapidly and by the 1890s was a good address. The streets to its west and south were of much lower status and quality and did not rise much above slums until after the 1st World War. The name Montpelier has no direct connection with Montpellier in France and first occurs in relation to the area in June 1825.

Montrose House *186 Petersham Road, Richmond, Surrey.* One of the least altered of the PETERSHAM mansions. It was built before 1707 for Sir Thomas Jenner, Justice of the Common Pleas under James II; he was arrested in 1688 but was released without charges being made. Inside there is a panelled room and a fine staircase. The house takes its name from the Dowager Duchess of Montrose who lived here in 1837–47. Even at that time complaints were being made about the notorious corner made by the Petersham Road rounding her property, complaints that were still being made in 1982. At the end of the 19th century J.H. Master lived here with his wife, Gertrude Emma; they were very active in the field of charities and education, founding a Coffee House and Mission for the Poor of Petersham in a building opposite Elm Lodge, popularly known as the Gem Palace and later as Trefoil House when it was taken over for the local Girl Guides after the 1st World War. It was bought by the entertainer, Tommy Steele, in 1969.

Monument *Monument Street and Fish Street Hill, EC2.* 'And the better to preserve the memory of this dreadful Visitation, Be it further enacted, That a Column or Pillar of Brase or Stone be erected on or as neere unto the place where the said Fire soe unhappily began as conveniently may be, in perpetual Remembrance thereof, with such inscription thereon, as hereafter by the Maior and Court of Aldermen in that behalfe be directed.' Thus the Act of Parliament, which provided for the rebuilding of the CITY after the GREAT FIRE, provided also for the commemoration of the Fire by a monument. The design of the column was entrusted to Wren and the responsibility for its erection was placed in the hands of the City Lands Committee of the CORPORATION OF LONDON which still maintains it today. Wren and his friend Robert Hooke prepared several designs, including one for a pillar with bronze flames leaping from holes in the shaft and a phoenix on the summit. But in the end the design of a simpler monument of the Doric order was chosen. It was constructed of Portland stone in 1671–7. Its total height is 202 ft, and it is the tallest isolated stone column in the world. At the summit is a flaming urn of gilt bronze symbolising the GREAT FIRE. Wren would have preferred a statue of Charles II, but Hooke had his way. The balcony beneath this urn is approached by a spiral staircase of 311 steps. The cost was £13,450 11s 9d. Three of the panels on the pedestal bear inscriptions in Latin. The inscription on the north panel reads in translation: 'In the year of Christ 1666, on 2 September, at a distance eastward from this place of 202 feet, which is the height of this column, a fire broke out in the dead of night which, the wind blowing, devoured even distant buildings, and rushed devastating through every quarter with astonishing swiftness and noise . . . . On the third day . . . at the bidding, we may well believe, of heaven, the fatal fire stayed its course and everywhere died out.' To these words were added in 1681, 'But Popish frenzy, which wrought such horrors, is not yet quenched.' This addition provoked Pope to write:

Where London's column pointing at the skies,
Like a tall bully, lifts the head, and lies.

This part of the inscription was removed in 1830. The inscription on the south panel records the part played by Charles II and Parliament in the rebuilding of the CITY. The inscription on the east panel records the names of the Lord Mayors who held office while the Monument was being built. The west panel contains a bas-relief by Caius Gabriel Cibber, an allegorical design representing Charles II in Roman costume, accompanied by the Duke of York, commanding his attendants to bring relief to the afflicted city. The four dragons at the base are by Edward Pierce the Younger.

When the column was completed it was used for certain experiments by Fellows of the ROYAL SOCIETY, but the vibrations caused by the traffic proved too much of an interference and they were abandoned.

Another Dreadful Suicide AT THE MONUMENT, BY A YOUNG WOMAN.

After many suicides at the Monument, the death of a maidservant in 1842 led to the enclosure of the gallery by a cage.

Like so many other visitors to London, James Boswell climbed to the gallery in 1762 soon after his arrival from Scotland. Halfway up he grew frightened and would have come down again had he not felt he would despise himself for his timidity. He persevered and mounted to the gallery where he found it 'horrid to be so monstrous a way up in the air, so far above London and all its spires'. He dared not look around him despite the rail, and he shuddered as every wagon passed down GRACECHURCH STREET, dreading that 'the shaking of the earth would make the tremendous pile tumble to the foundations.' In 1788 a baker threw himself from the gallery, the first of six people to commit suicide in this way. After the sixth of these suicides, a servant girl, had thrown herself off in 1842 the building was temporarily closed while the gallery was enclosed by an iron cage. The column was completely renovated in 1834 when the gilt-bronze urn was regilded. The urn was again regilded in 1954, the stone steam-cleaned and the scars caused by bomb fragments in the 2nd World War eradicated.

Monument Street *EC3*. Named after the MONUMENT which stands at the western end between FISH STREET HILL and PUDDING LANE. First formed in 1883–93 and later extended to take in the former Monument Square.

Moor Lane *EC2*. Built across the moor which lay outside the CITY wall (*see* MOORFIELDS). Between 1725 and 1843 the workhouse of ST GILES CRIPPLEGATE stood on the east side of the street. ST BARTHOLOMEW MOOR LANE was built on the site but was demolished in 1901.

Moorfields *EC2*. Runs parallel with MOORGATE and extends from Fox Street Avenue to Ropemaker Street. It takes its name from the moor outside the city walls which was drained in 1527. LAZARD BROTHERS are at No. 21.

Moorfields Eye Hospital *City Road, EC1*. Founded in 1805 under the name of the London Dispensary for the Relief of the Poor afflicted with Diseases of the Eye and Ear. Until that time there was no such specialist hospital in London and surgeons gave little attention to these diseases. The driving force of the project was a young man named John Cunningham Saunders, a student at GUY'S who became a protégé of and assistant to Sir Astley Cooper for whom he made dissections. This was at the time of the Napoleonic Wars during which a British occupying force was sent to Aboukir in Egypt. The force remained there from 1803 to 1805. Most of the troops were infected with trachoma and many went blind. On returning home they infected areas all over the country and an enormous number of people lost their sight. At that time most eye complaints were treated by itinerant quacks. No. 40 CHARTERHOUSE SQUARE was leased as premises for the new dispensary, the patron of which was a wealthy City merchant named Benjamin Travers. Within a year it was decided to treat eyes only and the name was changed to the London Infirmary for Curing Diseases of the Eye. In 1811 medical students and postgraduates were admitted to the Infirmary. Amongst them were two young Americans recently qualified in New York. They were so impressed by what they saw in London that, on returning home in 1820, they founded the New York Eye and Ear Infirmary which still exists.

The London Eye Infirmary immediately developed an international reputation and doctors came from all over the world to study here. It soon became apparent that larger premises would be needed and in 1821 Robert Smirke was commissioned to erect a building on a freehold site in the north-east corner of Lower Moorfields, near FINSBURY CIRCUS. The new building was called the Royal London Ophthalmic Hospital. It was more generally known as the Moorfields Eye Hospital, though it was not officially so designated until 1956. In 1868 a new wing was added. By 1887 it was obvious that the hospital's buildings were inadequate so it was decided to move. With the money obtained from the sale of the old site a new hospital was built in the CITY ROAD and opened in 1899, the architects being Keith Young and Hall. With the opening of the new hospital, a medical school was formed. There were then five ophthalmic hospitals in London. After Moorfields the most senior was the Royal Westminster Eye Hospital in HIGH HOLBORN, founded in 1816 and now known as the HIGH HOLBORN branch of Moorfields. The third hospital was the small Central London Eye Hospital in Judd Street, WC1. Shortly after the creation of the National Health Service in 1948, this hospital was dissolved and the building was converted into the Institute of Ophthalmology, part of the British Postgraduate Medical Federation under the UNIVERSITY OF LONDON. The fourth eye hospital – the Western Ophthalmic – amalgamated with ST MARY'S, PADDINGTON, and the fifth, the Royal Eye Hospital, St George's Circus, was absorbed by ST THOMAS'S HOSPITAL. In 1982 there were 252 beds in Moorfields and its branch in HIGH HOLBORN.

Moorgate *EC2*. Named after the postern gate in the CITY wall leading out to the fens which was built in 1415 by Thomas Falconer, mercer. It was repaired in 1472 and rebuilt in 1672. The gateway was made higher so that the TRAINED BANDS could march through with their pikes upright. It was demolished in 1762 and the stones used to prevent LONDON BRIDGE being washed away by the tide. The street was laid out in the 1840s to give easier access to the new LONDON BRIDGE. Some houses of that period survive; but Moorgate is now a centre of banking and insurance. The CHARTERED ACCOUNTANTS' HALL at No. 132 was designed by Whitfield Partners (1970). The Moorgate public house at No. 85 stands on the site of the Swan and Hoop where the poet John Keats was born in 1795.

Moravian Burial Ground *see* BURIAL GROUNDS.

Moray Lodge *Kensington*. Built by John Tasker in 1817. Its most interesting resident was Arthur James Lewis, silk mercer, who lived here from 1862. His evening entertainments, which featured a band of music-loving friends, 'The Moray Minstrels', attracted notable guests, amongst them Thackeray, Trollope, Millais, Leighton and Arthur Sullivan. In 1867 Lewis married the actress Kate Terry, the sister of Ellen. The house was demolished in 1955.

Morden *Surrey*. The parish of Morden was one of the smallest of the ancient Surrey parishes, covering only 1,475 acres. A Roman road, later called Stane Street, ran diagonally across the parish and crosses Morden Park 4 ft below the present surface. This park also contains what is believed to be a Romano-British burial mound. The first mention of Morden was in 968 when Edgar confirmed previous gifts of land, which included Morden, to WESTMINSTER ABBEY. The Abbot still held the manor at the *Domesday* survey. At the DISSOLUTION the manor was bought by Richard Garth, whose family retained possession until 1872, living for much of this time in Morden Hall. This is a 17th-century house substantially altered about 1840 and set in its own extensive deer park. Subsequently the manor was sold to Gilliat Hatfeild who was succeeded by his son, also Gilliat, upon whose death Morden Hall and its park was taken over by the NATIONAL TRUST. Both of the Hatfeilds were great local benefactors.

The parish church of ST LAWRENCE retains much of its rural charm, being little altered since its rebuilding in 1636. To the north is Church Farm Cottage, a weatherboarded building of 1813 and sole surviving relic of the old church farm (dating from 1331). To the south of the church is the George Inn which probably has 16th-century origins. Behind the church is Morden Park, within which is a Georgian villa built in 1770 for John Ewart, a distiller and merchant of London, who enclosed the park. After a succession of private owners it is now occupied by the Parks Department of the Borough. Across the road, opposite the church, is the Old School House built in 1731 for 12 poor children of the parish by Mrs Elizabeth Gardiner, widowed daughter of George Garth. Close by, in Green Lane, are the Haig Memorial Homes opened in 1931 for ex-servicemen and their widows.

Morden remained essentially a village centred upon the parish church until the terminus of the NORTHERN LINE Underground arrived in 1926 approximately half a mile north of the old village. This encouraged very substantial housing development.

Morden College *St German's Place, SE3*. To the south of BLACKHEATH lies what was originally the Wricklemarsh Estate. It was some 280 acres in extent and was probably so named from the Saxon word

writtle or *wrickle* which means 'chirp', describing the sound of the many brooks which intersected it. It has been roughly translated as 'babbling brooks'. The name appears in *Domesday Book*. It was then arable land. After passing through various hands, it was bought in 1669 by Sir John Morden. He was a 'Turkey Merchant', a man of wealth and evidently of philanthropic impulses. He went through a bad time when his ships were greatly delayed and he thought he was facing penury. When they at last arrived safely, he built Morden College, in 1695, as a thanks offering. This lovely Wren building, with its colonnaded courtyard and its beautiful gardens, was intended to house 'decayed Turkey Merchants' who had fallen on hard times through no fault of their own. The chapel on the west side contains a fine wood carving attributed to Grinling Gibbons. Sir John, who died in 1708, is buried there. He left his foundation, richly endowed with land, to be administered by trustees. Lady Morden, who lived till 1721, had a life interest. The College still exists, is still administered by trustees, and is a home for elderly people who pay according to their means.

Morgan Grenfell and Co. Ltd *23 Great Winchester Street, EC2*. The merchant house of Peabody, Riggs and Co. was established by George Peabody of Boston, Massachusetts, in 1838 (*see* PEABODY BUILDINGS). Originally located in MOORGATE, the firm moved to OLD BROAD STREET in 1854, when J.S. Morgan became a partner. In 1864 Peabody left the firm, which was renamed J.S. Morgan and Co. With his son J.P. Morgan (founder of J.P. Morgan and Co. of New York in 1871), Morgan developed the firm's banking business, notably in railway finance and international loans. The London and New York firms played major roles in Anglo-American finance in the 1st World War. Renamed Morgan Grenfell and Co. in 1910, the firm moved to its present address in 1926.

Morley College *61 Westminster Bridge Road, SE1*. Founded in the 1880s by Emma Cons, who, as a friend of the housing reformer Octavia Hill, was determined to raise the moral as well as the material standards of the WATERLOO ROAD district. A lease was taken of the OLD VIC which thereafter presented variety free of the coarseness and vulgarity which had previously characterised that theatre's productions, as well as concerts and lectures. Regular evening classes were started in the theatre dressing rooms in 1885; and in 1889 this educational side of the OLD VIC was formally organised as Morley College, the name being chosen in honour of Samuel Morley, a textile manufacturer and Member of Parliament who had supported the project from the beginning. In 1924, the premises available at the OLD VIC being no longer large enough, the College moved to a house on the present site to which a new wing, opened by Queen Mary, was added in 1937. The older building, destroyed in the BLITZ, was reconstructed in 1958; the Art Centre was opened in 1969; and an entirely new college was opened by Queen Elizabeth II in 1973.

Morley's Hotel *Trafalgar Square*. Built in 1831 on the south-east corner of TRAFALGAR SQUARE, it was one of the foremost older hotels. It had 100 bedrooms. It became South Africa House in 1921.

Mornington Crescent *NW1*. Part of the Fitzroy family estate (*see* FITZROY SQUARE). It was begun in 1821 and named after the Earl of Mornington whose daughter, Anne, had married the Hon. Henry Fitzroy, brother of the 2nd Baron Southampton. The north side of the crescent was originally known as Southampton Street, the name being changed in 1864. It was formerly a favourite residence of artists and writers. Clarkson Stanfield lived at No. 36 in 1834–41; F.R. Pickersgill succeeded him in the same house, Walter Sickert lived at No. 6. Frederick Henry Yates, the actor and father of the novelist Edmund Yates, died in the crescent in 1842. George Cruikshank lived just round the corner at No. 48 Mornington Place.

Mortimer Street *W1*. Takes its name from the title of Earl Mortimer bestowed upon the statesman Robert Harley (1st Earl of Oxford and Mortimer), whose son, husband of the heiress of MARYLEBONE Manor, built the street on her land. The Duke of Clarence, afterwards William IV, lived at No.32 in 1809 and Admiral Earl St Vincent at No.34 in 1804–9. Nollekens, the sculptor, had his studio in the street from 1771 until his death here in 1823. Samuel Johnson sat for his bust here. Johnson's friend Mrs Thrale stayed in the street for a short time in 1784 before her marriage to Piozzi. William Charles Macready, the actor, was born here in 1793. The MIDDLESEX HOSPITAL is on the north side. Cole and Son, the wallpaper manufacturers, are at No. 18.

Mortlake *and* **East Sheen** *SW14*. Mortlake was already so called in *Domesday Book* and the name (of obscure origin) has no connection with plague pits. The manor, which also included PUTNEY and WIMBLEDON and possessed certain rights over BARNES, was held by the Archbishop of Canterbury. Until at least 1348 the parish church was sited at WIMBLEDON and the priest's visits to Mortlake are perhaps perpetuated in 'Priest's Bridge' over the BEVERLEY BROOK. The manor house, rebuilt by Cardinal Bourchier on an impressive scale, stood near the river with its gatehouse facing Mortlake Green. Henry VIII persuaded Cranmer to relinquish it and bestowed it first on Thomas Cromwell and, after his fall, on Catherine Parr but it fell into disuse and no trace remains. By the late 16th century Mortlake had become a popular residential village, its most celebrated figure being the alchemist Dr John Dee. In 1619 the tapestry works was set up (*see* TAPESTRY COURT *and* SUTHREY HOUSE) and, in 1637, 732 acres of the common land were seized for enclosure in the New (later RICHMOND) PARK. After the Restoration, a Dissenting minister, David Clarkson, founded an independent church which has survived uninterrupted until the present day. During the 17th and 18th centuries, imposing mansions were built in the south of the parish in the area known as East Sheen although there is no formal boundary with Mortlake. These were largely superseded by ambitious late Victorian villas but they in turn were overtaken by the suburban development of the early 20th century. After the closure of the tapestry works, the main industries were market gardening and brewing, which still flourishes at Watney's; there was also a pottery and some of its wares are kept at the church. Until recently Mortlake was a riverside village but its character has been largely eroded with the widening of the High Street. A rare feature for the south bank is the presence of 18th-century houses with gardens on to the river (*see* THE LIMES). There is a further cluster of early houses at Thames Bank (*see* LEYDEN HOUSE). The former rural atmosphere of East Sheen is best recaptured in Christ Church Road where the Plough Inn and a group of early cottages face the grand mid-Georgian Percy Lodge with its fine brickwork and Venetian windows. Sir Arthur Blomfield, whose firm undertook the rebuilding of the parish church of ST MARY'S, also designed Christ Church, East Sheen (1862–4); the tower collapsed shortly before the church was due to be consecrated and had to be rebuilt to the design of J.B. Tolhurst. All Saints, East Sheen Avenue, was built in 1929, to serve a further increase in population.

Mortlake Tapestries Made from 1619 by Flemish weavers. The mark was a white shield with a red cross, Raphael's cartoons for *The Acts of the Apostles*, acquired for the workshop by Charles I in 1632, were the model for several tapestries as, later, were Mantegna's paintings now at HAMPTON COURT. After the Civil War the quality of the workshop's products declined; and the weavers began to leave soon after the Restoration. Some went to work in the SOHO factories. The Mortlake workshop was closed in 1703.

Moss Bros *21 Bedford Street, WC2*. Moses Moses started selling second-hand clothes in 1860. His two youngest sons, Alfred and George, opened a little shop in KING STREET, COVENT GARDEN, later extending it to BEDFORD STREET, and by 1917 had bought up other small shops till the firm occupied the whole corner site. They called themselves Moss Bros. Their famous hire service for weddings and other special occasions, including coronations, continues undiminished.

Mossop Street *SW3*. Originally known as Green Lettuce Lane – and more prosaically Green Lane – when it went between market gardens, it was renamed in 1935. Its new name commemorates Henry Mossop, an 18th-century actor buried in CHELSEA OLD CHURCH, and Charles Mossop, who was active in local politics in CHELSEA. Four small cottages still survive from the days when it was a country lane. The Admiral Codrington public house, which has some fine mirrors and wooden panelling and is still lit by gas, is one of the few Chelsea inns with a garden.

Motcomb Street *SW1*. Built on the GROSVENOR ESTATE and named after one of the family's properties in Dorset. It is first shown on a map of 1830 and named Kinnerton Mews. It became Motcomb Street soon afterwards. It was clearly designed for a slightly higher social class than its neighbour, KINNERTON STREET. It has one public house and is composed of pleasant 'third-rate' houses dating from the early 1830s. Many of them soon became shops and by 1854 the occupants included cowkeepers, bakers and grocers. Richard Gunter (*see* GUNTER'S) had his confectionary shop at the corner with LOWNDES STREET. On the north side of the street stood the famous Pantechnicon of almost 2 acres, a complex of 'fireproof' warehouses, stables, wine vaults and carriage houses built by Seth Smith to the designs of Joseph Jobling in 1830. It was almost totally destroyed by fire in February 1874, only the front remaining. Jobling also designed the arcade running south to WEST HALKIN STREET, both frontages of which still remain. The sculpture inside the entrance to Halkin Arcade is *Fountainhead* by Geoffrey Wickham (1971).

Motor Shows The first Motor Show in London was the International Horseless Carriage Exhibition which opened at the IMPERIAL INSTITUTE on 9 May 1896. In 1903 and 1904 the Society of Motor Manufacturers and Traders held shows at CRYSTAL PALACE. From 1905 shows were held annually at OLYMPIA in November, except for the war years, 1914–18. In 1937 the shows were transferred to EARL'S COURT where they were continued annually (except for 1939–47) until 1977 when they were transferred to Birmingham.

Mottingham *SE9*. Lies south of ELTHAM in the northernmost part of the London Borough of BROMLEY and borders the London Boroughs of LEWISHAM to the west and GREENWICH to the east. By the 9th century Modingahema was named and probably associated with someone called Moda. The area lay within the manor of LEWISHAM until 1290 when it passed to ELTHAM manor. By the 16th century a growing hamlet lay around Mottingham Place, built in 1560 on the site of the later Mottingham House, and the Porcupine Inn existed by the 17th century (rebuilt 1922). Until the 19th century there were a handful of residences on Mottingham Lane but following the arrival of the Dartford Loop Line in the 1860s development between the lane and the station began. The station was named Mottingham in 1927. St Andrew's church was built (E.C. Clark, 1880) and a separate parish was formed in 1884. In 1842 ELTHAM COLLEGE was founded in a building once called Fairy Hall, the home of Henry, Lord Bathurst, Lord Chancellor in 1771, and the Royal Naval College from 1889–1910. Geffreye's almshouses, for retired members of the IRONMONGERS' COMPANY, were built (George Hubbard, 1912; later converted into flats) following the closure of the original almshouses in SHOREDITCH, now the GEFFRYE MUSEUM. Between the Wars the LONDON COUNTY COUNCIL developed 244 acres of the Mottingham Estate, and development continued after the 2nd World War. In 1965 the London Borough of Bromley absorbed the Mottingham portion of CHISLEHURST and SIDCUP Urban District Councils. W.G. Grace lived at Fairmount from 1909 until his death in 1915.

Mount *Hampstead, NW3*. A side road running off HEATH STREET and above it. A house called The Mount was built here in the early 18th century (now No. 6 and called Cloth Hill) and here Romney stayed while his studio in Holly Bush Hill was being built. The painter Ford Madox Brown lodged in Heath Street, just across the road, in 1852 and used the Mount as the setting for his famous painting *Work* – now in the Manchester Art Gallery. It depicts, as the artist said, 'the British excavator or navvy . . . in the full swing of his activity, with his manly and picturesque costume'. The workmen, busy on drainage work, are watched by a group of onlookers who include Thomas Carlyle.

Mount Coffee House *Grosvenor Street*. First mentioned in 1727 as a place for Masonic lodge meetings; similar references continue for the next twenty years. Laurence Sterne apparently frequented the house while he was living in BOND STREET, and some of his love letters to Eliza, Mrs Draper, bear the address. In 1772 Boswell mentions taking breakfast here. Shelley's first wife, Harriet Westbrook, whom he married in 1811, was the daughter of the landlord, John Westbrook. The house is last mentioned in the 1833 edition of *Picture of London*.

Mount Pleasant *WC1*. Formerly a country path leading down to the FLEET RIVER and rising beyond the far bank. By 1720 Strype described the area as 'a dirty Place with some ill buildings', so the name was presumably ironic. Certainly rubbish was deposited on the river bank here and a laystall was formed. Hence also Laystall Street. The Apple Tree public house at No. 45 occupies the site of a tavern of the same name which was kept by one Topham, the 'strong man of Islington', in the middle of the 18th century and was frequented by prisoners released from COLDBATH FIELDS PRISON.

Mount Pleasant Sorting Office *WC1*. The principal sorting office served by the POST OFFICE RAILWAY. It is one of the largest letter-sorting offices in the world. It handles an average of three million letters every day.

Mount Royal Hotel *Bryanston Street, Marble Arch, W1*. Designed – an unusual design for its day – by Francis Lorne of Sir John Burnet, Tait and Lorne and built in 1932–3. In 1982 there were 705 bedrooms.

Mount Street *W1*. On the GROSVENOR ESTATE, it extends from BERKELEY SQUARE to PARK LANE. It takes its name from Mount Field, where (near the north end of Carpenter Street) formerly stood a small earthwork known as Oliver's Mount, said to be part of London's fortifications erected during the Civil War. The street was first built in about 1720–40, most of the houses being small and unpretentious, probably due to the presence of the parish workhouse on the south side. Shops were always numerous here, and also respectable lodging-houses, one of which was taken by Anthony Trollope's Archdeacon Grantly when he and his wife had occasion to come up to London. In 1880–1900 the whole street was rebuilt under the aegis of the 1st Duke of Westminster, chiefly in the pink terracotta Queen Anne style which he so greatly favoured. The workhouse was removed to PIMLICO, and east of SOUTH AUDLEY STREET arose several fine ranges of shops (now almost exclusively used for luxury trades), with residential accommodation above. The best of these are Nos 104–111 (consecutive) (1885–7) and Nos 112–113 (1891–2), both by Ernest George and Peto; and Nos 13–26 (consecutive) (1896–8) by Herbert Read and R.F. Macdonald. West of SOUTH AUDLEY STREET all trade was banished in favour of large private houses, those on the south side, Nos 68–69 and 78–79 Mount Street and 6, 7 Balfour Place (1891–7) being designed by Eustace Balfour (the estate surveyor) and Thackeray Turner. The finest house in the whole street was No. 54, at the north corner with PARK STREET, designed by Fairfax Wade for Lord Windsor (1896–9), a palatial affair now the residence of the Brazilian ambassador. John Baily and Son (Poulterers) Ltd were established at No. 116 in 1720.

Mount Vernon *NW3*. Takes its name from General Charles Vernon who bought property in the area in 1785. Sir Henry Dale, the physiologist, lived at Mount Vernon House, which was built in about 1800, in 1919–42.

Mulberry Garden (Corporation Row) *Clerkenwell*. In 1742 Mr Body gave notice that 'at six o'clock in the evening the garden would be opened and would continue open every evening during the summer season'. Rocque's map of 1746 shows a large pond, gravelled walks and an avenue of trees. There was a skittle alley, a long room, and an orchestra which consisted only of British musicians as the proprietor considered 'the manly vigour of our own native music is more suitable to the ear and heart of a Briton than the effeminate softness of the Italian.' Admission was free. Occasional firework displays were given. An advertisement for one display in 1744 promised 'the most curious fireworks ever seen in England including a rocket weighing 50 lb'. 1,600 people were admitted and 500 turned away. Fashionable gentlemen came here for an occasional game of skittles, but during its later years the garden was mainly patronised by tradesmen. Nothing is known of it after 1752. It lay on the south side of Corporation Row, east of Woodbridge Street.

Mulberry Walk *SW3*. Lies on what was the southern boundary of Chelsea Park which contained many mulberry trees. Several attempts, varying in success, were made to establish a silkworm industry nearby. There are still fruiting mulberry trees in some CHELSEA gardens.

Mumford Court *EC2*. The court is first marked on Ogilby and Morgan's map of 1667 and was probably named after its owner or builder. After the 2nd World War it was incorporated with Castle Court, named after a 17th-century tavern which stood in Lawrence Lane.

Museum of Artillery *Rotunda, Repository Road, Woolwich*. A circular tent-like structure designed by John Nash, it was first erected in the grounds of CARLTON HOUSE for the Prince Regent's reception of the allied sovereigns after Napoleon's abdication. A month later it held celebrations in honour of the Duke of Wellington. It was draped with white muslin. Two bands played in the centre beneath a temple and artificial flowers. Covered walks leading to the supper tents were decorated with transparencies. Having been given to the army as a military repository, it was re-erected on its present site in 1819. The museum exemplifies the development of artillery from the 14th century to the present day and contains the finest collection of ordnance in this country, both in original and model form. Its control is vested in the Royal Artillery Institution.

Museum of London *London Wall, EC2*. Opened in 1975 as an amalgamation of the LONDON MUSEUM and the GUILDHALL MUSEUM, its exhibits illustrate the history of London from prehistoric to modern times and range from a Roman pavement unearthed in BUCKLERSBURY and a 16th-century herb burner found in MOORGATE, to the LORD MAYOR'S COACH, the reconstruction of a Victorian barber's shop and the 1928 lift interiors from SELFRIDGE'S. The museum is financed by the Office of Arts and Libraries, the GREATER LONDON COUNCIL and the CORPORATION OF THE CITY OF LONDON. The building was designed by Powell and Moya.

Museum of Mankind *(Ethnography Department of the British Museum), 6 Burlington Gardens, W1*. The contents of the museum were formerly in the BRITISH MUSEUM. In 1970, because of lack of space, the exhibits were moved to the present location and renamed the Museum of Mankind. The elegant museum building, designed by Sir James Pennethorne, was first occupied (in 1869) by the UNIVERSITY OF LONDON who made it their adminstrative centre. From 1902 until 1970 it was used by the Civil Service. The permanent collections of the museum, which include their greatest treasures, came from the indigenous peoples of Africa, Australia and the Pacific Islands, North and South America and certain parts of Asia and Europe, and comprise objects from ancient as well as recent and contemporary cultures.

Museum of Manufactures *Marlborough House*. Opened on 6 September 1852 under the supervision of Henry Cole (*see* GREAT EXHIBITION) after £5,000 had been spent on buying items which were 'distinguished entirely for the excellence of their art of workmanship' and which had been displayed at the GREAT EXHIBITION the year before. Its aims were 'the improvement of public taste in design' and 'the application of fine art to objects of utility'. Subsequently known as the Museum of Ornamental Art, in 1857 its contents were moved to South Kensington (*see* VICTORIA AND ALBERT MUSEUM).

Museum of Practical Geology *Jermyn Street*. One of the earliest of the great national museums in England, it was designed by James Pennethorne and opened by the Prince Consort in 1851. Its contents were removed to SOUTH KENSINGTON in 1934 and it was demolished in 1936.

The Great Hall of the Museum of Practical Geology, designed by James Pennethorne, in 1851, the year of its opening by the Prince Consort.

Museum Street *WC1*. This used to be Peter Street, part of a series of streets between GREAT RUSSELL STREET and Broad Street (now gone). It was renamed after the BRITISH MUSEUM was built. At No. 40 are George Allen and Unwin, the publishers.

Musical Museum *368 High Street, Brentford, Middlesex.* Founded in 1963 by Frank W. Holland with the aim of allowing the public to hear the performances of automatic pianos. All kinds of pianos – from grand pianos and barrel pianos to cinema, jazz and miniature pianos – are to be heard as well as various sorts of organs including the only self-playing Wurlitzer in Europe. There are also ancient recording phonographs, the only known piano roll projector in the world and over 30,000 music rolls.

Musicians' Company *see* CITY LIVERY COMPANIES.

Muscovy Street *EC3.* Probably takes its name from the tavern, the Czar of Muscovy (*see* GREAT TOWER STREET).

Muswell Hill Formerly in the Borough of HORNSEY and now in the London Borough of HARINGEY, this hilly suburb is named after a mossy spring or well on land given in the 12th century by the Bishop of London to the Augustinian Priory of St Mary, CLERKENWELL for use by the nuns as a dairy farm. The well, dedicated to St Mary, and with a priest and chapel, was claimed to have miraculous curative properties and was the subject of pilgrimages. After the DISSOLUTION OF THE MONASTERIES this area of 63 acres to the east of Colney Hatch Lane came under the civil jurisdiction of the parish of ST JAMES CLERKENWELL and until the end of the 19th century was known as Clerkenwell Detached. A house in Muswell Road has a plaque marking the site of the well.

For most of its history Muswell Hill was a rural backwater and a favoured retreat with elegant villas, estates and scattered cottages. Notable among the estates was The Grove of 8 acres, owned in the 1770s by Topham Beauclerk and visited by his friend Dr Johnson. The house was demolished in the 1870s when the railway was extended from HIGHGATE to Muswell Hill to serve the newly opened ALEXANDRA PALACE and the estate incorporated into ALEXANDRA PARK. Attempts to develop roads after the coming of the railway met little success until in 1896 James Edmundson of Highbury bought The Limes estate on the death of C.E. Mudie, the circulating library pioneer, who owned it. Edmundson laid out avenues and shopping parades on this and other acquired estates and with another developer, W.J. Collins, largely created Muswell Hill as a suburb in the period 1897–1914. It has a unique Edwardian homogeneity of architectural style – substantial, stone-dressed, brick-built terraces with ornamental plasterwork, served by fine shopping parades.

Muswell Hill Broadway has a fine townscape, dominated at one end by the tall tower and spire of St James's church, built in 1901 to replace a smaller church of 1842. Designed by J.S. Alder in the Perpendicular style, it is in Ancaster stone with Bath stone dressings. The Broadway is distinguished by the former Presbyterian church of 1901 by George Baines and Son, a notable building in Art Nouveau Gothic of flint, terracotta and brick, now disused but saved from demolition by a public inquiry in 1978. At the other end of the Broadway is Baines's redbrick Baptist church in the Decorated style, of 1902.

Myatts Fields *SE5.* An area of 14·5 acres, acquired by the LONDON COUNTY COUNCIL in 1889. They were named after a market gardener called Myatt who was famous for his strawberries and rhubarb. The park provides sports facilities including tennis courts.

Myddelton Square *EC1.* Laid out in 1827 with large houses for the rich and smaller ones for the less well-off. Named after Sir Hugh Myddelton who planned and financed the NEW RIVER. In the centre is St Mark's church, built to the designs of W.C. Mylne in 1828. Edward Irving, the Scottish divine and mystic, lived here in the 1820s when Thomas Carlyle came to stay with him for some months. Fenner Brockway, later Lord Brockway, lived at No. 60 in 1908–10. Thomas Dibdin lived at No. 5.

——N——

Nag's Head *10 James Street, WC2.* First built in 1673 and rebuilt in 1700, this was originally a hotel for musicians at the ROYAL OPERA HOUSE. When COVENT GARDEN functioned as a market this inn had an early morning licence, which enabled the landlord to sell alcohol to the market porters only, between 6.30 a.m. and 9 a.m.

Nando's Coffee House *Fleet Street.* Probably stood at No. 15. It is first mentioned in 1696 when a John Jones directed in his will that a quarter of the house be given to trustees to pay for a Latin master at the Free School of HAMPTON. The house was frequented by lawyers. Joseph Cradock records in his memoirs, in about 1770, 'There was no-one who could supply coffee or punch better than Mrs Humphries; and her fair daughter was admired at the Bar and by the Bar.' The most distinguished legal patron was Edward Thurlow, the Lord Chancellor. He came to the house while still a student and formed an attachment to the barmaid which is said, by William Hickey, to have lasted as long as she lived, and produced two children. When Thurlow was overheard discussing the case of Douglas *v* the Duke of Hamilton here, in 1767, he was appointed as junior counsel for the appeal. The earliest stop-press, which appeared at the end of the 17th century as a handwritten postscript to the *Post Boy,* was available only at Nando's and the Black Boy near ST DUNSTAN'S CHURCH. The last mention of Nando's as a coffee house was in 1799. By 1897 there was a hairdresser's on the site.

Napier Terrace *N1.* Sir William Napier, the historian of the Peninsular War, was a brother of General Sir Charles Napier, conqueror of Sind, and cousin of Admiral Sir Charles Napier. The terrace runs between Waterloo Terrace and Almeida Street (the fortress of Almeida was the scene of fierce fighting in the Peninsular War). In a sunken garden here is a long frieze from the Hall of Commerce, LEADENHALL STREET, which was demolished in 1922. The frieze, sculpted by Musgrave Watson, was placed here in 1975.

National Army Museum *Royal Hospital Road, SW3.* Formerly at the Royal Military Academy, Sandhurst, and now housed in a purpose-built modern building, the museum was set up in 1961 with the object of displaying the history of the British Army from the reign of Henry VII until August 1914, the history of the Indian Army until Partition in 1947 and of other Commonwealth armies before their independence. This was a first phase of the building which was opened in 1971. A second phase, which has involved further building, will provide additional exhibition and administrative accommodation and continue the history of the army and land forces of the empire until the present day.

National Book League *Book House, 45 East Hill, Wandsworth, SW18.* Founded in 1925 to promote books and reading. It was first housed in COVENT GARDEN. In 1945 the NBL moved to 7 Albemarle Street, formerly Grillon's Hotel (*see* ALBEMARLE STREET); and in 1980 to its present address. In addition to its other activities, the NBL holds regular exhibitions and is responsible for the administration of many literary awards. In 1982 there were about 4,000 members. The Mark Longman Library, an important collection of books about books, is also housed at Book House, as well as a unique Children's Reference Library. The Book Information Service answers some 20,000 questions a year.

National Film Theatre *Belvedere Road, SE1.* The first cinema established by the BRITISH FILM INSTITUTE in 1953 was known as the Telekinema and was situated on the SOUTH BANK as part of the FESTIVAL OF BRITAIN a few yards from the present site of the National Film Theatre. Its main function was to demonstrate the latest technical developments in film, and it proved so successful that it continued to operate after the Festival was over. Five years later it moved to its present home under WATERLOO BRIDGE and became officially known as the National Film Theatre. A second auditorium (NFT2) was added in 1970. A members' clubroom was built in 1971. In 1982 there were some 45,000 members. A London Film Festival is held each year.

National Gallery *Trafalgar Square, WC2.* Founded in 1824 after King George IV and the connoisseur Sir George Beaumont had persuaded the government to buy 38 splendid pictures – among them works by Raphael, Rembrandt and Van Dyck – which had belonged to the Russian-born merchant and philanthropist John Julius Angerstein, who had died the year before. The government bought the collection for £57,000, added to it 16 pictures (including two Rembrandts, four Claudes, and works by Rubens, Wilkie and Richard Wilson, donated by Sir George Beaumont) and housed them all in Angerstein's house in PALL MALL until a more suitable gallery could be built. The site chosen for the new gallery was on the north side of TRAFALGAR SQUARE; and the building was constructed here in 1832–8 to the design of William Wilkins (*see* TRAFALGAR SQUARE). It was originally extremely narrow and has since been much enlarged.

The gallery's first director was Sir Charles Eastlake, President of the ROYAL ACADEMY, who travelled widely in Italy every year in 1854–65, buying pictures of the Italian Renaissance and of earlier date. In all he purchased 139 pictures, 'many of them of the greatest interest and value, and raised the gallery to a position of high rank among the public collections of Europe'. After Eastlake's death at Pisa in 1865, the collection

William Wilkins's National Gallery was built in 1832–8. A fountain was originally proposed where Nelson's Column now stands.

continued to grow. By 1870 both Rubens and Rembrandt were well represented; so, soon afterwards, were other Flemish and Dutch masters; and so, too, were painters of the Spanish school and British painters, Hogarth, Gainsborough, Stubbs and Constable among them. When the TATE GALLERY was opened in 1897, however, much of the British work, including those works of Turner which had remained in his possession at his death, was moved there.

Numerous important purchases were made in the 20th century; and the gallery now owns over 2,000 pictures (some of them on loan to provincial galleries) from the time of Giotto to that of Van Gogh. The government makes an annual purchase grant to the gallery of £480,000 and occasionally supplements this by special grants for the purchase of pictures which would otherwise go abroad, as, for instance, Titian's *Death of Actaeon*, which was bought by the government and public subscription in 1972.

National Heart Hospital *Westmoreland Street, W1*. Founded in 1857 in Margaret Street, MARYLEBONE, by Dr Eldridge Spratt who, unlike most of his colleagues, believed that diseases of the heart merited special study and treatment. The hospital moved first to SOHO SQUARE and then to its present site in 1914. The hospital, which has 85 beds, forms part of the National Heart and Chest Hospitals which is a postgraduate teaching group including the BROMPTON HOSPITAL and LONDON CHEST HOSPITAL.

National Hospital for Nervous Diseases *Queen Square, WC1*. In the 1850s the Chandlers, a closely knit, middle-class family living in ST PANCRAS, were faced with the predicament of caring for a relative who had sustained a stroke. Their doctor was at a loss to find nursing assistance. The family set out to remedy this state of affairs, even after their relative had died. Though their circumstances were modest, they had influential friends among whom was Alderman David Wire, then Lord Mayor. It is believed that he, too, had been afflicted with a minor stroke. A public meeting was called at the MANSION HOUSE in November 1859 and a committee appointed whose purpose it was to raise funds for the purchase and staffing of a hospital to be devoted to the treatment of patients who were paralysed or who were victims of epilepsy. The

sum of £800 was soon raised and early in 1860 a suitable house was rented in QUEEN SQUARE and a secretary, a matron, and a resident doctor were appointed. In June 1860 the first patient entered the hospital which was then known as the National Hospital for the Paralysed and Epileptics. It was not only the pioneer institution for the care of the neurologically sick, but was the first to levy contributions from the patients. These contributions, 7s a week, were waived in the case of those who were destitute. The hospital was the first to establish a gymnasium and facilities for balneotherapy. According to the *London Mirror*, the 'amenities of the hospital included day-rooms, pictures, books, music, manifold amusements, and, in summer, country drives'. Its fame extended far beyond London and even England, for within a relatively short time the National Hospital became internationally renowned as the cradle of neurological teaching and practice. Doctors from all parts of the world flocked to Queen Square to attend the clinical lectures of its brilliant staff which at one time included four Fellows of the ROYAL SOCIETY. The hospital was rebuilt in 1866 and 1885. The Rockefeller Wing was added in 1938 and the Brain Institute in 1978. After the 2nd World War the medical school amalgamated with the Postgraduate Medical Federation and became recognised by the UNIVERSITY OF LONDON as the Institute of Neurology. Soon afterwards the hospital was merged with the MAIDA VALE HOSPITAL FOR NERVOUS DISEASES; and the title of the parent hospital was changed to the National Hospital for Nervous Diseases.

National Liberal Club *Whitehall Place, SW1*. Built in the 1880s next to Whitehall Court to the designs of Alfred Waterhouse. The interior is decorated with much glazed patterned tiling. The 1st Lord Birkenhead, who used to visit the lavatory here, though not a member, affected to be surprised to learn that it was 'a club as well as a lavatory'. The wide marble staircase, which rises unsupported through three storeys, was designed by Clyde Young and Eagle (1950–1). The club was established in 1882 with Gladstone as President, and the club house opened in 1887. Members are still required to undertake not to engage in anti-Liberal political activities, but the connection with the Party is not so evident as it was. The

Gladstone Library has been removed to Bristol University; but the Club still possesses a Gladstone bag and an axe he used to chop down a tree at Hawarden.

National Library for the Blind Founded in SOUTH HAMPSTEAD in 1882. The library rapidly expanded from 50 volumes in 1882 to nearly 8,000 volumes in 1904, having become the Incorporated National Library for the Blind in 1898. Owing to its constant expansion it had many homes in London and finally settled in TUFTON STREET, WESTMINSTER in 1916. The library moved to Stockport in 1978.

National Maritime Museum *Romney Road, SE10.* Founded in 1934 when the QUEEN'S HOUSE and its wings were vacated by the Royal Naval Asylum, a school for sailors' orphans. It was opened in 1937. The QUEEN'S HOUSE, completed in 1635, was in need of extensive restoration which was undertaken by the Office of Works. It is now the central building of the museum and attracts visitors for its architectural interest as well as its 16th- and 17th-century exhibits. The entrance hall, with the earliest open-well staircase in England, the Tulip Staircase, still as Inigo Jones designed it, is the main feature of the house. The loggia, by John Webb, gives a fine panorama over GREENWICH PARK.

The wings, completed in 1809, are connected to the QUEEN'S HOUSE by colonnades, commissioned in 1807 to commemorate the battle of Trafalgar. The west wing houses mostly Georgian exhibits, also the celebrated Kneller and Dahl portraits of Queen Anne's admirals, including Kneller's of Admiral Benbow. There are also portraits by Hogarth and Reynolds. Two special collections commemorate Nelson and Cook. The Nelson collection was started in 1823 in the Painted Hall, now part of the ROYAL NAVAL COLLEGE, and includes Turner's *Victory*. The Navigation Room houses the finest collection of globes in the world, early charts and instruments. The exhibition in the east wing concentrates on the 19th and early 20th centuries. Two special collections deal with the fated Franklin expedition and the migration to America.

In 1953 the Museum took over the Octagon Room of the ROYAL OBSERVATORY; in 1960 Flamsteed House, completed for the first Astronomer Royal in 1675; and in 1967 the 19th-century Caird Planetarium and the 18th-century Meridian Building. In the 1970s redevelopment of the galleries took place. The Archaeological Gallery contains a fibreglass cast of the 7th-century burial ship discovered in 1939 at Sutton Hoo. The New Neptune Hall exhibition concentrates on the history of the steamship.

National Museum of Labour History *Limehouse Town Hall, Commercial Road, E14.* Sponsored by the Trade Union, Co-operative and Democratic History Society, which was founded in 1966. Its exhibits illustrate the history of the Labour and Trade Union movements and range from trade union banners and insignia to posters and handbills.

National Portrait Gallery *St Martin's Place, WC2.* Established in 1856 at the suggestion of Philip, 5th Earl of Stanhope, the historian, who proposed in the House of Lords 'that an humble Address be presented to Her Majesty, praying that Her Majesty will be graciously pleased to take into Her Royal Consideration the expediency of forming a Gallery of the Portraits of the most Eminent Persons in British History'. The next day Stanhope wrote to the Prince Consort who warmly approved of the motion which was accordingly carried through both HOUSES OF PARLIAMENT. A board of trustees was formed and Stanhope was elected chairman. (Sir) George Scharf, the antiquarian, book illustrator and lecturer, was appointed secretary. On 15 January 1859 the gallery opened at No. 29 GREAT GEORGE STREET where 57 portraits were on display. So many pictures were thereafter given to the gallery that there was soon no room to show them. In 1869 the gallery, which then owned 288 pictures, moved to the department of Science and Art at SOUTH KENSINGTON; and in 1885, after a fire in a neighbouring building, to BETHNAL GREEN MUSEUM. In May 1889 William Henry Alexander offered to build a gallery at his own expense if the government provided a site. A suitable area was found at the back of the NATIONAL GALLERY and the present building was erected here in 1890–5 at a cost of £96,000 to the designs of Ewan Christian. Scharf was appointed Keeper. The wing in ORANGE STREET was constructed in 1937 at the expense of the art dealer Lord Duveen.

The gallery now has over 8,000 portraits, any of which can be seen on request. It is thus a research institute on British historical portraiture as well as a panorama of British history. The portraits on display are arranged chronologically beginning with those of the late 15th century and ending with those of the 20th. Some are by great artists: Henry VII, Henry VIII and Sir Thomas More are by Holbein; Nelson by Sir William Beechey; Gladstone and Disraeli by Millais; Sir Winston Churchill by Sickert; T.S. Eliot by Sir Jacob Epstein. There are self-portraits by Hogarth, Reynolds and Gainsborough. Others are by unknown artists or by artists whose names are known but whose talents are minimal. The portrait of Jane Austen by her sister, Cassandra, is little better than a daub but it is the only authentic portrait of the great novelist from the life. The serious collection of photographs was begun belatedly – in 1960 the gallery declined the Gernsheim Collection which is now in Texas – but there are now over 500,000 photographs.

National Postal Museum *King Edward Building, General Post Office, King Edward Street, EC1.* Founded in 1965 on the initiative of Reginald M. Phillips of Brighton with the object of commemorating the history of British postage stamps of the reign of Queen Victoria and of creating a national home for postal history. To this end he presented to the nation his extensive collection of 19th-century British postage stamps, official documents, and artists' drawings and proofs, many of them unique. The collection was of immense philatelic and historic importance. He also donated a large sum of money to found the museum which was opened by the Postmaster General on 12 September 1966. Besides the Phillips Collection, it also houses the Post Office Collection, containing examples of all postage stamps issued by offices under the control of the British Post Office, both in Britain and overseas, including registration or proof sheets of practically every British postage stamp issued since 1840, as well as many original designs, essays and trials. The Museum also contains the Berne Collection of stamps from member countries of the Universal Postal Union, much of the De La Rue Philatelic Archives, and an extensive reference library.

National Sporting Club *66–68 Regent Street, W1*. Originated when prize fighting was one of London's most popular sports. The enthusiasm for it gave rise to the Corinthian and Pelican Clubs amongst others, and supporters formed a boisterous fraternity known as the 'fancy', which often clashed with the law, but the frequent attendance of the Prince Regent and his brothers prevented the magistrates from doing their duty. The National Sporting Club developed out of the wish of its more respectable supporters to regularise the sport and was officially founded in 1891. It enforced the Marquess of Queensberry's rules, stamped out fixed fights and by the turn of the century awarded the Lonsdale Belts. Boxing slowly became a recognised sport and control passed to the British Boxing Board of Control, the Amateur Boxing Association, the Olympic Committee and similar bodies. Thereafter the good of boxing, and the entertainment of its members by the arrangement of regular contests, became the prime function of the club.

National Temperance Hospital *Hampstead Road, NW1*. Founded in 1873 as an experiment to discover if alcohol, then being extensively used therapeutically in all hospitals as well as being too freely indulged in by their staffs, was really necessary for the treatment of patients. Newspapers ranged their criticism from sarcastic references to the adjacent cemetery of ST JAMES' CHURCH to strong comments that the doctors should be charged with manslaughter if the experiment failed. Then called the London Temperance Hospital, it was opened at small premises in GOWER STREET and in 1881 moved to its present site. At the opening of the east wing, Sir Wilfred Lanson Bart, MP, declared, 'I have no right to say whether alcohol is a useful or deleterious drug, but I want to see the question have a *bona fide*, fair straightforward practical trial.' The founders were ahead of their time in insisting on plenty of light and air, no overcrowding of patients, and as perfect sanitary conditions as possible. There was no rule against the prescribing of alcohol, but to this day, if alcohol is prescribed alone it is still entered in the same Register of Exceptional Cases which was started in 1873. In 1885 the west wing was opened, raising the number of beds to 100.

In 1892 a children's ward was added. Double glazing was provided for all the windows from the outset. By 1911 the UNIVERSITY OF LONDON recognised the hospital and in 1923 postgraduate teaching began. In 1932 private wards, special departments and nurses' accommodation were added and at that time the name was changed to the National Temperance Hospital. In 1948 the National Health Service took over its running. By then the experiment undertaken by the original Board of Governors had been more than vindicated, the prescribing of alcohol, which had been common in most hospitals up to 1939, having almost ceased. The hospital is now linked to UNIVERSITY COLLEGE HOSPITAL and in 1982 contained 133 beds.

National Theatre *South Bank, SE1*. The project of a National Theatre was first put forward in 1848 by Effingham Wilson, a London publisher. But the first practical proposals were made in 1904 in a privately printed document, *A National Theatre Scheme and Estimate*, which was written by H. Granville-Barker and William Archer and endorsed by several leading actors and playwrights. Soon afterwards, in 1907, the Shakespeare Memorial National Theatre Committee was formed with the object of keeping Shakespearian plays in repertory, reviving English classic drama and developing the potential of modern plays. National Theatre meetings were held over the years and appeals launched, and in 1930 Granville-Barker wrote insisting that the National Theatre should comprise two theatres under one roof, should pay its way and use the acting company to its maximum capacity. Various sites were proposed and rejected and foundation stones were laid on four separate occasions. A site in Cromwell Gardens was purchased but Granville-Barker refused the offer of appointment as director as it was too small to house the two theatres he considered essential. This project was shelved by the outbreak of the 2nd World War. In 1944 a meeting between the LONDON COUNTY COUNCIL and the Shakespeare Memorial National Theatre Committee took place. It was proposed that the latter and the OLD VIC should amalgamate and that the National Theatre should be built on land on the SOUTH BANK made available by the LONDON COUNTY COUNCIL between WESTMINSTER and WATERLOO BRIDGES. In 1949 the National Theatre Bill granted a sum of £1,000,000, and a building commission was set up under the joint chairmanship of Sir Laurence Olivier and Norman Marshall. Denys Lasdun was appointed to design the new theatre. In 1951 Princess Elizabeth, deputising for her father, King George VI, laid a foundation stone on the SOUTH BANK site. On 3 July 1962 the National Theatre Board was set up under the chairmanship of Lord Chandos. This was responsible for the creation and running of the National Theatre Company, of which Sir Laurence Olivier was appointed artistic director. In 1963 the company took over the OLD VIC as its temporary home and opened the same year with Olivier's production of *Hamlet* with Peter O'Toole. Kenneth Tynan was appointed literary manager. In 1969 Jennie Lee, Britain's first Arts Minister, initiated the building of the theatre. In 1975 Peter Hall, who had formed a London base for the Stratford-on-Avon Company at the ALDWYCH THEATRE, took over as artistic director from Sir Laurence Olivier. In 1976 the National Theatre Company moved from the OLD VIC to its new home.

There are three theatres: the Cottesloe, a small rectangular theatre with adjustable seating and largely concerned with experimental plays and available for fringe-theatre groups; the Lyttelton, a proscenium theatre; and the Olivier, which has an open stage. Each theatre opened as it was completed: the Lyttelton with the transfer from the Old Vic of Albert Finney's *Hamlet* in March 1976; the Olivier in October 1976 with Peter Hall's production of *Tamburlaine*, again starring Albert Finney; and the Cottesloe in March 1977 with Ken Campbell's Science Fiction Theatre of Liverpool with a cult show, *Illuminatus*. Apart from Shakespeare many other established as well as new and controversial plays have been produced. Somerset Maugham's collection of theatrical portraits, which had been presented to the National Theatre before its existence, were put on display here in February 1981. The seating capacity of the Cottesloe is about 400, of the Lyttelton 890, and of the Olivier 1,160.

National Training School of Music *Kensington Gore*. In 1866 the Society of Arts reported on the state of musical education in England and as a direct result the school was founded. The foundation stone of the building in KENSINGTON GORE was laid by the Duke of Edinburgh in 1873. The school was designed by Lieutenant H.H. Cole of the Royal Engineers and financed by C.J. Freake, a builder and friend of the Prince of Wales. Cole said, 'After mature consideration and consultation it was decided that the style of architecture to be adopted for the National Training School should be as different from that of the Royal Albert Hall as to provoke no comparison unfavourable to the school.' The exterior is decorated with two-tone plaster work by F.W. Moody. The frieze shows youths and maidens playing musical instruments. The site was leased from the Commissioners of the GREAT EXHIBITION. In 1876 the school opened with Sir Arthur Sullivan as Principal. In 1883 the ROYAL COLLEGE OF MUSIC took over the school's buildings, furniture and bank balance. Since 1904 the ROYAL COLLEGE OF ORGANISTS has occupied the building.

National Trust *42 Queen Anne's Gate, SW1.* Founded in 1895 as the National Trust for Places of Historic Interest or Natural Beauty by Octavia Hill, the philanthropist and housing reformer, Sir Robert Hunter, a solicitor and authority on commons and public rights, and Canon H.D. Rawnsley. They had all realised that the proliferation of industry, the growth of population and lack of planning were combining to spoil much of the country's beauty. The Trust was formed with the intention of halting this trend, educating public opinion, making the countryside more easily accessible to the people as a whole, and acquiring land and buildings in order to preserve them from neglect and ruin and from the hands of selfish speculators. In 1907 the Trust was granted by Parliament the unique power to declare its land inalienable. Most of its properties have been so declared and can neither be sold nor compulsorily acquired without Parliament's permission.

At the beginning of 1980 the Trust had 850,000 members who paid an annual subscription of £7 for ordinary membership and £125 for life membership. It owns about 400,000 acres (892 of these in London) and some 200 houses of architectural or historical importance. Buildings owned by the Trust and open to the public in the London area include CARLYLE'S HOUSE, FENTON HOUSE, HAM HOUSE, and OSTERLEY PARK. As well as its headquarters at No. 42 QUEEN ANNE'S GATE, the Trust also owns the other attractive early 18th-century houses on either side, Nos 40 and 44. Between 1839 and 1840 No. 42 was occupied by Sir James Pennethorne.

National Union of Journalists *Acorn House, 314 Gray's Inn Road, WC1.* Founded in Birmingham in 1907. It was affiliated to the TRADES UNION CONGRESS but broke away in 1923 to rejoin in 1940. It aims to protect the rights of journalists. In 1982 it had a membership of about 32,000.

National Westminster Bank Ltd *Lothbury, EC2.* In 1968 this bank was established to take over the clearing bank business of the National Provincial Bank of England, the Westminster Bank, and the District Bank. Both the National Provincial and the Westminster had strong London connections. Founded by the banking pioneer Thomas Japlin in 1833, the National Provincial was originally based upon a wide network of country banks. The bank retained an office in

BISHOPSGATE, but it was not until 1865 that it operated as a fully London-based bank. Two years later a new head office was opened at 15 BISHOPSGATE. The National Provincial's London business was greatly reinforced by the acquisition of the Union of London and Smith's Bank (*see* SMITH'S BANK) in 1918 and the affiliation of COUTTS AND CO. in 1920.

The Westminster Bank was first opened under the name of the London and Westminster Bank in THROGMORTON STREET in 1834. J.W. Gilbart, its general manager between 1834 and 1859, emerged as the leading professional banker of the early Victorian period. The Bank's many acquisitions included the Commercial Bank of London (founded in 1840 and acquired in 1863), Jones Lloyd and Co., LOTHBURY (established about 1771 and absorbed in 1864), and the multi-branch London and County Banking Co. of LOMBARD STREET (formed 1836, amalgamated 1909). The shorter title of Westminster Bank was adopted in 1923.

By the late 1970s, as the NATIONAL WESTMINSTER TOWER neared completion, the Bank operated through some 350 branches in the London area.

National Westminster Tower *Bishopsgate, EC2.* In 1959 the National Provincial Bank bought premises adjoining their own at No. 15 BISHOPSGATE. Four years later permission was sought to redevelop the site as well as that of the nearby CITY OF LONDON CLUB. But the LONDON COUNTY COUNCIL decreed that both the Club and No. 15 BISHOPSGATE (a good building by John Gibson, 1864–5) were of sufficient interest not to be demolished. Having appealed to the Minister of Housing and Local Government, the bank was told that they could demolish the club but not the banking hall. Outline planning permission was accordingly given by the CITY CORPORATION. But before work could begin the Government's 1964 regulations limiting the size of office developments in London came into force; and the proposed redevelopment had to be abandoned until 1969. R. Seifert and Partners then submitted plans for a tall tower to the CITY CORPORATION, which was known to favour a high focal point for the cluster of towers in the area. Building began in 1971 but was interrupted in 1974 when a decision to list the CITY OF LONDON CLUB as a building of historical or architectural interest entailed the redesigning of the ground area. On its completion in 1980 the tower had cost £72 million. Its 52 storeys rise to a height of 600 ft, making it the tallest building in Europe.

Natural History Museum *Cromwell Road, SW7.* On 21 January 1860, at a special general meeting of the Trustees of the BRITISH MUSEUM, the following resolution was proposed and carried: 'That it is expedient that the Natural History Collection be removed from the British Museum, inasmuch as such an arrangement would be attended with considerably less expense than would be incurred by providing a sufficient additional space in immediate contiguity to the present building of the British Museum.' A competition was subsequently held for a design for a new building at SOUTH KENSINGTON. The competition was won by Captain Francis Fowke, but Fowke died before his work was finished and the Trustees approached Alfred Waterhouse, whose variegated terracotta erection, opened in 1881, displays a characteristically Victorian determination to provide a fitting storehouse for the wonders of creation, with a central hall like the nave of a

The entrance hall of the Natural History Museum, from a perspective drawing by Alfred Waterhouse, its architect, executed in 1878.

cathedral, embellished externally with towers and spires. The inside is crowded with ornamentation in the 11th- and 12th-century Romanesque style of the Rhineland. It is at once a museum – containing a comprehensive collection of fossils and exhibits of all the main classes of animal and plant life, including many extinct species, as well as minerals, including meteorites – and a research institution with an extensive library of books and periodicals on all general and scientific aspects of natural history, together with works of reference, maps, manuscripts and drawings. There are, in addition to the central general library, specialised collections in each of the five departments of paleontology, zoology, entomology, botany and mineralogy, and a special library attached to the subdepartment of anthropology. Use of the library is limited to the museum staff, research workers and advanced students.

The specimens and exhibits displayed in the 4 acres of gallery space are only a small proportion of the museum's whole collection. The nucleus of this collection was the library, herbarium and natural history specimens of Sir Hans Sloane. These were originally displayed at the BRITISH MUSEUM where, in 1781, they were augmented by the ROYAL SOCIETY's 'repository' and, in 1820, by the huge botanical collection of Sir Joseph Banks. Several of the galleries were destroyed in the 2nd World War. The north block, containing the library, lecture theatre and the reference and study collections was opened in 1959 and the Botanical Gallery in 1963. A new wing, designed by a team of architects from the Department of the Environment led by James Ellis, with consultant architect John Pinckheard, was completed on the corner of EXHIBITION ROAD in 1977.

The first superintendent of the natural history department of the BRITISH MUSEUM was the zoologist Sir Richard Owen, appointed in 1856.

Naval and Military Club *94 Piccadilly, W1.* Founded in 1864 and often referred to as 'The In and Out' from the markings on the gateposts. The club house was designed by Matthew Brettingham in 1756–60 for Lord Egremont. In 1756–70 it was occupied by the Duke of Cambridge. From 1855–65 it was the home of Lord Palmerston. It was entirely refitted for the club.

Neasden *NW10, NW2.* Lies between WILLESDEN and CRICKLEWOOD, straddling the NORTH CIRCULAR ROAD. Until houses were built for workers of the Metropolitan Railway in 1876 it was a totally rural hamlet consisting of three or four large houses, a few cottages and a smithy. Two waves of development transformed Neasden. The first, and smaller, in the late 19th century, followed the extension of the Metropolitan Railway. The second, in the 1920s and 1930s when the NORTH CIRCULAR ROAD was built, turned Neasden into such a typical inter-war London suburb that the name Neasden, which means 'nose-shaped hill' and is familiar to readers of the satirical magazine *Private Eye*, is now synonymous with suburbia.

Neckinger A river which took its name from the 'Devil's Neckinger' or 'Neckerchief', the popular name for the hangman's noose on the gibbet, used for the execution of pirates, which stood on a wharf adjoining the point where it entered the THAMES. Its upper part was known as the Lock Stream, which rose in ST GEORGE'S FIELDS, passed near the ELEPHANT AND CASTLE, ran eastwards skirting the LOCK HOSPITAL, went on through the grounds of BERMONDSEY ABBEY and entered the THAMES at ST SAVIOUR'S DOCK to the east of the present LONDON BRIDGE.

Needlemakers' Company *see* CITY LIVERY COMPANIES.

Nelson Column *Trafalgar Square, WC2.* In 1838 the Nelson Memorial Committee was formed to raise

The stone statue of Nelson by E.H. Baily was placed upon the top of Railton's 145 ft column in 1843.

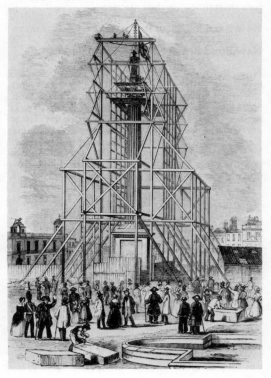

money by voluntary subscription for a monument in honour of Lord Nelson to commemorate his last and greatest victory at Trafalgar. William Railton won the competition for the design of the monument, 145 ft high, which now stands in the centre of the south side of Barry's formal TRAFALGAR SQUARE. The fluted Corinthian column of Devonshire granite from Foggin Tor, erected in 1839–42, supports a bronze capital cast from old guns from WOOLWICH ARSENAL. This is surmounted by the 17 ft high Craiglieth stone statue of Nelson, raised in 1843, the work of E.H. Baily. The bronze bas-reliefs at the base of the Column were completed in 1849, cast from cannon captured in Nelson's battles. They represent the Battle of Cape St Vincent (sculptor M.L. Watson), the Battle of the Nile (W.F. Woodington), the bombardment of Copenhagen (J. Ternout) and the death of Nelson (J.E. Carew).

The four bronze lions at the foot of the Column, 20 ft long and 22 ft high, were designed by Landseer and cast by Baron Marochetti. Though part of Railton's original design, they were not placed in position until 1867, nearly a quarter of a century after the Column itself, and indeed their perpetual non-appearance became something of a London joke. In 1873 they were decorated with mourning wreaths on the day of Landseer's funeral.

Netherhall Gardens *NW3.* Takes its name (adopted in 1877) from Netherhall in Sussex, a property of the Maryon-Wilson family (*see* HAMPSTEAD). In 1911–21 Edward Elgar, the composer, lived at Severn House, which was designed by Norman Shaw and demolished in 1938. A plaque on No. 42 commemorates Elgar's occupancy. Sidney and Beatrice Webb, the social scientists and political reformers, lived at No. 10 for a short time after their marriage.

New Barnet *see* HIGH BARNET *and* EAST BARNET.

New Bond Street *W1. See* BOND STREET.

New Bridge Street *EC4.* Built over the FLEET RIVER in 1764 between what is now LUDGATE CIRCUS and BLACKFRIARS BRIDGE which was then being built. No. 14 is on the site of the main entrance to BRIDEWELL PRISON. The building there now, the CHARTERED INSTITUTE OF SECRETARIES which was designed by James Lewis in about 1805, bears a keystone head of Edward VI who gave the Palace of BRIDEWELL to the CITY OF LONDON a few days before his death in 1553. The large office blocks in the street include Blackfriars House by F.W. Troup (1913) and the Unilever Building by J. Lomax-Simpson in association with Sir John Burnet, Tait and Lorne (1930–1). This carries huge pieces of sculpture by Sir William Reid Dick. The statue in the roadway is of Queen Victoria by C.B. Birch (*see* STATUES). On the west side of the approach to BLACK-FRIARS BRIDGE in what was then Chatham Place, the fourteen-year-old Emma Lyon, who was to become Lady Hamilton and Nelson's mistress, began work as under-housemaid in the family of Dr Budd. Dante Gabriel Rossetti lived in Chatham Place in the 1860s.

New Burlington Place *W1.* On the BURLINGTON ESTATE, it was until 1900 called Old Burlington Mews. Until the completion of the northward extension of SAVILE ROW to CONDUIT STREET, access to this mews was by a covered passage from REGENT STREET, but with the building of Fortress House in SAVILE ROW in 1950 a greatly improved entrance was provided from SAVILE ROW.

New Burlington Street *W1.* On the BURLINGTON ESTATE, it extends from REGENT STREET to SAVILE ROW. Building began here in about 1735, but only Nos 1 and 2 survive from the original development, and even they have been very much altered. The rest of the street is now occupied by uninteresting modern commercial buildings. Residents have included (Sir) Joseph Banks, scientist, in 1771–7; the 1st Earl Camden, Lord Chancellor, in 1778–84; and Henry Clutton, architect, in 1858–77.

New Cavendish Street *W1.* Built in 1775 on the PORTLAND ESTATE and named after the Cavendish family who were related to the ground landlords. Sir Alfred Waterhouse lived at No. 8 in 1871–2 and at No. 20 in 1872–1907. Henry George Mott, dancing master and manager of the Portland Ball Rooms in FOLEY STREET, lived and died in 1873 at No. 125. The College of Engineering and Science, Central London Polytechnic, designed by Lyons, Israel and Ellis, was completed in 1970.

New Change *EC4.* OLD CHANGE having been destroyed by bombs in 1941, New Change, a wider street, was built a little to the east of it.

New Court *St Swithin's Lane, EC4.* The site is shown as vacant on Ogilby and Morgan's map of 1676 and the name is merely mentioned by Strype in 1720. Seymour, writing in 1734, said it was, 'A very handsome large place, with an open passage into it for coach or cart. Here are very good buildings with inhabitants considerable and at the upper end is a very good large house inclosed from the rest by a handsome pale.' The German financier Nathan Meyer Rothschild, who had become a naturalised British subject in 1804 and had settled at St Helen's Place in 1805, soon afterwards moved his business here. His son, Lionel Nathan de Rothschild, who became the first Jewish MP, was born in New Court in 1808. In 1836 the street frontage was rebuilt and the rest was reconstructed in 1857–60 and again in 1963–5. New Court is still the headquarters of Messrs N. M. ROTHSCHILD AND SONS LTD.

New Covent Garden *Nine Elms Lane, SW8.* The original market in COVENT GARDEN dated from 1670 when Charles II granted a charter to the Earl of Bedford to hold a market in the area. Over the years the market increased in area and continued to spread, eventually extending to 30 acres surrounding the original area. In 1961 The Covent Garden Market Authority was created with the task of developing further the COVENT GARDEN area. Problems involving access and distribution, due to its increased size, had made modernisation imperative. After considering the diverse trading interests and problems concerned, in 1966 a site of 68 acres, formerly owned by British Rail, 2½ miles from COVENT GARDEN at NINE ELMS, VAUXHALL, was approved by Parliament. In November 1974, at a cost of over £40,000,000, the new market, designed by Gollins, Melvin, Ward and Partners, was opened. It is the most important fruit, flower and vegetable market in the United Kingdom, dealing in goods estimated at over 1,000,000 tons annually.

New Coventry Street *W1*. Built in the 1840s after a Select Committee of the House of Commons on Metropolitan Improvement had emphasised the need for a faster flow of traffic in the congested area between COVENTRY STREET and LEICESTER SQUARE where coaches, omnibuses and the carts of market gardeners frequently became entangled. On the south is Fanum House, the headquarters of the Automobile Association, and on the north the shops, restaurants, showrooms and offices of the Swiss Centre built in 1963–6 to the designs of David du R. Aberdeen.

New Cross *SE14*. A small district lying south of DEPTFORD, west of BLACKHEATH, north of BROCKLEY and east of PECKHAM within the London Borough of LEWISHAM. It was formerly in the parish of DEPTFORD, and it takes its name from an old hostelry and coaching house, bearing the sign of the Golden Cross, which was famous for centuries. Evelyn records in his diary how he accompanied Lord Berkeley in his carriage from Evelyn's home, Sayes Court at DEPTFORD, through 'New Crosse' on their way to Dover: 'my Lord being bound for Paris as ambassador with a retinue of three coaches, three wagons and 40 horses'. Some good Georgian houses survive in the area. The Royal Naval School was housed at New Cross in a building opened by Prince Albert in 1843, a grand symmetrical Wren pastiche. This school for the sons of impecunious naval officers began at CAMBERWELL in 1833 and moved from New Cross to CHISLEHURST in 1889. New Cross Gate refers to the toll gate established on the New Cross turnpike road in 1718. The district includes the ancient manor of Hatcham. At Hatcham House (where Hatcham Park Road is today), lived Joseph Hardcastle, the philanthropist and prominent supporter of the abolition of slavery. In the 1840s Robert Browning lived just south of New Cross Road at Telegraph Cottage, a house which he described as 'resembling a goose pie'. TELEGRAPH HILL PARK, formerly Plow Garlic Hill, was the site from 1795 of one of the signalling stations forming the Admiralty semaphore telegraph to Deal and Dover. Hatcham was noted in the last century for its market gardens; but from the 1870s the HABERDASHERS' COMPANY, who had purchased the manor in 1614, laid out their Hatcham Estate for houses of a 'superior class'. Strict insistence on a 'Haberdashers' style' (best seen in Jerningham, Pepys, Waller and Erlanger Roads) stamped the area with an identity it still retains. A plaque at No. 233 New Cross Road commemorates John Tallis, the publisher of *London Street Views*, who died here in 1876.

New Cross Hospital *Avonley Road, SE14*. Opened in 1877 'expressly for pauper patients afflicted with smallpox'. It remained a fever hospital until 1941. In 1883 its name was changed from Deptford Hospital to South Eastern Hospital. It was enlarged in 1902–6, was taken over in 1930 by the LONDON COUNTY COUNCIL from the Metropolitan Asylums' Board and in 1948 by the National Health Service which closed it temporarily. In 1952 it reopened as New Cross Hospital and is now attached to GUY'S. In 1982 there were 269 beds, mainly for geriatric patients.

New Cut *and* **Lower Marsh Markets** Among the most notorious of the Victorian street markets. In 1819 a map shows a few houses in the road. By the middle of the 19th century there was a thriving market stretching half a mile from Waterloo Road to Great Charlotte Street. The area was infamous for sneak thieves and prostitutes and became a centre for travelling costermongers. Mayhew in 1850 describes it as a riotous and noisy scene more like a fair than a market with over 300 stalls selling a multitude of goods including straw bonnets, night caps, brooms and brushes, marine stores, sheep's trotters, black lead, songs and almanacs, and hot eels as well as great piles of fruit and vegetables. The market began at 6 p.m. on Saturday and was mainly frequented by wives of mechanics and labourers who came to buy their Sunday dinner after pay day. Stalls were lit by naphtha flares and the air was filled with the sound of street cries. In 1849 the CHOLERA epidemic seriously diminished the market because of its customers' reluctance to buy fresh food and in the 1850s it was further reduced by the Police Act. By the 1870s it was thriving once again and spread to Lower Marsh. In 1872 it was curtailed by the Vestry who limited the opening hours. Today in the Cut there is still a busy lunchtime market selling food, clothing and household goods.

New End Hospital *New End, Hampstead, NW3*. In 1810 the Hampstead Board of Guardians bought a house in New End which was converted into a workhouse. In 1845 the workhouse was rebuilt. The stone-breaking cells where casual inmates earned their keep are still in existence. There was also a padded cell where refractory casuals, including alcoholics, were confined. Unusual circular wards were added in 1870. It was used by the Army in the 1st World War. In 1930 it was taken over by the LONDON COUNTY COUNCIL and gradually converted into a hospital. In 1948 it was taken over by the National Health Service and operated as an acute hospital. In 1968 it was attached to the ROYAL FREE HOSPITAL and has since been used as a geriatric hospital. In 1982 there were 143 beds.

New Exchange *Strand*. Built in 1608–9 on part of the gardens of DURHAM PLACE which had been leased to Robert Cecil. King James opened the exchange and gave it the name of 'Britain's Burse'. The exchange began to be popular after the Restoration, particularly after the GREAT FIRE when it took over much of the business previously enjoyed by the ROYAL EXCHANGE. Pepys bought gloves here for his wife, Mrs Pierce and Mrs Knipp. The Grand Duke Cosimo II on his travels through England 'went to see the New Exchange. . . . The building has a façade of stone, built after the Gothic style which has lost its colour from age and become blackish. It contains two long and double galleries, one above the other in which are distributed in several rows, great numbers of very rich shops of drapers and mercers filled with goods of every kind, and with manufactures of the most beautiful description. These are for the most part under the care of well dressed women who are busily employed in work, although many are served by young men called apprentices.' In 1720 Strype described it as 'a place of great resort and trade for the nobility and gentry' but its popularity rapidly declined after that. It was demolished in 1737 and shops were built on the site. One of these was leased by George Middleton and his partner, John Campbell, goldsmiths and bankers (*see* COUTTS AND CO.). Nos 54–64 STRAND now occupy the site.

New Fetter Lane *EC4*. The area around here was devastated by bombing in the 2nd World War. One of the few streets to survive was Bartlett's Buildings which had been so named after Thomas Bartlett, a printer, who owned property in the area. This street was widened and extended in a westerly curve from HOLBORN CIRCUS to meet FETTER LANE. The two streets meet where Neville's Court used to be. This was an old court which was named after Ralph Neville, Bishop of Chichester in 1222–4, who had his London house here. James Keir Hardie, the Labour leader, lived for several years in this court at No. 14 which was consequently, so one of his biographers says, 'the resort of all manner of British and foreign leaders of advanced thought and action'. The head office of W.H. SMITH AND SONS, the booksellers, is at Strand House, 10 New Fetter Lane, which was build in 1958–9 to designs by H.F. Bailey. The Daily Mirror Building (1958–60) is by Sir Owen Williams and Partners and Anderson, Forster and Wilcox.

New Gaiety Theatre *see* GAIETY THEATRE.

New Hall *and* **Library** *Lincoln's Inn, WC2*. The library, already formed in 1497 and said to be the oldest in London, now contains some 80,000 volumes. It is the most comprehensive collection of legal books in the country. The present tall structure was built to the romantic neo-Tudor designs of Philip Hardwick in 1843–5 on the site of the Cottrel Garden, a plot of land from which was dug the clay for the construction of the Gatehouse and the Old Hall. The building was extended in 1871–3 by Sir George Gilbert Scott who received much officious advice from that bossy lawyer and horologist Edmund Beckett Denison, later Lord Grimthorpe, a bencher who became the Inn's Treasurer in 1876. The interior of the hall, designed by Gilbert Scott, is graced by a statue of Lord Erskine by Westmacott (1830). In the hall is a large fresco by G.F. Watts, *The Lawgivers* (1859), depicting 33 of the world's great legislators, including Moses, Solomon, Charlemagne and Alfred the Great. The artist charged no fee but was presented with a gold cup and 500 sovereigns on its completion. He used several of his friends as models for the faces of his figures. The features of Holman Hunt, for example, may be seen representing those of the West-Saxon King Ine.

The New Hall and Library were opened by Queen Victoria, accompanied by Prince Albert, on 30 October 1845. The Prince was admitted a member of the Inn, to the evident pleasure of the Queen who, 'holding a glass of port in her hand . . . stood up all the time, and drank it off to the bottom.'

New Jonathan's *Threadneedle Street*. Established in 1773. In the same year it was renamed the Stock Exchange Coffee House when a group of stock-jobbers contributed 6d each to change the sign and christen the new one in punch. It stood above the STOCK EXCHANGE and retained its site even after the STOCK EXCHANGE'S move to CAPEL COURT in 1802. Stockjobbers continued to be the most regular patrons. Smollett wrote in his *Reproof*:

Nor has my Satire yet supplied a scourge
For that vile tribe of usurers and bites
Who sneak at Jonathan's, and swear at White's.

In 1816 the premises were destroyed by fire.

New King's Road *Fulham, SW6*. In 1894 the KING'S ROAD from CHELSEA, beyond No. 648, became the New King's Road. It differs in character from the KING'S ROAD in having more houses than shops, and shops which cater for local people rather than for visitors. Much of its north-west side is taken up with the open spaces of Eelbrook Common and PARSONS GREEN while the south-east side retains a number of early 19th-century houses with fanlights and other interesting details. Eelbrook Common (a corruption of hill-brook), once waste land on which local people had a right to pasture their cattle, gets its name from being at a slightly higher level than WALHAM GREEN. It is an open space of 14 acres used for recreation.

South of the New King's Road lies the Peterborough Estate, built on the grounds of Peterborough House, the home of Charles Mordaunt, 3rd Earl of Peterborough (the original house, in which Voltaire stayed, was demolished in 1798 and its replacement in about 1900). It is notable for its elaborately decorated houses, embellished with small lions, the trade-mark of its builder, J. Nichols.

Nos 247–249 New King's Road replaced Samuel Richardson's villa in 1805–6. No. 247, Aragon House, takes its name from the tradition that Catherine of Aragon, while widow of Prince Arthur, lived in the house then on the site. Both houses are now used by the Royal British Legion. Further to the south lies HURLINGHAM ROAD, once the southern boundary of the Fulham Nursery, which lay between it and the New King's Road and lasted from about 1700 until 1881. Opposite, on the north side, was Draycott Lodge, the home of William Holman Hunt, whose name is given to a nearby primary school. Further on are some attractive houses of the 18th and early 19th centuries, among which Elysium Row, built in 1738, still retains some original doors and balconies. The FULHAM POTTERY, founded in 1672, of which a 19th-century kiln is preserved in the new office development, is the last point of interest before PUTNEY BRIDGE is reached.

The King's Arms at No. 425 occupies a site where a tavern has stood since 1526; the previous building, a well-known coaching house and a resort of smugglers on their way into London from the south coast, was demolished in 1888. The actor Frederick Sullivan lived at No. 134 where his brother, Arthur, composed *The Lost Chord* while staying with him during his last illness. Nos 156–158 were converted in 1866 by Mrs Tait, wife of Bishop (afterwards Archbishop) Tait, into an orphanage for girls who had lost their parents in the CHOLERA epidemic of that year; the orphanage was removed to Broadstairs in 1869. The comedian Charles Mathews the Elder lived nearby in 1811–14.

New London Theatre *167 Drury Lane, WC2*. The West End's newest theatre, built on the site of the WINTER GARDEN THEATRE where there has been a place of entertainment since Elizabethan times. The New London Theatre was designed by Sean Kenny for the New London Theatre Centre Ltd. It opened on 2 January 1973 with Peter Ustinov's *The Unknown Soldier and His Wife*. The original seating capacity of the theatre was 952 but was increased to 1,102 for the musical *Cats*.

New Malden *Surrey*. Originally part of the parish of KINGSTON, New Malden had developed to a size large enough to become a separate authority under a

Local Board set up in 1866. This was due mainly to the coming of the railway and the statutory enclosure of the area known as Norbiton Common some 30 years before. Due to the energy and drive of its inhabitants, the town was drained, good roads were laid out, churches and solid houses were built, so that, in time, the place became known as 'The Montpelier of Surrey'. By annexing Coombe in 1894 and Old Malden a year later, the whole area became the Urban District of the Maldens and Coombe. In 1936 it achieved borough status, but in 1965, under the London Government Act, it was returned to KINGSTON.

New North Road *N1*. A highway financed in 1812 by a company of subscribers under a private Act, shortening the link between SHOREDITCH and north ISLINGTON via CITY ROAD and UPPER STREET by connecting the turnpike road near Highbury Place (now Highbury Corner) with SHOREDITCH at Haberdasher's Street. At the present Baring Street it crossed the new REGENT'S CANAL. About 1823, when CANONBURY began to be built up, another bridge was made between Canonbury Grove and Astey's Row, over the NEW RIVER whose course at the Horseshoe was here straightened to facilitate building development. For some 30 years the new road, crossing fields where old archers' marks or pillars still survived, was little used, but its existence stimulated building until by 1842 the area between ISLINGTON and HOXTON was covered with streets and houses. By abolition of subsidiary terrace names in 1863 the whole stretch south of Essex Road was named New North Road and the northern part Canonbury Road. It is now a busy lorry route to the CITY, THAMES and beyond, and many of its early houses have been demolished. On the corner of Eccleston Road is an early cinema building, the Victoria Cinema Theatre, opened in 1901.

New Oxford Street *WC1*. Completed in 1847 as an extension of OXFORD STREET, it cut through a notorious slum area and allowed traffic to reach HOLBORN without passing through ST GILES HIGH STREET. In 1852 Charles Edward Mudie moved into No. 510 which he rebuilt as a large book-hall in 1860. Mudie had started in business as a stationer and bookseller at No. 28 Upper King Street (now SOUTHAMPTON ROW) in 1840. He had begun by lending his own books on philosophy and science to students at the newly established LONDON UNIVERSITY nearby, but soon realised that there was a far larger public for novels. He changed the name of his establishment to Mudie's Select Library; and a subscription of one guinea a year enabled readers to borrow from him one volume at a time. Amongst early subscribers were Herbert Spencer, Edward Fitzgerald, Frederick and Charles Tennyson and Thomas Hughes. Although, as Robert Louis Stevenson said, 'the novel was the staff and stay of Mr Mudie', he covered a wide range of history and travel and, in 1855, took 2,400 copies of the third and fourth volumes of Macaulay's *History* and 2,000 copies of Livingstone's *Travels*. At one time he had 25,000 subscribers, and branches in Manchester, Birmingham and other parts of London. Mudie, a chapel preacher, exercised a strong control over the selection of books on his shelves and was castigated in a pamphlet by George Moore in 1885. He died in 1890 and the business was continued by his son.

At Nos 44–52 are M. Harris and Sons, the antique furniture dealers, established in 1868; and at 54–56 Camerer Cuss and Co., the jewellers and specialists in antique clocks and watches, founded on a permanent basis in 1788 opposite MOORFIELDS EYE HOSPITAL by Andrew Camerer, an itinerant German clockmaker; in the 1850s the firm moved to New Oxford Street where Andrew Cuss, a jeweller, joined the firm and where, until the 1st World War, the apprentices slept in the shop in hammocks. At Nos 112–116 until September 1981 was Imhof's (Retail) Ltd, dealers in television sets and records, founded in 1845 by Daniel Imhof who sold musical instruments, including his own invention, the orchestrion, a large clockwork instrument which played orchestral music. In 1896 his was the first shop to sell a gramophone; and in 1910 Mrs Kathleen Imhof gave the first gramophone recital at the QUEEN'S HALL. At No. 53 are James Smith and Sons (Sticks and Umbrellas Ltd) founded in 1830. This firm formerly had a tiny shop in a passageway off SAVILE ROW. Umbrellas were manufactured here in a space 4 ft wide. They were bought by, amongst others, Gladstone, Bonar Law and Lord Curzon. Centre Point, the towering 36-storey office block, which lay empty for so long at the junction with St Giles Circus, is by R. Seifert and Partners (1965–6). They also designed the fountain.

New Palace Yard *SW1*. The open space to the north of WESTMINSTER HALL which indicates the site of the extensions made to Edward the Confessor's palace by the Norman kings. It was for centuries a place of punishment like OLD PALACE YARD. Perkin Warbeck was put in the stocks here in 1498; and Titus Oates stood in the pillory in 1685. The last man to be pilloried was John Wilkes, the Fleet Street bookseller and publisher of the notorious No. 45 of the *North Briton*, who suffered the punishment in 1765. The houses on the south side of BRIDGE STREET were demolished in 1866–7 to open up the yard to public view. The House of Commons Members' Entrance and the public entrance to WESTMINSTER HALL are here. The Silver Jubilee Fountain, a steel sculpture of fauna emblematic of the six continents, surmounted by a gilt crown, is by Valenty Pytel (1977).

New Quebec Street *W10*. First rated in 1776 and called after Wolfe's victory of 1759 in Canada, it is today an attractive small shopping street.

New River *see* WATER SUPPLY.

New River Company *30 Myddelton Square, EC1*. The early history of this water company is obscured by the dearth of records, most of which were burnt in a fire in 1769. In 1606 and 1607 the LORD MAYOR and Commonalty of the CITY OF LONDON obtained two Acts of Parliament enabling them to construct a channel to bring water from fresh springs at Chadwell and Amwell in Hertfordshire. In 1608 Edmond Colthurst offered to carry out the works, but soon after he had started them, the COURT OF ALDERMEN refused his request for financial assistance. Work began again in 1609, however, after the Corporation had transferred the powers conferred upon them by the 1606 and 1607 Acts to Hugh Myddelton who undertook to complete the work within four years. Myddelton, a rich entrepreneur and goldsmith, had been a member of the Commons Committees into the WATER SUPPLY of London. Opposition to the

The New River Head waterworks and reservoirs at Islington in 1730, with the north London skyline in the distance.

scheme from landowners through whose estates the river had to pass was vociferous and determined. Since it attempted to follow the 100 ft contour line, flexible negotiations were limited and its sinuous path further irritated landowners. In 1610 opponents of the 1606 and 1607 Acts complained that their farms would be 'mangled' and that the river was little better than a ditch and as such dangerous to men and cattle. But, although their objections were overruled, the cost of the scheme proved beyond Myddelton's private means and he approached the King for help. James I had seen the work at Theobald's, his Enfield hunting estate, and Myddelton was his jeweller. He agreed to pay half the cost of the whole undertaking in return for half the profit as a sleeping partner. Articles of Agreement were drawn up in November and in May 1612 this was confirmed by a Grant under the Great Seal. On 29 September 1613 at a ceremony attended by Myddelton's brother, Thomas, as Lord Mayor elect, water was let into the Round Pond at New River Head, CLERKENWELL. There were ultimately four reservoirs, each about 10 ft deep, the largest 2 acres, and the other 1 acre. Water was then carried to the CITY in wooden pipes. Waste by leakage and bursts totalled one-quarter of that supplied. Small lead pipes then supplied houses. The original length of the channel was about 38·75 miles (only 20 as the crow flies) but was shortened in the mid-19th century by straightening many of the more tortuous loops. It was 10 ft wide and probably about 4 ft deep. From 1618 supplies were augmented by water from the River LEA. In 1619 the Company was incorporated by Royal Charter. (Half the 72 shares were owned by the King.) In 1622 Hugh Myddelton was created a Baronet. The King waived the customary fees in recognition of his enterprise. Myddelton died in 1631, bequeathing one share in the Company to the GOLDSMITHS' COMPANY for needy brethren, 'especially to such as should be of his name, kindred and country'.

From 1640 the Company steadily increased its profitability. By 1700 a single share paid about £200 a year, and by 1766 was worth £8,000. In 1768 steam power was first used at New River Head; and in 1805 water was supplied for the first time to first-floor premises. From 1811 the wooden pipes were replaced with cast-iron. In 1818 the YORK BUILDINGS WATER-WORKS were purchased, and in 1822 the rights of the LONDON BRIDGE WATERWORKS COMPANY. In 1831–3 two reservoirs were constructed at STOKE NEWINGTON. By 1850 the Company was deriving supplies in part from the springs at Amwell and Chadwell and in part from the River LEA, from wells at Cheshunt and TOTTENHAM, and from the THAMES at Broken Wharf, UPPER THAMES STREET. But about one-third of the population of 900,000 in the Company's area was still unsupplied. In *A Microscopic Examination of the Water Supplies to the Inhabitants of London*, Arthur Hassall condemned the various sources of supply as all being impure. Even the deep well water was then pumped into open reservoirs which had just been cleaned for the first time in 12 years. The New River Channel was 'accessible to the public, who use it as a resort for bathing in summer and at all times as a receptacle for refuse, animal and vegetable matter'. In addition, the gravity fall into London was so slow that it favoured 'the development of the lower forms of animal and vegetable life'.

After 1852 filtration works were established at STOKE NEWINGTON, HORNSEY and New River Head as a result of the Metropolis Water Act. The HAMPSTEAD WATER COMPANY was purchased in 1856. In 1873 a quarter of a share was sold for £12,240 (its income had been £448 the previous year); in 1891 one-twentieth part of a share was sold for £700; and in 1893 a single share for £94,900. In 1904 the operations of the New River Company were transferred to the Metropolitan Water Board whose new headquarters were opened on the site of the New River Head in 1920. Reconstructed within the new building was the Oak Room, the former

Council Room of the New River Company, with elaborately carved panelling and a florid moulded ceiling, surrounding a portrait of William III, and allegorical figures by Henry Croke. In 1946 the last of the filterbeds at New River Head was abandoned and the river ceased to flow there. It now ends at the reservoirs and filter beds at Green Lanes, STOKE NEWINGTON and is 24 miles long, falling 15·5 feet from New Grange, Hertford, to STOKE NEWINGTON. Stretches of the redundant New River Channel south of STOKE NEWINGTON have now been landscaped and opened as public amenities, notably at CANONBURY.

New River Estate *EC1, WC1.* In the 17th and 18th centuries the NEW RIVER COMPANY acquired property covering approximately the area bounded by St John Street and present-day PENTONVILLE ROAD, King's Cross Road and ROSEBERY AVENUE. Outside the New River Head and Upper Reservoir, this remained open fields, watered by ponds and springs, until in 1819 the company's surveyor, William Chadwell Mylne, laid out a handsome suburb, probably designing many of its houses himself.

The two squares, MYDDELTON – ISLINGTON's finest – and Claremont, were begun in 1821 and finished in 1827 and 1828 respectively, Claremont surrounding the Upper Reservoir, which was open water until 1856. Mylne's St Mark's church (1827–8) was gutted in 1941 and since restored. The north side of the square was also destroyed then, and rebuilt in replica by the Company (1947–8). Amwell Street's terraces were begun in 1824 along an old field path; at No. 69 lived George Cruikshank, who drew from its back windows his celebrated *March of Bricks and Mortar* in 1829. Near its southern end is the old Clerkenwell Parochial School, moved here in 1828 from Aylesbury Street. On the western hillside were Holford Square, destroyed in 1942 and now replaced by Bevin Court; and PERCY CIRCUS, one segment of which has been lost and another demolished for the Royal Scot Hotel with a fake replica façade.

Much of the estate retained genteel respectability until the late 19th century, though there was also multiple occupation by poorer artisans and clerks, and the properties were gradually run down. In 1974–5 the Company sold most of it – apart from three sides of MYDDELTON SQUARE and some commercial properties off ROSEBERY AVENUE – to ISLINGTON COUNCIL, which has restored many houses. The New River Head itself was taken over by the Metropolitan Water Board (now the Thames Water Authority) under the Metropolitan Water Act of 1904 (*see* WATER SUPPLY).

New Scotland Yard Part of the old precincts of the old WHITEHALL PALACE was originally made over for lodgings for the Kings of Scotland. By 1829, when Sir Robert Peel was casting about for a suitable headquarters for his newly formed METROPOLITAN POLICE FORCE, only Great Scotland Yard remained as a commemoration of these lodgings. The former alleys that had been known as Middle Scotland Yard and Little Scotland Yard had been merged into Whitehall Place. A row of houses had been built in Whitehall Place in 1820. One of these houses No. 4, was empty and was acquired for the new headquarters. The servants' quarters at the back of the house were converted into a police station for 'A' division and a recruiting office. The front of the building was turned into offices

New Scotland Yard, 'a very constabulary kind of castle', designed by Norman Shaw, became the police headquarters in 1890.

for the Receiver and the two Commissioners, with bachelor quarters for Colonel Rowan, the senior of the two. The house backed on to Great Scotland Yard and was approached through an archway from the street. Every day the six divisional superintendents would ride there to make their reports to the Commissioners. 'It was not much longer', according to Douglas G. Browne, 'before even those who had business with the Commissioners or the Receiver at No. 4 Whitehall Place ceased to refer to it as "the Metropolitan Police Office"; and, Middle and Little Scotland Yard having vanished, the epithet "Great" became redundant, and the whole headquarters was known, *tout court*, as Scotland Yard.' Gradually, as the force expanded, it outgrew the 'dingy collection of mean buildings' that it had acquired. The offices there were hopelessly muddled. *The Times* wrote, 'Innumerable books are piled up on staircases, so that they are almost impassable, piles of clothing, saddles and horse furniture, blankets and all manner of things are heaped up in little garrets in a state of what outside Scotland Yard would be called hopeless confusion.' In 1883 the Fenians began a new series of bomb attacks on the capital; and on 30 May 1884 a bomb explosion blew in a wall of Scotland Yard and wrecked the nearby Rising Sun public house. The police officer whose office had been wrecked commented philosophically, 'We could not console ourselves in the same way as the proprietor of the Rising Sun. Naturally thousands of people flocked to see the effects of the outrage. And he charged 3d a head for admitting spectators, and what with this and the increase of custom that accrued to him, he more than recouped himself for the damage done to his premises.'

The search for a new police headquarters had begun in the 1870s. When the completion of the VICTORIA EMBANKMENT brought with it about 30 acres of reclaimed land, interest focused on a site close to WESTMINSTER BRIDGE. This was to have been the site of the Grand National Opera House. The foundation stone had been laid in 1875 but the whole project had collapsed through lack of funds when the building was only partly completed. Because the ground was water-logged, extra money had to be spent on the foundations. The police wanted to convert this structure into a headquarters and police station for 'A' Division. They had put forward proposals in 1878, but there had been eight years of delay before the land was purchased; and by then the price had risen from £25,000 to £186,000.

The architect chosen to design the building was Norman Shaw who produced what A.P. Herbert subsequently described as 'a very constabulary kind of castle'. It was faced with granite, appropriately quarried by the convicts on Dartmoor. Shaw had been asked to provide 140 offices, more than 40 of them for the Criminal Investigation Department. The Commissioner had a turret office overlooking the river; senior officers were given rooms near ground level; for others, the lower the rank, the higher they had to climb. In the centre of the building was a quadrangle. The offices were linked by a warren of corridors, the whole resting on the water-logged foundations of the proposed Opera House. The headquarters were named New Scotland Yard by James Munro, the outgoing Commissioner. The police moved in in 1890. To ease the pressure, a new building was added to the south some five years later. As this was contrary to his original conception of a single building, Shaw had little to do with it and its construction was mostly in the hands of the Metropolitan Police Surveyor. This building was called Scotland House and was connected by a bridge to Shaw's building as there was no right of way between the two. A third building was added later. This, with nearby CANNON ROW police station, completed the complex. In the Commissioner's Annual Report (1935) the Commissioner complained that the staff were 'crowded together like warehouse clerks in a Christmas rush.'

In February–March 1967, in a move spread over 23 days, Scotland Yard moved to its present building on BROADWAY and VICTORIA STREET. This third headquarters, designed by Chapman Taylor and Partners, has 20 storeys, extends over 11 acres and contains nearly 700 offices housing the METROPOLITAN POLICE administration departments. The original New Scotland Yard has been renamed NORMAN SHAW BUILDING.

New Southgate Cemetery   *see* CEMETERIES.

New Square   *Lincoln's Inn, WC2*. A plain and elegant square laid out between 1685 and 1697 on the former Ficket's Field of the KNIGHTS TEMPLAR by the barrister and speculator Henry Serle and known formerly as Serle's Court. It was not originally intended to be part of the Inn. Sir Samuel Romilly, Lord Eldon, the Hon. Charles Yorke, who was Lord Chancellor for three days in 1770, and Dr Johnson's friend, Arthur Murphy, the dramatist, all had chambers here in the 18th century. In 1829, five years after Disraeli had unwillingly agreed to read for the law in the nearby OLD BUILDINGS, Dickens was, also unhappily, employed here in the offices of the solicitor, Charles Molloy. At the south end is Lincoln's Inn Archway, CAREY STREET, and at the north a splendid iron screen, made in 1863, with two stone water pumps in front of it.

New Wells   *(Rosoman Street), Clerkenwell*. An 18th-century spa which was established around a chalybeate spring whose existence had been known since the Middle Ages. The wells were then in open fields and the revellers were milkmaids and their sweethearts who danced to a fiddler. In about 1737 a theatre was built. Performances were given daily between 5 and 10 o'clock by acrobats, musicians and clowns. The public were admitted for the price of a pint of wine or punch. In 1739 'a rattlesnake with nineteen rattles' was on view 'along with a young crocodile from Georgia, flying squirrels and a cat between the tiger and the leopard perfectly tame'. FIREWORKS 're-enacted the siege of Portobello'. In 1744 Rosoman, later proprietor of SADLER'S WELLS, played Harlequin in the pantomime *The Sorceress*, Mr Dominique jumped over the heads of 24 men with drawn swords and Mme Kerman danced on stilts on a tight-tope. In 1745, 'The Youthful Giant not yet sixteen and 7 ft 4 ins high', made an appearance followed the next year by 'The Saxon Lady giantess who was 7 ft high and the wonderful little Polander who was only 2 ft 6 in high and 60 years old.' In 1746 the storming of Culloden House was re-enacted. The audience supported the English troops so enthusiastically that the manager had to rebuke them for damaging the benches with their canes. In 1747 the gardens were shut. When they were reopened in 1750 they had been much improved. Hannah Snell, the woman who had served under the name of James Gray at the siege of Pondicherry, was the star attraction. In 1752 the theatre was let to John Wesley and converted into a methodist tabernacle. In about 1756 it was demolished when Rosoman Street was built. Bowling Green Lane commemorates the pleasure gardens.

New Zealand House   *Haymarket, SW1*. This 18-storey glass and concrete building was designed for the offices of the New Zealand Commission by Robert Matthew, and opened by the Queen in May 1963. The upper storeys, except for the penthouse which is used for official New Zealand functions, are let. The top floor, used for receptions, is known as the Martini Terrace.

Newgate Bastion   *see* LONDON WALL.

Newgate Market   *Newgate Street*. According to John Strype, there was a general market in NEWGATE STREET before the GREAT FIRE. In about 1666 the main meat market was moved here from the parish of St Nicholas Shambles; 600 sheep and 50 bullocks were slaughtered daily. The market was closed in 1869 and demolished when its function was taken over by the Central Meat Markets, SMITHFIELD.

Newgate Prison   *Newgate Street*. A prison stood on the site since the 12th century and probably even earlier. In 1422 a licence was granted to the executors of Richard Whittington 'to re-edify the gaol of Newgate'. But by the end of the 16th century it was once more in a ruinous condition and had to be 'new fronted and new faced'. Soon after the restoration was completed, it was burned down in the GREAT FIRE and had to be rebuilt once more. The new prison, which was finished in 1672, was designed with 'great magnificence', decorated with emblematic figures and statues, including one of Richard Whittington and his cat. 'The sumptuousness of the outside', however, 'but aggravated the misery of the wretches within.' The water supply was quite inadequate, the ventilation

Newgate Market, which after the Great Fire had become a meat market, was closed in 1869, when the traders moved to Smithfield.

almost non-existent, the stench appalling; and during the frequent outbreaks of gaol fever, a virulent form of typhoid, the fumes bore the germs of the disease into every cell of the prison. Newly arrived prisoners were bullied and robbed not only by the other convicts, but also by the keeper and his turnkeys who made large profits from the sale of spirits and candles, food and water, and from obliging their charges to pay a variety of fees for such privileges as being released from irons and being allowed to approach the sea-coal fire. Henry Fielding observed that a London prison, of which Newgate was the most famous example, was both a 'prototype of hell' and, 'one of the dearest places on earth'. Prisoners who could afford to do so were allowed to sleep in less insalubrious parts of the prison; but those who could not were likely to be cast into such places as the Stone Hold which, according to a convict who was there in 1724, was 'a terrible stinking dark and dismal place situate underground into which no daylight can come. It was paved with stone; the prisoners had no beds and lay on the pavement whereby they endured great misery and hardship.'

In the 16th century several Roman Catholic

Condemned malefactors being hanged outside the Debtors' Door at Newgate Prison, soon after its reconstruction in 1780–3 after the Gordon Rioters had destroyed it.

martyrs, as well as the Protestant martyr, Anne Askew, were incarcerated here. So, in later times, were Titus Oates, William Penn and Daniel Defoe. So was the murderer, Major Strangeways who, in 1658, in that part of the prison known as the Press Yard, was pressed to death, a punishment which could then, and for more than a century afterwards, be inflicted on those who refused to plead in order to save their property for their heirs. Jonathan Wild, the 'Thief-Taker General' who was executed in 1725, was held here during his trial. So was Jack Sheppard, hero of Harrison Ainsworth's novel, the last of whose remarkable escapes was made from the Castle, a cell high up on the third floor of the 60 ft high tower above the gate which spanned Newgate Street. He had been handcuffed, manacled and chained to the floor, but got out through various other locked apartments and across the leads. On his recapture, Sheppard became one of the principal sights in London as he chatted away to the hundreds of curious visitors who came to see him in the Condemned Hold. He was painted there by Sir James Thornhill, the Serjeant Painter to the Crown; and inspired Daniel Defoe to write one of at least ten accounts of his life which appeared within a few months of his death by hanging at TYBURN. The 'ridiculous rage of going to Newgate', condemned by Horace Walpole, had begun. In 1813 Elizabeth Fry came here for a nobler purpose. Informed by an American Quaker that conditions in the prison were far worse than anything he had seen during his Continental travels, she visited the so-called female side where the sight of starving women, many of them drunk, lying on the stone floor without bedding, led her to undertake the work for which she will always be remembered.

By this time the prison from which Sheppard had escaped had been pulled down and a new one rebuilt in 1770–8 to the designs of George Dance the Younger, Clerk of the City Works, who was said to have been influenced by Giovanni Battista Piranesi, the architect and copper-engraver of Roman antiquities, whom Dance had met in Rome. It was as George Crabbe, the poet, told a friend, 'very large, strong and beautiful'. Soon after Newgate was completed it was attacked by the mob during the GORDON RIOTS. 'They did not proceed to storm', the *Gentleman's Magazine* reported, 'until they had given their terms [for the release of the prisoners] like regular assailants,' and had placed sentinels at every approach to the prison so that any prisoners who escaped could not be taken off to other gaols. The keeper of the prison refused their request, whereupon the mob hurled a cascade of stones at the window from which he had spoken, and while he and his wife and daughter rushed up to the attic and escaped over the roof, one of the assailants, a young man subsequently discovered to be a mad Quaker, the son of a rich and respectable corn factor, broke all the ground-floor windows of the keeper's house, using a scaffold pole like a battering ram. The upper windows were subsequently broken by a hysterical youth who climbed up on to the Quaker's shoulders and battered at them with his head. The furniture, doors and floorboards, together with 'a nice collection of pictures', were then thrown through the window frames and piled up against the walls and set alight. As this was being done there appeared a column of about a hundred nervous constables (*see* POLICE) who were set upon by the rioters 'with great fury'. Their staves were torn from their hands, broken in two, ignited at the now crackling fire and, with handfuls of tow dipped in turpentine, hurled about as brands towards other parts of the prison. The poet George Crabbe 'never saw anything so dreadful'. He watched the rioters break the gates with crowbars, and tear holes in the roof from which dark figures appeared, silhouetted against the flames. 'The prisoners escaped,' Crabbe wrote. 'They were conducted through the streets in their chains. You have no conception of the phrensy of the multitude.' About 300 prisoners escaped within an hour, while others in more inaccessible parts of the prison could be heard screaming in terror, 'expecting an instantaneous death from the flames or from the thundering descent of huge pieces of building.' A day or two later the prison was a smouldering shell through which, so Susan Burney said, 'everybody went in and out as freely as they walk under the Piazzas in Covent Garden', and around which groups of bewildered prisoners, frightened by the outside world, vainly looked for someone to take responsibility for them. The prison was rebuilt in 1780–3 and the new structure admitted Lord George Gordon who was held responsible for the riots and who died there of gaol fever in 1793. 'In consequence of the rebuilding of the prison . . . a great area' was opened up before it and, on the recommendation of the SHERIFFS the place of execution in London was transferred here from TYBURN. The scaffold was erected in front of the prison in OLD BAILEY and the condemned stepped on to it through the door nearest to NEWGATE STREET. As at TYBURN, enormous crowds collected and every window overlooking the scene was filled with people, many of whom paid extremely high prices for their places. The spectacle of hanging outside Newgate was brought to an end in 1868 in accordance with a Bill introduced by J.T. Hibbert (see EXECUTIONS). Thereafter the hangings took place behind Newgate's walls. Dickens, for whom Newgate had a 'horrible fascination', visited the prison on several occasions. It appears, of course, in *Barnaby Rudge*; in *Oliver Twist* in which Fagin waits for the end, sitting on the stone bed in the Condemned Hold, behind 'those dreadful walls'; and in *Great Expectations* in which Pip is shown inside 'the grim stone building', to view the yard where the gallows are kept and 'the Debtors' Door, out of which culprits come to be hanged'. The prison also appears in Thackeray's *Henry Esmond*. It was finally demolished in 1902 to make way for the CENTRAL CRIMINAL COURT.

Dance's second Newgate Prison shortly before its demolition in 1902 to make way for the Old Bailey.

Newgate Street *EC1*. Newgate was one of the principal gates in the CITY wall and so called because it was, as Stow says, 'latelier built than the rest'. Excavations in 1875, 1903 and 1909 revealed outlines of a Roman-type gateway built on over 4 ft of rubbish that had accumulated on the top of the wall, so it was clearly of later date than the Roman wall. It seems to have been in existence at least as early at 857. It is mentioned in 1188 as a prison. It was rebuilt in the 15th century, again in 1555–6, after its destruction by fire, once more in 1628–30 and finally in 1672 after its destruction in the GREAT FIRE. It was demolished in 1767. The street, which takes its name from the gate, extends from HOLBORN VIADUCT to ST MARTIN'S LE GRAND. It was originally known as Bladder Street, presumably because of its butchers' stalls and shambles, then as Mount Goddard Street, a name derived, so Stow suggested, from 'the tippling-house where goddards or goblets were in frequent use'.

Newham *E6, E7, E12, E13, E15, E16*. London Borough of about 8,500 acres formed in 1965 by the amalgamation of the County Boroughs of EAST HAM and WEST HAM together with the detached part of the Metropolitan Borough of WOOLWICH known as NORTH WOOLWICH. Ham ('low-lying pasture') appears in the *Domesday* survey, as EAST HAM and WEST HAM did not achieve separate identity until the late 12th century. Until the middle of the 19th century, modern Newham consisted of the town of STRATFORD and the villages or hamlets of WEST HAM, PLAISTOW, UPTON, and FOREST GATE in WEST HAM. EAST HAM, Green Street, Plashet and Wallend in EAST HAM, and the separate parish of LITTLE ILFORD which from Tudor times also included the manor of Aldersbrook. Arable land lay between the habitations, while south of PLAISTOW and EAST HAM between 2,000 and 3,000 acres of valuable marsh pasture land extended to the THAMES shore. From the 18th century, vegetable growing for the London market tended to replace arable farming. From about 1690 until the early 19th century the neighbourhood shared in suburban prosperity as richer Londoners began to develop south-west Essex as a residential retreat; but nearly all their large houses in Newham have now disappeared. Earlier industries were mainly in STRATFORD, with some in PLAISTOW.

The modern development of Newham came in two stages: industrial in the west and south from about 1840 and residential in the centre, east and north from about 1860, with a peak in 1880–1900. There were four interacting influences on industrial development. First was the expansion of the PORT OF LONDON. The south of Newham was made more accessible by the construction of the Barking Road in about 1810–12 to connect the EAST AND WEST INDIA DOCKS with the river port of BARKING and with Tilbury. The next development brought docks to Newham and the whole of the ROYAL GROUP are within the borough: Victoria (1855), Albert (1880), and King George V (1921). The second influence was railway development from the opening of the Eastern Counties line through STRATFORD in 1839. In 1939 the present Newham was served by 21 stations on seven lines. Closures have reduced these to 14 on six. The third influence was industrial expansion. The Metropolitan Buildings Act, 1844 restricted 'offensive trades' in metropolitan London and began to force manufacturers of such products as sulphuric acid, soap, paint

and varnishes first into western STRATFORD and then along the THAMES bank. The fourth and final influence was the availability of land near road, rail and river. Thus the period of the construction of the Victoria and Albert docks saw the development of shipbuilding, rubber and cable, gas and chemicals manufacture. The modern townships of CANNING TOWN, CUSTOM HOUSE, SILVERTOWN, NORTH WOOLWICH, Beckton and Cyprus grew up to house workers in the new industries in the south, and Stratford New Town to house the railway workers in the north. George Parker Bidder, civil and railway engineer, was a principal influence. He built the North Woolwich Railway and the Victoria Dock and he and his associates secured much of the land south of the Barking Road in WEST HAM.

While in the 19th century the west and south were developed with housing for workmen, new residential districts developed in the north and east – FOREST GATE, MANOR PARK, UPTON Manor, Upton Park – together with the great expansion of the older villages. This residential growth resulted from emigration out of the overcrowded East End of London, and from the building of houses for clerks working in the CITY. It was encouraged by good communications and the availability of building land as the estates of the Gurney, Pelly, Burges and Henniker families were sold off. Between the wars, the EAST and WEST HAM Councils were responsible for most of the housing development and a total of approximately 2,600 municipal dwellings were provided up to 1939. Since the 2nd World War both Corporations have promoted vigorous housing programmes and the Newham Council now provides some 30,000 homes – about one-third of the total – most of them built since 1945.

Nonconformity was very strong in Newham by the turn of the century and in 1904 there were about 90 chapels of all denominations in WEST HAM and 37 in EAST HAM and LITTLE ILFORD. The oldest nonconformist chapel in Newham is the Brickfields United Reformed Church, Welfare Road, E15. It was built in 1776 by a congregation which had been founded north of Stratford Broadway over a century earlier. The Quakers also have a long history and were established in PLAISTOW by at least 1671. A meeting house was built in North Street, PLAISTOW in 1704 and a larger building in 1823. This was attended by a number of famous families – Gurneys, Frys, Listers, Howards and Barclays. The meeting was mainly transferred to WANSTEAD in 1870 and the PLAISTOW meeting finally closed in 1924. The Roman Catholic Church has also been strong locally and there are two convents, two friaries and nine churches in the Borough.

The population of the Borough was between 7,700 and 7,800 in 1801. The period of largest growth was 1880–1900. In 1901 the aggregate population stood at 363,000 and rose to a peak of about 450,000 in the early 1920s. Decline, which began before the 2nd World War, was accelerated by war damage, evacuation and a general movement to newer suburbs.

Newington *SE1*. Lies within the London Borough of SOUTHWARK, north of WALWORTH, east of LAMBETH and west of BERMONDSEY. The first mention of Neweton (or New Town) occurs in the *Testa de Nevil* in the reign of Henry III wherein it is stated that 'the queen's goldsmith holds of the king one acre of land in Neweton, by the service of rendering a gallon of

A game of trap-ball in 1788 at Newington Butts, where in previous centuries young men practised archery.

honey'. In the Register of the Archbishop of Canterbury of 1313 the parish is named Newington *juxta* London. On its south it contains the ELEPHANT AND CASTLE, a confused meeting of roads, including Newington Causeway, Newington Butts, and the New Kent Road. West of this traffic-ridden conglomeration rises the classical front of Dr Spurgeon's METROPOLITAN TABERNACLE opened in 1861. Newington Butts, running south, is thought by some to have been a place where young men were trained in archery long ago, but others say the name derives from a family called Butts who owned an estate here at one time. The Elephant and Castle public house was a coaching house, its sign being the crest of the CUTLERS' COMPANY who dealt in ivory. A Victorian Elephant and Castle replaced the earlier building, but this was destroyed by bombing in the 2nd World War, and the public house has now been rebuilt on a new site. Near the inn, early in the 19th century, stood the meeting-house in which the deluded Joanna Southcott preached to her followers.

Newington Green *Stoke Newington, N16*. This square was enclosed in 1742, but the four houses Nos 52–55 Newington Green are much older. They are amongst the oldest houses in London and date from 1658. On the Albion Road corner of the Green is a set of fine wrought iron gates with the monogram 'W'. Behind these gates stood the house of the hymn writer, Isaac Watts. Also of interest in Newington Green are the Unitarian Chapel of 1708 on the north side and a group of 18th-century houses on the east side.

Newman Street *W1*. First rated in 1746 and called after Newman Hall, Quendon, Essex, which belonged to William Berners, the ground landlord. For the rest of the century, the list of residents reads like a roll call of artists and sculptors: No. 5, Thomas Banks, sculptor, 1779–1805; No. 14, Benjamin West, PRA, 1777–1820; No. 17, John Bacon, sculptor, 1774–99; No. 22, Charles Kemble, actor, 1809; No. 28, Thomas Stothard RA, 1806–23; No. 31, William Behnes, sculptor, 1818–22; No. 72, Luke Fildes, PRA, 1868; No. 87, Thomas Holcroft, actor and author, 1790–9.

Newport Court *WC2*. Laid out in the 1680s in the courtyard of Newport House (*see* NEWPORT MARKET). It was described by Strype in 1720 as 'a great passage into So-Ho, and those new-built places. It is for the generality inhabited by French; as indeed are most of these Streets and Alleys. It is a place of good trade' (*see* SOHO). Like the rest of this area its character deteriorated rapidly in the 19th century; and in 1872, when there were butchers in the court and it was consequently known as 'Butchers' Row', it was said to be a veritable 'fountain of foul odours'. The north side was demolished and reconstructed in the 1880s, and part of the south was replaced by the large, unsightly multi-storey artisans' dwellings which, with shops on the ground floor, can still be seen in CHARING CROSS ROAD.

Newport Market Named after Mountjoy Blount, the eldest natural son of Charles Blount, Earl of Devonshire, and Penelope, daughter of the Earl of Essex. He was created Earl of Newport in 1628 and died in 1665, having treacherously served both sides during the Civil War. His large house and grounds covered a considerable area north of the present

A mid-18th-century engraving of Newington Green, which still contains some fine houses of the 1650s.

LITTLE NEWPORT STREET. His grandson sold the estate to Nicholas Barbon who rapidly set out developing it and leased to one John Bland an area on which to build a market. Six years later, in 1692, the market rights were sold to Sir Nathaniel Curzon, the 2nd Baronet of Kedleston; and in 1720 John Strype described the market as being 'much eclipsed' by CLARE MARKET but as having 'a good Market-house, with Shambels for Butchers in the Midst, with Shops round about it.' Within five years of this description Defoe considered it one of the principal meat markets in London. Its reputation declined in the 19th century, however, and by the 1850s the area had deteriorated into one of the worst and most violent slums in London. The market-house was turned into a refuge for the destitute by a group of philanthropists with whom Mr Gladstone, much concerned with the reformation of prostitutes, was closely connected. But the area grew ever more sordid until, in the 1880s, a police report described it as 'a veritable focus of every danger which can menace the health and social order of a city. The houses, from their insanitary condition, are horribly disgusting; and can only be fitly designated as well prepared propagating ground for every kind of contagious and loathsome disease. ... The grossest immorality flourishes unabashed from every age downwards to mere children. ... It would be an act of true philanthropy to break up this reeking home of filthy vice ...' It was, therefore, a profound relief to the authorities when the METROPOLITAN BOARD OF WORKS was able to clear the foetid district for the construction of CHARING CROSS ROAD and SHAFTESBURY AVENUE.

Newspaper Library *Colindale, NW9.* National collection of daily and weekly newspapers and periodicals. The first section, then the BRITISH MUSEUM Newspaper Repository, was completed in 1903 to house English provincial, Scottish and Irish newspapers dating from about 1700. A bindery, reading rooms and further stacks were added in 1932, and the Library, which became part of the BRITISH LIBRARY on its formation in 1973, now holds the entire national collection of newspapers, apart from the Burney Collection (1603–1800) and the Oriental Collections, which remain in the BRITISH MUSEUM. It contains early London newspapers and journals which are not part of the Burney Collection, and those dating from 1801. There are also large collections of Commonwealth and foreign newspapers. About 15,000 provincial and Irish newspapers were destroyed when the original building was bombed in 1940, but the United Kingdom collections are very comprehensive from about 1840.

Newton Road *W2.* One of the best streets built by William Kinnaird Jenkins in the 1850s. It is lined with charming detached villas. Breaking the symmetry is No. 32, designed by Denys Lasdun in 1938, now well screened by trees.

Nicholas Lane *EC4.* Named after the church of ST NICHOLAS ACONS which was destroyed in the GREAT FIRE.

Nichols Square *Barbican.* Stood between WELL STREET and Castle Street and was probably named after an 18th-century landowner or builder. It was completely destroyed in the 2nd World War.

Nine Elms *Battersea, SW8.* First named in 1645 after a row of trees bordering the road. From that time it became a centre of industries, including brewing, lime kilns, potteries, woodyards and timber docks. Several windmills lined the riverbank, surrounded by fields and osier beds. Battersea New Town, begun in the 1790s, provided houses for the expanding labour force over the next hundred years. The railway, opened in 1838, had first its terminus at Nine Elms. Afterwards goods yards and works covered many acres. Its neighbours were the gasworks, established in 1833, and the waterworks, site of the later power station. Among the factories was the chapel of St George's-in-the-Fields, built in 1828 and destroyed during the 2nd World War. After the war, the area became neglected and the railway yards and many factories closed down. Then in 1974 the NEW COVENT GARDEN MARKET opened, followed, after further years of dereliction, by new factories, making Nine Elms again the industrial heart of BATTERSEA.

Nine Elms Station *Vauxhall, SW8.* Built as the London terminus of the London and Southampton Railway and opened in 1838. It was designed by Sir William Tite in an area south of the river described as 'a low, swampy district, occasionally overflowed by the Thames'. Nine days after the opening of the station the London and Southampton announced in the newspapers that eight special trains would run from NINE ELMS to a station near Epsom for Derby Day. The response was unexpectedly enthusiastic and more than 5,000 people besieged the station and swamped the trains. The station was closed to passengers in 1848 when the line was extended to WATERLOO but was still occasionally used by Queen Victoria and other notabilities. Garibaldi arrived here in 1864 by special train for his visit to London. Nine Elms was damaged in an air raid in 1941 and finally demolished in the 1960s. The flower section of the NEW COVENT GARDEN MARKET now stands on the site of the station.

Nine Worthies of London A chronicle in verse and prose by Richard Johnson, published in 1592 and recounting the exploits of nine distinguished Londoners, Sir William Walworth, Sir Henry Pritchard, Sir William Sevenoke, Sir Thomas Knight, Sir John Bonham, Christopher Croker, Sir John Hawkwood, Sir Hugh Calveley and Sir Henry Maleverer.

Noble Street *EC2.* Probably named after Thomas Le Noble who owned land here in the 14th century. In the 16th century Sir Nicholas Bacon had a house here; and in the 17th the Lord Mayor, Robert Tichborne, who signed Charles I's death warrant. SCRIVENERS' HALL was in the street from 1642 to 1730 and COACH-MAKERS' HALL until its destruction in the 2nd World War. At the corner of GRESHAM STREET is the site of ST JOHN ZACHARY, a church destroyed in the GREAT FIRE. ST ANNE AND ST AGNES was also burned but was rebuilt by Wren. West of Noble Street towards GRESHAM STREET is an exposed section of the old city wall which includes part of the Roman fort built in the 1st century (*see also* LONDINIUM).

Noel Street *W1.* Named after the Duchess of Portland who was Lady Elizabeth Noel before her marriage. The east end of the street, which had been built in 1706, was formerly known as Tweed Street in association with its neighbour, BERWICK STREET. Most of the street was rebuilt in the 1740s but from this time only two houses, Nos 5 and 18, remain. Nos 14–17 were built to the design of Sir Aston Webb in 1897–8 for L'Ecole de L'Eglise Protestante Française de Londres. It remained a school until 1939. Most of the north side of the street was demolished to make way for Waverley House, a modern block overlooking BERWICK STREET.

Nonsuch Palace Built in 1538 by Henry VIII as a hunting palace and guest house for foreign visitors. It was situated on the site of the village and church of Cuddington, which was cleared to make room for the palace. Merton Priory had been the patron of the church; the priory having been dissolved by Henry, its stones were used as foundations for the palace.

The name 'Nonesuch', as given in early records, indicates the desire by Henry to have a building without compare, and it was, in fact, a Tudor extravaganza. It consisted of two-storey buildings ranged round two interconnecting open courtyards. Although small, only 150 yds long, it was lavishly decorated in the Renaissance style. The workmen were mostly Italian, including Nicolas Belin (or Bellin) of Modena, who had worked at Fontainebleau. Belin's chief work at Nonsuch was a series of stucco reliefs, framed in elaborately carved slate, which went all round the walls of the Inner Court and along the South Front. The South Front had towers at each end topped by onion-shaped cupolas and ornamented with fanciful weather vanes. The gardens were formal and contained much statuary.

In 1556 Nonsuch was exchanged by Mary with Henry Fitzalan, 12th Earl of Arundel, for estates in Suffolk. Queen Elizabeth stayed at Nonsuch many times, her first visit being on a royal progress in 1559. In 1579 the estate was inherited by Arundel's son-in-law John, Lord Lumley, whose splendid library passed to James I's son Henry, and is now part of the Royal Library. By 1603 Nonsuch was back in royal hands. James I gave it to his queen, Anne of Denmark, and the palace was used again as a royal hunting lodge by James and his son Charles I. During the Commonwealth, a survey was made with a view to selling the property. Charles II reclaimed it, however, and then

Nonsuch Palace, from Hoefnagel's view of 1582. Built for Henry VIII in 1538, it was nearly all demolished by the end of the 17th century.

gave it to his extravagant mistress, Barbara Villiers, who in 1682 sold it to Lord Berkeley. He promptly demolished the palace, using some of the stone for his house, Durdans, at Epsom. By 1702 only a ruin remained.

The site, now part of Nonsuch Park, was excavated in 1959–60 when the ground plan was revealed, including the site of Cuddington church. Fragments of carved and gilded slate and stone were found, and much domestic refuse such as pottery, glass, pewter and bone. Most of the finds were given to the MUSEUM OF LONDON, while the site was filled in and is now under grass. The main building now in the park is the Mansion House, a 17th-century farmhouse rebuilt by Wyatville in the Georgian Gothic style in 1804.

Norbiton *Surrey*. The name derives from the Saxon *tun* or 'enclosure' i.e. the north enclosure (as opposed to SURBITON, the south enclosure) and applies to the area between the eastern end of London Road, KINGSTON and the lower slopes of Kingston Hill. Norbiton Common lay to the south-east and was enclosed as a result of the Enclosure Act of 1808. NEW MALDEN and the main-line railway now extend across the site. It was the first area to be made a separate ecclesiastical district from All Saints, Kingston. St Peter's church, at the junction of London and Cambridge Roads, was built by Gilbert Scott and Moffatt on behalf of the CHURCH COMMISSIONERS and opened in 1842. Built in yellow and white brick, it is designed in the Norman style. The interior displays Norman columns and three galleries, but lack of funds prevented the building being completed according to the architect's original conception, the present church ending at the chancel arch. The chancel itself was completed in 1869. The original foundation stone was reset in the north wall of this extension and has another stone above it recording the enlargement. In 1904 the chancel and sanctuary were floored with mosaics. The present pulpit was designed by J. Oldrid Scott.

On the hill above Norbiton Station stands Kingston Victoria Hospital, opened in 1898 by the Duke of Cambridge, cousin of Queen Victoria and a local landowner. It was designed by Major Macaulay, the Borough Surveyor, and built to commemorate the Diamond Jubilee of 1897. The Duke gave the site from part of his estate; it was KINGSTON's first hospital. In 1948, as a result of the National Health Service Act, it became the gynaecological section of Kingston (main) Hospital. This began as the Infirmary Section of Kingston Union Workhouse in Gloucester Road, but was separated in 1902. The new outpatients' department and new surgical unit were both opened by Princess Alexandra in 1963 and 1976 respectively. The whole hospital is now one of the largest in the district, extending from Kingston Hill along Wolverton Avenue and Galsworthy Road to Coombe Lane West.

Norbury *SW16*. Lies in the north-western part of the London Borough of CROYDON on the River GRAVENEY. The land rises from the GRAVENEY valley to over 200 ft at Pollards Hill. The Roman Road to the south coast branched off Stane Street and passed through present-day Norbury. The route to and from London continued in use and in 1264 a battle between Henry III's supporters and the barons took place nearby on what was subsequently called Battle Close or Green. In the 14th century Norbury's name probably referred to its position in CROYDON parish. The manor, a sub-manor of CROYDON, passed in 1359 to the Carew family of BEDDINGTON who held it virtually continuously until 1859. Sir Nicholas Carew, Henry VIII's favourite and Master of the Horse, was eventually beheaded. The medieval area was mainly agricultural and the road was kept by a hermit who lived by the river. Charcoal was burned on the common land of THORNTON HEATH which was plagued with highwaymen during the 17th and 18th centuries. In 1878 Norbury station was opened and by the end of the century there were about 30 buildings near the main road. With the electrified train system to THORNTON HEATH (1901) development accelerated. Between the World Wars shopping parades appeared along the London Road and estates were built. CROYDON Borough Council acquired land east of the railway between Norbury and THORNTON HEATH and built about 800 dwellings (1920–7). Norbury Hall (built 1802) became an old people's home in 1935 and the grounds became Norbury Park.

Norfolk College *Greenwich, see* TRINITY HOSPITAL.

Norfolk House *31 St James's Square, SW1*. A block of brick and stone offices, built by Grunton and Grunton in 1939 in the south-east corner of the Square, on the site of the first house to be erected here (*see* ST JAMES'S SQUARE). This house, originally owned by the Earl of St Albans, was bought by the 8th Duke of Norfolk in 1722 for £10,000 and it remained in the family until the time of the 16th Duke in 1938. In 1737, Frederick, Prince of Wales, described by his mother as 'a nauseous little beast' and by his father, George II, as 'the greatest ass and the greatest liar, the greatest *canaille* and the greatest beast in the whole world', rented the house furnished when he was turned out of ST JAMES'S PALACE by his father. The prince's eldest son, George III, was born here on 4 June 1738. According to the Julian calendar in use at the time, the date was 24 May. But after 1751, when the Gregorian calendar was adopted in England, George III followed contemporary usage and celebrated his birthday according to the new style. The custom of celebrating 4 June at Eton College, in whose traditions and history he took a deep interest, began in George III's time. Before the house was rented by his father, it was described by Lord Strafford's mother, who looked at it on behalf of her son while house-hunting for him, as 'soe strong it will last for ever'. In 1748, however, it had become so dilapidated that it was demolished and rebuilt for the 9th Duke of Norfolk on a larger site to the designs of Matthew Brettingham the Elder in 1748–52. After a reception to celebrate its completion, Horace Walpole wrote, 'All the earth was there . . . . You would have thought there had been a comet, everyone was gaping in the air and treading on one another's toes . . . . The lightness and novelty of the ornaments, and the ceilings, are delightful.' The interior, behind a plain brick façade, was indeed splendid. One of the rooms survived the demolition in 1938, the Music Room; and this can still be seen at the VICTORIA AND ALBERT MUSEUM. A portico was added in 1842. During the war the present building housed the headquarters of General Eisenhower's 1st Allied Army as a plaque on the wall testifies. The invasions of North Africa in 1942 (Operation Torch) and of Europe in 1944 (Operation Overlord) were both planned here.

Norland Estate *W11*. On the north side of Holland Park Avenue between Norland Road and Portland Road this estate, formerly in the ownership of the Greene and Vulliamy families, was bought in 1839 by Charles Richardson, a solicitor, and developed by him until his bankruptcy in 1851. Robert Cantwell was associated with the design of the southern half of the estate, including Royal Crescent with its distinctive 'pepperbox' end houses (about 1840–50) and Norland Square (1844–53). St Ann's Villas differs from the rest of the estate in having semi-detached villas in the Tudor-Gothic and Jacobean manner built in about 1846–50. St James church, Norlands, was built 1844–50 to the designs of Lewis Vulliamy. Norlands was the 'North lands' of the parish.

Norman Shaw Building *Victoria Embankment, SW1*. Formerly known as NEW SCOTLAND YARD when it was the headquarters of the METROPOLITAN POLICE. It was built to the designs of Norman Shaw in 1888–90. An annexe was constructed to the south in 1912 and another to the north, designed by W. Curtis Green, in 1935–40. The iron gates are by Sir Reginald Blomfield. Since the removal of NEW SCOTLAND YARD to BROADWAY, the building has been known by its present name and is used as offices for Members of PARLIAMENT. There is a commemorative plaque to the architect facing the river.

North Audley Street *W1*. Takes its name from Sir Hugh Audley, from whom the lands later comprising the GROSVENOR ESTATE descended through Mary Davies to the Grosvenor family. It extends northward from GROSVENOR SQUARE to OXFORD STREET and was originally laid out in the mid-1720s. The houses were generally small and by 1790 were chiefly occupied by tradesmen. In the late 19th and early 20th centuries most of the street was rebuilt in large blocks with shops beneath residential chambers or offices, and today there are only two notable buildings – ST MARK'S CHURCH and Nos 11 and 12. The latter were designed by Edward Shepherd and were in existence by 1730. No. 12, the larger of the two, was occupied from 1730–70 by the Huguenot refugee Jean Louis Ligonier, who later became Commander-in-Chief of the Army. The gallery at the rear, which still exists, has been described as 'perhaps the most beautiful early-Georgian room surviving in London'. It has been conjectured that the Irish Palladian architect, Sir Edward Lovett Pearce, may have had a hand in the embellishment of this fine house. From 1795 to 1814 both houses were occupied by the Gillow family of furniture makers and decorators; and in 1932 Samuel Courtauld, the industrialist and art-collector, employed Rex Whistler to decorate one of the bedrooms at No. 12. Notable residents of North Audley Street include Lord Palmerston in 1807, and Maria Edgeworth, the novelist, after 1830.

North Circular Road Unlike its southern counterpart, the SOUTH CIRCULAR ROAD, the North Circular road is, at least in parts, purpose-built. As the A406 it runs in a great loop through the northern suburbs for 23 miles between CHISWICK and WOODFORD. It then turns south and follows the A104, A114, A116 and A117 until it reaches the North Woolwich Ferry. From CHISWICK to SOUTHGATE it was planned and built as the North Circular Road, from the early 1930s onwards. From SOUTHGATE to WOOLWICH existing roads were used. Long stretches are now dual carriageway; nevertheless at times of heavy traffic there is considerable congestion.

North Cray *Kent*. Lies in the valley of the River CRAY, south of BEXLEY. The Roman road from London to Dover runs to the north and villa remains attest to Roman settlement at North Cray. The church of St James was founded during the Saxon era. By the 14th century the Gatton family, probably associated with Gatton's Wood and Plantation, were resident in the area. The surviving 15th-century yeoman's cottage (now re-erected in the Weald and Downland Museum, Singleton, West Sussex) was built at a time when North Cray together with RUXLEY to the south had passed to the Percy family. The two parishes were formally united in 1557. Ruxley church, in a dilapidated state, was used as a barn, which still stands in the grounds of the RUXLEY garden centre. From the 17th century mansions appeared around the village. Mount Mascal (demolished 1959) was the home of Sir John Leman and Sir Robert Ladbroke, Lord Mayors of London in 1616 and 1747 respectively. In about 1740 Vale Mascal was built on the estate and later became the home of Sir Francis Burdett and his wife Sophia, daughter of the banker Thomas Coutts. The ornamental bath-house, once in the grounds and reputedly used by Charles Wesley as a baptismal font, still stands nearby. In the early 19th century Castlereagh lived at North Cray Cottage. It was there that he killed himself in 1822, and the house is now Loring Hall, used by GOLDSMITHS' COLLEGE. The parish population was gradually increasing and in 1851 St James was rebuilt, but the village with its farmland changed little until the construction in 1968 of North Cray Road. Despite this development and that, for example, of Jacquets Court (taking its name from the once nearby Jacobean mansion) on the Mount Mascal estate, as well as industrial development in neighbouring FOOTS CRAY, North Cray remains a rural farming area, since 1965 within the London Borough of BEXLEY.

North-East London Polytechnic, *Romford Road, E15*. Formed in 1979 by the amalgamation of the BARKING Regional College of Technology, WALTHAM FOREST Technical College and School of Art, and WEST HAM College, thus continuing a tradition dating, in the case of WEST HAM College, back to the turn of the century.

North End Road *Fulham, SW6, W14*. Leads from FULHAM BROADWAY to HAMMERSMITH and is the site of the street market transferred from WALHAM GREEN. It was first settled in the 16th century although the road is mentioned as Gybbesgrene Lane in the previous century. The area became one of farms and market gardens with some fine houses, among which Normand House lay to the west. The name is a corruption of No Man's Land and the house was built between 1649 and 1661. It became St Katherine's Convent in 1885 but was extensively damaged in the 2nd World War, demolished and its site made into Normand Park, opened in 1952. Also on the west side amid the maze of streets, is ST THOMAS'S ROMAN CATHOLIC CHURCH, designed by Pugin and probably the most distinguished building now in the area. Across the busy West

Cromwell Road lay the last house of any importance to survive in North End: The Grange. Built in the time of Charles II, it was the home of Samuel Richardson before he moved to PARSONS GREEN, and from 1867 until his death in 1898, of Sir Edward Burne-Jones, painter and friend of William Morris; the house was demolished in 1958, amid a public outcry, and housing built in its place.

North London Collegiate School *Canons Drive, Edgware, Middlesex*. In 1850 Frances Mary Buss opened a model school for girls in Camden Street, CAMDEN TOWN. In a year, numbers increased from 35 (daughters of gentlemen and respectable tradesmen) to 115, paying fees of 2 guineas a quarter. The syllabus included natural philosophy, Latin and branches of science additional to basic subjects. Languages other than French were extra. In 1870 larger premises were acquired in Camden Road and in 1879, with considerable help from CITY LIVERY COMPANIES, new buildings were opened in Sandall Road. The establishment was run on the lines of a boys' public school, and the syllabus included swimming, skating and athletics as well as cookery, handicrafts and political economy. Discipline was strict. The educational aim was to prepare girls for public examinations and acceptance at universities, for training as teachers and for professional careers. In 1929, with help from the Middlesex County Council, the school bought CANONS, a Georgian house in EDGWARE built in the 1740s by a cabinet maker, William Hallett, on the site of a former mansion of the Duke of Chandos. Hallett and his wife Elizabeth were painted in 1786 by Gainsborough in *The Morning Walk* which hangs in the NATIONAL GALLERY. The house was later owned by Dennis O'Kelly, owner of the great racehorse, Eclipse. In 1939 new buildings were designed for the school by Sir Albert Richardson. In 1944 it became a direct grant school but reverted to private status in 1976. In 1981 there were 800 pupils.

North Middlesex Hospital *Edmonton, N18*. In 1731 the parish of EDMONTON built a workhouse near the parish church. In 1837 a new and larger workhouse was built to serve other parishes in addition to EDMONTON. Over the years more land was bought and additional buildings erected. In 1899 a medical block was added. In 1915 much of the hospital was taken over for war casualties. In the 2nd World War the buildings suffered severely from air raids. In 1948 the National Health Service took over. In 1982 there were 667 beds.

North Ockendon *Essex*. The village lies in a farming area. The church of St Mary Magdalene is a small but attractive flint structure comprising nave with north aisle (four bays), chancel with chapel, south porch and an embattled west tower. The building is of various styles from Romanesque to 14th-century Gothic. The Poyntz chapel (named after a family who held the manor from the time of Edward III to 1714) is filled with a remarkable family portrait gallery – their monuments and brasses. There are no fewer than eight marble tombs, each with kneeling effigies. The church was restored in 1858 and at the beginning of the 20th century. The Old Bakehouse and The Forge are 17th-century buildings of interest in Ockendon Road.

North Sheen *Surrey*. Lies west of MORTLAKE on the south bank of the THAMES. The civil parish of North Sheen was created in 1894, the name relating to its position north of the area comprised in the ancient manor of SHEEN. Until the early 20th century, when the FULHAM and HAMMERSMITH CEMETERIES were consecrated, the area consisted basically of market gardens on the outskirts of MORTLAKE. Development occurred between the two World Wars and a 300-year-old barn was re-erected as the Church of St Philip and All Saints. Since 1965 North Sheen has formed part of the London Borough of RICHMOND-UPON-THAMES.

North Villa *Regent's Park, NW1*. A delightful cottage *orné*, originally called Albany Cottage, on the eastern side of REGENT'S PARK built in about 1827 for Thomas Raikes, dandy and diarist, by C.R. Cockerill and Decimus Burton. Other, later, residents have included Russell Donithorne Walker, the cricketer (in residence 1895–1922), and Lady Ribblesdale (1928–41), *née* Ava Willing of Philadelphia, married first to Col J.J. Astor, the millionaire who perished in the *Titanic* disaster in 1912, and then to Lord Ribblesdale. She was an outstanding personality in London society, dying in 1958 at the age of 90. The house was extensively altered for her by W.E. Lord. Since 1946 it has been an Islamic Cultural Centre; the MOSQUE stands in its grounds.

North Woolwich *E16*. Industrial and residential area to the south-east of NEWHAM. Before it was incorporated in the London Borough of NEWHAM in 1965, it largely comprised two detached parts (totalling approximately 400 acres) of the Metropolitan Borough of WOOLWICH north of the THAMES. This anomaly of 'Kent in Essex', which existed for 900 years, was most probably due to Hamon, the 11th-century Sheriff of Kent, whose manorial lands extended both sides of the THAMES. It is reasonably certain that he annexed the Essex lands to his shrievalty and hence to his county of Kent. It appears that a medieval hamlet was destroyed by floods, and habitation did not return until the 19th century. The name North Woolwich was not given until the Eastern Counties and Thames Junction Railway (later called the North Woolwich Railway) extended its line from CANNING TOWN station to the THAMES bank in 1847 and so named its terminus. The name was then applied to the whole of the area, including the small tongue of EAST HAM which separated the two detached parts of WOOLWICH. The first habitation centred round the telegraph and cable works of W.T. Henley, opened in 1859. These were later joined by Standard Telephones. Both works are now closed. A steam ferry service to the south bank was inaugurated in connection with the railway in 1847. In 1889 a parallel, and free, public ferry service was opened by the LONDON COUNTY COUNCIL. Post-war diesel-driven vessels continue to operate under the GREATER LONDON COUNCIL. The railway ferry ceased in 1908. A foot-passenger tunnel was opened under the river in 1912. The ROYAL VICTORIA GARDENS, on the Thames frontage, opened as privately run pleasure gardens in 1851, were part of the manor of Hammarsh, owned by WESTMINSTER ABBEY from at least the 11th century until their sale in 1846. The gardens were acquired by public subscription and opened in 1890 under the control of the LONDON COUNTY COUNCIL. They are now maintained by NEWHAM Council.

Northcote *SW11*. Lies in the southern part of BATTERSEA between WANDSWORTH COMMON and CLAPHAM COMMON. Until the 19th century the area, within BATTERSEA parish, was rural with mansions such as Broomwood where William Wilberforce lived for many years. From the 1860s the Bolingbroke Park Estate was developed. Northcote Road and those running off it were planned and named apparently arbitrarily. By the end of the century the layout of the district was complete, with Northcote Road as a shopping centre. The churches of St Mark's (1874) and St Michael's (1881) were both designed by William White. In 1879 Bolingbroke House became a hospital, and later redevelopment involved the demolition of the house. In 1965 the area became part of the London Borough of WANDSWORTH.

Northern Line Consists mainly of the amalgamation of two separately built railways, the City and South London Railway (C & SLR) and the HAMPSTEAD Tube. The C & SLR, opened in 1890 from KING WILLIAM STREET to STOCKWELL, was the world's first electric tube railway. Its deep-level tube tunnels (over 40 ft) had been built using the Greathead shield (*see* UNDERGROUND RAILWAYS) and the three-car trains were hauled by electric locomotives. Although the cars were nicknamed 'padded cells' because they were upholstered nearly to the ceiling, the railway prospered as a quick, clean and cheap (2d) form of transport and carried 165,000 passengers in its first two weeks.

The success of this pioneer led to a wave of tube railway promotions, one of which was for a tube from CHARING CROSS to HAMPSTEAD. This finally received financial backing from C.T. Yerkes, an American, who bought powers for the Hampstead Tube in 1900 for £100,000. The whole line, from CHARING CROSS to GOLDERS GREEN, with a branch from CAMDEN to HIGHGATE, was opened by David Lloyd George on 22 June 1907, when 140,000 passengers took a free ride on it. The distinguishing feature of this line was the depth of the tunnels: the deepest point is about 900 ft north of HAMPSTEAD Station, where the rails are 250 ft below HAMPSTEAD HEATH; HAMPSTEAD Station also has the deepest lift shaft on the Underground – 181 ft. The line was extended to HENDON Central in 1823 and thence to EDGWARE in 1924. The Hampstead Tube and C & SLR were linked in 1924. The C & SLR by this time extended from CLAPHAM COMMON to EUSTON, but was still worked by electric locomotives. Its tunnels therefore had to be widened for modern tube rolling stock, and a link was built between the two railways between CAMDEN TOWN and EUSTON. After the extension from CLAPHAM COMMON to MORDEN and a link from CHARING CROSS to KENNINGTON, the two railways were effectively integrated into one system, named the Northern Line in 1937. Under the 1935–40 New Works Programme the Northern Line was extended to High BARNET and MILL HILL East, bringing its total length to 40 miles, which included the longest continuous tunnel in the world, 17 miles 528 yards between East FINCHLEY and MORDEN (*see also* UNDERGROUND RAILWAYS).

Northolt *Middlesex*. Now the north-west corner of the London Borough of EALING with HARROW to the north and HAYES to the south-west. For much of its history it was known by the name Northall which complements SOUTHALL, its neighbour. Until the 19th century it was an exclusively agricultural area and, as in many other MIDDLESEX suburbs, the first significant developments took place in the 1920s, building continued after the 2nd World War, particularly of council housing.

Wheat was grown in Northolt until the arrival of the PADDINGTON CANAL in 1801 and its closeness to the metropolis made hay for the rapidly expanding London market profitable. The canal also stimulated the exploitation of the brick earth that forms part of the soil of the area, and by the end of the century the sizeable New Patent Brick Co. occupied 36 acres beside the canal. The last brickworks closed in 1939.

Although a railway station was built at Northolt in 1907 sales of farms and their development for speculative building did not start until the 1920s. The widening of the existing roads and the building of Western Avenue east-west across the centre set the pattern for subsequent building. Some industry was set up in the 1930s near the canal but the area is predominantly residential. Council housing has extended the built-up area since the war but some large open spaces survive as parks, playing fields and the West London shooting grounds. In the 1930s a pony-racing track was built north of the railway, but this has since been built over as the Race Course housing estate.

The old parish had consisted of three hamlets: Northolt village, West End and Wood End. This last was obliterated in the housing development north of Whitton Avenue, and West End only retains its old inn, the White Hart, beside a busy roundabout. The village centre, now a conservation area, retains some charm, having been bypassed by the building of Mandeville Road in the 1930s. The tiny 14th-century church, ST MARY THE VIRGIN, and some old cottages overlook the remains of the Green. Beside the church are the remains of the moated medieval manor house, which has been excavated; evidence of occupation in Saxon times has also been found. Northolt Aerodrome was opened in 1915.

Northumberland Alley *EC3*. Marks the site of the house occupied by the Earls of Northumberland before they moved to NORTHUMBERLAND HOUSE, STRAND. A Roman pavement discovered here in 1787 is now in the possession of the SOCIETY OF ANTIQUARIES.

Northumberland Avenue *WC2*. Built in 1876 between CHARING CROSS and VICTORIA EMBANKMENT over the site of NORTHUMBERLAND HOUSE. It originally contained several smart hotels. Now the buildings are mostly offices. The ROYAL COMMONWEALTH SOCIETY and the Royal African Society are at No. 18; the Nigerian High Commission is at No. 9. The PLAYHOUSE THEATRE stood at the eastern end.

Northumberland House *Strand*. Built at the beginning of the 17th century for the Earl of Northampton on the site of a convent. It was designed by Bernard Jansen and Gerard Christmas. The Earl of Northampton died in 1614 and was succeeded by his nephew, Thomas Howard, Earl of Suffolk, whose daughter married Algernon Percy, 10th Earl of Northumberland. The house formed part of her dowry and became known as Northumberland House. In 1749 an art gallery was added and the Percy lion was placed on top of the STRAND façade. In 1770 Robert Adam remodelled some of the interiors. By the middle of the 19th century it was surrounded by shops and commercial buildings. TRAFALGAR SQUARE had been built on one side and the THAMES EMBANKMENT on another. After many protests it was demolished in 1874 to make way for NORTHUMBERLAND AVENUE, the Percy lion on the arch above the main gateway being removed to SYON HOUSE, the Duke of Northumberland's country house at ISLEWORTH.

Northumberland Street *W1*. Built in about 1770. De Quincey had lodgings here in 1808–9, during 'the calamities of [his] noviciate in London'. And during 1834–41 Anthony Trollope took rooms here 'opposite the back-door of Marylebone Workhouse'. Life for him was hard: 'How I got my daily bread I can hardly remember, but I do remember I was often unable to get myself a dinner.'

An engraving of 1753 after Canaletto shows the Percy Lion above Northumberland House, which was demolished in 1874.

Northwood *Middlesex*. Occupies the high ground of north-west MIDDLESEX bordering Hertfordshire. It originated as the northern settlement of the ancient manor of RUISLIP and was the site of a manorial grange referred to in a document of 1248. The sparse settlement was an agricultural community and grew up along the north side of the Rickmansworth–Pinner road with an extensive area of common and woodland to the south. The common was enclosed by the Ruislip Enclosure Act of 1804 but parts have been kept open by the Northwood golf course, on land leased in 1899 from King's College Cambridge, Lords of the Manor since 1451, and Haste Hill golf course, laid out in 1929. The remainder is taken up by the modern development of Northwood Hills, served by a railway station opened in 1933. The site of the manorial grange is now occupied by The Grange, a building with 15th-century timber framing enclosed in later additions and incorporating a flint buttress. It was purchased in 1934 for public use.

Old farmhouses still existing are Greenhill Farmhouse, Youngwood Farm (17th-century) and Ducks Hill Farm (1783). The Cottage in Jackets Lane and Gatehill Farm (much modernised) both date from the 16th century. Denville Hall was originally Maze Farm, one of whose owners was the judge, Sir John Vaughan. It was extended and renamed Northwood Hill in the early 19th century by Daniel Norton and in 1925 was bought by Alfred Denville MP and opened by the Princess Royal as a home for retired members of the theatrical profession. Holy Trinity Church, designed by S.S. Teulon, was built in 1854 with the help of Lord Grosvenor (1st Baron Ebury) of Moor Hall, Rickmansworth. It has a Burne-Jones window.

Northwood remained a farming area until in 1887 Northwood station on the Metropolitan railway was opened, and shortly after the first large-scale sale of land for building took place. This was to transform the area into the present-day suburb of pleasant streets and open spaces. One of the high parts of Northwood is occupied by Mount Vernon Hospital, which includes in its grounds one of the only two complete Art Nouveau churches in the country. It was built in 1905 to the design of F.H. Wheeler. In 1965 Northwood was absorbed into the London Borough of HILLINGDON.

Norwood *SE19, SE25, SE27*. The name of North Wood was recorded by the 12th century and referred to the ancient forest stretching north from CROYDON. It survived in parts as woodland into the 19th century when the urban development south of London began. West Norwood lies within the London Borough of LAMBETH, and UPPER and SOUTH NORWOOD and Norwood New Town within the London Borough of CROYDON.

Notre Dame de France *Leicester Square, W1*. Designed by Professor Hector O. Corfiato after the 2nd World War in the style known as Beaux Arts Modern, this church stands on the site of Robert Barker's PANORAMA. It replaces a church built in the 19th century which was badly damaged by bombs in 1940. In 1860, Cardinal Wiseman, aware of the need for a central church to serve the many Roman Catholic French residents in London, asked Père Charles Fauré of the Marist Fathers to undertake the task of establishing one. By 1865, with money collected in France, Père Fauré was able to purchase the lease of the PANORAMA in LEICESTER SQUARE, together with that of No. 5, the neighbouring house. Louis-Auguste Boileau, an architect who specialised in the use of iron ribs and columns in church building, was appointed to draw up plans. He erected a temporary chapel in the porch of the PANORAMA, and using the entrance of No. 5, he designed a cruciform church within the circular drum of Robert Barker's building. By 10 June 1896 the church was ready for Archbishop – later Cardinal – Manning to celebrate the first mass there. No. 4 and No. 6 LEICESTER SQUARE were purchased in 1903, enabling a larger porch to be built. The present church was begun in 1953. The first stone came from Chartres, and was laid by Maurice Schumann. The work was completed in 1955. The tapestry behind the high altar was designed by Jean Cocteau and made at Aubusson. Jean Cocteau is also responsible for the decoration of the walls of the Lady Chapel.

Notting Hill *W11*. Originally the name given to CAMPDEN HILL, it is now used as an alternative for NORTH KENSINGTON. Recorded as Knottynghull in 1356, its meaning has not been traced. Until the 19th century much of the area was farmland, the small settlement of Kensington Gravel Pits (Notting Hill Gate from about 1840) being grouped about the Uxbridge Road at its junction with KENSINGTON CHURCH STREET. Gravel and sand extraction had been carried on in the vicinity since at least the 17th century while the 'gate' was built in the 18th century for the Uxbridge Turnpike Trust.

With the development of the LADBROKE and NORLAND ESTATES from the 1830s building began to spread north. The prime sites on these estates were soon taken and the heavier clay lands to the north were more slowly developed; yet by 1879 only the northwest quadrant still remained unbuilt on. The two principal farms, Portobello and Notting Barns, were developed for building purposes from the 1860s onwards, the latter surviving until 1880. The area was one of extreme contrasts, fine houses and noxious slums existing in close proximity, and problems of social deprivation and poor housing conditions have continued to the present day. W.H. Hudson, the author and naturalist, died in 1922 at 40 St Luke's Road, 'a fantastically gloomy house', in the words of Ford Madox Ford, which his wife ran as a boarding-house. The Notting Hill Carnival, founded in 1966 as a local pageant and fair, has become a full-blooded Caribbean carnival held on August Bank Holiday.

Novello and Company Ltd *1–3 Upper James Street, W1*. Vincent Novello was born at 240 Oxford Road (later OXFORD STREET) in 1781, of an Italian father and English mother. He was a chorister at the SARDINIAN CHAPEL in DUKE STREET until, at the age of 16, he became organist of the Portuguese Embassy Chapel in SOUTH STREET, GROSVENOR SQUARE, which post he retained until 1822. He married in 1808, and at his home Charles and Mary Lamb, Hazlitt, Leigh Hunt, Shelley and his sister Mary, Mendelssohn, famous singers and other celebrated people gathered regularly. The music he and his choir performed was so popular that in 1811 he decided to print and publish some of it. Among his numerous engagements, he conducted the Italian Opera at the PANTHEON in 1812, and helped to found the London Philharmonic Society in 1813. In 1825 he published a series of Masses by

Notting Hill Gate turnpike c.1790, from a watercolour by Paul Sandby, a local resident.

Mozart and Haydn which appeared in print for the first time. As the music became readily available, choral singing became very popular. His son, J. Alfred Novello, started business as a music publisher in 1829 at 67 FRITH STREET. In 1834 they removed to DEAN STREET, to what was to become the great music warehouse of Novello and Company, then to the 1906 building designed by F.L. Pearson in WARDOUR STREET. In the 1960s they moved again to 27 SOHO SQUARE and in 1977 to UPPER JAMES STREET.

Nuffield Lodge *see* GROVE HOUSE, REGENT'S PARK.

Number Ten Club *10 Belgrave Square.* Founded in 1955 as a club for the Institute of Directors, all of whose members were entitled to join at no additional cost. In 1956 No. 9 BELGRAVE SQUARE was also acquired for the club whose membership soon reached over 40,000. By 1975 large debts necessitated the sale of the BELGRAVE SQUARE properties and the

Institute acquired 116 PALL MALL from the Crown Estate Commissioners, the former premises of the UNITED SERVICE CLUB.

Nunhead *SE15.* Lies south of PECKHAM in the London Borough of CAMBERWELL. By the 18th century a hamlet existed around a green with the 17th-century Nun's Head tavern as its focus. Tea gardens and dancing made this a summer country resort with a fine panorama towards London; but the consecration of the 51-acre NUNHEAD CEMETERY in 1840 marked the beginning of its urbanisation. Small industries developed, including Brock's FIREWORKS factory which supplied displays at the CRYSTAL PALACE. New homes served a growing population; the acre of the green became a playground; and St Antholin was built (Ewan Christian, 1877), housing Wren's oak reredos from its demolished namesake CITY church.

Nunhead Cemetery *see* CEMETERIES.

O

Oakley Square *NW1*. Built in about 1856 as part of Bedford New Town which was intended as a model suburb for the lower and middle classes. It was named after Oakley House near Bedford, one of the seats of the Duke of Bedford. At the north end is St Michael's Church, built to the Gothic designs of John Johnson in 1852–6. The south side of the square has been replaced by council flats.

Oakley Street *SW3*. Leading from the KING'S ROAD to ALBERT BRIDGE. Built in the 1850s on the CADOGAN ESTATE. William Cadogan had been created Baron Cadogan of Oakley in 1718. In 1851 Dr J.S. Phene, who built much of Carlton Terrace, Phene Street, planted the fine trees which still line this street. Queen Victoria and Prince Albert commented on them and in 1852 Prince Albert asked for trees to be planted beside the South Kensington Museum in a similar manner. Oscar Wilde's mother lived in Oakley Street. Robert Falcon Scott (of the Antarctic) lived at No. 5 from about 1905 to 1908. To the east is Oakley Gardens where, at No. 33, George Gissing, the novelist, lived in 1882–4, the longest period the impoverished author of *New Grub Street* ever spent in any one of the 13 houses in London at which he could at various times be found.

Oat Lane *EC2*. Oats used to be sold here. The church of ST MARY STAINING stood here until destroyed by the GREAT FIRE. PEWTERERS' HALL is on the north side.

Observatory Gardens *W8*. Laid out in 1870 on the site of New Campden House (formerly Phillimore House) which was built in 1762 by Robert Phillimore. From 1826–67 it was owned by Sir James South, one of the founder members of the (ROYAL) ASTRONOMICAL SOCIETY. He had his own observatory in the grounds, which boasted for a time the largest telescope in the world.

October Club A club of some 150 diehard Tory Members of Parliament who met in the reign of Queen Anne at the BELL, KING STREET, WESTMINSTER, and later at the nearby Crown tavern.

Odeon Cinema *Northfield Avenue, Ealing, W5.* Has one of the finest cinema interiors of the 1930s. It was designed by Cecil Masey and built in 1932. Originally called the Avenue, it was known as Spanish City because of its external detailing and its elaborate interior with Moorish influence, including roofs, balconies, turrets windows and grilles. This interior may have been designed by Komisarjevsky, who designed many elaborate auditoria in this period. It is now a listed building.

Old Bailey *see* CENTRAL CRIMINAL COURT.

Old Barrack Yard *SW1*. Originally the entrance to a cow pasture on which in 1758 a Foot Guards barracks was built. The yard was between the small houses lining KNIGHTSBRIDGE (St George's Place) and the north side of the barracks which stood on the site of part of the BERKELEY HOTEL, WILTON PLACE and ST PAUL'S, WILTON PLACE. In 1826 Thomas Phillips, a corn chandler and the licensee of the Fox, took a lease from Earl Grosvenor for much of the area surrounding the barracks. About this time the barracks became a depot and Phillips took over the northern part, which he turned into a museum. On the east side of the entrance from KNIGHTSBRIDGE to the yard stood the ALEXANDRA, a small, smart hotel opened in 1863 and demolished in the 1950s. Old Barrack Yard's present form dates from the 1830s when Phillips built most of the cottages and stables.

Old Battersea House *Vicarage Crescent, SW11.* There have been arguments as to whether or not Sir Walter St John, Lord of the Manor, commissioned Wren to design this house. No documentary proof exists, nor any exact date of building, although a sundial on the south front is dated 1699. The early rate books show it was occupied by various wealthy locals, the last being Sir John Shaw Lefevre. In 1840 it was acquired by Sir James Kay-Shuttleworth for St John's College, a teacher training establishment. The BATTERSEA council bought the freehold in 1930, planning to clear the site. Because of the public outcry the house was left standing but surrounded by flats. Mr and Mrs Stirling became life tenants, bringing with them the Pre-Raphaelite De Morgan Collection of paintings and pottery, later bequeathed to the public. When Mrs Stirling died in 1965, the house was rather dilapidated, and not until 1971 was it restored to its former glory.

Old Bell Inn *95 Fleet Street, EC4.* A much restored public house built in 1678 by Sir Christopher Wren to act as a hostel for workmen re-erecting ST BRIDE'S CHURCH which had been destroyed in the GREAT FIRE. It stands on the site of an earlier tavern, the Swan, part of whose ancient cellarage still exists. The inn, which has also been known as the Golden Bell and the Twelve Bells, is believed to have been the workshop of Wynkyn de Worde, assistant to William Caxton, who is reputed to have sold books on the premises. The rear entrance opens on to St Bride's Avenue and customers may drink their beer in the churchyard.

Old Bond Street *W1 see* BOND STREET.

Old Broad Street *EC2*. The ancient Broad Street used to run to LONDON WALL from the MANSION HOUSE along the route of the present THREADNEEDLE STREET. From the reign of Queen Elizabeth I until the 17th century it was a fashionable place to live. The

557

Lord Mayor, Sir William Cockayne; the Marquess of Winchester; and the Earl of Shrewsbury all had houses here. Alexander Pope's father was a linen draper here in the 1670s before moving to LOMBARD STREET. There was a well-known glasshouse in the street where Venetian glass was made from early in the 17th century until it was destroyed in the GREAT FIRE. On the west side was ST PETER LE POER until it was demolished in 1907. No. 24 partly occupies the site of Sir Thomas Gresham's handsome house which had gardens extending to BISHOPSGATE STREET. When Gresham's widow died the house became the first GRESHAM COLLEGE, then, in 1645, the first home of the ROYAL SOCIETY. The building was demolished in 1768. No. 19, which occupies part of the site of SOUTH SEA HOUSE where Charles Lamb worked as a clerk, is now the CITY OF LONDON CLUB, designed by Philip Hardwick and built in 1833–4. There are several banks in the street. The merchant bankers, MONTAGU SAMUEL, are at No. 114. BROAD STREET STATION is at the northern end. The STOCK EXCHANGE is on the corner of THROGMORTON STREET.

Old Brompton Road *SW5, SW7.* Extends from ONSLOW SQUARE to just beyond BROMPTON CEMETERY. It is one of the older thoroughfares of KENSINGTON. In the 19th century its rural aspect was emphasised by the number of market gardens and nursery grounds which bordered it although the Eagle Saw Mills once stood on the site between Cranley Gardens and Cranley Mews. A number of notable people have resided in the road, amongst them Jenny Lind, 'the Swedish nightingale', at No. 189; Beatrix Potter across the way in a house the site of which is now covered by Bousfield School; and Samuel Carter Hall in The Rosary, a house adjacent to Hereford Square. CHRISTIE'S, South Kensington, is at No. 85. The ROYAL SOCIETY OF BRITISH SCULPTORS is at No. 108.

Old Buildings *Lincoln's Inn, WC2.* Originally known as Gatehouse Court and built between 1490 and 1520 of dark red brick with blue diapering. Lord Mansfield, Lord Campbell, author of *The Lives of the Lord Chancellors*, and John Thurloe, Oliver Cromwell's Secretary of State, had chambers here. So, at the beginning of his career, did Disraeli who, under pressure from his father, was admitted as an unwilling student in November 1824. The offices of Kenge and Carboy in Dickens's *Bleak House* were here and in them that firm's clerk, Mr Guppy, spent his wearisome days blunting the blade of his penknife by sticking it into his desk, gyrating on his stool, putting his head into the office safe 'with a notion of cooling it', 'reclining his head on the window-sill in a state of hopeless langour', and sending his colleague, Young Smallweed, out for effervescent drinks which were stirred by the office rulers in the office tumblers.

Old Bull and Bush *North End Road, Hampstead, NW3.* Said to have once been a country home of William Hogarth, who is alleged to have planted the famous yew trees from which the Bush part of the name is derived. The Bull is derived from the fact that it was once a farmhouse as well as an inn. It was always popular among artists and writers, but it was made famous by Florrie Forde, one of the great 19th-century music-hall stars, who sang 'Down at the Old Bull and Bush' – a song composed at the inn.

Old Burlington Street *W1.* The principal street on the BURLINGTON ESTATE, it extends from BURLINGTON GARDENS to Boyle Street. Its layout began in 1718 and was completed within about a decade, the finest house being the small Palladian *palazzo* at No. 29 (designed in 1723 by Lord Burlington himself for General George Wade) which was demolished in 1935. Much of Old Burlington Street is now dominated by modern office blocks, with a few high-class tailors' shops. The most notable survivors of the original development are Nos 31 and 32, the southerly pair of a row of four houses designed by Colen Campbell and built in 1718–23 – a row of great importance, for the absence of any exterior articulation of the party walls here may well have provided the prototype for the uniform 18th-century terrace ranges prevalent throughout Georgian London. No. 31 still contains some good early Georgian work, though it is not thought to be by Campbell. Much less important are Nos 24, of about 1720, and Nos 22–23 of 1812, at the north end of the street. Henry Pelham, later Prime Minister, lived at No. 32 in 1722–32, and John, Lord Hervey, the memoir-writer, at No. 31 in 1725–30. Residents of houses now demolished include Major-General Edward Wolfe, father of General James Wolfe, who stayed here in 1743–51 (in his own words) 'in the idlest dissolute abandoned manner that could be conceived'; and the 1st Marquess Cornwallis, commander of the British force at Yorktown who lived here in 1802–5. Herbert Johnson, the hatters, at No. 13 were established at No. 38 NEW BOND STREET in 1889.

Old Change A CITY street destroyed in the 2nd World War. Formerly known as Old Exchange, it took its name from a 13th-century building used 'for the receipt of bullion to be coined'. The site of the building is now marked by a plaque in ST PAUL'S GARDENS. In the reign of James I, Lord Herbert of Cherbury lived 'in a house among gardens near the Old Exchange'. At the beginning of the 18th century, the street was mainly occupied by Armenian merchants and by the end of the 19th century by silk and woollen warehouses. NEW CHANGE has been built a little to the east of it.

Old Church Street *SW3.* The oldest street in CHELSEA, it extends from CHEYNE WALK to FULHAM ROAD. The section south of the KING'S ROAD was formerly known as Church Lane and to the north it was called the Road to the Cross Tree. To the south it is a street of offices, shops and public houses with some 18th- and 19th-century private houses – notably Nos 34–38. No. 34 was a tobacconist's where Carlyle bought his cigars. There is some light industry, a geological workshop and a sheepskin coat factory. All that remains of Wright's Dairy is the cow's head on the wall of No. 46. The fields behind the dairy were grazed by the proprietor's cows in the last century. A little further north on the opposite side may be seen the entrance to Hereford Buildings, an attractive block of flats built in 1878 and at one time owned by Octavia Hill, whose tenants were mostly elderly ladies whom she took on an outing every year. Sir Charles Wheeler, former President of the ROYAL ACADEMY, lived here at one time. On the same side of the street, past the modern development opposite CHELSEA RECTORY (where Charles Kingsley lived as a child when his father was rector), are the CHELSEA Red Cross offices. William De Morgan, the artist, inventor and author, died in 1917 at

No. 27, and his wife, the artist Evelyn De Morgan, died here two years later. Nos 64 (Mendelssohn and Chermayeff) and 66 (Gropius and Fry) are good examples of 1930s' architecture. Opposite these, set back from the road, is an attractive row of early 19th-century houses, Nos 129–139, formerly known as Bolton Terrace. No. 149, Sloane House, was from 1845 to 1881 an asylum for 'ladies suffering from the milder forms of mental disease'. No. 155 has a BLUE PLAQUE commemorating J.F. Sartorius, the animal and sporting painter. CHELSEA ARTS CLUB is at No. 143. Adrian Jones, the sculptor, lived at No. 147 from 1892 until his death in 1937.

Old Compton Street *W1*. SOHO's main shopping street, the first houses appeared in it in the 1670s, and by 1683 it was fully built. It was named after Henry Compton, Bishop of London. From the beginning, although the names of some ladies of title are to be found among the ratepayers, it was a shopping street and many of the inhabitants were foreign. In 1720 Strype wrote, 'This Street is broad, and the Houses well built, but of no great Account for its inhabitants which are chiefly French.' By the end of the 18th century, less than ten of the houses were without shop fronts; and in the middle of the 19th century, while there were some workshops, too, as well as restaurants and public houses, the ground floors of most of the houses were still used as shops. As the years passed the number of foreign occupants continued to grow and the street became a recognised meeting-place for exiles, particularly those from France: after the suppression of the Paris Commune, the poets, Rimbaud and Verlaine, were often to be encountered at a drinking-place here. Old Compton Street is still characterised by foreign provision shops, cafés and restaurants. The most distinguished restaurant, however, is English, No. 19, WHEELER's. Residents of the street have included Richard Wagner in 1839; Nicholas Sprimont, proprietor of the CHELSEA PORCELAIN factory in 1742–50; and Edward Inwood, the architect, in 1827–32. All the 18th-century houses have been much altered externally; and as the *London Survey* puts it, 'only two stuccoed fronts of the mid-19th century have any claim to stylishness, No. 50 and Nos 40–42.' At Nos 22–28 stands the PRINCE EDWARD THEATRE, formerly the London Casino.

Old Court House *Hampton Court Green, Middlesex*. In 1536 a wood and plaster house was built on this site for the Surveyor of the King's Works. Sir John Denham, on his appointment to the office at the Restoration, had the house partly rebuilt in brick. Denham's successor, Sir Christopher Wren, lived there as occasion required, mainly during the rebuilding of HAMPTON COURT PALACE by William and Mary. In 1708 Queen Anne granted Wren the lease of the house on condition that he rebuilt it or sufficiently repaired it. It has been suggested that the new house was designed by his assistant, William Dickinson. It is often said that Wren died there, but his biographer, Elmes, stated that he died at his house in London. On Wren's death the house went to his son, Christopher, and then to his grandson, Stephen Wren. In 1808 the house was combined with the house on the right. Several alterations were made in the 19th century. In 1960 the house was divided again and the right-hand part became the Paper House, so called because at the time of the grant to Wren the Old Court House was 'what is called a Paper Building, consisting chiefly of wood and plaister'.

Old Curiosity Shop *13 Portsmouth Street, WC2*. Alleged to be the home of Charles Dickens's child heroine, *Little Nell*, this picturesque house was built in about 1567. Now a listed building, it is thought to be the oldest shop in London. Today it sells gifts, antiques and mementoes.

Old Deer Park *Richmond, Surrey*. In the former garden and park of RICHMOND PALACE, Henry V founded a monastery for 40 Carthusian monks to pray for his father's atonement for his part in the murder of Richard II. In 1540 Henry VIII suppressed the monastery. In 1768–9 the observatory was built on its site by Sir William Chambers at the instigation of George III. The building, largely unaltered, was used by the Meteorological Office until 1981. The three obelisks nearby used to measure London's time. The park is now divided between the Royal Mid-Surrey golf course and playing fields. There are 250 acres.

Old Ford *E3*. A district of East London formerly situated in the parish of BOW. The River LEA is tidal as far north as Old Ford Locks and traces of the original ford have been found between Iceland and Bundock's Wharves. This is thought to have been the lowest point on the river where it was possible to cross regularly on foot and was used by the Roman road from the CITY to Colchester (*see* ROMAN ROADS). The Roman burials and evidence of occupation near here suggest that there was a Roman settlement in the 3rd and 4th centuries AD. However, in the Middle Ages, BOW became the local centre of population. The ford had become increasingly dangerous and the Empress Matilda is said to have narrowly escaped from drowning whilst attempting to cross here. After Bow Bridge was built traffic no longer passed through Old Ford. There was a fulling mill here in the 13th century and a large dye house around 1500. Scarlet dyeing remained an important local industry, using osiers and reeds growing on the banks of the LEA; but farming and market gardening predominated until the 19th century. A medieval gatehouse known as King John's Palace survived into the 1800s but by the end of the century factories and railways had changed the character of the locality into an industrial suburb of London, with poor housing and much poverty.

Old Ford Road *E2, E3*. Gascoyne's 1703 map shows it as Old Ford Lane, linking the hamlets of BETHNAL GREEN, OLD FORD and BOW. Netteswell House, at the western end, is a 17th-century building with traces of Tudor brickwork in the cellar. Israel Zangwill, author of the classic of East End Jewish life *Children of the Ghetto*, lived for a time at No. 288.

Old Gloucester Street *WC1*. Takes its name from Queen Anne's son, the Duke of Gloucester, who survived longer than any of his 16 brothers and sisters. Queen Square is to the north. Bishop Richard Challoner, Vicar Apostolic of the London District, lived at No. 44.

Old Grange *2 Church Street, Hampton, Middlesex*. Noticeable for its two gables in the Dutch style. It dates from the middle of the 17th century and still has a fireplace of that period. It was occupied for several generations by a well-known HAMPTON family, the Maceys. David Garrick acquired it as well as the adjoining ORME HOUSE. The Old Grange became a girls' school in about 1803 and remained so until 1910, when it again became a private house. Between about 1850 and about 1870 it was run jointly with the school at ORME HOUSE.

Old Hall *Lincoln's Inn, WC2.* Built in 1490–2, it has an open, arch-braced roof with collar beams, linenfold panelling and four bay windows, two at each end. On the interior south wall is a fine carved 17th-century screen, and on the north Hogarth's vast and disappointing painting, recently cleaned and restored, *Paul Preaching before Felix* (1750). It was commissioned by the Benchers for £200. The Court of Chancery sat here out of term-time from about 1737 to 1883. The exterior of the hall was stuccoed between 1790 and 1818 but was restored to its original condition under the supervision of Sir John Simpson, architect to the Inn, and reopened by Queen Mary in 1928. The chancery suit, Jarndyce v. Jarndyce, described by Dickens in *Bleak House*, took place here.

Old Jewry *EC2.* In the 12th century and probably before, this was an area set aside for Jews. Their synagogue was at the north-west corner of the street. The Jewry was ransacked in 1262 and more than 500 Jews were murdered because a Jew had charged a Christian more than the legal interest. This was just one of the persecutions which Jews in London suffered. Some were burned to death for allegedly crucifying Christian children and plotting to burn London. Others had to pay crippling taxes at the King's whim. Between 1263 and 1273 the Crown is known to have extorted £420,000. In 1291 Edward I expelled them. Stow said, 'The King made a mighty mass of money of their houses, which he sold, and yet the Commons of England had granted and gave him a fifteenth of all their goods to banish them.' The Jews returned in the 17th century and Ben Jonson laid several scenes of *Every Man in His Humour* in the street. His character, Kitely, was a merchant here.

Old Kent Road *SE1, SE15.* Follows the line of Roman Watling Street, the Dover road. The Canterbury Pilgrims halted at 'St Thomas a Watering', site of the Victorian public house, Thomas à Becket, now noted as a training place for boxers. The gasworks were founded in 1833. The LIVESEY MUSEUM, erected in 1890 as a library by Sir George Livesey, has varied exhibitions, often of local history. North Peckham Civic Centre and Library, opened in 1966, has an exterior mural by the Polish artist, Adam Kossowski, depicting the history of the Old Kent Road. The Victorian song, 'Knocked 'em in the Old Kent Road', evokes the period when costermongers' barrows lined the road.

Old Middlesex Sessions House *Clerkenwell Green, EC1.* Built in 1779–82 at MIDDLESEX County's expense, to the designs of Thomas Rogers. It replaced the Jacobean sessions house, Hicks Hall (1621), in St John Street. The old name was long still applied to the new building, in which a fireplace from the old house and a portrait of its founder, Sir Baptist Hicks, were

T.H. Shepherd's drawing, c.1828, of the Old Middlesex Sessions House of 1779–82. It was a magistrate's court until 1920.

installed though since removed. The pedimented front is adorned by sculptured plaques by Nollekens representing emblems of justice. In 1860–76 the building was greatly altered and enlarged by the County Surveyor, Frederick Pownall, to deal with increasing crime and a rising population. The courts removed to Newington Causeway in 1921 and the building, after some years' occupation by Avery and Co., the weighing machine manufacturers, and another period lying empty, was restored in 1979 for masonic use. It is now the Central London Masonic Centre.

Old Mitre Court *EC4.* On the south side of FLEET STREET between INNER TEMPLE LANE and SERJEANTS' INN. An old tavern called the Mitre used to stand slightly west of the Court in the 16th century and it is said that Shakespeare sometimes wrote here. Later the tavern moved to the Court itself and here Samuel Johnson was a frequent customer. The building was demolished in 1829 after the purchase of the site by HOARE AND CO.

Old Nichol Street *E2.* Forms the southern side of the Boundary Street Estate, built at the end of the last century as a major slum clearance scheme. The area included the 'Old Nichol', the criminal quarter portrayed in Arthur Morrison's novel, *A Child of the Jago*.

Old Park Lane *W1.* Extends from PICCADILLY to the western end of HERTFORD STREET, where it also joins PARK LANE itself. Until the widening of HAMILTON PLACE in 1809–71 all the traffic along PARK LANE passed through this narrow bottleneck, only 40 ft wide even today. The two most prominent buildings now are the LONDONDERRY HOTEL and the return front of the INN ON THE PARK, but the bowed front of No. 17, now the headquarters of the Women's Royal Voluntary Service, still indicates its Regency origin.

Old Palace Yard *SW1.* The open space to the south of WESTMINSTER HALL which indicates the site of the palace of Edward the Confessor. Chaucer had a house on the north side when Clerk of the King's Works. The house was demolished in 1503 to make way for Henry VII's Chapel (*see* WESTMINSTER ABBEY). Ben Jonson also had a house here. Guy Fawkes and

Queen Caroline crosses Old Palace Yard on her way from the House of Lords during her trial in 1820.

his fellow-conspirators were executed here in 1606; so was Sir Walter Raleigh in 1618. There is now a car park here used by Members of Parliament.

Old Pye Street *SW1*. Extends from STRATTON GROUND to St Ann's Street. Sir Robert Pye, John Hampden's son-in-law, lived here. Henry Purcell, the composer, son of Henry Purcell, 'master of the children' of WESTMINSTER ABBEY and music copyist there, was born in St Ann's Lane, Old Pye Street, in 1659.

Old Queen Street *SW1*. A continuation to the east of QUEEN ANNE'S GATE. Nos 9–11 date from about 1706, and most of the other houses are later 18th-century. The strange interloper at No. 20 is by F.W. Troup (1909).

Old Slaughter's Coffee House *St Martin's Lane*. Established as Slaughter's in 1692, it took its name from the proprietor, Thomas Slaughter, who died in 1740. The house provided a meeting place for players of whist, chess and various games of chance. The mathematician, de Moivre, ended his days here giving advice on play in order to 'pick up a pittance'. Sock, the head waiter in 1750, was so nicknamed by Fielding who frequented the house; he was otherwise called 'Punch Spiller', a reference to his habit of sipping the patrons' punch on the way from the bar and then apologising for having spilled it. Old Slaughter's position attracted many artists. Hogarth, Nathaniel Smith the engraver, Gravelot the illustrator, and Roubiliac the sculptor were patrons. B.R. Haydon, in his autobiography (1808), mentions dining here regularly with Wilkie: 'This period of our lives was one of great happiness; painting all day, then dining at Old Slaughter's Chop House.' It was also a lively house for discussion. Oliver Goldsmith, in 1765, advises 'If a man be passionate he may vent his rage among the old orators at Slaughter's Chop House and damn the

nation because it keeps him from starving'. Slaughter's was the scene of the inaugural meeting of the Royal Society for the Prevention of Cruelty to Animals in 1824. In 1843 it was demolished to make way for CRANBOURN STREET.

Old Street *EC1*. Extends from GOSWELL ROAD to SHOREDITCH and is so called, according to Stow, 'for that it was the old highway from Aldersgate for the north-east parts of England, before Bishopsgate was built.' ST LUKE'S CHURCH is on the corner of IRON-MONGER ROW. The granite obelisk at the junction of CITY ROAD and East Street was erected by the METROPOLITAN BOARD OF WORKS in 1876.

Old Swan *116 Battersea Church Road, SW11*. Public house built in 1969, incorporating timber from the old THAMES sailing barges. The original Old Swan was first mentioned in 1215, when it was patronised by King John's watermen. Large windows give extensive views over the river.

Old Swan House *17 Chelsea Embankment, SW3*. Mellow riverside house with latticed bow windows designed by Norman Shaw and built in 1875 on the site of the Old Swan Inn. This used to be the finishing post of the watermen's race for DOGGETT'S COAT AND BADGE.

Old Vic *Waterloo Road, SE1*. Designed in 1816–18 by Rudolph Cabanel of Aachen as a house of melodrama. The foundation stone and some other materials came from the SAVOY PALACE, then being demolished to make way for the approaches to WATER-LOO BRIDGE. It was named the Royal Coburg Theatre in honour of its chief of patrons, Prince Leopold and Princess Charlotte. During the 1820–1 season a curtain of 63 pieces of looking glass was installed. It became one of the sights of London but had to be taken

The Old Vic, originally known as the Royal Coburg Theatre, was completed in 1818 and opened as 'a house of melodrama'.

down soon after as the roof was not strong enough. In 1831 Edmund Kean gave six performances at £50 a night. In 1833 its name was changed to the Royal Victoria Theatre in honour of the young princess. A 4d gallery was introduced in 1845. For the next twenty years it was mainly patronised by local people. In 1858, during a false fire alarm, 16 people were trampled to death. After reconstruction of the interior, the theatre reopened in 1871 as the New Victoria Theatre. It closed in 1880 but, with a new interior designed by J.T. Robinson, it reopened later that year as a temperance music-hall for the working-class. It was run by Emma Cons, the social reformer, and first woman member of the LONDON COUNTY COUNCIL. In 1898 Lilian Baylis returned from South Africa to help her aunt with the management. In 1900 the theatre's first opera, *The Bohemian Girl* was produced. In 1912 Emma Cons died and Lilian Baylis became sole manager. She boldly set out to raise the standards of the theatre. In 1914 the first Shakespeare season at popular prices was a great success. Between then and 1923 new productions of all Shakespeare's plays were staged. By the end of the 1st World War it had become one of the leading London theatres. It was reconstructed in 1927–8 to meet LONDON COUNTY COUNCIL safety regulations. The Vic-Wells Ballet Company was formed in 1931 under the direction of Ninette de Valois. Opera, ballet and Shakespeare productions alternated between the Old Vic and SADLER'S WELLS. In 1935 opera and ballet became established at SADLER'S WELLS and drama at the Old Vic. Damaged by bombs in 1941, it was reopened in 1950 after repairs by D.W. Rowntree. The annexe in The Cut was designed by Lyons, Israel and Ellis (1958). Closed for rebuilding in 1963, it was reopened a few months later as the temporary home of the NATIONAL THEATRE under the direction of Sir Laurence Olivier. In 1977 the Prospect Theatre Company moved in but they failed in 1981.

Oldchurch Hospital *Romford, Essex.* Erected in 1839 to the designs of Francis Edwards. It was originally known as the Romford Union Workhouse and run by the Board of Guardians with two part-time medical research officers and a nurse. The original buildings still stand with additions from 1891. In 1948 the National Health Service took over the running and it is now an acute general hospital with, in 1982, 600 beds.

Olde Dr Butler's Head *Mason's Avenue, Coleman Street, EC2.* Tavern founded in the early 17th century by Dr William Butler who, despite having no medical qualifications, became Court Physician to James I after prescribing a cask of his medicinal ale for the royal sciatica. His other unorthodox prescriptions included a shock cure for epilepsy (he discharged firearms close to the patient's ear), and a cold water cure for sufferers from the ague (he threw them into the THAMES).

Olde Mitre Tavern *1 Ely Place, Hatton Garden, EC1.* Standing in a part of London which is still technically Cambridgeshire, the Mitre Tavern was built by Bishop Goodrich in 1546 for the use of his servants at ELY PLACE, the town residence of the Bishops of Ely. On the side of the inn an inscribed mitre records this fact. In 1576 the favourite of Elizabeth I, Christopher Hatton, acquired the lease in return for an annual rent of ten loads of hay and one red rose. Elizabeth I is said to have danced round a cherry tree, the preserved trunk of which is inside the tavern. During the Civil War the building – whose small rooms and dark panelling are preserved – became first a prison, then a hospital.

Olde Wine Shades *Martin Lane, EC4.* Claims have been made that it is the oldest wine house in the City, dating back to 1663, the date found on a lead cistern in the garret. Certainly enough of the building seems to have survived the GREAT FIRE for it to have been rebuilt on its original foundations. 'It is a wine house quite in the old style,' the *London Argus* reported in November 1900. 'No flaring gas jets and flaunting plate-glass windows showing a brilliant interior here, but simply a smoke-begrimed, time-stained building which might be a City warehouse or anything but a place of entertainment. You would have some trepidation in entering but for a dingy brass plate at the door bearing the legend "Sprague's Wine Shades". Passing through a narrow doorway you find yourself in a low-ceilinged room, the light in which is so dull that you have to wait some time before you can make out your surroundings. Gradually a singular scene is disclosed to view. On one side of the apartment is a bar counter flanked with casks of wine and an array of bottles and glasses. On the other side are a number of wooden pens with partitions about five feet high, and with cushioned seats bearing unmistakable evidences of long and constant service. A table black with age occupies a place in the centre of each pen ...' The place is less dark and grimy now but much of the atmosphere remains and the charming early Victorian front survives, an application to demolish the building having been turned down in 1972. The Shades was a popular name for drinking places in the 18th and 19th centuries; these places were usually underground or sheltered from the sun by an arcade.

Olde Wrestlers' Tavern *98 North Road, N6.* Supposedly the highest inn in London. There has been a tavern on the site since 1547, though the present building dates from 1921. Dick Turpin is alleged to have been here, and legend has it that a tunnel leads from the cellar to JACK STRAW'S CASTLE. 'Swearing on the Horns' takes place here on the last Friday in March. (For this ceremony, *see* the FLASK, Highgate West Hill.)

Olympia *Hammersmith Road, W6.* Built on a part of the grounds of the famous Vineyard Nursery of Lee and Kennedy and originally called the National Agricultural Hall, it was opened in 1884 but changed its name to Olympia in 1886 when it staged its first circus, the 'Paris Hippodrome', which included 400 animals, a chariot race and a stag hunt. From that time circuses were a regular feature, notably that of Bertram Mills. In 1891 Imré Kiralfy (later to be associated with the WHITE CITY and EARL'S COURT exhibitions) put on the first of a number of spectacular shows which combined education with entertainment. In 1895 the Grand Hall was extended. The first Motor Show was held in 1905, the International Horse Show in 1907. In 1911 C.B. Cochran transformed the interior into the representation of a cathedral to stage *The Miracle* which was produced by Reinhardt. During the 1st World War the buildings were taken over by the War Office. In 1923 the National Hall was built, and in 1929 the Empire Hall. Regular events included the Daily Mail Ideal Home Exhibition and CRUFT'S DOG SHOW together with countless exhibitions, prize fights and sporting events. In spite of its 500,000 sq ft of space, in recent years the larger exhibitions have gone to EARL'S COURT and Olympia has staged the smaller ones and conferences. The Empire Hall has become a furnishing centre.

Olympic Theatre *6–10 Wych Street, Strand.* Built in the form of a tent by Philip Astley, mainly from the timbers of an old French warship and with a tin roof. It opened as the Olympic Pavilion on 18 September 1806 with a display of horsemanship and a pantomime, *The Indian Chief.* Despite many changes of name and forms of entertainment, including boxing and pony racing, Astley lost and continued to lose money and in January 1813 he sold the theatre to Robert William Elliston who partly redesigned it and opened on 19 April 1813 with *Love's Perils,* or *The Hermit of St Kilda.* Mixed programmes of entertainment and a further renovation of the theatre in 1818 led to modest prosperity. But it was not until 1831 when Eliza Vestris took over and opened it with *Mary, Queen of Scots,* with Maria Foote as the Queen, that the theatre became established. On 13 March 1849 during the ownership of Walter Watts, the theatre was burned to the ground. The fire spread so rapidly that there was a rumour of incendiarism. Watts rebuilt the theatre (to the designs of F.W. Bushall) so quickly that

The intimate interior of the Olympic Theatre. Built in tent form by Astley, the circus proprietor, it opened in 1806.

it opened in December of the same year with *The Two Gentlemen of Verona,* but closed shortly afterwards when Watts was arrested for fraud. William Farren took over in 1851 with little success, and Frederick Robson, who made his first appearance under him, became the manager in 1857. He and his successor, Horace Wigan, ran romantic plays so successfully that a tradition of Olympic drama was established with Henry Neville and Kate Terry as the stars. The popularity of this form of entertainment began to fade, however, and the theatre closed in 1889. It was entirely rebuilt in 1890 under the direction of Wilson Barrett to the design of Bertie Crewe and W.G.R. Sprague. The presentations, however, had little appeal and revivals of *The Silver King, The Lights of London* and other old favourites proved unsuccessful. The theatre finally closed on 18 November 1899.

Omega Workshops *33 Fitzroy Square, W1.* Founded in 1913 by Roger Fry who aimed to revolutionise public taste by popularising Post-Impressionist design in the decorative arts. Many members of the BLOOMSBURY GROUP were closely involved. The workshops were financed by a legacy, and by contributions from Clive Bell, George Bernard Shaw and others. Young artists would paint and make furniture, pottery and carpets. They were paid a regular wage (7s 6d a day or 30s a week) and none of the work was signed, but all carried the Omega sign. It was sold mostly to private buyers, but the designs were often copied by commercial firms. During the 1st World War the workshops kept going with difficulty, but had to close in 1919. The building is now the London Foot Hospital.

Onslow Gardens *SW7.* Built in about 1846 by C.J. Freake and named after the Earl of Onslow who owned the land. James Froude, the historian, lived at No. 5 in 1865–92; Bonar Law, the Prime Minister, at No. 24 in 1921–3; W.E.H. Lecky, the historian, at No. 38 in 1874–1903; and E. Beresford Chancellor, the historian of London, at No. 65 in 1924–6.

Onslow Square *SW7.* Elegant stuccoed houses built in 1846 by C.J. Freake and named after the ground landlord, the Earl of Onslow. Edwin Lutyens, the architect, was born at No. 16 in 1896. Thackeray lived at No. 36 in 1854–62 and wrote *The Virginians* here. Admiral Robert Fitzroy, the hydrographer and meteorologist, commander of the *Beagle* in which Darwin sailed to the Galapagos Islands, lived at No. 38 from 1854 until in 1865 he committed suicide, overcome by remorse for the part he had played in casting doubt upon the truth of the Bible.

Open Air Theatre *Queen Mary's Gardens, Regent's Park, NW1.* Since 1900, when the Woodland Players performed here under the direction of the actor-manager, Ben Greet, Regent's Park has been used for open-air performances, mostly of Shakespeare. In 1932 permission was given to Sydney Carroll to put on four matinées of *Twelfth Night,* produced by Robert Atkins. In 1933 a licence was granted to Sydney Carroll and Lewis Schaverien and the theatre formally opened on 5 June 1933 with *Twelfth Night* under the direction of Robert Atkins. It soon became part of the London theatrical scene with distinguished casts including Gladys Cooper, Vivien Leigh and Jack

Hawkins, playing mainly Shakespearean pastoral comedies. Ballet and opera were also occasionally performed and Bernard Shaw wrote *The Six of Calais* for the theatre, where it had its world premiere in 1934. The theatre closed in 1961 when the stage was reconstructed. Subsequently the New Shakespeare Company, formed by David Conville, was extremely successful here, despite the uncertainty of the weather. The whole theatre was reconstructed in 1972–5 by Howell, Killick, Partridge and Amis. With conventional seating in the new amphitheatre. The seating capacity is 1,200.

Opera Comique *Aldwych*. Built mostly underground in 1870 by F.H. Fowler. Like its neighbour, the GLOBE, the theatre was put up quickly in the hope that the site would be acquired for redevelopment and heavy compensation paid. The pair were known as 'The Rickety Twins'. In 1871 the Comédie Française appeared here for the first time outside France and were followed by other foreign visiting companies. In 1877 Richard D'Oyly Carte became manager and that year produced the first Gilbert and Sullivan opera, *The Sorcerer*, followed by *The Pirates of Penzance* (1880) and *Patience* (1881) which transferred with the successful trio to the SAVOY THEATRE. In 1885 Marie Tempest made her début in *The Fay O'Fire*. Succeeding managements were unsuccessful. In 1899 the theatre closed and was demolished soon after in the ALDWYCH development scheme.

Operating Theatre of Old St Thomas's Hospital *Southwark Cathedral Chapter House, St Thomas's Street, SE1*. In 1862 ST THOMAS'S HOSPITAL moved to SOUTHWARK to make room for the railway line from LONDON BRIDGE STATION to CHARING CROSS. At that time the old hospital contained two operating theatres, one for male and one for female patients. The theatre for women was built in 1821 and was in use until 1862. It was sited beyond the Dorcas ward for women in the attic of what used to be the parish church of ST THOMAS and is now the Chapter House of nearby SOUTHWARK CATHEDRAL. Thanks to a generous donation from the Wolfson Foundation the theatre, which was rediscovered in 1957, has been restored to its original form: when found it was just an empty, bricked-up room. Much research was undertaken to achieve an accurate restoration. There are five tiers of standings from which the students used to watch the surgeons' work, a replica operating table copied from a contemporary table from UNIVERSITY COLLEGE HOSPITAL, and underneath it a box containing sawdust. Also included are a gas lamp, a small wash basin and ewer where the surgeons washed their hands after operating, and a row of pegs on which hang old purple frock coats, used as overalls then, and a carpenter's type of apron.

Orange Street *WC2*. Now extends from HAYMARKET to CHARING CROSS ROAD, but the part to the west of WHITCOMB STREET was, until 1905, called James Street. This part was built in the 1670s, probably by Colonel Thomas Panton, the speculator responsible for nearby PANTON STREET. A tablet inscribed 'Iames Street 1673' is still attached to the building (now a garage) erected in 1887 upon the site of the TENNIS court built by Simon Osbaldeston in about 1634 (*see* PANTON STREET). The rest of Orange Street was not built until the 1690s, part of it upon the site of the stables of the Duke of Monmouth, beheaded after the battle of Sedgemoor in 1685. These stables seem to have been sometimes called the Orange Mews, in reference to the colour of Monmouth's coat-of-arms and to distinguish them from the nearby Green Mews and Blue Mews; and it may be that this explains the name of the street. East of St Martin's Street the Orange Street Congregational Church stands upon part of the site of a Huguenot chapel established in 1693. In the 1770s and 1780s, when it was briefly a Church of England chapel, the Revd. Augustus Toplady, author of the hymn 'Rock of Ages', was a minister here. The present much smaller chapel was built in 1929. Thomas Holcroft, the playwright and novelist, was born in the street in 1743. Edmund Kean, the actor, went to a little school here. Constable, the publishers, are at Nos 10–12.

Orchard Street *W1*. First rated in 1760 and later named after Orchard in Somerset, seat of Lord Portman, the ground landlord. Richard Cosway, the miniature painter, lived here in 1767 and Sheridan in 1773–5.

Order of St John Museum *and* **Library** *St John's Gate, Clerkenwell, EC1*. The functions of the library and museum are 'to acquire, conserve, research and exhibit items concerned with the history of the Order and its foundations – the St John Ambulance [launched from ST JOHN'S GATE in 1877] and the St John Ophthalmic Hospital in Jerusalem [founded in 1882]' (*see* ST JOHN'S GATE *and* ST JOHN CLERKENWELL). The museum contains the most comprehensive collection of items relating to the Order outside Malta. It illustrates the ecclesiastical, hospitaller and military aspects of the Order and contains armour, insignia, coins, paintings, prints, books, manuscripts, sculptures, silver, furniture, jewellery and porcelain from the Order's churches, hospitals, palaces and other properties. Of special interest are two panels of a Flemish triptych, one of which shows the arms of John Weston, Prior in 1476–89; a 16th-century processional cross; the Rhodes Missal of 1504 upon which the Knights swore their oath of allegiance; and a group of majolica apothecary jars from the hospital in Valetta.

Ordnance Hill *NW8*. First rated in 1842, there had been a military riding school nearby 20 years earlier. A barracks was built here which, after the Crimean War, was occupied by the Royal Horse Artillery, hence the name of the street. The Royal Horse Artillery are still there in rebuilt barracks, with their splendid horses which are used on ceremonial occasions (*see* ST JOHN'S WOOD BARRACKS).

ORGANS Very little is known about the history of British organ-building before the restoration of the monarchy in 1660, and almost nothing survives. With the revival of music in religious worship and the consequent demand for organs, the principal makers were Renatus Harris and Bernard Smith: the latter, even in his lifetime, became known as 'Father Smith'. Although both men had received their training abroad, they continued the earlier British tradition of making organs without pedals and this lasted into the first quarter of the 19th century. The visits of Mendelssohn

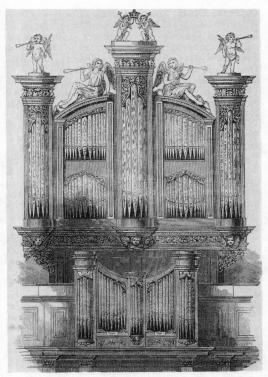

Renatus Harris's organ at St James's Piccadilly, originally built for James II in 1685, came from Whitehall Palace.

to England during the 1830s and his championing of the music of Bach led to a revitalisation of British organ-building and a consequent rebuilding of the archaic instruments whose musical scope was very small. Very few of them therefore survive, but there are some in London of which enough remains to form a fairly good idea of what they originally sounded like.

With the revival of the 1830s Britain entered upon its golden age of organ-building and of this era London is fortunate in possessing no less than four in original, or nearly original condition. These are at ST GILES, CAMBERWELL; ST PAUL, COVENT GARDEN; ST MARY-AT-HILL in the CITY; and ST ANNE, LIMEHOUSE.

This tradition continued throughout the 19th century, but with steadily diminishing merit in the face of declining musical taste, which saw the organ increasingly as a sort of one-man band. Nor was there any significant change throughout the first half of the 20th century, but on the continent there was a revived interest in the classical organ, with mechanical action, from about 1925 onwards. In London, the Willis organ of 1926 in the Jesuit church in FARM STREET, MAYFAIR, was a significant British recognition of this trend, and in 1939 the Harris organ from ALL HALLOWS, LONDON WALL, was rebuilt in the new church of ALL HALLOWS, TWICKENHAM (with all the other Wren-Gibbons furnishings from LONDON WALL), with mechanical action.

The construction of the new organ in the ROYAL FESTIVAL HALL in 1954, by Harrison and Harrison, to the design of Ralph Downes, set an altogether new standard for British organ-building, and its classical principles not only established it as a popular recital

instrument, but influenced all subsequent British organs to a greater or lesser extent. An almost equally strong contributory factor in this classical revival has been the sensitive restoration of many historical organs by Noel Mander. In addition to those mentioned the following are London organs of outstanding merit.

Surviving organs from before 1840: The Smith organ at ST JAMES, GARLICKHYTHE (3 manuals, 1697). The Harris organ at ST BOTOLPH, ALDGATE (2 manuals, 1707) was restored by Mander as a classical organ. A Harris organ with a chequered history was rebuilt in MERCHANT TAYLORS' HALL by Mander, as a 2-manual, in 1966, in a superb new case by Stephen Dykes-Bower. The John Byfield organ (3 manuals, 1764) at ST MARY, ROTHERHITHE, is unusually complete after restoration of the organ and case by Mander and is one of the finest in England. The Snetzler organ in MARLBOROUGH HOUSE Chapel (3 manuals) was well restored by Hill, Norman and Beard in 1939. George Pike England supplied a new organ to ST JAMES, CLERKENWELL, in 1792 and the restoration of the organ and case, with 2 manuals, by Mander, in 1978, must be accounted one of the finest restorations so far. By the same combination is the organ in ST MARY MAGDALENE, HOLLOWAY (3 manuals, 1814). Several original cases survive but without original instruments. Notable are ST PETER AD VINCULA (Smith), ST JAMES, PICCADILLY (Harris; the chair case added in 1852), CHELSEA ROYAL HOSPITAL (possibly Harris), ST PAUL, DEPTFORD, and ST ANDREW, ENFIELD (Bridge), ST MAGNUS-THE-MARTYR, LONDON BRIDGE (Jordan; this contained the first swell organ, 1712), ST VEDAST, FOSTER LANE (Harris and Byfield, but still containing a lot of old pipes in a Mander organ), and HAMPTON COURT PALACE (Shrider).

Organs subsequent to 1840 itemised by builder: *Bevington* – ST PAUL, COVENT GARDEN (3 manuals, 1862). *Bishop* – ST GILES, CAMBERWELL (3 manuals, 1844. Designed by S.S. Wesley. Exceptionally elaborate mixtures scheme. No visible pipes, behind a screen by Gilbert Scott). *Gray and Davison* – ST ANNE, LIMEHOUSE (3 manuals, 1851. A GREAT EXHIBITION organ. Completely original and exceptionally fine). *Harrison and Harrison* – ROYAL ALBERT HALL (4 manuals, 1924. Contains many pipes from the original Willis organ, but effectively a Harrison instrument). WESTMINSTER ABBEY (4 manuals, 1936. Cases by J.L. Pearson, 1899. Decorated in colour by S.E. Dykes-Bower in 1960). The TEMPLE CHURCH (4 manuals, 1924). The ROYAL FESTIVAL HALL (4 manuals, 1954). ST CLEMENT DANES (3 manuals, 1958. Reproduction of war-destroyed Smith case). *Hill* – ST MARY-AT-HILL, City (built in 1848 as a very fine and complete 2-manual, subsequently enlarged to 3-manual. Keyboards have black naturals and ivory sharps. Hill case in early 18th-century style). ST JOHN, Southwick Crescent (3 manuals, 1865). ALL HALLOWS, GOSPEL OAK (4 manuals, 1915. Exemplifies the adherence of Hill to classical principles long after most others had abandoned them). *Hill, Norman and Beard* – ROYAL COLLEGE OF ORGANISTS (3 manuals, 1966). *Lewis* – SOUTHWARK CATHEDRAL (4 manuals, 1897. An important return to earlier classical principles. Somewhat rebuilt, not to its advantage, by Henry Willis III). *Mander* – represented in London almost entirely by restorations of historic organs, already cited. The nearest approach to a new organ, although containing many old pipes and Willis reeds, is ST GILES, CRIPPLEGATE (3 manuals, mechanical action, 1971). The main case, by Bridge-Byfield, is from ST LUKE, OLD STREET, 1733. The chair case is new, and the west case is partly by Harris. At ST PAUL'S CATHEDRAL Mander restored the chancel organ as closely as possible to its 1872 state, with the addition of a Positive-type section. The dome section, with a new diapason chorus, became a separate, very powerful 2 manual instrument. A diapason chorus was added at the west end to overcome time-lag in leading large congregations, and a set of new fanfare trumpets, for processional use, projects from the west wall. All are controlled from a new 5-manual console above the south choir stalls. Mander also rebuilt the 'organ on wheels' with the addition of a mixture stop, and made for it a new classical case. *Walker* – The two outstanding organs in the earlier tradition of this firm – HOLY TRINITY, SLOANE STREET (4 manuals, 1891) and ST MARGARET, WESTMINSTER (3 manuals, 1897, designed by Edwin Lemare) – have unfortunately been altered by the firm and some of their character has disappeared. Walker has been prominent in the post-war classical revival, notably: BROMPTON ORATORY (3 manuals, 1953. Ralph Downes design) and ITALIAN CHURCH, HATTON GARDEN (3 manuals, 1959). *Henry Willis I ('Father Willis')* – ST PAUL'S CATHEDRAL is regarded as his *magnum opus*, built in 1872 with the dome section added in 1900. Also in ST PAUL'S is his remarkable 8-stop 'organ on wheels' of 1887. Both rebuilt by Mander. Of the many surviving organs by Henry Willis perhaps the finest are: ST DOMINIC'S PRIORY, HAVERSTOCK HILL (3 manuals, 1876). UNION CHAPEL, ISLINGTON (3 manuals, 1883). ST MICHAEL AND ALL ANGELS, CROYDON (3 manuals, 1882. Superb Bodley cases. Restored and enlarged by Mander). Willis also built an organ in 1873 for ALEXANDRA PALACE (4 manuals and 87 speakers tops). It was badly damaged in the 2nd World War. *Henry Willis III* – WESTMINSTER CATHEDRAL (4 manuals, 1923 and subsequently). FARM STREET, MAYFAIR (3 manuals, 1926, *see above*).

Orient Football Club   *see* FOOTBALL CLUBS.

Oriental Club   *Stratford House, Stratford Place, W1.* Founded in 1824 by officers in the service of the East India Company who were not eligible for the military clubs of PALL MALL. The clubhouse in HANOVER SQUARE was built to the design of Benjamin Dean Wyatt and Philip Wyatt in 1827–8 and was enlarged by Decimus Burton in 1852–4. It was sold in 1962 and has since been demolished, the club then moving to its present address. The club's members do not necessarily have any connection with the orient.

Orleans House   *Riverside, Twickenham.* Downriver from TWICKENHAM village stood a villa built in 1710 for James Johnston, Joint Secretary of State for Scotland under William III. All that remains today is the Octagon, added twenty years later by Johnston to entertain Caroline, Princess of Wales, wife of the future George II. The Octagon was designed by James Gibbs who also designed SUDBROOK PARK in PETERSHAM, and is a fine example of his work. It stands in a woodland garden. The house acquired its present name after it became the home of the exiled Duke of Orléans in 1815–70. He later became Louis-Philippe, King of the French (1830–48). The house, however, retained its French connections when his widow purchased it in 1852 and it passed to her son who owned it until 1877. TWICKENHAM became a popular place for Orleanist emigrés. Most of Orleans House was pulled down in 1926–7 but the Octagon Room was saved by the Hon. Mrs Ionides who left it and her collection of 18th- and 19th-century pictures to the Borough. On the site of the house a Gallery was built which now houses the collection and holds regular exhibitions on a variety of themes.

Orme House   *4 Church Street, Hampton, Middlesex.* Built about 1700, but without the pediment, which was added as recently as 1929. In 1770 it became a Young Ladies' Boarding Academy, with provision for a few small boys. The school closed in 1807, when Thomas Holloway came to live there. It was while living in the house that he engraved the Raphael Cartoons, which had recently been returned

Orleans House, Twickenham c.1850, showing James Gibbs's Octagon, built for Caroline, Princess of Wales, in 1730.

to HAMPTON COURT PALACE from Windsor Castle. After his removal from the house, it became the village doctor's home. By 1850 it had again become a school for girls in conjunction with neighbouring OLD GRANGE. In about 1870 it again became a private house.

Orme Square W2. Edward Orme, a Bond Street printseller, having made money from KENSINGTON gravel pits, reputedly selling two ship-loads of building gravel to Tsar Alexander I when he visited London in 1814, leased land here. He built Orme Square, Moscow Road and St Petersburgh Place with the Bayswater Chapel, now St Matthew's Church, in 1815–24. John Bank continued the development. At No. 1 Orme Square Sir Rowland Hill lived in 1839–42 while introducing the penny post. At No. 2 lived Lord Leighton in 1859–66 and Bernard Partridge, the cartoonist, in 1914–24, and at No. 10 Sir Max Beerbohm attended a preparatory school. At No. 12 Edward Dannreuther, the pianist and conductor, lived in 1874–94. Here, in 1877, he entertained Wagner and his wife Cosima, walking across the park with them for concerts. The eagle column of 1814 remains a mystery, representing neither Orme's family crest, nor the Russian imperial eagle. The sculptor is unknown.

Ormeley Lodge *Ham Gate Avenue, Ham, Surrey.* Built in 1714–16 on the site of a small cottage facing Ham Common for Thomas Hamond, son of a wealthy landowner. The architect is unknown but it is one of the most beautiful houses in the district with fine wrought-iron gates and railings leading to the brick-built house. The doorway with its Corinthian pillars opens on to an oak staircase with carved handrails. Extensions were made on either side later in the century; the name dates from 1845.

From 1763 to his death in 1767 the owner was Charles Townshend, the Chancellor of the Exchequer, whose import duties outraged the American Colonies; he was second husband to Lady Caroline Campbell, eldest daughter of the Duke of Argyll and occupant of SUDBROOK PARK. Mrs Fitzherbert and the Prince of Wales spent part of their honeymoon here after their secret marriage on 15 December 1785. From 1814 to 1819 another Cabinet Minister was the tenant – Sir John Sinclair, an authority on Highland language and customs; his daughter Catherine became a popular writer of children's stories such as *Holiday House*, novels and books about Scotland.

Orpington *Kent.* There is evidence of settlement in the Orpington district from the Stone Age onwards. Remains of Romano-British villas have been found at Crofton and Poverest, and, close to the Poverest site, an extensive Saxon cemetery has been excavated. The manor, belonging to the Archbishop of Canterbury at the time of *Domesday Book*, reverted to its former owners, Christ Church Canterbury, until the DISSOLUTION when it was granted to Sir Percival Hart. He built a house beside the church, where Queen Elizabeth I visited him; and local legend says that she gave the house the name of Bark Hart.

Orpington was described in 1820 as a pretty little village, with such local entertainments as laying bets on the length of the Sunday sermon, and getting drunk at cricket matches. This peaceful life changed with the coming of the railway, but it was still an agricultural district in the 1890s when a local farmer developed the famous Orpington breeds of poultry. Building development increased rapidly. During the 1st World War the Ontario Military Hospital (now ORPINGTON HOSPITAL) was built for Canadian servicemen, and there is a Canadian corner in the parish churchyard. Bark Hart, after being used for various purposes, was demolished in the 1950s to make way for the extension to All Saints church, designed by Gedder Hyslop. The hop gardens, strawberry fields and orchards have gone, and where there was once an avenue of walnut trees is now the Walnuts shopping precinct and civic centre.

Neighbouring ST MARY CRAY was the market and industrial centre for the district. Several famous bells were cast here at Hodson's Bell Foundry, and the paper mills here and at ST PAUL'S CRAY were well known. Today there are modern factories along Cray Avenue.

South and west of Orpington are CHELSFIELD, GREEN STREET GREEN, FARNBOROUGH, DOWNE, CUDHAM and BIGGIN HILL. Charles Darwin moved to Down House, in Luxted Road, Downe, in 1842, and did much of his work here, including writing *The Origin of Species*. The house, owned by the ROYAL COLLEGE OF SURGEONS, is now the Darwin Museum. Both DOWNE and CUDHAM are still completely rural. BIGGIN HILL is famous as a former fighter station of the RAF with its vital role in the Battle of Britain.

Orsett Terrace W2. George Wyatt was one of the architects of this terrace and of others close to it such as PORCHESTER SQUARE. They were built in 1845–55 and the sophisticated curved corner houses are particularly noticeable. The builder probably came from Orsett in Essex. Alexander Herzen, the Russian liberal thinker, lived at No. 1, a villa, in 1860–3, and was visited by many notable figures, including Dostoievsky and Bakunin.

Osnaburgh Street *NW1*. Like most of the streets in the REGENT'S PARK area, this takes its name from a member of George III's family. His second son Frederick, Duke of York, was Bishop of Osnabrück. St Saviour's Hospital here was built in about 1852 by Butterfield for the Anglican Order of the Holy Cross. The hospital was demolished in the 1960s and the fine choir stalls from Buxheim which had been installed in the 1880s were removed to another house belonging to the Order of the Holy Cross in Kent.

Osterley *Middlesex.* Borders the southern perimeter of OSTERLEY PARK. An area of farms, market gardens, and few houses before the GREAT WEST ROAD opened in 1925 and led to extensive suburban development. Further development followed the opening of Osterley Station on the Great West Road in 1934. This, designed by Adams, Holden and Pearson, replaced the Osterley and Spring Grove Station in Thornbury Road.

Osterley Park An 18th-century reconstruction of a country mansion built by Sir Thomas Gresham ' . . . in a parke . . . well wooded, and garnished with manie faire ponds'. For nearly a hundred years after Gresham's death, the house remained much in its original state, changed hands frequently, and was then bought in 1683 by the building speculator, Nicholas Barbon, who seems to have carried out some restoration work: a late Stuart staircase in the West Tower

Osterley Park, erected in the 16th century, was remodelled by Robert Adam in the 1760s for Child the banker.

and some 17th-century wood panelling still survive.

A bill of 1756, referring to the 'reposetory' at Osterley, suggests that the next owner, the banker, Sir Francis Child, may have bought it, in 1711, as a storage place for his bank's cash. He never lived there himself, and the capacious vaults beneath the raised courtyard, possibly dating from the time of Elizabeth, would have served his purpose well. He died in 1713, and the house passed to his sons, and then to his grandsons, Francis and Robert Child, who were successively responsible for transforming the Tudor house into its present classical grandeur. Before he died, in 1763, Francis had seen the completion of the Long Gallery and the remodelling of several of the principal rooms, begun under the direction of Sir William Chambers in the late 1750s. Several other architects, inspired like Chambers by classical models, may have contributed to the alterations before 1761, when Robert Adam first came on the scene.

Adam's plans of 1761 show a more ambitious scheme of rebuilding than was actually followed, for in 1763, when Robert Child inherited the house from his brother, a less radical if equally grand programme, based largely upon the existing fabric, was put into operation. Adam completely re-cased and enlarged the building, adapting the Elizabethan towers at each corner of the square courtyard, and rearranging the windows round the four sides to fit his classical designs. He moved the porch from the entrance hall on the north side to the old gateway opposite, where a double row of Ionic columns forms an open colonnaded screen across the gap, carved and painted inside and approached by a great flight of steps. There are classical models for this type of open portico (e.g. the Portico of Octavia in Rome) but Adam most probably took his idea from a similar feature at Witham Park, built by William Talman for Beckford earlier in the century.

Apart from this elegant relief, the exterior retains the severity of Chambers's original elevations. Not so the interior where, to use Adam's own words describing his beloved Roman interiors, 'all is delicacy, gaiety, grace and beauty'. The state rooms, with their 'great diversity of ceilings, friezes, decorated pilasters ...

painted ornaments, together with the flowing rainceau ... fanciful figures and winding foliage', and the inimitable 'grotesque' stucco, are still to be seen as Adam left them. The work took 19 years to complete, and illustrates to perfection the development of his style from early, relative simplicity to the elaboration of over-exuberance of his later years. Much of the furniture designed by Adam for the main rooms is preserved in the house, superb examples of pure neoclassical English cabinet-making.

Horace Walpole went to see the house in 1773 and was entranced: 'On Friday we went to see – oh, the palace of palaces .... The old house I have often seen, which was built by Sir Thomas Gresham; but it is so improved and enriched, that all the Percies and Seymours of Sion must die of envy. There is a double portico that fills the space between the towers of the front, and is as noble as the Propyleum of Athens. There is a hall, library, breakfast-room, eating-room, all chefs-d'oeuvre of Adam, a gallery one hundred and thirty feet long, and a drawing-room worthy of Eve before the Fall. Mrs Child's dressing-room is full of pictures, gold filigree, china and japan. So is all the house; the chairs are taken from antique lyres, and make charming harmony; there are Salvators, Gaspar Poussins, and to a beautiful staircase, a ceiling by Rubens. Not to mention a kitchen-garden that costs £1,400 a-year, a menagerie full of birds that come from a thousand islands, which Mr Banks has not yet discovered: and then, in the drawing-room I mentioned, there are door-cases, and a crimson and gold frieze, that I believe were borrowed from the Palace of the Sun.'

Robert Child died in 1782, two years after the house was finished. It passed, through his widow, to his granddaughter, whose husband, George Villiers, was to succeed in 1805 as 5th Earl of Jersey. From that time, Osterley was almost continuously occupied by the Jersey family until 1949, when the 9th Earl gave the house and grounds to the nation. They are now owned by the NATIONAL TRUST, maintained by the Department of the Environment to which they are leased, and administered by the VICTORIA AND ALBERT MUSEUM.

Other Club In 1911 Winston Churchill and F.E. Smith (Lord Birkenhead) failed to gain admission to The Club, one of the oldest of the Oxford dining clubs, and accordingly founded a similar club of their own. The rules of this began as follows: '(1) The club shall be called The Other Club. (2) The object of the club is to dine. (3) The club shall consist of no more than 50 members of which not more than 24 shall be members of the HOUSE OF COMMONS.' Rule (3) was broken within 12 months but no one seems to have minded. Rule (12) read: 'Nothing in the rules . . . shall interfere with the rancour or asperity of party politics.' Members have included famous men in all walks of life, including Lord Kitchener, David Lloyd George, Arnold Bennett, H.G. Wells, J.L. Garvin, Sir William Orpen, Sir Gerald Du Maurier and Lord Olivier.

Outwich Street *EC3*. Outwich in old English means street of Otto. People living in the area took it as a surname. The church of ST MARTIN OUTWICH in THREADNEEDLE STREET was rebuilt by Martin, Nicholas, William and John de Oteswich in the 14th century.

Oval Cricket Ground *Kennington, SE11*. The headquarters of the SURREY COUNTY CRICKET CLUB leased from the DUCHY OF CORNWALL. Nearly all Surrey's home fixtures are played here and traditionally it always stages the last of a full Test series in this country. Originally a market garden, a lease was secured from the DUCHY by the Montpelier Cricket Club of WALWORTH in 1845. In the same year at a meeting in an adjacent public house, The Horns, the decision to form the SURREY COUNTY CRICKET CLUB was made and the first notable match was played at the Oval between the Gentlemen versus the Players of Surrey. A new pavilion was built in 1858 but was replaced 40 years later by the present pavilion, the Long Room of which is on the ground floor and contains many trophies and cricket memorabilia. Many sports have been played at the Oval including rugby and association football. It was one of the principal grounds of football, staging the Football Association Cup semi-finals and most of the finals between 1870 and 1892. During this time C.W. Alcock, the journalist, was secretary of both the Football Association and the SURREY COUNTY CRICKET CLUB. He was largely responsible for the first Test Match between England and Australia which took place at the Oval on 6, 7 and 8 September 1880 and which England won by five wickets. In 1934 the Hobbs Gates, at the main entrance, were erected in honour of Sir John Berry (Jack) Hobbs, one of the greatest batsmen of all times (*see* SURREY COUNTY CRICKET CLUB). The Oval was used as a prisoner-of-war camp during the 2nd World War, but was restored immediately after with many improvements. Many cricket records have been made here. On 20, 22 and 23 August 1938, for instance, the highest innings in Test cricket was made (903 for 7 wickets declared) by England against Australia, during which Leonard Hutton scored the highest Test score in Tests between England and Australia, 364 runs (then the highest Test score of any kind) and England won by an innings and 579 runs. Percy Fender, captain of Surrey in 1921–31, scored the world's fastest century in a county match – in 35 minutes. The ground has a capacity of 31,000.

Overlord Embroidery *Whitbread's Brewery, Chiswell Street, EC1*. Commissioned in 1968 by Lord Dulverton to commemorate the invasion of Normandy in 1944 and the liberation of the continent of Europe by the Allies. It was designed by Sandra Lawrence and made, over a period of five years, by 20 women of the ROYAL SCHOOL OF NEEDLEWORK. It consists of 34 panels, each 8 ft long and 3 ft high and measures 272 ft in length. It is 41 ft longer than the Queen Mathilda Embroidery which, more familiarly known as the Bayeux Tapestry, commemorates William of Normandy's invasion of England in 1066, and is the largest work of art of its kind in the world.

Ovington Gardens *SW3*. A small estate, originally a single field with some small cottages facing Brompton Lane, which was developed by the Dyer family. The derivation of the name is obscure but it may well come from the small north Essex village near to which the Dyers once lived. When first developed there were three large houses facing BROMPTON ROAD with a curved common entrance drive and with large gardens. On their west side was Ovington Terrace, built in about 1845 and gradually extended down the whole length of the 'square'. The houses on the east side then followed and the parish boundary was breached (probably because a field entrance had always been there) by Vincent Place, a short street connecting the newly built WALTON STREET and named after a trustee of SMITH'S CHARITY which owned the land to the south of the boundary. The front houses did not survive long. After their demolition the street line was restored and over their gardens another line of houses was built with Ovington Mews at their back. The names of Ovington Terrace and Vincent Place were changed to Ovington Gardens in 1930. In the 1880s the gardens were clearly a good address and remained so for many years. All the houses were in time converted to flats.

Oxendon Street *SW1*. Extends southward from COVENTRY STREET to ORANGE STREET. It takes its name from Sir Henry Oxenden (*sic*), who in 1668 inherited a life interest in 3 or 4 acres of land here from his father-in-law, Robert Baker, the tailor of Piccadilly Hall (*see* PICCADILLY). Shortly afterwards he came to an arrangement with Colonel Thomas Panton, who also had an interest in this property, to exclude Baker's descendants, and building development took place in the 1670s. No. 8, a much restored house, probably dates mainly from the 18th century, and has a sundial dated 1679 and inscribed '*Vigila Oraque*'. At No. 7 is the Comedy Restaurant.

Oxford Circus *W1*. The four quadrants with identical facades were designed by Sir Henry Tanner and built in 1913 (the south-east), 1923 (the north-east), 1925 (the south-west), and 1928 (the north-west). PETER ROBINSON were originally established at 103 OXFORD STREET in 1833.

Oxford Court *EC4*. Site of OXFORD PLACE, a mansion once owned by the Earls of Oxford and destroyed in the GREAT FIRE.

Oxford Market A small arcaded building east of GREAT PORTLAND STREET and sometimes known as Portland Market. It was designed by James Gibbs and built in 1721 to stimulate development in CAVENDISH SQUARE. Meat, fish and vegetables were sold. It was closed and demolished in 1876.

Oxford Place A City mansion which originally belonged to Henry Fitzailwyn, the first mayor of London. In 1286 one Robert Aguillum left the property to the Priory of Tortington in Sussex. In 1539, at the DISSOLUTION OF THE MONASTERIES, Henry VIII granted it to John de Vere, 15th Earl of Oxford, who renamed it Oxford Place. The 17th Earl sold it in about 1580. In 1579–80 Sir Ambrose Nicholas kept his mayoralty here; in 1598 it was occupied by one of Nicholas's successors, Sir John Hart. In 1641 it was bought by the SALTERS' COMPANY for a livery hall. It was destroyed in the GREAT FIRE. SALTERS' HALL COURT and OXFORD COURT mark the site.

Oxford Street *W1*. On the route of a Roman road which ran from the Hampshire to the Suffolk coast. The street now runs from MARBLE ARCH to ST GILES CIRCUS. It was always used as a route to the west and was variously called 'The Waye from Uxbridge', 'The King's Highway' (1678), 'The Road to Oxford' (1682), and 'The Acton road' (1691). It was also sometimes called 'The Tyburn Way' as the TYBURN flowed across it from STRATFORD PLACE to DAVIES STREET. The TYBURN gallows were at the west end, near MARBLE ARCH. Oxford Street became established as its name in the 18th century due to the coincidence that the land on the north side had been acquired in 1713 by Edward Harley, 2nd Earl of Oxford. He married Lady Henrietta Cavendish-Holles, and their only daughter married William Bentinck, Duke of Portland. The three families gave their names to many streets on the north side (*see* PORTLAND ESTATE). Pennant, the traveller,

describes the area at the beginning of the century as 'a deep hollow road and full of sloughs; with here and there a ragged house, the lurking place of cut-throats'.

Development of the street was started in 1739 by Thomas Huddle, a gardener, who began to build on the north side at the east end. There was a further spate of development from 1763 to 1793 and by the end of the century Oxford Street stretched from ST GILES CIRCUS to PARK LANE unbroken. Places of entertainment were founded as it became a residential area. Figg's School of Arms (1720) stood opposite POLAND STREET. The PANTHEON (1772) was at No. 173, now MARKS AND SPENCER. (It was at an adjacent chemist's that Thomas de Quincey bought his first dose of opium.) The PRINCESS'S THEATRE (1840) stood on the site of the Oxford Walk shopping precinct. Regent Hall, No. 275, still survives. It was originally a skating-rink, but in 1882 was taken over by the SALVATION ARMY. The interior is little altered.

In the late 19th century Oxford Street began to change character and to develop into the shopping street it now is. Drapers, furniture shops and shoemakers gave way to the first departmental stores. The middle-price department stores have now been joined by cheap market-style complexes which attract thousands of tourists. Many of the remaining premises are used as offices, schools of English, or employment bureaux. A traditional characteristic of the street is the presence of illegal street-traders selling souvenirs and cheap jewellery. Some of the earlier street-traders, mostly fruiterers and greengrocers, have survived for decades and become established: one fruiterer in ARGYLL STREET was officially established in 1932; but the site was originally secured by his grandfather at the beginning of the century. He slept at night in Oxford Street to guard his site.

The Princess's Theatre in Oxford Street, one of the last places of entertainment left among the all-enveloping shops.

Firms with shops in Oxford Street include Boot's, BOURNE AND HOLLINGSWORTH, BURTON'S, Dunn and Co. (founded in SHOREDITCH in 1887), D.H. EVANS, JOHN LEWIS, His Master's Voice (said in 1982 to be the largest record shop in the world), MARKS AND SPENCER, PETER ROBINSON, Scotch House (see BROMPTON ROAD), SELFRIDGE'S and WOOLWORTH'S. Swears and Wells (established in the 1860s) and Marshall and Snelgrove (established in 1837) have now closed. Other shops to be found here (several with more than one branch) include Horne's, the outfitters, Dolcis Shoe Co.; Manfield and Sons, shoe retailers; C. and A. Modes in British Industries House with elevations designed by Sir Edwin Lutyens, 1927; John Collier, men's wear; Mothercare; Bally, shoe retailers; H. Samuel, jewellers; British Home Stores; Wallis and Co., ladies' clothing; K Shoe Shops; Lilley and Skinner, shoe retailers (the façade modelled on that of DERBY HOUSE at the end of STRATFORD PLACE); Richard Shops, ladies' outfitters; Littlewood's Department Store; Dorothy Perkins, ladies' outfitters; Claude Gill, booksellers; Anello and Davide, theatrical shoemakers; Saxone Shoe Co.; Freeman, Hardy and Willis, shoe retailers; and Penberthy's, the ladies' outfitters, who were established in 1883.

No. 151, Bata, is by Bronek Katz (1956); No. 181 by T.E. Collcutt (1885); Nos 363–367, HIS MASTER'S VOICE, by Joseph Emberton (1938–9); Nos 385–397 by T.C. Clarke (1889); No. 399, Lloyd's Bank, by Sir John Burnet, Tait and Partners (1969–70); No. 62, Evelyn House, by Charles Holden (1909); Nos 70–88 by Trehearne and Norman, Preston and Partners; and No. 385, National Westminster Bank, by R. Seifert and Partners (1969–70). The Academy Cinema is at No. 165. Plans to make Oxford Street a 'tree-lined paradise' with limited access to vehicles were drawn up in 1972.

Oxford Theatre *Corner of Tottenham Court Road and Oxford Street*. One of the best-known music-halls, opened in 1861 by 'the father of the halls', Charles Morton. It was designed by Finch, Hill and Paraire and built on the site of an old galleried inn, the Boar and Castle. Partially destroyed by fire in 1868, it was rebuilt the next year. Damaged by fire again in 1872, it was reconstructed in 1873 and completely rebuilt by Wylson and Long in 1892. Marie Lloyd topped the bill on the first night and sang 'Oh Mr Porter'. In 1917 C.B. Cochran converted it into a theatre and staged spectacular revues. In 1924 he brought Lilian Baylis's Shakespearian company from the OLD VIC to the West End for the benefit of visitors to the British Empire Exhibition. The theatre was closed and demolished in 1926. A LYONS' CORNER HOUSE was built on the site.

Oxford Walk *W1*. From No. 150 to No. 154 OXFORD STREET. A pedestrian shopping precinct built in 1978 in an attempt to simulate the atmosphere of the Lanes at Brighton. There are 52 shops, a cinema and cafés.

Oxgate *NW2*. Situated north of DOLLIS HILL, south of the junction of the NORTH CIRCULAR ROAD and EDGWARE ROAD. By the end of the 11th century it belonged to ST PAUL'S as the north-eastern prebend of the wooded manor of WILLESDEN, and contained the area known as DOLLIS HILL. The name existed by 1250 and probably referred to a gate to stop oxen straying onto WATLING STREET from the neighbouring pasture land. A track along the line of the present Oxgate Lane would appear to have linked WATLING STREET to the Oxgate farms from an early date. Farms existed by the early 15th century and the surviving Upper Oxgate Farm dates from the 16th century. From the 17th to the 19th centuries the boundaries of the farm fields changed little. Sheep and cattle were reared and there is evidence of a 17th-century tannery. Oxgate remained one of the last farming areas of WILLESDEN, being built up only with the arrival of industry in the area and the construction of the NORTH CIRCULAR ROAD in the 1920s and 1930s. As an increasing population spread northwards from DOLLIS HILL, council estates were established, the farm cottages on Oxgate Lane were demolished, and, in 1939, St Paul's Oxgate by N.F. Cachemaille-Day was opened to serve the new parish. It was closed in 1980 and united with St Catherine's, DOLLIS HILL.

Oxgate Farmhouse *Coles Green Road, NW2*. The oldest domestic building in WILLESDEN and the only building remaining of the Manor of OXGATE first mentioned in records of 1246. The house consists of two parallel ranges, a north wing surviving from the 16th century and a south wing added in the 17th century. The house is two-storied with attics in the gables beneath a roof of locally made tiles. The walls are timber framed, in part of wattle and daub, though the whole is now cement rendered. The upper storey originally projected to the east but has been under-built. A porch has been added. Within are many period features including exposed and moulded beams. The house is a private residence.

Ozinda's Chocolate House *St James's*. Established in 1694 and situated north of ST JAMES's PALACE. It was said 'to rank with White's as a Tory house'. John Macky, a Scottish customer, wrote, 'A Whig will no more go to the Cocoa-Tree or Ozinda's than a Tory will be seen at the Coffee house of St James's.' It was frequented by Swift who had 'a mighty fine' dinner here on 27 March 1712. William Byrd, a planter from Virginia, found that 'drinking chocolate, betting and reading the newspapers' were the main attractions of the establishment. In March 1724 Dominico Osenda, or Ozinda, 'being disposed to return to France', announced his intention to sell by auction his household goods, 'and likewise his Shop Goods, consisting of Several Sorts of Snuffs ... superfine Liquors of his own making ... with a Quantity of Hermitage Wine'. The house was demolished in 1748.

Paddington *W2, W9, W10.* One of the most varied areas in north London, with an unexpectedly rich historical past. An ancient parish and former metropolitan borough, since 1965 part of the City of WESTMINSTER, Paddington is believed to have originated from the followers of Padda, an Anglo-Saxon chieftain, who settled strategically near the junction of the EDGWARE and BAYSWATER ROADS, both of them important ROMAN ROADS which would have later remained tracks through the forest. Probably the settlement was at PADDINGTON GREEN, the likely site of all Paddington's early churches. Tucked into the triangle formed by this junction of roads, with a natural northern boundary at the top of MAIDA VALE, where the River WESTBOURNE crossed on its course south, Paddington's western boundary was changed in 1900, when KENSAL TOWN and QUEEN'S PARK, which by historical accident had previously been a detached part of CHELSEA, were after some argument divided between the new boroughs of Paddington and KENSINGTON. Initially a country village, surrounded by farms and springs (*see* BAYSWATER), Paddington did not really become part of London until the 19th century, when it expanded on a dramatic scale.

It is widely believed that most of Paddington belongs to the CHURCH COMMISSIONERS and that its building brought the Church a vast income. Neither belief is true, although for nearly 1,000 years Paddington was owned by the Church in one form or another. From the 10th century Paddington belonged to WESTMINSTER ABBEY. The Plantagenet kings eventually confirmed this in an important charter of 1222, which also referred to a chapel here and a farm at WESTBOURNE. Detailed records survive from between 1168 and 1485 of the activities of Richard, William and Gervaise 'de Padintune' and their descendants, the earliest tenant farmers of the land of whom

Paul Sandby's watercolour of his studio in Paddington, whose pastoral charms attracted many artists in the 18th century before the area was built over.

anything is known. After the Reformation the ABBEY's land was seized by the Crown, and in 1550 King Edward VI granted Paddington to the BISHOP OF LONDON. It remained with the See of London until 1836, when it passed into the hands of the Ecclesiastical Commissioners, who, in 1948, became the CHURCH COMMISSIONERS. However, by the 18th century the Frederick family (*see below*) and their descendants had acquired two thirds of the interest in the estate. In addition very long leases were granted. This has meant that only recently have the CHURCH COMMISSIONERS been in a position to improve property. In 1981 the decision was taken to sell their remaining property in MAIDA VALE, though they remain landlords of the south-eastern corner of BAYSWATER. WESTMINSTER ABBEY retained some of the area beyond the River WESTBOURNE after 1550, its land also being later administered by the ECCLESIASTICAL COMMISSIONERS or sold. Successive BISHOPS OF LONDON, like the Abbey before them, leased the farmland to a number of tenants, many of them CITY merchants. Few left any mark behind them. However, Sir Thomas North, son of Sir Edward, who leased land here from the King in the 1540s, translated Plutarch's *Lives* into English in 1579, and may be called Paddington's earliest literary figure. A little later Shakespeare, who used this work, is said to have performed with Burbage at taverns in the EDGWARE ROAD. After the Civil War, Sir Joseph Sheldon and his brother Daniel, nephews of the BISHOP OF LONDON, became tenants, and built a new church in 1679, the predecessor of ST MARY's. Sir John Frederick took the lease of the estate in 1740. His granddaughters Elizabeth and Selina married Sir John Morshead and Robert Thistlethwaite and it is from these three families and their country estates that many of Paddington's street names derive.

Despite its relative isolation from the rest of London, the 18th-century village of Paddington became a haven for a large number of French Huguenots. They included Claudius Amyand, principal surgeon to George II and nephew of the Revd Daniel Amyand, vicar of Paddington in 1698–1730, who had been imprisoned in La Rochelle for his public denunciation of Louis XIV as a wolf and the Pope as Anti-Christ. Many of the French immigrants were skilled craftsmen, among them Denis Chirac of PADDINGTON GREEN who was jeweller to Queen Anne. A carpet factory was set up for a few years in the 1750s. Some of the French nobility settled here too, and the gardens of the Count and Countess de Vandes in BAYSWATER became famous. Gardens in fact became a feature of Paddington which lasted well into the 19th century. But over the pastoral calm of 18th-century Paddington, which attracted artists such as George Morland and Paul Sandby to record its rural delights, hung the shadow of TYBURN. The presence near MARBLE ARCH of this public place of execution until 1783 was probably one reason for the delay in any extensive building. However, in 1795 the BISHOP OF LONDON'S trustees leased land to the GRAND JUNCTION CANAL Company for extending the canal from BRENTFORD to Paddington; also by the Paddington Estate Act it was at last made possible for building leases to be granted on the estate. This year, therefore, marks the time when real change began.

The new section of the GRAND JUNCTION CANAL was opened in 1801. The occasion was watched by a rejoicing crowd of 20,000 people, for the canal was not only a novelty but also a direct trade link between London and the Midlands, bringing business to the Paddington Basin, its terminus, and much needed employment to the growing number of inhabitants of Tomlin's Town, a shanty-town which had sprung up near the site of CONNAUGHT SQUARE in the 1790s. Paddington's monopoly on canal trade in London only lasted until 1820 , when the REGENT'S CANAL was completed; but by then building had started in earnest.

For various reasons Paddington developed in a disjointed manner, leaving it with no real centre, but a number of quite well-defined though separate districts (see BAYSWATER, MAIDA VALE, QUEEN'S PARK and WESTBOURNE PARK). Broadly speaking the growth took place from east to west and from south to north. CONNAUGHT PLACE, overlooking HYDE PARK, was built during the course of the Napoleonic Wars. After the wars it became easier to meet the need of London to expand, and the trustees of the BISHOP OF LONDON'S estate realised that the area north of HYDE PARK could seriously compete with BELGRAVIA. In the 1820s CONNAUGHT SQUARE and the streets around it were started. Samuel Pepys Cockerell was the architect. For the next 30 years development continued steadily under George Gutch's supervision, extending to the BAYSWATER terraces, the villas north and south of the canal, terraces along the EDGWARE and HARROW ROADS (almost all now demolished) and the streets north to Sutherland Avenue.

Other private builders were active to the north and west, where the enterprising Edward Orme laid out ORME SQUARE and the streets around it before 1820, and the Aldridge, Jenkins and Neald families together with small speculative builders developed the areas on either side of the canal and railway between 1850 and 1870. KENSAL TOWN was built in the 1840s and QUEEN'S PARK in the 1870s. The area north of Sutherland Avenue with its mansion blocks was finally completed by 1910.

PADDINGTON STATION first opened in 1838, and was followed in 1863 by the first underground line, the METROPOLITAN. This helped to give the area from the mid-19th century a cosmopolitan flavour which it has always kept. Greek and Jewish communities were present then, and more recently West Indians, Asians and Arabs have made Paddington their home. The railway together with the canal and now WESTWAY have also made an unfortunate geographical division between north and south.

Just as several of the fine Victorian churches in Paddington suffered bomb damage during the war and general structural decay leading to their demolition and replacement, in the same way much of the Victorian housing eventually developed into slums, giving Paddington an unsavoury reputation. However, the rebuilding which began in the 1930s is still continuing, bringing much needed housing improvement on a massive scale. Curiously, therefore, Paddington

remains, as it was in the 18th century, if in a rather different way, a residential area. The population leapt from 1,881 in 1801 to 46,305 in 1851 and continued to rise by well over 10,000 every decade to a peak of around 144,000 between 1910 and 1939. By 1971 the population had dropped to a more manageable 96,000. Apart from the railway, it has never experienced the shock of heavy industry.

In 1953 Sir John Betjeman deftly sketched some of the social changes:

Through those broad streets to Whiteley's once
The carriages would pass,
When ever-weeping Paddington
Was safely middle-class.
That silent land of stable smells,
High walls and flowering trees,
Is now rack-rented into flats
For busy refugees.

Stately Edwardian days gave way, in fact, to those of the appalling housing conditions exploited by Rachman in the late 1950s when Paddington became a byword for overcrowding, poverty and vice. The last 30 years, however, have seen a vast improvement. Paddington's legacy of Victorian architecture has remained, enriched on the whole by the mixture of 20th-century redevelopment. It is an area of lively and total contrasts, whose residents have shown a cheerful resilience to change.

Paddington Canal. Now part of the GRAND UNION CANAL system. It connects the REGENT'S CANAL at PADDINGTON with Bull's Bridge, whence the River BRENT runs south to the THAMES at BRENTFORD, and UXBRIDGE, and then it proceeds northwards as the GRAND UNION. It was opened in 1801 and runs parallel with the HARROW ROAD for part of its course. (See also GRAND JUNCTION CANAL).

Paddington Gardens. see BURIAL GROUNDS.

Paddington Green W2. The oldest part of PADDINGTON. North of the churchyard stood the manor house until 1824; around the Green was a cluster of big Georgian houses of which two remain. In 1782–6 the Hon. Charles Greville looked after the young Emma Hart nearby. She was adoringly painted here by Romney and later married Greville's uncle, Sir William Hamilton. Greville, a founder of the ROYAL HORTICULTURAL SOCIETY, lived on at Paddington Green

An 18th-century view of Paddington Green round which clustered a group of Georgian houses, of which only two survive nowadays.

until 1809. At the same period both John Symmons and Thomas Hogg had famous gardens here. In 1829 George Shillibeer overcame local protest and introduced his omnibus service to the CITY from Paddington Green, linking the growing village to the rest of London. West of ST MARY'S CHURCH stood Paddington's Town Hall designed by James Lockyer. It was demolished in 1966. The Children's Hospital dates from 1883. Ignatius Pollaky, the local private detective referred to in Gilbert and Sullivan's *Patience* ('the keen penetration of Paddington Pollaky'), would have seen the last thatched house in London demolished in the 1890s to make way for St David's Welsh church. Modern development to the north and ceaseless traffic now dominate the Green. The statue of Sarah Siddons is by Chavalliand (*see* STATUES). Dolamore Ltd, the wine and spirit merchants formerly at No. 16, were established at No. 38 BAKER STREET in 1842. In 1982 they moved to WATERLOO STATION Approach.

Paddington Green Children's Hospital *Paddington Green*. W2. Founded in 1883 as a successor to the children's dispensary in Bell Street begun in 1862. It was rebuilt in 1938 and is now a part of ST MARY'S HOSPITAL PADDINGTON. In 1982 there were 33 beds.

Paddington Station *Praed Street, W2*. The London terminus of British Rail, Western Region. It was opened in its original form – a wooden structure – on 4 June 1838, on a site near the Bishops Bridge Road, now a goods depot. Queen Victoria arrived at this station after her first railway journey, from Slough, in 1842. The 17-mile journey took 23 minutes – at an average 44 m.p.h., which Prince Albert thought too high. 'Not so fast next time, Mr Conductor', he is often said to have requested. When, in 1851, the Great Western decided to build a new station, Isambard Kingdom Brunel, the company's engineer, was given the task of designing it. There was at first a suggestion that, as the Great Western and the London and Birmingham's lines approached London very close together, they should combine and use EUSTON as a common terminal. This plan was abandoned for two reasons: first, because the companies could not agree

The coffee room of the Great Western Hotel, designed by Philip Hardwick and opened in 1854 as the largest hotel in England, with over 100 bedrooms.

on the financial arrangements, and secondly, because Brunel was resolute in his determination to continue using broad-gauge (7 ft 0¼ ins) tracks for the Great Western instead of standard (4 ft 8½ ins).

When the new Paddington Station was built, 1850–4, a quarter of a mile east of the old one, only broad-gauge tracks were laid; but mixed gauge (both broad and standard) trains were able to use the station from 1861, three years after Brunel's death, and the last broad-gauge trains ran in 1892. Brunel asked the architect, M.D. Wyatt, to provide the ornamentation of the station, and his elegant iron-work decoration embellishes the roof and the capitals of the columns. But Brunel himself was the station's designer. Taking ideas from Paxton's CRYSTAL PALACE, he built a triple roof of wrought iron and glass, supported on cast-iron pillars. The central aisle was 102 ft across, the side aisles 70 ft and 68 ft. A fourth aisle was added to the north side when extensions were being made to the station in 1909–16. The Great Western Hotel (later the GREAT WESTERN ROYAL HOTEL) was designed by Philip Hardwick. Now the station covers 13 acres. Seven named expresses leave each day for various destinations in the West Country, and 48,000 passengers, 27,000 parcels and 10,000 mail bags pass through the station each weekday. On the wall by Platform 1 is a plaque with a picture of Brunel, wearing a stovepipe hat. The plaque was put up to mark Paddington's Centenary in 1954.

Paddington Street *W1*. Extends from 79 MARYLEBONE HIGH STREET to 92 BAKER STREET. The Victorian stone statue, *The Street Orderly Boy*, in the gardens is by Donato Barcaglia. It was placed here in 1943. The gardens were St George's burial ground between 1731 and 1851; and an attractive mausoleum can still be seen here.

Page Street *SW1*. The large blocks of flats here were built for artisans in 1928–30 to the designs of Sir Edwin Lutyens.

Pageantmaster Appointed every year by 'the Alderman who is expected to be the next Lord Mayor' to organise his procession (*see* LORD MAYOR'S SHOW). The earliest named Pageantmaster was Richard Baker, of the PAINTER-STAINERS' COMPANY, in 1566. In recent years the position has been held by a practising architect and it takes him a year to co-ordinate the diverse elements which make up the LORD MAYOR'S SHOW.

Painter-Stainers' Company *see* CITY LIVERY COMPANIES.

Painter-Stainers' Hall *Little Trinity Lane, EC4*. Alderman John Brown, Serjeant-Painter to Henry VIII, bequeathed a Hall in LITTLE TRINITY LANE to the Company. The Relief Commission used this Hall during the GREAT PLAGUE in 1665. It was destroyed by the GREAT FIRE and rebuilt by 1670. The building was extensively repaired in 1776–7 and a new wing was added in 1880. The façade was reconstructed by H.D. Searles-Wood between 1914 and 1916. Bombing destroyed the Hall in 1940. The present Hall, designed by Denis Harrington, was opened in 1961. The dining capacity is 180. For the Company *see* CITY LIVERY COMPANIES.

Palace Court *W2.* On the site of the 18th-century house built for the Countess of Shaftesbury, and used in the 19th century by Dr Thomas Davidson as a mental asylum, this street was not built until the 1880s. Consequently it is a perfect microcosm for studying the fashionable architecture of this period, for the houses were built individually. Percy Macquoid, a furniture expert, lived at No. 8 in 1894–1924 and Leonard Stokes built No. 47 for Wilfred and Alice Meynell. They lived here in 1889–1905, and the house became a centre for writers and aesthetes, amongst them Aubrey Beardsley and Oscar Wilde, and the poet Francis Thompson, who was rescued from destitution by Alice Meynell.

Palace Gardens Terrace *W8.* Built in 1860. The Second Church of Christ, Scientist, was designed by Sir John Burnet in 1921. James Clerk Maxwell, the physicist, lived at No. 16 in 1860–6, Max Beerbohm at No. 57 in 1872, and Wyndham Lewis lived at No. 61 in 1923–6.

Palace Gate *W8.* Takes its name from the nearby gate into the grounds of KENSINGTON PALACE. A street of large, grand houses originally occupied by the kind of 'people of professional and social eminence' who lived in the nearby HYDE PARK GATE. In its original form No. IA was built in 1862–4 by Messrs William Cubitt and Co. for John Forster, who wrote his life of Dickens here. It was entirely rebuilt for William Alfred Johnstone, a young newspaper proprietor, by C.J. Harold Cooper, the idiosyncratic architect of 15 STRATTON STREET, who produced a building which *The Studio* described as having ' "distinction" written everywhere for those who know how to read' and of leaving the 'impression of a house built for gentlemen by gentlemen'. No. 2 was also built by Cubitts and designed by P.C. Hardwick (in the Italianate style more usually favoured in the area) for his friend John Everett Millais whose studio occupied an entire wing at the back. No. 6 was built in the 1870s for Colonel A.W.H. Meyrick, several pieces from whose splendid collection of armour, inherited from a cousin, can now be seen in the WALLACE COLLECTION. A huge house,

known as Thorney House and built 'regardless of cost', was constructed in the Elizabethan style for the 8th Duke of Bedford on the east side of Palace Gate in 1869–70. The Duke already had a town house in BELGRAVE SQUARE and it was said that he wanted to move to be nearer his mistress in Leonard Place, but she died before the house was finished and her lover never moved into it. It was demolished in 1904–5 and a block of flats was built on the site. These flats, Thorney Court, were themselves pulled down in 1972. The Korean Embassy is at No. 4.

Palace Green *W8.* Private road of large Victorian houses mainly built in the 1850s on the kitchen garden of KENSINGTON PALACE. Many are now embassies: the Israeli at No. 2; the Romanian at No. 4; the Laotian at No. 5; the Philippine at No. 9a. In 1722–4 a water tower for supplying the palace was built here, perhaps to the designs of Sir John Vanbrugh. It was demolished in about 1830. No. 1 was designed by Philip Webb for the Duke of Carlisle in 1863. No. 2 was designed by Thackeray for his own use. He had a special mirror put across his study window so that he would not be disturbed. He lived here from 1861 until his death in 1863.

Palace of Westminster *Westminster, SW1.* The first Palace of Westminster was built for Edward the Confessor on land between the THAMES and WESTMINSTER (now WESTMINSTER ABBEY), the comparatively modest monastery which he had renovated and enlarged. After he died in 1066 the Palace became the home of William the Conqueror and his court. William's son, William Rufus, built WESTMINSTER HALL but his plans for further enlarging the Palace were not realised after his violent death in 1100. Nevertheless the Palace remained the main residence of the kings of England, and the home of the Court until Henry VIII abandoned it for WHITEHALL PALACE in 1512. Even after that it remained the administrative centre of the kingdom. In early times the King's Council had met in WESTMINSTER HALL, and there the 'Model' Parliament was summoned by Edward I; but soon after his death the Lords and Commons held their deliberations

An early design for the Palace of Westminster by Charles Barry, published in the Stationer's Almanack *in 1837.*

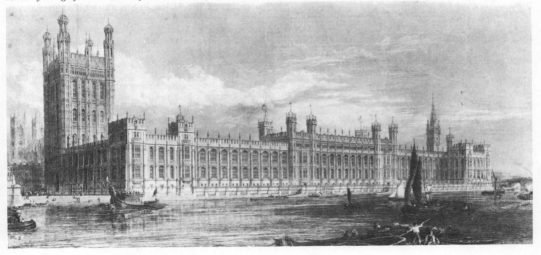

separately. After meeting in the presence of the King, usually in the Painted Chamber, where the Lord Chamberlain announced the reason for the summoning of Parliament, the Lords withdrew to the White Chamber. The Commons, however, had to meet wherever was convenient, sometimes in the Chapter House of the Abbey, or in the Refectory which the Abbot allowed them to use.

At the Reformation, under the Chantries Act of 1547, the Royal Chapel of St Stephen, like all other private chapels, was secularised, and by 1550 had become the meeting place of the Commons. This chapel, traditionally founded by St Stephen, had been burned down in 1298, rebuilt by Edward I, and finished in the reign of Edward III in 1347. The king had worshipped in St Stephen's, the courtiers in the crypt which had been built by Edward I in 1292. St Stephen's Chapel was a tall, two-storeyed building with high turrets at the four corners, and long stained-glass windows. As it had no aisle it was perfectly suitable for use as a debating chamber. The Members sat in the choir stalls on the north and south walls; the Speaker's chair was placed where the altar had been. (The tradition of Members bowing to the Speaker's chair probably derives from genuflexion to the altar.) The Mace, the Speaker's staff of office, was placed on a table where the lectern had been. The ante-chapel, separated from the main chapel by the choir-screen, served as a lobby in which Members registered their votes as Ayes, the Noes remaining in the Chapel. From the mid-16th century until its destruction by fire in 1834 St Stephen's was, in fact, the HOUSE OF COMMONS.

After 1547 St Mary Undercroft, the crypt of St Stephen's, was used as a parliamentary store-house, as were the Cloisters. It survived the 1834 fire (*see below*), after which it was carefully restored by Barry for use as a chapel by Members of both Houses. It is 90 ft long by 26 ft wide, and comprises five vaulted bays with a fine groined roof and four carved bosses. There is an unusual circular mural representing Judas Iscariot with silver coins above his head. In this chapel Members can be married and their children baptised, whatever their denomination, in the adjoining octagonal Baptistry, the work of Barry who also designed the font of alabaster and marble with its highly ornamented brass cover.

The only other parts of the Palace to survive the fire of 1834 are WESTMINSTER HALL; the Cloisters, with their fine fan vaulting and carved bosses, built early in the reign of Henry VIII by Dr John Chamber, Dean of St Stephen's College; and the JEWEL TOWER, built in 1365–6 as a royal treasure house and used from 1621 as the Parliament Office and as a storage place for the HOUSE OF LORDS records.

After 1547 the canons of St Stephen's were dismissed and as the Palace was no longer a royal residence, Members and officials of both Houses started to occupy the many vacant chambers. The Lords settled permanently in the White Chamber. In the cellars below, Guy Fawkes, a Roman Catholic convert, and his fellow conspirators were caught in their plot to blow up King James I and his ministers, and Members of both Houses on 5 November 1605 (*see* GUNPOWDER PLOT). The cellars are searched to this day by the YEOMEN OF THE GUARD before each State Opening of Parliament, as if in confirmation of the nursery rhyme:

I see no good reason
Why Gunpowder Treason
Should ever be forgot.

Sixteen years later the King angered the Commons by tearing out the pages in their Journal in which they had asserted their right to deal 'with all matters of grievance and policy'. Relations between the Crown and the Commons deteriorated over the years until the day in January 1642 when Charles I burst into St Stephen's demanding the arrest of five Members. Replying to the King who asked where the missing Members were, the Speaker, William Lenthall, said, 'I have neither eyes to see, nor tongue to speak in this place, but as this House is pleased to direct me.' The King had no alternative but to withdraw. Since then no monarch can set foot in the Commons Chamber. The throne, which is occupied during the ceremony of the STATE OPENING OF PARLIAMENT, is in the Lords' Chamber, to which the Commons repair to hear the Monarch's Speech from the Throne.

In the reign of Queen Anne, Sir Christopher Wren, the Surveyor General, was commissioned to build galleries in the former St Stephen's Chapel to accommodate the new Scottish Members, and in 1800, because of the admission of Irish Members, the new Surveyor General, James Wyatt, was required to enlarge it further by reducing the thickness of the walls. At the same time the Lords moved from the White Chamber, which they were overcrowding, to the Hall, formerly used by the Court of Requests, next to the House of Commons kitchen.

The fire of 1834 ended the makeshift accommodation in which Lords and Commons had worked for nearly 300 years. Until the Court of Exchequer was abolished in 1826 it had continuously kept records of accounts by a system of tallies and foils, notched elmwood sticks split in half, one half being retained by the Exchequer, the other half constituting a receipt to those who were required to pay money into the Court. 'The sticks were housed at Westminster', Charles Dickens told an audience at DRURY LANE, 'and it would naturally occur to any intelligent person that nothing could be easier than to allow them to be carried away for firewood by the miserable people who live in that neighbourhood. However, they never had been useful, and official routine required that they never should be, and so the order went forth that they should be privately and confidentially burned.' It was decided to burn them in the big furnace beneath the Lords' Chamber. By early next morning not only the House of Lords but the House of Commons and nearly all the conglomeration of buildings known as the Palace of Westminster lay in smoking ruins.

Thus the opportunity arose for buildings to be designed specifically to house Parliament. Architects were invited to submit plans 'in the Gothic or Elizabethan style'; 97 designs were submitted and of these Barry's was selected.

Charles Barry, knighted in 1852, son of a prosperous stationer, was born in WESTMINSTER and had been articled to a firm of surveyors in LAMBETH. With a modest inheritance from his father he travelled in Italy and became deeply influenced by Renaissance architecture. Conscious of his limitations as an architect in the Gothic style, he enlisted the help of Augustus Pugin who had been trained in the office of his father, the French architect, Auguste Pugin. He had spent much of his apprenticeship in making drawings for his father's books on Gothic architecture. Barry and Pugin made a perfect partnership, Barry providing the practical and commanding plans, Pugin the picturesque ornamentation. Construction began in 1837, Mrs Barry having the honour of laying the foundation stone. Ten years later the House of Commons was completed. The Clock Tower was not finished until 1858; it had presented even more problems than the extremely expensive heating and ventilation system which proved so inefficient that Lord Randolph Churchill once had no difficulty in persuading the House to adjourn in mid-debate in protest against the foulness of the atmosphere.

When the Clock Tower reached a height of 150 ft, work on it had to be suspended as it was discovered that the mechanism of the clock could not be raised inside it. The clockmaker, not Barry's choice, was E.J. Dent, whose clock for the ROYAL EXCHANGE was classed as 'the best public clock in the world'. In spite of his distinction and experience everything went wrong with the Westminster clock (*see* BIG BEN). When the Victoria Tower was roofed in 1860, however, and the Palace of Westminster was complete it was generally acclaimed as a building worthy to be the Houses of Parliament, and a splendid example of Perpendicular Gothic.

Prince Albert was greatly interested in art and ensured that the new buildings were richly furnished with painting and sculpture. In 1841, under his influence, a Select Committee was appointed 'to take into consideration the promotion of the Fine Arts . . . in connection with the rebuilding of the Houses of Parliament'. William Dyce was one of the winning artists of the resultant competitions, and his five huge frescoes of Arthurian legend can be seen in the Robing Room in which the Monarch assumes the Imperial Crown and Parliamentary Robes for the STATE OPENING OF PARLIAMENT.

The walls of the Royal Gallery, which leads from the Robing Room to the Prince's Chamber, are painted with two 45 ft long frescoes by Daniel Maclise, *The Death of Nelson* and *The Meeting of Wellington and Blücher*; the floor is patterned in buff, red and blue Minton tiles. In the Prince's Chamber is John Gibson's monument to Queen Victoria. The two fireplaces, with bronze bas relief panels by William Theed above them, are, like the one in the Robing Room, intricately patterned and ornamented.

There are more frescoes in the House of Lords by Dyce, Maclise, Charles Cope and John Calcott Horsley. Above the four doorways in the Central Lobby are mosaics of the patron saints of England, Scotland, Wales and Ireland by Sir Edward Poynter and Anning Bell, and there stand the life-size statues of four 19th-century statesmen, Earl Granville, William Ewart Gladstone, Earl Russell and the Earl of Iddesleigh by Sir Joseph Boehm, Sir William Hamo Thornycroft and Pomeroy. Barry's own statue in white marble by John Henry Foley is in the Lower Waiting Hall beneath a trefoiled window.

The whole interior of the Palace, except the part rebuilt after the bombing in 1941, is gorgeously and intricately ornamented to designs by Pugin, including panelled ceilings, tiled floors (the encaustic tiles by Herbert Minton), stained glass, wallpapers, clocks, fireplaces, door furniture and even umbrella stands and inkwells.

Barry's structure, described by James Pope-Hennessy as 'this great and beautiful monument to Victorian artifice', stood intact for nearly a century until 1940. Between September 1940 and May 1941 the Houses of Parliament were damaged 11 times during air raids. Bombs had fallen in OLD PALACE YARD, wrecking part of St Stephen's Porch, and in Cloister Court, demolishing part of the Cloisters. But on 10 May 1941 numerous incendiary bombs were dropped by a fleet of 500 German aircraft, and a high-explosive bomb fell near Victoria Tower, bringing tons of masonry crashing down into Royal Court. Such was the blaze that the Chief Superintendent of the LONDON FIRE BRIGADE said it was an 'impenetrable inferno of flames'. By the next morning the House of Commons and the adjoining Lobby were a heap of smouldering rubble.

Sir Giles Gilbert Scott was commissioned to rebuild the House of Commons in the tradition of the old Chamber. This he did between 1945 and 1950, retaining Barry's general plan but simplifying Pugin's extreme Gothic decoration.

Palace Street *SW1*. A street of hybrid character sweeping in a curve from the ROYAL MEWS to VICTORIA STREET. The Gothic buildings of the United Westminster Schools Foundation by R.R.Arntz (1876) are at Nos 51–53. The statue in the forecourt is of Sir Sidney Waterhouse (*see* STATUES). The WESTMINSTER THEATRE is at No. 12.

Palace Theatre *Cambridge Circus, WC2*. Formerly Royal English Opera House, 1891; Palace Theatre of Varieties, 1892–1910. A triple-decker Victorian theatre built as an opera house by T.E. Collcutt and G.H. Holloway in 1888–91 for Richard D'Oyly Carte. It opened with *Ivanhoe*, a grand opera by Sir Arthur Sullivan, which ran for six months but did not make a profit. The next production was Messager's *La Basoche* but that also was a financial failure and the theatre closed. It was reopened by Augustus Harris as a music-hall in 1892. In 1906 Marie Tempest made her first appearance in variety here. Pavlova's London debut was made here in 1910. Between 1914 and 1919 the various reviews staged included *The Passing Show* (1914), *Bric à Brac* (1915), *Vanity Fair* (1916), *Hullo America* (1918), and *The Whirligig* (1919). Between 1919 and 1923 it was used mainly as a cinema. It reopened as a theatre for musicals in 1924. The best remembered success was *No, No, Nanette* (1925) which had 655 performances. During the 2nd World War Jack Hulbert and Cicely Courtneidge appeared in the musical comedies *Under Your Hat* (1942), *Full Swing* (1942), and *Something in the Air* (1943). Since then the theatre's longest runs have mostly been musicals including *The Song of Norway* (1946) which had 526 performances, *Carissima* (1948), *King's Rhapsody* (1949) by Ivor Novello which had 839 performances, and *Zip Goes a Million* (1951). *The Love Match* (1953), a comedy by Glenn Melvyn, had 593 performances. From 1961 to 1967 Rodgers' and Hammerstein's *The Sound of Music* ran for 2,385 performances. The seating capacity is 1,450.

Palais de Danse *Shepherd's Bush Road, W6*. This dance-hall, colloquially known as the Hammersmith Palais, was built on the site of a tram garage, and opened on 28 October 1919. It was in many ways an innovator, being the first place in Britain at which a jazz band played (the Dixieland Jazz Band in 1921), the first dance-hall to have two bands playing each evening, the first to enable those who came alone to 'hire' partners and, in 1938, the first to be televised. Its maple floor can accommodate 2,000 dancers. In 1929 it became a skating rank, but returned to being a dance-hall in 1935.

Pall Mall *SW1*. Takes its name from a game something like croquet which had originated in Italy as *pallo a maglio* (ball to mallet) and had become highly popular in France. In his *View of France as it stoode in . . . 1598*, Sir Robert Dallington wrote of his enjoyment of the 'gentleman-like sport', which he preferred 'among all the exercises of France', and marvelled that it had not been introduced into England. It had already been introduced into Scotland, possibly by Mary, Queen of Scots, whose son, James I, recommended it to his son, Prince Henry. Prince Henry's brother, Charles I, played the game in London where it became popular in the reign of Charles II who could often be seen playing it with his mistresses in the park at ST JAMES'S. The royal pall mall alley was built just inside the park wall close to an existing one in St James's Field; but carriages on their way between the Palace and CHARING CROSS set up such clouds of dust in summer that the players could sometimes scarcely see the ball. So it was decided to block the existing thoroughfare and to build a new one to the north between two lines of elms on the old pall mall alley in St James's Field. This new road, which ran almost parallel with the former highway, was laid out 1661. It was at first officially known as Catherine Street in honour of the Queen, Catherine of Braganza; but it was familiarly known by the name which has survived to this day.

From the beginning Pall Mall was a highly fashionable street. Here lived the Countess of Ranelagh, whose husband, the 1st Earl, owned houses in KING STREET and ST JAMES'S SQUARE as well as a large country house in CHELSEA, being a most extravagant man who 'spent more money, built more fine houses, and laid out more on household furnishing and garden-

ing than any other nobleman in England.' Here also lived the King's vivacious mistress, Nell Gwynne, the site of whose house at No. 79 is the only ground on the south side of Pall Mall which does not belong to the Crown. The freehold has been in private hands since 1676 when King Charles had it conveyed to the trustees of his mistress who, so it was said, had crossly complained about being granted a lease, insisting that she 'had always conveyed free under the Crown and always would'. On Nell Gwynne's death in 1687 the house passed to her son whom the King created Earl of Burford and later Duke of St Albans, according to one version of the story, after his mistress had called to the boy, 'Come here, you little bastard!' and, reproached by her lover for using such a rude word, had replied that she had no other name by which to call him. The Duke was obliged to assign the house to his creditors in 1693. In the next century George III's brother, the Duke of Gloucester, was secretly married in the drawing-room to the Dowager Countess Waldegrave, a match that, combined with the Duke of Cumberland's marriage to Mrs Anne Horton, led to the passing of the Royal Marriage Act in 1772.

By the beginning of the 18th century Pall Mall had become renowned also for its expensive shops as well as its grand houses. Gay wrote in his *Trivia*:

Oh bear me to the paths of fair Pell Mell!
Safe are thy pavements, grateful is thy smell.
At distance rolls along the gilded coach,
Nor sturdy Carmen on thy walks encroach.
No louts would bar thy ways were chairs denied
The soft supports of laziness and pride.
Shops breathe perfumes, thro' sashes ribbons glow
The mutual arms of ladies and the beaux.

Among these shops could later be found, at No. 68, the premises of the clockmaking family of Vulliamy, successive members of which were here from 1765 to 1854. At No. 52 was the bookshop of Robert Dodsley, who suggested to Samuel Johnson that he should compile a dictionary.

Although still a 'fine long Street', in Strype's words, with houses on the south side having 'a Pleasant

Carlton House, behind its colonnade in Pall Mall, was rebuilt at vast expense for the Prince Regent by Henry Holland in 1783–96.

Prospect into the King's Garden', by 1746 it had been 'greatly disfigured by several mean houses of the lowest mechanicks being interspersed in it in several places'. Writers and artists had also begun to move in. Swift lodged here in 1710, Laurence Sterne in 1760, Edward Gibbon in 1769–70, 1772–3 and 1787, Gainsborough in 1774–88, and Richard Cosway, the miniaturist, in 1784–91. Mrs Fitzherbert, wife of George IV, lived at No. 105 in 1789–96 and William Cobbett at No. 11 in 1800–2. Both Cosway and Gainsborough (whose residence there is indicated by a BLUE PLAQUE) lived at SCHOMBERG HOUSE whose dark redbrick façade can still be seen at Nos 80–82 amidst the grey and yellow 19th-century premises which now occupy so much of the southern side of Pall Mall.

On 4 June 1807 part of the street was gaslit to celebrate the King's birthday, an experiment conducted by a pioneer of gas lighting, F.A. Winsor, who occupied a house on part of the site of Nos 93–95. 'The Mall continued crowded with spectators until near twelve o'clock, and they seemed much amused and delighted by this novel exhibition.' Gas light was not permanently installed in the street until 1820.

As well as for fine houses and shops Pall Mall was celebrated for its coffee-houses (such as the SMYRNA at No. 59) and for the clubs that developed from them. ALMACK'S, BROOKS'S, BOODLE'S, the CARLTON, the GUARDS, the JUNIOR NAVAL AND MILITARY, the MACARONI CLUB, the Ladies' Club, the Cocoa Tree Club, Goostree's and the MARLBOROUGH CLUB were all at one time in the street. The clubs that remain are, on the south side, the ATHENAEUM, the TRAVELLERS', the REFORM, the ROYAL AUTOMOBILE CLUB, the UNITED OXFORD AND CAMBRIDGE UNIVERSITY CLUB and, on the north side, the JUNIOR CARLTON and the ARMY AND NAVY CLUB. The premises of the UNITED SERVICE CLUB, which cover the site of the house where the ROYAL ACADEMY met until 1779, have been taken over by the INSTITUTE OF DIRECTORS. The STAR AND GARTER tavern was at No. 100 and the Shakespeare Gallery at No. 52. On part of the site of the REFORM CLUB stood the house of John Julius Angerstein where the NATIONAL GALLERY was first housed.

At the beginning of the 19th century Pall Mall was still a 'stately aristocratic-looking street', occupied by 'private mansions fit for the residence of the wealthy and noble'. Pre-eminent amongst these were CARLTON HOUSE, YORK HOUSE, MARLBOROUGH HOUSE and BUCKINGHAM HOUSE. But at the east end it was 'bordered with filthy alleys, inhabited by abandoned characters'. These alleys were swept away in later 19th-century developments, and Pall Mall was considered a desirable address by Princess Christian, daughter of Queen Victoria, who lived at Nos 77–78 in 1902–23 and whose daughters, Princess Helena Victoria and Princess Marie Louise, were here until 1947.

Pall Mall is no longer a residential street but one mainly of offices and some shops as well as clubs. John Harvey and Sons, the wine merchants (established in Bristol in 1796), are at No. 27, having moved there from King Street, St James's in 1965. Doulton and Co., the pottery manufacturers (see DOULTON), are at No. 46; Robson Lowe, the stamp auctioneers (founded in REGENT STREET in 1926), at No. 50; Churchill, Atkin, Grant and Lang, the gunmakers, at No. 61; Pimm's, the compounders, at No. 63; ROTHMANS, the cigarette manufacturers, at No. 65; and Hardy Brothers (Alnwick) Ltd, established at Alnwick as makers of fishing tackle in 1872 and at No. 61 since 1892. The Legal and General Assurance Society is at No. 52; the Eagle Star Insurance Co. at No. 79 in an elaborate Italianate building designed by David Brandon in the 1860s; and the Phoenix Assurance Co. at Nos 44–45. The Royal British Legion's headquarters are at No. 49.

Palmers Green *N13, N14*. A district in the former Borough of SOUTHGATE. Before the opening of the railway in 1871, it consisted merely of a cluster of cottages in Green Lanes. Large amounts of land became available for building in 1902 and extensive housing development followed. In its heyday, Palmers Green was one of the most solidly respectable suburbs in North London.

Pancras Lane *EC4*. Commemorates the church of ST PANCRAS SOPER LANE which was burnt in the GREAT FIRE. ST BENET SHEREHOG on the north side was also destroyed. Richard Abbey, who became the Keats children's guardian after the death of their parents, had his counting-house at No. 4.

Pancras Wells A 17th- and 18th-century spa which lay to the south of ST PANCRAS OLD CHURCH. In 1697 the proprietor of the Horns Tavern advertised the waters which he claimed to have found 'by long experience, a powerful antidote against rising of the vapours also against the stone and gravel'. They 'cleansed the body and sweetened the blood'. Admission cost 3d. During the summer there was dancing every Tuesday and Thursday. By 1769 it had become a tea-garden supplying 'hot loaves, syllabubs and milk from the cow'. 'Dinners and neat wine, curious punch, Dorchester, Marlborough and Ringwood beers' were also provided. By the time Daniel Lysons wrote his *Environs of London* (1792–6) the spa had closed and the well was part of a private garden. ST PANCRAS STATION partly covers the site.

Pandora Road *NW6*. Built in 1881 and named by its builder in honour of the first woman, created by Zeus. Lord Northcliffe, the newspaper proprietor, lived at No. 31 in 1888–91.

Panoramas Popular in the late 18th century, they were introduced before the DIORAMAS and outlived them. They were conceived when Robert Barker, an Irish artist, invented a system of curving lines of perspective in a scenic painting on a cylindrical surface so that they would appear correct when viewed from the centre of the cylinder. Barker opened his famous Panorama in 1793 on a site in LEICESTER PLACE that runs north from the north-east corner of LEICESTER SQUARE. It was a rotunda 90 ft in diameter divided into two rooms, a smaller above a larger to provide a double exhibition. Many huge scenes were exhibited up to 1865 when the building was converted to a French church; though damaged in the 2nd World War, it is still there and retains the original circular plan of the Panorama.

When Daguerre's DIORAMA was opened at Nos 9 and 10 Park Square East in 1823, another rotunda of Doric classicism, like a miniature Pantheon, was under construction on a site a few hundred yards to the north, facing REGENT'S PARK. This hall of entertainment, called the COLOSSEUM, was designed by Decimus Burton and consisted of a polygonal hall 126 ft across lit by

Artists completing the London panorama at the Colosseum, c.1829. Visitors climbed to a three-tiered viewing platform.

GARDENS presented its 'Diaphanic Panopticon', a huge display, 200 ft long, on the theme of war and peace. FIREWORKS and acrobatics often accompanied the shows, which attracted enormous crowds.

Pantheon *Oxford Street.* Designed by James Wyatt as the 'winter Ranelagh'. Its main room was a huge and beautiful rotunda based on Santa Sophia, Constantinople. There were smaller vestibules, card rooms, tea and supper rooms. It took more than two and a half years to build and was opened on 27 January 1772. Over 1,500 people were present on the occasion. A foreign nobleman said that it brought to his mind 'the enchanted palaces described in the French Romances, which are said to have been raised by the potent wand of some Fairy'. The less impressionable Horace Walpole was quite as impressed. 'It amazed me myself', he wrote. 'Imagine Balbec in all its glory! The pillars are of artificial *giallo antico*. The ceilings, even of the passages, are of the most beautiful stuccos in the best taste of grotesque .... Monsieur de Guisnes said to me, *"Ce n'est qu'à Londres qu'on peut faire tout cela."* ' After a subsequent visit Walpole decided that the Pantheon was 'the most beautiful edifice in England'. Gibbon was almost as entranced: it was, he thought, the wonder of the 18th century and of the British Empire. Charles Burney expressed an almost universal opinion when he wrote that it was 'regarded both by natives and foreigners as the most elegant structure in Europe, if not on the globe .... No person of taste in architecture or music, who remembers the Pantheon, its exhibitions, its numerous, splendid, and elegant assemblies, can hear it mentioned without a sigh.'

Yet although the masquerades, *ridottos*, fêtes and concerts were at first extremely well conducted and well attended, after about eight years their popularity declined. The price of admission to the assemblies, for which subscribers had previously paid 6 guineas for the twelve held during the season, had to be reduced in 1780; and the Pantheon began to be used for such purposes as the exhibition of Lunardi's Balloon which was shown here in 1784 and 1785 (*see* BALLOONING). In 1791 it was decided to turn the building into a

A masquerade at the Pantheon c.1809, from an aquatint after Rowlandson and Pugin.

a glazed dome, its first purpose being to display an enormous circular view of London as if seen from the top of ST PAUL'S CATHEDRAL. The artist was E.T. Parris, but other scenes were shown later such as Paris by moonlight and a view of Lake Thun, both painted by Danson. Viewers were elevated to galleries at different levels by a steam-driven lift within a central shaft. The building also contained an organ, a museum of sculpture, a hall of mirrors, and a refreshment room, a cyclorama theatre being added in 1848. In the grounds stood various beguiling structures including a Swiss chalet, a grotto and a Gothic aviary. The COLOSSEUM was demolished in 1875 and the existing block of Victorian flats was erected on the site.

By the year of the GREAT EXHIBITION of 1851, Panoramas had become a mania of the London public. Now appeared Cycloramas, Poeciloramas and Typoramas. Movement was introduced, as in ALBANY STREET, where the Lisbon earthquake of 1755 was represented with agitated waves and wildly rolling vessels to reproduce 'the appalling scene in all its attractive horrors'. Panoramas also moved across the field of vision between rollers, horizontally, vertically, in opposite directions, or outwards from a central parting; sometimes a series of up to 50 scenes were shown – a Grand Tour, a visit to the Holy Land, a climb up Mont Blanc, a balloon voyage above a great city. By 1860 the Panorama had lost its appeal, being weakened no doubt by the appearance of illustrated weekly magazines that dramatised topical events in their woodblock engravings.

Spectacles called Picture Models, a mixture of diorama, panorama and pantomime, displayed in three dimensions on a huge scale, were also staged in Victorian times at night in such pleasure gardens as CREMORNE and the SURREY GARDENS. In 1851 SURREY theatre. A licence was obtained for operatic productions, and the King's Theatre, Pantheon, opened on 17 February 1791 with a production of Sacchini's *Armida*. *The Times* considered it 'among the prettiest' theatres in Europe. But in January 1792, on a night of severe frost, it was almost completely destroyed by a fire which, rumour held, had been started by those interested in the success of the KING'S THEATRE, HAYMARKET. The next morning crowds of people gazed in astonishment upon the gutted building and the 'phenomenon of vast clusters of icicles, twelve and fifteen feet in length' hanging about the ruins, the frozen stream of the jets of water from the fire engines. In 1792 the Pantheon was rebuilt by Crispus Clagett, proprietor of the Apollo Gardens, WESTMINSTER BRIDGE ROAD, and reopened with a masquerade on 9 April 1795. But Clagett's venture was not a success. He himself disappeared, leaving many debts behind him. And in 1810 his building was leased to the 'National Institution for improving Manufactures of the United Kingdom, and the Arts connected therewith'. This institution, too, was also soon in debt; and the lease was sold to Henry Greville whose ARGYLL ROOMS were proving too small for his purposes. Greville, however, finding the cost of adapting the Pantheon too large for his means, agreed to sell his lease and licence to Nicholas Wilcox Cundy who wished to convert it into a new theatre but was soon in trouble with the Lord Chamberlain who declined to alter the existing licence which covered only music and dancing, *burlettas* and dramatic entertainments by children under 17. Defying the Lord Chamberlain, Cundy opened his English Opera House at the Pantheon on 22 July 1813, and the Lord Chamberlain retaliated by ordering it to be closed. In 1814 it was stripped of its fittings and left empty, and in 1833–4 converted into a bazaar to the designs of Sydney Smirke. The Pantheon Bazaar was bought in 1867 by Gilbey's, the wine merchants, who sold it to MARKS AND SPENCER LTD in 1937. MARKS AND SPENCER had it demolished and built in its place their shop in OXFORD STREET designed by W.A. Lewis and Partners and Robert Lutyens.

Panton Square Colonel Thomas Panton, a property speculator and one-time heavy gambler (*see* PANTON STREET), began building here in 1673. It was described by Strype in 1720 as 'a very large Place for Stabling and Coach-houses, there being one large Yard within another. This place is being designed to be built into Streets.' By 1746 houses had appeared; and one of these was occupied in 1762 by the Moroccan Ambassador who, when one of his attendants happened to displease him, had him brought up to the garret, and sliced his head off. An angry crowd then broke into his house, smashed the furniture, threw the pieces out of the windows, 'threshed and beat the grand Moor and his retinue down the Haymarket'. Benjamin West, the American painter, lived here in 1768–75; and in 1863, when several of the houses had been turned into small hotels, Stéphane Mallarmé, the French poet. After his death, Colonel Panton's estate passed into the hands of the Arundell family through his daughter's marriage to Henry Arundell, 5th Baron Arundell. In 1919 the family sold it to J. Lyons and Co. who demolished the buildings for an extension of their LYONS' CORNER HOUSE in COVENTRY STREET.

Panton Street *SW1*. Extends from HAYMARKET to LEICESTER SQUARE. It forms part of 3 or 4 acres of ground bought in 1619 by Robert Baker, the tailor of Piccadilly Hall (*see* PICCADILLY) and is where Simon Osbaldeston, barber to the Lord Chamberlain, later ran a popular eating-house (derisively known as Shaver's Hall) in conjunction with a tennis court and bowling green. In the 1660s Colonel Thomas Panton, a friend of Charles II and at the card table described as 'an absolute artist, either upon the square or at foul play', acquired an interest in this property by unscrupulous means, and in 1669 came to an arrangement with Robert Baker's son-in-law, Sir Henry Oxenden, who had a life interest in it, to exclude Baker's descendants. Building took place in the 1670s, but the only houses of any great age now are Nos 5 and 6, adjacent to the COMEDY THEATRE. Dean Swift lived in the street for a short time; in 1711–12 Addison wrote his *Campaign* in a garret lodging on the south side. On 9 June 1803 a violent hail and rain storm broke over OXENDON STREET, Panton Street, COVENTRY STREET and HAYMARKET. During it witnesses saw an electric cloud come down in the middle of the street forming a pit and giving off a sulphurous smell. G.A. Sala, the journalist and novelist, had his nose broken in a restaurant in the street during a quarrel over a bottle of wine. On the north side stood Stone's Chop House, the successor of Stone's Hotel which was often patronised by Thackeray. This closed in August 1981.

Panyer Alley *EC4*. The name is perhaps derived from the panyers or bread-baskets which were made here for sale to the bakers of nearby BREAD STREET. A stone relief dated 1688 and re-erected in 1964 depicts a naked baker's boy sitting on a panyer. It commemorates the Panyer Boy, an inn destroyed in the GREAT FIRE. It is let into the wall of a house in Panyer Alley Steps. Beneath it is the inscription

When ye have sought the City round
Yet still this is the highest ground.

In fact the claim is unjustified, as CORNHILL is one foot higher.

Paper Street *Barbican*. Warehouses for the paper trade were built in 1890–1 on the site of Three Tuns Court, Sun Court and several alleys between REDCROSS STREET and WHITECROSS STREET. Paper Street was completely destroyed in the 2nd World War.

Paradise Walk *SW3*. A narrow street between ROYAL HOSPITAL ROAD and DILKE STREET which takes its name from the fine small Georgian houses in Paradise Row which have long since disappeared. The name was strangely incongruous at the beginning of the 20th century as it was then a slum.

The Paragon *and* **Paragon House** *Blackheath, SE3*. When Lady Morden died in 1721 (*see* MORDEN COLLEGE) it was found that the trustees owed her £2,640. After obtaining the necessary authorisation from Parliament, they sold the land south and west of the College, together with Wricklemarsh House, in which Lady Morden had lived, to Sir Gregory Page, one of the richest men in England. He tore down Wricklemarsh House and built a new one, said to be one of the finest in the country. But his great-nephew, to whom his estate passed, did not wish to live there and sold the whole by auction to John Cator of

BECKENHAM. Cator vainly tried to find a use for the house and finally, in 1787, had it demolished. The building materials sold for £14,000 and his original investment of £22,500 certainly paid off as he sold leases on much of the freehold property for speculative building. On the west side he built a detached house, The Paragon. Wealthy merchants were beginning to realise that London was noisy, dirty and extremely unhealthy. BLACKHEATH was easily reached from the city by water and the Heath was beginning to lose some of its sinister reputation. The houses were to be of such dignity as would attract suitable tenants. There were strict conditions in the leases containing a long series of prohibitions against exercising the 'art, mystery or trade' of such varied occupations as schoolmaster or fishmonger. For his architect John Cator chose Michael Searles, who also designed Paragon House and COLONNADE HOUSE. The lovely crescent consisted of 14 semi-detached houses, forming seven blocks linked by single-storey colonnades. Each house contained a basement, ground floor, two upper floors and an attic. On the garden side most of them had bow windows though these did not extend above the ground floor. The leases sold quickly and for the most part to the sort of people for whom John Cator had planned the development. But one of the first occupants was a Miss Eliza Robertson who took possession of No. 3, still unfinished, in 1800. She was a very plausible adventuress and lived with her friend, Miss Charlotte Sharpe. A lesbian attachment was suspected and even referred to from the pulpit of the Congregational Chapel. She managed, somehow, to run up debts within a very short time to the enormous sum of some £15,000, or even more. In October 1801 she removed herself to the FLEET PRISON, where she lived in some comfort, attended by her maid, named, improbably, Frisk, for four years. She wrote a highly unconvincing story of her life and various pamphlets. As she had not been declared bankrupt, she could retain the proceeds of her writing and also sell what remained of her possessions. She died in the Fleet, still in her early thirties, in 1805.

Miss Robertson was, however, an exception. The houses in the Paragon were leased to solid respectable citizens who played no inconsiderable part in the life, not only of the community, but of the London world. Sir John Simon, who was born in No. 10, was the first officer of health for the CITY OF LONDON. Charles Harris, in No. 9, was one of the co-founders of the ROYAL NATIONAL ORTHOPAEDIC HOSPITAL.

It was not until the end of the 1st World War that the Paragon began to deteriorate. During the previous century many of the houses were seriously overcrowded, extra rooms had been built, even on the top of the colonnades, and extra buildings added in the gardens. In spite of the restriction in the leases, the junior department of the BLACKHEATH High School moved into No. 14. Several of the houses were converted into hotels, Paragon House among them, and the district became rather seedy. It was perhaps fortunate that it was badly damaged by bombs during the 2nd World War, as it gave a chance to Col. H. J. Cator, the ground landlord, and the architect, C. Bernard Brown, to restore the buildings to their original beauty.

Paris Garden *Southwark*. Paris Garden Manor, or Parish Garden Manor as it was once called, consisted of 100 acres of marshy riverside land. It was owned by the KNIGHTS TEMPLAR from the 12th century until the time of their suppression when it passed to the Knights Hospitallers. In Henry VIII's reign the 14th-century manor house which had belonged to Robert de Paris was owned for a time by the King's third wife, Jane Seymour, before it was acquired by William Baseley, Bailiff of Southwark, who opened it to the public for bowling and gambling. In the 16th and 17th centuries customers for the bear garden and the theatres landed at Paris Garden Stairs and often stopped for refreshment in Paris Garden. The thickly wooded gardens, unlit at night, were a favourite meeting place of conspirators and secret agents. Lupton, writing in 1632, said, 'This may better bee termed a foule dene then a faire garden . . . . Here come few that either regard their credit or losse of time; the swaggering Roarer, the cunning Cheater, the rotten Bawd and the bloudy Butcher have their rendezvous here.' During the Commonwealth the gardens were used for bleaching cloth and were built over at the end of the 17th century.

Park Crescent *W1*. Originally planned by Nash as a full circus, the main entrance into the new CROWN ESTATE, but only the southern semi-circle was realised. This was begun in 1812 by Charles Mayor who went bankrupt when he had completed just six houses in the south-eastern quadrant. The work was not taken up again till 1818 when three builders, William Richardson, Samuel Baxter and Henry Peto, finished it. Lord Lister, the surgeon, lived at No. 12 from 1877 to 1912 and Joseph Bonaparte stayed for a short while at No. 23. Other residents have included Dame Marie Tempest, the actress, at No. 24 and Sir Charles Wheatstone, the scientist and inventor, at No. 19. After the 2nd World War the Crescent was completely rebuilt with an exact copy of Nash's façade. The six easternmost houses are a students' hostel, and the rest accommodate learned societies and other bodies. The grace, proportion and elegance of Park Crescent make it the loveliest of all the terraces in REGENT'S PARK. The INSTITUTE OF CHARTERED SECRETARIES AND ADMINISTRATORS is at No. 12.

Park Lane *W1*. Extending from MARBLE ARCH to the western end of PICCADILLY, Park Lane was for centuries a narrow road bounded on its west side by a high brick wall enclosing HYDE PARK. When building began on the east side in the mid-18th century a few substantial houses were erected. The most important of these (all now demolished) were Breadalbane House, on the site of the modern GROSVENOR HOUSE, by James Paine for the 9th Baron Petre, 1766–70, and later occupied by the Marquesses of Breadalbane; Somerset House, at the corner with OXFORD STREET, by the master carpenter, John Phillips, for the 2nd Viscount Bateman, 1769–70, later occupied by Warren Hastings in 1789–97 and by successive Dukes of Somerset from 1808 to 1885; and CAMELFORD HOUSE. But elsewhere the first ranges of houses in Park Lane were either set back from the road (as at the present Nos 93–99) or had their entrances away from the park in Norfolk (now DUNRAVEN) STREET or PARK STREET.

Park Lane was not, in fact, particularly sought after until the 1820s, when Decimus Burton built his Ionic screen at the HYDE PARK CORNER entrance to the park, the view of which from Park Lane was improved by the building of new entrance lodges at

Stanhope, Grosvenor and Cumberland Gates and by the replacement of the old brick wall by iron railings. LONDONDERRY HOUSE (demolished in 1964) and APSLEY HOUSE were both reconstructed by Benjamin Dean Wyatt in about 1825–9; Dudley House was rebuilt by William Atkinson in 1827–8; and GROSVENOR HOUSE was enlarged. The old terrace houses were either rebuilt or drastically remodelled, often with the fronts and curved projecting bays then much in vogue. Park Lane thereafter became one of the most fashionable streets in London, all of its residents being rich and many of them titled. Its reputation at this time has been frequently celebrated in the works of Victorian novelists, particularly Thackeray and Trollope.

Today the most notable survivors of this period are Nos 93–99, all rebuilt in 1823–7 except No. 95 which was reconstructed in 1842–4. Benjamin Disraeli lived at No. 93 in 1839–72; Rufus Isaacs, MP (later Viceroy of India and 1st Marquess of Reading), at No. 96 in 1903–10; and Sir Moses Montefiore, stockbroker and philanthropist, at No. 99 in 1826–85. Another survivor is Dudley House (or No. 100 Park Lane), where the Earl of Dudley (whose family was associated with this site for over two centuries) added a splendid ballroom and picture gallery in 1855–8 to designs by S.W. Daukes. (Both these rooms were severely damaged by bombing in 1940, and in 1969–70 the whole house was remodelled by Sir Basil Spence for the Hammersmith group of companies.) But Dorchester House, built in 1851–7 by Lewis Vulliamy for R.S. Holford, with a façade derived from the Villa Farnese in Rome, was demolished in 1929, when the present DORCHESTER HOTEL took its place; GROSVENOR HOUSE was also replaced by a hotel in 1926–30 and BROOK HOUSE of 1867–9, by T.H. Wyatt, survived only until 1933.

In the second half of the 19th century the volume of traffic using Park Lane very greatly increased. After the re-erection of the MARBLE ARCH at the junction of PARK LANE and OXFORD STREET in 1851, a short stretch at the north end of Park Lane was widened. On 23 July 1866 a great demonstration in HYDE PARK in support of the second Reform Bill, then before Parliament, ended in the trampling down of the iron railings almost as far south as STANHOPE GATE, and shortly afterwards this section of the roadway was widened too. In 1870–1 the worst bottleneck, at the south end, was relieved by the opening up of HAMILTON PLACE as an auxiliary traffic outlet to and from PICCADILLY.

In the 20th century all the great houses (except Dudley House) have been demolished, the lesser ones now being used as offices, and in recent years three more hotels have been built near the south end – the LONDON HILTON (1961–3), the LONDONDERRY HOTEL (1964–7), both by Lewis Solomon, Kaye and Partners, and the INN ON THE PARK (1967–70) by Michael Rosenauer. In 1960–3 Park Lane was converted into a dual carriageway by the sacrifice of a broad swathe of HYDE PARK.

Park Lane Hotel *Piccadilly, W1*. Built in 1927 to the designs of Adie and Button. A large pillared portico in front of the hotel overlooks GREEN PARK. There are 325 bedrooms.

Park Mansions Arcade *SW1*. Dates from 1890 when the Park Mansions block was built. It is on the site of the yard of the Marquis of Granby public house (which was on the site of the Paxton's Head). In 1850 there was a plan to build a terminus for the Great Western Railway here, which did not materialise.

Park Place *SW1*. Laid out in the 1680s probably at the instigation of the Duchess of Cleveland (*see* CLEVELAND HOUSE) and her trustees. The Duchess's son, the Duke of Grafton, lived on the site of Nos 8 and 9 in the 1730s. None of the original houses remains. Distinguished occupants of the street have included Thomas Creevey in 1804–9; Frederick John Robinson, later Viscount Goderich and Earl of Ripon, the prime minister, in 1816–17; and Charles Kemble, the

Park Crescent, originally planned by Nash as a full circus, was built in 1812–18. From an engraving after T.H. Shepherd.

583

actor, in 1837–9. PRATT'S CLUB is at No. 14. The Royal Over-Seas League is in Over-Seas House. Part of this is the house, designed by Gibbs and built in 1736, which formerly belonged to Lord North and, later, the Duchess of Rutland.

Park Place *W2.* Some large villas in this area were built as early as the 1820s. Edward Calvert, artist and friend of Samuel Palmer, lived here in 1832–51, and has described Palmer painting the blossoming chestnut trees in St Mary's burial ground.

Park Road *NW1, NW8.* First rated in 1811, the road runs along the boundary of REGENT'S PARK, hence its name. José de San Martin, Argentinian soldier and statesman, stayed briefly at No. 23. On the corner with Ivor Place is the Francis Holland Church of England School, founded in 1879. The present building was designed by H.T. Hare (1915). Beside it is Rudolf Steiner House by Montague Wheeler (1926), with additions of 1932 and 1937.

Park Royal *Middlesex.* Twyford was selected to be the permanent showground for the ROYAL AGRICULTURAL SOCIETY under the fanciful name of Park Royal. The venture was not a success, however, and in 1905 the scheme was abandoned. Instead the Park Royal area proved ideal to meet the demand for extensive munitions factories during the 1st World War, and so what could have been an attractive amenity became an estate which established Park Royal as an industrial area.

Park Square *NW1.* Replaced the northern half of the circus which Nash had planned for this entrance into REGENT'S PARK. The 'square' consists of two terraces facing each other; they were designed by Nash and built by William Mountford Nurse in 1823–5. The middle three houses on the eastern side accommodated the DIORAMA. That early forerunner of the cinema was converted in 1854 into a Baptist chapel, which it remained until 1921. Its future was uncertain in 1982.

Park Street *SE1.* The name commemorates the parklands of the Bishop of Winchester's estate (*see* CLINK STREET). A plaque on Courage's bottling factory marks the approximate site of Shakespeare's GLOBE THEATRE where many of his plays had their first performance. Other nearby ELIZABETHAN PUBLIC THEATRES were the Rose, remembered in Rose Alley, and the Hope, used also for bear-baiting, on the approximate site of the BEAR GARDENS MUSEUM. Courage's Brewery, formerly Barclay Perkins, was owned in the 18th century by Henry Thrale, husband of Mrs Thrale, friend of Dr Johnson, who often visited them at their home in Park Street (*see* BREWERIES).

Park Street *W1.* Built between the 1720s and 70s, it extends from OXFORD STREET to SOUTH STREET and crosses several of the principal streets on the GROSVENOR ESTATE of which it forms part. Many of the original houses in Park Street were built on the shallow return frontages of plots in these greater streets, and they were therefore generally small, their occupants often being tradesmen. The surviving Nos 70–78 (even) are cases in point. But near the southern end of the west side, on the sites now occupied by Fountain House and Aldford House, PARK LANE, there were

larger houses with gardens overlooking HYDE PARK. At the north end, also on the west side near the corner with OXFORD STREET, formerly stood the house in which Mrs Fitzherbert married the Prince of Wales (later George IV) in 1785. Between the 1890s and the 1930s there was much rebuilding in Park Street, large private houses being at first the order of the day, and latterly blocks of flats. The former include Nos 37–43 (odd) by W.D. Caröe (1908–11), Nos 91–103a (odd), by Edward Wimperis and W.B. Simpson (1913–25), and the stone-fronted Nos 44–50 (even), by Detmar Blow and Fernand Billerey (1911–12), which originally overlooked the garden of old GROSVENOR HOUSE but which are now confronted by the great cliffs of the back of the new GROSVENOR HOUSE. Here, and further south on the west side, the scale of the rebuildings of the 1920s and 1930s in PARK LANE has given this part of Park Street a somewhat depressing aspect. Notable inhabitants include Sir Humphrey Davy, the scientist, in 1825–29; John Ruskin and his wife, in 1848–51; Thomas Hughes, author of *Tom Brown's Schooldays*, in 1861–85 (successively in two different houses); and George Otto Trevelyan, the statesman and historian, in 1870–2.

Park Villages East *and* **West** *NW1.* Lying in the north-eastern corner of the CROWN ESTATE, outside the boundary proper of REGENT'S PARK, this land was the hardest of all to place with a developer until Nash took up all the leases himself and began to build pretty but sophisticated cottages, reminiscent of those that he had planned for Blaise Hamlet in Gloucestershire many years before. James Pennethorne, Nash's pupil, planned Nos 1–7 Park Village West. Edmund Kean, the actor, lived in Bute Cottage, Dr James Johnson, physician to William IV, occupied 12 Park Village West; and James Wyld, the geographer, lived at No. 8. Half of Park Village East was obliterated when the Euston Railway cutting was enlarged in 1906, but the remaining houses in both halves have been restored and are now cherished.

Parkhill Road *NW3.* It takes its name from St John's Park over which the road was built. Piet Mondrian, the painter, had a studio at No. 60 in 1938–40. Barbara Hepworth, whose studio, like those of Ben Nicholson, Walter Gropius and Henry Moore, was nearby, wrote that Mondrian made his studio 'as exciting as the one in Montparnasse where he lived for so many years'.

Parkside *W1.* The first houses on the north side of KNIGHTSBRIDGE, west from HYDE PARK CORNER, were known as Parkside. They appear to have been built around 1600 and to have stretched as far west as Prospect Place. They were mostly small, narrow-fronted, two-storey buildings on either side of the ancient bridge with an old chapel in the centre of the row. The chapel, later known as Trinity Chapel, dated from the 14th century and had been rebuilt four times. It was finally demolished in 1904 and its site sold for £14,300. The east extension of the French Embassy was built over it. Three inns were also in the row, the Queen's Head, the White Hart, and the Fox. In 1796 Thomas Goding built the Cannon Brewery at the west end, extending it in 1830 as far as Prospect Place. A considerable number of small houses were demolished on each occasion. The brewery, whose black smoke gave offence to the Duke of Wellington, was demolished in 1842 for the creation of ALBERT GATE. Most of the other houses disappeared in 1908 when the Edwardian block of flats, also called Parkside (by Hart and Green), was built. The last houses at the east end, all refaced, survived until the underpass was built in the 1960s.

Parliament *see* PALACE OF WESTMINSTER.

Parliament Hill *N5, NW5.* Acquired for the public in 1887 at a cost of more than £300,000. It affords fine views of London and both HIGHGATE and HAMPSTEAD. There are several explanations of its name including the suggestion that it was from here that the GUNPOWDER PLOTTERS were to watch the destruction of Parliament in 1605. It was also called Traitors' Hill. Keats, Shelley, Leigh Hunt and Coleridge frequented the hill and before them Addison, Steele and Pope. The tumulus at the northern side was excavated but with little result. However, treasure-trove comprising several silver articles was later discovered by a child playing there in 1892. There are a number of small lakes which are popular for fishing, bathing, model yacht sailing, and skating in the winter. Kite flying is also popular. There are 270 acres.

Parliament Square *SW1.* Laid out by Sir Charles Barry in 1868 as a suitable approach to his Houses of Parliament, it resulted in the clearance of much slum property in the area. Always a busy traffic roundabout, particularly since its reconstruction in the 1940s by G.S. Wornum, it has long and unsuitably been a favourite site for statues of statesmen and soldiers. Commemorated are Lords Derby and Palmerston, Canning, Peel and Disraeli, Field-Marshal Smuts, Winston Churchill and Abraham Lincoln (*see* STATUES).

Parliament Street *SW1.* The original narrow way from CHARING CROSS to WESTMINSTER ran along the line of the western edge of the present WHITEHALL and Parliament Street. When the court abandoned WHITEHALL PALACE after the fire of 1698, it became possible in 1723–5 to use part of the Privy Garden to widen WHITEHALL southwards to the site of the present CENOTAPH. As part of the general approach improvements to the new WESTMINSTER BRIDGE the road was further extended in 1741–50 by making the new Parliament Street run southwards across the small courts and alleys that had replaced the Bowling Green of the Palace. The street first appears in the rate books in 1750. Nos 43 and 44 are original houses of about 1753. The street was widened when the government offices were built in it in the 19th-century and, at 130 ft, it is still the widest street in London. Charles James Fox lived for a time in a house on the site of No. 52. In 1820–56 the *Gentleman's Magazine* was published at No. 25, the office of John Nichols. In 1833–5 Isambard Kingdom Brunel had an office at No. 53 which was replaced by the present building in 1896. His friend Sir George Burke occupied chambers on the other side of the street. Burke recorded, 'To facilitate our intercourse it occured to Brunel to carry a string across Parliament Street from his chambers to mine, to be there connected with a bell, by which he could either call me to the window to receive his telegraphic signals, or more frequently to wake me up in the morning when we had occasion to go into the country together, and great was the astonishment of the neighbours at the device, the object of which they were unable to comprehend. On 26 January 1843 a would-be assassin of the Prime Minister, Sir Robert Peel, shot his private secretary, Drummond. The Red Lion public house at No. 48 is a mid-19th-century replacement of an earlier tavern, perhaps the one where Dickens, in an experience he ascribed to David Copperfield, called for 'a glass of Genuine Stunning Ale' and was given it with a kiss. No. 47, the former Whitehall Club, designed by C.O. Parnell, was built in 1865–6. The Treasury, designed by William Kent, Sir John Soane and Sir Charles Barry, was finally completed in 1845; the GOVERNMENT OFFICES next to it were designed by Sir George Gilbert Scott (1868–73), and those further north by J.M. Brydon (1898–1900).

Parsons Green *Fulham, SW6.* Lies to the north of the NEW KING'S ROAD. It gets its name from the parsonage or rectory, first mentioned in 1391, which stood on its western side and which was demolished in 1882. St. Dionis's Church, designed by Ewan Christian in Gothic style, was built on its site two years later with funds obtained from the sale of ST DIONIS'S BACK-CHURCH. Parsons Green was considered to be the aristocratic part of FULHAM. Bowack, in 1705, said that it was inhabited 'mostly by Gentry and Persons of Quality' who reside in 'several very handsome Houses all standing very airy upon a dry, clean Green'. Of these notable houses only three remain: Park House (now Henniker House), Elm House and Belfield House, which house Lady Margaret School. Elm House, while it was the property of Sir John Vaughan, was for six weeks the refuge of the disgraced Sir Francis Bacon. Later it was the home of Mrs Jordan, the mistress of the Duke of Clarence, later William IV. Hollybush House (later East End House) at the south-east corner was an Elizabethan house with 16 acres of gardens, for many years the property of the Child family of bankers and later the home of Mrs Fitzherbert, wife of the Prince Regent. It was demolished in 1884. Nos 17 to 41, flats, now mark its site. Samuel Richardson lived in a villa on the south side from 1756 until his death in 1761. The villa was demolished and Aragon House and Gosford Lodge, NEW KING'S ROAD were built on its site.

At its south-east corner Parsons Green had a large pond of which mention was made in 1559. It was filled in during drainage work in the late 19th century. From the reign of William III, until it was suppressed by the magistrates in 1823, an annual pleasure fair was held on the Green in August.

Passmore Edwards Museum *Romford Road, Stratford, E15.* The foundation stone of the building was laid in 1898 by J. Passmore Edwards who contributed half the construction cost of £6,000. The museum was opened in 1900 by the Countess of Warwick. It is concerned with the heritage of the geographical County of Essex, especially that area now administered by the five Greater London Boroughs north of the THAMES and east of the LEA, in the fields of archaeology and local history, biology and geology. The permanent displays reflect these interests. The Governors of the museum are developing the large churchyard of ST MARY MAGDALENE, EAST HAM as a nature reserve.

Patent Office *25 Southampton Buildings, WC2.* Applications made for patents are filed here, as well as applications for the registration of trade marks and of designs having an industrial application. The number of applications filed in 1980 were: patents 41,640, trade marks 20,102, designs 5,329.

Until the mid-19th century the patent system was directed by lawyers who advised the Crown whether patents should be granted. With the technological developments of the Industrial Revolution the system became overburdened and there was considerable pressure from industrialists for patent reform, leading to the Patent Law Amendment Act of 1852, which set up the Patent Office. It was housed in a Master in Chancery's office in Southampton Buildings, off CHANCERY LANE. The accommodation was expected to be temporary but the intention to build a new patent office was never carried out, though the office was reconstructed *in situ* at the end of the 19th century and extended across a site that previously formed a part of STAPLE INN. The publishing section is now at ST MARY CRAY in Kent, and is probably the largest technical publishing house in the country with 40,000–50,000 specifications and abstracts produced annually, as well as weekly Official Journals providing up-to-date patent, trade mark and registered design information.

Bennet Woodcroft, an inventor himself, has been called the Father of the Patent Office. He was appointed Superintendent of the Specifications on the establishment of the office and a few years later also became Clerk to the Commissioners of Patents and so Head of the Office. The Trade Marks Registry was set up in 1875, and the first Registrar, Reader Lack, succeeded Woodcroft when the latter retired in 1876. The poet A. E. Housman worked at the Trade Marks Registry from 1882 to 1892.

The Patents, Designs and Trade Marks Act of 1883 transferred responsibility for the Office from 'Commissioners of Patents' to the Board of Trade as from January 1884. Under this Act the head of the Office was styled Comptroller General of Patents, Designs and Trademarks, and for the first time Examiners of Patents were appointed.

Bennet Woodcroft had for a short while been Professor of Machinery at UNIVERSITY COLLEGE and had a fine collection of models. He had also been involved in setting up the GREAT EXHIBITION in 1851, when he had come into contact with the Prince Consort, who was very keen to have a Museum of Industry and Library associated with the Patent Office. The Patent Office Museum was opened at SOUTH KENSINGTON in 1857 and soon included the locomotives *Rocket, Sanspareil* and *Puffing Billy*, some of the earliest engines of James Watt, the second oldest clock in the country, the first reaping machine and some of the earliest telegraph apparatus. These and many other older exhibits are now to be found in the SCIENCE MUSEUM, with which the collection was later incorporated.

Patent Office Library *see* SCIENCE REFERENCE LIBRARY.

Paternoster Row *EC4*. 'So called,' wrote Stow in 1598, 'because of stationers or text writers that dwelt there who wrote and sold all sorts of books then in use.... There dwelt also turners of beads and they were called Pater Noster makers.' The name may also

be derived from the *paternoster* recited here by the medieval clergy of ST PAUL'S during their procession round the precincts, as with AVE MARIA LANE and Amen Corner. Mercers, silkmen and lacemen also lived here before the GREAT FIRE, according to Strype, 'and their shops were so resorted unto by the nobility and gentry in their coaches that oft times the street was so stop'd up that there was no passage for foot passengers.' The locality was additionally celebrated in the 16th-century for its taverns, particularly for the Castle which was kept by the comedian, Richard Tarlton. The Chapter Coffee House, later the Old Chapter tavern, was also there. The murder of Sir Thomas Overbury was planned by Lord Rochester (later the Earl of Somerset) and the Countess of Essex in a house in the street belonging to Mrs Anne Turner, a doctor's venerable widow who was a dressmaker and fortune-teller, procuress and apothecary and dealt in abortion, yellow starch, love-philtres and poison. From after the GREAT FIRE, when the mercers moved to COVENT GARDEN, Paternoster Row was a centre of bookselling and publishing. In 1719, at the sign of the Ship, William Taylor published *Robinson Crusoe*. In 1724 Taylor's business was purchased by Thomas Longman who founded the firm that still bears his family's name. The street was devastated in the 2nd World War when about 6 million books were destroyed. The northern end was rebuilt as PATERNOSTER SQUARE.

Paternoster Square *EC4*. For the derivation of its name *see* PATERNOSTER ROW. From the 17th century until 1889 it was the site of the Newgate Meat Market where 600 sheep and 50 bullocks were slaughtered daily. The market was demolished when the Central Meat Market at Smithfield was established. After the devastation of the 2nd World War it was rebuilt as a pedestrian precinct with shops and office blocks, at a cost of £9,000,000. The sculpture, *Paternoster – Shepherd and Sheep*, fibre glass with bronze finish, is by Elizabeth Frink (1975).

Pattenmakers' Company *see* CITY LIVERY COMPANIES.

Paul Pindar's House *Bishopsgate*. Sir Paul Pindar was sent to London from Northamptonshire as a boy and apprenticed to a merchant who employed him as his factor in Italy where he acquired a very plentiful estate. He was later British Ambassador in Turkey. On his return to London in the 1620s he built this fine mansion. In the 18th century the house became a tavern, Sir Paul Pindar's Head. It was demolished in 1890 by the Great Eastern Railway. The elaborately carved oak frontage may still be seen in the VICTORIA AND ALBERT MUSEUM.

Paul's Chain A street on the south side of ST PAUL'S CHURCHYARD leading to CARTER LANE, so called because of the chain which was hung across it during the time of services in ST PAUL'S CATHEDRAL.

Paul's Cross *see* ST PAUL'S CATHEDRAL.

Paultons Square *SW3*. Pleasant Georgian square built in the 1830s on a market garden and, like Paultons Steet, named after Paultons, Hampshire, the country seat of George Stanley, Sir Hans Sloane's son-in-law (*see* SLOANE ESTATE).

The Bishopsgate house of Sir Paul Pindar, merchant and diplomat, after it had become a tavern in the 18th century.

The Pavilion *Chelsea.* A large mansion of the 1790s designed by Henry Holland and intended as an advertisement for his architectural skills as well as a private residence for himself. It stood round three sides of a courtyard which was open to the north. The façade was decorated with Doric columns. The principal rooms on the ground floor were all intercommunicating and were built round an octagonal vestibule. The grounds of 21 acres were landscaped by Holland's father-in-law, 'Capability' Brown. They contained a serpentine lake and a Gothic ice-house built with stones from Cardinal Wolsey's palace at Esher. Holland called his house Sloane Place but it was generally known as The Pavilion after the Prince Regent's house at Brighton which Holland had designed. It was later divided into three and part of its land was leased to PRINCE'S CLUB. After its demolition PONT STREET and CADOGAN SQUARE were built over the site. It is commemorated by PAVILION ROAD.

Pavilion Road *SW1.* Part of the original HANS TOWN, it was created by Henry Holland in the 1780s as a service road to SLOANE STREET and then known as New Street. Very few of the occupants of SLOANE STREET in the early days were of the status to afford carriages so that by 1800 it was still largely a country lane running behind the gardens of SLOANE STREET and the large garden of Henry Holland's house, called originally Sloane Place, but always known as THE PAVILION. The street was only 20 ft wide and gradually became built up as the houses in SLOANE STREET became grander and were almost all refronted. No. 30 is a fascinating house built on the site of the Ebenezer Chapel and originally the power station of the local electricity company in the 1890s. It then became a warehouse, and eventually the interior was most skilfully converted by Searcy's, the caterers, in 1963. John Searcy, born in 1813, was the Duke of Northumberland's pastry cook and founded the firm in 1870. The five-sided car park was originally 'Wonder-What Place', then Pentagon Place, then a warehouse, until bought by HARROD's and connected to the store by a tunnel.

Paviors' Company *see* CITY LIVERY COMPANIES.

Paymaster General's Office *Whitehall, SW1.* Built in 1732–3 by John Lane, it is now the Parliamentary Counsel Office.

Peabody Buildings Austere housing blocks for 'the artisan and labouring poor of London' built from the Trust set up by the American philanthropist, George Peabody. Born in 1795 in Massachusetts, he spent most of his later life in London. In March 1862 he gave £150,000, later raised to £500,000, to endow a fund 'to ameliorate the condition of the poor and needy of this great metropolis and to promote their comfort and happiness.' This became known as the Peabody Donation Fund. It was not restricted to the provision of housing but the Trustees decided that a portion of the Trust should be applied to the provision of 'cheap, cleanly, well-drained and healthful dwellings for the poor'.

The first development in Commercial Street, SPITALFIELDS, was designed by H.A. Darbishire in 1862–4 and set the pattern for future blocks set up all over London. Nikolaus Pevsner described the block at Wild Street as 'familiar but nonetheless detestable'. Whatever the architectural quality of its buildings the Trust had, however, by 1890 provided more than 5,000 dwellings for the poor of London. After the establishment of local authorities with housing powers the Trust has complemented their services and since the 1974 Housing Act it has been agreed that the Fund should gradually revert to its original foundations as a general charity. The Peabody Housing Association deals with new development and the Peabody Donation Fund retains responsibility for existing estates.

There is a seated statue of George Peabody by his compatriot William Wetmore Story behind the ROYAL EXCHANGE (*see* STATUES).

Pearly Kings and Queens So called from their clothes which are studded with countless pearl buttons. The 'aristocracy' of the costermongers, they were originally elected by them to safeguard their rights from competitors and roughs. They maintain the Victorian costermongers' dressy traditions, but now devote their time to charitable activities. The Pearly Kings' and Queens' Association was founded in 1911.

Peasants' Revolt In the decade preceding the Peasants' Revolt, the English monarchy's unsuccessful prosecution of war against the French substantially increased the burden of taxation placed on the English people. The English population had already been weakened by the effects of the BLACK DEATH and subsequent plagues and famines. By 1381, confidence in the government was low, and the immensely powerful John of Gaunt, Duke of Lancaster, was particularly unpopular.

The most important outbreaks of revolt in 1381 occurred during May and early June in the eastern counties, from Norfolk south to Kent. These usually began with protests against the unpopular poll-tax and its bitterly resented, often corrupt, collectors. Politically most significant were the rebels of Kent and Essex. Their leaders, working possibly in concert, decided in favour of a march on London, where anti-government opinion was strong among the poorer classes and some City officials. The Kentish rebels set off for London after plundering Rochester and Canterbury. Their leader was Wat Tyler. It is uncertain whether he was originally from Essex or Kent, but he is thought to have been an ex-soldier. He maintained order among the rebels with the help of John Ball, a vagrant priest who had been persecuted for his egalitarian principles summarised in the contemporary rhyme which he made famous:

> When Adam dalf, and Eve span,
> Wo was thanne a gentilman?

By 12 June both groups had arrived in London. Tyler led the Kentish contingent to BLACKHEATH to await a meeting with the King, Richard II, while the Essex men camped at MILE END in the fields beyond ALD-GATE. Either panic, or the knowledge of widespread sympathy for the rebels among the London lower classes, led to a failure by the authorities to take adequate defensive action. The 14-year-old Richard II, from his refuge in the TOWER OF LONDON, courageously decided to attempt personal, conciliatory negotiations with the rebels. On 12 June, however, the size and passion of the crowds prevented him from landing at GREENWICH in the Royal Barge.

Wat Tyler, frustrated in his desire to speak to Richard, and aware that his men were running short of supplies, led them to SOUTHWARK. Here they opened the MARSHALSEA PRISON and destroyed one of the Marshal's houses. They proceeded to LAMBETH where they burnt Chancery records stored in the Archbishop's Manor there. Aided by London mobs, they crossed LONDON BRIDGE and headed west towards FLEET STREET. They then opened FLEET PRISON, and at NEW TEMPLE destroyed the rolls of the lawyers. The legal profession was generally hated because of its connection with John of Gaunt and the Treasurer, Hales. Meanwhile, the Londoners had begun an assault on Gaunt's luxurious SAVOY PALACE, where Kentish rebels joined in the destruction. Furnishings, jewels, clothes and plate were burnt or thrown in the THAMES. Tyler, however, insisted that there should be no looting. Justice, not profit, was declared to be the rebels' aim. All over London lawyers and other unpopular persons were summarily beheaded, while the hospital of the KNIGHTS HOSPITALLERS burned for several days.

Richard saw the flames rise from the TOWER which itself was in a state of near siege. But his policy continued to favour the dispersal of rebels by concession, rather than the use of force. On Friday 14 June, while one band of rebels, commanded by a man named Jack Straw, was attacking the Treasurer's house at HIGHBURY, King Richard, accompanied by a group of courtiers, had an arranged meeting with a body of Essex rebels at MILE END. He granted their requests for the abolition of feudal services; the right to rent land at 4d an acre; and an end to restrictions on the sale of land. He also promised an amnesty for all rebels and due punishment for proven traitors. Charters confirming these concessions were drawn up and many of the Essex camp began to disperse. But Richard's troubles were not over, for many of the Kentishmen, including their leader, Tyler, remained. The beheading, by the rebels, of Sudbury, Archbishop of Canterbury, and Hales, the Treasurer, spoke all too clearly of their determination to root out their enemies

themselves. Anarchy still ruled in London and bloodshed was increasing. Richard bravely resumed negotiations next day at SMITHFIELD with Wat Tyler personally. Tyler increased the rebels' demands with a disrespectful confidence, an attitude which provoked the Mayor, William Walworth, to stab him, pulling him from his horse to the ground where another of the King's party, Standish, dealt him a final blow. Richard, with admirable presence of mind for his age, offered himself as captain to the wavering, confused rebels who remained, and succeeded in leading them north towards the fields of CLERKENWELL. The Mayor, Walworth, was able to bring a body of loyal citizens to the King, and the rebels dispersed without bloodshed.

Risings in Norfolk, Suffolk, Cambridgeshire and Hertfordshire had followed the early successes of the rebels in London. By the end of June, however, the revolt had been overcome and many of its local leaders killed. But it had succeeded in ending the poll-tax, and the memory of peasants wreaking havoc in the streets of London endured in the minds of England's rulers for many years to come.

Peck A river which rose in PECKHAM RYE flowing through Peckham Park and joining the Earl's Sluice to enter the THAMES at DEPTFORD. The main part was enclosed as the Earl Main Sewer in 1820–3 and the lower portion in 1831. Its name derives from the 'peak' known today as TELEGRAPH HILL.

Peckham *SE15*. Situated between ROTHERHITHE in the north and FOREST HILL in the south. It is mentioned in *Domesday Book* where it is called Pecheha. The name is Anglo-Saxon and means 'village among the hills', referring to the nearby hills of HONOR OAK, NUNHEAD and Plow Garlick. During the reign of Henry I, Peckham belonged to the King who gave it to his illegitimate son Robert, 1st Earl of Gloucester, a connection remembered in the name of Gloucester Grove.

Until the 19th century, Peckham was a rural area of market gardens and pasture. Cattle drovers used the village as a stopping place before going on to the markets of London. Their herds were put out to graze whilst they themselves took refreshment in the inns. Those times are recalled by the names of the public houses along the High Street, the Red Cow (rebuilt about 1962), the Red Bull (a late 19th-century building replacing an earlier tavern of the same name), and the Kentish Drovers (closed in 1954 and now a shop).

Several grand houses were built and occupied by wealthy families. In the 17th century, Sir Thomas Bond, the builder of BOND STREET, erected a fine mansion on the site of the old Manor House. Nearby was Marlborough House, the residence of the Marlboroughs and possibly at one time of the 1st Duke. The house, which became a 'casual' workhouse of the CITY OF LONDON, was demolished in about 1860. Peckham House, the former mansion of the Spitta family which later became a lunatic asylum, was demolished as recently as 1954.

Peckham gained a reputation for education. Oliver Goldsmith taught at Dr Milner's Academy and the poet Robert Browning attended the Revd Thomas Ready's establishment in the High Street. St Mary's College once stood in Hanover Park and at Peckham Rye there was Manilla College. Peckham was also a centre for nonconformist religion. William Penn is said to have stayed at a house in Meeting House Lane (where a Puritan meeting place existed in 1658) before his imprisonment in the TOWER. The house was destroyed during the 2nd World War. John Wesley was also a frequent visitor to Peckham and is known to have preached to the local Methodists.

Dr Collyer, a Congregationalist, founded the Hanover Chapel in 1816. The Dukes of Kent and Sussex were regular worshippers there. The building, at the corner of Rye Lane, is now used as a shoe shop. The Society of Friends' Meeting House in Highshore Road was built in 1826. Elizabeth Taylor of Peckham Rye married George Cadbury, the head of the chocolate firm, there. The restored building is now a postman's office.

The canal was the first major development in the area and was to transform the village into a town. The GRAND SURREY CANAL Company was formed in 1801 and work started on the first stretch from ROTHERHITHE to the OLD KENT ROAD. The Peckham arm was cut in 1826 through the grounds of Peckham Manor. Sir Thomas Bond's mansion was demolished in 1797 in anticipation of the Metropolitan developments. The notorious fair which had been an annual event for centuries, was suppressed with the coming of the canal.

By 1842, a number of houses had appeared in Hill Street, their gardens leading down to the canal towpath. The South Metropolitan Gas Company established its business on the bank of the canal near the OLD KENT ROAD. Apart from these developments the district was still largely rural and the canal was used to transport local market garden produce. In the southern part of Peckham known as NUNHEAD, once a popular resort of 'smoke dried London artisans' who came to refresh themselves at the Nun's Head Tavern and tea gardens, the private 54-acre NUNHEAD CEMETERY had been laid out and consecrated in 1840.

Tommy Tilling started his omnibus service from the Adam and Eve to the West End in 1851 and the railways came to Peckham in 1862. Stations were built by the London, Brighton and South Coast Railway at Rye Lane and Queen's Road. The London, Chatham and Dover Railway opened its station at NUNHEAD in 1872. With the railways came the speculative builders and soon the remaining fields and market gardens were built over. PECKHAM RYE COMMON was purchased by the vestry in 1868 to save it from the developers. Homestall Farm was acquired for the public in 1890 at a cost of £51,000 and is now Peckham Rye Park.

Since 1960, most of the Victorian terraces of north Peckham have disappeared, replaced by massive council estates. The canal was drained in 1971 and is now a park. NUNHEAD, too, has been transformed by recent redevelopment, yet here and there remnants of the old village can be seen including No. 4 Queen's Road, built about 1700, and Peckham's oldest building, No. 2 Woods Road, built about 1690.

Peckham Road *SE5, SE15.* Southwark Town Hall was built in 1933. Other departments occupy Georgian houses adjoining and across the road, where the gardens form a public park. The SOUTH LONDON ART GALLERY, built in 1891, presents varied loan exhibitions and has permanent collections of Victorian and later paintings, original prints and local topography. The CAMBERWELL SCHOOL OF ART opened in 1898. The continuation of Peckham Road is Camberwell Church Street. ST GILES, the parish

church of CAMBERWELL, was rebuilt in 1844 by George Gilbert Scott.

Peckham Rye Common *SE15.* About 64 acres, opened in 1894 on the site of the ancient common. The local inhabitants had always maintained their rights, even against 32 vans of Wombwell's Wild Beast Show in 1864. The park now offers various sporting facilities. The Common adjoins Peckham Rye Park, SE22, which extends to 49 acres; 19th-century houses overlook the Rye. Elizabeth Cadbury, the Quaker and wife of George Cadbury, the chocolate manufacturer, lived here as a girl. William Blake as a child saw a vision of angels in an oak tree on Peckham Rye.

Peckham Rye in 1858, before its ancient common became a public park.

Peel Street *W8.* Built in 1824 and named after Sir Robert Peel who was then Home Secretary. Sir William Russell Flint, the artist, lived at No. 80 in 1925–9.

Peerless Pool *Finsbury.* In 1743 a swimming-bath was formed by a London jeweller named William Kemp from a natural pond caused by an overflowing spring. It had originally been known as 'Perillous Pond because divers youths by swimming therein have been drowned'. Beside it, Kemp built a large fish pond and stocked it with carp and tench, and opened both to subscribers for an annual payment of one guinea or to occasional visitors for 2s. In winter the ponds were used for skating. In about 1805 Joseph Watts acquired the lease, drained the fish pond and built Baldwin Street on part of the site. In 1826 William Hone found little change had been made: 'Trees enough remain to shade the visitor from the heat of the sun while on the brink. On a summer evening it is amusing to survey the conduct of the bathers; some boldly dive, others timorous stand and then descend step by step, unwilling and slow; choice swimmers attract attention by divings and somersets, and the whole sheet of water sometimes rings with merriment. Every fine Thursday and Saturday afternoon in the summer columns of bluecoat boys, more than three score in each, headed by their respective beadles, arrive and some half strip themselves ere they reach their destination. The rapid plunges they make into the Pool and their hilarity in the bath testify their enjoyment of the tepid fluid.' In about 1850 the pool was closed and soon afterwards built over. Peerless Street marks the northern boundary, Bath Street the western one.

Pelham Crescent *SW7*. Elegant stuccoed houses built by George Basevi in 1827–30 on the SMITH'S CHARITY ESTATE and named after Henry Thomas Pelham, Earl of Chichester, a former trustee. Nigel Playfair, the actor-manager lived at No. 26 in 1910–22.

Pemberton Row *EC4*. Formerly known as Three Leg Alley, it was renamed after Sir James Pemberton, Lord Mayor and a member of the GOLDSMITHS' COMPANY which owns much of the land in the area. Thomas Flaxman, the poet and miniature painter, lived here.

Pembridge Square *W8*. Built in the middle of the 19th century on land belonging to W.K. Jenkins who came from Herefordshire and used many names from that county and from Wales in his developments (Chepstow, Denbigh and Ledbury, as well as Pembridge). Field-Marshal Burgoyne lived at No. 5 in 1871.

Pembridge Villas *W11*. On part of the LADBROKE ESTATE developed by W.K. Jenkins, a Herefordshire landowner, building began in 1845. Its most famous resident was probably the artist, William Powell Frith, who occupied No. 7 in 1852–88.

Pembroke Lodge *Richmond Park, Surrey*. By 1754 there was a small house in RICHMOND PARK called the Molecatcher's after the humble occupation of its resident. In 1780 George III granted it to his friend, the Countess of Pembroke, who lived here until her death 50 years later; she added four rooms and gave her name posthumously to the house. Elizabeth, Countess of Errol, daughter of the Duke of Clarence and Mrs Jordan, lived here until 1847 when Queen Victoria granted it to her new Prime Minister, Lord John Russell – as a younger son of the Duke of Bedford he was otherwise unprovided for. Here he brought up his family and transacted much of his business as Prime Minister or Foreign Secretary, since he disliked the London social life. Cabinet meetings were held here; important Bills prepared; and ambassadors and heads of state received as well as workers' delegations or groups of children from the school Russell founded in Petersham Park in 1849. Most of the famous writers and politicians of his day were guests. When his heir, Lord Amberley, and his wife died in 1876, the three-year-old Bertrand Russell came to Pembroke Lodge where he was brought up until he went to Cambridge. When he revisited the place in 1953 he was saddened to see that his old home had become a public restaurant which it still is.

The house itself has no architectural pretensions – each generation added another two-storey wing with no attempt at unity – except that the whole rear front commands one of the finest views in the country. The gardens extend into the Park at either side and along the ridge where the New Terrace created by William IV in 1832 links the house to the King's Standing or Henry VIII's Mound from where it is possible to see ST PAUL'S CATHEDRAL on one side and Windsor Castle on the other.

Penge *Kent*. Lies to the west of BECKENHAM. A detached hamlet of BATTERSEA parish, it was recorded in *Domesday Book* as 'a wood for fifty hogs pannage'. The name probably means 'place at the end of the wood'. It remained a small hamlet until the second quarter of the 19th century. In 1839, Penge and Anerley stations on the South Eastern Railway were opened. Much of the old Anerley Station remains today. This brought the district within very easy reach of London, and it became a fashionable suburb by the middle of the century, especially after the CRYSTAL PALACE was re-erected here.

About 1840, Queen Adelaide's Cottages were built in St John's Road, being paid for by the Queen in memory of her husband, William IV. They were to be homes for twelve widows of naval officers. The Watermen's Almshouses were built in the same period, Queen Adelaide giving 100 guineas to this project. These housed 60 former THAMES watermen or lightermen or their widows. The Almshouses have been converted in recent years by the GREATER LONDON COUNCIL into cottages as part of a complex, and the naval cottages, too, were in 1982 in process of conversion to homes for the GREATER LONDON COUNCIL.

Penge's popularity as a fashionable place to live declined after a notorious murder case in 1877, when Harriet Staunton died of starvation at a house in Forbes Road. The name of the road was changed, but the stigma remained. Building development covered almost all the district by the end of the 19th-century, so that now it looks much older than the rest of BROMLEY Borough. The principal open spaces remaining are Betts Park, which contains the last remaining section of the old London to Croydon canal, and the CRYSTAL PALACE grounds.

Pennyfields–Limehouse Causeway *E14*. These two streets were the centre of the Chinese community that settled in LIMEHOUSE towards the end of the 19th century. The community was originally made up of seamen who had been employed by shipping lines using the nearby WEST INDIA DOCKS, but later other Chinese moved there. Few Chinese remain today, and the houses in both streets have been replaced by flats.

Pentonville *N1*. One of London's earliest planned suburbs, began to be laid out in 1773 on the rural estate of Henry Penton, MP for Winchester. The ground, adjoining the New Road (here renamed Pentonville Road in 1857), was separated from London by open land of the NEW RIVER COMPANY. Penton's estate originated as three fields of 66 acres between the north part of St John Street and the ANGEL belonging to the PRIORY OF ST JOHN and became known as Commandry Mantels after a later owner, Geoffrey de Mandeville. It was fertile, well endowed with springs (*see* WHITE CONDUIT). In his *Herball* of 1597 the botanist, John Gerard, records, among numerous plants found here, the orchid by 'a bouling place under a few old shrubby okes', and saxifrage 'in a great fielde ... called the Mantels'.

Pentonville as planned covered 134 acres, laid out on a rough grid system extending three quarters of a mile up the New Road but barely 300 yards in depth across the fields on Islington Hill. The first street completed (1773), appropriately named Penton Street and leading to Brunswick Place in front of White Conduit House, was the fashionable hub of the area – 'the Regent's Park of the City Road'. Many vacant sites still remained in 1810 and some streets were not built up until the 1840s.

The London Gymnastic Society give a display at their open-air gymnasium at Pentonville in 1826. From a drawing by G. Tytler.

In 1777 Penton secured a clause in an Act empowering the building of a church, but difficulties over responsibility for the stipend caused long delays, and the church, half-way up the hill, was begun only in 1787. Its architect, Aaron Hurst, also designed some adjoining houses.

At first CLERKENWELL parish refused responsibility for the church, which thus functioned independently. However, when the parish trustees were embarrassed for funds to rebuild Clerkenwell's now ruinous ST JAMES'S (1788), Pentonville parishioners negotiated purchase of their own church in exchange for a loan to the building fund. ST JAMES'S PENTONVILLE thenceforward became a chapel of ease for CLERKENWELL.

The purchase included the church's ground-lease, granted by Penton to three prominent residents typical of the prosperous CITY tradesmen and craftsmen who settled here. One of these was Alexander Cumming, an ingenious Scot employed in the 1750s by the 3rd Duke of Argyll as clock-maker and organ-builder at Inveraray, who later used his skills for Argyll's nephew, Lord Bute, George III's Prime Minister. Cumming, who made a barometric clock now in BUCKINGHAM PALACE, established a flourishing business in the STRAND, and he and his brother John eventually retired to live as gentlemen in Pentonville, where they speculated in building plots and generally promoted the area.

John Cumming built a large mansion named after himself at 166 PENTONVILLE ROAD, between Cumming and Southampton (now Affleck) Streets. In 1807, a year after his death, it was acquired for the London Female Penitentiary, where sincerely repentant 'fallen women' were rehabilitated. Additions to the house in 1811–12 extended its capacity from 35 inmates to 100. It removed in 1884 to STOKE NEWINGTON.

Of Cumming House nothing survives, and very little of old Pentonville either. Chapel Market, built in 1790 as a residential street but from the mid-19th century gradually taken over as a market and shops, contains several good original buildings, and between Penton Street and the ANGEL Pentonville Road has battered fragments of early 19th-century terraces. The latter include the former Claremont Chapel, opened in 1819 for Congregational Dissenters and altered in 1840 and 1860. At No. 36 was the manufactory of patented gadgets (including the famous 'tantalus') founded in 1820 by the 'fancy cabinet maker' George Betjeman, ancestor of the Poet Laureate and for years a Pentonville ward Councillor. The premises are now occupied by the Medici Company. Otherwise almost the only site not substantially rebuilt is an 1840s' range in Northdown (formerly North) Street, whose handsome pedimented Ionic group is centred on the bottom of Collier Street.

ST JAMES'S PENTONVILLE is now redundant. In 1981 a scheme was proposed for replacing it by a replica as offices. Notable residents buried in its precincts include Alexander Cumming, the architect Hurst, Charles Dibdin and the clown Grimaldi, who died aged 58 in 1837 at 33 Southampton Street (now Calshot Street; demolished). One celebrity whose house actually pre-dated the suburb was a versatile Swiss doctor who practised in London, Francis de Valangin, a one-time student of Boerhaave's at Leyden, awarded honours from several countries and a Licentiate of the ROYAL COLLEGE OF PHYSICIANS. He built his house, Hermes Hill, in 1772 with a roof-top observatory tower, between WHITE CONDUIT and Penny's Folly (BUSBY'S FOLLY), approximately on the site of Starcross School, and lived there in the growing suburb till his death in 1805. In 1811–13 the house was occupied by the fluent and eccentric lay preacher, William Huntington.

Pentonville, which by 1851 had 1,503 houses and 9,522 inhabitants deteriorated to a slum during the later 19th century. What little survived the war has since been mostly demolished and rebuilt with council flats.

Pentonville Prison *Caledonian Road, N7.* Built in 1840–42 as the model prison on the separate system, which had not been properly tried before in this country. It was planned by Sir Joshua Jebb on the radial pattern, based on Haviland's Eastern Penitentiary in Philadelphia. It had 'massive posterns in front, ... a frowning entrance-gateway, its arched head filled with portcullis-work and not altogether unpicturesque .... From the inspection or central hall [radiated] five wings or galleries, on the sides of four of which [were] the cells in three stories ...' There was a 'wondrous and perfectly Dutch-like cleanliness pervading the place'. Its distinctive feature, according to a contemporary account, 'is the extremely bright and cheerful and airy quality of the building; so that, with its long, light corridors, it strikes the mind, on first entering it, as a bit of the Crystal Palace, stripped of all its contents.' Selected male convicts underwent a term of probationary discipline, in which they were taught a trade and, it was hoped, made morally better members of society, prior to transportation. The crank, a hard-labour machine invented at Pentonville especially for cellular prisons, was said to 'grind the wind', producing nothing but exhaustion of body and boredom of mind. The period of confinement was 18 months, reduced to 12, then 9. At first there was 'an unusually large number of cases of mental affection among the prisoners', so the amount of exercise in the yards was increased and the plan of brisk walking introduced. The system was generally considered to be a success and at least one prisoner attested in 1845 to the beneficial changes wrought in him.

Pentonville now has convicted prisoners awaiting sentence, some unconvicted prisoners, non-criminal prisoners held for non-payment of rates, etc. There is a pre-release hostel: a small number of suitable prisoners, towards the end of their sentence, are able to live in it and work outside during the day. In 1982 Pentonville had 1,094 inmates (the certified normal accommodation is 840).

Pentonville Road *N1*. The last stretch of the New Road, built in 1756 to link the CITY with the western suburbs, avoiding the built-up area, was renamed Pentonville Road in 1857 after the suburb on Henry Penton's land on Islington Hill, which it skirted from KING'S CROSS to the ANGEL. The road-line from TOTTENHAM COURT ROAD to ISLINGTON had been disputed, a straight route being proposed through fields owned by, among others, the SKINNERS' COMPANY, the Revd Lloyd Baker (*see* LLOYD BAKER ESTATE) and the NEW RIVER COMPANY, but it was finally aligned farther north to Battle Bridge (now KING'S CROSS), thence taking a turn across Penton's fields from Bagnigge Wells Road, between Penny's Folly and Prospect House bowling-green on the north (*see* BUSBY'S FOLLY *and* DOBNEY'S) and the New River Head's Upper Reservoir (now Claremont Square) on the south. From the ANGEL it was continued in 1761 as the CITY ROAD. While it remained rural the road was patrolled at night by mounted escorts to protect homeward-bound playgoers on their way from SADLER'S WELLS to the West End or CITY.

Along the broad, straight thoroughfare, an obvious route for transport experiments, an unsuccessful attempt was made in 1798 to run a public coach between PADDINGTON and the BANK, and in 1829, George Shillibeer's famous pioneer omnibus service covered the same route. Until 1830 this was a toll-road, but with the abolition of tolls in CLERKENWELL, maintenance costs fell on the parish, which until 1882 also paid a ground rent to Penton's successors for the disused Pentonville toll-house at No. 274 (whose site was next to the Welsh Congregational church). The road contains the former ST JAMES'S CHURCH and some remnants of early terraces near the ANGEL. The handsome Cumming House also once stood here (*see* PENTONVILLE).

People's Palace Queen Victoria opened the Queen's Hall of the People's Palace in Mile End Road in 1887, but the origin of the project can be traced back nearly half a century before, when an endowment by the soldier, painter and philanthropist, Barber Beaumont, led to the founding of the New Philosophic Institute in MILE END. The Institute offered educational and recreational facilities for local working men. In 1884 the Trustees of the Institute became associated with the DRAPERS' COMPANY, who were the administrators of the nearby Bancroft Hospital, which included almshouses and a school. Agreement was reached in launching a project of interest to both, namely, a centre for social, educational and recreational activities for the benefit of East Londoners, to be housed in a building of distinction, and bearing comparison with the 'Palace of Delights' in Walter Besant's novel *All Sorts and Conditions of Men*. Plans by E.R. Robson (better known as architect to the School Board for London) were considerably altered before the building began on the site of the demolished Bancroft Hospital. At the opening ceremony Queen Victoria also laid the foundation stone for the East London Technical College. Originally providing evening classes, this developed in time into QUEEN MARY COLLEGE, which received its Royal Charter in 1934, forming a college of the UNIVERSITY OF LONDON. By this time the educational side of the project had become distinct from the social and recreational. The Queen's Hall had been burned down in 1931, and the rebuilt hall (by Campbell-Jones and Smithers), like the whole site, is today part of QUEEN MARY COLLEGE.

Percival David Foundation *53 Gordon Square, WC1*. Fine collection of Chinese ceramics of the Sung, Yuan, Ming and Ch'ing dynasties (10th to 18th centuries) presented to LONDON UNIVERSITY by Sir Percival David in 1951. The collection is renowned for the unique quality of the exhibits and for their detailed documentation and accurate dating.

Percy Circus *WC1*. Takes its name from Robert Percy Smith, Sydney Smith's brother, who worked for the NEW RIVER COMPANY. It was built on land which the Company had bought around the New River Head. Lenin and his wife, Nadia, stayed at No. 16 in 1905 for the third Congress of the Russian Social and Democratic Labour Party. The site of the house is commemorated by a plaque on the wall of the Royal Scot Hotel in KING'S CROSS ROAD.

Percy Street *W1*. Extends from RATHBONE PLACE to TOTTENHAM COURT ROAD. It was built in the 1760s on land belonging to Francis and William Goodge (*see* GOODGE STREET). It probably takes its name from the coffee-house on the corner of RATHBONE PLACE frequented by Boswell. George Rowney and Co. Ltd, the artists' colour manufacturers at No. 12, were established in Broad Street, St Giles in 1789. They moved to No. 51 RATHBONE PLACE in 1815 and in the 1850s to Percy Street. Frederick Gibberd and Partners, the architects, are at No. 8. There are several restaurants in the street, notably the White Tower at No. 1. Peter de Wint, the landscape painter, lived at No. 10 in 1817–26; E.H. Baily, the sculptor, at No. 8 in 1825–8; and Coventry Patmore, the poet and essayist, at No. 14 in 1863–4.

Perivale *Middlesex*. The name Perivale (pear tree valley) has been used only since the 16th century.

Before that the hamlet was known as Greenford Parva (Little Greenford). It lay to the east of GREENFORD itself (Greenford Magna). Within living memory it was only a cluster of houses near the church and only 60 people lived here in 1901. The Great Western Railway opened a station here in 1904, later part of London Transport's CENTRAL LINE. The building of WESTERN AVENUE brought industry to the area (principally Sanderson's Wallpaper Factory and the Hoover Factory) and a sizeable industrial estate was developed in the 1930s. Speculative house building followed and the area was built up by 1940. Shops were built along WESTERN AVENUE but Perivale continues dependent on other areas for amenities. Some open space remains in the shape of playing fields, golf courses and a nature reserve. Some factories have been replaced in recent years by warehouses but little otherwise has changed. The medieval church, ST MARY THE VIRGIN, survives, isolated from the rest of the area by WESTERN AVENUE.

Peter Street *W1*. Probably takes its name from a saltpetre house which was built in the middle of the 17th century between here and BREWER STREET. It was built between the 1670s and 1693. Strype described it in 1720 as a 'Street not over well inhabited'; by the 1830s it had evidently deteriorated into 'a short dirty street, without any thoroughfare'; and by 1878 it was composed of 'wretched hovels and [was] a disgrace to humanity'. None of the original houses remains, but there are a few late 18th- and early 19th-century houses of no great distinction. Westminster College on the corner of Hopkins Street was formerly the Pulteney London County Council School, erected for the London School Board in 1880.

Peterborough Court *EC4*. On the north side of FLEET STREET, between WINE OFFICE COURT and SHOE LANE. The site was owned by the Bishop of Peterborough from the 14th century until 1863, when it was acquired by the *Daily Telegraph*.

Peter's Hill *EC4*. Named after the Church of ST PETER PAUL'S WHARF which was destroyed in the GREAT FIRE.

Petersham *Surrey*. Variously known as Piterichesham, Patricesham, Petrosham and Pettresham, Petersham has over the centuries remained a village by the side of the THAMES. Now part of the London Borough of RICHMOND-UPON-THAMES, it still retains its individuality, helped by surroundings of superb parkland and the river. In 1086, the Abbot of Chertsey owned lands there and the *Domesday* entry mentions a church and fishery of 1,000 eels and 1,000 lampreys. But it was in the 17th century when Londoners, weary of the plague and the tensions of the city, discovered the peace of the rural THAMES, that Petersham, along with RICHMOND and TWICKENHAM, began to acquire the handsome houses which still give it a certain style today. In the 18th century it was described as the most elegant village in England. The most famous of its houses, Petersham Lodge, now no longer exists. It stood opposite the Dysart Arms and was finally demolished in 1834. The grounds were incorporated into RICHMOND PARK and included the mound where legend has it that Henry VIII stood to see the signal for the execution of Anne Boleyn.

Ham House, Petersham, c. 1830. Built in the early 17th century, it was the home of the Earls of Dysart until after the 2nd World War.

Charles I granted the lease of the Manor of Petersham to William Murray, 1st Earl of Dysart, who took up residence at HAM HOUSE. This brought to Petersham and HAM an influential family who remained at HAM HOUSE until 1948. Murray's daughter Elizabeth inherited HAM HOUSE. Her first marriage to Sir Lyonel Tollemache produced many children; her second to the Duke of Lauderdale in Petersham Church on 17 February 1672 produced a powerful political union and helped create HAM HOUSE as we know it today. One of Elizabeth's daughters, by her first husband, married the 1st Duke of Argyll. Their son, the 2nd Duke, was born at HAM HOUSE and around 1726 built for himself SUDBROOK PARK in the hamlet of Sudbrook which borders on Petersham. In Petersham Road there is an extremely sharp right-angled bend and the passing motorist might just glimpse a pair of handsome wrought-iron gates as he negotiates it. This is the entrance to MONTROSE HOUSE. After a spate of serious accidents on the bend in the road, the neighbours formed a group called Trustees of the Roads in the 1850s. The Hon. Algernon Tollemache of HAM HOUSE was their leader and they managed to persuade the owner of MONTROSE HOUSE to part with some land to reduce the sharpness of the bend. But various dents in the brick wall today reveal that motorists are still taken unawares by it. Another interesting house is DOUGLAS HOUSE just off the east drive to HAM HOUSE. One of its more notable inhabitants was Catherine, Duchess of Queensberry. She was an eccentric and quarrelled violently with the 4th Earl of Dysart, at HAM HOUSE. However, she was also a woman of some culture and a staunch patron of John Gay. Across the THAMES in TWICKENHAM, Horace Walpole looked out at HAM HOUSE and DOUGLAS HOUSE from STRAWBERRY HILL, but it was with relief that he wrote '. . . thank God, the Thames is between me and the Duchess of Queensberry'. Charles Dickens rented Elm Lodge in 1839 and wrote a large part of *Nicholas Nickleby* there. He seemed to enjoy living in Petersham and wrote to a friend '. . . Come down – come down – revive yourself with country air . . . . The roads about are jewelled after dusk with glow-worms, the leaves are all out and the flowers, too. Swimming feats from Petersham to Richmond Bridge have been achieved before breakfast. . . .'

Petersham Church, dedicated to ST PETER, is a beautiful example of an 18th-century country church complete with gallery and box pews. In 1778 the incumbent, distressed by its dilapidated condition, decided to attack his tight-fisted congregation from the pulpit. 'The House of God is almost the only house in the parish neglected, ruinous and sordid. ... I never enter this building, but I feel myself filled with astonishment – I had almost said, with indignation and terror – that it should be suffered to remain another year a disgrace, perhaps a calamity to the parish. ...' His appeal fell on deaf ears and the incumbent struggled on for almost 50 years on a stipend of under £100 from pew rents, while his church crumbled around him. Only after his death in 1788 was something done and over the next 100 years, the church was enlarged and improved. There are many interesting memorials on the walls, and in the churchyard is buried Captain George Vancouver who died in 1798 aged 40. Born in Norfolk, he sailed with Cook on two expeditions and discovered the island off the Pacific coast of Canada which is called after him. He returned to England in 1795 and lived in Glen Cottage in River Lane where he wrote his *Voyage of Discovery*. Also buried here are Mary and Agnes Berry who lived at Devonshire Cottage. As young women, they were friends of Horace Walpole, then in his 70s. After his death, the sisters' salons became famous. They both died in 1852 and lie in Petersham churchyard 'amidst scenes which in life they had frequented and loved'. Today, Petersham is a pleasant blend of small cottages, elegant terraces and imposing houses, bounded on one side by RICHMOND PARK and on the other by the THAMES.

Petersham House *143 Petersham Road, Richmond, Surrey*. Built about 1674 (it is not known by whom or for whom) with later additions such as the Regency circular portico and the 19th-century upper storey. Outside, the beautiful wrought-iron garden gates are remarkable. Inside there is a fine staircase with a large ceiling and wall paintings by Laguerre (about 1710) and in six rooms there are superb sculptured marble mantelpieces. In the 18th century the house was owned successively by the Rutland and Montrose families; in the 19th by local worthies such as Robert Thorley and Samuel Walker. The latter's daughter, Loetitia, has immortalised herself in Petersham by buying up the old Bute House property on the opposite side of the road in 1898 and building there the enormous All Saints' Church in bright red brick and in the style of the early North Italian basilicas, complete with Baptistry, marbles of all colours, 108 ft campanile, parish hall and institute.

Petersham Lodge *River Lane, Petersham, Surrey*. Built for Robert Ord, Chief Baron of the Exchequer of Scotland, in 1740, but considerably extended in 1762–1868. Because the white building is such a prominent feature of the view over PETERSHAM from RICHMOND HILL, it was given to the Borough of RICHMOND by Sir Max Waechter in order that the prospect might be preserved forever. It is now a private residence, but between 1902 and 1940 it was leased to the Princess of Wales (later Queen Mary)'s Holiday Homes for Governesses. There had been an earlier more famous Petersham Lodge; for James II granted Petersham Park to Edward Hyde and his uncle Laurence Hyde, Earl of Rochester, in 1686. They built a fine mansion that was first called 'New York' because Edward became Governor of the colony in 1701–8. The gardens were even more magnificent: formal, but landscaped to exploit the slopes of

RICHMOND PARK and the views across to the THAMES – gardens that foreshadowed the work of Kent and Bridgman.

In 1721 William Stanhope, later Earl of Harrington, bought the estate after a fire had destroyed the mansion with its library where many of Clarendon's manuscripts were kept. Here Lord Burlington designed one of the first Palladian houses in England – 'Harrington's Retreat' in the words of Richmond's poet, James Thomson. It belonged to the Duke of Clarence in 1790–5. It was demolished in 1834 when the property reverted to the Crown and was re-incorporated into RICHMOND PARK.

Peto Place *NW1*. A cul-de-sac running behind Park Square East and so originally providing a back entrance to the DIORAMA. It is named after Sir Samuel Mortimer Peto, the Victorian building contractor and politician whose firm, Grissell and Peto, were responsible for erecting the NELSON COLUMN.

Petre House *Aldersgate Street*. Until 1639 the town house of Lord Petre, then used as a prison until the end of the Commonwealth. Richard Lovelace was imprisoned here in 1648. In 1657 it was bought by the Marquess of Dorchester; and in 1666 by the See of London and renamed London House. It was demolished in 1871.

Petticoat Lane *E1*. A Sunday street market situated in and around MIDDLESEX STREET. In the Middle Ages the street was a tree-lined country road called Hog's Lane, presumably because of the pigs that were kept in the nearby fields. By the 1590s it was wound through a residential area of neat cottages and in 1608 Ryther's map shows it as Peticote Lane, its new name perhaps being derived from the sellers of old clothes who carried on business here, though it was still quite a fashionable area: the Spanish lived here in the reign of James I. In 1665 the GREAT PLAGUE drove out the well-to-do and a few years later Huguenot weavers and Jewish traders moved in. By the 1750s it was well established as a trading centre and a market had grown up. It was renamed Middlesex Street in about 1830 though it clung to the old name which was appropriate to the thriving business in old clothes. It was one of the largest of the Victorian street markets specialising in all kinds of second-hand goods. It was expanded in the 1900s when the street was widened and became enormously popular. Several attempts were made to stop Sunday morning trading even to the extent of buses and fire engines being driven through the crowds but it was allowed by Act of Parliament in 1936. It remains a busy Sunday morning cockney market today, covering a large area and spreading into the surrounding streets; Club Row has stalls specialising in fish, birds and reptiles; BRICK LANE is noted for both furniture and electrical equipment.

Petts Wood *Kent*. Possibly takes its name from William Pett, a master shipwright, who leased the wood in 1587. The railway station was opened in 1928, to the south of the main wood, and development thereby encouraged. Early houses were consistently in Tudor style and formed something of a 'garden suburb'. Meanwhile some 87.75 acres of the woodland were acquired by the NATIONAL TRUST in 1927 and a granite sundial erected at their north corner (near

Petticoat Lane in the 1890s. A thriving old clothes market since the beginning of the 17th century, it is still a busy general market.

Orpington Road, CHISLEHURST) as a memorial to William Willett, a local resident and campaigner for Daylight Saving. An adjoining 47 acres were added in 1958.

Petty France So called because French wool merchants used to live here. According to Stow, 'Cornelius Van Dun (a Brabander born, yeoman of the Guard to King Henry VIII, King Edward VI, Queen Mary, and Queen Elizabeth) built twenty houses for poor women to dwell rent free'. John Milton took 'a pretty-garden house ... opening into St James's Park' here in 1652 and remained until 1660. During this time he was Latin Secretary to Cromwell, wrote most of *Paradise Lost* and buried two wives. The house was demolished in 1877. Other residents here were Jeremy Bentham and Hazlitt, both in 1812—19. John Cleland, author of *Fanny Hill*, died in the street aged 82 in 1789, having been given an annuity by the Privy Council 'on his engaging to write nothing more of the same description'. The *Man and Woman* sculptures on either side of the entrance are by Willi Soukop (1963). The Passport Office is at Clive House, Nos 70–78.

Pewterers' Company *see* CITY LIVERY COMPANIES.

Pharmaceutical Society *1 Lambeth High Street, SE1.* Founded in 1841 by Jacob Bell, owner of a well-known pharmaceutical business, for the purpose of protecting the interests of the trade and of raising its status. Bell also established the Society's periodical, *Pharmaceutical Journal*, which he edited till his death in 1859. The first President, from 1841 to 1844, was William Allen, of the chemists Allen and Hanbury, and Bell himself was President from 1856 to 1859. In 1843 the Society was incorporated by royal charter. Its premises from 1841 were 17 BLOOMSBURY SQUARE, WC1, a fine Nash building to which the Society added its name along the frieze. Between 1860 and 1870, an attic storey, window pediments and porch were also added. The Society was obliged to move to its present address because of the compulsory purchase of its previous offices for the intended BRITISH LIBRARY.

The Pheasantry *King's Road, SW3.* A house has been on the site since 1769. It is now the centrepiece of a modern development. The ornate façade and portico are all that remain of the original building. Its name came from pheasants living in the garden in the middle of the 19th century. The Joubert family, upholsterers and furniture makers, took the house in 1881 and frenchified the façade. Princess Serafine Astafieva, dancer and teacher, lived in the first floor of the house in 1916–34 and taught there. Anton Dolin, Dame Alicia Markova, Dame Margot Fonteyn and Leonide Massine were among her pupils. In 1932 the basement became a club and restaurant which lasted for nearly 35 years and was patronised by many painters, writers, politicians and actors, including Augustus John and Pietro Annigoni.

Philharmonia Orchestra Formed by Walter Legge (a senior executive of EMI Records); the inaugural concert was conducted by Beecham on 28 October 1945. Legge, who maintained an autocratic control, employed the orchestra to make celebrated recordings with famous international soloists and such conductors as Richard Strauss and Toscanini. In 1964 the management collapsed but the members of the orchestra decided to take over as a self-governing body, renamed the New Philharmonia; finance was a problem at first but soon improved. In 1977 the orchestra resumed the original name and it is now regarded as one of the leading orchestras of the world.

Phillimore Estate Developed from the 1780s by William Phillimore whose ancestor, Joseph Phillimore, the son of a Gloucestershire clothier, had come to London and, in Kensington, had married Anne D'Oyley whose family owned much land there. Phillimore Gardens, Close, Place, Terrace and Walk, W8, cover a good deal of ground between KENSINGTON HIGH STREET and DUCHESS OF BEDFORD'S WALK. Sheldrake Place, W8, takes its name from Elizabeth Jane Sheldrake, wife of William Brough Phillimore.

Phillimore Gardens *W8*. Victorian terraced houses built in 1858 on the PHILLIMORE ESTATE. Lord Kitchener lived at No. 44 in 1875. In Phillimore Place to the east, Kenneth Grahame, author of *The Wind in the Willows*, lived at No. 16 (then 16 Durham Villas) in 1901–8 while working at the BANK OF ENGLAND.

Phillimore House *Kensington*. Built sometime before 1730 and occupied by the Phillimore family. It was later occupied by Sir James South, the astronomer, who called it Observatory House after the private observatory that he had built in the grounds and which for a few years boasted the largest telescope in the world. The house, which had also been known as New Campden House, was demolished about 1870. The site is now partly covered by Observatory Gardens.

Phillips *Blenstock House, New Bond Street, W1*. (Additional sale rooms at Hayes Place, Marylebone, NW1.) Fine art auctioneers and valuers, founded in 1796 by Harry Phillips, former head clerk to James Christie (*see* CHRISTIE, MANSON AND WOODS). Since Phillips had no premises of his own, sales took place in the vendor's house until, in 1797, he acquired 73 NEW BOND STREET and soon became a recognised figure in London society. In 1820 Harry was joined by his son, William Augustus, who, after Harry's death in 1840, remained head of the firm for many years. In 1881 William took into partnership his son-in-law, Frederick Neale, who was joined in 1924 by his own son, Philip. Thereafter the firm bore the name of Phillips, Son and Neale until in 1972 it reverted to the traditional 'Phillips'. Fire destroyed the NEW BOND STREET premises in 1939 whereupon the move to Blenstock House took place. After the 2nd World War the firm was joined by Glendinning and Co., dealers in coins and medals, and in 1954 Phillips absorbed the auctioneers Puttick and Simpson and now occupies the whole of Blenstock House. In 1980 turnover was £32,823,519.

Philpot Lane *EC3*. Named after Sir John Philpot, Lord Mayor of London in 1378–9 and owner of land in the area. A small sculpture of mice eating cheese on one of the buildings commemorates a fatal accident here when a workman on the roof quarrelled with one of his mates whom he suspected of having eaten part of his sandwiches. In the ensuing fight one of the men fell and was killed. It was afterwards discovered that mice were responsible.

Phoenix Theatre *Charing Cross Road, WC2*. Built for S.L. (later Lord) Bernstein in 1930 partly on the site of an old undistinguished music-hall, the Alcazar, it takes its name from Phoenix Street, the short street on its southern side. It was constructed to the design of Sir Giles Gilbert Scott and Bertie Crewe with interior decorations by Theodore Komisarjevsky. It opened on 24 September 1930, under the management of C.B. Cochran, with Noël Coward's *Private Lives*, the author, Gertrude Lawrence and Laurence Olivier being in the cast. For some time the theatre had a chequered career apart from *Late Night Final*, which

ran for 132 performances in 1931, and Noël Coward's *Tonight*, a programme of one-act plays, in 1936. During the War the most successful presentations were John Gielgud's revival of Congreve's *Love for Love* and Ivor Novello's musical play, *Arc de Triomphe*. Since then there have been intermittent successes from Chaucer's *Canterbury Tales* to Tom Stoppard's *Night and Day*.

PICCADILLY *W1*. Extending from PICCADILLY CIRCUS to HYDE PARK CORNER, this is one of the two ancient highways leading westward out of London, the other being OXFORD STREET. Building began near the eastern end in the early 17th century, when Robert Baker, a tailor with a shop in the STRAND who had made a fortune out of the sale of 'picadils', 'a kinde of stiff collar' then in vogue at Court, invested his new riches in the purchase of lands to the north of what is now PICCADILLY CIRCUS. There, on the east side of the modern GREAT WINDMILL STREET in about 1612, he built himself a country house which was promptly nicknamed Piccadilly Hall in derisive allusion to the source of his wealth. Widespread building began soon after the Restoration, when the street was first called Portugal Street after Charles II's Queen, Catherine of Braganza; but the name 'Piccadilly' was already commonly used to denote the eastern part near Piccadilly Hall, and by the middle of the 18th century this had become the generally accepted name for the whole street.

On the south side Charles II's companion in exile, Henry Jermyn, Earl of St Albans, had been rewarded in 1661 by the grant of a Crown lease of all the land between the HAYMARKET and ST JAMES'S STREET, and here development had been completed by the 1680s, most of the original buildings (apart from ST JAMES'S CHURCH) being inns or shops. On the north side as far as SWALLOW STREET, where the land was also granted to the Earl of St Albans (the painter Verrio being a resident here in 1675), there was very similar development, but to the west of SWALLOW STREET, half a dozen great noblemen's mansions were built in the 1660s, of which the most important were BURLINGTON HOUSE, CLARENDON HOUSE and BERKELEY HOUSE. Sir William Petty, the political economist, lived in another, on the site of the present SACKVILLE STREET, from 1673 until his death in 1687. To the west of STRATTON STREET, there were still open fields in the 1680s, but by the middle of the 18th century all this land had been built over as far as HYDE PARK CORNER, much of it in a higgledy-piggledy way with several masons' and statuaries' yards. The sole survivors of all this original development are ST JAMES'S CHURCH and BURLINGTON HOUSE, the latter building very substantially altered.

Rebuilding began in about 1760, when a town house with a rustic prospect became *à la mode* for the first time, and Lord Egremont and Sir Hugh Hunlock built themselves mansions overlooking GREEN PARK (later the NAVAL AND MILITARY CLUB and the ST JAMES'S CLUB). Also built at this time were Nos 79 and 80 Piccadilly (*see below*). These houses were followed in the 1770s and 1780s by Apsley House, later the house of the Duke of Wellington (*see* WELLINGTON MUSEUM). Thereafter this western part of Piccadilly became one of the most sought-after residential streets in London, particularly in Regency and early Victorian times, when its famous inhabitants included the following: at

No. 99, Sir William Hamilton, the antiquary, and his wife Emma, Nelson's mistress, in 1800–3; at No. 139, Lord Byron in 1815, shortly after his ill-fated marriage; at the west corner of Hamilton Place, Lord Chancellor Eldon (1820–38) who died in his front drawing-room from which, a little earlier, he had amused himself by counting the long and short petticoats that passed in Piccadilly, and had found the short ones greatly in the majority; at No. 110, 'Queenie' Thrale, for many years after her marriage to Admiral Viscount Keith; at No. 107, Nathan Mayer Rothschild from 1825 onwards; at No. 126, Louis Blanc in 1848; at No. 132 John Bright, the statesman, 1883–4; and at No. 145, much more recently, the Duke of York, who was living here at the time of his accession as George VI in 1936.

In late Victorian and Edwardian times many of the houses overlooking GREEN PARK were again rebuilt, and although they continued for a time in private occupation – Dorothy Sayers placed Lord Peter Wimsey in a flat in 'a new, perfect and expensive block' at No. 110A – the growing noise of the traffic in Piccadilly gradually drove most of the private residents elsewhere. Some of the houses which they vacated were then used as clubs, of which there were over a score at various times, and others as offices. But in more recent years clubs have fallen on hard times financially, and today the NAVAL AND MILITARY CLUB, the CAVALRY AND GUARDS CLUB, the American Club and the ROYAL AIR FORCE CLUB are almost the only survivors.

Offices and hotels now virtually monopolise this part of Piccadilly, some of them occupying recently erected buildings of no great architectural distinction. The PARK LANE HOTEL and the ATHENAEUM HOTEL are on the north side, the RITZ HOTEL is on the south. On the Park side of the street, towards the west end, is a 'porter's rest', put up in 1861 for the benefit of porters carrying heavy loads on their backs. Further east the handsome wrought-iron gates leading into the park were originally made in about 1735 for Lord Heathfield's house at TURNHAM GREEN. From 1898 to 1921 they stood in front of DEVONSHIRE HOUSE on the north side of Piccadilly; but after the demolition of that house they were placed in their present position. East of GREEN PARK, ST JAMES'S CHURCH and BURLINGTON HOUSE are the only exceptions in an otherwise wholly commercial street, dominated by shops, hotels, banks and air-line offices, none of which occupies a building erected before about 1860. The shops include or included such famous names as HATCHARD'S, FORTNUM AND MASON, SIMPSON'S (by Joseph Emberton 1935), SWAN AND EDGAR (by Sir Reginald Blomfield); the House of Bewlay (founded in 1780) at No. 214; Airey and Wheeler, tropical clothing specialists, at No. 44; Cording and Co., rainwear specialists, at No. 19; Dunn and Co., hatters, at Nos 228–229; Swaine, Adeney, Brigg and Son, whip manufacturers (founded in 1750), at No. 185; and Cogswell and Harrison, founded by Benjamin Cogswell in New Kent Road in 1770, at No. 168. At No. 213 Messrs J. Lyons opened their first tea shop in 1894. The hotels include Shaw's great PICCADILLY HOTEL (1905–8), its east wing unfortunately never built. And alongside ST JAMES'S CHURCH is Sir Edwin Lutyens's Midland Bank. At No. 193, above the huge window of Pan American World Airways, is the former house of the Royal Society of Painters in Water

Colours (by E.R. Robson 1881). The Iraqi Airways building at No. 188 is by Alison and Peter Smithson (1961).

Nos 79 and 80 Piccadilly These two adjoining houses (both now demolished; No. 79 was more commonly known as No. 1 Stratton Street) had long associations with the great banking family of Coutts. No. 79 Piccadilly was built in 1763 by Robert Mylne for the 10th Earl of Eglington, and No. 80 Piccadilly in 1764–6 by Matthew Brettingham for Sir Richard Lyttelton. In 1795 Thomas Coutts, bought No. 1 STRATTON STREET and two small adjoining houses at the back. In 1802 he bought No. 80 Piccadilly for the use of his daughter, Sophia, and her husband, Sir Francis Burdett, the radical MP for WESTMINSTER, and here their daughter, Angela (later Baroness Burdett-Coutts, the philanthropist) was born in 1814. It was in this house that Sir Francis barricaded himself for a few days in 1810 after the Speaker of the House of Commons had issued a warrant for his arrest for breach of privilege. When, after great popular demonstrations outside in his favour, forcible entry was finally made, he was found quietly instructing his son in the complexities of the text of *Magna Carta*. This did not prevent his being conveyed to the TOWER where he remained for a few weeks until Parliament was prorogued. In 1815 Thomas Coutts, then aged 80, married as his second wife the Irish actress Harriet Mellon, who was about 37. When he died in 1822 he left all his immense riches to his widow who five years later married the 9th Duke of St Albans aged 26, an event which provoked much public mirth, endured by the Duchess with great good humour. Duchess Harriet took a great fancy to her step-granddaughter, Angela Burdett, to whom, after her death in 1837, she bequeathed almost her entire fortune. The bereaved Duke subsequently lived at No. 80 Piccadilly for the remaining 12 years of his life, while Angela set up her own establishment at No. 1 STRATTON STREET. She continued to live here (being raised to the peerage in her own right in 1871 as Baroness Burdett-Coutts) until her death in 1906. It was from this house that she conducted her numerous philanthropic projects, and here she entertained her wide circle of friends, who included such varied people as the Duke of Wellington, Charles Dickens and General Gordon.

No. 106 Piccadilly A fine Palladian house at the west corner of Brick Street, it was built in 1761 for Sir Hugh Hunlock. He was soon succeeded by the 6th Earl of Coventry, who called in Robert Adam to remodel the interior in 1765–6, and much of this work still survives. In the mid-19th century No. 106 was occupied by the Coventry House Club, but in 1869 it became the house of the ST JAMES'S CLUB which remained here for over a hundred years.

Piccadilly Circus *W1*. Formed in 1819 by the intersection of PICCADILLY with John Nash's new REGENT STREET then in course of construction. It was thus originally a crossroads, but the frontages of the four corners were set back and lined with concave-curving stucco buildings to form a circular *place*. This elegant arrangement was destroyed in the mid-1880s, when the METROPOLITAN BOARD OF WORKS demolished the buildings in the north-east segment of the Circus for the formation of SHAFTESBURY AVENUE. Their replacement by the LONDON PAVILION and some undistinguished shops reduced the enlarged

Piccadilly Circus and Regent Street. On the left are the old premises of Swan and Edgar, which were rebuilt in 1910.

Circus to an ill-shaped vortex of converging streets, redeemed only by the statue of Eros in the centre (*see* MEMORIALS). But worse was to follow, for the shop-keepers on the new north-east side of the Circus soon discovered that the erection of electrically illuminated advertisements on their façades could provide them with very lucrative rentals. The LONDON COUNTY COUNCIL was powerless to prevent their doing so; and by 1910 the famous Bovril and Schweppe's signs, which dominated the Circus for many years, had been erected. These were followed in 1923 by gigantic advertisements covering much of the façade of the LONDON PAVILION, despite the fact that here the LONDON COUNTY COUNCIL was the ground landlord. And the only reason why the disease did not spread to the other three sides of the Circus was that the leases granted in Nash's day by the Crown as ground landlord had been so strictly worded as to enable all signs to be prohibited.

Piccadilly Hotel *Piccadilly, W1.* Built in 1905–8 to the designs of Norman Shaw, it has a screen of giant columns behind which the frontage recedes. The ST JAMES'S RESTAURANT of 1875 at Nos 24–26 and the ST JAMES'S HALL were both demolished for the building of the hotel. There are 294 bedrooms.

Piccadilly Line The Piccadilly line, which in December 1906 opened from FINSBURY PARK to HAMMERSMITH, was the second tube of C.T. Yerkes's comprehensive scheme of electric railways for London. When Lloyd George opened it, the Piccadilly was the longest tube railway in London and had graduated fares ranging from 1d. to 4d. Of its many distinctive features, the most remarkable was the first railway escalator in London, brought into use in October 1911 at EARL'S COURT. The public mistrusted it and a man with a wooden leg called 'Bumper' Harris was engaged to travel up and down all day to give passengers confidence. After the remaining section of the tube, which served passengers going to the theatres, was opened from HOLBORN to STRAND (ALDWYCH) in 1907, the

Piccadilly line did not increase its mileage for 25 years. Then the tube was extended northwards to COCKFOSTERS and westwards to UXBRIDGE making the through run of 32 miles longer than any previous electric train journey operated by LONDON TRANSPORT. At the same time, stations serving the WEST END were enlarged and improved to cater for a substantial increase in traffic. Finally, in December 1977 an extension was opened to HEATHROW Central making HEATHROW the world's first large international airport to be linked with the underground railway of a major capital city. New rolling stock was provided at a cost of £41 million with special features such as larger carriages and more floor space to accommodate luggage. With the HEATHROW extension, the Piccadilly line, which originally covered nine miles of route, now operates on 40.5 miles of route (*see also* UNDERGROUND RAILWAYS).

Piccadilly Place *W1.* A short, L-shaped street connecting SWALLOW STREET with PICCADILLY, the main east–west arm being known until 1939 as VINE STREET.

Piccadilly Theatre *Denman Street, W1.* Built in 1928 to the designs of Bertie Crowe and E.A. Stone. The interior was redecorated in 1955 and reconstructed in 1960 when the theatre became the first in London to be fully air-conditioned. After the opening show starring Evelyn Laye, it became a cinema. In 1960 it was bought by the Albery family and has since prospered.

Pickering Place *SW1.* Known as Pickering Court until 1812, it is approached by a narrow arched passageway beside Berry Brothers and Rudd in ST JAMES'S STREET. A plaque on the wall, erected by the Anglo-Texan Society, indicates that in 1842–5 a building here was occupied by the Legation from the Republic of Texas to the Court of St James's. The houses were built in the early 1730s by William Pickering, whose mother-in-law began the grocer's shop from which Berry Brothers and Rudd are descended.

Pilgrim Street *EC2.* Said to be the route taken by cathedral-bound pilgrims after disembarking at the FLEET RIVER. The name, however, does not appear until the middle of the 18th century. Parts of the old City wall have been found here. At the corner of NEW BRIDGE STREET was Ludgate Hill Station which was opened by the London, Chatham and Dover Railway Company in 1865 and which closed in 1929.

Pimlico *SW1.* The area lying roughly between Chelsea Bridge Road, EBURY STREET and VAUXHALL BRIDGE ROAD. The origin of the name is unknown. It has been suggested that it is that of a local drink whose recipe has been lost, or that it comes from the Pamlico tribe of Red Indians who exported timber to England from America in the 17th century, or is derived from the friar bird which was once to be seen here, or from Ben Pimlico, a 16th-century publican.

It seems to have been first used in 1626 to refer to a group of mean cottages called the Neat Houses, around RANELAGH GARDENS, which had been built on land originally forming part of a manor belonging to the Abbot of WESTMINSTER. In August 1667, after going backstage to see his actress friend Mrs Knipp, Pepys went with her and his wife 'to the Neat Houses in the way to Chelsy'; 'and there,' he recorded, 'in a box in a tree, we sat and sang, and talked and eat; my wife out of humour as she always is when this woman is by.' A century later, when the nearby BUCKINGHAM HOUSE had been sold to George III, the low-lying land of Pimlico had been little developed, apart from a brewery which was to become Watney's Stag Brewery (*see* BREWERIES) and the public house known as JENNY'S WHIM. Much of the area was taken up with osier beds, market gardens and waste land. So it remained until the middle of the 1830s when Thomas Cubitt obtained leases from the GROSVENOR ESTATE into whose hands much of the land had passed, and began to build here as he had done in BELGRAVIA, though in a less grand way and for less fashionable people, digging up clay from under the gravel to make bricks and depositing earth excavated from the ST KATHARINE DOCK. Several of the streets were called after Grosvenor names and estates: Lupus and Chester Streets, for example, after Hugh Lupus, Earl of Chester. The newly married Lady Alexandrina in Trollope's *The Small House at Allington* does not wish to live here, and makes her disinclination clear to her husband: 'If indeed they could have achieved Eaton Square, or a street leading out of Eaton Square – if they could have crept on to the hem of the skirt of Belgravia – the bride would have been delighted. And at first she was very nearly taken in with the idea that such a proposal was made to her. Her geographical knowledge of Pimlico had not been perfect, and she had very nearly fallen into a fatal error. But a friend had kindly intervened. "For heaven's sake, my dear, don't let him take you anywhere beyond Eccleston Square!"' Although never as smart as BELGRAVIA there are in Pimlico several delightful terraces of small early 19th-century houses which today's Lady Alexandrinas would find perfectly acceptable.

Pindar of Wakefield *328 Gray's Inn Road, WC1.* Originally built in 1517 when the landlord was George Green, one-time Pindar of Wakefield, who was supposed to have had connections with Robin Hood. The present house, built in 1878, was once patronised by Karl Marx and Lenin. It now houses a regular 'Old Time Music-Hall'.

Pine Street *EC1.* Formerly known as Wood Street after a carpenter, Thomas Wood, who leased a field here from the Lord of the Manor, the Marquess of Northampton (hence Northampton Road and Square), in 1776. The reason for the change of name is unknown. The Finsbury Health Centre is by Tecton (1938).

Pinner *Middlesex.* The name derives from Pinn or Pynn (a Saxon personal name) and *ora* (old English: river bank), hence 'Pynn's place by the river'. The first recorded reference to Pinner is in a charter of AD 793 when the chapel at Pinner Hill was given by Offa, King of Mercia, to the Abbey of St Albans. Parish and, indeed, county boundaries today are different and the little chapel on Pinner Hill, rebuilt in 1610 and still standing, is now in Oxhey in Hertfordshire. The monks at Pinner built a hedge to prevent their oxen from straying, hence ox-hedge, or Oxhey. The land was taken from the monks but restored to them by King Ethelred in a charter of 1007. The church of St John the Baptist in the High Street was built in 1321. The next major event in the history of Pinner was the granting of a charter by King Henry III to John, Archbishop of Canterbury, in 1336 for a market to be held every week on Wednesday and for two fairs every year. The tradition of one annual fair still survives on the first Wednesday following Whitsun when the streets are closed to traffic. Many old and historically important buildings still remain in Pinner. The oldest surviving house is possibly the four-bay timber-framed hall house, East End Farm Cottage, dating from the 15th or 16th centuries. This area of Moss Lane, containing also the 16th-century East End Farm, Tudor Cottage (1592) and the Georgian East End House, forms the nucleus of a proposed conservation area. Three other conservation areas are proposed, plus two already scheduled. The High Street conservation area contains the Queen's Head and Victory Hotels, both half-timbered and 16th-century, the 17th-century Church Farm House, the early 18th-century Pinner House and Chestnut Cottage, plus other buildings from the 16th to the 18th centuries, some of which are now shops or business premises. The Tooke's Green conservation area contains several old cottages, one of which (Elmdene) was once the home of Mrs Horatia Ward, daughter of Lord Nelson and Lady Hamilton. The focal point is a memorial fountain to William Arthur Tooke, who restored the parish church in 1880. Pinner Hill House, now the home of Pinner Golf Club, and the tower at Pinner Hill Farm, or Tooke's Folly as it is affectionately known, were both built by his father, Arthur William Tooke. Pinner Place (demolished in 1954) was the residence of the governor of Bengal, John Zephaniah Holwell, one of the few survivors of the Black Hole of Calcutta; and in Woodhall Drive, the 16th-century Woodhall Farm was once the residence of John Claudius Loudon, garden designer and author of encyclopaedias of agriculture, gardening, plants and architecture and numerous other related works. The early 18th-century Pinnerwood House in the proposed Pinner Wood conservation area was once the home of Lord Lytton, and it was here that he wrote *Eugene Aram*. Orchard Cottage, Bee Cottage, Waxwell Cottage, Manor Cottage and other timber-framed buildings in the proposed Waxwell

Lane conservation area date from the 16th to the 18th centuries, and Sweetmans Hall in West End Lane from the 17th century; 20th-century buildings of architectural interest include St Luke's Roman Catholic church in Love Lane, the Odeon Cinema and adjacent shopping area in Rayners Lane, and a 1925 development in neo-Georgian style in Waxwell Close. A plaque at No. 75 Moss Lane commemorates the residence here of the comic artist, W. Heath Robinson.

Pioneer Health Centre, Peckham *St Mary's Road, SE15.* Built in 1934–5 at a cost of £38,000 as the home of the 'Peckham Experiment'. It is a three-storey building of concrete and glass with six large bow windows. It was designed by Sir E. Owen Williams, to the requirements laid down for the Experiment by Dr Scott Williamson, as a laboratory for the study of human biology. All inner partition walls were of glass. Local people were invited to join on payment of a small weekly subscription. The facilities included a gymnasium; theatre; swimming pool; cafeteria; infants' nursery; and games and consulting rooms. The conditions of membership were that the entire family should join and attend for periodical medical examinations. At the outbreak of the 2nd World War the centre was closed down and the building was taken over by a munitions firm. After the war the 'Peckham Experiment' was resumed for a while until forced to close down due to lack of financial support in 1950. The building is now used for adult education. Part remains in use, however, as a general practitioners' clinic.

Pitshanger Manor *The Green, W5.* Architecturally the most interesting building in EALING and the only one with a Grade One listing (Pitshanger means 'wooded slope frequented by kites'). Ealing Green in the later 18th century was flanked by attractive gentlemen's residences, some of which still survive. In 1770 Thomas Gurnell, the owner of an estate to the north of EALING that included Pitshanger Farm, decided to build a house and he employed George Dance the Younger, later his son-in-law. This house seems to have been plain with a central block and projecting wings in redbrick. In 1800 the architect John Soane bought the house from Gurnell's executors and reconstructed it. He had been a pupil of Dance's and may have worked on the original house. He demolished all but the south wing and erected a central block linking this to a detached north wing with a colonnade and a low wall. Beyond this north wing he built sham Roman ruins. Soane kept the house only until 1810 and it passed through several owners until it was bought by Spencer Walpole, the Cabinet Minister, who lived next door. He let it to his sisters-in-law, the daughters of Spencer Perceval, who had lived on the opposite side of the Green. After the death of the last daughter in 1900 (Spencer Walpole having predeceased her) the house and grounds were sold to EALING District Council which uses them as a public library and public park respectively. The house has been much altered since Soane's rebuilding.

Pitt House *North End Road, NW3.* A substantial mansion stood on this site for many years and was the manor house of the hamlet known as North End. At various times it was known as North End Place, North End House, then Wildwoods House and Wildwoods, before becoming Pitt House in 1910. The name marks the stay in the mansion by William Pitt, Earl of Chatham, in 1767. Although a member of the Government of the day, the recently ennobled Earl shut himself away in North End in total seclusion whilst 'mentally incapacitated by suppressed gout'. He refused to see anyone, and his meals were served to him through a hatchway with double doors. The servant had to close the outer door before Chatham would open the inner one. The house was lived in from 1905 to 1908 by Harold Harmsworth, later Lord Rothermere, and was demolished in 1952, to be replaced by some undistinguished modern houses.

Pitt Street *W8.* Takes its name from Stephen Pitt who inherited estates in KENSINGTON from his mother and who purchased more land in the area from Edmund Lechmere in 1751. The street was laid out in 1878.

Pitt's Head Mews *W1.* Extends eastwards from PARK LANE towards SHEPHERD MARKET, and takes its name from a tavern commemorating William Pitt the Elder, which formerly stood hereabouts.

Plagues The first plague mentioned was in AD 664. Bede records that it depopulated the south east of England, so it must have affected London. A successor to this plague certainly killed the population of BARKING ABBEY shortly after its foundation in about 666. In early centuries leprosy was a greater problem than plague. The hospital and chapel of ST GILES-IN-THE-FIELDS was founded at the beginning of the 11th century to house 40 lepers. The leper hospital of ST JAMES dates from the same century. In 1346 an ordinance excluded lepers from London. By the reign of Henry VIII there were several leper hospitals in London, mostly used, however, for syphilitics since leprosy was less common by this time. Before the BLACK DEATH of 1348–9 London was struck by one major plague in 1258. This plague was compounded with, if not caused by, famine. As the price of imported corn rose to 15s a quarter it was the poor who were mainly affected, though not exclusively: Falk, the Bishop of London, was a victim. In 1361 and 1368–9 plagues that were considered to be related to the BLACK DEATH broke out. Another related plague in 1407 killed 30,000 people.

Henry IV sailed to an Essex port where he stayed until the danger had passed. The plague of 1426 was the first to be peculiar to London. In 1433–4 there was 'a grete pestilence and a grete frost' in London. The same strain of disease recurred in 1437 and in 1439 when the custom of kissing the King in PARLIAMENT was suspended lest he be infected by his subjects.

There was a further series of outbreaks in 1450, 1452 and 1454. PARLIAMENT was constantly being moved, if only as far as LUDGATE, to avoid WESTMINSTER's 'foul air'. From the middle of the 15th century when plagues began to be especially virulent, people began to take the precaution of leaving the city at the onset of an epidemic. This did not, however, prevent the Royal Household being amongst those worst hit by the 1474 plague. The plague of 1499–1500 killed 20,000 people. There appears to have been some cessation until 1517, although Erasmus mentions being 'shut up in the midst of pestilence' at various times in 1512–15. In 1517 the plague was accompanied by sweating sickness. The Court kept away from London until public criticism demanded its return in March, shortly after which three pages died and it withdrew again to Berkshire. Catherine of Aragon declared that, although she was no prophet, she feared greatly for the King's life. The disease recurred regularly until 1521. In 1531 plague forced the Court to move again and, feeling unsafe even in GREENWICH, it retired to Southampton. In the autumn of the next year WESTMINSTER and the areas around the INNS OF COURT were deserted by both nobles and lawyers. This was a particularly violent strain: Secretary Cromwell's gardener was in good health and working on the evening of Saturday 12 March, but was buried by the morning of Monday. In the summer of 1535 when two thirds of recorded deaths were the result of plague, the Court retired to Thornbury in Gloucestershire. So great was the alarm that a decision was taken in September to suspend PARLIAMENT for six months until cold weather should have eliminated the infection. The disease continued until 1548 when there was a respite. It was about this time that it became obligatory to mark the doors of plague-stricken houses with blue crosses. The return of the soldiers from Le Havre in 1563 was blamed for a violent outbreak of plague after 15 years of immunity, though the soldiers returned, in fact, after the first cases had broken out. Dr John Jones recorded some features of this plague in his *Dyall of Agues*: the problem was most acute in the areas around ST SEPULCHRE and Sea Coal Lane 'by reason of many fruiterers, poor people and stinking lanes'. He identified the contagious nature of the disease, and destroyed the myth of one attack giving the victim subsequent immunity by relating the case of a baker's wife at TEMPLE BAR: 'This sayde wyfe had the plague at Midsommer and at Bartholomewtide, and at Michaelmas, and the first time it brake, the second time it brake, but ran littel, the thirde time it appeared and brake not: but she died, notwythstanding she was twice afore healed.'

Towards the end of the century, attempts were made to improve records of deaths. Parish Clerks were to be responsible for inspecting BILLS OF MORTALITY and for isolation of infected areas. In 1581 it was decreed that 'two discreet matrons' be selected from each parish to confirm reports of the causes of death. 10,000 died in the plague of 1593, which had begun the previous year. Against these 10,000 deaths only 4,000 christenings are recorded. In his *Defensative* (1593), Simon Kellawaye advised isolating victims, washing the streets daily with cold water, burning fires with frankincense and herbs, restraining animals from running free, and keeping the water clear, particularly of waste from the shambles. Ordinances had been passed to ban shambles from the city when they were recognised as a health hazard as early as the reign of Edward III, but little action had been taken.

In 1603 London was afflicted with a plague so acute that 2,798 died in one week in the CITY alone. It spread from the East End, probably beginning in STEPNEY. Anyone who had the means fled, but they were not well received in the country: 'The sight of a Londoner's flat-cap was dreadful to a lot, a treble ruff threw a village into sweat. The physicians also fled; and quacks, herbalists (who sold rosemary at 8s a handful) and sextons alone stayed to reap the profits. Dr Thomas Lodge, who claimed to be the only orthodox physician left in London, recommended cakes of arsenic under the armpits and, again, pleaded for removal of the shambles. He also considered the idea of establishing pest houses to isolate victims, but was worried that the emotional shock of isolation might accelerate death. After a succession of mild autumnal plagues until 1610, London then enjoyed a 15-year immunity. An outbreak in the summer of 1625, however, killed 35,000 people. The life of the city came to a halt. John Taylor, the 'Water Poet', wrote:

All trades are dead, or almost out of breath,
But such as live by sickness and by death.

Again citizens fled and again they were ill-received in the country. According to Taylor:

Milk-maids and farmers' wives are grown so nice
They think a citizen a cockatrice.

Even the magistrates fled and looting and begging were rampant. The coronation of Charles I was postponed until the following year. After another outbreak compounded with typhus in 1636, London was struck by a new strain of fever in the years of 1638–43. The poor living in congested conditions were mainly affected. This was the last major epidemic before the GREAT PLAGUE after which the GREAT FIRE did much to destroy the conditions in which plague had thrived.

Plaisterers' Company *see* CITY LIVERY COMPANIES.

Plaistow *E13*. A postal and residential district in the centre of NEWHAM with a railway station (1858) serving the London, Tilbury and Southend line and the DISTRICT LINE. (The LT and SR company had a small works adjoining from about 1875 to 1934.) The name is first recorded in 1414 and means a place where people gathered for play. It does not derive from the manor of Plaiz which, with Bretts, centred on Plaistow. Until the mid-19th century it was a large, mainly agricultural, village which gave its name to the southernmost of the three wards of the ancient parish of WEST HAM. There was some early industry in the 16th and 17th century with evidence of silk weaving and leather trades. Cordwainer Street, the earliest name of Plaistow High Street, is mentioned in 1527. With the industrial development from about 1840 (*see* NEWHAM), the over 1,200 acres of marsh pasture land in the south of the ward were gradually covered by the new districts of CANNING TOWN, CUSTOM HOUSE and SILVERTOWN, the Victoria Dock, and the industries of Thames-side and Bow Creek. Luke Howard, the Quaker chemist, meteorologist, philanthropist and founder of Howard and Sons, lived at Chesterton House, Balaam Street, in the early 19th century, and John Curwen, educator and developer of the tonic *sol-fa* system of musical notation, was Congregational minister at Plaistow in 1844–64 and founded there the Curwen Press. Upton Manor, E13, to the north of the village, was developed on the estate of Sir John Henry Pelly, after his death in 1852. He had held a number of public offices including the Governorship of the Hudson's Bay Company.

Plaistow Hospital *Samson Street, Plaistow, E13.* Built in 1901 for patients suffering from infectious diseases. In 1948 under the National Health Service its use was changed to that of a hospital for acute cases and geriatrics. In 1981 there were 152 beds.

Planetarium *Marylebone Road, NW1.* Opened in 1958 next door to MADAME TUSSAUD'S. The Zeiss projector contains 29,000 separate parts and includes nearly 200 optical projectors. 9,000 stars are visible. On certain evenings the Planetarium is used as a Laserium, when a combination of sound and patterns of coloured light are produced by a laser beam.

Planning *and* **Building Regulations** The first building ordinances about which any information survived are of uncertain date but are usually ascribed to Henry Fitzailwyn, who was London's first mayor from *c.*1190 to 1212. 'Fitzailwyn's Assize', as it has come to be known, stipulated *inter alia* that party walls were to be of stone and at least 3 feet thick, and also required the construction of gutters to carry rainwater off buildings into the streets. Further regulations passed from time to time in the wardmotes specified that the overhanging projections or jetties on the upper floors of houses had to be at least high enough for a man on horseback to pass beneath, and that roofs were to be constructed of tile, stone or lead. Chimneys were to be faced with plaster, tile or stone, and, as a further precaution against fire and its consequences, the occupants of large houses were ordered to keep a ladder and a barrel of water outside their houses during the summer months. Other regulations guarding against encroachments on the highway can be seen as remote ancestors of the uniform building line.

The fourfold increase in the POPULATION of London during the Tudor period placed an enormous strain on the fabric of the capital. Unregulated expansion took place, chiefly to the east, while in the centre buildings were enlarged and heightened in an unsafe manner; ramshackle structures were erected in the courts of large buildings and tenements were piled up in alleys and passageways to the detriment of health and order. The result was a remarkable royal proclamation, issued in 1580 and enacted into law in 1592, which has been described as the birth of the concept of planning in London. The proclamation forbade the erection of any building on new foundations within 3 miles of the City and prohibited the subdivision of existing houses between families and the letting of rooms to lodgers.

Similar proclamations, which were issued at intervals up to 1630, also contained regulations about the manufacture of bricks and other structural matters such as the thickness of walls, and stipulated that any new houses built on old foundations were to be of brick and stone. The proclamations were singularly ineffective, however, both because the problems caused by the rapid growth of population could not be resolved by such crude and negative measures, and because the Stuart kings regarded the fines levied for contravening the regulations or the premiums exacted for granting building licences as convenient sources of income. The result was a haphazard application of the regulations which made matters even worse in the centre where flimsy structures were erected since these would entail no great loss if they had to be pulled down. Paradoxically, however, the worsening of conditions in the City and its immediate environs which followed this failure of centralised control helped to promote the development of well-planned layouts on the private estates of the great landowners in the West End, whose families and friends sought a haven from the disease and squalor in the centre. Two such developments of the

1630s – in COVENT GARDEN and LINCOLN'S INN FIELDS – are of cardinal importance in any consideration of the evolution of planning in London. Both were products of that peculiarly English, and often uneasy, compromise between central direction or exhortation and private initiative. COVENT GARDEN was the result of the enterprise of the 4th Earl of Bedford who obtained a special dispensation to erect new buildings on the site of the old convent garden of WESTMINSTER ABBEY by a royal licence of 1631, for which he had to pay a substantial fee. A condition of the granting of the licence was that the Earl should be directed in his building operations by the King and Council, in effect by the King's Surveyor General, Inigo Jones. The resulting Piazza in COVENT GARDEN, which was based on Italian and French models, has justly been described as the first of the great London squares.

The open ground on the west side of LINCOLN'S INN had long been used as recreation ground by the members of the inn, and attempts to erect buildings there had been stoutly resisted. When, in 1638, William Newton, a speculative builder, received a licence to build on the fields, however, a compromise was reached whereby he undertook to keep a 'square peece of ground' free of buildings, and in the course of long and complex negotiations LINCOLN'S INN FIELDS was given its present form. With its gravelled walks, grass plots and plantations, LINCOLN'S INN FIELDS corresponds more closely to the general idea of a London square than COVENT GARDEN'S Piazza, although the difference was less obvious at first. But it might be said that the development of the urban square of streets and houses surrounding a garden enclosure, which is London's principal contribution to town planning, arose from the fortuitous conjunction in time of a carefully planned piazza on the European model and an enclosure of fields which was preserved largely by accident.

After the Restoration in 1660 the square invariably became the principal unit of any major layout in the West End, beginning with BLOOMSBURY SQUARE (where the adoption of the word 'square' in leases of 1663 may be the first instance of its use in the topographical sense) and ST JAMES'S SQUARE, and reaching its apogee in the 18th and 19th centuries with GROSVENOR SQUARE and BELGRAVE SQUARE and their counterparts in KENSINGTON and further afield. The square itself became the centrepiece of a regular grid of wide, straight streets which embodied classical ideals of symmetry, order and proportion, but each orderly layout tended to be confined within the bounds of a great estate, with little or no communication over the boundaries.

If the layout of London's fashionable quarters in the West End can be seen as a logical progression from COVENT GARDEN and LINCOLN'S INN FIELDS, the development of building regulations, and thereby the types of houses erected in the new layouts, were profoundly affected by the GREAT FIRE. One immediate response to the fire was the preparation of plans for rebuilding the devastated area of a kind and on a scale not before seen in London. There were several such plans, of which those of Sir Christopher Wren and John Evelyn are the best known. All of them were grandiose schemes which envisaged London as a city of broad streets and piazzas of various shapes, recalling the great plan imposed on Rome during the pontificate of Sixtus V in the previous century. The realities of English property divisions made such schemes academic; and the most that could be achieved in the rebuilding was the widening of some streets, the creation of one or two new streets and quays, and the elimination of the worst overcrowding. The Act for the Rebuilding of the City of London, passed in 1667, was more important, however, for the comprehensive building regulations it contained. Houses were classified into four types, depending on which street they faced, and ranged in size from four storeys to two. They were to be built of brick and stone with a minimum of external timberwork; and the thickness of walls and heights of ceilings and timber scantlings were specified. There was little that was new in the regulations and the Act applied only to the CITY, but, perhaps because of the extent of the catastrophe of the GREAT FIRE, it was obeyed to a far greater degree than earlier building ordinances and was also taken as a model outside the City.

Two further Building Acts affecting the CITY OF LONDON and WESTMINSTER were passed in 1707 and 1709 and had a considerable effect on the appearance of the London terrace house. Both were concerned with the threat of fire: the first abolished the wooden eaves cornice, requiring the front wall to be carried up above the roof as a parapet, while the second required window frames to be recessed at least 4 ins from the external wall face (although this latter provision was by no means always obeyed). A number of further Acts were passed in the course of the 18th century on such matters as the construction of party walls and the standardisation of bricks; and in 1774 all previous legislation was consolidated into a major new Act. This divided all buildings into various 'rates' according to size and type and established standards of construction for each rate. It further affected the appearance of houses by requiring most of the window frame to be set within the brickwork of the reveals, so that only a thin strip of wood remained showing. The Act also applied to a wider area which embraced the districts covered by the BILLS OF MORTALITY and the parishes of ST MARYLEBONE, ST PANCRAS, PADDINGTON and CHELSEA. Moreover it established in embryo the office of district surveyor.

The Act of 1774 was replaced by a new Building Act in 1844. Under this, district surveyors were placed on a more professional footing and their authority strengthened. In addition an Office of Metropolitan Buildings was set up to oversee building matters. More specific provisions regulated the width of new streets and mews and laid down a ratio between the height of buildings and the width of streets. Most importantly, however, the area covered by the Act was greatly extended to include the whole of metropolitan London – defined, in fact, as slightly more extensive than the area which was incorporated into the County of London in 1889.

The Act of 1844 was superseded by another Building Act in 1855 when the METROPOLITAN BOARD OF WORKS was established. Practical changes were minimal, but a new office of Superintending Architect of Metropolitan Buildings was created. Under the METROPOLITAN BOARD OF WORKS a number of bylaws and amending Acts were passed regulating building lines and dealing with structural matters like the specifications for foundations.

Shortly after the METROPOLITAN BOARD OF WORKS was replaced by the LONDON COUNTY COUNCIL, a comprehensive new Building Act was passed in 1894.

This Act defined a relationship between the height of a building and the open space around it. It also restricted the height of buildings to 80 ft, apart from attic storeys, unless special consent was obtained. It was additionally concerned with the means of escape in case of fire and, naturally, with the prevention of the spread of fire. A clause limiting the cubic capacity of buildings without internal party walls held back the development of large modern steel-framed buildings such as department stores, but by recognizing the advance in fire precautions and the fire-resisting capacities of some materials the Act and the bylaws passed under its authority proved a liberating influence on the appearance of buildings, once more permitting, for instance, door and window frames to be fitted flush with the wall surface under certain circumstances. Amending Acts were passed in 1905 and 1909, while many bylaws tackled the problems raised by new materials and methods of construction until a new London Building Act was passed in 1930. This Act, together with amending Acts of 1935 and 1939 and subsequent bylaws, still forms the statutory basis of building regulations in inner London. Obvious changes from earlier Acts include the relaxation of restrictions on the height and internal planning of buildings. For the outer London BOROUGHS comprehensive sets of building regulations are from time to time issued by statutory instrument under the authority of several Acts of Parliament.

Throughout the 19th and much of the 20th century planning remained largely a private matter and depended on the conscientiousness, and far-sightedness, of the great landlords. Some major improvements were achieved on Crown land, such as the formation of REGENT STREET and REGENT'S PARK, and several new streets were cut through slum areas including VICTORIA STREET, and, under the METROPOLITAN BOARD OF WORKS, SHAFTESBURY AVENUE and CHARING CROSS ROAD.

It was not until the passing of the Town and Country Planning Act of 1932 that the LONDON COUNTY COUNCIL resolved to prepare a London-wide plan which received government approval as the Town Planning Scheme Number 19. Inquiries were held at which the representatives of the large estates stated with some justification that they had been managing their own planning in a perfectly satisfactory manner and should be allowed to continue doing so. Little was achieved before the outbreak of war in 1939 apart from the creation of the Green Belt. This consists of a broad band of mostly farmland, parkland and recreation ground around London in which any building development is carefully controlled, its purpose being both to provide the amenities of the countryside within easy access of the city-dweller and to prevent the unrestricted, tentacle-like spread of the metropolis into the surrounding countryside. During the war Sir Patrick Abercrombie was appointed to prepare plans for the County of London and Greater London, and the *County of London Plan* and *Greater London Plan* were published in 1943 and 1944 respectively. These recognised that problems of the administration of a wider area than that of the LONDON COUNTY COUNCIL were inextricably linked with planning matters. The creation of the GREATER LONDON COUNCIL was in part a response to such problems, and the GLC's most important statutory role was to prepare the *Greater London Development Plan,* which was published in

1969 but has scarcely been a subject of agreement, let alone implementation.

One aspect of post-war planning legislation which has had a marked impact on the appearance of London is the increased protection given to historic buildings, a vital matter for a city with a long history and a large number of fine buildings in a period when rebuilding has taken place on a large scale. Earlier legislation had provided a rudimentary means of protection for buildings of special architectural and historical interest, but it was not until the passing of the Town and Country Planning Acts of 1944 and 1947 that provision was made for compiling lists of buildings which would thereafter receive statutory protection. The control over the demolition and material alteration of such listed buildings has been strengthened by subsequent planning Acts, especially those of 1968 and 1971. The Civic Amenities Act of 1967 also introduced the concept of conservation areas which were defined as 'areas of special architectural or historic interest the character or appearance of which it is desirable to preserve or enhance'. While new developments are not entirely excluded from conservation areas, care is taken to ensure that they are of a type and on a scale which harmonise with the existing buildings. There are now nearly 30,000 listed buildings and over 300 conservation areas in Greater London.

London has steadfastly refused to submit to comprehensive replanning. The saga of the motorway box which was fundamental to the *Greater London Development Plan* but which has since been almost universally rejected is a case in point, and recent developments in COVENT GARDEN, where planning in London can be said to have begun, illustrates the present situation well. There a major planning scheme has been whittled away, largely through the opposition of local residents, and has been replaced by a programme of piecemeal renewal, including a splendid restoration of the market building, in which small-scale traditional uses are being retained alongside new ones which result from a process of organic growth rather than authoritarian imposition.

Platt's Lane *NW3*. It takes its name from Thomas Pell Platt, the orientalist, who lived at Child's Hill, HAMPSTEAD. T.G. Masaryk, the Czech statesman, lived at No. 21 during the 1st World War.

Players' Theatre Club *Villiers Street, WC2*. Began in 1927 as Playroom Six, in New Compton Street. Peggy Ashcroft made her first London appearance here. It was renamed the Players' Theatre in 1929. In 1934 it moved to KING STREET, COVENT GARDEN, formerly the home of EVANS MUSIC AND SUPPER ROOMS which had latterly been occupied by the NATIONAL SPORTING CLUB. But the theatre soon afterwards closed. It was reopened in 1936. The object of the new theatre club was to revive the early Victorian music-hall. It was taken over in 1940 by Leonard Sachs. In 1946 the club moved into premises consisting of two arches, Nos 173 and 174 VILLIERS STREET, which had been associated with music-hall since the early Victorian age. Most of the foremost music-hall artistes appeared here; but after renovation and structural changes Sandy Wilson's *The Boy Friend* (1953) opened the club to a different kind of audience. It subsequently reverted to music-hall, its players known as 'The Late Joys', a reference to Joy, Evan's predecessor whose rooms were colloquially known as 'Evans Late Joys'. Its seating capacity is 300 at tables and chairs.

Playhouse Theatre *Northumberland Avenue*. Built in 1882 by the speculator, Sefton Parry, who expected the site to be required by the South Eastern Railway Company. In 1891 George Alexander began his career as an actor-manager here. In 1894 the first production of Shaw's *Arms and the Man* was staged. From 1898 to 1900 the theatre was managed by Charles Hawtrey. In 1899 *A Message from Mars* had 544 performances. In 1905 part of CHARING CROSS STATION collapsed on the theatre, killing six people. It was rebuilt in 1907 by the French architects Blow and Billerey for Cyril Maude, who managed it until 1915. From 1917 to 1923 it was run by Frank Curzon and Gladys Cooper. In 1924 *White Cargo* began its run of 821 performances. From 1927 to 1933 it was managed by Gladys Cooper alone. It became a BBC studio in 1951, and in 1982 was empty. It seated 620.

Playhouse Yard *EC4*. The site of the BLACKFRIARS PLAYHOUSE which was constructed in the 1590s by James Burbage in some of the disused buildings of the BLACKFRIARS MONASTERY. The local residents protested and Burbage had to lease the theatre to the Children of the Chapel, a popular company of boy actors recruited from the choristers of the Chapel Royal. In 1608 Burbage resumed possession. William Shakespeare had a share in the theatre and his company, the King's Players, acted here. It was demolished in 1655.

Plough *27 Museum Street, WC1*. A late Victorian public house, much frequented by writers and artists before the war, when it was known as 'The Baby's Bottom', perhaps because it was once painted pink. It was renovated in 1967.

Plumbers' Company see CITY LIVERY COMPANIES.

Plumstead *SE18*. Although part of the seemingly endless riverside suburbs, it is a community of surprising contrasts. The lower levels by the river are dominated by industrial development and the encroachment of the new town of THAMESMEAD, but the higher ground to the south preserves aspects of its former rural character with its two commons and extensive open land on Shooters Hill. It is a community of considerable antiquity: two burial mounds, probably from the pre-Roman era, survive, one on Winns Common, the other in Brinklow Crescent on SHOOTERS HILL. Roman burials have been discovered in Wickham Lane beside the ancient riverside highway, and the southern boundary of the parish has always been the great Roman road, Watling Street, that runs over the steep slopes of Shooters Hill. In about 960 King Edgar granted four ploughlands in Plumstead to the Abbot and Convent of St Augustine at Canterbury. In 1023 the body of Archbishop Alfege, slain at GREENWICH 11 years previously, was brought through Plumstead on its way to Canterbury Cathedral and by the time of the *Domesday* survey the village had been divided into two manors.

It was always a prosperous village with extensive, well-drained marshes for sheep grazing and good soil for fruit growing (all place-name authorities agree that its name derives from the Old English word for plums). Until the last century when rapid and massive development took place, mainly because of its proximity to industrial WOOLWICH, its character remained unchanged – a long high street with the parish church of St Nicholas (the west and south walls of the south aisle of which date from the 12th century, the transept from the 13th, the north aisle from the 15th and the brick tower from 1664) and the now demolished manor house at the eastern end, the marshes and the river to the north, and fields and commonland on the uplands to the south. However, in the last century, WOOLWICH ARSENAL expanded further over the marshes and the arrival of the railway in 1849 prompted considerable suburban development, especially on the old Burrage Estate to the west of the village adjoining WOOLWICH. During 1801–61 the population increased from 1,166 to 24,502. As the land was developed so the eyes of developers were turned to the large expanse of open common land. Attempts at enclosure were resisted with increasing militancy until, in the 1870s, soldiers from the garrison at WOOLWICH began to use the common for drill and exercise. The riots that ensued and the imprisonment of the local leader, John De Morgan, provided the necessary stimulus for the METROPOLITAN BOARD OF WORKS to acquire Plumstead and Winns Commons in 1877 and preserve them as public open spaces.

In Old Mill Road on the common can be seen the remains of an 18th-century windmill, which ceased working in the 1840s and is now part of a public house, and not far away to the west in Vicarage Park is Bramblebury, a fine Georgian house, built in 1790, which became the vicarage of the now demolished St Margaret's Church on Plumstead Common.

In the High Street there are two 18th-century buildings of note, the Volunteer public house, formerly a vicarage, and the Plume of Feathers public house. Also in the High Street is the GREENWICH Borough Museum on the first floor of Plumstead Library. Here are displayed exhibitions relating to the local and natural history of the district drawn from the museum's extensive collections.

Poland Street *W1*. Building began here in the 1680s and continued until 1707. The street takes its name from the King of Poland tavern which stood on the north-west corner and which, after changing its name to the Wheatsheaf and then, in 1925, to the Dickens Wine House, was destroyed by a bomb in 1940. The street has been much rebuilt but there are still some 18th-century houses to be seen. No. 7, which has been refronted, was built for the Countess of Sandwich in 1707. No. 11 is of the same date and has also been refaced. No. 15 was also built at this time and has been considerably altered; the Earl of Suffolk was living here in 1717, and Percy Bysshe Shelley took lodgings here for a few weeks in the spring of 1811, having been sent down from Oxford after issuing his pamphlet, *The Necessity of Atheism*. No. 24 was built in 1707, No. 48 in about 1705 and refaced in 1750. No. 54 was built in 1705 and occupied from 1788 to 1792 by Elizabeth Billington, the lascivious and marvellously gifted singer, mistress of the Duke of Rutland and George, Prince of Wales, who was known as 'the Poland Street Man Trap'. Other notable occupants of the street when it was fashionable in the 18th

century were Giacomo Leoni (1744–6) and William Chambers (1758–66), the architects, Paul Sandby, the painter (1767–72), and William Blake who lived at No. 28 from 1785 to 1791 and who composed, designed, engraved and printed here his *Songs of Innocence, The Ghost of Abel, The Book of Thell, The Marriage of Heaven and Hell* and *The French Revolution*. In 1760–70 Dr Charles Burney, the musical historian, lived at No. 50 which has since been demolished.

At No. 23 is Ye Olde King's Arms public house which occupies a site where a tavern has stood since at least 1718. A plaque on the front announces: 'In this Old King's Arms Tavern The Ancient Order of Druids was revived 28th November 1781. This commemorative plaque was placed here on the 150th anniversary By the AOD.' At No. 62 is another public house, the Star and Garter, on which site there has been a tavern of this name since 1825.

In the 19th century the well-to-do inhabitants left the street which was taken over by tradesmen and craftsmen, many of them jewellers and engravers. There are still some of these left but there are more clothing manufacturers, textile agents and fashion wholesalers. The Academy Cinema is on the corner of OXFORD STREET. The Poland Street Garage, opened in 1934 (now Poland Street Autos), was the first multistorey car park in London in which the floors were interconnected by a shallow ramp.

Police The only general act of policing between the Norman Conquest and Peel's police bill of 1829 was the Statute of Winchester of 1285. This was fundamentally a consolidating act and reaffirmed the system of watch and ward, hue and cry, and what was termed an 'assize of arms' by which every male between 15 and 60 was to maintain a 'harness to keep the peace'. A separate *Statuta Civitatis* was passed the same year for the CITY OF LONDON. This seems merely to have confirmed existing practices going back to a time 'whereof the memory of man is not to the contrary'. It is probable that the CITY system at that time had evolved from an earlier form of defence system, possibly Roman, although there is no direct evidence for this. The CITY was divided into 200 precincts with one constable to each precinct. When curfew was rung at ST MARTIN'S-LE-GRAND the constables would put on quilted leather jackets or cuirasses and arm themselves with swords, halberds and longbows; half would go to the CITY gates and the other half to patrol Thames Street along the shoreline until the morning curfew was rung at ST THOMAS OF ACON in CHEAPSIDE. This was the 'standing and marching watch'.

By law, CITY freemen 'paying scot' and 'bearing lot' had to serve one year as constable, beadle and scavenger; out of office they had to serve by rotation in their ward watch; both posts were unpaid; refusal to serve could be punished by fine or imprisonment. The CITY was divided into WARDS, each of which had its own officers and watch. At first the watch mustered only at certain times of the year such as Christmas, Easter and Midsummer for periods of not more than one or two weeks. They were expected to maintain the peace but, judging from the records, much of their time seems to have been spent in closing down local bawdy houses by making them uninhabitable. In 1305 they broke into the house of William Cok of Cockes Lane and, using hammers and chisels, took away 11 doors and five windows. Gradually, as the CITY lost its defensive character, musters became more frequent, until by the beginning of the 16th century the watch was mustering nightly; and since it was no longer vital to protect the CITY from external attack, the constables and watch were reorganised on a WARD basis. Each watch stayed inside its own WARD boundary and, while nominally under the control of their WARD ALDERMAN, the direct control lay with the constable and BEADLE.

Because of the hostility to the system, which was unpaid, dangerous and time-consuming, the CITY was constantly looking for fresh sources of man-power. Foreign traders were pressed into service; freemen working in one WARD and living within another had to take office in both; traders investing in CITY businesses were technically 'paying scot' and were therefore liable to serve even though, as many protested and as the records confirm, they lived and worked many hundreds of miles away. Refusal to serve was punished with fines or imprisonment. Inevitably a blind eye was turned to the practice of sending a substitute. At first these were servants or apprentices but gradually it became the accepted practice to hire the old and generally unemployable as watchmen and constables. By Shakespeare's time they were notorious for 'abusing the time, coming very late to the watch, sitting down in some common place of watching, wherein some falleth on sleep by reason of labour or much drinking before, or else nature requireth a rest in the night. These fellows think every hour a thousand until they go home, home, home, every man to bed.' In 1705 the CITY came to terms with the hiring of substitutes. A new Watch Act officially recognised the practice and by doing so created the first professional paid watch force in the country.

The policing of WESTMINSTER was under the control of the Abbot. In 1584, when the Abbot was replaced by a Dean, an Act of Parliament divided WESTMINSTER into WARDS and gave it a form of civic government similar to that of the CITY. As in the CITY there was little or no co-operation between the WARDS, each of which acted in splendid isolation from the other. From the 1570s the CITY made several temporary appointments of a Provost Marshal to try to get the watch and constables to act together on a common basis. In 1603 the CITY appointed a CITY MARSHAL who, for the next 300 years, was to be the head of its police force. He was assisted by an Under-Marshal and six marshalmen. They were independent of the WARDS and answerable only to the LORD MAYOR and ALDERMEN. In 1663 an Act of the COURT OF COMMON COUNCIL for regulating the watch led to the watchmen in general being known from that time on as 'Charleys', perhaps because the Act was passed soon after the restoration of Charles II.

The end of the 17th century coincided with two unwelcome developments. In 1694 the CITY was made bankrupt by Act of Parliament because of overspending on rebuilding after the GREAT FIRE. To recoup its money it decided to auction its offices including such important ones as RECORDER, Keeper of NEWGATE and City Marshal. These changed hands for enormous sums and the system led to much corruption. This sale of offices coincided with the growth of the rewards system and the rise of the professional thief-takers. The most notorious of these was Jonathan Wild, the self-styled 'Thieftaker-General of Great Britain and Ireland'. Beginning as an unsworn marshalman, he quickly graduated to being a receiver of stolen pocket books; and by using the rewards system and the

Rowlandson's caricature of a watchman, known as a 'Charley', who fails to notice either the burglars or the lovers in his own watch-house.

general corruption of the time he gained a total mastery of the early 18th-century underworld. At the height of his powers he had specially-trained thieves to rob at Court and at fashionable levées, and his own gangs of highwaymen and an army of burglars, pickpockets and prostitutes working for him. He was frequently attacked, and when he died had the scars of 19 sword and pistol wounds on his body, and his skull was morticed together with silver plates where it had frequently been fractured. He was eventually hanged at TYBURN in 1725. In 1737 the CITY abolished the system of personal service for watchmen but not for constables. In 1748 the novelist and writer, Henry Fielding, was appointed magistrate at BOW STREET. Instead of exploiting his opportunities to earn 'the dirtiest money upon earth', he instigated a number of reforms which were to have a significant influence upon police development. Ill-health forced his premature retirement but these ideas were developed by his blind half-brother, John Fielding. The seven thief-takers known as 'Mr Fielding's people' were the spearhead of his war on the underworld, and they were the original BOW STREET runners. Sir John Fielding experimented also with the use of foot patrols on the main roads out of London. These continued even though the financial support for a mounted patrol, which was tried for a limited period, was discontinued.

In Fielding's time the word 'police' began to be used in its modern sense. Until then its French connotation of spies and *agents provocateurs* was the most widely accepted. By 1781, when Sheridan used it in a Parliamentary debate, he said, 'Gentlemen would understand what he meant by the term police; it was not an expression of our law, or of our language, but was perfectly understood.'

By 1778 the CITY had managed to buy back the offices of City Marshal, Under-Marshal and those of the six marshalmen. Two years later the GORDON RIOTS engulfed the capital in an orgy of looting and destruction. Many CITY constables openly sympathised with the rioters and flaunted the white cockade; indeed in WESTMINSTER they disappeared from the streets completely. Four years later the CITY formed a Day Police as an additional means of protection; the men were issued with a blue greatcoat every four years and a pair of boots every two. Blue was chosen, at the suggestion of Jonas Hanway, as being a sober and dignified colour to wear at the executions which they would have to attend.

In 1785 a police bill for the metropolis was introduced into Parliament. This was the short-lived London and Westminster police bill. It proposed that the CITY, WESTMINSTER, SOUTHWARK and adjacent parts should be merged into one police district and then split up into nine divisions. It has wrongly been suggested that this was an early version of the Metropolitan Police bill some years later. In practice the bill would have retained the old watch system which would have meant that half the total watch force would have been retained in the CITY. Equally unrealistic was the suggested number of foot and horse patrols; these would have totalled not more than 225 men who would have been portioned out in units of 25 to each division. The bill, which one newspaper called 'radically bad', antagonised several influential sections of the community and was never re-introduced. In 1798 the THAMES police force was formed to stop piracy on the river. The initial cost was borne by merchants trading to the West Indies, but the scheme proved so successful that in 1801 it was taken over by the government (*see* RIVER POLICE). In 1805 the BOW STREET horse patrol was organised to stop the increase in highway robbery. Because of their scarlet waistcoats the horsemen were known as the 'Robin Redbreasts'. The foot patrols begun by Sir John Fielding patrolled up to four miles out of town; this was where the horse patrol took over and patrolled up to 20 miles from London.

Parliamentary committees urged in 1812, 1816 and again in 1818 that reform of the so-called police in the metropolis was long overdue. The CITY with less than 12 per cent of the capital's population had more than 40 per cent of its police force. As far as the rest of the metropolis was concerned, excluding the watchmen who were a proverbial 'rope of sand' and the THAMES police, the Home Secretary of the day had fewer than 400 men with which to control a population of more than one million. The London watchmen were a scandal. In 1821 the following mock advertisement was published: 'Wanted, a hundred thousand men for London watchmen. None need apply for this lucrative situation without being the age of sixty, seventy, eighty, or ninety years; blind with one eye and seeing very little with the other; crippled in one or both legs; deaf as a post; with an asthmatical cough that tears them to pieces; whose speed will keep pace with a snail, and the strength of whose arm would not be able to arrest an old washerwoman of fourscore returned from a hard day's fag at the washtub. . . .'

In 1822 the Home Secretary, Robert Peel, was rebuffed by his Parliamentary Committee in an attempt to find a solution and it was not until 1828 that he tried again. The police reformers were in a minority. Public opinion was against any change in the system as it was thought that it would entail too great a loss of freedom. But Peel's main opposition was to come from the CITY which was against placing police powers in the hands of the representative of an unreformed House of Commons. Peel silenced this opposition by drafting a bill for a police force which included the CITY. When the CITY protested, as had been expected, he agreed to exclude it if the rest of his bill for a police force for the metropolis was given an unopposed reading. This was agreed to and Peel was enabled to steer his bill successfully past the opposition within his own party.

The Metropolitan Police Bill became law; on 29 September 1829 the first Metropolitan policemen stepped on to the streets. The old system was swept away except for BOW STREET and the THAMES police which maintained their independence for ten more years. Command of the force was in the joint control of two Commissioners, Colonel Charles Rowan, a Peninsular and Waterloo veteran, and the Irish barrister, Richard Mayne. Their headquarters was at 4 Whitehall Place, the back part of which was used as a police station, entered from SCOTLAND YARD from which the police station soon acquired its name. The initial strength of the force was about 3,000 men split among 17 divisions, each of which was designated by a letter of the alphabet. The blue uniform and top hat was deliberately chosen to emphasise its non-military character. Because of public suspicion it had to be worn even when the men were not on duty. The wages of 3s a day were just above charity level and were largely responsible for the abnormally high wastage: within four years fewer than one sixth of the original 3,000 remained. Peel's reply to criticisms was, 'No doubt three shillings a day will not give me all the virtues under heaven, but I do not want them. Angels would be far above my work.' Public opinion was hostile to Peel's 'Blue devils'. They were stoned, blinded, mutilated, spiked on railings and beaten up. In 1831 these demonstrations of hate and mistrust reached new heights when at the CLERKENWELL riots an unarmed police constable was stabbed to death and the coroner's jury brought in a verdict of 'Justifiable homicide'. For many years following an annual banquet was held to commemorate the event.

'The Real Blue Collarer in London.' Hostility to the new police is compared in this 1832 caricature to the dread of cholera.

In 1839 the THAMES police and the BOW STREET runners (who had become little more than a private detective agency) were absorbed into the new force. The same year, after a decade of attempted reform, the old watch system was finally abolished in the CITY and a separate police force, the CITY OF LONDON POLICE, was formed to patrol the one square mile. The passing of the runners was largely unmourned but left a gap. Three years later, in 1842, after two particularly sensational murders, a Detective Department was formed consisting of two inspectors and six sergeants. They caught the public imagination and served as models for both Dickens and Wilkie Collins.

The Commissioners steered the new force through the hostility that nearly destroyed them in those early years and when Rowan retired in 1850 they had a large measure of the public respect and the beginning of its affection. 'King' Mayne, as he became known, continued as Commissioner. As the force continued to expand it was broken down into departments dealing with problems as diverse as dangerous structures and public carriages, in addition to its chief role which was – and is – the prevention and detection of crime. In 1864 the old swallow-tail coat and top hat were replaced by a tunic and helmet. Public demands for Mayne's resignation mounted with police mishandling of the HYDE PARK riots (1866) and the CLERKENWELL explosion (1867). Much of the criticism was muted by Mayne's death in 1868.

Public suspicion, as well as professional jealousy from within the force itself, had restricted any expansion of the Detective Department. When Mayne died it numbered only 15 men in a force of 8,000. The new Commissioner, Colonel Edmund Henderson, began to expand the department. The uniformed men were allowed to wear plain clothes when off duty and beats were shortened. Henderson also started a Register of Habitual Criminals which was the genesis of the Criminal Records Office. But grievances over pay, a strike in 1872 and a trial in 1877 which exposed corruption in the Detective Department showed that all was far from well. The Home Office set up its own inquiry into the Detective Department and laid the seeds of future trouble by recommending that it should be separate from the uniformed branch and that its head should be independent of the Commissioner and have direct access to the Home Secretary. In 1878 it was renamed the Criminal Investigation Department.

From 1883 to 1885 acts of Fenian terrorism, including the bombing of SCOTLAND YARD, led to the forming of the Special Irish Branch which was soon renamed Special Branch. When uncontrolled rioting in 1886 forced Henderson's resignation he was succeeded by Sir Charles Warren, a 'soldier in jackboots', who gained some public applause with his handling of the TRAFALGAR SQUARE riots (1887), but his mishandling of the Jack the Ripper murders (1888), his differences with his colleagues and his quarrels with the Home Office brought about his resignation in November 1888. It was conflict again with the Home Office, this time over pensions, that compelled his successor, James Monro, to resign 19 months later and precipitated a strike which was quickly suppressed but which marked the beginning of a decade of slow reform.

By 1900 the force had grown to nearly 16,000 men. Its 21 divisions covered an area of nearly 700 square miles. And in the years following increased use was made of such aids as a Central Finger Print Bureau (1901), a detective training school (1902) and a police training school at Peel House, WESTMINSTER. But the morale of the force, which often felt itself to be ruled tyrannically by the military Commissioners of the Metropolitan Police, was not high. Part of the problem was the status of the policeman who was rated as little more than an unskilled labourer and paid accordingly. Policemen's other grievances included the long-standing complaint that they were not allowed any rest day but had to work the full seven days every week. This grievance was redressed in 1910 but not until after the men had complained that 'even convicts are given time for recreation'. As conditions worsened, the men's militancy grew. The 1st World War held it in check until the closing stages when 6,000 men came out on strike. Their action brought about the immediate capitulation of the Government and forced the resignation of the Commissioner. The Desborough Committee and the Police Act, 1919, dealt with police problems on a national basis and brought about a settlement which redressed some of the grievances. It also achieved the important aim of destroying the embryo Police Union which the men were forbidden to join. When the Union called a second strike in 1919 only 1,083 men out of a force of 19,004 obeyed the call and these were instantly dismissed. In 1919 the Women's Police Service, supposedly a temporary wartime creation, were absorbed into the force.

The 1920s and 1930s brought great mechanisation. Traffic patrols, wireless cars and radio rooms all became common, while vans, used to speed the police to the scenes of crimes, marked the beginnings of the Flying Squad.

The Metropolitan Police College at HENDON was begun in 1934 by the then Commissioner, Lord Trenchard. It was attacked as a supposed upholder of the class system and even as an encouragement to Fascism. When it was closed in 1939, on the outbreak of war, fewer than 200 men had passed through its doors, one of whom, in 1958, Joseph Simpson, was to be the first policeman to rise through the ranks to Commissioner. In 1946 a training school for probationers was opened at HENDON, and in 1951 a cadet scheme was started there with an initial intake of 160 entrants. Peel Centre, the new Metropolitan Police Training Centre, was opened by the Queen in 1974. Detectives as well as probationers and cadets are trained here. By 1945 the force was again under strength and the post-war decades were to see a growing number of problems calling for ever-increasing specialisation.

Special squads were formed, including those for Murder, Robbery, Fraud, Obscene Publications, Serious Crimes, Bombs and Drugs. A Criminal Intelligence Unit was also introduced. The policeman on the beat was given more sophisticated aids such as pocket radios, computers and videos, and found himself becoming involved in marches, demonstrations and riots on a scale unimagined by his Victorian predecessor. Public confidence, badly weakened by trials exposing the darker side of the force, brought about the merging of the CID with the uniformed branch, to which it was subordinated, and the creation of the Police Complaints Board.

The present establishment figure for the force is 26,577 men. Despite increased recruiting the force is still below strength: the 1981 figures show an actual strength of 22,251 men, 2,179 women and 865 cadets.

The Metropolitan Police area which they have to protect has now extended to 786 square miles. This is divided into 23 Districts with two more for HEATHROW AIRPORT and Thames Division. The total number of police stations inside this area is 200. Other statistics show that one day the civilian staff might be the same size as the uniformed branch: its present size is 16,965. There are, in addition, 1,225 traffic wardens, 1,632 part-time special constables, 187 horses, 369 dogs, 27 boats, 532 motor cycles, 1,171 miscellaneous vehicles and 2,054 police cars (*see also* CITY OF LONDON POLICE).

Polish Institute *and* **Sikorski Museum** *20 Prince's Gate, SW7.* Begun after 1945 as a collection of historical records, documents, regimental standards, uniforms, insignia and notable works of art and literature, to conserve and consolidate the heritage of exiled and dispossessed Polish citizens. The Sikorski Collection comprises personal belongings, books, press cuttings and the personal diary of General Sikorski, wartime Prime Minister and Commander-in-Chief of the Polish Forces.

Polka Children's Theatre *240 The Broadway, Wimbledon, SW19.* Dedicated to Charlie Chaplin, the theatre was opened by the Queen Mother in November 1979. It was the inspiration of Richard Gill who inherited his love of puppets from his father, an amateur puppeteer. With his wife, a scenic designer, Gill formed the Polka, presenting a mixture of clowning, mime, children's theatre and puppets.

Pollen Street *W1.* On the Millfield Estate (*see* HANOVER SQUARE), it is a short side street connecting HANOVER STREET and MADDOX STREET. It takes its name from Benjamin Pollen, the heir of Sir Benjamin Maddox, the ground landlord at the time of the estate's first development around 1720.

Pollock's Toy Museum *1 Scala Street and 41 Whitfield Street, W1.* Benjamin Pollock was one of the last publishers of toy theatre sheets which in Victorian times were sold for 'a penny plain and two pence coloured'. He also made toy theatres, a craft learned from his father-in-law, John Redington. 'If you love art, folly or the bright eyes of children,' wrote R.L. Stevenson, 'speed to Pollock's.' Pollock died in 1937 and his shop at HOXTON was bombed in the 2nd World War. But in 1956 the shop moved to 44 MONMOUTH STREET where a museum was created as an attraction and a sympathetic background to the shop. Having outgrown these premises, the collection was moved in 1969 to two little adjoining houses of 1760 with small rooms on four floors at its present address. Pollock's Toy Theatres Ltd is at 44 The Market, Covent Garden.

Polygon Road *NW1.* Originally formed the north side of Clarendon Square, where stood one of the first developments in SOMERS TOWN, The Polygon, a striking 15-sided building of 32 houses, three storeys high, built around gardens. William Godwin lived at No. 29, The Polygon, and here his wife died after giving birth to a daughter, later Mary Shelley. In 1828, by which time the area had become rather seedy, Dickens and his family lodged for a short time in No. 17. Years later, when he wrote *Bleak House*, he made The Polygon the home of Harold Skimpole, a character possibly modelled on Godwin. The Polygon was demolished in the 1890s (*see* SOMERS TOWN).

Polytechnic of Central London *309 Regent Street, W1.* Formed by the amalgamation of the Polytechnic, REGENT STREET, and the Holborn College of Law, Language and Commerce, following the White Paper 'A Plan for Polytechnics and Other Colleges', which was presented to Parliament in 1966. The Polytechnic, REGENT STREET received its Royal Charter as the Royal Polytechnic Institution in 1839. Holborn College of Law, Language and Commerce was founded by the LONDON COUNTY COUNCIL in 1958, by the amalgamation of the former Princeton College of Languages and Commerce with the Department of Law from Kennington College of Commerce and Law. Holborn College began in the former Princeton College building and moved to new premises in RED LION SQUARE in 1961. In 1971 the then Lord Chancellor, Lord Hailsham, who is the grandson of Quintin Hogg who had played such an important role in the life of the Polytechnic, REGENT STREET, during the 1880s, formally opened new buildings on sites in MARYLEBONE ROAD and NEW CAVENDISH STREET.

Polytechnic of North London *Holloway Road, N7.* Formed in 1971 by amalgamation of the Northern Polytechnic and the North Western Polytechnic. Though it operates from five sites in CAMDEN and ISLINGTON, its main buildings are located on the HOLLOWAY ROAD.

Polytechnic of the South Bank *Borough Road, SE1.* Formed in 1970 by bringing together four colleges of different types, the oldest being the Borough Polytechnic, established in 1892 and mentioned by George Bernard Shaw in *Man and Superman*. The main campus is in SOUTHWARK at the ELEPHANT AND CASTLE, while the older Polytechnic building, which houses the Faculty of Science and Engineering, is in Borough Road.

Pond Street *NW3.* Takes its name from a pond which was one of the sources of the FLEET RIVER. Sir Rowland Hill, originator of the penny post (*see* POSTAL SERVICES), lived in Bertram House, a large house on the site of the ROYAL FREE HOSPITAL, from 1848 until his death in 1879. Sir Julian Huxley, the biologist, Professor of Zoology at KING'S COLLEGE and secretary of the ZOOLOGICAL SOCIETY OF LONDON, lived at No. 31 in 1943–75.

Ponders End *Middlesex.* Lies in ENFIELD, west of the LEA river, with Enfield Highway to the north and EDMONTON to the south. The LEA was used for traffic from ancient times and formed a boundary between Saxon and Danish territory. At *Domesday* ENFIELD was woodland with marshes near the river – a section of the parish occupied by the Ponder family, probably keepers of a pond, from at least the 14th century. The land was used for common grazing, and by the 16th century some houses existed including Lincoln House, reputedly the residence of William Wickham, Bishop of Lincoln and then of Winchester. A moated manor house known as Durants (demolished 1910) to the north was frequently visited by James I and, later in the 17th century, by Judge Jeffreys. By the 18th century the nearby settlement was called Enfield

Highway, and further north Grove House near Enfield Wash (demolished) was visited by Thomas Rowlandson. The present PONDERS END MILL and the LEA NAVIGATION Canal were built. The convenience of the canal led to the development of light industry on the marshlands east of Hertford Road. Early in the 19th century an arms factory opened at Enfield Lock, becoming in 1854 the Royal Small Arms Factory. Baylis's crepe works was important, and Edison Swan United Electric Light Company (1886) was to be the pioneer of thermionic and commercial radio valves in the early 20th century. A long-standing brickworks continued until the 1930s and during the 1st World War a shell works operated. The population of Ponders End and Enfield Highway had increased dramatically by the end of the 19th century. In 1831 St James's Enfield Highway was built to the designs of William Lochner to serve all of eastern ENFIELD; and in 1878 St Matthew's chapel-of-ease for Ponders End was opened, becoming its parish church in 1899. J.H. Paull built the nave and north aisle, and, in 1900, J.E.K. and J.P. Cutts, the chancel and chapel. In the early 20th century the area became increasingly residential and industrial and private building took over former nursery land. There was much building to the east of the Great Cambridge Road of 1923, and the settlements of Ponders End, Enfield Highway and Enfield Wash gradually merged. By the 1970s industry predominated east of Hertford Road. In 1903 ENFIELD Urban District Council purchased 34 acres near St James's church to create Durants Park from the estate of the former manor house.

Ponders End Mill *Enfield, Middlesex*. There has been a mill on this site at least from the 11th century. A court case of 1235 tells of a dispute between two millers at Ponders End. The present building put up in the late 18th century is weatherboarded and painted white. It is still in use as a corn mill. The miller's house, of yellow stock brick, is attached.

Pont Street *SW1*. The name was originally given to the short street east of CADOGAN PLACE leading to the WESTBOURNE River. It was built some time after 1805. Greenwood's map of 1827 shows a bridge at this point leading to the new BELGRAVIA development. It probably derives its name from this bridge. The street was completed to the west of SLOANE STREET in 1878. It was laid out across the grounds of the demolished PAVILION. Lined with large gabled redbrick mansions, it inspired Osbert Lancaster's classification 'Pont Street Dutch'. Sir George Alexander, the actor manager, lived at No. 57 in 1896–1918. ST COLUMBA'S (CHURCH OF SCOTLAND) is on the south site. The offices of the Swaziland High Commission are at No. 58. The CADOGAN HOTEL, standing on the corner of SLOANE STREET, was the scene of Oscar Wilde's arrest. A BLUE PLAQUE commemorates the residence here of Lillie Langtry. The black cement *fondu* sculpture, *Jeeves*, the trademark of the shop outside which it stands, was designed by Derek Holmes and executed by Kate McGill (1971).

Pontack's *Abchurch Lane*. A famous French eating house which flourished in the 17th and 18th centuries. It took its name from its eccentric proprietor, Pontack, son of the President of Bordeaux. He was well read in philosophy, spoke several languages, but was an 'eternal babbler' and Evelyn reports that 'much learning had made him mad'. As his sign he used a portrait of his father. In 1697 a meal here cost 'one or two guineas a head'; and Swift, writing in 1711, cites 7s as Pontack's price for a flask of claret from his father's country. The ROYAL SOCIETY held their annual dinners here until 1746. Pontack's successor, Mrs Susannah Austin, was said to have 'acquired a considerable fortune' from the house, which was a byword for gourmandising and celebrated for its 'ragout of falled snails' and its 'chickens not two hours from the shells'.

Ponting Bros *Kensington High Street*. In 1873 Tom Ponting, one of four brothers from Gloucester, opened a fancy draper's shop in Westbourne Grove. His three brothers, Sydney, John and William, bought No. 125 HIGH STREET, KENSINGTON, expanding to 123, 123a and 127 and also to Scarsdale House, formerly the mansion of the Curzons of Kedleston. They soon established a good business in retail fancy goods and silks, everything for art needlework, and even a Needlework School. The original premises were replaced by a High Victorian building, designed by Sherrin. In 1907 JOHN BARKER AND CO. LTD. bought the business. The premises were demolished in the early 1970s and a new complex of shops built in their place.

Pool of London This reach of the Thames has two parts, the Lower Pool and the Upper Pool. The lower runs from Limekiln Creek to CHERRY GARDEN PIER (once the landing stage for the Cherry Garden, a popular resort in the 17th century). It contains, on its north bank, the entrance to LIMEHOUSE CUT (which returns to the LEA NAVIGATION), the entrance to REGENT'S CANAL DOCK, EXECUTION DOCK and WAPPING Police Station, and, on the south of the river, the SURREY DOCKS. Below it are the THAMES TUNNEL and ROTHERHITHE TUNNEL. The Upper Pool runs from Cherry Garden Pier to LONDON BRIDGE and contains on the north the entrance to the ST KATHARINE DOCK, the TOWER OF LONDON, the CUSTOM HOUSE, BILLINGSGATE MARKET, and, beside LONDON BRIDGE, Wren's church of ST MAGNUS THE MARTYR, and on the south the districts of BERMONDSEY and SOUTHWARK, HAY'S WHARF, and the permanently moored HMS BELFAST. Across it spans TOWER BRIDGE. In past times the Lower Pool was known as the river below the bridge and the Upper Pool as that just above it. Today it could be said that TOWER BRIDGE divides the two Pools. Although ships did penetrate above the bridge for a while, mostly to Queenhithe Dock, the river below the bridge was London's main port from Roman days up to the building of the enclosed docks in the 19th century. The Venerable Bede in the 7th century recorded that the Pool provided London's reason for existence; and when Charles I threatened to remove his Court from London, the CITY replied that they did not mind so long as he did not remove the Pool. Even in recent years the Pool was busy with shipping, but today it is virtually empty of ships, the Victorian warehouses are being pulled down and the area is being redeveloped. The bascules of TOWER BRIDGE are now rarely raised.

Henry Poole and Co. *10 Cork Street, W1*. In 1806 James Poole opened a draper's shop in Everett Street, BRUNSWICK SQUARE, having entered tailoring

An engraving after Allom of the Pool of London in 1839, when its waters were still crowded with shipping.

accidentally when he made his own military tunic to join the Volunteer Corps. This was so much admired that he had many requests to make uniforms, and set up as a military tailor. In 1822 he opened a shop in REGENT STREET and in 1823 moved to OLD BURLINGTON STREET. His son, Henry, started at the age of 15 in his father's sewing room. On his father's death in 1846 he altered and enlarged the premises and made the main entrance out of the back door in SAVILE ROW, thus establishing himself as the first of the skilful and fashionable tailors in a street which was to gain fame as the centre of tailoring. Henry Poole died in 1876 and the firm was carried on by a cousin, Samuel Cundey. The move to CORK STREET took place in 1961.

Pope's Villa *Twickenham, Middlesex* In 1719 Alexander Pope leased a house near TWICKENHAM on the London to Hampton Court road. Until his death in 1744 he devoted his life to creating one of the most famous riverside gardens of his time. Virtually nothing remains today. He employed the architect James Gibbs to remodel the house into a small English Palladian villa. Pope was content in TWICKENHAM away from 'the pomps of the town' and wrote to a friend, 'No ideas you could form in the winter, can make you imagine what Twickenham is in the summer season . . . . My building rises high enough to attract the eye and curiosity of the passenger from the river, when, upon beholding a mixture of beauty and ruin, he inquires what house is falling, or what church is rising.' But it was on the garden that Pope lavished his creative powers. Horace Walpole considered him one of the greatest influences on the evolution of the English landscape garden. Pope wrote to his friend, Edward Blount, 'From the river Thames you see through my arch up a walk of the wilderness, to a kind of open temple, wholly composed of shells in the rustic manner . . . .' This led to the famous grotto which was 'finished with shells interspersed with pieces of looking-glass in angular forms, and in the ceiling a star of the same material'. In 1736 Pope opened his 'little kingdom' to the public. After his death in 1744, the house had several owners, finally being bought by Sophia Howe in 1807. She became so irritated by the stream of visitors that she destroyed the house, the gardens and stripped the grotto, earning the title 'Queen of the Goths'. She built herself another house on the site

which was sold and partially pulled down in 1840. Around 1842, a tea merchant, Thomas Young, acquired the site and built a villa described by *The Times* as 'neither like Pope's nor any other, a Chinese erection for which his own chests must have been the model'. Parts of this house can still be seen incorporated in St Catharine's Convent, a school for girls which now occupies the site. The mutilated grotto still exists.

Poplar *E3, E14.* Poplar, including BLACKWALL and the ISLE OF DOGS, was a hamlet of STEPNEY until it became a separate parish in 1817. It is thought to have been named after the tree which would have flourished in the marshy ground nearby. A few fishermen lived here in medieval times; but the village, centred on the High Street, grew from the 16th century onwards because of its nearness to London by road and its ability to cater for ocean-going vessels at BLACKWALL. In Henry VIII's reign Sir Thomas Spert and 54 mariners lodged in Poplar while sails were made for the *Henri Grace Dieu*. The East India Company (founded in 1600) had many of its ships built in the Blackwall Yard and erected almshouses and a chapel in Poplar. The chapel, later dedicated to St Matthias and now closed for worship, is supported by oak pillars said to have been made from the masts of East Indiamen. By 1801 the population was only 4,500, but within ten years the opening of the EAST and WEST INDIA DOCKS linked to London by the new EAST INDIA DOCK ROAD and COMMERCIAL ROAD provided the opportunity for rapid expansion. In the first half of the 19th century many ship builders, merchants, dock officials and others formed a sizeable middle-class element; but later in the century a more industrial suburb, less dependent on maritime trades, developed as manufacturing and transport played increasingly important roles encouraged by the building of railways. The population reached about 55,000 by 1881 and the last portion of open space was built over soon afterwards. Highly skilled labour such as that employed in the engineering trades lived side by side with the vast mass of poorly paid unskilled workers. Poplar, which became a metropolitan borough in 1900 taking in BOW and BROMLEY, played a pioneering part in the development of socialism in London in the early 20th century, under local leaders such as Will Crooks and George Lansbury. Mass demonstrations supported the Poplar

Pope's House c.1753, remodelled into a Palladian villa by James Gibbs, had one of the finest riverside gardens in England.

councillors imprisoned during the 1921 Rates Dispute, and the councillors succeeded in gaining an increased measure of rates equalisation between the richer and poorer boroughs. Their generous treatment of the unemployed in the 1920s added a new word to the English language – 'Poplarism'. The high rate of unemployment and large number of badly paid workers in the area helped to make Poplar the poorest borough in London by 1930. Community spirit, however, was strong; and a local Methodist minister, W.H. Lax, claimed to have originated the idea of the street party, which first took place in 1919 for the peace celebrations. The 2nd World War had a catastrophic effect on Poplar. About half the houses were damaged in the BLITZ and the population also dropped by about half. Most of the area has been redeveloped since, the Lansbury Estate forming the 'live architecture' exhibit in the 1951 FESTIVAL OF BRITAIN. Much of the population has dispersed elsewhere, together with the major sources of employment.

Poppin's Court *EC4*. A small court in the triangle between SHOE LANE, FLEET STREET and ST BRIDE STREET. The Abbots of Cirencester, whose crest included a poppinjay or parrot, had a town house here in the early 14th century called Le Popyngaye. The court consequently came to be known as Popinjay Court. There is a relief of a parrot above the entrance.

Population All figures of the population of London are approximate. Before the first census of 1801 the estimates for most periods are little more than sophisticated guesswork, subject to a wide margin of error, although at some dates, as at the end of the 17th century, there is sufficient rudimentary evidence to enable statistical techniques to be used. Even the first census is now thought to have under-enumerated the population by as much as five per cent, and later ones are still subject to a degree of error, though small. More important by this later period is the problem of determining what is meant by London. Administrative boundaries rarely coincide with geographical realities although it is often necessary to use them for convenience in studying population. In London, in particular, the boundaries fixed at any one time are invariably a

belated and usually out-of-date recognition of an expansion that has occurred some time previously, and the detailed census returns, district by district, have to be used retrospectively to calculate a total for the past population of the city. Before the 19th century, however, uncertainty about the extent of the metropolis at any one time must be added to the imprecision of the basic figures to compound the guesswork.

The first London established in the wake of the Roman legions rapidly became a major trading and administrative centre (*see* LONDINIUM). On the basis of the figures given by Tacitus for casualties in Boudicca's revolt, it has been estimated that that city contained as many as 30,000 people by AD60. If this is correct, the population of the Roman city probably amounted to between 45,000 and 50,000 in the 3rd century. The ethnic composition of this teeming centre (certainly more populous than any other English town was to become until the 18th century) was richly varied, and one factor which dominates the demographic history of the city was present right from the beginning, namely the importance of immigration in maintaining and increasing the population. Of the Roman citizens who constituted the ruling class, a small number would have been of Italian origin, some were Gauls and others came from far-flung parts of the Roman Empire such as Spain or North Africa. The large group of people engaged in trade or commerce was equally cosmopolitan and included substantial and wealthy merchants from as far away as Athens. Slaves were mostly of British origin, but some were occasionally brought in from abroad to perform specialist functions such as clerical work; and the legions which were garrisoned in the city added to the variety of its peoples.

The decline of Roman power in the 4th century and its eventual withdrawal in the mid-5th century had a severe effect on LONDINIUM. Initially numbers may have been maintained as people from outside took refuge within its walls; but with the collapse of the economic foundations and the socio-economic superstructure necessary to support such a large centre, the population must have declined severely. There are no reliable estimates, but it is unlikely that London was ever entirely deserted and probable that a small but significant residential population remained throughout the so-called Dark Ages. Bede, writing of the 7th century, called London 'a mart of many peoples' and said that it was an important trading centre. In the mid-9th century it was under Danish control, but Alfred's reconquest towards the end of that century inaugurated a period of stability and growth. In the late 11th century, shortly after the Norman conquest when the building of the TOWER OF LONDON was a tangible manifestation of the city's importance, it held between 14,000 and 18,000 persons on the best available evidence. In 1199 Peter of Blois said that London had 40,000 inhabitants; but it is now thought that he was exaggerating wildly, and recent careful scholarship has led to the calculation that a figure of 20,000 to 25,000 is more likely at the end of the 12th century. The following century was one of prosperity and expansion when settlement spread well beyond the city walls into the extra-mural suburbs; and, at the probable peak of its medieval growth in about 1340, the population was at least 40,000, almost certainly nearer 50,000, and perhaps once more as high as the limit it had reached under the Romans. Natural increase is clearly insufficient to account for the doubling of population in over little more than a century, especially as the death rate must have been high in an increasingly crowded city. There is, in fact, a good deal of evidence to suggest that immigration was taking place on a large scale. Sizeable communities of foreign merchants were established, but the bulk of the migrants came from other parts of England, often from surprisingly far afield for an age in which travel was difficult and dangerous. Changes in the language used by Londoners indicate that there was a heavy influx from the prosperous trading areas of the East Midlands and East Anglia, and records show that most of the city's apprentices were born outside its limits, about half coming from the Home Counties and others principally from the east and north. It is important to put the medieval city into perspective, however. Three times as large as Bristol or York, the next in rank among English towns, London was still far outstripped by Paris, which had 200,000 inhabitants in the early 14th century, and by Venice, Naples and Milan which had double London's population in the later Middle Ages. Moreover, its proportion of the total population of an overwhelmingly rural nation was no more than one-seventieth.

How far the populace of London was reduced by the great plagues of the 14th century, especially the BLACK DEATH of 1348–9, is a matter of dispute, but it is clear that on balance the capital's overall population increased little, if at all, in the century and a half following the peak of about 1340. The great expansion of the Tudor period was as sudden as it was surprising. Before the death of Elizabeth in 1603 brought the Tudor dynasty to an end, the population of London may well have quadrupled. Much of this unprecedented growth was accommodated in the expanding suburbs to the east and south and in WESTMINSTER; but for the first time there was serious and potentially dangerous overcrowding in the centre. A proclamation against new building in 1580 – the first of many – recognised this state of affairs. Disease was feared as much as disaffection and one of the most remarkable aspects of London's population explosion in the 16th century is that little, if any, of the growth can be accounted for by natural increase at a time when the death rate was still very high. There was, though, a perceptible change in the nature of immigration as the

numbers flooding in from the provinces increased: the craftsmen who sustained the apprenticeship system were becoming progressively outnumbered by the unskilled labourers, the poor and the destitute.

The tendencies established in the 16th century became more pronounced in the 17th and took on a distinct geographical characteristic as the lower classes spread along the riverside to the east (where the population increased from some 20,000 to 90,000 in the course of the century), while the upper and middle classes increasingly sought refuge from the ravages of disease in the overcrowded alleys of the CITY and its liberties by establishing new suburbs in the west. In terms of sheer numbers the population of the metropolis increased from about 200,000 in 1600 to perhaps 350,000–400,000 in 1650 and 575,000–600,000 in 1700. By the beginning of the 18th century London contained ten per cent of the nation's population, had 20 times more inhabitants than the next largest English town, and was already the biggest city in western Europe.

In contrast to the end of the 17th century, when returns made for the purposes of taxation provided at least a basis for both contemporary and later demographers to calculate the capital's population, the 18th century is remarkably devoid of reliable statistics. Studies of parish registers and similar sources have indicated that the rise in population continued until about 1725, but thereafter received a severe check until the middle of the century or later. It was during this second quarter of the 18th century that gin drinking reached epidemic proportions among the poorer sections of the populace of the metropolis, and the burial rate exceeded the baptism rate, sometimes by as much as 2:1. In some years the excess of deaths over births was over 15,000, but there was certainly no massive depopulation during this period. Overall numbers were sustained by continuing immigration on a massive scale in which an influx of from 8,000 to 10,000 persons a year was required merely to keep the total population static. The effect of surplus births in the Home Counties, the Midlands and farther afield, was that thousands of people poured into London, often to die within a short time.

The bare statistic that London's population stood at about 650,000 in 1750 hides a grim story of misery and appalling waste in the previous half century. A slow improvement is discernible from the middle of the century as the death rate declined until, in 1790, recorded baptisms exceeded burials for the first time. With immigration continuing at its previous rate, the growth in the population was resumed until by the end of the 18th century London contained a little under one million inhabitants, over 11 times more than the next largest English city, Liverpool, and almost twice as many as the next most populous European centre, Paris.

The figures in the table below are taken from the decennial censuses (with the exception of 1941 when there was no census and an estimate for 1939 has to suffice), adjusted to cover the areas administered firstly by the LONDON COUNTY COUNCIL after 1889 and secondly by the GREATER LONDON COUNCIL from 1965. In general the figures in the first column are a reasonably accurate representation of London's population until 1861 when those for the wider area become increasingly more relevant.

The growth in population which had been resumed

in the late 18th century continued unabated throughout the 19th. The increase per decade hovered around the 20 per cent mark until by the middle of the century London had well over two million people and was six times as large as Liverpool, seven times the size of Manchester and ten times that of Birmingham, despite the prodigiously rapid growth of those provincial cities. As the death rate was falling and the birth rate rising, natural increase accounted for a significant proportion of the growth, but as always immigration was a potent force. It has been calculated that in the three decades between 1841 and 1871 an average of about 300,000 newcomers came into the capital in each decade; but against this should be balanced an exodus of some 100,000 to 150,000. Of the migrants into London about one-third came from the immediately neighbouring counties and a half from the Home Counties in general. Most of the remainder came from other parts of England and Wales, but a sizeable number were from Scotland or Ireland (where perhaps 15 per cent of all immigrants originated in the famine years of the 1840s) and the continent of Europe.

In the last quarter of the 19th century the number of immigrants from abroad increased as the dispossessed of eastern Europe settled in the East End, but most still came from nearby counties. More significant in numerical terms was the increase in migration out of the metropolitan area, as it was then defined, with a consequent slowing down in the overall rate of growth. But most of this movement was to the new outer suburbs and it soon became apparent to contemporaries that the population of London had spread well beyond its official boundaries.

The figures in the second column of the table have been calculated to provide comparisons between the population of the area of Greater London in each decade back to 1801. In that year this large area, which included all of MIDDLESEX and parts of Surrey, Kent and Essex and which stretched far beyond the then limits of the metropolis, contained only a little over one million inhabitants, that is to say not substantially more than London proper. Until the mid-19th century virtually the entire increase in the population of the larger region can be accounted for by that of the inner area, but thereafter the rates of increase begin to diverge. In the decade 1881–91, for instance, whereas the population of the centre grew by some 400,000, that of Greater London increased by 850,000. The outward movement continued in the 20th century as the population of the LONDON COUNTY COUNCIL area actually decreased from its peak of 4,536,267 in 1901 while that of Greater London expanded rapidly to reach an estimated peak of about 8,600,000 on the outbreak of war in 1939. The centrifugal flow gathered momentum after the war and, as the population of Greater London itself began to decline, planners introduced the concept of a new outer metropolitan area with a radius of about 40 miles from CHARING CROSS containing some 12,500,000 people by 1971.

Migration has been by far the most important factor in determining the changes of the present century. Until the mid-1950s the pattern of immigration into London retained its traditional character with the majority of the new inhabitants of the metropolis coming from the counties immediately surrounding the capital and most of the remainder from the rest of the British Isles. For a brief period, however, until the introduction of more restrictive immigration controls

in the mid-1960s, the pattern was dramatically changed by the advent of mass immigration from the new Commonwealth. Even after the imposition of controls, the virtual drying up of the historically predominant sources of migrants from within the country has meant that as many as a third of all newcomers to London within the last 20 years have come from overseas.

The report of the census of 1981 indicates that the rate of the depopulation of London is accelerating. The population of Greater London is now under 7,000,000, a decrease of ten per cent from 1971, and in inner London, where the population is now under 2,500,000, the lowest figures since 1851, the decrease from 1971 is as high as 17 per cent.

Population of London 1801–1981

	London*	Greater London**
1801	959,310	1,096,784
1811	1,139,355	1,303,564
1821	1,379,543	1,573,210
1831	1,655,582	1,878,229
1841	1,949,277	2,207,653
1851	2,363,341	2,651,939
1861	2,808,494	3,188,485
1871	3,261,396	3,840,595
1881	3,830,297	4,713,441
1891	4,227,954	5,571,968
1901	4,536,267	6,506,889
1911	4,521,685	7,160,441
1921	4,484,523	7,386,755
1931	4,397,003	8,110,358
1939	4,013,400 (est)	8,615,050 (est)
1951	3,347,982	8,193,921
1961	3,200,484	7,992,443
1971	3,031,935	7,452,356
1981	2,497,978***	6,713,165***

*The County of London as defined by the Local Government Act, 1888
**As defined by the London Government Act, 1963
***Provisional figures subject to correction

Porchester Terrace *W2.* Some 20 years older than the other BAYSWATER terraces, many of the large original villas have survived here. No. 3 was designed in 1823 by John Claudius Loudon who lived here until his death in 1843. Both he and his wife Jane were influential and prolific writers on horticultural matters. Loudon also invented a system for curving glass later used by Paxton for the CRYSTAL PALACE, and recommended the familiar plane tree for London streets and squares. His portrait was painted by his neighbour at No. 34, the artist, John Linnell, who lived here in 1829–52. Another artist, William Collins, lived at No. 26A in 1831–6. His more famous son, Wilkie, attended a local school. Many other artists, including Landseer and John Martin, belonged to this circle. Later inhabitants included the eccentric Russian, Prince Yury Golitsin, in 1860–2; the composer William Sterndale Bennett, at No. 18 in 1870–2; and, more recently, the Liberal statesman Viscount Samuel, who lived at No. 32 in 1934–63.

Port of London Authority Towards the end of the 19th century rivalry between the dock companies had become intense. Strikes by the dockers were frequent and competition between companies had become ruinous. John Burns, the dockers' leader and the first Labour MP to reach the Cabinet, began to urge the amalgamation of all the dock companies into one municipal enterprise. Drastic action was, indeed, imperative. A Royal Commission reported in 1902 that the Port of London was neglected, ill-equipped, inefficient, possessed too many separate authorities, charged exorbitant prices and was in danger of losing much of its trade to other ports, both British and foreign. It advised the formation of a new Port Authority. After long delays caused by disputes, an Act was eventually passed in 1908 and the following year the Port of London Authority took over full control of the tidal river and its docking – about a century after the first enclosed docks had been built. An important step taken by the Authority was the reduction and regularisation of docking charges, a boon to merchants and shipowners. Another was a thorough dredging of the river to depths navigable by modern ships of deep draught which had been needed for a long time. Dock facilities were also improved. The Authority took over the whole of the THAMES and its docks from Teddington to the Nore, a distance of 70 miles, from the Thames Conservators (see THAMES). The RIVER POLICE continued their independent watch, co-operating with the Authority's own force to police the docks; while TRINITY HOUSE retained its long-held supervision of pilotage, lights and sea-marks. Under the PLA the London docks were able to maintain the position they had held for two centuries as the world's largest port.

The Authority was first housed in a great stone structure in TRINITY SQUARE, overlooking TOWER HILL, 'a lasting monument to Edwardian optimism like a super-palace for an international exhibition, showy, happily vulgar and extremely impressive' as Pevsner has described it. Built between 1912 and 1922 to a design by Sir Edwin Cooper, it was sold in 1971 and, as the docks began to close, the PLA moved to smaller offices in the new World Trade Centre at the ST KATHARINE DOCK.

The Port of London Act had been passed under Winston Churchill who had taken over the Board of Trade from Lloyd George. Many regarded the Act as a dangerous step towards socialism, but the Authority has proved its worth. At first it consisted of elected members: two from the Board of Trade, four from the LONDON COUNTY COUNCIL, three from the CITY CORPORATION, one from the Admiralty and one from TRINITY HOUSE. An important item in the Act was the diminishing of the evil of casual labour in the docks, an evil finally eliminated by the influence of the Devlin Report of 1965. For six decades the PLA served as the greatest warehouse keeper in the world. Today, under diminished responsibilities, the board of the PLA consists of some 16 members each serving for three years and representing shippers, the LONDON CHAMBER OF COMMERCE, wharfingers, lightermen, the GREATER LONDON COUNCIL, the CITY CORPORATION, TRINITY HOUSE, the National Ports Council and organised labour.

By 1939 the PLA had constructed 80 new acres of dock water and 6 extra miles of quay and had dredged a 50-mile channel, 1,000 ft wide and 30 ft deep at low water, to take large ships. It had also undertaken considerable improvements at Tilbury Docks. Between 1909 and 1939 the total tonnage using the Port rose from less than 40 million to over 60 million, while the percentage of Britain's seaborne trade handled at the Port rose from 29 to 38. After the 2nd World War the PLA improved Tilbury Docks to deal with the new system of containerisation which can reduce turnaround time from a fortnight to 36 hours. Now the London docks lie moribund and the PLA is concentrating its efforts on Tilbury and on research into the potential of a new seaport at Maplin (see also DOCKS).

Portland Club *42 Half Moon Street, W1.* Originally called the Stratford Club, it was founded in 1816 in the STRATFORD PLACE house of the Duke of Portland. It was reconstituted to become the Portland Club in 1825. The first game of bridge was played here in 1894. The first bridge rules were not sanctioned, however, until 1895. It has had homes in ST JAMES'S SQUARE and CHARLES STREET and moved to its present address in 1969. It produced the latest rules on bridge in 1981.

Portland Estate This estate comprises the southern half of the manor of TYBURN (see ST MARYLEBONE). James I sold the land to Edward Forsett, JP, for £829 3s 4d; it passed to his daughter, Arabella, and then to her son, John Austen, who sold it to John Holles, Duke of Newcastle, for £17,500 in 1708. The Duke's heiress was his daughter, Henrietta, who, with her husband, Edward Harley, Earl of Oxford and Mortimer, began the development of the estate about 1719. The undertaking was continued by their daughter, Margaret, and her husband, William Bentinck, 2nd Duke of Portland. The estate remained in the possession of the Dukes of Portland until the 5th Duke died unmarried in 1879; the MARYLEBONE land passed to his sister, Lucy, Countess Howard de Walden, to whose descendants it still belongs today.

Portland Place *W1.* The grandest street of 18th-century London, it was laid out by Robert and James Adam in about 1778 and named after the ground landlord, the Duke of Portland. It owes its superb width to an undertaking given to Lord Foley that the view northwards from the windows of his house, which blocked the southern end of the street, should never be obscured. Nash took it as his example and adopted it as the northern part of his triumphal way between REGENT'S PARK and CARLTON HOUSE. Some of the original buildings remain but many are altered and the rest have been rebuilt; the street, however, retains its proper proportions. Admiral Lord Radstock died at No. 10 in 1825; his house has gone and the site is now covered by BROADCASTING HOUSE. At No. 20 is the Medical Research Council which was established here in 1913; at No. 26 the Central Council of Recreation, founded in 1935; at No. 28 the Royal Institute of Health and Public Hygiene, established in 1937. No. 29 is the Swedish Embassy; and No. 45 the Malaysian High Commission. Field-Marshal Lord Roberts lived at No. 47 in 1902–6. This house is now the Polish Embassy. No. 49, the office of the Chinese Chargé d'Affaires, was demolished for rebuilding in 1981. No. 63 was the home of Sir Ralph Milbanke whose daughter, Anne Isabella, was courted here by Lord Byron in 1812–14. THE ROYAL INSTITUTE OF BRITISH ARCHITECTS is at No. 66. No. 69 is the Turkish Embassy. In 1912–19 John Buchan lived at No. 76, now the CITY AND GUILDS OF LONDON INSTITUTE. No. 98 was the United States Embassy, between 1863 and 1866. Henry Brook Adams, the American historian, lived here while working for his father, Charles Francis Adams, who had been appointed Ambassador by Abraham Lincoln. Frances Hodgson Burnett, the author of *Little Lord Fauntleroy*, lived at No. 63 in 1893–8. The CHARTERED INSTITUTE OF TRANSPORT at No. 80 occupies a house which was once owned by Admiral Jellicoe.

Portman Estate In 1553 Sir William Portman, Lord Chief Justice of England, purchased 270 acres of land in MARYLEBONE which his collateral descendant, Henry William Portman, began to develop 200 years later. Family estates in Dorset, such as Bryanston, Blandford and Orchard Portman, have given their names to many London streets. Though portions of the estate have been sold during the present century, the 9th Viscount Portman still owns that half of the original area which lies north of the MARYLEBONE ROAD.

Portman Square *W1.* Built on the outskirts of the town in 1764–84 for the ground landlord Henry William Portman. At the north-west corner was MONTAGU HOUSE built by James (Athenian) Stuart in 1777–82 for Mrs Elizabeth Montagu. Every May Day she gave a dinner of roast beef and plum pudding to chimney-sweeps and their apprentices. One of them, David Porter, grew up to be a builder and named MONTAGU SQUARE after her. The house was bombed in the 2nd World War, and only its gate-piers survive, resurrected in the grounds of KENWOOD HOUSE. The Portman Inter-Continental Hotel stands on its site. No. 20, HOME HOUSE, which contains the COURTAULD INSTITUTE OF ART, is by Robert Adam (1773–7). Round the corner from it, but still numbered in Portman Square, is the HEINZ GALLERY where the RIBA's collection of architectural drawings is housed. The rest of the square has been mainly rebuilt with flats, offices and hotels, including the CHURCHILL. Daniel Neal, the children's clothes and school uniform suppliers established in 1837, have now closed.

Portman Street *W1.* Built on the PORTMAN ESTATE in 1758. The Mount Royal Hotel on the west side and the offices of Gulf Eastern Petroleum Company on the east now fill the street. Caroline of Brunswick, the discarded wife of George IV, lived at No. 22 on her return to England for his coronation in 1820.

Portobello Road *W10, W11.* A long street extending from PEMBRIDGE VILLAS to LADBROKE GROVE. It was originally a track leading to a farm which was called Porto Bello Farm in honourable allusion to Admiral Vernon's capture of Porto Bello in the Gulf of Mexico from the Spaniards in 1739. (Hence also Vernon Yard, W11.) In 1927–8 George Orwell lodged at No. 10 with a Mrs Craig, formerly a lady's maid, who, when she, her husband and Orwell were locked out of the house, declined to borrow a ladder from her neighbours to climb through an upstairs window. In the 14 years she had lived there she had never spoken to them; she did not wish to do so now in case they became familiar – one could not be too careful in NOTTING HILL. They walked a mile to fetch a ladder from a relative (*see also* PORTOBELLO ROAD MARKET).

Portobello Road Market *W10, W11.* Established by the early 1870s, amongst its first dealers were gipsies who came to buy and sell horses at the nearby Hippodrome and to offer herbs in the market. In 1893

the vestry minutes record complaints about the size of the costermongers' stalls; a long running battle over the extent of the market began between the authorities, street-traders and shop-keepers. In 1929 the first licence was officially granted. In 1948, after the closure of the CALEDONIAN MARKET, antique dealers came here in large numbers followed by bargain hunters. Today it is crowded with tourists. The main market is on Saturday and stretches the full length of Portobello Road.

Portsea Place *W2.* Takes its name from a Hampshire estate of the Thistlethwaites (*see* STANHOPE TERRACE). Olive Schreiner, the South African author, lived at No. 16 from August 1885 to January 1886.

Portugal Street *WC2.* The south side of LINCOLN'S INN FIELDS used to be known as Portugal Row in honour of Charles II's wife Catherine of Braganza, daughter of the Duke of Braganza, later John IV of Portugal. After the name was no longer used for that side of LINCOLN'S INN FIELDS it was transferred to Portugal Street. LINCOLN'S INN FIELDS THEATRE once stood here. John Wilmot, Earl of Rochester, lived next door to it. The street was the last place in London where stocks were set up. They remained here until 1820. The George public house at No. 28 is a successor to the Magpie and Stump which Pickwick visits in *The Pickwick Papers*.

Post Office Railway The problem of moving mail quickly across London was solved by going underground. The Post Office Railway was started in 1913, but work was interrupted by the 1st World War. The tunnels were completed in 1926 and in 1927 the railway was opened. It is 6 miles long and runs between PADDINGTON and WHITECHAPEL, connecting six sorting offices, including MOUNT PLEASANT. The railway carries up to 50,000 bags of mail each day. The trains are 27 ft long, powered by electricity, and have four containers which can carry 15 bags of letters or six bags of parcels. The original trains were replaced by 34 new ones in 1981. During peak periods there is a train each way every four minutes. The railway is the only one of its kind in the world.

Post Office Tower *see* LONDON TELECOM TOWER.

Postal Services Before 1635 there was no postal service for the general public. A City Post had been set up in 1526 in OLD JEWRY for the King's Letters, and in 1619 a Foreign Post was opened near the ROYAL EXCHANGE for collection and delivery of overseas letters. In 1635 the royal posts were made available to the public by the establishment of a General Post in the CITY to carry letters along the main post roads out of London. In 1680 these were the Kent road to Dover, which had its receiving office for letters at the Round House in LOVE LANE, and which ran every day; the Essex road to Yarmouth, which also ran every day; the west road to Plymouth; the road to Bristol; the Chester road via Holyhead to Ireland; and the north road to Edinburgh. The last four ran three times a week. Postage was charged according to the distance carried, and, until the development of cross posts, all mail had to be sent via London. Henry Bishop, who was made Postmaster General in 1660, gave his name to the Bishop Mark, a handstamp consisting of a divided circle showing the month and the day of the month, but not the year. The mark was applied in London to indicate the date of receipt in the London office. It was in use in London for 126 years from 1661.

There was still, however, no local delivery of letters in London, except by private messenger, until, in 1680, William Dockwra set up a private Penny Post service. In his first broadsheet he announced the new service for 'conveying of Letters or Pacquets under a Pound Weight, to and from all parts within the Cities of London and Westminster, and the Out Parishes within the Weekly Bills of Mortality, for One Penny'. In summer letters would be delivered from six in the morning to nine at night 'and at reasonable hours agreeable to the Winter Season'. To 'places of quick Negotiation within the City' delivery would be at least 15 times a day, but 'no letters that come after Nine at Night, to be delivered till next morning'. Dockwra opened seven sorting offices and between four and five hundred receiving houses, where letters were received and taken to the sorting office for delivery to the addressee in London for one penny to be paid by the sender. A triangular type of mark was applied to the letter, showing the sorting office where the letter was received, e.g. L for LIME STREET, W for WESTMINSTER, T for TEMPLE. Dockwra recorded details of all letters accepted, and gave compensation for loss.

Dockwra's London Penny Post was started with other associates, including William Murray. When Murray was arrested for distributing a seditious pamphlet, Dockwra operated the postal service on his own. It was so successful that in 1682 the Post Office stopped his operations as being an infringement of the Post Office monopoly and took over the system themselves. In 1689 Dockwra was granted a pension 'in consideration of his good service in inventing and setting up the business of the Penny Post Office'. The Government ran the service on much the same lines as Dockwra. It was very popular and widely used. One of the earliest literary references to the London Penny Post is in Sir John Vanbrugh's *The Provok'd Wife* (1697) when the servant enters and announces, 'Madam, here's a letter for your Ladyship by the Penny Post'. An extra penny was charged for delivery to the country area of the London Post, that is to say outside the CITIES OF LONDON and WESTMINSTER and the BOROUGH OF SOUTHWARK and their respective suburbs but within 10 miles of the General Letter Office. The 2d rate was increased to 3d in 1711. In the early part of the 18th century Ralph Allen, who had

Sorting and weighing letters in the Inland Letter Office in 1844.

been appointed Postmaster at Bath at the age of 18, reorganised the posts, increasing the revenue from bye posts and cross-posts, which enabled letters to be sent from one post town to another without having to go through London. He also appointed inspectors to check corruption; but the system was still a slow one, letters being carried by postboys or men riding horses. In 1784 John Palmer of Bath revolutionised the postal service with a scheme using special lightweight mail coaches. The London–Bath–Bristol service was quickly followed by others throughout the country. The mail coaches, and the horses, were hired; they carried a limited number of passengers, and an armed guard, and ran to a strict schedule. The horses were changed at the coaching inns, and if a passenger was not ready in time he was left behind. The coaches left London from the General Post Office in LOMBARD STREET. From 1830, however, the development of the railways led to the gradual decline of the mail coach service.

In 1794 Edward Johnson of the Postmaster General's Office was responsible for the reform of the London Post. One of the main changes which he proposed was that London letters could be sent unpaid in the Penny Post. This was to stop the letter-receivers from destroying the letter and keeping the penny which had been paid for delivery. Delivery walks were organised and seven Rides were set up serving BRENTFORD, EDMONTON, FINCHLEY, MITCHAM, MORTLAKE, WOODFORD, and WOOLWICH. In 1801 the 1d rate in the town area was increased to 2d, and the Penny Post became the Twopenny Post. In 1805 the 2d rate in the country area of the London Post was increased to 3d. The London Bye Post was introduced in 1809 to enable mails between one place and another on the same Ride to be sorted and exchanged without having to be passed through the Chief Office of the London Post. The London Cross-Post, introduced in 1834–6, further speeded the mails by enabling the London Post to exchange mails with the General Post at post stages at the edge of the London Post Boundary on all the main coaching roads out of London. Many people, however, could not afford to use the postal services, and many unpaid letters were refused because the addressee could not afford to pay the postage. In 1833 Robert Wallace, a Member of Parliament, started a campaign for a Penny Postage. This was taken up by Rowland Hill and eventually on 10 January 1840 a uniform Penny Post was established. Rowland Hill published a pamphlet on Post Office Reform, advocating a uniform rate, that letters should be charged by weight rather than the number of sheets, and postage should be paid by the sender instead of the recipient. The idea of an adhesive stamp to pay the postage was adopted by Rowland Hill, who was responsible for the introduction of the world's first adhesive postage stamp, the famous Penny Black, on 6 May 1840. The Treasury had run a competition for the design of the stamp, and many of the essays or entries in this competition can be examined in the NATIONAL POSTAL MUSEUM. (*See also* GENERAL POST OFFICE *and* POST OFFICE RAILWAY.)

Postman's Park *EC1*. So called because of the proximity of the GENERAL POST OFFICE. In the summer postal workers may be seen here feeding bits of their sandwiches to the pigeons. A sign in this small open space reads, 'Postman's Park which was opened in 1880 is made up of the churchyard of St Leonard's,

Foster Lane, St Botolph's, Aldgate and the graveyard of Christ Church, Newgate Street. More land bordering Little Britain was added in 1883. In 1887 Mr G[eorge] F[rederick] Watts [the painter and sculptor] conceived the idea of a national memorial to heroic men and women and dedicated a wall to this cause in 1900.' This wall bears numerous plaques briefly relating the deeds of these heroes: 'Alice Ayres, daughter of a bricklayer's labourer, who by intrepid conduct saved three children from a burning house in Union Street, Borough at the cost of her own young life.' 'Thomas Simpson died of exhaustion after saving many lives from the breaking ice at Highgate Ponds, Jan 25 1885.' 'Harry Sisley of Kilburn, aged 10, drowned in attempting to save his brother after he himself had just been rescued, May 24 1878.' 'Daniel Pemberton, aged 61, foreman LSWR, surprised by a train when gauging the line, hurled his mate out of the track, saving his life at the cost of his own, Jan 17 1903.' On the south side is Michael Ayrton's powerful bronze *Minotaur*, placed here in 1973 (*see* STATUES).

Poulters' Company *see* CITY LIVERY COMPANIES.

Poultry *EC2*. The continuation of CHEAPSIDE towards the BANK, named after the poulterers who used to live here. It was celebrated before the GREAT FIRE for its great number of taverns. One of the sheriff's prisons was in this street, and from it emanated a 'mixture of scents from tobacco, foul feet, dirty shirts, stinking breaths and unclean carcases'. It was demolished in 1817. In 1819–72 Congregationalists had a chapel on the site. Nos 24–25 is the site of ST MILDRED POULTRY. The bookshop of Edward and Charles Dilly, who published Boswell's *Life of Johnson*, was in the street. Thomas Hood, the poet and author of 'I remember, I remember the house where I was born', was born in a house on the site of No. 31 in 1799. On this site now is the Head Office of the MIDLAND BANK, designed by Sir Edwin Lutyens in 1924 and finally completed in 1939.

Poultry Compter The ancient sheriff's prison situated east of Grocer's Hall Court. It was the oldest of the three compters and mainly kept for prisoners committed by the LORD MAYOR. Conditions were extremely dirty and unhealthy and few prisoners were free from lice and scurvy. In 1628 Dr Lamb, who was said to have supplied the Duke of Buckingham with love potions, died here after a pelting from a mob for witchcraft. Other prisoners have included Dekker the dramatist, Boyse the Grub Street poet, and in 1772 James Somerset, the last slave in England. The prison was demolished in 1817.

Praed Street *W2*. The backbone of the GRAND JUNCTION CANAL Company's estate which served the Paddington Basin in the early 19th century, this street was named after the first Chairman of the company. Its seediness is outweighed by the presence of PADDINGTON STATION, the GREAT WESTERN ROYAL HOTEL and ST MARY'S HOSPITAL, all of which were first built in the early 1850s. On the sites of Norfolk Square, Talbot Square and St Mary's Hospital there were originally large reservoirs for water supply. The area was badly bombed, and the churches of St Michael, Star Street, and All Saints, Norfolk Square, have both

been demolished, but the remaining houses are now being restored. No. 144 Praed Street was the site of the first Baptist chapel in PADDINGTON, opened in 1816.

Pratt's *210 Streatham High Road, SW16*. At the age of 13, in 1840, George Pratt came from Hampshire to serve his apprenticeship with a linen draper, William Reynolds. In 1850 he bought him out, and had his own business at 5 Bedford Row on the High Road. His sons Henry and Charles expanded into neighbouring properties. In 1981 the department store formed part of the JOHN LEWIS PARTNERSHIP.

Pratts Bottom *Kent*. It is thought to derive its name from the family of a Stephen Pratt who is believed to have lived here in 1332. In 1791, however, it was referred to as Spratts Bottom. There are very few references to it in old documents. The CHELSFIELD Vestry built some poor houses here about 1628. In 1747 an Act was passed to establish a turnpike road through the area. At that time the main coach road went up Rushmore Hill. The present main road over Polhill was not built until 1836. A toll gate and turnpike man's cottage were built here by the Turnpike Trust. This cottage was not demolished until 1928 when road improvements took place. The village is now part of the London Borough of BROMLEY.

Pratt's Club *14 Park Place, SW1*. Takes its name from William Nathaniel Pratt, steward to the 7th Duke of Beaufort, who had been a croupier at CROCKFORD'S. He lived at 14 PARK PLACE where he let rooms. The Duke of Beaufort used to visit this house in the 1840s with friends to spend an informal evening gambling and drinking in the kitchen. Pratt's establishment was continued after his death by his widow, then by his son and in 1907 was purchased by William Walsh, later 4th Lord Ormathwaite, who assiduously attended dinners there until 1937 when he sold it to the 10th Duke of Devonshire. Members still dine in the small basement (the club is open only in the evenings), no more than 14 of the 600 members being able to sit down together at the single table at the same time. Club servants are all known as George. Members are mostly upper class. Ladies are not admitted.

Prehistoric London The CITY OF LONDON was founded by the Romans. Excavations in the city have not revealed any earlier occupation layers. There have been scattered finds of pre-Roman material, but only of isolated items such as might be found in any river valley area. There is nothing to suggest any settlement. Within Greater London, however, there are a few sites which would seem to indicate earlier settlement.

The classification and dating of prehistoric ages is at the moment under review. The distinctions between the different cultures may not be as rigid as at one time supposed, and much of the dating may have to be extended back further than was once thought. It is convenient, however, to use here the traditional labels and time scales.

The Palaeolithic Age lasted from about 50000 BC to 10000 BC. Man during this time was nomadic; if he constructed shelters they were probably of a wind-break type and very temporary. Worked stone tools, hand axes, scrapers and borers, have been found in the gravel terraces around London. At Swanscombe, Kent, the oldest known human skull in this country was found, and is possibly of a type of man between *Pithecanthropus* and *Homo sapiens*. Nearby at Gravesend and Ebbsfleet there is evidence of early tool making. There is also evidence of this at Creffield Road, ACTON, and at STOKE NEWINGTON. Scattered finds of Palaeolithic tools have also been made at CROYDON, WIMBLEDON, PUTNEY, EALING, HANWELL, BRENTFORD, and elsewhere around London. The Palaeolithic Age spanned the last of the Ice Ages, and the skeleton of a mammoth was found at SOUTHALL as well as hand axes of the Levalloisian type. At Waltham Abbey also, mammoth and other extinct animal remains have been found, with Palaeolithic implements.

Use of the ACTON, Ebbsfleet and STOKE NEWINGTON areas was continued in the Mesolithic Age (10000–4000 BC), distinguishable by the finer flint work and the use of microliths. Mesolithic finds have been made at Ewell, where several knapping floors have been found. At BRENTFORD there was a large collection of picks, such as were used in other areas for the mining of chalk. At HAMPSTEAD the finds included struck flints, tools, burnt flint, crazed stones and charcoal. Crazed stones are the result of dropping heated stones into water or liquid, the object being to heat the liquid. This was an ancient cooking method before the use of cooking pots.

The Neolithic Age (4000–2000 BC) brought a change in occupation. Farming and stock breeding began and with them developed a more settled way of life. The earliest surviving pottery dates from this period, as do the earliest funeral monuments or barrows. In the London area, Neolithic flints have been found at BRENTFORD, both beneath Roman layers and in the THAMES, at Waltham Abbey, PUTNEY, CROYDON, MITCHAM and PURLEY. In some of these places fragments of pottery known as Ebbsfleet Ware, from the site of the earliest finds, have also been found.

In the Bronze Age (2500–800 BC) the use of bronze made a whole new range of weapons and tools available. These have been found throughout the London area, and especially in the river. At BRENTFORD there was found a fine collection of swords, spears, gouges and horse harness trappings, some of which were typical products of the Urnfield and Hallstatt cultures. Stray finds have been made all round London; and, in the CITY, an axe known as a Celt was found at the TOWER (1834), a palstave in the MINORIES, and a number of spearheads fused together in THAMES STREET (1868). On HAMPSTEAD HEATH, between HAMPSTEAD and HIGHGATE Ponds, there is a round barrow, probably Bronze Age. When it was excavated in 1894 nothing was found in it. There are also round barrows on WIMBLEDON COMMON.

The final pre-Roman age, the Iron Age from about 800 BC to Roman times, not only introduced iron, but also the use of extensive earthworks. There are two hill forts in the London area both oddly enough known as Caesar's Camp, one at WIMBLEDON COMMON and the other, also known as Holwood Hillfort, at Keston, BROMLEY. Near to the Roman Keston Tombs a shaft was discovered which contained material suggestive of Celtic religious practices and may indicate a Celtic sanctuary. The nearest Iron Age dyke to London is the Grim's Ditch to be seen at intervals between Pinner Green and Brockley Hill, at HARROW and STANMORE. It has been suggested that this could be a boundary for the land of the Catuvellauni, the tribe whose capital was Prae Wood near St Albans. Iron age pottery,

swords, spears and other articles have been found all over the London area, and many items have been found in the THAMES. One of the most notable, known as the Battersea Shield, may be seen in the MUSEUM OF LONDON.

HMS President   Moored in KING'S REACH opposite THE TEMPLE, a sloop of the 1st World War which, with HMS CHRYSANTHEMUM, is now the headquarters of the London Division of the Royal Naval Reserve.

Press Club   *International Press Centre, 76 Shoe Lane, EC4.* Founded in 1882 at Anderton's Hotel, FLEET STREET, at an inaugural dinner of journalists presided over by George Augustus Sala, and first housed at 63 FLEET STREET. The club thereafter moved successively to CHANCERY LANE, LUDGATE CIRCUS, WINE OFFICE COURT, St Bride's House, FLEET STREET, and, in 1973, to the first and second floors of the International Press Centre which was officially opened the next year. In the Edgar Wallace Room (Wallace was chairman in 1923–4) is a collection of early newspapers. Only about a third of the members now are journalists. Women members are admitted to the club and the Women's Press Club has been merged with it.

Prestbury House   *Hampton Court Green, Middlesex.* Generally regarded as a Queen Anne house, but it was 1743 when George Lowe, the King's gardener, was granted the lease of the land on which he had recently built 'a very fair and commodious dwelling'. The house remained in the hands of George Lowe and his heirs until 1914, but none of them lived there. The first tenant was Henry Wise, son of the renowned Henry Wise who, with George London, remade the gardens of HAMPTON COURT PALACE and planted the Chestnut Avenue for William III. The tenants during 1788–1820 were Horace Walpole's second cousins, the Misses Philipps. Winifred Graham, who had made her reputation as a popular novelist, renamed the house Old Place when she lived there in 1914–24. During the 1st World War she conducted a fanatical campaign for the internment of all persons with German names, regardless of nationality. The wing and a corridor in front are additions to the original house.

Preston   *Middlesex.* Probably originated as 'the Priest's farm' and first recorded in 1194. Although the Metropolitan Railway passed near the hamlet in 1880, suburban growth did not begin until after the main access roads were improved for the British Empire Exhibition of 1924–5. On Preston Hill once lay the medieval farmhouse of John Lyon of HARROW SCHOOL. Rebuilt in 1708–9, it was demolished in 1960 for the construction of John Perrin Place. The railway station was opened in 1931–2, replacing a halt that had been provided there in 1908 for the Olympic Games clay pigeon shooting contests at Uxendon Farm (redeveloped for housing and the underground railway in the early 1930s). In the 16th century, Uxendon Farm was the home of the Bellamy family who, in 1586, sheltered Anthony Babington here, following the discovery of the plot to assassinate Queen Elizabeth.

Primrose Hill   *NW3, NW8.* Once covered with medieval forest 'full of the lairs and coverts of game, stags, bucks, boars and wild bulls'. The trees and

Isaac Cruickshank's 1791 caricature of a family struggling to the top of Primrose Hill to enjoy the prospect of the City.

undergrowth were cleared away in Elizabeth I's reign for meadowland. The hill is 206 ft high and has also been known as Battle and Greenberry Hill. The name Primrose Hill first occurs in the 15th century, probably after the flowers which then grew here in abundance. In the 16th century Mother Shipton prophesied that when London surrounded Primrose Hill the streets of the metropolis would run with blood. In October 1678 Sir Edmund Berry Godfrey, the magistrate who had heard Titus Oates's evidence on the Popish Plot, was found in a ditch, face downwards, transfixed with his own sword. In the ensuing panic three servants from SOMERSET HOUSE named Green, Hill and Berry were convicted and hanged. The ST PANCRAS Volunteers held their target practice here in 1799. In the early 19th century Primrose Hill was popular with duellists. The North Western Railway built a tunnel 3,500 ft long through the hill to connect CHALK FARM and ST JOHN'S WOOD in 1834. In 1842 a Bill was introduced to Parliament to establish a cemetery here but the vestry of ST PANCRAS objected and the project was dropped. In 1847 a gymnasium was built, and in 1852 the rifle range was filled in. In 1964 an oak tree was planted at the foot of the hill to commemorate the 400th anniversary of Shakespeare's birth. It is a successor to the Shakespeare Oak planted in 1864 by the actor Samuel Phelps which died in 1958. There are 112 acres.

Prince Albert Road *NW8.* First rated in the 1820s and called Albert Road till 1938, it was named after the Prince Consort. At the eastern end many of the original pretty villas remain, though those at the western end have been replaced by blocks of flats. The fibreglass, *St John the Baptist*, is by Hans Feibusch (1979).

Prince Charles Theatre *Leicester Place, WC2.* Opened on 26 December 1962 with a Canadian revue *Clap Hands*, directed by John Gray and transferred from the LYRIC, HAMMERSMITH. Built for Alfred Esdaile on the corner of LEICESTER PLACE and LISLE STREET as part of an office block designed by Carl Fisher and Associates, the foundation stone was laid by Dame Flora Robson on 18 December 1961. A long lease of the theatre was granted to Harold Fielding. It was modern in design but retained the traditional proscenium arch. It was proposed to present intimate entertainments of any kind for which there proved to

be a public. But as a theatre the Prince Charles was never completely successful. It opened and closed intermittently. In 1964 it was renovated and renamed Fielding's Music Hall. The attempt to create the old music-hall atmosphere by transferring from the PLAYERS' THEATRE their company of 'Late Joys' was, however, a failure. The theatre closed in 1965 and was sold for reconstruction as a cinema. It opened as the Prince Charles Cinema in 1969. Its capacity as a theatre was 420.

Prince Consort Road *SW7.* Formerly part of the Gore Estate purchased in 1852 for an academic centre with the profits of the GREAT EXHIBITION. It was built in 1887, cutting through the former grounds of the ROYAL HORTICULTURAL SOCIETY. Holy Trinity Church was built to designs by G.F. Bodley in 1901–4. The ROYAL COLLEGE OF MUSIC, the ROYAL SCHOOL OF MINES and buildings of IMPERIAL COLLEGE are on the south side; Beit Hall, the Imperial College Department of Zoology, and its Department of Botany are on the north. They are by Norman and Dawbarn (1959–65).

Prince Consort's Model Lodge *Kennington Park, SE1.* Erected in 1851 by the Society for Improving the Condition of the Labouring Classes on a site adjoining the GREAT EXHIBITION acquired for them through the influence of their president, the Prince Consort. The block was designed by Henry Roberts, a pioneer in model housing. It contained four dwellings, two on each floor, and each having a living room, three bedrooms, a lavatory and a scullery fitted with a sink, coal bin, plate rack, dust shaft and meat safe. An airing cupboard in the living room was heated with air from the fireplace. Hollow bricks were used in the construction which were claimed to be dry, warm, long lasting, sound-proof, fire-proof and cheap. The internal face of the walls was so smooth that plastering was unnecessary. The total cost of the building was £458 14s 7d. The design was later used in Cowley Gardens, STEPNEY and Fenelon Place, KENSINGTON. In 1852 the building was re-erected in Kensington Park by William Higgs to house two park attendants and a museum for articles relating to cottage economy. It is now used by the Park Superintendent. An inscription under the balcony reads 'Model houses for families erected by HRH Prince Albert'.

Prince Edward Theatre *22 Old Compton Street, W1.* Opened on 3 April 1930 with a musical comedy, *Rio Rita*, under the management of Lee Ephraim. It has been intermittently a cinema, a cabaret restaurant (known as the London Casino) and, during the war, a Services Club.

Prince Henry's Room *17 Fleet Street, EC4.* The house containing Prince Henry's Room was built in the early 17th century, but the site itself has a longer history. In the 12th century it formed part of the land owned by the Order of the KNIGHTS TEMPLAR. In 1312 their order was dissolved and a few years later the buildings were taken over by the KNIGHTS HOSPITALLERS of the Order of St John of Jerusalem. They in turn leased their property, the main part to lawyers and the buildings which faced on to FLEET STREET, including No. 17, to various other tenants. By the beginning of the 16th century the eastern half of

No. 17 was an Inn called the Hand, the rooms over the gate being known as the Prince's Arms. In 1592 the owner of the Hand was Zachary Bennett whose son, John, decided to rebuild the premises in 1610. The rebuilding was carried out in 1610–11 by William Blake who took over the inn from John Bennett and thereafter called it the Prince's Arms. The main room above the gateway, which can still be seen, was beautifully constructed with oak panelling all around and on the ceiling were the three feathers of the Prince of Wales together with the letters 'P.H.'. It seems likely that this was done because Prince Henry, son of James I, became Prince of Wales in 1610.

After 30 years the name of the inn seems to have been changed to the Fountain and then, in 1795, MRS SALMON'S WAXWORKS were moved here from the other side of the street. Some time during the 19th century the front was crudely covered over with paint and boards. In 1898 the LONDON COUNTY COUNCIL bought the premises which were then restored.

Prince of Wales Hospital *The Green, South Tottenham, N15.* Founded in 1855 as an orphanage for young boys and girls. It was enlarged in 1883 and converted to a hospital. Over the years extensions have been built and it now has 197 beds.

Prince of Wales Theatre *Coventry Street, W1.* Built in 1884 (as the Prince's Theatre) to the designs of C.J. Phipps for the actor-manager, Edgar Bruce, who financed the building with profits he had made on *The Colonel* at the SCALA THEATRE. Charles Hawtrey's farce, *The Private Secretary*, was first produced here with Beerbohm Tree in the title role. Since then the theatre has presented every kind of entertainment from Mrs Patrick Campbell and Forbes Robertson to André Charlot revues. In 1930 the theatre was for a short time under the management of Edith Evans, but mainly it has been the home of musicals, revues and, occasionally, farces. It seats 1,088.

Prince's Club *Knightsbridge.* The north-east end of the ground owned by the SMITH'S CHARITY ESTATE was a roughly triangular piece of land now mostly covered by LENNOX GARDENS and Mews and Clabon Mews. It was known as the Quail Field and was approximately 14 acres in extent. Late in the 18th century a celebrated market gardener, Mr Malcolm, leased the Quail Field and held it until he died in 1837. Its history from then until the 1850s is slightly obscure. The Prince brothers, George and James, were born in Lewes and were known to be interested in racehorse training and by the late 1860s were managing the 'Cigar Divan' in REGENT STREET and the Ottoman Club nearby. In the late 1850s they founded Prince's Sporting Club which was immediately a social and sporting success. They leased and laid out the Quail Field as a fine cricket ground and built a large pavilion on the west side of the 'Pavilion Gardens'. Cricket, TENNIS and lawn tennis were the principal games. By 1872 the club had 700 members. Lord Cadogan was Chairman. In that year the MARYLEBONE CRICKET CLUB moved their headquarters here and the ground was said to be the finest in England. In 1876, due to a financial argument, the MCC left and moved to LORD'S. But notwithstanding this, England played Australia on the Prince's Ground on their second tour in 1878. The club, which had introduced lawn tennis

in 1875, did more to formalize the rules than any other body in the early days. It established both the size of the court and the height of the net. Scoring in the modern manner was introduced after 1878. The Prince's and WIMBLEDON annual championships were on a par in 1881 when overhead service was first used at Prince's. The club held the same eminent position in racquets and later in squash racquets. A skating rink was built and ladies' 'skating teas' were very fashionable. The club acquired a considerable reputation for snobbishness and it was said that no lady could enter the club who had not been presented at court. But, after the extension of PONT STREET was authorised and Holland's PAVILION was demolished, the racquet courts were pulled down in 1886 and the cricket ground was closed.

The club moved to KNIGHTSBRIDGE in that year, the ground floors of Albert Court Mansions being converted for its use. The racquets and squash courts were built on the gardens to the south. In racquets and squash, the club retained a pre-eminent position. A brief revival of the skating club occurred on the site of the old floorcloth manufactury on the west side of TREVOR PLACE, but this was a financial disaster and it became the Daimler Hire Garage. The club was active until the 2nd World War but did not survive it.

Prince's Gardens *SW7.* Mostly large mid-Victorian mansions now converted into flats. The gardens, into which the public are admitted, are those of IMPERIAL COLLEGE. Weeks Hall at Nos 16–18, a hall of residence for IMPERIAL COLLEGE students, was presented by Vickers Ltd and opened by Viscount Knollys in 1959. Joseph Chamberlain lived at No. 40 in 1883–1914.

Prince's Gate *SW7.* In 1848 a new gate to HYDE PARK was opened by Edward, Prince of Wales. It stood on the site of the Halfway House, an old tavern which was notorious as a resort of footpads and highwaymen in the early 19th century. In 1848–55 five-storey stuccoed terraces were built opposite it. Leigh Hunt described them as being like a set of tall, thin gentlemen squeezing together to look at something over the way. In between the eastern and western terrace was Kingston House, built in about 1770 by Evelyn Pierrepoint, 2nd Duke of Kingston-upon-Hull, the husband of the notorious Elizabeth Chudleigh. It was demolished in the 1930s and replaced by a block of flats designed by M. Rosenauer. Field Marshal Earl Haigh lived at No. 21 in 1928; Lord Baden-Powell at No. 32 in 1903–14; Joseph Chamberlain at No. 72 in 1880–2. J.F. Kennedy stayed at No. 14 with his father Joseph P. Kennedy who lived here while American Ambassador in 1937–40. No. 49 held Whistler's Peacock Room from 1876 to 1904. It was the dining-room of a house owned by Frederick Leyland. He had commissioned various artists to decorate the interior. The centrepiece of the house was the grand staircase from NORTHUMBERLAND HOUSE, STRAND. Other rooms contained Beauvais tapestry, Renaissance bronzes, mosaic floors, Genoese velvet curtains, oriental china, inlaid French furniture, and paintings by both old masters and contemporary artists. Norman Shaw was in overall command of the project. The dining-room was assigned to Thomas Jeckyll who lined it with old Norwich leather costing £1,000 which was decorated with pomegranates and red flowers. Over the fireplace hung Whistler's *La Princesse du Pays de la Porcelaine*. Whistler complained that the colours of the flowers clashed with the painting and asked Leyland's permission to gild them. Leyland then went away, rashly giving Whistler leave to experiment with the room. With the help of Walter and Henry Greaves, Whistler covered the precious leather with an elaborate pattern of gold and blue peacocks. Leyland did not like it, nor did he like the bill for 2,000 guineas with which Whistler presented him. Having consulted other artists Leyland paid Whistler £1,000. Whistler was furious that the amount was in pounds not guineas and spitefully painted a pile of gold coins under one of the peacock's claws. In 1904 the whole room was taken to the Freer Gallery, Washington. The ROYAL SCHOOL OF NEEDLEWORK, designed by Fairfax B. Wade (1903), is at No. 25. THE ROYAL COLLEGE OF GENERAL PRACTIONERS is at No. 14. Embassies here are the Ethiopian at No. 17, Iranian at No. 27, Royal Thai at No. 28, Tunisian at No. 29, United Arab Emirates at No. 30, Afghanistan (closed) at No. 31, Liberian at No. 21. The POLISH INSTITUTE AND SIKORSKI MUSEUM is at No. 20. The Hyde Park Chapel of the Church of Jesus Christ of Latter Day Saints is at Nos 64–68. No. 6 is by Turner, Lansdown, Holt and Partners (1975).

Prince's Gate Mews *SW7*. An attractive mews behind the VICTORIA AND ALBERT MUSEUM developed by the rich builder C.J. Freake (*see* EXHIBITION ROAD.)

Princes Street *EC2*. Laid out after the GREAT FIRE. On the east side is the BANK OF ENGLAND, on the west GROCERS' HALL and the MIDLAND BANK by Sir Edwin Lutyens, designed in 1924. In 1929 the 'London Curse' was found here and is now in the MUSEUM OF LONDON. It is a piece of lead damaged by fire and with a hole in the middle suggesting that it was once fixed to a wall, and it is inscribed on both sides in Latin: 'Titus Egnatius Tyranus is hereby solemnly cursed, likewise Publius Cicereius Felix.'

Princes Street *W1*. On the Millfield estate (*see* HANOVER SQUARE), it extends from REGENT STREET to HANOVER SQUARE, and was probably so named in honour of the Prince of Wales (later George II) at the time of the first development of the estate around 1720. One or two of the original houses survive in much altered form on the north side.

𝔓𝔯𝔦𝔫𝔠𝔢𝔰𝔰'𝔰 𝔗𝔥𝔢𝔞𝔱𝔯𝔢 *Oxford Street, W1*. Built in 1830 as the Queen's Bazaar at the east end of OXFORD STREET by Thomas Hamlet who, in 1836, converted the bazaar into a theatre to the design of T.M. Nelson. It was named the Princess's Theatre in honour of Princess Victoria who had become Queen before it opened on 30 September 1840 – not, however, as a theatre but as a promenade concert hall with a resident orchestra of 65 musicians. The concert hall was not a success and Hamlet reverted to his original intention of staging theatrical productions. The theatre opened on 26 December 1842 with Bellini's *La Sonnambula* and, on the same bill, a burlesque, *The Yellow Dwarf*. Hamlet followed this with *Fra Diavolo*, *Lucia di Lammermoor* and a new opera by Balfe, but in 1843 (loans to eminent persons having been repudiated) he went bankrupt. One of his creditors, J.M. Maddox, took over the theatre and offered mixed entertainment: General Tom Thumb appeared in *Don Pasquale* and popular songs were

introduced into Shakespearean productions in which two world-famous tenors competed against each other in decibels.

Maddox handed over in 1850 to Charles Kean. There followed, for some nine years, one of the greatest periods of the English theatre. Kean's presentations, mostly Shakespeare and melodrama, were magnificiently produced, and his brilliant companies were rigidly disciplined. In 1852 *The Corsican Brothers* was first produced. Ellen Terry made her first stage appearance as a child in *The Winter's Tale*. Charles Reade, Douglas Jerrold and Boucicault contributed new plays.

After Kean's retirement in 1860 the theatre was under the direction of Augustus Harris but it was not until George Vining took over in 1863 that the theatre returned to its former greatness with Charles Reade's *It's Never Too Late to Mend* which was produced on 4 October 1865. This was done so realistically that in the prison scene, when a boy was flogged, the audience groaned and screamed and Oxenford, *The Times* critic, protested from a box. Vining came on the stage and argued with him that the play was itself a protest against what they were seeing. Under the same management Zola's play, *Drink*, with Charles Warner as Coupeau, was acted so vividly that the curtain came down on a silent audience so stunned with emotion that it was many seconds before the uproar of its reception began.

The following year, in 1880, the theatre caught fire and the new theatre designed by C.J. Phipps, who had also designed the GAIETY, was claimed to be the most up-to-date in London. It opened on 6 November 1881. This new theatre never achieved the renown of its predecessor, though it had some notable successes under the successive managements of Wilson Barrett, Charles Hawtrey and Lillie Langtry. The American actress, Grace Hawthorne, took over the direction of the theatre in 1887, producing amongst other melodramas *Uncle Tom's Cabin*, *The Mystery of a Hansom Cab* and *Hands Across the Sea*. Thereafter the fortunes of the theatre began to wane and the only further success was *Two Little Vagabonds* by George R. Sims in 1896. It closed in 1902. In 1905 part of the ground floor was converted into shops. The auditorium became a furniture store. It was demolished in 1931 and a branch of WOOLWORTH'S stood on the site until 1978 when the shopping complex, Oxford Walk, took its place. The seating capacity at the time of demolition was 1,750.

Printing House Square *EC4*. The site was originally part of the BLACKFRIARS MONASTERY. In the 17th century there were many printers in the area. At Hunsdon House the King's printers, Bonham Norton and John Bill, had established their press before 1627. The LONDON GAZETTE was first printed here, as was the edition of the Bible from which the word 'not' was omitted from the seventh commandment, an omission for which Archbishop Laud fined the STATIONERS' COMPANY very heavily. Norton's and Bill's successors continued printing here until 1769 when Charles Eyre and William Strachan move to New Street, GOUGH SQUARE. In 1784 John Walter, who had been bankrupted as a LLOYD'S underwriter, bought the Blackfriars premises, and in 1785 he established the *Daily Universal Register* which became *The Times* (price 3d) three years later. The great success of the paper under Walter's son, also John Walter, who adopted for its printing the recently invented double-cylinder steam-driven press, enabled the proprietor to take over the surrounding buildings including the site of the BLACK-FRIARS PLAYHOUSE. The buildings which were erected piecemeal, some of them designed by John Walter II, were replaced in the 1960s by a new *Times* building designed by Llewelyn-Davies, Weeks and Partners and Ellis, Clarke and Gallannaugh. The huge sundial which was set before it and bears the newspaper's motto, *'Tempus Fuis Est Et Fuerit'*, is by Henry Moore. In June 1974 *The Times* moved to NEW PRINTING HOUSE SQUARE, GRAY'S INN ROAD. Its building was taken over by the *Observer*, the Sunday newspaper founded in 1791.

The Priory *225 Bedford Hill, Balham, SW12*. Built about 1810 in the 'Strawberry Hill' Gothic style. In 1874, the Priory was leased by a young widow, Mrs Florence Ricardo. She brought a new husband, Charles Bravo, to the house in January 1876. The following April Charles was taken violently ill and after several days died. The doctors called to his aid knew poison was involved but not how it had been taken. The two inquests held at the nearby Bedford Arms threw suspicion on Florence, a Dr Gully, her lover, and a Mrs Cox, her companion-housekeeper. The question of murder or suicide was never answered but Florence soon left Balham, driven out by gossip. Except for a period as a school, the Priory continued as a private house until 1972. Then empty and in need of repair, its condition deteriorated and there was danger of demolition. The house has, however, now been fully restored externally and converted into flats inside.

The Priory *Church Hill, Orpington, Kent*. Never a monastic establishment, it is a good example of a pre-Reformation rectory. A rectorial court was recorded here in 1270. The building was enlarged several times, the timbered wing being added in the 17th century, and one of the 19th-century tenants gave it the name of The Priory. After use as Council offices, it was restored and a new library extension was added in 1960. The outbuildings, restored in recent years and now used as offices, date mostly from the 16th century. The hall of the restored building now houses the BROMLEY Borough Museum and the rooms are used for meetings of local societies.

Priory of St John of Jerusalem *Clerkenwell*. Headquarters of the Knights Hospitaller. It was a 12th-century foundation consecrated by Heraclius, Patriarch of Jerusalem, in 1185. Its church had the round nave of the Military Orders, the outline of which can still be seen in ST JOHN'S SQUARE. Its buildings and gardens covered 5 acres from the site of the present ST JOHN'S GATE in St John's Lane down to the River of Wells, a continuation of the FLEET RIVER, now covered by FARRINGDON STREET. Provision was made for the sick and infirm but the priory was not a hospital; it was a hospice or a house of refuge. Even a stranger could claim a share in the abundance of the house for three days. This was the rule of all monastic houses throughout Christian Europe. Nearness to London brought many guests to this priory, who earned their keep in bread, beef and beer by bringing news. The priory was razed to the ground in the PEASANTS' REVOLT of 1381 and the unpopular Prior Hales was beheaded. The restoration begun by Prior Redington was sufficiently advanced for Henry IV to stay here for two weeks before his coronation in 1399. The new

church had a rectangular nave and a superb bell tower, 'the glory of North West London' in the words of Stow. According to a 16th-century description of the priory the gate was covered with lead, and had three gardens attached to it with an orchard and a fish pond to east and north. Next came the sub-prior's lodging with gardens, the Turcopolier's house and garden, the great and little courts, woodhouse and yard, slaughter house, plumber's house, laundry and counting house. Camden says of this priory that it 'resembled a palace, had a very faire church, and a toure steeple raised to a great height with so fine workmanship that it was a singular beauty and ornament in the City.' At the DISSOLUTION, the monastery was parcelled up and sold. Protector Somerset blew up the tower and took the stone for SOMERSET HOUSE in the STRAND. By the 18th century most of the priory buildings had disappeared. Nothing remains today except ST JOHN'S GATE and the 12th-century crypt of ST JOHN'S, CLERKENWELL.

Prospect of Whitby *57 Wapping Wall, E1*. One of the oldest riverside public houses. It was originally built in 1520, when, because of its associations with river thieves and smugglers, it was known as the Devil's Tavern. Samuel Pepys was a regular visitor here and meetings of the Ancient Society of Pepys are still held here. In 1777 the name was changed to the present one after a ship named the *Prospect*, which was registered at Whitby, moored off the tavern and became a landmark. In the early 18th century a sailor sold an unknown plant here to a local market gardener – it became known as the fuchsia. Dickens was a customer, as were Whistler and Turner.

Prudential Assurance Co. *142 Holborn Bars, EC1*. Built partly on the site of FURNIVAL'S INN. A huge redbrick and red terracotta structure, it was designed by Alfred Waterhouse in 1879 and extended in 1899–1900. It is the last great Gothic Revival building in London. The 1879 section was rebuilt in 1932. In the museum there are memorabilia covering early HOLBORN, including FURNIVAL'S and STAPLE INNS, the history of the Prudential (which was founded in 1848) and of industrial life assurance which it pioneered.

Public Lavatories *and* **Public Baths** For such familiar institutions, the history of public baths and lavatories has been short. In the case of the former it seems destined to remain so, such is the current decline in their numbers. The Romans introduced public baths to London, but these hot and cold baths, showers and sweating rooms, followed by the application of ointment and oils, failed to survive their departure. The reasons were a combination of the practical and the spiritual: fear of catching the plague and religious disapproval of licentious mixed bathing. The first major sanitary act was passed in London in 1358 when the 'Chancellor of the University' was required by Royal Writ 'to remove from the streets and lanes of the town all swine and all dirt, dung, filth . . . and to cause the streets and lanes to be kept clean for the future'. That such a step was necessary is evidenced by a court case of 1347 in which two men were accused of piping ordure into their neighbour's cellar. Public latrines were built over rivers for the most part, those overhanging the FLEET RIVER apparently being particularly busy since their combined output stopped the river flowing. Lavatory paper did not exist, the alternative ranging from a sponge on a stick in a container of salt water to stones, shells, and bunches of herbs for the poor. The chamber-pot was the most popular device in the home and remained so well into the 18th century. The invention of the first flush lavatory is credited to Sir John Harington in 1596 but his enthusiasm for the device, which would 'keep all sweet and savourie', was shared only by a few, including his godmother, Queen Elizabeth I, who installed one in RICHMOND PALACE. Public latrines were periodically cleaned by 'rakers' and 'gongfermers' (cleansing gangs) who were amply rewarded with 40 shillings per 'job'. After the construction of the New River (see WATER SUPPLY) sanitation in London was improved, although the 'human lavatory' was still in evidence, offering, for a small fee, the use of a pail and his voluminous cape as a screen to passers-by. In 1775 Alexander Cummins, a watchmaker, patented a water-closet with an S-trap. After improvements effected by Thomas Prosser in 1777, the perfected version was produced by Joseph Bramah. But it was only in the middle of the next century that dramatic change occurred. In 1847 all cesspits were abolished and in 1858 the METROPOLITAN BOARD OF WORKS under Sir Joseph Bazalgette embarked upon the task of laying a new sewerage system beneath London. At its completion in 1875 over 1,000 miles of sewers had been built (see DRAINS). In 1851 George Jennings applied the new sanitary technology to public conveniences. At that year's GREAT EXHIBITION he introduced his quaintly named 'monkey closets' into the retiring rooms in HYDE PARK and later at SYDENHAM. Jennings's ideas were revolutionary; many conveniences were thereafter placed underground with cast iron arches, railings or pergolas to mark their whereabouts. Those above ground were decorated distinctively with finials, pillars, panels and lamps. The urinals themselves were built in slate and were often grouped around a central pillar for economy of space and water. Jennings subsequently took his pioneering ideas to Paris, Florence, Madrid, Frankfurt, Hong Kong and Sydney, and was presented with the gold medal of the Society of Arts by Prince Albert.

While Jennings was establishing London's network of conveniences, action was finally being taken with regard to public baths. On 16 October 1844, a 'Committee for Promoting the Establishment of Baths and Wash-Houses for the Labouring Classes' was set up. The first such establishment was opened in London in May 1845 at Glasshouse Yard in dockland. In its first year it attracted 35,000 customers for the baths and 49,000 for the washing and ironing facilities. In 1851 a far grander establishment was opened by the Prince Consort at Goulston Square, WHITECHAPEL; the Whitechapel Amenity Complex stands on its site today. Momentum was increased with the passing of the Baths and Wash-Houses Act of 1846-7. The first parish to adopt the recommendations contained therein was ST-MARTIN-IN-THE-FIELDS where the ORANGE STREET baths were opened in 1849. Typical charges at the time were 1d for a cold bath, 2d for a hot bath with clean towel; 2d for a cold bath, or 4d for a hot bath for up to four children under eight years old. Towards the end of the century the list of attractions was enhanced by the addition of Russian vapour and Turkish baths which had been introduced to Britain by

An 1860 poster advertising baths in the City Road where the 'purest spring water allowed the swimmer the lengthened enjoyment of his art'.

David Urquhart. The Victorian passion for the grandiose was increasingly reflected in the architecture of new baths. But this tended to deter the very poor for whom they had originally been built: 'the great unwashed' was both a scathing and a literal expression. While its embryonic partner, the public swimming pool, has gone from strength to strength, the London public bath is now in decline. Recently establishments in North End Road and Silchester Road have been closed despite public outcry. Notable examples of existing public baths include the following: Church Street Baths, E15 (Spalding and Cross, 1892; enlarged, 1910); Clissold Road Baths, N16 (1908-9; rebuilt by Hobden and Porri, 1930); Dulwich Public Baths (Spalding and Cross, 1892; enlarged, 1910); Englefield Road Baths, N1 (Percival Holt, 1932); Evelyn Baths, Clyde Street, SE8 (A.W.S. Cross, 1929); Finsbury Public Baths, Ironmonger Row, EC1 (A.W.S. and K.B.M. Cross, 1931; extended 1938); Greenwich New Baths, Trafalgar Road, SE10 (Horth and Andrew, 1898); Hornsey Road Baths, N7 (A. Hessell Tiltman, 1892; reopened after war damage, 1960); Island Baths, Tiller Road, E14 (Clarkson, 1900; rebuilt after war damage); Ladywell Baths, Lewisham (Wilson and Aldwinkle, 1885); Laurie Grove Baths, New Cross Road, SE14 (Thomas Dinwiddy, 1929; rebuilt 1980); Lower Clapton Road Baths, E5 (Harnor and Pinches, 1896-7; rebuilt by John Phillips and Harry Gibberd, 1937); Marshall Street Baths, W1 (Price Prichard Baly, 1851-3; extended, 1861 and 1893; rebuilt by A.W.S. and K.B.M. Cross, 1930); Plumstead High Street Baths, SE18 (Frank Summer and J.R. Dixon, 1907); Poplar Baths, East India Dock Road, E14 (Price Prichard Baly, 1851-2; reconstructed 1934); Porchester Baths, Paddington, W2 (H. Shepherd, 1921); Prince of Wales Baths, Kentish Town, NW5 (T.W. Aldwinkle, 1898-1901); Seymour Place Baths, W1 (A.W.S. and K.B.M. Cross, 1921; extended, 1935); Shacklewell Lane Baths, E8 (Percival Holt, 1932); Sherard Road Baths, SE9 (Adams, 1905; rebuilt by H.W. Tee, 1939); Town Hall Baths, Chelsea Manor Street, SW3 (E. Perrett, 1877; rebuilt by Wills and Anderson, 1907); Wells Way Baths, SE5 (Maurice Adams and William Oxtoby, 1902-3); Whiston Road Baths, Haggerston (A.W.S. Cross, 1903-4); Woolwich Baths, Bathway, SE18 (1894); York Hall Baths,

Old Ford Road, EC2 (A. Ernest Darby, 1929).

Notable public lavatories are not so numerous in London. The establishment on the EMBANKMENT has impressive glass cisterns, while the Star Yard conveniences, just off CHANCERY LANE, boast an impressive cast-iron urinal in the Parisian style. Other notable example include the public lavatories in front of BATTERSEA Town Hall and those adjacent to the old GUILDHALL LIBRARY. An indication of what the future holds is the 'Loomatic' opened in LEICESTER SQUARE in 1982, which combines austerity with high technology in a positively frightening manner. In 1982 the MUSEUM OF LONDON acquired the fine Victorian public lavatory from HOLBORN near KINGSWAY Station. In one of the glass cisterns above the urinals an attendant had kept goldfish in constantly changing water. (*See also* QUEENHITHE.)

Public Record Office *Chancery Lane, WC2*. The national repository of records (excluding certain classes maintained separately) deriving from the actions of central government and the courts of law, dating back to the Norman Conquest. By the beginning of the 19th century they were scattered among some 50 different buildings, including the TOWER OF LONDON, the ROLLS CHAPEL, the Treasuries at WESTMINSTER, the STATE PAPER OFFICE, the Chapter House of WESTMINSTER ABBEY, as well as casual wards, prisons and castles. To a Record Commission reporting in 1807, they were a growing national scandal 'unarranged, undescribed and unascertained ... exposed to erasure, alienation and embezzlement ... lodged in buildings uncommodious and insecure', urgently needing the central organisation established finally, by Act of Parliament, in 1838.

Sir James Pennethorne's massive mock-Tudor building in CHANCERY LANE received its first deposits in the 1860s. Two extensions by the same architect were added in the following ten years to house documents from the State Paper Office, demolished in 1862. The ROLLS CHAPEL, on the same site, was pulled down in 1895 to make way for two more blocks and a Museum, designed by Sir John Taylor and completed in 1902. A Record Commission of 1912–13 predicted, correctly, that existing accommodation, which included some of the old repositories, would be outgrown by 1917. The next 50 years saw temporary solutions to the problems of selecting, storing, preserving and making easily available to the public an increasing volume of documents: huts for binders, repairers and photographers were erected alongside the main buildings; records brought back from their wartime dispersal were stored in the underground station at CHANCERY LANE. Strong Rooms, including the Rolls Room, were converted to reading rooms.

The decision to divide the Records between CHANCERY LANE and an entirely new building was reached in 1968. The new Office, opened at KEW in 1977, houses records of modern government departments and public offices, some (from the Treasury and the Colonial Office, for example) dating back to the 16th century. Medieval records, State Papers domestic and foreign before 1782, legal records of all periods, and certain decennial census returns remain at CHANCERY LANE and its branch repositories. With few exceptions, Public Records are open to inspection after a lapse of 30 years from their creation.

The Museum, which incorporates glass and monuments from the ROLLS CHAPEL, contains, among other treasures, *Domesday Book* and Shakespeare's will.

Public Schools Club Founded in 1909, its first premises were in ALBEMARLE STREET whence it moved to CURZON STREET and then, in 1937, to 100 PICCADILLY, formerly the Badminton Club and before that the house of the Duke of Beaufort. So many members were killed in the 1st World War that for a time it had to close. In the 1960s, to improve a worsening financial situation, which the admission of women members had not solved, members were allowed to put forward the names of those who had not attended a public school. This measure did not answer the problem, however, and in 1972 the club was merged with the EAST INDIA AND SPORTS CLUB.

Pudding Lane *EC3*. Said to be named after animals' puddings (the medieval word for guts and entrails) which were brought down the lane from the butchers' shops in EASTCHEAP on the way to the THAMES dung barges. It was the starting point of the GREAT FIRE which began in Farryner's baking shop on 2 September 1666. A nonconformist minister attributed the fire to gluttony as it began in Pudding Lane and ended at Pie Corner, the corner of COCK LANE and GILSTPUR STREET, where a small gilt statue of a boy high on the wall marks the spot.

Puddle Dock A small inlet on the north bank of the THAMES just east of BLACKFRIARS RAILWAY BRIDGE and formerly east of the mouth of the FLEET RIVER which has for a long time served as a sewer. According to Stow the name comes 'of one Puddle that kept a wharf on the west side thereof and now Puddle Water by means of many horses watered there'. Ogilby's map, completed in 1677 after his death, shows it as having good wharving facilities. Hereabouts in the past stood the south-west corner of the City wall and the medieval BAYNARD'S CASTLE, not far from where the BLACK FRIARS' monastery was and where the Black Friars public house can now be found. An attempt was made to build a theatre here in 1616 but the City fathers banned it, fearing perhaps that the 'rogues and vagabonds' might be tempted to rob the nearby Royal Wardrobe. Since then the stage has become more respectable, and in 1956 the Lord Mayor, Sir Cuthbert Ackroyd, laid as a symbolic foundation of a new theatre, on the east bank of the dock, two bricks – one from a bombed London dock, the other from the bedroom in which Mozart was born. The MERMAID THEATRE arose within the walls of a bombed warehouse.

Pulteney Hotel *Piccadilly*. In Regency times one of the most fashionable hotels in London. Here the Grand Duchess Catherine, sister of the Tsar Alexander I, watched the exiled French King Louis XVIII enter London in state on his way back to Paris; and she warmly admired *'certains arrangements de commodité'* to be found there – almost certainly a reference to the new-fangled water-closets, for which the Pulteney was famous. Soon afterwards she was joined by her brother, the Tsar, much to the annoyance of the Prince Regent who had wanted to put him up at ST JAMES'S PALACE. At that time Alexander was a popular hero in England, and during his stay he had to appear on the balcony of the hotel to respond to the cheers of the crowds assembled below in PICCADILLY. In 1823 the Pulteney Hotel was removed to ALBEMARLE STREET.

Punch Tavern *99 Fleet Street, EC4*. A large public house in which the satirical magazine *Punch* was conceived in 1841. The FLEET STREET entrance leads into a long tiled and mirrored lobby. Inside is a copper bar top and original drawings and cartoons from *Punch*, as well as photographs of its various editors.

Purcell Room *see* QUEEN ELIZABETH HALL.

James Purdey and Sons Ltd *Audley House, 57–58 South Audley Street, W1*. Gunmakers founded in 1814 in LEICESTER SQUARE by James Purdey, himself the youngest child of a gunmaker. In 1826 he extended his business to premises in OXFORD STREET where he prospered. After his death in 1863 the firm was taken over by his son, James Purdey the Younger, who in 1881 built Audley House to accommodate its further expansion.

Purley *Surrey*. The Saxon *purley* was an open space in woodland with pear trees. With COULSDON, KENLEY, SANDERSTEAD and SELSDON, Purley in 1965 became part of the London Borough of CROYDON. In 1804 a member of the Royal Jennerian Society held an early vaccination session against smallpox for nine poor Coulsdon children at the Rose and Crown coaching inn below Riddlesdown. The Brighton Railway opened Godstone Road Station in 1841. This was renamed Purley in 1888. Branches extended to Caterham (1856) and Tattenham Corner (1897) for Epsom Downs racecourse. Trams to Purley via CROYDON also operated from 1901 to 1951. Reedham Orphanage, founded in 1844 by the Revd Andrew Reed, was demolished in 1980, following a shortage of orphans, but the school opened by the Prince of Wales on Russell Hill in 1866 still dominates the skyline. In West Purley from 1900 William Webb pioneered his spacious house and garden layouts forming the present fashionable estates. About every seven years the River Bourne rises mysteriously in the Caterham valley chalk to resubmerge between Purley and CROYDON, its appearance being traditionally considered a portent of national calamity.

Putney *SW15*. A THAMES-side settlement lying on the south side of a sweeping bend opposite FULHAM and between WANDSWORTH and BARNES. The name derives from Anglo-Saxon and means 'Putta's landing-place'. The first documentary reference is in *Domesday Book*, 1086, although only a toll from the fishery is mentioned. Archaeological work, however, has shown that there was some kind of settlement here in the Iron Age, and that the Romans were here near the THAMES from the 1st to the 4th centuries AD. It has been suggested that they may have had a wooden bridge here on the line of the ancient trackway from London to the south-west. Certainly Putney Ferry was important in the medieval period, both the short crossing to FULHAM and the long one to London and WESTMINSTER. Edward I used the latter in 1290.

Little is known of Putney before 1400, although it is likely that the farming and fishing community which survived into the 19th century had its roots in this period. By 1500, the existence of six open fields along with various enclosures for pasture is known. The parish church of St Mary by the river is first mentioned in 1291, and Archbishop Winchelsea held an ordination there in 1302. Until 1535, Putney formed part of the Archbishop of Canterbury's manor of WIMBLEDON, along with MORTLAKE and ROEHAMPTON. After that date, although the manor remained intact, it passed through a succession of lay hands until, in 1720, it was purchased by the Duchess of Marlborough. From her it came to the Earls Spencer in 1763, a long-standing association which is marked by several local street and public house names. Amongst the people of Putney in the Tudor period, Thomas West, later Bishop of Ely and servant of Henry VII and Henry VIII, and Thomas Cromwell stand out as the most important. At this time, it became common for London merchants and members of the Court to acquire property in convenient riverside parishes like Putney, a fashion which gradually worked its way down the social scale until the mass suburban building of the 19th and 20th centuries. Amongst the notable early 'commuters' was John Lacy, who entertained both Elizabeth I and James I at Putney Palace, his mansion by the THAMES. The 17th century was a time of rapid expansion locally, and was also marked during the Civil War by the famous Putney Debates, which were held in the parish church by the Parliamentary Army in 1647. It was at this time that Putney's daughter settlement, ROEHAMPTON, which had been founded on the far side of the Heath during a previous upsurge in population in the 13th century, began to attract grand houses, many of which still survive.

During the 18th century, Putney continued to grow as a fashionable outer suburb. In 1729 the ferry was replaced by a 15-arch wooden bridge and this attracted increased foot and carriage traffic, despite the tolls. It was much used by troops marching to reviews on the Heath, which was also notorious at this time for duels and, to a lesser extent, highwaymen. Edward Gibbon was born in Putney and spent his childhood there. By 1801 the population had increased to about 2,400, whereas on the eve of the 1st World War it was ten times that figure, eloquent testimony to the expansion of Cobbett's 'Great Wen' during the Victorian period. Growth was slow at first, with a scattering of modest villas and artisan cottages from the 1820s. The parish church was rebuilt in 1836 to the designs of Edward Lapidge, although the tower of about 1440 was suffered to remain (this building was gutted by fire in 1973, but is being rebuilt). In 1846 the railway arrived *en route* from WATERLOO to RICHMOND and made Putney even more accessible than hitherto. Building operations took place throughout the parish after 1860, even in remote ROEHAMPTON, where the Conservative Land Society built villas in spacious grounds, replaced when the leases fell in by giant blocks on the much-acclaimed Alton Estate. PUTNEY BRIDGE was freed from toll in 1880, the year that the District Railway arrived in FULHAM, giving direct access to the CITY. The bridge was rebuilt in stone in 1884–6, and this was followed by a spate of shop-building in the High Street, and also by a relentless march of small brick houses across the fields and market gardens. Even so, Putney was not fully built up by 1914, and there were few of the slums which characterised many other suburbs. After 1919, the pace of private speculative

Lime Grove, the house of Lady St Aubyn below Putney Hill, when the area was still a fashionable suburb.

building slackened, and the largest development was the Roehampton Estate of attractive small cottages built in 1921–5. Since 1925 there has been little housing development in Putney, neither has there been any large-scale clearance and rebuilding, so that the impression of the place is very much that of a Victorian – Edwardian suburb, consisting mainly of two-storey terrace and semi-detached houses, containing a population of between 40,000 and 50,000.

At The Pines, 11 Putney Hill, Algernon Charles Swinburne lived with his friend, Theodore Watts-Dunton. Ford Madox Ford described it as the most lugubrious London semi-detached villa it was ever his fate to enter. At No. 26 Gwendolen Avenue, Eduard Benes, President of Czechoslovakia, stayed with his nephew in 1938–40 before moving to the Czech Embassy at No. 9 GROSVENOR PLACE.

Putney *or* **Fulham Bridge**   *Fulham – Putney.* The first bridge was built of timber here in 1727–9 by the master carpenter, Thomas Phillips, to the design of Sir Joseph Acworth. Until 1750, when WESTMINSTER BRIDGE opened, it was the only bridge across the river west of LONDON BRIDGE. It had 26 spans varying in size from 14 to 32 ft and presented a serious obstruction to navigation. In 1870–72 the number of the spans was reduced to 23. The bridge was replaced by the present five-span granite bridge by Sir Joseph Bazalgette in 1882–6. Built upstream of the older structure, the new bridge also replaced an aqueduct belonging to the CHELSEA WATERWORKS COMPANY and the mains now run under the footways of the bridge. Since 1845 it has been the starting point of the UNIVERSITY BOAT RACE.

Putney Railway Bridge   *Fulham – Putney.* Built in 1887–9 for the London and South Western Railway with five spans of lattice-girder construction. It was built by William Jacomb, Brunel's assistant on the ship, the *Great Eastern*.

Putney Vale Cemetery   *see* CEMETERIES.

Q

Quaggy A river which rises on BROMLEY Common and flows through BROMLEY and MOTTINGHAM to ELTHAM, where it is joined by the Kidbrooke and turns westwards to join the RAVENSBOURNE.

Queen Alexandra Military Hospital *Millbank*. Constructed between 1903 and 1905 and opened by King Edward VII on 1 July 1905. It was originally intended to replace the three regimental hospitals of the BRIGADE OF GUARDS in VAUXHALL BRIDGE ROAD, ROCHESTER ROW and WARWICK WAY. Its scope was increased, however, as a result of the two World Wars, and became the central reference hospital for the Army. It was closed in 1977 and its functions taken over by the QUEEN ELIZABETH MILITARY HOSPITAL, WOOLWICH. The buildings have been taken over by the Trustees of the TATE GALLERY.

Queen Anne Street *W1*. Built from 1723 onwards on the PORTLAND ESTATE. Edmund Burke lodged here in 1764–5 and James Boswell in 1788. No. 47, now Nos 22 and 23, was the home of J. M. W. Turner in 1808–51. Hector Berlioz, the composer, stayed at No. 58 in 1851. A good proportion of 18th-century houses remain unspoiled. Queen Anne Street now takes the medical overflow from HARLEY STREET, the doctors mingling with architects, solicitors and chartered accountants.

Queen Anne's Gate *SW1*. Originally two closes separated until 1873 by a wall whose site is marked by a statue of Queen Anne (*see* STATUES). The western close was formerly known as Queen Square and the eastern as Park Street. The attractive brown brick and stone banded houses in the former Queen Square date from about 1704. Several of them have elaborate decorated wooden canopies with pendants. Most of the houses in the former Park Street are of the later 18th century. Nos 6–12 are by James and Harvey Lonsdale Elmes and were built in the 1830s. Two distinguished collectors lived in this part of the street in the last quarter of the 18th century, Charles Towneley at No. 14 in 1777–1805 and the Revd Clayton Cracherode at No. 32 in 1775–99. Towneley's marbles and Cracherode's books are now at the BRITISH MUSEUM. Lord Palmerston was born at No. 20 in 1784. Jeremy Bentham owned No. 40. He let it to his friend, James Mill, who lived here in 1814–31, for part of that time with his son, John Stuart Mill. Lord Haldane lived at No. 28 in 1907–28. William Smith, MP, 'pioneer of English liberty', lived at No. 16 which was occupied between 1904 and 1910 by Admiral of the Fleet Lord Fisher when he was 1st Sea Lord. Other residents have included William Windham, the statesman; Lord North, the Prime Minister; James Thomson, the poet; Peg Woffington, the actress; Sir Joshua Reynolds's sister, Frances, who died here in 1807; John St Loe Strachey, editor of the *Spectator*; and

Viscount Grey of Falloden, the Foreign Secretary. The Soldiers', Sailors' and Airmens' Families Association is at No. 27 in a house formerly occupied as the Westminster Training School and Home for Nurses founded in 1874 by Lady Augusta Stanley. No. 42 is the headquarters of the NATIONAL TRUST. The Director of Public Prosecutions is at Nos 4–12. The incongruous baroque building at No. 36 was built for the Anglo-American Oil Company in 1909 to the designs of Runtz. The bronze *Mother and Child* in the garden on the BIRDCAGE WALK side is by Henry Moore (1960–1, erected here 1966). *The Greek Boy* fountain in ST JAMES'S PARK nearby is by an unknown sculptor (1883).

Queen Anne's Mansions *Broadway, Westminster*. A massive block of flats, 14 storeys high, built for the developer, Henry Alers Hankey, in 1873–89. 'Black with the dirt of ages and without any external decoration', in the words of Harold Clunn, 'it is for real ugliness unsurpassed by any other great building in all London.' It was demolished in 1971.

Queen Charlotte's Maternity Hospital *Goldhawk Road, W6*. Founded in 1739 as the earliest lying-in hospital in the British Isles. That year Sir Richard Manningham, the foremost obstetrician of his time, opened a house in JERMYN STREET next to his own for 25 lying-in women. In 1752 the hospital moved to St George's Row; in 1754 to DUKE STREET, GROSVENOR SQUARE; in 1762 to Quebec Street; in 1773 back to St George's Row and in 1791 to Bayswater Gate. It was then variously known as Bayswater Lying-in Hospital, General Lying-in Hospital, Bayswater Hall and Queen's Lying-in Hospital, Bayswater Gate. In 1804 it came under the patronage of Queen Charlotte. Its purpose was 'to afford an asylum for indigent females during the awful period of childbirth and also to facilitate the repentance of suffering and contrite sinners'. In 1813 it was moved to the Old Manor House, Lisson Green, now the MARYLEBONE ROAD. It was rebuilt in 1856 to the designs of Charles Hawkins and a new wing was added in 1886. In 1929 a site of 5 acres was secured in Ravenscourt Park, HAMMERSMITH where initially a 30-bed isolation hospital was built for special research and treatment of puerperal fever. A team under Leonard Colebrook FRS demonstrated for the first time how germs of childbed fever spread. After the 2nd World War the new hospital was completed on that site. In conjunction with the CHELSEA HOSPITAL FOR WOMEN it forms the Institute of Obstetrics and Gynaecology of the British Postgraduate Federation. In 1982 there were 141 beds.

Queen Elizabeth College, University of London *Campden Hill Road, W8*. Its origins go back to 1881 when KING'S COLLEGE set up a Department for Higher Education of Women which, in 1885, opened in premises in KENSINGTON SQUARE. In 1908 this was incorporated into the UNIVERSITY OF LONDON with the title King's College for Women, and specialised in courses in Home Science and Economics. In 1915 it moved to CAMPDEN HILL ROAD, to a site (which it still occupies) and buildings provided by money raised by Sir John Atkins, a KENSINGTON doctor, concerned that provision be made for this form of women's education. In 1916 a Diploma in Household and Social Science was instituted, and in 1920 a degree of BSc. In 1928 the connection with KING'S COLLEGE was severed and it became an independent School of LONDON UNIVERSITY with the title of King's College of Household and Social Science. It had its own governing body of which Sir John Atkins remained Chairman for many years. During the 2nd World War the college was evacuated and its buildings suffered considerable bomb damage. It returned to CAMPDEN HILL in 1946.

Queen Elizabeth Hall *and* **Purcell Room** *Belvedere Road, SE1.* Built close to the ROYAL FESTIVAL HALL, the Queen Elizabeth Hall was opened by the Queen on 1 March 1967. It seats 1,100 and is used for small orchestral and chamber music concerts, solo recitals and poetry readings, as well as conferences and film performances. There is a small chamber organ. The Purcell Room, seating capacity 372, is a small intimate hall used mainly for recitals by soloists and chamber groups.

Queen Elizabeth Hospital for Children *Hackney Road, E2.* In 1868, following a CHOLERA epidemic, the East London Hospital for Children was established with ten beds in two old warehouses in Hackney Road. It was visited by Charles Dickens who described it as 'a Haven to the children who came from the length and breadth of East London' and 'the equally dreary districts over the water of Rotherhithe and Deptford'. In 1870, 327 Hackney Road was purchased. It is the site of part of the present hospital. Over the years extensions were built and in 1942 the hospital received its present name. In 1968 it was amalgamated with the HOSPITAL FOR SICK CHILDREN, GREAT ORMOND STREET. In 1982 there were 148 beds.

Queen Elizabeth Military Hospital *Stadium Road, Woolwich, SE18.* Opened by Queen Elizabeth, the Queen Mother, in 1978 to replace five old hospitals: the QUEEN ALEXANDRA MILITARY HOSPITAL, MILLBANK; the Military Maternity Hospital, WOOLWICH; the Royal Herbert Hospital, WOOLWICH; the Military Hospital, Colchester; and the Royal Victoria Hospital, Netley. The new hospital, designed by Messrs Powell and Moya, caters for all acute cases. In 1982 there were 464 beds.

Queen Mary College *Mile End Road, E1.* Became a School of LONDON UNIVERSITY in 1934, receiving its charter and name from Queen Mary. It incorporated both the Peoples' Palace Technical Schools, founded in 1887 with DRAPERS' COMPANY funds to give educational facilities and night classes for students of all kinds (*see* PEOPLE'S PALACE), and the East London Technical College founded in 1902 and given in 1907 provisional recognition in LONDON UNIVERSITY'S Faculty of Science and Engineering. Since 1948 the College has added new buildings.

Queen Mary's Hospital for Children *Carshalton, Surrey.* Opened in 1909 as a long-stay children's hospital. When taken over in 1948 by the National Health Service it became a general children's hospital. In 1959 the Fountain Hospital for Mentally Handicapped Children was transferred from TOOTING and amalgamated with Queen Mary's. This step produced the first comprehensive children's hospital in the country. It thus brought to an end the historical isolation of mental and physical illness. In 1982 there were 537 beds.

Queen Mary's Hospital for the East End *West Ham Lane, Stratford, E15.* The foundation stone of a new hospital, developed from a dispensary, was laid in 1888. When opened in 1890 the hospital housed 12 men, 12 women, a children's ward and an isolation ward. By 1903, with the addition of new buildings, the accommodation rose to 60 beds. A maternity wing was added in 1923. In 1948 the National Health Service took the hospital over. Now it is an acute general hospital with 128 beds.

Queen Mary's Hospital *Roehampton, SW15.* Founded in 1915 and originally intended to provide a hospital, a limb-fitting centre and a factory for the manufacture of limbs for men wounded in the War. Queen Mary actively supported the venture and the hospital was consequently named after her. The imposing building, Roehampton House, had been built in 1710–12 for Thomas Cary, a wealthy City merchant, to the designs of Thomas Archer, a pupil of Sir John Vanbrugh. Wings and pavilions were added by Sir Edwin Lutyens in 1912 for A. Morgan Grenfell, a subsequent owner. The building is of redbrick and is three storeys in height. Although artificial limbs were known to have been fitted since at least the 5th century BC in Greece, there was no centre in England before 1915, though there were a number of small private firms. In 1915 the Americans were the leaders in the art and American firms assisted in setting up the limb factory. Every serviceman who lost a limb, or limbs, was entitled to be fitted with an artificial limb and to have it looked after, repaired and renewed for as long as he lived. In 1917 a research department for artificial limbs was set up but closed later. It was reopened in 1945 and has continued since as the Biomechanical Research and Development Unit. Special facilities were provided for children after the use by expectant mothers of the drug thalidomide, which was responsible for numerous deformed babies. The hospital is now under the National Health Service and serves a wide area as a general hospital. In 1982 there were 465 beds.

Queen Square, *WC1.* Built in about 1708–20 and named after Queen Anne. No original buildings remain. It is on the site of an ancient reservoir excavated to supply the GREYFRIARS of NEWGATE STREET. An iron pump at the south end marked 'unfit for drinking' is a reminder of this. Until the early 19th century it was a very fashionable part of London. Dr Charles Burney and his daughter, Fanny, lived here in 1771–2 when the square was still open to the north. Fanny described the beautiful view of the verdant hills of HAMPSTEAD and HIGHGATE. Dr Burney entertained Captain Cook here shortly before his second voyage. From the mid-18th century until the mid-19th a girls' school

Engraving after Dayes of the fashionable Queen Square, Bloomsbury, in 1787, when it was still open to the north.

nicknamed the 'ladies' Eton' was on the east side. James Boswell's daughter, Veronica, was a pupil. The 'ladies' occupied a gallery in ST GEORGE THE MARTYR in the south-west corner of the square and always went by coach in order to practise getting in and out decorously. When the coach got too decrepit it was kept in the schoolroom and they practised there. In the gardens is a lead statue, placed there in about 1775, of Queen Charlotte, wife of George III (*see* STATUES). The King stayed privately in the square with Dr Willis when he began to be ill. Also in the gardens is a plaque commemorating the lucky escape of nearly 1,000 people sleeping in the area who were unhurt when a Zeppelin exploded there in 1915. Now the square is mostly taken up with medical buildings. On the west side are the examination halls of the ROYAL COLLEGES OF PHYSICIANS and SURGEONS. On the north, the Royal Institute of Public Health and Hygiene. On the east, the NATIONAL HOSPITAL FOR DISEASES OF THE NERVOUS SYSTEM (founded in 1859) occupies a building opened in 1885 by Prince Albert Edward, Prince of Wales. On the south is the ITALIAN HOSPITAL, founded in 1884 and rebuilt in 1898. Next to it is the Stanhope Institute (INNER LONDON EDUCATION AUTHORITY Adult Education). Faber and Faber, the publishers, are at No. 3. The ART WORKERS' GUILD is at No. 6. One of the Guild's founders was William Morris who lived in the square in 1865–82. Other inhabitants have included Dr William Stukely, the antiquarian rector of ST GEORGE THE MARTYR; Jeremy Bentham; and J. K. Jerome.

Queen Street EC4.

Built with KING STREET and Queen Street Place as a main road from the THAMES to the GUILDHALL after the GREAT FIRE. This section followed the line of Soper Lane where soapmakers and sellers used to live. There are fine 18th-century houses at Nos 27–28, two of the very few now remaining in the CITY.

Queen Street *Mayfair, W1*.

A short street leading from CURZON STREET to CHARLES STREET. On the east side Nos 2–11 (consecutively) have a pleasing irregularity and with one or two exceptions are predominantly 18th-century, as also is No. 19 on the west side. Mrs FitzGeorge, with whom the Duke of Cambridge, commander-in-chief of the British army, contracted a morganatic marriage in 1840, lived at No. 6 until her death in 1890.

Queen Victoria Memorial *and* Gardens

Opposite Buckingham Palace, SW1. Conceived in 1901 by the Queen Victoria Memorial Committee as part of a 'great architectural and scenic change' near BUCKINGHAM PALACE, the sculpture forms the nucleus of Aston Webb's design for the transformation of the MALL. Standing 82 ft high, the white marble memorial group was unveiled in 1911 by George V who knighted its creator, Thomas Brock, on the spot. A 13 ft high seated figure of Queen Victoria faces eastwards down the MALL. It was made from one block of marble. The Queen is surrounded by what Osbert Sitwell called 'tons of allegorical females in white wedding cake marble, with whole litters of their cretinous children'. Behind, marble groups representing Charity (west) Truth (south) and Justice (north) occupy the other three sides of the squat column that rises to a gold-leafed figure of Victory with figures of Courage and Constancy at her feet. This is set in the middle of a circular ponded podium approached by two flights of steps to the east and west flanked by figures of Progress and Peace (east) and Manufacture (west). To the north are Painting and Architecture, and to the south War and Shipbuilding. On the encircling ground-level podium wall and friezes are sea nymphs and deities with two aqueous bronze reliefs interposed. The group used 2,300 tons of marble.

A secondary creation was the Memorial Gardens around it designed by Aston Webb. These are enclosed by a low stone balustrade which links the three main ornamental exit gates: on the north side the entrance to GREEN PARK, the gift of Canada, the pillars therefore topped by wheat and fruit and a seal; on the east side the entrance to Constitution Hill, the gift of West and South Africa (West Africa is represented by

630

a leopard and an eagle, South Africa by an ostrich and monkey); on the south side the entrance to BIRDCAGE WALK, the gift of Australia, hence a kangaroo and ram. The gates on the east and south sites are by Alfred Drury. There are two less elaborate subsidiary gateways: at the junction of BIRDCAGE WALK and BUCKINGHAM GATE opposite the DUCHY OF CORNWALL office (two columns topped by urns given by the Malay States); and at the Constitution Hill exit (the gift of Newfoundland). Parts of both ST JAMES'S PARK and GREEN PARK were taken to create the garden space and the ST JAMES'S PARK lake was shortened. The intended plain grass counterpoint to the memorial was changed at the request of Edward VII and spectacular flower beds have been the tradition since. The present Portland stone façade of BUCKINGHAM PALACE was paid for with the money left over from the memorial.

Queen Victoria Street *EC4*. Cut through from the VICTORIA EMBANKMENT to the BANK OF ENGLAND in 1867–71. THE DISTRICT LINE was built underneath at the same time. Some of the Victorian offices still stand but most have been replaced by modern blocks. At the BLACKFRIARS end is the Black Friar, in Sir Nikolaus Pevsner's opinion, the 'best pub in the Arts and Crafts fashion in London. Bits of metalwork and enamel outside, the Saloon Bar inside, with pink and white veined marble slabs and monkish stories told in friezes of bronze figures. Inglenook in the grand manner, with plenty of copper. The whole by H. Fuller Clark. Sculpture by Henry Poole.' BLACKFRIARS STATION was officially opened in 1886 for the London, Chatham and Dover Railway. The MANSION HOUSE Underground Station was designed by Charles Holden in 1926. The church of ST ANDREW BY THE WARDROBE WITH ST ANN is next to the Baynard Castle public house at No. 148; ST BENET GUILD CHURCH next to No. 101; and ST NICHOLAS COLE ABBEY next to 110. The COLLEGE OF ARMS is on the corner of PETER'S HILL. The Faraday Building of 1932 covers the site of DOCTORS' COMMONS. Bucklersbury House at No. 3, which is one of the largest modern blocks in London and was built to the designs of O. Campbell Jones and Partners in 1953–8, is on the site of the TEMPLE OF MITHRAS. Near it in 1869 was found a splendid Roman tessellated pavement now in the MUSEUM OF LONDON. The British and Foreign Bible Society occupied No. 146 which was designed in 1866–7 by Edward I'anson. The aluminium sculpture, *Seven Ages of Man* in the wall of Baynard House is by Richard Kindersley.

Queenhithe *EC4*. An ancient quay of UPPER THAMES STREET where there has been a dock for at least eight centuries. It was originally known as Ethelredshythe after King Alfred's son-in-law, the Alderman of Mercia. Its present name is in honour of Queen Matilda, wife of Henry I, who in the early 12th century built here, for the 'common use of the citizens', London's first public lavatory which was repaired in 1237. Queen Matilda's great-grandson, King John, gave it to his mother Queen Eleanor who made herself unpopular by the strict manner in which her right to gather customs tolls here was enforced. Succeeding queens inherited this right. In the Middle Ages it was the most important docking place in London but it declined in the 15th century as boats became larger and went instead to BILLINGSGATE.

Queen's Bodyguard of the Yeomen of the Guard Founded in 1485 for the coronation of Henry VIII. It is the oldest royal bodyguard and the oldest military corps in the world. Its distinctive Tudor uniform of knee-length tunics, white ruffs and round black hats is distinguished from that of the Yeomen Warders of the TOWER OF LONDON (*see* BEEFEATERS) by a cross belt originally designed for supporting an arquebus. There are six officers and some 80 men.

Queen's Chapel *Marlborough Gate, SW1*. First classical church in England, designed by Inigo Jones for the Infanta of Spain who was intended to marry Charles I. Building began in 1623 but when the wedding negotiations stopped so did the construction work. It was completed for Henrietta Maria in 1626–7 and refurnished for Charles II's Catholic wife Catherine of Braganza, in about 1662–80. In 1761 George III married Charlotte of Mecklenburg-Strelitz here. As well as Roman Catholic services, Dutch Reformed services for William and Mary, German Lutheran for the Hanoverians and Danish for Queen Alexandra have been held here. From the 18th century until 1901 it was known as the German Chapel Royal.

Queen's Chapel of the Savoy *see* SAVOY CHAPEL.

Queen's College *43–49 Harley Street, W1*. Founded in 1848, it was the first school in the country established for the higher education of women. It originated in the concern of supporters of the Governesses' Benevolent Institution that women who educated others should themselves receive education. Its first premises were at No. 67 HARLEY STREET where lecturers from KING'S COLLEGE gave lessons to young women (admitted over the age of 14) who were accompanied by chaperones known as Lady Visitors. The outstanding figure in the early years was the Revd Frederick Denison Maurice, Christian socialist and Professor of Theology at KING'S COLLEGE, whose liberal and progressive views strongly affected the college's development and influenced its character. With him was associated Charles Kingsley, a close friend and admirer of Maurice who later became Professor of Modern History at Cambridge, and others with advanced ideas about women's education. The standard of education was high and range of subjects wide. At first the college granted its own certificates of proficiency, but later students were prepared for public examinations. Throughout the 19th century the organisation and teaching of the college was directed by men, women filling only subsidiary positions. The college received its charter in 1853 and took the name of Queen's College in 1860. It was inspected by the government's Schools' Inquiry Commission in 1868 which reported that its students were mostly from the upper middle class and that fees at £28 per annum (additional subjects extra) were comparatively high. In spite of sporadic criticism in the 19th century about its liberal attitudes, the college remained true to the principles of its foundation. Jewish girls were admitted from 1865. By the 20th century women were taking responsibility for some of the teaching and the college became an institution of pre-university standard. After the 1st World War the chaperonage of Lady Visitors was abolished and the first woman Principal was appointed in 1931. During the 2nd World War the college was affected by the bombing of London but resumed its teaching in 1944 after brief periods of evacuation and closure. After the war it continued as a small, single-sex, independent day school, and in 1980 it had 380 students and about 50 teaching staff. Amongst famous pupils of the college were the renowned educationalists, Dorothea Beale and Frances Mary Buss, later headmistresses respectively of Cheltenham Ladies' College and NORTH LONDON COLLEGIATE SCHOOL; Sophia Jex-Blake, a leader of the movement to open the medical profession to women; the writers, Gertrude Bell and Katherine Mansfield; and the actress, Cicely Courtneidge.

Queen's Elm *241 Fulham Road, SW3*. Named after an elm tree underneath which Queen Elizabeth I, visiting Lord Burleigh, took shelter during a shower. An earlier building on the site was first licensed in 1667. The present building dates from 1914. There is a large collection of antique pipes.

Queen's Gallery *Buckingham Palace Road, SW1*. Opened in 1962 in Buckingham Palace in what had formerly been a conservatory and was consecrated as a chapel by William Howley, Archbishop of Canterbury, in March 1843. There is still a small private chapel in the building, which is screened from public view. The gallery holds public exhibitions of art treasures from the royal collection.

Queen's Gardens *W2*. Built in about 1850. Herbert Spencer, the philosopher, lived in a boarding house at Nos 37–38 in 1866–87.

Queen's Gate *SW7*. Built on land purchased by the Royal Commissioners for the GREAT EXHIBITION under an agreement dated August 1855 between them, Henry Browne Alexander, whose family owned the land (mostly market gardens) through which part of the road was to pass, and William Jackson, a building speculator. The road was originally known as Albert's Road but was officially changed to Queen's Gate in 1859. The houses built in it were large family residences in an Italianate style; and – although many demolitions and much rebuilding have taken place and the older houses have mostly been divided into flats or converted into hotels – the expansive, expensive mid-Victorian atmosphere remains. Several of the houses built in the 1870s and 1880s were designed by Norman Shaw. No. 196 was designed by Shaw for J. P. Heseltine, a rich young stockbroker and connoisseur. No. 170 is also by Shaw and was designed for a friend of Heseltine, a cement manufacturer who was, like Heseltine, a member of the Society for the Protection of Ancient Buildings. Two other of Shaw's houses, Nos 180 and 185, have unfortunately been demolished. Sir Henry Campbell-Bannerman lived at No. 60 in 1870–2. Baden-Powell House was built in 1961 to the designs of Ralph Tubbs (*see* BADEN-POWELL HOUSE MUSEUM). There is a statue of Baden-Powell outside. There is also a statue of Lord Napier of Magdala at the northern end (*see* STATUES). St Augustine's Church is by William Butterfield. The ROYAL ENTOMOLOGICAL SOCIETY is at No. 41. Embassies here are those of the Republic of Haiti (17), Iraq (21–22), Thailand (28–30), Kuwait (45–46), Bulgaria (186–188). The Bangladesh High Commission is at No. 28.

Queen's Grove *NW8*. Built in 1841. Sir George Frampton, the sculptor, lived at No. 32 in 1894–1908.

Queen's Hall *Langham Place, W1*. Opened in 1893, under the management of Robert Newman, with a children's party in the afternoon and performances by professional and amateur musicians in the evening. The classical exterior of the building was based on the Pantheon at Rome. The florid Victorian interior had a colour scheme of gold, red and grey. T. E. Knightley, one of the architects, insisted that the grey should be the same as the belly of a London mouse and hung up a string of dead mice in the painters' workshop as a pattern. There were in fact two halls; a large one for orchestral concerts and a smaller one for chamber music. In December the inaugural concert was held. The choir sang Mendelssohn's *Hymn of Praise*. Margaret Hoare, Madame Albani and Edward Lloyd were soloists. Henry Wood played the organ. The hall did not do well during the first two years and was often let for civic and private functions. In 1894 the first Sunday afternoon concert was held here, in spite of opposition from the Lord's Day Observance Society. In 1895 Henry Wood was appointed conductor of the newly formed Queen's Hall Orchestra. At that time the only other permanent orchestra in London was based at CRYSTAL PALACE. In April Sunday evening concerts were begun and in October the first season of promenade concerts. 'Proms' were not an innovation in London as they had been given at VAUXHALL and RANELAGH in the 18th century and at COVENT GARDEN in the 19th. All the same, Wood's concerts were such a success that there was often little room left for promenading. Queen's Hall became the principal concert hall in London in 1905 when ST JAMES'S HALL was closed. After its destruction by bombing in 1941, the proms were moved to the ALBERT HALL. Sir Henry Wood wanted to rebuild the hall but there were never enough funds. St George's Hotel (85 bedrooms, opened in 1963) now stands on the site.

Queen's Head and Artichoke, *Marylebone Park*. Traditionally built by Queen Elizabeth's gardener. It is marked on Rocque's map (1745). This small inn had a ground for skittles and bumble-puppy, and bowers in which cream teas were served. It was demolished about 1811, and the COLOSSEUM covered the site. A public house at No. 30, Albany Street, bears the name.

Queen's House *Greenwich, SE10*. The surrounding GREENWICH PARK and GREENWICH PALACE were settled on Anne of Denmark by James I in 1605. In 1616 Inigo Jones was commissioned to design a house for her, but it had not progressed far by 1619 when she died. The unfinished building was given to Prince Charles. His Queen, Henrietta Maria, asked Inigo Jones to complete the house in 1629–40. He used the Palladian style and described the exterior as 'sollid, proporsionable according to the rulles, masculine and unaffected'. In the interior, however, he allowed himself 'licentious imaginacey'. The building, which pleased the Queen so much it was named the 'House of Delights', was H-shaped and built on either side of the muddy DEPTFORD to WOOLWICH road which passed through a bridge connecting the two sides of the house. Its main room was the entrance hall, a perfect 40 ft

The Queen's House, Greenwich, in 1781. Designed by Inigo Jones, it is now the central portion of the National Maritime Museum.

cube with a gallery at first-floor level. The painted ceiling was by Gentileschi. On the east side a graceful iron staircase, the 'Tulip Staircase', led up to the gallery, the Queen's bedroom and her drawing-room which was to have had panels painted by Rubens and Jacob Jordaens. Across the bridge was the loggia, 'the frontispiece in the midst', which looked out over GREENWICH PARK. In 1642 Henrietta Maria left for Holland to raise funds for arms and men on the pretext of taking the ten-year old Princess Mary to Prince William, her betrothed. On 3 November the house was searched for arms by Parliamentary forces. Nothing was found but the house was taken from royal keeping. When most Crown lands were disposed of, Greenwich was retained and the Queen's House was occupied by Bulstrode Whitelock. Paintings by Rubens, Raphael and Van Dyck from Charles I's collection, much of which had been kept here, were, however, sold. The house was used for the lying-in-state of Commonwealth generals. At the restoration of 1660 Henrietta Maria returned. In 1662, John Webb, pupil of Inigo Jones, added two first-floor rooms over the highway for her. In 1670 the house was given to Charles II's Queen, Catherine of Braganza; and in 1685 to James II's Queen, Mary of Modena, who rarely used it. William and Mary did not make use of the house either, prefering KENSINGTON PALACE and HAMPTON COURT. In 1690–7 it was occupied by the Earl of Dorset, the first Ranger of GREENWICH PARK, whose appointment included its use. In 1697 Dorset was succeeded by the Earl of Romney who diverted the WOOLWICH to DEPTFORD road to its present course between the old palace and the Queen's House.

In the 1690s the Royal Naval Hospital was designed by Wren, using the Queen's House as a central point at Queen Mary's insistence (see ROYAL NAVAL COLLEGE). In 1708 it was bought by Prince George of Denmark who probably intended to give it to the Hospital for use as the Governor's residence. The Hospital paid for its repairs but the Prince died before formal arrangements were completed. At about this time Queen Anne gave her favourite, the Duchess of

Marlborough, permission to remove the Gentileschi paintings from the entrance hall and take them to MARLBOROUGH HOUSE. From 1710 to 1729 the house was used by the Hospital governors, but it proved very expensive to maintain. On 18 September 1714 George I landed at Greenwich and held his first official reception in the house the next day. Queen Caroline owned the house in 1730–7 and commissioned the painting of the Queen's Bedroom, probably from James Thornhill. In 1743–80 Lady Catherine Pelham, Ranger of the Park, occupied the house. In 1795, Princess Caroline of Brunswick, who had come to marry the Prince of Wales, was received here by his mistress, Lady Jersey. In 1805 Princess Caroline was appointed Ranger and granted the house. It was sold to the Royal Naval Asylum the following year, for a school for sailor's orphans. The colonnades were added in 1809 to commemorate the Battle of Trafalgar. In the same year the wings were added to accommodate the school's 950 pupils. When the school moved to Suffolk in 1933 the house was left in a damaged condition. Partitions had been built, doorways knocked through walls, and floors, fireplaces, bathrooms and staircases put in. It was restored in 1934–6 by the Office of Works, and opened in 1937 as the central portion of the NATIONAL MARITIME MUSEUM, housing the Elizabethan and Stuart exhibits.

Queen's Park NW6. Laid out at a cost of £3,000 by the CORPORATION OF THE CITY OF LONDON who acquired the land from the ECCLESTIASTICAL COMMISSIONERS with money provided under the will of William Ward. The park was opened in 1887. It contained a well-treed area of 30 acres and an attractive cast-iron bandstand. The earlier Victorian housing development of QUEEN'S PARK, south of Kilburn Lane, gave its name to the football club and the later housing surrounding the park formed a natural expansion of Kensal Rise and KILBURN.

Queen's Park W10. At the time of Edward the Confessor, the area now known as Queen's Park, together with KENSAL TOWN, was woodland, forming a detached part of the manor of CHELSEA. The woods were described as being used to supply logs for the fires and acorns for the pigs of the new ABBEY at WESTMINSTER. The exact ownership of the land is difficult to trace, but in the 15th century Henry VI granted part of it to All Souls' College, Oxford (*see* CEMETERIES, Kensal Green). After changing hands again the land passed to Lady Margaret Beaufort, mother of Henry VII, who used it to found professorships at Oxford and Cambridge Universities. Subsequently Henry VIII gave it to Catherine Parr on their marriage and Queen Mary, in 1557, sold it to Thomas Hues, one of her physicians, who founded scholarships at Merton College, Oxford. The income from this land was therefore used in remarkable ways, but it remained a simple farm until the 19th century.

Queen's Park as it is today was purchased, built and named by the Artisans, Labourers and General Dwellings Company in 1875–81. The avenues, from which is named the fine new terrace behind Droop Street built by WESTMINSTER City Council to the designs of Yorke, Rosenberg and Mardall in 1978, are linked by streets originally called A Street to P Street, as in Washington DC, but this was evidently not popular and they were soon given names. The little Gothic houses, often decorated with the company's monogram in the brickwork, were bought by PADDINGTON Borough Council in 1964 (Queen's Park had become part of PADDINGTON in 1900). Today the houses are privately owned, and form one of the Conservation Areas within the City of WESTMINSTER.

Queen's Park is an example of solid Victorian enterprise. No public houses were allowed on the estate. In 1890 CHELSEA built the Queen's Park Public Library to the designs of Karslake and Mortimer. Opposite, there are gardens beside the canal. The Flora public house commemorates the pleasure gardens of that name which once stood here, and Kensal House marks the end of this section of the HARROW ROAD with dignity. Queen's Park, the park in Harvist Road further north, has no connection with the estate; it was laid out by the CITY OF LONDON in 1886.

Queen's Theatre *Long Acre*. Built in 1867 to the designs of C. J. Phipps for Lionel Lawson, proprietor of the *Daily Telegraph*, on the site of a former concert hall. It was the largest theatre in London next to DRURY LANE and the opera houses. Henry Irving, Ellen Terry and Charles Wyndham were among the company who acted here and for the first decade it was very successful. But it was closed in 1878 and the next year converted into storerooms. In 1911 it was offices for Odhams Press. The frontage was rebuilt in 1938.

Queen's Theatre *Shaftesbury Avenue, W1*. Built in 1907 to the designs of W. G. R. Sprague as a twin for the GLOBE. It opened under the management of J. E. Vedrenne. In 1913 'Tango Teas' were introduced. These cost 2s 6d for dancing, a dress parade and tea in the stalls. In 1914 *Potash and Perlmutter*, a comedy by Montague Glass and Charles Klein, had 655 performances and was the theatre's first big success. In 1929 Shaw's *The Apple Cart* was produced, with Cedric Hardwicke and Edith Evans, followed by *The Barretts of Wimpole Street*. In 1940 the theatre was bombed. It was rebuilt in 1959 to the designs of Brian Westwood, and since then has presented plays by Ronald Harwood, Alan Bennett, Simon Gray and others. The theatre seats 989.

Queen's Walk *SW1*. Laid out for George II's wife, Queen Caroline, along the eastern boundary of GREEN PARK. She had a little pavilion built here. In it she caught a severe chill while having breakfast in January 1737 and died ten days later.

Queen's Woods *N10*. Area of 52 acres named in honour of Queen Victoria and administered by the Borough of HARINGEY. It became a public open space in 1898 at a cost of £30,000 paid by the HORNSEY District Council. The area is mainly woodland.

Queensborough Terrace *W2*. Commemorates John Aldridge who was MP for Queensborough in the 18th century. He married Henrietta Busby, a rich widow, who owned land in the BAYSWATER area. This was developed by his grandson in the 1860s. C. P. Cavafy, the Greek poet, lived at No. 5 in 1873–6.

Queensbury *Middlesex*. The 1930s suburb was named as a result of a newspaper competition because of its proximity to KINGSBURY. The residential and shopping estates were largely planned by Percy H. Edwards Ltd and J. Laing. The station planned to serve Queensbury Circle in the London Borough of HARROW did not materialise and was resited instead in Beverley Drive in 1934, thus creating a separate shopping centre of Queensbury Station Parade.

Queensway *W2*. Soon after Queen Victoria's accession the former ancient Black Lion Lane was renamed Queen's Road, for here as a young Princess she rode out from KENSINGTON PALACE. Although now the centre for shops and restaurants in BAYSWATER, above street level can still be seen some of the terraces which were completed in the 1850s, replacing still earlier houses. 400 ft below Consort House lies an artesian well where sharks' teeth and other marine fossils were found during a bore taken in 1888. At Ivy Cottage, now demolished, lived Augustus Egg, the portrait painter; here he introduced Dickens to Wilkie Collins in 1851. G. H. Lewes and his wife separated in 1849 whilst living with the Thornton Hunts at a house close to Queensway. Lewes returned briefly to another house in this area, No. 8 Victoria Grove Terrace, with George Eliot on their return from Germany. The domes of the Coburg Hotel echo in a minor key the Greek Orthodox Cathedral of St Sophia. The former WHITELEY's was completed in 1925.

Quintin Kynaston School *Marlborough Hill, St John's Wood, NW8*. A comprehensive co-educational school formed by the amalgamation of two previous schools, Quintin and Kynaston. Quintin School was originally founded in 1886 as the Polytechnic Day School by Quintin Hogg, grandfather of the Conservative Lord Chancellor; Kynaston School took its name from Sir Kynaston Studd, former Lord Mayor of London and President of the MARYLEBONE CRICKET CLUB, who had been chairman of the Governors of Quintin School. The two schools were established on their present site in 1956 and were joined together to form Quintin Kynaston Comprehensive Boys' School in September 1969. Girls were first admitted in 1976. In 1982 there were about 1,150 pupils.

R

Radio London *35A Marylebone High Street, W1.*
Started on 6 October 1970 in HANOVER SQUARE, it
moved to its present address in 1975. It has two transmitters, one at CRYSTAL PALACE and the other at
Brookmans Park, Hertfordshire, enabling broadcasts
to be heard as far north as Huntingdon, as far west as
Birmingham and on the south and east coasts. Half its
programmes are devoted to providing a wide range of
music from classical to popular, the other half to
providing programmes about London, including
hourly news bulletins, documentaries, current affairs,
advice and programmes for minority groups. It has an
operating charter from the BRITISH BROADCASTING
CORPORATION.

Rag Fair A market rather than a fair, it was
situated in ROSEMARY LANE, which was renamed
ROYAL MINT STREET in 1850. Probably of 17th century
origin, it was flourishing in the early 18th century,
when Pope in the *Dunciad* referred to 'the tatter'd
ensigns of Rag Fair' and in a footnote described it as 'a
place near the Tower where old clothes and frippery
are sold'. When Pennant visited it he was surprised at
the poor state of the goods on sale, and their cheapness.
He met a merchant who had just fully clothed a man
for 14d. The street was surrounded by courts and
alleys that were inhabited by the very poor, many of
them Irish immigrants. When the Irish temperance
leader, Father Mathew, came to London in 1843 he
held one of his rallies in Cartwright Street, just off
Rosemary Lane, with 2,000 people taking the pledge.
A few years later Mayhew noted many Irish in the area,
some of them engaged, along with the Jews, in street
selling. A shoemaker pointed out to Mayhew that the
poor depended on places like the Rag Fair to keep
themselves clothed. The Rag Fair lingered on into the
present century, but an article in *The East End News*
in 1911 confirmed it had disappeared by that date, part
of the site having been used for a 'splendid approach to
that magnificent piece of engineering skill, the Tower
Bridge'.

Railways (*see also* TRANSPORT). London's main
railway termini, with the exception of St Paul's (now
BLACKFRIARS, built in 1886) and MARYLEBONE (1889)
were all built in the 40 years 1836–76. In 1834, work
had begun on the London and Birmingham Railway
under the direction of Robert Stephenson. Before this
line reached London, others had approached it from
the South. The London and Greenwich Railway
reached BERMONDSEY early in 1836 and ten months
later the first terminus in the capital opened at LON-
DON BRIDGE. This was quickly followed, in 1838, by
the building of EUSTON STATION, the earliest main-
line terminus, which completed the line from Birmingham. This was the beginning of a change that was to
affect the whole way of life of Victorian London.
    Railway companies scrambled to buy land. Tracks
and stations were planned, houses destroyed, bridges
and viaducts built, cuttings and tunnels dug and endless locomotive sheds and shunting areas laid out in a
frenzy of construction that changed the face of the
capital for ever. To the north the main companies, the
Great Northern and the Midland as well as the London
and Birmingham, concentrating their termini immediately north of the New Road (now the EUSTON
ROAD), brought chaos and destruction to the newly
developing, respectable inner suburbs. Charles
Dickens, who had himself witnessed the disruptive
effects in CAMDEN TOWN, describes, in *Dombey and
Son*, how the building of the railway wholly changed
the neighbourhood. In the poorer areas the effects
were even more devastating. In the slums of such
places as SOMERS TOWN and AGAR TOWN whole areas
were destroyed. Little or no attempt was made in the
early days to rehouse the population. By 1874, when
the Great Eastern Railway was extending its tracks
from SHOREDITCH to LIVERPOOL STREET, destroying
450 tenement dwellings and rendering about 7,000
people homeless as it went, legislation had required the
provision of cheap trains to the outer suburbs for the
benefit of displaced workers. But although these 2d
journeys benefited clerks and artisans, who moved in
large numbers to new suburbs such as TOTTENHAM,
EDMONTON and WALTHAMSTOW, they were of no
assistance to the slum-dwellers who could not afford to
move from the neighbourhood, thus adding to the desperate overcrowding. Other areas were equally affected: in the west, the Great Western on its route to
PADDINGTON; and, south of the Thames, the London,
Brighton and South Coast, the London, Chatham and
Dover, the South Eastern and the London and South
Western Railways, in their rush to reach both the West
End and the CITY, caused the same upheavals and left
the same scars. Although nothing, not even the increasing cost of land, seemed to halt the rush of tracks
into London, a Royal Commission decreed in 1846
that railways should not penetrate the inner city area.
The underground railway link between the termini
was not complete until 1884, so for decades the railways caused an immense increase to London's wheeled
traffic as passengers were carried from one terminus to
another across the centre of the capital.
    With the railways came hotels. Most of the com-
panies built hotels close to their stations for long-
distance travellers. At first, it was thought that
railways catered chiefly for such travellers, but the
possibilities for the transport of workers over short
distances were soon realised. Increasing rents had
made living near the centre of London far too expensive, and railways enabled people to travel further and
further to their place of work. 'The railways have set
us all moving away from London. . . . The upper ten
thousand and the abject poor still live and sleep in the
metropolis. The middle classes . . . betake themselves
to far off spots like Richmond, Watford, Croydon or

635

The building of the London-Birmingham railway at Camden Town in 1839, from a lithograph by J.C. Bourne.

Slough ... the smaller fry content themselves with semi detached boxes at Putney, Kilburn, New Cross or Ealing'. From wherever they came, they arrived in London over bridges and into stations designed by the Railway Companies' engineers, who magnificently met the challenges set them by this new form of transport. The imagination, skill and exuberance of these Victorian designers left London a collection of termini which have proved their fitness for their purpose for more than a century, and which, despite the attention of enemy bombers and 20th century developers, have in most cases continued to serve to this day. Three of them, KING'S CROSS, ST PANCRAS and PADDINGTON now have Grade 1 listing as buildings of architectural or historical merit.

Rainbow Coffee House *Fleet Street*. Stood near the INNER TEMPLE Gate. It succeeded the Rainbow Tavern, formerly on the site. The first proprietor, a Mr Farr, was accused in 1657 of causing 'Disorders and Annoys'; 'Item, we pr'sent James Ffar, a barber, for makinge and selling of a drink called coffee, whereby in makinge the same, he annoyeth his neighbours by evil smells.' Farr was also accused of creating a fire risk. In 1682, the Fire Office, later to be called the 'Phoenix', was founded in apartments over the coffee room. Ironically the Rainbow had escaped the GREAT FIRE. Addison criticised the house in the *Tatler* in 1710, for accommodating a great number of quacks: 'The Rainbow in particular I should have taken for a Quack's Hall or the parlour of some eminent mountebank.' Its history becomes obscure after 1825; it may have been merged with NANDO'S. It later reverted to a tavern. The building was demolished in 1859.

Raine's Foundation School *Arbour Square, E1*. Mixed secondary school founded in 1719 by a local brewer, Henry Raine, 'in gratitude to God', to provide an education for 50 boys and 50 girls. The original buildings were in what is now Raine Street, and still stand. In 1885 new buildings were erected in Cannon Street Road, and in 1913 construction of a new school on the present Arbour Square site began. In 1977 the

school was amalgamated with St Jude's School, BETH-NAL GREEN, and became a comprehensive. The school still possesses the 18th-century motto-stone bearing the words, 'Come in and learn your duty to God and Man', and the Charity Children statuettes from the original Raine Street building. In 1981 there were 900 pupils.

Rainham *and* **South Hornchurch** *Essex*. Objects unearthed in the Thames-side parish of Rainham, parts of which are marsh, span the history of man. For instance, stone tools of early man have been discovered and a Saxon burial ground has produced relics suggesting people of some importance. This ties in with one derivation of its name: 'settlement of the ruling people' (Roeginga-ham). Swords, spearheads, brooches, rings and shield bosses surfaced from the sand and gravel and were joined by small wooden buckets with bronze fittings and olive green drinking horns, wonderfully preserved. These are now at the BRITISH MUSEUM. In 1963 Roman remains were found on the Mardyke Farm housing site, hence the name Roman House for a block of flats. In Norman times there were four manors and roads of today carry their names – South Hall, Launders, Gerpins and Berwick. Rainham's church of St Helen and St Giles stands at the centre of the old village and is the oldest building in HAVERING. It remains a complete Norman building surviving from its construction 900 years ago. This is reflected in the sturdy walls and massive columns and ancient rough-hewn font. An oak chest of the 15th century is preserved. A drawing scratched on the rood-stairway wall dating from about 1500 of a ketch at anchor reminds us of a time when the Ingrebourne was navigable. In fact Rainham Creek was used from before 1200 until the 19th century as a trading port. John Harle, a sea-captain from South Shields, married a STEPNEY widow in 1718. About the same time he acquired Rainham Wharf. His trading business prospered and he had built RAINHAM HALL which stands next to the church, by 1729. Other buildings of interest in the centre are 18th-century Redbury and the 1710 Vicarage, both in the Broadway. Northward of the A13 (New Road) lie the more recently developed areas of South Hornchurch and Elm Park. These spread across what were acres of market gardens and farmland and since the 2nd World War across Hornchurch Aerodrome. Bretons is a late 17th-century house which lies just off the Rainham Road on the western fringes. It is owned by the council and used as a centre for sports and leisure facilities. Albyns farmhouse on the eastern side is 16th- to 17th-century, a timber-framed structure refronted in the 18th century.

Rainham Hall *Broadway, Rainham, Essex.* Built in 1729 for John Harle, a merchant and owner of Rainham Wharf. An attractive three-storeyed house of brown-red brick with red rubbed brick dressings, its interior which has many fine contemporary fittings, is largely unaltered. It is occupied by tenants of the NATIONAL TRUST.

Ranelagh Gardens *Chelsea.* In about 1690 a house was built for Lord Ranelagh, Paymaster General to the Forces, to the east of CHELSEA HOSPITAL. In 1741, some years after his death, the house and grounds were bought by a syndicate led by Mr Lacy, patentee of DRURY LANE THEATRE, and Sir Thomas Robinson, MP, and laid out as pleasure gardens. They were opened in 1742. The centrepiece was a large rococo rotunda built by William Jones, a Surveyor to the East India Company, into which 'everybody that loves eating, drinking, staring or crowding' was admitted for 12d. It was 150ft in diameter and was heated by a large fireplace in the centre. There was an orchestra stand in which Mozart once played, and around the outside walls were booths for tea and wine drinking. Booths for gentlemen to smoke in were provided outside. Ranelagh House stood to the north. To the west was an ornamental lake beside which a Chinese pavilion was built in 1750. Horace Walpole wrote soon after the gardens opened, 'It has totally beat VAUXHALL. . . . You can't set your foot without treading on a Prince, or Duke of Cumberland.' In Smollett's *Humphrey Clinker* Ranelagh is described as, 'the enchanted palace of a genius, adorned with the most exquisite performances of painting, carving and gilding, enlightened with a thousand golden lamps that emulate the noon-day sun; crowded with the great, the rich, the gay, the happy and the fair; glittering with cloth of gold, and silver lace, embroidery and precious stones.' Edward Gibbon thought it, 'the most convenient place for courtships of every kind – the best market we have in England'. Canaletto painted it. The

An engraving after Canaletto of the canal, Chinese pavilion and rotunda at Ranelagh Gardens during a masquerade at these fashionable pleasure grounds in 1751.

charge for admission was 2s 6d, 'Tea and Coffee included'. On FIREWORKS nights the charge was 5s. In 1803 the rotunda was used for the last time, and two years later it was demolished. The grounds are now part of CHELSEA HOSPITAL gardens.

Ranger's House *Greenwich, SE10.* An early 18th-century house occupied in 1748–72 by Philip, 4th Earl of Chesterfield, author of the celebrated letters. In 1807–14 the Duchess of Brunswick, mother of Caroline, Princess of Wales, lived here so as to be near her daughter who was then living at Montague House nearby. In 1815 it became the official residence of the Ranger of GREENWICH PARK. In 1888–92 Field-Marshal Viscount Wolseley was the occupant. The house was bought in 1902 by the LONDON COUNTY COUNCIL and turned into refreshment rooms. It now houses the Suffolk Collection of Jacobean and Stuart portraits.

Raphael Street *SW7.* An ancient little street originally a field path along which small houses were gradually built. It became a rookery and was noted for its houses of ill repute. Many of these houses were cleared away when PRINCE'S CLUB moved into Albert Court Mansions in 1886, to provide space for its racquets and squash courts. The rest were obliterated when large office blocks were erected in the 1950s and 1960s and the street became an access road to car parks and goods entrances.

Ratcliff *E1, E14.* A natural landing place on the north bank of the THAMES between the marshes of WAPPING and the ISLE OF DOGS, the reddish colour of the soil perhaps inspiring the Saxon name of 'red cliff'. The northern part of the hamlet of Ratcliff, which contained the parish church of ST DUNSTAN'S STEPNEY, was quite rural until the 19th century; the southern part grew rapidly at an early period because of its position on the riverside. In the 14th century ships were constructed here for use in the French wars but the village became increasingly devoted to the fitting out, repairing and victualling of ships rather than ship building. In Tudor times many voyages of discovery began at Ratcliff, notably those by Sir Hugh Willoughby in 1553 and Martin Frobisher in the 1570s. Stow, at the end of Elizabeth's reign, provides the first description of Ratcliff's development at this time: 'The first building at Ratcliff in my youth was a fair free school and almshouses founded by Avice Gibson: but of late years shipwrights and (for the most part) other marine men, have built many large and strong houses for themselves, and smaller for sailors from thence almost to Poplar.' The school was administered by the COOPERS' COMPANY and has moved to UPMINSTER. By 1610 Ratcliff was the most populous of the hamlets of STEPNEY with about 3,500 inhabitants. Several of the leading members of TRINITY HOUSE had houses in Ratcliff and, when its CITY offices were destroyed in the GREAT FIRE, the Elder Brethren transferred their meetings here. For a short period, around 1700, the Corporation of 'Shipwrights of Redrith' (ROTHERHITHE) also had their hall in Butcher Row. Ratcliff Cross was the most important station for watermen east of the TOWER. Pepys often hired a boat here to cross the river. The main street was Broad Street (now part of The Highway). On its south side the East India Company and others had wharves and warehouses, on the north side were to be found ship-chandlers, chart sellers, outfitters, ship and anchor smiths, mast and block makers. In 1794, however, this area was devastated by the worst of many fires which constantly swept through the riverside hamlets. Two buildings in Ratcliff date from just after this fire, the East India Company's saltpetre warehouse in The Highway, which later became a part of the Free Trade Wharf, and the Master's House of the ROYAL FOUNDATION OF ST KATHARINE in Butcher Row which contains some remarkable early 19th-century murals.

The part of Ratcliff destroyed in the fire was soon rebuilt, and COMMERCIAL ROAD from the WEST and EAST INDIA DOCKS was cut through the hamlet by 1810. Some of the land which the CORPORATION OF LONDON had purchased in 1616 but had not developed was acquired for the Limehouse Basin of the REGENT'S CANAL opened in 1820; and the agricultural land north of Commercial Road was soon laid out for housing. The population trebled from 1801 to 1861 when it reached its peak of about 17,000. Many poor Irishmen, who worked in the nearby docks, settled especially around Brook Street and London Street and the well-to-do tradesmen, merchants and sea captains who had previously lived here moved to less overcrowded areas of London. DR BARNARDO's established its headquarters in Stepney Causeway in 1870 where they remained for 100 years. Ratcliff became a part of the Borough of STEPNEY in 1900. The ROTHERHITHE TUNNEL, opened in 1908, cut through more of the districts. Bomb damage, slum clearance, road widening and demolition of the riverside wharves have given most of the area south of Commercial Road a desolate appearance relieved only by the oasis that is the ROYAL FOUNDATION OF ST KATHARINE.

Ratcliff Highway Murders Seven victims were murdered in these two incidents in December 1811. The first murder occurred at midnight on 7 December at 29 Ratcliff Highway. Mr Marr, a draper, sent his maid out for oysters before he and his shopboy closed the shop for the night. On her return, she could not rouse them to gain entry to the shop and summoned a watchman who also failed. A neighbour who finally managed to enter found the draper and shopboy murdered in a blood-spattered room downstairs, and Marr's wife and child dead upstairs. The weapons, a ripping chisel and maul, lay on the shop floor. A few days later, a nearly naked man escaped from a second-floor window of the nearby King's Arms shouting, 'They are murdering the people in the house.' The publican, his wife and the maid were found dead with fractured skulls and deep-cut throats. Terror spread from WAPPING throughout the country and rewards were offered by the Government and various public bodies. After more than 40 false arrests, John Williams, a lodger at the Pear Tree public house, was arrested. He hanged himself before the committal proceedings. As a result of the public outcry that ensued, all the watchmen at SHADWELL were discharged, and new patrols, armed with cutlasses and pistols, were established. Voluntary associations of 'gentlemen and respectable inhabitants' were also formed for police duties. Demands for a professional police force in London, loudly voiced at the time of the GORDON RIOTS, were repeated. But after a time these subsided, and it was not until 1829 that Peel's Metropolitan Police Act was passed (*see* POLICE).

Rathbone Place *W1*. Built in 1721–5 by Captain Thomas Rathbone, a local notability who had had a house here since 1684. William Hazlitt lived at No. 12 in 1802–5; John Constable at No. 50 in 1802; Gilbert Bayes, the sculptor, at No. 52 in 1899–1900. Winsor and Newton, the artists' colourmen, were established here at No. 38 in 1832 and are still flourishing. George Jackson and Sons, now at Rainville Road, W6, had premises at No. 49 from 1790 to the early 1930s. They were the first firm to use fibrous plaster known as *carton-pierre* which they are said to have worked in mouldings and ornaments for the Adam brothers.

Ravensbourne A river which rises in Farnborough and flows northwards through BROMLEY, LEWISHAM and DEPTFORD (where Lord Daubeny defeated the Kentish rebels for Henry VII in 1497) to enter the THAMES at GREENWICH. At Southend village, between BROMLEY and CATFORD, it was used by a cutler in 1789 to drive his machinery.

Ravenscourt Park *W6*. The remnant of the park that was attached to the ancient Manor House of Paddenswick. The manor was first heard of in the 14th century when owned by Alice Perrers, mistress of Edward III. In 1378 it was seized when she was banished by Richard II. In 1380 it was returned to her husband, Lord Windsor. It was heard of in Elizabeth's reign when it belonged to the Payne family. In 1631 it was sold to Sir Richard Gurney, royalist Lord Mayor, who died in the Tower in 1647. In 1650 it was bought by Maximilian Bard who had the old manor house pulled down and built another to the west of it. The estate remained in his family until 1747. It was sold then to Thomas Corbett, Secretary to the Admiralty. He changed the name to Ravenscourt because there was a raven on his coat of arms. In 1812 the manor was bought by George Scott. His descendants sold the house and 30 acres to the METROPOLITAN BOARD OF WORKS in 1887. From 1889 until bombed and destroyed in the 2nd World War the house was used as a public library. The park now contains various sporting facilities.

Rawthmell's Coffee House *Henrietta Street, Covent Garden*. First mentioned in TWINING's ledgers for 1710–29, it took its name from John Rawthmell, 'a respectable parishioner' and coffee man. The house had passed to his widow, Sarah, by 1743. On 22 March 1754, a group of men met here to form 'a Society for the encouragement of Arts, Manufactures and Commerce in Great Britain', later to become THE ROYAL SOCIETY OF ARTS.

Raymond Mander and Joe Mitchenson Theatre Collection *5 Venner Road, Sydenham, SE26*. In 1946, Raymond Mander and Joe Mitchenson, both actors, set about forming a collection of everything to do with the English theatre. Their collection today covers most branches of live entertainment, and comprises plays, printed and in manuscript, photographs, programmes and gramophone records as well as costumes and china figures representing actors and actresses past and present. It is particularly rich in illustrations relating to the 19th and 20th centuries. By 1977 the collection had become the largest of its kind in private hands, and was, and continues to be, extensively used for research purposes by writers and students, as well as stage, film and television producers. Now formed into a Charitable Trust, with the two founders as its Directors, the collection is to be housed in the Georgian mansion, BECKENHAM PLACE, by LEWISHAM Council which intend to establish a theatrical museum specifically for this collection.

Raynes Park *SW20*. Lies south of WIMBLEDON COMMON on the western boundary of the London Borough of MERTON. In 1855 Edward Rayne, a member of a west BARNES yeoman family, sold Bushey Mead, part of his estate in MERTON parish, to the South Western Railway for the construction of the Nine Elms to Woking line. As a result of Rayne's ready co-operation the railway station was named after him and in turn gave its name to the surrounding district. In 1907 the ecclesiastical parish of St Saviour's, Raynes Park was formed.

Reaches of the Thames On the estuarial and London THAMES most reaches have names of long standing, but two have no names. Starting from the mouth and proceeding up river, the reaches are: Sea Reach (from Yantlet Creek to West Blyth Buoy); Lower Hope (to Coalhouse Point); Gravesend (to Tilburyness); Northfleet Hope (to Broadness); St Clement's, or Fiddlers' (to Stoneness); Long (to Dartford Creek); Erith Rands (to Coalharbour Point); Erith (to Jenningtree Point); Halfway (to Crossness); Barking (to Tripcock Point); Gallions (to Woolwich Hoba Wharf) – the name may be a corruption of Galleons; Woolwich (to Lyle Park) – across this reach is the huge Thames Barrier (*see* FLOODS) – Bugsby's (to Blackwell Point) – this strange name may be the patronym of an erstwhile local landowner, or that of a captain of a prison hulk moored here, but some say it comes from Boggertsby, or 'by the Bogles'; Blackwall ('to Dudgeon's Dock); Greenwich (to Deptford Creek); Limehouse (to Limekiln Creek); Lower Pool (to Cherry Garden Pier); Upper Pool (to LONDON BRIDGE); London Bridge to WESTMINSTER BRIDGE (a reach without a name); Westminster Bridge to Vauxhall Bridge (also unnamed); Nine Elms (to CHELSEA BRIDGE); Chelsea (to BATTERSEA BRIDGE); Battersea (to WANDSWORTH BRIDGE). Reaches to the west are Wandsworth (to PUTNEY BRIDGE); Barn Elms (to HAMMERSMITH BRIDGE); Chiswick (to Chiswick Ferry); Corney (to Barnes Railway Bridge) and Mortlake (to Kew Bridge).

Recorder of London The City's senior law officer and senior judge at the CENTRAL CRIMINAL COURT. The first known Recorder was Geoffrey de Norton in 1298, and the subsequent list includes many famous names, among them Sir Edward Coke and Judge Jeffreys. He is elected Recorder and High Steward of SOUTHWARK by the Court of ALDERMEN but he must also be appointed by the Crown to exercise his judicial functions. He is listed among the ALDERMEN, taking precedence over all who have not served the office of LORD MAYOR. He plays an important part in City ceremonial, particularly the election and swearing in of the LORD MAYOR. It is his duty to present the Lord Mayor Elect to the Lord Chancellor for approval. A few weeks later he presents the new LORD MAYOR to the Lord Chief Justice and the Master of the Rolls in the great hall of the ROYAL COURTS OF JUSTICE on Lord Mayor's Day.

Red Bull Theatre *St John Street, Clerkenwell*. An open-air playhouse built in 1600 by Aaron Holland. The Queen's Men used it until 1617. In 1625 it was renovated and may then have been roofed in. Thomas Killigrew began his theatrical career here by playing the Devil. During the Commonwealth illegal performances were given. The theatre was officially reopened in 1660. Killigrew's company used it briefly. When Pepys visited the theatre in 1661 he found 'the clothes very poor and the actors but common fellows'. 'At last into the pit,' he recorded, 'where I think there was not above ten more than myself and not one hundred in the whole house. And the play (which is called 'All's Lost by Lust') poorly done – and with so much disorder; among others, that in the music room the boy that was to sing a song not singing it right, his master fell about his ears and beat him so that it put the whole house in uproar.' Some time during 1663–5 the theatre was demolished.

Red House *Bexleyheath, Kent*. Designed by Philip Webb for William Morris in 1859, the Red House marks a turning point in English domestic architecture. Morris thought it medieval in spirit, and his interior decorations show his Gothic romanticism. In fact Webb used a simplified Gothic style then not uncommon for workaday buildings like schools, but did it with brilliant originality. The result is a substantial redbrick house with steeply pitched roof and tall chimney stacks, unsymmetrical but a perfect unity. Morris lived here for about five years. It has remained in use as a private house.

Red Lion *23 Crown Passage, Pall Mall, SW1*. One of the oldest licensed houses in the WEST END, it has been in the hands of the same BREWERY since the early 18th century. The original lease mentions gardens which have long since disappeared. There used also to be a secret passage from ST JAMES'S PALACE. Charles II and Nell Gwynne are supposed to have met here.

Red Lion Court *EC4*. Named after the Red Lion tavern which stood here since at least 1592 and was destroyed in the GREAT FIRE. John Nichols, the printer, lived in the court and from 1781 published the *Gentleman's Magazine* here. The printing establishment of Richard Taylor and William Francis also stood here in the middle of the 19th century.

Red Lion Square *WC1*. South of THEOBALDS ROAD and named after the Red Lion Inn, HOLBORN, where the disinterred bodies of Cromwell, Ireton and Bradshaw lay the night before their desecration at TYBURN in 1661. The square was laid out in 1684 by Nicholas Barbon on a 17-acre paddock. The lawyers of GRAY'S INN objected to losing their rural vistas and there were pitched battles when 100 or so of them went to beat up the workmen; but, led by Barbon in person, the workmen won. No. 17 was the home of Dante Gabriel Rossetti in 1851 and of William Morris and Edward Burne-Jones in 1856–9. Rossetti's landlord stipulated 'that the models are kept under some gentlemanly restraint as some artists sacrifice the dignity of art to the baseness of passion'. The firm of Morris and Co. was set up at No. 8 and Ruskin often visited it there. The actress, Fay Compton, lived at No. 28 in 1928–9.

At the north-east corner is County Hall,

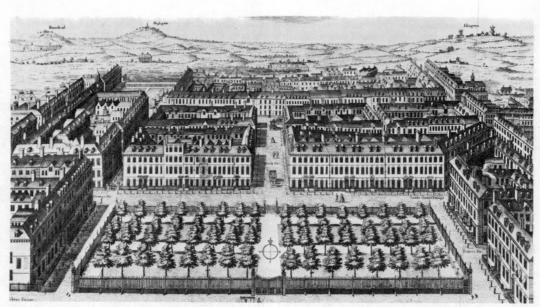

Red Lion Square, built after battles with neighbouring Gray's Inn lawyers. From an engraving by Sutton Nicholls c.1725.

headquarters of the South Place Ethical Society, a liberal religious body originally founded in 1793. On the wall of Cable and Wireless's Summit House is a BLUE PLAQUE to John Harrison, inventor of the marine chronometer, who lived and died on the site.

Jonas Hanway, the first man (as opposed to woman) to walk the streets of London with an umbrella, lived and died in a house on the square. Cassell's, the publishers, are at No. 35. Outside their offices is a statue of Pocahontas. There is a bust of Bertrand Russell in the gardens (*see* STATUES).

Redbridge   The London Borough created by the amalgamation of the former Municipal Boroughs of ILFORD and WANSTEAD-and-WOODFORD. The amalgamating authorities chose this neutral name because the old Red Bridge over the river RODING at the north end of Wanstead Park enabled Redbridge Lane to link WANSTEAD on the right bank with ILFORD on the left bank. The bridge itself was swept away in about 1922 when the Southend Arterial Road (now Eastern Avenue, part of A12) was built, but the name Redbridge was later chosen by London Transport to be the name of a nearby station on the CENTRAL LINE extension, and so has become, rather confusingly, the name of one of a dozen or so districts within the London Borough of the same name.

Redcliffe Gardens *SW10.* Formerly Walnut Tree Walk linking OLD BROMPTON ROAD with the FULHAM ROAD, it became part of the Redcliffe Estate developed by the builders Alexander and McClymont from the 1860s on land owned by the Gunter family. St Luke's, Redcliffe Square was designed by the Godwin brothers in 1873. The brothers had previously worked at Redcliffe in Bristol. Henry Austin Dobson, the poet and essayist, lived at No. 10 Redcliffe Street.

Redcross Street *Barbican.* Probably named after a red cross which stood outside a house belonging to the Abbot of Ramsay. It was often mentioned in deeds in the 13th century and Stow said it was still standing in his time. From 1728 to 1865 DR WILLIAMS'S LIBRARY occupied a house on the east side of the street adjoining WHITECROSS STREET PRISON. At the end of the 18th century several BREWERIES settled in Redcross Street and there was also a distillery here in the 19th century. In 1871–5 the Midland Railway Co. built a goods depot on the prison site. The street was completely destroyed in the 2nd World War.

Reeves Mews *W1.* On the Grosvenor Estate, it extends from PARK STREET to SOUTH AUDLEY STREET. It was laid out in the 1720s to provide stables and coach-houses for the mansions in nearby UPPER GROSVENOR STREET, and probably takes its name from one of its builders.

Reform Club *104–105 Pall Mall, SW1.* Founded for Radicals in 1832. In 1837 Charles Barry, Edward Blore, S. P. Cockerell and Sydney Smirke competed to design the club house. Barry's plans were chosen.

The kitchens of the Reform Club, which opened in 1841, were designed by the club chef, Alexis Soyer.

Alexis Soyer, the club chef, helped him plan the kitchens. The centrepiece was to have been an open courtyard but the club insisted it should be covered in. The interiors were richly decorated and the original estimate had doubled by the time the club house opened in 1841. Phineas Fogg, the Jules Verne character who went round the world in 80 days, took on the bet in the smoking-room. Most leading 19th-century Whigs were members. Membership, which is now social rather than political, has from 1981 been open to women.

Regency Place *SW1*. At the northern end of Regency Street where it joins HORSEFERRY ROAD. The church of the Sacred Heart was built in the 1960s for the Religion of the Eucharist to the design of H. G. Clacy. The stained glass windows are by Arthur Fleischman.

Regent Palace Hotel *12 Sherwood Street, W1. (Piccadilly Circus)*. A huge hotel built in 1912–15 for Montague Gluckstein and Alfred Salmon by Sir Henry Tanner, F.J. Wills and W.J. Ancell. It is faced with 'Burmantoft's Marmo', a kind of faience. It covers an area bounded by BREWER, SHERWOOD, GLASSHOUSE and AIR STREETS. Modestly priced, it has only public bathrooms. There are 1,069 bedrooms.

Regent Square *WC1*. A small square built in about 1820. Regency terraces survive only on the south side, the rest having been replaced by council flats. On the south was a lofty Gothic church designed by William Tite for the Presbyterians and built in 1824–5. Edward Irving preached here before his expulsion for heresy in 1837. The church was bombed in the 2nd World War and was replaced by a plain brick church, the United Reform Church. On the east side was St Peter's church, a Greek design by the Inwoods (1822–6), also destroyed in the 2nd World War and not replaced.

Regent Street *W1*. Part of John Nash's scheme to connect Marylebone Park, now REGENT'S PARK, to the Regent's palace, CARLTON HOUSE. The need for such a street had been voiced by others for some time before Nash. In *London and Westminster Improved* (1766) the architect John Gwynn complained of the lack of planning in the West End and suggested such a thoroughfare. Another influential figure in the planning of Regent Street was the Scottish civil servant, John Fordyce, who was appointed in 1793 to the post of Surveyor-General to the Department of Woods and Forests, which represented the interests of the Crown. He perceived the need for this new street in anticipation of 1811 when the lease for the 500-acre Marylebone Park, situated in the rural area north of PORTLAND PLACE, would revert to the Crown. Without such a road to reduce the travelling distance between the park and central London a profitable development of the lands would be impossible. It was also hoped that the new street would improve the value of the down-at-heel areas around PALL MALL and the HAYMARKET, much of which was also royal property. The traffic conditions around CHARING CROSS and the western end of the STRAND were becoming a major problem and such a street would alleviate this situation as well. Nash himself was appointed to the post of 'Architect in the Office of Woods and Forests' in 1806,

due, mainly, to the influence of the Prince Regent. In fact, Nash had been advising the Prince for several years before the appointment. After Fordyce died in 1810 Nash put forward his own report concerning the development of the 'New Street'. He felt his predecessor's plans were drawn too far to the east and proposed a route which would follow a social distinction already in existence: 'The whole communication from Charing-Cross to Oxford-Street will be a boundary and complete separation between the Streets and Squares occupied by the Nobility and Gentry, and the narrower Streets and meaner houses occupied by mechanics and the trading part of the community.' His plans also included a swerve to the east between OXFORD STREET and PICCADILLY in order to avoid penetrating the fashionable ST JAMES'S SQUARE area, and to bring the new street down to the east end of PALL MALL. The construction of circuses at the junctions with both OXFORD STREET and PICCADILLY would make the intersections less awkward and also provide the street with a visual continuity. The 'New Street' was intended to be the first in a series of improvements which would remove London's somewhat provincial image and enable it to rank with other European capitals.

Soon after the issuing of the report the Commissioners of Woods and Forests applied to Parliament to draft a bill which would empower the commissioners to borrow £600,000 for the building and development of the street. After several proposals and amendments of Nash's reports had been submitted, the New Street Act, which also authorised the purchase of houses and land not already owned by the Crown, was passed in 1813. Development of the street would still depend heavily on private capital, and Nash was to be responsible for valuing any ground or buildings to be purchased, and to prepare all designs for the new buildings.

Once development actually started, the disturbance to the life of the area was enormous: trade was disrupted, houses were left derelict or torn down, and clouds of dust from the builders' rubbish irritated eyes and throats. The Commissioners, however, did their best to reduce the inconvenience, and existing tenants were given the first opportunity to purchase new leases.

Nash's original scheme was much altered in practice; his early hopes for a perfectly balanced street came into collision with the individual requirements of those who undertook to build on it. However, Nash did succeed in imposing upon the whole street a kind of unity. The semi-residential LOWER REGENT STREET, which contained the fashionable UNITED SERVICE CLUB and the ATHENAEUM (as well as Nash's own house), was dominated by the County Fire Office, the design of which was influenced by the earlier SOMERSET HOUSE.

The central, curved portion between PICCADILLY and OXFORD STREET, known as the Quadrant, was to be devoted to 'shops appropiated to articles of fashion and taste'; the remainder of the street, to PORTLAND PLACE, was to be residential. Nash made the Quadrant his chief display piece, with sweeps of colonnades of cast-iron columns. His intention was that 'those who have daily intercourse with the Public Establishments in Westminster, may go two-thirds of the way on foot under cover, and those who have nothing to do but walk about and amuse themselves may do so everyday in the week, instead of being frequently confined many days

Part of the Quadrant, Regent Street, from an engraving after T.H. Shepherd c.1830.

together to their Houses by rain. . . . The Balustrades over the Colonnades will form Balconies to the Lodging-rooms over the Shops, from which the occupiers of the Lodgings can see and converse with those passing in the Carriages underneath, and which will add to the gaiety of the scene, and induce single men, and others who only visit Town occasionally, to give a preference to such Lodgings.' The façades of the buildings in the Quadrant were not uniform; the skyline was irregular and the façades a variety of different designs, sometimes formal, sometimes picturesque. Nash felt a genuine desire to break away from the formal street architecture of the 18th century; but the style of these buildings was also determined by what sites were available and by prospective clients' wishes. The buildings varied considerably in architectural quality and not all were designed by Nash; C. R. Cockerell, G. S. Repton, Sir John Soane, Robert Smirke and other less prominent architects and builders also contributed. It was Nash, however, who was responsible for co-ordinating the medley of designs and designers.

The Regent Street development shared a common problem with the scheme to develop REGENT'S PARK: to encourage fashion to 'cross the road', in this case the eastern end of Piccadilly. The north-south BOND STREET was long established as a commercial centre of the fashionable West End, but Regent Street was something new. After many setbacks, however, the surge to acquire premises in the new street began and by 1819 rents were being paid regularly to the Crown.

After Nash's time, the changes which took place in Regent Street concerned more the character of the shops situated on it than its architecture. The shops expanded to carry more imported and exotic delicacies and fineries. There was also a definite movement towards larger units spreading over three or more shops, quite often having distinct departments; even when large stores like SWAN AND EDGAR continued to call themselves 'silk mercers' they were offering a wide

range of other goods as well. Theatres, restaurants, photographers and other enterprises were also successful, although fashion remained the street's main business.

By the turn of the century Regent Street had enjoyed 80 years as the 'centre of fashion'. It was mainly dependent on the custom of society, and out of season it was often almost deserted. But by 1900 a change could be discerned in the nature of the Regent Street customer, partly due to a shift in the relative wealth of the aristocracy and middle classes. A shopkeeper, writing to the *Daily Telegraph*, describes this new breed of customers as coming 'from the suburbs and country visitors. A most valuable class of customer, as I said, but in the main they are ladies who want things in quite the most up-to-date style at a very moderate outlay. . . . One has to do at least five times the volume of business to get the same returns, and even then the net profits are less.'

At the same time that the shopkeepers' profits were diminishing, the Crown was making an initial attempt at a uniform rebuilding scheme for Regent Street. To many the need for redevelopment was clear: the shops were becoming cramped and overcrowded and the structural stability of the houses, never good, had been so tried by alterations that they were very near to becoming dangerous.

The first proposal for rebuilding in the Quadrant itself came with the plans for the PICCADILLY HOTEL between Regent Street and PICCADILLY. The Commissioners, wary of public outcry, suggested the appointment of an expert committee, led by the President of the ROYAL INSTITUTE OF BRITISH ARCHITECTS, Aston Webb, to advise them and to suggest a suitable architect. They chose Richard Norman Shaw whose plans for the hotel were conceived, revised and finally accepted. He was also asked by the committee to design a complete new layout for PICCADILLY CIRCUS. But his plans, especially his concept of a uniform style of façade spreading up Regent Street, were seen as a threat by the shopkeepers. They were against the expense Shaw's plans entailed and also disliked the height proposed for the new buildings, which would make the street dark and obscure their display windows. They were led by Walter Morford, managing director of SWAN AND EDGAR, who voiced their fears and declared to his shareholders: 'Your directors . . . are absolutely certain that to extend the building which exists . . . on the same elevation would spell ruin to us. . . . I would almost say that rather than have such a building . . . we would remove or shut up shop.'

The Commissioners, bowing to the storm of protest which was coming also from architectural circles and the public at large, appointed another advisory committee. This committee approved Shaw's plans, modified as much as possible to appease the shopkeepers, and decided that the 'general style and character of design should follow that of the hotel'. In 1916 it was decided that Aston Webb, Ernest Newton and Sir Reginald Blomfield should collaborate on designs for the Quadrant, although it was mainly Blomfield who was responsible for the appearance of the new Regent Street. The outbreak of the 1st World War deferred building, but by the 1920s the redevelopment had been completed.

In 1925 a group of Regent Street shopkeepers founded the Regent Street Association to help the tradesmen to deal with financial and other problems as a group. The street is still one of the major shopping centres in London. Among the more well-known establishments located in Regent Street are SWAN AND EDGAR, now closed (Nos 49–63); Veeraswamy's, one of London's earliest Indian restaurants (No. 99); Austin Reed, founded in FENCHURCH STREET in 1900 and moved to Regent Street in 1911 (Nos 103–113); Hedges and Butler, established in Hungerford Street, STRAND in 1667 and at their present address since 1819 (No. 153); VERREY'S RESTAURANT (No. 233); the CAFÉ ROYAL (No. 68); MAPPIN AND WEBB (No. 106); GARRARD AND CO. (No. 112); CARRINGTON AND CO.

(No. 130); Aquascutum, whose newly patented showerproof fabric was displayed at the GREAT EXHIBITION, 1851 (No. 100); HAMLEY's (Nos 200–202); LIBERTY AND CO. (Nos 210–220); and DICKINS AND JONES (Nos 224–244). The POLYTECHNIC OF CENTRAL LONDON is at No. 309. Boosey and Hawkes, the music publishers at No. 295, originated from a circulating library founded by John Boosey in the 1760s.

Regent's Canal Work began in 1812 on the Regent's (also called the North Metropolitan) Canal, and it opened in 1820, the engineer being James Morgan. It joins with the GRAND JUNCTION CANAL at Paddington Basin, from which it goes eastward through a tunnel under EDGWARE ROAD, MAIDA HILL and ST JOHN'S WOOD and on through CAMDEN TOWN and ISLINGTON. From here it runs through another tunnel to the City Basin, and thence by way of Kingsland, HACKNEY and STEPNEY to join the THAMES at LIMEHOUSE. It has 40 bridges over it and passes through 12 locks. As early as 1826 it had a steam tug working regularly through the Islington Tunnel (*see also* GRAND UNION CANAL).

Regent's Canal Dock The Regent's Canal and Dock Company was formed in 1812 for building and maintaining a canal between the GRAND JUNCTION CANAL terminus at PADDINGTON and LIMEHOUSE. It was opened in 1820 and part of it still runs along the edge of REGENT'S PARK. Later, a dock for vessels, called the Limehouse Basin, was constructed at LIMEHOUSE. This had 10 acres of water, some 4 acres of quays and wharfs, and a lock into the river that lies two miles below LONDON BRIDGE. The dock has been much used for coal shipment, and at one time was the entrance to the whole canal network of the country from the THAMES. It is not under the PORT OF LONDON AUTHORITY but is owned by the British Waterways Board. It ceased operating in 1969, apart from one

Barges entering the Regent's Canal at Limehouse, from a watercolour by T.H. Shepherd c.1828.

quay used by pleasure craft. Like most of the dock areas of London, the Regent's Canal Dock is now about to undergo redevelopment.

Regent's Park *NW1*. Originally part of the vast Forest of MIDDLESEX, by 1066 the area formed the northern half of the Manor of Tyburn (*see* ST MARYLEBONE), the property of the Abbess of BARKING. At the DISSOLUTION OF THE MONASTERIES, Henry VIII appropriated the land, ignoring the Abbey's claim and buying out the occupier, Thomas Hobson, with other church property. In July 1539, Geoffrey Chambers was sent to survey the manor, and 554 acres to the north were set aside as a hunting park, its roughly circular shape following no natural boundary or feature. A ditch and rampart, later surmounted by a fence, were constructed to keep the deer in and poachers out. Edward VI entertained the Maréschal de St André, the French ambassador, in Marylebone Park; and his sister, Elizabeth I, hunted here with the Duke of Anjou in 1582 and gave the Russian ambassadors leave to hunt here in 1601. In 1645, Charles I pledged the park to Sir George Strode and to John Wandesford as security for gunpowder, 'Musquette, Match and Pikes' with which to conduct the Civil War. At the King's execution in January 1649, the Park was sold with the rest of the Crown Estates; a survey had been made of it which records that there were standing some 16,297 trees – oak, ash, elm, whitethorn and maple – valued at £1,774 8s 0d. They were soon felled, some for the Navy, the rest for the purchasers' profit; the land was ploughed over and let out in small holdings. At the Restoration, it became Crown Land once more, Strode and Wandesford receiving the rents for a while as compensation. For a century and a half thereafter, the farms here helped to supply London's needs for hay and dairy produce.

By the 1790s, buildings were pressing against the boundary of the New Road (*see* MARYLEBONE ROAD). John Fordyce, a clear-sighted Scot who held the office of Surveyor-General for Crown Lands, realised that these 500 open acres afforded the Crown an exceptional opportunity both to increase its revenues and to enrich the appearance of the capital. The farm leases

were due to fall in in 1811 and a competition was held to determine the best design for the new estate and for a new street linking it with WESTMINSTER (*see* REGENT STREET). The most original, and most profitable, design was produced by John Nash, the architect intimately associated with the Prince Regent. Instead of extending northwards the chequer-board development of the PORTLAND ESTATE, he took advantage of the Park's curious shape and produced a lay-out based on two eccentric circles, lining them with terraces, each designed to appear to be a single, monumental palace, and scattering some 56 villas, each set in its own grounds and so screened by trees as to give the impression of unbroken parkland. The façades he iced with stucco, so that the whole Park seemed a gigantic wedding-cake; charm and variety were still further given to the landscape by a curiously-shaped lake on the south-western side and by a sweeping arm of the REGENT'S CANAL which embraced the northern boundary. The eastern sector Nash thoughtfully turned into a market area to provide the supplies and services needed by the residents of the terraces and villas. Though the component parts of the design, the terraces, villas, crescents and circuses, were the stock-in-trade of any 18th-century town planner or architect, Nash's use of them, his creation of a *rus in urbe*, his translation of town houses into an idyllic landscape, created something new, something totally unlike the rest of London. Its effects are being felt in town planning to this day.

The Park was planned during the Napoleonic wars, and it was not until peace came, and until numerous financial and practical problems had been solved, that the new estate began to develop. For seven long years, the Prince Regent supported Nash against all his critics: that the Park should today be called after him is only proper. PARK CRESCENT, begun in 1812 by a speculative builder, Charles Mayor, who went bankrupt, was at last completed in 1820, the same year in which the first terrace, CORNWALL TERRACE, was begun; whilst the first villa, THE HOLME, was constructed in 1817–18, and the Park was effectively completed by 1828. Of the 56 villas planned, only 8 were built – perhaps fortunately. The terraces, Munster and

Taking the air in Regent's Park , with Nash's Hanover Terrace in the background. From an 1827 engraving after Harvey.

Carrick, which were to have stood on the northern perimeter, were abandoned too and their place was taken, most delightfully, by the zoo. The double circus which was to have filled the INNER CIRCLE, was foregone as well, its place being filled by the gardens of the Royal Botanic Society during 1839–1932 and now, in our own day, by Queen Mary's Rose Garden. By 1841, the greater part of the Park had been opened to the public for recreation.

Though the Park remained comparatively unscathed during the 1st World War, the 2nd took a heavy toll. Bombs destroyed HOLFORD HOUSE and the western sector of PARK CRESCENT, and grievously damaged the market area to the east. More insidious harm was done by inevitable wartime neglect and by building regulations which made all but essential repairs illegal. Complete restoration and total redevelopment were urged by different parties. In 1946 the Gorell Commission wisely recommended that, since 'the Nash Terraces are of national interest and importance . . . they should be preserved as far as that is practicable and without strict regard to the economies of "prudent" estate management.' Twelve years later, the CROWN ESTATE COMMISSIONERS with Sir Malcolm Trustram Eve as their Chairman, and the gifted and imaginative Louis de Soissons as their architect, began the slow rehabilitation of the Park, which was at last, triumphantly, completed in the late 1970s. (For details see under individual terraces – CAMBRIDGE, CHESTER, CLARENCE, CORNWALL, CUMBERLAND, HANOVER, KENT, and YORK TERRACES, PARK CRESCENT and SQUARE, and SUSSEX PLACE – and the villas – ABBEY LODGE, the DORIC VILLA, GROVE VILLA, HANOVER LODGE, HERTFORD VILLA later ST DUNSTAN'S, HOLFORD HOUSE, THE HOLME, NORTH VILLA, ST JOHN'S LODGE, SOUTH VILLA, and SUSSEX LODGE). The total area of Regent's Park bounded by the OUTER CIRCLE is 487 acres. The bronze, *Conversations with Magic Stones*, is by Barbara Hepworth (1977); the *Triton Fountain* is by William Macmillan (1939, with additional work, 1950); the *Dolphin Fountain* in the Broad Walk by Alexander Munro (this was originally erected in HYDE PARK in 1862 and moved here in the 1960s); the *Boy with a Frog Fountain* in Queen Mary's Garden by Sir William Reid Dick (1936); the *Matilda* fountain by Gloucester Gate with the bronze figure of a girl shading her eyes with her hand and standing on a pile of cornish rocks is by Joseph Durham (1878); and the bronze of a boy with an arrow straddling a turkey, *The Lost Bow*, is by A. H. Hodge (1939) who also made the bronze of a boy with a goose, *The Mighty Hunter* (1939), in Queen Mary's Garden.

Regent's Park Explosion At 3 a.m. on 10 October 1874 the dumb barge *Tilbury*, third in a train of six vessels drawn by a steam tug, left the City Road wharf of the REGENT'S CANAL, bound westwards and laden with a cargo which included sugar, nuts, two or three barrels of petroleum and 5 tons of gunpowder for blasting purposes. At 5 a.m., as she passed under the bridge at North Gate, REGENT'S PARK, the gunpowder caught fire, and, in the explosion which followed, the barge and her crew of three men and a boy were wiped out, the bridge was destroyed, neighbouring houses were half ruined and windows were blown out a mile away. The POLICE and FIRE BRIGADE, and a detachment of HORSE GUARDS from Albany Barracks, were brought in to keep order and salvage as much as possible.

The scene in Regent's Park the morning after the explosion of October 1874, which devastated the area.

Regent's Park Road *N3*. The northern extension of FINCHLEY ROAD to Ballard's Lane. Friedrich Engels lived at No. 121 in 1870–94.

Regiments While the London regiments are associated essentially with the forces which have been raised from time to time, and in varying strengths, from among the citizens of the capital, largely on a voluntary basis, there are, nevertheless, regular units which have a London origin. Both the Royal Fusiliers – later amalgamated with other fusilier regiments – and the Buffs – subsequently amalgamated with others to form the Queen's Regiment – are in this category. The former began its history in the reign of James II as two independent companies of foot which formed the garrison of the TOWER. The latter, which formerly bore the designation of the Holland Regiment, was originally formed from the TRAINED BANDS. Apart from the HONOURABLE ARTILLERY COMPANY, the earlier citizen units had no lasting identity. The TRAINED BANDS were reorganised as the City of London Militia in 1794.

During the Napoleonic Wars citizens offered their services in large numbers and, in 1799, 65 volunteer units, headed by the HAC, were reviewed by George III in HYDE PARK: at the time of threatened invasion, during 1803–4, the peak of volunteer recruiting was reached. Thereafter, there was a decline in, and disbandment of, units.

A troop of yeomanry raised in UXBRIDGE in 1797 is claimed as a predecessor of the 1st County of London Yeomanry. Another unit, later to be designated the 9th London Regiment (Queen Victoria Rifles), claimed descent from a unit raised at the beginning of the 19th century. It maintained its existence as a rifle club and was officially recognised in 1853 as a rifle volunteer corps.

In 1859, due to fear of France's intentions towards England, there was a large scale revival of the volunteer movement and under an Act of 1804 many rifle corps were formed in the city and county of London. These corps bore titles indicating their place of origin.

Such famous regiments as the Artists' Rifles and the London Scottish were raised at this time.

In June 1860 Queen Victoria reviewed the Metropolitan Rifle Corps in HYDE PARK, together with other volunteer contingents from all over the country. Of the former, there were seventeen variously named units in a parade totalling over 13,000, the majority being infantry. The 1870s saw the affiliation of these volunteer units to regular regiments.

The Post Office Rifles have the distinction of bearing honours for the earliest campaign in which volunteers participated – the Egyptian campaign of 1882. During the South African War (1899–1902), volunteers from these units provided service companies for regular regiments, or individually joined the City Imperial Volunteers. The need for cavalry resulted in the raising of three Imperial Yeomanry regiments: the 2nd and 3rd County of London Regiments (Westminster Dragoons and Sharpshooters) and the City of London Yeomanry (Rough Riders).

In 1908 the Territorial Army was formed and infantry units became numbered London Regiments but still retained their titles. They were to distinguish themselves in the 1st World War when a varying number of battalions from each regiment were raised for the duration.

In 1937 the London Regiments became battalions named after regular regiments of the line, mainly those with whom they were already affiliated. The HAC, which included both artillery and infantry, was not included in this reorganisation. The yeomanry regiments, while including their original names in the new overall titles, were to become Royal Armoured Corps and Royal Artillery units.

Just before, and in anticipation of, the 2nd World War, territorial infantry regiments throughout the country doubled their strength.

After the war there were the usual reductions and amalgamations which follow a large-scale conflict. In the late 1960s, due to defence economies, most units had been reduced to cadre strength.

Realisation that what was now known as the Territorial and Army Volunteer Reserve (TAVR) was rapidly becoming an ineffective force led to a general strength increase and reorganisation over the next decade.

In London, the former yeomanry elements are now contained in a unit named The Royal Yeomanry and also in the Royal Corps of Signals. The infantry are represented in volunteer battalions of the Queen's Regiment (which also has artillery batteries), The Royal Regiment of Fusiliers and The Royal Green Jackets. The London Scottish and the London Irish are represented in the Highland Volunteers and North Irish Militia. The Artists Rifles live on in the 21st Special Air Service Regiment and the HAC is a TAVR unit of the Royal Artillery. There is also a volunteer parachute brigade based in the capital.

Overall, the picture of the London non-regular regiments is largely one of many subunits of squadron, battery and company strength whose headquarters may be located elsewhere, maintaining the tradition of their predecessors. In some cases they have their own small museums (see also HOUSEHOLD DIVISION).

Restoration Spring Gardens St George's Fields. The Restoration Tavern was in existence from the early part of the reign of Charles II. In 1714 it advertised cock-fighting; and by 1733 a spring in the garden was reputed to be a cure for 'all cancerous and scorbutic humors'. A second, chalybeate, spring was found shortly afterwards and the waters were sold at the tavern, or at EXETER CHANGE in the STRAND. In 1771 William Curtis, author of *Flora Londiniensis*, took over the tavern and laid out gardens which were open to subscribers.

Reuter's Ltd *85 Fleet Street, EC4*. A world news organisation founded in London in 1851 by Paul Julius Reuter who had formed a service for transmitting commercial news by telegraph at Aachen two years before. The company now has a full-time staff of 2,837 located in 86 countries. There are subscribers to its services in 159 countries.

Rhenish Wine House *Cannon Row, Westminster*. Pepys was a regular customer. He came here on 19 June 1663 with his lawyer friend, Henry Moore, and 'a friend of Captain [Robert] Ferrers who called for a red Renish wine called Bleakard, a pretty wine, and not mixt as they say. Here Mr Moore showed us the French manner when a health is drunk, to bow to him that drunk to you, and then apply yourself to him whose lady's health is drunk, and then to the person that you drink to; which I never knew before, but it seemed is now the fashion.'

Richmond *Surrey*. Lies on the banks of the THAMES. The original hamlet was probably a cluster of fishermen's cottages with a simple manor house. It was called Shene and didn't acquire its present name until the beginning of the 16th century when Henry VII rebuilt the manor house after a fire in 1499 and called it Rychemonde after his earldom in Yorkshire. The lands to the east and west of the manor were still called Shene, and today the name survives as SHEEN. The early history of Richmond revolves around the manor house and its royal owners. The first record of the house dates from the 12th century when it belonged to Henry I. It changed hands over the years, sometimes being leased to courtiers as a reward for services to the monarch. The village prospered with the manor as houses for members of the royal household and craftsmen were built nearby. After Henry VII had rebuilt it, it acquired the status of a palace. There were few industries in Richmond which were not connected in some way with the life of the Palace. As the splendour of the Palace grew, so did Richmond whence people moved from London to acquire homes in the country away from the plague-infested city. Pageants and spectacles were held on the Green which in medieval times had been the jousting ground. In 1492 Henry VII held a tournament on the Green: 'In the moneth of May following, was holden a great and valiant justing within the kinges manor of Shine, nowe called richmond, in Southerie, the which endured by the space of a moneth, sometime within the saide place and sometime without, upon the Greene . . . .' The Green was also common land where the villagers pastured their sheep. In 1649 a survey of the Palace was written and it noted that the Green '. . . conteyns twenty acres, more or less, excellent land, to be depastured only with sheep; it is well turfed, level, and a splendid ornament to the palace. One hundred and thirteen elm trees, forty-eight whereof stand all together on the west side, and include in them a very handsome walk.' There were a few houses round the Green in Elizabethan times but Queen Anne's reign saw the start of fine building, much of which remains.

Old Palace Terrace, Old Palace Place, MAIDS OF HONOUR ROW, and the Old Court House are superb examples of early 18th-century houses. In *Great Expectations* Dickens catches the flavour of the Green's 18th-century architecture in a passage in which Pip takes Estella to Richmond: 'We came to Richmond all too soon, and our destination there was a house by the Green: a staid old house, where hoops and powder and patches, embroidered coats, rolled stockings, ruffles, and swords, had had their court days many a time. Some ancient trees before the house were still cut into fashions as formal and unnatural as the hoops and wigs and stiff skirts . . . .' Behind Old Palace Yard off the Green is Trumpeters' House. Built in the early 17th century, it is one of the finest of its date. The architect was probably John Yemans who succeeded Sir Christopher Wren as Surveyor of Works. It is built on the site of the Middle Gate of the Palace and has an imposing façade facing towards the river with a columned portico surmounted by a pediment. One famous resident was Metternich, the Austrian statesman, who fled there from the upheavals in Vienna in 1848. The house was then called the Old Palace and in 1849 Disraeli visited it, afterwards writing to his sister, 'I have been to Metternich. He lives on Richmond Green in the most charming house in the world, called the Old Palace . . . . I am enchanted with Richmond Green, which, strange to say, I don't recollect ever having visited before, often as I have been to Richmond. I should like to let my house and live there. It is still and sweet, charming alike in summer and winter.' Further along the towpath is another house which was also built on the foundations of the Palace. This is Asgill House built in honey-coloured stone by Sir Robert Taylor in 1758 for Sir Charles Asgill, a banker.

The Green has long associations with the theatre. One of the most successful was the Theatre Royal, sometimes called the Theatre on the Green, built in the 1760s in the north-west corner. It was modelled on the THEATRE ROYAL, DRURY LANE and David Garrick wrote a prologue for its opening. In 1769, Boswell paid a visit to his friend, James Love, the manager: 'So I this morning set out in the Richmond Stage . . . . It was a most delightful day. Richmond seemed delicious. Mr Love's theatre is a very handsome one, having everything in miniature . . . .' Many famous London actors played there over the years, including Edmund Kean, Charles Macready and Mrs Siddons. The audience upset Kean after one of his performances as Richard III by applauding the rest of the cast as loudly as they did Kean. He wrote to the manager, 'I have the greatest respect for you, and the best wishes for your professional success; but if I play in Richmond Theatre again–I'll be damned.' However, in 1831 he became the lessee of the theatre. He was not to enjoy the peace of Richmond for long. He died in 1833 and was buried in Richmond churchyard. The Theatre on the Green survived until 1884 when it was pulled down and a villa built on the site. Richmond was without a permanent theatre until 1899 when the Theatre Royal and Opera House was opened on the Little Green, next to the Green. It is now known as the RICHMOND THEATRE. Surmounted by two green copper cupolas, it is an extravagant Victorian building of redbrick and shiny terracotta.

The parish church of St Mary Magdalene in the centre of Richmond is an amalgam of styles stretching from Tudor to 20th-century. Although there was probably a church on this site before, it was the rebuilding of the Palace by Henry VII which provided the impetus to build a new parish church. Henry himself gave £20 to 'the Parish Clerke of Richmond toward ye building of his new Church'. As the population of Richmond increased over the centuries, new additions were made. The most interesting features of the church today are the Tudor tower and the monuments inside the church. In the past Richmond was famous for its inns which sprang up to serve the villagers, watermen and those connected with the Palace. In 1634, of 25 inns licensed in the area, ten were in Richmond '. . . by reason of the Prince's Court often residing there and being a place of much resort and recreation for divers gentlemen and citizens.' Another attraction in the first half of the 18th century was Richmond Wells which were opened in 1696 in the grounds of what is now Cardigan House on RICHMOND HILL. A spring of iron-impregnated waters was the excuse for setting up what began as a respectable place of entertainment. People went there to 'play Quadrille, Ombre, Wisk, etc. And on Saturdays and Mondays during the summer season there will be dancing as usual.' But it soon deteriorated, attracting a loud and raffish crowd. Finally, two sisters who lived opposite, Rebecca and Susanna Houblen, could stand the noise no longer. They acquired the Wells and closed them down.

The increase in population at the end of the 18th century occasioned an application to build a bridge over the river. The only means of crossing the river was by ferry which ran from Ferry Hill (now Bridge Street) to TWICKENHAM. There was much argument about the kind of bridge and its position but it was finally begun in 1774 and followed the same route as the original ferry. RICHMOND BRIDGE was finished in 1777 and is still one of the most beautiful across the THAMES. The railway bridge was built in 1848 and further down is a footbridge connecting Richmond and St Margaret's. By the footbridge is a lock which became necessary when improvements to the THAMES in London meant that the tidal water disappeared more swiftly, leaving Richmond with nothing but mud at low tide. In 1890 it was decided to build a lock consisting of sluice gates which could be raised and lowered to control the tides. The footpath along the river was extended from KEW to Cholmondely Walk in 1774 and is still a delightful rural walk.

Richmond is surrounded by open spaces, with KEW GARDENS and the OLD DEER PARK on one side and RICHMOND PARK on the other. RICHMOND PARK is the largest urban park in Britain with over 2,500 acres of magnificent trees and bracken-covered rides. There had been a royal hunt there for many centuries but before Charles I's time much of the land was also common grazing or owned by farmers. Charles, however, determined to acquire all the land for his new hunting park and enclose it with a brick wall. This he did in spite of much opposition and hardship to the people. Today it is still a royal park, full of deer and other wildlife.

In April 1965, the Borough of Richmond became the London Borough of RICHMOND-UPON-THAMES and included TWICKENHAM, TEDDINGTON, the HAMPTONS and BARNES. It is the only London Borough with land on both sides of the THAMES.

Richmond Bridge in 1780, three years after its completion.

Richmond Bridge *Twickenham–Richmond.* A five-span masonry bridge faced in Portland stone, by James Paine and Kenton Couse, built in 1774–7. It was freed from tolls in 1859, and widened in 1937.

Richmond Hill *Richmond, Surrey.* 'Heavens! What a goodly prospect spreads around, of hills, and dales, and woods, and lawn and spires and glittering towns and gilded streams,' wrote James Thomson in 1727. From the 16th century wealthy gentlemen have built their houses here overlooking the Thames Valley. Most of those that survive are 18th century. No. 3 The Terrace was built in about 1769 by Sir Robert Taylor for Christopher Blanchard, George III's cardmaker. Mrs Fitzherbert is said to have been living here when she first met her future husband, the Prince of Wales. At the top of the hill is Wick House, built by William Chambers for Joshua Reynolds in 1771. Reynolds lived here from 1772 until his death in 1792 and painted the view. Across the road is the STAR AND GARTER HOME. Opposite, a fountain and arbour commemorate the Duchess of Teck, the mother of Queen Mary who lived for many years in RICHMOND PARK. Leonard McNally, W. Upton and W. Hudson have been credited as the writers of 'Sweet Lass of Richmond Hill', of which the following is probably the best-known verse:

This lass so neat, with smile so sweet,
Has won my right good will,
I'd crown resign to call thee mine,
Sweet lass of Richmond Hill

Richmond in Yorkshire is also said to have been the sweet lass's provenance.

Richmond House *Whitehall.* Built in about 1660 on the river bank south of the Privy Garden. In 1668 Charles Stuart, 3rd Duke of Richmond and his wife 'La Belle Stuart' came to live here. The Duke died in 1672 but the Duchess continued to live in the house until her death in 1702. It was then taken over for official use, first as the residence of the Secretary of State and later as the office of the Comptroller of Army Accounts. In 1710 another Richmond House, designed by Lord Burlington, was built adjoining it for Charles Lennox, 1st Duke of Richmond, an illegitimate son of Charles II. In 1738 the older Richmond House was granted to the 2nd Duke so that nobody could build on the site and spoil the view from his house. Soon after it was demolished. In 1749 the Peace of Aix la Chapelle was celebrated with a firework party on the river (*see* FIREWORKS). In 1758 the 3rd Duke, who had a collection of plaster casts of Roman and Florentine statues, set aside a room for their exhibition. Instruction was

The west view from Richmond Hill, with the Star and Garter on the right, from an engraving by Grignion, 1752.

given to students by Cipriani and Wilton and silver medals were awarded for designs and bas-reliefs. Alterations were made to the house by James Wyatt in 1782. A fire destroyed the building in 1791. In 1822–5 RICHMOND TERRACE was built on the site.

Richmond Palace The old palace of Shene was first used extensively by Edward III who enlarged the old manor house, adding magnificent chambers and kitchens. In 1377 he died here, deserted by even his servants who, led by his mistress Alice Perrers, had snatched the rings off his fingers. It was the favourite summer resident of Richard II and Anne of Bohemia. Each day they fed 10,000 guests. In 1394 Anne died of plague at the palace and her broken-hearted husband ordered it to be destroyed. But some of it was left for soldiers and servants to live in. Henry V, while still a prince, had it repaired and enlarged. Henry VI and Margaret of Anjou often held court at Shene. So did Edward IV and Elizabeth Woodville and in their time many jousts and tourneys were held on the Green.

Henry VII preferred Shene to all other royal residences. His two sons, Arthur and Henry, were brought up here. In 1499 the palace was destroyed by fire, but by 1510, it had been rebuilt as a grander palace still and renamed Richmond after the King's earldom of Richmond, in Yorkshire. In 1509 Henry VII died here and is said to have left hoards of gold hidden all over the palace. Catherine of Aragon had lived here, after Prince Arthur's death in 1502, until her marriage to Henry VIII in 1509. In 1510 Catherine came here for the birth of her child – a much wanted son, but he died the following year after catching a chill whilst being christened. In 1540 Anne of Cleves was given the palace on her divorce. Elizabeth often stayed here as a princess and even Henry himself paid cordial visits. Edward VI used it often and entertained both his sisters here. In 1554 Mary and Philip of Spain spent their honeymoon at the palace.

Elizabeth did not use Richmond much in the early days of her reign but later spent the summer here. Cecil had a house nearby, as did Walsingham, the Earl of Leicester, Ralegh, Christopher Hatton and Sir Philip Sidney. In 1603 the ailing Queen came to the palace on the advice of her astrologer, but died within a few months of a distemper. James I neglected it and in 1610 gave it to Prince Henry who built a gallery for his pictures and sculptures. After Prince Henry's death in 1612 Prince Charles was given the manor and often came here to hunt. In 1625 he gave it to Henrietta Maria on their marriage but later it was transferred to

Richmond Palace, the birthplace of Henry VIII, from an engraving of 1765. Only the gateway on the Green, and the restored Wardrobe buildings, now remain.

their son Charles. After the King's execution in 1649 most of the palace was destroyed. At the Restoration, Charles II repaired part of it for his mother, but she found it too bleak to live in. James II asked Wren to restore it, but nothing came of the plans and by the 18th century the palace was 'decayed and parcelled out in tenements'. All that is left is the gateway on the Green which bears the weatherbeaten arms of Henry VII and behind it, in Old Palace Yard, the restored buildings of the Wardrobe.

Richmond Park *Richmond, Surrey and SW15.* This park of 2,470 acres, 2½ miles across, was first enclosed in 1637 by Charles I to enlarge the grounds of RICHMOND PALACE. In 1649 the park was given to the CITY OF LONDON by the Commonwealth Government in return for support in the Civil War. The CORPORATION gave it back to Charles II in 1660. Ladderstile Gate commemorates the method of entry used by John Lewis who defended and finally won pedestrian public rights of way against the Crown in the reign of George II.

The two Pen Ponds, reserved for anglers, were formed in the 18th century and abound in many species of fish including pike, bream, carp, roach and eels. Adam's Pond is for model boats.

The herds number over 350 fallow deer and 250 red deer. Haunches of venison by Royal Warrants are still made available to certain officers of the Crown and Government and the Archbishops of Canterbury and York. Hares, rabbits and other wildlife are plentiful.

Sports facilities include five cricket pitches, two golf courses and 24 football grounds. The Isabella Plantation contains gardens of rhododendrons and other plants. The oaks in the park are very old and with those of EPPING FOREST represent the survivors of the medieval forests which surrounded London (*see also* PEMBROKE LODGE *and* THATCHED HOUSE LODGE).

Richmond Railway Bridge The original cast-iron bridge by Joseph Locke and John Errington, with Thomas Brassey as contractor, was built in 1848 to take the Windsor, Staines and South Western Railway from Richmond to WINDSOR. It was replaced in 1908 by the present steel bridge which is similar in appearance and was designed by J. W. Jacomb Hood.

Richmond Terrace *SW1.* Originally a modest brick terrace of 1822–5 built by George Harrison on the site of RICHMOND HOUSE. William Huskisson lived at No. 3 in 1770–1827 and at No. 4 in 1828–30. No. 3 was occupied in 1830 by Edward Ellice, brother-in-law of Lord Grey, the Prime Minister, and consequently became the headquarters of the Whigs and supporters of the Reform Bill. Quintin Hogg lived at No. 6 in 1873–7 and No. 4 in 1877–81. H. M. Stanley, the explorer, died in 1904 at No. 2. The whole terrace is now occupied by Government offices.

Richmond Theatre *The Green, Richmond, Surrey.* Built for F. C. Mouflet on open land known as the Little Green, it opened in 1899. Except for a lapse of a few years in the 1880s, there has always been a theatre in RICHMOND since the early 18th century. At one time the actor, Edmund Kean, lived in a house adjoining the then existing theatre and died there in 1833. An unlicensed theatre in the mid-18th century, it was used as a snuff warehouse and free entertainment was

An aquatint by James Winston of the Theatre Royal, Richmond, in 1804.

offered. The present theatre replaced one converted by Mouflet from the old Assembly Hall. This proved so popular, not only with the local community, but also the wider theatre-going public, that the present theatre had to be built. The interior was designed by Frank Matcham. The theatre provides a wide choice of entertainments and has included plays by Alan Ayckbourn, *The Danny La Rue Show* and pantomimes at Christmas. Its seating capacity is 920.

Rillington Place *Notting Hill.* A small cul-de-sac of ten shabby terraced houses on each side bounded by St Mark's Road on the east. During 1943–53 at least eight women were murdered in the south-westernmost house, No. 10. John Reginald Halliday Christie ('unattractive and insignificant', 'very much the gentleman', 'repulsive', 'a marvellous bloke', who collected women's pubic hairs in an old tobacco tin), moved into the ground-floor flat of No. 10 with his wife in 1938, and ten years later Timothy Evans, a likeable man with the intelligence of a ten-year-old, and his pregnant wife, moved into the second-floor flat. In 1949 Evans confessed to the murder of his wife and his adored baby girl, whose bodies were found in Christie's garden shed, and he was hanged. In 1953 were found the mouldering bodies of three young women in Christie's kitchen cupboard; soon afterwards his wife's body was discovered underneath the kitchen floorboards, and then the skeletons of two women buried some ten years earlier in the garden. Christie, a necrophiliac, confessed to these crimes, and to the murder of Mrs Evans. He was hanged, like Evans, in BRIXTON PRISON. Evans was granted a free pardon in 1966. The notoriety of the case led to Rillington Place being renamed Custom Close. It was later demolished.

Riots *and* **Demonstrations** 'Mere Mob', Fielding's Fourth Estate, have rarely been solely responsible for major outbreaks of violence in London. Until Stuart times such outbreaks were often the only way that certain grievances could be redressed. Protests were frequently led by normally law-abiding working men struggling to preserve a certain standard of life. With little or no democratic representation, rioting became a substitute for the ballot box. Groupings might be made of mass protests such as hunger riots, political riots and economic riots with further subdivisions into weavers' riots, GORDON RIOTS and 'BLOODY SUNDAY' riots. Then, in Burke's famous

phrase, there were those 'little lambent meteors that pass away in the evening', the minor disturbances that would accompany a fair, an execution procession, a price increase in gin or theatre tickets or the closing down of a bawdy house. Not until the 18th and 19th centuries did the *mobile vulgus* (Swift protested at the contraction to 'mob' and said that it should properly be called 'rabble') polarise into political parties and causes.

Medieval disturbances often stemmed from trade disputes particularly with foreign traders. The PEASANTS' REVOLT and CADE'S REBELLION were major outbreaks of unrest but without the element of xenophobia that seems to have been a feature in other disturbances. This bigotry can be seen at its worse in the anti-semitism which marred the coronation of Richard the Lion-heart (1189). JEWS had been banned from the ceremony and when some were found they were attacked. As they tried to withdraw it was said that the King had ordered them to be destroyed. Some were killed in the street and others in their homes which were looted and burned. Such pretexts were often an excuse for more widespread looting. In 1262 *Liber Albus* records that when 'the citizens kept watch and ward' they were joined by a multitude of persons some of whom, 'under pretext of searching for aliens' broke into many houses which they looted. A 15th-century Italian trader was forced to protest, 'Londoners have such fierce tempers and wicked dispositions that they not only despise the way in which Italians live, but actually pursue them with uncontrollable hatred . . . they sometimes drive us off with kicks and blows of the truncheon.' Such hatred of foreign traders made inevitable the EVIL MAY DAY riots.

The existence of a standing army from the time of Charles I gave the Crown a sword which it could draw in the people's defence. Pepys was an eye-witness of its early use. On 24 March 1668 he wrote 'of the tumult at the other end of town about Moorefields among the prentices, taking the liberty of these holidays to pull down bawdy-houses. And Lord, to see the apprehensions which this did give to all people at Court, that presently order was given for all the soldiers, horse and foot, to be in armes; and forthwith alarmes were beat by drum and trumpet through Westminster, and all to their colours and to horse, as if the French were coming into the town.' The army was used again in 1697 to help break up the FLEET STREET sanctuary of ALSATIA which was the last and biggest of the rookeries of crime. Interventions, like this, had to have the direct approval of the Crown or Government Minister concerned. Until the middle of the 18th century commanding officers could not go to the assistance of the civil power without this direct sanction. Helpless on his own, the average Londoner was well-advised to follow Edward Chamberlayne's advice which was given in 1702 '. . . to wit that if ever he happens to fall under the displeasure of the Mobile in a Tumult, that he doth not *vim vi repellere* oppose 'em by Force, but by kind Words, pitiable Harangues, Condescensions or some such resigning Method get free from 'em and leave them to themselves; for he who treats them so divides them, and hereupon they generally fall out one among another.' In 1710 riots in support of Henry Sacheverell, the political preacher, demonstrated how necessary it was to stiffen the magistrates' powers. These powers were increased by the 1715 Riot Act. Magistrates could thereafter order riotous assemblies of twelve or more persons to disperse within one hour of being so ordered; failure to do so was death. In the next few decades the growth of violence was so great that one magistrate is said never to have been without a copy of the act in his pocket. There were savage riots in 1743 (against an Act intended to stop the retailing of British spirits) during which two magistrates were seriously injured. SPITALFIELDS was one of the worse areas for violence. On one occasion in the middle of the century several thousand journeyman weavers 'in a riotous and violent manner broke open the house of one of their masters, destroyed his looms, and cut a great quantity of rich silk to pieces, after which they placed his effigy in a cart, with a halter about his neck, an executioner on one side and a coffin on the other. They then drove it through several streets, hung it on a gibbet and burnt it to ashes . . . .' Before the Wilkes riots of 1768 – which were caused by attempts to prevent the electorate choosing their own Member of Parliament and which continued intermittently for several months – the weavers rioted again, as did the tailors, coal heavers and other workers. Within three days of the Wilkes riots beginning the magistrates were asking for troops. When the Riot Act was read at the St George's Fields riots on 10 May at least five people were killed and fifteen wounded. One disturbing feature was that the magistrate who had ordered the Act to be read was himself brought to trial as were two soldiers charged with the killing of one of the rioters. Although acquitted the implications were such that when the GORDON RIOTS broke out in 1780 it was some time before a magistrate could be found to read the Act.

In the next century rioters had to contend not so often with soldiers as with the POLICE. Instead of swords and muskets the crowds were now faced with either passive police resistance or controlled baton charges such as were used with devastating effect in the Reform Riots (1831) and the Clerkenwell Riot (1832) (*see* CLERKENWELL) without the intervention of the military. The existence of this disciplined body delayed the expected confrontation with the Chartists until 1848, the year of revolution. Such were the fears of the anticipated meeting on KENNINGTON Common that 150,000 special constables were sworn in and the army held in reserve. Faced with this massive demonstration of strength the Chartists backed down and took their petition to the HOUSE OF COMMONS in a cab. It was again the question of Parliamentary reform which provoked the HYDE PARK riots of 1866 when police failure to control them forced the military to intervene once more. One consequence was the increasing militarisation of the police in equipment and training. Growing demands for political and social reform by the 'submerged nine-tenths of the population', led to the feeling that revolution was imminent. 'This mighty mob of famished, diseased and filthy helots is getting dangerous, physically, morally, politically dangerous,' wrote George R. Sims. 'The barriers which have kept it back are rotten and giving way . . . its lawless armies may sally forth and give us the taste of the lesson the mob has tried to teach now and again in Paris, when long years of neglect have done their work.' In 1886 the social unrest was such that about 3,000 demonstrators rioted and looted their way through the West End. The following year similar demonstrations culminated in the BLOODY SUNDAY riots which were provoked by the mass occupation of TRAFALGAR SQUARE by unemployed workers. The

In 1866 social unrest led to a riot in Hyde Park: 3,000 demonstrators tore up railings before looting the West End.

police were heavily reinforced with special constables and soldiers and ruthlessly crushed the massed demonstrators opposing them. Protests and demonstrations continued into the next century, some of them, such as those of the Suffragettes, achieving their aims with the ending of the 1st World War, others still pressing ahead with demands for political and social reforms which had been temporarily interrupted by that conflict. A new piece of legislation was the Public Order Act (1936) prompted by the provocative marches of the British Union of Fascists through the East End. The Act banned the wearing of uniforms on such marches but did not, and does not, prevent the continuing racial violence of NOTTING HILL in the 1950s and LEWISHAM in the 1970s. In the political demonstrations of the 1960s there was a sharp increase in violence against the police who themselves were no longer regarded by many demonstrators as politically neutral. Coupled with this feeling was an equally aggressive determination that demonstrators should be defended from arrest. The GROSVENOR SQUARE riots of 1967–8 and the BRIXTON riots of 1981 were confrontations of unparalleled violence between police and demonstrators. Violence has continued to increase in London not only against the police but against rival groups and rival political creeds.

Ritz Hotel *Piccadilly, W1.* Built for the Blackpool Building and Vendor Company Ltd on the site of the Walsingham House and Bath Hotels, to the specifications of the Swiss hotelier, César Ritz, and named after him. By then he was already retired. The architects were Mewès and Davis (of the Paris Ritz). The hotel opened on 24 May 1906. It was the first major steel-framed building in London. The exterior is of Norwegian granite and Portland stone and the noble arcade built into the PICCADILLY façade is purposely reminiscent of the Rue de Rivoli. The interior is in the style of Louis XVI and has a long gallery with marble floors and crystal chandeliers, a palm court and restaurant with opulent ceilings. The interior and furniture were executed by WARING AND GILLOW to the designs of the architects. The mural in the foyer depicting famous guests of the past is by Philip Core. 'Ritzy' has become a colloquialism for high-class, luxurious, or ostentatiously smart.

River Police The Marine Police Force was founded in 1798 by Patrick Colquhoun and John Harriott.

It was the first fully organised police force in the country and preceded the London police by 31 years. The new force was badly needed. By the end of the 18th century trade had grown tremendously and vessels too had grown in size and number. In the Upper Pool 1,775 ships were allowed to moor in a space allotted to 545 while some 8,000 vessels and boats of all kinds occupied the river for 4 miles below and 2 miles above LONDON BRIDGE. This, the greatest port in the world, was now accommodating two-thirds of the nation's seaborne trade. The congestion caused such chaos that a ship might be compelled to stay two months in port before it could depart. Ships were still moored in mid-stream and their cargoes were unloaded into open lighters which then transported the goods to the legal quays where supervision was lax and goods might lie about untended in the open for weeks on end. Adequate warehouses were few. The inefficiency led to pilfering on a huge scale. About a third of all men working in the port were known to be either thieves or receivers so that the shipping companies lost half their cargoes before they could be carted away up the narrow, crowded streets that ran down to the river. There were night plunderers or 'light horsemen', day plunderers or 'heavy horsemen', scuffle-hunters and river pirates. Smuggling too was rife. The total losses from pilfering were estimated to be £500,000 a year. Of this the West India Company alone was losing £150,000. It decided on action.

Dr Patrick Colquhoun, a successful merchant who had served as Lord Provost of Glasgow, became a London magistrate in 1792 and, as a result of his experiences, wrote his *Treatise on the Police of the Metropolis* which went into several editions. Impressed by the work, the West India merchants approached him for advice on how to deal with the criminal problems of the port. Colquhoun proposed, and then established, a force which was semi-official and paramilitary, having a resident magistrate in the person of John Harriott, a clerk and a chief constable commanding 200 armed men, all paid for by the government. The West India Company supplied and paid for police on the water and watchmen on the quays. The men were mostly recruited from seamen and WATERMEN and for a time they led dangerous and violent lives, being often forced into pitched and bloody battles with the plunderers. Nine hundred lumpers were recruited to discharge the West India ships and were required to wear special uniforms in which goods could not be concealed. Colquhoun's force brought some order to the port but the full solution to the problems of protection did not come until the building of the enclosed DOCKS. Then each dock company organised its own police protection until they were all united under the PORT OF LONDON AUTHORITY in 1909, when they co-operated with the official River Police, the Thames Division of the METROPOLITAN POLICE in which Colquhoun's force had been incorporated in 1839. The Thames Division continues to police London's River and banks and has its own fleet of fast cruisers, mostly based at WAPPING where there is a river police museum.

Rivercourt House *36 Upper Mall, Hammersmith, W6*. Built in about 1808 on the site of the house where the Queen Dowager, Catherine of Braganza, lived intermittently from 1687 until her return to Portugal in 1692. Her orangery remained until the late 19th century. Rivercourt House may include features from the previous house such as the fine entrance doorway. Its grounds once extended as far as KELMSCOTT HOUSE. The house is now part of LATYMER UPPER SCHOOL and linked to the main building in King Street by an underpass beneath the GREAT WEST ROAD.

Robert Street *WC2*. Named after Robert Adam (*see* ADELPHI). Robert Adam and his brother James both lived here in 1778–85 and William Adam in 1775–82. Thomas Rowlandson lived here in 1793–5; Thomas Hood, the poet, in 1828–30; Sir James Barrie in 1911–37; and John Galsworthy in 1917–18. Nos 1–3 are original Adam houses.

Robert Adam Street *W1*. First rated in 1780, it was originally called Adam Street, the name being changed in 1938. In it stands the rebuilt St Paul's Church, built as Portman Chapel in 1779. One terrace of houses, Nos 7–11, remain unspoilt, No. 11 having an engaging curved line, a spider's web pediment, at first-floor level.

Peter Robinson *Oxford Circus, W1*. In 1833 Peter Robinson, a Yorkshireman, opened a linen draper's shop at 103 OXFORD STREET, between OXFORD CIRCUS and GREAT PORTLAND STREET, still part of the present site. It had a dressmaking department, and in 1866 was advertising 'Waterproof Mantles'. Its lace department became famous. Peter Robinson also opened a 'Court and General Mourning House' at Nos 256, 258, 260 and 262 REGENT STREET, which became known as 'Black Peter Robinson's'. They had a brougham always ready-harnessed to hurry off to a house of mourning. The coachmen dressed in black, had whips adorned by black bows, and the lady fitters sat inside with their designs and pattern books. By 1900 almost all the island site on the north-west corner of OXFORD CIRCUS had been bought. The present building by H. A. Hall and Clarkson (1924) was part of the redevelopment scheme of REGENT STREET. The firm's branch at 214 OXFORD STREET is also by H. A. Hall and Clarkson (1924). The firm was bought by BURTON'S MENSWEAR in 1946.

Robson Lowe *50 Pall Mall, SW1*. Robson Lowe, who had begun collecting stamps in 1914, opened a postage stamp auctioneers' office at 93 REGENT STREET in 1926, moving to 96 REGENT STREET in 1933. These premises were bombed in 1940, when the firm moved to its present address. It was merged with the old-established firm of P. L. Pemberton and Son Ltd in 1957. The firm publishes *The Philatelist*, a centenary dinner for which was held at the CAFÉ ROYAL on 1 December 1966, and *The Philatectical Journal of Great Britain*, the oldest philatelic journal in unbroken production.

Rochester House *Little Ealing Lane, W5*. Built in the early 18th century for John Pearce, it took its name from his son, Zachary Pearce, who became Bishop of Rochester. It was probably built on the site of an earlier house which seems to have been moated. It was later occupied by a number of public figures including Lt-Col. John Drinkwater, Sir Thomas Plumer, Master of the Rolls, and the singer, Ann Catley, who bought the house out of the considerable fortune she had earned. In 1812 General Dumouriez moved there.

He had been Minister of Foreign Affairs in France during the Revolution (Louis Philippe, also in exile, lived in the neighbourhood and taught at Great Ealing School). The house is a simple redbrick block of five bays with two stories and an attic.

Rochester Row *SW1*. Named after the Bishops of Rochester, several of whom also held the Deanery of Westminster. The church of ST STEPHEN AND ST JOHN is on the south side. On the north at No. 42 are the United Westminster Almshouses designed by R. R. Arntz in 1881.

Roding River Rising near Dunmow, Essex, it enters Greater London north of WOODFORD Bridge, overshadowed by the M11 motorway and electricity pylons. It meanders south-eastwards over a quarter-mile flood plain, under REDBRIDGE and along the eastern edge of Wanstead Park, where it feeds 300-year-old artificial lakes and watercourses. Then, bisecting IL-FORD Golf Course, it becomes tidal and thereonwards is embanked. Vehicles parked on derelict wharves south of ILFORD Bridge, and a pair of sluice-gates within a couple of miles at the head of BARKING CREEK, mark the extent of the Roding Navigation (1737), now defunct, but carrying some 34,000 tons as recently as 1965. As watermills gave way to sewage works and factories, effluent and noxious waste extinguished life from the river for almost a century until it began to be cleaned about ten years ago.

Rodney Street *N1*. Begun in 1782, the year Admiral George Rodney defeated the French fleet in the Battle of the Saints. James Mill and his son, John Stuart Mill, lived at No. 39.

Roehampton *SW15*. The village of Roehampton is first recorded as a distinct community under the name of Hampton or East Hampton in the early 14th century, having apparently been established, perhaps only a generation or two earlier, as a secondary settlement by migrants from PUTNEY. The most spectacular and colourful phase of its development undoubtedly belongs to the 17th and 18th centuries when the influx into the area of politically influential and socially distinguished families helped to establish the village as an elegant and attractive London suburb: previously, it had been a tranquil but insignificant rural backwater, isolated from its neighbours by poor communications. The most dramatic and tangible expression of social transformation was architectural, and by the opening decades of the 19th century Roehampton was liberally adorned with country houses and villas, each reflecting the latest style of building and providing the focal point of an elegantly landscaped estate. The sequence of houses begins in about 1630 with Roehampton Great House (*see* GROVE HOUSE). And among those which appeared in the course of the next two centuries, particular mention should be made of Roehampton House (designed by Thomas Archer and built in 1710–12 for Thomas Cary, later enlarged by Lutyens and now QUEEN MARY'S HOSPITAL); MANRESA HOUSE (formerly Bessborough House, then Parkstead); Mount Clare (built in about 1772); and Downshire House (now GARNETT COLLEGE, built in about 1770 to the designs of Matthew Brettingham the Younger; the fibreglass figures now in the grounds here are copies of abstracts by Lynn Chadwick, erected in 1963). While traditional village life undoubtedly continued, it inevitably did so in a changed form and at a subordinate level, the older economic patterns suffering disruption and modification as the demands of a new, more cosmopolitan society exerted themselves. Indeed, one recent writer has argued that aristocratic penetration may have precipitated the wholesale migration of the medieval settlement from its original site to the present 'village' centre at what was then the southern end of Roehampton Lane.

Roehampton retained its reputation as a socially select London suburb until well into the 19th century, but more recent times have brought to the village a new and more diverse identity. Economic pressures have gradually prised most of the great houses from aristocratic hands, and those which survive have done so as the property of corporate bodies, mainly of a religious, educational or medical nature. At the same time, most of the accompanying estates have been broken up and sold to developers, whose influence may be seen in the profusion of private houses, apartment blocks and high-rise flats which now obscure the former rural landscape.

Roehampton Club *Roehampton Lane, SW15*. Founded in 1901 by Colonel Charles Miller and his two brothers in the grounds of Upper Grove House. Three polo grounds were laid out, as well as croquet lawns, tennis courts, a golf course and a sunken garden. During the 1st World War the land was requisitioned by the Royal Flying Corps. After the war squash courts and swimming pools were added to the attractions. And after the 2nd World War, under the continued direction of the Miller family, the club built a large new glass-walled club house. The sports grounds now extend to 102 acres. ROSSLYN PARK RUGBY FOOTBALL CLUB have a lease of part of them.

Roehampton Institute *Roehampton Lane, SW15*. Although a new venture in its present form, the Roehampton Institute is a federation which brings together the traditions and teaching expertise of four long-established Colleges of Education, two of which – Digby Stuart and Froebel Institute College – have been part of the local landscape for over half a century. Founded in the mid-1970s in the context of a national reorganisation of higher education, the Institute is no longer exclusively concerned with the training of teachers, but also provides a wide range of first degree courses in both arts and sciences, as well as some postgraduate courses. With about 2,500 students, the Institute,is one of the largest establishments of its kind in the country (*see also* WHITELANDS COLLEGE).

Rolls Chapel *Chancery Lane*. Originally served the Domus Conversorum founded by Henry III in 1232 for the reception of Jews converted to Christianity. In 1377 Edward III officially assigned it to the Keeper of the Rolls of Chancery, and in due course it became part lawyers' chapel, part record repository and part mortgage office. It was rebuilt in 1617 by Inigo Jones, again rebuilt in 1734 and altered in 1784. The records were transferred to the PUBLIC RECORD OFFICE in 1856 and the Chapel was demolished in 1895.

Roman Bath Street *EC1*. A Roman bath has never been found here despite the name it was given in 1885. It is, however, the site of the first Turkish baths in

London, built by Turkish merchants in 1679. John Strype, writing in 1733, said they were 'much resorted unto for sweating being found very good for aches and approved by our physicians'. The price was 4s per person. Ladies were admitted on Wednesdays and Saturdays. The baths stood here until 1876.

Roman Baths The major public bathing establishment of London lay in the area of CHEAPSIDE. Building operations in 1955 revealed a substantial part of the baths except for the exercise yard (*palaestra*) and dressing-rooms which both probably lie further towards the east. Built late in the 1st or early in the 2nd century, the baths were demolished in the 3rd century because of problems with the rising level of the WAL-BROOK to the east. The Sun Life Building, 110–116 CHEAPSIDE, now covers the site. Several private bath suites of Roman houses have been found (*see* COAL EXCHANGE), and there is also the controversial bath off the STRAND (*see* STRAND ROMAN BATH).

Roman Boats *and* **Barges** Two major finds of Roman vessels have been made in the THAMES at London this century, the County Hall boat in 1910 and the Blackfriars barge in 1962. The County Hall boat was carvel-built of oak and a section approximately 13 × 6 metres survived in the river mud. Probably the boat was around 20 metres in length. Dating evidence of coins found in or beneath the boat (one of Tetricus 1, 268–73; two of Carausius, 287–93; and one of Allectus, 293–6) point to late in the 3rd century. Because of the coins of the two British usurper Emperors present (Carausius and Allectus), and the fact that 'several large rounded stones' weighing just over 1½ kilos each

were found, one of them 'partially embedded in a strake', it has been suggested that this boat may have been one of those that the troops of the usurper Allectus were using to make good their escape from Constantius Chlorus (*see* ARRAS MEDALLION). However, as Sir Mortimer Wheeler rightly wrote in *London in Roman Times* (1946), this 'is a conjecture entirely unsupported by the evidence'.

The Blackfriars barge was found in 1962 when work was being carried out for a new riverside underpass. The following year the remains were enclosed in a coffer dam and successfully excavated. They were found to be those of a keelless, flat-bottomed, carvel-built barge, probably about 55 ft long. Her cargo had been of Kentish ragstone, obviously for use in building the LONDON WALL, and she had presumably sunk at her moorings. The mast, a valuable piece of timber, seems to have been retrieved and in the mast-step was found a worn copper coin (an *as*) of the Emperor Domitian (81–96) that had been struck in 88–89. Pottery indicated a late 2nd-century date, consistent with the postulated date for her cargo of stone. The coin, with its appropriate reverse type of the standing figure of the goddess Fortuna holding a ship's rudder, had probably been deliberately placed in the mast-step for good luck long after it had been struck. The remains of both vessels are stored in the MUSEUM OF LONDON.

Roman Fort *London Wall, EC1.* WOOD STREET and SILVER STREET still preserve the line of the Via Praetoria (main street) and Via Principalis (at right angles to it) of the fort. The fort, built at the northwest corner of the then unwalled city seems to have been a late afterthought following Boudicca's attack in

A Roman boat of the 3rd century was found preserved in the Thames mud in 1910. The remains are now in the Museum of London.

AD 60. It was built in the reign of Trajan (98–117) according to the coin and pottery evidence. Since it would have had little defensive effect it probably served as a barracks for the garrison attached to the GOVERNOR'S PALACE. Substantial portions of the barracks are buried under WOOD STREET Police Station. The area of the fort was about 12 acres with the usual playing-card shape associated with such forts – about 270 metres north to south by 220 metres east to west. Although the stone walls were quite substantial they were not felt to be strong enough when the fort was incorporated into the LONDON WALL at the end of the 2nd century. The north and west sides were thickened by an additional skin of brickwork and masonry and the two parts side by side can be seen in the remains in the public garden in NOBLE STREET. In a room at the west end of the underground car park (entrance from LONDON WALL) are the remains of the west gate of the fort and part of a guardroom that were excavated in 1956.

Roman London *see* LONDINIUM.

Roman Road *E2, E3*. Shown on Gascoyne's 1703 map as the Drift Way. The western end of the road, in BOW, acquired its present name in the mid-19th century when archaeological finds suggested it was on or near the Roman road from London to Colchester. The street market, an unauthorised one until the present century, also originated around the middle of the 19th century. The western end of the street, in BETHNAL GREEN, was previously known as Green Street. The bronze, *Blind Beggar and his Dog*, is by Elizabeth Frink (1957).

ROMAN ROADS London was the hub of the Roman road network in Britain, but to understand how the system developed it is necessary to go back a little farther, to pre-Roman times. The River THAMES was the most important factor. Before the embankments were built in the 19th century, it was wide and shallow. In the Roman period, the land level was higher than at present, and the tide would not have risen much above WESTMINSTER, which became a convenient fording place for traders wishing to cross the river. Travelling inland from the Kentish ports, travellers would have crossed the WESTMINSTER ford, and then struck north or west to the important tribal capitals at Wheathampstead (near St Albans) or Silchester, west of Reading. An east-west route would also have developed, aiming for the third of the main tribal centres, at Colchester, following a track which kept to high ground along the line of OXFORD STREET and OLD STREET. It is likely that the Roman engineers made use of these routes; the two main alignments of WATLING STREET north and south of the river converge on the early river crossing. When LONDON BRIDGE was built (within 15 years of the Roman invasion of AD 43), short connecting tracks would have been made to the nearest established roads.

The long straight alignments of the Roman roads resulted from the method of surveying used by the engineers who built them. The roads were set out by sighting between points on high ground, the actual lines being carefully chosen to avoid, if possible, steep inclines and marshy ground. Roads would deviate from the direct line if there were advantages such as better ground conditions; a good example is the diversion of Stane Street at Ewell, which follows the chalk formation and stays clear of the difficult London clay for several miles. Important Roman roads were usually about 24 ft wide, and were frequently set on an embankment about five ft high, known as an *agger*. Excavations of buried roads reveal the original surface layer of fine stone chippings.

For much of their length, the Roman roads in London are still in use as modern thoroughfares.
Watling Street approaches from Dover, Canterbury and Richborough along the line of SHOOTERS HILL, before taking a curving route through DEPTFORD and NEW CROSS much like the present road. Northward, the alignment is followed almost exactly by the present road from MARBLE ARCH to EDGWARE. The substantial construction of the original road has been disclosed by excavation for pipe-laying.
Ermine Street was the main artery to Lincoln and York, and its course from BISHOPSGATE is closely represented by Kingsland Road, Stoke Newington Road and Stamford Hill.
Colchester Road is followed by present roads east of STRATFORD. The River LEA was crossed at OLD FORD, where remains of Roman masonry have been found near Iceland Wharf. From this point, a road must have gone direct to Aldgate and the bridge. Remains have been found at Eastcheap, where a 16 ft wide roadway with massive retaining walls was uncovered.
Silchester Road was the main artery to the West of England. It is represented by the course of OXFORD STREET, NOTTING HILL (a possible surveying point), HOLLAND PARK and GOLDHAWK ROAD, where remains have been excavated. Eastward, the road must have connected to NEWGATE, with a branch to OLD STREET, OLD FORD and STRATFORD; much of this route is now lost.
Ludgate–Hammersmith A Romanised form of the early trackway followed the line of the STRAND through KENSINGTON, to join the main western road at CHISWICK.
Stane Street connected London with Chichester, the tribal capital of Sussex, and its course is approximately that of the present road from BOROUGH HIGH STREET to TOOTING. Traces have been found under buildings in BOROUGH HIGH STREET, and the buried road surface directly under Newington Causeway. With the passage of time, the modern road has deviated in places; BALHAM HIGH STREET is about 60 yards from the original line, and CLAPHAM COMMON South Side almost a quarter of a mile further west, but Clapham Road and Kennington Park Road are on the Roman line.
London–Brighton was an important road for the traffic in corn and iron from Sussex. It probably branched from Stane Street at Kennington Park, on the course of Brixton Road, Brixton Hill and Streatham Hill.
London–Lewes also served the corn-growing and iron-producing areas of Sussex. Its course in London has been traced by careful probing and digging in gardens and allotments. Branching from WATLING STREET at Asylum Road, PECKHAM, it followed an alignment of Blyth Hill, CATFORD, where the buried agger remains intact. It then ran through WEST WICKHAM to a point on the North Downs. The only section of this road in use today is the 3 mile straight length through Edenbridge, but the route survived in the form of parish boundaries and property divisions.

Thus, it is represented through PECKHAM and NUNHEAD by the alignment of back garden fences and walls.

London–Stevenage left the CITY at CRIPPLEGATE, and the course is marked by REDCROSS STREET and Golden Lane, Highbury Grove, HIGHBURY PARK and parts of Blackstock Road. Traces of an agger have been found in the grounds of ALEXANDRA PALACE, and there are more substantial remains north of Potters Bar.

Romford *Essex*. Situated on the great Roman road between London and Colchester. In the Roman road book, *The Antonine Itinerary*, Durolitum, the Roman station, is placed in the vicinity. The exact site is probably at Hare Street, a suburb south of GIDEA PARK. It is likely that Durolitum was not a town but a strategic barracks and posting station. Later in the Middle Ages, Romford appears to have grown in size through being an adjunct to the royal palace at HAVERING village, a few miles to the north. It also became the market for the area, mainly as an outlet for leatherware, originating at the then more important village of HORNCHURCH. The market was given a charter by Henry III in 1247. The early medieval site of Romford had been to the south of the present town at Oldchurch. It was moved to the higher ground around the present market place to avoid the frequent flooding of the River Rom, then named the Merchedyche at the Oldchurch end. The Church of St Edward appears to have been the first permanent building on the new site, a small wood being pulled down to clear the site. Permission to build it had been granted by Henry IV in 1406. The church lasted for over 400 years and was then demolished. The present St Edward's was opened in 1850 and is based on the Middle Pointed style of the 14th century. It contains some interesting monuments, for instance those commemorating members of the Hervey and Cooke families. Next to the church is 15th-century Church House. It once housed the priest who looked after the chantry at the church, in memory of Avery Cornburgh who had been an esquire of the body to Edward IV and to Richard III and Treasurer to Henry VII. In the upper room at the front of this house can be seen ship's timbers re-used in the construction. In the 19th century, when many coaches ran through Romford this house was used as an inn and called the Cock and Bell. The ground floor facing on to the market has recently reverted to church use after having been an estate agent's premises. Two other buildings still used as public houses are of interest. The Golden Lion dates from various periods from the 17th century onwards, the stucco frontage and side having been applied in the 19th century. The Lamb public house in the corner of the market is a pleasant pedimented building of early to mid-Victorian date.

Romilly Street *W1*. Building began here in 1678 and, like the streets in SOHO to the north, there were in its early years several foreign residents, though not as many aristocratic English families as in DEAN STREET and FRITH STREET. It was largely rebuilt in the 18th century and on the north side some houses of this period still remain. The south side, however, is occupied by the backs of buildings facing on to SHAFTESBURY AVENUE and by the featureless brick wall of the PALACE THEATRE. The premises occupied at Nos 28–31 by KETTNER'S RESTAURANT were built or reconstructed in the 1730s. The street, originally known as Church Street, was given its present name in 1937 in honour of Samuel Romilly, the law reformer, who was born at No. 18 FRITH STREET, the son of a well-to-do immigrant watchmaker and jeweller, Peter Romilly, and grandson of Etienne Romilly, a Huguenot of good family and estate who fled from Montpelier to England on the revocation of the Edict of Nantes. Thomas Rowlandson was living at No. 4 in 1775.

Romney Street *SW1*. Formerly known as Vine Street, a name that commemorated the vineyard of WESTMINSTER PALACE. It was renamed in 1869. Charles Churchill, the poet, was born here in 1731. His father became curate at the nearby ST JOHN THE EVANGELIST in 1733. He lost a legacy by writing the lines:

Famed Vine Street
Where Heaven the utmost wish of man to grant,
Gave me an old house and an older aunt.

Rood Lane *EC3*. Named after a crucifix which once stood in the churchyard of ST MARGARET PATTENS. Stow said that 'in the year 1538, about 23rd May, in the morning, the said rood was found to have been, on the night preceding, by people unknown, broken all to pieces.'

Rookfield Garden Estate Situated on the south side of MUSWELL HILL, the main road which climbs up to Muswell Hill Broadway. W.J. Collins, the Muswell Hill developer, with his two sons created this little-known garden estate on the sites of Avenue House, Rookfield House (once the home of A.W. Gamage, the proprietor of GAMAGE's) and Lalla Rookh (a cottage briefly occupied by the poet, Tom Moore, and named after one of his poems). The estate is based on the Garden City idea, first realised at Letchworth in 1903. Begun in 1906, it is contemporary with HAMPSTEAD GARDEN SUBURB and consists of two-storey domestic houses, many in vernacular Queen Anne style, set in short, tree-lined and grassy roads. Building was completed by about 1922. The Estate is now a Conservation Area and is additionally protected by an Article 4 Direction restricting what owners may do to the exteriors.

Ropemaker Street *EC2*. Named after the rope walks some of which survived until the middle of the 19th century. In 1731 Daniel Defoe died at his lodgings here.

Rosary Gardens *SW7*. Built in 1881 and named after a house called the Rosary which once stood at the corner of GLOUCESTER and OLD BROMPTON ROADS. Sir Herbert Beerbohm Tree, the actor manager, lived at No. 31 in 1886–8.

Rose and Crown Yard The large yard and stables of the oldest inn in KNIGHTSBRIDGE. Its site is now the parking area between 195 Knightsbridge (Mercury House) and the Normandie Hotel. In the mid-18th century it belonged to the Moreaus, a wealthy Huguenot family, who also owned land in the MONTPELIER SQUARE area.

Rose Street *WC2*. Built in the 1620s as a narrow alley, it took its name from a tavern. It was here in 1679 that John Dryden was beaten up by hired bullies on his way home from WILL'S COFFEE HOUSE. Samuel Butler, author of *Hudibras*, died here in 1680. Edmund Curll, the bookseller who quarrelled so bitterly with Pope, was living here in the 1730s. Much of the street was later absorbed by GARRICK STREET.

Rose Tavern *Russell Street, Covent Garden*. Stood next to DRURY LANE THEATRE and was much patronised by playgoers including Pepys who, feeling hungry, slipped out of a performance of Sir Charles Sedley's *The Mulberry Garden*, getting a boy to keep his place, and ate 'half a breast of mutton off the spit'. George Powell, the churlish, quarrelsome actor, 'spent great part of his time' here, according to Thomas Davies, 'and often toasted to intoxication, his mistress, with bumpars of Nantz [Nantes] brandy'. By the end of the 17th century, although respectable enough in daytime, the Rose had the reputation of being at night one of the most wild and dangerous taverns in London, a place that 'stood pre-eminent among the dangerous places of the neighbourhood . . . where murderous assaults were frequently occurring amongst the bullies of the time.' This is indicated by Thomas Shadwell in his play, *The Scourers*. Lord Gerard died here, possibly the victim of a gang known as the Hectors who came to this and other similar places in the area looking for a fight. In November 1712 in this tavern the seconds arranged the duel between the Duke of Hamilton and Lord Mohun in which both were killed. The site of the tavern is now covered by the THEATRE ROYAL, DRURY LANE.

Rose Theatre *Southwark*. The first of the Bankside playhouses. It was built in 1586-7 by Philip Henslowe and his partner, John Cholmley, on the site of an old house known as The Rose. It appears to have been an octagonal building of wood and plaster. Part of it was thatched. Edward Alleyn, founder of DULWICH COLLEGE made his reputation as an actor here. In 1605 Henslowe's lease ran out and soon after the theatre was demolished. Rose Alley marks its site.

Rosebery Avenue *EC1*. Built in 1889-93 under the auspices of the LONDON COUNTY COUNCIL and opened in 1895 by its first Chairman, Lord Rosebery. It linked CLERKENWELL ROAD with St John Street and the ANGEL by bridging the old FLEET valley, cutting diagonally across Exmouth Street beside the site of the newly demolished COLDBATH FIELDS PRISON where Mount Pleasant Post Office was at once built. At the western end are the gaunt tenement blocks of Rosebery Buildings, some of them rising from valley level. Opposite Mount Pleasant, the rebuilt Clerkenwell Fire Station is aligned with Exmouth Street. The latter was licensed as a costers' street market as soon as the Avenue was completed.

In 1895 a handsome brick English-Renaissance Town Hall with a finely decorated interior (C. Evans Vaughan) was built on the irregularly shaped site adjoining old Clerkenwell Vestry Hall, in Rosoman Street, which was demolished in 1899 to make way for an annexe. In 1900 it became Finsbury Town Hall, but lost its status with the merging of FINSBURY and ISLINGTON in 1965.

Old SADLER'S WELLS, by 1895 a decayed music-hall *cum* cinema, was replaced by the present theatre in 1931. Between the terraces at the eastern end of NEW RIVER formerly flowed to its destination at the Round Pond just south of SADLER'S WELLS. The pond's site is now largely covered by the headquarters of the Thames Water Authority, opened in 1920 as the Metropolitan Water Board in place of the original NEW RIVER COMPANY'S offices. The Spa Green Housing Estate is by Messrs Tecton (1950).

Rosemary Branch *Islington*. About half a mile east of ISLINGTON church, this appears on Hole's 1594 plan of Finsbury Fields, and was at first an alehouse used by archers near the SHOREDITCH boundary. In 1783 the old tavern was taken over by Champion, Fishwick and Co. for a white-lead works, powered by two windmills built in 1786 and 1792 which formed a great landmark, and the Rosemary Branch was rebuilt actually on the parish boundary. It adjoined ISLINGTON common and an ancient footpath leading to London, and its large tea-gardens were notable for a one-acre pond supplied by water from the NEW RIVER and popular for boating and skating among 'the lower order of people'. In 1836 it was still referred to as 'Islington Vauxhall', used for pony-racing and tightrope displays, but already by 1835 the windmills had given way to a steam-engine, and the pond had dried up because of land drainage for building. Rosemary Gardens, a small modern park, approximately marks the site, and the old tavern's name is retained by a Victorian public-house at No. 2 Shepperton Road.

Rosemary Lane *(Royal Mint Street since 1850)*. Once an infamous street market for old clothes and frippery, familiarly known as RAG FAIR. It was run by Jews and supplied by itinerant collectors who gathered discarded or stolen clothes and rags. It was open every day and frequented mainly by local inhabitants. In 1753 an anonymous observer described the 'dunghills of old shreds and patches' offered for sale in the market which he thought would be a good place for farmers to buy clothes for their scarecrows. In 1756 a newspaper story tells of a poor woman buying a pair of breeches for 7d. and a pint of beer and finding 11 gold guineas and a £30 note inside the lining. Richard Brandon, Charles I's executioner, having taken an orange stuck with cloves from the king's pocket, sold it in this market for 10s. It remained a large clothes market during Victorian times with a street trade greater even than PETTICOAT LANE.

Rosoman Street *EC1*. Takes its name from Thomas Rosoman, proprietor of SADLER'S WELLS in 1736-42. It was originally a path leading to the various places of entertainment he established near the wells.

Rosslyn Hill *NW3*. Links HAVERSTOCK HILL to HAMPSTEAD HIGH STREET. It was formerly known as Red Lion Hill, after the Red Lion Inn which stood half-way up the hill on the left hand side. The public house was demolished in 1868 and a police station built on the site. A drinking fountain now marks this spot. Near the present-day Unitarian Chapel (which was designed by John Johnson and built in 1862) stood the Chicken House, a Jacobean building. James I and the Duke of Buckingham stayed a night there in 1619 and this visit was commemorated in a remarkable ornamental window. The Chicken House was demolished in 1880. The middle of this century saw the destruction of Vane House, a 17th-century mansion which had extensive grounds and some noble trees. A plaque now recalls the residence there of Sir Harry Vane, who was executed for treason in 1662. The Royal Soldiers' Daughters Homes occupied Vane House for a time before moving into their new buildings just behind the house. Nos 22 and 24 Rosslyn Hill are the oldest houses here; they are dated 1702.

Rotherhithe *SE16*. Formerly called Redriffe (as it was by Pepys), it lies within a loop of the river on the north-east corner of the London Borough of SOUTH-WARK, east of BERMONDSEY and north of DEPTFORD. It faces WAPPING across the river. The SURREY COM-MERCIAL DOCKS occupied much of the area. Through Rotherhithe from the docks ran the GRAND SURREY CANAL. The docks and canal were closed in 1970 and the whole district is due for redevelopment. The name may derive from two Saxon words, *redhra*, a mariner, and *hyth*, a haven. It became a small maritime settlement along the river bank, and here Jonathan Swift decided that Lemuel Gulliver had been born. The first of London's enclosed wet docks, the HOWLAND, was built here in 1699. It is thought that King Canute began his trench to VAUXHALL at Rotherhithe when laying siege to London. At the time of the *Domesday* survey Rotherhithe was included in the royal manor of BERMONDSEY and here a fleet was fitted out by order of the Black Prince and John of Gaunt. Later Henry IV lived here when afflicted with leprosy. Near the river in St Marychurch Street stands the parish church of ST MARY. Other buildings of note are the former Peter Hills School to the south of the church with attractive carvings in the form of two 18th-century school children; to the west of the school a Watch House and Engine House of 1821; No. 141 Rotherhithe Street, a good warehouse of about 1800; No. 265 Rotherhithe Street, a ship-builder's house of the 18th century with a cupola on the roof. The Angel Inn on the river front dating from at least the 17th century, has a smugglers' trap door in the kitchen. Beneath the river, between Rotherhithe and WAPPING, runs Brunel's double tunnel, the first to be built beneath the THAMES. It was opened in 1843 as a thoroughfare but was converted in 1871 to railway use. Down river where Limehouse Reach begins, is Cuckold's Point which was at one time marked with a pair of horns on top of a pole commemorating HORN FAIR, the establishment of which, according to folklore, was a privilege accorded by King John to pacify an enraged local miller as

Ice-locked boats on the frozen Thames at Rotherhithe in 1789, from an engraving after G. Samuel.

compensation, together with some land here, for his seduction of the miller's pretty wife.

Rotherhithe Street *SE16*. One of London's longest streets following a great bend of the river, it formerly had water on both sides, the THAMES and the SURREY DOCKS. These are now closed and mostly filled in, but some bridges, once raised to let ships through, still survive. The MAYFLOWER, a riverside inn, commemorates the Pilgrim Fathers' ship which probably set sail from here on the first stage of her voyage (*see also* ST MARY CHURCH STREET). Neighbouring 19th-century warehouses have been converted to new uses including a picture library. The UNDERGROUND from ROTHERHITHE to WAPPING uses the first Thames Tunnel, designed by Marc and Isambard Kingdom Brunel. Their original engine house has been restored. Down river is Nelson Dock House, an 18th-century mansion and dry dock, once owned by shipbuilders. It was so named in the early 19th century, not long after Nelson's victory at Trafalgar. The Lavender Pond Nature Park, 2 acres of transformed dockland, is in the street.

Rotherhithe Tunnel *Shadwell–Rotherhithe*. Built in 1904–8 by Sir Maurice Fitzmarice and built partly with a tunnelling shield and partly by the cut and cover method. It is 4,860 ft long, excluding the approaches. The top of the tunnel is 48 ft below Trinity high-water mark to allow for the passage of large ships. Much street widening and extension was carried out in connection with the scheme and some 3,000 people had to be rehoused.

Rothman's of Pall Mall *64 Pall Mall, SW1*. In 1890, with only £40 behind him, 21-year-old Louis Rothman, whose family owned a tobacco factory in the Ukraine, bought the lease of a tiny shop at 55A FLEET STREET. Here, he sat up late every night making by hand the cigarettes which he sold the next day to the FLEET STREET journalists. He soon attracted a large clientele which included such influential figures as Lord Rothermere and Lord Northcliffe, and in 1900 he opened the showroom in PALL MALL. In 1905 he received a Royal Warrant from Edward VII, and five years later a special Royal Warrant was conferred on him by King Alfonso XIII of Spain. Demand grew rapidly, and during the 1st World War, having acquired a larger factory, Rothman replaced his handmade, exotically blended cigarettes with machinemade Virginia brands; later, together with his son, Sydney, who joined him in 1919, he greatly expanded the business which, in 1929, three years after his death, became a public company.

Today, although now part of a large group of companies which trade under the name of Rothmans International, Rothmans of Pall Mall still maintains a traditional custom. Special deliveries are made daily in London by a horse-drawn brougham. Resplendent in red and gold, this coach is 116 years old and is drawn by two dapple greys.

N.M. Rothschild and Sons Ltd *New Court, St Swithin's Lane, EC4*. One of London's most prestigious merchant banks; the business was founded by Nathan Meyer Rothschild at NEW COURT in 1809. Rothschild, from Frankfurt, had settled in England in 1798 and had built up a large textile export trade in

Manchester. He gave up the textile business in 1811 to concentrate (through the London firm) on bullion dealing and contracting for government loans. After spectacular financial successes during and after the Napoleonic Wars, often with the help of the Rothschilds in France and Germany, Rothschild's foreign loans and issues became a major factor in international banking and politics. The firm acted for Disraeli, for example, in Britain's purchase of Suez Canal shares. Rothschild's subsequently developed a wide range of merchant banking activities and the family remained in the front rank of the City's financiers. The firm is a member of the London Gold Market, and it continues to act as official gold broker to the BANK OF ENGLAND.

Round House *Chalk Farm Road, NW1.* Licensed as a theatre late in 1967, it opened in June 1968 with *Themes on the Tempest*, written and directed by Peter Brook. The Round House was built in 1847 to the designs of Stephenson, Dockray and Normandy to house the turntable at the terminus of the London and Birmingham Railway. When its use for this purpose ceased in 1869 it became a warehouse and factory until 1964 when it was listed as a building of architectural and historic interest. Its use as a centre for the arts was the brainchild of Arnold Wesker who founded Centre 42 in 1960. The name derived from the Resolution Number 42 of the Trades Union Congress conference which was held in that year and called upon the Trades Union movement to participate more fully in the arts. Centre 42 held festivals in many parts of the country; but in June 1964 Messrs Mintz and Coleman, who held the lease of the Round House, presented it to Centre 42 as a permanent home. Since then in spite of financial problems it has presented many good plays. It seats 600. In 1982 the future of the Round House was uncertain.

Roundshaw *Wallington, Surrey.* A housing estate built on part of the old CROYDON airport site, and occupying roughly the area on which once stood the buildings of the first CROYDON Aerodrome (the Plough Lane Aerodrome), which were demolished in 1928. A compact estate, housing some 8,000 people, Roundshaw was begun in 1965 and first occupied two years later. Dwellings on the estate are heated from a communal boiler house; and it has its own shops; a library and community centre; and a public house, the Merry-Go-Round. There is also a church, opened in 1981 and used by both the Church of England and the Free Churches, which before either had a place of worship, co-operated in a religious venture known as 'The Roundshaw Experiment'. There are several schools, including, since 1975, the Wilson's School which moved here from CAMBERWELL. All the roads, and the high-rise blocks of flats, Instone Close, are named after aircraft or people and firms famous in aviation, such as Mollison Drive and Lindberg Close. The name Roundshaw itself, however, comes from a 'round shaw' or circular grove of trees, some of which still stand in the small recreation ground, Roundshaw Park, opened in 1931 on the edge of the site.

Rowton House *(Now Rowton Hotels Ltd) 3–9 Bondway, SW8.* Founded by Montagu William Lowry, Lord Rowton. He had been private secretary to Disraeli and had helped to set up the GUINNESS TRUST in 1890. He made a survey of London's common lodging houses for the Trust and decided to set up working men's hostels. He put up the initial £30,000 and the first Rowton House was opened at VAUXHALL in 1892. It now houses 430 men. In the first year 140,105 beds were let at 6d a night. For this the customer received clean sheets, had the use of tiled wash rooms, foot baths and washing troughs for clothes, all with ample hot water. There was also a lodgers' kitchen so that he could cook his own food. In 1894 KING'S CROSS Rowton House opened with 678 beds. It was closed as a Rowton House in 1960 and reopened in October 1961 as the Mount Pleasant Hotel. In 1897 Parkview House at NEWINGTON BUTTS was opened with 800 beds at 7d per night. It was closed in 1970 and reopened as the London Park Hotel in 1972. Also in 1897 a hostel was opened at HAMMERSMITH but that was demolished in a Council redevelopment scheme. The Tower House, WHITECHAPEL was opened in 1902 and now houses 700; and the largest hostel, Arlington House in CAMDEN TOWN, was opened in 1905 and houses nearly 1,100. All accommodation is now in individual rooms. Prices rose to 1s in 1920, 1s 1d in 1940, 2s 3d in 1951 and 5s in 1960. In 1971 the nightly charge was 50p and now it is £1.80. The cheapest rate is £11.25 per week.

Roxeth *Harrow, Middlesex.* Modern nondescript South Harrow was once the hamlet of Roxeth, lying below the south-western slopes of Harrow Hill. The name Roxeth derives from Hroces Seath, the lake or spring where the rocks drank, or possibly the lake belonging to a man called Hroc. The earliest known reference to Hroces Seath is in a parchment which indicates that the marshy ground was first drained by the Christ Church monks from Canterbury who obtained the land in the year 845. The site of the ancient moated manor of Roxeth Grange is traditionally associated with King Stephen, who may have resided there at the time of the unrest arising from the rival claims of Stephen and Matilda to the throne. The farms that once abounded in old Roxeth, including the great 16th-century barn, have all gone. Only the 17th-century weatherboarded Roxeth Farm House in Lower Road survives to remind us of a once rural past. Christ Church on Roxeth Hill by G.S. Scott dates from 1862, and the more modern church of St Pauls in Corbin's Lane by A.W. Kenyon from 1937. The latter with its illuminated cross was built to serve a rapidly expanding suburbia following the coming of the railway. The naming of the station as South Harrow was perhaps the prime reason for Roxeth losing its identity and being swallowed up as part of HARROW.

Royal Academy of Arts *Burlington House, Piccadilly, W1.* Founded in 1768, it is the oldest society in the country devoted solely to the fine arts. When signing the Instrument of Foundation, George III declared that he would be the Academy's 'patron, protector and supporter'. The first President was Sir Joshua Reynolds, the first Treasurer the architect, William Chambers. Other Foundation Members were Thomas Gainsborough, Paul Sandby, Benjamin West and Richard Wilson. As well as holding exhibitions, the Academy conducted art schools; and among the early students were Lawrence, Constable and Turner. The first exhibitions were held in a house in PALL MALL, and the first pupils instructed in apartments made over to them in SOMERSET HOUSE where the

George III and his family visiting the Royal Academy, then at Somerset House, in 1788. From an engraving after Ramberg.

library was also situated. The old SOMERSET HOUSE was demolished in the 1770s when Chambers designed the present building which was built from 1776 onwards.

The Academy was given its own rooms here on the STRAND frontage. And it was, thereafter, able to hold much larger exhibitions. There had been room for only 136 works in the first exhibition in 1769, but when the rooms at SOMERSET HOUSE were ready, as many as 600 or 700 could be shown, though the pictures almost covered the walls with little space between the frames. In 1837 the Academy moved to TRAFALGAR SQUARE to a building shared with the NATIONAL GALLERY and in 1868, when this proved too small for both institutions, to BURLINGTON HOUSE. After the building had been adapted and extended, 17 main galleries were provided and two rows of studios for the Schools. Ever since the election of the Foundation Members, each new Academician has been obliged to present to the Academy 'a Picture, Bas-relief, or other specimen of his abilities'. This has led to the Academy's acquisition of a variety of valuable works whose interest is enhanced by their being the choice of their creators. Other works have been acquired over the years by purchase and by gift. Gifts have included splendid works by Reynolds, Gainsborough, Constable, Turner and Stubbs, and the beautiful Carrara marble tondo, the *Madonna and Child with the Infant St John* by Michelangelo, which is one of only four important sculptures by Michelangelo outside Italy.

The famous annual Summer Exhibition has been held every year for more than two centuries. At these exhibitions about 1,300 works – contemporary paintings, drawings, engravings, sculpture and architecture – are shown out of the 10,000 or so submitted by some 4,000 artists. All artists are eligible to submit work, irrespective of their nationality or training. There are also frequent Loan Exhibitions. These were started in 1870, and have since been extremely varied in scope.

Royal Academy of Dramatic Art *62–64 Gower Street, WC1.* The leading drama school in the country. It was founded in 1904 by the actor-manager, Sir Herbert Beerbohm Tree, in the dome of HIS MAJESTY'S THEATRE. Later that year the Academy was transferred to the Georgian house in GOWER STREET which it has occupied ever since. In 1906 the responsibility and management was invested in a Council of which Sir Squire Bancroft became the first president and the stability of the Academy was further assured in 1908 by the formation of a corporate body of Associates drawn from distinguished persons in the world of drama. In 1920 George V granted the Academy a Royal Charter; in 1921 the Prince of Wales, after opening its new theatre in MALET STREET, became Patron. In 1931 the GOWER STREET premises, incorporating a new little theatre (now called the GBS Theatre) were reconstructed with the help of an appeal launched by George Bernard Shaw who had become an active member of the Council. The MALET STREET theatre was destroyed in 1941 by enemy action and the present Vanbrugh Theatre, designed by Alister MacDonald, was opened by the Queen Mother in 1954. Shaw left RADA a third part of all his royalties while his copyright lasts.

Royal Academy of Music *Marylebone Road, NW1.* The oldest institution for advanced musical training in England. In 1774 Dr Charles Burney, impressed by the conservatories of Italy, proposed to convert the FOUNDLING HOSPITAL into a musical academy. He had the backing of the royal Dukes of Cumberland and Gloucester but the plan fell through as the Act of Parliament founding the Hospital did not allow for such expansion. In July 1822 John Fane, Lord Burghersh, later 11th Earl of Westmorland, held a meeting of noblemen at the THATCHED HOUSE TAVERN, ST JAMES'S STREET, where it was decided to form an academy which began its work in March 1823, under the patronage of King George IV, with William Crotch as Principal. The original intention was that there should be 80 resident students (40 boys and 40 girls) but, when the Academy opened, in a house in TENTERDEN STREET, HANOVER SQUARE, there were only 21, none of them more than 12 years old. One of the earliest pupils was Charles Dickens's sister, Fanny. The RAM was granted a Royal Charter in 1830, but for the first 40-odd years of its existence it was continually in financial straits. In 1845 Albert Gilbert, aged nine, entered the Academy. He wrote in his autobiography, 'Picture to yourself five iron bed-steads crowded so closely together that three of them were reached best by getting over the two outside ones. At the feet of these beds – which were covered with somewhat unsavoury coverlets – an old square pianoforte by Collard was placed for practice. Not a vestige of any other furniture was in the room. ... The Usher was supposed to take all boys who had been imperfectly educated for lessons in the three R's from eight to nine every evening except Wednesday and Saturday which were half-holidays. The Superintendent read prayers in the concert room every morning at seven in summer and eight in winter. On the door of each bedroom was nailed a practice paper accounting for the duties and whereabouts of the occupants of the room from 9 a.m. to 9 p.m. when all were supposed to be in bed ... There were three pianos in the dining room used simultaneously'.

In 1853 the boarding school system was discontinued. Gladstone awarded the Academy an annual government grant of £500 in 1864, but this was discontinued three years later when Disraeli came to power, and an attempt was made to close the institution. The grant was renewed, however, with the return of Gladstone's ministry in 1868, and from then onwards the RAM started to flourish.

In 1912 it moved to more spacious premises in MARYLEBONE ROAD, designed by Sir Ernest George and Albert B. Yates. This contained some 50 teaching rooms, a concert hall (the Duke's Hall), office accommodation, and a restaurant. A small theatre and a lecture hall were added in 1926. A new library was opened in 1968 and, with funds raised by a 150th anniversary appeal, an ambitious programme of renovation of the fabric was launched.

Royal Aero Club Formed in 1901 after a discussion in a balloon over the CRYSTAL PALACE between, amongst others F. Hedges Butler and Charles Rolls. Its object was to encourage 'aero automobilism and ballooning as a sport'. In addition to Rolls and Hedges Butler early members included Handley Page, Grahame-White, and Thomas Sopwith. Its premises were for some time at 119 PICCADILLY. The club then moved to the JUNIOR CARLTON, then to the Senior, and, from 1961 to 1968, was at the LANSDOWNE. In 1971 its members were admitted to the UNITED SERVICE CLUB.

Royal Aeronautical Society *4 Hamilton Place, W1*. Founded in 1866 at ARGYLL LODGE, CAMPDEN HILL. The 8th Duke of Argyll was the first President. Its headquarters in HAMILTON PLACE, where there is an extensive library, was once the home of the Duke of Wellington.

Royal Agricultural Hall *Liverpool Road, N1*. Founded by the Smithfield Club, which had held annual agricultural and livestock exhibitions since 1798

The Royal Aeronautical Society, founded at Argyll Lodge in 1866, held an exhibition at the Crystal Palace in 1868.

and needed a larger building than their BAKER STREET premises. It was built in 1861–2 on a cattle lair used for herds going to SMITHFIELD, to the designs of Frederick Peck of Maidstone, using 1,000 tons of cast-iron and having 130 ft roof-span flanked by two towers. Smaller halls were added including a music hall (the Blue Hall), increasing its area to 4.75 acres. Besides regular cattle shows it became the home of industrial exhibitions, the World's Fair (from 1873), walking and bicycle races (from 1877 and 1879), Sanger's and other circuses, the Grand Military Tournament (later the ROYAL TOURNAMENT), religious and missionary services, CRUFT'S (from 1891), concerts, motor shows and other large displays. So well patronised by royalty that from 1885 it was named Royal Agricultural Hall, its most splendid occasion was probably the Grand Ball of 1869 for nearly 5,000 guests, in honour of the visit of the Belgian Volunteers. The Hall closed in 1939; in 1943–71 it was used as the Parcels department of MOUNT PLEASANT SORTING OFFICE; and has since been empty. A public campaign to save 'Aggie' resulted in ISLINGTON Borough Council's buying it in 1976, and after various attempts to find a new use it was acquired in 1981 for a trade exhibition centre.

Royal Agricultural Society of England *35 Belgrave Square, SW1*. Founded in 1838. It is a registered charity possessing some 18,000 members.

Royal Air Force Club *128 Piccadilly, W1*. In October 1918 the 1st Lord Cowdray made a gift of £100,000 for the purpose of providing a building for the Club. The premises acquired were those of the LYCEUM CLUB on the PICCADILLY frontage and carriage stables on the OLD PARK LANE side. In 1982 the membership was 19,000.

Royal Air Force Museum *Grahame Park Way, NW9*. The Museum was established in 1963 and officially opened by the Queen in November 1972. It covers all aspects of the history of the RAF and its predecessors and much of the history of aviation generally. The Museum building is sited on 10 acres of the

661

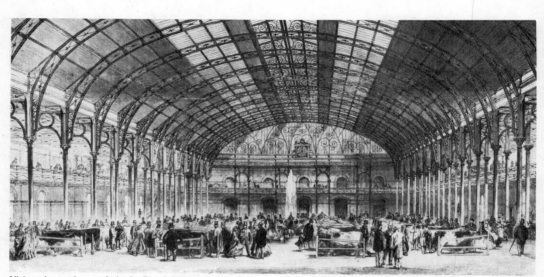

Visitors inspecting cattle in the Royal Agricultural Hall in 1861, the year of its opening.

former airfield at Hendon. Its aircraft hall, which occupies two hangars dating from the 1st World War, displays some 40 aircraft from the Museum's total collection of over 100 machines.

On a site adjacent to the main building the Battle of Britain Museum has been built. It was opened by the Queen Mother in November 1978 and contains a unique collection of British, German and Italian aircraft which were engaged in the great air battle of 1940.

Royal Amphitheatre *Dane Street, High Holborn.* Opened 25 May 1867 for circus performances under the direction of William Charmon and Thomas M'Collum with a mixed programme of equestrian entertainment and farce. It was converted into a conventional theatre and reopened on 11 October 1873 under the management of Frederick Strange with a farce and a new version of Offenbach's *Eurydice*. Strange's management was not a success and although the theatre was renamed the National Theatre of Novelties and used for miscellaneous entertainment of comedy, ballet and pantomime, it was closed for most of 1874. John Hollingshead took over, renamed the theatre the Holborn Amphitheatre and opened on 19 December 1874 with *Cinderella* which was described as 'a Musical Drama and Opera with a Christmas Pantomime ending'. Hollingshead, however, was running too many theatrical ventures to give the Holborn Amphitheatre his full support and it closed again in March 1875. Within a period of four years it became successively Newsome's Circus, the Grand Central Skating Rink, the Royal Amphitheatre and Hamilton's Royal Amphitheatre. In November 1879 it came under the management of J.W. Currans and, renamed the Connaught Theatre, it opened with a comic opera and ballet. The lack of success which dogged the theatre continued, however, and after a period of closures it reopened as the Alcazar on 12 April 1884 with a pantomime under the management of John Baum. This lasted for only a few nights as the theatre was refused a licence until certain repairs had been carried out. The necessary work was completed by

May but no tenant could be found until December 1883 when Marguerite Dinorben became the lessee and opened on the 22 December 1883 with *Mizpah: A Story of Today*, having changed the name of the theatre to the International. Nothing that the theatre presented ever met with success and on the 12 April 1884 it was again renamed the Holborn Theatre and, under the management of George Rignold, opened with Callender's American 'Nigger Minstrels' preceded by *A Silent Woman*, a one-act farce. Several unsuccessful plays followed and finally a burlesque called *Little Lohengrin*. After a few performances, however, a reasonably well-filled house waited a considerable time for the curtain to rise, which it failed to do as apparently one of the actors refused to perform until the whole of his salary, of which he had received only part, was paid. Incensed by the delay, the audience demanded their money back and proceeded to wreck parts of the theatre. The theatre closed on 30 August 1886, having given up the unequal struggle for success.

Royal Anthropological Institute *56 Queen Anne Street, W1.* The successor to the Ethnological Society of London formed in 1843. After disputes among members over racial issues in the middle of the century, the Anthropological Institute of Great Britain and Ireland was formed in 1871 and was permitted to add the prefix 'Royal' in 1907. Membership is opened to specialists and others interested in anthropology, ethnography and prehistoric archaeology. It has a large library at 6 Burlington Gardens (*see* MUSEUM OF MANKIND).

Royal Aquarium *Westminster.* A classical building of Portland stone designed by A. Bedborough in 1876 as a palace of Victorian entertainment. The main hall had palm trees, pieces of sculpture, tanks of curious sea creatures and an orchestra. There were rooms for reading, smoking, and eating, an art gallery, a skating rink and a theatre. The total cost was nearly £200,000. But the hoped-for intellectual clientele never came and by the 1890s the place had become 'a

The Royal Aquarium, which opened opposite Westminster Abbey in 1876 as a palace of entertainment, was demolished in 1906.

sort of magnified "music hall" in which scantily dressed females go through "exciting" acrobatic performances, or are shot out of cannons, "genuine Zulus" dance, and female swimmers exhibit "aquatic feats" in the great tank, or fasting men are exhibited to a gaping crowd.' In 1903 the site was sold to the Methodists for their CENTRAL HALL. All but the theatre was demolished, and that was pulled down in 1906. Its interior was built into the Imperial Theatre, CANNING TOWN which was destroyed by fire in 1931.

Royal Arcade *W1.* A shopping arcade between 28 OLD BOND STREET and 12 ALBEMARLE STREET. It was opened in 1879. Queen Victoria used to buy her handkerchiefs, riding shirts, vests and knitting wool from H.W. Bretell, hosiers and shirtmakers, still at No. 12. The Folio Society showrooms are at No. 5.

Royal Archaeological Institute *304 Addison House, Grove End Road, NW8.* Received a Royal Charter in 1961 and continued the work of an Institute founded some 120 years earlier.

Royal Army Medical College *Millbank, SW1.* Founded as the Army Medical School at Fort Pitt, Chatham in 1860. It moved to Netley in 1863 and in 1907 to its present neo-Georgian premises designed by Wood and Ainslie. The College provides postgraduate training in military surgery, medicine, army pathology, military psychiatry, preventive medicine, general practice and the dental sciences. In a room known as the VC Room are the names of medical Victoria Cross holders of whom there are 29, two of whom received the decoration twice, a distinction only achieved three times. There are also many portraits to be seen and pictures representing the actions in which VCs were won. Opposite the VC Room is the Barry Room, so called after General James Barry, discovered after death to have been a woman. Joined to the College by

a raised corridor is the Royal Army Medical Corps Officers' Headquarters Mess. In the mess courtyard can be seen the bollards to which were tied the barges that brought the convicts sentenced to transportation to the MILLBANK PENITENTIARY which formerly occupied the site. Also in the courtyard is a statue of Sir James McGrigor, Director General of the Army Medical Department, 1815–21 (*see* STATUES).

Royal Arsenal *see* WOOLWICH ARSENAL.

Royal Artillery Barracks *Woolwich, SE18.* The Royal Regiment of Artillery was formed at WOOLWICH in 1716 with barracks for the soldiers in the ROYAL ARSENAL. Conditions there by the mid-18th century were appalling because of overcrowding and poor sanitation and thus, in 1772, the Surveyor General was ordered to prepare plans for new barracks on Woolwich Common. The magnificent façade of nearly 1,000 ft with a triumphal arch in the centre was constructed in two stages, the eastern half in 1776–81, the western half being complete by 1802 except for the Chapel of 1808 which, from 1863 to 1954, served as the Garrison Theatre.

Royal Artillery Museum *Academy Road, Woolwich, SE18.* This small but very comprehensive museum has exhibits providing a historical background for the Royal Regiment of Artillery, as opposed to its weapons, which can be seen at the MUSEUM OF ARTILLERY at the Rotunda. The museum is divided into three main rooms set in chronological order, beginning in the early 18th century and followed by the Napoleonic Wars, the Indian artilleries, the Crimean War and Indian Mutiny. Next, there are sections relating to the colonial and Boer wars and the Royal Horse, Mountain and Volunteer Artillery. The role played by animals is also shown. The 1st and 2nd World Wars are adequately covered in bays devoted to land-based anti-aircraft, coast and maritime anti-aircraft artillery and observation posts. Below the museum there is an extensive library.

Royal Astronomical Society *Burlington House, W1*. Founded in 1820 for the encouragement and promotion of astronomy and geophysics.

Royal Automobile Club *89 Pall Mall, SW1*. Founded in 1897 'for the Protection, Encouragement and Development of Automobilism' and first housed at WHITEHALL COURT, then at 119 PICCADILLY. The present building, on the site of the old WAR OFFICE in PALL MALL, was completed in 1911 by Mewès and Davis, the architects of the RITZ. The least intimate of the gentlemen's clubs of London, it was selected by Burgess and Maclean as a suitable place to have lunch before fleeing the country. There are some 8,000 members who, in addition to the usual club amenities, have the use of a bookstall, a post office, Turkish baths, a rifle range and a swimming pool.

Royal Avenue *SW3*. A wide, leafy boulevard laid out in 1692–4 to connect CHELSEA HOSPITAL with KENSINGTON PALACE but never continued north of KING'S ROAD. It is now lined with attractive 19th-century terraces. It was the fictional home of James Bond. Open-air art exhibitions are held on Saturdays in the summer.

Royal Bagnio *Bath Street, Newgate Street*. Opened in 1679. It was built by Turkish merchants and was 'a neat and contrived building after the Turkish mode'. The main bath room had a cupola roof, Dutch-tiled walls and marble steps. Patrons could enjoy 'sweating, rubbing, shaving, cupping and bathing'. The baths continued as the Old Royal Baths until 1876 when they were demolished to make way for an office block.

Royal Ballet School *155 Talgarth Road, W14*. Founded in 1931 by Dame Ninette de Valois who, in 1926, had opened a school of dance, the Academy of Choreographic Art, and had established a working relationship between her school and Lilian Baylis's theatre, the OLD VIC. When Dame Lilian acquired the SADLER'S WELLS THEATRE, a special studio was built there; and there Dame Ninette began to create the dancers and repertory of the future Sadler's Wells Ballet. Certain of her most promising students were sent for further education to a tutor at the INNS OF COURT. This arrangement was not very satisfactory, but lack of means prevented the founding of a proper establishment until in 1947, with the help of the Arts Council, the present building in TALGARTH ROAD was acquired. The school then became fully educational with a syllabus of general education added to the dance syllabus for pupils up to the age of 16; for senior pupils (16–18) general education had to yield to specialisation in ballet. At first the school admitted girls only but in 1948 it became co-educational. In 1956 both the Sadler's Wells Ballet School and the Sadler's Wells Ballet were granted a Royal Charter, and they became the Royal Ballet School and the Royal Ballet respectively. The Upper School, which is non-residential, continued at TALGARTH ROAD, but by then a Lower School had been established at WHITE LODGE, RICHMOND PARK. This Lower School accommodates some

120 pupils most of whom, at the age of 16, move on to the Upper School – which now has about 150 students, including about 40 on a Teachers' Training Course – to complete their training as dancers for the Royal Ballet or, failing that, for other British and foreign companies. Almost without exception the members of the Royal Ballet are former students of the school.

Royal Botanic Gardens *Kew*. These unique gardens, extending to 300 acres, combine a scientific centre with an historic pleasure garden dating from the 18th-century, possibly earlier. The diarist, Sir John Evelyn, mentions a visit in 1678, to Sir Henry Capel in Kew, 'whose orangerie and myretetum are most beautiful and perfectly well kept.' In 1731, Frederick Prince of Wales, leased The White House, also known as KEW PALACE, together with its grounds from the Capel family, and this site now forms the eastern part of the present gardens. The Prince instituted a pleasure garden and, after his death, his widow, Augusta, Dowager Princess of Wales, continued to improve it. In 1759 she created a botanic garden of nine acres under the guidance of Lord Bute and the head gardener, William Aiton. The western part was attached to the now vanished Richmond Lodge, the favourite residence of George II. The grounds had been laid out by his wife, Queen Caroline (of Anspach), but they were extensively altered and improved, around 1770, by Lancelot 'Capability' Brown after the property had passed to George III in whose reign the two sites were united. Under the unofficial directorship of Sir Joseph Banks the Botanic Garden became famous and, in 1841, was handed over to the nation as the result of a Royal Commission.

Today, as well as being a public park, the Royal Botanic Gardens are primarily a scientific institution organised in several divisions principally concerned with the accurate identification of plants, living and dried, from worldwide sources. It acts as a centre for the distribution of economic and decorative plant material, and as a quarantine station, and is also increasingly involved in the conservation of endangered plant species.

Housed in a large block of buildings just outside the main gate, and not open to the public, is the Herbarium, consisting of a collection of between four and five million dried and pressed plants.

Also within the Royal Botanic Gardens stand a number of other buildings, many of them legacies of Royal Kew. In about 1756 Sir William Chambers was employed to instruct the Prince of Wales (soon to be George III) in architectural draughtsmanship, and shortly afterwards he was commissioned to design a series of garden buildings at Kew, which failed, however, to impress Horace Walpole, a neighbour and critic: 'Frederick, Prince of Wales, enlarged and ornamented the House, and began great works in the Garden. The Princess Dowager continued the improvements, and Lord Bute had the disposition of the ground. ... There is little invention or Taste shown. Being on a flat, Lord Bute raised hillocs [*sic*] to diversify the ground, and carried Chambers the architect thither, who built some temples, but they are all of wood and very small. Of his design was the round Temple in the middle ... called the Temple of Victory on the Battle of Minden; another with a Doric portico [the Temple of Bellona] ... the Roman Ruin, the Aviary, and a Chinese building in the Menagerie. The bridge and the round Temple were each erected in a night's time to surprise the Princess. . . .'

Of Chambers's classical temples, three survive: those of Arethusa, Bellona and Æolus. The Temple of War or Bellona stands 100 yards south-west of the Victoria Gate. Built in 1760, it has a projecting portico of four Doric columns, above which there is a frieze carved with alternating helmets and daggers, vases and *paterae*. Inside, the oval dome is painted blue and has in its centre a gilded wooded 'glory' or sun. On a hillock about 70 yards west of the Cumberland Gate stands the 'ring-temple' of Æolus which once contained a large semi-circular niche that could be pivoted to shield the occupants from the wind. This niche was removed when the structure was renovated and modified in 1845 by Decimus Burton. Built in 1785, the Temple of Arethusa is 100 yards north-west of the Victoria Gate and was designed by Chambers as a shelter for the Royal Family. Two other alcoves, built for this purpose, also survive; one, 100 yards north-west of the Lion Gate, and the other, a plain edifice, at the Brentford Gate.

The impressive Orangery, which stands about 200 yards south of Aroid House, was designed by Chambers in 1761. Reminiscent of Wren, it is a long, single storeyed building with shallow pedimented wings, lit by tall round-headed windows with very heavy glazing-bars. Of Chambers's design, also, is the Great Pagoda which was inspired by a visit to China in his youth. This stands ten storeys and 163 ft high, on a base 49 ft in diameter. Although formerly elaborately ornamented, it is a relatively simple structure which was erected in less than six months in the winter of 1761–2. Between the present Lion Gate and the Unicorn Gate stands Chambers's classical 'folly' in the form of a brick and stone gateway, resembling a Roman ruin. Of this structure Horace Walpole remarked, 'A solecism may be committed even in architecture. The ruin in Kew Gardens is built with Act-of-Parliament brick.'

A later building (standing about 350 yds from the Victoria Gate) is King William's Temple. Designed by Sir Jeffry Wyatville in 1837, it is constructed of Bath stone with a portico at either end.

In the south-west corner of the Gardens, amid 37 acres of woodland, stands the Queen's Cottage. Built as a summerhouse for Queen Charlotte around 1771, it was the scene of many a royal tea-party. It is a two-storeyed, thatched cottage *orné*, of brick framed with timber. With its surroundings it was retained by Queen Victoria, until she gave it to the nation to commemorate her Diamond Jubilee. It was first opened to public view on 1 May 1899.

Cambridge Cottage, on Kew Green, is approached from the Gardens, and houses the Wood Museum. Formerly the property of Lord Bute, advisor to Augusta, Dowager Princess of Wales, it was assigned by George III to his sixth son, Adolphus, whom he created Duke of Cambridge in 1801. After 1837 the Duke made the Cottage his permanent home, adding to it substantially during the following years. It was from here that his daughter, Princess Mary, was married in 1866. After the death of the last Duke of Cambridge in 1904, the Cottage was presented to the Gardens by Edward VII. The building is generally of yellow or red stock brick, and the central 18th-century portion is two-storeyed with a parapet.

Opposite the Aquatic Garden, and now closed to the public, stands a Georgian building which contained the first collection of economic botany. It was opened in 1847; the original exhibits were donated by Sir William Hooker, the first Director of the Gardens. On account of its popularity, a second Museum, now known as Museum 1, designed by Decimus Burton, was opened in 1857. This lies between Cumberland Gate and Victoria Gate. A third Museum, the Marianne North Gallery, lies on the eastern border of Kew, close to the Ruined Arch. It houses a collection of 848 oil paintings on botanical subjects by Marianne North, who gave them to Kew, together with the building designed by her architect friend, James Fergusson. It was opened on 9 July 1882.

Close to the Marianne North Gallery is the Flagstaff. The fourth on this site, it is 225 ft high and is made from a single trunk of Douglas Fir, which was about 370 years old when felled. Presented by the Government of British Columbia, it was put up by the Royal Engineers in 1959. South of this landmark is the Refreshment Pavilion, which was designed by R.D. Allison and erected in 1920, its predecessor having

The Palm House in Kew Gardens was built by Decimus Burton and the engineer Richard Turner in 1844–8.

been burnt in 1903 by Suffragettes. Not far away, and west of the Pagoda, is a replica, four-fifths natural size, of a famous Japanese Gate, 'The Gateway of the Imperial Messenger' of *Chokushi-Mon*, which was presented to the Gardens by the Kyoto Exhibitors' Association after it had been displayed at the Japanese-British Exhibition in SHEPHERDS BUSH in 1910.

Just within the main gate stands Aroid House (No. 1 Glasshouse). This is a plain stone building with an Ionic portico illuminated by many tall windows with glazing bars. Originally one of two pavilions designed by Nash to flank the garden façade of BUCKINGHAM PALACE, it was removed and re-erected (slightly altered) in its present position in 1836. Its companion remains *in situ*.

To the design of Decimus Burton and lying towards the southern end of the Gardens, is the Temperate House. Started in 1860 but not completed until 1899, this great glasshouse is solidly built and conventional in appearance with much ornamentation, unlike the celebrated Palm House, also ascribed to Decimus Burton but built in conjunction with Richard Turner, a civil engineer, in 1844–8. This original piece of architecture is composed of curved sheets of glass; one big curve in the wings up to the clerestory, another from there to the central dome. Among the 3,000 species here is a giant Chilean wine palm, the second oldest specimen at Kew. Another Chilean wine palm was planted in 1775. Connected to the Palm House by a tunnel is the Campanile. Built in brick, this water tower stands 107 ft high and was erected in the 1840s.

The main entrance, at the north-west end of Kew Green, consists of a semi-circular drive bordered by Portland stone piers with wrought-iron infilling, and ornamental iron gates bearing the arms and cypher of Queen Victoria, designed by Decimus Burton, and erected in 1848.

The Chinese Guardian Lions by the Pond, a pair of stone lions probably made in the 18th century, though possibly dating from the Ming period, resemble examples in the gardens of the Imperial Palace, Peking. François Joseph Bosio's *Hercules Fighting Achelous* in the Pond was first exhibited in plaster at the Paris salon in 1814 and in bronze in 1842. Acquired by George IV in 1826, it originally stood on the East Terrace at Windsor Castle. It was given by Elizabeth II in 1963. Hamo Thornycroft's bronze, *The Sower*, is near Museum 3.

Royal Botanic Society of London Incorporated in 1839, the Society had gardens occupying a portion of the INNER CIRCLE, in REGENT'S PARK, formerly Jenkins's Nursery. They consisted of 18 acres and were laid out by Robert Marnock with rock, winter and landscape gardens, also a lake and an artificial mound, all made in the style of the 'natural' school. There was a conservatory entirely of glass and iron covering 15,000 square feet, to accommodate 2,000 visitors. The Society held exhibitions and distributed prize medals. There was also a library and museum, illustrating the varieties of structure in the parts of plants, their products and uses. In several parts of the botanic ground were privet hedges, each forming a segment of a circle, and cut so as to make each look like a miniature green wall. These hedges were to shelter the tender plants from the wind. There was also a medical garden and a collection of British plants, arranged according to the Linnaean System. William

Robinson worked under Marnock and was in charge of the herbaceous border and a collection of English wild flowers. For 30 years the Society's Secretary was J. de C. Sowerby, eldest son of the author of Sowerby's *English Botany*. When KEW was in decline after the death of George IV it offered its rare plants to this Society and the then Horticultural Society at CHISWICK, but they both refused to break up the collection. Gertrude Jekyll, an exponent of 'wild' gardening like William Robinson, was a judge at the Botanic Show in REGENT'S PARK in 1881. The Society was wound up when the lease of the land in REGENT'S PARK terminated in 1931. A proposal that the ROYAL HORTICULTURAL SOCIETY should take over the garden never materialised, and in 1932 it became Queen Mary's Rose Garden (*see* GARDENS, Regent's Park).

Royal College of Art *Kensington Gore, SW7.* Founded in 1837 as the School of Design following the report of a select committee on art education. It was intended for teaching industrial design rather than fine arts which were then the province of the ROYAL ACADEMY Schools. Lectures were given in SOMERSET HOUSE. John B. Papworth, an architect, was the first principal. In 1841 the government founded provincial schools of design in industrial areas; and a teachers' training department was started at the school. The best students from the provincial colleges were sent to finish their training in London. In 1852 the school moved to MARLBOROUGH HOUSE and was renamed the Central School of Practical Art. A department of practical art was set up at the suggestion of Henry Cole. At MARLBOROUGH HOUSE the school had a library, museum, lecture room and later a collection of exhibits from the GREAT EXHIBITION. In 1853 it became part of the Government Department of Science and Art. In 1856 the Board of Education took over control of the school from the Board of Trade. In 1857 the school and museum moved to the 'Brompton Boilers' (*see* VICTORIA AND ALBERT MUSEUM). In 1863 permanent college buildings in EXHIBITION ROAD, designed by Gottfried Semper, were completed. In 1896 the college was renamed by Queen Victoria the Royal College of Art and given the right to grant diplomas. In 1961 an eight-storey teaching block, designed by H.T. Cadbury-Brown, Sir Hugh Casson and R.Y. Goodden, was built in KENSINGTON GORE. In 1967 the College was granted a royal charter whereby it became a post-graduate university institution empowered to award degrees. In 1981 there were 570 students.

Royal College of Defence Studies *Seaford House, Belgrave Square, SW1.* Founded in 1927 as the Imperial Defence College. Suspended during the 2nd World War, it reopened in 1946. It was given its present name in 1970. It aims to equip officers for high command, mainly brigadiers and equivalent rank of all services, and a number from overseas. About 75 officers attend a year-long course.

Royal College of General Practitioners *13, 14 and 15 Prince's Gate, SW7.* As early as 1830 Dr William Gaitskell wrote to the *Lancet* suggesting the formation of a College of General Practitioners. Nothing came of the suggestion and it was not until the National Health Service was planned in the 1940s that it was seriously considered again. Dr John Hunt (later Lord Hunt) was the driving force. He met with much obstruction and opposition, including that of the reigning Presidents of the ROYAL COLLEGE OF PHYSICIANS and of the ROYAL SOCIETY OF MEDICINE but he was not to be deterred. In 1952 the College was founded, but it had no home. Temporary offices were set up in three successive premises in the West End. In 1962 the College purchased 13–14 PRINCE'S GATE, a house once owned by John Pierpont Morgan and afterwards the home of the American Ambassador. President Kennedy spent part of his boyhood here. In 1976 the College expanded into No. 15 PRINCE'S GATE.

Royal College of Music *Prince Consort Road, SW7.* In 1882 the Prince of Wales called a meeting to found a music school on a sounder basis than the existing NATIONAL TRAINING SCHOOL OF MUSIC and in May the next year the college was incorporated by Royal Charter. It opened in the building in KENSINGTON GORE formerly occupied by the National Training School, and now by the ROYAL COLLEGE OF ORGANISTS. George Grove, compiler of *The Dictionary of Music*, was appointed the first Director. In 1890–4 the present building was designed by Sir Arthur Blomfield. It cost £48,000 and was financed by Samson Fox. There have been several additions since, including extensions in 1964 and 1973. In 1894 Sir Charles Hubert Parry succeeded Grove as Director, a post he held until his death in 1918. In 1894 Sir George Donaldson presented the college with his collection of over 300 old musical instruments including Haydn's clavichord, Handel's spinet and Rizzio's guitar. Jenny Lind was one of the first professors at the college. Walford Davies, Vaughan Williams, Clara Butt and Benjamin Britten were students here.

Royal College of Nursing *Henrietta Place, W1.* The College of Nursing, as it then was, was founded in 1916. In 1919 it moved into 7 Henrietta Street (now Henrietta Place) but by 1921 this building was already too small. At that time Lady Cowdray, who had always been interested in the college, acquired the mansion standing on the corner of Henrietta Place and CAVENDISH SQUARE. It had been the London home of the Prime Minister, Herbert Asquith. The building, designed by Sir Edwin Cooper, contains fine panelling and a mural by John Devoto (1729). In 1922 it became the Cowdray Club – a residential club for nurses. In the garden of the club new headquarters were constructed. These were opened in 1926. In 1939 the College received the title 'Royal'. In 1982 there were about 182,000 members.

Royal College of Organists *Kensington Gore, SW7.* Founded in 1864 by Richard Davidge Limpus, Organist of ST MICHAEL'S, CORNHILL. On 5 July that year the first general meeting took place at the FREEMASONS HALL. The college at first held only lectures and competitions. In 1865 the Archbishop of Canterbury became President and the Bishop of London, Vice-President. Examinations were first held in 1866 and successful candidates became Fellows of the College. From 1868 to 1875 Limpus's own house at No. 41 Queen's Square, BLOOMSBURY was used by the college. In 1875 Limpus died and the college moved to Hart Street, BLOOMSBURY. In 1893 a royal charter was granted and in 1904 the college moved to its present home which had been built for the NATIONAL TRAINING SCHOOL OF MUSIC.

Royal College of Physicians of London *11 St Andrew's Place, Regent's Park, NW1.* The oldest English medical society or institution, founded by a charter of Henry VIII in 1518. At this time medicine in England, compared with its practice in Italy, was very backward. The instigator and first President of the college was the King's physician, Thomas Linacre, a cleric and noted scholar and grammarian, a friend of Erasmus and Thomas More. He was known throughout Europe as a translator of Galen. The early meetings were held in Linacre's house in KNIGHTRIDER STREET near ST PAUL'S. After Linacre's death in 1524 the premises used by the college in his house were enlarged, if not completely rebuilt later in the century. In 1614 new premises were leased from the Dean and Chapter of ST PAUL'S at Amen Corner, PATERNOSTER ROW. The building was destroyed with most of its valuables in the GREAT FIRE. This was shortly after the death of William Harvey whose most famous discovery was the circulation of the blood which he described at the College in 1616. His portrait and a few other things were saved from the fire. The College's third home was in WARWICK LANE but the building was not completed until near the end of the century. Wren is usually credited with the designs, but Robert Hooke also had a hand in them. It was a distinguished building and served the College for over a century. It was imposing enough to be one of the regular sights for visitors to London, and a French guide-book of 1693 recommends tourists to give at least 3d to the person who shows them round. By then London was moving westward and the college began to look for a site nearer the new centre of practice and social life.

At the instigation of the president, Sir Henry Halford, who was physician and personal friend of the monarch, George IV, a site was obtained in PALL MALL East, in the north-west corner of the proposed site for TRAFALGAR SQUARE. Halford was a man of great energy and drive, physician to four monarchs (George III, George IV, William IV and Queen Victoria), and president of the College from 1820 until his death in 1844, longer than any other holder of the office. Sir Robert Smirke was appointed architect for the new building which was opened in 1825. It has an impressive portico with six Ionic columns. It sheltered in three niches, three statues by Henry Weekes – Linacre, Harvey and Sydenham, 'the founder of the art of clinical medicine'. Smirke's building, which still stands, served the College for over a century, as had its predecessor, but shortly after the 2nd World War it became obvious that it was too small for the much greater number of Fellows. It was sold and became part of Canada House (*see* TRAFALGAR SQUARE). The statues were taken down and found to be 'in extremely bad condition' and taken to a breaker's yard, from which they were rescued. That of Harvey was removed to the garden of the William Harvey public house at Willesborough, Ashford, Kent, which stands on the site of a cottage where Harvey spent part of his childhood. That of Sydenham was re-erected outside a doctor's surgery in Church Road, Ashford. The head of Linacre's was cut off and placed in the garden of 42 Choumet Square, SE15, the house of a member of his family, A.T. Linacre.

After the 2nd World War a site for a new College was found in the south-east corner of REGENT'S PARK where formerly had stood Someries House, once the Adult Orphan Asylum which had been designed free of charge by John Nash for the daughters of clergymen and officers. Sir Denys Lasdun was appointed architect. He was given two instructions: to reproduce the Censors' Room which was to be lined with the same Spanish oak which decorated that room in WARWICK LANE and had been transferred to PALL MALL East, and to reproduce the library as closely as possible. The contents of the library (which is historical only) had been almost entirely destroyed by the GREAT FIRE, but Dr Merrett, the librarian, had saved 140 volumes. These formed the nucleus of the present library. The Marquess of Dorchester, at his death in 1680, bequeathed his valuable library to the College. It was devoted to physic, mathematics, law, philology and many other subjects, including the first book on dancing. There is also a near-contemporary manuscript of Chaucer's *Canterbury Tales*, an early Caxton and the famous Wilton *Psalter* of about 1250. The new college was completed in 1964.

Royal College of Psychiatrists *17 Belgrave Square, SW1*. Established here in 1971 when it received a supplemental Charter, modifying that granted in 1926 to the Royal Medico-Psychological Association. In 1841, on the initiative of Dr Samuel Hitch, physician to the Gloucester Lunatic Asylum, a society was formed which at first bore the title of the Association of Medical Officers of Asylums and Hospitals for the Insane. In 1865 this name was changed to the Medico-Psychological Association.

Royal College of Radiologists *38 Portland Place, W1*. Developed from the Faculty of Radiologists which was established in 1939. It was granted its Royal Charter in 1975. After occupying various temporary premises, it moved to its present address in 1978. The house, built in 1777, was once the home in exile of the Empress Eugénie.

Royal College of Surgeons of England *Lincoln's Inn Fields, WC2*. The College was given its first Royal Charter in 1800, but its origins go back to the Middle Ages when there was a Guild of Surgeons in the CITY OF LONDON. In 1540 under Henry VIII the Surgeons were united with the Barbers (as happened in many parts of Europe). In 1745 the Surgeons left the Barbers to former a separate Company of Surgeons and it was to this Company that the Government under William Pitt entrusted the Hunterian Collection (*see* HUNTERIAN MUSEUM), this act in turn leading to the establishment of the Royal College in 1800.

In 1797 the Company of Surgeons had purchased a house at 41 LINCOLN'S INN FIELDS which was rebuilt between 1806 and 1813 and extended by George Dance and James Lewis for the new College. In 1835 most of the building, except for the portico, was demolished and a new building designed by Charles Barry was completed in 1835, additional premises at the rear being added in 1855. Later 19th-century additions were made by Stephen Salter, and in 1953–63, following the destruction by bombing in 1941 of much of the old building, the present College, greatly extended, was rebuilt by Alner W. Hall, with Sir Edward Maufe as consulting architect. The present building retains the entrance hall and library of Charles Barry, but new museums have replaced those destroyed in 1941 and many additional research laboratories and teaching facilities have been added, as well as the Nuffield College of Surgical Sciences, which houses post-graduate medical students from all over the world, most of them attending the courses provided by the College and its Institute of Basic Medical Sciences.

At the centre of the College, physically and spiritually, is the renowned collection of anatomical, pathological and physiological specimens collected by the great 18th-century surgeon-scientist, John Hunter. This collection illustrates Hunter's remarkable insight into the form and function of the human body, related to the animal kingdom, and predates many of Charles Darwin's theories on evolution. It contains specimens that testify to Hunter's interest in the possibilities of transplantation surgery. The College that has grown up around the Hunterian Collection has devoted itself in the 20th century to research, both fundamental and applied, which has pushed forward the boundaries of surgical, dental, and anaesthetic practice. In this direct involvement in research it is unique amongst medical colleges throughout the world (and it has been the model for the establishment of other surgical colleges in Canada, Australasia, South Africa and America, which share its objects of maintaining and advancing standards in the interests of patients by education, examination and training). In 1979 the College commissioned a new bronze bust of John Hunter which stands in the south-west corner of LINCOLN'S INN FIELDS gardens (*see* STATUES).

Most of the great surgeons, past and present, have been Fellows or Honorary Fellows of the College, which is rich in historical associations. Apart from John Hunter, Lord Lister, whose instruments are displayed in a special cabinet in the College, and Sir Arthur Keith and Richard Owen, both of whom worked for many years in the College museum, are worthy of special note. Horatio Nelson's name appears in a list of naval officers whose wounds were assessed for compensation by the Court of Examiners of the Company of Surgeons in 1797.

Dentistry emerged as a learned profession from within the College in 1869 and Sir John Tomes and his son, Sir Charles Tomes, two of the pioneers of dentistry, were both connected with the College. The reigning sovereign has been Visitor to the college since 1937, and its links with the throne go back to George III who presented the ceremonial mace. The college's library, built up by the Council since 1800, now has over 120,000 volumes.

Royal College of Veterinary Surgeons *32 Belgrave Square, SW1*. The governing body of the veterinary profession founded by Royal Charter in 1844. All veterinary surgeons practising in the United Kingdom and Northern Ireland must be registered members of the college.

Royal Commonwealth Society *Northumberland Avenue, WC2*. Founded as the Colonial Society in June 1868 to strengthen the bonds between Britain and her colonies. It was supported by Canadians and Australians resident in London, its first elected Fellow being Edward Wilson, the Australian newspaper proprietor. The Society's main activities were the building up of a library and publication of papers on colonial affairs. It was granted a Royal Charter in 1882 and opened a permanent headquarters in NORTHUMBERLAND AVENUE in 1885. In 1936 this was rebuilt on an extended site to include full-scale club facilities. The building was damaged by bombing in 1941 but fully restored by 1957. The following year the Society's name was changed from the Royal Colonial Institute to the Royal Commonwealth Society. The Society has a membership of some 23,000.

Royal Court Theatre *Sloane Square, SW1*. In 1870 a Dissenters' chapel on the south side of the square was converted into a small local theatre. The next year it was reconstructed by Walter Emden for Marie Litton. It was known as the New Chelsea, 1870–1, and as the Belgravia, 1871–88. In 1875–9 it became well known under the management of the Kendals and John Hare. Between 1885 and 1887 John Clayton staged a series of Pinero comedies here. These included *The Magistrate* (1885), *The Schoolmistress* (1886) and *Dandy Dick* (1887). In 1887–8 the present theatre, designed by Walter Emden and W.R. Crewe, was built on the east side of the square. It opened under the joint management of Mrs John Wood and Arthur Chudleigh. Pinero's *The Weaker Sex* (1889) and *The Cabinet Minister* (1890) were produced. Mrs Wood then left and, on his own, Chudleigh staged *The Amazons* (1893) and *Trelawny of the Wells* (1898). In 1904–7 the theatre was run by J.S. Leigh, J.E. Vendrenne and Granville-Barker. It is one of the most notable periods in the history of the London stage: 32 plays by 17 authors were produced. Many of Shaw's plays were first publicly performed here and rehearsed under his direction including *Candida* (1904), *John Bull's Other Island* (1904), *Major Barbara* (1905), *The Doctor's Dilemma* (1906), *The Philanderer* (1907) and *The Man of Destiny* (1907). In 1907 Otho Stuart produced *Lady Frederick* by Somerset Maughan. During the 1st World War the theatre was mainly occupied by visiting companies and amateur productions. The first production of Shaw's *Heartbreak House* was performed in 1921. In 1924–8 the theatre was managed by Barry Jackson. His outstanding success was *The Farmer's Wife* (1924) by Eden Phillpotts which ran for three years. Closed in 1932, the theatre became a cinema in 1934. Bombed in 1940, it was rebuilt in 1952 by Robert Cromie for the London Theatre Guild and Alfred Esdaile. In 1954 the revue, *Airs on a Shoestring*, began its run of 772 performances. In 1956 the English Stage Company under the direction of George Devine, took the theatre and it has since become known for its adventurous productions. Many new plays have been first staged here including Wesker's *Roots* (1959) and *Chips with Everything* (1962) and Osborne's *Look Back in Anger* (1956), *The Entertainer* (1957), *Inadmissible Evidence* (1964), *A Patriot for Me* (1965) and *Hotel in Amsterdam* (1968). The seating capacity is 401.

Royal Courts of Justice *see* LAW COURTS.

Royal Dock Commonly called King's Yard. It was created in 1513 at DEPTFORD south of the HOWLAND DOCK, for the building and maintenance of Henry VIII's navy. Its water covered 36 acres. Queen Elizabeth knighted Francis Drake there in 1581 when she was inspecting the *Golden Hind*. As Secretary to the Navy, Samuel Pepys often visited the place, and after one visit recorded in his *Diary:* 'Never till now did I see the great authority of my place, all the captains of the fleete coming cap in hand to us.' At the end

of the 17th century Peter the Great worked in the yard as a ship's carpenter for three months in order to understand ship-design; he then resided nearby at Sayes Court which belonged to John Evelyn, the diarist. In the 19th century the King's Yard became the Royal Marine Arsenal and in 1869 the CITY CORPORATION bought most of it for use as a market for imported cattle. Another naval shipyard was also built downriver at WOOLWICH.

Royal Entomological Society of London *41 Queen's Gate, SW7*. Founded in 1833 following other short-lived societies which dated back to 1745. Its first meetings were held in the THATCHED HOUSE TAVERN in ST JAMES'S STREET and other places until it bought its present premises in 1920. It received its Royal Charter in 1885 and in 1933 was permitted to add Royal to its title. The Society has one of the world's finest entomological libraries.

Royal Exchange *Threadneedle Street and Cornhill, EC3*. LOMBARD STREET was the traditional meeting place for merchants to conduct their business but, according to Stow, it had its shortcomings: 'The merchants and tradesmen, as well English as strangers, for their general making of bargains, contracts and commerce, did usually meet twice every day. But these meetings were unpleasant and troublesome, by reason of walking and talking in an open street, being there constrained to endure all extremes of weather, or else to shelter themselves in shops. . . .' From the early years of the 16th century plans to provide a proper exchange building were under discussion in the CITY. The English Merchant Adventurers, who received their charter in 1509, formed their headquarters in Antwerp, and when Sir Richard Gresham, a prominent Adventurer, visited Antwerp he was so impressed by the fine bourse there that he submitted to Thomas Cromwell designs for a similar building in London, asking Cromwell to enlist the King's help in obtaining a suitable site. Gresham wrote, 'The last year I showed your good Lordship a platte, that was drawn out for to make a goodly burse in Lombard Street for merchants to repair unto . . . which shall be very beautiful for the City and also for the honour of our soverign Lord the King.' But negotiations for a site proved unsuccessful, in spite of letters written by the King supporting the project.

In 1552 Sir Richard's son, Thomas Gresham, also a successful merchant, was appointed 'King's Merchant' or agent, at Antwerp, becoming virtually English Ambassador to Europe and chief of the foreign intelligence service. Sir Thomas was also impressed by Antwerp's bourse, and was determined to work towards a similar trading centre in London. His right-hand man and factor in Antwerp was Richard Clough of Denbighshire who wholeheartedly supported the idea of a London bourse. Enmity between England and Spain, resulting in mounting trading difficulties with Flanders, reinforced in Gresham's and Clough's minds the dire need for an Exchange in London; and after the death of his only son in 1564, Gresham determined to devote some of his vast wealth towards this end.

It was first planned to build the bourse between LOMBARD STREET and CORNHILL, but negotiations to purchase this site came to nothing and instead the CITY bought a site in CORNHILL. At Christmas 1565 warning

Hollar's 1644 engraving of the Royal Exchange, opened by Elizabeth I in 1570. Statues of monarchs decorate the courtyard.

was given to 45 householders – mostly clothworkers and drapers – occupying 36 houses and two gardens in BROAD STREET and Swan, New and St Christopher's Alleys in CORNHILL, that they must vacate the site by 25 March following. The purchase price of £3,737 0s 6d was raised by subscriptions from 750 leading merchants and citizens; materials from the demolished premises fetched £478. The bourse was built at the personal expense of Gresham, perhaps assisted by Richard Clough. The first brick was laid by Gresham on 7 June 1566, and most of the materials were imported from Antwerp under Clough's personal supervision – slates from Dort, wainscoting and glass from Amsterdam. The roof was slated by November 1567 and work completed shortly after. It was a long four-storeyed building resembling the bourses at Antwerp and Venice, its bell-tower surmounted by a huge grasshopper, an emblem from the Gresham crest. There were also grasshoppers at each corner of the main building and on top of each dormer window. A statue of Gresham was set up at the north end of the western piazza in 1622, and the niches above the covered walks facing the courtyard were filled with statues of English monarchs. A statue of Elizabeth I by Nicholas Stone, made for the Exchange, was rejected by the CITY as unsuitable; it may now be seen at the entrance to the old GUILDHALL LIBRARY. Above the piazza were small shops – milliners, armourers, apothecaries, booksellers and goldsmiths. On 23 January 1570, having dined with Sir Thomas Gresham, Queen Elizabeth toured the bourse and then caused it 'by an herald and trumpet to be proclaimed The Royal Exchange, and so to be called from henceforth and not otherwise.' Richard Clough never saw the completed Exchange, falling ill in Hamburg in January 1570 and dying there a few months later. Gresham himself died in 1579, leaving the Royal Exchange, after his wife's decease, jointly to his own livery company and the CITY OF LONDON.

The Exchange soon became a resort for idlers, and in 1570 women were prosecuted for selling fruit at the CORNHILL gate and 'amusing themselves in cursing and swearing to the great annoyance and grief of the inhabitants and passers-by.' But its worth as a trading centre became increasingly apparent until its destruction in the GREAT FIRE, when 'the fire ran around the galleries, filling them with flames, then descending the

A bird's eye view of the second Royal Exchange, 1674. Designed by Edward Jarman, it opened in 1669 and was burned down in 1838.

stairs ... giving forth flaming vollies, and filling the courts with sheets of fire.' Christopher Wren proposed making a new Exchange the central point of the CITY; Evelyn planned its removal to QUEENHITHE. Both plans fell through and Edward Jarman, the CITY surveyor, undertook the design. The foundation stone of the new, larger building was laid on 6 May 1667. Expenditure amounted to £69,979 11s 0d. It was opened to merchants on 28 September 1669. A second series of statues of monarchs in the niches round the courtyard was donated by CITY LIVERY COMPANIES, and additions were made to the series up to the time of George IV. A statue of Charles II by Grinling Gibbons, commissioned by the Merchant Adventurers, stood in the centre of the courtyard, but this was replaced by a statue by Spiller in 1792. There were also statues of Charles I and II and Gresham, by John Bushnell, on the CORNHILL face of the tower. It proved difficult to let all the shops, and the main part of the building was eventually occupied, during the 18th century, by the Royal Exchange Assurance, LLOYD'S, the Gresham Lecture Room, and the Lord Mayor's Court Office. The vaults were let to bankers and to the East India Company for the stowage of pepper. Fire, believed to have started in LLOYD'S rooms, destroyed the second Exchange on 10 January 1838. Some of the carvings and statuary survived the fire. The statue of Charles II by Spiller was repaired and replaced in the south-east corner of the courtyard; Bushnell's statues from the tower were removed and are now at the OLD BAILEY, and two reliefs by George Bubb, made in 1822, also from the tower, are now in the garden at Hatfield. Other carvings, including many of the series of monarchs, were sold by auction in April 1838, but cannot now be traced. Opening the third bourse on 28 October 1844, Queen Victoria, following the example of Elizabeth I nearly 300 years before, went to the central quadrangle and announced: 'It is my royal will and pleasure that this building be hereafter called The Royal Exchange.'

The classical building was designed by Sir William Tite, and involved the demolition of Christopher Wren's ST BENET FINK. The massive portico, with its eight Corinthian columns, has a pediment with sculpture by Richard Westmacott consisting of 17 figures carved in limestone, the central figure being that of Commerce. The large central court has a Turkish pavement, relic of the first Exchange, and the walls display scenes from London's history painted by Lord Leighton, Frank Owen Salisbury, Sir Frank Brangwyn, Sigmund Goetze and others. On the north side of the Exchange are statues of Richard Whittington by J.E. Carew, and of Sir Hugh Myddelton by S. Joseph. Against the tower, in a niche, is a statue of Gresham by William Behnes. A statue of Queen Victoria by T.G. Lough was placed in the centre of the courtyard, but this was replaced in 1896 by one by Hamo Thornycroft. In 1951 this was moved to the northwest corner of the Exchange. There are also statues of Prince Albert, of Elizabeth I by M.L. Watson, and a bust of Abraham Lincoln by Andrew O'Connor. In front of The Exchange is a memorial to London troops of the two World Wars by Sir Aston Webb with bronzes by Alfred Drury.

The Exchange ceased its original function in 1939. The offices are still occupied by the Guardian Royal Exchange Assurance Company and the courtyard is used mainly as an exhibition area. The outside steps are one of the places from which a new sovereign is proclaimed.

Congested horse-drawn traffic outside the third Royal Exchange. Designed by Tite, it was opened by Queen Victoria in 1844.

Royal Festival Hall *Belvedere Road, SE1*. A large concert hall – designed by Sir Robert Matthew and J.L. Martin (1949–51) and Sir Hubert Bennett (1962–5) – whose stage has room for 100 players. The hall can be used not only for choral and orchestral concerts and recitals but also for film and ballet performances (when a special proscenium arch is put up). The organ, designed by Ralph Downes, was installed in 1954. The seating capacity fluctuates according to the type of performance from 3,111 (recital) to 2,299 (ballet).

Royal Foundation of St Katharine *2 Butcher Row, E14*. Founded in 1148 by Queen Matilda on land adjoining the TOWER granted by the Augustinian priory at ALDGATE for the maintenance of 'thirteen poor persons' and for prayers to be said in perpetuity for her soul and those of her family. The foundation became independent of ALDGATE at the beginning of the 13th century and has ever since been under the patronage of the Queens of England. Queen Eleanor, wife of Henry III, was responsible for the grant of a charter establishing a chapter of brothers and sisters under religious vows who were to care for the old and ill, grant hospitality to strangers and provide education. St Katharine's escaped dissolution in the reign of Henry VIII, whose first wife, Catherine of Aragon, was allowed to remain its patron. The Master officiated at her funeral. During the next two centuries numerous foreigners, who were not allowed within the City walls, were admitted by the chapter into their extensive precincts where many of them worked in brew houses and glass works. By the end of the 18th century there were as many as 3,000 inhabitants.

In 1825 the whole of St Katharine's was demolished for new docks and the inhabitants were evicted. The Master obtained compensation from the ST KATHARINE'S DOCK Company; and the foundation was granted land in REGENT'S PARK for the building of houses, a school and a chapel. During the 1st World War the chapel was granted to her fellow Danes by Queen Alexandra and it is now the principal Danish church in London (*see* ST KATHARINE'S, Regent's Park). After the 2nd World War, when Queen Mary was patron, St Katharine's returned to a site near its original area in the EAST END where the church of St James had been destroyed by bombing. The Georgian vicarage of St James's became the Master's house and wings were added for those who were to come for retreats and conferences. A small chapel was built and in it were incorporated the finely carved 14th-century stalls from the earlier chapel. In 1968 the patron, Queen Elizabeth, the Queen Mother, offered the care of the Foundation to the Community of the Resurrection (a priest member of which serves as Master) and the Deaconess Community of St Andrew. The Eucharist is daily celebrated in the chapel; and the present-day brothers and sisters undertake all kinds of social and educational work. Every year hundreds of people are welcomed for conferences, retreats, training courses and as private guests in search of quiet and spiritual refreshment.

Royal Free Hospital *Pond Street, Hampstead, NW3.* Founded by William Marsden, a young surgeon who was inspired with the idea of free admissions to hospitals when he found a young woman dying on the steps of ST ANDREW'S CHURCH in HOLBORN and was unable to get admission for her at any of the London hospitals which all then demanded letters of recommendation from a subscriber. On 14 February 1828, Marsden met members of the CORDWAINERS' COMPANY at the Gray's Inn Coffee House where they resolved to found the first hospital to admit patients without payment or a subscriber's letter. The hospital opened on 17 April 1828 under the patronage of King George IV and with the Duke of Gloucester as its first President. It has continued to receive royal patronage ever since. The original site was a small rented house at No. 16 Greville Street, HATTON GARDEN, with only a few beds. The hospital, though familiarly called 'The Free Hospital', was officially known as The London General Institution for the Gratuitous Care of Malignant Diseases. In 1837, when Queen Victoria became Patron, she asked that it should henceforth be known as The Royal Free Hospital. In the first year 926 patients were treated. In the second year the hospital dealt with 1,551 cases. In 1832 over 700 cholera patients were treated. A matron and nurse were employed while the epidemic lasted. In 1839 another house was acquired and the number of beds rose from 30 to 72.

With rapidly growing public support, a larger building was necessary, and in 1843 the hospital moved to a site in GRAY'S INN ROAD which had formerly been the barracks of the Light Horse Volunteers. The lease was purchased on 31 August 1843. The hospital extended its facilities on the new site, the Sussex Wing being opened in 1856 in memory of the Duke of Sussex. In 1877 the teaching of students began, and thus the hospital became one of the first of the London undergraduate teaching hospitals. The Victoria Wing with an out-patient department was added in 1878; and the Alexandra Building was opened by the Prince of Wales in 1895. The numerous benefactors included Lord Riddell, Sir Albert Levy, Freemasons, and several of the CITY LIVERY COMPANIES. Apart from the pioneer principle of its inception, the Royal Free took a leading part in two other important aspects of hospital work, the introduction of women medical students in 1877 and of a Lady Almoner in 1895.

The admission of women to study medicine was the most momentous step in the history of the hospital and the provision of clinical facilities for women students marked the triumphant climax of a struggle for recognition that had been going on for some years by a small group of brave and determined women led by Elizabeth Garrett Anderson and Sophia Jex-Blake. Until 1894 all the medical members of the consultant and resident staff were men, but in that year Miss L.B. Aldrich-Blake was appointed as honorary anaesthetist. In the following year she obtained the MS London, the first woman to secure this qualification and she subsequently became a distinguished surgeon on the hospital staff. In 1901 women were accepted as resident medical officers.

In 1921 it became the first hospital in England to have an obstetrics and gynaecology unit. In 1926–30 the Eastman Dental Hospital was built to the designs of Burnet, Tait and Lorne. The Royal Free suffered severe damage in the 2nd World War, with considerable loss of beds.

In 1948, with the inception of the National Health Service, the Royal Free Hospital became the centre of a group of hospitals which included the HAMPSTEAD GENERAL HOSPITAL, the ELIZABETH GARRETT ANDERSON HOSPITAL, the London Fever Hospital (Liverpool Road), the North West Fever Hospital (Lawn Road) and subsequently also New End and Coppetts Wood Hospitals. The ELIZABETH GARRETT ANDERSON HOSPITAL later separated from the group while the Hampstead General, North West Fever and London Fever Hospitals were incorporated with the parent hospital and its medical school in the new Royal Free Hospital, which was built on its present site to the designs of Watkins, Gray, Woodgate International. The first patient was admitted in October 1974; the hospital was in full use by March 1975; and it was officially opened by the Queen on 15 November 1978. There are 1,070 beds comprising 852 in the new building, 144 at New End Hospital (New End, NW3) and 74 at Coppetts Wood Hospital (Coppetts Road, MUSWELL HILL, N10).

Royal Fusiliers *see* REGIMENTS.

Royal Fusiliers' Regimental Museum *Tower of London, EC3.* The TOWER OF LONDON was the birthplace of this regiment in 1685. In 1881 it was given the additional name of City of London Regiment. More recently it has amalgamated with other fusilier regiments and the overall title is the Royal Regiment of Fusiliers (*see* REGIMENTS). The Museum has an entrance hall and three main rooms where exhibits are displayed. These include oil paintings and uniforms of distinguished members, a number of Victoria Crosses, other medals and relics of various campaigns. There are also some dioramas of battles in which the regiment has fought.

Royal Garden Hotel *Kensington High Street, W8.* A T-shaped glass and steel building overlooking KENSINGTON GARDENS, built in 1965 to the designs of R. Seifert and Partners. There are 434 bedrooms.

Royal Geographical Society *Lowther Lodge, Kensington Gore, SW7.* Founded as the Geographical Society of London in 1830 by John Barrow, Secretary to the Admiralty; Robert Brown of the LINNEAN SOCIETY; John Britton, topographer; Mountstuart Elphinstone, diplomat; G.C. Renouard, scholar of oriental languages; Thomas Colby, Director of the Ordnance

Survey; John Hobhouse, MP for WESTMINSTER; Francis Baily of the ROYAL ASTRONOMICAL SOCIETY; W.H. Smyth, astronomer and oceanographer; and Roderick Murchison, geologist. The Society was an offshoot of the TRAVELLERS' CLUB (whose members must have travelled a distance of 500 miles outside the British Isles measured in a straight line) and the dining club, The Raleigh (which still survives as the Geographical Club). The new Society, of which William IV agreed to be Patron, absorbed the African Association which had been in existence since 1788. In 1859 Queen Victoria granted a Royal Charter to the Geographical Society of London which thereafter became the Royal Geographical Society. The Charter stated that the purpose of the Society was 'the Advancement of Geographical Science' and 'the improvement and diffusion of geographical knowledge'. The first meetings were held at the premises of the (ROYAL) HORTICULTURAL SOCIETY in LOWER REGENT STREET. In 1839 the Society moved to No. 3 WATERLOO PLACE; in 1854 to No. 15 WHITEHALL PLACE; in 1858 to BURLINGTON HOUSE; in 1870 to No. 1 SAVILE ROW; and in 1911 to Lowther Lodge which had been built as a private residence for the Hon. William Lowther by Norman Shaw in 1874 and was the first house in London to have a passenger lift. In 1921 a bronze bust of Sir Clements Markham, the geographer and explorer, by F.W. Pomeroy, was erected in the forecourt. In 1930, the Society's centenary, the building was extended to provide a library, lecture hall and council rooms. In 1932 a bust by C. Sargeant Jagger of Sir Ernest Shackleton, the Arctic explorer, was placed in a niche on the outside wall facing EXHIBITION ROAD. The statue of David Livingstone facing Kensington Gore is by J.B. Huxley-Jones and was erected in 1953 (see STATUES). The Royal Geographical Society sponsors and organises expeditions into the unknown. In the past notable expeditions have been led by Burton, Speke, Baker, Stanley, Livingstone, Scott and Hillary. Livingstone lay in state in the SAVILE ROW map room before being buried at WESTMINSTER ABBEY. More recent expeditions include one to southern Iran and in 1980 one to the frontier regions of Afghanistan, Pakistan, China and the USSR, in conjunction with scientists from China and Pakistan. Fellows of the Society, of whom there are about 7,500, need have no special qualifications other than their nomination by two existing Fellows. The Society publishes a journal three times a year. The Society's library has 130,000 books for Fellows' and Members' use only; but the map room, containing a large amount of old and new maps, is open to the public.

Royal Group of Docks Lying east of Bow Creek on the Plaistow Marshes, these docks consist of the Royal Victoria, the Royal Albert and the King George V. These were the last to be built in London and, at 245 acres in all formed the largest area of impounded dock water in the world. Lying farthest to the east and therefore nearest to the sea, they were able to accommodate the largest ocean-going ships which were built even in the 20th century. The Victoria was constructed by the St Katharine's Dock Company and opened by Prince Albert in 1855 at the time of the Crimean War, its soil having been carried up river to consolidate the marshy land of BATTERSEA PARK, which was opened in 1859. The Victoria was an immediate financial success and the St Katharine's Company, amalgamating with

The 35,655-ton Mauretania *just manages to enter the King George V Dock on 6 August 1939.*

the London Dock Company, extended the Victoria to the east to form the Royal Albert which was opened in 1880 by the Duke of Connaught acting for the Queen. Three-quarters of a mile long with 3 miles of quay, it was even larger than the Victoria and provided another entrance to the east from Gallions Reach, the Victoria havings its entrance to the west from Bugsby's Reach. When built it was the finest dock in the world. Finally, under the PORT OF LONDON AUTHORITY, came the King George V Dock with 64 acres of water. Begun in 1912 under the supervision of the engineer, Frederick Palmer, its construction was delayed by the 1st World War and it was not completed until 1921. It lay south of the Albert, was smaller than its huge parent, and had its own entrance from Gallions Reach; yet it could berth P & O liners, and there in 1939 arrived the 35,655-ton *Mauretania*.

Together the Victoria and the Albert contain 175 acres of water and share seven miles of quay. They handled bulk grain and later frozen meat, fruit and vegetables as refrigeration methods improved. They also handled many other goods, and during the 2nd World War served as a naval and arms base.

The Victoria was the first to use the new railways to the full and this compensated for its distance of four miles from the CITY. It was also the first to be built for the iron steamships that ousted the old sailers, and the first also to use hydraulic cranes and lifts for raising ships in a pontoon dock. The Royal Albert (designed by Sir Alexander Rendel) was the first large undertaking to be lit throughout by electricity and was well served by railways extending on both sides as branches of the Great Eastern Railway. Apart from goods it docked large passenger steam ships. During the General Strike of 1926, a serious danger arose that the electricity supply might be cut off from the Royal Group where three-quarters of a million carcases of meat were in refrigeration, but the situation was saved by the arrival of two naval submarines whose generators, when coupled, were able to supply the precise amount of power required. Today, the Royals, like the rest of London's docks, are virtually moribund and the area awaits redevelopment.

Royal Hammersmith Hospital *Du Cane Road, W12.* In 1910 the Haldane Commission advocated the foundation of a large hospital to teach advanced medicine on academic principles, but it was not until 1921 that the Minister of Health, Lord Addison, appointed the Athlone Committee to consider the suggestion and not until 1925, when Neville Chamberlain was Minister, that action was taken. The existing medical schools were not prepared to help, but Sir Frederick Menzies, chief medical member of the LONDON COUNTY COUNCIL, suggested that one of the Council's municipal hospitals might be the first to become a teaching hospital. Hammersmith Hospital was chosen, partly because of its large site and partly because it was a fine Art Nouveau building designed by J.E. Trollope in 1904 and known as 'The Paupers' Paradise'. Here in a new small building opened by George V in 1935 the school began its work which was soon recognised throughout the world. In 1947 all postgraduate teaching in London was organised by Sir Francis Fraser, who had been Professor of Medicine at Hammersmith. He initiated the British Postgraduate Medical Federation which became part of the UNIVERSITY OF LONDON. In addition to the Royal Hammersmith, 12 other hospitals, renowned for their specialist research, joined the Federation, among them the HOSPITAL FOR SICK CHILDREN and THE NATIONAL HOSPITAL FOR NERVOUS DISEASES. Students from all over the world flocked to the school at Hammersmith which was, however, ill-equipped to deal with such numbers until the Wolfson Foundation provided a large new building and over a million pounds was collected for the construction of the Commonwealth Building designed by T.B.H. Ellis. The school's research work is internationally renowned. In 1982 the hospital had 677 beds.

Royal Historical Society *University College London, Gower Street, WC1.* Founded in 1868 and granted its Royal Charter of Incorporation in 1889. In 1897 the Camden Society was amalgamated with the Society. A principal object of the Society is to promote the study of history by publishing documentary material and, from time to time, bibliographical and reference works. The Library consists mainly of primary sources of British history.

Royal Holloway College *Egham, Surrey.* Founded by the philanthropist, Thomas Holloway, for the higher education of women. Its buildings, designed in the French Renaissance style and set in large grounds, were opened by Queen Victoria in 1886. In 1900 it was incorporated as one of the original Schools of LONDON UNIVERSITY. It has 14 academic departments in Arts and Science and provides for studies in Management, Drama and Theatre. Men have been admitted since 1965. It was announced in 1982 that the college was to merge with BEDFORD COLLEGE.

Royal Horticultural Society *Horticultural Halls, Vincent Square, SW1.* Founded in 1804 as the Horticultural Society of London in a room above HATCHARD'S book shop by a group of enthusiastic gardeners and botanists called together by John Wedgwood, the eldest son of Josiah Wedgwood, the potter. Meetings were first held at the premises of the LINNEAN SOCIETY in PANTON SQUARE and later in GERRARD STREET. An experimental garden adjoining EDWARDES SQUARE and a nursery garden at KENSINGTON were established in 1818. The next year a house in LOWER REGENT STREET was bought. In 1821 the Society took a lease on 33 acres at CHISWICK from the Duke of Devonshire and the gardens in KENSINGTON were given up. Joseph Paxton worked at Chiswick as gardener and here came to the notice of the Duke of Devonshire. In 1826 Paxton was promoted head gardener at Chatsworth where he later designed the great conservatory, the prototype of the CRYSTAL PALACE. The first fête was held in the gardens at CHISWICK in 1827, and in 1831 the first floral exhibition was held in LOWER REGENT STREET, but the house was too small and in subsequent years the exhibitions were held at CHISWICK. In 1855 the Society found themselves in financial difficulties; and in 1859 the house in LOWER REGENT STREET had to be sold. But, through the influence of Prince Albert, who had become President in 1858, the commissioners of the GREAT EXHIBITION granted a lease of the central area of their South Kensington estate to the society.

The commissioners undertook to surround the whole ground with beautiful Italian arcades and execute extensive ground works at a cost of £50,000, provided the Society spent an equal amount on the layout of the gardens and the erection of a conservatory. The grounds were landscaped by Nesfield and the arcades and conservatory designed by Sydney Smirke and Captain Fowke under the supervision of Prince Albert. The Gardens were opened by Albert in 1861 when the society became the Royal Horticultural Society. Prince Albert saw the gardens as 'a valuable attempt . . . to reunite the science and art of gardening to the sister arts of Architecture, Sculpture and Painting.' The INTERNATIONAL EXHIBITION of 1862 was held in a large glass and iron building erected to the south of the gardens. Visitors could see the gardens for a small admission fee. The Exhibition building was demolished in 1864. From 1871 to 1874 a series of International Exhibitions was held in the gardens organised by Henry Cole, but these were not successful. And in 1882, the society having found the gardens too expensive to maintain, the Commissioners terminated the lease and they were dismantled.

The Fisheries Exhibition was held on the site in 1883 followed by the Health Exhibition in 1884, the Inventions Exhibition in 1885 and the Colonial and Indian Exhibition in 1886. PRINCE CONSORT and IMPERIAL INSTITUTE ROADS were built across the site in 1887. The gardens at Wisley, Surrey were presented to the society in 1903 by Sir Thomas Hanbury, and the garden at CHISWICK was given up. The Royal Horticultural Hall designed by E.J. Stebbs was built in VINCENT SQUARE for exhibitions and opened in 1904. A new hall, designed by Murray Easton, was built behind it in GREYCOAT STREET in 1927–8. Regular exhibitions are held in both of these halls and in May in the ground of the ROYAL HOSPITAL, CHELSEA (*see* CHELSEA FLOWER SHOW). The Lindley Library at VINCENT SQUARE, which was established in 1868, contains over 36,000 books and is one of the leading horticultural libraries in the world.

Royal Hospital, Chelsea see CHELSEA HOSPITAL.

Royal Hospital and Home for Incurables
West Hill, Putney, SW15. Founded in 1854 by Dr
Andrew Reed at CARSHALTON in Surrey. In 1855
Charles Dickens became Chairman. In 1863 the hospital moved to Melrose Hall, West Hill, which at that
time was in the country. The grounds, extending to
over 30 acres, had been planned by 'Capability' Brown
and improved by Repton. Six new wings were added
between 1868 and 1980. When the National Health
Service was formed in 1948 the hospital authorities
protested against being taken over. They won their
case and have remained a voluntary organisation ever
since.

Royal Hospital Burial Ground see BURIAL
GROUNDS.

Royal Hospital Road *SW3.* Formerly known as
Queen's Road, it extends westwards from CHELSEA'S
WESTMINSTER border to CHEYNE WALK. It contains
the whole of the northern frontage of the ROYAL HOS-
PITAL, hence its name, and that of Chelsea Physic
Garden. Between the two now stands the NATIONAL
ARMY MUSEUM, opened by HM the Queen in 1971 to
display the history of the British Army from the reign
of Henry VII. It also tells the story of the Indian Army
up to the partition of 1947, and of other Commonwealth armies up to their independence. Many fine
houses once stood in this road including Gough House
built in about 1707 and later lived in by the 3rd Earl of
Carbery, President of the ROYAL SOCIETY.

Royal Institute of British Architects *66 Portland Place, W1.* Founded in 1834 as the Institute of
British Architects. The first meeting of the Council
was held on 10 December of that year at the THATCHED
HOUSE TAVERN. By the following year the Institute
was established at No. 43 KING STREET, COVENT GAR-
DEN; and the first President, Earl de Grey, was elected
at a Council meeting on 3 February 1835. He continued in office until his death in 1859. A Royal Charter was granted by William IV in 1837, and in 1866 the
title Royal was conferred by Queen Victoria. The supplemental charter of 1887 made compulsory the
examination in architecture for associate membership;
and the first Code of Professional Conduct was
published in 1901. In 1837 the Institute moved to
No. 16 LOWER GROSVENOR STREET, and in 1859 to
No. 9 CONDUIT STREET where it remained until 1934
when it moved to its present address in PORTLAND
PLACE. The Institute comprises some 27,000 members
of which 5,000 are overseas. In addition there are
approximately 2,000 student members. The Institute
is governed by a Council of 60 members under the
chairmanship of the President whose term of office
is two years. Since the death of the first President,
Earl de Grey, there have been 58 Presidents including
such famous architects as C.R. Cockerell, Sir George
Gilbert Scott, Charles Barry, Alfred Waterhouse,
Sir Reginald Blomfield, H.S. Goodhart-Rendel, Sir
Edwin Lutyens, Sir Basil Spence, Professor Sir
Robert Matthew and Eric Lyons. The main aims and
objectives of the Institute were first stated in the 1837
Royal Charter as being for the general advancement of
Civil Architecture, and for promoting and facilitating
the acquisition of the knowledge of the various Arts

and Sciences connected therewith. These purposes
remain the same today. Although the RIBA is the main
professional body for architects, comprising 82 per
cent of practising architects for its membership, all
architects whether or not they are members of the
Institute must be registered with the Architects
Registration Council of the United Kingdom, an independent body set up by Act of Parliament in 1931.
No one may practise under the title 'architect' unless
his name is on the register. In 1971 a supplemental
Charter introduced a single class of corporate membership (RIBA) which replaced the three previous classes
of Fellow (FRIBA), Associate (ARIBA), and Licentiate (LRIBA), although these titles may continue to
be used by members who acquired them before the
new rule came into force. In order to assist clients in
the selection of architects for specific jobs, the RIBA
maintains a free Clients' Advisory Service. By means
of comprehensive records and modern retrieval
methods, lists of suitably qualified architects can be
provided for any design, planning or consultancy
requirement. As a learned society, the Institute's most
important aid to practice and scholarship is the British
Architectural Library which together with its Drawings Collection at the Heinz Gallery, 21 PORTMAN
SQUARE, is one of the most comprehensive collections
of architectural material in the world.

Royal Institute of International Affairs
Chatham House, 10 St James's Square, SW1. At the
end of the 1st World War, the need for better information and exchange of ideas about international affairs
was recognised by a group of experts who had attended
the Peace Conference. Amongst their number were
Viscount Cecil later President of the League of Nations Union, Lionel Curtis, one of the founders of the
Round Table and author of *Civitas Dei*, Philip Noel-
Baker, later Stevenson Professor of International History, LONDON SCHOOL OF ECONOMICS, Sir Charles
Webster, the Labour Member of Parliament and
former Cassel Professor of International Relations at
the UNIVERSITY OF LONDON, Lord Eustace Percy,
Lord Cecil's assistant at the Peace Conference,
Geoffrey Dawson, Editor of *The Times* and political
historian, and Sir James Headlam-Morley. They
decided to form a permanent organisation which was
inaugurated on 5 July 1920. Called the British Institute of International Affairs, its objects were 'to encourage and facilitate the study of international questions to promote the exchange of information and
thought on international affairs with a view to the creation of better informed public opinion and to publish
... works with these objects.' In July 1921, headquarters were opened in MALET STREET, BLOOMSBURY
where small meetings were held, larger meetings taking
place in the hall of the ROYAL SOCIETY OF ARTS. The
generosity of two Canadians, Mr and Mrs R.M. Leonard, allowed the Institute to purchase more suitable
premises in St James's Square in a house once
occupied by William Pitt, Earl of Chatham (*see* ST
JAMES'S SQUARE). Chatham House was opened in
1923 and the Institute received its Royal Charter from
George V in 1926. Further gifts allowed the Institute
to buy adjacent houses, No. 6 DUKE STREET and No. 9
ST JAMES'S SQUARE, so that it was able to have a large
meeting hall in addition to space for library and
research work. From the beginning the Institute had
maintained a policy of complete independence of

government or political influence. Membership was, and is, limited to 2,500 British subjects elected for their qualifications in some field of international affairs. In addition corporate subscribers of the Institute such as Shell, the Corporation of LLOYD'S and the BANK OF ENGLAND were allowed to nominate a number of members. Work of the Institute includes research into international problems and publication on such subjects, holding of meetings on current matters of interest which are from time to time addressed by men and women of international distinction. In addition, the Institute maintains a library and a press cuttings library.

Many distinguished people have been associated with the Institute, including the historians Dr Harold Temperley and Professor Arnold Toynbee. The library, which forms part of the Institute's information service, contains many thousands of books, pamphlets and documents on international affairs.

Royal Institute of Painters in Water Colours
17 Carlton House Terrace, SW1. Founded in 1831 as the New Society of Painters in Water Colours, two earlier and rival societies formed towards the beginning of the century having ceased to exist by the end of 1812. The Society held its first exhibition at 16 OLD BOND STREET in 1832. Fifty years later spacious galleries especially built for the Society were opened at 195 PICCADILLY; and soon afterwards Queen Victoria conferred upon the Society its present title which can be seen carved in the stone façade of the PICCADILLY building which also contains busts of the founders of the British school of water colour painting including those of Turner, Girtin and Cotman. The Institute's lease of the Piccadilly premises expired in 1970 and their MALL GALLERIES were opened by the Queen in 1971.

Royal Institution *Albemarle Street, W1.* Founded in 1799 by Benjamin Thompson, Count von Rumford for 'diffusing the knowledge and facilitating the general introduction of useful mechanical inventions and improvements, and for teaching by courses of philosophical lectures and experiments the application

Professor Tyndall, the Irish physicist, gives a lecture at the Royal Institution in 1870.

of science to the common purposes of life.' A house was taken in ALBEMARLE STREET and the library begun. In 1800 the institution was granted a royal charter by King George III. The next year Humphry Davy was engaged as assistant lecturer and director of the laboratory. He was made Professor of Chemistry in 1802 and held that post until 1823. Michael Faraday was engaged as Davy's assistant at 25s a week in 1812. In the 1830s Faraday conducted his experiments on electricity here, and in 1833 was made Professor of Chemistry, a post he held until 1867. The classical façade, based on the Temple of Antoninus, Rome, was added in 1838 by Lewis Vulliamy. In 1896 the Davy-Faraday Research Laboratory was set up at No. 20 ALBEMARLE STREET by Dr Ludwig Mond to develop chemical and physical science by original research. Many well known scientists have been Professors of the Royal Institution, including T.H. Huxley (1855–7 and 1865–8), Lord Rutherford (1921–27), Julian Huxley (1927–9) and John Haldane (1930–2).

Royal Institution of Chartered Surveyors *12 Great George Street, Parliament Square, SW1.* In 1794 a Surveyors Club was formed with 16 members who were principally architects and surveyors to the CITY LIVERY COMPANIES. The Institution of Surveyors was founded in 1868 and opened its headquarters at 12 GREAT GEORGE STREET. In 1881 Queen Victoria granted the first Royal Charter, although its present title was not adopted until 1946. Since that date, the Institution has amalgamated with many kindred associations.

Royal London Homeopathic Hospital *Great Ormond Street, WC1.* Founded in GOLDEN SQUARE in 1850 by Dr Frederick Quin, the first homeopathic physician in England. The hospital moved to its present site in 1859 and was rebuilt in 1893–6 to the designs of W.A. Pite, and extended in 1909 by E.T. Hall. In 1948 it was given the title 'Royal', by command of George VI.

Royal Marsden Hospital *Fulham Road, SW3.* Founded in 1851 as the Cancer Hospital (Free) by William Marsden, a doctor who was greatly moved by the plight of the sick poor in Victorian London and who, 23 years before, had founded what is now the ROYAL FREE HOSPITAL. The aims of the Cancer Hospital, for which no patient required a letter of introduction, were to treat the poor without charge, and to make a study of the disease. It was the first purely Cancer Hospital in the world and started as a small Outpatient's Dispensary in CANNON ROW, WESTMINSTER, but in 1862 the present buildings in FULHAM ROAD were opened. The Cancer Hospital began in the face of great official opposition. Queen Victoria refused her patronage, declining 'to contribute to a hospital devoted exclusively to a single malady when those who suffered from it were not excluded from general hospitals.' However, she eventually relented and in 1860 gave a donation of £100. From the 1890s on, the Queen headed the donation list in the Annual Report with a gift of 'pheasants and cast-off linen'.

To assist in the development of research a 'pathological anatomist' was appointed in 1856. This was Robert Knox of Edinburgh, a brilliant anatomist whose career had been blighted by being the undoubtedly innocent recipient for his Anatomy School of the wares of Burke and Hare in the 1820s. In 1909 the Cancer Hospital Research Institute was founded. In 1939 the Hospital used a donation given by Sir Chester Beatty to move much of the research work of the Institute a little way down FULHAM ROAD to the old Freemasons' Hospital, which had recently moved to BARON'S COURT, and it was named the Chester Beatty Research Institute. The building had, in fact, originally been the CHELSEA HOSPITAL FOR WOMEN.

In addition to its surgical work the hospital has a proud history of pioneer work in treatment with radiation and radioactive materials and more recently in the development of chemotherapy. There are now 385 beds, divided between FULHAM ROAD and SUTTON. Its research partner, the Institute of Cancer Research, operates on both those sites as well as at Pollards Wood in Buckinghamshire. The name was changed from Cancer to Royal Marsden in 1954.

Royal Mews *Buckingham Palace Road, SW1.* The Riding House was built to the designs of Sir William Chambers in 1763–6 and was ornamented with its acanthus frieze and pediment at the beginning of the 19th century. The spirited group on the pediment, *Hercules Capturing the Thracian Horses,* is by William Theed, the Elder. The Mews themselves were built in 1824–5. Here may be seen the carriage horses, royal cars and carriages including the Gold State Coach which was made for George III in 1762 and has been used at CORONATIONS ever since. It was designed by Sir William Chambers and painted by Cipriani with a series of emblematical subjects. It cost £7,661 16s 5d. The Irish Coach, made in Dublin in 1852, was bought by Queen Victoria for the STATE OPENING OF PARLIAMENT. The Glass State Coach was bought in 1910 by George V for royal weddings. The Royal Mews come under the jurisdiction of the Master of the Horse and are administered by the Crown Equerry who is responsible for the Queen's 30 horses (10 Greys and 20 Bays), her five coachmen, 15 grooms (who act as postilions on ceremonial occasions) and her 70 carriages, from state coaches to phaetons, all in working order. He also has charge of her 20-odd cars, including the £60,000 three-ton Phantom Six Rolls Royce which was presented to her in 1978 by the Society of Motor Manufacturers as a Jubilee present.

Royal Mews *Charing Cross, see* TRAFALGAR SQUARE.

Royal Mews *Hampton Court Green, Middlesex.* Consists of two buildings. The one on the left was built for Henry VIII in 1536 as the King's New Stable. The one on the right was built in 1570 for Queen Elizabeth and was formerly known as the Queen's New Stable. The King's New Stable had a characteristic Tudor archway and a courtyard with stables and coachhouses and accommodation for grooms on the floor above. Queen Elizabeth's extension consisted mainly of two barns and a coach-house with garrets above. On the abandonment of the PALACE as a royal residence, there was little for the Mewskeeper to do and he was allowed to convert the left-hand part of the King's Stable into an inn, known as the Chequers. The Mewskeeper had a windfall in 1794 when George III authorised the posting of 200 cavalrymen to HAMPTON COURT. The Chequers was given up about 1840. The Horse Rangers Trust now has its headquarters in the Royal Mews.

Royal Military Academy *Woolwich, SE18.* There was a school for potential officers of the artillery at WOOLWICH as early as 1719. In 1741 the Board of Ordnance took steps to 'institute, endow and support an academy': this was located in a convenient room in Woolwich Warren and in 1752 it moved into specially built barracks. The title 'The Company of Gentlemen Cadets' was applied from the mid-18th until the early 19th century when a new academy was built; the strength increased from 40 to 246 over that period. The academy was fully established by 1810. Following the Napoleonic Wars, the number of cadets was appreciably reduced and the position did not improve until the 1830s.

The Royal Military Academy, referred to as 'The Shop' over a long period, has trained potential officers for the Royal Artillery and Royal Engineers and, more recently, for the Royal Corps of Signals. It amalgamated with the Royal Military College at Sandhurst in 1947. The concept of amalgamation of the two institutions had been argued for more than a century.

Royal Mint *Tower Hill, EC3.* According to Herodotus there was a Mint in Lydia in about the 8th century BC. Coins were of gold and uninscribed. The art of coining passed to this country by way of the Romans. Native coins inscribed as in the Roman fashion have been identified bearing names of ancient British chiefs, but their use died out as they were superseded by Roman coinage. The right of coinage has always been a royal prerogative, exercised with varying degrees of honesty and efficiency, by successive monarchs; from the Anglo-Saxon period kings were in the habit of creating their own mints and of issuing coins bearing their own effigy and place of origin. The addition of the name of the moneyer gave proof of the coin's integrity. Severe punishment was meted out for offences against coinage, including cutting off the right hand and emasculation.

Evidence suggests that the London Mint was founded in AD 825. It was later established in the Treasury and Exchequer buildings and in 1300 transferred to a site between the inner and outer walls of the TOWER OF LONDON. Its pre-eminence was firmly established by the 14th century. Successive edicts had given it control over all designs and dies, and all coinage was eventually carried out in the Tower Mint. The appointment in 1279 of William de Turnemire as Master Moneyer throughout England completed its ascendancy. Operations were eventually governed by an Indenture between the King and the Master of the Mint – a post held with success and distinction by Sir Isaac Newton from 1699–1727. The office was eventually abolished in 1870 and the Chancellor of the Exchequer is now (*ex officio*) Master of the Mint. The employment of an artistengraver to design the coinage, and the royal effigy, led to improvements in appearance and portraiture. The model for Britannia on the Charles II coinage was said to have been Frances Stewart, afterwards Duchess of Richmond, mistress of the King. For some years the penny (its origin indirectly derived from the Roman *denarius*) was the only coin minted; small change being obtained by halving and quartering. From the 14th century onwards other coins were produced, all now made obsolete by decimalisation.

Pressure for space from the Tower garrison, and from machinery, compelled the Mint's removal at the beginning of the 19th century to a new building on

Little Tower Hill, designed and executed in the neo-classical style by James Johnson, and after his death, Sir Robert Smirke. Coins were first struck there in 1810. In 1798 a man named Turnbull successfully robbed the Mint of 2,804 guineas by holding the staff at gunpoint. In 1971 dock development excavations revealed a tunnel leading from the ST KATHARINE DOCK to the walls of the Mint. Thought to indicate a projected robbery, it proved to be part of a feasibility study on the possibility of a pedestrian underpass. The great increase in the demand for internal circulating coins and from commerce, and latterly for the whole process of decimalisation, resulted in the transfer of the Mint to large new buildings at Llantrisant in South Wales where coins were first minted in 1968. Since 1975 no coins have been minted in the Tower Hill buildings and the shop and exhibitions there were closed in 1980 because of the imminent redevelopment of the site.

Royal Mint Street *E1.* Previously known as Rose-mary Lane, it was renamed in 1850, 40 years after the MINT moved from the TOWER OF LONDON. (It moved again to Wales in 1968.) Mayhew found the lodgings in the street inhabited by workers employed along the riverside and in the clothing industry, and in the famous Rag Fair he noticed that Irish, rather than Jewish, street sellers were predominant.

Royal National Orthopaedic Hospital *234 Great Portland Street, W1.* Originated in 1907 as an amalgamation of three hospitals. These were the Royal, formerly the Infirmary for the Cure of Club Feet and other Contractions, which was opened in 1840 at No. 6 BLOOMSBURY SQUARE and moved to No. 15 HANOVER SQUARE in 1856; the City, which was opened at No. 26 HATTON GARDEN in 1851; and the National which was founded in 1864 at No. 234 GREAT PORTLAND STREET. With the amalgamation the National was rebuilt to the designs of Roland Plumbe. In 1921 4½ acres were bought at STANMORE where the Mary Wardell Convalescent Home for Scarlet Fever had been opened in 1884 in a house, once known as Verulam House and later East Gate House, which Miss Wardell had bought the year before. In 1891 a purpose-built block had been added to this Home. The

new buildings, created in the 1920s when the STAN-MORE institution became part of the Royal National Orthopaedic Hospital, were designed by Mountford Piggot. During the 2nd World War additional build-ings were erected for military patients. Besides the hospital there is now associated a boot and instrument workshop and a bio-engineering department.

Royal National Throat, Nose and Ear Hospital *Gray's Inn Road, WC1.* Opened in 1875 and then known as the Central London Throat and Ear Hos-pital. It originally had only ten beds. This was the era of the establishment of specialist hospitals. Formal postgraduate courses started in 1865. The scope of these was extended over the years and in 1944 the Institute of Laryngology and Otology was formed as a member of the British Postgraduate Medical Federa-tion. Also a professional chair in Otolaryngology was created by LONDON UNIVERSITY. In 1939 the hospital was amalgamated with the small Ear, Nose and Throat Hospital at GOLDEN SQUARE, W1, which had been founded in 1862. In 1982 there were 230 beds in the combined hospitals.

Royal Naval College *Greenwich, SE10.* Consists of four blocks, King Charles's building, Queen Anne's building, King William's building and Queen Mary's building. It was built on the site of GREENWICH PALACE which had fallen into disrepair in the Civil War. In 1694 Wren demolished all that remained of the original palace, except for the undercroft now under Queen Anne's building. In 1967 this was restored by the Ministry of Works. Sir John Summerson has discovered that it was not part of the original palace, but was added by James I to strengthen the founda-tions which had been damaged by inadequate drainage. The earliest building, King Charles's, was intended as a wing of the new palace to be built to the designs of John Webb, a pupil of Inigo Jones. The foundation stone was laid in 1664, but by 1669 the King had lost interest in the project and money had run out. In 1692 the sight of the wounded of the vic-torious naval battle of La Hogue inspired Queen Mary to order building to begin around King Charles's wing in order to provide a Naval Hospital corresponding to the recently finished CHELSEA HOSPITAL. Christopher

Nelson's funeral procession passes the Royal Naval Hospital at Greenwich. From a drawing by A.C. Pugin, 1806.

Wren gave his services as architect free, and Nicholas Hawksmoor was his assistant. Controversy arose over the original plans which would have obscured the QUEEN'S HOUSE. Queen Mary ordered that the house should remain visible from the waterfront. The buildings were, therefore, split to produce the effect that Samuel Johnson described as 'too much detached to make one great whole'. Queen Anne's building was completed in 1728. Vanbrugh, who succeeded Wren, used the original plans. In 1705 the structure of King William's building was completed. But the façade of the west front, by Vanbrugh, was not completed for a further 21 years. In 1708 James Thornhill began the decoration of the Painted Hall, which consists of three levels, the Great Hall, the Upper Hall and the vestibule with cupola. The celebrated ceiling of the Great Hall represents William and his Queen handing Liberty and Peace to Europe. In 1805 Nelson lay in state in the Hall. Queen Mary's building houses the Chapel, completed in 1742 to Wren's designs. In 1779 it was destroyed by fire and rebuilt to the designs of James 'Athenian' Stuart. The fine boxwood pulpit, with scenes from St Paul's life, and the painting above the altar, *St Paul at Melita*, are by Benjamin West. In 1778 the pavilions were constructed. In 1834 the gates were removed to their present position and the Celestial and Terrestrial globes were placed at the West entrance. The grand structure was not an ideal place for a hospital, and in 1771 Captain Baillie complained that 'Columns, colonnades and friezes ill accord with bully beef and sour beer mixed with water.' After many accusations of cruelty and corruption on the part of those administering the Hospital, the number of pensioners fell off and in 1869 the buildings were vacated. In 1873 the Royal Naval College moved here from Portsmouth. The College now provides training for Royal Naval Officers and some other specialist officers of the armed forces.

Royal Northern Hospital *Holloway Road, N7.* Founded in 1856 with his own money by a young surgeon named Sherard Statham who leased 11 York Road (now York Way). It was then called the Great Northern Hospital and lay near KING'S CROSS, the terminus for the Great Northern Railway, in a densely populated area. Sadly, Statham never worked there, dying of phthisis in 1858, aged 32. The Metropolitan Railway Company needed the site for their new railway, so in 1862 the hospital moved to combine with the Spinal Hospital at No. 84 Portland Road. In 1869 it moved again to Caledonian Road. In 1876 Dr Robert Bridges, later Poet Laureate, was appointed to the staff. In 1884 its name was changed to the Great Northern Central Hospital. In 1888 a new hospital was built in HOLLOWAY ROAD to the designs of Keith Young and Henry Hall. In 1924, after amalgamation with the Royal Chest Hospital, its name was changed again to the Royal Northern Hospital. In 1926 wireless was installed in the wards. In 1928 a private patients' wing (St David's) was built by the generosity of Sir Howell Williams. The National Health Service took the hospital over in 1948 since when much modernisation has been undertaken. There are 270 beds for acute cases.

Royal Observatory (Old) *Greenwich Park, SE10.* After his appointment in 1675 as the first Astronomer Royal, John Flamsteed wrote, 'The next

The Royal Observatory, Greenwich in 1848, from a print by George Baxter.

thing to be thought of was a place to fit the observatory in. Several were proposed: at Hyde Park and Chelsea College. I went to view the ruins of the latter and judged it might serve the turn, and the better because it was near the court. Sir Jonas Moore rather inclined to Hyde Park but Sir Christopher Wren, mentioning Greenwich Hill, it was resolved on. The King allowed £500 in money with bricks from Tilbury Fort where there was a spare stock; and some wood, iron and lead from a gatehouse demolished in the Tower; and encouraged us further with a promise of affording what more should be requisite.' Soon afterwards Flamsteed laid the foundation stone of the observatory and cast its horoscope. Wren designed a building 'for the observator's habitation and a little for pompe' and a Sextant House nearby. The Octagon Room in the house was given a high ceiling so that Thomas Tompion's pendulum clocks could be fitted in it. Charles II did not honour his commitment to buy instruments, so Flamsteed had to provide his own. At the observatory he made some 30,000 observations, the basis of his great star catalogue *Historia Coelestis Britannica* which was later published by his widow. He was succeeded in 1720 by Edmond Halley who, with a grant of £500 from the Board of Ordnance, bought a transit telescope. In 1725 an 8 ft iron quadrant and month clock were installed in Flamsteed's observatory. Halley was succeeded in 1742 by James Bradley who, in 1748, discovered the mutation of the earth's axis. In 1749 a new series of rooms, the 'New Observatory' was built to house the new instruments, including a transit telescope and an equatorial sector, which Bradley bought with a grant of £1,000 from George II. Further rooms were built to house newly acquired instruments in 1813. In 1833 the time ball was put up on the north-eastern turret of the Octagon Room. It was dropped daily (and indeed still is) at one o'clock precisely, as a signal to boats on the THAMES and to chronometer makers in CLERKENWELL. In 1833–6 the building was extended to the south and west of Wren's original structure. In 1840 a Meteorological and Magnetic Department was formed. And in 1848 the Circle Room was enlarged to house the Airy Transit Circle whose longitudinal centre line defines the Prime Meridian of the world. In 1857 the Great Equatorial Building was added; and in 1873 a Solar Department formed. In 1936 the Observatory began the control of (TIM) the Speaking Clock. Between 1948 and 1957 instruments and staff were gradually moved to Herstmonceux Castle in Sussex, as London fog and smoke made work here increasingly difficult. In 1953 the Octagon Room was opened as a museum under the care of the NATIONAL MARITIME MUSEUM; and in 1960 Flamsteed's House, whose rooms had been furnished with 17th-century furniture provided by the VICTORIA AND ALBERT MUSEUM, was also opened. In 1965 the Caird Planetarium was opened nearby; and in 1967 the Meridian Building. Among instruments now on view are Halley's 8 ft iron quadrant and 5 ft transit, Bradley's zenith sector and 8 ft transit, and Airy's transit circle.

Royal Opera Arcade *Pall Mall to Charles II Street, SW1*. London's earliest shopping arcade with pure Regency shop fronts built by John Nash and G.S. Repton in 1816–18 at the back of the Haymarket Opera House (now HER MAJESTY'S THEATRE).

Royal Opera House *see* COVENT GARDEN (ROYAL OPERA HOUSE).

Royal Panopticon of Science and Art *Leicester Square*. A large and most exotic structure erected in the square in the early 1850s with the declared purpose of holding 'Scientific Exhibitions' and 'Promoting Discoveries in Arts and Manufactures'. It was the brainchild of Edward Marmaduke Clarke, an Irishman who had some experience of exhibitions and who had founded the London Electrical Society. And it was in accordance with his wishes that the building was constructed in a Saracenic or Moorish style quite at variance with the restrained Georgian character of its neighbours. The architect had not at first been very happy with his commission but had comforted himself with the reflection that as 'the Saracens had not been in the habit of building Panopticon institutions,' he would have 'a tolerably free scope in working out the design.' The completed structure had a Moorish façade decorated with tiles made by Minton's and shields bearing the coats of arms of various scientists and artists, musicians and writers, including those of Sir Humphry Davy and Oliver Goldsmith, and the armorial bearings of the institution itself: Newton's apple, Galileo's lamp and Columbus's egg. Above the parapet soared two minarets. Inside were lecture rooms and a huge rotunda, its walls decorated with alabaster, enamelled slate and glass mosaics, 'the most splendid room ever appropriated to scientific and artistic purposes,' according to the *Illustrated Handbook*. Staircases led to the galleries, but there was also a hydraulic lift, described as an 'Ascending Carriage.' The organ was said to be the most powerful in the world.

Having cost its proprietors £80,000, the Royal Panopticon was opened on 16 March 1854, 11 days before England declared war on Russia. It aroused some initial curiosity, but it was not a success. Within less than two years the building was put up for sale and in May 1857 it was purchased by the showman, E.T. Smith, who turned it into the ALHAMBRA. The site is now covered by the ODEON cinema.

Royal Philatelic Society *41 Devonshire Place, W1*. Founded in 1869, it is the oldest philatelic society in the world. Her Majesty the Queen is Patron of the Society and previous Patrons have been King George V, King Edward VIII and King George VI.

Royal Philharmonic Orchestra Formed in 1946, this was one of the last big London orchestras to achieve self-governing status. It was firmly directed by its founder, Sir Thomas Beecham, from its inaugural concert on 15 September 1946 until his death in 1961. During this time the orchestra was financed largely by American recording contracts and engagements with the Royal Philharmonic Society, and was resident for the summer opera season at Glyndebourne (1948–63) as well as touring. After Beecham died the orchestra had artistic and financial problems but these were gradually solved with the formation of its own self-governing board in 1963.

Royal Philharmonic Society Founded for the purpose of giving regular orchestral concerts of a high standard. The first concert was given at the ARGYLL ROOMS on the 8 March 1813, bringing back the tradition of the subscription concerts of Handel's time. The second oldest society of its kind in the world, it was organised by professional musicians who engaged, as soloists and conductors, many of the greatest musicians of the 19th century, and also commissioned works by Mendelssohn, Dvořák, Tchaikovsky and others. The Society has always had a special affinity with Beethoven, commissioning his Ninth Symphony in 1822. A bust of him is placed on the platform at all concerts. Sir Thomas Beecham rescued the society from financial difficulties after the 1st World War and its series of concerts has flourished since, different artists and orchestras continuing the policy of commissions and of promoting new music as well as carrying a traditional orchestral repertoire. The Society's Gold Medal (commemorating the centenary) has been awarded to such musicians as Brahms, Rachmaninov, Casals, Sibelius, Stravinsky and Messiaen.

Royal Polytechnic Institution *309 Regent Street*. Originally known as the Royal Gallery of Arts and Sciences, it received its Royal Charter in 1839. It provided opportunities for inventors to display their machines and models and contained a large lecture hall. There were also an extraordinarily eclectic display of exhibits, including astronomical clocks, a pneumatic telegraph, a wax *tableau* of the Resurrection, a stuffed pig, and a diving tank in which Prince Albert descended in 1840. In 1841 a photographic studio was opened on the roof. In 1858 a stairway collapsed and there were several casualties. Suits were later brought against it for damages and the Royal Polytechnic was closed. The POLYTECHNIC OF CENTRAL LONDON is its successor.

Royal Russell School *Ballards, Addington, Croydon, Surrey.* An independent co-educational school of 495 pupils between nine and 18 years old, including about 120 day pupils. It was founded in 1853 by a committee of textile trade workers, with the support of Lord John Russell and Charles Dickens. In 1863, the Prince of Wales became the Patron of the school, and each succeeding monarch has occupied this position since 1901.

Royal School of Church Music *Addington Palace, Croydon, Surrey.* Founded as the School of English Church Music in 1927 by Sydney Nicholson who resigned as Organist and Master of Choristers at WESTMINSTER ABBEY to be the first Director. He understood the need for guidance for the musicians of ordinary parish churches. The School still works within this tradition. Churches of all denominations may now become affiliated. The school was originally at Chislehurst, Kent and moved to ADDINGTON PALACE in 1953.

Royal School of Needlework *25 Prince's Gate, SW7.* Princess Christian, third daughter of Queen Victoria, founded the school in 1872, in order to restore ornamental needlework 'to the high place it once held amongst the decorative arts'.

Royal Society *6 Carlton House Terrace, SW1.* From 1648 to 1659 meetings were held in the rooms of Dr Wilkins at Wadham College, Oxford to discuss natural philosophy. After 1659 the group met at GRESHAM COLLEGE, London where lectures were given by Laurence Rooke and Christopher Wren. In November 1660 the Society was formally constituted and in 1662 Charles II granted them a charter. John Evelyn, the diarist, is thought to have suggested the title 'The Royal Society'. In 1665 *Philosophical Transactions* was first published. In 1666 after the GREAT FIRE the Society moved to ARUNDEL HOUSE in the STRAND as the CITY authorities needed GRESHAM COLLEGE for administrative purposes. The Earl of Arundel presented the Society with his library which formed the basis of their scientific collection. In 1673 it moved back to GRESHAM COLLEGE. In 1710 it moved to Crane Court, FLEET STREET. In 1768–71 an expedition was organised to observe the transit of Venus. Joseph Banks, soon to be president, sailed with Captain Cook on *The Endeavour* to the Pacific, Hudson Bay and Madras. En route they explored the coast of Australia. In 1780 the Society was given rooms in SOMERSET HOUSE. In 1845 it organised Franklin's fatal expedition to find a north-west passage. In 1857 it moved to BURLINGTON HOUSE. From 1945 women were admitted as Fellows. In 1967 they moved to CARLTON HOUSE TERRACE. The Society is now the oldest scientific society in the world. It has organised many scientific expeditions and has advised the government on numerous subjects from the changing of the calendar in 1751 to the setting up of the National Physical Laboratory in 1901. It awards several medals annually for original research work in many scientific fields. Among the well known men who have been presidents of the Society are Wren (1680–1), Pepys (1684–5), Newton (1703–26), Sloane (1727–40), Banks (1778–1819), Hooker (1873–7), Huxley (1883–4), Lister (1895–9) and Rutherford (1925–30).

Royal Society for British Sculptors *108 Old Brompton Road, SW7.* Founded in 1904 to maintain professional standards and encourage public interest in sculpture. It was granted its Royal Charter in 1911. It acts as a professional body for its members and in an advisory capacity to governmental authorities and private companies.

Royal Society of Arts *8 John Adam Street, WC2.* Founded in 1754 by William Shipley, a drawing master from Northampton, as the Society for the Encouragement of Arts, Manufactures and Commerce. Its first meetings were held over a circulating library in CRANE COURT, FLEET STREET. In 1755–6 its meetings were held at Craig's Court, CHARING CROSS; in 1756–8 at Castle Court, STRAND; and in 1759–94 in Beaufort Buildings, STRAND. The society held the first organised art exhibition in the country in 1760. Reynolds, Wilson, Cosway, Morland, Roubiliac and 64 other artists exhibited. In 1774 the society moved to the present house which was built for the society as part of the Adam brothers, ADELPHI development. In 1777–83 the lecture hall was decorated with six large murals by James Barry. From 1843 to 1861 Prince Albert was President of the Society which was given its royal charter in 1847. The Society played a large part in organising the GREAT EXHIBITION. In 1852 the first photographic exhibition was organised and in 1854 the first educational exhibition. In 1856 the society began holding examinations in 16 subjects for the benefit of the working classes. In 1862 it helped to organise the International Exhibition. In 1864 its first Albert Medal was awarded to Rowland Hill. Later recipients have included Faraday in 1866, Pasteur in 1882, Lister in 1894, Bell in 1902, Madame Curie in 1910, Rutherford in 1928, Nuffield in 1937 and Fleming in 1946. In 1867 the Society put up the first memorial plaque on a London house to commemorate where Byron was born in HOLLES STREET. (This function was taken over by the LONDON COUNTY COUNCIL in 1901). In 1876 the Society played a large part in the setting up of the NATIONAL TRAINING SCHOOL OF MUSIC, the predecessor of the ROYAL COLLEGE OF MUSIC. In 1883–6 it organised the South KENSINGTON exhibitions on *Fisheries, Health and Education, Inventions and Music* and *British Colonies and India*. In 1908 Edward VII gave permission for the Society to call itself the Royal Society of Arts. In 1950–1 it helped to organise the FESTIVAL OF BRITAIN.

Royal Society of Chemistry *Burlington House, Piccadilly, W1 and 30 Russell Square, WC1.* Formed in 1980 on the integration of the Royal Institute of Chemistry (established 1877) with the Chemical Society. The latter had been started in 1841 when 25 men, including Sir Robert Grove, lawyer and physicist, Lyon Playfair later 1st Baron Playfair, and the chemist, Arthur Aikin, agreed to found a society for 'the promotion of chemistry and those branches of science connected with it, by communications, discussions and by collecting a library, museum ... etc'. Thomas Graham, Professor of Chemistry at UNIVERSITY COLLEGE, was elected first President. The Society was incorporated by charter in 1848 and in 1857 given rooms in BURLINGTON HOUSE where its premises were built in the south wing to the designs of R.R. Banks and E.M. Barry. During the next 100 years, the Society became a centre for scholars in all fields of chemistry. Its Fellows were chosen for their eminence in the science.

Royal Society of Literature of the United Kingdom *1 Hyde Park Gardens, W2.* Founded in 1823 by George IV on the suggestion of Thomas Burgess, Bishop of St David's. The King agreed to contribute the sum of 1,000 guineas towards its establishment and to make an annual grant of 100 guineas. The Bishop mistook the King's meaning and announced that the entire sum would be given annually. The King did not correct the mistake, and it was therefore settled that he would give 1,000 guineas a year from the Privy Purse as pensions to ten Associates to be elected to the Society and to donate an annual prize of 'two medals of 50 guineas each'. The first Fellows enrolled after the King himself were his brothers, the Dukes of York, Clarence and Cambridge; the first President was the Bishop of St David's; and at the top of the list of Associates was the name of Samuel Taylor Coleridge. One of the first medals to be awarded by the Society went to Sir Walter Scott. The Society's original headquarters were in a house designed for it by Decimus Burton in St Martin's Place, TRAFALGAR SQUARE. This house was demolished when the NATIONAL GALLERY was enlarged in the 1890s. The Society then moved to HANOVER SQUARE, then to BLOOMSBURY SQUARE, before settling in HYDE PARK GARDENS. In 1961 the Society inaugurated an honour known as the Companionship of Literature. The present Companions are Sir John Betjeman, Lord David Cecil, Sir Angus Wilson, Miss Ruth Pitter, Philip Larkin and Stephen Spender. Lord Clark, Dame Rebecca West and Arthur Koestler were also Companions at the time of their deaths in 1983.

Royal Society of Medicine *1 Wimpole Street, W1.* Founded in 1805 as the Medical and Chirurgical Society of London, it received its Royal Charter in 1834. In 1907 14 specialty societies merged with it, and the new body was called The Royal Society of Medicine. The present headquarters, designed by John Belcher and Joass, were occupied in 1912. The Society is renowned for its library – the best medical library in the country and one of the best in the world.

Royal Society of Musicians *10 Stratford Place, WC1.* Founded in 1738 to maintain 'aged and infirm musicians' and their families, its founder members included the composers Arne, Boyce and Handel. Funds were raised from concerts, especially with performances of Handel's works, the most famous of these being the Handel Commemorations held in WESTMINSTER ABBEY under the patronage of George III, who granted the Society a royal charter in 1790. In 1792 Haydn wrote a march for the society and other famous musicians, including Liszt and Mendelssohn, played to its members.

Royal Society of Painters in Water Colours *Bankside Gallery, 48 Hopton Street, Blackfriars, SE1.* Founded in 1804 at a meeting held in the Stratford Coffee House, OXFORD STREET. W.S. Gilpin was elected President. The Society's first exhibition was held at Vandergucht's Gallery, 20 Lower Brook Street. Its members have included Peter de Wint, John Sell Cotman, Samuel Palmer, John Singer Sargent, Sir William Russell Flint and Edward Seago. The 295th exhibition of the Society was held in 1982 at the Bankside Gallery.

Royal Statistical Society *25 Enford Street, W1.* Founded in 1834 under the title of the Statistical Society of London with the principal original objects of procuring, arranging and publishing 'Facts calculated to illustrate the Condition and Prospects of Society' limited, as far as possible, to 'Facts which can be stated numerically and arranged in table.' The Society, which was granted a Royal Charter in 1887, is now concerned with the development of statistical theory and methodology, together with the application of statistical methods in many fields.

Royal Strand Theatre, *Strand.* Opened in 1832 in a building formerly used as a panorama and a nonconformist chapel. In 1833 Fanny Kelly successfully staged her one-woman shows. During the theatre's early years it was frequently in trouble with the Lord Chamberlain and was often closed. Between 1836 and 1839 Douglas Jerold and his father-in-law, W.J. Hammond, staged *burlettas*. In 1858 William Swanborough took the theatre and refurnished it. He put on burlesques which were mostly written by H. J. Byron. With his profits he had the theatre reconstructed by John Ellis in 1865. In 1879 the comic opera, *Madame Favart*, was a success and was followed by *Olivette* (1880), *Manola* (1882) and *La Mascotte* (1882). In 1882 the theatre was rebuilt by C.J. Phipps to comply with fire regulations. Between 1888 and 1895 it was managed by Willie Edouin who staged the farces *Our Flat* (1888), *The Late Lamented* (1891) and *Niobe (All Smiles)* (1892). In 1901 *A Chinese Honeymoon*, a musical play by George Dance and Howard Talbot began its run of 1,075 performances which was the theatre's biggest ever success. It was demolished in 1905. ALDWYCH tube station was built on the site.

Royal Thames Yacht Club *60 Knightsbridge, SW1.* Founded in the 1770s, and first known as the Cumberland Fleet, after its patron the Duke of Cumberland, and for a short time from 1823 as His Majesty's Coronation Fleet, it is the oldest yacht club in England. After meeting for some hundred years in inns and hotels, the club acquired premises first in ST JAMES'S STREET, then in ALBEMARLE STREET, then in PICCADILLY and from 1923 has been in KNIGHTSBRIDGE. The club occupies the three lower floors at No. 60. Most of the 1,500-odd members are yachtsmen (or yachtswomen), but those who are not sailors are admitted provided they pay a higher fee.

Royal Tournament An annual display of military and naval expertise, musical drives, massed bands, field-gun races, tugs-of-war and physical training displays. Originally known as the Grand Military Tournament, and first held at the ROYAL AGRICULTURAL HALL, ISLINGTON, in 1880, it is now held at EARL'S COURT. In the year of its inception the Commander-in-Chief was George III's grandson, the Duke of Cambridge, who once declared, 'Change, at any time, for whatever purpose, is to be deprecated.' As though obedient to this precept the displays have not much changed in the past 100 years.

Royal United Services Institute for Defence Studies *Whitehall, SW1.* Founded in 1831 at a gathering of officers in the THATCHED HOUSE TAVERN, ST JAMES'S STREET. Major-General Henry Hardinge proposed the resolution that a 'Naval and Military

A programme for the 15th Royal Tournament, held at the Royal Agricultural Hall, Islington in 1894.

Library and Museum be now formed'. Captain Francis Beaufort RN, seconding the resolution, expressed the hope that the library and museum would 'detach many of our friends from the club house and billiard table'. Membership was open 'to all Officers of the Army, Navy, and Marines, the Militia (Regular and Local), the Yeomanry, the East India Company's Land and Sea Forces, and civil functionaries attached to those Departments'. Some 2,000 officers enrolled. The Institution's first premises were in WHITEHALL, in the small building known as Vanbrugh House. In 1839, the title 'United Service Institution' was assumed. Queen Victoria succeeded her uncle King William IV as Royal Patron, and in 1842 was joined by the Prince Consort as Joint Patron. In 1860, the United Services Institute was granted a Royal Charter with the title of 'Royal United Services Institution', and given an annual grant of £60 – half from the Navy and half from the Army.

In 1890, Queen Victoria granted the Institution the use of Inigo Jones's BANQUETING HOUSE to house its museum. (This was disbanded in 1962 when the Government took back the BANQUETING HOUSE for official entertainment.) But larger premises than those available at Vanbrugh House were required for the main work of the Institution – the provision of facilities for reading and study. So the Crown gave an eight-year lease on the site of what had been the DOVER HOUSE stables, almost adjoining the BANQUETING HOUSE. An Appeal for £23,000 was launched to erect a new building, the foundation stone of which was laid in June

1893 by the Prince of Wales. In February 1895 the Prince formally opened the Institution building as it now stands. The architect was Aston Webb.

Royal Veterinary College *Royal College Street, NW1.* In 1785 the Odiham Agricultural Society began to discuss possible ways of encouraging the study of scientific farriery in England, based on medical and anatomical principles. In continental Europe farriery had become more scientific and there were veterinary schools in Paris, Lyons, Vienna and Hanover. In 1791 it was decided to form a Veterinary College in London and M. de St Bel was appointed Principal. He came from Lyons, which at that time had the most famous of the veterinary schools. The college's first building was erected on the present site. In about 1872 diseases of cattle were included in the work of the college which, until then, had dealt only with horses. In 1937 the college was rebuilt on the same site to the designs of H.P.G. Maule. In the previous year the college was granted its Royal Charter and in 1949 became a School of the UNIVERSITY OF LONDON in the Faculty of Medicine. The Beaumont Animals' Hospital adjoins the college.

Royal Victoria Gardens *North Woolwich, E6.* Nine acres of gardens lying on the north shore of the THAMES in Essex and opened in 1851. In the 1850s William Holland provided open-air dancing, 'monster baby' shows and other popular amusements at the adjoining Pavilion Hotel. Holland escaped from his creditors here by balloon. Formerly the ground was liable to flooding and the treacherous swamp on the shore once reputedly claimed the lives of a couple who went boar-hunting here on their wedding day.

Royal Victoria Victualling Yard, *Deptford.* Founded in 1513 and originally called the Red House, it became known as the Royal Victoria Victualling Yard after 1858. Formerly an important naval centre, it closed in 1961 when the site became the GREATER LONDON COUNCIL's Pepys Estate. Some of the officers' houses and warehouses facing the river, all dating from about 1790, remain as part of the Estate.

Royalty Theatre *Dean Street, W1.* Opened in May 1840 as Miss Kelly's Theatre and Dramatic School. In 1850 it was redecorated and became the Royal Soho Theatre and in November of the same year the New English Opera House. In 1861 for a season it was the Théâtre Français and later the New Royalty Theatre, then in 1862 the New Royalty Operetta House. It was remodelled in 1906. In 1911 it became known as the Royalty Theatre. The Lord Chamberlain withdrew its licence in 1938, and its impecunious and century-long search for an identity was finally terminated by the BLITZ. Royalty House, built in 1959, is now on the site.

Royalty Theatre *Portugal Street, WC2.* In 1911 the London Opera House was built for Oscar Hammerstein in KINGSWAY as a rival to COVENT GARDEN. Designed by Bertie Crewe it cost £200,000 but was a complete failure. It was reopened in 1912 with variety shows and revues. Acquired by Sir Oswald Stoll in 1916, it became a cinema in 1917 and remained so until 1941 when, for six years, revivals of famous musicals, such as *Rose Marie* and *Lilac Time* were staged here.

In 1947–9 Tom Arnold's ice spectaculars were popular. In 1957–60 the theatre was rebuilt as part of an office block to fulfil LONDON COUNTY COUNCIL requirements. It reopened with *The Visit* by Friedrich Dürrenmatt, starring the Lunts. From 1961 it was used as a cinema; and in 1970 reopened again as a theatre with a revue, *Birds of a Feather*. In September that year the nude review *Oh! Calcutta* was transferred here from the ROUND HOUSE. This ran for four years until transferred to the DUCHESS in 1974. A more recent success was the American musical, *Bubbling Brown Sugar*. The seating capacity is 1,016.

RUGBY FOOTBALL CLUBS
The principal clubs in London (with their dates of foundation given in brackets) are:

Blackheath FC (1853), *Rectory Field, Blackheath, SE3*. Founded by former pupils of Blackheath Preparatory School, it is the oldest organised Rugby Club. In 1863 its members played their first game against RICHMOND with whom they were amongst the founders of the Rugby Union in 1871. In 1882 they acquired a tenancy of Rectory Field which has been their home ever since. Their longest playing international was C.N. Lowe of Cambridge and England who won 25 caps (1913–23). Their colours are red and black hoops.

Harlequin FC (1866), *Stoop Memorial Ground, Twickenham, Middlesex*. One of the founder members of the Rugby Football Union, it was installed in 1910 at TWICKENHAM, the Rugby Football Union's Headquarters, where it continues to play its home matches. It has exercised great influence on the game, particularly during the period preceding the 1st World War. Since then the most famous member has been W.W. Wakefield (now Lord Wakefield) (1920–7) captain in turn of Sedbergh, the Services, Harlequin, Middlesex and England. His 31 caps for England remained a record for 40 years. The Club colours are harlequin squares of light blue and magenta, chocolate and French grey with light green and black sleeves.

London Irish RFC (1898), *The Avenue, Sunbury-on-Thames*. The club's most capped player is K.W. Kennedy (1965–75) who won 45 caps. Club colours are emerald green jerseys and white shorts.

London Scottish RFC (1878), *Richmond Athletic Ground, Richmond, Surrey*. The club's most capped player (44 caps) is A.F. McHarg (1968–79). The Club colours are blue jerseys with a red lion on the left breast, white shorts and red stockings.

London Welsh RFC (1885), *Old Deer Park, Kew Road, Richmond, Surrey*. The club's most capped player is J.P.R. Williams (55 caps, 1969–81). The club colours are scarlet jersey with white shorts.

Metropolitan Police RFC (1923), *Police Sports Club, Imber Court, Embercourt Road, East Molesey, Surrey*. The club's most capped player is A.M. Rees 13 caps (Wales) (1934–8). The club colours are dark blue jerseys and white shorts.

Richmond FC (1861), *Athletic Ground, Richmond, Surrey*. One of the oldest clubs in the country. Its members played their first game against BLACKHEATH in 1863. The club founder was Edwin Ash who was responsible for the formation of the Rugby Union in 1871 and was its first secretary. Its most capped player was C.W. Ralston who played for England 22 times (1971–5). The club colours are old gold, red and black.

Rosslyn Park RFC (1879), *Priory Lane, Upper Richmond Road, Roehampton, SW15*. It was originally a section of a cricket club at HAMPSTEAD. A.G. Ripley, who played for England 24 times (1972–6), is their most capped player. The club colours are red and white hoops.

Saracens RFC (1876), *Bramley Sports Ground, Green Road, Southgate, N14*. V.S. Harding of Cambridge and England was capped six times for England (1961–2). The club colours are black jerseys with red star and crescent, black shorts and red stockings.

Wasps RFC (1867), *Repton Avenue, Sunbury, Middlesex*. Formed largely by students of UNIVERSITY COLLEGE HOSPITAL. The club's most capped player is R.M. Uttley. Club colours are black jerseys with golden wasp on the left breast and gold stripes down the sleeves, black shorts and black stockings with gold hoops on turnover.

Ruislip *Middlesex*. The manor of Ruislip, referred to in *Domesday Book* of 1086, was given by the Norman, Ernulf de Hesdin, to the Benedictine Abbey of Bec in about 1096 and the monks remained owners until 1404. There are still earthworks at Ruislip which mark the site of a motte and bailey. In 1451 Henry VI granted the manor to his foundation of King's College, Cambridge, which remained the Lord of the Manor until modern times.

Ruislip has retained almost the whole of its old village buildings grouped together at the end of the modern shopping High Street. The parish church of St Martin is a flint and stone building dating from 1250 with a battlemented tower of about 1500. The interior has a 15th-century roof and a 12th-century font, medieval wall paintings, 16th-century pews and two iron-bound chests of the same period. There is a finely carved bread cupboard of 1697. The brasses and monuments (one by the brothers Christmas) mostly commemorate the Hawtrey family of Eastcote House and there is a fine set of funeral hatchments. Manor Farmhouse, on the site of the Benedictine prior's house, is a handsome building with a front of close studded timber framing dating in part from the 16th century. Adjacent is the Great Barn. This dates back to the last decades of the 13th century and is the oldest barn in the county. It is a timber-framed, aisled building of seven bays, 116 ft long and 35 ft wide, with a tiled roof and weatherboarded walls standing on a low plinth, some of the original flints remaining. The timbers have their original medieval assembly marks and there are scarf joints in the arcade plates of a very early type. The Little Barn, converted into a public library, has a queen-post roof of 1600. On the west side of the High Street the village group continues with the 16th-century Swan public house, flanked by old cottages converted into offices. A pair of 17th-century cottages adapted as the village sweet shop and the old post office stand by the entrance to Manor Farm facing down the High Street. Backing on to the churchyard is a row of 16th-century cottages with a jettied first floor at the rear. The former alehouse is now a shop within the original Tudor timber framing. Ruislip almshouses of about 1570, have recently been skilfully restored. Converted farms and old houses include The Old House (16th-century), the timbered Mill House (17th-century) in Bury Street, and Woodmans Farm and the Plough public house (both 17th-century) and the Little Manor House in Arlington Drive opposite.

Cannons Bridge Farmhouse is 16th-century, much modernised. In Ducks Hill Road is the Old Workhouse of 1789 now privately owned. Old Clack Farmhouse (16th-century) in Tile Kiln Lane and Hill Farmhouse (17th-century) in Orchard Close still exist. The 17th-century Sherleys Farmhouse behind Ruislip Station remains as part of a motel. To the north of the village centre is an area of some 570 acres of woodland around Ruislip Common known as Park Wood, Copse Wood, Bayhurst Wood and Mad Bess Wood (the last name has never been satisfactorily explained). Oak from the woods was used in the 14th century for work on the TOWER OF LONDON, in 1344 for Windsor Castle and in 1346 and 1347 for WESTMINSTER PALACE. The woods are open to the public and include the Lido, a boating and sailing lake formed in 1811 as a feeder to the GRAND JUNCTION CANAL.

The economic and social life of Ruislip remained related to agriculture until the 19th century. In 1804 the Ruislip Enclosure Act was passed and from 1814 onwards the large open fields to the south were divided up into hedged fields with fenced access roads and alloted to various owners. New farms were built and a marked change took place in the landscape. It was not until 1904, however, when Ruislip station was opened, that agriculture began to give way to housing development. The increasing building estates necessitated a new station at Ruislip Manor in 1912. Northolt Airfield was opened in 1915. Ruislip is now a suburban dormitory and since 1965 has formed part of the London Borough of HILLINGDON.

Rule's *25 Maiden Lane, WC2*. A restaurant established by Thomas Rule at its present address in 1798 and first celebrated for its 'porter, pies and oysters'. The walls are covered with memorabilia – paintings, prints, playbills, statuettes – of its distinguished patrons, many of them actors and actresses. Those who dined here regularly include Charles Dickens, H.G. Wells, Edward VII as Prince of Wales and Lillie Langtry. The Prince and Mrs Langtry came so often, indeed, that a special door was made for him so that they could enter unobserved.

Rummer Tavern *Charing Cross*. A tavern kept in the reign of Charles II by Samuel Prior, uncle of Matthew Prior, the poet who, after the death of his father, came to live with his uncle who sent him to WESTMINSTER SCHOOL. While at the Rummer he attracted the notice of the Earl of Dorset who found him reading Horace and paid for him to go to Cambridge. In the 18th century the tavern was also known as the New Bagnio. It was here that Jack Sheppard, then apprenticed to a carpenter in WYCH STREET, committed his first theft by stealing two silver spoons. The tavern was burned down in 1750. The SALOPIAN afterwards appeared on the site.

Rupert Street *W1*. Built in 1680–2 on land which had been granted by Charles II to the Earl of St Albans in exchange for St Albans's surrender of his leasehold interest in Nell Gwynne's house in PALL MALL. St Albans sold the land immediately to three speculators including Nicholas Barbon. It was described by Strype in 1720 as 'a pretty handsome, well built Street'. In the 1880s it was bisected by SHAFTESBURY AVENUE. That part of it which extends south from SHAFTESBURY AVENUE to COVENTRY STREET contains some remnants of the early 18th-century buildings, but of the northern part which leads to BREWER STREET nothing earlier than SHAFTESBURY AVENUE itself remains. It is now an undistinguished street remarkable only for the number of its Chinese and Indian restaurants. The site of the White Horse public house at No. 45 has been occupied by a tavern of that name since at least 1739.

Ruskin Park *SE5*. Thirty-six acres maintained by the Borough of LAMBETH, and named after John Ruskin, who came to live nearby in 1823 at the age of four and spent most of his life in houses in HERNE HILL and in DENMARK HILL. In the early 19th century the area bordered on open country and Ruskin mentions that HARROW was 'conspicuous always in fine weather.' The commemorative fountain to Felix Mendelssohn is by an unknown sculptor.

Russell Court *SW1*. Takes its name from a family of Russells who lived in a house on the north side in the 17th century.

Russell Hotel *Russell Square, WC1*. Overlooking RUSSELL SQUARE, this fantasy 'François-premier château' hotel in redbrick and terracotta was designed by Charles Fitzroy Doll in 1898. It opened on Derby Day 1900. The main entrance and restaurant are resplendent with marble pillars and chandelier. There are 324 bedrooms.

Russell Road *W14*. On the HOLLAND ESTATE and named after Lord John Russell who was a frequent visitor to HOLLAND HOUSE. Mohammed Ali Jinnah Quaid i Azam, founder of Pakistan, stayed at No. 35 where he was a law student in London in 1895.

Russell Square *WC1*. One of London's largest Squares, it was laid out in 1800 by Humphry Repton and named after the ground landlords, the Russells, Dukes of Bedford (*see* BLOOMSBURY). On the west side some of the original houses by James Burton still remain; those on the north and south sides were altered in the 19th century. Those on the east were demolished for the RUSSELL HOTEL.

From the beginning the square was much favoured by lawyers and other professional men. Thackeray placed the home of the Sedleys and Osbornes of *Vanity Fair* here. Thomas Denman, afterwards Lord Denman and Lord Chief Justice, lived at No. 50 in 1818–34; and Sir Samuel Romilly, the great law reformer, killed himself at No. 21 in 1818 when distracted by grief at the death of his wife. Lord Tenterden, who presided at the trial of the CATO STREET conspirators, died at No. 28 in 1832. William Cowper, the poet, lived at No. 62 (later demolished for the IMPERIAL HOTEL) when a schoolboy at WESTMINSTER. Sir Thomas Lawrence had his studio at No. 67 (also later demolished for the Imperial Hotel) from 1805 until his death here in 1830. He painted in this studio the series of portraits of princes, generals and statesmen who contributed to Napoleon's downfall which hang in the Waterloo Chamber at Windsor Castle. When he was painting Platov the house was guarded by Cossacks 'on their small white horses with their long spears grounded'. Mrs Humphry Ward and her husband lived at No. 61 (a site later covered by the Imperial Hotel) in the 1880s. Henry Crabb Robinson, the witty journalist, occupied for many years a house at No. 30 later rebuilt for the ROYAL INSTITUTE OF CHEMISTRY. Mary Russell Mitford, the novelist and dramatist, was at No. 56 in 1836 when a dinner here was attended by Wordsworth, Browning, and 'quantities more of poets'. Sir George Williams, founder of the YMCA, lived at No. 13 from 1880 until his death in 1905. No. 67, now the Hotel President (447 bedrooms: designed by C. Lovett, Gill and Partners, 1962) occupies the site of BALTIMORE HOUSE. The statue on the south side is of Francis 5th Duke of Bedford by Westmacott (see STATUES). Several houses in the square are occupied by departments of LONDON UNIVERSITY. The Institute of Commonwealth Studies is at No. 27; the Institute of Germanic Studies is at No. 29. There is a large public garden with three fountains.

Russell Street *WC2.* Built in the 1630s and named after the Russells, Earls and Dukes of Bedford, the ground landlords. Strype in 1720 called it 'a fine broad street, well inhabited by tradesmen'. WILL'S COFFEE HOUSE was here; so were BUTTON'S, TOM'S COFFEE HOUSE and the ROSE TAVERN. In 1660 candidates who wished to be touched for the King's Evil were asked to go first to 'Mr Knight, the King's Surgeon, living at the Cross Guns in Russell Street, Covent Garden, over against the Rose Tavern'. John Evelyn took lodgings here in 1659; Thomas Betterton, the actor, died here in 1710. Tom Davies, the bookseller, began his business here in 1762 and it was in his shop that the celebrated meeting of Dr Johnson and Boswell took place. Charles Lamb took lodgings here in 1817. He said it was 'the individual spot' he liked best 'in all this great city'. And it was here that Edward Gibbon consulted a Roman Catholic bookseller when he had, at the age of 16, decided to join the Roman Catholic faith. The FORTUNE THEATRE is on the north-west side.

Russia Row *EC2.* The origin of the name is unknown but it first appears in *Lockie's Topography* of 1810 at a time when Russia and Britain were allied against Napoleon.

Ruston Mews *W11.* Takes its name from Ruston Parva, a village in Yorkshire, where the ground landlords, the St Quintin family, had a country house. It was built in 1869.

Rutland Gardens *SW7.* On the west side are the Rutland Court flats by Delissa Joseph (1902). A gateway by Rutland Lodge, occupied by the Consulate General of the Republic of Turkey, leads to Kent Yard.

Rutland Gate *SW7.* A square of large stuccoed Victorian houses and adjoining roads built in 1838–56 on the grounds of the Duke of Rutland's house. Sir Francis Galton, the scientist and explorer, lived at No. 42 in 1858–1910. Lord Lugard, the colonial administrator, lived at No. 51 in 1912–19. The gardens are private. The British Antique Dealers' Association is at No. 20.

Rutland Lodge *145 Petersham Road, Richmond, Surrey.* A beautiful redbrick building put up soon after the Restoration by Sir William Bolton who became Lord Mayor of London in 1666 but who was later disgraced for misappropriation of public funds

provided for rebuilding London after the GREAT FIRE. The first occupant was a London lawyer, Sir John Darnall. His son put in the magnificent rococo plaster overmantel in the saloon which with the fine old wall-panelling and carved staircase was destroyed in a fire on 25 February 1967. The exterior was saved but the house has now been converted into luxury flats. The name is taken from Lucy, Duchess of Rutland who lived here in 1741–51, though the owner was Sir William Yonge, Secretary at War in Walpole's ministry.

Rutland Street *SW7.* Originally St Michael's Terrace on the north, then Rutland Terrace, and finally Rutland Street. The lower part of the street was sold to William Farler, the developer of the neighbouring BROMPTON SQUARE, in 1830. He proceeded to build 30 cottages of the meanest type, a number of which still remain, though now much improved internally.

Ruxley *Kent.* The only real reminder of its past are the remains of its long disused and ruined church. The de Rokesle family, who owned land in this area, held high offices of state for hundreds of years in the early Middle Ages and Ruxley may have been an important centre. In 1557, in the reign of Mary, a petition from the patron, Sir Martin Bowes, to Archbishop Pole said that the church was much decayed and ruined, and clergy could not be found to perform the services. He asked, therefore, that Ruxley church should be incorporated with the church of NORTH CRAY, and this was agreed. The church was not however demolished as was intended but used as a barn for Ruxley Farm. It was damaged during the 2nd World War and by a gale in 1964. Considerable efforts have been made to preserve what remains. It is now within the grounds of the garden centre known as Ruxley Manor Nursery. Ruxley is now part of the London Borough of BROMLEY.

Ryder Street *SW1.* Built in the 1670s on land granted to Henry Jermyn, Earl of St Albans (see JERMYN STREET) and perhaps named after Captain Richard Rider, Master Carpenter to Charles II. (It was formerly spelled Rider Street.) The freehold of the whole street still belongs to the Crown. None of the original houses remains. At No. 11 is the ECCENTRIC CLUB. The Gothic building in red and black brick, designed by John Norton, was built in three stages between 1865 and 1915 and was formerly Dieudonné's Hotel.

Rye Lane *SE15.* One of south-east London's busiest shopping streets with market stalls in side-streets, Rye Lane developed largely thanks to public transport. Thomas Tilling started a bus service from PECKHAM in 1851. In 1933 Tilling's buses became an important component of London Transport. The railway station opened in 1865. The longest established business, formerly Jones and Higgins, the department store, now Houndsditch in Peckham, was founded in 1867. Rye Lane is also a through route to Central London but traffic diversion has eased congestion. Rye Lane West Conservation Area, reached via Holly Grove, is an early 19th-century oasis. The former Friends' Meeting House in Highshore Road was erected in 1835 and attended by many eminent 19th-century Quakers.

S

Sackville Street *W1*. Extends from PICCADILLY to VIGO STREET. It was originally laid out in the 1670s, when Captain Edward Sackville (from whom the street evidently takes its name), younger brother of the 5th Earl of Dorset, was one of the first residents in 1675–8. In the 1730s it was completely rebuilt at the instigation of the ground landlord, William Pulteney, later Earl of Bath, who in 1730 signed a building agreement with two famous West End master craftsmen, Thomas Phillips, carpenter, and John Mist, paviour. Within the next few years the whole street was reconstructed under their auspices, but only Nos 29–36 (consecutive) now survive. No. 29 has a ceiling by Robert Adam of 1770, and No. 36, of 1732, was probably designed by Henry Flitcroft. Most of the rest of the street has been rebuilt at various dates since the 1920s with large neo-Georgian blocks by (or based on designs by) George J. Skipper; and shops and offices predominate throughout. Notable inhabitants have included Arthur Young, writer on agriculture, in 1798–1820; Dr John Snow, who discovered that CHOLERA is water-borne, in 1853–8; Robert R. Banks and Charles Barry the Younger, architects, in 1855–64. Saccone and Speed, the wine merchants at No. 32, were established towards the end of the 18th century.

Saddlers' Company *see* CITY LIVERY COMPANIES.

Sadler's Wells *Rosebery Avenue, E1*. The first 'musick' house was built in 1683 by Thomas Sadler as a side attraction to a medicinal well. At the height of the spa's popularity 500 people visited it each day. After 1687 it was neglected. Rope dancers, jugglers and other similar entertainers appeared at the theatre. The audience was made up of 'strolling damsels, half-pay officers, peripatetic tradesmen, tars, butchers and others that are musically inclined'. In 1746 Thomas Rosoman, a local builder, took over the theatre and restored its former popularity. A regular company was engaged in 1753. The theatre was rebuilt in seven weeks in 1765. In 1772 Rosoman retired and was succeeded by Tom King, the ex-manager of Drury Lane, who brought with him a fashionable audience. In 1781 Joseph Grimaldi first appeared as an infant dancer. After his father's death in 1788 he regularly acted here, concluding with a benefit in 1828. Edmund Kean appeared here as a boy in 1804 when aquatic spectacles, including the Siege of Gibraltar, were staged by Thomas Dibdin. A false fire alarm in 1807 caused the death of 23 people. In 1844–62, following the breaking of the patent theatre's monopoly over drama in 1843, Samuel Phelps produced 34 of Shakespeare's plays, many of which had not been performed for years. During 1863–71 his successor, Robert Edgar, continued to stage Shakespeare. Afterwards the theatre became a skating rink, then a pickle factory and later a boxing arena. It was closed in 1878. The following year, Mrs Bateman of the LYCEUM opened it as a house of melodrama. After becoming a music-hall in 1893, it closed in 1906. The present theatre, designed by F.G.M. Chancellor, was built in 1927–31 with funds raised by Lillian Baylis and Sir Reginald Rowe. Ballet, opera and drama alternated between Sadler's Wells and the OLD VIC but after 1931 the ballet and opera companies settled permanently at the Wells. The theatre was closed in 1940. It reopened in 1945 with Britten's *Peter Grimes*. In 1946 the ballet company moved to COVENT GARDEN as the Royal Ballet. Another company was formed but this also went to COVENT GARDEN in 1957. In 1959 a second opera company was set up for touring. In 1968 the resident opera company moved to the COLISEUM. The original theatre is now used by foreign and touring companies. Sadler's well can still be seen under a trap door at the back of the stalls. The theatre's seating capacity is 1,500.

Saffron Hill *EC1*. Lies north of HOLBORN between LEATHER LANE and FARRINGDON ROAD. In 1272 John Kirkby, Treasurer of the Realm, acquired land in the then rural parish of ST ANDREW, HOLBORN. His estate included a great hall and chambers, a chapel later dedicated to St Ethelreda, stables, gardens and a vineyard. He was awarded the Bishopric of Ely in Cambridgeshire by Edward I, and, at his death in 1290, he bequeathed the estate to the see as a London palace. The gardens became famous for their fruits and for saffron which was probably first grown there soon after its introduction into Cambridgeshire in the 14th century. Saffron was essential to disguise the taste of the city-dwellers' rancid meat and eventually gave its name to the hilly road running through the estate. In 1575 Elizabeth I forced Bishop Cox to lease the gardens to her favourite, Sir Christopher Hatton, who built himself a residence there. The next bishop was obliged to grant the freehold and the latter's palace fell into disuse. In 1620 the Spanish Ambassador, Gondomar, resided here; and in 1642 it was used as a prison. In the 17th century Baron Hatton of Kirby had to sell the Hatton estate and its development followed swiftly; by the second half of the century HATTON GARDEN, Hatton Wall and Kirby Street had appeared. The remaining Ely estate had become dilapidated and 'thieves' houses' soon abounded among the ramshackle and overcrowded buildings. Towards the end of the 18th century ELY PLACE was developed leaving only the Chapel and a successor to the 1546 Mitre tavern as relics of the Bishop's palace complex.

Saffron Hill became notorious as a rookery. Poor immigrants, first the IRISH, then the Italians, were attracted to it. Crime and vice, immortalised in Dickens's *Oliver Twist*, flourished, the Fleet Ditch providing a getaway for criminals. The Ditch was a filthy open sewer and remained so into the 19th century, by which time the district was improving and social work started. Charles Barry's church, St Peter Saffron Hill, was opened in 1832, and a Catholic

Sadler's Wells Theatre, the original 'musick' house, in 1813. Built in 1683, it became celebrated for aquatic spectacles.

mission was established in the 1840s; the mid-century development of HOLBORN CIRCUS, HOLBORN VIADUCT and FARRINGDON ROAD, which covered the Fleet Ditch north of HOLBORN, required much demolition and warehouses replaced slum dwellings. A commercial character developed: HATTON GARDEN was already the centre of the diamond trade when the influx of European refugee traders in the 1930s confirmed this position. In 1900 Saffron Hill had been incorporated into the Borough of HOLBORN and in 1965 it became part of the London Borough of CAMDEN. ELY PLACE remains gated off and is still outside the jurisdiction of the METROPOLITAN POLICE.

J. Sainsbury Ltd *Stamford Street, SE1.* The head office of a firm controlling a large chain of supermarkets and freezer centres throughout much of England. It was founded in London in 1869 by John James Sainsbury, who opened his first modest shop at 173 DRURY LANE, selling butter, milk, eggs and, later, cheese. This shop prospered as did two others which followed it and in 1882 Sainsbury opened an experimental branch in CROYDON which, spacious and highly ornate, was a great success; it was soon followed by similar branches in different parts of London.

From the first, Sainsbury maintained exceptionally high standards of cleanliness and order, and perseveringly sought reliable suppliers of good produce, some of whom, such as Buismans, the Dutch butter merchants, supply the firm to this day. In 1896, his eldest son married Mabel Van den Bergh, thus forging a link with the famous margarine firm. By the early 1900s three sons had entered the firm, which continued to expand and to pioneer innovations. In 1982 there were 73 branches in the Greater London area.

St Aidan *Acton, W3.* Roman Catholic Church designed by John Newton and built in 1961. It has an open campanile with nine bells. The oil-on-canvas altarpiece, *The Crucifixion*, is by Graham Sutherland.

St Alban *Wood Street.* Built on the alleged site of the palace chapel of King Offa, the 8th-century ruler of Mercia. In penance for his part in the murder of Alban, the first English martyr, Offa founded St Alban's Abbey; and in 793 gave the patronage of the WOOD STREET church to the Abbey. It was rebuilt in the Gothic style in 1633–4, perhaps by Inigo Jones. Burned down in the GREAT FIRE, it was rebuilt in 1682–5 by Wren as a copy of the former church. It cost £3,165 0s 9d. The tower was added in 1697–8. It was modernised in 1858. After an air raid in 1940 only the tower was left standing. The ruins were demolished in 1955, leaving Wren's tower on an island in the roadway. The upper stage and pinnacles are Victorian. St Alban's churchyard was the place the Barber-Surgeons' Company used for burying the bodies of dissected felons.

St Alban the Martyr *Holborn (Brooke Street), EC1.* A noble church built in 1861–2 by William Butterfield amid the HOLBORN slums, a successor to a chapel over a fish shop and one in a cellar. Lord Leigh donated the site and J.G. Hubbard, MP, financed the building. It was a centre of 19th-century Catholic Revival controversies; prosecutions were brought for illegal ritual. Except for the saddle-back tower it was destroyed in the 2nd World War and rebuilt by Adrian Scott in 1945.

St Alban's Tavern *St Alban's Street, Pall Mall.* A fashionable 18th-century tavern frequented by rich young men, a party of whom in 1771, finding the noise of the coaches troublesome, so Horace Walpole told Sir Horace Mann, 'ordered the street to be littered with straw, as is done for women that lie in. The bill from the Haymarket amounted to fifty shillings apiece.' The African Association was formed here in 1788 by, amongst others, Sir Joseph Banks.

St Alfege *London Wall.* The glass walls of offices now tower above the ruins of a parish church dedicated

688

to an Archbishop of Canterbury, brutally murdered by the Danes in 1012 (*see* ST ALFEGE WITH ST PETER, GREENWICH). The earliest building was attached to the Roman City wall. In Tudor times, the Augustinian Priory across the road became vacant and was adapted for the use of the parish. This was rebuilt in 1777. In 1923, the church was demolished and the parish united with ST MARY ALDERMANBURY.

St Alfege Garden *EC2*. The former churchyard of ST ALFEGE LONDON WALL is now a public garden. In it is a large piece of the late medieval City wall.

St Alfege with St Peter *Greenwich High Road, SE10*. St Alfege, who had been appointed Archbishop of Canterbury in 1006 and had bravely refused to sanction a ransom for his release from captivity by the invading Danes, was murdered by them in GREENWICH in 1012. It seems that a church was built on the site soon afterwards. This was rebuilt, probably in the 13th century. John Morton, Henry VII's Chancellor, was vicar of this church in 1444–54. Henry VIII was baptised here and his sister, Mary, was married to Charles Brandon, Duke of Suffolk. Thomas Tallis, the composer, was buried here in 1585. (He probably used the existing organ console and his music is played at evensong on 23 November, the anniversary of his death.) The tower was rebuilt in 1617 but in 1710 destroyed by a storm during which part of the nave fell in. The parishioners could not afford to finance a new church themselves and suggested that Parliament should levy a coal tax to pay for one. This was the first of Queen Anne's 50 churches financed in this way. It was rebuilt in 1712–18 by Nicholas Hawksmoor who also designed a tower and steeple but the Church Commissioners rejected the plans and he later used them for ST GEORGE IN THE EAST. John James added the western tower in 1730. Badly damaged in the 2nd World War, the Church was restored in 1952 by Sir Albert Richardson. Sir James Thornhill's altarpiece was repainted by Glynn Jones and a new east window by F.H. Spear was installed. General Wolfe was buried here in the family vault in 1759 and the future General Gordon, hero of Khartoum, was christened here in 1833. St Peter's, which used to stand nearby, was destroyed in the 2nd World War and the parish united with St Alfege's.

St Andrew *Enfield Market Place, Middlesex*. A town church in the heart of ENFIELD. The nave and west tower date from the 16th century. There are several fine monuments including one by Nicholas Stone. An epitaph in the churchyard to Thomas Carter (d.1742) reads:

> Wail not our fate, wail for thy own;
> We rest in peace, while you drudge on.

St Andrew *Holborn (Holborn Circus), EC1*. First mentioned in 951. In 1348 John Thane left houses and shops 'to maintain for ever the fabric of St Andrews Church'. This benefaction still maintains the church and its buildings. The tower and the north and south aisles were rebuilt in about 1446. In 1545 Henry Wriothesley, Earl of Southampton, was baptised here with Henry VIII as his godfather. During the Civil War the rector, John Hacket, carried on using the prayer book. When soldiers entered the church and

held a pistol to his head he told them, 'I'm doing my duty. Now do yours.' They left without harming him. Repaired in 1632 the church escaped damage by the GREAT FIRE. Rebuilt by Wren in 1684–90, it was the largest of his parish churches, measuring 105 ft by 63 ft and costing £9,000. The 15th-century tower was refaced in Portland stone in 1703 and heightened. Dr Henry Sacheverell was rector in 1714–24. One winter's night in 1827 Dr William Marsden found a young girl dying from exposure in the churchyard. He could not get her into any hospital for treatment and she died. The incident so horrified him that he founded the ROYAL FREE HOSPITAL where the poor could be admitted without formality.

The creation of HOLBORN VIADUCT in 1863–9 resulted in the loss of part of the churchyard. Drastically restored by S.S. Teulon in 1871–2, the church was severely damaged by bombs in 1941; but rebuilt in its original form by Seely and Paget in 1960–1. The pulpit, font, organ case, chapel altarpiece, communion rails and the tomb of Thomas Coram were brought from the FOUNDLING HOSPITAL. The reredos in the Lady Chapel came from ST LUKE OLD STREET. The east window, depicting the Resurrection and Last Supper, is by Brian Thomas. In 1954 St Andrew's was made a guild church in charge of post-ordination training and youth work. The parish was united with ST BRIDE'S FLEET STREET. The church was reconsecrated in 1961. Richard Savage, the poet, was christened here in 1696 (the illegitimate son of Lady Macclesfield, he was baptised Richard Smith). Henry Addington was christened here in 1757 and Benjamin Disraeli in 1817. Sir Edward Coke, Lord Chief Justice, was married to Lady Elizabeth Hatton in 1598; Marc Brunel, father of I.K. Brunel, to Miss Sophia Kingdom in 1799; William Hazlitt to Sarah Stoddart in 1808. Charles Lamb was best man and his sister, Mary, a bridesmaid.

Dr Sacheverell was buried beneath the high altar in 1724. The Resurrection stone originally over the entrance to the SHOE LANE burial ground is now in the churchyard.

St Andrew *Kingsbury Old Church Lane, NW9*. First built in Wells Street, MARYLEBONE, by Samuel Dawkes in 1845–7, it became celebrated for the High Anglican services, during 1862–85, when the Revd Benjamin Webb was the incumbent. During these years G.E. Street designed the reredos, chancel screen and font. The litany desk is by William Burges (1867) who also designed the monument to the second incumbent which was shown at the INTERNATIONAL EXHIBITION OF 1862. The *sedilia* was by J.L. Pearson and the sacristy decorations by G.F. Bodley (1881). By 1932 the church had lost most of its congregation as the area had become less densely populated and it was therefore demolished. The stones were numbered and the whole building re-erected in Old Church Lane under the supervision of W.A. Forsyth, with as few changes as possible.

St Andrew by the Wardrobe *Queen Victoria Street, EC4*. First mentioned in about 1244 as St Andre de Castello, an allusion to the nearby BAYNARDS CASTLE. After 1361 its present name was used. This refers to the adjoining KING'S WARDROBE where ceremonial robes were kept. It was repaired and beautified in 1627 but destroyed in the GREAT FIRE. It was rebuilt by Wren at a cost of £7,000 16s 11d in

1685–95. It is a plain brick rectangular church with a plain tower and was the last and cheapest of Wren's city churches. The Rectory House in ST ANDREW'S HILL was built in about 1766. The construction of QUEEN VICTORIA STREET in 1871 removed most of the churchyard and created the church's present elevated position. The remains of the churchyard were laid out as a public garden in 1901. Three bells from Avenbury, Herefordshire, were installed in 1933. One is said to have tolled on its own accord on the death of an Avenbury rector. Except for the walls and tower, the church was destroyed by incendiary bombs in 1940 but was rebuilt in 1959–61 to the designs of Marshall Sisson who used Wren's original plans. Both north and south aisles were enclosed, the former being leased as offices to the British and Foreign Bible Society, the latter being converted into the Chapel of St Ann below and vestries for the rector and churchwardens above. The vaulting is an attempt to reproduce the original Wren motifs. The stained glass in the west window was originally made for Bulstrode Park House, Buckinghamshire, and installed here in 1967. The font and restored pulpit are 17th-century and are from another Wren church, long demolished, ST MATTHEW FRIDAY STREET. The parish now includes the parishes of ST NICHOLAS COLE ABBEY, ST NICHOLAS OLAVE, ST MARY SOMERSET, ST MARY MOUNTHAW, ST BENET PAUL'S WHARF and ST PETER PAUL'S WHARF as well as parts of other parishes.

St Andrew Hubbard First mentioned in 1202. Hubbard was probably a benefactor. Extensively repaired in 1630, it was burnt in the GREAT FIRE and not rebuilt. The parish was united with ST MARY AT HILL in 1670. A plaque at No. 16 EASTCHEAP marks the site.

St Andrew and St Michael *Blackwall Lane (Tunnel Avenue), SE10*. Built by Basil Champneys in 1900–2 of yellow stock brick with pantiled roofs. Despite being unfortunately sited on a busy approach road to BLACKWALL TUNNEL, the church is an appealing building with attractive wrought-iron bellcote. The interior has a barrel roof and the font came from ST MICHAEL'S, WOOD STREET in the CITY.

St Andrew Undershaft *Leadenhall Street, EC3*. First mentioned in 1147 as St Andrew Cornhill. Its present name was given it in the 15th century because an unusually tall maypole was put up annually beside the church. On EVIL MAY DAY 1517 there was a riot of City apprentices, resulting in the hanging of one man and the arrest of 300. The maypole was then stored under the eaves of houses in Shaft Alley until 1549 when it was denounced as a heathen idol by the curate of ST KATHARINE CREE and chopped into pieces and burnt. In 1520–32 the church was rebuilt in the Gothic style at the expense of Sir William Fitzwilliam, Sheriff, and Sir Stephen Jenyns, Lord Mayor. Jenyns's coat-of-arms is on the north aisle ceiling. The parish was united with that of ST MARY AXE in 1561. The church was restored in 1627. A new east window depicting Edward VI, Elizabeth I, James I and Charles I was presented by Sir Christopher Clitherow, Lord Mayor, in 1635. In 1634 the font by Nicholas Stone was installed. It cost £16. Having escaped damage in the GREAT FIRE, the church was restored in 1684. The organ by Renatus Harris dates from 1696. In 1704 the communion rails were made for the church by Jean Tijou as part of improve-ments that included wainscotting, new pews and new paving. In 1726 Henry Tombes paid for the paintings of apostles between the clerestory windows and for the painting over the chancel, *The Heavenly Choir*, by Robert Brown.

During the 18th and 19th centuries there were several interior restorations. The tower was partly rebuilt in 1830; and in 1875 the church was further 'improved': the wainscotting, sounding board, communion rails and west gallery were removed and the organ transferred to the chancel; the east window was moved to the west end and William III substituted for Charles II. The east window was then filled with glass showing the *Ascension* and the *Crucifixion* by Heaton Butler. The roof was renewed in 1949–52 and the original 125 bosses replaced. The bosses are all different and include Catherine of Aragon's pomegranate and Henry VIII's rose. John Stow, London's first historian, was buried here in 1605. A terracotta monument, erected by his widow, was replaced by the MERCHANT TAYLORS' COMPANY in 1905. Every year the LORD MAYOR attends a memorial service at the church and puts a new quill pen into Stow's hand, presenting the old one and a copy of Stow's book to the child who writes the best essay on London. Holbein the Younger may be buried here. He died in 1543 and lived in the parish but his remains could also be in nearby ST KATHERINE CREE. There is a 1534 brass of Nicholas Levison, his wife and 18 children. The parish was united with that of ST KATHERINE CREE in 1954. The damage caused by a bad fire in 1976 has been repaired.

St Andrew's Gardens *see* BURIAL GROUNDS.

St Andrew's Hospital *Devons Road, Bow, E3*. Opened in 1871 under the name of the Poplar and Stepney Sick Asylum for the Poor. Before 1867 no statutory provisions existed for the destitute sick. In most districts workhouses were adapted to house these people. The building consisted of eight separate blocks containing 572 beds and was staffed by 26 nurses. In 1895, following further building it was possible to house 789 patients. In the 1920s the hospital was given its present name, that of a nearby church destroyed by enemy action in the 2nd World War. In 1948 the National Health Service assumed control. It is now an acute general hospital with 372 beds.

St Ann *Blackfriars*. The Monastery of BLACKFRIARS was dissolved in 1538 and the church demolished. A temporary church was provided for the parishioners by Sir Thomas Cawarden to whom the buildings had been granted (*see* BLACKFRIARS MONASTERY). The roof of the church collapsed in 1597 and a more substantial church was built, but this was burned down in the GREAT FIRE and not replaced. The parish was united with ST ANDREW BY THE WARDROBE.

St Ann *Mortlake SW14*. Built in 1714, this church has been enlarged several times, first in 1766 to plans of J.J. Kirby; for the second time in 1810, under the direction of Robert Browne; again in 1837 by Sir Jeffry Wyatville; and the apsidal domed chancel, south chapel and vestry were added in 1884 by H. Stock.

St Anne *Kew Green, Surrey*. In an effective siting on the side of the beautiful green, lined with many

Georgian houses, St Anne's is chiefly noted for its intimate royal connections. Built in 1710–14 with Queen Anne's support, it was enlarged – mainly at the expense of George III – in 1770 when he bought KEW PALACE. In 1836 William IV provided 200 free seats in the north side, and in 1866 the parents of the future Queen Mary were married here.

The church in its present form dates from the 19th century when the portico and bell-turret were added at the west and the octagon, plus mausoleum, for the Duke and Duchess of Cambridge at the east end. There is a pleasing long interior with vaulted ceiling and timber columns. Thomas Gainsborough is buried on the south side of the churchyard.

St Anne *Limehouse (Commercial Road), E14.* Built in 1712–24 in open fields immediately to the north of the riverside colony of LIMEHOUSE, and consecrated in 1730. 'Afterwards the bishop drank a little hot wine and took a bit of ye sweetmeats and then ye clergy and ye laity scrambled for ye rest for they left not a bitt.' It is now known why the church was not consecrated for six years but the first rector, Robert Leybourne, was the rector of ST DUNSTAN AND ALL SAINTS, STEPNEY from which parish the new one had been formed. This may be significant. Certainly the Bishop of London in his address at the consecration spoke of the 'many oppositions' encountered by the ecclesiastical lawyer who dealt with the creation of the new parish.

The church was designed by Nicholas Hawksmoor. It is almost the shape of a Greek cross but has an elongated nave. There is a broad based tower at the west end. The main entrance is through an apsidal

Hawksmoor's St Anne Limehouse, completed in 1724, still has the highest clock in London. Engraving of c. 1855.

porch at the west end and there are side entrances from the north and south leading into lobbies. When the church was completed the parish of Limehouse had insufficient funds to pay the stipend of an incumbent. In 1850 the church was gutted by a fire which began when a roof timber fell and blocked the chimney flue. It was repaired in 1851–7 by John Morris and Philip Hardwick, at a cost of £13,000. The font and pulpit are theirs. The stained glass window of the *Crucifixion* at the east end was designed by Clutterbuck and dates from this time. Restored by Sir Arthur Blomfield in 1891, the church was badly damaged by bombing in 1941. The clock is the highest church clock in London.

St Anne *Soho (Wardour Street).* Built in 1677–86 to the designs of either Wren or William Talman, possibly both. The tower was added in 1717 and rebuilt by S.P. Cockerell in 1803. This survived an air raid in 1940 but the rest of the building was destroyed. George II worshipped here as Prince of Wales, having 'discovered an Inclination to come to this Church'. Theodore, the dethroned King of Corsica, was buried here in 1756. (Horace Walpole wrote his epitaph.) Hazlitt was buried in 1830. The tombstones of both can be seen at the foot at the tower. In 1976 an appeal to restore the tower was launched by the Poet Laureate, Sir John Betjeman, who declaimed lines written for the occasion:

High in the air two barrels interlock
To form the faces of this famous clock
Reduced to drawing-room size this clock would be
A Paris ornament of 1803.
Let's make it go again, let London know
That life and heart and hope are in Soho.

The church gardens had to be raised six feet above the pavement to accommodate the more than 10,000 corpses of parishioners who are buried here. In 1978 a plaque to commemorate Dorothy L. Sayers, the detective story writer, theologian and churchwarden here, was unveiled. Her ashes are buried beneath the tower.

St Anne *Wandsworth (St Anne's Hill), SW18.* WANDSWORTH developed rapidly in the early part of the 19th century, and in 1820 the CHURCH COMMISSIONERS considered the size of the parish necessitated a chapel-of-ease. Accordingly the vestry purchased this hill-top site in what was then open country to the east of the river WANDLE. Known affectionately by its parishioners as 'The Pepper Pot Church', it was designed by Sir Robert Smirke, the surveyor to the Commissioners and architect of the BRITISH MUSEUM. St Anne's was the fifth 'Waterloo Church' built to commemorate the victorious ending of the Napoleonic Wars. The Commissioners agreed to contribute a maximum sum of £15,000 towards the expense of the building. Smirke used his favourite Ionic order for the portico, but in this instance his proportions are not good, and the round tower rising uncomfortably behind it from a square base, is distinctly too tall. The body of the church is plainly built of stock brick. It has large round-headed windows over smaller ones. The galleried interior originally provided for 426 rented pews and 332 free seats. On 1 May 1824 the church was consecrated. It had cost £14,510 14s 9d. In 1822 a dispute arose between the vestry and the Bishop of Winchester, in whose diocese St Anne's was included, concerning the construction of the fence around the graveyard. Members of the vestry had been evenly divided in their opinion as to which was the most suitable material to use, iron or oak. When they informed the Bishop that they had agreed to compromise and proposed building the fence of equal quantities of both materials, he objected and ordered them to choose either one or the other. They ignored his injunction and he in turn refused to consecrate the ground. To this day no burials have taken place in the burial ground. St Anne's became a parish church in its own right in 1850. The chancel was added in 1896 and is the work of Edward Mountford, architect of Sheffield Town Hall.

The church was badly damaged in 1944. On the 129th anniversary of Wellington's victory over Napoleon at Waterloo, a flying bomb fell, causing havoc. It was soon after the beginning of the Sunday morning service and many members of the congregation were injured. After the war the church was repaired and in 1947 a ceremony of rehallowing took place 140 ft up on the scaffolding that surrounded the dome of the 'pepper-pot' tower. The vicar climbed a further 20 ft in order to bless the cross. Three years later, however, a disastrous fire destroyed the roof and so the work of restoration had to be embarked upon once again. The church was reopened in 1951.

St Anne and St Agnes *Gresham Street, EC2.* Also once known as St Anne, St Anne near Aldergate, St Anne in the Willows, St Anne and St Agnes within Aldersgate, it is first mentioned in 1137. In 1548 it was burnt down and rebuilt. The tower was repaired in 1629–30. The vicar in 1649 was beheaded for protesting against the execution of Charles I. The church was destroyed in the GREAT FIRE. The parish was joined to that of ST JOHN ZACHARY in 1670. Wren built the fabric in a charming domestic style in 1676–87 at a cost of £2,448 0s 11d. Badly damaged in 1940, it was made a guild church for Lutheran worship in 1954; and the parish was joined to that of ST VEDAST FOSTER LANE. The church was rebuilt by Bráddock and Martin-Smith in 1963–8.

St Ann's Hospital *St Ann's Road, N15.* Built about 1900 as an infectious diseases hospital. It is now an acute general hospital with an infectious diseases unit. It has 432 beds.

St Ann's Lane *SW1.* Between OLD PYE STREET and GREAT PETER STREET. Robert Herrick, the poet and devoted Royalist, having been ejected from his living of Dean Prior in Devonshire, lived here as 'Robert Herrick, Squire' from about 1647 until the Restoration. Henry Purcell, the composer, the son of Henry Purcell, 'master of children of Westminster Abbey' and music copyist there, was born in the Lane in about 1658.

St Ann's Villas *W1.* Possibly named after a church projected but never built. Albert Chevalier, the music-hall comedian, was born at No. 17, then numbered 21.

St Anselm and St Cecilia *Kingsway, WC2.* Roman Catholic church opened in 1909 to replace the SARDINIAN CHAPEL which was demolished for the creation of KINGSWAY. The architect was F.A. Walters. The south aisle was added and the façade rebuilt to

designs of S.C. Kerr Bate in 1951–4. There is a late 18th-century painting, *The Deposition of Christ*, which may have come from the SARDINIAN CHAPEL. The altar stone and altar certainly did. These were originally in the Lady Chapel of Glastonbury Abbey.

St Antholin *(St Anthony) Peckham, (Nunhead Lane) SE15.* The successor, built in 1877–8, to Wren's ST ANTHOLIN, WATLING STREET, regrettably demolished in 1875. Although of little architectural interest, the new church retains the City church's fine reredos. St Antholin's was badly damaged during the 2nd World War.

St Antholin *Watling Street. Named after St Anthony the Hermit and built in 1678 to replace an ancient church that had been gutted in the* GREAT FIRE. *It was considered to be one of Wren's finest buildings. It was thoughtlessly destroyed in 1875, the site sold for £44,990 and the money spent on a new church of St Antholin in Nunhead Lane,* PECKHAM. *Wren's spire was sold for £5. The top 15 ft of it still stand in the garden of* FOREST HILL *Social Club.*

St Anthony's Hospital *Threadneedle Street.* In 1242 Henry III gave a former synagogue on the north side of THREADNEEDLE STREET to brothers from the Hospital of St Antoine de Viennois. The brothers had come to England to collect alms for the French hospital where people were treated for ergotism (St Anthony's Fire) caused by eating poisonous grains of rye. They also prayed for souls and gave food, clothes and lodgings to passers-by. They relied entirely on charity and the CITY authorities let them have any pig which was considered unfit to be killed for food. The pigs used to follow those they knew would feed them which gave rise to the expression 'such an one will follow such an one and whine as it were an Anthony pig.' (There were still Anthony pigs in 1525 but they were extinct by 1545.) In 1310 the chapel was rebuilt. In 1389 Richard II appointed one of his clerks, John Macclesfield as Warden and in 1414 it became a royal free chapel under the Alien Priories Act. In 1429 the adjoining house and land were acquired for a garden, cemetery and hospice for the poor. In 1440 most of the revenues of ST BENET FINK were appropriated to found a grammar school which became one of the two main CITY schools. Every year boys from St Anthony's competed for prizes against their rivals from the school of St Thomas Acon in the churchyard of ST BARTHOLOMEW THE GREAT. The Anthony's boys usually won. Thomas More and Archbishop Whitgift were once pupils. In 1442 Henry VI endowed five scholarships to Eton and Oxford. In 1475 Edward IV gave the hospital to the Dean and Canons of St George's, Windsor. The hospital was not dissolved by Henry VIII or Edward VI. In the 1540s, however, Edmund Johnson, the schoolmaster, and a prebendary of Windsor, dissolved the choir, took away the plate, ornaments and bells and turned the almsmen out with a pension of 1s a week. Thereafter the school declined and in 1550 the chapel was let to become the French Protestant Church. All the buildings were destroyed in the GREAT FIRE.

St Augustine *Queen's Gate, SW7.* In 1865 the curate of Holy Trinity, BROMPTON, the Revd R.R. Chope had a temporary iron church put up in his garden off GLOUCESTER ROAD and there he would conduct services which, for one writer of the time, were 'the nearest approach to Romanism we have yet witnessed in an Anglican Church ... if indeed it be not very Popery itself under the thinnest guise of the Protestant name.' Finding Mr Chope's shed inadequate, a group of influential members of his congregation approached the CHURCH COMMISSIONERS later that year with a request for the formation of a new parish in SOUTH KENSINGTON to be known as St Augustine's. They offered a 'benefaction' of £100 per annum, stipulating that the first incumbent should be Mr Chope. As there was no shortage of churches in the neighbourhood, the Bishop of London, A.C. Tait, objected strongly to the proposal and it was not until he became Archbishop of Canterbury in 1869 that a site was purchased and the new parish formed. It was a difficult site, for although plans had been formulated to extend QUEEN'S GATE to OLD BROMPTON ROAD, at this time the road went no further than the crossing of Harrington Road. Access to the site had to be made through what is today Reece Mews, and the church plan was aligned with this. This accounts for the strange angle the church presents today in relation to QUEEN'S GATE. William Butterfield was appointed architect and the estimated cost of his plan was £18,000. As there was not enough money, it was proposed to build the church in two stages. The nave and adjourning aisles were ready for services in 1871. The chancel and sanctuary were completed in 1876. The seating capacity was for 853 people. The design is considered to be a robust example of Butterfield's work. His style, reminiscent of the great brick churches of northern Germany, is in striking contrast with the dull correctness of KENSINGTON street architecture for which he had a particular dislike. The tall, west façade is broken with bands of Bath stone and red brick. The large gabled bellcote for two bells dominates. The interior is composed of many different coloured materials: white, red and pink stone; red, yellow and blue bricks; Pether's patent moulded bricks; dark grey slate and many coloured marbles; there are unglazed tiles and mosaics, as well as glazed tile murals. In the 1920s these last were considered 'frightful' and were boarded up and all the colourful brickwork of the interior was whitewashed. This was removed in 1974 and Butterfield's colour scheme restored. The exhuberant baroque reredos (1928) is the work of Martin Travers who also altered the east window and designed the altar in the Lady Chapel.

St Augustine in the Wall *St Mary Axe*. A small parish church first mentioned in the 12th century and also known as St Augustine Papey. In 1442 it became the chapel of a hospital for poor priests because its population had dwindled to ten householders. The parish was amalgamated with ALL HALLOWS ON THE WALL. The hospital priests took the name already attached to the Church and became the Fraternity of the Papey. Edward VI suppressed it, and the church was demolished.

St Augustine of Hippo *South Bermondsey, (Lynton Road), SE1*. Built in the early 1880s, the interior is in the Early English Lancet style with arcades of pink Dumfries sandstone and finely carved Portland stone capitals.

St Augustine with St Faith *Watling Street*. Has also been known as St Augustine by St Paul's Churchyard, at St Paul's Gate, Old Change and Old Fish Street. It is first mentioned in 1148. It was enlarged and repaired in 1630–1. Burned down in the GREAT FIRE it was rebuilt in 1680–7 by Wren as a small church costing £3,145 3s. 10d. The spire was completed in 1695. It was restored in 1829 and again in 1866. R.H. Barham, author of *The Ingoldsby Legends*, was vicar in 1842–5. It was bombed in 1940 and only the tower and spire remained. The parish was united to ST MARY-LE-BOW in 1954, having already been united with that of St Faith's in 1670. The tower was restored in 1954 and a new spire, a copy of the old one, was erected. This was incorporated in 1965–7 by Architects' Co-Partnership into a new building for St Paul's Choir School.

St Augustine with St John *Kilburn (Kilburn Park Road), NW6*. A magnificent redbrick church with a vaulted interior designed by J.L. Pearson in 1871 and 1880. The tower and spire were not finished until 1898 and the decorations not until some years later. It is one of the largest Victorian churches in London. The altar in the Lady Chapel is by Sir Giles Gilbert Scott.

St Augustine with St Philip *Stepney, E1*. The largest church in the East End. It was built in 1888–92 to the designs of Arthur Cawston and largely financed by the extremely rich vicar, the Revd Sidney Vacher.

St Barnabas *Addison Road, W8*. In 1827, the CHURCH COMMISSIONERS asked Lewis Vulliamy to design a church for the people of WEST KENSINGTON, who had, they considered, too far to walk to their parish church of ST MARY ABBOTS. Lord Holland, the nephew of Charles James Fox, gave the site and the Commissioners contributed £7,983 towards the £10,938 it cost to build. There is a window designed by Sir Edward Burne-Jones on the south side of the sanctuary, and at the west end of the church, in the foyer, there is one by John Byam Shaw who was a choirboy at St Barnabas and a sidesman in 1905–19.

Several celebrated people have been married here: in January 1844, Ellen Terry married George Frederick Watts. On 4 June 1878 Teddy Kilvert, brother of the diarist, married Nellie Pitcairn, and in 1957 T.S. Eliot married his second wife.

The unusually large crypt is today the headquarters of the London Boy Singers, a choir formed in 1961 under the patronage of Benjamin Britten. In the early 1960s three pop musicians, later to achieve fame as The Who, also used the crypt for rehearsal.

St Barnabas *King Square, EC1*. The neighbouring churches of St Matthew by Gilbert Scott and St Clement by William Butterfield were both demolished and were absorbed into the parish of St Barnabas. The church was built in 1822–6.

St Barnabas *Pimlico (St Barnabas Street), SW1*. Small Gothic church designed by Thomas Cundy in 1846–9. It was the first London church to incorporate the ideas of the Oxford Movement. The *Ecclesiologist* hailed it as the most complete and sumptuous church dedicated since the Revival. It was the cause of anti-Papal riots in 1850. The reredos by Bodley and Garner was added in 1893; the Lady Chapel by Ninian Comper in 1900. The rood screen is by Bodley, 1906.

St Bartholomew *Moor Lane.* Built in 1848–50 to the designs of C.R. Cockerell as a facsimile of ST BARTHOLOMEW-BY-THE-EXCHANGE, which had been demolished a few years earlier. The CHURCH COMMISSIONERS paid £1,400 for the site which had formerly been that of St Giles's Workhouse. Some of the materials and fittings from Wren's church were used. The church was demolished in 1902, having lost much of its parish when the Metropolitan Railway was built. The site was sold for £20,400 and the church of St Bartholomew at Stamford Hill was erected with the proceeds. The pulpit, font and cover and altar rails were taken there. The reredos and other carvings are in ST GILES WITHOUT CRIPPLEGATE.

St Bartholomew-by-the-Exchange *Bartholomew Lane.* Once known as Little St Bartholomew and St Bartholomew the Less. First mentioned in 1150, it was rebuilt in 1438. The south chapel was added by Sir William Capel in 1509. Repaired in 1620, the church was destroyed in the GREAT FIRE. It was rebuilt by Wren at a cost of £5,077 1s 1d in 1674–9, but demolished, in 1840–1, to make way for new ROYAL EXCHANGE. The materials were sold for £483 15s 0d; the plate given to ST MARGARET LOTHBURY and the two parishes united. The pulpit, organ and woodwork were incorporated in a replica church, ST BARTHOLOMEW MOOR LANE, CRIPPLEGATE built to the designs of C.R. Cockerell in 1848–5. The site is now covered by the Sun Alliance Offices. Miles Coverdale, translator of the Bible, was buried here in 1568.

St Bartholomew-the-Great *West Smithfield, EC1.* London's oldest church. It is the only surviving part of the Augustinian priory founded in 1123 by Rahere, Henry I's court jester, after a vision in which St Bartholomew saved him from a winged monster. Rahere became the first prior and built a choir, ambulatory and Lady Chapel. In 1133 Henry I granted the prior and canons the right to hold ST BARTHOLOMEW'S FAIR. In the middle of the 12th century Rahere's successor added the transepts and crossing. The long nave was built in 1230–40. The timbered gateway leading to the church marks the site of the south door. The completed church measured approximately 300 ft by 86 ft and had a central tower at the crossing flanked by two turrets. The Lady Chapel was rebuilt in 1336; and in 1405–6 the east wall of the choir was rebuilt, as well as the bell tower, clerestory, cloister and chapter house. In 1515 Prior Bolton added the oriel window overlooking the choir, probably to keep an eye on the offerings on Rahere's tomb opposite. On it is his rebus, a crossbow in a cask (bolt and tun). In 1539 Prior Robert Fuller quietly surrendered to Henry VIII. The nave was pulled down but the Norman choir was left for parishioners. The remaining monastic buildings were sold in 1544 to Sir Richard Rich whose family owned them until 1862. In 1556 Mary I allowed some Dominican monks to return; but Elizabeth I expelled them in 1559.

The central tower was removed and a new one built at the west end in 1628. The monastic buildings were mostly leased out. The crypt was used as a coal and wine store. The Lady Chapel was in turn three private houses, a printer's office, where Benjamin Franklin worked in 1725, and a workshop. There were stables in the cloisters, a blacksmith's forge in the north transept, a non-conformist meeting house and school in the south triforium, a parish school in the north triforium and a carpenter's workshop and a hop store in the sacristy. In 1863–85 the church was restored by Aston Webb; and in 1893 the porch was rebuilt and the west front refaced under Webb's direction. The choir screen, decorated with paintings of the monks' daily routine by Frank Beresford, was erected in 1932. The font is 15th-century. The tomb of Rahere, who was buried here in 1143, is 16th-century. Sir Walter Mildmay, founder of Emmanuel College Cambridge, was buried here in 1589; and William Hogarth christened here in 1697. The BUTCHERS' COMPANY hold their annual service here.

St Bartholomew-the-Less *West Smithfield, EC1.* Founded in about 1184 as a chapel of ST BARTHOLOMEW'S HOSPITAL. Two 15th-century arches survive under the tower. It was made a parish church in 1547 when Henry VIII refounded the hospital. The interior was rebuilt in wood as an octagon within a square by George Dance the Younger in 1789. The nave was rebuilt in stone by Thomas Hardwick, following Dance's plan, in 1823–5. Most of the fittings are Victorian. The church was badly damaged in the 2nd World War, restored by Seely and Paget and reopened in 1956.

Inigo Jones was christened here in 1573 and numerous physicians, surgeons and treasurers from ST BARTHOLOMEW'S HOSPITAL are buried here.

St Bartholomew's Hospital *West Smithfield, EC1.* The oldest hospital in London. It was founded in 1123 by Rahere, an Augustinian of Frankish descent, who had suffered an attack of malarial fever on a pilgrimage to Rome and had made a vow to build a hospital in London on his return. For this purpose he was granted a strip of land in Smithfield, just outside the City wall, by Henry I. He founded a priory (*see* ST BARTHOLOMEW-THE-GREAT) as well as a hospital. The hospital was run by a master, eight brethren and four Augustinian nuns. The master had a servant who had to stay continuously in the infirmary 'to wait upon the sick with diligence and care in all gentleness'. The needy, orphans, outcasts and poor of the district were looked after, as well as the sick and travellers.

In 1381 Wat Tyler was brought here after being stabbed by the LORD MAYOR (*see* PEASANTS' REVOLT) but he was followed by the King's men and dragged out and beheaded on the spot. In 1537 the priory was dissolved by Henry VIII and its revenues confiscated. The hospital managed to keep going, although it had little money. In 1544 it was refounded by the King on the petition of Sir Richard Gresham. In 1548 the CITY authorities replaced the master and chaplains by a court of governors made up of four aldermen and eight commoners. The LORD MAYOR presided. In 1549 three surgeons were appointed and in 1551 the number of sisters was increased to 12, one of whom acted as matron. Among her duties was making sure that none of the sisters came out of the women's wards during the night, except for some 'great and special cause'. In 1568 Dr Roderigo Lopez became the hospital's first physician. (He was hanged at TYBURN in 1594 accused of trying to poison Elizabeth I.) In 1585 the surgeons asked for a garden where they could grow herbs. A surgery room for the poor was built in 1597. William Harvey was chief physician to the hospital in 1609–33.

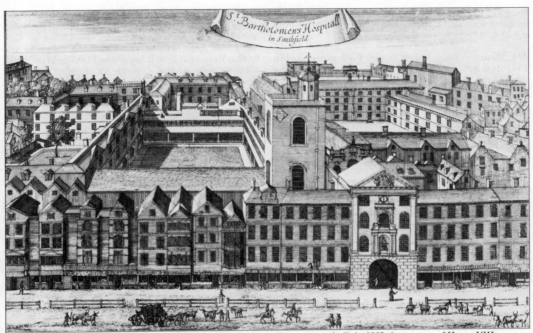

St Bartholomew's Hospital, the oldest in London, in 1725. Over the gateway, built in 1702, is a statue of Henry VIII.

The presence of medical students is first recorded in 1662 although it is probable that there were students before that date. By 1699 the surgeons were paid 6s 8d for every amputation they performed. To ensure that none were carried out unnecessarily the approval of the treasurer, governors and other surgeons had first to be obtained and the patient's friends notified.

In 1702 the gateway was built by Edward Strong. Over it is a stone statue of Henry VIII by Francis Bird. In 1714 stones taken from the patients during operations were ordered to be shown to the governors and then hung in the counting house. This was perhaps the beginning of the pathological museum. In 1722 the physicians and surgeons asked the governors to provide a dissecting room and hot and cold baths for the patients. The hospital was rebuilt in four blocks round a courtyard by James Gibbs in 1730–59. William Hogarth was appointed a governor in 1734. Three years later he received official thanks for painting *The Good Samaritan* and *The Pool of Bethesda* which now hang on the main staircase. In 1744 it was decreed that patients who did not attend church on Sunday or holidays should not be given any dinner. Percival Pott, diagnoser of Pott's disease and Pott's fracture, was surgeon to the hospital in 1749–87. A lecturer on midwifery was appointed in 1787 and in 1791 a new lecture hall was built for John Abernethy, lecturer on anatomy, physiology and surgery, for whom a larger dissecting room was built in 1822. A dentist was appointed in 1836. The out-patients' department was built in 1842; and a residential college for medical students was established in LITTLE BRITAIN that same year. In 1861, James Paget, who first described several medical and surgical disorders, was appointed surgeon. An opthalmic surgeon was appointed in 1870; and an anaesthetist engaged in 1875. The nurses' school was begun in 1877; and the electrical department opened in 1878. An aural surgeon was appointed in 1882; a pathologist in 1893; a laryngologist in 1906; a physician for diseases of the skin in 1908; and the orthopaedic department was opened in 1911. In 1912, Archibald Garrod, who made a fundamental contribution to medicine with his discovery of 'inborn errors of metabolism', was appointed to the staff. The medical school became a constituent college of the UNIVERSITY OF LONDON in 1900. It was the first medical school in London to introduce professional units in medicine and surgery with a full-time director and staff. These units were started in 1919, and in 1921 the first professors were appointed, Francis Fraser in medicine and George Gask in surgery. A new out-patient and casualty department was built in 1904–7 by I'Anson who also designed the pathological block (1907–9). A new nurses' home was built in 1921–9; and a new surgical block, designed by W.T.A. Lodge, was built in 1929–30. In 1933 the site of MERCHANT TAYLORS' SCHOOL, CHARTERHOUSE SQUARE was repurchased. (It had originally been given to the hospital in 1187 by Ermengarde, Prioress of ST MARY'S CLERKENWELL, and had been sold to Sir Walter de Manny in 1370 as a site for CHARTERHOUSE priory.)

In 1937 the George V Block, designed by Lodge, replaced the south block of Gibbs's hospital. The lecture theatre, operating theatres and medical students' residential college were all bombed in 1940–1. In 1947–57 the medical school was built in CHARTERHOUSE SQUARE by Easton and Robertson. The hospital continued under the Henry VIII charter until 1948 when it was absorbed into the National Health Service. The Board of Governors survived until 1974 when Bart's, as it is familiarly known, became part of the City and Hackney Health District together with the other hospitals in the area, of which the largest is

HACKNEY HOSPITAL. Bart's continues as a teaching hospital with many specialised departments. In 1982 it had 826 beds.

St Benet *Gracechurch Street*. First mentioned in 1181. It was repaired in 1630–3 and was destroyed in the GREAT FIRE. Rebuilt by Wren at a cost of £3,583 9s 5½d in 1681–7, it was closed in 1864 and the parish united with ALL HALLOWS LOMBARD STREET, and later also with ST EDMUND KING AND MARTYR. The church was demolished in 1867–8 and the site sold for £24,000. The *Illustrated London News*, which condemned its 'ugly spire', thought that the widening of the entrance of FEN-CHURCH STREET by the 'removal of the church [would be] a great improvement to the city and [would] prevent many of the accidents to which foot passengers [had] always been exposed at the junction of the two streets.' St Benet Mile End Road was built on the proceeds. The pulpit was given to ST OLAVE HART STREET and the plate divided between the new church of St Benet and ST PAUL SHADWELL. A plaque at No. 64 GRACECHURCH STREET marks the site.

St Benet Fink *Threadneedle Street*. First mentioned in 1216. Stow said it was named after the Robert Fink or Finch who paid for the building. Repaired in 1633, it was destroyed in the GREAT FIRE. It was replaced in 1670–81 by a ten-sided church built by Wren at the cost of £4,129 16s 10d. It was demolished in 1842–4 to make way for the new ROYAL EXCHANGE and the parish united to St Peter Le Poer. Part of the site was given to the CITY CORPORATION to widen Royal Exchange Avenue. On the proceeds of the sale a new church of St Benet Fink was built at TOTTEN-HAM and the church plate transferred there. In 1907 the parish was united with ST MICHAEL CORNHILL. John Henry Newman, the future cardinal, was christened here in 1801 and Richard Baxter, the nonconformist divine, married here in 1662.

St Benet Paul's Wharf *Upper Thames Street, EC4*. One of the prettiest of all Wren's churches. It stands on the site of an early-12th-century church – a victim of the GREAT FIRE. Wren started building in 1677, and the church was opened in 1683. It cost £3,328 18s 10d. It is of dark-red brick, with alternate courses of Portland stone at the corners. The carved garlands that festoon the windows are an unusual feature, for Wren believed in plain walls and 'lofty ornamental Towers and Steeples'. The charming tower is set to the north-west of the nave and is capped by a small lead dome, lantern and simple short spire. The interior is almost a square. Corinthian columns support the galleries, and there is a lovely altarpiece. The Royal Arms of Charles II carved over the doorcase to the tower are particularly fine. The panelled walls, flat ceiling and original stone floor, are all of a homely character.

There are many monuments: one to Inigo Jones, who was buried in the chancel of the old church, and a very good medallion bust in white marble of Sir Robert Wyseman, Dean of the COURT OF ARCHES and a benefactor of St Benet's who died in 1684. The institution of ecclesiastical lawyers, known as DOCTORS' COMMONS, had a special association with the church and this made it a convenient place for quick marriages in the 18th century. Henry Fielding married his first wife's former maid here in 1747.

In 1879 the parish was united with that of ST NICHOLAS COLE ABBEY and St Benet's, which had been scheduled for destruction under the Union of City Benefices Act, became the London Church of the Welsh Episcopalians. It is still the Metropolitan Welsh Church within the Church of England London Diocese. Services are conducted in Welsh. The church is also used by the ROYAL COLLEGE OF HERALDS.

St Benet Sherehog Built sometime before 1111 in the centre of the wool district (a shere hog is a ram castrated after its first shearing). It was destroyed in the GREAT FIRE and not rebuilt. In 1670 the parish was united with ST STEPHEN WALBROOK.

St Bernard's Hospital *Uxbridge Road, Southall, Middlesex*. The Middlesex County Asylum (commonly known as the Hanwell Lunatic Asylum) was built on a 44-acre site near Hanwell Bridge and completed in 1831. The first governor was Dr (later Sir) William Ellis who believed in humane methods for the treatment of mental patients and introduced employment therapy. In 1838, after a quarrel with the management committee, he resigned and was succeeded by Dr John Connolly (1839–44). Connolly abolished all form of physical restraint and became well-known for his lectures. Wings were added in 1838; there was further extension in 1859, when the number of patients rose to 1,743 and in 1916 to 2,750. The chapel in the early English style was built in 1880.

After the establishment of County Councils in 1888, Hanwell Asylum passed to the LONDON COUNTY COUNCIL and remained under its control until 1948. Its present name was adopted in 1937. In 1980 the number of patients was reduced to 1,200. A monumental brick gateway, recently cleaned, gives access from the Uxbridge Road. In 1979 the hospital was attached to the new EALING HOSPITAL.

St Botolph *Aldersgate, EC1*. One of four churches in London which were dedicated to the 7th-century Saxon Abbot Botolph who became the patron saint of travellers and which stood near the City's gates. This one was largely rebuilt in 1627. After suffering slight damage in the GREAT FIRE it was rebuilt by Nathaniel Wright in 1788–91. The west front was stuccoed in 1831. The interior is charming with sword rests, galleries, round-headed windows and an elaborate barrel-vaulted roof. In the east window there is a transparency, *The Agony in the Garden*, by John Pearson. It ceased to be a parish church in 1954 and became a Guild Church, the parish being divided between ST GILES CRIPPLEGATE and ST BARTHOLOMEW-THE-GREAT, Smithfield. The churchyard is laid out as a garden (*see* POSTMAN'S PARK).

St Botolph *Aldgate, EC3*. Four churches dedicated to St Botolph were built in the 10th and 11th centuries beside the City's main gates for the spiritual comfort of travellers. The original church on this site belonged to the Knighten Guild, a privileged company of men founded in the reign of King Edgar by 13 knights who, in return for certain duties, were granted land in this part of the City. In 1115 the Knighten Guild gave the church to the newly established Priory of Holy Trinity, Aldgate. The priors rebuilt it just before the Reformation. John Stow in his *Survey of London* describes this 'lately new-built church' and observes

The old tower of St Botolph Aldgate in c.1740 rises behind the charity school founded by John Cass.

that 'the parishioners of this parish being of late years mightily increased, the church is pestered with lofts and seats for them'. After the suppression of the Priory in 1532 it became the property of the Crown. In 1727 a churchwardens' report stated that, 'Our Parish Church and Steeple hath been lately well and sufficiently Repair'd, the floors, Pews and Seats in Good Order.' In 1740, however, the surveyor, Benjamin Franklin, pronounced the building unsafe and a new church was designed by George Dance, the Clerk of the City Works. It was completed in 1744 at a cost of £5,536 2s 5d. During the rebuilding the body of a boy was found in a standing position in one of the vaults. People paid 2d to have a peep. They were impressed by the well-preserved state of the intestines.

The present church is a plain brick building with stone dressings. The brick tower with its obelisk spire faces south on to Aldgate High Street. The church is well lit with venetian windows in the centre of three of its sides. The character of the interior was transformed in the 1880s by John Francis Bentley, the architect of WESTMINSTER CATHEDRAL. His treatment of the ceiling with its figured coves is notable for its originality. He retained the galleries on the three sides but altered their balustrade. The reredos is also by him. Restorations were carried out in 1958–66 by Rodney Tatchell, after which the church was rehallowed by the Bishop of London in the presence of the Queen Mother on 8 November 1966.

The church possesses a Renatus Harris organ, donated by a parishioner, Thomas Whiting, in 1676 (*see* ORGANS). There is also a peal of eight bells cast by Lester and Pack in 1744. The lovely carved panel in the gallery in the style of Grinling Gibbons comes from ST MARY'S WHITECHAPEL and is 17th-century. The most interesting monument is that of Thomas, Lord Darcy of the North, and Sir Nicholas Carew with members of their families. These two Knights of

the Garter were beheaded on TOWER HILL in 1537 and 1538 for their allegiance to the Roman Catholic faith. The monument shows a white marble recumbent corpse, covered by a winding sheet, on an albaster tomb. The coloured bust of Robert Dowe, a benefactor of the parish, was erected by the Company of MERCHANT TAYLORS in 1612.

Daniel Defoe was married here in 1683. In his description of the GREAT PLAGUE he mentions two pits dug in this churchyard being filled in four months with 5,136 plague victims. Sir James Cass was christened here in 1661; so too was Jeremy Bentham in 1747. White Kennett, the anti-Jacobite preacher and historian, was an incumbent, in 1700–7, before becoming Bishop of Peterborough. George Appleton, afterwards Archbishop of Perth in Western Australia, was responsible for the opening of the crypt to homeless men when he was the incumbent in the 1960s. The crypt is also used for an East End Youth Club.

St Botolph *Billingsgate (Lower Thames Street).* First mentioned in 1181. It was described by Stow as 'a proper church and hath had many fair monuments therein, now defaced and gone ... destroyed by bad and greedy men of spoil'. It was destroyed in the GREAT FIRE and not rebuilt. The parish was united with that of ST GEORGE BOTOLPH LANE.

St Botolph without Bishopsgate *EC2.* First mentioned in 1212. Stow said it overlooked the City ditch. In about 1307 the KNIGHTS TEMPLAR were examined here by an inquisition on charges of corruption. In 1413 a female hermit lived in the churchyard surviving on a pension of 40s. a year from the Sheriff. In 1571–2 the church was rebuilt at the expense of the Lord Mayor, Sir William Allen. It escaped damage in the GREAT FIRE, but had to be demolished in 1724 and was rebuilt in 1725–8 by George Dance the Elder and his father-in-law, James Gould, at the cost of £10,400. It was subsequently restored no less than seven times. In 1819–28 C.J. Blomfield, afterwards Bishop of London, was rector. In 1821 the glass dome was added by Michael Meredith to lighten the interior; in 1869 the west window was put in and in 1878 the chancel was remodelled by A.T. Carter. In 1897 it was said to be one of the richest livings in the CITY; the incumbent received £3,090 a year. After damage in the 2nd World War it was restored by N.F. Cachemaille-Day and a new east window *The Risen Christ* was installed. In 1954 the parish was amalgamated with that of ALL HALLOWS LONDON WALL. To the west of the church is the old school room, a mid-19th-century building which has statues of charity children in COADE STONE on the front. Edward Alleyn, founder of DULWICH COLLEGE, was christened here in 1566 and John Keats in 1795. Sir Paul Pindar (*see* PAUL PINDAR'S HOUSE) was buried here in 1650.

St Bride *Fleet Street, EC4.* After an air raid in December 1940 the archaeologist, Professor W.F. Grimes, was invited to excavate the site of the ruined church and to investigate the crypts. These had been used as burial chambers and a charnel house for many centuries. (Samuel Pepys mentions having to bribe the grave digger with sixpence to 'justle together' the bodies because 'of the fulness of the middle isle' to make room for his brother, Tom, when he died in 1664.) The discoveries made by Professor Grimes

St Bride, Fleet Street, rebuilt by Wren, with St Paul's in the background. From an engraving by Bowles, 1753.

took the history of St Bride's back to the Romans and the first Irish settlement in London. The remains of a substantial Roman house are preserved in the crypt. Many of the legends relating to St Bride's were proved to be true, and the antiquity of the spot as a place of Christian worship was confirmed. It was now possible for scholars to deduce that St Bridget, a 6th-century Irish saint from Kildare, founded the first Christian church here. The feast day of St Bridget used to be celebrated on the same day as that of Brigit – the pre-Christian Celtic goddess of fertility. Churches bearing her name are generally to be found near wells, and St Bride's Well is known to have had some religious significance. The Roman finds included a ditch and, within its boundary, the skeleton of a Roman woman who had been given a Christian burial. The foundations of seven different churches dating from the 6th to the 17th century were also revealed.

The traces of the first Saxon church show a marked resemblance to one of the same date at Kildare. The second church, built in the 6th century, may have been pillaged by the Danes. The Norman church, built in the late 12th century was a place of secular as well as religious importance. It had a separate tower and was one of four CITY churches appointed to ring the curfew. The *Curia Regis* met here in 1205, and King John held a parliament in the church in 1210. In the 15th century William Vyner, Warden of the FLEET PRISON, built a large perpendicular church. Fragments of the masonry and glass described by Stow as being 'wrought about' with grapes and vines as a pun on Vyner's name, have been uncovered. It was at this time that Caxton's apprentice, Wynkyn de Worde, brought the printing press to FLEET STREET. He was buried in St Bride's in 1535. Other parishioners of this date were the parents of Virginia Dare, the first English child born in colonial America in 1587. The parents of Edward Winslow, one of the leaders of the Pilgrim Fathers, were married here. In his youth Winslow worked as an apprentice in FLEET STREET.

Writer and poets, attracted by the printing press, now came to live in the neighbourhood. Dryden, John Milton, the poet, Richard Lovelace, and the diarist, John Evelyn, were all parishioners. So, too, was Thomas Tompion, 'father of the English clock'. Samuel Pepys and his eight brothers and sisters were christened in St Bride's. Pepys described how the parish suffered during the GREAT PLAGUE: 238 people died in one week. The following year the church was completely destroyed by the GREAT FIRE. The last entry in the church warden's accounts reads 'paid to the ringers for ringing that the Duch was routed . . . 6s'. Five years later Sir Christopher Wren designed one of his largest and most expensive churches to replace Vyner's. It cost £11,430 5s 11d, excluding the steeple, and took seven years to complete. Joshua Marshall, the master mason, carried out much of the work, but died before it was finished.

The spire, which been described as a 'madrigal in stone', was added in 1703. It consists of four octagonal arcades of diminishing size, capped by an obelisk and finished by a ball and vane. Mr Rich, a pastry cook who lived in Fleet Street until his death in 1811, became famous for his wedding cakes modelled on the spire. The tallest of Wren's steeples, it originally measured 234ft but it lost 8 ft after being struck by lightning in 1764. The form the new lighting conductor should take became a subject of national controversy. George III was deeply concerned. He consulted Benjamin Franklin among others. The fact that the King favoured a conductor with blunt ends, while the American felt a pointed one would be more effective led to such comments as 'good, blunt, honest King George' and 'those sharp-witted colonists'.

Meanwhile FLEET STREET and its parish church continued to be a place of consequence for men of letters. The Society of St Cecilia held its annual music festival here and Dryden composed the ode 'Alexander's Feast' for its members. From 1687 to 1798, the Spital sermon was preached at the church. Samuel Richardson, the novelist, was buried here in 1761 together with the other members of his family. (His crushed coffin and brass memorial plaque were found amongst the debris in 1940.) In 1824 parishioners contributed towards the cost of opening up the dramatic approach to the west door under the buildings of St Bride's Avenue. Godfrey Allen who, like Wren, held the Office of Surveyor of the Fabric of ST PAUL'S CATHEDRAL, was the architect commissioned to carry out the work of restoration after its damage in 1940.

The crypts with their wealth of history and relics have been made into a museum. The display cabinets were given by Sir Max Aitken, in memory of his father, Lord Beaverbrook. St Bride's was rededicated in the presence of Queen Elizabeth II and the Duke of Edinburgh 282 years to the day after the opening of Wren's church. It had taken 17 years to restore. Much of the work was paid for by the national newspapers and the glass doors under Wren's archway were presented by the Press Association whose nearby building provides the church's heating. So, although St Bride's is no longer a parish church, the link with the Press begun by Wynkyn de Worde still continues.

St Bride Foundation Institute *Bride Lane, EC4.* Created in 1891 from an amalgamation of parish churches; its building was completed in 1894 to the designs of R.C. Murray. It provided technical classes in letterpress printing and lithography. In 1891 the Foundation bought the library of William Blades, a CITY printer and author of the first serious study of William Caxton, who had assembled the major private collection of books on the history and practice of his trade. A modern technical library was provided for the printing school, and the two libraries were opened in 1895. To these were added that of Talbot Baines Reed (a typefounder as well as a writer of boys' stories), John Southward, and those of other benefactors, and in recent years type, presses,, blocks and plates, so that the collection now documents the whole history of printing and making books. Since 1966 it has been administered by the CITY OF LONDON. The technical classes moved in 1922 to become the London School of Printing in STAMFORD STREET. This in turn went in 1961 to the ELEPHANT AND CASTLE to become the London College of Printing.

St Bride Street *EC4.* Extends north-west from LUDGATE CIRCUS as far as SHOE LANE. It takes its name from St Bridget who was associated with the well near what is now BRIDEWELL PLACE when well worshipping was common practice.

St Bride's Passage *EC4.* Pedestrian pathway with deep steps cut from SALISBURY SQUARE to St Bride's Lane. It was once Blue Ball Court (on Strype's map of 1755), then Bell's Buildings and in 1909 was renamed St Bride's Passage. Its line represents the boundary between the Bishop of Salisbury's estate and the precincts of ST BRIDE'S CHURCH.

St Chad *Dunloe Street, E2.* Built in a slum area in 1868–9 to the plain Gothic designs of James Brooks, who also designed the vicarage (1873), the sole survivor of the Gothic Nichols Square, now demolished.

St Chad's Well *Gray's Inn Road by St Chad's Place.* Medicinal well dedicated to St Chad, the first

Bishop of Lichfield, who is said to have been cured of disease by drinking similar waters. It became popular in the middle of the 18th century and in 1772 it had 1,000 visitors every week. The subscription was £1 per annum. At the beginning of the 19th century its attraction as a spa declined and instead it became a Sunday pleasure garden for local people. Various attempts were made to rejuvenate the spa. In 1829 a theatre for equestrian events was erected. In 1830 St Chad's Place was built on part of the gardens. In 1832 a new pumproom was built. In 1841 William Hone visited it and found it rather derelict and patronised only by locals. In 1860 the last part of the gardens was swept away when the METROPOLITAN LINE was built.

St Charles Hospital *Exmoor Street, W10.* Designed by Saxon Snell and opened in 1881 as the St Marylebone Infirmary. It was given its present name in 1930. It now has strong links with ST MARY'S HOSPITAL, PRAED STREET. It is a District General Hospital with 384 beds.

St Christopher le Stocks *Threadneedle Street.* Built sometime before 1225 on the banks of the WALBROOK and dedicated to the patron saint of watermen. It was first known as St Christopher on Cornhill or St Christopher in Bread Street but after the 14th century it took its name from the nearby STOCKS MARKET. In 1462 it was rebuilt by Richard Shere. Damaged by the GREAT FIRE, it was rebuilt in 1670–6 by Wren who incorporated much of the medieval fabric, so it only cost £2,098 12s 7d. It was his first City church to be completed. During the GORDON RIOTS of 1780 troops were garrisoned in the church and tower to protect the BANK OF ENGLAND. The attack was repulsed but the incident showed the vulnerability of the Bank and a petition was sent to Parliament supported by the Bishop of London and the Prime Minister, Lord North, for the demolition of the church. It was demolished in 1782 and the parish united to ST MARGARET LOTHBURY. Most of the fittings are at St Margaret's but the reredos is at ST VEDAST FOSTER LANE. The Dividend Warrant Office, designed by Sir Robert Taylor, was built on the site. The churchyard was left an open space. Several Lord Mayors are buried here, also William Dan Jenkins, aged 31 and 6 ft 7 ins tall, by special permission, in the disused churchyard in 1798. Surgeons offered body snatchers 200 guineas for his skeleton.

St Clare Minoresses without Aldgate The Convent of Poor Clares was founded by Edmund, Earl of Lancaster, brother of Edward I, in 1293. The first sisters were brought to England by his wife, Blanche of Navarre, probably from France. The nunnery stood outside the City wall at ALDGATE and occupied the site of one of the principal Roman burial grounds. The sisters were not wealthy but were granted many privileges by the King and the Pope which freed them from paying taxes, from interference by bishops and from arrest, except for 'treason or felony touching our crown'. Edmund died in 1296 and his heart was buried under the high altar. In 1346 Queen Isabella gave the sisters the advowsons of three churches. In 1360 Elizabeth de Burgh, Countess of Clare and founder of Clare College, Cambridge, was buried in the nuns' church. Also buried here, in 1481, was Anne Mowbray, Duchess of York, wife of the younger prince

St Christopher Le Stocks, Threadneedle Street in 1781 with the Bank of England to its right. From an aquatint by Malton.

murdered in the TOWER. Her coffin was discovered in 1964 and reburied in WESTMINSTER ABBEY. Lady Anne's mother, Elizabeth Duchess of York, was buried here in 1507 and Edmund de la Pole in 1513. He was executed in the TOWER by order of Henry VIII because of his claim to the throne. His wife, Margaret, and his daughter, Elizabeth, who was one of the minoresses, were also buried here. The convent was burned down in about 1516 but, at the special request of Cardinal Wolsey, the COURT OF COMMON COUNCIL contributed 100 marks to its rebuilding and the LORD MAYOR, ALDERMEN and citizens a further 200. In 1538 the Abbess, Elizabeth Savage, surrendered the convent to the King and was granted an annual pension of £40. Four other nuns got £3 3s 8d, ten more received £2 13s 4d, nine others £2 and a novice received £1 6s 8d. Six lay sisters received nothing at all.

The nuns' church became parochial and was renamed HOLY TRINITY MINORIES. The parishioners continue to claim freedom from taxes, arrest and interference by bishops. In 1539 the Bishop of Bath and Wells was given the convent buildings in exchange for his town house near TEMPLE BAR. He lived in the great house and let the rest to such tenants as the Duchess of Norfolk and the Countess of Kildare. In 1548 his successor exchanged the property with Edward VI for several rectories. Edward granted it to Henry Grey, Duke of Suffolk, whose family sold it to the Marquess of Winchester. It was thereafter used as a residence for the Lieutenant General of the Ordnance and as a munitions' store. Sir Philip Sidney lay in state for three months here in 1586–7 before his funeral in ST PAUL'S. In 1601 John Stow wrote, 'Near adjoining to this abbey on the south side thereof was some time a farm belonging to the said nunnery; at the which farm I myself in my youth have fetched many a halfpenny worth of milk . . . always hot from the kine, as the same was milked and strained.' In 1642 Sir John Heydon, Lieutenant General of the Ordnance, was instructed by Charles I from York 'to send by sea hither or to Newcastle, in as much as it will not be safe to do so by land such cannon, arms, powder, shot and munition you can get out of our stores, ships or other-wise in such secret and close manner that the same may not be interrupted by those who wish not well to our safety and person.' Heydon did so and left soon after to join the King's forces as Lieutenant General of Artillery. The armoury was closed in 1673 and the building sold to private individuals.

According to Hatton there were 120 houses in the parish in 1708. In 1734 Robert Seymour wrote, 'The Minories of which there are the Great and the Little, the Great is a broad and spacious street . . . chiefly noted for the gunsmiths . . . . The Little Minories are the buildings erected upon the site of the Abbey of Nuns . . . containing two or three courts all pretty well inhabited.' In 1756 Maitland said there were 129 houses in the parish, six with coaches. In 1797 a fire destroyed the remaining convent buildings. In 1894 the MINORIES lost its privileges as a liberty by order of the Queen in Council. Clare Street and St Clare Street as well as the Minories commemorate the convent.

St Clement *Barnsbury (Westbourne Road), N7.* A Gilbert Scott church of 1864–5, built of stock brick with three redbrick portals. The tall steep west front is strongly buttressed and has a bellcote.

St Clement *Eastcheap (Clement's Lane and King William Street), EC4.* First mentioned in the 11th century. It is dedicated to the martyred Bishop of Rome who was thrown into the sea with an anchor round his neck. Repaired and beautified in 1632 it was destroyed by the GREAT FIRE. It was rebuilt by Wren at a cost of £4,365 3s 4d in 1683–7. The parishioners were pleased and sent Wren one third of a hogshead of wine. St Clement's is one of his plainest churches with a stuccoed exterior and a tower at the south-west corner. The interior is divided into nave and south aisle and there is a flat plaster ceiling. The 17th-century pulpit has an elaborate carved sounding board and the font an unusual cover of a caged dove. In 1872 there was drastic reorganisation by Butterfield who renewed the seating, removed the south gallery, filled the windows with stained glass and divided the altarpiece into three. In 1933 Sir Ninian Comper reassembled the altarpiece and painted it blue and gold. In 1936 the organ was replaced in the gallery at the west end in its 17th-century case. The church was badly damaged by bombing in 1940.

St Clement Danes, rebuilt by Wren in 1679 with a tower by James Gibbs. From an engraving by Kip, c. 1715.

St Clement Danes *Strand, WC2.* The reasons for the association of the site with the Danes are obscure. According to John Stow it is so called 'because Harold [Harefoot], a Danish King, and other Danes were buried here'. William Fleetwood, however, Recorder of London in 1581, contended that when Alfred the Great drove most of the Danes out of the kingdom, those residing in London who had married English women were allowed to live between WESTMINSTER and LUDGATE and 'they builded a synagogue the which being afterwards consecrated, was called *Ecclesia Clemtis Danorum*'. What at least is certain is that some time towards the end of the 10th or at the beginning of the 11th century, the wooden church was replaced by one of stone – the remains of whose tower are incorporated into the present building – and that in 1189 it was transferred by Henry II to the Order of the KNIGHTS TEMPLAR. After their expropriation it was held by the AUSTIN FRIARS, and in the 14th century the living was secularised and presented to Walter de Stapleton, Bishop of Exeter, whose London house was in the vicinity.

The church escaped destruction in the GREAT FIRE; but in 1679 the whole fabric, apart from the tower, was pronounced unsafe. Christopher Wren, who was then at the height of his powers, designed the new church. It is the only one of his churches, with the exception of ST PAUL'S, to have an apse. He faced the existing tower with Portland stone. In 1719 it was agreed that the tower should be raised 25 ft and that 'over the bells an ornamental steeple not less than 50 foot' should be built. James Gibbs was then commissioned to design his elegant addition to the tower, so making the west front with its domed vestries and projecting porch particularly pleasing. The interior was richly decorated with a profusion of ornate plasterwork. There was a scandal in 1725 when it was alleged that the picture of St Cecilia 'supposed to be beating time to the Musick' was a portrait of the wife of the Pretender, the Princess Sobieski. It was removed by order of the bishop.

Baptisms which have taken place here include those of Robert Cecil, later Earl of Salisbury, the son of Lord Burghley, on 6 June 1563 and Charles Sedley, the future dramatist, in 1639. The marriage of Sir Thomas Grosvenor to the heiress, Mrs Mary Davies of Ebury (*see* GROSVENOR ESTATE) was solemnised here on 10 October 1676.

Buried here are Ben Jonson's friend, Sir John Roe, who was the subject of some of his best verses; John Lowin, one of the most eminent of the original Shakespearean players; Marchmont Needham, the writer of the *Mercurius* papers during the Civil War; Thomas Otway, the poet; Bishop George Berkeley; and the wife of the poet, John Donne, whose death occurred soon after she had given birth to their twelfth child and whose splendid tomb, by Nicholas Stone, was lost when the church was rebuilt. The chains inside the door to the crypt are a relic of the days when coffins had to be secured from body snatchers. The church's burial ground in Portugal Street has been built over by KING'S COLLEGE.

In the 18th century Samuel Johnson was a regular member of the congregation. His seat was No. 18 in the north gallery close to the pulpit. There is a brass plate on a nearby pillar – against which he must often have leaned – which records this fact. On Good Friday 1773 he and James Boswell attended service here and Boswell records his devotion: 'His behaviour was, as I had imagined to myself, solemnly devout. I never shall forget the tremulous earnestness with which he pronounced the awful petition in the Litany: "In the hour of death, and at the day of judgement, Good Lord deliver us."' In 1784, in a letter to Mrs Thrale, Johnson wrote, 'After a confinement of 129 days, more than the third part of a year, and no inconsiderable part of human life, I returned this day thanks to God in St Clement's Church for my recovery.'

The church was bombed in December 1941 and, although the steeple was not much damaged and the walls remained largely intact, the interior was gutted and most of the bells were cracked. In 1958 W.A.S. Lloyd completed the reconstruction of the church to which £150,000 was contributed by members of the RAF and of Commonwealth and Allied Air Forces. It is now the central church for the RAF. At the entrance there is a memorial to the air forces of the Commonwealth who fought in the 2nd World War. Over 750 Welsh slate badges of the different squadrons and units of the RAF are let into the floor; and on pillars are the badges of all the Commands. The shrines of

701

remembrance contain rolls of honour with the names of the men who died in action. Beneath the west gallery is a book containing the names of 1,900 American airmen killed in the War while based in Britain. The windows at the east end are by Carl Edwards and the *Annunciation* on the reredos by Ruskin Spear. The pulpit has been assigned to Grinling Gibbons and the organ, designed by Ralph Downes, is one of the best in London. On the south side of the nave is a list of the rectors of the parish which includes the name of William Webb-Ellis, rector between 1843 and 1855, who as a schoolboy at Rugby, 'with a fine disregard of the rules of the game [football] as played in his time, first took the ball in his arms and ran with it, thus originating the distinctive feature of the Rugby game.'

The new peal of ten bells which were hung in 1957 play on occasions the tune traditionally associated with the nursery rhyme, *Oranges and Lemons*. An orange and a lemon are also given every year to each child of St Clement Danes Primary School after the annual service. The verses, which when sung are intended to imitate the sound of 'the bells of old churches of London Town', are in full:

Bull's eyes and targets,
Say the bells of St Marg'ret's

Brickbats and tiles,
Say the bells of St Giles'.

Oranges and lemons,
Say the bells of St Clement's

Pancake and fritters,
Say the bells of St Peter's

Two sticks and an apple
Say the bells at Whitechapel.

Old Father Baldpate,
Say the bells at Aldgate.

Maids in white aprons,
Say the bells at St Catherine's

Pokers and tongs,
Say the bells at St John's

Kettles and pans,
Say the bells at St Anne's

You owe me five farthings,
Say the bells of St Martin's

When will you pay me,
Say the bells at Old Bailey.

When I grow rich,
Say the bells at Shoreditch.

Pray, when will that be?
Say the bells at Stepney.

I'm sure I don't know,
Says the great bell at Bow.

Here comes a candle to light you to bed,
Here comes a chopper to chop off your head.

The St Clement's church referred to in the rhyme is, however, more likely to be ST CLEMENT EASTCHEAP which stands by the wharves where citrus fruit from the Mediterranean was unloaded.

St Clement's Lane *WC2*. This short street between Portugal Street and Grange Court was once a long country lane leading to the parish church of ST CLEMENT DANES from which it takes its name.

St Columba *Kingsland Road, N1*. Built in a slum area in 1868–73 to the French Gothic design of James Brooks and arranged in a group with the vicarage, clergy house and school.

St Columba's Church of Scotland *Pont Street, SW1*. The original St Columba's, built in 1883–4 to revive the waning fortunes of the Kirk in London, and to provide a central place of worship, was destroyed by an incendiary bomb in the heavy air raid of 10 May 1941. The present church was built in 1950–5, and designed by Sir Edward Maufe.

St Cuthbert *Philbeach Gardens, SW5*. Built in 1884–7. The church has relics of St Cuthbert. The foundation stone came from Holy Island. The furnishings in the Arts and Crafts style are by W. Bainbridge Reynolds. The reredos was made by the Revd E. Geldart in 1914.

St Cyprian *Clarence Gate, NW1*. Although the Bishop of London did not approve, the founder of this church, Charles Gutch, insisted on the dedication to St Cyprian, the 3rd-century Carthaginian martyr, renowned for his compassionate care for people. The church was designed by Sir Ninian Comper in 1903. It is in the medieval Gothic style and was described by the architect as 'the last development of a purely English parish church with lofty aisles and clerestory'.

St Dionis *Parsons Green, SW6*. Built in 1884–5 with the proceeds of the sale of ST DIONIS BACKCHURCH. It contains the 17th-century pulpit and font from the City church.

St Dionis Backchurch *Lime Street and Fenchurch Street*. First heard of in 1198. St Dionis is a

St Dionis Backchurch, built by Wren in 1670–84. From a watercolour by G. Shepherd, 1811.

corruption of St Denys, the patron saint of France who was beheaded when he tried to convert the Parisians in the 3rd century. The suffix Backchurch is thought to have been added either because the church stood back from FENCHURCH STREET or after someone named Bac. In 1450 it was rebuilt at the expense of John Bugge and in 1466 Alderman John Derby added a chapel of St John on the south side. A steeple was built in 1632. The church was destroyed by the GREAT FIRE. It was replaced in 1670–84 by a small but lofty church with nave and two aisles built by Wren at the cost of £5,737 10s 8d. From 1749–51 Dr Charles Burney was organist. The church was demolished in 1878 under the Union of City Benefices Act and the parish united with that of ALL HALLOWS LOMBARD ST. ST DIONIS PARSONS GREEN was built on the proceeds of the sale and the pulpit, woodwork, font and plate were given to the new church. In 1954 the parish was united with that of ST EDMUND KING AND MARTYR. A plaque on offices at the corner of FENCHURCH STREET and LIME STREET marks the site.

St Dominic's Priory   *Southampton Road, NW5.* Opened in 1867, on the edge of the rapidly developing area of KENTISH TOWN, this Dominican Priory consisted of 12 priests with a Prior at their head. In addition to a refectory, chapter house and cloisters, there was a large Priory Hall, where church services were held. The congregation from the surrounding areas, however, became so large that it was decided to build a church. The foundation stone of the Priory Church of Our Lady of the Rosary and St Dominic's was laid by Cardinal Wiseman in 1882. The architect was Charles Buckler.

St Dunstan   *Cranford Park, Middlesex.* A small building without aisles, possibly owing its origins to a chapel built by the KNIGHTS TEMPLAR who had been given the manor of Cranford St John in the 13th century. The chancel and lower parts of the tower, of flint and rubble with freestone dressings, date from the 15th century. The top of the tower is 17th-century. The nave was rebuilt in 1716 by Elizabeth, Dowager Countess of Berkeley, sister of the 1st Earl of Gainsborough. The south wall of the chancel contains an altar tomb to Elizabeth, widow of Sir Thomas Berkeley, who was buried in 1635, (*see* CRANFORD PARK). It is the work of Nicholas Stone the Younger, who was a pupil of Bernini in Rome. Opposite is the memorial to Sir Roger Aston, Gentleman of the Bedchamber to James I, who died in 1612. He is shown kneeling facing his two wives, while his four daughters kneel, two on either side. There are also tablets to Sir Charles Scarburgh (1694), physician to Charles II, and to Thomas Fuller, rector of CRANFORD, chaplain to Charles I and Charles II and author of *England's Worthies*. The church was restored in 1895 and again in 1935.

St Dunstan and All Saints   *Stepney (Stepney High Street), E1.* A church of great antiquity, it was rebuilt in the 10th century by St Dunstan, then BISHOP OF LONDON. Until the 13th century it was the only church for the whole of STEPNEY. Then a whitewashed chapel was built at WHITECHAPEL; and in the 14th century a chapel was built at STRATFORD. St Dunstan's was rebuilt, except for the 13th-century chancel, in the 15th century. Bishop Foxe, founder of Corpus Christi College, Oxford and John Colet, founder of ST PAUL'S SCHOOL, were vicars here. WAPPING got its own

church in 1617, POPLAR in 1654, SHADWELL in 1656, LIMEHOUSE in 1715, SPITALFIELDS in 1728 and BETHNAL GREEN in 1743. In 1871–2 the exterior of St Dunstan's was refaced, and stained glass was put in the west window. The Renatus Harris organ (made in 1678) was sold to DRURY LANE THEATRE. From the earlier churches a Saxon stone rood and a 13th-century relief of the *Annunciation* survive.

St Dunstan in the East   *Idol Lane.* After a hurricane had swept London in 1703, Sir Christopher Wren was told that the steeple of every City church had been damaged. He is said to have commented with quiet assurance, 'Not St Dunstan's, I am sure'. His confidence in its structure was not misplaced and today it is all that remains of this ancient church.

The CITY OF LONDON used to possess two churches dedicated to the great Saxon Archbishop of Canterbury, St Dunstan. The one on the west boundary still stands. St Dunstan's in the East, however, was destroyed in the 2nd World War. A wealthy and prosperous parish church, it had been built some time during the second half of the 13th century. The only incumbent in the City who was paid a higher stipend was the rector of ST MAGNUS THE MARTYR. In 1382 a southern aisle and porch were added at the expense of Lord Cobham, father-in-law of John Oldcastle, the leader of the Lollards. Extensive repairs were carried out in 1633 and Portland stone was used to reinforce the outer walls; as a result the main body of the church withstood the ravages of the GREAT FIRE. The tower and steeple, however, had to be rebuilt. There are many legends associating Christopher Wren's only daughter Jane, with the building of the steeple. Some say she suggested the design to her father, others that she went up with the mason to fix the last stones after he had lost his nerve and that she lay down beside it as the props were being removed to show her confidence in its stability. It is of Gothic design and resembles the spire of St Giles's Cathedral in Edinburgh. The four-storied tower is surmounted by tall pinnacles. From behind these pinnacles spring flying buttresses which support the lantern and the spire; the whole is topped by a ball and vane. With this striking construction, Wren achieved an effect of deceptive fragility and weightlessness. In 1817 it was discovered that the walls of the medieval nave had been forced 7ins out of the perpendicular by the pressure of the roof. The church was rebuilt in Gothic style by David Laing. It was bombed in the 2nd World War. In 1971 the tower and nave walls were restored and the site turned into a garden. The parish was amalgamated with that of ALL HALLOWS BARKING.

St Dunstan in the West   *Fleet Street, EC4.* First mentioned in 1185, it was known as St Dunstan's Over Against the New Temple in 1237, when the advowson, formerly in the hands of WESTMINSTER ABBEY, was granted by the King to the nearby DOMUS CONVERSORUM in CHANCERY LANE. But by 1278 it was called St Dunstan's West to differentiate it from ST DUNSTAN'S IN THE EAST near the TOWER. The Chapel of St Katherine was erected in 1421. In 1523 William Tyndale, later the translator of the *New Testament*, arrived in London and obtained brief employment as a preacher here. A cloth merchant, Humphrey Monmouth, heard his sermons and installed him in his house to pray for his 'father and mother and all Christian souls'. There is a bust of Tyndale on the west side

St Dunstan in the West, with Temple Bar in the distance. From an aquatint by Malton, 1797.

of the porch in the present church. In 1575–1624 the rector was Thomas White, the founder of SION COLLEGE. He was buried here in 1631. John Donne succeeded White as rector in 1624, and remained until his death in 1631. His bust is on the east side of the porch of the present church. He received the benefice from the Earl of Dorset but in his letters claimed that he never derived any income from the benefice despite diligently performing the duties whilst also Dean of ST PAUL'S. In 1629–44 Izaac Walton was 'scavenger, questman and sidesman'. His *Compleate Angler* was published in the churchyard by Richard Marriott in 1653. There is a memorial west window (1895) and plaque (1895) on the main entrance. In 1666 the GREAT FIRE was contained within yards of the church. On 18 August the following year Pepys '. . . walked towards Whitehall, but being weary, turned into St Dunstan's Church, where I hear an able sermon from the minister of the place. And stood by a pretty, modest maid whom I did labour to take by the hand and the body, but she would not, but got further and further from me, and at last I could perceive her to take pins out of her pocket to prick me if I should touch her again; which seeing I did forbear, and was glad I did espy her design. And then I fell to gaze upon another pretty maid in a pew close to me and she on me; and I did go about to take her by the hand, which she suffered a little and then withdrew. So the sermon ended and the church broke up, and my amours ended also; and so took coach and home.' As a thank offering by parishioners for the escape of the church from the GREAT FIRE the clock was erected in 1671. It comprises a bracket clock which originally projected over the street and an Ionic temple containing two figures with clubs that half-heartedly strike a bell every 15 minutes. The clock is said to have been the first London clock

to have the minutes marked on the dial and the first with a double face. Made for '£35 and the old Clock', by Thomas Harris of Water Lane, it was a notable London sight and is mentioned in Goldsmith's *Vicar of Wakefield*, Dickens's *Barnaby Rudge* and anachronistically, in Scott's *Fortunes of Nigel*. Cowper, also, refers to it in his *Table Talk* (1782):

When Labour and when Dullness, club in hand
Like the two figures of St Dunstan's stand
Beating alternately in measured time
The clock tintinnabulum of rhyme.

Strype (1720) calls the figures 'two savages or Hercules'. They have also been identified as GOG AND MAGOG. They may have been modelled on a pre-GREAT FIRE clock in ST PAUL'S. In 1701 the church was extensively repaired and the roof replaced. In 1749 the evangelical divine, William Romaine, was granted a double lectureship. He was so popular that parishioners complained that they had to force their way to their pews through a 'ragged unsavoury multitude', 'squeezing', 'shoving', 'panting', 'riding on one another's backs'. The rector sat in the pulpit to prevent Romaine occupying it, and the bitter dispute was referred to the KING'S BENCH COURT who deprived Romaine of one lectureship supported by voluntary contributors, but let him keep the other, which was endowed with £18 a year, and granted him the use of the church at 7 o'clock in the evening. The churchwardens, however, refused to open the church until the clock struck seven and then refused to light it. Romaine frequently preached by the light of a single candle, a situation that ended when the BISHOP OF LONDON chanced to observe a large crowd by the closed church door. He intervened to provide normal facilities for the services. Romaine continued at St

Dunstan's, once refusing a country living from Lord Dartmouth and a large church in Philadelphia from Whitefield. In 1766 he took the living of ST ANDREW BY THE WARDROBE. This design is now in the GUILD-HALL LIBRARY. In 1760 when LUDGATE was demolished the statute of Queen Elizabeth I was erected over the vestry door. The statues of King Lud and his two sons were initially deposited in the parish bone-house and can now be seen just inside the doorway to the east of the main church entrance. In 1830 the church was demolished and the site diminished by a widening of FLEET STREET by 30 ft. Part of CLIFFORD'S INN grounds was then purchased. The new octagonal church, built in 1829–33 by John Shaw, is an early London example of the Gothic revival. The tower, 130 ft high, is of yellow freestone from Ketton, Leicestershire. It is modelled on that of All Saints' Pavement at York. The eight bells are from the previous church. Shaw died 21 days after the completion of the outer shell and his son, John, completed the work. The altar is to the north. The clock was bought by the Marquess of Hertford for £210 and re-erected at his house, HERTFORD VILLA, in REGENT'S PARK. Moxon said the removal brought tears to Charles Lamb's eyes. In 1930 the Northcliffe Memorial, designed by Lutyens, was erected on the outside wall of the church. The bust is by Lady Hilton Young. In 1935 Lord Rothermere bought the clock and returned it to St Dunstan's. In 1954 St Dunstan's was created a Guild church and the parish was united with ST BRIDE'S. In 1966 an early 19th-century ikon screen from Antim Monastery, Bucharest was placed in the north-west chapel which is used by the Russian Orthodox Church. There are several good monuments from the earlier church; and there are two interesting epitaphs; one is to Alexander Layton, 'ye famed swordsman':

His thrusts like lightning flew, more skilful Death
Pairied 'em all, and beat him out of breath.

The other is:

To the Memory of Hobson Judkin Esq ...
The Honest Solicitor.

St Dunstan's *191 Old Marylebone Road, NW1.*
Founded in 1915, by Sir Arthur Pearson, who had himself recently become blind, this organisation looks after the welfare of men and women blinded on war (or active) service. The first blinded soldier of the 1st World War to arrive at an English hospital was a young Belgian, who was soon followed by many others, and Pearson set up a hostel for blinded soldiers and sailors in Bayswater Hill at the beginning of February 1915. Soon there were so many war-blinded men that the hostel had to be moved to HERTFORD VILLA, a house with 15 acres in REGENT'S PARK. In the grounds stood a huge clock which had been moved there from the Church of ST DUNSTAN IN THE WEST, FLEET STREET. This clock, ornamented by two giants who mark the hours by striking a bell, gave its name first to the house and then to the charitable organisation for the blind, which has been known ever since as St Dunstan's. The clock was later returned to its original home in FLEET STREET. By 1918, 1,000-2,000 men were being trained at St Dunstan's to work in the outside world, and the organisation's work has continued ever since, at hostels and training schools in many parts of the United Kingdom and the rest of the world. Some St Dunstaners

have become solicitors, chartered accountants, lecturers and university professors. The organisation holds annual reunions, is completely responsible for the welfare of its members and has branches in many parts of the world. In 1982 it had about 1,470 members, 976 of whom were in the United Kingdom.

St Dunstan's College *Stanstead Road, SE6.* The
parish school of St Dunstan in the East was recognised by Henry VI in 1446. It was refounded in 1888 in CATFORD, on land owned by St Dunstan's Church. It is an independent school with about 875 boys, aged 7 to 19 years.

St Dunstan's Court *EC4.* On the north side of
FLEET STREET, it is flanked on the west side by JOHNSON'S COURT and on the east by BOLT COURT, to which it provides access. The name derived from St Dunstan who was a Bishop of London in the 10th century and also Archbishop of Canterbury. ST DUNSTAN IN THE WEST is nearby.

St Edmund the King *Lombard Street, EC3.*
Founded in the 12th century and dedicated to the King of East Anglia who was tied to a tree and shot with arrows by Danes for refusing to renounce his religion. Destroyed in the GREAT FIRE it was rebuilt in 1670–9 by Wren and Robert Hooke. The spire was completed in 1708. Inside is some good 17th-century woodwork, especially the font cover and pulpit. Addison married the Countess of Warwick and Holland here in 1716.

St Ethelburga-the-Virgin within Bishopsgate
Bishopgate, EC2. There is no record of when St Ethelburga's was first built, but it was probably during the early part of the 13th century. It is dedicated to a 7th-century Abbess of BARKING the daughter of the first Saxon ruler – Ethelbert, King of Kent, who became a Christian. The smallest of the CITY's churches, it is situated just north of where the GREAT FIRE of London stopped, and it is of interest because from it we can see what so many of the CITY churches must have been like before the Fire. The parish which supported it covered just 3 acres. Before the DISSOLUTION OF THE MONASTERIES the patronage belonged to the nearby convent of St Helen's. The church was rebuilt in the 15th century and has been restored several times since. The little square 18th-century bell turret is topped by a beautifully elaborate weather vane dated 1671. Until 1933 access to the church was through a medieval porch under a 16th-century house, with shops of the same date on either side. These were pulled down by the CORPORATION in order to widen the pavement and so the humble, ragstone west façade of the church was revealed, with its 14th-century doorway and 15th-century window above.

The tiny modest interior is divided into a nave and south aisle by a perpendicular arcade. The south gallery – added in 1629 – was used, according to G. Godwin's account in his book *Churches of London* (1839), 'only for the daughters and maidservants of this parish to sit in'. On the north wall there is a 16th-century painting, *Christ healing Blind Bartimaeus*, attributed to the Flemish artist, van Aelst. The east window is 17th-century and shows the arms of the City and the MERCERS', SADDLERS' and VINTNERS' COMPANIES;

St Ethelburga-the-Virgin, the smallest City church, surrounded by shops in Bishopsgate. Engraving by Toms, 1736.

added the cloister where Henry VIII is said to have first met Cranmer. In 1620 Roman Catholics worshipped here under the protection of Gondomar, the Spanish ambassador, the living at ELY PLACE. In 1772 the bishops of Ely moved to DOVER STREET and St Etheldreda's became a proprietary chapel. In 1836 it was bought by Welsh Episcopalians, and in 1874 sold to Roman Catholics. The chestnut roof and the Victorian glass were badly damaged in the 2nd World War, but the west window of 1300 survived. The new glass in the east window is by Joseph E. Nuttgens. On 3 February, St Blaise's Day (he saved a boy from choking to death on a fish bone), lighted candles are held near those suffering from throat diseases.

St Etheldreda *Fulham (Fulham Palace Road), SW6.* The church, built to the designs of A.H. Skipworth in 1896–7, was seriously damaged during the 2nd World War and replaced in 1958 by a concrete and brick building designed by Guy Biscoe. The name was chosen by the then Vicar of Fulham because of his family connection with Ely, the Cathedral of which is dedicated to St Etheldreda. The copper font and baptistry glass are by Carter Shapland. The crucifix on the east wall by Rita Lang was made with wood from Brighton pier.

St Ewin *Newgate Street.* A small church of which almost nothing is known. It stood at the north-west corner of WARWICK LANE. Its existence is first recorded in about 1220. It was demolished in about 1583 and its parish became part of CHRIST CHURCH GREYFRIARS. St Ewin is an English version of St Ouën, a 7th-century Archbishop of Rouen.

St Faith with St Matthias *Wordsworth Road, N16.* Built in the middle of the 1850s to the designs of Butterfield, with a tall saddleback tower.

St Faith's under St Paul's The extension of the choir of old ST PAUL'S eastwards in 1256 necessitated the demolition of this small parish church which served the people of PATERNOSTER ROW and ST PAUL'S CHURCHYARD. In return, the parishioners were given space for their little church under the choir in the large, busy crypt (or Shrouds as it was often called) of the Cathedral. In 1551 St Faith's moved into a larger and lighter area of the crypt which had become vacant when the Chapel of Jesus was suppressed. People would fondly compare the position of St Faith's to that of a babe in the mother's womb. Even after its destruction in the GREAT FIRE, the playwright John Crowne makes a reference to it in his comedy *The Married Beau*, written in 1694:

> Our happy love may have a secret church
> Under the church, as Faith's under Paul's

At the time of the GREAT FIRE the publishers and booksellers of the parish, thinking that the massive walls of Normandy stone would be proof against the flames, filled the crypt with their stocks of books. However, they were all lost and according to Pepys were 'burning for a week'. The new ST PAUL'S did not provide space for the publishers and their parish was united with ST AUGUSTINE WITH ST FAITH, WATLING STREET. Traces of the old crypt church can be seen today at the east end

the font too, is 17th-century. Many of the fittings, including the screen, organ case, pulpit and lectern, were put in by Sir Ninian Comper in 1912. Three windows executed by Leonard Walker in 1928–30, commemorate Henry Hudson and his crew who took Communion here before setting out on their attempt to find the North-West Passage in 1607.

St Ethelburga's has had many notable rectors; amongst them was St Thomas More's friend, Blessed John Larke, who was hanged, drawn and quartered at TYBURN in 1544 for refusing to take Henry VIII's Oath of Supremacy. His successor, John Deye, during Mary Tudor's reign in 1553 had his ear nailed to the pillory for 'hannus wordes against the queen's magestie ... and for the up-rore that was ther don' after a sermon he had preached at ST PAUL'S CROSS. Luke Milburne, Dryden's critic, was rector here in 1704–20. Alexander Pope, in his *Essay on Criticism*, wrote of him, 'Luke Milburn, a clergyman the fairest of critics; who, when he wrote against Mr Dryden's *Virgil*, did him justice in printing at the same time his own translations of him, which were intolerable.' In 1860, St Ethelburga's displayed 'advanced' Roman tendencies by the use of vestments and incense and was the centre of controversy. It remained High Church up until 1939, and is the only City church to have a rood screen. In 1954 the parish was united with ST HELEN BISHOPGATE, and St Ethelburga became one of the new Guild churches.

St Etheldreda *Ely Place, EC1.* Built in about 1293 as a private chapel by William de Luda, Bishop of Ely, on the site of an earlier structure. St Etheldreda was a 7th-century abbess of Ely. Part of her hand is kept in the church. The crypt, dating from about 1251, incorporates still older walls which may have been part of the Roman basilica. In about 1373 Bishop Arundel of the present Cathedral crypt. The area has been defined by a brass strip. In 1954 the parish was united with ST MARY-LE-BOW.

St Francis of Assisi *Pottery Lane, Notting Hill, W11.* Built in 1859–60 to the designs of Henry Clutton. The site had been acquired for the English branch of the Oblates of St Charles Borromeo, a small community founded in BAYSWATER in 1857 by Dr H.E. (later Cardinal) Manning. Clutton's pupil, J.F. Bentley, was responsible for various alterations and additions, including the adjoining school, in 1861–3.

St Gabriel Fenchurch Street The first mention of this church is in 1315 when it is known as St Mary Fenchurch. John Stow, however, writing in 1598, refers to it as St Gabriel Fenchurch. It was burned in the GREAT FIRE and not rebuilt. In 1670 the parish was joined with that of ST MARGARET PATTENS. There is a plaque on Plantation House, 35 FENCHURCH STREET, to mark the site of the church, which, like ST MARY LE STRAND, was in the middle of the road. Part of the churchyard, now laid out as a garden, remains at Fen Court. The parish was united with ST MARY AT HILL in 1954.

St George *Bloomsbury Way, WC1.* In the early 18th century, respectable residents of the northern part of the parish of ST GILES-IN-THE-FIELDS, objected to having to pass through the notorious district known as the Rookery (scene of Hogarth's *Gin Lane*) in order to attend church. The Commissioners for the Fifty New Churches Act of 1711 acceded to their request for a new church; and, on a plot of land purchased from the widow of Lord John Russell for the sum of £1,000, Nicholas Hawksmoor built St George's. It was 15

Hawksmoor's St George, Bloomsbury. A statue of George I, in Roman dress, surmounts the steeple. Aquatint by Malton, 1799.

years before it was finished in 1731. The cost (which included the minister's house) of £31,000, so far in excess of the original estimate of £9,790 17s 4d, did not please the Whig Government.

The tower on the west of the church has an extraordinary steeple. Inspired by Pliny's description of the Mausoleum at Halicarnassus, it is stepped like a pyramid, at the base of which lions and unicorns used to cavort until they crumbled away in 1842. A STATUE of George I in Roman dress, posing as St George on the top of the steeple, was the gift of Mr Huck, brewer to the Royal Household.

Horace Walpole dismissed it as 'a masterpiece of absurdity'. In 1870 George Edmund Street did much to restore the interior to Hawksmoor's original intentions. A *London Guide* of 1876 was of the opinion, however, that St George enjoyed 'the privilege of being the most pretentious and ugliest edifice in the metropolis'. In the 18th and 19th centuries, BLOOMSBURY was a fashionable parish. Lord Mansfield, a vestryman, used the church to hide the guards he had engaged to protect his house at the time of the GORDON RIOTS in 1780 – a fruitless operation, as his house was burned by the rioters.

St George *Botolph Lane.* Stood on the west side of the lane on the south corner of St George's Lane. It is first mentioned in 1180. Repaired in 1360 and again in 1627, it was destroyed in the GREAT FIRE. It was rebuilt in 1671–4 by Wren who used rubble from ST PAUL'S CATHEDRAL. It was declared unsafe in 1903 and demolished the following year. The parish was united with that of ST MARY-AT-HILL. The sword rests, plate, royal crest, ironwork, organ and organ case were transferred to ST MARY'S. The pulpit went to ST GEORGE THE MARTYR, SOUTHWARK.

St George *Brentford. Middlesex.* Stands on the north of the High Street, in the shadow of a gasholder. The original building, made of brick, was erected by public subscription in 1762 to serve Old Brentford. The present building designed by A. Blomfield was built in 1887. It was closed in 1959 and the parish united with that of St Paul, using a church built in 1867–8. Since 1963 the church of St George has been occupied by a MUSICAL MUSEUM.

St George *Camberwell (Wells Way), SE5.* Now in ruins, this church, sited on the bank of the Grand Surrey Canal, was built in 1822–4 by Francis Bedford with a six-columned portico and west tower. It was altered by Basil Champneys in 1893 and 1909.

St George *Tufnell Park Road, N7.* Designed in 1868 by George Truefitt for the Islington Church Extension Society. The building was badly vandalized after the war and sold to the Elizabethan Theatre Ensemble in 1970. (*See* ST GEORGE'S THEATRE.)

St George Hanover Square *St George Street, W1.* One of the 50 new churches erected under the Act of 1711, it was built for the fashionable new residential area by John James in 1721–4. The portico was the first ever to be built for a London church. A statue of George I was intended for the pediment but never put there. The cast iron dogs by the main door are said to be copies of ones by Landseer. The east window contains 16th-century Flemish glass. The altar painting, *The Last Supper*, is by Sir James Thornhill.

St George, Hanover Square, built by John James in 1721–4, has the earliest portico on any London church.

In 1762 Boswell visited the church and heard a good sermon, yet he was rather cold in his devotion as the Duchess of Grafton 'attracted his eyes too much'. The church has always been a fashionable place for weddings. Among those married here were Lady Hamilton in 1791, Shelley in 1814, Disraeli in 1839, George Eliot to John Walter Cross in 1880 and Asquith in 1894. The two cast-iron dogs in the porch are by Adrian Jones. They were placed here in 1940 when the shop in CONDUIT STREET outside which they had formerly stood was bombed.

St George in the East   *Cannon Street Road, E1*. Built in 1714–26, with a massive 160 ft tower, to the designs of Nicholas Hawksmoor; the east windows are by Sir Joshua Reynolds. In the 1850s, when the rector and curate introduced what were considered Romish practices and when the Bishop of London, A.C. Tait, born a Presbyterian, appointed in retaliation a Low Church afternoon lecturer, there were riotous demonstrations with catcalls and horn blowing. Men came into the church with their hats on, smoking pipes and leading barking dogs. Refuse was thrown on to the altar. After the church had been closed in 1859, the rector, whose health had broken down, was persuaded by Tom Hughes, the author, to hand over his duties to a locum. The church interior was burned out during the Blitz. In 1960–4 the building was restored by Arthur Bailey.

St George the Martyr   *Queen Square, WC1*. Built at the beginning of the 18th century, it was drastically altered by S.S. Teulon in the 19th.

St George the Martyr   *Southwark (Borough High Street), SE1*. First mentioned in 1122 when it was given to BERMONDSEY ABBEY. It was rebuilt in the 14th century. From 1510 to 1527 Peter Carmelianus, Latin Secretary and Chaplain to Henry VII and Lute Player to Henry VIII, was rector. The church was enlarged, repaired and beautified in 1629. In 1658 according to Anthony à Wood, Oliver Cromwell's body was met here by friends, clergy and gentry who accompanied it to SOMERSET HOUSE for its lying-in-state. It was rebuilt by John Price in 1734–6. In 1897 Basil Champneys added the plaster ceiling of cherubs descending from clouds. The frieze bears the arms of the SKINNERS', GROCERS', FISHMONGERS' and DRAPERS' COMPANIES who contributed to the buildings. In 1951–2 the church was restored by T.F. Ford. The new east window of the *Ascension* was designed by Marion Grant. It includes the kneeling figure of Little Dorrit who was baptised and married in this church in Dickens's novel. General Monk was married here to his laundress Nan Clarges, in 1653. Bishop Bonner, who died in the MARSHALSEA PRISON in 1569, may be buried here, though some claim that his body is at Copford, Essex.

The Indigent Blind School, St George's Fields, Southwark, seen behind the Obelisk in c. 1825. From a lithograph after Haghe. Some 40 years earlier the area was still an open space where great crowds could assemble.

St George Street *W1.* Extends from HANOVER SQUARE to CONDUIT STREET and, until 1938, known as George Street. At the time of its building, soon after 1714, it formed part of the 1st Earl of Scarbrough's Millfield speculation (*see* HANOVER SQUARE), and with the building of ST GEORGE'S CHURCH on the east side in 1720–4 it at once became fashionable. Survivors of the original development include Nos 8, 9, 13, 16, 17 and 30, most of which have or had brick fronts and tall segmental-headed windows. Quite different in feeling, and the finest house in the street, is No. 15, five bays wide, with pedimented doorcase and first-floor windows, the front now stuccoed all over, designed by the Huguenot architect, Nicholas Dubois. At the south end is the Steinway Hall and Steinway's piano showrooms. Almost all of the buildings are now in commercial use and most of them have had shop windows inserted.

St George's Fields An extensive open space between SOUTHWARK and LAMBETH which took its name from the nearby church of ST GEORGE THE MARTYR and which has now been entirely built over. Notables were frequently received here, among them Catherine of Aragon, Charles II and William III. John Gerard, the herbalist, used to pick water violets here in the 16th century. The area was used for gatherings of large numbers of people, notably in 1780 of the Protestant Association whose march to WESTMINSTER provoked the GORDON RIOTS. According to Pennant writing in 1790 the fields were 'the wonder of foreigners approaching by road to our capital, through avenues of lamps, of magnificent breadth and goodness. I have heard that a foreign ambassador, who happened to make his entry at night, imagined that these illuminations were in honour of his arrival, and as he modestly expressed, more than he could have expected.' By day the fields were a training ground for soldiers and, on Sundays, a favourite resort of Londoners. They were also a place of execution. By the beginning of the 19th century, as James Smith wrote:

Saint George's fields are fields no more;
The trowel supersedes the plough;
Swamps, huge and inundate of yore,
Are changed to civic villas now.

By the end of the century the civic villas had mostly given way to the mean dwellings of the poor. The name survives in St George's Circus, SE1.

St George's Fields *see* BURIAL GROUNDS.

St George's Gardens *see* BURIAL GROUNDS.

St George's Hall *Langham Place.* Opened in 1867 as a concert hall for the New Philharmonic Society. From 1874 to 1895 Mr and Mrs German Reed entertained the Victorian middle classes here with polite sketches and popular music. In 1905–17 the magician, John Nevil Maskelyne, performed plate dancing, the floating lady and others of his well-known tricks. After his death in 1917 the shows were carried on first by his sons and then by his grandsons. From 1934–41 the hall was used as a BBC studio concert hall. It was bombed in 1941. ST GEORGE'S HOTEL and Henry Wood House now stand on the site.

St George's Hospital *Blackshaw Road, SW17.* Founded in 1733 by a group of Governors from WESTMINSTER HOSPITAL who considered their own building unequal to the needs of the charity. They looked at a number of buildings and settled on Lanesborough House at HYDE PARK CORNER, thus providing the patients with the benefit of a country air 'which in the general opinion of the physicians would be more effectual than physick in the cure of many distempers, especially such as mainly affect the poor, who live in close and confined spaces within these great cities.' The village of KNIGHTSBRIDGE had a reputation for healthiness. Lanesborough House was built in 1719 by James Lane, 2nd Viscount Lanesborough. The Governors rented it for £60 a year. It was a plain redbrick building, three storeys high. Wings were

St George's Hospital, originally the house of Lord Lanesborough, and Hyde Park Corner turnpike, in c. 1797.

added later by Isaac Ware. It faced north on to HYDE PARK. By 1745 it accommodated 250 patients and 20 nurses. A rustic cottage lay about 30 yards west of the hospital occupied by Huggitt, the cow-keeper, who supplied the hospital with milk. Originally there were six physicians, and three surgeons. The full diet was, Breakfast: one pint milk pottage; Dinner: 8 oz meat (four days), 1 pint pease pottage (other three days); Supper: 2 oz cheese or 1½ oz butter or 1 pint of broth; Daily: 14 oz bread, quart of small beer. Patients who died were buried in the burial ground of ST GEORGE'S, HANOVER SQUARE, hence also presumably the name of the hospital.

The greatest son of the hospital was John Hunter, father of scientific surgery and furtherer of all biological sciences, who was appointed in 1768, aged 40. He suffered from angina and often said that if his temper was roused he might die, which he did in a board meeting at the hospital. In the 1820s demand for a new hospital and more accommodation to house 350 patients led to a new structure, designed by William Wilkins, which was held to be remarkable for the use of square columns. Wilkins's building, which was begun in 1827, cost £40,000. The hospital has many other famous sons including Thomas Young, Professor of Natural Philosophy to the ROYAL INSTITUTION, and Henry Gray whose *Anatomy* (1858) has gone into over 30 editions. In 1834 a medical school was set up in KINNERTON STREET nearby. Previously teaching had been done at Lane's School, 1 Grosvenor Crescent across the road. In 1868 the school was moved to the hospital. In 1869 a convalescent home was established at WIMBLEDON on 28 acres with money left by Atkinson Morley (*see* ATKINSON MORLEY'S HOSPITAL).

The hospital and medical school moved to Tooting in 1980. In 1982 there were 450 beds.

St George's Hospital *Hyde Park Corner, see* ST GEORGE'S HOSPITAL, Blackshaw Road.

St George's Hotel *Langham Place, W1*. On the top six floors of a 14-storey block built to the designs of Burnet, Tait, Wilson and Partners on the site of the QUEEN'S HALL. The hotel opened in 1963.

St George's Lane *EC3*. Named after ST GEORGE BOTOLPH LANE which was demolished in 1904.

St George's Square *SW1*. A long, narrow square between GROSVENOR ROAD and Lupus Street. The church of St Saviour's was built in 1864 to the designs of Thomas Cundy the Younger. The vestry is by Nicholson and Corlette (1913–14). Pimlico School, known locally as 'the Glass School', was designed by Sir Hubert Bennett and Michael Powell and built in the 1960s. In 1982 there were 1,725 pupils.

St George's Theatre (The Elizabethan Theatre) *49 Tufnell Park Road, N7*. An Elizabethan theatre converted from a church built in 1866–7 to the designs of George Truefitt who modelled it on a 5th-century Crusaders' church. The St George's Elizabethan Theatre Limited was set up by George Murcell in 1968 with the intention of producing plays of Shakespeare's time as closely as possible to the original productions and in a recreated 16th-century atmosphere. The theatre was opened on Shakespeare's birthday, 23 April 1976.

St Giles *Camberwell, SE5*. Built in the 1850s to the designs of Sir George Gilbert Scott. The central tower with broach spire rises to a height of 210 ft. An early 14th-century church once stood on the site, and the *sedilia* and *piscina* from this church have been reinstalled on the south wall of the chancel.

St Giles *Ickenham, Middlesex*. Stands at the junction of Swakeleys Road and Long Lane in the centre of the old village. The walls are of flint rubble, mostly roughcast, and brick. The nave and chancel are 14th century. A timber bell-turret was added to the west end of the nave in the 15th century, and a large north aisle was built about 100 years later. A rustic timber-framed south porch adds to the rural character.

St Giles Circus *W1, WC1, WC2*. The crossroads at the junction of OXFORD STREET, TOTTENHAM COURT ROAD, NEW OXFORD STREET, and CHARING CROSS ROAD. It has been so known since 1921. The tower block which rises above it and remained empty for so long is Centre Point by R. Seifert and Partners (1971) who were also responsible for the fountain.

St Giles-in-the-Fields *St Giles High Street, WC2*. Here, in fields outside the city wall, in 1101, Matilda, the wife of Henry I, founded a leper hospital and dedicated it to St Giles, the patron saint of outcasts. At her behest a 'Cup of Charity' used to be given to condemned prisoners as they passed the door of the hospital chapel on their way to execution at TYBURN. By the 13th century this chapel had come to serve parishioners and patients. It continued in this parochial role even after the hospital had been closed by Henry VIII in 1539. In 1623 a handsome, new church was built on the site at a cost of £2,016. It was consecrated by Archbishop Laud. Alice, the pious daughter-in-law of Robert Dudley, Earl of Leicester, was a generous benefactor. However, many of her furnishings, including a lovely chancel screen, met with the disapproval of the Puritans and were consequently despoiled. The parish of St Giles was where the GREAT PLAGUE of 1665 started, and in one month 1,391 burials were recorded. The church suffered severe structural damage from the excessive number of burials, and in 1711, under The Fifty New Churches Act, a new church was proposed. A competition held to select an architect was won by Henry Flitcroft, the son of William III's gardener. Both James Gibbs and Nicholas Hawksmoor were unsuccessful candidates. The building cost £8,436 and was opened on Christmas Day 1733. The design was influenced by the newly completed church of ST MARTIN-IN-THE-FIELDS.

Apart from some alterations to the interior by Sir Arthur Blomfield in 1875 and Sir William Butterfield in 1896, the building has changed little since the 18th century. The unpretentious exterior is faced with Portland stone. The tower rises above the west pediment and becomes octagonal at clock-face level. The stone spire is banded and topped with a gilded ball and vane. The Resurrection gate, with its relief in wood of the *Day of Judgement*, was carved in 1687 and erected in 1800 as a lychgate. It was moved to its present position in 1865.

The 75 Volumes of Parish Registers dating from 1561 are full of interest. George Chapman, who translated Homer, was buried here in 1634. There is a memorial to him in the church which is said to have been designed by Inigo Jones. Wenceslaus Hollar, the

St Giles in the Fields, built in 1753 after a competition won by Henry Flitcroft, the son of William III's gardener.

engraver, was married here in 1653, and Sir William Temple married Mrs Dorothy Osborne in 1654. Catharine Sedley, the mistress of James II, was baptised in the church in 1657. There is a memorial to the poet, Andrew Marvell, who was buried in 1678. Five Jesuits, executed after the Popish Plot, were also buried in the same year. The murdered Archbishop of Armagh, the Blessed Oliver Plunket, was buried here in 1681. His body was later exhumed. In 1647 Mary, daughter of John Milton, was baptised here as was Henry Pelham, the future Prime Minister in 1694. The painter, Sir Godfrey Kneller, was buried in 1723. David Garrick married Eva Maria Violetti in 1749. Frances Kemble, the actress, was also married here in 1786. (Mrs Siddons signed as a witness.) Allegra, the daughter of Lord Byron, and two of Shelley's children were baptised at the same ceremony in 1818. Luke Hansard, printer to the House of Commons, was buried in 1828 and John Soane, the architect, in 1837. There is a tombstone to Richard Penderell (Pendrell), one of the five brothers who risked their lives by hiding Charles II in the Boscobel Oak after the Battle of Worcester in 1651.

There is a tradition that Claude Duval, the high-wayman, was buried here in 1670 after his body had lain in state at the Tangier Tavern following his execution at TYBURN. There is certainly an entry in the parish register of the interment of Peter de Val dated the day after the lying-in-state, whereas there is no entry in the register of ST PAUL'S COVENT GARDEN where a stone bears Duval's epitaph.

St Giles without Cripplegate *Fore Street, EC2.* Founded in the 11th century and dedicated to St Giles, the patron saint of cripples. It was rebuilt in 1537, and again in 1545–50 after being almost destroyed by fire. It escaped the GREAT FIRE, but, apart from the tower and walls, it was reduced to ruins by an air raid in the 2nd World War. In 1952–60 it was rebuilt by Godfrey Allen

as the parish church of the BARBICAN development. The interior is rectangular, divided into nave and aisles by 15th-century arcades. The 18th-century organ case and font came from ST LUKE OLD STREET. In the churchyard is a bastion of the CITY wall. Holman Hunt was christened here in 1827. Oliver Cromwell married Elizabeth Bourchier here in 1620. Buried here were John Foxe, the author of *The Book of Martyrs* (1587), Martin Frobisher (1594), John Speed, the cartographer in 1629 and John Milton in 1674. Milton's grave was opened in 1793: 'A journeyman named Holmes procured a mallet and chisel, and forcing open the coffin so that the corpse (which was clothed in a shroud, and looked as if it had only just been buried) might be seen. Mr Fountain, one of the over-seers, then endeavoured to pull out the teeth but, being unsuccessful, a bystander took up a stone and loosened them with a blow. There were only five in the upper jaw, but they were quite white and good. They, together with some of the lower ones Mr Fountain, [and two other men] divided between them. A rib bone was also taken and the hair from the head which was long and smooth was torn out by the handful. After this the caretaker Elizabeth Grant took the coffin under her care charging sixpence to anyone who wished to view it. Later she reduced her fee to threepence and finally to twopence.'

St Gregory by Paul's First mentioned in 1010, it stood at the south-west corner of ST PAUL'S CATHEDRAL. It was dedicated to Pope Gregory who sent Augustine to convert England. The body of St Edmund the Martyr is said to have been kept either here or at ST HELEN BISHOPSGATE to escape desecration by the Danes. From June to November 1561 the Cathedral services were held here while ST PAUL'S was being repaired after a fire. In 1631–2 the church was repaired and beautified. In 1641 Inigo Jones was brought before the HOUSE OF LORDS by the enraged parishioners for partly demolishing the church to make way for the Cathedral portico. He was compelled to put the stones back. In 1658 Dr John Hewet, the rector, was beheaded on TOWER HILL for collecting money for the exiled king. The church was destroyed by the GREAT FIRE and not rebuilt. In 1670 the parish was united with that of ST MARY MAGDALENE, KNIGHTRIDER STREET; in 1890 with ST MARTIN LUD-GATE; and in 1954 with ST SEPULCHRE HOLBORN.

St Helen Bishopsgate in 1817. It contains more monuments than any other London church except Westminster Abbey.

St Helen *Bishopsgate (Great St Helens), EC3.* Said to have been built by the Emperor Constantine on the site of a pagan temple when he was converted to Christianity in the 4th century. The dedication is to his mother, Helena. In 1010–13 the body of St Edmund is said to have been kept either here or at ST GREGORY BY PAUL'S to escape desecration by the Danes. In about 1204 a Benedictine nunnery was founded here by William Fitzwilliam, the son of a goldsmith. The parish church was rebuilt with a separate nave on the north for the nuns. In 1385 the nuns were scolded for the number of little dogs kept by their prioress, for kissing secular persons and for wearing ostentatious veils. In 1439 'dancing and revelling' were forbidden except at Christmas and then only among themselves. The nunnery was dissolved in 1538. The buildings were given to a relative of Thomas Cromwell who sold them to the LEATHERSELLERS' COMPANY; and the nuns' church became parochial. In it are 15th-century choir stalls, a 17th-century font, pulpit and doorways. The remaining furniture is Victorian. There is a memorial window to Shakespeare who is known to have lived in the parish. In the north wall a squint enabled nuns to watch Mass. St Helen's has been called 'the Westminster Abbey of the City' as it has more monuments than any other London church and several early brasses. Sir John Crosby of CROSBY HALL was buried here in 1475, Sir Thomas Gresham, founder of the ROYAL EXCHANGE in 1579, and the Lord Mayor, Sir John Spencer, in 1609.

St Helena Gardens *Rotherhithe.* Opened in 1770 with music and dancing in the evening. George IV occasionally came here as Prince of Wales. FIREWORKS were introduced in 1831. The gardens closed in 1869, but reopened in 1874, offering music, dancing and fireworks for 6d admission. They finally closed in 1881. St Helena's Road now marks the site.

St Helen's Place *EC3.* Takes its name from the Black Nuns of St Helen's whose hall was purchased by the LEATHERSELLERS' COMPANY soon after the surrender of the priory to Henry VIII. LEATHERSELLERS' HALL is on the west side.

St Helier *Surrey.* The St Helier Estate was built in 1928–36 by the LONDON COUNTY COUNCIL as a London overspill estate to rehouse people from decaying Inner London areas. The lay-out followed the 'Garden City' ideas of Sir Ebenezer Howard. As many as possible of the original trees were preserved; and greens and shrubberies were used to break up the monotony of rows of small houses. Many of the building materials came by rail, and were distributed over an extensive light railway system worked by six saddle-tank locomotives: the last of the LONDON COUNTY COUNCIL'S estate-construction railway systems. The estate was built west of MITCHAM and south of the River WANDLE on 825 acres of what is now the London Boroughs of SUTTON and MERTON (then the Urban Districts of CARSHALTON, MERTON and MORDEN, and SUTTON). The land was previously agricultural and much of it had been used for the local lavender and herb industry, originally based on MITCHAM. Designed to be self-contained, the estate was given its own shops, schools, churches, public houses, a cinema, and a railway station. There were also considerable open spaces, totalling 120 acres. The huge ST HELIER HOSPITAL was opened in 1938. The roads on St Helier were named after monastic establishments (108

of them, from Abbotsbury to Woburn) to commemorate the facts that MORDEN was once in the possession of WESTMINSTER ABBEY, SUTTON of Chertsey Abbey, and MERTON had a notable Priory. The Estate itself was named after Lady St Helier, a LONDON COUNTY COUNCIL alderman who died in 1931, and who had devoted much time to the problems and alleviation of poverty.

St Helier Hospital *Wrythe Lane, Carshalton, Surrey.* Opened in 1938 and run by the Surrey County Council. In 1948 it was taken over by the National Health Service. It is a district general hospital with, in 1982, 563 beds.

St James *Bermondsey (Thurland Road), SE16.* Designed by James Savage in 1827 and completed in 1829, this is one of the finest and one of the most expensive of the churches built to commemorate the victory of Waterloo. The total cost was £22,000; £5,330 of which was raised by the parishioners.

St James *Clerkenwell Green, EC1.* Once part of a Benedictine nunnery dedicated to St Mary, it was founded by Jordan Briset in about 1100. In about 1500 St James was included in the dedication. The nunnery was dissolved in 1539, and all but the church was demolished and the site built over. The church was rebuilt in 1625 and again, by James Carr, in 1778–82. The steeple was rebuilt by W.P. Griffith in 1849. Restoration was carried out by Sir Arthur Blomfield in 1882. Bishop Burnet, the historian, was buried here in 1715.

St James *Duke's Place.* After the suppression of Holy Trinity Priory, Aldgate the parishioners who had worshipped in the priory church joined the congregation of ST KATHARINE CREE. In 1622 they successfully petitioned King James for permission to build their own church. In the 17th century it was infamous for irregular marriages. Between 1644 and 1691 40,000 couples were married without licence, banns or parental consent. The nave was rebuilt in 1727, but in 1838 it was described by Godwin as 'very dilapidated and dirty and quite unworthy of description'. It was demolished under the Union of City Benefices Act in 1874 and the parish was reunited with that of ST KATHARINE CREE. The reredos and memorials were moved there. The site and materials were sold for £6,100 and St John, Red Lion Square was built on the proceeds. In 1954 the parish was united with ST ANDREW UNDERSHAFT. The SIR JOHN CASS SCHOOL now covers the site.

St James *Hampstead Road.* Built in 1791 as a burial chapel to serve the needs of the parish of ST JAMES, PICCADILLY. In 1788 Parliament granted the parish permission to acquire an additional burial ground covering some 4 acres, and to erect 'a Chapel adjoining thereto'. The surveyor, Thomas Hardwick, was commissioned to carry out the work, and in January 1793 the ceremony of consecration took place. Hardwick used a standard composition; the west façade had pilasters, a pedimented portico and a cupola; the interior was galleried with a flat ceiling. One of the first people to be buried here – in an unmarked grave – was Lord George Gordon, the instigator of the GORDON RIOTS of 1780. The Metropolitan Interment Act of 1852, which forbade burials 'to take place in populous places', caused the closure of the graveyard.

The Italian Gothic interior of G.E. Street's St James the Less. Built in a slum area in 1858–61, it was described as rising like 'a lily among weeds'.

One acre of the ground was sold to the London and North Western Railway in 1883 for £8,000 for their extensions to EUSTON STATION; the remainder was laid out as gardens for the public. (These have since given way to a car park for the TEMPERANCE HOSPITAL.) The chapel continued to serve the parish of ST JAMES'S, PICCADILLY as a chapel-of-ease until 1864. It then became the parish church of a newly formed parish. By 1954, however, the number of parishioners had dwindled to such an extent that this parish was once again united with that of ST PANCRAS and the church of St James was closed. It was demolished in 1964.

St James Garlickhythe *Garlick Hill, EC4.* Founded in the 12th century. Stow in his *Survey of London* (1598) says that garlic was once sold near here. The church was rebuilt in 1326 and, after its destruction in the GREAT FIRE, again rebuilt under the direction of Wren in 1676–83. The steeple was added in 1714–17. After being damaged in the 2nd World War, it was restored in 1954–63 by Lockhart Smith and Alexander Gale. Inside are sword rests, a pulpit with wig stand, a magnificent organ case containing a Father Smith organ of 1697 (*see* ORGANS), a painting of the *Ascension* by Andrew Geddes and a mummified body kept in a cupboard in the vestry. Several medieval LORD MAYORS were buried here. In the 2nd World War a 500 lb bomb fell on the church but did not explode.

St James *Pentonville (Pentonville Road), N1.* Designed by Aaron Hurst in 1787 as a proprietory chapel on the PENTONVILLE estate. In 1791 it became a chapel-of-ease to ST JAMES CLERKENWELL. It was given its own parish in 1854. It was restored by T. Murray Ashford in 1933. Aaron Hurst was buried here in 1799, Henry Penton, the developer of PENTONVILLE in 1812 and Grimaldi, the clown, in 1837. The church was much altered in 1920 and is now redundant.

St James in the Wall *Monkwell Street.* An ancient hermitage of CRIPPLEGATE. It was bought in 1543 by one William Lambe who left it to the CLOTHWORKERS' COMPANY. It was rebuilt in Wood Street Square, ST PANCRAS in 1825, but demolished in 1872. The 12th-century crypt was moved to the church of ALL HALLOWS STAINING.

St James *Sussex Gardens, W2.* By the middle of the 19th century, St Mary, PADDINGTON GREEN was found to be too small to hold the congregations of PADDINGTON; and in 1845, St James's was built to replace it as the parish church. It was designed by John Goldicutt and George Gutch, the architects of SUSSEX SQUARE and GLOUCESTER SQUARE. In 1881 the size of the parish necessitated an even bigger building, and George Edmund Street rebuilt and enlarged St James's in the most ingenious fashion using a 14th-century Gothic style. He retained the porches and tower of the original building and redesigned the church to face in the opposite direction with the new chancel at the west end of the building. The foundation stone was laid by Princess Christian in February 1882, but Street was not there to see it. He had died two months earlier and the work was carried out by Sir Arthur Blomfield. It was finished in 1883.

St James the Less *Thorndike Street, SW1.* A red-brick church patterned with black, designed in the Italian Gothic style by G.E. Street and built in 1858–61. It was financed by Jane, Mary and Penelope Monk in memory of their father, the Bishop of Gloucester. The red and black design carries on inside, but the chancel is decorated with marble and tiles. Over the chancel arch is a mural by G.F. Watts. The carved pulpit is by Thomas Earp. The short columns in the nave are of granite and there is a large and striking iron canopy over the font. The tower, built over the porch and away from the church and surmounted by a spire, is surrounded by railings decorated with iron arum lilies. At the time of completion the church was in an extremely poor neighbourhood, and *The Illustrated London News* said that it rose 'as a lily among weeds'.

St James Piccadilly *W1.* At the Restoration, Christopher Wren's friend and patron, Henry Jermyn, Earl of St Albans, obtained permission from the King to develop that part of the estate that had belonged to ST JAMES'S PALACE known as St James's Fields. In 1674, Wren was appointed the architect of the parish church which was to serve this new neighbourhood. In the spring of 1676 the foundation stone was laid and eight years later the building was consecrated. It is the only one of Wren's London churches to be built on an entirely new site. He was particularly pleased with the design and although he was not given to boasting, he wrote in a report to Parliament in 1708, 'I think it may be found beautiful and convenient.' It embodies all the

essentials that go to make a successful 'auditory' church, that is, one where the maximum number of people (in this case 2,000) may hear the preacher distinctly, in contrast to the Roman Catholic churches where, as Wren explained, 'it is enough if they hear the Murmer of the Mass, and see the Elevation of the Host'. Certainly St James's became the prototype for most of the 18th-century urban churches.

The exterior is modest. It is built of plain brick with Portland stone. The elaborate Ionic doorway in the middle of the south wall was removed in 1856. The outdoor pulpit was added in 1902 by Temple Moore. Wren had planned to put a small domed steeple on the tower, but the vestry preferred the spire designed by one of the carpenters, Edward Wilcox. Soon after it was erected, it had to be removed because of cracks in the tower. It lay about in Wilcox's yard and in 1696 ST ANNES SOHO would have liked to have had it. However, it was at last returned to the top of the tower of St James's in 1699. The interior of the church is in the best 18th-century tradition of quiet yet sumptuous elegance. The gallery curves round the west end, and from it Corinthian columns rise to support beautiful barrel vaults with rich plasterwork. The reredos, carved by Grinling Gibbons, is of limewood. John Evelyn, after visiting the church in 1684, wrote in his diary, 'There was no altar anywhere in England, nor has there been any abroad more handsomely adorned.' The marble font is also the work of Gibbons. (William Pitt, Earl of Chatham, and the poet and artist William Blake were baptised here.) The Renatus Harris organ is especially interesting. It was made for James II's Chapel Royal in WHITEHALL in 1685. At the request of the rector, Doctor Thomas Tenison, it was given to St James's church by Queen Mary in 1691. John Blow and Henry Purcell are known to have tested it on its installation in the church. The organ case is again the work of Grinling Gibbons. During the course of repairs in 1852, a miniature coffin containing a bird was discovered inside the instrument. The church suffered badly from bomb damage in the 2nd World War, but was afterwards restored by Sir Albert Richardson. It was rededicated in 1954.

Many distinguished names have been associated with St James's. In his play *The Relapse*, Vanbrugh has Lord Foppington reply to the question, which church does he 'most oblige with his presence', 'Oh! St James's, there's much the best company.' 'Is there good preaching too?' Amanda goes on to ask. 'Why faith, madam,' he replies, 'I can't tell. A man must have very little to do there, that can give an account of the sermon.' Many literary figures were buried here, among them Izaak Walton's friend Charles Cotton, James Dodsley, the brother and partner of Dr Johnson's publisher, Robert Dodsley, to whose memory there is a tablet by Flaxman in the north vestibule; and Tom d'Urfey, the writer of bawdy songs. The arts are represented by William Van de Velde, father and son, Dutch marine painters patronised by Charles II and James II; James Christie, the auctioneer; James Gillray, the caricaturist; and G.H. Harlow, the Regency portrait painter. Francis White, founder of the famous coffee house, was also buried here in 1711. The churchyard was converted into a garden of remembrance to commemorate the courage of Londoners during the BLITZ. It was opened by Queen Mary in 1946. Among those whose marriages were celebrated here was Sir Samuel Baker, the explorer, who in 1865

married the young Hungarian woman whom he had bought at a slave auction in a Turkish bazaar and whom he had subsequently taken with him on his journey up the Nile. The stone figure of Mary of Nazareth is by Charles Wheeler (1944, erected here 1975).

St James Spanish Place *George Street, W1*. A large Gothic Roman Catholic church designed by Joseph Goldie and built in 1887–90. It replaces the small chapel in SPANISH PLACE built by his grandfather in 1791. The alabaster Stations of the Cross and the baptistery gates are by Geoffrey Webb (1915). Many society weddings have been held here.

St James's Club *106 Piccadilly*. Founded in 1859 for members of the Diplomatic Service and housed until 1868 at 54 ST JAMES'S STREET. The PICCADILLY house was built for Sir Hugh Hunloke (*see* PICCADILLY), who sold it to the Earl of Coventry, and as Coventry House it became the home of the Coventry Club, a raffish gambling club. The lease was afterwards bought by Napoleon's former aide-de-camp, the Comte de Flahaut, French Ambassador in London, from the executors of whose widow it was purchased by the club. Until its demise in 1975 the club continued to have a good proportion of diplomats among its members, but most of its membership was drawn increasingly from other fields. From 1922 the meetings of the DILETTANTI SOCIETY were held here (and the Society's valuable pictures were hung on the walls); and during the 2nd World War hospitality was offered to the BACHELORS' CLUB with which the St James's was amalgamated in 1946. Financial difficulties led in 1975 to the merger of the St James's Club with BROOKS'S. The DILETTANTI SOCIETY also went to BROOKS'S.

St James's Coffee House *87 St James's Street*. Established in 1705 by John Elliott. It had the reputation of being a Whig house. Steele and Addison were patrons. Steele addressed his love letters to Mary Scurlock from here, and many items of the *Tatler* (1709–10) are dated from the St James's. Swift also used the house as an address. His letters were placed in a glass frame at the bar. The Whig reputation strengthened, and in 1724 it was stated that no Tory would allow himself to be seen at St James's. Garrick, Sir Joshua Reynolds and Goldsmith were regulars. It is said to be here that Garrick uttered the epitaph on Goldsmith to which Goldsmith replied in the posthumously published *Retaliation* (1774). Isaac d'Israeli, father of the statesman, travelled here from ENFIELD regularly to read the newspapers. The house closed towards the end of the 18th century.

St James's Fair Held outside the leper hospital dedicated to St James the Less where ST JAMES'S PALACE now is, on the eve of St James's Day and for six days afterwards. It was suppressed in 1664 as 'tending rather to the advantage of looseness and irregularity than to the substantial promotion of any good, common and beneficial to the people'.

The Earl of St Albans, who had been granted much of the area by the Crown, erected a market-house in the centre of what had been St James's Fair, intending it to become the centre of a resuscitated fair. In 1689 James II granted a licence for the holding of a fair on 1 May and the succeeding 14 days. Its booths and stalls spread in the streets as far as PICCADILLY and PARK LANE and a good way towards OXFORD STREET.

It soon began to rival ST BARTHOLOMEW AND SOUTHWARK FAIRS for its riotous nature and this reached a peak in 1702 when a watchman was killed in a riot and a butcher called Cook was arrested and eventually hanged at TYBURN. The Grand Jury of Middlesex suppressed the fair in 1708. An attraction of the fair had been the duck hunting on a nearby pond. Hounds were let loose and bets laid on which one would first catch a duck. Winners celebrated and losers consoled themselves in a nearby tavern called, inevit‚ ably, The Dog and Duck.

The fair was revived in 1738 by a Mr Shepherd who received a royal grant for a cattle market (hence SHEPHERD MARKET). The central building he erected had booths downstairs for butchers and other food shops and a theatre upstairs. The fair was in its heyday in the 1760s and John Carter, writing in 1816, recalled that 'in the areas encompassing the market building were booths for jugglers, prize-fighters ... boxing matches and wild beasts. The sports under cover were mountebanks, fire-eaters, ass-racing, dice-ditto, ups-and-downs, merry-go-rounds, bull-baiting, running for a shift, hasty pudding eaters, eel-divers and an infinite variety of other pastimes.' One of the great characters of the fair was Tiddy-Dol the Gingerbread Man, a great dandy who often dressed in white satin and got his nickname from the refrain of a song he sang to attract customers.

The Earl of Coventry secured the ending of the fair in 1764 because, having bought Sir Hugh Hunloke's residence in Piccadilly (afterwards ST JAMES'S CLUB) he was annoyed by the annual noise and disturbance at the rear of his premises. (*See also* MAYFAIR.)

St James's Gardens see BURIAL GROUNDS.

St James's Hall *Piccadilly, W1*. Built in 1857–8 to the designs of Owen Jones and financed by the St James's Hall Company. It had a large concert hall with two smaller halls upstairs. The acoustics were good but the seats were hard and smells from the kitchen sometimes seeped in. Dickens gave a series of six readings from his novels here in 1861 and, after all his heavy expenses had been paid, got 'upwards of £500. A very great result. We certainly might have gone on through the season, but I am heartily glad to be concentrated on my story [*Great Expectations*].' He again gave readings here in 1866, 1868 and 1870. When he read from *Oliver Twist* the audience stared at him with 'blanched and horror-stricken faces', so powerful was his acting. In 1880 the hall was established as London's premier concert hall. Dvořák, Grieg, Liszt, Sullivan and Tchaikovsky performed here. And in 1890 Paderewski made his London début. Competition from the QUEEN'S HALL and the WIGMORE HALL caused it to close. It was demolished in 1905. The PICCADILLY HOTEL covers its site.

St James's Hospital *Westminster*. Stow said that the hospital here was founded by some London citizens before the Norman Conquest but the first record of it is in the reign of Henry II. In about 1267 the Papal Legate and the Abbot of WESTMINSTER limited the inmates to eight brothers and 16 sisters. They laid down that the rule of St Augustine should be read in English to these brothers and sisters four times a year, and that a chapter should be held every week when faults were to be corrected. Everyone had to

confess once a week and attend all services. Brothers had to eat with the Master. If they were absent from the hospital they could eat, drink or sleep only at the house of a king, bishop or another religious order. Clothes were to be either russet or black. After a visitation by the Sub-prior of WESTMINSTER in 1277 the brothers were reminded that they were not to eat or drink with the sisters or enter their houses. Vigils at the death of a brother or sister were to be held 'without drinking or unseemly noise'.

In 1290 Edward I granted the hospital the right to hold an annual fair from the eve of St James's Day for seven days. In 1317 the Abbot of WESTMINSTER found that the Master had not been holding a weekly chapter and had been making special beer for himself, and that the Prior was often drunk, had embezzled funds and disclosed the secrets of the chapter. By 1319 there were no more than three brothers and six sisters, and by 1320 discipline had become utterly lax and the property neglected. The BLACK DEATH of 1349 killed all the inmates except William de Weston who became Master, but he was deposed two years later. By 1384 there were no inmates and Thomas Orgrave, the Master, let most of the building to Elizabeth le Despenser for life. In 1450 Henry VI gave the hospital, by then a leper hospital for young women, to Eton College. In 1532 Henry VIII acquired it as a site for ST JAMES'S PALACE. Eton College was recompensed with other lands and the four remaining sisters were granted an annual pension of £6 13s 4d each.

St James's Market Established after the suppression of St James's Fair in 1664. It was proclaimed as a thrice-weekly general market with a meat market to be held twice a week in the nearby HAYMARKET. In 1666 the Earl of St Albans erected the first market building which stood midway between Charles Street and Jermyn Street. In 1674 Richard Baxter, the nonconformist, preached his first sermon in an upstairs room. The main floor beam is said to have cracked under the weight of the audience. By the 1720s the market had grown to a good size and was supplying most of the West End tables. In 1669 Pepys describes visiting two Dutch painters in St James's Market – Loten and Varelst. Of one of Varelst's paintings he said he had never seen a better picture in his whole life. The market was demolished at the beginning of the 19th century to make way for Waterloo Place and REGENT STREET.

St James's Palace *SW1*. Built by Henry VIII on the site of ST JAMES'S HOSPITAL, WESTMINSTER, 'A goodly manor' of redbrick with blue diapering took its place. It had four courts. The present courts are named Ambassadors' Court, Friary Court, Engine Court and Colour Court. This last is approached through the gatehouse which is the only large part of the original palace to survive and which, with its flanking octagonal turrets, stands at the southern end of ST JAMES'S, a familiar landmark for some 15 generations. A large area of land to the south was annexed as a park and enclosed by a long brick wall. For over 300 years the palace remained one of the principal residences of the Kings and Queens of England. Henry VIII's daughter, Queen Mary, died here; his other daughter, Queen Elizabeth, held court here, as did her successor, James I. Several of Ben Jonson's masques were performed here at this time. And it was here that

The Tudor gateway of St James's Palace at the western end of Pall Mall. From an engraving by Bowles, c. 1750.

James's son, Charles I, spent the night before his execution in WHITEHALL. Charles's son, Charles II, was often to be seen playing bowls and pall-mall (*see* PALL MALL) with his mistresses and feeding ducks on the lake in the park to which he added 36 acres (*see* ST JAMES'S PARK).

After the destruction by fire of WHITEHALL PALACE in 1698, St James's became the principal royal residence in London. Queen Anne spent most of her time in London in the palace where nearly all her children were born. Her Hanoverian successors, the first three Georges, all spent long periods in the palace from which the future George II was expelled to LEICESTER HOUSE after a violent quarrel with his father. George II subsequently required his son, Frederick, Prince of Wales, to leave. George III was married here in 1761 and his eldest son, the future George IV, who was born here in 1762, was also married here on 8 April 1795; he was so drunk that night that, according to his indelicate wife, Queen Caroline, he collapsed into the fireplace of the bridal chamber where he remained till morning.

In 1809 a large part of the palace was destroyed by fire; but it was restored by 1814 when entertainments were held here in honour of various distinguished visitors who had come to London for the celebrations on the occasion of Napoleon's defeat at Leipzig. Among these was Marshal Blücher, who was provided with ground-floor apartments through the windows of which he could be seen smoking his pipe, bowing to the passers-by and accepting the compliments of ladies who called 'to congratulate him and kiss his moustachios'. At this time George IV, then Prince Regent, was living at CARLTON HOUSE; but his brothers, those royal dukes so tartly castigated by the Duke of Wellington, had apartments in the palace; and it was in one of them that the dislikeable Duke of Cumberland was assaulted and almost murdered by his Corsican valet whom he had taunted unmercifully for being a Roman Catholic, and to whom, it was said, he had made homosexual advances after having been found in bed with his wife.

After the Prince Regent's accession in 1820, two of his brothers were provided with houses within the palace precincts, the Duke of York with York House, later known as LANCASTER HOUSE and the Duke of Clarence, later William IV, with CLARENCE HOUSE. The King himself had a new palace built on the site of his parents' house. Thereafter the State Apartments were no longer lived in; although foreign ambassadors are still accredited in traditional style to the Court of St James's, they are received at BUCKINGHAM PALACE. Certain functions continued to be held at St James's, however. Queen Victoria, her eldest daughter, Princess Victoria, and her grandson, the future George V, were all married here. The accession of a new sovereign is still proclaimed at St James's and privy councillors still assemble here for the Accession Council as they did on 8 February 1952 in the entrée room to hear Elizabeth II make her first speech as Queen.

Next to the levée room is the throne room which has an overmantel of carved fruit and flowers by Grinling Gibbons as beautiful as any of his works. Other state rooms, none of which is open to the public, contain some fine doorcases by William Kent and are splendidly decorated in white, crimson and gold. The tapestry room contains tapestries woven for Charles II and a Tudor fireplace with the initials H and A. Like the armoury, which also contains an original fireplace, it was redecorated by William Morris's firm in the 1860s, a remarkably early period for the official acceptance of so revolutionary a style. The rest of the palace provides offices for the Lord Chamberlain's department and residences for various officers of the royal household.

St James's Park *SW1*. Takes its name from the hospital for leper women which was rebuilt as ST JAMES'S PALACE. The oldest of London's royal parks, it extends to about 90 acres with THE MALL as the northern boundary and BIRDCAGE WALK as the southern. The VICTORIA MEMORIAL is at its western end and Horse Guards Road forms its eastern boundary. It was originally a

716

marshy field attached to the hospital where the lepers fed their hogs. Henry VIII had the field drained and had a bowling alley and tilt yard made here and used the land as a nursery for his deer. Later he made it part of a chase which extended up to ISLINGTON, MARYLEBONE and HAMPSTEAD. The trees were gradually cut down during the reigns of Edward VI and Mary I. Elizabeth I hunted here. James I had formal gardens laid out with a menagerie (containing, amongst other strange beasts, two crocodiles) a physic garden and an aviary (*see* BIRDCAGE WALK). Charles I was escorted across the park to his execution on 30 January 1649, his dog, Rogue, running after him. 'The Park had several companies of foot drawn up,' Sir Thomas Herbert remembered. 'And a guard of halberdiers in company went, some before, and some followed; the drums beat, and the noise was so great as one could hardly hear what another spoke.'

During the Commonwealth the park was much neglected and most of the remaining trees were cut down by the citizens for fuel. Charles II extended it by 36 acres and laid it out afresh, advised, so it has been said, by André Le Nôtre, the great landscape gardener whose work at Versailles he so much admired. He planted it with fruit trees, stocked it with deer and built an avenue, lined with trees and covered with powdered cockleshells where he could play pall-mall (*see* PALL MALL). He also converted several small ponds into a long strip of water known as the Canal, leaving untouched the romantic pond known as Rosamond's Pond which was mentioned by both Congreve in *The Way of the World* and by Pope in *The Rape of the Lock*. (It was filled in in 1770.) The Canal became one of Charles II's favourite spots. He could often be seen, accompanied by his mistresses, walking his dogs around it, feeding the ducks and sometimes swimming in it. John Evelyn visited the park at this time and found it 'stored with numerous flocks of severall sorts of ordinary and extraordinary wild fowle, breeding about the Decoy, which for being neere so great a city and among such a concourse of soldiers and people, is a singular and diverting thing. There were

also deere of several countries – white, spotted like leopards, antelopes, an elk, red deere, roebucks, stags, etc.' There were also two pelicans, a present from the Russian ambassador, and a crane with a wooden leg. Pepys, too, came to see the birds 'walking, talking and fiddling with their hats and feathers'. One winter's day in 1662, he recorded, 'Over to the Parke, where I first in my life, it being a great frost, did see people sliding with their skeates, which is a very pretty art.' A fortnight later he accompanied the Duke of York into the park 'where though the ice was broken and dangerous, yet he would go slide upon his skeates.' 'I did not like it,' Pepys added, 'but he slides very well.' The readiness with which the royal family appeared among the people occasionally led to disorders. In 1677 one Deborah Lyddal was committed to BETHLEHEM HOSPITAL for 'she doth frequently intrude herself into St James's Park where she hath committed several disorders and particularly took a stone offering to throw it at the Queen.' A Richard Harris was similarly confined for 'throwing an orange at the King'.

Already the park was becoming a less pleasant place than it had been in earlier years; and after the death of Charles II in 1685 it ceased to be the haunt of the sovereign, although William III built himself a bird watching house on an island in the lake – a salient point at the east end still known as Duck Island – and could occasionally be seen here smoking his Dutch pipe. In Queen Anne's reign the park became notorious for prostitutes and for the depredations of those ruffianly aristocrats known as Mohocks; and in 1736 a writer in the *New Critical Review* complained of the stagnant water in the lake and the trees and shrubs all wanting attention. After the appointment of Lord Pomfret as Ranger in 1751 the condition of the park began to improve. The 1755 guidebook *London in Miniature* writes of it in complimentary vein: 'In this park are stags and fallow deer that are so tame as to take gently out of your hand and [at] each end of the Mall there are stands of cows, from whence the company at small expence, may be supplied with warm milk.' A French visitor of 1765 elaborated, 'The cows are driven about

The lake in St James's Park in c. 1830, when George IV had instigated a number of improvements to the Park, with the Horse Guards and Downing Street in the distance. From a lithograph by Baynes.

noon and evening to the gate which leads from the Park to the quarter of Whitehall. Tied in a file to posts at the extremity of the grass plot, they will swill passengers with their milk, which is being drawn from their udders on the spot [and which] is served with all the cleanliness peculiar to the English, in little mugs at the rate of 1d per mug.'

'If a man be splenetic' wrote Goldsmith at about this time, 'he may every day meet companions in the seats in St James's Park, with whose groans he may mix his own, and pathetically talk of the weather.' If, however, St James's park was not as rowdy as it had been in the earlier years of the century, and if fewer duels were fought here than in other parks (it was illegal to draw a sword within its boundaries), it remained a recognised haunt of whores. The gates were locked at night but 6,500 people were authorised to possess keys to them and thousands of others had keys unofficially. James Boswell was a frequent visitor here, sometimes in the afternoons when he liked to watch the soldiers on parade, but more often after dark when the gates were unlocked by girls who came in to stroll up and down the paths, and he was likely to be accosted, as he was one evening in 1762 'by several ladies of the town'.

In 1814 St James's, like the other parks, was the scene of a splendid gala, organised by the Regent and his favourite architect, John Nash, to celebrate the anniversary of the Battle of the Nile and the centenary of the accession to the English throne of the House of Hanover. A seven-storey Chinese pagoda was built and, across the Canal, a picturesque yellow bridge ornamented with black lines and a bright blue roof. It was a 'trumpery' affair, in the opinion of Canova who, when asked what had a struck him most forcibly during his visit to England, had replied that this bridge should have been the production of the Government whilst WATERLOO BRIDGE was the work of a private company. The 'trumpery' bridge, however, remained until 1825. The pagoda caught fire during the celebratory fireworks display, killing a lamplighter and injuring five other workmen.

After the accession of George IV further improvements were made to the park. It was lighted by gas in 1822 and in 1826–7 the canal was remodelled into its present graceful curvilinear shape. Trees were planted and new walks laid out. Improvements to the park were continued intermittently throughout the 19th century. In 1840–1 a lodge for the Ornithological Society was built on an island at the east end of the lake to the designs of J.B. Watson. It contained a council room, keepers' apartments and steam hatching apparatus. (This has recently been demolished.) In 1855 the lake was dredged, concreted and made a uniform 4 ft deep. In 1857 an iron suspension bridge, designed by James Meadows Rendel, and decorated by Sir Matthew Digby Wyatt, was built across the lake. (Although this was the only remaining early suspension bridge in London, it, too, was demolished and replaced by the present concrete bridge, designed by Eric Bedford, in 1956–7.) The Lake House north of Duck Island was built in 1922, demolished in 1968 and replaced in the 1970s by the present tent-like structure which has a hand-painted ceramic tile mural by Barbara Jones depicting the history of the park. In 1873 an ornithologist listed 28 species of birds in the park. Today there are over 30, pelicans, duck, geese and gulls among them. The Guards' Memorial (see MEMORIALS) is at the east end. The view across the lake to the spires, pinnacles and domes of WHITEHALL has been described as 'the most astonishing and romantic roofscape in London'.

St James's Place SW1. Laid out in two stages by John Rossington, the master builder, and other members of his family who bought CLEVELAND HOUSE. The east-west part of the L-shaped street was built in 1685–6 and the north-south part, originally known as Rossington Street, in the 1690s. Strype described the street in 1720 as 'a good Street' which received 'a fresh Air out of the Park'. A few of the original houses remain, though they have been much altered. SPENCER HOUSE is at No. 27. Samuel Rogers, who is better remembered for his breakfasts than for his poetry, rebuilt a house on the site of Nos 22–23 to the designs of James Wyatt. It was finished in 1803. After attending a breakfast in 1831 Macaulay wrote, 'What a delightful house it is! It looks out on the Green Park just at the most pleasant point. The furniture has been selected with a delicacy of taste quite unique.' After Rogers's death in 1855 this furniture and his collection of pictures and objets d'art were sold by CHRISTIE'S, over a period of 22 days, for £45,000. The house was destroyed by bombing in the 2nd World War. A block of flats by Denys Lasdun and Partners (1961), covers the site.

Other famous residents of the street have included Domenico Angelo, the fencing master, at No. 3 in 1758–62; Edward Gibbon at No. 2 (an 'indifferent lodging', costing him two guineas a week) in 1766; William Whitehead, the poet laureate, at No. 3 in 1768–72; Mrs Mary Delany, George III's friend, at No. 33 in 1771–88; the statesmen, the Earl of Moira and William Huskisson at Nos 21 and 28 respectively in 1790–1805 and 1804–6; and Robert Cruikshank, the caricaturist, at No. 11 in 1820–6. The house on the site of No. 25 was built for Lord Hervey's widow in 1748–59. Henry Flitcroft helped her but she was proud to claim the general design as her own. The house was restored by Sir Francis Burdett who lived here in 1816–44. It was destroyed by bombs in the 2nd World War. Chopin was staying at No. 4 in 1848 when he gave his last public performance at the GUILDHALL.

The STAFFORD HOTEL has been at Nos 16–18 since 1912. The Royal Ocean Racing Club, founded in 1925 and open to those who take part in one of the Club's 12 annual races, is at No. 20. Francis Chichester Ltd, the map and chart publishers, are conveniently close by at No. 9. No. 35, formerly chambers for wealthy bachelors, has been a hotel (Duke's Hotel) since 1908.

St James's Restaurant 24–26 Piccadilly. Built in 1875 by the owners of ST JAMES'S HALL; the Italianate front by Walter Emden was designed to blend with the Hall. There were small kitchens to each dining room to facilitate good service. The PICCADILLY HOTEL stands on the site of the hall and restaurant.

St James's Square SW1. A development carried out by Henry Jermyn, Earl of St Albans, in the fields to the north-east of ST JAMES'S PALACE. Soon after the Restoration in 1660, Jermyn persuaded the King to grant a lease of part of these fields for building. By 1665 Jermyn had obtained the freehold of half St James's Field including the central area where St James's Square was soon to appear. In co-operation with various associates, including Sir Thomas Clarges, Jermyn let plots of lands on building leases around the

St James's Square in 1812 with John Bacon's statue of William III, looking towards Wren's St James, Piccadilly.

west, north and east sides of a central piazza to several speculative builders prepared to put up houses for aristocratic occupiers, particularly for those whose duties required them to be near ST JAMES'S PALACE. In each side a space was left for the streets, KING STREET, CHARLES II STREET and DUKE OF YORK STREET, which were to lead into the square from ST JAMES'S STREET, HAYMARKET and JERMYN STREET. The houses, designed perhaps by Sir John Denham, the surveyor-general, were plain, redbrick with stone dressings, of three storeys and an attic. In its early days the square was perhaps the most fashionable address in London and remained so for half a century. When James Butler, who had been created Duke of Ormonde in the Irish peerage in 1661, was granted an English dukedom in 1682, he immediately bought a house in the square, a purchase which his son thought highly appropriate: 'How ill it would look now you are an English Duke to have no house there.' Forty years later there were no less than six other dukes in the square as well as seven earls. It was also an area much favoured by the richer foreign embassies. By the latter part of the 18th century nearly all the houses had been rebuilt or extensively altered, but the spacious simplicity of the square had not been impaired. 'Although the Appearance of the Square hath an Air of Grandeur,' an observer wrote in 1776, 'yet that by no Means resulteth from the Pomp and Greatness of the Structures about it; but rather from a prevailing Regularity throughout, joined to the Neatness of the Pavement.'

Soon tradesmen and clubs began to encroach and by the middle of the 19th century, when the centre of fashionable London had moved to BELGRAVIA, *The Builder* observed that St James's Square was 'rapidly losing caste'. Several large private houses remained, however, and in the 1920s the residential appearance of the square was still not essentially impaired. Soon afterwards the last private houses were successively taken over for business purposes. By the outbreak of war there were only three or four left and now there are none: the last to survive, No. 5, is occupied by representatives of the Libyan government.

The numbering begins on the west side of King Charles II Street. The house on the site of No. 1 was completed by January, 1673 and soon afterwards became known as Ossulston House after its owner Lord Ossulston, later Earl of Tankerville. This was demolished in 1753, and rebuilt for the 2nd Earl of Dartmouth. The 4th Earl sold the house in 1845 to the Westminster Bank; and in the 1950s the Bank demolished it for the rebuilding of their present premises at Nos 1 and 2, designed by Messrs Mewès and Davis. No. 3 was sold in 1710 by the Duke of Devonshire to Lord Ashburnham who seems to have commissioned Nicholas Hawksmoor to rebuild it for him. In 1716 Edward Harley, 2nd Earl of Oxford, the manuscript collector, was living here, as was Henry Temple, 2nd Viscount Palmerston in 1757–9. In 1818–19 the house was remodelled for the 3rd Earl of Hardwicke by John Soane. It remained in private occupation until 1852 when it became first a club, then offices, before being demolished in 1930 and rebuilt by Messrs Alfred and David Ospalek in 1933–4. No. 4 was built by the speculator Nicholas Barbon, and was soon afterwards sold to Anthony Grey, 10th Earl of Kent, whose descendants owned the site until 1908. The original house was burned down in 1725, and rebuilt by the Earl's son who had been created Duke of Kent in 1710. His kinsman, Earl de Grey, first President of the Institution of British Architects, lived here in 1854–9 when he died in the house. Waldorf Astor, 2nd Lord Astor, lived here in 1912–42; and in 1943–5 the house served as the headquarters of the Free French Forces. No. 5, which belonged to the 3rd Earl of Strafford in 1711 and is still owned by his family, was rebuilt in 1748–9 by Matthew Brettingham, the Elder. It was refaced in 1854, when a second storey was added, but the interior remains almost as it was. No. 6 was owned in 1677 by John Hervey, Treasurer of the Household to Queen Catherine of Braganza, whose descendants owned the house until 1955. It was demolished for an office block built to the designs of Fitzroy Robinson and Partners. No. 7 was bought by Richard Jones, Earl of Ranelagh, who was described as having 'spent more Money, built more fine Houses, and laid out more on Household Furniture and Gardening than any other Nobleman in England; he is a great epicure and prodigious Expensive.' Having passed through the lands of Lord Radnor and Earl Egerton, the house was bought in 1909 by three bachelor brothers who commissioned Edwin Lutyens to rebuild it for them. It was occupied as a private house until requisitioned by the Government in 1943. No. 8, having been occupied by the French Ambassador in the 18th century, was used as a showroom in 1796–1830 by the firm of Josiah Wedgwood who sold it to the Earl of Romney. Romney occupied it for a short time, but in 1840 it became a club. In 1893 the Sports Club took it over before moving in 1938 to No. 16, having amalgamated with the East India United Service Club (*see* EAST INDIA, DEVONSHIRE, SPORTS AND PUBLIC SCHOOLS CLUB). Nos 9, 10 and 11 are on the site of CHANDOS HOUSE. No. 10 was once occupied by William Pitt, Earl of Chatham, and two other prime ministers – Derby and Gladstone. No. 12 was built by Cyril Wyche, later President of the ROYAL SOCIETY, and occupied in 1686–1737 by the 8th Earl of Pembroke, the collector. In 1833 it was inhabited by Byron's son-in-law, Lord King, later Earl of Lovelace, who had it demolished in 1836 and rebuilt to the designs, it is supposed, of Thomas Cubitt. No. 13, which had been finished in 1676, was rebuilt in the 1730s for Lord Ravensworth, probably by Matthew Brettingham the Elder. It was sold in 1836 to the Windham Club which remained in occupation until 1941. It has been greatly changed in character inside; but, apart from the alterations to the third-storey windows and the parapet, the outside remains much as it was in Brettingham's day. It is now a branch of Grindlay's Bank. No. 14, which was built by the speculator, Richard Frith, was rebuilt in the 1770s and since 1845 has been the home of the LONDON LIBRARY. It was rebuilt in 1896–8 with a strange façade, part Georgian and part Elizabethan, to the designs of J. Osborne Smith. Extensions were made in 1920–2 to the designs of the same architect and further extensions at the back by Mewès and Davis in 1932–4. No. 15 is LICHFIELD HOUSE. No. 16 was occupied from 1705 until 1768 by Lady Elizabeth Germain, of whom the Duchess of Marlborough wrote, 'notwithstanding the great pride of the Berkeley family [she was a daughter of the 2nd Earl of Berkeley] she married an innkeeper's son', Sir John Germain. 'She was very ugly,' the Duchess added, 'without a portion, and in her youth had an unlucky accident with one of her father's servants.' She inherited a vast fortune from her husband, a handsome soldier of fortune, who had in turn inherited it from his first wife, only surviving child of the Earl of Peterborough; and when she lived in St James's Square, where she died in 1769, she was acknowledged to have 'outlived the irregularities of her youth, and she was esteemed for her kindness and liberality.' In 1815 the Prince Regent was attending a ball in the rebuilt house, which then belonged to Edmund Boehm, a rich merchant, when Major the Hon. Henry Percy, bloodstained and dirty, arrived to announce the victory at Waterloo and to lay the eagles of the French army at his feet. Mrs Boehm was 'much annoyed with the battle of Waterloo as it spoilt her party'; but 'the Prince delighted in the scene.' He asked the ladies to leave the room while Lord Liverpool, the Prime Minister, read out the despatch which Major Percy had brought with him. When Lord Liverpool had finished reading, the Regent turned to Major Percy and in his most good-natured, gracious manner said to him, 'I congratulate you, *Colonel* Percy.' In 1850 the inaugural dinner was held here of the East India United Service Club.

No. 17, then known as Halifax House, was successively occupied between 1673 and 1719 by the 1st and 2nd Marquesses of Halifax and by the widow of the 2nd Marquess who married as her second husband the 1st Duke of Roxburghe. In 1790 Sir Philip Francis, the reputed author of *The Letters of Junius*, bought the house which was taken in 1820 by Queen Caroline who, for convenience, moved here from BRANDENBURGH HOUSE, while the House of Lords were investigating her supposed adultery. On the day that the enquiry began she presented herself at a window in response to shouts of 'The Queen! The Queen!' from crowds of sympathisers in the square below. 'Her appearance called forth from the surrounding multitude the most unbounded marks of applause,' *The Times* reported. 'A short interval only had passed before the multitude again expressed their wish to see her.' She willingly responded to their calls. Soon afterwards she left for the House of Lords in a state carriage drawn by six bays, attended by liveried footmen. The crowds in the square that morning and on each subsequent day of the 'trial' – as most people referred to the proceedings in the House of Lords – were both noisy and immense. People clambered on to the roofs of carriages and rented standing room in carters' wagons for a shilling a day to catch a glimpse of the Queen as her postilions whipped the horses out of the Square, into PALL MALL and past CARLTON HOUSE (the King's house) where, to the delight of the mob, the guard presented arms. The site of the house, with that of its neighbour, No. 16, is now occupied by the EAST INDIA, DEVONSHIRE, SPORTS AND PUBLIC SCHOOLS CLUB.

No. 18 was occupied in 1727–33 by Philip, Earl of Chesterfield; and, at the beginning of the 19th century, by Lord Castlereagh, later 2nd Marquess of Londonderry. When Castlereagh's mind became deranged he was advised to leave the house and move to his country seat in Kent where, all his pistols and razors having been taken out of his dressing-room, he made use of 'a little nail-knife, which he carried in his pocket-book', to cut his carotid artery 'with anatomical accuracy'. In 1831 the house was let to the Oxford and Cambridge University Club then, in 1838 to the ARMY AND NAVY CLUB. It was rebuilt in 1846. No. 19 was first occupied by Arthur Capel, Earl of Essex, who, having been implicated in the Rye House plot, was either murdered or killed himself in the Tower in 1683. In 1720 the house was sold to the Duke of Cleveland whose family owned it until 1894. It was rebuilt in 1898–9 and, still known as CLEVELAND HOUSE, is now occupied as offices. No. 20 was built in 1771–5 by Robert Adam for Sir Watkin Williams Wynn, a gentleman of large fortune who professed himself delighted with Adam's designs which, indeed, the architect himself considered among his best. In 1935 the house was bought by the Distillers' Company which also bought the adjoining property, No. 21. This had once been the home of two of James II's ill-favoured mistresses, Arabella Churchill and Catharine Sedley, who, the King's brother, Charles II, once said, must surely have been inflicted on him by his priests as a penance. In 1791–5 it was rebuilt by Robert William Furze Brettingham for the 5th Duke of Leeds who immediately commissioned Sir John Soane to complete it, having fallen out with Brettingham. In 1829 it became the London residence of the Bishops of Winchester who held it for 46 years. The house was demolished in 1934, and the following year Messrs

St James's Street has been celebrated for its fine shops and gentlemen's clubs since the early 18th century.

Mewès and Davis were instructed by the DISTILLERS' COMPANY to construct on its site an addition to their offices to match the adjoining Adam façade. No. 31 stands on the site of NORFOLK HOUSE which was demolished in 1938. It bears a plaque stating that General Eisenhower formed the First Allied Force Headquarters here. No. 32 was the house of the BISHOPS OF LONDON between 1771 and 1919 and was rebuilt for William Howley, the then Bishop, in 1819–21 by Samuel Pepys Cockerell in association with his son, Charles Robert Cockerell. In 1939 the house was sold to the CALEDONIAN CLUB which had rented it for 20 years; and was sold by the club to the Prudential Assurance Company in 1949. No. 33 was rebuilt in 1770–2 by Robert Adam for the Hon. George Hobart, later 3rd Earl of Buckinghamshire. Adam's plans are in the SOANE MUSEUM. Sir John Soane supervised extensive alterations for a subsequent owner, the Earl of St Germans, in the early 19th century. From 1855 until his death in 1869 the house belonged to the 14th Earl of Derby, Prime Minister in 1852, in 1858–9 and in 1866–8. The statue in the garden in the centre of the square is of William III (*see* STATUES).

St James's Street *SW1*. Came into existence soon after Henry VIII's acquisition of ST JAMES'S HOSPITAL on whose site he built ST JAMES'S PALACE. It began to be built up at the beginning of the 17th century and first appears as St James's Street in the ratebook of 1660. At that time, however, it was, in John Evelyn's words, 'a quagmire'. It was placed under the control of paving commissioners in 1662. Thereafter it became celebrated for its coffee and chocolate houses and clubs, particularly so after the fire that almost destroyed WHITEHALL PALACE led to the transfer of the court to ST JAMES'S PALACE. WHITE'S was established in 1693, OZINDA'S in 1694, the COCOA TREE in 1698, the SMYRNA in 1702, the THATCHED HOUSE TAVERN in 1704 or 1705, the ST JAMES'S COFFEE HOUSE in 1705, Williams's at No. 86 in about 1710, Gaunt's at No. 88 in the 1730s and Saunders's at No. 85 in 1758.

Few noble or rich men lived here, it being better known for its fashionable shops than for its great houses, but the street has had several distinguished residents, most of them as lodgers. These included Sir Christopher Wren who probably died here in 1723; Alexander Pope in 1724; Edward Gibbon in 1793–4; Charles James Fox in 1781 when Horace Walpole saw his furniture being carried out by creditors; Lord Byron in 1811 when he awoke one morning to find himself famous after the publication of the first part of *Childe Harold*; James Gillray in 1808–15 when he threw himself to his death from an upper floor of Mrs Humphrey's print shop at No. 24; and Thomas Creevey in 1836.

Two 18th-century shops which still survive are Berry Brothers and Rudd, the wine merchants at No. 3, successors to the grocer and painter-stainer, William Pickering (*see* PICKERING PLACE), who took over the shop from one Widow Bourne in 1703–4; and LOCK's the hatters, who have occupied No. 6 since 1765. J. Lobb, the bootmakers at No. 9, were established by the grandfather of the present owners in about 1850; they have been bootmakers to the Crown since 1911. Wirgman's, the jewellers and goldsmiths at No. 71A, from whom Samuel Johnson, in the company of Boswell, bought a pair of silver shoe buckles in 1778, are no longer to be found. The St James's Bazaar, which was built in the 1830s to the designs of James Pennethorne on the site of No. 10 for William Crockford (*see* CROCKFORD'S), did not flourish. The building was converted into chambers in 1847, then, in 1882, taken over by the JUNIOR ARMY AND NAVY CLUB which remained there until 1904. In 1907 it was bought by the Parisian firm of Rumpelmayer and opened as a short-lived *confiserie*. In 1912 it was occupied as offices by the Motor Union Insurance Company. Chubb and Sons, the locksmiths and safemakers, have been at No. 68 since about 1875. D.R. Harris and Co., the chemists, at No. 29, were established in about 1790 at No. 11. Justerini and Brooks, the wine and spirit merchants established in PALL MALL in 1749, are at No. 61, and Leggatt Brothers, the picture dealers, at No. 30. Two well-known St James's Street hotels have disappeared: Fenton's Hotel, which was established in 1800 in premises on the site of No. 63, previously used as a *bagnio*, and which remained a fashionable hotel until 1886; and the St James's Royal Hotel which was at No. 88 during 1815–40. Prunier's restaurant, in its day one of the best fish restaurants in London, which was opened at Nos 71–73 in 1935, has now also gone. But Overton's Restaurant and Oyster Bar is still at No. 5.

Clubs which have now gone from St James's are the Union Club which, in 1951, moved into Nos 85–86, a building formerly occupied by the Thatched House Club; the Constitutional Club which occupied this same building from 1964; CROCKFORD's whose club-house by Benjamin Dean Wyatt was erected in 1827 on the site of Nos 50–53, later the premises of the DEVON-SHIRE CLUB; the Conservative Club which once occupied No. 74, a building constructed for them in 1843–5 to the designs of George Basevi and Sydney Smirke, and which was merged in 1950 with the BATH CLUB, now at 43 Brook Street. The clubs that survive are WHITE's at Nos 37–38, a building constructed in 1674, rebuilt in the 1780s, altered again in 1811 when the famous bow window was put in, and improved again in 1850 under the direction of James Lockyer; BOODLE's whose fine clubhouse at No. 28, built to the designs of John Crunden in 1775–6, was partially reconstructed by J.B. Papworth in the 1820s and 1830s and by Mayhew and Knight in the 1860s; the CARL-TON CLUB at No. 69, a building of 1827 by Thomas Hopper which was occupied until 1940 by ARTHUR's CLUB; and, on the corner of Park Place, BROOKS'S CLUB built in 1788 to the designs of Henry Holland.

Nos 87–88 is a distinguished building of 1904–5 designed by Norman Shaw for the Alliance Assurance Co. The building opposite it on the corner of PALL MALL was constructed in 1882–3 and is also by Norman Shaw. The Economist Building at No. 25, three stone-faced hexagonal towers in their own raised piazza, was built in 1964 to the designs of Alison and Peter Smithson.

St James's Theatre *King Street, SW1*. Built in 1835 to the designs of Samuel Beazley for John Braham, the tenor. Braham retired in 1838, having lost all his money. In 1842–54 the bookseller, John Mitchell, presented seasons of French theatre. In 1869–76 the theatre was run by Mrs John Wood who staged new dramas and revivals of old favourites such as *She Stoops to Conquer*. The interior was remodelled by Thomas Verity in 1879; and in 1880–8 the theatre was successfully managed by John Hare and W.E. Kendal. In 1890–1918 George Alexander was manager and staged for the first time *Lady Winder-mere's Fan* (1892) by Oscar Wilde, *The Second Mrs Tanqueray* (1893) by Pinero and *The Importance of Being Earnest* (1895) by Wilde. There were a number of notable productions in the 1920s including *The Green Goddess* (1923), *The Last of Mrs Cheyney* (1925), *Interference* (1927) and *Caprice* (1928). There was a celebrated production of *Pride and Prejudice* with sets by Rex Whistler in 1936. During the 2nd World War *A Month in the Country* (1943) by Tur-genev and *Ten Little Niggers* (1943) by Agatha Chris-tie both had long runs. During 1950–4 plays by Fry, Tyrone Guthrie, Shaw and Shakespeare were staged under the management of Laurence Olivier and Vivien Leigh. In 1954 Rattigan's *Separate Tables* ran for

almost two years. The theatre was closed in 1957 and, after considerable protest, demolished. Offices de-signed by R. Seifert were built on the site in 1959.

St John *Clerkenwell (St John's Square), EC1*. The priory church of the KNIGHTS HOSPITALLERS was built in about 1100 soon after the Order settled here. In 1185 it was consecrated by Heraclius, Patriach of Jerusalem. In 1381 Wat Tyler's rebels beheaded the Prior on TOWER HILL and burnt the priory (*see* PEASANTS' REVOLT). The priory was rebuilt soon afterwards but in 1540 the Order was dissolved. The Prior died of a heart attack when he heard the news. Many knights fled abroad. Some of those who stayed were executed.

The buildings were given to the Duke of Northum-berland but Henry VIII kept the church to store his hunting tents. In Edward VI's reign most of the priory was blown up to provide stone for Protector Somerset's new house in the STRAND (*see* SOMERSET HOUSE). The church was left to decay. Mary invited the knights back but Elizabeth banished them again and gave the church to the Master of the Revels. 30 of Shakespeare's plays were licensed here. In 1623 it was bought by one Simon Michel who restored and enlarged it. Two years later it was sold to the CHURCH COMMISSIONERS and given a parish. In 1931 it reverted to the Order of St John which had been revived in 1831 as the Protes-tant Most Venerable Order of the Hospital of St John of Jerusalem. After damage in the 2nd World War, restoration work, under the direction of Lord Mottis-tone, was completed in 1958. In the church are 15th-century altar paintings looted at the DISSOLUTION and returned in 1915. There is a well preserved 12th-century crypt containing an exceptionally fine alabas-ter effigy of a late 16th-century Proctor of the League of Castile in the Order of St John.

St John *East Dulwich Road, SE22*. Built in 1863–5 in French early Gothic style with a tower and broach spire on the south side. After bomb damage in the 2nd World War reconstruction was necessary; the nave was vaulted in concrete, a clerestory added to the nave, the interior was whitened and a colourful west gallery and *ciborium* were provided.

St John *Hampstead (Church Row), NW3*. Founded in the 14th century, it was rebuilt by John Sanderson in 1744–7. Henry Flitcroft offered his services free but they were refused. The wrought-iron gates were bought from the Duke of Chandos's house, CANONS at EDGWARE. In 1833–4 the nave was lengthened and the transepts were built by Robert Hesketh. The large chancel was built to the west by S.P. Cockerell in 1874. In 1874–5 the tower was threatened with demolition but was saved by a petition signed by Nor-man Shaw, William Butterfield, J.P. Seddon, Alfred Waterhouse, William Morris, Holman Hunt, An-thony Trollope, D.G. Rossetti and Sir Gilbert Scott, among others. It was this petition which fired Morris to organize opposition to the Victorian practice of destroying, altering and rebuilding early cathedrals, churches and other buildings. It led him to establish in 1878 the SOCIETY FOR THE PROTECTION OF ANCIENT

BUILDINGS. Buried here are John Constable, George Du Maurier, Sir Walter Besant, and Sir Herbert Beerbohm Tree.

St John *Hampstead (Downshire Hill), NW3.* This pretty, intimate, proprietary chapel with its white paint and wooden bell-turret evokes the religious and social atmosphere of village life in HAMPSTEAD during the early part of the 19th century. It is set in a garden enclosed by ornamental iron railings of that period. The building is made of stuccoed brick. The classical façade originally had a number of decorative features which have been lost over the years. The interior is light and cheerful with box pews which have stands for umbrellas and walking sticks on their doors. Elegant stairs on either side of the porch lead to the gallery. As the nature of the church is evangelical rather than sacramental there is no recessed chancel. Some historians have suggested that Samuel Pepys Cockerell may have been the architect. It is more likely, however, to have been the work of William Woods, a speculative builder, who, together with a clergyman, the Revd James Curry, and a lawyer, Edward Carlisle, bought the site in 1817 and erected the chapel to serve the residents of the new houses on Downshire Hill. Curry died before the chapel was completed in 1823 and the Revd William Harness was installed as the first minister. He was a life-long friend of Lord Byron and suffered from a similar lameness. At HARROW, Byron had often protected him from the bullies and later would have dedicated *Childe Harold* to him but for the fear of damaging the reputation of a man whose goodness he greatly admired.

In 1832 the chapel became the centre of an ecclesiastical storm. It had been bought by an evangelical clergyman, the Revd John Wilcox. The Vicar of HAMPSTEAD, Dr Samuel White – described by John Keats as 'the Parson of Hampstead quarrelling with all the world' – did not like Wilcox and, after appealing to the ecclesiastical courts, he succeeded in closing the chapel and silencing the preacher. A petition signed by many influential residents of Downshire Hill including Sara, the daughter of Samuel Taylor Coleridge, and her husband, was to no avail. The chapel closed until in 1835 an incumbent was found who met with Dr White's approval.

In 1916 the freehold of 'The Downshire Chapel' was bought by Mr Leslie Wright and leased to the congregation for a peppercorn rent. When he died in 1938 he directed in his will that his trustees should 'postpone the sale of the said chapel so long as there is sufficient congregation' to support a minister and pay for the upkeep of the building. He also placed the patronage in the hands of trustees who would ensure that St John's would continue on evangelical lines. It is today the only remaining proprietary chapel in the diocese of London.

St John *High Barnet, Hertfordshire.* The church crowns the ascent up Barnet Hill and stands at the junction of the historic Wood and High Streets. It was originally built as a chapel-of-ease to ST MARY THE VIRGIN, East Barnet, and still has traces of 13th-century remains in its north wall. In 1420 its enlargement and rebuilding was paid for by the brewer, John Beauchamp. In 1866 it became Barnet parish church and in 1870 it was enlarged and restored by William Butterfield.

St John *Hillingdon, Middlesex.* Built mostly of flint rubble with stone dressings. The oldest part of the building is the 13th-century chancel arch. The nave and north and south aisles date from the 15th century, while the west tower was rebuilt in 1629. A restoration by Sir George Gilbert Scott in 1847–8 produced a lengthened nave, transepts, and a new chancel with flanking chapels. Memorials in the church include a notable brass on the north wall of the south aisle to John, Lord Strange and his wife Jacquetta (1509).

St John *Waterloo Road, SE1.* Designed by Francis Bedford and built on piles in Lambeth Marsh in 1822–4. It was renovated by Sir Arthur Blomfield in 1885, and again repaired and altered by Ninian Comper in 1924. It was bombed in the 2nd World War. Only the walls, portico, steeple and an 18th-century Italian marble font survived. It was restored by Thomas Ford in 1950.

St John at Hackney *Mare Street, E8.* Designed in 1798 by James Spiller in the shape of a Greek cross to hold 4,000 people. It replaced the old church, dedicated to St Augustine, whose 16th-century tower still stands to the south. The spire and porch were added in 1812–13. It was restored after a fire in 1955. The parish stocks and whipping post are preserved in the churchyard.

St John-at-Wapping Built in the middle of the 18th century, this church, apart from the tower, was destroyed in the BLITZ. The tower, which has a charming clock storey and lead cupola, was subsequently restored.

St John on Bethnal Green *E2.* Built in 1825–8 to the designs of Sir John Soane. It was extensively repaired in 1871 after a fire.

St John of Jerusalem *South Hackney (Lauriston Road, Church Crescent), E9.* A large church on an island site, built 1845–8 by Henry Hakewith.

St John Street *EC1.* Mentioned as early as 1170, it was originally a road for pack-horses only. In the days of the stage-coach, when it was the starting point for BARNET and other towns and villages to the north, there were several taverns here, the Three Cups (mentioned in *Moll Flanders*) and the Bottle of Hay (mentioned by Pepys) among them. The Cross Keys, a favoured haunt of Johnson's wild friend, the poet, Richard Savage, is no longer at No. 16, but the Old Red Lion is still at No. 418, on a site occupied by a tavern of the same name since the beginning of the 15th century. Goldsmith, Johnson and Tom Paine were all frequent customers.

St John the Baptist *Chipping Barnet, Hertfordshire.* Largely rebuilt by William Butterfield in 1875. There are some fine 17th-century monuments.

St John the Baptist *Croydon (Church Street), Surrey.* On the night of Saturday, 5 January 1867, during a gale and blinding snowstorm the parish church of St John the Baptist, CROYDON – the largest in Surrey – was almost completely consumed by fire. Worshippers arriving the following morning found only the tower, south porch and charred walls still standing. The perpendicular style church is thought to have been erected at the end of the 14th and during the first part of the 15th century and its size was undoubtedly due to generous contributions by successive Archbishops of Canterbury who, until 1780, had a favourite summer residence at CROYDON, which is still, today, a peculiar of Canterbury. The Archbishop's Palace is now Palace School. Sir George Gilbert Scott rebuilt the damaged church to the original design, except for adding outsize pinnacles to the tower and the church was reconsecrated on 5 January 1870.

St John the Baptist *Pinner (High Street), Middlesex.* Built on the site of an earlier church, and consecrated in 1321. The west tower and south porch date from the 15th century. The church has been much restored on numerous occasions including a new chancel aisle and arcade in 1859 and a new vestry in 1880. Among the church treasures are a 15th-century octagonal font, 17th-century altar rails and an oak chest which must predate 1672 when it required a new lock. James Pye, poet laureate to George III, is buried in the church and William Skenelsby, who died at the reputed age of 118 years, in the churchyard. Also in the churchyard is the monument to William and Agnes Loudon with the coffin apparently above ground level protruding from a tall pyramid-style structure.

St John the Baptist upon Walbrook Built some time before 1150 on the banks of the WALBROOK which ran past its west wall. Repaired in 1649, it was burned down in the GREAT FIRE and was not rebuilt. The parish was united with that of ST ANTHOLIN in 1670, that of ST MARY ALDERMARY in 1873 and that of ST MARY LE BOW in 1954. During excavations for the DISTRICT LINE in 1884, a Saxon cross was found in the churchyard. Part of the churchyard remains in CLOAK LANE.

St John the Divine *Vassall Road, SW9.* Built in 1871–4 to the designs of G.E. Street. The tower and spire were added in 1888–9. After severe damage in the 2nd World War the church was restored by H.S. Goodhart Rendel.

St John the Evangelist *Blackheath (St John's Park), SE3.* A dignified church of 1852–3, situated in the Park, built in the Perpendicular style with western tower and spire.

St John the Evangelist *Finsbury Park (Queen's Drive), N4.* The church was built 1869–74, but the west end was not begun until 1877 and the projected central tower never was built.

St John the Evangelist *Friday Street.* Dedicated in the mid-13th century to St Wereburga, an 8th-century Princess of Mercia and Abbess of Ely. The parish was the smallest in the CITY being less than an acre in extent. By the middle of the 14th century the dedication had been changed to St John the Evangelist. In 1555 Laurence Saunders, the rector, was burned to death at Coventry for preaching against popery. In 1626 the church was repaired and beautified and a new gallery was built. It was burned down in the GREAT FIRE and not rebuilt. In 1670 the parish was united with ALL HALLOWS, BREAD STREET, and in 1876 with that of ST MARY-LE-BOW.

The churchyard survived until 1954 when the BANK OF ENGLAND extension was built over it.

St John the Evangelist *Great Stanmore, Middlesex.* There was a Saxon church in Old Church Lane, but all that now remains is the tomb of Baptist Willoughby, rector of Stanmore, 1563–1610. A brick church was built in 1632 at the sole expense of the merchant-adventurer, Sir John Wolstenholme, on land given by local benefactors. It was consecrated by Archbishop Laud. One of the earliest brick churches in the country, it had by 1845 become unsafe. Contractors were called in to demolish it. The roof was removed, but strong local resentment prevented further demolition. It is now a very picturesque ivy-covered ruin. The present church, designed by Henry Clutton, was completed in 1850. The foundation stone was laid by the Prime Minister, the Earl of Aberdeen, in the presence of the dowager Queen Adelaide, widow of William IV. Aberdeen is buried in the church and W.S. Gilbert, who lived at GRIMSDYKE, in the churchyard.

St John the Evangelist *Upper Norwood (Sylvan Road), SE19.* Almost by chance a young priest from Southampton heard in 1874 of the financial difficulties of a group of UPPER NORWOOD residents who had erected a small iron church to provide a form of worship more suited to their needs than was available elsewhere. The priest – Revd W.F. Bateman (later to be known as La Trobe-Bateman) – offered his services and so began a ministry which lasted 26 years. So successful were his efforts that the money needed to pay off the cost of the iron church was soon raised and thoughts began to turn towards the endowment and building of a permanent place of worship. Sympathy for the minister in the loss of his 29-year-old wife encouraged the fund until Bateman felt able to engage the eminent John Loughborough Pearson to build the new church. Although the foundation stone was laid in May 1878, work did not begin until 1881, consecration taking place in April 1887.

St John Zachary *Gresham Street and Noble Street.* First mentioned in about 1120 as the church of St John the Baptist. In about 1180 the canons of ST PAUL'S, who owned the living, gave it to a man named Zacharie. It was rebuilt in 1390 at the expense of Nicholas Twiford who also provided a tomb for himself and his wife. After being repaired several times in the 17th century it was destroyed in the GREAT FIRE. It was not rebuilt and the parish was united with ST ANNE AND ST AGNES, GRESHAM STREET. The churchyard is now a garden.

St John's Gate *St John's Lane, Clerkenwell, EC1.* Main gateway to the PRIORY OF ST JOHN OF JERUSALEM which was founded in the 12th century by a Norman Knight, Jordan de Briset. Only the gatehouse, dating from 1504, part of the chancel and the crypt, both incorporated in ST JOHN'S CLERKENWELL, survive. After the dissolution of the Priory in the reign of Henry VIII, the gatehouse fulfilled various functions. It housed the offices of Elizabeth I's Master of the Revels. From 1731–81 it was the printing works of Edward Cave's *Gentleman's Magazine* which numbered Johnson, Garrick and Goldsmith among its contributors. Johnson was provided with a room here in which to write his articles, poems and book reviews, and he locked himself in so that nobody could get in to

St John's Gate, Clerkenwell, the main gateway to the Priory of St John of Jerusalem, now houses the Order of St John Museum.

disturb him or to tempt him out. As the magazine prospered so did Cave who, in Johnson's words, bought himself 'an old coach and a pair of older horses; and, that he might not incur the suspicion of pride in setting up an equipage, he disclosed to the world the source of his affluence by a representation of St John's Gate, instead of his arms, on the door panel.' Later the gatehouse became the parish watch house, then a public house known as the Old Jerusalem Tavern. In 1874 it came into possession of the Most Venerable Order of the Hospital of St John of Jerusalem, a Protestant order established in 1831 to uphold the Hospitaller tradition of the medieval order. From here in 1877 was launched the St John Ambulance brigade. The gatehouse now contains the Museum and Library of the Order of St John.

St John's Hospital *St John's Hill, Battersea, SW11.* Opened in 1870 and then called the Wandsworth and Clapham Union Infirmary. In 1948 it was taken over by the National Health Service. It is mainly a geriatric hospital with, in 1982, 226 beds.

St John's Lodge Built in 1817–18 by John Raffield for Charles Augustus Tulk, MP, this was the second villa to be occupied in REGENT'S PARK. From 1829–33, it was the home of the Marquess Wellesley, the Duke of Wellington's eldest brother. In 1842–87 it belonged to the Goldsmid family; Sir Isaac Lyon Goldsmid was a banker, a President of the ROYAL SOCIETY and a philanthropist, and Sir Frances Goldsmid was MP for Reading and the first Jewish barrister. In 1889–1913 the Marquess of Bute lived there. In 1921 the villa became the headquarters of ST DUNSTAN'S and in 1937 the Institute of Archaeology. In 1959 the building was renovated and occupied by BEDFORD COLLEGE. The grounds of the villa have been made into a quiet rose garden for the public.

St John's Public Hall *Smith Square, SW1.* Built as a magnificent Baroque church. It cost £40,875 and was the most expensive of the 50 new churches which were required by the Act of Parliament of 1711. It was designed by Thomas Archer and built in 1713–28. The four towers in his original design were to have had pinnacles but during construction the plans were altered without his knowledge and the towers given cupolas, possibly for reasons of economy or because there had been trouble with the foundations. In 1742 the church was gutted by fire. In 1744–5 the interior was rebuilt by James Horne who omitted the 12 columns which had supported the original roof. It was refurnished by William Inwood in 1824–5. Most Victorians disliked the church. Dickens in *Our Mutual Friend* called it, 'a very hideous church with four towers at the corners, generally resembling some petrified monster, frightful and gigantic, on its back with its legs in the air'. It was gutted in the 2nd World War. The interior has since been rebuilt by Marshall Sisson for concerts.

St John's Wood *NW8.* When the *Domesday Book* was drawn up in 1086, the area known today as St John's Wood lay within the Manor of Lileston (*see* LISSON GROVE), and was held by a lady called Eideva from William the Conqueror himself. By the 13th century, it belonged to the KNIGHTS TEMPLAR. On the dissolution of that order in 1312, it was bestowed on another military order, the Knights of St John of Jerusalem – hence its subsequent and present name of St John's Wood. At the Reformation, the land changed hands a number of times and was eventually divided into two main estates – a long, narrow strip of land lying along the EDGWARE ROAD which John Lyon bequeathed to his foundation, HARROW SCHOOL in order to maintain the roads between London and HARROW in good repair, and a larger portion which Charles II bestowed at the Restoration on the 3rd Lord Wotton. (Charles had become indebted to him and his mother in his exile.) Lord Wotton left the estate to his nephew, Lord Chesterfield, whose heirs sold it in 1732 to Henry Simon Eyre, a City merchant. The EYRE ESTATE remains largely intact to this day.

Throughout the Middle Ages, the land was forest or woodland in more than name. Henry VIII appointed John Conway as its Keeper. Anthony Babington, following the discovery of his plot to murder Queen Elizabeth and place Mary, Queen of Scots, on the throne, hid there with his confederates. During the Commonwealth period, the trees were cut down. A Swedish botanist, Pehr Kalm, travelling through England in 1746, noted that there were market gardens along the EDGWARE ROAD and that the rest of the area, as far as HAMPSTEAD and beyond, was grassland – 'The meadow here is all their food and sustenance' – for quantities of hay were needed to provide for the horses kept in stables in the CITY and WESTMINSTER so that two, or even three, harvests were reaped each year by itinerant Irish labourers.

The 18th-century development of the PORTLAND and PORTMAN ESTATES scarcely affected the rural calm of St John's Wood. Thomas Lord, whose first cricket ground had opened in 1787 where DORSET SQUARE now stands, sought the calm of the Wood in 1811, though the projected development of the REGENT'S CANAL forced him to move his ground again, this time to its present site. It was from then onwards that the unbroken development of St John's Wood began. Even as early as 1794, a plan was issued by a firm of auctioneers (Messrs Spurrier and Phipps), recommending the laying-out of the estate with a grand circus ringed about with pairs of semi-detached houses – probably the first time that such a domestic arrangement had been suggested. The circus never materialised but the pairs of houses did, multiplying along the north and south banks of the canal, up Wellington Road towards HAMPSTEAD and FINCHLEY; they became an essential ingredient of the charm, at once urban and rural, that characterised St John's Wood. A chapel, designed by Thomas Hardwick, was erected in 1816. The Eyre Arms, on the west side of Wellington Road, opened its Assembly Rooms and Gardens, and an Artillery Barracks was built beside St John's Wood Farm.

For perhaps three generations, St John's Wood enjoyed, undisturbed, a character that was all its own and described as idyllic. The calm, the variety and charm of the comparatively inexpensive houses – Italianate villas, Victorian Gothic twins, the elegant uniformity of Abbey Gardens, each house adorned with pairs of Ionic pilasters – and the convenience of its proximity to London, combined with the purity of the air, made this an area chosen and inhabited by artists, authors, philosophers and scientists as well by more prosaic members of the middle classes. Mary Anne Evans, better known as the novelist George Eliot, residing with G.H. Lewes at 21 North Bank, held her Sunday receptions here; Sir Edwin Landseer spent most of his adult working life in St John's Wood Road; Thomas Henry Huxley, the naturalist, had half-a-dozen St John's Wood addresses, among them No. 48 Marlborough Place and No. 26 Abbey Place (now ABERCORN PLACE); the flamboyant Italian patriot and revolutionary, Ugo Foscolo, spent a short time at Digamma Cottage on the south bank of the REGENT'S CANAL before being arrested for debt; Thomas Hood wrote *The Song of the Shirt* when living in lodgings in ELM TREE ROAD before he moved a little further north to 28 Finchley Road. The artists J.J. Tissot and Sir Lawrence Alma-Tadema were successive owners of 17 (later 44) GROVE END ROAD; John MacWhirter lived in ABBEY ROAD, with the sculptor Onslow Ford as his neighbour, as well as the original seven members of the ST JOHN'S WOOD CLIQUE who used to meet to paint and draw and criticise each other's works together at the house of each one in turn. George Frampton, the sculptor, lived at 32 Queen's Grove.

The pretty villas were often establishments for courtesans. Elizabeth Anne Howard, whom Napoleon III created Comtesse Beauregard for her services both personal and political, lived at No. 23 (later No. 52) CIRCUS ROAD, whilst Mary Baker, later known as Mrs Meres, whose career and character may have provided the original inspiration for Thackeray's Becky Sharp in *Vanity Fair*, lived in Loudoun Road. Michael Sadleir's novels, *Forlorn Sunset* and *Fanny by Gaslight*, describe the milieu vividly.

The peaceful charm of the Wood was brutally disturbed, though not destroyed, when in 1894 the Great Central Railway was allowed to build in the area. 70 acres of the EYRE ESTATE and Harewood Square were wiped out and both the north and south banks of the CANAL were destroyed. It is true that two-thirds of St John's Wood remained unspoilt, but inevitably, once the great change had occurred, other smaller ones followed, each little alteration undermining the integrity of the rest of the area. By the 1920s and 1930s, the original leases on the EYRE ESTATE were falling in; individual houses or pairs of houses were pulled down

to make way for blocks of flats. The bombs of the 2nd World War continued the work of destruction begun by the railway. The magnificent houses in St John's Wood Park on the northern boundary lay almost derelict. Not a villa remained along the western side of Wellington Road.

Then, during the 1950s and 1960s, the remaining denizens of the Wood began to re-assert themselves. St John's Wood Park was redeveloped into smaller, but still very smart, town houses. Older properties along Carlton and Clifton Hills were granted new ground leases and their owners began to repaint and refurbish them. The almshouses in St John's Wood Terrace were modernised internally to the great benefit of the residents. In the High Street, the excellent butcher's and fishmonger's shops stand side by side with chic boutiques.

St John's Wood Barracks *Ordnance Hill, NW8.* Erected in 1832 as the Riding Department of His Majesty's Ordnance. Since its formation in 1946, the King's Troop, Royal Horse Artillery, has been quartered there. George VI decreed that this unit should be preserved with horses and full dress uniforms to act as a saluting battery to the HOUSEHOLD DIVISION. The troop is organised into three sections with an establishment of 182 men and 111 horses and has six 13-pounder quick-firing guns. Amongst its duties are firing salutes on the royal birthdays, state visits and other ceremonial occasions. During the summer it takes part in a number of military and civilian large-scale functions and, normally during September, provides relief guard duties at the HORSE GUARDS. The name of the King's Troop was not changed on the accession of Queen Elizabeth II, at her request.

St John's Wood Church *St John's Wood High Street, NW8.* A small Georgian church designed by Thomas Hardwick as a chapel-of-ease to the parish church of ST MARYLEBONE and built in 1813–14 on the site of a plague pit. Joanna Southcott, the religious fanatic, was buried here in 1814. In 1823 Morland, the murderer, was buried at the crossroads outside, with a stake driven through his stomach. In 1952 the church was given its own parish.

St John's Wood Clique A group of high-spirited artists living in and around the 'Wood' in the late 19th century, they were known sometimes as the Gridirons because of their badge, a miniature gridiron. They met every Saturday to draw given subjects together.

Conceived by David Wilkie Wynfield, the clique included P.H. Calderon, J.E. Hodgson, G.D. Leslie, H. Stacey Marks, G.A. Storey, and W.F. Yeames (best known for his painting *And When Did You Last See Your Father?*) Their work soon began to fetch high prices and to dominate the ROYAL ACADEMY. Yeames's first major work, *The Ambassadors*, was bought by Thomas Agnew. They all had a special knack for painting dramatic, pathetic or frivolous scenes. Val Prinsep and George Du Maurier were later admitted as honorary members, as were also F. Walker and Eyre Crowe. A collection of their work is now in the Hamburg Museum as part of a bequest made in 1897 on the death of G.C. Schwabe, a wealthy German art dealer, who frequently entertained the group at his home, Yewdon Manor, near Henley-on-Thames.

The hospital of St Katharine moved to Regent's Park in the 1820s, when a new chapel was designed by Ambrose Poynter.

St John's Wood Road *NW8.* Laid out from 1819 onwards on the EYRE ESTATE. Sir Edwin Landseer lived at No. 1 from 1828 until his death in 1873.

St Jude on the Hill *Hampstead Garden Suburb, (Central Square), NW11.* Named after St Jude, WHITECHAPEL, of which Canon Samuel Barnett had been vicar. HAMPSTEAD GARDEN SUBURB was his wife's idea. Part of Central Square, the church is the focal point of the suburb. With the Free Church opposite and the Institute (Adult Education Centre) between, all designed by Sir Edwin Lutyens in 1908–10, it forms one of the most harmonious architectural groups in London.

St Katharine *Regent's Park (Outer Circle), NW1.* ST KATHARINE'S BY THE TOWER was founded in 1148 by Queen Matilda. It was re-endowed and enlarged in 1273 by Eleanor, Queen of Henry III. In 1825 the buildings and grounds were acquired for ST KATHARINE'S DOCK. The hospital then moved to REGENT'S PARK, where, in 1829, Ambrose Poynter designed for it a stately Gothic chapel. This chapel was granted to her fellow-Danes by Queen Alexandra in the 1st World War and it is now the principal Danish church in London. The 17th-century wooden figures of Moses, and John the Baptist, carved by Caius Cibber, were brought from the old Danish church at LIMEHOUSE. Outside is a copy of the Rune stone set up at Jelling in about 980 by Harald Bluetooth, the first Christian King of Denmark.

St Katharine by the Tower *see* ROYAL FOUNDATION OF ST KATHARINE.

St Katharine Coleman *Fenchurch Street.* Originally built some time before 1346. It escaped destruction in the GREAT FIRE and was repaired in 1703. It was rebuilt in 1739 by James Horne. In his *Churches of London* (1838) George Godwin called it 'most ugly and inelegant' and illustrated it only 'to serve as evidence of the improvement which has taken place in public taste'. It was demolished in 1925–6, and the parish united with that of ST OLAVE HART STREET. Coleman was probably the name of the builder of the medieval church.

St Katharine Cree *Leadenhall Street, EC3.* Built in 1280 by the Prior of HOLY TRINITY ALDGATE for his parishioners so the 'canons be not disturbed by the presence of laity' at the services in the priory church. Cree is said to be corruption of Christchurch. It was rebuilt in 1504. The priory was dissolved in 1531. The church was rebuilt in 1628–30 and consecrated by Bishop Laud. (The popish manner of the services here was brought against him at his trial.) It escaped the GREAT FIRE and suffered only minor damage in the 2nd World War. It was restored by Marshall Sisson in 1962. At the east end is a rose window said to be modelled on the one in old ST PAUL'S. It is symbolic of the toothed wheel on which St Katharine was tortured by Emperor Maximilius in 307. The spectacular plaster ceiling is decorated with the arms of 17 CITY LIVERY COMPANIES. The font is 17th-century and was

St Katharine Cree in 1840. Rebuilt in 1628–30, this interior shows the influence of many contrasting styles.

presented to the church by the Lord Mayor, John Gayer. He also endowed the Lion Sermon preached annually on 16 October after surviving a face-to-face encounter with a lion. The Father Smith organ of 1686 was remade by Willis in 1866 and again by Lewis in 1906. Purcell, Wesley and Handel have played on it. The altar is 18th-century and ascribed to Robert Adam. In 1954 the parish was united with that of ST ANDREW UNDERSHAFT. St Katharine's is now a guild church. Temporary offices of the Industrial Christian Fellowship line the north and south aisles. Sir Nicholas Throckmorton was buried here in 1571.

St Katharine's *E1*. Queen Matilda, the wife of King Stephen, founded a hospital for the poor in the 12th century on 13 acres of land belonging to the Priory of Holy Trinity, Aldgate in the Portsoken Ward of the CITY OF LONDON. By the following century it was known as the Hospital of St Katharine (now the ROYAL FOUNDATION OF ST KATHARINE) and soon afterwards royal officials employed at the TOWER began to settle in its precincts. A Charter of Privileges granted in 1442 removed the residents from the civil jurisdiction of the CITY and the ecclesiastical jurisdiction of the BISHOP OF LONDON. St Katharine's became a royal peculiar with its own ecclesiastical court and in civil matters responsible only to the Master and Lord Chancellor. Trades and industries could therefore develop free from the jealously guarded rights of the CITY and its guilds; and evidence from the records of riots in 1451 suggest that a floating population of foreigners, seamen and criminals had already settled here. Originally all property was built on lease from the Hospital and control over development was stringent; but, when the leases were sold and tenements divided, the Hospital became 'inclosed about or pestered with small tenements and homely cottages', according to John Stow, writing at the end of the 16th century. A large number of foreigners, especially Flemish weavers and brewers, settled in the area about this time, attracted by its nearness to the CITY and the absence of restriction on immigrants. The few open spaces left were

soon occupied and wharves built along the riverside. Despite the rapid growth in buildings and population, which was estimated to have reached 3–4,000 inhabitants by 1640, St Katharine's appears to have been fairly well kept and comparatively healthy – mortality during the GREAT PLAGUE, for example, was about a half of that of neighbouring areas to the north and east. The promoters of the scheme to convert the area into wet docks described it as a collection of hovels inhabited by the lowest sections of the community, but more objective reports show that the houses were not ruinous and though most of the inhabitants were small tradesmen, manufacturers, and watermen, there were some wealthy residents. However, the Act to establish the ST KATHARINE'S DOCK was passed in 1825 and within a year all the buildings in the precinct were demolished. After this dock was closed in 1968, imaginative redevelopment has brought life to the area occupied by the World Trade Centre, the TOWER HOTEL, a marina, a collection of historic vessels and a housing estate.

St Katharine's Dock Built on 23 acres lying between LONDON DOCKS and the TOWER OF LONDON, conveniently near the CITY. On the site stood 1,250 insanitary small houses, a brewery, the old foundation of St Katharine's Hospital (*see* ROYAL FOUNDATION OF ST KATHARINE) with its river creek, and the 12th-century church of St Katharine, a royal peculiar, being the personal property of the queens of England. All were demolished in the face of protests and 11,300 inhabitants who did not own freeholds or leaseholds were dispossessed of their homes without compensation. After two and a half years of building, the docks were opened in 1828. The designer was Thomas Telford. This was his only complete work in London. The company's architect was Philip Hardwick, who was later to design the magnificent portico at EUSTON STATION. He collaborated with Telford on the designing of the warehouses and other buildings. The waters consisted of a large basin of 1½ acres leading to two docks of irregular shape of 4 acres each. These were

The opening of Thomas Telford's and Philip Hardwick's St Katharine's Dock in 1828. From an engraving after Huggins.

surrounded by sturdy warehouses of yellow brick-work, six floors high, supported by heavy Tuscan columns of iron and providing 1¼ million sq ft of storage area to house such commodities as tea, rubber, wool, marble, sugar, tallow, matches and live turtles. The warehouses were unusual in being built close to the water, having little unloading area for transit sheds in front of them so that goods could be immediately stored when unloaded. The lock to the river was somewhat narrow and could not admit large ships. The docks were never a great financial success and in 1864 the St Katharine Company merged with that of the LONDON DOCKS. After these no more docks were built in London for 25 years. The docks were closed in 1968, having been running at a loss, and were sold by the PORT OF LONDON AUTHORITY to the GREATER LONDON COUNCIL for £1½ million which was less than the original cost. The firm of Taylor Woodrow were granted a 125-year lease and there in 1973 they built the TOWER HOTEL. The magnificent warehouses have been disappearing and modern buildings for offices, flats and shops have been taking their place, while the waters have become a marina (see also HISTORIC SHIP COLLECTION OF THE MARITIME TRUST).

St Katharine's Way *E1*. The stainless steel sundial with bronze pointer is by Wendy Taylor (1973) and the bronze fountain, *Girl with a Dolphin*, by David Wynne (1973).

St Lawrence *Brentford, Middlesex*. Situated on the south side of the High Street, not far from BRENTFORD BRIDGE. It was originally the Chapel of New BRENTFORD. There was a church on this site in the 12th century but the tower dates from the 15th century, although the rest of the church was rebuilt in 1764 in brick. It contained a number of interesting memorials, some, including a 14th-century stone commemorating the burial at BRENTFORD of Maurice de Berkeley in 1189, transferred from the medieval church. It was closed in 1961, when the parish was united with that of St Paul. The monuments have been removed but may be returned. A trust has been formed which hopes to use the building as a theatre.

St Laurence *Catford (Bromley Road), SE6*. The architect of this circular church with its coroneted open-work spire, is Ralph Covell. It was built in 1968 and replaced a large 19th-century brick and stone church by H.R. Gough. The Lady Chapel contains a remarkable carving by a Kenyan artist, Samuel Wanjau, depicting the martyrdom of St Laurence.

St Lawrence *Morden*. A church has existed here since at least 1200. The present church, a rare example of a place of worship built in the reign of Charles I (others are ST PAUL, COVENT GARDEN; ST LUKE, CHARLTON; and ST KATHARINE CREE), dates from 1636. The brick exterior in English bond with stone quoins is thought to enclose the walls of an earlier structure. There is a plain castellated west tower containing a clock and three bells – the oldest is 1604. A vestry was added in 1805. The interior is an aisleless nave and chancel in one, separated only by a step. It has a barrel-vaulted roof supported by kingposts and tie-beams between which, on either side, is a series of 13 hatchments. These, together with the stained glass windows, provide a rich splash of colour against the plain plaster of the walls. The east window contains 17th-century glass together with some of later date. Furnishings include a pulpit of 1730 with original stair and sounding board, contemporary three-sided altar rails and wainscotting. The font by Legrew dates from about 1843.

St Lawrence *Whitchurch, Little Stanmore, Middlesex*. In 1710 Little Stanmore Manor passed by marriage to James Brydges, later Duke of Chandos. At an early age Brydges became Paymaster General to the Forces and soon amassed a considerable fortune, part of which he expended on CANONS and part on the rebuilding, except for the tower, of the 16th-century church of St Lawrence, Whitchurch. The palace was soon demolished, but the church is still in use and is unique. Its glory is in the magnificent paintings by the great masters of the day, including Laguerre. The showpiece is the vivid painting decorating the ceiling of the Ducal gallery: a magnificent reproduction of Raphael's *Transfiguration* attributed to Bellucci. The Duke appointed Handel as his music master at CANONS in 1718. According to local legend Handel's supposed inspiration for *The Harmonious Blacksmith* came whilst sheltering from a storm in a nearby blacksmith's forge. William Powell, the blacksmith, is buried in the churchyard.

St Lawrence Jewry *Gresham Street, EC2*. Founded in the 12th century and dedicated to the St Lawrence who, in 3rd-century Rome, was roasted alive on a gridiron. Little is known of earlier buildings. Burned down in the GREAT FIRE, it was rebuilt by Wren in 1671–7 with a handsome decorated east wall which lends classical dignity to the GUILDHALL approach. The stone façade consists of a pediment resting on four corinthian half-columns above five rounded arches above which are swags of fruits and flowers. After bomb damage in 1940, which left only the walls and the tower, the church was rebuilt by Cecil Brown in 1954–7. Most of the furniture was donated by CITY LIVERY COMPANIES but the font dates from 1620 and came from HOLY TRINITY MINORIES. Windows by Christopher Webb commemorate Sir Thomas More, who preached here, and Wren, flanked by his master-mason and master-carver. Since the GUILDHALL CHAPEL was demolished in 1820 the LORD MAYOR and CORPORATION have worshipped here. Behind the church is a Gothic drinking fountain erected in 1866 in memory of church benefactors.

St Laurence Pountney *Laurence Pountney Lane*. Mentioned in 1275 as St Laurence next the Thames, in 1277 as St Laurence in Candlewigstrate and in 1285 St Laurence de Lundenestane. At an unknown date Thomas Cole added the Chapel of Jesus. In about 1334 John de Poulteney converted the parish church and chapel into a college with a master and seven chaplains and gave it its present name. The advowson of the church seems to have passed into the hands of the college. From 1370 expatriate weavers from Flanders met in the churchyard. The college was dissolved in the reign of Edward VI when it was valued at £79 17s 11d. In 1634 major repairs included the provision of new bells and the releading of the spire which was one of the highest in the CITY. The church was destroyed in the GREAT FIRE and not rebuilt. The parish was amalgamated with that of ST MARY ABCHURCH.

St Leonard *Eastcheap*. First mentioned in 1214 and also known as St Leonard Milkchurch. Stow says its alternative name was derived 'of one William Melker, an especial builder thereof', but the designation EASTCHEAP was more common. The patron was the Prior of Christ Church Canterbury, thus it was a peculiar. In 1554 John Towner, the rector, was made to do penance for marrying. In 1618, after the steeple had been burned down, repairs included the enlargement of the church. In 1650–62 the rector was Matthew Barker who later founded the independent meeting house in MILES LANE. The church was burned down in the GREAT FIRE and was not rebuilt. The parish was united with ST BENET GRACECHURCH and the site of the church retained as a burial ground to serve it. In 1864 the parish of ST BENET GRACECHURCH was united with that of ALL HALLOWS LOMBARD STREET. In 1882 the remains from the burial ground were communally re-interred in the CITY OF LONDON CEMETERY at ILFORD. The parish of ALL HALLOWS LOMBARD STREET was united with that of ST EDMUND THE KING in 1937.

St Leonard *Foster Lane*. First mentioned in 1278. Stow said it was 'used by them of St Martin's le grand'. Enlarged and repaired in 1631, it was destroyed in the GREAT FIRE and not rebuilt. The parish was added to that of CHRIST CHURCH NEWGATE.

St Leonard *Shoreditch (Shoreditch High Street), E1*. Probably founded in the 12th century. After part of the tower had given way during a service in 1716, the church was rebuilt by George Dance the Elder, in 1736–40. He tried to imitate the spire of ST MARY-LE-BOW. The interior has sombre woodwork and a flat panelled ceiling. In 1857 the north and south galleries were removed. The rood beam was inserted in 1923. The church was damaged in the 2nd World War but has since been repaired. The whipping post and village stocks are in the churchyard. Three of Keats's brothers were baptised here in 1801 and Charles Bradlaugh, the atheist, in 1833. Buried here are Will Sommers, Henry VIII's jester, 1560; Gabriel Spencer, the actor who was killed by Ben Jonson in a duel in 1598; Elizabeth Benson, who has an outstanding monument by Francis Bird of two skeletons tearing at the Tree of Life, 1710; and Richard Burbage, Shakespeare's friend and the builder of the CURTAIN.

St Leonard *Streatham (Streatham High Street), SW16*. Shoddily built by J.T. Parkinson in 1830, this church replaced a 12th century one loved by Dr Samuel Johnson. He used to attend the services here when visiting his dearest friends, the Thrales, and when Mrs Thrale decided to leave STREATHAM after the death of her husband, Dr Johnson kissed this ancient parish church goodbye. The main interest of St Leonard's today lies in its many monuments. One in particular to John Howland, who died in 1686, is a rare example of English Baroque by John Van Nost. Two of the three memorials to members of the Thrale family bear Latin inscriptions by Dr Johnson. He would justify his praise of Mrs Thrale's mother because he held that 'in lapidary inscriptions a man is not upon oath.' The one to Sophia Hoare, a daughter of Henry and Hester Thrale who died in 1824, is by John Flaxman. A brass of an artist in front of an easel is to the Pre-Raphaelite painter, William Dyce, who

designed the chancel in 1862. The church has been restored after being damaged by fire in 1975.

St Leonard's Hospital *Nuttall Street, N1*. Began as a parish workhouse in 1777, but there was no proper organisation or treatment until Dr James Parkinson, a general practitioner in HOXTON, was appointed in 1813. He divided the wards into male and female, surgical and medical, maternity, incurable and insane. In 1817, he published an *Essay on the Shaking Palsy* in which he described the condition now known as Parkinson's Disease.

During the 19th century the workhouse was frequently enlarged and in 1872, with 503 beds, a matron was appointed. In 1903–6 Edith Cavell was the assistant matron before going to Belgium to found an institute for the training of nurses. In 1920 the workhouse was designated a hospital. In 1948, it was taken over by the National Health Service, and modernised. In 1982 it had 200 beds for acute cases.

St Leonard's Terrace *SW3*. Previously called Green's Row after its builder, a Westminster brewer. There are some charming 18th-century houses with gardens both front and back. Later a few were reconstructed and more erected by a builder, John Tombs, who was born near Upton St Leonards, Gloucestershire, whence probably the name. A BLUE PLAQUE at No. 18 commemorates Bram Stoker, author of *Dracula*, who lived here from 1896 to 1906.

St Luke *Charlton Village, SE7*. A church in CHARLTON is mentioned, before *Domesday*, in 1077. It came under BERMONDSEY ABBEY until the DISSOLUTION when the Manor passed into secular hands, being bought by Sir Adam Newton in 1607. After his death in 1630, money left by him largely helped towards the building of the present brick church, a rare example of a place of worship built in Charles I's reign. The area of CHARLTON near the church is still called 'The Village'. St Luke's homely brick exterior with Dutch gabled south porch makes an attractive vignette with the handsome CHARLTON HOUSE nearby.

The church has many notable monuments, especially those to Sir Adam and Lady Newton. On the south wall is a memorial to Edward Wilkinson, Master Cook to Queen Elizabeth and 'Yeoman of the Mouth' to King Henry VIII, Anne Boleyn and King Edward VI. On the west wall of the north aisle is a tablet, with a beautifully modelled portrait bust above to Spencer Perceval, assassinated in the HOUSE OF COMMONS in 1812. In the rector's vault lies another victim of assassination, the brother of the rector at the time, who was killed by a madman in mistake for Sir Robert Peel.

Because St Luke's was a landmark from the THAMES and used as a navigational aid in the past, the church is authorised on St George's and St Luke's Days to fly the British Ensign from a flagpole outside.

St Luke *Chelsea (Sydney Street), SW3*. A lofty stone church designed by James Savage in 1820–4. A spire was planned but never built. In 1872 Charles Eastlake called it 'the earliest groined church of the modern revival'. It cost £40,000 and seats 2,500. The altar painting, *The Entombment*, is by James Northcote. The east window is by Hugh Easton (1959). Charles Dickens was married here in 1836 to Catherine Hogarth, whose parents lived at 18 York

Place, FULHAM ROAD. The gardens of the rectory are, after those of BUCKINGHAM PALACE, the largest private gardens in central London. The rectory itself became disused in the 1970s.

St Luke *Kentish Town, (Caversham Road), NW5.* A large redbrick church built in 1868–70 to the designs of Basil Champneys.

St Luke *Old Street, EC1.* One of the last of the churches built under the Act of 1711 which provided for 50 new churches in London. St Luke's was built in 1727–33 to relieve ST GILES CRIPPLEGATE. George Dance the Elder was a member of the vestry; and the church has often been erroneously attributed to him. But, in fact, it was designed by the CHURCH COMMISSIONERS' surveyors, John James and Nicholas Hawksmoor. In 1959 the building was found to be unsafe and the roof was taken off leaving only the obelisk spire and the walls. The parish was reunited with ST GILES CRIPPLEGATE. Buried here are George Dance the Elder, in 1768 (a blackmarble slab was provided 20 years later by his children but has now gone), and the type founders, William Caslon, father and son, in 1766 and 1778 respectively.

St Luke *West Norwood, (Knights Hill), SE27.* One of four Commissioners' churches built in SOUTH LONDON, each dedicated to one of the four Evangelists, the others being ST JOHN, WATERLOO ROAD, ST MATTHEW, BRIXTON and ST MARK, KENNINGTON. They were known as Waterloo churches, being built out of funds set aside by Parliament, ostensibly as thanksgiving for victory. St Luke's was built by a woman contractor (Elizabeth Broomfield) to the designs of Francis Bedford in 1822–5 and, although very like St John's (also by him), St Luke's gains from its elevated site giving full effect to its six-columned portico. The interior was remodelled by G.E. Street in Italian Romanesque style in the 1870s.

St Magnus the Martyr *Lower Thames Street, EC3.* Founded sometimes before 1067. Originally built of stone, it stood at the foot of old LONDON BRIDGE. The St Magnus to whom the church is dedicated is probably the saintly Norwegian Earl of the Orkneys. St Magnus's Corner was an important meeting place of medieval London where notices were read and malefactors punished. In 1544 three of Wyatt's rebels were hanged here. In 1563–5 Miles Coverdale, translator of the New Testament, was vicar. In 1581 Pieter Morice, a Dutchman, harnessed the THAMES at the north end of LONDON BRIDGE to supply water to houses in Lower Thames Street. He demonstrated its force by sending a jet over the church tower. Burned down in the the GREAT FIRE, the church was rebuilt by Wren in 1671–6. The 185 ft high steeple was added in 1705. After a fire in 1760 the roof was replaced. In 1762 the vestries were demolished and a new one was built to the south. At the same time the aisles were shortened by George Dance to allow the pavement to pass under the tower when the road was widened. The northern windows were made circular in 1782. The interior is described in T.S. Eliot's *The Waste Land* as 'inexplicable splendour of Ionian white and gold'. Statues, shrines and gilded sword rests abound. The organ case, altarpiece and font are all 17th-century. The very grand organ was built by Abraham Jordan in 1712. In the churchyard are some stones from old LONDON BRIDGE and the remains of a Roman wharf. Henry Yevele, the architect of the nave of WESTMINSTER ABBEY, was buried here in 1400; and Miles Coverdale, first buried at ST BARTHOLOMEW-BY-THE-EXCHANGE, was reburied here in 1840.

St Margaret *Barking (Broadway), Essex.* Stands in splendid isolation on a large common, close to the site of BARKING ABBEY which included among its abbesses three queens, two princesses and the sister of Thomas Becket. Only the curfew tower of the ABBEY remains. The church is mainly of the 15th and 16th centuries, including the west tower, but parts go back to the 13th century and even earlier. Long and low, the exterior is dominated by the tower with higher stair-turret. Inside, although the nave arcade varies in date, the effect is of a medieval town church, double-aisled on the north side. The nave and aisle roofs are original, although timbers on the north aisle have had to be renewed, but the stuccoed vault in the chancel dates from 1772. There are many notable monuments. One of the most appealing is that on the south wall of the chancel to Sir Charles Montague who gazes pensively out of his tent flanked by musketeers, with more tents in the distance. In the outer north aisle is a fine memorial to Captain John Bennett showing him flanked by carvings of naval vessels in relief like huge epaulettes. Other monuments include one to Sir Orlando Humfreys in the south aisle and another in the north aisle to Sir Crisp Gascoyne, Lord Mayor of London in 1752 and the first to live in the MANSION HOUSE. Of much earlier date is the incised slab of 1328 on the north wall of the chancel to Martinus (first Vicar of BARKING) discovered above a culvert during ABBEY excavations in 1912. There are also 15th- and 16th-century brasses. The font, dating from about 1635, is encrusted with decoration and has a charming cover with bird paintings and a carved bird on top. The 18th-century pulpit has a staircase railing of finely twisted balusters. Like ALL SAINTS, WEST HAM, St Margaret's is unusual – for historical reasons – in having three churchwardens. Amongst its many associations, one of the most famous is that the great navigator, Captain James Cook, was married at St Margaret's on 21 December 1762. The incumbency of BARKING seems in recent years frequently to have been a path to preferment, for in the last 100 years or so no fewer than eight vicars have become bishops.

St Margaret *Lee (Lee Terrace), SE3.* Built in 1839–41 to replace an earlier church of 1813–14, of which the lower part of the tower remains. The west tower has an octagonal top-stage and tower, and is surmounted by a spire. There are some 16th-century brasses.

St Margaret *Lothbury, EC2.* First mentioned in 1197, it was rebuilt in 1440. Burned down in the GREAT FIRE it was rebuilt by Wren in 1686–90. The interior is cluttered with superb 17th-century woodwork from demolished Wren churches. The pulpit, with its elaborate sounding board and the rood screen, came from ALL HALLOWS THE GREAT; the reredos, communion rails and font, ascribed to Grinling Gibbons, from ST OLAVE OLD JEWRY; and the paintings of Moses and Aaron from ST CHRISTOPHER LE STOCKS. The bust of Sir Peter le Maire is probably by Le Sueur and that of Mrs Simpson by Nollekens.

St Margaret *New Fish Street Hill.* Stood so close to Pudding Lane that it must have been one of the first churches to burn in the GREAT FIRE. It was not rebuilt. The MONUMENT was erected on its site. The parish was later joined with that of ST MAGNUS THE MARTYR.

St Margaret *Uxbridge, Middlesex.* Stands on a crowded site at the junction of High Street and Windsor Street. The first church to be built here dates from about 1200, but it was largely rebuilt in the 15th century. The large south aisle, constructed as a chapel for the guild of St Mary and St Margaret, has a fine hammerbeam roof. Before the creation of St Margaret's parish in 1827, the building was a chapel-of-ease to HILLINGDON. A burial ground, opened in 1576, lies 150 yards south-west of the church.

St Margaret *Westminster (Parliament Square), SW1.* Founded by the Abbot of WESTMINSTER towards the middle of the 12th century, it was declared by the Pope in 1189 to be exempt from the jurisdiction of the BISHOP OF LONDON. The first church was demolished in the reign of Edward III. It was rebuilt in 1486–1523. Since then it has been restored many times. In about 1549 it was one of the buildings earmarked by Protector Somerset for demolition to provide stone for SOMERSET HOUSE. He had already razed the cloisters of ST PAUL'S and ST JOHN'S, CLERKENWELL. The angry parishioners, however, appeared in force with clubs and bows and the workmen had to beat a hasty retreat. In 1614 the Commons made it their parish church. The first service was on 17 April when the Commons attended a corporate Communion. It was probably to test Dissenters in their midst. Members remain *ex officio* parishioners of St Margaret's. Galleries were added in 1641 and 1681. Here in 1643 Members accepted the Solemn League and Covenant demanding the reform of the Church of England in return for military aid from Scotland. In 1647 the churchwardens were fined for observing Christmas Day. In 1661 the bodies of John Pym and other Parliamentarians were buried in a pit in the churchyard. During 1676–1708 Father Smith, the organ builder, was organist. In 1734 the walls were cased in Portland stone and the tower was rebuilt by John James. The 16th-century east window was installed in a neo-Gothic apse by Kenton Couse in 1758. The glass was made for Ferdinand and Isabella of Spain to celebrate the betrothal of Catherine of Aragon to Prince Arthur, and was intended for WESTMINSTER ABBEY, but by the time it arrived Arthur was dead and Catherine had married Henry VIII. The glass had been tactfully despatched to WALTHAM ABBEY. In 1840 the parish was incorporated in the Diocese of London. The rector is still normally a Canon of WESTMINSTER ABBEY. During restoration in the 1870s all the 18th- and the galleries' 19th-century woodwork and Couse's apse were removed and a new roof put on. The churchyard was cleared and grassed. In 1897 a new organ by Walker was installed. The east end was extended in 1905. The church was repeatedly damaged in the 2nd World War. It has since been repaired: the south aisle windows are by John Piper, 1967. The font is by Nicholas Stone, 1641, and the relief, *Christ at Emmaus,* above the altar is a copy done in about 1753 of Titian's masterpiece. Barbara Villiers, Duchess of Cleveland, was christened here in 1641. Among many distinguished men married here were Samuel Pepys in 1655, John Milton to his second wife, Katherine Woodcock in 1656, and Winston Churchill in 1908. Buried here were William Caxton, 1491; John Skelton the poet, 1529; Nicholas Udall, author of the first English comedy, *Ralph Roister Doister,* 1556; Sir Walter Ralegh, 1618; John Pym (reburied in 1661 after his death in 1643); Admiral Blake (reburied in 1661, after his death in 1657); Wenceslaus Hollar, the engraver, 1677.

St Margaret Moyses *Friday Street.* Nothing remains of this church, which was destroyed by the GREAT FIRE and never rebuilt. The derivation of the name, Moyses or Moses, is unknown. Possibly it is that of a benefactor. The parish was united with that of ST MILDRED, BREAD STREET.

St Margaret Pattens *Rood Lane, EC3.* First mentioned in 1216. Pattens, wooden soles worn to protect shoes from the mud, were made nearby. The church was rebuilt in 1530 and repaired in 1614–32. It was burned down in the GREAT FIRE and rebuilt by Wren with a 200 ft spire in 1684–7. Inside are some of the few remaining canopied pews in London. One of them has 'CW 1686' carved on its roof and was probably Wren's own. Beside the pulpit is an hour-glass for timing sermons. In the north transept is a beadle's pew and a punishment bench carved with the Devil's head where miscreants had to sit during the service. In the side chapel there are hooks where wigs were placed on hot days. The altar painting of *Christ in Gethsemane* is by Carlo Maratti. Since 1954 the church has been a Christian Study Centre.

St Mark *Dalston, (St Mark's Rise), E8.* Brick church with stone dressings built to the designs of Chester Cheston in 1864–6 and completed by E.L. Blackburne in 1877–80. The choirboys, mostly black, wear Eton collars and pinstriped trousers.

St Mark *Hamilton Terrace, NW8.* Built in 1846–7 to the designs of Thomas Cundy and Thomas Cundy the Younger. Goodhart-Rendel criticised it strongly, describing it as a 'large broad Gothic riding school'. In 1864 the tower and spire were completed. The chancel, designed by E.B. Ferrey, was completed in 1878 and new porches and lobbies added. The glass in the chancel is by Clayton and Bell and the painting of the cradle roof is by Edward Armitage. The church was restored after suffering damage in the 2nd World War. The spire was rebuilt in 1955.

St Mark *Kennington, SE11.* One of four Commissioners' churches built in SOUTH LONDON, each dedicated to one of the four evangelists. It was built in the 1820s and restored after damage in the 2nd World War. The 17th-century pulpit is from ST MICHAEL, WOOD STREET. (*See* ST LUKE'S, WEST NORWOOD.)

St Mark *Marylebone Road, NW1.* Brick church built in 1871–2, at a low cost, to the designs of Blomfield. The tower has a characteristic pyramid top. The church was redecorated at the beginning of the century, the walls whitened, and the pillars painted black.

St Mark *North Audley Street, W1.* Built in 1825–8 by J.P. Gandy-Deering as a chapel-of-ease to ST GEORGE HANOVER SQUARE, it was 'Normanised' by Sir Arthur Blomfield in 1878.

St Mark *Silvertown, E16.* Built to the designs of S.S. Teulon in 1862, it was badly damaged by fire in 1981 and is now redundant.

St Mark's Hospital *City Road, EC1.* Founded in 1835 by Frederick Salmon who received his medical education at ST BARTHOLOMEW'S nearby. Originally only out-patients were treated in a small room in ALDERSGATE STREET. In 1838 the hospital was moved to CHARTERHOUSE SQUARE where in-patient accommodation was available. In those days its name was The Infirmary for the Relief of the Poor Afflicted with Fistula and other Diseases of the Rectum. Salmon, who retired in 1859, published *A Practical Treatise on Stricture of the Rectum* which went to four editions and was beautifully illustrated. A new hospital, designed by John Wallen, was opened on the present site on St Mark's Day, 25 April 1854. It was given the name of St Mark's Hospital for Fistula and other Diseases of the Rectum. It was extended in 1898 to the designs of Rowland Plumbe. There were then about 40 beds. The operating theatre was heated by an open coal fire. There was one small steriliser which took only the instruments. (As was common practice then, the dressings, gowns and towels were not sterilised.) The operating table was an ordinary bedstead from which the ends had been removed. In 1926 a further extension brought the number of beds up to 72. In 1928, the old operating theatre was modernised. In 1948 the hospital was taken over by the National Health Service and recognised as a postgraduate teaching hospital for diseases of the colon and rectum. Its medical school became part of the Postgraduate Medical Federation of the University of London. It has recently been linked with ST BARTHOLOMEW'S HOSPITAL. In 1982 there were 93 beds.

St Martin *Vicar's Road, NW5.* Built in 1865–6 to the Gothic designs of E. Buckton Lamb for a glove manufacturer of strong evangelical tendencies. Lamb who, so the *Builder* said, 'constantly endeavoured to exhibit originality', produced a characteristically unorthodox structure.

St Martin *West Drayton, Middlesex.* There is a record of a church at WEST DRAYTON in the late 12th century but no trace of it now remains. Early in the 13th century a second church was built, of which the base of the tower, the *piscina* and the north chancel wall are incorporated in the present building which dates from the mid-15th century. A major restoration and reordering of the church took place in 1974–5 when the altar was resited at the west end. The font is a splendid example of mid-15th-century work and the parish chest is early 17th-century. There are monumental brasses to Richard Roos (Mercer, 1406, surviving from the second church); Margaret Burnell (1529), her son John Burnell (1551, Officer of the Cellar to Henry VIII); and Dr James Good (1581, one of Mary, Queen of Scots's physicians). A small mural tablet records the benevolence of Elizabeth I's cousin, Lord Hunsdon, Lord of the Manor.

St Martin-in-the-Fields *Trafalgar Square, WC2.* A small chapel was built on this site sometime between *Domesday Book* and Henry II's reign, possibly for the monks of WESTMINSTER ABBEY who came to work in their convent garden. By the 12th century it had its

St Martin-in-the-Fields, rebuilt by James Gibbs in 1722–4, with Hubert le Sueur's statue of Charles I in the foreground.

own parish. It was rebuilt in 1543–4, and a new chancel built and paid for by Henry, Prince of Wales, 1606–9. Thomas Tenison, later Archbishop of Canterbury, was vicar in 1680–92. It was rebuilt in 1722–4 by James Gibbs who wanted a circular building but the CHURCH COMMISSIONERS scotched the idea on the grounds of expense. So he built a large model of ST PETER VERE STREET, a rectangular church with a portico straddled by a high steeple – a design much copied in America. The interior was altered by Sir Arthur Blomfield in 1887. From 1914 to 1927 Dick Sheppard was vicar. After the 1st World War he opened the crypt for homeless soldiers coming back from France and then, until 1945, it was used as a shelter for down-and-outs. In 1924 Sheppard conducted the first broadcast service from the church. The crypt was used as an air raid shelter in the 2nd World War: several people were killed when it was hit by a bomb. It is now restored and is used for meetings and concerts. St Martin's has often been called the royal parish church. Several royal babies have been christened here. Mary I sometimes worshipped here and gave tapestries to the church. George I was appointed churchwarden but rarely attended and gave an organ to compensate. Christened here were Francis Bacon in 1561 and Charles II in 1630. Benjamin West, the painter, was married here in 1765. Buried here are Nicholas Hilliard, the miniature painter, 1619; Nicholas Stone, the sculptor, 1647; Nell Gwynne, 1687; Laguerre, the painter, 1721; Jack Sheppard, the highwayman, 1724; Hogarth, 1762; Sir Joshua Reynolds, 1762; Roubiliac the sculptor, 1762; James 'Athenian' Stuart, the architect, 1788; and

Thomas Chippendale, the cabinet maker, 1779. John Hunter the surgeon was also buried here in 1793, but his remains were moved to WESTMINSTER ABBEY in 1859.

St Martin-in-the-Fields High School *155 Tulse Hill, SW2.* Owes its origin to the SOCIETY FOR PROMOTING CHRISTIAN KNOWLEDGE which in 1699 proposed to the parish of ST MARTIN-IN-THE-FIELDS the formation of a committee to establish a charity school, first for boys and then for girls. The minute books of the girls' school committee from 1700–98 and 1873 onwards are in possession of the school. From 1873 to 1928 the school was situated in CHARING CROSS ROAD. The present building were opened in May 1928. In 1953 the Worshipful Company of Farriers (*see* CITY LIVERY COMPANIES) took up one of the eight Foundation Governorships of the school. Since then the school has maintained close links with the Company, with the church of ST MARTIN-IN-THE-FIELDS and with the SOCIETY FOR PROMOTING CHRISTIAN KNOWLEDGE. In 1982 there were about 600 pupils.

St Martin Orgar *Martin Lane, EC4.* First mentioned in the 12th century when the church was granted by Ordgar, the Deacon, to the Canons of ST PAUL'S. 'A small thing', according to Stow, it was destroyed, except for the tower and part of the nave, in the GREAT FIRE. The congregation abandoned it and moved to ST CLEMENT EASTCHEAP. However, French Protestants restored the tower and worshipped in it for more than a century and a half. It was demolished in 1820. In 1852 an Italianate tower, designed by J. Davies, was built as a rectory for ST CLEMENT'S. By 1871 it was being used as offices and it now houses the Diocesan Registry. Three Lord Mayors are buried here – John Mathew, William Crowmer and Sir William Huet.

The 15th century church of St Martin Outwich in 1736, just before it was burnt down in the fire which swept Cornhill.

St Martin Outwich *Threadneedle Street.* In 1403 Martin, Nicholas, William and John de Oteswich built a church dedicated to St Martin at the junction of THREADNEEDLE STREET and BISHOPSGATE. According to Stow the first patronage of this church was given to 'the master and wardens of tailors and linen armourers, keepers of the guild and fraternity of St John Baptist'. It escaped the GREAT FIRE only to be burnt down a century later in 1765 in a fire that swept through CORNHILL. Samuel Pepys Cockerell built a charming little church with an oval interior to replace it in 1796. A commentator in 1820 observed that 'a great neatness pervades the whole'. However, the population in the CITY OF LONDON declined sharply during the middle of the 19th century and money was needed for the building of churches in the new suburbs, so St Martin Outwich was demolished in 1874. The bones from the vaults were removed to ILFORD Cemetery. Among them were those of a medieval lady, a Mrs Abigail Vaughan, who left 4s a year to buy faggots to burn heretics. The parish was united with that of ST HELEN'S BISHOPSGATE.

St Martin Pomeroy *Ironmonger Lane.* This little parish church stood near an apple orchard – hence its name. The GREAT FIRE destroyed it and the parish was then united with that of ST MICHAEL AT CORN, PATERNOSTER ROW.

St Martin Vintry *College Hill.* Described by Stow as a 'fair parish church'. For some obscure reason it was referred to as St Martin de Beremand Church. Perhaps this had some connection with the 11th-century building. In 1399 the church was rebuilt by the executors of Matthew Columbars – a vintner from Bordeaux. In the middle of the 15th century, a wealthy fishmonger, Sir Ralph Austrie, restored the church and put in some beautiful windows. The GREAT FIRE destroyed it and it was not rebuilt. The parish was united with ST MICHAEL PATERNOSTER ROYAL.

St Martin within Ludgate *Ludgate Hill, EC4.* According to the unreliable Geoffrey of Monmouth, the church was founded by the Welsh hero Cadwallader in the 7th century. The first references to it in historical documents occur in 1174. Burned down in the GREAT FIRE, it was rebuilt by Wren in 1677–84. Inside a screen separates the nave from the entrance and from the noise of LUDGATE HILL. Much 17th-century woodwork survives, including the altarpiece, pulpit and organ case. The font is also 17th century and is inscribed with the Greek palindrome, *Niyon anomhma mh monan oyin* (cleanse my sin and not my face only). Hanging beside the altar is Benjamin West's *Ascension.* Above rises the most slender and graceful of Wren's lead steeples, mounted on an octagonal stone tower which itself rests upon a leaden ogee dome. It is now a guild church.

St Martin's Court *WC2.* Extends from ST MARTIN'S LANE to CHARING CROSS. Sheekey's Restaurant and Oyster Bar (established 1896) is at Nos 29–32. WYNDHAM'S THEATRE is at the CHARING CROSS corner.

St Martin's Gardens *see* BURIAL GROUNDS.

St Martin's Lane *WC2.* Building began in about 1610 on the west side when 5 acres were granted to the Earl of Salisbury. Until 1617–18 it was called West Church Lane. From the first it was fashionable. The large houses on the west side which had coach-houses and stables attached were most popular. Tradesmen were to be found on the east side. Among the 17th- and 18th-century residents were Daniel Mytens, the painter; Thomas Tenison, Vicar of ST MARTIN-IN-THE-FIELDS and, afterwards, Archbishop of Canterbury; Thomas Chippendale, the cabinet maker, Sir Kenelm Digby; General Charles Fleetwood; Henry Fuseli; Sir Joshua Reynolds; Sir James Thornhill and

St Martin's le Grand in 1819, before the building of Robert Smirke's General Post Office, from an engraving after Girton.

Louis Francis Roubiliac. (Ellen Terry later lived in Burleigh Mansions.)

In 1764 the child Mozart stayed in CECIL COURT with Mr Couzin, 'hare cutter'. Before TRAFALGAR SQUARE was built the lane went down to the STRAND. Opposite ST MARTIN-IN-THE-FIELDS were the stocks, whipping post and a small prison. One night 25 women were locked in there by some drunken constables and four of them suffocated. In 1720 Louis Chéron and John Vanderbank opened an Artists' Academy in a room reputed to have once been used as a meeting-house. Hogarth became a student during the first year, as did William Kent. In about 1735 the treasurer embezzled the funds and the landlord seized the furniture. Hogarth refounded it and, until it merged with the ROYAL ACADEMY in 1768, it was the main London art school. Gainsborough, Reynolds and Benjamin West worked there. OLD SLAUGHTER'S COFFEE HOUSE stood on the west side. The CHIPPENDALE WORKSHOP stood on the site of Nos 60–61. The SALISBURY PUBLIC HOUSE is at No. 90; Beoty's Restaurant at No. 79. There are three theatres in the street, the ALBERY, the DUKE OF YORK'S and the LONDON COLISEUM. J.B. Cramer and Co. Ltd, the music publisher's at No.99, was founded in 1824 in a warehouse at the junction of REGENT STREET and CONDUIT STREET.

St Martin's le Grand A monastery and college founded by Ingelric and Girard, two brothers, in the mid-11th century. Ingelric was a man of influence in the courts of Edward the Confessor and William I and, as all his fellow-canons were similarly well connected, the college prospered. The foundation was confirmed by charter in 1068. William I then endowed the college with land in CRIPPLEGATE in return for prayers for his parents' souls. The curfew was rung from St Martin's-le-Grand in the reign of Edward I. Anyone ignoring the bells, unless he were 'some great lord or other substantial person of reputation', was thrown into the TUN PRISON in CORNHILL. By the reign of Edward III the curfew was rung from the Church of Our Lady at BOW. Henry II gave the canons the right to hold their own court, answerable to the King and the Chief Justice. In 1360 the Dean, William of Wykeham, later Bishop of Winchester and Chancellor of England, restored the church and cloister and built a new chapter house. The precinct provided the largest and safest sanctuary in England: prisoners on their way from NEWGATE to TOWER HILL for execution passed the south gate and often managed to escape and enter it. Thieves and debtors were accepted, Jews and traitors turned away. Sir Thomas More reports that Miles Forrest, one of those accused of the murder of the princes in the TOWER, 'rotted away piece-meal' in the sanctuary. In 1447 the GOLDSMITHS' COMPANY, with the Dean's permission, confiscated the counterfeit jewellery made here and put the offenders into the college prison. In 1503 the college was given to WESTMINSTER ABBEY to endow the Henry VII chapel; but was finally suppressed in the 1540s, though the rights of sanctuary continued until 1697. In the reign of Elizabeth I the precinct was celebrated for its tailors: the famous St Martin's Lace was produced here. The tradition of making counterfeit jewellery continued throughout the 17th century. Today all that remains is the street that bears its name.

St Martin's School of Art *Charing Cross Road, WC2.* One of the oldest art schools in London. There were art academies in the neighbourhood in the middle of the 18th century, and it is probable that St Martin's developed from one of these. In the 1850s it was sponsored by the church of ST MARTIN IN THE FIELDS. It was first established in Shelton Street, then in Castle Street near LONG ACRE. It became an independent school in 1859 and in 1894 was aided by the LONDON COUNTY COUNCIL. In 1913 it moved to premises which had originally been occupied by St Mary's National Schools in CHARING CROSS ROAD. The adjoining site of St Mary's church and clergy house was acquired in 1935; and the school was rebuilt by E.P. Wheeler in 1937–9. As well as in CHARING CROSS ROAD, the school has premises at Nos 16–17 GREEK STREET (the fashion department) and at Nos 27–29 LONG ACRE (the graphic design department and the film and video unit).

St Martin's Street *WC2.* First built in the 1690s. None of the original houses remain. The City of WESTMINSTER Central Reference Library is on the east side. Opposite is the Pastoria Hotel (54 bedrooms).

St Martin's Theatre *West Street, WC2.* Built in 1916 to the designs of W.G.R. Sprague as a companion to the AMBASSADORS THEATRE. In 1916–20 Charles B. Cochran was lessee and manager and successfully produced *Houp La!* (1916), a revival of *Damaged Goods* (1917), Seymour Hicks's *Sleeping Partners* (1917) and *The Officers' Mess* (1918). In 1920–5 the theatre was under the joint control of Alec Rea and Basil Dean. Among the plays staged were Galsworthy's *The Skin Game* (1920); *A Bill of Divorcement* (1921), a play by Clemence Dane which had 401 performances; Galsworthy's *Loyalties* (1922) which had 407 performances; *The Likes of Her* (1923) and *Spring Cleaning* (1925). In 1925 *Ghost Train* by Arnold Ridley began its long run here. In 1928 Walter Hackett's *77 Park Lane* had 308 performances. The main successes of the 1930s and 1940s were *Petticoat Influence* (1930), *The Wind and the Rain* (1933), *Claudia* (1942), and *The Shop at Sly Corner* (1945). The seating capacity is 560.

St Mary *Barnes (Church Road), SW13.* Since the building was gutted by fire in 1978, a thorough arch-aeological survey has revealed that there was a church on this site a century earlier than the traditional con-secration date of 1216. In its final form, the medieval church consisted of the present south aisle with its chancel and tower. The south wall is built from widely disparate materials reflecting the sequence of its development and the earliest identifiable feature is the remnant of a Norman arch near the present south door. The chancel has three 13th-century lancets with a vesica window above; some wall painting in this area was destroyed in the fire although a further section was revealed on the south wall. The 15th-century roof timbers bore original carpenters' marks. The brick tower is also 15th-century. The church was considerably enlarged in the 19th and early 20th centuries.

St Mary *Battersea (Battersea Church Road), SW11.* Given to the monks of WESTMINSTER ABBEY by William I after the Norman Conquest. Henry Yevele rebuilt the east gable in 1379. The south aisle was added in 1400, the south chapel in 1489 and the north aisle in 1613. The tower was built in 1639, and the whole structure rebuilt as a simple village church in 1775–7. The east window is filled with 17th-century glass depicting Margaret Beauchamp (grandmother of Henry VII), Henry VIII and Elizabeth I in order to display the royal connections of the St Johns, a once important local family. Edward Hyde, later Earl of Clarendon, was married here in 1631; and William Blake married Catherine Boucher, the daughter of a local market gardener here in 1782. She signed the register with an 'X'. Henry St John, Viscount Boling-broke, was buried here in 1751.

St Mary *Bourne Street, NW1.* Brick Gothic church built in 1873–4 to the designs of Robert Jewell Withers and originally a chapel-of-ease to ST BARNABAS, PIM-LICO. Alterations and additions were carried out by H.S. Goodhart-Rendel in 1926–34.

St Mary *Bow, E3.* St Mary's was built as a chapel-of-ease to the parish church in 1311, when BOW was part of STEPNEY. Much of the ancient fabric still stands, though it has been restored many times over the centuries. It escaped demolition on three occasions during the 19th century, first in 1829, when the top of the tower fell off, then in 1882 when Sir Arthur Blomfield suggested rebuilding, and again in 1896 after the collapse of the chancel roof. On this last occasion, the Society for the Protection of Ancient Buildings saved St Mary's. They ignored the requests to rebuild and employed A.W. Hills of BOW to carry out the necessary repairs. After the 2nd World War Sir Albert Richardson rebuilt the top of the tower in brick. The church possesses a few interesting 17th- and 18th-century monuments and there is an early 15th-century font.

St Mary *Bryanston Square, W1.* Built in 1821–4 to the designs of Sir Robert Smirke. Various alterations were carried out by Sir Arthur Blomfield in 1875 and the church was redecorated by Sir Albert Richardson after the 2nd World War.

St Mary *Cable Street, E1.* A stone church built in 1849–50 at the instigation of the Revd William Quekett.

St Mary *Cadogan Street, SW3.* At the time of the Napoleonic Wars, the Abbé Voyaux de Franous, an émigré priest, built a small chapel here to serve the French prisoners-of-war lodged in CHELSEA. This was replaced in 1877 by a church designed in the Early English manner by John Francis Bentley. It was his first church and is of little merit. Lack of money prevented him carrying out the more ornate design which he had, at first, submitted. In order to comply with the directives of the Second Vatican Council, the sanctuary was altered in the 1970s to enable the priest to celebrate the Mass facing the people and other al-terations and restoration were carried out at a cost of £20,000. The rector at that time was Canon John Longstaff, a descendant of St Thomas More. Of his seven predecessors, five became bishops and one a cardinal.

St Mary *Chislehurst, Kent.* Built by the Bowden family in 1854, this Roman Catholic church was atten-ded by the French Imperial family. Napoleon III was buried here in 1873 – and six years later, his son, the Prince Imperial, killed in Zululand. Empress Eugénie had a side chapel added, but found it impracticable to enlarge the church as she wished, and her husband and son were later reburied at Farnborough, Hants.

St Mary *Finchley (Hendon Lane), N3.* Was so cal-led in 1356, but there is reference to a church in 1274 and evidence of a building before then. Fragments of 12th-century stonework are built into the north aisle's west wall. An aumbry, now in the north wall, and a font bowl, rescued in Victorian times from the rectory grounds, are both Norman. Alterations and additions from the 14th century until the repair of bomb damage in 1953 have left a 14th- to 15th-century tower and one north and two south aisles. A fine collection of brasses, now wall-mounted, date from about 1480 onwards; one, of Thomas Sanny, 1509, most unusually re-produces part of his will. Four hatchments are displayed and notable monuments include those to the Allen family of the MANOR HOUSE and a splendid one to an earlier Lord of the Manor, Alexander Kinge, Auditor to Queen Elizabeth I.

St Mary *Hammersmith Road, W14.* Built in 1814 and enlarged in 1881. It was destroyed by an air raid in 1944, and a new church by Lord Mottistone was opened in 1961.

St Mary *Hampton, Middlesex.* The earliest known Vicar of HAMPTON was presented in 1342, but the church had been founded some time before then by the Priory of Takeley in Essex, itself a cell of the Norman Abbey of St Valéry. Charles II contributed to the rebuilding of the tower of the old church in 1679 and George I to the addition of a north aisle, schoolroom and vestry room in 1726. By 1821 the church was too small for the growing population. After six years of hesitation the decision about its future was hastened by an 'Act of God' when the tower was struck by lightning in 1827 and the church was damaged. So the old church was pulled down in 1829 and the new church, designed by Edward Lapidge, was consecrated in the presence of Queen Adelaide on 1 September 1831. The sanctuary was added in celebration of Queen Victoria's Golden Jubilee in 1887.

St Mary *Hampstead (Holly Place), NW3*. A charming small church opened on 17 August 1816 to provide a place of worship for French refugees who had come over with the Abbé Morel in 1796. It was sited unobtrusively amongst a row of cottages (the Catholic Emancipation Act was not passed until 1829). The statue of the Virgin, carved from Caen stone, and the attractive open bellcote above the doorway were added in 1850.

St Mary *Harmondsworth, Middlesex*. A church of many periods. There is Norman work in the south doorway and south arcade pillars, while the north aisle and its arcade were constructed in the 13th-century, the north chapel being added a century later. There was a major reconstruction of the church during the early 15th century. The north chancel arcade was built and extended into the nave, ending abruptly in a split arch, the north chapel roof was raised and the tower rebuilt, partly in Tudor brick. The font is of the late 12th century and the *piscina* and *sedilia* are 15th-century work. Some pews survive from the early 16th century. On the external south wall may be seen an early mass dial. In the churchyard are the graves of Richard Cox, a former brewer, who in 1830 cultivated the orange pippin in his garden at The Lawn, Colnbrook, and Peggy Bedford, landlady of an inn on the Bath Road for over 50 years. She is remembered in the name of a modern hotel at the beginning of the Colnbrook by-pass.

St Mary *Harrow-on-the-Hill (Church Hill), Middlesex*. Founded in 1087 by Archbishop Lanfranc and consecrated in 1094 by his successor, Anselm. Becket was several times at HARROW, the last occasion being 12 days before his murder at Canterbury in 1170. The church spire dates from 1450. Charles II called it 'the visible church'. Widespread Victorian restoration by Gilbert Scott was carried out in 1847. The most interesting brass (1592) is that of John Lyon (*see* HARROW SCHOOL) and his wife Joan, both of whom were buried in the church. The earliest of the 13 brasses in the church commemorates the lord of the manor, Sir Edmund Flambard, and dates from 1370. Little is known of Sir Edmund (or when the family first settled in Harrow) except that he was descended from Ranulf Flambard, the chief minister of William Rufus. The nine clerestory windows trace the history of HARROW from the Council of Clovesho (825) (*see* HARROW-ON-THE-HILL) to the school tercentenary (1871). Church treasures include the 13th-century marble font, oak chest and north door, and the 17th-century carved pulpit. The church terrace, beloved of Byron who was at HARROW SCHOOL, is remembered in his poem 'Lines written beneath an elm in the churchyard of Harrow'.

St Mary *Hayes, Middlesex*. There is a *Domesday* reference to a priest at HAYES, but the existing parish

church of St Mary the Virgin has no trace of building earlier than the late 13th century, although the font is probably of about 1200. Flint and stone rubble construction is used, with ashlar dressings: there are nave, chancel, north and south aisles and a battlemented west tower. A vestry was added in the late 19th century. The south porch is 16th-century, as also is the lychgate. The nave and chancel are both originally 13th-century, although the chancel has a 15th-century east window. In plan, chancel and nave show the misalignment traditionally claimed to represent Christ on the cross. There are a 13th-century *sedilia* and *piscina* in the chancel and the splendid altar tomb of Sir Edward Fenner, a judge. There is also a half-effigy brass to Robert Lellee, rector in about 1370, surrounded by some medieval floor tiles.

St Mary *Hendon (Church End), NW4*. A 13th- to 15th-century building enlarged by Temple Moore in 1914–15.

St Mary *Islington (Upper Street), N1*. Founded in the 12th-century and rebuilt in the 15th. Charles Wesley was appointed unlicensed lecturer in 1738. In 1751–4 the church was rebuilt by Launcelot Dowbiggin. The chancel was added in 1902. After an air raid in the 2nd World War only the tower and steeple remained. Rebuilding was completed in 1956 under the supervision of Seely and Paget. The murals are by Brian Thomas. Buried here are Sir James Steward, godson of James I, and Sir George Wharton, both killed in a duel in 1609. James ordered them to be buried in the same grave at his expense. Launcelot Dowbiggin was buried here in 1759.

St Mary *Lewisham, SE13*. Built in the 1770s to the designs of George Gibson who added the crown to the 15th-century tower. The interior was heavily restored in the 19th-century.

St Mary *Merton, SW19*. There was a church here in 1086 and the present nave dates from 1115 and the chancel from early in the 13th century. Each appears to have its original roof beams. This church, dedicated to St Mary, remained unchanged until a south aisle was added in 1856 and a north aisle ten years later. The north doorway contains Norman decorative stonework surrounded by an excellent decorated 15th-century timber porch. Just inside the west door are the hatchments of Lord Nelson and Sir William Hamilton, each of whom was a parishioner (*see* MERTON). Outside the door is a free-standing Norman arch, dating from about 1175, which was discovered at the site of Merton Priory and rebuilt here in 1935.

St Mary *Mortlake (High Street), SW14*. A church was licensed first by Edward III in 1349 and originally stood within the curtilage of the manor house on the other side of the High Street until moved to the present site by Henry VIII in 1543. The font, presented by Cardinal Bourchier (Archbishop of Canterbury in 1454–86) remains from the earlier church and the tower, the only surviving part from the Tudor church, may also contain reused material from its predecessor. The bell chamber and cupola, as well as five out of the eight bells, date from 1694–5 but otherwise the building was mostly rebuilt in 1885 (chancel) and 1905 (nave). Some interesting wall monuments include those to Francis Coventry by William Kidwell, and Lady Sidmouth by Westmacott. Lord Sidmouth is buried in the churchyard. The vestry house of about 1670 was recently altered and extended. The church boasts an unusually complete series of registers, vestry minutes, churchwarden's accounts and other documents (now deposited at Surrey Record Office).

St Mary *Primrose Hill, NW3.* Built of redbrick in 1871–2 and enlarged in 1890.

St Mary *Putney (High Street), SW15.* Like so many medieval churches of riverside parishes, St Mary's is sited close to the bridge. It has only one point of architectural interest and that is the diminutive Chantry Chapel built in the early part of the 16th century by Bishop West of Ely. With its delicate fan-vaulting it is a miniature version of the one he gave to his great cathedral. Bishop West had been born in PUTNEY. With the exception of the heavily restored 15th-century tower, the rest of the building is 19th-century, erected in 1836 by Edward Lapidge. The old church had been renowned for the Council of War held there in 1647. It is said that the Cromwellian generals sat round the Communion Table defiantly wearing their hats. Daniel Lysons, the author of *Environs of London,* was the incumbent here from 1791–9. A fire in 1977 badly damaged the structure.

St Mary *Rotherhithe (Marychurch Street), SE16.* Stands beyond the crumbling warehouses that line the banks of the THAMES. Together with the old Charity School and the rectory it forms part of a pleasing group of 18th-century buildings. In 1710, the old church, whose history stretched far back into the Middle Ages, was found to be irreparably damaged from continual flooding. The Commissioners of the Fifty New Churches Act were petitioned for the money to build a new church. Despite the poignant wording of the petition, a copy of which can be seen at the foot of the stairs to the west gallery, their request was turned down. The parishioners – who described themselves as 'being chiefly seamen and watermen who venture their lives in fetching those coals from Newcastle which pay for the Rebuilding of the Churches in London' – were instructed to find the necessary money themselves. It was not easy and they were constantly in financial difficulties. The church was finished in 1715. The architect is not known, but it is well designed. The white stone quoins, the red dressing of the bricks, and the straightforward delineation of the windows and doors give the exterior a good sense of balance. Launcelot Dowbiggin was responsible for the stone spire which was erected in 1739.

William Butterfield carried out some restoration work in 1876: the north and south galleries were removed, new seating arrangements made and the pulpit was lowered. Nevertheless, the interior still retains its original character. The piers are ships' masts, thinly encased in plaster, and are of an order all their own; the altar in the Lady Chapel and the two bishop's chairs in the north aisle are constructed of timber from the *Fighting Temeraire*. The *Mayflower* sailed from ROTHERHITHE with a crew largely composed of Rotherhithe men. A wall plaque reminds us that the Master, Captain Christopher Jones, together with three of the part-owners of the ship were buried in the churchyard in 1622. Another wall plaque tells the extraordinary tale of Prince Lee Boo, the son of a kind cannibal chief, who rescued the shipwrecked sailors of the East India sloop *Antelope* off the Pelau Islands in 1783. In a mistaken act of gratitude, Captain Wilson brought the 20-year-old Prince back on a trip to ROTHERHITHE, where he died in the middle of December 1784 while a guest of the Wilson family in nearby Paradise Row. He too is buried in the churchyard.

St Mary *Walthamstow (Church Path), E17.* Founded by Ralph de Toni, Lord of Walthamstow Toni manor, the church was sited on an early cross-roads and also served the Manor of Higham in the north. It was dedicated in the mid-12th century. In the 16th century Sir George Monoux, benefactor of WALTHAMSTOW parish, and John Thorne financed rebuilding and extension. The tower was rebuilt and chapels, north aisle and porch were added. A storm that destroyed the vicarage in 1703 was probably the cause of restoration, some of it by Sir John Soane in 1784. During the 19th century the Thorne and Monoux chapels were lost in alteration and enlargement, and in the 20th century extensive restoration, following bomb damage, revealed Norman remains. There is a 17th-century monument to Gerard Conyers, and another to Sir Thomas Merry and his wife by Nicholas Stone, the verses on which are attributed to Sir William Davenant.

St Mary *Willesden (Neasden Lane), NW10.* In 937 King Athelstan defeated the Danes at the battle of Brunanburh, and as a thank offering gave the Royal Manors of Willesden-cum-Neasden to the Dean and Chapter of ST PAUL'S CATHEDRAL. A church was built, probably replacing a wooden Saxon church. As it stands today, the fabric dates from the mid-13th century, the oldest part being the south arcade. The tower, nave, chancel and chapel date from the end of the 13th century and the north aisle and vestries, added to accommodate the growing number of people living in WILLESDEN from the 19th. The windows were altered at the same time, replacing domestic sash windows inserted, some say, by Sir Christopher Wren. Within are a magnificent 14th-century door, the oldest Norman font in the county, a Reformation altar table and an Elizabethan dining-table converted into an altar. There are two hatchments to the Nicol and Courtenay families. There are a number of brasses including those of Bartholomew Wilsdon and his wife Margaret of Oxgate Manor. In the sanctuary are fine wall monuments to Richard and Margaret Paine and to Sir John Franklyn, carved by Cornelius Cure in 1606 and John Colt in 1647 respectively. Cure carved the monument to Queen Mary I and Colt that to Queen Elizabeth I in WESTMINSTER ABBEY. There are other monuments to the Barne family and to the Roberts family of Neasden House. The registers date from 1569. The Victorian novelist, Charles Reade, is buried in the churchyard.

St Mary Abbots *Church Street, Kensington, W8.* Founded in the 12th century by the Abbot of Abingdon on land given to him by Godfrey, son of Aubrey de Vere, Earl of Oxford. It was rebuilt in 1370 and, except for the 14th-century tower, again in 1696. William and Mary worshipped here as KENSINGTON PALACE then had no chapel. William contributed towards the new building and gave a pulpit and reading desk. The tower was rebuilt in 1772. The church was again rebuilt by Sir George Gilbert Scott in 1869–72. The spire is a copy of St Mary Redcliffe's, Bristol. Arthur Onslow, Speaker of the House of Commons, was christened here in 1691. Sir John Fielding, the magistrate, was married here in 1774. There is a grand monument to Edward, Earl of Warwick and Holland, Addison's stepson (*see* HOLLAND HOUSE).

St Mary Abbots Hospital *Marloes Road, Kensington, W8.* Began as the Kensington workhouse, designed by T. Allom in 1849. The building was in the Jacobean style and was known as Stone Hall. Additions were made over the years and in 1923 it was given its present name. It has been modernised since and in 1982 had 301 beds.

St Mary Abchurch *Abchurch Yard, EC4.* This is not only one of the prettiest of Wren's CITY churches, it is also the one that has altered least since it was built in 1686. It stands in a small cobbled yard, between CANNON STREET and KING WILLIAM STREET on the site of a 12th-century church that had belonged to the Prior of St Mary Overie (now SOUTHWARK CATHEDRAL). In early documents this medieval church is referred to as St Mary Upchurch, possibly because to those at the Priory it was the church 'up river'. In the reign of Elizabeth I, Archbishop Parker persuaded the Queen to give the patronage to Corpus Christi College, Cambridge, where he had been Master, and with whom it has remained to this day. After the destruction of the church in the GREAT FIRE, the parishioners had to wait 15 years before Sir Christopher Wren could find the time to design their new church. Work finally began in 1681. It took five years to build and cost £4,922 2s 4d. Constructed of dark redbrick with stone quoins, it exhibits, like ST BENET'S, PAUL'S WHARF, a Dutch influence. The tower to the north-west has a pierced lantern above which rises a slender lead-covered spire. The simple grace of the outside, with its hip roof, gives no hint of the rich splendour to be found within. Wren gathered together his most talented friends to decorate the interior of this church. A lovely, shallow dome painted by William Snow, rests, without the aid of buttresses, on eight arches and one column. Beneath it is to be found some of the finest 17th-century woodwork in the CITY, all retaining the original dark, oxblood stain. The doorcases and the Royal Coat of Arms of James II are the work of William Emmett. The font cover and rails are also by him. The font itself is by William Kempster, the brother of the master-mason of the building – Christopher Kempster. The pulpit by William Gray still has its original steps, and the carved pews are also unchanged with the exception of those on the south side which have had the dog kennels that used to be underneath them removed. The chief glory of the church, however, is the reredos. It is the only one in the CITY that is known with certainty to be by Grinling Gibbons. (Signed receipts were found in a chest in 1946). In 1940 it was found after a bombing raid to be broken into 2,000 pieces. It took five years to restore. Godfrey Allen carried out repairs to the fabric of the church after the 2nd World War and Professor Tristram and Walter Hoyle restored the painted dome with great skill. Today St Mary's is a guild church.

St Mary Aldermary *Queen Victoria Street, EC4.* Aldermary is Old English for older Mary and is taken to mean that this church is older than ST MARY-LE-BOW which was founded in the 11th century. It was rebuilt, except for the tower, in 1510–18. The tower was mostly rebuilt in 1626–9. Burned down in the GREAT FIRE, it was rebuilt by Wren at the expense of Henry Rogers in 1681–2. The fan vaulted ceiling was probably copied from the earlier church. The tower was completed in 1702–4. The church was restored in 1867–8 by Richard Tress and Charles Innes who threw out a great deal of the 17th-century woodwork, leaving only the pulpit, the font and a wooden sword rest. After damage in the 2nd World War, the church was restored by Arthur Nisbet. The new stained glass windows are by Lawrence Lee and John Crawford. St Mary's was made a guild church in 1954.

Since ST ANTHOLIN WATLING STREET was demolished in 1874 the St Antholin Lectures, instituted in 1559, have been read here. Milton and his third wife, Elizabeth Minshull, were married here in 1663.

St Mary-at-Hill *Lovat Lane, EC3.* Founded in the 12th century and rebuilt in the 15th. Damaged in the GREAT FIRE, it was rebuilt by Wren, who incorporated the old tower and parts of the walls, as a square, Dutch-like church. The tower and west end were rebuilt by George Gwilt in 1787–8. In 1827–8 the nave was partly rebuilt by James Savage who restored the church again in 1848–9 after a fire. Much of the woodwork was replaced by William Gibbs Rogers. His reproductions are so good that it is difficult to tell 17th- from 19th-century work. In 1892–1926 Wilson Carlile, founder of the Church Army, was rector. The interior is one of the best in the CITY with vaulted ceiling, magnificent organ case and pulpit, box pews and gilded sword rests. Every October BILLINGSGATE fish merchants hold their harvest festival here.

St Mary-at-Lambeth *Lambeth Palace Road, SE1.* At the time of the *Domesday Book* St Mary's was owned by Countess Goda, sister of Edward the Confessor. It was afterwards given to the Bishops of Rochester and in 1197 the living passed to the Archbishops of Canterbury. In 1374–8 the church was rebuilt in stone and, except for the tower, again rebuilt in the late 15th and early 16th centuries. In 1688 Mary of Modena sheltered here from a storm with her baby son on her flight to France. The church was yet again rebuilt in 1851–2 by Philip Hardwick whose designs were intended to match the 14th-century tower. A font for total immersion (the only one of its kind in London) was installed in about 1900 in memory of Archbishop Benson. Badly damaged in the 2nd World War, the church was restored by Godfrey Allen.

Adam and Eve in one panel and John Tradescant, father and son, in the other, are depicted in a new window (1981) designed and made by Lawrence Lee and commissioned for the Tradescant Trust by the Glaziers' and Painters of Glass Company. In the south chapel is the 'Pedlar's Window' designed by Francis Stephens. It commemorates a pedlar who left the parish an acre of land on the condition that he and his dog would always be remembered by a window in the church. Lambeth Borough Council sold the acre to the LONDON COUNTY COUNCIL in 1910 for £81,000. Buried here are Cuthbert Tunstall, Bishop of Durham, 1559; Archbishop Bancroft, 1610;

John Tradescant, Charles I's gardener, 1637 (also Tradescant's son); Elias Ashmole, the antiquary, 1692; Archbishop Tenison, 1715; Archbishop Hutton, 1758; Archbishop Secker, 1768; Archbishop Cornwallis, 1783; Archbishop Moore, 1805, and Captain Bligh of the *Bounty*, 1817. The Tradescant Trust is restoring the church 'as the first museum of garden history'. It will contain 'examples of plants and flowers introduced into this country from their world travels' by the Tradescants. This family is said to have introduced the pineapple as an ornamental motif to this country. There are examples of it on nearby LAMBETH BRIDGE.

St Mary Axe Built sometime before 1197, the church was suppressed in 1565 and converted into a warehouse. There was a legend attached to its strange dedication. A certain King of England gave his daughter and 11,000 of her handmaidens permission to travel abroad, and while journeying on the Lower Rhine, they met Attila the Hun who slaughtered them all with three axes, one of which was kept in the church. Stow mentions the full title of the church as St Mary the Virgin and St Ursula and the Eleven Thousand Virgins.

St Mary Axe *EC3*. Takes its name from the church of ST MARY AXE which once possessed an axe said to be one of the three with which the Eleven Thousand Virgins were beheaded. It was a largely residential street in the 18th and early 19th centuries: Henry Cline, the surgeon, was living and practising here when Astley Cooper, later to become surgeon to George IV, joined him as a resident pupil in 1784. The banker, Joseph Denison, father of the Marchioness of Conyngham, George IV's mistress, also lived in the street. Dickens placed 'Fascination' Fledgeby's money-lending business, Pubsey and Co., in *Our Mutual Friend* in St Mary Axe as well as the Golden Axe, on the corner of BEVIS MARKS, which Dick Swiveller recommends in *The Old Curiosity Shop*. The BALTIC EXCHANGE is at Nos 14–20. The street is now mainly occupied by shipbrokers, marine insurance companies and export merchants. The SHIPWRIGHTS' COMPANY is at Nos 24–28.

St Mary Bothaw *Cannon Street*. The old name of this church was St Mary Boatehaw by the Erber. *Haw* was another word for yard, so presumably it stood close to a boatyard. What remained of the church after the GREAT FIRE was used to help to build the new church of ST SWITHIN LONDON STONE.

St Mary Colechurch *Poultry*. Cole was the name of the man who built this medieval church. According to Stow it was 'upon a wall, above ground, so that men are forced to go to ascend up thereunto by certain steps'. Thomas Becket was baptised here. Henry IV granted the church a licence to found and maintain the Brotherhood of St Katherine. The church was not rebuilt after its destruction in the GREAT FIRE.

St Mary Coneyhope A chapel attached to the parish church of ST MILDRED POULTRY first mentioned in the 13th century. In the 14th century a fraternity of Corpus Christi was founded here to say mass for the souls of the dead. It was afterwards known as Corpus Christi Chapel. At the DISSOLUTION OF THE MONASTERIES the fraternity was suppressed and the chapel

sold to a haberdasher for a warehouse. The MIDLAND BANK, POULTRY now stands on the site.

St Mary Cray *Kent*. Was once a 'handsome populous village' whose Market House blew down in the great gale of 1703. Originally a chapelry of ORPINGTON, the 13th-century church (St Mary) with its shingled spire huddles under the railway arch amongst the scant remains of the waterside village which is interspersed with light industry. Northwards, beyond a housing estate, there is still some open country.

St Mary Graces A small Cistercian abbey, also known as East Minster and New Abbey, founded by Edward III to the east of Smithfield in 1349.

St Mary Haggerston *Shoreditch*. Built in 1826–7 to the designs of John Nash, and financed by the Waterloo Commissioners. The extremely tall tower and an unbroken gallery continued even over the altar were unusual features. In the 1860s James Brooks redesigned the interior. The building was destroyed in 1941.

Wren's magnificent steeple of St Mary-le-Bow, Cheapside, which houses the famous Bow Bells. From an engraving of c. 1680.

St Mary le Strand, built by James Gibbs, with Old Somerset House on the right. From an engraving by Bowles, 1753.

St Mary-le-Bow *Cheapside, EC2.* Famous for its bells (*see* BOW BELLS). The church is first mentioned in 1091 when its roof was blown off in a storm. In 1196 William Fitz Osbert escaped up the church tower, having protested against unevenly imposed taxes at PAUL'S CROSS and killed one of the Archbishop of Canterbury's guards. He was smoked out, tried and hanged in chains at SMITHFIELD. In 1271 the tower collapsed, killing 20 people. In 1284, Duckett, a goldsmith, was murdered here after seeking sanctuary: 16 men were hanged and one woman was burned. The church was closed until it could be reconsecrated. In 1331 a wooden balcony collapsed during a joust to celebrate the birth of the Black Prince. Queen Philippa and her ladies were hurled to the ground. The present balcony on the tower is a memento. During the 14th century the curfew was rung on Bow Bells, probably the origin of the idea that every true COCKNEY is born within hearing distance of them. The tower was rebuilt in 1521. The church burned down in the GREAT FIRE and was rebuilt in 1670–3 by Wren who modelled it on the Basilica of Maxentius at Rome. The dragon weathercock was put up on the steeple in 1674. The stuntman, Jacob Hall, climbed up on to its back. The spire, one of Wren's finest, is 217 ft high. Hatton in his *New View of London* (1708) said it was 'accounted by judicious artists an admirable piece of architecture, not to be paralleled by the steeple of any parochial church in Europe.' In 1818–20 the upper part of the spire was rebuilt by George Gwilt, and in 1878–9 the interior restored by Sir Arthur Blomfield.

After being bombed in the 2nd World War, the church was rebuilt in 1956–62 by Laurence King. The tower was reconstructed around a steel tube. The stained glass is by John Hayward. Under the church is a Norman crypt whose arches probably gave the church its name. St Mary-le-Bow used to be one of the 13 peculiars in the CITY owned by the Archbishop of Canterbury and exempt from the jurisdiction of the BISHOP OF LONDON. The Archbishop's COURT OF ARCHES (which took its name from the crypt) sat here until the peculiars were abolished in 1847.

St Mary le Strand *WC2.* In 1147 the site was occupied by the church of the Nativity of Our Lady and the Innocents. This was demolished in 1549 to make way for SOMERSET HOUSE. Protector Somerset promised to rebuild it but never did so and for nearly 200 years the parishioners had to use the SAVOY CHAPEL. A maypole used to stand on the green outside (*see* MAYPOLE IN THE STRAND). In 1714–17 the present small Baroque church, designed by James Gibbs, was built as the first of the 50 new churches which were built in London in accordance with the Act of 1711. It was Gibbs's first public building and 'got him great reputation'. He had recently returned from Rome where he had spent several years as Carlo Fontana's pupil. The walls of St Mary's show the influence of Michelangelo and the steeple that of Wren. The ceiling was inspired by Fontana's SS Apostoli and Pietro da Cortona's SS Lucia e Martina, the porch by Cortona's S Maria della Pace. A 250 ft column topped by a statue of Queen Anne was planned to stand in front of the church but the Queen died and a spire was built instead. The fate of the brass statue of the Queen which had been made in Florence by John Talman is unknown. In 1750 Bonnie Prince Charlie is said to have been received into the Church of England here during a five day secret visit. Charles Dickens's parents were married here in 1809. In 1871 the interior was refitted by R.J. Withers. Although large sums have been spent on the church since an appeal was launched in 1977, the structure was reported, in 1981, to be crumbling from the combined effects of time, weather, heavy traffic and the blast of a war-time bomb.

St Mary Magdalen *Bermondsey Street, SE1.* Like ST MARGARET, WESTMINSTER, St Mary Magdalen was built beside a monastery to cater for the spiritual needs of its servants and tenants but, of the important Cluniac BERMONDSEY ABBEY where two Queens of England died, all that remains is a pair of hinges from the south gate, a stone bearing a consecration mark in a local garage and some capitals in the church. After the DISSOLUTION the church became parochial but by the latter part of the 17th century it was considered unsafe and pulled down. There had been an earlier place of worship but no trace of this survives. The present building dates from 1675–7 but has been much altered since; galleries were added in 1793 and, in 1830, the top stage of the tower was removed and the present gabled structure capped with a diminutive lantern substituted; at the same time the west front was remodelled in Gothic style with stucco and projecting aisles terminating at the west end in castellated lean-to roofs. The interior is a confused composition but basically late 17th-century with entablature supported on Tuscan columns and galleries borne on separate spindly columns which do not harmonise with one another. A churchwardens' pew has all-round seating and a four-sided reading desk enabling the pew to be used as an office. There are two fine Dutch-type candelabra dating from 1698 and 1703 and an altar at the end of the south aisle which was rescued from bombed St John's, Horsleydown, made by the celebrated smith, Jean Tijou; it has unfortunately lost its marble top. It is recorded that a Puritan rector at St Mary Magdalen preached a sermon of 60 pages ending 'one hundred and twenty-seventhly'. In the register, under the date 4 January 1624–5, James Herriott is recorded 'as one of the forty children of his father, a Scotchman'. The Costermongers' Harvest Festival often attended by the PEARLY KINGS AND QUEENS is held in September.

St Mary Magdalen *Knightrider Street.* This church, designed by Sir Christopher Wren replaced a 12th-century structure gutted in the GREAT FIRE. The design for the top of the tower derived from Pliny's description of the Mausoleum at Halicarnassus. It was the only time Wren used an unpierced stone lantern. R.H. Barham, the author of The *Ingoldsby Legends,* was rector here in 1824–42. A fire damaged the church in 1886 and it was consequently demolished.

St Mary Magdalen *Milk Street.* Some of the material of this medieval church, destroyed in the GREAT FIRE, was used to rebuild ST MARY ALDERMARY.

St Mary Magdalen *Richmond, Surrey.* The tower of this church was built by a freemason, Henry Walton, in 1624. The rest of the church was largely rebuilt in 1750 with further additions in 1904 by G.F. Bodley. There are a number of 18th-century memorial tablets.

St Mary Magdalen *Enfield (Windmill Hill), Middlesex.* A fine late Victorian church built in 1883 to the designs of William Butterfield on a prominent hill-top site. The tall spire is a major local landmark and can be seen from as far away as parts of SOUTHGATE and EDMONTON. The chancel contains some of Butterfield's favourite coloured marblework, now discreetly hidden behind curtains.

St Mary Magdalene *East Ham (High Street South), E6.* A charming and probably unique example, in a London postal district, of a Norman parish church built about 1130 and still in use as a church.

Except for the addition of the west tower in the 16th century, porches and some alterations in the windows to admit more light, St Mary Magdalene has remained practically unaltered structurally since it was built. The greatest treasure is the Norman timber roof over the apse; it is held together by wooden pegs. There are also the monuments, especially one in the north-east of the sanctuary erected by Edmund Nevill, Lord Latimer, in 1613, in memory of his daughter; the interesting arches with zig-zag decoration on the north wall of the chancel; the double *piscina* in the south-east of the sanctuary dating from the 13th century; the font of 1639 (pedestal added later); and the church-wardens' prickers of 1805 used to awaken those lulled to sleep by the sermon. There is a fine Norman doorway at the west end and a notable semi-circular arch at the entrance to the apse. The 9-acre churchyard is being developed by the PASSMORE EDWARDS MUSEUM as a nature reserve. It is said to be the largest churchyard in England.

St Mary Magdalene *Munster Square, NW1.* In the middle of the 19th century this area of London was considered to be one of ill repute. Father Edward Stuart, a wealthy, young cleric serving on the staff of CHRIST CHURCH, ALBANY STREET, thought the district would improve if it had a church 'as nearly perfection as the handicraft of man, the skill of architects and the experience and ingenuity of ecclesiastical art could make it.' It should be accessible to all and have no rented seats. To implement this proposal, he chose Richard Carpenter as architect, and in July 1849, the work began. Three years later the church was ready for consecration and Father Stuart was installed as the first vicar. The *Ecclesiologist* deemed it 'the most artistically correct new church yet consecrated in London'. Even today it is of interest as an unspoilt example of the Gothic Revival – a style which at the time it was built was still in its infancy. The decorations were modest and the proportions good. There is no tower or spire. The interior is designed for the celebration of the High Church Catholic liturgy. The east window was designed by Augustus Welby Pugin.

St Mary Magdalene *Paddington, W2.* Built in 1868–78 to the designs of G.E. Street at the instigation of R.T. West, curate of ALL SAINTS, MARGARET STREET, who wanted to provide similar High Church services for the people of PADDINGTON. Street was a member of the congregation at ALL SAINTS.

St Mary Magdalene *Rowington Close, W2.* High-Victorian church designed by G.E. Street. Building started in 1867 but was not completed until 1878 due to a fire in 1872 which destroyed the roof and a decision to raise the tower and spire in 1873. Stone carving was executed by Thomas Earp and stained glass by Henry Holiday.

St Mary Magdalene *Woolwich (St Mary's Street), SE18.* In 1718, the 12th-century parish church, which St Mary Magdalene's replaced, was in danger of collapsing into the THAMES. As the parishioners were unable to raise sufficient money to save it a petition was presented to Parliament for the parish to be included in the Fifty New Churches scheme. The petition was granted, and in 1727, Matthew Spray, a DEPTFORD bricklayer, 'under the supervision of two gentlemen', began work on the foundations of the new church. However, work had to be halted in 1731 for want of money, and a second petition was necessary in order to procure the required sum. The church was completed in 1739 at a cost of £6,328. It is not known who the architect was.

The few monuments in and around St Mary Magdalene's, while of little interest in themselves, are evidence of the long associations of the parish with the army and navy. At one time the top of the tower used to boast a semaphore.

St Mary Magdalene with St James *Holloway, N7*. St Mary's was built in 1812–14; St James's in Chillingworth Road in 1837–8. The latter was bombed in 1944 and converted into a church hall for St Mary's.

St Mary Moorfields *Finsbury Circus (Eldon Street), EC2*. This is such an unobtrusive church that the architect, George Sherrin, might have designed it, not for the 20th century, but for those MOORFIELDS parishioners of another age, who had their LIME STREET church suppressed in 1688, and who then used to meet surreptitiously for Mass in a house in Ropemakers' Alley, MOORFIELDS. This chapel was destroyed in the GORDON RIOTS in 1780, and with the money they received in compensation, the Roman Catholics of MOORFIELDS built, in 1820, an imposing, Italianate church on a site occupied today by the MOORGATE underground station. This building, designed by John Newman, served as a pro-Cathedral until WESTMINSTER CATHEDRAL was built. By 1900, however, FINSBURY CIRCUS was no longer a residential area and the dwindling congregations called for a smaller church. Although Eldon Street is not part of MOORFIELDS, the present church, built in 1902, retained the name of its illustrious predecessor. The carved Madonna above the doorway and the related panels on either side are all that distinguish it from the neighbouring offices. Inside, the Corinthian columns from Newman's church cluster round the altar. But it is the apse, of Carnico marble from Verona, that catches the eye. The presbytery occupies the upper floors of the building.

St Mary Mounthaw *Fish Street Hill*. A tiny church built sometime before 1275 as a private chapel of the Montenhaut family. It was not rebuilt after its destruction in the GREAT FIRE. The parish was united with that of ST MARY SOMERSET.

St Mary of the Angels *Moorhouse Road, W2*. Built in 1857 to the designs of Thomas Meyer for the community of the Oblates of St Charles Borromeo (*see* ST FRANCIS OF ASSISI). For eight years this was the centre of the ministry of the future cardinal, Dr. H. E. Manning. Various additions to the church were made by J. F. Bentley in 1869–87.

St Mary of Eton *Hackney Wick, E9*. Built in the early 1890s, to the designs of G.F. Bodley, with funds provided by Eton College who then ran a mission in the area. The gate-tower (1911–12) is by Cecil Hare.

St Mary on Paddington Green *W2*. Built in 1788–91 to the designs of John Plaw on the site of two earlier demolished churches. It was much altered in

the 19th century but was expertly restored to its original character by Raymond Erith in the early 1970s. John Donne preached his first sermon in the original church; and William Hogarth was married in the second. William Collins, the painter and father of Wilkie Collins, and Sarah Siddons, the actress, were buried here.

St Mary Rouncivall *Charing Cross*. In 1199 Augustinian monks from the priory of St Mary Roncevalles in Navarre came to England to beg for alms. William Marshal, Earl of Pembroke, became their patron and gave them land by the river in the village of Charing so that they could build a hospital. Henry III confirmed the grant. In Chaucer's *Canterbury Tales* the Pardoner is 'of Rouncivale'. In 1414 the hospital came under the crown's jurisdiction when Henry V suppressed alien houses; but in 1432 the Master, one of the King's chaplains, was allowed official communication with the mother church and allowed to send ten marks a year. In 1475 Edward IV founded the fraternity of St Mary Rouncivall and in 1478 he granted the hospital and its properties to the fraternity for the maintenance of the chaplain, other clergy serving the chapel and the poor people flocking to the hospital which appears to have cared for sick wayfarers and pilgrims going to the shrine of Edward the Confessor at WESTMINSTER ABBEY. In 1544 the hospital was dissolved and the brethren pensioned off; and in 1550 the site was granted to Sir Thomas Cawarden, formerly Henry VIII's Master of the Revels. In 1608–13 Northampton House, later known as NORTHUMBERLAND HOUSE, was built nearby. The chapel was demolished in 1608 and the bones of those buried there were reinterred in ST-MARTIN-IN-THE-FIELDS's churchyard. The monastic quarters remained a private residence until they, too, were demolished in 1705. The site was thereafter gradually encroached upon for extensions to NORTHUMBERLAND HOUSE.

St Mary Somerset *Upper Thames Street*. The earliest references are in the 12th century. Somerset is probably derived from Somershithe, a nearby wharf. Having been repaired in 1624, the church was destroyed in the GREAT FIRE. It was rebuilt by Wren in 1686–95, but in 1872 an Act of Parliament was passed to demolish it. The tower was, however, preserved, owing to the efforts of the architect, Ewan Christian. The parish was united with that of ST NICHOLAS, COLE ABBEY.

St Mary Spital Founded in 1197 by Walter Brown and Rose, his wife, on the east side of BISHOPSGATE. In early records it appears as the New Hospital Without Bishopsgate, as also does the nearby BETHLEHEM HOSPITAL.

It was run by Austin canons with the help of lay brothers and sisters. In 1303 a visitation by the Archbishop of Canterbury revealed that lamps were no longer lit between the beds and the sisters had not received their allowance of food, money or clothes. The canons were reprimanded for disobedience and for 'frequenting the houses of Alice la Faleyse and Matilda, wife of Thomas'. In 1400 the hospital was so deeply in debt it had to borrow 300 marks from the parish of ST JAMES GARLICKHYTHE in exchange for an annual quitrent of 12 marks. In 1534 the Prior and 11 canons acknowledged the King's supremacy. But in

1538 the hospital was closed despite Sir Richard Gresham's petition to the King. At that time it had 180 beds with two patients in each. Spital Square now marks the site. In the churchyard was an outdoor pulpit called the Spital Cross where sermons were preached at Easter to the LORD MAYOR, ALDERMEN and others. The sermons continued after the suppression of the hospital and in 1559 Elizabeth I attended one. During the Commonwealth they were stopped but were revived at the Restoration. They no longer took place at Spital Cross, however, but at various city churches, usually ST BRIDE'S. From 1707 to 1940 they were preached at CHRISTCHURCH, NEWGATE STREET. Since that church was bombed they have been given at ST LAWRENCE JEWRY on the second Wednesday after Easter. The LORD MAYOR and ALDERMEN attend.

St Mary Staining *Staining Lane*. First mentioned in 1189, it was rebuilt in the late 16th century. Destroyed in the GREAT FIRE, it was not rebuilt. The parish was united with that of ST MICHAEL WOOD STREET.

St Mary the Virgin *Aldermanbury*. The medieval church was once famed for the enormous human bone displayed in the cloister. After the GREAT FIRE, Wren built a simple church here, without a spire. Although damaged in the 2nd World War it was not rebuilt. The ruins were shipped to Fulton, Missouri, USA where they have been re-erected as a memorial to Sir Winston Churchill. In the carefully planned garden which now covers the site, and which was opened in 1970, there is a memorial to Hemming and Condell, the Shakespearian actors who published the first folio of Shakespeare's plays and who were buried here.

St Mary the Virgin *East Barnet, Hertfordshire*. Built in the late 11th century, it is the oldest ecclesiastical structure in the neighbourhood. Part of the Norman nave's north wall still exists. During the 19th century the church developed its present form: in 1816 the vestry was built and the mid-17th-century gallery enlarged; in 1828 a new tower was added; in 1868 a south aisle was constructed; and in 1880 the 15th-century chancel was enlarged with an organ chamber. The register dates back to the 16th century, and there are monuments from the 17th century.

St Mary the Virgin *Leyton (Church Road), E10*. A church existed on the site by 1182 but the present building essentially dates back to the beginning of the 17th century when Sir William Ryder, the lord of LEYTON Manor, added a chapel on the north side of the existing chancel. Later in the century the tower was rebuilt and a north aisle added; and at the end of the century the minister, John Strype, the antiquary, lengthened the chancel. Alabaster effigies of Sir Michael Hickes, secretary to Lord Burghley, and his wife Elizabeth, of Ruckholt Manor, date from the 17th century. The cupola and clock were 19th-century additions and enlargements in 1822 by Thomas Cubitt to John Shaw's designs included a south aisle so that the original church was by then completely enclosed. The tower was raised and given battlements. Two early-19th-century monuments by John Flaxman commemorate William Bosanquet and John Hillers-

den. Another by John Soane, to Samuel Bosanquet, was vandalised and demolished. Restoration and repairs were carried out on the church in the late 18th century and again in 1951 as a result of bomb damage.

St Mary the Virgin *Little Ilford (Church Road), Essex*. A 12th-century church rebuilt in the early 18th century. There is a brass to a schoolboy, Thomas Heron, who died in 1517, the son of the Lord of the Manor. Thomas's brother, who succeeded to the estate, married Sir Thomas More's daughter and was, like More, executed for his opposition to Henry VIII.

St Mary the Virgin *Monken Hadley, Hertfordshire*. A sacred building existed on the site as early as 1136 when it passed to the Abbey of Walden with the 'Hermitage of Hadley'. The church existed by the beginning of the 15th century and the chancel and transepts were probably built by then. The flint and ironstone tower dates from 1494, probably built by Sir Thomas Lovell, Treasurer to Henry VII. The beacon on the tower, a rare surviving example, was apparently lit to guide travellers across ENFIELD CHASE. It also provided a means of communication, because of Hadley's high location, in times of danger like the Armada. During the 17th century Nicholas Stone provided the monument to the local benefactor, Sir Roger Wilbraham, and Sir Justinian Pagitt bought land for the building of the rectory, clerk's house and almshouses next to the church. In the 19th century these were rebuilt by J.R. Thackeray, cousin of the novelist, and the church was restored and enlarged by G.E. Street who removed much of the 17th- and 18th-century interior. The east window was replaced after a bomb blast in 1944.

St Mary the Virgin *Northolt (Ealing Road), Middlesex*. A very small church, the nave measuring only 44 ft by 25 ft. It is set on rising ground overlooking what remains of the old village centre and adjacent to the site, still visible, of the moated medieval manor house. The nave was built of clunch, flint and ironstone, the mouldings of doors and windows of Reigate stone. The nave of the church was built about 1300 and the chancel added between 1500 and 1540. The bell tower with its broach spire was added in the 16th century and, although the exterior has been much repaired, the internal beams are original and the bells date from the 17th century. A gallery was put up at the west end in 1703. The most distinctive feature of the exterior is the pair of buttresses erected against the west wall in about 1718 when it was feared the church was slipping down the hill. The Memorial Hall which stands beside the church was originally a National school, built in 1868.

St Mary the Virgin *Perivale (Perivale Lane), Middlesex*. Isolated from most of its parish by the construction of WESTERN AVENUE, it has not been used for regular worship since 1972. It is now preserved by the Friends of St Mary's. It is built of flint and rag rubble with stone dressings and, like its neighbour at GREENFORD, has a square wooden tower which was added to the original 13th-century building in 1510. Again like those of GREENFORD and NORTHOLT it is a small church but adequate for the small population of this hamlet until modern times. It has been much altered and restored throughout its history. The small but full graveyard was a fashionable rural spot for the graves of the middle classes of nearby EALING in the latter half of the 19th century.

St Mary the Virgin *Southall (Norwood Green), Middlesex*. The precinct of NORWOOD was part of the parish of HAYES until 1859, and the church at NORWOOD was originally a chapel-of-ease of HAYES. The earliest part of the existing building dates from the 12th century; the chancel was added or rebuilt in the 13th. The Manor of HAYES was held by the Archbishop of Canterbury and the 15th-century font was given by Archbishop Chichele. The church was built of flint rubble with Reigate stone dressings which were obliterated when the exterior was refaced in 1860–4 with black flint and multi-coloured brickwork. A gallery was erected by Francis Awsiter, Lord of the Manors of NORWOOD and SOUTHALL, but this was removed in 1862. The windows date from the 13th to 15th centuries and the roofs from the 15th. The last major rebuilding occurred in 1896 when the bellcote was demolished and the present tower erected.

St Mary the Virgin *Twickenham (Church Street), Middlesex*. Pleasantly set on the north bank of the THAMES. Apart from the medieval tower of Kentish rag, it was built in 1714–15 to the designs of John James, largely on the initiative of Sir Godfrey Kneller, the court painter, at a time when TWICKENHAM was developing as a country residence for nobility and gentry. The nave of the previous church had collapsed through neglect. The superb rubbed and gauged brickwork of the main fabric contrasts with the stone of the tower, the principal façades being on the north and south sides facing the village and the river with the central portions projecting and crowned with large pediments.

St Mary's is rich in associations but is probably best known for its links with Alexander Pope, TWICKENHAM's most famous resident. He is commemorated by a memorial in the form of a medallion portrait in the north gallery and on the nave floor by a brass plate given by three American scholars, although he was actually buried under the next stone (marked 'P'). In the north gallery there is also a tablet to his parents, and – outside on the east wall – one to his nurse. Sir Godfrey Kneller, who painted the portraits of six monarchs, was churchwarden and his arms are in the westernmost window of the north aisle.

The interior has, in recent times, been enriched with gilding and a lovely ceiling of Wedgwood blue with Adamesque decoration consisting of a large circle and rosettes for the light supports. There are galleries on each side. The door to the vestry at the east end of the south aisle is especially fine. Nearby is a monument to Francis Poulton, who died in 1642, and his wife with their portraits made of baked clay. Both reredos and altar-rails are 18th-century.

St Mary the Virgin *Wanstead (Overton Drive), E11*. The first mention of a rector of WANSTEAD is in 1207 but there is nothing left of his church. Altered, rebuilt and added to, it was pulled down in 1790, only some floor slabs, now looking like flat graves in the churchyard, mark where it stood. An Act of Parliament in 1787 authorised the building of a new church,

to be paid for partly by a tontine. This church stands in the park of the former Wanstead House. Designed by Thomas Hardwick it is worthy of the site. Five steps lead up to a west portico with two pairs of Doric columns. Above the rectangular nave rises a bell turret with double Ionic columns supporting a cupola and wind vane. The beautiful interior with the ceiling carried on tall Corinthian columns, which also support the original galleries, is renowned. The woodwork of the galleries, organ case and elegant box pews is of very high quality, as is the metalwork of the low screen and altar rail. The pulpit has its high sounding board carried on two slender columns, partly gilt, shaped as palm trees – an allusion to the East India Company connections of the Child-Tylney family. The Baroque monument, in white marble, probably by John van Nost, to Sir Josiah Child was re-erected from the old church in a bay specially designed for it between nave and altar. Sir Josiah stands in a Roman tunic oddly combined with a 1690s wig. There is also a Chantrey monument to George Bowles.

The large churchyard contains, besides the site of the former church, some interesting gravestones, including 'the Watcher's Box', apparently intended for a guard to prevent body-snatching.

St Mary the Virgin *Wimbledon (Church Road), SW19*. Perched prominently above the famous tennis courts, St Mary's has a long history, as evidenced by the Cecil Chapel which contains a plain black marble monument to Sir Edward Cecil, grandson of Elizabeth's Lord Burghley and a fine 14th-century stained glass figure of St George.

Most of the church, however, dates from 19th-century restoration which provided a light, airy interior with a notable hammerbeam roof in the nave.

St Mary the Virgin *Woodford (High Road), Essex*. The main structure with lancet windows is dated 1817 and the tower 1708, all of redbrick. The interior has recessed galleries on the north and south sides. The Raikes Mausoleum is in the churchyard.

St Mary Woolchurch First mentioned in the 11th century. It stood on the site of the MANSION HOUSE. According to Stow, wool was weighed in the churchyard. During the GREAT FIRE a churchwarden was so intent upon saving it that his own house burned down. The church was not severely damaged but it was demolished and the materials sold. The parish was united with that of ST MARY WOOLNOTH.

St Mary Woolnoth *Lombard Street and King William Street, EC4*. Said to have been founded by Wulfnoth, a Saxon prince, on the site of a Roman temple to Concord. First recorded in 1273, it was rebuilt in 1442. Damaged in the GREAT FIRE, it was repaired by Wren in 1670–7. In 1681 the organ, made by Father Smith, was installed. The church was rebuilt by Nicholas Hawksmoor in 1726–7 as one of Queen Anne's 50 new churches. John James had a hand in the original drawings. The interior is one of Hawksmoor's finest and is based on the Egyptian Hall of Vitruvius. William Butterfield 'restored' it in 1875–6, removing the galleries (whose fronts were stuck back on the wall later), cutting down the high pews and lowering the pulpit. The Bank tube station was built underneath the church in 1897–1900. St

Mary's is now a guild church. Edward Lloyd, owner of LLOYD'S COFFEE HOUSE, was buried here in 1712.

St Marychurch Street *SE16*. ST MARY, ROTHER- HITHE, a riverside landmark, rebuilt 1715, has interesting memorials to local seafarers and ship- wrights. Most famous was Christopher Jones, Master of the *Mayflower*, whose children's baptisms and own burial are in the parish registers. Across the road is the former Peter Hills School, with 18th-century charity school figures, and an old watch-house and engine house. This is a conservation area. Hope Sufferance Wharf has been converted to craft workshops.

St Marylebone *W1, NW1*. At the time of the Norman Conquest in 1066, the former Metropolitan Borough of St Marylebone (since 1965 a part of the City of WESTMINSTER) consisted of the manors of Lileston (Lisson) and TYBURN. The former, covering the western half, was held by a lady, Eideva; it later became the property of the KNIGHTS TEMPLAR and, on their suppression in 1312, passed to the KNIGHTS OF ST JOHN OF JERUSALEM (*see* ST JOHN'S WOOD). The latter, occupying the eastern half, took its name from the stream flowing southwards towards the THAMES and was the property of the abbess of BARKING ABBEY, who was confirmed in her rights by William the Con- queror. The Abbey, in its turn, leased the land to a suc- cession of owners, one of whom, Gilbert de Sanford, granted land on which to erect a water conduit in 1237 to the CITY OF LONDON (*see* STRATFORD PLACE). This land lay beside the parish church, dedicated to St John, which stood where Dolcis shoe shop now stands in OX- FORD STREET.

By the 14th century, the area had become dangerous and violent; in 1388, a gallows was set up at TYBURN and on several occasions the little church was broken open and its plate and vestments robbed. The parishioners therefore petitioned the BISHOP OF LON- DON for permission to move their place of worship northwards and a new church, dedicated to Our Lady, was erected ½ mile away close to TYBURN stream thus giving a new name – St Mary's by the bourne, which later compressed itself into Marylebone – to the whole area.

At the DISSOLUTION OF THE MONASTERIES, both Manors passed to the Crown. The greater part of Lileston was eventually acquired by the Portman family (*see* PORTMAN ESTATE). The northern half of Marylebone became a royal hunting park (*see* REGENT'S PARK) while the southern half was leased out to a series of tenants before James I sold it in 1611 to Edward Forsett, a justice of the peace, for £829 3s 4d. It passed to his daughter, Arabella, and in time to her son, John Austen. All these generations resided in the manor house at the north end of the High Street op- posite the parish church. The mansion was built at the beginning of the 16th century by a pre-Reformation owner, Thomas Hobson, and had been enlarged and beautified, and a bowling green, known as MARYLE- BONE GARDENS had opened behind it by 1659. Samuel Pepys visited it on 7 May 1668 and, finding it 'a pretty place . . . stayed till nine at night, and so home by moonlight'.

In 1708 John Austen sold the manor to John Holles, Duke of Newcastle, whose heiress was his daughter Henrietta, wife to Edward Harley, Earl of Oxford and Mortimer. He was an avid collector of books and for a while his library was accommodated in Oxford House

in the High Street. After his death in 1741, the manuscripts in his collection were bought for the nation and eventually became part of the original collection of the BRITISH MUSEUM. By this time the manor house had become a school for young gentle- men, run first by Dr Fountaine and then by his son-in- law.

Long before the Earl's death, he and his Countess had decided to develop their Marylebone estate. A plan was drawn up in 1719 by John Prince, and the architect, James Gibbs, designed the little chapel-of- ease, now ST PETER VERE STREET and gave his advice over the earliest houses. In one of them, No. 11 Hen- rietta Street, he made his home (a reception room, with a grandly painted ceiling from another room, is now in the VICTORIA AND ALBERT MUSEUM). The first house was built in CAVENDISH SQUARE in 1720 and a chequer-board of streets and squares soon began to spread across the fields. Clay was dug out and bricks were manufactured on the spot. A tile kiln occupied the site which SELFRIDGE'S covers today. Once again, a daughter, Margaret Cavendish Harley, inherited the estate; she became the wife of William Bentinck, 2nd Duke of Portland, and they continued the northward expansion of the buildings, the majority of the streets taking the names of members of the family – Margaret, Henrietta or Bentinck – or of their titles – Portland, Mortimer or Titchfield – or of estates – Wigmore, Wimpole or Welbeck – in their possession. The manor house was demolished and MARYLEBONE GARDENS closed in 1778 and was built over. The houses soon pressed against the New Road (*see* MARYLEBONE ROAD) which had been laid out in 1757 whilst the development of the PORTMAN ESTATE, begun just after 1760, soon fretted against the same limitation.

The development of REGENT'S PARK, projected by 1811 and virtually complete by the late 1820s, released the northern half of St Marylebone for development. The 1820 edition of Peter Potter's map of the parish shows the fields almost clear of houses but the 1832 edition marks their spread northwards into ST JOHN'S WOOD along Wellington Road and as far as Marl- borough Place, whilst the 1849 and 1856 editions of George Lucas's survey of Marylebone demonstrate that building proceeded steadily until the northern boundary with HAMPSTEAD was reached. Thomas LORD'S CRICKET GROUND, which had opened in 1787 where DORSET SQUARE now stands, removed in 1811 to ST JOHN'S WOOD. The market gardens of Lisson Green and the dairy farms of ST JOHN'S WOOD gave way to the advance of bricks and mortar. The ap- pearance of pairs of semi-detached villas on the EYRE ESTATE gave an elegance, a charm, and a variety to the layout of the area, qualities which, within three generations, were to be severely marred when the Great Central Railway smashed through 70 acres of this idyllic suburb to reach its new terminus at MARYLEBONE STATION.

Today Marylebone is increasingly an area of com- mercial and office development (for details see under individual street names), and blocks of flats replace pairs of villas but, in spite of the impersonal bustle of the 20th century along OXFORD STREET and the stream of cars filing along MARYLEBONE ROAD, per- fectly distinct village centres continue in Marylebone and ST JOHN'S WOOD High Street and an excellent street market flourishes in Church Street off LISSON GROVE.

746

St Marylebone Parish Church *Marylebone Road, W1.* The first parish church was built in about 1200 in what is now OXFORD STREET and dedicated to St John. Large numbers of human bones found at the bottom of Marylebone Lane probably mark the spot. In 1400 a second church was built on the present site and given the name of St Mary by the Bourne (the Bourne being the River TYBURN). It was rebuilt in 1740, and between 1770 and 1774 Sir William Chambers drew up six different plans for a new church but they were all rejected. In 1811 when John Nash was planning REGENT'S PARK, a new parish church was included. Nash wanted it to stand in the centre of a grand circus at the southern end of PORTLAND PLACE, but the vestry disagreed. Eventually the Duke of Portland said he would close up PORTLAND PLACE unless the church was built on his land so a fourth church by Chambers's pupil, Thomas Hardwick, in a style inspired by one of Chambers's rejected designs, was built on Portland's estate (1813–17). It was begun as a chapel-of-ease but when half completed, the vestry decided to make it the parish church and demote the old church to the status of parish chapel. It has a heavy portico and distinctive cupola supported by gilt caryatids. The chancel was reconstructed in 1885 by Thomas Harris. The altarpiece of the holy family is by Benjamin West. Byron was christened here in 1778 and Horatia, daughter of Nelson and Lady Hamilton in 1803. Francis Bacon was married here in 1606, Robert Browning and Elizabeth Barrett in 1746, and Sheridan in 1773. James Figg, the prize fighter, was buried here in 1734; George Stubbs, the painter, in 1806; and James Northcote, the painter, in 1831. The former church which became the parish chapel was badly damaged in the 2nd World War and was demolished in 1949. The site is now a garden. The graves of Charles Wesley and his nephew Samuel were moved from the graveyard and marked by an obelisk.

St Mary's Hospital *Praed Street, W2.* At the beginning of the 19th century London was spreading west across the EDGWARE ROAD towards the village of PADDINGTON. In 1795 the GRAND JUNCTION CANAL Company built the Paddington Basin, an offshoot of the main canal. In 1837 the Great Western Railway, built by Brunel to link London with Bristol, had its terminus at PADDINGTON. These factors made the area busy and thriving and the population grew rapidly. Since there was no hospital nearer than ST GEORGE'S HOSPITAL to the south of HYDE PARK and the MIDDLESEX HOSPITAL to the east, in 1842 several influential inhabitants of the 'North-Western quarter of the Metropolis' set their minds to building one. In 1844 Thomas Hopper drew up plans for a hospital of 380 beds to be known as the Paddington and Marylebone Hospital. The name was soon changed to St Mary's after the adjacent church by the canal. On 28 June 1845 Prince Albert laid the foundation stone. But the contractors went bankrupt and the first block of the hospital, designed by Hopper and Wyatt, was not opened until June 1851. One year later there were still only 150 beds in use.

There was then the problem of obtaining a competent consultant staff capable of teaching in the projected medical school. This was a difficult and delicate matter as they could not be obtained from the staffs of other teaching hospitals in London and there were only a limited number of distinguished medical men who were unattached to such hospitals. By 1854, however, medical school buildings for 300 students were completed. The school was formed largely through the efforts of Samuel Lane who had owned a private anatomy school in GROSVENOR PLACE near ST GEORGE'S HOSPITAL. It went out of business when the governors of ST GEORGE'S HOSPITAL decided to form a medical school of their own. Lane and several of his teachers joined the staff of St Mary's. In 1857 the Allcroft Accident Ward was opened, and in 1864 the Albert Edward Wing was built.

In 1875 and again in 1886 the hospital closed while the drains were rebuilt. In 1882–4 the out-patient wing and the Stanford Wing were added. Stanford was a barrister who was elected MP for Reading after promising the electorate he would marry a Reading lady before the year ended, but as he did not fulfil his promise he was ousted. His legacy to the hospital was £30,000. The wing was named after his mother, Mary Stanford. In 1887 Dr A. Waller, head of the Medical School's Physiology Department, invented the electrocardiograph. In 1902 Almroth Wright joined the staff and set up an Inoculation Department. It was he who introduced immunisation against typhoid fever. He was a friend of Bernard Shaw, another Irishman, who parodied him in *The Doctors' Dilemma*. In 1904 the Clarence Wing, designed by W. Emerson, was opened, and in 1907 the Department of Neurology was inaugurated. In 1909 the research wards were opened by Almroth Wright.

After the 1st World War there was a threat that LONDON UNIVERSITY would no longer recognise it as there were so few students. However, the new Dean, Charles Wilson (later Lord Moran) with the aid of benefactors revitalised the school.

In 1928 Alexander Fleming, working in the hospital's laboratories, first realised the significance of penicillin when a culture dish left near an open window became mouldy. He wrote, 'If my mind had not been in a reasonably perceptive state I would not have paid any attention to it.' In 1933 the Medical School and Pathological Institute, designed by Sir Edwin Cooper, were opened; and in 1936 the nurses' home, also designed by Cooper, was completed. In 1937 the Fleming family presented Joyce Grove, Nettlebed, as a convalescent home. Subsequently Lord Porritt, later President of the Royal College of Surgeons and Governor-General of New Zealand, was Senior Surgeon. With the introduction of the National Health Service, St Mary's was grouped with ST MARY'S HOSPITAL HARROW ROAD, the PADDINGTON GREEN CHILDREN'S HOSPITAL, Princess Louise Kensington Hospital for Children, the SAMARITAN HOSPITAL FOR WOMEN, the WESTERN OPHTHALMIC HOSPITAL and CHEPSTOW LODGE formerly ST LUKE'S HOSPITAL BAYSWATER. In 1982 there were 462 beds.

St Mary's New Church *Stoke Newington (Church Street), N16.* By the 1850s, the old church had become too small. STOKE NEWINGTON was a growing suburb, and a new rector, the Revd Thomas Jackson, was attracting congregations from all over London by his reputation as a preacher. The new church was consecrated in 1858, having been paid for by voluntary subscription. Sir George Gilbert Scott was the architect and the design, in 13th-century Gothic style, was loosely modelled on Salisbury Cathedral. The spire was not completed until 1890, and this gave rise to the rhyme:

Stoke Newington is a funny place
With lots of funny people
Thomas Jackson built a church
But could not build a steeple.

St Mary's Old Church *Stoke Newington (Church Street), N16*. There has been a church in STOKE NEWINGTON for at least 1,000 years. William Patten, Lord of the Manor 1550–71, was responsible for the present building, an almost total reconstruction of an earlier, medieval church. It dates from 1563, and is thus one of the very few churches built in the troubled period immediately after the Reformation. The exterior, in redbrick, is in the characteristic Tudor style, and it complements a charming interior with 18th-century box pews. Over the entrance is a plaque with the motto *ab alto* (from above). The timber spire was added at the time of the church's restoration by Sir Charles Barry in 1829.

St Matthew *Bethnal Green, E2*. Built in 1743–6 to the designs of George Dance the Elder. It was rebuilt in 1859 after a fire; and redecorated after severe damage in the 2nd World War.

St Matthew *Brixton, SW2*. Built in 1822 by William Porden with a portico at the west end and a steeple at the east. Much of the interior has been cleared for a community centre.

St Matthew *Friday Street*. First mentioned in 1261. In 1637 Henry Burton, the rector, preached an offensive sermon for which he was condemned to stand in the pillory at WESTMINSTER, lose his ears, pay a heavy fine and stay in prison for life. He was released in 1640. The church was rebuilt by Wren in 1681–7 at a cost of £2,301 8s 2d, having been destroyed by the GREAT FIRE. It was a small plain church with the east end backing on to the street. This façade had six circular headed plain glass windows and was topped by a balustrade. At the west end was a small brick tower. The church was repaired in 1861 but demolished in 1881 under the Union of City Benefices Act and the parish joined with that of ST VEDAST FOSTER LANE. The site was sold for £22,005 and some of the proceeds were used to build ST THOMAS FINSBURY PARK. The pulpit and the font from St Matthew's are now at ST ANDREW BY THE WARDROBE. The new BANK OF ENGLAND offices were built in the churchyard in 1954. Sir Hugh Myddelton, planner of the NEW RIVER, was a churchwarden and was buried here in 1631.

St Matthew *Great Peter Street, SW1*. Built in 1849–51 to the designs of Sir George Gilbert Scott. The Lady Chapel is by Sir Ninian Comper. The lectern is 15th-century Spanish. The church was badly damaged by fire in 1977.

St Matthew's Hospital *Shepherdess Walk, N1*. Founded in 1782 and then known as St Luke's Workhouse as it lay in the parish of St Luke in Hoxton Fields. It is mentioned in *David Copperfield*. Dr James Parkinson (who described the 'shaking palsy') practised in Hoxton and probably sent patients to the workhouse. It was rebuilt in 1871 to the designs of Saxon Snell. Visitors were forbidden to bring in anything except flowers, oranges, grapes and acid drops. Introduction of spiritous liquor led to a fine of £10 or

two months' imprisonment. In 1930 its name was changed to St Matthew's. There are still Dickens, Copperfield and Parkinson wards in the hospital. It is now administered by the National Health Service. In 1982 there were 205 beds, mainly for geriatric and rheumatic cases.

St Matthias *Poplar, E14*. Originally a private East India Company chapel of the 17th century. It was rebuilt in 1776, and restored in the 19th century by S.S. Teulon. The memorial to George Stevens is by Flaxman (1800). The church was closed in 1977 and has since been seriously damaged by vandals.

St Matthias *Stoke Newington (Matthias Road), N16*. An early work (1851) by William Butterfield. The church is a gaunt and massive brick structure with a tall tower capped by an unusual steep saddleback roof.

St Michael *Camden Road, NW1*. Plain stone and stock brick church with an impressive interior built in 1880–94 to the designs of George Frederick Bodley and Thomas James, both pupils of George Gilbert Scott.

St Michael *Chester Square, SW1*. At the time of its opening in 1846, St Michael's was criticised by *The Ecclesiologist* for being 'an attempt – but happily a most unsuccessful one – to find a "Protestant" development of the Christian styles.' It is in the late decorated style, with an exterior facing of Kentish ragstone. The architect was Thomas Cundy, who, like his father, was surveyor of the GROSVENOR ESTATE.

St Michael *Cornhill, EC3*. First mentioned in 1055. The tower was rebuilt in 1421. Burned down in the GREAT FIRE, the church was rebuilt in 1670–1 by Wren who incorporated the 15th-century tower. A new Gothic tower, designed by Wren, was begun in 1715–17 but work on this was suspended through lack of funds. In 1718–22 the tower was completed by Nicholas Hawksmoor to his own design based on the tower of Magdalen College, Oxford. The church was restored by Sir George Gilbert Scott in 1857–60. All the 17th-century furniture was thrown out except for a wrought-iron sword rest, a wooden pelican, the symbol of piety, and the Renatus Harris organ on which Purcell had once played. Outside a bronze statuette of St Michael by R.R. Goulden commemorates the dead of the 1st World War. Thomas Gray, the poet, was christened here in 1716.

St Michael *Crooked Lane*. First mentioned in 1271. In the 14th century William Walworth (the Lord Mayor who stabbed Wat Tyler) built on a choir, side chapels and a college for a master and nine priests. Burned down in the GREAT FIRE the church was rebuilt by Wren in 1684–9. The tower was completed in 1698. On 21 November 1703 27 vases from the steeple were blown down in the 'most violent storm known in the memory of any one now living; it was a South Westerley wind attended with small rain and some say an earthquake.' The church was demolished in 1831 to make way for KING WILLIAM STREET. The parish was united with that of ST MAGNUS THE MARTYR. William Walworth was buried here in 1385.

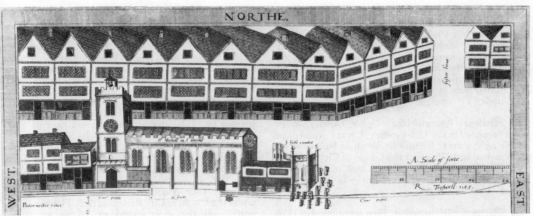

St Michael at Corn, after a drawing of 1585 by Ralph Treswell, showing the water jugs around the adjoining 'Lytle Cundit'.

St Michael *Highgate, N6.* In 1826 the Court of Chancery ruled that parishioners had no right to worship in the chapel of HIGHGATE SCHOOL and that it was unfair to expect the school to pay for its upkeep. Consequently in 1831–2 a Gothic parish church was built, designed by Lewis Vulliamy. It cost £8,171. In 1878 the chancel was extended eastwards by C.H. Mileham. In 1961 the remains of Samuel Taylor Coleridge, buried in the school chapel since 1834, were reinterred in the church.

St Michael at Corn *Paternoster Row.* First mentioned in 1181. A corn market was sometimes held in the churchyard. Destroyed in the GREAT FIRE, it was not rebuilt. The parish was united with that of ST VEDAST FOSTER LANE. John Leland, the antiquary, was buried here in 1552.

St Michael Bassishaw *Basinghall Street.* This small brick church, designed by Sir Christopher Wren in 1676, had to be demolished in 1899 because the foundations were seriously damaged when work was being done in accordance with the CITY Sanitary Authorities' order to clear the crypt of human remains. The site was bought by the CITY CORPORATION for £36,000 and the parish was joined to that of ST LAWRENCE JEWRY.

St Michael Paternoster Royal *College Hill, EC4.* First mentioned in 1219. Royal is a corruption of Reole, a nearby street inhabited by merchants of the vintry who imported wine from La Reole, near Bordeaux. In 1409 the church was rebuilt at the expense of Richard Whittington. Burned down in the GREAT FIRE it was rebuilt in 1689–94 by Wren. The steeple

St Michael Crooked Lane in 1830, with the Monument in the background. Watercolour by G. Scharf.

was completed in 1713. In 1866 the interior was re-arranged by William Butterfield. Bombed in 1944, it was restored in 1967. Much 17th-century woodwork had survived, including the pulpit, font cover, altar-piece, lectern, sword rests and statues of Moses and Aaron beside the altar. The east window and the Whittington window are by John Hayward. Whittington was buried here in 1423; and Peter Blundell, founder of Blundell's School, in 1601.

St Michael Queenhithe *Upper Thames Street.* First recorded in the 12th century, it was burned down in the GREAT FIRE. Rebuilt by Wren in 1676–7 it was demolished in 1876 under the Union of City Benefices Act. The parish was united with that of ST MICHAEL PATERNOSTER ROYAL. The pulpit was taken to ST JAMES GARLICKHYTHE.

St Michael *Wood Street.* First mentioned in 1170. It was burned down in the GREAT FIRE and rebuilt by Wren in 1670–5. In 1894 it was demolished under the Union of City Benefices Act. The parish was united with that of ST ALBAN, WOOD STREET. The head of James IV of Scotland, who was killed at Flodden Field in 1513, was said to have been buried in the church.

St Michael and All Angels *Bedford Park (Bath Road), W4.* An integral part of BEDFORD PARK, the earliest planned garden suburb. Norman Shaw designed the suburb and was responsible for the principal group of church, inn and bank opposite the common. The exterior of St Michael's, dating from 1880, is distinctive for its large porch with palisaded gates and delightful lantern over the crossing.

St Michael and All Angels *Blackheath Park, SE3.* Built by George Smith in 1828–30 as a chapel-of-ease to ST LUKE'S, CHARLTON.

St Michael and All Angels with St James *Croydon (Poplar Walk), Surrey.* Surrey's finest 19th-century church, designed by John Loughborough Pearson and built in 1880–3. Decoration and furnishings are by Sir Ninian Comper. The vicars of St Michael's seem to have been exceptionally enduring,

for in the first 99 years of the church's ministry there were only three incumbents.

St Mildred *Bread Street.* Built sometime before 1252. During 1485–8 Hugh Oldham, founder of Manchester Grammar School, was rector. Burned down in the GREAT FIRE it was rebuilt by Wren in 1677–83. Until the 2nd World War it was one of the best preserved of Wren's churches with its original pews and woodwork but it was bombed and completely destroyed in 1941. Shelley was married here to Mary Wollstonecraft in 1816.

St Mildred *Poultry.* First recorded in 1175. Burned down in the GREAT FIRE, it was rebuilt by Wren in 1670–6, although the tower was not completed until the early 18th century. It was demolished in 1872 under the Union of City Benefices Act. The parish was united with that of ST MARGARET, LOTHBURY.

St Mildred's Court *EC2.* Commemorates the Church of ST MILDRED POULTRY which was demolished in 1872. Before 1754 the court was called Scalding Alley after the scalding houses used by medieval poulterers. Mrs Elizabeth Fry, the prison reformer, lived here in 1800–9.

St Nicholas *Chislehurst, Kent.* This originally Saxon church was partly rebuilt in the 15th century, and further rebuilt and extended in the mid-1800s. The rector responsible for the extension, the Revd F. Murray, was one of the original editors of *Hymns Ancient and Modern.*

Tombs in the church include those of the Sydneys whose name was given to Sydney in Australia, and the Walsinghams. The tomb of Sir Thomas Walsingham, Marlowe's patron, was opened in 1956 to see whether manuscripts of Shakespeare's plays in Marlowe's writing might be buried there, thus proving Marlowe to be the author. No manuscripts were found.

St Nicolas *Chiswick (Church Street), W4.* The dedication to St Nicolas is a reminder that CHISWICK was once a fishing village. The tower used to stand beside a ford crossing the river and St Nicolas, among

Norman Shaw's St Michael and All Angels, Bedford Park, in 1882. From a lithograph after F. Hamilton Jackson.

his various patronages (including pawnbrokers), was the patron saint of sailors and fishermen. Of the medieval building, only the ragstone tower dating from 1446 remains; the rest was completely rebuilt in 1882. Fortunately the work was in the hands of one of the finest of Victorian architects, John Loughborough Pearson. In the churchyard the painter, William Hogarth, who lived nearby (see HOGARTH HOUSE), is commemorated by an urn on a massive pedestal. Two of Oliver Cromwell's daughters – Mary and Frances – and Charles II's mistress, Barbara Villiers, Duchess of Cleveland, are buried in the church without memorials.

St Nicholas *Deptford Green, SE8*. The late 17th-century church was gutted during the 2nd World War. An admirable restoration left it smaller by cutting off the eastern bay and sanctuary to provide a church hall and other amenities. Entrance is through a gate with pillars crowned by gruesome and much worn death's-head skulls but these are encircled with wreaths to symbolise victory over death. Apart from the top, the Kentish ragstone tower is medieval, dating from about 1500, but the walls which survived the bombing are of brick with stone quoins and dressings, the north and south sides having Dutch high-pointed gables.

The monuments include a striking one of 1615 in golden-brown alabaster to Roger Boyle who is shown praying in a tent. On the west wall, the death of Christopher Marlowe, the Elizabethan dramatist, killed on 20 May 1593 in a tavern brawl, is recorded. On a pew in the south-eastern part of the church, a tablet commemorates the men of Deptford Power Station, which overshadows the church, who lost their lives in the 2nd World War as a result of enemy action.

St Nicholas *Plumstead (Plumstead High Street), SE18*. Built in the 12th century on the edge of the THAMES marshes to serve a small community of fruit growers, St Nicholas has many times been close to ruin. John Gossage, a wealthy farmer, rescued it in 1662, after it had, according to the parish records, been 'above 20 years lying waste and ruinous'. He is responsible for the distinctive, dark brick tower, with its buttresses reaching to the battlements. By 1800, however, the church was once again open to the skies with trees growing in the aisles. Restoration was carried out by Charles H. Cooke in 1867, and in 1907 the church was considerably enlarged by the architects Greenaway and Newberry. It was badly damaged by bombs during the 2nd World War and was repaired yet again in 1959.

St Nicholas *Tooting (Church Lane), SW17*. A church has been on this site for over 1,000 years. The Saxon church was a small building with a nave, chancel and a round tower to one side, a rare example of its kind. When this became too small for the growing population a new church was built. This was completed in 1833. Designed in the Gothic style by T.W. Atkinson, it is of brick with a pinnacled tower. The Saxon church was then demolished. The new church retains 16th- to 18th-century monuments, including the funeral achievements of Sir James Bateman, Lord Mayor of London.

St Nicholas Acons *Between Lombard Street and Cannon Street*. Built in 1084 for Malmesbury Abbey. Acons is probably a corruption of Haakon, a benefactor. The church was repaired in 1520 but burned down in the GREAT FIRE and not rebuilt. The parish was united with that of ST EDMUND THE KING.

St Nicholas by the Shambles *Newgate Street*. Built some time before 1196 next to an abattoir. It was demolished in 1547 and the parish united with that of CHRIST CHURCH GREYFRIARS.

St Nicholas Cole Abbey *EC4*. According to Strype this was the first CITY church Sir Christopher Wren built after the GREAT FIRE. He completed it in 1677. Included in the total cost of £5,042 6s 11d are such items as 'Dinner for Dr Wren and other Company – £2 14s 0d' and 'Half a pint of canary for Dr Wren's coachmen – 6d'. Wren adopted a simple, classical design in radical contrast to the still fashionable decorated Gothic. The quaint steeple resembles an inverted funnel. It has a balcony and railings at the top. The pulpit, altar-rail and font cover, together with the tracery on the west doors and south entrance, are all 17th-century woodwork. So, too, is the royal Coat-of-Arms over the south door. Wren's church replaced one first mentioned in a letter of Pope Lucius in 1144. Land deeds in the reign of Richard I later record 'a new fish market' near the Church of St Nicholas; and in a Charter of 1272 it is referred to, affectionately, as '*Sci Nichi retro fihstrate*' or 'St Nick's behind Fish Street'. From the number of fishmongers buried here during the 16th century, it would appear to have maintained a close association with the fish trade which began in the reign of Richard I when a new fish market was established nearby. A wealthy fishmonger in the reign of Elizabeth I gave £900 'to bring Thames water to a tank on the north wall of the Church for the care and commodity of the Fishmongers in and about Old Fish Street'.

The BOWYERS, too, whose Worshipful Company still use the church, have links going back over many centuries. There is a brass plaque commemorating the burial, at St Nicholas in 1629, of a benefactor of their company – James Wood.

It was never an abbey. Its title probably derives from the medieval word *coldharbour*, meaning a shelter. Perhaps there was a lodging-house nearby. It is named after the patron saint of children, and an inventory of the church's possessions at the time of the Reformation describes some of the vestments being 'as for children', so possibly the ancient ceremony of the 'Boy Bishop' was celebrated here (see ST PAUL'S CATHEDRAL). The stark simplicity of the services which replaced such ceremonies in the reign of Edward VI were not popular in the parish according to one observer who rejoiced, in 1553, at the restoration of the Roman Rite under Queen Mary: 'Mass at St Nicholas Cole Abbaye goodly sung in Latin, tapers set on the altar and a cross, and all this not by commandment but by the people's devotion.'

It was here that the first Mass in London was celebrated after Mary's accession. The priest was said to have sold his wife to a butcher, for which he was pelted with rotten eggs. Later the patronage belonged to the Puritan, Colonel Hacker, who commanded the guard for the execution of Charles I. In 1737, John Wesley recorded that his friend and fellow Methodist, George Whitefield, preached a stirring sermon at St Nicholas on 'Profane Swearing in Church'. Under the rectorship of Henry Shuttleworth in the late 19th century, the church became a centre for lively discussion and debate. Shuttleworth is thought to be the model for Mr Morell, the socialist priest in Shaw's play *Candida*.

In 1941, on a Sunday morning in May, St Nicholas Cole Abbey was gutted by fire bombs. It was restored to Wren's original design in 1962. The shops no longer cluster against the south wall and so these windows have been opened up. The east windows are by Kenneth New.

St Nicholas Olave *Bread Street Hill*. First mentioned in 1188, it was burned down in the GREAT FIRE and not rebuilt. The parish was united with that of ST NICHOLAS COLE ABBEY.

St Olave *Hart Street, EC3*. When King Haakon VII of Norway laid the foundation stone for the restoration of this church in 1951, he was maintaining a link with another Norwegian king – Olaf, who fought beside Etheldred the Unready against the Danes in the Battle of London Bridge in 1014. King Olaf, who died in 1025, was canonised for his services to Christendom. Not long afterwards a wooden church was erected on this site and dedicated in his honour. This church was replaced in the 13th century with a stone construction, and the nave was then extended westwards in order to contain an ancient well. What remains of this early church forms the crypt of the present, mainly 15th-century building which, despite several restorations, has altered little over the centuries. It stands today like 'a country church in the world of Seething Lane' in the view of John Betjeman.

It was commissioned in 1450 by Robert and Richard Cely, wealthy fellmongers of the parish, and it is in the perpendicular style. The brick top to the tower was added in 1732. The projecting 18th-century clock comes from the church of ST OLAVE OLD JEWRY, which was demolished in 1888. The turret and vane, together with the south porch (the gift of the wine and spirit trade, who hold their Harvest Festival here in October) are part of the restoration executed by E.B. Glanfield in 1954 after the bomb damage of the 2nd World War.

The interior of the church has clustered columns of Purbeck marble with pointed arches which separate the north and south aisles from the clerestoried nave. The simple roof is oak-panelled with bosses. The communion rails are 17th-century. The pulpit is reputed to be the work of Grinling Gibbons, and was presented by the Brethren of TRINITY HOUSE in 1863. It was acquired from ST BENET GRACECHURCH. Pepys refers affectionately in his Diary to St Olave's as 'our own church'; and it was largely due to his vigilance in seeing that many of the wooden structures around the church were removed, that St Olave's survived the GREAT FIRE. He had an outside stairway and small gallery built in 1660 leading from the Navy Office in SEETHING LANE so that he could go to church without getting wet. This has since been removed; but a monument to Pepys by Sir Arthur Blomfield marks the place where the gallery used to be. The monument to his wife Elizabeth, which he put up after her death in 1669, is beautifully sculpted in white marble by John Bushnell. It is on the north wall of the Sanctuary. Pepys himself is buried in the nave beside his wife.

The burial registers are full of interest. There is a record of Mother Goose being buried here on 14 September 1586; and in 1665 on 24 July, Mary Ramsay, who is said to have brought the GREAT PLAGUE to London. Those who died from the plague of that year have a 'p' after their name. Dickens, in *The Uncommercial Traveller* called the church St Ghastly Grim, because of the gateway to the churchyard. It is of the late 17th century and abounds with skulls and crossbones and ferocious iron spikes. St Olave's is still an active parish church. The parishes of ALL HALLOWS STAINING and ST CATHERINE COLEMAN were added to it in 1870 and 1921 respectively.

St Olave *Manor House (Woodberry Down), N4*. Built of redbrick in 1893–4 from proceeds of the 1888–9 demolition of ST OLAVE'S OLD JEWRY, from which the stone baluster font and finely carved 17th-century pulpit were transferred.

St Olave Old Jewry *or* Upwell Old Jewry The first certain reference is in 1181. Stow says that there was a well at the east end of the churchyard, hence the name. In medieval times St Olave's bells summoned traders to BLACKWELL HALL. The church was restored in 1608 and again in 1628 but destroyed by the GREAT FIRE. It was rebuilt by Wren in 1670–6. It comprised a plain nave 18 ft long by 34 ft wide and 36 ft high, with a flat ceiling and medallion cornice and cost £5,588 4s 10d. Obelisk pinnacles are the only decoration of the plain tower. The parish was amalgamated with ST MARTIN POMEROY, which was not rebuilt. Despite restoration in 1879, the nave was demolished in 1888 under the Union of City Benefices Act and the site sold for £22,400. The remains of the dead were removed to the City of London Cemetery at ILFORD. A Roman pavement of red terracotta was found during demolition. Most of the wood furnishings and plate were transferred to ST MARGARET LOTHBURY; the clock to ST OLAVE HART STREET; and the Stuart coat of arms to ST ANDREW BY THE WARDROBE. The organ was later taken to Christchurch, PENGE.

The proceeds were used to build ST OLAVE, Manor House, and the pulpit and font were taken to the new church. The parish was amalgamated with ST MARGARET LOTHBURY and the surviving Wren tower is used as the rectory. Robert Large, the Lord Mayor to whom Caxton was apprenticed, was buried here in 1440; and John Boydell a subsequent Lord Mayor, in 1804. Boydell's bust, designed by Banks and carved by F.W. Smith, is now in ST MARGARET LOTHBURY.

St Olave Silver Street *Noble Street*. This was the parish church of the silversmiths and the figure of Christ on the Cross had silver shoes. The parish register records that in 1665–6 the bodies of 119 people hanged at TYBURN were given to the barber-surgeons to dissect for research purposes. The church was not rebuilt after being destroyed in the GREAT FIRE.

St Olave's Burial Ground *see* BURIAL GROUNDS.

St Olave's Court *EC2*. Commemorates the Church of ST OLAVE OLD JEWRY which was demolished except for its tower in 1888. Before 1916 it was known as Church Court.

St Pancras New Church in 1822 on its completion to designs by William and Henry Inwood, who had not long returned from Athens. This Greek Revival edifice was the most costly church to be built around this time.

St Pancras *NW1*. The cult of St Pancras (according to legend a 14-year-old convert to Christianity martyred by Diocletian) was propagated in England by St Augustine, and the old parish church of St Pancras existed by the Norman era. William and Henry W. Inwood's new parish church (1822) is further south and close to George Gilbert Scott's ST PANCRAS STATION. The Borough of St Pancras comprised CAMDEN TOWN, CHALK FARM, KENTISH TOWN and SOMERS TOWN, stretching from HIGHGATE to TOTTENHAM COURT ROAD and BLOOMSBURY. In 1965 it united with the Borough of CAMDEN to form the London Borough of CAMDEN.

St Pancras *Soper Lane*. First mentioned in 1257, the church was attached to the monastery of Christchurch Canterbury and was thus a peculiar of the Archbishop of Canterbury under the jurisdiction of the COURT OF ARCHES at ST MARY-LE-BOW. In 1374 the Archbishop granted 40 days' indulgence to all penitents who contributed towards the church bell, which was called 'Le Clok'. Stow records various monuments, 'all defaced and gone', including one of 1536 to Robert Packenton, a mercer, 'Slain with a gun shot at him ... as he was going to morrow mass'. The rector from 1593 to his death in 1607 was Abraham Fleming, poet and antiquary, the first translator of Virgil. The Vestry Minutes of 1641 record orders that inscriptions on gravestones 'tending to supersitition, be removed with images over the church porch'. The church was destroyed in the GREAT FIRE and the parish united with that of ST MARY LE BOW. The small churchyard remains in PANCRAS LANE.

St Pancras Hospital *4 St Pancras Way, NW1*. Formerly known as St Pancras South Hospital it was founded in 1805 for the general and chronic sick and as a mental observation ward. It is now a general hospital linked to UNIVERSITY COLLEGE HOSPITAL. In 1982 there were 264 beds.

St Pancras New Church *Upper Woburn Place, WC1*. A beautiful Greek Revival building and the most expensive church of its time. It was designed by Henry W. and William Inwood in 1819–22. Henry had only just returned from Athens with measured drawings. The church is based on the Erechtheion. A spacious Ionic portico runs the length of the western façade. The tower is a copy of the Tower of the Winds. At the east end are two pavilions whose roofs are supported by caryatids of terracotta modelled by Rossi.

St Pancras Old Church *Pancras Road, NW1*. A Saxon altar dating from 600 has been found here indicating this is one of the oldest Christian sites in Europe. The chancel was probably rebuilt in about 1350. In 1822 the church was made a chapel-of-ease to the new parish church of ST PANCRAS. In 1866 the Midland Railway Company began to build a tunnel through the churchyard but the disinterment of bodies caused such a public outcry that questions were asked in the HOUSE OF COMMONS and the project had to be abandoned. In 1847–8 the church was drastically restored by A.D. Gough and R.L. Roumieu. The nave was extended westwards, a new tower built, and the walls and windows 're-Normanised'. Jonathan Wild, the self-styled 'thief-taker general', was married here in 1718 and Joseph Grimaldi, the clown, in 1801. The burial ground was long popular with Roman Catholics who believed this to be the last parish church in England where Mass was said. Many refugees from the French Revolution were buried here. Also buried here were Jonathan Wild, who was hanged in 1725, exhumed two days later, and gibbeted; Ned Ward, author of *The London Spy*, in

1731; and, in 1797, Mary Wollstonecraft Godwin, whose remains were moved to Bournemouth in 1851. Over her grave in July 1814 Shelley and her daughter, Mary, confessed their love for each other.

General Pasquale de Paoli, the Corsican patriot, whose remains were removed to Corsica in 1889, was buried here in 1807. In the adjoining burial ground of ST GILES IN THE FIELDS were interred Flaxman, the sculptor, in 1826, and Sir John Soane, the architect in 1837. Soane's monument was designed by him for his wife who died in 1815.

St Pancras Station *and* **former Midland Grand Hotel** *Euston Road, NW1*. In 1863 the Midland Railway bought a site for their London terminus in the centre of the slums of AGAR TOWN. They had previously shared the Great Northern Railway's terminus at KING'S CROSS. In 1863–7 the 689 ft-long glass and iron train shed was built. It was designed by W.H. Barlow and executed by R.M. Ordish. The 55-ton ribs were made by the Butterley Iron Company. It spans 240 ft and is 100 ft above the rails at its apex, one of the wonders of Victorian engineering. The platforms had to be raised 20 ft above the level of EUSTON ROAD because of the proximity of the REGENT'S CANAL which the trains had to cross. The cellars beneath were designed for the brewers of Burton-on-Trent to use for storage. In 1865 a design competition was held between 11 architects for the Midland Grand Hotel which was to enclose the train shed to the south and form the façade to Euston Road. George Gilbert Scott entered under pressure from one of the company's directors after more than once declining, and won. His designs were produced during a visit to Hayling Island where his son was ill; the estimated cost was £316,000, far higher than those of the other entrants. In 1868–72 the hotel was built, a high Gothic design of pinnacles, towers and gables which was similar to Scott's rejected plans for government offices in WHITEHALL. Concerning this similarity Scott wrote in his *Personal and Professional Recollections*, 'It is often spoken of to me as the finest building in London; my own belief is that it is possibly too good for its purpose, but having been disappointed through Lord Palmerston of my ardent hope of carrying out my style in the Government Offices . . . I was glad to be able to erect one building in that style in London.' Its total frontage is 565 ft flanked by the 270 ft-high clock tower and the 250 ft west tower. The clock was made by John Walker of CORNHILL. The hotel had 250 bedrooms. George Augustus Sala thought it the most sumptuous and best conducted hotel in the empire. Its main internal features were a long curving dining-room and an imperial staircase. In 1890 the first ladies' smoking room in London was opened in it. Since 1935 it has been closed and used as offices, and is known as St Pancras Chambers.

St Pancras Way *NW1*. Known first as Longwich Lane and later as the King's Road, this was the ancient track winding beside the FLEET RIVER, which led from the north to OLD ST PANCRAS CHURCH and on into London. By 1760 it was said to be edged with 'dust heaps and open drains'. In 1809 the St Pancras Workhouse was opened near to where the ST PANCRAS HOSPITAL now stands, at the southern end. Most of the rest of the road is now flanked by warehouses and factories.

St Patrick *Soho Square, W1*. According to an 18th-century church manuscript, in 1791 'a very numerous and respectable body of Catholics conceived the wise and charitable project of establishing a Catholic Chapel' in the neighbourhood of ST GILES'S which was 'inhabited principally by the poorest and least informed of the Irish who resort to this country'. And so, under the inspiration of the energetic Father Arthur O'Leary, a small chapel was built in 1792 on the south-east side of SOHO SQUARE and dedicated to St Patrick. In 1891 this was demolished and replaced by the present Italianate church designed by John Kelly.

St Paul *Bow Common (Burdett Road), E3*. The first church here was designed by Rhode Hawkins in 1858 and financed by William Cotton of LEYTONSTONE. Bishop Blomfield presented the church with a gold communion service made for Queen Adelaide. Bombed in the 2nd World War, it was rebuilt in 1958–60 to the distinguished designs of Robert Maguire. The mosaics are by Charles Lutyens.

St Paul *Clapham (Rectory Grove), SW4*. The site of the first parish church, dedicated to the Holy Trinity, is first recorded in the 12th century. In 1775 a new parish church was built on the Common and the old one was demolished except for the north aisle and transept which were used for burial services. In 1815 these were also demolished to make way for a chapel-of-ease designed by Christopher Edmonds. Sir Arthur Blomfield added the chancel in 1879. William Hewer, Samuel Pepys's friend, was buried here in 1715.

St Paul *Covent Garden, WC2*. Designed by Inigo Jones for Francis Russell, 4th Earl of Bedford (*see* COVENT GARDEN), it was the first new Anglican church to be built in London since the Reformation. According to Horace Walpole, Bedford, a low churchman, did not want to go to 'any considerable expense; "In short" said he, "I would not have it much better than a barn." 'Well, then,' replied Jones, 'You shall have the handsomest barn in England.' And this, at a cost of nearly £5,000, is what he was given.

A Tuscan pastiche, at once plain and majestic, it was placed on the western side of the square, its three doors (two of them since removed) looking out through the smooth, tall columns which support the huge eaves of the roof, towards a sundial, surrounded by newly planted trees and painted benches, in the middle of the piazza. Work was begun in 1631 and completed in 1633, though the church was not consecrated until 1638. The main entrance facing on to the square beneath the portico has never been used, since the Bishop of London, William Laud, insisted that the altar must be given its traditional place against the east wall. So smaller side doors have to be used instead. The interior is a simple double square, 100 ft by 50 ft. The church was given its own parish in 1645.

In 1788 Thomas Hardwick began a major renovation which included refacing the interior with stone. A contemporary newspaper observed that a new church would have cost little more, but no one in the parish was 'so deficient in understanding as to propose rebuilding a church which for a century and a half has been the admiration of scientific men from all quarters of the globe!'. In September 1795 a fire destroyed nearly all the work which had been done, and the building had to be restored once more. Hardwick was put in charge and he reproduced the old church faithfully. In 1871 William Butterfield was commissioned

Thomas Archer's baroque St Paul, Deptford, of 1712–13, and the Rector's House (right). From an engraving by Toms, c. 1736.

to carry out alterations. He removed the galleries, raised the chancel and rearranged the furniture. This is when the east doors were blocked up. The organ is by Henry Bevington who made it in 1861, incorporating part of the case, which had been designed by Hardwick in 1795, and perhaps parts of William Gray's earlier organ.

Famous preachers who have given sermons here include John Wesley who wrote in his journal in 1784, 'It is the largest and best-constructed parish church that I have preached in for several years, yet some hundreds were obliged to go away, not being able to get in.' J.M.W. Turner was baptised here in 1775 and W.S. Gilbert in 1837. Those buried here include Samuel Butler in 1680; Sir Peter Lely in 1680; William Wycherley, 1715; Grinling Gibbons, 1721; Thomas Arne, composer of *Rule Britannia*, 1778; Charles Macklin, the actor, 1792; Thomas Rowlandson, 1827; and Ellen Terry in 1928. Her ashes are preserved on the south wall. Also perhaps buried here in 1670 after being hanged at TYBURN was the highwayman, Claude Duval, under a stone which is inscribed:

Here lies Du Vall: Reader, if male thou art
Look to thy purse; if female to thy heart.

There is, however, no entry to confirm the burial in the parish register and he may have been interred at ST GILES-IN-THE-FIELDS. There are monuments to Arne on the north wall and Macklin on the south. Above a notice recording the burial of Grinling Gibbons is an example of his work brought here from ST PAUL'S.

The church has always been associated with the theatre, since both the THEATRE ROYAL, DRURY LANE and the ROYAL OPERA HOUSE are in the parish. Garrick attended services here. There are numerous plaques inside commemorating well-known actors, actresses, playwrights and others connected with the theatre from C.B. Cochran, the impresario, to W. MacQueen-Pope, the theatrical historian. Leading actors read the lessons at most services.

The portico provides the setting for the opening scene of Shaw's *Pygmalion* in which pedestrians run under it for shelter from 'torrents of heavy summer rain' with 'cat whistles blowing frantically in all directions'. According to a plaque fixed to the wall of the portico, it was here, too, that Pepys on 9 May 1662 witnessed 'an Italian puppet play' which was 'very pretty, the best [he] ever saw'. But it seems more likely that the performance took place in the central open space within the piazza. There is, however, a special puppeteers' service in the church each year.

St Paul *Deptford (High Street), SE8*. A church of great distinction built by Thomas Archer in 1712–30. Tablets commemorate John Harrison who was the founder of, and first surgeon at, the LONDON HOSPITAL, Dr Charles Burney brother of Fanny Burney, the novelist, and a delightful inscription recalls a midwife, Margaret Hawtrees, in the following words:

She was an indulgent mother, and the best of wives. She brought into this world more than three thousand lives.

Because of its contribution to the wellbeing of the community in a deprived area, the church received £50,000 from local authorities and this, together with a further £50,000 privately raised, enabled much excellent restoration work to be carried out in 1975–6 so that St Paul's has good claim to be considered externally as one of the finest parish churches architecturally in the whole of London.

St Paul *Hammersmith, W6*. Replaces the 17th-century church which was in need of constant repair and too small. It was designed by H.R. Gough in

Gothic style. The foundation stone was laid in 1882, but, for lack of funds, the church was not finished until 1889.

Its most interesting monument is the bust of Charles II erected by Sir Nicholas Crisp. After the King's death in 1685, his heart, enclosed in a small urn, was placed upon this monument. The pulpit came from ALL HALLOWS THE GREAT, UPPER THAMES STREET and is reputed to be by Grinling Gibbons. The church, dominated by the flyover which runs a few yards from it, now stands in a garden formed from the grassed-over churchyard and still retains a few of the old tombs and some of the gravestones against a wall, although their inscriptions are rapidly becoming obliterated.

St Paul *Knightsbridge (Wilton Place), SW1*. A large brick church built to the perpendicular designs of Thomas Cundy the Younger in 1840–3. The first vicar, the Revd W.J.E. Bennett, resigned in 1851 after being constantly rebuked by Bishop Blomfield for his High Church practices. Alterations to the church were carried out under the supervision of R.J. Withers in the 1870s and improvements were made by Walter Sorel in 1933–40. Many fashionable weddings have been held here.

St Paul *Shadwell (The Highway), E1*. Built in 1656 as a chapel-of-ease to ST DUNSTAN'S STEPNEY. Thomas Neale, who owned property in SHADWELL, bore most of the cost. He had leased land from the Dean of ST PAUL'S, hence the dedication. In 1669 the chapel was augmented by a church and a parish 'distinct and separate from Stepney'. It served an almost exclusively nautical area and during 1730–90 over 175 names of sea captains and their wives appear in the registers. It was sometimes known as the Church of the Sea Captains. Wesley preached here on five occasions (in 1770, 1778, 1780, 1789 and 1790).

By 1811 the church had become dilapidated and was closed. Parishioners petitioned for a new church. The consequent Enabling Act of 1817 stated that there was a population of 10,000 souls 'the far greater part of them being labourers in the docks and on the river'. The present church, built in 1819–20, is by John Walters and cost £27,000, which was paid by the Waterloo

Commissioners. Only ST PANCRAS NEW CHURCH cost more. The chief expense was the impressive tower and spire. The body is brick with stucco dressings. Butterfield 'improved' the galleried interior in 1848 by removing the organ and an entrance from the east end and forming a sanctuary space by building flanking vestry rooms. A three-light window was cut and the 17th-century font replaced. The east window glass is by John Hayward.

St Paul *Wimbledon Park (Augustus Road), SW19*. Built of brick in two stages under one wagon roof. The chancel was built in 1888, using the nave of the temporary church; the new nave was built in 1896.

St Paul's Cathedral The fifth cathedral to be built on a site where, according to tradition and to evidence discovered after the GREAT FIRE, there once stood a Roman Temple dedicated to Diana. According to Bede, the 1st cathedral was founded and dedicated to St Paul in 604 by St Ethelbert, King of Kent, the first Christian King in England. At that time St Melitus became the 1st Bishop of London. This building, probably of wood, was destroyed by fire. It was rebuilt in stone between 675 and 685 by Eorconweald, 4th Bishop of London, whose tomb became a place of pilgrimage throughout the Middle Ages. The *Anglo-Saxon Chronicle* states that this 2nd St Paul's was destroyed by the Vikings in 961. The first great Ecclesiastical Council of the English Church was held, under the presidency of Archbishop Lanfranc, in the 3rd Saxon cathedral which was, in its turn, destroyed by fire in 1087.

The construction of the Norman cathedral began immediately afterwards under Maurice, Bishop of London, chancellor and chaplain to William the Conqueror, whose son, William II, was a generous benefactor. Built of Caen stone, brought by sea and up the Thames, 'Old St Paul's' became one of the largest buildings in England, considerably larger and higher than today's building, and topped by the tallest spire ever to have been built. (This spire was struck by lightning in 1447, and was not rebuilt until 15 years later.) At the west end were two great bell towers which were also used as prisons; at the east end was the

Old St Paul's Cathedral from Hollar's view of 1656. The steeple was struck by lightning in 1561 and not replaced.

DOMVS CAPITVLARIS S. PAVLI
Meridie Prospectus.

The Chapter House of Old St Paul's Cathedral was built by William Ramsay, the mason, in 1332. Etching by Hollar, 1656.

rose window, so renowned that the dandy Absolon in Chaucer's *Miller's Tale* had 'Powles window corven on his shoos'. In the 12th century William of Malmesbury contended that the cathedral was 'worthy of being numbered amongst the most famous of buildings'.

In the early Middle Ages there was a law school within the cathedral precincts, but in the 13th century Henry III forbade law to be taught within the City, intending thus to benefit the schools he had founded at Oxford. In 1284 the precincts were enclosed by walls to keep out robbers and marauders. The course of these walls is defined today by Creed Lane, Ave Maria Lane, Paternoster Row, Old Change and Carter Lane. There were six gates in the walls, the main one at Ludgate Hill. Within the precincts, over the years, were built the Chapter House surrounded by a two-storey cloister (remains of which can be seen in the gardens to the south side of the nave); St Gregory's parish church; the Bishop's Palace; the Pardon Churchyard, circumscribed by a cloister; a College of Minor Canons; and St Faith's Chapel which was demolished in the middle of the 13th century in order to lengthen the east end of the cathedral so that it could accommodate the increasing numbers of clergy. This chapel was rebuilt in the crypt where, more than 700 years later, it is still known as the Chapel of St Faith. Also built within the precincts in the early Middle Ages were ST PAUL'S SCHOOL; Paul's Cross; and the Jesus Bell Tower, a free-standing campanile, whose great bell summoned the citizens of London to a thrice-yearly folk-moot at Paul's Cross. Attendance was compulsory until the reign of Edward II at the beginning of the 14th century. Papal Bulls, announcements of victories, of royal marriages, of excommunications and of royal proclamations were issued from Paul's Cross; and for religious services the congregation sat or stood in the open air. The Cross was a wooden, lead-covered pulpit from which political orations were made on occasion and from which sermons were regularly preached. Among distinguished divines who preached there were Ridley, Latimer, Gardiner, Coverdale and Laud. In spite of being struck by lightning in 1382, it survived until the Civil War when it was destroyed in 1643 by order of Parliament. Jane Shore, mistress of Edward

IV, was forced to do penance 'before the Crosse ... with a taper in her hand'. In 1517 a maypole was 'denounced to death' here, and here, too, ten years later, Tyndale's translation of the *Bible* was publicly burned, as were Luther's works. Henry VIII ordered the 'preaching down' of the papal authority every Sunday, while in his Roman Catholic daughter, Mary's, reign, Bishop Gardiner anathematised the Protestants. Carlyle called Paul's Cross the 'Times newspaper of the Middle Ages'. A memorial designed by Sir Reginald Blomfield and sculpted by Sir Bertram Mackennal was erected almost on the site in 1910.

Old St Paul's was the focal point of many processions, services of thanksgiving, and ceremonies, including the Boy Bishop ceremony in which a boy was elected on St Nicholas Day (6 December) to fulfil various duties usually performed by the bishop, until Holy Innocents' Day (28 December). On that day the Boy Bishop sometimes even preached a sermon. The practice was abolished during the Reformation by Henry VIII, revived by Mary Tudor, and abolished finally by Elizabeth I. In 1400 the body of the deposed King Richard II lay in state here, and here Henry V prayed and made offerings before he embarked for France in the summer of 1415. Bishop Beaufort read the news of the victory at Agincourt from the Cathedral steps and a month later the King himself, bareheaded and wearing a purple robe, accompanied by a 'cavalcade of scarlet-clad aldormen, citizens and craftsmen' was met by bishops at the west door, whence he followed them to the high altar. Ten years later Henry's only child, the four-year-old Henry VI, was 'led upon his feet between the Lord Protector and the Duke of Exeter unto the choir, whence he was borne to the high altar'. After his murder in 1471 the body of this 'royal saint' was exposed in St Paul's 'and his face was open that every man might see it'. In 1501 Arthur, Prince of Wales, was married here in great splendour to Princess Catherine of Aragon who, after his death, became the wife of his younger brother, later Henry VIII.

It was Henry's determination to divorce Catherine, in the hope of begetting a son by a younger wife, which provoked the English Reformation during which the Cathedral suffered to such an extent that the Dean and Chapter could not afford to maintain the fabric. In 1549 the High Altar was demolished and an ordinary table was used to administer the sacrament. The reredos, too, was completely destroyed and the nave, known as Paul's Walk, became a 'common thoroughfare between Carter Lane and Paternoster Row for people with vessels of ale and beer, baskets of bread, fish, flesh and fruit, men leading mules, horses and other beasts'. Here servants were hired, lawyers received their clients, and the rood-loft, tombs and font were used as shop-counters; indeed the standard measure of a foot was derived from the carved foot of Algar, the first prebendary of Islington, which rested at the base of a pillar. Bishop Pilkington wrote of the nave in 1560 'The south side for Popery and Usury; the north for Simony; and the horse-fair in the middle for all kinds of bargains, meetings, brawlings, murders, conspiracies; and the font for ordinary payments of money.' In the midst of this traffic and commerce, services were held in the choir. In 1569 the first public lottery was drawn at the west door, the proceeds being used for the repair and reinforcement of the harbours of the kingdom rather than of the Cathedral.

Following the reign of Queen Mary Tudor – during which the pomp and splendour of Rome flourished in

St Paul's for the last time – Church of England services were again celebrated under the new Protestant dean, Alexander Nowell. Elizabeth I often attended services here. On one occasion she put Dean Nowell in his place, interrupting a diatribe against worship of images by saying, peremptorily and clearly, 'To your text, Mr Dean, we have heard enough.' Queen Elizabeth was a generous benefactor, contributing £6,000 towards the restoration of the roof after its destruction by fire in 1561. But this sum, and further money donated by Bishop Grindal, were sufficient only for makeshift repairs. The spire, which had been destroyed in the 1561 fire, was not replaced.

This was the state of affairs in 1620 when James I became interested in the cathedral. It was not, however, until 1628 that extensive repairs were begun. In this year William Laud became Bishop of London and Inigo Jones was appointed King's Surveyor. Jones cleared the precincts of the incongruous houses and shops; he refaced the walls of the transept and built a classic portico, for which Charles I paid from his own purse, in front of the west façade. By this time, in the opinion of John Webb, St Paul's 'contracted the Envy of all Christendom for a Piece of Architecture not to be paralleled in these last ages of the World'.

Work on the restoration continued during 1634–43 when it was interrupted by the Civil War. The £17,000 remaining in the restoration fund was seized by the Parliamentarians to pay their troops. The nave was used by Cromwell's army as a cavalry barracks, and the Lady Chapel, somewhat less unsuitably, as a preaching house. The porch of the cathedral was let to seamstresses, pedlars and other small traders. The ravages wrought by the Parliamentary army included the smashing of windows, mutilation of effigies, burning of carved woodwork and destruction of the statues of James I and Charles I which had stood on Inigo Jones's portico. The scaffolding supporting the roof of the nave was sold and the roof fell in. In 1647 the Bishop's Palace was demolished. By the end of the Civil War the Cathedral had fallen into decay.

In 1663, three years after the Restoration of the monarchy, the Dean and Chapter, having decided on yet another renovation of St Paul's, asked Christopher Wren to survey the Cathedral and to suggest how best to effect the repairs. Wren, then 31, had recently been appointed Professor of Astronomy at Oxford. Son of the Dean of Windsor, he had been educated at WESTMINSTER and at Wadham College, Oxford. A 'miracle of a youth', as John Evelyn called him, he was one of the founders of the ROYAL SOCIETY of which he became president in 1680. He very strongly recommended demolition and rebuilding, but as the commission adamantly rejected this he eventually drew up plans, one of which was accepted in 1666, only six days before the outbreak of the Great Fire. Samuel Pepys wrote that he had seen on 7 September 'a miserable sight of Paul's church, with all the roofs fallen, and the body of the quire fallen into St Fayth's'. About two months later he wrote that he had stopped 'at Paul's and in the Convocation House Yard did there see the body of Robert Braybrooke, Bishop of London, that died in 1404. He fell down in the tomb out of the great church into St Fayth's this late fire, and is here seen his skeleton with the flesh on; but all tough and dry like a spongy dry leather, or touchwood all upon his bones . . . Many flocking to see it'.

The only monument to survive the Fire was that of Dr John Donne, the poet, who had been Dean of St

Paul's for the last ten years of his life. It is now in the south choir aisle. As it was found impossible to restore what remained of the building after the Fire, it was decided to demolish it and rebuild from the very foundations. Wren tried using gunpowder in the demolition, frightening the inhabitants of Ludgate Hill, who thought London was undergoing an earthquake. Realising that explosives were too dangerous, he razed the remains of the walls with battering rams.

Wren designed three plans for the new cathedral. While he was working on the first, the so-called New Model, in 1669, he was appointed Surveyor General. It is said that when his second, his own favourite, the Great Model, approved by Charles II, was rejected, he burst into tears. The Great Model, 20 ft long and constructed of oak, is part of a collection of architectural models on display in the Trophy Room, so called because Nelson's trophies were exhibited there before his funeral. Wren's third design, the Warrant Design, was at last accepted. The royal warrant, issued in May 1675, fortunately contained a clause giving Wren 'liberty . . . to make some variations rather ornamental than essential, as from time to time he should see proper'. Between the laying of the foundation stone with Masonic rites (Wren was a Mason) the following month and the completion of the building in 1710, he considerably modified the Warrant Design, dispensing with the planned steeple and shortening the nave.

The new building was begun on a traditional cruciform Gothic ground plan with a long nave and choir. This Wren modified, so that the meeting of the nave, transept and chancel aisles is circular; but the design of the nave is conventional in having a triforium and clerestory. After 21 years of work on the building a problem arose over the supply of Portland stone; for, as Evelyn recorded in his diary in February 1696, 'an earth quake in Dorset-shire by Portland [hindered] the conveyance of that materi[a]ll for the finishing of St Paules'.

Alert to the probability that economies would be insisted on by the Commissioners, and even by Parliament, if he had started building at the east end and progressed to the west, Wren arranged for work to start on the overall ground plan, so that the whole building was to go up stage by stage. As a result it was not possible to hold the first service until 1697. He was, indeed, justified in taking precautions against the parsimony of the authorities, for in that same year, 1697, a Parliamentary committee, exasperated by the slow rate of progress, voted that his annual salary of £200 should be reduced by half; and not until 1711, after personally petitioning Queen Anne, did he receive his arrears, by which time he was nearly 80 years old.

When Wren had decided on the dome instead of the planned tall steeple, by a happy chance the stone which he asked a labourer to fetch to mark the exact centre of the dome proved to be a fragment of tombstone on which was incised *Resurgam*. Wren commissioned the sculptor, Caius Gabriel Cibber, to carve this motto beneath a phoenix rising from the flames in the pediment above the south door. The dome presented a constructional problem. As Wren envisaged it from the outside, it would be too lofty to be suitable for the inside of the cathedral. His solution was to build a smaller dome to be seen from the interior; over this he built a brick cone to support the weight of the lantern, which is surmounted by the ball and cross; and over the interior dome and brick cone he built the outer

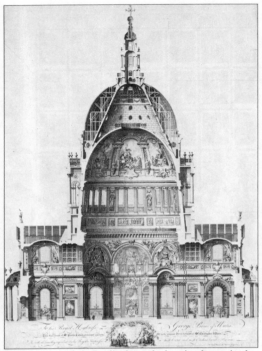

A section through St Paul's shows the interior decoration by James Thornhill and others. From an engraving of 1755.

dome, 60 ft taller, one of the most famous of London's landmarks. The cross is 365 ft above the pavement.

The outer dome consists of a timber frame covered with Derbyshire lead; the inner dome is brick-built and is painted in grisaille with frescoes of stories from the life of St Paul by Sir James Thornhill. There is a story that, while working on his frescoes, Thornhill stepped back to inspect the effect and was so close to the edge of the platform that his assistant was afraid to shout a warning. Instead, with great presence of mind, he started to besmear the painting, at which Thornhill angrily sprang forward towards him and was thus saved from probable death. Immediately below the 24 windows in the dome is the Whispering Gallery, the best place from which to view the Thornhill frescoes. It is 100 ft above the floor and is famous for its acoustics. If you whisper against the wall you can be heard clearly on the opposite side of the Gallery 107 ft away.

The dome is supported by eight massive floor-standing piers, faced with Corinthian pilasters, with eight arches. Above the columns is the Stone Gallery, which affords a fine view over London. Above this gallery, at the apex of the inner dome and the base of the lantern, is the Inner Golden Gallery. The Outer Golden Gallery, from which an even more extensive view can be enjoyed, is at the apex of the outer dome. The lantern, in the baroque style in contrast to the classical dome and its supporting columns, harmonises with the graceful west towers. These towers were an afterthought, designed by Wren at the age of 75. There was to have been a clock in each tower, but the space for the clock in the north-west tower still remains empty. In the lower part of the south-west tower is the elegant Geometrical Staircase, the work of the master-mason, William Kempster, with

Tijou's wrought-iron balustrade leading up to the Library. Much of the original collection of books was destroyed in the Great Fire. When Henry Compton, Bishop of London, died in 1713 he bequeathed half his collection of books to St Paul's, and this formed the nucleus of the Library, which also contains the Cathedral Archives, some dating back to the 11th century.

The clock room in the upper part of the south-west tower houses three old bells on which the clock strikes. The largest, on which the hours are sounded, is Great Tom, and on this bell are tolled the deaths and funerals of members of the royal family, of BISHOPS OF LONDON, of Deans of St Paul's and of the LORD MAYOR of London should he die in office. In the north-west campanile hangs the peal of 12 bells given to St Paul's in 1877 by Baroness Burdett-Coutts, the philanthropist, and seven CITY LIVERY COMPANIES. They ring out a full peal on Sundays and on certain other special days.

The imposing west front of the cathedral is approached by a wide flight of steps, above which is a portico of 12 columns in pairs; above this rises another portico of eight columns in pairs which support a high pediment surmounted by a statue of St Paul flanked on either side by statues of St Peter and St James, all the work of Francis Bird, who was also responsible for the font and the original monument to Queen Anne, a copy of which stands outside the west front (*see* STATUES).

Bird was one of several distinguished artists and craftsmen whom Wren was able to employ. Tijou, the French master-ironworker, all of whose known work is in England, wrought the gates to the north and south chancel aisles, as well as the balustrading for the Geometrical Staircase, and collaborated with Grinling Gibbons on the Quire Screens. The choir stalls are the work of Gibbons who carved them to perfection, front and back. John Evelyn had brought Gibbons to Wren's notice, and wrote about one of his carvings 'there being nothing even in nature so tender, and delicate as the flowers and festoones about it'. The organ on each side above the choir stalls designed by Wren, and played by Handel and Mendelssohn, is Gibbons's work. The mosaics in the choir, depicting the Creation, are of much later date; they were designed in the late 19th century by G.F. Watts, A. Brittan and Alfred Stevens. Also 19th-century is Holman Hunt's *Light of the World*, which hangs in the south aisle.

It is remarkable that St Paul's should have been built over a period of 35 years under the supervision of only one master-builder, Thomas Strong, and one architect. Although engaged in building more than 50 churches from 1666 onwards, Wren went every week, often on a Saturday, to superintend the progress. When the work was nearing completion, he used to be hoisted up to the lantern in a basket. Since he was reluctant to undertake the task himself, his son performed the ceremony of laying the last and highest stone in the lantern.

Fittingly, he was one of the first persons to be buried in the crypt. His tomb is marked by a plain black marble slab. Above it on the wall is the inscription composed by his son, *Lector, si monumentum requiris, circumspice*. R.H. Barham, a minor canon of St Paul's, described it irreverently in 'The Cynotaph':
Though I've always considered Sir Christopher Wren,
As an architect, one of the greatest of men;
And, talking of Epitaphs – much I admire his,
'*Circumspice, si monumentum requiris*';
Which an erudite Verger translated to me,
'If you ask for his Monument, Sir-come-spy-see!'

759

On return from one of his frequent visits to St Paul's, Wren died at his home at HAMPTON COURT at the age of 91. There is another memorial to him, a bronze plaque in the gallery over the north aisle, presented in 1924 by the Architectural League of New York as a tribute to his 'inspiration and enduring influence on American architecture'.

Also buried in the crypt is Lord Nelson whose tomb is placed immediately below the dome. The graceful black marble sarcophagus was designed originally for Cardinal Wolsey by the Florentine, Benedetto de Rovezzane, but it was confiscated by Henry VIII, and lay neglected at Windsor Castle for nearly three centuries until it was used for Nelson's interment in January 1806. Wellington's imposing tomb, towards the east end of the crypt, is a sarcophagus of Cornish porphyry on a granite base. Several other distinguished soldiers, as well as sailors and airmen, musicians, artists and men of letters, are interred in the crypt, which is believed to be the longest in Europe. The chapel for the knights and members of the Order of the British Empire is in the east end of the crypt.

There are comparatively few monuments in St Paul's. There was in fact none until 1795, when John Bacon's monument to John Howard, the pioneer of prison reform, was erected at the entrance to the choir. Bacon was also the sculptor of Samuel Johnson's statue. The third to appear was Flaxman's statue of Sir Joshua Reynolds.

The many ceremonies which have taken place in New St Paul's have included the thanksgiving service for victory at Blenheim in 1704, attended, according to Evelyn, by 'the Duchesse of Marlbrow, in a very plain garment, the Q [Queen Anne] full of Jewells'; Nelson's funeral in 1806; thanksgiving for peace after the Napoleonic Wars in 1814 when the Duke of Wellington carried the Sword of State before the Prince Regent; Wellington's own funeral in 1852; in 1872 a thanksgiving service was attended by Queen Victoria for the recovery of her son, the Prince of Wales, from typhoid, an event which marked the end of republicanism as a political force in England; and in 1981 the wedding of Charles, Prince of Wales and Lady Diana Spencer.

During the aerial bombardment in the 2nd World War, St Paul's, though particularly vulnerable by its size and height, was comparatively unharmed. The vigilant volunteers, St Paul's Watch, protected it from damage from the tons of incendiary bombs which were

Spectators outside the window of Bowles's print shop in St Paul's Churchyard. From a caricature of c. 1760.

dropped in its immediate vicinity. In one night alone, just after Christmas 1940, no less than 28 incendiary bombs fell. The high explosive bombs and the land mine which fell in the precincts were defused before they could go off, but a bomb fell in the north transept, much of which crashed through into the crypt, while another destroyed the Victorian high altar and damaged its marble reredos. The present high altar with its imposing *baldachino*, commemorating the Commonwealth dead of both World Wars, was consecrated in 1958. The former Jesus Chapel behind the High Altar, damaged in 1940, has been restored and refurnished as the American Chapel, a tribute to the 28,000 American citizens based in the United Kingdom who lost their lives in the 2nd World War.

St Paul's Churchyard *EC4*. Once a place of execution for martyrs to their faith; and, before the GREAT FIRE, the principal centre of the London book trade. From before the end of the 15th century there are records of stationers (the general term for booksellers) who had shops here. It was a central place for doing business and probably foreigners could trade without the permission of the CITY LIVERY COMPANIES. The *Sarum Missal*, of 1500, contains the earliest known imprint which is commonly met with in later books: 'sold by the booksellers in St Paul's Churchyard'. According to Gordon Duff, 'The native printers whose business premises were situated in other parts of the city soon saw the necessity, brought about by the competition of these foreign booksellers, of themselves setting up shops in the churchyard. Thus Wynkyn de Worde, who printed at the Sun in FLEET STREET, had a shop by the Cathedral with the sign of 'Our Lady of Pity'. Notary also had a small shop there (*cellula* he calls it) though his main place of

The north front of St Paul's Cathedral in 1798. From an aquatint by Malton.

business was outside TEMPLE BAR. Richard Faques who lived and printed in the STRAND had a shop in the churchyard called the ABC. The shops in St Paul's Churchyard were of two distinct classes. There were the substantial houses situated all round the churchyard in which the printer could both reside and carry on his business, and there were also a large number of booths clustered around the cathedral which were merely shops and had no accommodation for either living or printing.

Among those who had businesses here was John Newbery, who moved to the Bible and Sun in 1745. He was a bookseller, publisher and vendor of patent medicines of which 'Dr James's Fever Powder' was best known. He published several periodicals to which Johnson and Goldsmith contributed. He is, however, best remembered as the first to make a special business of publishing books for children. His 'Juvenile Library' of tiny volumes was bound in flowered and gilt Dutch paper. In *Little Goody Two Shoes* (probably written anonymously by Goldsmith) the heroine's father 'died miserably seized with a violent fever where Dr James's powder was not to be had'. Newbery's *Lilliputian Magazine* was the first children's periodical. He also published *The Christian Magazine*, edited by Dr Dodd (afterwards executed for forgery), and *The British Magazine*. Many of his children's books and his periodicals were written anonymously by Newbery's regular authors such as Goldsmith and Johnson and occasionally Smollett and also by Newbery himself. Goldsmith portrays him in *The Vicar of Wakefield* as 'the philanthropic publisher of Saint Paul's Churchyard' and describes him as 'a red-faced good-natured little man who was always in a hurry'. Dr Johnson also gently satirises him in the *Idler*. He died in 1767 and the business was continued by his son Francis Newbery who, in 1779, transferred the patent medicines to a new building by the architect John Crunden in the north east of Saint Paul's Churchyard, which was inscribed in large letters of stone 'The only Warehouse of Dr James's Powder'. John Newbery, some years before his death, had assisted his nephew (also called Francis Newbery) to set up at the Crown, PATERNOSTER ROW. It was to this Francis Newbery that Johnson sold for £60 the manuscript of the *Vicar of Wakefield* on behalf of his destitute friend, Oliver Goldsmith.

The cathedral Chapter House at No. 67 was built to the designs of Wren in 1712–14; it was gutted in the 2nd World War but has been restored. The deanery in DEAN'S COURT was also designed by Wren in 1670. The monument to Queen Anne (*see* STATUES) stands on the site of the Church of St Gregory (*see* ST PAUL'S). No. 37 is the site of the first ST PAUL'S SCHOOL. The Gunpowder Plot conspirators were hanged, drawn and quartered here. The bronze, *Young Lovers*, is by George Erlich (1973). The monument designed by Blomfield marks the site where the medieval Paul's Cross stood. It is a tall column surmounted by Mackennal's bronze of St Paul with a gilt cross (1910).

St Paul's Coffee House *St Paul's Churchyard.* First mentioned in 1702. An anecdote of 1764 relates how some poor parsons, who came here to compete for 'an occasional burial or sermon', were tricked when a group of bucks lured them in, pretending to have a curacy to offer them. In 1769 Boswell belonged to a club of clergymen, physicians and professional men which met here for conversation every Thursday. By

1772 the landlord had moved to the LONDON COFFEE HOUSE, LUDGATE HILL.

St Paul's Cray *Kent.* An area of contrasts: the church (St Paulinus) was originally Saxon, and the parish spread symmetrically up both sides of the Cray valley. Nowadays the west side is mostly a LONDON COUNTY COUNCIL estate of the 1950s and the east side comparatively unspoilt countryside. The Common (west) remains as it was, while traces of the village linger along the river. St Barnabas Church (1960s) stands on a Bronze Age site.

St Paul's Gardens, *EC4.* Small gardens on the corner of NEW CHANGE and CANNON STREET. A plaque marks the spot where the building from which OLD CHANGE took its name stood.

St Paul's Girls' School *Brook Green, W6.* An independent school which, like ST PAUL'S SCHOOL, BARNES, is part of the Christian Foundation originally provided by Dean Colet in 1509. The Foundation's Trustees are the Worshipful Company of MERCERS and it was their decision in 1895 to buy The Grange, Brook Green and three adjacent houses as premises for a girls' school which was opened there in 1904. The school's governors include, in addition to the trustees, representatives of the universities and 'lady members'. The school has always stressed sound academic education and prepared some girls for university entrance and for future training for the professions. It owed much to its early High Mistresses Frances Gray (1904–27) and Ethel Strudwick (1927–48). The school's high standard of music was established by its first Director of Music, Gustav Holst (1905–34). New buildings and 5½ acres for playing fields were added in 1916 and a science block in 1933.

The school was evacuated in 1939 but returned to Brook Green in 1940 and later suffered some bomb damage. Colet Girls' School became the official junior department of the school in 1944 and a new St Paul's Girls' Preparatory School building was opened in 1958. In 1965 a school consultative committee (with a pupil as chairman) was started and the prefect system was abolished. In 1982 there were 560 girls aged 11–18.

St Paul's Hospital for Urological Diseases *see* ST PETER'S HOSPITAL FOR STONE AND OTHER URINARY DISEASES.

St Paul's School *Lonsdale Road, Barnes, SW13.* Founded in 1509 by John Colet, Dean of ST PAUL'S CATHEDRAL who was also a Freeman of the MERCERS' COMPANY, which administered the school. At its foundation, the school was the largest in England, providing free education for 153 children (a number traditionally associated with the Gospel miracle of the draught of fishes; a fish was the school emblem) who were to be 'of all nations and countries indifferently'. Originally the school was opposite the east side of ST PAUL'S CATHEDRAL, and like it, was destroyed in the GREAT FIRE. It was rebuilt in 1670 at a cost of £6,000 and was replaced in 1822 with a new building costing £23,000. A 4th building was opened at HAMMERSMITH in 1884 (at a cost of £41,000 for the site and £116,000 for the building), and the school moved to its present buildings at BARNES in 1968.

In 1876 the Charity Commissioners approved a new scheme of management allowing the MERCERS'

COMPANY to retain control of estates and property (for the benefit of the school) whilst school management was administered by a Board of Governors consisting of representatives of the MERCERS' COMPANY and of the Universities of Oxford, Cambridge and London. Changed administration, and the new interest in education toward the end of the 19th century, brought a new spirit to the school which expanded rapidly, especially after its removal from the CITY. It became one of the foremost schools in the country. In the 2nd World War it was evacuated to Crowthorne and became a boarding school, the HAMMERSMITH buildings being used by the army. It was there that planning and final briefing for the 1944 invasion of Europe took place. The school (which had acquired Colet Court as a junior school in 1943) returned to London after the war, becoming again predominantly a day school.

Famous pupils include the poet John Milton, diarist Samuel Pepys, the general John Churchill, 1st Duke of Marlborough, Judge Jeffreys, the astronomer Edmond Halley, the poet and author G.K. Chesterton and Field-Marshal Lord Montgomery.

St Peter   *Brockley (Wickham Road), SE4*. A church of striking and unusual design dating from 1866–70. The tower and adjoining vestibules open into the nave with arches of equal height. There is much decoration and nearly all the stained glass is by Clayton and Bell.

St Peter   *Clerkenwell*. Built in 1869 as a memorial to the Smithfield Martyrs. It was badly damaged during the 2nd World War and demolished in 1955.

St Peter   *Ealing (Mount Park Road), W5*. A temporary church constructed of corrugated iron and dedicated to St Andrew was erected on this site in 1882. It was popularly referred to as 'the Iron Church'. When the Presbyterians started to build in Mount Park Road in 1889, the vestry felt 'that this Church should set the example of giving way in face of a threatened dispute about the Saint's name', and with commendable tact abandoned the Scottish saint in favour of St Peter. The present building was begun in 1891. The foundation stone was laid in 1892 by Princess Helena, and the ceremony of consecration was carried out by Frederick Temple, Bishop of London, on 15 July 1893. It was designed in the Italianate manner in white freestone by John D. Sedding. He died, however, before work on the building started and his assistant, Henry Wilson, was appointed his successor.

St Peter   *Eaton Square, SW1*. A Greek revival building designed by Henry Hakewill in 1824–7. In 1870 G.H. Wilkinson was appointed vicar and such was his popularity that, although the church had a capacity of 1,650, it could not hold all his congregation. In 1872–5 the chancel was added and the nave enlarged by Sir Arthur Blomfield. The stained glass in the nave is by John Hayward. Admiral Sir Edward Codrington was buried here in 1851.

St Peter   *Hammersmith (Black Lion Lane), W6*. Built in 1829 by Edward Lapidge in Grecian style with an octagonal tower, at a cost of £14,000. In 1958 the churchyard was laid out as a garden of rest. On the grass outside the church, facing the GREAT WEST ROAD, is a stoneware statue of a reclining woman, by Karel Vogel. It was placed there in 1959.

St Peter   *Kennington Lane, SE11*. Not far from KENNINGTON OVAL CRICKET GROUND, but little known, is a church of distinction by one of the most notable of Victorian architects, John Loughborough Pearson.

St Peter's, built in 1863–4, lies on the edge of what used to be VAUXHALL GARDENS and its main altar stands on the site of the Neptune Fountain. In 1761 when the Gardens were at the height of their popularity, VAUXHALL was a village but by the time the church was built, LAMBETH, of which VAUXHALL forms a part, had a population of 162,000, nearly all poorly housed, and St Peter's was built to help cater for their spiritual needs.

St Peter   *London Docks (Wapping Lane), E1*. Built for the Revd Charles Lowder, head of the St George's Mission and a tireless High Church worker in the slums of East London. The church, designed by Frederick Hyde Pownall in what Lowder described as 'later First Pointed Gothic', was begun on St Peter's Day 1865 and replaced a tin church which had been used for ten years. After Lowder's death in 1880 Maurice Bingham Adams was engaged to design extensions in his memory. In 1884–94 a mortuary, chapel and a baptistry were consequently added. Further work was completed in 1940, only to be immediately destroyed by a bomb. Repairs were completed in 1949.

St Peter   *Petersham (Church Lane), Surrey*. Although mainly 17th-century, the chancel is 13th-century whilst the upper half of the west tower with its attractive octagonal lantern was rebuilt in 1790 and the south transept enlarged in 1840. The interior consists of a small chancel and two transepts (with galleries) opening out like long arms on the north and south sides. Both transepts are fitted with box-pews; and, as the baluster font dates from 1740, the pulpit with delicately wrought handrail from 1796, and the reading desk opposite from probably the same date, the Georgian atmosphere is preserved intact.

On the north wall of the chancel is a monument to George Cole and his wife dating from 1624; they recline one above the other with their grandson in a kneeling position below. Opposite is a well-carved wall cartouche to Sir Thomas Jenner who in 1683 was made RECORDER of London. He left 11 sons ('nine . . . lived to be men') and two daughters. Petersham's most famous citizen is remembered more modestly with a tablet on the west side of the north transept and a simple grave against the wall to the south-east of the church. He was Captain George Vancouver who, in the years 1791–4, circumnavigated the world and discovered Vancouver Island.

Prince Rupert of the Rhine is said, on no very reliable evidence, to have married Lady Francesca Bard here on 30 July 1664. Certainly the Queen Mother's parents – the Earl and Countess of Strathmore – were married at St Peter's in 1881.

St Peter   *Regent Square, WC1*. Built in 1822–4 by the Inwoods, who also designed ST PANCRAS NEW CHURCH. It was destroyed in the 2nd World War.

St Peter   *Vere Street, W1*. Once the Oxford Chapel, designed by James Gibbs and decorated for Edward Harley, 2nd Earl of Oxford, and his wife, Henrietta, in 1721 on the newly formed Cavendish-Harley Estate. It was considered in its earlier days 'the most beautiful edifice of its class in the metropolis', but little of its former elegance remains. The Tuscan portico has gone and the exterior has been stripped of all ornamentation. The Burne-Jones windows remain; but the interior is covered with *eau-de-nil* paint and the floor with cheap carpeting. The large columns, which carry supports for the delicate vault, have been left standing awkwardly on their pedestals after the removal of all seating. The west end has been boxed off by plate glass and deal doors. The church is now a daughter church of ALL SOULS LANGHAM PLACE.

St Peter *Walworth (Liverpool Grove), SE17*. Sir John Soane's first church built in 1823–5 with a classical portico and domed tower. When a bomb fell directly on it in the 2nd World War, 84 people were killed while sheltering in the crypt. In 1953 the restoration was completed by T.F. Ford. The stained glass is by Clare Dawson.

St Peter *Westcheap*. Built in the 12th century and rebuilt in the 16th when it was known as St Peter's at the Crosse in Cheape because of the memorial cross erected here by Edward I in 1291 to Queen Eleanor to mark one of the places where her body rested on the journey from Nottinghamshire to WESTMINSTER ABBEY. It became a holy shrine, adorned with religious carvings, and was consequently removed by the Puritans. Musicians often performed on the leads of the church during processions; and it was here that Elizabeth I on her procession through the City was presented with a copy of the English translation of the Bible. The church was not rebuilt after the GREAT FIRE. In the churchyard, where three LORD MAYORS are buried, is a plane tree said to have been that mentioned in Wordsworth's poem, 'Poor Susan'.

St Peter ad Vincula *Tower Green, EC3*. Founded in the 12th century for the use of TOWER prisoners and aptly dedicated to St Peter in chains. The present building is mostly 16th-century and is full of royal and noble bones. Anne Boleyn was buried in a common oak chest here in 1536. Other persons buried here include Thomas Cromwell, Earl of Essex, 1540; Margaret, Countess of Salisbury, 1541; Katherine Howard, 1542; Thomas, Lord Seymour, 1549; Protector Somerset, 1552; the Duke of Northumberland, Bishop Fisher and Sir Thomas More, 1535; Lady Jane Grey and her husband, Lord Guilford Dudley, 1554; Robert Devereux, Earl of Essex, 1601; the Duke of Monmouth, 1685; and the Jacobite lords of the 1745 Rebellion.

St Peter-le-Poer *Old Broad Street*. First mentioned in 1181. Early references were to St Peter's, BROAD STREET and it does not appear to have been called 'poor' until the 16th century. Stow says the name was 'for a difference from the other of that name, sometime peradventure a poore parish', though the church had been rebuilt in 1540 and Stow noted that in the parish 'at this present there be many fair houses, possessed by rich merchants and others'. The church was enlarged and repaired in 1615–30. It escaped serious damage in the GREAT FIRE. In 1704–20 Benjamin Hoadly, later Bishop of Winchester, was rector. It was repaired in 1716 but by 1788 it had become ruinous; it also projected into Broad Street and obstructed traffic. So, in 1788–92 it was rebuilt by

Jesse Gibson at a cost of £4,500 on part of the church cemetery. The brasses were sold to a plumber in the MINORIES. The Gibson church was circular, 54 ft in diameter, and the interior was lit by a vast lantern in the domed ceiling. A plain gallery of oak, with organ, encircled the interior except for the slight altar recess. In 1888 it was restored and the gallery was removed; but a few years later, in 1907, it was demolished and the parish was united with that of ST MICHAEL'S, CORNHILL. The site and materials were sold for £96,000. A new St Peter-le-Poer was erected at FRIERN BARNET.

St Peter, Paul's Wharf *Upper Thames Street*. First mentioned in 1170 as St Peter the Little. Stow described it as 'a small parish church . . . no monuments do remain'. A churchyard had been added in 1430, the gift of one Robert Frankeleyn. In 1625 and 1655 the church was repaired. Throughout the Commonwealth the liturgy of the Church of England and dispensation of the sacraments continued. Many of the nobility resorted here at this time and Evelyn noted in his diary, 'I heard the Common Prayer (a rare thing in these days) in St Peter's at Paul's Wharf March 25, 1649'. According to Newcourt, 'its galleries were hung with turkey carpet for accommodation of the nobility'. It was destroyed in the GREAT FIRE and not rebuilt. In 1670 the parish was united with that of ST BENET'S PAUL'S WHARF; in 1879 with that of ST NICHOLAS COLE ABBEY, and in 1954 with that of ST ANDREW BY THE WARDROBE. On the construction of the new building for the SALVATION ARMY, the memorial stones were moved from the churchyard to that of ST ANN BLACKFRIARS.

At the foot of Peter's Hill in UPPER THAMES STREET is a stone tablet with this inscription:

Before ye late Dreadful Fire
This was ye Parish Church
Of St Peters Pauls Wharf
Demolished Sept 1666
And now erected
For a Church Yarde. Anno Domini 1675.

St Peter and St Paul *Dagenham, Essex*. Consists of a 13th-century chancel, 15th-century north chapel, nave and west tower. The chancel and chapel are all that remain of the medieval building, the tower having collapsed in 1800, destroying the nave and south aisle. The tower and nave had been rebuilt by 1805 in rag, brown brick and flint, with the architect's name, William Mason, over the west porch.

St Peter and St Paul *Harlington, Middlesex*. Stands at the top end of the High Street, now turned into a cul-de-sac by the M4 motorway. The oldest part is the 12th-century nave with its south doorway: the latter, with four decorative orders, is claimed to be the best Norman doorway in MIDDLESEX. The chancel is mid-14th-century, the west tower late 15th-century, and a north aisle was added in 1880. The walls are of flint rubble, with some ironstone conglomerate and Reigate-stone dressings. The timber south porch is early 16th-century. Monuments include a rare Easter sepulchre which once formed a canopy for the memorial to Gregory Lovell and his wife; a brass half-effigy to John Monemouthe, rector 1414–19; and the busts of Lord Ossulston and his two wives. In the churchyard is a living remnant of a yew which was, until 1825, clipped annually into elaborate shapes.

763

Gravediggers uncover skulls in the churchyard of St Peter upon Cornhill. From an engraving of c. 1819.

St Peter and St Paul

Mitcham, Surrey. The original church was built by Baldwin de Redvers, Earl of Wight, who lived locally and the advowson was presented by him to the Augustinian Canons of ST MARY OVERIE, SOUTHWARK in 1259. Lightning severely damaged the church in 1637 and it was repaired, but by 1819 it had fallen into disrepair and had to be demolished, although the original medieval tower was retained. The present church, dedicated to St Peter and St Paul, was completed in 1822 and is in 'Com-missioners' Gothic' style in brick rendered with Roman cement. The architect was George Smith, a local resident who was surveyor to the southern division of the CITY of London and to the MERCERS' COMPANY.

St Peter upon Cornhill

EC3. Allegedly founded on the site of the Roman basilica by Lucius, the first Christian King of Britain in AD 179. A large library and one of the few London grammar schools were attached to it in the Middle Ages. Burned down in the GREAT FIRE, it was rebuilt by Wren in 1677–8. In 1872 it was restored by J.D. Wyatt. Most of Wren's furniture was removed but Wyatt kept a wooden screen, a fine pulpit with sounding board, the font with its pre-fire cover and the Father Smith organ on which Mendelssohn had played in September 1840 and June 1842.

ST PETER'S HOSPITAL FOR STONE and OTHER URINARY DISEASES

27 Henrietta Street, WC2. The Hospital for Stone, as it was first called, was opened in 1860 at 42 GREAT MARL-BOROUGH STREET (now 34 NEW CAVENDISH STREET). It treated mainly out-patients. The hope of creating an in-patient department in a healthy suburban situation was not realised. A move to 54 BERNERS STREET was made in 1863 when the present name was adopted. A site for a new purpose-built hospital was found in Henrietta Street and there this new small hospital, designed by J.M. Brydon, was opened in 1882. In 1929 an adjacent house was purchased to accommodate a laboratory and sleeping quarters for nurses. This house had once been owned by Henry, brother of Jane Austen, who had stayed with him there when visiting London. By 1950 rats had invaded the sleeping quarters and nurses refused to sleep there any longer. The Board of Governors sold the building to the recently founded Institute of Urology whose architect, Jefferiss Mathews, supervised extensive alterations, reconstructing the entire interior apart from the 18th-century staircase.

The Board of Governors of St Peter's is responsible for three other hospitals which are collectively known as St Peter's Hospitals. These are St Paul's, St Philip's and the Shaftesbury and have a total of 145 beds:

St Paul's Hospital for Urological Diseases

24 Endell Street, WC2. Began with six beds at 13A RED LION SQUARE. It moved to its present address in 1923 and was taken over by the Board of Governors in 1948.

St Philip's Hospital

Sheffield Street, WC2. Built in 1870. It was taken over by the Board of Governors in 1951.

The Shaftesbury Hospital

172–176 Shaftesbury Avenue, WC2. Originally the French Hospital which had opened in 1867 for the treatment of French and other foreigners seeking medical help but had closed when the trustees had insufficient funds to maintain it. The Board of Governors of St Peter's took it over in 1969 and gave it its present name. The Institute of Urology is now housed here.

St Peter's Italian Church

4 Back Hill, Clerkenwell Road, EC1. A site was obtained in 1852 for the construction of an international Roman Catholic cathedral, and the architect Francesco Gualandi of Bologna was appointed to design it. Though some work was apparently started, it was soon abandoned. After some years a modified plan was revived and St Peter's, soon to be known as 'the Italian Church in Hatton Garden', was built to designs by J.M. Brydon and opened in 1863.

St Peter's Square *Hammersmith, W6.* Lies between the GREAT WEST ROAD and King Street and is said to have been designed by J.C. Loudon in the 1830s. The houses are mostly built in groups of three, with stucco fronts, pediments and Ionic porches; some still retain eagles and lions as decoration. The centre garden contains a bronze, *The Greek Runner*, by Sir William Richmond, erected as a memorial to him in 1926.

St Philip *Avondale Square, SE1.* Built in 1963 and faced with handmade bricks. The roof is of copper and the turret aluminium. The church is square with an octagonal upper part with four clerestory windows. The canvas paintings on the ceiling are by John Hayward.

St Philip *Turner Street, E1.* In 1888 a rich, extravagant vicar, the Revd Sidney Vacher, paid for the Commissioners' church on this site to be pulled down and replaced, at a cost of some £40,000, by the present impressive Gothic structure. It was designed by Arthur Cawston, author of *A Comprehensive Scheme for London Street Improvements*. He died in a shooting accident in 1894, two years after the consecration of the church.

St Philip's Hospital *see* ST PETER'S HOSPITAL FOR STONE AND OTHER URINARY DISEASES.

St Quintin Avenue *W10.* Takes its name from the St Quintin family who had owned land here since the 18th century. It was built in 1878.

St Saviour *Eltham (Middle Park Road), SE9.* Designed in 1932 by Welch, Cachemaille-Day and Lander, St Saviour's is a striking example of the modernistic movement in the architecture of that time. It is built of concrete with high narrow windows filled with blue glass. The pulpit is of brick and the reredos, with its commanding figure of Christ, of concrete.

St Saviour *Highbury (Aberdeen Park) N5.* Built of red, black, and white brick in 1865–6 to the Gothic designs of William White, a man of many interests; author, inventor, mountaineer and gymnast as well as idiosyncratic architect. The money was provided by a canon of Salisbury Cathedral intent upon bringing Anglo-Catholicism to HIGHBURY.

St Saviour's Almshouses *Hamilton Road, SE27.* The original almshouses were founded in the parish of St Saviour's, Southwark, from the 16th to the 18th centuries by Thomas Cure, Edward Alleyn (*see* DULWICH), Henry Jackson, Henry Spratt and Henry Young. With the purchases of their site by the Charing Cross Railway, the almshouses were moved in stages to NORWOOD. The first buildings were completed in 1863 to designs by Edward Habershon and included a chapel and 16 almshouses. They were rebuilt and added to at frequent intervals. In 1937 a new south block was completed and bomb damage resulted in the rebuilding of the east block in 1952. Further rebuilding took place in 1966–7. Although the present almshouses are of relatively modern appearance, they are still set round an attractive quadrangle with fine gates.

St Simon Zelotes *Milner Street, SW3.* Ragstone church built in 1858–9 to the Gothic designs of Joseph Peacock.

St Stephen *Gloucester Road, SW7.* Built in 1866–7. The interior (1903–4) was largely designed by G.F. Bodley. T.S. Eliot was churchwarden here for 25 years.

St Stephen *Rochester Row, SW1.* Financed by Baroness Burdett-Coutts and built of Northumbrian sandstone in 1845–50, to the designs of Benjamin Ferrey, a pupil of Pugin, on a site chosen for her by Charles Dickens. The capitals in the nave were carved by G.P. White who, on that nearest the pulpit, provided portraits of 12 people connected with the church at the time of its construction, including Queen Victoria and the BISHOP OF LONDON. In the south aisle is a stained glass window by Burne-Jones.

St Stephen *Rosslyn Hill, NW3.* Built in 1869 to the high Victorian Gothic designs of S.S. Teulon. The church was declared redundant in May 1977.

St Stephen Coleman *Coleman Street.* First mentioned in about 1214. Stow thought it had first been a synagogue. During the Civil War it was a low-church stronghold. Communion was only allowed to those thought virtuous enough by a committee comprising the vicar and 13 parishioners (among them two of the judges who condemned Charles I). It was rebuilt by Wren in 1674–6 after its destruction in the GREAT FIRE, but was bombed in 1940 and then demolished.

St Stephen Walbrook, described in 1734 as 'the masterpiece of the celebrated Christopher Wren'. Aquatint by Malton, 1798.

St Stephen Walbrook *EC4.* Founded on the west bank of the WALBROOK sometime before 1096. It was rebuilt on the east bank in 1429–39 at the expense of Richard Chicheley, a former Lord Mayor. Burned down in the GREAT FIRE it was rebuilt by Wren in 1672–9. Here he tested out some of the theories he later brought into practice at ST PAUL'S CATHEDRAL. It combines a cross-in-square plant with a large centralised dome. Lord Burlington, John Wesley and Canova, the Italian sculptor, all praised it highly. *The Critical Review of Publick Buildings in London* of 1734 recorded that it was 'famous all over Europe and justly reputed the masterpiece of the celebrated Sir Christopher Wren. Perhaps Italy itself can produce no modern buildings that can vie with this in taste or proportion'. Although badly bombed in 1940, the rich 17th-century fittings, the font, pulpit, sounding board, altar piece and communion rails all survived. They were the gift of the GROCERS' COMPANY and many of the original drawings for them are preserved in the GUILDHALL. On the north wall is *The Martyrdom of St Stephen* by Benjamin West. The post-war glass is by Keith New. Sir John Vanbrugh was buried here in 1726. The SAMARITANS started here.

St Stephen's Chapel *see* PALACE OF WESTMINSTER.

St Stephen's Constitutional Club *34 Queen Anne's Gate, SW1.* A merger of the Constitutional Club and the St Stephen's, the latter being founded in 1870 as a meeting place for Conservative Members of Parliament who were either not members of the CARLTON or who found the St Stephen's Club's premises on the corner of BRIDGE STREET and the EMBANKMENT more convenient for the HOUSES OF PARLIAMENT. Several consulting engineers, who were at that time often to be seen at WESTMINSTER advising on railway developments, were also elected to the club, whose membership was increased during the 1st World War when the premises of the Whitehall Club in STOREY'S GATE were requisitioned and many of those who had belonged to it joined St Stephen's. After the 2nd World War the club's premises in BRIDGE STREET were sold to the Government for £395,000, and St Stephen's bought its present house in QUEEN ANNE'S GATE which, once Lord Glenconner's, was opened as a clubhouse by Harold Macmillan in 1963.

St Stephen's Hospital *Fulham Road, SW10.* The foundation stone, which can still be seen by the original entrance at 369 FULHAM ROAD, was laid in 1876. The architect was E.T. Hall and the building, then known as the St George's Union Infirmary, was opened in 1878. It was erected for the accommodation of the sick poor of the parishes of ST GEORGE'S HANOVER SQUARE and ST MARGARET'S WESTMINSTER and contained the largest number of imates (808) of any infirmary or hospital in London. There were no bathrooms as it was deemed desirable that the baths should be on wheels and taken to the bedside of the patient for use. The name was changed to St Stephen's (the patron saint of WESTMINSTER) in 1925, at the suggestion of K.F.D. Waters, surgeon to the hospital and husband of the writer of children's stories, Enid Blyton.
The hospital was absorbed into the National Health Service in 1948, since when it has been largely rebuilt. It now has 502 beds and is an acute general hospital.

St Stephen's Tavern *10 Bridge Street, Westminster, SW1.* A mid-Victorian building on the corner of CANNON ROW and BRIDGE STREET. It was opened in 1867 by Henry Champness as the Swan Tavern and has always been a haunt of politicians and parliamentary correspondents. There is a division bell to recall MPs to the House for voting.

St Swithin London Stone *Cannon Street.* An unusual Wren masterpiece destroyed by bombs in 1941. An octagonal dome covered a cube-shaped building. The tower, beside the dome, supported an octagonal spire. It was a beautiful illustration of Wren's preoccupation with the geometry of domes. It was built in 1677. Some of the stones of the earlier church of 1420 were used in the building.

St Swithin's Lane *EC4.* Named after the Church of ST SWITHIN LONDON STONE which was bombed in the 2nd World War. At No. 13 is FOUNDERS' HALL.

St Thomas *Fulham (Rylston Road), SW6.* It is likely that this church's dedication came about through the brewing interest of the Bowden family, since St Thomas of Canterbury is the patron saint of brewers and it was Mrs Elizabeth Bowden, aunt of the poet Algernon Swinburne, who was the generous benefactor. A convert to Roman Catholicism, she was anxious to erect a church as a memorial to her husband, John Bowden, who had been the friend of John Henry Newman at Oxford. On hearing that Father William Kelly, the chaplain of the Benedictine Convent at HAMMERSMITH, had acquired a site for this purpose in the Market Gardens of Fulham Fields, on behalf of the Irish immigrants who worked there, she undertook to pay for the total cost of the building. The leading church architect of the day and master of the Gothic revival style, Augustus Welby Pugin, was commissioned to draw up plans. Work began in 1847. One year later the church was opened with great pomp and ceremony. Pugin, however, was not there to witness the distinguished gathering of Roman Catholic hierarchy, or to hear Father – later Cardinal – Newman preach. The relationship between architect and client had not been an entirely happy one. Mrs Bowden had specifically refused to have a rood screen; Pugin had, nevertheless, designed one. When it was half built, Mrs Bowden, to Pugin's fury, told the workmen to remove it and replace it with communion rails.

St Thomas *Southwark (St Thomas Street), SE1.* On the site of ST THOMAS'S HOSPITAL chapel, which was probably founded at the same time as the hospital in the 13th century. In Edward VI's reign it became the parish church. It was rebuilt in 1702. In 1862 the hospital moved to LAMBETH and most of the buildings were demolished to make way for LONDON BRIDGE STATION. In 1956 the 19th-century operating theatre was discovered in the garret over the church (*see* OPERATING THEATRE OF OLD ST THOMAS'S).

St Thomas *Woolwich (Maryon Road, Old Charlton), SE7.* A red-and-white-brick church built in 1849–50 in Romanesque style without a tower. Inside is a large open wooden roof with separate colonettes resting on the arcade below.

St Thomas the Apostle *Queen Street.* First mentioned in 1170. It was rebuilt by John Barnes,

The extensive blocks of St Thomas's Hospital were designed by Henry Currey and opened by Queen Victoria in 1871.

Lord Mayor, in 1371. Stow said it was 'a proper church but monuments of antiquity be there none, except some arms in the windows as also in the stone work which some suppose to be of John Barnes'. There were three chantries. In 1538 the rector, Nicholas Wilson, was committed to the TOWER for denying the King's supremacy. In 1636 his successor, William Cooper, was committed to Leeds Castle (where he died) for refusing to take the Oath of Conformity. And in 1658 the rector, John Rogers, one of the Fifth Monarchy Men, was committed to the TOWER by Cromwell. He had proclaimed a solemn day of humiliation for the sins of the rulers, and in a sermon had likened WHITEHALL to Sodom and demonstrated that Cromwell had broken the first eight commandments. He would have gone on to the other two had he not been interrupted. The church was destroyed in the GREAT FIRE and not rebuilt. The parish was united in 1670 to that of ST MARY ALDERMARY. Part of the burial ground was cleared in 1851 to enable QUEEN STREET to be widened. The human remains were put in a vault on the east side. Sir William Littlesbery, Lord Mayor, was buried here in 1487. He was nicknamed 'Horne' by Edward IV for his superlative horn blowing.

St Thomas Street *SE1.* Two great London hospitals originated here. St Thomas's, founded in the 13th century, moved out in 1865 to make way for railway extensions but the former chapel, a Queen Anne building, is now SOUTHWARK CATHEDRAL Chapter House. The OPERATING THEATRE OF OLD ST THOMAS'S is in the tower, which had access from the hospital. Adjoining is a Georgian terrace, formerly occupied by hospital officials. GUY'S was founded in 1725 by Thomas Guy, son of a wharfinger who made a fortune largely from the South Sea Bubble Co. His statue by Scheemakers stands in the 18th-century forecourt. More recent hospital buildings tower above. The statue of another benefactor, Lord Nuffield, is in an inner courtyard (*see* STATUES).

St Thomas's Hospital *Lambeth Palace Road, SE1.* Founded in about 1106, probably as part of the Priory of St Mary Overie, SOUTHWARK. Its name, The

Hospital of St Thomas the Martyr, cannot have been assumed until after Becket's canonisation in 1173. In 1207 or 1212 the Priory was destroyed by fire. It was soon afterwards rebuilt and the hospital obtained a new site on the east side of BOROUGH HIGH STREET from the Bishop of Winchester in whose diocese it lay. In the early 15th century the famous Lord Mayor of London, Richard Whittington, made 'a new chamber with eight beds for young women who had done amiss, in trust of a good amendment'. And he commanded 'that all things that had been done in that chamber should be kept secret ... for he would not shame no young woman in no wise, for it might be the cause of their letting [i.e. hindering] of their marriage'. In 1535 it was visited by Thomas Cromwell, who called it 'the bawdy hospital of St Thomas in Southwark'. It was alleged that the master kept a concubine and had sold the church plate. In 1540, at the DISSOLUTION OF THE MONASTERIES Henry VIII closed The Hospital of St Thomas the Martyr, and 'decanonised' Becket. In 1551 the buildings were granted to the LORD MAYOR and citizens of London by Edward VI. When the hospital was reopened that year its name was changed to the Hospital of St Thomas the Apostle. At that time the three royal hospitals – King Edward VI of Christ, BRIDEWELL, and St Thomas the Apostle – were administered jointly. By the end of the century St Thomas's had become independent.

The Governors were representatives of the CITY OF LONDON. A treasurer, hospitaller, clerk, butler, steward and surgeons were appointed. Patients were expected to attend a daily service in the chapel and if they did not they went without food. They were also punished for dicing, gambling, swearing and drunkenness. In 1561 unmarried pregnant women were refused admission because the hospital was erected for the relief 'of honest persons and not of harlottes'.

In 1566 Henry Bull was appointed the first physician to the hospital at an annual salary of £13 6s 8d. In 1583 the cook took on the duties of grave digger and made an extra £1 per year. In 1605 the Governors appointed an administration committee. In 1634 the number of patients was limited to 240 in summer and 280 in winter. In 1639 the hospitaller and matron were both sent to gaol. The hospitaller's offence is unknown but the matron had debts of over £100. The Governors had to pay £50 to free her. Between 1693 and 1709 the hospital was rebuilt largely at the expense of Sir Robert Clayton, who was Lord Mayor in 1679. Among the rules drawn up in 1700 were regulations that no patient was to be admitted more than once for the same disease, that no incurables or patients suffering from infectious diseases were to be admitted, that there was to be no suspicious talk or contracting matrimony or entering the wards of the opposite sex, that not more than one patient was to be allowed in a bed. In 1703 Richard Mead, physician to Queen Anne and later to George II, was appointed physician. In his efforts to improve the hospital's facilities, Mead was much helped by his rich friend, Thomas Guy, who founded the adjacent sister hospital, GUY'S. In 1859 the site of the hospital was acquired by Charing Cross Railway Company for LONDON BRIDGE STATION. A new site was found in Stangate at the foot of WESTMINSTER BRIDGE. The foundation stone was laid by Queen Victoria on 13 May 1868 and the hospital was opened in 1871. It was built to the designs of Henry Currey on a block principle which followed the current continental pattern and which was approved by Florence Nightingale who established here the Nightingale Training School of Nursing and thus revolutionised the profession. Before her time nurses in hospital were drawn from the lowest classes of domestics; drunkenness, illiteracy and ignorance restricted their efficiency. Miss Nightingale laid down strict rules: nurses were required to be sober, honest, truthful, trustworthy, punctual, quiet and orderly, clean and neat. Their notebooks were sent to her monthly for marking. To this day St Thomas's nurses are known as Nightingales.

Medicine developed rapidly at the hospital towards the end of the century. The medical school was opened in 1871. By 1900 there were 11 special departments for out-patients – ophthalmic, throat, skin, ear, teeth, electrotherapeutics, X-ray, vaccination, mental diseases, diseases of women and diseases of children. In the 1920s Saint Thomas's House was built on the other side of Lambeth Palace Road as a hostel for medical students. In the 2nd World War the hospital was heavily bombed and in 1956 W. Fowler Howitt was commissioned to design a new east wing which was completed in 1966. The north wing was subsequently built by Yorke, Rosenberg and Mardall. In 1974 the Board of Governors was abolished by Act of Parliament after nearly four and a half centuries. The hospital is now administered by the South-East Thames Regional Health Authority. In 1982 there were 997 beds.

The rotating steel fountain in the sunken garden is by Naum Gabo (1976).

St Vedast-alias-Foster *Foster Lane, EC2*. First mentioned in 1170, it was rebuilt in 1519 and repaired in 1614. Destroyed in the GREAT FIRE, it was rebuilt by Wren in 1670–3. The Baroque steeple was added in 1694–7. Bombed in 1941, it was restored by Stephen Dykes-Bower. Most of the furniture has been brought from other Wren churches – the magnificent organ case from ST BARTHOLOMEW BY THE EXCHANGE, the altar-piece from ST CHRISTOPHER LE STOCKS, the pulpit from ALL HALLOWS BREAD STREET, and the font and cover from ST ANNE AND ST AGNES. The east windows are by Brian Thomas.

St Vincent's Orthopaedic Hospital *Eastcote, Pinner, Middlesex*. The St Vincent's Cripples Home was founded in CLAPHAM by the Sisters of Charity in 1907 with 25 boys from poor law institutions. In 1912 a move was made to more extensive premises in PINNER. In 1924 the hospital was given its present name. Over the years many extensions have been made. In 1982 there were 127 beds.

Salesian College *Surrey Lane, SW11*. Secondary school for boys founded in 1888 by St John Bosco who had established the Society of St Frances of Sales for the education of the poor in Cowley, Oxford. Inspired by a prophetic vision of his pupil, Dominic Savio, who became the first schoolboy saint when he was canonised after his death at the age of 15, Bosco sent the first Salesians to BATTERSEA. He died in the same year and the Salesians established the school premises in Orbel Street in 1890. In 1895 they acquired an adjacent plot with a hunting lodge, now Surrey House, which they developed and extended. The old stables were converted into the college chapel in 1905.

Salisbury *90 St Martin's Lane, WC2*. Once known as the Coach and Horses and later as Ben Caunt's Head, this inn used to be well known for the prize fights organised here. It is now a magnificently preserved early Victorian inn, dating from 1852 when the lease was acquired from the Marquess of Salisbury. It has splendid brasswork, marble, red plush seating, Art Nouveau lamps and much glittering glasswork.

Salisbury Court *EC4*. Named after SALISBURY HOUSE, over whose grounds it was built (*see* SALISBURY SQUARE). Samuel Pepys was born here in 1632, the son of a tailor whose house stood on the site of the National Westminster Bank.

Salisbury Court Theatre *Salisbury Square*. A private theatre built in 1629 by Richard Gunnell and William Blagrove at a cost of £1,000. In 1629–31 it was used by the King's Revels, in 1631–5 by Prince Charles's Men, and in 1637–42 by the Queen's Men. During the Commonwealth plays were illegally performed and the interior was destroyed by soldiers in 1649.

At the Restoration it was restored by William Beeston and was one of the first theatres to reopen. D'Avenant acted here until LINCOLN'S INN FIELDS THEATRE was opened. Companies led by John Rhodes, George Jolly and Beeston himself used it briefly. On 9 September 1661 Pepys recorded, 'And thence to Salisbury Court Playhouse where was acted for the first time *Tis a pitty she's a Whore* a simple play and ill acted, only, it was my fortune to sit by a most pretty and most ingenious lady, which pleased me much'. The theatre was destroyed by the GREAT FIRE.

Salisbury Estate The Marquesses of Salisbury are descended from Sir William Cecil, Baron Burghley, who was Elizabeth I's principal minister, through his younger son Robert, Viscount Cranborne and Earl of Salisbury. The eldest son, Thomas, became Earl of Exeter. The father's property on the north side of the STRAND, now marked BURLEIGH STREET and EXETER STREET, where Cecil House and Robert's (Little) Cecil House stood, passed to Thomas at Burghley's death in 1598. Robert moved to the south side of the STRAND, where Shell-Mex House now stands, and proceeded to acquire and rebuild property. Here were erected SALISBURY HOUSE, Little Salisbury House and the NEW EXCHANGE. Subsequently SALISBURY STREET, CECIL STREET and the Middle Exchange were built on the site. (EXETER CHANGE was built on the family property on the north side of the STRAND.) None of this now belongs to the Salisbury Estates.

In 1609–10 Lord Salisbury also acquired part of St Martin's Field. Its development was undistinguished. It began in 1610 on the west side of ST MARTIN'S LANE and proceeded, after the laying out of LEICESTER SQUARE in the 1670s, with the filling in of the rest of the estate between the Leicester property and ST MARTIN'S LANE. The family's property in the area diminished in the 19th century as a result of the extension of CRANBOURN STREET, then famous for its milliners' shops, and the making of CHARING CROSS ROAD.

Salisbury House *Bury Street West, N9.* A late-16th-century house, timber-framed with jettied storeys and a gabled roof. Several of the rooms retain original panelling. The front room on the 1st floor has a fine fireplace and overmantel. In the attic the elaborate roof structure can be viewed at close quarters. After lying derelict for many years, the house was renovated by the former EDMONTON Borough Council and opened as an arts centre in 1959.

Salisbury House *(later called Dorset House), Fleet Street.* The Bishops of Salisbury owned land in the parish of ST BRIDE as early as the 12th century. Their inn was the largest and most important house in the district. It stood just to the south of today's St Brides Passage and its grounds extended down to the river. On the east was BRIDEWELL PALACE and west of the house and garden was the Bishop of Salisbury's Manor which extended to the line of the modern WHITEFRIARS and CARMELITE STREETS. The boundary wall between the garden and manor is represented by the line of SALISBURY COURT.

In the 15th century the house was often used for lodging princes and others of high rank, as when in 1498 Prince Arthur lodged here and received gifts from the Lord Mayor. In 1554 Corier, the Spanish envoy sent to arrange the marriage of Philip and Mary, stayed here. In 1564 the house was purchased under letters patent by Sir Richard Sackville and was briefly known as Sackville Place. Aubrey, the historian, was told by Seth Ward that the Sackville family had acquired the property in exchange for a piece of land near Cricklade, Wiltshire that proved not to be theirs. The Sackvilles were created Earls of Dorset in 1603 and continued to live here for a century. Edward, the 4th Earl, is said to have remained in the house after the execution of Charles I in 1649 until his own death in 1652. In 1666 the house was destroyed in the GREAT FIRE. It was not rebuilt. DORSET GARDEN THEATRE was built in its garden. Dorset Rise and SALISBURY SQUARE commemorate it.

Salisbury Square *EC4.* Known as Salisbury Court until the late 19th century, it was never an architecturally planned square. It partly covers the site of SALISBURY HOUSE, the town house of the Bishops of Salisbury from the 13th century until the 17th when it passed into the hands of the Earls of Dorset. The SALISBURY COURT THEATRE was here from 1629–66. In 1673–82 John Dryden lived in the square where he wrote *Amboyna* (1673), *Aurengzebe* (1676), *All for*

Love (1678), *The Spanish Fryar* (1681), *Absalom and Achitophel* (1681) and many other works. Thomas Shadwell is also said to have lived here. It was popular as a place of residence for actors from the nearby DORSET GARDEN THEATRE. Thomas Betterton and Henry Harris and the proprietress, Lady D'Avenant, had houses here. On the accession of George I there was an ale-house in the square where his supporters met. In July 1716 it was stormed by a Jacobite mob led by a man named Bean. In the fray the landlord shot a weaver. The landlord was later acquitted of manslaughter but five rioters were sentenced to be hanged at the end of Salisbury Court. In about 1724 Samuel Richardson set himself up as a printer in the court. He wrote *Pamela* here and probably parts of *Clarissa Harlowe* and *Sir Charles Grandison*. In 1755 'he took a range of old houses, eight in number, which he pulled down and built a commodious and extensive range of warehouse and printing offices'. In 1757 Goldsmith worked here correcting proofs. Boswell records the first meeting of Dr Johnson and Hogarth at the house. Hogarth 'perceived a person standing at a window in the room, shaking his head, and rolling himself about in a strange, ridiculous manner. He concluded that he was an idiot, whom his relations had put under the care of Richardson. To his great surprise, however, this figure stalked forward . . . and all at once took up the argument . . . He displayed such a power of eloquence that Hogarth looked at him in astonishment and actually imagined that this idiot had been at the moment inspired'. Richardson owned the house until he died in 1761; it was demolished in 1896.

In 1814 10,000 copies of *The Memoirs of Mrs Mary Anne Clarke,* the spurned mistress of the Duke of York, were burned at Gilbert's the printers', after the Duke had paid the lady's debts and awarded her a pension of £400 a year. In 1863 the Salisbury Hotel designed by John Giles replaced all the houses on the south side. This in turn was replaced in the 1960s by Salisbury Square House. Only the early 18th-century No. 1 now remains to hint at the former domestic scale and, except at pavement level, the square belies its name. An obelisk to Alderman Robert Waithman, formerly at LUDGATE CIRCUS, now stands in the centre. It was erected in 1833 to the memory of Waithman by his friends and fellow citizens: 'A Friend of Liberty in evil times'. The Press Council is at No. 1.

Mrs Salmon's Waxworks *Fleet Street.* Formerly at the Golden Ball, ST MARTIN'S-LE-GRAND, where there were 'six rooms full of all kinds of wax figures', Mrs Salmon's waxworks moved to the north side of FLEET STREET near CHANCERY LANE in 1711. She also exhibited her works at BARTHOLOMEW and SOUTHWARK FAIRS. They included the execution of Charles I, the 'Rites of Molock', 'Hermonia a Roman Lady, whose father offended the Emperor, was sentenced to be starved to death, but was preserved by sucking his Daughter's Breast', 'Margaret Countess of Heningbergh, Lying on a Bed of State, with her Three hundred and Sixty-Five Children, all born at one Birth', as well as numerous other figures and *tableaux* both horrific and comical, some of them operated by clockwork. Hogarth confessed to having 'frequently loitered at Old Mother Salmon's'. Boswell also visited the show. When she died, aged 90, in 1760, the exhibition was taken over by a surgeon named Clarke. It was moved to the south side of FLEET STREET by the corner of INNER TEMPLE LANE in 1795 and survived there well into Victorian times.

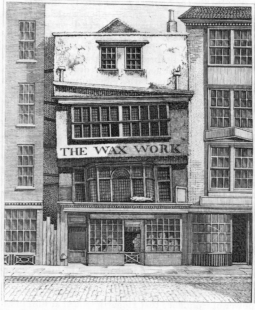

Mrs Salmon's Waxworks, established in Fleet Street in 1711, were a favourite haunt of William Hogarth.

Salopian *Charing Cross.* A tavern and coffee-house built on the site of the RUMMER after that tavern's destruction by fire in 1750. Thomas Telford, the Scottish engineer, used it as his London quarters for 21 years and, being a friendly, sociable, entertaining companion, full of anecdote, and with a wide circle of friends and acquaintances who came to see him here, he came to be considered a valuable fixture of the premises and was bought and sold by succeeding landlords as part of the business. When he decided to move to 24 Abingdon Street, WESTMINSTER, the landlord of the Salopian who had just acquired the business was horrified. 'What,' he exclaimed indigantly, 'leave the house! Why, Sir, I have just paid £750 for you.'

Salters' Company *see* CITY LIVERY COMPANIES.

Salutation Tavern *Newgate Street.* A popular tavern from the time of Queen Anne until the middle of the 18th century. It was a tradition of the house 'that Sir Christopher Wren used to smoke his pipe there whilst St Paul's was in course of rebuilding'. At the beginning of the 18th century, it was a recognised resort of printers and booksellers. Coleridge and Lamb used to meet here to talk over Welsh rarebit, egg-hot and orinoco. Southey was also a customer.

Salvation Army *International Headquarters, 101 Queen Victoria Street, EC4.* The Salvation Army originated in the Christian Revival Association, subsequently The Christian Mission, founded by the Revd William Booth in 1865. Its first headquarters were opened in WHITECHAPEL ROAD in 1867. In 1881 William Booth, helped by his son, Bramwell, and their small staff, moved their few effects in a fruiterer's horse-drawn van and a handcart to larger premises, formerly used as a billiards club, at the Army's present address. Here the

Army grew and its work prospered. William Booth, who had received the FREEDOM OF THE CITY of London at GUILDHALL in 1905, died in 1912. His funeral procession blocked all traffic in the CITY for most of the day. The LORD MAYOR took the salute at the MANSION HOUSE as the cortège proceeded to ABBEY PARK CEMETERY. Similar scenes were enacted when Bramwell Booth, who had succeeded his father as General, died in 1929.

The headquarters were destroyed in an air raid in 1941. New premises, designed by H. and H.M. Lidbetter, were opened by Queen Elizabeth, the Queen Mother in 1963. From this building the Army's work in more than 80 countries is co-ordinated. It is also the national headquarters for England, Wales and Ireland (Scotland has its own territorial headquarters in Glasgow). The International (William Booth Memorial) Training College was opened in Denmark Hill, SE5, in 1929; and the International College for officers at 34 Sydenham Hill, SE26 in 1950.

Samaritans An organisation of anonymous volunteers created to help the suicidal and desperate. It was started in 1953 at ST STEPHEN WALBROOK by the Revd Chad Varah. There are now almost 200 branches where those in need of help can seek advice and comfort.

Samaritan Hospital for Women *161–173 Marylebone Road, NW1.* Founded in 1847 by Dr William Jones as the Gynaepathic Institute Free Hospital in Gray Street, MANCHESTER SQUARE. There were eight beds for women and children. For the first three years men were also treated as out-patients. Later that year the hospital moved to No. 7 NORTH AUDLEY STREET. The lower part of the house was let to 'a medical gentleman' who acted as surgeon, supplied drugs at wholesale prices and prepared and dispensed them. In 1850 the hospital moved to No. 27 ORCHARD STREET; and in 1854 took over the Marylebone Dispensary in GEORGE STREET. In 1858 it moved to LOWER SEYMOUR STREET. By 1862 it had 50 beds. In 1869 the first block in Britain with pay-beds was opened for people of limited means. There were 23 beds, each costing one to three and a half guineas a week. In 1874 the hospital moved to No. 1 Dorset Street; and in 1889 to its present building which had five medical wards, 11 surgical wards and three for convalescents. In 1904 it was renamed the Samaritan Hospital for Women. Under the National Health Service it became part of ST MARY'S HOSPITAL PADDINGTON group and in 1982 had 79 beds.

Sam's *Cornhill.* Stood where LLOYD'S BANK head office is now situated. The damage it suffered in the CORNHILL fire 1748 was apparently repaired by 1749. In 1759–63 it was used as an address by 'Benjamin da Israeli', the statesman's grandfather, described as an 'Italian merchant'. The house seems to have been the scene of various kinds of trading. It was later known as the 'Old Jewellery Mart'.

Sanderstead *Surrey.* Sanderstede, the sandy place, was in 1876 a pretty, secluded village (population 267) on the Warlingham road with a fine view over CROYDON. The parish stretched to Foxley Hatch (now PURLEY crossroads), site of the last turnpike gates on the Brighton Road.

Sanderstead Pond, which in 1895 froze a foot thick, the Gruffy (a green open space) and All Saints Church, lie in the middle of the village. The church clock was donated in 1844 by George Smith of nearby Selsdon House (now SELSDON PARK HOTEL). He was a director of the East India Company, Member of Parliament for three rotten boroughs until 1832, and an ancestor of the Queen Mother, who recently contributed to the clock's repair.

One of Sanderstead's first policemen was a survivor of the charge of the Light Brigade at Balaclava on 25 October 1854. He died in 1908 aged 78. The village, which in 1798 boasted 'a pack of the best harriers in this country with every necessary appendage for rural diversion', had until 1925 only one village shop with a postmistress known for her mob cap and clay pipe. It now has a population of 20,000.

Sandford Manor House *Near King's Road, Fulham, SW6*. Probably got its name from John de Saundford who owned the estate in 1363. Tradition links the house, which dates from the 17th century (with subsequent alterations), with Nell Gwynne. In her time it was owned by the Maynard family and there is no proof that she had any connection with it. Joseph Addison, who wrote letters from 'Sany End' in 1708, may have lived here. From 1762 the house was used by manufacturers of saltpetre, cloth and pottery and for bleaching and dying. The property was purchased by the Imperial Gas Company in 1824 as a site for their works. The house remained in the hands of their successors and for 50 years was the home of one of the managers.

Sans Souci Theatre *Leicester Place*. Opened in 1796 by Charles Dibdin as a successor to his successful theatre in the STRAND (*see below*). The interior of the former Sans Souci was moved here. In 1804 Dibdin retired and it was afterwards used mostly by amateurs. In the 1830s it became a warehouse and eventually part of a hotel. It was demolished in 1898. An office block on the corner of LEICESTER PLACE and LEICESTER SQUARE marks the site.

Sans Souci Theatre *Strand*. A makeshift theatre opposite Beaufort Buildings where Charles Dibdin sang every night in 1791–6. He was so popular that when his lease ran out he opened another SANS SOUCI THEATRE in LEICESTER PLACE.

Saracen's Head *Snow Hill*. An ancient tavern which in 1522 had 30 beds and stabling for 40 horses. Stow described it in 1598 as 'a fair and large inn for the receipt of travellers'. Its sign was noted for the ferocity of the Saracen's face. In Dicken's day there were three signs, one on each side of the coachyard and one on the inn itself. It is here that Wackford Squeers, the dreadful schoolmaster, who has but one eye, though 'the popular prejudice runs in favour of two', is introduced to Nicholas Nickleby in the coffee-room depicted by Hablôt Browne.

Sardinian Chapel *Lincoln's Inn Fields*. Demolished in 1910, this was the oldest of the Embassy chapels. The probable date of foundation, taken from the stone of an adjacent arch, is 1648. In the reign of James II the house, later to be the presbytery, was occupied by Franciscans. During the Glorious Revolution, however, rioters attacked both the house and the chapel, burning books, vestments and altar ornaments in a bonfire in 'The Fields'. From 1720 the Sardinian ambassador occupied the house; and in 1729 the chapel registers begin. The chapel's interior was seriously damaged by fire in 1759 and it was not reopened until 1762.

In 1780 the chapel's fame and central position made it a prime target during the GORDON RIOTS. Joined by a mob from the London streets, the rioters set fire to the chapel and burnt the pews, vestments and altar ornaments in a bonfire in Duke Street. The fire was extinguished, the Catholics compensated, and the chapel saved. In 1798 the house was sold and the chapel closed. The devout Catholic who purchased the whole, however, gave both chapel and house to Bishop John Douglass, who had been appointed vicar-apostolic of the London district. The fabric was repaired and the chapel opened again in 1799. The chapel then enjoyed a quieter history until its demolition in 1910. The marriage of Fanny Burney to General d'Arblay was celebrated here in 1793.

Savage Club *9 Fitzmaurice Place, Berkeley Square, W1*. Founded in 1857 at the suggestion of the journalist George Augustus Sala. It is named after Richard Savage, the dissolute poet. It was initially peripatetic, but found a permanent home in 1888 in ADELPHI TERRACE. After the demolition of the ADELPHI TERRACE house, the club moved in 1907 to Lord Curzon's residence in CARLTON HOUSE TERRACE. They could not afford to renew the lease on these premises and moved again to share the premises of the NATIONAL LIBERAL CLUB. From there they went to COVENT GARDEN, and shortly afterwards moved again to the basement of the Constitutional Club in ST JAMES'S STREET. In 1975 they moved to their present home in the LANSDOWNE CLUB.

Distinguished members of this gregarious club, to which many actors, writers and lawyers have belonged, have included Harry Tate, Edward Elgar, Edgar Wallace, G.A. Henty, Gilbert and Sullivan, Norman Birkett and Somerset Maugham.

Savile Club *69 Brook Street, W1*. Founded in 1868, it first occupied rooms in the Medical Club, TRAFALGAR SQUARE when it was known as the New Club. It adopted its present name in 1891 when it moved to a house in SAVILE ROW. In 1882 it moved again, this time to PICCADILLY, into a house purchased from Lord Rosebery; and in 1927 it settled at its present address.

Its membership is largely drawn from the world of the arts. From the names of some of its members, past and present, its character may be inferred – R.L. Stevenson, George Saintsbury, W.E. Henley, Herbert Spencer, Compton Mackenzie, Frank Muir and Sir Ralph Richardson. Evelyn Waugh, referring to it as the Greville in a *Handful of Dust*, said that it had 'a tradition of garrulity'.

Savile House *Leicester Square*. Built in about 1683 possibly for the 2nd Earl of Ailesbury, a friend of Lord Leicester, the ground landlord. Certainly it was first known as Ailesbury House and occupied intermittently by Lord Ailesbury in 1686–98. In 1699 it was sold to Henry Portman, a kinsman of Lord Ailesbury and in 1717 leased to George, Prince of Wales (later George II) who had also taken the neighbouring LEICESTER HOUSE. In 1727 Queen Caroline acquired the house on George II's accession. In 1729 she sold it to Sir George Savile, a baronet of Rufford in Lancashire, and it was renamed Savile House. On the death of George II's heir, Frederick, Prince of Wales,

Sir George Savile's son leased the house to the new heir apparent, Prince George, and his brother, Prince Frederick, Duke of York. Prince George remained there until he came to the throne as George III in 1760 and his brother, the Duke of York, lived there until 1767 when he moved to the house designed for him by Matthew Brettingham in PALL MALL. In 1788 the younger Sir George Savile, an outspoken proponent of religious toleration, introduced the Catholic Relief Act to Parliament; and in consequence, in 1780, the house was attacked and looted in the GORDON RIOTS and his furniture burnt in the street.

In 1789 the house and grounds were bought as a site of a new opera house which, designed by Sir John Soane, was, however, never built. In 1806 it was partly rebuilt to house a carpet factory and a gallery of embroideries of famous paintings created by Mary Linwood, an artist in needlework. Other parts were let as wine cellars, a bazaar, a concert room, a shooting gallery, a wrestling arena, and for so many other purposes that 'few could tell whether it was a theatre, a wine vault, a billiard-room, a coffee-shop, a gunsmith's, or a Royal Academy; or, if they could, they never knew, amidst the ascending and descending steps, and doors, and passages, which one must take to get any where. ... A confusion of sounds further tends to bewilder the visitor: the noise of everything is heard every where else. The click of Billiard-balls, the music of *poses plastiques*, the thwacking of single-sticks, the cracking of rifles, and the stamping of delighted Walhallaists, all mingle with each other, and it is only by taking refuge in the lowest apartment, which partakes of a coffee-room, a cabin, and a cellar, that you will find repose'.

Not altogether surprisingly the building was destroyed in 1865 in a dramatic fire attended by the Prince of Wales, and his friend, the Duke of Sutherland, who both delighted in the sight of a good conflagration. The Empire Cinema now covers the site.

Savile Row *W1*. On the Burlington Estate, it takes its name from Lady Dorothy Savile, wife of the 3rd Earl of Burlington. It now extends from BURLINGTON GARDENS to CONDUIT STREET, but the portion north of Boyle Street is a modern extension, chiefly notable for its Metropolitan Police Station (formerly in VINE STREET) of 1939. Savile Row is now world-famous as the headquarters of many of the finest London tailors, but this reputation dates only from the mid-19th century, and when it was originally laid out in the 1730s it at once became a fashionable residential street. Surviving houses – all on the east side, because until the 19th century the back gardens of the houses in OLD BURLINGTON STREET occupied most of the west side of Savile Row – include Nos 3, 11–14, 16 and 17; and No. 1, although much altered outwardly, contains work by William Kent. This last house was occupied by the ROYAL GEOGRAPHICAL SOCIETY in 1870–1911, and here in 1874 the body of Dr Livingstone lay in state before its interment in WESTMINSTER ABBEY. Inhabitants of these surviving houses included at No. 11, Richard Bright, identifier of Bright's disease, in 1830–58; at No. 12 George Grote, the historian of Greece, in 1848–71; at No. 13, Lewis Vulliamy, the architect in 1838–49; at No. 14 Richard Brinsley Sheridan, the dramatist and politician, in 1813–16; at No. 17, George Basevi, the architect, in 1826–45; and at No. 7 (now demolished), another architect, S.P. Cockerell, in 1788–1801.

All of Savile Row is now in commercial or official occupation, much of it, of course, by gentlemen's tailors, among them Gieves and Hawkes (No. 1); Henry Huntsman and Sons (No. 11); Hardy Amies Ltd (No. 14); Strickland and Sons (No. 15); Welsh and Jefferies (No. 15); and Anderson and Sheppard (No. 30). Henry Maxwell and Co., the shoemakers' at No. 11, were established as spur-makers' in 1756 in RUPERT STREET where they had a forge in the garden. In 1820 they moved to No. 181 PICCADILLY, in 1907 to Nos 8 and 9 DOVER STREET, thence to No. 177 NEW BOND STREET and, in 1979, to their present address.

Saville Theatre *Shaftesbury Avenue*. Built to the design of T.P. Bennet and Sons on land at the upper end of SHAFTESBURY AVENUE, the theatre was leased to A.E. Fournier in 1930. The exterior frieze, *Drama through the Ages*, was sculpted by Gilbert Bayes. The theatre opened on 8 October 1931 with a musical play, *For the Love of Mike*. For much of its life it was the home of revues and musicals. The theatre closed in 1970 and was converted into a double cinema, ABC 1 and ABC 2, which opened in December of that year. As a theatre its seating capacity was 1,200.

Savory and Moore Ltd *13 Curzon Street, W1*. Chemists founded in 1799 at 143 NEW BOND STREET by Thomas Field Savory, an apothecary's apprentice and protégé of Dr Jenner. The shop was patronised by such fashionable neighbours as Emma, Lady Hamilton, and became well known for its sale of Dr Jenner's lozenges and Seidlitz powders. On Thomas's death it passed to his nephew, John Savory, a founder of the PHARMACEUTICAL SOCIETY, and by the mid-19th century had many distinguished customers, among them Florence Nightingale, the Duke of Wellington and Disraeli. During the Crimean War, Savory and Moore were the sole medical suppliers to the Army, and at about the same time they produced the first artificial baby food. The firm amalgamated with JOHN BELL AND CROYDEN in 1928, and in 1933 merged with William Martindale. In 1950 they acquired Squires of Oxford Street, a firm patronised by the Royal Family and the traditional suppliers of the royal anointing oil which was subsequently made by Savory and Moore for the coronation of Elizabeth II. In 1955 they held four royal Warrants. The firm also has a branch at 45 Craven Road, W2. The shops formerly in BOND STREET and GLOUCESTER ROAD ceased trading in 1981.

Savoy Chapel *Savoy Street, WC2*. In the SAVOY PALACE owned by John of Gaunt there was a chapel dedicated to St John the Baptist but it was destroyed with the rest of the building in the PEASANTS' REVOLT of 1381. In 1510 when the SAVOY was rebuilt as a hospital for the poor, a new chapel was dedicated to St John the Baptist. It had a 75 ft-high belfry. At the southern end was an antechapel, above which were two rooms, whose windows overlooked the chancel, for the use of women who wanted to hear mass and for the election of the masters of the hospital. The main window had a stained glass of the *Last Judgment* by Barnard Flower. On the walls were paintings of Henry VI, John the Baptist and other saints. The wooden ceiling was divided into 138 panels decorated with religious and heraldic bosses. A gallery was added in 1518. In 1642–3 Thomas Fuller author of the *Church History of Britain* and *Worthies of England*, was lecturer and packed the church. He returned at the Restoration but died a year later. Pepys heard some of the sermons but thought them poor and dry. Some time before the 18th century the window of the Last Judgment was removed and the embrasure bricked up. The chapel was extensively repaired in 1723. In 1754–6 illegal marriages were performed here by the incumbent, John Wilkinson, who advertised, 'There are five private ways by land to this chapel and two by water'. He was arrested, tried and transported.

The ceiling was whitewashed in about 1787 and in 1820–1 the south wall and tower were rebuilt by Robert Smirke. After a fire at the south end in 1843, restoration work was carried out by Sydney Smirke. In 1859–60 the gallery was removed and a south-east door made. In 1864 another fire left only the exterior walls standing, but the chapel was rebuilt as before by Smirke in 1864–5.

Thomas Willement designed the ceiling and the windows. In 1877 the vestry was rebuilt and a new eastern entrance made. In the 1880s the chapel became as fashionable as ST GEORGE'S, HANOVER SQUARE, for upper-class weddings. In 1890 it became the first place of worship to be lit by electricity. In 1909–33 Hugh Boswell Chapman was the incumbent; and, since he was vice-president of the Divorce Reform Union, both innocent and guilty parties in divorce cases could be remarried here. In 1937 the Savoy became the Chapel of the Royal Victorian Order. It was refitted in 1939 and given the title of the King's Chapel of the Savoy. Further alterations were carried out by A. B. Knapp-Fisher in 1957–8.

Savoy Hotel *Strand, WC2.* In 1884 Richard D'Oyly Carte decided to build a hotel adjoining the SAVOY THEATRE on land which Henry III had given to Peter, Count of Savoy, in 1264. Designed by T.E. Collcutt, the hotel opened in 1889. Another block was added in 1903–4. It is one of the earliest London hotels to provide a high ratio of bathrooms to bedrooms and to be fitted with electric lifts and electric lights.

César Ritz was the first manager and Auguste Escoffier the first chef. The hotel still possesses his pots and pans. Between them they created a card index of the rich and famous who were their guests, recording and catering for their extravagant or idiosyncratic tastes (or lack of them). Amongst the exuberant dishes they created was Pêche Melba in honour of Dame Nellie Melba's visit to London. Sir Henry Irving lived here; Sarah Bernhardt nearly died here; Edwardian millionaires flooded the courtyard with champagne and Caruso sang. Between the Wars 2LO broadcast dance music from their ballroom. The forecourt is the only street in the British Isles where traffic must keep to the right. The River Restaurant has recently been redecorated. The Grill Room remains one of the best hotel restaurants in London. There are 300 bedrooms.

Savoy Palace *Strand.* In the early 13th century the land on which the palace was built belonged to Brian de l'Isle, one of King John's counsellors, who died in 1233, and the land passed to his heir. In 1246 Henry III granted it, for an annual rental of three barbed arrows, to his wife's uncle Peter, the future Count of Savoy, who bequeathed it in 1268 to the monastery of St Bernard, Montjoux, Savoie. In 1270, Queen Eleanor bought it for 300 marks for her second son, Edmund, Earl of Lancaster. In 1293 Edward I gave his brother permission 'to strengthen and fortify his mansion called the Sauvoye with a wall of stone and mortar'. Between about 1345 and 1370 this mansion was rebuilt by Henry, 1st Duke of Lancaster, for £35,000, the proceeds of his French campaign. The house was said to be without equal in England.

Little is known of the building but there were stables, chapel, cloister, river gate, a vegetable garden and fish pond in addition to the Great Hall. The Duke added more land to the west which completed the boundaries of the future Savoy precinct – the STRAND to the north, the THAMES to the south, Ivy Bridge to the west and the TEMPLE to the east. In 1357 King John of France was conducted here after the Battle of Poitiers, accompanied by his captor, the Black Prince, and held here until 1360. In 1361 the palace was inherited by John of Gaunt through his wife, Blanche, Henry of Lancaster's daughter. In 1364 the French King, John, died here, having returned voluntarily after his son had broken parole. Geoffrey Chaucer

The Savoy Palace as it would have appeared in c. *1550, when it was largely a hospital. From an 18th-century engraving.*

married Phillipa Swynford, John of Gaunt's sister-in-law, in the chapel. In 1377 the palace was attacked by a mob because of Gaunt's support for Wycliffe but little damage was done. It was again attacked by Wat Tyler's followers in 1381 (*see* PEASANTS' REVOLT). The Duke escaped but his physician and serjeant-at-arms were killed. His gold and silver plate, furnishings and hangings were thrown on to a bonfire and his precious stones crushed and thrown into the river, as the assailants refused to steal from so hated a figure. One man who tried to pillage was also thrown on to the fire. There were 32 men trapped when the wine cellar in which they were drinking the Duke's wine collapsed on them and they were left there to starve. The explosion of a box of gunpowder, consigned to the flames in the belief that it contained gold, brought down the Great Hall. Afterwards the Palace was no longer usable, though many of the buildings were still standing. Between 1404 and 1405 a new stone wall was built along the STRAND frontage.

In 1505 Henry VII ordered the palace to be rebuilt as a hospital for the poor with 100 beds and he endowed it with land. Dormitories were built in the shape of a church in 1510–15. There were also three chapels including SAVOY CHAPEL and many outbuildings. The main gateway was at the west end. On the STRAND gate was a statue of St John the Baptist, the patron saint of the hospital, the date, 1505, and a Latin inscription which Weever translated in the 17th century as follows:

Henry the Seventh to his merite and honor
This hospital founded pore people to socor

It is not known when the hospital opened, but William Holgill was appointed Master in 1517. In 1535 an enquiry was held into its ill management. Holgill had many other interests and was probably often absent. In 1553 the hospital was suppressed by Edward VI, and its land given to the City to endow BRIDEWELL, the furniture and bedding being divided between BRIDEWELL and ST THOMAS'S HOSPITAL. Queen Mary refounded it in 1556 and reinstated the former master. Her maids-of-honour and the ladies of the court paid for new bedding and equipment and the Dean of ST PAUL'S gave plate for the chapel. It was endowed with land taken from dissolved monasteries. In 1559 Thomas Thurland was appointed Master. In 1570 a Bill of Complaint stated that Thurland's relations were maintained by the hospital, that he rarely went to church, that he had sexual relations with the hospital staff and that he owed the institution £2,500. However, he was not replaced and the hospital never recovered from his misrule. In the 16th and 17th centuries, houses in the precinct were occupied by noblemen and high-ranking clergy. The hospital itself continued to be misused. Stow wrote that vagabonds lay idly in the fields during the day, spending the night in the hospital. In 1581 Fleetwood, the Recorder of London, complained to Lord Burghley that the 'chief nurserie of evil men' was the Savoy because criminals claimed sanctuary here from the law.

During the second half of the 17th century tradesmen occupied the former houses of the nobility. Printers, glove-makers, leather-sellers and many others set up in business. In 1627 the hospital was used for soldiers wounded on the expedition to La Rochelle to help the Huguenots; and in 1642 a Parliamentary committee ordered the hospital to be vacated again for wounded soldiers. In 1653 sailors wounded in the Dutch War were admitted but they fought with the soldiers and were put under martial law. In 1661 the Conference of the Savoy was held here between 12 Anglican bishops and the same number of distinguished non-conformists to seek a compromise on religious problems but no agreement was reached. Subsequently French Protestants were given the use of the Little Chapel, and a Quaker meeting-house was established.

In 1670 a fire destroyed the west end of the precinct. In 1675 the hospital was taken over for wounded servicemen; and in 1679 the Great Dormitory and the Sisters' dwellings were requisitioned as a barracks for foot guards. In 1685 the French Protestant chapel was rebuilt by Wren. In 1687 a Jesuit school was founded for 400 boys. The children, irrespective of their religion, were taught free of charge but they had to pay for their books and writing materials. On the abdication of James II the following year the school was closed. In 1694 German Lutherans were given the former Sisters' Hall as a church. Princess Caroline, the future wife of George II, built them a schoolhouse. A Calvinist congregation moved to the Savoy about the same time. In 1695 a military prison was built here by Wren. In 1697 the right of sanctuary for criminals was abolished. In 1702 the hospital was formally dissolved, and in the 1730s the French Protestants moved to SOHO. The Lutheran Church was rebuilt in 1766–7, by Sir William Chambers, on the site of the former French chapel. In 1772 a long dispute over the ownership of the precinct was settled: the Crown took possession of the centre part and the DUCHY OF LANCASTER took the outer ring and the SAVOY CHAPEL. By now most of the buildings were in ruins. In 1775 Chambers made plans for building a barracks for 3,000 officers and men but they were never carried out. In 1776 the old barracks were burned down.

In 1816–20 the site was cleared to make way for the approach road to WATERLOO BRIDGE. By 1823 Savoy Street, Lancaster Place and two wharves were completed. In 1864–70 VICTORIA EMBANKMENT and EMBANKMENT GARDENS were made. Savoy Street and SAVOY HILL extended to the embankment. The Lutheran church and minister's house were demolished and rebuilt at the corner of Howland and Cleveland Streets. The only relic of the hospital is now the SAVOY CHAPEL. Most of the rest of the site is covered by the SAVOY HOTEL, the SAVOY THEATRE, the VICTORIA EMBANKMENT, EMBANKMENT GARDENS and the west wing of SOMERSET HOUSE.

Savoy Street WC2. Built over the site of SAVOY PALACE. The QUEEN'S CHAPEL OF THE SAVOY is between Savoy Hill and Savoy Row.

Savoy Theatre *Strand, WC2*. Built in 1881 to the designs of C.J. Phipps and financed by Richard D'Oyly Carte for the production of Gilbert and Sullivan's operas. The theatre was the first public building in London to be lit by electricity. It opened with *Patience*, transferred from the OPERA COMIQUE, and was followed by *Iolanthe* (1882), *Princess Ida*, *The Sorcerer* and *Trial by Jury* (1884), *The Mikado* (1885), *Ruddigore* (1887), *The Yeoman of the Guard* (1888) and *The Gondoliers* (1889). In 1890 Gilbert quarrelled with D'Oyly Carte over the expense of the production of *The Gondoliers*, being especially annoyed by a bill of £500 for new carpets. Sullivan supported Carte and the partnership broke up. In 1893 *Utopia Ltd* was produced. In 1896 *The Grand Duke*, their last joint effort, was a failure. From 1897 to 1903 comic operas by other composers were staged. In 1903 J.H. Leigh became lessee with J.E. Vedrenne as manager. In 1907 Vedrenne was joined by Granville-Barker with whom he had a highly successful partnership at the ROYAL COURT. In 1910–19 Henry Irving was the lessee and often appeared here, playing Hamlet in 1917. The first production of the children's play *Where the Rainbow Ends* was given in 1911. Between 1912 and 1914 a series of Shakespearian revivals were staged by Granville-Barker. In 1918 *Nothing but the Truth*, a farce by James Montgomery, began its run of 578 performances. From 1920 to 1929 the theatre was managed by Robert Courtneidge. During this time the most successful plays were *Paddy the Next Best Thing* (1920) which had 578 performances; Coward's comedy, *The Young Idea* (1923); *Young Woodley* (1928) by John Van Druten and *Journey's End* (1929) by R.C. Sherriff, which had 594 performances. In 1929 the theatre was entirely reconstructed by F.A. Tugwell and the interior redecorated by Basil Ionides. In 1941 *The Man Who Came to Dinner*, a comedy with Robert Morley, began its run of 709 performances.

Scadbury *Scadbury Park, Chislehurst, Kent*. A moated Saxon manorial site in a good defensive situation and still remarkably secluded today. The de Scathebury family were early owners and the Walsinghams lived here from 1425 to 1655. Queen Elizabeth I paid two visits and Christopher Marlowe also stayed. The Tudor house of 1540 was demolished in 1752, the widowed owner moving to FROGNAL, SIDCUP which he had just bought: his heir the 1st Viscount Sydney (after whom the Australian city is named) built a new house at Scadbury in 1870 adjacent to the moat (re-excavated in 1938) but that house was damaged by fire in 1976. The estate (about 300 acres) remains private, the previous orchards are now replaced by pasture.

Scala Theatre *(New Scala, 1923–38), Charlotte Street*. The King's Concert Rooms were opened on this site by Francis Pasquali in 1772. In 1776 they were leased by the Directors of Concerts of Ancient Music. George III took an interest in the concerts and they became very fashionable. They moved to HER MAJESTY'S THEATRE in 1794. In 1800 John Hyde hired the rooms for less ambitious concerts. In 1802 they were taken by the Pic Nics, a dramatic society; and in 1808 converted into a circus. In 1810 they were fitted up as a theatre by a gunsmith named Paul whose wife wanted to act, but he retired in 1814, having lost his money. Successive managers were equally unlucky.

The theatre was refurbished and reopened as the Prince of Wales Theatre under royal patronage in 1865. In 1867 Maria Wilton (the joint manager with H.J. Byron since 1865) married her leading man, Squire Bancroft, and between them they managed the theatre until 1880, producing Robertson's plays *Ours* (1866), *Caste* (1867), *Play* (1868), *School* (1869) and *MP* (1870). Ellen Terry, John Hare and Forbes Robertson acted in them. In 1880–2 the theatre was managed by Edgar Bruce. He made so much money out of *The Colonel* that he left to build his own theatre, THE PRINCE OF WALES in COVENTRY STREET. From 1866 to 1903 the theatre was used as a Salvation Army hostel. In 1905 the Scala Theatre was built on an enlarged site by F.T. Verity. Forbes Robertson managed it for a short time but was not particularly successful.

The earliest colour films were shown here in 1911–14. In the 1920s and 1930s the theatre was used by amateurs, and in the 2nd World War it became the United States Theatre Unit Base. In 1945 *Peter Pan* was first performed at the theatre and returned every Christmas. Otherwise it was still used by amateurs. It was demolished in 1970. No. 60 CHARLOTTE STREET stands on the site.

Scampston Mews *W10*. Takes its name from Scampston Hall in Yorkshire, the country house of William St Quintin (*see* ST QUINTIN'S AVENUE).

Schomberg House, Pall Mall, c. 1830, where Gainsborough died, was reconstructed behind its original façade in the 1950s.

Schomberg House *80–82 Pall Mall, SW1*. Reconstructed in 1698 for the 3rd Duke of Schomberg, whose father had been William III's second-in-command during the Glorious Revolution of 1688. It was divided into three in 1769. In 1771 the Scottish doctor, James Graham, who had established his Temple of Health at No. 4 ADELPHI TERRACE in 1779, opened his Temple of Health and Hymen here. It was famous for its 'Medico-Electrical Apparatus' and its 'Grand Celestial State Bed' which had a dome lined with mirrors, coloured sheets and mattresses 'filled with strongest, most springy hair, produced at vast expense from the tails of English stallions'. It also played music. From his 'Celestial Throne', Graham, who was ultimately confined in a lunatic asylum, delivered his 'very celebrated lecture on Generation' before his patients enjoyed the pleasures of his bed at a cost of £50 a night and, supposedly, conceived perfect babies as 'even the barren must do when so powerfully agitated in the delights of love'. In 1774–88 Thomas Gainsborough had an apartment in the house, and Richard Cosway, the miniature painter, lived here in 1784–9. The east wing was demolished in 1850. From 1859–1956 the rest was occupied by various departments of the War Office. In 1956–8 the house was reconstructed behind its original façade and the east wing rebuilt by C.H. Elsom and Partners for use as offices.

School of Design *Somerset House*. Established in 1837 in premises vacated by the ROYAL ACADEMY as a result of a recommendation by the Select Committee of the House of Commons of 1835. The painter, William Dyce, was Director from 1838–43, and the sculptor, Alfred Stevens, was employed as a master. In 1852 the Government established the Department of Practical Art which thereafter assumed responsibility for the school. Five years' later, the school was moved, with its collection of plaster casts, models, engravings and examples of contemporary manufacture, to the VICTORIA AND ALBERT MUSEUM.

School of Oriental and African Studies *Malet Street and Russell Square, WC1*. Originally established at FINSBURY CIRCUS in response to demands for improved teaching facilities for people taking up posts in Asia and Africa. The school was given its LONDON UNIVERSITY Charter in 1913, and lecturers working in associated fields at KING'S and UNIVERSITY COLLEGES moved there when it opened in 1917. When the UNIVERSITY acquired the BLOOMSBURY estate (*see* BLOOMSBURY), it was felt necessary to bring the school into closer proximity to the other colleges. Work began on a new building off RUSSELL SQUARE. Meanwhile, the teaching and administrative parts of the school moved to Vandon House and the library to CLARENCE HOUSE. The outbreak of the 2nd World War brought building to a halt. The school, however, provided much in the way of information and translation services once the War had spread to the Far East, and the number of people learning oriental languages rose steeply.

The school is now housed in two buildings: the older one, off RUSSELL SQUARE, was built by 1946, but was not brought into full working order until 1979; its extension, which houses the library of 500,000 books, was designed by Sir Denys Lasdun and completed in 1973. In 1982 there were approximately 450 undergraduates.

School of Pharmacy *29–39 Brunswick Square, WC1*. Founded in 1842 and admitted as a school of LONDON UNIVERSITY in the Faculty of Medicine in 1925. In 1952 it received its Royal Charter and was incorporated as the School of Pharmacy. In 1981 there was about 320 students.

J. Henry Schroder Wagg and Co. Ltd *Cheapside, EC2*. Henry Schroder, of the important merchant family of Schroders of Hamburg, established this banking firm in 1804. Schroders were amongst the first international houses to gain a foothold in London banking, and Henry Schroder quickly developed a large business in the acceptance of bills. More recently the firm built up a strong tradition in corporate finance and investment management. In 1962 it merged with Helbert, Wagg and Co., a merchant bank established in London in about 1800.

Science Museum *Exhibition Road, SW7*. In 1852 the Museum of Ornamental Art opened at MARLBOROUGH HOUSE. It consisted of the museum of the Central School of Practical Art, now the ROYAL COLLEGE OF ART, a collection of educational books and models, an animal products and food collection, and a number of exhibits from the GREAT EXHIBITION bought with a parliamentary grant of £5,000. In 1856 the museum moved to 'the Brompton Boilers', SOUTH KENSINGTON, where its collections gradually expanded.

In 1864 a collection of naval models was begun with a loan of exhibits from the ADMIRALTY; in 1874 a collection of scientific instruments; in 1883 the Science Library was formed by amalgamating the Educational Library at SOUTH KENSINGTON with the library of the MUSEUM OF PRACTICAL GEOLOGY; and in 1884 the collections of the Patent Office Museum were acquired. These collections had been formed by Bennet Woodcroft, Superintendent of Specifications at the PATENT OFFICE, and included *Puffing Billy*, constructed in 1813 and one of the world's oldest locomotives still in existence; Stephenson's *Rocket* of 1829; Arkwright's spinning machine and Wheatstone's electric telegraph. In 1898 a select committee recommended the division of the science and art sections of the museum. The following year the foundation stone of a new building was laid by Queen Victoria who requested it should be known as the VICTORIA AND ALBERT MUSEUM.

The science collections – further expanded by the acquisition of the Maudsley collection of machine tools and marine engines in 1900 and by the Woodcroft bequest of engine models and portraits in 1903 – were moved to buildings on their present site which were adapted and extended in stages between 1913, when Sir Richard Allison's east front was begun, and 1977 when the east block extension was opened. The museum, Britain's foremost museum of science and industry, now contains examples and illustrations of the machines, apparatus and scientific discoveries which formed the basis of Britain's industrial and scientific pre-eminence in the 19th century as well as extensive displays concerned with more recent international achievements in science and technology such as Fox Talbot's first camera, Edison's original phonograph, an early Bell telephone, the Vickers 'Vimy' aircraft in which Alcock and Brown made the first Atlantic air-crossing in June 1919 and Sir Frank Whittle's turbo-jet aeroengine.

The Science Museum Library, a national library of pure and applied science, which contains about half a million volumes, is housed in a new building adjacent to the museum, part of the extensions to the IMPERIAL COLLEGE OF SCIENCE AND TECHNOLOGY completed in 1969.

Scientific Instrument Makers' Company *see* CITY LIVERY COMPANIES.

Science Reference Library *25 Southampton Buildings, WC2*. Opened in 1855. It then contained the personal books and index of specifications of Bennet Woodcroft (*see* PATENT OFFICE) and the considerable collections of Richard Prosser. In 1857 it moved to improved but still cramped accommodation in the same building. 'The Free Library of the Commissioners of Patents' or PATENT OFFICE Library was for years the only free technical library in London. Today it is the Science Reference Library of the BRITISH LIBRARY. It is open to the public as the national library for modern science and technology and for patents, trade marks and designs. It contains nearly 25,000 different journals, 82,000 books and pamphlets and 19·5 million patents from all countries, as well as a world-wide collection of literature on trade marks, United Kingdom and other European reports and about 1,000 abstracting periodicals. As well as the literature on the inventive sciences, engineering and industrial technologies at HOLBORN there are some 70,000 books and pamphlets, 25,000 journals and 400 abstracting periodicals dealing with the life sciences and technologies, medicine, earth sciences, astronomy and pure mathematics in a library at 10, Porchester Gardens, QUEENSWAY, W2.

Scotch House Ltd *2–10 Brompton Road, SW1.* Founded by the Gardiner brothers who travelled from Glasgow to London to sell Scottish tweeds and tartans in the 1830s. The KNIGHTSBRIDGE shop was opened in 1900. The Tartan Room has a collection of over 300 tartans. There are now six branches in the Greater London area.

Scotland Yard *see* NEW SCOTLAND YARD.

Scottish Corporation This charity, originally nicknamed the Scottish Box, was more properly known as the Hall of the Scottish Hospital of his Majesty's Foundation situated in Water Lane, BLACK-FIARS, in 1676. It moved to new offices in CRANE COURT, FLEET STREET, in 1880 and the original site is now covered by the railway. Now known as the Scottish Corporation, it provides pensions and other funds for the relief of needy Scots in London.

Scott's *6 St James's Street.* Hatters founded in the early 1870s at 1 OLD BOND STREET where there had been a hat shop since 1851 and where a firm of outfitters, Bicknell, Jones and Griffiths, had been selling hats as early as 1758.

The firm was amalgamated with JAMES LOCK AND CO. LTD in the early 1970s.

Scott's Restaurant *20–22 Mount Street, W1.* The origins of the present restaurant lie in Coventry Street where in 1872 the proprietors of the London Pavilion Music Hall opened an 'oyster warehouse' at No. 18. In 1891 the business, which had by then changed hands and expanded into No. 19, became known as Scott's Oyster and Supper Rooms. Over the next two years both Nos 18 and 19, together with No. 20, were rebuilt of Bath stone in an Early French Renaissance style to the designs of Treadwell and Martin. For the next 50 years Scott's remained one of the best-known fish restaurants in Europe. The business moved to MAYFAIR in 1967.

Scriveners' Company *see* CITY LIVERY COMPANIES.

Seasons *17 Upper Mall, Hammersmith, W6.* May once have been one building with No. 19, the Dove Inn. Both probably date from the early 18th century. There is a tradition that it was here that James Thomson wrote the 'Winter' part of his *Seasons*, which was published in 1726. He is known to have met his death in 1748 by catching a chill on a river journey from HAMMERSMITH to KEW.

Secondary and Under-Sheriff and High Bailiff of Southwark Prothonotary An officer appointed and paid by the CORPORATION OF LONDON to carry out ceremonial and administrative duties at the CENTRAL CRIMINAL COURT. The post combines the duties of five former officers and was created in 1968 by a resolution of the COURT OF COMMON COUNCIL.

He is the deputy of the two SHERIFFS, is responsible for the CITY jurors and handles all ceremony within the CENTRAL CRIMINAL COURT. As High Bailiff of SOUTHWARK he attends the Court Leet which is held annually as a formality.

Sedley Place *W1.* On the Conduit Mead estate (*see* CONDUIT STREET), it is a short L-shaped side street connecting OXFORD STREET with Woodstock Street. The wrought-iron arch over the OXFORD STREET end, proclaiming 'Sedley Place 1873', was erected by Angelo Sedley, who in that year persuaded the METROPOLITAN BOARD OF WORKS to rename this alley (hitherto Hanover Place), thereby acquiring a valuable advertisment for his large furnishing business here.

Seething Lane *EC3.* Seething probably comes from Old English words meaning full of chaff. (The lane was near the cornmarket in FENCHURCH STREET.) Sir Francis Walsingham had a house here from 1580 until his death in 1590. In 1656 the Navy Office was built on the site. In 1660 Samuel Pepys was appointed Clerk of the Acts of the Navy and given a house in the lane. In 1672 the Navy Office was destroyed by fire. It was rebuilt in 1674–5 on the old site to the designs of either Wren or Robert Hooke. From 1673–9 Pepys was Secretary for the Affairs of the Navy but had to resign when unfounded charges for spying for the French were brought against him. He was appointed Secretary of the Admiralty in 1686 and held the post until his retirement three years later. In 1777 Nelson stayed at the Navy Office as a young man with his uncle who was Comptroller of the Navy. In 1788 the building was demolished when the Office moved to SOMERSET HOUSE.

In the lane now is ST OLAVE HART STREET, where Pepys worshipped in the Navy Office pew, and where he and his wife are buried. Also here are ALL HALLOWS BARKING and the offices of the PORT OF LONDON AUTHORITY.

Selfridge Hotel *Orchard Street, W1.* Built in 1973 to the designs of David Brookbank and Associates, behind the OXFORD STREET store on the site of the former Somerset Hotel. There are 298 bedrooms.

Selfridge's Ltd *400 Oxford Street, W1.* Harry Gordon Selfridge was born in Ripon, Wisconsin, USA. In 1877 at the age of 20 he worked in Marshall Field in Chicago, and later became a junior partner. In 1902 he bought his own store in Chicago but did not like competing with his old firm, so sold out and left for Europe. In 1906 he decided to build a store in OXFORD STREET. Sam Waring of WARING AND GILLOW backed him on condition that he did not sell furniture, a condition which Selfridge always honoured. On 15 March 1909 the store opened. It was conceived in a giant Ionic order to the original design of Daniel Burnham of Chicago, in consultation with Frank Swales, executed by the English architect R.F. Atkinson and completed in 1928 by Sir John Burnet. It had a clock with a figure 11 ft high called *The Queen of Time* (by Gilbert Bayes) over the main entrance. It was originally intended to have a colossal tower.

Gordon Selfridge retired in 1940. In 1952 Selfridge's was bought by Lewis's Investment Trust and Charles Clore of the British Shoe Corporation.

The huge Oxford Street store built by the American Gordon Selfridge, and which bears his name, was opened in 1909.

Selhurst *SE25 and Surrey*. Situated between UPPER NORWOOD and CROYDON. It was named thus by the 13th century – a willow wood – and remained little changed until the enclosure of common land in the area at the end of the 18th century. Following the construction of the London and Croydon Railway in 1838–9, residential development took place. In 1844 an experimental atmospheric railway system carried the Selhurst track over the main line but it was not used after 1846 (*see* ATMOSPHERIC RAILWAY).

In 1965 Selhurst became part of the London Borough of CROYDON.

Selsdon *Surrey*. The name probably originates from two Saxon words meaning mansion and hill. It is first mentioned as being bequeathed to his wife, Werburg, by Aelfrid in 861. It was later held by the KNIGHTS TEMPLAR and in 1347 by Sir John Gresham. Now a suburb between CROYDON and SANDERSTEAD, it became prominent in the 1970s after the Tory Party Special Conference had been held at SELSDON PARK HOTEL and the Press described a new type of Conservative as 'Selsdon Man'. In part of its former grounds – which contain cedars dating from Tudor times one of which is said to have been planted by Elizabeth I herself – stands CROYDON HIGH SCHOOL FOR GIRLS. From 1925 the adjoining Selsdon Court became a hotel annexe until, damaged by fire in 1944, it was demolished in 1958. Nearby also are Selsdon Woods, one of the earliest NATIONAL TRUST properties. This bird sanctuary, surrounded by expanding housing estate, is famous for its bluebells. The Church of St John is by Newberry and Fowler (1935–6).

Selsdon Park Hotel *Addington Road, Sanderstead, Surrey*. The original Tudor mansion was sold in 1805 to George Smith MP who was mainly responsible for redesigning the building with its 11 bays, outbuildings and castellated towers. In 1874 it was secured for Bishop Thorold of Rochester (later of Winchester). In 1925 it was bought by the father of the present owner and converted into an hotel, spectacularly enlarged by Hugh Macintosh in neo-Jacobean style.

Senate House *Malet Street, WC1*. The principal building of the UNIVERSITY OF LONDON. It was designed by Charles Holden, and built of Portland stone in 1932. There is a massive tower, 210 ft high. The building contains administrative offices and the University Library of about one million volumes and 4,500 current periodicals. There are special collections of Elizabethan literature, economics and music. The building also houses the School of Slavonic and East European Studies (founded 1933) and the Institute of Historical Research (founded 1921).

Serapis *see* TEMPLE OF MITHRAS.

Serbia House *West Norwood*. This house, now demolished, was once Knight's Hill Farm, one of the oldest houses in the area. It was built on land leased and later bought by Lord Thurlow from the Manor of Leigham Court (*see* WEST NORWOOD), and appears on Rocque's map of 1746. The house, which was near Norwood Road, became known as Thurlow Lodge and adjoined the site where Thurlow built his ill-fated mansion (*see* WEST NORWOOD). It was also lived in by Sir Hiram Maxim, inventor of the machine-gun, who apparently wrote to the *Norwood Press* to notify the public that he would be experimenting with the gun in his garden and if they kept their windows open there would be no danger of broken glass! Flying-machines were among his many interests and in the early 1900s he conducted experiments in his garden and at the CRYSTAL PALACE. During the 1st World War, Serbian refugees occupied the house, hence its final name.

Serjeants-at-Law A superior rank of barrister appointed by Royal Writ and dating from the very early Middle Ages. One is mentioned in the Prologue to Chaucer's *Canterbury Tales*. They were originally few in number, each being allocated a pillar in old ST PAUL'S CATHEDRAL where they would meet their clients. The name derives from the Latin *servientes ad legem* since they were originally envisaged as servants of the Crown. In the course of time appointments to the order came to be made as recognition of professional eminence. They were also known as the Order of the Coif from the rounded patch of black and white cloth worn on the top of their wigs by members. By the 14th century they had secured virtually complete control of the legal profession in England.

On appointment as a Serjeant, a barrister left his INN OF COURT and joined SERJEANTS' INN, his departure being marked by lavish feasting and ceremonial. Serjeants took precedence over all junior barristers. A Serjeant who became a King's Counsel was known as a King's Serjeant. Until 1846 they enjoyed a monopoly of advocacy in the Court of Common Pleas and, until 1875, they alone could be appointed judges in any of the superior courts. Any barrister who was not already a Serjeant was customarily created one before he took his seat on the bench. After 1868 appointments were confined to persons about to be created judges. The last appointment of a Serjeant was that of the future Lord Lindley who became a judge of the Common Pleas in 1875 and who died in 1921. In the 19th century the number of practising Serjeants never exceeded 28.

In Chapter xxxiv of *The Pickwick Papers* Charles Dickens, recounting the case of Bardell *v.* Pickwick, immortalised the names of Serjeant Buzfuz and Serjeant Snubbin, leading counsel in the celebrated action for preach of promise heard at the GUILDHALL.

Serjeants' Inn   Three different places at one time or other bore the name of Serjeants' Inn. The first was Scrope's Inn, situated on the north side of HOLBORN, which was in use in 1459–91. It was abandoned in 1498 and later came to be known as Scrope's Court. It was totally destroyed at the time of the construction of HOLBORN VIADUCT in the 19th century. The second, Fleet Street Inn, situated on the south side of FLEET STREET and at the north-east corner of the TEMPLE, was destroyed in the GREAT FIRE. The Inn was restored by 1670, but by 1732 when the Serjeants were refused a renewal of their lease, they moved to CHANCERY LANE and the premises were let as professional chambers. In the 2nd World War they were severely damaged and then rebuilt as offices. The entry today is through an archway in the frontage. Another Serjeants' Inn was situated at the south-eastern end of CHANCERY LANE where the site is now occupied by the premises of the Royal Insurance Group (No. 5 CHANCERY LANE). A plaque in the wall reads 'Site of Old Serjeants' Inn 1415–1910'. In the course of the 15th century the Serjeants occupied the Fleet Street Inn (1424–42), then the Chancery Lane Inn (1442–59), then Scrope's Inn (1459–96) and then the Chancery Lane Inn once more. By the 16th century both Fleet Street and Chancery Lane Inns were in occupation. The Serjeants sold the Chancery Lane Inn in 1877 and returned to their original INN OF COURT. The stained glass arms of the Serjeants can be seen in the LAW SOCIETY's Hall at No. 113 CHANCERY LANE, while portraits of the Serjeants are in the NATIONAL PORTRAIT GALLERY.

Serle's Coffee House   *Lincoln's Inn.* Named after Henry Serle, a bencher of LINCOLN'S INN, who was associated in the development of NEW SQUARE. He died in 1690 in debt, and it was never clear how he had raised the money in the first place. There is no evidence that the house existed in his lifetime and it is not mentioned before 1711 when, according to the *Spectator*, it was patronised by lazy law students.

There is no mention of the house after 1840; and the area was certainly cleared for office blocks before 1897.

Sermon Lane   *EC4.* Perhaps named after Adam Sermoncinarius, a 13th-century property owner, or, since it was once known as Sheremoiners' Lane, its name may have come from the sheremongers, who sheared, or cut, and rounded the silver plates used in the minting of coins. According to Stow there was a house here in the 13th century called the Blacke Loft where silver was melted down before it went to the King's bullion store in OLD CHANGE. In the 14th century Sir Nicholas Housebonde, a minor canon of ST PAUL's, was allotted a house here. He complained it was too far from the Cathedral and that he would be attacked at night in the surrounding streets by robbers and loose women.

Serpentine Gallery   *Hyde Park,* W2. A former tea-house designed by Sir Henry Tanner. Exhibitions of contemporary art are held here under the auspices of the ARTS COUNCIL.

Seven Dials   *WC2.* In October 1694 John Evelyn went to see 'the building beginning neare St Giles's where seaven streetes make a starr from a Doric Pillar plac'd in the middle of [a] Circular Area'. The seven streets were Great Earl Street, Little Earl Street, Great White Lion Street, Little White Lion Street, Great St Andrew's Street, Little St Andrew's Street and Queen Street. The column, which supported a clock with seven faces, was removed in 1773 in the false belief that a great sum of money had been lodged in the base. It was re-erected in 1882, on the green at Weybridge, Surrey, to commemorate Frederica, Duchess of York's long residence at Oatlands. The development of Seven Dials had been started in 1693 by Thomas Neale, Master of the MINT, and was completed in about 1710. In 1716 Gay wrote in *Trivia*:

> Where famed St Giles' ancient limits spread,
> An inrailed column rears its lofty head;
> Here to seven streets, seven dials count the day,
> And from each other catch the circling ray;
> Here oft the peasant with enquiring face
> Bewildered trudges on from place to place;
> He dwells on every sign with stupid gaze,
> Enters the narrow alley's doubtful maze,
> Tries every winding court and street in vain,
> And doubles o'er his weary steps again.

It was intended to be a fashionable residential area adjoining SOHO and COVENT GARDEN but in the 18th and 19th centuries it became the hideout of petty thieves and the haunt of the very poorest STREET VENDORS, including many street-ballad chapbook publishers one of whom, James Catnach, established his press at No. 2 Monmouth Court in 1814.

Dickens describes the area in his *Sketches by Boz*. Much of this area was cleared away when CHARING CROSS ROAD and SHAFTESBURY AVENUE were built. It is now the junction between Mercer, MONMOUTH and EARLHAM STREETS and Shorts Gardens.

Seven Sisters Road   *N7, N4, N15.* A long straggling road through dingy suburbs built in the 19th century to connect HOLLOWAY and TOTTENHAM. It is named after seven sisters who, when they were about to go their separate ways, planted seven elms outside a TOTTENHAM tavern.

Seven Stars *Carey Street, WC2*. A public house built in 1602. Originally known as the League of Seven Stars, after the seven provinces of the Netherlands; its first customers were Dutch sailors who settled in the area in the 17th century. As it is opposite to the rear entrance of the LAW COURTS, its present clientele consists mainly of members of the legal profession and their clients. The walls are decorated with 'Spy' cartoons of eminent lawyers.

Seville Street *SW1*. Made about 1843 to provide an entrance to the LOWNDES ESTATE. It had houses on both sides and Cubitt was worried that one on the main road had become a wine merchant's office which might offend the occupants of LOWNDES SQUARE. Known originally as Charles Street, in honour of Charles Lyall, a trustee and friend of William Lowndes, the reason for its change of name is unknown. The change took place shortly before the 2nd World War when air-raid precautions necessitated new names for several streets in London to avoid ambiguity.

Seymour Street *W1*. Built in about 1769 and named after Henry Seymour who inherited the PORTMAN ESTATE. Michael William Balfe, the composer, lived at No. 12 in 1861–4; Thomas Campbell, the poet, at No. 10 in 1822–8 and Edward Lear at No. 30 in 1857–8. Sir Robert Peel was married in the drawing-room of No. 45 to Julia Floyd in 1820. Seymour Place, laid out from 1810 onwards, runs north from Seymour Street. Halfway along it are the Seymour Hall Baths.

Shades *Upper Thames Street and Old Swan Stairs*. A tavern overlooking the river, with a coffeeroom built out from the old FISHMONGERS' HALL. It was said to be the last tavern in London to retain the custom of drawing the wine from the butt into old silver tankards.

Shadwell *E1*. A district of STEPNEY on the north bank of the THAMES which was virtually uninhabited until the 17th century, although evidence of Roman burials has been found here. Much of the area belonged to the Canons of ST PAUL'S who had been granted an estate in Shadwell in 1228; and by the 16th century a large part of their land was covered with ditches which fed a tide mill. A marine-centred industrial hamlet rapidly grew up, however, with roperies, tan yards, breweries, wharves, smiths and numerous taverns, when the riverside was developed in the 17th century. By 1674 it has been estimated that over 8,000 people lived here, many of whom were mariners, watermen or lightermen. Development had been greatly encouraged by the enterprising speculator, Thomas Neale, who built the chapel in 1656 (St Paul's which was rebuilt in 1821) and petitioned Parliament for the creation of a new parish in 1669. When established the following year, Shadwell was the first parish to be created from ST DUNSTAN'S STEPNEY since WHITECHAPEL in 1338. By 1681 Neale had also founded a market in Shadwell, which served the neighbouring hamlets, and built a waterworks which supplied about 8,000 houses by the 1790s with water drawn from the THAMES. Most of the

houses he built were small, wood-framed dwellings infilled with bricks. None of them survived into the 20th century and the area between the High Street and the river become one of the most wretched slums in Victorian London. At the beginning of the 19th century Malcolm claimed that 'thousands of useful tradesmen, artisans and mechanicks and numerous watermen inhabit [Shadwell] but their homes and workshops will not bear description'. The only open space left at this time was Sun Tavern Fields which had several ropewalks.

Captain Cook's first child was baptised in St Paul's Church close to where the Cooks had lodgings for a short time; and William Perkins, the discoverer of aniline dye, the mauve beloved of Victorians, lived in the parish. Many labourers, especially Irish, were employed in unloading coal here; and the Coal Whippers' Office was established in Lower Shadwell after the Act of 1843 which regulated their employment.

The population reached its peak of almost 12,000 in 1851 but dropped by a quarter the following decade because the extension of the LONDON DOCKS into the Shadwell Basin caused the demolition of numerous houses and drove their poor inhabitants to neighbouring areas. More streets near the riverfront were cleared for the short-lived Shadwell Fish Market which in turn was demolished with nearby streets to make way for the King Edward VII Memorial Park opened by George V in 1922. A monument there commemorates explorers who set sail from this reach of the THAMES in Tudor times – Sir Martin Frobisher, Sir Hugh Willoughby, William and Stephen Borough and others. Several large warehouses remain along Wapping Wall, as does the London Hydraulic Power Company's former pumping station; the PROSPECT OF WHITBY PUBLIC HOUSE has become a tourist attraction as one of the older riverside taverns and, since the closure of the LONDON DOCKS, it is intended to develop the Shadwell Basin as a centre for water sports.

Shadwell Waterworks Company Established in 1669 to serve the area from the TOWER to LIMEHOUSE and the THAMES to WHITECHAPEL. The works stood partly on the sites of Shadwell Basin and partly on the area which became the KING EDWARD VII MEMORIAL PARK, the land being leased from the Dean of ST PAUL'S.

In 1750 the horse mills were replaced by an atmospheric engine. And in 1756 reference was made to two engines which supplied 'two main pipes of six or seven inch bores with Thames Water, wherewith the neighbourhood is plentifully furnished'. In 1774 an engine which could raise more than 730,000 gallons in a 14-hour working day was installed. Before its demise the company was supplying water to about 8,000 houses and other buildings. In 1807 the London Dock Company needed the site and purchased the works for £50,000. They continued to operate, however, until the EAST LONDON WATERWORKS were complete.

Shaftesbury Avenue *W1, WC2*. After the completion of REGENT STREET, the need for additional improvements in communications between PICCADILLY CIRCUS and CHARING CROSS northwards to TOTTENHAM COURT ROAD and BLOOMSBURY became imperative. In 1877, therefore, Parliament granted the METROPOLITAN BOARD OF WORKS powers to form the thoroughfares to be known as CHARING CROSS ROAD and Shaftesbury Avenue. The route of the two streets was planned by the Board's architect, George Vulliamy, and their engineer, Sir Joseph Bazalgette. For reasons principally of economy, the street to be called Shaftesbury Avenue – in memory of the 7th Earl of Shaftesbury whose charitable work had been largely directed towards helping the poor in the areas through which it was to pass – was to a great extent to be formed by widening existing streets – Richmond Street, King Street and Dudley Street among them – so that the old street pattern of SOHO was not transformed and most of the new thoroughfare, like most of CHARING CROSS ROAD, follows the line of an ancient highway.

As well as easing the congested traffic in this part of London, the formation of Shaftesbury Avenue also resulted in the demolition of some of the most squalid slums whose horrors are glimpsed in the work of Dickens; but the need to provide new housing for the families displaced impeded the rate of the work and it was not until June 1886 that the road was opened and even then the pride which the public might have felt in its construction was marred by the indifferent quality of the architecture which looked down upon it and by the misdemeanors and peculations of some of the Board's officials which were to be the subject of enquiry by a Royal Commission. Between 1888 and 1907 six theatres opened in Shaftesbury Avenue, the LYRIC, THE APOLLO, the GLOBE, the SHAFTESBURY, the QUEEN's and the PALACE. All these, to be joined in 1931 by the SAVILLE THEATRE, remain, apart from the SHAFTESBURY which, severely damaged by bombing in 1941, has since been demolished; and Shaftesbury Avenue is still known as the 'heart of theatreland'. All the theatres are on the west side of the street. Also on this side is the Columbia Cinema, part of a handsome modern block built in 1958 to the designs of Sir John Burnet, Tait and Partners, and on the corner of Bucknell Street is the Bloomsbury Central Baptist Church. On the east side, which is largely occupied by restaurants, offices, employment agencies and shops selling musical instruments, practical joke kits, postcards and mementoes for tourists, are the FRENCH HOSPITAL and, at Nos 22–32, the former TROCADERO RESTAURANT. Arthur Beale Ltd, the yacht chandlers at No. 194, trace their origins to a company of ropemakers on the FLEET RIVER at the beginning of the 16th century.

Shaftesbury Hospital see ST PETER'S HOSPITAL FOR STONE AND OTHER URINARY DISEASES.

Shaftesbury Theatre *(Prince's, 1911–62), Shaftesbury Avenue, WC2*. Originally known as the New Prince's Theatre, it was designed by Bertie Crewe for Popular Playhouses Ltd whose directors, Walter and Frederick Melville, were, at the time, managing the Lyceum Theatre *(see LYCEUM DANCE HALL)*. Built in 1911 on the corner of SHAFTESBURY AVENUE and HIGH HOLBORN it opened on the 26 December 1911 with *The Three Musketeers*. Most of its presentations were melodramas until Seymour Hicks took over the management in 1916. His most successful production was *Monsieur Beaucaire* which ran for 221 performances.

In 1916–29, when it was entirely reconstructed, the theatre (for most of the time under the management of C.B. Cochran) staged many notable productions. Almost all D'Oyly Carte's Gilbert and Sullivan operas

were presented in 1919, 1921, 1924 and 1926. Sarah Bernhardt appeared as *Daniel* in 1921. Seasons of Diaghilev's Ballets Russes and plays presented by the Guitrys were followed by Sybil Thorndike and Henry Ainley in *Macbeth*. Gershwin's *Funny Face* with Leslie Henson, Sydney Howard and Fred and Adèle Astaire, which ran for 263 performances, was interrupted by a gas main's explosion in a nearby street which closed all passage to the theatre for several weeks.

George Robey took over the management in 1927 and was followed in 1929 by W.H. Berry, then by Firth Shephard, who had been associated with Robey. Thereafter many well-known stars appeared at the theatre, including Evelyn Laye, Richard Hearne, Douglas Byng and, later, Maurice Chevalier, Michael Redgrave and Peggy Ashcroft. In 1961 the freehold was purchased by Jack Hylton and the following year it was acquired by Charles Clore and EMI in partnership. The theatre was then reconstructed and reopened as the Shaftesbury Theatre, the name of a former theatre in Nassau Street destroyed by enemy action. The seating capacity is 1,300 (that of the Prince's was 1,726).

Shaftesbury Theatre *Shaftesbury Avenue*. Opened in 1888 with *As You Like It*, Forbes-Robertson playing Orlando. It was the first theatre to be built in SHAFTESBURY AVENUE. The early productions were not a success, though the *Middleman* (1889) and *Judah* (1890) had fairly long runs. In 1891 *Cavalleria Rusticana* had its London *première*. In 1896 £15,000 was lost. The fortunes of the theatre took a more hopeful turn with *The Belle of New York* which began its run of 697 performances in 1898. This was followed by *For Sword or Song* with Fred Terry and Julia Neilson, which was another failure. In 1903 the successful musical play with a black cast, *In Dahomey*, was followed six years later by another success, *The Arcadians*. These, however, were the last productions of note.

In 1933 the first-night appearance of the German actor, Werner Krauss, provoked disturbances; and in 1941 the theatre was destroyed by bombs.

Shakespeare Gallery *52 Pall Mall*. Opened in June 1789 by John Boydell, a rich print publisher who was to become Lord Mayor the following year. His idea had been to 'form an English School of Historical Paintings [depicting] scenes of the immortal Shakespeare'. These were to be exhibited in a permanent gallery and from them he would make engravings. He commissioned 35 artists including Reynolds, Romney, West, Fuseli, Opie and Kauffmann; 34 paintings were ready for the opening of the gallery and 33 more were added in 1790. The building in which they were displayed was designed by George Dance the Younger and on its façade was a relief of Shakespeare with the Dramatic Muse on one side and the Genius of Painting on the other. The cost of the building, paintings and engravings was over £100,000, a sum which proved beyond Boydell's means when his business was badly affected by the wars that broke out after the French Revolution, and Continental customers for his prints could not easily be found. He obtained an Act of Parliament to dispose of the paintings and thousands of his prints by lottery. The lease of the building was sold to an artists' group, the British Institution, which occupied it until it was demolished in 1868.

Shaw Theatre *Euston Road, NW1.* Named after George Bernard Shaw, once a St Pancras Councillor. Designed by Elidir Davies and Partners for CAMDEN Council, it is part of a complex including a library. It is the home of the National Youth Theatre and the Shaw Theatre Company. The seating capacity is 510. The sculpture outside is by Keith Grant.

Sheen *Surrey.* The ancient manor of Sheen – shelters – was associated with royalty from at least the 12th century. The manor house became Sheen Palace in the 14th century. Henry V established two religious houses nearby: a Carthusian monastery on the site of the OLD DEER PARK; and Syon monastery for the Bridgettine order (originally at TWICKENHAM), whose name may be related to the manor (*see* SYON HOUSE). The palace, destroyed by fire in 1499, was rebuilt by Henry VII, who renamed it Richmond after his Yorkshire earldom. In the centuries following the DISSOLUTION, Sheen's priory buildings became dilapidated and in the 18th century George III demolished those remaining to use the area as pasturage. The hamlet of West Sheen was also demolished so that only East Sheen and Sheen Common perpetuated the name.

NORTH SHEEN was named at the end of the 19th century and over 50 acres of the common were preserved, subsequently under the care of the NATIONAL TRUST. At Sheen Lodge in RICHMOND PARK, once part of the manor of Sheen, the physiologist Richard Owen entertained Dickens, Millais and Gladstone.

Sheffield Terrace *W8.* Built in 1849 and named after the Sheffield family of Sheffield House, Kensington Church Street. G.K. Chesterton was born at No. 32 in 1874. The family firm of auctioneers and estate agents, Chestertons, have offices in KENSINGTON HIGH STREET and elsewhere. Prebendary Wilson Carlile, curate of St Mary Abbots, and later founder of the Church Army, lived at No. 34.

Shepherd and Shepherdess *City Road.* A tavern built some time before 1745. Invalids stayed here to benefit from the pure country air and it was popular at holiday time for cream cakes and furmety. It was demolished in about 1825.

Shepherd Market *W1.* The area is best approached from CURZON STREET, by way of the covered passage at No. 47, which leads into the network of narrow streets and alleys which was laid out here in about 1735 by Edward Shepherd, the architect and builder active in so many parts of MAYFAIR. Previously this had been (since 1686–8) the site of the MAY FAIR, from which the whole district takes its name, and which was kept here annually from 1 May for 15 days. Very soon this event had become notorious for riotous and disorderly behaviour, and in 1708 it had been abolished, only to be revived again, with similar results. In the days before the existence of the METROPOLITAN POLICE such *saturnalia* were difficult to suppress permanently, and building on the site was probably the most effective way of doing so. The aristocratic residents of nearby streets must, at all events, have been glad when Shepherd built his two-storey market house, with butchers' shops below and a great room above, the latter used as a theatre in fair time during the years before the fair finally ceased to

exist. The original market house has been rebuilt or at any rate refurbished, for although the buildings on its island site bear the date 1860 they still have an 18th-century air about them. Most of them, and most of those facing them, are now either foodshops, antique shops, restaurants or pubs, particularly popular at lunchtime with people working in the offices which predominate in many nearby streets. Shepherd Market is the 'village centre' of Mayfair.

Shepherd Street *W1.* Extends westward from WHITE HORSE STREET along the south side of the island block which forms the core of SHEPHERD MARKET.

Shepherd's Bush *W12.* The area between West KENSINGTON and ACTON. The name 'Shepherd' is thought to be a personal one. Described by Faulkner in 1839 as a 'pleasant village', its common, a triangular space of 8 acres, remains an island in the traffic, with Uxbridge Road on the north and Goldhawk Road on the south side. Goldhawk was the name of a 15th-century family of landowners and the road is thought to have been a Roman one, although it fell out of use for centuries.

Development of Shepherds Bush was slow and confined to the sides of the main roads. It retained its brickfields and farms north of Uxbridge Road until the late 19th century, while, following the development of railways, the rest of the district gradually filled up with streets of small houses. The WHITE CITY EXHIBITION land was used for housing estates in the 1920s and for the BBC TELEVISION CENTRE. Some open spaces remain: RAVENSCOURT PARK of 32 acres, WORMWOOD SCRUBS of 190 acres, Wormholt Park of 8 acres, Hammersmith Park of 7 acres and the grounds of QUEEN'S PARK RANGERS at Loftus Road.

Shepherd's Bush Common *W12.* Triangular open space of 8 acres acquired by Act of Parliament 1871. It was formerly called Gagglegoose Green. Its present name is from the shepherd's practice of watching his sheep whilst lying in a thorn bush. The highwayman 'Sixteen String Jack' was finally captured here. It was here also that in 1657 Miles Syndercombe planned to assassinate Oliver Cromwell on his way to HAMPTON COURT, by discharging an early type of machine-gun firing 12 bullets. Syndercombe was betrayed by an accomplice and was found dead in the TOWER before his planned execution at TYBURN.

Shepherd's Bush Market A general market opened in 1914 on a site originally intended as an access road to the underground railway station. The same year the *West London Observer* recorded complaints from shopkeepers and the area was paved. The market expanded rapidly after the 1st World War. There were further extensions in 1932 and 1939. After heavy damage in the 2nd World War it was threatened with closure, but the traders joined together to clear the rubble and it was reopened within a few days. The food stalls cater largely for West Indians.

Shepherd's Tavern *50 Hertford Street, W1.* Built in 1708. It has Georgian bow windows and wooden panelling. It was named after Edward Shepherd of SHEPHERD'S MARKET. There is a sedan chair which was once owned by the Duke of Cumberland, son of George III, and is now used as a telephone kiosk.

During the 2nd World War the house was a meeting place for RAF pilots.

Sheraton Park Tower Hotel *101 Knightsbridge, SW1.* Built on the site of Wontland's department store, a fashionable shop which had formerly been a servants' bazaar. The building, which contains 295 bedrooms on 17 storeys, was designed by R. Seifert and Partners and opened in 1973.

Sheraton Street *W1.* Laid out in the 1690s and first known as Little Chapel Street because of the HUGUENOT chapel, La Petite Patente which once stood here. Its name was changed in 1937 to commemorate the furniture designer, Thomas Sheraton, who occupied houses nearby in the 1790s. None of the original houses survives.

Sherbourne Lane *EC4.* Stow thought it was named after the River LANGBOURN which, he said, broke up into small shews or streams here. A more recent theory is that it was named after a shittah tree which stood here: earlier versions of the name are Shitteborwelane (1272–3) and Shiteburn Lane (1303). ST MARY ABCHURCH is here.

Sheriffs The office of Sheriff is the oldest in the CITY OF LONDON, the name deriving from 'Shire Reeve' or County Justice. William the Conqueror's charter to London is addressed to William, the Bishop, and Godfrey, the Port-reeve; and Henry I in 1132 bestowed a charter on the CITY empowering the citizens to appoint their own SHERIFF and Justician not only for London but also for the County of MIDDLESEX. This right existed until the Local Government Act of 1888, by which the two sheriffs elected ceased to represent the County of MIDDLESEX but were appointed for the CITY only. Until the institution of the mayoralty in 1192 the Sheriffs governed the CITY.

They are today elected annually by the liverymen of the CITY COMPANIES on Midsummer Day, 24 June, in GUILDHALL, and take the oath of office on Michaelmas Eve, 28 September, before the LORD MAYOR, ALDERMEN and the courts of the LIVERY COMPANIES to which they belong. One of the Sheriffs elected is normally an ALDERMAN, who must serve the office of Sheriff if he aspires to the mayoralty: he is known as the Aldermanic Sheriff. The other, called the Lay Sheriff, need be neither ALDERMAN nor common councilman; but if he is not, he must retire from the CORPORATION at the end of his year of office.

Sheriffs attend the LORD MAYOR on most official occasions, including the meetings of the CORPORATION's various Courts. They attend the sessions at the CENTRAL CRIMINAL COURT in the OLD BAILEY, where they have their own chambers. They present petitions from the CITY to PARLIAMENT at the Bar of the HOUSE OF COMMONS. They no longer appoint their own Under-Sheriffs.

A Sheriff wears the same gown and hat as an ALDERMAN with a chain of office from which hangs a badge usually presented him by his ward or livery company.

Sherlock Holmes *10 Northumberland Avenue, WC2.* Previously known as the Northumberland Arms, this public house is now a shrine to the great detective. The walls are decorated with Holmes mementoes. Upstairs can be seen a reconstruction of the front room at

221b BAKER STREET, complete with Sherlock Holmes reading his *Times* in front of the fire. The collection originated with the Sherlock Holmes Society of London.

Sherwood Street *W1.* Built in the 1670s on land assigned by Sir William Pulteney to Francis Sherard, a younger brother of Lord Sherard of Leitrim. It was formerly known as Sherard Street but the present corruption of that name was more commonly used by the middle of the 18th century and it was officially designated Sherwood Street by the METROPOLITAN BOARD OF WORKS in 1862. Described by Strype in 1720 as 'a handsome, broad, well built and inhabited Place', none of its early character remains. Its west side is dominated by the REGENT PALACE HOTEL. On its east is the PICCADILLY THEATRE.

Ship *Ship Lane, Mortlake, SW14.* Although the present building is Georgian, the original tavern here, known as the Hart's Horn, was Elizabethan. In the 17th century it became the Blue Anchor, and received its present name in the 19th century. It provides a fine view of the UNIVERSITY BOAT RACE.

Ship and Shovel *2 Craven Passage, WC2.* An inn built in about 1700 and now almost under the arches of CHARING CROSS STATION. The unusual name derives from the stevedores, who, having unloaded the cargoes from the Thames barges which docked nearby, refreshed themselves here, leaving their long-handled shovels leaning against the wall outside.

Ship Tavern *27 Lime Street, EC3.* Originally built in 1447, the Ship has always been closely connected with shipowners and master mariners. The notices of the PORT OF LONDON AUTHORITY have been posted here since 1909.

Shipwrights' Company *see* CITY LIVERY COMPANIES.

Shirley *Surrey.* Lies south of ADDISCOMBE towards the eastern boundary of the London Borough of CROYDON. Neolithic remains and Roman coins have been found in the area which was named – bright wood or clearing – by the 14th century. Until enclosure at the end of the 18th century it was largely heath wasteland with some large mansions such as Coombe House (now St Margaret's School). The windmill in the grounds of the John Ruskin School (moved from CROYDON in 1955) dates in part from the 18th century and was restored in 1962. Within the parish of ADDINGTON, Shirley had no church building until Sir George Gilbert Scott's St John the Evangelist was opened in 1856. Its vicar during 1879–1912 was William Wilks, horticulturalist and propagator of the Shirley poppy.

In the early 20th century the district rapidly became residential, and in 1927 it was formed into a separate parish. The Monks Orchard and Spring Park Estates to the north and east were developed. The early 18th-century Spring Park Lodge survives as an estate office. In 1958 more than 1,000 houses and flats were built in Shrublands Estate by the CROYDON Corporation to replace prefabricated homes; and in 1959 the Governors of WHITGIFT SCHOOL bought Shirley Park Hotel – originally Shirley House built in 1721 and used as a convalescent home during the 1st World War – and

Trinity School was built on the site, opening in 1966. Much open space still lies around the residential core of Shirley: Lloyd Park extends over 114 acres and Addington Hills, which rise to 470 feet, over 130 acres.

Shoe Lane *EC4*. Named after the ancient Sho well which was at the north end of the street. In the 17th century it was known for its sign-writers, designers of broad-sheets and cockpit. Sir Henry Wotton visited the cockpit in 1633 and Pepys came in 1663 when the spectators included Members of Parliament as well as butchers, draymen and apprentices. John de Critz, serjeant-painter to James I and Charles I, lived here and Richard Lovelace, the poet, died in a mean lodging in Gunpowder Alley between Shoe Lane and FETTER LANE in 1657. Nearby another poet, Thomas Chatterton, poisoned himself with arsenic in 1770 and was buried in the Workhouse Cemetery swept away when HOLBORN VIADUCT was built in 1869.

At the Windmill Tavern in Shoe Lane, John Felton, having read the Parliamentary Remonstrance against the Duke of Buckingham, made up his mind to assassinate him. Paul Lovell, one of the few people to die in the GREAT FIRE, was burned to death in the lane because he refused to leave his house. Praise-God Barebone, who gave his name to Cromwell's 'Little Parliament' and was the father of the speculator, Nicholas Barbon, lived here in 1676. The *Standard* offices are at No. 47. This evening newspaper was established in 1980 on the amalgamation of the *Evening Standard* and the *Evening News*.

Shooters Hill *SE18*. A well-wooded suburb which because of its height (432 ft at the summit) commands fine views of London, Kent and Essex. Its steepness and remoteness in the past made it a place to be avoided by travellers even though the main road to Dover passed over it. Not only did highwaymen and footpads lie in wait but also the traveller had to pass the gallows by the cross-roads at the bottom of the hill and the gibbet where the bodies were displayed on the summit. The last execution to take place on the gallows here was in 1805.

Samuel Pepys wrote in 1661, 'I rode under a man that hangs at Shooters Hill and a filthy sight it was to see how the flesh is shrunk from his bones.' This road, also referred to in *A Tale of Two Cities* by Dickens, was originally laid out by the Romans as their principal road from London to Europe and has remained a major highway since that time although the A2 now runs around the base of the hill. Because of its height the hill has always been an important link in the national communications system: a beacon stood there in the 16th century, a shutter telegraph in the 18th and VHF radio transmitters stand there now. On top of the hill can be found the Bull Hotel adjacent to the site of an earlier hotel of the same name. This earlier inn was well known in the 18th century as a resort of the rich and famous and offered, according to the memoirs of William Hickey (published 1761), somewhat indecent entertainment.

In Castlewoods stands Severndroog Castle, a triangular folly 60 ft high, built by Lady James in 1784 in memory of her husband Sir William James who captured the fortress of Severndroog on the Malabar Coast in 1775. Fine views can be had from the top of the tower. Shrewsbury House, a GREENWICH Council community centre and library, was built in 1923 on the site of an earlier mansion constructed for the Earl of Shrewsbury in 1789. In 1799 Princess Charlotte, daughter of George IV, lived there in the care of the Dowager Duchess of Elgin. In the 1930s, when the grounds were developed by John Laing and Son as a smart estate, many pre-Roman burial mounds were destroyed but one, in Brinklow Crescent, was preserved and can still be seen.

Shoreditch *N1, N2*. The settlement grew up at the junction of two ROMAN ROADS, Kingsland Road and Old Street. It is first mentioned in manuscripts in 1148 as Scoredich which probably means ditch of Sceorf or

Shoreditch in 1827, with St Leonard's church, rebuilt by George Dance the Elder in 1738–40.

Scorre. ST LEONARD'S CHURCH was founded in the 12th century if not before and includes in its parish the hamlets of HOXTON and HAGGERSTON, both of which are mentioned in the *Domesday Book*. Between 1152 and 1158 the Augustinian priory of Holywell was established. The priory owned a large amount of land in the parish, as did the hospital at ST MARY SPITAL, the Canons of ST PAUL'S and the BISHOP OF LONDON. In 1539 Holywell priory was dissolved and most of its buildings were demolished.

In 1576 James Burbage founded the THEATRE in the vicinity. It was the first playhouse in England and lasted until 1598 when it was taken down and re-erected in SOUTHWARK as the GLOBE. In 1577 another theatre was begun nearby known as THE CURTAIN. It is not known who built it but one Henry Lanman, or Laneman, was the owner in March 1582. By 1625 it had fallen into disuse. Many actors lived in the area and some of them were buried in ST LEONARD'S CHURCH. In 1598 Stow wrote in his *Survey of London* that there were houses along the High Street and along Old Street as far as Golden Lane. In 1598 Ben Jonson fought a duel with Gabriel Spencer in Hoxton Fields and killed him.

In about 1683 development of the area began with Hoxton Square. No. 32 is said to date from this time. In 1695 Robert Aske bequeathed money for building Haberdashers' almshouses and a school in Pitfield Street (*see* HABERDASHERS' ASKE). In 1715 Robert Geffrye bequeathed money for building IRON-MONGERS' almshouses in the Kingsland Road. They now house the GEFFRYE MUSEUM.

The first houses in Charles Square appear to have been built between 1685 and 1687, on the east side. These were followed in 1726–7 by No. 16, which is the only Georgian house left; the rest have been replaced with modern housing blocks. By 1750 the population of the parish had reached an estimated 10,000. By 1801 it had risen to 35,000. About 1824 the former pleasure garden known as the Shepherd and Shepherdess was developed by Thomas Rouse as the EAGLE TAVERN in Shepherdess Walk. The Grecian Saloon was added in 1831, using fittings from the coronation of William IV. In 1822–6 the Church of St John the Baptist Hoxton, designed by Francis Edwards, was built by the Commissioners under the 1818 Act. St Mary Haggerston, designed by John Nash and also financed by the Commissioners, was built at the same time. This church was destroyed in the 2nd World War. By 1831 the population had reached 69,000 and by 1851 109,000. In 1965 Shoreditch was amalgamated with the borough of HACKNEY. Famous residents have included Richard Burbage, the actor who played at THE THEATRE with Shakespeare.

Shortlands *Kent*. The mill dam under Shortlands bridge on the river RAVENSBOURNE is believed to be that referred to in the *Domesday* survey. Traces of a Roman settlement have been found at Tootswood. Shortlands house was built in about 1702. George Grote, the author of *The History of Greece*, was born here in 1794. He was Member of Parliament for the CITY OF LONDON and helped to introduce the principle of secret voting at elections. He also helped to establish the UNIVERSITY OF LONDON and was a trustee of the BRITISH MUSEUM. About 1863 the estate, which then covered about 130 acres, was divided into building plots. The house later became a hotel and is now the

Bishop Challenor Roman Catholic School. Another large house was The Oakery at one time occupied by Dr James Scott, to whom patients came for treatment from all over London. This house was demolished and Oakwood House built in its place in 1847. During the 1st World War it was used as a military headquarters, and it in turn was demolished about 1930.

St Mary's church was consecrated in 1870. It was enlarged in 1888, but, together with its fine lych gate, was destroyed during the 2nd World War. The present church was built in 1956. Shortlands station, at first called Bromley station, was opened in 1858. There-after Shortlands developed into a London suburb. It is part of the London Borough of BROMLEY.

Shouldham Street *W1*. Laid out from 1801 on-wards and called after Admiral Lord Molyneux Shuld-ham [*sic*]. The whole street of tiny early-19th-century houses is virtually unspoilt. Arthur Orton, the claimant to the Tichborne inheritance, died at No. 21 on 1 April 1898.

Shrewsbury House The present modern block of flats of this name in CHEYNE WALK is on the site of the house built in about 1519 by George, 4th Earl of Shrewsbury. The house later passed to his grandson's widow, Bess of Hardwick. It was subsequently used as a school and as a paper manufactory. The major part of the property was demolished in 1813, the rest a century later.

Shroton Street *NW1*. Built in about 1785 on property belonging to Sir Edward Baker of Shroton, Dorset.

Sidcup *Kent*. First mentioned in 1254, it became a proto-suburb in the 18th century. Originally in the manor and parish of FOOTS CRAY, it spread into parts of BEXLEY and CHISLEHURST in the 19th century. Key dates were the turnpiking of the London road in 1781, the opening of the railway in 1866 and its electrifica-tion in 1926. The railway caused the creation of self-contained 'old' Sidcup to the south of the station.

Electrification brought about a housing boom to the north and west as farms and woods were covered with short terraces of inexpensive houses (the cheapest was £395) and the ever-popular chalet. Now urban renewal is demolishing even recently built property, replacing it with high-density flats and maisonettes and some office blocks, while the chalets lend themselves to ex-tension in all three dimensions. Traces of 'old' Sidcup remain, however, including a few double-fronted houses, shops, some public buildings, SIDCUP PLACE and the so-called MANOR HOUSE – unspoilt since its erection in the 1780s.

Sidcup Place *Kent*. Built in 1743 for 'an officer of Engineers', with a fine view of the Cray valley. The architect was probably Joseph Trought. Originally planned like 'a star fort with angle bastions' (traces of which are still identifiable), the house was extensively altered in 1853. Following two spells as a boys' board-ing school, it became Council offices in 1934.

Sidney Street *E1*. Scene of the famous siege on 3 January 1911 when two foreign revolutionaries bar-ricaded themselves into a house and fired at the police, fire brigade and a detachment of Scots Guards. They

Scots Guards in Sidney Street in 1911 when Anarchists barricaded themselves in a house and fired on police.

both died when the house caught fire. Winston Churchill, then Home Secretary, witnessed the battle and later gave evidence in court.

Silver Street *EC2*. According to Stow, silversmiths used to live here. The line of the street marked the west to east axis of a Roman fort, probably built in the 2nd century, which stood inside the north-west corner of the City wall. In about 1602 Shakespeare took lodgings at the corner of Monkwell Street over the shop of Christopher Mountjoy, a French Huguenot refugee who made jewelled head-dresses for the ladies of the Court. The street disappeared when LONDON WALL was widened.

Silvertown *E16*. Industrial and residential district of NEWHAM, south of the Royal Victoria and Albert Docks with a station, built in 1863, on the North Woolwich line. It was first developed in the 1850s round the rubber and telegraph works of S.W. Silver and Co. – hence the name. It gradually extended along the THAMES bank with chemical and engineering works, an oil refinery, and food and confectionery factories. Tate and Lyle have had their main works here since about 1880. It was the scene of the disastrous 'Silvertown Explosion' in 1917 when about 50 tons of TNT exploded in a fire at Brunner Mond's chemical works at West Silvertown. A large part of West Silvertown was wrecked. There were 450 casualties, including 69 killed and 72 seriously injured, and £2½ million worth of damage done. The church of ST MARK is by S.S. Teulon.

Simpson (Piccadilly) Ltd *203 Piccadilly, W1*. Designed by Joseph Emberton this department store, now a listed building, opened in 1936. It was the first welded steel building in London. Felix Samuely was the structural engineer. The building had been commissioned the previous year by Alexander Simpson to display men's wear produced by his own firm, S. Simpson Ltd of STOKE NEWINGTON, which had been founded by his father in 1894. When they opened Moholy Nagy, then a refugee in London, was engaged to design their first window displays.

Simpson's-in-the-Strand *100 Strand, WC2*. In 1818 Mr Reiss opened 'a home of chess' in the STRAND which later became known as the Grand Cigar Divan (the chess players sat on divans or sofas, the room being divided up into 'boxes'). In 1848 John Simpson, a caterer, joined Mr Reiss, rebuilt the premises and opened them as Simpson's Divan and Tavern. He consulted Alex Soyer, the famous chef, and produced a menu of good roast beef and saddles of mutton which were wheeled in on a dinner wagon. In 1862 E.W. Cathie took over the business just before Simpson's death. The premises were demolished to allow for the widening of the STRAND in 1900. T.E. Collcutt, who had built the SAVOY HOTEL in 1889, was responsible for the rebuilding of the new block which included Simpson's. The restaurant reopened in 1904 under the auspices of the SAVOY HOTEL. Ever a traditional meeting place for luncheon for gentlemen (ladies had a special separate dining-room for that meal), it has had the patronage of royalty from George IV onwards, as well as many famous literary figures such as Charles Dickens.

Sion College *Victoria Embankment, EC4*. Despite its name, it is not a college but a society of Anglican clergymen, which possesses a library that is largely, though not exclusively, theological. It was established in 1624 by the will of Dr Thomas White, rector of ST DUNSTAN-IN-THE-WEST who left £3,000 to found a college for the City clergy and an almshouse for 20 poor people, ten men and ten women. Land between Philip Lane and ST ALFEGE'S CHURCH in the LONDON WALL was purchased by the executors in 1627; and in 1630 a Royal Charter was obtained by which 'all the Rectors, Vicars, Lecturers and Clergy in or close to the City' were constituted Fellows of the College. It was to be governed by a President, two Deans and four assistants. In 1631 the College and almshouses were built. The inclusion of a library was at the instigation of the Revd John Simpson, rector of ST OLAVE HART STREET, one of White's executors, and was not specified in the original bequest. Several benefactors supplied the books.

The reason for the College's name is not known. The Common Seal, chosen in 1632, has in the centre a figure of the good Samaritan and two inscriptions *Vade fac similiter* and *Sigillum Collegii de Sion Londini*. In 1647 books from ST PAUL'S CATHEDRAL library were incorporated in that of the college, and it is assumed that these were lost in the GREAT FIRE which destroyed the College buildings and one third of the books. Gifts such as that from Pepys of £20 helped towards the rebuilding which cost more than £3,400 and was completed in 1678. There was a central courtyard and main entrance on LONDON WALL. The library was above the almshouses and was 121 ft long and 25 ft wide.

Under the Copyright Act of 1710 the library was entitled to claim a copy of every book printed in London. This arrangement ceased in 1836 and was replaced by an annual grant from the Treasury. In 1845 the almshouses were moved because of the fire danger to the library above in which, in 1850, there were estimated to be 40,000 volumes. In 1879 the College purchased the freehold site on the new VICTORIA EMBANKMENT from the CITY CORPORATION for £31,625 and the almshouse's affairs were wound up. The old buildings were sold in 1884 and the new building by Arthur Blomfield was opened by the Prince of Wales in 1886. At the opening ceremony the President stated that the college had been established by Dr White 'for the maintenance of truth in doctrine, love in conversing together and for the repression of such sins as do follow men'. And, 'with a view to encouraging sound learning', there had been added to the foundation a library containing over 62,000 books. Sir Walter Besant described it as 'a new and garish place'. The library has a large stained glass window with figures of Milton, Spenser, Caxton, Shakespeare, Coverdale, More, Chaucer, Bacon, Wycliffe and Erasmus.

About 6,000 books were destroyed and more damaged by water in the air raids of the 2nd World War; and there was substantial damage to the building, but most of the valuable books had been moved. In December 1944 the CITY LIVERY CLUB moved in to become the college's tenants, and now use the hall as a dining-room and the library as a club-room. Since 1958 two lay members have joined the Court. The library now contains about 100,000 volumes, including more than 30 medieval manuscripts.

Sipson *see* HARMONDSWORTH.

Sir John Cass Foundation School *Duke's Place, EC3.* Founded at HOUNDSDITCH by Zachary Crofton in 1669 with money provided by Sir Samuel Stamp for the education of 40 boys and 30 girls. In 1710 Alderman Sir John Cass agreed to provide further funds for the school but died suddenly before he could sign an endowment deed. In 1738 the school closed for 10 years until Chancery enforced the deed. In 1869 it moved to premises in JEWRY STREET. In 1895 revenues from Cass's endowment had increased sufficiently for the Chancery Commissioners to establish a new trust scheme to fund the Sir John Cass Technical Institute which was to share the school building. In 1908 the school moved to DUKE'S PLACE, leaving the Institute at JEWRY STREET. It is now a voluntary aided Church of England school with about 200 pupils aged three to 11.

Sir John Soane's Museum *13 Lincoln's Inn Fields, WC2.* John Soan, the son of a bricklayer, was born in 1753. He entered the office of George Dance the Younger, in 1768, that of Henry Holland two years later and, after travelling in Italy, he set up in practice as an architect on his own account in London in 1781. In 1784 he married the niece and heiress of George Wyatt, a rich builder, who left her his fortune. He began to spell his name Soane, and was appointed architect to the BANK OF ENGLAND in 1788; two years later, his wife now a wealthy woman, he started, at first in a modest way, the extraordinarily varied collections which can still be seen in his house. He bought 12 LINCOLN'S INN FIELDS, which had originally been built in 1658, and completely reconstructed it in 1792. Gradually his collection began to expand, both in LINCOLN'S INN FIELDS and in the classical villa which he built for himself at EALING in 1800. A number of antique marbles were bought at CHRISTIE's sale of the Earl of Bessborough's collection in 1801; the eight canvasses of Hogarth's *Rake's Progress* were purchased, also at CHRISTIE's, for £570 by Mrs Soane in 1802; and in the same year Soane himself purchased Watteau's *L'Accordée du Village* and 40 antique vases. In 1806 he was appointed Professor of Architecture at the ROYAL ACADEMY and between that date and 1813 – when he and his wife (having given up their EALING

Visitors in 1864 to the Sarcophagus Room of the museum in Lincoln's Inn Fields established by Sir John Soane.

villa in 1810) moved into 13 LINCOLN'S INN, which he had bought and rebuilt for their occupation and the display of their growing number of treasures – he had acquired works by Clérisseau and Canaletto, manuscripts, statues, casts, a number of cork models of classical buildings, and a cast of the Apollo Belvedere which was placed in the Dome, part of the extensions at the back of the house, where it still stands today. After the death of his wife in 1815, Soane continued to augment his collections and in 1824 he rebuilt No. 14 LINCOLN'S INN FIELDS, which he had bought some time before, and at the rear he added a picture-room and a mock medieval monastic suite, including the Monk's Parlour. By this time he had acquired numerous other casts, marbles, bronzes, busts, vases, books, antique fragments, Reynolds's *Snake in the Grass* together with the artist's notebooks, Hogarth's *Election* series, a book of drawings by Christopher Wren given to him by George Dance, and Robert Adam's library. In 1825 Soane held a three-day reception to celebrate one of his greatest purchases, the sarcophagus of Seti I, which had been discovered in 1815 by Giovanni Battista Belzoni and which he acquired for £2,000, after the Trustees of the BRITISH MUSEUM had declined it at that figure. Indian drawings were then bought, antique gems, an astronomical clock which had belonged to the Duke of York, a 13th-century *Bible*, Dance's architectural drawings, drawings by Piranesi, 52 volumes containing nearly 9,000 drawings from the office of Robert and James Adam, which were acquired for £200, and paintings from his ACADEMY colleagues and other contemporary artists, including Turner, Fuseli, Maria Cosway and Henry Howard. Before he died in 1837 Soane, who had been knighted in 1831, succeeded in obtaining an Act of Parliament which preserved the houses and their collections as a public museum. They have thus been open to the public ever since and are much as Soane left them, treasure troves of the beautiful, the instructive and the curious. Here may be seen, in addition to those objects already mentioned, Soane's furniture and his imposing portrait by Lawrence, Wren's watch, pistols belonging to Napoleon and Peter the Great, a scold bridle for nagging wives, shackles for slaves, a German cross-bow, a 'flint stone in the shape of a human foot' and a huge fungus from Sumatra.

The exterior of No. 13 is decorated with COADE-STONE versions of the caryatids of the Erechthion at Athens, which Soane placed there as counterparts of the figures which used to stand on the front of the ROYAL COLLEGE OF SURGEONS on the opposite side of the square. The Gothic pedestals between the windows come from niches on either side of the entrance in the 14th-century north front of WESTMINSTER HALL.

Sise Lane *EC4*. Corruption of St Sithe. The Church of ST BENET SHEREHOG, which was destroyed in the GREAT FIRE, was earlier dedicated to this saint.

Skinner Street *EC1*. Takes its name from the Worshipful Company of Skinners (*see* CITY LIVERY COMPANIES) who were left 8 acres in CLERKENWELL by John Meredith, a member of the Company, in 1630. In about 1830 the Skinners leased the land to James Whiskin who built Skinner Street, and Whiskin and Meredith Streets. A shop in the area belonging to Beckwith, a gunsmith, was plundered during the Spa Fields Riots in 1816. A sailor named Cashman was arrested with a gun in his hand. He was sentenced to death and hanged in front of Beckwith's shop. This was the last time in England that a criminal was executed on the site of his crime.

Skinners' Company *see* CITY LIVERY COMPANIES.

Slade Green *Kent*. One mile north of CRAYFORD, it dates from the early years of the present century but was originally part of the manor of Howbury (*see* HOWBURY MOATED GRANGE). The name means 'green place in low-lying meadow'.

Slade School of Fine Art *University College, WC1*. Named after Felix Slade who died in 1868 and founded chairs of fine art at Oxford, Cambridge and London. He also made UNIVERSITY COLLEGE LONDON a further gift by endowing six scholarships in fine art. UNIVERSITY COLLEGE added to Slade's gift by voting money to found a School of Art. The Slade School opened in the newly built north wing of the College quadrangle in 1871. Sir Edward Poynter became Slade Professor. He was succeeded in 1876 by Alphonse Legros who had come to London at the suggestion of Whistler. Among his pupils were W.R. Sickert and William Rothenstein. Legros was succeeded in 1892 by Frederick Brown in whose time Augustus John, William Orpen, Wyndham Lewis and Stanley Spencer attended the school. Brown was succeeded in 1919 by Henry Tonks who retired in 1930 and was succeeded by Randolph Schwabe. Schwabe's successor, William Coldstream, was appointed in 1949 and Coldstream's successor, Lawrence Gowing, in 1975.

Provision was made for the study of sculpture in 1893 and studios were later built for modelling and carving. Havard Thomas was appointed Professor of Sculpture in 1916. Reg Butler became Director of

Sculpture Studies in 1966. A course in the Study of Film was introduced in 1960 and directed by Thorold Dickinson who was appointed to a personal Chair in Film in 1967. Lectures in the History of Art were first delivered in 1890; and, after a lapse of a few years, D.S. MacColl was appointed to a lectureship in the History of Art to be succeeded in 1909 by Roger Fry, whose successor, Tancred Borenius, became Professor of the History of Art in 1922. In 1949 the Durning-Lawrence Chair was established by the UNIVERSITY and Rudolf Wittkower, who was appointed to it, was succeeded in 1956 by Ernst Gombrich who was succeeded, in turn, by L.D. Ettlinger. In 1965 a Department of History of Art was established. Professor Ettlinger was appointed its head and was succeeded in 1971 by Professor John White.

Sloane Avenue *SW3*. This was first laid out in the early 1920s after a large area of small houses had been demolished. It remained undeveloped for several years with most of the large blocks of flats and houses not built until the late 1930s. At the junction with FULHAM ROAD stands Michelin House with its fine tile panels showing early motor cars. George Seferis, the poet and Greek ambassador, lived at No. 7.

Sloane Court *SW3*. Two short streets of imposing Edwardian flats on the north side of ROYAL HOSPITAL ROAD which replaced a warren of small cottages in narrow courts, originally built to accommodate ex-soldiers who, as out-pensioners of the ROYAL HOSPITAL, had to collect pensions from there in person.

Sloane Estate Sir Hans Sloane, the physician, collector and President of the ROYAL SOCIETY, bought the Manor of CHELSEA in 1712 and went to live there in 1741 (*see* CHELSEA). His estate passed to his two daughters (*see* CADOGAN ESTATE). In addition to those of SLOANE STREET, SLOANE SQUARE and Sloane Avenue, Gardens and Terrace, SW3, Hans Crescent, Place and Street, SW1 and Hans Road, SW3, the name of TEDWORTH SQUARE also has family connections, and Ellis Street may be named after Anne Ellis, wife of Lord Mendip and sister of Hans Stanley, a descendant of Sir Hans Sloane.

Sloane Gardens *SW1*. Built by William Willett, the campaigner for daylight saving, in 1889.

Sloane Square *SW1*. Named after Sir Hans Sloane, Lord of the Manor of CHELSEA (*see* SLOANE ESTATE). The grassland was enclosed and cobbled in 1771 and houses were later built around it under the direction of Henry Holland. Sloane Square station was first opened in 1868. The River WESTBOURNE, running down from the SERPENTINE to the River THAMES, is carried over the station in a large iron pipe. Escalators were opened in March 1940 but were partially destroyed that November by a bomb. Two trains standing in the station at the time were hit and many killed, of whom a great number were never identified. The station, restoration of which took 11 years to complete, was opened in time for the FESTIVAL OF BRITAIN in 1951.

PETER JONES, the department store, originally opened by a young Welsh draper's assistant of that name in 1877, is on the west side. The War Memorial to both world wars stands in what is now the centre of the Square. It had to be moved from its original position when the Square was replanned in the early 1930s. Before that roads went criss-cross through the Square. Another important monument, the bronze *Venus Fountain* was unveiled in 1951. Designed by Gilbert Ledward, it was the prize winner of a ROYAL ACADEMY competition for a fountain.

The ROYAL COURT THEATRE stands on the east side next to the station. It is now the home of the English Stage Company. The Royal Court Hotel (103 bedrooms) is on the north side. Willett House, a block of flats, is named after William Willett, the originator of daylight saving, who also designed many houses in the neighbourhood.

Sloane Street *SW1*. Extends from KNIGHTSBIRDGE to SLOANE SQUARE. Planned by Henry Holland, it was built in 1780. Distinguished residents commemorated by BLUE PLAQUES are Sir Herbert Beerbohm Tree on the site of No. 76 and Sir Charles Wentworth Dilke at No. 75. Edgar Allen Poe attended a school on the east side in 1816. Count Cagliostro lived in the street in 1780; Mrs Inchbald in lodgings ('a situation for which she had always professed uncommon dislike') in 1812 and 1818; and the artist, Felix Moscheles, had a house on the east side from about 1862 until it was demolished in the early 1890s. Robert Browning was a regular visitor on Sundays. The Peruvian Embassy is at No. 52 and the Royal Danish Embassy at No. 55 in a building designed by Arne Jacobsen and completed in 1978. The CADOGAN HOTEL is at No. 75; and the Holiday Inn (Chelsea) at Nos 17–25. The General Trading Co. at No. 144 was established by Colonel Dealtry Part and his brothers in HOLBORN in 1920. Finnigan's, the leather goods retailers at No. 198, were founded by Brian Finnigan at No. 17 New Bond Street in 1830. TRUSLOVE AND HANSON, the booksellers, are at No. 205. HOLY TRINITY CHURCH is by John Dando Sedding (1890).

Sloane Terrace *SW1*. Lord Byron's mother took apartments here when she brought him to London in 1799 as a boy of 11 for treatment for his lameness by Dr Matthew Baillie. Byron came for weekends and holidays here when he was at school at DULWICH. The First Church of Christ Scientist, built to the designs of Robert Chisholm and dedicated in 1904, is on the corner of D'Oyley Street. The corner stone of granite is from Concord, New Hampshire, where Mary Baker Eddy, founder of Christian Science, had a house.

W.H. Smith and Son Ltd *Strand House, 10 New Fetter Lane, EC4*. Henry Walton Smith and his wife Anna opened a small news vendor's in Little Grosvenor Street in 1792. Smith died shortly afterwards, leaving his widow with two young sons, Henry Edward and William Henry. As H. and W. Smith the business flourished, however; and the two brothers, trading as newsagents and stationers, moved to larger premises at 42 DUKE STREET. In 1820 they opened branch offices at No. 192 STRAND (1849–55) and No. 186 (1855–1920). In 1828 the firm became known as W.H. Smith when the younger brother took charge. He built up the fastest, most efficient newspaper delivery service in London with a fleet of small carts and horses. When George IV died in 1830 W.H. Smith chartered a special boat to cross the Irish Sea and brought the news to Dublin 24 hours ahead of the Royal Messen-

ger. His son, also William Henry, worked with his father from the age of 17 and together they would go to the STRAND at four o'clock in the morning and pack and dispatch newspapers with their men. The firm became W.H. Smith and Son.

In 1848, with the growth of railways, they bought up the sole bookstall rights and opened the first WHS bookstall at EUSTON on 1 November 1848. They had contracts for 200 bookstalls on the Great Western and London and North Western Railways. W.H. Smith died in 1891 and his widow was created Viscountess Hambleden. Their son, the 2nd Viscount, became head of the firm, and when he died in 1928 his son, the 3rd Viscount, took over. On his death in 1948 it became a public company. In 1932 the WHS stables were finally closed and mechanical transport used. In 1936 the *Queen Mary* was launched with a W.H. Smith bookshop aboard.

As the contracts with the railways ran out, a shop would be opened, preferably near the station approach. This idea led to today's successful chain of retail shops. In 1982 there were 48 main shops in the Greater London Area, as well as 12 bookstalls at mainline railway terminals and three bookstalls at London Airport terminals.

Smith Square *SW1*. Laid out in about 1726 and named after the ground landlord, Henry Smith, probably the son of Sir James Smith who had built GREAT SMITH STREET in 1700. The centre is taken up by ST JOHN'S PUBLIC HALL. On the north side a few early 18th-century brick terraced houses remain. Others have been replaced by offices, including those of the Conservative and Unionist Central Office at No. 32, and Transport House, the headquarters of the Labour Party and the Transport and General workers' Union.

Smith Street *and* **Terrace** *SW3*. Built in about 1794 to 1807 by Thomas Smith. Nos 27 and 29 which, until the 2nd World War, were common lodging houses have been listed for preservation. The Chelsea Synagogue is on the corner of Smith Terrace.

Smithfield Market *EC1*. London's largest meat market covering an area of over 10 acres. Smithfield, or 'Smoothfield', a 'plain, grassy space just outside the City Walls', was well known in the Middle Ages for its horse market. In 1173 William FitzStephen, clerk to Thomas Becket, describes the area as 'a smoth field where every Friday there is a celebrated rendezvous of fine horses to be sold.' There was also trading in sheep, pigs and cattle. In 1305 oxen were being sold for 5s 6d each. In 1400 the CITY OF LONDON was granted the tolls from the market by charter. BARTHOLOMEW FAIR was held here from 1123 until its suppression for rowdiness and debauchery in 1855. As a convenient open space near the city, the field was used for tournaments, jousting and sporting events; and in 1357 a royal tournament was attended by the Kings of England and France. Another royal tournament was held in honour of Edward III's mistress, Dame Alice Perrers, in 1384 and lasted 7 days. Wat Tyler came here with his rebels in 1381 to meet Richard II. He was stabbed by Lord Mayor Walworth and executed in front of ST BARTHOLOMEW'S HOSPITAL (*see* PEASANTS' REVOLT). Smithfield was a place of public execution for over 400 years. Criminals were hanged 'betwixt the horse pool and the river of Wels' until the gallows were moved to

Smithfield Market in 1811. From an aquatint after Rowlandson and Pugin.

TYBURN in Henry IV's reign. Many witches and heretics were burned, roasted or boiled alive. In 1410 Henry, Prince of Wales (later Henry V) attended the execution of John Badly and endeavoured in vain to make him recant. And in 1538 John Forest, Prior of the Observant Convent at Greenwich, was put in a cage and roasted alive for refusing to recognise the King's supremacy. In 1554–8 in the reign of Mary Tudor, over 200 martyrs were burned, and as late as 1652 Evelyn records seeing a woman burned at Smithfield for poisoning her husband. Excavation outside the doorway of ST BARTHOLOMEW THE GREAT in 1849 uncovered burnt stone and charred human bones – many were taken away as relics. By the early 17th century the area was notorious for fighting and duelling and was commonly known as 'Ruffians Hall'. In 1615, in an attempt to bring order, the area was paved and provided with sewers and railings. In 1638 the CITY OF LONDON CORPORATION formally established a cattle market on the site under Royal Charter. Over the next 100 years the City spread to surround the market and at the beginning of the 17th century complaints were made against unruly cattle and drunken herdsmen. Drovers were inclined to have fun stampeding cattle on the way to market; tormented beasts took refuge in shops and houses. (This is probably the origin of the phrase 'a bull in a china shop'). In 1789 the LORD MAYOR issued a proclamation against these 'loose idle and disorderly persons' but the situation had not improved by the middle of the 19th century. Live cattle were still being driven through Sunday congregations and slaughtered in the market. Facilities were inadequate, blood flowed through the streets and entrails were often dumped in the drainage channels. Dickens give a graphic description in *Oliver Twist*: 'The ground was covered, nearly ankle-deep, with filth and mire; a thick steam perpetually rising from the reeking bodies of the cattle . . . the unwashed, unshaven, squalid and dirty figures constantly running to and fro, and bursting in and out of the throng, rendered it a stunning and bewildering scene, which quite confounded the senses.'

Despite its impracticability the market was not moved until 1855 when the sale of live cattle and horses was transferred to the Metropolitan Cattle Market in ISLINGTON. In 1851–66 Henry Jones built a new market modelled on Paxton's CRYSTAL PALACE, which had an underground railway linking Smithfield with the main railway stations. It was opened in 1868 as the London Central Meat Market and further extensions were made in 1875 and 1899. The entire poultry section was burned out in 1958 and a new market hall was erected by the CITY OF LONDON CORPORATION at a cost of £2,000,000 in 1963. Today the market employs nearly 3,000 people and sells over 350,000 tons of meat every year. It has its own police force and public house (which is licensed from 6.30 a.m.).

Smith's Bank *1 Lombard Street, EC3*. This bank, now the Smith's Office of the NATIONAL WESTMINSTER BANK, was launched by Abel Smith II and John Payne in 1758. Closely linked to Smith and Co. of Nottingham (established in 1658, the oldest of the country banks), it was renamed Smith, Payne and Smiths in 1758. The bank had originally opened in LOTHBURY but by 1806 it had settled at the present address. In 1902 Smith's Bank was merged with the Union Bank of London, a constituent company of the NATIONAL WESTMINSTER BANK.

Smith's Charity Estate About 70 acres in KENSINGTON which provide most of the income of Smith's Charity founded by the will of Alderman Henry Smith who died in 1627. Many of the streets in the area are named after former trustees of the charity as, for instance, Egerton Crescent, Gardens, Place and Terrace, SW3 (the Hon Francis Egerton), Evelyn Gardens, SW7 (the Revd John Evelyn), LENNOX GARDENS, Pelham Street, SW7 (Henry Thomas Pelham, Earl of Chichester), and also SUMNER PLACE, SYDNEY PLACE and WALTON STREET.

Smyrna Coffee House *Pall Mall*. Founded in 1702 on the site of No. 59 and soon renowned for its political discussions. It is mentioned in both *The Tatler* and *The Spectator* and was frequented by both Swift and Prior, and later by Boswell. According to Steele, porters and chairmen were 'much edified' as they listened to the arguments through a broken window. In his life of Beau Nash, Goldsmith wrote that he had 'known him wait a whole day at a window in the Smyrna Coffee House, in order to receive a bow from the Prince or the Duchess of Marlborough as they passed by . . . and he would then look round upon the company for admiration and respect'.

Snaresbrook *E11, E18*. The northern part of the old parish of WANSTEAD. It has retained its identity largely because in 1856 the Great Eastern Railway gave that name to its new station at the bottom of Wanstead High Street. The earlier focal point had been the Spread Eagle coaching inn on the Woodford Road (which is also the Newmarket Road). Now the Eagle, it still retains something of its former elegance. Opposite the inn is the famous Eagle Pond, once beloved of fishermen. Across the road is the 18th-century Snaresbrook House, now the home of municipal departments; and in this area, especially along Snaresbrook Road, there are still a few of the villas of City gentlemen.

South of the pond are the splendid buildings erected in 1843 for the Infant Orphan Asylum, which had been established in east London in 1827. In its later years it was known as the Royal Wanstead School, but the children have moved on yet again and the buildings now house Snaresbrook crown court.

In Hermon Hill is another fine building of red brick in the Venetian style, with a similar history. Designed by G. Somers Clarke, it was opened in 1862 as the Merchant Seamen's Orphan Asylum. This foundation, too, came from east London and is now, as the Royal Merchant Navy School, in Berkshire. The buildings at Snaresbrook were later occupied by a religious order but today they constitute the WANSTEAD HOSPITAL. At the very top of Hermon Hill, right on the Woodford border, is the noble but uncompleted Holy Trinity church, designed by James Fowler in 1881. This serves a parish cut out partly from WANSTEAD and partly from WOODFORD.

Snow Hill *EC1*. A steep winding hill extending from CENTRAL MARKETS to HOLBORN VIADUCT. Before the viaduct was built wild young men used to capture elderly women at the top and roll them down to the bottom in barrels, a practice much enjoyed by the 18th-century gangs known as Mohocks. In 1715 a Jacobite mob congregated at the bottom to drink a toast to the memory of King James and stripped passers-by who refused to join them. John Bunyan died in 1688 at the house of his friend, John Strudwick, who kept a grocer's and chandler's shop at the sign of the Star. Oliver Cromwell's great-grandson, Thomas Cromwell, also had a grocer's shop on Snow Hill where he died in 1748. The Star Inn and the SARACEN'S HEAD were celebrated coaching inns here.

Sobell Centre *Hornsey Road, N7*. Established in 1973 by ISLINGTON Council so that residents in the borough could enjoy a variety of sports facilities. Ice-skating, squash, badminton, volleyball, table tennis, judo, snooker, weight-lifting and a sauna are some of the attractions. Outdoor activities arranged through the Sobell are subaqua, pony trekking, camping and canoeing. Occasionally mime and dance classes are also arranged. The architect was R. Seifert and the centre was donated by Michael Sobell, a local resident.

Society for Promoting Christian Knowledge *Holy Trinity Church, Marylebone Road, NW1*. Founded in 1698 'to promote religion and learning' both at home and overseas, the SPCK today is a Christian publisher and bookseller in the United Kingdom and a missionary society helping the Church throughout the world to write, publish, and distribute Christian literature.

The Society draws support from all denominations. It moved its headquarters from NORTHUMBERLAND AVENUE to MARYLEBONE ROAD in 1956. HOLY TRINITY CHURCH now houses most of its administrative departments as well as its warehouse and London bookshop.

Society for the Protection of Ancient Buildings *37 Spital Square, E1*. Started by William Morris in 1877. He had protested three years before about the rebuilding of the church tower of ST JOHN HAMPSTEAD, but it was the sight of Burford church being pulled down and the news that the Minster at Tewkesbury was being drastically restored by Sir Gilbert Scott which prompted a vigorous letter to the *Athenaeum* in March 1877. His letter promptly brought about the founding of a society. Its first committee included Thomas Carlyle, James Bryce, Lord Houghton, Leslie Stephen, Holman Hunt and Burne-Jones, and its purpose was not only to defend old churches against destruction and Gothic rebuilding, but also to save them from the current practice of scraping medieval plaster and age-old weathering from the walls, leaving them smooth, clean and devoid of character. They were consequently referred to as the 'anti-scrape' people, and Scott himself dismissed their propaganda as the 'do nothing system'.

Philip Webb, the architect of Morris's RED HOUSE and his life-long friend, was a foundation member and directed the interest of the Society into much wider fields than churches. Very soon they were involved in the care and preservation of every kind of historic building that was neglected or threatened with demolition or over-restoration. Webb, and later W.R. Lethaby, instructed and trained architects to report and advise on buildings; then on the basis of their information public opinion and pressure would be organised. Out of their informed approach to conservation grew what Lethaby called 'the school of rational builders'. The Society became the prototype for all subsequent preservation societies not only in Britain but in the rest of the world, and it is due to them that the nation now accepts responsibility for its building heritage.

In 1877 William Morris was Secretary and its first address was at his house at No. 26 QUEEN SQUARE. In 1880 it moved to the office of Eustace Balfour at No. 9 BUCKINGHAM STREET, and in 1905 to an office of its own at No. 20 in the same street. In 1936 it took over a pair of fine 18th-century houses at 55–57 GREAT ORMOND STREET, and in 1983 it moved to its present address.

Society of Antiquaries of London *Burlington House, Piccadilly, W1*. Founded in 1707 when a group of men with antiquarian tastes began to meet weekly at the Bear Tavern in the STRAND and subsequently at other taverns in FLEET STREET. The minutes of the Society are unbroken since 1717. In 1751 the Society obtained its Royal Charter. From 1753 it gave up its old meeting place at the MITRE in FLEET STREET and rented a house in CHANCERY LANE. In 1781 it was granted apartments in SOMERSET HOUSE where its monogram can still be seen in the ceiling of its old meeting room. The Society moved once more, in 1875, to the apartments in BURLINGTON HOUSE which it occupies today. The library contains more than 130,000 books and periodicals. The Queen is Patron of the Society; there are four Royal Fellows, 60 Honorary Fellows and about 1,500 ordinary Fellows. Women Fellows were first admitted in 1921 and in 1959 Dr Joan Evans became the first woman President.

Society of Authors *84 Drayton Gardens, SW10*. Founded in 1884 by Walter Besant to promote the interests of authors and defend their rights. Many distinguished writers including Shaw, Galsworthy, Hardy, Wells, Barrie, Masefield, Forster and A.P. Herbert have assisted the activities and campaigns of the Society. The Society is a limited company and has been certified as an independent trade union, not affiliated to the Trades Union Congress. The Society's journal *The Author* is published quarterly. Various awards including the Hawthornden Prize are administered by the Society which in 1982 had over 3,000 members under the Presidency of Sir Victor Pritchett.

Society of Engineers *21–23 Mossop Street, SW3*. Formed in 1854 and then known as the Putney Club as it was set up by students of Putney College, one of the few institutions then existing for the education of engineers, and amalgamated in 1910 with the Civil and Mechanical Engineers' Society (established in 1859). There are about 4,000 members of the Society.

Soho *W1*. During the Middle Ages this most cosmopolitan area of London was farmland belonging to the Abbot and Convent of Abingdon and to the Master of the Hospital of Burton St Lazar in Leicestershire, who was custodian of the leper hospital of St Giles in the Fields. In 1536 both owners surrendered their land, then known as St Giles's Field, to King Henry VIII so that a royal park could be formed for WHITEHALL PALACE. Parts of the land were subsequently granted, leased or sold to a variety of owners including the Earls of Portland, Newport, Leicester and Salisbury, Lord Gerard and Sir William Pulteney. Hunting took place in the area; and, since 'So-ho!' is an ancient hunting cry, this is presumably the origin of the name by which it became known.

One of its earliest residents was Charles II's illegitimate son, the Duke of Monmouth, whose forces at the Battle of Sedgemoor are said to have been rallied by the cry and to have used it as a password. As well as MONMOUTH HOUSE, other large mansions which were built in the neighbourhood included LEICESTER HOUSE, FAUCONBERG HOUSE, CARLISLE HOUSE and NEWPORT HOUSE. Building on a more modest scale had begun in the earlier part of the century: in 1641 'a lewd woman' named Anna Clerke was bound over to keep the peace after 'threteninge to burne the houses at Soho'. In the 1670s and 1680s building progressed rapidly; and, at the same time, foreign immigrants began to settle here, many of them French HUGUENOTS who took over a chapel which had originally been built in 1677–80 for Greek Christians who had sought refuge in England. This chapel was in Hog Lane which later became known as Crown Street, its site now being covered by the ST MARTIN'S SCHOOL OF ART in CHARING CROSS ROAD. It was used by the Huguenots until 1822. By their thrift and industrious craftsmanship they had overcome the poverty that had burdened the *émigrés* of their grandfathers' day. By this time the foreign character of Soho had been stamped permanently upon it. Writing in 1720 John Strype had observed, 'Abundance of French people, many whereof are voluntary exiles for their Religion, live in these Streets and Lanes, following honest Trades; and some Gentry of the same Nation'. 19 years later, William Maitland, the Scottish topographer who had settled in London, wrote in his history of his adopted city, 'Many parts of this parish [ST ANNE'S] so greatly abound with French that it is an easy Matter for a Stranger to imagine himself in France'. When Maitland wrote his book, most of the English aristocratic residents who had formerly lived in the area, particularly in DEAN, FRITH, GREEK and GERRARD STREETS and SOHO SQUARE, had left it; and the artists, who later came to live here in large numbers, had begun to move in.

In the 19th century the population increased rapidly: by 1851 there were 327 inhabitants per acre, a figure higher than that in almost every other area of London. Houses had been divided into tenements; overcrowding was common. In 1854 there was a serious outbreak of CHOLERA; and after this most of the remaining wealthier families moved away from the area which, at the same time, became distinguished for the number of hospitals built here – no less than six appeared between 1851 and 1874. It was during these years also that Soho consolidated its reputation as a place of entertainment. Theatres and music halls opened, some of the smaller ones of a rather disreputable character; and prostitutes established themselves here in large numbers. The reputation of the area as one in which good restaurants could be found was, however, a somewhat later development. There were some hotels with excellent restaurants in and around LEICESTER SQUARE including the Sablonière. But, although KETTNER'S was established in Church Street (*see* ROMILLY STREET) in 1868, this was in those days a rare exception in the neighbourhood where the best eating-places are now to be found: the many small establishments here were, according to the guide-books, to be avoided by all but the most impecunious. 'Of all quarters in the queer adventurous amalgam called London', wrote John Galsworthy in *The Forsyte Saga*, writing from the viewpoint of a well-to-do family of the late 19th century, 'Soho is perhaps least suited to the Forsyte spirit. ... Untidy, full of Greeks, Ishmaelites, cats, Italians, tomatoes, restaurants, organs, coloured stuffs, queer names, people looking out of upper windows, it dwells remote from the British Body Politic'. 'It is therefore not surprising', comments the writer of the introduction to volume XXXIII of the *Survey of London*, that, although restaurants in the area were patronised by such writers as G.K. Chesterton and Hilaire Belloc who first met in a French restaurant in GERRARD STREET, the chapters on 'Where to Dine' in the guidebooks of the period barely mention any places outside Leicester

Square 'where the old-established foreign hotels began to enjoy the patronage of theatre-goers . . . At about the turn of the century there was "a remarkable change in the habits of London society" and public restaurants were for the first time used "for many luncheon, dinner and supper parties that would formerly have been given at home". This change in social habits, and the building of new theatres in SHAFTESBURY AVENUE and CHARING CROSS ROAD, greatly enlarged the clientèle of the hitherto dingy and often second-rate eating-houses of Soho. . . . In the restless, epicurean years after the 1st World War, when the decline in the number of domestic servants increased the habit of "eating out", Soho's gastronomic reputation was finally established. A guidebook published in 1924 listed 24 restaurants there, excluding those in LEICESTER SQUARE, and stated that, "Of late years the inexpensive restaurants of Soho have enjoyed an extraordinary vogue, and this fact seems to have somewhat modified the previously exclusive foreign air of the district".'

In fact, the inhabitants of the area were still largely of foreign extraction, though not now, as the extract from *The Forsyte Saga* suggests, mostly French. Germans and Italians had arrived, many of them cooks and waiters, and considerable numbers of Russian and Polish Jews as well as Greeks and Swiss. Since then, however, the resident population of the area, both British and foreign, has rapidly declined: in 1951 there were less than a sixth as many inhabitants as there had been 80 years earlier. Very few of the people who now crowd its streets at night live here. Most of them come because Soho, as well as a 'noted centre for foreign restaurants and delicatessen shops', has in recent years, in the words of Brewer's *Dictionary*, become a centre, too, for 'strip-tease shows, near-beer clubs and clip-joints'. In 1981, when there were no less than 164 'sex establishments', the resident population of Soho had declined to less than 3,000, while over 70,000 moved in every day or night to work here. An increasing number of the residents are Chinese and Bengali.

Soho Academy A boarding school for boys established by Martin Clare (author of *Youth's Introduction to Trade and Business*) at 1 SOHO SQUARE in 1717, and then moved to No. 8 in 1725. It became one of the most successful and well-known private boarding schools of the time, renowned for the Shakespeare plays which were performed by the boys, several of whom achieved distinction in later life as actors, and for the high quality of its drawing and painting instruction. Thomas Rowlandson and J.M.W. Turner were both pupils; so were Philip Hardwick, architect of EUSTON RAILWAY STATION, Henry Angelo, the fencing master (*see* CARLISLE HOUSE, CARLISLE STREET), John Horne Tooke, and the sons of Edmund Burke and James Boswell. Described as 'the first academy in London' in 1801, it closed a few years later, the Shakespearian productions for which it had become famous having been discontinued by one of Clare's successors, the Revd William Barrow, on the grounds that they exposed the boys to moral danger.

Soho Bazaar In 1801–4 John Trotter, the army contractor, rebuilt Nos 4, 5 and 6 SOHO SQUARE as a warehouse. Having made a fortune in the Napoleonic Wars, he turned the warehouse into a bazaar which was opened in 1816 and intended primarily to enable the widows and daughters of Army officers to dispose of their handiwork. Stalls and mahogany counters, which were hired by the day at 3d a foot, were arranged as in a closed market. The goods sold were mostly jewellery, millinery, gloves, lace and potted plants. The venture proved a great success and was described in 1839 as 'a very extensive, novel and curious establishment' and in 1843 as still standing 'at the head of its class', it then having inspired various imitators including the PANTHEON in OXFORD STREET. It remained in existence until 1885 when the building was purchased by the Edinburgh publishers, Adam and Charles Black.

Soho Square *W1*. Laid out in the 1680s on land formerly known as Soho Fields which had been granted by Charles II and Henrietta Maria to the Earl of St Albans. St Albans leased part of the fields to a brewer who obtained a royal licence to build there. The brewer sold his lease and licence to Richard Frith, a bricklayer, who put up the first houses. By 1691 there were 41 houses including MONMOUTH HOUSE, which had been built for the Duke of Monmouth on the south side of the Square. It was then called King Square in honour of Charles II whose statue seems to have stood in the centre. At this time it was an extremely fashionable place and several noble families had fine houses here. FAUCONBERG HOUSE and CARLISLE HOUSE were on the east side, as was the mansion of Viscount Preston. MONMOUTH HOUSE was on the south side. When Richard Steele wanted to suggest a likely neighbourhood for that Worcestershire gentleman, Sir Roger de Coverley, it seemed appropriate to name Soho Square which, in the words of John Strype in 1720, 'hath very good Buildings on all Sides, especially the East and South, which are well inhabited by Nobility and Gentry'. Of these buildings only two now survive, No. 10, which was adapted from two separate houses in the late 17th century, and No. 15 which was at that time occupied by the Countess of Mountrath. All the others were rebuilt in the 18th and 19th centuries. Some were turned into hotels like FAUCONBERG HOUSE and several were afterwards demolished to make way for offices, like No. 22, where the rich Alderman William Beckford, Lord Mayor of London, lived in 1751–70 and where his son, the author of *Vathek* and creator of Fonthill, was born in 1759; and No. 32, where the botanist, Sir Joseph Banks, having inherited a great fortune from his father, lived as a young man and housed his scientific collections and library which were freely available to all scientific men of every nation who gathered here for Banks's famous breakfasts. Arthur Onslow, Speaker of the House of Commons in 1728–61, lived in a house on the site of FAUCONBERG HOUSE.

Most of the rich aristocratic residents had left the square by the 1770s for the, by then, more fashionable areas in MAYFAIR and north of PICCADILLY. But several country gentlemen retained their houses here, while others were occupied by foreign diplomatic missions, including at various times in the century those of Venice, Spain, France, Russia and Sweden, and by Members of Parliament and wealthy merchants. Towards the end of the 18th century and at the beginning of the 19th century, however, professional men were more commonly to be found as occupants. There were several doctors and lawyers, a few auctioneers, dentists and architects; and, in 1837–41, a newspaper editor, Thomas Barnes of *The Times*.

A bird's eye view of 1731 from the south of Soho Square looking towards Tiborn Road (Oxford Street) and Hampstead.

Later came several musical instrument makers, booksellers and publishers. Routledge, publisher of *Uncle Tom's Cabin*, was at No. 36 in 1843–58. Until recently Adam and Charles Black (now at 35 BEDFORD ROW) were at Nos 4–6 which they had occupied since 1885. No. 8 had already been turned into a school; Nos 4, 5 and 6 into a warehouse; and No. 21 was rebuilt for Messrs Edmund Crosse and Thomas Blackwell whose firm extended into No. 20 in 1858 and No. 18 in 1884. In the 19th century, also, ST PATRICK'S ROMAN CATHOLIC CHURCH was built on part of the site of CARLISLE HOUSE which had seen the rise and fall of Mrs Cornelys's assembly rooms (*see* CARLISLE HOUSE), and the FRENCH PROTESTANT CHURCH on the site of Nos 8 and 9. In 1867 No. 29 was demolished for extensions to the HOSPITAL FOR WOMEN which had occupied No. 30 since 1852.

In 1924 the appearance of the Square changed dramatically when No. 20 was demolished by Messrs Crosse and Blackwell and a tall office building replaced it. Other high office buildings followed in the 1930s and after the 2nd World War, including Gordon Jeeves's Twentieth-Century House (1936–7) for the Twentieth Century-Fox Film Company.

The garden, however, remains much as it was in the 19th century. It was described by Strype in 1720 as 'a very large and open place, enclosed with a high Pallisado Pale, the Square within neatly kept, with Walks and Grass-plots, and in the midst is the Effigy of King Charles the Second, neatly cut in Stone to the Life, standing on a Pedestal'. The garden was not well maintained, and in 1748 a new wall and railings were erected round it. Further alterations were made in the 1870s when the wooden arbour and tool shed replaced the statue of Charles II which, removed to the grounds of GRIMSDYKE, the home of Frederick Goodall, the artist, was returned to the square in 1938 (*see* STATUES).

Soho Tapestries After the decline of the MORTLAKE Workshops the 18th-century tapestry weavers of SOHO and the surrounding areas became the most skilful in the craft. In the early 1740s the yeomen arras-workers were Richard Chillingworth and John Ellys, who had taken over from Moses Vanderbank, son of John Vanderbank, the most prominent tapestry weaver in the country. Other fine tapestry makers were Joshua Morris, whose workshops, on the corner of FRITH and BATEMAN STREETS, were renowned for his Arabesque and Chinoiserie designs; and William Bradshaw and Tobias Stranover who took over Morris's premises before going their separate ways, Stranover to another address in FRITH STREET and Bradshaw to SOHO SQUARE and GREEK STREET. In 1753 a relative of William Bradshaw, George Smith Bradshaw, opened workshops at CARLISLE HOUSE in partnership with Paul Saunders, a weaver who specialised in oriental landscapes. Two years later they also took over William Bradshaw's workshops in GREEK STREET and a house in DEAN STREET. Many workers were employed in the trade which, however, by the end of the century was extinct.

Solicitors' Company *see* CITY LIVERY COMPANIES.

Somers Town Lies between ST PANCRAS STATION and the HAMPSTEAD ROAD, with CROWNDALE ROAD in the north and EUSTON ROAD in the south. Totenhele Manor, one of the four manors in the old parish of ST PANCRAS CHURCH, stood near the angle formed by present day HAMPSTEAD ROAD and EUSTON ROAD. The manor was in the hands of the Crown in 1591 when the house was described as 'a very slender building of timber and brick', and a century later it was noted that the property covered 7 acres, with the manor-house and 1½ acres enclosed by a moat.

Totenhele Manor seems to have disappeared by the end of the 18th century, and until then there was little in the eastern part of the area except fields. The land belonged to the Somers family, descendants of the 1st Baron Somers of Evesham, Lord Chancellor in 1697. The oldest building on the Somers's land was the Brill Farm, which stood near the junction of what are now Ossulton Street and Phoenix Road; and there was a Brill Tavern in the same area from the 17th century. The opening of the New Road (EUSTON ROAD) in 1757 divided Somers Town from the spacious developments in BLOOMSBURY, and as the irresistible spread of London crept ever nearer, the pastures slowly turned to brickfields and dust-heaps and barren land 'whither resorted many roughs from London to witness dog-fighting, bull-baiting and other rude sports'. In 1784, the then Lord Somers leased land on the Brill Farm to a Frenchman, Jacob Leroux. Leroux and others planned to build a pleasant suburb, and a 15-sided building, 3 storeys high and containing 32 houses, known as the Polygon, was built in a large square, later Clarendon Square (*see* POLYGON ROAD). The construction of houses 'seemed to proceed prosperously, when some unforeseen cause occurred which checked the fervour of building and many carcases of houses were sold for less than the value of materials'. From then on Somers Town was predominantly inhabited by the working classes, though crowds of *émigrés* from the French Revolution swelled the poorer population. In 1808 the Abbé Carron, a great benefactor to these Frenchmen, founded St Aloysius Church in Phoenix Street for them. And by 1813, the Abbé, living in Clarendon Square, presided 'over four schools, for young ladies, poor girls, young gentlemen and poor boys'. In 1821–31 building activity continued throughout the area.

The population was further increased, in 1823, by Spanish liberal refugees. These Spaniards, many of them professional men, settled in substantial numbers in Somers Town. They included Alcala Galiano, once a member of the Spanish Cortés and later to become Professor of Spanish at UNIVERSITY COLLEGE. He wrote, 'Many of our fellow countrymen . . . knew the name of Somers Town as a miniature constitutional Spain which made room for a great number of homeless Spaniards.' These refugees were mostly very poor and they suffered dreadfully from the cold and from hunger; they eked out a living by teaching, writing and translating. Some of them opened printing presses and publishing houses.

In 1824, Charles Dickens lived briefly in a house (demolished) in Johnson Street, now Cranleigh Street, and later lodged for a short time in the Polygon. The building of St Mary's Eversholt Street, designed by William Inwood, started in 1824. In 1838, the London and Birmingham Railway reached London and EUSTON STATION was built on land owned by the Rhodes family. Somers Town was to be dominated by the railways from then on.

By the 1850s the Brill Tavern was the site of a flourishing Sunday-morning market, noted for the 'uproarious conduct' of its habitués, and there was a costermongers' colony nearby. By then the district was a slum area of narrow streets and 'filthy, ill-drained, ill-ventilated courts'. The building of ST PANCRAS STATION in 1868 cleared a large area of the slums (and the Brill Tavern) but the population, rendered homeless, poured into the rest of the area and created worse

overcrowding. In 1840 public baths and washhouses were opened near a reservoir which had been constructed early in the century to supply water to west London. The baths, a 'model establishment' provided by the Society for Establishing Baths and Washhouses for the Labouring Classes, were closed in 1859, and in 1861 the reservoir was filled in and Tolmers Square (demolished in 1979) was built on the site. In 1875, the London Temperance Hospital (now the NATIONAL TEMPERANCE HOSPITAL) was built on the Hampstead Road and the New Hospital for Women (later ELIZABETH GARRETT ANDERSON HOSPITAL) was opened on EUSTON ROAD in 1890. The Polygon was demolished in the same year and later Polygon Buildings were put up, to be occupied mainly by railway employees. This was part of an attempt to improve the area, but by 1904 there were 'portions yet to wipe out, which are still centres of wickedness and vice'.

In 1906, Goldington Buildings were built, the first Borough Council Housing Scheme in the area and Ethel le Neve, the mistress of the murderer, Crippen, lived at No. 17. A 'School for Mothers', one of the first Maternity and Child Welfare Centres (*see* CHARITIES) opened in 1907. In 1924, the St Pancras Housing Improvement Society was formed largely to get rid of the slums, and during the 1920s and 1930s many of them were cleared away and replaced by blocks of flats. The Unity Theatre flourished in Goldington Crescent during the 1930s. Huge Council redevelopments of the 1960s and 1970s included big blocks of flats and planned open spaces. Sir William Collins School, Chalton Street, the St Pancras Library and the SHAW THEATRE on the EUSTON ROAD, were all opened in 1971. Since 1979 there has been a plan to build the BRITISH LIBRARY on old railway land on the corner of Pancras Road and EUSTON ROAD.

Somerset Coffee House *Strand*. First mentioned in 1744. Boswell frequented the house. The notorious *Junius* letters of 1769–72, anonymous letters to the *Publick Advertiser*, criticising George III and his Ministers, were sometimes deposited with waiters either here or at Munday's. By 1838 the Somerset had become a hotel.

Somerset House *Strand, WC2*. Site of the first Renaissance palace in England built in 1547–50 for Lord Protector Somerset. Pennant said the architect was John of Padua, others Sir John Thynne. To clear a site for it, the inns of the Bishops of Chester and Worcester were demolished, as were Strand Inn, an INN OF CHANCERY, and the Church of the Nativity of Our Lady and the Innocents. The Priory Church of ST JOHN CLERKENWELL and St Paul's Charnel House and Cloister were pulled down to provide stone. Attempts were made to take stone also from ST MARGARET'S, WESTMINSTER but the parishioners drove the Duke's men off. The entrance gate was carved by Nicholas Cave, Henry VIII's master mason at NONSUCH. In 1552 Somerset was executed, and the house was later given to Princess Elizabeth in exchange for DURHAM HOUSE. She used it occasionally and rode out from here to welcome her sister Mary to London as Queen. Soon after the house was searched and anti-Catholic literature was found. Elizabeth's tutor and governess were taken to the TOWER but later released. In 1558, on her accession, part of the house was given back to the Protector's son, Edward Seymour. The rest was

Somerset House in the Strand, designed by William Chambers, showing the Adam brothers' Adelphi beyond. From an engraving after Farington of 1790.

kept as a meeting-place for the Council, and for grace and favour residences and apartments for foreign ambassadors. The Queen herself stayed here from time to time before starting on long journeys.

In 1603 the house was given to Anne of Denmark. During her residence it was the scene of many spectacular masques organised by Ben Jonson and Inigo Jones. (Jones had apartments here.) In 1604 the peace conference between England, Spain and Spanish Netherlands was held here. A painting of this occasion hangs in the NATIONAL GALLERY. In 1604 John Gerard, the herbalist, was granted a lease on a 2-acre site to the east of the house on condition that he supplied the Queen with plants, herbs, flowers and fruit. In 1605 he parted with it to Robert Cecil, Earl of Salisbury. In 1606 the house was renamed Denmark House in honour of Anne's brother, Christian IV of Denmark, who was staying with her. In 1619 Anne's embalmed body lay in state for two months while the Countesses of Arundel, Nottingham and Northumberland argued over who was to be the chief mourner. Soon after the funeral the house was given to Prince Charles but he preferred to live at ST JAMES'S PALACE and so the late Queen's household stayed on. In 1623 a Catholic chapel was built in anticipation of the Spanish Infanta's marriage to Prince Charles. After the death of James I at Theobalds in 1625, his body was brought to Denmark House to lie in state for a month. £50,000 was spent on the funeral, the greatest ever known in England. 8,000 mourners followed the coffin to the Abbey. In 1625 the house was given to Henrietta Maria. To compensate for sending her French attendants home, Charles built her a large new chapel designed by Inigo Jones in 1630–5. The consecration ceremonies lasted for three days. In 1645 Henrietta Maria left for the Netherlands, and the house was taken over by Members of Parliament and the Army and was once more known as Somerset House. The chapel was wrecked. Inigo Jones died there in 1652, and in September 1658 Cromwell lay in

state. 'This folly and profusion so far provoked the people that they threw dirt in the night on his escutcheon that was placed over the great gate of Somerset House'. His body was badly embalmed and had to be buried quietly. The official funeral was held a fortnight later. After Richard Cromwell's abdication Parliament decided to sell Somerset House to pay the Army but there were no bidders. In February 1660 the garrison mutinied and surrendered to General Monk.

At the Restoration the house was put in order for Henrietta Maria who went to France the following year to attend her daughter's wedding. While she was away a gallery along the water front was built, probably to the designs of John Webb. After Henrietta Maria's departure from England in 1665 Catherine of Braganza often retired here. On Charles II's death in 1685 she lived here permanently, amusing herself with cards and music. With her encouragement Italian opera was performed for the first time in England. It was mentioned in an advertisement in 1676 that Somerset House was the first English building to have parquet flooring. In 1693 Catherine left to become Regent of Portugal. Successive Queen Consorts took little interest in the house and it was mostly let out as grace and favour residences until 1775. Queen Charlotte considered living there but chose BUCKINGHAM HOUSE instead. The house was then demolished and its site was allocated for government offices, the first large block ever built. William Robinson was asked to draw up designs. Meanwhile Sir William Chambers, the Surveyor General, went to Paris to study new buildings, presumably intending to get the commission for himself. Fortunately for him, Robinson died in 1775 and he was appointed architect. The imposing building he designed is built round a large courtyard with a free-standing north wing. The unembanked river used to lap against the south terrace. In 1788 the statue of George III was erected in the courtyard (*see* STATUES). The ornamented Keystones are by Joseph Nollekens, Agostino Carlini, Joseph Ceracchi, John Bacon the Elder,

Visitors to Somerset House passing through the vestibule in 1796 when Chambers's building was almost complete.

and Nathaniel Smith. In 1796 when Chambers died, the building was still not complete. In 1835 the east wing was added by Robert Smirke, and the west wing by James Pennethorne.

The ROYAL ACADEMY was here during 1771–1836, the ROYAL SOCIETY in 1780–1857 and the SOCIETY OF ANTIQUARIES in 1781–1873. These were allotted the north wing. The Navy had the west wing and part of the river wing, with the Stamp Office occupying the rest. In the remaining parts were many smaller offices, for example the Hackney Coach and Barge Master. In 1836–1973 the offices of the General Register of Births, Deaths and Marriages were there and the Inland Revenue Office occupied most of the building.

Somerset Street *W1*. Built in about 1763 on the PORTMAN ESTATE and named after the county of Somerset where the family owned land. George Stubbs, the painter, lived at No. 24 in 1764–1806. The original house has long since gone but a plaque to the painter can be seen inside SELFRIDGE's store.

Sotheby Parke Bernet *34–35 New Bond Street, W1 and 19 Bloomfield Place, W1*. Fine art auctioneers and valuers, established in 1744 by Samuel Baker, a London bookseller and auctioneer of 'Literary Properties'. Initially only one sale a year was held until, in 1754, Baker opened sale rooms in Yorke Street, COVENT GARDEN where, at first in collaboration with Abraham Langford, more frequent sales of general objects were held. In 1767 Baker took into partnership George Leigh and retired from the business. In 1776 the first Sotheby, Baker's nephew John, joined the firm, to be succeeded by three generations of the family until the connection was broken in 1861 with the death of Samuel Leigh Sotheby. In 1818 the firm was transferred to 13 WELLINGTON STREET, STRAND, and thence in 1917 to its present address. From the 1860s to 1913, Sotheby's were book auctioneers. It was only with their move to BOND STREET, under the chairmanship of Montague Barlow, that they began seriously to challenge CHRISTIE's as art auctioneers.

The purchase of Parke Bernet, the New York firm of auctioneers, took place in 1964. Notable and record-breaking sales in libraries, paintings and *objets d'art* occur continually. In 1978–9 international sales totalled £181,500,000 and London sales £82,370,000. In 1967 Sotheby's acquired the firm of Hodgson's, book auctioneers of CHANCERY LANE, where sales were held until May 1981. New premises were then opened for the sale of books, manuscripts, coins, medals and jewellery in Bloomfield Place, formerly part of the AEOLIAN HALL.

South Audley Street *W1*. Extends from GROSVENOR SQUARE to CURZON STREET. The section north of HILL STREET forms part of the GROSVENOR ESTATE and the street was named after Hugh Audley, from whose heirs the estate was acquired by the marriage of Sir Thomas Grosvenor in 1677. Building began in 1720, with small houses (probably used as shops) at the north end and larger ones further south. The most important of these was Chesterfield House, designed by Isaac Ware for the 4th Earl of Chesterfield in 1747–50. (This was demolished in the 1930s.) In addition to the GROSVENOR CHAPEL, survivors include Nos 9–16 (consecutive) and 71–75 (consecutive), all built in the 1730s, the latter (mostly now refronted) by or under the aegis of Edward Shepherd, the builder-architect, with very fine Georgian plasterwork inside. Sir Richard Westmacott, the sculptor, lived at No. 14 in 1818–56; the Comte d'Artois (later Charles X of France) at No. 72; and the 3rd Earl of Bute, Prime Minister, at No. 75 in 1754–92. In 1927 No. 75 became the Egyptian Legation (now Embassy), and in 1969 a ceiling painting in one of the drawing-rooms

South Audley Street, c. 1860. From its earliest days, in 1720, there were shops as well as houses in this part of Mayfair.   ·

was identified as by Tiepolo and sold to the NATION-AL GALLERY; it had probably been installed in the house by H.L. Bischoffsheim, a banker and art collector who had lived here in 1873–1908. Between about 1875 and 1900 almost all the buildings north of SOUTH STREET were rebuilt, generally in the Queen Anne manner, with shops and residential chambers above. The most notable of these is Thomas Goode's china-and-glass shop at Nos 17–22 (consecutive), designed for Goode's by Ernest George and Peto and built piecemeal in 1875–91. James Boswell often stayed with his friend General Paoli at a house in this street, and Queen Caroline was at No. 77 for a short while on her return from Italy in 1820.

South Bank The THAMES-side area on the 'Surrey' side of the river between WATERLOO BRIDGE and HUNGERFORD BRIDGE. Development began with the FESTIVAL OF BRITAIN in 1951, but has extended considerably since. Besides the ROYAL FESTIVAL HALL (R.H. Matthew and J.L. Martin, 1951), the area contains the QUEEN ELIZABETH HALL AND PURCELL ROOM, the NATIONAL THEATRE (Sir Denys Lasdun and Partners, 1977), the NATIONAL FILM THEATRE, the HAYWARD GALLERY (GREATER LONDON COUNCIL architects, 1967); and, beside all these, the 25-storey Shell Centre (*see* BELVEDERE ROAD). The tall spiral bronze fountain in the gardens was commissioned by the Shell Company and is by Franta Belsky (1961). The two sculptures outside the ROYAL FESTIVAL HALL, the bronze *The Motorcyclist* (1962) and the cement and fibreglass *The Cellist* (1958) are by Siegfried Charoux. The stainless-steel abstract, *Zemran*, outside the QUEEN ELIZABETH HALL is by William Pye (1972). The wooden peacock at the end of the waterfront terrace is by Brian Yale (1978).

South Circular Road The South Circular Road (A205) has been marked out through the maze of streets and roads in the built-up area south of the THAMES. On its looping 20-mile route from KEW BRIDGE in the west to WOOLWICH in the east, it passes through no fewer than seven suburban towns. A count in 1977 revealed that some parts of the route were carrying 36,000 vehicles a day.

South Croydon *Surrey*. Situated south of ADDISCOMBE. The area of South Croydon, south of CROYDON manor, belonged to Haling manor, Crown property until the 16th century. Development occurred towards the end of the 19th century following the opening of South Croydon Station. In 1851 Sir George Gilbert Scott's St Peter's church was built, and in 1884 its daughter church of St Augustine (John Oldrid Scott) was opened. Development included shops along Selsdon Road, although 19th-century cottages survive on Drovers Road.

South Eaton Place *SW1*. Between EATON SQUARE and EBURY STREET. Viscount Cecil of Chelwood, who was largely responsible for the creation of the League of Nations, lived at No. 16.

South End Road *NW3*. On the Prompt Corner Restaurant at No. 1 is a plaque which reads, 'George Orwell writer (1903–50) lived and worked in a bookshop on this site 1934–5'.

South Hornchurch *see* RAINHAM.

South Lodge *Ham Common, Surrey*. A large yellow brick building in the late Classical style with an Italianate cupola facing Ham Common. The central portion was erected in 1856–61 to house a National Orphanage which had been founded by local philanthropists in 1849 for 36 girls orphaned by a recent CHOLERA outbreak. It was soon extended to orphans of all kinds and the two wings were added in 1868 and 1872.

The girls were given an education and trained to be nurses or domestic servants. After the closure of the orphanage in 1922 the building was used for adult education, a British restaurant during the War, and other purposes until it was converted into luxury flats.

Previously the site was occupied by two buildings which housed a school started in 1838 by W. Oldham and H. Wright to put into practice the ideas pioneered at Pestalozzi. It was named Alcott House after the American educationalist who visited the school in 1842 by which time there were 12 children under 12, both boys and girls, with a number of local day pupils. Adults could attend classes or special lectures. The place was already growing into a fully fledged Commune. The inspiration came from James Pierrepoint Greaves, a mystic who had broken away from Robert Owen. He was joined by a number of disillusioned Owenites from Harmony Hall, Queenwood, Hampshire where Owen had set up one of his practical but unsuccessful experiments in socialism. All these new members shared 'the idea of founding an Industrial Harmonic Educational College for the benefit of such parties as were ready to leave the ignorant selfish strife of the antagonistic world', and the belief that 'pure air, simple food and cold water are much more beneficial to man than any national doctrinal creeds, or any churches, chapels or cathedrals'.

They hoped their example of vegetarianism, austerity, celibacy and self-sufficiency would spread to all society and make the world a better place. But by 1848 they had dispersed, some going to America, and some to join other 'protest' movements which were a feature of mid-19th-century Britain.

South London Art Gallery *Peckham Road, SE5*. Founded by William Rossiter, a parishioner of CAMBERWELL who had originally exhibited a small collection of pictures and engravings in his shop in Camberwell Road. Unable to accommodate his growing number of visitors, in 1868 he purchased Lion House in Peckham Road and opened a small gallery at the rear of the building, insisting that it should open on Sundays, as no other gallery then did. Later he enlisted the help of well-known figures in the art world, including Lord Leighton and G.F. Watts, to raise money for a purpose-built gallery designed by Morris Adams in 1891. In 1898, after Rossiter's death, Lion House was demolished and replaced by the Camberwell School of Art with which the gallery still has close ties. The collection now has over 300 Victorian paintings including works by Ruskin, Millais, Opie and Prinsep, and a growing 20th-century section, together with an interesting pictorial history of SOUTHWARK.

South London Botanical Institute *323 Norwood Road, SE24*. Established and endowed in 1911 by Allan Octavian Hume, who pursued a distinguished career as an administrator in India and was one of the leading naturalists of his time. Among the many other well-known botanists associated with it were A.B. Rendle and J. Ramsbottom, both of whom held the post of Keeper of Botany at the BRITISH MUSEUM (NATURAL HISTORY). The purpose of the Institute is to encourage the study of botany among the residents of SOUTH LONDON and meetings, courses and field excursions are organised on all branches of the subject. It occupies a large three-storey house, with a meeting room, herbarium of over 100,000 specimens, botanic garden and fine botanical library.

South London College *Knight's Hill, SE27*. In 1859 the Lower Norwood Working Men's Institute was built 'to promote the moral, intellectual and social improvement of the Inhabitants residing within a radius of five miles'. It became known as the Norwood Technical Institute in 1895, and later the Norwood Technical College. In 1905 it was taken over by the LONDON COUNTY COUNCIL Education Committee. The first major additions were made in 1939; and in 1956 the Jackson building, now known as the Centre Block, was opened. The older buildings were pulled down and rebuilt and the college – now a College of Further Education – became the South London College in 1974.

South London Hospital for Women and Children *Clapham Common, SW14*. Founded in 1912 on the inspiration of Dr Maud Chadburn, one of the pioneer women surgeons who worked with Elizabeth Garrett Anderson at her hospital and who felt that London should have a second women's hospital on the south side of the river. There was considerable opposition from the almost entirely male medical profession. Dr Chadburn's father, the Revd James Chadburn, was also very disapproving. When she had expressed a wish to become a doctor he had said, 'I would rather see Maud in her coffin before becoming a doctor'. The hospital began with four beds. A larger purpose-built hospital, designed by Marcus Collins and containing 80 beds, was opened in 1916. In the 1930s it was enlarged to its present size, the architect being Sir Edwin Cooper. In 1982 there were 187 beds.

South Molton Lane *W1*. Extending from DAVIES STREET to BROOK STREET, it marks the course of the TYBURN which here formed the boundary between the GROSVENOR ESTATE and the CORPORATION OF THE CITY OF LONDON's Conduit Mead Estate (*see* CONDUIT STREET). In the mid-18th century it was known as Poverty Lane, but by the 1790s had acquired its present name, the reason for which is not known.

South Molton Street *W1*. Extends from OXFORD STREET to BROOK STREET and at the time of its building in the mid-18th century it formed part of the COR-PORATION OF LONDON's Conduit Mead Estate (*see* CONDUIT STREET). The origin of the name is not known. Despite a considerable amount of rebuilding around 1900 many of the original small Georgian houses survive, the best one being No. 63, which bears a plaque of the CORPORATION's arms and is almost the only one still having its original ground-floor windows. South Molton Street is now a pedestrian precinct, and the small shops (mostly dealing in food, jewellery or women's clothes) which occupy almost the whole

length of both sides, provide a very agreeable promenade. Rigby and Pellier, the corsetières at No. 12, make the Queen's foundation garments. William Blake and his wife moved into a 2nd floor flat at No. 17 in 1803. They were reported to be 'still poor [and] durtyer than ever'. They removed to a house off the STRAND, No. 3 Fountain Court, which was demolished in 1821. Blake died six years later and was buried at BUNHILL FIELDS.

South Norwood *SE25*. The southern part of the area once covered by the Great North Wood of Surrey (*see* UPPER NORWOOD), which lies between UPPER NORWOOD and CROYDON. References in *Domesday Book* and the writings of John Aubrey in the 17th century suggest that large sections of land were owned by the Archbishops of Canterbury, who may have hunted in the area. Whitehorse Road and Whitehorse Lane are present-day roads commemorating the Whitehorse family who had land here in the 14th century. A Walter Whitehorse was the shield-bearer of Edward III in 1368 and a leather bag of gold and silver coins dating from his reign was unearthed in a garden on BEULAH HILL in 1953.

By the middle of the 18th century the lower slopes of the wooded hills had begun to thin out into areas of common land, largely due to the activities of woodmen and charcoal burners. The area has been described as an immense furze-clad waste, dotted with the occasional woodman's hut, the only other inhabitants being the gipsies who gave their name to Beggar's Hill (now BEULAH HILL and South Norwood Hill). The Croydon Enclosure Acts of 1797–1802 brought the commons into the existing Manors, including the Manor of Whitehorse, and land was soon made available for building. The enclosure maps show a number of existing lanes, and as CROYDON developed and communications with London improved, the population gradually increased. In 1803 the GRAND SURREY IRON RAILWAY linked West Croydon with the THAMES at WANDSWORTH; in 1809, the Croydon Canal opened (*see* SOUTH NORWOOD LAKE) and in 1839 the London and Croydon Railway line opened a track which now runs through Norwood Junction and Anerley stations. A shortlived phase of building homes for the wealthy soon gave way to the rapid growth of smaller suburban homes. CRYSTAL PALACE football ground is south of Whitehorse Lane. At No. 30 Dagnall Park, the composer, Samuel Coleridge-Taylor, lived in 1900–2. And Sir Arthur Conan Doyle lived at No. 12 Tennison Road in 1891–4, where he wrote the first Sherlock Holmes stories.

South Norwood Lake This was once a reservoir for the CROYDON canal, which was opened in 1809 and linked West Croydon with the GRAND SURREY at NEW CROSS, via SOUTH NORWOOD, PENGE WOODS, SYDENHAM, FOREST HILL and BROCKLEY. It was built by John Rennie and was 9¼ miles long. It became a popular place for picnics, boat trips and fishing in attractive wooded surroundings, but by 1836 had been closed and drained, its use having been superseded by the railways. The London and Croydon Railway bought it and replaced it with a railway line.

South Sea House *Threadneedle Street*. Once the place of business of 'The Governor and Company of Merchants of Great Britain trading to the South

Seas and other parts of America'. The Company was incorporated in 1711 and assigned a monopoly of British trade with Spanish America. The trade, however, did not materialise and in 1719, in order to retrieve its fortunes, the Company put forward a highly speculative scheme which resulted in the notorious collapse known as the 'South Sea Bubble' and the ruin of many investors.

Charles Lamb was employed as a clerk by the Company on leaving CHRIST'S HOSPITAL in 1789. One of his fellow-clerks was an Italian, Ellia, whose name, shortened to Elia but pronounced as originally spelled, he chose as his *nom de plume*. His first essay as 'Elia' was entitled *Recollections of the Old Sea House* in which the place, a huge building whose grounds stretched back as far as OLD BROAD STREET, is described as it was in 1820: 'The throng of merchants was here – the quick pulse of gain. . . . Here are still to be seen stately porticos, imposing staircases, offices as roomy as the state apartments in palaces . . . the still more sacred interiors of court and committee rooms, with venerable faces of beadles, doorkeepers – directors seated on forms on solemn days . . . at long wormeaten tables, that have been mahogany, with tarnished gilt-leather coverings, supporting messy silver inkstands. . . . The oaken wainscot hung with pictures of deceased Governors . . . huge charts, which subsequent discoveries have antiquated; dusty maps of Mexico, dim as dreams. . . .'

Parts of the interiors were remodelled in 1855–6 and by 1891 the building had become 'a nest of mercantile offices'. The British Linen Bank designed by John MacVicar Anderson was built in 1902 over part of the site.

South Street *W1*.

On the GROSVENOR ESTATE, it extends from PARK LANE to FARM STREET. Building began here in the 1730s, the houses (all now demolished) on the south side near PARK LANE having fine views over the garden of DORCHESTER HOUSE towards HYDE PARK. Inhabitants included the 2nd Earl (later 1st Marquess) Cornwallis, commander at Yorktown in 1766–8; the Duke of Orleans (Philippe Égalité), intermittently in 1788–93; Mrs Elizabeth Armistead, successively mistress and wife of Charles James Fox, in 1787–92, Fox himself being the ratepayer in 1793–8; the Duke of Sussex, son of George III, in 1832–43; the 3rd Earl of Lucan, cavalry commander in the Crimea, in 1862–88; Florence Nightingale, in 1865–1910. Farther east lived the architect, J.P. Gandy-Deering, in 1830–50 (he designed a range of large houses here of which only No. 26 survives); and the 2nd Viscount Melbourne, the Prime Minister, in 1830–48. No. 28, built to the designs of Detmar Blow, in 1902–3 was the birth place of another Prime Minister, Alec Douglas-Home.

East of South Audley Street are Nos 39–47 (odd) by J.J. Stevenson (1896–8) and a school by Philip A. Robson (1897–8). On the south side is No. 38, built in 1919–22 to the designs of Edward Wimperis and W.B. Simpson for Henry McLaren, the industrialist (later 2nd Baron Aberconway). The last great private house to be built in MAYFAIR, it backs on to an attractive communal garden designed by Wimperis in about 1914. Catherine Walters, known as Skittles, the last of the great Victorian courtesans, died at No. 15 in 1920, aged 81.

South Villa

Built in 1827 by Decimus Burton for William Henry Cooper, it was, during 1834–61, the home of George Bishop, a London wine merchant, who built and maintained an astronomical observatory from which notable observations of double stars were made. This building was demolished during the 2nd World War.

In 1879–83, the villa was rebuilt in a florid late Victorian manner by Paull and Bonella. In 1908 it was acquired by BEDFORD COLLEGE and was eventually demolished to make way for the present academic buildings.

Southall *Middlesex*.

Has become well known in recent years because of the settlement there of a large number of Commonwealth immigrants, notably Sikhs, since the 2nd World War. As the name of an administrative area Southall is quite recent, the area previously being part of the civil parish of Norwood, Norwood Green still being the name of that area south of the canal. Norwood Parish itself only came into being in 1859, the Precinct of Norwood previously forming part of the Parish of HAYES. Norwood-Southall was largely agricultural until the 19th century but enjoyed a local significance by virtue of its market, whose charter had been granted by William III. In the early 19th century it became the chosen site of the County Lunatic Asylum, now ST BERNARD'S HOSPITAL and of a number of private institutions as well. Industrialisation followed the opening of the GRAND JUNCTION CANAL in 1796 and the PADDINGTON CANAL in 1801, which meet at Bulls Bridge. The Great Western Railway main line to the west was built across Southall between the canal and the Uxbridge Road in the 1830s. Brickmaking became a significant occupation, as it did in the neighbouring districts of HAYES and NORTHOLT and in the latter half of the 19th century a number of factories were built adjacent to the railway line or the canal, including a vast margarine works. Industrialisation continued into the 1920s and 1930s and companies that settled in the area included Quaker Oats, the Crown Cork Co. Ltd and AEC whose old premises have recently closed. Industry is largely confined to the area south of the Uxbridge Road, the area to the north having been developed in the 20th century for housing, which stretches to Greenford Broadway; there is no obvious point where Southall ends and GREENFORD begins.

Little now survives of the agricultural past of Southall, though the livestock market still continues (*see* SOUTHALL MARKET). The only buildings of any age still standing are the MANOR HOUSE and the much rebuilt Norwood church. Most of the architecture is undistinguished and the industrial buildings are the most striking.

The Martin brothers, the art potters, had their works in Southall from 1877 to 1923 and a good collection of their work is displayed in the public library (*see* MARTINWARE POTTERY COLLECTION). The ASIAN influx of the 1950s and 1960s has, despite the problems that it has caused, also resulted in the brightening up of the shopping centre. It has also resulted in the cinemas in the area, including the LIBERTY, showing Asian films and to the establishment of Sikh and Hindu temples amongst the close-packed houses. In July 1981 there were riots in Southall where race relations are usually harmonious and trouble is caused by outsiders.

Southall Market *Southall, Middlesex*. London's oldest horse auctions are held here weekly in the livestock market. Sales have been held on the site since 1698, when William III granted a charter following an application by Francis Therrick, head of an influential local family.

Southampton House, Bloomsbury Square, in c. 1750. Later Bedford House, it was demolished in 1800.

Southampton House *Bloomsbury Square*. Built in about 1657 for Thomas Wriothesley, 4th Earl of Southampton, on the north side of BLOOMSBURY SQUARE. It was a long low house of brick with two short wings. The servants occupied the wings and the ground floor, the principal rooms were on the first floor and the family's bedrooms and dressing rooms on the second. The architect is unknown. In 1667 Southampton died without a male heir. In 1669 his widow remarried and the house passed to one of her stepdaughters, Rachel, wife of William Russell, the second son of the 5th Earl of Bedford. It may briefly have been known as Russell House. In 1700 their child William inherited the title and estates of the Dukes of Bedford and in 1734 the name was changed to Bedford House. In 1800 Francis, 5th Duke of Bedford, had the house demolished. The chapel altar-piece is in ST GEORGE BLOOMSBURY. In 1800–14, James Burton built Nos 18–27 BLOOMSBURY SQUARE on the site of the house. BEDFORD PLACE was laid out northwards through the site and across the garden. The southern half of RUSSELL SQUARE fills the rest of the garden.

Southampton Place *WC1*. South of BLOOMSBURY SQUARE, it is named after the 1st Earl of Southampton. There are some fine, well-preserved Georgian houses of the 1740s by Henry Flitcroft. The actor and poet, Colley Cibber, was born here in 1671. Cardinal John Henry Newman lived on the west side in his early life.

Southampton Row *WC1*. The continuation north of KINGSWAY from HIGH HOLBORN to RUSSELL SQUARE. The uncle of the poet Cowper lived in this street and Cowper 'spent my days there'. Edgar Allen Poe lived here and so did Sir John Barbirolli. At Nos 17–23 is the CENTRAL SCHOOL OF ARTS AND CRAFTS. On the building there is a BLUE PLAQUE to William Richard Lethaby, the architect and first principal, 1896–1911. The JEANETTA COCHRANE THEATRE next door was opened in 1963. The Baptist Church House (1903) by Arthur Keen has a statue of John Bunyan (*see* STATUES). On the west side is Sicilian Avenue (1905) by W.S. Wortley, a pretty, planned, shopping street with colonnaded screens. It is paved with Sicilian marble.

Southampton Street *WC2*. Built on part of the site of the grounds of BEDFORD HOUSE in 1706–10 and named after the Earl of Southampton who was related to the Duke of Bedford, the ground landlord. Colley Cibber, the actor, dramatist and Poet Laureate, lived here in 1714–20. The street was mainly residential until the 19th century. A gate prevented it being used as a short cut to COVENT GARDEN MARKET. In the 19th century many of the houses were taken over as newspaper offices or by societies. No. 3 was the publishing office of William Cobbett's short-lived *Porcupine*. David Garrick lived at No. 27 in 1750–72.

Southend *SE6*. A quiet country village, surrounded by farmland, until the 1920s. The River RAVENSBOURNE powered two water mills at Southend, known as the Upper and Lower Mills. The Lower Mill, the mill pond of which survives as Peter Pan's Pool, was famous in the early 18th century for the cutlery which John and Ephraim How made there. Both mills were still functioning as corn mills in the early years of this century. The Bromley Road, which was once a narrow lane bordered with deep ditches, connected Southend with LEWISHAM. Southend was dominated in the 19th century by the Forster family, who lived at Southend Hall, and whose family chapel served the parishioners before St John's was built in 1926. The Forsters also acquired lands in neighbouring Bellingham. Lord Forster gave the site of Forster Park to LEWISHAM Borough Council, in memory of his two sons who were killed in the 1st World War.

The railway came to Southend in 1892, but the Ordnance Survey map of 1916 shows the village still surrounded by fields, allotments and sports grounds. Gradually new streets were developed along Bromley Road, and in the 1920s and 1930s the LONDON COUNTY COUNCIL built large housing estates at Bellingham and Downham, on land which had previously been farmland. The name Downham derives from Lord Downham, who was chairman of the LONDON COUNTY COUNCIL in 1919–20. These estates, which boasted solid, low-density housing, were partly tenanted by people from the EAST END where the slums were being cleared. Further municipal housing has been built in the Southend area since the 2nd World War. Downham was once the home of one of the world's heaviest men, Richard Harrow of Glenbow Road, who weighed over 40 stone.

Southfields *SW18*. The name is derived from the south field of Durnsford Manor, although the modern political ward covers a larger area. The manor house, later Durnsford Farm, was probably on the site of the present Territorial Army depot in Merton Road. The land was used mainly for agriculture well into the 18th century, except for Anthony Rucker's West Hill estate, now the ROYAL HOSPITAL AND HOME FOR INCURABLES, and the 2nd Earl Spencer's WIMBLEDON PARK, landscaped by 'Capability' Brown. The 3rd Earl found, on his succession in 1835, that family financial difficulties necessitated the selling of much of his land in the area, including half of the park, on which estates were created for wealthy merchants and bankers.

George Eliot finished *The Mill on the Floss* whilst living at Holly Lodge, No. 31 Wimbledon Park Road. In 1889, the railway was extended from PUTNEY BRIDGE to WIMBLEDON, Southfields Station being set in rural surroundings. Development was a slow, piecemeal affair, the area known as 'the Grid' not being completed until 1905. Industry in early times was represented by the flour mills on the WANDLE, some used later to produce calico, paper, copper utensils and dyes. At the end of the 19th century, light industry began to move in both sides of Merton Road, followed in the 1920s by two small industrial estates. The same years saw the start of municipal housing, although the greatest change came after the 2nd World War, when western Southfields was redeveloped with massive, tower-block estates, most of the 19th-century houses being swept away.

Southgate *N14.* Before 1881 Southgate formed part of EDMONTON parish. It occupies high ground overlooking the LEA valley on the east and BARNET valley on the west. It was formerly heavily wooded and in the 16th century the coppices were exploited for timber, firewood, charcoal and bark (used by tanners). Scraps of the former coppices remain in Grovelands Park. The area was thinly populated with scattered settlements such as BOWES, PALMERS GREEN, WINCH-MORE HILL, SOUTHGATE and COLNEY HATCH. The area had a substantial number of large country houses of which BROOMFIELD, GROVELANDS and ARNOS GROVE remain. Lord Lawrence, later Viceroy of India, lived at Southgate House (now Minchenden School) in 1861–4.

The Great Northern Railway arrived in 1871 and development began. The first area to be built up was Bowes Park, on the Wood Green border, in the late 1890s. It was followed early in the 20th century by extensive developments in PALMERS GREEN and WINCHMORE HILL. The opening of the PICCADILLY LINE extension in 1933 produced massive housing developments along the hitherto rural western side of the district from New Southgate to COCKFOSTERS. The area was virtually fully developed by 1939. The population reached a peak of 73,000 in 1951. In 1965 Southgate joined with ENFIELD and EDMONTON forming the London Borough of ENFIELD.

Southlands *The Green, West Drayton, Middlesex.* Stands at the south-eastern corner of The Green. In the early 18th century George Cowdery enlarged his Tudor farmhouse by adding the attractive Queen Anne frontage. The Tudor house was replaced by the present rear portion in 1864. A Sun firemark on the front of the building was placed there in 1743 when the house was insured for £500 and the outbuildings for £300. Early this century Southlands was the home of Cosmo Hamilton, the author, and his actress wife, Beryl Faber. In 1963 the property was acquired by the YIEWSLEY and WEST DRAYTON Urban District Council and it is now used as an Arts Centre.

Southwark *SE1.* A large London borough extending from the area around LONDON BRIDGE and BLACK-FRIARS BRIDGE as far south as SYDENHAM HILL and the Crystal Palace Parade. It was formed in 1965 by the amalgamation of the Metropolitan Boroughs of SOUTHWARK, BERMONDSEY and CAMBERWELL, and en-compasses NEWINGTON, the ELEPHANT AND CASTLE, ROTHERHITHE, WALWORTH, PECKHAM, NUNHEAD, HERNE HILL and DULWICH. Southwark began at the south end of the wooden bridge which the Romans probably built soon after they landed in Britain in AD 43. Evidence of this Roman bridge was discovered in 1834 when oak piles were uncovered as old LONDON BRIDGE was being demolished – the piles having shoes of the hard iron which the Romans forged. The name obviously comes from South Warke or Work. Here a Roman settlement developed, as evidenced by many finds in archaeological excavations. Two ROMAN ROADS met in BOROUGH HIGH STREET, Stane Street on the line of Newington Causeway and Watling Street, now OLD KENT ROAD. As the main entry to London from the south, Southwark was noted for its inns, especially the TABARD, meeting place of Chaucer's pilgrims and the GEORGE INN of 1677 now preserved by the NATIONAL TRUST and built on the site of an earlier inn. The GEORGE became an important coaching inn towards the end of the 18th century when it was the London terminus for traffic and mail from south-eastern England. Many other inns stood in Southwark; and Stow in 1598 mentions eight celebrated ones, including the White Hart which appears in both Shakespeare's *Henry VI* and the *Pickwick Papers*. Another

Southwark Bridge and Toll Gate, c. 1859, looking towards the church of St Antholin, which was demolished in 1874.

vanished inn was the Queen's Head, the sale of which provided John Harvard with funds for the founding of Harvard University. The finding of a gladiator's trident in Southwark suggests that a circus or an arena may have existed here in Roman days, establishing an association of the SOUTH BANK with entertainment and pleasure which continued through the years up to the 17th century. The association has been revived recently by the FESTIVAL HALL and NATIONAL THEATRE, upriver in LAMBETH. Southwark was originally not only a travellers' terminus but a position of defence. The *Olaf Sagas* record a battle by the bridge between Danes and Saxons who were allied with the Norsemen under St Olaf. As the *Sagas* tell 'on the other side of the river is a great cheaping town called Southwarke'. It remained a cheaping-town, or market town, through the centuries but was never a serious commercial rival to the CITY itself. It also became, through the convenience of sanctuary at the church by the bridgehead, the abode not only of prelates but also of debtors, criminals and prostitutes. The church, on the site of a Roman building, was known after the Reformation as St Saviour's and in 1905 became SOUTHWARK CATHEDRAL. A medieval church stood east of the bridgehead, ST OLAVE'S in TOOLEY STREET, dedicated to Norway's warrior king who died in 1030. This was rebuilt in 1740 in Classical style to a design by Henry Flitcroft but was demolished in 1928 to make way for new offices for the Hay's Wharf Company. An important Cluniac abbey existed in BERMONDSEY from 1082 until the DISSOLUTION.

Wyngaerde's great 10 ft panorama of London in the mid-16th century shows a complex of buildings around the bridgehead, including Suffolk House and the tall, square tower of ST SAVIOUR'S. In the Agas map of about the same date the south bank is shown built up with houses to the west as far as PARIS GARDENS and beyond a point lying opposite the TEMPLE, and to the east to a point opposite the TOWER. To the west can be seen 'The Bearebayting' ring, also used for bull-baiting. Here in 1598 on BANKSIDE arose Shakespeare's GLOBE Playhouse which survived until the Puritans pulled it down in 1644. Wyngaerde marks WINCHESTER HOUSE and Rochester House west of ST SAVIOUR'S, where the bishops had their London homes, and far to the west is shown LAMBETH PALACE belonging to the Archbishops of Canterbury. At one time the Abbots of St Augustine, Canterbury, Battle and Hyde and the Prior of Lewes had their houses in Southwark, down river from LONDON BRIDGE. Near WINCHESTER HOUSE, Wyngaerde marks a group of buildings called the Stewes. These were the brothels which Henry VIII closed down. Until then they had been increasing the revenues, through fines and rents, of the Bishops of Winchester who owned this liberty, and so the women of easy virtue on BANKSIDE became known as Winchester Geese.

In the early 17th century the street still named BANKSIDE was described as a 'continued ale-house' and since Chaucer's time Southwark maintained a reputation for its good, strong beer made with THAMES water. Here grew up the large brewery of Barclay Perkins (*see* BREWERIES). No less than seven prisons existed in Southwark, the most notable being the CLINK (recalled by CLINK STREET). The MARSHALSEA was another. BANKSIDE retained its notoriety up to the 19th century.

In 1550 the CITY bought a large area of Southwark from the King and in 1556 the whole of it came under the jurisdiction of the CITY as the 26th ward, called Bridge Ward Without to distinguish it from Bridge Ward Within which consisted of the bridge itself and the area around the north bridgehead. Even when it ceased to be a Liberty the traditional laxity of Southwark continued. Southwark had four special sorts of buildings: houses of prelates, pleasure resorts, prisons and inns. The prelates' houses completely disappeared with the Reformation except for WINCHESTER HOUSE, vestiges of which may still be seen in CLINK STREET. The GLOBE and the other ELIZABETHAN PUBLIC THEATRES of BANKSIDE came to an end with the Civil War and the bear-baiting soon after. The prisons were known to Dickens but were closed and mostly demolished by the mid-19th century. The medieval inns were largely destroyed in Southwark's own conflagration of 1676, ten years after the GREAT FIRE. They were rebuilt but went out of business in the 19th century when railways replaced coaches and horses. Except for parts of the GEORGE INN, all have vanished. As the 17th century progressed, Southwark became more and more built up, especially along the riverside to both east and west of the bridgehead. Defoe describes the south bank in his *Tour* as it was in 1728: 'A long street of about 9 miles in length ... reaching Vauxhall to London Bridge and from the Bridge to Deptford, all up to Deptford Bridge, which parts it from Greenwich, all the way winding and turning as the river winds and turns'. Rocque's map of 1746 shows great changes, for by then the riverside was built up as far west as NINE ELMS, beyond which were the open fields of BATTERSEA in which were several windmills. NEWINGTON and WALWORTH are marked on Rocque's map of 1746 but much open land and market gardens can still be seen south of the river. Scattered buildings extend for about a mile south of LONDON BRIDGE. North of WESTMINSTER BRIDGE, which was then under construction, and round the river bend, lie many timber yards. Opposite the mouth of the FLEET several coal wharfs are shown. More wharfs and warehouses lie all the way to Cuckold's Point on Limehouse Reach and, where the SURREY DOCKS were later dug, are some shipyards and more timber yards. South of them the HOWLAND GREAT WET DOCK is clearly shown and south of that is a small wet dock, and the northern part of the ROYAL DOCK, or King's Yard, DEPTFORD. In the mid-18th century the main area of Southwark consisted of BANKSIDE, the High Street running south to the parish church of St George of 1736, the side-streets off it, and some ribbon development on the two coaching roads south of the parish church.

WESTMINSTER BRIDGE was completed in 1750 and BLACKFRIARS BRIDGE in 1769, and SOUTH LONDON began its expansion. In the 19th century more roads were built and the railways with their river bridges and their viaducts of arched brickwork. In 1800 the population of old Southwark was around 66,000; a century later, thanks to these increased communications, it had more than trebled.

Today the most important monuments of the former Metropolitan Borough of Southwark are the CATHEDRAL; ST GEORGE'S parish church, CHRIST CHURCH in BLACKFRIARS ROAD (1738); Pugin's ST GEORGE'S CATHOLIC CATHEDRAL in St George's Road (1841); Soane's ST PETER'S, Liverpool Grove; Bedford's HOLY TRINITY, Trinity Church Square (1824); Searle and Haye's METROPOLITAN TABERNACLE,

Newington Butts where Spurgeon preached (1861); the IMPERIAL WAR MUSEUM, Lambeth Road; the old part of GUY'S HOSPITAL, St Thomas's Street (1728–80); some relics of the old ST THOMAS'S HOSPITAL, notably the chapel of 1703, now the Chapter House of SOUTHWARK CATHEDRAL, and the GEORGE INN, BOROUGH HIGH STREET. Important elements in Southwark are LONDON BRIDGE terminal station, London's earliest, and the ELEPHANT AND CASTLE complex, where some eight roads converge. Large-scale redevelopments of the Southwark riverside are now being constructed (*see also* CAMBERWELL, BERMONDSEY, ROTHERHITHE and WALWORTH).

Southwark and Vauxhall Water Company

Established in 1845 on the amalgamation of the Southwark Water Company and the VAUXHALL WATER COMPANY. BATTERSEA POWER STATION stands on part of the works' site. The reservoirs covered nearly 18 acres of ground; and the steam engines had the power to force water to a perpendicular height of 175 ft thus enabling a supply at BRIXTON. In 1850 Arthur Hassall, in his *Microscopic Examination of the Water Supplied to the Inhabitants of London*, described the water as being 'in the worst condition in which it is possible to conceive any water to be, as regards its animalcular contents. ... A curious fact in connexion with the water of the Southwark Company has been mentioned to me by Mr Hett, Surgeon of Bridge Street, viz: ... that a gauze bag tied to the tap of the water cistern is found at the end of a few days to contain a mass sufficient to fill an eggshell, consisting principally of the hairs of mammalian animals'. Of the Vauxhall Water Company's supply, Hassall wrote, 'It is water the most disgusting which I have ever examined. When I first saw the water of the Southwark Company, I thought it as bad as it could be, but this far exceeded it in the peculiarly repulsive character of living contents'. In 1855 new works were established at HAMPTON as required by the 1852 Metropolis Water Act. Four reservoirs were constructed to the north of NUNHEAD CEMETERY with a capacity of 18 million gallons. Water was pumped from HAMPTON to BATTERSEA and on to NUNHEAD. In 1894 work began on a covered reservoir at HONOR OAK and in 1898 a storage reservoir was constructed at Walton. The operations of the Company were taken over by Metropolitan Water Board in 1902 (*see also* WATER SUPPLY).

Southwark Bridge *Mansion House–Southwark*.

The Southwark Bridge Company was formed in 1813 in response to urgent demands for a new bridge between LONDON and BLACKFRIARS. There was much opposition to the scheme because of the impediment to shipping of a bridge at this narrow point in the river. In 1814–19 John Rennie built his three-arch cast-iron bridge with a central span of 240 ft, the largest bridge ever constructed of this material. The ironwork was cast by Walker's of Rotherham, whom it bankrupted. Robert Stephenson described the bridge as being 'unrivalled as regards its colossal proportions, its architectural effects and the general simplicity and massive character of its details'. It was replaced in 1912–21 by the present five-span steel bridge of Mott and Hay, with Sir Ernest George as architect.

Southwark Cathedral *Southwark, SE1*.

The Cathedral Church of St Saviour and St Mary Overie is the 4th church to have been built on this site, the three earlier ones having been destroyed by fire. The

George Cruikshank's caricature of 1832 condemns the notoriously unhealthy supplies of the Southwark Water Company.

1st is said to have been built in the 7th century by the ferryman whose trade made him wealthy at a time when there was no bridge over the THAMES between the CITY and SOUTHWARK. In the 9th century the Bishop of Winchester, St Swithun, rebuilt the church which was within his diocese, adding a monastery to replace the original convent. Both church and monastery were rebuilt in the early 12th century by the Augustinian Canons, who also built and administered ST THOMAS'S HOSPITAL as part of their priory. Traces of this Norman Priory church, St Mary Overie (St Mary over the water), survive, including some 13th-century blank arcading in the south aisle and the internal arch in the doorway of the north aisle of the nave.

Destroyed by fire in 1206, the new St Mary Overie was begun in 1220 in the Gothic style, and is now the earliest Gothic church in London. Cardinal Beaufort, Bishop of Winchester, helped to finance restoration after further damage by fire in 1385, and in 1424 his niece, Joan Beaufort, married James I, King of Scotland, here. The Cardinal's hat and coat-of-arms are carved on a pillar in the south transept. After its collapse in 1469, the stone-vaulted roof of the nave was rebuilt in wood. Some of its bosses can be seen today in the north-west end of the nave. In 1539, at the Reformation, the Priory was suppressed and the buildings surrendered to Henry VIII; St Mary Overie became the parish church of St Saviour, Southwark, incorporating also the parish of St Margaret's and the Chapel of St Mary Magdalene. During the reign of Mary Tudor another Bishop of Winchester, Stephen Gardiner, held a consistory court in the retro-choir in which he tried and condemned to death seven of the Marian martyrs. After his death in the reign of Elizabeth I the retro-choir fell into disuse and was leased as a bakery and even as pig-sties. The conventual buildings, too, decayed until eventually they were in ruins. In 1614 the church was bought from James I by the parishioners whose property it thereafter remained. In 1616, when most of London's theatres were situated in this area, Sutton, the chaplain of the parish, preached a sermon denouncing those 'who dishonour God . . . by penning and acting of plays'.

St Saviour's escaped damage during the Civil War; and its new tower was completed by 1689 with the four pinnacles we see today. Early in the 19th century extensive repair work to the choir and the tower was executed under the supervision of George Gwilt the Younger, who also restored the retro-choir (which had been threatened with demolition) free of charge. The old and unsafe wooden roof of the nave was taken down in 1831, leaving the nave open to the heavens, and seven years later its walls were demolished.

Towards the end of the century it was decided that St Saviour's should become the Cathedral church of a new diocese for the increased population south of the THAMES. This prompted the building, to designs by Sir Arthur Blomfield, of the present nave, the foundation stone of which was laid by the Prince of Wales in 1890. During the reorganisation of the boundaries of the medieval sees, SOUTHWARK was transferred from the See of Winchester to the See of Rochester for a time. In 1897 St Saviour's became the pro-Cathedral of SOUTH LONDON, and in 1905 Edward Stuart Talbot, 1st Bishop of Southwark, was enthroned.

Among the furnishings are a modern bronze sculpture, *The Holy Family* by Kenneth Hughes, at the west end of the nave, a great brass candelabrum hanging in the crossing under the central tower, the gift in 1680 of 'Dorothy ye relict of Jno. Applebye Esqe' and the altar screen rising above the High Altar, the gift in about 1520 of Richard Fox, Bishop of Winchester. This three-tiered stone altar screen, carved with niches, divided the High Altar and the Sanctuary from the retro-choir. The statues in the niches are 19th century. The lower part of the screen was gilded and repainted by Sir Ninian Comper who, in 1950, designed the stained glass east window behind and above the screen, depicting the Lord in Glory.

The Cathedral is rich in monuments. Among the earliest is an oak effigy of a knight, ankles crossed, one hand on the pommel of his sword, about 1275. Another is the effigy of John Gower, poet and friend of Chaucer, on a tomb-chest, gilded and painted, with the inscription *Angl. poeta celeberrimus*. In the south aisle is a memorial to Shakespeare carved in 1912 by Henry McCarthy. Above this is the memorial window designed by Christopher Webb in 1954 to replace the earlier one destroyed in the 2nd World War. Every year a birthday service is held here in Shakespeare's honour. St Saviour's was the place of worship of many of his friends and colleagues, for there were no less than five theatres at BANKSIDE, including 'the great Globe itself'. His youngest brother, Edmund, and John Fletcher and Philip Massinger the dramatists, are buried here, as is Lawrence Fletcher, the co-lessee of the GLOBE.

John Harvard, the founder of Harvard University, was born in SOUTHWARK in 1607 and baptised in St Saviour's. He is commemorated in the Harvard Chapel off the north transept, which is entered by a heavy studded oak door. Its reconstruction in 1907, from the Chapel of St John the Evangelist, was paid for by members of Harvard University.

In the south choir aisle is the tomb of Lancelot Andrews, Bishop of Winchester, scholar and court preacher, who died in 1626, a staunch supporter of the reformed Church of England, and the last Bishop to live at WINCHESTER HOUSE.

Southwark Fair The right to hold a fair at SOUTHWARK was granted to the Corporation of London by a charter of Edward IV in 1402 and confirmed by Edward VI in 1551. With ST BARTHOLOMEW FAIR and Stourbridge, Cambridgeshire, it was, for a long time, one of the great annual English fairs. Originally lasting three days from 7 September it grew to two weeks' duration and was known as Our Lady Fair. It was held in what is now BOROUGH HIGH STREET near the famous TABARD INN and ST GEORGE'S CHURCH. As no large open space existed, all the nearby streets, courts, and inn-yards were requisitioned for booths and shows, seriously inconveniencing local shop-keepers. Both Pepys's and Evelyn's diaries record visits. In 1660 Evelyn saw monkeys dancing on ropes. 'They saluted one another with as good grace as if instructed by a dancing-master; they turned heels over head with a basket having eggs in it without breaking any; also with lighted candles in their hands and on their heads without extinguishing them and with vessels of water without spilling a drop'. Evelyn also saw a weight-lifter and an Italian female rope-dancer and mentions that 'all the Court went to see her'. In 1668 Pepys records: 'To Southwark Fair, very dirty, and there saw the puppet show of Whittington which was pretty to see;

Hogarth's Southwark Fair, *1733, features all the best-known performers and booth proprietors of the day.*

and how that idle thing do work upon people that see it, and even myself, too! And thence to Jacob Hall's dancing on the ropes, where I saw such action as I never saw before and mightily worth seeing.' He later met Hall in a tavern and asked if he ever had accidents to which the reply was, 'Yes, many, but never to the breaking of a limb'.

In 1733 Hogarth produced his great picture of Southwark Fair, peopled by all the famous performers and booth-proprietors of the day. They include Lee and Harper's acting booth where Elkanah Settle's *Siege of Troy* was playing; a waxwork show of *The whole court of France*; Miller, the German giant; Violante, the tumbler; Mr Fawkes, a conjuror with his 'curious Indian birds'; Cadman, a slack-rope performer; and James Figg, the famous pugilist who entertained the crowds with 'foil-play, back-sword, cudgeling and boxing'. At this time SOUTH-WARK entertainments ranged from polished theatrical performances such as Timothy Fielding's production of *The Beggar's Opera* with actors from the HAY-MARKET THEATRE to exhibits of freaks of all kinds. Pick-pockets and prostitutes abounded and in 1743 the fair was ordered to be 'cried down' by the bellman. In 1762 it was prohibited by the COMMON COUNCIL and in 1763 the CORPORATION finally suppressed it.

Southwark Park *SE16.* Comprising 63 acres opened in 1869 by the METROPOLITAN BOARD OF WORKS which had acquired it four years before. It lies on former market gardens near ROTHERHITHE docks. Facilities include a cricket ground and a bandstand.

Southwark Pottery Tin-glazed earthenware made here from 1618 in a workshop opened by Christian Wilhelm, a Dutchman. Much of his work in blue and white is decorated with motifs copied from Ming porcelain. LAMBETH POTTERY resembled it.

Southwood Lane *N6.* Extends north from HIGH-GATE HIGH STREET to ARCHWAY ROAD. Mary Kingsley, the traveller and ethnologist, lived at No. 22 as a girl.

Spa Fields Chapel *Clerkenwell.* Stood at Nos 22–24 EXMOUTH STREET on the site of a pond where dogs were set to hunt ducks (*see* ROSOMAN STREET). It was the first chapel of the Dissenters known as 'the Countess of Huntingdon's Connection'. It opened in 1779. The Countess, who played a large part in making non-conformism acceptable to the aristocracy, was a close friend of the Wesleys. She took up residence next door to the chapel from the year of its opening. The building was demolished in 1879.

Spa Fields Chapel was opened in 1779 by the Wesleys' friend, the Countess of Huntingdon, who lived in the house next door.

Spaniards *Hampstead Lane, NW3.* A 16th-century weatherboarded house said to have been named after a Spanish Ambassador to James II or after two Spanish brothers, joint proprietors, who killed each other in a duel over a woman. It was used by Dick Turpin, who stabled his horse, Black Bess, in the toll house opposite. In 1780 a party of Gordon Rioters, on their way to destroy KENWOOD, were invited in for

The Spaniards, Hampstead, which has been a tavern since the 16th century. From an engraving of c. 1855.

drinks and kept there until a detachment of soldiers arrived and subsequently disarmed them. The rifles can be seen in the saloon bar. It has been much used by literary men, among them Shelley, Keats and Byron; Charles Dickens made it the place where Mrs Bardell and her friends plotted the downfall of Mr Pickwick.

Special Operations Executive This organisation, normally referred to as SOE, had its headquarters at No. 64 BAKER STREET during the 2nd World War and was known as the Baker Street Irregulars. It was an independent British secret service organisation set up in July 1940 and disbanded in 1946. Its main role was to conduct subversive warfare and to co-ordinate worldwide clandestine and sabotage activity against Germany and her allies.

Spanish Place *W1*. A turning out of MANCHESTER SQUARE, it owes its name to the Spanish Ambassador's tenancy of Manchester House (*see* WALLACE COLLECTION). Captain Frederick Marryat lived at No. 3 in 1793, and the house was later the home of the younger George Grossmith, the actor-manager. ST JAMES'S Roman Catholic church stands in George Street, opposite its junction with Spanish Place.

Spanish and Portuguese Synagogue *Bevis Marks, EC3*. This uniquely preserved and well-appointed synagogue, built in 1700–1, took the place of an earlier one in Creechurch Lane, the first to be opened after the Jews were allowed to return to England by Cromwell in 1657. The builder was Joseph Avis, a Quaker. Queen Anne gave one of the main beams. The design is a plain rectangle with two tiers of windows, a flat ceiling and three galleries. The original Jewish furnishings are not dissimilar from those one would find in other City churches; the seven chandeliers from Amsterdam (some with eight others with six sconces) are exceptionally fine. The birth of Benjamin Disraeli in 1804 is recorded in the synagogue register. His father, Isaac D'Israeli, was a devout conformist member of the Sephardi congregation here.

Spectacle Makers' Company *see* CITY LIVERY COMPANIES.

Spencer House *27 St James's Place, SW1*. Henry Bromley, 1st Baron Montfort, had intended building a new house on the site of an older one here to the designs of John Vardy but he got into financial difficulties and shot himself while his lawyer, to whom he had read over his will, was still on the stairs. A lease of the site was then sold to John Spencer, heir to Sarah, Duchess of Marlborough, who was created Earl Spencer in 1765. The design of the house seems largely to have been the work of Vardy, but Spencer's friend and fellow-member of the DILETTANTI SOCIETY, General Sir George Gray, also had a hand in it. Another member of the Dilettanti Society, James Stuart, worked on the interior of the house and was responsible for the painted room. Robert Adam also worked here. The house was completed in 1766. 'I do not apprehend,' wrote Arthur Young, 'there is a house in Europe of its size, better worth the view of the curious in architecture, and the fitting up and furnishing great houses, than Lord Spencer's in St James's Place . . . I know not in England, a more beautiful piece of architecture.' Henry Holland made alterations to the house for the 2nd Earl Spencer in the 1780s. Philip Hardwick was employed in the 1840s. After 1927 Spencer House was no longer used as a private residence. Some of the furniture may be seen at KENWOOD. Other pieces and the mahogany doors were taken to the Spencers' country house, Althorp, to be followed later by the chimney piece and other fittings. The house was used by the Ladies' Army and Navy Club until 1943 when it was taken over by the Government. CHRISTIE'S, the auctioneers, moved in in 1948, while their KING STREET premises were being rebuilt. In 1956 the house was leased to British Oxygen Gases Ltd for whose use it was adapted by Robert Atkinson and Partners. In 1980 it was occupied by the Economist Intelligence Unit Ltd. It is the property of the trustees of the 8th Earl Spencer's marriage settlement. In December 1982 the NATIONAL TRUST was negotiating to take over the lease.

John Vardy, James Stuart and Robert Adam all worked on Spencer House, completed for Earl Spencer in 1766.

Spink and Son Ltd *5, 6 and 7 King Street, St James's, SW1*. In 1666 John Spink set up as a goldsmith in LOMBARD STREET and four years later his cousin, Elwes Spink, joined him. By 1703 their business in plate and jewellery was so successful they moved to GRACECHURCH STREET where they remained for over 100 years. They moved to PICCADILLY CIRCUS after this, and later to the present site in ST JAMES'S. The firm expanded its interests to include fine

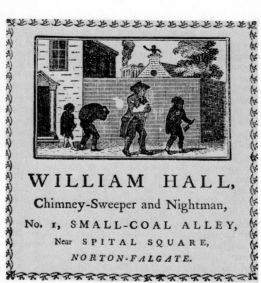

The trade card of William Hall, 'Chimney-Sweeper and Nightman', of Small-Coal Alley, Spital Square.

paintings and drawings, antique silver and jewellery and an oriental department specialising in mid- and far-Eastern works of art, coins, orders and medals. Spink Coin Auctions are held in London and abroad. Their factory designs and makes orders, decorations and medals for many countries.

Spital Square   *E1*. Built on the site of the precinct of ST MARY SPITAL, the development of the square began in the late 17th century, but most of the building took place in the 1720s and 1730s. Occupied by the silk merchants and master weavers, it retained its seclusion in the 18th century by having obstacles erected to prevent through traffic. Only a tiny section survives today.

Spital Yard   *E1*. In the 17th century SPITAL SQUARE was known as Spital Yard, but the name now refers only to the cul-de-sac leading off the square. The yard is thought to run along the line of an entrance to the Priory of ST MARY SPITAL. John Wesley's mother was born in a house in the Yard in 1669.

Spitalfields   *E1*. The fields to the east of the medieval priory and hospital of ST MARY SPITAL, where a Roman cemetery was discovered in the 16th century. Daniel Defoe claimed that Spitalfields became 'all town' in his lifetime. In his childhood, 'the lanes were deep, dirty and unfrequented, the part now called Spitalfields Market was a field of grass with cows feeding on it. Brick Lane, which is now a long well paved street, was a deep dirty road, frequented chiefly by carts fetching bricks that way into Whitechapel from brick kilns in those fields.' By 1640, however, there had already been some building along the southern and eastern fringes spreading from WHITE-CHAPEL and the CITY. Nicholas Culpepper, the herbalist and physician, lived in Red Lion Street in the 1640s. The most rapid period of development occurred in the next three decades. By 1675 there were over 1,300 houses, mostly small tenements crowded into narrow streets and alleyways. The area was noted

as a stronghold of nonconformity – the first Baptist church in England had been founded there in 1612 and Spitalfields was described in 1684 as 'the most factious hamlet of all the Tower Division, having had many conventicles in it'. The magnificent CHRIST CHURCH SPITALFIELDS was erected in 1714–29 to combat nonconformity and cater for the rapidly growing population. Foreigners in large numbers, including French weavers, were present by the time of the greatest influx of HUGUENOT refugees from France after the Revocation of the Edict of Nantes in 1685. Their skill in silk weaving gave Spitalfields its reputation in the 18th century as the centre of production of fine quality silks. Although the Georgian buildings that remain, notably around FOURNIER STREET and ELDER STREET, recall the prosperity of some of the silk merchants, master weavers, dyers and retailers, much of vanished Spitalfields was always the home of poorer working weavers subject to the vagaries of an uncertain trade. In 1807 when the population had reached over 15,000 the Vestry claimed that Spitalfields and MILE END New Town were inhabited almost entirely by poor persons, and streets had been taken over by common lodging-houses offering wretched accommodation to an impoverished and partly criminal population.

Slums had been cleared away when Commercial Street was constructed in 1848, and the erection of blocks of artisans' dwellings, beginning with the first PEABODY BUILDINGS in COMMERCIAL STREET in 1864, hastened the rebuilding of an area made more notorious by the activities of Jack the Ripper. The blocks of new dwellings were mostly occupied by Jewish immigrants who came into the area in increasing numbers from the 1880s. The almost defunct weaving trade was replaced by small furriers' and clothiers' workshops; but by the 19th century employment had considerably diversified especially with the development of Truman's BREWERY and SPITALFIELDS MARKET. Extensions to the market in the 1920s and 1930s destroyed many of the finest buildings; but Spitalfields still retains one of the largest concentrations of early Georgian buildings in London, ironically saved from demolition and redevelopment by 19th-century economic decline. One building at the corner of Fournier Street and BRICK LANE particularly reflects the social changes that have occurred in Spitalfields. Built as a Huguenot chapel in 1743, it later became a synagogue and is now a mosque, catering for the latest immigrants to settle here, the Bangladeshi.

Spitalfields Market   *Commercial Street, E1*. An important market for bulky vegetables established in 1682, under licence granted by Charles II to John Balch. In 1708 it was described by Hatton as a fine market for flesh, fowl and roots. After the revocation of the Edict of Nantes there was an influx of Huguenot refugees to the area. Spitalfields became a centre for silk weaving and the market flourished. Balch sold the market to the Goldschmidt family and in 1856 they sold it to Robert Horner, a self-made man who had once worked in the market as a porter. Horner spent £80,000 on the construction of new buildings. In 1920 these were bought by the CITY OF LONDON CORPORATION who spent £2 million on modernisation. The new market was opened in 1928. It was carefully designed as a fruit and vegetable market specialising in bananas with heated cellars for ripening and an aggregate floor space of 10½ acres.

Spitalfields Silks The industry was established in the early 17th century and was soon employing many Huguenot refugees (*see* SPITALFIELDS). By the beginning of the 18th century damasks and velvets were being produced as well as figured silk brocades mainly for women's clothes and men's suits and waistcoats. The industry flourished under a system of government protection which included the prohibition of the import of French silks. Patterns were usually supplied by independent designers such as the naturalist, Joseph Dandridge, and Anna Maria Garthwaite, a Lincolnshire parson's daughter who came to work in SPITALFIELDS. Designs by both can be seen, among several others, at the VICTORIA AND ALBERT MUSEUM. Silk weaving in SPITALFIELDS began to decline after the end of the Napoleonic Wars and by the late 1830s it had become a sweated industry.

Sprimont Place *SW3*. Commemorates Nicholas Sprimont, a silversmith by training, who was manager of the Chelsea china factory in LAWRENCE STREET in 1747–69 (*see* CHELSEA PORCELAIN WORKS).

Spring Garden *Mile End Road, Stepney*. Short-lived 18th-century pleasure garden, sometimes known as the Jews' Spring Garden, which existed from 1702 until about 1764. Globe Road marks the eastern boundary and Mile End Road the southern one.

Spring Gardens *Charing Cross*. Gardens shown on Morden and Lea's map of 1682 as immediately behind Wallingford House, now the ADMIRALTY. Access to the gardens was through the present SPRING GARDENS. The gardens seem to have been originally part of the royal ST JAMES'S PARK, and it is not clear from what date they were open to the public. They are probably the gardens described by Hentzner in 1598. They had butts, a bathing-pond and a pheasant yard. They are first mentioned by name in 1610–11. In 1629 a bowling green, laid with turf from BLACKHEATH, and a garden house for Charles I to rest in were constructed

by William Walker. By 1634 the gardens were certainly in public use, since Garrard wrote to Lord Strafford describing 'an ordinary of six shillings a meal (when the King's proclamation allows but two elsewhere), continual bibbing and drinking wine under the trees'. The place had 'grown scandalous and insufferable'. Charles suppressed the bowling green for a time, but it was reprieved after the Queen's intercession, though its use for bowling was no longer allowed. A new green was, therefore, established on the other side of what is now TRAFALGAR SQUARE where the NATIONAL GALLERY stands today. By 1649 the original green was reopened, but was closed again in 1654 by Cromwell. It had reopened yet again by 1659 when it was described in *A Character of England*: 'For it is usual here to find some of the young company till midnight; and the thickets of the garden seem to be contrived to all advantages of gallantry'. The refreshment available is also mentioned: 'The forbidden fruits are certain trifling tarts, neats' tongues, salacious meats, and bad Rhenish; for which the gallants pay sauce'. After the Restoration the gardens were built over, and the entertainments removed to VAUXHALL.

Spring Gardens *SW1*. On the site of a pleasure-ground laid out at the beginning of the 17th century, closed during the Commonwealth and reopened at the Restoration. Prince Rupert had a house nearby from 1670 until his death in 1682. The Blue Posts, a tavern much frequented by Jacobites in the time of William III, was here. It is the scene of romantic intrigues in Vanbrugh's *The Provok'd Wife*. In the 18th century it was known mainly for its Great Room used at different times as a concert hall, exhibition room and museum (*see* COX'S MUSEUM). George Canning lived here in a house, since demolished, on the corner of COCKSPUR STREET in 1799. Sir Robert Taylor, architect of the BANK OF ENGLAND, also had a house here in which he died in 1788; and Sir George Gilbert Scott, an equally prosperous architect, lived here in 1834–44 and had an office here until his death. The BRITISH COUNCIL are

A fête in the grounds of John Penn's mansion in Spring Gardens, held in 1830 for the benefit of Charing Cross Hospital.

at No. 10. The bronze, *Large Spindle Piece*, is by Henry Moore (1980).

Spring Grove *Osterley, Middlesex*. A development of large villas intended for London merchants and professional men, built from about 1850 by Henry Davies. Building ceased in 1870 as Davies lost his money. The District Railway came in 1883, leading to more building, and there was further building after the opening of the GREAT WEST ROAD in 1925. Blocks of flats have now replaced many villas. St Mary's Church, Osterley Road, was built and financed by Davies in 1853. The spire collapsed in 1861, was replaced, and collapsed again in 1867. On the second rebuilding the spire's height was reduced by 8 ft. Three houses called Spring Grove have occupied the site of the present building in London Road. The first house was built for Sir John Offley in 1645 and the second was occupied by Sir Joseph Banks. The third was built in 1892–4 for Andrew Pears, owner of Pears Soap, and is now part of Hounslow Borough College.

Springfield Hospital *61 Glenburnie Road, SW17*. Opened in 1841, it was originally called the Surrey County Lunatic Asylum. 294 patients were admitted from workhouses, private mad-houses and BETH-LEHEM. The numbers of patients rapidly rose to 500 and later to 940, additional buildings having been erected. The chapel was built in 1879. In 1889 the Asylum was transferred to the MIDDLESEX County Council. It was later administered by the LONDON COUNTY COUN-CIL and finally by the National Health Service.

Spurgeon's College *South Norwood Hill, SE25*. Theological training college named after Charles Haddon Spurgeon, the famous Baptist preacher, who lived in a large house called Westwood on BEULAH HILL and is buried in the SOUTH METROPOLITAN CEMETERY in WEST NORWOOD. After his death in 1892, a place was sought for a residential training college and in 1923 Falkland Park was given for this purpose by its owner Hay Walker. This large mansion, built at the end of the 19th century, took its name from Admiral Carey, Viscount Falkland, who lived in the original house on the estate. Other college buildings have been added subsequently.

Square Rigger *King William Street, EC4*. Public house standing directly opposite the MONUMENT. The owners have re-created an 18th-century ship-of-the-line, complete with masts, rigging, timbers and stuffed seagulls. The four bars have nautical names and the whole gives a remarkably authentic impression.

Squire's Coffee House *Fulwood's Rents, Holborn*. First mentioned at the beginning of the 18th century, it took its name from a Mr Squire, 'a noted coffee man', who died in 1717. Most of the patrons were students and benchers of GRAY'S INN. In 1711 a writer in the *Spectator* comments on, 'the young fellows at the Grecian, Squire's, Searle's and all other coffee houses adjacent to the law, who rise early for no other purpose but to publish their laziness'. Addison describes a visit to Squire's with Sir Roger de Coverley in 1712, during which the knight's 'air of cheerfulness and good humour' charmed the servants.

Stafford Hotel *16 St James's Place, SW1*. No. 17, once a private lodging house, became the Public Schools' Club, then The Phoenix Club and in 1870 Richmond Club Chambers which existed here until 1886. In 1873 the building became Green's Private Hotel, later the St James's Place Hotel. And in 1886 The Stafford Club was founded in the hotel and probably named after the family who lived in the area. In 1902, No. 16, a private residence since the 17th century, and No. 17 were joined to form one building. In 1912 Simon Harwath became the first owner of the new Stafford Hotel. During the 2nd World War it was used as a club for American and Canadian officers. In 1947 it was bought by Sir Richard Costain. There are 67 bedrooms.

Stafford House *St James's, SW1 see* LANCASTER HOUSE.

Stafford Place *SW1*. Takes its name from William Howard, Lord Stafford, who, falsely accused by Titus Oates, was executed on TOWER HILL in 1680. He lived at Tart Hall, now demolished, in the grounds of which Stafford Place was built. Lord Hore-Belisha, who introduced 'Belisha beacons' to London when Minister of Transport, lived at No. 16, which was altered for him by Lutyens.

Stafford Street *W1*. Extends from OLD BOND STREET to DOVER STREET and takes its name from Margaret Stafford, one of Sir Thomas Bond's partners in 1684 in the development of Albemarle Ground (*see* ALBEMARLE STREET).

Stafford Terrace *W8*. Built on the PHILLIMORE ESTATE in 1868–74 by Joseph Gordon Davis, a builder who had been active in PIMLICO. LINLEY SAMBOURNE HOUSE is at No. 18.

Stag Place *SW1*. Takes its name from the Stag BREWERY, on the site of which beer was being brewed since at least 1641. The 7-acre site was redeveloped in 1959 by Trehearne and Norman, Preston and Partners. The aluminium figure *The Stag* is by E. Bainbridge Copnall (1962) and marks the site of the brewery.

Staining Lane *EC2*. Possibly, as Stow thought, named after painter-stainers or perhaps after people from Staines who had lived here. In the adjacent Oat Lane was the church of ST MARY STAINING which burnt down in the GREAT FIRE. HABERDASHERS' HALL is here.

Stamford Brook The name is said to mean 'stony ford', and the ford which gave its name to Stamford Brook was on the GREAT WEST ROAD. The brook was formed by three streams. One rose at WORMWOOD SCRUBS and flowed down Old Oak Common Lane; another ran down to RAVENSCOURT PARK and a third – the BOLLO – rose in West ACTON and flowed through TURNHAM GREEN, where all joined and turned south to enter the THAMES at HAMMERSMITH Creek. By the end of the 19th century it had been completely covered in and turned into a sewer.

Stamford Hill *N16*. The earliest record dates from the 13th century, when it was called Sanford Hill, the hill by the sandy ford. A map of 1745 shows a small hamlet at the junction of Hackney Lane and the Cambridge Road; but by 1795, the Cambridge Road was lined with select villas in spacious grounds, homes of wealthy City bankers and merchants. Little more was built until the railway arrived in 1872, when the surrounding fields were quickly developed with terraced houses for the middle classes. Between the two world wars, most of the 18th-century villas were demolished to make way for large blocks of flats for the working classes, but little has changed since.

Stamford Hill has long been a centre for the orthodox Jewish community: men belonging to the Hassidic movement can be seen wearing long black coats and wide-brimmed fur hats, a style derived from 18th-century Poland, and the area is notable for Jewish scholarship. Egerton Road is the third home of the New Synagogue; the building contains the interior of the synagogue first erected in LEADENHALL STREET in 1760, which moved to GREAT ST HELEN'S in 1838 and finally came to Stamford Hill in 1915. In Rookwood Road stands the former Ark of the Covenant of the Agapemonites, built in 1892. The head of this notorious and bizarre sect, the 'Revd' J.H. Smyth-Piggott, announced in 1902 that he was God, and a crowd of 6,000 people greeted the self-styled messiah with hisses, catcalls and a shower of stones and umbrellas when he arrived in his carriage. The Agapemonites have gone but their 'church' remains.

Stamford Street *SE1*. Extends from Waterloo Road to BLACKFRIARS ROAD. It was built across LAMBETH Marsh. John Rennie, the engineer and builder of WATERLOO and SOUTHWARK BRIDGES, lived at No. 18 from 1793 until his death there in 1821. Cox's Horse Repository, where Queen Victoria is believed to have bought her first horse, was in this street.

Stanhope Gate *W1*. A short broad street extending from PARK LANE to SOUTH AUDLEY STREET which it enters almost opposite the site formerly occupied by the mansion built by Philip Stanhope, 4th Earl of Chesterfield, in 1747–50 – hence its name. Several large Georgian houses of about 1760 still survive (all now used as offices or banks), and at No. 5 there is a plaque commemorating the residence there of Lord Raglan, commander-in-chief during the Crimean War.

Stanhope Street *NW1*. Named after William Stanhope, 2nd Earl of Harrington who married Lady Caroline Fitzroy, daughter of the 2nd Duke of Grafton (*see* FITZROY SQUARE). William Macready, the actor, was born at No. 45 in 1793.

Stanhope Terrace *W2*. Takes its name from Arthur Stanhope, brother-in-law of Robert Thistlethwaite of Southwick Park and inheritor of land leased in PADDINGTON from the BISHOPS OF LONDON. Thistlethwaite had married Selina, younger daughter of Elizabeth Bathurst of Clarendon Park, Wiltshire, whose elder daughter married Sir John Morehead, father-in-law of Jane Warwick of Warwick Hall, Cumberland – hence Southwick Street and Place, Bathurst Street, Clarendon Close, Gardens, Place and Terrace, Morehead Road and Warwick Avenue, CRESCENT and Place. Sir Edwin Chadwick, the social reformer, lived at No. 9.

Canons, Stanmore, now the North London Collegiate School, was built by William Hallet in c. 1747.

Stanmore *Middlesex*. The Celtic tribe of the Catuvellauni displaced the original neolithic inhabitants of Hertfordshire about 100 BC. The southern limit of their territory extended to the northern heights of Stanmore with a settlement on Brockley Hill. Legend has it that it was on Brockley Hill that the Catuvellauni, under their leader Cassivellaunus, joined battle with Julius Caesar in 54 BC. The battle is commemorated by an obelisk erected in 1750 on what was then common land, but which is today in the grounds of THE ROYAL NATIONAL ORTHOPAEDIC HOSPITAL. It is now generally agreed that the victory was Caesar's, not that of the Catuvellauni as recorded on the obelisk. The Romans later established the Belgic settlement on Brockley Hill as Roman Sulloniacae. It was a posting station on Watling Street, with an entry in the Antonine Itinerary and developed as a major centre of the pottery industry.

The name Stanmore derives from 'Stony mere' or 'Stones by the mere'. The 'stones' may refer to the stony nature of the ground, or to the ruins of Sulloniacae; the 'mere' was the pond on Stanmore Common still called by the older inhabitants Caesar's Pond. Local legend tells us that it was also on Stanmore Common that Boudicca was defeated after her bloody uprising. A mound in the grounds of Lime's House has always been traditionally known as Boudicca's Grave. In AD 793 land in Stanmore was granted by Offa, King of Mercia, to the Abbey of St Albans. With the Norman invasion the two manors of Great and Little Stanmore (Stanmore Magna and Stanmore Parva) changed hands. Great Stanmore passed from Edmer Atule to Robert, Count of Mortain, a half-brother of William the Conqueror; Little Stanmore passed from Algar to Roger de Rames.

The two Stanmores remained largely rural until the present century, but in the words of Defoe (1720) there were in the vicinity 'a great many very beautiful seats of the nobility and gentry'. The finest were undoubtedly CANONS and BENTLEY PRIORY. Stanmore Park, home of Andrew Drummond, founder of DRUMMOND'S BANK, was demolished in 1938 when the RAF took possession. Stanmore Hall, the finest work of the architect J.M. Derrick, with ceilings painted by Edward Burne-Jones, was recently devastated by fire. It

811

was the home of Robert Hollond, remembered in *The Ingoldsby Legends* for his adventure in the 'Monstre Balloon' which took him, in 1836, on an 18-hour flight to southern Germany. Warren House (now Springbok House) was the home of the architect, Robert Smirke, and later of the Keyser family. Charles Keyser was a founder member and first chairman of the Colne Valley Water Company; his sister Agnes founded the KING EDWARD VII HOSPITAL FOR OFFICERS. LIMES HOUSE, dating from the Victorian era, was once the home of the aircraft pioneer, Handley Page; and the recently demolished Grove on Stanmore Common, was the home of the naturalist and author, Mrs Eliza Brightwen. The naturalist, Edward Wilson, who died with Scott on the ill-fated expedition to the South Pole in 1912, lived for a time in an 18th-century house still on Stanmore Hill. The area around ST JOHN'S CHURCH with its timber-framed Church House and Tithe Barn is now a designated conservation area. Much of Stanmore Hill with its historic Abercorn Arms, the meeting place in 1814 of the Prince Regent and Louis XVIII of France, is a second conservation area; whilst Little Common with its two delightful ponds and ornate cottages, one with a particularly fine chimney and Dutch gable, is a third. Much of the northern part of Stanmore is GREEN BELT land open to the public. Prominent in Stanmore village is what is perhaps the finest group of 16th-century jettied cottages in MIDDLESEX.

Star and Garter *Pall Mall*. A fashionable and expensive 18th-century tavern mentioned by Smollett in *Humphrey Clinker* and patronised by Swift and the Brothers' Club of which he was a member. George Selwyn's Thursday Club of which Reynolds and Lord March were members met here to dine and play whist. The DILETTANTI SOCIETY also met here occasionally. So also did the Nottinghamshire Club at one of whose meetings a quarrel broke out between William, Lord Byron and his cousin, Mr Chaworth, about the game on their neighbouring estates. They asked a waiter to show them to an empty room where they fought a duel in which Chaworth was mortally wounded. Lord Byron was tried for murder but acquitted. He felt no remorse for having killed his cousin, according to his great-nephew, the poet. 'He always kept the sword which he used upon that occasion in his bedchamber, and there it still was when he died'. Meetings of the Jockey Club were also held here and of the smart *Je ne sais quoi* Club of which the Prince of Wales, later George IV, was a member and from which the Duke of Orléans was expelled at the Prince's insistence for his 'disgraceful conduct' in supporting the Jacobins against the King in the Revolution. In 1774 a committee, whose members included the Duke of Dorset, Lord Tankerville and Sir Horace Mann met here, under the presidency of Sir William Draper, to amend the rules of the game of cricket which were revised here in 1755 (*see* WHITE CONDUIT CLUB). The inn was said to serve the 'best claret in England'.

Star and Garter Home *Richmond Hill, Surrey*. The famous view of the THAMES from the top of RICHMOND HILL made this the ideal spot for an inn. The site was leased by John Christopher in 1738 from the Earl of Dysart of HAM HOUSE and, as the Earl was a Member of the Noble Order of the Garter, Star and Garter became the inn's name. In the early 1800s the inn was enlarged to accommodate overnight guests but its real success came after 1822 when the Ellis family took it over. Joseph Ellis ran it as a flourishing and fashionable meeting place. In 1825 the inn was described in glowing terms: 'A little beyond the Terrace is the renowned tavern and hotel, the Star and Garter, more like the mansion of a nobleman than a receptacle for the public; looking down with stately aspect from the adjoining valley, and seen to advantage from every point of the horizon. Hither, in the summer season, crowd visitants from the overgrown Metropolis, to inhale the pure air and exhilarate their spirits by contemplating a wide-spreading circumference of rural scenery.' The Assembly Room was the fashionable place to hold wedding receptions and balls. Louis-Philippe stayed here for six months after his flight from Paris. Napoleon III had apartments here. Dickens gave a dinner for friends every year in a private room to celebrate his wedding anniversary. By the 1850s as many as 560 dinners were served on Sundays.

In 1864 the inn was purchased by a limited liability company and rebuilt in the style of a French renaissance château designed by Edward Middleton Barry. In a letter to *The Times* it was described as 'gross, pretentious, common, impudently obtrusive, it stood out, a great disfiguring wart or wen on the face of Richmond Hill'. In 1870, all that remained of the original Star and Garter except for the coffee room was destroyed by fire and its passing was mourned with a poem in the *Graphic*. The author ended with a plea to the architects:

> Don't mimic London's monsters, hang 'em –
> Stiff Charing Cross, and lumbering Langham
> Build nothing vaster, nothing smarter –
> Give us back our own old Star and Garter.

The plea fell on deaf ears and the monster remained. The coffee room burned down in 1888 and the last traces of the old hotel disappeared. By the end of the century the hotel was unused.

It became a temporary hospital for troops in the 1st World War and in 1916 a home for disabled soldiers. The war over, the hotel was now inadequate and it was pulled down to make way for a new home which was completed in 1924. It was designed by Sir Edwin Cooper in a sub-Lutyens style and the massive redbrick building still dominates the brow of the hill, a heavy-handed reminder that there stood one of England's most historic hotels.

State Opening of Parliament A ceremonial which has changed little since the 16th century. The monarch rides in the Irish State Coach (*see* ROYAL MEWS) from BUCKINGHAM PALACE to the PALACE OF WESTMINSTER through the MALL and WHITEHALL. At WESTMINSTER the monarch and accompanying members of the Royal Family are greeted by a salute of guns fired by the KING'S TROOP of the ROYAL HORSE ARTILLERY. The royal party enters the HOUSES OF PARLIAMENT by Victoria Tower, and the sovereign enters the Robing Room before proceeding to the House of Lords whose members are present. When the Commons have been summoned by the official known as the Gentleman Usher of the Black Rod, the monarch reads the speech which is, in fact, a summary of the Government's intentions.

Stationers' and Newspaper Makers' Company
see CITY LIVERY COMPANIES.

Stationers' Company's School *Mayfield Road, Hornsey, N8.* Founded by the STATIONERS' COMPANY in 1858 in BOLT COURT. It moved to HORNSEY in 1895 and became comprehensive in 1967. There are about 1,300 boy pupils.

STATUES All the statues listed may be seen out of doors and all, unless otherwise stated, are full length.

Achilles *Park Lane, W1.* 20 ft-high bronze by Sir Richard Westmacott (1822). Derived from one of the horse tamers on the Monte Cavallo in Rome, it was cast from captured French guns and erected by 'the women of England to Arthur Duke of Wellington and his brave companions in arms'. The site overlooks APSLEY HOUSE. Leigh Hunt described the figure as 'manifesting the most furious intentions of self defence against the hero whose abode it is looking at'.

Prince Albert *Steps of Albert Hall, SW7.* A 42 ft-high memorial by Joseph Durham (1863). It was originally intended to commemorate the GREAT EXHIBITION. The Prince is surrounded by 'Europe', 'Asia', 'Africa' and 'America'. The statue was paid for from a public fund and was first put up in the gardens of the ROYAL HORTICULTURAL SOCIETY. It was moved to its present site in 1899.

Prince Albert *Holborn Circus, EC1.* Equestrian bronze by Charles Bacon erected in 1874. The Prince is in field-marshal's uniform. On either side of the oblong plinth are bronze plaques of Britannia and of Prince Albert; and at either end are bronze figures of Commerce and Peace. Presented to the CITY OF LONDON by Charles Oppenheim, it cost £2,000.

Sir John Alcock *London Airport, Heathrow.* Stone statue by William Macmillan of Sir John and Sir Arthur Brown, the first men to fly the Atlantic. They wear flying kit. Originally erected in 1954 it was moved in 1966 and was finally placed in its present position between Terminals 2 and 3 in 1974.

Dame Louisa Aldrich-Blake *Tavistock Square, WC1.* Twin bronze busts by A.G. Walker (1927) placed on either side of a column, rising from the centre of a circular stone seat, designed by Edwin Lutyens. This is the only example in London of twin busts on one plinth.

Queen Alexandra *London Hospital, Mile End Road, E1.* Bronze by George Edward Wade (1908). The Queen is depicted in coronation robes with crown and sceptre. According to the inscription she 'introduced to England the Finsen Light cure for lupus and presented the first lamp to this hospital'.

King Alfred *Trinity Church Square, SE1.* 14th-century stone figure removed from the site of WESTMINSTER HALL in 1822 and placed here in 1824. The identification with King Alfred is uncertain.

Queen Anne *Market Hall, Kingston-on-Thames, Surrey.* Gilt-leaden statue by Francis Bird (1706).

Queen Anne *In front of St Paul's Cathedral, EC4.* Marble statue by Richard Belt, 1886, a bad copy of the one by Francis Bird which was erected in 1712 to commemorate the completion of the cathedral and which deteriorated badly over the years. Around the Queen are statues of women who depict England, France, Ireland and North America. Lampoonists made the most of the statue's position and the Queen's love of brandy:

Brandy Nan, Brandy Nan, you're left in the lurch,
Your face to the gin shop, your back to the church.

Bird's original sculpture was rescued from a

Richard Westmacott's huge bronze Achilles, erected by the 'women of England', was the first public nude statue in England.

Children watch a Punch and Judy show beneath Richard Westmacott's bronze of the Duke of Bedford in Russell Square, c. 1829.

stonemason's yard by Augustus Hare, the writer of guides to London and Rome, and can still be seen in St Leonard's-on-Sea.

Lord Ashfield *St James's Park underground station, Broadway, SW1.* Bronze medallion by A. Pallitser (1959) commemorating the 'Creator of Modern Transport'.

Robert Aske *Haberdashers' Aske's Boys' School, Pepys Road, SE14.* Copy in COADE STONE by William Croggan (c.1825) of the original statue from Aske's almshouses in HOXTON.

Sir Francis Bacon *City of London School, Victoria Embankment, EC4.* Stone figure between the windows on the 2nd floor facing BLACKFRIARS BRIDGE. By J. Daymond and Son (1882).

Sir Francis Bacon *South Square, Gray's Inn, WC1.* Bronze by F.W. Pomeroy (1912). Erected to mark Bacon's tercentenary as Treasurer of GRAY'S INN. He wears the robes of Lord Chancellor.

General Lord Baden-Powell *Queen's Gate, SW7.* Granite by Donald Potter (1961) outside the Boy Scout headquarters (*see* BADEN-POWELL HOUSE MUSEUM).

Sir Joseph Bazalgette *Victoria Embankment, WC2.* Bronze bust, set in highly decorated surround, by George Simonds. The inscription reads, 'Engineer of the London Main Drainage System and of this Embankment'.

Admiral Earl Beatty *Trafalgar Square, SW1.* Bronze bust by William Macmillan (1948). One of three busts on the north wall of the square.

St Thomas Becket *St Paul's Churchyard, EC4.* Recumbent bronze of Becket in his death agony by E. Bainbridge Copnall (1973).

5th Duke of Bedford *Russell Square, WC1.* Bronze by Sir Richard Westmacott, erected in 1809, facing south down Bedford Place. The Duke's interest in farming is indicated by the ploughshare on which he rests his right hand and by the corn in his left, as well as by the reliefs of agriculture and dairy farming on the plinth.

Alfred Beit *College of Mines, Prince Consort Road, SW7.* Stone bust of the gold and diamond merchant by Paul Montford (1910).

Joseph René Bellot *River front near Greenwich Pier, SE10.* Obelisk of red Aberdeen granite by Philip Hardwick, commemorating the distinguished French sailor (1855).

Lord (William) George Bentinck *Cavendish Square, W1.* Bronze by Thomas Campbell (1851).

Sir Walter Besant *Victoria Embankment, WC2.* Bronze plaque and bust of the historian of London and founder of the SOCIETY OF AUTHORS by Sir George Frampton, erected on the river wall in 1904.

Ernest Bevin *Tooley Street, SE1.* Bronze bust on a stone column by E. Whitney-Smith (1955).

Colonel Samuel Bourne Bevington *Tooley Street, SE1.* Bronze of first Mayor of BERMONDSEY by Sydney Marsh, erected in 1910.

Simon Bolivar *Belgrave Square, SW1.* Bronze of 'the liberator of Venezuela, Colombia, Ecuador, Peru and Panama . . . . Erected on behalf of the countries of Latin America liberated and founded by Simon Bolivar.' On the plinth are also inscribed Bolivar's words, 'I am convinced that England alone is capable of protecting the world's precious rights as she is great, glorious and wise.' By Hugo Daini (1974).

General William Booth *Mile End Road, E1.* Bronze bust by G.E. Wade (1927). Erected on the spot where Booth held his first open-air service (*see* SALVATION ARMY).

General William Booth *Mile End Road, E1.* Fibreglass copy of statue by Wade at Denmark Hill (1979).

General and Mrs William (Catherine) Booth *Champion Park, Denmark Hill, SE5.* Bronze statues by G.E. Wade (1929) to mark the centenary of their birth.

Queen Boudicca *Victoria Embankment, SW1.* Bronze group of the Queen and her daughters in a chariot. Made in the 1850s by Thomas Thornycroft and unveiled in 1902. Prince Albert lent horses as models.

Reginald Brabazon, 12th Earl of Meath *Lancaster Gate, W2*. Stone bust of the Brigadier General set into the front of a stone column on top of which kneels the figure of a boy. By Herman Cowthra (1934).

The Brontë Sisters *32 Cornhill, EC3*. Deep relief of the novelists in conversation with William Makepeace Thackeray, carved in mahogany. Designed by B.P. Arnold and carved by Walter Gilbert (1939).

Sir Arthur Brown *see* SIR JOHN ALCOCK.

Isambard Kingdom Brunel *Victoria Embankment and Temple Place, WC2*. Bronze by Baron Carlo Marochetti (1877). The pedestal and surround were designed by Norman Shaw.

John Bunyan *Baptist Church House, Southampton Row, WC1*. Stone by Richard Garbe (1901) in a niche on the first floor. Beneath the statue are the first lines of *Pilgrim's Progress*: 'As I walked through the wilderness I lightened on a certain place.'

Sir John Fox Burgoyne *Waterloo Place, SW1*. Bronze of the Field Marshal by Sir Joseph Boehm, erected in 1877 by fellow-officers of the Royal Engineers.

Robert Burns *Victoria Embankment Gardens, WC2*. Bronze by Sir John Steel (1884), the gift of John Gordon Crawford. The inscription, by Burns, reads, 'The poetic genius of my country found me at the plough . . . I turned my artless notes as she inspired.'

George Gordon Byron, 6th Baron Byron *Hamilton Gardens, W1*. Bronze by Richard Belt (1880). The *rosso antico* plinth was a gift from the Greek government. According to Byron's friend, Trelawny, the statue bears no resemblance to the subject.

George Gordon Byron, 6th Baron Byron *John Lewis, Holles Street, W1*. Bronze medallion by Tom Painter (1960) erected in commemoration of Byron's birth in a house on the site.

Field-Marshal HRH George, Duke of Cambridge *Whitehall, SW1*. Equestrian bronze of Queen Victoria's cousin who was Commander-in-Chief for many years. By Adrian Jones (1907).

Sir Colin Campbell, 1st Baron Clyde *Waterloo Place, SW1*. Bronze by Carlo Marochetti of the Field Marshal in uniform (1867).

George Canning *Parliament Square, SW1*. Bronze of the statesman in a toga by Richard Westmacott. Removed from PALACE YARD, where it was erected in 1832, to its present site in 1867.

Thomas Carlyle *Chelsea Embankment, SW3*. Bronze by Sir Joseph Boehm (1882). Carlyle sits in an armchair in his long overcoat. The statue is a replica of one owned by Lord Rosebery.

Thomas Carlyle *24 Cheyne Row, SW3*. Portland stone medallion designed by C.F.A. Voysey and sculpted by Benjamin Creswick (1900) on the façade of CARLYLE'S HOUSE.

Major John Cartwright *Cartwright Gardens, WC1*. Seated bronze of the reformer and political writer by George Clarke (1831). Cartwright lived at No. 37.

Edith Cavell *St Martin's Place, WC2*. Marble statue by Sir George Frampton (1920) stands in front of a 25 ft high granite background. Inscribed are her own last words, 'Patriotism is not enough.' It is a very ugly monument. At its unveiling a General murmured to Margot Asquith, 'The Germans will blush when they see this.' She is said to have replied, 'Won't the British?'

Charlie Chaplin *Leicester Square, W1*. Bronze by John Doubleday. Unveiled by Sir Ralph Richardson in April 1981. It portrays the comedian in his characteristic costume with bowler hat and walking stick. The legend on the plinth reads: 'The comic genius who gave pleasure to so many.'

King Charles I *Banqueting House, Whitehall, SW1*. Lead bust by an unknown sculptor over the entrance, placed here in 1950.

King Charles I *St Margaret Westminster, SW1*. Lead bust by an unknown sculptor over the east door, placed here in 1949.

King Charles I *Trafalgar Square, SW1*. Bronze equestrian statue by Hubert le Sueur (1633) ordered by Lord Weston, High Treasurer, but not erected immediately. In 1649 John Rivett, a brazier, was ordered to destroy it, but buried it in his garden and made a fortune by selling souvenirs allegedly from the metal. In 1660 he refused to give it up to Lord Weston's son and by purchase or gift it came into the hands of Charles II. It was erected on its present site in 1765–7. The pedestal is said to have been designed by Wren and carved by Grinling Gibbons. The Royal Stuart Society lays a wreath here on the anniversary of the King's death, 30 January.

King Charles II *Soho Square, W1*. Stone statue by Caius Gabriel Cibber. For a time it was in private ownership, the last owner being the librettist W.S. Gilbert, whose widow returned it to SOHO SQUARE where it was erected in 1938.

King Charles II *South Court, Chelsea Hospital, Royal Hospital Road, SW3*. Bronze by Grinling Gibbons (1676) of the King in Roman costume presented to Charles by Tobias Rustat, a member of the Court. It was not erected here until 1692. On Oak Apple Day (29 May) it is wreathed in oak leaves to celebrate King Charles's birthday and to commemorate his escape from the Battle of Worcester when he took refuge in the Boscobel Oak.

Sedan chairs parked beneath Hubert Le Sueur's statue of Charles I. From an engraving by Sutton Nicholls, c.1750.

Queen Charlotte (of Mecklenburg-Strelitz)
Trinity House, Trinity Square, EC3. COADE STONE
medallion by M.J. Baker (1776).
Queen Charlotte (of Mecklenburg-Strelitz)
Somerset House, Strand, WC2. Stone medallion on the
façade. By Joseph Wilton (1780).
Queen Charlotte *Queen Square, WC1.* A lead
statue by an unknown sculptor, believed to represent
the consort of George III (*c.*1780).
Major-General Lord Cheylesmore *Victoria Em-
bankment Gardens, WC2.* Stone memorial with family
crest by Sir Edwin Lutyens above a fountain and lily
pond (1930).
Frederic Chopin *Beside the Festival Hall, SE1.*
Bronze by his fellow-Pole, B. Kubica (1975). The
money was subscribed almost entirely by Poles in
Britain and Poland.
Sir Winston Churchill *Bracken House, Cannon
Street, EC4.* Bronze mask over the entrance by Frank
Dobson (1959).
Winston Churchill *Parliament Square, SW1.* In
naval overcoat and leaning on a stick, Churchill looks
towards WESTMINSTER BRIDGE. Bronze by Ivor
Roberts-Jones (1973).
Winston Churchill *Woodford Green, E18.* 8½ ft-
high bronze of the Member for Woodford on a Cornish
granite plinth. By David McFall, it was unveiled by
Field Marshal Montgomery in the presence of Sir
Winston and Lady Churchill in October 1959.
Sir Winston and Lady Churchill *Kensington Gar-
dens (near Hyde Park Gate), SW7.* Bronze by Oscar
Nemon (1981).
Sir Robert Clayton *St Thomas's Hospital, SE1.*
The only outdoor stone statue by Grinling Gibbons.
The hospital's benefactor is shown in contemporary
dress and long wig. The statue originally stood in Clay-
ton Court, SOUTHWARK outside the first hospital and
was moved to its present position in 1976.
Robert Clive *King Charles Street (on the steps at St
James's Park end), SW1.* Bronze figure in uniform by
John Tweed (1912). Bronze reliefs on the plinth
depict Clive at the siege of Arcot, 1751, and Clive
receiving the grant of Bengal, Behar and Orissa at
Allahabad, 1765.
Richard Cobden *Camden High Street, NW1.*
Marble by W. and T. Wills (1868). Napoleon III
made the largest contribution to the cost of £320.
Dean John Colet *St Paul's School, Barnes, SW13.*
Bronze by Sir Hamo Thornycroft (1898) of the foun-
der of ST PAUL'S SCHOOL with two kneeling scholars.
Captain James Cook *The Mall (near Admiralty
Arch), SW1.* 'Circumnavigator of the globe, explorer
of the Pacific Ocean, he laid the foundations of the
British Empire in Australia and New Zealand ...'
Bronze by Sir Thomas Brock unveiled in 1914.
Thomas Coram *40 Brunswick Square, WC1.*
Stone bust by D. Evans (1937) over the entrance.
Thomas Coram *Brunswick Square, WC1.* Bronze
by William Macmillan (1963) of the founder of the
FOUNDLING HOSPITAL. The pose is taken from the
portrait by Hogarth.
Oliver Cromwell *Outside Westminster Hall, SW1.*
Bronze figure by Sir Hamo Thornycroft (1899).
Cromwell carries a Bible in one hand, in the other a
sword. After strong opposition to its erection by the
Irish Party, Parliament declined to pay for it. Lord
Rosebery, Prime Minister when the statue was first
proposed, paid for it himself.

Admiral Viscount Cunningham *Trafalgar
Square, SW1.* Bronze bust by Franta Belsky (1967).
One of three busts on the north wall of the Square.
**George Nathaniel Curzon, Marquess Curzon of
Kedleston** *Carlton Gardens, SW1.* Bronze by Sir
Bertram Mackennal (1931) of the statesman and Vice-
roy of India, whose pomposity was ridiculed by his
fellow members of Balliol College in the famous lines:

> My name is George Nathaniel Curzon
> I am a most superior person.
> My face is pink, my hair is sleek,
> I dine at Blenheim once a week.

Edward Stanley, 14th Earl of Derby *Great Windmill Street, W1.* Stone bust in first-floor niche adjacent
to St James's and St Peter's school (1871). Derby laid
the foundation stone of the Church of St Peter which
stood here until its demolition in 1954 (*see* GREAT
WINDMILL STREET).
Edward Stanley, 14th Earl of Derby *Parliament
Square, SW1.* Bronze figure wearing the Garter. The
bronze reliefs on the plinth depict him speaking in the
old HOUSE OF COMMONS in 1833, in the Sheldonian
Theatre, Oxford as Chancellor of the University in
1853 and at a Cabinet Council in 1867. By Matthew
Noble (1874).
**Spencer Compton Cavendish, 8th Duke of
Devonshire** *Whitehall, SW1.* Bronze by Herbert
Hampton (1910). The statue of the Duke, who was
Secretary of State for War, appropriately stands opp-
osite the old WAR OFFICE.
Bartolomeu Diaz *South Africa House, Trafalgar
Square, SW1.* Large stone figure of the Portuguese
navigator by Coert Steynberg (1934).
Charles Dickens *Ferguson House, Marylebone
High Street, W1.* Sculptured panel of the author and
various characters from his novels by Eastcourt J.
Clark (1960). Dickens lived in a house on this site.
Charles Dickens *Prudential Assurance Building,
Holborn, EC1.* Cupronised plaster bust by Percy Fitz-
gerald (1907) marks the site of FURNIVAL'S INN where
Dickens lived from 1834 to 1837.
Charles Dickens *Red Lion, Parliament Street,
SW1.* Terracotta head of the author at 2nd-floor level
(1900).
Major-General Sir Alexander Dickson *Royal
Artillery Mess, Woolwich, SE18.* Bronze medallion
on tall grey granite quadrilateral by Sir Francis
Chantrey, originally erected near the Rotunda in 1844
and moved to its present site in 1912.
Benjamin Disraeli, Earl of Beaconsfield *Parlia-
ment Square, SW1.* Bronze figure in Garter robes by
Mario Raggi, unveiled in 1883 on the second anniversary of the statesman's death.
King Edward I *National Westminster Bank, 114
High Holborn, WC1.* Elevated stone by Richard Garbe
(1902).
King Edward VI *North wing of St Thomas's Hos-
pital, SE1.* Two statues of Henry VIII's only son, who
refounded ST THOMAS'S HOSPITAL after its closure
during the DISSOLUTION. The bronze by Peter
Scheemakers was cast in 1737 and the earlier one in
stone was sculpted by Thomas Cartwright in 1681.
King Edward VII *Caxton Hall, SW1.* Terracotta
statue on the façade. Queen Victoria stands by him.
King Edward VII *Edward VII Memorial Park,
Shadwell, E1.* Bronze medallion by Sir Bertram
Mackennal (1922) on the memorial pillar.

King Edward VII *55 Knightsbridge, SW7*. Small stone bust, almost obscured under a second-floor window (1902).

King Edward VII *Mile End Road, E1*. Opposite the LONDON HOSPITAL stands a column supporting a winged angel and bearing a bronze medallion of the King. The column is flanked by fountains and sculptures of Justice and Liberty. The memorial, the work of W.S. Frith, was the gift of the Jews of East London (1911).

King Edward VII *National Westminster Bank, 114 High Holborn, WC1*. Elevated stone by Richard Garbe (1902).

King Edward VII *Temple Bar Memorial, Fleet Street, EC4*. Marble by Sir Joseph Edgar Boehm (1918). Edward faces Queen Victoria.

King Edward VII *Tooting Broadway, SW17*. Bronze statue by L.F. Roselieb (1911).

King Edward VII *University College School, Frognal, NW3*. Stone statue, in a niche above the school doorway (1907).

King Edward VII *Waterloo Place, SW1*. Bronze equestrian statue by Sir Bertram Mackennal (1922).

Queen Elizabeth I *St Dunstan in the West, Fleet Street, EC4*. Stone by William Kerwin (1586) over the vestry porch. The statue originally stood on LUDGATE and was moved to ST DUNSTAN's after the gate's demolition.

Robert Devereux, Earl of Essex *Devereux Court, WC2*. Painted stone bust of the last Earl of Essex on the second floor of the Devereux Inn (1676).

Stephen Fairbairn *Mile post on Surrey bank of the Putney to Mortlake footpath*. Bronze medallion on granite obelisk of the distinguished Australian oarsman and rowing coach by George Drinkwater, himself an Oxford rowing blue (1963).

Henry Fawcett *Victoria Embankment Gardens, WC2*. Bronze medallion by Mary Grant, part of Basil Champney's fountain (1886). The memorial to the blind Postmaster General was 'erected . . . by his grateful countrywomen'.

Henry Fitzailwyn *25 Holborn Viaduct, EC1*. On the first house adjoining the viaduct on the west side, by H. Bursill (1868).

Marshal Ferdinand Foch *Grosvenor Gardens, SW1*. Bronze equestrian figure by G. Mallisard (1930), a copy of the one in Cassel, France, 'erected by public subscription on this site, presented by the 2nd Duke of Westminster. On the north side of the plinth is inscribed, 'I am conscious of having served England as I served my own country.'

Onslow Ford *Corner of Abbey Road and Grove End Road, NW8*. Bronze bust of the sculptor on a column by A.C. Lacchesi (1903).

William Edward Forster *Victoria Embankment Gardens (south of Temple Place), WC2*. Bronze by H.R. Pinker (1890), inscribed: 'To his wisdom and courage England owes the establishment throughout the land of a national system of elementary education.'

Charles James Fox *Bloomsbury Square, WC1*. Bronze by Westmacott (1816) of the orator in the robes of a Roman senator. In one hand he holds the Magna Carta. The statue was erected with surplus money inscribed for the monument in WESTMINSTER ABBEY

Sir John Franklin *Waterloo Place, SW1*. Bronze statue of the Arctic explorer and discoverer of the North-west Passage, by Matthew Noble (1866). On the front of the plinth is a bronze high relief of Sir John's funeral.

Sir Bartle Frere *Victoria Embankment Gardens, SW1*. Bronze statue of the colonial administrator by Sir Thomas Brock (1887).

Sigmund Freud *Adelaide Road, Swiss Cottage, NW3*. Bronze by Oscar Nemon from the original plaster model cast as early as 1930. The statue was unveiled in 1970 by five of the great-grandchildren of the founder of psycho-analysis who spent his last years in Elsworthy Road and Maresfield Gardens nearby.

Elizabeth Fry *Wormwood Scrubs Prison, W12*. Medallion over the prison entrance (1874). A second medallion shows John Howard.

Mahatma Gandhi *Tavistock Square, WC1*. Bronze by Fredda Brilliant (1968), unveiled by Sir Harold Wilson. The hollow of the plinth on which the cross-legged figure sits is used for tributes of flowers.

David Garrick *27 Southampton Street, WC2*. Bronze medallion by H.C. Fehr (1901). Commemorates Garrick's residence in the house, 1750–76.

Sir Robert Geffrye *Kingsland Road, E2*. 6ft lead by James Mande and Co. (1913). Replica of an original by John Van Nost (1723), commemorating the merchant and Lord Mayor of London who built these almshouses.

King George I *Leicester Square*. Modelled by C. Burchard in about 1716 and cast by John Nost the Elder. It originally stood in the garden of the Duke of Chandos's house, CANNONS. It was removed to LEICESTER SQUARE, then known as Leicester Fields, in 1784. It depicted the King on horseback in armour. As the condition of the garden deteriorated so did that of the statue. Children clambered over it and rode on the horse's back. Both mount and rider lost a leg; and on an October night in 1866 practical jokers painted the horse with spots, placed on its head a dunce's hat

A sketch drawn in 1866 after practical jokers had made a mockery of the statue of George I in Leicester Square.

acquired from the property room of the ALHAMBRA THEATRE, and pushed the handle of a broomstick through a hole in the King's armour. The statue was sold for £16 in 1872 and removed from the Square.

King George I *St George's Church, Bloomsbury, WC1.* Figure, placed at the top of the church steeple, representing the King in a toga. William Hicks, brewer, gave the statue for the steeple, built in 1730 by Nicholas Hawksmoor. Horace Walpole satirised the arrangement:

When Henry VIII left the Pope in the lurch,
The Protestants made him head of the church,
But George's good subjects, the Bloomsbury people
Instead of the Church, made him head of the steeple.

King George II *Golden Square, W1.* This Portland stone figure is attributed to John Van Nost and is supposed to represent George II, the monarch at the time of its erection in the Square in March 1753. It was said to have come from the Duke of Chandos's seat at CANONS and to have been bought at the auction there in 1748 by an anonymous bidder, who presented it to the public. Certainly there were several allegorical figures by Van Nost on the roof of CANONS before its demolition and this 'George II' may, perhaps, be one of these. Dickens described it in *Nicholas Nickleby* as 'a mournful statue of Portland stone, the guardian genius of a little wilderness of shrubs'.

King George II *Greenwich Hospital, SE10.* Marble, by J.M. Rysbrack. The marble was found in a French ship, captured in the Mediterranean, and the statue was presented by Sir John Jennings, Prefect of GREENWICH HOSPITAL. It was placed on the river side of the hospital in 1735.

King George III *Cockspur Street, SW1.* Bronze equestrian figure of the King, by Matthew Cotes Wyatt (1836). In 1820 a subscription for the statue was started. On the eve of its unveiling an unspecified 'calamity' causing 'loss and distress' to the artist occurred. After three months it was restored and unveiled, prompting the verse:

> Here stands a statue at which critics rail
> To point a moral and to point a Tail.

The horse's tail is extended horizontally.

King George III *Somerset House, Strand, WC2.* Baroque fountain in bronze, including a figure of the King, by John Bacon the Elder (1788). Neptune is represented in the foreground. When Queen Charlotte asked Bacon why he had created such a frightful figure, he replied, 'Art cannot always effect what is ever within reach of Nature, the union of beauty and majesty.'

King George III *Somerset House, Strand, WC2.* Stone medallion on the façade by Joseph Wilton (1780).

King George III *Trinity House, EC1.* Medallions on COADE STONE of the King and his wife, by M.J. Baker (1796).

King George IV *Somerset House, Strand, WC2.* Stone medallion on the façade by Joseph Wilton (1780, when its subject was Prince of Wales).

King George IV *Trafalgar Square, SW1.* Bronze equestrian statue by Chantrey (1834). Ordered by George IV in 1829 for the top of MARBLE ARCH which then stood in front of BUCKINGHAM PALACE. The King died before the statue was finished and it was finally erected 'temporarily' in TRAFALGAR SQUARE.

King George V *Old Palace Yard, SW1.* Stone statue by Sir William Reid Dick of the bareheaded King in Garter robes, holding the Sword of State. The plinth was designed by Sir Giles Gilbert Scott. King George VI unveiled the statue in 1947.

King George VI *Carlton House Terrace, SW1.* Stone statue of the King in the uniform of Admiral of the Fleet and Garter robes, by William Macmillan (1955).

W.S. Gilbert *Victoria Embankment (near Hungerford railway bridge), WC2.* Bronze plaque with head of the 'Playwright and Poet. His foe was folly and his weapon wit.' By Sir George Frampton (1914).

W.E. Gladstone *Bow Churchyard, E3.* Bronze by Albert Bruce-Joy, erected in 1882, when Gladstone was still alive.

W.E. Gladstone *Strand (west of St Clement Danes), WC2.* The four bronze female allegorical figures represent Education, Courage, Aspiration, and Brotherhood. By Sir Hamo Thornycroft (1905).

F.C. Goodenough *London House, Mecklenburgh Square, WC1.* Bronze medallion by William Macmillan (1936) on the wall of the hall of residence which he gave to the UNIVERSITY OF LONDON.

General Charles George Gordon *Victoria Embankment Gardens, SW1.* Bronze by Sir Hamo Thornycroft, removed to the present site in 1953 from TRAFALGAR SQUARE where it had stood since 1887. The General is standing holding a Bible and with the cane he habitually carried under one arm.

Thomas Gray *39 Cornhill, EC3.* Bronze medallion of the poet, by F.W. Pomeroy, placed in 1917 to commemorate the poet's birthplace.

Richard Green *East India Dock Road, E14.* Bronze, outside the public baths, of the head of the shipping family whose works were in Blackwall Yard. By E.W. Wyon (1866).

Sir Thomas Gresham *Gresham House, Holborn Viaduct, EC1.* By H. Bursill (1868).

Sir Thomas Gresham *Royal Exchange, EC2.* Stone, by William Behnes, of the City merchant and Lord Mayor of London who built the ROYAL EXCHANGE. The statue was placed in a niche at the east end of the EXCHANGE when it was rebuilt in 1845.

Lord Grey of Fallodon *Foreign Office, SW1.* Stone plaque by Sir William Reid Dick of the Secretary of State for Foreign Affairs. It was unveiled by Stanley Baldwin (1937).

Thomas Guy *Guy's Hospital, SE1.* Brass by Peter Scheemakers, erected in about 1733. The only brass outdoor statue in London. The panels on the base depict scenes of the Good Samaritan and the Pool of Bethesda.

Guy of Warwick *Newgate Street and Warwick Lane, EC1.* Stone figure by an unknown sculptor of the 15th-century romantic hero who had a house here (1668).

Field-Marshal Earl Haig *Whitehall, SW1.* Equestrian bronze of the Commander-in-Chief of the British Armies in France, 1915–18. By Alfred Hardiman (1937). Parliament granted £5,000 for the bronze. This is the third version of the statue, the first two having been rejected. It was criticised by the public at its unveiling but won the ROYAL SOCIETY OF BRITISH SCULPTORS' award in 1939.

Sir Augustus Harris *Drury Lane Theatre, WC2.* Bronze bust by Sir Thomas Brock of the theatre manager. The bust is in the centre of an ornate fountain beside the main portico.

818

Sir Henry Havelock *Trafalgar Square, SW1.* Bronze by William Behnes (1861).

King Henry VIII *St Bartholomew's Hospital, EC1.* Stone, by Francis Bird (1702). Henry VIII founded the hospital. The figure stands over the gateway.

Sidney Herbert (Lord Herbert of Lea) *Waterloo Place, SW1.* Bronze by John H. Foley, first erected in front of the old War Office, PALL MALL, in 1857, and moved to its present site in 1915. It stands by the GUARDS' CRIMEAN MEMORIAL near the statue of Florence Nightingale.

Rowland Hill *King Edward Street, EC1.* Granite figure, by R. Onslow Ford (1881), of the founder of the Penny Post, standing in his frock coat and gazing across the street. First erected at the ROYAL EXCHANGE in 1882 and moved to its present site in 1923.

William Hogarth *Leicester Square, WC2.* Stone bust by Joseph Durham (1875).

Quintin Hogg *Langham Place, W1.* Bronze group by Sir George Frampton (1906). The founder of the nearby POLYTECHNIC OF CENTRAL LONDON is shown seated, a boy on either side, one with a football. On the pedestal are inscriptions to his wife, Alice Hogg, and to members of the Polytechnic who were killed in the 1st World War.

3rd Lord Holland *Holland Park, W1.* Bronze by G.F. Watts and Joseph Boehm (1872). The statue stands in the former park of HOLLAND HOUSE.

John Howard *Wormwood Scrubs Prison, W12.* Medallion over the prison entrance (1874). A second medallion commemorates Elizabeth Fry.

John Hunter *Leicester Square, WC2.* Stone bust of the surgeon, who lived in the Square from 1785–93, by Thomas Woolner (1874).

William Huskisson *Pimlico Gardens, SW1.* Stone statue by John Gibson of the President of the Board of Trade, the first person to be killed in a railway accident. In 1848, 18 years after his death, his widow presented the statue to LLOYD'S, who, in turn, presented it to the LONDON COUNTY COUNCIL in 1915 when it was erected on its present site. The figure in a Roman toga is inscribed 'Opus Iannis Gibson 1836'.

Sir Henry Irving *Charing Cross Road (by St Martin's Place), WC2.* Bronze by Thomas Brock (1910). This statue of the first actor to be knighted was paid for by donations from fellow-members of his profession.

King James II *Trafalgar Square, SW1.* Bronze by Grinling Gibbons (and/or his pupils) of the King in Roman dress. It is a companion piece to the statue of Charles II at the ROYAL HOSPITAL, CHELSEA. It stands on the grass in front of the NATIONAL GALLERY, its fourth resting place, having previously stood in two places just off WHITEHALL and in ST JAMES'S PARK. It was commissioned by Tobias Rustat, Page of the Backstairs, 'a very simple, ignorant but honestly loyal creature'.

Admiral Earl Jellicoe *Trafalgar Square, SW1.* Bronze bust by Sir Charles Wheeler at the foot of the north wall of the Square (1948).

Dr Edward Jenner *Kensington Gardens, W8.* Bronze of the discoverer of vaccination against smallpox, by W. Calder Marshall. First erected in TRAFALGAR SQUARE in 1858, it was moved to its present site in the Italian Garden in 1862.

Dr Samuel Johnson *Strand (east of St Clement Danes), WC2.* Bronze by Percy Fitzgerald (1910), the gift of the sculptor. On the front of the pedestal is a bronze plaque of James Boswell, and on the side

another of Mrs Thrale. Johnson worshipped at this church.

Inigo Jones *Chiswick House, W4.* Stone statue by Rysbrack (1729).

John Fitzgerald Kennedy *Marylebone Road, NW1.* Bronze bust by Jacques Lipchitz of the 34th President of the United States, unveiled in 1965 by his brothers Robert and Edward Kennedy, and paid for by readers of the *Sunday Telegraph*.

Edward Augustus, Duke of Kent *Park Crescent, W1.* Bronze of Queen Victoria's father by S.S. Gahagen (1827). Erected by the charities he had supported.

Sir John Kirk *31 John Street, WC1.* Bronze medallion of the philanthropist by an unknown artist (c.1926).

Field Marshal Earl Kitchener *Horse Guards Parade, SW1.* Bronze figure in uniform by John Tweed (1926).

Field Marshal Earl Kitchener *73 Knightsbridge, SW1.* Stone bust by an unknown artist (1902) in the 1st-floor pediment.

Charles Lamb *Giltspur Street, EC1.* Bronze bust by William Reynolds-Stephens of the essayist. It was placed on the wall of a restored watch-house in 1962. Formerly outside CHRIST CHURCH, NEWGATE.

Charles Lamb *Inner Temple, EC4.* Figure of a youth, known as the Lamb statue because Charles Lamb was born in Crown Office Row and lived in the Temple until 1817.

George Lansbury *Serpentine Pavilion, SW1.* Bronze medallion of the Labour politician by H. Wilson Parker (1953). Lansbury started public bathing in the Serpentine. The medallion was unveiled by Clement Attlee.

Lord Lawrence (John Laird Mair, 1st Baron Lawrence) *Waterloo Place, SW1.* Bronze (1884) by Sir Joseph Boehm of the Governor General of India, inscribed: 'How youngly he began to serve his country, how long continued.' This is a replacement of the original which portrayed Lawrence with a sword and quill and bore the inscription: 'Will you be governed by the pen or the sword?' Boehm, disturbed by criticism and not satisfied himself, produced this version.

Sir Wilfrid Lawson *Victoria Embankment Gardens, WC2.* Bronze by David McGill of the orator and temperance advocate (1909).

Abraham Lincoln *Parliament Square, SW1.* Bronze figure in a frock coat standing in front of his Grecian chair, a copy of the statue by Augustus Saint-Gaudens in Chicago.

Joseph Lister (Lord Lister) *Upper Portland Place, W1.* Bronze bust by Thomas Brock (1924). The surgeon lived nearby at No. 12 PARK CRESCENT from 1877 to 1909.

David Livingstone *Royal Geographical Society, Kensington Gore, SW7.* Bronze figure by T.B. Huxley-Jones (1953) in a niche on the façade.

Margaret Macdonald *Lincoln's Inn Fields (north side), WC2.* Bronze group by Richard Goulden (1914). The social worker and wife of Ramsay MacDonald kneels holding out her arms to nine little children. The inscription reads: 'She brought joy to those with whom she lived and worked'. She lived at No. 3 LINCOLN'S INN FIELDS in 1896–1911.

Sir James McGrigor *Atterbury Street, SW1.* Bronze figure of the 'Director General of the Army Medical Department, 1815–51' by James Noble.

Erected in the grounds of CHELSEA HOSPITAL in 1865, it was moved to its present site in 1909.

Sir Clements Markham *Royal Geographical Society, SW7.* Bronze bust of the geographer and explorer by F.W. Pomeroy. Gift of the Peruvian government.

Karl Marx *Highgate Cemetery, Fortune Green Road, NW6.* Bronze bust by Laurence Bradshaw (1956) on the tombstone on which is inscribed: 'Workers of all lands unite.'

Queen Mary *Marlborough House, The Mall, SW1.* Bronze medallion by· Sir William Reid Dick (1967).

Mary, Queen of Scots *143–144 Fleet Street, EC4.* Stone, placed here in a first floor niche by Sir John Tollemache Sinclair, an admirer (c.1880).

Lord Melchett *ICI Building, Millbank, SW1.* Head of the company's first chairman, over the centre window of the 7th floor, by W.B. Sagan (1929).

Krishna Menon *Fitzroy Square, W1.* Bronze head of the Indian statesman by Fredda Brilliant (1977).

John Stuart Mill *Victoria Embankment Gardens, WC2.* Seated bronze figure of the economist and philosopher by Thomas Woolner (1878).

Sir John Everett Millais *Millbank, SW1.* Bronze by Sir Thomas Brock (1904). The statue of the artist, palette in one hand and brush in the other, stands in the forecourt of the TATE GALLERY.

Viscount Milner *Toynbee Hall, E1.* Bronze medallion of the statesman, set in a circular wreath; this is a replica of the original Milner Memorial in the Henry VII chapel of WESTMINSTER ABBEY. The original was by Gilbert Ledward (1930).

John Milton *City of London School, Victoria Embankment, EC4.* Figure of the poet, at 1st-floor level nearly opposite BLACKFRIARS BRIDGE. It was erected in 1882.

'Monty', Field Marshal Viscount Montgomery of Alamein *Whitehall, SW1.* Bronze figure in battledress and beret staring sternly towards DOWNING STREET. By Oscar Nemon. Unveiled by the Queen Mother in 1980. It cost over £30,000. The names of more than 7,000 contributors are recorded in a book in the IMPERIAL WAR MUSEUM.

Sir Thomas More *Carey Street (on the corner of Serle Street), WC2.* Stone figure by Robert Smith (1866), inscribed, 'The faithful servant both of God and the King. Martyred July 5th 1535'. More was a member of LINCOLN'S INN nearby.

Sir Thomas More *Chelsea Embankment, SW3.* The seated bronze (1969) by L. Cubitt Bevis is opposite CHELSEA OLD CHURCH. The robes are black but the saint's face and hands are golden.

Sir Thomas More *City of London School, Victoria Embankment, EC4.* Stone figure facing BLACKFRIARS BRIDGE. Erected in 1882.

Sir Hugh Myddelton *Islington Green, N1.* Marble weather-worn figure by John Thomas (1862) of Sir Hugh Myddelton, holding a scroll with plans for the NEW RIVER (*see* WATER SUPPLY). 'Presented by Sir Samuel Morton Peto. Pedestal and fountain contributed by voluntary subscription.' The pedestal is decorated with aquatic emblems such as dolphins, water flowers and shells. The statue was unveiled by Gladstone.

Sir Hugh Myddelton *Royal Exchange, EC2.* Stone, by Samuel Joseph (1845). The figure stands at 1st-floor level, next to a representation of Dick Whittington.

Field Marshal Lord Napier of Magdala *Queen's Gate, SW7.* Equestrian bronze by Sir Joseph Boehm, erected in CARLTON HOUSE GARDENS in 1891 and moved to its present position in 1920. It is a replica of the one in Calcutta.

General Sir Charles Napier *Trafalgar Square, SW1.* Bronze by George Canon Adams (1855).

John Nash *3 Chester Terrace, NW1.* Expressive marble head of the architect, by William Behnes (1831). In about 1930 Lord Gerald Wellesley set the head into a bust and placed it outside his house, at 1st-floor level. A larger bust, by Cecil Thomas, taken from a plaster cast of the original, was placed in the colonnade of ALL SOULS in 1956.

Cardinal Newman *Brompton Oratory, SW3.* Marble by Léon-Joseph Chavalliaud (1896).

Sir Isaac Newton *City of London School, Victoria Embankment, EC4.* Stone figure between the windows on the 2nd floor facing BLACKFRIARS BRIDGE. By J. Daymond and Son (1882).

Sir Isaac Newton *Leicester Square, WC2.* Stone head by William Calder Marshall (1874).

Florence Nightingale *St Thomas's Hospital, SE1.* Figure of the nurse with lamp, by Frederick Mancini. Stands on the north wing terrace. The bronze original was stolen in 1970 and this replica is of a composite material.

Florence Nightingale *Waterloo Place, SW1.* Figure of Miss Nightingale with her lamp by Arthur Walker. It stands in front of the GUARDS' CRIMEAN MEMORIAL next to a figure of Lord Herbert of Lea.

Alfred Harmsworth, Viscount Northcliffe *St Dunstan in the West, Fleet Street, EC4.* Bronze bust of the newspaper magnate in the forecourt, by Lady Scott (1930).

T.P. O'Connor *72 Fleet Street, EC4.* Bronze bust by F. Doyle-Jones of the Irish journalist and politician (1934). The plaque bears the inscription, 'His pen could lay bare the bones of a book or the soul of a statesman in a few vivid lines'.

General Sir James Outram *Victoria Embankment Gardens, WC2.* Bronze standing figure of the soldier and administrator by Matthew Noble (1871).

Viscount Palmerston *Parliament Square, SW1.* Bronze figure in a frock coat by Thomas Woolner (1876).

Dame Christabel Pankhurst *Victoria Tower Gardens, SW1.* Bronze medallion by Peter Hills added in 1959 to the memorial to her mother, Emmeline Pankhurst, with whom she was joint founder of the Women's Social Political Union.

Emmeline Pankhurst *Victoria Tower Gardens, SW1.* Bronze of the leader of the militant suffragettes by A.G. Walker (1930).

Sir Joseph Paxton *Crystal Palace, SE19.* Huge marble bust by W.F. Woodington (1869) on a redbrick plinth.

George Peabody *Royal Exchange, EC2.* Large seated figure of the American philanthropist by W.W. Story. Peabody is the only American to have been buried · in WESTMINSTER ABBEY. The statue was erected in 1869, the year of his death.

Sir Robert Peel *Metropolitan Police Training Centre, Hendon Way, NW2.* Bronze by Sir William Behnes (1855). First erected at the west end of CHEAPSIDE, it was moved to POSTMAN'S PARK in 1935 and unveiled in its present position by the Queen in 1971.

Sir Robert Peel *Parliament Square, SW1.* Bronze figure in a frock coat by Matthew Noble (1876).

Captain Sir William Peel *Outside door to east wing, National Maritime Museum, Greenwich, SE10.* Marble by William Theed (1860).

Admiral Sir Edward Pellew *Outside door to east wing, National Maritime Museum, Greenwich, SE10.* Marble by Patrick MacDowell (1846).

Admiral Arthur Philip *25 Cannon Street, EC4.* Bronze bust by Charles Hartwell. The bust and plaques were placed here in 1968, but were originally presented by Lord Wakefield in 1932.

William Pitt the Younger *Hanover Square, W1.* Bronze by Francis Chantrey (1831). Peter Cunningham, who was present at the unveiling ceremony, wrote, 'The statue was placed on its pedestal between 7 and 8 in the morning, and while the workmen were away at their breakfasts a rope was thrown around the neck of the figure and a vigorous attempt made by several sturdy reformers [Whigs] to pull it down. When word of what they were about was brought to my father [Chantrey's secretary], he exclaimed with a smile on his face, "The cramps are leaded and they may pull till doomsday."' The inscription reads, 'William Pitt 1759–1806'.

Samuel Plimsoll *Victoria Embankment Gardens (opposite Whitehall Court), SW1.* Bronze bust flanked by two supporters, one a representative of those seamen to whose welfare Plimsoll devoted most of his parliamentary life. 'Erected by members of the National Union of Seamen.' By F.V. Blundstone (1929).

Princess Pocahontas *Red Lion Square, WC1.* Bronze recumbent nude by David McFall opposite the office of Cassell's, the publishers, who presented it.

Viscount Portal of Hungerford *Victoria Embankment Gardens, SW1.* Bronze of the Marshal of the Royal Air Force by Oscar Nemon (1975).

Joseph Priestley *Royal Institute of Chemistry, 30 Russell Square, WC1.* Seated stone statue over the entrance of the building by Gilbert Bayes (1914). Priestley was a Presbyterian Minister, but his statue here commemorates his achievements as a chemist.

Robert Raikes *Victoria Embankment Gardens, WC2.* Bronze standing figure of the founder of Sunday Schools by Sir Thomas Brock (1880). It was erected by Sunday School teachers and pupils.

Sir Walter Ralegh *Whitehall, SW1.* Bronze figure in Elizabethan dress by William Macmillan (1959). It was unveiled by John Hay Whitney, the American Ambassador.

Baron Paul Julius Reuter *Alley behind the Royal Exchange, EC2.* Granite column and head of the German-born founder of the worldwide news agency, by Michael Black (1976).

Sir Joshua Reynolds *Burlington House, W1.* Bronze of the artist holding brushes and palette in his left hand and a brush in his right. By Alfred Drury (1931). It was erected by the ROYAL ACADEMY.

Sir Joshua Reynolds *Leicester Square, WC2.* Stone bust by Henry Weekes (1874). Sir Joshua lived in the Square at No. 47, now demolished.

King Richard I *Old Palace Yard, SW1.* Equestrian bronze figure by Carlo Marochetti (1861), a cast of the plaster figure made for the ROYAL ACADEMY.

Field Marshal Earl Roberts *Horse Guards Parade, SW1.* Bronze equestrian figure in tropical uniform with topee. By Harry Bates (1923).

Field Marshal Earl Roberts *69 Knightsbridge, SW1.* Stone bust by an unknown artist (1902) in the 1st-floor pediment.

Franklin D. Roosevelt *Grosvenor Square, W1.* Bronze by Sir William Reid Dick, unveiled by Mrs Roosevelt in 1948 on the third anniversary of her husband's death. The cost was raised in a day by 200,000 donations of not more than 5s each from British subscribers.

D.G. Rossetti *Cheyne Walk, SW3.* Memorial fountain designed by J.P. Seddon with bronze medallion of Rossetti by his fellow Pre-Raphaelite, Ford Madox Brown (1887).　　　　　·

Bertrand Russell *Red Lion Square, WC1.* Bronze bust of the philosopher and mathematician by Marcelle Quinton (1980). Unveiled by Mrs Dora Russell, the bust stands near CONWAY HALL where her former husband lectured.

Marquess of Salisbury *87 Knightsbridge, SW1.* Stone bust over a 1st-floor window. Placed to commemorate Edward VII's coronation during Salisbury's term of office as Prime Minister (1902).

Admiral James Saumarez *Outside door to west wing, National Maritime Museum, Greenwich, SE10.* Marble by Sir John Steel.

Count Peter of Savoy *Savoy Hotel, WC2.* Gilt bronze by Frank Lynn Jenkins (1904). The figure is in medieval dress and holds a shield and spear; it stands on the canopy (*see* SAVOY HOTEL).

Captain Robert Falcon Scott *Waterloo Place, SW1.* Bronze by Lady Scott of her husband in full Arctic kit (1915). Erected by officers of the Royal Navy.

Sir Ernest Shackleton *Royal Geographical Society, Exhibition Road, SW7.* Bronze by C. Sarjeant Jagger (1932).

William Shakespeare *City of London School, Victoria Embankment, EC4.* Stone figure between the windows on the 2nd floor facing BLACKFRIARS BRIDGE. By J. Daymond and Son (1882).

William Shakespeare *Leicester Square, WC2.* Marble by Giovanni Fontana (1874), a copy of the one by Scheemakers in WESTMINSTER ABBEY.

William Shakespeare *Churchyard of St Mary, Aldermanbury, EC2.* Monument with bronze bust by Charles J. Allen (1895).

William Shakespeare *Shakespeare's Head, Great Marlborough Street, W1.* Bust representing Shakespeare as if leaning out of the window. The public house probably takes its name from the brothers Thomas and John Shakespeare, landlords in 1735–44, not from the playwright.

Norman Shaw *Shaw Building, SW1.* Stone medallion by Sir Hamo Thornycroft (1914). Commemorates the architect of the building.

Sarah Siddons *Paddington Green, W2.* Marble by Léon-Joseph Chavalliaud of the actress as the Tragic Muse (1897). It was unveiled by Sir Henry Irving. Mrs Siddons is buried nearby in ST MARY's churchyard.

Sir Hans Sloane *Apothecaries' Garden, Royal Hospital Road, SW3.* White marble, by John Rysbrack, commissioned in 1732 by the Apothecaries' Company to whom Sloane gave the garden for botanical research.

Captain John Smith *Cheapside, EC2.* Bronze by Charles Rennick (1960), a copy of the statue in Jamestown, Virginia. Smith was Governor of the colony.

Field-Marshal Jan Christian Smuts *Parliament Square, SW1.* Uniformed figure striding purposefully forward with fists clasped firmly behind his back. Bronze by Jacob Epstein (1958).

Sir John Soane *Bank of England, EC2*. Stone by Sir William Reid Dick (1937), commemorating the architect who remodelled the building.

W.T. Stead *Victoria Embankment (opposite Temple underground station), WC2*. Bronze plaque with head of the journalist near the spot where he worked for 30 years. Flanked by figures of Fortitude and Sympathy. By Sir George Frampton (1920).

Robert Stephenson *Euston Station, NW1*. Bronze of the engineer of the London-Birmingham line by Baron Marochetti (1871).

Major-General Sir Herbert Stewart *Hans Place, SW1*. Bronze medallion by Sir Joseph Boehm (1886), above a red granite basin with fountain at the south end of HANS PLACE.

Sir Arthur Sullivan *Victoria Embankment Gardens, WC2*. Bronze bust of the composer by W. Goscombe John (1903). The plinth is inscribed with Gilbert's lines:

> Is life a boon?
> If so it must befall
> That death when e'er he call
> Must call too soon.

A bronze mourning female figure, Music, weeps against the plinth.

Sir Henry Tate *Effra Road (opposite Lambeth Town Hall), SW2*. Bronze bust on a tall column by Sir Thomas Brock.

Archbishop Temple *87 Knightsbridge, SW1*. Small bust of the first Archbishop Temple, on the pediment of a 1st-floor window (1902).

William Makepeace Thackeray *32 Cornhill, EC3*. Deep relief of the author in conversation with the Brontë sisters, carved in mahogany. Designed by B.P. Arnold and carved by Walter Gilbert (1939).

Dr Bentley Todd *Denmark Hill, SE5*. Marble statue by Matthew Noble of one of the founders of KING'S COLLEGE HOSPITAL. Erected in 1862, it moved with the Hospital from the STRAND to DENMARK HILL in 1913.

Viscount Trenchard *Victoria Embankment Gardens, SW1*. Bronze by William Macmillan (1961) which stands in front of the former AIR MINISTRY.

Richard Trevithick *University College London, WC1*. Bronze tablet with a medallion of Trevithick by L.S. Merrifield (1933). He was a pioneer of high-pressure steam, and below the medallion is a model of his engine. The tablet was erected to commemorate his centenary.

Joseph Mallord William Turner *23 Queen Anne Street, W1*. Stone medallion of the painter by W.C.H. King (1937). Placed to commemorate the site of Turner's house.

Madame Tussaud *Madame Tussaud's, Marylebone Road, NW1*. Fibreglass medallion of the exhibition's founder by Arthur Pollen (1969).

William Tyndale *Victoria Embankment Gardens, WC2*. Bronze by Sir Joseph Boehm (1884) of the first translator of the Bible into English.

Queen Victoria *Broad Walk, Regent's Park, NW1*. Stone bust by unknown artist (1869) on the Parsee Fountain in REGENT'S PARK.

Queen Victoria *Caxton Hall, SW1*. Terracotta, by an unknown artist (1902). A figure of Edward VII stands next to her.

Queen Victoria *Kensington Gardens*. Marble seated statue of the newly crowned Queen by Princess Louise, her daughter (1893). In the Broad Walk near the Round Pond.

Queen Victoria *121 Mount Street, W1*. White marble bust, standing in a niche over the shop entrance. A bust of the Duke of Westminster, who presented both pieces, stands round the corner. They commemorate the Queen's Jubilee (1887).

Queen Victoria *New Bridge Street, EC4*. Bronze figure with sceptre and orb by C.B. Birch (1896).

Queen Victoria *Temple Gardens, Victoria Embankment, EC4*. Marble medallion in the railings of the Gardens by C.H. Mabey (1902) commemorating the Queen's last visit to the CITY in 1900.

Queen Victoria *Warwick Gardens, W14*. Bronze medallion by F.L. Florence (1904) on a red granite column, formerly on the corner of KENSINGTON HIGH STREET and CHURCH STREET and moved here in 1934.

Viscount Wakefield of Hythe *41 Cooper's Row, EC3*. Bronze medallion by Cecil Thomas (1937) on the façade of the headquarters of TOC H, in commemoration of the man who 'gave this house for good to church and people'.

Edgar Wallace *Ludgate Circus (at the junction with Fleet Street), EC4*. Bronze medallion of the writer by F. Doyle-Jones (1934) inscribed, 'He knew wealth and poverty yet had walked with kings and kept his bearing. Of his talents he gave lavishly to authorship – but to Fleet Street he gave his heart.'

George Washington *Trafalgar Square, SW1*. Bronze statue standing in front of the NATIONAL GALLERY, a copy of the original in Richmond, Virginia, by Jean-Antoine Houdon, and presented in 1921 by the 'Commonwealth of Virginia'.

Sir Sidney Waterlow *Palace Street, SW1*. Bronze by Frank Taubman, standing in front of Westminster City School, Palace Street, a replica of the one in WATERLOW PARK (1901).

Sir Sidney Waterlow *Waterlow Park, Highgate Hill, N19*. Bronze by Frank Taubman in the park, which Waterlow gave to London. He is carrying a hat and an umbrella in one hand and a key in the other, symbolising his gift of WATERLOW PARK to the public.

George Frederick Watts *Postman's Park, EC1*. Small wood figure by T.H. Wren (1905), of the artist who planned the memorials here (*see* POSTMAN'S PARK).

Duke of Wellington *(Formerly at Hyde Park Corner)*. Colossal bronze statue modelled by Matthew Cotes Wyatt and his son, James, representing the Duke of Wellington upon his horse, Copenhagen, at the field of Waterloo, was begun in 1840 and took three years to construct. The weight is 40 tons, the height 30 ft and the measurement from nose to tail 26 ft. In 1846 it was placed on the Triumphal Arch at HYDE PARK CORNER with much ceremony. By 1882 town planners were concerned about the future of HYDE PARK CORNER and moved the Triumphal Arch to a position at the top of CONSTITUTION HILL. As a result of this, the Wellington statue was moved to Round Hill at Aldershot and handed over to the Aldershot Division in August 1885 by the Prince of Wales, later Edward VII (*see also* HYDE PARK CORNER *and* CONSTITUTION ARCH).

Duke of Wellington *Hyde Park Corner, SW1*. Bronze figure of the Duke in uniform mounted on his favourite horse, Copenhagen. At each corner of the polished granite plinth are bronze figures of soldiers: 1st Guards and 42nd Royal Highlanders to the north,

Punch's cartoon of 1846 of the 'cortège' accompanying the colossal 40-ton statue of the Duke of Wellington to Hyde Park Corner.

the 23rd Royal Welsh Fusiliers and the 6th Inniskilling Dragoons to the south. The plinth is inscribed simply 'Wellington' on the west side and '1769–1852' on the east. By J.E. Boehm (1888). The statue was originally intended to replace the large and ugly equestrian statue of the Duke by Mathew Cotes Wyatt, which stood on CONSTITUTION ARCH and was moved to Aldershot in 1883. A Frenchman who saw it is said to have exclaimed, 'We have been avenged!'.

Duke of Wellington *Royal Arsenal, Woolwich, SE18.* Stone figure by Thomas Milnes (1848). First erected at the TOWER, it was brought here in 1863 to commemorate the Duke's Master-Generalship of the Ordnance.

Duke of Wellington *Royal Exchange, EC2.* Equestrian bronze by Chantrey, who died soon after he had made the maquette, and Henry Weekes, who completed the work in 1844. The bronze is from captured French guns. The Duke is the only person to whom two equestrian bronzes have been erected in London. The statue was erected by the Corporation in recognition of the Duke's support of the Bill for the rebuilding of LONDON BRIDGE. He attended the unveiling himself.

Sir Julius Wernher *College of Mines, Prince Consort Road, SW7.* Stone bust of the diamond and gold merchant by Paul Montford (1910).

John Wesley *Wesley's Chapel, City Road, EC1.* Bronze by J. Adams Acton (1891). The inscription reads, 'Erected with Funds Collected by the Children of methodism'.

Duke of Westminster *Carpenter Street, W1.* White marble bust, presented by the Duke himself to commemorate the Jubilee of Queen Victoria (1887). A bust of the Queen stands round the corner at No. 121 MOUNT STREET.

Field-Marshal Sir George White *Portland Place, W1.* Equestrian bronze by John Tweed (1922) of the soldier who was twice awarded the Victoria Cross.

Richard Whittington *Royal Exchange, EC2.* Stone figure in a niche on the THREADNEEDLE STREET side by J.E. Carew (1845).

Richard Whittington *Whittington College, Highgate.* Stone figure (c.1827).

King William III *Bank of England, EC2.* Stone figure by Sir Henry Cheere (1735) in the Princes Street entrance.

King William III *St James's Square, SW1.* Bronze equestrian statue commissioned, probably by CHRIST'S HOSPITAL, from John Bacon the Elder, and executed to his designs by his son, John Bacon the Younger. It was placed in its present position in the square in 1808. The King is portrayed as a Roman General, as he is in Rysbrack's statue of him in Queen Square, Bristol, which seems to have been the principal influence of Bacon's work. Under the horse's hooves is the molehill (in bronze) which caused the King's fatal accident while he was riding at HAMPTON COURT.

King William III *Kensington Palace, W8.* Bronze by Heinrich Baucke (1907). Presented by Kaiser Wilhelm II to his uncle, Edward VII, 'for the British nation'.

King William IV *William Walk, Greenwich, SE10.* Foggit Tor granite by Samuel Nixon, removed to GREENWICH PARK in 1938 from KING WILLIAM STREET where it had been erected in 1844.

General James Wolfe *Greenwich Park, SE10.* Bronze by Tait Mackenzie (1930). It stands on the high point of GREENWICH PARK on the axis of the ROYAL NAVAL COLLEGE and the QUEEN'S HOUSE. The plinth is scarred by a landmine which fell nearby in the 2nd World War. Wolfe lived intermittently at McCartney House, GREENWICH in 1752–7 and is buried in ST ALFEGE'S CHURCH. The statue was presented by the Canadian people and unveiled by the Marquis de Montcalm, a descendant of the General whom Wolfe defeated at Quebec.

Field-Marshal Viscount Wolseley *Horse Guards Parade, SW1.* Bronze equestrian figure in uniform carrying a baton. By Sir William Goscombe John (1920). Cast from captured cannon.

Andrew Young *Bush House, Aldwych, WC2.*

Samuel Nixon's Foggit Tor granite statue of William IV on its original site in King William IV Street, c.1845.

Bronze relief of the first Valuer to the LONDON COUNTY COUNCIL, 1889–1914. 'He laboured to beautify the London he loved.'

Steelyard *Upper Thames Street, EC4.* Took its name from the big scales used in the weighing of imported goods. This was the London trading centre of the merchants of the Hanseatic League, originally a grouping of ports in Germany, which had come to agreements with each other for mutual protection against pirates; but by 1370 it had become a trading league comprising 66 cities and 44 confederates. The merchants are first heard of in England during the reign of King Ethelred in the 10th century. The first record of their house in London, which was probably near or on the site of the Steelyard, is dated 1157. In 1194 Richard I gave the merchants a charter freeing them from paying rent on the house and giving them freedom to trade throughout the country. King John and his successors confirmed the privilege, probably in exchange for the use of the merchants' ships in war time. Throughout the 13th and 14th centuries the merchants enlarged their property around UPPER THAMES STREET. Holding themselves aloof from all unnecessary contact with the Londoners, drinking their own Rhenish wine from stone bottles, electing their own aldermen in their own guildhall, issuing their own currency, refusing to allow women within their walls or even to play games with Englishmen for fear of quarrels, they led a life apart. And this withdrawal, coupled with their extensive privileges, aroused the jealousy of the English trade guilds. In 1551 Edward VI was persuaded to take over the Steelyard and to revoke the merchants' privileges. They continued to live here, however, until 1598 when Elizabeth banished them. The Steelyard Hall for which Holbein had painted two large pictures, now lost (*The Triumph of Riches* and the *Triumph of Poverty*), was turned into a naval storehouse. During James I's reign some of the merchants returned to the Steelyard but their privileges were not reinstated and, weakened by the 30 Years' War, they never regained their former supremacy. The Steelyard was destroyed by the GREAT FIRE. Some merchants rebuilt their houses and were helped to do so by being exempted from taxes. German merchants continued to operate

The Steelyard in Upper Thames Street, covered over since 1865 by Cannon Street Station. From a watercolour by C. Shepherd, 1811.

here until 1853 when their premises and Steelyard Lane were sold to the Victoria Dock Company for a central warehouse. In 1865 CANNON STREET STATION was built on the site.

Stephen Street *W1.* Built in about 1767 on the site of his house by Peter Gaspard Gresse (*see* GRESSE STREET) in conjunction with his neighbour, Stephen Caesar Lemaistre.

Stepney *E1, E3, E4.* Although Roman remains have been found in various parts of the area which was later known as Stepney, the name originally referred to the Saxon settlement of 'Stebba's landing place'. This was probably at RATCLIFF but the name became applied to a site about ½ mile inland on higher ground where the church of ST DUNSTAN'S STEPNEY was erected. In medieval times the parish extended from the CITY to the RIVER LEA and from HACKNEY to the RIVER THAMES. Some 67 daughter parishes were created within this extensive area by the end of the 19th century, the first of which was WHITECHAPEL, built in the 14th century. By the year 1000 the BISHOP OF LONDON possessed the manor of Stepney which then included HACKNEY. In Edward VI's reign the manor passed to the Wentworth family. The *Domesday Book* of 1086 portrays Stepney as a mostly arable area with some mills, good meadows, rich pastures and woodlands and a peasant population of about 900, including HACKNEY. The first period of rapid growth in population began at the end of the 16th century with the development of the riverside and the eastern suburbs of the CITY. For civil purposes the parish of Stepney had formerly been divided into four hamlets – RATCLIFF, LIMEHOUSE, POPLAR and MILE END, but such was the increase in buildings and inhabitants that the new hamlets of SHADWELL (in 1645) and Wapping-Stepney (*see* ST GEORGE-IN-THE-EAST) (in 1670) were taken out of RATCLIFF; and BETHNAL GREEN (in 1597), SPITALFIELDS (in 1662) and MILE END new town (in 1691) were taken out of MILE END. WHITECHAPEL and BROMLEY ST LEONARD were already separate parishes and BOW became one in 1719. Once these districts had been given autonomy for rating purposes, the term Stepney became little more than a geographical expression loosely applied to the area around ST DUNSTAN'S church but revived in the 19th century as the name of a registration district. In 1900 the Metropolitan Borough of Stepney was formed by amalgamating numerous civil vestries, parishes and liberties in a wide area bounded by the CITY, BETHNAL GREEN and POPLAR to cover one of London's largest industrial suburbs with a population of almost 300,000, many of whom lived in poverty and overcrowded conditions. The chief industries were dock labour and the manufacture of clothing with considerable numbers employed in warehouses and shops. It was one of the most cosmopolitan boroughs in London with many JEWS, IRISH, Germans, Scandinavians and CHINESE living there. However, the BLITZ rendered more than one third of the houses uninhabitable and almost all of the others were damaged by bombing, as were much of the docks, warehouses, factory and business premises. Most of the population has moved away and industries closed or left. Large-scale slum clearances and redevelopment have tranformed the appearance of Stepney which was absorbed into the new London Borough of TOWER HAMLETS in 1965.

Stepney Causeway *E1*. Running north from CABLE STREET, the name suggests the waters of the THAMES once came up this far. In 1870 Dr Barnardo opened his refuge for 25 homeless boys at No. 18. Now demolished, the headquarters of DR BARNARDO'S HOMES remained in the street until 1969.

Stepney Green *E1*. Shown as Mile End Green in Gascoyne's 1703 map, it is the last remaining part of the fields where Richard II met the rebels in the PEASANTS' REVOLT. By Gascoyne's time it had become a pleasant country retreat. Some early 18th-century houses remain, Nos 29–35 forming an interesting terrace, and No. 37, now an INNER LONDON EDUCATION AUTHORITY Careers Centre, is an excellent example of a Queen Anne house.

Sterling Street *SW7*. Part of the MONTPELIER development, it is the southern extension of the west side of MONTPELIER SQUARE. It was originally called Alfred Street and dates from 1835. Its name commemorates Edward Sterling, contributor to *The Times* between 1811 and 1840, who lived nearby at No. 2 South Place. Bruce Bairnsfather, the cartoonist, lived and had a studio at No. 1 in 1919–21.

Stew Lane *EC4*. Said to have been the embarking place of whores for their places of business across the river on BANKSIDE where stews and brothels were licensed until Henry VIII closed them in 1546. Many of these houses of ill-fame belonged to the Bishops of Winchester.

Stock Exchange *Capel Court, EC2*. Joint stock companies first appeared in the middle of the 16th century with the setting up of the Russia and Africa Companies. Shares were usually bought and sold privately but were occasionally auctioned. After the Restoration of 1660 several more companies were formed and by 1688 there were about 15. The war with France at the end of the 17th century brought about rapid inflation and the first great commercial boom.

The Trading Floor of the Stock Exchange shortly after the new building was erected to the designs of J.J. Cole in 1882–8, replacing the one of 1801–2.

By 1695 there were at least 140 companies and enough activity for brokers to specialise in stocks and shares. In 1694 John Houghton in the *Second Collection of Letters for the Improvement of Husbandry and Trade* wrote, 'The manner of managing the trade is this: the monied man goes among the brokers which are chiefly upon the Exchange and at JONATHAN'S COFFEE HOUSE sometimes at GARRAWAY'S and at some other coffee houses and asks how stocks go and upon information bids the broker buy or sell so many shares of such and such stocks'. At this period the functions of broker (a man who buys and sells for a client) and jobber (one who acts as a middle man between brokers and who trades in shares on his own account) were inseparable. Jobbers were held in low esteem and continued to be so in the time of Dr Johnson who defined one in his *Dictionary* as 'a low wretch who makes money by buying and selling shares in funds'. In 1696 a Parliamentary enquiry was held into 'the pernicious art of stock jobbing'. This led, the following year, to a Bill passed to restrain the number and ill practice of brokers and stock jobbers, many of whom had 'lately set up and carried on most unjust practices and designs in selling and discounting of talleys, bank stock, bank bills, shares and interests in joint stocks and other matters and things, and had, unlawfully combined and confederated themselves together to raise or fall from time to time the value of such talleys, bank stock and bank bills most convenient for their own private interest and advantage'. The Act laid down that all brokers had to be licensed and approved by the LORD MAYOR and Court of ALDERMEN and a register of their names kept at GUILDHALL and the ROYAL EXCHANGE. Brokers had to take an oath, pay admission fees, wear a silver medal, enter into a bond of £500 which would be forfeited for misconduct, and keep a register of deals. Their number was limited to 100. Contracts for options were to cover a period of no longer than three days. Commissions were limited to 10 per cent. Brokers were not allowed to deal on their own account on pain of perpetual banishment from the EXCHANGE. A broker practising without licence was fined £500 for each offence. Stock brokers also had to spend one hour in the pillory for three days.

In 1698 *The Course of the Exchange and Other Things*, the direct ancestor of the present Stock Exchange list, was first published by John Broker. On the expiration of the 1697 Act in 1707 there was no longer a limitation on the number of brokers. Soon afterwards 12 Jews were licensed as brokers. The 'Bull' and 'Bear' date from 1714 and 1709 respectively. Their origin is uncertain but 'Bear' is possibly from the proverb, 'You must not sell the bear skin until you have shot the bear'. Thomas Mortimer in *Every Man His Own Broker*, published in 13 editions between 1761 and 1810, defines the Bear as 'a person who has agreed to sell any quantity of the public funds, more than he is possessed of and often without being possessed of any at all which nevertheless he is obliged to deliver against a certain time. Before this time arrives he is continually going up and down seeking . . . whose property he may devour'. The Bull is defined as 'the name by which the gentlemen of CHANGE ALLEY choose to call all persons who buy any quantity of government securities without the intention or ability to pay for it and are consequently obliged to sell it again either at a profit or a loss before the time comes when they have contracted to take it'. Mortimer also calls a Bull a man now known as a Stag, that is to say one 'who has bought and actually paid for a large quantity of any new fund commonly called subscription while there is no more than one or two payments made on it but who is unable to pay in the whole of the sum and consequently is obliged to part with it again before the next pay day'. The Lame Duck was 'a name given in CHANGE ALLEY to those who refuse to fulfil their engagements'.

In August 1720 the South Sea Bubble burst and shares which had stood at £1,000 in June, tumbled to £150. Numerous people, including several members of the Government, were ruined. Two years later 150 of the more respectable brokers formed themselves into a club and agreed to rent JONATHAN'S COFFEE HOUSE for their exclusive use at £1,200 per annum. This scheme was shortlived as one of the ejected brokers brought a law suit against them and won access. In 1773 a group of brokers bought a building in THREADNEEDLE STREET which they called the Stock Exchange. Anybody could use it on payment of 6d a day. It was governed by a Committee of Proprietors and a Committee for General Purposes. In 1801 the proprietors decided to close the Stock Exchange and open a private subscription room. Squabbles followed over the rules and over election of members and committees. So 11 brokers, chaired by William Hammond, decided to build another Stock Exchange, in CAPEL COURT, on the site of Daniel Mendoza's boxing saloon which they bought for the purpose. This new exchange, a 'neat plain building fronted in stone', was built in 1801–2 to the designs of George Dance's assistant, James Peacock. Most of the interior was taken up by a large high rectangular room where the brokers congregated. A gallery ran round it fitted with desks for the clerks. At the south end of the room hung a board showing defaulters' names.

The new exchange started with 550 members including most of the substantial members from the old exchange. Management was vested in a Committee of Proprietors made up of nine trustees who held office for life. Their duties were to invest reserve funds and fix the price of admission. A Committee for General Purposes represented the brokers' interests and they dealt with all other matters, including election of members. The first rule book was published in 1812. By the middle of the 19th century the number of brokers had reached 864. So, in 1853–4, a larger exchange was built by Thomas Allason and his son. In it a telegraph line was installed. By 1872 there was a tickertape machine and, soon afterwards, a telephone. By 1878 there were over 2,000 brokers. In 1882–8 a new building was erected to the south east of the site to the designs of J.J. Cole. In 1882 Burdett's *Official Intelligence* was first published, the forerunner of the *Stock Exchange Year Book*. In 1885 a ban on advertising was incorporated in the rules; and the next year brokers' rents were abolished. In 1904, in order to restrict numbers, new members had to be nominated by a retiring member, except for clerks who had worked in the exchange for four years. By 1905 membership had reached a peak of 5,567. In 1908 members were barred from acting as both brokers and jobbers. In 1912 a scale of minimum commission was agreed. In 1945 both management committees were abolished and replaced by the Council which has 46 unpaid members. From 1971 new members have had to pass an examination in general financial knowledge. In 1973 women were admitted and the Stock Exchanges of the United Kingdom and the Irish Republic were amalgamated to form a new organisation called simply The Stock Exchange. This brought together the London Stock Exchange and the six so-called Country Exchanges, the Irish, Belfast, Provincial Brokers', Scottish Northern, and Midlands and Western Stock Exchanges. There are now about 4,000 members grouped into 275 separate firms. Each member has to acquire a nomination which can cost up to £2,000, and be proposed and seconded by existing members. The entrance fee and the annual subscription is £300. The attendants of the exchange are called waiters, a relic of the coffee-house days, and wear a livery of blue coats with red collars. The Stock Exchange now has the largest number of securities listed in the world and is bigger than all the European stock exchanges combined.

The present building, on the site which the Exchange has occupied since 1801, was opened in 1972. It was designed by Messrs Llewelyn-Davies, Weeks, Forestier-Walker and Bor and Fitzroy Robinson and Partners. It has an electronic paging system, a complex telephone network, and a closed circuit television with 22 channels of prices and information operated by computer. No stranger is allowed on the floor of the house but visitors can watch the conduct of business from the public gallery.

Stocks Market Established in the 13th century by the Lord Mayor, Henry Wallis, on the site of the present MANSION HOUSE under the terms of a charter granted by Edward I and authorising the construction of a market next to ST MARY WOOLCHURCH. The rents were to be used for the maintenance of LONDON BRIDGE. The first building was called Les Stokkes after what were at that time the only fixed pair of stocks in the City. In 1319 William Sperlynge 'of West Hamme' was pilloried for trying to sell rotten meat. The carcasses were burned under his nose. During the 15th century the Stocks became firmly established as a fish and flesh market. It was rebuilt several times and in 1633 was described as a great stone house. It was burned down in the GREAT FIRE after which the Court of Aldermen were ordered to sell the materials for the best advantage of the City. In 1668 ST MARY WOOLCHURCH was demolished to make way for the construction of a new market. It was rebuilt as a general market for fruit, vegetables and other articles and flourished. Strype describes it as 'surpassing all other markets in London'. In the centre of the market stood a famous equestrian statue of Charles II erected by Sir Robert Vyner, Lord Mayor in 1675. The statue was brought back from the continent as an unfinished statue of John Sobieski, King of Poland, trampling on a Turk. Vyner had some alterations made so that the head of Sobieski was replaced by that of Charles II and the head of the Turk by that of Oliver Cromwell. The statue was later presented by the Common Council to a descendant of Sir Robert Vyner who removed it to his country house in Lincolnshire. In 1737 the market was cleared for the construction of MANSION HOUSE and moved to the present Farringdon Street where it was renamed FLEET MARKET.

Stockwell *SW9*. The name (first recorded in 1197) means the well by the stump or wood. There seems to have been a Stockwell Wood, which disappeared, like others in the LAMBETH area, during the 17th century.

The Stocks Market, held beneath the statue of Charles II, in c.1737. The site was later cleared for the Mansion House.

The manor of Stockwell was formed at the end of the 13th century, when King Edward I acquired the manor of south LAMBETH and divided it into the two manors of VAUXHALL and Stockwell. The manor lay on the west side of the Brixton Road, extending as far south as the top of Brixton Hill. The medieval manor house stood in 4 acres of gardens on the north-east side of Stockwell Road, the last parts surviving until 1801.

The oldest surviving building is St Andrew's Church, Stockwell Green, built in 1767 on land provided by the Duke of Bedford, and much altered 100 years later to the designs of H.E. Coe. Stockwell Congregational Church is also of early date (1798) and remodelled to a lesser extent in the mid-19th century. Of four Stockwell inns known in the 18th century, the New Queen's Head in Stockwell Road retains its original building, contemporary with the adjoining terrace, Queen's Row (1786). The remaining buildings on the west side of Stockwell Green were erected at various dates between 1790 and 1840, while the land between them and Stockwell Road was the original village green, not built on until 1876.

Stockwell remained a rural village until well into the 19th century. A Cockney on a September outing in 1825 described how he breakfasted at the Swan on the Green and pressed on to BLACKHEATH by way of BRIXTON without 'meeting anything beyond yellow-hammers and sparrows'. But the growing demand for country houses for CITY merchants led to development along the Clapham Road and Stockwell Road frontages even before the break-up of the manor into small lots in 1802, and several examples survive from this period. Residential streets were laid out off Clapham and Brixton Roads in the 1830s, and most of the Stockwell Park area was developed during the 1840s, with some later, denser infilling on the Stockwell Road side. The small triangle on which the clock tower stands opposite the underground station is all that remains of South Lambeth Common, the rest having been covered with houses in 1843.

Construction of the London Chatham and Dover Railway in 1862–3 formed an effective southern boundary to the Stockwell area, and accelerated the building of humbler houses in dense layouts around the present Landor Road. Commercial development tended to drift towards Clapham and Brixton Roads, leaving Stockwell Green itself as a backwater, with horse-bus and tram services being introduced along the main roads, and the first London Tube – the City and South London Railway – connecting Stockwell with the CITY in 1890.

While there has been extensive redevelopment for local authority housing, at high densities, a high proportion of the original fabric survives, safeguarded by conservation areas and housing improvement schemes. A BLUE PLAQUE at No. 18 Burnley Road reads: 'Violette Szabo G.C. (1921–45), secret agent lived here. She gave her life for the French Resistance'.

Stockwell Ghost The supposed phantom whose eerie noises were eventually traced to Anne Robinson, a maidservant, in STOCKWELL in 1722.

Stoke Newington *N16.* The Roman road to York, Ermine Street, left the CITY at BISHOPSGATE and ran in a straight line northwards, climbing steadily for the first three miles to reach a low ridge and then dropping to the valley of the Hackney Brook. On this ridge, the Saxons chose to build their village; the name means 'new town in the wood', and tradition has it that the manor of Stoke Newington was given by King Athelstan to the Canons of ST PAUL'S CATHEDRAL in about 939. The Saxon settlers were not, however, the first to live in Stoke Newington, for palaeolithic remains have been found on a site where the Hackney Brook ran through Stoke Newington Common. Stoke Newington is thus one of the ancient villages engulfed in the tide of London's growth, but a rural atmosphere persists, especially around the old church, set in a picturesque churchyard with 18th-century tombstones. Stoke Newington Church Street is the old village street, and its interesting and varied collection of 18th-century buildings has survived largely intact, if neglected. From the 17th century onwards, the village fell into London's orbit. At first, it was a refuge for Dissenters, who were forbidden to live in the CITY, and in the 18th century there were many nonconformist chapels and meeting houses; Daniel Defoe is perhaps the most famous of the inhabitants of this time. There is a BLUE PLAQUE commemorating him at No. 95 Stoke Newington Church Street on the corner of Defoe Road. There are still many nonconformists in the area. Many Jewish immigrants came here during the 19th century and, more recently, there has been an influx from the Caribbean, India and Cyprus. Four main periods of development can be distinguished. The first was in the 18th century, when the medieval half-timbered buildings were replaced by grand houses in redbrick, of which the best preserved example is No. 171 Church Street, where ancient timbers re-used from earlier buildings can be seen inside. On the north side of Church Street large mansions standing in their own ground were built: Manor House on the site of the Town Hall, Fleetwood House and Abney House of 1676, of which the entrance gates remain. Abney House was demolished when ABNEY PARK CEMETERY was opened in 1840. Towards the end of the period, new terrace houses were built on virgin sites, marking the encroachment of the Georgian suburbs.

1830 saw the start of the Cubitt development in Stoke Newington, the precursor of the larger and better known projects in BELGRAVIA and PIMLICO. Streets were laid out to a spacious plan and large villas erected, mostly in white stucco in the contemporary Greek Revival style.

The third distinct period of development took place in the 30 years from 1860 onwards, which saw the remaining open land disappear under bricks and mortar. Some of the area had previously been worked for the brick-earth deposits used in brickmaking, and now they were filled up with streets of two- and three-storey terrace houses of modest scale and neat appearance, built in yellow stock brick. By the end of the period, only CLISSOLD PARK, ABNEY PARK CEMETERY and

Stoke Newington Common remained undeveloped, and even the Common had been sliced in half by a railway cutting.

After 1947, houses destroyed during the 2nd World War were replaced by council flats in sporadic developments, and some small areas were similarly rebuilt in the mid-1970s. Stoke Newington is now shabby and run-down and it is hard to discern the underlying quality of the place. Nevertheless, it still does not quite belong to London and at times presents the aspect of an 18th-century village with a hinterland of Victorian suburb (*see also* NEWINGTON GREEN).

Stoll Theatre *Kingsway, WC2.* Opened as the London Opera House on 13 November 1911 with Nouguès and Cain's *Quo Vadis?* It was built by the American impresario Oscar Hammerstein to the design of Bertie Crewe on a vast and opulent scale to rival the ROYAL OPERA HOUSE, COVENT GARDEN. The ending of its first season and the opening of the new Covent Garden season coincided in the spring of 1912 and Hammerstein's venture could not compete with COVENT GARDEN's virtual monopoly of operatic works and stars. It was never wholly a theatre again, presenting from Christmas 1912, films, variety and revue. It opened and closed intermittently until Oswald Stoll obtained control in 1916. He produced *Look Who's Here*, a pantomime, *Cinderella* and other unsuccessful shows for about a year and then converted the theatre into a cinema which was renamed the Stoll Picture Theatre and had a resident orchestra and organist. Having reverted to a theatre, it closed in 1957 and the ROYALTY THEATRE together with an office block now stands on the site. At the time of its closure, the theatre's capacity was 2,420.

Stone Buildings *Lincoln's Inn, WC2.* Built to the severely Classical designs of Sir Robert Taylor in 1774–80. The south wing was added in 1845. William Pitt the Younger had his chambers here, as did Mr Wharton in Trollope's *The Prime Minister*. Of the 151

The Red Lion at the corner of Lordship Road and Church Street, Stoke Newington, in c.1900.

occupants now listed in the *Post Office London Directory* only 19 are not barristers and nearly all of these are solicitors.

Stone Grove *Middlesex*. Situated to the north of EDGWARE on the east side of the EDGWARE ROAD. In the early Middle Ages, Stone Grove was part of the manor of EDGWARE. Its name may well refer to a largely wooded area around the 10-mile stone along WATLING STREET and thus probably antedates the surviving 19th-century references. The area remained agricultural until the 19th century: an 18th-century part-timbered barn survives at Mill Ridge. And among the inns that served travellers on the road north, an earlier Leather Bottle is known to have existed in the mid-18th century. It was replaced by the present public house in the 20th century. The Samuel Atkinson (1680, rebuilt 1957) and Charles Day (1828, restored 1959) almshouses existed on WATLING STREET before the residential development of the area began with the coming of the Great Northern Railway in 1867. The resulting Victorian mansions were replaced in the early 20th century by blocks of flats and in their grounds were developed roads of smaller houses following the arrival of, first, the Metropolitan Electric tramways, and, 20 years later, the underground to EDGWARE. The Park remains as open space on the site of what was once the pound.

Stonebridge *NW10*. Now a residential area of mainly high-rise flats. It was here that the HARROW ROAD was carried across the River BRENT and the local inn – the Coach and Horses – was frequented by the painter, Morland, at the end of the 18th century. The Stonebridge Palace of Varieties next to it was rebuilt in 1907–8 but is now converted into commercial premises. The development of the Stonebridge Park estate in the 1870s and 1880s was intended to set the tone of the area and two of its attractive Italianate Victorian properties remain.

Store Street *WC1*. Between TOTTENHAM COURT ROAD and GOWER STREET. The origin of the name is unknown. The publishers, Routledge and Kegan Paul, are at No. 39. Keith Prowse and Co., the theatre ticket agents, are at No. 24. Robert Keith had been making musical instruments in RATHBONE PLACE in 1780 and had moved in 1800 to CHEAPSIDE where he took in as partner William Prowse, and began music publishing as well. Runners were first used in the ticket agency until the telephone came into use in the 1870s. The firm took over Ashton Mitchell (established in about 1790 by William Sams) in 1970.

Storey's Gate *SW1*. Laid out in the 17th century and probably named after either its builder, Abraham Storey, one of Wren's master masons, or Edward Storey, Keeper of Charles II's aviary in BIRDCAGE WALK. The METHODIST CENTRAL HALL was built in 1905–11.

Stornoway House *13 Cleveland Row, SW1*. Built in the 1790s for Lord Grenville, Prime Minister in 1806–7, probably to the designs of Samuel Wyatt. Grenville remained here until 1800. In 1801 Miles Peter Andrews, the playwright and owner of powder-magazines, moved in and gave several memorable parties here. During the occupancy of a later resident, John George Lambton, 1st Earl of Durham, the house became known as Durham House. The crown lease was bought from Durham's family in 1844 by Sir James Matheson, MP who gave it its present name. From 1926 it was occupied by the newspaper owner, Lord Beaverbrook, until it was badly damaged by bombing in the 2nd World War. It was rebuilt in 1958–9, the outer walls being retained.

Samuel Straker and Sons *25 Lime Street, EC3*. Printers, lithographers and stationers established in George Yard, LOMBARD STREET in about 1820 by Samuel Straker who was succeeded by his sons and grandsons. The firm, which printed the banknotes known as Green Backs, used in America during the Civil War, was the first to erect lithographic and letter-press and ruling machines. It moved from No. 49 FEN-CHURCH STREET to LIME STREET in 1982.

Strand *WC2*. The street, just over ¾ mile long, which extends from CHARING CROSS to the LAW COURTS and thus links WESTMINSTER to the CITY. Now a hybrid street of shops, offices, theatres, restaurants and hotels, it was originally a bridle path running alongside the river, hence its name. As early as the 12th century there were several large mansions whose gates opened on to it. These were later overshadowed by the SAVOY PALACE and later still by SOMERSET HOUSE. In 1532 the Strand was still, however, 'full of pits and sloughs, very perilous and noisome'; and an order was issued for its being paved at the expense of the owners of the land bounding it. At this time many of these owners were bishops; others were noblemen and courtiers who soon outnumbered them. Their houses or families are commemorated by the names of streets which lead off the Strand. DURHAM HOUSE STREET, for instance, commemorates DURHAM PLACE, EXETER STREET, EXETER HOUSE, BEDFORD STREET, the Earls, later Dukes, of Bedford, who lived at BEDFORD HOUSE, NORTHUMBERLAND AVENUE, NORTHUMBERLAND HOUSE, ARUNDEL STREET, ARUNDEL HOUSE, while BUCKINGHAM STREET derives its name from the owner of YORK HOUSE. Those not commemorated are WIMBLEDON HOUSE and WORCESTER HOUSE. The house next door to NORTHUMBERLAND HOUSE was for many years the official residence of the Secretary of State. Sir Henry Vane lived here in the reign of Charles I and Sir Edward Nicholas in that of Charles II. It later became known as No. 1, the Strand and was said to be the first house in London to be numbered. The YORK WATERGATE is the only relic of these great Strand mansions. Indeed, in the early 17th century the large mansions had been replaced by smaller houses for fairly well-to-do citizens and shops had begun to appear.

The NEW EXCHANGE which Robert Cecil, Earl of Salisbury, had built in the grounds of DURHAM PLACE, had become a fashionable shopping centre. Thomas Twining, supplier of tea to Queen Anne, established his business at No. 216 in 1706. The family firm is still there. It claims to be the oldest rate-payer in WESTMINSTER, occupying premises on the same site where it was established and carrying on its original business. At the time of its foundation this part of the Strand was becoming well known for its coffee-houses and chop-houses, such as the New Church chop-house, where the young James Boswell often had his shilling dinner, and the Somerset Coffee House where he sometimes

The cobbled Strand in c.1824, looking east towards St Mary le Strand, from a painting by C.R. Stanley.

had breakfast. The GRECIAN COFFEE HOUSE stood in Devereux Court from about 1702 to 1813. TOM'S, another haunt of literary men, was established nearby in about 1706 and remained until about 1775. In the heyday of TOM'S, the Strand, and the alleys leading off it, were also a favourite haunt of pickpockets and prostitutes. Boswell picked up several of his girls here, both ordinary whores to whom he paid 6d, and such unusual ones as 'the fine fresh lass', the officer's daughter whom he encountered after watching the annual race between the watermen who rowed against each other from LONDON BRIDGE TO CHELSEA (*see* DOGGETT'S COAT AND BADGE RACE). It was here that he and Johnson were, 'in the usual enticing manner', accosted by one of these girls while they were walking home one night arm in arm. 'No, no, my girl,' said Johnson, though not harshly, 'No, it won't do.'

In the 1830s improvements, planned by John Nash, were made to the west end of the street which Disraeli was to consider 'perhaps the finest street in Europe'. These improvements included Decimus Burton's CHARING CROSS HOSPITAL in the triangle formed by AGAR STREET, WILLIAM IV STREET and CHANDOS PLACE, and COUTTS' BANK, the ground floor of which has been mostly occupied by small shops since its redevelopment in the 1970s to the designs of Sir Frederick Gibberd and Partners. The huge glass front of the new bank replaces a building of 1903 designed by J. MacVicar Anderson which, in turn, replaced the LOWTHER ARCADE. Other interesting buildings of the 19th and early-20th centuries on this south side are, from the east, BUSH HOUSE; the STRAND PALACE HOTEL and ZIMBABWE HOUSE.

Buildings of the same periods on the north side are, from the west, the CHARING CROSS HOTEL; Val Myers's Halifax Building Society (1933) at Nos 51–55; Shell-Mex House which was originally the Cecil Hotel (designed by Perry and Reed), the largest hotel in Europe

when it was opened with 600 rooms in 1886; the SAVOY HOTEL; and Lloyds Bank Law Courts Branch at Nos 222–225, once a restaurant designed by F.W. Hunt in 1897 and still containing its majolica vestibule. SIMPSONS'S RESTAURANT is in a building reconstructed at the beginning of the 20th century when the adjoining building, Savoy Court, designed by T.E. Collcutt, was erected in 1903–4. In those days the Strand was renowned for its restaurants, jolly public-houses, music-halls and smoking-rooms. Harry Castling's song, *Let's all go down the Strand*, gave rise to a familiar proposition. William Hargreaves's Burlington Bertie, rose at 10.30, walked up the Strand with his gloves on his hand, and walked down again with them off.

Of the many theatres in the Strand (which in the 1890s contained more than any other street in London) now only three remain: the ADELPHI, the VAUDEVILLE and the SAVOY. The Tivoli music-hall at No. 65 adjoined the Tivoli Restaurant. Both have now gone. The two fine churches, however, still stand, more or less unchanged in the middle of the street: ST MARY LE STRAND and ST CLEMENT DANES. A bronze statue of Samuel Johnson stands outside the latter, and to the west of the former is a statue of Gladstone (*see* STATUES).

Within recent years there has been extensive redevelopment of the street. On the north side Norman Shaw's GAIETY THEATRE has been demolished to make way for Citibank House, originally designed for the English Electric Company by Adams, Holden and Pearson. On the south side a huge new office block, Villiers House, designed by Trehearne and Norman, Preston and Partners was built in 1957–9 to the east of the CHARING CROSS HOTEL. Also in 1957–9 New South Wales House (formerly Peter Robinson's) was built to the pleasing designs of Denys Lasdun. A new block by E.D. Jefferiss Mathews has appeared in front of Smirke's KING'S COLLEGE by whose office has also appeared an abstract bronze by Barbara Hepworth.

These and other developments have cost the Strand almost the last of those remaining timber-framed 17th-century houses, reminders that it was once a residential street. Among its residents in the 18th and 19th centuries were Rudolph Ackermann, the print-seller, at No. 101 in 1797–1827, one of the first shopkeepers to have his premises lighted by GAS in 1810 (see ACKERMANN'S); Mrs Siddons, the actress, a lodger at No. 149 in 1782; Mrs Inchbald, the actress, at No. 163 in 1809; William Godwin, the bookseller, Shelley's father-in-law, at No. 191; S.T. Coleridge at No. 348; and GeorgeEliot in 1851–5 at No. 142. This was the house of Frederic Chapman of Chapman and Hall, Dickens's publishers, a firm which was founded in 1834, and which was at No. 186 Strand until 1850 when it was removed to No. 193 PICCADILLY before moving to Henrietta Street, COVENT GARDEN in 1881. Mme de Staël was one of many distinguished guests who stayed at the Golden Cross, the celebrated coaching tavern whose site was later occupied by the hotel of the same name and is now occupied by Golden Cross House at the most westerly end of the Strand. The WIG AND PEN CLUB is at Nos 229–230; Stanley Gibbons Ltd (founded in Plymouth in the 1850s and moved to London in 1874) are at Nos 391 and 399. No. 399 was formerly Romano's Restaurant, opened in 1885 by an ex-waiter from the CAFÉ ROYAL, and closed in 1948.

Strand on the Green *W4.* A riverside path in Chiswick stretching eastwards from Kew Bridge and containing some particularly attractive 18th-century houses, notably those at Nos 45, 56, 60, 61, 63–66 and 71–72. John Zoffany lived at No. 65 in 1790–1810. Other distinguished residents have included the writers Nancy Mitford (at Rose Cottage), Margaret Kennedy (at No. 1), Geoffrey Household (at Post House) and Jerrard Tickell (at the Moorings). Dylan Thomas once occupied Ship House Cottage, Goronwy Rees lived at No. 5, Lord Cudlipp at No. 14 Magnolia Wharf, and Air-Marshal Sir John Slessor at Carlton House. The City Barge public house is next to Post Office Alley. The Bull's Head is at No. 15.

Strand Palace Hotel *Strand, WC2.* Built by F.J. Wills in 1925–30 and faced with artificial stone. It stands on the site of EXETER HALL. The original exciting entrance of 1929–30 by Oliver Bernard (who did many interior designs for Lyons' restaurants) was replaced in 1968 by Dennis Lennon and Partners. The dismantled entrance is now at the VICTORIA AND ALBERT MUSEUM. There are 786 bedrooms.

Strand 'Roman' Bath *Strand Lane, WC2.* Although built of red bricks that initially look to be of Roman date the true date of this 'antiquity' is not known. It is a plunge bath, 4¾ by 2 metres, with an apsidal end and was probably fed by water from the adjacent Holy Well. First mentioned in 1784 it is several times thereafter referred to as an 'old Roman bath' (as, for instance, by Charles Dickens in *David Copperfield*), but until such time as more reliable archaeological evidence is forthcoming from the area it must remain 'unproven'.

Strand Theatre *(Waldorf, 1905–8; Strand, 1909–10; Whitney, 1911–12), Aldwych, WC2.* Built to the designs of W.G.R. Sprague in 1905 to match the ALDWYCH THEATRE. It opened with a season of Italian opera, alternating with plays presented by Eleanora Duse and her company. In 1905 it temporarily housed Beerbohm Tree's company while alterations were made to HER MAJESTY'S THEATRE. In 1905–7 Cyril Maude's company used it while the PLAYHOUSE THEATRE was being rebuilt. In 1911–12 it was managed by F.C. Whitney. In 1913 *Mr Wu*, by H.M. Vernon and Harold Owen had 403 performances. In 1919–23 Arthur Bourchier was in control and staged many outstanding productions including *At the Villa Rose* (1920), *A Safety Match* (1921) and *Treasure Island* (1922), adapted from Robert Louis Stevenson's book which was revived every Christmas from 1923–6 and in 1929. Between 1930 and 1934 Leslie Henson and Firth Shepard were co-lessees and began with the farce *It's a Boy* which had 366 performances. In 1935 the musical comedy *1066 and All That* began its run of 387 performances. During the BLITZ Donald Wolfit kept the theatre open with lunch-time performances of Shakespeare. In the 1940s and 1950s the main successes were *Arsenic and Old Lace* (1942), which had 1,337 performances, the farce *Fifty-Fifty* (1946); and *Sailor Beware* (1955), a comedy by Philip King and Falkland Cary which ran for 1,082 performances. Since then *A Funny Thing Happened on the Way to the Forum* (1963), *An Ideal Husband* (1965) and *Not Now Darling* (1968) have all had long runs. These have been followed by *No Sex Please We're British* which, transferred to the GARRICK, was in its 12th year in 1982. The seating capacity is 1,076.

Stratford *E15.* Postal and industrial and residential district in the north west of NEWHAM. Stratford station (originally built in 1839) is an important junction on the Eastern Region, including an interchange with the CENTRAL LINE. A modern bus station and Stratford Centre – a covered shopping area – adjoin it. Maryland station (1874) is at Maryland Point. The latter, first recorded in the late-17th century, is generally held to derive from a Stratford merchant who emigrated to America, made his fortune in Maryland, and returned to that area of his native town. Stratford Market station (originally Stratford Bridge, 1846) in the High Street served the North Woolwich line until its closure in 1957. Stratford's name (street by the ford), first recorded in the second half of the 11th century, was given to the northernmost of the three wards of the ancient parish of WEST HAM and, during 1918–48, to a parliamentary constituency. From at least the 19th century it was the administrative centre of WEST HAM and the new Municipal Offices, being built by stages in The Grove under the direction of the Borough architect, Kenneth Lund, will be the civic centre for NEWHAM.

There were two formative influences in the 12th century. The first was Queen Matilda's building of Bow Bridge in about 1110 over the River LEA, a further bridge over the tributary Channelsea, and her raising of a causeway along the line of the present Stratford High Street. The line of the Roman road out of ALDGATE to the eastern counties, which crossed the LEA at OLD FORD, was thus turned southward and two townships developed on either side of Bow Bridge – Stratford-atte-Bow, the modern BOW in TOWER HAMLETS, and Stratford Langthorne, the modern Stratford. Langthorne derived from the tall thorn which grew in the neighbourhood, mentioned in a charter of 958. The second formative influence in the development of Stratford was the foundation in 1135 by William de Montfichet, the most influential manorial lord in Ham, of the Cistercian STRATFORD LANGTHORNE ABBEY by the Channelsea River. This foundation grew in wealth and influence until, by the 15th century, it owned most of modern NEWHAM with other properties in Essex and elsewhere. The Abbey was dissolved in 1538 and much of its buildings demolished. A few survived until the early 19th century but nothing now remains except two minor relics in ALL SAINTS, WEST HAM.

Western Stratford was an early industrial area. The eight mills in Ham, the largest group in Essex, recorded in the *Domesday* survey, were on the tributary streams of the LEA in Stratford. Other industries were gunpowder manufacture, distilling, and oil and timber milling. From about 1676 to about 1870 there were, successively, calico and silk printing industries; and from about 1749 to 1776 the BOW PORCELAIN works operated on the Stratford High Street just east of Bow Bridge. The Eastern Counties Railway established its main locomotive and rolling stock works at Stratford in 1847. They closed in 1963. The southern part of Stratford New Town was built by the railway company from 1847 to house its workers and was first called Hudson Town after George Hudson the 'railway king', then chairman of the ECR. Part of this southern area has been affected by the Newham Council's developments north of Stratford Broadway and The Grove. The northern part of New Town was built later on the lands of Lord Henniker's manor of Chobhams and most of its road names derive from Henniker family connections. The Stratford fruit and vegetable market, still operating alongside the North Woolwich railway line, south of the High Street, was established by the Great Eastern Railway in 1879.

An obelisk (1861) in Stratford Broadway commemorates Samuel Gurney, the Quaker banker and philanthropist of Ham House, Upton and a memorial (1879) in the churchyard of St John's, the 18 Protestants burned at the stake at Stratford and BOW in 1555–6. They included the largest group martyrdom of the Marian persecutions when 13 were burned together on Stratford Green in 1555–6. The former West Ham Town Hall (1869) in the Broadway now serves as Newham's Education Offices. Stratford House (demolished in the late 19th century), seat of the Lords Henniker, stood on the north side of The Grove. Gerard Manley Hopkins, the Jesuit poet, was born in 1844 in a house on the south side where the New Municipal Offices now stand. QUEEN MARY'S HOSPITAL FOR THE EAST END in West Ham Lane was first founded in 1861 by Dr William Elliot as a dispensary for the sick poor at 30 Romford Road. This 18th-century boarded building is now used as an annexe of the PASSMORE EDWARDS MUSEUM. The dispensary moved to the present site in 1879 and from 1890, as West Ham Hospital, developed accommodation for in-patients. It adopted its present name when Queen Mary became patron in 1916.

Two small areas – Stratford Marsh and Mill Meads – stand between the Stratford rivers, respectively north and south of the High Street. Christ Church, Stratford Marsh served the area in 1852–1961. The church is now demolished. ABBEY MILLS PUMPING STATION of the Thames Water Authority adjoins Mill Meads.

Stratford House *Stratford Place, W1*. The site of the water conduit which stood here beside the LORD MAYOR'S BANQUETING HOUSE. When its supply was no longer needed, the land was sold by the CITY OF LONDON to Edward Stratford, 2nd Earl of Aldeborough, whose Adam-style house was built in the 1770s to the design of Richard Edwin. The east wing with ballroom was added in 1909 by G.H. Jenkins and Sir Charles Allom. For a time the house was known as Derby House. It was occupied in the early 20th century by the 17th Earl who was War Secretary in 1916–18 and Ambassador to France in 1918–20. After the 2nd World War it was occupied for a time by Hutchinson, the publishers. It is now the ORIENTAL CLUB.

Stratford Langthorne Abbey One of the richest Cistercian houses in England, this abbey, founded by William de Montfichet, flourished from the 1130s to 1538. Most of the buildings were demolished after the DISSOLUTION; and a late 18th-century owner of the site sold nearly all the stone that remained. Part of the main gateway survived into the 19th century and the remains of a stone window can be seen in the south porch of ALL SAINTS, WEST HAM; but the site is now covered by railways and factories and is commemorated by a street name – Langthorne Road, SE11.

Stratford Place *W1*. Built in 1775 on the site of the LORD MAYOR'S BANQUETING HOUSE where he and the CORPORATION feasted after hunting and inspecting the local springheads. At the northern end is STRATFORD HOUSE, now the ORIENTAL CLUB. Gates used to separate the cul-de-sac from OXFORD STREET; they have gone but a single gate-pier remains, topped by a COADE STONE lion. Richard Cosway, the miniature painter, had a house here in 1798–1806; Charles, 3rd Earl Stanhope, the reformer and inventor, lived at No. 2 in 1804–9; Sydney Smirke, the architect, at No. 5 in 1820; Sydney Smith at No. 18 in 1771–1845; and Martin Van Buren, later 8th President of the United States, in 1831. At No. 10 is the Royal Society of Musicians founded in 1738 to help their needy brethren.

Stratton Street *W1*. Originally part of the estate of the 1st Lord Berkeley of Stratton (*see* BERKELEY SQUARE), it extends northward from PICCADILLY. Until 1924 it was a cul-de-sac, its eastern side bounded by the garden wall of DEVONSHIRE HOUSE; but after the demolition of DEVONSHIRE HOUSE the north end was extended eastwards across the site of the garden to BERKELEY STREET. Building (on the west side only) began in about 1693 and in 1720 the houses were said to be 'very gentily built, and well inhabited'. No. 6, of the late-18th century, is now the only house of any age, and its projecting 1st-floor bow window, supported on a cast-iron column, must have had a beautiful view over the Dukes of Devonshire's garden. Today it looks out at the great modern blocks which now dominate the rest of the street. Residents include Thomas Campbell, the poet; General Thomas Graham, Lord Lynedoch, Peninsular War commander; and Baroness Burdett-Coutts, the philanthropist. Langan's Brasserie, originally the Coq d'Or, was established in 1976. Peter Langan had formerly worked at Odin's, No. 27 Devonshire Street, where he had done the cooking himself.

Strawberry Hill *Twickenham, Middlesex.* 'It is a little plaything of a house, the prettiest bauble you ever did see'; so Horace Walpole described his new house on the TWICKENHAM riverside in 1748. Giving himself a lifetime of pleasure, he transformed an unpretentious little villa into a Gothic castle of great charm and originality, adding to it at whim for over 44 years and opening it to the public on request. To assist him in his research he set up A Committee of Taste including Richard Bentley, a gifted illustrator, and John Chute, owner of the Vyne in Hampshire; later Thomas Pitt, Lord Camelford, replaced Bentley. Their method of work was to take various details from Gothic buildings, known to them from illustrations in topographical books, and adapt them to Walpole's needs. (Their approach was not the scholarly one which was to typify the 19th-century Gothic Revival.)

Initially content to Gothicise the exterior with battlements, Tudor chimneys and quatrefoil windows, Walpole eventually extended the house with a Long Gallery (the ceiling modelled on that of Henry VII's Chapel at WESTMINSTER) and two towers, the Round and the Beauclerc Towers. Bookcases, doors and screens all had medieval prototypes, designs for chimneyplaces ranging from Archbishop Wareham's tomb at Canterbury to Edward the Confessor's at WESTMINSTER. Walpole commissioned his friends to find him furnishings, thereby accumulating a large and famous collection which was sold at the Great Sale of 1842. All his letters, which stretch to many volumes, have been edited by the American scholar W.S. Lewis. Walpole kept meticulous building accounts and inventories, printing them on his own private press which he installed in the house.

After his death the house passed through several hands until it was inherited in 1846 by Frances, Countess Waldegrave. Like Walpole, both a leading figure in society and a passionate builder, she immediately began to restore the house. As it was too small for entertainment on a lavish scale, Frances Waldegrave constructed an entirely new wing linking the main body of the original house to the domestic offices.

A castellated wall and entrance gate were added to the north side and the picturesque silhouette accentuated by raising the height of both towers. To improve accessibility from London she had the railway extended to her door. Under her tutelage Strawberry Hill became a focal point of political influence; her receptions were legendary and her guest lists renowned.

The house was sold after her death in 1879 and in 1923 was bought by the Catholic Education Council. It is now a Roman Catholic teachers' training college, St Mary's College, which has some 1,200 students, both men and women.

Strawberry House *Church Road, SW13.* Barnes Rectory until 1939, it was largely rebuilt during the incumbency of Francis Hare from 1717–27. Later in the 18th century the upper storey was heightened and the present parapet constructed. The interior includes a fine staircase with triple twisted balusters to each tread and crisply carved tread-ends. The rectors have included Hezekiah Burton; the famous preacher, Henry Melvill; and the hymn-writer, John Ellerton. It is now a private house.

Streatham *SW16.* Although there was believed to have been a small Roman settlement here during the construction of the road from London to the Sussex coast, the name Streatham is of Saxon origin, meaning 'the dwellings by the street'. In the years preceding the Norman conquest, Streatham is mentioned in documents as being under the jurisdiction of the Abbey of Chertsey in Surrey. In *Domesday Book* the Saxon chapel was assessed at 8s.

After the Conquest, Streatham, together with TOOTING, part of which lay within the former's parish boundaries, was given to William's cousin, Richard of Tonbridge, who later bestowed both estates on the Benedictine Abbey of Saint Mary of Bec in Normandy. Owners of Streatham land in following years included Eton College, Edward VI, Lord Thurlow, the Russells, Dukes of Bedford, and the Du Cane family.

Strawberry Hill, Horace Walpole's 'prettiest bauble', at Twickenham. From an engraving after Paul Sandby, 1774.

As the halfway point between London and CROYDON and, therefore, an ideal resting place, the development of Streatham in the Middle Ages followed that of CROYDON where the Archbishops of Canterbury had a palace (*see* ADDINGTON PALACE). A charter giving the right to hold a fair and a market was granted in the 13th century, and the rebuilding of the parish church of ST LEONARD in the mid-14th century reflected the increasing well-being of the village. For the next two centuries it remained, however, a small village straggling the main road for a mile, with a few hundred inhabitants.

City merchants were amongst those who, after the GREAT FIRE, found the village a pleasant rural setting for their country residences. In Elizabethan and Stuart times Edmund Tilney, Master of the Revels at Court; the architect, John Bodley, who was used as a money-lender by Charles I; and Robert Livesay, twice Sheriff of Surrey, all had strong associations with Streatham. The discovery of a medicinal spring near the Common in 1659 further increased the attraction of the village. A spa was soon established and people flocked to take the waters (*see* STREATHAM SPA). In the 1680s a small colony of Huguenot silk weavers was established near the common and, following the accession of William of Orange, a number of Dutch families also settled in the village.

The turnpike road from KENNINGTON, through BRIXTON and Streatham, to CROYDON was authorised in 1717 and the Horse and Groom inn at the top of BRIXTON Hill was one of the official stops for the stage coaches en route to the developing towns on the south coast. The inn gained a reputation for gambling and cock-fighting and was often used by the Prince of Wales, later George IV, on his way to Brighton. The area became increasingly attractive to highwaymen, who had frequented the surrounding heath and shrubland for centuries, necessitating the erection of a gallows on Brixton Hill in the 1720s.

Maps of the 18th century show that the village was concentrated in two main areas, one around the parish church and the other stretching south from the common to Green Lane, together with the High Road and Greyhound Lane. Between and beyond were farms and smallholdings.

During the Georgian period a family of SOUTHWARK brewers, the Thrales, acquired over 100 acres of common land from the Duke of Bedford, whose manor house stood near the High Road, overlooking the common. Two of the Duke's other houses were used as homes by Lord William Russell – Russell House and Bedford House. The latter survives as Pratt's Department Store.

On their estate, known as Streatham Park, the Thrales built a large mansion overlooking Tooting Bec Common and made it a centre of social and intellectual life (*see* STREATHAM PLACE). Between 1766 and 1782 Dr Samuel Johnson spent much of his time here, becoming a familiar figure around the village.

Streatham, whose population numbered 2,729 in 1811, continued to attract the wealthy who built fine Georgian mansions and Regency villas. By the early 1800s regular coach services provided easy access to WESTMINSTER and the CITY. William Dyce, the Pre-Raphaelite painter, had a house in the High Road and was buried in the churchyard in 1864. Another notable resident was Sir Henry Tate whose house, Park Hill, overlooked the common and who presented the Tate Library to Streatham in 1890.

The changes which took the population from 6,000 in 1841 to 20,000 in 1881 and 70,000 by the turn of the century were accelerated by the expansion of the railways and the opening of Streatham Hill station in 1856. Within 12 years two more stations were opened. The old manorial estates were rapidly being broken up for commercial and residential development and large new estates were built to accommodate the growing population: Telford Park in the 1870s and Coventry Park and the Leigham Court estate in the following decade. Shops and businesses also continued to expand. Until after the 1st World War, Streatham retained a good deal of open land, fields and woods; but, following the War, many of the 19th-century mansions were demolished for the construction of thousands of smaller houses. Following the 2nd World War, new private and council estates were built to replace those damaged in air raids. Cinemas, dance halls, theatres, an ice-rink and a swimming pool helped to make Streatham an entertainment centre for south London. To some extent it remains so now; and the High Street continues as a major route for the traffic bound from London to the south coast (*see also* STREATHAM COMMON).

Streatham Common *SW16*. Streatham Common, which now comprises 36 acres in all, was once part of a vast tract of land stretching from NORBURY to TULSE HILL. There were once a number of ponds which were fed by a chain of springs from NORWOOD via BEULAH SPA but most were filled in by the early years of the 20th century. In medieval times the Common belonged to the Liberty of Lower Streatham whose inhabitants had the rights of grazing and collecting furze. A cage was erected on the Common in the mid-18th century 'for the confinement of loose and disorderly persons' but a happier scene followed in 1887 when the Common was the site for one of the beacon fires lit to celebrate Queen Victoria's JUBILEE. Cricket was played on the Common from the 1830s and those whose houses bordered the Common had private access gates to the cricket ground.

Streatham Place The Thrales, a brewing family from SOUTHWARK, bought over 100 acres of common land from the Duke of Bedford. The estate extended from ST LEONARD'S CHURCH in the village centre to TOOTING BEC COMMON and was known as Streatham Park. There Ralph Thrale, MP for SOUTHWARK, built a large white Georgian mansion – Streatham Place – in 1740. During the lifetime of his son, Henry Thrale, a lake of 3 acres with an island was formed which, in the winter, was used for skating. The arbor in the garden near to the house was a favourite retreat of Doctor Samuel Johnson, who did much of his writing here. Other frequent guests of Henry and Hester Thrale were Burke, David Garrick, Fanny Burney and Joshua Reynolds.

On display in the house were a number of portraits painted by Reynolds for the Thrales. The extensive grounds also included stables, paddocks and large hot houses. The toll bar at the north-western corner of the Park was once the scene of a dramatic incident when the gate-keeper fired at the carriage carrying the Chancellor, Lord Thurlow, and William Pitt the Younger because they had not stopped to pay the toll.

After the death of Henry Thrale the Prime Minister, Lord Shelburne, rented the house for three years. It then passed through many hands and, on its sale in

1816, the gallery of portraits by Reynolds was dispersed. It was finally pulled down in 1863 and a private estate, also called Streatham Park, was built on the land. This was taken over by the LONDON COUNTY COUNCIL in 1946.

Streatham Spa A spring was first discovered on rising ground near Streatham Common by a ploughman in 1659. The waters were found to have medicinal properties with 'a mawkish taste' and were declared to be good for worms and for the eyes. Rich and poor alike flocked to take the waters which were also sold fresh each morning at ST PAUL'S CHURCHYARD, TEMPLE BAR and ROYAL EXCHANGE. The usual dose was apparently about three cups which was said to be equivalent to nine cups of Epsom waters. At the beginning of the 18th century, when the reputation of the Spa was at its highest, concerts were held twice a week. It was said that the Common and the High Street 'became fashionable promenades where all the leaders of society might be met'. No accommodation was built for the visitors, however, and the Spa had closed by about 1792. By this time a second mineral spring had been discovered nearer to the village centre in Valley Road. A Georgian well-house was built here and the waters were pumped, sold and distributed until the 2nd World War. The tea gardens attached to the well were in use until the 1860s.

Street Cries Until the second half of the 19th century, it was itinerant street sellers, rather than shopkeepers and market traders, who supplied Londoners with their material needs. Their street cries were the equivalent of modern advertising, alerting the public to the traders' presence, and to the type and quality of their wares. Fortunately the sights and sound of this aspect of street life inspired the work of artists, writers and musicians over the centuries, thus providing us with a full record of this fascinating aspect of economic history.

Possibly the earliest literary reference comes in Langland's *Piers Plowman*. This work includes a street scene featuring traders crying 'Hot Pyes Hote!' and taverners reciting their wine lists to passers-by.

A richly detailed description of street-traders' cries and their bewildering effect on a newly arrived stranger, comes in the ballad *London Lyckpenny* attributed to John Lydgate, a monk who lived in Bury St Edmunds, at some time in the 15th century. Legal business took him to the capital:

> Then unto London I dyd me hye,
> Of all the land it beareth the pryse:
> Hot pescodes, one began to cry,
> Strabery rype, and cherryes in the ryse;
> One bad me come hear and buy some spyce
> Peper and Safforne they gan me bede
> But for lack of money I myght not spend

By 'the Chepe' he is offered fine materials from Paris; and he continues:

> Throughout all Canwyke [Candlewick] Streete
> Drapers mutch cloth offred anone
> Then comes me one cryed hot shepe's feete;
> One cryde makerell, ryster [rushes] grene . . .
> . . . Then I hyed me into Est-chepe
> One cryes rybbs of befe, and many a pye.

Almost any commodity could, from Lydgate's time,

until less than 150 years ago, be bought on the streets; and the din of vendors' voices, competing for attention and custom, formed an integral part of London life throughout that period. All types of food were offered as the following cries record: 'Hott baked Wardens [stewed pears] Hott!'; 'Crab, Crab, any Crab?'; 'Ripe Speragras! [asparagus]'; 'Buy my fat Chickens!'; 'Buy my Flounders?'; 'Fair Lemons and Oranges!'; 'Twelve pence a peck, Oysters!'; 'Sixpence a pound, Fair Cherryes!'.

All these foodstuffs were carried and 'cried' by individual sellers, as were the vast range of goods other than food: 'Buy a fine singing bird!'; 'Fine Writeing Ink!'; 'Small Coale!'; 'Oh Rare Shoes!'; 'Old Cloaks, Suits or Coats!'; 'Long thread laces, long and strong!'. Most vendors repeated a phrase sing-song, with emphasis on the appropriate word; 'Buy my four ropes of hard *onions*!', 'Delicate *cucumbers*!', 'Buy my Dish of Great *Eeles*!'. Others recited or sang a verse, like the 17th-century vendor of marking stones, which preceded the wood-encased lead pencil:

> Buy marking stones, marking stones buy,
> Much profit in their use doth lie;
> I've marking stones of colour red,
> Passing good, or else black lead!

Sometimes music was incorporated in a trader's cry. Newspaper sellers in the late 18th and early 19th centuries made their progress round the city streets known by the sound of a trumpet. The dustman's cry of, 'Dust O!' was generally accompanied by a bell. Dustmen were not the only street traders who offered services rather than goods: 'Knives or Scissors to Grind?'; 'A Brass pot or an Iron Pot to mend?'; 'Wood to Cleave?'; 'Old Chaires to Mend?'; 'Any Cornes to Pick?'. There were also two famous public-service street criers: the Public Cryer and the Belman or Nightwatchman. These criers, traditionally bearing staff and keys, gave news and asked for information.

Andrew Tuer, who made a detailed and entertaining study of the subject in *Old London Street Cries* (1885), provides one example:

> O is, any man or woman that
> Can tell any tydings of a little
> Mayden childe of the age of 24 [sic]
> Yeares. Bring worde to the cryer
> And you shal be pleased for
> Your labor,
> And God's blessinge.

Until the 18th century, the Belman walked the streets at night with lantern, halberd and dog, singing out the time and the state of the weather.

Tuer again gives us an example:

> Mayds in your smocks, looke
> Wel to your locke –
> Your fire
> And your light
> And God
> Give you Good-night
> At
> One o'clock.

Sometimes, however, the Belman's efforts irritated rather than reassured his listeners. One of Ben Jonson's characters wore a 'huge turban of night-caps' against this nocturnal noise; while Addison complained, 'The watchman's thump at midnight startles us in our beds

835

'Knives Combs or Inkhornes', an engraving from Lauron's
The cryes of the city of London drawne after the life, 1687.

produced by the Industrial Revolution led to the
establishment of a more permanent, sophisticated and
shop-based retailing system.

Beggars may have got itinerant traders a bad name,
using as they did the same vocal means of attracting
attention. Mayhew wrote that street criers covered the
complete range from shameless impostors to 'Marvels
of ingenuity and industry'. J.T. Smith, in his
Vagabondia (1817), catalogued the activities of some
of them. He includes a list drawn up by a 16th-century
Justice of the Peace, Thomas Harman, of the various
categories of beggars and 'vagabones' attempting to
earn a living on the streets of London at that time.
'Rufflers' pretended to be wounded soldiers recently
returned from war; 'Pallyards' sported artificial sores
to encourage donations, and were alleged to be chiefly
Welsh; 'Abraham Men' sought public sympathy by
pretending to be lunatics. Smith also gives a 19th-
century example of a begging cry emphasising the
similarity between street trading and street begging:
'My worthy heart, stow a copper in Jack's locker – for
poor Jack has not had a quid today'. Sailors, who had
great appeal for the English public, used this cry
frequently. But, as Smith points out, such 'criers' included many 'freshwater sailors' who had never seen a
ship 'but from London Bridge'. Many petty criminals
used street selling as a cover for their nefarious
activities. Tuer gives us several examples from his own
experiences of the 19th-century capital. One 'shivering
coatless vagabond' persuaded him to purchase a tract
by displaying 'an eruption of biceps perfectly appalling
in its magnitude'. He also tells of a toy seller who used
ventriloquism to persuade his customers that his Jack-
in-the-Box had a voice, which, as they discovered on
purchase, it did not. Mispronunciation was similarly
employed for the purpose of deception. 'Three un-
derd an' fifty songs for a penny' was really 'three under
fifty songs for a penny'.

Tuer concludes, however, that 'Street criers are
honest enough ... in the main. If vegetables are
sometimes a little stale, or fruit is suspiciously over-
ripe, they do not feel absolutely called upon to mention
these facts; but they give bouncing penn'orths, and
their clients are generally shrewd enough to take care
of themselves'.

The humour and eccentricity of the street criers was
generally appreciated by the London public. Tuer
writes of 'a jovial rogue whose beat extends to
numerous courts and alleys on either side of Fleet
Street, who regularly and unblushingly cries, "Stinking Shrimps" and by way of addenda, "Lor 'ow they do
stink today, to be sure". His little joke is almost as
much relished as his shrimps and bloaters and they
appear to be always of the freshest'.

Mispronunciation, too, could amuse, as well as
deceive, as in the case of the Cockney boot-lace-man's
cry: 'Lice, lice, penny a pair boot-lice!'. In some cases
wit and eccentricity secured some traders celebrity
status among the London public. 'Tiddy Diddy Doll'
was a celebrated vendor of gingerbread in the 18th
century, whose stylish clothing – ruffled shirt, silk
stockings, and fashionably laced suit of clothes – made
his name a byword for a dandified or overdressed appearance, and confirmed his reputation as king of
itinerant salesmen. He was in attendance at every
public occasion amusing the crowd with a constant
stream of humorous 'patter': 'Here's your nice gingerbread, your spiced gingerbread, which will melt in

as the breaking in of a thief'. In the same article he
continued to describe the disturbing effects on newcomers to London: 'My good friend Sir Roger [De
Coverley] often declares that he cannot get them out
of his head or go to sleep for them for the first Week
that he is in Town'. Residents also had problems with
the noise. Addison tells of a man who paid a card-
match maker to stay away from his house because her
cries distracted him. Next day, however, a 'whole
tribe' of vendors passed by hoping for similar easy
earnings. Addison also complained of the incom-
prehensibility of some cries, citing the case of 'the
country boy who ran out to buy apples of a Bellows
Mender; and Gingerbread from a grinder of knives
and scissors'. He also noted the occasional discrepancy
between a cry's volume and the quality of the goods
offered.

Coleridge, irritated whilst working by an old Jewish
street trader's constant repetition, 'Ogh clo', Ogh clo',
asked him to explain his mispronunciation. 'Sir,'
replied the Jew, 'I can say "old clothes" as well as you
can, but if you had to say so, ten times a minute for an
hour together, you would say "Ogh clo" as I do now.'
Coleridge gave him a shilling.

There was also a long history of official hostility to
street vendors. An Act of Common Council in
Elizabeth I's reign attempted to keep the lanes of the
City for use as highways only; but this met with little
success. During Charles I's reign, street traders were
denounced as 'unruly people' and accused with 'framing themselves a way whereby to live a more easy life
than labour'. In fact street traders survived the
authorities' hostility, until the economic changes

your mouth like a red-hot brickbat, and rumble in your inside like Punch in a wheelbarrow.' He always ended by singing, 'Tiddy Diddy Doll, Lol, Lol Lol', hence his nickname. So great was the fame of one gingerbread seller who went by the name of Ford, that when he missed a week from his usual stand in the HAYMARKET to visit the country, a 'Catchpenny' account of his alleged murder was printed and sold in thousands.

As mentioned earlier, street traders and their cries have found a lasting place in European art and music. Orlando Gibbons, Richard Dering and Thomas Weekes are among the musicians who incorporated street cries in their compositions. Pictorial studies of London's 'Criers' first appeared in the 17th century, probably based originally on Hogenberg's series, *Cologne Cries*. In 1687 a Dutch-born artist Marcellus Lauron drew a set of 74 street cries, which were engraved by Pierce Tempest and copied for the next two centuries. Tiddy Diddy Doll featured in this series, as did the London milkmaids in their festive May-time dress. In the 1760s, Paul Sandby's *Twelve London Cries* gave a topical French taste to the subject. In the 1790s perhaps the two most popular portrayals of street criers were made. These were Francis Wheatley's *The Itinerant Trades of London* (1793–7) and Thomas Rowlandson's *London Street Cries*. Both works have been reproduced ever since. An extract from John Gay's *Trivia*, Book II (1716) provides a striking example of the pathos of the street-vendors' picturesque but precarious existence.

> The cracking crystal yields
> She sinks, she dies,
> Her head chopt off from her lost shoulders, flies.
> Pippins! she cry'd;
> But Death her voice confounds
> And Pip – Pip – Pip!
> Along the ice resounds.

(*See also* STREET MUSIC and STREET VENDORS).

Street Lighting   Up to the end of the 18th century London was the worst lit capital in Europe. Most of the light at night came either from the moon, from candles shining through windows, or from the occasional moving torch made of tow dipped in pitch. Some light came also from lamps which citizens were obliged to hang outside their houses between certain hours on dark nights in accordance with a law of 1416 – a law that was reinforced by an Act of 1661. An attempt to organise public lighting came in 1685 when Edward Hemming was granted a monopoly on condition that he placed oil lamps outside every tenth house along the main thoroughfares between six o'clock and midnight on moonless nights from Michaelmas until Lady Day. In prosperous districts sporadic lighting was provided either by lamps burning whale oil on cotton wicks suspended over the entrances to the larger houses, or from an occasional lamp hung from a wall or a pole and protected by a glass globe. The moving torches of the linkmen also helped the pedestrian on his way to avoid pot holes and dunghills. Iron cones for extinguishing the torches can still be seen above the railings of a number of 18th-century houses.

Linkmen and linkboys formed a disorderly class, for as Gay wrote in his *Trivia*:

> Though thou art tempted by the linkman's call,
> Yet trust him not along the lonely wall:

In the midway he'll quench the flaming brand,
And share the booty with the pilfering hand.

The WESTMINSTER Paving and Lighting Act of 1792 improved street lighting to some degree, but London did not become adequately lit until coal-gas could be commercially exploited. In that year of 1792, William Murdock inaugurated a pilot scheme of gas lighting in Cornwall, and a few years later he extended it to Birmingham and Manchester. Then in 1804 F.A. Winsor (a German, born Winzer) established the New Light and Heat Company and lit the LYCEUM THEATRE with gas. In 1807 the north side of PALL MALL was lit by Windsor's Patent Gas, supplied along pipes of lead, to honour the King's birthday. Then came the turn of BISHOPSGATE in the CITY. In 1814 WESTMINSTER BRIDGE was lit by gas supplied by the Gas-Light and Coke Company which had just erected its works in CANNON ROW, WESTMINSTER. At the peace rejoicings that took place the same year, the ceremonial Chinese Bridge with its pagoda in ST JAMES'S PARK was lit by gas – and caught fire.

By 1842 most of London's main streets were gas-lit, the last locality to adopt the method being GROSVENOR SQUARE where the carriage folk had for long been resisting the vulgar intrusion. Many had, indeed, mocked the new lighting, including Sir Humphry Davy who asked if it were intended to take the dome of ST PAUL'S for a gasometer? By the 1840s 12 gas companies existed in London consuming nearly 200,000 tons of coal a year and employing 380 lamp-lighters. By the 1860s the iron pipes of the London Gas Company at

A lamplighter and his young apprentice attend to an oil lamp. Engraving from Pyne's Costume of Great Britain, *1805.*

VAUXHALL extended as far north as HIGHGATE, 7 miles away, and throughout the metropolis over 2,000 miles of piping had been laid below ground. By 1880, the year the gas fire was introduced, the gas companies were consuming 6½ million tons of coal a year and London streets had acquired a million gas lamps. The effects of this improvement were remarkable: street crime was much reduced, shops could remain open long after dark (on Saturdays often up to midnight), and indoors it was an aid to literacy.

By the turn of the century most of London's gas was being supplied by two corporations: the old Gas-Light and Coke Company, which was supplying 22 billion cubic feet of gas a year to some 60 square miles of territory, and the South Metropolitan which was supplying 11 billion to South London. A number of smaller companies also existed. Gas was stored in gigantic telescopic cylinders of iron, some of which still stand. One example was the famous Jumbo erected at VAUXHALL in 1906 with a capacity of over 5 million cubic feet; another, with twice that capacity, stood on the GREENWICH marshes.

The early gas lamps were called Bengal Lights and were simply open burners. Later burners were based on the Argand lamp with its ring of holes that formed a cylinder of flame. Batwing and fishtail burners were also common, but not until Welsbach had invented the incandescent gasmantle of cotton saturated with certain chemicals in 1885, did gas lighting become fully effective.

Electric lighting first appeared in London on WEST-MINSTER BRIDGE in 1858, but it did not come into wider use until two more decades had passed. In 1878, for instance, electric arc lighting was installed in some large workshops at WOOLWICH and in the machine room of *The Times*, while the following year Siemens's electric lighting was applied successfully in the interior of the ALBERT HALL, on the north side of the EMBANKMENT and on WATERLOO BRIDGE. In 1880 more electric lights appeared on the EMBANKMENT and also at VICTORIA STATION.

Between 1878 and 1880 Edison and Swan independently produced the first vacuum bulbs with incandescent carbon filaments. The electric-light revolution had begun. In 1887 the first station of the Kensington and Knightsbridge Electric Lighting Company was opened and two years later the first large power station began operating at DEPTFORD under the London Electricity Supply Company. The same year the CITY was lit electrically from FLEET STREET to ALDGATE.

Electricity superseded gas very slowly. The first London Electric Supply Act was not passed until 1908, and not until 1925 did London and the Home Counties achieve a joint electricity authority. By then lamps had much improved. Today London is lit almost entirely by electricity. The new light sources bring extra lumens but to some they also bring nostalgic regret that the romantic years of the lamp-lighter have gone for ever – the years when, in T.S. Eliot's words:

> The winter evening settles down
> With smells of steaks in passageways ...
> And at the corner of the street
> A lonely cab-horse steams and stamps.
> And then the lighting of the lamps.

Street Music Successive conquests have influenced the development of music heard in London from the earliest times. Military music was well developed by the Romans whose bands of brass instruments and percussion provided a spur to soldiers on the march. By the time of the Norman conquest, public and court entertainments, especially long narrative poems, were accompanied by groups of musicians, often able to perform also as jugglers and dancers. Such troubadours and minstrels flourished in the streets and taverns of the CITY, and later formed a guild from which can be traced the origins of the Worshipful Company of Musicians (*see* CITY LIVERY COMPANIES). Itinerant musicians settled in London; and Chaucer and Shakespeare describe vividly both their performance and personality. From the Middle Ages the shouts of street hawkers advertising wares became associated with appropriate melodies, gradually becoming stereotyped and evolving into a folk music of the streets. Many of these cries were notated and incorporated into music by composers such as Weekes, Deering and Orlando Gibbons whose *Cries of London* is well known. The tunes of similar street cries have been used in more formal works by later composers such as Handel, Elgar and Vaughan Williams, as well as being commemorated visually by artists like Wheatley and Hogarth. During the Middle Ages nightwatchmen of the CITY had become associated with musicians who formed small bands known as Waits. These, maintained at CITY expense, would welcome travellers with instrumental music on shawms and trumpets, and celebrate Christmas with carols. More particular celebrations might accompany the arrival of royalty, when elaborate ritual and pageantry accompanied the procession of the monarch, such as occurred on Henry V's return to London after Agincourt.

Extension of patronage by others such as noblemen and tavern-keepers resulted in the composition of doggerel directed towards political targets, as well as commentary on contemporary events. The street ballad continued to be popular throughout the 17th and 18th centuries, although it was suppressed temporarily by Cromwell. Publication became centred in the locality of *Seven Dials*; one of the most prolific writers was John Gay, whose enormously successful *The Beggar's Opera* (1728) was based on a series of popular ballads, well known to the public by street performance.

Such activity continued well into the 19th century; and by 1850 Mayhew recorded more than 250 ballad singers in London, and even more street instrumentalists, including hurdy-gurdy, bagpipes, violin and wind players. From the Continent came others, including brass bands from Germany, and from Italy, mechanical organs mounted on a cart. Whilst these undoubtedly attracted a meagre living from public support, many Londoners considered street musicians a nuisance, both as beggars and as producers of unwelcome noise to disturb the peace.

This was no recent problem, for in 1642 Puritan control of London had forbidden the City waits from playing at the ROYAL EXCHANGE on Sundays; and Hogarth, in his *Enraged Musician* (1741) depicts Castrucci, principal violin of the Italian opera, with hands to ears to stifle the sound of itinerant musicians outside his window. Early in Queen Victoria's reign, London householders were given power to require street musicians to withdraw on 'grounds of illness or other reasonable cause', but this was not a sufficient control for M.T. Bass, MP who objected in

Hogarth's Enraged Musician, *1741. A professional violinist stops his ears against the cacophony of a street band.*

particular to German bands and organ-grinders, probably because they were louder than most. In 1864 he introduced a Metropolitan Police Act which had the support of a large number of writers, including Dickens and Tennyson, whose work was allegedly disturbed by passing street-musicians. Some of these were thought to annoy purposely by playing out of tune, to extract money in return for silence on their departure. The 1864 Act strengthened the grounds upon which a complainant could make a charge, but required the complaint to be made in person at a police station. Clearly this Act did not deter performers, for in 1880 the *Musical Times* records the formation of a Society for the Regulation of Street Music and of Street Musicians. An enraged correspondent listed a whole range of performers of varying sorts who had caused his displeasure in a single day. These included a 'Brass Band, two organs, Punch and Judy, organ driven by donkey, bagpipes, organ with two babies attached . . .'

In the present day the most effective music heard on the streets of London is that of military bands, especially those of the HOUSEHOLD DIVISION on state and ceremonial occasions, such as the TROOPING THE COLOUR ceremony to commemorate the Queen's Official Birthday in June, held on HORSE GUARDS PARADE, and at the daily Changing the Guard ceremony at BUCKINGHAM PALACE. SALVATION ARMY bands are, however, heard nowadays much less frequently than hitherto.

Street processions of ethnic minorities may be accompanied by the music of their cultures. For example, steel bands at the West Indian Carnival held annually in August in NOTTING HILL GATE, and oriental music at the Chinese New Year celebrations in central London. At Christmas larger organised choirs may be heard singing carols in such public places as TRAFALGAR SQUARE. Street musicians, often with music-hall pretensions as entertainers, and known as buskers, were until the 1950s a frequent accompaniment to theatre queues. More often seen now are student musicians who, defying the laws which inhibit their performances, play in sheltered streets, in the UNDERGROUND subways, and lately in organised sites such as the new COVENT GARDEN. They may attract modest financial reward from the passers-by until moved on by the police. Recently the GREATER LONDON COUNCIL has agreed to consider the licensing of performers of suitable musical standard. Some present-day street musicians have had commercial success both as recording artists and in the concert-hall. Among these are the Cambridge Buskers who, while not finding the streets of London particularly hospitable, have become well known on the Continent (*see also* STREET PERFORMERS).

Street Performers London's street performers probably owed their origin to the earliest FAIRS that were formed to cater for the needs of worshippers and pilgrims who gathered round sacred places, and on the feast-days of the saints enshrined in them. Twelfth century descriptions of the FAIR that grew up outside the Norman Priory OF ST BARTHOLOMEW at SMITHFIELD tell of an intrepid woman who balanced herself to the music of tabor and pipes, head downwards, by the palms of her hands upon sword points. Another woman walked on high stilts, baby in arms and jug of water on her head. '. . . Entertainments of a devout kind' at the early fairs, described by Fitzstephen, were forerunners of the popular street 'mummers' of later times. Round the abbeys, priories and churches grew up graveyards full of traders, and places of jesting where men and women applauded the performers and curiosities provided for their entertainment. These entertainers, 'monsters', troupes of actors and animals making their way to the many fairs all over London at all seasons, became an established part of street life and as much of a draw as in their appointed sites. Some of them, realising their popularity with the ordinary Londoners, did not restrict their appearances to the fairs but laid claim to certain streets and areas for their performances.

The closure of abbeys and priories at the DISSOLUTION, and the dispersal of large numbers of monks and employees, added to the already growing army of unemployed; and many of these tried their hand at 'street entertaining' – not always too successfully.

John Evelyn, in the 17th century, often went out of his way to see such things as '. . . a sort of Cat with a monkey's body' or 'The Hairy Woman' whose eyebrows covered her forehead, whose ears sprouted hair, and whose face was adorned with a thick beard and moustaches. Rope-dancing was a very popular street act from early times; Samuel Pepys reported that Jacob Hall's performance was '. . . mightily worth seeing'. Another performer, 'The Turk', climbed with his toes up an almost perpendicular rope attached to a church steeple, then slid down head first, arms and legs extended. On one occasion, Evelyn watched fascinated as 'The Turk' danced blindfold on a high tightrope, a small boy attached to one foot, then did a head-stand atop a lofty mast. Richardson, the 'fire-eater', was another hero of 17th-century London streets. He chewed and swallowed hot coals, then melted glass and, as a finale, put a hot coal on his tongue, heated it with bellows until it flamed, then cooked an oyster placed on it, swallowing the lot. To restore himself after this act, Richardson drank flaming pitch, wax and sulphur. In the mid-17th century the puppet-show Punch and Judy arrived from Italy, and soon became an integral part of London street entertainment, its popularity reaching its height in Queen Anne's reign; Addison gave a criticism of a performance in *The Spectator*. Shows required two persons, one to carry 'the frame' and work the figures, the other to transport the box of puppets and, when

'Big Ben's Telescope Man' beneath Boudicca's statue on Westminster Bridge in c.1912.

Hombres, was a Shadow Show invented in China and first performed in London about 1835 by Thomas Paris. Many 'Punch and Judy' showmen switched to this performance at night. Three candles were lighted behind the curtains, and ½d to 1d was considered a fair price per show. From Germany came the exhibition of mechanical figures moved by wheels and springs, performing on a round table; favorite subjects were The French Emperor's Carriage, and the elephant which moved its legs, trunk and tail, rolling its eyes from side to side. Two men accompanied the operator who carried the table, one playing the organ, the other transporting the heavy box of figures. Winter fogs as well as rain also badly affected the 'Telescope Operator' who charged 1d a peep. The exhibitor gave an initial short lecture on the wonders of the heavens. The 'Microscope Exhibitor' did not have to worry about rain so much, and could operate as easily by night as by day. Objects were placed on a wheel at the back of the microscope and inspected in turn, the most popular being a flea, human hair, a drop of water, a cheese mite or a section of cane. A favorite day-stand was opposite the LONDON HOSPITAL in WHITECHAPEL where light was good; and WESTMINSTER BRIDGE was favoured at night.

Regular Victorian street entertainers were the Italian mechanical orchestras, the Italian woman with her cage of fortune-telling budgerigars or parakeets, and the street-acrobats with clowns on high stilts covered in long striped trousers, who cheerfully collected pennies from excited children leaning out of high nursery windows. Conjurors out busking reckoned to earn 20s weekly, and sometimes more in

Street performers on stilts dancing to the music of a barrel organ, from Henry Mayhew's London Labour and the London Poor, *1861.*

possible, play the drum and pipes. Operators walked 12 to 20 miles daily, heavily laden, always collecting an unwelcome following of small boys who parted with no money. Early performances of 'Punch' were sentimental and moralistic, much being made of the killing of the Devil accompanied by Punch's shouts of 'Bravo!'. When played in the open street – known as 'short showing' – Punch and Judy earned an average 3d a performance; shows of half an hour or more, confined to street corners, were 'long pitches' and earned about 1s a show. Spring, mid-summer and Christmas were known as 'Punch's seasons' and wet weather, though damaging street shows, helped private house visits, aimed at entertaining bored children. LEICESTER SQUARE, with its continuous passing crowds of all classes, proved 'Punch''s best pitch with REGENT STREET a close second.

The 'Fantoccini Man', a show on four wheels four times as big as 'Punch and Judy', was an exhibition of dancing dolls whose name was later changed to 'Marionettes' after an exhibition under that name at the ADELAIDE GALLERY. A Scotsman named Gray first introduced the show to London's streets with dancing figures 9 inches high; these were at a later date superseded by dolls of 2 ft or more, performing in a mobile theatre about 10 ft by 6 ft. Gray performed before George IV, and the show for a time took away 'Punch and Judy''s popularity. Programmes usually included quadrille dancers, representation of the clown, Grimaldi, tumblers, an enchanted Turk and dancing skeletons.

The 'Chinese Shades', originally known as *Les*

return for teaching some gentleman their tricks. The snake-swallower gave small boys ½d for each snake brought from the woods, scraping the reptiles with his fingernail to clean them. The same performer daily swallowed swords and knives. The 'Street Clown', often accompanying acrobats, habitually wore red striped cotton stockings with trunks dotted red and black, tight-fitting bodice with full sleeves and frills, and a cox-comb wig sewn on a white cap. His dead-white face was painted with dry white lead and enlivened with vermilion cheeks and mouth. Many old 'Street Clowns' ended their days, ill and destitute, in the workhouse. 'Silly Billy' and 'Billy Barlow' were two comic characters who roamed the streets in their individual attire, in company with dancers and acrobats. Bands of strolling actors often risked prosecution by erecting their canvas theatres and giving impromptu performances of dumb acting, singing and dancing. The 'mummers' had their own very individual slang, a compound of broken Italian and French. Children as young as two and a half were trained, often with great cruelty, to perform on stilts, playing tambourines as they danced. The Jellini family was famed for its ballets on stilts, accompanied by its own barrel-organ. WALWORTH and COMMERCIAL ROADS, near LIMEHOUSE, were popular haunts of the 'Street Reciter', who knew Shakespeare backwards and earned a regular wage of 10s weekly in fine weather. The 'Blind Reader' was limited to the Scriptures – the only literature converted to Braille – and some varied the performance by 'blind writing'.

The performing bear could still be found with its trainer in some quiet side street in the early years of this century, but increasing congestion of vehicles, the growth of other forms of entertainment and a family life which tended to be spent more in the home, steadily drove entertainers off the streets. The 1st World War despatched the remaining few acrobats, sword-swallowers and showmen from the pavements, and when peace returned they were only a memory. But the recent advent of 'street theatre' is enlivening London's squares and alleys once again, while many a theatre or sale queue is enlivened by some enterprising performer. (*See also* STREET MUSIC.)

Street Signs The earliest tradesmen's signs were bas-reliefs in stone. Introduced by the Romans, they were adopted by the British in London. Symbols included mermaids, eagles, astrological devices, the boar, which was originally the emblem of the 20th Legion, and the dolphin, which was frequently used in Roman mosaics and was used in the arms of the FISH-MONGERS' COMPANY. The signs, usually set up high on the building and containing the date of their erection, eventually became incorporated into the façade ornamentation. These stone signs gradually gave way to the gaudy wooden signboards which, of inestimable help to the illiterate, became so striking a feature of the London streets in the 17th and 18th centuries. The earliest signs were quite simple with a single device closely related to the occupant's trade. By the 18th century, however, they often contained double or triple devices which bore little or no relevance to the tradesmen's occupation. These wooden signs were always brightly painted and often gilded, with an ornately carved wooden frame. They hung out at right angles to the street on heavy wrought iron brackets. Competing for recognition, they grew bigger and bigger in size until they almost completely blocked off both sun and air from London's narrow streets. Often they became far too heavy for their brackets and crashed down to earth, killing and maiming pedestrians. When the brackets did hold, entire fronts of buildings sometimes collapsed under the weight of the boards which, as well as sign boards, showed pawnbrokers' premises advertised by the familiar three balls, undertakers' by coffins, barbers' by striped poles, taverns by tankards, opticians by spectacles. It was not, however, until 1762 that an Act was passed forbidding these hanging signboards in the CITY OF LONDON and WESTMINSTER. The signs were now required to be fixed flat to the building, and those that were so heralded the birth of the shop front fascia of today. Tavern keepers seemed generally to have defied the law with impunity, as did certain other tradesmen.

In 1765 another Act was passed requiring the Court of Common Council to affix name tablets to the corners of each street, square and lane. Three years later only 12 streets had complied; but by 1770 three quarters of all streets were named and their buildings

Street signs all along Cheapside. Detail from an engraving by Bowles, c.1752.

numbered. Both trade signs and numbers were displayed. By 1800 signboards had almost completely given way to shop fascias, often with gilded and carved lettering. The last signboard, depicting a half moon, hung outside the premises of George III's official stay-maker in HOLYWELL STREET. But many streets, courts and passages still bore, and continue to bear, the names of the most prominent signs that were once displayed there. The best examples of sign painting were those done by the highly skilled coach painters of LONG ACRE. As early as 1700 there is a record of £500 being paid to one of these craftsmen for a sign. This would include the actual sign plus an elaborately carved and gilded frame and the wrought iron brackets. The less prosperous tradesmen bought their boards at the sign of the Blackamoor's Head in SHOE LANE and FLEET STREET. The sign makers and painters held large stocks of all the standard signs, already painted with the usual trade devices and carved frames. However, many signboards were extremely complicated, for when a tradesman bought an existing business he often incorporated the sign of that business, whose customers he hoped to retain, with his own. Also, when apprentices set up on their own, they frequently used their former masters' devices and combined them with others of their own devising. Moreover, since certain streets were known for the particular trades practised there, it became essential to make variations in the signs and symbols used. Shared premises, too, led to further variations and to the necessity of the pairing of devices when one sign served for two tradesmen occupied in quite different trades. This explains some of the more incongruously paired tradesmen's signboards such as the Bull and Bedpost, the Three Nuns and Hare, the Whale and Gate and the Goat and Compasses (sometimes supposed to be a corruption of God Encompasseth Us). Adding to these confusions in design were mistakes in heraldry, a growing taste for puns, and ignorance of what was intended to be represented: this led, for instance, to the Order of the Garter sign being known colloquially as the Leg and Star.

Devices most commonly used in London street signs were those connected with royalty, heraldic and religious symbols, national heroes and patron saints, fauna, flora and buildings. Besides the familiar white and red roses of Lancaster and York, there were the Portcullis of John of Gaunt, the White Swan of Edward III, the Blue Boar of Richard III and the White Horse of the House of Hanover. The incidence of the Feathers denoted the popularity of the current heir apparent; and the numbers of Royal Oaks the affection in which Charles II was held, particularly among innkeepers, after the Restoration. The sign of the Highlander, favoured by tobacconists, was used originally to denote a Jacobite rendezvous. Many tradesmen used heraldic devices based on the crests of their livery companies.

Portraits of well-known people were sometimes used as trade signs for related professions. Shakespeare, Virgil and Pope were used by booksellers. Archimedes or Isaac Newton graced the premises of the makers of scientific instruments. Apothecaries used likenesses of Galen and Glauber; and artists, colourmen and printsellers, portraits of Hogarth and Rembrandt. Popular military and naval heroes, such as Lord Nelson and the Duke of Marlborough, were frequently to be seen outside taverns and inns. Likenesses of Blackamoors and

Red Indians were also common. Soon after the return of the first Crusaders, the Saracen's Head became a favourite sign. And during the ages of discovery, Red Indian braves smoking pipes were as commonly seen outside tobacconists as Highlanders. Dyers, mercers and drapers often used the Indian Queen; distillers the Noble Savage; and Goldsmiths the Morocco Head. When Negro slaves became common as servants and pages, the coffee houses that employed them to serve their beverages in gaily coloured uniforms and turbans often advertised themselves with signs such as the Blackamoor's Head, the Black Boy or the Black Girl. Angels appeared as early as 1200 on tradesmens' signs in BISHOPSGATE and were used in signs for the FLETCHERS' COMPANY in 1486 and again by the TALLOW CHANDLERS in 1602. The anchor, the Christian symbol of Hope, became part of the Hope and Anchor device used for the sign of the MASTER MARINERS' COMPANY. The Bell is one of the oldest recorded inn signs and usually denoted the proximity of a church. Adam and Eve appeared on fruiterers' trade signs: the Bible was used by booksellers; and Noah's Ark for the arms of the SHIPWRIGHTS' COMPANY. Most traders and craftsmen had their personal patron saint. Woolcombers used St Blaise; shoemakers had the choice of either St Crispin or St Hugh; St Peter protected locksmiths; St Luke looked after painters; St George was used by all and sundry. The sign of the Three Kings was used regularly by inns, since the Magi were the patron saints of travellers. Each king had his own astrological sign and these, in turn, were used on inn signs, giving rise, for instance, to the Seven Stars, the Half Moon, and the Sun.

Animals were equally popular. Some were obviously related to the trades which adopted them: the beaver to the hatters, the civet cat to perfumers and the leopard to the skinners. Ironmongers and armourers sometimes advertised their presence with a lobster because of the similarity between the soldier in his armour and the lobster in his shell. Scallop shells, a favourite decorative motif with carvers, was a popular sign with joiners. Animals were particularly common on inn signs. At the sign of the Dog and Bear or at the Bull, bear- and bull-baiting were usually offered as occasional supplementary entertainment. Sometimes live animals in cages were used as signs. A vulture was used in this way outside an inn in CORNHILL. The sign of the Swan with Two Necks has an interesting origin: in the 16th century swans were all branded on their beaks by the marks of one of their three legally entrusted groups of owners, the DYERS' COMPANY, the Crown and the VINTNERS' COMPANY. Most of the latter were tavern keepers and their particular mark was two nicks which, in time, became two necks.

Trees and plants, when depicted in tradesmen's signs, were, like animals, usually related to their trades. Cabinet makers used walnuts; silk merchants, mulberries; Italian warehousemen, olives and lemons; grocers, figs; and confectioners, pineapples. Certain other plants and fruits were used because of their connection with the patron saints of particular traders. Many famous artists, for example Richard Wilson, started their careers as sign painters. Others painted signs to cancel out debts to landlords and tradesmen. William Hogarth was not only an adept painter of signs but he also engraved tradesmen's cards and billheads which generally reproduced the tradesman's sign or a detail from it.

Oysters being sold from a Billingsgate stall in 1861, when 'prices ruled very high' at the equivalent of 5p per pint.

Street Vendors Plied their trade in London from very early times, the word 'coster' appearing in an English manuscript of 1292. In the 15th century John Lydgate, a Benedictine monk from Bury St Edmunds, wrote of the numbers and noise of the street vendors in London; and by Shakespeare's time costers were so much part of London life that they appear in many of his plays.

Because they could not afford to patronise shops and were, in any case, discouraged from entering them in case they put off wealthy customers, thousands of poor Londoners had to be supplied with the necessities of life where they lived, cheaply and in small quantities; and only traders willing to work long hours pushing laden barrows through miles of squalid courts and alleys supplied this need. Accepting this, authorities turned a blind eye to unlicensed traders so long as they kept moving. Merchandise of almost every description was 'carried and cried' in the streets, and 'What d'ye lack, what d'ye lack, my masters? . . .' was daily heard, together with colourful descriptions of goods, resulting in an almost deafening hubbub that amazed country visitors. Vendors kept rigidly to their own wares – wet, dry or shell fish, poultry, game and cheeses; vegetables, fruit, flowers and 'greenstuff'; eatables and drinkables such as hot eels, pickled whelks, sheep's trotters, hot wine and asses' milk; stationery and literature including ballad sheets and playbills; livestock such as dogs, squirrels, and birds; manufactured articles – matches, rat poison, razors and shirt buttons; and second-hand clothing and other items. Costermongers, who got their name from 'costard', a large ribbed apple, sold only fish, fruit and vegetables. Always regarded as the cream of the traders, they were noted for their colourful language and fierce independence. From the Middle Ages a well defined form of 'coster regional royalty' sprang up resulting, in the 1880s, in the PEARLY KINGS AND QUEENS. The highly competitive trade of costermongering attracted bullies attempting to seize good pitches leading to fights and trouble with authority.

Being unlicensed, the costers could not expect legal protection, so in each borough was chosen a strong, quick-witted representative or local 'king', ready to protect their rights. These coster 'monarchies' were hereditary, the 'royal children' being trained for later responsibilities.

The nave of OLD ST PAUL'S was a favorite haunt of Tudor street vendors, until the COMMON COUNCIL passed an Act forbidding the carrying of baskets of bread, fish, flesh or fruit, or the leading of mules or horses through the Cathedral. In 1590 women were prosecuted for making a nuisance as they sold oranges at the gates of the ROYAL EXCHANGE. Women selling fruit and nosegays in HYDE PARK in the 17th century always found willing customers among the *beaux* who paraded there. One of the earliest travelling salesmen in the HAYMARKET was a vendor of sea-coals whose trade token, now in the BRITISH MUSEUM, bears the inscription: 'Nathaniel Robins, the sea-coal seller 1666', and on the reverse, 'HAY MARKET in PICCADILLA, his half-penny'. The HAYMARKET was also the haunt of 'Tiddy Diddy Doll', the gingerbread man.

London's street vendors developed their own individual way of life, with their own superstitions, ceremonies, secret language and a fierce loyalty to their own kind. Unemployment was a serious problem in the mid-19th century, so that traders' ranks were swelled by newcomers. Costermongering attracted the most recruits, and Henry Mayhew reckoned there were at least 30,000 on the streets in 1851, all the time being increased as unemployed mill-hands, servants, farm labourers and even actors 'took to the barrow'. Surprisingly, the regular costers never resented these newcomers competing for valuable sites; in fact they expressed pity for them, knowing what lay ahead of them. Although a good new barrow could be bought for £2 12s in the mid-19th century, barrows were usually hired at 3d a day (6d on Saturdays). Donkeycarts were rarely hired, £3 10s being the average buying price; but donkeys were frequently hired from fellow costers at 2s 6d to 3s weekly. Shallows (baskets), used

The Muffin Man announced his presence in the streets by ringing a handbell.

mostly by flower girls, were hired for 1d daily, even when they could be bought for as little as 1s 6d. A pewter quart pot for measuring onions cost 2s to buy, 2d a day to hire. The costers' trade was seasonal. In winter time sprats and herrings sold best. March heralded the arrival of spring flowers and May brought fish and rooted plants. New potatoes, peas and beans arrived in June, and in July cherries and soft fruit were in abundance, though CHOLERA epidemics – thought to be spread by dirty fruit – damaged trade. September brought apples and pears and good daily profits. October was the month for oysters, a staple working-class food. December and Christmas meant demand for oranges and lemons, imported from abroad.

The 19th-century trader usually rose at 4 a.m. and hurried to the central market to load his barrow – average weight of load 13 cwt – or his basket. In his 12- to 14-hour day he would walk about 10 miles, crying his wares and hitting a tin box with a stick until his voice gave out, when a boy apprentice took over. Any goods left over at the end of the day were sold cheap, or dumped, to avoid pushing a heavy barrow home. A succession of wet days spelt ruin for the traders in perishable goods.

Ballad sellers were almost as frequently seen as costermongers. Newness was the great attraction, though old favorites were always available. Once a crowd had formed, the ballad seller would sing his numbers lustily, to teach the tunes, before selling the sheets for ½d to 1d. As William Chappell reported, 'Tinkers sang catches; milkmaids sang ballads . . . even the beggars had their special songs'. Ballad selling was a comparatively profitable trade, often resulting in a day's takings of 20s when ½d bought ¼lb meat. 'Running patterers' were mostly concerned with news ballads, especially reports of murders and executions.

One of the most famed of all street vendors was Thomas Britton, the 'musical small-coal man', who lived in one room above a stable at a corner of JERUSALEM PASSAGE. Educated through his own efforts in the highest branches of music, he attracted around him the greatest musicians of the day including Handel. He founded a musical club which met at his humble room for 40 years, coffee being sold to members at 1d a cup. Handel played the harpsichord, Bannister or Medler first violin, while Britton performed skilfully on the viol da gamba. Having completed his coal round by midday, Britton would join his friends at Bateman's, the booksellers, still in his smutty blue smock.

Up until the 1st World War London's streets remained crowded with traders. The traditional dress of female vendors remained sternly conventional, consisting, in 1903, of black cloth or plush jacket, large white apron, black hat of either feather or sailor variety, slovenly down-at-heel boots and, most important of all, large gold earrings. The 'flower girls' were usually elderly married women, shawled and befeathered, and were to be seen in their dozens in the early morning at COVENT GARDEN, sitting on doorsteps or upturned baskets, making their buttonholes for the day, and anxiously scanning the weather. By the 1920s the STREET CRIES of the traders had greatly diminished, at least in the politer areas of London. Even the muffin-man's bell, so welcome in a winter afternoon's gloom, was seldom heard, though ex-servicemen, selling anything from matches to marzipan, were all too frequent. HATTON GARDEN, SAFFRON HILL and CLERKENWELL

were the chief haunts of the Italian ice-cream traders, the suspect hygiene of whom was said to prompt the frequent question, 'What'll you 'ave, Strabry, Vanniller or Microbe?' Other Italians modelled and sold stucco figures. Old ladies who had seen better days still knocked on doors, selling recipes for furniture restoration, and men pushed barrowloads of tortoises. Curbside hawkers were to be found wherever queues or crowds congregated, HOLBORN at Christmas time being a favorite haunt. With their nodding dolls and acrobatic toys they were more exciting to children than the smartest shops, and the chestnut-seller's glowing coals and succulent aroma cheered up gloomy days. From tree tops and from behind dustbins London's cats trotted after the regular 'cat's meat man' with his horse flesh on skewers. The firewood vendor, itinerant tinker, 'Old Clo' Man' and rag, bone and bottle man or woman were some of the longest surviving traders.

The Boat Race mascot-sellers, the quack medicine-seller in mortar-board and faded barrister's gown, the cheap-jack and mistletoe merchant have disappeared. Prohibitions, rules, regulations and bye-laws have persistently pushed the traders off the streets.

But the traditions of centuries die hard; and once again unemployment is providing new recruits to this ancient, historic occupation. One can still buy chestnuts fresh from the glowing coals, rosettes, the colours of football teams, spring's first daffodils and summer's first strawberries from laden barrows. A van has replaced the ice-cream vendor's cart but children still listen for his bell or recorded jingles. (*See also* STREET CRIES.)

Strombolo House *and* **Gardens**   *Chelsea*. Tea gardens which stood on the south side of PIMLICO ROAD. They were open by 1762. The gardens, unusually, offered no entertainments and were celebrated mainly for a fine fountain and their position opposite the CHELSEA BUN HOUSE. The house was still standing in 1829, but was no longer a place of amusement. The grounds were later occupied by the Orange Tavern and Tea Gardens and the gardens were used by the Orange Theatre in 1831–2 for amateur dramatics. In the 1840s ST BARNABAS CHURCH covered part of the site.

Stroud Green   *N4*. Formerly in the southern part of the Borough of HORNSEY, and now in the London Borough of HARINGEY, Stroud Green is more commonly referred to as FINSBURY PARK, an area which also embraces parts of the Boroughs of ISLINGTON and HACKNEY. Stroud Green was marshy, neglected land, overgrown with brushwood till the 19th century, with only two, large houses, Japan House, which was demolished in 1870 when Crouch Hill station was built, and Stapleton Hall, a farm building dating from the 17th century, part of which survives in Stapleton Hall Road and is used as a Conservative Club. SEVEN SISTERS ROAD to the south, named after a group of elms at the TOTTENHAM end, was cut through in 1832 as a new road into London. A wayside railway station was opened on the Great Northern Railway in 1861 and named Seven Sisters but was renamed Finsbury Park in 1869 when the adjacent Hornsey Wood was opened to the public. As a sop to the electors of the City district of FINSBURY, who wanted an open space, it was named Finsbury Park, although Hornsey Park would have been a more appropriate name. Finsbury

Park station became an important suburban rail junction with branch lines to East FINCHLEY (1866) and ALEXANDRA PALACE (1873) and underground lines beneath it in 1904 (NORTHERN to MOORGATE) and 1906 (PICCADILLY to the WEST END). In the 1960s the VICTORIA LINE was added and in the 1970s the suburban, overland lines were electrified. Crouch Hill station was opened in 1870 and Stroud Green station in 1881 and in consequence Stroud Green was rapidly built up. This Victorian housing largely survives although there has been some rebuilding by the Council and the Victorian properties are often in multiple occupancy. One building of note is the dairy at the junction of Stroud Green Road, Hanley Road and Crouch Hill which is distinguished by seven incised wall panels depicting dairy farming scenes. They were executed in the 1890s in an old method called *sgraffito*. North of Stroud Green the land rises to the Hog's Back, a ridge which extends to HIGHGATE. Fine views can be obtained from Ridge Road.

Strutton Ground *SW1*. The continuation of HORSEFERRY ROAD into VICTORIA STREET, its name is a corruption of Stourton Ground from Stourton House, the mansion of the Lords Dacre of the South. The street market here, the only one in the area, is bounded by VICTORIA STREET, VAUXHALL BRIDGE ROAD and MILLBANK.

Strype Street *E1*. Formerly known as Strype's Yard, it takes its name from the house of John Strype, silk merchant, whose house stood nearby (*see* MIDDLESEX STREET). His son, John, the historian who edited and enlarged Stow's *Survey of London*, was born in the house in 1643.

Sudbrook Park *Petersham, Surrey*. Built 1717–26 by James Gibbs (fresh from his studies of the Baroque in Rome) for John Campbell, 2nd Duke of Argyll and Greenwich after his marriage to the humble Jane Warburton. He had played a prominent part in securing the Union with Scotland, the defeat of Louis XIV and the Hanoverian Succession. George I rewarded him somewhat tardily in 1726 by leasing him 30 acres of RICHMOND PARK. Special features are the panelled Cube Room with a marble mantelpiece carved by J.M. Rysbrack and a gilt mirror bearing the Argyll coat of arms; and the south front with elegant steps up to the garden entrance. The main, or north entrance was altered by bringing forward the portico too prominently. Extensions were made by the Duke to the west where a separate annexe was built for his 'useless pack' of five daughters – 'the bawling Campbells' who could then be left to be brought up by the servants. The youngest of these daughters, Lady Mary Coke, after death had mercifully removed an appalling husband, achieved fame as writer of a journal (1766–91) which gives an intimate account of life not only at Sudbrook but also in Court circles.

By 1842 the family had given up Sudbrook which was bought back by the Crown and then promptly leased for a hydropathic spa where the fashionable 'water cure' could be practised – successfully in the case of Charles Darwin, disastrously in that of Richard Dresser who died from 'assault by water'. The doctor, James Ellis, was tried for manslaughter but was acquitted. By 1891 Sudbrook had become an hotel and since 1898 it has been the home of the Richmond Golf

Club which maintains the building and grounds in an excellent state (*see also* GOLF CLUBS).

Sudbury *Middlesex*. Here was the principal demesne farm of the Archbishop of Canterbury until Headstone, PINNER replaced it as the Archbishop's main MIDDLESEX residence in the 14th century.

Hundred Elms farmhouse survives in Elms Lane, Sudbury to the rear of modern housing development. It is a square two-storey building constructed in the middle of the 19th century but adjoining it is a 16th-century outbuilding. This is built with very fine quality red bricks cut and rubbed to make mullioned windows. Its original use remains as a mystery although various theories have been suggested, including a chapel.

Thomas Trollope, father of the novelist, came to Ilotts farm, Sudbury in 1813–15 and his son used it as a model for 'Orley Farm'. Sudbury was also the home of Sir William H. Perkin, the inventor of aniline dyes. Victorian development reflected Sudbury's proximity to HARROW SCHOOL and the railway line into EUSTON. Further development was encouraged at the beginning of the 20th century by the PICCADILLY LINE whose station (Sudbury Town) was rebuilt by Charles Holden in 1930–1 in a then new style of architecture. The Great Central line was opened across the settlement in 1905–6 and a further significant improvement in communications occurred with the coming of the trams in 1910.

Suffolk Lane *EC4*. Named after the Duke of Suffolk who had a house here in the 15th century. The MERCHANT TAYLORS bought it and converted it into a school. It was destroyed by the GREAT FIRE but new buildings were put up and the school continued to exist here until its removal to the CHARTERHOUSE in 1875. No. 22 was built in the late 1780s. Excavations in 1964–5 between Suffolk and Bush Lanes uncovered a warren of walls some 22 ft thick which were thought to be the remains of an important civic building of Roman London.

Suffolk Place *SW1*. Extends eastward from HAYMARKET to SUFFOLK STREET, and takes its name from the Earls of Suffolk, who had stables on this site in the 17th century. The whole street was rebuilt in the 1820s by John Nash as part of his metropolitan improvement schemes, and the stucco-faced range on the north side, extending round to Nos 3 and 4 HAYMARKET and to the west side of SUFFOLK STREET, is one of the few surviving examples of his smaller-scaler street architecture. The matching range on the south side of Suffolk Place was demolished when Nos 1 and 2 PALL MALL EAST were rebuilt by Sir Reginald Blomfield in 1915–22.

Suffolk Street *SW1*. So-called because the Earls of Suffolk had stables on this site in the early 17th century. It is a short cul-de-sac extending northward from PALL MALL EAST; off its west side SUFFOLK PLACE leads to HAYMARKET. On the east side No.1, now occupied by the British School of Osteopathy, is by Sir Reginald Blomfield in his Parisian style and dates from 1906, with a northward extension in 1924. The rest of Suffolk Street is virtually all that still survives south of OXFORD CIRCUS of John Nash's rebuildings made during the formation of REGENT STREET in the 1820s. All of the houses are faced with stucco, and several are by Nash himself. No. 5 is by G. Ledwell Taylor and No. 6 by Edward Cresy. Nos 6½ and 7 (the Gallery of the Royal Society of British Artists), by Nash, has a Roman Doric pedimented giant portico on an arched ground floor. Nos 8–11 are also by Nash, but Nos 12–17 (now partly rebuilt) are by Lewis Wyatt. Part of the west side is occupied by the attractive rear elevation of the HAYMARKET THEATRE, and much of the rest by the block designed by Nash which extends along the north side of SUFFOLK PLACE and round to Nos 3 and 4 HAYMARKET. Samuel Foote, the actor, lived here from about 1770. Dean Swift had lodgings here in 1771 and No. 29 was occupied by James Barry, the Irish historical painter, in 1773–6. The Marquess of Winchilsea was living at No. 7 in 1829 when he was challenged by the Duke of Wellington (*see* BATTERSEA PARK). Richard Cobden was living at No. 23 in 1865. Anthony Trollope, while staying at No. 14 in 1882, quarrelled so violently with a group of rowdy street musicians that he had a stroke and died a few days later in WELBECK STREET. Richard Dadd, the painter, lived at No. 15 where his father ran a silver-gilding and ormolu business. Richard murdered his father in 1843 and was later admitted to BETHLEM HOSPITAL.

Summerstown *SW17*. Lies between TOOTING and WIMBLEDON and is bisected by Garratt Lane, the main road connecting TOOTING with WANDSWORTH. As 'Sumerton' it is mentioned in *Domesday Book* and was probably then just a mill which in the 12th century belonged to Merton Priory. In the 15th century the area was densely wooded and was a favourite hunting ground of King Henry VII. It was during his reign that the woods were destroyed by fire. The road known as Burntwood Lane is a present-day reminder of that event. The River WANDLE, which flows through Summerstown, made the area an attraction both as a good fishing ground and for industry. From early times there are records of mills along the river banks.

During the reign of Elizabeth I the hamlet of Garratt, as Summerstown was then known, comprised one house called Garratt. The following years saw gradual cottage growth for the estate tenants, manor servants and the workers from the mills. It was then possible to sail directly into the area from the THAMES. The arrival of Huguenot refugees in 1572 saw the establishment of mills for calico and print dyeing. In the following century copper mills played an important part in the life of the area. In the mid-18th century the inhabitants found it necessary to elect a 'mayor' to protect their rights on the Common. A 6 ft long wooden sword was used to 'knight' the mayor (*see* MAYOR OF GARRATT). In the early 1800s there were still only 50 houses in the hamlet of Garratt. The Leathern Belle was the prominent inn. It faced the Common which is today known as Garratt Green. There were, however, enough inhabitants to warrant the opening of a School of Industry for girls in 1805. The first railroad sanctioned by Parliament, the SURREY IRON RAILWAY of 1801, passed directly through Garratt Lane on its route from CROYDON to WANDSWORTH, and by 1865 a fuse match factory and a silk printing works had been established, the population then being about 700.

In 1835 Dr Joshua Stanger erected a hall for use as a place of worship on Sundays and a school during the week. He built separate school premises in 1841, and in 1845 the original hall was consecrated as the Church

of St Mary the Virgin. The ecclesiastical district then took the name of Summerstown. Unfortunately, due to insecure foundations, the church had to be demolished. After some years in a temporary church, the new St Mary's was opened in 1904. In 1847 a National Day School connected with the church was opened. This was handed over to the London School Board in 1878 – the first Board school in WANDSWORTH. In 1853 a large works for Messrs Heath, print manufacturers, was built in Summerstown at a time when the old hamlet of Garratt was rapidly disappearing with the advent of the train and the tram. At the turn of the century the watercress beds were a marked feature of Summerstown. By then the area had been expanded with new streets and houses and the population had risen to about 3,000. Today the banks of the River WANDLE are still the scene of industry, but the area in general is no longer the attraction it was in past times, although an open space known as Garratt Park remains on the river's east bank. A large scrapyard pollutes the river which was once the source of good fishing and the whole area has a run-down and depressed appearance.

Sumner Place *SW7*. Built in 1851 on the SMITH'S CHARITY ESTATE, it probably takes its name from William Holme Sumner, once a trustee of the charity. Joseph Aloysius Hansom, architect and inventor of the hansom cab, lived at No. 27 in 1873–7.

Sun Inn *Church Road, Barnes, SW13*. Although this building was erected in 1750 there was previously a much older establishment on the same site. There was a bridge over the THAMES here in Tudor times and legend has it that Drake and Walsingham taught Queen Elizabeth I to play bowls here.

Sundridge Park *Kent*. Its earliest history shows that it was the property of the Bishop of Rochester. It is known that in 1301 'The manor of Sundresshe near Bromlegh' was owned by John le Blunt, draper of London. The estate remained in the ownership of the Blunt (or Blound) family for many years. In 1680 it came into the possession of Thomas Washer of LINCOLN'S INN. It was whilst in the hands of this family that it became known as 'Washers in the Wood'. In 1801, Claude Scott, a cornfactor, who later became a banker and Member of Parliament, bought the estate. The old house was demolished and the mansion, which still stands, built. The layout of the parklands and the building of the mansion were the combined work of Humphry Repton, John Nash and Samuel Wyatt. It is a large mansion with three giant porticos, and stuccoed a brilliant white, surrounded by beautiful parklands. The estate was occupied by the Scott family for over 100 years. In the 1870s the then novel idea of breeding pheasants was started here and the Prince of Wales came for the shooting. One of the Scotts bred racehorses and the horse Sundridge, bred and trained at Sundridge Park, was a famous sprinter and sire. The spread of the neighbouring BROMLEY created a demand for land for houses and eventually part of the parkland was sold as building land. In 1901 about 125 acres of the park were converted into a golf course. The Scotts left Sundridge Park soon after this and eventually the mansion became a hotel. It has since become the Sundridge Park Management Centre.

Sunnydene *108 Westwood Hill, Sydenham, SE26.* Built in 1868–70 to the designs of John Francis Bentley for the millionaire carrier, W.R. Sutton. The imposing redbrick house in the Tudor and Jacobean styles has now been converted into flats.

Surbiton *Surrey.* Created as a result of KINGSTON's refusal to accept the railway, which was forced to cut through rising ground to the south. Known at first as Kingston New Town or Kingston-on-Railway, the area was thus on the main line between London and Southampton and the south west. It became a very fashionable and desirable residential neighbourhood, earning itself the name 'Queen of the London Suburbs'. The bankers, COUTTS AND CO., made generous donations of land and money. Under an Improvement Act of 1855 Surbiton became independent of KINGSTON and became an urban district in 1894. It spread rapidly in area, particularly after the opening of the Kingston by-pass in 1927. In 1936 it achieved borough status, by which time it included TOLWORTH, HOOK and CHESSINGTON, but in 1965, as a result of the London Government Act, it was returned to KINGSTON.

Today Surbiton is very representative of good Victorian architecture, its churches of St Mark, St Matthew and St Andrew being typical of the Gothic style of the period. The districts around St Andrew's Square and Langley Avenue to Ditton Hill are both scheduled conservation areas. The Seething Wells district beside the THAMES was celebrated for its therapeutic springs; and the Water Works were erected here on the Portsmouth road in 1852, and are still noted for their embattled Romanesque towers.

Surrey Commercial Docks Built on the peninsula between the Lower Pool and Limehouse Reach 2 miles east of LONDON BRIDGE, as the only enclosed docks lying on the south bank of the THAMES. Their nucleus was the HOWLAND GREAT DOCK of 1697, later named Greenland Dock. The system finally consisted of nine docks, six timber ponds and a canal 3½ miles long. Covering 300 acres in all the docks belong to four companies and that is the reason for the irregular congeries of waters. The earliest of the enterprises there was that of the Surrey Canal Company which was formed to dig a navigable cut from ROTHERHITHE to Epsom with the aim of linking up with the Wey Navigation and having branches to various small towns on the way, mainly to transport to London the produce of market gardens in the low-lying countryside through which it passed. The Company obtained its Act in 1801 and Ralph Dodd, the speculator, was its engineer. Although the shortlived Croydon Canal was linked with it for a time, it became in the end less of a waterway than a very long dock. In 1802 a plan was evolved for a shipping basin with a lock into the THAMES; and in 1807 the first ship entered this Grand Surrey Basin which was 3 acres in extent and in effect a widening of the terminus of the canal. The enterprise was then being run by the Commercial Dock Company, and two years later another group called the Baltic Dock Company was formed. In 1825 a Grand Ship Canal, without locks, was projected to start from the Basin and run down to Portsmouth, but the scheme did not even reach Parliament. Even the relatively modest GRAND SURREY CANAL never reached further then PECKHAM. In 1855 another company was formed called the Grand Surrey Docks and Canal Company and a new Act was obtained, the result being a dock of 16 acres called the Albion, a basin of 3 acres, and a new lock, all completed by 1860. In 1864 the company merged with its competing neighbour as the Surrey Commercial Dock Company, and, after several decades of poor profits, the docks became more prosperous than they had been in the past.

At the end of the century the Greenland Dock was enlarged to 22 acres in order to accommodate larger vessels. It came into operation in 1904. The engineer responsible was Sir John Wolf-Barry. When the whaling industry at the Greenland Dock declined, the chief trade became softwood from Scandinavia and the Baltic and so it remained until the whole 120-acre complex was closed in 1970. The place had developed a special breed of dockers with their own slang and special hats for carrying planks of wood. With the closure, a whole local and traditional way of life vanished.

The Surrey Docks suffered severely from air attacks during the 2nd World War, but the South Dock was pumped dry and used for the construction of some of the concrete caissons needed for D-Day's Mulberry Harbour. A scheme of redevelopment for a community, covering an area larger than HYDE PARK and using some of the dock waters as a landscape element, designed by R. Seifert and Partners, was accepted by the GREATER LONDON COUNCIL and SOUTHWARK Council in 1981.

Surrey County Cricket Club Founded in 1845 by a committee under the chairmanship of William Ward, MP for the CITY OF LONDON and a director of the BANK OF ENGLAND. Surrey was one of the original nine counties which competed in the County Championship of 1873. It is generally accepted that the Championship began in that year although a county competition without any formal structure had been in existence for many years before. Surrey's headquarters and home ground have always been the OVAL, KENNINGTON, a ground, originally a market garden, leased from the DUCHY OF CORNWALL. The first game played there was in 1845 between the Gentlemen of Surrey and the Players of Surrey. The club has produced many famous cricketers. Surrey have won the county championship 18 times, more than any county apart from Yorkshire. Their colours are chocolate and their badge the Prince of Wales's feathers.

Surrey Gardens Music Hall *Walworth.* Built in 1856 in the SURREY ZOOLOGICAL GARDENS by Horace Jones. It was an exotic building with a roof decorated with minarets and pagodas. It could hold 10,000 people and cost £18,000. A few months after it opened seven people were trampled to death after a false fire alarm was given at a service taken by the Revd Charles Spurgeon, the Baptist preacher. It was rebuilt after a fire in 1861. In 1868 it was temporarily used to house patients of ST THOMAS'S HOSPITAL until their new buildings on the ALBERT EMBANKMENT were completed. It was closed and demolished in 1872. Small terraced houses were built on the site.

Surrey Iron Railway Horse-drawn railway which ran from Ram Creek, WANDSWORTH through MERTON, MITCHAM and Waddon to Pitlake, CROYDON. It was authorised by an Act of Parliament in 1801 and is notable because it was the first public railway and the first

The Surrey Gardens Music Hall, built in 1856 to the designs of Horace Jones, was demolished in 1872.

railway company in the world. Previously horse-drawn railways had been owned by firms for transporting only their own goods, but the Surrey Iron Railway worked on a toll principle with users providing their own horses and carts. One horse could pull ten wagons, each carrying 3½ tons of coal, lime or grain. The WANDSWORTH to CROYDON line was opened in 1803 and branch lines were built to CARSHALTON and MERSTHAM by 1805. It closed down in 1846 in the face of competition from steam railways.

Surrey Theatre *Blackfriars Road*. Opened in 1782 as the Royal Circus and Equestrian Philharmonic Academy by Charles Hughes and Charles Dibdin. Burned down in 1803, it was rebuilt by Rudolph Cabanel, architect of the OLD VIC. In 1809 it was converted into a theatre and renamed the Surrey. In 1816–23 it was run by Thomas Dibdin who retired a ruined man. In 1829 Douglas Jerrold's *Black Eyed Susan* was staged here. In 1845 Sir Arthur Sullivan's father was violinist. It was then rebuilt by J. Ellis after a fire in 1865, and used as a cinema in 1920–4, then left empty and used as a scenery paint shop. It was demolished in 1934 to make way for an extension to the ROYAL OPHTHALMIC HOSPITAL.

Surrey Zoological Gardens The Surrey Literary, Scientific and Zoological Institution was founded by Edward Cross at a meeting at the Horns Tavern, KENNINGTON in 1831. Cross agreed to sell to the Institution the menagerie which he had established at EXETER CHANGE, and Lord Holland agreed to let a 13-acre site east of VAUXHALL GARDENS. For some time the Surrey Gardens proved more popular than their rivals, those of the Zoological Society in REGENT'S PARK (*see* ZOO). The Regent's Park zoo was, however, subsidised whereas the Surrey Gardens had to rely mainly upon the 1s admission charge. So, in addition to the animals, the Surrey Gardens soon offered other attractions – flower shows, exhibitions, fireworks, 'Colossal Pictorial Typorama', representations of such dramatic events as the Siege of Gibraltar and the storming of Badajoz, volcanic eruptions and those other shows for which London's pleasure gardens were celebrated. These rendered the Gardens extremely popular for some years – in 1850 *Punch* referred to 'that grand shilling's worth of beasts, flowers, music, and fireworks – the Surrey Zoological' but the competition of the CRYSTAL PALACE proved formidable; and when Nathaniel Hawthorne visited the Gardens in

1855, to see a panoramic spectacle of the Battle of Sebastopol, he was disappointed. They were, to be sure, 'provided with lions and lionesses, also a giraffe or two, some camels, a polar bear who plunges into a pool of water for bits of cake, and two black bears who sit on their haunches or climb poles; besides a wilderness of monkies, some parrots and macaws, an ostrich . . . and an aquarium, but the menagerie, though the ostensible staple of the Gardens', was 'rather poor and scanty', while the resort as a whole proved 'a rather poor place of suburban amusement'.

The animals were sold by auction that year, part of the proceeds being used to build a large, new concert hall in which, in addition to musical performances, the evangelical preacher, Charles Spurgeon, delivered his fiery sermons during one of which, in 1856, a false report of fire resulted in a panic and seven deaths in his audience. A few years later a fire did break out and the concert hall was burned down. It was rebuilt but only to be used soon afterwards as temporary accommodation by ST THOMAS'S HOSPITAL, whose own buildings were being reconstructed. The Surrey Gardens were sold for development in 1877. Penton Place covers part of the site (*see also* SURREY GARDENS MUSIC HALL).

Sussex Gardens *W2*. Known until 1938 as Grand Junction Road, this broad avenue was an important feature of the original layout of BAYSWATER. On the north side, formerly Cambridge Terrace, lived Barry O'Meara, surgeon to Napoleon on St Helena, at No. 32, in 1830–6; and at No. 34, in 1833–64, John Doyle, political cartoonist, and his son, Richard, who designed the famous cover for *Punch*. Sir Arthur Conan Doyle was his nephew. On the south side, formerly Oxford Terrace, Henry Buckle, author of *The History of Civilisation*, lived at No. 115 in 1843–6. At the western end stands the church of St James, parish church of PADDINGTON since 1845.

Sussex House *12 and 14 Upper Mall, Hammersmith, W6*. A large three-storey house which dates from about 1726. It may contain parts of an earlier house which was on the site in 1628. The entrance has fluted pilasters, curved pediment and a patterned fanlight. The name may come from the occasional residence of Augustus Frederick, Duke of Sussex, but, more probably, from his association with the district. He laid the foundation stone of HAMMERSMITH BRIDGE in 1825.

Admission ticket, issued for 1s, for the Surrey Zoological Gardens. Founded in 1831, they were sold for redevelopment in 1877.

Sussex Lodge A detached house, also known as 27 SUSSEX PLACE, built by William Smith from designs by John Nash. In 1840–78 it was the home of Sir Francis Grant, and later became the property of his granddaughter, Mabel, who married Lord Annesley and lived there till 1906. In 1908–33 Lord Wavertree, a noted sportsman who bred the Derby winner, Minoru, lived here. The house was demolished in 1957 and replaced by the headquarters of the ROYAL COLLEGE OF OBSTETRICIANS AND GYNAECOLOGISTS.

Sussex Place *NW1.* So called after Augustus, Duke of Sussex, George IV's younger brother. This extraordinary terrace has curved wings; its 26 houses have bow windows. Along the roofline there are ten pointed cupolas; the façade is adorned with 56 Corinthian columns. The terrace looks on to the Lake and probably enjoys the most agreeable views of any in REGENT'S PARK. John Lockhart, Sir Walter Scott's son-in-law and biographer, lived at No. 24 in 1828–55; Herbert and Cynthia Asquith occupied No. 8 in 1913–40. During the 1960s, the terrace was rebuilt behind the original façade as premises for the London Graduate School of Business Studies. The Royal College of Obstetricians and Gynaecologists is at No. 27.

Sussex Square *W2.* One of the recently rebuilt squares of Tyburnia. Sir Winston Churchill lived at the former No. 2 in 1920–4 and Admiral Jellicoe at the former No. 26, after the Battle of Jutland. The square was originally built in 1843, the year of the death of the Duke of Sussex, King George III's sixth son.

Suthrey House *119 Mortlake High Street, SW14.* A curious L-shaped building of which the projecting larger section is 17th-century. The miniature courtyard, early 18th-century railings and extension are particularly attractive. Wilfrid Scawen Blunt, the poet, lived here as a boy. It is still a private house.

Sutton *Surrey.* Derives its name from the Saxon Sudtuna, meaning southern farmstead, and was probably a 6th- or 7th-century settlement. Throughout the Middle Ages it was an agricultural village. The turnpike road from London to Brighton was constructed through it in 1755, but its real expansion came in the period 1850–80 after the construction of the railway from London to Epsom in 1847. During that period Sutton became an early commuter town with large numbers of Victorian houses of all sizes from mansions for the well-to-do to smaller houses for city clerks and their families. The first expansion, to the north of the village in what was called and still is Sutton New Town, started in 1850 with an early Victorian public house called the Jenny Lind after the Swedish opera singer. When a covered reservoir was built on the chalk just south of the railway in 1861, expansion started on the chalk lands. Stowford, one of the first houses built there (in 1865), still stands. In late Victorian times Sutton possessed several institutions set up by the private philanthropy of its richer citizens, such as the Public Hall built in 1878, the Adult School built in 1895 and one of the earliest Nursery Schools founded in 1909. The last two were founded by T.B. Walls, the founder of the Walls's food firm.

During the early 20th century, the town continued to grow. The area is still predominantly a residential one. It has lost all but one of its cinemas, but it possesses in the new Central Library, opened in 1975, one of the finest local libraries in Europe. A municipal theatre, by conversion of the 1930s brick Christian Science Church, is planned. Sutton's mile-long shopping street is a centre for shoppers from a considerable area around. St Nicholas, the original parish church, probably founded in the 7th century, was rebuilt to the designs of Edwin Nash in 1862 in Romanesque revival style, and All Saints on the northern edge is a fine Victorian Gothic Church, built in 1865 to the designs of S.S. Teulon, to serve the fast growing New Town

The pointed cupolas and curved wings of Sussex Place in c.1829 from an engraving after T.H. Shepherd.

area. Apart from the Baptist Church in Cheam Road, an Art Deco building of 1933 by N.F. Cachemaille-Day, and the two Anglican Churches mentioned above, Sutton has only four other listed buildings: Trinity Methodist Church near St Nicholas, a 1909 Gothic revival building; the Cricketers Inn at the Sutton Green end of the High Street, an early 19th-century boarded building; the National Westminster Bank at 26–28 High Street built in 1901 with fine Art Nouveau stone carving on its façade; and Sutton Lodge, a Georgian chalkland farmhouse on the Brighton Road near the site of the old southern tollbar.

Sutton Court *Chiswick, W4.* The manor house of the manor of Sutton, it was rebuilt in the late 18th century and demolished, to be replaced by flats, in 1896. Among its occupiers were Chaloner Chute, Speaker of the House of Commons for a few months before his death in 1659, and the Earl and Countess (Mary, daughter of Oliver Cromwell) of Fauconberg. Later owners were Lord Burlington and the Dukes of Devonshire.

Swakeleys *Ickenham, Middlesex.* Takes its name from Robert Swalcliffe, who had acquired land here by 1329. The present mansion, built by Sir Edmund Wright in 1629–38, was probably erected on the site of an earlier manor house. It is H-shaped, and built of redbrick with stone or plastered dressings. Internal features of note are a mid-17th century painted wooden screen in the hall, and mural paintings over the staircase attributed to Robert Streater. Samuel Pepys came here in September 1665 to call upon Sir Robert Vyner, the London financier and later Lord Mayor. He recorded: 'A very pleasant place bought by him of Sir James Harrington's lady. He took us up and down with great respect, and showed us all his house and grounds; and it is a place not very moderne in the garden or house, but the most uniforme in all that ever I saw; and some things to excess. Pretty to see over the screene of the hall (put up by Sir J. Harrington, a Long parliament man) the King's head, and my Lord of Essex on one side and Fairfax on the other; and upon the other side of the screene, the parson of the parish and the lord of the manor and his sisters. The window-cases, door-cases, and chimneys of all the house are marble. He showed me a black boy that he had, that died of a consumption, and being dead, he caused him to be dried in an oven, and lies there entire in a box.' In 1981 Swakeleys belonged to the London Postal Region Sports Club who used it as a clubhouse and changing rooms. It was converted to offices in 1982.

Swallow Passage *W1.* On the Millfield Estate (*see* HANOVER SQUARE), it is a short alley connecting OXFORD STREET with PRINCES STREET. It marks the northern extremity of SWALLOW STREET, which, until the formation of REGENT STREET upon most of its old course, was the principal thoroughfare between PICCADILLY and OXFORD STREET.

Swallow Street *W1.* Now a short street extending northward from PICCADILLY to the REGENT STREET Quadrant. It takes its name from Thomas Swallow, the tenant in the 16th century of a field here, and is first mentioned as a street in 1671. Within the next 50 years building had extended Swallow Street northward all the way to OXFORD STREET, but all of it except the

southern end was swallowed up in 1813–21 by the formation of REGENT STREET along its course. At its northern extremity the line of Swallow Street also survives as the short passageway between PRINCES STREET and OXFORD STREET, now called Swallow Passage.

Swan *66 Bayswater Road, W2.* First established in 1775 as a coaching inn and the first stop past Tyburn gallows. In 1819 it became the Floral Tea Gardens, complete with skittle alley, but later reverted to use as a tavern.

Swan and Edgar Ltd *49 Regent Street.* William Edgar had a stall selling haberdashery in ST JAMES'S MARKET when he came to London, and used to sleep under it at night. He met Mr Swan and together they ran a shop in the LUDGATE area. They moved in 1812–14 to No. 20 PICCADILLY and then, after the redevelopment of PICCADILLY CIRCUS, went to No. 49 REGENT STREET which had been the Western Mail Coach Offices and also the Bull and Mouth (Swan and Edgar retained the inn licence until the late 1970s). Mr Swan died in 1821 though his name was still upon the shop 150 years later. In 1841 a fine new shopfront appeared in PICCADILLY CIRCUS and Mr Edgar flourished. He used to ride his horse to work from Kingston Hill. He was always asked to help when Queen Victoria's family visited the store. By 1848 the business occupied Nos 45–51 The Quadrant and nearly all the corner of PICCADILLY CIRCUS. The premises were rebuilt in 1910–20 to Sir Reginald Blomfield's design. They were a place of assignation for several generations. In 1927 the store was taken over by The Drapery Trust and later by the Debenham Group. It was closed in 1982.

Swan Tavern *Charing Cross.* A fashionable tavern in the 15th century, patronised in the 1460s by John Howard, Duke of Norfolk. According to John Aubrey whose account is confirmed by the actor George Powell, Ben Jonson once said this extempore grace before King James I:

> Our King and Queen, the Lord God blesse,
> The Palsgrave and the Lady Besse;
> And God blesse every living thing
> That lives and breathes and loves the King.
> God bless the council of Estate,
> And Buckingham the fortunate
> God blesse them all, and keepe them safe,
> And God blesse me, and God blesse Ralph.

'The King', Aubrey comments, 'was mighty inquisitive to know who this Ralph was'. Ben told him ''twas the drawer at the Swanne Tavern by Charing Crosse, who drew him good canary. For this drollery, his Matie gave him an hundred poundes'.

Swan Theatre *Southwark.* Built in 1594–6 by Francis Langley, a prominent citizen and draper in PARIS GARDEN. In 1596 John de Witt from Utrecht made a sketch of the interior and wrote, 'Of all the theatres, however, the largest and most distinguished is that whereof the sign is a Swan . . . since it contains 3,000 persons and is built of a concrete of flint stones (which greatly abound in Britain) and supported by wooden columns painted in such exact imitation of marble that it might deceive even the most cunning'. It did not have a regular company of actors and was

The Swan with Two Necks, Lad Lane (now Gresham Street) a busy coaching inn. Engraving after Pollard, 1831.

sometimes used for fencing matches. After Langley's death in 1601 it was rarely used. The last record of it was in 1632. Its site was west of HOPTON STREET.

Swan Walk *SW3*. Contains some of the most charming houses in CHELSEA with gardens at front and back. It faces the eastern wall of CHELSEA PHYSIC GARDEN. The Swan Tavern, frequented by Samuel Pepys, stood at the river end and gave the Walk its name. Elizabeth Blackwell, author and illustrator of *A Curious Herbal* (1737) probably lived in Swan Walk and worked in the PHYSIC GARDEN. Osbert and Edith Sitwell lived in Swan Walk in 1917–19. Walton's *Façade* was first performed here.

Swan with Two Necks *Lad Lane*. A busy inn and coaching, wagon and parcel office in the 17th and 18th centuries. The name is a corruption of Swan with Two Nicks, the mark (*cygnita*) by which the birds belonging to the VINTNERS' COMPANY were distinguished.

Swans on the Thames Legend has it that the first swans came to England as a gift to Richard I from Queen Beatrice of Cyprus, and the species known as *Cygnus olor* still haunts the river. Paul Hentzner, who visited England during the reign of Elizabeth I, noted in his journal that many companies of swans frequented the THAMES. 'They live', he wrote, 'in great security, nobody daring to molest, much less kill, any of them, under penalty of a large fine'. That was because the swan was, and still is, regarded as a royal

Swanherds marking the beaks of swans in 1874 during the annual ceremony known as Swan Upping.

bird. The swan was sacred to Apollo and Venus in ancient Greece. Swans have thus survived through the centuries under strong legal protection, and the owning of swans on an English river has always been a privilege. In 1483 anyone who did not own a freehold valued at an annual income of at least 5 marks could not own any swans. In 1496 it was ordained that anyone stealing a swan's egg should be imprisoned for one year and be fined at the monarch's will, and the stealing or snaring of swans was even more severely punished. At the same time it was ordered that on every river in the kingdom all the swans were to be counted, examined and recorded each year. Henry VIII decreed that no one who owned swans could appoint a new swanherd without a licence from the royal swanherd, and he instituted the marking of cygnets with nicks on their beaks with the proviso that any bird not so marked became Crown property. Queen Elizabeth supported these injunctions and the *Order of Swannes* of 1570 also laid down that those who erased or counterfeited any owner's marks should be imprisoned for a year.

For some time only those of royal or noble blood were allowed to keep swans, but later the CITY LIVERY COMPANIES, among others, were given the concession to do so as a royal gesture towards the encouragement of trade. Eton College was also accorded the privilege. For centuries the THAMES swans were regarded, not only as decorative in a majestic way, but as a delicacy at royal feasts, while swan feathers were used for palace upholstery. Their economic value has declined, and it is their decorative effect that is now most valued. Today on the THAMES all the swans belong either to the sovereign or to the DYERS' and the VINTNERS' COMPANIES. The Queen still employs her Keeper of the Swans, a title which has descended from that of the Middle Ages: 'Keeper of the Swans in the Thames from the town of Graveshende to Cicester'. That official still presides over the ceremony of Swan Upping or Swan Hopping, when, assisted by the swanherds of the DYERS' and VINTNERS', he rounds up the new cygnets each year in late July or early August to mark their beaks – one nick for the DYERS, two for the VINTNERS', and none for the Queen. A small fleet of boats with banners flying and bearing the Royal Swan Keeper, his assistants and the swanherds of the two CITY COMPANIES, travels up river to 'up' the birds, sometimes in lively scrimmages, the men all in colourful garments of red, green, blue, white and gold. The voyage concludes with a traditional banquet at a riverside inn when the main course is a dish of swan meat. In 1980 the length of the journey, which once began at SOUTHWARK BRIDGE, was curtailed. It now starts at SUDBURY and ends at Pangbourne. In the early 1950s there were almost 1,000 swans on the THAMES; but owing to lead poisoning, probably from anglers' weights, the numbers have fallen drastically.

Swinton Street *WC1.* Named after James Swinton, a builder and surveyor, who bought the land from Henry Calthorpe (*see* CALTHORPE ESTATE). A few houses from the 1830s and 1840s remain.

Swiss Cottage *NW3.* Situated in the London Borough of CAMDEN, north of REGENT'S PARK. In 1826 the FINCHLEY ROAD from REGENT'S PARK to Ballard's Lane was established by Act of Parliament at the instigation of Colonel Henry Samuel Eyre. To help pay for what was to be one of the most imposing highways

Swiss Cottage in c.1845. It takes its name from one of the first buildings there, a tavern resembling an Alpine chalet.

to London of its time, Eyre launched a turnpike trust. One of the first buildings by the Junction Road Toll Gate was a Swiss-style tavern designed in line with a contemporary fashion. In 1859 it became a bus terminus and in 1868 a station on the METROPOLITAN underground line, and at the end of the 19th century the surrounding area was developing from the rural to the urban. After the 2nd World War the tavern was reconstructed as the present Swiss Cottage. In 1964, on the site opposite, Sir Basil Spence's Hampstead public library block was opened, forming part of SWISS COTTAGE CENTRE.

Swiss Cottage Centre *Adelaide Road, NW3.* Opened in 1964 as part of CAMDEN Council Civic Centre. Facilities include a gymnasium, swimming pool, squash and badminton courts. There is also a library. The architect was Sir Basil Spence. Occasional exhibitions are held in the library.

Swordbearer The first of the three Household Officers of the LORD MAYOR. He shares the administration of engagements and daily attendance upon the LORD MAYOR with the COMMON CRYER and SERJEANT-AT-ARMS and the CITY MARSHAL. His office was no doubt in existence in the 14th century, but is first mentioned in 1419 when it was recorded that the MAYOR should have an Esquire to bear his sword before him, 'a man well bred . . . one who knows how in all places . . . to support the honour of his Lord and of the City'. He wears a beaver fur hat and bears the State Sword before the LORD MAYOR.

Sydenham *SE26.* Originally a wild, isolated area, consisting partly of Westwood Forest and partly of Westwood Common, it is a large open tract of land more than 500 acres in size. The local people grazed their animals and cut firewood on the common; and in 1615 they went to court to stop an attempt to enclose it, after marching to London to present a petition to James I. At that time there were weather-boarded cottages along what is now Sydenham Road, surrounded by orchards and market gardens. In the mid-17th century, medicinal springs were discovered at the site of Wells Park; and crowds flocked to drink the bitter waters, until they lost favour in the early 19th century. The short-lived Croydon Canal passed through Sydenham. After it closed, the London–Croydon Railway was laid along its line. Trains driven by atmospheric pressure also ran along special tracks through Sydenham in the mid 1840s, but they proved so unreliable that the experiment failed.

The common land was enclosed in 1810, and most of Sydenham became built up in the 19th century. Upper Sydenham was a smart area, where well-off people built large family houses on the healthy high ground, while working people lived in meaner housing in Lower Sydenham. Sydenham became particularly fashionable after the CRYSTAL PALACE moved there in 1854. Very popular at first, the Palace had been in decline for some years when it burned down in 1936. By the late 19th century Sydenham's affluent residents had begun to move out, and in this century Sydenham has changed from a quiet, prosperous place into a busy suburb. New shops and blocks of flats have replaced some of the older buildings since the 2nd World War. Famous people who have lived in Sydenham in the past include Thomas Campbell, the poet, Sir Ernest Shackleton (at No. 12 Westwood Hill) and W.G. Grace, who practised as a doctor in Lawrie Park Road. John Logie Baird, the television pioneer, was living at No. 3 Crescent Wood Road at the time of his death in 1946.

Sydenham High School *19 Westwood Hill, SE26.* Opened in 1887 by the GIRLS' PUBLIC DAY SCHOOL TRUST in the premises of a former hotel on Westwood Hill. The original 20 pupils increased ten-fold in less than three years and there are now about 630 girls who occupy larger premises across the road from the original building.

Sydney Street *SW3.* Built in 1845 on the SMITH'S CHARITY ESTATE. Probably named after a former trustee, the 3rd Viscount Sydney. In 1864 'The Flying Man', who had intended to descend from a balloon 5,000 ft up into CREMORNE GARDENS (with the aid of bat's wings and a tail) crash-landed here. ST LUKE'S CHURCH is on the east side.

Syon House *Isleworth, Middlesex.* Home of the Percys, Dukes of Northumberland, since 1594. A stone-built, turreted quadrangle, it stands on the site of the Bridgettine monastery which was founded at TWICKENHAM in 1415 by Henry V. The monastery was annexed by Henry VIII in 1534 and it was here that his fifth wife, Katherine Howard, was confined before her execution in 1542. Five years later a gruesome incident occurred when Henry VIII's coffin, resting at Syon on its way from WESTMINSTER to Windsor, burst open in the night and dogs were discovered in the morning licking up certain remains. After the accession of Edward VI, Edward Seymour, Duke of Somerset, Protector of the Realm, acquired the monastry and estate and started to construct a house, the basic design of which forms the present building. After Somerset's execution for felony in 1552, Syon passed to John Dudley, Duke of Northumberland, and it was here that his daughter-in-law, Lady Jane Grey, was offered the Crown and began her nine days' reign. Following Dudley's execution, Syon reverted to the monarch.

In 1594 Elizabeth I granted the lease of Syon to Henry Percy, 9th Earl of Northumberland, known as the Wizard Earl because of his interest in scientific experiments. After his death in 1632, his son,

Algernon Percy, the 10th Earl, employed Inigo Jones to make repairs and improvements to the house, including the addition of an arcade along the east side. During the Civil Wars three of Charles I's children were placed in the charge of this Earl who took them to Syon in 1646 to escape the plague. Their father visited them here, and the picture in the red drawing-room by Lely of Charles I and the Duke of York, for which, it is recorded, the Earl paid £30, was probably painted at this time. In the following year an historic Council was held at Syon, attended by Cromwell, who was supported in his martial policies.

During the early 1660s, accompanying Charles II on a visit to Syon, John Evelyn observed, 'I viewed that seat belonging to the Earl of Northumberland, builte, out of an old Nunnerie, of stone, and faire enough; but more celebrated for the garden than it deserves; yet there is excellent wall fruit and a pretty fountain ...' A century later the 1st Duke of Northumberland of the third creation, considering his property to be 'ruinous and inconvenient', engaged Robert Adam to improve the house, and 'Capability' Brown to landscape the grounds. Beginning in 1762, Adam worked for several years, creating within the existing architectural framework a magnificent suite of rooms which include the great hall, where a clever arrangement of steps embellished with a screen of Doric columns disguise the uneven floor levels; the ante-room, lavishly gilded and adorned in Roman style; the dining-room with its richly ornamented half-domes screened by columns at each end; the red drawing-room with its crimson silk walls, which contains many famous Stuart portraits of royalty; and the long gallery, interestingly proportioned with a length of 136 ft and a height and width of only 14 ft. He also constructed the fine entrance gates on the London road, with archway, colonnades and lodges.

Adam was unable to complete the work,, and it was not until the 19th century that the north side was rebuilt and the walls refaced with Bath stone by the 3rd Duke, who also added the Great Conservatory, which was designed by Charles Fowler. Constructed of gunmetal and Bath stone, this edifice is said to have inspired Joseph Paxton, who studied it before designing the CRYSTAL PALACE. The impressive ceilings by Monteroli in the north range were added by the 4th Duke in 1863–4.

In 1874, after the demolition of NORTHUMBERLAND HOUSE to make way for NORTHUMBERLAND AVENUE, much of the furniture and the family portraits were removed by the 6th Duke to Syon, together with the Percy Lion (after a model by Michelangelo) which had surmounted the London house for 125 years and now stands above the east front of Syon.

Approached by an old avenue of limes, Syon House stands in a spacious setting of lawns and parkland. In 1837, the already famous botanical gardens were opened to the public. These contained, among many rare horticultural specimens, two mulberry trees, planted in the reign of Edward VI, which can be seen today. In 1965, with the co-operation of ICI, the 10th Duke formed the Gardening Centre Ltd, the first national centre of gardening.

Tabard *Southwark*. The scene of the meeting of the pilgrims in Chaucer's *The Canterbury Tales*.

In Southwerk at the Tabard as I lay
Ready to wende on my pilgrimage
To Caunterbury with ful devout corage
At night was come in-to that hostelrye
Wel nyne and twenty in a companye,
Of sondry folk, by aventure y-falle
In felawshipe, and pilgrims were they alle,
That toward Canterbury Wolden ryde;
The chambres and the stables weren wyde,
And wel we weren esed atte beste.

The tabard was a short sleeveless jacket, open at the sides, worn by a knight over his armour and emblazoned with his arms, also by heralds, emblazoned with the royal arms. After Chaucer's day the tavern fell into disrepair but by the end of the 16th century was 'newly repaired, and with convenient rooms much encreased, for the receipt of many guests'. Destroyed by fire in 1676, it was soon afterwards rebuilt in the same style with galleries and a Pilgrims' Room, though the landlord changed the name to the Talbot. For fear lest the change cost him business a subsequent landlord had a notice fixed to the wooden arch which transversed the road: 'This is the inn where Sir Jeffry Chaucer and the nine and twenty pilgrim's lay, in the journey to Canterbury, anno 1383.' During the time of SOUTHWARK FAIR in the 18th century plays were performed in the courtyard. In the 19th century, with the coming of the railways, the inn fell again into disrepair and was used as storerooms. Eventually, in 1873, it was sold by auction and soon afterwards demolished. TALBOT YARD, BOROUGH HIGH STREET marks the site.

Tachbrook Street *SW1*. Built on land acquired in PIMLICO by Henry Wise, gardener to William III, Queen Anne and George I. Wise also bought land at Lillington and Tachbrook, Warwickshire and at Charlwood, Surrey and Moreton, Warwickshire. He died at Warwick Priory in 1738. Other streets on his PIMLICO land are hence called Lillington Gardens; Moreton Place, Street and Terrace; Charlwood Place and Street; Warwick Place North, Warwick Square and Way.

Talbot Inn *Southwark, see* TABARD.

Talbot Road *W2*. Named after the Talbot family who had owned a large estate mainly in KENSINGTON until the 1850s, part of this road was recently demolished to build the Wessex Gardens estate, including No. 60, where the Indian nationalist and journalist, Lokamanya Tilok, had lived, being visited there in 1915 by Gandhi.

Talgarth Road *W6, W14*. Extends from the HAMMERSMITH FLYOVER to WEST CROMWELL ROAD. It takes its name from Talgarth in Brecon, the county in which James Gunter, the ground landlord, was born. Gunter bought several fields in EARL'S COURT, CHELSEA and FULHAM at the beginning of the 19th century, and a number of other roads in these areas commemorate places in Brecon. Among them are Tregunter, Gwendwr, Gilston and Glazbury Roads and Gunter Grove. James Gunter's son, Robert, was the founder of the caterers, Gunter's, formerly of 13 BRUTON PLACE. Having tea at Gunter's was once a fashionable treat. The Gunters' house in EARL'S COURT was known as Currant Jelly Hall. Robert's son, Colonel Sir Robert Gunter, developed the family lands in the 1860s and 1870s. His country house was in Yorkshire where he represented Knaresborough and Barkston in PARLIAMENT. His wife came from Gledhow Hall, Yorkshire. Hence Knaresborough Place, Barkston Gardens, Gledhow Gardens and several other streets and squares with Yorkshire names in the neighbourhood. The ROYAL BALLET SCHOOL is at 155 Talgarth Road.

Tallis Street *EC4*. Named in 1893 after Thomas Tallis, the English 16th-century composer, because of the adjoining GUILDHALL SCHOOL OF MUSIC which has Tallis's name inscribed on the façade.

Tallow Chandlers' Company *see* CITY LIVERY COMPANIES.

Tate Almshouses *Cricket Green, Mitcham, Surrey*. Tudor-style almshouses built and endowed in 1829 by Miss Mary Tate to accommodate 12 poor widows or spinsters who originally lived rent-free and received a small weekly pension. The Tate family had lived in Mitcham since 1705, occupying a large mansion which stood on this site. This was inherited by Mary Tate in 1822, and having moved away from MITCHAM, it was let as a 'House of Recovery' for ladies. In 1829 she had the house demolished and, since the family had connections with Magdalen College, Oxford, the college bailiff, John Buckler, the watercolour artist, was asked to design the almshouses.

Tate Gallery *Millbank, SW1*. Built on the site of the MILLBANK PENITENTIARY to the designs of Sidney R.J. Smith. It was opened in 1897, the cost of its erection, £80,000, being defrayed by Sir Henry Tate, the sugar refiner, who also offered to the nation his collection of 67 paintings and three sculptures which were mostly the work of his fellow-Victorians. Sir Joseph Duveen, the art dealer and benefactor, paid for a wing to house the Turner Bequest, a fine collection of paintings by J.M.W. Turner which were left by him to the nation and previously accommodated in the NATIONAL GALLERY. In 1926 Duveen's son, later Lord Duveen of Millbank, paid for a further extension for the modern foreign collection. Lord Duveen also defrayed the cost of a third enlargement, the long sculpture gallery which was built in 1937. Work began on a fourth extension in 1971.

The gallery contains two main collections, the British Collection, comprising paintings, sculpture, drawings and engravings by British artists from the 16th century up to about 1900, and the Modern Collection consisting of works by British artists from 1850 and foreign works from the time of the Impressionists. There are works by all the greatest British artists, Hogarth, Blake, Turner and the Pre-Raphaelites being particularly strongly represented. The Modern Collection is the most comprehensive collection of British art over the last century and a quarter, its foreign works being a necessarily more selective collection but including representative examples which trace the main developments from impressionism and post-impressionism to cubism, futurism, vorticism, expressionism, surrealism, abstract expressionism, and optical, kinetic and 'pop' art. Displays are changed constantly; and there are frequent exhibitions, incorporating works on loan from other galleries.

The gallery contains works bought under the terms of the bequest made by Sir Francis Chantrey, the sculptor (who left most of his fortune for the purchase of British works of art for the nation), works bought from the fund provided by Samuel Courtauld (*see* COURTAULD INSTITUTE OF ART) and gifts from the National Art Collection Fund, the Contemporary Art Society and private individuals. The Friends of the Tate was founded in 1958 to raise funds to purchase works to fill gaps in the collection. The gallery also receives an annual purchase grant from the Treasury.

The Tate has a good restaurant whose walls were charmingly decorated by Rex Whistler with the story of the *Pursuit of Rare Meats*. The large bronze to the left of the entrance, *Circe and the Bull*, is by Charles Lawes-Wittewronge, a copy of his original work in marble (1908, placed here 1911). The bronze on the right is *Perseus and Andromeda* by H.C. Fehr (1897). In the garden are Henry Moore's bronzes, *Two-piece Reclining Figure* (1963, placed here 1979) and *Upright Motive Nos 1, 2, 7* (1956, placed here 1979), and his *Totem Head* (1968).

Tattersall's *Hyde Park Corner*. Richard Tattersall, a former groom to the 2nd Duke of Kingston, established himself as an auctioneer in 1766 and soon afterwards opened premises near Hyde Park Turnpike. There were stables and loose boxes and a large circular enclosure for trying out horses, in the centre of which was a cupola surmounted by a bust of Tattersall's friend, the Prince of Wales, who is said to have made him 'his almoner for the relief of certain decayed turfites'. There were also two subscription rooms for members of the JOCKEY CLUB and these became not only a resort of well-known figures of the racing fraternity but also the recognised centre for the regulation of betting upon the turf. The business was carried on by Tattersall's descendants until the 99-year lease expired in 1865, when the buildings were pulled down and the site covered by a new wing for ST GEORGE'S HOSPITAL. The business was moved to Knightsbridge Green. It remained there until 1939 and is now at Newmarket.

Tavistock Clinic *120 Belsize Lane, NW3*. Established in 1920 as one of the first out-patient clinics in Great Britain to provide systematic major psycho-therapy for those suffering from psychoneurosis and allied disorders who were unable to afford private fees. It was founded by Dr H. Crichton-Miller who, with other doctors, had been working on men suffering from so-called 'shell-shock' (battle neurosis) in the 1st World War, and who wished civilian patients to benefit from their experience. The clinic began in some disused mews in Malet Place at the corner of

Prospective buyers await an auction in Tattersall's enclosure at Hyde Park Corner c. 1865, just before its demolition. From an engraving after T.M. Joy.

Torrington Place. In 1948 it became part of the National Health Service. In 1967 it moved to the site of the bombed Marie Curie Hospital at the corner of Belsize Lane and Fitzjohn's Avenue. The new building was designed by F.A.C. Maunder.

Tavistock Hotel *4–10 Great Piazza, Covent Garden*. The last of Inigo Jones's houses in the Piazza, the Tavistock was demolished in 1928 and rebuilt as offices. The great dining-room occupied the whole of the first floor. It had 200 bedrooms.

Tavistock Place *WC1*. Runs from TAVISTOCK SQUARE to REGENT SQUARE. Built in about 1807 and named after the ground landlord, the Duke of Bedford, Marquess of Tavistock. The west end was designed by James Burton and one or two of his houses, heavily restored, remain. John Galt, the novelist, lived here in 1815–23. Zachary Macaulay, father of Thomas Babington Macaulay and member of the CLAPHAM SECT, lived here in 1835–7. Francis Baily, the physicist, lived at No. 37 in 1825–44. He held meetings of scientists, known as the Baily Club. Jerome K. Jerome lodged at No. 33 (the house has gone) in 1889 with George Wingrave, whom he immortalised in *Three Men in a Boat*. He wrote *Thoughts of an Idle Fellow* here. The MARY WARD CENTRE is at No. 9.

Tavistock Square *WC1*. Named after the Marquess of Tavistock who was also Duke of Bedford. James Burton built the east side in about 1803 including old Tavistock House which was demolished in 1901. The rest of his work was demolished in 1938. Thomas Cubitt began work in 1820 and completed the square in about 1826. The west side was particularly fine and has been well preserved. Behind the Georgian façade are the Connaught Hall of Residence of LONDON UNIVERSITY and other university institutions. On the east side Tavistock House was designed by Edwin Lutyens in 1938. It was originally intended for the Theosophists, but became the home of the BRITISH MEDICAL ASSOCIATION. In the courtyard is a memorial fountain designed by S. Rowland Pierce to medical men and women who died in the 2nd World War. The statues are by James Woodford who sculpted the Queen's Beasts for the Coronation of Queen Elizabeth II. Dickens lived in part of the old Tavistock House in 1851–60 and wrote *Bleak House, Little Dorrit, Hard Times, A Tale of Two Cities* and part of *Great Expectations* here. He also built a little theatre in the garden in which he acted himself. A plaque in the library garden wall commemorates his stay here. Charles Gounod lived for a while in the same house. At No. 52 in 1924–39 were Leonard and Virginia Woolf and the Hogarth Press, whose first book they themselves had printed in 1919 in the kitchen of Hogarth House, RICHMOND. During these years they published not only Virginia's novels but the English translations of Freud and many other influential works. On the north is Adler House, the Court of the Chief Rabbi, and Adolph Tuck Hall which houses the JEWISH MUSEUM. In the beautiful, shady garden square is a statue of Mahatma Gandhi and a bust of Louisa Brandreth Aldrich-Blake, the surgeon (*see* STATUES). There is a copper beech planted by President Nehru of India in 1953 and a cherry tree in memory of the victims of Hiroshima planted in 1967. The Tavistock Hotel (301 bedrooms) is by C. Lovett, Gill and Partners (1951).

Tavistock Street *WC2*. The eastern part (known as York Street until 1937) was built in 1631–2. The street was extended west to SOUTHAMPTON STREET in 1706–14. This later part has always been known as Tavistock Street after the ground landlord the Duke of Bedford, Marquess of Tavistock. The firm moved to the STRAND in 1804. The magazine *Country Life* was first published by Edward Hudson in 1897 at Nos 2–10. A new building was designed for the magazine by Sir Edwin Lutyens in 1904–5. Thomas de Quincey, author of *Confessions of an English Opium Eater*, was living at No. 36 in 1821.

Teddington *Surrey*. Lies south of TWICKENHAM on the southern bank of the THAMES. A farm or estate associated with *Tuda* existed by the 10th century. By the Middle Ages the hamlet belonged to WESTMINSTER ABBEY and had its own church dedicated to St Mary. In the 17th century residents included Sir Orlando Bridgeman, Charles II's Lord Keeper of the Great Seal, and the poet Thomas Traherne. In the 18th century St Mary's was rebuilt as it now stands, and the scientific laboratory of the vicar, the Revd Stephen Hales, was visited by Frederick, Prince of Wales. The actress Peg Woffington lived in Teddington Place House and was buried in the church. BUSHY PARK to the south, which had been a royal hunting preserve when the house was built by the Earl of Halifax, was the home of Lord North, and later of the Duke of Clarence and Mrs Jordan. The Chestnut Avenue was originally planned as an approach to HAMPTON COURT. Queen Victoria opened the Park to the public. A 19th-century resident of Teddington was the writer R.D. Blackmore who ran a market garden. Farming continued in the area until the 19th century when the railway arrived and development followed. By the end of the century the population had increased more than tenfold and five new churches were built. St Mary combined with the unfinished St Albans (W. Niven, begun 1887). In 1900 the National Physical Laboratory moved into Bushy House. In 1937 the Urban District of Teddington became part of the Borough of TWICKENHAM which in 1965 was incorporated into the London Borough of RICHMOND-UPON-THAMES. THAMES TELEVISION Studios occupy a riverside mansion formerly belonging to Teddington Film Studios.

Teddington Weir Suspension Bridge *Teddington–Kingston-upon-Thames*. The footbridge below the weir was built in 1888 by G. Pooley, with steel towers protected by concrete.

Tedworth Square *SW3*. The daughter-in-law of William Sloane-Stanley of Paultons (*see* PAULTON'S SQUARE) came from Tedworth (or Tidworth) in Hampshire. Mark Twain lived at No. 23 in 1896–7. No. 15, now rebuilt and subdivided, was the home of two well-known actresses, first Lillie Langtry, then Mrs Patrick Campbell. The correspondence between Bernard Shaw and Mrs Patrick Campbell was addressed to No. 15 Tedworth Square. Later the cricketer Sir Pelham (Plum) Warner lived at No. 15.

Telegraph Hill Park *NW3*. Recreation grounds totalling 9½ acres near NEW CROSS opened in 1895. Wellington's victory at Waterloo in 1815 was flashed to London from the telegraph station which linked the capital with Dover and the Continent.

Telegraph Street *EC2*. Takes its name from the English Telegraph Company which opened a branch here in 1859. The Post Office's Central Telegraph Station opened here in 1872 and remained until 1933. Robert Blomfield, the poet, lived in a house on the site of Nos 11–16.

Television Centre *Shepherd's Bush, W12*. The BBC acquired 13½ acres of the White City site of the Franco-British Exhibition of 1908 at SHEPHERD'S BUSH in 1949. It is 4 miles from the centre of London. A large circular main building of seven storeys, designed by Graham Dawbarn, covers 3½ acres – twice the area covered by ST PAUL'S CATHEDRAL. Surrounding blocks radiate from it. Beyond a colonnade flanking the front entrance is a central court dominated by a fountain and a 40 ft obelisk with a bronze figure of Helios, the all-seeing Greek sun god. The first of the new studios came into use in 1960 – 24 years after the BBC ran its first television service from two studios at ALEXANDRA PALACE. There are now seven major production studios at the Centre, two news studios and Eurovision and satellite complexes providing an international focal point and one of the most up-to-date telecommunication centres in the world. Altogether nearly 8,000 staff work in BBC television – not all at the Centre. There are two colour studios at Lime Grove and the Television Theatre is at SHEPHERD'S BUSH.

Temple Bar *Fleet Street–Strand, EC4*. Used to mark the western limits of the CITY. When first mentioned in 1293 it was no more than a chain between wooden posts. By 1351 a gate had been built with a prison above it. It was repaired and painted for the coronation of Anne Boleyn and further repaired in 1547–54. Elizabeth I passed through it on her way to ST PAUL'S to give thanks for the defeat of the Armada and since then a brief ceremony has always been performed here on state occasions when the Sovereign wishes to enter the CITY: permission is asked of the LORD MAYOR who offers his Sword of State as a demonstration of his loyalty. It is immediately returned to him and carried before the royal procession to show that the Sovereign is in the CITY under the LORD MAYOR's protection. In the 1630s Inigo Jones drew up plans for a new gate but they were never carried out. The old gate survived the GREAT FIRE. Nevertheless it was rebuilt in Portland stone by Wren in the early 1670s with a central arch for carriages and a foot postern at either side. On top of it on the west side were placed figures of Charles I and Charles II and on the east figures of James I and Anne of Denmark. From 1684, when parts of the body of Sir Thomas Armstrong (boiled in salt so birds would not eat them), were displayed here, Temple Bar was used to show the remains (usually the heads) of traitors to the populace. The heads of the Rye House Plotters were thus displayed on spikes. Telescopes could be hired for ½d a look. The last head exhibited was that of Francis Towneley the Jacobite in 1746. Beside the gate was a pillory where Titus Oates in 1685 and Daniel Defoe in 1703 spent uncomfortable days. In 1806 the gate was repaired and covered in black velvet for the funeral of Nelson. In 1870 it was removed because of traffic congestion and for ten years lay in pieces in a yard in FARRINGDON ROAD until Sir Henry Bruce Meux re-erected it on his estate at Theobalds Park, Cheshunt,

Temple Bar, which was rebuilt by Wren in the early 1670s, shortly before its removal in 1870 to ease traffic flow.

Hertfordshire. It is now in a very dilapidated condition. It has been suggested that it should be restored and removed to the north-west corner of ST PAUL'S CHURCHYARD. In 1880 a memorial designed by Horace Jones was set up opposite THE LAW COURTS to mark the site. It is surmounted by Charles Birch's bronze griffin, the unofficial badge of the CITY. The bronze panels on the side are by Sir Edgar Boehm.

Temple Church *EC4*. Although the ground plan of the Temple Church is unchanged since its foundation, it is difficult to capture the ancient romance of the building, since the restorers, particularly those of the 19th century, have seen to it that, in the words of the architect, Walter Godfrey, 'every ancient surface was repaired away or renewed'. The name derives from the Order of the KNIGHTS TEMPLAR, that powerful order whose white tunics with the red cross proclaimed them to be immune from all jurisdiction save that of the Pope. They were formed in 1118 for the purpose of protecting pilgrims in the Holy Land, and were brought back to England by Henry I. In 1162 they built their first church and, in 1185, their great house, together with the Round Church on the banks of the THAMES which they named the New Temple. The church, usually said to have been modelled on that of the Holy Sepulchre in Jerusalem, is more probably modelled on the Dome of the Rock (*see* KNIGHTS TEMPLAR).

It is a fine example of the Transitional style, the new pointed arch being cleverly used with the interlacing semi-circular of the Romanesque. There is a lavish use of Purbeck marble and some interesting carved grotesque stone heads. The ceremony of consecration was carried out by Heraclius, the Patriarch of Jerusalem, in the presence of Henry II. It is dedicated to the Blessed Mary. The rectangular choir was added in 1204 and at the same time a small chapel was built against the south side of the Round Church and dedicated to St Anne. The crypt, where the secret initiation ceremonies were performed, is all that remains of this chapel today. Another basement chamber was discovered underneath the south aisle in 1950. This could have been the Knights' Treasury. Another relic from the days of the Crusaders is the penitential cell next to the wheel window in the Round Church. Here Walter-le-Bacheler, the Grand Preceptor of Ireland, was left to starve to death for disobeying the Master of the Order.

When the TEMPLARS were discredited in the 14th century their property was given to the KNIGHTS HOSPITALLERS. They in turn leased the Temple to the lawyers who continued as tenants until Henry VIII appropriated the property. In 1608 James I presented the freehold of the church to the lawyers, presenting the southern half to the INNER TEMPLE and the northern half to the MIDDLE TEMPLE on condition they maintained the church and its services for ever. The appointment of the chaplain or Master remains the prerogative of the monarch and is independent of the BISHOP OF LONDON. A series of controversial sermons caused a stir in 1585, when Richard Hooker was Master and Walter Travers, a Calvinist, Reader. According to Isaac Walton 'the forenoon sermon spake Canterbury and the afternoon Geneva.' In 1682, Wren was called upon to 'beautify' the Temple, and battlements and buttresses were added. By this time the Round Church was being used as a meeting place for lawyers and their clients, and in the west porch, John Playford, a clerk of the Temple, had a music shop where Samuel Pepys bought copies of the latest songs. Decimus Burton and Sydney Smirke refurbished the church in the 19th century. Most of their work, however, was destroyed in the BLITZ. The bombs also severely damaged the figures of the Crusader knights which had lain in the Round Church for so many centuries. These have been skillfully repaired and Walter Godfrey and his son have restored the fabric of the building with admirable simplicity. The reredos, carved by William Emmett in the 17th century, and removed by the Victorians to the Bowes Museum near Barnard Castle, has been reinstated under the great east window. Charles Lamb was baptised in the church in 1775.

The north window carries the crest of the MIDDLE TEMPLE and the south window that of the INNER TEMPLE. By custom members of these Inns sit separately, members of the INNER occupying the stalls in the southern half of the Choir and those of the MIDDLE occupying the northern. The east windows (1842) were destroyed in the bombing and have been replaced by new work in the medieval idiom by Carl Edwards. The central window was presented to the Church by the GLAZIERS' COMPANY after the 2nd World War.

Temple of Flora *Lambeth*. Pavilion and pleasure gardens which stood on the north side of WESTMINSTER BRIDGE ROAD. The grounds were elaborate, embellished with cascades, alcoves and statuary. The temple was constructed after the style of the rotunda in RANELAGH GARDENS. There was also a hot-house with a transparency of Flora and fountains. From 1788–91 the garden preserved a good reputation, but by 1796 it was said that the company that assembled there were 'as neatly painted' as the alcoves in the grounds. In that year the proprietor was sentenced to six months' imprisonment for keeping a disorderly house, and the gardens seem to have been closed.

Temple of Isis The worship of the oriental cults, as those of Egypt, Syria and the Near East were called, was popular under the Roman Empire. They tended to spread with trade. The Egyptian deities Isis and Serapis are represented in Roman London (the latter by a fine marble head from the TEMPLE OF MITHRAS). A temple to the goddess Isis was presumed to exist from the inscription found scratched on a wine jug from TOOLEY STREET, SOUTHWARK: LONDINI AD FANVM ISIDIS – 'at London at the temple of Isis'. Other slight indications of the cult had been the finding of a steelyard weight representing the goddess, and a silver statuette of her son, Harpokrates, from the THAMES at LONDON BRIDGE in 1825. The temple has still not been found but further evidence for it came to light in 1975 when the river wall was discovered, incorporating within its fabric many sculptures from earlier monuments. The silver statuette of Harpokrates is in the BRITISH MUSEUM, the other finds in the MUSEUM OF LONDON.

Temple of Mithras *Temple Court, 11 Queen Victoria Street, EC4*. The existence of a temple to the essentially Persian god Mithras had been suspected since the discovery in 1889 in the WALBROOK of a relief of the god ritually slaying the bull. It had been dedicated by Ulpius Silvanus, a veteran of the II Legio Augusta. At the same time part of a sculpture of a reclining river god was also found 'in the middle of the WALBROOK at a depth of about 20 ft'. After the 2nd World War, when the area had suffered heavy bomb damage, excavation began under the direction of Professor W.F. Grimes in 1954 in advance of redevelopment of the area for Bucklersbury House.

All the sculptures from the 1889 and 1954 finds and the superb small silver incense box decorated with scenes in relief (found hidden in a wall) are exhibited in the MUSEUM OF LONDON.

Temple Place *WC2*. The Howard Hotel (137 bedrooms) was originally built in 1894 to the designs of John Dunn. It was rebuilt in 1975 by Jackson and Partners.

Tenter Street *Barbican*. Extended from MOORFIELDS to MOOR LANE through the old tenter-grounds where cloth was stretched out on tenter-hooks. In the 2nd World War the street was bombed and no longer exists.

Tenter Streets (North, South, East and West) *E1*. Built in the middle of the 19th century, the streets surround what was once a tenter ground, where tenters, or wooden frames, were used to stretch woven cloth so that it dried evenly. Earlier still it formed part of Goodman's Fields, where Stow in his youth used to go to fetch milk 'always hot from the kine'.

Tenterden Street *W1*. On the Millfield Estate (*see* HANOVER SQUARE), it is a short street connecting HANOVER SQUARE with Dering Street. It was laid out in about 1720. The origin of the name is not known.

Terry's Theatre *105–106 Strand*. Built to the designs of Walter Emden for actor Edward Terry in

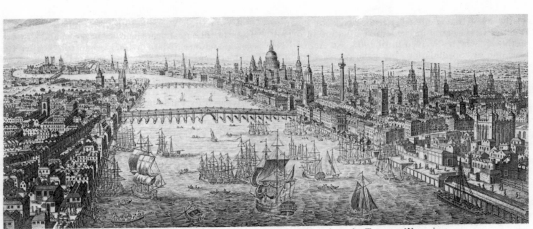

The Thames in c. 1750 from an engraving by Bowles, showing the river front from the Tower to Westminster.

1887. It usually staged comedies but its biggest successes were *Sweet Lavender* (1888) by Pinero and *The French Maid* (1897), a musical comedy. From 1910 until it was demolished in 1923 it was used as a cinema. Offices were built on the site.

THAMES The origin of the name is obscure but Caesar called the river Tamesis. It is the second oldest place name in England, the oldest being Kent.

As well as providing fish for food and water for drinking, rivers afford an easy means of travel and an economical means of transport. The Thames became, and remained until our day, important as a highway running east towards the Continent and Scandinavia, its swinging tides helping the merchant ships along. Moreover, its non-tidal but navigable length ran across the island through the most fertile and, for centuries, most productive regions. While a river is a useful defensive barrier, it can also form a barrier to communication and must therefore be bridged at the nearest possible point to its mouth so as to avoid detours inland to a crossing or a ford. Along the whole stretch of the tidal Thames only one place exists where two spurs of high, dry and gravelly land face each other on the river's banks on which a pair of bridgeheads could stand securely – on the south bank at SOUTH-WARK and on the north bank at the foot of the twin hills on which the CITY stands. Here the engineers of the Roman army built the most important crossing of the Thames. Around this wooden bridge a settlement grew up, a port and meeting place of roads from every quarter. Until 1750, when the first bridge at WESTMIN-STER was completed, LONDON BRIDGE was the only one spanning the Thames in London.

Control and ownership The conservancy of the Thames was handed over in a vague way to the CITY CORPORATION in 1197 for a consideration of 1,500 marks by Richard I, who had returned from the Crusades and was short of money. The agreement mainly concerned fishing rights. In the CITY's hands it remained jealously, if inefficiently, guarded until 1857. Its jurisdiction extended all the way from the mouth of the Medway, right up to Staines where, above the town on the north bank, was set a stone inscribed 'God Preserve ye City of London'. For centuries the legal position on the ownership and control of the river was never very clear and frequent disputes

arose, especially about fishing rights. In 1613 a court decided that the CITY and its LORD MAYOR were, indeed, the legal conservators of the Thames. Although a Select Committee reported in 1836 on the state of the river, including the bad effects of the new steam vessels on lighters, barges and banks, condemning the laxity of control by the City, and recommending the removal of that control, nothing was done for 20 years. Then, when the proposed EMBANKMENTS and new outfall sewers were being considered, a dispute arose between the CITY and the Crown about the rightful ownership of the bed and banks of the river within the ebb and flow of the tides. That argument lasted for 17 years. Since early times, control of the Thames and of the other royal rivers had been a prerogative of the Crown, yet between 1197 and 1857 the CITY OF LON-DON had been under the impression that ownership and control of the Thames lay in its hands, quite definitely up to Staines and somewhat uncertainly beyond. Now the solicitor of Her Majesty's Woods and Forests claimed that the position of the CITY was not one of ownership but merely one of ministry, and he demanded that the title of the Crown to the bed and banks of the tidal Thames should be admitted. In its traditional manner of standing firmly for its rights against the Sovereign, the CITY CORPORATION refused to do so and produced old documents from the GUILD-HALL archives to prove its right to full ownership. The Crown remained adamant and it is said that Queen Victoria herself was determined on the matter. So the Crown proceeded, by way of Chancery, against the LORD MAYOR and CORPORATION. The dispute continued while the revenue from the river rapidly declined as railways developed and the CITY refused to advance adequate funds for the benefit of navigation. Finally the CITY gave way and agreed to withdraw all claim to ownership and admitted the claim of the Crown. So the first Thames Conservancy Act was passed in 1857. The next year a new Board of Conservancy was formed. The Thames Commissioners consisted of the LORD MAYOR, two ALDERMEN, four nominees of the Common Council, two of the Lord High Admiral, one of the Privy Council, the Deputy Master of TRINITY HOUSE, and a TRINITY HOUSE nominee. This body lasted only nine years and, under an Act of 1866, a new body was formed called the Thames Conservancy Board which was given control of the whole navigable river from Cricklade down to Yantlet Creek, an unprecedented situation of overall authority which survived until 1908. An Act of 1894 was one of consolidation, but gave representation to the LONDON COUNTY COUNCIL and to riparian county councils; it also resulted in some radical dredging of the river. In 1909 the new PORT OF LONDON AUTHORITY came into being and took over the tidal river between TEDDINGTON and the sea, while the Conservancy was reconstituted to look after the whole of the 135 miles of tideless river and its watershed above Teddington. In 1974 the Thames Water Authority acquired full control of all the river's waters and its catchment area of 5,000 square miles with authority over the three other bodies concerned: the METROPOLITAN WATER BOARD, the Thames Conservancy and the PORT OF LONDON AUTHORITY. The new organisation indicates a change of emphasis on the river's uses: water supply, control and drainage of the Thames valley have become more important than navigation. The TWA controls all uses of water resources, including a flow of about one million gallons of water as well as sewerage, recreation and improvement of the environment in the tidal area. Among its responsibilities is the overcoming of a predicted shortage of water threatening southern England (*see also* BARKING CREEK, FLOODS, PORT OF LONDON AUTHORITY, REACHES OF THE THAMES, RIVER POLICE, STAIRS, SWANS, WATER GATES *and* WATERMEN AND LIGHTERMEN).

Thames Barrier   *see* FLOODS.

Thames Police   *see* RIVER POLICE.

Thames Polytechnic *Wellington Street, Woolwich, SE18.* Formed in 1970 by the amalgamation of the Woolwich Polytechnic and the Department of Architecture and Surveying of Hammersmith College of Art and Building and by its merger in 1976 with Dartford College of Education.

Thames Rowing Club *Embankment, Putney, SW15.* Formed in 1860. It came into prominence in the period between the 1st and 2nd World Wars under the coaching of J. Beresford Snr and the Australian, Stephen Fairburn. Jack Beresford, one of the world's greatest oarsmen, was a member of the club. In 1867 the club formed the Hare and Hounds Cross Country Club for the purpose of ensuring the fitness of members by regular exercise during the winter months. The club colours are red white and black.

Thames Television *306 Euston Road, NW1.* Founded in 1967 to offer a 'comprehensive output of different sorts of programme to the London Region' from Monday to Friday evening. The building was designed by the Sidney K. Firman Partnership, the architects of the technical designs being the Ware MacGregor Partnership.

Thames Tunnel *Wapping–Rotherhithe.* The first underwater tunnel in the world. In 1802 Robert Vazie, a Cornish mining engineer nicknamed 'The Mole', produced a plan for a tunnel between ROTHERHITHE and LIMEHOUSE. The Thames Archway Company was authorised to build the tunnel in 1805 and a shaft was sunk at ROTHERHITHE. In 1807 Richard Trevithick

took over from Vazie and drove a timbered driftway 1,000 ft. The next year the river broke in and all work was abandoned. Marc Brunel began to consider the problem and in 1818 patented a tunnelling shield. In 1823 he published a description of such a shield in the *Mechanic's Magazine*; and that year his plan for a tunnel between ROTHERHITHE and WAPPING was authorised by Parliament. Henry Maudslay built the shield with which it was to be constructed. The idea of the tunnelling shield was that only a small proportion of the excavation face should be exposed at any one time, thus considerably reducing the dangers of caving in. It had 12 cast-iron frames supporting rows of poling boards attached to them by screw jacks. One by one each board was removed and the earth in front of it excavated 4½ inches. The board was then screwed forward by the same amount. When this process had been completed with all the boards of a frame, that frame was itself jacked forward and the space behind it lined with brick. Even so, there were to be five major inundations, the first in 1827 just after Isambard Brunel became resident engineer under his father. The resulting cavities in the riverbed were filled with bags of clay. There was much loss of life during the building of the tunnel, though this was due more to the serious pollution in the river than to drowning. During 1828–35 all work was suspended through lack of funds. But by 1843 the work was completed with a new improved shield built by the Rennies and with much financial aid from the Government. Thomas Page, the builder of WESTMINSTER BRIDGE, was Marc Brunel's assistant throughout this period. Although it had been intended for vehicular traffic, there was not enough money to build the necessary carriage ramps and the tunnel remained a foot-tunnel until the 1860s, when it was converted into a railway tunnel for the East London Railway. It still carries underground trains. The tunnel is 1,200 ft long and has elegant twin horse-shoe shaped archways interconnected at intervals and lined throughout with brick. It was famous throughout its long years of building and many commemorative souvenirs were produced. Of lasting and world-wide significance, however, is Marc Brunel's ingenuity in solving the crucial problem of boring through soft ground or under water, for tunnelling shields, in more developed forms, have been used ever since.

A commemorative broadsheet with 'an account and perspective view of the two archways' of the Thames Tunnel.

Thames Tunnel Paper,
PRINTED BY AUTHORITY, 76 FEET BELOW HIGH-WATER MARK.
To commemorate the day of opening the Tunnel as a Thoroughfare for Foot Passengers,
March 25, 1843.

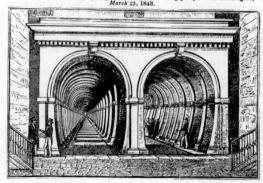

Thamesmead *Plumstead, SE18*. An award-winning new town, begun in 1967 to the designs of the GREATER LONDON COUNCIL architects. It is still rapidly expanding to cover the 1,300 acres of former marshlands at PLUMSTEAD. The development includes 200 acres of parkland, two lakes, a yacht basin and a magnificent health centre by Derek Stow and Partners. The population of 11,000 in 1976 is expected to reach about 50,000 when stage 3 is complete.

Thatched House Lodge *Richmond Park, Surrey*. Built about 1673 as a house for two keepers of RICHMOND PARK, it came to be known as Aldridge's Lodge after Charles Aldridge, one of the keepers. In 1727 Sir Robert Walpole's son was made Ranger and took over the Lodge. His father, already building The Old Lodge in the Park for himself, soon spent £14,000 enlarging and redesigning it. The special feature is a summer house or gazebo in the garden which commands a fine view over the Thames Valley below. This has a high-pitched thatched roof – hence the present name given to the house from 1771 – and consists of two octagonal rooms whose ceilings and walls are beautifully decorated with paintings considered to be the work of Antonio Zucchi and P.M. Borgnis who were both working at OSTERLEY in 1775–8. The commission probably came from General Sir William Medows and his wife, who were tenants from 1769 to 1785. The Lodge has continued to be leased to courtiers and servicemen – including General Eisenhower who was allotted a suite during the 2nd World War. Since 1963 it has been the home of Princess Alexandra and her husband, the Hon. Angus Ogilvy.

Thatched House Tavern *St James's Street*. A fashionable tavern from 1704 or 1705 and frequented by Swift. It was later the meeting-place of the DILETTANTI SOCIETY whose collection of portraits was then kept here. The building was demolished in 1814, rebuilt, then demolished again in 1843 when the CONSERVATIVE CLUB designed by George Basevi and Sydney Smirke was erected on the site. The Thatched House Club, known affectionately as 'the ale house', occupied adjoining premises. Its members included Sheridan and the art collector, George Salting, who had rooms over the club premises.

Theatre *Shoreditch*. London's first playhouse, opened in 1576 by James Burbage, the son of a carpenter and travelling player, stood at the corner of Great Eastern Street and New Inn Yard. No description exists (*but see* ELIZABETHAN PUBLIC THEATRES). It was taken down in 1598 and its timber used for the GLOBE on BANKSIDE.

Theatre Museum *Victoria and Albert Museum*. Due to move to COVENT GARDEN in 1983. The museum was first suggested in 1955 by Laurence Irving, grandson of Sir Henry. In 1960 the Coulthurst Trust and other bodies made funds available, and the British Theatre Museum was able to open in 1963, in an annexe at LEIGHTON HOUSE, KENSINGTON. The basis of the museum was the Irving Collection, but this was added to by gifts and donations, funds also being raised from various institutes and London boroughs. In 1968 a collection of Diaghilev ballet material came on the market, and it was felt that this should not be dispersed but bought for the nation. The Friends of the Museum of Performing Arts was formed by Richard Buckle, and enough funds were raised for important acquisitions to be made.

In 1971 it was decided to merge these collections with the large department at the VICTORIA AND ALBERT MUSEUM and establish the Theatre Museum as a branch of the VICTORIA AND ALBERT MUSEUM.

Theatre Royal Drury Lane *Catherine Street, WC2*. The first theatre was built in 1663 for Thomas Killigrew and the King's Company as one of the two patent theatres. It cost £2,400. Nell Gwynne made her début here in Dryden's *Indian Queen* in 1665. From 1665 until November 1666 it was closed because of the GREAT PLAGUE and the GREAT FIRE. Burned down in 1672, it was rebuilt by Wren in 1672–4 at a cost of £4,000. Quarrels with the other patent company, LINCOLN'S INN FIELDS THEATRE, marred the theatre's success until both companies joined forces in 1682. After Killigrew's death in 1684 there were disagreements between the actors and his successor, Christopher Rich, which culminated in Betterton, the leading actor, forming his own company at LINCOLN'S INN FIELDS in 1695. In 1711 the management of Colley Cibber, Robert Wilkes and Thomas Doggett brought stability again to the theatre. In 1716 a man named Freeman tried to shoot the future George II in the theatre. In 1737 there was a riot when footmen were refused free admission to the gallery. In 1742 David Garrick made his debut here; and in 1747 he went into partnership with James Lacey and acquired the patent. During his management Drury Lane became famous for Shakespearian revivals. In 1775 the Adam brothers altered the theatre inside and out. In that year Mrs Siddons made her début as Portia in *The Merchant of Venice* but she was not a great success and retired temporarily to the country. In 1776 Garrick retired and Richard Brinsley Sheridan took over as manager; and in 1777 Sheridan's *School for Scandal* was first produced here. In 1779 Mary Robinson (one of Gainsborough's favourite models) was discovered here by the Prince of Wales while playing Perdita in *A Winter's Tale*. The next year the theatre was attacked in the GORDON RIOTS because 'papists and Frenchmen' had appeared here. A guard was consequently posted outside until 1896. In 1783 John Kemble made his début as Hamlet and in 1788 took over the management. It was here, in 1791, that the Duke of Clarence, later William IV, first saw Mrs Jordan, the Irish actress who became his mistress and companion and bore him several children. The theatre being declared unsafe in 1791, a new one designed by Henry Holland was built on the site. It opened in Lent 1794 with sacred music by Handel. In 1800 there was an attempt upon the life of George III in the theatre, as there had been in 1716 upon the life of his grandfather. The theatre was again destroyed by fire in 1809. The blaze could be seen from the HOUSE OF COMMONS where Sheridan was attending an important debate. A motion was made to adjourn but he protested that whatever the extent of the present calamity he hoped it would not interfere with the public business of the country. Later he was seen sipping a glass of port watching the flames. 'Surely,' he commented, 'a man may take a glass of wine by his own fireside.' In 1811–12 a new theatre, modelled on the great theatre at Bordeaux, was built to the designs of Benjamin Wyatt. It cost £151,672 and opened under the

The Adam brothers' new front for the Theatre Royal Drury Lane in 1775, when Mrs Siddons made her début as Portia.

management of Samuel Arnold. Edmund Kean first appeared here in 1814, and Grimaldi's farewell benefit was held in 1818. In 1820 the portico was added; and in 1822 Samuel Beazley remodelled the interior. Charles Kean made his début here in 1826. The colonnade was added in 1831. The pillars came from Nash's Quadrant in REGENT STREET. In 1841–3 William Charles Macready managed the theatre and, although he made a financial loss, he added to its prestige. In 1879 Augustus Harris was made manager at the age of 27 and remained in charge of the theatre until his death in 1896. He made Drury Lane famous for spectacular dramas in which snowstorms, earthquakes, avalanches and horse races took place. A pantomime was performed annually in which Dan Leno and Herbert Campbell appeared. Sir Henry Irving's last London season was given here in 1905; and in June that year Ellen Terry's stage jubilee was celebrated. Forbes-Robertson's farewell performance was given in 1913. That year and the next there were seasons of Diaghilev's Ballets Russes and opera. Films were shown in 1915; and in 1916 the revue *Razzle Dazzle* ran for 408 performances. In 1921 the interior was reconstructed by J. Emblin Walker. It reopened in 1922 with *Decameron Nights*, a romantic play by Robert McLaughlin which ran for 371 performances. From 1919–31 Alfred Butt had a part in the management and produced many memorable productions including the musicals *Rose Marie* (1925) which had 851 performances, *The Desert Song* (1927) and *Show Boat* (1928). Noël Coward's play *Cavalcade* began its run of 405 performances in 1931. In 1935 Marie Tempest's golden jubilee was celebrated at Drury Lane. In 1935 Ivor Novello's musical *Glamorous Night* was a big success and was followed by his *Careless Rapture* (1936), *Crest of the Wave* (1937)

and *The Dancing Years* (1939). In the 2nd World War the theatre was the headquarters of the Entertainment National Service Association. Since the war it has been the home of many well-known musicals including *Oklahoma* (1947); *Carousel* (1950); *South Pacific* (1951); *The King and I* (1953); *My Fair Lady* (1958) which had 2,281 performances; *Camelot* (1964); *Hello Dolly* (1965); *The Four Musketeers* (1967) and *Mame* (1969). More recent notable productions have been the musicals *Billy* and *A Chorus Line* and *The Pirates of Penzance* with George Cole, Pamela Stephenson, Tim Curry and Annie Ross. Drury Lane has a phantom which appears in the Circle (mostly at matinées) and is thought to be the ghost of a man whose bones were found with a knife in his ribs behind one of the walls in 1840. The seating capacity is 2,245.

Theatre Royal Haymarket *see* HAYMARKET THEATRE.

Theatre Royal Stratford East *Gerry Raffles Square, Stratford, E15.* Built for William Charles Dillon to the design of James George Buckle in 1884, the theatre had an unprepossessing exterior but an attractive auditorium. It opened – with some misgivings in view of its location – on 17 December 1884 with *Richelieu* by Bulwer Lytton. Although the first-night audience had to be reprimanded from the stage by Dillon, the play's producer, the standard of productions was considerably higher than anticipated. In 1953 the theatre was taken over by Theatre Workshop under the direction of Joan Littlewood. There followed *A Taste of Honey* (1958), *Fings Ain't Wot They Used t'Be* (1959), and *Oh! What a Lovely War* (1963). The seating capacity is 477.

Theatre Upstairs *Royal Court, Sloane Square, SW1.* Originally the old rehearsal room of the ROYAL COURT THEATRE, it opened as the Theatre Upstairs on 23 November 1971. It has become a fringe theatre with the aim of promoting experimental productions and new writers.

Theobalds Road *WC1.* Extends from SOUTHAMPTON ROW to GRAY'S INN ROAD and once formed part of King James I's route to his house at Theobalds, Hertfordshire. It was built up in the 18th century with homes for city merchants and professional men. When KINGSWAY was cut through in 1906 it became an important thoroughfare. Severely damaged in the 2nd World War, it was rebuilt with modern office blocks.

Thirties Society *c/o Country Life, Stamford Street, SE1.* Founded in 1979 to encourage appreciation of the architecture of the period between the two World Wars, from Art Deco to Classical, and neo-Tudor to Modern Movement.

Thomas Coram Foundation for Children *40 Brunswick Square, WC1.* At the instigation of William Hogarth, several other distinguished artists gave paintings to Thomas Coram's FOUNDLING HOSPITAL for display in the Governor's Court Room in the hope that this would attract visitors and funds to the hospital. Hogarth's fine portrait of Coram was the first gift; many other splendid works of art, including some by Gainsborough and Reynolds, followed it. When the hospital moved to Berkhamstead the buildings were demolished and a new house built nearby. In this the Foundation's treasures are displayed. The Court Room is an exact representation of the original.

Thorney Island The ancient name, meaning Isle of Brambles, for the area by the river on which WESTMINSTER ABBEY stands. After the Romans departed, WESTMINSTER became a wild, marshy and deserted place and there Sebert, King of the East Saxons, is believed to have founded a monastery. According to tradition, Sebert's foundation was destroyed by the Danes and rebuilt by Bishop Dunstan; the church was restored again by Edgar, King of the English, in 958, only to fall into disrepair again. The devout Edward the Confessor established the Abbey firmly, regardless of cost, and in 1060 built his own palace close by. The land around the abbey was thereafter cultivated and was no longer the inhospitable site which an 8th-century charter of King Offa had described as 'loco terribili'. Thorney was called an island on account of the ditches that surrounded and defined the precinct, and these can be seen on old maps. One ditch formed the southern boundary along what is now College Street, and its current turned the Abbot's millwheel by the river at MILLBANK. Another ditch took the line of Gardener's Lane down to the THAMES, and a third ditch running north and south along PRINCES STREET joined the other two. The waters of the TYBURN stream no doubt helped to fill the ditches. The precise outline of Thorney Island, however, is uncertain. It may have been bounded by the present lines of TACHBROOK STREET on the south-west and the line south of the lake in ST JAMES'S PARK on the north. John Rocque's map shows that it lay at least up to the mid-18th century among open fields and market gardens.

Thornton Heath *Surrey*. Situated between NORBURY and CROYDON. There was Saxon settlement around Thornton Heath which became the common land of medieval NORBURY manor. By the 16th century it was named as the Heathland by Thornhill, and charcoal burning took place, commemorated in the name of Colliers Water Lane. Although the practice declined with the arrival of Newcastle coal it continued into the 18th century when the Heath was notorious for highwaymen and a gibbet existed at the junction of London and Thornton Roads where several were hanged. Buildings survive from the 18th and early 19th centuries, including part of the Wheatlands public house. Towards the end of the 19th century there was some residential development following the construction of Thornton Heath station in 1862, but the transformation of the rural area followed the introduction of an electrified train in 1901. In addition to private building the LONDON COUNTY COUNCIL bought 30 acres to build estates. With NORBURY it became part of the London Borough of CROYDON in 1965.

Thornwood Lodge *Kensington*. First occupied in 1813, the house was built by John Tasker. Aristocratic residents included the Marchioness of Hastings (1817–23) and the 4th Earl of Glasgow (1824–30). During 1867–98 it was the home of the noted railway engineer, Sir John Fowler. Scophony

Ltd, used it as a television research centre in 1936–40. The house was demolished in about 1956.

Threadneedle Street *EC2*. Probably takes its name either from the three needles which appear in the arms of the NEEDLEMAKERS' COMPANY or the thread and needle employed by the MERCHANT TAYLORS who were a guild long before a charter was granted to them in 1327. (Merchant Taylors' Hall is still in the street at No. 30.) It was Sheridan who referred to the BANK OF ENGLAND, which occupies the area formed by Threadneedle Street, PRINCES STREET, LOTHBURY and BARTHOLOMEW LANE, as 'The Old Lady of Threadneedle Street'. On the north side of the street used to stand the Hospital of St Anthony, a community of French protestants, founded in 1243 to give aid to travellers and to collect alms for the hospital of St Antoine in the Dauphiné. In the 15th century a grammar school was attached to it and both Sir Thomas More and Archbishop John Whitgift were educated here. The buildings were burned down in the GREAT FIRE and were not replaced. The chapel, however, survived until 1840 when the street was widened. Four churches once stood here: ST CHRISTOPHER LE STOCKS (demolished 1794); ST BARTHOLOMEW BY THE EXCHANGE (demolished 1841); ST MARTIN OUTWICH (demolished 1874); and ST BENET FINK (demolished 1844) on whose site, now an open space, stands a statue of the American philanthropist George Peabody (*see* STATUES) and a fountain surmounted by a statue of a mother with two children by the French sculptor, Jules Dalou. The father and grandfather of Sir Philip Sidney lived in the street in a house known as Lady Tate's House on the site now occupied by the National Westminster Bank at No. 52. At No. 37, now the Bank of Scotland, was SOUTH SEA HOUSE. On the south side of the street is the ROYAL EXCHANGE. And on the corner of OLD BROAD STREET stands the STOCK EXCHANGE. On the corner of Finch Lane at No. 5 is a building designed by William and Andrew Moseley in 1856. This, formerly the City Bank, is now occupied by the MIDLAND BANK. The drinking fountain at the corner of the ROYAL EXCHANGE was erected by the METROPOLITAN DRINKING FOUNTAIN AND CATTLE TROUGH ASSOCIATION in its jubilee year; it is by J. Whitehead.

Three Cranes in the Vintry *Upper Thames Street*. A 16th-century tavern which, according to Stow, took its name from the 'three strong cranes of timber placed on the Vintry Wharf by the Thames side to crane up wines there'. It was a favourite haunt of Ben Jonson and his friends, but Pepys's opinion of it was most unfavourable. It was the scene of his unfortunate dinner with his poor relations in 1661. And the following year, on 23 January, he recorded: 'We all went over to the Three Cranes Tavern and, though the best room in the house, in such a narrow dogg-hole we were crammed and I believe were were near forty, that it made me loath my company and victuals, and a sorry poor dinner it was too.' A character in Sir Walter Scott's *Kenilworth* described it as 'the most topping tavern in London'.

Three Greyhounds *25 Greek Street, W1*. There has been an inn on this site for over 500 years. The present public house, a Tudor-style building with a

863

frieze depicting greyhound racing, is the subject of a preservation order.

Three Hats *Islington*. An ancient inn on the site of 39 Islington High Street near the then turnpike, its name possibly deriving from the three helmets on the Northampton family arms. Besides such outdoor pleasures as skittles and a game called 'double stick', from 1758 it pioneered summer equestrian displays, where the 'Irish Tartar', Thomas Johnson, galloped round the field standing on one, two, then three horses – even riding on his head till spectators complained that he gave them 'pain'. In July 1766 he performed to the Duke of York and an audience of 500.

In 1767–70 Mr and Mrs Sampson rode here to musical accompaniment in a specially constructed amphitheatre, demonstrating 'that the fair sex are by no means inferior to the male, either in courage or agility'. Sampson became a drunkard under the malign influence of his rival Price, of DOBNEY'S. Recovering, he returned as performer and riding master in 1772–3, but the Three Hats was then outshone by a new rival, ASTLEY'S.

Its tea gardens continued until the grounds were built over in the 19th century, when it became a tavern. In 1839, after a serious fire, it was completely rebuilt as a bank, which it still is.

Three Kings Yard *W1*. On the GROSVENOR ESTATE, it is a T-shaped mews cul-de-sac leading off the west side of DAVIES STREET, and takes its name from a tavern which formerly stood near the entrance. At the west end a picturesque brick archway surmounted by a cupola closes the vista from DAVIES STREET.

Three Nuns Inn *Aldgate High Street*. A busy coaching inn in the 17th and 18th centuries celebrated for its punch. It was later rebuilt as the Three Nuns Hotel.

Three Tuns *Guildhall Yard*. The tavern which General Monk made his headquarters when he marched into the CITY in February 1660. The name was commonly given to taverns as three tuns were the arms of the VINTNERS' COMPANY. In the following century Jeremy Bentham used to dine here 'for 13d including a penny to the waiter'.

Three Tuns Tavern *St Margaret's Hill, Southwark*. The tavern to which John Wilkes's coach was dragged by his supporters on 27 August 1768 when he was arrested and ordered to be committed to KING'S BENCH PRISON. He made a speech from one of the upper windows, after which he asked the crowd to disperse and delivered himself up to justice. Three Tuns Court marks the site.

Throgmorton Avenue *EC2*. Like THROGMORTON STREET, named after Nicholas Throgmorton, Elizabeth I's ambassador to France and Scotland. It was built across the gardens of DRAPERS' HALL into which Macaulay was taken as a child by his nurse. CARPENTERS' HALL is on the east side at No. 1, the corner of LONDON WALL.

Throgmorton Street *EC2*. Henry VIII's minister, Thomas Cromwell, had a house here, and made himself very unpopular with his neighbours because of his encroachments against which 'no man durst argue'. One of these neighbours was John Stow's father, a tailor, whose house Cromwell had dug out of the ground, placed on rollers and pulled over 20 feet away from his boundary so that he could extend his garden further down the street. After Cromwell's execution in 1540 the DRAPERS' COMPANY took over his house for their hall; and their present hall stands on the site. The STOCK EXCHANGE is on the south side.

Thurloe Estate Developed in the 1820s by John Alexander, godson of Harris Brace whose father, John Thurloe Brace, had through his wife inherited land in BROMPTON from John Thurloe, who, it is said, had been presented with it by Oliver Cromwell for services rendered during the Commonwealth. The architect of the houses was George Basevi. Several of the streets on the estate, including Thurloe Close, Place, Square and Street, SW7, derive their names from the Thurloe family connections.

Thurloe Place *SW7*. Extends from BROMPTON ROAD to Cromwell Place. BROMPTON ORATORY and the VICTORIA AND ALBERT MUSEUM are on the north side. The Rembrandt Hotel (169 bedrooms) is at No. 11. For the Yalta Memorial *see* MEMORIALS.

Thurloe Street *SW7*. Elegant terraced houses built on the Thurloe Estate by George Basevi in 1820–43.

Tiger Tavern *Tower Hill, EC3*. A modern public house built on a site where a tavern has stood since the 16th century. In the upper bar can be seen the mummified remains of a cat said to have been stroked by the young Princess Elizabeth when a prisoner in the TOWER. There is still a tunnel from the house to the TOWER, although this has now been blocked off. Every ten years the LORD MAYOR OF LONDON, together with his SHERIFFS and ALDERMEN come here to test the beer. Some beer is poured on to a stool and the beer-tester invited to sit. If his trousers stick to the seat all is well: a laurel wreath is hung outside the door and a garland round the neck of the landlord.

Tigris *or* **Tygris** A small stream which rose near the site of the ELEPHANT AND CASTLE and followed the course of BLACKFRIARS ROAD on its way to the THAMES. It is called the Tigris by Robert Bowers and the Tygris by William Kent, but neither gives any explanation of the name. It is said to be part of a canal cut by King Canute, through the marshes from ROTHERHITHE to CHELSEA, to enable his fleet to by-pass LONDON BRIDGE when he besieged London in the 11th century.

Tilbury Docks In the 1880s the EAST and WEST INDIA DOCK Company was not prospering, partly due to the competition from the new Royal Albert Dock. So it decided to build new docks at Tilbury that would take the larger modern ships. It achieved its Act in 1882 and the Tilbury Docks were opened in 1886 with celebrations at the new Tilbury Hotel. The site was 450 acres of marshland opposite Gravesend, 26 miles down river from TOWER BRIDGE. Under its engineer, A. Manning, the area of dock water achieved was 56 acres, which was entered by an open tidal basin of 19 acres. Instead of the usual long quays it had three branch docks and it was linked to London by the London, Tilbury and Southend Railway. Houses for police officers, foremen and executives, and tenement dwellings for the dock workers, were built near the docks. Custom was expected from ships which normally arrived at Gravesend and might have to wait there at anchor for the flood tide to help them up river but could now berth at Tilbury at any state of the tide and could thereby save a day as well as the cost of towage and pilotage and the risks of navigating narrow, crowded waters. The early years were disappointing. The expected business did not arrive and considerable expense was incurred by the continuous silting up of the tidal entrance. There was financial mismanagement, some costly litigation with the contractors, and trouble with the lightermen and wharfingers who were boycotting the new docks. The company had to offer such ruinous rates that it ran at a loss. Early in 1888 came financial disaster and stock fell from a nominal £100 to £9. The next year a major dock strike occurred. Competition between dock companies was now so intense that in 1888 the London and St Katharine Dock Company, which owned the VICTORIA and ALBERT, and the EAST and WEST INDIA DOCK Company were compelled to amalgamate in a working union through a joint committee, though full amalgamation was not achieved until 1900.

When it took over the docks the PORT OF LONDON AUTHORITY improved those at Tilbury, an addition being a huge passenger landing stage that could be used at any state of the tide. In the early 1930s a 750 ft long dry dock and a new entrance lock 1,000 ft long were constructed; and an innovation came in the form of a new Customs Baggage Hall, opened by the Prime Minister Ramsay MacDonald. During the 2nd World War the dock was used for converting luxury liners into armed merchantmen. The docks have been greatly improved in recent years. There are new techniques of containerisation, trailer handling, fork lifting, 'roll-on-roll-off' systems, new cranes, and giant grain silos, on which the PORT OF LONDON AUTHORITY has spent in all £30 million.

Tilney Street *W1*. A short street extending from the south end of DEANERY STREET to SOUTH AUDLEY STREET. On the north side No. 3 and the houses eastward of it form a pleasantly variegated Georgian range, now partly stuccoed, and one having a projecting bow at first- and second-floor levels – added, no doubt, to obtain an oblique view to HYDE PARK.

Tin Plate Workers' Company alias Wireworkers *see* CITY LIVERY COMPANIES.

Tite Street *SW3*. Named after Sir William Tite, MP, who, as a member of the METROPOLITAN BOARD OF WORKS, played a large part in building the CHELSEA EMBANKMENT. It was much favoured by artists and writers in the late 19th century. E.W. Godwin designed the White House for James McNeill Whistler in 1877. The designs embodied all Whistler's ideas of elegance but it was too plain for the METROPOLITAN BOARD OF WORKS who insisted on ornamental moulding before granting a building licence. Whistler had to leave the house after a few months when financially crippled by his libel case with John Ruskin. The day before he left he inscribed over the door 'Except the Lord build the house, they labour in vain that build it.' He lived later at Nos 13 and 46. The house was demolished and the present White House was built on its site. John Singer Sargent lived and died at No. 31. No. 33 contains studios used by Augustus John, Simon Elwes and others. Oscar Nemon sculpted his statue of Winston Churchill here. Oscar Wilde lived at No. 16 (now No. 64) from his marriage in 1884 until his arrest in 1895. *Lady Windermere's Fan* and *The Importance of Being Earnest* were both written here. 'I have,' wrote Wilde, 'a dining room done in different shades of white, with white curtains embroidered in yellow silk: the effect is absolutely delightful and the room beautiful.' His study was red and yellow. The walls of the drawing room were buttercup yellow; the ceiling was blue and painted with dragons; there were two brilliant peacock's feathers let into the plaster; there were blue and white curtains of a William Morris design and black and white bamboo chairs. Wilde liked Tite Street because it was in easy reach of his mother, who lived in OAKLEY STREET (then No. 46, afterwards No. 87, now demolished), and because one morning he saw Ellen Terry going to sit for her portrait in Whistler's studio: 'The street that on a wet and dreary morning had vouchsafed the vision of Lady Macbeth in full regalia magnificently seated in a four-wheeler can never be as other streets: it must always be full of wonderful possibilities.' Edwin Abbey, the American artist, lived at Chelsea Lodge, Tite Street, which he vainly wished would become a museum for the ROYAL ACADEMY.

Tithe Barn *Manor Farm, Harmondsworth, Middlesex*. The most important secular building in the London Borough of HILLINGDON, it is listed as an Ancient Monument. Erected probably towards the end of the 14th century, its base is of a local pudding stone conglomerate and its pillars consist of complete tree trunks. Not a single iron nail was used in its construction. Its approximate size is 190 ft by 36 ft. Within living memory the village 'harvest home' was held in the barn. In 1972 a fire seriously damaged the southern bay of the barn but expert restoration has left little trace of this near disaster.

Tivoli Music Hall *65–70½ Strand*. Erected in 1890 to the designs of C.J. Phipps at a cost of £300,000, twice that of the PALACE, CAMBRIDGE CIRCUS which was built at approximately the same time and had an equivalent seating capacity. It comprised not only a theatre but also a restaurant and private dining-rooms. It became a popular social resort and one of London's most famous music halls under the management of Charles Morton. It closed in 1914 and a cinema was built on the site in 1923.

Tobacco Pipe Makers' and Tobacco Blenders' Company *see* CITY LIVERY COMPANIES.

Toc H During the 1st World War the Revd P.B. (Tubby) Clayton established at Poperinghe near Ypres a centre, Talbot House, for the physical and spiritual needs of troops temporarily withdrawn from the battle front. This was referred to by the men as 'Toc H' from the term used by signallers to avoid misreading of the letter 'T'. It was the beginning of a world-wide Christian charity which had its headquarters on TOWER HILL and does good work among the youth of the nation. It has adopted ALL HALLOWS BY THE TOWER as its special church.

Tokenhouse Yard *EC2*. Built in the reign of Charles I by Sir William Petty, the economist and one of the first members of the ROYAL SOCIETY, on the site of the mansion of the Earl of Arundel. It takes its name from a house where farthing tokens were coined. Thomas Hood, the poet, went to a school here kept by the Misses Hogsfleash.

Tolworth *Surrey*. Known until the 1880s as Talworth, this was originally a small hamlet. When the Local Government Act of 1894 set up urban districts, it was joined to SURBITON. Much residential development took place from then on, and this was accelerated when the Kingston by-pass was completed in 1927. The tram service had reached Red Lion Road in 1906, although the Southern Railway branch line was not completed until 1938. The Broadway office and shopping area had begun at this time and was completed between 1962–4. This includes the 22-storey Tolworth Tower by R. Seifert and Partners.

The parish church of St Matthew stands at the junction of St Matthew and Ewell Roads. It was designed by Charles Lloyd Luck and built in 1874–5. In Ashcombe Avenue is Southborough House, designed by John Nash for Thomas Langley in 1808.

Tom King's Coffee House *Covent Garden*. Mentioned by Fielding in 1732: 'What rake is ignorant of King's coffee house.' Tom King, the landlord, had been a scholar of Eton in 1715, but left when he realised he was unlikely to become a fellow. The house was a rudimentary shed under ST PAUL'S, 'one of the old night houses of Covent Garden', frequented by 'gentlemen to whom beds are unknown'. After King's death the house was retained by his notorious widow, Moll, 'renowned for her good humour and repartee'. She was constantly before the King's Bench for keeping a disorderly house. In *Roderick Random* (1748) Smollett describes a visit to the house: 'Banter and I accompanied Bagwell to Moll King's Coffee House, where, after he had kicked half a dozen hungry whores, we left him to sleep on a bench.' After Moll King's death in 1747 the history of the house becomes obscure.

Tom's Coffee House *Russell Street, Covent Garden*. Established in about 1700 by Thomas West, who died in 1722, throwing himself from a second-storey window in a delirium occasioned by gout. The house was used by theatregoers. Mackay describes his pleasure in the conversation, in the hours after a play, when nobles mixed with commoners and enjoyed 'the universal liberty of Speech of the English Nation'. Amongst regular patrons listed in 1763 are Dr Johnson, Garrick, Sir Joshua Reynolds, the Duke of Northumberland, the Marquess of Granby, Admiral Lord Rodney and George Steevens, the Shakespearian commentator. In 1768 Tom's became a subscription club and the premises were altered to accommodate a large cardroom. The building was demolished in 1865.

Toole's Theatre *William IV Street*. Opened in 1869 as a variety house in a converted building under the title The Royal Charing Cross Theatre. It was reconstructed by Thomas Verity in 1876. Thereafter for two years burlesques were staged under the management of Alexander Henderson. His greatest success was *Les Cloches de Corneville* (1878). During 1879–95 the theatre was managed by the actor, John Toole, who staged comedies and farces until he was forced to retire with gout. The theatre was demolished in 1896. The Out-patient Department of CHARING CROSS HOSPITAL stood on the site.

Tooley Street *SE1*. The name is a corruption of St Olave's Street which was so called after the nearby Church of St Olave. It was once known as Short Southwark to distinguish it from Long Southwark, now BOROUGH HIGH STREET, and was inhabited in the Middle Ages by wealthy citizens and prelates including the Priors of Lewes, the Abbots of Battle and the Priors of St Augustine, Canterbury. St Olave's Grammar School, founded in 1560, formerly stood in the street. One of the Governors was Robert Harvard whose son, John (after whom Harvard University is named) spent part of his youth in the street. Keats lived in Dean Street off Tooley Street when a student at ST THOMAS'S HOSPITAL. Today it is lined with warehouses owned by HAY'S WHARF, whose headquarters stands near LONDON BRIDGE on the former site of St Olave's Church. Until the closure of the docks in 1970 it was known as 'London's larder'. Much of the area now awaits redevelopment. There is a bronze bust of the former Foreign Secretary, Ernest Bevin, by E. Whitney-Smith (1955).

Tooting *SW17*. Of the two common theories about the origin of the name Tooting, one suggests that it means 'the dwelling of the sons of Totas' – a Saxon name; while the other claims that it is derived from *theou* meaning a slave and *ing*, a dwelling, thus – 'the dwelling of villeins'. The *Domesday* survey shows two distinct areas of Tooting, Tooting Bec (later also known as Upper Tooting) and Tooting Graveney (Lower Tooting). The former was part of the parish of STREATHAM and was held by the Benedictine Abbey of Saint Mary of Bec in Normandy, whose Abbot set up a gallows in Tooting Bec in 1258. During the wars with France Edward II seized all the land held by alien priories, but Tooting Bec was restored to the French Abbey by Edward III. Later holders of the land included the Earls of Warwick in the 16th century, the Russell family in the 17th century and Lord Thurlow, the Lord Chancellor, in the late 1700s.

At the time of the Survey some of the land at Tooting Graveney was held by WESTMINSTER ABBEY but the majority was in the hands of Chertsey Abbey and had been so held since 675 AD. Before the Conquest most of the land was cultivated for the benefit of Chertsey Abbey. *Domesday* also records the existence of a church which probably dated from shortly after the death of Edward the Confessor. After the Conquest the land was leased to the nobility and in 1394 most of the Manor went to the Dymoke family who held it for two centuries until Elizabeth I granted it to Lord Burleigh's secretary Henry Maynard. The De Gravenells, who held the land for a time, gave the name Graveney to this part of Tooting. Elizabeth I visited Sir Henry Maynard at Tooting in 1600 and it is said that an avenue of trees was planted on the Common in her honour. Another tradition concerns a house called Knapdale which was supposedly occupied, during the Civil War, by a commander of Lord Fairfax while General Fairfax himself was encamped on Putney Heath.

Although, contrary to tradition, there is no evidence that Daniel Defoe actually lived in Tooting he did have strong connections with the area towards the end of the 17th century. From 1688 there was a strong group of Dissenters based on Tooting and led by Joshua Gearing, which met secretly in private houses. Defoe played a large part in forming the local Dissenters into a regular congregation (*see* DEFOE CHAPEL).

Throughout the 17th century the ancient rights of the inhabitants to cut furze and to dig gravel on the two commons caused many difficulties. Fines were imposed on the inhabitants of Tooting Bec for cutting furze on Tooting Graveney Common instead of the one at Tooting Bec; and in 1668 a three-year ban on any furze cutting on Tooting Graveney Common was imposed. Fifteen years later it was deemed necessary to appoint a Common keeper to exercise control. Problems continued throughout the following century and in 1709 it was decreed that no one should take more furze than could be carried on their shoulders. The use of carts was banned completely. The Duke of Bedford who owned much land in STREATHAM, adjoining TOOTING BEC COMMON, ordered his agent to fence off the Common and to sell the furze. The riot which resulted caused the Duke to change his mind and the fences were removed.

Like neighbouring STREATHAM, but to a much lesser extent, Tooting became known as a desirable place for a country residence; and the 18th century saw the erection of some large mansions for the rich of the CITY. Richard Blackmore, court physician and poet, was one of those who made his home at Tooting and, in 1714, the Lord Mayor, Sir James Bateman, bought the manor of Tooting Graveney. His funeral at Tooting Church in 1718 needed 20 coaches, each of which was drawn by six horses.

Settlement was centred around the church at Tooting Graveney with a few houses at Tooting Bec. The High Street at Tooting Bec was part of Stane Street, one of the original roads in Roman Britain, which ran from the city to Chichester. The inhabitants of Tooting, as in nearby localities, suffered from the activities of highway robbers and, in 1700, strict regulations were brought into force for their protection between Mitcham Road and the churchyard. By 1770 Tooting Graveney had a constable, a pound keeper, a common field keeper and an ale taster. But the population of Tooting remained small, numbering only 1,189, housed in 168 dwellings, in 1801.

In 1823 the parishioners of Tooting Graveney financed the sinking of an artesian well with a fountain above. This provided a constant and abundant supply of water to several small fountains in the village.

In the first half of the 19th century there was a considerable growth of villa-type housing in Tooting Bec which was then described as a 'very pretty district of hills and woods and tiny streams'. A few shops had opened in the High Road. The census of 1841 shows that there was also a brewery, although this is not recorded in the census of 1851. The Surrey County Lunatic Asylum was opened in 1840 and is, today, the Springfield Hospital.

At this time Tooting was the centre of a notorious Poor Law scandal. Many neighbouring Poor Law Unions sent some of the children in their care to the Infant Pauper Asylum at Tooting, where the Master, Bartholomew Drouet, offered to clothe, feed and instruct them at a weekly cost of 4s 6d. In the 1840s an average of 1,500 children lived at the institution at any one time. During a CHOLERA epidemic in 1849, 118 children died between 5 and 18 January. 'That most infamous and atrocious enormity committed at Tooting,' as Charles Dickens described the tragedy in 'A Walk in a Workhouse', was attributed by the Coroner to insufficient food, defective clothing and impure air. Contemporary accounts show that the children were, in fact, kept in the most appalling conditions. Drouet was, nevertheless, found not guilty on a charge of manslaughter. Many contemporaries believed that murder would have been a more appropriate charge.

By the mid-19th century there were six daily omnibus services to the CITY but the population had only risen to 2,122 by 1851, in direct contrast to the very rapid growth of neighbouring STREATHAM. In 1878–81 Thomas Hardy was living at No. 172 Trinity Road, then No. 1 Arundel Terrace. But it was not until after the creation of the LONDON COUNTY COUNCIL in 1889 that the growth of Tooting really began, particularly after the COUNCIL turned the Totterdown area into a building estate. One of those who moved here at this time was Sir Harry Lauder, the music-hall performer who lived at No. 46 (then No. 24) Longley Road in 1903–11. Today Tooting, retaining its two adjacent Commons, is a typical London suburban area, although there is a greater feeling of openness than is to be found in many of the capital's boroughs.

Tooting Bec Common *SW12*. Extends to about 150 acres. Samuel Johnson was for 15 years until the death of Henry Thrale in 1781 a frequent visitor to the Thrales' house which formerly overlooked the Common.

Topsfield Hall *Crouch End*. The seat of the Lord of the Manor of Topsfield, one of the ancient holdings in HORNSEY. A London merchant, Richard of Topsfield, who allegedly paid rent for the manor in 1342, may have given it its name; but the first undoubted Lord was Stephen Maynard of ISLINGTON in 1347. A house built on the estate in the late 18th century (*see* CROUCH END) passed into the hands of the Booth distilling family whose executors sold it in 1853 to Henry Weston Elder, a bristle merchant in the City, the final occupant, who had bought the manor some years before. After the death of Elder's widow the house was demolished in 1895. Middle and Tottenham Lanes were then widened and part of the site developed with shops. Two roads are named after Henry Weston Elder: Weston Park, N8, and Elder Avenue, N8.

Torrington Square *WC1*. Built in 1821–5 by James Sim and named after Lord Torrington, father of the 6th Duke of Bedford's first wife. The area was formerly known as the FIELD OF FORTY FOOTSTEPS. One dignified terrace is left, the rest is now mostly

BIRKBECK COLLEGE of LONDON UNIVERSITY. Charles Kean lived at No. 3 in 1853–6; Christina Rossetti at No. 30 in 1876–94. Round the corner in Torrington Place is Dillon's University Bookshop in a building by Fitzroy Doll (1907). This bookshop was opened in Store Street in 1936 by Una Dillon. It moved to its present address in 1956.

Tothill Fields *Westminster*.

Once lay between WESTMINSTER ABBEY and MILLBANK. A toot hill was the highest ground in an area which could be used as an observation post or for the erection of a beacon. (Thus Wycliffe rendered the authorised version of the Second Book of Samuel's 'Nevertheless David toke the stronghold of Zion' as 'Forsooth David took the tote hill Syon'). Some have maintained, however, that this was a place where the Druids worshiped Teut. Tournaments were held in the fields by early kings living in the PALACE OF WESTMINSTER. In 1236 Queen Eleanor's coronation was celebrated by one. The fields were also used for pasturing cattle, for growing vegetables and herbs, for horse racing, for archery practice and military parades, until 1793 for bear baiting and until 1820 for bull baiting. St Edward's Fair was held annually. There was also a maze which was drawn by Hollar. Duels were often fought here and punishments inflicted, particularly for witchcraft and necromancy. In 1618 a prison was built. This served as a model for Hogarth when he was working on *The Rake's Progress*. It was rebuilt in Francis Street in 1834 and demolished in 1885. (WESTMINSTER CATHEDRAL covers the site.) Victims of the GREAT PLAGUE were buried in pits in the fields as the city churchyards were so overcrowded; and over 1,000 Scottish prisoners, taken at the Battle of Worcester, were also buried here. The fields were developed in 1832–50. TOTHILL STREET preserves the name.

Tothill Street *SW1*.

Takes its name from TOTHILL FIELDS. In the 16th and early 17th centuries it was lined with the houses of aristocratic families. Thomas Betterton, the actor, was born here in 1635; in about 1658 much of the street was rebuilt with smaller houses, some of which were used as inns. Soon after the Restoration, the office of the Revels was established at Lincoln House here by Sir Henry Herbert, Master of the Revels to Charles II. Edmund Burke lived in the street for a time. The ROYAL AQUARIUM stood here between 1876 and 1906. Steel House at No. 11 is by Sir John Burnet, Tait and Lorne (1936).

Tottenham *N17*.

Lies about 7 miles to the northeast of central London. Its name perhaps originally meant Totta's village. In Saxon times it was evidently a clearing in the forest. The forest was gradually cleared until, by the 17th century, all that remained of it was the area known as WOOD GREEN. *Domesday Book* of 1086 suggests that the population of Tottenham consisted of one priest, renting 50 to 60 acres, six villeins with 50 acres and 24 villeins having 6–7 acres each. There were two 'francig' (Frenchmen) with about 100 acres each and some 29 bordars' cottages. In 1254 Tottenham was divided into seven lordships. In the 16th century Henry VIII hunted deer here; and it was at 'Maister Comton's House by Totnam', now BRUCE CASTLE, that he met his sister Margaret Queen of Scots in 1516 when she came to reside at her brother's court at Bayford Castle, having been exiled from Scotland. By 1600 Tottenham was said to be a prosperous area with numerous almshouses, endowments and charities for the poor. In 1724 Defoe commented in his *Tour of England and Wales* that the increase in buildings was so great that it appeared 'to be one continued street'. At that time and subsequently Tottenham was famous for its greens and taverns. Izaak Walton is said to have stayed at the Swan when he came to fish here. By 1800 the wood had completely disappeared. Tottenham, however, still continued to be a rural community, despite the founding of rubber and crêpe factories.

In 1843 shocking housing conditions prevailed and references were made about 'Tottenham High Crosse' where they kept 'tippling houses without licences' amongst the tumble-down cottages. In 1840 the Great Eastern Railway was built but this had little effect initially. In 1872, however, when the line from ENFIELD TO LIVERPOOL STREET opened, offering cheap workmens' tickets on certain trains, great building activity resulted; and from 1890 onwards light industry developed. In 1868 the PRINCE OF WALES HOSPITAL was founded, and in 1880 TOTTENHAM HOTSPURS FOOTBALL CLUB. Many of today's familiar buildings were built in the 1890s, including Tottenham Palace where Marie Lloyd appeared. This is now a Mecca Social Club. In 1894 a local historian claimed that Tottenham had become the most populous distict in MIDDLESEX. In 1912 the town hall was opened and the development of the area became complete by the end of the 1st World War. In the survey of 1971 Tottenham had a population of 78,400. The area is mainly residential though light industry remains. Tottenham

Hollar's view of the maze in Tothill Fields, Westminster, where bull-baiting took place until 1820.

Hale has recently been declared an industrial development area.

Tottenham Court Road *W1*. Originally a market road leading from OXFORD STREET to Tottenham Court. The manor of Tothele, which was north of the present EUSTON ROAD, was mentioned in *Domesday Book*. It passed through the hands of the Crown and many others, and finally to the Dukes of Grafton. Tottenham Court and Tottenham fields were a popular place of entertainment for Londoners. Now it is a busy street best known for furniture dealers, including HEAL'S, MAPLES and Habitat (an international concern founded by Terence Conran in the 1960s) with a concentration of audio and video dealers at the south end. It is difficult to imagine that it was once so rural that when HEAL'S was established in 1840 on land belonging to Capper's Farm, the lease provided for 'the proper accommodation of 40 cows at least'. The cowsheds burned down in 1877.

There was an old boundary stone in ST GILES CIRCUS at the junction of TOTTENHAM COURT ROAD and OXFORD STREET, where charity boys of ST GILES beating the bounds were themselves beaten if they were considered to have deserved a flogging. Nearby there was Meux's Brewhouse, on the site of which was built the DOMINION CINEMA; and next to it is the Horseshoe Tavern, dating from the 17th century, now the Horseshoe public house in a very elaborate 19th-century building. On the west side facing Torrington Place is WHITEFIELDS TABERNACLE, built in 1756.

Tottenham Hotspur Football Club *see* FOOTBALL CLUBS.

Totteridge *Hertfordshire*. Situated between FINCHLEY and HIGH BARNET, one mile west of the Great North Road. The earliest reference to it dates from the 13th century when it was called Tatarige, possibly connected with someone called Tata or derived from the Saxon *tot*, a small grove of trees, hence 'wooded ridge'. Before the Reformation Totteridge manor, an area of woodland and pasture, had belonged, together with Hatfield, to the Bishop of Ely. By the 13th century it was an established hamlet with a chapel of Hatfield serving its needs.

Over the centuries its rural qualities attracted well-to-do families to Totteridge. Many members of the Pepys family are buried in St Andrew's churchyard in the heart of the village. The site may have been occupied by a church for 1,000 years, as suggested by the age of the great yew standing in front of it. The present church dates to the beginning of the 18th century although it has been suggested that the nave still contains much medieval masonry. In 1789 it was decided to rebuild the church completely except for the upper part of the steeple. It was also enlarged, and extended eastwards.

The parish grew in population with the opening of the Great Northern Railway to BARNET. Late Victorian and Edwardian mansions were built around the village, along Totteridge Lane (which was already named by the 17th century) and Common. Harry Vardon, the professional golfer, lived at No. 35 Totteridge Lane in 1903–37. Cardinal Manning was born at the since-demolished Copped Hall. Between the wars further estates were developed so that by 1951 the district of Totteridge had a population of 4,500.

Having been incorporated into BARNET Urban District in 1914, Totteridge came part of the London Borough of BARNET in 1965. In 1968 Totteridge village and much of Totteridge Lane and Common were designated a conservation area.

Tower Armouries *Tower of London, EC3*. While armour has always been kept in the TOWER, the present collection took shape in the reign of Henry VIII, who was personally interested. Later, Charles II had the King's armour concentrated here; but before this the armouries had for some time been a showplace to which the royal nucleus of armour gave a special character, closely associating it with the history of England. The displays consist essentially of armour and weapons of offence. The former covers the development of body armour to the full armour of the 15th century and its later virtual disappearance as a result of the development of gunpowder. The latter are divided into four categories which consist of swords and daggers, weapons relying on percussion, like the club and mace, staff weapons, such as the lance and pike and all forms of projectile, ranging from javelins, slings and bows to firearms.

In the White Tower are found the Sporting Gallery, with weapons used for sport throughout the ages; the Tournament Gallery, displaying jousting and tournament equipment; the Medieval Gallery, which has arms and armour from the Viking period to the end of the 15th century; the 16th-century Gallery, containing the personal armour of Henry VIII and prominent Elizabethans; the 17th-century Gallery, with its Stuart royal armours; and the mortar and cannon rooms, containing a variety of the earlier heavy firearms. The late 17th-century red brick building, known as the New Armouries, provides additional display and contains oriental arms and armour and firearms of foreign countries.

Tower Bridge *Tower Hill–Bermondsey*. The first and only bridge below LONDON BRIDGE. In 1879 Sir Joseph Bazalgette put forward a design for a single-arch road bridge. It was rejected because of insufficient headroom. In 1884 it was decided to build a bascule bridge, and John Wolfe-Barry was appointed engineer with Sir Horace Jones as architect. The Act authorising its building was passed in 1885. It stipulated an opening span with 200 ft clear width and headroom of 135 ft. It was also required to be in the Gothic style. The first stone was laid by the Prince of Wales in 1881. The next year Jones died and the detailing was not carried out exactly to his original design. The bridge was opened with great ceremony in 1894 by the Prince of Wales. London's best-known bridge, its towers are constructed with a steel frame clothed in stone in order to support the great weight of the bascules. They also contain lifts to convey pedestrians to the high-level footbridge which was in use when the bridge was opened. The two side-spans are on the suspension principle, the decks being hung from curved lattice girders. The hydraulic machinery to raise and lower the bridge, supplied by Armstrong-Mitchell Ltd, was preserved after electrification in 1976.

Tower Hamlets *E1, E2, E3, E4*. The London Borough created in 1965 when the former Metropolitan Boroughs of BETHNAL GREEN, POPLAR

Tower Bridge nearing completion in the 1890s.

and STEPNEY were amalgamated; but the name originally related to a wider area and was in use by the 16th century. In 1554 the Council ordered a muster of men of the hamlets 'which owe their service to the Tower'. This right of the Lieutenant of the Tower to exact guard duty was extended in 1605 to include the right to muster the militia, and EAST LONDON was made a distinct military unit with the official name of 'Tower Hamlets'. The term became increasingly used in civil affairs in the 17th century with the Justices of the Peace being described as for the 'Tower Hamlets' in 1636. In 1684 it was claimed that the inhabitants mostly 'consist of Weavers, and other Manufacturers, and of Sea-men, watermen and such . . . and are generally very factious and poor'. There were 21 hamlets, listed by Strype in 1720: HACKNEY, Norton Folgate, SHOREDITCH, SPITALFIELDS, WHITECHAPEL, Trinity Minories, East Smithfield, Tower Liberty Within, Tower Liberty Without, ST KATHARINE'S, WAPPING, RATCLIFF, SHADWELL, LIMEHOUSE, POPLAR, BLACKWALL, BROMLEY, BOW, OLD FORD, MILE END and BETHNAL GREEN. This was the area covered by the new parliamentary borough of Tower Hamlets, established in 1832 with a population of about 400,000. HACKNEY, SHOREDITCH and BETHNAL GREEN were later separated, and the name ceased to exist from 1918 until revived again in 1965 for the new London Borough and in 1974 for the two parliamentary constituencies of Tower Hamlets (BETHNAL GREEN AND BOW) and Tower Hamlets (STEPNEY AND POPLAR).

Tower Hamlets Cemetery *see* CEMETERIES.

Tower Hill *EC3.* Principal place of execution by beheading for the traitors who have been imprisoned in the TOWER. 75 people in all have been known to be executed here surrounded by thousands of spectators. The first was Sir Simon de Burley, tutor to Richard II (1388). Among the others were Sir Thomas More (1535); Thomas Cromwell (1540); the Duke of Somerset, Protector in the reign of Edward VI (1552); John Dudley, Duke of Northumberland (1553); Thomas Wentworth, Earl of Strafford (1641); Archbishop Laud (1645); the Duke of Monmouth (1685); and the Jacobite, Lord Lovat (1747). Lord Lovat was the last man to be executed by beheading in England. 'God save us!' he exclaimed when he saw the immense numbers of people who had come to witness the event. So overladen, in fact, was one of the spectators' stands overlooking the scaffold that a support cracked and broke, bringing it tumbling to the ground and crushing several people to death. 'The more mischief, the better sport,' Lovat grimly commented. For a time, after Lovat's death, a gallows stood on Tower Hill. The last people to be hanged there were two prostitutes and a one-armed soldier who had been arrested during the GORDON RIOTS in 1780 for leading an attack by a drunken mob on the tavern of a foreign Roman Catholic. The execution site is marked by a stone in the pavement at the west end of the gardens of TRINITY SQUARE.

Tower Hotel *St Katharine's Way, E1.* Built in 1973 to the designs of the Renton Howard Wood Partnership as part of the ST KATHARINE'S DOCK development. It has magnificent views of the THAMES and TOWER BRIDGE. There are 826 bedrooms.

Tower Liberties *EC3, E1.* Before 1686 the liberties of the TOWER were restricted to the area within its walls and the land on TOWER HILL immediately outside, which the TOWER authorities were anxious to keep unoccupied for its protection. They made every effort in the 16th and 17th centuries to prevent encroachment, and disputes over jurisdiction with the CITY authorities were frequent. However, three further areas were added by James II's charter of 1686, the MINORIES, the Old Artillery Ground and Wellclose, all former monastic lands which had been acquired by the Crown and previously used for the storage of ordnance. By 1686 these three sites had been sold for redevelopment, and privileged status as Tower Liberties was claimed and granted. Thus the inhabitants were freed from jury service at assizes and county sessions and exempted from the jurisdiction of the CITY OF LONDON and COUNTY OF MIDDLESEX. Rates were levied only occasionally. The Tower Liberties had their own courthouse and prison, originally

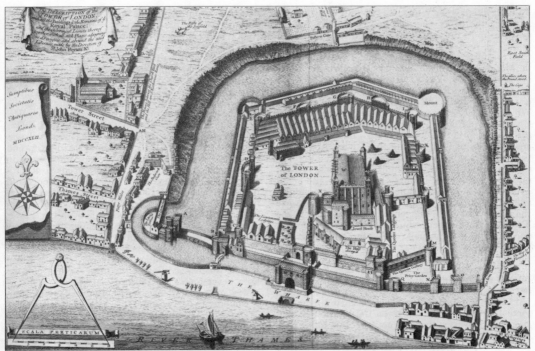

The Tower Liberties in 1597, when they were restricted to an area within the walls, and the land on Tower Hill.

situated on TOWER HILL and later in Wellclose Square. From the mid-19th century the autonomy of the liberties was progressively eroded by the Police Acts which removed their criminal jurisdiction; and some administrative powers were transferred to the LONDON COUNTY COUNCIL. For local government purposes the TOWER OF LONDON and its liberties were included in the WHITECHAPEL Board of Works from 1855 and the Metropolitan Borough of STEPNEY from 1900, when their last vestiges of independence were finally taken away.

TOWER OF LONDON *Tower Hill, EC3.* The most perfect medieval fortress in Britain, begun by William I and added to by successive monarchs until Edward I completed the outer wall, enclosing an area of 18 acres. It has been a palace, prison and place of execution and has housed the royal armouries, the mint, the royal observatory, the royal menagerie, the Public Records, and still guards the Crown Jewels (*see below*).

Soon after the Battle of Hastings in 1066 William I ordered a temporary fort to be built on a strategic site outside the city wall to awe the people into submission. He later required a stone tower and this was probably designed by Gundulf, a tearful, emotional monk from the Abbey of Bec in Normandy who became Bishop of Rochester and was much respected as a designer of both churches and fortresses. Caen limestone, Kentish ragstone and local mudstone were used in the building.

The walls range from 15 ft thick at the bottom to 11 ft at the top. They are 90 ft high and although the building looks square, in fact the sides vary between 107 ft and 118 ft long. The only entrance to the keep

was on the south side, about 15 ft above ground, with a flight of steps which would be removed in times of danger. Inside there were four floors. The ground floor was originally intended as a store but was later used as dungeons. Here is the Little Ease, a dark unventilated cell 4 ft square, where the prisoner could neither stand nor lie down. The first floor was used as the soldiers' and servants' quarters; the second floor contained the banqueting hall, ST JOHN'S CHAPEL and sleeping accommodation for the nobility; and on the third floor were the royal bedrooms and the council chamber. The only staircase was in the north-east corner. It spiralled in a clockwise direction so defenders could have the advantage of holding their swords in their right hand. From every apartment the garrison could keep watch on the city and surrounding countryside. There were three large fireplaces, two on the first floor and one in the banqueting hall. Water was supplied by three wells. The top three floors each had two garderobes, or latrines, with seats and chutes. When the keep was completed is uncertain – it is not mentioned in the *Domesday* Survey carried out in 1086. Some authorities maintain that it was finished in the reign of William Rufus (1087–1101); others in that of Henry I (1101–35). It can be said with more certainty that the Chapel of ST PETER AD VINCULA was built in Henry I's reign for the use of the Tower's garrison, servants and prisoners. Some other buildings were also built at that time.

In 1101 Ralf Flambard, Bishop of Durham, became the Tower's first prisoner when he was arrested for selling benefices. He escaped from a window by a rope, having first made his guards drunk. The Tower was first used as a royal residence by King Stephen at Whitsun 1140; but as his cousin Matilda, the other claimant to the throne, had so much support only one bishop dared to attend upon him. The next year Londoners supporting Stephen tried to capture the Constable of the Tower, Geoffrey de Mandeville, Queen Matilda's man, but he broke out and escaped.

During Henry II's reign (1154–89) a kitchen, bakery and gaol were built. In 1189 Richard I appointed William of Longchamp, a Norman of humble birth, Chancellor of England, Bishop of Ely and Constable of the Tower in his absence abroad. Longchamp spent enormous sums on fortifying the Tower. A wall was thrown round the keep; the Bell Tower and perhaps the Wardrobe Tower were built, and a ditch was dug on the west and north sides. Longchamp also spent £100 on mangonels, machines for hurling large stones, when he heard that Prince John was plotting to seize the throne. In 1191 Longchamp was besieged in the Tower by the Council, who were jealous of his power, and by John's supporters. After three days he surrendered and was exiled to France, and John took over the kingdom.

During John's reign (1189–99) the Tower was further strengthened: the Bell Tower seems to have been finished and the northern ditch deepened. In 1215 the Barons seized the Tower in their attempts to force John to accept the Magna Carta. After he had signed it, however, they did not trust him to keep his word and continued to occupy the Tower. When John did break faith they offered the throne to the French Dauphin. Louis arrived in 1216 and held court in the Tower for a year.

During Henry III's reign (1216–72) there was a great spate of building: repairs were carried out on what are referred to as the King's Houses, the first mention of the royal palace south of the White Tower. A new kitchen and great hall were also built at this time; work began on building or rebuilding the inner wall; and a new moat was dug under the expert advice of a Fleming. In 1235 the Holy Roman Emperor gave Henry three leopards, an allusion to the leopards on the Plantaganet coat of arms. Thus the royal menagerie was begun. The animals were open to public viewing and the expression 'going to see the lions' probably dates from this time. On the occasion of Henry's marriage to Eleanor of Provence in 1236 the coronation procession set out from the Tower for the first time. Four years later the Keep was whitewashed and thereafter became known as the White Tower. In 1252 the SHERIFFS of London were ordered to provide 4d a day for food for a polar bear, a gift from the King of Norway, and to buy the animal a chain so that he could fish in the THAMES. Three years later the menagerie was further expanded when an elephant house was built to accommodate a present which had arrived from the King's French cousin, Louis IX. The public were allowed to see the great animal until its death and burial in the Tower precincts. In 1261 Henry, having almost lost control of the country, shut himself up in the Tower and summoned PARLIAMENT who refused to attend. His Queen, Eleanor, was besieged by both Barons and Londoners in 1263. She tried to escape by river but was pelted with rubbish at LONDON BRIDGE and had to return. On regaining control after the Battle of Evesham in 1265 Henry imprisoned the MAYOR and SHERIFFS and gave the Queen the

revenues from the shops and houses on LONDON BRIDGE.

At the coronation of Edward I the procession set off from the Tower through streets hung with tapestries. The conduits ran with wine and the King flung coins to the crowd. Feasting continued for a fortnight. Between 1275 and 1285 the western inner wall was built between the Bell and Devereux Towers. This included the construction of what later became known as the Beauuchamp Tower probably because Thomas, Earl of Warwick, of the Beachamp family, was held here for a time in the reign of Richard II. The Outer Wall was also built including the Byward and Lion Towers and Traitors' Gate. In 1278 600 JEWS were imprisoned in the sub-crypt of ST JOHN'S CHAPEL, accused of clipping coins. The next year 267 of them were hanged and the rest banished. In 1300 the MINT was moved here from WESTMINSTER; and in 1303 it was decided that the CROWN JEWELS should also be kept in the Tower after various valuables had disappeared mysteriously at WESTMINSTER. The Abbot of WESTMINSTER, 48 monks and 32 other suspects were brought here as prisoners. Miles Podlicote, Keeper of the Royal Palace, was hanged for the theft but the true culprits were never found. In 1308 several suspects were arrested and tortured, accused of offences ranging from blasphemy to perversion.

During the troubled reign of Edward II the defences were strengthened: two new portcullises and a gate were installed, and five springalds for throwing missiles were set up. Edward's Queen, Isabella, gave birth to Princess Jean in the Tower in 1322. The royal apartments were in such bad repair by this time that the Constable was dismissed for endangering the health of the mother and child. That same year Roger Mortimer, a rebellious Welsh baron, was imprisoned here. He escaped in 1324, aided by his paramour, the Queen. Two years later, he and the Queen, at the head of an invading army, seized the Tower, released the prisoners, and gave the keys to the citizens of London. After Edward II was murdered at Berkeley Castle in 1327, Mortimer and Isabella governed, while Edward III, still a minor at the time, was kept a virtual prisoner in the Tower. Before he was 18, however, the new King, with the support of the Barons, had Mortimer arrested and executed, and had his mother banished to Castle Rising in Norfolk.

During the long war with France which began in 1345, 300 burghers from Caen were imprisoned here. The next year, David II of Scotland was taken prisoner at the Battle of Neville's Cross. He was paraded through the streets of London and imprisoned in the Tower, but was moved later to Oldham Castle to make way for the large numbers of French prisoners taken at Crécy. In 1356 King John II of France was taken prisoner by the Black Prince at Poitiers as well as his son Philip, an archbishop, 13 counts, five viscounts, 21 barons and nearly 2,000 knights; 11 were freed on payment of ransom, but it took France three years to raise the money for their King's release.

In 1377 the ten-year-old Richard II rode from the Tower to his coronation clad in white robes, looking 'as beautiful as an angel'. The procession took three hours to reach WESTMINSTER, pageants being performed along the way. The conduits and fountains once more flowed with wine. During the PEASANTS' REVOLT in 1381, Richard left the Tower to speak to a rabble gathered at MILE END. While the King was making promises of pardons and emancipation some of the more violent rebels, led by Wat Tyler, managed to break through the open gate to the Tower. Once inside they ransacked the kitchens, bedchambers and armoury. They broke down the door to the Queen Mother's private apartments, seized and mockingly kissed her, and destroyed her furniture and wall hangings. The Queen herself, aided by her pages, escaped, but the King's ministers did not. The mob sought out Archbishop Sudbury, Treasurer Hales, John Legge, a royal sergeant-at-arms who was notorious as a collector of taxes, and John of Gaunt's physician who were praying in ST JOHN'S CHAPEL. All four were dragged from the altar to TOWER HILL and beheaded.

Five years later TOWER HILL was the scene of the first of many official executions when Richard II's tutor, Sir Simon de Burley, was beheaded. Richard had displayed great courage and an aptitude for statesmanship in the early years of his reign, but after the death of his wife and most of his close friends his strength and powers of judgement began to fail. In 1399, at the age of 32, he was forced to abdicate in favour of his cousin, Henry Bolingbroke, and was kept prisoner in the Tower. Henry IV spent the eve of his coronation in the Tower and initiated the Ceremony of the Bath: 46 of his followers were selected. As a symbol of their spiritual cleansing they first had to climb into baths in the hall adjoining ST JOHN'S CHAPEL. While they were in the bath the King made a cross on each man's back and knighted him. After a token rest in 46 separate beds, representing ease after labour, the new knights spent the night in prayer in the chapel. At the end of their vigil they offered up a taper to God and a penny to the King on the altar. In 1400 Richard II's body lay in state for one night in the chapel, having been fetched from Pontefract, Yorkshire, where he had died a mysterious death.

The young Prince James of Scotland was imprisoned here in 1406, having been captured when on his way to France to be educated. His father died when he heard the news and the Prince became King. He lived in the Tower for two years and was then moved to Nottingham where he was kept for 16 years before his ransom was paid.

Henry V's coronation procession set off from the Tower in 1413. Even though it was April there was a snowstorm, which was taken as a sign that the King 'had put off the Winter of his Youth'. Soon afterwards the persecution of the Lollards began and many were imprisoned, including Sir John Oldcastle, Shakespeare's Falstaff who had been the King's closest friend while he was still a prince. Oldcastle, under sentence of death, escaped in 1414, probably with the King's help. He was subsequently recaptured and found guilty of heresy and treachery; after being hanged in St Giles's Fields, his body was burned. Captives brought here after the Battle of Agincourt in 1415 included Charles, Duke of Orléans, the French King's nephew.

In 1446, John Holland, Duke of Exeter, held the post of Constable of the Tower and introduced the rack, thenceforth known as the Duke of Exeter's daughter. Edward IV was received ceremoniously at the Tower gates in 1461, having defeated Henry VI at the Battle of Towton, and was escorted to the royal palace. Three months later his coronation took place. In 1464, however, Henry was captured at Clitheroe, Lancashire. He was brought to London and made to sit on a sickly horse with his legs tied to the stirrups. A straw hat was put on his head and a placard on his back, and he was led into the Tower. He was imprisoned in the Wakefield Tower and had with him a Bible, breviary, a pet dog and a pet sparrow. He told the chaplain, 'I do not mind, so long as I can have the Sacrament. I am not worried about the loss of my earthly kingdom.' After six years of imprisonment he was rescued from his prison by Warwick, the King Maker, supported by the Archbishop of York and Bishop Wainfleet, and proclaimed King at WESTMINSTER. Recaptured at the Battle of Tewkesbury, he was returned to the Tower; and in May 1471 murdered at his prayers in the Wakefield Tower. Edward IV announced that he died of pure displeasure and melancholy. Every year, on the anniversary of his death, the institutions which he founded remember him, Eton College by laying lilies at the place of his death, and King's College Cambridge white roses.

During Edward's reign the Tower became the centre of a gay and relatively informal court. Though every royal activity was precisely ordered there were many games, picnics and competitions on the Tower lawns. The handsome and sensual king was popular with the citizens of London in the early years of his reign but later his increasing debaucheries turned them against him. In 1478 his brother, the Duke of Clarence, was arrested for plotting against him. He was found guilty and died, under mysterious circumstances, in the Tower. Upon Edward's death in 1483, Richard of Gloucester took charge of the boy king Edward V and brought him to London, appointing himself Protector. According to Sir Thomas More, the Protector had Lord Hastings immediately executed for defending Queen Elizabeth Woodville and Jane Shore, the late King's mistress, against Richard's accusation of sorcery. The Queen, who had taken sanctuary with her children at WESTMINSTER, was persuaded to part with her younger son to keep his brother company in the Tower. Richard, declaring the children illegitimate, left the Tower by river for his own coronation at WESTMINSTER. The next month the two princes were found dead in the Garden Tower, thereafter known as the Bloody Tower. It is thought they were smothered by two men named Green and Forest on the orders of Sir James Tyrrell, Master of the Horse. Their bodies were said to have first been buried in the Wakefield Tower and later reburied by a priest in consecrated ground. In Charles II's reign two skeletons were found under the staircase leading to ST JOHN'S CHAPEL and were reburied in WESTMINSTER ABBEY. Exhumation in 1933 suggested that they were those of the young Edward V and his brother, the Duke of York.

In 1485, Henry, Earl of Richmond, ascended to the throne after the Battle of Bosworth Field. At his coronation Henry VII was attended by the newly formed YEOMEN OF THE GUARD. Soon afterwards, to show the unity of the factions which had fought each other during the Wars of the Roses, representatives from York and Lancaster rode, two on a horse, through the CITY in procession from the Tower. As a pledge to the country that the rivalry between the two

Tower Hill in 1641, when the Earl of Strafford was executed before a large crowd. From an engraving by Hollar.

families was truly over, Henry married Elizabeth of York, daughter of Edward IV, in 1486. In 1501 Catherine of Aragon stayed at the Tower before her marriage to Prince Arthur, Henry VII's elder son, and was entertained with feasts and tournaments. Two years later Prince Arthur's mother, Queen Elizabeth of York, gave birth to a daughter and died nine days later. She lay in state for three days in ST JOHN'S CHAPEL before her funeral procession set out for WESTMINSTER ABBEY. 'The body was put in a carriage covered with black velvet with a cross of white cloth of gold . . . and an image exactly representing the Queen was placed in a chair above in her rich robes of state . . . and at every end of the chair knelt a gentlewoman usher by the coffin which was in this manner drawn by six horses trapped in black velvet.'

In 1509 the joint coronation procession of Henry VIII and Catherine of Aragon was an occasion of great splendour. Following precedent, Henry created 24 new Knights of the Bath. The streets were decorated with tapestries, the goldsmiths' houses in CHEAPSIDE were hung with cloth of gold, and pageants were performed along the route. Soon afterwards Empson and Dudley, Henry VII's despised tax collectors, were sent to the Tower and the following year executed on TOWER HILL. The chapel of ST PETER AD VINCULA was destroyed by fire in 1512, and rebuilt three years later. During Henry's reign part of the royal palace was also rebuilt and the half-timbered houses which still survive on Tower Green were constructed. These included the Lieutenant's Lodgings, which have been known since about 1880 as the Queen's House.

The palace was redecorated for the coronation of Henry VIII's second wife, Anne Boleyn, in 1533 and for a fortnight there were great festivities. On the day of the coronation she set out in a litter decked in damask, accompanied by the nobles of the land. She wore a robe of crimson brocade covered with precious stones, pearls and diamonds round her neck, and a coronet of rubies. However, she was coldly received by the people, who were still loyal to Henry's first wife, Catherine.

Although a great number of prisoners had been detained in the Tower since its construction five centuries earlier, it was not until the Reformation brought Henry VIII's victims to the Tower that harsh treatment of prisoners became almost normal policy. Two of the first victims were Thomas More and John Fisher, who were imprisoned in the Bell Tower for refusing to take the Oath of Supremacy. More was at first allowed writing materials, but later these were taken away from him. Fisher wrote to Thomas Cromwell, 'I beseech you to be good Master, unto me in my necessity; for I have neither shirt nor suit, nor yet other clothes that are necessary for me to wear, but that be ragged and rent so shamefully. Notwithstanding I mighte easily suffer that, if they would keep my body warm. But my diet also, God knoweth how slender it is at times, and now in mine age my stomach may not away with but a few kinds of meats, which if I want, I decay forthwith, and fall into coughs and diseases of my body, and cannot keep myself in health.' By 1535 John Fisher was so weak he had to be carried to the scaffold. After praying, he said that he forgave both the executioner and the King. A fortnight later More was told he was to be executed that day, but the traitor's fate of being drawn and quartered was commuted to beheading. On this he commented, 'God forbid the king shall use any more such mercy on any of my friends.' More asked for help to mount the scaffold, 'I pray you, Mr Lieutenant to see me safe up and for my coming down let me make shift for myself.' He prayed and at the last moment moved his beard from the block, saying, 'Pity that should be cut that has not committed treason.'

The next year Anne Boleyn was brought to the Tower accused of adultery with her brother, Lord Rochford, one of the court musicians, Mark Smeaton, and three courtiers. All were found guilty and were executed. Anne herself was tried in the Great Hall of the palace by 26 peers presided over by her uncle, the Duke of Norfolk. He wept as he pronounced the sentence of death. Anne asked to be executed with a sword instead of an axe and an executioner expert in the art was brought over from France. Three years to the day after her coronation she was led to the scaffold on Tower Green. She said, 'I am not here to preach to you but to die. Pray for the King, for he is a good man and has treated me as good could be. I do not accuse anyone of causing my death, neither the judges nor anyone else for I am condemned by the law of the land and die willingly.' She knelt to pray and was blindfolded. The executioner crept up to her, snatched out the sword from under a pile of straw and cut off her head. Her body was thrown into an old arrow chest and buried in ST PETER AD VINCULA.

In 1540 Thomas Cromwell, the King's Minister, was imprisoned, and six weeks later beheaded on TOWER HILL. The next year the Countess of Salisbury was executed with difficulty, as she refused to put her head on the block but ran around shouting that she was no traitor. Arthur Plantagenet, Viscount Lisle, former Governor of Calais, was imprisoned in 1542 for plotting to hand over the port to the French, and died of a heart attack when told he was to be released. That year the King's fifth wife, Catherine Howard, was also brought to the Tower, accused of infidelity. As she passed under LONDON BRIDGE she saw the heads of her lovers, Culpepper and Dereham, on the spikes. On 12 February she was told she was to die the next day and coolly asked for the block to be brought to her so that she could practise putting her head on it. On the scaffold she said, 'If I had married the man I loved instead of being dazzled with ambition all would have been well. I die a Queen but I would rather have died the wife of Culpepper.' Afterwards her body – like that of her predecessor, Anne Boleyn, and of all the other five people known to have been executed on Tower Green – was buried in the Chapel of ST PETER AD VINCULA. In 1547 the Duke of Norfolk and his son, the Earl of Surrey, were accused of treason and imprisoned. Surrey was beheaded on TOWER HILL in January. But on the eve of the day set for his father's execution Henry died and Norfolk remained a prisoner throughout the reign of Henry's son, Edward VI.

Edward was nine years old at the time of his father's death and, according to custom, was taken to live in the royal apartments of the Tower until the day of his coronation. His uncle, the Duke of Somerset, became Lord Protector. The Duke of Somerset, however, did not live long to enjoy his new position of power. In 1551 he was imprisoned for plotting to overthrow John Dudley, Duke of Northumberland, his successor as Lord Protector. The next year he was beheaded on TOWER HILL surrounded by a thousand soldiers to prevent a rescue attempt. In 1553, after six years of rule, young Edward VI became seriously ill. The Duke of Northumberland, determined to retain his power, arranged for his son, Lord Guilford Dudley, to marry the King's cousin Lady Jane Grey. He then persuaded the dying King to nominate Lady Jane as his successor in place of his elder half-sister, Princess Mary, daughter of Henry VIII by his first wife, Catherine of Aragon. Most Londoners, however, supported the claims of Princess Mary, and eventually the Tower was deserted except for the Northumberland family. Shortly after Lady Jane's arrival at the Tower, the Duke was arrested and imprisoned.

Mary entered London in triumph accompanied by her sister, Elizabeth. At the Tower gates she was met by four Roman Catholic prisoners, the Duke of Norfolk, Bishop Gardiner, Edward Courtenay, and the Duchess of Somerset, all of whom she released. In August Northumberland was sentenced to death. He tried to save himself by becoming a Roman Catholic and celebrated mass in the presence of the Council in ST JOHN'S CHAPEL, but to no avail. He was executed on TOWER HILL. The next month Archbishop Cranmer was imprisoned; and in September Hugh Latimer, Bishop of London. Both of them were later burned for heresy in Oxford.

Mary arrived at the Tower to take part in the festivities that preceded her coronation. The usual pageants were performed on the route and a Dutch acrobat bravely balanced on the top of the spire of ST PAUL'S. In November Lady Jane Grey and her husband, Lord Guilford Dudley, were tried at GUILD-HALL and found guilty of treason; but they were allowed to live separately in comparative comfort in the Tower.

In January 1554, however, Mary announced that she would marry Philip of Spain. Rebellions broke out all over the country, one in Leicester led by the Duke of Suffolk, another in Devon, and a third in Kent, led by Thomas Wyatt. Wyatt reached London and created a great deal of panic before he was arrested and brought to the Tower. Under torture he incriminated Princess Elizabeth and orders for her arrest were made. On 12 February Lady Jane Grey and Guilford Dudley were executed, as they were now too dangerous to keep alive. Dudley asked to say farewell to Jane but she refused him, saying their separation would be temporary. He was taken out to TOWER HILL early in the morning, and from the window Jane saw his headless body being brought back in a cart. She herself was executed in the relative privacy of Tower Green. She wore a simple black gown and carried a prayer book in which she had written. 'As the preacher sayeth, there is a time to be born and a time to die.' She spoke briefly, admitting she had been the unwilling tool of others, but accepted the justice of her sentence.

On 18 March Princess Elizabeth was brought through the Traitors' Gate and conducted to the Bell Tower. Mass was celebrated in her cell every day, but she refused to be converted to Roman Catholicism. The close confinement affected her health and she was allowed to walk in the Lieutenant's garden and on the part of the ramparts between the Bell and Beauchamp Towers, which is still known as Princess Elizabeth's Walk. At the end of the month, when order had been restored, Mary was betrothed by proxy in ST JOHN'S CHAPEL to Philip of Spain. On 19 May Princess Elizabeth was released, as no further evidence of her complicity in the plots could be discovered. Mary and Philip rode from WHITEHALL to the Tower in August 1555, to dispel the rumour that Mary had died of dropsy.

When Mary did die in 1558 the new Queen, Elizabeth, rode from Hatfield to the Tower. When she arrived she patted the earth and said, 'Some have fallen from being princes of this land to be prisoners in this place. I am raised from being prisoner in this place to be the prince of the land.' She stayed for a week while she appointed her ministers; and returned in January 1559, three days before her coronation, for the usual festivities. The day before her coronation she rode from the Tower to WHITEHALL seated in a golden chariot, wearing a blue velvet robe covered in precious stones. The streets were decorated with triumphal archways, and tableaux were performed at the street corners.

From 1565 to 1567 Lady Lennox was imprisoned for arranging the marriage of her son, Lord Darnley, to Mary Queen of Scots without Elizabeth's consent. She was released just after Darnley's murder, but again imprisoned between 1574 and 1577 for allowing her younger son to marry without the Queen's consent. In prison she wove some lace from the grey hairs on her head and sent it to Mary Queen of Scots as a token of her sympathy. Until Mary's execution in the great hall of Fotheringay Castle in 1587 there were almost as many of her supporters being held in the Tower as there were Jesuit prisoners. In 1581 Edmund Campion was arrested for his book *Decem Rationes* attacking the Anglican Church. He was tried and sentenced to be hanged, drawn and quartered at TYBURN. Two years later Francis Throgmorton was executed for plotting to gain the throne for Mary Queen of Scots through an invasion by Spanish troops. And in 1585, under the threat of the Spanish Armada, many Roman Catholic priests and noblemen were imprisoned, among them Henry Percy, Earl of Northumberland, who was later found stabbed in the Bloody Tower. The next year John Ballard, a Jesuit priest, and Anthony Babington conceived a plan for a general uprising of Catholics, the murder of Queen Elizabeth, and the accession of Mary to the English throne. They were discovered, tried, and condemned to traitors' deaths. The 12 other conspirators were also executed. Mary's own complicity was discovered and this hastened her own execution. In 1592 Sir Walter Ralegh was briefly imprisoned for seducing Elizabeth Throgmorton, one of the Queen's ladies-in-waiting. Robert Devereux, Earl of Essex, was imprisoned after his ineffectual rebellion in 1601. He was tried at WESTMINSTER and executed six days later on Tower Green rather than on TOWER HILL, a privilege granted him by the Queen. His body was buried in the chapel of ST PETER AD VINCULA.

King James I, son of Mary Queen of Scots, who succeeded to the throne at the death of Queen Elizabeth, was the last monarch to occupy the Tower as a palace. He was very interested in the royal menagerie, an interest which mainly took the form of staging trial-of-strength spectacles. To observe the lions fighting the mastiffs, James had a viewing gallery built above the Lion Tower. Animal fights were staged regularly until 1609 when one of the Tower bears killed a small child. The King, hoping for a grand battle, ordered the culprit to be forced into the lions' den, but the lions only cowered in the corners; the bear was finally given to the dogs to be baited to death. At this time the inventory of the zoo was recorded as 11 lions, two leopards, three eagles, two owls, two mountain cats, and a jackal.

In 1603 Sir Walter Ralegh was imprisoned again, this time for plotting to place on the throne Arabella Stuart. He was found guilty and sentenced to death but was reprieved on the eve of his execution. He lived in the Tower fairly comfortably during his long imprisonment. He was allotted the upper floors of the Bloody Tower, and his wife and son lived with him. He was often visited by Henry, Prince of Wales, who encouraged him to write his *History of the World* and

to carry out scientific experiments in a makeshift laboratory.

In 1605 Guy Fawkes and some of his accomplices were arrested after being caught in their attempt to blow up the HOUSES OF PARLIAMENT (*see* GUNPOWDER PLOT) and were taken to the Lieutenant's Lodgings to be interrogated. The King himself wrote out the questions he wanted answered, but they refused to say anything. They were taken to the dungeons and the next year Fawkes, Winter, Rookwood and Keyes were executed in Palace Yard, WESTMINSTER.

In 1610 Arabella Stuart and William Seymour were imprisoned for marrying secretly. He escaped to France soon after; but she remained a prisoner until dying, insane, in 1615. Sir Thomas Overbury was imprisoned in 1612, ostensibly for refusing to go on a diplomatic mission to Russia, but actually because he opposed the marriage of his friend, Robert Carr, to the Countess of Essex. The Countess had the Lieutenant of the Tower replaced by an ally, Sir Gervase Helwys, and, with his connivance, poison was administered to Overbury for three months before his death. Two years later one of the apothecaries' apprentices confessed to the crime and Carr and his wife, now the Earl and Countess of Somerset, were sent to the Tower. They were convicted but received the King's pardon. They were, however, obliged to live together for seven years before they were released, and by the end of that time they hated each other. Four of their accomplices, including Helwys, were hanged.

In 1617 King James granted permission for Sir Walter Ralegh to leave the Tower to conduct an expedition to South America where he believed they would find rich deposits of gold. The expedition, however, was a disaster and when they returned to England the next year Ralegh was again arrested and taken to the Tower. No new trial was held as he had already been sentenced to death for treason years before. He was executed in Palace Yard, WESTMINSTER.

In 1629 nine Members of Parliament, including Sir John Eliot, were imprisoned for their harsh attacks on the King's favourite, the Duke of Buckingham. The conditions under which Eliot was kept were so squalid that he contracted tuberculosis and died three years later. Eliot's son asked permission of King Charles to remove his father's body for burial in the Cornish churchyard where his ancestors lay, but this was denied.

The split between the King and Parliament was becoming deeper. In 1641 Thomas Wentworth, Earl of Strafford, the King's principal adviser, and Archbishop Laud were impeached by Parliament and sent to the Tower. Strafford was found guilty of high treason and, with regret, Charles was forced to sign his death warrant. On the way to his execution Strafford saw Archbishop Laud standing at the window and received his blessing. Laud was afterwards executed on TOWER HILL. In the face of a civil war Charles determined to retain control of the Tower. He dismissed the Constable and appointed in his place Colonel Thomas Lunsford, a desperately patriotic man who could be depended upon to defend the Tower to the death. He was condemned by the House of Commons as a dangerous man, and among the citizens of London was rumoured to be a cannibal. At length Charles agreed to remove him, and replaced him with Sir John Byron.

On 10 January 1642, after a disastrous attempt to arrest five of his leading opponents in Parliament,

Charles fled London, leaving Byron to defend the Tower. Philip Skippon, commander of the TRAINED BANDS, was ordered by the Commons to blockade the Tower and the Constable was eventually forced to surrender control of it. At Stow-on-the-Wold, on 26 March 1646, the commander of the King's last army surrendered to Cromwell's men and Parliament's control over London and the Tower was confirmed. Early the next year Charles was delivered back from Scotland by his enemies and arrested. In 1649 he was tried by a parliamentary high court, found guilty of treason, and executed at WHITEHALL. After the war the buildings were neglected and in 1672–4 the Jewel House and Coldharbour Gate were demolished. Most of the CROWN JEWELS were seized.

With the restoration of the monarchy in 1660 several of the regicides were imprisoned before being executed. Charles II returned from exile on the Continent and spent the eve of his coronation in the Tower in April 1661. Pepys found it 'impossible to relate the glory' of the following day. A new collection of CROWN JEWELS was made for the occasion, but the monks of WESTMINSTER produced the ampulla, the anointing spoon and Queen Elizabeth's salt cellar which they had hidden during the Commonwealth.

An attempt was made to steal these jewels by Colonel Blood, an Irishman. Blood disguised himself as a clergyman to gain the confidence of the Jewel House Keeper, and the unsuspecting man invited Blood and his supposedly wealthy nephew to supper, hoping that the nephew would take a fancy to his daughter. During the evening the Keeper sold a pair of pistols they affected to admire, thus leaving himself unarmed. The next morning Blood arrived with some friends to view the jewels. Once inside the Jewel House they gagged and bound the Keeper. However, they were disturbed. One of Blood's accomplices stuffed the orb down his breeches and ran off but was caught on Tower Wharf. Another grabbed the sceptre and escaped from the Tower but was caught when he was knocked off his horse by a barber's pole. Blood flattened the crown with a mallet and placed it in a bag, but he too was caught by one of the Tower's garrison. He refused to speak to anyone but the King and was taken to WHITEHALL. Charles was much taken with his charm and impudence and not only pardoned him but gave him estates in Ireland and a pension of £500 a year. His accomplices were also released. The Keeper's daughter married Captain Beckman who had captured Blood.

Samuel Pepys was imprisoned in the Tower in 1679, accused by Titus Oates of giving naval secrets to the French. He was released on bail and a few years later cleared his name.

At the coronation of James II the ceremony of the procession from the Tower was abandoned. In 1685 James, Duke of Monmouth, was imprisoned after the Battle of Sedgemoor. He was executed on TOWER HILL on 15 July. The axe was blunt and after the first blow he got up and rebuked the executioner, John Ketch. After two more attempts Ketch had to resort to a knife. Between 1688 and 1692 the Grand Storehouse was built, possibly to the designs of Wren who also probably supervised the alterations to the windows of the White Tower.

The Jacobite, Lord Nithsdale, escaped from the Tower on the eve of his execution in 1716, dressed as his wife's maid. The next day Robert, Earl of Kenmure, and an English sympathiser, the Earl of Derwentwater, were beheaded on TOWER HILL. Over the next few years many more Jacobites were detained as prisoners in the Tower for their attempts to restore the Stuarts. Many Scots were imprisoned after the Jacobite defeat at Culloden in 1745, among them Lords Tullibardine, Cromarty, Kilmarnock and Balmerino. Tullibardine died in prison; Cromarty was pardoned as he was only 19; but the others were executed the following year on TOWER HILL. In 1747 another Jacobite, Simon Fraser, Lord Lovat, was also beheaded on TOWER HILL. He was the last man in England to be thus executed.

In 1763 John Wilkes was imprisoned after publishing the forty-fifth copy of the *North Briton* in which he criticised George III's speech at the prorogation of Parliament; and in 1780 Lord George Gordon, instigator of the GORDON RIOTS, was held here for eight months. In 1798 James Turnbull, a worker in the MINT, held up the rest of the employees and made off with 2,804 newly minted guineas. He was caught after nine days and sentenced to death. The Mint was moved to Little Tower Hill 12 years later (*see* ROYAL MINT).

By 1822 the royal menagerie had dwindled to 'a grizzly bear, an elephant and one or two birds'. However, in that year Alfred Copps was appointed as the Royal Keeper. He had an excellent knowledge of animal behaviour and in a short time assembled 59 different species. Unfortunately, in 1835 one of his lions attacked some members of the garrison, and the animals were moved to the ZOOLOGICAL GARDENS. Only the ravens still remain at the Tower.

The moat was drained in the 1840s when Waterloo Barracks were built on the site of the old armouries. On 24 January 1885 Fenians planted a bomb on the second floor of the White Tower. The explosion occurred almost simultaneously with others in the HOUSES OF PARLIAMENT and WESTMINSTER HALL. Fire broke out but the Tower's fire brigade soon brought the flames under control and no one was killed, though several people were seriously injured.

During the 1st World War Sir Roger Casement was imprisoned in St Thomas' Tower. He was found guilty of planning the Easter Rising with German help, and was hanged at PENTONVILLE. Eleven spies were shot in the outer ward by the Martin Tower. In the 2nd World War Rudolf Hess was imprisoned in the Lieutenant's House for four days. Two bombs fell near the White Tower, killing five people and exposing an underground tunnel thought to have been built in Charles II's reign.

The ancient Ceremony of the Keys still takes place at the Tower every night at ten o'clock when the Chief Yeoman Warder, in long red cloak and Tudor bonnet, carrying a lantern, marches out toward the Byward Tower with the keys of the fortress in his hand, and calls out: 'An escort for the Keys.' Four armed soldiers of the garrison fall into step beside him, and march through the gates of the Byward Tower and over the causeway to the entrance gate beyond the Middle Tower. The gate is locked; the escort marches back in the darkness toward the towers of the outer ward; the gates of the Byward Tower are locked. As the Chief Yeoman Warder and his escort approach the Bloody Tower, the sentry on guard comes forward with the challenge:

'Halt, who goes there?'

The Chief Yeoman Warder replies, 'The Keys.'

A Yeoman Warder of the Tower escorts visitors round the Great Horse Armoury in 1841.

'Whose Keys?'

'Queen Elizabeth's keys.'

The sentry presents arms, the Chief Yeoman Warder removes his bonnet and calls out, 'God preserve Queen Elizabeth!'

The whole guard replies, 'Amen!'

Crown Jewels   The regalia, the ornaments of the sovereigns of England, date for the most part from the 17th century. After the execution of Charles I in 1649 the Parliamentary party ordered the destruction of the existing crowns and sceptres, and a new set was made for the coronation of Charles II in 1661. As well as these, a few individual pieces which appear to go back to the Middle Ages, or before, are preserved and displayed in the Tower.

One of the most important pledges William the Conqueror made to the citizens of London was to preserve the constitution of the saint-king Edward the Confessor. It is probable that by the end of the 13th century certain ancient robes and ornaments, taken from Edward's body when Henry III transferred it to a new shrine, were actually placed upon the king at his coronation. Even when the actual crown was destroyed by the Parliamentary Commissioners the name and tradition survived, and the name of St Edward's Crown is still given to the coronation crown of the kings of England.

The Ampulla and Spoon, the oldest objects among the regalia, are not actually royal ornaments, and this is probably why they survived the Commonwealth when all things 'royal' were destroyed. They are, however, connected with the most solemn moment of the coronation ceremony, when the holy oil is poured from the beak of the golden eagle into the spoon and is applied by the officiating bishop to the new sovereign's head, breast and palms. The Spoon probably dates from the late 12th century, and the Ampulla was probably first used at the coronation of Henry IV in 1399.

St Edward's Crown, the name given to the crown made for Charles II, is still used for the coronation ceremony. It is likely that it was made from one of the old crowns broken up during the Commonwealth. Because of its great weight – nearly 5 lb – it is worn only for the ceremony of coronation, and is afterwards changed for the lighter Crown of State.

This crown was made for the coronation of Queen Victoria and was used by her and by Edward VII. It has been used at every coronation since then and is worn when the sovereign appears in state, as at the STATE OPENING OF PARLIAMENT. The frame, remade for the coronation of George VI, is of fine gold, and thickly set with over 3,000 precious stones, mainly diamonds and pearls. The largest is the irregular ruby given to the Black Prince in the 14th century.

As well as being anointed and crowned, the monarch is invested with sword and spurs, the attributes of knighthood. The Golden Spurs, made for the coronation of Charles II, are not actually buckled on, but applied for a moment to the monarch's heels and then placed upon the altar. The Sword, however, is still girt about the monarch, then offered on the altar by the monarch. It is then 'redeemed' for a fee and carried before the Sovereign for the rest of the ceremony.

The Jewelled Sword now used was originally made for the coronation of George IV, and has been so used since the coronation of Edward VII. Clusters of precious stones are set into the hilt and scabbard, making up a pattern that incorporates the national emblems of England, Scotland and Ireland.

The Bracelets, also made for the coronation of Charles II, were not worn but carried at later coronations, their place being now taken by the stole that forms part of the Coronation Robes. They are decorated with the fleur-de-lis, a reminder that, until the early 19th century, the royal title was 'King of England, Scotland, France and Ireland'. The new Bracelets were presented by the Commonwealth countries and were first used for the coronation of Queen Elizabeth in 1953.

The officiating bishop emphasises the symbolism of the Orb, a globe of the world dominated by the emblem of Christianity, when he presents it to the

878

Sovereign, who then gives it back so as to leave his or her hands free for the Ring and the two Sceptres.

The 'ring of kingly dignity' is a sapphire with the Cross of St George set on it in rubies. The ring made for William IV was not used by Queen Victoria, who had a smaller one made for her, but has been used by all her successors.

The Sceptre with the Cross, symbolic of the king's role as ruler of his people, is described, at its delivery, as the 'Ensign of Kingly Power and Justice'. The sovereign's paternal function as guardian and guide is symbolized by the Rod with the Dove, the dove suggesting divine inspiration. In the present century the great diamond, weighing 530 carats, has been added to the Sceptre with the Cross; it was the largest of the four 'Stars of Africa' presented by the Union of South Africa to Edward VII. The second of these stones is in the State Crown and the other two, previously in the Crown of Queen Mary, are now in the Crown of the Queen Consort.

St Edward's Staff is another sceptre, traditionally carried in the coronation procession but not used in the actual ceremony. It is longer than the others, and its golden shaft ends in a steel ferrule. The original Staff was probably used as a walking stick.

The Great Sword of State, representing the king's own personal sword, is of the late 17th century, decorated with a lion and unicorn supporting the Royal Arms. During the coronation ceremony this sword is actually delivered to the Sovereign; but there are three others carried before him in token of his power. The custom of bearing these swords, named the Swords of Justice, can be traced as far back as 1189, when Richard I was crowned. The three swords stood for Mercy, Justice and the championship of the Church.

The oldest crown preserved at the TOWER is one worn by Mary of Modena, the second wife of James II, at her coronation in 1685. It has a cap of purple velvet and ermine, surrounded by a gold band set with diamonds and pearls. Another small crown is also known as Mary of Modena's, but was most probably made for the coronation of Queen Anne in 1702. The Prince of Wales's crown was probably made for Frederick Louis, son of George II. Queen Victoria had a small diamond crown made, and is shown wearing it in her statue at Windsor. It was preserved for a long time at BUCKINGHAM PALACE, but is now exhibited at the TOWER. Conspicuous in the crown made for the coronation of George VI and Queen Elizabeth in 1937 is the famous Indian diamond known as the Koh-i-Noor. It has been worn by all the queens of England since Queen Victoria, and is traditionally supposed to bring good luck to the woman who wears it but ill-luck to the man.

When a king and queen are crowned together, the queen's coronation ornaments are normally those of a consort, but in 1689 the queen, as well as the king, was invested as a Queen Regent. Mary II, daughter of the deposed James II, was heiress to the throne in her own right, but her husband, William of Orange, insisted that he be crowned on terms of absolute equality with her as King William III.

Most of the silver-gilt plate preserved among the Crown Jewels was made at the Restoration. One piece, however, the great cylindrical 'salt', bears a hallmark for the year 1572–3. It is set with rubies, sapphires, emeralds and amethysts and was popularly supposed to be a model of the White Tower, although it bears no real resemblance to it. It was a Restoration gift to Charles II from the city of Exeter. The city of Plymouth presented a silver-gilt wine fountain. The font and basin, first used for the christening of James, known later as the Old Pretender, was made in 1600. They were subsequently used for the christening of George IV, William IV, and the other children of George III. The great alms dish used at the ceremony of the Royal Maundy (*see* CEREMONIES) is another piece of Restoration plate, though it has subsequently been inscribed with the arms of William and Mary. Of the 13 Royal Maces still in existence, ten are at the TOWER, two at the HOUSE OF LORDS and one at the HOUSE OF COMMONS. Most of these are composites, made from parts of other maces, probably numbering 30 in all, which were made during the period 1660 to 1695.

Tower Place *EC3*. 'A very successful piece of replanning,' in the words of Sir Nikolaus Pevsner and Bridget Cherry, 'by the City Corporation, the former London County Council and the former borough of Stepney.' The architect was Anthony Beckles Willson (of George, Trew, Dunn) in association with CLRP Architects (1962–5). Sir Basil Spence acted as consultant on the lay-out. The bronze, *The Hammer-thrower*, in front of the Bowring Buildings is by John Robinson (1973).

Tower Royal *Cannon Street*. First heard of in the 13th century, it was named after the wine merchants, from Le Riole near Bordeaux, who lived in the area. In 1320 it came into the possession of Edward III who granted it in 1331 to Queen Philippa, who enlarged it and established her wardrobe here. On her death the King gave it to the Dean and Canons of WESTMINSTER. But in 1371 Joan, Princess of Wales, mother of the future Richard II, was living here. In 1381 her son rode here to tell her of the suppression of the PEASANTS' REVOLT. By 1598 it was, according to Stow, neglected and used for stabling the King's horses. It was burned down in the GREAT FIRE.

Tower Subway *Tower Hill–Bermondsey*. Built in 1869 by P.W. Barlow, with J.H. Greathead, this was the precursor of the London tubes, deep bored through clay using Greathead's cylindrical tunnelling shield and lined with cast-iron segments. Originally intended for use by cable-hauled trams, it was soon converted to a foot tunnel and closed in 1896 after the opening of TOWER BRIDGE. It now carries water mains. There is a small round entrance building on TOWER HILL.

Town Clerk A High Officer of the CORPORATION OF LONDON elected by the COURT OF COMMON COUNCIL. The first Town Clerk of the CITY was appointed in 1274. He is the CORPORATION's Chief Executive Officer and co-ordinates the work of all committees and departments. In the name of the LORD MAYOR he conducts the business of the Courts of ALDERMEN and Common Council, and of Common Hall. He is Keeper of the CITY Records, assisted by a Deputy who is a qualified archivist, and the Electoral Registration Officer for the CITY. He attends the LORD MAYOR and ALDERMEN in procession, administers civic declarations and oaths, and advises the LORD MAYOR on CITY laws, customs and privileges.

Town of Ramsgate *62 Wapping High Street, E1.* Previously known as the Red Cow after, it is said, a red-haired barmaid. The present name derives from the Ramsgate fishermen who landed their catch at Wapping Old Stairs nearby. It was here, in 1688, that Judge Jeffreys was captured as he attempted to escape to Hamburg on a collier. He was recognised by a scrivener, who had appeared before him, and had to be rescued from a lynch mob by a company of soldiers who took him to the TOWER OF LONDON where he later died. In the cellars of the inn are the dungeons where convicts were chained before deportation to Australia.

Toynbee Hall *28 Commercial Street, E1.* The Universities' Settlement in East London, named after the social philosopher, Arnold Toynbee, opened its doors to the first two settlers on Christmas Eve 1884. Its founder, Canon Samuel Barnett, aimed 'to educate citizens in the knowledge of one another, to provide teaching for those willing to learn and recreation to those who are weary'. From their programme of educational and social activities grew the Workers' Educational Association, the Workers' Travel Association and many other organisations. The Youth Hostels Assocation had its first offices at Toynbee Hall; the settlement's art exhibitions led to a subscription to build the WHITEHALL ART GALLERY; and the HAMPSTEAD GARDEN SUBURB was planned at the hall. Among famous past residents have been William Beveridge, R.H. Tawney and Clement Attlee. Today there are 50 residents all of whom assist with voluntary social work.

Trades Union Congress *Congress House, 23–28 Great Russell Street, WC1.* The national organisation of British trade unions which was founded in 1868 and which now has 11 million members in 108 affiliated unions. The building was designed as a memorial to trade unionists who died in the two World Wars, and was first occupied in 1957 by the TUC which had previously shared offices with the Labour Party and Transport and General Workers' Union in SMITH SQUARE. The bronze sculpture in front of the building, *The Spirit of Trade Unionism*, is by Bernard Meadows (1958). Epstein's memorial to trade unionists who suffered in the two World Wars is in the courtyard (*see* MEMORIALS).

Trafalgar Square *WC2, SW1.* Not so named until about 1835, it was laid out on the site of the King's Mews. Edward I was probably the first monarch to maintain the Mews in which the royal hawks were kept, falconers lodged, and daily services held in the 'Chapel of the Muwes'. Chaucer was at one time Clerk of the Mews. By the time of Henry VII they were used as stables. Burned down in 1534, they were rebuilt as stables during the reign of Elizabeth I. During the early Stuart period for the first time some of the buildings were used as lodgings by Court officials. During the Civil War the Mews became barracks for the Parliamentary army, and after the battle of Naseby about 4,500 Cavalier prisoners were incarcerated here. After the Restoration of the monarchy reconstruction was started in and around the Mews, but Wren's plan for rebuilding them 'to house 388 Horses and 42 Coaches' was never carried out. William Kent, however, did rebuild the main stable block in 1732 on the site where the NATIONAL GALLERY now stands, making the shabby adjacent buildings 'look like a common inn-yard'. By the end of the 18th century most of the frontages on the east and west were let to private individuals. In its last years the main building was used as a menagerie and a store for public records. In 1830 this building and much of the adjoining property was demolished in John Nash's CHARING CROSS Improvement Scheme which provided for the building of Trafalgar Square, though Nash did not live to execute his plan.

Because the land was on a slope the architect, Sir Charles Barry, levelled and paved the central area in 1840, building a terrace on the north side with a broad shallow flight of steps on either side leading down into the square. At the foot of this north wall, in the middle, are set out in metal the standard linear measures: inch, foot and yard. In each of the sloping east and west walls is a drinking fountain, given in 1960 by the METROPOLITAN DRINKING FOUNTAIN AND CATTLE TROUGH ASSOCIATION, and each wall is terminated by a cylindrical granite plinth surmounted by a splendid octagonal bronze lamp.

The NELSON COLUMN which dominates the square is one of London's most famous landmarks. In front of the column on an island in the road is an equestrian statue of Charles I (*see* STATUES) facing down WHITEHALL. There is an equestrian bronze of George IV (*see* STATUES) at the north-east corner of the

The King's Mews, Charing Cross, in c.1830, the year of its demolition for the development of Trafalgar Square.

square; the corresponding plinth in the north-west corner still awaits a monument. Between these on the north wall are bronze busts of Admirals Cunningham, Beatty and Jellicoe. On either side of the NELSON COLUMN are bronze statues of Generals Napier and Havelock (*see* STATUES). The NELSON COLUMN and the fountains are floodlit at night.

The two granite fountains and basins were not part of Barry's original design. Completed in 1845, they were remodelled in 1939 by Lutyens as memorials to Beatty and Jellicoe. The fountain pools were tiled in blue to give light and colour to the water, and inner basins were built of Portland Stone. Sir Charles Wheeler and William Macmillan further decorated them after the War with mermen, mermaids and dolphins in bronze. The water to supply the fountains according to a mid-19th-century contributor to *The Builder* 'is obtained from two wells, one in front of the National Gallery, and the other behind it, which are connected by means of a tunnel, that of course passes directly under the National Gallery, behind which is also placed the engine house for raising the required water into the tanks, etc., before it is forced through the fountains.' As this water supply eventually dried up, it was replaced at the end of the 19th century by a town mains. Since then powerful new jets have been installed, worked by electrically-driven pumps, and a fine spray is dispersed over the bronze groups in each fountain, helping to maintain the patina. The jets spring up into the air at ten o'clock every morning, startling the pigeons into flight.

The east and west sides of the square are gracefully flanked by plane trees. Beyond the terrace above the north side stands the NATIONAL GALLERY; on the lawns in front of the Gallery stands a statue of James II, to the west of the main entrance, and to the east a statue of George Washington (*see* STATUES). Among other important buildings surrounding the square are the church of ST MARTIN-IN-THE-FIELDS; the building designed in 1871 by F.W. Porter for the National Provincial Bank; the ADMIRALTY ARCH; Canada House, designed by Sir Robert Smirke for the UNION CLUB and the ROYAL COLLEGE OF PHYSICIANS, and converted in 1925 by Septimus Warwick for the Canadian High Commission; and Herbert Baker's South Africa House, 1935. On the corner of STRAND and CHARING CROSS ROAD there is a plaque indicating the central point of London from which all distances on signposts are measured. In the south-east corner of the square, contained inside a lamp-post, is the smallest police station in Britain. It has a direct telephone link with SCOTLAND YARD.

Trafalgar Square has long been the place for political meetings and demonstrations, including those of the Chartists who began their march here in 1848. More recently it has become the terminal point of protest marches. Every year at Christmas time an enormous Christmas tree is erected, the annual gift, since the 2nd World War, of the Norwegian people. On New Year's Eve Trafalgar Square is always the scene of boisterous celebrations.

The bronze *Horses of the Sun* over the entrance to Australia House is by Bertram Mackennal (1919); the stone groups on either side of the entrance at ground level, *Awakening of Australia* and *Prosperity of Australia*, are by Harold Parker (1918). The gilt springbok over the entrance of South Africa House is by Charles Wheeler (1934). In December 1982, after a competition in which 79 firms of architects had competed, it was announced that Ahrends, Burton and Koralek were to design an extension for the NATIONAL GALLERY on a site to the west of it, which had been vacant since 1949.

Trafalgar Tavern *Park Row, Greenwich, SE10*. A THAMES-side inn built in 1837 on the site of the George Tavern and frequented by the Cabinet who came here for their WHITEBAIT DINNERS. Thackeray, Wilkie Collins, Captain Frederick Marryat, George Cruikshank and Dickens were all occasional customers. So was Macaulay who was once observed by an American journalist enjoying a dinner of whitebait, spitchcocked eels and stewed carp. He broke a decanter but, not in the least discomfited by the accident, called for the bill as though nothing untoward had occurred. In *Our Mutual Friend*, Dickens set the wedding feast of Bella Wilfer and John Rokesmith here: 'What a dinner! Specimens of all the fishes that swim in the sea, surely had swum their way to it.' The tavern closed in 1915 and became successively an institution for aged merchant seamen, a working men's club and flats. It was restored and reopened in 1965.

Trained (Train) Bands The London Trained Bands, formed in the reign of Henry VIII, were considered to be the élite of the 'General Levey' of the Tudor period. They owed their commendable degree of efficiency and discipline to their affiliation to the Artillery Company of London, which survives as the HONOURABLE ARTILLERY COMPANY. They were the forerunners of the Militia and Territorial Forces. The Bands later served as a standard for militia training in the counties. In 1585 the first line of the London Trained Bands, all musketeers, said to be some 4,000 in number, were exercised and later reviewed at GREENWICH by Queen Elizabeth I. Under James I there was a reorganisation into companies and then into four regiments under the LORD MAYOR'S command. Strengths greatly increased during the Civil War when, in 1643, two regiments of London Trained Bands and three of Auxiliaries marched to the relief of Gloucester and fought in other engagements, including the Battle of Newbury. When their charter was renewed by William III he specifically ordered that the officers must be members of the HAC. The London Trained Bands continued until 1794, when they were reorganised as the City of London Militia.

TRANSPORT
Water Transport Examples of primitive 'dug-out' canoes of pre-Roman date have been found in the London area at ISLEWORTH, NORTH WOOLWICH, ERITH, WALTHAMSTOW, HAMPTON COURT, SHEPPERTON and STRAND-ON-THE-GREEN. The NORTH WOOLWICH example, found during the excavations for the ROYAL ALBERT DOCK, was 17 ft long and is now in the BRITISH MUSEUM, while one of the Isleworth specimens is in the MUSEUM OF LONDON. It is to be presumed that on the THAMES, as elsewhere in England, coracles made of animal skins stretched over a wicker framework were used for the conveyance of goods and passengers about 2,000 years ago.

During the building of COUNTY HALL part of a Roman ship was excavated. In it were found coins of the Emperor Tetricus the elder – the Gallic Emperor – and a section of its mast was found in the vicinity.

The Roman galleys were almost certainly the models for the English ships which followed them, but in Saxon times the latter show the influence of the Viking 'Gogstad' ships, with a single mast and square sail and auxiliary propulsion by oars. In time the various THAMES craft developed different hull forms and sail rigs according to the uses to which they were put.

By the 15th century caravels with two and three masts were bringing cargo from overseas up the Thames to LONDON BRIDGE, and in the Elizabethan era the early examples of what was to be known as the square-rigged full-rigged ship appeared in the POOL OF LONDON. In 1600 Elizabeth I granted a charter to the Honourable East India Company, and from then on the great 'full-riggers' of the Company became regular visitors to the Port of London with cargoes from India and the East. Meanwhile the Dutch, who were advanced seafarers at that time, had solved the problem of navigating their coastal and inland waters by inventing the fore-and-aft rig, in which the sails of small vessels were set in line with the keel instead of at right angles to it, and were in consequence easier to handle. The main sail was supported by a 'sprit' to its upper after corner from the foot of the mast, and on either side of the hull were slung 'lee-boards' which were lowered in deep water to prevent the shallow-draught vessels from drifting to leeward in a wind. Dutch vessels of this type were regular visitors to London, and continued to be so long after their influence had inspired the development of the THAMES sailing barges. These splendid vessels had a large mast carrying a big triangular foresail and a huge main spritsail and gaff topsail, and also a tiny mizzen mast and sail right aft, and could if necessary be operated by two men. Up to the 1940s large fleets of them were a familiar and impressive sight as they tacked across the river.

Thames sailing barges in the 1930s. Modelled on Dutch vessels, they were common on the Thames up to the 1940s.

Until the opening of WESTMINSTER BRIDGE in 1750 LONDON BRIDGE was the only bridge across the THAMES in the metropolis. The only other way to cross the river was by ferry, and both banks were lined at intervals with stairs or landing places for picking up and setting down passengers or in some cases horses and carts. It is uncertain when the THAMES WATER-MEN first appeared on the scene, but in 1372 the CITY CORPORATION ordered them to limit their fare between London and WESTMINSTER to 2d. They only became organised by degrees, and during the 17th century much of their business was poached on by the lightermen, whose main business was the carriage of goods. In 1700 the watermen and lightermen were formed into one guild or company, which is not and has never sought to be a LIVERY COMPANY, thus differing from all the other City guilds. Its Hall in ST MARY-AT-HILL was built in 1776 and is the fourth to fulfil its purpose. From the ranks of the licensed watermen came the Sovereign's Bargemasters and the crews of the state, civic and livery company barges which formerly lent splendour to processions on the THAMES.

The 19th century brought with it the introduction of steam propulsion for passenger traffic on the river, and the *Margate Hoy* and other sailing vessels formerly conveying passengers from BILLINGSGATE gradually gave way to steamers. The THAMES continued to be used as a highway, and in the 1850s the City Steamboat Company of BATTERSEA maintained a large fleet of smart little paddle steamers carrying passengers up and down the river. The smoke-belching tug with its string of dumb barges became as much a feature of the river as the great red sails of the sailing barges, and all figure in the lively paintings of William Wyllie, Charles Dixon and other leading marine artists of the Victorian era. Larger excursion steamers plied between the POOL OF LONDON and seaside resorts on the Kent and Essex shores of the Thames Estuary. Those operated by the General Steam Navigation Company continued until the late 1950s. Most were paddle steamers but the last ones were twin-screw vessels.

With the enormous improvements in the London streets during the late Victorian and Edwardian period the small steamboats became outmoded, and it was not until 1938 that a Mr C. Odell revived water transport on the Thames with his 'river buses' plying between WESTMINSTER and GREENWICH. The boats were comfortable and clean and their crews the soul of courtesy. They never seriously competed with road traffic, but have survived as a form of pleasure trip and are even now used for 'commuting' by those to whom time on the journey is not of paramount importance. A more recent and more rapid form of THAMES commuting is the hydrofoil, introduced in the 1970s between GREEN-WICH, TOWER PIER and CHARING CROSS.

The large and ornate state barges formerly paraded by the Crown, the LORD MAYOR and the LIVERY GUILDS have disappeared from the scene, as has also the CITY CORPORATION's navigation barge, the *Maria Wood*, a large and luxurious craft in which members of the CORPORATION and their ladies were rowed up the THAMES on tours of inspection in their former capacity as conservators of the river. A touch of elegance is still supplied, however, by the handsome modern motor river-boats which accommodate expensive dinner parties or other functions on festive occasions like a royal jubilee or a UNIVERSITY BOAT RACE.

Excursion steamers take on passengers in the Pool of London. From a lithograph by Parrott, 1841.

Road Transport

Began when men decided that they would rather ride than walk. How early this happened in London is not certain, but the Romans were accustomed to riding horses when they colonised London in the first century AD, and such of the local inhabitants as were able would no doubt have adopted the practice. They would also have adopted the carriage of passengers by litter – a light carriage body with shafts in front and behind, between which horses or men formed the motive power. Ownership of a horse was a sign of affluence and privilege, and the animal was a sturdy working beast strong enough to carry its owner and possibly one or two additional passengers. The breeding of swift and fragile racehorses and other specialist animals was to come much later. The horse was expensive to maintain, but it was more of a necessity than a luxury, and its use gradually spread down the social scale, though not to the extent that the use of the motor car has done in our own day. The poorer citizens of London still went on foot.

The limited carrying capacity of a horse's back led to the development of more economical use of horse power by the construction of wheeled carriages, in which a small group of passengers might sit more or less comfortably while being drawn along the road by one or more horses. Less economical were the litters, which required two horses but could not carry more than two passengers; but they were still in use in medieval and Tudor times along with the wheeled horse carriages. Dogs are said to have been used for drawing small carriages, but no details of the breed of dog employed appear to have survived.

During the middle of the 16th century Walter Rippon introduced into London from the Continent the coach – a four-wheeled carriage with a roof and more or less protection at the sides, drawn by one or more horses. Like the horse in earlier times, its use started at the upper end of the social scale and spread downwards, so that two hundred years later we find the London traffic jam featured in the engravings of Thomas Rowlandson and other artists. Private coaches varied from such magnificent vehicles as the LORD MAYOR'S COACH, which was drawn in procession by six horses, to the plain and modest conveyance kept by the City merchant.

Public transport was introduced to London by Captain Baily – previously one of Ralegh's sea-captains –

with the hackney coach (named from the French *haquenée* – an ambling nag), a two-seater vehicle drawn by two horses, one of which was ridden by the driver. The THAMES watermen rightly foresaw a drop in their income as the hackney coaches captured their trade, but were powerless to prevent their operation. There was a certain amount of dishonesty and overcharging in both groups, so that from about 1720 makers of London maps adopted the practice of printing tables of hackney coach and watermen's fares on the maps which they published.

The fact that a man could get soaked with rain or fall down his own steps between leaving his coach and entering his front door led to the introduction in 1711 of the sedan chair. This could be described as a descendant of the litter, since it was a one-seater coach body with shafts back and front, borne by men, and its advantage was that it could be taken through a man's front door into his hall. The chair was completely enclosed and padded all round. The roof could be lifted and the sides folded back to allow the passenger to board and alight. The whole structure was stout and heavy, and took the combined efforts of two strong

Sedan chairs, which were introduced in 1711, survived until well into the 19th century. From an engraving of 1761.

men to carry it when loaded – especially if the occupant happened to be of aldermanic proportions. It was no doubt for this reason that two-seater sedan chairs never came into use. Until adequate STREET LIGHTING was introduced in London at the beginning of the 19th century link boys or torch bearers accompanied hackney coaches and sedan chairs on their journeys on dark nights, partly as a guide through the darkened streets and partly to discourage footpads. At the entrance to many houses were fitted conical extinguishers, in which the link boys might dowse their torches on arrival. Sedan chairs survived well into the 19th century, and the last active one is said to have been seen in Church Lane, HAMPSTEAD, not many years before the age of the railways began. Charles Knight reported one in MAYFAIR in 1841.

The more wealthy Londoners continued to maintain their own private carriages and their own coach horses and stables, while those less affluent but still well-to-do kept their carriages at the local livery stables, and those who could not keep carriages of their own hired them from the same source. Coach hire persisted until about 1920.

As London spread outwards in the late 18th and early 19th centuries the stage coach, which had come into use as the inter-city transport of those days, began to be used for short stages in the metropolitan area. It was a heavy and capacious carriage with room for half a dozen people inside and two or three outside, and was drawn by two or more horses. With the coming of the Post Office mail service in 1840 (*see* POST OFFICE) the coaches developed into very elegant well-sprung vehicles, drawn by a team of horses which had to be changed at certain distances along the route, where coaching inns afforded suitable facilities in addition to those required by the passengers. The driver and guard were required to adhere to a strict time table, with an astonishingly brief time for changing horses; and, on turning over duty to their reliefs, they handed over their watches at the same time.

Alongside the stage coach developed the short stage carriage – the public transport service between central London and places like GREENWICH, CROYDON and EALING. The vehicles used were at first traditional coaches, but by 1791 some at least of them were more akin to the omnibuses which came on the scene some four decades later, with long hearse-like bodies to accommodate inside passengers and room on the top for a few people who did not mind some discomfort. The number of passengers on top was limited to seven if less than four horses were used, or 12 if four or more hauled the vehicle.

The transport of goods into and out of London in the 18th century was effected in large stage wagons with hoods of tarpaulin, mounted on axles with wide-tread roller-like wheels to negotiate the rough or muddy roads, drawn by teams of six or more horses.

Short stage carriages were not allowed to pick up or set down passengers within the London area covered by the 17th-century BILLS OF MORTALITY, in order that traffic jams should not develop and in order also that the monopoly of the hackney coaches should not be disturbed.

The omnibus appears in London prints of the last years of the 18th century, but not under that name, which originated in France. A service of large-capacity passenger vehicles had a terminus in the town of Nantes, at the shop of a Monsieur Omnès, who adopted as a business slogan the Latin pun on his own names – *Omnes omnibus* ('All for every one'). The name 'omnibus' was applied to the vehicles and persisted in England until the 1920s, when the 'omni' was officially sloughed off and the abbreviation 'bus', already in colloquial use for many years, became the usual term. The credit for the introduction of the omnibus to London is generally given to George Shillibeer. He had seen its success in Paris, and on 4 July 1829 launched his own version on the London streets. It was routed from PADDINGTON to the BANK along the New Road in order to avoid the BILLS OF MORTALITY area, and the fare for the journey was 1s 6d for passengers inside the omnibus and 1s for those on top. (In the 1920s a journey of this length would have cost half the smaller of these two fares, but in 1980 it cost four times the larger.) The 'Shillibus' accommodated 16 or 18 passengers in a wide van-like vehicle with windows on three sides, which was drawn by three bay horses harnessed abreast. The arrangement

Shillibeer's Omnibus, 'A new carriage on the Parisian Mode', was introduced to London in 1829.

Horse-drawn traffic at the busy junction of Princes Street and Threadneedle Street.

of the horses made it unsuitable for narrow streets, but the width of the carriage made it more comfortable, and the courtesy and efficiency of the conductors – some of whom were said to be sons of naval officers – were apparently of a very high order. As other bus operators entered the scene the conductors or 'cads' lost their quarter-deck image and became notorious for their anxiety to crowd as many passengers as possible into their vehicles.

In 1832 the monopoly of the hackney coachmen in the BILLS OF MORTALITY area was terminated and the number of omnibuses in central London rapidly increased. Drivers and conductors were required to be licensed from 1838 onwards. Thomas Tilling began an omnibus business in PECKHAM in the late 1840s and in 1855 the Compagnie Générale des Omnibus de Londres was established in Paris with a board of British and French directors. It subsequently became the London General Omnibus Company and the word 'GeneraL' (*sic*) appeared on the side of most of London's buses until the coming of the LONDON PASSENGER TRANSPORT BOARD in 1933, when it was replaced by 'London TransporT' (*sic*).

The 'outside' of the buses became more of a top deck, with transverse seats, in 1881. The first motor bus was licensed in 1897, but horse buses did not finally disappear until 1916. Until 1919 the body of the bus rested between the back wheels, like that of a horse bus, and the driver sat in front of the body and behind the engine as if he were driving a horse – the 'B' or 'Old Bill' type. But in 1919 the 'K' bus appeared, with the body placed over the wheels and the driver seated behind a shield alongside the engine on the off side. The 'K' seated 46 passengers and a larger version, the 'S', 54. In 1923 a new type, the 'NS', seating 52 passengers, was set on a specially designed chassis which gave it a low centre of gravity and allowed the boarding platform to be a mere 9 inches from the ground. Its stability enabled a roof to be fitted on the upper deck and pneumatic tyres to replace the solid tyres previously in

use; and in 1925 the first covered-top bus made its appearance on the London streets. About 1930 the first 'pirate buses' appeared. These were buses operated by independent owners who obtained permission to run along routes which, while differing slightly from the 'General' services, covered mostly the same ground and captured much of the trade. The situation was resolved in 1933, when the London Passenger Transport Board assumed control not only of all the bus services in the metropolis, but also of the UNDERGROUND RAILWAYS and certain tramway undertakings already associated with the 'General', and the extensive network of tramways previously operated by the LONDON COUNTY COUNCIL.

Meanwhile in 1929 the 'General' had introduced a wide-bodied bus of a more luxurious type – the 'LT' – on six wheels, and the following year they produced an improved version with an enclosed staircase, and a four-wheeled variant, the 'ST'. Improved versions of these came out, and diesel fuel gradually replaced petrol. But the next major development was the 8ft wide 'RTW', which entered service in 1949. This was followed by the vastly superior Routemaster about 1960 and eventually by the rear-engined 'DM'.

One form of transport already mentioned and now completely vanished from the London streets is the tramcar, which should be referred to here rather than with railways, although for most of its existence it ran on metal tracks. It was introduced to London by George Francis Train in 1861. Intended to take advantage of the lack of friction between wheels and iron rails as compared with macadamised road surfaces, it was at first a failure owing mainly to the fact that the rails slightly projected above the road surface and obstructed other traffic, but also to the experimental tracks being laid in fashionable rather than working districts. In 1869, however, three tramways were authorised on the fringes of London, and these lines expanded into a large system covering all of London except the central area. In 1899 almost the whole network became

One of London County Council's last horse-drawn tram-cars on its way to Bricklayers Arms in c.1905.

the responsibility of the LONDON COUNTY COUNCIL, and remained so until the formation of the LONDON PASSENGER TRANSPORT BOARD in 1933.

The tramcar itself changed comparatively little except in size. At first a single-decked carriage on four wheels with a slightly American appearance, it developed into a sort of double-decker date box with a vertical iron ladder at each end. With the coming of electric traction in 1900 (after experimental use of cable traction in some places in the 1870s and 1880s), larger and heavier vehicles became possible and in most cases the upper deck was roofed in. Cars were lengthened and were mounted on two four-wheel bogies for greater safety on curved tracks. Current was supplied to the motors from overhead power lines in the outer districts and from live rails set in a conduit between the rails in central London. On some of the longer routes cars had to change from one method to another at some stage on the way, by heaving down the overhead 'trolley' and sliding the under-carriage 'shoe' into position and reversing the process on the return journey. The LONDON COUNTY COUNCIL's type of car tended to pitch at speed like a ship in a head sea, but the Feltham pattern cars introduced by London

United Tramways were very much more comfortable and appeared to be more stable.

By the middle of the 1930s the tramcar had given place on many routes to the trolley-bus or 'trackless tram', as it was at first called. In form it was a large omnibus, silent in action except for the swish of the sheaves of the collector arms or trolleys against the overhead power lines. It had, however, certain disadvantages in that it needed a network of wires above the street and was prone to delay when the trolleys accidentally slipped off the wires at junctions. After 1945 tram routes which were closed were replaced by diesel-driven bus services. By 1953 the last tram had been ceremonially burnt at CHARLTON, and soon afterwards the valuable steel rails had been dug out of the London streets and sold for scrap. Trolley-buses themselves have since been 'phased out' and the motor bus reigns supreme.

Rail Transport London's first railway was authorised by Parliament in 1833 to run the four miles from LONDON BRIDGE to GREENWICH on a continuous viaduct of which the first brick was laid in 1834. The section from LONDON BRIDGE to DEPTFORD began operating in December 1836, but it was 1840 before a permanent station opened at GREENWICH. The London and Croydon Railway opened in 1839 and the London and Brighton in 1841. In due course these lines became part of the London, Brighton and South Coast Railway, while the Greenwich grew into the South Eastern Railway, and they all brought passengers from the south and south-east into LONDON BRIDGE STATION. The London and Birmingham Railway opened EUSTON STATION in 1838 and the South Western extended inwards to WATERLOO from NINE ELMS in 1848. A more modest venture, the Blackwall Railway, was opened from BLACKWALL to the MINORIES in 1840 and extended to FENCHURCH STREET in 1841. It was at first operated by cables hauled by stationary engines and the gauge of the track was 5 ft, but about 1848 the gauge was changed to the standard 4ft 8½ ins and steam locomotives were introduced. The Eastern Counties Railway, subsequently the Great Eastern,

London's first railway opened in 1836 and covered the 4 miles from London Bridge to Greenwich on a continuous viaduct.

Cables operating the Blackwall Railway, which opened in 1840 to take passengers to the Minories.

was opened with its London terminus at MILE END in 1839, extending to SHOREDITCH in 1840, but did not reach LIVERPOOL STREET STATION until 1875. In 1853 the East and West India Docks and Birmingham Junction Railway was authorised. It took a somewhat circuitous route to the north of central London to link the western suburbs with the DOCKS, and was subsequently named the North London Railway. In 1865 a spur was run south from DALSTON to BROAD STREET in the CITY.

PADDINGTON STATION, which was built in 1838 as the metropolitan terminus of the Great Western Railway, could hardly at that time be said to be in London at all, and this may probably have hastened the coming of the capital's first underground railway. The idea of running a line underground originated when the first schemes for the Holborn Valley Improvement were being discussed, and a scheme by Charles Pearson, Solicitor to the CITY OF LONDON, in 1851 envisaged a large area under the viaduct carrying the road across the valley, with stations connecting north and south railway lines. His plan was rejected by the CITY in 1853, but in the meantime the Bayswater, Paddington and Holborn Railway, later the North Metropolitan, was approved, and took over a modification of the Pearson scheme. To avoid expensive compensation to property owners the new line was laid in 'cut and cover' tunnels under the New Road linking PADDINGTON and ISLINGTON. The clay excavated was used to make the bricks with which the tunnels were lined, and in 1863 the first section of the Metropolitan Railway was opened between PADDINGTON and KING'S CROSS. It was subsequently extended in both directions. The District Railway, likewise a 'cut and cover' line, opened between SOUTH KENSINGTON and WESTMINSTER in 1868, extending to the MANSION HOUSE in 1871 and eventually linking up with the Metropolitan line. By 1884 the Inner Circle, known today as the CIRCLE LINE, was in operation.

The Metropolitan opened in 1879 a line northwards from BAKER STREET, and this had reached Aylesbury by 1892. Steam was still the motive power, locomotives being fitted with a device to enable them to 'consume their own smoke'. In 1890 electric traction was introduced with the opening of London's first 'Tube', which ran through tunnels excavated far below the surface by means of a 'Greathead Shield' from KING WILLIAM STREET to STOCKWELL – the City and South London Railway. The Great Northern and City 'Tube' from MOORGATE opened in 1904 and the Baker Street and Waterloo Railway or BAKERLOO in 1906. More recent developments include the pushing of the City and South London line south to MORDEN and linking it with the Hampstead and Highgate Railway to become the Edgware, Highgate and Morden line and later, when the Highgate line was extended to BARNET, the Northern Line – the longest tunnel in the world. The Central London Railway between EALING and LIVERPOOL STREET was extended eastwards to Epping and Ongar. The PICCADILLY tube was opened from HAMMERSMITH to COCKFOSTERS in the late 1920s and a non-stop service has recently been provided westward between HAMMERSMITH and LONDON AIRPORT. Main line termini and other London stations have recently been linked by the VICTORIA LINE, and a further 'link' tube line is the JUBILEE LINE.

Until 1860 the main surface lines from the south and south-east of London terminated on the south side of the THAMES, but in that year the London, Brighton and South Coast line crossed the river to VICTORIA where it was joined two years later by the London, Chatham and Dover Railway. The latter and its rival the South Eastern reached BLACKFRIARS in 1864 (extending to HOLBORN VIADUCT in 1874) and the South Eastern entered CANNON STREET STATION in 1866. (The SER and the LC and D amalgamated in 1899 to become the South Eastern and Chatham, nicknamed the 'Slow, Easy and Comfortable'.) More lines appeared to the north of the river, including the Midland running into ST PANCRAS in 1868, the Great Northern into KING'S CROSS in 1852 and the Great Central into MARYLEBONE in 1899. The London, Tilbury and Southend Railway brought passengers into FENCHURCH STREET from the Essex riverside, and the District underground line broke surface at Bow Road to run alongside it to BARKING and subsequently to UPMINSTER.

Private Motor Cars The history of the private motor car is epitomised today in the ROYAL AUTOMOBILE CLUB VETERAN CAR RUN from London to Brighton which has taken place annually in November since 14 November 1896. This event was then organised by Harry J. Lawson, motor engineer, to celebrate the raising by Parliament of the speed limit for cars from 4 miles to 12 miles per hour, and on that occasion included the latest machines rather than the earliest.

Private motoring in London during the 2nd World War was severely limited owing to the strict rationing of petrol, and even after the war was slow to recover; but the politician's promise of a car for every family and the growing practice of providing a company car as a staff perquisite rapidly filled the streets again, and in 1979 the number of private cars crowding the roads into central London was greater than ever before – 173,000 between 7 and 10 a.m. on a working day and an estimated 531,000 over the 24 hours. This situation has brought its own problems, and street parking has had to be regulated by meter and extensive off-street parking spaces above and below ground provided in the central London area. In the City of WESTMINSTER, which now covers most of central London apart from the CITY OF LONDON, there are 21 official car parks containing 7,408 parking spaces, six of which are leased to a car parking group. It also has 10,020 meters for on-street parking plus 16,160 residents' parking bays. Parking in the City of London is provided by six off-street car parks with a total capacity of 2,428 cars and 56 lorries or coaches, parking space for about 2,250 solo motor cycles and 1,550 parking meters for on-street parking and 11 coach parking bays. National Car Parks also operate a number of car parks in the CITY with a capacity of 3,100 vehicles.

Bicycles In 1979 the number of pedal bicycles entering central London between 7 and 10 a.m. on a working day was 7,000 and the figure for the 24 hours was 18,200 – 42 per cent more than in 1977. For motor cycles the numbers were 15,000 and 37,570 – 2 per cent up on 1977. During the latter year 31 pedal bicyclists and 102 motor cyclists were killed in accidents in London, and no fewer than 17,975 bicycles were stolen.

Cabs and Taxis In 1639 the Corporation of Coachmen obtained a licence to ply for hire in London; and in 1654 Parliament found it necessary to limit the number of hackney coaches in London and WESTMINSTER to 300. In 1661 Charles II authorised a maximum of 400 hackney coach licences in London and the fare across the CITY from the TOWER to the INNS OF COURT was 1s 6d. After the rebuilding of the streets following the GREAT FIRE the coachman sat on a 'box' on the coach instead of on one of the horses. In 1694 the behaviour of a coachload of unruly ladies in HYDE PARK led to a ban on coaches in the Park which lasted for 230 years. The number of hackney licences was increased to 700 in 1694. By 1768 it was 1,000; by 1805 it was 1,100. But, thanks to the arrival in 1823 of the *cabriolet*

de place or 'cab' from Paris, the hackney coach had practically disappeared by 1850.

The first cabs were drawn by a single horse and carried two passengers under a hood while the driver had a seat on what is now called the off-side of the vehicle, but outside the hood. In 1834 Joseph Harrison patented a cab with the driver seated on top, and this was improved by John Chapman in 1836 by seating the driver behind the cab and putting a window in the roof for communication with his passengers. At this time also appeared the four-wheeled cab or 'growler', drawn by a single horse and seating a third passenger alongside the driver.

By 1860 there were 4,600 cabs in London, and by 1904 the total had risen to 7,499 hansoms and 3,905 growlers – far too many for the amount of custom available. The number of cabs cruising in the central London area in search of fares caused so much traffic congestion that the police introduced regulations to

Cabmen eat a meal in one of London's 64 shelters, such as the one in Acacia Road, St John's Wood, shown (top) in 1875. The last cab was still in use after the 2nd World War.

compel them to remain on their 'ranks' until someone hired them. The coming of the motor-cab drove both hansom and four-wheeler off the roads, but, surprisingly, 12 hansoms and 100 'growlers' survived as late as 1927 and the last cab did not disappear until 1947.

In mid-Victorian times cabmen had a reputation for heavy drinking, and this led to the building – at the expense of various philanthropists – of the distinctive London cabmen's shelters, where drivers could restore their flagging spirits with a cheap meal and a hot, but non-alcoholic, drink. 64 of these shelters were built in London, but, due partly to enemy bombing and partly to street improvements, their number had dwindled to 12 by 1972.

The first mechanically driven cabs in London were electric, powered by batteries, illuminated by electric lamps and having a range of 30 miles between battery rechargings. They were introduced in 1897 and weighed two tons each, as against the hansom's 8 cwt. Quiet and smooth-running in comparison with horse cabs, they developed various faults including vibration and excessive tyre wear, and by the middle of 1900 had vanished from the London streets. Petrol-engined cabs were not licensed by the METROPOLITAN POLICE until 1904, and some of the earlier ones were constructed like a hansom, with the driver seated above and behind, with steering column and control handles instead of reins and the bonnet in front representing the horse. This arrangement was somewhat unnerving for the passengers, and in due course the design was changed and the driver took his place behind the bonnet, where he has remained ever since.

In 1906 the METROPOLITAN POLICE drew up a set of regulations for motorcab design and construction, one of which stipulated a maximum turning circle of 25 ft diameter, and by 1914 more than 45 car makers had designs officially approved. From 1920 to 1930 12 makes only were licensed and from 1930 to 1940 only four. The taximeter, which gave the cab its modern name, was in general use from 1907. Its purpose was to indicate to both driver and passenger the distance travelled, and so avoid arguments between them about payment due. But even before the advent of the motor cab it also registered fare, extras and information for the driver. Its metal flag, pulled down when the cab was hired (and usually covered with one of the cabby's gloves until then) survived until 1959, when it was replaced by an illuminated sign on the meter.

London's single motor cab of 1904 had multiplied to 8,397 by the beginning of 1914, but by the end of that year, presumably owing to the outbreak of war and the consequent petrol shortage, the figure was reduced to 7,260. By the end of the war in 1918 there were only 3,000 taxis in London, but the number increased rapidly under peace-time conditions and settled down to an annual figure of around 8,000 up to 1939. During the same period the London taxi became standardised and only three makers produced it. The driver had a vacant space on his left for luggage, and on his right there was no window to interfere with his hand signals.

The 2nd World War again brought down the number of London's taxis to 3,000. Both cabs and cabmen were requisitioned in large numbers for military and support services. After the War, improved vehicles were designed by the leading car makers and the number of cabs rose to 8,000 by 1950. Rising costs, including that of petrol, brought the total down to 5,443 by

1953, but the introduction of diesel engines saved the situation and by the end of 1966 there were 7,490 cabs in service. Numbers continued to increase and by the end of 1977 reached 12,452. The figure for the end of 1982 showed a slight increase at 12,560 including 3,340 with two-way radio. All are diesel-driven with the exception of 17 cabs.

London taxi drivers are required to satisfy high requirements of physical fitness, topographical knowledge, driving capability and personal character.

Air Transport Men had dreamed of air transport for centuries, but it may be said to have begun as far as London is concerned with the ascent of Signor Lunardi's BALLOON from MOORFIELDS in 1784. Mechanisation followed in due course and the first journey by powered airship took place in 1902 from the CRYSTAL PALACE at SYDENHAM to EASTCOTE in MIDDLESEX.

By 1910 the heavier-than-air machine – the aeroplane – had arrived and HENDON aerodrome was established, the first air mail service being operated from it to Windsor the following year to celebrate the Coronation of King George V and Queen Mary. Two years after the outbreak of the 1st World War in 1914 an aerodrome was opened at CROYDON as a fighter base for defence against attacks by German Zeppelin airships. After the War it was transferred to commercial use and developed by Imperial Airways as the London airport for their passenger services to the Continent. During the 2nd World War it became an obvious target for attacks by German aircraft, but it was brought back into use after the cessation of hostilities. With the rapid advances in the development of passenger aircraft and the need for longer runways it eventually became unsuitable and was closed in 1959.

Meanwhile on the other side of London the Fairey Aviation Company's Great Western aerodrome had been opened at HEATHROW in 1928. Next in importance of London's airports today is Gatwick, 25 miles south of the capital. Used at first by the Surrey Aero Club, it was acquired in 1936 by a company called British Airways – not the state airline, which in those days was known as Imperial Airways – which put up an airport building on it. The Southern Railway built a station there, its existing station at Gatwick Racecourse being too far away. After 1945 Gatwick became London's official charter airport and since 1952 it has been London Airport No. 2.

By this time air travel in, as distinct from that into, London had become a viable proposition, thanks to the improvements in the helicopter, and experiments began in 1952 for the building of a helicopter pad on the south bank of the THAMES in LAMBETH. From July 1955 to May 1956 the state-owned British European Airways operated a helicopter service from the SOUTH BANK to the airport at HEATHROW, but an adequate payload could not be carried owing to the excessive weight of safety equipment which was required by law. Between 1956 and 1959 'heliports' were proposed at ST KATHARINE'S DOCK, CANNON STREET STATION and NINE ELMS (VAUXHALL). Of these the NINE ELMS site was considered most suitable, but when the removal of the flower, fruit and vegetable market from COVENT GARDEN became urgent the market was given priority and the heliport had to go elsewhere. In the meantime the firm of Westland Aircraft Ltd, had obtained planning permission for the establishment of a heliport at BATTERSEA, and began operating it on 23 April 1959. Permission was granted for short periods of seven years or less, and night flights (between 11 p.m. and 7 a.m.) were allowed only during the summer months. The 'port' was situated on the south bank of the THAMES between BATTERSEA and WANDSWORTH BRIDGES and consisted of one acre of ground and a car park. Air traffic control was carried out by International Aeradio Ltd, and up to 4,000 flights were handled each year. Other sites considered suitable for heliports include Shadwell Basin, SURREY DOCKS, a site near Swan Lane and Knight's Wharf, NEWHAM. Civil helicopters are mainly chartered or private, but one company was considering the operation of a scheduled service. In the London area helicopter runs serve a number of localities which include LONDON BRIDGE, BARNES, BEDFONT, HEATHROW, NORTHOLT, and NORTHWOOD, but they seem unlikely seriously to compete with surface transport.

(*See also* DOCKS, RAILWAYS, RAILWAY STATIONS, UNDERGROUND RAILWAYS, *and entries for individual Underground lines*).

Travellers' Club *106 Pall Mall, SW1*. Founded in 1819, possibly at the suggestion of Lord Castlereagh, then Foreign Secretary, to form a point of reunion for gentlemen who have travelled abroad. Palmerston and the Earl of Aberdeen were members of the first club committee. The first premises were at No. 12 WATERLOO PLACE. In 1822 the club moved to No. 49 PALL MALL, 'a shabby low-roomed house'. In 1828 part of the grounds of CARLTON HOUSE were acquired as a site for a new club house. Wilkins, Deering, Harrison, Hopper, Barry, Blore and Benjamin Wyatt all competed in the first architectural competition held by a London club. Charles Barry's plans were chosen. His club house, completed in 1832 at a cost of £64,189, was built as a sumptuous Italian Renaissance palace round three sides of a central court. It was damaged by bombs in 1940 and restored in 1952–3 by F. Rowntree. It is a social and non-political club whose members are no longer necessarily travellers, though there are still many Foreign Office officials and diplomats among them.

Treasury *Whitehall, SW1*. Completed in 1845 to the designs of Kent, Soane and Barry. The interior was completely reconstructed in 1960–4 when various remains of Henry VIII's WHITEHALL PALACE were revealed, including the walls of the Great and Small Tennis Courts (*see* TENNIS COURTS). The south end was designed by Kent as the new Treasury in 1733–6. A public passageway, called Cockpit Alley, which links DOWNING STREET with HORSEGUARDS PARADE, runs underneath it. From 1824–7 Soane built a new Board of Trade and Privy Council towards WHITEHALL. This soon proved too small and was dismantled in 1844. Sir Charles Barry replaced it with his new Treasury building into which he incorporated Soane's columns and frieze.

Tredegar Square *E3*. Built in the 1830s on land owned by Lord Tredegar, the houses were designed for prosperous merchants rather than artisans. Many of the houses are now divided into flats, but the square still retains its grace, with the palatial aspect of the north side (Nos 24–31) particularly striking.

Tregunter Road *SW10*. Built in 1852 on the Gunter Estate (*see* TALGARTH ROAD) and named after a family home. Dame Emma Albani, the singer, lived at No. 61 in 1908–30.

Trent Park *Barnet, Hertfordshire*. Formerly part of the ancient royal hunting forest of ENFIELD CHASE. 200 acres were given to Dr Richard Jebb, physician to George III, as a reward for having gone to save the life of the King's brother, the Duke of Gloucester at Trento in the Austrian Tyrol. A lodge on the land was converted for Jebb by Sir William Chambers. Subsequently the Sassoon family acquired a total of 900 acres. Sir Philip Sassoon, the 3rd Baronet, spent part of his immense fortune on improving the magnificent gardens in which he employed 18 gardeners. After his death in 1939 the house was requisitioned as an interrogation centre for enemy airmen. After acquisition by the former MIDDLESEX County Council in 1952, 688 acres became Green Belt (*see* PLANNING), while the mansion and 200 acres adjoining it became a teacher's training college.

Trevor Place, Square, Street and **Terrace**. *SW7*. Take their name from Sir John Trevor, the corrupt Master of the Rolls and Speaker of the House of Commons and cousin of Judge Jeffreys, who built a house on the site of Nos 235–241 KNIGHTSBRIDGE in about 1700. His estate was developed by his grandson, Arthur Trevor Hill, in the early 19th century. Trevor Square was said to house the mistresses of officers of the HOUSEHOLD BRIGADE. The houses were originally three-storey but many had an attic storey added at the end of their first leases. By the 1880s the houses in Trevor Street were mainly in working-class occupation; and the south end of Trevor Square had become a slum. In 1909 the estate was sold to J. S. Humphreys for £200,000. Humphreys leased the southern two acres to HARROD's in 1913. HARRODS demolished the slums, including 44 cottages, and built their warehouse and garage on the site. The warehouse is connected by two tunnels under BROMPTON ROAD to the main building.

Trig Lane *EC4*. Named after the Trigge family, local residents and fishmongers in the 14th and 15th centuries. It was known earlier as Fish Wharf. Excavations in 1974, when THAMES STREET was being redeveloped, revealed an oak waterfront of the mid-14th century well preserved in the THAMES subsoil.

Trinity Almshouses *Mile End Road, E1*. The almshouses 'wherein 28 decayed Masters and Commanders of Ships or ye widows of such are maintain'd' were built in 1695 by the Corporation of TRINITY HOUSE on land provided by Captain Henry Mudd. In the 1890s the Corporation petitioned the Charity Commissioners to have the almshouses demolished, but, partly due to protests, permission was refused in 1896. In the same year C. R. Ashbee published *The Trinity Hospital in Mile End: An object Lesson in National History* as the first report of the Committee for the Survey of the Memorials of Greater London, later to grow into the *Survey of London* series. Ashbee considered the building to have been a 'joint creation' of John Evelyn and Christopher Wren, but his evidence was far from convincing. Bombed in 1941, the redbrick cottages have since been modernised by the LONDON COUNTY COUNCIL, and the chapel relined with 18th-century panelling from Bradmore House, HAMMERSMITH.

Trinity Church Passage *Fetter Lane, EC4*. Commemorates the church of HOLY TRINITY, GOUGH SQUARE which stood in Pemberton Row between 1838

Trinity Almshouses, Mile End Road, in 1696, the year after they were opened for 'decayed Masters and Commanders of ships'.

and 1905. The passage was earlier known as Three Leg Alley, Pemberton's Row, and Featherbed Lane.

Trinity College of Music *11 and 13 Mandeville Place, W1*.
Founded by the Revd H.G. Bonavia Hunt in 1872 as the School for the Study and Practice of Music for the Church, but it quickly extended its activities to include all fields of music. In 1875, the College was incorporated by special Act of Parliament as Trinity College of Music and is thus second only to the ROYAL ACADEMY OF MUSIC in length of establishment amongst the music colleges of London.

Trinity Hospital *Riverside Walk, Greenwich, SE10*.
Attractive 17th-century almshouses now dwarfed by a power station (1906). They were built in 1613 by Henry Howard, Earl of Northampton, for 20 male pensioners. The Earl was born in Norfolk, as, supposedly, were eight of the pensioners; so the almshouses are also known as Norfolk College. They were restored in 1812. In the charming small chapel is part of the Earl's tomb carved by Nicholas Stone and brought here from Dover Castle in the 1770s. The fine stained glass depicting the Crucifixion, the Agony in the Garden and the Ascension is 16th-century Flemish.

Trinity House *Trinity Square, EC3*.
The lighthouse authority for the coast of England and Wales. Its origin is obscure as early records have been lost. One theory is that it derives from a Guild of Mariners known to have existed in King Alfred's reign and another theory has it that it is the successor of a corporation founded by Archbishop Stephen Langton in the reign of King John. This later fraternity was made up of 'godley disposed men who, for the actual suppression of evil disposed persons bringing ships to destruction by the showing forth of false beacons, do bind themselves together in the love of Lord Christ in the name of the Masters and Fellows of Trinity Guild, to succour from the dangers of the sea all who are beset upon the coasts of England to feed them when ahungered and athirst, to bind up their wounds and to build and light proper beacons for the guidance of mariners'. By the 14th century there were several Trinity Guilds established in the main ports. In 1512 the DEPTFORD Guild of Mariners petitioned the King to grant them a charter since, as they put it, 'the practise of pilotship in rivers by young men who are unwilling to take the labour and advantage of learning the shipman's craft on the high seas, is likely to cause scarcity of mariners; and so this your Realm, which heretofore hath flourished with a Navy to all other lands dreadful, shall be left destitute of cunning masters and mariners; also that Scots, Flemings and Frenchmen have been suffered to learn as lodesmen the secrets of the King's streams, and in time of war have come as far as Gravesende and fette owte English shippes to the great rebuke of the Realm.' Credit for drawing up this petition has been given to Sir Thomas Spert who became the first Master. His monument of 1725 in ST DUNSTAN'S CHURCH, STEPNEY is unequivocal: 'By the Company of Trinity House, this monument was erected 81 years after the decease of their founder.'

In 1514 Henry VIII granted a charter to the 'Master, Wardens and Assistants of the Guild, Fraternity Brotherhood of the Most Glorious and Undivided Trinity and of St Clement in the parish of Deptford-Stronde in the County of Kent.' The title of St Clement has caused speculation as to whether there was a subsidiary guild at Leigh, as many early pilots are buried there in the parish church of St Clement. Possibly Leigh pilots guided the homeward-bound ships and the DEPTFORD pilots the outward-bound ones. The charter said the brotherhood was to be administered by a Master, four wardens and eight assistants who were to be elected annually. They were given the

891

duties of the defence and pilotage of the Thames and powers to make laws, for the 'relief, increase and augmentation of the shipping of this our realm of England'. Women were also included in the early Fraternity. In 1520 the Admiralty and Navy Board was established. But DEPTFORD Dockyard was placed under the jurisdiction of the Fraternity. In 1547 Edward VI renewed the charter but called it a Corporation instead of a Fraternity, its full title being The Corporation of Trinity House on Deptford Strand. The charter was renewed by Mary I in 1553 and by Elizabeth I in 1558. In 1566 Parliament authorised Trinity House to set up buoys at dangerous parts of the coast and to levy dues on shipping for their maintenance. This extended the jurisdiction of Trinity House beyond the PORT OF LONDON. In 1573 Trinity House was granted a coat of arms; and in 1588 30 ships were made available to the Navy to fight the Armada. In 1593, to ensure steady revenue, the right of ballastage, beaconage and buoyage from the THAMES, valuable sources of income, were given to the Corporation on the recommendation of Lord Howard of Effingham. When the charter was renewed by James I in 1604 the Corporation was divided for the first time into Elder and Younger Brethren and the number of the court was again raised. The Corporation was also given the exclusive right to licence pilots in the THAMES.

In 1609 the Corporation's first lighthouse was built at Lowestoft. In 1616 an additional meeting house was acquired at RATCLIFF. By 1636 the Brethren were raising wrecks from the THAMES, recommending Masters for the Navy (they examined them until 1874) and helping to suppress pirates off the English coast. Charles II granted a new charter in 1660 but he also granted individuals patents to erect lighthouses so that Trinity House never regained its former dominance of naval affairs. Although a new headquarters was acquired in Water Lane, LOWER THAMES STREET in 1660, the Corporation continued to return to DEPTFORD each year on Trinity Monday to attend a church service and elect the Court. The Water Lane house was burnt down in the GREAT FIRE, together with all the Corporation's records, and the headquarters were moved temporarily to Whitehorse Lane, STEPNEY. In 1667 at the King's request, the Corporation sank ships in Gallion's Reach to prevent Dutch ships from sailing up the THAMES. In 1670 'a stately building of brick and stone adorned with ten bustos' was completed in Water Lane. When the Mathematical School was founded at CHRIST'S HOSPITAL by Charles II in 1673 the examination of the boys was entrusted to the Brethren. Samuel Pepys was elected Master in 1676. It was he who drafted the charter which was granted by James II in 1685 and which, with a few minor alterations, is the one used today. The governing body was increased. In 1695 the Trinity Almshouses for '28 decayed masters and commanders of ships or the widows of such' were built in MILE END ROAD possibly to the designs of Christopher Wren.

In 1714 the headquarters in Water Lane were again burned down. They were rebuilt on the same site. In 1732 the first light vessel was established at the Nore. In 1786 a new hall was built at DEPTFORD for the Trinity Monday meeting. And in 1793–6 the present building on TOWER HILL was built to the designs of Samuel Wyatt. The foundation stone was laid by William Pitt, then Master of the Corporation. In 1797 the Corporation removed buoys during the mutiny of the fleet at the Nore so the mutineers could not sail out to sea; and in 1803, under its direction, 1,200 volunteers manned ten ships as a barrier at the Lower Hope to prevent Napoleon sailing up the river.

In 1836 the Corporation was given control of all English lighthouses and navigation marks, and a government loan of £1¼ million financed the purchase of all private lighthouses. In 1852 the annual court at DEPTFORD on Trinity Monday was discontinued and the event was moved to London. In 1894 the rights of ballastage were surrendered to the THAMES CONSERVANCY and a uniform for pilots replaced their former silk hats and frock coats.

In 1910 the number of Elder Brethren which had been reduced to 20 in 1822 and to 13 in 1870 was further reduced to ten and they were compulsorily retired at 70. In the 2nd World War, during which the Corporation helped to evacuate Dunkirk and to guide the Mulberry Units for the invasion of Normandy, both the headquarters on TOWER HILL and the almshouses in MILE END ROAD were bombed. In 1953 the headquarters were rebuilt by Richardson and Houfe behind the 18th-century façade which had survived the bombing. Trinity House today is the principal lighting, buoying and pilotage authority in Britain. The elder Brethren also sit as nautical assessors in the High Courts. It is run by ten Elder Brethren and a Secretary. The annual court is held on Trinity Monday when the Corporation walks in procession to ST OLAVE HART STREET for the service of rededication. At the Court the Master, the deputy Master and the Rental and Nether Wardens are elected by the Younger Brethren.

Trinity School *Shirley Park, Croydon, Surrey*. Established in 1856 as a 'poor school' by the Whitgift Foundation (*see* WHITGIFT SCHOOL). It became Whitgift Middle School in 1882, and in 1954 the name was changed to Trinity School. In 1931 it occupied Sir Arthur Blomfield's Whitgift Building in North End, Croydon, and in 1965 moved to the new school designed by G. Lowe at Shirley Park.

Trinity Square *EC3*. The former headquarters of the PORT OF LONDON AUTHORITY which dominate the square were built in 1912–22 to the flamboyantly Edwardian designs of Sir Edwin Cooper. Beside it is the small and attractive TRINITY HOUSE designed by Samuel Wyatt (1792–4) but severely damaged in the 2nd World War, and now restored to its original design. The gardens contain Lutyens's Mercantile Marine Memorial (*see* MEMORIALS) and a stone in the pavement indicating the site of the scaffold for those who were beheaded outside the TOWER's walls. More than 125 people were executed here.

Trocadero Restaurant *Shaftesbury Avenue and corner of Great Windmill Street*. In 1851 Robert Bignell, then a wine merchant, opened the Argyll Rooms (named after the famous rooms in ARGYLL STREET which burned down in 1832) for music and dancing on the corner of WINDMILL STREET and SHAFTESBURY AVENUE. He made a fortune; but because of the rooms' notoriety his licence was not renewed and they closed in 1878. He re-opened them in 1882 as a music hall called the Trocadero Palace. The bar occupied one side of the auditorium. It was here that Charles Coburn sang 'Two Lovely Black Eyes'. When Bignell died in 1888 the rooms were leased to a succession of theatrical agents until 1894. Meanwhile, the construction of SHAFTESBURY AVENUE in 1885–6 had placed the Trocadero at the obtuse angle formed by the new street with WINDMILL STREET; and a block of shops and residential mansions known as Avenue Mansions were built here in 1888–9. In 1895 Bignell's grand-daughter granted a 99-year lease of the adjoining Trocadero to J. Lyons and Co. Ltd who rebuilt it to the designs of W.J. Ansell and J. Hatchard Smith as an elaborately decorated restaurant with a frieze 6ft deep and 90ft long inside the new main entrance in SHAFTESBURY AVENUE. The famous 'Long Bar' of variegated marbles in neo-classical style by Davis and Emanuel, opened in 1901. In 1899 Lyons acquired the Crown Lease of Avenue Mansions, and by 1930 the firm had purchased the freehold of both Avenue Mansions and the original Trocadero in WINDMILL STREET. Additions were designed by F.J. Wills. In 1982 a complex of shops, restaurants and entertainment areas was being built mainly behind the façade of the existing buildings to the designs of Fitzroy Robinson with Ove Arup and Partners as structural engineers. The Electricity Supply Nominees are the present landlords.

Trooping the Colour A ceremony which takes place annually on the monarch's official birthday in early June. First performed in 1755, and regularly since 1805, it is commemorative of the ancient military practice of parading flags and banners in front of troops so that they were made familiar with the colours – later emblems of regimental honour – around which they were to rally in the chaos of battle. The ceremony takes place on HORSE GUARDS PARADE; and the colours trooped are those of a battalion of one of the five regiments of Foot Guards (*see* HOUSEHOLD DIVISION). The Queen takes the salute on horseback, wearing the uniform of whichever Guards regiment is trooping and a specially designed tricorn hat. She rides side-saddle which, since she normally rides astride, requires previous practice.

Truefitt and Hill *23 Old Bond Street, W1*. Francis Truefitt set up business as a hair cutter and head dresser at No. 40 BOND STREET in 1805. His firm is mentioned in Thackeray's *The Four Georges* as being wigmakers to George IV. Mr Hill joined the firm at the beginning of the 20th century. Some of the staff have been with the firm for up to 60 years.

Trump Street *EC2*. Built after the GREAT FIRE. Its present name dates from the middle of the 18th century and was probably derived from a nearby tavern, the Trumpeter Inn.

Truslove and Hanson *205 Sloane Street, SW1*. Booksellers founded in 1890 by Joseph Truslove at 143 OXFORD STREET. About three years later Truslove took on Frank Hanson as a partner and they opened a branch at 6B SLOANE STREET. Another branch was opened at 14A CLIFFORD STREET in 1916. On Hanson's death in 1923 W.H. SMITH AND SON became the principal shareholders of the company. The CLIFFORD STREET branch was closed in the 1950s and in 1965 a new branch was opened at 94 BROMPTON ROAD. In February 1969 control of the Truslove shops came under Bowes and Bowes, a subsidiary of W.H. SMITH, and in that same month the Times Bookshop was acquired and run as one branch from 6B SLOANE STREET

with new premises at 29 SLOANE STREET. These two shops were closed in 1972 when the firm acquired its present premises.

Tudor Hall *Wood Street, Barnet, Hertfordshire*. In 1573 Queen Elizabeth granted a charter for the building of 'a grammar school which shall be called The Free Grammar School of Queen Elizabeth for the education, bringing up and instruction of boys and youth, to be brought up in grammar and other learning, and the same to continue for ever, and the said School for one Master and one Usher for ever to continue and remain and that there shall be for ever four-and-twenty discreet, honest men who shall be called The Governors of the said Free Grammar School.' Money was raised by the first Governors of the school and by collections in London churches; and the building erected in about 1577 opposite the Church of ST JOHN THE BAPTIST. It was repaired in 1597 and again in 1637. During the 17th century the fabric was neglected and further extensive repairs were carried out.

The trustees of Elizabeth Allen's Charity, which had been established by her will dated 10 February 1725, gave financial assistance to save it from a state 'very ruinous and unfit for habitation'. It then became a private boarding school. It was closed in 1872 and restored in 1874 with many additions. The school was transferred in 1932 to a new site in Queen's Road, and the old building was completely restored in 1968 by The London Borough of BARNET. It is now part of Barnet College.

Tudor Street *EC4*. Extends east from the TEMPLE to NEW BRIDGE STREET, parallel with FLEET STREET. It is so named because of the nearby Tudor palace of BRIDEWELL. The offices of the magazine *Punch* are at No. 23. *The Daily Mail* is at Northcliffe House, built in 1926 to the designs of Ellis and Clarke.

The Tudors *25–27 Halfway Street, Sidcup, Kent*. A timber-framed 'wealden' house of about 1475. Originally it consisted of an unusual single-bay hall with open fire and, at each end, double storeys, together with the usual entry passage. In about 1550 a large chimney was inserted and the east end lengthened to compensate. There is an original horn window. The house is still in private occupation.

Tufnell Park *N7, N19*. According to tradition, Tufnell Park Road is an old Roman road: its straightness makes the story likely. The country atmosphere of the area remained undisturbed for many centuries, and, as London extended, this northern part of IS-LINGTON provided its share of the 'very extensive dairies for supplying the inhabitants of the metropolis with milk'. In 1753 the Manor of BARNSBURY came into the possession of William Tufnell, a brewer's son who attracted several legacies from rich relations, including this from his godfather on condition he changed his name to Joliffe. The medieval manor house (demolished in about 1840) stood at the junction of the Tufnell Park and Holloway Roads, on the site of the present Odeon Cinema. William Tufnell Joliffe obtained a private Act of Parliament in 1768 enabling him to grant building leases, but these do not appear to have been immediately taken up as, in the early 19th century, the painter J.M.W. Turner was still able to enjoy sketching a group of elms on the Old Roman

Road. By 1835, however, a prospectus was circulating for the building of 'superior residences' on the estate, about which it was said 'from the present rather retired character of the spot it is not perhaps so generally known as most parts within the same distance of London'. From about the 1850s, and for the next 30 or 40 years, building continued. George Truefitt, surveyor to the Tufnell Park Estate, designed many of the villas and himself lived in Middleton Grove in the 1860s. Later villas were not so 'superior' as the earlier ones and in the 1890s, Charles Booth reported, 'Of the Tufnell Park area, from which the rich are now going, it is said that if the new houses are of the same kind as have been put up in Corinne and Hugo Roads, the whole neighbourhood will inevitably go down rapidly, for the poor and the rough will press into it from all sides'. Much of Tufnell Park has remained as laid out by Victorian builders, though there has been Council redevelopment. ST GEORGE'S THEATRE was opened in Trufitt's Church in 1971. HOLLOWAY PRISON, and the site of Dr Crippen's murder of his wife, both stand on the borders of Tufnell Park and LOWER HOLLOWAY. The Manor of BARNBURY passed to William Tufnell Joliffe's brother, George Forster Tufnell, whose son 'obtained a considerable accession of wealth' by his marriage in 1804 to Mary Carleton, hence Carleton Road, N7, and Carleton Gardens, N19.

Tufton Street   *SW1.* Named after Sir Richard Tufton who lived in TOTHILL STREET. It was known in the 17th century as Bowling Alley or Bowling Street, and was famous in the early 19th for the Royal Cockpit, one of the last cockpits in London and, in its heyday, one of the most fashionable. Colonel Blood, who stole the Crown Jewels (*see* TOWER OF LONDON), died in a house here in 1680. The street now has a decidedly religious flavour. At No. 15 are the church furnishers, J. Wippell and Company, who were established in the 18th century; at No. 7 Watts and Company, also church furnishers. The United Society for the Propagation of the Gospel are at No. 15 in a house with the inscription, 'To the Glory of God and in furtherance of the work of the Society for the Propagation of the Gospel in foreign parts this stone was laid by HRH George, Prince of Wales on 27 April 1907.'

Tulse Hill   *SW2.* Once an area of undulating farmland on the southern borders of the parish of ST MARY LAMBETH, which, with what is now BROCKWELL PARK, was part of the Manor of Bodley, Upgrove and Scarlettes. After changing hands many times, it belonged to the Tulse family during the Commonwealth, hence the name. The manor passed from Sir Henry Tulse, a former Lord Mayor of London, to his daughter Elizabeth and her husband Arthur Onslow (Speaker of the House of Commons from 1708–10). It was owned by a series of their descendants until a large part of it was sold to William Cole in 1789. After Cole's death the property was divided between Richard Ogbourne, who received Brockwell Hall, and Mercy Cressingham, who received the western portion. Her husband, Dr Thomas Edwards, saw possibilities in its pleasant situation and set out to develop it into a desirable private estate for the wealthy. In 1810, Tulse Hill Farm was the only house on his land, but by 1813 building plots were being parcelled out, and by 1821 two private roads, now Tulse Hill and Upper Tulse Hill, had been built, opening up the area for develop-

ment. Although an earlier plan to cooperate with John Blades (who purchased Brockwell Hall in 1809) and use a scheme based on Nash's designs for REGENT'S PARK had come to nothing, a flourishing suburb soon grew up. Plots of land were leased, with provisions to ensure that the exclusive nature of the estate was retained. By 1843, there were 125 houses on Edwards's land, many of which were detached and designed to accommodate large families with servants. Their occupants were prosperous business and professional men. In 1856, Holy Trinity Church, built in Early Geometric Decorated style by T.D. Barry, was completed. Other popular sites for substantial houses, on the edges of the exclusive estate, were Palace Road and Christchurch Road. In 1869 a spur of the suburban railway connected Tulse Hill with HERNE HILL and, as with other parts of SOUTH LONDON, encouraged rapid population growth and urban development. Although large houses continued to be built towards the end of the 19th century, the area began to lose its appeal for the well-to-do. The original houses at the BRIXTON end of Tulse Hill have since been demolished and have largely been replaced by modern blocks of flats. ST MARTIN-IN-THE-FIELDS HIGH SCHOOL has occupied one of the few remaining mid-19th-century mansions further up the hill, since 1928, and Carisbrooke in Upper Tulse Hill is an existing example of the estate's detached villas.

Tun   *Cornhill.* So called because it was the shape of a tun (a large wine cask) standing on one end. It was built as a prison for night-walkers by Henry le Waleis, LORD MAYOR, in 1282, after an ordinance was issued against armed persons or those of suspicious appearance wandering the streets after dark. It was also used for bakers and millers caught stealing flour and for priests found in illicit intercourse with women. The priests were taken to the tun with minstrels playing before them. In 1297 an order was issued for its disuse but there were still inmates in 1311; and in 1475 the building was enlarged.

Turf Club   *5 Carlton House Terrace, SW1.* Founded in 1868 and originally housed in the Duke of Grafton's former house, No. 85 PICCADILLY, and then known as the Arlington. A committee of members of the club codified the rules of whist which were accepted by the PORTLAND CLUB. An aristocratic club, it recently had 16 dukes among its members, and most leading race-horse owners belong to it. The late Aga Khan is believed to have been blackballed. Maurice Baring, after enjoying a meal there with the Earl of Westmorland, said to the waiter, 'Please thank the chef for this delicious meal, and thank you for your splendid service.' The waiter burst into tears. 'I have been employed here man and boy forty years, sir,' he said, 'and that's the first kindly word I have ever had.' In 1975 the club sold the freehold of its PICCADILLY house and moved to its present address, a house once occupied by Lord Palmerston.

Turin Street   *E2.* Extends south from Gosset Street to Bethnal Green Road. It was given this name in the 1860s by the METROPOLITAN BOARD OF WORKS when the enthusiasm for a United Italy was at its height. At the same time another Bethnal Green street, or group of streets, was renamed Menotti Street in honour of the Italian patriot, Ciro Menotti. The bronze, *The*

Lesson, a mother teaching her baby to walk, is by Franta Belsky (1958).

Turk's Head Coffee House *Strand*. Stood at No. 142. Boswell and Johnson went to the house as Johnson expressed a wish to help its mistress, 'a good civil woman' in need of custom. In 1838 the house was converted into a hotel.

Turnagain Lane *EC4*. Used to run from SNOW HILL to the FLEET RIVER but there was no bridge across and carts and pedestrians had to turn round and go back. The northern section disappeared when HOLBORN VIADUCT was built in 1869.

Turners' Company *see* CITY LIVERY COMPANIES.

Turner's House *119 Cheyne Walk, SW3*. To this small house, when it was one of a small group of buildings on the road leading towards CREMORNE GARDENS, the painter J.M.W. Turner used to retreat from the crowds in London. In an attempt to remain unknown he adopted his landlady's surname and was known locally as Admiral or 'Puggy' Booth. He died here in 1851.

Turnham Green *Chiswick, W4*. Formerly a hamlet in the north of the parish of CHISWICK, situated along the main Western Road, now Chiswick High Road. It is probable that Chiswick, or Back, Common and Acton Green north of Chiswick High Road were all one at the time of the Battle of Turnham Green (1642). Throughout the 17th century highwaymen are recorded as attacking travellers in the area. E.M. Forster, the novelist, lived at No. 9 Arlington Park Mansions, Turnham Green Common.

Turnpikes By the middle of the 17th century the roads leading into London, whose upkeep was the responsibility of the usually reluctant parishes through which they passed, had become so deplorable that some more reliable method of maintaining them had to be devised. Parliament was, therefore, eventually induced to pass an Act authorising the establishment of Turnpike Trusts to erect gates and tollbars where passengers would be required to pay a toll in order to pass through. By the middle of the 18th century there were numerous Trusts controlling turnpikes on roads all round London; but, although there was a general improvement in the condition of the roads by the end of the century, many Trusts were more intent upon personal profit than on upkeep. Profits, indeed, were high and Turnpike Trusts, which could be sold like any other business, fetched extremely high sums when they were sold at auction. Lewis Levi, a rich stockbroker, paid over £12,000, for instance, for the lease of the Tyburn turnpike which stood on the site of the old TYBURN gallows and at which carriages drawn by one or two horses paid 10d, horsemen 4d, and drovers 5d for 20 oxen and 2d for 20 pigs. At this and other turnpikes mail-coaches were exempt, as were members of the Royal Family, soldiers in uniform, parsons on parish duties, funeral processions and prison carts.

A toll-keeper's was not an enviable appointment. Most were provided with a small house by the gate or bar and many contrived to cheat their employers and the road users; but the pay at the principal gates was usually no more than 5s for a 24-hour day and there was the constant inconvenience of being awoken in the middle of the night and the danger of robbery and assault.

Among the busiest turnpikes, in addition to that at TYBURN, were those at HYDE PARK CORNER, the ELEPHANT AND CASTLE, ISLINGTON, TOTTENHAM COURT ROAD, and MILE END ROAD. In the 1850s a Toll Reform Committee recommended that all turnpikes should be removed when their various leases expired and the Metropolitan Turnpike Act came into operation in 1864. The last main turnpike, that in MILE END ROAD, came down in 1866; but several smaller tollgates continued into the 20th century. That at DULWICH was still in operation after the 2nd World War (*see also* TRANSPORT).

Tottenham Court Road Turnpike and St James's Chapel (left). From an aquatint after Rowlandson, 1809.

Turret House *South Lambeth*. A garden and museum of natural history established in the 1620s and 1630s by John Tradescant, a professional gardener who had been in the service of the Duke of Buckingham and James I and had been as far as Russia and Algiers in pursuit of specimens. 'Tradescant's Ark', as it was called, was regarded in its day as the best museum of its kind in the world. Its collections were increased by Tradescant's son, also named John, whose *Musaeum Tradescantium* (1656) was the first printed catalogue of an English collection. It included, as well as birds, fishes, shells, fossils, stones, fruits and exhibits of that nature, such curiosities as 'a natural dragon, above two inches long', 'Blood that rained in the Isle of Wight', and 'a Brazen-ball to warm the Nunnes hands'. After the younger Tradescant's death in 1662 his will, by which he had left his 'closet of Rarities' to his widow, was challenged by the antiquary, Elias Ashmole, who claimed that he had been promised them and that Mrs Tradescant was selling some of the more valuable items to individual collectors. He built a house next door to 'Tradescant's Ark' whose harassed owner later drowned herself in a pond. Ashmole acquired the collection which he handed over to Oxford University.

Twickenham *Middlesex*. 'The village of Twickenham is agreeably seated on the margin of the Thames, at the distance of rather more than ten miles from London. The banks of the great English river are particularly beautiful in this neighbourhood. The Thames here flows in its happiest vein; broad, gentle, and lucid. Nature and art unite to render the scenery attractive; and at various points of the Middlesex shore we find mansions admirable for elegance of construction, or still more interesting, from a former connexion with men whose names adorn the historic pages of our country.' So wrote *The Gleaner* in 1823, and although today Twickenham is hardly a village, the description is still recognisable. The THAMES swings in a series of large curves from ISLEWORTH to TEDDINGTON, dotted with several willow-covered islands. The original settlement at Twickenham was probably opposite Twickenham Ait, now known as Eel Pie Island, where the ground was high enough to escape the worst floods. A stone set in the wall near the churchyard in 1774 shows that even the extremely high flood of that year did not reach the church. By 1086 it formed part of the manor of ISLEWORTH. The river contained a number of fish weirs and these and the river traffic probably provided the settlement's livelihood. The medieval village clustered round the church and in King Street, Church Street and Riverside, and in various small alleyways leading down to the river.

Just downriver from Eel Pie Island is the Twickenham Ferry, linking Twickenham to HAM. There is no evidence for the story that the ferry was established by Royal Charter in the time of King John and it probably began sometime in the 17th century when there was an increase in the number of important houses on both sides of the river. The Dysarts of HAM HOUSE claimed it as one of their manorial rights until a rival ferry was started by Walter Hammerton from Orleans Road to HAM HOUSE to cope with the increase of visitors to MARBLE HILL.

Eel Pie Island itself used to be a favourite spot for boating parties. In *Nicholas Nickleby* Charles Dickens related that 'Miss Morleena Kenwigs had received an invitation to repair next day, per steamer from Westminster Bridge, unto the Eel-pie Island at Twickenham: there to make merry upon a cold collation, bottled-beer, shrub, and shrimps, and to dance in the open air to the music of a locomotive band.' In 1853, John Fisher Murray wrote an account of his tour of the THAMES: '... Upon this ait a house of entertainment has been erected; and here the river steamers are accustomed to land great numbers of holiday folks, desirous of the delights of pure air, and solicitous to banquet upon eel-pies, for which the tavern is famed.' Today the tavern has gone and the island is covered in bungalows connected to the mainland by a bow-shaped footbridge.

By 1720 enough people wanted to live in Twickenham to enable a speculative builder to put up a terrace

Riverside houses at Twickenham, from an engraving after Muntz, 1756.

of houses, Montpelier Row. A 'well-mannered, well-proportioned' terrace, it is built of brown and red brick with original iron work and looks little changed. Another smaller terrace was built in Sion Row in 1721, which also preserves much fine work. The parish church of ST MARY THE VIRGIN was rebuilt in 1714–15 to the designs of John James. There are some remarkable 17th- and 18th-century monuments inside the church, including two memorials to Alexander Pope who is buried there, and on the outside of the church is a tablet to Mary Beach: 'Mary Beach . . . Alex Pope, whom she nursed in his infancy and constantly attended for thirty-eight years, in gratitude to a faithful old servant erected this stone.' A BLUE PLAQUE at No. 40 Sandycombe Road commemorates J.M.W. Turner who lived here in 'an unpretending little place', then known as Solus Lodge, which he built for £400. Another plaque at No. 160 Twickenham Road indicates that Vincent Van Gogh lived here in 1876.

Modern Twickenham is mainly residential with much late 19th- and early 20th-century building. The expansion began with the coming of the railway when the bridge from RICHMOND was built in 1848. The line to KINGSTON was opened in 1863 and the loop line to HOUNSLOW in 1883. It became a suitable commuter district when the tram service to SHEPHERD'S BUSH started in 1902. In 1933 TWICKENHAM BRIDGE was opened amid complaints that it led nowhere. Now, however, it is the start of the Chertsey Road, a feed road for the M3. Its approach has finally severed the OLD DEER PARK from Richmond Green.

Twickenham Bridge *Twickenham–Richmond*.
Built in 1933 by A. Dryland, with Maxwell Ayrton as architect, this bridge, like CHISWICK BRIDGE, was constructed to take the Great Chertsey Road (A316) over the river. It was the first large-scale bridge in this country to use three-hinged reinforced concrete arches. The bronze balustrading is by Aubrey Watson Ltd.

Twickenham Rugby Football Ground
Middlesex. The headquarters of the Rugby Football Union. The original site of 10.25 acres was purchased by William Williams in 1907, for £5572 12s 6d, and became known as 'Billy Williams's Cabbage Patch'. Stands, each seating 3,000, were erected on the west and east sides of the ground and terracing was built at the south end to accommodate a further 7,000. The standing accommodation was 24,000, giving a total capacity of 30,000. Although at that time the motor car was still an object of some curiosity, a car park to hold 200 vehicles was provided at the rear of the south terracing. The cost of the whole project was £20,000. A further 7 acres was acquired in 1921; and in 1924–5 the north stand with a seating capacity of 3,582 was completed. Later an upper deck was added to the east stand and the enclosures and terraces were extended to hold an additional 13,000. In 1931–2 the west stand was entirely rebuilt as a double-decker with new dressing rooms, baths, tea rooms, bars and offices. A Royal Retiring Room was furnished with a gift of £400 from the Shanghai RFC when this was disbanded. A new south stand accommodating 12,854 was opened in 1981. The total capacity of the ground is now 61,500.

Tyburn
The principal place of public execution in London from 1388 until 1783, when hangings began to take place outside NEWGATE. The first permanent gallows, 'made in triangular manner', were erected here in June 1571 for the execution of John Story, 'a Romish Canonical Doctor'. Condemned prisoners were driven here in a cart. It became customary to give them a nosegay of flowers at the gates of ST SEPULCHRES HOLBORN while the bellman rang his bell, chanted a traditional verse calling for repentance and asked for the people's prayers for the 'poor sinner' going to his death. Later, the condemned were given their last mug of ale at ST-GILES-IN-THE-FIELDS.

A foreign observer in the 17th century wrote, 'The English are a people that laugh at the delicacy of other nations who make it such a mighty matter to be hanged. He that is to be takes care to get himself shaved and handsomely dressed either in mourning or in the dress of a bridegroom. . . . Sometimes the girls dress in white with great silk scarves and carry baskets full of flowers and oranges, scattering these favours all the way they go.' At Tyburn the executioner stopped the cart 'under one of the cross beams of the gibbet and fastened to that ill-favour'd beam one end of the rope while the other went round the wretch's neck. This done he gives the horse a lash with his whip, away goes the cart and there swings my gentleman, kicking in the air. The hangman does not give himself the trouble to put them out of their pain but some of their friends or relations do it for them. They pull the dying person by the legs and beat his breast to despatch him as soon as possible.'

The victim's clothes were the perquisite of the hangman. (In 1447 five men had already been hanged, cut down while still alive, stripped, and marked out for quartering when their pardon arrived, but the hangman declined to give them back their clothes and they were obliged to walk home naked.) When the body had been cut down the spectators moved forward to touch it in the superstitious belief that it held some peculiar medicinal qualities. Women lifted up the hand to brush it against their cheeks; and a French visitor once noticed 'a young woman, with an appearance of beauty, all pale and trembling, in the arms of the executioner, who submitted to have her bosom uncovered in the presence of thousands of spectators and the dead man's hand placed upon it.' The bodies were buried nearby or carried away for dissection. Afterwards the executioner customarily repaired to an alehouse in FLEET STREET where the rope was sold at 6d an inch.

Hanging days were public holidays, as it was considered that the sight of an execution would prove a deterrent. However, a Scottish clergyman wrote 'Among the immense multitude of spectators, some at windows, some upon carts, thousands standing and jostling one another in the surrounding fields – my conviction is that, in a moral view, a great number were made worse, instead of better, by the awful spectacle. Of the ragamuffin class a large proportion were gratified by the sight; and within my hearing many expressed their admiration of the fortitude, as they termed the hardness and stupidity, of one of the sufferers. "Well done, little coiner!" "What a brave fellow he is!"'

In confirmation of this view, Henry Fielding wrote in his *Inquiry into the Causes of the Late Increase of Robbers* (1751), 'The day appointed by law for the thief's shame is the day of glory in his own opinion. His procession to Tyburn and his last moments there are all triumphant; attended with the compassion of the

The triangular gallows at Tyburn, on which 21 people could be hanged at once. From an engraving by Hogarth, 1747.

weak and tender-hearted, and with the applause, admiration and envy of all the bold and hardened.' The scene of an 18th-century hanging day is depicted in plate 11 of Hogarth's *Industry and Idleness*. The foreground is filled with rowdy spectators including vendors of gingerbread and gin, ballad and orange sellers, pickpockets and women of the town. Beyond them are the grandstand seats where sat the well-to-do. To the right of the gallows, a structure so large that 21 bodies could be suspended from it at the same time, a man releases the pigeon which flew back to the prison to inform the authorities there of the victims' arrival.

Among those who perished at Tyburn were Perkin Warbeck, the Flemish impostor and pretender to the throne (1499); Elizabeth Barton, the Maid of Kent, who denounced Henry VIII's marriage to Anne Boleyn (1534); Oliver Plunket, the last English martyr (1681); William Dodd, the forger (1777); the master criminal, Jonathan Wild (1725); and the highwaymen Claude Duval (1670), Jack Sheppard – whose death in 1714 was witnessed by an estimated 200,000 people – and James McClean (1750). After the Restoration of 1660 the exhumed bodies of Ireton, Bradshaw, and Cromwell were gibbeted at Tyburn from sunrise to sunset, beheaded, then buried at the foot of the gallows in a deep pit.

The approximate site of the gallows is marked by a stone in the traffic island at the junction of EDGWARE ROAD and BAYSWATER ROAD. The gallows were often referred to as Tyburn Tree and the hangman as Lord

of the Manor of Tyburn. A Tyburn Ticket was a certificate which was granted to prosecutors who were instrumental in securing a criminal's capital conviction and which exempted the holder from serving as a constable and other duties within the parish in which the crime had been committed. These tickets, and the privileges which they conferred, could be sold once only. They fetched prices between £200 and £300. They were introduced in the reign of William III by an Act which was repealed in 1818.

Tyburn A stream which rose from the Shepherd's Well, South HAMPSTEAD, and flowed south to REGENT'S PARK, borne by an aqueduct over the REGENT'S CANAL. Thence it followed the line of MARYLEBONE LANE, crossed under OXFORD STREET and PICCADILLY, finally emptying in ST JAMES'S PARK, whence in Tudor times it was continued south as the Old Ditch and the Marflete to join the THAMES near the site of VAUXHALL BRIDGE. Its name, originally *Teoburna* – said to mean 'boundary stream' – is also used to describe a tributary of the WESTBOURNE, the Tyburn Brook. The Tyburn itself gave its name to Tyburn Manor, Tyburn Road (now OXFORD STREET), Tyburn Lane (now PARK LANE), and TYBURN, the gallows on the site of MARBLE ARCH.

Tylers' and Bricklayers' Company *see* CITY LIVERY COMPANIES.

U

Ulster Terrace *NW1*. A small group of houses linking PARK SQUARE with REGENT'S PARK. It was designed by Nash and built by William Mountford Nurse in 1824. Its most distinguished resident was perhaps Elizabeth Anne Bostock who lived at No. 5; she was the close friend and supporter of Elizabeth Reid, the founder of BEDFORD COLLEGE. The terrace takes its name from the title of Frederick, Earl of Ulster and Duke of York, one of George IV's younger brothers.

Underground Railways The first underground passenger railways were built partly to ease congested roads in inner London and partly to enable working people to live in healthier districts outside London. They were also, of course, commercial enterprises. The first one, the METROPOLITAN RAILWAY, was built by the 'cut and cover' method, which consisted of digging a trench (usually along a road to avoid paying for property), supporting the soil with side walls, roofing over the railway track, and restoring the road surface. The four-mile line from PADDINGTON to FARRINGDON STREET was opened in 1863 and was steam-operated. Despite the initial suspicions of the public, the railway was an instant success and in 1864 no fewer than 259 projects for railways in and around London were presented. The METROPOLITAN was soon extended and its plans for an 'Inner Circle' led to the formation of the DISTRICT and CIRCLE LINES, also built by the 'cut and cover' method.

The next major development in underground railway construction was the use of a tunnelling shield, originally patented by Marc Brunel in 1818. The shield consisted of 12 massive frames, each 3 ft wide and 21 ft 4 ins high, in cast iron; each frame was divided into three compartments in which a man would work, cutting away the ground behind. Isambard Brunel used this shield to build a tunnel beneath the THAMES which was opened in 1843. It was then adapted to a circular shield which was used to build the first tube railway in the world, between TOWER HILL and BERMONDSEY. Opened in 1870, this cable-operated railway ran for a few months only; but the contractor, James Greathead, recognised the potential of the shield and used it to construct the world's first underground electric tube railway, The City and South London (*see* NORTHERN LINE) opened in 1890; and it is with his name that the shield is now associated. Small electric locomotives were used to pull the trains, and hydraulic lifts removed the disadvantages of a deep line (over 40 ft deep); the railway was safe, clean and quick and it prospered. The success of this pioneer led to a number of electric tube railways, the most popular of which was the Central London Railway, opened in 1900. With its flat fare of 2d for a ride along an extremely busy route and its smartly painted locomotives and white tunnels, it was London's first really modern tube.

In spite of enthusiasm and schemes for many more tube railways, the British were unwilling to invest in railways and it was left largely to an American, Charles Tyson Yerkes, to exploit the new invention. He bought the District Railway, electrified it, and then added the beginnings of the BAKERLOO, PICCADILLY and NORTHERN LINES to his planned railway empire. He also built a huge power station at LOTS ROAD, CHELSEA, to provide the electricity for his lines. The BAKERLOO was the first of the new lines to be opened, in March 1906, followed by the PICCADILLY in December of that year, and lastly HAMPSTEAD tube (later part of the NORTHERN LINE) called 'The Last Link', in June 1907. Yerkes did not live to see his tubes transform the pattern of London Transport (he died in 1905), but his company, the Underground Electric Railway Company of London, provided the basis of much of today's system. Single ownership of several lines obviously led to greater co-ordination between them, with increased interchange facilities, and in 1907 the London Passenger Traffic Conference, organised by the Chairman of the Underground group, agreed to use a distinctive symbol at all stations: 'UNDERGROUND'. Unification of the Underground was completed when, in 1933, the LONDON PASSENGER TRANSPORT BOARD took over all the underground railways and large-scale planning began. This took the form of the 1935–40 New Works Programme, a Government-assisted scheme set up partly to provide employment at a time of depression. There were some extensions to lines under the programme, principally the NORTHERN and CENTRAL LINES, but it mainly consisted of improving existing services by electrification, provision of new stock, widened tunnels, lengthened platforms and modernised stations with escalators replacing lifts.

During the 2nd World War tube stations were specially equipped and used by the public as air-raid shelters, and some of the unused tunnels were converted into war material factories and bomb-proof stores. Unfortunately, there were some direct hits from bombs on tube stations, one of the worst being at BALHAM station in 1940, when 68 people were killed. After the war, old rolling stock on the lines was gradually replaced by new stock made of aluminium alloy, left unpainted, with open saloons, instead of compartments, and fluorescent lighting.

The next major event in Underground history was the VICTORIA LINE, started in 1962 and opened in stages between 1968 and 1972. With its automatically operated trains, automatic signalling system and ticket issue and control, it was one of the most technically advanced railways in the world, and provided a standard against which modernization of the other lines could be measured. In the 1960s there were also changes in the structure and financing of London Transport, following the recognition that the Underground served an important social and economic function, and that an adequate service must be provided

Excavating a 'tube' for the underground railway in 1901 with the help of a shield, originally patented by Marc Brunel.

even if it was unprofitable. On 1 January 1970 the GREATER LONDON COUNCIL was therefore given overall responsibility for public transport in London, with the LONDON TRANSPORT EXECUTIVE, appointed by the Council, responsible for day-to-day management of the Underground and buses. After the MOORGATE disaster on 28 February 1975, when a passenger train ran into the end wall of Moorgate station, killing 41 people and injuring 74, a £1 million programme of speed control and other safety measures was introduced.

London's underground railway, which stretches over an area of 630 square miles, is one of the most extensive in the world. London Transport trains operate over 260 route-miles of railway, of which 101 are underground: 81 in tube tunnels and 20 in cut-and-cover tunnels. In 1980 the revenue from the Underground totalled £250 million, although losses from ticket evasion are estimated at £12 million a year. In 1980 559 million passenger journeys were made (*see also entries on individual lines*).

Unicorn Theatre for Children *Great Newport Street, WC2*. Formed by Caryl Jenner in 1948, it toured for many years before becoming resident in its present accommodation in 1967. Fully professional, the theatre caters for children from four to 12 years.

Union Chapel *Compton Terrace, Upper Street, N1*. A strikingly designed Congregational chapel by James Cubitt, completed in 1876. The large tower is a local landmark and the octagonal interior seats 1,800. It replaced a classical-style chapel of 1806, the central feature of a flanking terrace built by Jacob Leroux as

part of CANONBURY's earliest development. In 1981 an attempt was defeated to demolish the chapel and replace it by a pastiche façade of the original. The chapel contains a piece of the rock on which the Pilgrim Fathers landed in America.

Union Club *10–11 Carlton House Terrace*. Founded in about 1799 'when the Union of the Parliament of England and Ireland was in agitation'. 'The gentlemen of the latter nation and many of the former, resolved to establish a club in honour of the event.' The club's first house was Cumberland House, PALL MALL, originally the residence of the Duke of York and afterwards of his brother, the Duke of Cumberland. Among the early members were the Dukes of Bedford and Norfolk, Richard Brinsley Sheridan, Charles James Fox and Sir Francis Burdett. On vacating Cumberland House, the club moved to No. 21 ST JAMES'S SQUARE, then, in about 1818, to REGENT STREET. In 1821 it was re-established as a members' club. A club house was built for it by Robert Smirke in COCKSPUR STREET. This is now Canada House (*see* TRAFALGAR SQUARE). In 1923 another move was made, this time to Nos 10–11 CARLTON HOUSE TERRACE. The club closed in 1964 when 400 of its members were admitted into the UNITED SERVICE CLUB.

United Oxford and Cambridge University Club *71 Pall Mall, SW1*. Formed by the amalgamation in 1972 of the Oxford and Cambridge University Club (founded 1830) and the United University Club (founded 1921) which had earlier merged, in 1938, with the New University Club (founded 1864). The club still draws its membership solely from members of the universities of Oxford and Cambridge. Its fine neo-classical club house was built in 1836 to the designs of Sir Robert Smirke and was completely refurbished in 1973. The Library contains 20,000 volumes and is supervised by a full-time librarian. There are 2,950 members and 405 lady associates who have their own dining-room and drawing-room.

United Service Club *Pall Mall, SW1*. In 1815 a meeting of senior army officers, chaired by Lieutenant-General Lord Lynedoch, was held at the THATCHED HOUSE TAVERN, ST JAMES'S STREET where a decision was taken to form the General Military Club. Temporary premises were taken in ALBEMARLE STREET. In 1816 the club was renamed the United Service Club when the Navy Club joined them. In 1817–19 a club house, designed by Sir Robert Smirke, was built in CHARLES STREET. It was the first club house to be built in London. In 1825 a larger site in PALL MALL was acquired on the demolition of CARLTON HOUSE. The present building was built by John Nash in 1827–8. It incorporates the main staircase from CARLTON HOUSE, presented to the club by George IV. In 1858–9 the exterior was remodelled by Decimus Burton to look more like the ATHENEUM opposite. The main entrance was moved from the west to the south and a frieze added to the upper storey. Gas *flambeaux* were put round the building. They are only lit now on state visits, Waterloo Day, Trafalgar Day and Battle of Britain Day. In 1912 the building was extended eastwards by Thompson and Walford who reconstructed the roof in 1929–30. In 1953 the club was amalgamated with the Junior United Service Club. In 1964 400 civilian members of the UNION CLUB were admitted, and in 1971 members of the ROYAL AERO CLUB; but these attempts to overcome the club's financial difficulties were not successful. It closed in 1976. The United Service was the Duke of Wellington's favourite club. The horse blocks in WATERLOO PLACE were put there specially for him. The building is now occupied by the INSTITUTE OF DIRECTORS.

United States Embassy *Grosvenor Square, W1*. Apart from the residence of John Adams at No. 9 GROSVENOR SQUARE in 1785–8 and of Ambassador Page at No. 6 in 1913–18, the American presence in GROSVENOR SQUARE dates only from 1938, when the embassy was established in unpretentious quarters on the east side. During the 2nd World War several nearby buildings were occupied by American forces and missions, and soon afterwards the American government requested the ground landlord, the Grosvenor trustees, to sell the freehold of the whole west side of the square for a new embassy. At last the trustees reluctantly agreed, subject to one proviso – the return of 'the Grosvenor Family's 12,000 acres in East Florida confiscated by the American nation at the time of the War of Independence'. This condition being unacceptable, the new American embassy on the west side of the square is therefore, it is said, the only one in the world of which the United States Government does not own the freehold. It was built to the designs of Eero Saarinen in 1957–60. There are some 600 rooms for about 700 staff. The massive gilded aluminium eagle on the roof was made by Theodor Roszak (1960). It stands 8 ft high and has a wing span of 35 ft. Its white marble predecessor was brought back from Italy by Whitelaw Reid and stood over the doorway of DORCHESTER HOUSE during his ambassadorship.

United Wards Club The United Wards Club of the CITY OF LONDON was founded in 1877 by Joseph Newbon, a Common Councilman of the City, as a general and central ward club for the consideration and discussion of public matters affecting imperial, civic, guild and general interests, the promotion of the spirit of citizenship and maintenance of the high traditions of the CITY OF LONDON and the furtherance of unity between the motherland and overseas dominions and goodwill with foreign countries. Its membership consists of FREEMEN, Liverymen and members of City of London ward clubs, its meetings and lectures are held at TALLOW CHANDLERS' HALL, 4 DOWGATE HILL and its annual banquet takes place at the CONNAUGHT ROOMS, GREAT QUEEN STREET.

University Boat Race Oxford (Dark Blues) and Cambridge (Light Blues) first raced each other from Hambleden Lock to Henley in 1829. Oxford won. The present 4½ mile course from PUTNEY TO MORTLAKE was first used in 1845. The race became an annual event in 1856. In Victorian times towpaths, terraces, bridges and trees swarmed with people. 'Every tint and shade and film of shade of Gainsborough's Blue Boy was patched upon the myriads who covered the Thames Valley from Putney to Mortlake.' The race's popularity has somewhat declined. In 1982 Oxford, with Susan Brown as cox for the second time, had their seventh successive win (one of the crew, Boris Rankov, was the first oarsman to have been in the winning eight in five Boat Races). By then Cambridge had won 68 of the 127 races, Oxford 59 and there had been one dead heat. Cambridge still hold the record number of successive wins, 13 between 1924 and 1936. In 1912 both boats sank.

University College *Gower Street, WC1*. Founded in 1826 by lovers of religious toleration – Lord Brougham, Thomas Campbell, James Mill – and others to provide university education for non-Anglicans who were excluded from Oxford and Cambridge. It was called by its detractors 'the godless college in Gower Street'. The first stone was laid in 1827; it received a charter in 1836 and was incorporated in the UNIVERSITY OF LONDON in 1907.

The main building is in the classical style and built in 1827–9 by William Wilkins, the architect of the NATIONAL GALLERY. Flights of steps lead to a fine Corinthian portico. The dome was recast by T.L. Donaldson in 1848. Restoration after heavy war damage was completed in 1954. Incorporated in the buildings are the SLADE SCHOOL OF FINE ART, established in 1871; the Galton Laboratory, set up by Sir Francis Galton, founder of eugenics; and the School of Librarianship and Archives.

In the South Wing by Sir Albert Richardson (1954) is the Mocatta Library and Museum of the Jewish Historial Society. The Gustave Tuck Lecture Theatre is also by Richardson. The new buildings for Engineering and Biological Sciences are by H.O. Corfiat. There is also the Collegiate Theatre (1968), and the new School of Environmental Studies, incorporating the former Bartlett School of Architecture in Wates House.

The College contains a fine collection of work by John Flaxman, the sculptor, bought by public subscription in 1858. The Egyptology collection was formed by Sir Flinders Petrie. The most unusual

The University Boat Race in 1846, the second year in which the present 4½-mile course from Putney to Mortlake was used.

exhibit is the clothed skeleton of the philosopher, Jeremy Bentham, which he bequeathed to the College.

University College Hospital   *Gower Street, WC1.*

In 1828 the University Dispensary was opened at No. 4 George Street, EUSTON SQUARE, now 171 GOWER STREET. Two years earlier the UNIVERSITY OF LONDON had been founded. The UNIVERSITY insisted on the importance of a medical school being linked to it. Up to that time medical degrees could be obtained only at Oxford and Cambridge. Most medical practitioners were licentiates of the society of Apothecaries and had no university degree. Only out-patients were treated in the Dispensary. In 1834 the hospital was built, to the designs of William Wilkins. It was first called North London Hospital and had 130 beds. In 1837 it was renamed University College Hospital. In 1846 the first major operation under ether in Europe was performed here. The ether was given by William Squire, a medical student aged 21. The surgeon was Robert Liston who wrote, having amputated the patient's leg, 'Not the slightest groan was heard from the patient nor was the countenance at all expressive of pain.' Liston had heard of ether being used for an anaesthesia in Boston, Mass., earlier that year. After the successful anaesthetic he turned to the students and said, 'This yankee dodge, gentlemen, beats mesmerism hollow.' In 1844 Joseph Lister (later Lord Lister) was a student, being unable to enter Oxford or Cambridge as he was a Quaker. He became famous for introducing antiseptic surgery in 1867 based on Pasteur's work.

The hospital was gradually enlarged during the second half of the 19th century, and in 1870 about 200 operations were performed each year, nearly half of them amputations. In 1884 the Medical Committee decided that connecting the hospital to the telephone exchange would not be of any advantage. In 1897 Sir John Blundell Maple, the head of the furnishing business in TOTTENHAM COURT ROAD, gave about £200,000 for extensive rebuilding. When the work was completed there was room for 300 beds. Many distinguished consultants held appointments, among them

Sir William Gowers, one of the most famous neurologists of all time, who in 1880 published a two-volume text book on the nervous system, still known as 'the neurologists' bible'. Gowers also made great contributions to ophthalmology, being one of the first to use the ophthalmoscope. In 1884 Sir Rickman Godley, Lister's nephew, performed the first operation for the removal of a cerebral tumour. In 1887 his colleague Sir Victor Horsley removed the first spinal tumour. Horsley was one of the fathers of neurosurgery, as well as a great medical and social reformer and a crusader against alcohol. Sir Thomas Lewis, physician in charge of the Medical Research Unit at the hospital, did fundamental work on the heart, publishing in 1911 *The Mechanism of the Heart Beat.* He was one of the pioneers of electrocardiography.

In 1906 the foundation stone of a new medical school (designed by Paul Waterhouse) was laid by Sir Donald Currie who provided the funds. Currie also gave money for a new nurses' home. In 1920 the Rockefeller Foundation granted the Medical School £400,000 for its building programme and £435,000 for maintenance. This money allowed the building of an 85-bed Obstetric Hospital in Huntley Street. In 1927 the Royal Ear Hospital (41 beds) was added and in 1937 the Private Patients' Wing (77 beds) in which charges were then from six to twelve guineas a week. One of the most skilful surgeons of the century was Wilfred Trotter who operated on King George V in 1929, curing him of a prolonged illness and characteristically refusing the honour of a baronetcy. In 1970 a new Out-patient and Accident Clinic was opened. Medicine at the hospital has the unique advantage over the other great medical schools of London in being next door to UNIVERSITY COLLEGE where so much good basic research is undertaken. In 1982 there were 418 beds.

University College School   *Frognal, NW3.*

Founded in GOWER STREET as a school for UNIVERSITY COLLEGE. The aim of the school was to foster academic excellence and independent thought without religious or denominational barriers. It moved to HAMPSTEAD in 1905 with less than 300 pupils. There are now about 770 boys between seven and 18 years old. Distinguished old boys include Joseph Chamberlain, John Morley, Richard D'Oyley Carte, Lord Leighton and W.R. Sickert. The junior school is at No. 11 Holly Road, NW3.

University of London *Malet Street, WC1.* Grew out of the need to provide undenominational higher education for Dissenters who were excluded from the older universities in Great Britain. Led by the poet, Thomas Campbell, a group of Dissenters with support from most denominations made plans for a University of London, which was opened in 1826 and later became known as UNIVERSITY COLLEGE. In 1828 KING'S COLLEGE was founded as a rival by supporters of the Church of England. In 1836 Lord Melbourne's Government founded the University of London 'for the purpose of ascertaining by means of examination the persons who have acquired proficiency in Literature, Science and Art.' UNIVERSITY COLLEGE became a separate teaching institution, receiving a new charter, and with KING'S COLLEGE and other approved institutions could submit students for examination by the University. London University's charter stated that the King 'deems it to be the duty of his royal office to hold forth to all classes and denominations of his faithful subjects, without any distinction whatsoever, an encouragement for pursuing a regular and liberal course of education.'

The first university examinations were held in 1838 with 23 students. William Cavendish, 2nd Earl of Burlington, was appointed Chancellor and among 26 members of the governing body, the Senate, were Dr Arnold, Headmaster of Rugby; the scientist, Michael Faraday; and the Whig Lord Chancellor, Henry Brougham. The University started in rooms in SOMERSET HOUSE, moving in 1853 to BURLINGTON HOUSE and thirteen years later to buildings designed by James Pennethorne in Burlington Gardens (now the MUSEUM OF MANKIND). In 1858 certificates of studentship for those sitting for examinations were abolished in all faculties except medicine, allowing anyone to sit university examinations and be awarded a degree. In 1878 women were allowed to sit for degrees. By the University of London Act of 1898 and the university statutes that followed (1900), the University was reorganised with a Senate (the Chancellor and 54 members) as its supreme governing body

James Pennethorne's Burlington Gardens buildings, designed in the 1860s for London University, now house the Museum of Mankind.

and three (later increased to six) standing committees, for 'internal' students, 'external' students and an academic council.

Provision was made for the University to appoint professors and teachers and for the recognition of professors and others in recognised colleges and institutions. These included at that time UNIVERSITY COLLEGE, KING'S, BEDFORD, ROYAL HOLLOWAY, WESTFIELD, the IMPERIAL COLLEGE OF SCIENCE AND TECHNOLOGY, the LONDON SCHOOL OF ECONOMICS AND POLITICAL SCIENCE, the Medical Schools of the principal London hospitals, Wye College, the Central Technical College of the City and Guilds of London, the East London College and several theological colleges. By 1980, a considerable number of other colleges (such as BIRKBECK, GOLDSMITHS' and JEWS COLLEGE) and institutes for specialised studies (as for example the School of Slavonic and East European Studies, the Institute of Historical Research and the COURTAULD INSTITUTE OF ART) were included.

In 1911 it was decided that the University should have appropriate permanent buildings and a site in BLOOMSBURY was procured. New buildings for the Senate and university administration were completed in 1936. During the 2nd World War these were occupied by the Ministry of Information but returned in 1945 to use as main university offices, lecture halls and library. In 1981 Princess Anne became Chancellor of the University, the office which had previously been held by her grandmother, the Queen Mother.

University of London Observatory *Mill Hill Park, Watford Way, NW7.* Built to the designs of L. Rome Guthrie and opened by the Astronomer Royal, Sir Frank Dyson, on 8 October 1929. Additional buildings were subsequently erected and opened by the Astronomer Royal, Sir Harold Spencer Jones, in 1938. The observatory with its local annexe and supporting department at UNIVERSITY COLLEGE is pre-eminent in Britain for the study of optical astronomy. In addition it has strong research links with foreign observatories in the study of interstellar physics, star and planet formation theory, geological surveying of planetary surfaces and cosmic abundance studies.

Upholders' Company *see* CITY LIVERY COMPANIES.

Upminster and Corbets Tey *Essex.* It is thought that a church stood at Chafford (as it was originally called) in the 7th century. The earliest parts of the present St Laurence, standing at the crossroads amidst its ancient trees, date from about AD 1100. The base of the tower remains from the original church. The pillars and arches of the nave are 13th-century as is the wooden framework of the tower. William Denham, the Rector in 1689–1735, was a scientist as well as a theologian, writing a book on the theory of Clockwork. He used the belfry for experiments into the speed of light and sound, as it was visible from WOOLWICH ARSENAL, south of the THAMES. Up Hall Lane stands UPMINSTER TITHE BARN, a masterpiece of medieval timber construction. Next to it, lying back from the road, is UPMINSTER HALL. The most famous building in Upminster is the smock mill of 1803 sited at the back of its field (*see* UPMINSTER WINDMILL).

The Clock House in St Mary's Lane is a two-storey red brick building of about 1775. In the centre of the façade is a small turret with circular clock-face dating from 1774. This was formerly the stable block to New Place, seat of the Esdaile family, now demolished. To the north of the parish in Tomkyn's Lane near Upminster Common is Great Tomkyns, a 16th-century house with two-storeyed, jettied wings. There are several other listed buildings on the rural fringe of Upminster, the earliest being Frank's Farmhouse, a two-storey colourwashed timber-framed building with parts dating from the 15th–17th centuries. Nearer to Upminster, the southern hamlet of Corbets Tey has a dozen listed properties, mainly 17th- and 18th-century cottages and farms. Harwood Hall was built about 1782 for Sir James Esdaile and altered around 1840 to a Gothic design. It contains some late 18th-century chimneypieces. The grounds now house an equestrian centre.

Upminster Hall *Hall Lane, Upminster, Essex.* Dates back to the 15th and 16th centuries, the wing to the north being probably of the 17th century. It was once the hunting seat of the Abbot of Waltham Abbey. It is now the club house of the Upminster GOLF CLUB.

Upminster Tithe Barn *Hall Lane, Upminster, Essex.* Dates from about the middle of the 15th century. It stands near the drive to UPMINSTER HALL and was probably used by the monks of Waltham Abbey. It consists of nine bays and has recently been re-thatched. It has been made into a museum of agricultural and local history.

Upminster Windmill *St Mary's Lane, Upminster, Essex.* A fine smock mill in excellent condition, built in 1803 by James Noakes. A steam engine had been installed by 1811. Purchased by the Abraham family in 1857, it remained in use until 1934. In 1937 it was bought by the Essex County Council, later passing into the hands of the London Borough of HAVERING. Under the auspices of these two bodies it has been extensively repaired.

Upper Belgrave Street *SW1.* Built in the 1840s between KING'S ROAD and BELGRAVE SQUARE. Walter Bagehot, the author of *The English Constitution*, lived at No. 12 in the 1860s. The house had formerly been owned by James Wilson, proprietor of *The Economist*, whose daughter Bagehot married.

Upper Berkeley Street *W1.* Built in about 1771 and named after William Berkeley, heir to the Portman estate. Elizabeth Garrett Anderson, the first British woman doctor, lived at No. 20 from about 1860 to about 1874. The West London Synagogue by Davis and Emanuel (1870) is at No. 34. The Masons' Arms at No. 51 is a well-restored 18th-century public house.

Upper Brook Street *W1.* Extends from GROSVENOR SQUARE to PARK LANE and is one of the principal streets on the GROSVENOR ESTATE. Building began in about 1721, but was not completed at the west end until 1759 when about a quarter of the houses in the street were occupied by people of title. Upper Brook Street remained almost entirely residential until 1939, and over 20 18th-century houses still survive in some form. The finest of these are No. 33, remodelled by Robert Taylor in 1767–8, and Nos 35 and 36. Elsewhere there have been many rebuildings or refront-

ings, chiefly in the 1850s and 1860s and in 1905–15, when a dozen houses were rebuilt with stone façades. More recently several blocks of flats in the neo-Georgian manner have been put up, and most of the houses are now used as offices or by foreign diplomatic missions. Notable residents include, on the north side, Anne Damer, sculptress, in 1799–1878, and Stanley Baldwin, the Prime Minister, in 1930–2. On the south side lived David Ricardo, the economist, in 1812–51; Lord Ashley, later 7th Earl of Shaftesbury, philanthropist, in 1835–51; Sir Henry Meux, the brewer, in 1845–57; and Sir William Jowitt, later Earl Jowitt, Lord Chancellor, in 1921–42. Le Gavroche at No. 43, founded in 1967 at No. 61 Lower Sloane Street (now Gavvers), became in 1982 the first British restaurant to be awarded three stars in the *Guide Michelin*.

Upper Cheyne Row *SW3.* Nos 16–28 were built in about 1716, a lovely row of houses facing the CHURCH OF THE HOLY REDEEMER. No. 22 was the home of Leigh Hunt from 1833–40. He was visited by Carlyle who described the house as 'poetical tinkerdom'. Further west the scale of the houses and the width of the street diminishes to charming cottages built in about 1840. At the opposite end, No. 2 is on the site of Dr J.S. Phene's house, built in 1903 and considered one of the most fantastic mansions ever built in London, with mystic devices and figures decorated in extraordinary colours. It was demolished in 1924. Dr Phene, who died in 1912 aged 90, was a familiar and eccentric figure in CHELSEA and there are many stories about him. His bride died on her wedding day, and he kept the room in which the reception was held just as it had been on the morning of the wedding.

Upper Grosvenor Street *W1.* One of the principal streets on the GROSVENOR ESTATE, it extends from GROSVENOR SQUARE to PARK LANE, and was first built in about 1724–41. About a dozen of the original houses still survive, though much altered; and another dozen now have stone fronts dating from 1905–14. GROSVENOR HOUSE, the town residence of the Grosvenor family from 1808 to 1916, stood on the south side of the street, which was said in 1918 to be still 'one of the finest residential properties' in MAYFAIR. Today much of it is overshadowed by the return elevation of the GROSVENOR HOUSE HOTEL and the UNITED STATES EMBASSY, and most of the remaining houses are now used as offices. Notable residents include, on the north side, Sir Robert Peel, the father of the Prime Minister, in 1800–22; and Captain David Beatty, later Admiral of the Fleet Earl Beatty, in 1903–10; and, on the south side, John Walter, chief proprietor of *The Times*, in 1847–94.

Upper Ground *SE1.* Extends from BLACKFRIARS ROAD to BELVEDERE ROAD. The IBM Central London Marketing Centre was under construction in 1982 to the designs of Denys Lasdun, Redhouse and Softley. LONDON WEEKEND TELEVISION is at Kent House.

Upper Harley Street *NW1.* The continuation of HARLEY STREET north of EUSTON ROAD. F.D. Maurice, the Christian philosopher and educationist, lived at No. 2 in 1862–6. He was at various times chaplain to GUY'S HOSPITAL, Professor of English Literature and History at KING'S COLLEGE, and minister at ST PETER, VERE STREET. He helped to found QUEEN'S COLLEGE.

Upper Holloway *N7, N19.* 'Holloway may be said to comprehend what lies on either side of the high road up to Highgate'; and the history of this area is closely linked with that of the HOLLOWAY ROAD which had been used as a northward route from the CITY since the 14th century. What lay on either side of the road for many years was undisturbed countryside, though by the 17th century the highwayman Claude Duval was making life uncomfortable for travellers in the northern areas. Duval 'made Holloway one of the chief scenes of his predatory exploits' and Duval's Lane (now Hornsey Lane) was 'so notoriously infested with highwaymen that few people would venture to peep into it even at midday'. Duval was executed at TYBURN in 1670.

After the GREAT FIRE John Evelyn 'went towards Islington and Highgate' where he found '200,000 people of all ranks and degrees, dispersed and laying along by their heapes of what they could save from the Incendium, deploring their loss.' By this time the HOLLOWAY ROAD had been chosen as a main coaching route to the north, and during the next century it began to be lined with houses, and lanes led off the road to tea gardens in the surrounding countryside. There was a growth of public houses, notably the Mother Red Cap and the Half Moon, whose famous Holloway cheese-cakes were widely sold by vendors on horseback.

By the early 19th century it had been decided that too much traffic was having to toil up HIGHGATE HILL, and the ARCHWAY ROAD was cut to by-pass HIGHGATE. Hornsey Lane had to be carried over the road and a brick arched tunnel was built for this purpose; but it collapsed in 1812, and was replaced by a cutting and an archway designed by John Nash. This became the northern gateway to the CITY. Edward Lear was born in Holloway in 1812, and spent his early years in Bowman's Lodge where Bowman's Mews now stands. On the north side of the HOLLOWAY ROAD, in the 1820s, there were still 'a few ancient houses, which it is probable were formerly occupied by persons of note'; but the rural atmosphere was soon to disappear. Charles Barry designed St John's, Upper Holloway in 1828 as one of four churches built to cater for the increasing population; and as coaching services and the droving of cattle down the HOLLOWAY ROAD were diminished and eventually destroyed by the coming of the railway and the short distance omnibus, so it became practicable to live in Holloway and work in London. The mid-19th-century developments covered the surrounding fields with rows of small villas where the respectable Mr Pooter and his family of the Grossmiths' *Diary of a Nobody* were provided with 'the perfect environment for being absurdly conventional'.

In 1897, a new iron bridge designed by Sir Alexander Binnie replaced Nash's ARCHWAY. By this time, 60 buses an hour were running down the HOLLOWAY ROAD, and Holloway had become a major shopping centre, served by many public houses. There were 25 in the HOLLOWAY ROAD in 1880. One of them, the Nag's Head, built in a key position at the junction of Seven Sisters, Holloway and Parkhurst Roads, gave its name to this central part of Holloway. Among the large, well-known establishments was Beale's Restaurant which opened as a baker's shop in 1861 but had grown by 1889 into a five-storey building with balconies and a turret, containing four banqueting suites. A friendly rivalry grew up between Beale's and Jones Brothers, a large shop across the Tollington Road. Holloway also became a centre of entertainment. The Parkhurst Grand Hall and Theatre opened in 1890; the Holloway Empire, a variety theatre, in 1899 and the Marlborough Theatre (with a seating capacity of 2,612) in 1903. All later became cinemas; none now survives. In 1888 the Great Northern Central Hospital (now the ROYAL NORTHERN) opened, also in the HOLLOWAY ROAD.

So, at the turn of the century, Holloway was drawing large crowds. The crowds still throng the pavements, but they come to shop in branches of popular multiple stores (Beale's was demolished in 1970 and replaced by a branch of SAINSBURY's; Jones Brothers is now part of the JOHN LEWIS group).

Upper James Street *W1 see* LOWER JOHN STREET.

Upper Mall *Hammersmith, W6.* Probably formed in the middle of the 17th century. Before that the path ran to the north and the gardens of the houses probably extended to the waterside. Of the earlier buildings that remain the most interesting are No. 15, an early 18th-century house which contained the Doves Press and Bindery of T.J. Cobden-Sanderson; THE SEASONS; No. 19, the Dove Inn; and, on the north side, SUSSEX HOUSE; Nos 22 and 24, River House, late 17th-century with curved balconies; KELMSCOTT HOUSE; RIVERCOURT HOUSE; and LINDEN HOUSE. Beyond this is the Old Ship Inn and 'Upper Mall Open space' which extends to the east end of HAMMERSMITH TERRACE. This was opened in 1970 on land purchased from the METROPOLITAN WATER BOARD.

Upper Norwood *SE19.* Takes its name from the Great North Wood, which covered what was once north Surrey and stretched from CROYDON nearly as far as CAMBERWELL. *Domesday Book* records that an area of woodland near CROYDON belonged to the Archbishop of Canterbury for his 'pleasure-hunting, fuel and pannage for 200 swine' and the first certain mention of the wood seems to have been in the Assize Rolls of 1272. In the reign of Edward III the land passed into the hands of the Whitehorse family. In Tudor times, its pollard oaks provided valuable timber for the DEPTFORD ship-builders and two of Sir Francis Drake's ships, the *Pelican* (later the *Golden Hind*) and the *Revenge*, were built of Norwood oak. An enormous tree, known as the 'Vicar's Oak', marked the meeting-point of the four parishes of LAMBETH, CROYDON, CAMBERWELL and BATTERSEA and regular BEATING OF THE BOUNDS ceremonies took place. It remained a significant landmark for centuries. In 1662 Norwood is described by John Aubrey as 'A great wood . . . belonging to the See of Canterbury'. It appears to have been seized from the Archbishops during the Commonwealth. Defoe's *Journal of the Plague Year* mentions it as a place of refuge for those fleeing the plague.

Although the wood was crossed by many tracks, it was wild and dangerous, and local people and travellers lived in fear of highwaymen and footpads. In 1652 the diarist, John Evelyn, was dragged from his horse, tied to a tree and robbed. Dick Turpin is supposed to have lived in nearby Thornton Heath and to have gone into hiding in Leather Bottle Lane, now Spa Hill. Smugglers also used this secluded route to the capital, bringing spirits, tea, laces and silk from the coast, and in 1846 a local mansion called Smugglers' Hall is known to have existed. Rocque's map of 1746

Beulah Spa, Upper Norwood, in 1831. It attracted a fashionable clientele who built substantial villas in the area.

shows the wood covering an area about three miles wide and thinning out into many commons. A major source of fuel for London, it was quickly losing its trees to woodmen and the CROYDON charcoal-burners. At the end of the 18th century there were few buildings apart from farmhouses and cottages, and possibly two hunting lodges in what is now Church Road, but the wood had shrunk to a few coppices; roads were becoming established; and in 1797 the first of several enclosure acts prepared for later development. The floating population of gipsies (*see* GIPSY HILL) who had once been the area's major inhabitants, had to integrate with a growing local community.

As the land was divided up for building, three different districts began to develop, becoming known as Upper, Lower (now WEST) and SOUTH NORWOOD. By the 1820s, Upper Norwood had become a small suburb, as 'neat, commodious villas' were built and communications improved between CROYDON and London, and it acquired its own church in 1829 (*see* ALL SAINTS). However, Dr Leese on Central Hill fired a pistol from his window on winter nights to make sure that it was known that he had firearms in the house. Ruskin describes the view from his parents' home in HERNE HILL, with 'the Norwood Hills, partly rough with furze, partly wooded with birch and oak, partly in pure green bramble copse, and rather steep pasture ...' The area was popular with COCKNEY day trippers, who visited the tea-gardens and The Woodman public house, had their fortunes told by gipsies and indulged in the sport of 'tumbling' down the hillsides. In 1831, BEULAH SPA opened, attracting the rich and fashionable, and substantial villas began to be built around its perimeter. There were even plans to develop a New Town of Beulah, along the lines of Bath. In 1849 the area was still remote enough for Mr Leach, an amateur naturalist, to disappear without trace on his rambles.

In 1854 the CRYSTAL PALACE was reconstructed on SYDENHAM HILL, chosen for its magnificent position on a high ridge overlooking London and its proximity to the London, Brighton and South Coast Railway, which passed through SYDENHAM. Norwood retained its reputation as a health resort, recommended by London physicians, but the Palace became the centre of its existence. Visitors flocked to the Palace's varied attractions, many of them brought by the Crystal Palace and West End Railway Line, opened in 1856. Extensive building began, of large family homes for the affluent, hotels and inns to cater for the crowds, and shops to serve an expanding population. Charles Barry's High Level Railway Station was constructed up to Crystal Palace Parade to bring people to the doors of the Palace itself. Many of the area's distinguished residents occupied large houses on BEULAH HILL; Vice-Admiral Robert Fitzroy (captain of the *Beagle*) lived in Church Road; Madame Tussaud lived on Central Hill; and Camille Pissarro lived and painted here for a time. The German Emperor, Frederick III, who was among many royal visitors to the area, stayed at the Queen's Hotel in 1887.

By the end of the 19th century there was a town of some size, with some well-known institutions including the Royal Normal College for the Blind founded in 1872, and the British Home and Hospital for Incurables, which moved to Crown Lane in 1894. The declining popularity of the CRYSTAL PALACE and its ultimate destruction by fire in 1936 meant the end of an era for Norwood. Badly damaged by air-raids in the 2nd World War, it then suffered from neglect. Its substantial houses became too large for modern needs and were demolished or divided into flats, and its narrow Victorian side streets and lanes fell into disrepair. Action by preservationists has done something to arrest this process, and steep, leafy streets such as Fox Hill and Cintra Park retain something of Norwood's original charm. The National Sports Centre opened in Crystal Palace Park in 1964, as a training centre for athletes, but in no way replaced the Palace as a hub for the local community. The top of Anerley Hill, the site of the Vicar's Oak, is still the junction of several boroughs – since 1965, LAMBETH, CROYDON, SOUTHWARK and BROMLEY.

Upper Richmond Road *SW15 and* **Upper Richmond Road West** *SW14*. Extends for just over two miles from EAST SHEEN to PUTNEY, north of RICHMOND PARK and WIMBLEDON COMMON. Lawrence Oates, the Antarctic explorer, lived as a boy at No. 309 in 1885–91.

Upper St Martin's Lane *WC2*. Part of the ancient highway which led north from CHARING CROSS, it was formerly known either as Cock Lane, presumably from the nearby Cock and Pye Inn, or Little St Martin's Lane. Its present name was in general use by the late 1860s. Houses had appeared on both sides by 1681. Aldridge's 'Horse Bazaar', or 'Repository for Horses and Carriages' as the premises were also called, stood on the west side of the lane in the later years of the 18th century and throughout the 19th century. It was described in 1895 as 'a well-known mart for nearly all kinds of horses, except racers. It is, however, specially famous for the sale of middle-class and tradesmen's horses.' The last horse sale was held in 1926; and the firm, which had begun to sell motor-cars in 1907, left for ST PANCRAS in 1940. The buildings were demolished in 1955–6. On its site now stands the tower block known as Thorn House which, designed for Thorn Electrical Industries by Basil Spence and Partners, was completed in 1959. The large bronze sculpture, *Spirit of Electricity*, on the tower's east face is by Geoffrey Clarke (1961).

Upper Street *N1*. Islington's main street, the start of the GREAT NORTH ROAD, runs from the High Street at Liverpool Road, where the tollgate stood, to Highbury Corner. Until the mid-19th century it contained handsome Tudor houses and gardens, one of them (now the Pied Bull, No. 98) associated with Sir Walter Ralegh. Its earliest houses now are 18th-century; and of old terraces only Compton Terrace remains. The street had its high causeway, its Green (part of the 'waste' of CANONBURY manor), stocks, watch-house and cattle pound.

Chief of the public buildings today is ST MARY'S CHURCH. An early 19th-century Baptist chapel in Providence Place is now a factory, and a sophisticated-looking former Congregational chapel (Bonella and Paull, 1888–9) on the corner of Gaskin Street succeeded another a little farther north.

At the Green's south tip is a statue of Sir Hugh Myddelton (*see* STATUES). COLLINS' MUSIC HALL, north of the Green, was gutted in 1963. The fashionable Screen on the Green is an old cinema modernised, and the domed 'Electric' 'has become one of south ISLINGTON's many antique shops. The Little Angel Puppet Theatre has operated since 1960 in a former temperance hall behind the church, while the King's Head launched Islington's first public house theatre in 1971. This public house's ancient predecessor was probably so named to commemorate James I's progress to London via Islington in 1603.

Beyond the Northern District Post Office of 1906, on the site of another Elizabethan house was once Shield's Academy, whose pupils included William Hawes, founder of the Royal Humane Society, and

John Nichols, the biographer. Behind this, after Dr Pitcairn's botanic garden (*see* BARNSBURY) was laid out for building, the Islington Literary and Scientific Institute provided an early adult education centre for nearly 40 years, with a lecture-room, library and museum. Built in 1837 by Roumieu and Gough, its later uses included a SALVATION ARMY citadel. In 1981 it was acquired for restoration as the Almeida Theatre.

Near here at No. 147 (formerly 119), Kate Greenaway lived in the 1850s, attending art classes at the one-time vicarage on the corner, Myddelton Hall (demolished). Terrett's Place is a fine 18th-century survival, generally identified with the house of Tom and Ruth Pinch in *Martin Chuzzlewit*, 'a singular little old-fashioned house, up a blind street'. At Hornsey Row, a long-vanished terrace south of Canonbury Lane, lived John Quick, the comedian; and Thomas Topham, 'the strong man of Islington', kept the Duke's Head at Gadd's Row – now St Alban's Place – by the Green. Among Topham's achievements was lifting three hogsheads of water, weighing 1,831 lbs at Cold Bath Fields in 1741.

At the corner of Florence Street, the petrol station is the site of the Vestry Hall of 1859 which became a cinema when superseded by the new Town Hall in 1925. Clearance (in 1980) of a large space opposite Compton Terrace – site of Roberts's noted department store, destroyed in the 2nd World War – was made with the intention of building yet another Town Hall. Sutton Dwellings, opposite the present building, replaced the large Church Missionary College which existed from 1825 to 1915.

Upper Thames Street *EC4*. The western part of what used to be Thames Street, LOWER THAMES STREET forming the eastern part below LONDON BRIDGE. In the Middle Ages, as well as BAYNARD'S CASTLE and the STEELYARD, there were many fine houses in Thames Street: Geoffrey Chaucer's father was a vintner here. Hugh Herlan, chief carpenter to Edward III, Richard II and Henry IV, and designer of WESTMINSTER HALL roof, lived in a house on the site of Nos 24–25. These houses were destroyed in the GREAT FIRE. In March 1668 Pepys recorded: 'Walked all along Thames Street, which I have not done since it was burned, as far as Billingsgate; and there do see a brave street likely to be, many brave houses being built . . . The raising of the street will make it mighty fine.' By the 19th century these fine mansions were much decayed and the street is often mentioned in the literature of the time as a peculiarly dingy and ramshackle place: Mrs Nickleby and her daughter Kate were conducted by Newman Noggs to a 'large old dingy house' here; and Mrs Clennam lived here, in *Little Dorrit*, in a house that afterwards tumbled down. The churches which once stood in Thames Street, ST PETER PAUL'S WHARF, ST MARY MOUNTHAW, ST MARY SOMERSET, ST NICHOLAS OLAVE, ST MICHAEL QUEENHITHE, ALL HALLOWS THE GREAT, ALL HALLOWS THE LESS and ST MARTIN VINTRY, have all now disappeared, although the tower of ST MARY SOMERSET remains and the lower part of the tower of ALL HALLOWS THE GREAT can still be seen on the east side of All Hallows Lane. ST ANDREW BY THE WARDROBE is on the corner of Lambeth Hill. VINTNERS' HALL is at No. 68½ and the MERMAID THEATRE at the western end by PUDDLE DOCK.

Upton *E7*. Former village or hamlet now a residential district in the centre of NEWHAM. Although it is first mentioned in the 13th century it was not greatly populated until the 17th century when, for a time, it was a fourth ward in the ancient parish of WEST HAM. Soon after the Restoration it was included in the Church Street ward. From at least the 16th century it contained the estate which is now WEST HAM PARK – first as Rooke Hall, then as Upton House and finally as Ham House. Dr John Fothergill, Quaker physician and botanist, owned the estate in 1762–80, doubled its size to about 80 acres (slightly larger in area than the present park) and developed botanic gardens esteemed second only to KEW. In the 18th and 19th centuries Upton was the residence of several notable Quaker families. Samuel Gurney held the Ham House estate in 1812–56; his sister lived in Upton Lane House (later The Cedars which was demolished in 1960) from 1829 until her death in 1845; and Lord Lister, founder of modern antiseptic surgery, was born of Quaker parents in (the second) Upton House, Upton Lane in 1827. Upton also contains the oldest inn in NEWHAM – the Spotted Dog, Upton Lane, dating from the 16th century – although now much modernised and enlarged. Adjoining is the home ground of the Clapton Football Club, one of London's oldest amateur teams (founded in 1878). Upton Cross is a small district centred on the cross-roads by the main gates of WEST HAM PARK. It has given its name to a primary school, a Baptist chapel and to the parish of St Peter. The church was demolished in the 1960s and the parish united with Emmanuel, Forest Gate. (*For* Upton Manor *see* PLAISTOW *and for* Upton Park *see* EAST HAM.)

Uxbridge *Middlesex*. Formerly Wxebruge, it is said to derive its name from a Saxon tribe called the Wixan who built a bridge across the Colne river here. In *Domesday Book* Uxbridge does not merit a mention, being a mere hamlet of Colham Manor, but by the end of the 12th century it had emerged as the market centre of the district. A chapel to HILLINGDON Church was erected in the town about this time (*see* ST MARGARET'S). By 1600 Uxbridge was the principal corn market for West Middlesex and much of south Buckinghamshire. Flour mills operated on the waterways which form the western boundary of the town. During the Civil War a Commonwealth garrison was established here, and in 1645 meetings were held in a mansion, today known as The Treaty House between Parliamentary and Royalist representatives (*see* CROWN AND TREATY). The Story of this abortive 'treaty' is given in Clarendon's *History of the Great Rebellion*. The period from 1790 to 1840 was one of great prosperity. The corn trade developed steadily throughout the 18th century, and led to the erection of a large Market-House. The GRAND JUNCTION CANAL, ready in 1805, brought further commercial development. In the 1830s approximately 40 stage-coaches passed through each way daily on the London to Oxford route. The opening of the Great Western Railway in 1838 about 2½ miles to the south soon brought a dramatic fall in stage-coach traffic. Corn-growing declined during the remainder of the century, and although market-gardening and fruit-growing took its place, the importance of Uxbridge as a market centre was much reduced. By 1900 the growing of cut-flowers for the London market was developing steadily. A branch line of the GWR was opened to the town in 1856. The Metropolitan Railway reached Uxbridge in 1904, and the GWR added another branch line in 1907 from their new PADDINGTON to Wycombe route. A fourth terminus had appeared in 1904, when the electric cars of the London United Tramways reached the town, and Uxbridge now had a distinctly 'end of the line' look. These changes heralded the outward sprawl of London, and since that time much of the surrounding countryside has been swallowed up by building. A Royal Flying Corps base was established in 1917, and during the BLITZ most of the fighter squadrons in South-East England were controlled from an underground operations room here. In the post-war period BRUNEL UNIVERSITY has been built to the south of the town. Uxbridge achieved Borough status in 1955, but became part of the London Borough of HILLINGDON ten years later. The new Civic Centre is by Robert Matthew, Johnson-Marshall and Partners (1979).

V

Vale of Health *NW3*. Situated at the south-west corner of East Heath in the HAMPSTEAD HEATH. The Vale of Health comprises about six acres of the Heath which in *Domesday Book* belonged to the Abbot and Monks of WESTMINSTER. Probably inhabited by the 10th century, by the 18th century it was notorious as a malarial marsh and paupers' haunt, known as Gangmoor. It became known as Hatches or Hatchett's Bottom after a Samuel Hatch who owned a cottage there before 1770. In 1777, in order to meet the growing demand for water from the fast increasing London population, the HAMPSTEAD WATER COMPANY, which supplied the CITY from the Hampstead Ponds, drained the malarial marsh. The Vale began to undergo a change from wasteland to a pleasant area of fashionable residences. By 1802 the name 'Vale of Health' had appeared, perhaps reflecting its dramatic change and also intended to attract residents, who numbered 112 by 1841. In the early 19th century James Henry Leigh Hunt was among them, evidently entertaining Hazlitt, Keats and Shelley in his home. In the later part of the 19th century the Vale attracted many visitors, catered for by two hotels; and its own fair was held at weekends. The 1871 Act for the Preservation of the Heath ensured that the Vale's development could not spread on to the Heath and consequently very few additional buildings have appeared. The unsystematic development of the Vale is still reflected in its warren-like character and its service by one road only from East Heath Road. In addition to Leigh Hunt, residents have included Alfred Harmsworth, the father of Lords Northcliffe and Rothermere, at Hunt Cottage in 1870–3; J.C. and Barbara Hammond, the social historians, at Hollycot in 1906–13; and D.H. Lawrence at No. 1 Byron Villas in 1915. Rabindranath Tagore, the Indian poet, stayed at No. 3 Villas on the Heath in 1912.

Valence House *Dagenham, Essex*. Occupies a medieval moated site and is an L-shaped, timber-framed and plastered house of two storeys, with attic dormers in the west wing. It is mainly 17th-century with possibly earlier work incorporated. The name comes from Aymer de Valence, Earl of Pembroke, who inherited a life interest in the manor in 1309. The house was bought by DAGENHAM Urban District Council in 1926 and now accommodates a small local history museum, including portraits of the Fanshawe family, Lords of the Manor of BARKING for several generations. These portraits include works by Gheeraedts, Lely and Kneller amongst others.

Vanbrugh's Castle *3 Westcombe Park Road, SE3*. Sir John Vanbrugh's own house designed by him like a medieval castle and built in 1717–26. It is known locally as the Bastille, a name which was given to it by Vanbrugh himself who was imprisoned in the Bastille in 1692 on suspicion of being a spy. It was privately occupied after Vanbrugh's death, auctioned in 1845, then used by schools until its conversion into flats.

Vaudeville Theatre *Strand, WC2*. Built in 1870 by C.J. Phipps. It opened under the management of three popular actors: H.J. Montague, David James and Thomas Thorne. In 1870 James Albery's comedy *Two Roses* brought fame to Henry Irving who played the part of Digby Grant. Montague left the management in 1871. In 1875–9 *Our Boys*, a comedy by H.J. Byron, had 1,362 performances. James left the management in 1882. The next year Joseph Derrick's farce *Confusion* began its run of 437 performances. In 1897 the theatre was reconstructed by Phipps, and Ibsen's *Rosmersholm* and *Hedda Gabler* had their English *premières* here. In 1892 Thomas Thorne handed over the management to Agostino and Stephano Gatti. In 1896 *A Night Out*, a musical play by George Grossmith and Arthur Miller, had 531 performances. In 1900–6 Seymour Hicks and his wife, Ellaline Terris, acted in a series of long runs at the theatre. These were followed from 1915 to 1923 by André Charlot's revues. Since the reconstruction of the theatre in 1925–6 the theatre has housed several successful comedies and musicals, including *Salad Days*, which had 2,329 performances in 1954–60, and *Move Over Mrs Markham* with Moira Lister, Tony Britton, Lana Morris and Terence Alexander. The seating capacity is 659.

Vauxhall Derived its names from Falkes de Breauté (second husband of Margaret, widow of Baldwin de Redvers) who built a house here in the reign of King John. It was formerly known as Fulke's Hall, Faukeshall and Foxhall. Sir Samuel Morland, the diplomatist, mathematician, and inventor, also had a house here in the 1660s. It was later converted into a distillery and was still a distillery in 1790. Vauxhall remained a village throughout the 18th century but by the time ST PETER'S, KENNINGTON LANE, had been built in the 1860s it had been swallowed up by the streets of LAMBETH. VAUXHALL BRIDGE was opened in 1816 and VAUXHALL BRIDGE ROAD built the same year. The village is also commemorated by Vauxhall Street, Walk and Gardens East. VAUXHALL PARK was opened in 1890 (*see also* VAUXHALL GARDENS).

Vauxhall Bridge *Pimlico–Lambeth*. In 1811 Rennie began to build a masonry bridge at this site; but two years later the Vauxhall Bridge Company decided to adopt James Walker's cheaper cast-iron bridge design. The Regent's Bridge, as it was first called, opened in 1816 and was the first iron bridge over the THAMES in London. In 1881 the two central piers were removed, converting three of its nine arches into one to aid navigation. In 1895–1906 the structure was replaced by the present bridge, designed by Sir Alexander Binnie, with five steel arches on granite piers. F.W. Pomeroy and Alfred Drury were responsible for the bronze figures of heroic size representing *Pottery*, *Engineering*, *Architecture* and *Agriculture* upstream, and *Science*, *Fine Arts*, *Local Government* and *Education* downstream. It was freed from tolls in 1879.

Vauxhall Bridge Road *SW1*. Constructed in 1816 as an approach to the new VAUXHALL BRIDGE. A few of the original houses remain. The New Victoria Cinema by Trent and Lewis (1929) is now the Apollo Victoria, a theatre which stages musical and comedy shows. The Gordon Hospital is at No. 126; a large block of flats of the Peabody Trust is on the corner of Francis Street. The CROWN ESTATE COMMISSIONERS' office development, Drummond Gate, on the corner of Rampayne Street is by Whitfield Partners (1980–1). The immense Lillington Gardens Estate on the west side is a residential development by John Darbonne of Messrs Darbonne and Darke, completed in 1972. ST JAMES THE LESS in Thorndike Street behind this estate is by G.E. Street.

Vauxhall Gardens The New Spring Garden, as it was called until 1785, probably opened just before the Restoration of 1660. Admission was free. The gardens could be reached only by water until WESTMINSTER BRIDGE was built in 1750. 'A pretty contrived plantation', was Evelyn's first impression on 2 July 1661. Pepys was a frequent and admiring visitor: 'A great deal of company and the weather and garden pleasant . . . It is very cheap going thither, for a man may go to spend what he will, or nothing, all is one – but to hear the nightingales and other birds, and here fiddles and there a harp, and here a jews trump, and here laughing, and there fine people walking, is mighty divertising. Among others, there were two pretty women alone, that walked a great while; which [being] discovered by some idle gentlemen, they would needs take them up; but to see the poor ladies, how they were put to it to run from them, and they after them; and sometimes the ladies put themselfs along with other company, then the others drew back; at last, the ladies did get off out of the house and took boat and away.' (28 May 1667). On a later visit Pepys once again observed: 'How rude some of the young gallants of the town are become, to go into people's arbors where there are not men, and almost force the women – which troubled me, to see the confidence of the vice of the age: and so we away by water, with much pleasure home.' (27 July 1668).

The main walks were lit at night by hundreds of lamps, but there were also dark walks with windings and turnings so intricate that 'the most experienced mothers often lost themselves in looking for their daughters.' Vauxhall appealed to all sections of society. As a contemporary ballad put it:

> Now the summer months come round,
> Fun and pleasure will abound,
> High and low and great and small,
> Run in droves to view Vauxhall.
> See the motley crew advance,
> Led by Folly in the dance,
> English, Irish, Spanish, Gaul
> Drive like mad to dear Vauxhall.
>
> Each profession, ev'ry trade
> Here enjoy refreshing shade,
> Empty is the cobbler's stall,
> He's gone with tinker to Vauxhall,
> Here they drink, and there they cram
> Chicken, pasty, beef and ham,
> Women squeak and men drunk fall.
> Sweet enjoyment of Vauxhall.

In 1728–67 Jonathan Tyers managed the gardens, buying a share in them in 1752 and the balance in 1758. Originally the only building had been the proprietor's

A general prospect of Vauxhall Gardens, then known as New Spring Gardens, in c.1751. From an engraving after Wale.

Mrs Weichsel sings to visitors, including the Prince of Wales, at Vauxhall Gardens. From an aquatint after Rowlandson, 1784.

house which he turned into a footman's waiting-room and cloakroom. Tyers added supper boxes decorated with paintings by Francis Hayman, ruins, arches, statues, a cascade, a music-room, Chinese pavilions and a Gothic orchestra which accommodated 50 musicians. Out in the gardens was another orchestra housed in an underground pit but it had to be abandoned because the damp ruined the musical instruments. In 1732 a fancy-dress ball attended by Frederick, Prince of Wales, established the gardens as the fashionable resort of the day. Soon afterwards they were opened every day except Sundays from May until September. A shilling admission was charged. At about this time the young and then unknown Louis François Roubiliac was returning from Vauxhall when he found a pocket-book containing bank notes and valuable papers belonging to Sir Edward Walpole. He returned it and Walpole, impressed by his honesty, and subsequently by specimens of his sculpture, arranged his employment as assistant to Henry Cheere. In 1737 Roubiliac received 300 guineas and his first independent commission from Jonathan Tyers for the statue of Handel for the entrance to Vauxhall. (This is now in the VICTORIA AND ALBERT MUSEUM).

On 21 April 1749 a rehearsal of Handel's *Music for the Royal Fireworks* was held here by 100 musicians in front of an audience of over 12,000. LONDON BRIDGE was impassable for three hours. In 1764 the infamous dark walks were fenced off but the barriers were broken down soon afterwards by a gang of young men. In 1767 Tyers died, leaving the management in the hands of his sons, Tom and Jonathan. Tom was a great friend of Dr Johnson who frequently came to the gardens. Johnson is shown here in Rowlandson's famous print which was taken from a watercolour exhibited at the ROYAL ACADEMY in 1784, a faintly satirical social panorama. He is shown in a supper-box with Boswell, Goldsmith (who in fact died in 1774) and Mrs Thrale. Also in the picture are the Prince of Wales depicted whispering to his former mistress, Perdita Robinson, (who is arm-in-arm with her little husband); the Duchess of Devonshire and her sister; the foppish Major Topham; and Mrs Weichsel, singing to the

strains of the orchestra from a box. Boswell commented, 'Vauxhall Gardens is peculiarly adapted to the taste of the English nation; there being a mixture of curious show, – gay exhibition, musick, vocal and instrumental, not too refined for the general ear; – for all which only a shilling is paid [this was raised to two shillings in 1792 after 'more expensive decorations' had been introduced]. And, though last, not least, good eating and drinking, for those who wish to purchase that regale.'

Vauxhall is frequently mentioned in 17th- and 18th-century literature: Wycherley's *The Gentleman Dancing Master*, Fanny Burney's *Evelina*, Congreve's *Love for Love*, Vanbrugh's *The Provok'd Wife*, Swift's *Journal to Stella* and Fielding's *Amelia*. In 1785 Tom sold his share of the management to his brother and the gardens became officially known for the first time as Vauxhall Gardens. In 1786 a jubilee was held four years late to celebrate their 50th anniversary: 61,000 people in fancy dress, including the Prince of Wales, attended. Tickets cost half a guinea each. In 1792 Jonathan Tyers died and was succeeded by his son-in-law, Bryant Barrett. Six years later the first fireworks display was held here. In 1802 Mr Garnenin made an ascent in a fire balloon and a fortnight afterwards, made another accompanied by his wife. In 1809 Barrett died and his son, George, took over as manager. He raised the admission to 3s 6d and opened only three nights a week. In 1813 a grand fête was held to celebrate Wellington's victory at Vittoria. It was attended by the Prince Regent and all the royal dukes. The crush was so great that it took three hours for a carriage to get from WESTMINSTER BRIDGE. In 1816 Mme Saqui gave her first performances, ascending and descending a tightrope tied to a sixty foot mast amidst a cloud of fireworks. In 1821 the gardens were bought by the London Wine Company and admission was raised to 4s 6d. In 1825 magistrates insisted that the dark walks be lit. In 1827 the Battle of Waterloo was re-enacted by 1,000 soldiers. In November 1836 Charles Green, a fruiterer's son, Monck Mason, the lessee of HER MAJESTY'S THEATRE and Robert Holland, a Member of Parliament, ascended in the *Royal Vauxhall* balloon. They took with them three weeks' provisions: 40 lb of beef, ham and tongue, 40 lb of bread, sugar and biscuits, 45 lb of fowls and preserves and two gallons each of sherry, port and brandy as well as a device for making coffee. Despite their elaborate preparations, they descended next day in Nassau, Germany. In 1837 the balloonist, Robert Cocking, was killed when he tried to descend by parachute. In 1840 the owners went bankrupt and the gardens closed. They were reopened the following year, but at the end of the season they were auctioned. Some of the furniture and fittings were sold, including 24 of Hayman's paintings which fetched between £1 10s and £9 15s each. The gardens were reopened in 1842 but soon afterwards closed again. No less than seven 'farewells' were held in 1859. The final one took place on 25 July with a concert, equestrian performance, dancing and fireworks. This was followed by a sale of the remaining furniture which fetched £800. The gardens were then built on. The site is now marked by Goding Street on the west, St Oswald's Place on the east, Leopold Street and Vauxhall Walk on the north and Kennington Lane on the south. The early managers are commemorated by Jonathan Street and Tyers Street.

Vauxhall Park *SW8*. About 8 acres off South Lambeth Road between Lawn Lane and Fentiman Road. It was opened by the Prince of Wales in July 1890. It included the garden of Henry Fawcett, the statesman, who lived in LAMBETH from 1874.

Vauxhall Water Company Incorporated in 1805 as the South London Waterworks Company. The works were on the site of the present gasworks at KENNINGTON OVAL. Its intake was from both the THAMES and VAUXHALL Creek and it supplied the parish of ST GILES, CAMBERWELL, that part of LAMBETH parish not supplied by the LAMBETH WATERWORKS CO. and other parts of Surrey. By the early 1830s the VAUXHALL Creek supply was so polluted that it was handed over to the jurisdiction of the Sewer Commissioners. In 1834 the company was renamed the Vauxhall Water Company. It took over the area formerly served by the LAMBETH WATERWORKS. In 1845 it was amalgamated with the Southwark Water Company to form the SOUTHWARK AND VAUXHALL WATER COMPANY. The works at KENNINGTON were abandoned in 1847 when the gasworks were built.

Vere Street *W1*. First mentioned in the Overseers' Report for 1723, the street was one of the first to be laid out by Edward Harley. He called it after the de Vere family, who had been Earls of Oxford of an earlier creation than his own. Michael Rysbrack, the sculptor, lived at No. 3 in 1726–69. ST PETER'S, Vere Street, was designed by James Gibbs, as a miniature ST MARTIN-IN-THE-FIELDS.

Vere Street Theatre *Clare Market*. Gibbon's Tennis Court was first used as a theatre during the Commonwealth. In 1660–3 Thomas Killigrew and his company acted here while DRURY LANE THEATRE was being rebuilt. From 1663 to 1671 it was a drama school; and in 1675–82 a nonconformist meeting house. Afterward it was a carpenter's shop and a slaughter house. It was destroyed by fire in 1809.

Verge of the Court Originally denoted the area comprised within a radius of twelve miles around the sovereign's palaces. It was later limited to the area within twelve miles of WHITEHALL PALACE only. It takes its name from the Latin *verga*, rod, the white wand of office of the Lord Steward. All taverns within the Verge were subject to the Lord Steward's licence, issued by the BOARD OF GREEN CLOTH, since it was unseemly that 'any brawling, drunkenness, thieving and so on, should take place within the immediate neighbourhood of the King's person.' The premises still licensed by the Board include three public houses in WHITEHALL – the Silver Cross, Old Shades and the Clarence Tavern – CROCKFORD'S CLUB, the NATIONAL GALLERY, the ROYAL SOCIETY and WHITEHALL COURT. The Old Ship public house, which had stood on the site of the present WHITEHALL THEATRE since the 14th century and moved to the other side of the road in 1926, used also to be licensed by the BOARD, but it ceased to trade in 1959.

Vernon Gallery *50 Pall Mall*. Robert Vernon, who had made a fortune during the Napoleonic Wars by providing horses for the British Army, and coaches and drivers, as well as horses, for the Royal Mail, lived at 50 PALL MALL from 1820 to 1849. He assembled here a fine collection of works by such artists as Constable, Gainsborough, Reynolds and Landseer. He commissioned works from numerous contemporary artists and bought many more earlier paintings at CHRISTIE'S, then at No. 125 PALL MALL. He donated his collection to the nation and it subsequently became a substantial basis for the NATIONAL GALLERY. No. 56, which was completely rebuilt in 1930, is now occupied by ROBSON LOWE LTD.

Verrey's Restaurant *233 Regent Street, W1*. Charles Verrey, a resident at No. 231, started his first shop at No. 218 with his daughter Fanny, selling ice cream. By 1848 their shop, by then at No. 229, was also a restaurant. It became one of the leading Victorian restaurants, its customers including the Prince of Wales, Disraeli, and Charles Dickens. Sherlock Holmes used to send here for sweetmeats when he got tired of Mrs Hudson's cooking.

Vestries In the Middle Ages local government in London was run by parish 'vestries' of householders, so named because they usually met in the church vestry. Sometimes the 'vestry' would consist of all the ratepayers, but in some parishes a select vestry of office holders and their nominees were in control. In the CITY OF LONDON local government developed early in the WARDS and in the CORPORATION so the vestries dealt mainly with church matters. When London started to spread outside the walls, particularly after the GREAT FIRE the CORPORATION refused to take responsibility for the new suburbs. So in places like MARYLEBONE, CAMDEN and LAMBETH local government was left to the vestries. They dealt with the ever-increasing problems of relief of the poor, road mending, paving, cleansing and lighting, and the maintenance of law and order. They employed paviors, lamplighters, scavengers and watchmen. There was great confusion as their responsibilities often overlapped those of the Turnpike Trusts, Paving Boards and Square Trustees. In the 19th century legislation progressively transferred the duties of local government to metropolitan and national bodies in the Metropolitan Board of Works Act 1848, and the Metropolitan Management Act

1855. Finally the London Government Act of 1899 (which excluded the CITY OF LONDON) ended the vestries as instruments of local government and set up 27 Metropolitan Boroughs together with Westminster City Council to run local government in the capital. In 1907 the Union of Parishes Act officially transferred the power of the vestry in the CITY OF LONDON to the COURT OF COMMON COUNCIL for all except charity and ecclesiastical purposes.

Vestry Hall *Cricket Green, Mitcham, Surrey*. Built in the middle of the Cricket Green on what was clearly common land. In 1765 leave was granted to MITCHAM Vestry by the Lords of the Manor, the Dean and Chapter of Canterbury Cathedral, to erect here a watch-house or lock-up. The manorial pound, village stocks (last used in 1810) and pump stood nearby. In the 1850s the building housed the hand-operated fire-engine. The architect of the present building, which was constructed in 1887 and enlarged in 1930, was Robert Masters Chart, who in 1934 became the first Mayor of MITCHAM. His family hold the unique distinction of serving continuously for five generations (1762–1955) as Vestry Clerks and later Town Clerks.

Vestry House Museum *Vestry Road, E17*. Housed in the parish workhouse which was built in 1729 by the WALTHAMSTOW Vestry. The workhouse was also used by the Watch and a cage for prisoners stood outside. In 1836 the paupers were moved to the STRATFORD Workhouse; and from 1840 to 1870 the buildings were used as the local police station. A cell dating from 1840 is preserved. From 1870 to 1891 the former workhouse was the armoury of the WALTHAM-STOW Volunteers; and from 1882 to 1892 it was also the WALTHAMSTOW Literary and Scientific Institute. The Museum was opened in 1930. Its exhibits illustrate the history of WALTHAMSTOW and include bones of mammoths and bison from WALTHAMSTOW Marshes, stone age flints, bronze age spears and axe heads, a Roman sarcophagus, and a 16th-century room from the manor house of Higham Benstead which was demolished in 1933. A series of dioramas show the development of WALTHAMSTOW from a country village to a Victorian suburb with the coming of the railway in 1870. There is also the first British motor car with an internal combustion engine which was made by a local resident, Frederick Bremer, in 1892–5.

Veteran Car Run Began in 1896 when the law compelling motorists to have a man carrying a red flag walking in front of them was abolished. Motorists celebrated by destroying their flags and driving off to Brighton. The first organised run was in 1933. Cars made between 1895 and 1905 take part in the run which starts at HYDE PARK CORNER and ends at Madeira Drive, Brighton (*see also* TRANSPORT).

Viaduct Tavern *126 Newgate Street, EC1*. Built in 1869 and named after the HOLBORN VIADUCT. It has a magnificent Victorian interior with a beaten metal ceiling, beautiful woodwork and glass. The cellars were once part of NEWGATE PRISON.

Victoria *SW1*. Situated east of BELGRAVIA and north of PIMLICO. Part of the manor of Ebury held at *Domesday* by WESTMINSTER ABBEY, and from the 17th century by the GROSVENOR ESTATE, the low-lying unhealthy swamp-land near the THAMES changed little until the 19th century, becoming a refuge for the poor and criminals who sought the traditional sanctuary of the ABBEY. In 1816 VAUXHALL BRIDGE was opened and the arterial VAUXHALL BRIDGE ROAD followed, heralding a series of developments. The GROSVENOR CANAL was opened in 1825 and industrial estates built up. Willow Walk, owned by a Warwickshire clergyman, was widened and drained, becoming WARWICK WAY, and the area south of the Canal was developed during the 1840s and 1850s by Thomas Cubitt, builder of BELGRAVIA (*see* GROSVENOR and LOWNDES ESTATES). By 1851 a new street – VICTORIA STREET, named after the Queen – cut through the slums of WESTMINSTER as part of a programme that included Cubitt's extension of BUCKINGHAM PALACE. The street provided a vista of the ABBEY and the new HOUSES OF PARLIAMENT, and along it large buildings were raised, housing public institutions and shops such as the ARMY AND NAVY STORES.

As the canal fell into disrepair, proposals for a railway in the basin were put forward and this was built forming part of the London, Chatham and Dover Railway and the Great Western Railway. In 1862 a station was opened at the west end of VICTORIA STREET taking its name from the street and in turn giving it to the surrounding area. Redevelopment of VICTORIA STREET in the 1960s demolished the Stag BREWERY – a brewery site for 300 years – and transformed the area in front of WESTMINSTER CATHEDRAL, providing a piazza where Victorian shops had formerly stood. Today the area still focusses on VICTORIA STATION; it is the travellers' quarter of the CITY OF WESTMINSTER with its hotels and rail, coach and air terminals.

Victoria and Albert Museum *Cromwell Road, SW7*. A museum of fine and applied art of all countries, styles and periods. Its origins lie with the MUSEUM OF MANUFACTURES, which had opened at MARLBOROUGH HOUSE in September 1852 (and became known as the Museum of Ornamental Art in 1853) and with the School of Design, a forerunner of the ROYAL COLLEGE OF ART, which had collected at SOMERSET HOUSE a number of plaster casts, models, engravings and examples of contemporary manufacture for study by its students. In 1857 both the School and the Museum were removed to SOUTH KENSINGTON where, with the help of funds voted by Parliament, and with the active encouragement of Prince Albert, the royal Commissioners for the GREAT

The 'Brompton Boilers', built in the 1850s to house exhibits which later became part of the Victoria and Albert Museum.

EXHIBITION of 1851 had bought over 80 acres of land to further the aims of the Exhibition and to extend 'the influence of Science and Art upon Productive Industry' by building various museums, concert halls, colleges, schools and premises for learned societies. While plans were being made for this development, the School of Design was temporarily accommodated in wooden sheds and the Museum of Ornamental Art in an immense structure of corrugated sheet iron, cast-iron and glass built by William Cubitt and soon to be universally and irreverently known as the 'Brompton Boilers'. This building which, on Prince Albert's advice, was painted with green and white stripes to make it less forbidding, was opened by Queen Victoria on 22 June 1857.

Its first director was Sir Henry Cole, whose declared policy was 'to assemble a splendid collection of objects representing the application of Fine Art to manufactures'. With this end in view he had already arranged for the purchase of the Bandinel Collection of Pottery and Porcelain, part of the Bernal Collection of glass, plate and china, enamels, armour, medals, jewellery, ivories and furniture, as well as objects from the Paris Exhibition of 1856. He had also begun negotiations for the acquisition of the Soulages Collection at Toulouse which included Bellini's St Dominic. By then the scope and intent of the Museum had already begun to change: Gladstone, while Chancellor of the Exchequer, had in 1855 authorized the purchase of the Gherardini collection of models for sculpture, and in 1857 John Sheepshanks, a rich Yorkshire cloth manufacturer, offered to the nation his large collection of British paintings by Etty, Landseer, Stanfield, Naysmyth, Constable and others. To house this collection a red brick picture gallery, designed by Francis Fowke, a brilliantly inventive captain in the Royal Engineers, was annexed to the 'Brompton Boilers'. To the Sheepshanks Gallery other picture galleries and display areas, as well as refreshment rooms, lecture rooms, courts, quadrangles and staircases, were added, while the Museum's acquisitions continued to grow with increasing disregard to its original purpose. 'Future purchases should be confined to objects wherein Fine Art is supplied to some purpose of utility,' the Museum was instructed in 1863, 'and works of Fine Art not so only be permitted as exceptions and so far as they may tend directly to improve Art applied to objects of utility'. But, as Sir Roy Strong, the Museum's director, has since observed, the advice was 'totally ignored... the pull between a practical museum of the arts of manufacture and design, with its aim to educate the masses, as against a museum of masterpieces, the resort of antiquarians and connoisseurs, has never been resolved to this day ... Any visitor to the Victoria and Albert Museum today is likely to be bemused as to what exactly is the central thread that animates these discrepant if marvellous collections. The answer is that there is none. For over a century the Museum has proved an extremely capacious handbag.' Into this handbag were deposited, amongst numerous other items, the Tapestry Cartoons of Raphael which had been purchased for the Royal Collection by King Charles I when he was Prince of Wales in 1623 and which, lent by Queen Victoria, are still lent by the Queen today; fine collections of British watercolours and 18th-century French paintings; numerous canvases by William Dyce and John Constable: and the

contents of the India Museum, transferred from the India Office. In 1884 the National Art Library was opened in the Museum.

By then it had been realised that the various structures in which all these treasures were congested were quite inadequate for their purpose. And at last, in 1890, the Chancellor of the Exchequer authorised a competition for a new design. Eight architects, each to be paid 300 guineas, were invited to enter the competition which was won, on the recommendation of Alfred Waterhouse (whose NATURAL HISTORY MUSEUM had already appeared nearby), by Aston Webb. It was not until 1899, however, that the foundation stone was laid by the Queen who, in this last important public engagement of her reign, directed that the Museum should be given its present name; and it was not until 1909 that the new building, which had cost over £600,000 including its fittings and furniture, was officially opened by King Edward VII. The terracotta brick is surmounted by a central tower 185 ft high, shaped at the top like an imperial crown. Above the ornate main entrance are statues of Queen Victoria and Prince Albert by Alfred Drury and, on either side of them, statues by W. Goscombe John of Edward VII and Queen Alexandra who, to the disgust of *The Gentlewoman*, was carved 'wielding an enormous fan! Could bathos descend lower!' Around the building are other sculptures representing British artists made by students of the ROYAL COLLEGE OF ART.

Under the Museum's aegis have now come HAM HOUSE, OSTERLEY PARK and the WELLINGTON MUSEUM. The Museum's collection of dolls, toys and games may be seen at the BETHNAL GREEN MUSEUM; and its theatrical collections have been amalgamated with those of the British Theatre Museum and the Museum of Performing Arts to create the THEATRE MUSEUM.

In 1982 the Boilerhouse was opened in an underground section of the museum's old boilerhouse yard. The exhibition room is used to show works of modern functional design. The project was conceived and sponsored by Terence Conran of Habitat Designs Ltd.

Victoria Dock *see* ROYAL GROUP.

Victoria Embankment *SW1, WC2 and EC4.* A riverside road running from WESTMINSTER to BLACKFRIARS was first proposed by Christopher Wren after the GREAT FIRE, and later by Sir Frederick Trench and John Martin, the painter; but not until 1864–70 was it built by Sir Joseph Bazalgette. Thirty-seven acres were reclaimed from the river, a wall was built 14 ft below the low water mark and another up to 20 ft above the high. The total cost was over £1,260,000. The western boundary of the CITY is marked by a stone tablet with a relief of Queen Victoria who was here presented with the City Sword on 7 March 1900 by the LORD MAYOR. It has since 1963 also been marked by two cast iron dragons, painted silver and red. These dragons, which represent a constituent part of the armorial bearings of the CITY OF LONDON, were made in 1849 and formerly stood above the entrance to the COAL EXCHANGE. Victorian buildings still remaining include, from the Westminster end, the Norman Shaw Building (*see* NEW SCOTLAND YARD); WHITEHALL COURT and the NATIONAL LIBERAL CLUB; Hamilton House by W. Emerson (1898–1901); SION COLLEGE; and the CITY OF LONDON SCHOOL. The elaborate iron lamp standards along the riverside, with fierce-looking dolphins coiled round their bases, are by Timothy Butler and were erected in 1870. The Ministry of Defence Building by Vincent Harris was completed in 1957. The New Adelphi on the site of the Adams brothers' ADELPHI is by Collcutt and Hamp (1936–8). Unilever House on the corner of New Bridge Street is by J. Lomax Simpson and Sir John Burnet, Tait and Lorne (1930–31). The sculptures are by Sir William Reid Dick, the mermaids and mermen by Gilbert Ledward and the fourteen painted resin statues, seven sets of identical twins on the cornice, by Nicholas Munro. CLEOPATRA'S NEEDLE stands between WATERLOO BRIDGE and HUNGERFORD RAILWAY BRIDGE. Moored between WATERLOO BRIDGE and BLACKFRIARS BRIDGE are HMS WELLINGTON, HMS PRESIDENT, and HMS CHRYSANTHEMUM. Captain Scott's ship, the DISCOVERY, which was moored here until recently, has now been moved to ST KATHARINE'S DOCK. On the west side opposite WHITEHALL COURT there is a memorial to Samuel Plimsoll and on the riverside bronze busts and plaques of W.T. Stead (opposite Temple underground station), Sir Walter Besant (opposite Savoy Place), W.S. Gilbert (by HUNGERFORD BRIDGE), Sir Joseph Bazalgette (by HUNGERFORD BRIDGE), a memorial to the submariners of the British Navy and a memorial to the officers and men of the Royal Air Force (*see* MEMORIALS *and* STATUES).

Victoria Embankment Gardens *SW1, WC2.*

To the west of VICTORIA EMBANKMENT on either side of HUNGERFORD BRIDGE. They contain the YORK WATERGATE, the Belgian war memorial, memorials to Fawcett, Sullivan, Plimsoll, Lady Henry Somerset, and statues of Burns, Lawson, Brunel, Forster, Mill, Tyndale, Frere and Outram (*see* STATUES *and* MEMORIALS).

Victoria Hotel *Northumberland Avenue.* Built to

the designs of Isaacs and Florence in 1882–5. There were only four bathrooms for its 500 guests. It is now Northumberland House.

Victoria Line The first new tube route across

central London to be built since 1907. Although proposals showed that the line would not be directly profitable, it was considered vital to ease the peak-hour overload on other lines in central London, improve access to the West End and links between main-line stations, and ease road congestion. Work began on 20 September 1962 and the first part of the line, from WALTHAMSTOW Central to HIGHBURY and ISLINGTON, was opened to the public in 1968. The tunnels had been built in record time using new techniques, including a rotary type of shield called a 'drum digger', but the reconstruction of stations, particularly OXFORD CIRCUS, proved more time-consuming. On 7 March 1969 the Queen opened the third stage of the line from WARREN STREET to VICTORIA and Princess Alexandra opened the final section, from VICTORIA to BRIXTON, on 23 July 1971. The Victoria line is one of the most highly automated and technically advanced railways in the world. (*See also* UNDERGROUND RAILWAYS.)

Victoria Palace Theatre *Victoria Street, SW1.*

Built as a music-hall by Frank Matcham for Alfred Butt in 1911. Butt had introduced Pavlova to London and a statue of the ballerina stood on top of the theatre

until the 2nd World War, but Pavlova would never look at it and always drove past with the car blinds pulled down. In 1929–34 revues were staged here; and in 1935 it was taken for a season by Seymour Hicks who revived some of his earlier successes. Revues were resumed in 1936–7. In 1937–9 *Me and My Gal*, a musical comedy by L. Arthur Rose and Douglas Furber, featuring the LAMBETH WALK ran until the outbreak of war. After the war, it was the home of the Crazy Gang from 1947 to 1962, and the Black and White Minstrels, whose show ran for 4,344 performances until 1970. It seats 1,565.

Victoria Park *Hackney, E9.* The idea of a public

park in the EAST END was probably first put forward by Joseph Hume. In 1842 YORK HOUSE, ST JAMES'S was sold to finance the project. About 290 acres were acquired, including the site of the Manor House of STEPNEY (owned by the BISHOPS OF LONDON until the 15th century and demolished in 1800) and Bonner's Fields where heretics had been burned in the time of Bishop Bonner. In 1845 the park, laid out by James Pennethorne, was opened to the public, and in 1846 the lakes were excavated. In 1848 the Chartists' demonstrations caused 80 mounted police, 1,100 constables and 400 pensioners to be called out but the crowds dispersed peacefully in a thunderstorm. In 1861 the Gothic drinking fountain, designed by H.A. Darbishire, was presented by Angela Burdett-Coutts, and an arcade, designed by Pennethorne, was erected near the boating lake. In 1936 an open-air swimming bath was built; and in 1940 a refreshment pavilion designed by H.A. Rowbotham and Bone. Opposite the cricket pitch are two of the recesses from old LONDON BRIDGE and on the island in the boating lake a Chinese pagoda which formed the entrance to the Chinese Exhibition held in KNIGHTSBRIDGE in 1847.

A Chinese pagoda in Victoria Park, Hackney, which was opened to the public in 1845.

Victoria Road *W8.* Follows the course of an ancient track known as Love Lane. It was built up as part of Kensington New Town in 1837–55. At the southern end is Christchurch designed by Ferrey in 1851. George Robey, the comedian, lived at No. 10 in 1926–32.

Victoria Square *SW1.* Designed by Matthew Wyatt and built in 1838–9. Thomas Campbell, the poet, lived at No. 8 in 1841–3. When he left to live in France and sold his books, his grocer bought those containing sermons, one leaf of which would 'wrap up a whole pound of raisins'.

Victoria Station *Victoria Street, SW1.* Two stations now made one. In the 1850s the London, Brighton and South Coast Railway realised that they should extend their line, from the then terminus at PIMLICO, across the THAMES and closer to the WEST END. The Grosvenor Bridge, designed by J. Fowler, and opened in 1860, was the first railway bridge over the THAMES in the London area. At its northern end, and at the end of the newly created VICTORIA STREET, the LB and SCR opened its new station. The GROSVENOR HOTEL, one of the earliest of the railway hotels, was built beside it. The London, Chatham and Dover Railway were also looking for a West End Terminus, and they built theirs on the Eastern side of the Brighton terminus. The stations had separate entrances for the Brighton line and the Chatham line. Both were used extensively for holiday travel to South Coast resorts, and from 1862 the Chatham station handled a steady traffic in boat trains for travellers to and from the continent. The 1899 the two companies formed a partnership, though they remained separate businesses and each retained its part of the terminus. Both stations were remodelled and considerably enlarged, 1905–8, and the GROSVENOR HOTEL was also rebuilt. After 1908 more and more boat trains used the station.

Victoria has seen the arrival of more Royalty and visiting Heads of State than any other terminus. For the funeral of King Edward VII in 1910, an Emperor and Empress, seven Kings, more than 20 Princes and five Archdukes were welcomed here. The continental platforms took on sterner duties between 1914–18 when the station was used for the transport of troops to France. In 1921 the Southern Railway took over the two stations, and the wall between the two was first breached in 1924. The two parts have, however, retained their separate identities.

Victoria Street *SW1.* First projected in 1844 by the architect, H.R. Abraham, it was largely built in the 1850s and 1860s, though not finally completed until the 1880s. It extended from VICTORIA STATION to BROAD SANCTUARY and involved the clearance of much slum property and, at the Victoria end, Palmer's Village, so called after the Revd James Palmer who built several almshouses here in the middle of the 17th century (Palmer Street is named after him). The street was remarkable in its time for the even height and scale of the buildings. In 1861 an American entrepreneur, George Train, put down tram lines along its length from WESTMINSTER ABBEY to PIMLICO. The trams ran every five minutes and carried 48 passengers, half of them outside; but as the lines stood 14 ins above the ground and were strongly objected to by the owners of carriages and the drivers of vans he was obliged to

remove them that same year. Among the first large buildings to appear was the Westminster Palace Hotel, built in 1860 on the corner of TOTHILL STREET at the cost of five lives when the scaffolding fell. In its day it was one of the most luxurious hotels in London. It was later used by the NATIONAL LIBERAL CLUB before being converted into shops and offices. The old ARMY AND NAVY STORES was built in 1864 and ARTILLERY MANSIONS to the designs of John Calder, in 1895. With those in Morpeth Terrace and Ashley Gardens, these were amongst the earliest blocks of flats to be built in London. In the 1890s the street was described as being 'lined with lofty "mansions" let out in "flats" as residences [at the time of their erection a novelty in London] and large blocks of chambers.' Sir Arthur Sullivan died at No. 1 Queen's Mansions in 1900. Apart from Artillery Mansions, the Albert public house and the VICTORIA PALACE, a late Edwardian music-hall built to the designs of Frank Matcham and Company, there are few of the older buildings still left in the street. It is now remarkable mainly for its modern blocks. On the south side by GREAT SMITH STREET is a huge block by Ronald Fielding and Partners. Opposite it is Monsanto House by Sir John Burnet, Tait and Partners (1954–6) who also designed Westminster City Hall and Mobil House. Ashdown House at the VICTORIA STATION end and British Petroleum House next to it are by Elsom, Pack and Roberts (1975) who also designed the new ARMY AND NAVY STORES. Esso House is by T.P. Bennett and Son.

Victoria Tower Gardens *SW1.* These triangular gardens lie beside the THAMES between the HOUSES OF PARLIAMENT and LAMBETH BRIDGE and are popular with tourists. There is a fine view of Victoria TOWER which looks down on to a bronze of Rodin's six burghers of Calais (*see* STATUES). The Gothic fountain which used to stand in the north-west corner of PARLIAMENT SQUARE is a memorial to Sir Thomas Fowell Buxton, the brewer and social reformer. It commemorates the emancipation of slaves in the British Empire. There is also a statue by A.G. Walker of Emmeline Pankhurst, the suffragette (*see* STATUES), and a children's play area.

Victorian Society *1 Priory Gardens, Bedford Park, W4.* Founded in 1958 to encourage the study and protection of buildings created in the period of 1840–1914 and of other Victorian and Edwardian arts. There are over 3,000 members. It has campaigned successfully to save several buildings, including in London Norman Shaw's NEW SCOTLAND YARD and Sir George Gilbert Scott's ST PANCRAS STATION.

Vigo Street *W1.* A short street extending from REGENT STREET to SAVILE ROW. It is named after the naval victory of 1702 at Vigo Bay, off the coast of Spain. Most of the buildings here – all shops – provide the return fronts to blocks in REGENT STREET, SACKVILLE STREET and SAVILE ROW.

Villiers Street *WC2.* Built by Nicholas Barbon in the 1670s on the site of YORK HOUSE which had formerly belonged to George Villiers, Duke of Buckingham. John Evelyn, the diarist, spent a few months here in 1682; and Sir Richard Steele had a house in the street in 1712–24. Most of the west side of the street was demolished in the 1860s for CHARING CROSS

RAILWAY STATION. Rudyard Kipling lived at No. 43 in 1889–91 and here wrote *The Light That Failed*. The PLAYERS' THEATRE is on the west.

Vincent Square *SW1*. Large square built in the 18th century on the BEAR GARDENS of TOTHILL FIELDS and named after Dr William Vincent, Dean of Westminster and headmaster of WESTMINSTER SCHOOL. Together with the streets leading off it, it has recently been declared a conservation area. A few of the original houses remain. On the south-west side is WESTMINSTER CHILDREN'S HOSPITAL; on the north-west King's College Hostel by A.C. Martin (1913); and on the north-east the ROYAL HORTICULTURAL SOCIETY's Old Hall by E.J. Stebbs (1904). Behind this, on the corner of Greycoat Street and Elverton Street, is the Society's New Hall built in 1923–8 to the designs of Murray

Easton. In the middle of the square are WESTMINSTER SCHOOL playing fields. The square is popular with Members of Parliament. Sir Harold Wilson, Richard Crossman and Lord Duncan-Sandys all lived here. In 1981 the new Westminster Under School opened in the former Grosvenor Hospital, a building designed by George Aitchison and used until 1976 by ST THOMAS'S HOSPITAL as a gynaecological unit.

Vintners' Company *see* CITY LIVERY COMPANIES.

Virginia and Maryland Coffee House *Newman's Court, Cornhill*. So called because it was frequented by 'merchants, brokers, owners and commanders of ships, and all persons concerned in the trade to Virginia and Maryland.' Many masonic lodges held meetings here. By 1838 it had become a tavern.

W

Waddon *Surrey*. Situated south of CROYDON. Neolithic, Roman and Romano-British relics have been found at Waddon, and the name itself – woad hill – was in use by the beginning of the 2nd century. In the 12th century the manor of Waddon, a sub-manor of CROYDON, was given by Henry I to the monks of BERMONDSEY from whom it passed to the Archbishop of Canterbury. Lying on the Roman road to the south coast, Waddon was already a township by the 14th century. Its rural character changed little until the end of the 19th century when Victorian villas such as those in Rectory Grove appeared following the arrival of the London Bridge and South Croydon Railway. The footbridge over the railway to Wandle Park was built in 1888–90. In the early 20th century industrial buildings and blocks of flats to the east of Purley Way were built and Waddon Ponds was opened as a public park. The control tower of CROYDON airport, the first purpose-built airport in the country, still stands to the south of Waddon. In 1965 Waddon became part of the London Borough of CROYDON.

Waithman Street *EC4*. Built in 1891 and named after Alderman Robert Waithman who was MP for the CITY five times and Lord Mayor in 1823. For many years he had a linen draper's shop at the corner of FLEET STREET and Ludgate Circus. He died in 1833 and was buried in ST BRIDE'S FLEET STREET. An obelisk memorial to Waithman stands in SALISBURY SQUARE. The street was destroyed in the 2nd World War and has since been rebuilt.

Walbrook The stream of the Ancient Britons which rose in FINSBURY and flowed along the line of Curtain Road and Apollo Street, through the City wall by ALL HALLOWS CHURCH to the BANK and then west of the street called WALBROOK and into the THAMES. The Romans built their settlement around the stream and used it as their main water supply. A temple to MITHRAS stood on its banks. It was never navigable being only 12 ft to 14 ft wide and very shallow. ST MARGARET LOTHBURY, ST MILDRED POULTRY, ST. JOHN THE BAPTIST UPON WALBROOK, and ST STEPHEN WALBROOK were all built on the banks. In 1288 it had to be 'made free from dung and other nuisances'. But by 1383 it was 'stopped up by divers filth and dung thrown therein by persons who have houses along the said course'. The Lord Mayor, Robert Large, contributed to the cost of covering over part of the stream in 1440 when ST MARGARET LOTHBURY was rebuilt. When Stow compiled his *Survey of London* in 1598 it was completely hidden and its course hardly known.

Walbrook *EC4*. 'Called Walbrooke because it standeth on the east side of the same brooke by the bank thereof' (*see previous entry*). In the 14th century it was decreed that 'all the freemen of the said trade

(pelterers, that is to say furriers and skinners) shall dwell in Walebroke, Cornehulle [Cornhill] and Bogerowe [Budge Row].' ST STEPHEN'S CHURCH is on the east side. Bucklersbury House, built to the designs of O. Campbell Jones and Partners in 1953–8, is one of the largest office blocks in London. The TEMPLE OF MITHRAS was discovered when excavations were being dug for Bucklersbury House.

Walbrook Mithraeum *see* TEMPLE OF MITHRAS.

Waldorf Hotel *Aldwych, WC2*. A steel-framed, stone-cased hotel with French pavilion roofs, built in 1906–8 to the designs of A. G. R. Mackenzie for his father's firm of A. Marshall Mackenzie and Son, at the time of the replanning of the ALDWYCH. It has giant Ionic columns rising in the middle, with carved cherubs between the windows. The handsome public rooms surround an elegant Palm Court. There are 310 bedrooms.

Walham Green *Fulham, SW6*. The old name for the area round FULHAM BROADWAY. First mentioned in 1383 as Wandangrene or Wendenesgrene, it may derive its name from a personal name or refer to the original appearance of the area as an open depression in the ground (*dene*, from the middle part of the trisyllabic name). At first a sparsely populated settlement with a green, a pond, a pound, a market (now moved to NORTH END ROAD) and, by the 17th century, stocks and a whipping post, it gradually became an urban centre in which St John's church, designed by J. H. Taylor, was built in 1828 on the site of the pond; the Town Hall, designed by George Edwards, in 1888–90; the Granville Theatre in 1898 as well as four cinemas, all now closed. The Granville Theatre, founded by Dan Leno and associates, was designed by Frank Matcham. The interior was decorated with DOULTON majolica work. Leno called it his 'Drawing Room Music Theatre'. Demolished in 1971, it has been replaced by a commercial building.

Wallace Collection *Hertford House, Manchester Square, W1*. Takes its name from Sir Richard Wallace, who at his death in 1890 left all his property to his widow who, in her turn, left it to the nation on condition it should always be kept in central London. Richard Wallace was the last of a long line of discriminating collectors whose interests ranged from English and European paintings to Oriental and Continental armour, Sèvres porcelain and Limoges enamels. The collection was begun by the first Marquess of Hertford, patron of Sir Joshua Reynolds and Allan Ramsay. The 2nd Marquess added to the collection of English portraits with his purchase of Romney's *Mrs Robinson* and Reynolds's *Nelly O'Brien*.

In 1797 the 2nd Marquess, in his time British Ambassador in Berlin and Vienna, bought the present

Hertford House, Manchester Square, in 1813. This great house, the home of the Wallace Collection, was opened as a national museum in 1900.

house, then called Manchester House after the 4th Duke of Manchester who had had it built 20 years before because of the good duck shooting available nearby. The flamboyant 3rd Marquess became a legendary figure in London society and is portrayed as the mysterious Marquis de Steyne by Thackeray in *Vanity Fair*. He married a girl who was claimed as a daughter by the Duke of Queensberry and George Selwyn, each of whom, disregarding the other's claim, left her a fortune. A close friend of the Prince Regent, the 3rd Marquess would frequently advise him on the acquisition of works of art, with the result that several pictures and objects in the collection are similar to those in the Royal Collections. His particular interests were Sèvres porcelain and Dutch 17th-century painting. The 4th Marquess lived the life of an eccentric recluse in the Château de la Bagatelle in the Bois de Boulogne in Paris. Buying at a time when French 18th-century art, following the Revolution, was unfashionable, he was able to buy to great advantage and by 1855 had one of the finest collections of paintings by Fragonard, Boucher, Watteau and Lancret. His purchases of 18th-century furniture, sculpture and objets d'art were on the same lavish scale. In all these transactions it was his illegitimate son, Richard Wallace, who acted for him. By his death the 4th Marquess had augmented and transformed his inheritance into one of the greatest and most varied collections ever formed. All this was left unconditionally to Richard, his constant companion of 30 years.

Wallace, a complete contrast in character to his father, was knighted in 1871 for his philanthropic work for the British community in Paris during the Franco-Prussian War. Anxious for the future stability of France, Wallace decided to take the greater part of his collection over to London and to install it in Hertford House. While the house was being renovated part of the collection was exhibited at the newly founded BETHNAL GREEN MUSEUM, where it was visited by five million people. Another part of the collection was stored at the Pantechnicon in MOTCOMB STREET and was destroyed in a fire in 1874. Wallace's additions redressed the balance of the collection, which was then almost entirely of the 17th and 18th centuries, with the purchase of Italian majolica and Renaissance goldsmiths' work, bronzes and armour. After Wallace's death in 1897 it was decided that the collection should remain at Hertford House, and on 22 June 1900 it was opened as a national museum by the Prince of Wales.

Wallington *Surrey*. Until 1867 a hamlet in the parish of BEDDINGTON, it nevertheless in Saxon times gave its name to the local Hundred of the County of Surrey. The *Wal* element in its name is probably the same as the *Wel* in Welsh – the name applied to the Britons by the Saxons and therefore indicating a Celtic enclave. At *Domesday* in 1086 the manor was held by the king, and included two WANDLE water-mills. In the 15th and 16th centuries, Wallington was owned by the Dymokes, hereditary King's Champions, required to challenge at a CORONATION any rival claimant to the Crown to personal combat. In 1596 Wallington passed to the Carews of Beddington. By 1714 it was in the hands of the Bridges family, with whom it remained. In 1847 the steam railway came to Wallington; which was then a cluster of houses, mainly small (but including two separate manor houses, now lost) and an inn, grouped around a green. The station, built out in the fields, was called CARSHALTON after the largest nearby settlement it was meant to serve. A new community quickly began to grow around the station (renamed Wallington in 1868), outgrowing its old partner, BEDDINGTON, to which the railway never came. Wallington was created a separate Civil Parish in 1867, following the building of a church. It became the dominant partner in the Urban District of BEDDINGTON and Wallington in 1915. The horse-drawn SURREY IRON RAILWAY (the first public railway in the world) entered Hackbridge, at the northern end of Wallington, in 1803; and Woodcote, at the southern end, was claimed as the 'lost' Roman city of Noviomagnus on the strength of ruins now suspected to have been a deserted medieval village.

Walnut Tree Tavern *Tooley Street, Southwark*. 'A common hostelrie for travellers', in the words of John Stow, which 'was sometime one great house built of stone, with arched gates, pertaining to the Prior of Lewes in Sussex, and was his lodging when he came to London.' Walnut Tree Alley, which later covered the site, was pulled down to make way for the approaches to the new LONDON BRIDGE.

Waltham Forest *Essex*. Situated east of the River LEA with EPPING FOREST to the north-west. The London Borough of Waltham Forest was created in 1965 and comprises the former municipal boroughs of CHINGFORD, LEYTON and WALTHAMSTOW. It is called after an earlier name of EPPING FOREST, referring to that part of the ancient forest of MIDDLESEX and Essex which extended around Waltham Abbey. Roman and Saxon settlement took place and the parish churches of ALL SAINTS, CHINGFORD, ST MARY THE VIRGIN, LEYTON, and ST MARY WALTHAMSTOW existed in the 12th century. From the 16th century wealthy city merchants built their mansions; agriculture flourished; and there was little topographical change. Only with 19th-century improvement in transport to London did the population grow rapidly, a large proportion commuting for employment (as it still does); and within a century suburban development was complete. Works and factories were built along the LEA and reservoirs excavated from its marshes so that only limited areas such as LEYTON and WALTHAMSTOW MARSHES were left as open land. Encroachment on EPPING FOREST resulted in the Act of 1878 which continues to preserve it undeveloped for the public. Although many of Waltham Forest's fine 18th- and 19th-century buildings have disappeared, from the 1960s there have been efforts to protect surviving examples, and by 1981 47 buildings and two monuments were listed. A further substantial number await approval. In 1967 the Lea Valley Regional Park was established with the intention of developing 23 miles of the LEA Valley for the leisure and recreation of inhabitants of Essex, Hertfordshire and Greater London. From Bromley-by-Bow to Ware (Herts) the Park Authorities control about 2,000 acres including reservoirs where fishing, birdwatching and sailing take place.

Walthamstow *E17*. Situated between LEYTON and CHINGFORD, 6½ miles north-east of the CITY. The ancient parish lay wholly in the Royal Forest of Waltham (later EPPING FOREST) on the route from London to Waltham Abbey, but the name (a place where strangers are welcome) has no connection with these. The western boundary is the ancient course of the LEA, and the Walthamstow Marshes originally stretched along its whole length. Here were settlements from the Bronze and early Iron Ages, followed by those of Romans and Saxons. At *Domesday* the manor of Walthamstow Toni included all but the north, Higham Hill and HIGHAMS PARK, of the later parish. It belonged to descendants of Ralph de Toni, standard-bearer to William I, until 1427 and they were responsible for the foundation of ST MARY WALTHAMSTOW in the 12th century. By the 15th century much forest had been cleared and the population consisted of yeomen and small farmers. The timber-framed Ancient House (restored 1934) dates from that time.

By 1513 the northbound Hoe (ridge) Street was named and during the 16th century more wealthy and cultured residents arrived. Amongst these were the navigator, Sir Martin Frobisher, the poet, George Gascoigne, and the parish benefactor, Sir George Monoux, draper and Lord Mayor of London in 1514, who lived at Moons on the site of the present Monoux Grove. He built the Monoux Almshouses (rebuilt from the 18th century) and School (rebuilt 1889). During the 17th century Pepys was entertained by Admiral Sir William Penn when Walthamstow village at Church End was spreading outwards on to streets such as Shernhall which lay on the course of an earlier open sewer (Shernwell = filth stream). Shern Hall, the home of Cardinal Wiseman in 1849 (demolished 1896), replaced High Hall as the manor house. Eighteenth-century mansions included The Chestnuts, WATER HOUSE (now the WILLIAM MORRIS GALLERY), home of William Morris, and Cleveland House, which was probably altered by Sir John Soane in 1781–3. Still within a rural environment, with flourishing market gardens, the Coppermill struck copper coins during the Napoleonic Wars on a mill site dating back to 1066. It was still used as a pumping station in the 20th century.

The 19th century transformed Walthamstow into a heavily populated and industrialised urban area. At the beginning of the century Benjamin Disraeli attended Dr Cogan's Essex Hall Academy; but by its end the Midland Railway to Blackhorse Road had attracted industry north of Ferry Lane, and the first British car with an internal combustion engine, the Brewer Car,

had been produced in Walthamstow (1892–5). From the mid-century 120 acres of marshland were flooded to create reservoirs and the railways brought speculative land societies, such as the Tower Hamlets Society, intent on development. As the population increased twentyfold the new parishes of St John, St James and St Peter were created, and with the increasing urban pressures the Epping Forest Act ensured a continuous belt of forest from Chingford Hatch to Whipp's Cross, LEYTONSTONE. Following the arrival of the NORTH CIRCULAR ROAD in 1930 northern Walthamstow – the manor of Hecham which had given its name to HIGHAMS PARK – was developed: Essex Hall estate was built by the Council, an old people's home taking the name. Forest Road became the civic centre, replacing the High Street where the WALTHAMSTOW MARKET was held, and tower-block and shopping developments followed severe bomb damage in the 2nd World War. In 1965 Walthamstow became part of the London Borough of WALTHAM FOREST and in the following years conservation orders were placed on many deserving buildings: examples are those in Church End, and Forest School, founded in 1834, its chapel embellished in 1875–80 with stained glass windows by William Morris.

Walthamstow Market *E17*. A large and noisy general market with more than a mile of stalls in the High Street.

Walthamstow Marshes *E17*. The total area of 990 acres (apart from a small triangular central plot leased from British Railways), was purchased by Lea Valley Regional Park Authority in 1972. The greater part is open marsh supporting some interesting wildlife, but there is also a marina on the LEA River frontage, a riding school and football pitches. It was there that in July 1909 A. V. Roe performed the first powered flight in Great Britain.

Walton Place *and* **Walton Street** *SW3*. The north-east part of the SMITH'S CHARITY ESTATE was a 14-acre field known as the Quail Field. Originally a grazing pasture, it became the celebrated market garden of Mr Malcolm. After he left in 1840 it became the cricket ground of PRINCE'S CLUB. Development of the extreme north end began in 1836 when the CHURCH COMMISSIONERS approached the trustees for the site of a new church. The trustees offered the site for £300. The plot was fenced in and a small street, Walton Place, was laid out to approach it in 1843. The church, St Saviour's (1839–40), is the work of George Basevi. Walton Place, two terraces of nine houses, has remained almost exactly as it was when completed in 1844. Walton Street was laid out in 1847 and the first 16 houses on the north side are the work of William Pocock. The street was later extended along the parish boundary as a result of the Chelsea Improvements Bill. The names were given in honour of George Walton Onslow, a trustee of the SMITH'S CHARITY ESTATE.

Walworth *SE17*. Has the ELEPHANT AND CASTLE and NEWINGTON BUTTS on its north-west corner, is bounded on the north by the New Kent Road, on the west by Kennington Park Road, on the south by KENNINGTON and CAMBERWELL, on the east by the OLD KENT ROAD and PECKHAM. It lies within the London Borough of SOUTHWARK, and contains little of architectural interest except some early 19th-century houses in Walworth Road and in its continuation as Camberwell Road. To the east of Walworth Road in Liverpool Grove, is Soane's church of ST PETER, and in Wells Way, CAMBERWELL'S ST GEORGE'S CHURCH by Bedford in the Greek Revival style (now disused and vandalised). To the north of ST GEORGE'S CHURCH lay the terminus of the GRAND SURREY CANAL. In Cobourg Road stands St Mark's Church of 1880, designed by Norman Shaw. Walworth was important in the 19th century as a pleasure resort, for here flourished for a while the SURREY ZOOLOGICAL GARDENS with entrances from Penton Place and Manor Place. The grounds, at one time attached to the manor house here, covered 15 acres. In 1856 the Gardens were put up for sale by auction and the arcaded Surrey Gardens Music-Hall holding 12,000 was erected. Here on Sundays Dr Spurgeon preached his interminable but passionate sermons to huge congregations up to the year 1861 when the METROPOLITAN TABERNACLE was opened. The popularity of the gardens thereafter declined. After their closure ST THOMAS'S HOSPITAL took up temporary accommodation in the music-hall before moving to its new buildings by WESTMINSTER BRIDGE.

Walworth Road *SE1*. WALWORTH was a manor recorded before *Domesday Book*. A main thoroughfare and crowded shopping street, catering for a working-class neighbourhood, the main attraction today, especially on Sundays, is East Street Market. Liverpool Grove leads to ST PETER'S CHURCH. The CUMING MUSEUM of Local History and Archaeology originated in a collection built up during 1782–1902 by the Cumings, a WALWORTH family. Next door is the former Newington Vestry Hall, erected in 1866. Ruskin attended a chapel in John Ruskin Street, formerly Beresford Street. His tutor came from an academy in Walworth Road.

Wandle A river which rises near CROYDON and is fed by springs at CARSHALTON. It flows through BEDDINGTON and MERTON and is joined by the River GRAVENEY in TOOTING, going on to join the THAMES

to the west of WANDSWORTH Bridge. During its 11 miles it drops 100 feet in level, and in the early 18th century it drove 68 waterwheels in its course. Preservation bodies have restored its upper course in CARSHALTON, BEDDINGTON and MITCHAM, and purchased part of the walls of Merton Abbey adjoining it, but it enters the THAMES in a dreary waste of ruined buildings. On the riverside, however, some conversion to recreation space has been achieved. Admiral Nelson used to fish in the Wandle where part of it flowed in Lady Hamilton's garden at MERTON PLACE, she having diverted it and called it 'the Nile' in his honour. The SURREY IRON RAILWAY, intended to run from WANDSWORTH to Portsmouth, followed the Wandle valley as far as MERSTHAM and never went any further.

Wandsworth *SW18*. A Saxon noble called Wendle is thought to have given his name to the little tributary of the THAMES known as the River WANDLE: hence Wandsworth, the village by the Wandle. In Saxon times the land was divided into four manors, Wandsworth, Allfarthing, Down and Dunsford. The first of these, recorded in *Domesday Book* as Wandelesorde or Wendles-orde, survives as the name of one of London's largest boroughs. Two others survive, less significantly, in the street names Allfarthing Lane and Dunsford Way. Wandsworth has long been an industrial area. Bleaching cloth and hat-making were popular as early as the 13th century. In 1376 there was apparently a dispute between the fullers who bleached cloth and the hurrers who made hats, as to who had the rights to the waters of the WANDLE. The fullers successfully claimed a monopoly and managed to oust the hurrers from Wandsworth altogether. However, the Huguenot refugees who settled in Wandsworth in the 18th century were skilled hatters and dyers and were able to vindicate their profession. When the cardinals in Rome began to order hats from them, their industry made Wandsworth famous for its hats throughout Europe. The Huguenots were also renowned for their iron and copperware. Recalling their contribution to the industrial growth of the area, Aubrey wrote that 'there was a manufacture of brass plates for kettles, frying pans etc. by Dutchmen who kept it a great

The River Wandle at Wandsworth, from a watercolour by J.B. Watson of c.1819.

mystery.' Street names such as Dutch Yard and Coppermill Lane commemorate these Flemish settlers to this day and they have a memorial, erected in 1911, in the Parish Cemetery of Mount Nod in East Hill. Other industries have included calico printing and fur-making and in the 19th century the manufacture of war munitions was added. A large mill, famous for its 600 lb hammer, stood in what is now Ironmill Road. Brewing in Wandsworth was well established by the middle of the 16th century, and with Young's Brewery now based in Wandsworth it is well established there still.

In 1539, the vicar of Wandsworth together with his chaplain and two members of his household were hanged, drawn and quartered for refusing to acknowledge the Act of Supremacy. But during the Civil War, Wandsworth residents were loyal to the monarchy, as is clear from the ballad thought to be by Lovelace which runs:

Hark the clamour of fife and drum
Three Thousand Surreymen marching come
Their van by a snow white banner is lead
And the Miller of Wandsworth he walks at their head.
An humble petitition they come to present
At the doors of the houses of Parliament
And the windows fly open to catch up the strain
King Charles! King Charles! shall be brought home again.

The growth of industry in Wandsworth encouraged wealthy businessmen to settle there and to build large houses near what is now WANDSWORTH COMMON. In the 18th century they attempted to enclose and thereby to appropriate this land. The more lowly citizens rebelled and formed a society to protect their interests. The president of this society became known as the MAYOR OF GARRATT. Eventually the common land was released, but the mock election of a MAYOR OF GARRATT survived for many years, developing into a local festival.

Like the whole of SOUTH LONDON, the development of Wandsworth in the 19th century was greatly influenced by the railways. In 1801 the building of the SURREY IRON RAILWAY was sanctioned by Act of Parliament. The formal opening of the railway which connected all the various factories took place in 1803. In Victorian times several large institutions were built, most notably WANDSWORTH PRISON, then known as the Surrey House of Correction, and the Royal Victoria and Patriotic Asylum which was opened by the Queen in 1857. Another typical Victorian institution was the Friendless Boys Home in Spanish Road, built for boys 'who have lost their characters or are in danger of doing so'.

Famous past inhabitants of Wandsworth include Daniel Defoe, Edward Gibbon and Thackeray. Voltaire lived there in 1726–9 on a visit to England. The Methodist reformer Wesley also spent some time there, recording in his diary in 1769: 'I preached today at Wandsworth. For many years the people here were most dead but are now the most alive of any about in London.' David Lloyd George's first house in London was No. 179 Trinity Road. He moved to No. 3 Routh Road in 1904 and lived there until 1908. In its 13¼ sq. miles Wandsworth today has a population of approximately 260,000.

Wandsworth Bridge *Fulham–Wandsworth*. The first bridge on site was built by J. H. Tolmé in 1870–3.

It was a continuous lattice-girder bridge of five spans. It was freed from tolls in 1880. In 1936–40 it was replaced by the present three-spanned bridge of steel-plate girder cantilever construction, designed by Sir T. Pierson Frank, with E. P. Wheeler and F. R. Hiorns as architectural consultants.

Wandsworth Prison *Heathfield Road, SW18*. Originally a Surrey House of Correction, it was designed by D. R. Hill of Birmingham, on the separate system and the radial plan, to hold 1,000 prisoners. Five wings radiating from a central block formed the male part of the prison, a smaller compact building with three radiating wings formed the female section. Building began in 1849, male prisoners being admitted in 1851, female in 1852. For hard labour 100 labour machines or cranks were installed; from these prisoners were transferred to the pump house. A contemporary said that externally it had 'little to recommend it to the eye, having none of the fine gloomy solemnity of Newgate, nor any of the castellated grandeur of the City Prison at Holloway. . . . The central mass rising behind the stunted gateway is heavy even to clumsiness, and the whole aspect of the structure uncommanding as a Methodist college. Nevertheless the situation is admirably chosen for the health of the inmates . . . it is now, in an architectural point of view, so far as regards completeness of its arrangements, one of the best correctional prisons, if not the best, in the United Kingdom.' It was for those with short sentences. Oscar Wilde spent the first six months of his sentence here in 1895. Ronald Biggs, one of the 'Great Train Robbers', escaped in 1965. It now holds convicted persons awaiting sentence and is the long-term allocation centre in the south of England (except for life) – prisoners are eventually allocated to a training prison outside the London area. Its population in 1982 was 1,374 (the certified normal accommodation is 1,258).

Wanstead *E11*. Unlike most suburbs, Wanstead is still clearly identified. Separated from WALTHAMSTOW, LEYTONSTONE, FOREST GATE and MANOR PARK by continuous portions of EPPING FOREST and from ILFORD by golf links and Wanstead Park, it is only to the north, where Wanstead meets WOODFORD, that building straddles the boundary (*see* SNARESBROOK). The meaning of the name Wanstead is uncertain.

The mosaic pavement of a villa was disturbed in Wanstead Park in 1715 and other Roman remains have come to light in several places. In Saxon days the manor belonged to WESTMINSTER ABBEY and later to the BISHOPS OF LONDON, but there is no mention of a rector until 1207. Henry VII, Henry VIII, Mary I and Elizabeth I all visited Wanstead House, the glittering circle in Elizabeth's reign including her favourite, the Earl of Leicester, who owned Wanstead, his stepson, the young Earl of Essex, Lord Pembroke (a neighbour at Aldenbrook), Sir Philip Sidney and Penelope, Lady Rich, sister of Essex and the 'Stella' of Sidney's sonnets, *Astrophel and Stella*. James I several times stayed at Wanstead; some of his state papers are dated from it. Sir Josiah Child, Governor of the East India Company, bought the estate in 1667 and his grandson, the first Earl Tylney, commissioned from Colen Campbell a great Palladian mansion to replace the old house. In 1790 the parish church was replaced by the present elegant St Mary the Virgin. The heiress of

Wanstead House, the seat of the 1st Earl Tylney, in 1781. It was demolished in 1824 and sold for building stone.

Wanstead married a profligate nephew of the Duke of Wellington who squandered his wife's inheritance, with the result that in 1824 the mansion, which rivalled Blenheim and Holkham in size and spendour, was pulled down and sold for building stone. The stables survive, now the clubhouse of golfers and bowlers, and a little classical summer house, called the Temple, is still to be seen in Wanstead Park, together with the infamous but now dilapidated Grotto, reputed to have been the scene of various orgies.

The 18th and 19th centuries saw the building of pleasant villas; of these, only Manor House, now the Conservative Club, exists in recognisable form. The building of streets of small houses began with the coming of the railway in 1856, and development was then rapid: the population rose from 2,742 in 1861 to 31,657 in 1901. No medieval buildings remain. Later buildings of interest are: Christ Church, 1861; the WEAVERS' COMPANY almshouses (Joseph Jennings, 1859); the Roman Catholic church of Our Lady of Lourdes, 1929. The United Reformed Church, standing back from the High Street, was once the parish church of St Luke, KINGS CROSS, which had to be demolished when ST PANCRAS station was built. It was bought and re-erected on its present site as Wanstead Congregational Church in 1867.

Public reaction to attempted enclosures of parts of Epping Forest, notably of part of WANSTEAD FLATS, led to the CITY OF LONDON's spirited defence of commoners' rights and to the Epping Forest Act 1878, by which the City Corporation were made conservators for ever. The grounds of Wanstead Park were afterwards added. The Flats, the southernmost stretches of the Forest, are mostly laid out as sports pitches but still accommodate a traditional fair thrice a year. The Friends' Burial Ground, surrounded by Forest land, was formerly the Becontree Archery, in whose assembly rooms Dickens gave readings and, later, Elizabeth Fry addressed the Quakers of Wanstead.

Other notable Wanstead residents include the Quaker, William Penn; the Revd James Pound, rector of Wanstead, the astronomer, and his nephew, the Revd James Bradley, who became Astronomer Royal; Richard Brinsley Sheridan, the dramatist; and Thomas Hood, the poet.

Wanstead Flats *E7, E11, E12.* An area of 113 acres between WANSTEAD and FOREST GATE.

Wanstead Hospital *Hermon Hill, Wanstead, E11.* Originally an orphan asylum founded in 1861. The foundation stone was laid by the Prince Consort. In 1937 it was bought by Essex County Council as a hospital. It is now administered by the National Health Service which has undertaken many improvements. It has 160 beds for acute cases.

Wapping *E1.* The original Saxon settlement of 'Waeppa's people' was probably to the north of the present day Wapping in an area which later became known as Wapping-Stepney or ST GEORGE-IN-THE-EAST. A new hamlet in the parish of WHITECHAPEL called Wapping-on-the-Wose developed on the embankment of the THAMES when this section of the waterfront began to be developed. Wapping therefore acquired a peculiarly narrow and serpentine shape which followed the line of the river. It was hemmed in to the north by Wapping Marsh drained by a Dutchman,

The Gun Dock, Wapping, from a watercolour by T.H. Shepherd, 1850.

Cornelius Vanderdelft, in the early 16th century. The reclaimed land became rich meadow and garden ground until acquired for the LONDON DOCKS. At the end of the 16th century, Stow described Wapping High Street as 'a continual street, or filthy strait passage, with alleys of small tenements or cottages, built, inhabited by sailors' victuallers'. EXECUTION DOCK was moved a little further downstream. By 1617 the hamlet was sufficiently populated for a chapel, St John's, Wapping, to be erected. This was rebuilt in 1760 on the other side of the road, but only the tower remains. The 1694 Act which created the new parish of Wapping stated that 'the inhabitants have for some years past been much lessened in number by great fires which happened there and also by the present and former wars, the inhabitants thereof being chiefly seamen and depending on sea trade and several of the more wealthy of them are removed into new houses built in other parts of the said parish', that was to say WHITECHAPEL. Many of the seamen of Charles II's navy lived in Wapping and Pepys often described the disturbances they made. In 1688 the notorious Judge Jeffreys was captured at the Red Cow, one of many alehouses in Wapping, while trying to escape to France. The following century Dr Johnson recommended his listeners to 'explore Wapping' to see 'such modes of life as very few could even imagine'. Boswell, however, was not impressed by what he saw; and in the 19th century the lively maritime character of the small village began to disappear as the mastmakers, boatbuilders, blockmakers, mathematical instrument-makers and lodging-houses gave way to giant warehouses which towered above the narrow streets.

The LONDON DOCKS, besides destroying many of the houses, isolated Wapping once more, making it an island surrounded by high walls, with few exits, although Brunel's THAMES TUNNEL eventually provided Wapping with an underground link to the rest of London. The population of about 6,000 in 1801 had dropped by almost two-thirds 80 years later. Bomb damage in the 2nd World War, and the closure of the docks and many of the riverside wharves and warehouses, brought an appearance of dereliction to the area from which it is only just recovering as new housing estates, leisure facilities and industries are brought to the former LONDON DOCKS, old buildings such as Wapping Pier Head and Oliver's Wharf are converted to flats, and public gardens are created on waste land.

Wapping High Street *E1*. Stow saw it being built up in the late 16th century. It became known for industries related to shipping and as a centre of entertainment for sailors: there were 36 taverns in the street in 1750. Pennant found it 'well paved and handsomely flagged' but in 1879 the METROPOLITAN BOARD OF WORKS had it widened because only one vehicle could pass along at a time. The fine houses on Wapping Pierhead were built in 1811 for officials of the London Dock Company. The stainless steel sundial *Timepiece* at the end of St Katherine's Way is by Wendy Taylor (1973), and the bronze fountain is by David Wynne (1973).

Wapping Recreation Ground *E1*. The 2½ acres of gardens acquired in 1875 and eventually opened to the public in 1891. Charles I once hunted a stag from Wanstead which was finally killed at WAPPING.

War Office *Whitehall, SW1*. Built between 1899 and 1906 from designs by William Young, in a Victorian baroque style. The four circular towers at the corners disguise the fact that none of the angles is a right-angle. The building contains approximately 1,000 rooms and 2½ miles of corridor. It now forms part of the MINISTRY OF DEFENCE.

S.G. Warburg and Co. Ltd *Gresham Street, EC2*. Siegmund Warburg, a partner in the old-established Hamburg bank of M.M. Warburg and Co., moved to London and formed the New Trading Co. in 1934. Initially the company financed small and medium-sized firms. Renamed S.G. Warburg and Co. in 1946, it acquired in 1957 Seligman Bros, merchant bankers since 1864. After its success as an adviser to Reynolds in the takeover of British Aluminium in the late 1950s, the firm's reputation as a creative merchant bank was strengthened by its early entry into the Eurocurrency and Eurobond markets in the 1960s.

Warburg Institute *Woburn Square, WC1*. Part of the UNIVERSITY OF LONDON, the Institute is concerned with the study of the classical tradition and its influence on European thought, art, literature and institutions. It is named after its founder, Aby Warburg, who was born in Hamburg in 1866. He built up his private library and, with Fritz Saxl, turned it into a research institute. Saxl guided the development of the Institute after Warburg's death in 1929. When the Nazis rose to power he transferred the Institute to London. In 1934 it was housed in Thames House and in 1937 moved to the SOUTH KENSINGTON IMPERIAL INSTITUTE buildings. In 1944 it was incorporated with LONDON UNIVERSITY and in 1958 moved into its present building, by Charles Holden, next to the COURTAULD INSTITUTE GALLERIES in WOBURN SQUARE. There is a library, a photographic collection and a publications department. Undergraduate and postgraduate courses are held. It was originally at No. 1. GORDON SQUARE, the residence of Charles Fowler, the architect of COVENT GARDEN and HUNGERFORD MARKETS. This building was decorated with a relief panel of the Nine Muses, which is preserved in the entrance hall of the Institute.

Wardour Street *W1*. Marked on a plan of 1585 as a lane called Commonhedge Lane leading from the Uxbridge Road (OXFORD STREET) to the King's Mews (in TRAFALGAR SQUARE). It was built upon in the 1680s when the northern part was known as Wardour Street after Edward Wardour who owned land thereabouts, the southern part being then known as Prince's Street, evidently in honour of Prince Rupert, the 'Mad Cavalier', who died in 1682. In 1878 this part of the street also became known by its present name. Most of the 17th-century houses were rebuilt in the early 18th century and were later occupied by antique dealers and furniture-makers. Thomas Sheraton lived at No. 106 (now 103) in 1793–5, as a plaque on the wall indicates. In 1798–1800 he lived at No. 98 (now 147). The Intrepid Fox public house at No. 99 was given its name in 1784 by its proprietor, who was a most enthusiastic supporter of Charles James Fox during the Westminster election of that year. In the 19th century, when Gladstone came here to look for china, the antique shops had acquired a rather dubious reputation and Wardour Street was a term used to signify ornate gothic revival furniture and fake antiques generally as well as the style of writing employed in meretricious historical novels. In the early 20th century the street became better known for its music publishers. Nos 152–160 were designed by Frank Loughborough Pearson for Novello and Co., a firm that had begun publishing music in OXFORD STREET in 1811. Nos 41 and 43 were designed for Willy Clarkson, the theatrical costumier and wig maker. Sarah Bernhardt laid the foundation stone in 1904 and Sir Henry Irving the coping stone in 1905. Since the 1930s Wardour Street has been known for offices of film companies.

Wardrobe Place   *EC4*. In 1720 Strype wrote, 'The Garden of the King's Wardrobe is converted into a large and square court, with good houses.' Nos 3–5 are of this date. Part of the east side and half of the north side of Wardrobe Place were demolished in 1982 for redevelopment.

Wards *and* **Wardmotes**   From very early times the CITY OF LONDON has been divided into Wards for the purposes of government. They go back to Norman times more or less in their present form. In 1130 20 Wards were listed and by 1206 there were 24. In 1394 the Ward of FARRINGDON was divided into Farringdon Within and Farringdon Without because 'the governance thereof is too laborious and grievous for one person to occupy and duly govern the same.' In 1550 the Ward of Bridge Without was created as a sinecure for the Senior ALDERMAN past the chair (that is to say those who had served the office of LORD MAYOR), but this was abolished in 1978, so there are now 25.

The Wards used to have responsibilities for the preservation of the peace, supervision of trading, sanitation and local upkeep; the Ward Beadles were employed full-time on these duties. Now the BEADLES are just ceremonial attendants of the ALDERMEN and the Wards are units of election only. Their meetings are called Wardmotes and these are held annually on St Thomas's Day, 17 December, when they elect a varying number of 'good and discreet citizens' to be their representatives on the COURT OF COMMON COUNCIL for one year. Each Ward also meets when a vacancy occurs to elect their own Alderman (whose election must be approved by the Court of ALDERMEN). The votes are all those who occupy premises as tenants or owners and those who qualify for the parliamentary franchise by residence. The Wards vary in size and character and have such ancient names as Bassishaw, Cordwainer and Portsoken. Most of them have their own clubs and there is also a United Wards Club; all of them hold social events.

Warehouse (Donmar Theatre),   *41 Earlham Street, Covent Garden, WC2*. Originally a vat room of a large brewery, it was acquired in 1920 by a film company, the first to use colour. After a few years it was taken over by a market trader as a warehouse for ripening bananas. In 1960 Donald Albery bought and converted it into a theatre, naming it the Donmar after himself and Margot Fonteyn. It was used largely for rehearsals, but Peter Brook staged scenes here from the Royal Shakespeare Company's Theatre of Cruelty season. Renovated early in 1977, it is now leased to the Royal Shakespeare Company under the joint directorship of Terry Hands and Trevor Nunn. The stage is an open space and the seating accommodation is 200.

Waring and Gillow Ltd   *191 Brompton Road, SW3*. Robert Gillow, joiner, established a business in Lancaster in about 1731. His son, Robert, in partnership with his father, leased some land about 1765, in OXFORD STREET (now SELFRIDGE'S site) and erected premises. His two brothers joined him. They made furniture from fine imported woods and Richard Gillow designed and patented in 1800 the telescopic dining table, and worked on many other fine pieces. In the 1850s S.J. Waring began a cabinet-making enterprise in Liverpool, and in 1895 opened a retail branch at 181 OXFORD STREET. In 1897 the Gillow lease near MARBLE ARCH expired, and Waring and Gillow merged. The large new store designed by R.F. Atkinson opened in 1906 at Nos 164–182 OXFORD STREET. It continued the tradition of fine furniture making, catering for BOODLE'S, the GARRICK, the REFORM and other gentlemen's clubs and for the private apartments at Windsor Castle. It also made furniture and fittings for the best hotels, such as the CARLTON and the RITZ. The firm formerly had a store at 188 REGENT STREET which closed in December 1980.

Warley Hospital   *Warley Hill, Brentwood, Essex*. Opened in 1851 as the first 'Essex County Lunatic Asylum', designed by Kendall and Pope. Subsequent blocks were opened in 1860 and 1936 in extensive grounds. In 1982 there were 1,024 beds.

Warren Street   *W1*. Built in 1790–1 and named after Sir Peter Warren, father-in-law of the ground landlord, the 1st Baron Southampton. Charles Turner, the mezzotint engraver, lived at No. 56 in 1799–1803 and at No. 50 from 1803 to 1857.

Warren's Hotel   *Lower Regent Street*. Built in about 1820–30, it became the Continental and was closed down after a raid by the police in 1906.

Warrington Hotel   *93 Warrington Crescent, Maida Vale, W9*. A splendid example of an Edwardian public house with Art Nouveau stained glass, chandeliers and ornate lamp standards. It was at one time a resort for jockeys and other racing men, one of whom is said to have won a bet of £100 for riding a horse up the steps and into the pub.

Warwick Avenue   *W2*. Lined with classical mansions which are set out on an almost American scale of spaciousness, this was one of the first roads to be built in this area, dating from the early 1840s. George Ledwell Taylor, architect to the BISHOP OF LONDON's estate, probably designed Nos 2–16. In Warwick Place are the popular Warwick Castle public house and one of the few bookshops in Paddington.

Warwick Court   *WC1*. Robert Rich, an Elizabethan lawyer of GRAY'S INN, had his mansion here. He was made Earl of Warwick. His grandson, Earl of Warwick and Holland and Baron Kensington, abandoned Warwick House for HOLLAND HOUSE and the former was demolished in 1688 to make room for the street.

Warwick Crescent   *W2*. Demolished and rebuilt in 1966 for the GREATER LONDON COUNCIL. The former No. 19 was famous as the house of the poet, Robert Browning, in 1861–87. Here he wrote among other works *The Ring and The Book*, and he is said to have had trees planted on what is now known as Browning's Island. No. 2, Beauchamp Lodge, still stands on the corner beside the canal. Used for many years for charitable purposes, it was a musicians' hostel when the writer Katherine Mansfield stayed there briefly in 1908–9, before her unfortunate marriage. For the derivation of the name *see* STANHOPE TERRACE.

Warwick Gardens *W14*. Begun as Warwick Square in 1829, its entry from KENSINGTON HIGH STREET is now marked by the memorial to Queen Victoria (*see* STATUES). Originally erected at the junction with KENSINGTON CHURCH STREET in 1904, it was moved in 1934. Close by at No. 11 Gilbert Keith Chesterton lived with his family from about 1880 until 1901. It takes its name from the Earls of Warwick, once owners of the manor of EARL'S COURT.

Warwick House *St James's Stable Yard, SW1*. Built in 1770–1 to the designs of Sir William Chambers for Henry Errington, a Northumberland landowner, who in 1769 had married Dame Mary Broughton Delves, owner of buildings which were demolished for the new house. Henry Errington died in 1819 and the crown lease was then bought by the Earl of Warwick, who enlarged and largely rebuilt what then became known as Warwick House. The Earl's family occupied the house until 1907; and from 1924 it was occupied by the newspaper owner, Lord Rothermere.

Warwick House Street *SW1*. Takes its name from Warwick House which was built, possibly to the designs of Sir Roger Pratt, for Sir Philip Warwick, the Royalist memoir writer, in the 1660s. In 1805–7 it was the gloomy London home of the Prince Regent's hoydenish daughter, Princess Charlotte. It was from here that she fled to her mother's house in CONNAUGHT PLACE in 1814 when her father was so angry with her for flirting with other young men instead of considering marriage to the Prince of Orange. The house was demolished in 1827.

Warwick Lane *EC4*. Named after the Earls of Warwick who had a house here in the 14th century. When the GREAT FIRE destroyed the COLLEGE OF PHYSICIANS (later the Royal College of Physicians) in AMEN CORNER, another was built here to the designs of Wren; but it was demolished when the college moved to TRAFALGAR SQUARE. The street was badly damaged in the 2nd World War and has since been rebuilt. CUTLERS' HALL which was built on the site of the ROYAL COLLEGE OF PHYSICIANS, survived the bombing and still stands at No. 4.

Warwick Road *W14, SW5*. Dating from 1847, it was not extended to the OLD BROMPTON ROAD until the 1870s. At No. 175 (now demolished) the French poet, Jules Laforgue, stayed for a short time and was married from there in 1886. The Council depot was designed by Arup Associates and opened in 1975.

Warwick Square *EC4*. Named after the Earls of Warwick (*see* WARWICK LANE). In the 13th century it was largely inhabited by wax chandlers who supplied tapers to ST PAUL'S. Strype described it in 1720 as handsome, spacious and airy. The CORPORATION OF LONDON Office of Sheriffs is here.

Warwick Square *SW1*. A characteristic development by Thomas Cubitt in PIMLICO. There are six tall iron lamp standards happily preserved. The garden is private. St Gabriel Pimlico, designed by Thomas Cundy the Younger, was consecrated in 1853.

Warwick Street *W1*. Built in the 1670s and 1680s. The origin of the name is not known. It was described by Strype in 1720 as 'a Place not over well built or inhabited', though 'at the upper End it hath some good Houses on both Sides'. None of the original buildings remains and there is little of interest in the street today, other than the CHURCH OF OUR LADY OF THE ASSUMPTION AND ST GREGORY and No. 20, a five-storey building of 1907 with an attractive Art Nouveau front designed by J.N. Randall Vining.

Water Gates, River Stairs *and* **Piers** From Roman times until the 19th century, the river was the citizens' main highway, and up to 1856 the annual LORD MAYOR'S SHOW took place on the river. As London expanded in Victorian times and after, transport took to the land so that today London's river is used to a very limited extent. The recent closure of the docks has further reduced its activities downstream. Most of London's bridges belong to the 19th and 20th centuries. Indeed from Roman times until 1751 when Labelye's WESTMINSTER BRIDGE was opened, London possessed only one bridge. Many ferries were therefore needed through the centuries to carry people, horses, cattle, carts and carriages from bank to bank, and ferries needed landing places – quays, piers and river steps. Skiffs and wherries for hire also required landing places. The first specific landing place in London on record is BILLINGSGATE, adjoining LONDON BRIDGE, and the spot may have served as a landing stage with gateway for ferry before the bridge was built.

In his famous pictorial 'map' of Tudor London of about 1560, Agas shows over 30 landing places between WESTMINSTER and the TOWER, and both that map and the slightly earlier one of 1543 by Wyngaerde show the landing steps and river gates to the gardens of the big houses along the STRAND which were not built over until the 18th century. An engraving of the 17th century by Kuyp shows a splendid river gateway with steps at old SOMERSET HOUSE in the STRAND and Hollar's etching of 1647 of WESTMINSTER seen from the river reveals six gates with steps to the water set in the riverside walls. A long pier or 'bridge' extends into the river, while in the foreground eight boats, one with a cabin, are being rowed along. In his great map of London of 1746 John Rocque marks over 100 river stairs between CHELSEA HOSPITAL and SHADWELL; he also marks the old horse ferry between LAMBETH and WESTMINSTER and another upstream between VAUXHALL and Neat House Gardens. Wren's ROYAL HOSPITAL, CHELSEA, had its grand iron gates and river steps until the CHELSEA EMBANKMENT was built, but most of such ornamental gates belonged to the private palaces by the river where the prelates and magnates could board their gilded barges. One perfect little example is YORK WATERGATE.

By 1827 London had seven Thames bridges, yet Mogg's map of that year notes 66 river stairs between BATTERSEA and the ISLE OF DOGS, and many are still marked on Wyld's map of 1851. On Cassell's large-scale map of 1867, however, only some 25 stairs are marked, but more than 20 piers are there, many used

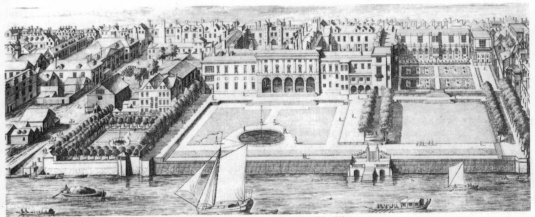

The steps at Old Somerset House in c.1720, from an engraving after Knyff by Kip.

by the Penny-Steamers, the river buses of the time, for until the new railways captured the market, the Penny-Steamer traffic was considerable. In 1861, for example, over three million passengers embarked and landed at Old Shades Pier to travel on the vessels of the London and Westminster Steamboat Co. A particularly charming jetty named Cadogan Pier projected into the river from CHEYNE WALK before the CHELSEA EMBANKMENT was formed. Built in the early 19th century; it had two solid towers with an iron suspension hanging between in the style of the old Brighton Chain Pier and Clark's existing Marlow Bridge. When Bazalgette built his VICTORIA EMBANKMENT, he incorporated a solid, noble, arched gateway and steps into the river wall opposite the TEMPLE, and that remains today. Now large housed caissons with bridge-like approaches float on the river here and there, notably the Cadogan Pier beside the ALBERT BRIDGE, while broad stone quays exist at WESTMINSTER BRIDGE and HUNGERFORD BRIDGE, mostly used by tourist passenger boats that ply the river in summer.

Water House *Forest Road, Walthamstow.* Built in about 1750. The estate had been known at various times as Hawkes, Copp, Cricklewood and Whynnes. From 1848 to 1856 it was the home of William Morris and the interior of the house remains basically as it was then. After the departure of the Morris family it was bought by the Lloyds, publishers of the DAILY CHRONICLE, and the house, gardens and grounds were given by them to the WALTHAMSTOW Council in 1898. Lloyd Park of about 19 acres was created from the grounds, and in 1950 the house was opened as the WILLIAM MORRIS GALLERY.

Water Supply Early water supplies came directly from wells or rivers. Fitzstephen commented in 1183 on the 'most excellent wells, whose waters are sweet, wholesome and clear'. Most of the early settlements in the London area were on water-bearing gravel terraces. But by 1236 'the fresh waters that were in and about the city, in process of time by encroachment buildings and heightenings of grounds, utterly decayed, and the number of citizens being mightily increased, they were forced to seek sweet water abroad'. So work began 'to convey water from the Tybourne by pipes of lead into the City'. Royal letters

patent approved the scheme 'for the profit of the City and good of the whole realm thither repairing, to wit for the poor to drink, and the rich to dress their meat'. In 1245 work was started on building a conduit house in CHEAPSIDE. According to Stow its pipes ran from the source 'to James Head . . . from James Head on the Hill to the Mewsgate . . . from the Mewsgate to the Cross in Cheape'. James Head seems to have been on the site of the churchyard of ST JAMES'S CHURCH, PICCADILLY and the term head implies a spring augmenting the supply. Mewsgate alludes to the Royal Mews on the site of the NATIONAL GALLERY (see TRAFALGAR SQUARE). The total distance was about 3065 yards. This was the first of the London conduit supplies. Others soon followed. The fall from the source to the distant point of consumption was always by gravity and natural pressure alone and, given the habitual leaks, the supply was never very efficient. Distribution pipes were very small hence Shakespeare's reference to the 'pissing conduit' in *Henry VI*, Part II. The water was free to all, but trade uses were assessed and charged. Keepers or Warders were appointed to manage conduits which were financed by rates levied on houses in the vicinity, by legacies and by benefactors. Private supplies ('quills') to houses were permitted only on specific authority. In 1260 there is the first mention of 'St Edward's Watercourse' of WESTMINSTER ABBEY. This was supplied from the WESTBOURNE. At the Coronation in 1273 of Edward I, the CHEAPSIDE conduit flowed all day with red and white wine. Twelve years later, Stow says, a head conduit with stone castellations was built in CHEAPSIDE. This appears to have been a rebuilding of the 40-year-old original conduit.

The quality of the river waters was a matter of constant concern in medieval London. In 1297 the Earl of Lincoln complained to Parliament that river water was unfit for drinking due to filth running into it from tanneries on the banks of the stream. In 1326 there were numerous complaints from citizens concerning the saltiness of THAMES water, caused by a lack of rainwater to dilute the tidal flow. Trade users were sometimes resented, as in 1337 when there was a complaint in the Hustings Court that water supply at the conduit in CHEAPSIDE was inadequate because 'men who keep breweries in the streets and lanes near the conduit send, day after day and night after night, their brewers with their tynes and make the ale which they sell with the water thereof'. Before the end of the 14th century the original conduit supply had clearly proved inadequate. In 1401 a cistern was erected in CORNHILL. And in 1423 two additions to the CITY supplies were created at the expense of Sir Richard Whittington. The first, at BILLINGSGATE, was a boss served by a spring on the site of the COAL EXCHANGE. The other boss was at the churchyard wall of ST GILES CRIPPLEGATE and was possibly served by spring at Crowder's Wells. The 'Standard in Cheapside', formerly a place of execution, was fitted up in 1430 with a small cistern of fresh water having one small cock continually running 'when the same was not turned or locked'.

Wine flowed through the CHEAPSIDE conduit in 1432 to welcome Henry VI after his coronation in Paris. In the same year CHARTERHOUSE received a water supply by aqueduct from ISLINGTON, and the gaols at LUDGATE and NEWGATE were first supplied with water at the same time. Their water may also have come from ISLINGTON, but it could equally well have been derived from the ancient supply to ST BARTHOLOMEW'S PRIORY which is mentioned in Letters Patent of 1433 as having 'run of old'. This supply came from the priory's Manor at CANONBURY, and was shared by the priory and hospital, for which the hospital paid the priory 6s 8d per year. Private philanthropy was always useful in defraying the costs of the conduits. For example, in 1437 John Pope, citizen and barber, willed his estates for the upkeep of the city conduits. And in 1438 the Lord Mayor, Sir William Esfeld, paid for the conversion of the boss created 15 years earlier by Whittington at Cripplegate. Esfeld became the driving force behind the improvement of London's water supplies. He inspired the first major extension in 1439 when springs at PADDINGTON were leased to the city by WESTMINSTER ABBEY at two peppercorns a year. These springs adjoined the WESTBOURNE. About 200 tons of lead were purchased for the pipes. Between 1453 and 1471 Esfeld's estate paid to extend the pipes carrying the PADDINGTON water from TYBURN to a new standard in FLEET STREET.

The City authorities granted 1,000 marks in 1441 for building and restoring conduits, and the following year the Little Conduit at CHEAPSIDE was built. Thereafter the original Cheapside conduit was known as the Great Conduit. The conduit in ALDERMANBURY was completed in 1471 as part of the Esfeld bequest. In 1478 William Campion of FLEET STREET was imprisoned for secretly tapping the nearby conduit supply into a private well, thus depriving his fellow citizens. He was paraded around each of the CITY conduits on horseback with a perforated vessel on his head. Water was constantly poured into the vessel and his offence was proclaimed at each point. In 1479 the Great Conduit in CHEAPSIDE was rebuilt and enlarged. A conduit in GRACECHURCH STREET was built in 1491, halfway between FENCHURCH STREET and EASTCHEAP. 1496 saw the incorporation of the 'Rulers Wardens and Fellowship of the Brotherhood of St Christopher of the Waterbearers of London'. Their Hall stood until 1568 on the west side of BISHOPSGATE on a site now covered by LIVERPOOL STREET STATION. New sources were required as London grew, and in 1543–4 the CITY obtained an Act of Parliament authorising the conveyance of water from springs found at HAMPSTEAD

HEATH, MARYLEBONE, HACKNEY, MUSWELL HILL and 'dyvers places within fyve miles of the said citie'. CITY representatives had authority to 'entre into grounds and possession of every other parsone and there to dig pittes, trenches and dytches and to erect heddes, lay pipes ... without interrupcion'. The Act also gave powers to repair damaged conduits and erect new ones. A new conduit in LOTHBURY followed in 1546. Every year there was a formal inspection of the TYBURN and PADDINGTON springs by the CITY dignitaries. 'The Lord Mayor ... Aldermen, and many worshipful Persons, and divers of the masters and wardens of the twelve companies, rid to the Conduit heads for to see them after the old custom', according to a description of this ceremony written in 1362. 'And afore Dinner they hunted the Hare, and killed her, and thence to dinner at the head of the Conduit. There was a good Number, entertained with good cheer by the Chamberlain. And after Dinner they went Hunting the fox. There was a great cry for a mile, and at length the hounds killed him at the end of St Giles's. Great hallowing at his death and Blowing of horns: and thence the Lord Mayor, with all his Company rode through London to his place in Lombard Street'. The dinner was probably in the LORD MAYOR'S BANQUETING HOUSE that stood on the site of STRATFORD PLACE. In 1577 William Lamb rebuilt the HOLBORN conduit, hence LAMB'S CONDUIT STREET.

The first pumped supply began in 1581 when the CITY CORPORATION granted Pieter Morice a 500-year lease at 10s annually on the first arch of LONDON BRIDGE (see LONDON BRIDGE WATERWORKS). Pumped supplies were gradually thereafter to oust the inefficient gravity conduits. The first major mechanical supply comprising a chain pump worked by horses and supplying a tower about 120ft high, was established by a mining engineer, Bevis Bulmer, at Broken Bridge near ST PAUL'S. This served the CHEAPSIDE and ST PAUL'S area. In 1589 COMMON COUNCIL resolved to spend 1,000 marks to draw 'diverse sprynges about Hampstead Heath into one head and course' in order to improve the flow of the FLEET. The expedient failed; as did an attempt in 1592 to increase the conduit supply by the erection of a windmill at fountain head. In about 1600 a petition was presented to the HOUSE OF COMMONS from 'the whole Company of the poore Water Tankard Bearers of the Cittie of London and the suburbs thereof, they and their families being 4000 in number'. It complained of legal and illegal diminution of the conduit supplies by private quills. The trade of the Water Carriers had also been affected by the new pumped supplies. 'We have water companies now instead of water carryers', Ben Jonson had written in 1598.

The supply to ESSEX HOUSE, STRAND which was permitted in 1601, was cut off in 1608 because the water was wastefully used. Two Acts were obtained by the CITY in 1606 and 1607 enabling the cutting of a channel almost four miles long from Amwell and Chadwell in Hertfordshire to supply London with spring water. At this date there were about 16 conduit supply points in the CITY. The new scheme differed from the previous piped supplies in that it was neither a benefaction nor an undertaking of the CITY authorities. It was a speculation privately financed by Sir Hugh Myddelton and, later, the King (see NEW RIVER COMPANY). And since it was a commercial enterprise, only paying customers received the supplies which cost some 26s annually. A petition of 1631 by the CITY to the Privy Council complained that the CITY's conduit water supply had been 'taken away by diverse persons inhabiting in the Strand and in or near the comon garden' – presumably the new COVENT GARDEN estate. Following this petition, CITY officers were given the right to enter any house or grounds to inspect pipes, providing they gave due notice to 'persons of eminent quality'. Further safeguards were sanctioned concerning possible damage to conduit pipes by building activity. In 1633 the Earl of Bedford was granted a royal licence to obtain water from springs in SOHO for his new estate and other landowners in the area. The last recorded applications to tap the CITY conduits are dated 1662–4. By this time their functions of supply to the wealthier London residents had been taken over by the NEW RIVER COMPANY and the LONDON BRIDGE WATERWORKS. So the era of free water as of right gave way to the era of commercial water.

In 1665 a licence to supply the new ST JAMES'S area (and PICCADILLY and HAYMARKET) was given to Francis Williams and Ralph Wayne. Their springs and water house were probably a few yards north of the junction of modern REGENT STREET and BEAK STREET where there was a messuage known as the Waterhouse in 1673.

In the rebuilding of London after the GREAT FIRE few changes in supply were made. The NEW RIVER COMPANY and LONDON BRIDGE WATERWORKS extended their supply pipes and the decline of conduits was hastened. Several outlets, including even the Great Conduit in CHEAPSIDE, were not rebuilt. The SHADWELL WATERWORKS COMPANY was formed in 1669; the YORK BUILDINGS WATERWORKS was established in 1675; and the HAMPSTEAD WATER COMPANY incorporated in 1692. The proven ability of these commercial water companies to supply adequate quantities of water accelerated the decline of CITY interest in conduit supplies. The essential difference that one was a free supply and the other paid for was ignored. The poor were therefore thrown back to the ancient system of well supply. In areas supplied by a communal pump linked to a company supply, the arrival of water usually depended on the payment of water rates by an absentee landlord; and the supply was never constant, coming on for a few hours daily if at all. In 1708 the *New View of London* commented on the change: 'Conduits were formerly many, being much used, but since there is such plenty of clean, wholesome water brought to people's houses from the New River, Thames, Marrowbone &c. the conduits as the Stock Market, Snow Hill, Cheapside, etc. are of little use'. In 1712 the YORK BUILDING WATERWORKS became the first to use steam power with 'a machine for raising water by fire'. Chelsea Waterworks Company was formed in 1723. And two years later the Swiss visitor de Saussure, gave his general impressions of the London water supply: 'One of the conveniences of London is that everyone can have an abundance of water. The big reservoir or cistern near Islington, the York Buildings machinery near the Strand and that of the bridge supply every quarter abundantly. In every street there is a large principal pipe made of oak wood, and little leaden pipes carry water into all the houses. Every private individual may have one or two fountains in his house, according to his means, and pays so much a year for each – these fountains giving three

hours water in every 24. Besides the pipes, there are in many streets, pumps and wells where poor people who cannot afford to pay for water can obtain it for nothing. Absolutely none is drunk. The lower classes, even the pauper, do not know what it is to quench their thirst with water'.

One of the problems of competitive commercial water supply was the unco-ordinated pipelaying and repairing by rival companies. A street recently excavated for the laying of new pipes could be immediately dug again by another company. During a Parliamentary debate on poor street surfaces in 1728, an MP observed that 'the Public Companies for raising the Thames Water [were] perpetually laying down their pipes or amending them and such a Bill [would] prove to little or no purpose.' This observation provoked the sour response that 'if the water companies Pipe, the members of both Houses must Dance.' In 1746 the Chelsea Company laid the first iron main, though it was to be some time yet before iron took the place of wood and lead. The LONDON BRIDGE WATERWORKS, for example, had 54,000 yards of wood pipe and 3,860 of lead. Elm was usually used since it did not rot. By about 1750 conduits were no longer used.

After the formation of the Southwark Water Company in 1760, and that of the LAMBETH WATER WORKS Company in 1785, several other companies were established between 1805 and 1811: the VAUXHALL WATER COMPANY (1805), the WEST MIDDLESEX WATERWORKS COMPANY (1806), the EAST LONDON WATERWORKS COMPANY (1807), the KENT Waterworks Company (1809) and the GRAND JUNCTION WATERWORKS COMPANY (1811). With the rapid increase in the number of water companies, competition became fierce and bitter. There was no demarcation of company areas. For instance, an 1808 Act extended the HAMMERSMITH-based WEST MIDDLESEX WATER COMPANY to serve MARYLEBONE and KENSINGTON from their new CAMPDEN HILL reservoir and allowed them also to supply the parishes of ST JAMES'S, WESTMINSTER; ST MARY LE STRAND; ST CLEMENT DANES; ST ANNE, SOHO; ST PAUL, COVENT GARDEN; and PADDINGTON. Thus rival pipelines proliferated in streets, while water rates fell sharply. But in 1815 the EAST LONDON COMPANY and the NEW RIVER COMPANY agreed boundaries for creating monopolies within their own areas, and by 1817 all the companies had agreed that competition had depressed water rates and charges to an uneconomic level and acted to increase their profits. Consumer complaints at the new intercompany arrangements resulted in the appointment in 1821 of a committee of the HOUSE OF COMMONS to enquire into 'the state of supply of water to the Metropolis'. This committee concluded that the supply of water should not be subject to the usual laws which govern supply and demand and that 'mutual destruction' of the companies was likely if unfettered competition was allowed to continue. It further endorsed 'the delimitation of areas' and recommended a statutory control of water rates. A bill proposing this and the establishment of referees to arbitrate in disputes between the public and companies did not, however, become law. And, considering themselves vindicated by the committee's observations that 'the present supply of water from London is very superior to that enjoyed by every other city in Europe,' the water companies continued as before. Speculative

'The freshest fruits of microscopical research are the wonders which have been reveald in a drop of London water', Punch, 1849.

enthusiasm spawned several abortive water schemes such as a proposed Thames Water Company (1824) to supply 'pure and unpolluted Thames Water from near Brentford' and a Metropolitan Water Company 'for the supply of the Metropolis with pure and wholesome soft spring water' from a 300 ft deep well.

Since most of the companies still supplied unfiltered water from the THAMES, which was also London's main drain, there was increasing concern over the quality of the water supplied. An 1827 pamphlet was entitled 'The Dolphin or Grand Junction Nuisance, proving that several thousand families in Westminster or its suburbs are supplied with water in a state offensive to the sight, disgusting to the imagination, and destructive to health.' Even the NEW RIVER and LEA supplies were polluted by sewage. In 1827 a Royal Commission was appointed to enquire into the sources of London's water following a petition by the radical, Sir Francis Burdett. This Commission's report concluded that the supply 'ought to be derived from other sources than those now resorted to'. The CHELSEA WATERWORKS COMPANY consequently introduced slow sand filtration in 1829. But this, the first attempt to purify the water supplied, was only gradually adopted by others. And in 1830 a Select Committee of the Commons ordered a survey of alternative sources of supply. As this was being prepared, London's first CHOLERA outbreak occurred in 1831. Even so, the estimated cost of providing alternatives was so high that the report was shelved. Nor were there any significant steps taken after another Select Committee, this time of the Lords, reported its conclusions in 1840.

The Poor Law Commissioner's Sanitary Report of 1842 was a powerful indictment of existing living conditions, of inadequate drains and water supply. It considered a constant water supply to every house an essential element in improved sanitation, and the cost was calculated at 2d per week per house. But too many vested interests were involved for rapid government action, though to satisfy public opinion, a Health of Towns Commission (1844) reinforced the earlier Sanitary Report. The first contained the evidence of the engineer of the EAST LONDON WATERWORKS COMPANY

who contended that it was impossible to keep water at pressure in all the mains and service pipes at the same time and that, therefore, a constant supply was impossible. In contradiction of this opinion, the report instanced the Trent Waterworks which supplied 8,000 Nottingham houses and 35,000 inhabitants with unlimited water and yet paid 5 per cent dividends. The Commission concluded in their second report: 'The results of our enquiries have convinced us that much disease, and many of the inconveniences under which the poorer classes labour, may be alleviated by a plentiful supply of this great necessity of life. All medical men wrote an opinion of the great advantages that a better supply of water will effect in the health of the working classes.' A public water authority was consequently recommended. Chadwick wrote late in 1844, 'The cause is progressing, the evidence is telling and in due time a fullness of opinion will be manifested to carry the measure which can only be carried with the strength of a strong opinion.' In 1845 Chadwick registered a Town Improvements Company to take over public utilities such as drains and water in London and other towns. Despite verbal backing from financiers and the appointment of Thomas Hawksley and Chadwell Milne as water engineers, the company floundered. Yet with the new public knowledge of the consequences of inefficient water supply, the companies were hereafter fighting a defensive battle. In 1847 the Waterworks Clauses Act limited the profits of water companies to 10 per cent and compelled them to provide a constant supply. It also obliged them to supply water for public services, such as baths and washhouses, and for cleaning the sewers and streets.

In 1849 Dr John Snow's pamphlet 'The Mode of Communication of Cholera', was published. It expanded his theory that CHOLERA was caused by 'a poison extracted from a diseased body and passed on through drinking water which had been polluted by sewage.' At the same time conditions in the poorer areas of London shocked Charles Kingsley who wrote, 'I was yesterday . . . over the cholera districts of Bermondsey, and oh God! What I saw! People having no water to drink – hundreds of them – but the water

Despite contrary evidence, the authorities consistently reported that the Thames water was 'of a high standard of excellence'. Caricatures were nearer the truth.

HOW DIRTY OLD FATHER THAMES WAS WHITEWASHED.

of the common sewer . . . full of . . . dead fish, cats and dogs.' In 1850 there were still 80,000 houses in London, inhabited by 640,000 persons, still not with water. Arthur Hassall's *Microscopic Examination of the Water supplied to the Inhabitants of London* revealed 'that the waters supplied by those Metropolitan Companies whose source is the Thames, are in a high degree impure and, therefore, unfit for use, and detrimental to health: in this condemnation the waters of the Companies which supply the Surrey side of London, viz. the Vauxhall, Southwark and Lambeth ought to stand first. The only Thames water supplied to the public in a condition *approaching* even to purity is that (as it would appear) by the Chelsea Company. The waters supplied by the remaining companies, although purer than the former, are yet by no means in the condition required for comfort, health or even safety.' Hassall noted the coincidence of CHOLERA in those areas with the most polluted supplies, the stagnation of water in reservoirs and cisterns, and he summarised the indispensable conditions for a proper supply to London as 'an unpolluted source: an unlimited supply: perpetual renewal: filtration: the abolition of modification of reservoirs and cisterns and: moderate cost.' He continued, 'It is beyond dispute that, according to the present system of London Water Supply, a portion of the inhabitants of the metropolis are made to consume, in some form or other, a portion of their own excrement, and moreover, to pay for the privilege. Shall this state of things be permitted to last? Is it possible that a system so infamous can long prevail? In the name of decency so outraged and the laws of health so violated, I trust not.'

In 1850 Edwin Chadwick's *Report on the Supply of Water to the Metropolis* contained three main recommendations: 'That the London water supply should be derived from new sources: that the water companies should be bought out on behalf of the public: and that an executive commission should be appointed to administer the combined water supply and drainage services.' But the new Bill for the Metropolitan Water Supply was sponsored by the Home Office and the General Board of Health was only formally consulted. The Bill attempted to vest the capital of the water companies in the public while guaranteeing the existing proprietors an annual dividend of 5 per cent on £4,800,000 which was the capital value of the Companies as assessed by the proprietors themselves. After being passed at its second reading by 95 votes to 79, the Bill floundered in a Select Committee faced with a plethora of conflicting advice and issues. The Prime Minister, Lord John Russell, then announced that the Government did not intend to legislate on water supply during the present session. A letter subsequently published in *The Times* (14 July 1851) illustrates the uncertainty and irregularity of London water supplies: 'Monday – water six inches. Cook and housemaid on short allowance. Master's bath relinquished. Tuesday – water one inch. Boiled vegetables and teas strictly forbidden. Wednesday – cistern dry; water no where. Thursday – the water on. Hurrah. Listen to that rushing sound. We shall drink – we shall wash – we shall bathe! Ah, in five minutes the stream ceases, and all our hopes are blighted.' At the GREAT EXHIBITION the authorities were required 'to supply *gratis*, pure water in glasses to all visitors demanding it'. *Punch* commented, 'whoever can produce in London a glass of water fit to drink will contribute the best and most universally useful article in the whole exhibition.' In 1852 the Metropolitan Water Act was passed, which

tackled some of the most blatant abuses of the water companies. Those companies supplying THAMES water were forced to move their intakes above TEDDINGTON Lock into the non-tidal river. All reservoirs within five miles of ST PAUL'S were to be covered and all domestic water was to be filtered. A constant supply of water was made obligatory if it was requested. The Companies were allowed a generous three years to move their intakes except the CHELSEA WATERWORKS COMPANY which was given four years, and a very generous five years to comply with the other measures. Maximum penalties were only £250. Clauses proscribing competition between the companies and scheduling uniform rates were dropped at the committee stage of the Bill. Joseph Hume observed in the debate on the Bill that 86 MPs were shareholders in water companies. In the previous year Sir Benjamin Hall's estimate was 70. Chadwick had complained that in Parliament his board's measures were discussed in 'an atmosphere of shareholders' and that 'shareholders and shareholders' agents appeared as impartial public representatives.' In 1853 the LAMBETH WATERWORKS COMPANY became the first to move its intake above the tideway as required by the Act. Its death rate fell to 37 deaths per 10,000 compared with that of the SOUTHWARK AND VAUXHALL WATER COMPANY of 130 deaths per 10,000. Sir John Simon accused the SOUTHWARK AND VAUXHALL WATER COMPANY of 'criminal indifference'.

The problem of constant supply had yet to be solved. In 1862 the Medical Officer of Health for WHITECHAPEL reported that in 48 of the 133 courts in the district the water supply was only by stand taps which supplied water daily (except on Sundays) for a period varying from a quarter to half an hour. These 48 courts comprised 388 houses occupied by 3,233 persons. Nor had the problem of polluted water been solved. CHOLERA was still rife and many Londoners still relied on well supplies. In 1866, 35 public well pumps remained in use in the CITY OF LONDON. In 1866 the Richmond Commission, which was appointed to investigate the water supply of the metropolis, recommended that the work of the water companies should be transferred to a public body. But this recommendation was not implemented. The completion of the Bazelgette sewage scheme did, however, at last remove one danger of pollution to the water supplies:

In the early 1860s water was still supplied to many London streets only by stand taps for the briefest periods.

931

the last major epidemic of CHOLERA was in 1868. But water continued to be a matter of major public concern, though the diversity of views on sources of supply, what constituted purity and the strong vested interest of the Companies militated against reform. A Royal Commission recommended the introduction of a constant service under public control in 1869 and Sir John Simon noted the 'colossal power of life and death' of the companies. At last the 1871 Metropolis Water Act attempted remedies. It obliged companies to supply water on Sundays, but merely empowered the METROPOLITAN BOARD OF WORKS to request a constant supply of water to any area and under certain conditions empowered the Board of Trade to compel a company to give a constant supply. The companies were still permitted to cut off the supply if the water rates were not paid. The Medical Officer of Health for WANDSWORTH wrote, 'Perhaps there never was an Act of Parliament so completely ignored in many districts as the one in question.' But the Act did provide for an impartial water examiner to submit monthly and annual reports to the Local Government Board and periodically to inspect the companies' work. A government auditor was also appointed to report on the water companies' accounts. In 1874 the Rivers Pollution Commission recommended the abandonment of the THAMES and LEA as sources of supply. By 1875 only four public well pumps remained in the CITY OF LONDON. The Commissioners of Sewers for the City recommended these should be closed and warned of 'the danger that may arise from the water being used for drinking purposes.'

Little progress had yet been made in the matter of constant supply. Only 53 per cent of houses in London had a constant supply of water, according to a Select Committee on Fire Brigades in 1876, although an estimated 116,250,000 gallons of water daily were supplied by the nine water companies in 1877. In 1878 a conference on water supplies was sponsored by the Prince of Wales at the ROYAL SOCIETY OF ARTS. The following year the Prince wrote to the Earl of Beaconsfield suggesting the appointment of a Royal Commission on water supply. This Commission recommended that the supply should be placed in the hands of a public body. But again the recommendation was not implemented. And in 1884 a Metropolitan Water Bill curbing the water companies, whose revenue was estimated to be well over £1,500,000 a year, was rejected by the Commons. There were further abortive Water Bills in 1885–6. However, the Water Companies (Regulation of Power Act) of 1877 prohibited the companies from cutting off the water supply from any dwelling house for non-payment of the water rate, if such rate were payable by the owner and not the occupier of the premises. In 1890 the new LONDON COUNTY COUNCIL and the CITY CORPORATION jointly recommended the replacement of the water companies by a public body. But there were two more abortive Water Bills in 1891; and in 1893 the Balfour Commission on Water Supplies reported: 'We are strongly of the opinion that the water supplied to the consumer of London is of a very high standard of excellence and of purity and that it is suitable in quality for all household purposes ... We do not believe that any danger exists of the spread of disease by the use of this water, provided that there is adequate storage and that the water is efficiently filtered before delivery to the consumers.' The Commission, did, however recommend the construction of reservoirs in the Thames Valley.

Although the Water Companies continued to receive adverse publicity throughout 1895 it was not until 1897 that yet another Commission, the Llandaff Commission, was appointed to review the problems. As a result of this Commission's recommendations the Metropolis Water Act was passed in 1902. And by this Act a METROPOLITAN WATER BOARD was at last created to take over the eight private water companies at a cost of about £40 million. The board became operational in 1904, and its headquarters were established in the NEW RIVER COMPANY's offices in ROSEBERY AVENUE at New River Head. The board comprised 66 delegated members, 14 from the LONDON COUNTY COUNCIL, 31 from the Metropolitan Borough Councils and CITY CORPORATION and 21 from the authorities of localities outside the water companies' areas. From 1907 widespread reservoir and waterworks building was carried out. The Round Pond, New River Head was abandoned in 1914, and in 1920 the rebuilt New River Company's headquarters were opened in ROSEBERY AVENUE. The Queen Mary Reservoir, with a capacity of 6,679 million gallons, was opened in 1925. In 1947 the King George VI reservoir was inaugurated at Staines, and the William Girling reservoir at CHINGFORD. In April 1974 the administration of the Metropolitan Water Board was transferred to the new Thames Water Authority. The Authority now supplies about 2,000 million litres of water a day in the London area. Natural sources are usually sufficient, but when the flows of the THAMES and the LEA are diminished water is drawn from the 169,000 million litre reservoir capacity in the authority's area. The principal treatment works in the London area are at HAMPTON, Ashford Common, and Coppermills near Lea Bridge.

Waterloo Bridge *Victoria Embankment–Waterloo*. The first bridge constructed on this site was designed by John Rennie and built in 1811–17 by the contractors Joliffe and Banks. It was opened by the Prince Regent on the second anniversary of the Battle of Waterloo, 18 June 1817. Described by Canova as 'the noblest bridge in the world, worth a visit from the remotest corners of the earth,' it was a granite bridge with nine elliptical arches and pairs of Doric columns at the piers. Originally it was known as the Strand Bridge, but in 1816 an Act of Parliament changed its name to Waterloo Bridge, since 'the said bridge when completed will be a work of great stability and magnificence, and such works are adapted to transmit to posterity the remembrance of great and glorious achievements.' It was freed from tolls in 1877. In 1923 two of its piers settled alarmingly and a temporary bridge was built alongside. Despite strong protests, it was demolished in 1936, and in 1937–42 replaced by the present bridge of cantilevered reinforced concrete box girders by Rendel, Palmer and Tritton, with Sir Giles Gilbert Scott as architect.

Waterloo Place *SW1*. Begun in 1816 as a termination of Nash's REGENT STREET by opening a vista of CARLTON HOUSE which stood on the south side of PALL MALL. Named in honour of the recent battle, it is shown on an 1818 plan marked as 'Square', though only marginally wider than REGENT STREET itself. CLEOPATRA'S NEEDLE was mentioned in 1821 as a possible central feature. In 1826 CARLTON HOUSE was demolished. On the southern part of the site CARLTON HOUSE GARDENS were laid out, and Waterloo Place was extended to link PALL MALL and the new development. The ATHENAEUM and UNITED SERVICES CLUB purchased the flanking sites with frontages to PALL MALL. The CROWN COMMISSIONERS originally insisted that the Waterloo Place façades of the clubs should be identical, but a prolonged and complicated wrangle between the various parties, including Nash himself as architect to the United Services, resulted only in similar elevations. The DUKE OF YORK COLUMN and steps were completed by 1833 at the south end. Outside the ATHENAEUM is the horse mount of the hero of Waterloo inscribed, 'This horse block was erected by desire of the Duke of Wellington 1830.' During 1902–25 the northern end of Waterloo Place was gradually rebuilt with Portland stone elevations, but the arrangement is symmetrical. It is now the resting place of a number of statues: the Guards Crimean Memorial (see MEMORIALS) group is to the north of PALL MALL and the equestrian Edward VII to the south (the latter ousted the statue of Field Marshal Napier, now at the north end of QUEENSGATE, in 1920). On the east side are statues of Lord Lawrence, Colin Campbell (Lord Clyde), and Captain R.F. Scott. On the west are Sir John Burgoyne and Sir John Franklin (see STATUES).

Waterloo Station   *York Road, SE1*. In 1845 the London and South Western Railway (the new name, since 1840, of the London and Southampton) obtained powers to build a terminus in York Road, near WATERLOO BRIDGE. The line was extended over the LAMBETH Marsh from NINE ELMS by means of a curved brick viaduct of 290 arches. Waterloo Station was opened in 1848. It was at first laid out as a through station, since it was intended to extend the line into the CITY, and the station buildings were described as 'temporary'. More permanent buildings were erected in 1853. Until the end of the 19th century more platforms were constantly and somewhat haphazardly added, as a result of increasing traffic. In 1864 the South Eastern Railway extended their line from London Bridge and opened another station at Waterloo, on the eastern side of the main terminus. It was originally connected with the main station by rail; a bridge across Waterloo Road now links the two. From 1854 the London Necropolis Company's funeral traffic to Brookwood Cemetery left from 'the Necropolis Station' just outside Waterloo and for many years there was a 'daily funeral express, down and back.' An early price list shows a charge of 2s 6d per coffin. In 1899 a link with the CITY was at last made by the construction of an underground 'tube' railway from Waterloo to the BANK. Still in use today, it is known as the 'Drain' and is the only underground railway in London not owned and operated by London Transport. By the end of the 19th century, Waterloo was handling about 700 trains a day from a random collection of platforms. It was described as 'the most perplexing railway station in London,' and the South Western decided to pull it all down and build a new station. Plans were drawn up by J.W. Jacomb-Hood and the work went on from 1900 to 1922. After Jacomb-Hood's death in 1914, rebuilding was continued by A.W. Szumper and J.R. Scott. Little of the earlier station remains, except the roof over platforms 18–21, with its supporting walls and columns, which date from 1885. In 1922 Queen Mary opened the new

Waterloo Station, with its 21 platforms in a west-facing crescent, served by a broad concourse 120 ft wide and 770 ft long. The main pedestrian entrance arch serves as a memorial to staff killed in 1st World War. Air raid shelters were made in the arches under the station during 2nd World War. The station itself suffered considerably from bombing (including the Necropolis Station which was demolished by a land-mine). A few main-line steam trains ran to and from Waterloo until as late as 1967, the last in southern England. Waterloo remains an important Southern Region terminus, handling in 1982 1,272 trains a day.

Waterlow Park   *N6*. An area of 29 acres on the south of HIGHGATE HILL named after Sir Sidney Waterlow, Lord Mayor of London and philanthropist. Lauderdale House was built in these grounds in 1660 for the Duke of Lauderdale. He intrigued both against Charles I and, after the Restoration, against the Covenanters. While he was away pursuing Charles II's enemies, Charles borrowed his house for Nell Gwynne. In 1666 Pepys visited the house for dinner where 'there played one of their servants upon the viollin some Scotch tunes only . . . but Lord! the strangest ayre that I ever heard in my life and all of one cast.'

In 1872 Lauderdale House and its grounds were presented by Sir Sidney Waterlow to ST BARTHOLOMEW'S HOSPITAL for use as a convalescent home. It was converted and furnished for this purpose at his expense and opened by the Prince and Princess of Wales. After its disuse by the hospital, both house and grounds were given by Waterlow to the LONDON COUNTY COUNCIL in 1889. There is a statue of Waterlow in the park (see STATUES). Naomi Blake's bonded bronze abstract *Image* (1979) is also here.

Waterman's Arms   *1 Glenaffric Avenue, E14*. Once owned by the writer Daniel Farson, this public house was originally the Newcastle Arms. It has been converted into an exact reproduction of a Victorian public house.

Watermen *and* **Lightermen**   From early times up to the 19th century the THAMES served as London's main thoroughfare. It was filled with craft of every kind. So lightermen to carry loads from ships to quays and watermen to carry passengers formed an important fraternity in London's economic and social life. Travel on the river was for centuries the cheapest, safest, most pleasant and most rapid means of transport, even for long journeys down to Gravesend or up to Windsor. Thousands of wherries plied the river and carried passengers from bank to bank or up and down the tideway. The cry for 'Oars' from river stairs and piers (see WATER GATES) reverberated down the years. As well as conveying commoners on their daily rounds, watermen were also needed to row the carved and gilded grand barges of the Sovereign, the LORD MAYOR, and dignitaries of the CITY LIVERY COMPANIES on state occasions and festivities. The tradition began in 1454 when Sir John Norman, Lord Mayor elect, built himself a magnificent rowing barge by which he could proceed to WESTMINSTER from the CITY and back on the water instead of by carriage or on horseback along the STRAND, as Lord Mayors had hitherto travelled, an event that so elated the watermen that they caused a commemorative song to be composed for the occasion which began 'Row thy boat, Norman.'

Rowlandson in 1812 caricatures one of the 'miseries of London' – being assailed by watermen crying 'Oars, Sculls, Sculls, Oars, Oars'.

Watermen have always been a sturdy, rough breed with their own jargon and as quick with raillery and repartee as with their fists. Their ribaldry was proverbial and often so indecent that an order was issued by their Company in 1761 imposing a fine of 2s 6d for each verbal offence, the fines to benefit 'the poor, aged, decayed, and maimed members of the Company, their widows and children'. The aim of all watermen was to be buried at their deaths in fraternal comradeship on the south side of the churchyard of ST MARTIN'S-IN-THE-FIELDS. Before 1514 watermen were nominally controlled by the CITY CORPORATION, but that year the earliest Act dealing with them was passed, mainly designed to suppress extortionate charges. A more important Act came in 1555 by which the CITY CORPORATION was to appoint annually eight selected watermen to be called overseers or rulers to redress any abuses that occurred between GREENWICH and Windsor. It also stipulated that all watermen were to serve their apprenticeships, become licensed and to row wherries of minimum sizes of 20 ft 6 ins long and 4 ft 6 ins wide amidships, such craft to be properly built, registered, numbered and regularly inspected. Fares were to be fixed by the CITY CORPORATION, subject to endorsement by the Privy Council, while any waterman avoiding impressment into the Navy were to be imprisoned for two weeks and banished from the river for a year and a day thereafter. The Act brought about the formation of the WATERMEN'S COMPANY, which was referred to in an Act of 1603 when its Hall stood at Coldharbour in the Vintry. Burnt down in the GREAT FIRE, the Hall was rebuilt on the same site, but in 1780 the Company moved to ST MARY-AT-HILL near BILLINGSGATE, where it still stands today. The building has a handsome front of stone with coupled Ionic pilasters and a large tripartite Palladian window.

Inside hangs the portrait of the Company's most renowned member, the water poet, John Taylor. In Taylor's time, during the reign of Elizabeth I, some 40,000 watermen earned their livings on the river between Gravesend and Windsor, 3,000 of them between WESTMINSTER and LONDON BRIDGE. By the close of the 18th century there were only about 20,000 of whom 4,000 were enrolled for spells in the Navy.

Watermen have always voiced their grievances, a frequent one being impressment. In 1667 they were at odds for a while with the lightermen for carrying passengers as well as goods, a dispute which was settled by the Act of 1700 when the two groups were united into one body. An earlier grievance had arisen at the beginning of the 17th century when hackney coaches and sedan chairs were beginning to clutter the London streets threatening the watermen's virtual monopoly of passenger conveyance. John Taylor called attention to the plight of his fellows in 'a rattling, rowling and rumbling age' and broke into his customary doggerel thus:

Carroaches, coaches, jades and Flanders mares
Do rob us of our shares, our wares, our fares;
Against the ground we stand and knock our heeles,
Whilst all our profit runns away on wheels.

In fact, the real threats to the watermen did not arrive until late in the Georgian period when the building of new bridges reduced the need for ferries. When BLACKFRIARS BRIDGE was opened and the ferry there, which had been producing revenue for the Watermen's Poor Fund, became redundant, the bridge committee in sympathy compensated the WATERMEN'S COMPANY with £13,650 Consolidated Three Per Cents. The building of the enclosed docks reduced the need for lightermen, and finally, the arrival of steam boats on the river and the increase of land traffic rendered the watermen increasingly unnecessary. With the growth of the PORT OF LONDON, lightermen suffered less than watermen, whose occupation almost vanished. In 1900 the trade was thrown open to any worker and in 1909 the new PORT OF LONDON AUTHORITY took over most of the old powers of the Master Wardens and Commonalty of Watermen and Lightermen of the River Thames as the Company had become entitled in an Act of 1827. Yet watermen and lightermen are an enduring race and some will always be needed on the river. The surviving COMPANY still examines new apprentices and, if they are successful, admits them to its Freedom. (*See also* TRANSPORT.)

Watermen and Lightermen's Hall *18 St Mary-at-Hill, EC3.* The Company's first hall was in UPPER THAMES STREET in the 17th century. This was destroyed in the GREAT FIRE and rebuilt in 1670 and again in 1720. The move to St Mary-at-Hill took place in 1780. After damage in the 2nd World War, the hall was repaired and improved in 1951 and 1961, the architect being Henry V. Gordon. (*See also* WATERMEN AND LIGHTERMEN.)

Watling Street *EC4.* First mentioned in 1230. The earliest form of the name was Athelyngestrate. It was probably an offshoot of the main Roman Watling Street between Dover and St Albans. In it once stood the TOWER ROYAL which was destroyed in the GREAT FIRE. The church of ST ANTHOLIN was demolished in 1874 and the St Antholin lectures, formerly given there, are now given at ST MARY WOOLNOTH, ST BARTHOLOMEW-THE-GREAT and ST MARY ALDERMARY. The tower of ST AUGUSTINE remains and it attached to ST PAUL'S CHOIR SCHOOL.

Wax Chandlers' Company *see* CITY LIVERY COMPANIES.

Wealdstone *Harrow, Middlesex.* Derives its name from a sarson stone embedded in the pavement outside the Red Lion at Harrow Weald. The stone, on a pre-Roman trackway, is one of several in the area and may have marked the boundary between the parish of HARROW and ancient Waldis (HARROW WEALD). Modern Wealdstone owes its origin and subsequent development to the coming of the London and Birmingham Railway in 1837. The station was completely rebuilt in 1911 to designs by G. Horsley; the pierced parapet still displays the inscription of the old London and North-Western Railway. Wealdstone is now largely industrial. It was in the hall of the extensive Kodak factory (*see* KODAK MUSEUM) that HARROW received its borough status in 1954. Whitefriars Glass Works, founded in 1667, moved to Wealdstone in 1923 but closed in 1980. Wealdstone High Street has three churches: the parish church of Holy Trinity (1881) by Roumieu and Aitchison; the Baptist Church (1905) in redbrick with a 75 ft tower by John Wills; and St Joseph's Catholic Church (1931) by A.G. Scott.

Weavers' Company *see* CITY LIVERY COMPANIES.

Webber Douglas Academy of Dramatic Art Ltd *Chanticleer Theatre, 30–36 Clareville Street, SW7.* Opened in 1926 by Amherst Webber and W.J. Douglas as a School of Singing, by the end of the 2nd World War it has become associated principally with acting and in 1966 assumed its present title. The Chanticleer Theatre, one of the first specifically designed for a drama school, was constructed in 1932 in the gardens behind houses dating from 1842.

Weeks's Mechanical Museum *3 Tichborne Street, Haymarket.* Opened in about 1803 as a successor to COX'S MUSEUM some of whose mechanical exhibits were displayed here. The exhibition room was designed by James Wyatt and contained musical clocks, life-size automaton musicians, mechanical mice, birds and other animals including a steel tarantula whose 115 pieces convincingly demonstrated the spider's movements 'much to the alarm of lady visitors'. After the death of Weeks's last surviving son most of these exhibits, by then much dilapidated, were sold at CHRISTIE'S.

Welbeck Street *W1.* Built about 1720 by John Price and named after Welbeck, Nottinghamshire, the family seat of the Cavendishes who were related to the ground landlords. Many 18th-century houses remain. Anthony Trollope lived at No. 34 in 1862; Thomas Young, scientist and writer on many subjects, who deciphered the Rosetta Stone, lived at No. 48 in 1802–25; Thomas Woolner, the sculptor and poet, at No. 29 in 1860–92. The Clifton-Ford Hotel on the west side has 229 bedrooms.

Well Hall *Well Hall Road, Eltham, SE9.* A converted barn probably built in the early 16th century (the date-stone of 1568 is thought to be a later addition). It was part of the Elizabethan manor house of William Roper, Sir Thomas More's son-in-law and biographer. The house remained in the Roper family until 1733 when it was sold to Sir Gregory Page, who pulled it down and built his own house. From 1899 to 1922 the house was occupied by Edith Nesbit and was featured in some of her children's stories. In 1930 it was bought by WOOLWICH Borough Council and was demolished the following year. The surrounding park was also bought by the Council. The barn was converted into an art gallery and restaurant.

Well Street *EC1.* Extended from JEWIN STREET to Nicholl Square. Stow said it was named after Crowder's Well, 'a fair pool of clear water near unto the parsonage on the west side'. It was laid waste by bombs in the 2nd World War and the site now forms part of the BARBICAN redevelopment.

Well Walk *Hampstead, NW3.* For the first 20 years of the 18th century, HAMPSTEAD was famous as a Spa (*see* HAMPSTEAD WELLS). Here in Well Walk, near the entrance to the present day Gainsborough Gardens, stood the Great Room, a huge building, 80 ft long, containing the Assembly Room, for dances and concerts, and the Pump Room where visitors came to drink the waters. But the spa became somewhat disreputable as undesirable visitors crowded in for gambling sessions, and the Great Room was finally sold and turned into a chapel. (The building was demolished in 1882). Later a new building known as the Long Room was constructed near BURGH HOUSE and a second spa was launched; and this was visited by, among others, Dr Johnson, Garrick, Fielding and Fanny Burney. Toward the beginning of the 19th century this spa in its turn became unfashionable and the Long Room

Well Walk, Hampstead, takes its name from the chalybeate spring which brought fame and fashion to the area.

became a private residence, Weatherall House. John Masefield lived here for a time; the house was demolished in 1948 and Wells House – a block of council flats – was built on the site. The Wells Hotel stands on the site of the Green Man public house, near which was the house were John Keats lodged and devotedly nursed his younger brother, Tom, until the latter's death from consumption in 1818. Constable also lived in Well Walk, at No. 40, where a BLUE PLAQUE is on the wall. 'A comfortable little house in Well Walk,' he called it, but it was a sad house after his wife died in 1828, leaving him with seven children.

Other distinguished inhabitants of Well Walk include H.M. Hyndman, the Socialist leader (No. 13); D.H. Lawrence (No. 32), the architect Ewan Christian (No. 50) and J.B. Priestley (No. 27).

A Victorian fountain marks the spot where flowed the chalybeate spring which brought fame to the area. The fountain, was recently restored. The water is now considered unfit for drinking.

Wellclose Square *E1*. One of the liberties of the TOWER. The square was laid out towards the end of the 17th century, with many sea captains making their homes there. A Danish church, designed by C.G. Cibber, was built in 1696 and stood on the site now occupied by St Paul's school. Wilton's Theatre, a music hall in Grace's Alley leading off the square, was opened in 1859 and is to be preserved.

Wellcome Institute for the History of Medicine *183 Euston Road, NW1*. Houses the remarkable library originally amassed by Sir Henry Wellcome, the manufacturing chemist and patron of science. It is devoted to all aspects of the history of medicine and cognate fields. It contains more than 400,000 printed books (650 incunabula), 5,000 Western and 9,000 Oriental manuscripts, 100,000 autograph letters, over 100,000 prints and drawings, 900 oil paintings and a photographic archive of 38,000 prints, negatives and slides. The Collection continues to grow through the support of the Wellcome Trustees. The Institute also contains an academic staff with joint appointments at UNIVERSITY COLLEGE. The Library is free and open to students and persons doing private research.

Wellcome Museum of the History of Medicine *Science Museum, Exhibition Road, SW7*. In addition to acquiring a large library (see WELLCOME INSTITUTE), Sir Henry Wellcome amassed a vast collection of artifacts – Western and non-Western – reflecting his vision of medicine as essentially an anthropological science. In 1976 this collection was transferred on permanent loan to the SCIENCE MUSEUM, SOUTH KENSINGTON, where two Wellcome Galleries display a selection of the artefacts illustrating many facets of the history of medicine.

Welling *Kent*. Originally a staging post of coaches on the Dover Road. It lies half in BEXLEY and half in neighbouring EAST WICKHAM.

Wellington Barracks *Birdcage Walk, SW1*. These barracks, long associated with the Foot Guards, were in 1982 undergoing extensive reconstruction. The chapel, replacing the one destroyed by a German flying bomb in 1944, is in use (see GUARDS' CHAPEL); so also is the main parade ground. The buildings,

Apsley House at Hyde Park Corner, home of the Duke of Wellington, became the Wellington Museum in 1952.

expected to be completed in 1983, provide accommodation for a regimental headquarters staff of the five regiments of Foot Guards, a museum, and a Guards battalion.

Wellington Museum *Hyde Park Corner, SW1*. Housed in Apsley House, which was built in 1771–8 by Robert Adam for Henry Bathurst, the Lord Chancellor, universally recognised as the most inefficient holder of that office in the 18th century. His father had married the daughter of Sir Allen Apsley, and Baron Apsley is the second title of the Earls Bathurst. It was the Duke of Wellington who faced the brick walls with Bath stone, added the Corinthian portico and enlarged the house to the designs of Benjamin and Philip Wyatt. The house was presented to the nation in 1947 by the 7th Duke of Wellington, and opened as the Wellington Museum in 1952. On account of its great Waterloo Gallery, wide range of rooms and finely proportion architecture and appointments, it provides an admirable setting for the numerous exhibits associated with the famous soldier and statesman, the 1st Duke of Wellington. With a setting of appropriate furniture, the exhibition includes many fine paintings, trophies, uniforms, decorations, batons and weapons, plate and porcelain. A colossal marble statue of Napoleon by Canova is of special note and, among the busts, one of the Duke himself by Nollekens is considered an excellent likeness. The large collection of pictures, in which over 90 painters are represented, has been acquired in two ways: there are those bought by, or given to, the Duke and those captured from Joseph Bonaparte at the Battle of Vittoria.

Wellington Square *SW3*. Small square built in about 1830 and named after the Duke of Wellington whose brother was rector of CHELSEA 1805–36.

HMS Wellington Moored in KING'S REACH opposite THE TEMPLE, the floating livery hall of the Honourable Company of Master Mariners.

Wellington Street *WC2*. The north part between RUSSELL and TAVISTOCK STREETS was built in 1631–5 and named Charles Street after King Charles I. In 1691–5 Robert King and Johann Franck gave vocal and instrumental concerts in an auction room here. In

1721–40 Colley Cibber had a house in the street. Next door lived Barton Booth, the actor, in 1721–33. Wellington Street was built from TAVISTOCK STREET to the STRAND in 1833–5 over the site of the English Opera House which had been burned down in 1830. In 1844 Charles Street had become notorious for brothels, and an attempt was made to clothe it in respectability by renaming it Upper Wellington Street. On the site of No. 18 stood Bielefeld's papier mâché works in 1839–61. The present building was designed by C.O. Parnell in 1863–4 for the now defunct Victorian Club. The portico of the LYCEUM DANCE HALL on the west side is all that remains of the Lyceum Theatre. Penhaligon's, the perfumers, are at No. 41. W.H. Penhaligon was Court Barber toward the end of the reign of Queen Victoria. He had a shop in JERMYN STREET at the back of which he made perfumes, toilet water and pomades. He moved to OLD BOND STREET in 1870. The firm moved to Wellington Street in 1975.

Welsh Harp Reservoir On the borders of HENDON, KINGSBURY and WILLESDEN, it is named after an old alehouse which stood on the EDGWARE ROAD. It is one of several water supplies for the GRAND UNION CANAL. The dam head was built across the River BRENT in 1834–5 to give greater effect to the canal feeder which had been constructed through STONEBRIDGE earlier in 1810. From about 1860 to 1910 the reservoir and its public house were very popular places of recreation and entertainment and figure in Victorian music-hall songs. The first mechanical hare was tried out here in a greyhound race in 1876. It is also known as the Brent Reservoir.

Wembley *Middlesex*. In appearance Wembley is a suburb of the 1920s and 1930s but on closer examination there are Victorian cores to most of its districts (*see* ALPERTON, PRESTON *and* SUDBURY) and some older buildings as well. Wembley was first recorded as Wemba Lea in 825. Its early development lay around Wembley Green and Wembley Hill. Present-day Wembley Central to the west is the offspring of the London to Birmingham railway which passed through what had been an agricultural landscape in 1837. A station was built in 1844 but its effect on development was slow and Wembley Central did not begin to grow until 1880–95. The coming of the trams in 1908 brought with it improved communications encouraging further expansion of the village community.

Wembley Park to the north originated as a private estate owned by Richard Page for whom it was landscaped by Humphry Repton in 1793. The Metropolitan Railway passed through the Park in 1880 and the whole estate was acquired by the Railway Company in 1889 for a leisure centre for north-west London. For this new venture a station was opened at Wembley Park in 1894. Later, the site was chosen for the British Empire Exhibition of 1924–5. The Exhibition which attracted 27 million people to Wembley required the reconstruction and realignment of many of the country lanes, thus opening up a rural backwater to bus traffic and motor cars alike and encouraging suburban development (*see also* WEMBLEY STADIUM). Arthur Lucan, the entertainer and creator of 'Old Mother Riley', lived at 11 Forty Lane.

Wembley Stadium *Wembley, Middlesex*. Built in 1922–3 as a multipurpose athletics and entertainments centre for the British Empire Exhibition of 1924–5. It was completed in time for the 1923 Football Association Cup Final in which Bolton beat WEST HAM. Most of the Exhibition buildings were designed by Sir John Simpson and Maxwell Ayrton (Sir Owen Williams being the engineer) and built in ferroconcrete. The open-air Stadium had a capacity of 120,000, now reduced to 100,000. Notable additions to the Exhibition buildings include Wembley Arena, built in 1933–4 as the Empire Pool by Sir Owen Williams and now used for entertainments such as ice shows, as well as sport. The 14th Olympic Games were held at Wembley in 1948. Fanny Blankers-Koen of the Netherlands, winner of four gold medals, was the *Victrix Ludorum* – the first time a woman had won the title. The stadium is now used for international football and hockey matches, greyhound racing, speedway racing, the Football Association Cup Final and Rugby League finals. The Palace of Industry (which at the time of the 1924–5 Exhibition displayed products from chemicals to cotton and from furniture to pottery) and the Palace of Arts (which contained art from Hogarth's age onwards – including furnished rooms of different periods) both survive today as industrial warehousing units.

Near the Wembley Arena is the Wembley Conference Centre, designed by R. Seifert and Partners, and built in 1973–6. The seating capacity of the main auditorium is 2,700.

Wennington *Essex*. Recorded as Winintune in AD 969. The original manor at the extreme south-east of HAVERING BOROUGH belonged to Edward the Confessor and later to WESTMINSTER ABBEY. It was eventually subdivided – into the manors of Wennington Hall, Leventhorpe and Noke. The marsh beside the THAMES known as Wennington Level stretches from the village on the edge of the modern London-Tilbury road right down to Great Coldharbour on the Thames bank. The small church of St Mary and St Peter is much restored. A doorway with diapered work has survived from the original church erected just after the Norman Conquest. Outside is the amazing mathematical tomb of Henry Perigal.

Wesley's Chapel *and* **House** *City Road, SE1*. The foundation stone of Wesley's Chapel was laid by John Wesley on 21 April, 1777 when he was 74 years old, the site being part of a field recovered from swamp by dumping soil from the excavations for ST PAUL'S CATHEDRAL. The Chapel was opened for public worship on 1 November, 1778. Damaged by fire in 1879 and considerably altered in 1891 on the centenary of Wesley's death, this mother-church of world Methodism survived the 2nd World War but was in such a bad state of repair by 1972 as to be declared unfit for public use. Between 1972 and 1978, nearly a £1 million was raised from all over the world, enabling the restored building to be reopened in the presence of the Queen and the Duke of Edinburgh on 1 November, 1978 – 200 years to the day after it was originally brought into use by John Wesley.

John Wesley is buried in a grave behind the Chapel and, beside the front courtyard (No. 47 City Road) lies the house, full of Wesleyana, where he lived when in London.

West Cromwell Road *SW5, W15*. Extends westward from CROMWELL ROAD to North End Road, crossing the railway between EARL'S COURT and OLYMPIA. Like CROMWELL ROAD it contains numerous small hotels.

West Drayton *Middlesex*. Lies between UXBRIDGE and HEATHROW AIRPORT. It was originally known as Draegtun – a place where boats were dragged across land in order to avoid a river bend. The Manor was owned by the Dean of ST PAUL'S at the time of the Conquest and remained so until 1546 when it was surrendered to the Crown. Henry VIII then granted it to his Secretary of State, Sir William Paget. Part of the site of Paget's manor house was excavated by the MUSEUM OF LONDON in 1979–80. In 1838 the Great Western Railway held its first trials at West Drayton and the station, the first stop from PADDINGTON, was opened. This was an important event for West Drayton as it opened up the district to London. The area was mainly an agricultural and brickmaking district until the beginning of the 20th century when a few factories were opened. Its residential development was slow until the 1920s when its easy access to London encouraged the development of private housing estates and also a certain amount of council house building following a slum clearance scheme. The opening of HEATHROW AIRPORT brought a demand for housing in west MIDDLESEX and a consequent increase in council house building. The Airport and the opening of the M4 Motorway in 1965 have presented the district with considerable traffic and parking problems. Today what was once a peaceful and isolated village has become a busy metropolitan suburb, but a certain amount of West Drayton's former rural charm still exists in the area around The Green.

West Ferry Road *E14*. It was known as the Deptford and Greenwich Ferry Road in the early 19th century. The ferries have closed, but the abandoned WEST INDIA and MILLWALL DOCKS, the names of side streets and blocks of flats (e.g. Cuba Street, Spinnaker House), and the site of the launching of Brunel's *Great Eastern* are all reminders of the area's association with ships and shipping.

West Halkin Street *SW1*. Built on the GROSVENOR ESTATE and named after a family property in Flintshire, Halkyn Castle. It does not appear on the original lay-out plans for the BELGRAVIA estate but is clearly an early modification to give improved access to the north-west corner of BELGRAVE SQUARE. It was not built as a very grand street and became less grand as it was extended west. There was a coach manufactury in Halkin Place. The chapel at No. 118 (now the Belfry, a luncheon club) first Presbyterian and then Spiritualist, dates from the 1860s. The Halkin Arcade of expensive shops is continued into LOWNDES STREET and MOTCOMB STREET.

West Ham *E7, E13, E15, E16*. Ancient parish, former county and parliamentary borough and industrial and residential town in the county of Essex, it was incorporated into the London Borough of NEWHAM in 1965. The present small area round the parish church designated West Ham is within the STRATFORD postal district but the county borough also included the western half of FOREST GATE, the whole

of PLAISTOW, and the majority of VICTORIA DOCKS and NORTH WOOLWICH. From medieval times West Ham was one of the more populous parishes in the county. West Ham's earlier industry is dealt with under STRATFORD and PLAISTOW, its general industrial and residential development under NEWHAM and its constituent 19th-century districts under CANNING TOWN, CUSTOM HOUSE and SILVERTOWN. Between the 1801 and the 1901 census its population rose from 6,500 to 267,400 and reached a peak of 320,000 in the 1920s.

Its parish administration was taken over successively by a Local Board of Health in 1856; a Borough Council in 1886; a County Borough Council in 1889; and from 1894 to 1965 it had its own Recorder and Court of Quarter Sessions. It became a parliamentary borough in 1885 with two seats – North and South. From 1918 to 1948 there were four constitencies – STRATFORD, UPTON, PLAISTOW and SILVERTOWN – and then there was a reversion to the original two. The county borough played an important part in Socialist history: the London Co-operative Society, partly orginated from the Stratford Society, was founded in 1862 by railway workers; one of the first of the 'new unions' – now the National Union of General and Municipal Workers was founded in CANNING TOWN in 1889; West Ham, South, elected the Labour MP – J. Keir Hardie – in 1892; The county borough had the first Socialist municipal administration in the country in 1898–1900; The Board of Guardians of the Union was suspended by Neville Chamberlain in 1926–9 for what the Government regarded as over-generous poor relief.

West Ham Park *E15, E7*. Formerly a private estate. From 1762 to 1780 it was owned by Dr John Fothergill, a Quaker philanthropist and botanist who established a botanical garden here. In 1812 Samuel Gurney, the banker, acquired the property. His sister, Elizabeth Fry, the prison reformer, lived there for the last 16 years of her life. The house was demolished in 1872 and the park of 77 acres sold to the CITY CORPORATION in 1874 for £25,000.

West Ham United Football Club *see* FOOTBALL CLUBS.

West Harding Street *EC4 see* EAST HARDING STREET.

West India Dock Road *E14*. Completed in 1810 to link the WEST INDIA DOCKS with COMMERCIAL ROAD, then a new highway to London. Seamen from all over the world gave the street a cosmopolitan air. Though the WEST INDIA DOCKS are now closed (the new BILLINGSGATE MARKET is being built on part of the site) what remains of John Rennie's original warehouses can be seen from the eastern end of the road.

West India Docks Stretching across the ISLE OF DOGS, the peninsula formed by a river loop, these were the first and the finest of those enclosed and protected docks of the 19th century which had become imperative if London's port was to function effectively. They were built on the basis of the West India Dock Act of 1799, the first legislation of its kind in being a parliamentary and not a municipal Act. William Pitt, as Prime Minister, attended the laying of the foundation stone in 1800. Opened in 1802, the docks consisted of an Import Dock of 30 acres of water, and an

Repairing ships at West India Docks in 1830. From a lithograph by Parrott.

Export Dock of about 24 acres, lying to the south. At each end was a basin connecting both with the river through the locks. Locks were also built in the cuts that joined the docks with the basins. Ships entered at the BLACKWALL shore of the ISLE OF DOGS and lighters at the LIMEHOUSE end. Wasteful journeys of three miles around the ISLE were thus avoided, and so was congestion. The purpose of the basins was to allow up to 20 vessels to gather there at high tide through the open lock, so that delays caused by locking through each vessel separately were avoided. A continuous line of three-quarters of a mile of warehouses, five storeys high, was built around the Import Dock, but the Export Dock needed fewer buildings since the cargoes were loaded aboard on arrival. The warehouses were superbly constructed and over a century later were showing no signs of deterioration. The designer was William Jessop, a great early engineer of canals and docks, who constructed the GRAND UNION CANAL between London and the Midlands; he allowed most of the credit for the West India Docks to go to his resident assistant, Ralph Walker. John Rennie acted as a consultant for the scheme.

The Docks were an immediate success, for now West India merchants could discharge their ships in four days instead of the four weeks that had previously been needed.

Three years after the docks were opened, the City Canal, lying south of both of the docks, was completed by the CITY with locks at both ends as a short cut across the ISLE OF DOGS between BLACKWALL and WAPPING. No dues were payable for its use, the cost of running it was therefore high and in 1829 it was sold to the West India Dock Company. It was later widened into a dock for discharging timber, and in the late 1860s it was reconstructed as the South West India Dock. The Docks were all closed in 1980.

West Lodge Park *Cockfosters Road, Hadley Wood, Hertfordshire.* Henry IV (then Duke of Lancaster)

acquired the Manor and Chase of ENFIELD when he married Mary de Bohun. It remained in the hands of the DUCHY OF LANCASTER for 500 years. In 1399 three lodges were built, West Lodge, the official residence of the Chief Ranger, South Lodge and East Lodge. In 1547 Edward VI granted the land to his sister, Princess Elizabeth (later Queen Elizabeth I) who often hunted in ENFIELD CHASE. In 1618–86 Henry Coventry, Secretary of State, lived at West Lodge; and in 1676 John Evelyn, 'went with my Lord Chamberlain to see a garden at Enfield towne, thence to Mr Sec Coventry's lodge in the Chase. It is a very pretty place, commodious the gardens handsome, and our entertainment very free . . . that which I most admired was that in all the Chace within 14 miles of London there is not a house, barn, church or building besides these three lodges.'

In 1689 Sir Robert Howard leased West Lodge from William III after Henry Coventry's death in 1686. In 1718 the lease was bought by James Brydges, Lord Chandos, who was Chief Ranger until he died in 1744. Henry (2nd Duke of Chandos) succeeded his father in the ownership of West Lodge Park and was Chief Ranger for 27 years until 1771. James (3rd Duke of Chandos) became Chief Ranger until his death in 1789. His widow owned the Lodge until 1808. It then fell into disrepair and was unoccupied until rebuilt in the 1830s. In about 1865 Dr Leonard Mosley, merchant and philanthropist, lived here, and planted many of the ornamental trees. It was converted to an hotel in 1922 when the north wing was built. A west wing was added in 1972 by the present owners.

West London Hospital *Hammersmith Road, W6.* Opened in 1856 at a small house in Queen Caroline Street, HAMMERSMITH and then known as the Fulham and Hammersmith General Dispensary. Due to the rapid growth of the western district of London larger premises were soon needed. In 1860 a lease was taken of Elm Tree House, HAMMERSMITH ROAD where in-patients could be cared for. In 1863 the hospital took on its present title. In 1868 the house was purchased and extensions to the building were made. Active teaching of students began in 1883 but not until 1937 was a medical school founded for undergraduates. Preference was given to women students who at that time were admitted to only three London hospitals. With the advent of the National Health Service the medical school was closed. It is now linked to the CHARING CROSS HOSPITAL, FULHAM PALACE ROAD, and has 150 beds.

West London Institute of Higher Education
Gordon House, 300 St Margaret's Road, Twickenham, Middlesex. The institute came about as a result of the amalgamation of Borough Road and Maria Grey Colleges, together with the advanced work of the Chiswick Polytechnic. In 1798 Joseph Lancaster founded his famous monitorial school in Borough Road, SOUTHWARK. Lancaster's policy of national education led in 1814 to the founding of the British and Foreign School Society supported by such reformers as William Wilberforce and James Mill. The Society took over Lancaster's school and so founded the oldest college in the country for the training of masters for its schools at home and abroad. The Borough Road College moved to ISLEWORTH in 1890. The original CHISWICK School of Art and Craft was predominantly a liberal arts college serving BEDFORD PARK garden suburb. Taken over by MIDDLESEX County Council in 1899, it broadened its interests until it became a leading institution for courses in public service, mainly health, social studies and public administration. Maria Grey College was founded in 1878 by the Teachers' Training and Registration Society, a group dedicated to the needs of the disadvantaged and to the education of teachers for the new secondary schools. Established originally in BISHOPSGATE, the college eventually settled in ISLEWORTH.

West Middlesex Hospital *Twickenham Road, Isleworth, Middlesex.* Built as a workhouse in 1837 and rebuilt in 1902. It was given its present name in 1920. In 1948 the hospital was taken into the National Health Service and much redevelopment has taken place since then. In 1982 there were 893 beds, mainly for acute cases.

West Middlesex Waterworks Company
Hammersmith. Founded in 1806. From 1808 cast-iron pipes were used and an extension to supply MARYLEBONE and PADDINGTON fed a 3.5-million gallon reservoir at CAMPDEN HILL. In 1825 a new reservoir was constructed on Barrow Hill, adjoining PRIMROSE HILL. In 1838 water began to be pumped into filter beds and reservoirs extending over about 110 acres at BARNES, (the present site of ST PAUL'S SCHOOL) before continuing via the HAMMERSMITH works to the supply points in north-west and west London. In 1835 the Hammersmith intake was closed, and the pumping works were established at HAMPTON. But the supply line remained as before through the BARNES filter beds. The Barrow Hill and CAMPDEN HILL reservoirs were covered over in 1860. In 1866 the Company's area was extended to cover HENDON, WILLESDEN and parts of ACTON and HAMPSTEAD. By 1872 there was a constant supply in most districts. In 1896 construction began of two reservoirs at Staines in co-operation with

the NEW RIVER and GRAND JUNCTION Companies, and four new reservoirs at BARN ELMS were completed. The Company was absorbed by the Metropolitan Water Board in 1902 (*see* WATER SUPPLY).

West Norwood *SE27.* The lower-lying area bordering the hills once covered by the Great North Wood (*see* UPPER NORWOOD), which, as a suburb developed in the mid-19th century, became known as Lower Norwood. It fell into the LAMBETH portion of Norwood and the land was owned by three Manors: the Archbishop of Canterbury's Manor of LAMBETH to the south, a detached part of the parish of STREATHAM and the Manor of Leigham Court to the north and east, and the Manor of Levehurst to the west. Much of the land south of ST LUKE'S CHURCH was wooded, but the area known as Lambeth Dean, stretching from the church to HERNE HILL, was more open, with farmland, common land and smaller sections of woodland. Two places existed with the same name – Knight's Hill – which causes some confusion in tracing land ownership. One, to the south, is still a road name, the other, a mile away, lay in the Manor of Levehurst and an area of allotments retains the name. Both take the name from the Knight family, who held the land in the 16th century and both later came to be owned by Lord Thurlow, Lord Chancellor from 1778–92. Thurlow bought land in Lambeth Manor in 1772 and over a period of 23 years acquired a large estate. His name is commemorated in several local street names, but he is particularly remembered for commissioning Henry Holland to build him a mansion and refusing to live in it after a dispute about the cost. The house, which was handsome and set in large grounds near the present Thurlow Park Road and Elmcourt Road, was eventually pulled down in 1810. Thurlow stayed in Knight's Hill Farm, a less impressive building nearby (*see* SERBIA HOUSE). Another individual with influential connections, who set up house in the area in 1775, was Mary Nesbitt, mistress of the third Earl of Bristol, once painted as Circe by Joshua Reynolds. The house was on the site of Virgo Fidelis School on Central Hill. At that time Norwood was remote and rural, but the death of Lord Thurlow in 1806 helped to bring about its development. In the same year the Lambeth Manor Enclosure Act was passed and subsequent legislation facilitated the break-up of the estate. A number of roads date from this time, together with various types of housing. ST LUKE'S CHURCH was consecrated in 1825 and a number of large houses were built on Crown Lane in the 1820s. In 1837, the South Metropolitan Cemetery was consecrated. St John's Lodge, originally an 18th-century building, was rebuilt as a magnificent mansion in the 1830s, but demolished by the end of the century. However, despite ambitious plans for the area, which included a scheme for a select development along the lines of the TULSE HILL Estate, on a splendid site at Royal Circus, Lower Norwood was soon covered by suburban homes. The West End of London and Crystal Palace Railway opened in 1856 and in 50 years the houses in the St Luke's district had increased from 647 to 6,431. Many were built by small private landowners (some of whom went bankrupt), others by building societies. Among the institutions that were founded or developed in this busy Victorian suburb were Elderwood, Norwood House and Wood Vale; Norwood Technical College (*see* SOUTH LONDON COLLEGE); the Jewish Hospital and Orphan

Asylum; and ST SAVIOUR'S ALMHOUSES, Hamilton Road. Norwood High Street, in its present state something of a misnomer, failed to become the main shopping area, the centre of gravity moving to the Broadway on Norwood Road which was built in 1888–90. In the 1880s there was considerable pressure to change the name Lower Norwood and in 1885 it took the name West Norwood. In 1911 Norwood Park was opened. Bomb damage during the 2nd World War and a constant process of change and redevelopment has left little of architectural interest.

West Street WC2. Originally laid out in the 1680s by Nicholas Barbon on the Earl of Newport's estate (*see* NEWPORT MARKET). Until the first quarter of the 18th century it was more commonly known as Hog Lane, the ancient throughfare of which it was a continuation and which was eventually absorbed by CHARING CROSS ROAD. In about 1700 the HUGUENOTS built a chapel here to the designs of E.A. Eden. Young's Chinese Restaurant – with its striking fibre glass panel of writhing dragons, waves and clouds which covered the windows of two upper storeys and was made in Hong Kong to the designs of Gene Wong – was a striking feature of the street at Nos 13–15 in the 1960s. The Ivy Restaurant is on the south side at Nos 1–5. Established in 1911, it was a favourite haunt of Noël Coward. Lloyd George and Winston Churchill were also to be seen here.

West Wickham *Kent*. A Saxon manor with adjacent church (St John the Baptist) and formerly a long parish along the county boundary. The manor (Wickham Court, Layham's Road) was rebuilt as a fortified residence in 1480 by Henry Heydon who married Anne Boleyn, great-aunt of the later queen. It is now a college for foreign students of business studies. Although the railway opened in 1882 there was little development until the 1920s and even today there are green fields towards the south.

Westbourne A river which rose in West HAMPSTEAD, fed by five streams which joined near KILBURN, crossed MAIDA VALE and ran south-east to PADDINGTON across the HARROW ROAD and south across the BAYSWATER ROAD into HYDE PARK, where it was joined by the TYBURN Brook. From here it flowed under KNIGHTSBRIDGE and southwards to the THAMES through the grounds of CHELSEA HOSPITAL. In 1730, at the suggestion of Queen Caroline of Anspach, consort of George II, the Westbourne valley in HYDE PARK was dammed up to form the Serpentine. On leaving the Serpentine the Westbourne now becomes the RANELAGH Sewer, and is carried across the District Railway at SLOANE SQUARE Station in a huge iron pipe.

Westbourne Grove W2. Full of character, much of it now Oriental, Westbourne Grove was scarcely a track before the 1850s, unlike QUEENSWAY. However, it rapidly developed into a prosperous shopping street in spite of its early pseudonym 'bankruptcy row'. At No. 26, where today the only Arabian bookshop in London has opened, was Westbourne Hall, originally an extension of the Bayswater Athenaeum, built in 1860, and still decorated with theatrical busts, for it became a music-hall. Just off Westbourne Grove, in Monmouth Road, the unusual Jehovah's Witnesses'

Kingdom Hall was for many years the French Eglise Réformée Evangélique. Prince Louis Lucien Bonaparte, nephew of Napoleon, lived a quiet life as a philologist between 1854–91 at a house demolished when the Odeon cinema was built; and A.J. Cronin, the novelist, had a medical practice at No. 152, in 1925–30.

Westbourne Park W2. Westbourne Park or Green lies in the centre of PADDINGTON between Great Western Road, Westbourne Park Road and the Warwick Estate. Until 1846 a large house known as Westbourne Place or Park with extensive grounds stood near Lord Hill's Bridge just north of Westbourne Park Road. However, Westbourne is mentioned as a farm belonging to WESTMINSTER ABBEY in a charter of 1222, the name being taken from the river which bounded it to the east. Westbourne was long ago sometimes linked with KENSINGTON but it has always been properly part of PADDINGTON. After the Reformation it was granted back to WESTMINSTER ABBEY, and was farmed by its tenants until the mid-19th century.

Westbourne Park Road and Great Western Road are built on the line of an ancient track known as the Green Lane, running between the fields, and Westbourne Park Passage, with the foot-bridge over the railway, perpetuates another old right of way. The building of the railway in 1832–8 brought an end to the isolated rural community of Westbourne Park. Westbourne Place, a 16th-century house belonging to Thomas Hues (*see* QUEEN'S PARK) was rebuilt in about 1740 by Isaac Ware, a chimney-sweep who became a successful architect; another architect, Samuel Pepys Cockerell, lived there in 1800–27. He was followed by Viscount Hill, Commander-in-Chief of the Army, who occupied the house until 1836. At Westbourne Farm, which stood near Woodchester Square, the actress, Sarah Siddons, lived in 1805–17, and her brother, Charles Kemble, close by in Desborough Lodge, in 1814–16. In the 1840s more actors, Charles James Matthews and his wife, Madame Vestris, lived at Westbourne Farm. Across the canal, south of Marylands Road, stood Westbourne Manor House until 1866; this was probably the site of the medieval farm.

Soon after 1850 building followed the railway. Many of the little detached houses of Westbourne Park Road and the terraces in this attractive area have survived. Thomas Hardy, the novelist, lived at 16 Westbourne Park Villas in 1863–7 and later, more briefly, at other addresses nearby. Hence the name of the new Wessex Gardens Estate, north of Talbot Road. Westbourne Park station opened in 1871 and a century later the Brunel Estate was built on the site of disused railway sidings. Both these undertakings are straightforward compared with the complex redevelopment now known as the Warwick Estate lying between the canal and the HARROW ROAD. It was carried out by the LONDON COUNTY COUNCIL in the early 1960s. This area was densely populated from the time it was built and by 1890 parts of it had already become a slum. The new estate has retained some of the Victorian houses, opened up the view of the church of ST MARY MAGDALENE and managed to balance tower blocks with areas of open space. Since the arrival of WESTWAY, football pitches and adventure playgrounds have ingeniously been set out underneath the motorway, but it is a very urban playground. The enormous mural here was painted by David Bonnington and Desmond Rochfort in 1977, and depicts 'Man and Mechanical Energy'. Near Bourne Terrace in about 1850 was an unusual public garden called the Maze, and on the site of the present Railway Tap public house on the corner of Porchester Road and Bishop's Bridge Road, stood the popular 18th-century tavern with gardens called the Royal Oak, from which the station is named. Beyond the municipal Porchester Hall stood Dr John Clifford's famous Westbourne Park Baptist church, bombed, but since rebuilt. This church was originally built in 1877 to house the enormous congregations attracted by Clifford's preaching in the Praed Street Chapel (*see* PRAED STREET). During Clifford's ministry in Paddington from 1858 to 1915, this church became one of the most important religious centres in London.

Westbourne Terrace *W2*. Once described as 'the finest street in London', this is certainly the grandest of the BAYSWATER terraces. It was built in 1840–52 mainly by William King and William Kingdom. The latter lived at No. 32 in 1844–9. The first house to be completed was No. 17, which was taken by John Constable, eldest son of the painter. George Ledwell Taylor, the architect, designed and lived briefly at No. 140 in 1852–3; and amongst other distinguished residents here have been Charles Manby, a leading civil engineer, at No. 60 in 1870–7; and Aldous Huxley, at No. 155 in 1921–2.

Westbury Hotel *Conduit Street, W1*. Designed by Michael Rosenauer, it was opened on 1 March 1955 by the American Ambassador and the President of the Board of Trade. The first hotel to be operated by an American company in Britain, it had several innovations, including an ice-making machine producing 16,000 cubes a day. Within six months a new wing with penthouse and garden terraces was added, and a second extension in 1961 brought the total of bedrooms to 280, including 19 suites. The site, partially cleared by bombing in the 2nd World War, was occupied in the mid-19th century by Dr Culverwell's Bathing Establishment, an 'Importer of Havannah Segars and Foreign Snuff's, by 'Thos. Cooper, Parasol

and Umbrella Maker to Her Majesty', and from 1918 to 1938 by Maggs Bros, the antiquarian booksellers who in 1931 bought the 4th-century *Codex Sinaiticus*, the earliest extant codex of the Old and New Testament, from the USSR on behalf of the British Museum for £100,000.

Westcott Lodge *22 Lower Mall, Hammersmith, W6*. Its present name is derived from J.T. Westcott, a member of Hammersmith Council who died in 1936, but it was built before 1746, when it was known as The Turret House. In 1860 it became the vicarage. It is now used as council offices but retains its attractive appearance with a balcony and porch with Adam-style details. Having lost its neighbours it stands, rather isolated on the edge of the open space of Furnivall Gardens (*see* HAMMERSMITH).

Western Avenue *W3, W5*. One of the arterial roads proposed in 1912 and designed to by-pass part of the London-Oxford road. Work began at the London end (Wood Lane, SHEPHERDS BUSH) in 1921 and continued throughout the 1920s and 1930s reaching Denham in 1943. Cycle tracks were provided on some stretches but were later removed. Factories were built beside the road (the A40), particularly in ACTON, the best known being the Hoover building at PERIVALE.

Western Ophthalmic Hospital *Marylebone Road, NW1*. Founded in 1856 as the St Marylebone Eye and Ear Institution in St John's Place, LISSON GROVE by Henry Obré and John Woolcott. Only outpatients were treated at first. In 1859 patients with ear trouble were no longer treated. Renamed the St Marylebone Eye Institution, it moved in 1860 to MARYLEBONE ROAD to a former shooting box of George III's built in about 1764. In 1866 it was renamed the Western Ophthalmic Hospital. In 1929–30 a new hospital was built on the site with 35 beds. Since the introduction of the National Health Service it has been grouped with ST MARY'S HOSPITAL PADDINGTON. In 1982 it had 56 beds.

Western Pumping Station *Grosvenor Road, SW1*. Built in 1872–5 by the METROPOLITAN BOARD

Westbourne Terrace, built in 1840–52, was once described as the finest street in London.

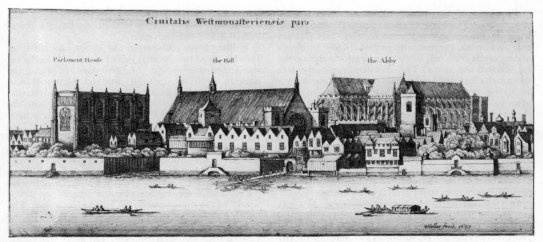

Hollar's 1647 etching of Westminster, showing St Stephen's ('Parliament House'), Westminster Hall and the Abbey.

of works as part of Sir Joseph Bazalgette's scheme for the drainage of London (*see* DRAINS AND SEWERS). *The Builder* in 1873 described it as 'Italian of simple character'. It was included in 1970 in the statutory list of Buildings of Architectural or Historic Interest.

Westfield College *Kidderpore Avenue, NW3.* Founded in 1882 to provide higher education for women, it obtained its Royal Charter in 1932. It is now a co-educational multi-faculty college whose 1,200-odd students read for degrees of the UNIVERSITY OF LONDON in the Faculties of Arts and Science. The marble, *La Fileuse Arabe*, is by Enrico Astori (1971).

Westminster During the construction of the Collegiate Church of St Peter, soon to be known as WESTMINSTER ABBEY, Edward the Confessor decided to move his main royal residence from the CITY to a riverside site further upstream south of the Abbey walls, a move which had far-reaching effects on the history of London and which separated the commercial centre of the capital from the seat of royal power and justice. No trace remains of King Edward's Saxon palace, nor of the additions which his Norman successor, William the Conqueror, no doubt made to it. WESTMINSTER HALL, built by the Conqueror's son, William II, still stands, however, while NEW PALACE YARD to the north of it and OLD PALACE YARD to the south commemorate the former royal residence as does the name the PALACE OF WESTMINSTER by which the Houses of Parliament are known.

There were a number of shops in the precincts of WESTMINSTER ABBEY and William Caxton rented one of them from 30 September 1476 until his death in 1491. He paid an annual rent of ten shillings. Later, when it was occupied by others in the book trade, it was described as 'adjoining the Chapter House' and 'near the south door', that is, just to the right of the door by the 'Poets Corner'. It was thus on the main path from the royal PALACE OF WESTMINSTER and WESTMINSTER HALL to the Abbey Church and the Chapter House where the HOUSE OF COMMONS met at that time. Caxton also rented two houses and later three houses, or tenements, in the Almonry which stood on a site which is now the corner of GREAT SMITH

STREET and VICTORIA STREET. Probably, this is the place where he displayed his sign of the 'Red Pale'. It was in his shop adjoining the Chapter House that he set up the first press in England. His first piece of printing was an Indulgence, dated 13 December 1476 (of which one copy survives in the PUBLIC RECORD OFFICE). Altogether, Caxton printed 107 separate books and pieces; 74 were books in English and 20 of these he translated himself. He printed the first edition of Chaucer's *Canterbury Tales* in 1478 and a second edition in 1483, and Malory's *Morte D'Arthur* in 1485. This great work had only been completed in 1469 or 1470 and we know from the extant manuscript that Caxton not only printed but also edited and rewrote some of it, replacing the archaic words with those currently in use. On the final leaf he prints: 'Thus endeth this noble and joyouse book . . .' He was responsible for many other great books and, as G.M. Trevelyan says, 'his diligence and success as a translator did much to lay the foundation of literary English.' His shop was kept on by Wynkyn de Worde, who probably came to England with Caxton as an assistant in 1476. All Caxton's printing materials passed to de Worde; but in 1493 he started a typeface of his own and in 1494 his name is first found in a printed book. De Worde lived in Caxton's house in Westminster until 1500 and, in the nine years of his tenancy, printed at least 110 different books. He moved then into FLEET STREET.

By the 15th century, Westminster, although it contained several decent lodging-houses for country gentlemen who came to attend Parliament and for those with business at the royal courts, was already a noisy, crowded area frequented by thieves and pickpockets; and, because of the marshy ground upon which much of it was built, its inhabitants were uncommonly susceptible to the plague. As was discovered by the misused hero of *London Lickpenny*, once attributed to John Lydgate, the streets were full of Flemish merchants selling hats and spectacles, of other street vendors loudly shouting their wares, of cooks' shops where London ale spiced with pepper, hot meat pies and porpoise tongues were displayed on trestle tables, and of footpads looking for an opportunity to snatch a purse. A century later Westminster had further degenerated. The long absences of the

943

peregrinating Court reduced those who made an uncertain living from its presence to poverty and crime; while the temptations offered by rich and unwary courtiers, when present, and pilgrims drew hundreds of dangerous criminals to the narrow streets around the PALACE and the ABBEY. This deterioration in the area was much increased by the custom of affording sanctuary to fugitives from the law not only within the ABBEY precincts but also in the area to the north-west of them; the streets known today as BROAD SANCTUARY and Little Sanctuary commemorate this practice while Thieving Lane indicates the kind of inhabitants with which the district was plagued. The construction of VICTORIA STREET in 1845–51 resulted in the demolition of part of this rookery; and the laying out of PARLIAMENT SQUARE resulted in the disappearance of many more unsavoury streets and passages.

In 1900 Westminster received its charter as a city and for the first time had a mayor. The city then comprised the parishes of ST MARGARET WESTMINSTER, St John the Evangelist Westminster, ST MARTIN IN THE FIELDS, ST ANNE SOHO, ST PAUL COVENT GARDEN, St John the Baptist Savoy, ST MARY-LE-STRAND and ST CLEMENT DANES. It also incorporated the LIBERTY OF THE ROLLS and the close of WESTMINSTER ABBEY. The City of Westminster, which now has a Lord Mayor, had a population in 1981 of 211,900 and an estimated rateable value of £313,427,950. The municipal offices are at City Hall, VICTORIA STREET, SW1.

WESTMINSTER ABBEY *SW1.*

Legend has it that the first church on THORNEY ISLAND in the THAMES was built by King Sebert, of the East Saxons, in the 7th century on the instructions of St Peter who materialised at its consecration by Melitus, first Bishop of London. The designs of salmon in the Chapter House floor are said to relate to the tradition that St Peter rewarded the ferryman who transported him across the river with the promise of plentiful catches. No mention of such a church is made by Bede, however, in his *Ecclesiastical History* although THORNEY was undoubtedly a suitable place for such a foundation, since it had fresh-water springs and the food resources of the River THAMES at hand.

A Charter purporting to be of King Offa of Mercia in 785, now in the Abbey Muniments, granted land 'to St Peter and the needy people of God in Thorney in the terrible place which is called Westminster'. St Dunstan is also said to have obtained a charter from King Edgar in the 10th century and to have restored the Benedictine Abbey to which he brought monks. Undoubtedly a substantial foundation existed here when, in 1040, Edward the Confessor became king.

He had vowed to make a pilgrimage to the tomb of the Apostle Peter in Rome but his Great Council dissuaded him for political reasons, and the Pope, Leo IX, was prepared to release the King from his vow if he would found or restore a monastery to St Peter. Edward moved his palace to WESTMINSTER and began building a church on a site east of the previous building. He also planned a new monastery for a greatly increased number of monks. Nothing now remains above ground of Edward's solid cruciform structure which was built to an advanced Continental design, although traces of it were discovered in the 19th century in the nave and sanctuary of the present Abbey. The church is depicted in the Bayeux Tapestry as having a central tower and transepts, covered with a lead roof. On 28 December 1065 the church was consecrated and eight days later Edward died and was buried before the high altar.

William I was crowned in the Abbey on Christmas Day 1066 and the Saxons, gathered around the doors, shouted in acclamation. The Normans, believing the noise to signify an uprising, attacked the crowds and several nearby houses were set on fire. This coronation was the first in a long line: all kings thereafter with the exception of Edward V and Edward VIII, have been crowned in the Abbey (*see* CORONATIONS). In 1139, Edward the Confessor was canonised and successive kings, anxious to be associated with the Saint, showered the Abbey with gifts, endowments and privileges. Henry III added a Lady Chapel in 1220 and in 1245 began rebuilding the Abbey. To demonstrate his veneration for the Saint he was determined that it would be the most sumptuous building possible. The old church was pulled down as far west as the nave, the new building being started from the east, as was the custom with medieval builders. The work was supervised in turn by three master masons: Henry de Reyns to 1253, Master John of Gloucester to 1260 and Master Robert of Beverley to 1284. Mystery surrounds the identity of Henry de Reyns. It is probable that the King found him at Rheims which he visited in 1243 but whether he was an Englishman who had gone to France to work, or a Frenchman, is uncertain. Many details about the early building are obscure but it was certainly influenced greatly by the buildings the King himself had seen at Rheims and by those at Amiens and the Sainte-Chapelle in Paris. 'The Abbey,'comments Pevsner, 'is the most French of all English Gothic churches.' The nave is 103 ft high, far higher than that of any other English church. The plan of the apse, with its radiating chapels, derives from Amiens, as do the recessed portals of the north transept, resembling those of Amiens's west front. The form of the apsidal chapels with tall windows and wall arcades, comes from Rheims, although the gallery in the ambulatory is entirely English. The flying buttresses, rose windows in the transepts, bar-tracery of the other windows and iron tie-bars connecting the columns are all French. Indeed, the whole design of the church is based on the French system of geometrical proportion. There are many English features incorporated into this Continental plan, however, notably single not double aisles, a long nave and widely projecting transepts, the elaborate moulding of the main arches, lavish use of polished Purbeck marble, the method of filling the stone vaults and the overall sculptured decoration.

The work proceeded rapidly, at the King's own expense, and by 1254 the transepts, north front, rose windows, parts of the cloisters and the Chapter House had been finished. By 1269, the choir and one bay of the nave were completed and the body of St Edward was moved to a special shrine in the chapel bearing his name. The Roman pavement before the high altar was also laid in this year by Abbot Ware. In 1272 Henry III died and, no longer ruler of Anjou, was buried before the high altar in the Abbey at the spot made available by the removal of the Confessor's body to its new site. His heart, however, was transported to Fontevrault Abbey in France to join his dead Angevin ancestors.

Little further building was undertaken until the middle of the following century. In 1303 while Henry's successor, Edward I, was fighting in Scotland, the Treasury, kept in the crypt of the Chapter House, was robbed, despite the thickness of its walls and its supposed impregnability. Richard de Podlicote, Keeper of the PALACE OF WESTMINSTER, was executed for his part in the theft, although it is generally believed that the ecclesiastics themselves must have been implicated.

Abbot Nicholas Littlington began the continuation of the nave in 1376, using money given by Simon Langham, a former Abbot and efficient administrator who had succeeded in putting the financial affairs of the Abbey in order. Littlington also rebuilt the Abbot's house which included a fine parlour, the Jerusalem Chamber. Richard II gave £1,685 towards the cost of building and under the direction of the master mason, Henry de Yevele, the original plan of Henry de Reyns was continued after 100 years with only very minor alterations of architectural design, giving the Abbey a unity of style rare in English cathedrals. Henry IV had a fit when praying one day in the Abbey before the Confessor's shrine and was carried into the Jerusalem Chamber where he died on 20 March 1413, thus fulfilling the prophesy that he would die in Jerusalem. Under Henry V, the Abbey received regular royal financing once more, to the generous extent of 1,000 marks (£666 13s 4d) annually. When Henry died in 1422, a new chantry chapel was built under the direction of John Thirske over the King's grave at the entrance to Edward the Confessor's Shrine. Prior Thomas Millyng gained royal support from Edward IV after his recovery of the throne in 1461, for having offered sanctuary to his queen, Elizabeth Woodville, in the preceding year. She built the chapel of St Erasmus adjoining the Lady Chapel and Millyng was made a bishop.

Henry VII, the fourth great royal benefactor of the Abbey, conceived the idea of building a new chapel where the body of his murdered uncle, Henry VI, would lie. Henry VI had been buried at Windsor and miracles were recorded as happening at his tomb, so that Henry VII wished to have him canonised. The Pope agreed to this but demanded an enormous sum of money before the canonisation process could be completed. This caused the parsimonious Henry VII to modify his building plans and he decided to erect a chapel in honour of the Virgin Mary instead. So, in 1503, the foundation stone of this *'orbis miraculum'* was laid, the building eventually being completed in 1519. The master mason was probably Robert Vertue and the skill of his builders was praised many years later by Washington Irving: 'Stone seems, by the winning labour of the chisel, to have been robbed of its weight and density, suspended aloft, as if by magic and the fretted roof achieved with the wonderful minuteness and airy security of a cobweb.' The fan-vaulting is, undoubtedly, one of the greatest achievements of Tudor building. When he died in 1509, Henry was buried in the chapel beside his queen, a magnificent monument by Torrigiano subsequently being erected over their tomb. The chapel is estimated to have cost Henry £14,000. By 1532, when he died, the chantry chapel of Abbot Islip, who had supervised Henry VII's building, had been completed as had the nave of the Abbey itself. The great building begun by Henry III in 1245 had at last been finished.

The monastery was dissolved in 1540 but its royal associations saved it from the destruction of statuary which occurred elsewhere. Part of the Abbey revenues were transferred to ST PAUL'S CATHEDRAL, the origin of the expression: 'Robbing Peter to pay Paul'. The Abbey became the cathedral of the new diocese of WESTMINSTER and Edward VI appointed a Dean and Chapter to replace Bishop Thomas Thirlby, accused of embezzling Abbey revenues. Mary restored the monks but they were turned out again under Elizabeth who reinstalled the Dean. During the Civil War, Cromwell's army camped in the church and 'broke down the rails before the Table and burnt them in the very place in the heat of July but wretchedly profaned the very Table itself by setting about it with their tobacco and all before them.' Cromwell, Bradshaw and Ireton were all buried in the Abbey but, at the Restoration, their bodies were

Westminster and St Margaret's church in 1753, after the Abbey's west towers had been completed by Hawksmoor.

disinterred, hanged at TYBURN, beheaded and then buried at the foot of the gallows.

From 1698 to 1723 Sir Christopher Wren was Surveyor. He undertook restoration work and designed the West Towers. His designs were subsequently modified by Nicholas Hawksmoor and completed in 1745. From the early 18th century onwards, the Abbey became increasingly crowded with monuments of all kinds to all sorts of men and women. So prolific are they that they obscure the lines of the actual building. In 1849, Sir George Gilbert Scott was appointed Surveyor and carried out the restoration of the Chapter House in 1866. Further restorations were carried out in the north transept by John Oldrid Scott from 1878 and his successor as Surveyor, J.L. Pearson.

Tombs and Monuments

> Think how many royal bones
> Sleep within these heaps of stones
> Here they lie, had realms and lands
> Who now want strength to stir their hands

When Francis Beaumont (himself buried in the Abbey) wrote these lines, few had been buried here who were not of royal blood, but since then an extraordinary variety of people have been interred within its walls. Of royal graves those reputed to be of King Sebert, his queen and sister are the earliest. Edward the Confessor lies in the shrine in the chapel bearing his name behind the High Altar. The base of the shrine is all that remains of the magnificent structure of gold erected by Henry III, and ornately bejewelled. Near Edward lies Henry III in the elaborate marble tomb prepared for him by his son, Edward I, who, in his turn, was buried in this chapel, but in a very simple tomb-chest so that his body could be taken out at any time, and his flesh removed by boiling in case his bones were needed to carry before an army invading Scotland. Edward's beloved first wife, Eleanor of Castile – for whom 'Eleanor crosses' were erected between Nottinghamshire and London to mark the stopping-places of her funeral cortège (*see* CHARING CROSS) – was buried in 1290, her tomb surmounted by an effigy by William Torel, the goldsmith who had also made Henry III's effigy. Edward III died in 1377 and his tomb, erected by his grandson Richard II, was by Henry Yevele. Nearby are the tombs of his queen, Philippa of Hàinault, and their son, Thomas, Duke of Gloucester, youngest of 14 children. Richard II and his wife, Anne of Bohemia, lie in one tomb, their effigies once represented with holding hands, now, sadly, with the arms broken off. The king's jawbone was removed through a hole in the tomb by a boy of WESTMINSTER SCHOOL in 1776 but was restored in 1916. Henry V has his own chantry chapel at the eastern end of St Edward's Chapel. The figure of the King was stripped of its decoration and even its head over the years, but a new one of polyester resin was installed in 1971. In the Abbey Museum are the shield, saddle and tilting helmet the King used at Agincourt in 1415. A riot of statuary depicting scenes from the King's life decorates every niche and surface of the tomb and the chantry chapel above it which are consequently among the principal sights of the Abbey. Henry's queen, Catherine de Valois, her body embalmed before burial, lay in an open tomb for 300 years. An entry in Pepys's diary for 23 February 1669 records that he 'did see by particular favour the body of Queen Catherine of Valois; and I had the upper part of her body in my hands, and I did kiss her mouth, reflecting upon it that I did kiss a queen, and that this was my birthday, 36 years old, that I did first kiss a queen.' In 1776 the Queen's body was hidden from sight beneath the Villiers monument in the chapel of St Nicholas.

After the building of Henry VII's chapel, royal burials regularly took place there. Elizabeth of York, Henry himself, Anne of Cleves, Edward VI, Queen Mary I and her half-sister, Queen Elizabeth, Mary Queen of Scots, all found resting-places here. They were later to be joined by James I, Anne of Denmark, James' daughter, Elizabeth of Bohemia, Charles II, Mary II, William III, Prince George of Denmark, Queen Anne, George II and Queen Caroline.

A host of other persons of royal and noble blood have tombs here. In the sanctuary are three of the finest, those of Edmund Crouchback, youngest son of Henry III, his wife, the heiress Aveline of Lancaster, and Aymer de Valence, Earl of Pembroke. Edmund and Aveline were the first couple to be married in Henry's church in 1269 and after her death, Aveline's wealth endowed the future house of Lancaster which Edmund founded by his second marriage. In 'Innocent's Corner' – Dean Stanley's name for part of the north aisle of Henry VII's chapel – are two small monuments of children of James I: Princess Sophia, only 3 days old, lies in her cradle, while Princess Mary aged 2 years, reclines on her elbow on a small altar tomb. In another small tomb lie the bones of two children, found in the Tower and placed here by order of Charles II in 1674. They are believed to be those of Edward V and his brother Richard, sons of Edward IV, allegedly murdered by order of their uncle, Richard III, in 1483. In the south aisle of this chapel lie buried Lady Margaret Beaufort, mother of Henry VII and founder of Christ's and St John's Colleges, Cambridge, and Margaret, Countess of Lennox, niece to Henry VIII, a famous beauty, mother of Lord Darnley and grandmother of James I. Another notable lady, Frances Sidney, has her tomb in St Paul's Chapel. Wife to the Earl of Sussex and Philip Sidney's aunt, she founded Sidney Sussex College, Cambridge and was noted as a woman of learning, beauty and wisdom in her lifetime.

Richard II began the custom of burying great commoners in the Abbey when he ordered the burials here of John of Waltham, Bishop of Salisbury, and Sir John Galoppe. The Islip chantry chapels in the sanctuary commemorate Abbot John who supervised the building of Henry VII's chapel and the completion of the nave. One of the many statesmen to be honoured in the Abbey is Charles II's Lord Chancellor, Clarendon, buried here like Queen Mary and Queen Anne, Charles II's granddaughters and nearly 20 more of his relatives and descendants. Both Pitt the Elder and Younger are here, the latter having a splendid monument by Westmacott above the west door depicting Pitt the Orator declaiming as the muse, History, records his words and Anarchy crouches at his feet. His rival, Charles James Fox, leader of the Whig opposition to Pitt, also has a Westmacott monument: he lies dying in the arms of Liberty while Peace mourns his parting and a Negro slave at his feet thanks him for his efforts to abolish the slave trade. The same sculptor was also commissioned to complete a monument to Spencer Perceval which shows him being assassinated in the HOUSE OF COMMONS in 1812. Many of the other great figures of 19th-century political life are also here: George Canning, Viscount

Castlereagh, Sir Robert Peel, Lord Palmerston and W.E. Gladstone. Disraeli, who was buried at Hughenden, his country estate in Buckinghamshire, has a memorial, as has Lord Salisbury who was buried at Hatfield. There are busts of Campbell-Bannerman and Joseph Chamberlain and a tablet in memory of Asquith. Reformers, including William Wilberforce and Anthony Ashley-Cooper, Lord Shaftesbury, are honoured, as are the two men chiefly responsible for establishing British rule in India, Robert Clive and Warren Hastings. Stones cover the ashes of Bonar Law, Neville Chamberlain, Clement Attlee and Ernest Bevin. Ramsay MacDonald and David Lloyd George have commemorative floor stones. Many of these monuments are in the nave with a special concentration of them in the north aisle, sometimes known as Statesman's Aisle, but one of the most splendid, that of James, Earl of Stanhope, George I's Chancellor of the Exchequer, stands against the choir screen.

The first poet to be buried in the south transept commonly known as Poet's Corner was Geoffrey Chaucer in 1400 and, after this, other poets sought to be buried near him. At Spenser's funeral, various poets are said to have thrown unpublished works of their own into the grave in tribute to him. Ben Jonson lived on the Abbey premises and when he was old and impoverished, the Dean asked what he could do to help. Jonson asked for a grave in the Abbey saying, 'Six feet long by two feet wide is too much for me; two feet by two feet will do for all I want'. So when he died, Jonson was buried upright. His epitaph – O rare Ben Jonson – is as economical in words as his grave is in space. Few of the poets honoured in this spot are actually buried here; but Dryden, Prior, Samuel Johnson, Sheridan, Browning and Tennyson all were. Many poets, often because of the unconventional lives they led, were considered undesirable by successive Deans and have only

Monuments in the nave of Westminster Abbey in 1809. From an aquatint after Rowlandson and Pugin.

been given memorials many years after their deaths. Shakespeare had to wait until 1740 for his memorial, Burns until 1885 and William Blake until the bicentenary of his birth in 1957, when a splendid Epstein memorial to him was erected. Keats, Byron and Shelley, too, had to wait a considerable time for recognition in the Abbey. Other poets and writers honoured are Milton, Samual Butler, Joseph Addison, William Congreve, Thomas Gray, Oliver Goldsmith, Samuel Taylor Coleridge, Robert Southey, William Wordsworth, Lord Macaulay, Thackeray, Charles Dickens, Thomas Hardy and Rudyard Kipling. Of 20th-century poets, T.S. Eliot has a memorial and John Masefield's ashes are beneath a stone near another commemorating W.H. Auden. Jane Austen, buried in Winchester Cathedral, and the Brontë sisters, Charlotte, Emily and Anne have memorials. Handel's monument by Roubiliac stands amidst these monuments to men and women of letters. A plaque nearby records that William Caxton set up his printing press in the Abbey precincts nearby. In Poet's Corner are also, incongruously, the graves of old Parr, said to be 152 years old when he died, and 'Spot' Ward who cured George II of a thumb injury and received a vote of thanks from the HOUSE OF COMMONS.

Many famous scientists and engineers have memorials. Sir Isaac Newton was buried in the Abbey and has a splendid monument against the choir screen, designed by Kent and executed by J.M. Rysbrack. Thomas Tompion and George Graham, the great clockmakers, are buried together, as are three great physicists, J.J. Thomson, Lord Rutherford and Lord Kelvin. Michael Faraday has a memorial tablet and Robert Stephenson and Thomas Telford are buried in the nave. Both William (the discoverer of Uranus) and John (the inventor of the finger-printing identity system) Herschel are here and James Watt has a monument. Joseph Lister, the pioneer of antiseptic treatment, is also remembered. The explorer David Livingstone was buried in the Abbey in 1874, his body having been brought back from Africa. The architects, Robert Adam, Sir William Chambers, Sir Charles Barry and Sir George Gilbert Scott are here with Thomas Banks, the sculptor. Dr Arnold, Headmaster of Rugby School, and Dr Busby of WESTMINSTER SCHOOL are commemorated, as are Dean Stanley who wrote *Memorials of Westminster Abbey* and William Tyndale who translated the Bible into English. Godfrey Kneller is the only painter commemorated in the Abbey although, because of his dying words – 'By God, I will not be buried in Westminster . . . they do bury fools there' – he was interred elsewhere. Several actors and actresses are buried here, however, among them David Garrick and Henry Irving.

Other notable memorials include that of Jonas Hanway, founder of the Marine Society and the first man in London to carry an umbrella; and that of Lady Elizabeth Russell who is erroneously supposed to have died by pricking her finger with a needle and who is mentioned in the works of Addison, Richardson, Johnson, Goldsmith and Dickens. The famous monument by Roubiliac to Lady Elizabeth Nightingale, who died in 1731, was erected by her son in 1761 and has been the subject of much criticism, Horace Walpole calling it 'more theatric than sepulchral'.

One of the most famous and visited of all tombs is that in the nave, of the Unknown Warrior whose body was brought back from France after the 1st World War and buried on 11 November 1920 as a representative of the thousands of dead. The soil for his grave was brought from the battlefields and the marble slab from Belgium. On a pillar to the north is the Congressional Medal of Honour bestowed on the soldier in 1921 and above it is the Padre's Flag which had been used to cover the coffins of many soldiers buried in France and was laid over that of the Unknown Warrior at his burial. Winston Churchill, buried at Bladon, has a marble slab beside the Unknown Soldier and Franklin D. Roosevelt, one of the very few foreigners so honoured, a plaque on the wall of the nave nearby.

Many other great soldiers are buried or commemorated in the Abbey. One of the most splendid memorials is that by Roubiliac to Field Marshal George Wade who died in 1748. Major-General James Wolfe has a colossal monument erected by the King and Parliament 13 years after his death; and General Gordon, slain at Khartoum, has a bronze bust given in 1892 by the Royal Engineers. Lieutenant-General Sir James Outram, hero of the defence of Lucknow, has a monument depicting scenes at the Residency during the siege. Two great RAF leaders, Trenchard and Dowding, are buried in the RAF Chapel in Henry VII's Chapel. Field Marshal Allenby's ashes are buried in St George's Chapel, known as the Warriors' Chapel, along with many other famous men.

Some of the most interesting monuments are those commemorating whole families. The Duke of Buckingham, favourite of James I and Charles I, has a monument by Le Sueur which also commemorates his wife and children. The large and fine Norris family memorial is by Isaac James. As Elizabeth I's guardian while her sister Mary was Queen, Norris earned her respect and affection and was raised to the peerage in 1572. The monument has the figures of Lord and Lady Norris and the kneeling figures of six of their sons. Other notable family monuments are those of the Speaker of the HOUSE OF COMMONS, Sir James Pickering, and the Percy family's private vault, the Percys still being the only family with the right to be buried in the Abbey. Baroness Burdett-Coutts was the last person to be buried there in 1906. Since then only ashes have been accepted.

Notable Features of the Abbey

Glass. There is very little old glass left except of the east windows of the clerestory, two windows at the east and west ends of the nave and the plain glass with the initials H R in Henry VII's Chapel. In the Jerusalem Chamber, Jericho Parlour and vestibule, old fragments of glass have been collected together. The glass in the west window was designed by Thornhill and completed in 1735. It depicts Abraham, Isaac and Jacob with 14 prophets. The Rose or Wheel Window in the south transept, the largest of this type, has painted glass completed in 1902. Glass of a different kind is seen in the 16 Waterford chandeliers in the nave, presented by the Guinness family in 1965 to mark the 900th anniversary of the consecration of the Abbey.

Paintings. When the Abbey building was completed, many of its interior surfaces were covered with paintings, very few traces of which now remain. On the *sedilia* are two portraits of kings, possibly Henry III and Edward I, and behind them are two more pictures, one of the Confessor giving a ring to a pilgrim, possibly St John, and part of an *Annunciation*. A painting of particular significance which hangs in the Abbey is the portrait of Richard II by Andre Beaneve of Valenciennes, the first reliable portrait of an English monarch. Paintings of St Christopher and the *Incredulity of St Thomas* appear on the end wall of the south transept. They date from 1280–1300 and are possibly by Walter of Durham.

The Coronation Chair was made for Edward I to enclose the Stone of Scone which he seized in Scotland and brought to the Abbey in 1277. Since 1308 this chair has been used for every coronation performed in the Abbey.

The Choir. The Choir Screen was designed by Edward Blore in 1834 although the inner stonework is 13th-century. The choir stalls date only from 1847, the original ones being destroyed by the Abbey Surveyor in 1775. The black and white marble pavement was given by Dr Busby, headmaster of WESTMINSTER SCHOOL for 55 years, before his death in 1695. The 13 shields carved in the choir aisles commemorate those who contributed money to Henry II's building.

The Organ was originally built in 1733 but has been much rebuilt, modified and added to over the years (*see* ORGANS). Famous organists at the Abbey include Orlando Gibbons and Henry Purcell.

Sculpture. Among the glories of the Abbey are the superbly crafted angels in the south transept. Other notable sculptures appear in Henry V's chantry chapel and seem to cover every available surface in Henry VII's chapel where saints, kings and philosophers appear to jostle one another for space. Among them is St Wilgefort who was so beautiful that she was constantly being pestered with offers of marriage. She prayed to God for protection and, overnight, grew a beard.

The Cloisters. These date from the 13th and 14th centuries. The Eastern Walk is the oldest. It was here that the Abbot washed the feet of 13 aged men each Maundy Thursday while the monks washed the feet of children in the South Walk. The stone bench they used to sit on is still there. Eight Abbots are buried beneath the South Cloister. A passage leads past the Deanery to Dean's Court, a cobbled courtyard surrounded by the 16th-century rooms built for Abbot Islip, including the Jericho Parlour.

The Chapel of the Pyx. Part of the early monastic buildings, this chamber was completed between 1065 and 1090 and a 'pyx' or box was kept in it, containing the standard pieces of gold and silver. The trial of the pyx took place once a year (*see* CEREMONIES).

The Undercroft Museum. This 11th-century room, 110 ft long and 45 ft wide, was probably originally the monks' Common Room. Many of the Abbey treasures are displayed here and the wax effigies of sovereigns, their consorts and important commoners, which were carried on top of the hearse in the funeral cortège.

The Chapter House. Built in 1245–55, the first meeting of Henry III's Great Council took place here on 26 March 1257 and, from the middle of the next century onwards till 1547, it was used for the meetings of the HOUSE OF COMMONS. Subsequently, it was used to store public records until 1866. It is octagonal in shape, 50 ft in diameter with a vaulted roof of eight bays with huge 4-light windows, each 39 ft high. The sculptures, though worn, are fine; and paintings, dating from about the 14th century, represent the *Last Judgement* and the *Apocalypse*. Later paintings, dating from about 1500 are of animals. The Chapter House has one of the finest tiled floors in England.

Westminster Bridge *Westminster–Lambeth.* The first suggestions for a bridge at WESTMINSTER were made soon after the Restoration but were quashed by opposition from the CITY CORPORATION and the THAMES watermen. The growth of WESTMINSTER in the 18th century urgently increased the need. Anybody wanting to cross the river had to go round by PUTNEY BRIDGE or LONDON BRIDGE, take a boat or use the horse ferry. So, in 1721 the Westminster Bridge project was revived; and the next year Colen Campbell produced a design. Other designs were submitted including one in 1736 by Hawksmoor. Bt these were rejected, and in 1738 Charles Labelye was appointed engineer and building began. The watermen were paid £25,000 in compensation, and the Archbishop of Canterbury, who owned the horse ferry, received £21,025. The second masonry bridge over the THAMES in London, its piers were founded in caissons, the first example of their use in this country. In 1747 there was an alarming settlement of one of the piers. In the controversy that ensued, Batty Langley castigated Labelye as an 'unsolvent, ignorant arrogating Swiss.' But in November 1750 the bridge was opened with a grand procession of gentlemen and the chief artificers responsible for the work, preceded by trumpets and kettledrums. No dogs were allowed on the bridge, and anybody found defacing the walls was threatened with death without benefit of clergy. In 1802 Wordsworth observed, while standing on it:

Earth has not anything to show more fair:
Dull would he be of soul who could pass by
A sight so touching in its majesty:
The City now doth, like a garment, wear
The beauty of the morning; silent, bare,
Ships, towers, domes, theatres, and temples lie
Open unto the fields, and to the sky;
All bright and glittering in the smokeless air . . .

In 1823 Telford carried out the first major technical examination, using Labelye's own papers and other early manuscript material. A Parliamentary committee was convened in 1836 to discuss continuing problems with foundations. The next year James Walker began to encase all the piers in cofferdams and rebuild them on piled foundations. But no sooner was this work completed than a parliamentary committee decided to build a new bridge. The present cast-iron bridge of seven arches was consequently built in 1854–62 by Thomas Page, with Sir Charles Barry as architectural consultant. Its width of 84 ft between the parapets was exceptional for the time. The COADE STONE LION on the south bank is by W.F. Wordington. The statue of Queen Boudicca on the north side is by Thomas Thornycroft (*see* STATUES).

Westminster Cathedral *Francis Street, SW1.* Not until more than 300 years after the Reformation was government by diocesan bishops restored to Roman Catholics in Britain. After the death of Cardinal Wiseman, who became the first Archbishop of Westminster in 1850, a large sum of money was raised in his memory and this was the nucleus of the building fund for the proposed cathedral. But it was not until 1884 that Cardinal Manning, the second Archbishop, bought the site on which this cathedral was to be built. The plot, known in medieval times as Bulinga Fen, was originally marshland reclaimed by the Benedictine monks of WESTMINSTER ABBEY and used as a market.

St Mary's Fair was held here yearly on 22 July. After the Reformation the place became a pleasure garden with a bull-baiting ring. Here Scottish prisoners were confined during the Civil War, and in 1826 a women's prison was built here, the Middlesex County Prison. When it was demolished the re-use of the deep foundations proved a considerable economy.

Cardinal Manning caused a storm of protest when, in 1867, he appointed as architect a relation by marriage, Henry Clutton, who devoted six years to designing a Gothic cathedral without asking for remuneration. But the Cardinal decided against starting to build until they had considerably more money, which he was eventually offered in 1882 by a wealthy and eccentric Yorkshireman, Sir Tatton Sykes, on condition that the architect should be Baron von Herstel. On the death of von Herstel in 1884, however, Cardinal Manning proceeded no further with the building project.

When Herbert Vaughan (later Cardinal Vaughan) became Archbishop in 1892 he appointed John Francis Bentley as architect, for Clutton's ambitious Gothic cathedral would have been enormously expensive to build and funds were limited to £45,000. Bentley rejected the Gothic in favour of an Early Christian Byzantine style of architecture. Although the fabric of the building was completed in 1903, only seven years after the foundation stone was laid, economy was made by leaving the decoration of the interior to future generations, and this work is still in progress. The first public religious service was the Requiem Mass for Cardinal Vaughan who, like the architect, Bentley, died very shortly before the completion of their project.

The Cathedral, dedicated to the Precious Blood of Our Lord Jesus Christ, is built entirely of brick with contrasting bands of Portland stone, and without steel reinforcement. The extreme length of the exterior is 360 ft, the width 156 ft, while the campanile on the north-west corner stands 273 ft high and is surmounted by a cross 11 ft in height, containing what is supposed to be a relic of the True Cross. The campanile, which can be ascended by a lift, is dedicated to St Edward the Confessor. The single bell, 'Edward', the gift in 1910 of Gwendolen, Duchess of Norfolk, is inscribed 'St Edward, pray for England'. Unfortunately the once celebrated panorama from the campanile is now partially obscured by the many high buildings in the area.

The interior of this Metropolitan church is ablaze with mosaic and *opus sectile* in true Byzantine tradition, and is ornamented with more than 100 different kinds of marble from quarries all over the world. The eight columns of dark green marble in the nave (the widest nave in England) were hewn from the same quarry which provided the marble for St Sophia, Istanbul, in the 6th century. As they were being transported across Thessaly in 1897 they were seized by the Turks who held them as spoils of war, and not until 1899 were they erected in the nave. On the piers of the nave are Eric Gill's bas-reliefs of the Fourteen Stations of the Cross, beneath one of which stands an early 15th-century statue of *Our Lady and Child*, a work of the Nottingham school of alabaster. An anonymous donor had it brought back from its 500-year sojourn in France and presented it to the Cathedral. From the main arch of the nave hangs the great Rood by Christian Symons who designed many of the mosaics in the various chapels. The marble pulpit, the gift of Cardinal Bourne in 1934, is an adaptation of the original, considerably smaller, one and contains an *opus sectile* panel by John Trivick representing Our Lady of Walsingham.

In the Sanctuary the massive *baldacchino* over the High Altar stands on eight columns of yellow marble from Verona, its vaulting lavishly inlaid with mosaic. The High Altar is cut from a single block of marble granite. In the Sanctuary, too, is the Metropolitan throne, the *cathedra*, given by the Catholic Bishops in England in memory of Cardinal Vaughan. To the north and south beyond the aisles of the Sanctuary are the Blessed Sacrament Chapel with the Sacred Heart shrine, and the Lady Chapel, the most richly decorated of all the Chapels in the Cathedral.

A flight of steps behind the High Altar leads into the retro-choir in the apse. Here is housed the Small Organ, one of two, the other, the Grand Organ, being situated in the narthex at the west end, 320 ft away. This compound organ is unique among cathedral organs in Britain because a dual control system enables it to be played from either end of the Cathedral. On 6 June 1903, the oratorio setting of Newman's poem *The Dream of Gerontius* had its first London performance here: the composer, Sir Edward Elgar, conducted. The singing today is by a choir of men and the boys of the Cathedral Choir School.

The Baptistry and the seven chapels flanking the nave all contain elaborate mosaic work, and in each of the chapels an altar encloses the relics of appropriate saints. In a shrine in the Chapel of St George and the English Martyrs lies the body of St John Southworth, martyred in 1654. Other tombs in these Chapels are those of Bishop Richard Challoner who died in 1781 and whose body was moved here in 1946 from Milton in Berkshire; and of Cardinals Hinsley and Vaughan (although his body lies at ST JOSEPH'S COLLEGE, MILL HILL.) In accordance with ancient tradition their Cardinal's Red Hats hang over their tombs. Cardinals Wiseman, Manning, Griffin and Godfrey are buried in the crypt. Wiseman's neo-Gothic tomb, not in keeping with the Byzantine style predominating in the Cathedral, is by Edward Pugin, while the bronze effigy of Manning is by John Adams-Acton. Other artists and sculptors whose work enriches the Cathedral include Robert Anning Bell, Lindsay Clarke, Boris Anrep, L.H. Shuttock, Gilbert Pownall, Giacomo Manzu, Justin Vulliamy, Sterling Lee, George Jack, Arthur Pollen, Henry Holliday and David Partridge.

The years in which the Archbishops of Westminster were in office are: Cardinal Wiseman, 1850–65; Cardinal Manning, 1865–92; Cardinal Vaughan, 1892–1903; Cardinal Bourne, 1903–1935; Cardinal Hinsley, 1935–43; Cardinal Griffin, 1943–56; Cardinal Godfrey, 1956–63; Cardinal Heenan, 1963–75. The present Archbishop is Cardinal Basil Hume.

Westminster Fair There were two separate fairs in WESTMINSTER, St Edwards's and St Magdalen's. The former was originally held in ST MARGARET'S churchyard but later removed to TOTHILL FIELDS in Edward III's reign and later still to ROCHESTER ROW between the Emery Hill Almshouses and what became the church of ST STEPHEN THE MARTYR. It lasted for fifteen days and survived until 1820. Henry III's charter of 1257 to the abbot and canons of St Peter's is preserved in ST MARGARET'S. St Magdalen fair, also held in TOTHILL FIELDS, was founded by a charter of Edward III and survived until the end of the 16th century.

Westminster Hall *Parliament Square, SW1.* The only surviving part of the original PALACE OF WESTMINSTER. The Hall was built as an extension of Edward the Confessor's palace in 1097 by William Rufus who originally intended to build an entire new palace. When the Hall was completed, William professed himself disappointed, saying it was a 'mere bedchamber' compared to what he had envisaged. The Hall, first used as a banqueting hall, then consisted of a central nave, divided from the aisles by timber ports. It was 240 ft long and nearly 40 ft high, with walls 6 ft 8 ins thick. Along the plastered and painted walls was a row of Norman round-headed windows. A wide railed gallery ran around the Hall at a height of 20 ft. The building was damaged by fire in 1291 and restored by Edward II. Further alterations were made by Richard II, between 1397 and 1399, to the design of Henry Yeve. The walls were elevated by 2 ft and a stately porch installed. Richard II's motif, a white hart couchant, was incorporated into the moulding surround. The most striking addition was the oak hammer-beam roof by Hugh Herland; it springs to a height of 92 ft in the centre and has the widest unsupported span in the country. Steel reinforcement was needed, however, by 1920.

The Hall became the centre of administrative life, outside the City walls. Grand Councils and, later, some early PARLIAMENTS were held here.

From the 13th century until 1882 the building housed the Law Courts. In the early days men were hired as witnesses here; the sign of their trade was a straw protruding from their shoe – hence the expression 'straw bail'. Later, in 1820–4, the courts were arranged by Sir John Soane along the west side of the Hall. These were the Court of Chancery, Court of the Queen's Bench, Court of Common Pleas and Court of Exchequer. From the time of Cromwell until the middle of the 18th century, justice lived alongside commerce here. Books, particularly law books, prints, toys, trinkets and the wares of seamstresses were sold in stalls inside the building. Wycherley captured the contrast of activities in *Epilogue to a Plain Dealer*:

In Hall of Westminster
Sleek sempstress vends amidst the Courts her ware.

In his *Amusements*, Tom Brown describes the surprise of an Indian gentleman taken to visit the Hall in

Westminster Hall in 1738, when the building still housed the Law Courts as well as booksellers' stalls.

1700: 'My Indian was surprised to see in the same place men on the one side with baubles and toys, and on the other taken up with the fear of judgement, on which depends their inevitable destiny.' The combination of activities inevitably made this a fashionable lounging place. But the crowded stalls constituted a risk to the building: a fire started amongst them in February 1630. The building has also survived floods which are recorded in 1621, 1625 and 1812. Speaker Abbott mentioned the 1812 flood in his diary: 'The tide soon rose to the door of Westminster Hall; flowed into it; and three or four boats full of men went into the Hall.'

The Hall has seen power change hands many times. In 1327 Edward II abdicated and presented his fourteen-year-old son, Edward III, as King. The barons interviewed Richard II here in 1387 after their rebellion, and in 1399 the Lords of the Council deposed Richard, then in the TOWER, and put Henry VI on the throne. Edward IV proclaimed himself King here in 1461. In 1649 Charles I was tried and condemned in the Hall; and Cromwell was installed as Lord Protector here in 1653. After the Restoration, Cromwell's head was placed, with those of Ireton and Bradshaw, on the roof; it remained there for 25 years before it was finally blown down.

Amongst those condemned here were Sir John Old-castle (Shakespeare's Falstaff) in 1417; Sir Thomas More and Bishop Fisher in 1535; Queen Anne Boleyn in 1536; the Duke of Somerset, the Great Protector, in 1552; Robert Devereux, Earl of Essex and Henry Wriothesley, Earl of Southampton in 1601; Guy Fawkes in 1606; and the Earl of Strafford in 1641. The trials of Lord Melville in 1806 and Warren Hastings in 1788–95 were also held here. The bodies of Gladstone, Edward VII and Churchill lay in state here.

The Hall has witnessed happier events, too. Since 1099, when William Rufus celebrated the completion of the Hall with a banquet, English monarchs have held coronation festivals here. Traditionally the Royal Champion would ride to the centre of the Hall, throw down his gauntlet, and challenge any man denying the right of the sovereign, to single combat. The last coronation festival held here was in celebration of George IV's coronation in 1821. Of this the Earl of Denbigh wrote, 'It exceeded all imagination and conception. Picture to yourself Westminster Hall lined beneath with the peers in their robes and coronets, the Privy Councillors, Knights of the Bath and a multitude of different attendants and chief officers of State in most magnificent dresses, and with a double row of galleries on each side above, filled with all the beauty of London, the ladies vying with each other in the magnificence of their apparel and the splendour of their head-dresses. Some of them being literally a blaze of diamonds.'

Charles Dickens, having seen his first contribution published in the *Monthly Magazine*, walked here for half-an-hour to overcome his emotion. The Hall is now the vestibule of the HOUSE OF COMMONS; it was retained by Sir Charles Barry in his design for the PALACE OF WESTMINSTER and is connected to the rest of the palace by St Stephen's Hall.

Westminster Hospital *St John's Gardens, Horse-ferry Road, SW1.* The first hospital in London to be founded by voluntary contributions. On 14 January 1715 four men met at St Dunstan's Coffee House, FLEET STREET to discuss a 'Charitable Proposal for Relieving the Sick and Needy and other Distressed Persons'. The minutes of the meeting and of subsequent ones are still extant, written in a beautiful hand. The leader of the four men was Henry Hoare of HOARE'S BANK. In 1720 a house in PETTY FRANCE was rented and patients were admitted. In 1724 the hospital moved to Great Chapel Street. In 1733 disagreement amongst the Trustees resulting in a split led to the founding of ST GEORGE'S HOSPITAL. Meanwhile the Westminster Infirmary, as it was then called, rented three houses in Castle Lane and moved there on 24 February 1735 (where they remained for almost 100 years). London now had five hospitals, the monastic foundations of ST BARTHOLOMEW'S and ST THOMAS'S, the Westminster, GUY'S and ST GEORGE'S.

The most famous medical men at the Westminster in the early days were the physician, Richard Mead, and the surgeon, William Cheseldon. Cheseldon was particularly skilled at removing stones from the bladder, an operation he was said to be able to perform within a minute of the first incision. In 1842 Sir Alexander Crichton, the physician, wrote that lower WESTMINSTER 'had not then been well drained and as many parts of it were lower than the river at high water, it partook at times of the unhealthy malaria of marsh land, so that malaria and bad intermittents [fevers] prevailed among the poor.' Many of these cases were treated at the infirmary. The first mention of medical students was in 1734. They were frequently called 'cubs', three being allowed to each surgeon. 'Cubs' were at first regarded with suspicion and not allowed to stay in the infirmary in the absence of their masters. In the 1820s there was pressure to establish a medical school. In 1834 the Westminster School of Medicine was opened in Dean Street. In 1885 it moved to CAXTON STREET where it remained until 1938. In 1831 a site was bought for a new hospital in BROAD SANCTUARY, opposite the west door of the ABBEY. This hospital was built by William and Charles Inwood at a cost of £40,000. Patients were first admitted in 1834.

Perhaps the most notable medical man that the hospital produced was Dr John Snow who qualified at the Westminster in 1838. In 1846 he was the first to study anaesthesia scientifically, initially with ether and later with chloroform. He is said to have given 4,000 chloroform anaesthetics without a death. He administered chloroform to Queen Victoria in April 1852 at the birth of Prince Leopold and in April 1857 at the birth of Princess Beatrice. He was also a brilliant epidemiologist and controlled the CHOLERA epidemic in 1854, a generation before bacteria were known to be the cause. The Matron (1847–73), Miss Elizabeth Eager, was the first (before Florence Nightingale) to use the term 'trained nurse'. In 1933 a site at St John's Gardens was obtained for rebuilding. The architect chosen was Lionel Pearson of Adams, Holden and Pearson. In 1938 the new medical school was opened, and in 1939 the new hospital. During the 2nd World War much of the hospital and many of its students were evacuated to suburban hospitals. The building suffered some bombing. From 1948 the Westminster Hospital has been administered by the National Health Service with the Infants' Hospital, Vincent Square (now WESTMINSTER CHILDREN'S HOSPITAL) GORDON HOSPITAL and ALL SAINTS' HOSPITAL in the same group. In 1960 QUEEN MARY'S HOSPITAL, ROEHAMPTON was added to the group. There are 422 beds. The hospital's old premises in BROAD SANCTU-ARY were demolished in 1951.

Westminster Palace *see* PALACE OF WESTMINSTER.

Westminster Palace Hotel *2–8 Victoria Street.*
Built in the French-Renaissance style in 1859 by W. and A. Moseley, it was the first hotel in London to have lifts. It was much frequented by Members of Parliament, and was noted for its good English fare. It had 300 bedrooms, but only 14 bathrooms. One half of the building was let to the India Board. It is now Abbey House.

Westminster School *Little Dean's Yard, SW1.*
Evolved from a school for clerks attached in early medieval times to the Benedictine ABBEY OF WESTMINSTER. When Henry VIII dissolved that monastery in 1540, the school continued under the headmastership of Alexander Nowell (1543–55), who was noted for his foundation of an annual Latin play which, with one interlude (1939–53), has continued until today. Elizabeth I refounded the school in 1560 providing for a headmaster, an undermaster and 40 scholars with fee-paying pupils known as 'town boys' admitted for the first time.

During the Civil War the school was loyal to Charles I and the Dean of Westminster told Cromwell that 'it would never be well with the nation till Westminster School was suppressed.' At the coronation of James II in 1685 King's scholars were the first to acclaim the sovereign with cries of '*Vivat Rex*', a privilege they still retain. The poet William Cowper mentions rebellions and disorder at the school in the 18th century. Under the 1868 Public Schools Act the school was made financially and administratively independent of the ABBEY and a new Board replaced the Dean and Chapter as governors. The school was given legal possession of all its buildings except College Hall.

School buildings, of varied architectural styles, date from different periods. Oldest is the School (1090–1100) which includes part of the old monastic dormitory. This was partly rebuilt in 1914 by Benjamin Wyatt and, after bombing in the 2nd World War, was rebuilt in 1959. Between 1602 and 1884 the entire school was taught in this room. Here, on Shrove Tuesday, the school cook tosses a pancake which is fought over by pupils; the one who grabs the largest piece after a minute's scrum receives a guinea from the Dean of WESTMINSTER. Another early building is College Hall Cloisters (1369–76), built as the abbot's state dining-hall, and now used as the school refectory. It has a musicians' gallery built about 1600. In the 18th-century, College, modelled on Palladio's Teatro Olimpico at Vicenza, was built by Lord Burlington (1722–30) who also built the School Gateway (1734). Through the centuries the size of the school remained restricted, because its buildings are almost entirely within the Abbey's precincts. In 1980 the numbers of pupils totalled 570, of whom 70 were girls (admitted to the sixth form since 1972).

Distinguished headmasters have included Nicholas Udall, author of the first English comedy, *Ralph Royster Doyster* (1555–6) and the antiquary, William Camden (1593–7). Numerous famous pupils include Ben Jonson, Christopher Wren, George Herbert, John Dryden, William Cowper, Judge Jeffreys,

Warren Hastings, Edward Gibbon, Charles Wesley, Lord John Russell and Peter Ustinov. The new Westminster Under School opened in 1981 in the former Grosvenor Hospital in VINCENT SQUARE.

Westminster Theatre *Palace Street, SW1.* On
this site stood the Charlotte Chapel, a chapel-of-ease to ST PETER EATON SQUARE, where Cardinal Manning attended his last Anglican service in a congregation which included W.E. Gladstone. Manning stole out before the service was over. In 1924–31 it was a cinema, the St James's Picture Theatre. It opened as a theatre with *The Anatomist*, produced by Tyrone Guthrie. Anmer Hall managed it for the next seven years and staged plays by Ibsen, Shaw, Eliot, Granville-Barker and others. From 1938–40 it was used by the Mask Theatre directed by J.B. Priestley. His own play *Music at Night* (1939) was first performed here. In 1943–5 it was managed by Robert Donat. In 1949 *Black Chiffon* by Lesley Storm began its run of 409 performances. In the 1950s the main successes were *Dial M for Murder* (1952) and *Carrington VC* (1953). After 1961 it was used for moral rearmament plays, mostly written by Peter Howard. In 1966 the theatre was rebuilt as part of an arts centre. The seating capacity is 588.

Wetherby Gardens *SW5.* Takes its name from
Wetherby Grange, Yorkshire, the country house of Colonel Sir Robert Gunter (*see* GUNTER ESTATE). Field Marshal Viscount Allenby lived at No. 25 in 1928–36.

Weymouth Street *W1.* Built in 1775 and named
after the Marquess of Bath, Viscount Weymouth, who married into the landowning Portland family. Bryan Waller Proctor, the writer, better known by his pseudonym, Barry Cornwall, lived at No. 13. Michael Faraday lived at No. 18 with his family from 1809 until Sir Humphry Davy sent for him to become his assistant in 1813.

Wheatley Street *W1.* Laid out in 1793 and until
1935 called Chesterfield Street after the Derbyshire estate of the Duke of Devonshire, a relation of the ground landlords, the Portland family. The new name was chosen in honour of the artist, Francis Wheatley, who was buried in MARYLEBONE PARISH CHURCH in 1801, having lived at a number of local addresses including No. 23 WELBECK STREET in 1785–93. Charles Wesley lived at No. 1 Chesterfield Street in 1771–88.

Wheeler's Restaurant *19 Old Compton Street,
W1.* One of London's leading fish restaurants it was founded at its present address in 1929 by Bernard Walsh, originally an oyster wholesaler, whose father had owned a shell-fish bar known as Wheeler's in Whitstable. There are now ten other Wheeler's restaurants in London. The Alcove, 17 KENSINGTON HIGH STREET; Antoine, 40 CHARLOTTE STREET; Braganza, 56 FRITH STREET; Carafe, 15 LOWNDES STREET; George and Dragon, 256 BROMPTON ROAD; Sovereign, 17 HERTFORD STREET; Vendôme, 20 DOVER STREET; Wheeler's, 12a DUKE OF YORK STREET; Wheeler's City Restaurant, 19–21 GREAT TOWER STREET and Wheeler's, 9–13 Fenchurch Buildings, FENCHURCH STREET. The menus in all are the same; and most of the chefs, like Bernard Walsh's first, are CHINESE.

Wheelwrights' Company *see* CITY LIVERY COMPANIES.

Whetstone *N20*. Whetstone High Road is on the old FINCHLEY–FRIERN BARNET boundary and part of the GREAT NORTH ROAD. Inn-keepers, brewers, wheelwrights, harness-makers, smiths and other tradesmen from at least the 15th-century stamped their characters on the district. But after 1875, the development of Oakleigh Park and other estates brought suburban respectibility to a somewhat raffish neighbourhood. Baxendale, a modern development, perpetuates the name of a one-time head of Pickfords, the carriers. Here, about 1820, he built a fine house and provided a hospital for 100 horses and fields for 200. An important 18th-century horse-dealing centre at Coleharbour was engaged in exporting animals to the continent.

Whitcomb Street *WC2*. Extends from PALL MALL east to COVENTRY STREET. Originally known as Hedge Lane, it takes its present name from William Whitcomb, a brewer who began building on the west side in the 1670s, and Nos 27–31 (odd) perhaps date from about this time. At the corner with ORANGE STREET the Hand and Racquet public house commemorates the tennis court which formerly stood nearby, and the narrowness of the carriageway hereabouts – little more than 10 feet–proclaims the rustic origin of this ancient highway.

White City *Wood Lane, W12*. In 1908 140 acres were laid out here by the Kiralfy brothers for the Franco-British Exhibition. There were 40 acres of gleaming white-stuccoed buildings and half-a-mile of waterways. The centrepiece was the Court of Honour which had a lake and illuminated fountains surrounded by exotic Indian-style pavilions. The exhibition was the largest held in Britain up to that date and there were more than 8 million visitors. The same summer the 4th Olympic Games were held in the stadium: 1500 competitors from 19 nations took part. The hero of the games was Doronado Pietri who collapsed just before the finishing line of the marathon. He was disqualified for being helped over the line but Queen Alexandra awarded him a special cup. In 1910 a Japanese-British exhibition was held to celebrate the Anglo-Japanese alliance. The grounds and buildings were taken over by the government in 1914; and after the war they were derelict. Greyhound racing was introduced in 1927. The AA Championships were first held here in 1932. In 1931–3 the stadium was used as the home ground of Queens Park Rangers (*see* FOOTBALL CLUBS). In 1936 50 acres were acquired by the LONDON COUNTY COUNCIL for housing. The Greyhound Derby is held here. The 52nd Derby was run in 1982.

White Conduit *Islington*. The junction of Barnsbury Road and Maygood Street marks the place where, by royal licence of 1431, a conduit on ISLINGTON hill supplied piped water to the CHARTERHOUSE. Later the lead cistern was arched with brick and flint with a loft above and enclosed in a small white building. A dated stone bearing the initials and arms of Thomas Sutton, founder of CHARTERHOUSE SCHOOL, commemorated a restoration of 1641. At its last survey in 1654 the supply was found so reduced that it was abandoned for NEW RIVER water. The cistern was stolen when PENTONVILLE was built, and in about 1810 vandals choked the springhead, in hostility to the controversial lay preacher William Huntington, who had tried to restore it for local use. Finally, as BARNSBURY developed, the masonry was stolen, and its last remains taken away in 1831 by pauper labour from Clerkenwell Workhouse, for use in repairing the NEW (PENTONVILLE) ROAD.

White Conduit Club A number of distinguished members of the STAR AND GARTER TAVERN, PALL MALL, including the Earl of Winchilsea and Charles Lennox, played cricket matches on White Conduit Fields at ISLINGTON and in 1752 formed a club under the name of the White Conduit Club. On becoming an exclusive club they considered it undignified to play on public land and instructed an employee, Thomas Lord, a Yorkshireman, to arrange a lease of private land which he obtained, apparently in his own name, on what is now the site of DORSET SQUARE. The ground was opened in 1787, in which year some members of the White Conduit Club formed the MARYLEBONE CRICKET CLUB. The latter played its first game in 1788 against the White Conduit Club, winning by 83 runs. The clubs then merged under the name of the MARYLEBONE CRICKET CLUB, more familiarly known as the MCC.

White Conduit House *Islington*. A tavern beside the WHITE CONDUIT, said to have opened on the very day of Charles I's execution, is shown on a view of 1731 by Lemprière. In 1754 Robert Bartholomew, a rich farmer who also owned the Angel Inn, advertised it as a coffee and tea room with fresh milk and hot loaves ('White Conduit loaves' were cried in London as late as 1825). Cricket was played in the next field. The 'shrubby maze' and fishpond on 'fair Islington plain' provided respectable diversion for well-dressed CITY families and their apprentices, as lauded by William Woty's facetious poem in the *Gentleman's Magazine* of 1760. Goldsmith, who mentions it in *The Citizen of the World*, came here after dinners at HIGHBURY BARN, and – according to Washington Irving – was embarrassingly caught out with no money after treating three young ladies to tea. Wroth reports that it had special customs: 'A White Conduit method of affecting an

The White Conduit House, opened as a tavern in the 1640s, became a favourite resort of City families by the 18th century. Cricket was played in White Conduit Fields.

A coach leaving the White Horse Cellars, later known as Hatchetts, Piccadilly. From a caricature by Cruickshank, 1836.

introduction was for the gallant 'prentice to tread on the lady's train, to apologise profusely, and finally to suggest an adjournment for tea in one of the arbours.' Bartholomew's son Christopher, a young man 'of gentlemanly manners and a superior turn of mind', who in 1766 inherited his father's extensive properties in ISLINGTON and HOLLOWAY, created the distinctive circular-ended tea-rooms on two floors, with an organ and a fine prospect. He laid out the grounds (says the *Sunday Rambler* in 1774) with 'pleasing walks prettily disposed' and 'genteel boxes for company, curiously cut into the hedges', adorned with paintings. A miniature steeple held a set of chimes, while a *trompe l'oeil* painting at the end lengthened the gardens' apparent extent. Abraham Newland, Cashier to the BANK OF ENGLAND, was a visitor, and much later, George Cruikshank, who used to sketch the company. But Bartholomew wrecked his prosperity by lottery losses, sold out in 1795, and died in 1809 in poverty.

Sharpe and Warren, proprietors till 1828, built the 'Apollo' dancing- and tea-room at the northern corner. They altered the boxes, drained the fishpond, and introduced an unruly element with spectacular shows such as Chamart, the fire-eater, balloon ascents, a bandstand and small theatre. In 1825 they launched a 'Minor Vauxhall' whose risque shows and low habitués lost them the licence. George Bowles took over, converted the Apollo room for billiards, and in December 1828 built a completely new house, stuccoed and pilastered, with a grand upper room. It survived for several more years, offering the attractions of juggling, tight rope walking, farces and ballet. Five of the Tolpuddle martyrs were welcomed back here with a dinner on their return from Australia. But BARNSBURY streets were closing in; entertainments were garish; the views had gone; and the now artisan clientele of 'Vite Cundick Couse' were finally displaced when in 1849 the whole site was built over, the present White Conduit Tavern rising on one small corner.

White Hart Inn *Bishopsgate Street Without.* Described by Stow as 'a fair inn for the receipt of travellers', it was a big, rambling building demolished in 1829 to make way for LIVERPOOL STREET.

White Hart Inn *Southwark.* The place where Sam Weller is introduced to the reader cleaning boots in Chapter 10 of *The Posthumous Papers of the Pickwick Club*. 'There still remain [in Southwark] some half dozen old inns, which have preserved their external features unchanged, and which have escaped alike the rage for public improvement, and the encroachments of private speculation. Great, rambling, queer, old places they are, with galleries, and passages, and staircases, wide enough and antiquated enough to furnish material for a hundred ghost stories.' This one, which had 'a double tier of bed-room galleries, with old clumsy balustrades . . . and a double row of bells to correspond, sheltered from the weather by a little sloping roof,' was in existence in 1406 and served as Jack Cade's headquarters in 1460. It was partially rebuilt after a fire in 1669, and demolished in 1889.

White Horse Cellars *Piccadilly.* Later known as Hatchett's White Horse Cellars. Coaches started here for Oxford and the Western Counties. Joshua Reynolds arrived here from Plymouth in 1740. The American painter, Thomas Sully, spent the night here on his arrival in London in 1837 and was justifiably annoyed to be charged 5s for two eggs for breakfast. Samuel Pickwick and his friends take the coach here for Bath and Sam Weller is much annoyed to find the coach named 'Pickwick'. Dickens borrowed the name from Moses Pickwick whose coaches were often to be seen on the road between the White Horse Cellars and the West Country and whose White Hart Hotel stood opposite the Pump Room in Bath. In *Bleak House* Esther Summerson is met at the White Horse Cellars by Mr Guppy off the coach from Reading and escorted to Messrs Kenge and Carboy.

White House *Albany Street, NW1*. A star-shaped nine storey block built in 1936 to the designs of R. Atkinson as self-contained service apartments. In 1975 after expensive conversions, it began to be run mainly as a hotel with 600 bedrooms; 150 apartments are leased separately.

White Lodge *Richmond Park, Surrey*. Palladian villa commissioned by George II from the Earl of Pembroke and Roger Morris. The original house of five bays and two storeys has been much extended. A favourite residence of Queen Caroline and later of her daughter, Princess Amelia (during her controversial Rangership–of Richmond Park), it was granted by George III to Lord Sidmouth, Prime Minister in 1801–4. Once more a royal residence, it was the home of the Duke and Duchess of Teck when their grandson, the future Edward VIII was born here in 1894. The Duke and Duchess of York (later George VI and Queen Elizabeth the Queen Mother) lived there for a few years following their marriage. It is now the ROYAL BALLET SCHOOL.

White Street *Barbican*. Until the mid-19th century known as White's Alley. In about 1745 a Roman Catholic chapel opened here. The door was fitted with a spyhole where lookouts kept watch during divine service. In the GORDON RIOTS of 1780 the chapel was wrecked and the priest so badly beaten up that he died. The congregation were compensated by the government and with the money built another chapel on the same site. In 1820 Arthur Thistlewood, leader of the CATO STREET conspirators, was arrested in White Street. The street was bombed in the 2nd World War and no longer exists.

White Swan *1 New Row, Covent Garden, WC2*. A pleasant, four-storied 17th-century building, mentioned by Charles Dickens in several of his books. Samuel Pepys recorded coming here for a 'morning draft' after going to WHITEHALL to see the return of Charles II from exile. Nell Gwynne, who is buried nearby in ST MARTIN-IN-THE-FIELDS, is also reputed to have been a customer here.

White Tower *1 Percy Street, W1*. Formerly a hotel and restaurant known as the Tour Eiffel, it was taken over by Rudolf Stulik, an Austrian, in 1910. It became extremely popular with successful artists and writers. In 1914 Ezra Pound and Wyndham Lewis and other Vorticists celebrated the launching of their magazine *Blast* here. Augustus John was a frequent customer in the 1930s. It was renamed The White Tower in 1943 when it changed hands and became a fashionable Greek restaurant.

Whitebait Dinners Annual banquets attended by Cabinet Ministers and held generally at The Ship (closed in 1908) on or near Trinity Sunday, the Sunday after Whit Sunday, at BLACKWALL or GREENWICH, where the best whitebait were to be had. The custom originated with dinners held at DAGENHAM by the commissioners for the engineering works carried out there in 1715–20 to save the lowlands from flooding. To one of these dinners the Prime Minister was invited and was afterwards accompanied by some of his colleagues. The dinners continued until 1868, were revived in 1874–80 and held for the last time in 1894.

Whitechapel *E1*. Originally in STEPNEY, Whitechapel soon developed as a suburb of the CITY OF LONDON because of its position along the main route into and out of the CITY from Essex. The chapel that gave the district its name was built in the 13th century and became the parish church of St Mary Whitechapel in about 1338. WAPPING was separated in 1694. Trades, particularly in metalwork, considered a nuisance in the congested CITY moved into Whitechapel; the WHITECHAPEL BELL FOUNDRY is still working in Whitechapel Road and the Gunmakers' Company Proof House is still in COMMERCIAL ROAD. Stow complained at the end of the 16th century that 'without the bars boths sides of the street be pestered with cottages and alleys even up to Whitechapel Church'. The poverty of the inhabitants, which was to be so much commented upon by the Victorians, was already present: the hearth tax returns of 1664, for example, show that almost three-quarters of the households occupied houses worth less than £1 a year – the highest proportion in East London. Rather more substantial houses were erected in the Leman Estate towards the end of the 17th century in an area popular among the Sephardic Jews, many of whom settled here. Nearby the GOODMAN'S FIELDS THEATRE was founded in 1733; and when the LONDON HOSPITAL moved to its new site in Whitechapel Road in the 1750s it was backed by fields. Nearer the CITY, WHITECHAPEL HIGH STREET was lined with coaching inns, the road was full of traffic, carts with garden produce, market women with baskets of fruit, flocks of sheep, herds of cattle, brewers' drays and haywains for the haymarket that survived until 1928. The offshoots were a maze of disreputable yards and courts. COMMERCIAL ROAD brought more traffic from the EAST and WEST INDIA DOCKS, including quantities of sugar to refineries in Whitechapel, especially around Blackchurch Lane. Germans were mostly employed at this trade; the Irish were concentrated around ROSEMARY LANE (later renamed Royal Mint Street). According to Mayhew in the middle of the 19th century, 'the lodgings here are occupied by dredgers, ballast heavers, coal whippers, watermen, lumpers and others whose trade is connected with the river as well as the slopworkers and sweaters working for the Minories. The poverty of these workers compels them to lodge wherever the rent of the rooms is lowest.' Mayhew also observed that the headquarters of the second-hand clothes trade which had formerly been in the MONMOUTH STREET area moved to Whitechapel when control was taken over by the Jews. The Old Clothes Exchange off CUTLER STREET became the wholesale centre of the trade and PETTICOAT LANE (officially renamed MIDDLESEX STREET in 1832) became the retail market. Thus by the end of the century Whitechapel was, in the words of Charles Booth, 'the Eldorado of the East, a gathering together of poor fortune seekers; its streets full of buying and selling, the poor living on the poor.' To help raise the standard of living and the level of education, Samuel Barnett, the Vicar of St Jude's in COMMERCIAL STREET, founded TOYNBEE HALL, the first university settlement and the WHITECHAPEL ART GALLERY. The first purpose-built Board School in London was Old Castle Street School which was opened in 1873.

Into this area of low rents and a rapidly changing population, where many Jews had previously settled, came the largest influx of Jewish refugees from Eastern

Europe during 1880–1914. For a short time parts of Whitechapel had the appearance of a foreign town as the new arrivals introduced their own language, dress, food, societies and synagogues. The second generation soon became a part of the community and moved to less crowded districts of London. Attempts by Fascists to stir up anti-immigrant feeling were rebuffed, most notably in the Battle of CABLE STREET. In recent years Bangladeshi immigrants have taken the place of the JEWS, especially in the clothing industry, but in far fewer numbers. Whitechapel is undergoing considerable redevelopment as the old centre at Gardiner's Corner is replaced by a large traffic roundabout, and as the offices of CITY firms move into much of the area.

Whitechapel Art Gallery *80–82 Whitechapel High Street, E1.* In 1881 Canon Barnett (then vicar of St Jude, WHITECHAPEL) held the first of a series of exhibitions to bring good art to the EAST END. The art gallery was built in 1897–9, financed by private individuals, notably John Passmore Edwards. It is a most interesting Art Nouveau building designed by C.H. Townsend. The mosaic over the door, *The Sphere and Message of Art*, is by Walter Crane. It was established by its first director, Charles Aitken, as a gallery devoted to avant-garde exhibitions.

Whitechapel Bell Foundry *32 and 34 Whitechapel Road, E1.* Established in 1420 in HOUNDSDITCH, the foundry moved to WHITECHAPEL in 1583. Soon afterwards bells were cast here for WESTMINSTER ABBEY. In 1738 the foundry moved to its present site, using the ground and buildings of the 17th-century Artichoke Inn, the cellars of which still survive. Here many of the world's great bells have since been cast, including BIG BEN, America's original Liberty Bell, and the Bicentennial Bell presented to the people of America by the Queen on behalf of the people of Great Britain.

Whitechapel High Street *E1.* Although paved, according to Maitland, in the reign of Henry VIII, Stow found the shabbiness of this street east of ALDGATE 'no small blemish to so famous a city'. The WHITECHAPEL GALLERY on the north side was founded by Canon Barnett. In the foyer of Whitechapel Library next door there is some tiling taken from a demolished house in the street. It shows a view of the haymarket in the street in 1788. This market continued down to 1927. Bloom's, a long-established kosher restaurant, is at No. 90. Bloom's also have a restaurant at No. 130 Golder's Green Road, NW11 which opened in 1963. Morris Bloom started his business at No. 58 Brick Lane, STEPNEY in 1920. He moved in 1924 to No. 2 Brick Lane, Stepney (which was bombed in the BLITZ) and had a factory in Wentworth Street. A connoisseur of table delicacies, he developed a new method of pickling salt beef which drew customers from all over London.

Whitechapel Market One of the largest Victorian street markets. William Besant describes it as selling books, boots, shoes, cutlery, hats and caps, rat traps, birdcages, flowers and skittles amongst many other things. The market was mainly run by Jewish and Irish traders and there was much competition between them. The numbers of Irish street sellers swelled during the famine in the 1850s. The area was surrounded by slaughter houses and there was a large area in the market for the sale of hay and straw. It was a local saying that you could furnish a house, feed a family and plant a garden from Whitechapel Market.

Whitechapel Murders It has never been established for certain whether or not Jack the Ripper committed all the murders attributed to him, but he is generally thought to have had six victims. All were killed within one square mile in the WHITECHAPEL district of London; all were killed within a period of three months; and all but one were prostitutes soliciting at the time of his assault. His methods were as consistent as his choice of victims: each body was found with a slashed throat and in various degrees of mutilation. The murderer's work was done with such horrific precision that the investigating police believed him to have studied surgery.

His first victim, Martha Turner, a 35-year-old prostitute, was found, stabbed repeatedly, on 7 August 1888, on the first floor of George Yard Buildings off WHITECHAPEL ROAD. A few weeks later, on 31 August, the body of Mary Ann Nicholls was found, by two

Whitechapel High Street, from an engraving after J.H. Shepherd, 1837.

THE PENNY ILLUSTRATED PAPER AND ILLUSTRATED TIMES

The body of Catherine Eddowes, a victim of Jack the Ripper, was discovered in Mitre Square, Whitechapel, in 1888.

carters, in a similar condition on the pavement of Buck's Row. The victim, 42 years old and penniless, had been staying in a room in Flower and Dean Street. The pathetic last remark to the lodging-house keeper – 'Don't let my doss, I'll soon be back with the money. See what a fine new bonnet I've got!' – has been attributed both to her and to the Ripper's next prey, Annie Chapman.

Annie Chapman, whose mutilated body was found in a backyard off Hamburg Street on 8 September, could be considered the most hopeless and helpless of all the victims. She had been married to a veterinary surgeon and had three children. The family, however, was broken up by her alcoholism and she eventually became a prostitute.

It was with her murder that the great Ripper scare really started. Then, on 30 September, he achieved his most frightening effect with two murders in one night. First, the body of Elizabeth Stride was discovered in the backyard of a working men's club in Berner Street. Her throat had been slashed but it appeared that her murderer had been interrupted before he could carry out his usual procedure of mutilation. Hers was another desperately tragic story. She had been married and had children but had lost her entire family when the pleasure steamer, the *Princess Alice*, sank in the THAMES. This loss, she claimed, had driven her to drink and prostitution.

At the time that Elizabeth Stride's body was discovered, Catherine Eddowes, aged 43, was being released from the Bishop's Gate police station where she had been taken earlier on charges of drunkenness. Most likely she was approached by the Ripper and suggested Mitre Square for their meeting. She was found there, her body mutilated, early next morning.

For five weeks there were no further attacks and WHITECHAPEL began to relax. Then, on November 9, the most appalling and revolting murder of all was discovered. Since it was the Ripper's only murder committed indoors, he had been able to work undisturbed and with thoroughness. His victim was Marie Kelly, a 24-year-old widow who lived alone. Her body, which had been dismembered and strewn about the room, was discovered by her rent collector. In the fireplace where the remains of charred clothing. This gave rise to one of the numerous theories concerning the murderer's identity – that he wore women's clothes as a disguise.

Every possible means of investigation was employed by the police to find the killer: bloodhounds were brought out on the streets of WHITECHAPEL, hundreds of suspects were interviewed and even the eyes of one of the victims were photographed on the theory that the image of the murderer might be recorded on the retinas of the murdered woman. Throughout the investigation the police received taunting notes from a person claiming to be the murderer. On one occasion the writer of the note enclosed half a human kidney, supposedly removed from a victim. The search for the Ripper proved futile though; and, so great was the public outcry over the failure to arrest the murderer, the London Police Commissioner was forced to resign.

Jack the Ripper disappeared into obscurity but his legend did not. Great interest was aroused over the case, in America as well as in England, and it provided themes for many literary and dramatic productions, perhaps the most notable being Mrs Belloc Lowndes's *The Lodger* (1913). Many theories have been advanced as to the Ripper's identity but none is entirely convincing.

Whitechapel Road *E1*. Runs east from the site of the original white chapel, built in the 14th century, that gave the area its name. Stow regretted the building that had taken place 'almost half a mile beyond it, into the common field'. The origins of the WHITECHAPEL BELL FOUNDRY, which moved to its present site in 1738, can be traced to late medieval times. Further east, opposite the LONDON HOSPITAL, the inscription on a memorial fountain to Edward VII records that it was 'erected from subscriptions raised by Jewish inhabitants of East London': the area was once a centre of Jewish life in London.

Whitecross Street *EC1*. Named after a cross painted white which stood outside a house belonging to HOLY TRINITY PRIORY, ALDGATE in the 13th century. The street once ran from FORE STREET to OLD STREET but the southern half was obliterated in the 2nd World War. WHITECROSS STREET PRISON for debtors stood at the corner with FORE STREET between 1813–70. In 1876–7 the Midland Railway Company built a goods terminus on the site which was also destroyed in the war.

Whitecross Street Market A Victorian street market between Old Street and Upper Whitecross Street. In 1861 Mayhew counted 150 stalls here. It was cleared in the 1890s to make way for a housing development.

Whitecross Street Prison *Whitecross Street, EC1*. Built in 1813–15 by the CORPORATION OF LONDON as a prison for debtors after a campaign fought by Sir Richard Phillips for separating debtors from ordinary criminals. It was designed by William Mountague to hold 500 prisoners. It was closed in 1870 as imprisonment for debt had become rare before being finally abolished and the last 27 prisoners were transferred to HOLLOWAY. In 1876–7 the Midland Railway Company built a good terminus on the site. This was destroyed in the 2nd World War and the site is now covered by the redeveloped BARBICAN.

Whitefields Ground *see* BURIAL GROUNDS.

Whitefield's Tabernacle *Tottenham Court Road, W1*. Built in 1756 for George Whitefield, the Methodist preacher. In 1760 the front was extended to make it the largest Nonconformist church in the world, capable of seating 7,000–8,000 people. It was known derisively as 'Whitefield's soul trap'. Lord Bolingbroke, Horace Walpole and David Hume were among the many distinguished admirers of his preaching. The hall was rebuilt after a fire, in 1857; and again, in 1898–90, after a general collapse. Damaged in the 2nd World War, it was again rebuilt as the Memorial Chapel under the direction of E.C. Butler. It is now the American church.

Whitefriars So called because of the white mantle worn over a brown habit. They were also known as Carmelites. A Carmelite Priory was erected in FLEET STREET in the middle of the 13th century. The events which led up to the foundation are as follows: Richard, Earl of Cornwall, brother of Henry III, returned to England from the Holy Land in 1241; he brought with him a colony of hermits who had been driven from their monastery on Mount Carmel by the Saracens. They were introduced into the presence of the King by William Vesey and Richard Grey; and since they were in search of silence and retirement, foundations were made for them in remote parts of Northumberland and Kent. But their strictly eremitical rule proved unsuitable in the new surroundings and in 1247, a prior general called Simon, who is probably to be identified with St Simeon Stock, obtained from Pope Innocent IV a new rule.

By this the Carmelites ceased to be hermits and became mendicants, following a rule similar to that of the preachers. Their vocation was now to live and work among the people in towns and cities. The move to London was the first one after the revision of the rule. Richard Grey and his wife, Lucy, were the patrons who gave land in Aylesford and 'in the suburbs of London'. Oaks for timber were given by Henry III in 1267 and by Edward I in 1282 and 1299. The site was within the Ward-of-Farringdon-Without. It was an easy five minutes' walk from ST PAUL'S CATHEDRAL on a busy thoroughfare connecting London and WESTMINSTER. The first church was a small one, built in about 1253. A much larger one was built in the middle of the 14th century. The life of the friars was one of deep poverty, as is shown by some of the inventories extant. They were popular with the people and were left unmolested during the PEASANTS' REVOLT. Upon the fall of the KNIGHTS TEMPLAR, they became increasingly important and their buildings were used for large meetings and as a depository for treasure. John

of Gaunt was a devoted patron and left the friars a special cloak and 15 marks of silver in his will. Sir John Paston, in his will made in 1476, requested that if he died in London his body should be brought 'to the chapel of ower Lady of the White Frerys, at the northest corner of the body of the church'. Other people of distinction made similar requests: William Montacute, Earl of Salisbury, was buried here in the 14th century. Whitefriars is mentioned in Shakespeare's *Richard III* in which the Duke of Gloucester commands that the body of the murdered Henry be borne away to Whitefriars.

The house had a right of sanctuary which remained even after the DISSOLUTION. At the time of the DISSOLUTION the site extended in terms of modern streets from FLEET STREET in the north to the THAMES in the south, from WHITEFRIARS and Carmelite streets in the east to the TEMPLE in the west. The library, *frater*, kitchen and other buildings were given to the king's armourer. The great hall was converted into WHITEFRIARS PLAYHOUSE. The chapter house and other parts were conferred on the king's physician.

Not a trace of the priory remains above ground. But considerable remains were found underground in excavations in 1927. These included, buried beneath eight feet of accumulated soil under the *News of the World* building in BOUVERIE STREET, the tiled paving of the cloister walk and a 14th-century vaulted crypt of great beauty.

Whitefriars Playhouse 'There was a theatre in the refectory of the former monastery, for more than 30 years used for plays, last by the Children of Her Majestie,' an observer wrote in 1616. 'It hath little or no furniture for a playhouse saving an old tattered curten, some decayed benches, and a few worn out properties and pieces of Arras for hangings and the stage and tire house. The rain hath made its way in . . . .' Until 1609 it was probably used by the Children of Pauls, a company of boy actors recruited from the choristers of ST PAUL'S CATHEDRAL. Between 1610–13 it was used by a rival company, the Children of the Queen's Revels. Jonson, Beaumont and Fletcher wrote plays for them. By April 1614 it was abandoned.

Whitefriars Street *EC4*. Extends southwards off FLEET STREET between BOUVERIE STREET and HOOD COURT. The site, including the area as far west as the TEMPLE, was once occupied by the Friars of Our Lady of Mount Carmel (*see* WHITEFRIARS). Their premises included a cemetery, cloisters, a church and a garden which went down to the north bank of the THAMES. Whitefriars later became known as an area of fencing-masters. The street used to extend to the river and until 1844 was known as Water Lane. William Filby, the tailor who made Oliver Goldsmith's celebrated plum-coloured coat, had his shop here at the sign of the Harrow.

Whitehall *SW1*. The name 'Whitehall' is of Tudor origin (*see* WHITEHALL PALACE) and was originally applied only to the northern part of the present thoroughfare between HOLBEIN GATE and CHARING CROSS. The narrow central section was known simply as 'The Street', whereas the part south of the point where Henry VIII built KING STREET GATE in 1532 was called KING STREET.

A prospect of Whitehall, showing Inigo Jones's Banqueting House and Holbein Gate. From an engraving by Maurer, 1740.

A route connecting CHARING CROSS to WESTMINSTER existed in medieval times. By the 16th century it was a residential street and several eminent men lived here in the 17th and 18th centuries, including Lord Howard of Effingham, Edmund Spenser, and, from 1647, Oliver Cromwell. Charles I was carried through this street in a sedan chair on his way to WESTMINSTER HALL on the first and last days of his trial. The narrowness of KING STREET caused congestion of traffic in the 17th century. In 1628 an act was passed, ordering that 'stalls of all fishmongers and sellers of hearbes, rootes, or any other things' and any 'trash in the street' that might 'stopp or hinder the passage' should be removed. But Pepys's diary for 27 November 1660 records: 'in King Street, there being a great stop of coaches, there was a falling out between a drayman and my Lord Chesterfield's coachman, and one of his footmen killed.'

The section called Whitehall was, however, of considerable width. There was space enough for a scaffold to be built outside the BANQUETING HOUSE at the time of Charles I's execution, and for the erection of a gun platform in the Civil War and again in 1688. The buildings between HOLBEIN GATE and the BANQUETING HALL were burned down in the fire of 1698, and were replaced by the new house of William van Huls, Clerk of Queen Anne's Robes and Wardrobes.

By the early 18th century, increasing pressure of traffic led to new proposals to clear and broaden the thoroughfare. Thus, in 1723, KING STREET GATE and the gun platform were demolished, to be followed by HOLBEIN GATE and the adjoining house of van Huls in 1759. KING STREET disappeared altogether when, as a result of the destruction of two blocks of houses between DOWNING STREET and GREAT GEORGE STREET, it was finally merged with PARLIAMENT STREET in 1899.

Whitehall is today dominated by Government offices. These include DOVER HOUSE, GWYDYR HOUSE, the MINISTRY OF DEFENCE, the MINISTRY OF HOUSING, the PAYMASTER GENERAL'S OFFICE (now the Parliamentary Counsel Office), the TREASURY. The WAR OFFICE (now part of the MINISTRY OF DEFENCE), Sir George Gilbert Scott's GOVERNMENT OFFICES and

J.W. Murray's Ministry of Agriculture and Fisheries (1909). On the west side are the HORSE GUARDS and the WHITEHALL THEATRE at No. 14. On the west side are the ROYAL UNITED SERVICES INSTITUTE and the OLD SHADES public house. The CENOTAPH is by Lutyens and was erected in 1919–20. There are statues of the Duke of Cambridge, Earl Haig, the 8th Duke of Devonshire and Field Marshal Montgomery (*see* STATUES). Cocks, Biddulph and Co., now the Cocks Biddulph branch of BARCLAY'S BANK, was founded by Francis Biddulph in 1757.

Whitehall *1 Malden Road, Cheam, Surrey.* An early two-storied continuous-jettied timber-framed house, built in about 1500. Additions and alterations made in the 16th century included a two-storied porch, a staircase tower and an attic floor. Whitehall is believed to have been the building where CHEAM SCHOOL was started. For over 200 years, until 1963, it was in the hands of a single family, the Killicks. A recent restoration revealed much of the original construction, and the house was opened to the public by the London Borough of SUTTON in 1978 and is run with the help of a voluntary Friends Society.

Whitehall Court *SW1.* A large block, eight storeys high, built in the French Renaissance Style in 1884 to the designs of Messrs Archer and Green. Of the many clubs which used to have premises here only the Farmers' Club remains at No. 3. The Royal Horse Guards Hotel (285 bedrooms) is at No. 2.

Whitehall Palace This name for the former YORK PLACE may be derived either from the light stone of some of the new buildings, or, more probably, from the custom of naming any festive hall a 'White-Hall' (an example of this is Kenilworth). Henry VIII carried out an extensive rebuilding programme; a turreted gateway, known as the Whitehall Gate which gave access to the palace from the street, was built in 1531–2, and two new sets of stairs led down to the river. New gardens and orchards were set out, and Henry acquired more land towards ST JAMES'S PARK on which he built a cockpit, tennis courts, and the Tiltyard where tournaments and bear-baiting were arranged as royal entertainments. The new property was connected to the old by the HOLBEIN GATE and the KING STREET GATE which spanned the street. Whitehall became the chief London residence of the court. Henry celebrated his marriage to Anne Boleyn here in 1533, and to Jane Seymour in 1536. He issued a set of strict rules, governing the behaviour of those who lived at the palace. They were to be 'loving together, of good unity and accord', and, most important, they were to avoid all 'grudging, rumbling or talking of the King's pastime'. Henry died at Whitehall in 1547. Latimer preached to the boy King, Edward VI, in the courtyard of the palace, and the Great Hall was frequently used for dramatic performances in Elizabeth's time. During James I's reign, Inigo Jones and John Webb drew up plans for a huge new palace, but only the BANQUETING HOUSE was ever completed. Even so, by this time, the palace comprised some 2,000 rooms. Charles I built up a magnificent art collection in Whitehall. He left more than 460 paintings, including 28 Titians and 9 Raphaels. Most of these were dispersed during the Commonwealth when Oliver Cromwell lived in Whitehall as Lord Protector, and died here in 1658.

The court returned after the Restoration, and Charles II restored masques and merrymaking to the palace. He had a laboratory built, and provided accommodation for two of his mistresses. Barbara Castlemaine took possession of a suite over HOLBEIN GATE, while the Duchess of Portsmouth's rooms were, according to Evelyn, 'twice or thrice pulled down to satsfy her prodigal and expensive pleasures'. The Queen lived in a far simpler apartment overlooking the river. Another important resident was James, Duke of Monmouth, who inhabited the converted tennis court, and was to return here as a defeated rebel during the reign of his uncle, James II. James replaced the old Privy Gallery with a three-storey building of brick, designed by Wren, and also added a Roman Catholic Chapel. In 1688, after the arrival of William of Orange in England, James II 'stole away from Whitehall by the Privy Stairs'.

The following year, in the last great ceremonial event at the palace, the crown was offered to William and Mary. The new rulers transferred their royal residence to KENSINGTON PALACE, as William found that the river air of Whitehall exacerbated his asthma. The old palace was damaged by fire in 1691. Wren designed the graceful new terrace which was built for Queen Mary, before her death in 1695. In 1698, apparently through the carelessness of a Dutch laundry woman, the old palace was burned to the ground, with only the BANQUETING HOUSE surviving.

Whitehall Theatre *Whitehall, SW1.* Built in 1930 to the designs of E.A. Stone. Walter Hackett was the lessee and the theatre opened with his play *The Way to Treat a Woman*. He left it in 1934. Since then it has had many lessees and presented many reviews, light comedies and farces. It seats 662.

Whitelands College *West Hill, SW15.* Founded by the National Society of the Church of England in 1841 as a training college for women teachers. Housed in a former girls' boarding school in the KING'S ROAD, CHELSEA, it grew from 12 students in 1841 to over 200 at the end of the century. Angela, later Baroness, Burdett-Coutts became closely associated with the college in the 1850s and 1860s, acting not just as a generous benefactor but also affecting changes in the curriculum. Charles Dickens helped her with this work and visited the college and drew upon it in his writing. In the last quarter of the 19th century John Ruskin also took a close personal interest in Whitelands, gave it hundreds of books, pictures and other objects, and with the principal of the college, inaugurated the Whitelands College May Queen Festival in 1881. This is the origin of the children's May Day celebrations throughout England. One student was elected May Queen, dressed appropriately and handed special editions of Ruskin's books to give away as presents. The festival is still celebrated at the college. As a result of Ruskin's connection with the college, William Morris and Edward Burne-Jones were involved with the decoration of its chapel. When the college moved to its new buildings on West Hill, PUTNEY, in 1930, the architect incorporated 13 Burne-Jones stained-glass windows designed for Whitelands in the 1880s and 1890s. The reredos designed in gold gesso by Morris and created by Faulkner was also incorporated. In 1948 Whitelands became a constituent college of the UNIVERSITY OF LONDON Institute of Education. In 1965 it became co-educational. In 1975 the college was a founder member of the ROEHAMPTON INSTITUTE of Higher Education and diversified its courses. In 1982, Whitelands, along with the Institute, transferred to the University of Surrey which now awards the degrees to the college's students.

William Whiteley Ltd *Queensway, Bayswater.* Born in Leeds in 1831 William Whiteley came to London 20 years later and went to the GREAT EXHIBITION at CRYSTAL PALACE. Excited by all he saw, he determined to build a vast emporium. First working for R. Willey and Co. of LUDGATE, he moved from one firm to another to learn the drapery trade, saving money all the time. Soon he had £700 and set up a business in WESTBOURNE GROVE, then nicknamed 'Bankruptcy Avenue'. In 1863 he opened new premises selling ribbons, lace and fancy goods. By 1872 he had bought up premises all along the street and had so many items in his store that he styled himself 'The Universal Provider', offering to supply 'from a pin to an elephant at short notice'. He had 'living in' accommodation for his staff who worked from 7 a.m. till 11 p.m. As he infringed all agreed retail demarcations by selling goods other than haberdashery, he was unpopular with local tradesmen, and BAYSWATER butchers burnt his effigy on Guy Fawkes night in 1876. His store suffered a number of fires, the most spectacular being in 1897. It burnt for several days and was attended by 34 steam fire engines.

He rebuilt once more, and in his new premises employed 6,000 staff. In 1896 when HYDE PARK was opened to bicycle riding, he bought 500 bicycles and sold out in a day. On 24 January 1907 Whiteley was shot dead in his office by a young man who claimed to be his bastard son. In 1911 a new store designed by J.J. Joass was opened in Queen's Road (now QUEENSWAY) and further extended in 1925. Bought in 1927 by Gordon Selfridge it later came under control of the United Drapery Stores Group which was forced to close it as 'unviable' in 1981, the district in which it was situated no longer being able to support such a shop.

White's Club *37–38 St James's Street, SW1.* The oldest and grandest of the St James's gentlemen's clubs. Its list of members over two-and-a-half centuries is replete with the names of the richest and most distinguished members of society. George IV, William IV and Edward VII were all members. Of the 32 administrations from the time of Sir Robert Walpole to that of Peel every prime minister was a member. Anson and Rodney, the admirals, were members; so were Clive and Wellington, Fox, Horace Walpole, George Selwyn, Lord Chesterfield, Edward Gibbon, Beau Brummell and the great recorders of their times, Charles Greville and Captain Gronow.

The club was founded at WHITE'S CHOCOLATE HOUSE, which had been opened in 1693 on the site of what is now BOODLE'S CLUB by an Italian, Francis White, whose real name was presumably Francesco Bianco. Business prospered and in about 1697 the Chocolate House was moved across the street to a house which was to become part of the premises of ARTHUR'S CLUB. John Arthur was White's assistant manager and after the death of Mrs White became proprietor. It was an expensive house charging twopence for entry when most others were known as 'penny universities'. Steele frequented it and in the first *Tatler* in 1709 readers are informed, 'all accounts of gallantry, pleasure and entertainment shall be under the article of White's Chocolate House.' Gay also mentions it and for Pope in the *Dunciad* (1728) it is where one may 'Teach oaths to youngsters and to nobles wit'. A correspondent informed Swift that 'at White's in St James's Street young noblemen were fleeced and corrupted by fashionable gamblers and profligates'; it was 'the bane of the English nobility'. Swift shook his fist at it every time he passed. In 1711 the house was burned to the ground in a dramatic fire which was started in a gaming-room called 'Hell'. Soon afterwards the *Daily Post* announced that Mr Arthur wished to 'acquaint all noblemen and gentlemen that having had the misfortune to be burnt out of White's Chocolate House, he has removed to Gaunt's Coffee House, next to St James's Coffee House in St James's Street, where he humbly begs that all will favour him with their company as usual.' As with other establishments an inner club developed in the house, admittance to which was given only to approved customers; but its evolution is obscure since the earliest records date from 1736 when White's Chocolate House moved back to its rebuilt premises on the east side of the street and a club (of 82 members) is mentioned for the first time. In 1743 a 'Young Club' was formed by members waiting to join the 'Old Club'. In this year, in the words of the Hon. Algernon Bourke, a 19th-century member and historian of the club, a typical night might involve 'dinner say at seven o'clock, play all night, one man unable to sit in his chair at three o'clock, break up at six the next morning and the winner going away drunk with a thousand guineas.'

White's famous betting book dates from this time. 'There is nothing, however trivial or ridiculous, which is not capable of producing a bet,' noted the *Connoisseur* magazine in May 1754. In the early years bets as to longevity figure prominently: 'Ld Lincoln bets Ld Winchilsea One Hundred Guineas to Fifty Guineas that the Dutchess Dowager of Marlborough does not survive the Dutchess Dowager of Cleveland.' There were also bets on births, marriages, sport, politics, public events, indeed on anything that cropped up in conversation or led to argument. One wet day Lord Arlington bet £3,000 on which of two raindrops would first reach the bottom of a window pane. And in 1750 Walpole related a newspaper report of a man who collapsed at the door of the club and, upon being carried up the steps, was immediately the object of bets as to whether he were dead or not. In more recent times Duff Cooper bet Ivor Guest £10—£1 that Mrs Barney was 'not hanged for the murder of Mr Stevens'.

Throughout most of the 18th and the early decades of the 19th centuries, White's was a byword for gambling for high stakes. Lord Lyttelton wrote in 1750, 'I tremble to think that the rattling of a dice box at White's may one day or other (if my son should be a member of that noble academy) shake down all our fine oaks.' Fortunes were lost. In 1755 Sir John Bland, who at one stage in an evening found himself £32,000 down, shot himself after being ruined at the club.

In that year White's moved again. Robert Arthur had made so much money by now that he was able to buy the freehold of a 'great house in St James's Street' which belonged to Sir Whistler Webster. Both the Old Club (now with 120 members) and the Young Club (with 230 members) moved to the new premises. The chocolate house was no more. In 1781 the two clubs amalgamated; and in 1787–8 the house which they occupied was rebuilt in its present form, probably to the designs of James Wyatt. Soon afterwards the club, which had hitherto welcomed both Tories and Whigs, became involved in the violent political animosities of the time. Pitt and his supporters congregated at White's; Fox, the Prince of Wales and *their* friends at BROOKS'S.

In 1811 the physical appearance of the club-house changed also. The celebrated bow window was created in the middle of the façade and the front door moved to its left. Immediately Beau Brummell made the bow window his own, and here could be seen the great dandy and his friends disporting themselves in their finery. Once pressed for the repayment of a debt of £500, Brummell airily replied, 'I paid you when I was standing at the window of White's and said as you passed, "How do you do?".'

The year after this window was put in, the club was taken over by George Raggett who made a fortune from it, as Arthur had done. It was Raggett's practice to sit up late when gambling for high stakes was in progress, so that he could personally sweep the floor on which he almost invariably found a few dropped sovereigns or gaming counters. In 1814 the number of members had risen to 500 and the waiting list was longer than ever. But political enmities led to so much blackballing – despite Harriette Wilson's assertion that White's blackballed no gentleman who tied a good knot in his neckerchief and kept his hands out of his breeches pockets – that the club rules had to be changed in 1833 when a committee took over from members the election of candidates. By that time, however, the CARLTON CLUB had been formed for committed Conservatives in opposition to BROOKS'S, and thereafter White's became less of a political and more the social club that it had been in the past and is today.

In 1852 the façade of the club-house was altered by James Lockyer and the sculptural decorations of the Four Seasons were added by Sir George Scharf. At this time the question of whether or not members should be allowed to smoke in the club aroused fierce passions. Up till 1845 no form of tobacco was used at the club other than snuff; and when the smoking of cigars became commonplace there were many older members who strongly disapproved of the habit. A smoking-room was eventually and grudgingly provided. Even after the election of the Prince of Wales, a heavy smoker, a resolution that members should be allowed to smoke in the drawing-room was defeated. The Prince consequently helped to establish another club, the MARL-BOROUGH, where members could smoke anywhere they liked except the coffee-room.

Many London clubs were by now owned by their members. But when the Raggett family decided to put up White's for auction, the members' bid of £38,000 was outmatched by a bid of £46,000 made by Henry William Eaton, afterwards 1st Baron Cheylesmore, who was said to have once been an omnibus driver and had made a fortune in a city firm which one of his regular passengers, struck by his appearance and manner, had invited him to join. Eaton had been put up for membership of White's some years before and had been blackballed. As owner of the premises he now increased the rent. His son, Major-General Lord Cheylesmore, an old Etonian guards officer, was elected to the club but, out of loyalty to his father, refused to take up membership; and he further increased the rent. It was not until 1927, when the 1st Lord Cheylesmore's grandson went to live in Canada, that the members were able to buy the club-house.

Whitewebbs Park *Middlesex*. Situated on the northern boundary of the London Borough of ENFIELD to the west of the line of the Roman ERMINE STREET. In 1570 Elizabeth I granted her physician, Dr Huicks, White Webbs House at the edge of ENFIELD CHASE. Its water was supplied by the NEW RIVER from Hertfordshire to the north and the old Conduit House still exists; at the beginning of the 17th century the river was diverted to serve the CITY. James I visited the area frequently – he is said to have knighted a tinker at the King and Tinker tavern – and he incorporated the land north of White Webbs Road into Theobalds Park. The Glasgow Stud Farm dates from the 17th century. In 1605 White Webbs House was reputedly used by the GUNPOWDER PLOT conspirators, and White Webbs Lane to the south was formerly called Rome Lane. The house was demolished in about 1790 and a year later Dr Abraham Wilkinson, an innovator of agricultural techniques, built a house, called White Webbs, on land south of the Lane. The house and estate were subsequently enlarged and the attached woodland also came to be known as Wilkinson's Woods. In 1955 EN-FIELD Urban District Council acquired the estate, creating Whitewebbs Park, and in 1973 the house became an old people's home.

Whitfield Street *W1*. Takes its name from George Whitefield who founded WHITEFIELD'S TABERNACLE in TOTTENHAM COURT ROAD nearby in 1756.

Whitgift School *Haling Park, South Croydon*. Founded by John Whitgift, Archbishop of Canterbury, in 1599 in a building next to the almshouses (which still exist) at the corner of North End and George Street (then Pond Street). In 1871 a new building in North End was designed by Sir Arthur Blomfield. In 1931 the school moved again, to Haling Park, once the estate of Lord Howard of Effingham, to

a school designed by Leathart and Granger. The Blomfield buildings were taken over by Whitgift middle school, now TRINITY SCHOOL, who sold them in 1965. The area has since been redeveloped as a vast complex of shops and offices called the Whitgift Centre.

Whittington Avenue *EC3*. Named after Sir Richard Whittington who owned property in the nearby LEADENHALL STREET. The LONDON METAL EX-CHANGE is on the corner of LEADENHALL AVENUE.

Whittington Club, Arundel Street, *Strand*. Founded in 1846 at the CROWN AND ANCHOR TAVERN. Douglas Jerrold, the journalist, was its first president. Dickens, Thackeray and Mark Lemon, editor of *Punch*, and Herbert Spencer, assistant editor of the *Economist*, were all members. Spencer used to dine here every day and visit the club's library.

Whittington College *Archway Road, Islington*. A charming row of almshouses built about 1822 by the MERCERS' COMPANY. A rare example of the early Gothic revival in London. They were demolished by the LONDON COUNTY COUNCIL after the 2nd World War for a road-widening scheme.

Whittington College *College Hill*. After the death of Richard Whittington in 1423, the executors of his estate obtained a charter from King Henry VI, for the foundation of a College of Priests and an almshouse close to ST MICHAEL PATERNOSTER in College Hill. The two were jointly known as Whittington College, and when the college of priests was suppressed at the Reformation, the almshouse (administered by the MERCERS COMPANY) kept on the name. The almshouses moved to HIGHGATE HILL early in the 19th century (*see* HIGHGATE) and after 1970 were rebuilt in East Grinstead.

Whittington Hospital *Highgate Hill, N19*. The original Smallpox Hospital had been on the site of KING'S CROSS STATION. The first building on the present site was erected in 1846 as a smallpox and vaccination hospital, some of the isolation rooms still being extant. Three other hospitals for the treatment of fevers were built nearby. All were designed by Saxon Snell. In 1929 these were taken over by the LONDON COUNTY COUNCIL and converted to ordinary hospitals, smallpox by then being very rare. After the 2nd World War all the hospitals were amalgamated into one and various names were suggested for the unified hospital. Whittington was chosen in memory of the Lord Mayor who was reputed to have nearly turned back at Highgate Hill (*see* WHITTINGTON STONE).

In 1948 the National Health Service assumed responsibility and several modern blocks have since been built. The hospital now has 1,041 beds and it assists in the teaching of students from UNIVERSITY COLLEGE HOSPITAL.

Whittington Stone *Highgate Hill, N6*. Stands near the foot of the hill on the west side of the road and traditionally marks the spot where Richard Whittington heard BOW BELLS chiming, 'Turn again, Whittington, thrice Lord Mayor of London.' The source of this well-known legend cannot, however, be traced to a date earlier than 1605, almost 200 years after Whittington's death, when a play called *The History of Richard Whittington* was produced in London. The stone now standing here is at least the third on the site. The original stone may have been the base of a pre-Reformation wayside cross which stood outside the Lazar House of St Anthony founded in 1473. It seems to have been removed in 1795 to ISLINGTON, cut in half and placed on either side of Queen's Head Lane. It was replaced with another stone, which was removed in 1821 and replaced by the present stone which is inscribed:

Whittington Stone
Sir Richard Whittington
Thrice Lord Mayor of London
1397 Richard II
1406 Henry IV
1420 Henry V
Sheriff in 1393

This stone was restored, the railing fixed and lamp erected in 1821. (There are two errors here: Whittington was never knighted; and he was four times Mayor.) A later inscription on a metal plaque records that the figure of the cat on top of the stone was placed there in 1964 by 'Mrs Paul Crosfield, Donald Basset and friends'.

Whitton *Surrey*. Situated near HOUNSLOW Heath and west of TWICKENHAM. By the 11th century Whitton – white farm – was a small out-settlement of TWICKENHAM parish. Whitton House, decorated by Laguerre, was the home of Sir Godfrey Kneller from 1703–9, later becoming a teachers' training college, with Francis Palgrave a vice-principal from 1847, and, in 1857, the Royal Military School of Music (*see* KNELLER HALL). Lord Islay, later the 3rd Duke of Argyll, lived at Whitton Place where in 1725 he planted from seed a great number of Cedar of Lebanon trees. Many of his trees were transplanted to KEW GARDENS. William Chambers, designer of KEW GARDENS, was one of the subsequent owners of the house. From about 1800 a park was developed on the site of the Duke's greenhouse, and the house demolished (1847). The grounds were extended into the present Whitton Park. In 1862 the Church of SS Philip and James was consecrated, and gradually the local market gardens disappeared under housing estates. In 1965 Whitton, with TWICKENHAM, became part of the London Borough of RICHMOND-UPON-THAMES.

Widow's Son *75 Devons Road, Bow, E3*. Down among the wharves and warehouses this inn was built in 1848 on the site of a cottage owned by a widow who made a hot cross bun for her missing sailor son every year. The custom has been carried on for over 150 years and every Easter a sailor is invited to add another bun to the collection, which hangs from the wooden ceiling.

Wiener Library *see* INSTITUTE OF CONTEMPORARY HISTORY.

Wig and Pen Club *229–230 Strand, WC2*. A club, intended for lawyers and writers, housed in two adjoining timber-framed and stuccoed buildings, No. 229 of the early 17th and No. 230 of the early 18th century. The gate-keeper of the TEMPLE once lived here.

Wigmore Hall *Wigmore Street, W1*. A concert hall built in 1901 by Friedrich Bechstein, adjoining his London pianoforte showrooms. The Bechstein Hall, as it was first known, seated 550 and cost nearly £100,000. It had excellent acoustics. The first public concert was given here by Evelyn Stuart in June 1901. On the outbreak of war with Germany in 1914 Bechstein's property was taken over and run by a receiver and manager. In 1916 the Board of Trade ordered it to be auctioned. The hall, studios, offices, showrooms and 137 pianos were sold for £56,000 to an agent of DEBENHAM'S. It was reopened as the Wigmore Hall in 1917.

Wigmore Street *W1*. Built in 1719–46 and named after one of the titles, Baron Wigmore of Herefordshire, of the ground landlord, Edward Harley, Earl of Oxford. The street dips sharply about the middle where it passes down and up the banks of the TYBURN, now concealed in a culvert. Sir William and Lady Hamilton had their first marital home in Wigmore Street in 1791. No. 9 was the childhood home of Marie Tempest in 1860. Matthew Cotes Wyatt, the sculptor, lived at No. 21 in 1803–4. Nos 23–37, the former premises of Debenham and Freebody, a terracotta building with beautiful windows, is by Clark and Russell (1907–8). The WIGMORE HALL is at No. 36. St Christopher's Place, an alleyway off Wigmore Street, is one of London's smartest shopping purlieus. Bendick's, the chocolate manufacturers at No. 53, were founded soon after the 1st World War by Captain Benson and Mr Dickson. The firm, which also has shops in GROSVENOR STREET, SLOANE STREET and ROYAL EXCHANGE, was granted a royal warrant in 1952.

Wilderness House *Hampton Court Palace, Middlesex*. Lies within the walls of the Palace. It was built about 1700 for the King's Master Gardener, Henry Wise, and occupied by him and his successors, including Charles Bridgeman, George Lowe and Lancelot ('Capability') Brown. During Lancelot Brown's time the famous vine was planted and the kitchen garden was expanded to produce peaches, pineapples, cherries and strawberries for the royal table. He was responsible for the grey brick extension on the left-hand side of the house. In 1881 it became a 'grace and favour' residence. Lady White, widow of Field Marshal Sir George White, the British Army commander at the siege of Ladysmith, had it from 1910 until her death in 1935, when King George V offered it as a home to the Grand Duchess Xenia of Russia.

Wilkinson Sword Ltd *287 Acton Lane, W4*. Founded in 1772 by Henry Nock, a gunmaker, in LUDGATE HILL. His partner, James Wilkinson, inherited the business in 1805. In 1825 James's son, Henry, took over the firm which began to make swords in 1840. In 1887 the name of the firm was changed to the Wilkinson Sword Company and a specially designed factory was opened in CHELSEA. Larger premises were acquired at Acton in 1903. Gardening tools and razors were first made in 1920. Showrooms were opened at No. 27 PALL MALL in 1825. These were moved to No. 53 PALL MALL, thence to No. 16 before being closed in 1969.

Willesden *NW2, NW10*. Lies to the north-west of Central London, bounded to the south by the HARROW

ROAD, to the east by the EDGWARE ROAD and to the north and west by the River BRENT which gave its name to the new Borough formed by the amalgamation of the Boroughs of WILLESDEN and WEMBLEY.

Until the 19th century it was a rural area of exceptional charm, with small hamlets such as NEASDEN and HARLESDEN, a few large houses, farms and the village of Willesden itself. They were strung along the High Road, between Chapel End at Willesden Green and Church End, and grouped round the Parish Church of ST MARY. The population grew from 751 in 1811 to over 100,000 in 1901, an increase largely brought about by the spread of the network of public transport services.

To begin with the development was for prosperous, commuting Victorian businessmen whose large villas still stand in Craven Park and Nicol Road, but subsequent development was of a humbler nature, and row upon row of small terraced houses were laid out over the woods and fields. The fact that the whole of Willesden had been given to the Dean and Chapter of ST PAUL'S CATHEDRAL by King Athelstan in AD938 is recalled by street names like Chapter Road and St Paul's Avenue. Much of the land was sold to landowners whose vanished estates are commemorated by roads like Mapesbury Road or Brondesbury Park. All Soul's Avenue and College Road recall the fact that another large landowner was All Souls College, Oxford.

Much of Willesden's past has been swept away, but there are survivals, including the parish church, grouped with the Vestry Hall and Church Cottages, OXGATE FARMHOUSE and THE GRANGE. Standing high above Willesden is the early 19th-century DOLLIS HILL HOUSE. There are some old cottages behind the Spotted Dog in the High Road, Willesden Green and there are agricultural labourers' cottages (originally attached to Willesden Green Farm and sadly dilapidated) in Pound Lane. Also in Pound Lane stand the old Church Infant Schools built in 1858. The complex of St Andrew's Church, Clergy House and Schools in the High Road, Willesden Green were built by James Brooks in 1896. These buildings are now listed, as is the State Cinema at the Kilburn end of Willesden Lane. At the time of its construction in 1937 this cinema was the largest in Europe, and is still a superb example of grandiose cinema design.

William Ellis School *Highgate Road, NW5.* Secondary school for boys, founded by the marine insurer and philanthropist, William Ellis in 1862. The school's education was based on the utilitarian principles of John Stuart Mill and George Birkbeck, and was one of ten so-called Birkbeck schools. The school moved to its present site in 1937. In 1982 there were about 700 pupils.

William Morris Gallery and Brangwyn Gift *Lloyd Park, Forest Road, E17.* Housed in a mid-18th-century house, originally called WATER HOUSE, the home of William Morris between 1848 and 1856. The first proposal to use it as a museum to commemorate Morris's work was in the 1900s. It was not, however, until the 1930s that any definite plan was formed. Both Arthur Heygate Mackmurdo and Frank Brangwyn gave donations forming the nucleus of the gallery. It was opened by Clement Attlee in 1950, the war having interrupted its progress. Between the beginning of 1981 and May 1982 extensive repair work and enlarge-

ments were carried out. It exhibits all aspects of the work of William Morris and Co, including displays of textiles and wallpaper, stained glass, ceramics, furniture, embroidery and tapestry with a special section on his book designs. There are also displays of ceramics by William De Morgan and the Martin Brothers, furniture by Ernest Gimson and Sidney Barnsley. The first floor rooms include work by the Pre-Raphaelites, late 19th-century sculpture, Sir Frank Brangwyn and A.H. Mackmurdo and the Century Guild.

William Street *SW1.* An entrance to the LOWNDES ESTATE and named after the developer, William Lowndes (as is William Mews, its service road). It was created in 1830, the east side being built considerably earlier than the west side. Lady Morgan, the Irish authoress, took No. 11 in 1838 shortly after it was built. She knew Cubitt and encouraged him to build an easy way into the Park.

William IV Street *WC2.* Named after the king during whose reign the West STRAND improvements were carried out. The publishers, Chatto and Windus and the Hogarth Press, are at No. 40. The old CHARING CROSS HOSPITAL is on the north side.

Williams and Glyn's Bank Ltd *Birchin Lane, EC3.* As successor to some of the oldest banks in London, Williams and Glyn's was established in 1970 by the merger of three banks owned by the Royal Bank of Scotland. Glyn, Mills and Co. had begun business as Vere, Glyn and Hallifax at 70 LOMBARD STREET in 1753. The firm moved to BIRCHIN LANE in 1757 and to the present site at 20 BIRCHIN LANE in 1788. Specialising in bank agencies, the business was strengthened by the acquisition of Currie and Co. of CORNHILL (founded in 1773) in 1864, HOLT AND CO. in 1923 and CHILD AND CO. in 1924. Control passed to the Royal Bank of Scotland in 1939. William Deacon and Co. founded in 1771 as Raymond, Williams, Vere, Lowe and Fletcher of 81 CORNHILL, also developed a large agency business. In 1890 it was absorbed by the Manchester and Salford Bank, which was renamed William Deacon's Bank in 1901 and acquired by the Royal Bank in 1930. In 1970 Glyn, Mills and William Deacon's, together with the National Bank (established in 1835), were amalgamated. Williams and Glyn's Bank emerged as the fifth largest London clearing bank, with over 30 branches in the London area.

Williamson's Tavern *Groveland Court, Bow Lane, EC4.* This building dates back to the 17th century. It was the official residence of the LORD MAYOR OF LONDON and it was here that the then occupant of that office entertained William III and Mary. They presented him with a pair of wrought iron gates, which can be seen at the end of the alleyway. It was bought in 1739 by one Robert Williamson who turned it into a public house. A stone in the parlour marks the centre of the CITY OF LONDON.

Will's Coffee House *1 Bow Street.* Established by William Urwin shortly after the Restoration. It became known as the 'Wits' Coffee House' and was celebrated for its literary patrons. Much of its reputation rested on the patronage of Dryden. 'The great press was to get near the chair where John Dryden sate. In the winter that chair was always in the warmest nook by the fire; in summer it stood in the balcony.' The Wits took the opportunity to criticise Dryden's latest plays here, as well as to curry favour with him. In 1679 he was attacked walking home by a gang hired by the Earl of Rochester who thought Dryden had written the anonymous *Essay on Satire* attacking Rochester and the Duchess of Portsmouth. Pepys also frequented the house, finding 'witty and pleasant discourse' here. Wycherley introduced Pope to Will's, 'out of pure compassion for his exotick Figour, narrow circumstances and humble appearance.' Although the house is supposed to have lost popularity after Dryden's death in 1700, literary anecdotes and references continue to abound. The *Tatler* (1709–10), however, records a change; 'Where you used to see songs, epigrams and satires in the hands of every man you met, you have now only a pack of cards.' After Addison established BUT-TON'S, Will's began to lose popularity and surrendered the title of 'Wits' Coffee House' to that establishment. It closed towards the middle of the 18th century.

Wilton Crescent *SW1*. An elegant and very grand crescent constructed in 1827 by W.H. Seth-Smith, and Thomas Cubitt and named after the 1st Earl of Wilton, father-in-law of the 1st Marquess of Westminster, who owned the land. It was refaced in stone in the early 1900s. At No. 2 is the High Commission of the Republic of Singapore; at No. 9 the Embassy of the Republic of Argentina; and at No. 27 the Luxembourg Embassy. Alfonso Lopez-Pumarejo, twice President of the Republic of Columbia, lived at No. 33. Many MPs have lived in it and no fewer than nine had houses here in 1854. Algernon Charles Swinburne lived here in 1856. It is part of the GROSVENOR ESTATE.

Wilton Place *SW1*. A short street built in 1825 to connect the BELGRAVIA development of the Grosvenors with KNIGHTSBRIDGE (Grosvenor Crescent was not cut through until much later). The houses on the west side are of the same date and KINNERTON STREET was made as their service road. The houses and church on the east side date from the late 1840s. The original entrance was to a cow yard named Porter's Lane. Amongst the earliest occupants was Sir James Macdonnel, the defender of Hougoumont at the battle of Waterloo, who lived No. 15 and died there in 1857. The Marquess of Westminster married Lady Eleanor Egerton, daughter of the first Earl of Wilton in 1794. This gives the area its name. The BERKELEY HOTEL was completed in 1971. This is mainly on GROSVENOR ESTATE land and is part of the original estate which Mary Davies brought to the Grosvenors on her marriage. In 1759 about half the site was leased to the Army and a barracks for foot guards was built here. This was demolished in 1840. The houses subsequently built on the site were pulled down to make way for the hotel. St Paul's Church is by Thomas Cundy the Younger (1840–3). St Paul's Victorian vicarage at No. 32 contrasts strongly with the earlier houses in the street. George Bentham, the botanist, lived at No. 25 until his death in 1884.

Wilton Row *SW1*. Originally Crescent Mews, the service road to the east side of WILTON CRESCENT and built in 1828–30, although it does not show on the 1830 maps.

The public house, The Grenadier, was built in 1830 and, despite the stories, was never an officer's mess. It has a sentry box outside.

Wilton Street *SW1*. Built in 1817. Henry Gray, author of *Gray's Anatomy*, lived at No. 8 in 1827–61.

Wimbledon *SW19*. No mention of Wimbledon occurs in the *Domesday* Survey as it was assessed under the extensive Manor of MORTLAKE. From 1328 until 1536 a Manor of Wimbledon appears among the possessions of the Archbishop of Canterbury. In 1588, after passing through a number of royal hands, Queen Elizabeth granted it to Sir Thomas Cecil, 1st Earl of Exeter, who immediately built Wimbledon House which stood on high ground where Home Park Road is today. This was replaced in 1732 by a house built for Sarah, Duchess of Marlborough, who left it to her grandson, the Hon. John Spencer, and the manor has remained with the Earls Spencer ever since. This house was burned down in 1785 and its successor remained in Arthur Road until 1949.

Wimbledon Village grew at the top of the hill surrounding Wimbledon House and the CHURCH. Immediately to the north of the Church is the Old Rectory, built about 1500 but with considerable, mainly Victorian, additions. The High Street is part of the medieval village and at one end contains EAGLE HOUSE built in 1613 and adjacent, the Rose and Crown, dating from the late 17th century. This was one of the chief inns of the village and it is known that a bowling alley existed here in 1670. The Dog and Fox stands at the junction of Church Road and High Street and although comparatively modern, stands on a site occupied by an inn since at least Tudor times. Most of the remainder of High Street was redeveloped in the late 19th century and the former buildings demolished or substantially converted. The railway came to Lower Wimbledon in 1838 and was one of the first in South London. Because of high ground in the village, the station was situated in open country half a mile away at the foot of the hill. The original station is now the Railway Tavern public house. Very slowly housing development surrounded the station and most residential roads were not laid out until the 1880s.

Wimbledon Common (1,100 acres) is still unenclosed and contains an impressive restored WINDMILL at its centre. The Common was used for reviews of Army Volunteers throughout the 19th century and for competitions by the National Rifle Association from 1860 until 1890 when they moved to Bisley. Distinguished residents of Wimbledon have included William Wilberforce, Charles James Fox, Frederick Marrgat, the novelist, and John Murray, the publisher (*see also* WIMBLEDON CHAMPIONSHIPS).

Wimbledon Championship The premier Lawn Tennis Competition in the world. It has always been played on the lawns of the All England Club. These were originally at Worple Road; and since 1922 have been at the Club's new ground in Church Road. Improvements are continually being made and the seating capacity increased. The accommodation now exceeds 30,000, the capacity of the Centre Court being 14,000 and that of Court No. 1 approximately 8,000. There are 16 outside grass courts and ten clay, though the grass is used only during the Championship. The club was originally founded as the All England Croquet

Club in 1869; but in 1877 it became the All England Croquet and Lawn Tennis Club, and finally, in 1882, the All England Lawn Tennis and Croquet Club (still its official title) as lawn tennis gained ascendancy. It is a private club of which the winner of the Men's Singles title in any year is usually invited to become an honorary member. The Lawn Tennis Association, founded in 1888, became the governing body of the game in Britain and shared in its organisation with the All England Club at Wimbledon.

Wimbledon Football Club *see* FOOTBALL CLUBS.

Wimbledon House *Strand*. Built in the late 16th century to the east of EXETER HOUSE by Sir Edward Cecil, later Viscount Wimbledon. Inigo Jones is said to have designed it. It was burned down in 1628, the day after Wimbledon's country house had been accidentally blown up with gunpowder.

Wimbledon Lawn Tennis Museum *Church Road, SW19*. Opened by the Duke of Kent, President of the All England Lawn Tennis and Croquet Club, in 1977, the centenary of the WIMBLEDON Championships. The idea of such a museum had been inspired by the success of an exhibition held in 1972 at Leamington Spa to commemorate the centenary of the world's first lawn tennis club. Between then and the museum's opening, the growing number of exhibits were stored at the Lawn Tennis Association's premises in Palliser Road, BARON'S COURT. The exhibits include the large private collection of the tennis historian, Tom Todd, held here on permanent loan; life-size models of famous players; ladies' tennis clothes of different periods; a late Victorian racquet-maker's workshop; a reconstruction of the men's dressing-room at Worple Road (*see* WIMBLEDON); court-side equipment; tennis bric-à-brac displayed in reconstructed rooms of the Victorian era and the 1930s; a blazer worn by a member of the English team at the 1924 Olympics, the last time tennis was included in the Games events; and equipment for playing 'Sphairistike', one of tennis's progenitors. There is also a library of tennis books and periodicals, the Kenneth Ritchie Wimbledon Library, named after Lord Ritchie of Dundee, a former Chairman of the STOCK EXCHANGE, who took a keen interest in the game.

Wimbledon Theatre *Broadway, Wimbledon, SW19*. Designed by Cecil Masey and Roy Young for J.B. Mulholland under whose management the theatre opened on 26 December 1910 with the pantomime, *Jack and Jill*. It was a successful house until the 1930s, many famous artists appearing in it, including Gracie Fields. The original pantomime was the start of a tradition of family Christmas shows which despite the general decline in theatre business still continues successfully. In the mid-1930s the theatre turned to repertory and managed to keep open until 1965. When ultimately it faced closure a local campaign to save it resulted in its purchase from the Mulholland family by the local authority in 1965. Renovations were completed in 1968 and it opened in November of that year. Since then many notable companies and stars have performed in the theatre including the National Theatre, D'Oyly Carte, the Royal Ballet, Marlene Dietrich, Danny La Rue and the Actors' Company.

Wimpole Street *W1*. Built in about 1724 by John Prince and named after Wimpole, the Cambridgeshire estate of the ground landlord, Edward Harley, Earl of Oxford. Edmund Burke had a house here in 1757. At No. 1 is The Royal Society of Medicine, which was founded in 1907 by amalgamating the Royal Medical Chirurgical Society with 16 smaller ones. Sir John Belcher designed the building in 1912. Admiral Lord Hood lived at No. 12; and Elizabeth Barrett at No. 50 from 1841 till she eloped with Robert Browning on 12 September 1846. Henry Hallam, the historian, lived at No. 67 in 1819–40. Alfred, Lord Tennyson, was engaged to his daughter when her brother, his friend, died. For him he wrote 'In Memoriam', speaking of 'The dark house by which once more I stand, Here in the dark unlovely street'. Wilkie Collins lived at No. 82 in 1889.

Winchester House *Southwark*. The large palace of the Bishops of Winchester for over 500 years. It had a long river frontage and a park of some 70 acres (*see* LIBERTY OF THE CLINK *and* BANKSIDE). It was built for William Giffard, Bishop of Winchester, in 1109. The bishops usually held high office from the 14th century until 1550 and many important visitors were entertained here. In 1424 James I of Scotland and Joan Beaufort held their wedding reception here after their marriage in SOUTHWARK CATHEDRAL. In 1540 Henry VIII probably met Catherine Howard, his fifth bride, at the house. The last bishop to live there was the saintly Lancelot Andrewes who died in 1626. In 1642, when the episcopacy was suppressed by order of Parliament, it was converted to a prison for royalists. While imprisoned here Sir Kenelm Digby wrote his *Critical Remarks on Sir Thomas Browne's Religio Medici*. It remained a prison for five years and was then sold to Thomas Walker of CAMBERWELL. At the Restoration it was returned to the see of Winchester but was in such a bad state that the Bishop let it out as tenements and it gradually deteriorated. In 1663 the park was leased for building. In 1814 a fire revealed the rose window of the great hall, 13 ft in diameter, in a warehouse in CLINK STREET.

Winchester House *Southwark Bridge Road, SE1*. The former house of Captain Eyre Massey Shaw, Superintendent of the LONDON FIRE BRIGADE. It was built in 1823–6 as two houses by Harrison Rawlings, MP who had already bought the workhouse behind it which he converted into a hat factory. He gave the house its name because it stands on the old Bishop of Winchester's Estate. It was purchased in 1870 by the METROPOLITAN BOARD OF WORKS as a residence for the Chief Officer of the Metropolitan Fire Brigade who had asked for accommodation of 'not less than 20 rooms'. The two houses were converted into one. In 1886 the Fire Brigade headquarters moved here from WATLING STREET. Shaw would emerge from his house in the early hours of the morning and ring a bell to parade his men. With the completion of the new ALBERT EMBANKMENT building, Winchester House ceased to be the headquarters of the Fire Brigade. It now houses the LONDON FIRE BRIGADE MUSEUM.

Winchester Palace *see* WINCHESTER HOUSE, SOUTHWARK.

Winchester Road *NW3*. Takes its name from William Waynflete, Bishop of Winchester, the first Provost of Eton College which was endowed with the manor of Chalcots (*see* CHALK FARM) by Henry VI. The abstract bronze is by F.E. McWilliam (1964).

Winchmore Hill *N21*. A district in the former Borough of SOUTHGATE. Before the coming of the railway in 1871 it was a remote hamlet. The centre of the old settlement was at Winchmore Hill Green and is still clearly recognisable as such. The Friends' Meeting House of 1790 stands on Church Hill. The area was largely swamped by middle-class suburban housing before and after the 1st World War.

Windham House Club *Pall Mall*. Established in 1828 as 'a place of meeting for a Society of Gentlemen all connected with each other by a common bond of literary or personal acquaintance.' It was for a short time housed at 106 PALL MALL, a building which had been occupied by Dr Johnson's friend, William Windham, the statesman and member of the Literary Club (*see* THE CLUB). It then moved to 10 ST JAMES'S SQUARE, having changed its name to the Windham Club; and in 1836 move yet again to No. 13 (*see* ST JAMES'S SQUARE). It left here in 1941 and its members were accommodated by the TRAVELLERS' until 1945 when the club was amalgamated with the MARLBOROUGH and Orleans Clubs to form the Marlborough-Windham Club.

Windmill *Wimbledon Common, SW19*. Believed to be the only remaining example of a hollow-post flour mill in this country. In this type of mill the shaft driving the machinery passes through the hollowed-out core of the main supporting post. A post mill was erected by Edward Hall in 1613 on the common near Tibbett's Corner, but this had been removed by the end of the 17th century. Charles March of ROEHAMPTON, who built the present mill in 1817, was a carpenter rather than a mill-wright which may account for the unusual design. Two pairs of 4 ft 6 ins diameter stones were used for grinding. The mill fell into disuse after 1865 and was used only for residential accommodation. It was

The Windmill on Wimbledon Common, built in 1817, was restored as a museum in 1975.

substantially restored in 1893 and also in 1975 when a museum was established here.

Windmill Hill *NW3*. Takes its name from a windmill which stood at the top of the hill from at least the 14th until the early 18th century. Joanna Baillie, the poet and dramatist, lived at Bolton House for almost 50 years.

Windmill Street *W1*. In FITZROVIA, it takes its name from an old windmill, probably that of the manor of Tottenham Court, which stood at the junction with CHARLOTTE STREET and was still there in the middle of the 18th century. Originally a farm track, leases for building on it were granted to John Goodge in the 1720s. Development was complete by about 1770. Henry Morland, the portrait painter and father of George Morland, was living at No. 36 in 1779. The Fitzroy Tavern at No. 43 (built to the designs of W.M. Brutton in 1897) was, in the 1930s, a favourite haunt of Augustus John and his friends and, in the 1940s, of writers, including Cyril Connolly, John Lehmann, George Orwell, Dylan Thomas and J. Maclaren-Ross.

Windmill Tavern *Old Jewry*. According to Stow it was originally a synagogue, made over to an order of friars when the Jews were banished from England by Edward I, 'then a nobleman's house, after that a merchant's house, wherein mayoralties have been kept, and now a wine tavern.' It is mentioned in Ben Jonson's *Everyman in his Humour*. It was here in 1628 that Dr Lambe, an astrologer consulted by the unpopular Duke of Buckingham, tried to take shelter from an angry mob that had chased him from the FORTUNE THEATRE. The landlord, refusing to protect him, pushed him out into the street where the mob set upon him, injuring him so badly that he died the next day.

Windmill Theatre *Great Windmill Street, W1*. Takes its name from a windmill which stood here until the late 18th century. Originally a small cinema, known as the Palais de Luxe, it was built in 1910. Unable to compete with the subsequent growth of larger cinemas, it became the property of Mrs Laura Henderson who converted it into a theatre. Her architect, Howard Jones, redeveloped the interior. It opened in December 1931 with *Inquest*, a play by Michael Barrington. Its lack of success as a theatre led to its being used again as a cinema temporarily.

But in 1932 Mrs Henderson gave her general manager, Vivian Van Damm, a free hand. And on 3 February 1932 he introduced 'revuedeville', a French innovation of non-stop variety which proved immensely successful, running daily from 2.30 p.m. to 11 p.m. The theatre became celebrated for its (almost) nude girls who were required to remain motionless in accordance with the then law. Apart from compulsory closure between 4 and 16 September 1939 it was the only London theatre to remain open during the whole of the war, adopting the proud slogan, 'We never closed'. It was a nursery for comedians. Many, who subsequently achieved great success, Harry Secombe, Jimmy Edwards and Tony Hancock among them, owed their start to the Windmill. The policy continued under the direction of Vivian Van Damm until his death in 1960 and thereafter, until 1964 under that of his daughter Sheila. It closed on 31 October 1964 and was reconstructed as a cinema. Paul Raymond bought the lease in 1973 and re-adapted it to its 'revuedeville' form but presenting sex revues lacking the former element of comedy.

Windsor Castle   *114 Campden Hill Road, W8*. This country-style, cottage-like inn was built in 1835 and has remained virtually unchanged. There are three small, plain bars. The walls are decorated with John Leech prints. There is a small garden. The name originated from a legend that on a clear day Windsor Castle could be seen – recent building has made this impossible.

Wine Office Court   *Fleet Street, EC4*. First shown on Ogilby and Morgan's map in 1676, it was so named because licences for selling wine were issued at premises here. The London house of the Bishops of Peterborough once stood in the Court. The house's extensive vaults still exist and are used as wine cellars by the CHESHIRE CHEESE. The part of Wine Office Court that runs eastward into SHOE LANE was once known as King's Head Court, and here could be found the shop of John Ogilby, the writer, translator, printer and, with his wife's grandson, William Morgan, compiler of the map of London. In 1760–2 Oliver Goldsmith lived in lodgings at No. 6 with a relation of John Newberry's the bookseller, and here began work on *The Vicar of Wakefield*. Johnson came to supper with him one evening, dressed with an astonishing scrupulousness because he had heard it said that Goldsmith, who spent far more money on clothes than he could well afford, had quoted him as an example of slovenly habits.

Winter Garden Theatre   (*New Middlesex Theatre of Varieties, 1911–19*) *Drury Lane*. Built in 1911 by Frank Matcham as a music-hall on the site of the Mogul Saloon, a Victorian music-hall affectionately known as 'The Old Mo'. It was acquired in 1919 by George Grossmith and Edward Laurillard. The theatre was then completely redecorated and reopened with *Kissing Time*, a musical by Guy Bolton and P.G. Wodehouse, which had 430 performances. In 1921–6, it was managed jointly by Grossmith and J.A.E. Malone. They had a string of musical successes, the chief being *Sally* (1921) and *The Cabaret Girl* (1922). In 1927 *The Vagabond King* began its run of 480 performances. In the 1930s and 40s the theatre was often closed, though *No Room at the Inn* (1946), by Joan Temple, had 425 performances. In 1952 it was taken for a season by Alec Clunes for the Arts Theatre Club productions. Afterwards there were long runs of *Witness for the Prosecution* (1953) by Agatha Christie, *The Water Gypsies (1955)* and *Hotel Paradiso* (1956). The theatre closed in 1960.

Witanhurst   *Highgate West Hill, N6*. This neo-Georgian mansion was built for Sir Arthur Crosfield in 1913, on the site of an early 18th-century house, Parkfield. It was used as a hospital during the 1st World War but in the inter-war years, and after the 2nd World War, it was the scene of much social entertainment, notably the annual pre-WIMBLEDON tennis parties which were held here for more than 30 years. After the death of Lady Crosfield in the 1960s, the house was put up for sale, being advertised as 'London's largest private residence', only the royal palaces being larger. Witanhurst's colonnades can be seen from many parts of HAMPSTEAD HEATH, and its extensive wooded grounds adjoin the Heath.

Woburn Square   *WC1*. This used to be an elegant square of Georgian houses built in 1828 by James Sim and named after Woburn Abbey, seat of the Duke of Bedford. It was demolished in 1969, amid protests, to make way for the LONDON UNIVERSITY Institute of Education and of Law, and the SCHOOL OF ORIENTAL AND AFRICAN STUDIES by Denys Lasdun and Partners. At the north-west corner is a building by Charles Holden (1958) shared by the WARBURG INSTITUTE and the COURTAULD INSTITUTE GALLERIES.

Woburn Walk   *WC1*. Formerly called Woburn Buildings, it was designed by Thomas Cubitt in 1822 as a small shopping centre. The bow-fronted shops on both sides are beautifully preserved. There is a plaque to mark W.B. Yeats's lodging here in 1865–1919. Dorothy Richardson, the first 'stream of consciousness' novelist, lived across the street from Yeats.

Wood Green   *N22*. Lies seven miles to the north of central London. It has a history as a rural hamlet originating as a small settlement at the foot of a wooded hill in the heart of which was a green, and it is from this that the village derived its name, Tottenham Wode Green and, subsequently, Wood Leigh. Until 1888 Wood Green was part of TOTTENHAM. The manor house comprised 300 to 400 acres and was known as The Ducketts. It had many owners and was a farm when it was destroyed in 1870. In 1609 the construction of the NEW RIVER between Amwell and London began and with the building of the river the peace of Wood Green was temporarily broken by an onslaught of navvies. In 1619, when the Earl of Dorset made a survey, Wood Green consisted of a few farms, ten houses and a population of 50. 110 years later, when the next survey was made in 1798, this had only increased to 100. In 1843, when the population had reached 400, a parish church was erected but this was too small to meet the needs of a growing parish and a new one was constructed in 1873, the year of the building of ALEXANDRA PALACE. The major turning point for Wood Green was the building of its railway station in 1859 and with the consequent development its character became more that of suburb. In 1888 Wood Green gained its own board of health and in 1894 it became an urban district, finally being granted its charter in 1933. Today its is best known for its shopping city, a complex designed by Richard, Sheppard, Robson and Partners which took seven years to build and was officially opened by the Queen on 13 May 1981.

Wood Street   *EC2*. Where wood was sold in medieval London. One of the sheriffs' prisons, WOOD STREET COMPTER, used to be in this street. Also the churches of St Michael, St Peter West Cheap and St Alban. St Peter's was destroyed in the GREAT FIRE. Only the churchyard remains. The plane tree in it is mentioned by Wordsworth in 'The Reverie of Poor Susan':

At the corner of Wood Street when daylight appears
Hangs a thrush that sings loud, it has sung for three years.
Poor Susan has passed by the spot, and has heard
In the silence of morning, the song of the bird.

St Michael's was demolished in 1897 and St Alban's bombed in 1940. St Alban's tower has been preserved. From the middle of the 19th until into the 20th century

Wood Street was noted for its drapers, milliners and haberdashers. The MITRE in Wood Street was a favourite resort of Ben Jonson and later of Pepys. Also here was the Cross Keys, the posting inn where the young Dickens arrived from Rochester and where Pip arrives in *Great Expectations*. HABERDASHERS' HALL is nearby in STAINING LANE. In the 2nd World War the street was devastated. It is now lined with new blocks, among them the City of London Police Station designed by Donald McMorran and George Whitby (1966). This station has a small museum of exhibits relative to the history of the CITY OF LONDON POLICE. Hill Samuel and Co., merchant bankers at No. 100, were formed in 1965 by the merger of M. Samuel and Co. (founded 1878) and Philip Hill (founded 1907).

Wood Street Compter *Wood Street, EC2*. The compter was a prison under the control of the SHERIFFS usually used for debtors but sometimes for other prisoners when NEWGATE was full. In 1555 prisoners were transferred here from the ancient BREAD STREET COMPTER. The Wood Street Compter, built as a prison at that time, stood on the east side of the street a few yards from CHEAPSIDE. There was room for 70 inmates. The compter was divided into three sections – 'the masters' side' for the wealthy, 'the knights' side' for the comfortably off and 'the hole' for the poor. On admission prisoners' names were entered in the Black Book. In 1617 an actor named Fennor wrote, 'When a gentleman is brought in by the watch for some misdemeanour committed he must pay at least an angell before he be discharged, he must pay twelve pence for turning the key at the master-side door, two shillings to the chamberlain, twelve pence for his garnish for wine, ten pence for dinner whether he stay or no, and when he comes to be discharged at the book, it will cost at least three shillings and sixpence more, besides sixpence for the book-keepers pains, and sixpence for the porter . . .' The office of keeper was a profitable post and until 1766 was acquired by purchase. In 1791 the prisoners were moved to GILTSPUR STREET COMPTER. Wood Street Compter was demolished in 1816.

Woodall House *Lordship Lane, N22*. Built in 1863 as a school by the Royal Masonic Society. In 1903 the school moved to Bushey and the building became a teachers' training college. In 1931 it was sold to the Tottenham District Gas Company, now the Eastern Gas Board, who named it after Sir Corbet Woodall, a former chairman of the company. The Eastern Gas Board left in 1981. A crown court and driving test centre have been built in its grounds.

Woodbridge Estate *EC1*. Thomas Sekforde, Master of the Court of Requests to Queen Elizabeth and patron of the mapmaker, Christopher Saxton, spent his last years in about 1581 on his country estate in CLERKENWELL. Its limits were the present St James's Walk (from 1708–74 called New Prison Walk), Aylesbury Street, St John Street and Corporation Row. Sekforde bequeathed the estate revenues to almshouses he had founded in Woodbridge, Suffolk, where he was born and buried. By 1767 the land value had so increased that the governors demolished Sekforde's mansion and carved out six plots on 60-year leases. When these expired the estate was developed on 99-year building leases; most of the existing houses were razed and the present streets laid out and built in

1827–8. One survivor was a Skinner Street terrace of about 1770. Another was Woodbridge House about (1807), built by the Vestry Clerk, William Cook, to replace an earlier house and workshops of George Friend, gentleman dyer to the East India Company. But the new Sekforde and Woodbridge Streets cut straight across the rear of the house, which now backs directly on to the corner, its original front hidden by a high brick wall. In 1848–70 it was used by the Finsbury Dispensary, a charity founded in 1780.

Clerkenwell Sunday School in St James's Walk was rebuilt in 1828 by a PENTONVILLE surveyor, William Lovell, and the Finsbury Savings Bank, founded 1816, removed in 1840 from Jerusalem Passage to a pretty Venetian-style building in Sekforde Street (now offices) by Alfred Bartholomew, another local architect.

The estate was largely restored in 1980–1 by ISLINGTON Borough Council. Its streets are distinguished by well-proportioned brick terraced cottages with string-courses and a diglyph frieze, and by the high curve of the back wall (1828) of Nicholson's former distillery, closed in the 1970s. Woodbridge Chapel (1833) in Sekforde Street, used from 1898 by John Groom's Crippleage, also known as the Watercress and Flower-Girls' Mission, is now the Clerkenwell and Islington Medical Mission, part of the National Health Service. The Crippleage later removed to Watford.

Woodfall Street *SW3*. An attractive street of small 19th-century cottages off Smith Street. It is named after Henry Woodfall, printer of the political *Letters of Junius*, who died in 1805 and was buried at CHELSEA OLD CHURCH.

Woodford *E18*. The earliest settlement was in the Forest of Essex where a minor Roman road from London crossed a ford over the River RODING. Tracks led to other settlements which became known as Woodford Row and Woodford Church End. The parish was controlled from Saxon times up to the 16th century by the Abbot of Waltham and the first known reference to a church in Woodford dates from the 12th century. After various alterations the church was destroyed by arson in 1969 and completely rebuilt in 1971–2. WALTHAM ABBEY was dissolved in 1540 and the monastic lands passed to laymen. Woodford provided attractive estates for wealthy London merchants and retired East India Company officials who built big houses there and provided employment for cottagers. Harts on Woodford Green was occupied by Richard Warner who cultivated the first gardenia to flower in England and in 1771 compiled *Plantae Woodfordienses* for his friends. The Rookery was built for Michael Godfrey, brother of Sir Edmund Berry Godfrey. Michael's son, also Michael, was one of the founders of the BANK OF ENGLAND of which he became the first Deputy Governor in 1695.

Village life, which depended upon the big houses, was rapidly changed after the railway to Loughton was built in 1856. Roads were cut through the private estates for housing developments and Woodford became a dormitory suburb. In 1980 the only big house in private occupation was the Naked Beauty built in 1714 for Henry Raine, a WAPPING brewer and the founder of Raine's Foundation Schools in East London. Close by is a statue to Sir Winston Churchill, once Member of Parliament for Woodford (*see* STATUES). Of other Woodford mansions, Harts is now a hospital, Higham's is part of Woodford County High School, Elmhurst a hostel of QUEEN MARY COLLEGE, and Gwynne House is part of DR BARNARDO'S HOMES.

Woodlands *Blackheath, SE3.* A beautiful Georgian villa commissioned in 1774 by John Julius Angerstein, and considerably enlarged in 1880. Angerstein was said to be the son of the Empress Anne of Russia and Poulett Thomson, a 'Russian Merchant'. The name is supposedly derived from the German doctor who delivered him and afterwards adopted him. He lived in Russia until he was 15 and then came to London to serve his apprenticeship in his reputed father's house, Thomson and Peters. At 21 he became an underwriter at LLOYD'S. His chief interest, outside of his business was in art. He helped Lawrence over some difficult years and was an early patron of Turner. In accumulating his magnificent collection of pictures he was advised by both Lawrence and Benjamin West. The collection was bought by the nation after his death in 1823 and became the nucleus of the NATIONAL GALLERY.

Woodlands was a most hospitable house, and among its visitors were Dr Johnson, Garrick, Reynolds and George III. Princess Caroline, then living in Montague House just outside GREENWICH PARK was a constant guest. The colony of French *emigrés* then established at Juniper Hall, Mickleham, Surrey which had been taken by Mme de Staël were cordially welcomed. Mme D'Arblay (better known as Fanny Burney) was a particular intimate. Angerstein was something of a hypochondriac and had a room fitted with hot air flues that kept the temperature at 65 degrees. He invited George III to come and see it. The King said he preferred an open fire. At the time of her trial in 1820, Queen Caroline tried to rent the house but Angerstein refused her.

Woodlands remained in the family until 1876 when John Julius's grandson sold it to an estate company.

Much of the estate was built over and the house was altered by various occupants. It was bought, carefully restored by the Greenwich Borough Council and opened as the Local History Centre and Art Gallery in 1972.

Woodside House *N22.* Built in the 1860s for a rich merchant. In 1888 the Borough of WOOD GREEN took it over as their town hall and enlarged it in 1913. In 1965 a new civic centre was built. It is now occupied by a day centre for the elderly, council offices and Department of Health and Social Security Offices. It is surrounded by a small park.

Woodstock Street *W1.* Built in 1720–45 and named after the ground landlord, the 1st Duke of Portland, also Viscount Woodstock. Dr Johnson lodged here in 1737 and George Morland in 1773.

Woolmen's Company *see* CITY LIVERY COMPANIES.

Woolsack *Without Aldgate.* A tavern popular in the days of Ben Jonson who mentioned it in both *The Alchemist* and *The Devil is an Ass*. Its pies were famous.

Woolwich *SE18.* A riverside town of considerable character, it is probably best known for its extensive ordnance works and for being the birthplace of the Woolwich ARSENAL FOOTBALL CLUB, founded in 1886.

The origins of the town are obscure, but from the presence of a Roman burial ground discovered in the ARSENAL in 1853 it can be assumed that a community existed here during the Roman occupation. Records of the Saxon period offer clearer evidence: in AD 918 Vuluvic was part of a gift by Aelstrudis, the daughter of King Alfred, to the Abbey of St Peter in Ghent. Hulviz appears in the *Domesday* Survey and *Textus Roffensis* of similar date records a church at Vulewic.

The present free ferry service, established in 1889,

The Royal Foundry, Woolwich, with ships' cannon in the foreground. From an engraving of 1779 after P. Sandby.

continues a tradition of ferry crossings dating back to at least the early 14th century, and is one possible explanation of why the town owned land on the north bank of the THAMES from very early times until the reorganisation of local government in 1965 (*see also* NORTH WOOLWICH).

However, Woolwich first came to prominence in 1512 when Henry VIII established a Royal Dockyard here to build the *Great Harry*, the flagship of his new royal navy. This yard, where many famous ships were built, including the *Sovereign of the Seas* in 1637, saw many royal visits and the departure of voyages of exploration. But having been expensively converted for the building and repair of steam ships in the first half of the 19th century it was closed in 1869 causing great distress and unemployment in the town. Part of the yard is now used for municipal housing but two fine Georgian buildings, two graving docks and gun bastions have been retained.

Industry came to Woolwich early: England's first salt-glazed stoneware kiln was set up here, near to the present ferry, in the early 17th century, and soon after glassworks were established on an adjacent site. And in 1694 the Royal Laboratory was built on Woolwich Warren at the east end of the town, adjacent to land previously used for the testing of guns and shot. This was the beginning of WOOLWICH ARSENAL, part of which is still in operation today. Several of the original buildings survive and can be seen from Warren Lane: the Brass Foundry of 1717, the original Royal Military Academy building of 1719 and part of Dial Square, all attributed to Sir John Vanbrugh and, in addition, derelict parts of the Royal Laboratory and the well preserved 18th-century house of the Verbruggen family. Within the walls of the ARSENAL were founded in 1716 the first two regiments of artillery. The artillerymen were later to move to the present barracks with its magnificent façade built in 1776–1802 on Woolwich Common. The Royal Military Academy began in the ARSENAL in 1721. The cadets lived in barracks, now threatened with demolition, adjoining the ARSENAL wall and attended lectures in the John Vanbrugh building. Lack of space forced the Academy to move south to Woolwich Common into quarters designed by Wyatt in 1808. This splendid building, where many famous soldiers received their instruction, (including Kitchener, General Gordon and Orde Wingate), is now the home of the ROYAL ARTILLERY INSTITUTION MUSEUM.

Close to the Royal Artillery Barracks on Woolwich Common can be seen the Rotunda, a strange building that began life as a tent in ST JAMES'S PARK in 1814. In 1819 it was brought to Woolwich and in 1822 it was converted into a permanent building by Nash. Then, as now, it housed the Royal Artillery Museum's collection of guns.

The town today is the centre of local government for the Borough of GREENWICH with a large and much admired town hall built to the design of Brumwell Thomas in 1905. The old market, created by a charter of 1619, still flourishes in Beresford Square close to the massive main gate of the ROYAL ARSENAL. The riverside area shows many signs of decay due to the exodus of riverside business and much of the ancient centre of the town near the parish church of ST MARY MAGDALENE consists of sites awaiting redevelopment.

Woolwich Arsenal Developed from the Royal Laboratory, Carriage Department and Powder House,

the arsenal dates from Tudor times and is the oldest and largest establishment of its kind in Britain. For generations it has been a centre for the manufacture and testing of arms, the main government foundry having moved here from MOORFIELDS in 1715–17. At that time it was called the Warren and in 1805 it was renamed the Royal Arsenal by George III. Up to 40,000 workers were employed here during the 2nd World War. The size of the Arsenal has been appreciably reduced in recent years and much of its site has been developed for housing.

Woolwich Dockyard *SE18*. The Royal Dockyard was created by Henry VIII in 1512–13, on a small sloping piece of THAMES foreshore, in order that a magnificent new flagship, the *Great Harry* might be built here. At about 1,500 tons, the largest ship of its day, it was destroyed by fire at WOOLWICH in 1553. In April 1581 Queen Elizabeth came here to welcome Sir Francis Drake after his circumnavigation of the globe and knighted him aboard the *Golden Hind*. Ralegh, Frobisher, Franklin and Cook all set out from here on their expeditions, and Peter the Great worked for a time as a ship's carpenter in the yard. By 1637 when the famous *Sovereign of the Seas* was constructed here by Peter Pett, the yard had been expanded, and levelled and had easy access to the nearby Woolwich Ropeyard founded in 1574. The abuses and maladministration which prevailed in the yard in the 17th century are vividly described by Pepys in his diary. In 1780–9 the present Gatehouse and the beautifully restored Clockhouse were built on land newly taken in to the yard. In the first half of the 19th century much rebuilding and further expansion took place in order that steam ships might be built and repaired here. In the 1840s two graving docks (now the Aquatic Centre) and the gun bastions were constructed. However, in 1869 the yard was closed, causing great distress in the town. In 1969 work began on a fine GREENWICH Council housing estate in which the modern buildings contrast pleasantly with the old dockyard features which have been retained.

Woolwich Free Ferry *North Woolwich – South Woolwich*. Opened for vehicles, passengers and goods in 1889. It was the first successful attempt to provide additional means of communication across the THAMES for eastern districts.

The paddle-steamers were replaced by end-loading diesel boats in 1963. And in 1964–6 the original floating landing stages were replaced by terminals with steel-trussed ramps designed by Husband and Co. The ferry is maintained free of charge by the GREATER LONDON COUNCIL.

F.W. Woolworth and Co Ltd *242–246 Marylebone Road, NW1*. Frank Winfield Woolworth paid his first visit to Europe in 1900. It was subsequently decided that the trading methods of 'walk around shopping' which had worked well in America (and were to inspire the present-day supermarkets) would succeed in Britain also. The first shop was opened at Liverpool in 1909. Other branches, in which the prices of all goods was clearly marked at 1d, 3d and 6d, soon followed. London's first store was opened at No. 311 OXFORD STREET in 1924. In 1982 there were 96 shops in the Greater London area.

Sailors cheer the launch of the Nelson *at Woolwich on 4 July 1814. From an engraving after Clennell.*

Worcester House *Strand*. In the Middle Ages the Bishop of Carlisle's town house stood here. At the Reformation Henry VIII gave it to the 1st Earl of Bedford. In 1552 Bedford was given another piece of land on the north side of the STRAND where the 3rd Earl built BEDFORD HOUSE. He sold the bishop's house to the 3rd Earl of Worcester. During the Civil war it was seized by Parliamentarians and after Charles I's execution it was used to store confiscated valuables. At the Restoration Lord Clarendon rented the house for six years until CLARENDON HOUSE was finished. In 1660 James, Duke of York, secretly married Anne Hyde, Clarendon's daughter, here. After Clarendon's departure the house was only used occasionally for official functions and was demolished soon after 1674.

Worcester Park *Surrey*. Lies north of Nonsuch Park and was originally part of the great park of NONSUCH PALACE. It takes its name from the large house, Worcester House, where the 4th Earl of Worcester lived when keeper of the Great Park in Jacobean times. When Nonsuch Park was broken up, it became Worcester Park Farm and here the Pre-Raphaelite artists, Millais and Holman Hunt, stayed and here, in the orchard in front of an abandoned gunpowder-making shed, with Millais as the model for Jesus, Hunt painted *The Light of the World*. When the London to Leatherhead railway came in 1865 and Worcester Park Station was opened, moderate expansion started in the area. The oldest surviving buildings apart from Worcester Park farmhouse near the station (now part of a furniture dealer's warehouse), are some wooden-boarded cottages in Longfellow Road, also near the station. 19th-century development on the farmlands was slow, although by Edwardian times there was a shopping street and a church, St Philip's. There was further development in the 1930s and after the 2nd World War.

World's End *SW10*. An area at the western end of the KING'S ROAD, CHELSEA, where a tavern and tea gardens stood about 1666. It was known to King Charles II and celebrated in Congreve's *Love for Love* (1695). The surrounding area was farmland; and market gardens still existed here earlier this century. The public house bearing the name World's End was built about 1901 on the site of a much earlier tavern. Nearby a very large council development of tower blocks and a shopping complex was built recently to the designs of Eric Lyons, Cadbury-Brown, Metcalf and Cunningham (1977). The Chelsea Community Centre stands in World's End Place.

Wormwood Scrubs *Du Cane Road, W12*. A prison designed by Sir Edmund Du Cane, on the separate system. In order to eliminate the lighting and ventilating difficulties of earlier radial plans, the buildings were arranged in four parallel blocks making every cell accessible to the sun. It was built by prison labour between 1874 and 1890. Contractors erected the shell of a small prison of corrugated iron with a wall one brick thick, a fence or hoarding with wooden gates and a small temporary lodge. Nine specially selected prisoners were then housed in the only cells with doors and locks. They completed the first block enabling 50 more prisoners to be brought in – enough to erect a second wing and increase the population to 100. 'So the work proceeded steadily ... the felon bees industriously adding cell to cell in the hive, and presently the four great parallel blocks were pushed forward towards completion. Each building was a self-contained prison.' Originally for both men and women, from 1902 it has been a male prison and is the largest in Britain. It has a surgical and psychiatric hospital, the main medical facility for the prison service in the south of England. It is one of seven dispersal prisons: prisoners in the top security category A are dispersed in it in the ratio of one category A to nine category B prisoners. It is the life-sentence centre for the south, the first years being spent here. It has a long-term training wing and is the centre to which young prisoners in the London area are allocated. George Blake, the master spy, escaped in 1966. In 1979 it was the scene of riots about conditions. In 1982 it had 1,075 prisoners (the certified normal accommodation is 1,224, but one wing is being altered).

Wormwood Street *EC2*. Probably takes its name from the plant which readily springs up on waste land and may well have grown over the CITY wall in early days.

Woronzow Road *NW8*. Laid out in 1843 and called after Count Simon Woronzow, Russian Ambassador to England who, dying in 1823, bequeathed £500 for charitable uses in MARYLEBONE. The money was spent in building a group of almshouses which, much modernised, still provide good accommodation today in St John's Wood Terrace.

Worship Street *EC2*. Formerly known as Hog Lane, the name was probably changed to commemorate a foundry which was used for the casting of cannon during the Civil War and which was afterwards leased by John Wesley as a place of worship. When the lease expired a chapel was built in CITY ROAD. Nos 91–101 were designed as workshops and shops by Philip Webb in 1861–2.

Wright's Lane *W8*. Formerly a country path, it takes its name from the houses at the southern end built for Gregory Wright in the 1770s. The Kensington Close Hotel (540 bedrooms) was formerly a block of flats built in 1939. It was gutted and converted to its present use after the 2nd World War.

Wych Street The south-eastern extension of DRURY LANE (formerly known as Via de Aldwych). New Inn was on the north side and Lyon's Inn on the south (*see* INNS OF CHANCERY). Mark Lemon, for many years editor of *Punch*, was for a time landlord of the Shakespeare's Head at No. 31 which consequently became a favoured resort of actors and journalists. The street disappeared when ALDWYCH was constructed.

Wycombe Lodge *Kensington*. Built in 1829, it formerly stood to the east of Aubrey House. It took its name from the first occupant, the Dowager Marchioness of Lansdowne, whose husband, the 2nd Marquess, was also Lord Wycombe. The house was demolished in 1868 and the site occupied by the covered reservoirs of the Grand Junction Water Works Co., the tops now being used as tennis courts.

Wyldes Farm An area of land between HAMP-STEAD and GOLDERS GREEN which was granted to Eton

College by Henry VI in 1449. It was an estate held in trust to provide funds for ST JAMES'S HOSPITAL which Henry VIII demolished for ST JAMES'S PALACE. Eton kept the Wyldes estate which in the 1890s covered 323 acres. It was sold in 1907 by Eton to form the extension to HAMPSTEAD HEATH and HAMPSTEAD GARDEN SUBURB. The farmhouse, in its early 17th-century form, still exists behind the Bull and Bush as the central section of a larger building. In 1820 it was known as Collins Farmhouse after the farmer who occupied part of it. He let another part to John Linnell, the painter, who was visited here by Morland, Constable, William Blake and others. In 1832 Charles Dickens stayed at Wyldes after the death of his beloved sister-in-law, Mary Hogarth. In 1907 Raymond Unwin leased and lived in Wyldes Farmhouse whilst working on HAMPSTEAD GARDEN SUBURB which he designed with Barry Parker. He remained here till 1940. A plaque to Unwin was unveiled in 1967 on the front of Wyldes Farmhouse by the Hampstead Garden Residents' Association and in 1975 a GREATER LONDON COUNCIL BLUE PLAQUE, reading 'John Linnell (1792–1882) lived here; William Blake (1757–1827) poet and artist, stayed here as his guest.'

Wyndham's Theatre *Charing Cross Road, WC2*. Built in 1899 to the designs of W.G.R. Sprague for Charles Wyndham, the only man the Marquess of Salisbury would allow to build a theatre on his estate. In 1902–9 Frank Curzon was sole manager and produced J.M. Barrie's *Little Mary* (1903), *When Knights were Bold* (1907), a farce by Charles Marlow, which had 579 performances, and *An Englishman's Home* (1909) by 'a patriot' later found to be Guy du Maurier. It filled the theatre for six months and substantially swelled the number of recruits for the Territorial Army. In 1909 Charles Hawtrey briefly joined Curzon in the management. In 1910–25 Gerald du Maurier was joint manager with Curzon. Their partnership produced many successful productions including a revival of *Diplomacy* (1913) which had 455 performances, *A Kiss for Cinderella* (1916), *A Fancy* and *Dear Brutus* by Barrie, *The Law Divine* (1918), *The Choice* (1919) by Alfred Sutro, *Bulldog Drummond* (1921) which had 430 performances and *The Dancers* (1923). A series of plays by Edgar Wallace was then staged by Curzon beginning with *The Ringer* (1926) which ran for four years, followed by *The Calendar* and *Smoky Cell* (1930), *The Old Man* and *The Case of the Frightened Lady* (1931) and *The Green Pack* (1932). Howard Wyndham and Bronson Albery took over the management in 1932 and produced *Clive of India* (1934) which had 409 performances. Since then the theatre has had several successes including *George and Margaret* (1937), which had 799 performances; *Quiet Weekend* (1941; 1,059 performances); Sandy Wilson's *The Boy Friend* (1954; 2,078 performances); and *The Prime of Miss Jean Brodie* (1966; 588 performances). The seating capacity is 759.

Y

Yacht *Crane Street, Greenwich, SE10.* A tavern originally licensed in the early 17th century. Charles II occasionally came here when the Court was at GREENWICH. The house was bombed in the 2nd World War and has since been rebuilt. It is decorated inside with nautical prints and photographs. The GREENWICH MERIDIAN line runs through the building. There are fine views of the river.

Yardley of London Ltd *33 Old Bond Street, W1.* In 1801 William Yardley took over a business which had obtained a concession to manufacture soap for the whole of London in 1625 and had long been purveyors of lavender water. At the beginning of the 20th century the firm began to concentrate on perfumery. 33 OLD BOND STREET was acquired in 1931. The gilt metal door is by Ruehlmann of Paris.

Yarmouth Place *W1.* A short cul-de-sac leading off the eastern extremity of BRICK STREET, it was known in the mid-18th century as Snead's Court. It doubtless acquired its present name from the subsequent residence of the Earl of Yarmouth in one of the great houses in PICCADILLY which back on to this rather sad little yard.

Ye Olde Watling *29 Watling Street, EC4.* Built by Sir Christopher Wren in 1668, it is said to have been used by him as an office while designing ST PAUL'S. It is named after the Roman Road, Watling Street, on which it stands. Ships' timbers were used in its construction.

Yeading *Middlesex.* Lies between NORTHOLT and SOUTHALL within the western boundary of the London Borough of HILLINGDON. Saxon settlement by the people or followers of Geddi resulted in the name of Geddinges, and by the 14th century Yeading existed as a sub-manor of HAYES. The agrarian environment changed little until the 19th century. In 1801 the GRAND UNION CANAL was continued north past Yeading; and brick-fields were worked until the end of the century. Then industries began developing, and factory and house building took place in the 1920s and 1930s. In 1957 the Catholic parish of St Raphael was created to serve a large Catholic community. In 1961 St Edmund's, Yeading (J. Anthony Lewis), was opened; it has a carved crucifix, a figure of St Edmund and an altar by Robin Dawson. In 1965 Yeading became part of the London Borough of HILLINGDON.

Yeoman's Row *SW3.* One of the oldest streets in the area, it appears as a line of small cottages in 1768. Mr Yeoman was probably a speculative builder who constructed his row along the uncertain north-east boundary of the SMITH'S CHARITY ESTATE. By 1780 the cottages stretched half way down and about 1790 a large house, The Hermitage, was built on the east side

and The Grange (*see* EGERTON TERRACE) on the west side. Both these were demolished in 1843 and a further line of cottages was built down the east side. On the west side remained a few stables and small cottages, most of which were replaced by the rather grand mews and stables built for Egerton Place in the 1880s. These buildings have now been converted to small houses or offices. The earliest row of cottages was torn down in 1960 and was replaced by modern counterparts.

Yiewsley *Middlesex.* Derives its name from Wivesleg (probably 'wife's clearing') It lay within Colham Manor (which included much of the London Borough of HILLINGDON) and formed part of Hillingdon Parish. The opening of the GRAND JUNCTION CANAL in 1805 provided cheap transport for its chief industry, bricks, and the coming of the railway in 1838 encouraged its industrial development. In 1858 St Matthew's chapel-of-ease was consecrated and was extended in 1898 to meet the needs of the growing population. Yiewsley became an ecclesiastical parish in 1874 and a civil parish in 1896, achieving urban district status in 1911. Apart from Yiewsley Grange and the De Burgh Arms (both 17th-century) its buildings are of the 19th and 20th centuries. This former village of brickmakers is now a crowded London suburb.

York Buildings Waterworks *Villiers Street.* In 1675 Ralph Bucknall and Ralph Wayne obtained a licence to erect waterworks at York Buildings – a general name then in use for the streets and houses erected on the site of YORK HOUSE. The 90-year licence was approved by Wren in his capacity as Surveyor-General. He had 'seene the designe of the Engine and did not conceive it would be any annoyance, the Worke moving easily and without noise.' The waterworks was erected on the west side of VILLIERS STREET closing the river end of the street. At its zenith the company was said to be supplying about 2500 houses. In 1684 fire damaged the waterworks and in 1690 they were totally destroyed in a conflagration. In 1691–2 the company was incorporated by Act of Parliament and a water tower about 70 ft high was built. In 1712 the company was the first to use steam power with 'a machine for raising water by fire'. After the early 1720s, when the company ventured disastrously into land speculation, life insurance and assurance, its finances were always precarious and frequent litigation was a feature of its existence. In about 1725 de Saussure, a Swiss visitor, described the engine: 'Smoke issuing with force through a little tube, and corresponding with a large piece of machinery, composed of wheels, counterpoise, and pendulum, which in their turn cause two large pumps to work continually. . . . At the summit of [the] tower, which is octagonal, there is a small lead cistern or bath, which received the water the pumps send up, and from thence it flows into the great reservoir or pond of Marylebone.' The steam engine ceased

The terrace and stairs at York Buildings in c. 1750, with Westminster Bridge (left) and the waterworks tower (right).

working in 1731 but was exhibited for several years thereafter as a curiosity. One pamphlet referred to it as the York Buildings Dragon. In 1783 the last properties of the company, forfeited Scottish estates bought after the 1715 rebellion, were sold for £102,537. And in 1818 the Company itself was sold for £32,000 to the NEW RIVER COMPANY. It was dissolved by Act of Parliament in 1829.

York Gate *NW1*. Takes its name from the Prince Regent's brother, the Duke of York. Francis Taylor Palgrave, compiler of *The Golden Treasury*, lived at No. 5 in 1867–75. Rotary International and the Rotary Club of London are at No. 6.

York House *Pall Mall*. One of the great Pall Mall mansions, it was built in the early 1760s by Matthew Brettingham the Elder, perhaps with the assistance of his son, for Edward Augustus, Duke of York and Albany, brother of George III. It was renamed Cumberland House when it passed to the Duke's brother, Henry Frederick, Duke of Cumberland who employed Robert Adam to refurbish it in the 1780s. The War Office occupied the central part of the house from 1807 and the side wings from 1811. The eastern half was demolished in 1908, and the western half in 1911–12. THE ROYAL AUTOMOBILE CLUB occupies the site.

York House *St James's, SW1 see* LANCASTER HOUSE.

York House *Strand*. Built some time before 1237 for the Bishops of Norwich and at first known as Norwich Place. In 1536 Henry VIII installed his brother-in-law, Charles Brandon, Duke of Suffolk, here, compensating the Bishop with a lesser house in CANNON ROW, WESTMINSTER, The Duke surrendered the house to Mary I who, in 1556, gave it to her Arch-

bishop of York, Nicholas Heath. In 1558 it became the official residence of the Lord Keeper of the Great Seal. Sir Nicholas Bacon was the first Lord Keeper to live here. In 1561 his son, Francis, was born here. In 1597 the Earl of Essex, Queen Elizabeth's favourite, was tried here before the Privy Council after his disastrous Irish expedition and kept prisoner here until another trial in 1600 deprived him of his offices. From 1617 Francis Bacon lived here as Lord Keeper until, in 1621, he was dismissed following his trial before the House of Lords for corruption. James I's favourite, George Villiers, Duke of Buckingham, took the house over. He seems to have repaired it and certainly built the fine YORK WATERGATE. After Buckingham's murder in 1628 his widow continued to live at York House, by then more commonly known as Buckingham House, and in 1635 she married Randal Macdonnell, 2nd Earl and 1st marquess of Antrim. In the Civil War the property was confiscated and afterwards taken over by General Fairfax. In 1657 the 2nd Duke of Buckingham married Fairfax's daughter, Mary, and at the Restoration the house was given back to his family. He used it, however, only for ceremonial occasions, leasing it for the rest of the time to foreign ambassadors.

Except for the Watergate it was demolished in the 1670s and the site was developed by the property speculator, Nicholas Barbon. The Duke insisted on being remembered by having his name and every syllable of his title used in the naming of Barbon's new streets – George Street, Villiers Street, Duke Street, Buckingham Street, even Of Alley, though this last has now been renamed York Place. York Buildings also occupies part of the site.

York House *Twickenham, Middlesex*. A handsome example of a late 17th-century mansion built in traditional red brick. The Central block is a symmetrical three-storey building with shuttered windows. The wings were added later during the 18th century. The exact date of the house is not known but the estate belonged to the Yorke family who were associated with TWICKENHAM since the 14th century. Originally called Yorke's Farm, it was granted by Queen Elizabeth in 1566 to John Jermyn and James Waifers, 'valets of our chamber', for 21 years. After several more residents, it was acquired by Sir Henry Hyde, son and heir of Edward, Earl of Clarendon, Lord Chancellor. There is no direct evidence that Lord Clarendon himself lived in the house, though it was in the possession of members of his family until 1689, and he certainly lived somewhere in TWICKEN-HAM when the king was in residence at HAMPTON COURT. Lord Clarendon's will bequeathed to his son, Laurence Hyde, 'a house at Twiknam'. The next notable resident of York house was Ludwig, Graf von Stahremberg, the Austrian Ambassador who built a theatre in the left wing and gave theatrical performances at the end of the 18th century with his family and friends as actors. In 1817 the house was bought by Anne Seymour Damer, the sculptress of, among other works, the masks of Thames and Isis on Henley Bridge. She was a close friend of Horace Walpole who left her STRAWBERRY HILL and £2,000 a year for its upkeep. The exiled French royal family acquired the house in 1864 and their connection with it continued on and off almost the end of the 19th century. The last private resident was the Indian merchant prince, Sir Ratan Tata, who built in the garden near the river the remarkable fountain in which several naked marble nymphs climb in and out of the water and up the rocks. The house was acquired in 1923 by the civic authority of TWICKENHAM and is now the municipal offices of the London Borough of RICH-MOND UPON THAMES. Its character has been carefully preserved. There is a large walled garden as well as rose and formal gardens.

York Minster   *49 Dean Street, W1*. Also known as 'the French Pub', it was taken over by M. Berlemont in 1914; and in the 2nd World War it became the official headquarters of the Free French Forces. On the walls hang many signed photographs of famous Frenchmen. Originally built in the 16th century, it was rebuilt in 1936. It has recently been renamed the French House.

York Place   *Whitehall*. In 1245 Walter de Grey, Archbishop of York, gave 'our house in the street of Westminster' (which he had acquired five years earlier), to the See of York, whereupon it became the Archbishop's official London residence. York House was greatly extended and altered by Wolsey, Archbishop of York in 1514–29, who bought adjoining land and built the Great Hall in 1528. Here he lavishly entertained Henry VIII and his court. After Wolsey's fall, the King took over York Place, which he found far more agreeable than the ancient and decaying PALACE OF WESTMINSTER, and renamed it WHITEHALL. Shakespeare refers to this change in *Henry VIII* (Act IV, Scene 1):

You must no more call it York Place, that's past:
For since the Cardinal fell, that title's lost;
'Tis now the King's and called Whitehall.

(*See also* WHITEHALL PALACE.)

York Road   *SE1*. Built in 1824 in connection with the construction of WATERLOO BRIDGE and named after York House which was erected nearby in about 1475 by Lawrence Booth, Archbishop of York, and used by his successors until the 17th century. Henry VIII is said to have met Anne Boleyn here. From 1753–6 it housed the BATTERSEA ENAMELS factory. Transfer printing was invented here by John Brooks. Examples of the fine enamels are in the VICTORIA AND ALBERT MUSEUM. The house was last heard of at the end of the 18th century. COUNTY HALL and the Shell Centre (*see* BELVEDERE ROAD) border the street.

York Street   *W1*. Built in about 1801 and probably named after Frederick, the 'Grand Old' Duke of York. There is a complete row of early 19th-century bow-windowed houses at Nos 78–84. George Richmond, the artist, lived at No. 20 from 1843 till his death in 1896.

York Terrace   *NW1*. Takes its name from the title of Frederick, Duke of York, younger brother of George IV. Nash designed it as two separate groups of twenty houses apiece, split by an open vista down to Hardwick's MARYLEBONE PARISH CHURCH. The houses have their main entrances in the mews on their south side and present an uninterrupted façade to REGENT'S PARK so that they seem to be two long palaces. The eastern half was built by James Burton and the western by William Mountford Nurse. At the easternmost end stand, separately, the DORIC VILLAS. William Charles Macready, the manager of the THEATRE ROYAL, DRURY LANE, lived at No. 1 York Gate nearby. Mrs Elizabeth Jesser Reid, the founder of BEDFORD COLLEGE, the oldest establishment for the university education of women, lived at No. 21 from 1846–65. Sir Charles Wyndham, the actor manager, died at No. 43. Hugh Walpole occupied No. 24 in 1922–3.

York Watergate   *Watergate Walk, WC2*. All that remains of YORK HOUSE, STRAND. Once the gateway leading from the Duke of Buckingham's garden to the river steps, it has now been separated from the THAMES by the reclaimed land of the VICTORIA EM-BANKMENT and EMBANKMENT GARDENS. Built in 1626, it has been variously attributed to Nicholas Stone, who erected it, Inigo Jones and Balthasar Gerbier, the talented agent of the Duke of Buckingham who lived at YORK HOUSE at the time. It is in stone of three bays with rusticated bands on the side facing the river. On this side also are the Villiers arms and on the other side their motto: *Fidei coticula crux* (the touchstone of faith is the cross). The two lions on the top hold shields with anchors to symbolise Buckingham's service as Lord High Admiral. Today it lacks its stone-paved landing stage, balustrade and steps.

Yorkshire Stingo   *Lisson Grove*. Tavern which stood where Chapel Street joins the MARYLEBONE ROAD. Stingo was a name for strong beer. Tea gardens and a bowling green were added before 1770. In 1790 a cast-iron bridge designed by Thomas Paine and only the second to be built, was brought here from Rotherham and set up on the bowling green. It was soon returned to Rotherham. In the early 19th century the Yorkshire Stingo found popularity with the middle classes. The Apollo Saloon, a hall for vaudevilles and comic *burlettas*, was in existence here from 1836. In about 1848 the gardens and

The Yorkshire Stingo, Marylebone, in c. 1770, when the tea gardens and bowling green were added behind the tavern.

bowling green were closed and the County Court and Baths were built on the site.

Young Men's Christian Association *112 Great Russell Street, WC1.*

Founded on 6 June 1844 at a meeting held in Hitchcock and Rogers's drapery store in ST PAUL'S CHURCHYARD. The prime mover was one of the shop's assistants, George Williams, the 23-year-old son of a West Country farmer. He was knighted for his work for the YMCA in 1894, and on his death in 1905 was buried in the crypt of ST PAUL'S CATHEDRAL. There are portraits of him in a stained glass window in WESTMINSTER ABBEY. The first premises were rooms rented at St Martin's Coffee House, LUDGATE HILL. Having outgrown this and a number of other rented premises, the lease of 156 ALDERSGATE STREET was acquired in 1854. In 1880 the London Association purchased the lease of EXETER HALL in the STRAND. And in 1895 the London Association was combined with the ALDERSGATE STREET and CORNHILL branches to form the Central Association whose headquarters were at EXETER HALL. The YMCA's premises on the present site were constructed in 1912. This building, one of the first to be constructed of ferro-concrete in London, was demolished in 1971; and the present building, erected to the designs of the Elsworth Sykes Partnership, was opened in August 1976. There is a hotel as well as a club and a residence known as George Williams House. The building, which cost £15.6 million and at its highest is 15 storeys above ground and five storeys below, is one of the largest of its kind in the world.

Young Women's Christian Association *2 Weymouth Street, W1.*

A hostel for Florence Nightingale's nurses, en route to and from the Crimea, was opened in Upper Charlotte Street by the Hon Mrs Arthur Kinnaird in 1855. This was continued after the war for girls working in London 'who could only afford 10s 6d for board and lodging'. A lending library and other advantages were offered without charge. Three further hostels were opened in London in 1863 to provide a 'home life based on Christian principles and at moderate charges for girls from the country working in London.' These were united in 1877 with a Prayer Union of several branches which had originally been formed in 1855 in BARNET by Miss Emma Roberts for young women willing to 'offer their service with their prayers'. Lord Shaftesbury became first President of this joint association, the YWCA in 1878.

In 1884 the first YWCA restaurant in London (and the first restaurant for women in the country) was opened. The first World YWCA Conference was held in London in 1897, with representatives from 20 countries and all five continents. In 1919 the Working Women's College was founded by the YWCA at Beckenham, Kent. This later became independent and is now Hillcroft College, SURBITON. In 1953 Bedford House, BAKER STREET was reconstructed and opened as the National Headquarters of the YWCA. The headquarters moved to WEYMOUTH STREET in 1967.

Young Street *SW3.*

Built in 1729 by Thomas Young. Thackeray lived at No. 16 in 1846–53 while writing *Vanity Fair*, *Pendennis* and *Henry Esmond*. The last novel mentions Lady Castlewood's house 'over against the Greyhounds'. This public house, rebuilt, still exists. Thackeray gave a party in his house for Charlotte Brontë, whom he found so shyly formidable that he went off to his club.

Young Vic *The Cut, SE1.*

Founded in 1970 by Frank Dunlop as part of the NATIONAL THEATRE, of which he was also the director. It became independent in 1974 with its own board of management. Designed by Howell, Killick, Partridge and Amis it was built in 1971 on a bomb-site near the OLD VIC. Its intention is to provide good theatre for young people at cheap prices with emphasis on the classics and outstanding modern plays. Included in the building is a studio theatre for dancing and small productions. Dame Sybil Thorndike officially opened the theatre in August 1970. The seating capacity of the theatre is 450 and of the studio 100.

Z

Zimbabwe House *Strand, WC2*. Formerly Rhodesia House, it was originally the Western Insurance Office, designed by C.R. Cockerell, and was rebuilt in 1907 for the BRITISH MEDICAL ASSOCIATION by Charles Holden. It is notable for the figures between the second-storey windows, the work of Jacob Epstein and his first important commission in this country. These larger than life figures depicting the Ages of Man caused an outcry of protest when they were unveiled in their nudity in 1908. It has been said that the windows of a building opposite were replaced with frosted glass so the figures could not be seen from inside, and that an offending part of one of the statues fell off and almost struck a passer-by on the head. It has also often been reported that when the Southern Rhodesian High Commission took the building over in the 1930s orders were given for the statues to be mutilated by the removal of their controversial appendages. But on 4 September 1980 Mr Alfred Baker wrote to *The Times*: 'I remember going up on the scaffold with my father (Sir Herbert Baker) to report on the Epstein figures and recommend treatment. We found that the stones had been laid with their natural bed vertical and the carver had left pockets for rain to collect. Frost action had followed. Removal of the figures was ruled out, so the only course was to make them safe by cutting away projections. *Not* vandalism, but putting right the sculptor's mistakes in his handling of stone.'

Zoological Gardens *Regent's Park, NW1*. The ZOOLOGICAL SOCIETY OF LONDON was founded in 1826. The next year an area in REGENT'S PARK was laid out for the Society by Decimus Burton. The Society's collection of animals was opened in 1828 with, amongst other animals, monkeys, bears, emus, kangaroos, llamas, zebras and turtles. There were 30,000 visitors within the first seven months. Whips had to be left at the gate, but ladies, who were allowed to keep their parasols, had to be restrained from poking them through the bars. The collections of animals were augmented in 1830, when the royal menagerie arrived from Windsor, and in 1832–4 when the animals from the TOWER were transferred here. These included an Indian elephant, an alligator, a boa, an anaconda and over a hundred rattlesnakes. In 1835 there arrived Tommy, the zoo's first chimpanzee, of whom Theodore Hook wrote:

The folks in town are nearly wild
To go and see the monkey-child
In gardens of Zoology
Whose proper name is Chimpanzee.
To keep this baby free from hurt
He's dressed in a cap and Guernsey Shirt;
They've got him a nurse and he sits on her knee
And she calls him her Tommy Chimpanzee

The next year saw the arrival of four giraffes, which gave rise to fashion for ladies' dresses patterned like their skin. The female gave birth to six babies between 1840 and 1851. In 1840 a lion and lioness arrived from Tunis; but the lioness died after tripping on a fence and the lion pined away, and died a few weeks later. The world's first reptile house was opened in 1843 (the reptile keeper tried to charm a cobra but was bitten between the eyes and died within hours). The world's first aquarium was opened in 1853; and the world's first insect house in 1881. Meanwhile a pair of bison had been presented by the Tsar of Russia in 1847; the first hippopotamus came in 1850, the first orang-utan in 1851; a giant ant-eater, which consumed 50 eggs a day, in 1853; the first sealion in 1856; and two African elephants, Jumbo and Alice, in 1867. A few years later, in mysterious and gruesome circumstances, Alice lost a foot of her trunk during a Bank Holiday. The first baby hippopotamus was reared in 1874; and the first koala bear to live outside Australia arrived in 1880. By then the Society's gardens had become universally known as the zoo, a name popularised in 1867 by the music-hall performer 'The Great Vance', who sang, 'Walking in the zoo is the OK thing to do'.

After 1913, when the Mappin Terraces for bears and goats were built by Belcher and Joass, various new animal houses and compounds were constructed. The aquarium was rebuilt by Joass in 1924; the reptile house in 1927; Pets' Corner was formed in 1934; and the penguin pool, designed by Lubetkin and Tecton, was constructed in 1936. Solly Zuckerman, later to become Lord Zuckerman and President of the ZOOLOGICAL SOCIETY, who was appointed Research Anatomist to the Society in 1928, afterwards helped to raise large sums of money for further improvements. A giant panda arrived in 1938 and soon afterwards the toyshops were filled with cuddly versions of it.

During the 2nd World War most of the dangerous animals were killed but some were evacuated to Ireland. The snakes were decapitated and the edible fish eaten. Soon after the War the first polar bear cub was reared at the zoo and in 1958 the giant panda, Chi-Chi, arrived from China to become, in its day, the most famous animal in England.

Since 1959 the gardens and their buildings and enclosures have been gradually remodelled by Sir Hugh Casson, Sir Peter Shepheard, the landscape architect, and F.A.P. Stengelhofen and J.W. Toovey, architects to the LONDON ZOOLOGICAL SOCIETY. New buildings include the Snowdon Aviary (1963–4); the Elephant and Rhino Pavilion, designed by Casson, Conder and Partners (1965); a small mammal house, designed by Black, Bayes and Gibson (1967); a new Primate House (1972) and the New Lion Terraces (1976), designed by J.W. Toovey.

The London Zoo is not only one of the biggest tourist attractions in London, it is also a major centre for research and the only national zoo in the world which receives no regular financial support from central or local government. The statue of Winnie-the-Pooh is by

The Regent's Park Zoological Gardens were laid out by Decimus Burton in 1827, and opened to Fellows of the Society the next year. From an engraving after T.H. Shepherd, 1851, by which time the 'Zoo' had become a popular attraction.

Lorne McKean and was unveiled by Christopher Milne, A.A. Milne's son, in September 1981.

Zoological Society of London *Regent's Park, NW1*. Founded on 29 April 1826 by Sir Stamford Raffles and a number of other influential men, including Sir Humphry Davy, President of the ROYAL SOCIETY. The ZOOLOGICAL GARDENS in REGENT'S PARK were opened to Fellows of the Society in 1828. The objects of the Society were set out in its Royal Charter of Incorporation granted in 1829: 'the advancements of Zoology and Animal Physiology, and the introduction of new and curious subjects of the Animal Kingdom'. A museum and library were established in the Society's offices in BRUTON STREET and a farm was purchased at RICHMOND. The farm was closed in 1834 and it was not until 1931 that another country branch was opened at Whipsnade. The museum was closed in 1855 and its exhibits distributed between the National History section of the BRITISH MUSEUM and other collections. At the Society's offices there was a dissecting room where work has been carried out by many distinguished anatomists, including Professor Richard Owen who performed a post-mortem on the Zoo's first orang-utan in 1829. Also at the Society's offices scientific meetings have been held since 1827, and the papers read at these meetings are published in the Society's main scientific journal, *The Journal of Zoology*. At the end of 1982 there were 2,541 Fellows and 4,463 Associates in the Society's membership.

981

Bizet, Georges, 374
Black, John N., 50
Black, Michael, 821
Black Prince, *see* Edward the Black
  Prince
Blackburne, E.L., 732
Blackmore, R.D., 856
Blackmore, Richard, 867
Blackstone, Sir William, 121, 142, 447,
  459, 514
Blackwell, Dr Alexander, 120
Blackwell, Elizabeth, 147, 851
Blades, John, 94, 894
Blagrave, John, 418
Blagrove, William, 768
Blake, George, 973
Blake, James, 114
Blake, Dame Louisa *see* Aldrich Blake
Blake, Naomi, 282, 933
Blake, Philip, 84
Blake, Admiral, Robert, 732
Blake, William, 2, 94, 105, 329, 334,
  342, 358, 374, 499, 589, 605, 621,
  714, 736, 799, 855, 947, 973
Blake, William, philanthropist, 379
Blanc, Louis, 266, 597
Blanchard, Christopher, 648
Blanche of Lancaster, 55, 773
Blanche of Navarre, 699
Bland, Sir John, 961
Blanke, Sir Thomas, 485
Blankers-Koen, Fanny, 937
Blashill, Thomas, 71
Blee, Michael, 412
Blemond, William, 74
Blessington, Countess of, 316, 425
Bliss, Sir Arthur, 205
Bligh, William, 186, 444, 474
Blizard, Sir William, 43, 474
Blomfield, Sir Arthur, 7, 35, 153, 214,
  298, 326, 364, 390, 525, 528, 691,
  707, 710, 712, 713, 723, 732, 733,
  736, 741, 752, 754, 762, 786, 805,
  892, 962
Blomfield, Charles James, 74, 697
Blomfield, Sir Reginald, 101, 122, 123,
  313, 425, 443, 507, 509, 551, 597,
  643, 675, 757, 845, 850
Blondin, Charles, 131, 378
Blood, Colonel, 44, 877, 894
Bloodworth, Sir Thomas, 324
Bloom, Morris, 956
Bloom, Ursula, 444
Blore, Edward, 103, 156, 301, 374, 441,
  444, 455, 640, 895, 948
Blount, Henry, 86
Blow, Detmar, 341, 342, 584, 604, 800
Blow, John, 39, 714
Blücher, Marshal, 716
Blundell, Peter, 750
Blundstone, F.V., 821
Blunt, Gerald, 148
Blunt, Wilfrid Scawen, 101, 849
Blyton, Enid, 766
Boadicea, *see* Boudicca
Bodley, G.F., 157, 391, 566, 620, 689,
  693, 742, 743, 748, 765
Bodley, John, 834
Boehm, Edmund, 720
Boehm, Sir Joseph, E., 387, 577, 815,
  817, 819, 820, 822, 823, 857
Boghurst, William, 327
Bohun, 2nd and 6th Earls of Hereford,
  Humphrey de, 245
Boileau, Louis-Auguste, 555
Bolesworth, Edmund, 296
Boleyn, Anne, *see* Anne Boleyn
Bolingbroke, 2nd Earl of, 326
Bolingbroke, Henry St John, 1st
  Viscount, 222, 321, 736
Bolingbroke, 5th Viscount, 958
Bolton, 1st Duke of, 77
Bolton, 6th Duke of, 35
Bolton, Lavinia Fenton, afterwards
  Duchess of, 239
Bolton, Prior, 694
Bolton, Sir William, 686
Bolton, William, 76, 120
Bonaparte, Joseph, 582, 936
Bonaparte, Prince Louis Lucien, 941
Bonar, Thomas, 115
Bond, Sir Thomas, 10, 77, 180, 588,
  810
Bond, William, 77
Bondfield, Margaret, 249
Bonham, Sir John, 549
Bonham, William Charles, 78
Bonhoeffer, Dietrich, 290
Boniface IX, Pope, 59
Bonner, Bishop, 345, 499, 708, 915
Bonnin, James, 14, 254
Bonnington, David, 942
Bonomi, Joseph, 108, 330, 446
Boone, Christopher, 450
Boone, Daniel, 450
Booth, Barton, 42, 206, 287, 937
Booth, Charles, 7, 61, 338, 894, 955
Booth, John and William Joseph, 464

Booth, Lawrence, Archbishop of York,
  976
Booth, Dame Margaret, 514
Booth, Webster, 296
Booth, General William, 129, 224, 246,
  517, 770, 814
Boreman, Sir William, 337
Borenius, Tancred, 788
Borgnis, P.M., 861
Bor-Komorowski, General Tadeus, 131
Borough, William, 456, 780
Borrow, George, 130, 374
Bosanquet, B.J.T., 515
Bosanquet, Samuel, 455
Boscawen, Admiral, 524
Bosco, St John, 768
Bostock, Elizabeth Anne, 899
Boswell, James, 76, 77, 81, 115, 138,
  152, 185, 192, 202, 206, 236, 295,
  308, 329, 335, 352, 371, 389, 407,
  418, 451, 471, 486, 522, 526, 529,
  592, 618, 628, 647, 686, 701, 708,
  718, 761, 768, 791, 793, 795, 798,
  819, 829, 830, 895, 911, 924
Boswell, Levi, 466
Boswell, Urania, 273, 466
Boswell, Veronica, 630
Botley, George Frederick, 748
Botolph, St, 696
Bott, James, 374
Bottomley, Horatio, 446
Boucher, Catherine, 94
Boucher, Francis, 919
Boucicault, Dion, 374
Boucicault the Younger, Dion, 12
Boudicca, Queen, 261, 279, 355, 392,
  466, 654, 811, 814
Boult, Sir Adrian, 476
Bourchier, Arthur, 304, 831
Bourchier, Basil, 79
Bourchier, Cardinal, Thomas, 528, 737
Bourdon, William, 79
Bourgeois, Sir Francis, 243
Bourke, Algernon, 961
Bourne, Cardinal, Francis, 949, 950
Bouton, Charles-Marie, 227
Bouwens Van Der Boijen, W.O.W., 98
Bowack, John, 585
Bowden, Elizabeth, 766
Bowden, John, 766
Bowen, Edward, 367
Bowen, Emanuel, 496
Bowers, Robert, 864
Bowes, Sir Jerome, 309
Bowes, Sir Martin, 155, 686
Bowler, Thomas and William, 465, 496
Bowles, Carington, 496
Bowles, Derek Parker, 291
Bowles, John, 418, 496
Bowman, Christopher, 81
Box, Simon, 106
Boyarsky, Alvin, 24
Boyce, William, 425, 682
Boyd, John, 220
Boydell, John, 411, 752, 781
Boyes, Henry C., 340
Boyle, Robert, 414, 477
Boyse, Samuel, 618
Brabazon, Reginald, *see* Meath, Earl of
Brace, Harris, 864
Brace, John Thurloe, 864
Bracebridge, E.L., 396
Bracegirdle, Anne, 398, 460
Bracken (Bratton or Bretton), 322
Bradbury, Thomas, 275, 276
Bradford, A.T., 67
Bradford, John, 184, 434
Bradlaugh, Charles, 730
Bradley, James, 679, 680, 923
Bradshaw, George Smith, 794
Bradshaw, H.C., 508
Bradshaw, Laurence, 820
Bradshaw, William, 794
Brazdys, Antanas, 43
Braganza, Catherine of, 633
Braham, John, 254, 722
Brahms, Johannes, 680
Braid, James, 313-315
Braidwood, James, 129, 279, 473, 507
Brain, Dennis, 130
Bramah, Joseph, 624
Bramwell, Sir Frederick Joseph, 410
Brandenburg-Anspach, Margrave of, 82
Brandon, David, 420, 498, 579
Brandon, John R., 18
Brandon, Richard, 427, 657
Brangwyn, Sir Frank, 144, 171, 671,
  964
Brassey, Thomas, 486, 649
Bravo, Charles, 623
Brawne, Fanny, 236, 421
Bray, Joel, 425
Bray, John, 462
Bray, Sir Reginald, 144
Braybrooke, Robert, 758
Brayley, Edward Wedlake, 478
Breakespear, W.H., 30

Breame, Richard, 249
Brearley, J.M., 176, 515
Bremer, Frederick, 913
Brereton, Cuthbert, 430
Brereton, William, 337, 454
Brettingham, Matthew the Elder, 537,
  551, 597, 719, 720, 772, 975
Brettingham, Robert William Furze, 720
Brettingham the Younger, Matthew, 653
Brett-James, Norman, 383
Breugel, *see* Bruegel
Brewer, Alfred, 372
Brewer, Cecil, 500
Bridgeman, Charles, *see* Bridgman
Bridgeman, Sir Orlando, 264, 856
Bridges, Robert, 679
Bridgewater, 3rd Duke of, 183
Bridgewater, 4th Earl of, 183
Bridgman, Charles, 154, 301, 373, 424,
  426, 497, 963
Bright, John, 597
Bright, Richard, 347, 772
Brightwen, Eliza, 812
Brilliant, Fredda, 817, 820
Briset, Jordan, 712
Bristow, T.L., 94
Brittain, Vera, 490
Britten, Sir Benjamin, 205, 667, 693
Britton, John, 91, 478, 672
Britton, Thomas, 31, 182, 844
Broadbent, E.R., 104
Broadwood, John, 104, 329, 425
Brock, Charles Thomas, 281
Brock, Sir Thomas, 630, 816–822
Brockway, Fenner Brockway, later
  Lord, 112, 531
Brontë, Anne, 46, 138, 947
Brontë, Charlotte, 46, 138, 197, 977
Brontë, Emily, 947
Brontë sisters, 815, 822
Brook, Edward, 30
Brooke, Christopher, 384, 499
Brooke, 1st Baron, *see* Greville, Sir
  Fulke
Brookes, Joshua, 326
Brooks, Alfred, 420
Brooks, James, 16, 17, 159, 394, 699,
  702, 740, 964
Brooks, John, 44, 976
Brooks, William, 98, 475
Broomfield, Elizabeth, 731
Brougham, Eleanor L. ('Tullia'), 458
Brougham and Vaux, Henry, Lord, 9,
  52, 57, 66, 320, 382, 386, 458, 459,
  901, 903
Broughton, John, 187
Brown, Sir Arthur, 776, 813, 815
Brown, Cecil, 509
Brown, Charles Armitage, 421
Brown, Ford Madox, 282, 290, 428,
  529, 821
Brown, Frederick, 290
Brown, H.T. Cadbury, *see* Cadbury-
  Brown
Brown, James, 99
Brown, John, 68
Brown, John, Alderman, 574
Brown, Lancelot, 'Capability Brown', 5,
  62, 220, 282, 301, 302, 313, 361, 367,
  563, 587, 664, 675, 801, 853, 963
Brown, Robert, 672, 690
Brown, Rose, 743
Brown, Sarah, 99
Brown, Susan, 81
Brown, Tom, 950
Brown, Walter, 743
Brown, Sir William, 43
Browne, Dr Edward, 206
Browne, Hablot Knight, 441, 771
Browne, James, 81
Browne, Robert, 690
Browning, Louisa, 70
Browning, Robert, 114, 222, 225, 463,
  539, 588, 686, 747, 789, 925, 947, 966
Brownlow, Lord, 53
Brownlow, William, 234
Brownrigg, Elizabeth, 268, 276
Bruce, Edgar, 406, 621, 775
Bruce-Joy, Albert, 818
Bruckner, Anton, 11, 279
Brudenell-Bruce, Lady Augusta
  Georgiana, 19
Bruegel the Elder, Pieter, 275
Bruges, William, 427
Brummell, George, 'Beau Brummell',
  14, 25, 78, 140, 294, 961
Brummell, William, 109
Brunel, H.M., 69
Brunel, Isambard Kingdom, 57, 83, 99,
  131, 139, 152, 364, 410, 519, 574,
  585, 658, 747, 815, 860, 899, 915, 924
Brunel, Sir Marc Isambard, 44, 131,
  152, 689, 860, 899
Brunswick, Duchess of, 637
Brunt, John, 128
Brutton, W.M., 967
Bryant, Sir Arthur, 9

Bryce, James, Viscount, 88, 791
Brydges, James, 729
Brydges, William, 428
Brydon, J.M., 145, 147, 256, 325, 521,
  585, 764, 765
Bubb, George, 217, 671
Bubb, J.H., 344
Buchan, John, Baron Tweedsmuir, 615
Buckingham, 1st Duke of, 8, 28, 48,
  618, 657, 784, 876, 896, 916, 948,
  967, 976
Buckingham 2nd Duke of, 101, 126,
  916, 975
Buckingham, 3rd Duke of, 30, 245
Buckingham and Chandos, 2nd Duke of,
  282
Buckingham and Chandos, 3rd Duke of,
  137
Buckingham, 1st Marquess of, 101
Buckingham and Normanby, 1st Duke
  of, 101
Buckinghamshire, George Hobart, 3rd
  Earl of, 721
Buckland, Francis Trevelyan, 9
Buckle, Henry, 848
Buckle, James George, 862
Buckle, Richard, 861
Buckler, Charles, 703
Buckler, John, 854
Buckley, Samuel, 104, 286, 462
Buckmaster, H.J., 184
Bucknall, Ralph, 974
Bucknall, Thomas, 84
Buckstone, J.B., 371
Bugge, John, 703
Bull, Henry, 767
Bull, John, 169
Bullein, William, 209
Bullock, William, 255, 463
Bulmer, Bevis, 95, 928
Bulwer-Lytton, *see* Lytton
Bunning, J.B., 65, 131, 132, 186, 344,
  346, 381, 388, 485
Bunsen, Christian, Freiherr Von, 1, 307
Bunyan, John, 105, 791, 801, 815
Buonaiuti, Serafino, 387
Burbage, Cuthbert, 310
Burbage, James, 67, 68, 257, 604, 785,
  861
Burbage, Richard, 69, 310, 730, 785
Burberry, Thomas, 105
Burbidge, Sir Richard, 366
Burchard, C., 453, 817
Burdett, Sir Francis, 148, 552, 597, 718,
  826, 900, 930
Burdett, Lady Sophia, 597
Burdett-Coutts, Angela, Baroness, 61,
  190, 202, 389, 597, 759, 765, 832,
  915, 960
Burges, William, 367, 436, 507, 689
Burgess, Guy, 664
Burgess, James, 234, 326
Burgess, Thomas, 682
Burgh, Allatson, 105
Burghley, William Cecil, Lord, 270,
  321, 722, 738
Burgon, John, 106
Burgoyne, Sir John Fox, 375, 590, 815
Burke, Edmund, 93, 140, 185, 203, 308,
  351, 451, 471, 514, 628, 650, 677,
  793, 834, 868, 966
Burke, Sir George, 585
Burke, Thomas, 178, 457
Burleigh, William Cecil, Lord, 96, 107,
  264, 308
Burley, Sir Simon de, 873
Burlington, 1st Earl of, 108, 766
Burlington, 2nd Earl of, 903
Burlington, 3rd Earl of, 88, 117, 154,
  184, 558, 594, 648, 772, 952
Burne-Jones, Edward, 282, 391, 427,
  456, 552, 555, 639, 693, 763, 765,
  791, 811, 960
Burnell, John, 733
Burnell, Margaret, 733
Burnet, Gilbert, Bishop, 182, 712
Burnet, Sir John, 91, 438, 575, 777
Burnett, Frances Hodgson, 616
Burney, Charles, senior, 107, 580, 629,
  703
Burney, Charles, junior, 755
Burney, Fanny, 75, 77, 81, 122, 149,
  150, 220, 233, 358, 451, 629, 755,
  771, 834, 911, 935, 970
Burney, Susan, 546
Burnham, Daniel, 777
Burns, John, 44, 178, 614
Burns, Robert, 219, 259, 815, 915, 947
Burr, Alfred, 293
Burrell, Peter, 348
Bursill, H., 385, 817, 818
Burton, Decimus, 1, 29, 50, 62, 115,
  138, 179, 190, 193, 197, 343, 362,
  367, 386, 389, 402, 403, 427, 429,
  553, 579, 582, 665, 666, 682, 800,
  830, 858, 901, 978
Burton, Sir Edmund, 109
Burton, Henry, 748

Burton, Hezekiah, 833
Burton, James, 51, 59, 75, 109, 126, 150, 346, 389, 685, 801, 856, 976
Burton, Sir Richard, 33, 453, 507, 673
Bury, John, 88
Busby, Christopher, 110
Busby, Henrietta, 634
Busby, Dr Richard, 947
Bush, Irving T., 110
Bushall, F.W., 563
Bushnell, John, 671, 752
Buss, Frances Mary, 116, 552, 632
Butcher, A.J., 121
Bute, 3rd Earl of, 284, 342, 428, 446, 591, 664, 665, 797
Bute, 1st Marquess of, 110
Bute, 2nd Marquess of, 110, 664
Bute, 4th Marquess of, 725
Butler, E.C., 958
Butler, F. Hedges, 661
Butler, H. Montagu, 367
Butler, J.D., 326
Butler, James, 327
Butler, John, 285
Butler, Reg, 429, 788
Butler, Samuel, 408, 657, 755, 947
Butler, Timothy, 915
Butler, William, 502, 562
Butt, Alfred, 862, 915
Butt, Dame Clara, 365, 667
Butte, William, 20
Butterfield, William, 17, 18, 52, 107, 155, 234, 367, 436, 497, 567, 632, 688, 693, 701, 710, 722, 738, 742, 745, 748, 750, 754, 756
Button, Daniel, 111
Buxton, Sir Thomas Fowell, 85, 262, 507, 916
Buzas, Stefan, 372
Bydell, John, 285
Byfield, John, 565
Byng, John, Admiral, 382
Bynns, Anne, 39
Byrd, William, 137, 370, 571
Byron, Lord, 9, 10, 24, 56, 57, 76, 165, 242, 270, 272, 356, 367, 368, 379, 386, 387, 395, 428, 597, 615, 681, 711, 721, 723, 728, 737, 747, 789, 807, 812, 877, 947
Byron, H.J., 212, 775
Byron, Sir John, later 4th Baron, 876
Byron, Lady, née Anne Isobella Milbanke, 457
Bywaters, Frederick, 133

Cabanel, Rudolph, 561, 848
Cachemaille-Day, N.F., 571, 697, 850
Cadbury, Elizabeth, 589
Cadbury, George, 589
Cadbury-Brown, H.T., 666
Cade, Jack, 69, 79, 143, 279, 469, 478, 954
Cadogan, Margaretta, Countess of, 112
Cadogan, 1st Baron and 1st Earl, 112
Cadogan, 4th Earl, 363
Cadogan, 5th Earl, 144, 621
Cadogan, 6th Earl, 144
Cadogan of Oakley, 1st and 2nd Barons, 112
Cadwallader, 734
Caesar, Julius, 44, 154, 181, 811, 859
Cagliostro, Count, 789
Caines, John, 171
Caius, John, 506
Calcraft, William, 269
Caldecott, Randolph, 330, 453
Calder Marshall, William, 12, 109, 402, 453, 819, 820
Calderon, P.H., 342, 726
Cale, Judith, 113
Calthorpe, Henry, 852
Calthorpe, 3rd Lord, 114
Calthorpe, 5th Lord, 293
Carlton, Francis, 241
Calton, Thomas, 241
Calveley, Sir Hugh, 549
Calvert, Edward, 584
Calvert, Robert, 85
Calvert, Sir William, 85
Cambridge, Adolphus, Duke of, 115, 411, 537
Cambridge, Duchess of, 402, 691
Cambridge, 2nd Duke of, 130, 194, 307, 311, 439, 550, 630, 665, 682, 691, 815
Camden, William, 109, 115, 158, 312, 321, 623, 952
Camden, 1st Earl, 116, 538
Camelford, 1st Baron, 116, 833
Camelford, 2nd Baron, 386
Camerer, Andrew, 541
Campbell, Colen, 98, 108–109, 341, 426, 493, 558, 949
Campbell, 1st Baron Clyde, Sir Colin, 815
Campbell, John, 201, 539
Campbell, Lord, 98, 440, 458, 558
Campbell, Neville, 113
Campbell, Mrs Patrick, 427, 856

Campbell, Thomas, 780, 814, 832, 853, 901, 903, 916
Campbell-Bannerman, Sir Henry, 341, 632, 947
Campden, Sir Baptist Hicks, later Lord, 355
Campden, 1st Viscount, 117, 425
Campeggio, Cardinal, 126
Campion, Edmund, 158, 249, 876
Campion, Henry, 85
Campion, Richard, 85
Campion, William, 928
Canaletto (Antonio Canale), 47, 637, 787
Canning, George, 9, 57, 100, 117, 154, 167, 192, 311, 368, 386, 408, 458, 809, 815, 946
Canning, Lord, 118
Canning, Sir Stratford, later 1st Viscount Stratford de Radcliffe, 91
Canova, Antonio, 480, 718, 766, 932, 936
Cantwell, Robert, 551
Canute, King, 346, 396, 658, 864
Capel, Sir Henry, 430, 664
Capel, Sir William, 121, 694
Caractacus, 507
Carausius, 467, 654
Carbery, 3rd Earl of, 675
Carden, George Frederick, 129
Carew, Sir Francis, 121
Carew, J.E., 160, 538, 671, 823
Carew, Sir Nicholas, 49, 190, 200, 551, 697
Carew, Richard, 286
Carey, Nicholas, 121
Carleton, Edward, 125
Carleton, John, 234
Carleton, Lord, 234
Carlile, Wilson, 739, 782
Carline, Hilda, 236
Carlini, Agostino, 796
Carlisle, 1st Earl of, 326
Carlisle, 2nd Earl of, 121
Carlisle, Duke of, 122, 575
Carlisle, Edward, 723
Carlton, Henry, Lord, 123
Carlyle, Alexander, 313
Carlyle, Jane, 21, 124, 347
Carlyle, Thomas, 5, 91, 124, 144, 145, 147, 151, 260, 418, 427, 475, 529, 531, 558, 757, 791, 815, 904
Carmelianus, Peter, 708
Carnarvon, Earl of, 2
Carnegie, Andrew, 125
Caro, Anthony, 78
Caröe, W.D., 156, 519, 584
Caroline, Princess, 414
Caroline of Anspach, Queen, 145, 148, 426, 430, 490, 566, 634, 664, 771, 774, 941, 946, 955
Caroline of Brunswick, Queen, 82, 193, 198, 223, 337, 427, 616, 633, 716, 720, 798, 970
Caron, Sir Noel, 421
Carpenter, John, 176, 417
Carpenter, Richard, 742
Carpenter, William Boyd, 156
Carr, E., 170
Carr, H., 68
Carr, James, 181, 712
Carr, Jonathan, 51
Carr, Robert, 876
Carr, Thomas, 304
Carré, Jean, 309
Carrington, Nathan, 125
Carroll, Sydney, 563
Carron, Abbé, 795
Carson, Lord, 251
Carte, Richard D'Oyley, 7, 564, 577, 773, 774, 781, 963
Carter, A.T., 697
Carter, John, 715
Cartwright, John, 126, 815
Cartwright, Thomas, 40, 816
Caruso, Enrico, 773
Cary, Henry Francis, 384
Cary, John, 496
Cary, Thomas, 629, 653
Casals, Pablo, 680
Casanova, Giovanni, 121, 332
Casement, Sir Roger, 877
Caslon, William, 61, 731
Cass, Sir James, 697
Cass, Sir John, 787
Cassel, Sir Ernest, 98, 160, 342, 498
Casson, Sir Hugh, 50, 666, 978
Casson, Sir Lewis, 189
Castlemaine, Lady, 384, 401, 960
Castlereagh, Lord, 127, 552, 720, 890, 947
Castling, Harry, 830
Caswell, Richard, 304
Catalani, Angelica, 48
Catesby, Robert, 346
Catherine, Grand Duchess, 625
Catherine of Aragon, 68, 86, 121, 126, 228, 244, 259, 267, 336, 389, 540, 601, 649, 671, 690, 709, 732, 757, 874

Catherine of Braganza, 127, 578, 596, 616, 631, 796
Catherine Howard, Queen, 763, 853, 875, 966
Catherine Parr, Queen, 68, 144, 146, 528, 634
Cathie, E.W., 786
Catley, Ann, 652
Catnach, James, 779
Cator, H.J., 582
Cator, John, 49, 257, 581, 582
Caunt, Benjamin, 64
Cavafy, C. P., 634
Cavanagh, John, 195
Cave, Edward, 724, 725
Cave, Nicholas, 795
Cave, Walter, 105
Cavell, Edith, 730, 815
Cavendish, Lord George, 107, 109
Cavendish, Lady Henrietta, 121, 387
Cavendish, Henry, 51, 178, 328
Cavendish, Lady Margaret, 497
Cawarden, Sir Thomas, 68, 690, 743
Cawston, Arthur, 693, 765
Caxton, William, 128, 168, 345, 557, 668, 698, 732, 752, 787, 943, 947
Cayley, Sir George, 375
Cecil, Algernon, 100
Cecil of Chelwood, Viscount, 675, 798
Cecil, Lord David, 682
Cecil, Sir Edward, 745
Cecil, Lady Elizabeth, 369
Cecil, Robert, Earl of Salisbury, 539
Cecil, William, Lord Burghley, 31
Cedda, St, 66
Cely, Robert and Richard, 752
Cenwulf, King 367
Ceracchi, Joseph, 796
Chadburn, Dr Maud, 799
Chadwick, Sir Edwin, 126, 238, 506, 811, 930, 931
Chadwick, Lynn, 653
Chadwick, Spencer, 220
Chadwick, William, 131
Challoner, Richard, 559, 950
Chamber, John, 576
Chamberlain, Sir Austen, 8, 132
Chamberlain, Joseph (Senior), 517
Chamberlain, Joseph, 114, 115, 271, 377, 621, 903, 947
Chamberlain, Neville, 130, 252, 411, 674, 938, 947
Chamberlayne, Edward, 650
Chamberlin, Peter, 345
Chambers, Ephraim, 120
Chambers, Geoffrey, 644
Chambers, Sir William, 7, 9, 9, 88, 220, 273, 303, 341, 493, 498, 559, 568, 605, 648, 659, 664, 665, 677, 747, 774, 796, 890, 926, 947, 963
Chamier, Anthony, 222
Champness, Henry, 766
Champneys, Basil, 50, 425, 518, 690, 707, 708, 731, 817
Champneys, Sir John, 352
Chancellor, Beresford, 383, 563
Chancellor, F.G.M., 687
Chandler, Arthur, 18
Chandos, 1st Duke of, 120, 128, 137, 312, 376, 729, 939
Chandos, 2nd Duke of, 939
Chandos, 3rd Duke of, 137, 939
Chandos, 1st Lord, 535
Chandos, 3rd Lord, 137
Changeur, Louis Léon, 254
Chantrey, Sir Francis, 100, 142, 252, 362, 496, 745, 816, 818, 821, 823, 855
Chaplin, Charlie, 364, 422, 453, 815
Chapman, Annie, 957
Chapman, Frederic, 831
Chapman, George, 710
Chapman, Hugh Boswell, 773
Chapman, John, 888
Chappell, William, 844
Charatter, Stephen and Thomas, 126
Charbonnel, Mlle, 78
Chare, Henry, 494
Charles I, 23, 28, 37, 135, 137, 138, 146, 188, 197, 234, 242, 243, 322, 345, 352, 360, 376, 377, 382, 402, 421, 433, 453, 458, 459, 513, 528, 550, 576, 578, 593, 610, 631, 633, 644, 647, 649, 671, 690, 692, 700, 716, 717, 736, 758, 796, 809, 815, 834, 853, 857, 876, 877, 878, 886, 924, 936, 951, 952, 959, 960
Charles II, 26, 32, 37, 44, 50, 66, 70, 74, 79, 90, 117, 126, 135, 145-147, 180, 183, 194, 235, 264, 272, 280, 282, 296, 320, 322, 323, 327, 328, 329, 331, 333, 335, 337-339, 353, 360, 361, 370, 401, 416, 421, 432, 433, 436, 447, 456, 459, 461, 466, 467, 469, 493, 513, 525, 538, 550, 578, 631, 639, 647, 671, 677, 678, 679, 681, 685, 690, 696, 709, 711, 714, 716, 717, 720, 725, 733, 736, 737, 756, 758, 793, 794, 796, 808, 815,

826, 842, 853, 857, 869, 877-879, 888, 892, 946, 960, 972, 974
Charles, Prince of Wales, 760
Charles Edward Stuart, the Young Pretender, 67
Charles V, Emperor, 68, 86
Charles X of France, 797
Charlotte, Princess, d. of George IV, 116, 124, 193, 499, 561, 784, 926
Charlotte of Mecklenburg-Strelitz, Queen of George III, 86, 140, 145, 153, 186, 342, 363, 368, 431, 565, 628, 631, 665, 796, 816, 818
Charmilly, Colonel, 254
Charmon, William, 662
Charoux, Siegfried, 379, 798
Charraton, Gordon, 66
Charrington, John and Frederick, 84
Chart, Robert Masters, 913
Chatham, William Pitt the Elder, Earl of, 36, 57, 98, 167, 344, 356, 370, 600, 675, 714, 720, 946, 961
Chattaway, W.H., 275
Chatterton, Thomas, 98, 784
Chaucer, Geoffrey, 14, 84, 96, 143, 173, 258, 275, 285, 345, 382, 560, 668, 743, 757, 773, 778, 787, 854, 880, 943, 947
Chaucer, Geoffrey (Senior), 907
Chavalliaud, Léon-Joseph, 820, 821
Cheere, Sir Henry, 823, 911
Chéron, Louis, 735
Chermayeff, Serge, 115
Cherry, Bridget, 879
Cheseldon, William, 951
Chesham, Lord, 107
Chester, Earl of, 599
Chester, Eliza, 421
Chesterfield, Countess of, 55
Chesterfield, 4th Earl of, 150, 637, 720, 725, 797, 811, 961
Chesterton, G.K., 51, 117, 131, 254, 308, 368, 762, 782, 792, 926
Cheston, Chester, 732
Chevalier, Albert, 692
Cheylesmore, Lord, 816, 962
Cheyne, Charles, 146
Cheyne, Lady Jane, 147
Chichele, Archbishop, 443, 745
Chichele, Elizabeth, 33
Chichele, John, 33
Chicheley, Richard, 766
Chichester, 3rd Earl of, 590, 790
Chichester, Sir Francis, 309
Child, Aylwin, 57, 58
Child, Francis, 152, 517, 568
Child, Sir Francis, 166, 568
Child, Sir Josiah, 745, 922
Child, Robert, 568
Chillingworth, Richard, 794
Chippendale, Thomas, 122, 153, 480, 734
Chirac, Denis, 572
Chisholm, Robert, 789
Chlorus, Constantius, 654
Cholmley, John, 657
Cholmley, Sir Richard, 267
Cholmley, Sir Roger, 379, 381
Chope, R.R., 693
Chopin, Frédéric, 235, 252, 445, 718, 816
Christian, Ewan, 16, 24, 156, 534, 585, 936
Christian IV of Denmark, 796
Christian, Princess, 579, 681, 713
Christie, Agatha, 21
Christie, J.R., 133
Christie, James, 144, 157, 596, 714
Christie, James J.B., 157
Christie, John Reginald Halliday, 650
Christie, William Douglas, 475
Christmas, Brothers, 684
Christmas, Gerard, 554
Christopher, John, 812
Christy, Henry, 90
Chudleigh, Arthur, 669
Chudleigh, Elizabeth, Countess of Bristol, 261, 621
Church, Richard, 301, 375
Churchill, Arabella, 720
Churchill, Charles, 186, 202, 656
Churchill, Lady (Clementine), 132, 816
Churchill, Lady Randolph, 128
Churchill, Lord Randolph, 193, 490, 577
Churchill, Sir Winston, 8, 12, 74, 88, 112, 123, 174, 202, 252, 260, 267, 344, 367, 403, 404, 534, 569, 615, 732, 744, 816, 849, 865, 941, 948, 951
Churchman, John, 218
Chute, Chaloner, 850
Chute, John, 833
Cibber, Caius Gabriel, 60, 525, 727, 758, 815, 936
Cibber, Colley, 373, 801, 861, 937
Cibber, Theophilus, 433
Cicero, Marcus Tullius, 154
Cipriani, Giovanni, 6, 363, 436, 482, 649, 677

985

986

Goss, Sir John, 151
Gossage, John, 751
Gosse, Sir Edmund, 223, 363
Gough, A.D., 374, 753
Gough, H.R., 127, 729, 755
Gough, Sir Richard, 318
Gould, James, 697
Goulden, Richard, 460, 748, 819
Goulding, Richard and William, 413
Gounod, Charles, 71, 856
Gower, John, 805
Gowers, Sir William, 902
Gowing, Lawrence, 768
Grace, W.G., 26, 95, 209, 484, 529, 853
Grafton, Duchess of, 708
Grafton, 1st Duke of, 282, 320, 583
Grafton, 2nd Duke of, 282, 320
Grafton, 3rd Duke of, 320, 342
Graham, George, 947
Graham, James, 7, 775
Graham, Raynold, 158
Graham, Susannah, 158
Graham, General Thomas, see
  Lynedoch, 1st Baron
Graham, Thomas, Professor of
  Chemistry, 681
Graham, Winifred, 619
Grahame, Kenneth, 596
Grahame-White, Claude, 320, 372, 661
Granby, Marquess of, 416, 866
Grant, Albert, 453
Grant, Duncan, 75, 100
Grant, Sir Francis, 849
Grant, John, 274
Grant, Keith, 265, 782
Grant, Marion, 708
Grant, Mary, 817
Grantham, Earl of, 79
Grantham, Thomas and John, 321
Granville, 1st Earl of, 353
Granville, 2nd Earl of, 577
Granville-Barker, Harley, 438, 535, 669,
  775
Grattan, Henry, 514
Gravelot, Hubert François, 561
Gray, Edward, 366
Gray, Frances, 761
Gray, Sir George, 807
Gray, Henry, 710, 965
Gray, John, 75
Gray, Thomas, 196, 416, 748, 818, 947
Gray, Walker, 343
Gray, William, organ-builder, 755
Gray, William, sculptor, 739
Greathead, James Henry, 879, 899
Greaves, James Pierrepoint, 798
Greaves, Sam, 252
Greaves, Walter and Henry, 152, 622
Green, Charles, 34, 208, 911
Green, John, 334, 433
Green, John Richard, 49, 427
Green, Richard, 818
Green, William Curtis, 39, 233, 551
Greenaway, Kate, 130, 296, 356, 399,
  460, 907
Greene, Graham, 9
Greene, Thomas, 85
Greene, William, 76
Greene, Sir William, 86
Greenhough, George Bellas, 343
Greenwell, James Hugo, 334
Greenwood, Christopher and John, 496
Greet, Sir Ben (Sir Philip Barling
  Greet), 444, 563
Gregory, John, 420
Gregory, 1st Pope and Saint, 711
Greig, David, 394
Grenville, Dorothy, 338
Grenville, 1st Baron, 246, 829
Grenville, Thomas, 8, 90
Gresham, Sir John, 778
Gresham, Richard, 387
Gresham, Sir Richard, 228, 396, 669,
  694, 744
Gresham, Sir Thomas, 39, 67, 79, 168,
  173, 338, 385, 510, 558, 567, 568,
  669, 670, 671, 712, 818
Gresse, J.A., 295
Gresse, John Alexander, 295, 339
Gresse, Peter Gaspard, 339, 824
Greville, Charles, 25, 339, 427, 573, 961
Greville, Francis, 24
Greville, Sir Fulke, later 1st Baron
  Brooke, 24, 30, 33, 98, 179, 384
Greville, Henry, 581
Grews, Robert, 51
Grey, 2nd Earl of, 8, 254, 375, 386
Grey, 3rd Earl of, 53, 124
Grey, Lady Jane, 126, 142, 244, 344,
  763, 853, 875
Grey, Maria, 309
Grey, Richard, 958
Grey of Falloden, Viscount, 628, 818
Gribble, Herbert, 97
Grieg, Edward, 715
Griffin, Bernard William, 950
Griffith, John W., 131
Griffith, W.P., 712

Grillon, Alexander, 192
Grimaldi, Joseph, 29, 136, 591, 687,
  713, 753, 862
Grimes, W.F., 697, 858
Grimthorpe, 1st Baron, 19, 540
Grindal, Edmund, 301, 381, 758
Grisi, Giulia, 205
Gronow, Rees Howell, 212, 343, 961
Groom, John, 182
Gropius, Walter, 584
Grossmith, George, the Elder, 119, 234
Grossmith, George, the Younger, 300,
  807, 968
Grosvenor, 2nd Earl, 340
Grosvenor, Lord Robert, later 1st Baron
  Ebury, 402
Grosvenor, Sir Robert, 518
Grosvenor, Sir Thomas, 221, 340, 701,
  797
Grote, George, 142, 772, 785
Grove, Sir George, 667
Grove, Sir Robert, 123
Gruner, Lewis, 330
Gualandi, Francesco, 764
Guardi, Francesco, 429
Guest, Ivor, later Viscount Wimborne,
  961
Guinness family, 948
Guinness, Sir Edward, see Iveagh, 1st
  Earl of
Gulbenkian, Calouste Sarkis, 414
Gumley, John, 413
Gundulf, 871
Gunhilda, 346
Gunne, Gregory, 404
Gunnell, Richard, 768
Gunning, Elizabeth, 150, 218
Gunter, James, 247, 854
Gunter, Richard, 528
Gunter, Robert, 40, 346
Gunter, Sir Robert, 854, 952
Gurnell, Thomas, 600
Gurney, Elizabeth, 1
Gurney, Geoffrey, 171
Gurney, Sir Goldsworthy, 9
Gurney, Mary, 309
Gurney, Sir Richard, 638
Gurney, Samuel, the Elder, 832, 908,
  938
Gurney, Samuel, the Younger, 289, 512
Gutch, Charles, 310, 702
Gutch, George, 46, 489, 573, 713
Guthrie, L. Rome, 903
Guy of Warwick, 818
Guy, Thomas, 138, 196, 347, 768, 818
Gwilt, George, 395, 739, 741
Gwilt, George, the Younger, 805
Gwilt, Joseph, 340
Gwydyr, Baron, 348
Gwynn, John, 641
Gwynne, Nell, 26, 32, 144, 235, 239,
  335, 447, 459, 518, 578, 639, 685,
  733, 771, 861, 933, 955
Gwynne, Patrick, 402
Gye, Frederick, the Younger, 205
Gyfford family, 86

Haakon VII, King of Norway, 752
Habershon, Edward, 79, 765
Habershon, W.G. and E., 55
Hacker, Colonel, 751
Hacket, John, 689
Hackett, Walter, 960
Hackman, James, 50
Hadrian, Emperor, 29, 291, 467
Haggard, Sir (Henry) Rider, 408
Haggerty, Owen, 269
Hahn, Otto, 375
Haigh, Earl, 621, 818
Haile Selassie, Emperor, 446
Hailsham, Baron, 458, 609
Hailsham, 1st Viscount, 458
Haines, Joe, 287
Hakewill, Henry, 762
Hakewill, J., 381
Hakewith, Henry, 723
Haldane, John, 676
Haldane, Viscount, 458, 628
Haldimand, George and William, 53
Hale, Sir Matthew, 3, 458
Hale, Warren Stormes, 176
Hales, Sir Robert, 588, 873
Hales, Stephen, 856
Halford, Sir Henry, 515, 667
Halhed, John, 477
Halifax, 1st Earl and 1st Marquess of,
  326, 720
Halifax, George Montagu Dunk, 2nd
  Earl of, 359
Halifax, 2nd Marquess of, 720
Hall, Alner W., 459, 515, 668
Hall, Anmer, 952
Hall, Austen, 281
Hall, Sir Benjamin, later Baron
  Llanover, 64, 931
Hall, E.S., 326, 456
Hall, E.T., 128, 326, 456, 676, 766
Hall, Edward, 967

Hall, H. Austen, 164, 244
Hall, Henry, 679
Hall, Jacob, 741, 806, 839
Hall, Peter, 535
Hall, Samuel Carter, 558
Hall, Stanley, 395
Hall, Susanna, 411
Hall, William, 342
Hallam, Arthur Henry, 408
Hallam, Henry, 100, 352, 475, 966
Hallett, William, 480, 552
Halley, Edmond, 331, 332, 351, 450,
  679, 680, 762
Halsey, John, 352
Halton, Sir William, 41
Hambleden, Viscountess, 789
Hambro, Sir Everard Alexander, 370
Hamilton, Cosmo, 802
Hamilton, 4th Duke of, 398, 401, 657
Hamilton, 6th Duke of, 150, 218
Hamilton, James, 353
Hamilton, Lady (Emma), 7, 77, 180,
  311, 511, 538, 708, 747, 772, 921, 963
Hamilton, Sir William, 90, 189, 511,
  573, 596, 737, 963
Hamlet, Thomas, 622
Hamley, William, 353
Hammerstein, Oscar, 683, 828
Hammerton, Walter, 896
Hammett, Benjamin, 355
Hammond, J.C. and Barbara, 909
Hammond, William, 826
Hamon, 553
Hamond, Thomas, 567
Hamp, Stanley H., 83, 293
Hampton, Herbert, 816
Hanbury, Sampson, 84
Hanbury, Sir Thomas, 674
Hancock, Tony, 967
Hand, Richard, 145
Handley, Tommy, 130, 207
Hands, Terry, 925
Hanff, Helene, 139
Hankey, Henry Alers, 628
Hanna, Maurice, 128
Hannay, James Oliver, 391
Hansard, Luke, 76, 711
Hansom, Joseph Aloysius, 846
Hanson, Frank, 893
Hanson, J.F., 117
Hanson, Robert, 483
Hanway, John, 363
Hanway, Jonas, 180, 607, 640, 947
Harald Bluetooth, King of Denmark,
  727
Harben, Henry Andrade, 383
Harcourt, Sir William, 320
Harcourt, 3rd Earl, 364, 407
Harcourt, 1st Viscount, 407, 476
Hardacanute, King of England, 177, 442
Hardcastle, Joseph, 539
Hardie, James Keir, 540, 938
Hardiman, Alfred, 200, 818
Harding, V.S., 684
Harding, Agas, 249
Hardinge, Sir Henry, later 1st Viscount
  Hardinge, 682
Hardwick, Bess of, 785
Hardwicke, 1st Earl of, 126, 283, 459
Hardwicke, 3rd Earl of, 719
Hardwick, Philip, 6, 53, 156, 175, 200,
  265, 293, 313, 502, 558, 728, 793
Hardwick, Philip Charles, 11, 108, 265,
  331, 441, 540, 574, 691, 739, 814
Hardwick, Thomas, 59, 222, 326, 694,
  712, 726, 745, 747, 754
Hardy, Thomas, 7, 435, 867, 792, 941,
  947
Hardy, Thomas, the shoemaker, 471
Hare, Augustus, 225, 814
Hare, Cecil, 743
Hare, Francis, 833
Hare, H.T., 584
Hare, Sir John, 303, 310, 669, 722
Hare, Sir Nicholas, 364, 407
Hare, William, 677
Harewood, 5th Earl of, 365
Harewood, 6th Earl of, 150
Hargreaves, Francis, 90
Hargreaves, William, 830
Harington, Sir John, 237, 624
Harle, John, 636, 637
Harley, Edward, 2nd Earl of Oxford,
  89, 128, 288, 365, 373, 387, 419, 570,
  615, 719, 762, 912, 963, 966
Harley, Margaret Cavendish, 746
Harley, Robert, 1st Earl of Oxford, 10,
  81, 89, 104, 528
Harlow, G.H., 714
Harman, Thomas, 836
Harmer, H.R., 77
Harmsworth, Alfred, senior, 909
Harmsworth, Alfred, see Northcliffe, 1st
  Viscount
Harmsworth, Cecil, 1st Baron, 418
Harmsworth, Geraldine Mary, 60
Harness, William, 723
Harold I, Harefoot, King, 701

Harold II, King, 197, 262
Harold Bluetooth, King of Norway, 727
Harper, Richard, 42
Harpur, William, 51
Harrington, Denis, 574
Harrington, 1st Earl of, 594
Harrington, 2nd Earl of, 811
Harrington, 5th Earl of, 271
Harrington, 11th Earl, of, 366
Harriott, John, 651, 652
Harris, Augustus Glossop, 622
Harris, Sir Augustus, 205, 260, 577,
  818, 862
Harris, Bumper, 598
Harris, Charles, 582
Harris, E.Vincent, 117
Harris, Frank, 446
Harris, Henry, 205, 234, 769
Harris, John R., 311
Harris, Renatus, 564, 690, 697, 703,
  714, 748
Harris, Thomas, architect, 747
Harris, Thomas, clockmaker, 704
Harris, Thomas, theatre manager, 204,
  205
Harris, S.J., 220
Harris, Vincent, 241, 915
Harrison, Benjamin, 347
Harrison, George, 649
Harrison, Jack, 252
Harrison, J.T., 367
Harrison, John, horologist, 640
Harrison, John, surgeon, 474, 755
Harrison, Joseph, 888
Harrison, Thomas, 138
Harrod family, 366
Harrow, Richard, 801
Harrowby, 1st Earl, 127
Hart, Emma, 573
Hart, Sir John, 570
Hart, Napthali, 496
Hart, Sir Percival, 567
Harte, Bret, 444
Hartnell, Norman, 100
Hartwell, Charles, 343, 821
Harvard, John, 803, 805, 866
Harvard, Robert, 866
Harvest, William, 85
Harvey, Benjamin, 368
Harvey, George, 149
Harvey, Richard, 394
Harvey, William, 447, 667, 694
Harwath, Simon, 810
Harwood, H.M., 21
Hasculf de Tania, 104
Hassall, Arthur, 358, 542, 804, 931
Hastings, Baron, 873
Hastings, Sir Charles, 89
Hastings, Marchioness of, 863
Hastings, Warren, 242, 582, 947, 951,
  952
Hatch, F. Brook, 509
Hatch, Samuel, 909
Hatchard, John, 368
Hatcliffe, William, 126
Hatfeild, Gilliat, 527
Hatton, Sir Christopher, 259, 369, 470,
  562, 649, 687
Hatton, Edward, 33, 217, 741, 808
Hatton, Lady Elizabeth, 689
Hatton, 3rd Viscount, 259
Haugwitz-Reventlow, neé Barbara
  Hutton, Countess, 375
Havelock, Sir Henry, 142, 819, 881
Hawes, William, 264, 907
Hawker, Harry, 393
Hawkesworth, John, 95
Hawkins, Charles, 628
Hawkins, Sir John, author, 76, 93, 185,
  414
Hawkins, Sir John, naval commander,
  360, 514
Hawkins, Rhode, 754
Hawkins, Waterhouse, 216
Hawkshaw, Sir John, 118, 119, 138, 139
Hawksley, Thomas, 930
Hawksmoor, Nicholas, 88, 156, 157,
  302, 335, 425, 426, 456, 679, 689,
  691, 707, 710, 719, 731, 745, 748,
  818, 946, 949
Hawkwood, Sir John, 549
Hawthorne, Grace, 622
Hawthorne, Nathaniel, 71, 848
Hawtrey, Sir Charles, 604, 622, 973
Hawtrey, Ralph, 251
Hay, Alexander, 58, 371
Haydn, Josef, 109, 329, 362, 556, 667,
  682
Haydon, Benjamin Robert, 59, 76, 253,
  255, 308, 326, 461, 561
Haydon, Sir Henry, 49
Hayek, Friedrich von, 477
Hayes, Catherine, 269
Hayman, Francis, 222, 911, 912
Haynau, Julius, Freiherr von, 37
Hayter, Sir William, 489
Hayward, C.F., 330, 367
Hayward, John, 741, 750, 756, 765

989

990

Maclise, Daniel, 140, 151, 459, 577
Macmanus, Frederick, 436
Macmillan, Daniel, 264
Macmillan, Harold, 123, 322, 766
Macmillan, William, 292, 407, 423, 645, 813, 814, 816, 818, 821, 822, 881
Macneice, Louis, 179
Macpherson, James, 118
Macqueen-Pope, W., 755
Macquoid, Percy, 575
Macready, William Charles, 179, 205, 295, 528, 647, 811, 862, 976
Macwhirter, John, 1, 726
Madden, H.H., 317
Maddox, J.M., 622
Maddox, Sir Benjamin, 108, 362, 489, 609
Magus, St, Earl of the Orkneys, 731
Maguire, Robert, 105, 754
Mahler, Gustav, 205
Mainwaring, Boulton, 474, 475
Mair, George, 439
Maire, Sir Peter le, 731
Maitland, F.W., 88
Maitland, William, 38, 349, 383, 700, 792
Makins, W.T., 113
Malcolm, James Peller, 283, 383, 780
Malcome, Sarah, 275
Malet, Sir Edward, 491
Maleverer, Sir Henry, 549
Mallarmé, Stéphane, 97, 581
Mallett, Edward, 275
Mallisard, G., 817
Mallowan, Sir Max, 88
Malmesbury, William of, 757
Malone, Edmond, 446
Malone, J.A.E., 968
Man, Alexander, 493
Man, Edmund, 493
Manby, Charles, 942
Manchester, 4th Duke of, 492, 919
Manchester, 4th Earl of, 308
Mancini, Frederick, 820
Mander, Noel, 565, 566
Mander, Raymond, 638
Mandeville, Geoffrey de, 590
Mann, Sir Horace, 812
Mann, James, 84
Manners-Sutton, Charles, 5
Manning, A., 864
Manning, Frederick and Marie, 270, 395
Manning, Henry Edward, 97, 122, 132, 160, 194, 249, 381, 493, 555, 707, 743, 869, 949, 950, 952
Manning, William, 65
Manningham, Sir Richard, 628
Manny, Sir Walter de, 141
Mansell, Sir Robert, 309
Mansfield, 1st Earl of, 75, 153, 355, 356, 428, 429, 436, 458, 558, 707
Mansfield, 2nd Earl of, 429
Mansfield, 6th Earl of, 429
Mansfield, Katherine, 249, 319, 632, 926
Manson, Sir Patrick, 218, 395
Manson, William, 157
Mantegna, Andrea, 360, 528
Manzu, Giacomo, 950
Maple, John, 494
Maple, Sir John Blundell, 179, 396, 495, 902
Mapp, Sarah, 332
Mappin, Jonathan, 495
Maratti, Carlo, 732
March, Charles, 967
March, Lord, 812
March, R.B., 447
Marchant, Hugh, 497
Marconi, Guglielmo, 306, 374
Margaret of Anjou, 212, 336, 649
Margaret, Lady, Countess of Richmond, 441
Margaret, Princess, 179, 198, 404, 427
Margaret Queen of Scots, 868
Margaret, Queen, widow of James IV, 330
Margaret, 2nd Queen of Edward I, 155
Marie Louise, Princess, 579
Marjoribanks, Sir Dudley Coutts, 98
Markham, Frederick, 510
Markham, Sir Clements, 673, 820
Markova, Dame Alicia, 139, 595
Marks, H. Stacey, 726
Marks, Michael, 498
Marks, 1st Baron, 498
Marlborough, 1st Duchess of, 74, 426, 498, 499, 626, 633, 720, 965
Marlborough, 1st Duke of, 42, 71, 326, 416, 439, 499, 762
Marlowe, Christopher, 153, 751, 775
Marnock, Robert, 666
Marochetti, Baron, 12, 538, 815, 821, 822
Marquand, John, 348
Marrable, Frederick, 303
Marriott, Richard, 436, 704
Marriott, Thomas, 525

Marryat, Frederick, 183, 807, 881, 965
Marsden, William, 132, 672, 676, 689
Marsh, Sydney, 814
Marshall, James, 499
Marshall, James C., 499
Marshall, Joshua, 159, 698
Marshall, Norman, 305, 535
Marsham, Thomas, 461
Marston, John, 286
Martin, A.C., 917
Martin Brothers, 800
Martin, G.D., 109
Martin, J.L., 671
Martin, John ('Mad'), 238, 260, 614, 914
Martin, Marius, 113
Martin, Richard, 447
Martin, Robert Wallace, 235, 500
Martin, Samuel, 402
Martin-Smith, D.F., 518, 692
Martin of Tours, St, 149
Martyn, John, 152, 436
Marvell, Andrew, 343, 381, 490, 711
Marwood, William, 269
Marx, Eleanor, 500
Marx, Karl, 91, 222, 282, 332, 381, 428, 599, 820
Mary I, 126, 795, 922
Mary, Princess, daughter of Charles I, 633
Mary, Princess, daughter of Malcolm III of Scotland, 58
Mary of Modena, 443, 739, 879
Mary, Queen of George V, 78, 158, 256, 286, 302, 427, 437, 499, 527, 560, 629, 671, 714, 820, 832, 933
Mary Queen of Scots, 142, 360, 578, 733, 820, 876, 946
Mary Stuart, Queen, 104, 288, 335, 361, 424, 425, 633, 678, 679, 714, 879, 946, 960
Mary Tudor, Queen, 14, 86, 120, 173, 188, 215, 228, 244, 245, 261, 262, 294, 311, 334, 336, 360, 369, 430, 443, 521, 550, 634, 649, 694, 715, 722, 733, 751, 757, 774, 790, 805, 875, 892, 945, 946, 975
Masaryk, T.G., 604
Masefield, John, 293, 356, 489, 792, 936, 947
Masey, Cecil, 557, 966
Masham, Abigail, 196
Masham, 1st Baron, 196
Maskelyne, John Nevil, 709
Mason, Hugh, 290
Mason, Isaac, 488
Mason, Monck, 911
Mason, William, 763
Massine, Leonide, 595
Massinger, Philip, 37, 805
Master, J.H. and Gertrude Emma, 525
Masterman, John, 175
Matcham, Frank, 127, 188, 206, 385, 474, 476, 488, 513, 650, 915, 918, 968
Mather, Andrew, 452
Mather, Rick, 52
Matheson, Sir James, 829
Mathew, John, 734
Mathew, Theobald, 635
Mathews, C.J., 487
Mathews, Charles, 303
Mathews, E.D.J., 167, 171, 435
Mathews the Elder, Charles, 540
Matilda, Empress, 671, 727, 872
Matilda (Maud), Queen Consort of Henry 1, 40, 80, 134, 631, 710, 831
Matilda, Queen Consort of King Stephen, 40, 728
Matthay, Tobias, 25
Matthew, Sir Robert, 425, 671, 675
Matthews, Captain, 373, 402
Matthews, Charles James, 941
Matthews, E.D. Jefferis, 764, 830
Matthews, Samuel, 242
Matthews, Tom, 208
Matyear, William, 299
Maud, daughter of Henry II, 40
Maud, daughter of King John, 40
Maud, wife of Henry I, see Matilda
Maude, Cyril, 604
Maudlay, Henry, 860
Maudsley, Henry, 502
Maufe, Sir Edward, 4, 243, 321, 322, 364, 509, 514, 515, 668, 702
Maugham, Somerset, 151, 352, 368, 535, 771
Maule, H.P.G., 683
Maunder, F.A.C., 856
Maurice, Bishop, 756
Maurice, F.D., 365, 435, 458, 631, 904
Maxim, Sir Hiram, 208, 369, 778
Maximilius, Emperor, 727
Maxwell, James Clerk, 435, 575
May, Baptist, 32
May, Hugh, 56, 108, 258, 259
May of Teck, Princess, see Mary, Queen of George V
Mayerne, Sir Theodore, 460

Mayhew, Henry, 9, 57, 79, 121, 211, 273, 382, 397, 444, 523, 539, 635, 678, 836, 843, 955, 957
Maynard, Sir Henry, 866
Maynard, Sir John, 346
Maynard, Stephen, 867
Mayne, Sir Richard, 607, 608
Mayor, Charles, 582, 644
Mazarin, Duchess of, 427
Mazzini, Giuseppe, 124, 319, 369
McAdam, John Loudon, 376
McArthur, William, 470
McCarter, Keith, 14
McCarthy, Henry, 805
McCarthy, Lillah, 438
McClean, James, 898
McFall, David, 816, 821
McGill, Kate, 610
McGill, David, 819
McGill, Donald, 71
McGrigor, Sir James, 663, 819
McHarg, A.F., 684
McKean, Lorne, 979, 980
McMillan, Margaret and Rachel, 384, 454
McMorran, Donald, 969
McNeile, H.C. (Sapper), 352
M'cOllum, Thomas, 662
McWilliam, F.E., 967
Mead, Richard, 347, 395, 768, 951
Meade, Jacob, 393
Meadows, Bernard, 880
Meard, John, 505
Mears, George, 64
Meath, Reginald Brabazon, 12th Earl of, 815
Medows, Sir William, 861
Meeson, Alfred, 15
Melbourne, 1st Viscount, 9, 235
Melbourne, 2nd Viscount, 66, 386, 458, 800, 903
Melchett, 1st Baron, 286, 820
Melitus, St, 66, 756, 944
Mellon, Harriet, 597
Melnotte, Violet, 241
Melvill, Henry, 833
Melville, 1st Viscount, 951
Melville, Walter and Frederick, 781
Mendelssohn-Bartholdy, Felix, 25, 61, 114, 555, 564, 632, 680, 682, 759, 764
Mendes, Fernando, 246
Menon, Krishna, 820
Menotti, Ciro, 894
Menpes, Mortimer, 113
Menuhin, Yehudi, 342, 407
Menzies, Sir Frederick, 674
Meredith, George, 152, 384
Meredith, John, 788
Meredith, Melchizedeck, 308
Meredith, Michael, 697
Merlin, John Joseph, 511
Merrick, Mrs, 308
Merrifield, L.S., 822
Messel, Oliver, 233
Messiaen, Oliver, 680
Messina Brothers, 212
Methuen, 2nd Baron, 271
Metternich, Prince von, 252, 280, 647
Meux family, 85, 857, 904
Mewès, Charles, 123
Meyer, Bertie A., 115
Meyers, Barnett, 417
Meynell, Alice, 132, 575
Meynell, Francis and Vera, 308, 326
Meynell, Wilfrid, 332, 575
Meyrick, A.W.H., 575
Michael, Grand Duke, 130
Michelangelo, 109, 660, 741, 853
Michelhain, 1st Baron, 194
Michell, Simon, 182
Micklethwaite, John Thomas, 159
Middlesex, Earl of, 226
Middleton, George, 201, 539
Middleton, William, 285
Milbanke, Anne Isabella, later Lady Byron, 615
Milbanke, Sir Ralph, 615
Mildmay, Sir Henry St John, 25
Mildmay, Sir Walter, 694
Mileham, C.H., 749
Miles, Bernard, (Baron Miles), 511
Miles, Jonathan, 418
Miles, Henry and Emma, 223
Mill, James, 250, 628, 653, 901, 940
Mill, John Stuart, 250, 427, 449, 475, 628, 653, 820, 915, 964
Millais, Sir John Everett, 49, 319, 527, 534, 575, 782, 798, 820, 972
Millar, Andrew, 436
Millburn, William and T.R., 233
Miller, Andrew, 436
Miller, Charles, 653
Miller, Sanderson, 25
Miller, Thomas, 422
Mills, Bertram, 563
Mills, Peter, 174, 329
Millyng, Thomas, 945

Milman, Sir Francis, 25
Milman, William, 519
Milne, A.A., 427, 492
Milne, Chadwell, 930
Milne, Oswald, 180
Milner, Viscount, 492, 820
Milnes, Richard Moncton, 1st Baron Houghton, 791
Milnes, Thomas, 823
Milton, John, 13, 16, 38, 42, 83, 104, 105, 330, 376, 384, 392, 417, 462, 595, 698, 711, 732, 739, 762, 787, 820, 947
Minet family, 521
Mingay, James, 51
Minoprio, Anthony, 46
Minshaw, Charles Stuart, 492
Mist, John, 687
Mitchell, F.J., 214
Mitchell, John, 722
Mitchell, Leslie, 15
Mitchell, R.J., 383
Mitchenson, Joe, 638
Mitford, Mary Russell, 363, 686
Mitford, Nancy, 831
Mitchell, Robert, 451
Modena, Mary of, 633
Moffatt, W.B., 114, 364, 474
Mogg, Edward, 926
Moholy-Nagy, Laszlo, 786
Mohun, 4th Baron, 398, 401, 402, 657
Moira, 2nd Earl of, 279, 718
Mollere, Nicholas, 143
Molloy, Charles, 544
Monck, General, 82, 167, 323
Monckton-Milnes, Richard, 476
Mond, Ludwig, 676
Mondrian, Piet, 584
Money-Coutts, David, 202
Monk, General, see Albemarle, 1st Duke of
Monk, James Henry, 113
Monk, Jane, Mary and Penelope, 713
Monmouth, Duchess of, 524
Monmouth, Duke of, 13, 269, 514, 523, 564, 763, 792, 793, 870, 877, 960
Monmouth, Humphrey, 703
Monoux, Sir George, 152, 738, 920
Monro, James, 608
Montagu, Duchess of, 524
Montagu, 1st Duke of, 436, 523, 524, 525
Montagu, 2nd Duke of, 524
Montagu, Edward, 296
Montagu, Edward Wortley, 4
Montagu, Elizabeth, 370, 382, 524, 525, 616
Montagu, Lady Mary Wortley, 4, 25, 128, 340, 414
Montagu, Sir Samuel, later 1st Baron Swaythling, 523
Montague, H.J., 909
Montague, Sir Charles, 731
Montcalm, Marquis de, 823
Monteagle, Baron, 251, 346
Montefiore, Sir Moses, 583
Monteroli, 853
Montez, Lola, 352
Montford, Paul, 814, 823
Montfort, 1st Baron, 807
Montgomery, 1st Viscount, 762, 816, 820
Moodie, T.A., 241
Moody, F.W., 61, 536
Moody, John, 41
Moorcroft, R.L., 266
Moore, A.W., 275
Moore, Francis J., 344
Moore, G.E., 75
Moore, George, architect, 144, 171
Moore, George, novelist, 252, 408, 541
Moore, Henry, 2, 45, 66, 94, 148, 194, 338, 403, 415, 519, 584, 623, 628, 810
Moore, John, 740
Moore, Sir John, 339
Moore, Mary, later Lady Wyndham, 212
Moore, L. Temple, 19, 714
Moore, Thomas, 124, 307, 386
Moore, Tom, 109, 416, 656
Moran, 1st Baron, 747
Mordaunt, Viscount, 187
Morden, Lady, 581
Morden, Sir John, 527
Morden, Robert, 495, 809
More, Alice, 147
More, Anne, 239, 499
More, Hugh, 458
More, Sir George, 283
More, Sir Thomas, 48, 104, 141, 144, 146, 147, 159, 168, 213, 214, 285, 345, 384, 409, 443, 458, 460, 469, 517, 534, 692, 729, 735, 744, 763, 787, 820, 863, 870, 873, 874, 951
Morehead, Sir John, 811
Morel, Abbé, 737
Moret, Dr, 34

992

1004

1005

Church of the Holy Redeemer, 151, 159
Church of the Holy Redeemer and St Thomas More, 159
Church of the Holy Sepulchre, Holborn, 5
Church of the Holy Sepulchre Without Newgate, 136, 159
Church of the Immaculate Conception, 159, 273
Church of the Most Holy Trinity, Dockhead, 58, 415
Church of the Nativity of Our Lady and the Innocents, 795
Church of Our Lady, Lisson Grove, 461
Church Road, Barnes, 846
Church Road, Wimbledon, 745, 965, 966
Church Row, 160, 456, 722
Church Street, Chiswick, 750
Church Street, Croydon, 724
Church Street, E1, 261
Church Street, Greenwich, 335
Church Street, Kensington, 738
Church Street, NW8, 160
Church Street, Soho, 656, 792
Church Street, Stoke Newington, 747
Church Street, Twickenham, 745
Church Street Baths, 624
Churchill, Atkin, Grant and Lang, 579
Churchill Gardens, 160
Churchill Gardens Estate, 148
Churchill Hotel, 160, 616
Churchill Theatre, 95, 160
Circle Line, 160, 227, 513, 645, 887, 899
Circus, 21, 160, 209, 355
Circus Road, 160
Citadel, 161
Citibank House, 300, 830
City Aldermen, 267
City and Guilds College, 405
City and Guilds of London Art School, 161, 165, 169
City and Guilds of London Institute, 161-168, 169, 170, 172, 405, 615
City Bank, 516, 863
City Barge, 161, 831
City Basin, 643
City Canal, 939
City Chamberlain, 161, 199
City Commissioners of Sewers, 516
City Corporation, 174, 190, 195, 203, 229, 230, 302, 318, 320, 338, 345, 358, 449, 462, 480, 511, 669, 696, 749, 786, 859, 882, 932, 934, 938
City Hall, 944
City Imperial Volunteers, 646
City Livery Club, 161, 787
City Livery Companies, 13, 47, 135, 161, 173, 174, 191, 193, 196, 201, 293, 344, 345, 383, 396, 467, 481, 552, 671, 672, 727, 729, 759, 783, 852, 882
City Marshal, 134, 135, 172, 191, 199, 494, 852
City of London, 12, 38, 47, 48, 65, 68, 69, 72, 79, 85, 86, 118, 130, 134, 135, 141, 142, 152, 155, 158, 160, 161, 165, 166, 169, 171, 172, 175, 176, 191, 192, 196, 199-201, 212, 227, 237, 239, 241, 250, 259, 264, 275, 279, 282, 289, 291, 293, 301, 302, 304, 323, 324, 325, 327, 328, 330, 337, 338, 345, 347, 358, 383, 384, 385, 393, 396, 407, 412, 445, 447, 456, 462, 465, 466, 470, 472, 480-482, 487, 494, 495, 504-506, 507, 511, 517, 526, 542, 547, 565, 601, 603, 605-608, 610, 613, 616, 619, 630, 637, 649, 656, 668, 669-671, 694, 697, 698, 699, 703, 711, 724, 728, 734, 746, 751, 764, 767, 770, 777, 783, 789, 803, 838, 841, 857, 859, 870, 873, 879, 901, 913, 932, 964
City of London Brewery, 85, 188
City of London Cemetery, 16, 130, 730
City of London Club, 175, 558
City of London Coat of Arms, 175
City of London College, 176
City of London Corporation, 790
City of London Freemen's School, 175, 293
City of London Lying-in Hospital, 278
City of London Militia, 645, 881
City of London Police, 13, 175, 318, 608, 969
City of London Polytechnic, 66, 176, 417
City of London Real Property Company, 497
City of London Regiment, 672
City of London School, 17, 163, 165, 167, 176, 234, 392, 814, 820, 821
City of London School for Girls, 38, 163, 175, 176
City of Westminster, 407, 463
City Remembrancer, 176
City Road, 13, 105, 176, 278, 293, 392, 474, 526, 561, 733, 782, 937, 973

City Sheriff, 83
City Temple, 177, 385
City Terminus Hotel, 177, 410
City University, 164, 169, 170, 172, 175, 177, 212, 338, 481
City University Club, 177
Civil and Mechanical Engineers' Society, 792
Civil Service Club, 330
Civil Service Commission, 108
Civil Service Stores, 177
Civil Service Supply Association, 177
Clabon Mews, 621
Clapham, 177, 389, 390, 442, 479, 754, 768
Clapham Brewery, 85
Clapham Common, 177, 178, 179, 389, 390, 553, 655, 799
Clapham High Street, 179
Clapham Junction, 45, 178, 272
Clapham Road, 254, 655
Clapham Sect, 178, 179, 389
Clapton, 179
Clapton Football Club, 908
Clare Market, 7, 104, 179, 477, 549, 912
Clare Street, 700
Claremont Chapel, 591
Clarence House, 179, 716, 776
Clarence Gate, 702
Clarence Tavern, 912
Clarence Terrace, 179
Clarendon Close, 811
Clarendon coaching inn, 354
Clarendon Cross, 446
Clarendon Gardens, 811
Clarendon House, 10, 179, 596, 972
Clarendon Place, 811
Clarendon Road, 446
Clarendon Terrace, 811
Clareville Cottage, 180
Clareville Grove, 180
Clareville Street, 180, 935
Clarges Street, 180
Claridge's, 98, 180
Clark and Russell, 963
Clark (Joseph) and Sons, 223
Clarke (Ellis) and Gallannaugh, 623
Clark's Place, 172, 180
Clattern Bridge, 180
Clayhill, 180
Clayton and Bell, 732, 762
Clayton Court, 816
Cleaves Almshouses, 180
Clement's Inn, 408
Clements Lane, 180, 410, 701
Clement's Passage, 408
Cleopatra's Needle, 181, 932
Clerical, Medical and General Life Assurance Society, 456
Clerkenwell, 22, 87, 181, 211, 228, 270, 316, 477, 518, 542, 564, 588, 607, 608, 623, 680, 722, 732, 762, 806, 844
Clerkenwell and Islington Medical Mission, 969
Clerkenwell Close, 183
Clerkenwell Craftsmen, 183
Clerkenwell Green, 183, 712
Clerkenwell House of Detention, 183
Clerkenwell Parochial School, 543
Clerkenwell Priory, 377
Clerkenwell Riot, 651
Clerkenwell Road, 85, 183, 764
Clerkenwell Sunday School, 969
Clerkenwell Workhouse, 273
Clermont Club, 57
Cleveland House, 183, 920
Cleveland Row, 87, 183, 829
Cleveland Street, 183, 774
Cliefden House, 258
Clifford Street, 104, 108, 184, 893
Clifford's Inn, 408, 705
Clifford's Inn Passage, 408
Clifton Gardens, 184, 489
Clifton Hill, 184
Clifton-Ford Hotel, 935
Clink Prison, 21, 184
Clink Street, 184, 966
Clipstone Street, 184
Clissold Park, 184
Clissold Road Baths, 624
Clive House, 595
Cloak Lane, 175, 176, 184, 219, 724
Clock House, 49, 903
Clockmakers' Company, 51, 63, 164, 345
Cloth Fair, 184
Clothworkers' Company, 17, 162, 164, 264, 345, 413, 520, 713
Clothworkers' Hall, 244
Cloudesley Estate, 184
Clowns' Service, 136
CLRP Architects, 879
Club Row, 61, 185, 594
Club, the, 185, 222, 308, 451
Clyde Street, 624
Clyde Young and Eagle, 533
Clydesdale Bank, 466
Coach and Horses, Great Marlborough Street, 326

Coach and Horses, Greek Street, 332
Coach and Horses, St Martin's Lane, 64, 768
Coach and Horses, Stonebridge, 829
Coachmakers' and Coach Harness Makers' Company, 164, 170
Coachmakers' Hall, 549
Coade Lion, 185
Coade Stone, 51, 85, 180, 185, 301, 442, 697, 788
Coal Exchange, 186, 914, 928
Coal Hole, 186
Coburg Hotel, 47, 122, 192, 634
Coburn School, 164
Cock, 431
Cock and Bell, 656
Cock and Pye Inn, 907
Cock Lane, 186, 308, 625, 907
Cock Lane Ghost, 186
Cock Pit, 186
Cock Tavern, 186, 187, 286
Cockes Lane, 605
Cockfosters, 187, 598, 887
Cockfosters Road, 939
Cockney, 80, 187, 741
Cockney School, 187
Cockpit Alley, 890
Cockpit Theatre, 187, 239
Cocks, Biddulph and Co., 959
Cockspur Street, 124, 187, 818, 900
Cocoa Tree Chocolate House, 187
Coffee houses, 202
Coffee Terminal Market Association of London Ltd, 471
Cogers' Hall, 187
Cogswell and Harrison, 597
Colchester Road, 655
Colcutt and Hemp, 7
Cold Bath Fields Prison, 187
Coldharbour, 85, 187, 188, 244, 934
Coldstream Guards, 397
Cole and Son, 528
Coleherne Court, 374
Coleman Street, 25, 81, 162, 188, 212, 562, 765
Colet Court, 762
Colet Girls' School, 761
Colfe's School, 168
Colham, 188, 382
Colham Green, 188
Colindale, 91, 188, 549
Coliseum Theatre, 188
Collard and Collard, 310
Collcutt and Hemp, 915
College Hill, 171, 188, 734, 962
College Hill Chambers, 166
College House, 155
College Lane, 381
College of All Saints, 516
College of Arms, 188, 631
College of Commerce and Law, Kennington, 609
College of God's Gift at Dulwich, 243, 244, 416
College of Mines, 814, 823
College of Physicians, 506, 926
College of Preceptors, 75, 188
College of St John, 189
College of St Mark, 189
College of St Mark and St John, 145, 189
College of Surgeons, 506
College Place, 53
College Road, 189, 242, 243, 313
College Street, 189, 863
Collet's International Bookshop, 139
Collier (John) Men's Wear, 571
Colliers Wood, 189
Collingham Gardens, 346
Collingwood's, 192
Collins Farmhouse, 973
Collins' Music Hall, 190
Colney Hatch, 190, 294, 295
Colney Hatch Asylum, 294
Colney Hatch Lane, 294
Colonnade, 420
Colonnade Hotel, 489
Colonnade House, 190
Colonnades, 46
Colosseum, 115, 190, 579, 580, 632
Columbia Cinema, 781
Columbia Market, 61, 190
Columbia Road, 61, 190, 346
Columbia Square, 61
Combe's Brewery, 86
Combs's Brewery, Mr, 85
Comedy Restaurant, 569
Comedy Theatre, 190
Commercial and General Travel Service, 84
Commercial Bank of London, 536
Commercial Dock Company, 321, 847
Commercial Road, 167, 191, 250, 456, 534, 611, 638, 691, 841, 955
Commercial Road Co., 191
Commercial Street, 191, 587, 808, 880
Commercial Union, 449
Commissioner of the City of London Police, 191, 192

Commissioners of Sewers, 496
Common Cryer and Serjeant-at-Arms, 47, 135, 172, 191, 199, 493, 494, 852
Common Hall, 161, 191, 192, 879
Common Serjeant, 191
Commonhedge Lane, 924
Commons, Open Spaces and Footpaths Preservation Society, 192, 262
Commonwealth Foundation, 499
Commonwealth Hall, 126
Commonwealth Institute, 192, 425
Communist Party of Great Britain, 433, 463
Companies Without Livery, 172
Company of Parish Clerks, 66
Comptroller and City Solicitor, 192, 199
Comyn Ching and Co., 523
Conduit Mead, 100, 320, 503
Conduit Mead Estate, 31, 77, 98, 192, 777, 799
Conduit Street, 24, 184, 192, 675, 942
Coney Wood, 49
Congregational Chapel, Highgate, 379
Congregational Church, Lambeth, 442
Congregational Church, Wanstead, 923
Congregational Memorial Hall, 274
Congregational Memorial Hall Trust, 192
Congregational Park Chapel, 214
Congress House, 330
Connaught Hall of Residence, 856
Connaught Hotel, 122, 192
Connaught Place, 193, 926
Connaught Rooms, 193, 293, 487, 901
Connaught Square, 46, 193, 573
Connaught Street, 46
Connaught Theatre, 193, 662
Connoisseur, 43, 50, 961
Conservative and Unionist Central Office, 789
Conservative Club, 43, 193, 861
Conservatoire of Music, 71
Consort House, 634
Consort Road, 53
Constable, 564
Constance Fund, 333, 402
Constance Spry Flower School, 502
Constitution Arch, 193
Constitution Hill, 194, 333, 630, 631
Constitutional Club, 722, 766, 771
Consulate General of the Republic of Turkey, 686
Contemporary Art Society, 855
Convent of Holy Trinity, off Basinghall Street, 168
Convent of the Daughters of Charity of St Vincent de Paul, 122
Convent of the Holy Child, 128
Convent of the Sacred Heart, Hammersmith Road, 194
Convent of the Sisters of Providence, 369
Convoy's Wharf, 224
Conway Hall, 194, 821
Cook and Maple, 494
Cook (Thomas) Ltd, 57, 516
Cooks' Company, 13, 164
Cooks Ground, 310
Cook's Road, 194
Coombe, 194, 541
Coombe House, 194
Coombe Hill Golf Club, 313
Coombe Wood House, 194
Cooney-Marsh Group, 29
Cooper (Thos.), Parasol and Umbrella Maker, 942
Co-operative Societies, 194
Coopers, 43
Coopers and Lybrand, 75
Coopers' Company, 164, 637
Coopers' Company and Coborn School, 165
Cooper's Row, 173, 479, 822
Cope Castle, 386
Cope Place, 386
Copenhagen Fields, 485, 512
Copenhagen House, 195, 471
Cope's Castle, 386
Copped Hall, 195
Coppermill, 920
Coppermills, 932
Coppetts Road, 672
Coppetts Wood Hospital, 672
Copt Hall, 262
Copthall Avenue, 195
Coptic Street, 195
Coq d'Or, 832
Coram Fields, 195
Coram Street, 196
Corbets Tey, 196, 903
Cording and Co, 597
Cordon Bleu Cookery School (London) Ltd, 502
Cordwainer Street, 80, 143
Cordwainers' College, 170
Cordwainers' Company, 118, 162, 164, 272, 517, 672
Cordwainers' Technical College, 164

1013

1019

1022

Stansfield House, 207
Stanstead Road, 705
Staple Inn, 169, 384, 385, 409, 410, 418, 623
Staple Inn Hall, 410
Stapleton Hall, 844
Star Alley, 497
Star and Garter, Pall Mall, 57, 812, 953
Star and Garter, Poland Street, 605
Star and Garter Home, 21, 812
Star Inn, 791
State Barge, 484
State Cinema, 964
State House, 376
State Opening of Parliament, 346, 392, 677, 812
State Paper Office, 625
Stationers' and Newspaper Makers' Company, 171, 813
Stationers' Company, 135, 622, 813
Stationers' Company's School, 813
Stationers' Hall, 90, 135, 171, 486
Stationers' Hall Court, 486
Statistical Society of London, 682
Steel House, 868
Steelyard, 391, 824, 907
Steelyard Lane, 824
Steinway, 192
Stephen (Douglas) and Partners, 207
Stephen Street, 824
Stepney, 61, 72, 272, 327, 411, 456, 506, 516, 517, 601, 611, 637, 638, 643, 693, 703, 736, 780, 824, 870, 871, 892, 915, 955
Stepney Causeway, 231, 638, 825
Stepney Green, 517, 825
Stepney High Street, 703
Stepney Marsh, 411
Sterling Guards Ltd, 477
Sterling Street, 825
Stevens and Munt, 97, 367
Stew Lane, 825
Steward and Head, 84
Stew's Bank, 37
Stickleton, 334
Stifford Estate, 415
Stinking Lane, 432
Stock Exchange, 121, 540, 558, 825, 863, 864, 966
Stock Exchange Coffee House, 540
Stocks Market, 143, 203, 273, 282, 284, 493, 699, 826
Stockwell, 91, 174, 442, 553, 826, 827, 887
Stockwell Ghost, 827
Stoke Newington, 158, 184, 350, 542, 591, 619, 747, 748, 786, 827
Stoke Newington Common, 828
Stoke Newington Road, 655
Stoll Picture Theatre, 828
Stoll Theatre, 828
Stone Buildings, 409, 458, 828
Stone Grove, 829
Stone House, 454
Stone, Toms and Partners, 160
Stonebridge, 829, 937
Stone's Chop House, 581
Stone's Hotel, 581
Stoop Memorial Ground, Twickenham, 684
Store Street, 104, 829, 868
Storey's Gate, 133, 766, 829
Stornoway House, 829
Stowford, 849
Stow's Quill Pen Ceremony, 136
Straker (Samuel) and Sons, 456, 829
Strand, 2, 6-8, 14, 24, 28, 30, 52, 66, 89, 94, 127, 131, 135, 137-139, 142, 177, 192, 201, 202, 217, 225, 233, 239, 244, 255, 263, 270, 296, 300, 306, 307, 345, 408, 409, 418, 434, 435, 447, 458, 465, 484, 486, 487, 539, 554, 563, 596, 623, 646, 654, 655, 660, 701, 722, 761, 768, 769, 771, 773, 774, 786, 789, 792, 795, 818, 819, 829, 831, 856-858, 881, 895, 909, 926, 963, 966, 972, 975-978
Strand Bridge, 932
Strand House, 477, 540, 789
Strand Inn, 409
Strand Magazine, 225
Strand Music Hall, 300
Strand Palace Hotel, 107, 270, 830, 831
Strand Theatre, 14, 831
Strand 'Roman' Bath, 831
Strand-on-the-Green, 153, 161, 831, 881
Strangers' Home for Asiatics, 457
Strangways Terrace, 386
Stratford, 67, 80, 238, 547, 655, 703, 831, 862, 913
Stratford Coffee House, 682
Stratford House, 566, 832
Stratford Langthorne, 80
Stratford Langthorne Abbey, 19, 832
Stratford New Town, 547
Stratford Place, 406, 566, 615, 682, 832, 928
Stratford Street, 311

Stratheden House, 440
Stratton Street, 56, 504, 596, 597, 832
Strawberry Hill, 116, 383, 833
Strawberry House, 833
Strawberry Lodge, 349
Streatham, 69, 442, 730, 833
Streatham Common, 834, 835
Streatham High Road, 618
Streatham Hill, 444, 655
Streatham Manor, 19
Streatham Place, 834
Streatham Spa, 835
Streatham Street, 245
Street Cries, 835
Street lighting, 837, 884
Street music, 838
Street performers, 839
Street signs, 841
Street, the, 958
Street vendors, 843
Strickland and Sons, 772
Strombolo Gardens, 844
Strombolo House, 844
Stroud Green, 394, 844
Strutton Ground, 845
Strype Street, 516, 845
Strype's Yard, 845
Studio, the, 575
Sudbrook Lodge, 352
Sudbrook Park, 314, 593, 845
Sudbury, 845
Sudbury Golf Club, 315
Suffolk House, 447
Suffolk Lane, 110, 510, 845
Suffolk Place, 78, 521, 845
Suffolk Street, 138, 303, 845
Suffragettes, 128, 651
Summer Exhibition, 660
Summerstown, 846
Summit House, 640
Sumner Place, 846
Sun, 41, 80
Sun Alliance Offices, 694
Sun Court, 581
Sun Fire Office, 206
Sun Inn, 846
Sun Life Assurance Co, 17
Sun Life Assurance Co. of Canada, 187
Sun Life Building, 654
Sun Tavern Fields, 780
Sunbury, 684
Sunbury Lock, 250
Sunday Ramble, 213
Sunday Telegraph, 819
Sundridge Park, 846
Sundridge Park Golf Club, 315
Sundridge Park Mansion, 95
Sunnydene, Westwood Hill, Sydenham, 847
Sunset Avenue, 315
Surbiton, 62, 149, 150, 393, 847, 866, 977
Surrey, 28, 230
Surrey Canal Company, 847
Surrey Chapel, 69
Surrey Commercial Dock Company, 847
Surrey Commercial Docks, 72, 230, 250, 321, 398, 658, 847
Surrey County Cricket Club, 422, 569, 847
Surrey County Lunatic Asylum, 867
Surrey Gardens, 580
Surrey Gardens Music Hall, 847, 921
Surrey House, 768
Surrey Institution, 69
Surrey Iron Railway, 50, 200, 846, 847, 919, 921, 922
Surrey Lane, 768
Surrey Literary, Scientific and Zoological Institution, 848
Surrey Mount, 290
Surrey Street Market, 215
Surrey Theatre, 848
Surrey Walking Club, 478
Surrey Zoological Gardens, 270, 847, 848
Survey of London, 105, 309, 792, 890
Sussex Gardens, 713, 848
Sussex House, 848
Sussex Lodge, 849
Sussex Place, 849
Sussex Square, 713, 849
Sutherland Avenue, 489, 490
Suthrey House, 849
Sutton, 49, 62, 349, 677, 712, 849, 959
Sutton Court, 154, 850
Sutton House, 350
Sutton Lodge, 850
Sutton to Epsom Downs Railway, 55
Sutton's, 686
Swaine, Adeney, Brigg and Son, 597
Swain's Lane, 380, 381
Swakeleys, 850
Swakeleys Road, 710
Swallow Passage, 850
Swallow Street, 596, 850
Swan, Bayswater Road, 47, 850
Swan, Hammersmith Broadway, 354

Swan, Knightsbridge, 440
Swan, Ruislip, 684
Swan, Tottenham, 868
Swan and Edgar Ltd, 223, 597, 642, 643, 850
Swan and Hoop, 527
Swan Court, 286
Swan Tavern, Bridge Street, 766
Swan Tavern, Charing Cross, 850
Swan Tavern, Swan Walk, 851
Swan Theatre, 257, 850
Swan Walk, 147, 851
Swan with Two Necks, 319, 338, 851
Swans on the Thames, 171, 851
Swaziland High Commission, 610
Swedish Embassy, 615
Sweeting's Rents, 21
Sweetmans Hall, 600
Swinton Street, 852
Swiss Centre, 539
Swiss Church of London, 260
Swiss Cottage, 356, 817, 852
Swiss Cottage Centre, 852
Swithin's Lane, St, 658
Swordbearer, 135, 172; 191, 199, 493, 494, 852
Sydenham, 215, 281, 324, 624, 638, 852, 889
Sydenham High School, 853
Sydenham Hill, 216, 770
Sydney Street, 391, 730, 853
Sylvan Road, 723
Symon's Wharf, 53
Syon, 142, 229
Syon House, 228, 412, 479, 554, 853
Syon House Gardens, 302

Tabard, Southwark, 805, 854
Tabard Inn, Bedford Park, 51
Tabernacle Street, 163
Tachbrook Street, 854, 863
Talbot Road, 854
Talbot Square, 618
Talbot Yard, Borough High Street, 854
Talgarth Road, 664, 854
Talk of the Town, 206
Tallis Street, 854
Tallow Chandlers' Company, 170, 171, 842
Tallow Chandlers' Hall, 235, 901
Tanner Street, 59
Tanners Lane, 230
Target Records, 84
Tarrant Crawford, 207
Tasel Close, 27
Tate Almshouses, 854
Tate and Lyle, 786
Tate Gallery, 132, 533, 628, 820, 854, 855
Tatler, 332, 493, 636, 714, 791, 961, 965
Tattersall's, 440, 855
Tavern, 484
Tavistock Chambers, 75
Tavistock Clinic, 855
Tavistock Hotel, 856
Tavistock House, 856
Tavistock Place, 500, 856
Tavistock Repertory Company, 119, 120
Tavistock Row, 51, 202
Tavistock Square, 89, 500, 509, 813, 817, 856
Tavistock Street, 51, 127, 856
TAVR, 646
Taylor Woodrow, 20, 729
Taylors, 162
Tecton, 380, 599, 657, 978
Teddington, 647, 856, 931
Teddington Film Studios, 302
Teddington Theatre Club, 359
Teddington Weir Suspension Bridge, 856
Tedworth Square, 788, 856
Telegraph Hill, 150, 355, 588
Telegraph Hill Park, 856
Telegraph Street, 857
Telekinema, 532
Telephone Cables, 220
Telephone Exchange, Broadway, 94
Television Centre, 857
Temperance Hospital, 713
Templar House, 376
Temple, 165, 172, 225, 228, 259, 296, 302, 324, 617, 773, 779, 927, 936
Temple Bar, 134, 135, 158, 172, 210, 268, 273, 284, 285, 407, 483, 619, 700, 761, 835, 857
Temple Bar Memorial, 817
Temple Church, 272, 407, 514, 565, 857
Temple Gardens, 260, 822
Temple Gardens Building, 408
Temple Mills, 455
Temple of Flora, 858
Temple of Isis, 467, 858
Temple of Mithras, 467, 631, 858, 918
Temple Place, 815, 858
Templeton Place, 254
Tenter Ground, 858

Tenter Street, Barbican, 858
Tenter Streets, E1, 858
Tenterden Street, 661, 858
Terminus Place, 104
Terrett's Place, 907
Territorial Army, 392, 646
Territorial Auxiliary Volunteer Reserve, 646
Territorial Auxiliary Volunteer Reserve Association, 240
Terry's Theatre, 858
Tessier Ltd, 77
Tetcott Road, 436
Thai Embassy, 622, 632
Thames, 37, 40, 43, 44, 55, 58, 64, 67-69, 71, 72, 84, 87, 93, 132, 144, 148, 171-173, 187, 208, 220, 235, 237, 238, 250, 254, 259, 261, 263, 272, 275, 280, 284, 287, 291, 296, 297, 304, 320, 321, 327, 329, 330, 336, 359, 384, 398, 411, 423, 437, 444, 449, 450, 457, 466, 467, 479, 497, 506, 537, 542, 549, 573, 588, 607, 619, 625, 637-639, 643, 647, 654, 655, 658, 680, 730, 731, 738, 742, 745, 756, 780, 788, 803, 805, 810, 846, 847, 857-859, 864, 872, 881-883, 889, 890, 892, 898, 899, 909, 912, 916, 918, 921, 923
Thames and Hudson, 75
Thames Archway Company, 860
Thames Barrier, 639, 860
Thames Conservancy Board, 859, 860, 892
Thames Embankment, 554
Thames House, 519, 924
Thames Ironworks and Shipbuilding Co., 118
Thames Police, 860
Thames Polytechnic, 860
Thames Rowing Club, 860
Thames Street, 196, 218, 221, 471, 485, 605, 619, 890, 907
Thames Television, 856, 860
Thames Tunnel, 610, 860, 924
Thames Water Authority, 238, 543, 657, 860, 932
Thamesmead, 40, 420, 861
Thanet House, 13, 74, 329, 330
Thatched House Club, 722
Thatched House Lodge, 861
Thatched House Tavern, 193, 264, 660, 669, 675, 682, 861, 901
Thavies Inn, 409, 410, 457
Thayer Street, 382
Theatre, 257, 310, 785, 861
Théâtre Français, 683
Theatre Museum, 861, 914
Theatre on the Green, 647
Theatre Royal and Opera House, Richmond, 647
Theatre Royal, Bridges Street, 460
Theatre Royal Drury Lane, 127, 239, 303, 371, 647, 657, 755, 861
Theatre Royal English Opera House, 487
Theatre Royal Haymarket, 862
Theatre Royal, New Adelphi, 7
Theatre Royal Stratford East, 862
Theatre Upstairs, 862
Theobalds Road, 74, 322, 862
Thieves' Kitchen, 33, 98
Thieving Lane, 944
Third Church of Christ, Scientist, 218
Thirties Society, 862
Thomas à Becket, 560
Thomas and Wilson, 299
Thomas Coram Foundation For Children, 100, 195, 292, 862
Thomas More House, 163
Thomas's Hotel, 57
Thompson and Walford, 901
Thorn Electrical Industries, 907
Thorn House, 907
Thorney Court, 311, 575
Thorney House, 575
Thorney Island, 863, 944
Thorney Isle, 323
Thornhill Terrace, 113
Thornton Heath, 863
Thornwood Lodge, Kensington, 863
Thorpe Close, 480
Thorpe Lodge, 116, 387
Threadneedle Street, 35, 36, 169, 516, 540, 569, 692, 696, 734, 799, 826, 863
Three Blue Posts, 296
Three Castles, 186
Three Cranes in the Vintry, 863
Three Cups, 724
Three Greyhounds, 863
Three Hats, 22, 229, 864
Three Kings, 56
Three Kings' Piece, 521
Three Kings Yard, 864
Three Leg Alley, 590, 891
Three Nuns Hotel, 864
Three Nuns Inn, 864
Three Pigeons, 296

1025

1028

Picture Acknowledgements

Maurice B. Adams, *Artists' Homes*, 1883: 453, 507. BBC Hulton Picture Library: 73, 112. W.H. Blanch, *Ye Parish of Camberwell*, 1875: 241, 243. *The British Architect* xxiii, 1885: 296. British Architectural Library, RIBA, London: 265, 537 above, 574. By courtesy of the Trustees of the British Museum: 572. *The Builder*, 1867 and 1862: 448, 713. *Cassell's Family Magazine*, 1877: 66. Cassell's *Old and New London*, 1897, Vols 6 and 2: 114, 435. The Directors of Coutts and Company: 486. T. Dawtrey Drewitt, *Romance of the Apothecaries Garden*, 1922: 147. Devonshire Collection, Chatsworth. Reproduced by permission of the Trustees of the Chatsworth Settlement: 154. Fotomas Index: 8, 19, 20, 22, 28, 38, 46, 48, 53, 58, 60, 78, 90, 101, 102, 108, 123, 127, 133 left/right, 141, 146, 156, 176, 180, 195, 198, 201, 204 above/below, 209, 218, 221 above, 225, 232, 254, 263 left, 268 above, 270, 280, 283, 292, 297, 306 right, 314, 317, 320, 322, 323, 333, 336, 341, 355, 362, 365, 373, 377, 379, 396, 399, 400, 401, 403, 412, 414, 426 above/below, 433, 452, 469, 497, 501, 503, 510, 514, 524 above/below, 533, 537 below, 542, 543, 545 below, 548 below, 573, 580 above/below, 583, 587, 595, 607, 611, 620, 636, 637, 670 below, 688, 695, 697, 702, 704, 706, 707, 708 above, 716, 734, 740, 741, 755, 757, 760 left/right, 784, 794, 804, 806 above, 807 right, 813, 817, 825, 828, 841, 862, 868, 874, 883 below, 885, 888 below, 895, 923 below, 943, 945, 947, 950, 953, 954, 957, 977. Greenwich Local History Library: 679. Guildhall Library, City of London: 3, 5, 23, 68, 84, 99, 103, 110, 117, 119, 125, 134, 143, 151, 185, 188, 189, 214, 221, 226, 230, 236, 240, 246, 249, 262, 267, 268 below, 269, 276, 278, 279, 284, 288, 298, 311, 316, 325 above, 344, 345, 347, 354, 374, 385, 398, 402, 419, 428, 431, 464, 482, 500, 502, 504, 508, 512, 526, 566, 591, 612, 624, 633, 642, 648 above, 650, 658, 660, 661, 670 above, 700, 708, 711 above/below, 717, 727 above/below, 728, 734, 749 below, 753, 756, 759, 765, 797 left/right, 802, 806 below, 807 left, 809, 811, 823 right, 824, 827, 833, 848 right, 851 above/below, 855, 859, 860, 883 above, 891, 896, 898, 903, 906, 934, 939, 956, 967, 970, 972. George Hennelle, *Album of Taste and Fashion and Book of Commercial and General Information*, 1878: 319. Thomas Holmes, *Holmes' Great Metropolis or Views and History of London in the 19th century*, c. 1855: 186 left, 691, 733. *Illustrated London News* (1842–1893): 1, 11, 29 right, 34, 61, 63, 69, 139, 191, 196, 237, 256, 260, 266, 325 below, 406, 445 right, 466, 473, 495, 530, 617, 645, 651, 662, 787, 843 left, 913. Islington Libraries: 378. Peter Jackson: 255. Courtesy of the London Oratory: 97. London Transport Executive: 313. Mansell Collection: 72, 80, 93, 105, 231 left, 274, 324, 356, 366, 367, 415, 422, 434, 438, 440, 442, 445 left, 457, 459, 513, 520, 523, 550, 565, 568, 570, 589, 593, 598, 627, 640 above/below, 649, 663, 665, 683, 721, 775, 778, 786, 801, 814, 839, 843 right, 848 left, 852, 857, 870, 871, 878, 880, 886 above, 888 above, 900, 902, 915, 919, 930 left/right, 935, 936, 975. Henry Mayhew and John Binny, *The Criminal Prisons of London and Scenes of Prison Life*, 1862: 183, 187. Museum of London: 7, 15, 26 right, 29 left, 32, 36, 37, 45, 49, 51, 55, 65, 70, 82, 87, 92, 129, 149, 157 above, 178, 181, 186 right, 190, 193, 197 above, 208, 215, 216, 231 right, 257, 261, 263 right, 277, 281, 285, 289, 306 left, 328, 337, 357, 359, 380, 387, 390, 394, 424, 430 above, 443, 450, 468, 470, 472, 475, 481, 491, 494, 495 right, 545 above, 548 above, 554, 556, 560, 561, 578, 630, 643, 644, 648 below, 654, 671, 673, 676, 678, 698, 701, 709, 716, 750, 767, 770, 773, 790, 796, 808, 815, 830, 836, 837, 840 left/right, 882, 884, 886 below, 910, 911, 921, 923 above, 927, 931, 942, 959. National Portrait Gallery: 430 below. R. Nevill, *London Clubs, Their History and Treasures*, 1909: 26 left. W.J. Pinks, *History of Clerkenwell*, 1880: 109. Popperfoto: 725, 979. *Prospects of the Most Remarkable Places in and about the City of London. Printed and Sold by Hen. Overton*, c. 1725: 157, 173. A.W. Pugin, *Select Views of Islington etc*, 1819: 120. *Punch*, 1846: 823 left. Donald Rumbelow: 546, 606. Science Museum, London: 6, 305, 350, 887 (Crown Copyright). T.H. Shepherd and James Elmes, *London and it's Environs in the 19th century*, 1829: 197 below, 217, 245, 389, 518, 849. Victoria and Albert Museum (Crown Copyright): 16. Westminster Public Libraries: 461. H.B. Wheatley, *Bond Street Old and New*, c. 1911: 77, 107. Robert Wilkinson, *Londinia Illustrata* (2 Vols), 1825: 290, 371, 409, 460, 465, 562, 563, 749 above, 764. W. Wroth, *Cremorne and the Later London Gardens*, 1907: 441. Endpapers: Guildhall Library, City of London.